20°E 40°E 60°E 80°E 100°E 120°E 140°E 160°E 180°

ARCTIC OCEAN 80°N

60°N

EUROPE
ALPS

Volga URAL MTS. Ob

ASIA 40°N

GOBI DESERT

HINDU KUSH HIMALAYA MTS. Yangtze

Indus Ganges

SYRIAN
DESERT

SAHARA

Nile

AFRICA

DECCAN
PLATEAU

Tropic of Cancer

20°N

PACIFIC OCEAN

Equator 0°

INDIAN OCEAN

NAMIB DESERT

KALAHARI
DESERT

GREAT
SANDY
DESERT

20°S

Tropic of Capricorn

AUSTRALIA

Cape of
Good Hope

0	1000	2000	3000 Km.
0	1000	2000	3000 Mi.

60°S

Antarctic Circle

ANTARCTICA

80°S

180°

A HISTORY OF
WORLD
SOCIETIES

A HISTORY OF WORLD SOCIETIES

THIRD EDITION

John P. McKay
UNIVERSITY OF ILLINOIS AT URBANA-CHAMPAIGN

Bennett D. Hill
GEORGETOWN UNIVERSITY

John Buckler
UNIVERSITY OF ILLINOIS AT URBANA-CHAMPAIGN

HOUGHTON MIFFLIN COMPANY   BOSTON   TORONTO

DALLAS   GENEVA, ILLINOIS

PALO ALTO   PRINCETON, NEW JERSEY

Sponsoring Editor: John Weingartner
Senior Development Editor: Lance Wickens
Project Editor: Christina Horn
Electronic Production Specialist: Karla K. Grinnell
Production Coordinator: Frances Sharperson
Manufacturing Coordinator: Priscilla Bailey
Marketing Manager: Diane Gifford

Chapter Opener Credits appear on page C-1.

Cover Credit Chen Hongshu, "The Four Pleasures." 1649. Handscroll; ink and color on silk, 9 ft. 6⅛ in. × 12¼ in. Rietberg Museum, Zurich.

Printed in the U.S.A.

Library of Congress Catalog Card Number: 91–71973

ISBN: 0-395-47293-8

CDEFGHIJ—VH—98765432

Text Credits Figures 1.1, 13.1, 21.1, 21.2, 26.1, 28.1, 28.2, 28.3, 28.4, 30.1, 30.2, 30.3, 30.4, and 32.1: from John P. McKay, Bennett D. Hill, and John Buckler, *A History of Western Society,* Fourth Edition. Copyright © 1991 by Houghton Mifflin Company. Used with permission. Page 20: Figure based on information from *The Sumerians: Their History, Culture and Character* by S. N. Kramer, pp. 302–306. Copyright © 1964 by The University of Chicago Press. Used with permission. Pages 20, 22, and 25: excerpts from *The Sumerians: Their History, Culture and Character* by S. N. Kramer, pp. 150, 238, and 251. Copyright © 1964 by The University of Chicago Press. Used with permission. Page 96: excerpts from *Lao Tzu* by Tao Te Ching, translated with an introduction by D. C. Lau (Penguin Classics, 1963), copyright © D. C. Lau, 1963. Reprinted with permission of Penguin Books Ltd. Pages 230, 234, 235–236, and 238–239: excerpts from *The Jerusalem Bible,* copyright © 1966 by Darton, Longman & Todd, Ltd., and Doubleday, a division of Bantam Doubleday Dell Publishing Group, Inc. Reprinted with permission of the publisher. Pages 237–238: excerpt from J. T. McNeil and H. Gamer, translators, *Medieval Handbooks of Penance,* Octagon Books, New York, 1965. Reprinted by permission of Columbia University Press. Pages 303 and 304: excerpts from *The Wonder That Was India,* translated by A. L. Basham (Grove, 1954), pp. 161, 459–460. Reprinted with permission of Sidgwick & Jackson, London. Page 318: excerpts from *Translations from the Chinese,* translated by Arthur Waley. Copyright © 1919. Reprinted with permission of HarperCollins Publishers. Pages 406 and 418: excerpts from *English Historical Documents,* Vol. 2, edited by D. C. Douglas and G. E. Greenaway (London: Eyre & Spottiswoode, 1961), pp. 853, 969–970. Reprinted with permission of Methuen, an imprint of Octopus Publishing Group.

About the Authors

John P. McKay Born in St. Louis, Missouri, John P. McKay received his B.A. from Wesleyan University (1961), his M.A. from the Fletcher School of Law and Diplomacy (1962), and his Ph.D. from the University of California, Berkeley (1968). He began teaching history at the University of Illinois in 1966 and became a professor there in 1976. John won the Herbert Baxter Adams Prize for his book *Pioneers for Profit: Foreign Entrepreneurship and Russian Industrialization, 1885–1913* (1970). He has also written *Tramways and Trolleys: The Rise of Urban Mass Transport in Europe* (1976) and has translated Jules Michelet's *The People* (1973). His research has been supported by fellowships from the Ford Foundation, the Guggenheim Foundation, the National Endowment for the Humanities, and IREX. His articles and reviews have appeared in numerous journals, including *The American Historical Review, Business History Review, The Journal of Economic History,* and *Slavic Review.* He edits *Industrial Development and the Social Fabric: An International Series of Historical Monographs.*

Bennett D. Hill A native of Philadelphia, Bennett D. Hill earned an A.B. at Princeton (1956) and advanced degrees from Harvard (A.M., 1958) and Princeton (Ph.D., 1963). He taught history at the University of Illinois at Urbana, where he was department chairman from 1978 to 1981. He has published *English Cistercian Monasteries and Their Patrons in the Twelfth Century* (1968) and *Church and State in the Middle Ages* (1970); and articles in *Analecta Cisterciensia, The New Catholic Encyclopaedia, The American Benedictine Review,* and *The Dictionary of the Middle Ages.* His reviews have appeared in *The American Historical Review, Speculum, The Historian, The Catholic Historical Review,* and *Library Journal.* He has been a fellow of the American Council of Learned Societies and has served on committees for the National Endowment for the Humanities. Now a Benedictine monk of St. Anselm's Abbey, Washington, D.C., he is also a Visiting Professor at Georgetown University.

John Buckler Born in Louisville, Kentucky, John Buckler received his B.A. from the University of Louisville in 1967. Harvard University awarded him the Ph.D. in 1973. From 1984 to 1986 he was the Alexander von Humboldt Fellow at Institut für Alte Geschichte, University of Munich. He is currently a professor at the University of Illinois. In 1980 Harvard University Press published his *The Theban Hegemony, 371–362 B.C.* He has also published *Philip II and the Sacred War* (Leiden 1989), and co-edited *BOIOTIKA: Vorträge vom 5. International Böotien-Kolloquium* (Munich 1989). His articles have appeared in journals both here and abroad, like the *American Journal of Ancient History, Classical Philology, Rheinisches Museum für Philologie, Classical Quarterly, Wiener Studien,* and *Symbolae Osloenses.*

Contents in Brief

1 ORIGINS — 3

What Is History and Why? — 4

The First Human Beings — 6

The Paleolithic Age — 8

The Neolithic Age — 9

Rivers, Resources, and Civilizations — 13

Mesopotamian Civilization — 15

The Spread of Mesopotamian Culture — 18

Daily Life in Mesopotamia — 23

Egypt, the Land of the Pharaohs (3100–1200 B.C.) — 25

The Hittite Empire — 32

The Fall of Empires (1200 B.C.) — 35

2 SMALL KINGDOMS AND MIGHTY EMPIRES IN THE NEAR EAST — 39

Migrations — 40

Egypt, a Shattered Kingdom — 40

The Children of Israel and Their Neighbors — 42

Assyria, the Military Monarchy — 49

The Empire of the Persian Kings — 52

3 ANCIENT INDIA TO CA A.D. 200 — 63

The Land and Its First Tamers (ca 2500–1500 B.C.) — 64

The Ascendancy of the Aryans (ca 1500–500 B.C.) — 68

India's Spiritual Flowering — 73

India and the West (ca 513–298 B.C.) — 78

The Mauryan Empire (ca 322–232 B.C.) — 80

4 THE RISE AND GROWTH OF CHINA TO CA A.D. 200 — 87

The Land and Its Challenge — 88

The Shang Dynasty (ca 1523–1027 B.C.) — 89

The Triumph of the Chou (ca 1027–221 B.C.) — 92

The Birth of Chinese Philosophy — 94

Confucianism — 94

The Age of Empire — 99

5 THE LEGACY OF GREECE — 115

Hellas: The Land — 116

The Minoans and Mycenaeans (ca 1650–ca 1100 B.C.) — 118

Homer and the Heroic Past (1100–800 B.C.) — 120

The Polis — 121

The Lyric Age (800–500 B.C.) — 123

The Classical Period (500–338 B.C.) — 128

6 HELLENISTIC DIFFUSION — 147

Alexander and the Great Crusade — 148

The Spread of Hellenism — 150

The Economic Scope of the Hellenistic World — 155

Religion in the Hellenistic World — 158

Philosophy and the Common Man — 159

Hellenistic Women — 161

Hellenistic Science — 162

Hellenistic Medicine — 165

7 THE RISE OF ROME — 171

The Land and the Sea — 172

The Etruscans and Rome (753–509 B.C.) — 174

The Roman Conquest of Italy (509–290 B.C.) — 175

The Roman State — 176

Social Conflict in Rome — 178

The Age of Overseas Conquest (282–146 B.C.) — 179

Old Values and Greek Culture   182

The Late Republic (133–27 B.C.)   187

8   THE PAX ROMANA   195

Augustus's Settlement (31 B.C.–A.D. 14)   196

The Coming of Christianity   202

The Julio-Claudians and the Flavians (27 B.C.–A.D. 96)   207

The Age of the "Five Good Emperors" (A.D. 96–180)   208

Life in the "Golden Age"   210

Rome and the East   214

Civil Wars and Invasion in the Third Century   217

Reconstruction Under Diocletian and Constantine (A.D. 284–337)   218

9   THE MAKING OF EUROPE   229

The Growth of the Christian Church   230

Christian Attitudes Toward Classical Culture   238

Monasticism and the Rule of Saint Benedict   241

The Migration of the Germanic Peoples   244

Germanic Society   248

The Byzantine East (ca 400–1000)   252

10   THE ISLAMIC WORLD, CA 600–1400   263

The Arabs Before Islam   264

Muhammad and the Faith of Islam   265

The Expansion of Islam   268

Consolidation of the Islamic State   273

Decentralization of the Islamic State   277

The Life of the People   279

11   TRADITION AND CHANGE IN ASIA, CA 320–1400   297

India, from Triumph to Invasion (ca 320–1400)   298

China's Golden Age (580–ca 1400)   309

Japan, Dawn of the Rising Sun   322

12   EUROPE IN THE EARLY AND HIGH MIDDLE AGES   333

The Frankish Aristocracy and the Rise of the Carolingian Dynasty   334

The Empire of Charlemagne   336

The Carolingian Intellectual Revival   341

Health and Medical Care in the Early Middle Ages   344

Division and Disintegration of the Carolingian Empire (814–987)   346

Feudalism   347

Great Invasions of the Ninth Century   350

Political Revival   352

Revival and Reform in the Christian Church   355

The Gregorian Revolution   359

The Crusades   362

13   LIFE IN CHRISTIAN EUROPE IN THE HIGH MIDDLE AGES   373

Those Who Work   374

Those Who Fight   385

Those Who Pray   392

14   CREATIVITY AND CRISIS IN THE HIGH AND LATER MIDDLE AGES   403

Medieval Origins of the Modern State   404

Economic Revival   417

Medieval Universities   426

The Creative Outburst   429

Heresy and the Friars   434

The Black Death   437

The Hundred Years' War (ca 1337–1453)   441

The Decline of the Church's Prestige   446

The Life of the People   448

15 AFRICA BEFORE EUROPEAN INTRUSION, CA 400–1500   461

The Land and Peoples of Africa   462

Early African Societies   464

African Kingdoms in the Western Sudan
(ca 1000 B.C.–A.D. 200)   465

The Trans-Saharan Trade   466

African Kingdoms and Empires
(ca 800–1450)   468

16 THE AMERICAS BEFORE EUROPEAN INTRUSION, CA 400–1500   485

The Geography and Peoples
of the Americas   486

Mesoamerican Civilizations from the
Olmec to the Toltec   487

Aztec Society: Religion and War   493

The Incas of Peru   498

17 EUROPEAN SOCIETY IN THE AGE OF THE RENAISSANCE AND REFORMATION   507

The Evolution of the Italian Renaissance   508

Intellectual Hallmarks of the Renaissance   512

Art and the Artist   515

Social Change   519

The Renaissance in the North   524

Politics and the State in the Renaissance
(1450–1521)   528

The Condition of the Church
(1400–1517)   535

Martin Luther and the Birth of
Protestantism   537

The Growth of the Protestant
Reformation   545

The Catholic and the Counter-
Reformations   553

18 THE AGE OF EUROPEAN EXPANSION AND RELIGIOUS WARS   563

Discovery, Reconnaissance, and
Expansion   565

Politics, Religion, and War   579

Changing Attitudes   593

Elizabethan and Jacobean Literature   599

Baroque Art and Music   601

19 ABSOLUTISM AND CONSTITUTIONALISM IN EUROPE, CA 1589–1725   607

Absolutism: An Overview   608

France: The Model of Absolute
Monarchy   609

The Decline of Absolutist Spain
in the Seventeenth Century   619

Lords and Peasants in Eastern Europe
(ca 1050–1650)   621

The Rise of Austria and Prussia   624

The Development of Russia   633

Absolutism and the Baroque in
Eastern Europe   639

Constitutionalism: An Overview   643

England: The Triumph of Constitutional
Monarchy   643

The Dutch Republic in the
Seventeenth Century   649

20 TOWARD A NEW WORLD VIEW IN THE WEST   659

The Scientific Revolution   660

The Enlightenment   669

The Development of Absolutism   679

21 THE LIFE OF THE PEOPLE IN EUROPE   691

Agriculture and Population   692

Marriage and the Family   699

Women and Children   704

Food and Medicine   709

Religion and Christian Churches   717

22 AFRICAN KINGDOMS AND SOCIETIES, CA 1450–1800   725

Senegambia and Benin   726

The Sudan: Songhay, Kanem-Bornu,
and Hausaland   728

Ethiopia   731
The Swahili City-States   732
The Transatlantic Slave Trade   734

23 THE MIDDLE EAST AND INDIA, CA 1450–1800   743

The Splendor of the Ottoman State   744
The Persian Theocratic State   751
India: From Mughal Domination to British Dominion (ca 1498–1805)   753

24 CHINA AND JAPAN, CA 1400–1800   767

China: From the Ming to the Mid-Manchu Dynasty (ca 1368–1795)   768
Japan (ca 1400–1800)   782

25 THE REVOLUTION IN WESTERN POLITICS, 1775–1815   795

Liberty and Equality   796
The American Revolution (1775–1789)   798
The French Revolution (1789–1791)   802
World War and Republican France (1791–1799)   810
The Napoleonic Era (1799–1815)   817

26 THE INDUSTRIAL REVOLUTION IN EUROPE   827

The Initial Breakthrough in England   828
Energy and Transportation   839
Industrialization in Continental Europe   846
Capital and Labor   852

27 IDEOLOGIES AND UPHEAVALS IN EUROPE, 1815–1850   863

Peace Settlement   864
Radical Ideas and Early Socialism   871
The Romantic Movement   876
Reforms and Revolutions   881
The Revolutions of 1848   887

28 LIFE IN EUROPEAN URBAN SOCIETY   897

Taming the City   898
Rich and Poor and In Between   906
The Family   914
Science and Thought   921

29 THE AGE OF NATIONALISM IN EUROPE, 1850–1914   929

Napoleon III in France   930
Nation Building in Italy and Germany   933
The Modernization of Russia   942
The Responsive National State (1871–1914)   945
Marxism and the Socialist Movement   953

30 THE WORLD AND THE WEST   959

Industrialization and the World Economy   960
The Great Migration   968
Western Imperialism   972
Responses to Western Imperialism   981

31 NATION BUILDING IN THE WESTERN HEMISPHERE AND IN AUSTRALIA   991

Latin America (1800–1929)   992
The United States (1789–1929)   1006
Canada: From French Colony to Nation   1023
Australia: From Penal Colony to Nation   1026

32 THE GREAT BREAK: WAR AND REVOLUTION   1037

The First World War   1038
The Home Front   1049
The Russian Revolution   1054
The Peace Settlement   1060

33 NATIONALISM IN ASIA, 1914–1939   1071

The First World War and Western Imperialism   1072
The Middle East   1075

Toward Self-Rule in India 1084

Turmoil in East Asia 1090

34   THE AGE OF ANXIETY IN THE WEST 1105

Uncertainty in Modern Thought 1106

Modern Art and Culture 1113

The Search for Peace and Political Stability 1118

The Great Depression (1929–1939) 1123

35   DICTATORSHIPS AND THE SECOND WORLD WAR 1133

Authoritarian and Totalitarian States 1134

Stalin's Russia 1138

Mussolini's Italy 1145

Hitler's Germany 1148

Nazi Expansion and the Second World War 1155

36   RECOVERY AND CRISIS IN EUROPE AND THE AMERICAS 1169

The Cold War (1942–1953) 1170

The Western European Renaissance 1174

Soviet Eastern Europe 1187

The Western Hemisphere 1200

37   ASIA AND AFRICA IN THE CONTEMPORARY WORLD 1213

The Resurgence of East Asia 1214

New Nations in South Asia and the Muslim World 1222

Imperialism and Nationalism in Black Africa 1234

Black Africa Since 1960 1241

38   LIFE IN THE THIRD WORLD 1253

Defining the Third World 1254

Economic and Social Challenges in the Third World 1255

The Growth of Cities 1266

Mass Culture and Contemporary Thought 1273

39   ONE SMALL PLANET 1283

World Politics 1284

Global Interdependence 1293

Patterns of Thought 1304

Contents

Contents in Brief   vi

Maps   xxiii

Timelines/Genealogies   xxvi

Preface   xxviii

Acknowledgments   xxxii

Expanding Horizons: Mapmaking in the World   xxxiii

1

ORIGINS   3

What Is History and Why?   4

The First Human Beings   6

The Paleolithic Age   8

The Neolithic Age   9

Rivers, Resources, and Civilizations   13

Mesopotamian Civilization   15
     Environment and Mesopotamian Culture · Sumerian Society

The Spread of Mesopotamian Culture   18
     The Triumph of Babylon · The Invention of Writing and the First Schools · Mesopotamian Thought and Religion

Daily Life in Mesopotamia   23

Egypt, the Land of the Pharaohs (3100–1200 B.C.)   25
     The God-King of Egypt · The Pharaoh's People · The Hyksos in Egypt (1640–1570 B.C.) · The New Kingdom: Revival and Empire (1570–1200 B.C.) · Akhenaten and Monotheism

The Hittite Empire   32
     The Rise of the Hittites · Hittite Society · The Era of Hittite Greatness (ca 1475–ca 1200 B.C.)

The Fall of Empires (1200 B.C.)   35

Summary   36

Notes   36

Suggested Reading   36

2

SMALL KINGDOMS AND MIGHTY EMPIRES IN THE NEAR EAST   39

Migrations   40

Egypt, a Shattered Kingdom   40

The Children of Israel and Their Neighbors   42
     The Evolution of Jewish Religion · Daily Life in Israel

Assyria, the Military Monarchy   49
     The Rise of Assyrian Power · Assyrian Rule

The Empire of the Persian Kings   52
     The Land of Mountains and Plateau · The Coming of the Medes and Persians · The Creation of the Persian Empire · Thus Spake Zarathustra · Persia's World Empire

Summary   60

Notes   60

Suggested Reading   60

3

ANCIENT INDIA TO CA A.D. 200   63

The Land and Its First Tamers (ca 2500–1500 B.C.)   64

The Ascendancy of the Aryans (ca 1500–500 B.C.)   68
     The Shaping of Indian Society · Early Indian Religion

India's Spiritual Flowering   73
     Hinduism · Jainism · Siddhartha Gautama and Buddhism

India and the West (ca 513–298 B.C.)   78

The Mauryan Empire (ca 322–232 B.C.)   80
     The Reign of Ashoka (ca 269–232 B.C.) · India and Its Invaders (ca 250 B.C.–A.D. 200)

Summary   84

Notes   84

Suggested Reading   84

4

THE RISE AND GROWTH OF CHINA TO CA A.D. 200   87

The Land and Its Challenge   88

The Shang Dynasty (ca 1523–1027 B.C.)   89
Social Organization · Origins of Chinese Writing

The Triumph of the Chou (ca 1027–221 B.C.)   92
The Rule of the Chou · Social Change and Cultural Advancement in the Chou Period

The Birth of Chinese Philosophy   94

Confucianism   94
Taoism · Legalism · *I Ching* and Yin and Yang

The Age of Empire   99
The Ch'in and Unification of China · Foreign Danger and Internal Unrest · The Glory of the Han Dynasty (206 B.C.–A.D. 220) · Han Confucianism and Intellectual Revolt · Daily Life During the Han Dynasty · The Fall of Han China

Summary   110
Notes   110
Suggested Reading   111

5

THE LEGACY OF GREECE   115

Hellas: The Land   116

The Minoans and Mycenaeans (ca 1650–ca 1100 B.C.)   118

Homer and the Heroic Past (1100–800 B.C.)   120

The Polis   121

The Lyric Age (800–500 B.C.)   123
Overseas Expansion · Lyric Poets · The Growth of Sparta · The Evolution of Athens

The Classical Period (500–338 B.C.)   128
The Deadly Conflicts (499–404 B.C.) · Athenian Arts in the Age of Pericles · Daily Life in Periclean Athens · The Flowering of Philosophy · The Final Act (403–338 B.C.)

Summary   144

Notes   144
Suggested Reading   144

6

HELLENISTIC DIFFUSION   147

Alexander and the Great Crusade   148

The Spread of Hellenism   150
Cities and Kingdoms · The Greeks and the Opening of Asia and Africa · Greeks and Easterners

The Economic Scope of the Hellenistic World   155
Commerce · Industry · Agriculture

Religion in the Hellenistic World   158

Philosophy and the Common Man   159
Cynics · Epicureans · Stoics

Hellenistic Women   161

Hellenistic Science   162

Hellenistic Medicine   165

Summary   168
Notes   168
Suggested Reading   168

7

THE RISE OF ROME   171

The Land and the Sea   172

The Etruscans and Rome (753–509 B.C.)   174

The Roman Conquest of Italy (509–290 B.C.)   175

The Roman State   176

Social Conflict in Rome   178

The Age of Overseas Conquest (282–146 B.C.)   179

Old Values and Greek Culture   182
Cato and the Traditional Ideal · Scipio: Greek Culture and Urban Life

The Late Republic (133–27 B.C.)   187

Summary   192
Notes   192
Suggested Reading   192

8

THE PAX ROMANA   195

Augustus's Settlement (31 B.C.–A.D. 14)   196
  The Principate and the Restored Republic · Augustus's Administration of the Provinces · Roman Expansion into Northern
  and Western Europe · Literary Flowering

The Coming of Christianity   202

The Julio-Claudians and the Flavians
(27 B.C.–A.D. 96)   207

The Age of the "Five Good Emperors"
(A.D. 96–180)   208
  The Antonine Monarchy · Changes in the
  Army

Life in the "Golden Age"   210
  Imperial Rome · The Provinces

Rome and the East   214
  Romans Versus Iranians · Trade and
  Contact

Civil Wars and Invasion in the Third
Century   217

Reconstruction Under Diocletian and
Constantine (A.D. 284–337)   218
  Inflation and Taxes · The Legalization of
  Christianity · The Construction of Con-
  stantinople

Summary   224
Notes   224
Suggested Reading   224

9

THE MAKING OF EUROPE   229

The Growth of the Christian Church   230
  The Church and the Roman Emperors ·
  Inspired Leadership · Missionary Activ-
  ity · Conversion and Assimilation

Christian Attitudes Toward Classical
Culture   238
  Hostility · Compromise and Adjust-
  ment · Synthesis: Saint Augustine

Monasticism and the Rule of
Saint Benedict   241
  Beginnings · The Rule of Saint Benedict · The Success of Benedictine Monasticism

The Migration of the Germanic Peoples   244
Germanic Society   248
  Kinship, Custom, and Class · Law ·
  German Life · Anglo-Saxon England

The Byzantine East (ca 400–1000)   252
  The Separation of Byzantine East and Ger-
  manic West · External Threats and Internal
  Conflicts · The Law Code of Justinian ·
  Intellectual Life · Private Life

Summary   259
Notes   260
Suggested Reading   260

10

THE ISLAMIC WORLD, CA 600–1400   263

The Arabs Before Islam   264
Muhammad and the Faith of Islam   265
The Expansion of Islam   268
  Expansion to the West · Expansion to the
  East · Reasons for the Spread of Islam

Consolidation of the Islamic State   273
  The Caliphate · Administration of the
  Islamic State

Decentralization of the Islamic State   277
  Decline of the Abbasids · The Assault of
  the Turks and Mongols

The Life of the People   279
  The Classes of Society · Women in Classical
  Islamic Society · Sufism · Trade and Com-
  merce · Urban Centers · Intellectual
  Life · The Muslim View of the West

Summary   293
Notes   294
Suggested Reading   295

11

TRADITION AND CHANGE
IN ASIA, CA 320–1400   297

India, from Triumph to Invasion
(ca 320–1400)   298
  The Gupta Empire (ca 320–480) · Daily
  Life in India · India and Southeast Asia ·
  India Under Siege

China's Golden Age (580–ca 1400) 309

    Buddhism Reaches China · The T'ang Dynasty (618–907) · The Sung Dynasty (960–1279) · Cultural Blossoming of the T'ang and Sung · The Mongol Conquest (1215–1368)

Japan, Dawn of the Rising Sun 322

    The Japanese Islands · Early Japan and the Yamato State · The Heian Era (794–1185) · The Land and the Samurai · The Kamakura Shogunate (1185–1333)

Summary 330
Notes 330
Suggested Reading 330

12
EUROPE IN THE EARLY AND HIGH MIDDLE AGES 333

The Frankish Aristocracy and the Rise of the Carolingian Dynasty 334
The Empire of Charlemagne 336

    Territorial Expansion · The Government of the Carolingian Empire · The Imperial Coronation of Charlemagne (800)

The Carolingian Intellectual Revival 341

    Northumbrian Culture · The Carolingian Renaissance

Health and Medical Care in the Early Middle Ages 344
Division and Disintegration of the Carolingian Empire (814–987) 346
Feudalism 347

    The Two Levels of Feudalism · Manorialism

Great Invasions of the Ninth Century 350
Political Revival 352

    The Decline of Invasion and Civil Disorder · Increasing Population and Mild Climate

Revival and Reform in the Christian Church 355

    Monastic Decline and Revival · Reform of the Papacy

The Gregorian Revolution 359

Pope Gregory VII's Ideas · The Controversy over Lay Investiture · The Papacy in the High Middle Ages

The Crusades 362
Summary 367
Notes 367
Suggested Reading 368

13
LIFE IN CHRISTIAN EUROPE IN THE HIGH MIDDLE AGES 373

Those Who Work 374

    Slavery, Serfdom, and Upward Mobility · The Manor · Agricultural Methods · Life on the Manor · Popular Religion

Those Who Fight 385

    Infancy and Childhood · Power and Responsibility

Those Who Pray 392

    Recruitment · The Nuns · Prayer and Other Work · Economic Difficulties

Summary 398
Notes 399
Suggested Reading 400

14
CREATIVITY AND CRISIS IN THE HIGH AND LATER MIDDLE AGES 403

Medieval Origins of the Modern State 404

    Unification and Communication · Finance · Law and Justice

Economic Revival 417

    The Rise of Towns · Town Liberties · Town Life · The Revival of Long-Distance Trade · The Commercial Revolution

Medieval Universities 426

    Origins · Instruction and Curriculum

The Creative Outburst 429

    From Romanesque Gloom to "Uninterrupted Light" · Community Expression · Vernacular Literature

Heresy and the Friars 434

The Black Death 437

Pathology · Social and Psychological Consequences

The Hundred Years' War (ca 1337–1453) 441

The Popular Response · The Course of the War to 1419 · Joan of Arc and France's Victory · Costs and Consequences

The Decline of the Church's Prestige 446

The Babylonian Captivity · The Great Schism · The Conciliar Movement

The Life of the People 448

Marriage · Life in the Parish · Peasant Revolts

Summary 456

Notes 456

Suggested Reading 458

15

AFRICA BEFORE EUROPEAN INTRUSION, CA 400–1500 461

The Land and Peoples of Africa 462

Early African Societies 464

African Kingdoms in the Western Sudan (ca 1000 B.C.–A.D. 200) 465

The Trans-Saharan Trade 466

African Kingdoms and Empires (ca 800–1450) 468

The Kingdom of Ghana (ca 900–1100) · The Kingdom of Mali (ca 1200–1450) · The East African City-States · Ethiopia: The Christian Kingdom of Axum · South Africa

Summary 482

Notes 482

Suggested Reading 482

16

THE AMERICAS BEFORE EUROPEAN INTRUSION, CA 400–1500 485

The Geography and Peoples of the Americas 486

Mesoamerican Civilizations from the Olmec to the Toltec 487

The Olmec · The Maya of Central America · Teotihuacán and Toltec Civilizations

Aztec Society: Religion and War 493

War and Human Sacrifice · The Life of the People · The Cities of the Aztecs

The Incas of Peru 498

Inca Imperialism · Inca Society

Summary 503

Notes 503

Suggested Reading 504

17

EUROPEAN SOCIETY IN THE AGE OF THE RENAISSANCE AND REFORMATION 507

The Evolution of the Italian Renaissance 508

Communes and Republics · The Balance of Power Among the Italian City-States

Intellectual Hallmarks of the Renaissance 512

Individualism · The Revival of Antiquity · A New Secular Spirit

Art and the Artist 515

Art and Power · The Status of the Artist

Social Change 519

Education and Political Thought · The Printed Word · Women in Renaissance Society · Blacks in Renaissance Society

The Renaissance in the North 524

Politics and the State in the Renaissance (1450–1521) 528

France · England · Spain · Germany and the Rise of the Habsburg Dynasty

The Condition of the Church (1400–1517) 535

Signs of Disorder · Signs of Vitality

Martin Luther and the Birth of Protestantism 537

The Ninety-five Theses · Protestant Thought · The Social Impact of Luther's Beliefs · The Political Impact of Luther's Beliefs

The Growth of the Protestant Reformation 545

Calvinism · The Anabaptists · The English
Reformation

The Catholic and the Counter-
Reformations   553

    The Slowness of Institutional Reform · The
Council of Trent · New Religious Orders ·
The Sacred Congregation of the Holy
Office

Summary   557

Notes   558

Suggested Reading   559

18

THE AGE OF EUROPEAN EXPANSION AND RELIGIOUS WARS   563

Discovery, Reconnaissance, and Expansion   565

    Overseas Exploration and Conquest · The
Explorers' Motives · Technological Stimuli
to Exploration · The Conquest of Aztec
Mexico and Inca Peru · The South American Holocaust · Colonial Administration ·
The Economic Effects of Spain's Discoveries
in the New World · Seaborne Trading Empires · The Chinese and Japanese Discovery
of the West

Politics, Religion, and War   579

    The Origins of Difficulties in France
(1515–1559) · Religious Riots and Civil
War in France (1559–1589) · The Nether-
lands Under Charles V · The Revolt of the
Netherlands (1566–1587) · Philip II and
the Spanish Armada · The Thirty Years'
War (1618–1648) · Germany After the
Thirty Years' War

Changing Attitudes   593

    The Status of Women · The Great Euro-
pean Witch Hunt · European Slavery and
the Origins of American Racism · The Origin of Modern Skepticism: Michel de Montaigne

Elizabethan and Jacobean Literature   599

Baroque Art and Music   601

Summary   603

Notes   603

Suggested Reading   604

19

ABSOLUTISM AND CONSTITUTIONALISM IN EUROPE, CA 1589–1725   607

Absolutism: An Overview   608

France: The Model of Absolute
Monarchy   609

    The Foundations of French Absolutism:
Henry IV and Richelieu · The Absolute
Monarchy of Louis XIV · Financial and
Economic Management Under Louis XIV:
Colbert · Revocation of the Edict of
Nantes · French Classicism · Louis XIV's
Wars

The Decline of Absolutist Spain in the
Seventeenth Century   619

Lords and Peasants in Eastern
Europe (ca 1050–1650)   621

    The Medieval Background · The Consoli-
dation of Serfdom

The Rise of Austria and Prussia   624

    Austria and the Ottoman Turks · Prussia in
the Seventeenth Century · The Consolidation of Prussian Absolutism

The Development of Russia   633

    The Vikings and the Kievan Principal-
ity · The Mongol Yoke and the Rise of
Moscow · Tsar and People to 1689 · The
Reforms of Peter the Great

Absolutism and the Baroque in Eastern
Europe   639

    Palaces and Power · Royal Cities · The
Growth of St. Petersburg

Constitutionalism: An Overview   643

England: The Triumph of Constitutional
Monarchy   643

    The Decline of Royal Absolutism in Eng-
land (1603–1649) · Puritanical Absolutism
in England: Cromwell and the Protectorate · The Restoration of the English Monarchy · Constitutional Monarchy and
Cabinet Government

The Dutch Republic in the Seventeenth
Century   649

Summary   653

Notes   654

Suggested Reading   655

20

TOWARD A NEW WORLD VIEW IN THE WEST 659

The Scientific Revolution 660
Scientific Thought in 1500 · The Copernican Hypothesis · From Tycho Brahe to Galileo · Newton's Synthesis · Causes of the Scientific Revolution · Some Consequences of the Scientific Revolution

The Enlightenment 669
The Emergence of the Enlightenment · The Philosophes and Their Ideas · The Later Enlightenment · The Social Setting of the Enlightenment

The Development of Absolutism 679
The "Greats": Frederick of Prussia and Catherine of Russia · Absolutism in France and Austria · An Overall Evaluation

Summary 688
Notes 688
Suggested Reading 689

21

THE LIFE OF THE PEOPLE IN EUROPE 691

Agriculture and Population 692
Working the Land · The Balance of Numbers · The Growth of Cottage Industry

Marriage and the Family 699
Extended and Nuclear Families · Work Away from Home · Premarital Sex and Birth-Control Practices · New Patterns of Marriage and Illegitimacy

Women and Children 704
Child Care and Nursing · Foundlings and Infanticide · Attitudes Toward Children · Schools and Education

Food and Medicine 709
Diets and Nutrition · The Impact of Diet on Health · New Foods and New Knowledge · The Medical Professionals · Hospitals and Mental Illness · Medical Experiments and Research

Religion and Christian Churches 717
The Institutional Church · Catholic Piety · Protestant Revival

Summary 722
Notes 722
Suggested Reading 722

22

AFRICAN KINGDOMS AND SOCIETIES, CA 1450–1800 725

Senegambia and Benin 726
The Sudan: Songhay, Kanem-Bornu, and Hausaland 728
Ethiopia 731
The Swahili City-States 732
The Transatlantic Slave Trade 734

Summary 740
Notes 741
Suggested Reading 741

23

THE MIDDLE EAST AND INDIA, CA 1450–1800 743

The Splendor of the Ottoman State 744
The Persian Theocratic State 751
India: From Mughal Domination to British Dominion (ca 1498–1805) 753
The Rule of the Mughals · European Rivalry for the Indian Trade · Factory-Fort Societies · The Rise of the British East India Company

Summary 762
Notes 763
Suggested Reading 763

24

CHINA AND JAPAN, CA 1400–1800 767

China: From the Ming to the Mid-Manchu Dynasty (ca 1368–1795) 768
The Ming Agricultural and Commercial Revolutions · The Government of Hung Wu · Maritime Expansion · Decline of the

Ming Dynasty · Manchu Rule · The Life
of the People

Japan (ca 1400–1800)   782
Feudalism in Japan · Nobunaga and
National Unification · The Tokugawa
Regime · The Life of the People

Summary   791

Notes   791

Suggested Reading   792

25

THE REVOLUTION IN WESTERN POLITICS, 1775–1815   795

Liberty and Equality   796
The Roots of Liberalism · The Attraction
of Liberalism

The American Revolution (1775–1789)   798
The Origins of the Revolution · Independ-
ence · Framing the Constitution · The
Revolution's Impact on Europe

The French Revolution (1789–1791)   802
The Breakdown of the Old Order · Legal
Orders and Social Realities · The Forma-
tion of the National Assembly · The Revolt
of the Poor and the Oppressed · A Limited
Monarchy

World War and Republican France
(1791–1799)   810
Foreign Reactions and the Beginning of
War · The Second Revolution · Total War
and the Terror · The Thermidorian
Reaction and the Directory (1794–1799)

The Napoleonic Era (1799–1815)   817
Napoleon's Rule of France · Napoleon's
Wars and Foreign Policy

Summary   823

Notes   823

Suggested Reading   824

26

THE INDUSTRIAL REVOLUTION IN EUROPE   827

The Initial Breakthrough in England   828

Eighteenth-Century Origins · The Agricul-
tural Revolution · The Cost of Enclosure ·
The Growth of Foreign Trade · Land and
Wealth in North America · The First
Factories

Energy and Transportation   839
The Problem of Energy · The Steam
Engine Breakthrough · The Coming of
the Railroads · Industry and Population

Industrialization in Continental Europe   846
National Variations · The Challenge of
Industrialization · Agents of Industrial-
ization

Capital and Labor   852
The New Class of Factory Owners ·
The New Factory Workers · Condi-
tions of Work · The Sexual Division of
Labor

Summary   860

Notes   860

Suggested Reading   861

27

IDEOLOGIES AND UPHEAVALS IN EUROPE, 1815–1850   863

Peace Settlement   864
The Congress of Vienna · Intervention
and Repression · Metternich and Conservatism

Radical Ideas and Early Socialism   871
Liberalism · Nationalism · French Utopian
Socialism · The Birth of Marxian Socialism

The Romantic Movement   876
Romanticism · Literature · Art and Music

Reforms and Revolutions   881
National Liberation in Greece · Liberal
Reform in Great Britain · The Revolution
of 1830 in France

The Revolutions of 1848   887
A Democratic Republic in France · The
Austrian Empire in 1848 · Prussia and the
Frankfurt Assembly

Summary   894

Notes   894

Suggested Reading   894

28

LIFE IN EUROPEAN URBAN SOCIETY 897

Taming the City 898
Industry and the Growth of Cities · The Public Health Movement · The Bacterial Revolution · Urban Planning and Public Transportation

Rich and Poor and In Between 906
Social Structure · The Middle Classes · The Working Classes

The Family 914
Premarital Sex and Marriage · Prostitution · Kinship Ties · Women and Family Life · Child Rearing

Science and Thought 921
The Triumph of Science · Social Science and Evolution · Realism in Literature

Summary 925
Notes 926
Suggested Reading 926

29

THE AGE OF NATIONALISM IN EUROPE, 1850–1914 929

Napoleon III in France 930
The Second Republic and Louis Napoleon · Napoleon III's Second Empire

Nation Building in Italy and Germany 933
Italy to 1850 · Cavour and Garibaldi · Germany Before Bismarck · Bismarck Takes Command · The Austro-Prussian War of 1866 · The Taming of Parliament · The Franco-Prussian War of 1870 to 1871

The Modernization of Russia 942
The "Great Reforms" · The Industrialization of Russia · The Revolution of 1905

The Responsive National State (1871–1914) 945
The German Empire · Republican France · Great Britain and Ireland · The Austro-Hungarian Empire

Marxism and the Socialist Movement 953
The Socialist International · Unions and Revisionism

Summary 956
Notes 956
Suggested Reading 956

30

THE WORLD AND THE WEST 959

Industrialization and the World Economy 960
The Rise of Global Inequality · Trade and Foreign Investment · The Opening of China and Japan · Western Penetration of Egypt

The Great Migration 968
The Pressure of Population · European Migrants · Asian Migrants

Western Imperialism 972
The Scramble for Africa · Imperialism in Asia · Causes of the New Imperialism · Critics of Imperialism

Responses to Western Imperialism 981
Empire in India · The Example of Japan · Toward Revolution in China

Summary 988
Notes 988
Suggested Reading 988

31

NATION BUILDING IN THE WESTERN HEMISPHERE AND IN AUSTRALIA 991

Latin America (1800–1929) 992
The Origins of the Revolutions · Race in the Colonial Period · The Comunero Revolution · Independence · The Consequences of Independence · Neocolonialism · The Impact of Immigration

The United States (1789–1929) 1006
Manifest Destiny · The Fate of the Indians · Black Slavery in the South · Westward Expansion and Civil War · The Black Family · Industrialization and Immigration

Canada: From French Colony to Nation 1023

British Colony (1763–1839) · The Age of
Confederation (1840–1905) · Growth,
Development, and National Maturity

Australia: From Penal Colony
to Nation   1026

Penal Colony · Economic Development ·
From Colony to Nation

Summary   1033

Notes   1033

Suggested Reading   1034

32

THE GREAT BREAK: WAR AND
REVOLUTION   1037

The First World War   1038

The Bismarckian System of Alliances · The
Rival Blocs · The Outbreak of War · Re-
flections on the Origins of the War · The
First Battle of the Marne · Stalemate and
Slaughter · The Widening War

The Home Front   1049

Mobilizing for Total War · The Social
Impact · Growing Political Tensions

The Russian Revolution   1054

The Fall of Imperial Russia · The Provisional Government · Lenin and the Bolshevik Revolution · Trotsky and the Seizure of
Power · Dictatorship and Civil War

The Peace Settlement   1060

The End of the War · Revolution in Germany · The Treaty of Versailles · American
Rejection of the Versailles Treaty

Summary   1066

Notes   1066

Suggested Reading   1067

33

NATIONALISM IN ASIA, 1914–1939   1071

The First World War and Western
Imperialism   1072

The Middle East   1075

The First World War and the Arab Revolt · The Turkish Revolution · Iran and
Afghanistan · The Arab States and Palestine

Toward Self-Rule in India   1084

Promises and Repression (1914–1919) ·
Hindu Society and Mahatma Gandhi · The
Roots of Militant Nonviolence · Gandhi
Leads the Way

Turmoil in East Asia   1090

The Rise of Nationalist China · China's
Intellectual Revolution · The Changing
Chinese Family · From Liberalism to Ultra-
nationalism in Japan · Japan Against
China · Southeast Asia

Summary   1102

Notes   1102

Suggested Reading   1103

34

THE AGE OF ANXIETY IN THE WEST   1105

Uncertainty in Modern Thought   1106

Modern Philosophy · The Revival of Christianity · The New Physics · Freudian Psychology · Twentieth-Century Literature

Modern Art and Culture   1113

Architecture and Design · Modern Painting · Modern Music · Movies and Radio

The Search for Peace and Political
Stability   1118

Germany and the Western Powers · The
Occupation of the Ruhr · Hope in Foreign
Affairs (1924–1929) · Hope in Democratic
Government

The Great Depression (1929–1939)   1123

The Economic Crisis · Mass Unemployment · The New Deal in the United
States · The Scandinavian Response to Depression · Recovery and Reform in Britain
and France

Summary   1130

Notes   1130

Suggested Reading   1130

35

DICTATORSHIPS AND THE SECOND
WORLD WAR   1133

Authoritarian and Totalitarian States   1134

Conservative Authoritarianism · Modern
Totalitarianism · Totalitarianism of the Left
and the Right

Stalin's Russia — 1138

From Lenin to Stalin · The Five-Year
Plans · Life in Stalinist Society · Women in
Soviet Russia

Mussolini's Italy — 1145

The Seizure of Power · The Regime in
Action

Hitler's Germany — 1148

The Roots of Nazism · Hitler's Road to
Power · The Nazi State and Society ·
Hitler's Popularity

Nazi Expansion and the Second
World War — 1155

Aggression and Appeasement
(1933–1939) · Hitler's Empire
(1939–1942) · The Grand Alliance · The
Tide of Battle

Summary — 1166

Notes — 1166

Suggested Reading — 1167

36

RECOVERY AND CRISIS IN EUROPE
AND THE AMERICAS — 1169

The Cold War (1942–1953) — 1170

The Origins of the Cold War · West Versus
East

The Western European Renaissance — 1174

The Postwar Challenge · Economic "Miracles" · Toward European Unity · Decolonization · The Changing Class Structure ·
Political Upheaval in the Late 1960s · The
Troubled Economy in Recent Times

Soviet Eastern Europe — 1187

Stalin's Last Years · Reform and De-Stalinization · Brezhnev and Stagnation · The
Gorbachev Era · The Revolutions of 1989

The Western Hemisphere — 1200

Postwar Prosperity in the United
States · The Civil Rights Revolution · The
Vietnam Trauma and Beyond · Economic
Nationalism in Latin America · The Cuban
Revolution · Authoritarianism and Democ-
racy in Latin America

Summary — 1209

Notes — 1210

Suggested Reading — 1210

37

ASIA AND AFRICA IN THE
CONTEMPORARY WORLD — 1213

The Resurgence of East Asia — 1214

The Communist Victory in China · Mao's
China · The Limits of Reform · Japan's
American Revolution · "Japan, Inc."

New Nations in South Asia and the
Muslim World — 1222

The Indian Subcontinent · Southeast
Asia · The Muslim World

Imperialism and Nationalism in Black
Africa — 1234

The Imperial System (1900–1930) · The
Growth of African Nationalism · Achieving
Independence with New Leaders · Ghana
Shows the Way · French-speaking Regions

Black Africa Since 1960 — 1241

Building National Unity · Nigeria, Africa's
Giant · The Struggle in Southern Africa

Summary — 1250

Notes — 1250

Suggested Reading — 1250

38

LIFE IN THE THIRD WORLD — 1253

Defining the Third World — 1254

Economic and Social Challenges in the
Third World — 1255

Poverty · The Medical Revolution and the
Population Explosion · The Race to Industrialize (1950–1970) · Agriculture and Village Life

The Growth of Cities — 1266

Urbanization in the Third World · Overcrowding and Shantytowns · Rich and
Poor · Migration and the Family

Mass Culture and Contemporary
Thought — 1273

Education and Mass Communications · Interpreting the Experiences of the Emerging World

Summary	1277
Notes	1278
Suggested Reading	1278

39
ONE SMALL PLANET   1283

World Politics	1284

Nation-States and the United Nations · Complexity and Violence · The Arms Race and Nuclear Proliferation

Global Interdependence	1293

Pressure on Vital Resources · North-South Relations · The Multinational Corporations

Patterns of Thought	1304

Secular Ideologies · Religious Belief: Christianity and Islam · Searching for Mystical Experience

Summary	1310
Notes	1310
Suggested Reading	1310
Chapter Opener Credits	C-1
Notes on the Illustrations	C-2
Index	I-1

Maps

1.1	Spread of Cultures in the Ancient Near East	11
1.2	River-Valley Civilizations	12
1.3	Ancient Egypt	26
1.4	Balance of Power in the Near East	33
2.1	Small Kingdoms in the Near East	42
2.2	The Assyrian Empire	50
2.3	The Persian Empire	53
3.1	The Development of India, ca 2500 – ca 250 B.C.	65
4.1	China Under the Shang and Chou Dynasties, 1523–221 B.C.	89
4.2	China Under the Han Dynasty, 206 B.C. – A.D. 220	101
5.1	Ancient Greece	117
5.2	Colonization of the Mediterranean	123
5.3	The Peloponnesian War	130
5.4	Ancient Athens	132
6.1	Alexander's Conquests	149
6.2	The Hellenistic World	152
7.1	Italy and the City of Rome	173
7.2	Roman Expansion During the Republic	180
8.1	Roman Expansion Under the Empire	200
8.2	Roman Britain	210
8.3	The Economic Aspect of the Pax Romana	213
8.4	The Major Empires of Central and Southern Asia, ca 250 B.C.	215
8.5	The Roman World Divided	219
9.1	The Spread of Christianity	234
9.2	The Germanic Migrations	246
9.3	Anglo-Saxon England	251
10.1	The Expansion of Islam to 733	270
10.2	Islamic Expansion to 1500	271
11.1	Political Map of India, ca 400–ca 1294	299
11.2	The States of Southeast Asia	305
11.3	The Political Divisions of China from the T'ang to Yuan Dynasties, 618–1368	312
11.4	The Islands of Japan, ca 1185	323
12.1	The Carolingian World	338
12.2	Division of the Carolingian Empire, 843	347
12.3	The Great Invasions of the Ninth Century	351
12.4	The Routes of the Crusades	364
14.1	Domesday Population and Agriculture, 1086	406
14.2	The Growth of the Kingdom of France	408
14.3	The Holy Roman Empire, ca 1200	410
14.4	Trade and Manufacturing in Medieval Europe	422
14.5	Intellectual Centers of Medieval Europe	427
14.6	The Course of the Black Death in Fourteenth-Century Europe	437

14.7   English Holdings in France During the Hundred
        Years' War   443
14.8   Fourteenth-Century Peasant Revolts   454
15.1   Africa Before 1500   463
15.2   The Kingdom of Mali   473
15.3   Trade Routes Between East Africa and India   479
16.1   The Maya World, A.D. 300–900   489
16.2   The Aztec Empire, 1519   493
16.3   The Inca Empire, 1463–1532   499
17.1   The Italian City-States, ca 1494   511
17.2   The Christianization and Unification of Spain   532
17.3   The European Empire of Charles V   534
17.4   The Protestant and the Catholic Reformations   544
18.1   Overseas Exploration and Conquest in the
        Fifteenth and Sixteenth Centuries   566
18.2   Seaborne Trading Empires in the Sixteenth and
        Seventeenth Centuries   576
18.3   The Netherlands, 1578–1609   584
18.4   Europe in 1648   590
18.5   The African Slave Trade   597
19.1   The Acquisitions of Louis XIV, 1668–1713   618
19.2   Europe in 1715   620
19.3   The Growth of Austria and Brandenburg-Prussia
        to 1748   627
19.4   The Expansion of Russia to 1725   632
19.5   Seventeenth-Century Dutch Commerce   652
20.1   The Partition of Poland and Russia's Expansion,
        1772–1795   683
21.1   Industry and Population in Eighteenth-Century Europe   700
21.2   Literacy in France on the Eve of the French Revolution   709
22.1   West African Kingdoms and Slave Trade, ca 1500–1800   727
22.2   East Africa, Sixteenth Century   732
23.1   The Ottoman Empire at Its Height, 1566   748
23.2   The Safavid Empire   751
23.3   India, 1707–1805   758
24.1   China: Ch'ing Empire, 1759   778
24.2   Tokugawa Japan   787
25.1   Napoleonic Europe in 1810   820
26.1   Cottage Industry and Transportation in
        Eighteenth-Century England   829
26.2   The Economy of the Atlantic Basin in 1701   834
26.3   European Claims in North America Before and After
        the Seven Years' War, 1756–1763   837
26.4   The Industrial Revolution in England, ca 1850   845
26.5   Continental Industrialization, ca 1850   849
27.1   Europe in 1815   866
27.2   Peoples of the Habsburg Monarchy, 1815   870
28.1   European Cities of 100,000 or More, 1800 and 1900   899
28.2   The Modernization of Paris, ca 1850–1870   905
29.1   The Unification of Italy, 1859–1870   934
29.2   The Unification of Germany, 1866–1871   939

30.1	European Investment to 1914	964
30.2	The Partition of Africa	974
30.3	Asia in 1914	976
30.4	The Expansion and Modernization of Japan, 1868–1918	986
31.1	Latin America Before Independence	994
31.2	Latin America in 1830	998
31.3	Territorial Growth of the United States	1008
31.4	Indian Cession of Lands to the United States	1011
31.5	Slavery in the United States, 1860	1014
31.6	Australia	1027
32.1	The Balkans After the Congress of Berlin, 1878	1043
32.2	The Balkans in 1914	1043
32.3	The First World War in Europe	1048
32.4	Shattered Empires and Territorial Changes After the First World War	1065
33.1	The Partition of the Ottoman Empire, 1914–1923	1078
33.2	The Chinese Communist Movement and the War with Japan	1099
34.1	The Great Depression in the United States, Britain, and Europe	1124
35.1	The Growth of Nazi Germany, 1933–1939	1156
35.2	The Second World War in Europe	1160
35.3	The Second World War in the Pacific	1164
36.1	Europe After the Second World War	1175
36.2	European Alliance Systems	1179
36.3	The New States in Africa and Asia	1180
36.4	Soviet Peoples	1193
36.5	Democratic Movements in Eastern Europe, 1989	1196
37.1	The Partition of British India, 1947	1224
37.2	Modern Islam, ca 1990	1230
37.3	Palestine, Israel, and the Middle East, 1947–1990	1231
37.4	Nationalism and Independence in West Africa	1244
37.5	The Republic of South Africa and Apartheid, ca 1960	1247
38.1	World Population Density	1259
39.1	The Persian Gulf War	1288
39.2	OPEC and the World Oil Trade	1297
39.3	World Drug Trade	1298
39.4	Estimated GNP per Capita Income in the Early 1980s	1300

Timelines/Genealogies

Periods of Egyptian History	31
Ancient Near East	57
India to ca A.D. 200	79
China to ca A.D. 400	109
Africa and the Middle East, the Americas, East Asia, *India and Southeast Asia, and Europe: 10,000 B.C.–500 B.C.*	112–113
Periods of Greek History	142
Spread of Hellenism	165
The Roman Republic	189
Roman History After Augustus	222
Africa and the Middle East, the Americas, East Asia, *India and Southeast Asia, and Europe: 500 B.C.–A.D. 200*	226–227
The Origins of Europe	255
The Islamic World, ca 600–1258	275
India, ca 320–ca 1400	309
China, ca 320–ca 1400	316
Japan, ca 320–ca 1400	328
Europe in the Middle Ages	363
Africa and the Middle East, the Americas, East Asia, *India and Southeast Asia, and Europe: A.D. 200–1200*	370–371
The Emergence of States	415
Africa, ca 400–1500	480
The Americas, ca 400–1500	500
The Later Middle Ages, Renaissance, and Protestant and Catholic Reformations, 1300–1600	548–549
The French Bourbon Succession, 1515–1715	583
The Habsburg Succession, 1493–1637	589
The Rise of Western Absolutism and Constitutionalism	628
The Rise of Absolutism in Eastern Europe	629
The Enlightenment	686
Africa and the Middle East, the Americas, East Asia, *India and Southeast Asia, and Europe: 1200–1700*	764–765
The French Revolution	816
The Napoleonic Era	818
The Prelude to 1848	884
The Revolutions of 1848	891
The Spread of Nationalism in Europe, 1850–1914	952
The Spread of Western Imperialism	980
Latin America, ca 1760–1900	1004
The Russian Revolution	1058
Africa and the Middle East, the Americas, East Asia, *India and Southeast Asia, and Europe: 1700–1920*	1068–1069
The Middle East, 1914–1939	1084
East Asia, 1911–1939	1095
Events Leading to World War Two	1154

Asia Since 1945   1227
Nationalism in Black Africa   1239
Africa and the Middle East, the Americas, East Asia,
   India and Southeast Asia, and Europe: 1920–1990   1280–1281

Note: *Italics* indicate comparative tables.

Preface

A HISTORY OF WORLD SOCIETIES grew out of the authors' desire to infuse new life into the study of world civilizations. We knew full well that historians were using imaginative questions and innovative research to open up vast new areas of historical interest and knowledge. We also recognized that these advances had dramatically affected the subject of economic, intellectual, and, especially, social history, while new research and fresh interpretations were also revitalizing the study of the traditional mainstream of political, diplomatic, and religious development. Despite history's vitality as a discipline, however, it seemed to us that both the broad public and the intelligentsia were generally losing interest in the past. The mathematical economist of our acquaintance who smugly quipped "What's new in history?"— confident that the answer was nothing and that historians were as dead as the events they examine—was not alone.

It was our conviction, based on considerable experience introducing large numbers of students to the broad sweep of civilization, that a book reflecting current trends could excite readers and inspire a renewed interest in history and the human experience. Our strategy was twofold. First, we made social history the core element of our work. Not only did we incorporate recent research by social historians, but also we sought to re-create the life of ordinary people in appealing human terms. A strong social element seemed to us especially appropriate in a world history, for identification with ordinary people of the past allows today's reader to reach an empathetic understanding of different cultures and civilizations. At the same time we were determined to give great economic, political, intellectual, and cultural developments the attention they unquestionably deserve. We wanted to give individual readers and instructors a balanced, integrated perspective, so that they could pursue on their own or in the classroom those themes and questions that they found particularly exciting and significant.

Second, we made a determined effort to strike an effective global balance. We were acutely aware of the great drama of our times—the passing of the European era and the simultaneous rise of Asian and African peoples in world affairs. Increasingly, the whole world interacts, and to understand that interaction and what it means for today's citizens we must study the whole world's history. Thus we adopted a comprehensive yet realistic global perspective. We studied all geographical areas and the world's main civilizations, conscious of their separate identities and unique contributions. Yet we also stressed the links between civilizations, for these links eventually transformed multicentered world history into a complex interactive process of different continents, peoples, and civilizations in recent times. Finally, it was our place neither to praise nor to vilify our own civilization's major role in the growth of global integration, accepting it rather as part of our world heritage and seeking to understand it and the consequences for all concerned. Four years ago, in an effort to realize fully the potential of our fresh yet balanced perspective, we made many changes, large and small, in the second edition.

Changes in the New Edition

In preparing the third edition we have worked hard to keep our book up-to-date and to make it still more effective. First, we have carefully examined the entire book and each of its sections for organization, clarity, and balance. Above all, the treatment of non-European societies has been expanded and enriched, while the history of European developments has been tightened and condensed. In the new edition, therefore, the history of Africa from 400 to 1500 receives a full chapter-length treatment in Chapter 15, permitting a more extensive analysis of early African kingdoms, and an expanded discussion of Mesoamerican civilizations is included in Chapter 16, the Americas before European intrusion. Similarly, in order to do justice to the complex developments occurring in Africa and western Asia in the early modern period, Africa is discussed in Chapter 22 of the new edition and the Middle East and India are the subject of Chapter 23.

As for Europe, Chapter 14 now brings together the history of the high and later Middle Ages in a single chapter. The emergence of royal absolutism and constitutionalism in western and eastern Europe in the early modern period is similarly combined in a reorganized and more sharply focused Chapter 19. For greater clarity, recent social developments in the West have been integrated into the larger, fully up-dated discussion of recovery and crisis in Europe after 1945 in Chapter 36. This chapter covers the transforming events in eastern Europe of recent years, including the revolutions of 1989.

Other major changes include a new section on the study of history and the meaning of civilization in Chapter 1. Islam and Islamic societies receive expanded and reworked coverage throughout the book. Chapter 34 contains a revised discussion of twentieth-century intellectual trends that emphasizes the connection between these movements and subsequent political developments, and Chapter 35 provides a unified account of the Second World War. With these changes and with numerous modifications highlighting cross-cultural linkages, we feel we have improved the geographical and cultural balance of our text and written a more integrated and effective world history.

Second, every chapter has been carefully revised to incorporate recent scholarship. Many of our revisions relate to the ongoing explosion in social history, and once again important findings on such subjects as class relations, population, and the family have been integrated into the text. We have made a special effort to keep up with the rapidly growing and increasingly sophisticated scholarship being done in women's history, adding or revising sections on women in early Jewish society and in the Crusades, as well as in the Renaissance, the Reformation, and the Industrial Revolution. The roots of modern feminism have been explored. The revised discussion of the origins and early development of Islam reflects recent scholarship, as does the extended reconsideration of the Ottomans and their cultural and intellectual achievements. Japanese feudalism is also reconsidered in the light of current scholarly thinking.

A major effort has also been made to improve the treatment of economic development and accompanying social changes in the light of new re-

search and fresh concepts. We are proud of the resulting changes, which include a consideration of early Islamic capitalism and agricultural innovation in Chapter 10, a new discussion of early modern crises in Chapter 19, a reexamination of the social and demographic effects of the slave trade in Africa in Chapter 22, and a fundamental rethinking of European industrialization in Chapter 26 and its global significance in Chapter 30. Other subjects not mentioned above that incorporate new scholarship in this edition include early human evolution, Germanic tribes, the Inquisition, industrial progress in early modern China, French industrialization and utopian socialism, and the development of modern Arab nationalism. New topics designed to keep the work fresh and appealing include *I-Ching* thinking in ancient China, Greek federalism, Sufism in the Islamic world, the early European reaction to knowledge of China and Japan, the settlement and the emergence of Australia, reform and revolution in the Soviet Union and eastern Europe in the 1980s, and the recent breakthrough in the struggle for racial equality in South Africa.

Third, the addition of more problems of historical interpretation in the second edition was well received, and we have continued in that direction in this edition. We believe that the problematic element helps the reader develop the critical-thinking skills that are among the most precious benefits of studying history. New examples of this more open-ended, more interpretive approach include the significance of Chinese economic development in the eighteenth century (Chapter 24), the social costs of English enclosure and the impact of industrialization on women and the standard of living (Chapter 26), and the impact of slavery on the black family in the United States (Chapter 31).

Finally, the illustrative component of our work has been completely revised. There are many new illustrations, including nearly two hundred color reproductions that let both great art and important events come alive. As in earlier editions, all illustrations have been carefully selected to complement the text, and all carry captions that enhance their value. Artwork remains an integral part of our book, for the past can speak in pictures as well as in words.

The use of full color throughout this edition also serves to clarify the maps and graphs and to enrich the textual material. Again for improved clarity, maps from the second edition have been completely redesigned to provide easily read and distinguished labels and prominent boundaries and topographical relief. We have also added new maps that illustrate social as well as political developments, including maps on Europe at 1715, the Safavid Empire, the ethnic and political boundaries of the Soviet republics, the reform movements of 1989 in eastern Europe, the world drug trade, and the Persian Gulf War.

In addition to the many maps that support text discussion, we offer a new, full-color map essay at the beginning of each volume. Our purpose is twofold. First, by reproducing and describing such cartographic landmarks as the Babylonian world map, the Islamic al-Idrisi map, the medieval Ebstorf map, the twelfth-century map of China, maps of the Americas and Africa based on Ptolemy and Mercator, the Japanese world map of 1645, and contemporary global projections and satellite images, we hope to demonstrate for students the evolution of cartography and to guide them toward an understanding of the varied functions and uses of maps. Second, the map essay is intended to show depictions of the world from different cultural perspectives and to reveal the changing concepts of our world and its interrelated parts from antiquity to the present. In a real sense, the map essay may serve as an introduction to the course as well as to cartography.

Distinctive Features

Distinctive features from earlier editions remain in the third. To help guide the reader toward historical understanding we have posed specific historical questions at the beginning of each chapter. These questions are then answered in the course of the chapter, each of which concludes with a concise summary of the chapter's findings. The timelines have proved useful, and the double-page comparative timelines, which allow students to compare simultaneous developments within different world areas, have been revised and updated.

We have also tried to suggest how historians actually work and think. We have quoted extensively from a wide variety of primary sources and have demonstrated in our use of these quotations how historians sift and weigh evidence. We want the reader to think critically and to realize that history is neither a list of cut-and-dried facts nor a sense-

less jumble of conflicting opinions. It is our further hope that the primary quotations, so carefully fitted into their historical context, will give the reader a sense that even in the earliest and most remote periods of human experience, history has been shaped by individual men and women, some of them great aristocrats, others ordinary folk.

Each chapter concludes with carefully selected suggestions for further reading. These suggestions are briefly described to help readers know where to turn to continue thinking and learning about the world. The chapter bibliographies have been revised and expanded to keep them current with the vast and complex new work being done in many fields.

World civilization courses differ widely in chronological structure from one campus to another. To accommodate the various divisions of historical time into intervals that fit a two-quarter, three-quarter, or two-semester period, *A History of World Societies* is published in three versions, each set embracing the complete work:

One-volume hardcover edition, A HISTORY OF WORLD SOCIETIES; a two-volume paperback, A HISTORY OF WORLD SOCIETIES *Volume I: To 1715* (Chapters 1–19), *Volume II: Since 1500* (Chapters 18–39); and a three-volume paperback, A HISTORY OF WORLD SOCIETIES *Volume A: From Antiquity Through the Middle Ages* (Chapters 1–16), *Volume B: From 1100 Through the French Revolution* (Chapters 14–25), *Volume C: From the French Revolution to the Present* (Chapters 25–39).

Note that overlapping chapters in the two- and three-volume sets permit still wider flexibility in matching the appropriate volume with the opening and closing dates of a course term.

Ancillaries

Learning and teaching ancillaries, including a *Study Guide, MicroStudy Plus* (a computerized version of the *Study Guide*), *Instructor's Resource Manual, Test Items, MicroTest* (a computerized version of the *Test Items*), and *Map Transparencies,* also contribute to the usefulness of the text. The excellent *Study Guide* has been thoroughly revised by Professor James Schmiechen of Central Michigan University. Professor Schmiechen has been a tower of strength ever since he critiqued our initial prospectus, and he has continued to give us many valuable suggestions and his warmly appreciated support. His *Study Guide* contains chapter summaries, chapter outlines, review questions, extensive multiple-choice exercises, self-check lists of important concepts and events, and a variety of study aids and suggestions. New to the third edition are study-review exercises on the interpretation of visual sources and major political ideas as well as suggested issues for discussion and essay and chronology reviews. Another major addition is the section, Understanding the Past Through Primary Sources. Seven primary source documents widely used by historians are included, each preceded by a description of the author and source and followed by questions for analysis. The *Study Guide* also retains the very successful sections on studying effectively. These sections take the student by ostensive example through reading and studying activities like underlining, summarizing, identifying main points, classifying information according to sequence, and making historical comparisons. To enable both students and instructors to use the *Study Guide* with the greatest possible flexibility, the guide is available in two volumes, with considerable overlapping of chapters. Instructors and students who use only Volumes A and B of the text have all the pertinent study materials in a single volume, *Study Guide, Volume 1* (Chapters 1–25); likewise, those who use only Volumes B and C of the text also have all the necessary materials in one volume, *Study Guide, Volume 2* (Chapters 14–39).

The multiple-choice sections of the *Study Guide* are also available as *MicroStudy Plus,* a computerized, tutorial version that tells students not only which response is correct but also why each of the other choices is wrong and provides the page numbers of the text where each question is discussed. *MicroStudy Plus* is available for both IBM and Macintosh computers.

The *Instructor's Resource Manual,* prepared by Professor John Marshall Carter of Oglethorpe University, contains learning objectives, chapter synopses, suggestions for lectures and discussion, paper and class activity topics, and lists of audiovisual resources. Professor Carter also offers suggestions for the instructor who is teaching world history for the first time. The accompanying *Test Items,* by Professor Charles Crouch of St. John's University in Collegeville, Minnesota, offer identification, multiple-choice, and essay questions for a total of approximately two thousand test items. These test items are available to adopters in both IBM and Macintosh versions, both of which include editing capabilities. In addition, a set of full-color *Map Transparencies* of all the maps in the text is available on adoption.

JOHN P. MCKAY

BENNETT D. HILL

JOHN BUCKLER

Acknowledgments

It is a pleasure to thank the many instructors who have read and critiqued the manuscript through its development:

Martin Berger
Youngstown State University

Elton Daniel
University of Hawaii, Manoa

Ronald Davis
Western Michigan University

Joseph Dorinson
Long Island University

Surjit Dulai
Michigan State University

Bruce Garver
University of Nebraska, Omaha

Robert Gowen
East Carolina University

Bruce Haight
Western Michigan University

Hines Hall
Auburn University

Deanna Haney
Lansing Community College

Eugene Huck
Kennesaw State College

Margaret Hutton
Jackson State University

Jim Jackson
Point Loma Nazarene College

Gregory Kozlowski
DePaul University

Glenn Nichols
Sul Ross State University

William Ochsenwald
Virginia Polytechnic Institute and State University

Donathan Olliff
Auburn University

Oliver Pollak
University of Nebraska, Omaha

Donald Reid
Georgia State University

John Ruedy
Georgetown University

Lowell Satre
Youngstown State University

Martin Seedorf
Eastern Washington University

Anita Shelton
Eastern Illinois University

Sara Sohmer
University of Hawaii, Manoa

Alexander Sydorenko
Arkansas State University

Joanne Van Horne
Fairmont State College

James Weland
Bentley College

Many colleagues at the University of Illinois provided information and stimulation for our book, often without even knowing it. N. Frederick Nash, Rare Book Librarian, gave freely of his time and made many helpful suggestions for illustrations. The World Heritage Museum at the University continued to allow us complete access to its sizable holdings. James Dengate kindly supplied information on objects from the museum's collection. Caroline Buckler took many excellent photographs of the museum's objects and generously helped us at crucial moments in production. We greatly appreciate such wide-ranging expertise. Bennett Hill wishes to express his sincere appreciation to Ramón de la Fuente of Washington, D.C., for his support, encouragement, and research assistance in the preparation of this third edition.

Each of us has benefited from the generous criticism of his co-authors, although each of us assumes responsibility for what he has written. John Buckler has written Chapters 1–8 and 11; Bennett Hill has continued the narrative in Chapters 9–10, 12–18, part of 19, 23–24, and 31; and John McKay has written part of 19 and Chapters 20–21, 25–30, and 32–39. Finally, we continue to welcome from our readers comments and suggestions for improvements, for they have helped us greatly in this ongoing endeavor.

Expanding Horizons: Mapmaking in the World

Today cartography, the art of making maps, is as widespread as typography, the process of printing. Maps are so much a part of daily life that people take them for granted. But people are not born with maps in their heads, as they are with fingers on their hands. The very concept of a map is a human invention of vast intellectual and practical importance. Like writing itself, cartography depends on people's use of visual and symbolic means to portray reality. Earth is not a flat table. Instead it is marked by features such as mountains, valleys, rivers, and oceans and by the distances that separate them all. Knowledge of these physical features and the accurate mapping of them allow people to understand their relationship to the planet on which they live.

Cartographers contribute something singular to the understanding of peoples. Human beings, no matter where they live, have a natural curiosity about their world and find joy in discovering new parts of it or in learning more about regions not well known. The Roman statesman and orator Cicero once asked, "Ubinam gentium sumus?" ("Where in the world are we?") Although he used this question as a figure of speech, many people have been quite serious about finding an accurate answer to it. Such curiosity and desire have led people to examine not only the earth but its relation to the cosmos of which it is a part. Early cartographers learned to use the stars as fixed points for the measurement of place and distance. Even today American nuclear submarines depend on

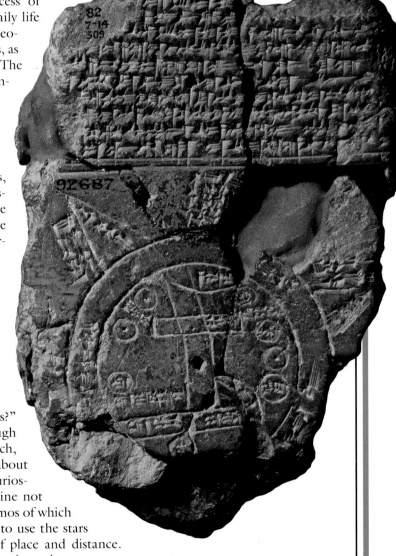

MAP 1 Babylonian world map, ca 600 B.C. (*Source: Courtesy of the Trustees of the British Museum*)

celestial navigation, transmitted by satellite, to determine their course and position. Once people looked to the stars, they began to wonder about the shape, nature, and content of the universe itself. Mapping of the earth was no longer enough; people began to chart the cosmos. The Hubble space satellite, launched in May 1990, is a sign that the quest continues today.

For ordinary purposes cartography fills a host of practical needs. Maps were first used to describe people's immediate environment—to illustrate the shape of villages and the boundaries of fields. As knowledge of the earth grew, maps became indispensable for travel, both on land and at sea. It was necessary for people to know where their destination lay, how to reach it, and what to expect along the way. Mariners used the geographical knowledge provided by maps to sail from one port to another.

Other uses of early maps were economic. As people came into contact with one another, they saw new opportunities for barter and trade. It was no longer enough to know how to travel to different locations. Merchants needed to understand the geography of their markets and to know what foreign lands produced and what trading partners wanted in return for their goods. In short, economic contact itself increased knowledge of the face of the land, and that knowledge could be preserved on maps by symbols to indicate the natural resources and products of various lands.

Another important function of early maps was military. Rulers and generals needed information about distances and the terrain through which their armies would move and fight. This need spurred interest in *topography,* the detailed description and representation of the natural and artificial features of a landscape, and led to greater accuracy of maps and better definition of the physical environment.

The demands of empire were not only military but also administrative. An area cannot be governed effectively unless the ruler knows where each part of it is located and what its importance is. Rulers need precise maps to enforce their authority, dispatch commands, collect taxes, and maintain order. Thus the value to historians of some maps lies in their illustration of people's knowledge of the world in relation to the needs of government and the exercise of authority over broad distances.

Those are only a few of the uses of cartography. But what of the maps themselves? How do cartographers visually and accurately depict large sections of land or the entire face of the globe? The ways are numerous and some more exact than others.

The earliest maps are pictures of towns showing spatial relationships within a very limited area. A more accurate way of making a map was derived from land surveys. Beginning about 1500 B.C., surveyors trained in geometry and trigonometry began to study the land in question and to divide its physical features into a series of measured angles and elevations. Cartographers then placed this information on a grid so that they could represent visually, according to a consistent and logical system, relations among areas. Although the method sounds simple, it presented a daunting problem, one that still exists. Mapmakers must represent on a two-dimensional surface the face of a three-dimensional globe. To complicate matters even further, the earth is not a perfect sphere. How cartographers have grappled with these problems can be seen from the maps reproduced here.

Since maps are basically visual, it is best to trace their evolution in their own context. People of all cultures have mapped their lands, and in many cases their approaches have been strikingly similar. The earliest known representation of the world is a Babylonian world map that dates to about 600 B.C. (Map 1). It is not a map of the entire globe, for the Babylonians were ignorant of the existence of many people beyond their immediate frontiers. Instead, Babylon, with its neighbors around it, lies at the center of the world. Surrounding the land is the ocean, depicted as a circle. The triangles beyond the ocean indicate that the Babylonians knew something of the peoples beyond the ocean. Here for the first time is evidence of a people who attempted to put themselves geographically into the context of their larger world.

The greatest geographer of the Greco-Roman period was Claudius Ptolemaeus, better known as Ptolemy, who lived in Alexandria in the second century A.D. He advanced far beyond the schematic Babylonian world map to produce a scientific atlas based on data. He knew from previous scholars that the world was spherical, so he devised a way of using conic lines of *longitude,* angular distances east and west, and *latitude,* angular distances north and south, to plot the positions and distances of the earth's features. Despite its distortions, Ptolemy's *Geographia* became the standard Western work on geography until Europeans sailed out to explore the broader world around them (ca 1450–1650). The best illustration of Ptolemy's brilliant vision actually dates much later than its first representation. It dates to a manuscript produced in the German city of Ulm in 1482 (Map 2). Ptolemy put cartography on a scientific basis.

Some of the fruits of Ptolemy's labor can be seen in the series of maps known as the Peutinger Table, which probably dates to ca A.D. 500. The Table is a good example of how cartography served the Roman Empire. The section shown here is typical of the entire series: it indicates roads, rivers, mountains, cities, and towns in Greece (Map 3). In that respect it is an ancient road map, for its purpose was not to define the known world, as Ptolemy had done, but to inform the emperor and his bureaucracy how they could most easily administer and communicate with the provinces. Although alien to modern notions of the shape of Europe, the Peutinger Table is a remarkably accurate atlas of routes and distances and thus displays vividly and beautifully one of the most practical functions of cartography. The table received its name from Konrad Peutinger of Augsburg, an owner of the maps in the sixteenth century.

Islamic cartographers also drew heavily on Ptolemy's research, but they relied on exploration as well. The most famous of them as al-Idrisi, who lived in the twelfth century. His atlas depicted the entire known world and was accompanied by a

MAP 2 Map from Ptolemy's *Geographica (Source: Michael Holford)*

MAP 3 Section of the Peutinger Table illustrating Greece, ca A.D. 500 *(Source: Oster-reichische Nationalbibliothek)*

MAP 4 Portion of the map of al-Idrisi, thirteenth century *(Source: Reproduced by per-mission of Norman J. W. Thrower, Department of Geography, UCLA)*

MAP 5 Ebstorf Map, thirteenth century *(Source: Niedersächsische Landesbibliothek Hannover)*

written commentary about the places illustrated. The portion shown here represents the eastern Mediterranean and the Middle East (Map 4). As in the Peutinger Table, physical features such as rivers and mountains are stylized, but al-Idrisi made a serious effort to delineate the general features of the landmass. His map looks different from modern maps because he used south as his basic point of orientation, not north as do modern cartographers. As a result, the atlas appears upside down to our eyes, with south being at the top of the map.

Europeans in the Middle Ages, like their predecessors, drew maps of the world, but religion became an ingredient of cartography. Ptolemy's concepts of geography remained in force, but maps also served another and different purpose for society. The Ebstorf Map, drawn during the thirteenth century, shows the world surrounded by the ocean, a conception dating to antiquity (Map 5). Yet the map has several novel features. In its background is the crucified Jesus. His head, portrayed at the top, signifies the east. His outstretched arms point north and south. His feet, at the bottom, signify the west. Jerusalem occupies the center of the map to represent the place of Jesus's death as the center of the Christian world. The Ebstorf Map, unlike the practical maps of the Peutinger Table, was intended to convey a religious message, a declaration of faith.

Like the Romans, the Chinese early found it necessary to draw maps to administer efficiently the vast tracts of land under their control. The Chinese so successfully mastered the problem of reducing a huge amount of territory into a visually manageable scale that in the twelfth century they produced the Yü Chi Thu Map (Map of the Tracks of Yü the Great) (Map 6). Although the name of the geographer is unknown, his achievement is monumental. He used a system of uniform square grids to locate features of the land in exact and measured relationship to one another. The outline of the coast and the courses of the rivers are remarkably accurate. As in the case of early European maps of Africa (see Map 10), knowledge of the interior was somewhat scanty. Nonetheless, the geographer devised a reliable system in which new discoveries could be easily fitted into what was already known.

In the Americas, maps were sometimes put to a novel use. The pre-Columbian picture map (Map 7) at first sight does not look like a map at all. Dating from sometime before the sixteenth century, it portrays the history of the Mixtec people of Mexico, who can be traced from about 800. Geographical features are incidental to the historical narrative. Nevertheless, the map amply demonstrates the originality of the pre-Columbian Americans in the art of mapmaking.

Meanwhile, the people of the European Middle Ages continued to draw maps along the lines set out by Ptolemy, yet they made improvements on the work of the master. Indeed, they explored the concept of triangulation to survey the land and to navigate the seas. Cartographers chose several major points to serve as hubs of a series of lines extended to other major points. The face of the globe was thereby cut up into a pattern of triangles, rectangles, and occasionally squares. Al-

Map 6 After the Yü Chi Thu Map, twelfth century *(Source: Pei Lin Museum, Sian, China)*

MAP 7 The Dominions of Quetzalcoatl 9 Wind, *Lord of the Toltecs. From the Codex Zouche-Nuttall (Source: Courtesy of the Trustees of the British Museum (Museum of Mankind))*

though this system proved complicated and unwieldy, triangulation did improve the utility of maps for explorers. An excellent example of a triangulated map comes from the Catalan Atlas of 1375 (Map 8). The atlas is more functional than other early maps because the cartographer indicated orientation, so that users could locate their position according to the points of a compass.

Only when the Europeans began to explore the broader world around them did they make significant advances over Ptolemy's view of the world. Sailors and navigators who voyaged to find new lands or to learn more about familiar places had to be able to calculate where they were. They knew that the world was curved, and they used the stars as fixed points to guide them. It is thus ironic that one of the most important advances in geographic knowledge came by mistake. In 1492 Christopher Columbus, looking for a sea passage to India, discovered the New World by sailing westward from Europe. Although Columbus himself did not immediately recognize the full significance of his achievement, his discovery revolutionized geographical thinking: there was more to the world than Ptolemy had known; and the basic features of the earth had to be explored, relationships rethought, and a new way of looking at the globe found.

Perhaps nothing better indicates the fluid state of geography and cartography at the end of the fifteenth century than Juan de la Cosa's map of Columbus's second voyage to the Americas (Map 9). A navigator and an explorer, de la Cosa charted the newly found coast of Central America using the points of the compass to orient the fall of the land and triangulation to project his findings inland. Although he could depict the coastline accurately because of direct observation, he could reveal little about the land beyond.

The discoveries of the European explorers opened a new era in the West and throughout the rest of the world, both in how people thought of the world and in how mapmakers depicted the new findings. These pioneers were also on the threshold of uniting European, American, and Asian traditions of cartography. The real breakthrough came with Geradus Mercator (1512–1594). Mercator improved Ptolemy's system of latitude and longitude by substituting straight lines for Ptolemy's curved lines. In that respect, Mercator's cartographic organization was similar to that used by the Chinese geographer of the Yü Chi Thu Map, but Mercator's plan applied over the face of the globe. Mercator used this grid to incorporate the discoveries in a completely new atlas. Admittedly, his method distorts the actual physical relations of the landmasses over broad spaces. Areas in the polar regions appear larger than lands near the equator. For instance, Greenland on his grid is larger than South America. More important, however, Mercator showed that every portion of the world may be portrayed as possessing four right angles to orient users of any one of his maps to any portion of his other maps. Mercator's grid, in one form or another, endures as a cartographic staple to this day.

The cumulative effects of the advance of knowledge in geography and cartography can best be

MAP 8   Catalan Atlas of 1375 *(Source: Bibliothèque Nationale, Paris/Photo Hubert Josse)*

MAP 9 Juan de la Cosa's map of Columbus's discoveries, 1493 *(Source: Museo Naval de Madrid)*

MAP 10 Blaeu's map of Africa, from *Grooten Atlas*, 1648–65 *(Source: The British Library, Department of Maps)*

seen in two maps that demonstrate increasing familiarity with Africa. The map of Dutch cartographer Willem Blaeu, dating to the early seventeenth century, brings together the concepts of scale maps and picture maps (Map 10). Explorers had an accurate idea only of the shape of the continent. The inland was *terra incognita,* unknown territory where dwelt fabulous beasts and peoples. The amazing progress of human knowledge of the land and how to map it can be seen by comparing Blaeu's map of Africa with the one of French cartographer Jean-Baptiste d'Anville published in 1747 (Map 11). D'Anville made excellent use of Mercator's system to produce a profile of Africa that could find its place in any modern atlas. Yet

d'Anville was intellectually honest enough to leave the interior of Africa largely blank. D'Anville's map is not so visually delightful as Blaeu's, but in terms of cartography it is far more important. It showed its users what was yet to be discovered and how to proceed with finding it.

European penetration of Asia excited another desire for maps. In 1822 the Frenchman J. B. J. Gentil published a map of India (Map 12) that bears some slight similarity to Blaeu's earlier map of Africa. The map, which dates from 1770, is actually a drawing by an Indian of Chadjeanabad province. Like Blaeu's map, it contains drawings of animals, fruits, and costumes of the local natives. It is also similar to the pre-Columbian map of the

MAP 11 D'Anville's map of Africa, 1747 *(Source: Library of Congress, Department of Maps)*

MAP 12 Map of Chadjeanabad province, India, 1770 *(Source: The British Library, Oriental and India Office Collections)*

MAP 13 Shanawdithit's map of central Newfoundland, 1829 *(Source: Newfoundland Museum)*

MAP 14 Kiangsi province in southeast China, eighteenth century *(Source: The British Library, Department of Maps)*

dominions of Quetzalcoatl (see Map 7) in that it possesses little geographical significance. Yet it portrays many of the salient human, zoological, and botanical features of the region.

An excellent example of the combination of pictorial and geographical features of a landscape comes from a map drawn in 1829 by Shanawdithit, a woman who was the last of the Beothuk Indians of Newfoundland (Map 13). This historico-pictorial map depicts the trek of her tribe crossing an ice-covered lake along the Exploits River in central Newfoundland. It tells the story of the journey while giving an impression of the geographical features of the land through which she and her people passed.

A beautiful early-eighteenth-century Chinese map of Kiangsi province (Map 14) shows a single prefecture, at the center of which is a walled town. The mapmaker carefully depicted the features of Kiangsi, to the point of showing individual buildings in their geographical setting. Thus the nature of the landscape, both rivers and mountains, is pictorially displayed, not as on a map but rather as a view seen from above. Although this is a picture-map, unlike the more technical map by al-Idrisi (see Map 4), it gives the user a vivid sense of the landscape.

Interesting by contrast is the Bankoku Sozu (or World Map) drawn in Japan in 1645, a half-century earlier than the Chinese map of Kiangsi.

MAP 15 Bankoku Sozu, Map of the World, 1645 *(Source: Kobe City Museum)*

This map (Map 15) resembles Ptolemy's map of the world in its definition of landmasses, their configurations, and their major features. Like d'Anville (see Map 11), the Japanese cartographer indicated candidly—in the legends at the top and bottom of the map—that geographical knowledge of these regions was hazy because few people had explored them. Yet in its basics the concept behind this map is Ptolemy's. Both were more interested in portraying the nature of the landmass and the physical relation of one place to another than in drawing a picture of the landscape.

Mapmakers still grapple with the problem of accurately depicting landmasses—their shapes and their spatial relationships—on an earth that is not a perfect sphere. No matter what projection they use, some geographical areas are distorted. In struggling with this problem, cartographers have used circles, ovals, and rectangles to display regions of the earth on a flat surface. The orthographic projection (the circular maps at the four corners of Map 16) uses circles and is one of the oldest projections. Because it shows only one hemisphere at a time, distortion is minimized, especially at the center of the map, where attention is focused. It allows a realistic view of the globe, but it makes possible the display of only one hemisphere at a time. One way to minimize distortion while showing more than one hemisphere is to represent the tops of the poles as lines rather than as points, as shown in the Robinson projection (the center image of Map 16). There is still some distortion (note how large Antarctica is), but cutting off the poles diminishes it. The Robinson projection is a compromise because it sacrifices some accuracy in area to achieve less distortion in shape.

Modern attempts to depict visually the nearly spherical earth on flat maps remind people that the problems first perceived by early cartographers remain to be solved. Yet contemporary cartographers enjoy the use of a new and unusual tool for

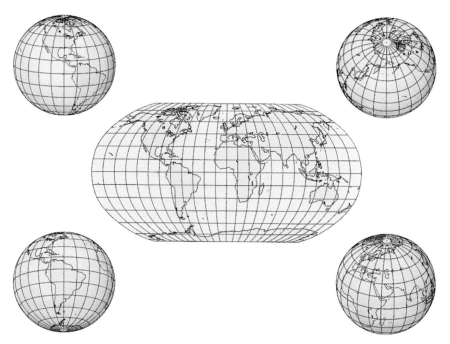

MAP 16 The Robinson projection (*Source: Reproduced with permission from WHICH MAP IS BEST? © 1988, by the American Congress on Surveying and Mapping*)

MAP 17 Landsat image of Brazil *(Source: GEOPIC™, Earth Satellite Corporation)*

mapping the globe and exploring the universe: the orbiting satellite. Technology has become so precise within the past ten years that the parts of the earth difficult to enter or too remote and forbidding to explore can be examined with minute accuracy from space. The Landsat satellite image of Brazil (Map 17) gives an excellent idea of how much more there is to learn about the earth.

JOHN BUCKLER

SUGGESTED READING

Bagrow, Leo. *History of Cartography.* 2d ed. Chicago: Precedent Publishing, 1985. Brown, Lloyd A. *The Story of Maps.* New York: Dover, 1979. Dilke, O. A. W. *Greek and Roman Maps.* Ithaca: Cornell University Press, 1985. Harley, J. B., and D. Woodward, eds. *The History of Cartography,* Vol. 1: *Cartography in Prehistoric, Ancient and Medieval Europe and the Mediterranean.* Chicago: University of Chicago Press, 1967. Harvey, Paul D. A. *The History of Topographical Maps.* London: Thames & Hudson, 1980. Hodgkiss, Alan G. *Understanding Maps: A Systematic History of Their Use and Development.* Folkestone, England: Dawson, 1981. Skelton, Raleigh A. *Decorative Printed Maps of the Fifteenth to Eighteenth Centuries.* London: Staples Press, 1952, reprinted by Spring Books, 1970. Skelton, Raleigh A. *Explorers' Maps: Chapters in the Cartographic Record of Geographical Discovery.* London: Routledge and Kegan Paul, 1958, reprinted by Spring Books, 1970. Thrower, Norman J. W. *Maps & Man: An Examination of Cartography in Relation to Culture and Civilization.* Englewood Cliffs, N.J.: Prentice-Hall, 1978, Tooley, R. V., Cand Bricker, and G. R. Crone. *A History of Cartography: 2500 Years of Maps and Mapmakers.* London: Thames & Hudson, 1969.

1

Origins

Peace panel from the Royal Standard of Ur

*B*efore the dawn of history, bands of people across the earth gradually developed numerous cultures, each unique in some ways while at the same time having features in common. Especially important to the history of the world are events that took place in the ancient Near East (Mesopotamia, Anatolia, and Egypt), India, and China, where human beings abandoned the life of roaming and hunting to settle in stable agricultural communities. From these communities grew cities and civilizations, societies that invented concepts and techniques now integral to contemporary life. Fundamental is the independent development of writing by the Sumerians in Mesopotamia and by the Chinese, an invention that enabled knowledge to be preserved and facilitated the spread and accumulation of learning, lore, literature, and science. Mathematics, astronomy, and architecture were all innovations of ancient civilizations. So, too, were the first law codes and religious concepts, which still permeate daily life across the globe.

- How did nomadic hunters become urban dwellers?
- What geographical factors influenced this change?
- How do geographical factors explain both the elements common to different cultures and the features that differentiate them?

These questions serve as themes for the first four chapters. Chapters 1 and 2 look at how ancient Near Eastern civilizations helped to shape modern Western society. Chapters 3 and 4 explore the response of the peoples of ancient India and China to these same questions.

WHAT IS HISTORY AND WHY?

History is an effort to reconstruct the past to discover what people thought and did and how their beliefs and actions continue to influence human life. In order to appreciate the past fully, we must put it into perspective so that we can understand the factors that have helped to shape us as individuals, the society in which we live, and the nature of other peoples' societies. Why else should we study periods so separated from ours through

time, distance, and culture as classical Greece, medieval India, early Japan, and modern Russia and Africa? Although most of the people involved in these epochs are long dead, what they did has touched everyone alive today.

The matter of perspective is more important than simple. In a perfect world all human experience would be equally valuable for its own sake, even if it had little or no impact on the mainstream of history. Yet the evidence on which historians depend for their understanding of the past is far from perfect. Some peoples have left so few traces of themselves that they cannot be understood even in their own right, much less in connection with others. Excellent examples of this problem are the Tocharians, an Indo-European-speaking people who lived in central Asia during the first millennium A.D. What they were doing there in the first place and how they related to their neighbors are complete mysteries. Such peoples for the moment remain historical enigmas, best left to specialists while other historians examine the principal currents of human development. Historical perspective demands that most attention be devoted to peoples who are best known in their own context and to how they have contributed to history.

Historians begin to reconstruct the past by posing questions about it. How and why, for example, did cities emerge? How did the political system of a particular society evolve? How did people create an economic system to sustain a complex society? What were a society's religious beliefs, and how did they influence daily life? Historians ask these kinds of questions to guide their research and focus their approach to the past.

To answer such questions, historians examine *primary sources,* the firsthand accounts of people who lived through the events—men and women who were in the best position to know what happened. Thus historians most commonly rely on the written record of human experience because, no matter how extensive the physical remains of a civilization may be, much of its history remains a mystery if it has not left records that we can read. Until we are able to decipher the written texts left by the ancient civilization of Minoan Crete, for example, we can draw only vague conclusions about its history. Nonetheless, the historian's responsibility is to examine all of the evidence, including visual evidence. Examined properly, visual sources provide a glimpse of the world as contemporaries saw it. Especially in conjunction with written documents, art can be a valuable and striking means of understanding the past. Similarly, archeology has proved a valuable avenue to the past, whether an excavation uncovers an ancient Greek city, a medieval temple, or a modern factory building. Things as dissimilar as beautiful paintings and ordinary machines tell historians much about the ways in which people have lived and worked.

In the fifth century B.C., a Greek named Herodotus wrote the first truly historical account of people and events in an effort to understand a great conflict between the Persians and the Greeks. Herodotus, now considered the "father of history," wrote that he was publishing an "inquiry" into the past. The Greek word that he used for "inquiry" was *historia,* from which we derive the word *history.* The two concepts of inquiry and history, first joined by Herodotus, became inseparable, and their connection is as valid today as when Herodotus wrote.

When studying sources—the most basic activity in research—historians assess the validity and perspective of each account. They try to determine whether sources are honest and accurate, generally by comparing and contrasting the testimony of several different observers. They criticize sources externally, to attempt to uncover forgeries and errors; and they criticize sources internally, to find an author's motives for writing, inconsistencies within a document, biases, and even cases of outright lying. Some contemporary written accounts, especially from ancient and medieval periods, have been lost; they are known to posterity only because people who read the originals later incorporated the information into their own writings. Historians analyze the viewpoints and accuracy of such *secondary sources* very carefully; these derivative writings have preserved much history that otherwise would have been lost. For the modern period historians have a vast supply of contemporary accounts of events, memoirs, personal letters, economic statistics, and government reports, all of them useful for an understanding of the past.

Once historians have pieced together what happened and have determined the facts, they interpret what they have found. Understanding the past does not necessarily come easily. Because no two historical events are precisely alike, history, unlike the exact physical sciences, cannot reproduce experiments under controlled conditions. A historian cannot put people into test tubes. Men, women, and children—the most complex organisms on this planet—are not as predictable as atoms or hydrocarbons.

To complicate matters, for many epochs only the broad outlines are known, so interpretation is especially difficult. For example, historians know that the Hittite Empire collapsed at the height of its power, but interpretations of the causes of the collapse are still speculative. On the other end of the spectrum, some developments are so vast and complex that historians must master mountains of data before they can even begin to venture an interpretation. Events as diverse as the end of the Roman Empire, the causes of the French Revolution, and the rise of communism in China are very complicated because so many people brought so many different forces to bear for so many different reasons. For such developments, one simple explanation will never satisfy everyone, and this fact itself testifies to the complexity of life.

Still another matter stands in the way of an accurate understanding of the past. The attempt to understand history is a uniquely human endeavor. Interpretations of the past sometimes change because people's points of view change. The values and attitudes of one generation are not necessarily shared by another. Despite such differences in interpretation, the effort to examine and understand the past can give historians a perspective that is valuable in the present. By analyzing and interpreting evidence, historians come to understand not only the past but the relationship of the past to life today.

Social history itself, an important subject of this book, is an example of historians' reappraisal of the meaning of the past. For centuries historians took the basic facts, details, and activities of life for granted. Obviously, people lived in certain types of houses, ate certain foods that they either raised or bought, and reared families. These matters seemed so ordinary that few serious historians gave them much thought. Yet within this generation a growing number of scholars have demonstrated that the ways in which people have lived over the years deserve as much study as the reigns of monarchs, the careers of great political figures, and the outcomes of big battles.

The topics of history and human societies lead to this question: What is civilization? *Civilization* is easier to describe than to define. The word comes from the Latin adjective *civilis,* which refers to a citizen. Citizens willingly and mutually bind themselves in political, economic, and social organizations in which individuals merge themselves, their energies, and their interests in a larger community. In the course of time, *civilization* has come to embrace not only a people's social and political organization but also its particular shared way of thinking and believing, its art, and other facets of its culture—the complex whole that sets one people apart from other peoples who have different shared values and practices. One way to understand this idea is to observe the origins and development of major civilizations, analyzing similarities and differences among them. At the fundamental level, the similarities are greater than the differences. Almost all peoples in the world share some values, even though they may live far apart, speak different languages, and have different religions and political and social systems. By studying these shared cultural values, which stretch through time and across distance, we can see how the various events of the past have left their impression on the present and even how the present may influence the future.

A further word about culture is in order. *Culture* is often defined as a particular type or stage of the intellectual, moral, artistic, and communal practices of a civilization. All people on this planet confront elemental challenges such as how to feed and shelter themselves (the economic aspect of culture) and how to govern their lives in harmony with others (the political and social aspects of culture). These basic economic, political, and social aspects of culture are inseparable from other aspects. All cultures have felt the need to transmit what they have learned to future generations. Sometimes the content of the transmission is intellectual—for example, the preservation of astronomical information. Sometimes it is religious—for example, beliefs about the gods and their relation to humanity. The artistic appreciation of life and the surrounding world has led all peoples to create their own forms of art and music. Historians note not only the common themes to be found among various peoples but also various peoples' unique response to the realities they face. Historians also study the differences among peoples. In short, the study of history is the examination of how various peoples confronted and responded to the circumstances of their lives, what their responses had in common with the responses of others, and how they remained individual over the space of time and across the planet earth.

THE FIRST HUMAN BEINGS

On December 27, 1831, young Charles Darwin stepped aboard the H.M.S. *Beagle* to begin a voyage to South America and the Pacific Ocean. In the course of that five-year voyage, he became convinced that species of animals and human beings had evolved from lower forms. At first Darwin was reluctant to publicize his theories because they ran counter to the biblical account of creation, which claimed that God had made Adam in one day. Finally, however, in 1859 he published *On the Origin of Species.* In 1871 he followed it with *The Descent of Man,* in which he argued that human beings and apes are descended from a common ancestor. Even before Darwin had proclaimed his theories, evidence to support them had come to light. In 1856 the fossilized bones of an early form of human were discovered in the Neander Valley of Germany. Called "Neanderthal man" after the place of his discovery, he was physically more primitive than modern man (*Homo sapiens,* or thinking man). But he was clearly a human being and not an ape. Neanderthal man offered proof of Darwin's theory that *Homo sapiens* had evolved from less developed forms.

The theories of Darwin, supported by the evidence of fossilized remains, ushered in a new scientific era in which scientists and scholars have re-examined the very nature of human beings and their history. Men and women of the twentieth century have made many discoveries, solved some old problems, but raised many new ones. Although the fossil remains of primitive unicellular organisms can be dated back roughly two and a half billion years, the fossil record is far from complete. Thus the whole story of evolution cannot yet be known.

Ideas of human evolution have changed dramatically, particularly in the past few years. Generations of paleoanthropologists—better remembered as fossil-hunters—have sought the "missing link." Ever since Darwin published his theories of evolution, scholars have tried to find the one fossil that would establish the point from which human beings and apes went their own different evolutionary ways. In 1974 an American team of scholars working in Africa discovered extensive remains of a skeleton that they named "Lucy." Lucy was an ape that had walked upright some three million years ago and had displayed human characteristics. Had the missing link finally been found? No. Lucy was an intriguing step along the road of development between human beings and apes, but she was only a step, not the missing link.

Since the discovery of Lucy, many other less spectacular but nonetheless instructive finds have caused scholars to question the very concept of the missing link and its implications. Fossil remains in China and Southeast Asia suggest that evolution was more complicated than paleoanthropologists previously thought and even that human beings may not have originated in Africa. It is not simply that paleoanthropologists, like historians, must interpret their data; they must rethink everything that they have discovered in the light of their latest findings.

Many contemporary paleoanthropologists working in widely separated parts of the world have proposed some startling ideas. Some suggest that the search for a missing link is itself a blind alley. They point out that the fossil record, extensive but incomplete, suggests that thousands of missing links may have existed, no one of them more important than any other. Given the small numbers of these primates and the extent of the globe, there is an almost infinitesimal chance of finding a skeleton that can be considered the missing link between other primates and human beings. Instead, contemporary scholars stress the need to study all of these fossil remains to open new vistas for the understanding of evolution. That conclusion should not be surprising. A number of years ago Loren Eiseley, a noted American anthropologist, offered the wisest and humblest observation: "The human interminglings of hundreds of thousands of years of prehistory are not to be clarified by a single generation of archeologists."[1]

Despite the enormous uncertainty surrounding human development, a reasonably clear picture can be drawn of two important early periods: the Paleolithic, or Old Stone Age; and the Neolithic, or New Stone Age. The immensely long Paleolithic Age, which lasted from about 400,000 to 7000 B.C. takes its name from the crude stone tools that the earliest hunters chipped from flint and obsidian, a black volcanic rock. During the much shorter Neolithic Age, which lasted from about 7000 to 3000 B.C., human beings began using new types of stone tools and, more important, pursuing agriculture.

Paleolithic Cave Painting   All Paleolithic peoples relied primarily on hunting for their survival. This scene, painted on the wall of a cave in southern France, depicts the animals that this group normally hunted. Paleolithic peoples may have hoped that by drawing these animals they gained a magical power over them. *(Source: Douglas Mazonowicz/ Gallery of Prehistoric Art)*

THE PALEOLITHIC AGE

Life in the Paleolithic Age was perilous and uncertain at best. Survival depended on success of the hunt, but the hunt often brought sudden and violent death. Paleolithic peoples hunted in a variety of ways, depending on the climate and environment. Many hunters stationed themselves at river fords and waterholes and waited for prey to come to them. Paleolithic hunters were thoroughly familiar with the habits of the animals on which they relied and paid close attention to migratory habits. Other hunters trapped their quarry, and those who lived in open areas stalked and pursued game. Paleolithic peoples hunted a huge variety of animals, ranging from elephants in Spain to deer in China.

Success in the hunt was likely to depend more on the quality and effectiveness of the hunters' social organization than on bravery. Paleolithic hunters were organized—they hunted in groups. They used their knowledge of the animal world and their power of thinking to plan how to down their prey. The ability to think and act as an organized social group meant that Paleolithic hunters could successfully feed on animals that were bigger, faster, and stronger than themselves.

Paleolithic peoples also nourished themselves by gathering nuts, berries, and seeds. Just as they knew the habits of animals, so they had vast knowledge of the plant kingdom. Some Paleolithic peoples even knew how to plant wild seeds to supplement their food supply. Thus they relied on every part of the environment for survival.

Home for Paleolithic folk also varied according to the environment. Particularly in cold regions, they sought refuge in caves from the weather, predatory animals, and other people. In warmer climates and in open country they built shelters, some no more elaborate than temporary huts or sunscreens.

The basic social unit of Paleolithic societies was probably the family, but family bonds were no doubt stronger and more extensive than those of families in modern urban and industrialized societies. It is likely that the bonds of kinship were strong not just within the nuclear family of father, mother, and children but throughout the extended family of uncles, aunts, cousins, nephews, and nieces. People in nomadic societies typically depend on the extended family for cooperative work and mutual protection. The ties of kinship probably also extended beyond the family to the tribe. A *tribe* was a group of families, led by a *patriarch*, a dominant male who governed the group. Tribe members considered themselves descendants of a common ancestor. Most tribes probably consisted of thirty to fifty people.

As in the hunt, so too in other aspects of life—group members had to cooperate to survive. The adult males normally hunted and between hunts made stone weapons. The women's realm was probably the camp. There they made utensils and—the likely inventors of weaving—fashioned skins into clothing, tents, and footwear. They left the camp to gather nuts, grains, and fruits to supplement the group's diet. The women's primary responsibility was the bearing of children, who were essential to the continuation of the group. Women also had to care for the children, especially the infants. Part of women's work was tending the fire, which served for warmth, cooking, and protection against wild animals. Paleolithic peoples were also world travelers. Before the dawn of history, bands of *Homo sapiens* flourished in Europe, Africa, and Asia and had crossed into the continents of North and South America and Australia. By the end of the Paleolithic Age, there were very few "undiscovered" areas left in the world.

Some of the most striking accomplishments of Paleolithic peoples were intellectual. The development of the human brain made abstract concepts possible. Unlike animals, whose lives are conditioned by instinct and learned behavior, Paleolithic peoples used reason to govern their actions. Thought and language permitted the lore and experience of the old to be passed on to the young. An invisible world also opened up to *Homo sapiens*. The Neanderthalers developed the custom of burying their dead and leaving offerings with the body, perhaps in the belief that somehow life continued after death.

Paleolithic peoples produced the first art. They decorated cave walls with paintings of animals and scenes of the hunt. They also began to fashion clay models of pregnant women and of animals. Many of the surviving paintings, such as those at Altamira in Spain and at Lascaux in France, are located deep in caves, in areas not easily accessible. These areas were probably places of ritual and initiation, where young men were taken when they joined the ranks of the hunters. They were also places of magic. The animals depicted on the walls were those either hunted for food or feared as predators. Many are shown wounded by spears or arrows; others are pregnant. The early artists may have been expressing the hope that the hunt would be successful and game plentiful. By portraying the animals as realistically as possible, the artist-hunters may have hoped to gain power over them. The statuettes of pregnant women seem to express a wish for fertile women to have babies and thus ensure the group's survival. The wall paintings and clay statuettes represent the earliest yearnings of human beings to control their environment.

Despite their many achievements, Paleolithic peoples were sometimes their own worst enemies. At times they fought one another for control of hunting grounds, and some early hunters wiped out less aggressive peoples. On rare occasions Paleolithic peoples seem to have preyed on one another, probably under the threat of starvation. One of the grimmest indications that Neanderthal man was at times cannibalistic comes from a cave in Yugoslavia, where investigators found human bones burned and split open. Nevertheless, the overriding struggle of the Paleolithic Age was with an unforgiving environment.

THE NEOLITHIC AGE

Hunting is at best a precarious way of life, even when the diet is supplemented with seeds and fruits. If the climate changes even slightly, the all-important herds might move to new areas. As recently as the late 1950s the Caribou Eskimos of the Canadian Northwest Territories suffered a severe famine when the caribou herds, their only source of food and bone for weapons, changed their migration route. Paleolithic tribes either moved with the herds and adapted themselves to new circumstances or, like the Caribou Eskimos, perished. Several long ice ages—periods when huge glaciers covered vast parts of Europe and North America—subjected small bands of Paleolithic hunters to extreme hardship.

Not long after the last ice age, around 7000 B.C. some hunters and gatherers began to rely chiefly on agriculture for their sustenance. This development has traditionally been called the "Agricultural Revolution." Yet contemporary scholars point out that ancient peoples had long practiced

agriculture. The real transformation of human life occurred when hunters and gatherers gave up their nomadic way of life to depend primarily on the grain they grew and the animals they domesticated. Agriculture enabled a more stable and secure life. Neolithic peoples thus flourished, fashioning an energetic, creative era.

They were responsible for many fundamental inventions and innovations that the modern world takes for granted. First, obviously, is systematic agriculture. Neolithic peoples relied on agriculture as their primary, not merely subsidiary, source of food. Thus they developed the primary economic activity of the entire ancient world and the basis of all modern life. From the settled routine of Neolithic farmers came the evolution of towns and eventually cities. Neolithic farmers usually raised more food than they could consume, and their surpluses permitted larger, healthier populations. Population growth in turn created an even greater reliance on settled farming, as only systematic agriculture could sustain the increased numbers of people. Since surpluses of food could also be bartered for other commodities, the Neolithic era witnessed the beginnings of large-scale trade. In time the increasing complexity of Neolithic societies led to the development of writing, prompted by the need to keep records and later by the urge to chronicle experiences, learning, and beliefs.

The transition to settled life also had a profound impact on the family. The shared needs and pressures that encourage extended family ties in nomadic societies are less prominent in settled societies. Bonds to the extended family weakened. In towns and cities the nuclear family was more dependent on its immediate neighbors than on kinfolk.

Meanwhile the nomadic way of life and the family relationships it nurtured continued to flourish alongside settled agriculture. But nomadic life did change. Neolithic nomads traveled with flocks of domesticated animals, their main source of wealth and food. Often farmers and nomads bartered peaceably with each other, one group trading its surpluses for those of the other. Still, although nomadic peoples existed throughout the Neolithic period and exist in modern times, the future belonged to the Neolithic farmers and their descendants. The development of systematic agriculture may not have been revolutionary, but the changes that it ushered in certainly were.

Until recently, scholars thought that agriculture originated in the ancient Near East and gradually spread elsewhere. Contemporary work, however, points to a more complex pattern of development. For unknown reasons people in various parts of the world all seem to have begun domesticating plants and animals at roughly the same time, around 7000 B.C. Four main points of origin have been identified. In the Near East, people in places as far apart as Tepe Yahya in modern Iran, Jarmo in modern Iraq, Jericho in Palestine, and Hacilar in modern Turkey (Map 1.1) raised wheat, barley, peas, and lentils. They also kept herds of sheep, pigs, and possibly goats. In western Africa, Neolithic farmers domesticated many plants, including millet, sorghum, and yams. In northeastern China, peoples of the Yangshao culture developed techniques of field agriculture, animal husbandry, pottery-making, and bronze metallurgy. Innovations in Central and South America were equally striking: Indians domesticated a host of plants, among them corn, beans, and squash. From these wide-ranging areas, knowledge of farming techniques spread to other regions.

The deliberate planting of crops led to changes in plants' genetic structure. The plants and animals cultivated by Neolithic farmers gradually evolved to the point where most of them could no longer survive in the wild. Thus human beings and the plants and animals they domesticated depended on one another for survival. Contemporary work on the origins of farming has led to a chilling revelation: the genetic base of most modern domesticated plants, such as wheat and corn, is so narrow that a new pest or plant disease could destroy many of them. The result would be widespread famine. Human society depends on a precarious food base.

Once people began to rely on farming for their livelihood, they settled in permanent villages and built houses. The location of the village was crucial. Early farmers chose places where the water supply was constant and adequate for their crops and flocks. At first, villages were small, consisting of a few households. As the population expanded and prospered, villages usually developed into towns. Between 8000 and 7000 B.C. the community at Jericho grew to at least two thousand people. Jericho's inhabitants lived in mud-brick houses built on stone foundations, and they surrounded their town with a massive fortification wall. The Neolithic site of Çatal Hüyük in Anatolia (modern Turkey) covered thirty-two acres. The outer houses of the settlement formed a solid wall of mud brick, which served as a bulwark against attack. At Tepe Yahya as well, the Neolithic farmers surrounded their town with a wall.

Walls offered protection and permitted a more secure, stable way of life than that of the nomad. They also prove that towns grew in size, population, and wealth, for these fortifications were so large that they could have been raised only by a large labor force. They also indicate that towns were developing social and political organization. The fortifications, the work of the whole community, would have been impossible without central planning.

One of the major effects of the advent of agriculture and settled life was a dramatic increase in population. No census figures exist for this period, but the number and size of the towns prove that Neolithic society was expanding. Early farmers found that agriculture provided a larger, much more dependable food supply than did hunting and gathering. No longer did the long winter months mean the threat of starvation. Farmers raised more food than they could consume and learned to store the surplus for the winter. Because the farming community was better fed than ever before, it was also more resistant to diseases that kill people suffering from malnutrition. Thus Neolithic farmers were healthier and lived longer than their predecessors. All these factors explain the growth of towns like Jericho and Jarmo.

The surplus of food had two other momentous consequences. First, grain became an article of commerce. The farming community traded surplus grain for items it could not produce itself. The community thus obtained raw materials such as precious gems and metals. In Mesopotamia the early towns imported copper from the north, and eventually copper replaced stone for tools and weapons. Trade also brought Neolithic communities into touch with one another, making possible the spread of ideas and techniques.

Second, agricultural surplus made possible the division of labor. It freed some members of the community from the necessity of raising food. Artisans and craftsmen devoted their attention to making the new stone tools that farming demanded—hoes and sickles for working in the fields and mortars and pestles for grinding grain. Other artisans began to shape clay into pottery vessels, which were used to store grain, wine, and

MAP 1.1 Spread of Cultures in the Ancient Near East This map illustrates the spread of Mesopotamian and Egyptian culture through a semicircular stretch of land often called the "Fertile Crescent." From this area knowledge and use of agriculture spread throughout the western part of Asia Minor.

oil and served as kitchen utensils. Still others wove baskets and cloth. People who could specialize in particular crafts produced more and better goods than any single farmer could.

Until recently it was impossible to say much about these goods. But in April 1985 archeologists announced the discovery near the Dead Sea in modern Israel of a unique deposit of Neolithic artifacts. Buried in a cave were fragments of the earliest cloth yet found, the oldest painted mask, remains of woven baskets and boxes, and jewelry. The textiles are surprisingly elaborate, some woven in eleven intricate designs. These artifacts give eloquent testimony to the sophistication and artistry of Neolithic craftsmanship.

Prosperity and stable conditions nurtured other innovations and discoveries. Neolithic farmers improved their tools and agricultural techniques. They domesticated bigger, stronger animals, such as the bull and the horse, to work for them. To harness the power of these animals, they invented tools such as the plow, which came into use by

3000 B.C. The first plows had wooden shares and could break only light soils, but they were far more efficient than stone hoes. By 3000 B.C., the wheel had been invented, and farmers devised ways of hitching bulls and horses to wagons. These developments enabled Neolithic farmers to raise more food more efficiently and easily than ever before, simply because animals and machines were doing a greater proportion of the work.

In arid regions such as Mesopotamia and Egypt, farmers learned to irrigate their land and later to drain it to prevent the build-up of salt in the soil. By diverting water from rivers, they were able to open new land to cultivation. River waters flooding the fields deposited layers of rich mud, which increased the fertility of the soil. Thus the rivers, together with the manure of domesticated animals, kept replenishing the land. One result was a further increase in population and wealth. Irrigation, especially on a large scale, demanded group effort. The entire community had to plan which land to irrigate and how to lay out the canals.

Then everyone had to help dig the canals. The demands of irrigation underscored the need for strong central authority within the community. Successful irrigation projects in turn strengthened such central authority by proving it effective and beneficial. Thus corporate spirit and governments to which individuals were subordinate—the makings of urban life—began to evolve.

The development of systematic agriculture was a fundamental turning point in the history of civilization. Farming gave rise to stable, settled societies, which enjoyed considerable prosperity. It made possible an enormous increase in population. Some inhabitants of the budding towns turned their attention to the production of goods that made life more comfortable. Settled circumstances and a certain amount of leisure made the accumulation and spread of knowledge easier. Finally, sustained farming prepared the way for urban life.

RIVERS, RESOURCES, AND CIVILIZATIONS

The development of systematic agriculture made possible a huge leap in human development, a leap that took place in several different parts of the world at roughly the same time (Map 1.2). In the ancient Near East, India, and China, Neolithic farmers created the conditions that permitted the evolution of urban civilization.

Certain geographical features were common to these early civilizations. The most important were the mighty river valleys in which they developed. The Egyptians relied on the Nile, which flows some 4,000 miles before reaching the Mediterranean Sea. To the east the Euphrates, roughly 1,675 miles in length, and the Tigris, a mere 600 miles long, created Mesopotamia, the Greek name for the land between them. The Indus River, flowing about 1,980 miles before reaching the ocean, nourished ancient Indian civilization; and the

MAP 1.2 River-Valley Civilizations Although systematic agriculture developed in four great river valleys, variations in geography and climate meant that different crops were grown and societies emerged in distinct but similar ways.

great Yellow River, some 2,700 miles long, made the birth of Chinese civilization possible. Thus all four ancient civilizations could depend on a steady source of water, which also brought nutrients to the soil and fish as a source of food. Except for the violent Tigris and Yellow, the rivers also served as an easy means of communication. It was safer and simpler to use the Nile as a highway than to travel across the deserts surrounding Egypt. Likewise the Indus offered the fastest, most convenient path through the jungle. The rivers enabled people throughout a large area to keep in touch with one another, and easy communications facilitated the exchange of ideas while breaking down the barriers of isolation. The size and fertility of the broad valleys made possible a vast increase in the land that could be cultivated, which in turn meant a vast increase in wealth and population, necessary ingredients to the development of large sophisticated social structures.

Although great rivers were a common feature of these civilizations, soil and climate differed, and these differences left a significant imprint on human development. The rich African mud carried by the Nile allowed abundant crops of wheat, and the dry desert air made it simple to preserve surpluses of grain. The Indus flows through rich subtropical land well suited to growing a large variety of crops, but the humid climate quickly brought rot. Different climates meant that the rivers nurtured different crops and required different methods of agriculture. Geography and the means by which people turned it to their uses, then, influenced the way in which societies evolved.

The rivers themselves are different. The Nile is gentle and predictable, the source of Egyptian life; the Tigris and Yellow rivers are violent and unpredictable, at times bringing floods and destruction. The nature of the rivers demanded differences in the ways they were used. In Egypt and China, the peoples employed irrigation to bring water to arid land, enabling them to cultivate more fields. That was true in Mesopotamia too, but the farmers there also relied on irrigation to drain land to reclaim it for cultivation. In India farmers protected themselves against the flood waters of the Indus while taking advantage of the rich alluvium that the river deposited. Whatever the differences, the rivers challenged early peoples to work together to make the best use of their geographical gifts, whether to divert water to new soil, to draw water from uncultivated fields, or to prevent water from destroying land already being farmed.

The effort needed to make the rivers useful to human life had several by-products. First, and most important, the more land brought under cultivation, the larger the population grew and the richer in material goods it became. As the river-valley societies in the ancient Near East, India, and China outgrew their Neolithic past, they were forced to diversify their activities and abilities. New, centrally organized forms of government were required on a regular, permanent basis, to coordinate massive irrigation projects, to administer the land, to govern the people, and to defend them in time of war. Specialization in government and defense was part of a larger division of labor. Some members of society abandoned the plow to master the technology of metalworking, while others devoted themselves to the study of mathematics and architecture to meet the building needs of society. In the firm belief that they belonged to a world inhabited by gods, some people tried to explain the origin and workings of these higher beings, both to honor them and to teach their mysteries to others so that the divine and human could live in harmony. In the process they preserved traditions not only about their beliefs but also about their own lives—traditions that linked them to the past and helped them shape the future.

Knowledge had become too valuable to lose and too complicated to be mastered easily. Whatever their specialization, people increasingly found it necessary to preserve knowledge and experience in a permanent form. To meet this need, they invented writing, which enabled them not only to record their accumulated wisdom but also to pass essential information about the past and the present to future generations. They extended the experience of humanity beyond the individual's lifetime and created the foundations of an intellectual continuity that defied both time and death.

North and South America, Europe, sub-Saharan Africa, and Southeast Asia can all boast of many rivers. Yet only the peoples of Mesoamerica and the Incas of Peru in South America established civilizations comparable to those in the Near East, India, and China, and even they came many centuries after the rise of the river-valley civilizations. Factors other than rivers were obviously essential to the development of civilization. Climate may be a limiting factor in places such as equatorial Africa and Southeast Asia. But why did nothing similar to Egyptian, Mesopotamian, Indian, and Chinese advances occur in areas of North America and Europe where the climate is relatively mild?

North America and sub-Saharan Africa are rich in raw materials, but often those raw materials were inaccessible. Early peoples lacked the tools and the technology to mine the coal in Kentucky or the diamonds in South Africa. Tools were primitive and totally inadequate. Instead of plowing the soil, early farmers not living in the river valleys of the Near East, India, or China mainly used hoes and digging-sticks, and they lacked the work animals necessary to haul burdens, pull plows, and grind grain. They relied on their own labor, not on animal power, to sow, harvest, and process grain. They worked hard to get crop yields that were so small that they could not expect sizable surpluses. That in turn made it hard for them to develop specialization of labor, to expand population, to build cities, and to accumulate knowledge in a durable form. Furthermore, areas such as parts of sub-Saharan Africa and the Caribbean are so naturally rich in readily available natural food resources that people did not have to toil for a living. Seldom did peoples in such areas develop sophisticated urban cultures.

Thus, something more than geography, natural resources, climate, sustained agriculture, and population is needed to constitute a civilization. Though important in themselves, together they permit people to live in villages, towns, and cities. The significance of urban life to the growth of civilization cannot be overestimated. By banding together and observing common laws and values of life, people could pool their resources. While some people were farmers or craftsmen, others magistrates or priests, all cooperated to sustain the community and to protect it. The invention of writing enabled them to hand on knowledge of values, law, religion, and history to later generations. Urban life provided the wealth, security, and stability to create civilization in its many forms.

Among the river-valley societies, nowhere can these abstractions be better seen than in the urban culture that flowered in the demanding environment of Mesopotamia, the first of the four societies to attain a level of development that can reasonably be called a civilization.

Map of Nippur The oldest map in the world, dating to ca 1500 B.C., shows the layout of the Mesopotamian city of Nippur. Inscribed on a clay tablet, the map has enabled archeologists to locate ruined buildings: (A) the ziggurat, (B) canal, (C) enclosure and gardens, (D) city gates, and (E) the Euphrates River. *(Source: The University Museum, University of Pennsylvania)*

MESOPOTAMIAN CIVILIZATION

Mesopotamia, an area roughly equivalent to modern Iraq, drew its life from the Euphrates and Tigris rivers. Both rivers have their headwaters in the mountains of Armenia in modern Turkey. Both are fed by numerous tributaries, and the entire river system drains a vast mountainous region. Overland routes in Mesopotamia usually followed the Euphrates because the banks of the Tigris are frequently steep and difficult. North of the ancient city of Babylon the land levels out into a barren expanse. The desert continues south of Babylon and still farther south gives way to a 6,000-square-mile region of marshes, lagoons, mud flats, and reed banks. At last, in the extreme south, the Euphrates and the Tigris unite and empty into the Persian Gulf.

This area became the home of many folk and the land of the first cities. The region around Akkad, near modern Baghdad, was occupied by bands of Semitic nomads, people related to one another by their language, Semitic, a family of languages that includes Hebrew and Arabic. Into the south came the Sumerians, farmers and city builders who probably migrated from the east. By 3000 B.C. they had established a number of cities in the southernmost part of Mesopotamia, which became known as Sumer. As the Sumerians pushed north, they came into contact with the Semites, who readily adopted Sumerian culture and turned to urban life. The Sumerians soon changed the face of the land and made Mesopotamia the source of values and techniques that fundamentally influenced the societies of their immediate neighbors, both in the West and the East (see Map 1.2).

In the context of world history, the capitalized terms "Western" and "Eastern" and "West" and "East" are *Eurocentric,* which means that they describe events and culture from the viewpoint of European experience and values. The concept behind these terms goes back to the ancient Greeks, who contrasted their life with the lives of their non-Greek neighbors in Africa and western Asia. Peoples in Asia and Africa would probably have dismissed the notion, and no one today uses the categories "West" and "East" to indicate the superiority of one set of historical developments to the other. Despite their flaws, however, the terms have come into general use as a useful but artificial way to distinguish historical developments in Europe and the Americas from those in Asia.

Another term already used in these pages, "the ancient Near East," also requires some explanation. It refers to a specific area of western Asia and northeastern Africa. In the north the ancient Near East included the western part of modern Turkey, extending south through the area now called the "Middle East" to Egypt in Africa. The major justification for this term is historical, not geographical. Although various peoples in this area developed their own civilizations to some extent independently, they did not develop in complete isolation but formed a well-defined unit.

Environment and Mesopotamian Culture

From the outset, geography had a profound effect on the evolution of Mesopotamian civilization. In this region agriculture is possible only with irrigation and good drainage. Consequently, the Sumerians and later the Akkadians built cities along the Tigris and Euphrates and their branches. Major cities such as Ur and Uruk took root on tributaries of the Euphrates, while others, notably Lagash, were built on tributaries of the Tigris (see Map 1.1). The rivers supplied fish, a major element of the city dwellers' diet. The rivers also provided reeds and clay for building materials. Since this entire area lacks stone, mud brick became the primary building block of Mesopotamian architecture.

The rivers sustained life, and simultaneously they acted as a powerful restraining force, particularly on Sumerian political development. They made Sumer a geographical maze. Between the rivers, streams, and irrigation canals stretched open desert or swamp where nomadic tribes roamed. Communication between the isolated cities was difficult and at times dangerous. Thus each Sumerian city became a state, independent of the others and protective of its independence. Any city that tried to unify the country was resisted by the other cities. As a result, the political history of Sumer is one of almost constant warfare. The experience of the city of Nippur (see Map 1.1) is an example of how bad conditions could become. At one point in its history Nippur was conquered eighteen times in twenty-four years. Although Sumer was eventually unified, unification came late and was always tenuous.

The harsh environment fostered a grim, even pessimistic, spirit among the Mesopotamians. They especially feared the ravages of flood. The Tigris can bring quick devastation, as it did to Baghdad in 1831, when flood waters destroyed seven thousand homes in a single night. The same tragedy occurred often in antiquity. Vulnerability to natural disaster deeply influenced Mesopotamian religious beliefs.

Sumerian Society

The Sumerians sought to please and calm the gods, especially the patron deity of the city. Encouraged and directed by a traditional priesthood long dedicated to understanding the ways of the gods, people erected shrines in the center of each city and then built their houses around them. The best way to honor a god was to make the shrine grand and impressive, for a god who had a splendid temple might think twice about sending floods to destroy the city.

The temple had to be worthy of the god, a symbol of his power, and it had to last. Special skills and materials were needed to build it. Only stone was suitable for its foundations, and only precious metals and colorful glazed tiles were fit for its decoration. Since the Mesopotamians had to import both stone and metals, temple construction encouraged trade. Architects, engineers, craftsmen, and workers had to devote a great deal of thought, effort, and time to build the temple. By 2000 B.C. the result was Mesopotamia's first monumental architecture—the *ziggurat,* a massive stepped tower that dominated the city.

Once the ziggurat was built, the traditional priesthood assumed the additional duty of running it and performing the god's rituals. The people of the city met the expenses of building the temple and maintaining both the temple and its priests by setting aside extensive tracts of land. The priests took charge of the produce of the temple lands and the sacred flocks. Part of the yield fed and clothed them and the temple staff. Part was used as offerings to the gods, and part was sold or bartered to obtain goods, such as precious metals and stone, needed for construction, maintenance, and ritual.

Until recently, the dominant position and wealth of the temple had led historians to consider the Sumerian city-state an absolute *theocracy,* or government by an established priesthood. According to this view, the temple and its priests owned the city's land and controlled its economy. Newly discovered documents and recent work, however, have resulted in new ideas about the Sumerian city. It is now known that the temple owned a large fraction, but not all, of the city's territory and did not govern the city. A king *(lugal)* or local governor *(ensi)* exercised political power, and most of the city's land was the property of individual citizens.

Sumerian society was based on a complex arrangement of freedom and dependence. It was divided into four categories: nobles, free clients of the nobility, commoners, and slaves. The nobility consisted of the king and his family, the chief priests, and high palace officials. Generally the king rose to power as a war leader, elected by the citizenry. He established a regular army, trained it, and led it into battle. The might of the king and the frequency of warfare in Mesopotamia quickly made the king the supreme figure in the city, and

Aerial View of Ur   This photograph gives a good idea of the size and complexity of Ur, one of the most powerful cities in Mesopotamia. In the lower right-hand corner stands the massive ziggurat of Urnammu. *(Source: Georg Gerster/Comstock)*

kingship soon became hereditary. The symbol of his status was the palace, which rivaled the temple in grandeur.

The king and the lesser nobility held extensive tracts of land that, like the estates of the temple, were worked by clients and slaves. Clients were free men and women who were dependent on the nobility. In return for their labor the clients received small plots of land to work for themselves. Although this arrangement assured the clients of a livelihood, the land they worked remained the possession of the nobility or the temple. Thus, not only did the nobility control most—and probably the best—land, they also commanded the obedience of a huge segment of society. They were the dominant force in Mesopotamian society.

Commoners were free citizens. They were independent of the nobility; however, they could not rival the nobility in social status and political power. Commoners belonged to large patriarchal families who owned land in their own right. Commoners could sell their land, if the family approved, but even the king could not legally take their land without their approval. Commoners had a voice in the political affairs of the city and full protection under the law.

Slavery has been a fact of life throughout history, until comparatively recent times. Some Sumerian slaves were foreigners and prisoners of war. Some were criminals who had lost their freedom as punishment for their crimes. Still others served as slaves to repay their debts. They were more fortunate than the others because the law required that they be freed after three years. But all slaves were subject to whatever treatment their owners might mete out. Although they could be beaten and even branded, they were not considered dumb beasts. Slaves engaged in trade and made profits. Indeed, many slaves bought their freedom. They could borrow money and received at least some legal protection.

THE SPREAD OF MESOPOTAMIAN CULTURE

The Sumerians established the basic social, economic, and intellectual patterns of Mesopotamia, but the Semites played a large part in spreading Sumerian culture far beyond the boundaries of Mesopotamia. Despite the cultural ascendancy of the Sumerians, continual wars wasted their strength. In 2331 B.C. the Semitic chieftain Sargon conquered Sumer and created a new empire. The symbol of his triumph was a new capital, the city of Akkad. Sargon, the first "world conqueror," led his armies to the Mediterranean Sea. Although his empire lasted only a few generations, it spread Mesopotamian culture throughout the Fertile Crescent, the belt of rich farmland that extends from Mesopotamia in the east up through Syria in the north and down to Egypt in the west (see Map 1.1).

Sargon's impact and the extent of Mesopotamian influence even at this early period have been dramatically revealed at Ebla in modern Syria. In 1964 archeologists there unearthed a once-flourishing Semitic civilization that had assimilated political, intellectual, and artistic aspects of Mesopotamian culture. In 1975 the excavators uncovered thousands of clay tablets, which proved that the people of Ebla had learned the art of writing from the Mesopotamians. Eblaite artists borrowed heavily from Mesopotamian art but developed their own style, which in turn influenced Mesopotamian artists. The Eblaites transmitted the heritage of Mesopotamia to other Semitic centers in Syria. In the process, a universal culture developed in the ancient Near East, a culture basically Mesopotamian but fertilized by the traditions, genius, and ways of many other peoples.

When the clay tablets of Ebla were discovered, many scholars confidently predicted that they would shed fresh light on the Bible. Some even claimed to recognize in them biblical names like Jerusalem and the "Five Cities of the Plain," which included Sodom and Gomorrah. Careful study since then suggests that these claims were more often optimistic than accurate. So far the Ebla tablets have added very little to biblical scholarship, yet they are a gold mine of data on the ancient history of northern Syria. They confirm the existence and importance of direct contact between Mesopotamia and Syria as early as the third millennium B.C. Moreover, they demonstrate the early influence of Mesopotamian civilization far beyond its own borders.

The Triumph of Babylon

Although the empire of Sargon was extensive, it was short-lived. The Semites, too, failed to solve the problems posed by Mesopotamia's geography and population pattern. It was left to the Babylonians to unite Mesopotamia politically and culturally. The Babylonians were Amorites, a Semitic people who had migrated from Arabia and settled on the site of Babylon, along the middle Euphrates. Babylon enjoyed an excellent geographical position and was ideally suited to be the capital of Mesopotamia. It dominated trade on the Tigris and Euphrates rivers: all commerce to and from Sumer and Akkad had to pass by its walls. It also looked beyond Mesopotamia. Babylonian merchants followed the Tigris north to Assyria and Armenia. The Euphrates led merchants to Syria, Palestine, and the Mediterranean. The city grew great because of its commercial importance and soundly based power (see Map 1.1).

Babylon was also fortunate in its farseeing and able king Hammurabi (1792–1750 B.C.). Hammurabi set out to do three things: make Babylon secure, unify Mesopotamia, and win for the Babylonians a place in Mesopotamian civilization. The first two he accomplished by conquering Assyria and Akkad in the north and Sumer in the south. Then he turned to his third goal.

Politically, Hammurabi joined in his kingship the Semitic concept of the tribal chieftain and the Sumerian idea of urban kingship. Culturally, he encouraged the spread of myths that explained how Marduk, the god of Babylon, had been elected king of the gods by the other Mesopotamian deities. Hammurabi's success in making Marduk the god of all Mesopotamians made Babylon the religious center of Mesopotamia. Through Hammurabi's genius the Babylonians made their own contribution to Mesopotamian culture—a culture vibrant enough to maintain its identity while assimilating new influences. Hammurabi's conquests and the activity of Babylonian merchants spread this enriched culture north to Anatolia and west to Syria and Palestine.

The Invention of Writing and the First Schools

Mesopotamian culture spread as rapidly as it did because of the invention and evolution of writing. Until recently, scholars have credited the Sumerians with the invention of writing in the Western world. Recent work, however, suggests that the Sumerian achievement, a form of writing called

Stele of Naramsin Naramsin, the grandson of Sargon, was one of the greatest of the Akkadian kings. The topmost figure on this stele, or commemorative tablet, he displays his power by defeating his enemies in battle. Naramsin's horned crown suggests that he considered himself divine. *(Source: Louvre/Cliché des Musées Nationaux, Paris)*

cuneiform—from the Latin term for "wedge-shaped" (used to describe the strokes of the stylus) may have been a comparatively late stage in the development of writing. The origins of writing probably go back thousands of years earlier than previously thought. As early as the ninth millennium

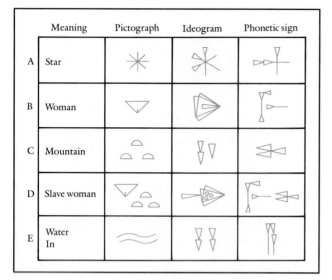

	Meaning	Pictograph	Ideogram	Phonetic sign
A	Star			
B	Woman			
C	Mountain			
D	Slave woman			
E	Water / In			

Figure 1.1 Sumerian Writing *(Source: Excerpted from S. N. Kramer,* The Sumerians: Their History, Culture and Character, *University of Chicago Press, Chicago, 1963, pp. 302–306)*

B.C., Near Eastern peoples used clay tokens as record-keeping counters. By the fourth millennium B.C., people had realized that drawing pictures of the tokens on clay was simpler than making tokens. This breakthrough in turn suggested that more information could be conveyed by adding pictures of still other objects. The result was a complex system of *pictographs,* in which each sign pictured an object. Pictographs were the forerunners of cuneiform writing.

How did this pictographic system work and how did it evolve into cuneiform writing? At first, if a scribe wanted to indicate "star," he simply drew a picture of a star on a wet clay tablet (see line A of Figure 1.1), which became rock hard when baked. Anyone looking at the picture would know what it meant and would think of the word for "star." This complicated and laborious system had serious limitations. It could not represent abstract ideas or combinations of ideas. For instance, how could it depict a slave woman?

The solution appeared when the scribe discovered that he could combine signs to express meaning. To refer to a slave woman, he used the sign for "woman" (line B) and the sign for "mountain" (line C)—literally, "mountain woman" (line D). Since the Sumerians regularly obtained their slave women from the mountains, this combination of signs was easily understandable.

The next step was to simplify the system. Instead of drawing pictures, the scribe made conventionalized signs. Thus the signs became *ideograms:* they symbolized ideas. The sign for "star" could also be used to indicate "heaven," "sky," or even "god."

The real breakthrough came when the scribe learned to use signs to represent sounds. For instance, the scribe drew two parallel wavy lines to indicate the word "a" or "water" (line E). The word "a" in Sumerian also meant "in" (as well as "water"). The word "in" expresses a relationship that is very difficult to represent pictorially. Instead of trying to invent a sign to mean "in," some clever scribe used the sign for "water" because the two words sounded alike. This phonetic use of signs made possible the combining of signs to convey abstract ideas.

The Sumerian system of writing was so complicated that only professional scribes mastered it, and even they had to study it for many years. By 2500 B.C. scribal schools flourished throughout Sumer. Most students came from wealthy families and were male. Each school had a master, teachers, and monitors. Discipline was strict, and students were caned for sloppy work and misbehavior. One graduate of a scribal school had few fond memories of the joy of learning:

My headmaster read my tablet, said:
"There is something missing," caned me.

. . .

The fellow in charge of silence said:
"Why did you talk without permission," caned me.
The fellow in charge of the assembly said:
"Why did you stand at ease without permission,"
*   caned me.*[2]

The Sumerian system of schooling set the educational standards for Mesopotamian culture, and the Akkadians and Babylonians adopted its practices and techniques. Students began by learning how to prepare clay tablets and make signs. They studied grammar and word lists and solved simple mathematical problems. Mesopotamian education always had a practical side because of the economic and administrative importance of scribes. Most scribes took administrative positions in the temple or palace, where they kept records of business transactions, accounts, and inventories. But scribal schools did not limit their curriculum to business affairs. They were also centers of culture and learning. Topics of study included mathematics, botany, and linguistics. Advanced students copied and studied the classics of Mesopotamian literature. Talented students and learned scribes wrote compositions of their own. As a result, many literary, mathematical, and religious texts survive today, giving a surprisingly full picture of Mesopotamian intellectual and spiritual life.

Mesopotamian Thought and Religion

The Mesopotamians made significant and sophisticated advances in mathematics using a numerical system based on units of sixty. For practical purposes they also used factors of ten and six. They developed the concept of *place value*—that the value of a number depends on where it stands in relation to other numbers. Mesopotamian mathematical texts are of two kinds: tables and problems. Scribes compiled tables of squares and square roots, cubes and cube roots, and reciprocals. They wrote texts of problems that dealt not only with equations and pure mathematics but also with practical problems such as how to plan irrigation ditches. The Mesopotamians did not consider mathematics a purely theoretical science. The building of cities, palaces, temples, and canals demanded practical knowledge of geometry and trigonometry. In not turning their knowledge into theories, the Mesopotamians were different from the Greeks, who enjoyed theorizing.

Mesopotamian medicine was a combination of magic, prescriptions, and surgery. Mesopotamians believed that demons and evil spirits caused sickness and that magic spells could drive them out. Or, they believed, a physician could force a demon out by giving the patient a foul-tasting prescription. As medical knowledge grew, some prescriptions were found to work and thus were true medicines. The physician relied heavily on plants, animals, and minerals for recipes, often mixing them with beer to cover their unpleasant taste. Surgeons practiced a dangerous occupation, and the penalties for failure were severe. One section of Hammurabi's law code (see page 23) decreed: "If a physician performed a major operation on a seignior with a bronze lancet and has caused the seignior's death, or he opened up the eye-socket . . . and has destroyed the . . . eye, they shall cut off his hand."[3] No wonder that one medical text warned physicians to avoid a dying person.

Sumerian Clay Tablet This Sumerian clay tablet dating from about 3000 B.C. shows Sumerian writing in transition. The scribe has begun to use pictures of things to represent abstractions, which is an advance from pictographs to ideograms (see Figure 1.1). *(Source: Courtesy of the Trustees of the British Museum)*

Mesopotamian thought had its profoundest impact on theology and religion. The Sumerians originated many beliefs, and the Akkadians and Babylonians added to them. Although the Mesopotamians thought that many gods ran the world, they did not consider all gods and goddesses equal. Some deities had very important jobs, taking care of music, law, sex, and victory, while others had lesser tasks, overseeing leatherworking and basket weaving. The god in charge of metalworking was hardly the equal of the god of wisdom.

Divine society was a hierarchy. According to the Sumerians the air-god Enlil was the king of the gods and laid down the rules by which the universe was run. Enki, the god of wisdom, put Enlil's plans into effect. The Babylonians believed that the gods elected Marduk as their king and that he assigned the lesser gods various duties. Once the gods received their tasks, they carried them out forever.

Mesopotamian gods lived their lives much as human beings lived theirs. The gods were *anthropomorphic,* or human in form. Unlike men and women, they were powerful and immortal and could make themselves invisible; otherwise, they were very human. They celebrated with food and drink, and they raised families. They enjoyed their own "Garden of Eden," a green and fertile place.

They could be irritable, and they were not always holy. Even Enlil was punished by other gods because he had once raped the goddess Ninlil.

The Mesopotamians considered natural catastrophes to be the work of the gods. At times the Sumerians described their chief god, Enlil, as "the raging flood which has no rival." The gods, they believed, even used nature to punish the Mesopotamians. According to the myth of the Deluge, which gave rise to the biblical story of Noah, the god Enki warned Ziusudra, the Sumerian Noah:

A flood will sweep over the cult-centers;
To destroy the seed of mankind . . .
Is the decision, the word of the assembly of the
    gods.[4]

The Mesopotamians did not worship their deities because the gods were holy. Human beings were too insignificant to pass judgment on the conduct of the gods, and the gods were too superior to honor human morals. Rather, the Mesopotamians worshiped the gods because they were mighty. Likewise, it was not the place of men and women to understand the gods. The Sumerian equivalent to the biblical Job once complained to his god:

The man of deceit has conspired against me,
And you, my god, do not thwart him,
You carry off my understanding.[5]

The motives of the gods were not always clear. In times of affliction one could only pray and offer sacrifices to appease them.

The Mesopotamians had many myths to account for the creation of the universe. According to one Sumerian myth (echoed in Genesis, the first book of the Old Testament), only the primeval sea existed at first. The sea produced heaven and earth, which were united. Heaven and earth gave birth to Enlil, who separated them and made possible the creation of the other gods.

These myths are the earliest known attempts to answer the question "How did it all begin?" The Mesopotamians obviously thought about these matters, as about the gods, in human terms. They never organized their beliefs into a philosophy, but their myths offered understandable explanations of natural phenomena. They were emotionally satisfying, and that was their greatest appeal.

Mesopotamian myths also explained the origin of human beings. In one myth the gods decided to make their lives easier by creating servants, whom they wanted made in their own image. Nammu, the goddess of the watery deep, brought the matter to Enki. After some thought, Enki instructed Nammu and the others:

Mix the heart of the clay that is over the abyss.
The good and princely fashioners will thicken the
    clay.
You, do you bring the limbs into existence.[6]

In Mesopotamian myth, as in Genesis, men and women were made in the divine image. However, human beings lacked godlike powers. The myth "The Creation of the Pickax" gives an idea of their insignificance. According to this myth, Enlil drove his pickax into the ground, and out of the hole crawled the Sumerians, the first people. As Enlil stood looking at them, some of his fellow gods approached him. They were so pleased with Enlil's work that they asked him to give them some people to serve them. Consequently, the Mesopotamians believed it their duty to supply the gods with sacrifices of food and drink and to house them in fine temples. In return, they hoped that the gods would be kind.

In addition to myths, the Sumerians produced the first epic poem, the *Epic of Gilgamesh.* The epic recounts the wanderings of Gilgamesh—the semihistorical king of Uruk—and his companion Enkidu, their fatal meeting with the goddess Ishtar in which Enkidu is killed, and Gilgamesh's subsequent search for eternal life. Although Gilgamesh finds a miraculous plant that gives immortality to anyone who eats it, a great snake steals it from him. Despite this loss, Gilgamesh visits the lower world to bring Enkidu back to life, thereby learning of life after death. The *Epic of Gilgamesh* is not only an excellent piece of literature but also an intellectual triumph. It shows the Sumerians grappling with such enduring questions as life and death, mankind and deity, and immortality. Despite its great antiquity, it addresses questions of importance to men and women today.

These ideas about the creation of the universe and of human beings are part of the Mesopotamian legacy to modern civilization. They spread throughout the ancient Near East and found a home among the Hebrews, who adopted much of

Mesopotamian religious thought and made it part of their own beliefs. Biblical parallels to Mesopotamian literary and religious themes are many. Such stories as the creation of Adam, the Garden of Eden, the Deluge, and the trials of Job can be traced back to Mesopotamian originals. Through the Bible, Mesopotamian as well as Jewish religious concepts influenced Christianity and Islam. Thus these first attempts by women and men to understand themselves and their world are still alive today.

DAILY LIFE IN MESOPOTAMIA

The law code of King Hammurabi offers a wealth of information about daily life in Mesopotamia. Hammurabi's was not the first law code in Mesopotamia; indeed the earliest goes back to ca 2100 B.C. Yet, like earlier lawgivers, Hammurabi proclaimed that he issued his laws on divine authority to "establish law and justice in the language of the land, thereby promoting the welfare of the people." His code may seem harsh, but it was no harsher than the Mosaic law of the Hebrews, which it heavily influenced. Hammurabi's code inflicted such penalties as mutilation, whipping, and burning. Today in parts of the Islamic world these punishments are still in use. Despite its severity, a spirit of justice and a sense of responsibility pervade the code. Hammurabi genuinely felt that his duty was to govern the Mesopotamians as righteously as possible. He tried to regulate the relations of his people so that they could live together in harmony.

Hammurabi's code has two striking characteristics. First, the law differed according to the social status of the offender. Aristocrats were not punished as harshly as commoners, nor commoners as harshly as slaves. Even slaves had rights, however, and received some protection under the law. Second, the code demanded that the punishment fit the crime. Like the Mosaic law of the Hebrews, it called for "an eye for an eye, and a tooth for a tooth," at least among equals. However, an aristocrat who destroyed the eye of a commoner or slave could pay a fine instead of losing his own eye. Otherwise, as long as criminal and victim shared the same social status, the victim could demand exact vengeance.

Gilgamesh The epic hero Gilgamesh here holds two bulls with human faces. Gilgamesh is not being an animal lover. The scene probably depicts his epic battle with these monstrous and powerful enemies. *(Source: The University Museum, University of Pennsylvania)*

Hammurabi's code began with legal procedure. There were no public prosecutors or district attorneys, so individuals brought their own complaints before the court. Each side had to produce written documents or witnesses to support its case. In cases of murder, the accuser had to prove the defendant guilty; any accuser who failed to do so was put to death. This strict law was designed to prevent people from lodging groundless charges. The Mesopotamians were very worried about witchcraft and sorcery. Anyone accused of witchcraft, even if the charges were not proved, underwent an ordeal by water. The gods themselves would decide the case. The defendant was thrown into the Euphrates, which was considered the instrument of the gods. A defendant who sank was guilty; a defendant who floated was innocent. (In medieval Europe and colonial America, accused witches also underwent ordeals by water, but they were considered innocent only if they sank.) Another procedural regulation covered the conduct of judges. Once a judge had rendered a verdict, he could not change it. Any judge who did so was fined heavily and deposed. In short, the code tried to guarantee a fair trial and a just verdict.

Consumer protection is not a modern idea; it goes back to Hammurabi's day. Merchants and

Law Code of Hammurabi Hammurabi ordered his code to be inscribed on a stone pillar and set up in public. At the top of the pillar Hammurabi is depicted receiving the scepter of authority from the god Shamash. (*Source: Louvre/Cliché des Musées Nationaux, Paris*)

businessmen had to guarantee the quality of their goods and services. A boatbuilder who did sloppy work had to repair the boat at his own expense. A boatman who lost the owner's boat or sank someone else's boat replaced it and its cargo. Housebuilders guaranteed their work with their lives. Careless work could result in the collapse of a house and the death of its inhabitants. If that happened, the builder himself was put to death. A merchant who tried to increase the interest rate on a loan forfeited the entire amount. Hammurabi's laws tried to ensure that consumers got what they paid for and paid a just price.

Crime was a feature of Mesopotamian urban life just as it is in modern cities. Burglary was a serious problem, hard to control. Because houses were built of mud brick, it was easy for an intruder to dig through the walls. Hammurabi's punishment for burglary matched the crime. A burglar caught in the act was put to death on the spot, and his body was walled into the breach that he had made. The penalty for looting was also grim: anyone caught looting a burning house was thrown into the fire.

Mesopotamian cities had breeding places of crime. Taverns were notorious haunts of criminals, who often met at taverns to make their plans. Tavernkeepers were expected to keep order and arrest anyone overheard planning a crime. Taverns were normally run by women, and they also served as houses of prostitution. Prostitution was disreputable but neither illegal nor regulated by law. Despite their social stigma, taverns were popular places, for Mesopotamians were fond of beer and wine. Tavernkeepers made a nice profit, but if they were caught increasing their profits by watering drinks, they were drowned.

Because farming was essential to Mesopotamian life, Hammurabi's code dealt greatly with agriculture. Tenant farming was widespread, and tenants rented land on a yearly basis, paying a proportion of their crops as rent. Unless the land was carefully cultivated, it quickly reverted to wasteland. Thus tenants faced severe penalties for neglecting the land or not working it at all. Since irrigation was essential to grow crops, tenants had to keep the canals and ditches in good repair. Otherwise the land would be subject to floods and farmers to crippling losses. Anyone whose neglect of the canals resulted in damaged crops had to bear all the expense of the lost crops. A tenant who could not pay the costs was sold into slavery.

The oxen that farmers used for plowing and threshing grain were ordinarily allowed to roam the streets. If an ox gored a passer-by, its owner had to pad its horns, tie it up, or bear the responsibility for future damages. Sheep raising was very lucrative because textile production was a major Mesopotamian industry. (Mesopotamian cloth was famous throughout the Near East.) The shepherd was a hired man with considerable responsibility. He was expected to protect the flock from wild animals, which were a standing problem, and to keep the sheep out of the crops. This strict regulation of agriculture paid rich dividends. The Mesopotamians often enjoyed bumper crops of grain, which fostered a large and thriving population.

Hammurabi gave careful attention to marriage and the family. As elsewhere in the Near East, marriage had aspects of a business agreement. The prospective groom and the father of the future bride arranged everything. The man offered the father a bridal gift, usually money. If the man and his bridal gift were acceptable, the father provided his daughter with a dowry. After marriage the dowry belonged to the woman (although the husband normally administered it) and was a means of protecting her rights and status. Once the two men agreed on financial matters, they drew up a contract; no marriage was considered legal without one. Either party could break off the marriage, but not without paying a stiff penalty. Fathers often contracted marriages while their children were still young. The girl either continued to live in her father's house until she reached maturity or went to live in the house of her father-in-law. During this time she was legally considered a wife. Once she and her husband came of age, they set up their own house.

The wife was expected to be rigorously faithful. The penalty for adultery was death. According to Hammurabi's code: "If the wife of a man has been caught while lying with another man, they shall bind them and throw them into the water."[7] The husband had the power to spare his wife by obtaining a pardon for her from the king. He could, however, accuse his wife of adultery even if he had not caught her in the act. In such a case she could try to clear herself before the city council, which investigated the charge. If she was found innocent, she could take her dowry and leave her husband. If a woman decided to take the direct approach and kill her husband, she was impaled.

The husband had virtually absolute power over his household. He could even sell his wife and children into slavery to pay debts. Sons did not lightly oppose their fathers, and any son who struck his father could have his hand cut off. A father was free to adopt children and include them in his will. Artisans sometimes adopted children to teach them the family trade. Although the father's power was great, he could not disinherit a son without just cause. Cases of disinheritance became matters for the city to decide, and the code ordered the courts to forgive a son for his first offense. Only if a son wronged his father a second time could he be disinherited.

Hammurabi's law code centered on social problems; it provides a bleak view of things. Other Mesopotamian documents give a happier glimpse of life. Although the code dealt with marriage shekel by shekel, a Mesopotamian poem tells of two people meeting secretly in the city. Their parting is delightfully modern:

Come now, set me free, I must go home,
Kuli-Enlil . . . set me free, I must go home.
What can I say to deceive my mother?[8]

Countless wills and testaments show that husbands habitually left their estates to their wives, who in turn willed the property to their children. All this suggests happy family life. Hammurabi's code restricted married women from commercial pursuits, but financial documents prove that many women engaged in business without hindrance. Some carried on the family business; others became wealthy landowners in their own right. Mesopotamians found their lives lightened by holidays and religious festivals. Traveling merchants brought news of the outside world and swapped marvelous tales. Despite their pessimism the Mesopotamians enjoyed a vibrant and creative culture, a culture that left its mark on the entire Near East.

EGYPT, THE LAND OF THE PHARAOHS (3100–1200 B.C.)

The Greek historian and traveler Herodotus in the fifth century B.C. called Egypt the "gift of the Nile." No other single geographical factor had such a fundamental, profound impact on the shap-

MAP 1.3 Ancient Egypt Geography and natural resources provided Egypt with centuries of peace and abundance.

areas, the Nile served to unify Egypt. The river was the principal highway and promoted easy communication throughout the valley. As individual bands of settlers moved into the Nile Valley, they created stable agricultural communities. By about 3100 B.C. there were some forty of these communities in constant contact with one another. This contact, encouraged and facilitated by the Nile, virtually ensured the early political unification of Egypt.

Egypt was fortunate in that it was nearly self-sufficient. Besides the fertility of its soil, Egypt possessed enormous quantities of stone, which served as the raw material of architecture and sculpture. Abundant clay was available for pottery, as was gold for jewelry and ornaments. The raw materials that Egypt lacked were close at hand. The Egyptians could obtain copper from Sinai and timber from Lebanon. They had little cause to look to the outside world for their essential needs, which helps to explain the insular quality of Egyptian life.

Geography further encouraged isolation by closing Egypt off from the outside world. To the east and west of the Nile Valley stretch grim deserts. The Nubian Desert and the cataracts of the Nile discourage penetration from the south. Only in the north does the Mediterranean Sea leave Egypt exposed. Thus geography shielded Egypt from invasion and from extensive immigration. Unlike the Mesopotamians, the Egyptians enjoyed centuries of peace and tranquillity during which they could devote most of their resources to the development of their distinctive civilization.

Yet Egypt was not completely sealed off. As early as 3250 B.C. Mesopotamian influences, notably architectural techniques and materials and perhaps even writing, made themselves felt in Egyptian life. Still later, from 1680 to 1580 B.C., northern Egypt was ruled by foreign invaders, the Hyksos. Infrequent though they were, such periods of foreign influence fertilized Egyptian culture without changing it in any fundamental way.

The God-King of Egypt

The geographical unity of Egypt quickly gave rise to political unification of the country under the authority of a king whom the Egyptians called "pharaoh." The details of this process have been lost. The Egyptians themselves told of a great

ing of Egyptian life, society, and history as the Nile (Map 1.3). Unlike the Tigris in Mesopotamia, it rarely brought death and destruction. The river was primarily a creative force. The Egyptians never feared the relatively tame Nile in the way the Mesopotamians feared the Tigris.

Whereas the Tigris and Euphrates and their tributaries carved up Mesopotamia into isolated king, Menes, who united Egypt into a single kingdom around 3100 B.C. Thereafter the Egyptians divided their history into dynasties, or families of kings. For modern historical purposes, however, it is more useful to divide Egyptian history into periods (see page 31). The political unification of Egypt ushered in the period known as the "Old Kingdom," an era remarkable for prosperity, artistic flowering, and the evolution of religious beliefs.

In religion, the Egyptians developed complex, often contradictory ideas about an afterlife. These beliefs were all rooted in the environment itself. The climate of Egypt is so stable that change is cyclical and dependable: though the heat of summer bakes the land, the Nile always floods and replenishes it. The dry air preserves much that would decay in other climates. Thus there was an air of permanence about Egypt; the past was never far from the present.

This cyclical rhythm permeated Egyptian religious beliefs. According to the Egyptians, Osiris, a fertility god associated with the Nile, dies each year, and each year his wife Isis brings him back to life. Osiris eventually became king of the dead, weighing human beings' hearts to determine whether they had lived justly enough to deserve everlasting life. Osiris's care of the dead was shared by Anubis, the jackal-headed god who annually helped Isis resuscitate Osiris. Anubis was the god of mummification, so essential to Egyptian funerary rites.

The focal point of religious and political life in the Old Kingdom was the pharaoh, who commanded the wealth, resources, and people of all Egypt. The pharaoh's power was such that the

Narmer Palette   This ceremonial object celebrates the deeds of Narmer, but it also illustrates several of the attributes of the pharaoh in general. On left at top, the conquering pharaoh views the decapitated corpse of an unknown enemy, showing his duty to defend Egypt by defeating its enemies. This same theme recurs on the right where the pharaoh—also represented by the falcon, symbol of Horus—is about to kill a captive. *(Source: Jean Vertut)*

Egyptians considered him to be the falcon-god Horus in human form. The link between the pharaoh and the god Horus was doubly important. In Egyptian religion Horus was the son of Osiris (king of the dead), which meant that the pharaoh, a living god on earth, became one with Osiris after death. The pharaoh was not simply the mediator between the gods and the Egyptian people. He was the power that achieved the integration between gods and humans, between nature and society, that ensured peace and prosperity for the land of the Nile. The pharaoh was thus a guarantee to his people, a pledge that the gods of Egypt (unlike those of Mesopotamia) cared for their people.

The king's surroundings had to be worthy of a god. Only a magnificent palace was suitable for his home; in fact, the word *pharaoh* means "great house." The king's tomb also had to reflect his might and exalted status. To this day the great pyramids at Giza near Cairo bear silent but magnificent testimony to the god-kings of Egypt. The pharaoh's ability to command the resources and labor necessary to build a huge pyramid amply demonstrates that the god-king was an absolute ruler.

The religious significance of the pyramid is as awesome as the political. The pharaoh as a god was the earthly sun, and the pyramid, which towered to the sky, helped him ascend to the heavens after death. The pyramid provided the dead king with everything that he would need in the afterlife. His body had to be preserved from decay if his *ka*, an invisible counterpart of the body, was to survive. So the Egyptians developed an elaborate process of embalming the dead pharaoh and wrapping his corpse in cloth. As an added precaution, they carved his statue out of hard stone; if anything happened to the fragile mummy, the pharaoh's statue would help keep his ka alive. The need for an authentic likeness accounts for the naturalism of Egyptian portraiture. Artistic renderings of the pharaohs combine accuracy and the abstract in an effort to capture the essence of the living person. This approach produced the haunting quality of Egyptian sculpture—portraits of lifelike people imbued with a solemn, ageless, serene spirit.

To survive in the spirit world, the ka required everything that the pharaoh needed in life: food and drink, servants and armed retainers, costly ornaments, and animal herds. In Egypt's prehistoric period, the king's servants and herdsmen and their flocks were slaughtered at the tomb to provide for

the ka. By the time of the Old Kingdom, artists had substituted statues of scribes, officials, soldiers, and servants for their living counterparts. To remind the ka of daily life, artists covered the walls of the tomb with scenes ranging from agricultural routines to banquets and religious festivities, from hunting parties to gardens and ponds. Designed to give joy to the ka, these paintings, models of furniture, and statuettes today provide an intimate glimpse of Egyptian life 4,500 years ago.

The Pharaoh's People

Because the common folk stood at the bottom of the social and economic scale, they were always at the mercy of grasping officials. The arrival of the tax collector was never a happy occasion. One Egyptian scribe described the worst consequences of such a visit:

And now the scribe lands on the river-bank and is about to register the harvest-tax. The janitors carry staves and the Nubians rods of palm, and they say, Hand over the corn, though there is none. The cultivator is beaten all over, he is bound and thrown into a well, soused and dipped head downwards. His wife has been bound in his presence and his children are in fetters.[9]

That was an extreme situation. Nonetheless, taxes might amount to 20 percent of the harvest, and tax collection could be brutal.

On the other hand, everyone, no matter how lowly, had the right of appeal, and the account of one such appeal, "The Tale of the Eloquent Peasant," was a favorite Egyptian story. The hero of the tale, Khunanup, was robbed by the servant of the high steward, and Khunanup had to bring his case before the steward himself. When the steward delayed his decision, Khunanup openly accused him of neglecting his duty, saying, "The arbitrator is a spoiler; the peace-maker is a creator of sorrow; the smoother over of differences is a creator of soreness."[10] The pharaoh himself ordered the steward to give Khunanup justice, and the case was decided in the peasant's favor.

Egyptian society seems to have been a curious mixture of freedom and constraint. Slavery did not become widespread until the New Kingdom. There was neither a caste system nor a color bar, and humble people could rise to the highest posi-

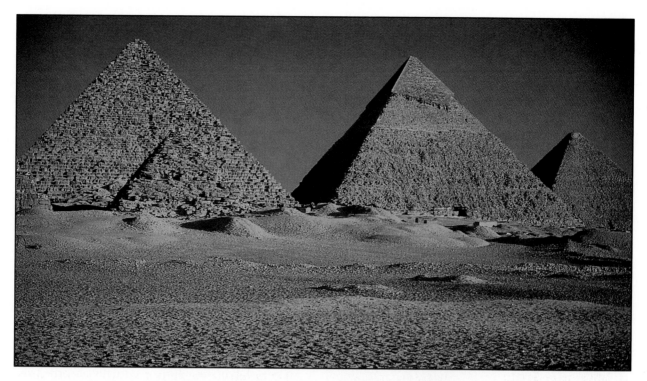

The Pyramids at Giza Giza was the burial place of the pharaohs of the Old Kingdom and of their aristocracy, whose rectangular tombs are visible behind the middle pyramid. The small pyramids at the foot of the foremost pyramid probably belong to the pharaohs' wives. *(Source: Geoffrey Clifford/Woodfin Camp)*

tions if they possessed talent. The most famous example of social mobility (which, however, dates to the New Kingdom) is the biblical story of Joseph, who came to Egypt as a slave and rose to be second only to the pharaoh. Most ordinary folk, however, were probably little more than serfs who could not easily leave the land of their own free will. Peasants were also subject to forced labor, including work on the pyramids and canals. Young men were drafted into the pharaoh's army, which served both as a fighting force and as a labor corps.

The Egyptian view of life and society is alien to those raised on the concepts of individual freedom and human rights. To ancient Egyptians the pharaoh embodied justice and order—harmony among humans, nature, and the divine. If the pharaoh was weak or allowed anyone to challenge his unique position, he opened the way to chaos. Twice in Egyptian history the pharaoh failed to maintain rigid centralization. During these two eras, known as the "First and Second Intermediate periods," Egypt was exposed to civil war and invasion. Yet even in the darkest times the monarchy survived,

and in each period a strong pharaoh arose to crush the rebels or expel the invaders and restore order.

The Hyksos in Egypt (1640–1570 B.C.)

While Egyptian civilization flourished behind its bulwark of sand and sea, momentous changes were taking place in the ancient Near East, changes that would leave their mark even on rich, insular Egypt. These changes involved enormous and remarkable movements, especially of peoples who spoke Semitic tongues.

The original home of the Semites was probably the Arabian peninsula. Some tribes moved into northern Mesopotamia, others into Syria and Palestine, and still others into Egypt. By 1640 B.C., people whom the Egyptians called *Hyksos*, which means "Rulers of the Uplands," began to settle in the Nile Delta. Egyptian tradition, as later recorded by the priest Manetho in the third century B.C., depicted the coming of the Hyksos as a brutal invasion:

Although the Egyptians portrayed the Hyksos as a conquering horde, they were probably no more than nomads looking for good land. Their entry into the delta was probably gradual and generally peaceful. The Hyksos "invasion" was one of the fertilizing periods of Egyptian history; it introduced new ideas and techniques into Egyptian life. The Hyksos brought with them the method of making bronze and casting it into tools and weapons that became standard in Egypt. They thereby brought Egypt fully into the Bronze Age culture of the Mediterranean world, a culture in which the production and use of bronze implements became basic to society. Bronze tools made farming more efficient than ever before because they were sharper and more durable than the copper tools they replaced. The Hyksos' use of bronze armor and weapons as well as horse-drawn chariots and the composite bow, made of laminated wood and horn and far more powerful than the simple wooden bow, revolutionized Egyptian warfare. However much the Egyptians learned from the Hyksos, Egyptian culture eventually absorbed the newcomers. The Hyksos came to worship Egyptian gods and modeled their monarchy on the pharaoh's.

The New Kingdom: Revival and Empire (1570–1200 B.C.)

Politically, Egypt was only in eclipse. The Egyptian sun shone again when a remarkable line of kings, the pharaohs of the Eighteenth Dynasty, arose to challenge the Hyksos. The pharaoh Ahmose (1558–1533 B.C.) pushed the Hyksos out of the delta. Thutmose I (1512–1500 B.C.) subdued Nubia in the south, and Thutmose III (1490–1436 B.C.) conquered Palestine and Syria and fought inconclusively with the Hurrians, who had migrated into the upper Euphrates from the north and created there the kingdom of Mitanni. These warrior-pharaohs inaugurated the New Kingdom—a period in Egyptian history characterized by enormous wealth and conscious imperialism. During this period, probably for the first time, widespread slavery became a feature of Egyptian life. The pharaoh's armies returned home leading hordes of slaves, who constituted a new labor force for imperial building projects. The Hebrews, who according to the Old Testament migrated into Egypt during this period to escape a

Hippopotamus Hunt This wall painting depicts the success of two men in a small boat who have killed a hippopotamus, seen in the lower right-hand corner. Behind the hippopotamus swims a crocodile hoping for a snack. *(Source: Egyptian Museum SMPK, Berlin/Bildarchiv Preussischer Kulturbesitz)*

In the reign of Toutimaios—I do not know why—the wind of god blew against us. Unexpectedly from the regions of the east men of obscure race, looking forward confidently to victory, invaded our land, and without a battle easily seized it all by sheer force. Having subdued those in authority in the land, they then barbarously burned our cities and razed to the ground the temples of the gods. They fell upon all the natives in an entirely hateful fashion, slaughtering them and leading both their children and wives into slavery. At last they made one of their people king, whose name was Salitis. This man resided at Memphis, leaving in Upper and Lower Egypt tax collectors and garrisons in strategic places.[11]

PERIODS OF EGYPTIAN HISTORY

Period	Dates	Significant Events
Archaic	3100–2660 B.C.	Unification of Egypt
Old Kingdom	2660–2180 B.C.	Construction of the pyramids
First Intermediate	2180–2080 B.C.	Political chaos
Middle Kingdom	2080–1640 B.C.	Recovery and political stability
Second Intermediate	1640–1570 B.C.	Hyksos "invasion"
New Kingdom	1570–1075 B.C.	Creation of an Egyptian empire
		Akhenaten's religious policy

drought, were soon enslaved and put to work on imperial construction projects.

The kings of the Eighteenth Dynasty created the first Egyptian empire. They ruled Palestine and Syria through their officers and incorporated the African region of Nubia. Egyptian religion and customs flourished in Nubia, making a huge impact on African culture there and in neighboring areas. The warrior-kings celebrated their success with monuments on a scale unparalleled since the pharaohs of the Old Kingdom had built the pyramids. Even today the colossal granite statues of these pharaohs and the rich tomb objects of Tutankhamen ("King Tut") testify to the might and splendor of the New Kingdom.

Akhenaten and Monotheism

One of the most extraordinary of this unusual line of kings was Akhenaten (1367–1350 B.C.), a pharaoh concerned more with religion than with conquest. Nefertiti, his wife and queen, encouraged his religious bent. The precise nature of Akhenaten's religious beliefs remains debatable. During his own lifetime his religion was often unpopular among the people and the traditional priesthood, and its practice declined in the later years of his reign. After his death, it was condemned and denounced; consequently, not much is known about it. Most historians, however, agree that Akhenaten and Nefertiti were *monotheists*—that is, they believed that the sun-god Aton, whom they worshiped, was universal, the only god. They consid-

ered all other Egyptian gods and goddesses frauds and disregarded their worship.

The religious notions and actions of Akhenaten and Nefertiti were in direct opposition to traditional Egyptian beliefs. The Egyptians had long worshiped a host of gods, chief among whom was Amon-Re. Originally Amon and Re had been two distinct sun-gods, but the Egyptians merged them and worshiped Amon-Re as the king of the gods. Besides Amon-Re, the Egyptians honored such other deities as Osiris, Osiris's wife Isis, and his son Horus. Egyptian religion had room for many gods and an easy tolerance for new gods.

To these genuine religious sentiments were added the motives of the traditional priesthood. Although many priests were genuinely scandalized by Akhenaten's monotheism, many others were concerned more about their own welfare. What were the priests of the outlawed gods to do? Akhenaten had destroyed their livelihood and their reason for existence. On grounds of pure self-interest, the established priesthood opposed the pharaoh. Opposition in turn drove Akhenaten to intolerance and persecution. With a vengeance he tried to root out the old gods and their rituals.

Akhenaten celebrated his break with the past by building a new capital, Akhetaten, the modern El-Amarna (see Map 1.3). There Aton was honored with an immense temple and proper worship. Worship of Aton focused on truth (as Akhenaten defined it) and a desire for the natural. The pharaoh and his queen demanded that the truth be carried over into art. Unlike Old Kingdom painting and sculpture, which blended the actual and the abstract, the art of this period became relentlessly realistic. Sculptors molded exact likenesses of Akhenaten, despite his ugly features and misshapen body. Artists portrayed the pharaoh in intimate family scenes, playing with his infant daughter or expressing affection to members of his family. On one relief Akhenaten appears gnawing a cutlet of meat; on another he lolls in a chair. Akhenaten was being portrayed as a mortal man, not as the dignified pharaoh of Egypt.

Akhenaten's monotheism was imposed from above and failed to find a place among the people. The prime reason for Akhenaten's failure is that his god had no connection with the past of the Egyptian people, who trusted the old gods and felt comfortable praying to them. Average Egyptians were no doubt distressed and disheartened when their familiar gods were outlawed, for they were the heavenly powers that had made Egypt powerful and unique. The fanaticism and persecution that accompanied the new monotheism were in complete defiance of the Egyptian tradition of tolerant *polytheism,* or worship of several gods. Thus, when Akhenaten died, his religion died with him.

THE HITTITE EMPIRE

At about the time the Hyksos entered the Nile Delta, other parts of the Near East were also troubled by the arrival of newcomers. Two new groups of peoples, the Hurrians and Kassites, carved out kingdoms for themselves. Meanwhile the Hittites, who had long been settled in Anatolia (modern Turkey), became a major power in that region and began to expand eastward (Map 1.4). Around 1595 B.C. a century and a half after Hammurabi's death, the Hittites and the Kassites brought down the Babylonian kingdom and established Kassite rule there. The Hurrians created the kingdom of Mitanni on the upper reaches of the Euphrates and Tigris.

The Hittites were an Indo-European people. The term *Indo-European* refers to a large family of languages that includes English, most of the languages of modern Europe, Greek, Latin, Persian, and Sanskrit, the sacred tongue of ancient India. During the eighteenth and nineteenth centuries, European scholars learned that peoples who spoke related languages had spread as far west as Ireland and as far east as central Asia. In the twentieth century, linguists deciphered the language of the Hittites and the Linear B script of Mycenaean Greece. When both languages proved to be Indo-European, scholars were able to form a clearer picture of these vast movements. Archeologists were able to date the migrations roughly and put them into their historical context.

Despite the efforts of many scholars, the original home of the Indo-Europeans remains to be identified. Judging primarily from the spread of the languages, linguists have suggested that the migrations started from the steppes region north of the Black and Caspian seas. Although two great waves began around 2000 B.C. and 1200 B.C., these

The Goddess Selket Selket appears in this statuette dressed as a queen. The goddess was originally a water scorpion who later assumed human form. She was the goddess who healed stings and bites. *(Source: Egyptian Museum, Cairo/Lee Boltin)*

MAP 1.4 Balance of Power in the Near East This map shows the regions controlled by the Hittites and Egyptians at the height of their power. The striped area represents the part of Mesopotamia conquered by the Hittites during their expansion eastward.

migrations on the whole followed a sporadic and gradual progression. The Celtic-speaking Gauls, for example, did not move into the area of present-day France, Belgium, and Germany until the seventh century B.C., long after most Indo-Europeans had found new homes.

Around 2000 B.C. Indo-Europeans were on the move on a massive scale. Peoples speaking the ancestor of Latin pushed into Italy, and Greek-speaking Mycenaeans settled in Greece. The Hittites came into prominence in Anatolia (modern Turkey), and other folk thrust into Iran, India, and central Asia. At first the waves of Indo-Europeans and other peoples disrupted already existing states, but in time the newcomers settled down.

The Rise of the Hittites

Until recently, scholars thought that as part of these vast movements the Hittites entered Anatolia only around 1800 B.C. Current archeological work and new documents, however, prove that the Hittites had settled there at least as early as 2700

B.C. Nor did they overrun the country in a sweeping invasion, burning, looting, and destroying. Their arrival and diffusion seem to have been rather peaceful, accompanied by intermarriage and alliance with the natives. So well did the Hittites integrate themselves into the local culture of central Anatolia that they even adopted the worship of several native deities.

Their mastery of iron technology set the Hittites apart. Although it is not yet known whether the Hittites were first to discover the possibilities of iron and the ways to use it, they mastered iron technology before anyone else in the Near East. Their knowledge permitted them to craft weapons and tools far superior to those of their neighbors, which gave them a decided advantage in both war and commerce.

Although much uncertainty still surrounds the earliest history of the Hittites, their rise to prominence in Anatolia is well documented. During the nineteenth century B.C. the native kingdoms in the area engaged in warfare that left most of Anatolia's once-flourishing towns in ashes and rubble. Taking advantage of this climate of exhaustion, the Hittite king Hattusilis I built a hill citadel at Hattusas, the modern Boghazköy, from which he led his people against neighboring kingdoms. Although the Hittites extended their arms as far as Babylon, where they snuffed out the dynasty of Hammurabi, they were themselves vulnerable to attack by vigilant and tenacious enemies. Yet once the Hittites were united behind a strong king, they were a power with which to be reckoned.

Hittite Society

The geography of central Anatolia encouraged the rise of self-contained agricultural communities. Each group was probably originally ruled by a

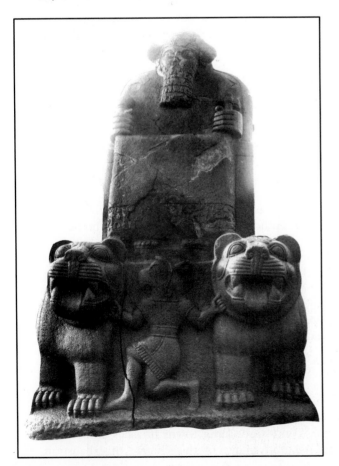

The Hittite God Atarluhas This statue of the god Atarluhas, with two lions at his feet, was set up near the gateway of the Hittite city of Carchemish. A bird-headed demon holds the lions. In 1920 this statue was destroyed during a war between Turkey and Syria. *(Source: Courtesy of the Trustees of the British Museum)*

petty king, but under the Hittites local officials known as "Elders" handled community affairs. Besides the farming population, a well-defined group of artisans fashioned the pottery, cloth, leather goods, and metal tools needed by society. Documents also report that traveling merchants peddled goods and gossip, reminding individual communities that they were part of a larger world. As in many other societies, ancient and modern, the Hittites held slaves, who nonetheless enjoyed certain rights under the law.

At the head of Hittite society stood the king and queen. The king was supreme commander of the army, chief judge, and supreme priest. He carried on all diplomatic dealings with foreign powers and in times of war personally led the Hittite army into the field. The queen, who was highly regarded, held a strong, independent position. She had important religious duties to perform, and some queens even engaged in diplomatic correspondence with foreign queens.

Below the king and queen was the aristocracy, among whom the relatives of the king constituted a privileged group. The king's relations were a mighty and often unruly group who served as the chief royal administrators. The royal family was often a threat to the king, for some members readily resorted to murder as a method of seizing power. Hittite nobles often revolted against the king, thereby weakening central authority and leaving Hittite society open to outside attack. At the base of society stood the warriors, who had the right to meet in their own assembly, the *pankus*. The pankus met to hear the will of the king but could not vote on policy. It was, however, a court of law, with the authority to punish criminals.

The Hittites, like many newcomers to the ancient Near East, readily assimilated the cultures that they found, such as Anatolia's. Soon they fell under the powerful spell of the superior Mesopotamian culture. The Hittites adopted the cuneiform script for their own language. Hittite kings published law codes, just as Hammurabi had done. Royal correspondence followed Mesopotamian form. The Hittites delighted in Mesopotamian myths, legends, and epics. Of Hittite art, one scholar has observed that "there is hardly a single Hittite monument which somewhere does not show traces of Mesopotamian influence."[12] To the credit of the Hittites, they used these Mesopotamian borrowings to create something of their own.

The Era of Hittite Greatness (ca 1475–ca 1200 B.C.)

The Hittites, like the Egyptians of the New Kingdom, eventually produced an energetic and capable line of kings who restored order and rebuilt Hittite power. Once Telepinus (1525–1500 B.C.) had brought the aristocracy under control, Suppiluliumas I (1380–1346 B.C.) secured central Anatolia, and Mursilis II (1345–1315 B.C.) regained Syria. Around 1300 B.C. Mursilis's son stopped the Egyptian army of Rameses II at the battle of Kadesh in Syria. Having fought each other to a standstill, the Hittites and Egyptians first made peace, then an alliance. Alliance was followed by friendship; friendship, by active cooperation. The two greatest powers of the early Near East tried to make war between themselves impossible.

The Hittites exercised remarkable political wisdom and flexibility in the organization and administration of their empire. Some states they turned into vassal-kingdoms, ruled by the sons of the Hittite king; the king and his sons promised each other mutual support in times of crisis. Still other kingdoms were turned into protectorates, where native kings were allowed to rule with considerable freedom. The native kings swore obedience to the Hittite king and had to contribute military contingents to the Hittite army. Although they also sent tribute to the Hittites, the financial burden was moderate. The common people probably felt Hittite overlordship little if at all.

Although the Hittites were often at war, owing to the sheer number of enemies surrounding them, they did seek diplomatic and political solutions to their problems. They were realistic enough to recognize the limits of their power and far-sighted enough to appreciate the value of peace and alliance with Egypt. Together the two kingdoms provided much of the ancient Near East with a precious interlude of peace. Unfortunately, however, both were seriously weakened in the process.

THE FALL OF EMPIRES (1200 B.C.)

This stable and generally peaceful situation endured until the cataclysm of the thirteenth century B.C., when both the Hittite and the Egyptian empires were destroyed by invaders. The most famous

Temple of Rameses II These colossal statues of Rameses II, carved literally out of the side of a hill, guard the entrance of a temple itself created by tunneling through rock. The statues of the last great pharaoh measure about 40 feet in height. *(Source: Geoffrey Clifford/Woodfin Camp)*

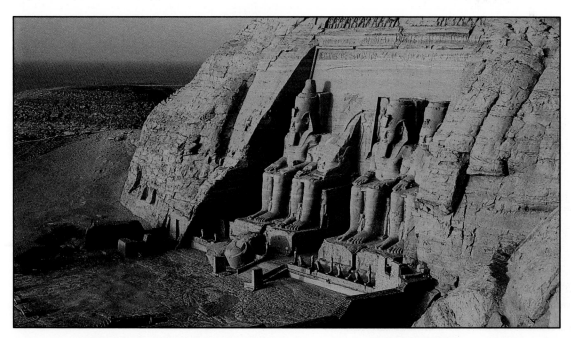

of these marauders, called the "Sea Peoples" by the Egyptians, remains one of the puzzles of ancient history. Despite much new work, modern archeology is still unable to identify the Sea Peoples satisfactorily. It is known, however, that they were part of a larger movement of peoples. Although there is serious doubt about whether the Sea Peoples alone overthrew the Hittites, they did deal both the Hittites and the Egyptians a hard blow, making the Hittites vulnerable to overland invasion from the north and driving the Egyptians back to the Nile Delta. The Hittites fell under the external blows, but the Egyptians, shaken and battered, retreated to the delta and held on.

In 1200 B.C. as earlier, both Indo-European and Semitic-speaking peoples were on the move. They brought down the old centers of power and won new homes for themselves. In Mesopotamia the Assyrians destroyed the kingdom of Mitanni and struggled with the Kassites; the Hebrews moved into Palestine; and another wave of Indo-Europeans penetrated Anatolia. But once again these victories were political and military, not cultural. The old cultures—especially that of Mesopotamia—impressed their ideas, values, and ideals on the newcomers. Although the chaos of the thirteenth century B.C. caused a serious material decline throughout the ancient Near East, the old cultures lived on through a dark age.

Although the societies of the Near East suffered stunning blows in the thirteenth century B.C., more persisted than perished. The great achievements of Mesopotamia and Egypt survived to enhance the lives of those who came after.

NOTES

1. L. Eiseley, *The Unexpected Universe* (New York: Harcourt Brace Jovanovich, 1969), p. 102.
2. Quoted in S. N. Kramer, *The Sumerians* (Chicago: University of Chicago Press, 1964), p. 238.
3. J. B. Pritchard, ed., *Ancient Near Eastern Texts,* 3d ed. (Princeton: Princeton University Press, 1969), p. 175. Hereafter called *ANET.*
4. *ANET,* p. 44.
5. *ANET,* p. 590.
6. Kramer, *The Sumerians,* p. 150.
7. *ANET,* p. 171.
8. Kramer, *The Sumerians,* p. 251.
9. Quoted in A. H. Gardiner, "Ramesside Texts Relating to the Taxation and Transport of Corn," *Journal of Egyptian Archaeology* 27 (1941): 19–20.
10. A. H. Gardiner, "The Eloquent Peasant," *Journal of Egyptian Archaeology* 9 (1923): 17.
11. Manetho, *History of Egypt,* frag. 42.75–77.
12. M. Vieyra, *Hittite Art 2300–750 B.C.* (London: Alec Tiranti, 1955), p. 12.

SUMMARY

During the long span of years covered by this chapter, human beings made astonishing strides, advancing from primitive hunters to become builders of sophisticated civilizations. Four great rivers provided the natural conditions necessary to sustain settled life. Yet because the rivers presented different problems to different peoples, developments across the globe were not identical. By mastering the plant and animal worlds, human beings prospered dramatically. With their basic bodily needs more than satisfied, they realized even greater achievements, including more complex social groupings, metal technology, and long-distance trade. The intellectual achievements of these centuries were equally impressive. Ancient Near Eastern peoples created advanced mathematics, monumental architecture, and engaging literature.

SUGGESTED READING

Those interested in the tangled and incomplete story of human evolution will be rewarded by a good deal of new work, much of it difficult. C. E. Oxnard, *Fossils, Teeth and Sex* (1987), uses current information to conclude that the very search for the "missing link" is the wrong approach. R. Singer and J. K. Lundy, *Variation, Culture and Evolution in African Populations* (1986)—especially chap. 16—discusses recent developments in Africa. C. Gamble, *The Palaeolithic Settlement of Europe* (1986), covers both methodology and recent finds to offer a new interpretation of how early peoples spread through Europe. I. Rouse, *Migrations in Prehistory* (1989), uses information from cultural remains to study population movements. A much broader book is T. C. Champion et al., *Prehistoric Europe* (1984). See also G. Lerner, *The Creation of Patriarchy* (1986), for recent findings of anthropologists. F. Dahlberg, *Woman the Gatherer* (1981), demonstrates the importance for primitive societies of women's role in gathering. A broader and newer study is M. Ehrenberg, *Women in Prehistory* (1989). A study of how primitive peoples depended on both hunting and gathering for survival is provided by T. D. Price and J. A. Brown, *Prehistoric Hunter-Gatherers* (1985), which also studies how hunting and gathering led to a more complex culture.

The origins of agriculture and the Neolithic Age have recently received a great deal of attention. J. R. Harlan's conclusions are set out in a series of works including "Agricultural Origins: Centers and Noncenters," *Science* 174 (1971): 468–474; *Crops and Man* (1975); and "The Plants and Animals That Nourish Man," *Scientific American* 235 (September 1976): 89; F. Wendorf and R. Schild, "The Earliest Food Producers," *Archaeology* 34 (September–October 1981): 30–36.

G. Barker, *Prehistoric Farming in Europe* (1984), and P. S. Wells, *Farms, Villages and Cities* (1984), treat the problem of commerce and urban origins in late prehistoric Europe. A very readable study, A. Ferrill, *The Origins of War* (1985), treats the topic of warfare from the Neolithic Age to Alexander the Great. Ferrill makes the interesting suggestion that more organized methods of warfare influenced the trend toward urbanization.

For the societies of Mesopotamia, see A. Leo Oppenheim, *Ancient Mesopotamia,* rev. ed. (1977); M. E. L. Mallowan, *Early Mesopotamia and Iran* (1965); and H. W. F. Saggs, *The Greatness That Was Babylon* (1962). H. W. F. Saggs, *Everyday Life in Babylonia and Assyria* (1965), offers a delightful glimpse of Mesopotamian life. S. Dalley, ed., *Myths from Mesopotamia* (1989), is a good translation of such prevailing myths as the Creation, the Flood, Gilgamesh, and many others. The best recent synthesis of the finds at Ebla can be found in G. Pettinato, *Ebla* (1991); the author has been a participant in the excavations since their beginnings.

C. B. Kemp, *Ancient Egypt: Anatomy of a Civilization* (1988), is a comprehensive reassessment of Egyptian society. D. B. Redford, *Akhenaten: The Heretic King* (1984), puts Akhenaten into his historical context, both political and religious. B. S. Lesko, *The Remarkable Women of Ancient Egypt,* 2d ed. (1987), a brief survey of aristocratic and ordinary women, concludes that Egyptian women led freer lives than the women of the Greco-Roman period. The title of L. Manniche, *Sexual Life in Ancient Egypt* (1987), aptly describes the book's subject. J. M. White, *Everyday Life in Ancient Egypt* (1963), provides a broad survey of Egyptian society. M. Lichtheim, *Ancient Egyptian Literature,* 3 vols. (1975–1980), is a selection of readings covering the most important periods of Egyptian history. D. B. Red-

ford, *Akhenaton* (1987), with illustrations, offers the most recent assessment of this complex pharaoh.

Introductions to problems and developments shared by several Near Eastern societies can be found in the studies edited by T. A. Wertime and J. D. Muhly, *The Coming of the Age of Iron* (1980), as well as in J. B. Pritchard, *The Ancient Near East,* 2 vols. (1958, 1976). The latter work is a fine synthesis by one of the world's leading Near Eastern specialists. A sweeping survey is C. Burney, *The Ancient Near East* (1977). Pioneering new work on the origins of writing appears in a series of pieces by D. Schmandt-Besserat, notably "An Archaic Recording System and the Origin of Writing," *Syro-Mesopotamian Studies* 1–2 (1977): 1–32, and "Reckoning Before Writing," *Archaeology* 32 (May–June 1979): 23–31.

O. R. Gurney, *The Hittites,* 2d ed. (1954), is still a fine introduction by an eminent scholar. Good also is J. G. MacQueen, *The Hittites and Their Contemporaries in Asia Minor,* 2d ed. (1986). J. P. Mallory, *In Search of the Indo-Europeans* (1989), uses language, archeology, and myth to study the Indo-Europeans. The 1960s were prolific years for archeology in Turkey. A brief survey by one of the masters of the field is J. Mellaart, *The Archaeology of Modern Turkey* (1978), which also tests a great number of widely held historical interpretations. The Sea Peoples have been the subject of two recent studies: A. Nibbi, *The Sea Peoples and Egypt* (1975), and N. K. Sandars, *The Sea Peoples* (1978).

A truly excellent study of ancient religions, from those of Sumer to those of the late Roman Empire, is M. Eliade, ed., *Religions of Antiquity* (1989), which treats concisely but amply all of the religions mentioned in Chapters 1 through 6. For Near Eastern religion and mythology, good introductions are E. O. James, *The Ancient Gods: The History and Diffusion of Religion in the Ancient Near East and the Eastern Mediterranean* (1960), and J. Gray, *Near Eastern Mythology* (1969). A survey of Mesopotamian religion by one of the foremost scholars in the field is T. Jacobsen, *The Treasures of Darkness: A History of Mesopotamian Religion* (1976).

Surveys of Near Eastern art include R. D. Barnett and D. J. Wiseman, *Fifty Masterpieces of Ancient Near Eastern Art* (1969); and J. B. Pritchard, *The Ancient Near East in Pictures,* 2d ed. (1969). For literature, see S. Fiore, *Voices from the Clay: The Development of Assyro-Babylonian Literature* (1965); W. K. Simpson, ed., *The Literature of Ancient Egypt* (1973); and, above all, J. B. Pritchard, ed., *Ancient Near Eastern Texts,* 3d ed. (1969).

2

Small Kingdoms and Mighty Empires in the Near East

Audience hall of King Darius, Persepolis

The migratory invasions that brought down the Hittites and stunned the Egyptians in the late thirteenth century B.C. ushered in an era of confusion and weakness. Although much was lost in the chaos, the old cultures of the ancient Near East survived to nurture new societies. In the absence of powerful empires, the Phoenicians, Syrians, Hebrews, and many other peoples carved out small independent kingdoms. During this period Hebrew culture and religion evolved under the influence of urbanism, kings, and prophets.

In the ninth century B.C. this jumble of small states gave way to an empire that for the first time embraced the entire Near East. Yet the ferocity of the Assyrian Empire led to its downfall only two hundred years later. In 550 B.C. the Persians and Medes, who had migrated into Iran, created a vast empire stretching from Anatolia in the west to the Indus Valley in the east. For over two hundred years the Persians gave the ancient Near East peace and stability.

- How did Egypt, its political greatness behind it, pass on its cultural heritage to its African neighbors?

- How did the Hebrew state evolve, and what was daily life like in Hebrew society?

- What forces helped to shape Hebrew religious thought, still powerfully influential in today's world?

- What enabled the Assyrians to overrun their neighbors, and how did their cruelty finally cause their undoing?

- How did Iranian nomads create the Persian Empire?

In this chapter we seek answers to these questions.

MIGRATIONS

The migrations of peoples on a huge scale during this period were merely a single aspect of a larger picture of human movement that has continued over the course of history, from the Paleolithic Age to the present day. Just as Indo-European and Semitic-speaking peoples sought new land around 1200 B.C., so in the nineteenth and twentieth centuries peoples from Europe and Asia came to North America seeking new opportunities for a more prosperous life. In antiquity, however, the picture is especially complex and the reasons for movement are varied and unclear. The Hyksos moved into Egypt looking for new land (see pages 29–30). The later onslaught of the Sea Peoples on Egypt seems more like random raids than migrations, even though many of the Sea Peoples established permanent homes elsewhere in the Mediterranean (pages 35–36). The Hebrews left Egypt to escape a harsh government (pages 43–44). In short, one major reason for migrations is poverty of the environment, sometimes combined with overpopulation, which forces people to seek better land. Another is the reaction to such vast movements. Weaker folk were pushed ahead of the newcomers and sought new homes elsewhere. In the process, they created for others the same problems and challenges that they themselves confronted. Still other migrants simply tried to escape cruel or oppressive governments to find a place of their own. In many instances several or all of these factors lay behind the migrations. Each case must be studied individually.

The effects of migrations are as varied as the reasons for them. In these instances, the various peoples involved assimilated aspects of the others' culture. Some newcomers, like the Hyksos and the Hittites, who came peaceably, drew important lessons from the established peoples whom they encountered and contributed something of their own to the cultural environment. In the process, both the new arrivals and the native inhabitants found their cultures mutually but differently enriched. Other migrations resulted in the obliteration of the native population so that some peoples are known today only by name. No one has yet studied this vast historical phenomenon on its own massive scale, but it can be safely said that many of these migrations were a combination of destruction and fertilization. Intellectually and socially enriched cultures often grew out of them.

EGYPT, A SHATTERED KINGDOM

An example of the complexities involved in large movements of peoples comes from the invasions that ended the Hittite Empire and from the Sea Peoples' onslaught on Egypt. The invasions of the Sea Peoples brought the great days of Egyptian power to an end. One scribe left behind a somber portrait of Egypt stunned and leaderless:

The land of Egypt was abandoned and every man was a law to himself. During many years there was no leader who could speak for others. Central government lapsed, small officials and headmen took over the whole land. Any man, great or small, might kill his neighbor. In the distress and vacuum that followed . . . men banded together to plunder one another. They treated the gods no better than men, and cut off the temple revenues.[1]

No longer able to dream of foreign conquests, Egypt looked to its own security from foreign invasion. Egyptians suffered a four-hundred-year period of political fragmentation, a new dark age known to Egyptian specialists as the Third Intermediate Period (eleventh to seventh centuries B.C.).

The decline of Egypt was especially sharp in foreign affairs. Whereas the pharaohs of the Eighteenth Dynasty had held sway as far abroad as Syria, their weak successors found it unsafe to venture far from home. In the wake of the Sea Peoples, numerous small kingdoms sprang up in the Near East, each fiercely protective of its own independence. To them Egypt was a memory, and foreign princes often greeted Egyptian officials with suspicion or even contempt. In the days of Egypt's greatness, petty kings would never have dared to treat Egyptian officials in such a humiliating fashion.

Disrupted at home and powerless abroad, Egypt fell prey to invasion by its African neighbors. Libyans from North Africa filtered into the Nile Delta, where they established independent dynasties. Indeed, from 950 to 730 B.C. northern Egypt was ruled by Libyan pharaohs. The Libyans built cities, and for the first time a sturdy urban life grew up in the delta. Although the coming of the Libyans changed the face of the delta, the Libyans genuinely admired Egyptian culture and eagerly adopted Egypt's religion and way of life.

In southern Egypt, meanwhile, the pharaoh's decline opened the way to the energetic Africans of Nubia, who extended their authority northward throughout the Nile Valley. Nubian influence in these years, though pervasive, was not destructive. Since the imperial days of the Eighteenth Dynasty (see pages 30–32), the Nubians, too, had adopted many features of Egyptian culture. Now Nubian kings and aristocrats embraced Egyptian culture wholesale. The thought of destroying the heritage of the pharaohs would have struck them as stupid and barbaric. Thus the Nubians and the Libyans repeated an old phenomenon: new peoples conquered old centers of political and military power but were nevertheless assimilated into the older culture.

The reunification of Egypt occurred late and unexpectedly. With Egypt distracted and disorganized by foreign invasions, an independent African state, the Kingdom of Kush, grew up in modern Sudan with its capital at Nepata. These Africans, too, worshiped Egyptian gods and used Egyptian hieroglyphs. In the eighth century B.C. their king Piankhy swept through the entire Nile Valley from Nepata in the south to the delta in the north. United once again, Egypt enjoyed a brief period of peace during which Egyptians continued to assimilate their conquerors. In the Kingdom of Kush, Egyptian methods of administration and bookkeeping, arts and crafts, and economic practices became common, especially among the aristocracy. Nonetheless, reunification of the realm did not lead to a new Egyptian empire. In the centuries between the fall of the New Kingdom and the recovery of Egypt, several small but vigorous kingdoms had taken root and grown to maturity in the ancient Near East. By 700 B.C. Egypt was once again a strong kingdom but no longer a mighty empire.

Yet Egypt's legacy to its African neighbors remained vibrant and rich. By trading and exploring southward along the coast of the Red Sea, the Egyptians introduced their goods and ideas as far south as the land of Punt, probably a region on the Somali coast. As early as the New Kingdom, Egyptian pharaohs had exchanged gifts with the monarchs of Punt, and contact between the two areas persisted. Egypt was the primary civilizing force in Nubia, which became another version of the pharaoh's realm, complete with royal pyramids and Egyptian deities. Egyptian religion penetrated as far south as Ethiopia. Just as Mesopotamian culture enjoyed wide appeal throughout the Near East, so Egyptian culture had a massive impact on northeastern Africa.

THE CHILDREN OF ISRAEL AND THEIR NEIGHBORS

The fall of the Hittite Empire and Egypt's collapse created a vacuum of power in the Near East that allowed for the rise of numerous small states. No longer crushed between the Hittites in the north and the Egyptians in the south, various peoples—some of them newcomers—created homes and petty kingdoms in Syria, Phoenicia, and Palestine. After the Sea Peoples had raided Egypt, a branch of them, known in the Bible as Philistines, settled along the coast of modern Israel (Map 2.1). Establishing themselves in five cities somewhat inland from the sea, the Philistines set about farming and raising flocks.

MAP 2.1 Small Kingdoms in the Near East   This map illustrates the political fragmentation of the Near East after the great wave of invasions that occurred during the thirteenth century B.C.

Another sturdy new culture was that of the Phoenicians, a Semitic-speaking people who had long inhabited several cities along the coast of modern Lebanon. They had lived under the shadow of the Hittites and Egyptians, but in this period the Phoenicians enjoyed full independence. Unlike the Philistine newcomers, who turned from seafaring to farming, the Phoenicians took to the sea and became outstanding merchants and explorers. In trading ventures they sailed as far west as modern Tunisia, where in 813 B.C. they founded the city of Carthage, which would one day struggle with Rome for domination of the western Mediterranean. Phoenician culture was urban, based on the prosperous commercial centers of Tyre, Sidon, and Byblos. The Phoenicians' overwhelming cultural achievement was the development of an alphabet: they, unlike other literate peoples, used one letter to designate one sound and vastly simplified writing and reading. This streamlined alphabet was handed on to the Greeks in the late eighth century B.C. to apply to their own language.

The Phoenicians made another significant contribution by spreading the technical knowledge of ironworking. The Hittites were the first people in the Near East to smelt iron, but the Phoenicians passed the complex technique west to the Greeks and south to the Africans. Once in Africa, the technology spread farther south, though gradually. Most of West Africa had acquired the process by 250 B.C., and sub-Saharan Africa produced steel by A.D. 500.

South of Phoenicia arose the kingdom of the Hebrews or ancient Jews. Although smaller, poorer, less important, and less powerful than neighboring kingdoms, the realm of the Hebrews was to nourish religious ideas that underlie much of world civilization. Who were these people, and what brought them to this new land? Early Mesopotamian and Egyptian sources refer to people called "Habiru" or "Hapiru," which seems to mean a class of homeless, independent nomads. One such group of Habiru were the biblical Hebrews. Their original homeland was probably northern Mesopotamia, and the most crucial event in their historical development was enslavement in Egypt. According to the Old Testament, the Hebrews followed their patriarch Abraham out of Mesopotamia into Canaan, in modern Israel, where they became identified as the "Children of

Phoenician Cargo Vessels An Assyrian artist has captured all of the energy and vivacity of the seafaring Phoenicians. The sea is filled with Phoenician cargo ships, which ranged the entire Mediterranean. These ships are transporting cedar from Lebanon, some of it stowed on board, while other logs float in their wake. *(Source: Louvre/Giraudon/Art Resource)*

Israel" after the patriarch Jacob, who was also called "Israel."

The Old Testament, the first part of the Bible, is the major literary source for many events involving the early Hebrews. A mere reading of the Bible proves that the Old Testament was composed in various stages. Modern scholars have demonstrated that the origins of the earliest books go back to a time between 950 and 800 B.C. In this period literate people collected oral traditions of the Hebrew past, which included legends, myths, songs, proverbs, and laws, and wove them into a narrative account. Later prophets, priests, and historians added to the narrative until the Old Testament took its final form. Archeologists can help to clarify biblical events by trying to ascertain what happened around the time of the Hebrew exodus from Egypt. The archeological record indicates that the thirteenth century B.C. was a time of warfare, disruption, and destruction and seems to confirm the biblical portrayal of the exodus as a long period of turmoil. It also shows that the situation in Palestine was far more complicated than the Bible suggests.

Many different peoples rubbed shoulders in Palestine in the thirteenth century B.C. Amorites, distant relatives of Hammurabi's Babylonians, had entered the area around 1800 B.C. There they found a Semitic-speaking people, the Canaanites, with whom they freely mingled. Hebrew tribes also arrived, an event about which there is great uncertainty as to time and detail. During the Eighteenth Dynasty of Egypt, some Hebrews were either taken to Egypt or migrated there voluntarily. Meanwhile, other Hebrews remained behind in Palestine. In Egypt the Hebrews were enslaved and forced to labor on building projects. During the thirteenth century B.C. Moses, who may be a mythical figure, led a group of Hebrews from Egypt. According to the biblical book of Exodus, this group consisted of twelve tribes, believed to be descended from the twelve great-grandsons of Abraham. Their wanderings took them to Palestine, where in a series of vicious wars and savage slaughters they slowly won a place (see Map 2.1). Success was not automatic, and the Hebrews suffered defeats and setbacks; but gradually they spread their power northward. Some assimilated

Nomadic Semitic Tribe This Egyptian fresco captures the essentials of nomadic life. These Semites have captured a gazelle and an ibex. The four men behind the leaders are portrayed with their weapons, a bow and spears, which were used for both hunting and defense. Bringing up the rear is a domesticated burro. *(Source: Erich Lessing Culture and Fine Arts Archive)*

themselves to the culture of the natives, even going so far as to worship Baal, an ancient Semitic fertility god. Striking confirmation of this came in July 1990 from an American excavation in Israel. The excavators found in a temple a statuette of a calf, which lends physical support to the notion that the Hebrews derived some of their religious practices from the Canaanites. In other instances, the Hebrews carved out little strongholds and enslaved the natives. Even after the conquest, nearly constant fighting was required to consolidate their position.

The greatest danger to the Hebrews came from the Philistines, whose superior technology and military organization at first made them invincible. In Saul (ca 1000 B.C.), a farmer of the tribe of Benjamin, the Hebrews found a champion and a spirited leader. In the biblical account Saul carried the war to the Philistines, often without success, yet in the meantime he established a monarchy over the twelve Hebrew tribes. Thus, under the peril of the Philistines, the Hebrew tribes evolved from scattered independent units into a centralized political organization in which the king directed the energies of the people. Saul's work was carried on by David of Bethlehem, who repulsed the Hebrews' enemies and established his capital at Jerusalem. His work in consolidating the mon-

archy and enlarging the kingdom paved the way for his son Solomon (ca 965–925 B.C.), who applied his energies to creating a nation out of a collection of tribes. Solomon built and dedicated a great temple in Jerusalem that was to be the religious heart of the kingdom and the symbol of Hebrew unity. At Solomon's death, the Hebrews broke into political halves (see Map 2.1). The northern part of the kingdom of David and Solomon became Israel, with its capital at Samaria. The southern half was Judah, and Solomon's city of Jerusalem remained its center. This political division mirrored a religious one. In Israel, the northern kingdom, the people worshiped Yahweh and other gods; in Judah, the southern kingdom, they worshiped only Yahweh. Within two centuries Israel was wiped out by the Assyrians, but Judah survived through several more centuries of war and unrest. The people of Judah came to be known as "Jews" and gave their name to *Judaism,* the worship of Yahweh.

The Evolution of Jewish Religion

While evolving politically from fierce nomads to urban dwellers, the Hebrews were also evolving spiritual ideas that still permeate contemporary societies. Their chief literary product, the Old Testament, has fundamentally influenced both Christianity and Islam and still exerts a compelling force on the modern world.

Fundamental to an understanding of Jewish religion is the concept of the *Covenant,* a formal agreement between Yahweh and the Hebrew people. According to the Bible, the god Yahweh, later often called "Jehovah," appeared to Moses on Mount Sinai. There Yahweh made a covenant with the Hebrews that was in fact a contract: if the Hebrews worshiped Yahweh as their only god, he would consider them his chosen people and protect them from their enemies. The Hebrews believed that Yahweh had led them out of bondage in Egypt and had helped them conquer their new land, the promised land. In return, the Hebrews worshiped Yahweh and Yahweh alone. They also obeyed Yahweh's Ten Commandments, an ethical code of conduct revealed to them by Moses.

Yahweh was unique because he was a lone god. Unlike the gods of Mesopotamia and Egypt, Yahweh was not the son of another god, nor did he have a divine wife or family. Initially anthropomorphic, Yahweh gradually lost human form and became totally spiritual. Although Yahweh could assume human form, he was not to be depicted in any form. Thus the Hebrews considered graven images—statues and other physical representations—idolatrous.

At first Yahweh was probably viewed as no more than the god of the Hebrews, who sometimes faced competition from Baal and other gods in Palestine. Enlil, Marduk, Amon-Re, and the others sufficed for foreigners. In time, however, the Hebrews came to regard Yahweh as the only god. This was the beginning of true monotheism.

Yahweh was considered the creator of all things; his name means "he causes to be." He governed the cosmic forces of nature, including the movements of the sun, moon, and stars. His presence filled the universe. At the same time Yahweh was a personal god. Despite his awesome power, he was neither too mighty nor too aloof to care for the individual. The Hebrews even believed that Yahweh intervened in human affairs.

Unlike Akhenaten's monotheism, Hebrew monotheism was not an unpopular religion imposed from above. It was the religion of a whole people, deeply felt and cherished. Some might fall away from Yahweh's worship, and various holy men had to exhort the Hebrews to honor the Cov-

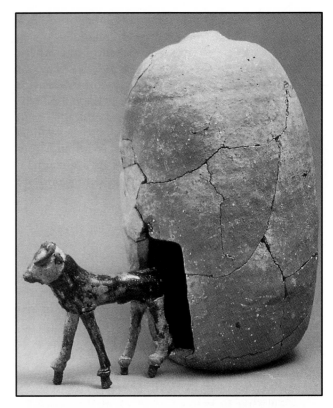

The Silver Calf The worship of calves was common among many of the peoples of Palestine, including the Hebrews sometimes. In August 1990 American archeologists from Harvard University discovered this small figurine of a calf in the ancient city of Ashkelon in modern Israel. It provides evidence for the cult practice before the biblical Exodus. *(Source: Ashkelon Excavations: Leon Levy Expedition. Carl Andrews, photographer)*

enant, but on the whole the people clung to Yahweh. Yet the Hebrews did not consider it their duty to spread the belief in the one god. The Hebrews rarely proselytized, as later the Christians did. As the chosen people, their chief duty was to maintain the worship of Yahweh as he demanded. That worship was embodied in the Ten Commandments, which forbade the Hebrews to steal, murder, lie, or commit adultery.

From the Ten Commandments evolved Hebrew law, a code of law and custom originating with Moses and built on by priests and prophets. The earliest part of this code, the Torah or Mosaic law, was often as harsh as Hammurabi's code, which had a powerful impact on it. Later tradition, largely the work of prophets who lived from the eleventh to the fifth centuries B.C., was more humanitarian.

The evolution of Hebrew monotheism resulted in one of the world's greatest religions, which deeply influenced the development of two others. Many parts of the Old Testament show obvious debts to Mesopotamian culture. Nonetheless, to the Hebrews goes the credit for developing a religion so emotionally satisfying and ethically grand that it has not only flourished but also profoundly influenced Christianity and Islam. Without Moses there could not have been Jesus or Muhammad. The religious standards of the modern world are deeply rooted in Judaism.

Daily Life in Israel

Historians generally know far more about the daily life of the aristocracy and the wealthy in ancient societies than about the conditions of the common people. Jewish society is an exception be-

cause the Old Testament, which lays down laws for all Jews, has much to say about peasants and princes alike. Comparisons with the social conditions of Israel's ancient neighbors and modern anthropological work among Palestinian Arabs shed additional light on biblical practices. Thus the life of the common people in ancient Israel is better known, for instance, than is that of ordinary Romans or ancient Chinese.

Initially life centered around the tribe, numerous families who thought of themselves as related to one another. At first good farmland, pasture, and water sources were held in common by the tribe. Common use of land was—and still is—typical of nomadic peoples. Typically each family or group of families in the tribe drew lots every year to determine who worked which fields. But as formerly nomadic peoples turned increasingly to settled agriculture, communal use of land gave way to family ownership. In this respect the experi-

Aerial View of Hazor Hazor was a Jewish citadel built in the ninth century B.C. Organized on a rectangular plan, Hazor commanded the surrounding countryside and was well fortified. Nonetheless, the Assyrians destroyed the citadel in 732 B.C. *(Source: From HAZOR II, Y. Yadin, Pl. XIII.)*

ence of the ancient Hebrews seems typical of that of many early peoples. Slowly but surely the shift from nomad to farmer affected far more than just how people fed themselves. Family relationships reflected evolving circumstances. The extended family, organized in tribes, is even today typical of nomads. With the transition to settled agriculture, the tribe gradually becomes less important than the extended family. With the advent of village life and finally full-blown urban life, the extended family in turn gives way to the nuclear family.

The family—people related to one another, all living in the same place—was the primary social institution among the Jews. At its head stood the father, who, like the Mesopotamian father, held great powers. The father was the master of his wife and children, with power of life and death over his family. By the eighth century B.C. the advent of full-blown urban life began to change the shape of family life again. The father's power and the overall strength of family ties relaxed. Much of the father's power, especially the power of life and death over his children, passed to the elders of the town. One result was the liberation of the individual from the tight control of the family.

Marriage was one of the most important and joyous events in Hebrew family life. When the Hebrews were still nomads, a man could have only one lawful wife but any number of concubines. Settled life changed marriage customs, and later Jewish law allowed men to be polygamous. Not only did kings David and Solomon have harems, but rich men also could have several wives. The chief reason for this custom, as in Mesopotamia, was the desire for children. Given the absence of medical knowledge and the rough conditions of life, women faced barrenness, high infant mortality, and rapid aging. The presence of several women in the family led to some quarrelsome households; the first wife, if she were barren, could be scorned and ridiculed by her husband's other wives.

Betrothal and marriage were serious matters in ancient Israel. As in Mesopotamia, they were left largely in parents' hands. Many boys and girls were married when they were little more than children, and the parents naturally made the arrangements. Rarely were the prospective bride and groom consulted. Marriages were often contracted within the extended family, commonly among first cousins—a custom still found among Palestinian Arabs today. Although early Jewish custom per-

mitted marriage with foreigners, the fear of alien religions soon led to restrictions against mixed marriages.

The father of the groom offered a bridal gift to the bride's father. This custom, the marriage price, also existed among the Mesopotamians and survives among modern Palestinian Arabs. The gift was ordinarily money, the amount depending on the social status and wealth of the two families. In other instances, the groom could work off the marriage price by performing manual labor. At the time of the wedding the man gave his bride and her family wedding presents; unlike Mesopotamian custom, the bride's father did not provide her with a dowry.

As in Mesopotamia, marriage was a legal contract, not a religious ceremony. At marriage a woman left her own family and joined the family and clan of her husband. The occasion when the bride joined her husband's household was festive. The groom wore a crown and his best clothes. Accompanied by his friends, also dressed in their finest and carrying musical instruments, the bridegroom walked to the bride's house, where she awaited him in her richest clothes, jewels, and a veil, which she removed only later when the couple was alone. The bride's friends joined the group, and together they all marched in procession to the groom's house, their way marked by music and songs honoring the newlyweds. Though the wedding feast might last for days, the couple consummated their marriage on the first night. The next day the bloody linen was displayed to prove the bride's virginity.

Divorce was available only to the husband; the right to initiate a divorce was denied the wife. Even adultery by the husband was not necessarily grounds for divorce. Jewish law, like the Code of Hammurabi, punished a wife's adultery with death. Jewish custom generally frowned on divorce, and the typical couple entered into marriage fully expecting to spend the rest of their lives together.

The newly married couple was expected to begin a family at once. Children, according to the Book of Psalms, "are an heritage of the lord: and the fruit of the womb is his reward."[2] The desire for children to perpetuate the family was so strong that if a man died before he could sire a son, his brother was legally obliged to marry the widow. The son born of the brother was thereafter considered the offspring and heir of the dead man. If the brother refused, the widow had her revenge by denouncing him to the elders in public:

Then shall his brother's wife come unto him in the presence of the elders, and loose his shoe from off his foot, and spit in his face, and shall answer and say, So shall it be done unto that man that will not build up his brother's house.[3]

Sons were especially desired because they maintained the family bloodline and kept the ancestral property within the family. The first-born son had special rights, honor, and responsibilities. At his father's death he became the head of the household and received a larger inheritance than did his younger brothers. Daughters were less highly valued because they would eventually marry and leave the family. Yet in Jewish society, unlike other cultures, infanticide was illegal; Yahweh had forbidden it.

The Old Testament often speaks of the pain of childbirth. Professional midwives frequently helped during deliveries. The newborn infant was washed, rubbed with salt, and wrapped in swaddling clothes—bands of cloth that were wrapped around the baby. Normally the mother nursed the baby herself and weaned the infant at about the age of three. The mother customarily named the baby immediately after birth, but children were free to change names after they grew up. Eight days after the birth of a son, the ceremony of *circumcision*—removal of the foreskin of the penis—took place. Circumcision signified that the boy belonged to the Jewish community and, according to Genesis, was the symbol of Yahweh's covenant with Abraham.

As in most other societies, in ancient Israel the early education of children was in the mother's hands. She taught her children right from wrong and gave them their first instruction in the moral values of society. As boys grew older, they received more education from their fathers. Fathers instructed their sons in religion and the history of their people. Many children were taught to read and write, and the head of each family was probably able to write. Fathers also taught sons the family craft or trade. Boys soon learned that inattention could be painful, for Jewish custom advised fathers to be strict: "He that spareth his rod hateth his son: but he that loveth him chasteneth him betimes."[4]

Once children grew to adulthood, they entered fully into economic and social life. For most that meant farm life, for which demands and rhythm changed little over time. Young people began with light tasks. Girls traditionally tended flocks of sheep and drew water from the well for household use. At the well, which was a popular meeting spot, girls could meet other young people and travelers passing through the country with camel caravans. After the harvest, young girls followed behind the reapers to glean the fields. Even this work was governed by law and custom. Once the girls had gone through the fields, they were not to return, for Yahweh had declared that anything left behind belonged to the needy.

Boys also tended flocks, especially in wild areas. Like the young David, they practiced marksmanship with slings and entertained themselves with music. They shared light work such as harvesting grapes and beating the limbs of olive trees to shake the fruit loose. Only when they grew to full strength did they perform the hard work of harrowing, plowing, and harvesting.

With the success of the first Hebrew kings, the future of many family farms was endangered. With peace, more settled conditions, and increasing prosperity, some Jews began to amass larger holdings by buying out poor and struggling farmers. Far from discouraging this development, the kings created their own huge estates. In many cases slaves, both Jewish and foreign, worked these large farms and estates shoulder to shoulder with paid free men.

In still later times, rich landowners rented plots of land to poor free families; the landowners provided the renters with seed and livestock and normally took half the yield as rent. Although many Old Testament prophets denounced the destruction of the family farm, the trend continued toward large estates that were worked by slaves and hired free men.

The development of urban life among the Jews created new economic opportunities, especially in crafts and trades. People specialized in occupations such as milling flour, baking bread, making pottery, weaving, and carpentry. All these crafts were family trades. Sons worked with their father, daughters with their mother. If the business prospered, the family might be assisted by a few paid workers or slaves. The practitioners of a craft usually lived in a particular street or section of the town, a custom still prevalent in the Middle East. By the sixth century B.C. craftsmen had joined together in associations known as "guilds," intended like European guilds in the Middle Ages (see page 419) to protect and aid their members. By banding together, craftsmen gained corporate status within the community.

Commerce and trade developed later than crafts. In the time of Solomon, foreign trade was the king's domain. Aided by the Phoenicians, who ranked among the leading merchants of the Near East, Solomon built a fleet to trade with Red Sea ports. Solomon also participated in the overland caravan trade. Otherwise, trade with neighboring countries was handled by foreigners, usually Phoenicians. Jews dealt mainly in local trade, and in most instances craftsmen and farmers sold directly to their customers. Many of Israel's wise men disapproved of commerce and, like the ancient Chinese, considered it unseemly and immoral to profit from the work of others.

Between the eclipse of the Hittites and Egyptians and the rise of the Assyrians, the Hebrews moved from nomadism to urban life and full participation in the mainstream of ancient Near East-

ern culture. Keeping their unique religion and customs, they drew from the practices of other peoples and influenced the lives of their neighbors.

ASSYRIA, THE MILITARY MONARCHY

Small kingdoms like those of the Phoenicians and the Hebrews could exist only in the absence of a major power. The beginning of the ninth century B.C. saw the rise of such a power: the Assyrians of northern Mesopotamia, whose chief capital was at Nineveh on the Tigris River. The Assyrians were a Semitic-speaking people, heavily influenced, like so many peoples of the Near East, by the Mesopotamian culture of Babylonia to the south. They were also one of history's most warlike peoples.

The Rise of Assyrian Power

For over two centuries the Assyrians labored to dominate the Near East. Year after relentless year, their armies hammered at the peoples of the west,

Siege of a City Art here serves to glorify horror. The Assyrian king Tiglath-pileser III launches an assault on a fortified city. The impaled bodies shown at center demonstrate the cruelty of Assyrian warfare. Also noticeable are the various weapons and means of attack used against the city. *(Source: Courtesy of the Trustees of the British Museum)*

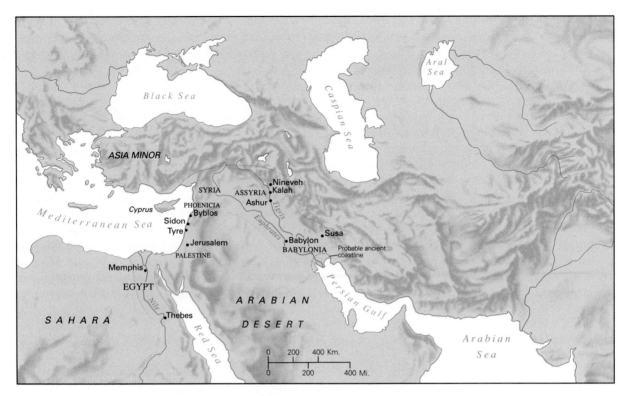

MAP 2.2 The Assyrian Empire The Assyrian Empire at its height included almost all of the old centers of power in the ancient Near East. As comparison with Map 2.3 shows, however, its size was far smaller than that of the later Persian Empire.

to overcome the constant efforts of Syria and the two Jewish kingdoms to maintain or recover their independence. Eventually the Assyrians conquered both Babylonia and northern Egypt. By means of almost constant warfare, they carved out an empire that stretched from east and north of the Tigris River to central Egypt (Map 2.2).

Although empire certainly was an objective of the Assyrian people, their preoccupation with war was in large part a response to the threat of incursion by their neighbors. Living in an open, exposed land, the Assyrians experienced frequent devastating attacks at the hands both of the wild war-loving tribes to the north and east and of the Babylonians to the south. These constant threats promoted political cohesion and military might among the Assyrians. That cohesion was critical to their survival, as evidenced by the immediate stirrings of freedom throughout the Near East in the occasional periods of Assyrian political instability.

An empire forged with so much blood and effort was vulnerable to revolt, and revolt provoked brutal retaliation. Though atrocity and terrorism

struck unspeakable fear into Assyria's subjects, Assyria's success was actually due to sophisticated, far-sighted, and effective military organization. By 716 B.C. the Assyrians had invented the mightiest military machine the ancient Near East had ever seen. The mainstay of the Assyrian army, the soldier who ordinarily decided the outcome of battles, was the infantryman armed with spear and sword and protected by helmet and armor. The Assyrian army also featured archers, some on foot, others on horseback, still others in chariots—the last ready to wield lances once they had expended their supply of arrows. Some infantry archers wore heavy armor, strikingly similar to the armor worn much later by William the Conqueror's Normans. These soldiers served as a primitive field artillery, whose job was to sweep the enemy's walls of defenders so that others could storm the defenses. Slingers also served as artillery in pitched battles. For mobility on the battlefield, the Assyrians organized a corps of chariots.

Assyrian military genius was remarkable for the development of a wide variety of siege machinery and techniques, including excavation to undermine city walls and battering-rams to knock down walls and gates. Never before in the Near East had anyone applied such technical knowledge to warfare. The Assyrians even invented the concept of a corps of engineers, who bridged rivers with pontoons or provided soldiers with inflatable skins for swimming. Furthermore, the Assyrians knew how to coordinate their efforts, both in open battle and in siege warfare. They were too powerful and well organized and far too tenacious to let themselves be defeated by isolated strongholds, no matter how well situated or defended.

Assyrian Rule

Not only did the Assyrians know how to win battles, they also knew how to use their victories.

As early as the reign of Tiglath-pileser III (774–727 B.C.), Assyrian kings began to organize their conquered territories into an empire. The lands closest to Assyria became provinces governed by Assyrian officials. Kingdoms beyond the provinces were not annexed but became dependent states that followed Assyria's lead. Assyrian kings chose their rulers either by regulating the succession of native kings or by supporting native kings who appealed to them. Against more distant states the kings waged frequent war in order to conquer them outright or make their dependent status secure.

Royal roads linked the Assyrian Empire, and Assyrian records describe how swift, mounted royal messengers brought the king immediate word of unrest or rebellion within the empire. Because of good communications, Assyrian kings could generally move against rebels at a moment's notice.

Royal Lion Hunt This relief from the palace of Ashurbanipal at Nineveh, which shows the king fighting two lions, is a typical representation of the energy and artistic brilliance of Assyrian sculptors. The lion hunt, portrayed in a series of episodes, was a favorite theme of Assyrian palace reliefs. *(Source: Courtesy of the Trustees of the British Museum)*

Thus, though rebellion was common in the Assyrian Empire, it rarely got the opportunity to grow serious before meeting with harsh retaliation from the king.

In the seventh century B.C. Assyrian power seemed secure. From their capitals at Nineveh, Kalah, and Ashur on the Tigris River, the Assyrians ruled a vast empire. An efficient army, calculated terrorism, and good communications easily kept down the conquered populations. With grim efficiency the Assyrians sacked rebellious cities, leaving forests of impaled prisoners or piles of severed heads to signal their victory. In other cases they deported whole populations, wrenching them from their homelands and resettling them in strange territories. The Assyrians introduced systematic terror tactics into warfare. Their ferocity horrified their subjects and bred a vast hatred.

Yet the downfall of Assyria was swift and complete. The burden of Assyrian taxation and the terror of Assyrian oppression at last prompted an alliance between the Medes, a new Indo-European-speaking folk from Iran, and the Babylonians for the primary purpose of destroying Assyrian rule. Together the allies conquered the Assyrian Empire in 612 B.C., paving the way for the rise of the Persians. The Hebrew prophet Nahum spoke for many when he proclaimed: "Nineveh is laid waste: who will bemoan her?"[5] Their cities destroyed and their power shattered, the Assyrians disappeared from history, remembered only as a cruel people of the Old Testament who oppressed the Hebrews. Two hundred years later, when the Greek adventurer and historian Xenophon passed by the ruins of Nineveh, he marveled at their extent but knew nothing of the Assyrians. The glory of their empire was forgotten.

THE EMPIRE OF THE PERSIAN KINGS

Like the Hittites before them, the Iranians were Indo-Europeans from the steppes north of the Black and Caspian seas who migrated into a land inhabited by more primitive peoples. Once settled in the area between the Caspian Sea and the Persian Gulf, the Iranians, like the Hittites, fell under the spell of the more sophisticated cultures of their Mesopotamian neighbors. Yet the Iranians went on to create one of the greatest empires of antiquity, an empire that encompassed scores of peoples and cultures. The Persians, the most important of the Iranian peoples, had a far-sighted conception of empire. Though as conquerors they willingly used force to accomplish their ends, they normally preferred to depend on diplomacy. They usually respected their subjects and allowed them to practice their native customs and religions. Thus the Persians gave the Near East both political unity and cultural diversity. Never before had a conquering people viewed empire in such intelligent and humane terms.

The Land of Mountains and Plateau

Persia—the modern country of Iran—is a land of towering mountains and flaming deserts, with a broad central plateau in the heart of the country (Map 2.3). Iran stretches from the Caspian Sea in the north to the Persian Gulf in the south. Between the Tigris-Euphrates Valley in the west and the Indus Valley in the east rises an immense plateau, surrounded on all sides by lofty mountains that cut off the interior from the sea.

The central plateau is very high, a landscape of broad plains, scattered oases, and two vast deserts. The high mountains, which catch the moisture coming from the sea, generate ample rainfall for the plain. This semitropical area is fertile, in marked contrast to the aridity of most of Iran. The mountains surrounding the central plateau are dotted with numerous oases, often very fertile, which have from time immemorial served as havens for small groups of people.

At the center of the plateau lies an enormous depression—a region devoid of water and vegetation, so glowing hot in summer that it is virtually impossible to cross. This depression forms two distinct grim and burning salt deserts, perhaps the most desolate spots on earth. These two deserts form a barrier between East and West.

Iran's geographical position and topography explain its traditional role as the highway between East and West. Throughout history nomadic peoples migrating from the broad steppes of Russia and central Asia have streamed into Iran. Confronting the uncrossable salt deserts, most have turned either eastward or westward, moving on until they reached the advanced and wealthy urban centers of Mesopotamia and India. When cities emerged along the natural lines of East-West communication, Iran became the area where no-

MAP 2.3 The Persian Empire   The Persian Empire not only included more of the ancient Near East than had the Assyrian Empire, but it also extended as far east as western India. With the rise of the empire, the balance of power in the Near East shifted east of Mesopotamia for the first time.

mads met urban dwellers, a meeting ground of unique significance for the civilizations of both East and West.

The Coming of the Medes and Persians

The history of human habitation in Iran is long and rich: traces of prehistoric peoples date back as far as 15,000 to 10,000 B.C. About the prehistoric period historians and archeologists still have much to learn. The Iranians entered this land around 1000 B.C. The most historically important of them were the Medes and the Persians, related peoples who settled in different areas. Both groups were part of the vast movement of Indo-European-speaking peoples whose wanderings led them in many successive waves into Europe, the Near East, and India. These Iranians were nomads who migrated with their flocks and herds. Like their kinsmen the Aryans, who moved into India, they were horse breeders, and the horse gave them a decisive

military advantage over the prehistoric peoples of Iran. The Iranians rode into battle in horse-drawn chariots or on horseback and easily swept the natives before them. Yet, because the influx of Iranians went on for centuries, cultural interchange between victorious newcomers and conquered natives proved constant.

Excavations at Siyalk, some 125 miles south of present-day Tehran, provide a valuable glimpse of the encounter of Iranian and native. The village of Siyalk had been inhabited since prehistoric times before falling to the Iranians. The new lords fought all comers: natives, rival Iranians, even the Assyrians, who often raided far east of the Tigris. Under the newly arrived Iranians, Siyalk became a fortified town with a palace and perhaps a temple, all enclosed by a wall that was strengthened by towers and ramparts. The town was surrounded by fields and farms because agriculture was the foundation of this evolving society.

The Iranians initially created a patchwork of tiny kingdoms, of which Siyalk was one. The chief-

Jug of Siyalk   Though later the Persians derived their art primarily from their neighbors, this jug, which dates to ca 1000 B.C., demonstrates that the early settlers possessed a vigorous sense of art themselves. While some features of this jug were borrowed from neighboring artistic traditions, others are solely Persian. This jug was probably used to pour wine. *(Source: The Ancient Art and Architecture Collection)*

tain or petty king was basically a warlord who depended on fellow warriors for aid and support. This band of noble warriors, like the Greek heroes of the *Iliad,* formed the fighting strength of the army. The king owned estates that supported him and his nobles; for additional income the king levied taxes, which were paid in kind and not in cash. He also demanded labor services from the peasants. Below the king and his warrior nobles were free people who held land and others who owned nothing. Artisans produced the various goods needed to keep society running. At the bottom of the social scale were slaves—probably both natives and newcomers—to whom fell the drudgery of hard labor and household service to king and nobles.

This early period saw some significant economic developments. The use of iron increased. By the seventh century B.C. iron farm implements had become widespread, leading to increased productivity, greater overall prosperity, and higher standards of living. At the same time Iranian agriculture saw the development of the small estate. Farmers worked small plots of land, and the general pros-

perity of the period bred a sturdy peasantry, who enjoyed greater freedom than their peers in Egypt and Mesopotamia.

Iran had considerable mineral wealth, and its iron, copper, and lapis lazuli attracted Assyrian raiding parties. Even more important, mineral wealth and Iranian horse breeding stimulated brisk trade with the outside world. Kings found that merchants, who were not usually Iranians, produced large profits to help fill the king's coffers. Overland trade also put the Iranians in direct contact with their neighbors.

Gradually two groups of Iranians began coalescing into larger units. The Persians had settled in Persis, the modern region of Fars, in southern Iran. Their kinsmen the Medes occupied Media, the modern area of Hamadan in the north, with their capital at Ecbatana. The Medes were exposed to attack by nomads from the north, but their greatest threat was the frequent raids of the Assyrian army. Even though distracted by grave pressures from their neighbors, the Medes united under one king around 710 B.C. and extended their control over the Persians in the south. In 612 B.C.

the Medes were strong enough to join the Babylonians in overthrowing the Assyrian Empire. With the rise of the Medes, the balance of power in the area for the first time shifted east of Mesopotamia.

The Creation of the Persian Empire

In 550 B.C. Cyrus the Great (559–530 B.C.), king of the Persians and one of the most remarkable statesmen of antiquity, threw off the yoke of the Medes by conquering them and turning their country into his first *satrapy,* or province. In the space of a single lifetime, Cyrus created one of the greatest empires of antiquity. Two characteristics lifted Cyrus above the common level of warrior-kings. First, he thought of Iran, not just Persia and Media, as a state. His concept has survived a long, complex, often turbulent history to play its part in the contemporary world.

Second, Cyrus held an enlightened view of empire. Many of the civilizations and cultures that fell to his armies were, he realized, far older, more advanced, and more sophisticated than his. Free of the narrow-minded snobbery of the Egyptians, the religious exclusiveness of the Hebrews, and the calculated cruelty of the Assyrians, Cyrus gave his subject peoples and their cultures his respect, toleration, and protection. Conquered peoples continued to enjoy their institutions, religion, language, and way of life under the Persians. The Persian Empire, which Cyrus created, became a political organization sheltering many different civilizations. To rule such a vast area and so many diverse peoples demanded talent, intelligence, sensitivity, and a cosmopolitan view of the world. These qualities Cyrus and many of his successors possessed in abundance. Though the Persians were sometimes harsh, especially with those who rebelled against them, they were for the most part

Tomb of Cyrus For all of his greatness Cyrus retained a sense of perspective. His tomb, though monumental in size, is rather simple and unostentatious. Greek writers reported that it bore the following epitaph: "O man, I am Cyrus the son of Cambyses. I established the Persian Empire and was king of Asia. Do not begrudge me my memorial." (*Source: The Oriental Institute, University of Chicago*)

enlightened rulers. Consequently, the Persians gave the ancient Near East over two hundred years of peace, prosperity, and security.

With Iran united, Cyrus looked at the broader world. He set out to achieve two goals: first, to win control of the west and thus of the terminal ports of the great trade routes that crossed Iran and Anatolia. Second, Cyrus strove to secure eastern Iran from the pressure of nomadic invaders. In

Funeral Pyre of Croesus This scene, an excellent example of the precision and charm of ancient Greek vase painting, depicts the Lydian king Croesus on his funeral pyre. He pours a libation to the gods while his slave lights the fire. Herodotus has a happier ending when he says that Cyrus the Great set fire to the pyre but that Apollo sent rain to put it out. (*Source: Louvre Cliché des Musées Nationaux, Paris*)

550 B.C. neither goal was easy. To the northwest was the young kingdom of Lydia in Anatolia, whose king Croesus was proverbial for his wealth. To the west was Babylonia, enjoying a new period of power now that the Assyrian Empire had been crushed. To the southwest was Egypt, still weak but sheltered behind its bulwark of sand and sea. To the east ranged tough, mobile nomads, capable of massive and destructive incursions deep into Iranian territory.

Cyrus turned first to Croesus' Lydian kingdom, which fell to him around 546 B.C., along with the Greek cities on the coast of Anatolia. For the first time the Persians came into direct contact with the Greeks, a people with whom their later history was to be intimately connected. Then Cyrus turned eastward to Parthia, Bactria, and even the most westerly part of India. Finally, in 540 B.C., Cyrus moved against Babylonia, now isolated from outside help. The Persian king treated all of these conquered peoples with magnanimity. He respected their religions, which he often subsidized, and their cultures, which he nurtured. Seldom have conquerors been as wise, sensitive, and far-sighted as Cyrus and his Persians.

Thus Spake Zarathustra

Iranian religion was originally simple and primitive. Ahuramazda, the chief god, was the creator and benefactor of all living creatures. Yet, unlike Yahweh, he was not a lone god. The Iranians were polytheistic. Mithra, the sun-god, whose cult would later spread throughout the Roman Empire (page 206), saw to justice and redemption. Other Iranian deities personified the natural elements: moon, earth, water, and wind. As in ancient India, the god of fire was particularly important. The sacred fire consumed the blood sacrifices that the early Iranians offered to all of their deities.

Early Iranian religion was close to nature and unencumbered by ponderous theological beliefs. A priestly class, the Magi, developed among the Medes to officiate at sacrifices, chant prayers to the gods, and tend the sacred flame. A description of this early worship comes from the great German historian Eduard Meyer:

Iranian religion knew neither divine images nor temples. On a hilltop one called upon god and his man-

ANCIENT NEAR EAST

ca 1700 B.C.	Covenant formed between Yahweh and the Hebrews; emergence of Hebrew monotheism
ca 1570–ca 1075 B.C.	New Kingdom in Egypt
ca 1475–ca 1200 B.C.	Rise and fall of the Hittite Empire
13th century B.C.	Moses leads Exodus of the Hebrews from Egypt into Palestine
ca 1100–700 B.C.	Founding of numerous small kingdoms, including those of the Phoenicians, Syrians, Philistines, and Hebrews
ca 1000 B.C.	Saul establishes monarchy over Hebrew tribes, under threat of Philistines
	Persians and Medes enter central plateau of Persia
10th century B.C.	David captures Jerusalem, which becomes religious and political center of Judah; Solomon inherits the throne and further unites Hebrew kingdom
925 B.C.	Solomon dies; Hebrew kingdom is divided politically into Israel and Judah
ca 900–612 B.C.	Rise and fall of the Assyrian Empire
813 B.C.	Phoenicians found Carthage
774–705 B.C.	Assyrian kings Tiglath-pileser III and Sargon II conquer Palestine, Syria, Anatolia, Israel, Judah, and Egypt
ca 710 B.C.	Medes unite under one king and conquer Persians
626 B.C.	Babylonia wins independence from Assyria
612 B.C.	Babylonians and Medes destroy Assyrian capital of Nineveh
ca 600 B.C.	Zoroaster revitalizes Persian religion
550 B.C.	Persian king Cyrus the Great conquers Medes, founds Persian Empire
546 B.C.	Cyrus defeats Croesus, wins Lydia
540 B.C.	Persian soldiers under Cyrus enter Babylon
525 B.C.	Cambyses, Cyrus's heir to the throne, conquers Egypt
521–464 B.C.	Kings Darius I and Xerxes complete Persian conquest of ancient Near East, an area stretching from Anatolia in the west to the Indus Valley in the east; Persian attempts to invade Greece unsuccessful

ifestations—sun and moon, earth and fire, water and wind—and erected altars with their eternal fire. But in other appropriate places one could, without further preparation, pray to the deity and bring him his offerings, with the assistance of the Magi.[6]

In time the Iranians built fire temples for these sacrifices. As late as the nineteenth century, fire was still worshiped in Baku, a major city on the Russian-Iranian border.

Around 600 B.C. the prophet Zarathustra—or Zoroaster, as he is more generally known—breathed new meaning into Iranian religion. So little is known of Zoroaster that even the date of his birth is unknown, but it cannot be earlier than

around 1000 B.C. Whatever the exact dates of his life, his work endured long afterward.

The most reliable information about Zoroaster comes from the Zend Avesta, a collection of hymns and poems, the earliest part of which treats Zoroaster and primitive Persian religion. Like Moses, Zoroaster preached a novel concept of divinity and human life. Life, he taught, is a constant battleground for two opposing forces, good and evil. Ahuramazda embodied good and truth but was opposed by Ahriman, a hateful spirit who stood for evil and falsehood. Ahuramazda and Ahriman were locked together in a cosmic battle for the human race, a battle that stretched over thousands of years. But, according to Zoroaster, people

Darius and Xerxes This relief from the Persian capital of Persepolis shows King Darius and Crown Prince Xerxes in state. Behind them the royal bodyguard stands at attention, as the royal pair receives the guard's commander. *(Source: The Oriental Institute, University of Chicago)*

were not mere pawns in this struggle. Each person had to choose which side to join—whether to lead a life of good behavior and truthful dealings with others or of wickedness and lies.

Zoroaster emphasized the individual's responsibility in this decision. He taught that people possessed the free will to decide between Ahuramazda and Ahriman and that they must rely on their own consciences to guide them through life. Their decisions were crucial, Zoroaster warned, for there would be a time of reckoning. He promised that Ahuramazda would eventually triumph over evil and lies and that at death each person would stand before the tribunal of good. Ahuramazda, like the Egyptian god Osiris, would judge whether the dead had lived righteously and would weigh their lives in the balance. Then good and truth would conquer evil and lies. In short, Zoroaster taught the concept of a Last Judgment at which Ahuramazda would decide each person's eternal fate on the basis of that person's deeds in life.

In Zoroaster's thought the Last Judgment was linked to the notion of a divine kingdom after death for those who had lived according to good and truth. They would accompany Ahuramazda to a life of eternal truth in what Zoroaster called the "House of Song" and the "Abode of Good Thought." There they would dwell with Ahuramazda forever. Liars and the wicked, denied this blessed immortality, would be condemned to eternal pain, darkness, and punishment. Thus Zoroaster preached a Last Judgment that led to a heaven or a hell.

Though tradition has it that Zoroaster met with opposition and coldness, his thought converted Darius (521–486 B.C.), one of the most energetic men ever to sit on the Persian throne. The Persian royal family adopted Zoroastrianism but did not try to impose it on others. Under the protection of the Persian kings, Zoroastrianism swept through Iran, winning converts and sinking roots that sustained healthy growth for centuries. Zoroastrianism survived the fall of the Persian Empire to influence religious thought in the age of Jesus and to make a vital contribution to Manicheanism, a theology that was to spread through the Byzantine Empire and pose a significant challenge to Christianity. A handful of the faithful still follow the teachings of Zoroaster, whose vision of divinity and human life has transcended the centuries.

Persia's World Empire

Cyrus's successors rounded out the Persian conquest of the ancient Near East. In 525 B.C. Cyrus's son Cambyses (530–522 B.C.) subdued Egypt. Darius (521–486 B.C.) and his son Xerxes (486–464

B.C.) invaded Greece but were fought to a standstill and forced to retreat (see pages 128–129); the Persians never won a permanent foothold in Europe. Yet Darius carried Persian arms into India. Around 513 B.C. western India became the Persian satrapy of Hindu Kush, which included the valley of the Indus River. Thus within thirty-seven years the Persians transformed themselves from a subject people to the rulers of an empire that included Anatolia, Egypt, Mesopotamia, Iran, and western India. They created an empire encompassing all of the oldest, most honored kingdoms and peoples of the ancient Near East, which never before had been united in one such vast political organization (see Map 2.3).

The Persians knew how to use the peace they had won on the battlefield. The sheer size of the empire made it impossible for one man to rule it effectively. Consequently they divided the empire into some twenty huge satrapies measuring hundreds of square miles, many of them kingdoms in themselves. Each satrapy had a governor, drawn from the Median and Persian nobility and often a relative of the king; the governor or *satrap* was directly responsible to the king. An army officer, also responsible to the king, commanded the mili-

The Royal Palace at Persepolis   King Darius began and King Xerxes finished building a grand palace worthy of the glory of the Persian Empire. Pictured here is the monumental audience hall, where the king dealt with ministers of state and foreign envoys. *(Source: George Holton/Photo Researchers)*

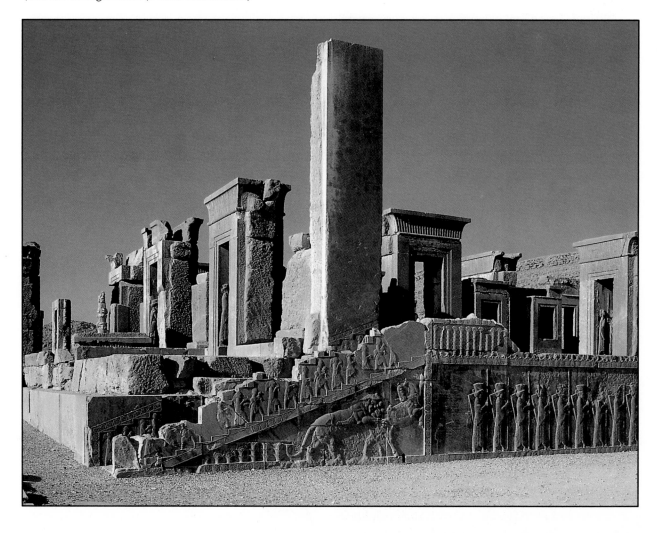

tary forces stationed in the satrapy. Still another official collected the taxes. Moreover, the king sent out royal inspectors to watch the satraps and other officials.

Effective rule of the empire demanded good communications. To meet this need the Persians established a network of roads. The main highway, known as the "Royal Road," spanned some 1,677 miles from the Greek city of Ephesus on the coast of western Asia to Susa in western Iran (see Map 2.3). The distance was broken into 111 post stations, each equipped with fresh horses for the king's messengers. Other roads branched out to link all parts of the empire from the coast of the Mediterranean to the valley of the Indus River. This system of communications enabled the Persian king to keep in touch with his subjects and officials. He was able to rule efficiently, keep his ministers in line, and protect the rights of the peoples under his control.

Conquered peoples, left free to enjoy their traditional ways of life, found in the Persian king a capable protector. No wonder that many Near Eastern peoples were, like the Jews, grateful for the long period of peace they enjoyed as subjects of the Persian Empire.

Meanwhile, farther east the Indians and Chinese were confronting many of the same problems that the peoples farther west were solving. The direction of developments in India and China differed from that in the Near East, largely, but not entirely, because of geography. The results, however, were essentially the same: sophisticated civilizations based on systematic agriculture, complex social structures, cultures, and religions.

NOTES

1. J. H. Breasted, *Ancient Records of Egypt,* vol. 4, (Chicago: University of Chicago Press, 1907), para. 398.
2. Psalms 128:3.
3. Deuteronomy 25:9.
4. Proverbs 13:24.
5. Nahum 3:7.
6. E. Meyer, *Geschichte des Altertums*, 7th ed., vol. 4, part 1 (Darmstadt: Wissenschaftliche Buchgesellschaft, 1975), pp. 114–115. Unless otherwise credited, all quotations from a foreign language in this chapter are translated by John Buckler.

SUMMARY

Between around 1200 and 500 B.C. the Near East passed from fragmentation to political unification under the Persian Empire. On the road from chaos to order, from widespread warfare to general peace, peoples in many areas wrought vast and enduring achievements. The homeless Hebrews laboriously built a state and entered the broader world of their neighbors. Simultaneously they evolved religious and ethical beliefs that permeate the modern world.

Although the Assyrians made the Near East tremble in terror of their armies, they too contributed to the heritage of these long years. Their military and, particularly, political abilities gave the Persians the tools they needed to govern a host of different peoples. Those tools were to be well used. For over two hundred years Persian kings offered their subjects enlightened rule. The Persians gave the ancient Near East a period of peace and stability in which peoples enjoyed their native traditions and lived in concord with their neighbors.

SUGGESTED READING

Although late Egyptian history is still largely a specialist's field, K. A. Kitchen, *The Third International Period in Egypt* (1973), is a good synthesis of the period from 1100 to 650 B.C. Valuable, too, is M. L. Bierbrier's monograph, *Late New Kingdom in Egypt, c. 1300–664 B.C.* (1975). More general is R. David, *The Egyptian Kingdoms* (1975). A. H. Gardiner, ed., *Late Egyptian Stories* (1973), contains other pieces of late Egyptian literature.

G. Herm, *The Phoenicians: The Purple Empire of the Ancient World* (1975), treats Phoenician seafaring and commercial enterprises. A more general treatment of the entire area is R. Fedden, *Syria and Lebanon*, 3d ed. (1965).

The Jews have been one of the best studied peoples in the ancient world; the reader can easily find many good treatments of Jewish history and society. A readable and balanced book is J. Bright, *A History of Israel,* 2d ed. (1972). Other useful general books include G. W. Anderson, *The History and Religion of Israel* (1966), a solid, scholarly treatment of the subject. The archeological exploration of ancient Israel is so fast paced that nearly any book is quickly outdated. Nonetheless, A. Negev, *Ar-*

chaeological Encyclopedia of the Holy Land (1973), which is illustrated, is still a good place to start.

M. R. de Vaux, *Ancient Israel, Its Life and Institutions,* 2d ed. (1965), which ranges across all eras of early Jewish history, is especially recommended because of its solid base in the ancient sources. The period of Jewish kingship has elicited a good deal of attention. B. Halpern, *The Constitution of the Monarchy in Israel* (1981), makes the significant point that the Jews are the only ancient Near Eastern people to have recorded the decision to adopt monarchy as a form of government. For an excellent discussion of the evolution of the Old Testament, see M. Smith, *Palestinian Parties and Politics That Shaped the Old Testament,* 2d ed. (1987). G. W. Ahlstrom, *Royal Administration and National Religion in Ancient Palestine* (1982), treats secular and religious aspects of Hebrew history. Last, W. D. Davis et al., *The Cambridge History of Judaism,* vol. 1 (1984), begins an important new synthesis with work on Judaism in the Persian period. R. Hachlili, *Ancient Jewish Art and Archaeology in the Land of Israel* (1988), attempts to trace the development and meaning of Jewish art in its archeological context.

The Assyrians, despite their achievements, have not attracted the scholarly attention that the ancient Jews and other Near Eastern peoples have. Even though outdated, A. T. Olmstead, *History of Assyria* (1928), has the merit of being soundly based in the original sources. More recent and more difficult is J. A. Brinkman, *A Political History of Post-Kassite Babylonia, 1158–722 B.C.* (1968), which treats the Babylonian response to the rise of Assyria. M. Cogan, *Imperialism and Religion: Assyria, Judah and Israel in the Eighth and Seventh Centuries B.C.* (1973), traces the various effects of Assyrian expansion on the two Jewish kingdoms.

A new edition of an earlier work, H. W. F. Skaggs, *Everyday Life in Babylonia and Assyria,* rev. ed. (1987), offers a general and well-illustrated survey of Mesopotamian history from 3000 to 300 B.C. Those who appreciate the vitality of Assyrian art should start with the masterful work of R. D. Barnett and W. Forman, *Assyrian Palace Reliefs,* 2d ed. (1970), an exemplary combination of fine photographs and learned, but not difficult, discussion.

Several new general works on ancient Iran have lately appeared. A comprehensive survey of Persian history is given by one of the leading scholars in the field, R. N. Frye, *History of Ancient Iran* (1984). I. Gershevitch, ed., *The Cambridge History of Iran,* vol. 2 (1985), offers a full account of ancient Persian history, but many of the chapters are already out of date. E. E. Herzfeld, *Iran in the Ancient East* (1987), puts Persian history in a broad context, as does M. A. Dandamaev, *A Political History of the Achaemenid Empire* (1989).

J. H. Moulton, *Early Zoroastrianism: The Origins, the Prophet, and the Magi* (1972), is a sound treatment of the beginnings and early spread of Zoroastrianism. R. C. Zaehner, *The Dawn and Twilight of Zoroastrianism* (1961), discusses the whole course of Zoroastrianism's history. Zaehner also provides a good introduction to the basic teachings of Zoroastrianism in his *Teachings of the Magi: A Compendium of Zoroastrian Beliefs* (1975). Finally, M. Boyce, a leading scholar in the field, offers a sound and readable treatment in her *Zoroastrianism* (1979).

3

Ancient India to
ca A.D. 200

King Vidudabha visiting the Buddha, from the Bharhut Stupa

While the peoples of the ancient Near East were spreading their cultures and grappling with the demands of political administration of large tracts of land, people in India were wrestling with similar problems—taming the land, improving agricultural techniques, building cities and urban cultures, and asking basic questions about social organization and the nature of human life.

The earliest Indian civilization, like those of Mesopotamia and Egypt, centered on a great river, in this case the Indus. The people of ancient India also were confronted with challenging climate and topography. They suffered monsoons; they faced jungle in some areas and desert in others. The fertile but undeveloped and underpopulated territory offered Neolithic pioneers and their descendants either prosperity or extinction, depending on how well they met the varied demands of the land. As in the ancient Near East, so too in India agricultural exploitation of the land promoted an increase in population, and the needs of metal technology encouraged wider contacts.

- How did the ancient Indians respond to the problems that ancient Near Eastern peoples were confronting?

- How did they meet the challenge of the land itself?

- What kind of social and political organization developed in India?

- What intellectual and religious values did this society generate?

These questions are the central concern of this chapter.

THE LAND AND ITS FIRST TAMERS
(CA 2500–1500 B.C.)

Ancient India—which encompassed modern Pakistan, Nepal, and part of Afghanistan as well as the modern state of India—was a geographically protected and relatively self-contained land. The subcontinent of India, a land mass as large as western Europe, juts southward into the warm waters of the Indian Ocean. India is a land of contrasts.

Some regions are among the wettest on earth; others are dry and even arid desert and scrub land. High mountain ranges in the north drop off to the low river valleys of the Indus and Ganges. These geographical variations greatly influenced the pattern of human development within India.

Three regions of India are of overriding geographical significance: (1) the ring of mountains in the north that separates India from its neighbors, (2) the great river valleys of the Indus and Ganges and their tributaries, and (3) the southern peninsula, especially the narrow coastal plains and the large Deccan Plateau (Map 3.1). The lower reaches of the Himalaya Mountains—the northern geographical boundary of the subcontinent—are covered by some of India's densest forests, sustained by heavy rainfall. Immediately to the south the land drops away to the fertile river valleys of the Indus and Ganges. These lowland plains, which stretch all the way across the subcontinent, are the most fertile parts of India. Here Indian agriculture has traditionally flourished. Furthermore, the flat terrain enabled invaders to sweep across and beyond the northern Indian plain, once they passed the area of Delhi. South of these valleys rise the Vindhya Mountains and the dry, hilly Deccan Plateau. Only along the coasts do the hills give way to narrow plains. In short, geography sets India off from its neighbors and simultaneously divides the country into many subregions, some of them huge, fertile, and capable of sustaining large and vigorous populations.

The Himalayas, which in many places exceed 25,000 feet in height, protected ancient India from wandering peoples in search of new lands to settle. The Indian Ocean, later a busy avenue to the outside world, served throughout much of antiquity as an immense moat, keeping out invaders while fostering maritime trade with both the Near East and China. Only in the northwest—the area between modern Afghanistan and Pakistan—was India accessible to outsiders. This region, penetrated by the famous Khyber Pass, has traditionally been the highway of invaders—a highway whose other terminus was the flourishing cultures of the ancient Near East. Thus geography segregated India, but it also made possible contact with the ideas, practices, and technology of the earliest civilizations.

The Himalayas shield the subcontinent from the northern cold. They also hold in the monsoon

MAP 3.1 The Development of India, ca 2500–ca 250 B.C. This map shows the development of India from the days of the Indus Valley civilization to the reign of Ashoka. Although northwestern India might fall to foreign conquerors like the Persians or Alexander the Great, most of India was unscathed by these incursions. Ashoka created the first real Indian empire.

rains that sweep northward from the Indian Ocean each summer. The monsoons in the south and the melting snows of the Himalayas in the north provide India with most of its water. In some areas the resulting moistness and humidity created vast tracts of jungle and swamp; the Ganges was a particularly forbidding region, and only gradually did settlers move there from the tamer west. Much of India, however, is not blessed with abundant water: instead of jungle, the environment is subtropical and dry. In general, the monsoon area of southeastern India experiences the heaviest rainfall, while the driest region is the northwest. Geography and climate, and especially good water resources, combined to make the Pun-

jab and the valley of the Indus River—now in Pakistan—the most attractive regions for India's first settlers.

The story of the first civilization in India, known as the Indus civilization, is one of the most dramatic in the entire ancient world. In 1921 archeologists discovered astonishing evidence of a thriving and sophisticated urban culture dating to about 2500 B.C. Until that time India had been the home of primitive tribes of hunters and food gatherers; then some newcomers began to develop a truly revolutionary way of life. About the tantalizing problem of the origin of the Indus civilization, the eminent English archeologist Sir Mortimer Wheeler has commented:

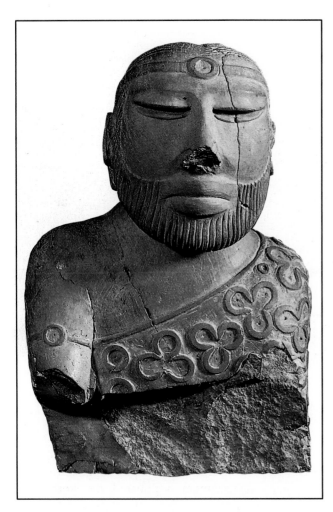

Figurine from Mohenjo-daro   Part of the heritage of the Indus civilization was its artistic creations, such as this figurine of a bearded man. The composition is at once bold and sophisticated. Yet even such glimpses as this give little clue to the origins of the creators of the Indus civilization. *(Source: National Museum, Karachi)*

By the middle of the 3rd millennium, something very important was happening in the Indus valley, and happening probably at great speed. Then or rather earlier, certain of the little communities in the Baluch foothills of modern Pakistan were emboldened to experiment. Who the first leaders were who led their people, however hesitantly, down to the wide and jungle-ridden plain we shall never know, nor why they ventured; but they were bold men, pioneers in the fullest sense, no mere ejects from the highland zone. Some, perhaps many of them, led forlorn hopes and perished. . . . Seemingly the attempted colonization of the valley continued intermittently, failure succeeding failure,

until at last a leader, more determined and far-sighted and fortunate than the rest, won through.[1]

These hardy adventurers created an urban culture based on large-scale agriculture. Like the Mesopotamian city, the Indian city was surrounded by extensive farmland, which fed its inhabitants. These pioneers also developed a script, which is still undeciphered. Contact was early and frequent between the Indus civilization and the great cultures of Mesopotamia. As early as the reign of Sargon of Akkad in the third millennium B.C. (see page 18), trade between India and Mesopotamia carried goods and ideas between the two cultures, probably by way of the Persian Gulf.

The Indus civilization extended over fully 1.25 million square kilometers in the Indus Valley, an area that exceeded the boundaries of modern Pakistan. Its two best-known cities were Mohenjo-daro in southern Pakistan and Harappa some four hundred miles to the north in the Punjab. Other sites have since been found in southern Pakistan, at Sutkagendor in the west, as far east as Alamgirpur near modern Delhi, and as far north as Ropar (see Map 3.1). Numerous sites are still being excavated, and a full portrait of this vast civilization will have to await archeologists' findings. It is already clear, however, that the Indus civilization was marked by a striking uniformity of culture and, simultaneously, by regional variation.

Some important new linguistic work suggests that other peoples were also filtering into India from western Asia while the Indus civilization was flourishing. The ancestors of the Dravidians, who are usually considered natives of central and southern India, probably moved through the Indus Valley at about this time. In short, the movement of ancient peoples into India was a far more complex process than anyone imagined even a few years ago. Only future work in a variety of fields can clarify this immense phenomenon.

Mohenjo-daro and Harappa are currently the best-understood keys to the Indus civilization. Both cities were huge, over three miles in circumference, and housed large populations. Built of fired mud brick, Mohenjo-daro and Harappa were largely unfortified, although both were defended by great citadels that towered 40 or 50 feet above the surrounding plain. Both cities were logically planned from the outset, not merely villages that grew and sprawled haphazardly. In both, blocks of houses were laid out on a grid plan, centuries be-

Mohenjo-daro The architectural vision and engineering expertise of the Indus civilization are obvious in this view of Mohenjo-daro. The central planning and huge scale of the city reflect a flourishing community. *(Source: Josephine Powell, Rome)*

fore the Greeks used this method of urban design. Streets were straight and wide, varying from 9 to 34 feet. The houses of both cities were substantial, many two stories tall, some perhaps three. The focal point of the Indus houses was a central open courtyard, onto which the rooms opened. The houses' brick exteriors were bland and blank, and the city streets must have presented a monotonous face to pedestrians.

Perhaps the most surprising aspect of the elaborate planning of these cities is their complex system of drainage, well preserved at Mohenjo-daro. Each house had a bathroom with a drain connected to municipal drains located under the major streets. These brick-built channels, which carried off refuse, had openings to allow the clearing of blockages. This system not only demonstrates a sophisticated appreciation of hygiene but also attests to the existence of a strong central authority capable of urban planning.

Centralized government is also apparent in both cities' numerous large structures, which excavators think were public buildings. One of the most important is the state granary, a large storehouse for the community's grain. Moreover, a set of tene-

ment buildings next to a series of round working-floors near the granary at Harappa suggests that the central government dominated the storage and processing of the city's cereal crops. The citadel at Mohenjo-daro further testifies to the power of the city's rulers: here stood monumental buildings, including a marketplace or place of assembly, a palace, and a huge bath featuring a pool some 39 feet by 23 feet and 8 feet deep. The Great Bath, like later Roman baths, was an intricate structure with spacious dressing rooms for the bathers. Because the Great Bath at Mohenjo-daro resembles the ritual purification pools of later Indian society, some scholars have speculated that power was in the hands of a priest-king. They also suggest that the Great Bath played a role in the religious rituals of the city; if so, the dressing rooms may have served the priests who performed the rituals. But little is yet known about the religious life of Mohenjo-daro and Harappa or about their government. Lacking readable written records, archeology cannot answer these questions. Nonetheless, the power and authority of the government, whether secular or religious, are apparent in the intelligent central planning of these cities.

The prosperity of the Indus civilization depended on constant and intensive cultivation of the rich river valley. The Indus, like the Nile, provided farmers with fertile alluvial soil enriched by annual floods. Farmers built earth embankments to hold the flood waters. The results of this labor were abundant crops of wheat, barley, vegetables, and cotton. The Indus people also domesticated cattle, buffalo, fowl, and possibly pigs and asses. Their efforts led to a high standard of living and to the surpluses that they traded with Mesopotamia. They were also in contact with neighbors closer to home, trading with the peoples of southern India for gold and with the ancient Afghans for silver.

Despite tantalizing glimpses of a serene and stable society, the intellectual and religious life of the Indus people is largely unknown. Fertility was a major concern to them, as it is to most agricultural people: they apparently worshiped a mother-goddess who looked after the welfare of the community. Some later Indian religious beliefs may have originated in this period. One of the most engaging of the early Indian deities—who is depicted at Mohenjo-daro with his customary three faces, surrounded by wild animals—closely resembles Siva, a major Hindu god. The Indus people's great fondness for animals is apparent in the popularity of terra-cotta animal figurines. Their attitude prefigures the deep respect for the animal world that Indians have traditionally felt. Indeed they give the impression of having been a people in tune with the world around them, a world they understood and enjoyed. The Indus people maintained their equilibrium with nature for hundreds of years, spreading their culture throughout the valley and enjoying a tranquil development.

Yet this civilization, which appeared in history so suddenly, perished just as mysteriously. After years of prosperity, Mohenjo-daro and Harappa suffered a long decline, perhaps as a result of deforestation, a change in climate, and their huge demands on the land. The first excavators of Mohenjo-daro concluded that the city met a violent end: they found some skeletons of men, women, and children, many with ax or sword wounds, scattered across the ground. Contemporary archeologists, however, have reinterpreted these findings. Some point out that too few skeletons at Mohenjo-daro showed signs of violence to indicate wholesale slaughter. Others suggest that the population may have fallen prey to diseases such as malaria. Thus the reasons for the disappearance of this intriguing civilization are obscure and disputed. It is known, however, that many of the Indus people lived on, though disrupted and scattered. With them they carried the accomplishments and values of their culture, which became an important element in the development of later Indian civilization.

Toy Ram The people of Mohenjo-daro not only respected animals, but they also enjoyed them. Here is a terra cotta ram on wheels that a child could pull around on a string. *(Source: Jehangir Gazdar/Woodfin Camp & Associates)*

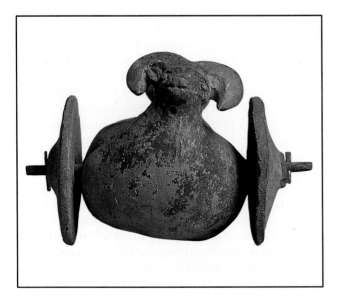

THE ASCENDANCY OF THE ARYANS (CA 1500–500 B.C.)

Many scholars think that the Indus civilization fell at the hands of the Aryans, an Indo-European people who entered India from the northwest. There is, however, no sound evidence to support this view. In fact, the Aryans may not have reached India until many years after the fall of the Indus civilization. Nevertheless, the Aryans, like the Hittites and later the Greeks, formed part of the widespread migrations that transformed the face of much of the ancient world. In any case, the arrival of the Aryans was a turning point in Indian history, an event that forever changed the face of India. The Aryans were part of the enormous movement of Indo-Europeans described in Chapter 1 (see page 4). Nomadic wanderers, they came in search of land; the Indus Valley, with its rich plains and predictable climate, lured them on.

Most knowledge of the early Aryans comes from the Rigveda, the oldest and most sacred of the Hindu "scriptures." The Rigveda is not a history but a collection of hymns in praise of the Aryan gods. Even so, the hymns contain some historical information that sheds light on the Aryans and on native Indians. The Rigveda and the other Vedas, which were also sacred writings, are crucial to understanding the social evolution of India during this period, sometimes called the "Dark Ages of India."

The Rigveda portrays the Aryans as a group of battle-loving pastoral tribes, at war with one another and with the native population of India. In that respect, they can be seen as conquerors of the local peoples. Their use of horses and bronze weapons in warfare gave them superiority over the natives. At the head of the Aryan tribe was its chief, or *raja,* who led his followers in battle and ruled them in peacetime. Next to the chief was the priest, entrusted with sacrifices to the gods and the knowledge of sacred rituals. In time, as Aryan, also called "Vedic," society laid increasing emphasis on proper performance of the religious rituals, priests evolved into a distinct class possessing precise knowledge of the complex rituals and of the invocations and formulas that accompanied them. The warrior nobility rode to battle in chariots and perhaps on horseback and expressed their will in assemblies. The commoners supported society by tending herds and, increasingly as conditions settled, working the land. To the non-Aryan slaves fell the drudgery of menial tasks. Women held a more favorable position in this period than in later times: they were not yet given in child marriage, and widows had the right to remarry. In brief, the Rigveda portrays the early Aryans, with their pride of conquest and delight in battle, as a heroic folk.

Gradually the Aryans pushed farther eastward into the valley of the Ganges River, a land of thick jungle populated by tribes. The jungle was as stubborn an enemy as its inhabitants, and clearing it presented a tremendous challenge. For the next six hundred years, the Aryans migrated eastward, finally founding the important city of Delhi. During this time the Aryans and their Indian predecessors blended their cultures, each influencing the other. If the Aryans brought new customs, they themselves adopted traditional ones. The re-

sulting synthesis constituted an entirely new Indian society.

The Shaping of Indian Society

Because the push into the jungle demanded a larger and more tightly organized political entity than before, tribes merged under strong rulers whose power grew increasingly absolute. As rulers claimed sovereignty over specific territory, political rule shifted from tribal chieftainship to kingship. The priests, or *Brahmans,* supported the growth of royal power in return for royal confirmation of their own religious rights, power, and status; the Brahmans also served a political function as advisers to the kings. In the face of this royal-priestly alliance, the old tribal assemblies of warriors withered away.

Development of the newly won territory led to further changes in Aryan society and its political structure. Once conquered and cleared, the land was ready for cultivation. However, constant work was needed to keep the land from reverting to jungle. The typical response to this challenge was the village. In this period India evolved into the land of villages it still is today. Even the later growth of cities did not eclipse the village as the hallmark of Indian society. Yet villages did not conform to a single social pattern. In the south the typical village consisted of groups of families who considered themselves related to one another. Each family was a large patriarchal joint or extended family composed of several nuclear families who lived and worked together. In the north, by contrast, marriage outside the village was common, and families' kinship ties extended over wider areas than in the south. What all Indian villages had in common was a tradition of mutual cooperation born of common interests and obligations. The close-knit society of the village has consistently been a stabilizing element in Indian history.

Sustained agriculture and settled conditions promoted prosperity and population growth, which in turn gave rise to the growth of towns and eventually cities. Thus the Aryans gradually transformed themselves from a tribal organization into an urban, as well as a village, society. Prosperity further enhanced royal power. Another feature of this process was frequent warfare among territorial states, the smaller and weaker of which were con-

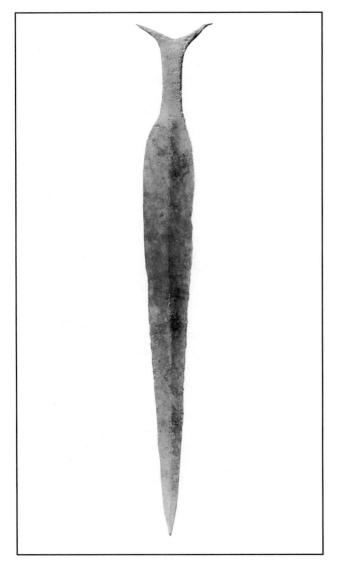

Bronze Sword A striking example of the quality of Aryan arms is this bronze sword, with its rib in the middle of the blade for strength. Native Indians lacked comparable weapons. *(Source: Courtesy of the Trustees of the British Museum)*

tem." A *caste* is a hereditary class of social equals who share the same religion, pursue a specific trade or occupation, and avoid extensive social intercourse with members of other castes. Initially this system had two goals: to distinguish Aryans from non-Aryans and to mark birth or descent. The caste system was fluid at first and allowed for a surprising amount of social mobility. Even in the early days of conquest the Aryans mixed with the conquered population, and that slow mingling eventually resulted in the Indian society that emerged into the full light of history. The blending was intellectual and religious as well as social. Only as conditions stabilized over the years did the system become strict and the number of castes grow.

By about 500 B.C. four main groups of Indian society—the priests *(Brahman)*, the warriors *(Kshatriya)*, the peasants *(Vaishya)*, and the serfs *(Shudra)*—were steadily evolving. Indians themselves ascribed this stratification to the gods, as the Rigveda testifies:

When they divided the [primeval] Man
*   into how many parts did they divide him?*
What was his mouth, what were his arms,
*   what were his thighs and his feet called?*
The Brahman was his mouth, of his
*   arms was made the warrior.*
His thighs became the Vaishya, of
*   his feet the Shudra was born.*[2]

According to this division of duties, the priests conducted religious sacrifices and treasured the religious lore. The warriors defended society on the battlefield, and the peasants grew the food and paid the taxes. The serfs, who were originally the property of the tribe, served the others by performing hard labor. Those without places in this tidy social division—that is, those who entered it later than the others or who had lost their caste status through violations of ritual—were *outcastes.* These people probably earned their livings by performing such undesirable jobs as slaughtering animals and dressing skins. Although their work was economically valuable, it was considered unworthy and socially polluting. These "impure" people were the *untouchables.*

This convenient summary of the caste system fails to do full justice to its complexity. For example, in southern India there were only two orders of caste, Brahman and Shudra; and throughout

quered and absorbed, giving rise to a number of large kingdoms. By about 500 B.C. the Aryans had created a new political map of India characterized by larger kingdoms, village life, and islands of urban culture.

As the Aryans struggled to dominate the land of India, they increasingly had to contend with its people. Social contact between Aryans and natives led to the development of the complicated system of social organization known as the "caste sys-the subcontinent variations of the system were common. Yet in one aspect the caste system was uniform: it severely limited social mobility, not only among individuals but also among groups of people.

Slavery was also a feature of social life, as it was elsewhere in antiquity. The scanty evidence available suggests that slavery in Aryan society resembled Mesopotamian slavery. In India there was no caste of slaves, although in practice most slaves would have come from the lower castes, which were economically disadvantaged. In the Vedic period, slaves were often people captured in battle, but these captives could be ransomed by their families. Still later, slavery was less connected with warfare; it was more of an economic and social institution. Slave children automatically at birth became the slaves of their parents' masters. Indian slaves could be bought, used as collateral, or even given away. As in ancient Mesopotamia, a free man might sell himself and his family into slavery because he could not pay his debts. And, as in Hammurabi's Mesopotamia, he could, if clever, hard working, or fortunate, buy his and his family's way out of debt.

Slaves in India performed tasks similar to those of slaves in other societies. Like Joseph in ancient Egypt, a man might serve as a royal counselor, having more actual authority than many a free man. Otherwise slaves served in their masters' fields, mines, or houses. Whatever their economic function, socially they were members of their master's household. Indian masters were legally responsible for the last rites of their slaves and were obliged to perform the customary duties necessary for the welfare of the soul of a deceased slave. Indian law forbade a master from abandoning slaves in their old age; it also recommended manumission of slaves as an act of piety. Nonetheless, in Indian literature there is ample evidence of the abuse of slaves; and as in other societies—both ancient and modern—it is sometimes impossible to determine to what extent laws and social injunctions were actually put into practice.

Early Indian Religion

In religion and intellectual life, a momentous revolution was occurring in Indian society. The Aryan gods represented natural phenomena. Some of them were great brawling figures, like Agni, the god of fire; Indra, wielder of the thunderbolt and god of war; and Rudra, the divine archer who spread disaster and disease by firing his arrows at people. Others were shadowy figures, like Dyaus, the father of the gods, who appears in Greek as Zeus and in Latin as Jupiter. Varuna, the god of order in the universe, was a hard god, quick to punish those who sinned and thus upset the balance of nature. Ushas, the goddess of dawn, was a refreshingly gentle deity, who welcomed the birds, gave delight to human beings, and kept off evil spirits. Although the Aryan gods had their duties, they differed from the Greek deities and Mesopotamian gods in that they rarely had distinctive personalities or extensive mythologies. All the Aryan gods enjoyed sacrifices, however, and ritual was an essential ingredient in early Aryan religion. Gradually, under the priestly monopoly of the Brahmans, correct sacrifice and proper ritual became so important that most Brahmans believed a properly performed ritual would force a god to grant a worshiper's wish. These beliefs became known as "Brahmanism." Religion became sterile and unsatisfying to many, even among the priestly class.

In search of a faith richer and more mystical, some Brahmans retreated to the forests to seek a personal road to the gods. Through *asceticism*— severe self-discipline and self-denial—and meditation on the traditional teachings of the Vedas, these pioneers breathed new life into the old rituals. They concluded that disciplined meditation on the ritual sacrifice could produce the same results as the physical ritual itself. Thus they reinterpreted the ritual sacrifices as symbolic gestures with mystical meanings. Slowly Indian religion was changing from primitive worship to a way of thought that nourished human needs and eased human fears. Two cardinal doctrines prevailed: *samsara,* the transmigration of souls by a continual process of rebirth, and *karma,* the tally of good and bad deeds that determined the status of an individual's next life. Karma was more than a concept of retribution for people's acts in life; it also embraced the human and animal worlds. Good deeds led to better future lives, but evil, to worse, even to reincarnation as an animal. The concept of samsara, when joined with that of karma, provided the Hindus with two methods of escape from continual reincarnation: extreme asceticism and yoga, or intense meditation. Either method, if pursued successfully, allowed the individual to be absorbed into a timeless and changeless state. Thus gradually arose the concept of a wheel of life that included human beings, animals, and even gods.

To most people, especially those on the low end of the economic and social scale, these concepts were attractive. All existence, no matter how harsh and bitter, could be progress to better things. By living righteously and doing good deeds, people could improve their lot in the next life. Yet there was another side to these ideas: the wheel of life could be seen as a treadmill, giving rise to a yearning for release from the relentless cycle of birth and death. Hence the new concepts created tension in religious thought.

The solution to this baffling problem appears in the Upanishads, a collection of sacred texts created by ascetics who opened up new vistas in religious speculation. The authors of the Upanishads fostered the concept of *moksha*, or release from the wheel of life. All people, they taught, have in themselves an eternal truth and reality called *atman*, which corresponds to a greater all-encompassing reality called *Brahma*. The truth in each person and the universal truth are eternal and identical. These mystics and ascetics claimed that life in the world is actually an illusion, and the only way to escape it and the wheel of life is to realize that reality is unchanging. By studying the Vedas, by penance, and by meditation, one could join one's individual self with the universal reality. This profound and subtle teaching they summed up in one sentence: "Thou art That." What does this sentence mean? The Chandogya Upanishad tells the story of a father explaining it to his son:

"Believe me, my son, an invisible and subtle essence is the Spirit of the whole universe. That is Reality. That is Atman. THOU ART THAT."

"Explain more to me, father," said Svetaketu.

A Brahman and the Vedas   Here a Brahman reads from a manuscript of the holy book of the Vedas. For centuries, however, knowledge of these poems was preserved only by oral tradition. *(Source: Francis Watson)*

"So be it, my son.

"Place this salt in water and come to me tomorrow morning."

Svetaketu did as he was commanded, and in the morning his father said to him: "Bring me the salt you put into the water last night."

Svetaketu looked into the water, but could not find it, for it had dissolved.

His father then said: "Taste the water from this side. How is it?"

"It is salt."

"Taste it from the middle. How is it?"

"It is salt."

"Taste it from that side. How is it?"

"It is salt."

"Look for the salt again and come again to me."

The son did so, saying: "I cannot see the salt. I only see water."

His father then said: "In the same way, O my son, you cannot see the Spirit. But in truth he is here.

"An invisible and subtle essence is the Spirit of the whole universe. That is Reality. That is Truth. THOU ART THAT." [3]

These great religious thinkers gave society a transcendent means to escape the problems presented by the wheel of life. These revolutionary ideas appealed to those who were dissatisfied with the old Brahman religion of sacrifice, and they even won the support of the Brahmans and kings. The thought of the Upanishads gave Brahmans a high status to which the poor and lowly could aspire in future life; consequently the Brahmans greeted these concepts, and those who taught them, with tolerance and understanding. They made a place for them in traditional religious practice. The rulers of Indian society had excellent practical reasons to encourage the new trends. The doctrines of samsara and karma encouraged the poor and oppressed to labor peacefully and dutifully. The revolutionary new doctrines actually promoted stability in social and political life.

By about 500 B.C., all these trends—political, social, and religious—had led to a society, shaped by conqueror and conquered, in which all had a place. Urban life flourished alongside a vigorous village life, both sustained by agriculture. Gone were the warrior chieftains, their place taken by hereditary kings who ruled large territorial states with the support of a hereditary priestly class. Many of India's basic values already had taken shape at this early date.

INDIA'S SPIRITUAL FLOWERING

India's spiritual growth came into full bloom in the sixth and fifth centuries B.C., a period of stunning moral and philosophical thought that gave rise to three of the world's greatest religions: Hinduism, Jainism, and Buddhism. The evolution of these sects is complex and somewhat obscure. Hinduism is the most direct descendant of the old Vedic religion. Jainism and Buddhism shared that heritage but reacted against it and against Hinduism. Jainism and Buddhism originated as schools of moral philosophy, preoccupied with the nature of ultimate reality and with ethical conduct.

Hinduism

Hinduism may be the world's oldest flourishing religion. It is certainly one of the world's largest faiths, with millions of adherents in India and other Asian countries, the West Indies, and South Africa; it is also a complex of social customs, doctrines, and beliefs.

Although influenced by Jainism and Buddhism, Hinduism was most firmly rooted in traditional Indian religion. The bedrock of Hinduism is the belief that the Vedas are sacred revelations and that a specific caste system is implicitly prescribed in them. Thus Hinduism is both a collection of religious beliefs and a sacred division of society with each part having its own moral law. Religiously and philosophically, Hinduism is diverse. It assumes that there are innumerable legitimate ways of worshiping the supreme principle of life. Consequently it readily incorporates new sects, doctrines, beliefs, rites, and deities. The numerous Hindu gods are all considered aspects of Brahma, the supreme and undefinable principle of life. According to Hinduism, Brahma suffuses all things and at the same time transcends all things. The various deities are considered specific manifestations of Brahma, each of whom helps people to reach Brahma by means of rituals.

Hinduism is a guide to life, whose goal is to reach Brahma. There are four steps in this search, progressing from study of the Vedas in youth to complete asceticism in old age. In their quest for Brahma, people are to observe *dharma,* a moral law nearly as complex as Hinduism itself. Dharma stipulates the legitimate pursuits of Hindus: material

Siva   One of the three most important Vedic gods, Siva represented both destruction and procreation. Here Siva, mounted on a bull and carrying a spear, attacks the demon Andhaka. Siva is seen as a fierce and bloodthirsty warrior. *(Source: C. M. Dixon/Photo Resources)*

gain, so long as it is honestly and honorably achieved; pleasure and love, for the perpetuation of the family; and moksha, release from the wheel of life and unity with Brahma. The society that a scrupulous observance of dharma could create is depicted in the Mahabharata, a long epic poem in which the law is personified as King Dharma, the bull of the Bharatas:

All the people, relying on King Dharma, lived happily like souls that rely on their own bodies that are favored with auspicious marks and deeds. The bull of the Bharatas cultivated Law, Profit, and Pleasure alike, like a family man honoring three kinsmen alike to himself. To Law, Profit, and Pleasure, now incarnated on earth in equal proportions, the king himself appeared as the fourth. In this overlord of men the Ve-

das found a superb student, the great sacrifices a performer, the four classes a pure guardian. Luck had found her place, wisdom its apex, all Law its kinsman with this lord of the earth.[4]

In short, Hinduism spells out the goals of life and how to attain them.

After the third century B.C., Hinduism began to emphasize the roles and personalities of powerful gods—especially Siva, the cosmic dancer who both creates and destroys, and Vishnu, the preserver and sustainer of creation. Since these gods are personal manifestations of Brahma, Brahma can be known through them. Thus people could reach Brahma by devotion to personal gods. From this emphasis on a god-force in all life came a tradition of nonviolence to all living creatures.

India's best-loved sacred hymn, the Bhagavad Gita, is a spiritual guide to the most serious problem facing a Hindu—how to live in the world and yet honor dharma and thus achieve release. The heart of the Bhagavad Gita is the spiritual conflict confronting Arjuna, a human hero about to ride into battle against his own kinsmen. As he surveys the battlefield, struggling with the grim notion of killing his relatives, Arjuna voices his doubts to his charioteer, none other than the god Krishna himself. When at last Arjuna refuses to spill his family's blood, Krishna—who is a manifestation of the great god Vishnu—instructs him, as he has instructed generations of Hindus, on the true meaning of Hinduism:

Interwoven in his creation, the Spirit Brahma is beyond destruction. No one can bring to an end the Spirit which is everlasting. For beyond time he dwells in these bodies, though these bodies have an end in their time; but he remains immeasurable, immortal. Therefore, great warrior, carry on thy fight. If any man thinks he slays, and if another thinks he is slain, neither knows the ways of truth. The Eternal in man cannot kill; the Eternal in man cannot die. He is never born, and he never dies. He is in Eternity: he is for evermore. Never born and eternal, beyond times gone or to come, he does not die when the body dies. When a man knows him as never-born, everlasting, never-changing, beyond all destruction, how can that man kill a man, or cause another to kill?[5]

Krishna then clarifies the relation between human reality and the eternal spirit. He explains compassionately to Arjuna the duty to act—to live

Kali Ma was the consort of Siva. Like him, she represented both destructive and procreative powers. Here she assumes her role as the mother goddess, but the necklace of skulls reminds the viewer of her ferocity. *(Source: C. M. Dixon/Photo Resources)*

in the world and carry out his duties as a warrior. Indeed, the Bhagavad Gita urges the necessity of action, which is essential for the welfare of the world.

The intimate relation between Hindu religion and the social structure of Indian life merits special attention. They are inseparable parts of a unity that forms the core of Indian civilization. The caste system on the social and economic side forms one part of the equation, and Hinduism on the religious side forms the other. Religion justifies the caste system, and that social system in turn stands as visible proof of the validity of religious teaching. The stability of the village is proof of the strength of this social and religious bond, which allows each village to be almost a complete universe in itself. The village, and not higher forms of social and political organization, was absolutely basic to Indian civilization.

Early in India's history Hinduism provided a complex and sophisticated philosophy of life and a religion of enormous emotional appeal. Hinduism also inspired and preserved, in Sanskrit and the major regional languages of India, the vast literature that is India's priceless literary heritage.

Jainism

The founder and most influential thinker of Jainism, Vardhamana Mahavira (ca 540–468 B.C.), the son of an aristocrat, accepted the doctrines of karma and rebirth but developed the animistic philosophy that human beings, animals, plants, and even inanimate objects and natural phenomena all have living souls. Mahavira taught that the universe and everything in it are composed of souls, usually mixed with matter. These souls, though infinite in number, are finite in nature, having definite limits. Souls float or sink, according to Mahavira, depending on the amount of matter with which they are mixed. The only way for any soul to reach eternal happiness is to rid itself of all matter so that it can float to the top of the universe.

Mahavira's followers, known as Jains, believed that people could achieve eternal bliss only by living lives of asceticism and avoiding evil thoughts and actions. The Jains considered all life too sacred to be destroyed. Yet if everything in the world possesses a soul, how can one live without destroying other life? The rigorously logical answer is that one cannot. Strictly speaking, the Jains could adhere to their beliefs only by starving to death. Instead of going to this extreme, the Jains created a hierarchy of life, with human beings at the apex, followed by animals, plants, and inanimate objects. A Jain who wished to do the least possible violence to life became a vegetarian. Nonviolence became a cardinal principle of Jainism and soon took root throughout Indian society. Although Jainism never took hold as widely as Hinduism and Buddhism, it has been an influential strand in Indian thought, and numbers several million adherents in India today.

Siddhartha Gautama and Buddhism

Siddhartha Gautama (ca 563–483 B.C.), better known as the Buddha, meaning the "Enlightened One," lived at the time when Jainism and Hinduism were evolving. The Buddha, like Mahavira, the founder of Jainism, was a Kshatriya, from a class likely to resent Brahman privilege. They both became dissatisfied with settled life and abandoned it for a wandering ascetic existence. The Buddha was so distressed by human suffering that he abandoned his family's Hindu beliefs in a quest for a more universal, ultimate enlightenment. He tried techniques of extreme asceticism, including fasting, but found that they led nowhere. Only through meditation did he achieve the universal enlightenment in which he comprehended everything, including how the world of samsara actually worked. His followers later believed that the Buddha taught them only what was necessary, but that he had seen much more. In this view, what he considered necessary were the "Four Noble Truths" contained in his first sermon. The message of the Four Noble Truths is that pain and suffering, frustration, and anxiety are ugly but inescapable parts of human life; that suffering and anxiety are caused by the human weaknesses of greed, selfishness, and egoism; that people can understand these weaknesses and triumph over them; and that this triumph is made possible by following a simple code of conduct, which the Buddha called the "Eightfold Path."

First, Buddha explained, people have to understand the evils they are suffering. Ultimate release can be achieved only if one has a clear view of the pain and misery of one's life. Next, one has to decide firmly to free oneself from suffering. This one can do by means of what Buddha called "right conduct" and "right speech," a way of living in which one practices the virtues of love and compassion, joy, and serenity in daily life. The fifth step on the Eightfold Path is to choose "right livelihood," a means of earning a living that does not interfere with the attainment of ultimate enlightenment. The sixth step is "right endeavor," the conscious effort to eliminate distracting and harmful desires. People can most readily see the worthlessness of desires, according to Buddha, by recognizing that everything and everyone in the world will pass away. Nothing is permanent. The seventh step is "right awareness," constant contemplation of one's deeds and words, giving full

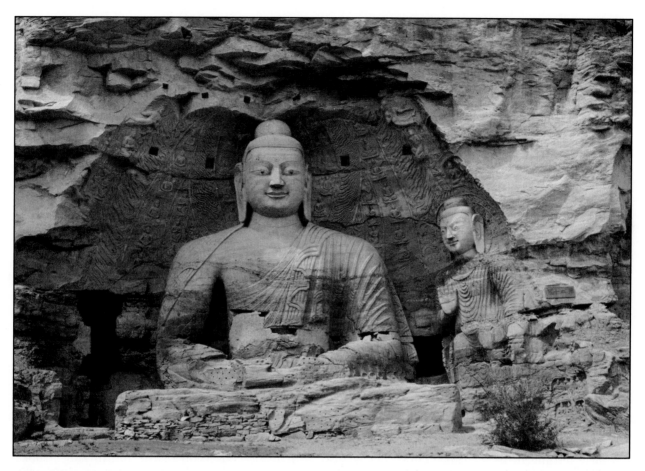

The Great Buddha   This figure of Buddha sits grandly and serenely in a cave in Jung-Kang. Here Buddha is typical of Theravada Buddhism, in which individuals sought their salvation alone through asceticism, meditation, and monasticism. *(Source: Werner Forman Archive)*

thought to their importance and whether or not they lead to enlightenment. "Right contemplation" is the last step expected of travelers on the Eightfold Path. This step entails deep meditation on the impermanence of everything in the world. With the attainment of the eighth step, the traveler achieves *nirvana*, a state of happiness gained by the extinction of self and desires and the release from the effects of karma. Thus Buddha propounded his own version of karma and how it worked. Though rooted in Hinduism, Buddhism set off on a road of its own, a road that eventually led out of India, into Ceylon and parts of Southeast Asia, through central Asia, into China, Korea, Japan, and Vietnam.

Buddha also taught that if people understand that everything changes with time, they will neither cling to their egos nor worry about what they believe to be their eternal souls. To Buddhists a human being is a collection of parts, physical and mental. As long as the parts remain combined, that combination can be called "I." When that combination changes, as at death, the various parts remain in existence, ready to become the building blocks of different combinations. According to Buddhist teaching, life is passed from person to person as a flame is passed from candle to candle.

Buddhism placed little emphasis on gods. The gods might help people out of difficulties like illness, but they could never help people achieve enlightenment. In Buddhist teachings, the gods are not judges who monitor human life and reign beyond the grave. Like human beings, the gods are subject to the laws of change. Nevertheless, Buddha was not strictly an atheist. He conceived of a divine power that was infinite and immortal. As he told his followers: "There is an unborn, an unoriginated, an unmade, an uncompounded; were there not . . . there would be no escape from the world of the born, the originated, the made and the compounded."[6] This unborn and unmade power had nothing to do with the journey to nirvana. That was entirely up to the individual.

The success of Buddhism largely resulted from Buddha's teaching that everyone, noble and peasant, educated and ignorant, could follow the Eightfold Path. Moreover, Buddha was extraordinarily undogmatic. Convinced that each person must achieve enlightenment alone, he emphasized that the Path was important only because it led the traveler to enlightenment, not for its own sake. He compared it to a raft, essential to cross a river but useless once on the far shore. Buddha warned his followers not to let dogma stand in the way of the journey. Buddhism differed from Hinduism by its willingness to accept anyone who wished to join, and in effect it tacitly rejected the caste system.

Buddha welcomed everyone, regardless of social status or sex, to join him in his exalted journey. He also formed a circle of disciples, the *Sangha*—an order of Buddhist monks. Buddha continually reminded his followers that each must reach ultimate fulfillment by individual effort, but he also recognized the value of a group of people striving for the same goal.

After Buddha's death, the Sangha met to decide exactly what Buddhist doctrine was and to smooth out differences of interpretation. The result was the split of Buddhism into two great branches: the Theravada (or Hinayana, School of the Elders, or Lesser Vehicle) and the Mahayana (or Larger Vehicle). The Theravada branch, which found its greatest popularity in Southeast Asia, from Ceylon to Kampuchea (modern Cambodia), asserted that its tenets rested on the authentic teachings of Buddha—in short, that it represented the oldest and purest form of Buddhism. By ca 20 B.C. the monks of the Theravada branch met to write down what they considered the authentic teachings of Buddha and Buddhist tradition. Theravada Buddhism is called the "Lesser Vehicle" because of its conservative and strict doctrines. Followers believed that the individual is saved only through a rigorous monastic life; because monasticism was the way for both men and women to follow Buddha's injunction to seek their own salvation, Theravada Buddhism created codes of monastic conduct for communal life.

Mahayana Buddhism, far more liberal than the Theravada branch, believed that Buddhism was a vast system capable of saving many living things. It also held that the teachings of Buddha were fluid and would evolve over time according to different cultures and climates. Mahayana doctrine differed from Theravada teachings by maintaining that not all of Buddha's message was included in the canon of sacred teachings. Mahayana Buddhism emphasized the compassionate side of Buddha's message. It was known as the "Larger Vehicle" because it maintained that there were many ways to salvation. Mahayana Buddhism stressed the possibility of other buddhas yet to come and taught that all buddhas follow a path open to everyone in the world. Mahayana held that Buddha in his previous lives had been a *bodhisattva*—a wise being, a buddha-in-becoming. Bodhisattvas have achieved enlightenment but decline the reward of nirvana to help others. Later Mahayana Buddhism created a huge pantheon of heavenly buddhas and bodhisattvas to whom people could pray for help toward enlightenment. Mahayana Buddhism eventually won the hearts and minds of the Chinese, Japanese, Koreans, and Vietnamese. Yet not until the dramatic conversion of the Indian king Ashoka, some two centuries after the death of the Buddha, did Buddhist teachings spread much beyond India.

INDIA AND THE WEST (CA 513–298 B.C.)

Between the arrival of the Aryans and the rise of Hinduism, India enjoyed freedom from outside interference. In the late sixth century B.C., however, western India was swept up in events that were changing the face of the ancient Near East. During this period the Persians were creating an empire that stretched from the western coast of Anatolia to the Indus River (see page 59). India became involved in these events when the Persian emperor Darius conquered the Indus Valley about 513 B.C.

Persian control did not reach eastward beyond the banks of the Indus. Even so, as part of the Persian Empire, western India enjoyed immediate contact not only with the old cultures of Egypt

INDIA TO CA A.D. 200

ca 2500–1500 B.C.	Indus civilization
ca 1500–500 B.C.	Arrival of the Aryans and development of Vedic society
6th–5th centuries B.C.	Development of Hinduism, Janism, and Buddhism
ca 513 B.C.	Persian conquest of northwestern India and the Indus Valley
326 B.C.	Alexander the Great conquers northwestern India and the Indus Valley
322–298 B.C.	Reign of Chandragupta
ca 269–232 B.C.	Reign of Ashoka
ca 261 B.C.	Ashoka conquers Kalinga, leading to spread of Buddhism in India
ca 183–145 B.C.	Greek invasion of India
ca 140 B.C.	First Chinese ambassadors to India
1st century A.D.	Shaka and Kushan invasions of India
A.D. 25–3rd century	Kushan rule in northwestern India
ca A.D. 78	Kushan emperor Kanishka promotes Buddhism

and Mesopotamia but also with the young and vital culture of the Greeks. What effects did contact with Persia and the lands farther west have on India?

Culturally the Persian conquest resembled the Hyksos period in Egypt (see page 29) in that it was a fertilizing event, introducing new ideas, techniques, and materials into India. In fact, the period of Persian rule was one of thoroughgoing innovation. As members of the vast Persian Empire, Indians learned the administrative techniques of ruling large tracts of land and huge numbers of people. The adoption of coined money for economic transactions was a far-reaching innovation. From the Persians the Indians learned the technique of minting silver coins, and they adopted the Persian standard to facilitate trade with other parts of the empire. Even states in the Ganges Valley, which were never part of the empire, adopted the use of coinage. Another innovation was the introduction of the Aramaic language and script, the official language of the Persian Empire. Indians adapted the Aramaic script to their needs and their languages—enabling them to keep records and publish proclamations just as the Persians did.

Likewise, India participated in the larger economic world created by the Persians. Trade increased dramatically with other regions under Persian rule. Once again hardy merchants took the sea route to the West, as had their predecessors of the Indus civilization. Caravan cities grew in number and wealth, as overland trade thrived in the peace brought about by Persian rule. New prosperity and new techniques also gave rise to rough-stone architecture, notably at the important city of Taxila in the northern Indus Valley (see Map 3.1). In short, the arrival of the Persians drew India into the mainstream of sophisticated urban, commercial, and political life in the ancient world.

Into this world stormed Alexander the Great, who led his Macedonian and Greek troops through the Khyber Pass into the Indus Valley in 326 B.C. (see pages 148–150). What he found in India is most readily apparent in Taxila, a major center of trade in the Punjab. The Greeks described Taxila as "a city great and prosperous, the biggest of those between the Indus River and the Hydaspes the modern [Jhelum River]—a region not inferior to Egypt in size, with especially good pastures and rich in fine fruits."[7] Modern archeology has shed light on Indian urban life in this period and in the process has proved the Greeks' praise excessive: despite its prosperity and importance as a seat of Hindu learning, Taxila was an unassuming town, a poor town when compared with the cities of the Near East.

From Taxila, Alexander marched to the mouth of the Indus River before turning west and leaving India forever. A riot of bloodshed and destruction, Alexander's invasion facilitated the rise of the first kingdom to embrace all of India.

THE MAURYAN EMPIRE
(CA 322–232 B.C.)

Alexander disrupted the political map of western India and died without organizing his conquests, leaving the area in confusion. Chandragupta, the ruler of a small state in the Ganges Valley, took advantage of this situation by defeating his enemies

Lion Capital of Ashoka This lion capital from a column of Ashoka handsomely represents the emperor's political power. It also illustrates significant Near Eastern and Greek influences on the Indian art of this period. *(Source: Raghubir Singh)*

piecemeal until, by 322 B.C., he had made himself sole master of India. He justified his position as king of India in 304 B.C. by defeating the forces of Seleucus, a general of Alexander the Great who founded the Seleucid monarchy. In the wake of this battle, Seleucus surrendered the easternmost provinces of his monarchy and concluded a treaty of alliance with Chandragupta. Hence Chandragupta not only defeated one of the mightiest of Alexander's lieutenants, he also entered the world of Hellenistic politics (see Chapter 5).

The real heir to Alexander's conquest, Chandragupta created the great Mauryan Empire, which stretched from the Punjab and Himalayas in the north almost to the tip of the subcontinent, from modern Afghanistan in the west to Bengal in the east. In the administration of his empire, Chandragupta adopted the Persian practice of dividing the area into provinces. Each province was assigned a governor, most of whom were drawn from Chandragupta's own family. The smallest unit in this system was typically the village, the mainstay of Indian life. From his capital at Pataliputra, in the valley of the Ganges, the king sent agents to the provinces to oversee the workings of government and to keep him informed of conditions in his realm. Chandragupta also enjoyed the able assistance of his great minister Kautilya, who wrote a practical treatise on statecraft. For the first time in Indian history, one man governed most of the subcontinent, exercising control through delegated power.

Chandragupta applied the lessons learned from Persian rule with stunning effectiveness. He established a complex bureaucracy to see to the operation of the state and a bureaucratic taxation system that financed public services. Chandragupta also built a regular army, complete with departments for everything from naval matters to the collection of supplies. He exercised tight control, to some degree repressing the people in order to retain power.

Megasthenes, a Greek ambassador of King Seleucus, left a lively description of life at Chandragupta's court. Like many other monarchs, Chandragupta feared treachery, especially assassination, but nonetheless refused to leave government to others. Therefore he took elaborate precautions against intrigue. According to Megasthenes:

Attendance on the king's person is the duty of women, who indeed are bought from their fathers. Outside the gates of the palace stand the bodyguards and the rest of the soldiers. . . . Nor does the king sleep during the day, and at night he is forced at various hours to change his bed because of those plotting against him. Of his non-military departures from the palace one is to the courts, in which he passes the day hearing cases to the end, even if the hour arrives for attendance on his person. . . . When he leaves to hunt, he is thickly surrounded by a circle of women, and on the outside by spear-carrying bodyguards. The road is fenced off with ropes, and to anyone who passes within the ropes as far as the women death is the penalty.[8]

These measures worked: after resigning the kingship, Chandragupta died the peaceful death of a Jain ascetic in 298 B.C.

Chandragupta left behind a kingdom organized to maintain order and defend India from invasion. India enjoyed economic prosperity and communications with its neighbors. At a time when many of the major cultures of the world were in direct touch with one another, the Indians, who had created much from their own experience and had learned much from others, could proudly make their own contributions in both cultural and material spheres.

The Reign of Ashoka (ca 269–232 B.C.)

The years after Chandragupta's death in 298 B.C. were an epoch of political greatness, thanks largely to Ashoka, one of India's most remarkable figures. The grandson of Chandragupta, Ashoka extended the Mauryan Empire to its farthest limits. The era of Ashoka was enormously important in the religious and intellectual history of the world. A man in search of spiritual solace, Ashoka embraced Buddhism and helped to establish it as an important religion. Buddhism would take deep and lasting root throughout much of the East, but not in India itself.

As a young prince, Ashoka served as governor of two important provinces, both seats of Buddhism—at this time still solely an Indian religion—and both commercially wealthy. While governor, Ashoka met and married Devi, a lady of the merchant class who would later end her life spreading Buddhism to Ceylon. The young prince spent his leisure hours hunting, horseback riding, and enjoying lavish feasts. Yet he was a sensitive and perceptive young man, known for his fondness for

and study of birds. In religion Ashoka was deeply influenced by Brahmanism and Jainism, which pointed him toward a broad religious outlook.

At the death of his father about 274 B.C., Ashoka rebelled against his older brother, the rightful king, and after four years of fighting succeeded in his bloody bid for the throne. Crowned king of India, he extended Mauryan conquests, initiated or renewed friendly relations with neighboring powers, and reorganized his empire. Ashoka ruled intelligently and energetically. He was equally serious about his pleasures, especially those of the banquet hall and harem. In short, Ashoka in the early years of his reign was an efficient and contented king whose days were divided between business and pleasure.

The change that occurred in the ninth year of his reign affected not just Ashoka and his subjects but the subsequent history of India and the world. In that year Ashoka conquered Kalinga, the modern state of Orissa on the east coast of India; in a grim and savage campaign, Ashoka reduced Kalinga by wholesale slaughter. As Ashoka himself admitted, "In that (conquest) one hundred and fifty thousand were killed (or maimed) and many times that number died."[9]

Yet instead of exulting like a conqueror, Ashoka was consumed with remorse and revulsion at the horror of war. On the battlefield of Kalinga, the conquering hero looked for a new meaning in life; the carnage of Kalinga gave birth to a new Ashoka. The king embraced Buddhism and used the machinery of his empire to spread Buddhist teachings throughout India. Ashoka's remarkable crisis of conscience has been the subject of considerable debate, much like the later conversion to Christianity of the Roman emperor Constantine. No one will ever know the content of Ashoka's mind, but the practical results of his conversion led to a more humane governance of India.

Ashoka emphasized compassion, nonviolence, and adherence to dharma. He may have perceived dharma as a kind of civic virtue, a universal ethical model capable of uniting the diverse peoples of his extensive empire. Ashoka erected inscriptions to inform the people of his policy. In one edict, he spoke to his people like a father:

Whatever good I have done has indeed been accomplished for the progress and welfare of the world. By these shall grow virtues namely: proper support of mother and father, regard for preceptors and elders,

Sanchi Topa This great monument of Mauryan architecture is the north gate of a stupa, or large mound built to house Buddhist relics. Standing eighteen feet high, the gateway is richly carved and decorated with Buddhist motifs. *(Source: BBC Hulton/The Bettmann Archive)*

proper treatment of Brahmans and ascetics, of the poor and the destitute, slaves and servants.[10]

Ashoka's new outlook can be seen as a form of *paternalism,* well-meaning government that provides for the people's welfare without granting them much responsibility or freedom. He appointed new officials to oversee the moral welfare of the realm and made sure that local officials administered humanely.

Ashoka felt the need to protect his new religion and keep it pure. Warning Buddhist monks that he would not tolerate schism—divisions based on differences of opinion about doctrine or ritual—he threw his support to religious orthodoxy. At the same time, Ashoka honored India's other religions. Hinduism and Jainism were revered and respected, and the emperor even built shrines for their worshipers. Buddhism, though royally favored, competed peacefully with Hinduism and Jainism for the hearts and minds of the Indian people.

Despite his devotion to Buddhism, Ashoka never neglected his duties as emperor. He tightened the central government of the empire and kept a close check on local officials. He also built roads and rest spots to improve communications within the realm. Ashoka himself described this work:

On the highways Banyan trees have been planted so that they may afford shade to men and animals; mango-groves have been planted; wells have been dug at an interval of every half a kos, approximately every two miles; resting places have been set up; watering-places have been established for the benefit of animals and men.[11]

These measures also facilitated the march of armies and the armed enforcement of Ashoka's authority. Ashoka's efforts were eminently successful: never before his reign and not again until the modern period did so much of India enjoy peace, prosperity, and humane rule.

India and Its Invaders (ca 250 B.C.–A.D. 200)

Ashoka's reign was the high point of ancient India's political history. Ashoka's successors remained on the throne until about 185 B.C.; there-

after India was subject to repeated foreign invasions, confined principally to the northwest, that constantly changed the political map of the country. For many years the history of India was a tale of relentless war between invaders and Indians and among native Indian kings as well. The energy consumed by these internal wars prevented the Indians from driving out the invaders, from bringing peace and prosperity to the land. Still, even though each wave of newcomers left its mark on the cultural heritage of India, Indian civilization triumphed, changing the invaders as well as being fertilized by them.

The Kushans, whose authority in India lasted until the third century A.D., were particularly significant because their empire encompassed much of central Asia as well as northwestern India. The Kushans put India in closer contact with its eastern neighbors. The Kushan invaders were assimilated into Indian society as Kshatriyas, of higher status than native Vaisya, Shudra, outcastes, and untouchables, and once again a backward nomadic people fell under the spell of a more sophisticated civilization.

The political map of India after Ashoka was fragmented: the Kushans and earlier invaders held northwestern India, and petty Indian kings ruled small realms in the rest of India. For many years the political history of India was a tale of relentless war among local Indian kings. The energy these wars consumed did nothing for India's capacity to resist foreign invaders.

Although the Kushans were the final nail in the coffin of Ashoka's political efforts to unite India, they played a valuable role by giving northwest India a long period in which to absorb the newcomers and adapt the cultural innovations introduced by the various invaders. The Kushans were receptive to external influence and were subject to many of the influences that acted on the Indians. Kushans and Indians alike absorbed Greek ideas. Greek culture made its greatest impression on Indian art. Greek artists and sculptors working in India adorned Buddhist shrines, modeling the earliest representation of Buddha on Hellenistic statues of Apollo, and were the leading force behind the Gandhara school of art in India. Only the form, however, was Greek; the content was purely Buddhist. In short, India owes a modest cultural debt to Hellenism. Just as Ashoka's Buddhist missionaries made no impression on the Greek world, so Hellenism gave India some fresh ideas but had no lasting impact on the essence of Indian life. Only Buddhism, which addressed itself to all human beings rather than to any particular culture, was at all significant as a meeting-ground for the Greeks, Indians, and Kushans. Otherwise, the outlooks and values of Greek and Indian cultures were too different and too tenacious for one to assimilate the essence of the other.

The most significant and lasting gift of these years was the spread of Buddhism to China. India's invaders embraced Buddhism enthusiastically and protected the Buddhist order. They preferred the teachings of the Mahayana sect, more compassionate and flexible than its rival Theravada branch. In the course of their commercial dealings, they carried Mahayana Buddhism across inner Asia to China, transforming it from a purely Indian sect into an international religion.

SUMMARY

By roughly 250 B.C. India had developed a highly accomplished urban civilization sustained by systematic agriculture. Many of the fundamental ideals, beliefs, customs, and religious practices that would leave their mark on succeeding generations had already taken shape. These early years of Indian history were especially rich in religion. Not only did the Indians form several different views of the nature of life and visions of an afterlife, but they also made a fundamental impact on life in China by the spread of Buddhism. Hinduism, both religious and social in nature, was for the Indians themselves perhaps the most important development of this period, an ancient heritage that is still a vital factor in Indian life.

NOTES

1. M. Wheeler, *Early India and Pakistan to Ashoka* (London: Thames and Hudson, 1959), pp. 106–107.
2. Rigveda 10.90, translated by A. L. Basham, in *The Wonder That Was India* (New York: Grove Press, 1959), p. 241.
3. J. Mascaro, trans., *The Upanishads* (London: Penguin Books, 1965), pp. 117–118.
4. J. A. B. van Buitenen, trans., *The Mahabharata,* vol. 1, *The Book of the Beginning* (Chicago: University of Chicago Press, 1973), 214.1–7.
5. J. Mascaro, trans., *The Bhagavad Gita* (London: Penguin Books, 1962), 2.17–21.
6. Quoted in N. W. Ross, *Three Ways of Asian Wisdom* (New York: Simon and Schuster, 1966), p. 94.
7. Arrian, *Anabasis* 5.8.2; Plutarch, *Alexander* 59.1. Translation by John Buckler.
8. Strabo 15.1.55. Translation by John Buckler.
9. Quoted in B. G. Gokhale, *Asoka Maurya* (New York: Twayne Publishers, 1966), p. 157.
10. Pillar Edict 7, quoted ibid., p. 169.
11. Quoted ibid., pp. 168–169.

SUGGESTED READING

Much splendid work has been done on the geographical background of ancient Indian society. Two fine works are O. H. K. Spate and A. T. A. Learmouth, *India and Pakistan: A General and Regional Geography,* 3d ed. (1967); and B. L. C. Johnson, *South Asia: Selective Studies of the Essential Geography of India, Pakistan, and Ceylon* (1969). A masterpiece in its own right is J. Schwartzberg, ed., *An Historical Atlas of South Asia* (1978), the epitome of what a historical atlas should be. Its contents range well into contemporary times.

General histories of India are too numerous to list, with the exception of A. L. Basham, *The Wonder That Was India* (1959), one of the monuments of the field and a good introduction to nearly every aspect of ancient Indian history. Solid too are R. Thapar's two books, *History of India,* vol. I (1966), and *Ancient Indian Social History* (1978). Both are highly recommended. Especially rewarding are Z. Liu, *Ancient India and Ancient China* (1988); S. F. Mahmud, *A Concise History of Indo-Pakistan,* 2d ed. (1988); and H. Scharff, *The State in Indian Tradition* (1989), which covers the period from the Vedic to the Muslims.

Work on the Indus civilization continues at a rapid pace. A good recent survey is D. P. Agrawal, *The Archaeology of India* (1982), which is marked by good sense and sound judgment. Equally recent is G. L. Possehl, ed., *Harappan Civilization: A Contemporary Perspective* (1982), which combines excavation reports and analysis of material. His *Ancient Cities of the Indus* (1979) reprints articles by a number of scholars, thus providing a variety of perspectives on early Indus developments. Trade between the Indus and Mesopotamian civilizations is treated in E. C. L. During Caspers, "Sumer, Coastal Arabia and the Indus Valley in Protoliterate and Early Dynastic Eras," *Journal of Economic and Social History of the Orient* 22 (1979): 121–135. See also G. L. Possehl and M. H. Ravel, *Harappan Civilization and*

Rojdi (1989), which uses the newest archeological findings to explore the Harappan civilization.

For the arrival of the Aryans and subsequent developments, N. R. Banerjee, *The Iron Age in India* (1965), and C. Chakraborty, *Common Life in the Rigveda and Atharvaveda* (1977), treat the period from different points of view. More difficult but rewarding is F. Southworth, "Lexical Evidence for Early Contacts Between Indo-Aryan and Dravidian," in M. M. Deshpande and P. E. Hook, eds., *Aryan and Non-Aryan in India* (1979), pp. 191–234; the book contains a number of stimulating articles on the period.

Early Indian religion is a complex subject, but a series of books provides a good introduction to the topic. Old but still a classic is A. B. Keith, *Religion and Philosophy of the Vedas and Upanishads,* 2 vols. (1925). P. S. Jaini, *The Jaina Path of Purification* (1979), and T. Hopkins, *Hindu Religious Tradition* (1971), cover two of the major religions, to which should be added K. K. Klostermaier, *A Survey of Hinduism* (1989), and K. H. Potter, *Guide to Indian Philosophy* (1988).

Buddhism is such a popular topic that the bibliography is virtually endless. A valuable introduction by a leading scholar is E. Zurcher, *Buddhism: Its Origins and Spread in Words, Maps, and Pictures* (1962). A shorter and more spiritual approach is E. Conze, *A Short History of Buddhism* (1980). Also enlightening is W. Rahula, *What the Buddha Taught* (1971), which sheds light on the Theravada tradition, and R. Robinson and W. Johnson, *The Buddhist Religion,* 3d ed. (1982), which is more comprehensive. Still unsurpassed for its discussion of the relations between Buddhism and Hinduism is the grand work of C. N. Eliot, *Hinduism and Buddhism,* 3 vols. (reprinted 1954), which traces the evolution of theistic ideas in both religions. C. Humphreys has written extensively about Buddhism. The student may wish to consult *Buddhism* (1962), *Exploring Buddhism* (1975), or *The Wisdom of Buddhism* (new ed., 1979).

More recent is D. Fox, *The Heart of Buddhist Wisdom* (1985).

A stimulating and far-reaching discussion of intellectual developments in India is R. Thapar, "Ethics, Religion, and Social Protest in the First Millennium B.C. in North India," *Daedalus* 104 (Spring 1975): 119–132. Good translations of Indian literature discussed in the chapter are listed in the Notes.

Among the numerous works describing India's relations with the Persian Empire and Alexander the Great are several titles cited in Suggested Reading for Chapters 2 and 6. P. H. L. Eggermont, *Alexander's Campaigns in Sind and Baluchistan* (1975), focuses solely on Alexander's activities in India, as does E. Badian in I. Gershevitch, ed., *The Cambridge History of Iran* (1985). A. J. Dani, *The Historic City of Taxila* (1988), uses anthropological and historic evidence to study this important city and its influence.

Chandragupta's reign is treated in R. K. Mookerji, *Chandragupta Maurya and His Times,* rev. ed. (1966). J. C. Heesterman, "Kautilya and the Ancient Indian State," *Wiener Zeitschrift* 15 (1971): 5–22, analyzes the work and thought of Chandragupta's great minister of state.

The kingdom of Ashoka has attracted much attention. In addition to Gokhale's book cited in the Notes, R. Thapar's excellent *Asoka and the Decline of the Mauryas* (1961) is still an indispensable work on the subject.

For the Greek invasions, see W. W. Tarn, *The Greeks in Bactria and India* (1951), a difficult book but still valuable. A. K. Narain's more recent treatment, *The Indo-Greeks* (1967), is equally valuable and a bit more readable. For contact between the Hellenistic world and India, see J. W. Sedlar, *India and the Greek World* (1980), which approaches the problem of cultural transmission between the two civilizations. C. Drekmeier, *Kingship and Community in Early India* (1968), takes a broader approach to early developments.

4

The Rise and Growth of China to ca A.D. 200

Clay Warriors from the tomb of the First Emperor

Ancient China provides another example of an early people confronting a formidable geographical challenge in order first to survive and then to build a complex and sophisticated civilization. The Chinese had inhabited this region of eastern Asia from the beginning of human existence. Like the Egyptians, they prospered along a great river. But the Yellow River was hardly the gentle Nile. It needed to be tamed before it would sustain life, and taming it called for group effort on a massive scale. The success of the Chinese in meeting this awesome challenge is reflected in the flowering of Chinese culture, in the overall political stability of the area and the prosperity of its people. As in Mesopotamia, Egypt, and India, so in China there were wars, and dynasty followed dynasty, but political disruption never crippled Chinese cultural evolution. Moreover, the Chinese were remarkably successful in governing a huge population settled over a vast area. Their success resulted in political and social stability seldom, if ever, found elsewhere in the ancient world.

- How did the early Chinese confront the geographical factors of climate, soil, and land?
- What did their response share with the solutions of ancient Near Eastern and Indian peoples to these same problems, and how did it differ?
- What form did Chinese success take in the shaping of society?

These are the questions addressed in this chapter.

THE LAND AND ITS CHALLENGE

While geography had left India an opening to the northwest and thus to the civilizations of the ancient Near East, terrain and distance made China's links to the broader world tenuous (Map 4.1). Between India and China towered the ice-clad and forbidding peaks of the Himalayas and the Pamirs, and beyond lay the vast expanses of Tibet and Chinese Turkestan. Geography isolated China in other directions as well. To the north stretched the Gobi Desert, some 500,000 square miles of desolate waste, and the Mongolian Plateau. To the south

rose mountains covered with forests and tracts of jungle. Beyond the shores of China lay Japan, inhabited at this early period by primitive peoples; the islands of the South China Sea; and the huge and then-uncharted expanse of the Pacific Ocean. China's main avenue to the major civilizations of the outside world was a threadlike corridor to the northwest, through the vastness of central Asia, past India, and ultimately to Mesopotamia. Though isolated, China was not sealed off completely. Like India, it enjoyed a link to other seats of civilization.

China encompasses two immense river basins: those of the Yellow River in the north and the Yangtze in the south. Both rivers rise in the mountains of Tibet and flow eastward across China (see Map 4.1). The Yellow River carries tons of loess, a fine light-colored dust whose color gives the river its name. Loess is exceptionally fertile and easy to cultivate, and this basin was the site of China's earliest agricultural civilization in the Neolithic Age (see page 13). Yet like the Tigris in Mesopotamia, the Yellow River can be a rampaging torrent, bringing disastrous floods and changing course unpredictably. Frequently called "China's Sorrow," the Yellow River had to be tamed with dikes. The taming of the river allowed China's great northern plain to be farmed, eventually nurturing a huge population.

The basins of the Yellow and Yangtze rivers are separated in the west by mountains, which give way to hills and finally disappear altogether in the flat country near the coast. The two basins are quite distinct, however, when it comes to farming. Dry farming of wheat and millet characterizes the Yellow River basin in the north; irrigated rice agriculture predominates in the warmer and wetter basin of the Yangtze. In the extreme south is the valley of the Hsi, or West, River, an area of mild climate and fertile soil that would later form the southern boundary of China. Within this enormous expanse of land the climate varies greatly from north to south and from east to west, with milder and wetter conditions prevailing in the south. Except for the river valleys, China is largely mountainous or semidesert land, which meant that people could thrive only in certain areas. Geography thus helped to ensure that human development in China would cling to the mighty river systems.

MAP 4.1 China Under the Shang and Chou Dynasties, 1523–221 B.C. The heartland of Chinese development is illustrated by this map, which shows the importance of the Yellow River in early Chinese life. Under the Chou, Chinese authority reached the Yangtze.

THE SHANG DYNASTY
(CA 1523–1027 B.C.)

At about the time the Aryans were transforming Indian life, the kings of the Shang Dynasty rose to power in northern China. Unlike the Aryans, the Shang were natives, very closely linked to indigenous Neolithic peoples. Chinese Neolithic farmers had long ago settled into a life of sustained agriculture and animal domestication. Asian scholars dispute the nature and degree of outside influence on early Chinese development, but most agree that ancient Chinese culture was largely a native

growth. China did not suffer massive foreign invasion. To this relatively self-contained society, the Shang gave a long period of political rule. Once considered legendary rather than historical, the Shang Dynasty has been verified from its own written records and the work of modern archeologists.

Social Organization

The excavations at the modern cities of Anyang, the Shang capital, and Chengchou, perhaps the oldest city in China, have shed surprisingly bright

Shang House   The ordinary farming family of Shang lived in a house very much like its Neolithic ancestors. The house was dark, close, and cramped, but the central hearth provided warmth and light. *(From John Hay,* Ancient China, *London: The Bodley Head, 1973, p. 41)*

light on the Shang kings and the society they ruled. Social divisions among the Shang were apparently simple but sharp: a ruling class of aristocrats, headed by a king and an incipient bureaucracy, directed the work and lives of everyone else. Warfare was a constant feature of Shang life, and the nobles were the warriors of Shang, those who enforced Shang rule. The Shang kings ruled northern China as a kind of family patrimony. The kings and the aristocracy owned slaves, many of whom had been captured in war. They also controlled the peasants, who served as semifree serfs.

The common people—serfs and slaves—performed all the economic functions of society. Most were farmers, whose way of life was basically Neolithic. Even in this remote period, however, Shang farmers knew how to cultivate the silkworm. Silken threads were woven into fine cloth, and under later emperors silk became China's prime export. Nonetheless, Shang farmers worked their fields with Neolithic tools and methods. Their homes too were Neolithic in construction. Each family dug in the ground a pit that served as the living area. Often they dug an entrance passage with a small platform inside the pit to keep water from running down the passage into the house. The central feature of the house was the hearth, which was dug out of the floor of the pit. Beside the hearth were wooden roof supports, against

which the roof timbers sloped. The family thatched the roof with reeds and clay, making a conical hutlike house. Although they helped create the wealth of Shang, peasant farmers enjoyed little of it themselves.

Other commoners were artisans. Dependent on the nobles, they manufactured the weapons, ritual vessels, jewelry, and other items demanded by the aristocracy. Shang craftsmen worked in stone, bone, and bronze but are best known for their bronze work. These early Chinese artists created some of the world's most splendid bronze pieces. Among the Shang, bronze was considered a noble metal, fit for weapons and ceremonial vessels but much too precious to be made into tools.

At the top of Shang society lived the king and his nobles, mighty figures elevated far above the common people. They lived in palatial houses built on huge platforms of pounded earth. The architecture of these houses set a pattern for house building that has flourished into modern times. The king and nobles enjoyed the magnificent bronze work of the artisans and carried bronze weapons into battle. Even after death, the king and his relatives had crucial social roles to play. The living worshiped and entreated them to intercede with the great gods, especially Shang-ti, the supreme god, to protect the lives and future hopes of their descendants. At first only the king and his family were worthy of such honors, but this custom was the forerunner of Chinese ancestor worship, an abiding element of Chinese religious belief.

Origins of Chinese Writing

The origins of Chinese writing appear to be deeply rooted in Shang religion. The kings of Shang were also high priests and frequently wanted to ask questions of the gods. Their medium was oracle bones, generally the shoulder bones of oxen or the bottom shells of tortoises. On one side of the bone or shell the king or priest wrote his message; on the other side he drilled a small hole, to which he applied a heated point. When the bone or shell split, the priest interpreted the cracks in relation to the writing.

Writing developed considerably later in China than in Sumer or India, but the Shang system was already highly developed and sophisticated. Originally pictographic, the signs used by the Shang contained phonetic values. Even so, the Shang and their successors created thousands of signs, resulting in a very complex system. Yet despite this complexity, like Sumerian cuneiform, mastery of even a few signs enabled people to keep records. Fluent literacy, however, demanded dedication, time, leisure, and thus wealth.

This system of writing proved popular and enduring. Later, when the script was simplified and standardized, it could be written and understood readily by literate Chinese who spoke different dialects. This accessibility was important, since many Chinese dialects were mutually unintelligible. The standardization of the written language, once achieved, proved to be indispensable for political, social, and cultural stability for centuries to come. The script spread throughout China and eventually to Korea and Japan, where it was adapted to local needs. The Koreans adopted the entire Chinese written language, including an approximation of the Chinese pronunciation of the signs. The Japanese went further than the Koreans, evolving a system in which the Chinese characters served as ideographs that had wholly Japanese pronunciations. In addition, they fashioned two other purely phonetic systems.

Literary mastery required such an effort that those who achieved it were a learned elite. Literacy

Shang Oracle Bone On one side of the bone the Shang diviner wrote his questions to the gods, and on the other side he applied a hot point. When the cracks in the bone led to the writing, the interpreter read the gods' message. Most questions dealt with the harvest, weather, travel, and hunting. (*Source: The Peabody Museum, Harvard University*)

was so politically important and socially valuable that education and scholarship were revered; the literate elite was essential to the king and deeply respected by the peasants. Literacy made possible a bureaucracy capable of keeping records and conducting correspondence with commanders and governors far from the palace. Hence literacy became the ally of royal rule, facilitating communication with and effective control over the realm. Literacy also preserved the learning, lore, and experience of early Chinese society, a precious historical heritage for future ages.

THE TRIUMPH OF THE CHOU
(CA 1027–221 B.C.)

Some Shang oracle bones mention the king of Chou, a small realm in the basin of the Wei River, a tributary of the Yellow River on the western frontier of the Shang domains. The Chou were an agricultural people who had emigrated into the region, perhaps from the northwest. They were also culturally sophisticated masters of bronze and of horse-drawn chariots. In the eleventh century B.C. the Chou king, a dependent of the Shang, became increasingly rebellious and ultimately overturned the Shang Dynasty.

The Rule of the Chou

When the Chou overthrew the Shang, they led China into the historical period. They extended Chinese rule beyond the boundaries of the Shang, and they grappled with the problems of governing the newly won territory. Because their contact with the Shang resulted in their adoption of much of Shang culture, the political victory of the Chou caused no cultural break. Nevertheless, the Chou made significant social and cultural strides. They succeeded in giving China a long period in which to consolidate these advances.

To justify their conquest ideologically, the Chou founders declared that the last Shang king had forfeited his right to rule because of his excesses and incompetence. They asserted that Heaven itself had transferred its mandate to rule China from the Shang house to its worthier rivals, the Chou. The justification belief of the Chou later served as the basis of the broader concept of the Mandate of Heaven (see page 104).

The victorious Chou confronted the formidable challenge of governing enormous areas of land. Communication within the realm was poor, and one king could not administer it all effectively. Moreover, the original Chou capital was near Sian in western China, too remote for efficient rule of the new domain. The Chou solved these problems by building a second capital at Loyang in the North China Plain (see Map 4.1) and by creating something resembling a loosely governed state.

The king of the Chou gave huge tracts of land to members of the royal family and to others who had demonstrated their talent and loyalty. At the outset, the newly appointed lords received their authority from the king. In a formal ceremony the king handed the new lord a lump of earth, symbolizing the king's gift of land to the lord. The lord pledged loyalty to the king and usually promised to send the king military forces if he requested them. A written record was made of the grant and the new lord's obligations and rights—an unprecedented secular use of writing. In effect, the Chou king was the political overlord of the land. He was also the supreme religious leader, who interceded with the gods for the welfare of Chinese society.

At first the Chou kings exercised strong control over their political dependencies. Gradually, however, the lords tried to strengthen their own positions, even at the expense of the king. Furthermore, the power of the lords grew with the prosperity of their holdings. The dependencies of the Chou were actually small islands of settlement scattered all over northern China, separated by wide tracts of undeveloped land. Over several centuries the growing populations of these settlements cleared new land, and eventually permanent cities arose. Once small and vulnerable, these settlements began to coalesce into compact regional states and then to fight among themselves over borders and territories. In this conflict the states in the interior of China were eclipsed by those on the borders, which took advantage of their geographical position to expand. The expansion spread Chinese culture ever wider. While conquering new territory, the lords of the border states were also wringing the most they could from their traditional seats of power. They became absolute rulers in their own right. Around them developed a hereditary class of aristocratic ministers of state, warriors, administrators, and tax collectors. China was gradually becoming a land of numerous independent kingdoms.

Along with the growing independence of the lords went a decline in the power and stature of the Chou kings. The lords used their troops to realize their own ambitions and stopped sending forces to the kings, disregarding their political obligations. In 771 B.C. a Chou king was defeated and killed by rebel lords. After that the Chou abandoned their western capital and made Loyang, the eastern capital, their permanent seat.

During the period known as the "Era of the Warring States" (402–221 B.C.), the entire political organization of the Chou Dynasty disintegrated. The Chou kings were little more than figureheads. The dreary cycle of warfare finally ended in 221 B.C., when the ruler of Ch'in, who had forced the abdication of the last Chou king in 256 B.C., conquered all the other states.

Social Change and Cultural Advancement in the Chou Period

The political events of the Chou period were to have a lasting impact on Chinese society. As the older interior states declined in stature, the aristocracies of these states lost their wealth. Educated, literate, and talented people were forced to seek their fortunes far from home. And the border states, dependent as they were on military and administrative efficiency, needed capable people to keep the wheels of government turning. The upshot was that impoverished aristocrats gravitated to the border states, where their much-needed talents opened the door to careers as ministers and officials. Merit, not birth, made the difference. This period saw the origins of a trained and able civil service, a group who saw to the daily workings of government and, later, gave a warm reception to the great philosophies of the Chou period. The rise of Chinese philosophy was largely a response to the political turmoil and warfare that wracked the country, which helps to explain its secular orientation.

Despite the long years of warfare and slaughter, the Chou period could boast of some remarkable cultural achievements. Cities grew up around the walled garrisons that the Chou established to hold down the Shang people. They evolved from army camps into genuine cities, some with huge populations. The roads and canals built to import food and goods to the city dwellers stimulated trade and agriculture. Trade was also stimulated and made easier by the invention of coined money.

A surge in technology during the Chou period permanently altered warfare, agriculture, and ultimately urban life. Under the Chou, craftsmen and artisans discovered the use of iron and rapidly developed its uses. Chou metalsmiths produced both wrought and cast iron—a remarkable achievement not matched in Europe until the fourteenth century. Chou craftsmen turned out an imposing number of weapons, especially dagger-axes and

Ritual Vessel This Shang bronze vessel excellently demonstrates the sophistication and technical mastery of early Chinese artists. The usual interpretation of the piece is that the tiger is protecting the man who is the head of his clan. Or the tiger may be having breakfast. *(Source: Michael Holford)*

swords (a mute commentary about life in the period). Use of the chariot in warfare led to improved harnesses for horses. The Shang had harnessed horses with bands around their girths and throats—a primitive arrangement that choked the horse when the harness was pulled hard. The Chinese did not perfect the harness until a later era, but they did so centuries before the medieval Europeans.

In agriculture the Chinese under the Chou Dynasty progressed from Neolithic farming methods to a metal technology. In place of the stone and bone tools of the Shang, Chou farmers used iron. Plows with iron shares broke the ground easily. Iron sickles, knives, and spades made the raising

Chou Ritual Vessel   This bronze vessel is ample proof that Chou bronzesmiths could rival their Shang predecessors. Although not as richly decorated as the vessel on page 93, the bronzeworking is complicated and the fanciful animal shape delightful. *(Source: Robert Harding)*

and harvesting of crops easier and far more efficient than ever before. By increasing productivity, metal technology gave Chou farmers the tools to support a thriving urban culture.

THE BIRTH OF CHINESE PHILOSOPHY

The Chou period was an era of intellectual creativity. Many thoughtful and literate people turned their minds to the basic question of how people could live the happiest and most productive lives in the most efficiently run society. Chinese thinkers were more secular than religious in their outlook. While Indian mystics were creating a complex socioreligious system, the Chinese were

exploring philosophies of political development. Fascinated by political, social, and economic problems, they sought universal rules for human conduct. This period gave rise to three branches of thought—Confucianism, Taoism, and Legalism—and the popular belief represented by *I Ching* that left an indelible stamp on the history of China.

CONFUCIANISM

Of the three schools of thought, Confucianism has had the most profound impact on China. The historical K'ung Fu-tzu (551–479 B.C.)—better known in the West as Confucius—was primarily a teacher and did not put his thoughts into writing. His fame comes largely from his students, who collected his sayings in a book called the *Analects*.

Confucius's family was aristocratic but poor, and the young man had few immediate prospects of success. His family had him educated so that he could take his place in the civil service, yet he achieved fame as a teacher, not as a minister of state, an irony that failed to satisfy him. Confucius taught the sons of nobles but yearned to advise lords. Setting out with a small band of students, he sought employment from the lords of the emerging regional states in northeastern China. He served intermittently as a minor official and continued to spread his ideas. At last Confucius returned home to die among his students, considering himself a failure because he had never held high office.

Confucius's thought centered on the duties and proper behavior of the individual within society. He was far more interested in orderly and stable human relationships than in theology or religious matters. For all his fame, Confucius was not so much an original thinker as a brilliant synthesizer of old ideas. He taught that there is a universal law that even the sun, moon, and stars follow and that human beings too should live according to this law. Confucius considered the family the basic unit of society. Within the family, male was superior to female, age to youth. Thus husband was obeyed by wife, father by son, elder brother by younger. The eldest male was the head of the family. This order was to be respected even when those in authority were wrong:

The Master said, In serving his father and mother a man may gently remonstrate with them. But if he sees that he has failed to change their opinion, he should resume an attitude of deference and not thwart them; he may feel discouraged, but not resentful.[1]

Order in the family was the essential building block of order in society at large.

A man of moderation, Confucius was an earnest advocate of gentlemanly conduct. Only such conduct, which involved a virtuous and ethical life, could bring about peaceful social relations and well-run government. The Confucian gentleman was a man of integrity, education, and culture, a man schooled in proper etiquette. Asked to evaluate Tzu-ch'an, a minister of the Cheng state, Confucius discussed the virtues of a "gentleman":

In him were to be found four of the virtues that belong to the Way of the true gentleman. In his private conduct he was courteous, in serving his master he was punctilious, in providing for the needs of the people he gave them even more than their due; in exacting service from the people, he was just.[2]

The way in which a gentleman disciplined himself is apparent in the conduct of Master Tseng, the most important of Confucius's followers:

Master Tseng said, Every day I examine myself on these three points: in acting on behalf of others, have I always been loyal to their interests? In intercourse with my friends, have I always been true to my word? Have I failed to repeat the precepts that have been handed down to me?[3]

Confucius pointed out that aristocratic birth did not automatically make a man a gentleman. Even men of humble birth could reach this exalted level through education and self-discipline. Confucius did not advocate social equality, but his teachings minimized the importance of class distinctions and opened the way for intelligent and talented people to rise in the social scale. The Confucian gentleman was made, not born.

This gentleman found his calling as a civil servant: he advised the ruler wisely, administered the kingdom intelligently, and dealt with the people humanely. Confucianism urged good government, emphasizing the duty of a good ruler to rule his people wisely and with compassion. Confucius commented on the qualities of a good ruler:

A country of a thousand war-chariots cannot be administered unless the ruler attends strictly to business, punctually observes his promises, is economical in expenditure, shows affection towards his subjects in general, and uses the labour of the peasantry only at the proper times of year.[4]

Confucianism was a vital ingredient in the evolution of an effective civil service. As a social movement, Confucianism was a distinct and specially recruited community, whose membership was ideally restricted to learned and talented people who embraced high standards of ethical awareness and conduct. Confucianism offered those in authority a body of expertise on the creation and consolidation of a well-ordered, sound, and powerful state. That expertise, like medical knowledge, demanded to be taken on its own innate merits and was thus offered in the form of advice and persuasion; it could not legitimately be imposed by violence. Neither revolutionaries nor toadies, Confucian scholar-bureaucrats opposed bad government by upholding in nonviolent ways the best ideals of statecraft. The Confucian ideal proved so powerful that it continued to shape Chinese society nearly to the present day.

Taoism

The later Chou period was a time of philosophical ferment. Many others besides Confucius were grappling with the problems of humanity, society, and the universal. Especially significant were the Taoists, followers of a school of thought traditionally ascribed to Lao-tzu. Little is known about Lao-tzu's life; he is supposed to have lived in the sixth century B.C., but his very existence has been questioned. The book attributed to him, *Tao Te Ching (Book of the Way and Its Power)*, is probably the work of several people and dates only from the fourth century B.C.

Where Confucian political thought was practical and humanistic, Taoism argued that political authority cannot bestow peace and order if it restricts itself to the rules and customs of society. The only effective social control stems, according to Lao-tzu, from adherence to the ultimate nature of reality. The Taoist sage points the way to that nature, and without his mystic vision of nature effective rule is impossible. The only way to achieve this end, Lao-tzu taught, is to follow Tao, or the Way of Nature. *Tao Te Ching* portrays the Way as the creative force of nature:

There is a thing confusedly formed,
Born before heaven and earth.
Silent and void
It stands alone and does not change,
Goes round and does not weary.
It is capable of being the mother of the world.
I know not its name
So I style it "the way." [5]

According to Taoists, people could be happy only if they abandoned the world and reverted to nature, living simply and alone. Those who followed the Way had no further need of human society. If the philosophy of Taoism had ever been car-

ried to its logical extreme, Taoism would have created a world of hermits.

Taoism treated the problems of government in a dramatically different way from Confucianism. In essence, the Taoists were convinced that government could do most for people by doing as little as possible. *Tao Te Ching* boldly declares that people are better-off left to themselves:

Exterminate the sage, discard the wise,
And the people will benefit a hundredfold;
Exterminate benevolence, discard rectitude,
And the people will again be filial;
Exterminate ingenuity, discard profit,
And there will be no more thieves and bandits. [6]

Lao-tzu argued that public works and services, from road building to law courts, led to higher taxes, which in turn led to unhappiness and even popular resistance. The fewer laws and rules, the better, Taoists urged. The Taoists also spelled out how, if there had to be a government at all, the people should be ruled:

Therefore in governing the people, the sage
empties their minds but fills their bellies,
weakens their wills but strengthens their
bones. He always keeps them innocent of
knowledge and free from desire, and ensures
that the clever never dare to act. [7]

The people are to be well treated, according to the Taoists, but they will be happiest if they remain uneducated and materially satisfied.

Taoism was most popular among the rulers and ministers who actually governed Chinese society. It gave them a safety valve in a rough-and-tumble world, a way of coping with the extreme pressures they faced. If a ruler suffered defeat or a minister fell out of favor, he could always resign himself to his misfortune by attributing it to the chaos of the world. In this respect Taoism became a philosophy of consolation—but only for a chosen few. The elite often adopted Taoism for consolation and Confucianism for serious everyday affairs.

Legalism

More pragmatic than Confucianism was Legalism, the collective name later given to a number of distinct but related schools of practical political theory that flourished during the late Chou period. Among the founders of Legalism were Han Fei-tzu (d. 233 B.C.) and Li Ssu (d. 208 B.C.), both former Confucians who had been heavily influenced by Taoism. Both were pragmatic realists who thought that the state should possess as much power as possible and extend it relentlessly. Their ideal state was authoritarian: the sensible ruler, in their view, should root out all intellectual dissent or resistance and all competing political ideas. Since human nature is evil, according to the Legalists, the ruler must keep the people disciplined and even suppressed if they are rebellious. The people should be well treated but need not be educated. The ruler should appropriate their labor to feed his armies and their wealth to fill his coffers. No frivolity is to be tolerated: people are to work and produce; they should not waste their time on the

A Meeting of the Minds The three figures here—representing a Confucian, a Buddhist, and a Taoist—discuss their philosophies in an atmosphere of peace and harmony. *(Source: China Classic Publishing Company)*

study of history, philosophy, and other unproductive pursuits. Legalism was ruthless in its approach to the problems of government. Rather than refute Confucian political ideas, it repressed or dismissed them, as many twentieth-century ideologies have done to conflicting ideas. Nonetheless, Legalism was realistic and offered Chinese rulers practical solutions to the problems of governing large populations over great distances.

Legalism was at first influential in practical affairs. Both Han Fei-tzu and Li Ssu were high officials, in a position to put Legalist theories into practice. Though Legalism offered an effective, if harsh, solution to the problems confronting Chou society, it was ultimately too narrow to compete successfully as an independent school with Confucianism and Taoism.

I Ching and Yin and Yang

Chinese thought was not entirely tied to philosophical schools or outlooks. It remained greatly influenced, especially at the popular level, by a belief that individuals were integral parts of a cosmic whole that they could understand. One aspect of this attitude was the belief that people could learn profound truths and receive dependable guidance to successful lives through interpretations of oracles. The Shang had much earlier used oracle bones to learn the will of the gods. At this period in the Han Dynasty, *I Ching (The Book of Changes)* fulfilled a similar purpose. *I Ching* directs readers in how to lead an ethical life and how to live in harmony with the universe. It is thus more ethical than philosophical, yet its philosophical content and importance should not be denied.

The *I Ching* is essentially a book of oracles, and readers used its contents by reading the result of randomly tossed coins. When people wanted answers to questions troubling them, they read the results of the throw of the coins and consulted the appropriate oracle. For instance, for those seeking to understand the continuous flow of life, the appropriate oracle was the following:

Creativity is a constant—flowing through our lives and our world; the very essence of all things. It is one moment built upon its predecessor, the continuous flow of existence. From this, the cosmic example, one must model his inner self, aspiring to consistency in his moments of cosmic unity. It is in this construct of

persistent contact and identification with the ceaseless power of heaven that the goal is realized.[8]

For those who wanted to be in harmony with this flow, the best oracle was this:

If one is to be in touch with the cosmic flow, he must develop a consciousness that will permit communication. Through the wide gate of his spirit's awareness, the sage receives the earth-intended force and humbly puts it to use for all men. Through this attitude of serving, he builds cooperation so that men may learn to work together in the shaping of their destinies.[9]

These two examples are enough to demonstrate that the *I Ching* uses ethics, philosophy, and plain common sense to enable people to live a happy, moral life. The *I Ching* did not demand acceptance of any particular philosophical or political doctrine; it simply provided sound advice.

Another attempt to understand the relationship between cosmic forces and human life led to the concept of Yin and Yang. Han thinkers developed the idea that these two elementary powers were a constant cosmic process, with Yang representing the strong, radiant, dry, and manly, while Yin was weak, dark, moist, and womanly; yet they constantly work together to bring about a changing but predictable relation of power in the world, a power that is related to the four seasons. Yang becomes strong in spring and comes to fullest strength in summer, only to decline in autumn and still further in winter. Yin reigns supreme in autumn and winter. Together they represent the powers and natural rhythms of the year, those of birth, growth, and death. Both are essential to the process of life, for they are in essence dual. Yin and Yang are not opponents like good and evil. Rather they are complementary. Neither can exist alone.

The concept of Yin and Yang attempted to put the observable facts of human life into an intelligible form. It accounts for the changes in the seasons, their natures, their fruits, the climates of each, and the place of human beings in this natural and eternal cycle. Unlike Hindu religion, which held out the opportunity to escape from the burdens of life, Yin and Yang helped people to think of themselves as a legitimate part of a natural order, and not necessarily as an alien or unfortunate part. They belonged just as much as did spring or winter and the fruits of the earth. Both *I Ching* and Yin and Yang gave people a simple and unsophisticated way of orienting themselves in the world, and the very simplicity of the two contributed to their popularity in ways that the more learned philosophies could not.

THE AGE OF EMPIRE

The leader of the state of Ch'in deposed the last Chou king in 256 B.C. Within thirty-five years he had made himself sole ruler of China, taking the title Ch'in Shih Huang Ti, or First Emperor. Thus began the Ch'in Dynasty. Although the Ch'in Dynasty lasted only some fifteen years, the work of its emperors endured for centuries. Indeed, the Western name for China is derived from the Ch'in. The First Emperor unified China under a central government, and the Han Dynasty, which replaced the Ch'in, maintained this unity for centuries. Under the emperors of the Ch'in and Han, China flourished economically, culturally, and socially.

The Ch'in and Unification of China

The ancient Chinese historian Ssu-ma Ch'ien left this vivid description of the victory of the First Emperor:

With its superior strength Ch'in pressed the crumbling forces of its rivals, pursued those who had fled in defeat, and overwhelmed and slaughtered the army of a million until their shields floated upon a river of blood. Following up the advantages of its victory, Ch'in gained mastery over the empire and divided up its mountains and rivers. The powerful states begged to submit to its sovereignty and the weaker ones paid homage at its court.[10]

The Ch'in extended their sway as far south as modern Hong Kong and the South China Sea, introducing Chinese influence into vast new areas. Ch'in armies even penetrated as far as northern Vietnam. With this hard-won victory came political unity, which the First Emperor was determined to maintain.

The First Emperor considered a highly centralized state necessary to ensure a united China. He and his prime minister, Li Ssu, a founder of Legalism, embarked on an imaginative, sweeping, and rigorous program of centralization that touched the lives of nearly everyone in China. At the head of the state stood the emperor, an autocrat possessing absolute power. His first act was to cripple the nobility. As Louis XIV of France was to do many centuries later, the First Emperor ordered the nobles to leave their lands and appear at his court. Aristocratic families all across China were torn from their estates and transported to Hsien-yang, the capital of Ch'in, where they built new homes around the court. The emperor took over their estates and organized China into a system of large provinces subdivided into smaller units.

The emperor controlled the provinces by appointing governors and lesser administrators, as well as other officials to keep watch on them. These officers were not drawn from the old aristocracy; they owed their power and position entirely to the favor of the emperor. Unlike the old aristocracy, they could not claim hereditary rights to their positions. The governors kept order in the provinces, enforcing laws and collecting taxes. One of their most important and least popular duties was to draft men for the army and for work on huge building projects.

In the interest of harnessing the enormous human resources of his people, the First Emperor ordered a census of the entire population. This information helped the imperial bureaucracy to plan its activities, estimating the costs of public works and the tax revenues needed to pay for them. The census also enabled the emperor to calculate the labor force available for military service and building projects.

A highly centralized empire needs good communications. Yet communication over an area as vast as China presented huge challenges, which the emperor met in several ways. First there was the problem of language itself. During the Chou period, states often spoke their own distinct dialects, which frequently borrowed words from other dialects. Written language also varied from dialect to dialect, with some people using signs that were unintelligible to others. These variations in language made central administration difficult. However literate, a governor might find himself transferred to a province whose dialect and script were unfamiliar; in such a case, he would be handicapped in carrying out his duties. The First Emperor and his ministers solved this problem by standardizing the written script.

Next the First Emperor standardized the weights, measures, and coinage of the realm. The

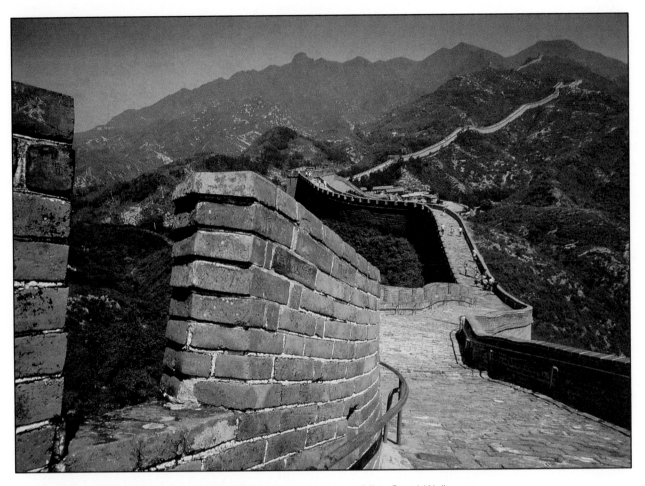

The Great Wall of China   The size and sheer awesomeness of the Great Wall comes through strikingly in this print. Over hill and through valley the Great Wall spanned some 3,000 miles of northern China. *(From D. Mennie and P. Weale,* The Pageant of Peking, *1922)*

old coinage was abolished in favor of new round coins with square holes in the center. The new coinage and system of weights and measures made it much easier for the central government to collect taxes. The emperor also standardized the axle lengths of carts. Most Chinese roads at the time were nothing more than deep tracks cut by the wheels of carts. Uniform axle lengths meant that all carts could use the same ruts, improving communications, strengthening imperial control, and making travel quicker and more convenient.

The First Emperor initiated land reforms that gave peasant farmers greater rights. He furthered irrigation projects and encouraged land reclamation to bring more soil under cultivation. These efforts, together with the widespread use of iron tools, increased agricultural production and fostered prosperity. The emperor also promoted the weaving of textiles, especially silk, which remained the aristocrat of Chinese fabrics. Thanks to the new road system, goods moved more easily than ever before and trade increased. Merchants became important figures, although their social status remained low; the First Emperor looked down on them as distinctly less than gentlemen. The growth of trade stimulated the growth of towns. Ch'in reforms and centralization helped to broaden the economy and thus enlarged the tax base for the government.

Foreign Danger and Internal Unrest

While the First Emperor was working to bring China unity and prosperity, he faced constant peril

MAP 4.2 China Under the Han Dynasty, 206 B.C.–A.D. **220** The glory of the Han Dynasty is evident from this map. Unlike China under the Chou, frontiers have been pushed far into central and southeastern Asia. The Han ruled over far more territory than any previous dynasty.

on the northern border. For years the Chinese had pushed northward, driving out the nomads and taking over their grassy pasture lands. These nomads were the Huns, who in later centuries would carry death, destruction, and terror to the decaying Roman Empire. Chinese encroachment endangered the very survival of the Huns, each of their scattered tribes led by its own chieftain. In retaliation the Huns, on horseback and armed with swords and bows, struck back at the Chinese. In quick and repeated raids, they plundered prosperous towns and farms and disappeared into the vastness of the north.

Since Chinese expansion in the north had all along met stiff opposition, the northern states had built long walls for self-protection as early as the fourth century B.C. The First Emperor ordered

these various stretches of wall to be linked together in one great wall, extending from the sea some 1,400 miles to the west (see Map 4.2). The number of laborers who worked on the wall and the sheer amount of construction material needed are stunning tribute to the First Emperor's power. The Great Wall of China is probably humanity's most immense ancient creation. The Great Wall and the huge numbers of troops guarding the frontier gave the north a period of peace.

Despite their innovations and achievements and the peace they brought to the north, the Ch'in were unpopular rulers. The First Emperor was no altruist. Primarily interested in his own wealth and power, he was determined to reap the profits of his work. Nor was he a man to tolerate opposition: as a Legalist, he distrusted Confucian scholars, some

460 of whom he reportedly had buried alive. He tried without success to destroy Confucian literature and China's ancient literary heritage by a massive campaign of book burning. He enforced the tenets of Legalism vigorously and ruthlessly in an effort to wipe out any system of thought that might challenge his autocratic position. The Ch'in demanded obedience, not intelligence.

The common people fared no better than the Confucian scholars. The Ch'in took advantage of the new prosperity to levy heavy taxes, especially on the peasants. Taxation and forced labor on the Great Wall and on other projects mercilessly ground down the peasantry. Forced labor and military service disrupted many peasant households; while the men were away, their families worked long, dreary hours to feed themselves and meet the staggering burden of taxes.

The oppressiveness of the Ch'in bred fierce hatred among the people, one of whom described the First Emperor as a monster who "had the heart of a tiger and a wolf. He killed men as though he thought he could never finish, he punished men as though he were afraid he would never get around to them all."[11] The death of the First Emperor in 210 B.C. sparked massive revolts. Huge bands of peasants took up arms against the new emperor. In the ensuing struggle for power, Liu Pang, a peasant and petty official of the Ch'in, defeated his opponents and in 206 B.C. established the Han Dynasty.

The Glory of the Han Dynasty (206 B.C.–A.D. 220)

The Han Dynasty marked the beginning of China's early imperial age. The dynasty also gave the Chinese their own name: they have traditionally called themselves "men of Han." Liu Pang, the victorious rebel, was no revolutionary. Because he, as a former Ch'in official, retained the main features of Ch'in administration and made no social reforms, there was no serious break in politics or culture between the two dynasties. The extreme political centralization of the Ch'in was relaxed, but the Han did not revive the feudalism of the Chou emperors. At least in theory, the Han Empire had an autocratic emperor aided by an educated but nonaristocratic bureaucracy. The basis of the empire, as always, was China's vigorous and hard-working peasants.

Under capable emperors like Liu Pang (206–195 B.C.) and his immediate successors, China recovered from the oppression and turmoil of the Ch'in period. Unable to conquer the Huns, who were renewing their threats on the northern border, the Chinese first tried to buy them off with lavish presents and stirred up internal trouble among Hun chieftains. In 133 B.C., however, Emperor Han Wu Ti changed this policy and went on the attack. In fourteen years of fighting, the Han drove the Huns still farther north. Chinese armies advanced into western Turkestan, where they opened up direct relations with the subcontinent of India. Equally impressive were the Han emperors' gains in the east. Chinese armies conquered western Korea, where they took over trade with Japan. The Han also extended their rule to modern-day Canton and the southeastern coast of China. By 111 B.C. when the emperor Han Wu Ti conquered northern Vietnam, Chinese rule had spread far beyond the natural boundaries of China (Map 4.2).

Han military conquests brought the Chinese into closer contact with distant peoples, which resulted in a dramatic increase in trade with the outside world. After Wu Ti conquered northern Vietnam, Chinese and foreign merchants moved in and set up trading stations under the supervision of Chinese officials. Southern China and northern Vietnam became meeting grounds for different cultures. The people of northern Vietnam accepted Chinese culture, and regions not far to the south were falling under the influence of Indian culture carried there by Indian merchants. Indeed, an independent state, called Funan by the Chinese, arose in modern southern Vietnam and Kampuchea among Malayan people who adopted many aspects of Indian culture.

Chinese rule in the south stimulated trade, and under the Han emperors Chinese merchants opened a new route from southwestern China via the rivers of Vietnam and Burma to ports on the Bay of Bengal. At first the Chinese were content to leave maritime trade in the hands of foreigners, but a later Han emperor sent an ambassador direct to the West (see page 216). Trade between China and its neighbors, together with the political and social stability of Han rule, gave China an unparalleled time of peace and prosperity. The Han historian Ssu-ma Ch'ien left a glowing report of Han administration as it existed around the year 136 B.C.:

The nation had met with no major disturbances so that, except in times of flood or drought, every person was well supplied and every family had enough to get along on. The granaries in the cities and the country-side were full and the government treasuries were running over with wealth. In the capital the strings of cash had stacked up by the hundreds of millions until the cords that bound them had rotted away and they could no longer be counted. In the central granary of the government, new grain was heaped on top of the old until the building was full and the grain over-flowed and piled up outside, where it spoiled and became unfit to eat. . . . Even the keepers of the community gates ate fine grain and meat.[12]

By excelling in the art of government, the Han emperors ruled a huge expanse of territory and improved vastly the quality of life for their subjects.

Han Confucianism and Intellectual Revolt

Confucianism made a comeback during the Han Dynasty, but it was a changed Confucianism. Many Confucian texts had fed the First Emperor's bonfires, never to be recovered. Some dedicated scholars had hidden their books, and others had memorized whole books: one ninety-year-old man

The Army of the First Emperor   When the grave of the First Emperor was recently discovered, an army of ceramic soldiers came to light. Six thousand statues, armed with spears, swords, bows, and crossbows, were found intact in a huge pit, here seen still in excavation. The statues give a vivid idea of the army that unified China. *(Source: Xinhua News Agency)*

was able to recite two books virtually in their entirety. These heroic efforts saved much of China's ancient literature and Confucian thought from the Ch'in holocaust. Yet there was extensive corruption of traditional Confucian texts, and non-Confucian elements were introduced into them.

While trying to reconstruct the past, the new Confucianism was influenced by other schools of thought, even by the hated Legalism. Strengthened by these influences, Confucianism again took hold—a hold so strong that Confucianism endured as the intellectual and cultural basis in China until the twentieth century.

During the Han era Confucian scholars pondering China's past put into systematic form a concept that went back to the Chou. They elaborated the related theories of the *dynastic cycle* and the *Mandate of Heaven*. The link between the cycle and the mandate was divine approval of the performance of a dynasty. Rule of China was the gift of Heaven, which was considered a deity. With Heaven's blessing the duty of the emperor and his successors was to expand the borders, if possible, or at least to foster prosperity and maintain order for noble and peasant alike. Once emperors failed in their duty, whether through weakness or corruption, conditions deteriorated, and the empire was left prey to foreign invasion and internal unrest. At that point, Confucian scholars argued, the dynastic cycle came full circle. By failing to maintain the Mandate of Heaven, the last emperor of the dynasty lost his authority to the first man who could restore order and prosperity. That man succeeded because Heaven transferred the mandate to him. Dynasties waxed and waned according to how well they served the requirements of Heaven; thus the Confucians accounted for the rise and fall of dynasties.

According to Han Confucianism, the emperor was the intermediary between his subjects and Heaven. He served this function by performing all the sacred rites to the deities correctly and scrupulously and by watching for signs that Heaven was displeased. He was also responsible for protecting the empire from outside threats and invasions and for maintaining order with as little interference as possible in the lives of the people. If the emperor failed in these tasks, he lost the Mandate of Heaven and risked losing his throne to a worthier claimant. Confucianism explained history by looking to the virtues and vices of individuals, especially emperors and dynasties. Confucian histo-

rians saw history not as progressive but as cyclical, as repetitions of the same kinds of events.

In this climate of thought, the study of history flourished. Generations of Chinese scholars devoted their efforts to studying particular dynasties and events and individual rulers, ministers, and generals. The Chinese, like the Greeks, conceived of history as broader and more complex than the mere chronicling of events. Indeed, during the Han Dynasty China produced one of its finest historians, Ssu-ma Ch'ien (ca 145–86 B.C.), who can be seen as the Chinese equivalent of the Greek Thucydides. Like Thucydides, he believed fervently in visiting the sites where history was made, examining artifacts, and questioning people about events. Ssu-ma was also interested in China's geographical variations, local customs, and local history. As an official of the emperor, he had access to important people and documents and to the imperial library. Having decided to write a history of China down to his own time, Ssu-ma set about interviewing eyewitnesses and those who had shaped events. He also reviewed official documents and written records. The result, ten years in the making, was his classic *Records of the Grand Historian,* a massive work of literary and historical genius.

Nor did Ssu-ma's work die with him. The Pan, a remarkably creative family, took up his study of the Han. Among the most eminent of them was Pan Chao, China's first woman historian and scholar. Pan Chao also wrote poems and essays, notably *Lessons for Women* on the education of women. Taking up Ssu-ma Ch'ien's history, the Pan family wrote the first history of a Chinese dynasty. Thereafter, official court historians wrote the history of every dynasty. Like their Greco-Roman counterparts, Chinese historians considered recent and current history important in their investigations.

Han intellectual pursuits were not limited to history. In medicine, the Han period produced its own Hippocrates, Ching Chi, a practicing physician whose *Treatise on Fevers* became a standard work in Chinese medicine. Chinese surgeons grappled with the problem of reducing the pain of surgery, and the Han physician Hua To developed a drug that, mixed with wine, would render a patient unconscious.

The career of Chang Heng (A.D. 78–139), the great mathematician, was strikingly similar to that of the Hellenistic philosopher Eratosthenes. Both delved deeply into astronomy and concluded that

Village Life These tomb figures depict an ordinary scene of village life in Han China. The two mounted figures represent wealthy men, for most villagers were too poor to keep horses. *(Source: The St. Louis Art Museum, Gift of the heirs of Berenice Ballard)*

the world is round, not flat as many of their contemporaries assumed. Chang Heng was not content to speculate; he also built models to test his theories. He even designed a seismograph capable of discerning the direction in which an earthquake was taking place, though not its severity. The brilliance of Han intellectual activity shone in its breadth and achievements.

Daily Life During the Han Dynasty

Because the people who chronicled events in Han China were an elite writing for other elites, more is known about the upper levels of society than about the lower levels. The lives of the common people were taken for granted or considered too vulgar to write about. Yet, though a complete portrayal is beyond reach, it is possible to sketch the outlines of daily life in Han China.

The peasant farmer was the backbone of Han society. Agriculture was considered an important and honorable human activity that distinguished the civilized Chinese from their barbaric and nomadic neighbors. Small households of farmers worked the land and generated most of the revenue of the empire. The Chinese peasant family was probably small, four or five people, frequently including a grandparent. Women were significant economic assets to poor farmers: both husband and wife performed hard manual labor in the fields. Men were typically required to spend time each year in the service of the emperor; and while they were away, their wives ran the farm. Farmers' existence was tenuous, for floods, drought, and unduly harsh taxes could wipe them out completely. Especially injurious was harsh, inefficient and sometimes corrupt government. When severely oppressed, the peasants revolted, turned to a life of begging or banditry, or they put themselves under the protection of powerful landlords. Thus it is easy to understand why the Han emperors were so proud of the peace and security of their reigns, which spared Chinese farmers the worst evils.

The staple grain under cultivation varied with the soil and climate. In the warm and wet south, rice was the traditional crop; in the north, farmers raised millet and wheat wherever possible. In northwestern China, peasants raised barley, which thrived on land too poor for wheat. Farmers also grew hemp, which was woven into coarse clothing for the common people. Some fortunate farmers had groves of timber or bamboo to supplement their crops. Most fortunate of all were those who grew mulberry trees, the leaves of which nourish silkworms, or groves of lac trees, which produced decorative lacquer. Wherever possible, farmers grew fruit and nut trees; farmers near cities found ready profit growing vegetables and ginger and other spices for city folk. Tea and sugar cane were raised in southern China but were still luxury items during the Han period.

Land use became systematic and effective under the Han, probably as a result of experience and of innovations recommended by Chao Kuo, a Han minister. Chao Kuo introduced a systematic ridge-and-furrow system of planting, with seeds planted in lines along the furrows. This method yielded fairly regular harvests and facilitated crop rotation because the position of the ridges and furrows would change annually. To maintain the fertility of the soil farmers treated their land with manure and crushed bones. The intensive character of Chinese agriculture meant that very little land was available for pasturage. Unlike his Indian counterpart, the Chinese farmer seldom raised cattle, horses, or donkeys. Dogs, pigs, and chickens were the typical domestic farm animals. The lack of draft animals meant that most farm work was done by hand and foot.

Farmers used a variety of tools, but the most important was the plow. The earliest wooden plow was a simple tool, more often pulled by humans than by animals. The new and more effective plow introduced during the Han period was fitted with two plowshares and guided by a pair of handles. This plow too could be pulled by manpower, but was typically pulled by a pair of oxen. The Chinese also developed an elaborate system using long hammers to mill grain and pound earth. At first the hammers were driven by people working pedals; later they were operated by animals and waterpower. Farmers used fans to blow the chaff from kernels of grain, and they used either mortar and pestle or hand mills to grind grain into flour. Irrigation water was pumped into the fields with devices ranging from a simple pole with attached

bucket and counterweight to a sophisticated machine worked by foot.

The agricultural year began in mid-February with the breaking up of heavy soil and manuring of the fields. February was also the beginning of the new year, a time of celebration and an important religious festival. This was the time to sow gourds, onions, melons, and garlic and to transplant oak, pine, and bamboo trees. Besides grain, farmers sowed beans and hemp and a variety of herbs. During the second and third months of the year, farmers practiced their archery to defend themselves against the bandits who infested the countryside; as a further precaution, they repaired the gates and locks of their houses. The fifth month was the time to cut the hay; the sixth, to hoe the fields. Meanwhile the women of the family were hard at work nurturing silkworms and making silk cloth, which they would later dye. Women also worked the hemp into coarse cloth. With the harvest, processing, and storage of the crop, farmers were ready for winter and the coming year.

City life was varied and hectic compared with the regularity of farming. The wealthiest urbanites lived in splendid houses of two or more stories, surrounded by walls and containing at least one courtyard. These palatial homes had such features as storage rooms and rooms for animals in the courtyard. The rooms or outhouses used for grain storage were built on stilts to protect against rats and moisture, which could cause rot or mildew.

The house itself was usually four-sided, with the door in one wall. The floors of the poor were covered with animal skins and mats of woven grass; those of the rich, with finely embroidered cushions and wool rugs. The bedrooms of wealthy homes were furnished with wooden beds, embroidered draperies, and beautiful screens for privacy. Fine furniture of expensive wood and beautifully lacquered bowls graced the houses of the wealthy.

Wealthy urban dwellers loved costly clothes, and everyone who could afford to bought fine and brightly colored silks. The wealthy also spent money on furs, usually fox and squirrel and sometimes badger. Expensive shoes lined with silk and decorated with leather became extremely popular. Wealthy women wore jewelry of jade and other precious and semiprecious stones, as well as gold earrings and finger rings. The urban poor probably had easier and somewhat cheaper access to silk garments than their rural neighbors, but their clothing was primarily made of coarse hemp cloth.

The diet of city folk, like their clothing, could be rich and varied. Owing to general prosperity, people during the Han period began to eat meat more frequently. Demand increased dramatically for wild game and young animals and fish, which were seasoned with leeks, ginger, and herbs. No longer was rice wine, like meat, a luxury for festival days. It began to be consumed avidly, and wealthy Chinese began to age vintages for twenty to thirty years. The Chinese were especially fond of pork, and roast pig was one of the most popular gourmet dishes. Other favorites were minced fish prepared in herbs and spices and fowl served in orange sauce, together with pickles and a variety of relishes. The Chinese also enjoyed liver and dog meat. Wood and pottery utensils were standard features of common households, but rich people relegated wood and pottery to the kitchen and dined on dishes decorated with gold and silver.

People with money and taste patronized music, and the rich often maintained private musical troupes consisting of small choirs, bells, drums, and pipes. Flutes and stringed instruments were also popular. People of more common taste flocked to puppet shows and performances of jugglers and acrobats. Magic shows dazzled the impressionable, and cockfighting appealed to bloody tastes. Gambling was popular but considered decidedly vulgar. Archeologists have found several board games.

As gangs of bandits infested the countryside, so crime plagued the cities. Officials were open to corruption and sometimes connived with criminals and gangs of thugs who had the support of wealthy and powerful families. At times the situation got so far out of hand that private armies roamed the streets, wearing armor and carrying knives and preying on the weak and helpless. Poor people who lacked influence suffered outrages and violence with no hope of justice or retribution.

Silk was in great demand all over the known world during the Han period, and strings of caravans transported bales of it westward. Another distinctive Chinese product was lacquered ware. Parts of China nourish the lac tree, which secretes a resinous fluid refinable to a hard and durable varnish. Han craftsmen developed lacquer work to a fine art. Because lacquer creates a hard surface that withstands wear, it was ideal for cups, dishes, toilet articles, and even parts of carriages. Lacquered boxes and other articles were often decorated with ornamental writing or inlaid with precious metals. Such works of art were only for the rich; poor people contented themselves with plain lacquered ware at best. Some of the most splendid examples of lacquer work are elaborately carved; Chinese craftsmen loved geometric designs, and some of their work is so accurate that it suggests that they used mechanical tools.

Perhaps the most momentous product of Han imagination was the invention of paper, which the Chinese traditionally date to A.D. 105. Scribes had previously written on strips of bamboo and wood. Fine books like those in the royal library were written on silk rolls, but only the wealthiest could afford such luxury. Ts'ai Lun, to whom the Chinese attribute the invention of paper, worked the fibers of rags, hemp, bark, and other scraps into sheets of paper. Though far less durable than wood, paper was far cheaper than silk. As knowledge of papermaking spread, paper became a cheap and convenient means of conveying the written word. By the fifth century, paper was in common use, preparing the way for the invention of printing.

Han craftsmen continued the Chinese tradition of excellent metallurgy. By the beginning of the first century A.D., China had about fifty state-run ironworking factories. These factories smelted iron ore, processed it with chemicals, and fashioned the metal into ingots before turning it over to the craftsmen who worked it into tools and other articles. The products of these factories demonstrate a sophisticated knowledge of metals. Han workmen turned out iron plowshares, agricultural tools with wooden handles, and such weapons as swords, spears, armor, and arrowheads. Han metalsmiths were mass-producing superb crossbows long before the crossbow was dreamed of in Europe.

Iron was replacing bronze in tools, but bronzeworkers still turned out a host of goods. Bronze was prized for jewelry, dishes, and spoons. It was the preferred metal for crossbow triggers and ornate mirrors. Bronze was also used for minting coins and for precision tools such as carpenters' rules and adjustable wrenches. Bronze and wood were used for wagon and carriage wheels; Han wheels were made either convex or concave to give a smooth ride. Surviving bronze gear-and-cog wheels bear eloquent testimony to the sophistication of Han machinery.

Distribution of the products of Han craftsmen was in the hands of merchants, whom Chinese aristocrats, like ancient Hebrew wise men, considered necessary but lowly. In the Chinese scale of values, agriculture was honorable because farmers worked to win the gifts that nature bestowed. Merchants, however, thrived on the toil of others, and the art of winning profits was considered ungentlemanly and not quite legitimate. The first Han emperor took action to put merchants in their place, as the great historian Ssu-ma relates:

After peace had been restored to the empire, Kao-tsu [Liu Pang's posthumous name as emperor] issued an

order forbidding merchants to wear silk or ride in carriages, and increased the taxes that they were obliged to pay in order to hamper and humiliate them.[13]

Yet the emperors and ministers of Han China realized that merchants had become indispensable. One outcome of this ambiguity was the conclusion that merchants ought to be regulated. Another was an early form of limited socialism—state monopolies on essential commodities like iron and salt, which made for price stability.

Retail merchants set up shop in stalls in the markets, grouped together according to their wares. All the butchers, for example, congregated in one part of the market, each trying to outsell the others. Nearly everything could be found in the markets, from food to horses and cattle, from ox carts and metal hardware to fine silks. The markets were also the haunts of entertainers and fortunetellers. The imperial government stationed officials in the markets to police the selling of goods and to levy taxes on the merchants. The imperial government also chose markets for the public execution of criminals: the rolling of heads served as an example and a warning to would-be criminals and political agitators in the crowd.

The transportation of goods in bulk was still difficult and expensive. Roads were primitive, but the Han developed several sturdy and effective types of carts and wagons, and a new harness for horses came into widespread use. Where earlier harnesses had fitted around the horse's neck, choking the animal when it pulled a load, the new harness fitted around the horse's chest and over its back, enabling it to pull heavier loads with less effort. This efficient horse collar finally reached medieval Europe in the eighth century A.D., a product of Asian technology that vastly influenced the history of the West.

Because of the difficulty of overland travel, the Chinese relied heavily on water transport. Since the major rivers of China run from east to west, canals were cut between the rivers to make north-south traffic possible. Bulk foodstuffs and goods could be transported fairly cheaply and swiftly on river boats, which also provided reasonably comfortable living quarters for crew and passengers. Maintenance of canals and dikes was expensive and made huge demands on the labor force, but these waterways allowed China to establish a flexible and effective network of communications.

Jade Burial Suit Made from thousands of jade pieces connected by gold thread, this suit totally clothed the body of Lady Tou, the wife of Liu Sheng, a Han prince. Jade was especially esteemed because the Chinese believed that it preserved the corpse. In fact, the contents of the suit consisted of only a few teeth. *(Source: Robert Harding Picture Library)*

CHINA TO CA A.D. 400

ca 1523–ca 1027 B.C.	Shang Dynasty and invention of writing
ca 1027–221 B.C.	Chou Dynasty
551–479 B.C.	Confucius and rise of Confucianism
4th century B.C.	Lao-tzu and development of Taoism
ca 250–208 B.C.	Han Fei-tzu and Li Ssu and development of Legalism
221–210 B.C.	Establishment of the Ch'in Dynasty and unification of China
	Construction of the Great Wall
	Destruction of Confucian literature
202 B.C.–A.D. 220	Establishment of the Han Dynasty
111 B.C.	Chinese expansion to the South China Sea and Vietnam
A.D. 221–280	Three Kingdoms Era
4th–5th centuries	Barbarian invasions

The Fall of Han China

The Han Empire was an imposing political edifice. Eventually, however, wars on the frontiers and the emperors' enormous building projects put an intolerable strain on society. The emperors drew so heavily on the peasants as soldiers and workers that agricultural production declined severely. Great landlords saw their chance to expand their holdings and to shift the burden of taxation onto the already hard-pressed peasantry. Ground down by ambitious emperors and unscrupulous landowners, many peasants lost their land and sold their children, farm animals, and tools to the landowners, ending as tenants, hired laborers—or outlaws.

The emperor Wang Mang (A.D. 9–23), who was a usurper, attempted to reverse these trends. He tried to re-establish a state monopoly on grain so that private speculators could not exploit famines and shortages to make huge profits. He set about redistributing land to the peasants and wanted to abolish slavery. Unfortunately, Wang Mang's commendable efforts did little to improve conditions, and he was killed in a peasant uprising. Han Kuang Wu in turn defeated the rebels and established the later Han Empire in A.D. 25.

After a century of peace, the later Han emperors found themselves facing the same problems that Wang Mang had tried to solve. Once again, excessive demands were made on the peasants. Great landlords took over peasants' land and burdened

them with heavy taxes. Disorder, intrigue, and assassination at court distracted the government, making intelligent leadership nearly impossible. A murderous rivalry developed between the old scholar-officials, who had traditionally administered political affairs, and the palace eunuchs, men usually of lowly origin who wielded huge influence from their lair among the women of the imperial harem. Turmoil and palace revolt meant that the great landlords were left unhindered. Once again the peasants staged massive uprisings. When the imperial armies were dispatched to put down the unrest, the victorious generals used their forces to carve out petty kingdoms for themselves. The palace eunuchs revolted against the emperor and his scholar-officials, and the Han Empire collapsed in general turmoil.

In the years that followed, known as the "Three Kingdoms Era" (A.D. 221–280), the empire was broken into three separate kingdoms. These kingdoms conformed to the natural geographical divisions of the land: the kingdom of Wei held the north; Shu, the upper Yangtze River Valley; and Wu, the lower Yangtze River Valley (see Map 4.2). Throughout this period, China experienced further disorder and barbarian trouble.

The difficulties with barbarians increased in later years, with catastrophic invasions from the north. Most significant were the conquests by the nomadic Toba from Mongolia, who created their own northern dynasty. Early in the fifth century the Toba assumed control of northern China,

Trieu Au Although Chinese armies were mighty, the Vietnamese held out against them. Trieu Au, seen here riding into combat on an elephant, played her part in the war against China in the third century. Having suffered defeat in battle, she committed suicide, but she is still revered today in Vietnam. *(Source: Yale University)*

Chinese elite. The Toba adopted Chinese agricultural techniques and the bureaucratic method of administering the empire. Chinese culture withstood the impact of invasion so well that it remained vital and essentially unshaken. China's political system was so excellently suited to the land and its people that no barbarian invader could have done without it. That system encompassed not just a bureaucracy fully dependent on the Chinese language, but the culture, religion, and outlook of Chinese society. In that respect, China absorbed its invaders more successfully than had India.

SUMMARY

Chinese mastery of the land led to the harnessing of China's resources. A vital aspect of this triumph was the development of a systematic method of agriculture capable of sustaining a huge population. Prosperity and growth in population allowed the Chinese to shape their lives as never before. One result was a vibrant and sophisticated intellectual life. Whereas Indian society was largely permeated by religion, Chinese thought was for the most part secular in orientation. Although China sometimes experienced internal disorder and the threat of invasion, political upheaval never destroyed China's cultural heritage. By the end of the Han Dynasty, writing, Confucianism, and complex political organization of a huge region had left an enduring mark on the Chinese people.

making the Great Wall their northern boundary. They extended their sway into central Asia and stopped further barbarian invasions of China. Southern China, which remained under Chinese rule, actually benefited from these invasions: thousands of Chinese, among them many scholar-officials, fled to the south, where they devoted their energies and talents to developing southern China economically and culturally.

Barbarian invasions caused China distress and disruption, but the Toba and other nomads quickly came under the spell of Chinese culture linguistically, politically, and economically. The Toba emperor ordered the Toba nobility to speak Chinese at his court and to dress and act like the

NOTES

1. A. Waley, trans., *The Analects of Confucius* (London: George Allen and Unwin, 1938), 4.18.
2. Ibid., 5.15.
3. Ibid., 1.4.
4. Ibid., 1.5.
5. D. C. Lau, trans., *Lao Tzu, Tao Te Ching* (London: Penguin Books, 1963), 1.25.56.
6. Ibid., 1.19.43.
7. Ibid., 1.3.9.
8. Anonymous, *Change* (Virginia Beach: A.R.E. Press, 1971), p. 1.
9. Ibid., p. 2.
10. B. Watson, trans., *Records of the Grand Historian of China Translated from the Shih chi of Ssu-ma Ch'ien*

(New York: Columbia University Press, 1961), 1.31.
11. Ibid., 1.53.
12. Ibid., 2.81.
13. Ibid., 2.79.

SUGGESTED READING

The Shang Dynasty, once considered legendary, is now the subject of considerable attention. The best place to start is K. C. Chang, *Shang Civilization* (1981). D. Keightley, "The Religious Commitment: Shang Theology and the Genesis of Chinese Political Culture," *History of Religions* 17 (1978): 211–223, studies the development of Shang royal bureaucracy. Early Chinese agriculture is a hotly debated topic. Scholars like Ho Ping-ti, "Loess and the Origins of Chinese Agriculture," *American Historical Review* 75 (1969): 1–36, argue that Chinese technological and agricultural methods occurred without any significant outside influence; others, like W. Watson, *Cultural Frontiers in Ancient East Asia* (1971), maintain that the Chinese imported techniques from the West. See also Z. Liu, *Ancient India and Ancient China* (1988). Other solid general treatments of East Asia include C. Schirokauer, *A Brief History of Chinese and Japanese Civilizations,* 2d ed. (1989), and A. Craig, *East Asia, Tradition and Transformation,* rev. ed. (1989).

For the development of the Chinese language, B. Karlgren, *The Chinese Language* (1949), is a clear discussion, although it ignores the Shang. Newer and more comprehensive in its discussion of earlier writing is Ho Ping-ti, *The Cradle of the East* (1975). A lively and readable account of early life and the origins of writing, told primarily from an archeological standpoint, is J. Hay, *Ancient China* (1973). More technical are K. C. Chang, *The Archaeology of Ancient China,* 3d ed. (1977), and *Food in Chinese Culture* (1977), an edited volume containing historical and anthropological material. A somewhat dated but still useful survey of the early periods is provided by T. Cheng, *Archaeology in China,* 3 vols. (1957–1963), which treats the prehistoric, Shang, and Chou periods. H. G. Creel, one of the foremost scholars of early Chinese thought, in *The Origins of Statecraft in China* (1970), argues forcefully that early Chou emperors maintained firm control over their political dependencies in the first centuries of their dynasty.

A fascinating starting point for the study of early Chinese thought is B. I. Schwartz, "Transcendence in Ancient China," *Daedalus* 104 (Spring 1975): 57–68, which argues that the emphasis in ancient China was on social and political rather than religious themes. So much has been written on Confucius and the Confucian tradition that only a few works can be singled out for mention. A. Waley's translation of the *Analects of Confucius* (1938) is an eminently readable version of the work attributed to Confucius. H. G. Creel, *Confucius and the Chinese Way* (1960), deals with both the historical and the mythological Confucius.

The complexities of Taoism are lucidly set out by H. G. Creel, *What Is Taoism?* (1970), which discusses the differences between purposive and contemplative Taoism. One of the most significant of the contemplative Taoists was Chuang-tzu, whose career is studied by A. C. Graham, *Chuang-tzu: The Seven Inner Chapters* (1981). D. C. Lau's *Lao-Tzu, Tao Te Ching* (1963) is a vigorous translation of Lao-tzu's classic. H. G. Creel provides a sound introduction to Legalism in *Shen Pu-hai* (1974), which demonstrates that, far from being monolithic, Legalism consisted of a number of schools of practical political theory. On the careers of Han Fei-tzu and Li Ssu, see D. Bodde, *China's First Unifier* (1938).

The political and military success of the Ch'in is the subject of D. Bodde, *China's First Unifier: A Study of the Ch'in Dynasty as Seen in the Life of Li Ssu (280?–208 B.C.)* (1958). P. Nancarrow, *Early China and the Wall* (1978), discusses the importance of the Great Wall of China to early Chinese society. A good account of Ch'in road building is J. Needham, *Science and Civilization in China,* vol. 4, part 3 (1970).

The Han Dynasty has been amply treated by a master scholar, H. H. Dubs, whose *History of the Former Han Dynasty,* 3 vols. (1938–1955), is comprehensive. The turmoil of Confucianism in this period is ably treated in a series of studies, among them E. Balazs, *Chinese Civilization and Bureaucracy* (1964); H. Welch and A. Seidel, eds., *Facets of Taoism* (1979), which ranges more broadly than its title might suggest; and especially C. Chang, *The Development of Neo-Confucian Thought* (1957), a solid discussion of Han Confucianism. B. Watson has provided two good studies of Ssu-ma Ch'ien and his historical work: *Records of the Grand Historian of China* (1961) and *Ssu-ma Ch'ien: Grand Historian of China* (1958). China's most important woman scholar is the subject of N. L. Swann, *Pan Chao: Foremost Woman Scholar of China* (1950). K. Frifelt and P. Sorensen, eds., *South Asian Archaeology* (1988), contains a number of papers devoted to South Asia and its broader connections.

M. Loewe, *Everyday Life in Early Imperial China* (1968), paints a vibrant picture of ordinary life during the Han period, a portrayal that attempts to include all segments of Han society. Last, W. Zhongshu, *Han Civilization* (1982), excellently treats many aspects of material life under the Han, including architecture, agriculture, manufacture, and burial.

PERIOD (CA 10,000–CA 500 B.C.)	AFRICA AND THE MIDDLE EAST	THE AMERICAS
10,000 B.C.	New Stone Age culture, ca 10,000–3500	Migration into Americas begins, ca 11,000
5000 B.C.	"Agricultural Revolution" originates in Tigris-Euphrates and Nile river valleys, ca 6000 First writing in Sumeria; Sumerian city-states emerge, ca 3500 Egypt unified under Narmer, 3100–2660 Metal-working in Caucasuses, 3000	Maize domesticated in Mexico, ca 5000
2500 B.C.	Old Kingdom in Egypt; construction of the pyramids, 2660–2180 Akkadian Empire, 2370–2150 Middle Kingdom in Egypt, 2080–1640 Hyksos "invade" Egypt, 1640–1570 Hammurabi, 1792–1750 Hebrew monotheism, ca 1700	First pottery in Americas, Ecuador, ca 3000 First metal-working in Peru, ca 2000
1500 B.C.	Hittite Empire, ca 1450–1200 Akhenaten institutes worship of Aton, ca 1360 New Kingdom in Egypt; creation of Egyptian empire, ca 1570–1075 Moses leads Hebrews out of Egypt, ca 1300–1200	Olmec civilization, Mexico, ca 1500 B.C.–A.D. 300
1000 B.C.	Political fragmentation of Egypt; rise of small kingdoms, ca 1100–700 United Hebrew kingdom, 1020–922: Saul, David, Solomon Iron-working spreads throughout Africa, ca 1000 B.C.–A.D. 300 Divided Hebrew kingdom: Israel (922–721), Judah (922–586) Assyrian Empire, 745–612 Zoroaster, ca 600	Olmec center at San Lorenzo destroyed, ca 900; power passes to La Venta in Tabasco Chavin civilization in Andes, ca 1000–200 B.C.
500 B.C.	Babylonian captivity of the Hebrews, 586–539 Cyrus the Great founds Persian Empire, 550 Persians conquer Egypt, 525	

EAST ASIA	INDIA AND SOUTHEAST ASIA	EUROPE
"Agricultural Revolution" originates in Yellow River Valley, ca 4000		
Horse domesticated in China, ca 2500	Indus River Valley civilization, ca 2500–1500; capitals at Mohenjo-Daro and Harappa	Greek Bronze Age, 2000–1100 Arrival of Greeks in peninsular Greece
Shang Dynasty, first writing in China, ca 1523–ca 1027	Aryans arrive in India; Early Vedic Age, ca 1500–1000 *Vedas,* oldest Sanskrit literature	Height of Minoan culture, 1700–1450 Mycenaeans conquer Minoan Crete, ca 1450 Mycenaean Age, 1450–1200
Chou Dynasty, promulgation of the Mandate of Heaven, ca 1027–221	Later Vedic Age; solidification of caste system, ca 1000–500 *Upanishads;* foundation of Hinduism, 800–600	Trojan War, ca 1180 Fall of the Mycenaean Kingdom, 1100 Greek Dark Age, ca 1100–800 Greek Lyric Age; rise of Sparta and Athens, 800–500
Confucius, 551–479 First written reference to iron, ca 521	Siddhartha Gautama (Buddha), 563– 483	Roman Republic founded, 509 Origin of Greek *polis,* ca 500 Persian wars, 499–479 Growth of Athenian Empire; flowering of Greek drama, philosophy, history, fifth century Peloponnesian War, 431–404 Plato, 426–347

5

The Legacy of Greece

The Erechtheum, Parthenon

The rocky peninsula of Greece was the home of the civilization that fundamentally shaped the civilization of Europe and later the rest of the world. The Greeks were the first to explore most of the questions that continue to concern thinkers to this day. Going beyond myth making and religion, the Greeks strove to understand, in logical, rational terms, both the universe and the position of people in it. The result was the birth of philosophy and science in Europe—subjects that were far more important to most Greek thinkers than religion. The Greeks speculated on human beings and society and created the very concept of politics.

The history of the Greeks is divided into two broad periods. The Hellenic (the subject of this chapter) spanned roughly the time between the arrival of the Greeks (approximately 2000 B.C.) and the victory over Greece in 338 B.C. of Philip of Macedon. The Hellenistic (the subject of Chapter 6) began with the remarkable reign of Philip's son Alexander the Great (336–323 B.C.) and ended with the Roman conquest of the Hellenistic East (200–148 B.C.).

- What geographical factors helped to mold the evolution of the city-state and to shape the course of the Greek experience?

- What was the nature of the early Greek experience, the impact of the Minoans and Mycenaeans, which led to the concept of a heroic past?

- How did the Greeks develop basic political forms—forms as different as democracy and tyranny—that have influenced all of later Western and much of modern Asian history?

- What did the Greek intellectual triumph entail, and what were its effects?

- How and why did the Greeks eventually fail?

These profound questions, which can never be fully answered, are explored in this chapter.

HELLAS: THE LAND

Hellas, as the ancient and modern Greeks called their land, encompassed the Aegean Sea and its islands as well as the Greek peninsula (Map 5.1).

The Greek peninsula itself is an extension of the Balkan system of mountains stretching in the direction of Egypt and the Near East. Greece is mountainous; its rivers are never more than creeks, and most of them go dry in the summer. It is, however, a land blessed with good harbors, the most important of which look to the east. The islands of the Aegean continue to sweep to the east and serve as steppingstones between the peninsula and Asia Minor (Anatolia). As early as 1000 B.C., Greeks from the peninsula had settled along the coastline of Asia Minor; the heartland of these eastern Greeks was in Ionia. Thus geography encouraged the Greeks to turn their attention to the old civilizations of Asia Minor and Egypt.

Despite the poverty of its soil, Greece is strikingly beautiful, as the eminent German historian K. J. Beloch has written:

Greece is an alpine land, which rises from the waters of the Mediterranean sea, scenically probably the most beautiful region in southern Europe. The noble contours of the mountains, the bare, rocky slopes, the dusty green of the conifer forests, the white cover of snow which envelops the higher summits for the greatest part of the year, added to which is the profound blue surface of the sea below, and above everything the diffused brightness of the southern sun; this gives a total picture, the charm of which impresses itself unforgettably on the soul of the observer.[1]

The Greeks gloried in their land, and its beauty was one of the factors that elicited their loyalty to the soil of this hard peninsula. The climate of Greece is mild; though hot in summer, the air is dry and stirred by breezes. In winter snow may blanket the mountain slopes but rarely covers the lowlands.

Simultaneously, geography acted as an enormously divisive force in Greek life. The mountains of Greece dominate the landscape, cutting the land into many small pockets and isolating areas of inhabitation. Innumerable peninsulas open to the sea, which is dotted with islands, most of them small and many uninhabitable. The geographical

MAP 5.1 Ancient Greece In antiquity the home of the Greeks included the islands of the Aegean and the western shore of Asia Minor as well as the Greek peninsula itself.

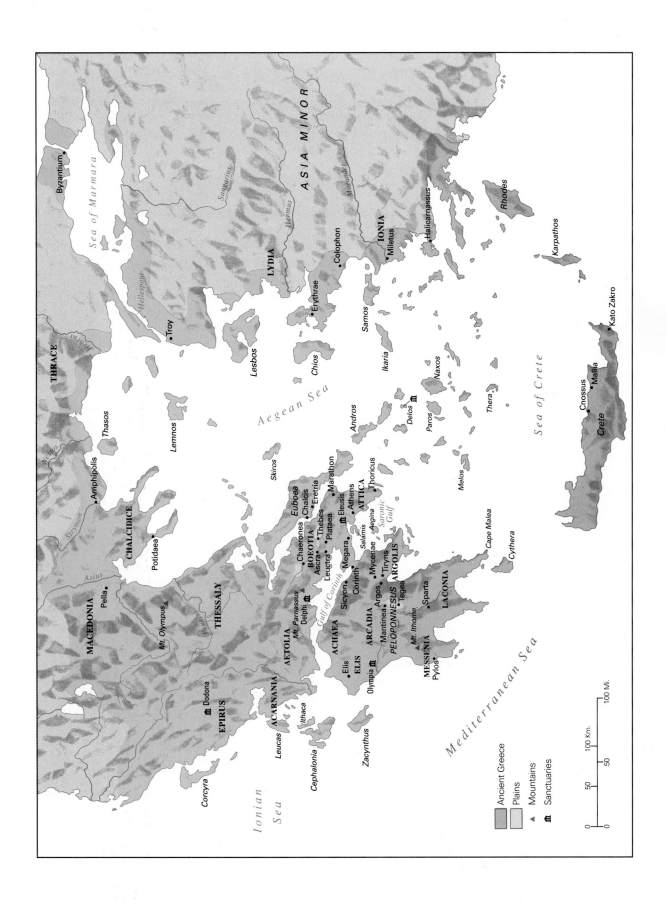

Byzantium

Sea of Marmara

ASIA MINOR

Hellespont

Sangarius

Rhodes

Karpathos

Hermus

LYDIA

Colophon

Erythrae

IONIA

Miletus

Halicarnassus

Maeander

Troy

THRACE

Samos

Ikaria

Sea of Crete

Lesbos

Chios

Kato Zakro

Strymon

Thasos

Aegean Sea

Naxos

Mallia

Cnossus

Crete

Lemnos

Andros

Paros

Delos

Thera

Amphipolis

CHALCIDICE

Skiros

Melos

Potidaea

Axius

THESSALY

Euboea

Marathon

Thoricus

Cape Malea

Cythera

Pella

MACEDONIA

Chaeronea

Chalcis

Eretria

Athens

ATTICA

Aegina

Saronic
Gulf

Mt. Olympus

AETOLIA

Mt. Parnassus

Delphi

Thebes

Plataea

Eleusis

Salamis

Peneus

Ascra

Leuctra

Megara

BOEOTIA

Corinth

Mycenae

Tiryns

ACARNANIA

ACHAEA

Sicyon

Gulf of Corinth

ARCADIA

Argos

ARGOLIS

Mantinea

Tegea

EPIRUS

Dodona

Leucas

Ithaca

ELIS

Elis

Olympia

PELOPONNESUS

Mt. Ithome

Sparta

LACONIA

MESSENIA

Pylos

Mediterranean Sea

Corcyra

Cephalonia

Zacynthus

Ionian
Sea

Ancient Greece

Plains

Mountains

Sanctuaries

0   50   100 Mi.

0   50   100 Km.

fragmentation of Greece encouraged political fragmentation. Furthermore, communications were extraordinarily poor. Rocky tracks were far more common than roads, and the few roads were unpaved. Usually they were nothing more than a pair of ruts cut into the rock to accommodate wheels. The small physical units of Greece discouraged the growth of great empires.

THE MINOANS AND MYCENAEANS (CA 1650–CA 1100 B.C.)

Neither historians, archeologists, nor linguists can confidently establish when Greek-speaking peoples made the Balkan peninsula of Greece their homeland. Yet it can safely be said that they, like the Hittites, Persians, and Aryans, were still another wave of Indo-Europeans who were expanding throughout many parts of Europe and Asia during much of antiquity. By ca 1650 B.C. Greeks had established themselves at the great city of Mycenae in the Peloponnesus and elsewhere in Greece. Before then the area from Thessaly in the north to Messenia in the south was inhabited by small farming communities. Quite probably the Greeks merged with these natives and from that union emerged the society that modern scholars call "Mycenaean," after Mycenae, the most important site of this new Greek-speaking culture.

Of this epoch the ancient Greeks themselves remembered almost nothing. The *Iliad* and the *Odyssey,* the magnificent epic poems of Homer (eighth century B.C.), retain some dim memory of this period but very little that is authentic. One of the sterling achievements of modern archeology is the discovery of this lost past. In the nineteenth century Heinrich Schliemann, a German businessman, fell in love with the *Iliad* and decided to find the sites it mentioned. He excavated Troy in modern Turkey, Mycenae, and sites in Greece to discover the lost past of the Greek people. At the turn of this century the English archeologist Sir Arthur Evans uncovered the remains of an entirely unknown civilization at Cnossus in Crete, to which he gave the name "Minoan" after the mythical Cretan king Minos. Scholars since then have further illuminated this long-lost era, and despite many uncertainties a reasonably clear picture of the Minoans and Mycenaeans is possible.

By ca 1650 B.C. the island of Crete was the home of the flourishing, vibrant, and charming Minoan culture. The Minoans occupied Crete from at least the Neolithic period and developed a written language, now called "Linear A," which has never been deciphered. Only archeology and art offer clues to Minoan life, but they cannot provide a history of it. The symbol of Minoan culture was the palace. The palace was the political and economic center of Minoan society, which, like many ancient Near Eastern societies, was rigorously controlled from above. By ca 1650 B.C. Crete was dotted with palaces, such as those at Mallia on the northern coast and Kato Zakro on the eastern tip of the island. Towering above all others in importance was the main palace at Cnossus.

Nothing very definite can be said of Minoan society except that at its head stood a king and his nobles, who governed the lives and toil of Crete's farmers, sailors, shepherds, and artisans. The implements of the Minoans, like those of the Mycenaeans, were bronze, so archeologists have named this period the "Bronze Age." Minoan society was wealthy and, to judge from the absence of fortifications on Crete, peaceful. The Minoans were enthusiastic sailors and merchants who traded with Egypt and the cities of the Levant, the general area of the eastern Mediterranean. Their ships also penetrated the Aegean Sea, throughout which they established trading posts. Their voyages in this direction brought them into contact with the Mycenaeans on the Greek peninsula.

By ca 1650 B.C. Greek speakers were firmly settled at Mycenae, which became a major city and trading center. Later other Mycenaean palaces and cities grew at Thebes, Athens, Tiryns, and Pylos. The political unit of the Mycenaeans was also the kingdom. The king and his warrior-aristocracy stood at the top of society. The seat and symbol of the king's power and wealth was his palace, which was also the economic center of the kingdom. Within its walls royal craftsmen fashioned jewelry and rich ornaments, made and decorated fine pottery, forged weapons, prepared hides and wool for clothing, and manufactured the goods needed by the king and his retainers. Palace scribes kept records in Greek with a script known as "Linear B," which was derived from Minoan Linear A. The scribes kept account of taxes and drew up inventories of the king's possessions. From the palace, as at Cnossus, the Mycenaean king directed the lives

Minoan Naval Scene This fresco, newly discovered at Thera, probably depicts the homecoming of a Minoan fleet of warships. Though later Greeks thought that the Minoans had ruled the sea, fleets such as the one pictured here probably protected Minoan maritime interests and suppressed piracy. Despite its military nature, the scene displays a general air of festivity, characteristic of Minoan art. *(Source: National Archaeological Museum, Athens/Ekdotike Athenon)*

of his subjects. Little is known of the king's subjects except that they were artisans, tradesmen, and farmers. The Mycenaean economy was marked by an extensive division of labor, all tightly controlled from the palace. At the bottom of the social scale were the slaves; normally owned by the king and aristocrats, they also worked for ordinary craftsmen.

Contacts between the Minoans and Mycenaeans were originally peaceful, and Minoan culture flooded the Greek mainland. The two peoples at first engaged in peaceful commercial rivalry, but around 1450 B.C. the Mycenaeans attacked Crete, destroying many Minoan palaces and taking possession of the grand palace at Cnossus. For about the next fifty years the Mycenaeans ruled much of the island until a further wave of violence left Cnossus in ashes. These events are more disputed than understood, and the fate of Cnossus in particular has sparked fiery controversy.

There is no question, however, that the Mycenaean kingdoms in Greece benefited from the fall of Cnossus and the collapse of Minoan trade. Mycenaean commerce quickly expanded throughout the Aegean, reaching as far abroad as Asia Minor, Cyprus, and Egypt. Throughout central and southern Greece Mycenaean culture flourished. Palaces became grander, and citadels were often protected by mammoth stone walls. Prosperity, however, did not bring peace, and between 1300 and 1000 B.C. kingdom after kingdom suffered attack and destruction. Later Greeks accused the Dorians, who spoke a dialect of Greek, of overthrowing the Mycenaean kingdoms. Yet some modern linguists argue that the Dorians dwelt in Greece during the Mycenaean period. Archeologists generally conclude that the Dorians, if not already present, could have entered Greece only long after the era of destruction. Furthermore, not one alien artifact has been found on any of these sites; there is no indication that any alien invader was responsible for the damage. Instead legends preserved by later Greeks told of grim wars between Mycenaean kingdoms and of the fall of great royal families. Apparently Mycenaean Greece destroyed itself in a long series of internecine wars, a pattern that later Greeks would repeat.

The fall of the Mycenaean kingdoms ushered in a period of such poverty, disruption, and backwardness that historians usually call it the "Dark Age" of Greece (1100–800 B.C.). Even literacy was a casualty of the chaos. Still, this period was important to the development of Greek civilization. It was a time of widespread movements of Greek-speaking peoples. Some sailed to Crete, where they established new communities. A great wave of Greeks spread eastward through the Aegean to the coast of Asia Minor. These immigrations turned the Aegean into a Greek lake. The people who stayed behind on the mainland gradually rebuilt Greek society. They thus provided an element of continuity, a link between the Mycenaean period and the Greek culture that emerged from the Dark Age.

Funeral Games   At the end of the *Iliad* Homer describes the funeral games given in honor of Patroclus, the companion of Achilles. The main event was the chariot race. Here the race has begun, and the painter states in the Greek inscription that one of the chariots seen here belonged to Achilles. *(Source: National Archaeological Museum, Athens/Ekdotike Athenon)*

HOMER AND THE HEROIC PAST (1100–800 B.C.)

The Greeks, unlike the Hebrews, had no sacred book that chronicled their past. Instead they had the *Iliad* and the *Odyssey,* which described a time when gods still walked the earth. For all his importance to Greek thought and literature, Homer was a shadowy figure. Later Greeks knew little about him and were not even certain when he had lived. This uncertainty underscores the fact that the Greeks remembered very little of their own past, especially the time before they entered Greece. They had also forgotten a great deal about the Bronze and Dark ages.

Instead of authentic history the poems of Homer offered the Greeks an ideal past, a largely legendary heroic age. In terms of pure history these poems contain scraps of information about the Bronze Age, much about the early Dark Age, and some about the poet's own era. Chronologically, then, the heroic age falls mainly in the period between the collapse of the Mycenaean world and the rebirth of literacy. Yet it is a mistake to treat the *Iliad* and the *Odyssey* as history; they are magnificent blendings of legends, myth, and a little authentic tradition.

The *Iliad* recounts an expedition of Mycenaeans, whom Homer called "Achaeans," to besiege the city of Troy in Asia Minor. The heart of the *Iliad,* however, is the quarrel between Agamemnon, the king of Mycenae, and Achilles, the tragic hero of the poem, and how their quarrel brought suffering to the Achaeans. Only when Achilles put away his anger and pride did he consent to come forward, face, and kill the Trojan hero Hector. The *Odyssey,* probably composed later than the *Iliad,* narrates the adventures of Odysseus, one of the Achaean heroes who fought at Troy, during his voyage home from the fighting.

The splendor of these poems does not lie in their plots, though the *Odyssey* is a marvelous adventure story. Rather, both poems portray engaging but often flawed characters who are larger than life and yet typically human. Achilles, the hero of the *Iliad,* is capable of mastering Trojan warriors but can barely control his own anger. Agamemnon commands kings yet is a man beset by worries. Hector, the hero of the Trojans, is a formidable, noble, and likable foe. Odysseus, the

The Shape of the Athenian Polis This print of the Athenian acropolis shows clearly the geographical requirements of the polis. Early Greeks desired an elevated spot, or acropolis, for refuge; later it became the seat of the polis' temples. At the foot of the citadel spread the agora, public buildings, and private homes. *(Source: Caroline Buckler)*

hero of the *Odyssey,* trusts more to his wisdom and good sense than to his strength. Odysseus's wife Penelope faithfully endures the long years of war and separation, patiently waiting for her beloved husband to return from Troy.

Homer was strikingly successful in depicting the deeds of the great gods, who sit on Mount Olympus and watch the fighting at Troy as if they were spectators at a baseball game. Sometimes they even participate in the action. Homer's deities are reminiscent of Mesopotamian gods and goddesses. Hardly a decorous lot, the Olympians are raucous, petty, deceitful, and splendid. In short, they are human.

THE POLIS

After the upheavals that ended the Mycenaean period and the slow recovery of prosperity during the Dark Age, the Greeks developed their basic political and institutional unit, the *polis,* or city-state. The details of this development are largely lost, but by the end of the Dark Age the polis was common throughout Greece. Rarely did there occur the combination of extensive territory and political unity that allowed one polis to rise above others. Only three city-states were able to muster the resources of an entire region behind them (see Map 5.1): Sparta, which dominated the regions of Laconia and Messenia; Athens, which united the large peninsula of Attica under its rule; and Thebes, which in several periods marshaled the resources of the fertile region of Boeotia. Otherwise, the political pattern of ancient Greece was one of many small city-states, few of which were much stronger or richer than their neighbors.

Physically the term *polis* designated a city or town and its surrounding countryside. The typical polis consisted of people living in a compact group of houses within the city. The city's water supply came from public fountains and cisterns. By the fifth century B.C. the city was generally surrounded by a wall. The city contained a point, usually elevated, called the "acropolis," and a public square or marketplace *(agora)*. On the acropolis, which in the early period was a place of refuge, stood the temples, altars, public monuments, and various dedications to the gods of the polis. The agora was originally the place where the warrior assembly met, but it became the political center of the polis. In the agora were porticoes, shops, and public buildings and courts.

The unsettled territory of the polis was typically its source of wealth. This territory consisted of arable land, pasture land, and wasteland. Farmers left the city each morning to work their fields or tend their flocks of sheep and goats, and they returned at night. On the wasteland men often quarried stone, mined for precious metals, or at certain times of the year obtained small amounts of fodder. Thus the polis encompassed a combination of urban and agrarian life.

Regardless of its size or wealth, the polis was fundamental to Greek life. Aristotle, who lived in the fourth century B.C. and was perhaps Greece's greatest thinker, could not envisage civilized life apart from the polis. "The polis," he wrote, "exists by nature, and man is by nature a being of the polis."[2] Aristotle was summing up the Greek view that the life of men and women in the polis was the only way to live according to nature. The polis was far more than a political institution. Above all it was a community of citizens, and the affairs of the community were the concern of all citizens. The intimacy of the polis was an important factor, one hard for modern city dwellers to imagine.

The mild climate of Greece meant that much of Greek life was spent outdoors. In a polis, as in a modern Greek village, a person might easily see most other citizens in the course of a day. Similarly, the citizen would normally see the public buildings and the temples of the polis daily. The monuments of past victories, the tombs of dead warriors, all would be personal and familiar. In short, life in the polis was very public. The smallness of the polis enabled Greeks to see how the individual fitted into the overall system—how the human parts made up the social whole. These simple facts go far to explain why the Greek polis was fundamentally different from the great empires of Persia and China. The Greeks knew their leaders and elected them to limited terms of office. They were unlike the subjects of the Mauryan Empire or the Han Dynasty, who might spend their entire lives without ever seeing their emperors. One result of these factors is the absence in Greek politics of a divine emperor. Another is the lack of an extensive imperial bureaucracy and a standing army. The Classical Greeks were their own magistrates, administrators, and soldiers.

The customs of the community were at the same time the laws of the polis. Rome later created a single magnificent body of law, but the Greeks had as many law codes as they had city-states. Though the laws of one polis might be roughly similar to those of another, the law of any given polis was unique simply because the customs and the experience of each polis were unique.

The government of a polis could take any of several forms. It could be a *monarchy*, a term derived from the Greek for "the rule of one man." In a monarchy, a king represented the community, reigning according to law and respecting the rights of the citizens. In an *aristocracy*, the nobility governed the state. In an *oligarchy*, which literally means "the rule of a few," the running of the polis was the duty and prerogative of a small group of wealthy citizens, regardless of their status at birth. In a *democracy*, which means "the rule of the people," all citizens, without respect to birth or wealth, administered the workings of government. How a polis was governed depended on who had the upper hand. When the wealthy held power, they usually instituted oligarchies. When the people could break the hold of the rich, they established democracies. In any case, no polis ever had an iron-clad, unchangeable constitution.

Still another form of Greek government was *tyranny*. Under tyranny the polis was ruled by a *tyrant*, a man who had seized power by unconstitutional means. The Greeks did not in theory consider tyranny a legitimate form of government, but in practice it flourished from the seventh century B.C. to the end of the Classical period (338 B.C.). By the Classical Age, however, the Greeks considered tyranny a political perversion.

Ironically, the very integration of the polis proved to be one of its weaknesses. Because the bonds that held the polis together were so intimate, Greeks were extremely reluctant to allow foreigners to share fully in its life. An alien, even someone Greek by birth, could almost never expect to be made a citizen. Nor could women play an active political role. Women participated in the civic cults and served as priestesses, but the polis had no room for them in state affairs. Thus the exclusiveness of the polis doomed it to a limited horizon.

The individualism of the polis proved to be another serious weakness. The citizens of each polis were determined to remain free and autonomous. Rarely were the Greeks willing to unite in larger political bodies. When they did, they preferred leagues or confederations in which each polis insisted on its autonomy. The political result in

Greece, as in Sumer, was almost constant warfare. The polis could dominate, but unlike Rome it could not incorporate.

THE LYRIC AGE (800–500 B.C.)

The maturation of the polis coincided with one of the most vibrant periods of Greek history, an era of extraordinary expansion geographically, artistically, and politically. Greeks ventured as far east as the Black Sea and as far west as Spain (Map 5.2). Politically these were the years when Sparta and Athens—the two poles of the Greek experience—rose to prominence.

Overseas Expansion

During the years 1100 to 800 B.C., the Greeks not only recovered from the breakdown of the Mycenaean world but also grew in wealth and numbers.

MAP 5.2 Colonization of the Mediterranean   Though both the Greeks and the Phoenicians colonized the Mediterranean basin at roughly the same time, the Greeks spread over a far greater area.

Mosaic Portrait of Sappho The Greek letters in the upper left corner identify this idealized portrait as that of Sappho. The mosaic, which was found at Sparta, dates to the late Roman Empire and testifies to Sappho's popularity in antiquity. *(Source: Caroline Buckler)*

This new prosperity brought new problems. Greece is a small and not especially fertile country. The increase in population meant that many men and their families had very little land or none at all. Land hunger and the resulting social and political tensions drove many Greeks to seek new homes outside of Greece. Other factors—the desire for a new start, a love of excitement and adventure, and natural curiosity about what lay beyond the horizon—played their part as well.

The Mediterranean offered the Greeks an escape valve, for they were always a seafaring people. To them the sea was a highway, not a barrier. Through their commercial ventures they had long been familiar with the rich areas of the western Mediterranean. Moreover, the geography of the Mediterranean basin favored colonization. The land and climate of the Mediterranean region are remarkably uniform. Greeks could travel to new areas, whether to Cyprus in the east or to Malta in the west, and establish the kind of settlement they had had in Greece. They could also raise the same crops they had raised in Greece. The move to a new region was not a move into totally unknown conditions. Once the colonists had established

themselves in new homes, they continued life essentially as in Greece.

From about 750 to 550 B.C., Greeks from the mainland and from Asia Minor poured onto the coasts of the northern Aegean, the Ionian Sea, and the Black Sea, and into North Africa, Sicily, southern Italy, southern Gaul, and Spain (see Map 5.2). Just as the migrations of the Dark Age had turned the Aegean into a Greek lake, this later wave of colonization spread the Greeks and their culture throughout the Mediterranean. Colonization on this scale had a profound impact on the course of world civilization. It meant that the prevailing culture of the Mediterranean basin would be Greek, the heritage to which Rome would later fall heir.

Lyric Poets

Two individuals can in many ways stand as symbols of the vital and robust era of colonization. Surprisingly, they were both poets: Archilochus, who had himself been a colonist, and Sappho, who seldom left her native island of Lesbos. What made them symbolic was their individualism. For the first time in Western civilization, men and women like Archilochus and Sappho began to write of their own experiences, and in so doing they set a new tone in Greek literature. To them poetry did not belong solely to the gods or the great heroes on the plain of Troy. In effect, they helped to liberate the individual emotionally, just as colonization opened new physical vistas to the Greeks. In their poetry they reveal two sides of Greek life in this period. Archilochus exemplifies the energy and adventure of the age, while Sappho expresses the intensely personal side of life. The link connecting the two poets is their individualism, their faith in themselves, and their desire to reach out to others to share their experiences, thoughts, and wisdom.

The Growth of Sparta

During the Lyric Age the Spartans expanded the boundaries of their polis and made it the leading power in Greece. Like other Greeks, the Spartans faced the problems of overpopulation and land hunger. Unlike other Greeks, the Spartans solved these problems by conquest, not by colonization.

The Hoplite Phalanx When the Greeks adopted heavy armor, weapons, and shields, their lack of mobility forced them to fight in several dense lines, each behind the other. Cohesion and order became as valuable as courage. To help the hoplites maintain their pace during the attack, a flute player here plays a marching tune. *(Source: Villa Giulia Museum/Ministero per i Beni Culturali e Ambientali, Rome)*

To gain more land the Spartans set out in about 735 B.C. to conquer Messenia, a rich, fertile region in the southwestern Peloponnesus. This conflict, the First Messenian War, lasted for twenty years and ended in a Spartan triumph. The Spartans appropriated Messenian land and turned the Messenians into *helots,* or state serfs.

In about 650 B.C., Spartan exploitation and oppression of the Messenian helots led to a helot revolt so massive and stubborn that it became known as the Second Messenian War. The Spartan poet Tyrtaeus, a contemporary of these events, vividly portrayed the ferocity of the fighting:

For it is a shameful thing indeed
* When with the foremost fighters*
An elder falling in front of the young men
* Lies outstretched,*
Having white hair and grey beard,
Breathing forth his stout soul in the dust,
Holding in his hands his genitals
* Stained with blood.*[3]

Confronted with such horrors, Spartan enthusiasm for the war waned. Finally, after some thirty years of fighting, the Spartans put down the revolt. Nevertheless, the political and social strain it caused led to a transformation of the Spartan polis.

It took the full might of the Spartan people, aristocrat and commoner alike, to win the Second Messenian War. After the victory the non-nobles, who had done much of the fighting, demanded rights equal to those of the nobility. These men were called "hoplites" because of their heavy armor, or *hopla.* Unlike modern soldiers who receive their equipment from the state, the Greek hoplite provided his own weapons. For this he needed a certain amount of wealth. He took his place in the battle line next to his aristocratic neighbors but lacked the social prestige and political rights of his noble companions. The agitation of the hoplites disrupted society until the aristocrats agreed to remodel the state. Nor were the Spartans alone in these developments. In other Greek city-states where hoplites came to the fore, they sought greater political rights and a larger role in society.

Although the Spartans later claimed that the changes brought about by this compromise were the work of Lycurgus, a legendary, semidivine law-giver, they were really the work of the entire Spartan people. The "Lycurgan regimen," as these reforms were called, was a new political, economic, and social system. Political distinctions among the Spartans were officially eliminated, and all citizens became legally equal. In effect the Lycurgan regimen abolished the aristocracy and made the government an oligarchy. Actual governance of the polis was in the hands of two kings, who were primarily military leaders. The kings and twenty-eight elders made up a council that deliberated on foreign and domestic matters and prepared legislation for the assembly, which consisted of all Spartan citizens. The real executive power of the polis was in the hands of five *ephors,* or overseers, elected from and by all the people.

To provide for their economic needs the Spartans divided the land of Messenia among all citizens. Helots worked the land, raised the crops, provided the Spartans with their living, and occasionally served in the army. The Spartans kept the helots in line by means of systematic terrorism, hoping to beat them down and keep them quiet. Spartan citizens were supposed to devote their time exclusively to military training.

In the Lycurgan system every citizen owed primary allegiance to Sparta. Suppression of the individual together with emphasis on military prowess led to a barracks state. Family life was sacrificed to the polis. If an infant was deformed or handicapped at birth, the polis could demand that it be put out to die. In this respect the Spartans were no better or worse than other Greeks. Infanticide was common in ancient Greece and Rome; many people resorted to it as a way of keeping population down. In other Greek states, however, the decision to kill a child belonged to the parents, not to the polis.

Once a Spartan boy reached the age of seven, he lived in barracks with other boys his age. Spartan youth all underwent rugged physical and military training until they reached age twenty-four, when they became front-line soldiers. For the rest of their lives, Spartan men kept themselves prepared for combat. Their military training never ceased, and older men were expected to be models of endurance, frugality, and sturdiness to the younger

men. In battle Spartans were supposed to stand and die rather than retreat. An anecdote about one Spartan mother sums up Spartan military values. As her son was setting off to battle, the mother handed him his shield and advised him to come back either victorious, carrying the shield, or dead, being carried on it. In short, in the Lycurgan regimen Spartans were expected to train vigorously, disdain luxury and wealth, do with little, and like it.

Yet it is too easy to see the Spartans as merely a military people. The Lycurgan regimen instilled the civic virtues of dedication to the state and provided a code of moral conduct. These aspects of the Spartan system were generally admired throughout the Greek world.

The Evolution of Athens

Like Sparta, Athens faced pressing social and economic problems during the Lyric Age, but the Athenian response was far different from that of the Spartans. Instead of creating an oligarchy, the Athenians extended to all citizens the right and duty of governing the polis. Indeed, the Athenian democracy was one of the most thoroughgoing in Greece.

In the seventh century B.C., however, the aristocracy still governed Athens oppressively. The aristocrats owned the best land, met in an assembly to govern the polis, and interpreted the law. Noble landowners were forcing small farmers into economic dependence. Many families were sold into slavery; others were exiled and their land was pledged to the rich. Poor farmers who borrowed from their wealthy neighbors put up their land as collateral. If a farmer was unable to repay the loan, his creditor put a stone on the borrower's field to signify his indebtedness and thereafter took one-sixth of the annual yield until the debt was paid. If the farmer had to borrow again, he pledged himself and at times his family. If he was again unable to repay the loan, he became the slave of his creditor. Because the harvests of the poor farmer were generally small, he normally raised enough to live on but not enough to repay his loan.

The peasants, however, were strong in numbers and demanded reforms. They wanted the law to be published so that everyone would know its contents. Under pressure, the aristocrats relented and turned to Draco, a fellow aristocrat, to codify the law. In 621 B.C. Draco published the first law code of the Athenian polis. His code was thought harsh, but it nonetheless embodied the ideal that the law belonged to all citizens. The aristocrats hoped in vain that Draco's law code would satisfy the peasants. Many of the poor began demanding redistribution of the land, and it was obvious that broader reform was needed. Unrest among the peasants continued.

In many other city-states conditions such as those in Athens led to the rise of tyrants. The word *tyrant* brings to mind a cruel and bloody dictator, but the Greeks seem at first to have used the word only to denote a leader who seized power without legal right. Many of the first tyrants, though personally ambitious, were men who kept the welfare of the polis in mind. They usually enjoyed the support of the peasants because they reduced the power of the aristocrats. Later tyrants were often harsh and arbitrary; when they were, peasants and aristocrats alike suffered—the Greeks then began to use the word in the modern sense.

Only one person in Athens had the respect of both aristocrats and peasants: Solon (ca 638–ca 559 B.C.), himself an aristocrat and poet, but a man opposed to tyrants. Solon used his poetry to condemn the aristocrats for their greed and dishonesty. He recited his poems in the Athenian agora, where everyone could hear his relentless call for justice and fairness. The aristocrats realized that Solon was no revolutionary, and the common people trusted him. Around 594 B.C. the aristocrats elected him *archon*, chief magistrate of the Athenian polis, and gave him extraordinary power to reform the state.

Solon immediately freed all people enslaved for debt, recalled all exiles, canceled all debts on land, and made enslavement for debt illegal. He also divided society into four legal groups on the basis of wealth. In the most influential group were the wealthiest citizens, but even the poorest and least powerful group enjoyed certain rights. Solon allowed them into the old aristocratic assembly, where they could take part in the election of magistrates. In all his work Solon gave thought to the rights of the poor as well as the rich. He gave the commoners a place in government and a voice in the political affairs of Athens. His work done, Solon insisted that all swear to uphold his reforms. Then, since many were clamoring for him to become tyrant, he left Athens.

Although Solon's reforms solved some immediate problems, they did not bring peace to Athens. Some aristocrats attempted to make themselves tyrants, while others banded together to oppose them. In 546 B.C. Pisistratus, an exiled aristocrat, returned to Athens, defeated his opponents, and became tyrant. Pisistratus reduced the power of the aristocracy while supporting the common people. Under his rule Athens prospered, and his building program began to transform it into one of the splendors of Greece. His reign as tyrant promoted the growth of democratic ideas by arousing in the Athenians rudimentary feelings of equality.

Athenian acceptance of tyranny did not long outlive Pisistratus, for his son Hippias ruled harshly, and his excesses led to his overthrow. After a brief period of turmoil between factions of the nobility, Cleisthenes, a wealthy and prominent aristocrat, emerged triumphant in 508 B.C., largely because he won the support of the people. Cleisthenes created the Athenian democracy with the full knowledge and approval of the Athenian people. He reorganized the state completely but presented every innovation to the assembly for discussion and ratification. All Athenian citizens had a voice in Cleisthenes' work.

Cleisthenes used the *deme,* a local unit, to serve as the basis of his political system. Citizenship was tightly linked to the deme, for each deme kept the roll of those within its jurisdiction who were admitted to citizenship. Cleisthenes also created ten new tribes as administrative units. All the demes were grouped in tribes, which thus formed the link between the demes and the central government. The central government included an assembly of all citizens and a new council of five hundred members. The council prepared legislation for the assembly to consider, and it handled diplomatic affairs. Cleisthenes is often credited with the institution of *ostracism*, the banishment by means of a vote of the Athenian people of a citizen considered dangerous to the polis. The man receiving the most votes went into exile. The goal of ostracism was to rid the state peacefully of a difficult or potentially dangerous politician. The result of Cleisthenes' work was to make Athens a democracy with a government efficient enough to permit effective popular rule.

Athenian democracy was to prove an inspiring ideal in civilization. It demonstrated that a large group of people, not just a few, could efficiently run the affairs of state. By heeding the opinions, suggestions, and wisdom of all its citizens, the state enjoyed the maximum amount of good counsel. Since all citizens could speak their minds, they did not have to resort to rebellion or conspiracy to express their desires.

Athenian democracy, however, must not be thought of in modern terms. In Athens democracy was a form of government in which poor men as well as rich enjoyed political power and responsibility. In practice, though, most important offices were held by aristocrats. Furthermore, Athenian democracy denied political rights to many people, including women and slaves. Foreigners were seldom admitted to citizenship. Unlike modern democracies, Athenian democracy did not empower citizens to vote for others who then ran the state. Instead, every citizen was expected to be able to perform the duties of most magistrates. In Athens citizens voted and served. The people were the government. They enjoyed equal rights under the law, and the voice of the majority determined law. This union of the individual and the state—the view that the state exists for the good of the citizen, whose duty is to serve the state well—has made Athenian democracy so compelling an ideal.

THE CLASSICAL PERIOD (500–338 B.C.)

In the years 500 to 338 B.C., Greek civilization reached its peak in politics, art, and thought. In this period the Greeks beat back the armies of the Persian Empire. Then, turning their spears against one another, they destroyed their own political system in a century of warfare. Some thoughtful Greeks recorded and analyzed these momentous events; the result was the creation of history in Europe. This era also saw the flowering of philosophy, as thinkers in Ionia and on the Greek mainland began to ponder the nature and meaning of the universe and human experience. Not content to ask *why*, they used their intellects to explain the world around them and to determine humanity's place in it. The Greeks invented drama, and the Athenian tragedians Aeschylus, Sophocles, and Euripides explored themes that inspire audiences today. Greek architects created buildings whose very ruins still inspire awe. Because Greek intellectual and artistic efforts attained their fullest and finest expression in these years, this age is called

the "Classical Period." Few periods in the history of the world can match it in dynamism and achievement.

The Deadly Conflicts (499–404 B.C.)

One of the hallmarks of the Classical Period was warfare. In 499 B.C. the Ionian Greeks, with the feeble help of Athens, rebelled against the Persian Empire. In 490 B.C. the Persians struck back at Athens but were beaten off at the Battle of Marathon, fought on a small plain in Attica. This failure only prompted the Persians to try again. In 480 B.C. the Persian king Xerxes led a mighty invasion force into Greece. In the face of this emergency the Greeks united and pooled their resources to resist the invaders. The Spartans provided the overall leadership and commanded the Greek armies. The Athenians, led by the wily Themistocles, provided the heart of the naval forces.

The first confrontation between the Persians and the Greeks occurred at the pass of Thermopylae and in the waters off Cape Artemisium in northern Greece (see Map 5.1). At Thermopylae the Greek hoplites—the heavily armed troops—showed their mettle. Before the fighting began, a report came in that when the Persian archers shot their bows the arrows darkened the sky. One gruff Spartan merely replied, "Fine, then we'll fight in the shade." The Greeks at Thermopylae fought to the last man, but the Persians took the position. In their next two battles, the Greeks fared better. In 480 B.C. the Greek fleet smashed the Persian navy at Salamis, an island south of Athens. The following year, the Greek army destroyed the Persian forces at Plataea, a small polis at Boeotia.

The significance of these Greek victories is nearly incalculable. By defeating the Persians, the Greeks ensured that a Near Eastern monarchy would not stifle the Greek achievement. The Greeks were thus able to develop their particular genius in freedom. The decisive victories at Salamis and Plataea meant that Greek political forms and intellectual concepts would be the heritage of the West.

After turning back the invasion, the Greeks took the fight to the Persian Empire. In 478 B.C. the Greeks decided to continue hostilities until they had liberated the Ionians from Persian rule. To achieve that goal a strong navy was essential. The Greeks turned to Athens, the leading naval power in the Aegean, for leadership. Athens and other states, especially those in the Aegean, responded by establishing the Delian League. Athens controlled the Delian League, providing most of the warships for operations and determining how much money each member should contribute to the league's treasury.

Over the next twenty years Athens drove the Persians out of the Aegean and turned the members of the Delian League into an Athenian empire. Athenian rule became severe, and the Athenian polis became openly imperialistic. Although all members of the Delian League were supposed to be free and independent states, Athens reduced them to the status of subjects. A sense of the harshness of Athenian rule can be gained from the regulations the Athenians imposed on their subject allies. After the Athenians had suppressed a revolt in Euboea, they imposed an oath on the people:

I will not revolt from the people of Athens either by any means or devices whatsoever or by word or deed, nor will I be persuaded by anyone who does revolt. And I will pay the tribute to the Athenians that I can persuade the Athenians to levy. I will be to them the best and truest ally possible. I will help and defend the people of Athens if anyone wrongs them, and I will obey the people of Athens.[4]

The Athenians dictated to the people of Erythrae, a polis on the coast of Asia Minor, their form of government:

There will be a council of 120 men chosen by lot. . . . The Athenian overseers and garrison commander will choose the current council by lot and establish it in office. Henceforth the council and the Athenian garrison commander will do these things thirty days before the council goes out of office.[5]

The Athenians were willing to enforce their demands by armed might, and they were ready both to punish violations and to suppress discontent.

The expansion of Athenian power and the aggressiveness of Athenian rule alarmed Sparta and its allies. While relations between Athens and Sparta cooled, Pericles (ca 494–429 B.C.) became the leading statesman in Athens. An aristocrat of solid intellectual ability, he turned Athens into the wonder of Greece. But like the democracy he led, Pericles was aggressive and imperialistic. He made

Greek Family in Mourning This funeral relief commemorates the death of a young girl. She stands on the right as though still living, bidding farewell to her mother, who is seated. Her father stands in the background. The scene is subdued but serene. Any Greek who saw this relief would know that parents and daughter were saying "XAIPE," which in Greek means "hello" as well as "good-bye." *(Source: Caroline Buckler)*

no effort to allay Spartan fear and instead continued Athenian expansion. At last, in 459 B.C. Sparta and Athens went to war over conflicts between Athens and some of Sparta's allies. The war ended fourteen years later with no serious damage to either side and nothing settled. But this war had divided the Greek world between two great powers.

Athens continued its severe policies toward its subject allies and came into conflict with Corinth, one of Sparta's leading allies (Map 5.3). Once again Athens and Sparta were drifting toward war. In 432 B.C. the Spartans convened a meeting of their allies, who complained of Athenian aggression and demanded that Athens be stopped. With

MAP 5.3 The Peloponnesian War This map, which shows the alignment of states during the Peloponnesian War, vividly illustrates the large scale of the war and its divisive impact.

a show of reluctance, the Spartans agreed to declare war. The real reason for war, according to Thucydides, the Athenian historian who also fought as a general in the war, was simple: "The truest explanation, though the one least mentioned, was the great growth of Athenian power and the fear it caused the Lakedaimonians [Spartans] which drove them to war."[6]

At the outbreak of this, the Peloponnesian War, a Spartan ambassador warned the Athenians: "This day will be the beginning of great evils for the Greeks." Few have ever spoken more prophetically. The Peloponnesian War lasted a generation (431–404 B.C.) and brought in its wake fearful plagues, famine, civil wars, widespread destruction, and huge loss of life. Thucydides described its cataclysmic effects:

For never had so many cities been captured and destroyed, whether by the barbarians or by the Greeks who were fighting each other. . . . Never had so many men been exiled or slaughtered, whether in the war or because of civil conflicts.[7]

As the war dragged on for years, older leaders like Pericles died and were replaced by men of the war generation. In Athens the most prominent of this new breed of politicians was Alcibiades (ca 450–404 B.C.), who was an aristocrat, a kinsman of Pericles, and a student of the philosopher Socrates. Alcibiades was brilliant, handsome, charming, and popular with the people. He was also self-seeking and egotistical; a shameless opportunist, his first thoughts were always for himself.

Alcibiades' schemes helped bring Athens down to defeat. Having planned an invasion of Sicily that ended in disaster, he deserted to the Spartans and plotted with the Persians, who had sided with Sparta, against his homeland. In the end, all of Alcibiades' intrigues failed. The Spartans defeated the Athenian fleet in the Aegean and blockaded Athens by land and sea. Finally, in 404 B.C. the Athenians surrendered and watched helplessly while the Spartans and their allies destroyed the walls of Athens to the music of flute girls. The Peloponnesian War lasted twenty-seven years, and it dealt Greek civilization a serious blow.

Athenian Arts in the Age of Pericles

In the last half of the fifth century B.C., Pericles turned Athens into the showplace of Greece. He appropriated Delian League funds to pay for a huge building program, planning temples and other buildings to honor Athena, the patron goddess of the city, and to display to all Greeks the glory of the Athenian polis. Pericles also pointed out that his program would employ a great many Athenians and bring economic prosperity to the city.

Thus began the undertaking that turned the Athenian acropolis into a monument for all time. Construction of the Parthenon began in 447 B.C., followed by the Propylaea, the temple of Athena Nike (Athena the Victorious), and the Erechtheion (Map 5.4). Even today in their ruined state they still evoke awe. Plutarch, a Greek writer who lived in the first century A.D., observed:

In beauty each of them was from the outset antique, and even now in its prime fresh and newly made. Thus each of them is always in bloom, maintaining its appearance as though untouched by time, as though an ever-green breath and undecaying spirit had been mixed in its construction.[8]

Mosaic Portrait of Alcibiades The artist has caught all the craftiness, intelligence, and quickness of Alcibiades, who became a romantic figure in antiquity. Besides the artistic merit of the portrait, the mosaic is interesting because Alcibiades' name in the upper right corner is misspelled. *(Source: Caroline Buckler)*

MAP 5.4 Ancient Athens By modern standards the city of Athens was hardly more than a town, not much larger in size than one square mile. Yet this small area reflects the concentration of ancient Greek life in the polis.

Even the pollution of modern Athens, although it is destroying the ancient buildings, cannot rob them of their splendor and charm.

The planning of the architects and the skill of the workers who erected these buildings were very sophisticated. Visitors approaching the Acropolis first saw the Propylaea, the ceremonial gateway, a building of complicated layout and grand design whose Doric columns seem to hold up the sky. On the right was the small temple of Athena Nike, whose dimensions harmonize with those of the Propylaea. The temple was built to commemorate the victory over the Persians, and the Ionic frieze above its columns depicted the battle of the Greeks and the Persians. Here for all the world to see was a tribute to Athenian and Greek valor—and a reminder of Athens' part in the victory.

Ahead of the visitors as they stood in the Propylaea was the huge statue of Athena Promachus (the Frontline Fighter), so gigantic that the crest of

Athena's helmet and the point of her spear could be seen by sailors entering the harbor of Athens. This statue celebrated the Athenian victory at the Battle of Marathon and was paid for by the spoils taken from the Persians. To the left stood the Erechtheion, an Ionic temple that housed several ancient shrines. On its southern side is the famous Portico of the Caryatids, a porch whose roof is supported by statues of Athenian maidens. The graceful Ionic columns of the Erechtheion provide a delicate relief from the prevailing Doric order of the massive Propylaea and Parthenon.

As visitors walked on they obtained a full view of the Parthenon, thought by many to be the perfect Doric temple. The Parthenon was the chief monument to Athena and her city. The sculptures that adorned the temple portrayed the greatness of Athens and its goddess. The figures on the eastern pediment depicted Athena's birth; those on the west, the victory of Athena over the god Poseidon for the possession of Attica. Inside the Parthenon stood a huge statue of Athena, the masterpiece of Phidias, one of the greatest sculptors of all time.

In many ways the Athenian acropolis is the epitome of Greek art and its spirit, which exhibits the rational side of Greek art. There is no violent emotion in this art, but instead a quiet intensity. Likewise, there is nothing excessive, for "nothing too much" was the canon of artist and philosopher alike. Greek artists portrayed action in a balanced, restrained, and sometimes even serene fashion, capturing the noblest aspects of human beings: their reason, dignity, and promise.

Other aspects of Athenian cultural life were as rooted in the life of the polis as were the architecture and sculpture of the Acropolis. The develop-

ment of drama was tied to the religious festivals of the city. The polis sponsored the production of plays and required that wealthy citizens pay the expenses of their production. At the beginning of the year dramatists submitted their plays to the archon. He chose those he considered best and assigned a theatrical troupe to each playwright. Although most Athenian drama has perished, enough has survived to prove that the archons had superb taste. Many plays were highly controversial, but the archons neither suppressed nor censored them.

The Athenian dramatists were the first artists in Western society to examine such basic questions as the rights of the individual, the demands of society on the individual, and the nature of good and

Sectional View of the Parthenon This figure both indicates what the Parthenon looked like in antiquity and explains the complex nature of Greek temple-building. As the illustration shows, the Parthenon's apparently simple façade is a work of great architectural sophistication. *(Source: Guide to Sculptures of the Parthenon, a British Museum publication)*

evil. Conflict is a constant element in Athenian drama. The dramatists used their art to portray, understand, and resolve life's basic conflicts.

Aeschylus (525–456 B.C.), the first of the great Athenian dramatists, was the first to express the agony of the individual caught in conflict. In his trilogy of plays, *The Oresteia,* Aeschylus deals with the themes of betrayal, murder, and reconciliation. Sophocles (496–406 B.C.), too, dealt with matters personal and political. In *Antigone* he examined the relationship between the individual and the state by exploring a conflict between the ties of kinship and the demands of the polis. As the play progresses, Antigone comes to stand for the precedence of divine law over human defects. Sophocles touches on the need for recognition of, and adherence to, the law as prerequisites for a tranquil state. Sophocles' masterpieces have become classics of literature, and his themes have inspired generations of playwrights. In his famous plays *Oedipus the King* and *Oedipus at Colonus*

Sophocles seems to be saying that human beings should do the will of the gods, even without fully understanding it, for the gods stand for justice and order.

Euripides (ca 480–406 B.C.), the last of the three great Greek dramatists, also explored the theme of personal conflict within the polis and sounded the depths of the individual. With Euripides drama entered a new, in many ways more personal, phase. To him the gods were far less important than human beings. Euripides viewed the human soul as a place where opposing forces struggle, where strong passions such as hatred and jealousy conflict with reason. The essence of Euripides' tragedy is flawed character—men and women who bring disaster on themselves and their loved ones because their passions overwhelm reason. Although Euripides' plays were less popular in his lifetime than those of Aeschylus and Sophocles, Euripides was a dramatist of genius whose work later had a significant impact on Roman drama.

The Parthenon   Stately and graceful, the Parthenon symbolizes the logic, order, and sense of beauty of Greek architecture. The Parthenon was also the centerpiece of Pericles' plan to make Athens the artistic showcase of the Greek world. *(Source: Caroline Buckler)*

Writers of comedy treated the affairs of the polis bawdily and often coarsely. Even so, their plays, too, were performed at religious festivals. The comic playwrights dealt primarily with the political affairs of the polis and the conduct of its leading politicians. Best known is Aristophanes (ca 445–386 B.C.), an ardent lover of his city and a merciless critic of cranks and quacks. It is a tribute to the Athenians that such devastating attacks could openly and freely be made on the city's leaders and foreign policy. Even at the height of the Peloponnesian War, Aristophanes proclaimed that peace was preferable to the ravages of war. Like Aeschylus, Sophocles, and Euripides, Aristophanes used his art to dramatize his ideas on the right conduct of the citizen and the value of the polis.

Perhaps never were art and political life so intimately and congenially bound together as at Athens. Athenian art was the product of deep and genuine love of the polis. It aimed at bettering the lives of the citizens and the quality of life in the state.

Daily Life in Periclean Athens

In sharp contrast with the rich intellectual and cultural life of Periclean Athens was the simplicity of its material life. The Athenians—and in this respect they were typical of Greeks in general—lived very happily with comparatively few material possessions. There were few material goods to own. The thousands of machines, tools, and gadgets considered essential for modern life had no counterparts in Athenian life. The inventory of Alcibiades' goods, which the Athenians confiscated after his desertion, is enlightening. His household possessions consisted of chests, beds, couches, tables, screens, stools, baskets, and mats. Other necessities of the Greek home included pottery, metal utensils for cooking, tools, luxury goods such as jewelry, and a few other things. These items the Athenians had to buy from craftsmen. Whatever else they needed, such as clothes and blankets, they produced at home.

The Athenian house was rather simple. Whether large or small, the typical house consisted of a series of rooms built around a central courtyard, with doors opening onto the courtyard. Many houses had bedrooms on an upper floor. Artisans and craftsmen often set aside a room to use as a shop or work area. The two principal rooms were

A Greek God Few pieces of Greek art better illustrate the conception of the gods as greatly superior forms of human beings than this magnificent statue, over six feet, ten inches in height. Here, the god, who may be either Poseidon or Zeus, is portrayed as powerful and perfect but basically human in form. *(Source: National Archaeological Museum, Athens)*

the men's dining room and the room where the women worked wool. Other rooms included the kitchen and bathroom. By modern standards there was not much furniture. In the men's dining room were couches, a sideboard, and small tables. Cups and other pottery often hung on the wall from pegs.

In the courtyard were a well, a small altar, and a washbasin. If the family lived in the country, the stalls of the animals faced the courtyard. Countryfolk kept oxen for plowing, pigs for slaughtering, sheep for wool, goats for cheese, and mules and donkeys for transportation. Even in the city, chickens and perhaps a goat or two roamed the courtyard together with dogs and cats.

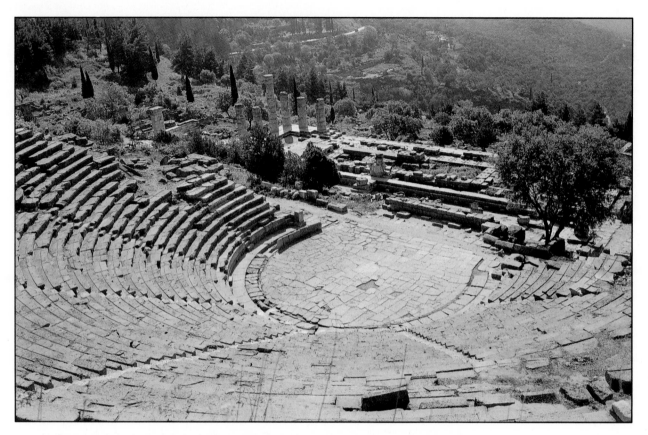

Theater of Delphi This scene admirably illustrates the religious quality of Greek drama. The theater, in which the great plays of Aeschylus, Sophocles, and Euripides were performed, overlooks the rest of the sanctuary of Apollo of which it is a significant part. The theater stands as a monument to the importance of drama to Greek cultural life. (*Source: Ekdotike Athenon*)

Cooking, done over a hearth in the house, provided welcome warmth in the winter. Baking and roasting were done in ovens. Food consisted of various grains, especially wheat and barley, as well as lentils, olives, figs, and grapes. Garlic and onion were popular garnishes, and wine was always on hand. These foods were stored at home in large jars; with them the Greek family ate fish, chicken, and vegetables. Women ground wheat into flour, baked it into bread, and on special occasions made honey or sesame cakes. The Greeks used olive oil for cooking, as families still do in modern Greece; they also used it as an unguent and as lamp fuel.

On special occasions, such as important religious festivals, the family ate the animal sacrificed to the god and gave the god the exquisite delicacy of the thighbone wrapped in fat. The only Greeks who consistently ate meat were the Spartan warriors. They received a small portion of meat each day, together with the infamous Spartan black broth, a ghastly concoction of pork cooked in blood, vinegar, and salt. One Greek, after tasting the broth, commented that he could easily understand why the Spartans were so willing to die.

In the city a man might support himself as a craftsman—a potter, bronzesmith, sail maker, or tanner—or he could contract with the polis to work on public buildings, such as the Parthenon and Erechtheion. Men without skills worked as paid laborers but competed with slaves for work. Slaves—usually foreigners, barbarian as well as Greek—were paid the same amount for their employment as were free men.

Slavery was commonplace in Greece, as it was throughout the ancient world. In its essentials Greek slavery resembled Mesopotamian slavery. Slaves received some protection under the law and could buy their freedom. On the other hand, masters could mistreat or neglect their slaves short of killing them, which was illegal. The worst-treated slaves were those of the silver mines at Laurium, who lived, worked, and died in wretchedness. Yet slavery elsewhere was not generally brutal. One crusty aristocrat complained that in Athens one could not tell the slaves from the free. Most slaves in Athens served as domestics and performed light labor around the house. Nurses for children, teachers of reading and writing, and guardians for young men were often slaves, whose lives were much like those of their owners. Other slaves were skilled workers, who could be found working on public buildings or in small workshops.

The importance of slavery in Athens must not be exaggerated. Apart from those who leased from Athens the right to operate the Laurium mines, Athenians did not own huge gangs of slaves as did Roman owners of large estates. Slave labor competed with free labor and kept wages down, but it never replaced free labor, which was the mainstay of the Athenian economy.

Most Athenians supported themselves by agriculture, but unless a family was fortunate enough to possess holdings in a plain more fertile than most of the land, reaping a good crop from the soil was difficult. Wealthy landowners sold their excess produce in the urban marketplace, but many people must have consumed nearly everything they raised. The plow, though wooden, sometimes had an iron share and was pulled by oxen. Attic farmers were free men. Though hardly prosperous, they were by no means destitute. Greek farmers could usually expect yields of five bushels of wheat and ten of barley per acre for every bushel of grain sown. A bad harvest meant a lean year. In many places farmers grew more barley than wheat because of the soil. Wherever possible farmers also cultivated vines and olive trees. In Greece arable land was much smaller in extent and less fertile than in Egypt, Mesopotamia, India, and China. Thus Greece could not provide sustenance for a population nearly so large as its Eastern neighbors. The economic basis for an empire resembling that of the Mauryan Empire or the Chou Dynasty did not exist for the Greeks. Although the Greeks also looked to the sea for their livelihood, even this economic resource was limited. Geography placed its own physical limits on Greek growth.

For sport both countryman and city dweller often hunted for rabbits, deer, or wild boar. A successful hunt supplemented the family's regular diet. Wealthy men hunted on horseback; most others hunted on foot with their dogs. Hunting also allowed a man to display to his fellows his bravery and prowess in the chase. If wild boar were the prey, the sport could be dangerous, as Odysseus discovered when a charging boar slashed open his foot.

The social condition of Athenian women has been the subject of much debate and little agreement. One thing is certain: the status of a free woman of the citizen class was strictly protected by law. Only her children, not those of foreigners or slaves, could be citizens. Only she was in charge of the household and the family's possessions. Yet the law protected her primarily to protect her husband's interests. Raping a free woman was a lesser crime than seducing her because seduction involved the winning of her affections. This law was concerned not with the husband's feelings but with ensuring that he need not doubt the legitimacy of his children.

Ideally, respectable women lived a secluded life in which the only men they saw were relatives. How far this ideal was actually put into practice is impossible to say. Athenian women seem to have enjoyed a social circle of other women of their own class. They also attended public festivals, sacrifices, and funerals. Nonetheless, prosperous and respectable women probably spent much of their time in the house. A white complexion—a sign that a woman did not have to spend her days in the fields —was valued highly.

Courtesans lived the freest lives of all Athenian women. Although some courtesans were simply prostitutes, others added intellectual accomplishments to physical beauty. In constant demand, cultured courtesans moved freely in male society. Their artistic talents and intellectual abilities appealed to men who wanted more than sex. The most famous of all courtesans was Aspasia, mistress of Pericles and supposedly friend of Socrates. Under Pericles' roof, she participated in intellectual discussions equally with some of the most stimulating thinkers of the day. Yet her position, like that of most other courtesans, was precarious. After Pericles' death, Aspasia fended for herself, ending her days as the madam of a house of prostitution.

A woman's main functions were to raise the children, oversee the domestic slaves and hired labor, and together with her maids work wool into cloth. The women washed the wool in the court-yard and then brought it into the women's room, where the loom stood. They spun the wool into thread and wove the thread into cloth. They also dyed wool at home and decorated the cloth by weaving in colors and designs. The woman of the household either did the cooking herself or directed her maids. In a sense, poor women lived freer lives than did wealthier women. They performed manual labor in the fields or sold goods in the agora, going about their affairs much as men did.

A distinctive feature of Athenian life and of Greek life in general was acceptance of homosexuality. No one has satisfactorily explained how the

Women Working The scene on this vase represents the women of the household at work. It shows how they produced woolen cloth, from the spinning of yarn to the completion of the cloth itself, here held by two women. (*Source: The Metropolitan Museum of Art, Fletcher Fund, 1931*)

Greek attitude toward homosexual love developed or determined how common homosexual behavior was. Homosexuality was probably far more common among the aristocracy than among the lower classes. It is impossible to be sure, simply because most of what the modern world knows of ancient Greece and Rome comes from the writings of aristocrats. Since aristocratic boys and girls were often brought up separately, the likelihood of homosexual relationships was very great. This style of life was impossible for the common folk because every member of the family—husband and wife, son and daughter—got out and worked. Among the poorer classes the sexes mingled freely.

Despite some modern speculation to the contrary, relations between Athenian husbands and wives were probably close. The presence of female slaves in the home could be a source of trouble; men were always free to resort to prostitutes; and some men and women engaged in homosexual love affairs. But basically husbands and wives depended on each other for mutual love and support. The wife's position and status in the household were guaranteed by her dowry, which came from her father and remained her property throughout her married life. If the wife felt that her marriage was intolerable, she could divorce her husband far more easily than could a Mesopotamian wife.

One particularly important aspect of social life in Athens and elsewhere in Greece was religion. Yet Greek religion is extremely difficult for modern people to understand, largely because of the great differences between Greek and modern cultures. In the first place, it is not even easy to talk about "Greek religion," since the Greeks had no uniform faith or creed. Although the Greeks usually worshiped the same deities—Zeus, Hera, Apollo, Athena, and others—the cults of these gods and goddesses varied from polis to polis. The Greeks had no sacred books, such as the Bible, and Greek religion was often a matter more of ritual than of belief. Nor did cults impose an ethical code of conduct. Greeks did not have to follow any particular rule of life, practice certain virtues, or even live decent lives in order to participate. Unlike the Egyptians, Hebrews, and Indians, the Greeks lacked a priesthood as the modern world understands the term. In Greece priests and priestesses cared for temples and sacred property and conducted the proper rituals but did not make religious rules or doctrines, much less enforce them.

In short, there existed in Greece no central ecclesiastical authority and no organized creed.

Although temples to the gods were common, they were unlike modern churches, temples, or synagogues in that they were not normally places where a congregation met to worship as a spiritual community. Instead the individual Greek either visited the temple occasionally on matters of private concern or walked in a procession to a particular temple to celebrate a particular festival. In Greek religion the altar was important; when the Greeks sought the favor of the gods, they offered them sacrifices. Greek religious observances were generally cheerful. Festivals and sacrifices were frequently times for people to meet socially, times of high spirits and conviviality rather than pious gloom. By offering the gods parts of the sacrifice while consuming the rest themselves, worshipers forged a bond with the gods.

Besides the Olympian gods, each polis had its own minor deities, each with his or her own local cult. In many instances Greek religion involved the official gods and goddesses of the polis and their cults. The polis administered the cults and festivals, and all were expected to participate in this civic religion, regardless of whether they believed in the deities being worshiped. Participating unbelievers, who seem to have been a small minority, were not considered hypocrites. Rather they were seen as patriotic, loyal citizens who in honoring the gods also honored the polis. If this attitude seems contradictory, an analogy may help. Before baseball games Americans stand at the playing of the national anthem, whether they are Democrats, Republicans, or neither, and whether they agree or disagree with the policies of the administration in authority. They honor their nation as represented by its flag. In somewhat the same way ancient Greeks honored their polis and demonstrated their solidarity with it by participating in the state cults.

Though Greek religion in general was individual or related to the polis, the Greeks also shared some pan-Hellenic festivals, the chief of which were held at Olympia in honor of Zeus and at Delphi in honor of Apollo. The festivities at Olympia included the famous games, athletic contests that have inspired the modern Olympic games. Held every four years, these games were for the glory of Zeus. They attracted visitors from all over the Greek world and lasted well into Christian times. The Pythian games at Delphi were also held every four years, but these contests differed from the Olympic games by including musical and literary contests. Both the Olympic and the Pythian games were a unifying factor in Greek life, bringing Greek citizens together culturally as well as religiously. Finally, there were some mystery cults, like that of Eleusis in Attica, which were open only to Greeks, who first had to master a body of arcane and secret ritual and who then purified themselves for initiation into the cult. Once admitted, they were not permitted to reveal any details of the cult. Though few in Classical Greece, other and new mystery cults grew up and became common in the Hellenistic period.

The Flowering of Philosophy

The myths and epics of the Mesopotamians and Indians are ample testimony that speculation about the origin of the universe and of humankind did not begin with the Greeks. The signal achievement of the Greeks was willingness to treat these questions in rational rather than mythological terms. Although Greek philosophy did not fully flower until the Classical Period, Ionian thinkers had already begun in the Lyric Age to ask what the universe was made of. These men are called the "Pre-Socratics," for their work preceded the philosophical revolution begun by the Athenian Socrates. Though they were born observers, the Pre-Socratics rarely undertook deliberate experimentation. Instead they took individual facts and wove them into general theories. Despite appearances, they believed, the universe was actually simple and subject to natural laws. Drawing on their observations, they speculated about the basic building blocks of the universe.

The first of the Pre-Socratics, Thales (ca 640–546 B.C.), learned mathematics and astronomy from the Babylonians and geometry from the Egyptians. Yet there was an immense and fundamental difference between Near Eastern thought and the philosophy of Thales. The Near Eastern peoples considered such events as eclipses as evil omens. Thales viewed them as natural phenomena that could be explained in natural terms. In short, he asked *why* things happened. He believed the basic element of the universe to be water. Although he was wrong, the way in which he asked the question was momentous: it was the beginning of the scientific method.

Thales' follower Anaximander continued his work. Anaximander was the first of the Pre-Socratics to use general concepts, which are essential to abstract thought. One of the most brilliant of the Pre-Socratics, a man of striking originality, Anaximander theorized that the basic element of the universe is the "boundless" or "endless"—something infinite and indestructible. In his view, the earth floats in a void, held in balance by its distance from everything else in the universe.

Anaximander even concluded that humankind had evolved naturally from lower organisms: "In water the first animal arose covered with spiny skin, and with the lapse of time some crawled onto dry land and breaking off their skins in a short time they survived."[9] This remarkable speculation corresponds crudely to Darwin's theory of the evolution of species, which it predated by two and a half millennia.

Another Ionian, Heraclitus (ca 500 B.C.), declared the primal element to be fire. He also declared that the world had neither beginning nor end: "This world, the world of all things, neither any god nor man made, but it always was and it is and it will be: an everlasting fire, measures kindling and measures going out."[10] Although the universe was eternal, according to Heraclitus, it changed constantly. An outgrowth of this line of speculation was the theory of Democritus that the universe is made of invisible, indestructible atoms. The culmination of Pre-Socratic thought was the theory that four simple substances make up the universe: fire, air, earth, and water.

With this impressive heritage behind them, the philosophers of the Classical Period ventured into new areas of speculation. This development was partly due to the work of Hippocrates (ca 460–ca 377 B.C.), a pioneer in the science of medicine.

Like Thales, Hippocrates sought natural explanations for natural phenomena. Basing his opinions on empirical knowledge, not on religion or magic, he taught that natural means could be employed to fight disease. In his treatise *On Airs, Waters, and Places,* he noted the influence of climate and environment on health. Hippocrates and his followers put forth a theory that was to prevail in European medical circles until the eighteenth century. The human body, they declared, contains four *humors,* or fluids: blood, phlegm, black bile, and yellow bile. In a healthy body the four humors are in perfect balance; too much or too little of any particular humor causes illness. Hippocrates and his pupils shared the Ionian belief that they were dealing with phenomena that could be explained purely in natural terms. But Hippocrates broke away from the mainstream of Ionian speculation by declaring that medicine was a separate craft—just as ironworking was—that had its own principles.

Socrates According to tradition, Socrates was homely at best. Yet this Roman copy of a fourth-century Greek statue has captured the simplicity and the thoughtfulness of the man. It also gives a sense of his intellectual exploration of basic human values. *(Source: Courtesy of the Trustees of the British Museum)*

The distinction between natural science and philosophy, on which Hippocrates insisted, was also promoted by the Sophists, who traveled the Greek world teaching young men. Despite differences of opinion on philosophical matters, the Sophists all agreed that human beings were the proper subject of study. They also believed that excellence could be taught, and they used philosophy and rhetoric to prepare young men for life in the polis. The Sophists laid great emphasis on logic and the meanings of words. They criticized traditional beliefs, religion, rituals, and myth and even questioned the laws of the polis. In essence they argued that nothing is absolute, that everything—even the customs and constitution of the state—is relative. Hence many Greeks of more traditional inclination considered them wanton and harmful, men who were interested in "making the worse seem the better cause."

One of those whose contemporaries thought him a Sophist was Socrates (ca 470–399 B.C.), who sprang from the class of small artisans. Socrates spent his life in investigation and definition. Not strictly speaking a Sophist because he never formally taught or collected fees from anyone, Socrates shared the Sophists' belief that human beings and their environment are the essential subjects of philosophical inquiry. Like the Sophists, Socrates thought that excellence could be learned and passed on to others. His approach when posing ethical questions and defining concepts was to start with a general topic or problem and to narrow the matter to its essentials. He did so by continuous questioning, a running dialogue. Never did he lecture. Socrates thought that by constantly pursuing excellence, an essential part of which was knowledge, human beings could approach the supreme good and thus find true happiness. Yet in 399 B.C. Socrates was brought to trial, convicted, and executed on charges of corrupting the youth of the city and introducing new gods.

Socrates' student Plato (427–347 B.C.) carried on his master's search for truth. Unlike Socrates, Plato wrote down his thoughts and theories and founded a philosophical school, the Academy. Plato developed the theory that all visible, tangible things are unreal and temporary, copies of "forms" or "ideas" that are constant and indestructible. Only the mind, not the senses, can perceive eternal forms. In Plato's view the highest form is the idea of good.

In *The Republic* Plato applied his theory of forms to politics in an effort to describe the ideal polis. His perfect polis is utopian; it aims at providing the greatest good and happiness to all its members. Plato thought that the ideal polis could exist only if its rulers were philosophers. He divided society into rulers, guardians of the polis, and workers. The role of people in each category is decided by the education, wisdom, and ability of the individual. In Plato's republic men and women are equal to one another, and women can become rulers. The utopian polis is a balance, with each individual doing what he or she can to support the state and with each receiving from the state his or her just due.

In a later work, *The Laws,* Plato discarded the ideal polis of *The Republic* in favor of a second-best state. The polis of *The Laws* grimly presages the modern dictatorship. At its head is a young tyrant who is just and good. He meets with a council that sits only at night, and together they maintain the spirit of the laws. Nearly everything about this state is coercive; the free will of the citizens counts for little. The laws speak to every aspect of life; their sole purpose is to make people happy.

Aristotle (384–322 B.C.) carried on the philosophical tradition of Socrates and Plato. A student of Plato, Aristotle went far beyond him in striving to understand the universe. The range of Aristotle's thought is staggering. Everything in human experience was fit subject for his inquiry. In *The Politics* Aristotle followed Plato's lead by writing about the ideal polis. Yet Aristotle approached the question more realistically than Plato had done and criticized *The Republic* and *The Laws* on many points. In *The Politics* and elsewhere, Aristotle stressed moderation, concluding that the balance of his ideal state depended on people of talent and education who could avoid extremes.

Not content to examine old questions, Aristotle opened up whole new fields of inquiry. He tried to understand the changes of nature—what caused them and where they led. In *Physics* and *Metaphysics* he evolved a theory of nature that developed the notions of matter, form, and motion. He attempted to bridge the gap between abstract truth and concrete perception that Plato had created.

In *On the Heaven,* Aristotle took up the thread of Ionian speculation. His theory of cosmology added ether to air, fire, water, and earth as building blocks of the universe. He concluded that the universe revolves and that it is spherical and eter-

PERIODS OF GREEK HISTORY

Period	Significant Events	Major Writers
Bronze Age 2000–1100 B.C.	Arrival of the Greeks in Greece Rise and fall of the Mycenaean kingdoms	
Dark Age 1100–800 B.C.	Greek migrations within the Aegean basin Social and political recovery Evolution of the polis Rebirth of literacy	Homer Hesiod
Lyric Age 800–500 B.C.	Rise of Sparta and Athens Colonization of the Mediterranean basin Flowering of lyric poetry Development of philosophy and science in Ionia	Archilochus Sappho Tyrtaeus Solon Anaximander Heraclitus
Classical Age 500–338 B.C.	Persian Wars Growth of the Athenian Empire Peloponnesian War Rise of drama and historical writing Flowering of Greek philosophy Spartan and Theban hegemonies Conquest of Greece by Philip of Macedon	Herodotus Thucydides Aeschylus Sophocles Euripides Aristophanes Plato Aristotle

nal. He wrongly thought that the earth is the center of the universe, with the stars and planets revolving around it. The Hellenistic scientist Aristarchus of Samos later realized that the earth revolves around the sun, but Aristotle's view was accepted until the time of the fifteenth-century Polish astronomer Nicolaus Copernicus.

Aristotle's scientific interests also included zoology. In several works he describes various animals and makes observations on animal habits, anatomy, and movement. He also explored the process of reproduction. Intending to examine the entire animal kingdom, he assigned the world of plants to his follower Theophrastus (see page 165).

Aristotle possessed one of the keenest and most curious philosophical minds of civilization. While rethinking the old topics explored by the Pre-

Socratics, he also created whole new areas of study. In short, he tried to learn everything possible about the universe and everything in it. He did so in the belief that all knowledge could be synthesized to produce a simple explanation of the universe and of humanity.

The Final Act (403–338 B.C.)

Immediately after the Peloponnesian War, with Athens humbled, Sparta began striving for empire over the Greeks. The arrogance and imperialism of the Spartans turned their former allies against them. Even with Persian help Sparta could not maintain its hold on Greece. In 371 B.C. the Spartans met their match on the plain of Leuctra in Boeotia. A Theban army under the command of

Epaminondas, one of Greece's most brilliant generals, destroyed the flower of the Spartan army on a single summer day. The victory at Leuctra left Thebes the most powerful state in Greece. Under Epaminondas the Thebans destroyed Sparta as a first-rank power and checked the ambitions of Athens, but they were unable to bring peace to Greece. In 362 B.C. Epaminondas was killed in battle, and a period of stalemate set in. The Greek states were virtually exhausted.

The man who turned the situation to his advantage was Philip II, king of Macedonia (359–336 B.C.). Throughout most of Greek history Macedonia, which bordered Greece in the north (in modern Greece and Yugoslavia), had been a backward, disunited kingdom, but Philip's genius, courage, and drive turned it into a major power. One of the ablest statesmen of antiquity, Philip united his powerful kingdom, built a redoubtable army, and pursued his ambition with drive and determination. His horizon was not limited to Macedonia, for he realized that he could turn the rivalry and exhaustion of the Greek states to his own purposes. By clever use of his wealth and superb army Philip won control of the northern Aegean and awakened fear in Athens, which had vital interests there. Demosthenes, an Athenian patriot and a fine orator, warned his fellow citizens against Philip. Others, too, saw Philip as a threat. A comic playwright depicted one of Philip's ambassadors warning the Athenians:

Do you know that your battle will be with men
Who dine on sharpened swords,
And gulp burning firebrands for wine?
Then immediately after dinner the slave
Brings us dessert—Cretan arrows
Or pieces of broken spears.
We have shields and breastplates for
Cushions and at our feet slings and arrows,
And we are crowned with catapults.[11]

Finally the Athenians joined forces with Thebes, which also appreciated the Macedonian threat, to stop Philip. In 338 B.C. the combined Theban-Athenian army met Philip's veterans at the Boeotian city of Chaeronea. Philip's army won a hard-fought victory. Philip conquered Greece and put an end to Greek freedom. Because the Greeks could not put aside their quarrels, they fell to an invader.

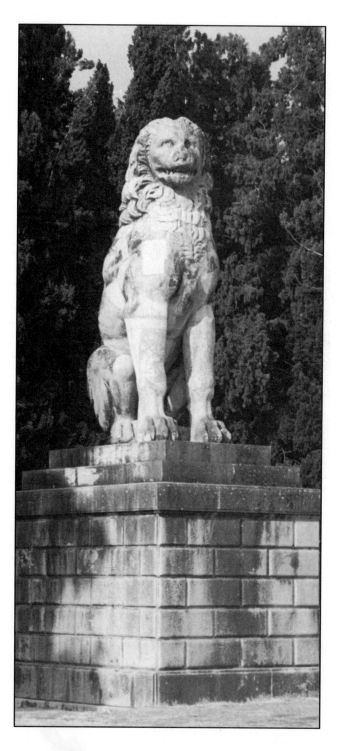

The Lion of Chaeronea This stylized lion marks the mass grave of nearly 300 elite Theban soldiers who valiantly died fighting the Macedonians at the Battle of Chaeronea. After the battle, Philip said: "May those who suppose that these men did or suffered anything dishonorable perish wretchedly." *(Source: Caroline Buckler)*

SUMMARY

In a comparatively brief span of time the Greeks progressed from a primitive folk, backward and rude compared with their Near Eastern neighbors, to one of the most influential peoples of history. These originators of science and philosophy asked penetrating questions about the nature of life and society and came up with deathless responses to many of their own questions. Greek achievements range from the development of sophisticated political institutions to the creation of a stunningly rich literature. Brilliant but quarrelsome, they were their own worst enemies. As the Roman historian Pompeius Trogus later said of their fall:

The states of Greece, while each one wished to rule alone, all squandered sovereignty. Indeed, hastening without moderation to destroy one another in mutual ruin, they did not realize, until they were all crushed, that every one of them lost in the end.[12]

Nonetheless, their achievements outlived their political squabbles to become the cornerstone of all later Western development.

NOTES

1. K. J. Beloch, *Griechische Geschichte,* vol. I, pt. I (Strassburg: K. J. Trubner, 1912), p. 49. Unless otherwise credited, all quotations from a foreign language in this chapter are translated by John Buckler.
2. Aristotle, *Politics* 1253a3–4.
3. J. M. Edmonds, *Greek Elegy and Iambus* (Cambridge, Mass.: Harvard University Press, 1931), 1.70, frag. 10.
4. R. Meiggs and D. Lewis, *A Selection of Greek Historical Inspirations* (Oxford: Clarendon Press, 1969), 52. 21–32.
5. Ibid., 40. 9–11.
6. Thucydides, *History of the Peloponnesian War* 1.23.
7. Ibid.
8. Plutarch, *Life of Pericles* 13.5.
9. E. Diels and W. Krantz, *Fragmente der Vorsokratiker,* 8th ed. (Berlin: Weidmannsche Verlagsbuchhandlung, 1960), Anaximander frag. A30.
10. Ibid. Heraclitus frag. B30.
11. J. M. Edmonds, *The Fragments of Attic Comedy* (Leiden: E. J. Brill, 1971), 2.366–369, Mnesimachos frag. 7.
12. Justin, 8.1.1–2.

SUGGESTED READING

Translations of the most important writings of the Greeks and Romans can be found in the volumes of the Loeb Classical Library published by Harvard University Press. Paperback editions of the major Greek and Latin authors are available in the Penguin Classics. Recent translations of documents include two volumes of *Translated Documents of Greece and Rome:* volume 1, by C. Fornara, *Archaic Times to the End of the Peloponnesian War* (1977); and volume 2, by P. Harding, *From the End of the Peloponnesian War to the Battle of Ipsus* (1985).

Among the many general treatments of Greek history is that of H. Bengtson, *Griechische Geschichte,* 4th ed. (1969), which is now available in an English translation by E. F. Bloedow under the title *History of Greece* (1988); the translation is additionally valuable because of the added bibliography. Another sound general treatment is J. Fine, *The Ancient Greeks* (1984).

A number of books on early Greece are available in addition to those cited in the Notes. A good, careful, and learned synthesis can be found in Lord W. Taylour, *The Mycenaeans,* rev. ed. (1983). More recent and wider in coverage is R. Drews, *The Coming of the Greeks* (1988), which puts the movements of the Greeks in the broader context of Indo-European migrations. M. Mueller, *The Iliad* (1984), discusses both the historical and the heroic aspects of one of the world's great poems. No finer introduction to the Lyric Age can be found than A. R. Burn, *The Lyric Age* (1960). Its sequel, *Persia and the Greeks,* 2d ed. (1984), which is also unsurpassed, carries the history of Greece to the defeat of the Persians in 479 B.C. More recent is J. Boardman et al., *The Cambridge Ancient History,* 2d ed., vol. 4 (1988), which is profusely illustrated. C. Roebuck, *Economy and Society in the Early Greek World* (1984), treats several aspects of early Greek developments. A. J. Graham, *Colony and Mother City in Ancient Greece,* rev. ed. (1984), gives a good account of Greek colonization.

A good survey of work on Sparta is P. Cartledge, *Sparta and Lakonia* (1979), which can be warmly recommended. J. F. Lazenby, *The Spartan Army* (1985), studies the evolution and performance of the Spartan army somewhat apart from its social setting. The Athenian democracy and the society that produced it continue to attract scholarly attention. Interesting and important are two studies by R. Osborne. His *Demos* (1985) deals with many political and social aspects of early Athenian history. His *Classical Landscape with Figures* (1987) takes a new look at the relation of the polis to its surrounding territory, part of a growing trend in ancient history to blend archeological and literary evidence to understand ancient society. A series of new studies re-evaluates aspects of the Athenian democracy: M. Ostwald, *From Popular Sovereignty to the Sovereignty of Law* (1986); M. H. Hanson, *The Athenian Assembly* (1987); and J. Ober, *Mass and Elite in Democratic Athens* (1989); and P. B. Manyville, *The Origins of Citizenship in Ancient Athens* (1990).

The Athenian Empire and the outbreak of the Peloponnesian War are covered by R. Meiggs, *The Athenian Empire* (1972), and M. McGregor, *The Athenians and Their Empire* (1987). The best account of the outbreak of the Peloponnesian War, despite its defects, is G. E. M. de Ste. Croix, *The Origins of the Peloponnesian War* (1972). A concise treatment of the Peloponnesian War from a military point of view can be found in A. Ferrill, *The Origins of War* (1985), chap. 4. A. Forde, *The Ambition to Rule* (1989), places Thucydides' treatment of Alcibiades in the context of politics and imperialism.

The fourth century has been one of the most fertile fields of recent research. G. Proietti, *Xenophon's Sparta* (1987), and P. Cartledge, *Agesilaos and the Crisis of Sparta* (1987), both treat Spartan government and society in its period of greatness and collapse. J. Buckler, *The Theban Hegemony, 371–362 B.C.* (1980), treats the period of Theban ascendancy, and Buckler, *Philip II and the Sacred War* (1989), studies the ways in which Philip of Macedonia used Greek politics to his own ends. J. Cargill, *The Second Athenian League* (1981), a significant study, traces Athenian policy during the fourth century. J. R. Ellis, *Philip II and Macedonian Imperialism* (1976), and G. Cawkwell, *Philip of Macedon* (1978), analyze the career of the great conqueror.

Greek social life has recently received a great deal of attention. R. Just, *Women in Athenian Law and Life* (1988), explores such topics as daily life, the family, and women's role in society. W. K. Lacey, *The Family in Classical Greece* (1984), is the place to start for those who wish to learn more about ordinary family relations, and B. Zimmermann, *Greek Tragedy* (1990). D. Sansone, *Greek Athletics and the Genesis of Sport* (1988), well illustrated, provides a good and far-ranging treatment of what athletics meant to the classical Greek world. The topic of ancient Greek slavery is one of frequent interest, and two books address it in different but interesting ways: Y. Garlan, *Slavery in Ancient Greece* (1988), is sound; more adventurous is E. M. Wood, *Peasant-Citizen and Slave* (1988), which links the two groups to the founding of the Athenian democracy.

For Greek literature, culture, and science, see A. Lesky, *History of Greek Literature* (English translation, 1963); M. Golden, *Children and Childhood in Classical Athens* (1990); J. Burnet, *Early Greek Philosophy,* 4th ed. (1930); M. Clagett, *Greek Science in Antiquity* (1971); and E. R. Dodds, *The Greeks and the Irrational* (1951).

The classic treatment of Greek architecture is W. B. Dinsmoor, *The Architecture of the Ancient Greeks,* 3d ed. (1950). More recent (and perhaps more readable) is A. W. Lawrence, *Greek Architecture,* 3d ed. (1973). J. Boardman, *Greek Art,* rev. ed. (1973), is both perceptive and sound, as is J. J. Pollitt, *Art and Experience in Classical Greece* (1972). D. Haynes, *Greek Art and the Idea of Freedom* (1981), traces the evolving freedom of the human personality in Greek art.

J. Pinsent, *Greek Mythology* (1969), is a handy introduction. G. S. Kirk, *The Nature of Greek Myths* (1974), examines Greek religion and myth in the contemporary context. Newer treatments of Greek religion include E. Simon, *Festivals of Athens* (1983), which describes Athenian religious festivals in their archeological context; and W. Burkert, *Greek Religion* (1987), which gives a masterful survey of ancient religious beliefs.

6

Hellenistic Diffusion

Detail from the Alexander Sarcophagus at Sidon, Phoenicia

Two years after his conquest of Greece, Philip of Macedon fell victim to an assassin's dagger. Philip's twenty-year-old son, historically known as "Alexander the Great" (336–323 B.C.), assumed the Macedonian throne. This young man, one of the most remarkable personalities in history, was to have a profound impact on history. By overthrowing the Persian Empire and by spreading *Hellenism*—Greek culture, language, thought, and the Greek way of life—as far as India, Alexander was instrumental in creating a new era, traditionally called "Hellenistic" to distinguish it from the Hellenic. As a result of Alexander's exploits, the individualistic and energetic culture of the Greeks came into intimate contact with the venerable older cultures of Africa and Asia.

The impact of Philip and Alexander was so enormous that the great German historian Hermann Bengtson has recently commented:

Philip and his son Alexander were the ones who opened the door of the world to the Macedonians and Greeks. With Macedonian imperialism was joined the diffusion of the Greek spirit, which permeated the entire ancient world. Without the achievement of these two kings neither the Roman Empire nor the diffusion of Christianity would have been conceivable.[1]

- Is Bengtson's estimation correct or is it mere rhetoric?
- What did the spread of Hellenism mean to the Greeks and the peoples of Asia?
- What did the meeting of West and East hold for the development of economics, religion, philosophy, women's concerns, science, and medicine?

These questions are explored in this chapter.

Bust of Alexander This Roman portrait of Alexander the Great is a copy of a Greek original. Alexander's youth and self-confidence are immediately apparent. Yet the style is surprisingly simple for a bust of someone who had conquered the Persian Empire. The Greek inscription is equally simple: "Alexander, the son of Philip, Macedonian." *(Source: Louvre/Giraudon/Art Resource)*

ALEXANDER AND THE GREAT CRUSADE

In 336 B.C. Alexander inherited not only Philip's crown but also his policies. After his victory at Chaeronea, Philip had organized the states of Greece into a huge league under his leadership and announced to the Greeks his plan to lead them and his Macedonians against the Persian Empire. Fully intending to carry out Philip's designs, Alexander proclaimed to the Greek world that the invasion of Persia was to be a great crusade, a mighty act of revenge for the Persian invasion of Greece in 480 B.C. Despite his youth, Alexander was well prepared to lead the attack. In 334 B.C. he led an army of Macedonians and Greeks into western Asia. In the next three years he won three major battles—at the Granicus River, at Issus, and at Gaugamela—victories that stand almost as road signs marking his march to the east (Map 6.1). Having overthrown the Persian Empire, he crossed the Indus River in 326 B.C. and entered India, where he saw hard fighting. Finally, at the Hyphasis River his troops refused to go farther. Still eager to explore the limits of the world, Alexander turned south to the Indian Ocean and then turned west. In 324

MAP 6.1 Alexander's Conquests This map shows the course of Alexander's invasion of the Persian Empire and the speed of his progress. More important than the success of his military campaigns was his founding of Hellenistic cities in the East.

B.C. a long, hard march brought him back to his camp at Susa. The great crusade was over, and Alexander himself died the next year in Babylon.

The political result of Alexander's premature death was chaos. Since several of the chief Macedonian officers aspired to Alexander's position as emperor and others opposed these ambitions, civil war lasting forty-three years tore Alexander's empire apart. By the end of this conflict, the most successful generals had carved out their own small and more or less stable monarchies.

Ptolemy immediately seized Egypt and transformed the native system of administration by appointing Greeks and Macedonians to the chief bureaucratic positions. Meanwhile, Seleucus won the bulk of Alexander's empire; his monarchy extended from western Asia to India. In the third

century B.C., however, the eastern parts of Seleucus's monarchy gained their independence, with the Parthians coming to power in Iran and the Greeks creating a monarchy of their own in Bactria. Antigonus maintained control of the Macedonian monarchy in Europe. Until the arrival of the Romans in the eastern Mediterranean in the second century B.C., these great monarchies were often at war with one another, but without winning any significant political or military advantage. In that respect, the Hellenistic monarchy was no improvement on the Greek polis.

Despite the disintegration of his empire, Alexander was instrumental in changing the face of politics in the eastern Mediterranean. His campaign swept away the Persian Empire, which had ruled the East for over two hundred years. In its

Alexander at the Battle of Issus At left, Alexander the Great, bareheaded and wearing a breastplate, charges King Darius, who is standing in a chariot. The moment marks the turning point of the battle, as Darius turns to flee from the attack. *(Source: National Museum, Naples/Alinari/Scala/Art Resource)*

place he established a Macedonian monarchy. More important in the long run was his founding of new cities and military colonies, which scattered Greeks and Macedonians throughout the East. Thus the practical result of Alexander's campaign was to open the East to the tide of Hellenism.

THE SPREAD OF HELLENISM

When the Greeks and Macedonians entered Asia Minor and Egypt, they encountered civilizations older than their own. In some ways the Eastern cultures were more advanced than the Greek, in others less so. Thus this third great tide of Greek migration differed from preceding waves (see pages 119 and 124), which had spread over land that was uninhabited or inhabited by less developed peoples.

What did the Hellenistic monarchies offer Greek immigrants politically and materially? More broadly, how did Hellenism and the cultures of the East affect one another? What did the meeting of West and East entail for the history of the world?

Cities and Kingdoms

Although Alexander's generals created huge kingdoms, the concept of monarchy never completely replaced the ideal of the polis. Consequently the monarchies never won the deep emotional loyalty that Greeks had once felt for the polis. Hellenistic kings needed large numbers of Greeks to run their kingdoms. Otherwise royal business would grind to a halt, and the conquerors would soon be swallowed up by the far more numerous conquered population. Obviously, then, the kings had to encourage Greeks to immigrate and build new homes. To these Greeks monarchy was something out of the heroic past, something found in Homer's *Iliad*, not in daily life. The Hellenistic kings thus confronted the problem of making life in the new monarchies resemble the traditional Greek way of life. Since Greek civilization was urban, the kings continued Alexander's policy of establishing cities throughout their kingdoms in order to entice Greeks to immigrate. Yet the creation of these cities posed a serious political problem that the Hellenistic kings failed to solve.

To the Greeks civilized life was unthinkable without the polis, which was far more than a mere city. The Greek polis was by definition *sovereign*— it was an independent, autonomous state run by its citizens and free of any outside power or restraint. Hellenistic kings, however, refused to grant sovereignty to their cities. In effect these kings willingly built cities but refused to build a polis. Instead they attempted a compromise that ultimately failed.

Hellenistic monarchs gave their cities all the external trappings of a polis. Each had an assembly of citizens, a council to prepare legislation, and a board of magistrates to conduct the city's political business. Yet, however similar to the Greek city-state they appeared, these cities could not engage in diplomatic dealings, make treaties, pursue their own foreign policies, or wage their own wars. None could govern its own affairs without interference from the king, who, even if he stood in the background, was the real sovereign. In the eyes of the king the cities were important parts of the kingdom, but the welfare of the whole kingdom came first. The cities had to obey royal orders, and the king often placed his own officials in the cities to see that his decrees were followed.

A new Hellenistic city differed from a Greek polis in other ways as well. A Greek polis had enjoyed political and social unity even though it was normally composed of citizens, slaves, and resident aliens. A polis had one body of law and one set of customs. In a Hellenistic city, Greeks represented an elite class of citizens. Natives and non-Greek foreigners who lived in Hellenistic cities usually possessed rights inferior to those of the Greeks and often had their own laws. In some instances the disparity spurred natives to assimilate Greek culture in order to rise politically and socially. Other peoples, including many Jews, firmly resisted the essence of Hellenism. A Hellenistic city was not homogeneous and could not spark the intensity of feeling inspired by a polis.

In many respects a Hellenistic city resembled a modern city. It was a cultural center with theaters, temples, and libraries. It was a seat of learning, home of poets, writers, teachers, and artists. It was a place where people could find amusement. A Hellenistic city was also an economic center that provided a ready market for grain and produce raised in the surrounding countryside. The city was an emporium, scene of trade and manufacturing. In short, a Hellenistic city offered cultural and economic opportunities but did not foster a sense of united, integrated enterprise.

There were no constitutional links between city and king. A city was simply his possession. Its citizens had no voice in how the kingdom was run. A city had no rights except for those the king granted, and even those he could summarily take away. Ambassadors from a city could entreat the king for favors and petition him on such matters as taxes, boundary disputes, and legal cases. But a city had no right to advise the king on royal policy and enjoyed no political function in the kingdom.

Hellenistic kings tried to make the kingdom the political focus of citizens' allegiance. If the king could secure the frontiers of his kingdom, he could give it a geographical identity. He could then hope that his subjects would direct their primary loyalty to the kingdom rather than to a particular city. However, the kings' efforts to fix their borders led only to sustained warfare. Boundaries were determined by military power, and rule by force became the chief political principle of the Hellenistic world (Map 6.2).

Border wars were frequent and exhausting. The Seleucids and Ptolemies, for instance, waged five wars for the possession of southern Syria. Other kings refused to acknowledge boundaries at all. They followed Alexander's example and waged wars to reunify his empire under their own authority. By the third century B.C., a weary balance of power was reached, but only as the result of stalemate. It was not maintained by any political principle.

Though Hellenistic kings never built a true polis, that does not mean that their urban policy failed. Rather, the Hellenistic city was to remain the basic social and political unit in the Hellenistic East until the sixth century A.D. Cities were the chief agents of Hellenization, and their influence spread far beyond their walls. These cities formed a broad cultural network in which Greek language, customs, and values flourished. Roman rule in the Hellenistic East would later be based on this urban culture, which facilitated the rise and spread of Christianity. In broad terms Hellenistic cities were remarkably influential and successful.

The Greeks and the Opening of Asia and Africa

If the Hellenistic kings failed to satisfy the Greeks' political yearnings, they nonetheless succeeded in giving the Greeks unequaled economic and social opportunities. The ruling dynasties of the Hellenistic world were Macedonian, and Greeks filled all important political, military, and diplomatic positions. Macedonians and Greeks constituted an upper class that sustained Hellenism in the East. Besides building Greek cities, Hellenistic kings offered Greeks land and money as lures to further immigration.

The opening of the East offered ambitious Greeks opportunities for well-paying jobs and economic success. The Hellenistic monarchy, unlike the Greek polis, did not depend solely on its citizens to fulfill its political needs. Talented Greeks could expect to rise quickly in the government bureaucracy. Appointed by the king, these administrators did not have to stand for election each year, as had many officials of a Greek polis. Since they held their jobs year after year, they had ample time to evolve new administrative techniques. Naturally they became more efficient than the amateur officials common in Hellenic Greek city-states. The

MAP 6.2 The Hellenistic World After Alexander's death, no single commander could hold his vast conquests together, and his empire broke up into several kingdoms and leagues.

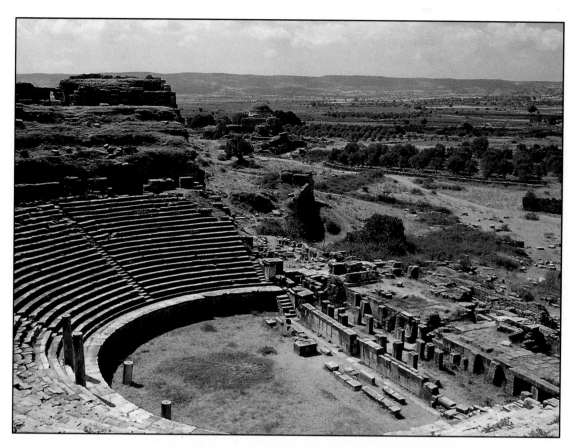

Priene The city of Priene in Asia Minor is an excellent example of the new Greek cities that sprang to life during the Hellenistic period. Greek architects designed the city of Priene to fit the slope of a hill that dominated the plain below. From the theater the spectator can see much of the city and the surrounding countryside. *(Source: Robert Harding)*

needs of the Hellenistic monarchy and the opportunities it offered thus gave rise to a professional corps of Greek administrators.

Greeks and Macedonians also found ready employment in the armies and navies of the Hellenistic monarchies. Alexander had proved the Greco-Macedonian style of warfare to be far superior to that of the Easterners, and Alexander's successors, themselves experienced officers, realized the importance of trained Greek and Macedonian soldiers. Moreover, Hellenistic kings were extremely reluctant to arm the native population or to allow them to serve in the army, fearing military rebellions among their conquered subjects. The result was the emergence of professional armies and navies comprising only Greeks and Macedonians.

Greeks were able to dominate other professions as well. In order to be truly philhellenic, the king-

doms and cities recruited Greek writers and artists to create Greek literature, art, and culture on Asian and African soil. Architects, engineers, and skilled craftsmen found their services in great demand because of the building policies of the Hellenistic monarchs. If Hellenistic kingdoms were to have Greek cities, those cities needed Greek buildings—temples, porticoes, gymnasia, theaters, fountains, and houses. Architects and engineers were sometimes commissioned to design and build whole cities, which they laid out in checkerboard fashion and filled with typical Greek buildings. An enormous wave of construction took place during the Hellenistic period.

Despite the opportunities they offered, the Hellenistic monarchies were hampered by their artificial origins. Their failure to win the political loyalty of their Greek subjects and their policy of wooing Greeks with lucrative positions encouraged a feeling of uprootedness and self-serving individualism among Greek immigrants. Once a Greek had left home to take service with, for instance, the army or the bureaucracy of the Ptolemies, he had no incentive beyond his pay and the comforts of life in Egypt to keep him there. If the Seleucid king offered him more money or a promotion, he might well accept it and take his talents to Asia Minor. Why not? In the realm of the Seleucids he, a Greek, would find the same sort of life and environment that the kingdom of the Ptolemies had provided him. Thus professional Greek soldiers and administrators were very mobile and apt to look to their own interests, not their kingdom's.

As long as Greeks continued to replenish their professional ranks, the kingdoms remained strong. In the process they drew an immense amount of talent from the Greek peninsula, draining the vitality of the Greek homeland. However, the Hellenistic monarchies could not keep recruiting Greeks forever, in spite of their wealth and willingness to spend lavishly to attract and keep the Greeks coming. In time the huge surge of immigration slowed greatly. Even then the Hellenistic monarchs were reluctant to recruit Easterners to fill posts normally held by Greeks. The result was at first the stagnation of the Hellenistic world and finally, after 202 B.C., collapse in the face of the young and vigorous Roman Republic.

Greeks and Easterners

The Greeks in Asia and Africa were a minority, and Hellenistic cities were islands of Greek culture in an Eastern sea. But Hellenistic monarchies were remarkably successful in at least partially Hellenizing Easterners and spreading a uniform culture throughout the East, a culture to which Rome eventually fell heir. The prevailing institutions, laws, and language of the East became Greek. Indeed, the Near East had seen nothing comparable since the days when Mesopotamian culture had spread throughout the area.

Yet the spread of Greek culture was wider than it was deep. At best it was a veneer, thicker in some places than in others. Hellenistic kingdoms were never entirely unified in language, customs, and thought. Greek culture took firmest hold along the shores of the Mediterranean, but in central

Asia, in Persia and Bactria, it eventually gave way to Eastern cultures.

The Ptolemies in Egypt made no effort to spread Greek culture, and unlike other Hellenistic kings, they were not city builders. Indeed, they founded only the city of Ptolemais near Thebes (see Map 6.2). At first the native Egyptian population, the descendants of the pharaoh's people, retained their traditional language, outlook, religion, and way of life. Initially untouched by Hellenism, the natives continued to be the foundation of the state: they fed it by their labor in the fields and financed its operations with their taxes.

Throughout the third century B.C., the Greek upper class had little to do with the native population. Many Greek bureaucrats established homes in Alexandria and Ptolemais, where they managed finances, served as magistrates, and administered the law. Other Greeks settled in military colonies and supplied the monarchy with fighting men.

In the second century B.C. Greeks and native Egyptians began to intermarry and mingle their cultures. The language of the native population influenced Greek, and many Greeks adopted Egyptian religion and ways of life. Simultaneously natives adopted Greek customs and language and began to play a role in the administration of the kingdom and even to serve in the army. Although many Greeks and Egyptians remained aloof from one another, the overall result was the evolution of a widespread Greco-Egyptian culture.

Meanwhile, in order to nurture a vigorous and large Greek population, the Seleucid kings established many cities and military colonies in western Asia and along the banks of the Tigris and Euphrates rivers. Especially important to the Seleucids were the military colonies, for they depended on Greeks to defend the kingdom. The Seleucids had no elaborate plan for Hellenizing the native population, but the arrival of so many Greeks was bound to have an impact. Seleucid military colonies were generally founded near native villages, thus exposing Easterners to all aspects of Greek life. Many Easterners found Greek political and cultural forms attractive and imitated them. In western Asia and Syria, for instance, numerous native villages and towns developed along Greek lines, and some of them became Hellenized cities. Farther east the Greek kings who replaced the Seleucids in the third century B.C. spread Greek culture to their neighbors, even into the Indian subcontinent.

For Easterners the prime advantage of Greek culture was its pervasiveness. The Greek language became the common speech of the East. A common dialect called *koine* even influenced the speech of peninsular Greece itself. Greek became the speech of the royal court, bureaucracy, and armed forces. It was also the speech of commerce: any Easterner who wanted to compete in business had to learn it. As early as the third century B.C., some Greek cities were giving citizenship to Hellenized natives.

The vast majority of Hellenized Easterners, however, took only the externals of Greek culture while retaining the essentials of their own way of life. Though Greeks and Easterners adapted to each other's ways, there was never a true fusion of cultures. Nonetheless, each found useful things in the civilization of the other, and the two fertilized each other. This fertilization, this mingling of Greek and Eastern elements, is what makes Hellenistic culture unique and distinctive.

THE ECONOMIC SCOPE OF THE HELLENISTIC WORLD

Alexander's conquest of the Persian Empire not only changed the political face of the ancient world, it also brought the East fully into the sphere of Greek economics. Yet the Hellenistic period did not see a revolution in the way people lived and worked. The material demands of Hellenistic society remained as simple as those of Athenian society in the fifth century B.C. Clothes and furniture were essentially unchanged, as were household goods, tools, and jewelry. The real achievement of Alexander and his successors was linking East and West in a broad commercial network. The spread of Greeks throughout the East created new markets and stimulated trade. The economic unity of the Hellenistic world, like its cultural bonds, would later prove valuable to the Romans.

Commerce

Alexander's conquest of the Persian Empire had immediate effects on trade. In the Persian capitals Alexander found vast sums of gold, silver, and other treasure. This wealth financed the creation of new cities, the building of roads, and the development of harbors. Most of the great monarchies coined their money on the Attic standard. Thus much of the money used in Hellenistic kingdoms had the same value, and traders were less in need of moneychangers than in the days when each major power coined money on a different standard. As a result of Alexander's conquests, geographical knowledge of the East increased dramatically, making the East far better known to the Greeks than previously. The Greeks spread their law and methods of transacting business throughout the East. Whole new fields lay open to Greek merchants, who eagerly took advantage of the new opportunities. Commerce itself was a leading area where Greeks and Easterners met on grounds of common interest. In bazaars, ports, and trading centers Greeks learned of Eastern customs and traditions while spreading knowledge of their own culture.

The Seleucid and Ptolemaic dynasties traded as far afield as India, Arabia, and Africa. Overland trade with India and Arabia was conducted by caravan and was largely in the hands of Easterners. The caravan trade never dealt in bulk items or essential commodities; only luxury goods were transported in this very expensive fashion. Once the goods reached the Hellenistic monarchies, Greek merchants took a hand in the trade.

In the early Hellenistic period the Seleucids and Ptolemies ensured that the caravan trade was efficient. Later in the period—a time of increased war and confusion—they left the caravans unprotected. Taking advantage of this situation, Palmyra in the Syrian desert and Nabataean Petra in Arabia arose as caravan states. Such states protected the caravans from bandits and marauders and served as dispersal areas of caravan goods.

The Ptolemies discovered how to use monsoon winds to establish direct contact with India. One hardy merchant, who sailed from Egypt, left a firsthand account of sailing this important maritime link:

Hippalos, the pilot, observing the position of the ports and the conditions of the sea, first discovered how to sail across the ocean. Concerning the winds of the ocean in this region, when with us the Etesian winds begin, in India a wind between southwest and south, named for Hippalos, sets in from the open sea. From then until now some mariners set forth from Kanes and some from the Cape of Spices. Those sailing to

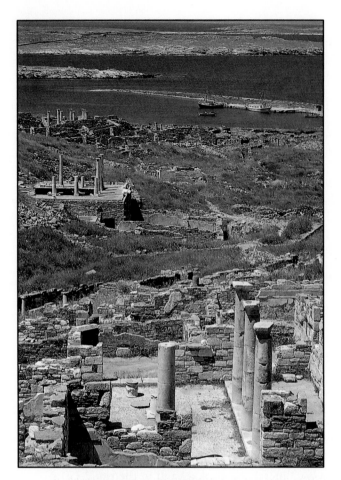

Harbor and Warehouses at Delos During the Hellenistic period Delos became a thriving trading center. Shown here is the row of warehouses at water's edge. From Delos cargoes were shipped to virtually every part of the Mediterranean. *(Source: Adam Woolfitt/Woodfin Camp)*

Dimurikes in southern India throw the bow of the ship farther out to sea. Those bound for Barygaza and the realm of the Sakas in northern India hold to the land no more than three days; and if the wind remains favorable, they hold the same course through the outer sea, and they sail along past the previously mentioned gulfs.[2]

Although this sea route never replaced overland caravan traffic, it kept direct relations with Europe alive, stimulating the exchange of ideas as well as goods.

More economically important than exotic trade were commercial dealings in essential commodities like raw materials, grain, and industrial products. The Hellenistic monarchies usually raised enough grain for their own needs as well as a surplus for export. For the cities of Greece and the Aegean this trade in grain was essential because many could not grow enough. Fortunately for them, abundant wheat supplies were available nearby in Egypt and in the Crimea in southern Russia.

The large-scale wars of the Hellenistic period often interrupted both the production and the distribution of grain. This was especially true when Alexander's successors were trying to carve out kingdoms. In addition natural calamities, such as excessive rain or drought, frequently damaged harvests. Throughout the Hellenistic period famine or severe food shortage remained a grim possibility.

Most trade in bulk commodities was seaborne, and the Hellenistic merchant ship was the workhorse of the day. Maritime trade gave rise to other industries and trades: sailors, shipbuilders, dock workers, merchants, accountants, teamsters, and pirates. Piracy was always a factor in the Hellenistic world and remained so until Rome extended its naval power throughout the eastern Mediterranean.

Slaves were a staple of Hellenistic trade. The wars provided prisoners for the slave market; to a lesser extent so did kidnapping and capture by pirates. The number of slaves involved cannot be estimated, but there is no doubt that slavery flourished. Both old Greek states and new Hellenistic kingdoms were ready slave markets, as was Rome when it emerged triumphant from the Second Punic War (see page 181). The war took a huge toll on Italian manpower, and Rome bought slaves in vast numbers to replace fieldworkers.

Throughout the Mediterranean world, slaves were almost always in demand. Only the Ptolemies discouraged both the trade and slavery itself, and they did so only for economic reasons. Their system had no room for slaves, who would only have competed with free labor. Otherwise, slave labor was to be found in the cities and temples of the Hellenistic world, in the factories and fields, and in the homes of wealthy people. In Italy and some parts of the East, slaves performed manual labor for large estates and worked the mines. They constituted a vital part of the Hellenistic economy.

Industry

Although demand for goods increased during the Hellenistic period, no new techniques of production appear to have developed. The discoveries of Hellenistic mathematicians and thinkers failed to produce any significant corresponding technological development. Manual labor, not machinery, continued to turn out the raw materials and few manufactured goods used by the Hellenistic world. Human labor was so cheap and so abundant that kings had no incentive to encourage the invention and manufacture of labor-saving machinery.

Pottery remained an important commodity, and most of it was made locally. The pottery used in the kitchen, the coarse ware, did not change at all. Indeed, it is impossible to tell whether specimens of this type of pottery are Hellenic or Hellenistic. Fancier pots and bowls decorated with a shiny black glaze came into use during the Hellenistic period. This ware originated in Athens, but potters in other places began to imitate its style, heavily cutting into the Athenian market. In the second century B.C., a red-glazed ware, often called "Samian," burst on the market and soon dominated it. Athens still held its own, however, in the production of fine pottery. Despite the change in pottery styles, the method of production of all pottery, whether plain or fine, remained essentially unchanged.

Although new techniques of production and wider use of machinery in industry did not occur, the volume of goods produced increased in the Hellenistic period. Small manufacturing establishments existed in nearly all parts of the Hellenistic world.

Agriculture

Hellenistic kings paid special attention to agriculture. Much of their revenue was derived from the produce of royal land, rents paid by the tenants of royal land, and taxation of agricultural land. Some Hellenistic kings even sought out and supported agricultural experts. The Ptolemies, for instance, sponsored experiments on seed grain, selecting seeds that seemed hardy and productive and trying to improve their characteristics. Hellenistic authors wrote handbooks discussing how farms and large estates could most profitably be run. These handbooks described soil types, covered the proper times for planting and reaping, and discussed care of farm animals. Whether these efforts had any impact on the average farmer, however, is difficult to determine.

The Ptolemies made the greatest strides in agriculture, but their success was largely political. Egypt had a strong tradition of central authority dating back to the pharaohs. The Ptolemies inherited this tradition and tightened the centralization. They could decree what crops Egyptian farmers would plant and what animals would be raised, and they had the power to carry out their commands. The Ptolemies recognized the need for well-planned and constant irrigation, and much native labor went into the digging and maintenance of canals and ditches. The Ptolemies also reclaimed a great deal of land from the desert, including the Fayum, a dry lake bed near the Nile.

The centralized authority of the Ptolemies accounts for the occurrence of agricultural advances

Scene from Daily Life Art in the Hellenistic period often pursued two themes: increased realism and scenes from daily life. This statuette illustrates both. Here a peasant follows his donkey, which has fallen, to sell his grapes in the city. The peasant saves his grapes with one hand while trying to pull the donkey to its feet with the other. *(Source: National Archaeological Museum, Athens)*

at the local level in Egypt. But such progress was not possible in any other Hellenistic monarchy. Despite royal interest in agriculture and a studied approach to it in the Hellenistic period, there is no evidence that agricultural productivity increased. Whether Hellenistic agricultural methods had any influence on Eastern practices is unknown.

RELIGION IN THE HELLENISTIC WORLD

In religion Hellenism gave Easterners far less than the East gave the Greeks. At first the Hellenistic period saw the spread of Greek religious cults throughout the East. When Hellenistic kings founded cities, they also built temples and established new cults and priesthoods for the old Olympian gods. The new cults enjoyed the prestige of being the religion of the conquerors, and they were supported by public money. The most attractive aspects of the Greek cults were their rituals and festivities. Greek cults sponsored literary, musical, and athletic contests, which were staged in beautiful surroundings among impressive Greek buildings. In short, the cults offered bright and lively entertainment, both intellectual and physical. They fostered Greek culture and traditional sports and thus were a splendid means of displaying Greek civilization in the East.

Despite various advantages, Greek cults suffered from some severe shortcomings. They were primarily concerned with ritual. Participation in the civic cults did not even require belief (see page 139). On the whole, the civic cults neither appealed to religious emotions nor embraced matters such as sin and redemption. Greek mystery religions helped fill this gap, but the centers of these religions were in old Greece. Although the new civic cults were lavish in pomp and display, they could not satisfy deep religious feelings or spiritual yearnings.

Even though the Greeks participated in the new cults for cultural reasons, they felt little genuine religious attachment to them. In comparison with the emotional and sometimes passionate religions of the East, the Greek cults seemed sterile. Greeks increasingly sought solace from other sources. Educated and thoughtful people turned to philosophy as a guide to life; others turned to superstition, magic, or astrology. Still others might shrug

and speak of *Tyche,* which meant "Fate" or "Chance," "Doom," or "Fortune"—a capricious and sometimes malevolent force.

In view of the spiritual decline of Greek religion, it is surprising that Eastern religions did not make more immediate headway among the Greeks, but at first they did not. Although Hellenistic Greeks clung to their own cults as expressions of their Greekness rather than for any ethical principles, they did not rush to embrace native religions. Only in the second century B.C., after a century of exposure to Eastern religions, did Greeks begin to adopt them.

Nor did Hellenistic kings make any effort to spread Greek religion among their Eastern subjects. The Greeks always considered religion a matter best left to the individual. Greek cults were attractive only to those socially aspiring Easterners who adopted Greek culture for personal advancement. Otherwise Easterners were little affected by Greek religion. Nor did native religions suffer from the arrival of the Greeks. Some Hellenistic kings limited the power of native priesthoods, but they also subsidized some Eastern cults with public money. Alexander the Great actually reinstated several Eastern cults that the Persians had suppressed.

The only significant junction of Greek and Eastern religious traditions was the growth and spread of new "mystery religions," so called because they featured a body of ritual not to be divulged to anyone not initiated into the cult. The new mystery cults incorporated aspects of both Greek and Eastern religions and had broad appeal for both Greeks and Easterners who yearned for personal immortality. Since the Greeks were already familiar with old mystery cults, such as the Eleusinian mysteries in Attica, the new cults did not strike them as alien or barbarian. Familiar, too, was the concept of preparation for an initiation. Devotees of the Eleusinian mysteries and other such cults had to prepare themselves mentally and physically before entering the gods' presence. Thus the mystery cults fitted well with Greek usage.

The new religions enjoyed one tremendous advantage over the old Greek mystery cults. Whereas old Greek mysteries were tied to particular places, such as Eleusis, the new religions spread throughout the Hellenistic world. People did not have to undertake long and expensive pilgrimages just to become members of the religion. In that sense the new mystery religions came to the people, for temples of the new deities sprang up wherever Greeks lived.

The mystery religions all claimed to save their adherents from the worst that fate could do and promised life for the soul after death. They all had a single concept in common: the belief that by the rites of initiation devotees became united with the god, who had died and risen from the dead. The sacrifice of the god and his or her victory over death saved the devotee from eternal death. Similarly, all mystery religions demanded a period of preparation in which the convert strove to become holy—that is, to live by the religion's precepts. Once aspirants had prepared themselves, they went through an initiation in which they learned the secrets of the religion. The initiation was usually a ritual of great emotional intensity, baptism into a new life.

The Eastern mystery religions that took the Hellenistic world by storm were the Egyptian cults of Serapis and Isis. Serapis, who was invented by King Ptolemy, combined elements of the Egyptian god Osiris with aspects of the Greek gods Zeus, Pluto (the prince of the underworld), and Asclepius (god of medicine). Serapis was believed to be the judge of souls, who rewarded virtuous and righteous people with eternal life. Like Asclepius, he was a god of healing. Serapis became an international god, and many Hellenistic Greeks thought of him as Zeus. Associated with Isis and Serapis was Anubis, the old Egyptian god who, like Charon in the Greek pantheon, guided the souls of initiates to the realm of eternal life.

The cult of Isis enjoyed even wider appeal than that of Serapis. Isis, wife of Osiris, claimed to have conquered Tyche and promised to save any mortal who came to her. She became the most important goddess of the Hellenistic world, and her worship was very popular among women. Her priests claimed that she bestowed on humanity the gift of civilization and founded law and literature. She was the goddess of marriage, conception, and childbirth—like Serapis, a deity who promised to save the souls of her believers.

There was neither conflict between Greek and Eastern religions nor wholesale acceptance of one or the other. Nonetheless, Greeks and Easterners noticed similarities among one another's deities and assumed that they were worshiping the same gods in different garb. These tendencies toward religious universalism and the desire for personal immortality would prove significant when the Hellenistic world came under the sway of Rome, for Hellenistic developments paved the way for the spread of Christianity.

PHILOSOPHY AND THE COMMON MAN

Philosophy during the Hellenic period was the exclusive province of the wealthy, for only they had leisure enough to pursue philosophical studies. During the Hellenistic period, however, philosophy reached out to touch the lives of more men and women than ever before. The reasons for this development were several. Since the ideal of the polis had declined, politics no longer offered people a satisfying intellectual outlet. Moreover, much of Hellenistic life, especially in the new cities of the East, seemed unstable and without venerable traditions. Greeks were far more mobile than they had ever been before, but their very mobility left them feeling uprooted. Many people in search of something permanent, something unchanging in a changing world, turned to philosophy. Another reason for the increased influence of philosophy was the decline of traditional religion and a growing belief in Tyche. To protect against the worst that Tyche could do, many Greeks looked to philosophy, particularly to the Cynics, Epicureans, and Stoics.

Cynics

Undoubtedly the most unusual of the new philosophers were the Cynics, who urged a return to nature. They advised men and women to discard traditional customs and conventions (which were in decline anyway) and live simply. The Cynics believed that by rejecting material things people become free and that nature will provide all necessities.

The founder of the Cynics was Antisthenes (b. ca 440 B.C.), but it was Diogenes of Sinope (ca 412–323 B.C.), one of the most colorful men of the period, who spread the philosophy. Diogenes came to Athens to study philosophy and soon evolved his own ideas on the ideal life. He hit on the notion that happiness was possible only by liv-

Tyche This statue depicts Tyche as the city-goddess of Antioch, a new Hellenistic foundation of the Seleucid king Antiochus. Some Hellenistic Greeks worshiped Tyche in the hope that she would be kind to them. Philosophers tried to free people from her whimsies. Antiochus tried to win her favor by honoring her. *(Source: Photo Vatican Museums)*

the streets and marketplaces. They more than any other philosophical group tried to reach the common people. As part of their return to nature they often did without warm clothing, sufficient food, or adequate housing, which they considered unnecessary. The Cynics also tried to break down political barriers by declaring that people owed no allegiance to any city or monarchy. Rather, they said, all people are cosmopolitan—that is, citizens of the world. The Cynics reached across political boundaries to create a community of people, sharing the common traits of all humanity and living as close to nature as humanly possible. The Cynics set a striking example of how people could turn away from materialism. Although comparatively few men and women could follow such rigorous precepts, the Cynics influenced all the other major schools of philosophy.

Epicureans

Epicurus (340–270 B.C.), who founded his own school of philosophy at Athens, based his view of life on scientific theories. Accepting Democritus's theory that the universe is composed of indestructible particles, Epicurus put forth a naturalistic theory of the universe. Although he did not deny the existence of the gods, he taught that they had no effect on human life. The essence of Epicurus's belief was that the principal good of human life is pleasure, which he defined as the absence of pain. Epicurus did not advocate drunken revels or sensual dissipation, which he thought actually cause pain. Instead, he warned that any violent emotion is undesirable. Drawing on the teachings of the Cynics, he advocated mild self-discipline. Even poverty he considered good, as long as people have enough food, clothing, and shelter. Epicurus also taught that individuals can most easily attain peace and serenity by ignoring the outside world and looking inward, to their personal feelings and reactions. Thus Epicureanism led to quietism.

Epicureanism taught its followers to ignore politics and issues, for politics led to tumult, which would disturb the soul. Although the Epicureans thought that the state originated through a social contract among individuals, they did not care about the political structure of the state. Content to live in a democracy, oligarchy, monarchy, or whatever, they never speculated about the ideal state. Their ideals stood outside all political forms.

ing according to nature and forgoing luxuries. He attacked social conventions because he considered them contrary to nature. Throughout Greece he gained fame for the rigorous way in which he put his beliefs into practice.

Diogenes did not establish a philosophical school in the manner of Plato and Aristotle. Instead he and his followers took their teaching to

Stoics

Opposed to the passivity of the Epicureans, Zeno (335–262 B.C.), a philosopher from Citium in Cyprus, advanced a different concept of human beings and the universe. When Zeno first came to Athens, he listened avidly to the Cynics. Concluding, however, that the Cynics were extreme, he stayed in Athens to form his own school, the Stoa, named after the building where he preferred to teach.

Stoicism became the most popular Hellenistic philosophy and the one that later captured the mind of Rome. Zeno and his followers considered nature an expression of divine will; in their view people could be happy only when living in accordance with nature. They stressed the unity of man and the universe, stating that all men were brothers and obliged to help one another. Stoicism's science was derived from Heraclitus, but its broad and warm humanity was the work of Zeno and his followers.

Unlike the Epicureans, the Stoics taught that people should participate in politics and worldly affairs. Yet this idea never led to the belief that individuals ought to try to change the order of things. Time and again the Stoics used the image of an actor in a play: the Stoic plays an assigned part and never tries to change the play. To the Stoics the important question was not whether they achieved anything, but whether they lived virtuous lives. Through virtuous living they could triumph over Tyche, for Tyche could destroy achievements but not the nobility of their lives.

Although the Stoics developed the concept of a world order, they thought of it strictly in terms of the individual. Like the Epicureans, they were indifferent to specific political forms. They believed that people should do their duty to the state in which they found themselves. The universal state they preached about was ethical, not political. The Stoics' most significant practical achievement was the creation of the concept of natural law. The Stoics concluded that since all men were brothers, partook of divine reason, and were in harmony with the universe, one law—a part of the natural order of life—governed them all.

The Stoic concept of a universal state governed by natural law is one of the finest heirlooms that the Hellenistic world passed on to Rome. The Stoic concept of natural law, of one law for all people, became a valuable tool when the Romans began to deal with many different peoples with different laws. The ideal of the universal state gave the Romans a rationale for extending their empire to the farthest reaches of the world. The duty of individuals to their fellows served the citizens of the Roman Empire as the philosophical justification for doing their duty. In this respect, too, the real fruit of Hellenism was to ripen only under the cultivation of Rome.

HELLENISTIC WOMEN

With the growth of monarchy in the Hellenistic period came a major new development: the importance of royal women, many of whom played an active part in political and diplomatic life. In the Hellenic period the polis had replaced kingship, except at Sparta, and queens were virtually unknown apart from myth and legend. Even in Sparta queens did not participate in politics. Hellenistic queens, however, did exercise political power, either in their own right or by manipulating their husbands. Many Hellenistic queens were depicted as willful or ruthless, especially in power struggles over the throne, and in some cases those charges are accurate. Other Hellenistic royal women, however, set an example of courage and nobility.

The example of the queens had a profound effect on Hellenistic attitudes toward women in general. In fact, the Hellenistic period saw a great expansion in social and economic opportunities for women. More women than ever before received educations that enabled them to enter medicine and other professions. Literacy among women increased dramatically, and their options expanded accordingly. Some won fame as poets, while others studied with philosophers and contributed to the intellectual life of the age. These developments, however, touched only wealthy women. Poor women—and probably the majority of women—were barely literate, if literate at all.

Women began to participate in politics on a limited basis. Often they served as priestesses, as they had in the Hellenic period, but they also began to serve in civil capacities. For their services to the state they received public acknowledgment. Women sometimes received honorary citizenship from foreign cities because of aid given in times of crisis. Few women achieved these honors, how-

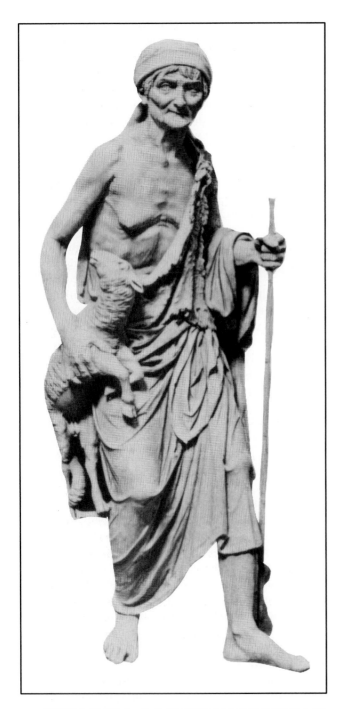

Old Shepherdess Daily life for the poor and elderly was as hard in the Hellenistic period as in other times. Here a tough, old, scantily clothed shepherdess brings a sheep to market. Such scenes were common during the period; but art, not written sources, has preserved them for posterity. *(Source: Alinari/Art Resource)*

ever, and those who did were from the upper classes.

This major development was not due to male enlightenment. Although Hellenistic philosophy addressed itself to many new questions, the position of women was not one of them. The Stoics, in spite of their theory of the brotherhood of man, thought of women as men's inferiors. Only the Cynics, who waged war on all accepted customs, treated women as men's equals. The Cynics were interested in women as individuals, not as members of a family or as citizens of the state. Their view did not make much headway. Like other aspects of Cynic philosophy, this attitude was more admired than followed.

The new prominence of women was largely due to their increased participation in economic affairs. During the Hellenistic period some women took part in commercial transactions. Nonetheless, they still lived under legal handicaps. In Egypt, for example, a Greek woman needed a male guardian to buy, sell, or lease land, to borrow money, and to represent her in other transactions. Yet often such a guardian was present only to fulfill the letter of the law. The woman was the real agent and handled the business being transacted. In Hellenistic Sparta, women accumulated large fortunes and vast amounts of land. As early as the beginning of the Hellenistic period women owned two-fifths of the land of Laconia. Spartan women, however, were exceptional. In most other areas, even women who were wealthy in their own right were formally under the protection of a male relative.

These changes do not amount to a social revolution. Women had begun to participate in business, politics, and legal activities. Yet such women were rare and labored under handicaps unknown to men. Even so, it was a start.

HELLENISTIC SCIENCE

The area in which Hellenistic culture achieved its greatest triumphs was science. Here, too, the ancient Near East made contributions to Greek thought. The patient observations of the Babylonians, who for generations had scanned the skies, had provided the raw materials for Thales' speculations, which were the foundation of Hellenistic astronomy. The most notable of the Hellenistic astronomers was Aristarchus of Samos (ca 310–230 B.C.), who was educated in Aristotle's school. Aristarchus concluded that the sun is far larger than the earth and that the stars are enormously distant from the earth. He argued against Aristotle's view that the earth is the center of the universe. Instead Aristarchus propounded the *heliocentric theory*— that the earth and planets revolve around the sun. His work is all the more impressive because he lacked even a rudimentary telescope. Aristarchus had only the human eye and brain, but they were more than enough.

Aristarchus's theories, however, did not persuade the ancient world. In the second century A.D., Claudius Ptolemy, a mathematician and astronomer in Alexandria, accepted Aristotle's theory of the earth as the center of the universe, and that view prevailed for 1,400 years. Moreover, Ptolemy based his conclusions on extensive observations of the stars and planets, which formed the scientific basis of his work. Aristarchus's heliocentric theory lay dormant until resurrected by the brilliant Polish astronomer Nicolaus Copernicus (1473–1543).

In geometry Hellenistic thinkers discovered little that was new, but Euclid (ca 300 B.C.), a mathematician who lived in Alexandria, compiled a valuable textbook of existing knowledge. His book *The Elements of Geometry* has exerted immense influence on European civilization, for it rapidly became the standard introduction to geometry. Generations of students, from the Hellenistic period to the present, have learned the essentials of geometry from it.

The greatest thinker of the Hellenistic period was Archimedes (ca 287–212 B.C.), who was a clever inventor as well. He lived in Syracuse in Sicily and watched Rome emerge as a power in the Mediterranean. When the Romans laid siege to Syracuse in the Second Punic War (see page 181), Archimedes invented a number of machines to thwart the Roman army. His catapults threw rocks large enough to sink ships and disrupt battle lines. His grappling devices lifted warships out of the water. In the Hellenistic period the practical applications of principles of mechanics were primarily military, for the building of artillery and siege engines. In a more peaceful vein, Archimedes invented the Archimedean screw and the compound pulley. Plutarch described Archimedes' dramatic demonstration of how easily his pulley could move huge weights with little effort:

A three-masted merchant ship of the royal fleet had been hauled on land by hard work and many hands. Archimedes put aboard her many men and the usual freight. He sat far away from her; without haste, but gently working a compound pulley with his hand, he drew her towards him smoothly and without faltering, just as though she were running on the surface of the sea.[3]

Archimedes was far more interested in pure mathematics than in practical inventions. His mathematical research, covering many fields, was his greatest contribution to thought. In his book *On Plane Equilibriums* Archimedes dealt for the first time with the basic principles of mechanics, including the principle of the lever. He once said that if he were given a lever and a suitable place to stand, he could move the world. In his treatise *Sand-Counter* Archimedes devised a system to express large numbers, a difficult matter considering the deficiencies of Greek numerical notation. *Sand-Counter* also discussed the heliocentric theory of Aristarchus. With his treatise *On Floating Bodies* Archimedes founded the science of hydrostatics. He concluded that whenever a solid floats in a liquid, the weight of the solid is equal to the volume of liquid displaced. The way he made his discovery has become famous:

When he was devoting his attention to this problem, he happened to go to a public bath. When he climbed down into the bathtub there, he noticed that water in the tub equal to the bulk of his body flowed out. Thus, when he observed this method of solving the problem, he did not wait. Instead, moved with joy, he sprang out of the tub, and rushing home naked he kept indicating in a loud voice that he had indeed discovered what he was seeking. For while running he was shouting repeatedly in Greek, "eureka, eureka" ("I have found it, I have found it").[4]

Archimedes was willing to share his work with others, among them Eratosthenes (285–ca 204 B.C.), a man of almost universal interests. From his native Cyrene in North Africa, Eratosthenes traveled to Athens, where he studied philosophy and mathematics. He refused to join any of the philosophical schools, for he was interested in too many things to follow any particular dogma. Hence his thought was eclectic, taking doctrines from many schools of thought. Around 245 B.C. King Ptolemy invited Eratosthenes to Alexandria. The Ptolemies

The Celestial Globe In Greek mythology the god Atlas held the world on his strong shoulders, thereby preventing it from falling. Hellenistic scientists formed a very accurate idea of the shape and dimension of the earth. Here Atlas holds the globe, which rests on its axis and displays the skies, with figures representing constellations, as well as the equator, tropics, and polar circles. *(Source: National Museum, Naples/Alinari/Art Resource)*

had done much to make Alexandria an intellectual, cultural, and scientific center. They had established a lavish library and museum, undoubtedly the greatest seat of learning in the Hellenistic world. At the crown's expense, the Ptolemies maintained a number of distinguished scholars and poets. Eratosthenes came to Alexandria to become librarian of the royal library, a position of great prestige. While there he continued his mathematical work and by letter struck up a friendship with Archimedes.

Unlike his friend Archimedes, Eratosthenes did not devote his life entirely to mathematics, although he never lost interest in it. He used mathematics to further the geographical studies for which he is most famous. He calculated the circumference of the earth geometrically, estimating it as about 24,675 miles. He was not wrong by much: the earth is actually 24,860 miles in circumference. Eratosthenes also concluded that the earth is a spherical globe, that the land mass is roughly four-sided, and that the land is surrounded by ocean. He discussed the shapes and sizes of land and ocean and the irregularities of the earth's surface. He drew a map of the earth and used his own system of explaining the divisions of the earth's land mass.

Using geographical information gained by Alexander the Great's scientists, Eratosthenes tried to fit the East into Greek geographical knowledge. Although for some reason he ignored the western Mediterranean and Europe, he declared that a ship could sail from Spain either around Africa to India or directly westward to India. Not until the great days of Western exploration did sailors such as Vasco da Gama and Magellan actually prove Eratosthenes' theories. Like Eratosthenes, Greek geographers also turned their attention southward to Africa. During this period the people of the Mediterranean learned of the climate and customs of Ethiopia and gleaned some scant information about equatorial Africa.

In his life and work Eratosthenes exemplifies the range and vitality of Hellenistic science. His varied interests included the cultural and humanistic as well as the purely scientific. Although his chief interest was in the realm of speculative thought, he did not ignore the practical. He was quite willing to deal with old problems and to break new ground.

In the Hellenistic period the scientific study of botany had its origin. Aristotle's pupil Theophras-

SPREAD OF HELLENISM

338 B.C.	Battle of Chaeronea: Philip II of Macedon conquers Greece
336 B.C.	Assassination of Philip II; Alexander III (the Great) inherits Macedonian crown
334–330 B.C.	Alexander overthrows the Persian Empire
334 B.C.	Battle of Granicus River
333 B.C.	Battle of Issus: Alexander conquers Asia Minor
331 B.C.	Battle of Gaugamela: Alexander conquers Mesopotamia
330 B.C.	Fall of Persepolis, principal Persian capital
	Fall of Ecbatana, last Persian capital
330–326 B.C.	Alexander conquers Bactria
326 B.C.	Alexander enters India; mutiny of his troops at the Hyphasis River
323 B.C.	Alexander dies in Babylon at the age of 32
323–275 B.C.	Empire divided into three monarchies; new dynasties founded by Ptolemy I (Egypt), Antigonus Gonatar (Macedonia, Asia Minor), and Seleucus I (Mesopotamia)
3d century B.C.	Development of the Hellenistic city
ca 300 B.C.	Euclid, *The Elements of Geometry*
ca 300–250 B.C.	Diffusion of philosophy; new schools founded by Epicurus (Epicureans) and Zeno (Stoics)
	Medical advances by Herophilus, Erasistratus, Philinus, and Serapion
263 B.C.	Eumenes of Pergamum wins independence from the Seleucids, establishes the Pergamene monarchy
ca 250–200 B.C.	Scientific advances by Archimedes, Eratosthenes, and Aristarchus of Samos

tus (ca 372–288 B.C.), who became head of the Lyceum, the school established by Aristotle, studied the botanical information made available by Alexander's penetration of the East. Aristotle had devoted a good deal of his attention to zoology, and Theophrastus extended his work to plants. He wrote two books on the subject, *History of Plants* and *Causes of Plants*. He carefully observed phenomena and based his conclusions on what he had actually seen. Theophrastus classified plants and accurately described their parts. He detected the process of germination and realized the importance of climate and soil to plants. Some of Theophrastus's work found its way into agricultural handbooks, but for the most part Hellenistic science did not carry the study of botany any further.

Despite its undeniable brilliance, Hellenistic science suffered from a remarkable weakness almost impossible for practical-minded Americans to understand. Although scientists of this period invented such machines as the air gun, the water organ, and even the steam engine, they never used their discoveries as labor-saving devices. No one has satisfactorily explained why these scientists were so impractical, but one answer is quite possible: they and the rest of society saw no real need for machines. Slave labor, which was abundant, made the use of labor-saving machinery superfluous. Science was applied only to war. Principles of physics were used to build catapults and other siege machinery. Even though Hellenistic science did not lead the ancient world to an industrial revolution, later Hellenistic thinkers preserved the knowledge of these machines and the principles behind them. In so doing, they saved the discoveries of Hellenistic science for the modern age.

HELLENISTIC MEDICINE

The study of medicine flourished during the Hellenistic period, and Hellenistic physicians carried the work of Hippocrates into new areas. Herophilus, who lived in the first half of the third century

B.C., worked at Alexandria and studied the writings of Hippocrates. He accepted Hippocrates' theory of the four humors and approached the study of medicine in a systematic, scientific fashion. He dissected corpses and measured what he observed. He discovered the nervous system and concluded that two types of nerves, motor and sensory, exist. Herophilus also studied the brain, which he considered the center of intelligence, and discerned the cerebrum and cerebellum. His other work dealt with the liver, lungs, and uterus. His younger contemporary, Erasistratus, also conducted research on the brain and nervous system and improved on Herophilus's work. He, too, followed in the tradition of Hippocrates and preferred to let the body heal itself by means of diet and air.

Tower of the Four Winds This remarkable building, which still stands in Athens, was built by an astronomer to serve as a sundial, water-clock, and weather vane. It is one of the few examples of the application of Hellenistic science to daily life. *(Source: Ekdotike Athenon)*

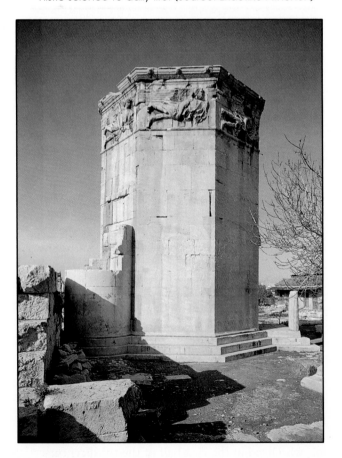

Both Herophilus and Erasistratus were members of the Dogmatic school of medicine at Alexandria. In this school speculation played an important part in research. So, too, did the study of anatomy. To learn more about human anatomy Herophilus and Erasistratus not only dissected corpses but even vivisected criminals whom King Ptolemy contributed for the purpose. *Vivisection*—cutting into the body of a living animal or person—was seen as a necessary cruelty. The Dogmatists argued that the knowledge gained from the suffering of a few evil men benefited many others. Nonetheless, the practice of vivisection seems to have been short-lived, although dissection continued. Better knowledge of anatomy led to improvements in surgery. These advances enabled the Dogmatists to invent new surgical instruments and techniques.

In about 280 B.C. Philinus and Serapion, pupils of Herophilus, led a reaction to the Dogmatists. Believing that the Dogmatists had become too speculative, they founded the Empiric school of medicine at Alexandria. Claiming that the Dogmatists' emphasis on anatomy and physiology was misplaced, they concentrated instead on the observation and cure of illnesses. They also laid heavier stress on the use of drugs and medicine to treat illnesses. Heraclides of Tarentum (perhaps first century B.C.) carried on the Empirical tradition and dedicated himself to observation and the use of medicines. He discovered the benefits of opium and worked with other drugs that relieved pain. He also steadfastly rejected magic as pertinent to the application of drugs and medicines.

Hellenistic medicine had its dark side, for many physicians were money grubbers, fools, and quacks. One of the angriest complaints comes from the days of the Roman Empire:

Of all men only a physician can kill a man with total impunity. Oh no, on the contrary, censure goes to him who dies and he *is guilty of excess, and furthermore* he *is blamed.... Let me not accuse their [physicians'] avarice, their greedy deals with those whose fate hangs in the balance, their setting a price on pain, and their demands for down payment in case of death, and their secret doctrines.*[5]

Abuses already existed in the Hellenistic period. As is true today, many Hellenistic physicians did not take the Hippocratic oath very seriously.

Hellenistic Medicine   During the Hellenistic period, the practice of medicine expanded greatly, and medical research made huge strides. Despite much harm done by quacks and dishonorable physicians, Hellenistic medicine made substantial progress in healing. In this relief, the physician at left treats a patient while other patients wait to the right. The invention of the waiting room also belongs to classical antiquity. *(Source: National Archaeological Museum, Athens)*

The Hellenistic world was also plagued by people who claimed to cure illnesses through incantations and magic. Their potions included such concoctions as blood from the ear of an ass mixed with water to cure fever, or the liver of a cat killed when the moon was waning, and preserved in salt. Broken bones could be cured by applying the ashes of a pig's jawbone to the break. The dung of a goat mixed with old wine would heal broken ribs. One charlatan claimed that he could cure epilepsy by making the patient drink, from the skull of a man who had been killed but not cremated, water drawn from a spring at night. These quacks even claimed that they could cure mental illness. The treatment for a person suffering from melancholy was calf dung boiled in wine. No doubt the patient became too sick to be depressed.

Quacks who prescribed such treatments were very popular but did untold harm to the sick and injured. They and greedy physicians also damaged the reputation of dedicated doctors who honestly and intelligently tried to heal and alleviate pain. The medical abuses that arose in the Hellenistic period were so flagrant that the Romans who later entered the Hellenistic world developed an intense contempt for physicians. The Romans considered the study of Hellenistic medicine beneath the dignity of a Roman, and even as late as the Roman Empire few Romans undertook the study of Greek medicine. Nonetheless the work of men like Herophilus and Serapion made valuable contributions to the knowledge of medicine, and the fruits of their work were preserved and handed on to the world.

SUMMARY

It can safely be said that Philip and Alexander broadened Greek and Macedonian horizons, but not in ways that they had intended. Although Alexander established Macedonian and Greek colonies across western and central Asia for military reasons, they resulted in the spread of Hellenism as a side effect. In the Aegean and Near East the fusion of Greek and Eastern cultures laid the social, intellectual, and cultural foundations on which the Romans would later build. In the heart of the old Persian Empire, Hellenism was only another new influence that was absorbed by older ways of thought and life. Yet overall, in the exchange of ideas and the opportunity for different cultures to learn about one another, a new cosmopolitan society evolved. That society in turn made possible such diverse advances as broadened trade and agriculture, the creation of religious and philosophical ideas that paved the way for Christianity, and greater freedom for women. People of the Hellenistic period also made remarkable advances in science and medicine. They not only built on the achievements of their predecessors, but they also produced one of the most creative intellectual eras of classical antiquity.

NOTES

1. H. Bengtson, *Philipp und Alexander der Grosse* (Munich: Callwey, 1985), p. 7. Unless otherwise credited, all quotations from a foreign language in this chapter are translated by John Buckler.
2. *Periplous of the Erythraian Sea* 57.
3. Ibid., 14.13.
4. Vitruvius, *On Architecture* 9. Pref. 10.
5. Pliny the Elder, *Natural History* 29.8.18, 21.

SUGGESTED READING

General treatments of Hellenistic political, social, and economic history can be found in F. W. Walbank et al., *The Cambridge Ancient History,* 2d ed., vol. 7, pt. 1 (1984). Shorter is F. W. Walbank, *The Hellenistic World* (1981), a fresh appraisal by one of the foremost scholars in the field. The undisputed classic in this area is M. Rostovtzeff, *The Social and Economic History of the Hellenistic World,* 3 vols. (1941). A leading American scholar, E. S. Gruen, has recently chronicled the Roman expansion into the Hellenistic East in *The Hellenistic World and the Coming of Rome,* 2 vols. (1984). Good selections of primary sources in accurate and readable translation can be found in M. M. Austin, *The Hellenistic World from Alexander to the Roman Conquest* (1981), and S. M. Burstein, *The Hellenistic Age from the Battle of Ipsos to the Death of Kleopatra III* (1985).

Each year brings a new crop of biographies of Alexander the Great. Still the best, however, is J. R. Hamilton, *Alexander the Great* (1973). Old but still useful is U. Wilcken, *Alexander the Great* (English translation, 1967), which has had a considerable impact on scholars and students alike. Although many historians have idealized Alexander the Great, recent scholarship has provided a more realistic and unflattering view of him. The foremost expert on Alexander is E. Badian, who has reinterpreted Alexander's career in a variety of journal articles: *Historia* 7 (1958): 425–444; *Classical Quarterly* 52 (1958): 144–157; *Journal of Hellenic Studies* 81 (1961): 16–43; and *Greece and Rome* 12 (1965): 166–182. Badian's analysis of Alexander also appears in *The Cambridge History of Iran,* vol. 2 (1985), chap. 8. Recent political studies of the Hellenistic period include A. B. Bosworth, *Conquest and Empire* (1988), which sets Alexander's career in a broad context, and F. L. Holt, *Alexander the Great and Bactria* (1988), which discusses the formation of a Greco-Macedonian frontier in central Asia. A. K. Bowman, *Egypt After the Pharaohs* (1986), is a readable account of the impact of the Greeks and Macedonians on Egyptian society. The same topic is treated by N. Lewis, a major scholar in the field, in his *Greeks in Ptolemaic Egypt* (1986); and a brief, new study comes from the pen of another major scholar, A. E. Samuel, *The Shifting Sands of History: Interpretations of Ptolemaic Egypt* (1989), which deals with history and historiography. E. V. Hansen, *The Attalids of Pergamon,* 2d ed. (1971), though dated, is still the best treatment of that kingdom. B. Bar-Kochva, *Judas Maccabaeus* (1988), treats the Jewish struggle against the Seleucids and Hellenistic influences. A good portrait of one of the busiest ports in the Hellenistic world can be found in R. Garland, *The Piraeus* (1987).

Much new work has focused on the spread of Hellenism throughout the Near East. Very extensive is A. Kuhrt and S. Sherwin-White, eds., *Hellenism in the East* (1988), which touches on a broad range of topics, including biblical studies, Christianity, and Islam. A. E. Samuels, *The Promise of the West* (1988), studies the connections among Greek, Roman, and Jewish culture and thought and their significance for Western history. P. McKechnie, *Outsiders in the Greek Cities of the Fourth*

Century (1989), provides an interesting study of the so-cial dislocation of the Greeks in the time of Philip II and Alexander the Great.

No specific treatment of women in the Hellenistic world yet exists, but two recent studies shed light on certain aspects of the topic. The first, an illustrated collection of essays covering the whole of the ancient world, is I. van Sertima, ed., *Black Women in Antiquity,* 2d ed. (1985). S. B. Pomeroy, *Women in Hellenistic Egypt* (1984), studies women in the kingdom from which the most ancient evidence has survived.

Two general studies of religion in the Hellenistic world are F. Grant, *Hellenistic Religion: The Age of Syncretism* (1953), and H. J. Rose, *Religion in Greece and Rome* (1959). For the effects of Hellenistic religious developments on Christianity, see A. D. Nock, *Early Gentile Christianity and Its Hellenistic Background* (1964). R. van den Broek et al., eds., *Knowledge of God in the Graeco-Roman World* (1988), is a difficult but rewarding collection of essays that points out how similarly pagans, Hellenistic Jews, and Christians thought about human attempts to know god. R. E. Witt, *Isis in the Graeco-Roman World* (1971), an illustrated volume, studies the origins and growth of the Isis cult; and more specifically, S. K. Heyob, *The Cult of Isis Among Women in the Graeco-Roman World* (1975), explores its popularity among women. The cult of Isis's consort Osiris is the subject of J. G. Griffiths, *The Origins of Osiris and His Cult* (1980); and for the mystery cults in general, see W. Burkert, *Ancient Mystery Cults* (1987), written by one of the finest scholars in the field.

Hellenistic philosophy and science have attracted the attention of a number of scholars, and the various philosophical schools are especially well covered. A new general treatment can be recommended because it deals with the broader question of the role of the intellectual in the Classical and Hellenistic worlds: F. L. Vatai, *Intellectuals in Politics in the Greek World from Early Times to the Hellenistic Age* (1984). Broader is S. Blundell, *The Origin of Civilization in Greek and Roman Thought* (1986), a survey of classical political and social theories through a period of ten centuries, from Aristotle to the Stoics and their Roman successors. A convenient survey of Hellenistic philosophy is A. A. Long, *Hellenistic Philosophy* (1974). F. Sayre, *The Greek Cynics* (1948), focuses on Diogenes' thought and manners; and C. Bailey, *Epicureans* (1926), though decidedly dated, is still a useful study of the origins and nature of Epicureanism. Three treatments of Stoicism are J. Rist, *Stoic Philosophy* (1969); F. H. Sandbach, *The Stoics* (1975); and M. L. Colish, *The Stoic Tradition from Antiquity to the Early Middle Ages,* 2 vols. (1985), which devotes a great deal of attention to the impact of Stoicism on Christianity. A good survey of Hellenistic science is G. E. R. Lloyd, *Greek Science After Aristotle* (1963). Specific studies of major figures can be found in T. L. Heath, *Aristarchos of Samos* (1920), still unsurpassed, and E. J. Dijksterhuis, *Archimedes,* rev. ed. (1987).

7

The Rise of Rome

The Pont du Gard, Roman aqueduct at Nîmes in southern France

*W*ho is so thoughtless and lazy that he does not want to know in what way and with what kind of government the Romans in less than 53 years conquered nearly the entire inhabited world and brought it under their rule—an achievement previously unheard of?"[1] This question was first asked by Polybius, a Greek historian who lived in the second century B.C. With keen awareness Polybius realized that the Romans were achieving something unique in world history.

What was that achievement? Was it simply the creation of a huge empire? Hardly. The Persians had done the same thing. For that matter, Alexander the Great had conquered vast territories in a shorter time. Was it the creation of a superior culture? Even the Romans admitted that in matters of art, literature, philosophy, and culture they learned from the Greeks. Rome's achievement lay in the ability of the Romans not only to conquer peoples but to incorporate them into the Roman system. In other words, Rome succeeded where the Greek polis had failed. Unlike the Greeks, who refused to share citizenship, the Romans extended their citizenship first to the Italians and later to the peoples of the provinces. With that citizenship went Roman government and law. Rome created a single state that embraced the entire Mediterranean area.

Nor was Rome's achievement limited to antiquity. Rome's law, language, and administrative practices were a precious heritage to medieval and modern Europe. London, Paris, Vienna, and many other modern European cities began as Roman colonies or military camps. When the founding fathers of the United States created the American Republic, they looked to Rome as a model. On the dark side, Napoleon and Mussolini paid their own tribute to Rome by aping its forms. Whether founding fathers or modern autocrats, all were acknowledging admiration for the breadth of Roman achievement.

Roman history is usually divided into two periods: the Republic, the age in which Rome grew from a small city-state to ruler of an empire, and the Empire, the period when the republican constitution gave way to constitutional monarchy.

■ How did Rome rise to greatness?

■ What effects did the conquest of the Mediterranean have on the Romans themselves?

■ Why did the republic collapse?

These questions are addressed in this chapter.

THE LAND AND THE SEA

To the west of Greece the boot-shaped peninsula of Italy, with Sicily at its toe, occupies the center of the Mediterranean basin. As Map 7.1 shows, Italy and Sicily thrust southward toward Africa. The distance between southwestern Sicily and the northern African coast is at one point only about a hundred miles. Italy and Sicily literally divide the Mediterranean in two and form the focal point between the halves.

Like Greece and other Mediterranean lands, Italy enjoys a genial, almost subtropical climate. The winters are rainy, but the summer months are dry. Because of the climate, the rivers of Italy usually carry little water during the summer, and some go entirely dry. Clearly these small rivers were unsuitable for regular, large-scale shipping. Italian rivers never became major thoroughfares for commerce and communications.

Geography encouraged Italy to look to the western Mediterranean. In the north Italy is protected by the Apennine Mountains, which break off from the Alps and form a natural barrier. The Apennines retarded but did not prevent peoples from penetrating Italy from the north. Throughout history, in modern times as well as ancient, various invaders have entered Italy by this route. North of the Apennines lies the Po Valley, an important part of modern Italy. In antiquity this valley did not become Roman territory until late in the history of the Republic. From the north the Apennines run southward the entire length of the Italian boot. They virtually cut off access to the Adriatic Sea and further induced Italy to look west to Spain and Carthage rather than east to Greece.

MAP 7.1 Italy and the City of Rome The geographical configuration of the Italian peninsula shows how Rome stood astride north-south communications and how the state that united Italy stood poised to move into Sicily and northern Africa.

ALPS

APENNINES

Po

Arno

UMBRIA

ETRURIA

PICENUM

SABINI

AEQUI VESTINI

Veii

Rome

SAMNIUM

LATIUM

CAMPANIA

APULIA

CALABRIA

Tarentum

LUCANIA

CORSICA

SARDINIA

Tyrrhenian Sea

BRUTTIUM

Messana

SICILY

Syracuse

Mediterranean Sea

Carthage

Cape
Bon

NORTH AFRICA

Adriatic Sea

Rome

0   500   1000 M.

0   1500   3000 Ft.

FIELD OF MARS

QUIRINAL HILL

VIMINAL HILL

CAPITOLINE MT.

Tiber

Senate House

Forum

Regia

ESQUILINE MT.

Temple of
Jupiter

JANICULUM

PALATINE MT.

CAELIAN MT.

Circus
Maximus

AVENTINE MT.

0   50   100 Km.

0   50   100 Mi.

——— Roman boundary before the Punic wars

——— Roman boundary before Augustus

——— Major road

Even though most of the land is mountainous, the hill country is not as inhospitable as are the Greek highlands. In antiquity the general fertility of the soil and its extent provided the basis for a large population. Nor did the mountains of Italy so carve up the land as to prevent the development of political unity. Geography proved kinder to Italy than to Greece.

In their southward course the Apennines leave two broad and fertile plains, those of Latium and Campania. These plains attracted settlers and invaders from the time when peoples began to move into Italy. Among these peoples were the Romans, who established their city on the Tiber River in Latium. This site enjoyed several advantages. The Tiber provided Rome with a constant source of water. Located at an easy crossing point on the Tiber, Rome thus stood astride the main avenue of inland communications between northern and southern Italy. The famous seven hills of Rome were defensible and safe from the floods of the Tiber. Rome was in an excellent position to develop the resources of Latium and maintain contact with the rest of Italy.

THE ETRUSCANS AND ROME (753–509 B.C.)

In recent years archeologists have found traces of numerous early peoples in Italy. The origins of these cultures and their precise relations with one another are not yet well understood. In fact, no clear account of the prehistory of Italy is yet possible. In the period between 1200 and 753 B.C., before the appearance of the Etruscans, one fundamental fact is indisputable: peoples speaking Indo-European languages were moving into Italy from the north, probably in small groups. They were part of the awesome but imperfectly understood movement of peoples who spread the Indo-European family of languages from Spain to India (see page 32). Only with the coming of the Greeks does Italy enter the light of history. A great wave of Greek immigration swept into southern Italy and Sicily during the eighth century B.C. (see pages 123–124). The Greeks brought urban life to these regions, spreading cultural influence far beyond their city-states.

In the north the Greeks encountered the Etruscans, one of the truly mysterious peoples of antiqu-

ity. Who the Etruscans were, where they came from, and what language they spoke are unknown. Nonetheless, this fascinating people was to leave an indelible mark on the Romans. Skillful metalworkers, the Etruscans amassed extensive wealth by trading their manufactured goods in Italy and beyond. The strength of their political and military institutions enabled them to form a loosely organized league of cities whose dominion extended as far north as the Po Valley and as far south as Latium and Campania (see Map 7.1). In Latium they founded cities and took over control of Rome. Like the Greeks, the Etruscans promoted urban life, and one of the places that benefited from Etruscan influence was Rome.

The Etruscans found the Romans settled on three of Rome's seven hills. The site of the future Forum Romanum, the famous public square and center of political life, was originally the cemetery of the small community. According to Roman legend, Romulus and Remus founded Rome in 753 B.C. During the years 753 to 509 B.C. the Romans embraced many Etruscan customs. They adopted the Etruscan alphabet, which the Etruscans had adopted from the Greeks. The Romans later handed on this alphabet to medieval Europe and thence to the modern Western world. Indeed, the great and deep influences of the Etruscans on the Romans have provided historians with particular and perhaps insoluble problems. No one can now determine whether the social, political, and military systems found later in the early Republic were indigenous to the Romans, an Etruscan creation imposed on the Romans, or a combination of the two. Most authentic Roman documents were destroyed in the Gallic raid of 390 B.C., and the first true history of the earliest periods was written some seven hundred years after the event. Thus there is very little authentic information about the origins of Rome.

Etruscan power and influence at Rome were so strong that Roman traditions preserved the memory of Etruscan kings who ruled the city. Under the Etruscans Rome enjoyed contacts with the larger Mediterranean world, and the city began to grow. In the years 575 to 550 B.C. temples and public buildings began to grace the city. The Capitoline Hill became the religious center of the city when the temple of Jupiter Optimus Maximus (Jupiter the Best and Greatest) was built there. The Forum ceased to be a cemetery and began its history as a public meeting place, a development parallel to that of the Greek agora. Trade in metal-work became common, and the wealthiest Roman classes began to import large numbers of fine Greek vases. The Etruscans had found Rome a collection of villages and made it a city.

THE ROMAN CONQUEST OF ITALY (509–290 B.C.)

Early Roman history is an uneven mixture of fact and legend. Roman traditions often contain an important kernel of truth, but that does not make them history. In many cases they are significant because they illustrate the ethics, morals, and ideals valued by Roman society. According to Roman tradition, the Romans expelled the Etruscan king Tarquin the Proud from Rome in 509 B.C. and founded the Republic. They did so in reaction to the harshness of Etruscan rule. In the years that followed, the Romans fought numerous wars with their neighbors on the Italian peninsula. They became soldiers, and the grim fighting bred tenacity, a prominent Roman trait. War also involved diplomacy, at which the Romans became masters. At an early date they learned the value of alliances and how to provide leadership for their allies. Alliances with the Latin towns around them provided them with a large reservoir of manpower. Their alliances involved the Romans in still other wars and took them farther afield in the Italian peninsula.

The growth of Roman power was slow but steady. Not until roughly a century after the founding of the Republic did the Romans try to drive the Etruscans entirely out of Latium. In 405 B.C. they laid siege to Veii, the last neighboring Etruscan city. After its destruction, they overshadowed their Latin allies and enemies alike. Yet about 390 B.C. they suffered a major setback when a new people, the Celts—or "Gauls," as the Romans called them—swept aside a Roman army and sacked Rome. More intent on loot than on land, the Gauls agreed to abandon Rome in return for a thousand pounds of gold.

During the century from 390 to 290 B.C., Romans rebuilt their city and recouped their losses. They also reorganized their army to create the mobile legion, a flexible unit capable of fighting on either broken or open terrain. The Romans finally brought Latium and their Latin allies fully under their control and conquered Etruria. In 343 B.C.

Etruscan Apollo A masterpiece of Etruscan art, this statue of Apollo testifies both to the artistic and the religious influence of the early Greeks. Yet Etruscan sculptors were not mere imitators, and they adapted Greek art to serve their own tastes. *(Source: Villa Giulia Museum, Rome/Art Resource)*

they grappled with the Samnites in a series of bitter wars for the possession of Campania and southern Italy. The Samnites were a formidable enemy and inflicted serious losses on the Romans. But the superior organization, institutions, and manpower of the Romans won out in the end. Although Rome had yet to subdue the whole peninsula, for the first time in history the city stood unchallenged in Italy.

Rome's success in diplomacy and politics was as important as its military victories. Unlike the Greeks, the Romans did not simply conquer and dominate. Instead, they shared with other Italians both political power and degrees of Roman citizenship. With many of their oldest allies, such as the Italian cities, they shared full Roman citizenship. In other instances they granted citizenship without the franchise (*civitas sine suffragio*). Allies who held this status enjoyed all the rights of Roman citizenship but could not vote or hold Roman offices. They were subject to Roman taxes and calls for military service but ran their own local affairs. The Latin allies were able to acquire full Roman citizenship by moving to Rome.

By their willingness to extend their citizenship, the Romans took Italy into partnership. Here the political genius of Rome triumphed where Greece had failed. Rome proved itself superior to the Greek polis because it both conquered and shared the fruits of victory with the conquered. The unwillingness of the Greek polis to share its citizenship condemned it to a limited horizon. Not so with Rome. The extension of Roman citizenship strengthened the state, gave it additional manpower and wealth, and laid the foundation of the Roman Empire.

THE ROMAN STATE

The Romans summed up their political existence in a single phrase: *senatus populusque Romanus,* "the Roman senate and the people." The real genius of the Romans lay in politics and law. Unlike the Greeks, they did not often speculate on the ideal state or on political forms. Instead they realistically met actual challenges and created institutions, magistracies, and legal concepts to deal with practical problems. Change was consequently commonplace in Roman political life, and the constitution of 509 B.C. was far simpler than that

of 27 B.C. Nonetheless, the political framework of the state can be sketched.

In the early Republic, social divisions determined the shape of politics. Political power was in the hands of the aristocracy—the *patricians,* who were wealthy landowners. Patrician families formed clans, as did aristocrats in early Greece. They dominated the affairs of state, provided military leadership in time of war, and monopolized knowledge of law and legal procedure. The common people of Rome, the *plebeians,* had few of the patricians' advantages. Some plebeians formed their own clans and rivaled the patricians in wealth. Many plebeian merchants increased their wealth in the course of Roman expansion, but most plebeians were poor. They were the artisans, small farmers, and landless urban dwellers. The plebeians, rich and poor alike, were free citizens with a voice in politics. Nonetheless, they were overshadowed by the patricians.

Perhaps the greatest institution of the Republic was the senate, which had originated under the Etruscans as a council of noble elders who advised the king. During the Republic the senate advised the consuls and other magistrates. Because the senate sat year after year, while magistrates changed annually, it provided stability and continuity. It also served as a reservoir of experience and knowledge. Technically the senate could not pass legislation; it could only offer its advice. But increasingly, because of the senate's prestige, its advice came to have the force of law.

The Romans created several assemblies through which the people elected magistrates and passed legislation. The earliest was the *comitia curiata,* which had religious, political, and military functions. According to Roman tradition, King Servius Tullius (578–535 B.C.), who reorganized the state into 193 *centuries* (military and political units) for military purposes, created the *comitia centuriata,* which served as a political body to decide Roman policy. Since the patricians shouldered most of the burden of defense, they dominated the comitia centuriata and could easily outvote the plebeians. In 471 B.C. the plebeians won the right to meet in an assembly of their own, the *concilium plebis,* and to pass ordinances. In 287 B.C. the bills passed in the concilium plebis were recognized as binding on the entire population.

The chief magistrates of the Republic were two *consuls,* elected for one-year terms. At first the consulship was open only to patricians. The consuls commanded the army in battle, administered state business, convened the comitia centuriata, and supervised financial affairs. In effect, they and the senate ran the state. The consuls appointed *quaestors* to assist them in their duties, and in 421 B.C. the quaestorship became an elective office open to plebeians. The quaestors took charge of the public treasury and prosecuted criminals in the popular courts.

In 366 B.C. the Romans created a new office, that of *praetor,* and in 227 B.C. the number of praetors was increased to four. When the consuls were away from Rome, the praetors could act in their place, primarily dealing with the administration of justice. When he took office, a praetor issued a proclamation declaring the principles by which he would interpret the law. These proclamations became important because they usually covered areas where the law was vague and thus helped clarify the law.

Other officials included the powerful *censors,* created in 443 B.C. They had many responsibilities, the most important being supervision of public morals, the power to determine who lawfully could sit in the senate, the registration of citizens, and the leasing of public contracts. Later officials were the *aediles,* four in number, who supervised the streets and markets and presided over public festivals.

After the age of overseas conquest (see pages 179–182), the Romans divided the Mediterranean area into provinces governed by ex-consuls and ex-praetors. Because of their experience in Roman politics, these officials were well suited to administer the affairs of the provincials and to fit Roman law and custom into new contexts.

The Roman Forum   The forum was the center of Roman political life. From simple beginnings it developed into the very symbol of Rome's imperial majesty. *(Source: Josephine Powell, Rome)*

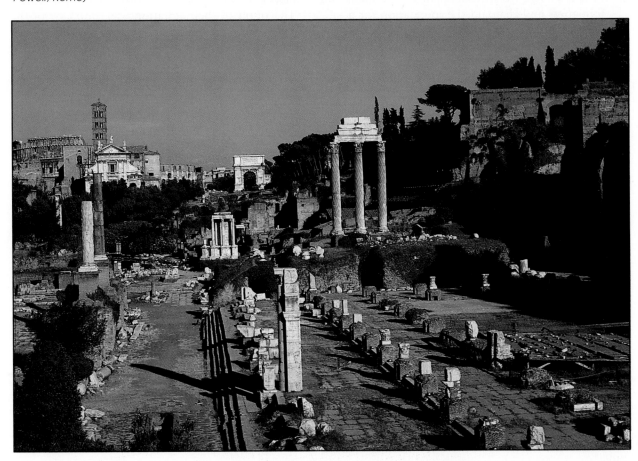

One of the most splendid achievements of the Romans was their development of law. Roman law began as a set of rules that regulated the lives and relations of citizens. This civil law, or *ius civile,* consisted of statutes, customs, and forms of procedure. Roman assemblies added to the body of law, and praetors interpreted it. The spirit of the law aimed at protecting the property, lives, and reputations of citizens, redressing wrongs, and giving satisfaction to victims of injustice.

As the Romans came into more frequent contact with foreigners, they had to devise laws to deal with disputes between Romans and foreigners and between foreigners under Roman jurisdiction. In these instances, where there was no precedent to guide the Romans, the legal decisions of the praetors proved of immense importance. The praetors adopted aspects of other legal systems and resorted to the law of equity—what they thought was right and just to all parties. Free in effect to determine law, the praetors enjoyed a great deal of flexibility. By addressing specific, actual circumstances, the praetors developed a body of law, the *ius gentium,* "the law of peoples," that applied to Romans and foreigners and that laid the foundation for a universal conception of law. By the time of the late Republic, Roman jurists were reaching decisions on the basis of the Stoic concept of *ius naturale,* "natural law," a universal law that could be applied to all societies.

SOCIAL CONFLICT IN ROME

War was not the only aspect of Rome's early history. In Rome itself a great social conflict, usually known as the "Struggle of the Orders," developed between patricians and plebeians. What the plebeians wanted was real political representation and safeguards against patrician domination. The plebeians' efforts to obtain recognition of their rights are the crux of the Struggle of the Orders.

Rome's early wars gave the plebeians the leverage they needed: Rome's survival depended on the army, and the army needed the plebeians. The first confrontation between plebeians and patricians came, according to tradition, in 494 B.C. To force the patricians to grant concessions, the plebeians seceded from the state; they literally walked out of Rome and refused to serve in the army. The plebeians' general strike worked, and because of it the patricians made important concessions. One of the first was social. In 445 B.C. the patricians passed a law, the *lex Canuleia,* which for the first time allowed patricians and plebeians to marry one another. Furthermore, the patricians recognized the right of plebeians to elect their own officials, the *tribunes.* The tribunes in turn had the right to protect the plebeians from the arbitrary conduct of patrician magistrates. The tribunes brought plebeian complaints and grievances to the senate for resolution. In 471 B.C., when the plebeians won the right to hold their own assembly, the *concilium plebis,* and enact ordinances that concerned only themselves, the plebeians became a state within a state. This situation could have led to chaos, but Rome was not a house divided against itself. The plebeians were not bent on undermining the state. Rather they used their gains only to win full equality under the law.

The law itself was the plebeians' next target. Only the patricians knew what the law was, and only they could argue cases in court. All too often they had used the law for their own benefit. The plebeians wanted the law codified and published. The result of their agitation was the "Law of the Twelve Tables," so called because the laws, which covered civil and criminal matters, were inscribed on large bronze plaques. The plebeians had broken the patricians' legal monopoly and henceforth enjoyed full protection under the law.

The decisive plebeian victory came with the passage of the Licinian-Sextian rogations (or laws) in 367 B.C. Licinius and Sextus were plebeian tribunes who led a ten-year fight for further reform. Rich plebeians, like Licinius and Sextus themselves, joined the poor to mount a sweeping assault on patrician privilege. Wealthy plebeians wanted the opportunity to provide political leadership for the state. They demanded that the patricians allow them access to all the magistracies of the state. If they could hold the consulship, they could also sit in the senate and advise the senate on policy. The senate did pass a law that stipulated that one of the two consuls, elected annually, must be a plebeian. Though decisive, the Licinian-Sextian rogations did not automatically end the Struggle of the Orders. That happened only in 287 B.C. with the passage of a *lex Hortensia,* a law that gave the resolutions of the concilium plebis the force of law for patricians and plebeians alike.

The Struggle of the Orders resulted in a Rome stronger and more tightly united than before. It

The Town of Terracina The Romans founded numerous colonies, first in Italy and later throughout the Mediterranean. Roman colonies, which often grew into cities, were intended to be self-sufficient. This ancient drawing shows the colonia Axurnas, now Terracina, with its walls and towers for protection of the population sitting astride the Appian Way, the famous road to Rome. The lines to the left show how Roman surveyors had marked out the land for cultivation. *(Source: Bibliotheca Apostolica Vaticana)*

could have led to anarchy, but again certain Roman traits triumphed. The values fostered by their social structure predisposed the Romans to compromise, especially in the face of common danger. Resistance and confrontation in Rome never exploded into class warfare. Instead, both sides resorted to compromises to hammer out a realistic solution. Important, too, were Roman patience, tenacity, and a healthy sense of the practical. These qualities enabled both sides to keep working until they had resolved the crisis. The Struggle of the Orders ended with a new concept of Roman citizenship. All citizens shared equally under the law. Theoretically, all could aspire to the highest political offices. Patrician or plebeian, rich or poor, Roman citizenship was equal for all.

THE AGE OF OVERSEAS CONQUEST (282–146 B.C.)

In 282 B.C. Rome embarked on a series of wars that left it the ruler of the Mediterranean world. There was nothing ideological about these wars. Unlike Napoleon or Hitler, the Romans did not map out grandiose strategies for world conquest. They had no idea of what lay before them. If they could have looked into the future, they would have stood amazed. In many instances the Romans did not even initiate action; they simply responded to situations as they arose. Nineteenth-century Englishmen were fond of saying, "We got our empire in a fit of absence of mind." The Romans could not go quite that far. Although they sometimes declared war reluctantly, they nonetheless felt the need to dominate, to eliminate any state that could threaten them.

Rome was imperialistic, and its imperialism took two forms. In barbarian western Europe, the home of fierce tribes, Rome resorted to bald aggression to conquer new territory. In areas such as Spain and later Gaul, the fighting was fierce and savage, and gains came slowly. In civilized eastern Europe and western Asia, the world of Hellenistic states, Rome tried to avoid annexing territory. The east was already heavily populated, and those people would have become Rome's responsibility. New responsibilities meant new problems, and such headaches the Romans shunned. In the east the Romans preferred to be patrons rather than masters. Only when that loose policy failed did

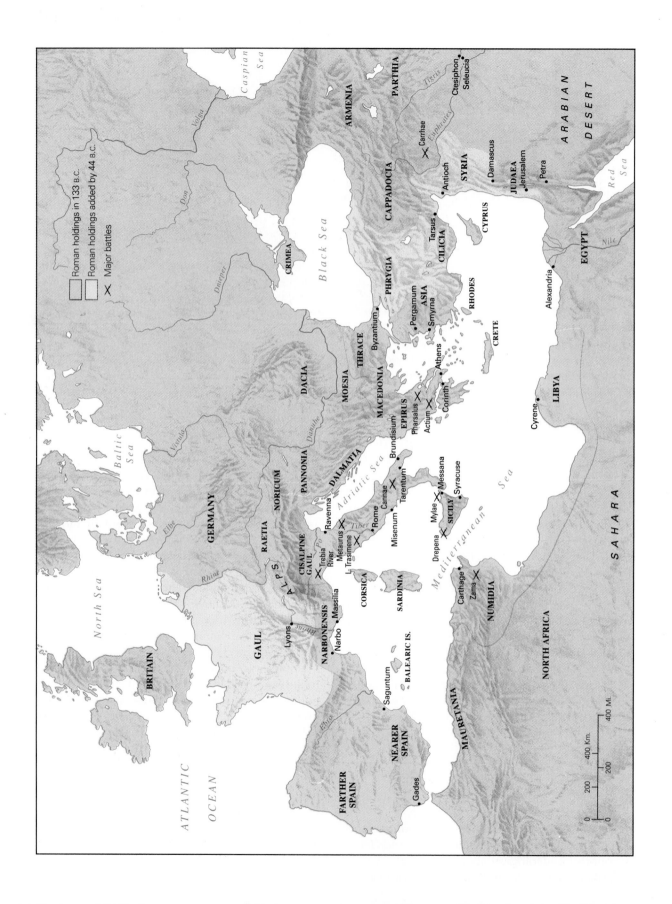

Roman holdings in 133 B.C.

Roman holdings added by 44 B.C.

✗ Major battles

ATLANTIC OCEAN

North Sea

Baltic Sea

BRITAIN

GERMANY

GAUL

Lyons

NARBONENSIS
Narbo
Massilia

ALPS

RAETIA

NORICUM

CISALPINE GAUL

PANNONIA

DALMATIA

Ravenna
Trebia River
Metaurus
L. Trasimene
Rome
Cannae
Tarentum
Misenum

Adriatic Sea

Brundisium

EPIRUS
Pharsalus
Actium

MACEDONIA

THRACE
Byzantium

MOESIA

DACIA

Danube

CRIMEA

Black Sea

Caspian Sea

Volga

Don

Dnieper

Vistula

Elbe

Rhine

Rhone

Po

Tiber

Ebro

FARTHER SPAIN

Gades

NEARER SPAIN

Saguntum

BALEARIC IS.

CORSICA

SARDINIA

Mylae
Drepena
SICILY
Messana
Syracuse

Mediterranean Sea

Carthage
Zama

NUMIDIA

MAURETANIA

NORTH AFRICA

SAHARA

Athens
Corinth

ARMENIA

PARTHIA

Tigris

Carrhae

Euphrates

CAPPADOCIA

PHRYGIA
Pergamum
ASIA
Smyrna

Tarsus
CILICIA

RHODES

CRETE

CYPRUS

SYRIA
Antioch
Damascus

JUDAEA
Jerusalem
Petra

ARABIAN DESERT

EGYPT

Nile

Alexandria

Red Sea

LIBYA

Cyrene

Ctesiphon
Seleucia

400 Mi.
400 Km.
200
200
0
0

they directly annex land. But in 282 B.C. all this lay in the future.

The Samnite wars had drawn the Romans into the political world of southern Italy. In 282 B.C., alarmed by the powerful newcomer, the Greek city of Tarentum in southern Italy called for help from Pyrrhus, king of Epirus in western Greece. A relative of Alexander the Great and an excellent general, Pyrrhus won two furious battles but suffered heavy casualties—thus the phrase "Pyrrhic victory" for a victory involving severe losses. Against Pyrrhus's army the Romans threw new legions, and in the end manpower proved decisive. In 275 B.C. the Romans drove Pyrrhus from Italy and extended their sway over southern Italy. Once they did, the island of Sicily became key for them.

The Phoenician city of Carthage, in North Africa (Map 7.2), had for centuries dominated the western Mediterranean. Sicily had long been a Carthaginian target. Since Sicily is the stepping-stone to Italy, the Romans could not let it fall to an enemy. In 264 B.C. Carthage and Rome came to blows over the city of Messana, which commanded the straits between Sicily and Italy. This conflict, the First Punic War (the word "Punic" refers to the Carthaginians), lasted for twenty-three years (264–241 B.C.). The Romans quickly learned that they could not conquer Sicily unless they controlled the sea. Yet they lacked a fleet and hated the sea as fervently as cats hate water. Nevertheless, with grim resolution the Romans built a navy and challenged the Carthaginians at sea. The Romans fought seven major naval battles with the Carthaginians and won six. Twice their fleet went down in gales. But finally the Romans wore down the Carthaginians. In 241 B.C., the Romans defeated them and took possession of Sicily, which became their first real province. Once again Rome's resources, manpower, and determination proved decisive.

The First Punic War was a beginning, not an end. Carthage was still a formidable enemy. After the First Punic War the Carthaginians expanded their power to Spain and turned the Iberian Peninsula into a rich field of operations. By 219 B.C. Carthage had found its avenger—Hannibal (ca 247–183 B.C.). In Spain, Hannibal learned how to lead armies and to wage war on a large scale. A brilliant general, he realized the advantages of swift mobile forces, and he was an innovator in tactics.

In 219 B.C. Hannibal defied the Romans by laying siege to the small city of Saguntum in Spain. When the Romans declared war the following year, he gathered his forces and led them on one of the most spectacular marches in ancient history. Hannibal carried the Second Punic War to the very gates of Rome. Starting in Spain, he led his troops—infantry, cavalry, and elephants—over the Alps and into Italy on a march of more than a thousand miles. Once in Italy, he defeated one Roman army at the Battle of Trebia (218 B.C.) and another at the Battle of Lake Trasimene (217 B.C.). At the Battle of Cannae in 216 B.C. Hannibal inflicted some forty thousand casualties on the Romans. He spread devastation throughout Italy but failed to crush Rome's iron circle of Latium, Etruria, and Samnium. The wisdom of Rome's political policy of extending rights and citizenship to its allies showed itself in these dark hours. Italy stood solidly with Rome against the invader. And Rome fought back.

The Roman general Scipio Africanus (ca 236–ca 183 B.C.) copied Hannibal's methods of mobile warfare. Scipio gave his new army combat experience in Spain, which he wrested from the Carthaginians. Meanwhile the Roman fleet dominated the western Mediterranean and interfered with Carthaginian attempts to reinforce Hannibal. In 204 B.C. the Roman fleet landed Scipio in Africa, prompting the Carthaginians to recall Hannibal from Italy to defend the homeland.

In 202 B.C. near the town of Zama (see Map 7.2), Scipio Africanus defeated Hannibal in one of the world's truly decisive battles. Scipio's victory meant that the world of the western Mediterranean would henceforth be Roman. Roman language, law, and culture, fertilized by Greek influences, would in time permeate this entire region. The victory at Zama meant that Rome's heritage—not Carthage's—would be passed on to the Western world. The Second Punic War contained the seeds of still other wars. Scipio Aemilianus, grandson of Scipio Africanus, completed the conquest of North Africa and Spain by 133 B.C.

MAP 7.2 Roman Expansion During the Republic The main spurt of Roman expansion occurred between 264 and 133 B.C., when most of the Mediterranean fell to Rome, followed by the conquest of Gaul and the eastern Mediterranean by 44 B.C.

Coin of Hannibal This Carthaginian coin bears one of the few profiles of Hannibal. The style of the profile is Roman, but the artist has captured the actual likeness of the arch-enemy of Rome. *(Source: Courtesy of the Trustees of the British Museum)*

When the Romans intervened in the Hellenistic East, they went from triumph to triumph. The Romans dealt with the Greeks in a relatively civilized fashion. There were hard-fought battles in the east, but the bloodletting and carnage that marked the battles in the west were not generally repeated in the more cultured east. Nevertheless, the consequences were essentially the same. The kingdom of Macedonia fell to the Roman legions, as did Greece and the Seleucid monarchy. By 146 B.C., the Romans stood unchallenged in the eastern Mediterranean, and they had turned many states and kingdoms into provinces. In 133 B.C., the king of Pergamum, which was in Asia Minor, left his kingdom to the Romans in his will. The Ptolemies of Egypt meekly obeyed Roman wishes. By 146 B.C., however, the work of conquest was largely done. The Romans had turned the entire Mediterranean basin into *mare nostrum,* "our sea."

OLD VALUES AND GREEK CULTURE

Rome had conquered the Mediterranean world, but some Romans considered that victory a misfortune. The historian Sallust (86–34 B.C.), writing from hindsight, complained that the acquisition of an empire was the beginning of Rome's troubles:

But when through labor and justice our Republic grew powerful, great kings defeated in war, fierce nations and mighty peoples subdued by force, when Carthage the rival of the Roman people was wiped out root and branch, and the seas and lands lay open, then fortune began to be harsh and to throw everything into confusion. The Romans had easily borne labor, danger, uncertainty, and hardship. To them leisure, riches—otherwise desirable—proved to be burdens and torments. So at first money, then desire for power grew great. These things were a sort of cause of all evils.[2]

Sallust was not alone in his feelings. At the time, some senators had opposed the destruction of Carthage on the grounds that fear of their old rival would keep the Romans in check. Yet in the second century B.C., Romans learned that they could not return to what they fondly considered a simple life. They were rulers of the Mediterranean world. The responsibilities they faced were complex and awesome. They had to change their institutions, social patterns, and way of thinking to meet the new era. They were in fact building the foundations of a great imperial system. It was an awesome challenge, and there were failures along the way. Roman generals and politicians would destroy one another. Even the republican constitution would eventually be discarded. But in the end Rome triumphed here just as it had on the battlefield, for out of the turmoil would come the *pax Romana*, "Roman peace."

How did the Romans of the day meet these challenges? How did they lead their lives and cope with these momentous changes? Obviously there are as many answers to these questions as there were Romans. Yet two men of different generations represent the major trends of the second century B.C. Cato the Elder shared the mentality of those who longed for the good old days and idealized the traditional agrarian way of life. Scipio Aemilianus led those who embraced the new urban life, with its eager acceptance of Greek culture. Forty-nine years older than Scipio, Cato was the product of an earlier generation, one that confronted a rapidly changing world. Cato and Scipio were both aristocrats and neither of them was typical, even of the aristocracy. But they do exemplify the opposing sets of attitudes that marked Roman society and politics in the age of conquest.

Battle Between the Romans and Barbarians   All of the brutality and fury of Rome's wars with the barbarians of western Europe come to life in this decoration for a horse's harness. Even the bravery and strength of the barbarians were no match for the steadiness and discipline of the Roman legions. *(Source: Museo Archeologico, Aosta/Scala Art Resource)*

Cato and the Traditional Ideal

Marcus Cato (234–149 B.C.) was born a plebeian, but his talent and energy carried him to Rome's highest offices. He cherished the old virtues and consistently imitated the old ways. In Roman society ties within the family were very strong. In this sense Cato and his family were typical. Cato was *paterfamilias,* a term that meant far more than merely "father." The paterfamilias was the oldest dominant male of the family. He held nearly absolute power over the lives of his wife and children as long as he lived. He could legally kill his wife for adultery or divorce her at will. He could kill his children or sell them into slavery. He could force them to marry against their will. Until the paterfamilias died, his sons could not legally own property. At his death, his wife and children inherited his property.

Despite his immense power, the paterfamilias did not necessarily act alone or arbitrarily. To deal with important family matters, he usually called a council of the adult males. In this way the leading members of the family aired their views. They had the opportunity to give their support to the paterfamilias or to dissuade him from harsh decisions. In these councils the women of the family had no formal part, but it can be safely assumed that they played an important role behind the scenes. Although the possibility of serious conflicts between a paterfamilias and his grown sons is obvious, no one in ancient Rome ever complained about the institution. Perhaps in practice the paterfamilias preferred to be lenient rather than absolute.

Like most Romans, Cato and his family began the day early in the morning. The Romans divided the period of daylight into twelve hours and the darkness into another twelve. The day might begin as early as half past four in summer, as late as half past seven in winter. Because Mediterranean summers are invariably hot, the farmer and his wife liked to take every advantage of the cool mornings. Cato and his family, like modern Italians, ordinarily started the morning with a light breakfast, usually nothing more than some bread and cheese. After breakfast the family went about its work.

Cato's wife also followed the old ways, and she ran the household. She spent the morning spinning and weaving wool for the clothes they wore. She supervised the domestic slaves, planned the meals, and devoted a good deal of attention to her son. In wealthy homes during this period the matron had begun to employ a slave as a wet nurse. Cato's wife refused to delegate maternal duties. Like most ordinary Roman women, she nursed her son herself and bathed and swaddled him daily. Later the boy was allowed to play with toys and terra-cotta dolls. Roman children, like children everywhere, kept pets. Dogs were especially popular and valuable as house guards. Children played all sorts of games, and games of chance were very popular. Until the age of seven the child was under the matron's care. During this time the mother began to educate her daughter in the management of the household. After the age of seven, the son—and in many wealthy households the daughter, too—began to undertake formal education.

In the country, Romans like Cato continued to take their main meal at midday. This meal included either coarse bread made from the entire husk of wheat or porridge made with milk or water; it also included turnips, cabbage, olives, and beans. When Romans ate meat, they preferred pork. Unless they lived by the sea, the average farm family did not eat fish, an expensive delicacy. Cato once complained that Rome was a place where a fish could cost more than a cow. With the midday meal the family drank ordinary wine mixed with water. Afterward, any Roman who could took a nap. This was especially true in the summer, when the Mediterranean heat can be fierce. Slaves, artisans, and hired laborers, however, continued their work. In the evening, Romans ate a light meal and went to bed at nightfall.

The agricultural year followed the sun and the stars—the farmer's calendar. Spring was the season for plowing. Roman farmers plowed their land at least twice and preferably three times. The third plowing was to cover the sown seed in ridges and to use the furrows to drain off excess water. The Romans used a variety of plows. Some had detachable shares. Some were heavy for thick soil, others light for thin, crumbly soil. Farmers used oxen and donkeys to pull the plow, collecting the dung of the animals for fertilizer. Besides spreading manure, some farmers fertilized their fields by planting lupines and beans; when they began to pod, farmers plowed them under. The main money crops, at least for rich soils, were wheat and flax. Forage crops included clover, vetch, and alfalfa. Prosperous farmers like Cato raised olive trees chiefly for the oil. They also raised grapevines for the production of wine. Cato and his neighbors harvested their cereal crops in summer and their grapes in autumn. Harvests varied depending on the soil, but farmers could usually expect yields of 5,112 bushels of wheat or 10,112 bushels of barley per acre. Roman farmers were much more fortunate than their Greek counterparts in that they generally enjoyed more fertile land and larger tracts of it.

An influx of slaves resulted from Rome's wars and conquests. Prisoners from Spain, Africa, and the Hellenistic East and even some blacks from Hannibal's army came to Rome as the spoils of war. The Roman attitude toward slaves and slavery had little in common with modern views. To the Romans slavery was a misfortune that befell some people, but it did not entail any racial theories. Races were not enslaved because the Romans thought them inferior. The black African slave was treated no worse—and no better—than the Spaniard. Indeed, some slaves were valued because of their physical distinctiveness: black Africans and blond Germans were particular favorites. For the talented slave, the Romans always held out the hope of eventual freedom. *Manumission*—the freeing of individual slaves by their masters—became so common that it had to be limited by law. Not even Christians questioned the institution of slavery. It was just a fact of life.

Slaves were entirely their master's property and might be treated with great cruelty. Many Romans were practical enough to realize that they got more out of their slaves by kindness than by severity. Yet in Sicily slave owners treated their slaves viciously. They bought slaves in huge numbers, branded them for identification, put them in irons, and often made them go without food and clothing. In 135 B.C. these conditions gave rise to a major slave revolt, during which many of the most brutal masters died at their slaves' hands. Italy, too, had trouble with slave unrest, but conditions there were generally better than in Sicily.

For Cato and most other Romans, religion played an important part in life. Originally the Romans thought of the gods as invisible, shapeless natural forces. Only through Etruscan and Greek influence did Roman deities take on human form. Jupiter, the sky god, and his wife, Juno, became equivalent to the Greek Zeus and Hera. Mars was the god of war but also guaranteed the fertility of the farm and protected it from danger. The gods of the Romans were not loving and personal. They were stern, powerful, and aloof. But as long as the

Manumission of Slaves During the Republic some Roman masters began to free slaves in public ceremonies. Here two slaves come before their master or a magistrate, who is in the process of freeing the kneeling slave by touching him with a manumission-rod. The other slave shows his gratitude and his good faith with a handshake. *(Source: Collection Waroque, Mariemont, Belgium, © A.C.L. Brussels)*

Romans honored the cults of their gods, they could expect divine favor.

Along with the great gods the Romans believed in spirits who haunted fields, forests, crossroads, and even the home itself. Some of these deities were hostile; only magic could ward them off. The spirits of the dead, like ghosts in modern horror films, frequented places where they had lived. They, too, had to be placated but were ordinarily benign. As the poet Ovid (43 B.C.–A.D. 17) put it:

The spirits of the dead ask for little.
They are more grateful for piety than for an expen-
sive gift.
Not greedy are the gods who haunt the Styx below.
A rooftile covered with a sacrificial crown,
Scattered kernels, a few grains of salt,
Bread dipped in wine, and loose violets—
These are enough.
Put them in a potsherd and leave them in the middle
of the road.[3]

A good deal of Roman religion consisted of rituals such as those Ovid describes. These practices lived on long after the Romans had lost interest in the great gods. Even Christianity could not entirely wipe them out. Instead Christianity was to incorporate many of these rituals into its own style of worship.

Scipio: Greek Culture and Urban Life

The old-fashioned ideals that Cato represented came into conflict with a new spirit of wealth and leisure. The conquest of the Mediterranean world and the spoils of war made Rome a great city. Roman life, especially in the cities, was changing and becoming less austere. The spoils of war went to build baths, theaters, and other places of amusement. Romans and Italian townsmen began to spend more of their time in the pursuit of leisure. But simultaneously the new responsibilities of governing the Mediterranean world produced in Rome a sophisticated society. Romans developed new tastes and a liking for Greek culture and literature. They began to learn the Greek language. It became common for an educated Roman to speak both Latin and Greek. Hellenism dominated the cultural life of Rome. Even diehards like Cato found a knowledge of Greek essential for political and diplomatic affairs. The poet Horace (64–8 B.C.) summed it up well: "Captive Greece captured her rough conqueror and introduced the arts into rustic Latium."[4]

One of the most avid devotees of Hellenism and the new was Scipio Aemilianus (185–129 B.C.), the destroyer of Carthage. Scipio realized that broad and worldly views had to replace the old Roman narrowness. The new situation called for new ways. Rome was no longer a small city on the Tiber; it was the capital of the Mediterranean world, and Romans had to adapt themselves to that fact. Scipio was ready to become an innovator in both politics and culture. He broke with the past in the conduct of his political career. He embraced Hellenism wholeheartedly. Perhaps more than anyone else of his day, Scipio represented the new Roman: imperial, cultured, and independent.

In his education and interests, too, Scipio broke with the past. As a boy he had received the traditional patrician training, learning to read and write Latin and becoming acquainted with the law. He mastered the fundamentals of rhetoric and learned how to throw the javelin, fight in armor, and ride a horse. But later Scipio also learned Greek and became a fervent Hellenist. As a young man he formed a lasting friendship with Polybius, who actively encouraged him in his study of Greek culture and in his intellectual pursuits. The new Hellenism profoundly stimulated the growth and development of Roman art and literature. The Roman conquest of the Hellenistic East resulted in wholesale confiscation of Greek paintings and sculpture to grace Roman temples, public buildings, and private homes. Roman artists copied many aspects of Greek art, but their emphasis on realistic portraiture carried on a native tradition.

Fabius Pictor (second half of the third century B.C.), a senator, wrote the first *History of Rome* in Greek. Other Romans translated Greek classics into Latin. Still others, such as the poet Ennius (239–169 B.C.), the father of Latin poetry, studied Greek philosophy, wrote comedies in Latin, and adapted many of Euripides' tragedies for the Roman stage. Ennius also wrote a history of Rome in Latin verse. Plautus (ca 254–184 B.C.) specialized in rough humor. He, too, decked out Greek plays in Roman dress but was no mere imitator. The Roman dramatist Terence (ca 195–159 B.C.) wrote comedies of refinement and grace that owed their essentials to Greek models, but his plays lacked the energy and the slapstick of Plautus's rowdy plays. All of early Roman literature was derived from the Greeks, but it managed in time to speak in its own voice and to flourish because it had something of its own to say.

The conquest of the Mediterranean world brought the Romans leisure, and Hellenism influenced how they spent their free time. During the second century B.C., the Greek custom of bathing became a Roman passion and an important part of the day. In the early Republic Romans had bathed infrequently, especially in the winter. Now large buildings containing pools and exercise rooms went up in great numbers, and the baths became an essential part of the Roman city. Architects built intricate systems of aqueducts to supply the bathing establishments with water. The baths included gymnasia, where men exercised and played ball. Women had places of their own to bathe, generally sections of the same baths used by men; for some reason, women's facilities lacked gymnasia. The baths contained hot-air rooms to induce a good sweat and pools of hot and cold water to finish the actual bathing. They also contained snack bars and halls where people chatted and read. The baths were socially important places where men and women went to see and be seen. Social climbers tried to talk to "the right people" and wangle invitations to dinner; politicians took advantage of the occasion to discuss the affairs of the day.

This period also saw a change in the eating habits of urban dwellers. The main meal of the day shifted from midday to evening. Dinner became a more elaborate meal and dinner parties became fashionable. Although Scipio Aemilianus detested fat people, more and more Romans began to eat excessively. Rich men and women displayed their wealth by serving exotic dishes and gourmet foods. After a course of vegetables and olives came the main course of meat, fish, or fowl. Pig was a favorite dish, and a whole suckling pig might be stuffed with sausage. A lucky guest might even dine on peacock and ostrich, each served with rich sauces. Dessert, as in Italy today, usually consisted of fruit. With the meal the Romans served wine, and in this era vintage wines became popular.

Although the wealthy gorged themselves whenever they could, poor artisans and workers could rarely afford rich meals. Their dinners resembled Cato's. Yet they, too, occasionally spent generously on food, especially during major festivals. The Roman calendar was crowded with religious festivals, occasions not of dreary piety but of cheerful celebration.

Did Hellenism and new social customs corrupt the Romans? Perhaps the best answer is this: the Roman state and the empire it ruled continued to exist for six more centuries. Rome did not collapse; the state continued to prosper. The golden age of literature was still before it. The high tide of Rome's prosperity still lay in the future. The Romans did not like change but took it in stride. That was part of their practical turn of mind and their strength.

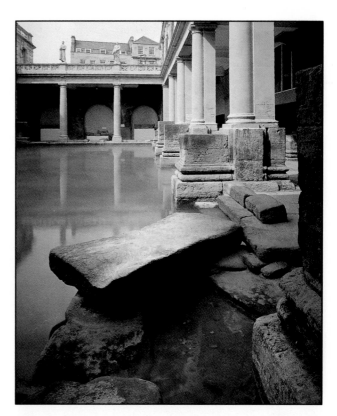

Roman Baths Once introduced into the Roman world, social bathing became a passion. These baths, which date to the Roman Empire, are located in Bath, England, to which they gave their name. A triumph of sophisticated engineering, they also demonstrate how Roman culture and institutions influenced life even on the perimeters of the Roman Empire. (*Source: Michael Holford*)

THE LATE REPUBLIC (133–27 B.C.)

The wars of conquest created serious problems for the Romans, some of the most pressing of which were political. The republican constitution had suited the needs of a simple city-state but was inadequate to meet the requirements of Rome's new position in international affairs (see Map 7.2). Sweeping changes and reforms were necessary to make it serve the demands of empire. A system of provincial administration had to be established. Officials had to be appointed to govern the provinces and administer the law. These officials and administrative organs had to find places in the constitution. Armies had to be provided to defend the provinces, and a system of tax collection had to be created.

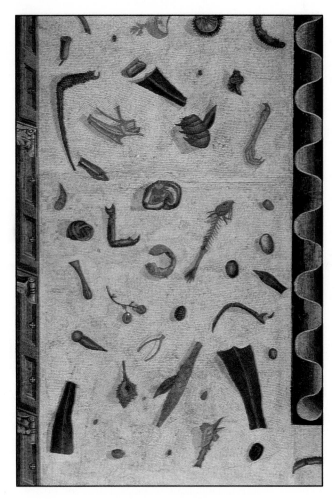

Roman Table Manners This mosaic is a floor that can never be swept clean. It whimsically suggests what a dining room floor looked like after a lavish dinner and also tells something about the menu: a chicken head, a wishbone, remains of various seafood, vegetables, and fruit are easily recognizable. *(Source: Museo Gregoria-Profano/Scala/Art Resource)*

Other political problems were equally serious. During the wars Roman generals commanded huge numbers of troops for long periods of time. Men such as Scipio Aemilianus were on the point of becoming too mighty for the state to control. Although Rome's Italian allies had borne much of the burden of the fighting, they received fewer rewards than did Roman officers and soldiers. Italians began to agitate for full Roman citizenship and a voice in politics.

There were also serious economic problems. Hannibal's operations and the warfare in Italy had

left the countryside a shambles. The movements of numerous armies had disrupted agriculture. The prolonged fighting had also drawn untold numbers of Roman and Italian men away from their farms for long periods. The families of these soldiers could not keep the land under full cultivation. The people who defended Rome and conquered the Mediterranean world for Rome became impoverished for having done their duty.

These problems, complex and explosive, largely account for the turmoil of the closing years of the Republic. The late Republic was one of the most dramatic eras in Roman history. It produced some of Rome's most famous figures: the Gracchi, Marius, Sulla, Cicero, Pompey, and Julius Caesar, among others. In one way or another each man attempted to solve Rome's problems. Yet they were also striving for the glory and honor that were the supreme goals of the senatorial aristocracy. Personal ambition often clashed with patriotism to create political tension throughout the period.

When the legionaries returned to their farms in Italy, they encountered an appalling situation. All too often their farms looked like the farms of people they had conquered. Two courses of action were open to them. They could rebuild as their ancestors had done. Or they could take advantage of an alternative not open to their ancestors and sell their holdings. The wars of conquest had made some men astoundingly rich. These men wanted to invest their wealth in land. They bought up small farms to create huge estates, which the Romans called *latifundia*.

Most veterans migrated to the cities, especially to Rome. Although some found work, most did not. Industry and small manufacturing were generally in the hands of slaves. Even when there was work, slave labor kept the wages of free men low. Instead of a new start, veterans and their families encountered slum conditions that matched those of modern American cities.

This trend held ominous consequences for the strength of Rome's armies. The Romans had always believed that only landowners should serve in the army, for only they had something to fight for. Landless men, even if they were Romans and lived in Rome, could not be conscripted into the army. A large pool of experienced manpower was going to waste. The landless former legionaries wanted a new start, and they were willing to support any leader who would provide it.

THE ROMAN REPUBLIC

509 B.C.	Expulsion of the Etruscan king and founding of the Roman republic
471 B.C.	Plebeians win official recognition of their assembly, the *concilium plebis*
ca 450 B.C.	Law of the Twelve Tables
390 B.C.	The Gauls sack Rome
390–290 B.C.	Rebuilding of Rome; reorganization of the army; Roman expansion in Italy
367 B.C.	Licinian-Sextian rogations
287 B.C.	Legislation of the *concilium plebis* made binding on entire population
282–146 B.C.	The era of overseas conquest
264–241 B.C.	First Punic War: Rome builds a navy, defeats Carthage, acquires Sicily
218–202 B.C.	Second Punic War: Scipio defeats Hannibal; Rome dominates the western Mediterranean
200–148 B.C.	Rome conquers the Hellenistic east
149–146 B.C.	Third Punic War: savage destruction of Carthage
133–121 B.C.	The Gracchi introduce land reform; murder of the Gracchi by some senators
107 B.C.	Marius becomes consul and begins the professionalization of the army
91–88 B.C.	War with Rome's Italian allies
88 B.C.	Sulla marches on Rome and seizes dictatorship
79 B.C.	Sulla abdicates
78–27 B.C.	Era of civil war
60–49 B.C.	First Triumvirate: Pompey, Crassus, Julius Caesar
45 B.C.	Julius Caesar defeats Pompey's forces and becomes dictator
44 B.C.	Assassination of Julius Caesar
43–36 B.C.	Second Triumvirate: Marc Antony, Lepidus, Augustus
31 B.C.	Augustus defeats Antony and Cleopatra at Actium

One man who recognized the plight of Rome's peasant farmers and urban poor was an aristocrat, Tiberius Gracchus (163–133 B.C.). Appalled by what he saw, Tiberius warned his countrymen that the legionaries were losing their land while fighting Rome's wars:

The wild beasts that roam over Italy have every one of them a cave or lair to lurk in. But the men who fight and die for Italy enjoy the common air and light, indeed, but nothing else. Houseless and homeless they wander about with their wives and children. And it is with lying lips that their generals exhort the soldiers in their battles to defend sepulchres and shrines from the enemy, for not a man of them has an hereditary altar, not one of all these many Romans an ancestral tomb, but they fight and die to support others in luxury, and though they are styled masters of the world, they have not a single clod of earth that is their own.[5]

Until his death Tiberius Gracchus sought a solution to the problems of the veterans and the urban poor.

After his election as tribune of the people, Tiberius in 133 B.C. proposed that public land be given to the poor in small lots. His was an easy and sensible plan, but it angered many wealthy and noble people who had usurped large tracts of public land for their own use. They had no desire to give any of it back, and they bitterly resisted Tiberius's efforts. Violence broke out in Rome when a large body of senators killed Tiberius in cold blood. It was a grim day in Roman history. The very people who directed the affairs of state and administered the law had taken the law into their own hands. The death of Tiberius was the beginning of an era of political violence. In the end that violence would bring down the republic.

Although Tiberius was dead, his land bill became law. Furthermore, Tiberius's brother Gaius

(153–121 B.C.) took up the cause of reform. Gaius was a veteran soldier with an enviable record, but this fiery orator also made his mark in the political arena. Gaius too became tribune, and demanded even more extensive reform than his brother. To help the urban poor Gaius pushed legislation to provide them with cheap grain for bread. He defended his brother's land law and suggested other measures for helping the landless. He proposed that Rome send many of its poor and propertyless people out to form colonies in southern Italy. The poor would have a new start and lead productive lives. The city of Rome would immediately benefit because excess and nonproductive families would leave for new opportunities abroad. Rome would be less crowded, sordid, and dangerous.

Gaius went a step further and urged that all Italians be granted full rights of Roman citizenship.

Roman Legionary   The backbone of the Roman army was the legionary, shown here in battle. His basic equipment—shield, sword, spear, and armor—is simple and allowed great flexibility of movement. *(Source: Laurie Platt Winfrey, Inc.)*

This measure provoked a storm of opposition, and it was not passed in Gaius's lifetime. Yet in the long run he proved wiser than his opponents. In 91 B.C., many Italians revolted against Rome over the issue of full citizenship. After a brief but hard-fought war the senate gave Roman citizenship to all Italians. Had the senate listened to Gaius earlier, it could have prevented a great deal of needless bloodshed. Instead, reactionary senators rose against Gaius and murdered him and three thousand of his supporters. Once again the cause of reform had met with violence. Once again it was Rome's leading citizens who flouted the law.

More trouble for Rome came from an unexpected source. In 112 B.C. war broke out in North Africa, when a Numidian king named Jugurtha rebelled against Rome. The Roman legions made little headway against him until 107 B.C., when Gaius Marius, an Italian "new man" (a politician not from the traditional Roman aristocracy), became consul. A man of fierce vigor and courage, Marius saw the army as the tool of his ambition. To prepare for the war with Jugurtha, Marius reformed the Roman army. He took the unusual, but not wholly unprecedented, step of recruiting an army by permitting the landless to serve in the legions. Marius thus tapped Rome's vast reservoir of idle manpower. His volunteer army was a professional force, not a body of draftees, and in 106 B.C. it handily defeated Jugurtha.

There was, however, a disturbing side to Marius's reforms, one that later would haunt the Republic. To encourage enlistments, Marius promised land to his volunteers after the war. Poor and landless veterans flocked to him, but when Marius proposed a bill to grant land to his veterans, the senate refused to act, in effect turning its back on the soldiers of Rome. This was a disastrous mistake. Henceforth, the legionaries expected their commanders—not the senate or the state—to protect their interests. By failing to reward the loyalty of Rome's troops, the senate set the stage for military rebellion and political anarchy.

Trouble was not long in coming. The senate's refusal to honor Marius's promises to his soldiers and a brief but bitter war between the Romans and their Italian allies (91–88 B.C.) set off serious political disturbances in Rome. In 88 B.C. the Roman general and conqueror Sulla (138–78 B.C.) marched on Rome with his army to put an end to the turmoil. Sulla made himself dictator, put his enemies to death, and confiscated their land. The constitution thus disrupted never was put back together effectively.

In 79 B.C. Sulla voluntarily abdicated as dictator and permitted the republican constitution to function once again. Yet his dictatorship cast a long shadow over the late Republic. Sulla the political reformer proved far less influential than Sulla the successful general and dictator. Civil war was to be the constant lot of Rome for the next fifty years, until the republican constitution gave way to the empire of Augustus in 27 B.C. The history of the late Republic is the story of the power struggles of some of Rome's most famous figures: Julius Caesar and Pompey, Augustus and Marc Antony. One figure who stands apart is Cicero (106–43 B.C.), a practical politician whose greatest legacy to the Roman world and to civilization is his mass of political and oratorical writings.

Pompous, vain, and sometimes silly, Cicero was nonetheless one of the few men of the period to urge peace and public order. As consul in 63 B.C. he put down a conspiracy against the Republic but refused to use force to win political power. Instead he developed the idea of "concord of the orders," an idealistic, probably unattainable, balance among the elements that constituted the Roman state. Yet Cicero commanded no legions, and only legions commanded respect.

In the late Republic the Romans were grappling with the simple and inescapable fact that their old city-state constitution was unequal to the demands of overseas possessions and the problems of governing provinces. Once the senate and the other institutions of the Roman state had failed to come to grips with the needs of empire, once the authorities had lost control of their own generals and soldiers, and once the armies put their faith in their commanders instead of in Rome, the Republic was doomed.

Sulla's real political heirs were Pompey and Julius Caesar, who realized that the days of the old republican constitution were numbered. Pompey (106–48 B.C.), a man of boundless ambition, began his career as one of Sulla's lieutenants. After his army put down a rebellion in Spain, he himself threatened to rebel unless the senate allowed him to run for consul. He and another ambitious politician, Crassus (ca 115–53 B.C.), pooled their political resources and both won the consulship. They dominated Roman politics until the rise of Julius Caesar, who became consul in 59 B.C. Together the

Julius Caesar   Both the majesty of empire and the way in which it was won shine forth from this statue of Julius Caesar. The famous conqueror wears the armor of the Roman legionary. His pose, however, is derived from that common among representations of Hellenistic kings. *(Source: Giraudon/Art Resource)*

three concluded an unofficial political alliance, the First Triumvirate, in which they agreed to advance one another's interests.

The man who cast the longest shadow over these troubled years was Julius Caesar (100–44 B.C.). More than a mere soldier, Caesar was a cultivated man. Born of a noble family, he received an excellent education, which he furthered by studying in Greece with some of the most eminent teachers of the day. He was also a shrewd politician of unbridled ambition, to which he added a successful military career.

In 58 B.C., Caesar became governor of Gaul, the region of modern France (see Map 7.2), a huge area that he had conquered in the name of Rome. Caesar's account of his operations, his *Commentaries* on the Gallic wars, became a classic in Western literature and most schoolchildren's introduction to Latin. By 49 B.C. the First Triumvirate had fallen apart. Crassus had died in battle, and Caesar and Pompey, each suspecting the other of treachery, came to blows. The result was a long and bloody civil war, which raged from Spain across northern Africa to Egypt. Although Pompey enjoyed the official support of the government, Caesar finally defeated Pompey's forces in 45 B.C. He had overthrown the Republic and made himself dictator.

Julius Caesar was not merely another victorious general. Politically brilliant, he was determined to make basic reforms, even at the expense of the old constitution. He took the first long step to break down the barriers between Italy and the provinces, extending citizenship to many of the provincials who had supported him. Caesar also took measures to cope with Rome's burgeoning population. By Caesar's day perhaps 750,000 people lived in Rome. Caesar drew up plans to send his veterans and some 80,000 of the poor and unemployed to colonies throughout the Mediterranean. He founded at least twenty colonies, most of which were located in Gaul, Spain, and North Africa. These colonies were important agents in spreading Roman culture in the western Mediterranean. Caesar's work would eventually lead to a Roman empire composed of citizens, not subjects.

In 44 B.C. a group of conspirators assassinated Caesar and set off another round of civil war. Caesar had named his eighteen-year-old grandnephew, Octavian—or Augustus, as he is better known to historians—as his heir. Augustus joined forces with two of Caesar's lieutenants, Marc Antony and Lepidus, in a pact known as the Second Triumvirate, and together they hunted down and defeated Caesar's murderers. In the process, however, Augustus and Antony came into conflict. Antony, "boastful, arrogant, and full of empty exultation and capricious ambition," proved to be the major threat to Augustus's designs.[6] In 33 B.C. Augustus branded Antony a traitor and a rebel. He painted lurid pictures of Antony lingering in the eastern Mediterranean, a romantic and foolish captive of the seductive Cleopatra, queen of Egypt and bitter enemy of Rome. In 31 B.C., with the might of Rome at his back, Augustus met and defeated the army and navy of Antony and Cleopatra at the Battle of Actium in Greece (see Map 7.2). Augustus's victory put an end to an age of civil war that had lasted since the days of Sulla.

SUMMARY

The final days of the Republic, though filled with war and chaos, should not obscure the fact that much of the Roman achievement survived the march of armies. The Romans had conquered the Mediterranean world only to find that conquest required them to change their way of life. Socially, they imbibed Greek culture and adjusted themselves to the superior civilization of the Hellenistic East. Politically, their city-state constitution broke down and expired in the wars of the Republic. Even so, men like Caesar and later Augustus sought new solutions to the problems confronting Rome. The result, as Chapter 8 describes, was a system of government capable of administering an empire with justice and fairness. Out of the failure of the Republic arose the pax Romana of the empire.

NOTES

1. Polybius, *The Histories* 1.1.5. Unless otherwise credited, all quotations from a foreign language in this chapter are translated by John Buckler.
2. Sallust, *War with Catiline* 10.1–3.
3. Ovid, *Fasti* 2.535–539.
4. Horace, *Letters* 2.1.156.
5. Plutarch, *Life of Tiberius Gracchus* 9.5–6.
6. Plutarch, *Life of Antony* 2.8.

SUGGESTED READING

H. H. Scullard covers much of Roman history in a series of books: *The Etruscan Cities and Rome* (1967), *A History of the Roman World, 753–146 B.C.,* 3d ed. (1961), and

From the Gracchi to Nero, 5th ed. (1982). R. T. Ridley, *The History of Rome* (1989), is a new, undogmatic history of Rome, firmly based in the sources. A. E. Astin, ed., *The Cambridge Ancient History,* 2d ed., vol. 7 (1988), discusses the rise of Rome and its relations with other Mediterranean powers. The Etruscans have inspired a great deal of work, most notably R. M. Ogilvie, *Early Rome and the Etruscans* (1976), an excellent account of Rome's early relations with those people from the north; and G. Dennis, *Cities and Cemeteries of Etruria,* rev. ed. (1985). K. Christ, *The Romans* (English translation, 1984), is a general treatment by one of Germany's finest historians. A very broad study, J. Ch. Meyer, *Pre-Republican Rome* (1983), treats the cultural relations of early Rome chronologically between 1000 and 500 B.C.

E. T. Salmon, *The Making of Roman Italy* (1982), analyzes Roman expansion and its implications for Italy. Roman expansion is also the subject of R. M. Errington, *The Dawn of Empire* (1971); and W. V. Harris, *War and Imperialism in Republican Rome 327–70 B.C.* (1979). J. F. Lazenby, *Hannibal's War: A Military History of the Second Punic War* (1978), is a detailed treatment of one of Rome's greatest struggles. One of the best studies of Rome's political evolution is the classic by A. N. Sherwin-White, *The Roman Citizenship,* 2d ed. (1973), a work of enduring value. S. L. Dyson, *The Creation of the Roman Frontier* (1985), deals with the process by which the Romans established their frontiers. Two other works concentrate on Rome's penetration of the Hellenistic East: A. N. Sherwin-White, *Roman Foreign Policy in the Near East* (1984), and the far better but longer book by E. S. Gruen, *The Hellenistic World and the Coming of Rome,* 2 vols. (1984). A. Keaveney, *Rome and the Unification of Italy* (1988), treats the way in which the Romans put down the revolt of their Italian allies and then integrated them into the Roman political system.

The great figures and events of the late Republic have been the object of much new work. E. S. Gruen, *The Last Generation of the Roman Republic* (1974), treats the period as a whole. Very important are the studies of E. Badian, *Roman Imperialism in the Late Republic* (1968), and *Publicans and Sinners* (1972). R. Syme, *The Roman Revolution,* rev. ed. (1952), is a classic. Valuable also are P. A. Brunt, *Social Conflicts in the Roman Republic*

(1971); A. J. Toynbee, *Hannibal's Legacy,* 2 vols. (1965); and A. W. Lintott, *Violence in the Roman Republic* (1968).

Many new works deal with individual Romans who left their mark on this period. H. C. Boren, *The Gracchi* (1968), treats the work of the two brothers, and A. M. Eckstein, *Senate and Generals* (1987), discusses how the decisions of individual generals affected both the senate and Roman foreign relations. A. Keaveney, *Sulla: The Last Republican* (1983), is a new study of a man who thought of himself as a reformer. A. E. Astin has produced two works that are far more extensive than their titles indicate: *Scipio Aemilianus* (1967) and *Cato the Censor* (1978). J. Leach, *Pompey the Great* (1978), surveys the career of this politician, and C. Habicht, *Cicero the Politician* (1989), offers a sensible view of Cicero, one that emphasizes both his laudable patriotism as well as his political weaknesses. M. Gelzer, *Caesar, Politician and Statesman* (English translation, 1968), is easily the best study of one of history's most significant figures. E. G. Huzar, *Marc Antony* (1987), offers a new assessment of the career of the man who challenged Augustus for control of the Roman world. Caesar's one-time colleague Marcus Crassus is studied in A. Ward, *Marcus Crassus and the Late Roman Republic* (1977).

K. D. White, *Roman Farming* (1970), deals with agriculture, and J. P. V. D. Balsdon covers social life in the Republic and the Empire in two works: *Life and Leisure in Ancient Rome* (1969) and *Roman Women,* rev. ed. (1974). Greek cultural influence on Roman life is the subject of A. Wardman, *Rome's Debt to Greece* (1976). F. Schulz, *Classical Roman Law* (1951), is a useful introduction to an important topic. H. H. Scullard, *Festivals and Ceremonies of the Roman Republic* (1981), gives a fresh look at religious practices. Work on Roman social history has advanced in several areas. G. Alfoeldy, a major scholar, has written *The Social History of Rome* (1985), an ambitious undertaking. R. M. Ogilvie, *Roman Literature and Society* (1980), uses literature to examine the development and achievements of Roman society. Work on Roman women, with emphasis on the aristocracy, includes J. P. Hallett, *Fathers and Daughters in Roman Society* (1984). S. Dixon, *The Roman Mother* (1988), focuses specifically on women's role as mothers within the Roman family.

8

The Pax Romana

Hadrian's Wall, Cuddy's Crag, Northumberland

*H*ad the Romans conquered the entire Mediterranean world only to turn it into their battlefield? Would they, like the Greeks before them, become their own worst enemies, destroying one another and wasting their strength until they perished? At Julius Caesar's death in 44 B.C. it must have seemed so to many. Yet finally, in 31 B.C. Augustus (63 B.C.–A.D. 14), restored peace to a tortured world, and with peace came prosperity, new hope, and a new vision of Rome's destiny. The Roman poet Virgil expressed this vision most nobly:

You, Roman, remember—these are your arts:
To rule nations, and to impose the ways of peace,
To spare the humble and to war down the proud.[1]

In place of the Republic, Augustus established what can be called a constitutional monarchy. He attempted to achieve lasting cooperation in government and balance among the people, magistrates, senate, and army. His efforts were not always successful. His settlement of Roman affairs did not permanently end civil war. Yet he carried on Julius Caesar's work. It was Augustus who created the structure that the modern world calls the "Roman Empire." He did his work so well and his successors so capably added to it that Rome realized Virgil's hope. For the first and second centuries A.D. the lot of the Mediterranean world was peace—the pax Romana, a period of security, order, harmony, flourishing culture, and expanding economy. It was a period that saw the wilds of Gaul, Spain, Germany, and eastern Europe introduced to Greco-Roman culture. By the third century A.D., when the empire began to give way to the Western medieval world, the greatness of Rome and the blessings of Roman culture had left an indelible mark on the ages to come.

- How did the Roman emperors govern the empire, and how did they spread Roman influence into northern Europe?

- What were the fruits of the pax Romana?

- Why did Christianity, originally a minor local religion, sweep across the Roman world to change it fundamentally?

- How did the Roman Empire meet the grim challenge of barbarian invasion and subsequent economic decline?

This chapter focuses on the answers to these questions.

AUGUSTUS'S SETTLEMENT (31 B.C.–A.D. 14)

When Augustus put an end to the civil wars that had raged since 88 B.C., he faced monumental problems of reconstruction. He could easily have declared himself dictator, as Julius Caesar had done, but the thought was repugnant to him. Augustus was neither an autocrat nor a revolutionary. His solution, as he put it, was to restore the Republic. But was that possible? Years of anarchy and civil war had shattered the republican constitution. It could not be rebuilt in a day. Augustus recognized these problems but did not let them stop him. From 29 to 23 B.C., he toiled to heal Rome's wounds. The first problem facing him was to rebuild the constitution and the organs of government. Next he had to demobilize the army and care for the welfare of the provinces. Then he had to face the danger of barbarians at Rome's European frontiers. Augustus successfully met these challenges. His gift of peace to a war-torn world sowed the seeds of a literary flowering that produced some of the finest fruits of the Roman mind.

The Principate and the Restored Republic

Augustus claimed that in restoring constitutional government he was also restoring the Republic. One of the biggest challenges in that effort was creating for himself an official place in the new government. Typically Roman, he preferred not to create anything new; he intended instead to modify republican forms and offices to meet new circumstances. Augustus planned for the senate to take on a serious burden of duty and responsibility. He expected it to administer some of the provinces, continue to be the chief deliberative body of the state, and act as a court of law. Yet he did not give the senate enough power to become his partner in government. As a result, the senate could not live up to the responsibilities that Augustus assigned, and many of its prerogatives shifted by default to Augustus and his successors.

Augustus's own position in the restored Republic was something of an anomaly. He could not simply surrender the reins of power, for someone else would seize them. But how was he to fit into a republican constitution? Again Augustus had his own answer. He became *princeps civitatis,* the "first citizen of the state." This prestigious title carried no power; it indicated only that Augustus was the most distinguished of all Roman citizens. In effect it designated Augustus as the first among equals and a little more equal than anyone else. His real power resided in the magistracies he held, the powers granted him by the senate, and above all his control of the army, which he turned into a permanent, standing organization. Clearly, much of the *principate,* as the position of First Citizen is known, was a legal fiction. Yet that need not imply that Augustus, like a modern dictator, tried to clothe himself with constitutional legitimacy. In an inscription known as *Res Gestae (The Deeds of Augustus),* Augustus described his constitutional position:

In my sixth and seventh consulships [28–27 B.C.], I had ended the civil war, having obtained through universal consent total control of affairs. I transferred the Republic from my power to the authority of the Roman people and the senate. . . . After that time I stood before all in rank, but I had power no greater than those who were my colleagues in any magistracy.[2]

Augustus was not exactly being a hypocrite, but he carefully kept his real military power in the background. As consul he had no more constitutional and legal power than his fellow consul. Yet in addition to the consulship Augustus held many other magistracies, which his fellow consul did not. Constitutionally, his ascendancy within the state stemmed from the number of magistracies he held and the power granted him by the senate. At first he held the consulship annually; then the senate voted him proconsular power on a regular basis. The senate also voted him *tribunicia potestas*—the "full power of the tribunes." Tribunician power gave Augustus the right to call the senate into session, present legislation to the people, and defend their rights. He held either high office or the powers of chief magistrate year in and year out. No other magistrate could do the same. In 12 B.C. he became *pontifex maximus,* "chief priest of the state." By assuming this position of great honor, Augustus became chief religious official in the state. Without specifically saying so, he had created the office of emperor, which included

Augustus This statue portrays Augustus as the Pontifex Maximus, "chief priest of the state." The emperor thereby emphasized his peaceful role and his position as the intermediary between the Roman people and the gods. *(Source: Alinari/Art Resource)*

many traditional powers separated from their traditional offices.

The main source of Augustus's power was his position as commander of the Roman army. His title *imperator,* with which Rome customarily honored a general after a major victory, came to mean "emperor" in the modern sense of the term. Augustus governed the provinces where troops were needed for defense. The frontiers were his special concern. There Roman legionaries held the German barbarians at arm's length. The frontiers were also areas where fighting could be expected to break out. Augustus made sure that Rome went to war only at his command. He controlled deployment of the Roman army and paid its wages. He granted bonuses and gave veterans retirement benefits. Thus he avoided the problems with the army that the old senate had created for itself. Augustus never shared control of the army, and no Roman found it easy to defy him militarily.

The size of the army was a special problem for Augustus. Rome's legions numbered thousands of men, far more than were necessary to maintain peace. What was Augustus to do with so many soldiers? This problem had constantly plagued the late Republic, whose leaders never found a solution. Augustus gave his own answer in the *Res*

Gestae: "I founded colonies of soldiers in Africa, Sicily, Macedonia, Spain, Achaea, Gaul, and Pisidia. Moreover, Italy has 28 colonies under my auspices."[3] At least forty new colonies arose, most of them in the western Mediterranean. Augustus's veterans took abroad with them their Roman language and culture. His colonies, like Julius Caesar's, were a significant tool in the further spread of Roman culture throughout the West.

What is to be made of Augustus's constitutional settlement? Despite his claims to the contrary, Augustus had not restored the Republic. In fact, he would probably have agreed with the words of John Stuart Mill, the nineteenth-century English philosopher: "When society requires to be rebuilt, there is no use in attempting to rebuild it on the old plan." Augustus had created a constitutional monarchy, something completely new in Roman history. The title *princeps,* "first citizen," came to mean in Rome, as it does today, "prince" in the sense of a sovereign ruler.

Augustus also failed to solve a momentous problem. He never found a way to institutionalize his position with the army. The ties between the princeps and the army were always personal. The army was loyal to the princeps but not necessarily to the state. The Augustan principate worked well at first, but by the third century A.D. the army would make and break emperors at will. Nonetheless, it is a measure of Augustus's success that his settlement survived as long and as well as it did.

Augustus's Administration of the Provinces

To gain an accurate idea of the total population of the empire, Augustus ordered a census to be taken in 28 B.C. In Augustus's day the population of the Roman Empire was between 70 and 100 million people, fully 75 percent of whom lived in the provinces. In the areas under his immediate jurisdiction, Augustus put provincial administration on an ordered basis and improved its functioning. Believing that the cities of the empire should look after their own affairs, he encouraged local self-government and urbanism. Augustus respected local customs and told his governors to do the same.

To create a spiritual bond between the provinces and Rome, Augustus encouraged the cult of Roma, goddess and guardian of the state. In the Hellenistic East, where king-worship was an estab-

Roma et Augustus   The nature of the cult of *Roma et Augustus* is immediately obvious from this cameo. Seated to the left is Augustus, who holds a scepter, which symbolizes his right to reign. He speaks with Roma, who personified Rome and who holds in her lap a shield, a symbol of her protection of the city of Rome and its empire. *(Source: Kunsthistorisches Museum, Vienna)*

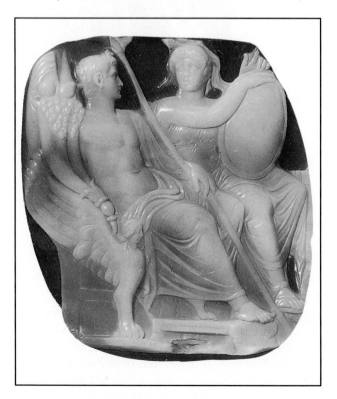

lished custom, the cult of *Roma et Augustus,* "Roma and Augustus," grew and spread rapidly. Augustus then introduced the concept of the cult in the West. By the time of his death in A.D. 14, nearly every province in the empire could boast an altar or shrine to *Roma et Augustus.* In the West it was not the person of the emperor who was worshiped but his *genius*—his guardian spirit. In praying for the good health and welfare of the emperor, Romans and provincials were praying for the empire itself. The cult became a symbol of Roman unity.

Roman Expansion into Northern and Western Europe

For the history of Western civilization a momentous aspect of Augustus's reign was Roman expansion into the wilderness of northern and western Europe (Map 8.1). In this Augustus was following in Julius Caesar's footsteps. Between 58 and 51 B.C., Caesar had subdued Gaul and unsuccessfully attacked Britain. Carrying on his work, Augustus pushed Rome's frontier into the region of modern Germany. The Germanic tribes were tough opponents, and the Roman legions saw much bitter fighting against them in the north.

Augustus began his work in the north by completing the conquest of Spain. In Gaul, apart from minor campaigns, most of his work was peaceful. He founded twelve new towns. The Roman road system linked new settlements with one another and with Italy. But the German frontier, along the Rhine River, was the scene of hard fighting. In 12 B.C. Augustus ordered a major invasion of Germany beyond the Rhine. Roman legions advanced to the Elbe River, and a Roman fleet explored the North Sea and Jutland. The area north of the Main River and west of the Elbe was on the point of becoming Roman. But in A.D. 9 Augustus's general Varus lost some twenty thousand troops at the Battle of the Teutoburger Forest. Thereafter the Rhine remained the Roman frontier.

Meanwhile, more successful generals extended the Roman standards as far as the Danube. Roman legions penetrated the area of modern Austria and western Hungary. The regions of modern Serbia, Bulgaria, and Romania fell. Within this area the legionaries built fortified camps. Roads linked these camps with one another, and settlements grew up around the camps. Traders began to frequent the frontier and to traffic with the barbarians. Thus Roman culture—the rough-and-ready kind found in military camps—gradually spread into the northern wilderness.

The achievements of Augustus in the north were monumental. For the first time in history, Greco-Roman culture spread beyond the sunny Mediterranean into the heart of Europe. Amid the vast expanse of forests, Roman towns, trade, language, and law began to exert a civilizing influence on the barbarians. The Roman way of life attracted the barbarians, who soon recognized the benefits of assimilating Roman culture. Many military camps became towns, and many modern European cities owe their origins to the forts of the Roman army. For the first time, the barbarian north came into direct, immediate, and continuous contact with Mediterranean culture.

Literary Flowering

The Augustan settlement's gift of peace inspired a literary flowering unparalleled in Roman history. With good reason this period is known as the "golden age" of Latin literature. Augustus and many of his friends actively encouraged poets and writers. The poet Horace summed up Augustus and his era:

With Caesar Augustus the guardian of the state
Not civil rage nor violence shall drive out peace,
Nor wrath which forges swords
And turns unhappy cities against each other[4]

These lines are not empty flattery, despite Augustus's support of many contemporary Latin writers. To a generation that had known only vicious civil war, Augustus's settlement was a blessing.

The tone and ideal of Roman literature, like that of the Greeks, was humanistic and worldly. Roman poets and prose writers celebrated the dignity of humanity and the range of its accomplishments. They stressed the physical and emotional joys of a comfortable, peaceful life. Their works were highly polished, elegant in style, and intellectual in conception. Roman poets referred to the gods frequently and treated mythological themes, but always the core of their work was human, not divine.

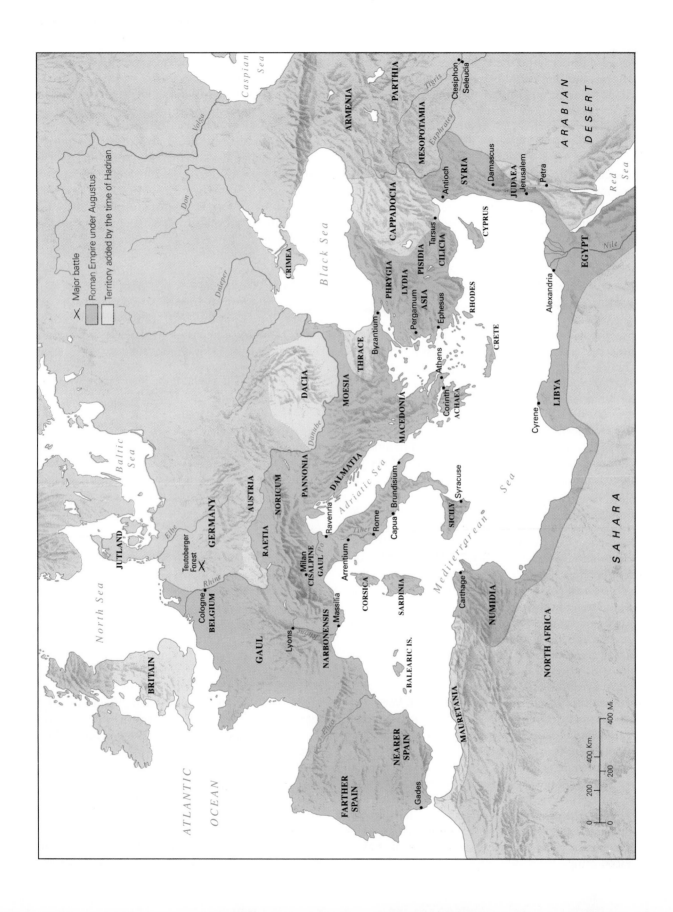

Major battle ✗

Roman Empire under Augustus

Territory added by the time of Hadrian

ATLANTIC OCEAN

North Sea

Baltic Sea

Caspian Sea

BRITAIN

JUTLAND

GERMANY

Elbe

Rhine

Teutoberger Forest ✗

Cologne

BELGIUM

GAUL

Lyons

Rhône

NARBONENSIS

Massilia

GAUL, CISALPINE

Milan

RAETIA

AUSTRIA

NORICUM

PANNONIA

Danube

DACIA

MOESIA

THRACE

Byzantium

CRIMEA

Dnieper

Don

Volga

Black Sea

ARMENIA

PARTHIA

Tigris

Euphrates

Ctesiphon
Seleucia

MESOPOTAMIA

CAPPADOCIA

SYRIA

Damascus

Antioch

JUDAEA

Jerusalem

Petra

ARABIAN DESERT

Red Sea

PHRYGIA

LYDIA

PISIDIA

CILICIA

Tarsus

ASIA

Pergamum

Ephesus

RHODES

CYPRUS

CRETE

Alexandria

EGYPT

Nile

MACEDONIA

Athens

Corinth

ACHAEA

LIBYA

Cyrene

Arrentium

Ravenna

Tiber

Rome

Capua

Brundisium

DALMATIA

Adriatic Sea

Syracuse

SICILY

Mediterranean Sea

CORSICA

SARDINIA

BALEARIC IS.

Carthage

NUMIDIA

NORTH AFRICA

MAURETANIA

SAHARA

NEARER SPAIN

FARTHER SPAIN

Gades

Ebro

400 Mi.

400 Km.

200

200

0

0

Virgil (70–19 B.C.) celebrated the new age in the *Georgics,* a long poetic work on agriculture. Virgil delighted in his own farm, and his poems sing of the pleasures of peaceful farm life. The poet also tells how to keep bees, grow grapes and olives, plow, and manage a farm. Throughout the *Georgics* Virgil wrote about things he himself had seen, rather than drawing his theme from the writings of others. Virgil's poetry is robust yet graceful. A sensitive man who delighted in simple things, Virgil left in his *Georgics* a charming picture of life in the Italian countryside during a period of peace.

Virgil's masterpiece is the *Aeneid,* an epic poem that is the Latin equivalent of the Greek *Iliad* and *Odyssey.* In the *Aeneid* Virgil expressed his admiration for Augustus's work by celebrating the shining ideal of a world blessed by the pax Romana. Virgil's account of the founding of Rome and the early years of the city gave final form to the legend of Aeneas, the Trojan hero who escaped to Italy at the fall of Troy. The principal Roman tradition held that Romulus was the founder of Rome, but the legend of Aeneas was also very old; it was known by the Etruscans as early as the fifth century B.C. Although Rome could not have had two founders, Virgil linked the legends of Aeneas and Romulus and kept them both. In so doing, he also connected Rome with Greece's heroic past. Recounting the story of Aeneas and Dido, the queen of Carthage, Virgil made their ill-fated love affair the cause of the Punic wars. But above all, the *Aeneid* is the expression of Virgil's passionate belief in Rome's greatness. It is a vision of Rome as the protector of the good and noble against the forces of darkness and disruption.

In its own way Livy's history of Rome, entitled simply *Ab Urbe Condita (From the Founding of the City),* is the prose counterpart of the *Aeneid.* Livy (59 B.C.–A.D. 17) received training in Greek and Latin literature, rhetoric, and philosophy. He even urged the future emperor Claudius to write history. Livy loved and admired the heroes and great deeds of the Republic, but he was also a friend of

MAP 8.1 Roman Expansion Under the Empire   Following Roman expansion during the Republic, Augustus added vast tracts of Europe to the Roman Empire, which the emperor Hadrian later enlarged by assuming control over parts of central Europe, the Near East, and North Africa.

Augustus and a supporter of the principate. He especially approved of Augustus's efforts to restore republican virtues.

The poet Horace (65–8 B.C.) rose from humble beginnings to friendship with Augustus. The son of a former slave and tax collector, Horace nonetheless received an excellent education. He loved Greek literature and finished his education in Athens. After Augustus's victory he returned to Rome and became Virgil's friend. Horace acquired a small farm north of Rome, which delighted him. He was as content as Virgil on his farm and expressed his joy in a few lines:

Strive to add nothing to the myrtle plant!
The myrtle befits both you, the servant,
And me, the master, as I drink under the
Thick-leaved vine.[5]

Horace happily turned his pen to celebrating Rome's newly won peace and prosperity. One of

Virgil and *The Aeneid*   Virgil's great epic poem, *The Aeneid,* became a literary classic immediately on its appearance and has lost none of its power since. The Roman world honored Virgil for his poetic genius not only by treasuring his work but also by portraying him in art. Here two muses, who inspired artists, flank the poet while he writes his epic poem. *(Source: C. M. Dixon)*

Ara Pacis Augustae This scene from the Ara Pacis Augustae, the Altar of Augustan Peace, celebrates Augustus's restoration of peace and the fruits of peace. Here Mother Earth is depicted with her children. The cow and the sheep under the goddess represent the prosperity brought by peace, especially the agricultural prosperity so highly cherished by Virgil. *(Source: Bildarchiv Foto Marburg/Art Resource)*

his finest odes commemorates Augustus's victory over Cleopatra at Actium in 31 B.C. Cleopatra is depicted as a frenzied queen, drunk with desire to destroy Rome. Horace saw in Augustus's victory the triumph of West over East, of simplicity over Oriental excess. One of the truly moving aspects of Horace's poetry, like Virgil's, is his deep and abiding gratitude for the pax Romana.

For Rome, Augustus's age was one of hope and new beginnings. Augustus had put the empire on a new foundation. Constitutional monarchy was firmly established, and government was to all appearances a partnership between princeps and senate. The Augustan settlement was a delicate structure, and parts of it would in time be discarded. Nevertheless it worked, and by building on it later emperors would carry on Augustus's work. The solidity of Augustus's work became obvious at his death in A.D. 14. Since the principate was not tech-

nically an office, Augustus could not legally hand it to a successor. Augustus had recognized this problem and long before his death had found a way to solve it. He shared his consular and tribunician powers with his adopted son, Tiberius, thus grooming him for the principate. In his will Augustus left most of his vast fortune to Tiberius, and the senate formally requested Tiberius to assume the burdens of the principate. All the formalities apart, Augustus had succeeded in creating a dynasty.

THE COMING OF CHRISTIANITY

During the reign of the emperor Tiberius (A.D. 14–37), perhaps in A.D. 29, Pontius Pilate, prefect of Judaea, the Roman province created out of the

Jewish kingdom of Judah, condemned Jesus of Nazareth to death. At the time a minor event, this has become one of the best-known moments in history. How did these two men come to their historic meeting? The question is not idle, for Rome was as important as Judaea to Christianity. Jesus was born in a troubled time, when Roman rule aroused hatred and unrest among the Jews. This climate of hostility affected the lives of all who lived in Judaea, Roman and Jew alike. It forms the backdrop of Jesus's life, and it had a fundamental impact on his ministry. Without an understanding of this age of anxiety in Judaea, Jesus and his followers cannot fully be appreciated.

The entry of Rome into Jewish affairs was anything but peaceful. The civil wars that destroyed the Republic wasted the prosperity of Judaea and the entire eastern Mediterranean world. Jewish leaders took sides in the fighting, and Judaea suffered its share of ravages and military confiscations. Peace brought little satisfaction to the Jews. Although Augustus treated Judaea generously, the Romans won no popularity by making Herod king of Judaea. King Herod gave Judaea prosperity and security, but the Jews hated his acceptance of Greek culture. He was also a bloodthirsty prince, who murdered his own wife and sons. Upon his death, the Jews broke out in revolt. For the next ten years Herod's successor waged almost constant war against the rebels. Added to the horrors of civil war were years of crop failure, which caused famine and plague. Men calling themselves "prophets" proclaimed the end of the world and the coming of the Messiah, the savior of Israel.

At length the Romans intervened to restore order. Augustus put Judaea under the charge of a prefect answerable directly to the emperor. Religious matters and local affairs became the responsibility of the *Sanhedrin,* the highest Jewish judicial body. Although many prefects tried to perform their duties scrupulously and conscientiously, many others were rapacious and indifferent to Jewish culture. Often acting from fear rather than cruelty, some prefects fiercely stamped out any signs of popular discontent. Pontius Pilate, prefect from A.D. 26 to 36, is typical of such incompetent officials. Although eventually relieved of his duties in disgrace, Pilate brutally put down even innocent demonstrations. Especially hated were the Roman tax collectors, called "publicans," many of whom pitilessly gouged the Jews. *Publicans* and *sinners*— the words became synonymous. Clashes between

Roman troops and Jewish guerrillas inflamed the anger of both sides.

Among the Jews two movements spread. First was the rise of the Zealots, extremists who worked and fought to rid Judaea of the Romans. Resolute in their worship of Yahweh, they refused to pay any tax other than the tax levied by the Jewish temple. Their battles with the Roman legionaries were marked by savagery on both sides. As usual, the innocent caught in the middle suffered grievously. As Roman policy grew tougher, even moderate Jews began to hate the conquerors. Judaea came more and more to resemble a tinderbox, ready to burst into flames at a single spark.

The second movement was the growth of militant apocalyptic sentiment—the belief that the coming of the Messiah was near. This belief was an old one among the Jews. But by the first century A.D. it had become more widespread and fervent than ever before. Typical was the Apocalypse of Baruch, which foretold the destruction of the Roman Empire. First would come a period of great tribulation, misery, and injustice. At the worst of the suffering, the Messiah would appear. The Messiah would destroy the Roman legions and all the kingdoms that had ruled Israel. Then the Messiah would inaugurate a period of happiness and plenty.

This was no abstract notion among the Jews. As the ravages of war became more widespread and conditions worsened, more and more people prophesied the imminent coming of the Messiah. One such was John the Baptist, "The voice of one crying in the wilderness, Prepare ye the way of the lord."[6] Many Jews did just that. The sect described in the Dead Sea Scrolls readied itself for the end of the world. Its members were probably Essenes, and their social organization closely resembled that of early Christians. Members of this group shared possessions, precisely as John the Baptist urged people to do. Yet this sect, unlike the Christians later, also made military preparations for the day of the Messiah.

Jewish religious aspirations were only one part of the story. What can be said of the pagan world of Rome and its empire into which Christianity was shortly to be born? To answer that question, one must first explore the spiritual environment of the pagans, many of whom would soon be caught up in the new Christian religion. Paganism at the time of Jesus's birth can be broadly divided into three spheres: the official state religion of Rome, the traditional Roman cults of hearth and countryside, and the new mystery religions that flowed from the Hellenistic East. The official state religion and its cults honored the traditional deities: Jupiter, Juno, Mars, and such newcomers as Isis (see page 159). This very formal religion was conducted on an official level by socially prominent state priests. It was above all a religion of ritual and grand spectacle, but it provided little emotional or spiritual comfort. The state cults were a bond between the gods and the people, a religious contract to ensure the well-being of Rome. Most Romans felt that the official cults must be maintained, despite their lack of spiritual content, simply to ensure the welfare of the state. After all, observance of the traditional official religion had brought Rome victory, empire, security, and wealth.

For emotional and spiritual satisfaction, many Romans observed the old cults of home and countryside, the same cults that had earlier delighted Cato the Elder (see page 185). These traditional cults brought the Romans back in touch with nature and with something elemental to Roman life. Particularly popular were rustic shrines—often a small building or a sacred tree in an enclosure—to honor the native spirit of the locality. Though familiar and simple, even this traditional religion was not enough for many. They wanted something more personal and immediate. Many common people believed in a supernatural world seen dimly through dreams, magic, miracles, and spells. They wanted some sort of revelation about this supernatural world and security in it during the hereafter. Some people turned to astrology in the belief that they could read their destiny in the stars. But that was cold comfort, since they could not change what the stars foretold.

Many people in the Roman Empire found the answer to their need for emotionally satisfying religion and spiritual security in the various Hellenistic mystery cults. Such cults generally provided their adherents with an emotional outlet. For example, the cult of Bacchus was marked by its wine drinking and often drunken frenzy. Although the cult of the Great Mother, Cybele, was celebrated with emotional and even overwrought processions, it offered its worshipers the promise of immortality. The appeal of the mystery religions was not simply that they provided emotional release. They gave their adherents what neither the traditional cults nor philosophy could—above all, security. Yet at the same time, the mystery religions

were by nature exclusive, and none was truly international, open to everyone.

Into this climate of Roman religious yearning and political severity, fanatical zealotry, and messianic hope came Jesus of Nazareth (ca 5 B.C.–A.D. 29). Raised in Galilee, stronghold of the Zealots, Jesus himself was a man of peace. Jesus urged his listeners to love God as their father and one another as God's children. The kingdom that he proclaimed was no earthly one, but one of eternal happiness in a life after death. Jesus's teachings are strikingly similar to those of Hillel (30 B.C.–A.D. 9), a great rabbi and interpreter of the Scriptures. Hillel taught the Jews to love one another as they loved God. He taught them to treat others as they themselves wished to be treated. Jesus's preaching was in this same serene tradition.

Jesus's teachings were Jewish. He declared that he would change not one jot of the Jewish law. His orthodoxy enabled him to preach in synagogues and the temple. His only deviation from orthodoxy was his insistence that he taught in his own name, not in the name of Yahweh. Was he then the Messiah? A small band of followers thought so, and Jesus revealed himself to them as the Messiah. Yet Jesus had his own conception of the Messiah. Unlike the Messiah of the Apocalypse of Baruch, Jesus would not destroy the Roman Empire. He told his disciples flatly that they were to "render unto Caesar the things that are Caesar's." Jesus would establish a spiritual kingdom, not an earthly one. Repeatedly he told his disciples that his kingdom was "not of this world."

Of Jesus's life and teachings the prefect Pontius Pilate knew little and cared even less. All that concerned him was the maintenance of peace and order. The crowds following Jesus at the time of Passover, a highly emotional time in the Jewish year, alarmed Pilate. Some Jews believed that Jesus was the long-awaited Messiah. Others were disappointed because he refused to preach rebellion against Rome. Still others hated and feared Jesus and wanted to be rid of him. The last thing Pilate wanted was a riot.

Christian tradition has made much of Pontius Pilate. In the medieval West he was considered a monster. In the Ethiopian church he is considered a saint. Neither monster nor saint, Pilate was simply a hard-bitten Roman official. He did his duty, at times harshly. In Judaea his duty was to enforce the law and keep the peace. These were the problems on his mind when Jesus stood before him. Je-

Pontius Pilate and Jesus   This Byzantine mosaic from Ravenna illustrates a dramatic moment in Jesus' trial and crucifixion. Jesus stands accused before Pilate, but Pilate symbolically washes his hands of the whole affair. *(Source: Scala/Art Resource)*

sus as king of the Jews did not worry him. The popular agitation surrounding Jesus did. To avert riot and bloodshed, Pilate condemned Jesus to death. It is a bitter historical irony that such a gentle man died such a cruel death. After being scourged, he was hung from a cross until he died in the sight of family, friends, enemies, and the merely curious.

Once Pilate's soldiers had carried out the sentence, the entire matter seemed to be closed. Yet on the third day after Jesus's crucifixion, an odd rumor began to circulate in Jerusalem. Some of Jesus's followers were saying he had risen from the dead, while others accused the Christians of having stolen his body. For these earliest Christians and for generations to come, the resurrection of Jesus became a central element of faith and, more than that, a promise: Jesus had triumphed over

death, and his resurrection promised all Christians immortality. In Jerusalem the tumult subsided. Jesus's followers lived quietly and peacefully, unmolested by Roman or Jew. Pilate had no quarrel with them, and Judaism already had many minor sects. Peter (d. A.D. 67?), the first of Jesus's followers, became the head of the sect, which continued to observe Jewish law and religious customs. A man of traditional Jewish beliefs, Peter felt that Jesus's teachings were meant exclusively for the Jews. Only in their practices of baptism and the sacrament of the *Eucharist,* the communal celebration of the Lord's Supper, did the sect differ from normal Jewish custom. Meanwhile, they awaited the return of Jesus.

Christianity might have remained a purely Jewish sect had it not been for Paul of Tarsus (A.D. 5?–67?). The conversion of Hellenized Jews and of

Gentiles (non-Jews) to Christianity caused the sect grave problems. Were the Gentiles subject to the law of Moses? If not, was Christianity to have two sets of laws? The answer to these questions was Paul's momentous contribution to Christianity. Paul was unlike Jesus or Peter. Born in a thriving, busy city filled with Romans, Greeks, Jews, Syrians, and others, he was at home in the world of Greco-Roman culture. After his conversion to Christianity, he taught that his native Judaism was the preparation for the Messiah and that Jesus by his death and resurrection had fulfilled the prophecy of Judaism and initiated a new age. Paul taught that Jesus was the son of God, the beginning of a new law, and he preached that Jesus's teachings were to be proclaimed to all, whether Jew or Gentile. Paul thus made a significant break with Judaism, Christianity's parent religion, for Judaism was exclusive and did not seek converts.

Paul's influence was far greater than that of any other early Christian. He traveled the length and breadth of the eastern Roman world, spreading his doctrine and preaching of Jesus. To little assemblies of believers in cities as distant as Rome and Corinth he taught that Jesus had died to save all people. Paul's vision of Christianity won out over Peter's traditionalism. Christianity broke with Judaism and embarked on its own course.

What was Christianity's appeal to the Roman world? What did this obscure sect give people that other religions did not? Christianity possessed many different attractions. One of its appeals was its willingness to embrace both men and women, slaves and nobles. Many of the Eastern mystery religions with which Christianity competed were exclusive in one way or another. Mithraism, a mystery religion descended from Zoroastrianism, spread throughout the entire empire. Mithras, the sun-god, embodied good and warred against evil. Like Christianity, Mithraism offered elaborate and moving rituals including a form of baptism, a code of moral conduct, and the promise of life after death. Unlike Christianity, however, Mithraism permitted only men to become devotees. Much the same was true of the ancient Eleusinian mysteries of Greece, which were open only to Greeks and Romans.

Indeed, Christianity shared many of the features of mystery religions. It possessed a set of beliefs, such as the divinity of Jesus, and a literary history. Paul's *epistles,* or letters, to various Christian com-munities were the earliest pieces of literature dealing with Christian beliefs and conduct. Shortly thereafter some of the disciples wrote *gospels,* or accounts of Jesus's life and teachings. Once people had prepared themselves for conversion by learning of Jesus's message and committing themselves to live by it, they were baptized. Like initiates in mystery religions, they entered the community of believers. The Christian community of believers was strengthened by the sacrament of the Eucharist. Christianity also had more than a priesthood to officiate at rituals; it had an ecclesiastical administration that helped to ensure continuity within the new church.

Christianity appealed to common people and to the poor. Its communal celebration of the Lord's Supper gave men and women a sense of belonging. Christianity also offered its adherents the promise of salvation. Christians believed that Jesus on the cross had defeated evil and that he would reward his followers with eternal life after death. Christianity also offered the possibility of forgiveness. Human nature was weak, and even the best Christians would fall into sin. But Jesus loved sinners and forgave those who repented. In its doctrines of salvation and forgiveness alone, Christianity had a powerful ability to give solace and strength to believers.

Christianity was attractive to many because it gave the Roman world a cause. Hellenistic philosophy had attempted to make men and women self-sufficient: people who became indifferent to the outside world could no longer be hurt by it. That goal alone ruled out any cause except the attainment of serenity. The Romans, never innovators in philosophy, merely elaborated this lonely and austere message. Instead of passivity Christianity stressed the ideal of striving for a goal. Each and every Christian, no matter how poor or humble, supposedly worked to realize the triumph of Christianity on earth. This was God's will, a sacred duty for every Christian. By spreading the word of Jesus, Christians played their part in God's plan. No matter how small, the part each Christian played was important. Since this duty was God's will, Christians believed that the goal would be achieved. The Christian was not discouraged by temporary setbacks, believing Christianity to be invincible.

Christianity gave its devotees a sense of community. No Christian was alone. All members of the

Christian community strove toward the same goal of fulfilling God's plan. Each individual community was in turn a member of a greater community. And that community, the Church General, was indestructible. After all, Jesus himself had promised, "Thou art Peter, and upon this rock I will build my church; and the gates of hell shall not prevail against it."[7]

Christianity's attractions, therefore, were many, from forgiveness of sin to an exalted purpose for each individual. Its insistence on the individual's importance gave solace and encouragement, particularly to the poor and meek. Its claim to divine protection encouraged hope in the eventual success of the Christian community. Christianity thus made participation in the universal possible for everyone. The ultimate reward promised by Christianity was eternal bliss after death.

THE JULIO-CLAUDIANS AND THE FLAVIANS (27 B.C.–A.D. 96)

For fifty years after Augustus's death the dynasty that he established—known as the Julio-Claudians because all members were of the Julian and Claudian clans—provided the emperors of Rome. Some of the Julio-Claudians, such as Tiberius and Claudius, were sound rulers and able administrators. Others, Caligula and Nero, were weak and frivolous men who exercised their power stupidly and brought misery to the empire. Yet even their occasional weaknesses cannot obscure the fact that Julio-Claudians were responsible for some notable achievements, among them the conquest of Britain in A.D. 43, and that during their reigns the empire prospered.

One of the most momentous achievements of the Julio-Claudians was Claudius's creation of an imperial bureaucracy composed of professional administrators. Even the most energetic emperor could not run the empire alone. Numerous duties and immense responsibilities prompted Claudius to delegate power. He began by giving the freedmen of his household official duties, especially in finances. It was a simple, workable system. Claudius knew his former slaves well and could discipline them at will. The effect of Claudius's innovations was to enable the emperor to rule the empire more easily and efficiently.

One of the worst defects of Augustus's settlement—the army's ability to interfere in politics—became obvious during the Julio-Claudian period. Augustus had created a special standing force, the Praetorian Guard, as an imperial bodyguard. In A.D. 41 one of the praetorians murdered Caligula while others hailed Claudius as the emperor. Under the threat of violence, the senate ratified the praetorians' choice. It was a bloody story repeated all too frequently. During the first three centuries of the empire the Praetorian Guard all too often murdered emperors they were supposed to protect and saluted emperors of their own choosing.

In A.D. 68 Nero's inept rule led to military rebellion and his death, thus opening the way to widespread disruption. In A.D. 69, known as the "Year of the Four Emperors," four men claimed the position of emperor. Roman armies in Gaul, on the Rhine, and in the east marched on Rome to make their commanders emperor. The man who emerged triumphant was Vespasian, commander of the eastern armies, who entered Rome in 70 and restored order. Nonetheless, the Year of the Four Emperors proved the Augustan settlement had failed to end civil war.

Not a brilliant politician, Vespasian did not institute sweeping reforms, as had Augustus, or solve the problem of the army in politics. To prevent usurpers from claiming the throne, Vespasian designated his sons Titus and Domitian as his successors. By establishing the Flavian (the name of Vespasian's clan) dynasty, Vespasian turned the principate into an open and admitted monarchy. He also expanded the emperor's power by increasing the size of the budding bureaucracy created by Claudius.

The Flavians carried on Augustus's work on the frontiers. Domitian, the last of the Flavians, won additional territory in Germany and consolidated it in two new provinces. He defeated barbarian tribes on the Danube frontier and strengthened that area as well. Nonetheless, Domitian was one of the most hated of Roman emperors because of his cruelty, and he fell victim to an assassin's dagger. Still, the Flavians gave the Roman world peace and kept the legions in line. Their work paved the way for the era of the "five good emperors," the golden age of the empire.

Triumph of Titus After Titus, the son of Vespasian and later himself emperor, conquered Jerusalem, he ordered his soldiers to carry off as spoils of war the sacred objects of the rebellious Jews, most notably in this scene the seven-branched candlestick. (*Source: Art Resource*)

THE AGE OF THE "FIVE GOOD EMPERORS" (A.D. 96–180)

In the second century A.D. a line of emperors, usually called the "five good emperors," gave the Roman Empire its last burst of summer before an autumn of failure and a winter of barbarism. It was a period of almost unparalleled prosperity and victorious wars generally confined to the frontiers.

The Antonine Monarchy

The age of the Antonines was the age of full-blown monarchy. Augustus had claimed that his influence arose from the collection of offices the senate had bestowed on him. However, there was in law no such office as emperor. Augustus was merely the First Citizen. Under the Flavians the principate became a full-blown monarchy, and by the time of the Antonines the principate was an office with definite rights, powers, and prerogatives. In the years between Augustus and the

Antonines, the emperor had become an indispensable part of the imperial machinery. In short, without the emperor the empire would quickly have fallen to pieces. Augustus had been monarch in fact but not in theory; during their reigns, the Antonines were monarchs in both.

The Antonines were not power-hungry autocrats. The concentration of power was the result of empire. The easiest and most efficient way to run the Roman Empire was to invest the emperor with vast powers. Furthermore, Roman emperors on the whole proved to be effective rulers and administrators. As capable and efficient emperors assumed new tasks and functions, the emperor's hand was felt in more areas of life and government. Increasingly the emperors became the source of all authority and guidance in the empire. The five good emperors were benevolent and exercised their power intelligently, but they were absolute kings all the same. Lesser men would later throw off the facade of constitutionality and use this same power in a despotic fashion.

Typical of the five good emperors is the career of Hadrian, who became emperor in A.D. 117. He was born in Spain, a fact that illustrates the importance of the provinces in Roman politics. Hadrian received his education at Rome and became an ardent admirer of Greek culture. He caught the attention of his elder cousin Trajan, the future emperor, who started him on a military career. At age nineteen Hadrian served on the Danube frontier, where he learned the details of how the Roman army lived and fought and saw for himself the problems of defending the frontiers. When Trajan became emperor in A.D. 98, Hadrian was given important positions in which he learned how to defend and run the empire. At Trajan's death in 117, Hadrian assumed power.

Roman government had changed since Augustus's day. One of the most significant changes was the enormous growth of the imperial bureaucracy created by Claudius. Hadrian reformed this system by putting the bureaucracy on an organized, official basis. He established imperial administrative departments to handle the work formerly done by imperial freedmen. Hadrian also separated civil service from military service. Men with little talent or taste for the army could instead serve the state as administrators. Hadrian's bureaucracy demanded professionalism from its members. Administrators made a career of the civil service. These innovations made for a more efficiently run empire and increased the authority of the emperor—the ruling power of the bureaucracy.

Changes in the Army

The Roman army had also changed since Augustus's time. The Roman legion had once been a mobile unit, but its duties under the empire no longer called for mobility. The successors of Augustus generally called a halt to further conquests. The army was expected to defend what had already been won. Under the Flavian emperors (A.D. 69–96), the frontiers became firmly fixed. Forts and watch stations guarded the borders. Behind the forts the Romans built a system of roads that

Scene from Trajan's Column From 101 to 107 Trajan fought the barbarian tribes along the Danube. This scene depicts Roman soldiers unloading supplies at a frontier city. Such walled cities serve as Roman strong points, as well as centers of Roman civilization, with shops, homes, temples, and amphitheaters. *(Source: Alinari/Art Resource)*

MAP 8.2 Roman Britain Although the modern state of Great Britain stands squarely in the center of current international affairs, Britain was a peripheral part of the Roman Empire, a valuable area but nonetheless on the frontier.

allowed the forts to be quickly supplied and reinforced in times of trouble. The army had evolved into a garrison force, with legions guarding specific areas for long periods.

The personnel of the legions was changing, too. Italy could no longer supply all the recruits needed for the army. Increasingly, only the officers came from Italy and from the most Romanized provinces. The legionaries were mostly drawn from the less civilized provinces, especially the ones closest to the frontiers. A major trend was already obvious in Hadrian's day: fewer and fewer Roman soldiers were really Roman. In the third century A.D., the barbarization of the army would result in an army indifferent to Rome and its traditions. In the age of the Antonines, however, the army was still a

source of economic stability and a Romanizing agent (Map 8.2). Men from the provinces and even barbarians joined the army to learn a trade and to gain Roman citizenship. Even so, the signs were ominous. Veterans from Julius Caesar's wars would hardly have recognized Hadrian's troops as Roman legionaries.

LIFE IN THE "GOLDEN AGE"

If a man were called to fix the period in the history of the world during which the condition of the human race was most happy and prosperous, he would without hesitation name that which elapsed from the death of Domitian to the accession of Commodus.[8]

Thus, according to Edward Gibbon, the age of the five good emperors was a golden age in human history. How does Edward Gibbon's picture correspond to the popular image of Rome as a city of bread, brothels, and gladiatorial games? If the Romans were degenerates who spent their time carousing, who kept Rome and the empire running? Can life in Rome be taken as representative of life in other parts of the empire?

Truth and exaggeration are mixed in Gibbon's view and in the popular image of Rome. Rome and the provinces must be treated separately. Rome no more resembled a provincial city like Cologne than New York resembles Keokuk, Iowa. Rome was unique and must be seen as such. Only then can one turn to the provinces to obtain a full and reasonable picture of the empire under the Antonines.

Imperial Rome

Rome was truly an extraordinary city, especially by ancient standards. It was also enormous, with a population somewhere between 500,000 and 750,000. Although it could boast of stately palaces, noble buildings, and beautiful residential areas, most people lived in jerrybuilt apartment houses. Fire and crime were perennial problems, even after Augustus created fire and urban police forces. Streets were narrow and drainage was inadequate. Under the empire this situation improved. By comparison with medieval and early modern

European cities, Rome was a healthy enough place to live.

Rome was such a huge city that the surrounding countryside could not feed it. Because of the danger of starvation, the emperor, following republican practice, provided the citizen population with free grain for bread and, later, oil and wine. By feeding the citizenry, the emperor prevented bread riots caused by shortages and high prices. For the rest of the urban population who did not enjoy the rights of citizenship, the emperor provided grain at low prices. This measure was designed to prevent speculators from forcing up grain prices in times of crisis. By maintaining the grain supply, the emperor kept the favor of the people and ensured that Rome's poor and idle did not starve.

The emperor also entertained the Roman populace, often at vast expense. The most popular forms of public entertainment were gladiatorial contests and chariot racing. Gladiatorial fighting was originally an Etruscan funerary custom, a blood sacrifice for the dead. Many gladiators were criminals; some were the slaves of gladiatorial trainers; others were prisoners of war. Still others were free men who volunteered for the arena. Even women at times engaged in gladiatorial combat. Although some Romans protested gladiatorial fighting, most delighted in it. Not until the fifth century did Christianity put a stop to it.

The Romans were even more addicted to chariot racing than to gladiatorial shows. Under the empire, four permanent teams competed against one another. Each had its own color—red, white, green, or blue. Some Romans claimed that people cared more about their favorite team than about the race itself. Two-horse and four-horse chariots ran a course of seven laps, about five miles. A successful driver could be the hero of the hour. One

Apartment Houses at Ostia   At heavily populated places such as Rome and Ostia, which was the port of Rome, apartment buildings housed urban dwellers. The brick construction of this building is a good example of solid Roman work. In Rome some apartment buildings were notoriously shoddy and unsafe. *(Source: Art Resource)*

charioteer, Gaius Appuleius Diocles, raced for twenty-four years. During that time he drove 4,257 starts and won 1,462 of them. His admirers honored him with an inscription that proclaimed him champion of all charioteers.

But people like the charioteer Diocles were no more typical of the common Roman than Babe Ruth is of the average American. Ordinary Romans were proud of their work and accomplishments. They dealt with everyday problems and rejoiced over small pleasures. Ordinary Romans left their mark in the inscriptions that grace their graves. The funerary inscription of Paprius Vitalis to his wife is particularly engaging:

If there is anything good in the lower regions—I, however, finish a poor life without you—be happy there too, sweetest Thalassia . . . married to me for 40 years.[9]

As moving is the final tribute of a patron to his former slave:

To Grania Clara, freedwoman of Aulus, a temperate freedwoman. She lived 23 years. She was never vexatious to me except when she died.[10]

Most Romans went about their lives as people have always done. Though fond of brutal spectacles, they also had their loves and dreams.

The Provinces

In the provinces and even on the frontiers, many men and women would have agreed with Gibbon's opinion of the second century. The age of the Antonines was one of extensive prosperity, especially in western Europe. The Roman army had beaten back the barbarians and exposed them to the civilizing effects of Roman traders. The resulting peace and security opened Britain, Gaul, Germany, and the lands of the Danube to immigration. Agriculture flourished as large tracts of land came under cultivation. Most of this land was in the hands of free tenant farmers. From the time of Augustus, slavery had declined in the empire as had the growth of latifundia (see page 188). Augustus and his successors encouraged the rise of free farmers. Under the Antonines this trend continued, and the holders of small parcels of land

throve as never before. The Antonines provided loans on easy terms to farmers. These loans enabled them to rent land previously worked by slaves. It also permitted them to cultivate the new lands that were being opened up. Consequently the small tenant farmer was becoming the backbone of Roman agriculture.

Since the time of Augustus, towns had gradually grown up around the camps and forts. The roads that linked the frontier with the rearward areas served as commercial lifelines for the new towns and villages. Part Roman, part barbarian, these towns were truly outposts of civilization, much like the raw towns of the American West. In the course of time, many of them grew to be Romanized cities, and emperors gave them the status of full Roman municipalities, with charters and constitutions. This development was pronounced along the Rhine and Danube frontiers. Thus, while defending the borders, the army also spread Roman culture. This process would go so far that in A.D. 212 the emperor Caracalla would grant Roman citizenship to every free man within the empire.

The eastern part of the empire also participated in the boom. The Roman navy had swept the sea of pirates, and eastern Mediterranean merchants traded throughout the sea. The flow of goods and produce in the East matched that of the West. Venerable cities like Corinth, Antioch, and Ephesus flourished as rarely before. The cities of the East built extensively, bedecking themselves with new amphitheaters, temples, fountains, and public buildings. For the East, the age of the Antonines was the heyday of the city. Life there grew ever richer and more comfortable.

Trade among the provinces increased dramatically. Britain and Belgium became prime grain producers, much of their harvests going to the armies of the Rhine. Britain's famous wool industry probably got its start under the Romans. Italy and southern Gaul produced wine in huge quantities. The wines of Italy went principally to Rome and

MAP 8.3 The Economic Aspect of the Pax Romana The Roman Empire was not merely a political and military organization but also an intricate economic network through which goods from Armenia and Syria were traded for Western products from as far away as Spain and Britain.

Roman Empire at its height, ca. A.D. 200

☐ Roman Empire at its height, ca. A.D. 200
━━ Principal trade routes by sea
━━ Principal trade routes by land
Grain Principal products

ATLANTIC OCEAN

North Sea

Baltic Sea

Caspian Sea

JUTLAND

BRITAIN
Deva — Lead
London — Grain
Tin — Lead — Cloth

GERMANY
Amber
Hides
Horses
Metals
Wool

BELGIUM
Cloth
Grain
Cologne — Slaves
Iron

GAUL
Pottery
Wine
Lyons — Glass — Pottery
Narbo — Grain
Wine — Olives
Massilia

SPAIN
Brigantium — Lead — Gold
Horses
Gades — Olives
New Carthage — Silver
Tarraco — Grain
Gold

Rhine
Rhône
Ebro

ALPS
Aquileia
Iron
Luna — Pottery
Ancona — Olives
Rome
Ostia
Puteoli — Wine

ITALY
Po

CORSICA
SARDINIA — Wool — Fish

DALMATIA
Salonae — Silver
Horses
Dyrrhachium

DACIA
Potaissa — Gold
Grain
Copper

Danube
Vistula
Elbe
Volga
Dneper
Don

MOESIA
THRACE
Byzantium — Fish — Horses

Black Sea

CRIMEA
Panticapeum
Dioscurias — Slaves
Salt
Olbia — Grain
Grain

CAUCASUS MTS. — Iron — Silk
Routes to China and India

ARMENIA

Trapezus
Amisus — Timber
Sinope
Grain

CAPPADOCIA
Horses
Melitene

Tigris
Euphrates

Ctesiphon
Seleucia

ARABIAN DESERT
Routes to southern Arabia, eastern Africa, and India

ASIA
Wool
Marble
Wine
Ephesus
Myra
Carpets
Tarsus
Copper

CYPRUS

CRETE

MACEDONIA
Thessalonica
Olives
Corinth — Marble
ACHAEA — Pottery
Olives

Mediterranean Sea

SICILY — Grain
Syracuse

Carthage — Olives — Grain
NUMIDIA
Olives
Slaves — Grain
Salt
Caesarea — Fish
Copper

MAURETANIA
NORTH AFRICA

Cyrene — Silphium
Leptis — Olives
LIBYA

NORTH AFRICA

SAHARA

Timber

Ivory and incense from Africa

Antioch — Wine
SYRIA
Damascus — Olives
Glass
Caesarea — Cloth
JUDAEA
Aelana

Alexandria
EGYPT — Glass — Grain — Cloth
Memphis — Grain
Papyrus
Gold and Ivory from Africa

Nile
Red Sea

0   200   400 Km.
0   200   400 Mi.

the Danube; Gallic wines were shipped to Britain and the Rhineland. Roman colonists had introduced the olive to southern Spain and northern Africa, an experiment so successful that these regions produced most of the oil consumed in the western empire. In the East, Syrian farmers continued to cultivate the olive, and oil production reached an all-time high. Egypt was the prime grain producer of the East, and tons of Egyptian wheat went to feed the Roman populace. The Roman army in Mesopotamia consumed a high percentage of the raw materials and manufactured products of Syria and Asia Minor. The spread of trade meant the end of isolated and self-contained economies. By the time of the Antonines, the empire had become an economic as well as a political reality (Map 8.3).

One of the most striking features of this period was the growth of industry in the provinces. Cities in Gaul and Germany eclipsed the old Mediterranean manufacturing centers. Italian cities were particularly hard hit by this development. Cities like Arretium and Capua had dominated the production of glass, pottery, and bronze ware. Yet in the second century A.D., Gaul and Germany took over the pottery market. Lyons in Gaul became the new center of the glassmaking industry. The technique of glass blowing spread to Britain and Germany, and later in the second century, Cologne replaced Lyons in glass production. The cities of Gaul were nearly unrivaled in the manufacture of bronze and brass. Gallic craftsmen invented a new technique of tin-plating and decorated their work with Celtic designs. Their wares soon drove Italian products out of the northern European market. For the first time in history, northern Europe was able to rival the Mediterranean world as a producer of manufactured goods. Europe had entered fully into the economic and cultural life of the Mediterranean world.

The age of the Antonines was generally one of peace, progress, and prosperity. The work of the Romans in northern and western Europe was a permanent contribution to the history of Western society. The cities that grew up in Britain, Belgium, Gaul, Germany, Austria, and elsewhere survived the civil wars that racked the empire in the third century A.D. Likewise, they survived the barbarian invasions that destroyed the western empire and handed on a precious cultural and material heritage to the medieval world. The period of the Antonine monarchy was also one of consolidation.

Roads and secure sea lanes linked the empire in one vast web. The empire had become a commonwealth of cities, and urban life was its hallmark.

ROME AND THE EAST

Their march to empire and their growing interest in foreign peoples brought the Romans into contact with a world much larger than Europe and the Mediterranean. As early as the late Republic, Roman commanders in the East encountered peoples who created order out of the chaos left by Alexander the Great and his Hellenistic successors. This meeting of West and East had two immediate effects. The first was a long military confrontation between the Romans and their Iranian neighbors. Second, Roman military expansion to the east coincided with Chinese expansion to the west, and the surprising result was a period when the major ancient civilizations of the world were in touch with one another. For the first time in history, peoples from the Greco-Roman civilization of the Mediterranean and peoples from central Asia, India, and China met one another and observed one another's cultures at first hand. This was an era of human exploration, and key figures in the process were the peoples of cental Asia, especially the Parthians and Sassanids of Iran.

Romans Versus Iranians

When Roman armies moved into Mesopotamia in 92 B.C., they encountered the Parthians, a people who had entered the Iranian plateau from central Asia in the time of the Persian kings. The disintegration of Alexander's eastern holdings enabled them to reap the harvest of his victory. They created an empire that once stretched from Armenia and Babylonia in the west to the Hellenistic kingdom of Bactria in the east (Map 8.4). They divided their realm into large provinces, or satrapies, and created a flexible political organization to administer their holdings. Unlike China, however, Parthia never had a sophisticated bureaucracy. Nonetheless, the loose provincial organization enabled the Parthians to govern the many different peoples who inhabited their realm. The Romans marveled at Parthia's success, as the Greek geographer Strabo (ca 65 B.C.–A.D. 19) attests:

MAP 8.4 The Major Empires of Central and Southern Asia, ca 250 B.C. From Anatolia in the west to the Himalayas in the east, three great empires ruled western, central, and southern Asia. During these years, frontiers fluctuated, but the Silk Road served as a thread connecting them all.

Now at first he [the Parthian king] Arsaces was weak, carrying the war to those whose land he had taken, both he and his successors. In this way the Parthians subsequently became mighty, taking neighboring territory through success in wars, so that accomplishing these feats, they established themselves as lords within the entire area east of the Euphrates. They also took part of Bactria . . . and now they rule so much territory and so many people that they have become in a way rivals of the Romans in the greatness of their empire.[11]

In the process the Parthians won their place in history as the heirs of the Persian Empire.

Although Augustus sought peace with the Parthians, later Roman emperors, beginning with Nero in A.D. 58, struggled to wrest Armenia and

Mesopotamia from them. The great military emperors Trajan, in 114 and 115, and Septimius Severus, between 197 and 199, threw the Parthians eastward beyond the Tigris River, but their victories were short-lived. Until their downfall in 226, the Parthians met the Roman advance to the east with iron and courage.

The Romans found nothing to celebrate in the eclipse of the Parthians, for their place was immediately taken by the Sassanids, a people indigenous to southern Iran, who overthrew them. As early as 230 the Sassanids launched a campaign to the west, which the Romans blunted. The setback was only temporary, for in 256 the great Persian king Shapur overran Mesopotamia and the Roman province of Syria. Four years later Shapur defeated the legions of the emperor Valerian, whom he took prisoner. Thereafter, the Romans and Sassanids fought long, bitter, and destructive wars in western Asia as the Romans battled to save their eastern provinces. Not until the reign of Diocletian did the Romans solidly anchor their eastern frontier on the Euphrates. Constantine followed up Diocletian's victory, and again Roman rule was firmly established in western Asia.

Trade and Contact

Although warfare between Roman emperors and Iranian kings disrupted western Asia, it did not prevent the major empires of the ancient world from coming and staying in direct contact with one another. Essential to the process was the geographical position of Iran as a link between East and West, a position that facilitated communications between the Roman and Chinese empires, the two wealthiest and most commercially active realms in the ancient world. The overland lines of communication stretched from China across the vast lands under Parthian control to the eastern provinces of the Roman Empire. Maritime routes linked the Romans to India and even to China. As the middlemen in this trade, the Parthians cleverly tried to keep the Chinese and Romans from making direct contact—and thus from learning how large a cut the Parthians took in commercial transactions.

An elaborate network of roads linked Parthia to China in the east, India in the south, and the Roman Empire in the west. The many branch roads even included routes to southern Russia. The most important of the overland routes was the famous Silk Road, named for the shipments of silk that passed from China through Parthia to the Roman Empire. Many other luxury items also passed along this route: the Parthians exported exotic fruits, rare birds, ostrich eggs, and other dainties to China in return for iron and delicacies like apricots. Other easily portable luxury goods included gems, gold, silver, spices, and perfumes. From the Roman Empire came glassware, statuettes, and slaves trained as jugglers and acrobats.

Rarely did a merchant travel the entire distance from China to Mesopotamia. Chinese merchants typically sold their wares to Parthians at the Stone Tower, located at modern Tashkurghan in Afghanistan. From there Parthian traders carried goods across the Iranian plateau to Mesopotamia or Egypt. This overland trade fostered urban life in Parthia as cities arose and prospered along the caravan routes. In the process, the Parthians themselves became important consumers of goods, contributing to the volume of trade and reinforcing the commercial ties between East and West.

More than goods passed along these windswept roads. Ideas, religious lore, and artistic inspiration also traveled the entire route. A fine example of how ideas and artistic influences spread across long distances is a Parthian coin that caught the fancy of an artist in China. The coin bore an inscription—a practice the Parthians had adopted from the Greeks—and although the artist could not read it, he used the lettering as a motif on a bronze vessel. Similarly, thoughts, ideas, and literary works found ready audiences; Greek plays were performed at the court of the Parthian king. At a time when communication was difficult and often dangerous, trade routes were important avenues for the spread of knowledge about other societies.

This was also an era of exciting maritime exploration. Roman ships sailed from Egyptian ports to the mouth of the Indus River, where they traded local merchandise and wares imported by the Parthians. Merchants who made the voyage had to contend with wind, shoal waters, and pirates, as the Roman writer Pliny the Elder recounts:

For those bound for India the most advantageous sailing is from Ocelis [a city in Arabia]. From there with the wind Hippalos blowing, the voyage is forty days to Muziris, the first port in India. It is not a desirable spot because of neighboring pirates, who occupy a place by the name of Nitrias. Nor is there an abundance of merchandise there. Besides, the anchorage for ships is a far distance from land. Cargoes are brought in and carried out by lighters [barges].[12]

Despite such dangers and discomforts, hardy mariners pushed into the Indian Ocean and beyond, reaching Malaya, Sumatra, and Java.

Direct maritime trade between China and the West began in the second century A.D. The period of this contact coincided with the era of Han greatness in China. It was the Han emperor Wu Ti who took the momentous step of opening the Silk Road to the Parthian Empire. Indeed, a later Han emperor sent an ambassador directly to the Roman Empire by sea. The ambassador, Kan Ying, sailed to the Roman province of Syria, where during the reign of the Roman emperor Nerva

(96–98) he became the first Chinese official to have a firsthand look at the Greco-Roman world. Kan Ying enjoyed himself thoroughly, and in A.D. 97 delivered a fascinating report of his travels to his emperor:

The inhabitants of that country are tall and well-proportioned, somewhat like the Chinese, whence they are called Ta-ts'in. *The country contains much gold, silver, and rare precious stones ... corals, amber, glass ... gold embroidered rugs and thin silk-cloth and asbestos cloth. All the rare gems of other foreign countries come from there. They make coins of gold and silver. Ten units of silver are worth one of gold. They traffic by sea with An-hsi (Parthia) and T'ien-chu (India), the profit of which trade is ten-fold. They are honest in their transactions and there are no double prices. Cereals are always cheap.... Their kings always desired to send embassies to China, but the An-hsi (Parthians) wished to carry on trade with them in Chinese silks, and it is for this reason that they were cut off from communication.*[13]

The sea route and to a lesser extent the Silk Road included India in this long web of communications that, once established, was never entirely broken.

CIVIL WARS AND INVASION IN THE THIRD CENTURY

The age of the Antonines gave way to a period of chaos and stress. During the third century A.D., the empire was stunned by civil wars and barbarian invasions. By the time peace was restored, the economy was shattered, cities had shrunk in size, and agriculture was becoming manorial. In the disruption of the third century and the reconstruction of the fourth, the European medieval world had its origins.

After the death of Marcus Aurelius, the last of the five good emperors, his son Commodus, a man totally unsuited to govern the empire, came to the throne. Misrule led to Commodus's murder and a renewal of civil war. After a brief but intense spasm of fighting, the African general Septimius Severus defeated other rival commanders and established the Severan dynasty (A.D. 193–235). Although Septimius Severus was able to stabilize the empire, his successors proved incapable of disciplining the legions. When the last of the Severi was killed by one of his own soldiers, the empire plunged into still another grim, destructive, and this time prolonged round of civil war.

Over twenty different emperors ascended the throne in the forty-nine years between 235 and 284, and many rebels died in the attempt to seize power. At various times, parts of the empire were lost to rebel generals, one of whom, Postumus, set up his own empire in Gaul for about ten years (A.D. 259–269). Yet other men like the iron-willed Aurelian (A.D. 270–275) dedicated their energies to restoring order. So many military commanders seized rule that the middle of the third century has become known as the age of the "barracks emperors." The Augustan principate had become a military monarchy, and that monarchy was nakedly autocratic.

The disruption caused by civil war opened the way for widespread barbarian invasions. Throughout the empire, barbarian invasions and civil war devastated towns, villages, and farms and caused a catastrophic economic depression. Indeed, the Roman Empire seemed on the point of collapse.

The first and most disastrous result of the civil wars was trouble on the frontiers. It was Rome's misfortune that this era of anarchy coincided with immense movements of barbarian peoples, still another example of the effects of mass migrations in ancient history, this time against one of the best organized empires of antiquity. Historians still dispute the precise reason for these migrations, though their immediate cause was pressure from tribes moving westward across Asia. In the sixth century A.D., Jordanes, a Christianized Goth, preserved the memory of innumerable wars among the barbarians in his *History of the Goths*. Goths fought Vandals, Huns fought Goths. Steadily the defeated and displaced tribes moved toward the Roman frontiers. Finally, like "a swarm of bees"—to use Jordanes's image—the Goths burst into Europe in A.D. 258.

When the barbarians reached the Rhine and Danube frontiers, they often found huge gaps in the Roman defenses. Through much of the third century A.D., bands of Goths devastated the Balkans as far south as Greece. They even penetrated Asia Minor. The Alamanni, a German people, swept across the Danube. At one point they entered Italy and reached Milan before they were beaten back. Meanwhile the Franks, still another German folk, hit the Rhine frontier. The Franks then invaded eastern and central Gaul and north-eastern Spain. Saxons from Scandinavia entered the English Channel in search of loot. In the east the Sassanids, of Persian stock, overran Mesopotamia. If the army had been guarding the borders instead of creating and destroying emperors, none of these invasions would have been possible. The barracks emperors should be credited with one accomplishment, however: they fought barbarians when they were not fighting one another. Only that kept the empire from total ruin.

Diocletian's Tetrarchy   The emperor Diocletian's attempt to reform the Roman Empire by dividing rule among four men is represented in this piece of sculpture, which in many features illustrates the transition from ancient to medieval art. Here the four tetrarchs demonstrate their solidarity by clasping one another on the shoulder. Nonetheless each man has his other hand on his sword—a gesture that proved prophetic when Diocletian's reign ended and another struggle for power began. *(Source: Alinari/Art Resource)*

RECONSTRUCTION UNDER DIOCLETIAN AND CONSTANTINE (A.D. 284–337)

At the close of the third century A.D., the emperor Diocletian (284–305) put an end to the period of turmoil. Repairing the damage done in the third century was the major work of the emperor Constantine (306–337) in the fourth. But the price was high.

Under Diocletian, Augustus's polite fiction of the emperor as first among equals gave way to the emperor as absolute autocrat. The princeps became *dominus,* "lord." The emperor claimed that he was "the elect of God"—that he ruled because of God's favor. Constantine even claimed to be the equal of Jesus's first twelve followers. No mere soldier but rather an adroit administrator, Diocletian gave serious thought to the empire's ailments. He recognized that the empire and its difficulties had become too great for one man to handle. He also realized that during the third century provincial governors had frequently used their positions to foment or participate in rebellions. To solve the first of these problems Diocletian divided the empire into a western and an eastern half (Map 8.5). Diocletian assumed direct control of the eastern part; he gave the rule of the western part to a colleague, along with the title *augustus,* which had become synonymous with "emperor." Diocletian and his fellow augustus further delegated power by appointing two men to assist them. Each man was given the title of *caesar* to indicate his exalted rank. Although this system is known as the *Tetrarchy* because four men ruled the empire, Diocletian was clearly senior partner and final source of authority.

Each half of the empire was further split into two prefectures, each governed by a prefect responsible to an augustus. Diocletian organized the prefectures into small administrative units called "dioceses," which were in turn subdivided into small provinces. He reduced the power of the old provincial governors by dividing provinces into

MAP 8.5 The Roman World Divided   Under Diocletian, the Roman Empire was first divided into a western and an eastern half, a development that foreshadowed the medieval division between the Latin West and the Byzantine East.

Prefecture of Gaul
Prefecture of Italy
Prefecture of Illyricum
Prefecture of the East

ATLANTIC OCEAN

North Sea

Baltic Sea

BRITAIN

GERMANY

GAUL

Rhine

Elbe

NARBONENSIS

Massilia

Lyons

Rhône

RAETIA

NORICUM

CISALPINE GAUL

Po

Ravenna

Rome

Tiber

Brundisium

PANNONIA

DALMATIA

Adriatic Sea

NEARER SPAIN

FARTHER SPAIN

Ebro

CORSICA

SARDINIA

BALEARIC IS.

Carthage

NUMIDIA

NORTH AFRICA

MAURETANIA

SICILY

Syracuse

Mediterranean Sea

SAHARA

Line of division between East and West

DACIA

MOESIA

THRACE

Danube

MACEDONIA

Corinth

Athens

Byzantium

Black Sea

CRIMEA

Don

Dnieper

Volga

Caspian Sea

ARMENIA

CAPPADOCIA

PHRYGIA

LYDIA

ASIA

Pergamum

Smyrna

Tarsus

CILICIA

CYPRUS

RHODES

CRETE

Antioch

SYRIA

Damascus

JUDAEA

Jerusalem

Petra

Tigris

Euphrates

ARABIAN DESERT

Red Sea

EGYPT

Nile

Alexandria

LIBYA

Cyrene

0   200   400 Km.

0   200   400 Mi.

A Large Roman Villa   During the third and fourth centuries, when the Roman Empire was breaking up, large villas such as this one in Carthage became the focus of daily life. The villa was at once a fortress, as the towers at the corners of the building indicate, and the economic and social center of the neighborhood. *(Source: Courtesy, German Archaeological Institute)*

smaller units. Provincial governors were also deprived of their military power and were left with only civil and administrative duties.

Diocletian's political reforms were a momentous step. The Tetrarchy soon failed, but Diocletian's division of the empire into two parts became permanent. Constantine and later emperors tried hard to keep the empire together, but without success. Throughout the fourth century A.D., the east and the west drifted apart. In later centuries the western part witnessed the fall of Roman government and the rise of barbarian kingdoms, while

the eastern empire evolved into the majestic Byzantine Empire.

The most serious immediate matters confronting Diocletian and Constantine were economic, social, and religious. They needed additional revenues to support the army and the imperial court. Yet the wars and the barbarian invasions had caused widespread destruction and poverty. The fighting had struck a serious blow to Roman agriculture, which the emperors tried to revive. Christianity had become too strong either to ignore or to crush. How Diocletian, Constantine, and their successors dealt with those problems helped to create the economic and social patterns inherited by medieval Europe.

Inflation and Taxes

The barracks emperors had dealt with economic hardship by depreciating the currency, cutting the silver content of coins until money was virtually worthless. As a result the entire monetary system fell into ruin. The immediate result was crippling inflation throughout the empire.

The empire was less capable of recovery than in earlier times. Wars and invasions had disrupted normal commerce and the means of production. Mines were exhausted in the attempt to supply much-needed ores, especially gold and silver. War and invasion had hit the cities especially hard. Markets were disrupted, and travel became dangerous. Craftsmen, artisans, and traders rapidly left devastated regions. The prosperous industry and commerce of Gaul and the Rhineland declined markedly. Those who owed their prosperity to commerce and the needs of urban life likewise suffered. Cities were no longer places where trade and industry thrived. The devastation of the countryside increased the difficulty of feeding and supplying the cities. The destruction was so extensive that many wondered whether the ravages could be repaired at all.

The response of Diocletian and Constantine to these problems was marked by compulsion, rigidity, and loss of individual freedom. Diocletian's attempt to curb inflation illustrates the methods of absolute monarchy. In a move unprecedented in Roman history, he issued an edict that fixed maximum prices and wages throughout the empire. The measure proved a failure because it was unrealistic as well as unenforceable.

The emperors dealt with the tax system just as strictly and inflexibly. As in the past, local officials bore the responsibility of collecting imperial taxes. Constantine made these officials into a hereditary class; son followed father whether he wanted to or not. In this period of severe depression, many localities could not pay their taxes. In such cases these local officials had to make up the difference from their own funds. This system soon wiped out a whole class of moderately wealthy people.

With the monetary system in ruins, most imperial taxes became payable in kind—that is, in goods or produce instead of money. The major drawback of payment in kind is its demands on transportation. Goods have to be moved from where they are grown or manufactured to where they are needed. Accordingly, the emperors locked into their occupations all those involved in the growing, preparation, and transportation of food and essential commodities. A baker or shipper could not go into any other business, and his son took up the trade at his death. The late empire had a place for everyone, and everyone had a place.

The Legalization of Christianity

In religious affairs Constantine took the decisive step of recognizing Christianity as a legitimate religion. No longer would Christians suffer persecution for their beliefs. Constantine himself died a Christian in 337. Constantine has been depicted both as a devout convert to Christianity and as a realistic opportunist who used the young religion to his own imperial ends. Certainly Constantine was realistic enough to recognize and appreciate Christianity's spread and hold on his subjects. He correctly gauged the strength of the Christian ecclesiastical organization and realized that the new church could serve as a friend of his empire. Yet there is no solid reason to doubt the sincerity of his conversion to the Christian religion. In short, Constantine was a man personally inclined toward Christianity and an emperor who could bestow on it a legal and legitimate place within the Roman Empire.

Why had the pagans—those who believed in the Greco-Roman gods—persecuted Christians in the first place? Polytheism is by nature tolerant of new gods and accommodating in religious matters. Why was Christianity singled out for violence? These questions are still matters of scholarly debate, but some broad answers can be given.

Even so educated and cultured a man as the historian Tacitus opposed Christianity. He believed that Christians hated the whole human race. As a rule early Christians, like the Jews, kept to themselves. Romans distrusted and feared their exclusiveness, which seemed unsociable and even subversive. Most pagans genuinely misunderstood Christian practices. They thought that the Lord's Supper, at which Christians said they ate and drank the body and blood of Jesus, was an act of cannibalism. Pagans thought that Christians

ROMAN HISTORY AFTER AUGUSTUS

Period	Important Emperors	Significant Events
Julio-Claudians 27 B.C.–A.D. 68	Augustus 27 B.C.–A.D. 14 Tiberius, 14–37 Caligula, 37–41 Claudius, 41–54 Nero, 54–68	Augustan settlement Beginning of the principate Birth and death of Jesus Expansion into northern and western Europe Creation of the imperial bureaucracy
Year of the Four Emperors 68–69	Nero Galba Otho Vitellius	Civil War Major breakdown of the concept of the principate
Flavians 69–96	Vespasian, 69–79 Titus, 79–81 Domitian, 81–96	Growing trend toward the concept of monarchy Defense and further consolidation of the European frontiers
Antonines 96–192	Nerva, 96–98 Trajan, 98–117 Hadrian, 117–138 Antoninus Pius, 138–161 Marcus Aurelius, 161–180 Commodus, 180–192	The "golden age"—the era of the "five good emperors" Economic prosperity Trade and growth of cities in northern Europe Beginning of barbarian menace on the frontiers
Severi 193–235	Septimius Severus, 193–211 Caracalla, 211–217 Elagabalus, 218–222 Severus Alexander, 222–235	Military monarchy All free men within the empire given Roman citizenship
"Barracks Emperors" 235–284	Twenty-two emperors in forty-nine years	Civil war Breakdown of the empire Barbarian invasions Severe economic decline
Tetrarchy 284–337	Diocletian, 284–305 Constantine, 306–337	Political recovery Autocracy Legalization of Christianity Transition to the Middle Ages in the west Birth of the Byzantine Empire in the east

indulged in immoral and indecent rituals. They considered Christianity one of the worst of the Oriental mystery cults, for one of the hallmarks of many of those cults was disgusting rituals.

Even these feelings of distrust and revulsion do not entirely account for persecution. The main reason seems to have been sincere religious convic-tion on the part of the pagans. Time and again they accused Christians of atheism. Indeed, Chris-tians either denied the existence of pagan gods or called them evil spirits. For this same reason many Romans hated the Jews. Tacitus no doubt ex-pressed the common view when he said that Jews despised the gods. Christians went even further than Jews: they said that no one should worship pagan gods.

At first some pagans were repelled by the fanaticism of these monotheists. No good could come from scorning the gods. The whole community might end up paying for the wickedness and blasphemy of the Christians. Besides—and this is important—pagans did not demand that Christians believe in pagan gods. Greek and Roman religion was never a matter of belief or ethics. It was purely a religion of ritual. One of the clearest statements of pagan theological attitudes comes from the Roman senator Symmachus in the later fourth century A.D.:

We watch the same stars; heaven is the same for us all; the same universe envelops us: what importance is it in what way anyone looks for truth? It is impossible to arrive by one route at such a great secret.[14]

Yet Roman religion was inseparable from the state. An attack on one was an attack on the other.

The Romans were being no more fanatical or intolerant than an eighteenth-century English judge who declared the Christian religion part of the law of the land. All the pagans expected was performance of the ritual act, a small token sacrifice. Any Christian who sacrificed went free, no matter what he or she personally believed. The earliest persecutions of the Christians were minor and limited. Even Nero's famous persecution was temporary and limited to Rome. Subsequent persecutions were sporadic and local.

The stress of the third century, however, seemed to some emperors the punishment of the gods. What else could account for such anarchy? With the empire threatened on every side, a few emperors thought that one way to appease the gods was by offering them the proper sacrifices. Such sacrifices would be a sign of loyalty to the empire, a show of Roman solidarity. Consequently, a new wave of persecutions began. Yet even they were never very widespread or long-lived; by the late third century, pagans had become used to Chris-

The Arch of Constantine   To celebrate the victory that made him emperor, Constantine built this triumphal arch in Rome. Rather than decorate the arch with the inferior work of his own day, Constantine plundered other Roman monuments, including those of Trajan and Marcus Aurelius. *(Source: C. M. Dixon)*

tianity. Although a few emperors, including Diocletian, vigorously persecuted Christians, most pagans left them alone. Nor were they very sympathetic to the new round of persecutions. Pagan and Christian alike must have been relieved when Constantine legalized Christianity.

In time the Christian triumph would be complete. In 380 the emperor Theodosius made Christianity the official religion of the Roman Empire. At that point Christians began to persecute the pagans for their beliefs. History had come full circle.

The Construction of Constantinople

The triumph of Christianity was not the only event that made Constantine's reign a turning point in Roman history. Constantine took the bold step of building a new capital for the empire. Constantinople, the New Rome, was constructed on the site of Byzantium, an old Greek city on the Bosporus. Throughout the third century, emperors had found Rome and the West hard to defend. The eastern part of the empire was more easily defensible and escaped the worst of the barbarian devastation. It was wealthy and its urban life still vibrant. Moreover, Christianity was more widespread in the East, and the city of Constantinople was intended to be a Christian center.

SUMMARY

The Roman Empire created by Augustus nearly collapsed before being restored by Diocletian and Constantine. Much was lost along the way but much was at the same time gained. Constantine's legalization and patronage of Christianity and his shift of the capital from Rome to Constantinople marked a new epoch in Western history as the ancient world gave way to the medieval. In the process the Roman Empire came into direct contact with its Asian neighbors, sometimes in anger but more often in peace. Never before in Western history and not again until modern times did one state govern so much territory for so long a time.

The true heritage of Rome is its long tradition of law and freedom. Under Roman law and government, the empire enjoyed relative peace and security for extensive periods of time. Through Rome the best of ancient thought and culture was preserved to make its contribution to modern life. Perhaps no better epitaph for Rome can be found than the words of Virgil:

While rivers shall run to the sea,
While shadows shall move across the valleys of
* mountains,*
While the heavens shall nourish the stars,
Always shall your honor and your name and your
* fame endure.*[15]

NOTES

1. Virgil, *Aeneid* 6.851–853. Unless otherwise credited, all quotations from a foreign language in this chapter are translated by John Buckler.
2. Augustus, *Res Gestae* 6.34.
3. Ibid., 5.28.
4. Horace, *Odes* 4.15.
5. Ibid., 1.38.
6. Matthew 3:3.
7. Ibid., 16:18.
8. E. Gibbon, *The History of the Decline and Fall of the Roman Empire* (New York: Modern Library, n.d.), 1.70.
9. *Corpus Inscriptionum Latinarum,* vol. 6 (Berlin: G. Reimer, 1882), no. 9792.
10. Ibid., vol. 10, no. 8192.
11. Strabo, 11.9.2.
12. Pliny, *Natural History* 6.26
13. Quoted in W. H. Schoff, *The Periplus of the Erythraean Sea* (London: Longmans, Green, 1912), p. 276.
14. Symmachus, *Relations* 3.10.
15. Virgil, *Aeneid* 1.607–609.

SUGGESTED READING

Some good general treatments of the empire include B. Levick, *The Government of the Roman Empire: A Source Book* (1984), a convenient collection of sources illustrating the workings of Roman imperial government; P. Garnsey and R. Saller, *The Roman Empire* (1987); and J. Wacher, ed., *The Roman World,* 2 vols. (1987), which attempts a comprehensive survey of the world of the Roman Empire. The role of the emperor is superbly treated by F. Millar, *The Emperor in the Roman World* (1977), and the defense of the empire is studied by E. N. Luttwak, *The Grand Strategy of the Roman Empire* (1976). The army that carried out that strategy is the subject of G. Webster, *The Roman Imperial Army* (1969).

G. W. Bowersock, *Augustus and the Greek World* (1965), is excellent intellectual history. C. M. Wells, *The German Policy of Augustus* (1972), uses archeological findings to illustrate Roman expansion into northern Europe. H. Schutz, *The Romans in Central Europe* (1985), treats Roman expansion, its problems, and its successes in a vital area of the empire. In *The Augustan Aristocracy* (1985), one of the great Roman historians of this century, R. Syme, studies the new order that Augustus created to help him administer the empire. Rather than study the Augustan poets individually, one can now turn to D. A. West and A. J. Woodman, *Poetry and Politics in the Age of Augustus* (1984). J. B. Campbell, *The Emperor and the Roman Army, 31 B.C.–A.D. 235* (1984), stresses the reliance of the Roman emperor on the army throughout the empire's history. Recent work on the Roman army includes M. Speidel, *Roman Army Studies,* vol. 1 (1984), and L. Keppie, *The Making of the Roman Army from Republic to Empire* (1984). Even though Augustus himself still remains an enigma, F. Millar and E. Segal, eds., *Caesar Augustus: Seven Aspects* (1984), is an interesting volume of essays that attempts, not always successfully, to penetrate the official facade of the emperor. N. Hannestad, *Roman Art and Imperial Policy* (1988), examines the way in which the emperors used art as a means of furthering imperial policy. M. Hammond, *The Antonine Monarchy* (1959), is a classic study of the evolution of the monarchy under the Antonines.

The commercial life of the empire is the subject of an interesting book by K. Greene, *The Archaeology of the Roman Economy* (1986), which offers an intriguing way in which to picture the Roman economy through physical remains. The classic treatment, which ranges across the empire, is M. Rostovtzeff, *The Economic and Social History of the Roman Empire* (1957). P. W. de Neeve, *Colonies: Private Farm-Tenancy in Roman Italy* (1983), covers agriculture and the styles of landholding from the Republic to the early years of the empire.

Social aspects of the empire are the subject of R. Auguet, *Cruelty and Civilization: The Roman Games* (English translation, 1972); P. Garnsey, *Social Status and Legal Privilege in the Roman Empire* (1970); and A. N. Sherwin-White, *Racial Prejudice in Imperial Rome* (1967). A general treatment is R. MacMullen, *Roman Social Relations, 50 A.D. to A.D. 284* (1981), and a recent contribution is L. A. Thompson, *Romans and Blacks* (1989). N. Kampen, *Image and Status: Roman Working Women in Ostia* (1981), is distinctive for its treatment of ordinary Roman women. An important feature of Roman history is treated by R. P. Saller, *Personal Patronage Under the Early Empire* (1982). J. Humphrey, *Roman Circuses and Chariot Racing* (1985), treats a topic very dear to the hearts of ancient Romans. K. R. Bradley, *Slaves and Masters in the Roman Empire* (1988), discusses social controls in a slave-holding society. Lastly, B. Cun-liffe, *Greeks, Romans and Barbarians* (1988), uses archeological and literary evidence to discuss the introduction of Greco-Roman culture into western Europe.

Christianity, paganism, Judaism, and the ways in which they all met have received lively recent attention. K. Wengst, *Pax Romana and the Peace of Jesus Christ* (English translation, 1987), is an interesting study of the social atmosphere of the lower classes at the time when Christianity was spreading. More recent is A. Chester, *The Social Context of Early Christianity* (1989). J. Liebeschuetz, *Continuity and Change in Roman Religion* (1979), emphasizes the evolution of Roman religion from the late Republic to the late Empire. M. P. Speidel, *Mithras-Orion, Greek Hero and Roman Army God* (1980), studies the cult of Mithras, a mystery religion that was an early competitor with Christianity. The evolution of Christianity in its Hellenistic background, both pagan and Jewish, can be traced through a series of recent books: R. H. Nash, *Christianity and the Hellenistic World* (1984); T. Barnes, *Early Christianity and the Roman Empire* (1984); S. Benko, *Pagan Rome and Early Christians* (1985); and R. L. Wilken, *The Christians as the Romans Saw Them* (1984). Last, R. MacMullen, *Christianizing the Roman Empire* (1984), treats the growth of the Christian church as seen from a pagan perspective.

Convenient surveys of Roman literature are J. W. Duff, *Literary History of Rome from the Origins to the Close of the Golden Age* (1953), and Duff, *Literary History of Rome in the Silver Age,* 3d ed. (1964).

Ever since Gibbon's *Decline and Fall of the Roman Empire,* one of the masterpieces of English literature, the decline of the empire has been a fertile field of investigation. S. Perowne, *Hadrian* (1987), is a new assessment of the emperor who attempted to limit Roman expansion. Broader are A. M. H. Jones, *The Decline of the Ancient World* (1966); F. W. Walbank, *The Awful Revolution* (1969); and R. MacMullen's two books: *Soldier and Civilian in the Later Roman Empire* (1963) and *Enemies of the Roman Order: Treason, Unrest, and Alienation in the Empire* (1966). S. N. C. Lieu and M. Dodgeon, *Rome's Eastern Frontier, A.D. 226–363* (1988), relies primarily on documents to trace Rome's policy in the East during this difficult period. Two studies analyze the attempts at recovery from the breakdown of the barracks emperors: T. D. Barnes, *The New Empire of Diocletian and Constantine* (1982), which, as its title indicates, concerns itself with the necessary innovations made by the two emperors; and, more narrowly, S. Williams, *Diocletian and the Roman Recovery* (1985). A. Ferrill, *The Fall of the Roman Empire* (1986), with plans and illustrations, offers a military explanation for the "fall" of the Roman Empire. R. MacMullen, *Constantine* (1988), written by a leading scholar, provides a broad and lucid interpretation of Constantine and the significance of his reign.

PERIOD (CA 500 B.C.–A.D. 200)	AFRICA AND THE MIDDLE EAST	THE AMERICAS
500 B.C.	Babylonian captivity of the Hebrews, 586–539 Cyrus the Great founds Persian Empire, 550 Persians conquer Egypt, 525 Darius and Xerxes complete Persian conquest of Middle East, 521–464	Olmec civilization, ca 1500 B.C.–A.D. 300 Fall of La Venta; Tres Zapotes becomes leading Olmec site
300 B.C.	Alexander the Great extends empire, 334–331 Death of Alexander (323): Ptolemy conquers Egypt, Seleucus rules Asia	
200 B.C.	Scipio Africanus defeats Hannibal at Zama, 202	
100 B.C.	Dead Sea Scrolls Pompey conquers Syria and Palestine, 63	
A.D. 100	Jesus Christ, ca 4 B.C.–A.D. 30 Paul, d. ca 65 Bantu migrations begin Jews revolt from Rome, Romans destroy Hebrew temple in Jerusalem: end of the ancient Hebrew state, 70	
A.D. 200	Camel first used for trans-Saharan transport	Classic age of the Maya, ca 300–900

EAST ASIA	INDIA AND SOUTHEAST ASIA	EUROPE
Confucius, 551–479 First written reference to iron, ca 521	Siddhartha Gautama (Buddha), 563–483	Roman Republic founded, 509 Origin of Greek polis, ca 500 Growth of Athenian Empire; flowering of Greek drama, philosophy, history, fifth century
Lao–tzu and development of Taoism, fourth century Han Fei-tzu and Li Ssu and development of Legalism, ca 250–208	Alexander invades India, 327–326 Chandragupta founds Mauryan Dynasty, 322–ca 185 Ashoka, 273–232 King Arsaces of Parthia defeats Seleucid monarchy and begins conquest of Persia, ca 250–137	Peloponnesian War, 431–404 Plato, 426–347 Gauls sack Rome, ca 390 Roman expansion, 390–146 Conquests of Alexander the Great, 334–323 Punic wars, destruction of Carthage, 264–146
Ch'in Dynasty and unification of China; construction of the Great Wall, destruction of Confucian literature, 221–210 Han Dynasty, 202 B.C.–A.D. 220	Greeks invade India, ca 183–145 Mithridates creates Parthian Empire, ca 171–131	Late Roman Republic, 133–27
Chinese expansion to South China Sea and Vietnam ca 111 Silk Road opens to Parthian and Roman empires; Buddhism enters China, ca 104	First Chinese ambassadors to India and Parthia, ca 140 *Badhavadgita,* ca 100 B.C.–A.D. 100	Formation of First Triumvirate (Caesar, Crassus, Pompey), 60 Julius Caesar killed, 44 Formation of Second Triumvirate, (Octavian, Antony, Lepidus), 43 Octavian seizes power, 31
First written reference (Chinese) to Japan, A.D. 57 Chinese invent paper, 105 Emperor Wu, 140–186	Shakas and Kushans invade eastern Parthia and India, first century A.D. Roman attacks on Parthian Empire, 115–211	Octavian rules imperial Rome as Augustus, 27 B.C.–A.D. 14 Roman Empire at greatest extent, 117
Three Kingdoms era, 221–280	Fall of Parthian Empire; rise of the Sassanids	End of the *Pax Romana;* civil wars, economic decline, invasion, 180–285 Reforms by Diocletian, 285–305

9

The Making of Europe

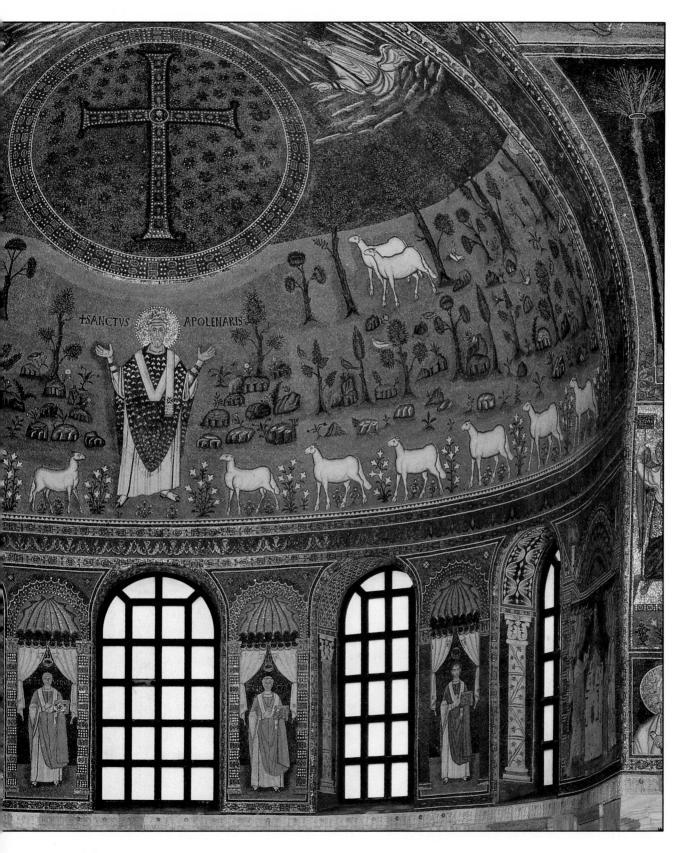

Apse mosaic of S. Apollinare in Classe, Ravenna

*T*he centuries between approximately 400 and 1000 present a paradox. They witnessed the disintegration of the Roman Empire, which had been one of humanity's great political and cultural achievements. But they were also a creative and important period, during which Europeans laid the foundations for medieval and modern Europe. Thus, this period saw the making of Europe.

The basic ingredients that went into the making of a distinctly European civilization were the cultural legacy of Greece and Rome, the customs and traditions of the Germanic peoples, and the Christian faith. The most important of these was Christianity, because it absorbed and assimilated the other two. It reinterpreted the classics in a Christian sense. It instructed the Germanic peoples and gave them new ideals of living and social behavior. Christianity became the cement that held European society together.

During this period the Byzantine Empire, centered at Constantinople, served as a protective buffer between Europe and regions to the east. The Greeks and the Muslims (see Chapter 10) preserved the philosophical and scientific texts of the ancient world—texts that later formed the basis for study in science and medicine and produced the Justinian *Code,* a great synthesis of Roman law. In urbane and sophisticated Constantinople, the Greeks set a standard far above the primitive existence of the West.

European civilization resulted from the fusion of the Greco-Roman heritage, Germanic traditions, and the Christian faith.

- How did these components act on one another?
- How did they cause the making of Europe?
- What influence did the Byzantine culture have on the making of European civilization?

This chapter will focus on these questions.

THE GROWTH OF THE CHRISTIAN CHURCH

While many elements of the Roman Empire disintegrated, the Christian church survived and grew. What is the church? According to scriptural scholars, the earliest use of the word *church* (in Greek, *ekklesia*) in the New Testament appears in Saint Paul's First Letter to the Christians of Thessalonica in northern Greece, written about A.D. 51. By *ekklesia* Paul meant the local community of Christian believers. In Paul's later letters, the term *church* refers to the entire Mediterranean-wide assembly of Jesus's followers. After the legalization of Christianity by the emperor Constantine (see page 221) and the growth of institutional offices and officials, the word *church* was sometimes applied to those officials—much as the terms *the college* or *the university* are used to refer to academic administrators. The bishop of Rome—known as "pope" from the Latin word *papa,* meaning "father"—claimed to speak and act for all Christians. The popes claimed to be the successors of Saint Peter and heirs to his authority as chief of the apostles—Christ's first twelve followers. Their claim was based on Jesus's words to Peter:

You are Peter, and on this rock I will build my church, and the jaws of death shall not prevail against it. I will entrust to you the keys of the kingdom of heaven. Whatever you declare bound on earth shall be bound in heaven; whatever you declare loosed on earth shall be loosed in heaven.[1]

Roman bishops used that text, which is known as the "Petrine Doctrine," to support their assertions of authority over other bishops in the church. The popes maintained that they represented "the church." The word *church,* therefore, has several connotations. Modern Catholic theology frequently defines the church as "the people of God" and identifies the church with local and international Christian communities. In the Middle Ages, the institutional and monarchial interpretations of the word tended to be stressed.

The church possessed able administrators and leaders and highly literate and creative thinkers. Having gained the support of the fourth-century emperors, the church gradually adapted the Roman system of organization to church purposes. Christianity, moreover, had a dynamic missionary policy, and the church slowly succeeded in *assimilating*—that is, adapting—pagan peoples, both Germans and Romans, to Christian teaching. These factors help to explain the survival and growth of the Christian church in the face of repeated Germanic invasions.

The Church and the Roman Emperors

The church benefited considerably from the emperors' support. In return, the emperors expected the support of the Christian church in maintaining order and unity. Constantine had legalized the practice of Christianity within the empire in 312. Although he was not baptized until he was on his deathbed, Constantine encouraged Christianity throughout his reign. He freed the clergy from imperial taxation. At the churchmen's request, he helped settle theological disputes and thus preserved doctrinal unity within the church. Constantine generously endowed the building of Christian churches, and one of his gifts—the Lateran Palace in Rome—remained the official residence of the popes until the fourteenth century. Constantine also declared Sunday a public holiday, a day of rest for the service of God. As the result of its favored position in the empire, Christianity slowly became the leading religion.

In 380 the emperor Theodosius (r. 379–395) went further than Constantine and made Christianity the official religion of the empire. Theodosius stripped Roman pagan temples of statues, made the practice of the old Roman state religion a treasonable offense, and persecuted Christians who dissented from orthodox doctrine. Most significant, he allowed the church to establish its own courts. Church courts began to develop their own body of law—*canon law*. These courts, not the Roman government, had jurisdiction over the clergy and ecclesiastical disputes. At the death of Theodosius, the Christian church was considerably independent of the authority of the Roman state. The foundation for the power of the medieval church had been laid.

What was to be the church's relationship to secular powers? How was the Christian to render unto Caesar the things that were Caesar's while returning to God God's due? This problem had troubled the earliest disciples of Christ. The toleration of Christianity and the coming to power of Christian emperors in the fourth century did not make it any easier. Striking a balance between responsibility to secular rulers and loyalty to spiritual duties was difficult.

In the fourth century, theological disputes frequently and sharply divided the Christian community. Some disagreements had to do with the nature of Jesus Christ. For example, Arianism, which originated with Arius (ca 250–336), a priest

The Council of Nicaea (A.D. 325) In this ninth-century pen-and-ink drawing, sixty-six bishops and theologians sit around the presiding bishop while scribes record the proceedings. The Council produced the Nicene Creed, drawn up to defend the orthodox faith against the Arians. *(Source: Bibliotheek der Rijksuniversitet, Utrecht)*

of Alexandria, denied two tenets of orthodox Christian belief: that Christ was divine and that he had always existed with God the Father. Arius held that God was by definition uncreated and unchangeable and that he had created Christ as his instrument for the redemption of humankind. Because Christ was created, Arius reasoned, he could not have been co-eternal with the Father. Orthodox Christians branded Arianism a *heresy*—the denial of a doctrine of faith. Nevertheless, Arianism enjoyed such popularity and provoked such controversy that Constantine, to whom religious disagreement meant civil disorder, interceded. In 325 he summoned a council of church leaders to Nicaea in Asia Minor and presided over it personally. The council produced the Nicene Creed, which defined the orthodox position that Christ is "eternally begotten of the Father" and of the same substance as the Father. Arius and those who refused to accept the creed were banished (this was the first case of civil punishment for heresy). The participation of Emperor Constantine in a theological dispute within the church paved the way for later emperors to claim that they could do the same.

So active was the emperor Theodosius's participation in church matters that he eventually came to loggerheads with Bishop Ambrose of Milan (339–397). Theodosius ordered Ambrose to hand over his cathedral church to the emperor. Ambrose's response had important consequences for the future:

> At length came the command, "Deliver up the Basilica"; I reply, "It is not lawful for us to deliver it up, nor for your Majesty to receive it. By no law can you violate the house of a private man, and do you think that the house of God may be taken away? It is asserted that all things are lawful to the Emperor, that all things are his. But do not burden your conscience with the thought that you have any right as Emperor over sacred things. Exalt not yourself, but if you would reign the longer, be subject to God. It is written, God's to God and Caesar's to Caesar. The palace is the Emperor's, the Churches are the Bishop's. To you is committed jurisdiction over public, not over sacred buildings."[2]

Ambrose's statement was to serve as the cornerstone of the ecclesiastical theory of state-church relations throughout the Middle Ages. Ambrose insisted that the church was independent of the state's jurisdiction. He insisted that, in matters relating to the faith or to the church, the bishops were to be the judges of emperors, not the other way around. In a Christian society, harmony and peace depended on agreement between the bishop and the secular ruler. But if disagreement developed, the church was ultimately the superior power because the church was responsible for the salvation of all (including the emperor). Theodosius accepted Ambrose's argument and bowed to the church. In later centuries, theologians, canonists, and propagandists repeatedly cited Ambrose's position as the basis of relations between the two powers.

Inspired Leadership

The early Christian church benefited from the brilliant administrative abilities of some church leaders and from identification of the authority and dignity of the bishop of Rome with the grand imperial traditions of the city. Some highly able Roman citizens accepted baptism and applied their intellectual powers and administrative skills to the service of the church rather than the empire. With the empire in decay, educated people joined and worked for the church in the belief that it was the one institution able to provide leadership. Bishop Ambrose, for example, was the son of the Roman prefect of Gaul, a trained lawyer and governor of a province. He is typical of those Roman aristocrats who held high public office, were converted to Christianity, and subsequently became bishops. Such men later provided social continuity from Roman to Germanic rule. As bishop of Milan, Ambrose himself exercised considerable responsibility in the temporal as well as the ecclesiastical affairs of northern Italy.

During the reign of Diocletian (r. 284–305), the Roman Empire had been divided for administrative purposes into geographical units called "dioceses." Gradually the church made use of this organizational structure. Christian *bishops*—the leaders of early Christian communities, popularly elected by the Christian people—established their headquarters, or *sees,* in the urban centers of the old Roman dioceses. A bishop's jurisdiction extended throughout all parts of a diocese. The center of a bishop's authority was his cathedral (the word derives from the Latin *cathedra,* meaning "chair"). Thus church leaders capitalized on the

Roman imperial method of organization and adapted it to ecclesiastical purposes.

After the removal of the capital and the emperor to Constantinople (page 224), the bishop of Rome exercised vast influence in the West because he had no real competitor there. Successive bishops of Rome began to identify their religious offices with the imperial traditions of the city. They stressed that Rome had been the capital of a worldwide empire and emphasized the special importance of Rome in the framework of that empire. Successive bishops of Rome reminded Christians in other parts of the world that Rome was the burial place of Saint Peter and Saint Paul. Moreover, according to tradition, Saint Peter, the chief of Christ's apostles, had lived and been executed in Rome. No other city in the world could make such claims.

In the fifth century, the bishops of Rome began to stress Rome's supremacy over other Christian communities and to urge other churches to appeal to Rome for the resolution of complicated doctrinal issues. Thus Pope Innocent I (r. 401–417) wrote to the bishops of Africa:

[We approve your action in following the principle] that nothing which was done even in the most remote and distant provinces should be taken as finally settled unless it came to the notice of this See, that any just pronouncement might be confirmed by all the authority of this See, and that the other churches might from thence gather what they should teach.[3]

The prestige of Rome and of the church as a whole was also enhanced by the courage and leadership of the Roman bishops. According to tradition, Pope Leo I (r. 440–461) met the advancing army of Attila the Hun in 452 and, through his power of persuasion, saved Rome from destruction. Three years later Leo persuaded the Vandal leader Gaiseric not to burn the city, though the pope could not prevent a terrible sacking.

By the time Gregory I (r. 590–604) became pope, there was no civic authority left to handle the problems pressing the city. Flood, famine, plague, and invasion by the Lombards made for an almost disastrous situation. Pope Gregory concluded a peace with the Lombards, organized relief services that provided water and food for the citizens, and established hospitals for the sick and dying. The fact that it was Christian leaders, rather than imperial administrators, who responded to

Pope Gregory I (590–604) and Scribes   One of the four "Doctors" (or Learned Fathers) of the Latin Church, Gregory is shown in this tenth-century ivory book cover writing at his desk while the Holy Spirit in the form of a dove whispers in his ear. Below, scribes copy Gregory's works. (*Source: Kunsthistorisches Museum, Vienna*)

the city's dire needs could not help but increase the prestige and influence of the church.

Missionary Activity

The word *catholic* derives from a Greek word meaning "general," "universal," or "worldwide." Christ had said that his teaching was for all peoples, and Christians sought to make their faith

MAP 9.1 The Spread of Christianity Originating in Judaea, the southern part of modern Israel and Jordan, Christianity spread throughout the Roman world. Roman sea lanes and Roman roads facilitated the expansion.

catholic—that is, believed everywhere. This goal could be accomplished only through missionary activity. As Saint Paul had written to the Christian community at Colossae in Asia Minor:

You have stripped off your old behavior with your old self, and you have put on a new self which will progress towards true knowledge the more it is renewed in the image of its creator; and in that image there is no room for distinction between Greek and Jew, between the circumcised or the uncircumcised, or between barbarian or Scythian, slave and free man. There is only Christ; he is everything and he is in everything.[4]

Paul urged Christians to bring the "good news" of Christ to all peoples. The Mediterranean served as the highway over which Christianity spread to the cities of the empire (Map 9.1).

During the Roman occupation, communities were scattered throughout Gaul and Britain. The effective beginnings of Christianity in Gaul were due to Saint Martin of Tours (ca 316–397), a Roman soldier who, after giving half of his cloak to a naked beggar, had a vision of Christ and was baptized. Martin founded the monastery of Ligugé, the first in Gaul, which became a center for the evangelization of the surrounding country districts. In 372 he became bishop of Tours and introduced a rudimentary parish system. A parish is a subdivision of a diocese, under the jurisdiction of a priest who is responsible for the spiritual welfare of the Christians living in the area.

Tradition strongly identifies the conversion of Ireland with Saint Patrick (ca 385–461), one of the most effective missionaries in history. Born in western England to a Christian family of Roman citizenship, Patrick was captured and enslaved by Irish raiders and taken to Ireland. He worked there for six years as a herdsman then escaped and returned to England, where a vision urged him to Christianize Ireland. In preparation, Patrick studied in Gaul and in 432 was consecrated a bishop. He landed in Ireland, and at Tara in present-day County Meath—seat of the high kings of Ireland—he made his first converts. From Tara, Patrick first baptized the king and then converted the Irish, tribe by tribe. In 445 with the approval of Pope Leo I, Patrick established his see in Armagh.

The ecclesiastical organization that Patrick set up differed in a fundamental way from church structure on the Continent: Armagh was a monastery, and the monastery, rather than the diocese, served as the center of ecclesiastical organization. Local tribes and the monastery were interdependent. The tribes supported the monastery economically, and the monastery provided religious and educational services for the tribes. Patrick introduced the Roman alphabet and supported the codification of traditional Irish laws. By the time of his death, the majority of the Irish people had received Christian baptism.

A strong missionary fervor characterized Irish Christianity. Perhaps the best representative of Irish-Celtic zeal was Saint Columba (ca 521–597), who established the monastery of Iona on an island in the Inner Hebrides off the west coast of Scotland. Iona served as a base for converting the pagan Picts of Scotland. Columba's proselytizing efforts won him the title "Apostle of Scotland," and his disciples carried the Christian Gospel to the European continent.

The Christianization of the English really began in 597, when Pope Gregory I sent a delegation of monks under the Roman Augustine (d. 604?) to Britain to convert the Angles and Saxons. Augustine's approach, like Patrick's, was to concentrate on converting the king. When he succeeded in converting Ethelbert, king of Kent, the baptism of Ethelbert's people took place as a matter of course. Augustine established his headquarters, or cathedral seat, at Canterbury, the capital of Kent. Kings who converted, such as Ethelbert and the Frankish chieftain Clovis (see page 247), sometimes had Christian wives. Besides being a sign of the personal influence that a Christian wife exerted on her husband, conversion may have indicated that barbarian kings wanted to enjoy the cultural advantages that Christianity brought, such as literate assistants and an ideological basis for their rule.

In the course of the seventh century, two Christian forces competed for the conversion of the pagan Anglo-Saxons: Roman-oriented missionaries traveling north from Canterbury and Celtic monks from Ireland and northwestern Britain. Monasteries were established at Iona, Lindisfarne, Jarrow, and Whitby (see Maps 9.1 and 9.3).

The Roman and Celtic traditions differed completely in their forms of church organization, types of monastic life, and methods of arriving at the date of Easter, the central feast of the Christian calendar. At the Synod (ecclesiastical council) of Whitby in 664, the Roman tradition was completely victorious. The conversion of the English and the close attachment of the English church to Rome had far-reaching consequences because Britain later served as a base for the Christianization of the Continent. Between the fifth and tenth centuries, the great majority of peoples living on the European continent and the nearby islands accepted the Christian religion—that is, they received baptism, though baptism in itself did not automatically transform people into Christians.

Religion influenced all aspects of tribal life. All members of a tribe participated in religious observances because doing so was a social duty. Religion was not a private or individual matter; the religion of a chieftain or king determined the religion of the people. Thus missionaries concentrated their initial efforts not on the people but on kings or tribal chieftains. According to custom, tribal chiefs negotiated with all foreign powers, including the gods. Because the Christian missionaries represented a "foreign" power (the Christian god), the king dealt with them. If a ruler accepted Christian baptism, his people also did so. The result was mass baptism.

Once a ruler had marched his people to the waters of baptism, the work of Christianization had only begun. Baptism meant either sprinkling water on the head or immersing the body in water. Conversion, however, meant mental and heartfelt acceptance of the beliefs of Christianity. What does it mean to be a Christian? This question has troubled sincere people from the time of Saint Paul to the present. The problem rests in part in the basic teaching of Jesus in the Gospel:

Then fixing his eyes on his disciples he said: "How happy are you who are poor: yours is the kingdom of

God. Happy you who are hungry now: you shall be satisfied. Happy you who weep now: you shall laugh."

"Happy are you when people hate you, drive you out, abuse you, denounce your name as criminal, on account of the Son of Man. Rejoice when that day comes and dance for joy, then your reward will be great in heaven. This was the way their ancestors treated the prophets."

The Curses

"But alas for you who are rich: you are having your consolation now. Also for you who have your fill now: you shall go hungry. Alas for you who laugh now: you shall mourn and weep."

Love of Enemies

"But I say this to you who are listening: Love your enemies, do good to those who hate you, bless those who curse you, pray for those who treat you badly. To the man who slaps you on one cheek, present the other cheek too; to the man who takes your cloak from you, do not refuse your tunic. Give to everyone who asks you, and do not ask of your property back from the man who robs you. Treat others as you would like them to treat you." [5]

These ideas are among the most radical and revolutionary that the world has heard.

The German peoples were warriors who idealized the military virtues of physical strength, ferocity in battle, and loyalty to the leader. Victors in battle enjoyed the spoils of success and plundered the vanquished. Thus the Germanic tribes found the Christian notions of sin and repentance virtually incomprehensible. In Christian thought, sin meant disobedience to the will of God as revealed in the Ten Commandments and the teachings of Christ. To the barbarians, good or "moral" behavior meant the observance of tribal customs and practices, and dishonorable behavior led to social ostracism. The inculcation of Christian ideals took a very long time.

Conversion and Assimilation

In Christian theology, conversion involves a turning toward God—that is, a conscious effort to live according to the Gospel message. How did missionaries and priests get masses of pagan and illiterate peoples to understand and live by Christian ideals and teachings? Through preaching, through assimilation, and through the penitential system. Preaching aimed at instruction and edification. Instruction presented the basic teachings of Christianity. Edification was intended to strengthen the newly baptized in their faith through stories about the lives of Christ and the saints. Deeply ingrained pagan customs and practices could not be stamped out by words alone or even by imperial edicts. Christian missionaries often pursued a policy of assimilation, easing the conversion of pagan men and women by stressing similarities between their customs and beliefs and those of Christianity. A letter that Pope Gregory I wrote to Augustine of Canterbury beautifully illustrates this policy. Sent to Augustine in Britain in 601, it expresses the pope's intention that pagan buildings and practices be given a Christian significance:

To our well beloved son Abbot Mellitus: Gregory servant of the servants of God. . . . Therefore, when . . . you reach our most reverent brother, Bishop Augustine, we wish you to inform him that we . . . have come to the conclusion that the temples of the idols among that people should on no account be destroyed. The idols are to be destroyed, but the temples themselves are to be aspersed with holy water, altars set up in them, and relics deposited there. For if these temples are well-built, they must be purified from the worship of demons and dedicated to the service of the true God. In this way . . . the people, seeing that their temples are not destroyed, may abandon their error and, flocking more readily to their accustomed resorts, may come to know and adore the true God. [6]

How assimilation works is perhaps best appreciated through the example of a festival familiar to all Americans, Saint Valentine's Day. There were two Romans named Valentine. Both were Christian priests, and both were martyred for their beliefs around the middle of February in the third century. Since about 150 B.C. the Romans had celebrated the festival of Lupercalia, at which they asked the gods for fertility for themselves, their fields, and their flocks. This celebration occurred in mid-February, shortly before the Roman New Year and the arrival of spring. Thus the early church "converted" the old festival of Lupercalia into Saint Valentine's Day. (Nothing in the lives of the two Christian martyrs connects them with lovers or with the exchange of messages and gifts.

The Pantheon (Interior)   Originally a temple for the gods, the Pantheon later served as a Christian church. As such, it symbolizes the adaptation of pagan elements to Christian purposes. *(Source: Alinari/Art Resource)*

That practice began in the later Middle Ages.) The fourteenth of February was still celebrated as a festival, but it had taken on Christian meaning.

Probably more immediate in its impact on the unconverted masses was the penitential system. *Penitentials* were manuals for the examination of conscience. Irish priests wrote the earliest ones, which English missionaries then carried to the Continent. An illiterate penitent knelt beside a priest, who questioned the penitent about sins he or she might have committed. The recommended penance was then imposed. Penance usually meant fasting for three days each week on bread and water, which served as a "medicine" for the soul. Here is a section of the penitential prepared by Archbishop Theodore of Canterbury (r. 668–690), which circulated widely at the time:

If anyone commits fornication with a virgin he shall do penance for one year. If with a married woman, he shall do penance for four years, two of these entire, and in the other two during the three forty-day periods and three days a week.

A male who commits fornication with a male shall do penance for three years.

If a woman practices vice with a woman, she shall do penance for three years.

Whoever has often committed theft, seven years is his penance, or such a sentence as his priest shall determine, that is, according to what can be arranged with those whom he has wronged....

If a layman slays another with malice aforethought, if he will not lay aside his arms, he shall do penance for seven years; without flesh and wine, three years....

Women who commit abortion before the fetus has life, shall do penance for one year or for the three forty-day periods or for forty days, according to the nature of the offense; and if later, that is, more than forty days after conception, they shall do penance as murderesses, that is, for three years on Wednesdays and Fridays and in the three forty-day periods. This according to the canons is judged punishable by ten years. . . .

If a poor woman slays her child, she shall do penance for seven years. In the canon it is said that if it is a case of homicide, she shall do penance for ten years.[7]

As this sample suggests, writers of penitentials were preoccupied with sexual transgressions. Penitentials are much more akin to the Jewish law of the Old Testament than to the spirit of the New Testament. They provide an enormous amount of information about the ascetic ideals of early Christianity and about the crime-ridden realities of Celtic and Germanic societies. Penitentials also reveal the ecclesiastical foundations of some modern attitudes toward sex, birth control, and abortion. Most important, the penitential system contributed to the growth of a different attitude toward religion: formerly public, corporate, and social, religious observances became private, personal, and individual.[8]

CHRISTIAN ATTITUDES TOWARD CLASSICAL CULTURE

Probably the major dilemma faced by the early Christian church concerned Greco-Roman culture. The Roman Empire as a social, political, and economic force gradually disintegrated. Its culture, however, survived. In Greek philosophy, art, and architecture, in Roman law, literature, education, and engineering, the legacy of a great civilization continued. The Christian religion had begun and spread within this intellectual and psychological milieu. What was to be the attitude of Christians to the Greco-Roman world of ideas?

Hostility

Christians in the first and second centuries believed that the end of the world was near. Christ had promised to return, and Christians expected to witness that return. Thus they considered knowledge useless and learning a waste of time. The important duty of the Christian was to prepare for the Second Coming of the Lord.

Early Christians harbored a strong hatred of pagan Roman culture—in fact, of all Roman civilization. Had not the Romans crucified Christ? Had not the Romans persecuted Christians and subjected them to the most horrible tortures? Did not the Book of Revelation in the New Testament call Rome the great whore of the world, filled with corruption, sin, and every kind of evil? Roman culture was sexual, sensual, and materialistic. The sensual poetry of Ovid, the political poetry of Virgil, even the rhetorical brilliance of Cicero represented a threat, in the eyes of serious Christians, to the spiritual aims and ideals of Christianity. Good Christians who sought the Kingdom of Heaven through the imitation of Christ believed they had to disassociate themselves from the "filth" that Roman culture embodied.

As Saint Paul wrote, "The wisdom of the world is foolishness, we preach Christ crucified." Tertullian (ca 160–220), an influential African Christian writer, condemned all secular literature as foolishness in the eyes of God. "What has Athens to do with Jerusalem," he demanded, "the Academy with the Church? We have no need for curiosity since Jesus Christ, nor for inquiry since the gospel." Tertullian insisted that Christians would find in the Bible all the wisdom they needed.

Compromise and Adjustment

At the same time, Christianity encouraged adjustment to the ideas and institutions of the Roman world. Some biblical texts clearly urged Christians to accept the existing social, economic, and political establishment. Specifically addressing Christians living among non-Christians in the hostile environment of Rome, the author of the First Letter of Saint Peter had written about the obligations of Christians:

Toward Pagans
Always behave honourably among pagans, so that they can see your good works for themselves and, when the day of reckoning comes, give thanks to God for the things which now make them denounce you as criminals.

Toward Civil Authority

For the sake of the Lord, accept the authority of every social institution: the emperor, as the supreme authority, and the governors as commissioned by him to punish criminals and praise good citizenship. God wants you to be good citizens. . . . Have respect for everyone and love for your community; fear God and honour the emperor.[9]

Christians really had little choice. Greco-Roman culture was the only culture they knew. Only men received a formal education, and they went through the traditional curriculum of grammar and rhetoric. They learned to be effective speakers in the forum or law courts. No other system of education existed. Many early Christians had grown up as pagans, been educated as pagans, and been converted only as adults. Toward homosexuality, for example, according to a recent controversial study, Christians of the first three or four centuries simply imbibed the attitude of the world in which they lived. Many Romans indulged in homosexual activity, and contemporaries did not consider such behavior (or inclinations to it) immoral, bizarre, or harmful. Several emperors were openly homosexual, and homosexuals participated freely in all aspects of Roman life and culture. Early Christians, too, considered homosexuality a conventional expression of physical desire and were no more susceptible to antihomosexual prejudices than pagans were. Some prominent Christians experienced loving same-gender relationships that probably had a sexual element. What eventually led to a change in public and Christian attitudes toward sexual behavior was the shift from the sophisticated urban culture of the Greco-Roman world to the rural culture of medieval Europe.[10]

Even if early Christians had wanted to give up classical ideas and patterns of thought, they would have had great difficulty doing so. Therefore, they had to adapt their Roman education to their Christian beliefs. Saint Paul himself believed there was a good deal of truth in pagan thought, as long as it was correctly interpreted and understood.

The result was a compromise. Christians gradually came to terms with Greco-Roman culture. Saint Jerome (340–419), a distinguished theologian and linguist, remains famous for his translation of the Old and New Testaments from Hebrew and Greek into vernacular Latin. Called the "Vulgate," his edition of the Bible served as the official translation until the sixteenth century; even today, scholars rely on it. Saint Jerome was also familiar with the writings of such classical authors as Cicero, Virgil, and Terence. He believed that Christians should study the best of ancient thought because it would direct their minds to God. Jerome maintained that the best ancient literature should be interpreted in light of the Christian faith.

Synthesis: Saint Augustine

The finest representative of the blending of classical and Christian ideas, and indeed one of the most brilliant thinkers in the history of the Western world, was Saint Augustine of Hippo (354–430). Aside from the scriptural writers, no

The Antioch Chalice This earliest surviving Christian chalice, which dates from the fourth century A.D., combines the typical Roman shape with Christian motifs. The chalice is decorated with figures of Christ and the apostles, leaves, and grapes, which represent the sacrament of the Eucharist. *(Source: The Metropolitan Museum of Art; The Cloisters Collection. Purchase, 1950 (50.4))*

one else has had a greater impact on Christian thought in succeeding centuries. Saint Augustine was born into an urban family in what is now Algeria in North Africa. His father was a pagan, his mother a devout Christian. Because his family was poor—his father was a minor civil servant—the only avenue to success in a highly competitive world was a classical education.

Augustine's mother believed that a good classical education, though pagan, would make her son a better Christian, so Augustine's father scraped together the money to educate him. The child received his basic education in the local school. By modern and even medieval standards, that education was extremely narrow: textual study of the writings of the poet Virgil, the orator-politician Cicero, the historian Sallust, and the playwright Terence. At that time, learning meant memorization. Education in the late Roman world aimed at appreciation of words, particularly those of renowned and eloquent orators.

At the age of seventeen, Augustine went to nearby Carthage to continue his education. There he took a mistress with whom he lived for fifteen years. At Carthage, Augustine entered a difficult psychological phase and began an intellectual and spiritual pilgrimage that led him through experiments with several philosophies and heretical Christian sects. In 383 he traveled to Rome, where he endured illness and disappointment in his teaching: his students fled when their bills were due.

Finally, in Milan in 387, through the insights he gained from reading Saint Paul's Letter to the Romans, Augustine received Christian baptism. He later became bishop of the seacoast city of Hippo Regius in his native North Africa (see Map 9.1). He was a renowned preacher to Christians there, a vigorous defender of orthodox Christianity, and the author of over ninety-three books and treatises.

Augustine's autobiography, *The Confessions*, is a literary masterpiece and one of the most influential books in the history of Europe. Written in the form of a prayer, its language is often incredibly beautiful:

Too late have I loved thee, O beauty ever ancient and ever new, too late have I loved thee! And behold! Thou wert within and I without, and it was without that I sought thee. Thou wert with me, and I was not with
thee. Those creatures held me far from thee which, were they not in thee, were not at all. Thou didst call, thou didst cry, thou didst break in upon my deafness; thou didst gleam forth, thou didst shine out, thou didst banish my blindness; thou didst send forth thy fragrance, and I drew breath and yearned for thee; I tasted and still hunger and thirst; thou didst touch me, and I was on flame to find thy peace.[11]

The Confessions describes Augustine's moral struggle, the conflict between his spiritual and intellectual aspirations and his sensual and material self. *The Confessions* reveals the change and development of a human mind and personality steeped in the philosophy and culture of the ancient world.

Many Greek and Roman philosophers had taught that knowledge and virtue are the same: a person who really knows what is right will do what is right. Augustine rejected this idea. He believed that a person may know what is right but fail to act righteously because of the innate weakness of the human will. People do not always act on the basis of rational knowledge. Here Augustine made a profound contribution to the understanding of human nature: he demonstrated that a learned person can also be corrupt and evil. *The Confessions,* written in the rhetorical style and language of late Roman antiquity, marks the synthesis of Greco-Roman forms and Christian thought.

Augustine also contributed to the discussion on the nature of the church that arose around the Donatist heretical movement. Promoted by Donatus, the North African bishop of Carthage, Donatism denied the value of sacraments administered by priests or bishops who had denied their faith under persecution or had committed grave sin. For the Donatists, the holiness of the minister was as important as the sacred rites he performed. Donatists viewed themselves as a separate "chosen people" who had preserved their purity and identity in a corrupt world. Thus they viewed the church as a small spiritual elite that was an alternative to society. Augustine responded to Donatism with extensive preaching and the treatise *On Baptism and Against the Donatists* (A.D. 400), written in the best classical Latin. He argued that, through the working of God's action, the rites of the church have an objective and permanent validity, regardless of a priest's spiritual condition. Being a Christian and a member of the church, Augustine maintained, meant striving for holiness, and rather than seeing oneself as apart from society, the Christian must live in and transform society. The notion of the church as a special spiritual elite, distinct from and superior to the rest of society, recurred many times in the Middle Ages. Each time it was branded a heresy, and Augustine's arguments were marshaled against it.

When the Visigothic chieftain Alaric conquered Rome in 410, horrified pagans blamed the disaster on the Christians. In response, Augustine wrote *City of God*. This profoundly original work contrasts Christianity with the secular society in which it existed. *City of God* presents a moral interpretation of the Roman government—in fact, of all history. Written in Latin and filled with references to ancient history and mythology, it remained for centuries the standard statement of the Christian philosophy of history.

According to Augustine, history is the account of God acting in time. Human history reveals that there are two kinds of people: those who live according to the flesh in the city of Babylon and those who live according to the spirit in the City of God. The former will endure eternal hellfire, the latter eternal bliss.

Augustine maintained that states came into existence as the result of Adam's fall and people's inclination to sin. The state is a necessary evil, responsible only for providing the peace and order that Christians need in order to pursue their pilgrimage to the City of God. The particular form of government—whether monarchy, aristocracy, or democracy—is basically irrelevant. Any civil government that fails to provide justice is no more than a band of gangsters.

Since the state results from moral lapse, from sin, it follows that the church, which is concerned with salvation, is responsible for everyone, including Christian rulers. Churchmen in the Middle Ages used Augustine's theory to defend their belief in the ultimate superiority of the spiritual power over the temporal. This remained the dominant political theory until the late thirteenth century.

Augustine had no objection to drawing on pagan knowledge to support Christian thought. Augustine used Roman history as evidence to defend Christian theology. In doing so, he assimilated Roman history, and indeed all of classical culture, into Christian teaching.

MONASTICISM AND THE RULE OF SAINT BENEDICT

Christianity began and spread as a city religion. Since the first century, however, some especially pious Christians had felt that the only alternative to the decadence of urban life was complete separation from the world. All-consuming pursuit of material things, gross sexual promiscuity, and general political corruption disgusted them. They believed that the Christian life as set forth in the Gospel could not be lived in the midst of such immorality. They rejected the established values of Roman society and were the first real nonconformists in the church.

Beginnings

Intellectual currents widespread in Syria, Egypt, and Palestine in the first and second centuries influenced the development of monasticism. One such current was *gnosticism,* a religious and philosophical movement that combined astrology, magic, elements of the Jewish tradition, Persian mysticism, and the Platonic dualism of mind and spirit (see page 141). The term *gnosis* means "knowledge," and some Christian gnostic sects claimed to possess a secret tradition that Jesus had taught the apostles in private. Gnostics believed in a dualism of spirit and matter, of mind and body; they stressed that all matter was evil and that the soul must strive through knowledge *(gnosis)* to free itself from family ties, material possessions and worldly obligations, and sexual desires. Gnostics held to a fierce determinism or predestinarianism. They believed that the vast majority of people were earthly clods damned to destruction but the few gnostics were the elect, their souls containing elements of the divine. Orthodox Christian teaching condemned these ideas, but they permeated monastic thought as it evolved in the West and later Sufi mysticism as that movement grew in Islam (see page 284).

The fourth century witnessed a significant change in the relationship of Christianity and the broader society. Until Constantinople's legalization of Christianity, Christians were a persecuted minority. The persecutions of Decius in 250 and Diocletian in 304 were especially severe. Christians greatly revered the men and women who suffered and died for their faith, the *martyrs*. They, like Jesus, made the ultimate sacrifice. The martyrs were the great heroes of the early Church. When Christianity was legalized and the persecutions ended, a new problem arose. Where Christians had been a suffering minority, now they came to be identified with the state: non-Christians could not advance in the imperial service. And if Christianity had triumphed, so had "the world," since secular attitudes and values pervaded the church. The church of martyrs no longer existed. Some scholars believe that the monasteries provided a way of life for those Christians who wanted to make a total response to Christ's teachings, people who wanted more than a lukewarm Christianity. The monks became the new martyrs. Saint Anthony of Egypt (d. 356), the first monk for whom there is concrete evidence and the father of monasticism, went to Alexandria during the last persecution in the hope of gaining martyrdom. Christians believed that monks, like the martyrs before them, could speak for God and that their prayers had special influence with God.

At first individuals and small groups left the cities and went to live in caves or rude shelters in the desert or mountains. These people were called "hermits," from the Greek word *eremos*, meaning "desert." There is no way of knowing how many hermits there were in the fourth and fifth centuries, partly because their conscious aim was a secret, hidden life known only to God.

In western Europe, several factors worked against the eremitical variety of monasticism. The cold, snow, ice, and fog that covered much of Europe for many months of the year discouraged isolated living. Dense forests filled with wild animals and wandering barbaric German tribes presented obvious dangers. Furthermore, church leaders did not really approve of eremitical life. Hermits sometimes claimed to have mystical experiences, direct communications with God. No one could verify these experiences. If hermits could communicate directly with the Lord, what need had they for the priest and the institutional church? The church hierarchy, or leaders, encouraged *coenobitic monasticism*—that is, communal living in monasteries. Communal living provided an environment for training the aspirant in the virtues of charity, poverty, and freedom from self-deception. The Egyptian ascetic Pachomius (290–346/7) organized the first successful coenobitic community at

Tabennisi on the Upper Nile. It drew thousands of recruits.

In the fifth and sixth centuries, many experiments in communal monasticism were made in Gaul, Italy, Spain, Anglo-Saxon England, and Ireland. After studying both eremitical and coenobitic monasticism in Egypt and Syria, John Cassian established two monasteries near Marseilles in Gaul around 415. One of Cassian's books, *Conferences,* based on conversations he had had with holy men in the East, discussed the dangers of the isolated hermit's life. The abbey or monastery of Lérins on the Mediterranean Sea near Cannes (ca 410) also had significant contacts with monastic centers in the Middle East and North Africa. Lérins encouraged the severely penitential and extremely ascetic behavior common in the East, such as long hours of prayer, fasting, and self-flagellation. It was this tradition of harsh self-mortification that the Roman-British monk Saint Patrick carried from Lérins to Ireland in the fifth century. Church organization in Ireland became closely associated with the monasteries, and Irish monastic life followed the ascetic Eastern form.

Around 540 the Roman senator Cassiodorus retired from public service and established a monastery, the Vivarium, on his estate in Italy. Cassiodorus wanted the Vivarium to become an educational and cultural center and enlisted highly educated and sophisticated men for it. He set the monks to copying both sacred and secular manuscripts, intending this task to be their sole occupation. Cassiodorus started the association of monasticism with scholarship and learning. This association developed into a great tradition in the medieval and modern worlds. But Cassiodorus's experiment did not become the most influential form of monasticism in European society. The fifth and sixth centuries witnessed the appearance of many other monastic lifestyles.

The Rule of Saint Benedict

In 529 Benedict of Nursia (480–543), who had experimented with both the eremitical and the communal forms of monastic life, wrote a brief set of regulations for the monks who had gathered around him at Monte Cassino between Rome and Naples. Recent research has shown that Benedict's *Rule* derives from a longer, more detailed and anonymously written document known as *The Rule*

St. Benedict Holding his *Rule* in his left hand, the seated and cowled Patriarch of Western Monasticism blesses the abbot of Monte Cassino with his right hand. The monastery is in the background. *(Source: Biblioteca Apostolica Vaticana)*

of the Master, which was actually suitable only for the place for which it was written. Benedict's guide for monastic life proved more adaptable and slowly replaced all others. *The Rule of Saint Benedict* has influenced all forms of organized religious life in the Roman church.

Saint Benedict conceived of his *Rule* as a simple code for ordinary men. It outlined a monastic life of regularity, discipline, and moderation. Each monk had ample food and adequate sleep. Self-destructive acts of mortification were forbidden. In an atmosphere of silence, a monk spent part of the day in formal prayer, which Benedict called the "Work of God." This consisted of chanting psalms and other prayers from the Bible in the part of the monastery church called the "choir." The rest of the day was passed in study and manual labor. After a year of probation, a monk made three vows. First the monk vowed stability: he promised to live his entire life in the monastery of his profession.

The vow of stability was Saint Benedict's major contribution to Western monasticism; his object was to prevent the wandering so common in his day. Second, the monk vowed conversion of manners—that is, to strive to improve himself and to come closer to God. Third, he promised obedience, the most difficult vow because it meant the complete surrender of his will to the *abbot,* or head of the monastery.

The Rule of Saint Benedict expresses the assimilation of the Roman spirit into Western monasticism. It reveals the logical mind of its creator and the Roman concern for order, organization, and respect for law. Its spirit of moderation and flexibility is reflected in the patience, wisdom, and understanding with which the abbot is to govern and, indeed, with which life is to be led. The *Rule* could be used in vastly different physical and geographical circumstances, in damp and cold Germany as well as in warm and sunny Italy. The *Rule* was quickly adapted for women, and many convents of nuns were established in the early Middle Ages.

Saint Benedict's *Rule* implies that a person who wants to become a monk or nun need have no previous ascetic experience or even a particularly strong bent toward the religious life. Thus it allowed for the admission of newcomers with different backgrounds and personalities. From Chapter 59, "The Offering of Sons by Nobles or by the Poor," and from Benedict's advice to the abbot in Chapter 2—"The abbot should avoid all favoritism in the monastery. . . . A man born free is not to be given higher rank than a slave who becomes a monk"—it is clear that men of different social classes belonged to his monastery. This flexibility helps to explain the attractiveness of Benedictine monasticism throughout the centuries. *The Rule of Saint Benedict* is a superior example of the way in which the Greco-Roman heritage and Roman patterns of thought were preserved.

At the same time, the *Rule* no more provides a picture of actual life in a Benedictine abbey of the seventh or eighth (or twentieth) century than the American Constitution of 1789 describes living conditions in the United States today. A code of laws cannot do that. *The Rule of Saint Benedict* had one fundamental purpose: to draw the individual slowly but steadily away from attachment to the world and love of self and toward the love of God.

The Success of Benedictine Monasticism

Why was the Benedictine form of monasticism so successful? Why did it eventually replace other forms of Western monasticism? The answer lies partly in its spirit of flexibility and moderation and partly in the balanced life that it provided. Early Benedictine monks and nuns spent part of the day in prayer, part in study or in some other form of intellectual activity, and part in manual labor. The monastic life as conceived by Saint Benedict did not lean too heavily in any one direction; it struck a balance between asceticism and idleness. It thus provided opportunities for persons of entirely different abilities and talents—from mechanics to gardeners to literary scholars. Benedict's *Rule* contrasts sharply with Cassiodorus's narrow concept of the monastery as a place for aristocratic scholars and bibliophiles.

Benedictine monasticism also suited the social circumstances of early medieval society. The German invasions had fragmented European life: the self-sufficient rural estate replaced the city as the basic unit of civilization. A monastery, too, had to be economically self-sufficient. It was supposed to produce from its lands and properties all that was needed for food, clothing, shelter, and liturgical service of the altar. The monastery fitted in—indeed, represented—the trend toward localism.

Benedictine monasticism also succeeded partly because it was so materially successful. In the seventh and eighth centuries, monasteries pushed back forest and wasteland, drained swamps, and experimented with crop rotation. For example, the abbey of Saint Wandrille, founded in 645 near Rouen in northwestern Gaul, sent squads of monks to clear the forests that surrounded it. Within seventy-five years, the abbey was immensely wealthy. The abbey of Jumièges, also in the diocese of Rouen, followed much the same pattern. Such Benedictine houses made a significant contribution to the agricultural development of Europe. The communal nature of their organization, whereby property was held in common and profits pooled and reinvested, made this contribution possible.

Finally, monasteries conducted schools for local young people. Some learned about prescriptions and herbal remedies and went on to provide medical treatment for their localities. A few copied manuscripts and wrote books. This training did not go unappreciated in a society desperately in need of it. Local and royal governments drew on the services of the literate men and able administrators produced by the monasteries. This was not what Saint Benedict had intended, but the effectiveness of the institution that he designed made it perhaps inevitable.

THE MIGRATION OF THE GERMANIC PEOPLES

The migration of peoples from one area to another has been a dominant and continuing feature of European history. Mass movements of Europeans occurred in the fourth through sixth centuries, in the ninth and tenth centuries, and in the twelfth and thirteenth centuries. From the sixteenth century to the present, such movements have been almost continuous, involving not just the European continent but the entire world. The causes have varied and are not thoroughly understood by scholars. But there is no question that migration profoundly affects both the regions to which peoples move and the ones they leave behind.

The *Völkerwanderungen,* or migrations of the Germanic peoples, were important in the decline of the Roman Empire. Many twentieth-century historians and sociologists have tried to explain who the Germans were and why they migrated, but scholars have not had much success at answering these questions. The surviving evidence is primarily archeological, scanty, and not yet adequately explored. As an authority on the Ostrogoths recently wrote, "Despite a century of keen historical investigation and archaeological excavation, the cause and nature of the *Völkerwanderung* challenge the inquirer as much as ever." Perhaps overpopulation and the resulting food shortages caused migration. Perhaps victorious tribes forced the vanquished to move southward. Probably the "primary stimulus for this gradual migration was the Roman frontier, which increasingly offered service in the army and work for pay around the camps."[12]

The answers that do exist rest on archeological evidence—bone fossils, cooking utensils, jewelry, instruments of war, and other artifacts—found later inside the borders of the Roman Empire. Like the Vikings, who first terrorized and then settled in many sections of Europe in the ninth and tenth centuries, the Germans inhabited the regions of present-day northern Germany, southern Sweden and Denmark, and the shores of the Baltic. At the time of their migrations, they had little ethnic solidarity.

Since about 150, Germanic tribes had pressed along the Rhine-Danube frontier of the Roman Empire. Depending on their closeness to that border, these tribes differed considerably from one another in level of civilization. Some tribes, such as the Visigoths and Ostrogoths, led a settled existence, engaged in agriculture and trade, and accepted Arian Christianity. Tribes such as the Anglo-Saxons and the Huns, who lived far from the Roman frontiers, were not affected by the civilizing influences of Rome. They remained nomadic, even barbaric, peoples.

Visigothic Eagle   (Sixth century) The eagle was a standard symbol of nobility and power among the Germanic peoples. A fine example of Visigothic craftsmanship, this richly jewelled eagle—worn as a cloak clasp or as a brooch—could be afforded only by the wealthiest and most powerful members of the nobility. *(Source: Walters Art Gallery, Baltimore)*

Historians do not know exactly when the Mongolian tribe called the Huns began to move westward from China, but about 370 they pressured the Goths living along the Rhine-Danube frontier. The Huns easily defeated the Ostrogoths, and the frightened Visigoths petitioned the emperor to be allowed to settle within the empire. Once inside, however, they revolted. In 378 a Visigothic army decisively defeated the emperor's army. This date

MAP 9.2 The Germanic Migrations   The Germanic tribes infiltrated and settled in all parts of western Europe. The Huns, who were not German ethnically, originated in central Asia. The Huns' victory over the Ostrogoths led the emperor to allow the Visigoths to settle within the empire, a decision that proved disastrous for Rome.

marks the beginning of massive Germanic invasions into the empire (Map 9.2).

Some tribes that settled within the borders of the Roman Empire numbered perhaps no more than ten thousand individuals. Others, such as the Ostrogoths and Visigoths, were about twenty or thirty times larger. Because they settled near and quickly intermingled with Romans and Romanized peoples, it is impossible to specify numbers of original migrators. Dense forests, poor soil, and inadequate equipment probably kept food production low. This meant that the Germans could not increase very rapidly in their new locations.

Except for the Lombards, whose conquests of Italy persisted into the mid-eighth century, the movements of Germanic peoples on the Continent ended about 600. Between 450 and 565, the Germans established a number of kingdoms, but none except the Frankish kingdom lasted very long. Since the German kingdoms were not states with definite geographical boundaries, their locations are approximate. The Visigoths overran much of southwestern Gaul. Establishing their headquarters at Toulouse, they exercised a weak domination over Spain until a great Muslim victory at Guadalete in 711 ended Visigothic rule. The Vandals, whose destructive ways are commemorated in the word *vandal,* settled in North Africa. In northern and western Europe in the sixth century, the Burgundians established rule over lands roughly circumscribed by the old Roman army camps at Lyon, Besançon, Geneva, and Autun.

In northern Italy, the Ostrogothic king Theodoric (r. 474–526) pursued a policy of assimilation between Germans and Romans. He maintained close relations with the Roman emperor at Constantinople and drew Roman scholars and diplomats into the royal civil service. He was a crude German, however, whose reign was disliked by pagan Roman aristocrats. Moreover, he was an Arian Christian, so Roman Catholics disliked him as heretical. His royal administration fell apart during Justinian's sixth-century reconquest of Italy. War and plague then made northern Italy ripe for Lombard conquest in the seventh century.

The most enduring Germanic kingdom was established by the Frankish chieftain Clovis (r. 481–511). Originally only a petty chieftain with headquarters in the region of Tournai in northwestern Gaul (modern Belgium), Clovis began to expand his territories in 486. His defeat of the Gallo-Roman general Syagrius extended his jurisdiction to the Loire River. Clovis's conversion to orthodox Christianity in 496 won him the crucial support of the papacy and the bishops of Gaul. As the defender of Roman Catholicism against heretical German tribes, he went on to conquer the Visigoths, extending his domain as far as the Pyrenees and making Paris his headquarters. Because he was descended from the half-legendary chieftain Merovech, the dynasty founded by Clovis has been called "Merovingian." Clovis's sons subjugated the Burgundians in eastern Gaul and the Ostrogothic tribes living north of the Alps.

Baptism of Clovis (A.D. 496)   In this ninth-century ivory carving, St. Remi, bishop of Reims, baptizes the Frankish chieftain by immersing him in a pool of water. Legend holds that on this occasion a dove brought a vial of holy oil from heaven, later used in the coronations of French kings. *(Source: Musée Condé. Chantilly/Laurie Platt Winfrey, Inc.)*

GERMANIC SOCIETY

The Germans replaced the Romans as rulers of most of the European continent, and German customs and traditions formed the basis of European society for centuries. What patterns of social, political, and economic life characterized the Germans?

Scholars are hampered in answering this question because the Germans could not write and thus kept no records before their conversion to Christianity. The earliest information about them comes from moralistic accounts by such Romans as the historian Tacitus, who was acquainted only with the tribes living closest to the borders of the empire. Furthermore, Tacitus wrote his *Germania* at the end of the first century A.D., and by the fifth century German practices differed from those of Tacitus's time. Current knowledge of the Germans depends largely on records written in the sixth and seventh centuries and projected backward.

Kinship, Custom, and Class

The Germans had no notion of the *state* as the term is used in the twentieth century; they thought in social, not political terms. The basic Germanic social unit was the *folk,* or tribe. Members of the folk believed that they were all descended from a common ancestor. Blood united them. Kinship protected them. Law was custom—unwritten, preserved in the minds of the elders of the tribe, and handed down by word of mouth from generation to generation. Custom regulated everything. Every tribe had its customs, and every member of the tribe knew what they were. Members were subject to their tribe's customary law wherever they went, and friendly tribes respected one another's laws.

Germanic tribes were led by kings or tribal chieftains. The chief was that member of the folk recognized as the strongest and bravest in battle, elected from among the male members of the strongest family. He led the tribe in war, settled disputes among its members, conducted negotiations with outside powers, and offered sacrifices to the gods. The period of migrations and conquests of the western Roman Empire witnessed the strengthening of kingship among the Germanic tribes. Tribes that did not migrate did not develop kings.

Closely associated with the king in some southern tribes was the *comitatus,* or war band. Writing at the end of the first century, Tacitus described the war band as the bravest young men in the tribe. They swore loyalty to the chief, fought with him in battle, and were not supposed to leave the battlefield without him; to do so implied cowardice and disloyalty and brought social disgrace. Social egalitarianism existed among members of the war band.

During the *Völkerwanderungen* of the fourth century, however, and as a result of constant warfare, the war band was transformed into a system of stratified ranks. For example, among the Ostrogoths a warrior nobility and several other nobilities evolved. Contact with the Romans, who produced armbands for trade with the barbarians, stimulated demand for armbands. Ostrogothic warriors wanted armbands because of the status and distinctiveness that they conferred. Thus armbands, especially the gold ones reserved for the "royal families," promoted the development of hierarchical ranks within war bands. During the Ostrogothic conquest of Italy under Theodoric, warrior-nobles also sought to acquire land, both as a mark of prestige and as a means to power. As land and wealth came into the hands of a small elite class, social inequalities emerged and were gradually strengthened.[13] These inequalities help to explain the origins of the European noble class (see page 334).

Law

As long as custom determined all behavior, the early Germans had no need for written law. Beginning in the late sixth century, however, German tribal chieftains began to collect, write, and publish lists of their customs. Why then? The Christian missionaries who were slowly converting the Germans to Christianity wanted to know the tribal customs, and they encouraged German rulers to set down their customs in written form. Churchmen wanted to read about German ways in order to assimilate the tribes to Christianity. Augustine of Canterbury, for example, persuaded King Ethelbert of Kent to have his folk laws written down: these *Dooms of Ethelbert* date from 601 to 604, roughly five years after Augustine's arrival in Britain. Moreover, by the sixth century the German kings needed rules and regulations for the

Romans living under their jurisdiction as well as for their own people.

Today if a person holds up a bank, American law maintains that the robber attacks both the bank and the state in which it exists—a sophisticated notion involving the abstract idea of the state. In early German law, all crimes were regarded as crimes against a person.

According to the code of the Salian Franks, every person had a particular monetary value to the tribe. This value was called the *wergeld,* which literally means "man-money" or "money to buy off the spear." Men of fighting age had the highest wergeld, then women of child-bearing age, then children, and finally the aged. Everyone's value reflected his or her potential military worthiness. If a person accused of a crime agreed to pay the wergeld and if the victim and his or her family accepted the payment, there was peace (hence the expression "money to buy off the spear"). If the accused refused to pay the wergeld or if the victim's family refused to accept it, a blood feud ensued. Individuals depended on their kin for protection, and kinship served as a force of social control.

Historians and sociologists have difficulty applying the early law codes, partly because they are patchwork affairs studded with additions made in later centuries. For example, the Salic Law—the law code of the Salian Franks issued by Clovis—offers a general picture of Germanic life and problems in the early Middle Ages and is typical of the law codes of other tribes, such as the Visigoths, Burgundians, Lombards, and Anglo-Saxons.

The Salic Law lists the money fines to be paid to the victim or the family for such injuries as theft, rape, assault, arson, and murder:

If any person strike another on the head so that the brain appears, and the three bones which lie above the brain shall project, he shall be sentenced to 1200 denars, which make 300 shillings. . . .

If any one have hit a free woman who is pregnant, and she dies, he shall be sentenced to 2800 denars, which make 700 shillings.

If any one have killed a free woman after she has begun bearing children, he shall be sentenced to 2400 denars, which make 600 shillings.

If any one shall have drawn a harrow through another's harvest after it has sprouted, or shall have gone through it with a wagon where there was no road, he shall be sentenced to 120 denars, which make 30 shillings.[14]

This is really not a code of law at all but a list of tariffs or fines for particular offenses. German law aimed at the prevention or reduction of violence. It was not concerned with abstract justice.

At first, Romans had been subject to Roman law and Germans to Germanic custom. As German kings accepted Christianity and as Romans and Germans increasingly intermarried, the distinction between the two laws blurred and, in the course of the seventh and eighth centuries, disappeared. The result was a new feudal law, to which Romans and Germans were subject alike.

German Life

How did the Germans live? The dark, dense forests that dotted the continent of Europe were the most important physical and psychological factor in the lives of the Germanic peoples who were not quickly Romanized. Forests separated one tribe from another. The pagan Germans believed that gods and spirits inhabited the forests. Trees were holy, and to cut them down was an act of grave sacrilege. Thus the Germans cut no trees. They also feared building a mill or a bridge on a river, lest the river spirit be offended. This attitude prevented the clearing of land for farming and tended to keep the Germans isolated.

In the course of the sixth through eighth centuries, the Germans slowly adapted to Greco-Roman and Christian attitudes and patterns of behavior. Acceptance of Christianity and the end of animistic beliefs that spiritual forces live in natural objects had profound consequences. In fact, the decline of animistic beliefs marks a turning point in the economic and intellectual progress of the West. A more settled, less nomadic way of life developed as people no longer feared to make use of natural resources such as rivers and forests. Once animistic beliefs were dispelled, the forests were opened to use, and all members of the community had common rights in them. Trees provided wood for building and for fuel; the forests served as the perfect place for grazing animals. The steady reduction of forest land between the sixth and thirteenth centuries was a major step in the agricultural development of Europe.

Vandal Landowner The adoption of Roman dress—short tunic, cloak, and sandals—reflects the way the Germanic tribes accepted Roman lifestyles. Likewise both the mosaic art form and the man's stylized appearance show the Germans' assimilation of Roman influences. (Notice that the rider has a saddle but not stirrups.) *(Source: Courtesy of the Trustees of the British Museum)*

Migrating Germans clustered in small settlements of a few families each. For example, the groups of Ostrogoths who settled in Moldavia in present-day central Romania lived in small, one-room huts in widely scattered villages near rivers. The huts were constructed of mud, wood, or *wattle* (poles intertwined with twigs or reeds) and were scattered over small clearings without alignment or evidence of town planning.

The closer they settled to sites of Roman civilization, such as Roman towns or army camps, the more quickly the Germans were Romanized. Most Germans were farmers, and all members of the community assisted in cultivation. They grew oats and rye for bread and hops for beer. Tribes such as the Ostrogoths also raised sheep, horses, pigs, and chickens. Archeological evidence dating from the

fifth century, from areas of Roman Dacia where the Goths frequently came in contact with Roman outposts and towns, reveals the steady acculturation of the Germans to Roman practices. Dietary habits shifted toward Roman tastes, as the Germans increasingly grew to prefer wheat bread and wine. German dress, especially among the warrior elite, copied Roman military garb. German nobles imitated the Roman fashion of multiple neck chains, though they clung to the traditional cloisonné *fibula*, or clasps, that fastened a cloak to the shoulders. Along the Rhine-Danube frontiers of the Roman Empire, Goths and other German peoples lived in sight of or within Roman army camps and towns. Many Germans found employment in the Roman army. As the Germans were Romanized, the Roman army was Germanized. Army officers gave their orders in military Latin, but talk and jokes around the evening campfires were in Germanic tongues.[15]

Anglo-Saxon England

The island of Britain, conquered by Rome during the reign of Claudius (r. A.D. 41–54), shared fully in the life of the Roman Empire during the first four centuries of the Christian era. A military aristocracy governed, and the official religion was the cult of the emperor. Towns were planned in the Roman fashion, with temples, public baths, theaters, and amphitheaters. In the countryside, large manors controlled the surrounding lands. Roman merchants brought Eastern luxury goods and Eastern religions—including Christianity—into Britain. The native Britons, a gentle Celtic people, had become thoroughly Romanized. Their language was Latin. Their lifestyle was Roman. Then an event in the distant eastern province of Thrace changed all this.

In 378 the Visigoths inflicted a severe defeat on the Roman emperor Valens at Adrianople. Even Britain felt the consequences. Rome was forced to retrench, and in 407 Roman troops were withdrawn from the island, leaving it unprotected. The savage Picts from Scotland harassed the north. Teutonic tribes from Scandinavia and modern-day Belgium—the Angles, Saxons, and Jutes—stepped up their assaults, attacking in a hit-and-run fashion. Their goal was plunder, and at first their invasions led to no permanent settlements.

As more Germans arrived in Britain, however, they took over the best lands and humbled the Britons. Increasingly the natives fled to the west and settled in Wales. Sporadic raids continued for over a century and led to Germanic control of most of Britain. Historians have labeled the period from 500 to 1066 "Anglo-Saxon." Except for the Jutes, who probably came from Frisia (modern Belgium), the Teutonic tribes came from the least Romanized and least civilized parts of Europe. They destroyed Roman culture in Britain. Tribal custom superseded Roman law.

The beginnings of the Germanic kingdoms in Britain are very obscure, but scholars suspect they came into being in the seventh and eighth centuries. Writing in the eighth century, the scholar Bede (see pages 341–342) described seven kingdoms: the Jutish kingdom of Kent; the Saxon

kingdoms of the East Saxons (Essex), South Saxons (Sussex), and West Saxons (Wessex); and the kingdoms of the Angles, Mercians, and Northumbrians (Map 9.3). The names imply that these peoples thought of themselves in tribal rather than geographical terms. They referred to the "kingdom of the West Saxons," for example, rather than simply to "Wessex." Because of Bede's categorization, scholars call the seven kingdoms the "Heptarchy" of Anglo-Saxon Britain. The suggestion of total Anglo-Saxon domination, however, is not entirely accurate. Germanic tribes never subdued Scotland, where the Picts remained strong, or Wales, where the Celts and native Britons continued to put up stubborn resistance.

Thus Anglo-Saxon England was divided along racial and political lines. The Teutonic kingdoms

MAP 9.3 Anglo-Saxon England The seven kingdoms of the Heptarchy—Northumbria, Mercia, East Anglia, Essex, Kent, Sussex, and Wessex—dominated but did not subsume Britain. Scotland remained a Pict stronghold, and the Celts resisted invasion of their native Wales by Germanic tribes.

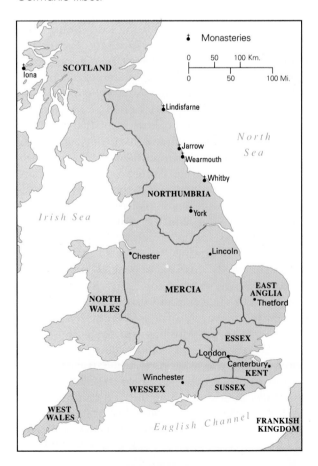

in the south, east, and center were opposed by the native Britons in the west, who wanted to get rid of the invaders. The Anglo-Saxon kingdoms also fought among themselves, causing boundaries to shift constantly. Finally in the ninth century, under pressure of the Danish, or Viking, invasions, the Britons and the Germanic peoples were molded together under the leadership of King Alfred of Wessex (r. 871–899).

THE BYZANTINE EAST (CA 400–1000)

Constantine (r. 306–337) had tried to maintain the unity of the Roman Empire, but during the fifth and sixth centuries the western and eastern halves drifted apart. Later emperors worked to hold the empire together. Justinian (r. 527–565) waged long and hard-fought wars against the Ostrogoths and temporarily regained Italy and North Africa, but his conquests had disastrous consequences. Justinian's wars exhausted the resources of the Byzantine state, destroyed Italy's economy, and killed a large part of its population. The wars paved the way for the easy conquest of Italy by another Germanic tribe, the Lombards, shortly after Justinian's death. In the late sixth century, the territory of the western Roman Empire came under Germanic sway, while in the East the Byzantine Empire continued the traditions and institutions of the caesars.

Latin Christian culture was only one legacy that the Roman Empire bequeathed to the Western world. The Byzantine culture centered at Constantinople—Constantine's New Rome—was another. The Byzantine Empire maintained a high standard of living, and for centuries the Greeks were the most civilized people in the Western world. The Byzantine Empire held at bay, or at least hindered, barbarian peoples who could otherwise have wreaked additional devastation on western Europe, retarding its development. Most important, however, is the role of the Byzantines, together with the Muslims (see pages 289–292), as preservers of the wisdom of the ancient world. Throughout the long years when barbarians in western Europe trampled down the old and then painfully built something new, Byzantium protected and then handed on to the West the intellectual heritage of Greco-Roman civilization.

The Separation of Byzantine East and Germanic West

As imperial authority disintegrated in the West during the fifth century, civic functions were performed first by church leaders and then by German chieftains. Meanwhile in the East, the Byzantines preserved the forms and traditions of the old Roman Empire and even called themselves "Romans." Byzantine emperors traced their lines back past Constantine to Augustus. The senate that sat in Constantinople carried on the traditions and preserved the glory of the old Roman senate. The army that defended the empire was the direct descendant of the old Roman legions. Even the chariot factions of the Roman Empire lived on under the Byzantines, who cheered their favorites as enthusiastically as had the Romans of Hadrian's day.

The position of the church differed considerably in the Byzantine East and the Germanic West. The fourth-century emperors Constantine and Theodosius had wanted the church to act as a unifying force within the empire, but the Germanic invasions made that impossible. The bishops of Rome repeatedly called on the emperors at Constantinople for military support against the invaders, but rarely could the emperors send it. The church in the West steadily grew away from the empire and became involved in the social and political affairs of the West. Nevertheless, until the eighth century, the popes, who were often selected by the clergy of Rome, continued to send announcements of their elections to the emperors at Constantinople—a sign that the Roman popes long thought of themselves as bishops of the Roman Empire.

The popes were preoccupied with conversion of the Germans, the Christian attitude toward classical culture, and relations with German rulers. Because the Western church concentrated on its missionary function, it took centuries for the clergy to be organized. Most church theology in the West came from the East, and the overwhelming majority of popes were of Eastern origin.

Tensions occasionally developed between church officials and secular authorities in the West. The dispute between Bishop Ambrose of Milan and Emperor Theodosius (see page 232) is a good example. A century later, Pope Gelasius I (r. 492–496) insisted that bishops, not civil authorities, were responsible for the administration

Justinian and His Court   The Emperor Justinian (center) with ecclesiastical and court officials personifies the unity of the Byzantine state and the orthodox church in the person of the emperor. Just as the emperor was both king and priest, so all his Greek subjects belonged to the orthodox church. *(Source: Scala/Art Resource)*

of the church. Gelasius maintained that two powers governed the world: the sacred authority of popes and the royal power of kings. Moreover, because priests have to answer to God even for the actions of kings, the sacred power was the greater.

Such an assertion was virtually unheard of in the East, where the emperor's jurisdiction over the church was fully acknowledged. The emperor in Constantinople nominated the *patriarch,* as the highest prelate of the Eastern church was called. The emperor looked on religion as a branch of the state. Religion was such a vital aspect of the social life of the people that the emperor devoted considerable attention to it. He considered it his duty to protect the faith, not only against heathen enemies but also against heretics within the empire. In case of doctrinal disputes, the emperor, following Constantine's example at Nicaea, summoned councils of bishops and theologians to settle problems.

The steady separation of the Byzantine East and the Germanic West rests partly on the ways Christianity and classical culture were received in the two parts of the Roman Empire. In the West, Christians initially constituted a small, alien minority within the broad Roman culture; they kept apart from the rest of society. They condemned, avoided, and demystified Roman society and classical culture—as Saint Augustine's *City of God* shows. In Byzantium, by contrast, most Greeks were Christian. *Apologists,* or defenders, of Christianity insisted on harmony between Christianity and classical culture: they used Greek philosophy to buttress Christian tenets. Politically, emperors beginning with Constantine worked for unanimity between church and state.

Distinctive attitudes toward holy persons illustrate the differences between the two societies. A *holy person* was a kind of hero whose life and character embodied the spiritual ideals of the group. *Confessors* publicly manifested their faith in Christ. *Martyrs* held to their Christian faith, even suffering death for it and revealing unique courage and fortitude. *Virgins* displayed outstanding qualities of earthly and sexual renunciation. Christians believed that spiritual ideals existed in the physical body of the holy person. The dead body of the holy person, or *saint,* as he or she came to be recognized, became an object of veneration. Saints were *ministers,* who carried people's prayers and petitions to God and interceded with God on behalf of the living. Completely contrary to pagan and Jewish attitudes toward holy persons, the dead saints, because of their intercessory powers, played an extremely important role in Christian worship.

In the Germanic West, many saints had been socially prominent persons, such as nobles or bishops, and had exercised real power during their lifetimes. The locus of the supernatural power associated with a Western saint was fixed with precision. People knew exactly where a saint's body was buried because that place was the source of his or her holiness and intercessory influence. Relatively few such sites existed in the Germanic West.

In the Byzantine East, by contrast, the saints during their lifetimes had usually shunned human contact and avoided society and those who exercised power; they had fulfilled no social function. Eastern saints drew their spiritual power and influence from outside of society—from a retreat in the desert and from the ability to speak directly to God. In the East, Christians accepted many people as bearers or agents of the holy, and the locus of spiritual power was more ambiguous than in the West; holiness often touched socially marginal persons such as monks, prostitutes, and soldiers. In the West, holiness was vested in those who had known how to rule, and their posthumous holiness tended to be concentrated in cathedral, monastery, or shrine.[16] Holiness in the West, therefore, could be utilized for political or economic purposes. In the East the socially marginal role of the holy person made it very difficult to use his or her reputation for political purposes.

External Threats and Internal Conflicts

The wars of Justinian's reign left the Byzantine Empire economically and demographically weakened. Over the next two centuries, two additional troubles threatened its very survival: foreign invasion and internal theological disputes.

Beginning around 560, the Avars, a mounted Asiatic nomad group, and the Slavs, an Indo-European people probably originating in Galicia (southeastern Poland and the western Ukraine), burst into the Balkan peninsula. In the meantime, the Sassanid Persians threatened the eastern provinces. By 602 both the northern and the eastern frontiers of the Byzantine Empire had collapsed. In 626 a combined force of Persians and Avars attacked Constantinople itself. Only Byzantine control of the sea and the superhuman exertions of the emperor Heraclius (r. 610–641) saved the empire. But this effort so thoroughly exhausted both the Persians and the Greeks that they proved no match for the Arabs, who overran the eastern provinces of the empire between 632 and 640 (see pages 268–269).

Arab armies pushed into Asia Minor while Arab navies seized the Greek islands of Cyprus, Rhodes, and Chios and attacked the coastal cities of the empire. Again Constantinople faced sieges between 674 and 678 and from 717 to 718. Again Byzantine naval supremacy and the use of "Greek fire" (see page 258) saved the day. The Balkans, however, were lost to the Slavs; the eastern provinces, to the Arabs.

From all of these military disruptions certain benefits did result. First, the territories lost to the empire contained peoples of very diverse ethnic origins, languages, and religions. The territories that continued under imperial authority gradually achieved a strong cultural unity. They were Greek in culture and administration, orthodox in religion.

Second, foreign invasions created the need for internal reorganization. Since the third century, the imperial administration had been based on Diocletian's separation of civil and military authority (see pages 218, 220). In times of crisis, such as during the Arab invasions, this structure had led to paralysis. Heraclius and his successors militarized the administration. The empire was divided into *themes,* or military districts, governed by *strategoi,* or generals, who held both civil and military authority. The strategoi were responsible directly to the emperor. This reorganization brought into being a new peasant army. Foreign invasion had broken up the great landed estates of the empire, and the estate land was distributed to peasant soldiers, who equipped and supported

THE ORIGINS OF EUROPE

312	Constantine legalizes Christianity
ca 315	Constantine removes capital of the Roman Empire to Constantinople
325	Nicene Creed
ca 370	Huns defeat the Ostrogoths
380	Theodosius recognizes Christianity as the official imperial religion
	Bishop Ambrose refuses to yield cathedral church of Milan to Theodosius, thereby asserting church's independence from state
ca 390	Publication of *The Confessions* of Saint Augustine
ca 400	Donatist heretical movement reaches its height
5th century	Germanic raids of western Europe
476	Death of Roman emperor Romulus Augustus signals end of empire in the West
ca 490	Clovis issues Salic Law of the Franks
496	Clovis adopts Roman Christianity
529	Publication of the *Rule* of Saint Benedict
	Publication of the *Law Code* of Justinian
ca 560–720	Foreign invasion of the Byzantine Empire
597	Pope Gregory I sends missionaries to convert the Britons
7th century	Monasteries established throughout Anglo-Saxon England
ca 602	Publication of the *Dooms of Ethelbert*
664	Roman Christianity upheld over Celtic tradition at Synod of Whitby
730	Leo III orders destruction of icons throughout the Byzantine Empire, thereby initiating the iconoclastic controversy
843	Byzantine icons restored; civil wars cease

themselves from the profits of the land. Formerly the Byzantine state had relied on foreign mercenaries. Now each theme had an army of native soldiers with a permanent (landed) interest in the preservation of the empire. The government saved the costs of hiring troops and was assured the loyalty of native soldiers. The elevation of peasants to military status revitalized the social structure.

Third, some scholars maintain that the military disasters of the period led to an increase in popular piety and devotion to icons. An *icon* is an image or representation in painting, bas-relief, or mosaic of God the Father, Jesus, the Virgin, or the saints that is venerated (revered) in religious devotion. Since the third century, the church had allowed people to venerate icons. Although all prayer had to be directed to God the Father, Christian teaching held that icons representing the saints fostered reverence and that Jesus and the saints could most effectively plead a cause to God the Father.

Iconoclasts, those who favored the destruction of icons, argued that people were worshiping the image itself, rather than what it signified. This, they claimed, constituted *idolatry,* a violation of the Mosaic prohibition of graven images in the Ten Commandments. Moreover, said iconoclasts, people's belief that certain icons had spiritual and magical powers was gross superstition.

The result of the controversy over icons was a terrible theological conflict that split the Byzantine world for a century. In 730 the emperor Leo III (r. 717–741) ordered the destruction of the images. The removal of icons from Byzantine churches provoked a violent reaction: entire provinces revolted, and the empire and Roman papacy severed relations. Since Eastern monasteries were the fiercest defenders of icons, Leo's son Constantine V (r. 741–775), nicknamed "Copronymous" ("Dung-name") by his enemies, took the war to the monasteries. Constantine seized their properties, executed some of the monks, and forced others into the army. Theological disputes and civil disorder over the icons continued intermittently until 843, when the icons were restored.

The implications of the iconoclastic controversy extended far beyond strictly theological issues. Iconoclasm raised the question of the right of the emperor to intervene in religious disputes, a central problem in the relations of church and state. Iconoclasm antagonized the pope and served to encourage him in his quest for an alliance with the Frankish monarchy (see page 336); iconoclasm thus contributed to the end of Byzantine political influence in central Italy. Arab control of the Mediterranean in the seventh and eighth centuries furthered the separation of the Roman and Byzantine churches by dividing the two parts of Christendom. Separation bred isolation. Isolation, combined with prejudice on both sides, bred hostility. In 1054 a theological disagreement led the bishop of Rome and the patriarch of Constantinople to excommunicate each other. The outcome was a continuing *schism*, or split, between the Roman Catholic and the Greek Orthodox churches. The bitterness generated by iconoclasm contributed to that schism. Finally, the acceptance of icons profoundly influenced subsequent religious art. That art rejected the Judaic and Islamic prohibition of figural representation and continued in the Greco-Roman tradition of human representation.

In spite of wars and internal theological disputes, the empire recovered with new vitality. Turning from conflict to peace, the Byzantines set about converting the Slavs. In antiquity the Slavs had lived as a single people in central Europe. With the start of the mass migrations of the late Roman Empire, the Slavs moved in different directions and split into several groups. Between the fifth and ninth centuries, the eastern Slavs, from whom the Ukrainians, the Russians, and the White Russians descend, moved into the vast and practically uninhabited area of present-day European Russia and the Ukraine (see Map 19.4). This enormous area consisted of an immense virgin forest to the north, where most of the eastern Slavs settled, and an endless prairie grassland to the south. Probably organized as tribal communities, the eastern Slavs, like many North American pioneers much later, lived off the great abundance of wild game and a crude "slash and burn" agriculture. After clearing a piece of the forest to build log cabins, they burned the stumps and brush. The ashes left a rich deposit of potash and lime, and the land gave several good crops before it was exhausted. The people then moved on to another untouched area and repeated the process.

In the ninth century, the Vikings (see pages 350–352) appeared in the lands of the eastern Slavs. Called "Varangians" in the old Russian chronicles, the Vikings were interested primarily in international trade, and the opportunities were good because the Muslim conquests of the eighth century had greatly reduced Christian trade in the Mediterranean (see page 269). Moving up and down the rivers, the Vikings soon linked Scandinavia and northern Europe with the Black Sea and with the Byzantine Empire, whose capital was at Constantinople. They built a few strategic forts along the rivers, from which they raided the neighboring Slavic tribes and collected tribute. Slaves were the most important article of tribute, and *Slavs* even became the word for "slave" in several European languages.

In order to increase and protect their international commerce, the Vikings declared themselves the rulers of the eastern Slavs. According to tradition, the semilegendary chieftain Ruirik founded the princely dynasty about 860. In any event, the Varangian ruler Oleg (r. 878–912) established his residence at Kiev. He and his successors ruled over a loosely united confederation of Slavic territories—the Kievan state—until 1054. The Viking prince and his clansmen quickly became assimilated into the Slavic population, taking local wives and emerging as the noble class.

Byzantine missionaries preached Christianity to the Vikings and local Slavs and in the process speeded up the assimilation of the two peoples. The missionary Cyril invented a Slavic alphabet using Greek characters, and this script (the Cyrillic alphabet) is still used. Cyrillic script made possible the birth of Russian literature. Similarly, Byzantine art and architecture became the basis and inspiration of Russian forms. In the realm of government, the Byzantines, in converting the Slavified Vikings, contributed to the unity of early Russia. So powerful was the Byzantine impact on Russia that the Russians claimed to be successors of the Byzantine Empire. For a time, Moscow was even known as the "Third Rome" (the second Rome being Constantinople).

The Law Code of Justinian

One of the most splendid achievements of the Byzantine emperors was the preservation of Roman law for the medieval and modern worlds. Roman law had developed from many sources—decisions by judges, edicts of the emperors, legislation passed by the senate, and the opinions of jurists expert in the theory and practice of law. By the fourth century, Roman law had become a huge, bewildering mass. Its sheer bulk made it almost unusable. Some laws had become outdated; some repeated or contradicted others. Faced with this vast, complex, and confusing hodgepodge, the emperor Theodosius decided to clarify and codify the law. He explained why:

When we consider the enormous multitude of books, the diverse modes of process and the difficulty of legal cases, and further the huge mass of imperial constitutions, which hidden as it were under a rampart of gross mist and darkness precludes men's intellects from gaining a knowledge of them, we feel that we have met a real need of our age, and dispelling the darkness have given light to the laws by a short compendium.[17]

Theodosius's work was only a beginning. He left centuries of Roman law untouched.

A far more sweeping and systematic codification took place under the emperor Justinian. Justinian intended to simplify the law and make it known to everyone. He appointed a committee of eminent jurists to sort through and organize the laws. The result, published in 529, was the *Code,* which distilled the legal genius of the Romans into a coherent whole, eliminated outmoded laws and contradictions, and clarified the law itself. Not content with the *Code,* Justinian set about bringing order to the equally huge body of Roman *jurisprudence,* the science or philosophy of law.

During the second and third centuries, the foremost Roman jurists, at the request of the emperors, had expressed learned opinions on complex legal problems, but often these opinions differed from one another. To harmonize this body of knowledge, Justinian directed his jurists to clear up disputed points and to issue definitive rulings. Accordingly, in 533 his lawyers published the *Digest,* which codified Roman legal thought. Finally, Justinian's lawyers compiled a handbook of civil law, the *Institutes.*

These three works—the *Code, Digest,* and *Institutes*—are the backbone of the *corpus juris civilis,* the "body of civil law," which is the foundation of law for nearly every modern European nation. The work of Justinian and his dedicated band of jurists still affects the modern world nearly fifteen hundred years later.

Intellectual Life

Among the Byzantines, education was highly prized, and because of them many masterpieces of ancient Greek literature survived to fertilize the intellectual life of the modern world. The literature of the Byzantine Empire was predominantly Greek, although Latin was long spoken among top politicians, scholars, and lawyers. Indeed, Justinian's *Code* was first written in Latin. Among the large reading public, history was a favorite subject. Generations of Byzantines read the historical works of Thucydides and others. Some Byzantine historians abbreviated long histories, such as those of Polybius, while others wrote detailed narratives of their own days.

The most remarkable Byzantine historian was Procopius (ca 500–ca 562), who left a rousing account of Justinian's reconquest of North Africa and Italy. Proof that the wit and venom of Aristophanes and other ancient writers lived on in the Byzantine era can be found in Procopius's *Secret History,* a vicious and uproarious attack on Justinian and his wife, the empress Theodora. The Byzantines are often depicted as dull and lifeless, but such opinions are hard to defend in the face of Procopius's descriptions of Justinian's character:

For he was at once villainous and amenable; as people say colloquially, a moron. He was never truthful with anyone, but always guileful in what he said and did, yet easily hoodwinked by any who wanted to deceive him. His nature was an unnatural mixture of folly and wickedness.[18]

The *Secret History* may not be great history, but it is robust literature.

Later Byzantine historians chronicled the victories of their emperors and the progress of their barbarian foes. They were curious about foreigners and left striking descriptions of the Turks, who eventually overwhelmed Byzantium. They sometimes painted unflattering pictures of the uncouth and grasping princes of France and England, whom they encountered on the Crusades.

In mathematics and geometry the Byzantines discovered nothing new. Yet they were exceptionally important as catalysts, for they passed

Woman Carrying Pitcher This detail from a floor mosaic in the Great Palace at Constantinople shows a buxom peasant woman balancing a huge water ewer on her shoulder. Notice the large earrings. *(Source: Scala/Art Resource)*

Greco-Roman learning on to the Arabs, who assimilated it and made remarkable advances with it. The Byzantines were equally uncreative in astronomy and natural science, but at least they faithfully learned what the ancients had to teach.

Only when science could be put to military use did the Byzantines make advances. The best-known Byzantine scientific discovery was chemical—"Greek fire," a combustible liquid that was the medieval equivalent of the flame thrower. In mechanics the Byzantines continued the work of Hellenistic and Roman inventors of artillery and siege machinery. Just as Archimedes had devised machines to stop the Romans (see page 163), so did Byzantine scientists improve and modify devices for defending their empire.

The Byzantines devoted a great deal of attention to medicine, and the general level of medical competence was far higher in the Byzantine Empire than it was in the medieval West. The Byzantines assimilated the discoveries of Hellenic and Hellenistic medicine but added very few of their own. The basis of their medical theory was Hippocrates' concept of the four humors (see page 140). Byzantine physicians emphasized the importance of diet and rest and relied heavily on herbal drugs. Perhaps their chief weakness was excessive use of bleeding and burning, which often succeeded only in further weakening an already feeble patient. Hospitals were a prominent feature of Byzantine life, and the army, too, had a medical corps.

Private Life

In the tenth century Constantinople was the greatest city in the Christian world. The seat of the imperial court and administration, a large population center, and the pivot of an extensive volume of international trade, Constantinople held Christian supremacy. As a natural geographical entrepôt between East and West, the city's markets offered goods from many parts of the world. About 1060 the Spanish Jew, Benjamin of Tudela, reported that Constantinople had merchant communities from Babylon, Canaan, Egypt, Hungary, Persia, Russia, Sennar (in the Sudan), and Spain, plus two thousand Jews.

Not that Constantinople enjoyed constant political stability. Between the accession of Heraclius in 610 and the fall of the city to Western Crusaders in 1204 (see page 365), four separate dynasties ruled at Constantinople. Imperial government involved such intricate court intrigue, assassinations, and military revolts that the word *byzantine* is sometimes used in English to mean extremely entangled and complicated politics. For example, in 963 the emperor Nicephorus I Phocas married Theophano, the widow of the emperor Romanus II. In 969 Nicephorus was murdered and replaced by his nephew John I Tzimisces, Theophano's lover and an exceptionally able general.

In commerce, Jewish, Muslim (see pages 286–288), and Italian merchants controlled most foreign trade. Beginning in the eleventh century, the Venetians acquired important commercial concessions in Byzantium, thereby laying the foundations for future Venetian prosperity (see pages 508, 510). Among the Greeks, commerce faced ancient prejudices, and aristocrats and monasteries usually invested their wealth in real estate, which involved little risk but brought little gain. As in the medieval West and early modern China, rural ideals permeated Byzantine society. The landed aristocracy always held the dominant social position in the empire. Greek merchants and craftsmen, even when they acquired considerable wealth, never won social prominence.

The monasteries represented one of the most important elements in the social structure of the Byzantine Empire. Deriving from the ascetic ideals of the ancient hermits (see page 242), monasticism spread rapidly in the Byzantine world during the third and fourth centuries and again in the eighth and ninth centuries. Many of the bishops in the Greek church and most of the patriarchs of Constantinople came from the monasteries. The people respected the monks, and the emperors consulted them and sought their blessings before important undertakings. Everyone believed that the monks' prayers constituted a spiritual force on which the security of the state depended. The monasteries, consequently, possessed great influence and acquired considerable wealth.

Behind the public life of the imperial court with its assassinations and proverbially complicated politics, beyond the noise and bustle of the marketplaces thronged with Venetian and Eastern merchants, and behind the monastery walls enclosing the sophisticated theological debates of the monks, what do we know of the private life of the Constantinopolitan Greeks? Recent research has revealed a fair amount about the Byzantine *oikos,* or household. The Greek household included family members and servants, some of whom were slaves. Artisans lived and worked in their shops. Clerks, civil servants, minor officials, business people—those who today would be called "middle class"—commonly dwelled in multistory buildings perhaps comparable to the apartment complexes of modern American cities. Wealthy aristocrats resided in freestanding mansions that frequently included interior courts, galleries, large reception halls, small sleeping rooms, reading and writing rooms, baths, and *oratories,* chapels where all members of the household met for religious services. A complicated system of locks protected most houses from intrusion.

In the homes of the upper classes, the segregation of women seems to have been the first principle of interior design. Private houses contained a *gynaikonitis,* or women's apartment, where women were kept strictly separated from the outside world. (The Muslim harem, discussed on page 284, probably derives from this Greek institution.) The fundamental reason for this segregation was the family's honor: "An unchaste daughter is guilty of harming not only herself but also her parents and relatives. That is why you should keep your daughters under lock and key, as if proven guilty or imprudent, in order to avoid venomous bites," as an eleventh-century Byzantine writer put it.[19] Women did not receive outside guests, at least in theory. Although they were allowed at family banquets, they could not attend if wine was served or questionable entertainment was given. To do so gave a husband grounds for divorce.

Marriage served as part of a family's strategy for social advancement. The family and the entire kinship group participated in the selection of brides and grooms. Wealth and social connections were the chief qualities sought in potential candidates. Weddings could take place at home, in the oratory of the bride's house, or in the local church.

Scholars know a great deal about the sleeping arrangements of the imperial couples. The emperor Romanus III (r. 1028–1034), for example, shared the bed of his wife, the empress Zoe; she shared the bed of her lover, later the emperor Michael IV (r. 1034–1041). The domestic arrangements of Byzantine rulers, however, were hardly typical, and little is known about the sleeping and sexual practices of lesser mortals. The church prescribed periods of abstinence, especially during Lent (the forty days before Easter) and on Saturday and Sunday. How closely practice conformed to precept is not known. The availability of relatively good medical attention suggests that those who could afford a physician secured his services. Women delivered children seated or standing up.

SUMMARY

Saint Augustine died in 430 as the Vandals approached the coastal city of Hippo. Scholars have sometimes described Augustine as standing with one foot in the ancient world and one in the Middle Ages. Indeed, Augustine represents the end of ancient culture and the birth of what has been called the Middle Ages. A new and different kind of society was gestating in the mid-fifth century.

The world of the Middle Ages combined Germanic practices and institutions, classical ideas and patterns of thought, Christianity, and a significant dash of Islam (see Chapter 10). Christianity, because it creatively and energetically fashioned the Germanic and classical legacies, was the most powerful agent in the making of Europe. Saint Augustine of Hippo, dogmatic thinker and Christian bishop, embodied the coming world view. In the Byzantine Empire a vigorous intellectual life, which preserved Greek scientific and medical knowledge and Roman law, flourished.

NOTES

1. Matthew 16:18–19 *(Jerusalem Bible)*.
2. Quoted in R. C. Petry, ed., *A History of Christianity: Readings in the History of Early and Medieval Christianity* (Englewood Cliffs, N.J.: Prentice-Hall, 1962), p. 70.
3. Quoted in H. Bettenson, ed., *Documents of the Christian Church* (Oxford: Oxford University Press, 1947), p. 113.
4. Colossians 3:9–11 *(Jerusalem Bible)*.
5. Luke 6:20–32 *(Jerusalem Bible)*.
6. Quoted in L. Sherley-Price, trans., *Bede: A History of the English Church and People* (Baltimore: Penguin Books, 1962), pp. 86–87.
7. J. T. McNeill and H. Gamer, trans., *Medieval Handbooks of Penance* (New York: Octagon Books, 1965), pp. 184–197.
8. L. White, "The Life of the Silent Majority," in *Life and Thought in the Early Middle Ages*, ed. R. S. Hoyt (Minneapolis: University of Minnesota Press, 1967), p. 100.
9. I Peter 2:11–20 *(Jerusalem Bible)*.
10. See J. Boswell, *Christianity, Social Tolerance, and Homosexuality: Gay People in Western Europe from the Beginning of the Christian Era to the Fourteenth Century* (Chicago: University of Chicago Press, 1980), chaps. 3 and 5, esp. pp. 87, 127–131.
11. F. J. Sheed, trans., *The Confessions of St. Augustine* (New York: Sheed & Ward, 1953), 1, 3.
12. T. Burns, *A History of the Ostrogoths* (Bloomington, Ind.: Indiana University Press, 1984), pp. 18, 21.
13. Ibid., pp. 108–112.
14. Quoted in E. F. Henderson, ed., *Select Historical Documents of the Middle Ages* (London: G. Bell & Sons, 1912), pp. 176–189.
15. Burns, pp. 113–119.
16. P. Brown, *Society and the Holy in Late Antiquity* (Berkeley: University of California Press, 1982), pp. 166–195.
17. Quoted in J. B. Bury, *History of the Later Roman Empire,* vol. 1 (New York: Dover, 1958), pp. 233–234.
18. R. Atwater, trans., *Procopius: The Secret History* (Ann Arbor: University of Michigan Press, 1963), 8.
19. Quoted in E. Patlagean, "Byzantium in the Tenth and Eleventh Centuries," in *A History of Private Life,* ed. P. Aries and G. Duby, vol. 1, *From Pagan Rome to Byzantium,* ed. P. Veyne (Cambridge, Mass.: Harvard University Press, 1987), p. 573. This section leans on Patlagean's article.

SUGGESTED READING

In addition to the studies listed in the Notes, students may consult the following works for a more detailed treatment of the early Middle Ages. Both M. Grant, *The Dawn of the Middle Ages* (1981), which emphasizes innovation and development, and P. Brown, *The World of Late Antiquity, A.D. 150–750* (1971), which stresses social and cultural change, are lavishly illustrated and lucidly written introductions to the entire period. Grant has especially valuable material on the Germanic kingdoms, Byzantium, and eastern Europe. B. Lyon, *The Origins of the Middle Ages: Pirenne's Challenge to Gibbon* (1972), is an excellent bibliographical essay with extensive references.

There is a rich literature on the Christian church and its role in the transition from ancient to medieval civilization. F. Oakley, *The Medieval Experience: Foundations of Western Cultural Singularity* (1974), emphasizes the Christian roots of Western cultural uniqueness. W. Meeks, *The First Urban Christians: The Social World of the Apostle Paul* (1983), provides fascinating material on the early Christians and shows that they came from all social classes. J. Richards, *Consul of God: The Life and Times of Gregory the Great* (1980), is the first major study in seventy years of this watershed pontificate. History, archeology, and language are critically examined in C. Thomas, *Christianity in Roman Britain to A.D. 500* (1981), a very learned study emphasizing the continuity in Britain's Christian history. P. Brown, *The Cult of the Saints: Its Rise and Function in Latin Christianity* (1982), describes the significance of the saints in popular religion. Students seeking a thorough treatment of Christianity through the sixth century should consult W. H. C. Frend, *The Rise of Christianity* (1984), an almost exhaustive treatment by a leading scholar-theologian.

For the synthesis of classical and Christian cultures, see C. N. Cochrane, *Christianity and Classical Culture* (1957), a deeply learned monograph. T. E. Mommsen, "Saint Augustine and the Christian Idea of Progress," *Journal of the History of Ideas* 12 (1951): 346–374, and G. B. Ladner, *The Idea of Reform* (1959), examine ideas of history and progress among the early church fathers. The best biography of Saint Augustine is P. Brown, *Augustine of Hippo* (1967), which treats him as a symbol of change.

The phenomenon of monasticism has attracted interest throughout the centuries. L. Doyle, trans., *St. Benedict's Rule for Monasteries* (1957), presents the monastic guide in an accessible, pocket-size form; a more learned edition is J. McCann, ed. and trans., *The Rule of Saint Benedict* (1952). The best modern edition of the document is T. Fry et al., eds., *RB 1980: The Rule of St. Benedict in Latin and English with Notes* (1981), which contains a history of Western monasticism and a scholarly commentary on the *Rule*. L. Eberle, trans., *The Rule of the Master* (1977), offers the text of and a commentary on Benedict's major source. Especially useful for students is O. Chadwick, *The Making of the Benedictine Ideal* (1981), a short but profound essay that emphasizes the personality of Saint Benedict in the development of the Benedictine ideal. G. Constable, *Medieval Monasticism: A Select Bibliography* (1976), is a useful research tool. Two beautifully illustrated syntheses by leading authorities are D. Knowles, *Christian Monasticism* (1969), which sketches monastic history through the middle of the twentieth century, and G. Zarnecki, *The Monastic Achievement* (1972), which focuses on the medieval centuries. L. J. Daly, *Benedictine Monasticism* (1965), stresses day-to-day living, and H. W. Workman, *The Evolution of the Monastic Ideal* (1962), shows the impact of the monastic ideal on later religious orders. For women in monastic life, see S. F. Wemple, *Women in Frankish Society: Marriage and the Cloister, 500–900* (1981), an important book with a good bibliography.

For the Germans, see, in addition to Burns's work cited in the Notes, J. M. Wallace-Hadrill, *The Barbarian West: The Early Middle Ages* A.D. *400–1000* (1962), and A. Lewis, *Emerging Europe,* A.D. *400–1000* (1967), both of which describe German customs and society and the Germanic impact on the Roman Empire. F. Lot, *The End of the Ancient World* (1965), emphasizes the economic and social causes of Rome's decline. On Rome itself and the Germans' impact on it, C. Hibbert, *Rome: The Biography of a City* (1985), contains instructive and entertaining material. G. Le Bras, "The Sociology of the Church in the Early Middle Ages," in S. L. Thrupp, ed., *Early Medieval Society* (1967), discusses the Christianization of the barbarians.

For Byzantium, the best starting point is probably the articles by Peter Charanis, "Byzantine Economy and Society," and T. E. Gregory, "Byzantine History (330–1025)," in J. R. Strayer, ed., *Dictionary of the Middle Ages,* vol. 2 (1983), pp. 475–491. G. Ostrogorsky, *History of the Byzantine State,* rev. ed. (1969), is probably the most useful one-volume introduction, but see also A. A. Vasiliev, *History of the Byzantine Empire* (1968); J. Hussey, *The Byzantine World* (1961); and S. Runciman, *Byzantine Civilization* (1956). For the reign of Justinian, see R. Browning, *Justinian and Theodora* (1971), and A. Bridge, *Theodora: Portrait in a Byzantine Landscape* (1984), a romantic and amusing biography of the courtesan who became empress. The best studies of the difficulties of the eighth and ninth centuries are probably A. Bryer and J. Herrin, eds., *Iconoclasm* (1977), and S. Gero, *Byzantine Iconoclasm During the Reign of Leo III* (1973). For the conversion of the Slavs, see F. Dvornik, *Byzantine Missions Among the Slavs* (1970).

10

The Islamic World,
ca 600–1400

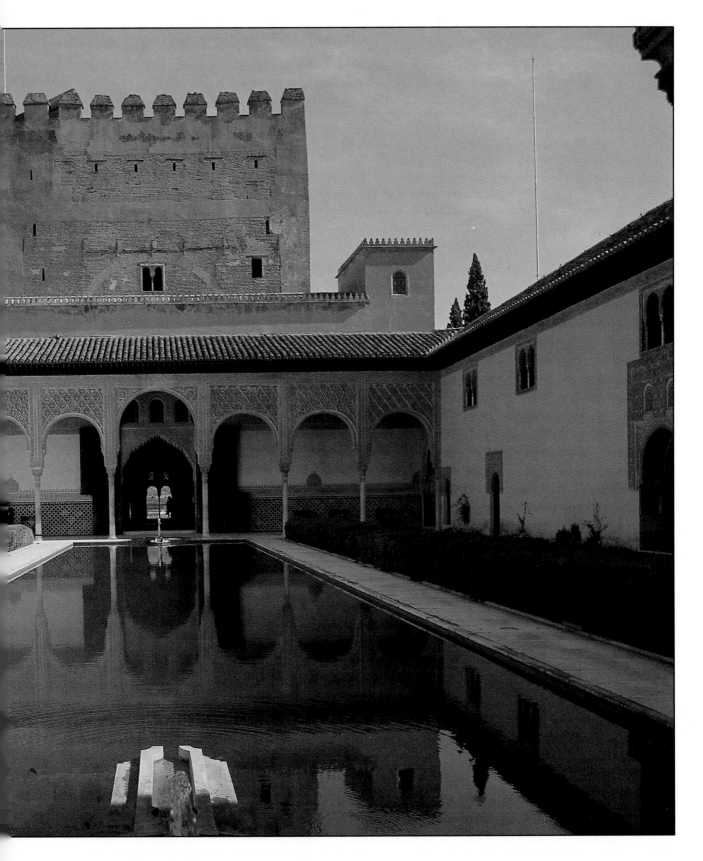

Alhambra Palace, Granada

Around 610, in the important commercial city of Mecca in what is now Saudi Arabia, a merchant called Muhammad began to have religious visions. By the time he died in 632, most of Arabia had accepted his creed. A century later, his followers controlled Syria, Palestine, Egypt, Iraq, Persia (present-day Iran), northern India, North Africa, Spain, and part of France. Within another century Muhammad's beliefs had been carried across central Asia to the borders of China. In the ninth, tenth, and eleventh centuries the Muslims created a brilliant civilization centered at Baghdad in Iraq, a culture that profoundly influenced the development of both Eastern and Western civilizations.

- Who were the Arabs?
- What are the main tenets of the Muslim faith?
- What factors account for the remarkable spread of Islam?
- How did the Muslims govern the vast territories they conquered?
- Why did the Shi'ite Muslim tradition arise, and how did the Shi'ite/Sunni split affect the course of Islam?
- What position did women hold in Muslim society?
- What features characterized the societies of the great Muslim cities of Baghdad and Cordoba?
- How did the Muslims view Western society and culture?

This chapter explores those questions.

THE ARABS BEFORE ISLAM

The Arabian peninsula, perhaps a third of the size of Europe or the United States, covers about a million square miles. Ancient Greek geographers named the peninsula *Arabian* after the Bedouin Arabs, nomads who grazed their animals in the sparse patches of grass that dotted the vast, semi-arid land. Thus *Arab* originally meant a native of Arabia. After Islam spread and peoples of various ethnic backgrounds attached themselves to or intermarried with the Arabs, they assumed an Arab identity. Today, the term *Arab* refers to an ethnic identity; *Arabic* means a linguistic and cultural heritage.

In the sixth century A.D. most Arabs were not nomads; most led a settled existence. In the southwestern mountain valleys of the Arabian peninsula, plentiful rainfall and sophisticated irrigation techniques resulted in highly productive agriculture that supported fairly dense population settlements. In other areas scattered throughout the peninsula, the presence of underground water prompted the digging of wells. Oasis towns based on the cultivation of date palms grew up around the wells. Some oasis towns sustained sizable populations including artisans, merchants, and religious leaders. Some, such as Mecca, served as important trading outposts. The presence of the Ka'ba, a temple containing a black stone thought to be a god's dwelling place, attracted pilgrims and enabled Mecca to become the metropolis of western Arabia. Mecca combined economic and religious/cultic functions.

Thinly spread over the entire peninsula, the nomadic Bedouins migrated from place to place, grazing their sheep, goats and camels. Although Bedouins were always small in number, they were the most important political and military force in the region because of their toughness, solidarity, fighting traditions, and ability to control trade and lines of communication. Between the peoples settled in oasis towns and the Bedouin nomads were semi-nomads who, as the agricultural conditions around them fluctuated, practiced either settled agriculture or nomadic pastoralism.

For all Arabs the basic social unit was the tribe—a group of blood relations that descended in the male line. The tribe provided protection and support and in turn received members' total loyalty. Like the Germanic peoples in the age of their migrations (see pages 244–247), Arab tribes were not static entities but continually evolving groups. A particular tribe might include both nomadic and sedentary members.

Strong economic links joined all Arab peoples. Nomads, seminomads, and settled peoples were economically interdependent. Nomads and seminomads depended on the agriculturally productive communities for food they could not produce, cloth, metal products, and weapons. Nomads paid for these goods with the livestock, milk and milk products, hides, and hair wanted by oasis towns. Nomads acquired income by serving as desert guides and as guards for caravans. Plundering caravans or extorting "protection money" also yielded funds.

In northern and central Arabia, tribal confederations dominated by a warrior aristocracy characterized Arab political organization. The warrior aristocrats possessed several assets that help to explain their power. They had tremendous physical toughness. They possessed a few horses, which though difficult to maintain in desert conditions gave them great speed and mobility. Warriors paid tribute to no one and claimed blood descent from some great chief. Within a confederation, tribes competed for pre-eminence.

In the southern parts of the peninsula in the early seventh century, religious aristocracies tended to hold political power. Many oasis or market towns contained *harams,* sacred enclaves controlled or dominated by one holy family. Members of the holy family claimed to be servants or priests of the deity who resided in the town, and they served as guardians of the deity's shrine. The family imposed rules for behavior at the shrine. Murder was forbidden at the shrine, and a tribesman knew that even his bitterest enemy would not attack him there. At the haram, a *mansib,* or cultic leader, adjudicated disputes and tried to get agreements among warrior tribes. All Arabs respected the harams because they feared retribution if the gods' shrines were desecrated and because the harams served as neutral places for arbitration among warring tribes.

The power of the northern warrior aristocracy rested on its fighting skills. The southern religious aristocracy, by contrast, depended on its cultic and economic power. Located in agricultural areas that were also commercial centers, the religious aristocracy had a stronger economic base than the warrior aristocrats. Moreover, recent scholarship has shown that the arbitrator role of the mansib marks a step toward a society governed by law.[1] The political genius of Muhammad was to bind together these different tribal groups into a strong unified state.

MUHAMMAD AND THE FAITH OF ISLAM

A fair amount is known about Jesus after he began his public ministry at about age thirty, but little is known about his early life. Similarly, a good deal is known about Muhammad after his "call" as God's

messenger at age forty, but little is known about him before then. Except for a few vague remarks in the Qur'an, the sacred book of Islam, no contemporary account of Muhammad's life (ca 570–632) survives. Arabic tradition accepts as historically true some of the sacred legends that developed about him, but those legends were not written down until about a century after his death. (Similarly, the earliest accounts of the life of Jesus, the Christian Gospels, were not written down until forty or fifty years after his death.)

Orphaned at the age of six, Muhammad was brought up by his paternal uncle. As a young man he became a merchant in the caravan trade. Later he entered the service of a wealthy widow, Khadija, and their subsequent marriage brought him financial security while she lived. Muhammad apparently was an extremely pious man, self-disciplined, and devoted to contemplation. At about forty, in a cave in the hills near Mecca where he was accustomed to pray, Muhammad had a profound religious experience. In a vision an angelic being (whom Muhammad later interpreted to be Gabriel, God's messenger) commanded him to preach the revelations that God would be sending him. Muhammad began to preach to the people of Mecca, urging them to give up their idols and submit to the one indivisible God. During his lifetime Muhammad's followers jotted down his revelations haphazardly. After his death scribes organized the revelations into chapters. In 651 they published the version of them that Muslims consider authoritative, the *Qur'an* (from an Arabic word meaning "reading" or "recitation"). Muslims revere the Qur'an for its sacred message and for the beauty of its Arabic language.

Islam, the strict monotheistic faith that is based on the teachings of Muhammad, rests on the principle of the absolute unity and omnipotence of Allah, God. The word *Islam* means "submission to God," and *Muslim* means "a person who submits." Thus the community of Muslims consists of people who have submitted to God by accepting his teachings as revealed by Muhammad. Muhammad, the Prophet, preached God's word and carried his message. Muslims believe that Muhammad was the last of the prophets, completing the work begun by Abraham, Moses, and Jesus. Muslims believe that they worship the same God as Jews and Christians. Islam's uncompromising monotheism—the oneness of God—spelled the end of paganism everywhere that Islam was accepted.

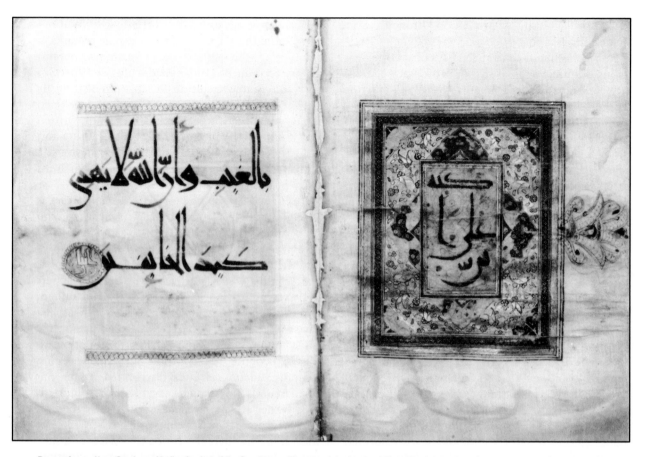

Page from the Qur'an. Kufic Script, 9th Century   The Arabic text of the Qur'an was always written with a slant-cut reed pen in a calligraphy intended not only to convey the message of Allah but also, through its beauty, to reflect the glory of God. The Kufic script, developed in the seventh century, stressed horizontal and vertical strokes and used loops sparingly. *(Source: Courtesy of the Freer Gallery of Art, Smithsonian Institution)*

Western writers have tended to place the origins of Islam in seventh-century Arabia. Recent research stresses that this view is historically inaccurate and from a Muslim perspective theologically wrong. Monotheism flourished in Middle Eastern Semitic and Persian cultures for centuries before Muhammad. "Muhammad was not the founder of Islam; he did not start a new religion." Like the Old Testament prophets, Muhammad came as a reformer. In Jewish, Christian, and Muslim theology, a prophet is not someone who predicts the future; a prophet speaks the word of God. Muhammad insisted that he was not preaching a new message; rather, he was calling people back to the one, true God, urging his contemporaries to reform their lives, to return to the faith of Abraham, the first monotheist.[2]

Likewise, Western secular scholars have distinguished between Muhammad's religious and his sociopolitical ideas. For a Muslim, this distinction is nonsensical because Muhammad's social and political views are inseparable from his religious ideas. Muhammad displayed genius as both political strategist and religious teacher. He gave Arabs the idea of a unique and unified *umma,* or community, which consisted of all those whose primary identity and bond was a common religious faith and commitment, not a tribal tie. The *umma* was to be religious and political community led by Muhammad for the achievement of God's will on earth.

In the early seventh century southern Arab society was characterized by tribal confederations centered around sacred enclaves. These confederations lacked cohesiveness and unity and were constantly warring; they recognized no single higher authority. Muhammad's goal was a Muslim community that rejected all paganism, a universal community of Muslim believers. The Islamic notion of an absolute higher authority fostered the political consolidation of the tribal confederations. Islam teaches that God is not only all-powerful and all-knowing but has set forth a law against which *all* human actions are measured. The *umma* regulated the behavior of community members by means of rules that transcended the boundaries of individual tribal units. Within the *umma*, authority was centralized in Muhammad. The fundamental tenet of Islam, to which any believer must subscribe, is "There is no God but God and Muhammad is his Prophet." If one accepts the idea of God's oneness and Muhammad's claim to be his Prophet, then it follows that all authority comes from God *through Muhammad*. Within the *umma*, the law of God was discerned and applied through Muhammad. Thus, in the seventh century, Islam centralized authority, both political and religious, in Muhammad's hands.[3]

The Qur'an is much holier to Muslims than the Torah and the Gospels are to Jews and Christians. The Qur'an prescribes a strict code of moral behavior. A Muslim must recite a profession of faith in God and in Muhammad as his prophet: "There is no God but God and Muhammad is his Prophet." A believer must also pray five times a day, fast and pray during the sacred month of Ramadan, make a pilgrimage to the holy city of Mecca once during his or her lifetime, and give alms to the Muslim poor. The Qur'an forbids alcoholic beverages and gambling. It condemns *usury* in business—that is, lending money at interest rates—and taking advantage of market demand for products by charging high prices. Some foods, such as pork, are forbidden, a dietary regulation perhaps adopted from the Mosaic law of the Hebrews.

By earlier Arab standards, the Qur'an sets forth an austere sexual code. Muslim jurisprudence condemned licentious behavior by both men and women, and the status of women improved. About marriage, illicit intercourse, and inheritance, the Qur'an states:

Of . . . women who seem good in your eyes, marry but two, three, or four; and if ye still fear that ye shall not act equitably, then only one. . . .

The whore and the fornicator: whip each of them a hundred times. . . .

The fornicator shall not marry other than a whore; and the whore shall not marry other than a fornicator. . . .

They who defame virtuous women, and fail to bring four witnesses to swear that they did not, are to be whipped eighty times. . . .

Men who die and leave wives behind shall bequeath to them a year's maintenance. . . . And your wives shall have a fourth part of what you leave, if you have no issue; but if you have issue, then they shall have an eighth part.

With regard to your children, God commands you to give the male the portion of two females; and if there be more than two females, then they shall have two-thirds of what their father leaves; but if there be one daughter only, she shall have the half.[4]

By contrast, Western law has tended to punish prostitutes, not their clients.

With respect to matters of property in the seventh and eighth centuries, Muslim women were more emancipated than Western women. Islamic law gave a woman control of all the property she brought to her marriage, except for the dowry. Half of the dowry went to the husband; the other half remained hers in case the marriage failed. A Muslim woman could dispose of her property in any way she wished. A Western woman had no such power.

Islam warns about the Last Judgment and the importance of the life to come. The Islamic Last Judgment bears striking resemblance to the Christian one: on that day God will separate the saved and the damned. The Qur'an describes in detail the frightful tortures with which God will punish the damned: scourgings, beatings with iron clubs, burnings, and forced drinking of boiling water. Muhammad's account of the heavenly rewards of the saved and the blessed are equally graphic but are different in kind from those of Christian theology. The Muslim vision of heaven features lush green gardens surrounded by refreshing streams. There, the saved, clothed in rich silks, lounge on brocaded couches, nibbling ripe fruits, sipping delicious beverages, and enjoying the companionship of physically attractive people.

How did the Muslim faithful merit the rewards of heaven? Salvation is by God's grace and choice alone. Because God is all-powerful, he knows from the moment of conception whether a person will be saved. Nevertheless, predestination should not take from the believer the will and courage to try to achieve heaven. Muslims who suffered and died for the faith in battle were ensured the rewards of heaven. For others, the Qur'anic precepts were the path to salvation.

THE EXPANSION OF ISLAM

Muhammad's preaching at first did not appeal to many people. Legend has it that for the first three years he attracted only fourteen believers. Because he preached a revelation that attacked the undue accumulation of wealth and social stratification, a revelation that held all men as brothers within a social order ordained by God, Muhammad's teaching constituted social revolution. The bankers and merchants of Mecca fought him. Moreover, he urged the destruction of the idols in the Ka'ba at Mecca, a site that drew thousands of devout Arabs annually and thus brought important revenue to the city. The townspeople turned against him, and he and his followers were forced to flee to Medina. This *hijra,* or emigration, occurred in 622, and Muslims later dated the beginning of their era from that event. At Medina, Muhammad attracted increasing numbers of believers, and his teachings began to have an impact.

Expansion to the West

By the time Muhammad died in 632, he had welded together all the Bedouin tribes. The crescent of Islam, the Muslim symbol, controlled most of the Arabian peninsula. In the next hundred

Jonah and the Whale The story of Jonah in the Old Testament describes a prophet who tried to avoid his responsibilities and is swallowed up by a whale; it is a parable of divine mercy, urging people to repent and seek forgiveness. The Chinese artist who executed this superb painting had never seen a whale but he possessed imagination, delicacy, and mastery of movement. *(Source: Edinburgh University Library)*

years, one rich province of the old Roman Empire after another came under Muslim domination—first Syria, then Egypt, then all of North Africa (Map 10.1).

In 711 a Muslim force crossed the Strait of Gibraltar and at the Guadalete River easily defeated the weak Visigothic kingdom in Spain. A few Christian princes supported by the Frankish rulers held out in the Pyrenees Mountains, but the Muslims controlled most of Spain until the twelfth century. The political history of Christian Spain in the Middle Ages is the history of the *reconquista,* the Christian reconquest of that country.

In 719 the Muslims pushed beyond the Pyrenees into the kingdom of the Franks. At the Battle of Tours in 733, the Frankish chieftain Charles Martel defeated the Arabs and halted their northern expansion. The Muslims had greatly overextended their forces. Ultimately, Charlemagne expelled them from France.

Expansion to the East

Between 632 and 640, the Arabs surged to the east into the Sassanid kingdom of Persia (see page 254). Between 635 and 651, one city after another fell to them. When they defeated the Persians at Nihawand in 651, Muslim control of the Persian Empire was completed. The wealth seized at the Persian capital, Ctesiphon, astounded the victorious, uneducated Bedouin tribesmen, who according to one modern scholar did not understand what they had won:

Some of the warriors, unfamiliar with gold pieces, were willing to exchange them for silver ones. Others, who had never seen camphor before, took it for salt and used it in cooking. When blamed at Hira for selling an aristocratic woman who had fallen as his share of booty for only a thousand silver pieces, an Arabian replied that he never thought there was a number higher than ten hundred.[5]

The government headquarters of the vast new empire was transferred from Medina to Damascus in Syria. A contemporary proverb speaks of the Mediterranean as a Muslim lake.

The Muslims continued their drive eastward. In the mid-seventh century, they occupied the province of Khorasan, where the city of Merv became

The Hijra from Mecca to Medina   Muhammad's career gave rise to a rich body of legends that became a permanent part of Islamic lore and culture. This Turkish illustration of the hijra shows the Prophet and his friend Abu Bakr having been pursued and found by a man from Mecca. When the Meccan tried to approach, he was thrown from his horse (at right). Muhammad has granted the repentant Meccan a written pardon, which he receives from Abu Bakr (foreground). (*Source: The New York Public Library, The Spenser Collection*)

the center of Muslim control over eastern Persia (Map 10.2) and the base for campaigns farther east. By 700 the Muslims had crossed the Oxus River and swept toward Kabul, today the capital of Afghanistan. From the city of Balkh, they launched raids into Transoxiana as far as the Jaxartes River. Crossing that river, they penetrated Kazakhstan and then seized Tashkent, one of the oldest cities in central Asia. The clash of Muslim horsemen with a Chinese army at the Talas River in 751 seems to mark the farthest Islamic penetration into central Asia.

From Makran in southern Persia a Muslim force marched into the Indus Valley in northern India and in 713 founded an Islamic community at Multan. This settlement became isolated from the rest of the Islamic world and did not expand. Beginning in the eleventh century, however, Muslim dynasties from Ghazni in Afghanistan carried Islam

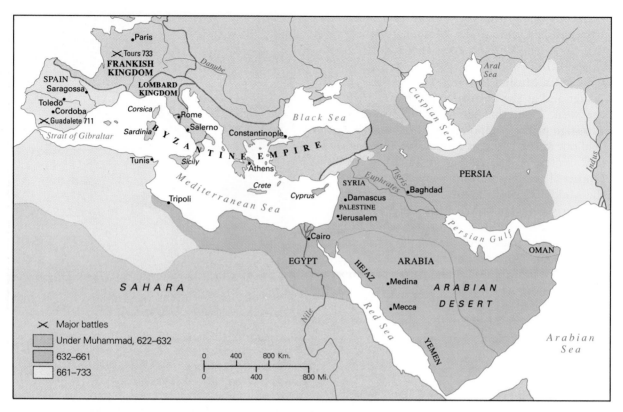

MAP 10.1 The Expansion of Islam to 733   Political weaknesses in the territories they conquered, as well as superior fighting skills, help explain the speed with which the Muslims expanded.

deeper into the Indian subcontinent (see pages 307–309).

Reasons for the Spread of Islam

By the beginning of the eleventh century the crescent of Islam flew from the Iberian heartlands to northern India. How can this rapid and remarkable expansion be explained? Muslim historians attribute Islamic victories to God's support for the Muslim faith. True, the Arabs won their military successes because they possessed a religious fervor and loyalty that their enemies could not equal. They were convinced of the necessity of the *jihad,* or holy war. The Qur'an does not explicitly mention this subject, but because the Qur'an does suggest that God sent the Prophet to establish justice on earth, it follows that justice will take effect only where Islam triumphs. Just as Christians have the missionary obligation of spreading their faith, so Muslims have the obligation, as individuals and as a community, to strive to lead a virtuous life and to

extend the Islamic community. *Jihad* also came to mean the struggle for the defense of Islam. Those who waged it were assured happiness in the world to come.

The Muslim outburst from Arabia and subsequent successes had strong economic, political, and military, as well as religious, causes. The Arab surge reflects the economic needs of a tough people squeezed into a semibarren, overpopulated area and the desire to share in the rich life of the Fertile Crescent. Arab expansion in the seventh and eighth centuries was another phase of the infiltration that had taken the ancient Hebrews to the other end of the Fertile Crescent (see Map 1.1). Also, recent conflicts between the Byzantine and Sassanid empires had left both weak and divided. Byzantine and Sassanid armies, composed of many diverse peoples scattered over vast territories, could not be easily assembled at a threatened place.

In the Byzantine provinces of Egypt and Syria, moreover, theological squabbles and factional divisions helped the Muslim advance. Groups alien-

MAP 10.2 Islamic Expansion to 1500 Islam spread along the commercial arteries that extended from the eastern Mediterranean all the way to China, Southeast Asia, and Malaysia.

ated from Byzantine rule expressed their dissatisfaction by quickly capitulating to the Arabs in return for promises of religious freedom and the protection of their property. In the period between 642 and 643, an Arab army officer recorded his pledges to the people of Qum, in Persia:

In the name of God, the Merciful and the Compassionate. This is what Suwayd ibn Muqarrin gave to the inhabitants of Qumis and those who are dependent on them, concerning safe-conduct for themselves, their religions and their property, on condition that they pay the jizya *[a poll tax] from the hand of every adult male, according to his capacity, that they show goodwill and do not deceive, that they guide the Muslim traveler, and that they accommodate Muslims who make a halt with them for a day and a night with their average food. If they change this or make light of their obligations, the pact* [dhimma] *with them is void.*[6]

The Muslim conquest of Syria provides an example of the combination of motives—economic, religious, and political—that propelled early Muslim expansion. Situated to the north of the Arabian peninsula, Syria had been under Byzantine-Christian (or Roman) rule for centuries. Arab caravans knew the market towns of southern Syria and the rich commercial centers of the north, such as Edessa, Aleppo, and Damascus. Syria's economic prosperity attracted the Muslims, and perhaps Muhammad saw the lands as a potential means of support for the poor who flooded Medina. Syria also contained sites important to the Muslim faith: Jerusalem, where Jesus and other prophets mentioned in the Qur'an had lived and preached; and Hebron, the traditional burial place of Abraham, the father of monotheism. Finally, a practical political reason encouraged expansion. Muhammad and the ruling elite insisted that all Arab tribes accept Muslim leadership. The centralization of the Islamic state depended on the control of the nomadic tribes of the Arabian and Syrian deserts. In the 630s the Byzantine state, barely recovering from a long war with the Sassanid empire of Persia over Syria, was trying

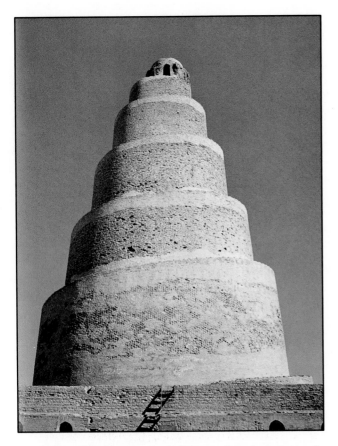

Muezzin Calling People to Prayer A mosque is usually surrounded by an open courtyard containing a fountain for ritual ablutions and a *minaret,* or lofty tower surrounded by projecting balconies from which an official, the muezzin, summons the faithful to prayer. *(Source: Ian Graham)*

to forge alliances with the nomadic tribes. From the Muslim perspective, the Islamic state had to win over these peoples before the Byzantines did so. Expansion in Syria, therefore, was absolutely essential.[7]

Military organization also helps account for the Muslims' rapid success. The leadership maintained a cohesive hold on the troops, and internal conflicts did not arise initially to slow their advances. The military elite solved the problem of recruitment for the army. Fixed salaries, regular pay, and the lure of battlefield booty attracted the rugged tribesmen. In the later campaigns to the east, many recruits were recent converts to Islam from Christian, Persian, and Berber backgrounds. The assurance of army wages secured the loyalty of

these very diverse men. Here is an eleventh-century description of the Egyptian army (remember that medieval numbers were always greatly exaggerated):

Each corps has its own name and designation. One group are called Kitamis [a Berber tribe]. These came from Qayrawan in the service of al-Mu'izz li-Din Allah. They are said to number 20,000 horsemen. . . . Another group is called Masmudis. They are blacks from the land of the Masmudis and said to number 20,000 men. Another group are called the Easterners, consisting of Turks and Persians. They are so-called because they are not of Arab origin. Though most of them were born in Egypt, their name derives from their origin. They are said to number 10,000 powerfully built men. Another group are called the slaves by purchase. . . . They are slaves bought for money and are said to number 30,000 men. Another group are called Bedouin. They are from the Hijaz [Hejaz] and are all armed with spears. They are said to number 50,000 horsemen. Another group are called Ustads. These are servants [?eunuchs], black and white, bought for service. They number 30,000 horsemen.[8]

In classical Islam, concepts of nation, country, and political sovereignty played a very small role. Before the nineteenth century, Islamic peoples rarely defined political power and authority in territorial or ethnic terms. For Muslims, religion was the core of identity. They divided the world into two fundamental sections: the House of Islam, which consisted of all those regions where the law of Islam prevailed, and the House of War, which was the rest of the world. "As there is one God in heaven, so there can be only one ruler on earth." By the logic of Islamic law, no political entity outside of Islam can exist permanently. Every Muslim, accordingly, has the religious duty of the *jihad*—carrying out the war of conversion. Consequently, a state of war exists permanently between the House of Islam and the House of War. With the conversion or conquest of all humankind, the war will end.

In practice, of course, Muslims did recognize divisions among unbelievers. The most basic distinction was between those who possessed revealed religions—Jews and Christians, whose faiths are based on the revelations in the Scriptures—and those who did not. Jews and Christians who submitted to Islam enjoyed the protection of the state because they were people of the book. They were known as *dhimmis,* or "protected people" (see page 292). Theoretically, Islam offered atheistic and polytheistic peoples the choice of conversion or death. In practice, Islam also accommodated Zoroastrians, Hindus, Buddhists, and other polytheists. Muslims' policy was far more liberal and tolerant than the policy of medieval Europeans toward Muslims. Europeans regarded Muslims as "heretics" or "infidels" who when conquered had to choose between conversion and death.[9] There were, of course, many exceptions, but in general the Christian attitude toward Islam was far more bigoted than was the attitude of Islam toward Christianity (see page 292).

Finally, the Muslim practice of establishing camp cities in newly conquered territories facilitated expansion. New military towns, such as Al-Fustat in Egypt and Basra in Iraq, became sites from which future conquests were planned and directed. They safeguarded Muslim identity and prevented the Muslim conquerors, at first a small minority, from being assimilated into the larger indigenous population. As the subject peoples became Muslim, the army towns became major centers for the spread of Islamic culture.

CONSOLIDATION OF THE ISLAMIC STATE

Although centered in towns, Islam arose within a tribal society that lacked stable governing institutions. When Muhammad died in 632, he left a large Muslim *umma,* but this community stood in danger of disintegrating into separate tribal groups. Some tribespeople even attempted to elect new chiefs. What provisions did Muhammad make for the religious and political organization of his followers? How was the vast and hastily acquired empire that came into existence within one hundred years of his death to be governed?

The Caliphate

Muhammad fulfilled his prophetic mission, but his religious work remained. The Muslim *umma* had to be maintained and Islam carried to the rest of the world. In order to achieve these goals, political and military power had to be exercised. But nei-

ther the Qur'an nor the *Sunna,* the account of the Prophet's sayings and conduct in particular situations, offered guidance for the succession (see page 274).

In this crisis, a group of Muhammad's ablest followers elected Abu Bakr (573–634), a close supporter of the Prophet, and hailed him as *khalifa,* or caliph, an Arabic term combining the ideas of leader, successor, and deputy (of the Prophet). This election marked the decisive victory of the concept of a universal community of Muslim believers. The selection of Abu Bakr showed that Muslims agreed that the faith revealed to Muhammad should continue as a unifying religious system that would reshape society. The goals of the Muslim *umma* were to promote the faith set down in the Qur'an and to make those revelations the cornerstone of Muslim law, government, and personal behavior.

When Muhammad died, Muslim "law" was still very primitive. It consisted of the tribal customs of Medina as corrected or altered by Qur'anic revelation and the decisions of the Prophet. Because the law of the Qur'an was to guide the community, there had to be an authority to enforce the law. Muslim teaching held that the law was paramount. According to Islam, God is the sole source of the law, and the ruler is bound to obey the law; the law is independent of the ruler and the ruler's will. Government exists not to make law but to enforce it. Muslim teaching also maintained that there is no distinction between the temporal and spiritual domains: social law is a basic strand in the fabric of comprehensive religious law. Thus religious belief and political power are inextricably intertwined: the first sanctifies the second, and the second sustains the first.[10] The creation of Islamic law in an institutional sense took three or four centuries and is one of the great achievements of medieval Islam.

In the two years of his rule (632–634), Abu Bakr governed on the basis of his personal prestige within the Muslim *umma.* He sent out military expeditions, collected taxes, dealt with tribes on behalf of the entire community, and led the community in prayer. His small group of advisers and scribes did not constitute an administrative structure, nor did his office become an institution.

Gradually, under Abu Bakr's first three successors, Umar (r. 634–644), Uthman (r. 644–656), and Ali (r. 656–661), the caliphate did emerge as an institution. The three continued Abu Bakr's policies and expanded on them. Umar succeeded in exerting his authority over the Bedouin tribes involved in ongoing conquests. Uthman asserted the right of the caliph to protect the economic interests of the entire *umma.* Uthman's publication of the definitive text of the Qur'an showed his concern for the unity of the *umma.* But Uthman's enemies accused him of nepotism—of using his position to put his family in powerful and lucrative jobs—and of unnecessary cruelty. Opposition coalesced around Ali, and when Uthman was assassinated in 656, Ali was chosen to succeed him.

The issue of responsibility for Uthman's murder troubled Ali's reign: it raised the question of whether Ali's accession was legitimate. Uthman's cousin Mu'awiya, a member of the Umayyad family, who had built a power base as governor of Syria, refused to recognize Ali as caliph. In the ensuing civil war, Ali was assassinated, and Mu'awiya (r. 661–680) assumed the caliphate. The Umayyads were the wealthiest and most powerful family of Mecca; they had bitterly fought Muhammad's ministry. Mu'awiya's victory and assumption of the caliphate, therefore, constituted social and political counterrevolution. The political and economic forces that had initially opposed Muhammad had now won. Mu'awiya founded the Umayyad dynasty and shifted the capital of the Islamic state from Medina to Damascus in Syria. From 661 to 750 Damascus served as the center of Muslim governmental bureaucracy.

The first four caliphs were elected by their peers, and the theory of an elected caliphate remained the Islamic legal ideal. Three of the four "patriarchs," as they were called, were murdered, however, and civil war ended the elective caliphate. Beginning with Mu'awiya, the office of caliph was in fact, but never in theory, dynastic. Two successive dynasties, the Umayyad (661–750) and the Abbasid (750–1258), held the caliphate.

From its inception with Abu Bakr, the caliphate rested on the principle that Muslim political and religious unity transcended tribalism. Mu'awiya, a consummate diplomat, bided his time. He always took care to confer periodically with the sheiks, or tribal leaders. He also, at least initially, behaved with them only as a *sayyid,* or first among equals. Mu'awiya sought to enhance the power of the caliphate by making the tribal leaders dependent on him for concessions and special benefits. At the same time, his control of a loyal and well-disci-

plined army enabled him to develop the caliphate in an authoritarian direction. Through intimidation he forced the tribal leaders to accept his son Yazid as his heir—thereby establishing the dynastic principle of succession. By distancing himself from a simple life within the *umma* and withdrawing into the palace that he built at Damascus, and by surrounding himself with symbols and ceremony, Mu'awiya laid the foundations for an elaborate caliphal court. Many of Mu'awiya's innovations were designed to protect him from assassination. A new official, the *hajib,* or chamberlain, restricted access to the caliph, who received visitors seated on a throne surrounded by bodyguards. Beginning with Mu'awiya, the Umayyad caliphs developed court ritual into a grand spectacle.

The assassination of Ali and the assumption of the caliphate by Mu'awiya had another profound consequence. It gave rise to a fundamental division in the *umma* and in Muslim theology. Ali had claimed the caliphate on the basis of family ties—he was Muhammad's cousin and son-in-law. When Ali was murdered, his followers argued—partly because of the blood tie, partly because Muhammad had designated Ali *imam,* or leader in community prayer—that Ali had been the Prophet's designated successor. These supporters of Ali were called *Shi'ites,* or *Shi'at Ali,* or simply *Shi'a,* Arabic terms all meaning "supporters" or "partisans" of Ali. In succeeding generations, opponents of the Umayyad dynasty emphasized their blood descent from Ali and claimed to possess divine knowledge that Muhammad had given them as his heirs.

Other Muslims adhered to the practice and beliefs of the *umma,* based on the precedents of the Prophet. They were called *Sunnis,* a term derived from the Arabic word *Sunna.* When a situation arose for which the Qur'an offered no solution, Sunnite scholars searched for a precedent in the Sunna, which gained an authority comparable to the Qur'an itself.

What basically distinguished Sunni and Shi'ite Muslims was the Shi'ite doctrine of the *imamate.* According to the Sunnites, the caliph, the elected successor of the Prophet, possessed political and military leadership but not Muhammad's religious authority. In contrast, according to the Shi'ites, the *imam* (leader) is directly descended from the Prophet and is the sinless, divinely inspired political leader and religious guide of the community. Put another way, both Sunnites and Shi'ites main-

THE ISLAMIC WORLD, CA 600–1258

610	Muhammad preaches reform, monotheism
610–733	Spread of Islam across Arabia, southern Europe, Africa, and Asia as far as India
622	The hijra—Muhammad and his followers are forced to leave Mecca and emigrate to Medina
632	Muhammad dies
632–661	Caliphate emerges as an institution
642	Muslims' victory at Nehawand signals their control of the Persian Empire
651	Publication of the Qur'an, the sacred book of Islam
661–750	The Umayyad dynasty
661	Umayyads move Muslim capital from Medina to Damascus
713	Spread of Islam to India, with the founding of a Muslim community at Multan
733	Charles Martel defeats Arabs at Battle of Tours, halting spread of Islam in northwestern Europe
750–1258	The Abbasid dynasty
751	Battle at Talas River ends Islamic penetration of central Asia
762	Abbasids move Muslim capital from Damascus to Baghdad
945	Buyids occupy Baghdad
946	Blinding of Caliph al-Muslakfi signals the practical end of the Abbasid dynasty
1055	Baghdad falls to the Seljuk Turks
1258	Mongols destroy Baghdad and kill the last of the Abbasid caliphs

tain that authority within Islam lies first in the Qur'an and then in the Sunna. Who interprets these sources? Shi'ites claim that the *imam* does, for he is invested with divine grace and insight. Sunnites insist that interpretation comes from the consensus of the *ulema,* a group of religous scholars.

The Umayyad caliphs were Sunnis, and the Shi'ites constituted a major source of discontent throughout the Umayyad period. Shi'ite rebellions expressed religious opposition in political terms. The Shi'ites condemned the Umayyads as worldly and sensual rulers, in contrast to the pious and true "successors" of Muhammad.

The Abbasid clan, which based its claim to the caliphate on the descent of Abbas, Muhammad's uncle, exploited the situation. The Abbasids agitated the Shi'ites, encouraged dissension among tribal factions, and contrasted Abbasid piety with the pleasure-loving style of the Umayyads. Finally, through open rebellion in 747, the Abbasids overthrew the Umayyads. In 750 the Abbasids won recognition as caliphs and later set up their capital at Baghdad in Iraq. The Abbasid dynasty lasted until 1258, but its real power began to disintegrate in the mid-ninth century.

Scholars agree that the Abbasid revolution established a basis for rule and citizenship more cosmopolitan and *Islamic* than the narrow, elitist, and Arab basis that had characterized Umayyad government. Abbasid rule had a strong impact on the Islamizing of the entire Middle East. Moreover, under the Umayyads the Muslim state had been governed by one ruler; during the Abbasid caliphate, steady disintegration occurred as provincial governors gradually won independent power. Although at first Muslims represented only a small minority of the conquered peoples, Abbasid rule provided the political and religious milieu in which Islam gained, over the centuries, the allegiance of the vast majority of the population from Spain to Afghanistan.

Administration of the Islamic State

The Islamic conquests brought into being a new imperial system that dominated southwestern Asia and North Africa. The Muslims adopted the patterns of administration used by the Byzantines in Egypt and Syria and by the Sassanids in Persia. Arab *emirs,* or governors, were appointed and given overall responsibility for good order, the maintenance of the armed forces, and tax collecting. Below them, experienced native officials—Greeks, Syrians, Copts (Egyptian Christians)—remained in office. Thus there was continuity with previous administrations.

The Arab conquerors developed devices to meet the changing needs of their empire. Tradition holds that the second caliph, Umar, established the *diwan*, or financial bureau. This agency recorded the names of soldiers, together with their salaries from state revenues. The *diwan* converted payments in kind to monetary equivalents and dispersed sums to tribal chieftains for distribution to their followers. All later departments of Muslim administration derive from this core.

The Umayyad caliphate witnessed the further development of the imperial administration. At the head stood the caliph, who led the holy war against unbelievers. Theoretically, he had the ultimate responsibility for the interpretation of the sacred law. In practice, the *ulema*, a group of scholars outstanding in learning and piety, interpreted the law as revealed in the Qur'an and in the Sunna. In the course of time the *ulema's* interpretations constituted a rich body of law, the *shari'a*, which covered social, criminal, political, commercial, and ritualistic matters. The *ulema* enjoyed great prestige in the Muslim community and was consulted by the caliph on difficult legal and spiritual matters. The *qadis*, or judges, who were well versed in the sacred law, carried out the judicial functions of the state. Nevertheless, Muslim law prescribed that all people had access to the caliph, and he set aside special times for hearing petitions and for the direct redress of grievances.

The central administrative organ was the *diwan al-kharaj*, which collected the two basic taxes on which the state depended. All persons paid the *kharaj*, a tax on land and movables. "Protected people"—Jews, Christians, and Zoroastrians—also paid the *jizya*, a poll tax. Revenues from these sources paid soldiers' salaries and financed charitable and public works that the caliph undertook, such as aid to the poor (as the Qur'an prescribed) and construction of mosques, irrigation works, and public baths.

As Arab conquests extended into Spain, central Asia, and Afghanistan, lines of communication had to be kept open. Emirs and other officials, remote from the capital at Damascus and later Baghdad, might revolt. Thus a relay network known as the *barid* was established to convey letters and intelligence reports between the capital and the various outposts. The *barid* employed a special technical vocabulary, as had similar networks used by the Byzantine and Sassanid empires.

The early Abbasid period witnessed considerable economic expansion and population growth, and the work of government became more complicated. New and specialized departments emerged, each with a hierarchy of officials. The most important new official was the *vizier*, a position that the Abbasids adopted from the Persians.

Initially, the vizier was the caliph's chief assistant—advising the caliph on matters of general policy, supervising the bureaucratic administration, and, under the caliph, superintending the army, the provincial governors, and relations with foreign governments. As the caliphs withdrew from leading Friday prayers and other routine functions, the viziers gradually assumed power. Khalid ibn-Barmak, vizier during the caliphate of Harun al-Rashid (r. 786–809), tried to make the office hereditary, as did some other viziers. But the authority and power of the vizier usually depended on the caliph's personality and direct involvement in state affairs. Many viziers used their offices for personal gain and wealth. Although some careers ended with the vizier's execution, there were always candidates seeking the job.

The vizier al-Fustat (d. 924) set down some of his reflections on government. They sound more like cynical aphorisms than serious policy principles:

The basis of government is trickery; if it succeeds and endures, it becomes policy.

It is better to keep the affairs of government moving on the wrong path than to stand still on the right one.

If you have business with the vizier and can settle it with the archivist of the diwan *or with the privy secretary, do so and do not bring it to the vizier himself.*[11]

In theory, the caliph and his central administration governed the whole empire. In practice, the many parts of the empire enjoyed considerable local independence; and as long as public order was maintained and taxes were forwarded to the *diwan al-kharaj*, the central government rarely interfered.

In theory, Muslim towns did not possess the chartered self-governing status of the towns and cities of medieval Europe (see pages 418–420). In practice, although a capable governor kept a careful eye on municipal activities, wealthy merchants and property owners had broad local autonomy.

DECENTRALIZATION OF THE ISLAMIC STATE

The Umayyad state virtually coincided with all Islamic states. Under the Abbasids, decentralization began nearly from the start of the dynasty. In 755 a Umayyad prince who had escaped death at the hands of the triumphant Abbasids and fled to Spain set up an independent regime at Cordoba (see Map 10.2). In 800, the emir in Tunisia in North Africa set himself up as an independent ruler and refused to place the caliph's name on the local coinage. In 820, Tahir, the son of a slave who had supported the caliphate, was rewarded with the governorship of Khorasan. Once there, Tahir ruled independently of Baghdad, not even mentioning the caliph's name in the traditional Friday prayers in recognition of caliphal authority.

This sort of decentralization occurred all over the Muslim world. The enormous distance separating many provinces from the imperial capital enabled the provinces to throw off the caliph's jurisdiction. Particularism and ethnic or tribal tendencies, combined with strength and fierce ambition, led to the creation of local dynasties. Incompetent or immature caliphs at Baghdad were unable to enforce their authority over distant and strong local rulers. This pattern led to the decline of the Abbasids and invasion by foreign powers.

Decline of the Abbasids

To check the power of the provincial governors, the caliph al-Mu'tasin (r. 833–842) expanded his military guard with a large corps of Turkish slaves loyal to him alone. The Turkish guard soon realized the degree of the caliph's dependence and vied with him for power. The guards' murder of one of al-Mu'tasin's successors, the caliph al-Mutawakkil (r. 847–861), reduced the caliphate to virtual insignificance.

In the later ninth century, rebellions shook Arabia, Syria, and Persia, and a slave revolt devastated Iraq. These disorders hurt agricultural productivity and in turn cut tax receipts. Having severely taxed the urban mercantile groups, the caliphate had already alienated the commercial classes. Disorder and the danger of disintegration threatened the Muslim state.

In the meantime, the luxury and extravagance of the caliphal court imposed a terrible financial burden. The caliphs lived in surroundings of awesome and ostentatious ceremony and wealth. In the palace complexes, maintained by staffs numbering in the tens of thousands, an important visitor would be conducted through elaborate rituals and confronted with indications of the caliph's majesty and power: rank upon rank of lavishly appointed guards, pages, servants, slaves, and other retainers; lush parks full of exotic wild beasts; fantastic arrays of gold and silver objects, ornamented furniture, precious carpets and tapestries, pools of mercury, and ingenious mechanical devices. The most famous of the mechanical devices was a gold and silver tree with leaves that rustled, branches that swayed, and mechanical birds that sang as the breezes blew.[12]

Some caliphs in the early tenth century worked to halt the process of decay. But by the time that ibn-Ra'ig, the governor of Wasit, a city in Iraq, compelled the caliph to give him the title *amir al-umara,* emir of emirs—which in effect bestowed precedence over other generals in Iraq—the caliphate had been reduced to a titular office symbolizing only the religious unity of Islam.

In 945, the Buyids, a Shi'ite clan originating in Daylam, the mountainous region on the southern shores of the Caspian Sea, overran Iraq and occupied Baghdad. The caliph, al-Mustakfi, was forced to recognize the Buyid leader Mu'izz al-Dawla as *amir al-umara* and to allow the celebration of Shi'ite festivals—though the caliph and most of the people were Sunnites. A year later the caliph was accused of plotting against his new masters. He was snatched from his throne, dragged through the streets to Mu'izz al-Dawla's palace, and blinded. Blinding was a practice that the Buyids adopted from the Byzantines as a way of rendering a ruler incapable of carrying out his duties. This incident marks the practical collapse of the Abbasid caliphate, although the caliphs remained as puppets of the Buyids and symbols of Muslim unity until the Mongols killed the last of them in 1258.

The Assault of the Turks and Mongols

In the mid-tenth century, the Islamic world began to be besieged by the Seljuk Turks. Originating in Turkestan in central Asia and displaying great physical endurance and mobility, the Turks surged westward. They accepted Sunnite Islam near Bukhara (then a great Persian commercial and intellectual center), swarmed over the rest of Persia, and pushed through Iraq and Syria. Baghdad fell to them on December 18, 1055, and the caliph became a puppet of the Turkish *sultan*—literally, "he with authority." The sultan replaced the Buyids as masters of the Abbasid caliphate. Caliphs retained their office, but Turkish sultans held the power. The Turks did not acquire all of the former Abbasid state. To the west, the Shi'ite Fatimids, so-called because they claimed descent from Muhammad's daughter Fatima, had conquered present-day central Algeria, Sicily, and, in 969, Egypt.

Thus by the middle of the eleventh century, there were three centers of Muslim power: Cordoba in Spain, Cairo in Egypt, and Baghdad in Iraq. Within the Baghdad caliphate the construction of mosques, schools, canals, and roads for commerce and pilgrimages by Nizam al-Mulk (1018–1092), the vizier of three sultans, signaled new intellectual and spiritual vitality. A Turkish sultan, rather than an Arab caliph, ruled the Baghdad caliphate, but it remained a Muslim state.

Into this world in the early thirteenth century exploded the Mongols, a people descended from an ethnic group that originated in the area that is present-day Siberia. The Mongols adhered to shamanism, a religion in which unseen gods, demons, and ancestral spirits are thought to be responsive only to *shamans,* or priests. In 1206 their leader Jenghiz Khan (1162–1227), having welded the Mongols and related Turkish tribes into a strong confederation, swept westward.

Whether the Mongols were driven by economic or military pressures, or were attracted by the sophisticated life to the west, scholars do not know. With perhaps sixty thousand highly disciplined soldiers, the Mongols left a trail of blood and destruction. They used terror as a weapon, and out of fear the rich commercial centers of central Asia—Khwarizm, Bukhara (whose mosques were turned into stables), Herat, Samarkand, Baikal

Embassy to the Court of Ethiopia   Describing an event that happened centuries before, a fourteenth-century artist depicts a Muslim embassy to the king of Ethiopia to arrange for the extradition of early converts to Islam who had fled to Ethiopia. The easy movement of the figures suggests the influence of Chinese artists who immigrated to Baghdad and Persia during the Mongol period. Both Chinese and Muslim artists believed the blacks dressed very simply. *(Source: Edinburgh University Library)*

(whose peoples were all slaughtered or enslaved)—fell before them. When Jenghiz Khan died, his empire stretched from northern China and Korea to the Caspian Sea, and from the Danube River to the Arctic. In 1242 the Mongols sacked Kiev. By 1250 they controlled all of southern Russia under the title "Khanate of the Golden Horde," and they ruled it for two hundred years (see page 634).

Under Jenghiz Khan's grandsons, Hulagu (1217–1265) and Kublai Khan (1216–1294), the Mongol Empire expanded farther. In the west, Hulagu sacked and burned Baghdad and killed the last Abbasid caliph (1258). His hordes captured Damascus in 1260, and only a major defeat at Ayn Jalut in Syria saved Egypt and the Muslim lands in North Africa and perhaps Spain. In the east, meanwhile, Kublai Khan campaigned in China. His defeat of the Sung Dynasty and establishment of the Yuan Dynasty (see page 320) marked the greatest territorial extent of the Mongol Empire. Kublai Khan ruled China from his capital at Peking.

Hulagu tried to eradicate Muslim culture, but his descendant Ghazan embraced Islam in 1295 and worked for the revival of Muslim culture. As the Turks had done earlier, so the Mongols, once converted, injected new vigor into the faith and spirit of Islam. In the Middle East the Mongols governed through Persian viziers and native financial officials.

THE LIFE OF THE PEOPLE

When the Prophet appeared, Arab society consisted of independent Bedouin tribal groups loosely held together by loyalty to a strong leader and by the belief that all members of a tribe were descended from a common ancestor. Heads of families elected the *sheik,* or tribal chief. He was usually chosen from among aristocratic warrior families whose members had a strong sense of their superiority. Birth determined aristocracy.

According to the Qur'an, however, birth counted for nothing; zeal for Islam was the only criterion for honor: "O ye folk, verily we have created you male and female. . . . Verily the most honourable of you in the sight of God is the most pious of you."[13] The idea of social equality

founded on piety was a basic Muslim doctrine. As a thirteenth-century commentator explained:

We have created everyone of you by means of a father and mother. All are equal in this and there is no reason therefore for boasting of one's lineage (the old Arab view being that in lineage lay honour). Through piety are souls brought to perfection and persons may compete for excellence in it; and let him who desires honour seek it in piety.[14]

When Muhammad defined social equality, he was thinking about equality among Muslims alone. But even among Muslims a sense of pride in ancestry could not be destroyed by a stroke of the pen. Claims of birth remained strong among the first Muslims; and after Islam spread outside of Arabia, full-blooded Bedouin tribesmen regarded themselves as superior to foreign converts.

The Classes of Society

In the Umayyad period, Muslim society consisted of four classes. At the top were the caliph's household and the ruling Arab Muslims. Descended from Bedouin tribespeople and composed of warriors, veterans, governing officials, and town settlers, this class constituted the aristocracy. Because birth continued to determine membership, it was more a caste than a class. It was also a relatively small group, greatly outnumbered by villagers and country people.

Converts constituted the second class in Islamic society. In theory, converts gained full citizenship when they accepted Islam. In practice, they did not: converts had to attach themselves to one of the Arab tribes as clients. This they greatly resented doing on economic, social, and cultural grounds, for they believed that they represented a higher culture than the Arab tribespeople. From this class of Muslim converts eventually came the members of the commercial and learned professions—merchants, traders, teachers, doctors, artists, and interpreters of the *shari'a.* Second-class citizenship led some Muslim converts to adopt Shi'ism (see page 274) and other unorthodox doctrines inimical to the state. Over the centuries, Berber, Copt, Persian, Aramaean, and other converts to Islam intermarried with their Muslim conquerors. Gradually assimilation united peoples of

Harvesting Dates Dates played a major part in fruit cultivation, and the Arabs developed many varieties with certain species famous for flavor, sweetness, or moisture. This detail from an ivory casket given to a Cordoban prince reflects the importance of fruit cultivation in the Muslim-inspired agricultural expansion in southern Europe during the ninth and tenth centuries. *(Source: Louvre/Cliché des Musées Nationaux, Paris)*

various ethnic and "national" backgrounds. However, "an Arabian remained a native of the peninsula, but an Arab became one who professed Islam and spoke Arabic, regardless of national origin."[15]

Dhimmis, or "protected people"—Jews, Christians, and Zoroastrians living under Muslim rule—formed the third class. The term *dhimmis* derives from an Arabic word meaning "pact." The pact allowed Christians and Jews to practice their religions, maintain their houses of worship, and conduct their business affairs, provided they gave unequivocal recognition to Muslim political supremacy. Here is a formula drawn up in the ninth century as a pact between Muslims and their nonbelieving subjects:

If the Iman wishes to write a document for the poll tax [jizya] of non-Muslims, he should write:

. . . I accord to you and to the Christians of the city of so-and-so that which is accorded to the dhimmis *. . . safe-conduct . . . namely:*

You will be subject to the authority of Islam and to no contrary authority. You will not refuse to carry out any obligation which we think fit to impose upon you by virtue of this authority.

If any one of you speaks improperly of Muhammed, may God bless and save him, the Book of God, or of His religion, he forfeits the protection [dhimma] of God, of the Commander of the Faithful, and of all the Muslims; he has contravened the conditions upon which he was given his safe-conduct; his property and his life are at the disposal of the Commander of the Faithful. . . .

If any one of them commits fornication with a Muslim woman or goes through a form of marriage with her or robs a Muslim on the highway or subverts a Muslim from his religion or aids those who made war against the Muslims by fighting with them or by showing them the weak points of the Muslims, or by harboring their spies, he has contravened his pact . . . and his life and his property are at the disposal of the Muslims. . . .

We shall not supervise transactions between you and your coreligionists or other unbelievers nor inquire into them as long as you are content. . . .

You may not display crosses in Muslim cities, nor proclaim polytheism, nor build churches or meeting places for your prayers . . . nor proclaim your polytheistic beliefs on the subject of Jesus [beliefs relating to the Trinity]. . . .

Every adult male of sound mind among you shall have to pay a poll tax [jizya] of one dinar, in good coin, at the beginning of each year. . . . Poverty does not free you from any obligation, nor does it abrogate your pact.[16]

Restrictions placed on Christians and Jews were not severe, and they seem to have thrived under Muslim rule. Rare outbursts of violence against Christians and Jews occurred only when Muslims felt that the *dhimmis* had stepped out of line and broken the agreement. The social position of the "protected people" deteriorated during the Crusades (see pages 362–367) and the Mongol invasions, when there was a general rise of religious loyalties. At those times Muslims suspected the *dhimmis,* often rightly, of collaborating with the enemies of Islam.

At the bottom of the social scale were slaves. The Qur'an's acceptance of slavery parallels that of the Old and New Testaments. The Qur'an forbids the enslavement of Muslims or "protected peoples," and Muhammad had recommended the humane treatment of slaves. Emancipation was a meritorious act, but the Qur'an did not grant freedom to slaves who accepted Islam. The Muslim duty of the holy war ensured a steady flow of slaves. Prisoners of war or people captured in raids or purchased in the slave markets, slaves constituted very large numbers in the Muslim world. The great Muslim commander Musa ibn-Nusayr, the son of a Christian enslaved in Iraq, is reputed to have taken 300,000 prisoners of war in his North African campaigns (708–718) and 30,000 virgins from the Visigothic nobility of Spain, though these numbers are surely greatly inflated. Every soldier, from general to private, had a share of slaves from the captured prisoners. In the slave markets of Damascus and Baghdad in the tenth and eleventh centuries, a buyer could select from white slaves brought from Spain, Sicily, and southeastern Europe, yellow slaves from central Asia, brown slaves from India, and black slaves from sub-Saharan Africa.

Most slaves in the Islamic world went into the army or worked as household servants. Some were

Muslim Slave Market Slaves of several races were available at this thirteenth-century market at Zabid in Yemen. Women and children were wanted more than men: boys for military or administrative service, attractive women for the harem. Emancipation or the attainment of high political or military positions worked against the growth of class consciousness among slaves. *(Source: Bibliothèque Nationale, Paris)*

entrusted with business or administrative responsibilities. Few performed the kinds of agricultural labor commonly associated with slavery in the Western Hemisphere. Islamic law declared the children of a female slave to be slaves, but the offspring of a free male and a slave woman were free because lineage was in the paternal line. Many Muslims took slave women as concubines; the children belonged to the father and were free. In classical Islamic civilization, slaves played a large and sometimes distinguished role in the military, politics, religion, and the arts and sciences. Many caliphs were the emancipated sons of Turkish, Greek, and black slave women.

By the beginning of the tenth century, Islamic society had undergone significant change. The courtier al-Fadl b. Yahya, writing in 903, divided humankind into four classes:

Firstly, rulers elevated to office by their deserts; secondly, viziers, distinguished by their wisdom and understanding; thirdly, the upper classes, elevated by their wealth; and fourthly, the middle classes to which belong men marked by their culture. The remainder are filthy refuse, a torrent of scum, base cattle, none of whom thinks of anything but his food and sleep.[17]

The last category hardly reflects compassion for the poor and unfortunate. However, it is clear that birth as a sign of social distinction had yielded to wealth and talent.

Women in Classical Islamic Society

Arab tribal law gave women virtually no legal status. According to tribal law, at birth girls could be buried alive by their fathers. They were sold into marriage by their guardians for a price. Their husband could terminate the union at will. And women had virtually no property or succession rights. The Qur'an sought to improve the social position of women.

The Qur'an, like the religious writings of all traditions, represents moral precept rather than social practice, and the texts are open to different interpretations. Yet modern scholars tend to agree that the Islamic sacred book intended women as the spiritual and sexual equals of men and gave women considerable economic rights. In the early Umayyad period, moreover, women played an active role in the religious, economic, and political

life of the community. They owned property. They had freedom of movement and traveled widely. They participated in the politics of the caliphal succession. With men, women shared in the public religious rituals and observances. But this Islamic ideal of women and men of equal value to the community did not last.[18] As Islamic society changed, the precepts of the Qur'an were interpreted to meet different circumstances.

In the later Umayyad period, the status of women declined. The rapid conquest of vast territories led to the influx of large numbers of slave women. As wealth replaced birth as the criterion of social status, men more and more viewed women as possessions, as a form of wealth. The increasingly inferior status of women is revealed in three ways: in the relationship of women to their husbands, in the practice of veiling women, and in the seclusion of women in harems.

On the rights and duties of a husband to his wife, the Qur'an states that "men are in charge of women because Allah hath made the one to excel the other, and because they (men) spend of their property (for the support of women). So good women are obedient, guarding in secret that which Allah hath guarded."[19] A tenth-century interpreter, Abu Ja'far Muhammad ibn-Jarir al-Tabari, commented on that passage as follows:

Men are in charge of their women with respect to disciplining (or chastising) them, and to providing them with restrictive guidance concerning their duties toward God and themselves (i.e., the men), by virtue of that by which God has given excellence (or preference) to the men over their wives: i.e., the payment of their dowers to them, spending of their wealth on them, and providing for them in full. This is how God has given excellence to (the men) over (the women), and hence (the men) have come to be in charge of (the women) and hold authority over them.[20]

A thirteenth-century commentator on the same Qur'anic passage goes into more detail and argues that women are incapable of and unfit for any public duties, such as participating in religious rites, giving evidence in the law courts, or being involved in any public political decisions.[21] Muslim society fully accepted this view, and later interpreters further categorized the ways in which men were superior to women.

Interpretations of the Qur'an's statements on polygamy give another example of the declining

Man Playing a Lyre   Major Persian pottery centers at Rayy and Kashan produced ceramic masterpieces, often in styles influenced by imported Chinese porcelains. In this delicate bowl of off-white paste with an opaque cobalt glaze from the early twelfth century, a gentleman serenades a lady on a lyre. *(Source: Courtesy of the Freer Gallery of Art, Smithsonian Institution)*

status of women. The Qur'an permitted a man to have four wives, provided "that all are treated justly. . . . Marry of the women who seem good to you, two or three or four; and if ye fear that you cannot do justice (to so many) then one (only) or the captives that your right hand possess. Thus it is more likely that you will do injustice."[22] This passage suggests the availability of large numbers of slave women. Where the Qur'an permitted polygamy, Muslim jurists interpreted the statement as having legal force. The Prophet's emphasis on justice to the several wives, however, was understood as a mere recommendation.[23] Although the Qur'an allowed polygamy, only very wealthy men could afford several wives. The vast majority of

Muslim males were monogamous because women could not earn money, and it was all men could do to support one wife.

In contrast to the Christian view of sexual activity as something inherently shameful and even within marriage only a cure for sexual desire, Islam maintained a healthy acceptance of sexual pleasure for both males and females. Islam held that sexual satisfaction for both partners in marriage was necessary to prevent extramarital activity. A sexually frustrated person was considered dangerous to the community. Thus Islam opposed asceticism and required believers with pious vocations to acquire pious wives. Abstinence and chastity were vehemently discouraged.

Although men and women were thought to have similar sexual instincts, men were entitled to as many as four legal partners but women had to be content with one. Because satisfaction of the sexual impulse for males allows polygamy,

one can speculate that fear of its inverse—one woman with four husbands—might explain the assumption of women's insatiability, which is at the core of the Muslim concept of female sexuality. Since Islam assumed that a sexually frustrated individual is a very problematic believer and a troublesome citizen, . . . the distrust of women is even greater.[24]

Modern sociologists contend that polygamy affects individuals' sense of identity. It supports men's self-images as primarily sexual beings, whereas—by emphasizing wives' inability to satisfy their husbands—it undermines women's confidence in their sexuality. The function of polygamy as a device to humiliate women is evident in an aphorism from Moroccan folklore: "Debase a woman by bringing in (the house) another one."[25]

In many present-day Muslim cultures, few issues are more sensitive than those of veiling and the seclusion of women. These practices have their roots in pre-Islamic times, and they took firm hold in classical Islamic society. The head veil seems to have been the mark of free-born urban women; wearing the veil distinguished free women from slave women. Country and desert women did not wear veils because they interfered with work.

Probably of Byzantine or Persian origin, the veil indicated respectability and modesty. As the Arab conquerors subjugated various peoples, they adopted some of the vanquished peoples' customs, one of which was veiling. The Qur'an contains no specific rule about the veil, but its few vague references have been interpreted as sanctioning the practice. Gradually, all parts of a woman's body were considered *pudendal* (shameful because they were capable of arousing sexual desire) and were not allowed to be seen in public.

Even more restrictive of the freedom of women than veiling was the practice of *purdah*, literally seclusion behind a screen or curtain—the harem system. The English word *harem* comes from the Arabic *haram*, meaning "forbidden" or "sacrosanct," which the women's quarters of a house or palace were considered to be. The practice of secluding women in a harem also derives from Arabic contacts with other Eastern cultures. Scholars do not know precisely when the harem system began, but within "one-and-a-half centuries after the death of the Prophet, the (harem) system was fully established. . . . Amongst the richer classes, the women were shut off from the rest of the household."[26] The harem became another symbol of male prestige and prosperity, as well as a way to distinguish and set apart upper-class women from peasants.

Sufism

In the ninth and tenth centuries, in Arabia, Syria, Egypt, and Iraq, a popular religious movement arose within Islam. For some especially devout individuals within the community, the traditional way of religious life through observance of the precepts of the Qur'an was not fully satisfying. They rejected what they considered the increasing materialism of Muslim life and sought a return to the simplicity of the Prophet's time. Called *Sufis* from the simple coarse woolen *(suf)* garments they wore, these men and women followed an ascetic lifestyle, dedicating themselves to fasting, prayer, and meditation on the Qur'an. Through asceticism and a deep love of God, Sufis sought a direct or mystical union with God. Sufi ideals—careful following of the Qur'an, the avoidance of sin, and a humble yearning toward God—were embodied in the word *zuhd*, renunciation.

The woman mystic Rabia (d. 801) epitomizes this combination of renunciation and devotionalism. An attractive woman who refused marriage so that nothing would distract her from a total commitment to God, Rabia attracted followers, whom she served as a spiritual guide. Her poem in the form of prayer captures her deep devotion:

O my lord, if I worship thee from fear of hell, and if I worship thee in hope of paradise, exclude me thence, but if I worship thee for thine own sake, then withhold not from me thine eternal beauty.

Sufism grew into a mass movement that drew people from all social classes. Though its sources were the Qur'an and the Sunna, Sufism accepted ideas from Christian and Buddhist monasticism and from Hindu devotionalism. Consequently, the *ulema*, the religious scholars who interpreted the Qur'an and Muslim law, looked on Sufism as a heretical movement and an unnecessary devi-

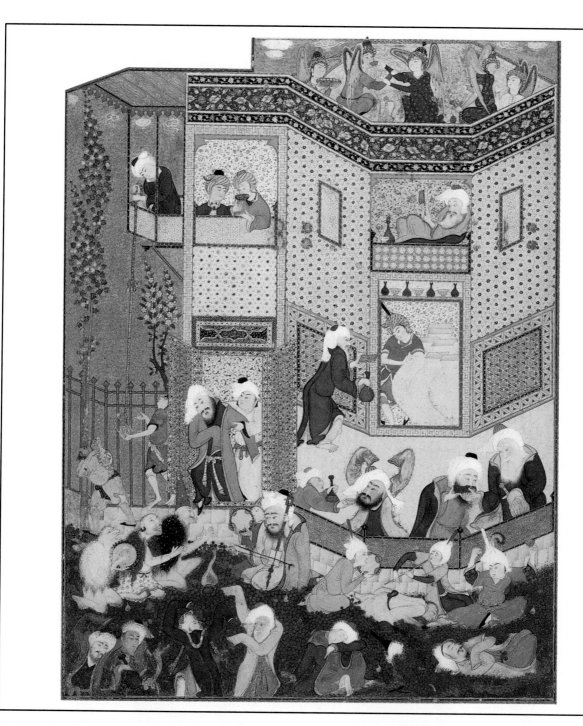

Sufi Collective Ritual   Collective or group rituals, in which sufis tried through ecstatic experiences to come closer to God, have always fascinated outsiders, including non-sufi Muslims. Here the sixteenth-century Persian painter Sultan Muhammad illustrates the writing of the fourteenth-century lyric poet Hafiz. Just as Hafiz's poetry moved back and forth between profane and mystical themes, so it is difficult to determine whether the ecstasy achieved here is alcoholic or spiritual. Many figures seem to enjoy wine. Note the various musical instruments and the delicate floral patterns so characteristic of Persian art. *(Source: Courtesy of The Arthur M. Sackler Museum, Harvard University)*

ation from orthodoxy. The *ulema* also felt that the Sufis challenged their religious authority. Just as ecclesiastical authorities in Europe looked on Christian mystics with suspicion because the direct mystical union with God denied the need for the institutional Church, so the Muslim *ulema* condemned and persecuted extreme Sufis for their rejection of religious formalism.

Trade and Commerce

Trade and commerce played a prominent role in the Islamic world. Muhammad had earned his livelihood in business as a representative of the city of Mecca, which carried on a brisk trade from south-ern Palestine to southwestern Arabia. Although Bedouin nomads were among the first converts to Islam, Islam arose in a mercantile, not an agricultural, setting. The merchant had a respectable place in Muslim society. According to the sayings of the Prophet:

The honest, truthful Muslim merchant will stand with the martyrs on the Day of Judgment.

I commend the merchants to you, for they are the couriers of the horizons and God's trusted servants on earth.

If God permitted the inhabitants of paradise to trade, they would deal in cloth and perfume.[27]

Muslim Dhow Hundreds of these lateen-rigged Arab vessels gave Islam mastery of the Indian Ocean. The Muslim fleet in the Mediterranean never equaled the one in the Indian Ocean, a circumstance that helps to explain Venetian and Genoese power in the Mediterranean in the thirteenth century. *(Source: Bibliothèque Nationale, Paris)*

In contrast to the social values of the medieval West and of Confucian China, Muslims tended to look with disdain on agricultural labor and to hold trade in esteem. The Qur'an, moreover, had no prohibition against trade with Christians or other unbelievers.

Western scholars have tended to focus attention on the Mediterranean Sea as the source of Islamic mercantile influence on Europe in the Middle Ages. From the broad perspective of Muslim commerce, however, the Mediterranean held a position much subordinate to other waterways: the Black Sea; the Caspian Sea and the Volga River, which gave access deep into Russia; the Aral Sea, from which region caravans departed for China; the Gulf of Aden; and the Arabian Sea and the Indian Ocean, which linked the Arabian gulf region with eastern Africa, the Indian subcontinent, and eventually Indonesia and the Philippines. These served as the main commercial seaways of the Islamic world.

By land Muslim traders pushed south from North Africa across the Sahara Desert into west central Africa (see Map 10.2) and by the tenth century had penetrated as far east as China and possibly Korea. They were pursuing silk, which was the earliest Chinese gift to the world. Travelers called the land route going through Samarkand, Bukhara, and other Turkestan towns the "great silk way," and along that way caravans collected the merchandise of Transoxiana and Turkestan. The following is a selection from a private ninth-century list of commodities transported into and through the Islamic world by land and by sea:

Imported from India: tigers, leopards, elephants, leopard skins, red rubies, white sandalwood, ebony, and coconuts

From China: aromatics, silk, porcelain, paper, ink, peacocks, fiery horses, saddles, felts, cinnamon

From the Byzantines: silver and gold vessels, embroidered cloths, fiery horses, slave girls, rare articles in red copper, strong locks, lyres, water engineers, specialists in plowing and cultivation, marble workers, and eunuchs

From Arabia: Arab horses, ostriches, thoroughbred she-camels, and tanned hides

From Barbary and Maghrib (the Arabic name for northwest Africa, an area that included Morocco, Algeria, and Tunisia): leopards, acacia, felts, and black falcons

From the Yemen: cloaks, tanned hides, giraffes, breastplates, cornelian incense, indigo, and turmeric

From Egypt: ambling donkeys, fine cloths, papyrus, balsam oil, and, from its mines, high-quality topaz

From the Khazars (a people living on the northern shore of the Black Sea): slaves, slave women, armor, helmets, and hoods of mail

From the land of Khwarizm (a state in central Asia): musk, ermine, sable, squirrel, mink, and excellent sugar cane

From Samarkand: paper

From Isfahan (a city in central Persia): honeycombs, honey, quinces, Chinese pears, apples, saffron, potash, white lead, antimony (a metallic element), fine cloths, and fruit drinks

From Ahwaz (a city in southwestern Persia): sugar, silk brocades, castanet players and dancing girls, kinds of dates, grape molasses, and candy.[28]

What made long-distance land transportation possible? Camels. Stupid and vicious, camels had to be loaded on a daily, sometimes twice-daily, basis. Nevertheless, they proved more efficient for desert transportation than horses or oxen. The use of the camel to carry heavy and bulky freight facilitated the development of world commerce.

Between the eighth and twelfth centuries, the Islamic world functioned virtually as a free-trade area in which goods circulated freely. The Muslims developed a number of business techniques that facilitated the expansion of trade. For example, they originated the concept of the bill of exchange, which made the financing of trade more flexible. The Muslims also seem to have come up with the idea of the joint stock company—an arrangement that lets a group of people invest in a venture and share in its profits and losses in proportion to the amount each has invested. Also, many financial and business terms—check, coffer, cipher, nadir, zenith, zero, and risk—entered the English language from Arabic.

Vigorous long-distance trade had significant consequences. Commodities produced in one part of the world became available in many other places, providing a uniformity of consumer goods among diverse peoples living over a vast area. Trade promoted scientific advances in navigation, shipbuilding, and cartography. For example, from the Chinese, Arabic sailors seem to have learned about the compass, an instrument used by mariners to determine directions on the earth's surface by means of a magnetic needle. Muslims carried the compass to Europe, and in the twelfth century it came into wide navigational use. Muslim mariners also developed the astrolabe, an instrument used to determine latitude and the time of day.

Long-distance trade brought some merchants fabulous wealth. A jeweler in Baghdad remained rich even after the caliph al-Muqtadir (r. 908–937) had seized 16 million dinars of his property. A long-distance trader in Bashr had an annual income of over 1 million dirhams. Many merchants in Siraf owned homes worth 30,000 dinars and had fortunes of 4 million dinars.[29] To appreciate the value of these sums in terms of present-day buying power, more information about the cost of living in tenth- and eleventh-century Muslim cities is needed. Nevertheless, it can be said that the sums represent very great riches.

Did Muslim economic activity amount to a kind of capitalism? If by capitalism is meant private (not state) ownership of the means of production, the production of goods for market sale, profit as the main motive for economic activity, competition, a money economy, and the lending of money at interest, then, unquestionably, the medieval Muslim economy had capitalistic features. Students of Muslim economic life have not made a systematic and thorough investigation of Muslims' industries, businesses, and seaports, but the impressionistic evidence is overwhelming:

despite all the uncertainty of our knowledge, a level (of economic development) does seem to have been reached in the Muslim world which is not to be found elsewhere at the same time or earlier. The density of commercial relations within the Muslim world constituted a sort of world market . . . of unprecedented dimensions. The development of exchange had made possible regional specialization in industry as well as in agriculture, bringing about relationships that some-
times extended over great distances. A world market of the same type was formed in the Roman Empire, but the Muslim "common market" was very much bigger. Also, it seems to have been more "capitalist," in the sense that private capital played a greater part in forming it, as compared with the part played by the state, than was the case in the Roman Empire. Not only did the Muslim world know a capitalist sector, but this sector was apparently the most extensive in history before the establishment of the world market created by the Western European bourgeoisie, and this did not outstrip it in importance until the sixteenth century.[30]

Urban Centers

Long-distance trade also provided the wealth that made possible a gracious and sophisticated culture in the cities of the Muslim world. Although cities and mercantile centers dotted the entire Islamic Empire, the cities of Baghdad and Cordoba at their peak in the tenth century stand out as the finest examples of cosmopolitan Muslim civilization. Founded in 762 by the second Abbasid caliph, al-Mansur, on the Tigris river, astride the major overland highways, Baghdad became the administrative, strategic, and commercial capital of the Muslim world. The presence of the caliph and his court and administration, caliphal patronage of learning and the arts, and Baghdad's enormous commercial advantages gave the city international prestige. On its streets thronged a kaleidoscope of races, creeds, costumes, and cultures, an almost infinite variety of peoples: returning travelers, administrative officials, slaves, visitors, merchants from Asia, Africa, and Europe. Shops and marketplaces offered the rich and extravagant a dazzling and exotic array of goods from all over the world.

The caliph Harun al-Rashid (r. 786–809) presided over a glamorous court. His vast palace with hundreds of officials, his harems with thousands of slave girls, his magnificent banquets, receptions, and ceremonies—all astounded foreign visitors. Harun al-Rashid invited writers, dancers, musicians, poets, and artists to live in Baghdad, and he is reputed to have rewarded one singer with 100,000 silver pieces for a single song. This brilliant era provided the background for the tales that appear in *A Thousand and One Nights*, the great folk classic of Arabic literature.

The central plot of the tales involves the efforts of Scheherazade to keep her husband, Schariar, legendary king of Samarkand, from killing her. She entertains him with one tale a night for 1,001 nights. The best-known tales are "Aladdin and His Lamp," "Sinbad the Sailor," and "Ali Baba and the Forty Thieves." Also known as *The Arabian Nights,* this book offers a sumptuous collection of caliphs, viziers, and genies, varieties of sexual experiences, and fabulous happenings. *The Arabian Nights,* although fictional, has provided a large store of the words and images that Europeans have used since the eighteenth century to describe the Islamic world. *The Arabian Nights* remains one of the great works of world literature.

Cordoba in southern Spain competed with Baghdad for the cultural leadership of the Islamic world. In the tenth century, no city in Asia or Europe could equal dazzling Cordoba. Its streets were well paved and lighted, and the city had an abundant supply of fresh water. With a population of about 1 million, Cordoba contained 1,600 mosques, 900 public baths, 213,177 houses for ordinary people, and 60,000 mansions for generals, officials, and the wealthy. In its 80,455 shops, 13,000 weavers produced silks, woolens, and brocades that were internationally famous. The English language has memorialized the city's leather with the word *cordovan.* Cordoba invented the process of manufacturing crystal. Cordoba was a great educational center with 27 free schools and a library containing 400,000 volumes. (By contrast, the great Benedictine abbey of Saint-Gall in Switzerland had about 600 books. The use of paper—whose manufacture the Muslims had learned from the Chinese—instead of vellum, gave rise to this great disparity.) Through Iran and Cordoba the Indian game of chess entered western Europe. Cordoba's scholars made contributions in chemistry, medicine and surgery, music, philosophy, and mathematics. Cordoba's fame was so great it is no wonder that the contemporary Saxon nun Hrosthwita of Gandersheim (d. 1000) could describe the city as the "ornament of the world."[31]

Intellectual Life

The wealth of Baghdad, the generous patronage of Harun al-Rashid, and the "international" character of Islamic culture launched a period of intellectual vitality. The cosmopolitan nature of the Mus-

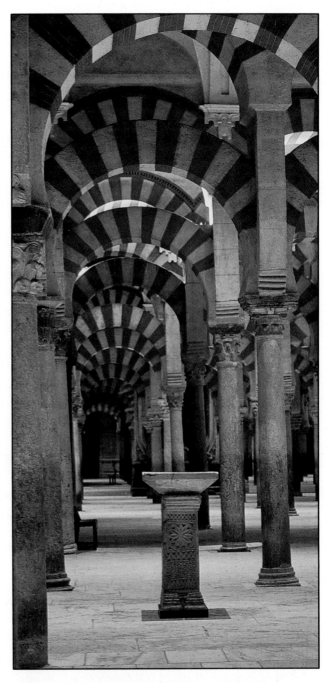

Mosque of Cordoba Ordered by Abd al-Rahman (r. 756–768), founder of the independent Umayyad dynasty in Spain, the mosque at the market city and river port of Cordoba is located on the site of a Roman temple and Visigothic church. The vaulting is supported by twelve aisles of columns rhythmically repeated in every direction. Some architectural historians consider this mosque the most spectacular Islamic building in the world. (*Source: MAS, Barcelona*)

Public Library at Hulwan near Baghdad In this scene from everyday life, the teacher, second from left with open book, instructs students by commenting on the text. Library books rest on the shelves in the background. *(Source: Bibliothèque Nationale, Paris)*

lim world facilitated this development. In spite of schism, warfare, and dynastic conflicts, several factors promoted Islamic unity: the sacred Arabic language of the Qur'an, the obligatory pilgrimage to Mecca, and dedication to scholarship and learning that combined Semitic, Hellenic, and Persian knowledge. "A scholar might publish in Samarkand the definitive work on arithmetic used in the religious schools of Cairo. Or, in a dialogue with colleagues in Baghdad and Hamadan, he could claim to have recovered the unalloyed teachings of Aristotle in the libraries of Fez and Cordoba."[32] Modern scholars consider Muslim creativity and vitality from about 900 to 1200 one of the most brilliant periods in the world's history.

Translations from Greek, Syrian, and Persian sources enabled Muslim scholars to absorb the major features of Semitic, Hellenic, Indian, and Persian civilizations. The Persian scholar al-Khwarizmi (d. ca 850) harmonized Greek and Indian findings to produce astronomical tables that formed the basis for later Eastern and Western research. Al-Khwarizmi also studied mathematics, and his textbook on algebra (from the Arabic *al-Jabr*) was the first work in which the word *algebra* is used to mean the "transposing of negative terms in an equation to the opposite side."

Muslim medical knowledge far surpassed that of the West. By the ninth century, Arab physicians had translated most of the treatises of Hippocrates. The Baghdad physician al-Razi (865–925) produced an encyclopedic treatise on medicine that was translated into Latin and circulated widely in the West. Al-Razi was the first physician to make the clinical distinction between measles and smallpox. The prevalence of eye diseases in the Muslim world encouraged medical people to study the eye. One result was the earliest book on ophthalmology. The great surgeon of Cordoba, al-Zahrawi (d. 1013), produced an important work in which he discussed the cauterization of wounds (searing with a branding iron) and the crushing of stones in the bladder. In Ibn Sina of Bukhara (980–1037), known in the West as "Avicenna," a physician, philologist, philosopher, poet, and scientist, Muslim science reached its peak. His *al-Qanun* codified all Greco-Arabic medical thought, described the contagious nature of tuberculosis and the spreading of diseases, and listed 760 pharmaceutical drugs. Muslim scholars also wrote works on geography and jurisprudence.

Likewise, in philosophy the Muslims made significant contributions. The Arabs understood philosophy not as a separate and distinct discipline but as a branch of theology related, like theology, to the study of the Qur'an. The Abbasid caliph al-Ma'mun (r. 813–833) established at Baghdad in 830 the House of Wisdom, a center for research and translation. Under the direction of Humayn ibn-Ishaq (d. 873), the House of Wisdom made a systematic effort to acquire and translate the chief works of ancient Greek philosophy and science. Humayn supervised the translation of almost all of Aristotle's works and the complete medical writings of Hippocrates. At the same research center al-Kindi (d. ca 870) was the first Muslim thinker to try to harmonize Greek philosophy and the religious precepts of the Qur'an. Al-Kindi sought to

Man Bitten by a Mad Dog   Alert to the dangers of diseases transmitted by animals, such as rabies, the author of this text discusses pharmaceutical remedies. Medical manuscripts were greatly valued. *(Source: Courtesy of the Freer Gallery of Art, Smithsonian Institution)*

integrate Islamic concepts of human beings and their relations to God and the universe with the principles of ethical and social conduct discussed by Plato and Aristotle. Inspired by Plato's *Republic* and Aristotle's *Politics,* the distinguished philosopher al-Farabi (d. 950) wrote a political treatise describing an ideal city whose ruler is morally and intellectually perfect and who has as his goal the citizens' complete happiness. Avicenna maintained that the truths found by human reason cannot conflict with the truths of revelation as given in the Qur'an.

Ibn Rushid, or Averroës (1126–1198), of Cordoba was perhaps Islam's greatest Aristotelian philosopher. A judge in Seville and later royal court physician, Averroës paraphrased and commented on the works of Aristotle. He insisted on the right to subject all knowledge, except the dogmas of faith, to the test of reason.

The profound significance of these Muslim philosophers lies in the fact that through Latin translations of their Arabic and Hebrew writings, Greek philosophy was transmitted to the European West (see page 428). The leading philosophical system of medieval Europe, Scholasticism (see page 428), leaned heavily on Aristotelian thought. Europeans gained their knowledge of Aristotle primarily from Muslim translators and commentators.

The Muslim View of the West

Europeans and Muslims of the Middle East were geographical neighbors. The two peoples shared a common cultural heritage from the Judeo-Christian past. But a thick psychological iron curtain restricted contact between them. The Muslim assault on Christian Europe in the eighth and ninth centuries—with villages burned, monasteries sacked, and Christians sold into slavery (see page 352)—left a legacy of bitter hostility. Europeans' fierce intolerance also helped form the barrier between the two peoples. Christians felt threatened by a faith that acknowledged God as creator of the universe but denied the doctrine of the Trinity; that accepted Christ as a prophet but denied his divinity; that believed in the Last Judgment but seemed to make sex heaven's greatest reward. Popes preached against the Muslims; theologians penned tracts against them; and church councils condemned them. Europeans' perception

of Islam as a menace helped inspire the Crusades of the eleventh through thirteenth centuries (see pages 362–367). The knightly class believed that it had a sacred obligation to fight the Muslims, as a popular song during the Second Crusade put it:

God has brought before you his suit against the Turks and Saracens [Crusaders' hostile term for Muslims], who have done him great despite [injury]. They have seized his fiefs, where God was first served [that is, the holy places in Palestine] and recognized as Lord.[33]

During the Crusades, Europeans imposed Christianity on any lands they conquered from Islam, and they compelled Muslims to choose among conversion, exile, and death.

By the thirteenth century, Western literature portrayed the Muslims as the most dreadful of Europe's enemies, guilty of every kind of crime. In his *Divine Comedy,* the great Florentine poet Dante (see pages 432–433) placed the Muslim philosophers Avicenna and Averroës with other virtuous "heathens," among them Socrates and Aristotle, in the first circle of Hell, where they endured only moderate punishment. Muhammad, however, Dante consigned to the ninth circle, near Satan himself, where Muhammad was condemned as a spreader of discord and scandal. His punishment was to be continually torn apart from his chin to his anus.

Muslims had a strong aversion to travel in Europe. They were quite willing to trade with Europeans, but they rejected European culture. Medieval Europe had no resident Muslim communities where a traveler could find the mosques, food, or other things needed for the Muslim way of life. Muslims generally had a horror of going among those they perceived as infidels, and often when compelled to make diplomatic or business contacts, they preferred to send Jewish or Christian intermediaries, the *dhimmis.* Commercially, from the Muslim perspective, Europe had very little to offer. Apart from fine English woolens, which the Muslims admired, there was only a trickle of slaves from central and southeastern Europe.

Did Western culture have any impact on Islam? Muslims considered Christianity to be a flawed religion superseded by Islam. "For the Muslim, Christ was a precursor, for the Christian Muhammad was an impostor. For the Muslim, Christianity was an early, incomplete, and obsolete form of the true religion."[34] Religion dominated the Islamic perception of Europe. Muslims understood Europe not as Western, European, or white, but as Christian. And the fact that European culture was Christian immediately discredited it in Muslim eyes. Christians were presumed to be hostile to Islam and were thought to be culturally inferior. Thus Muslims had no interest in them.

An enormous quantity of Muslim historical writing survives from the period between about 800 and 1600. Although the material reflects some knowledge of European geography, it shows an almost total lack of interest among Muslim scholars in European languages, life, and culture. Before the nineteenth century, not a single grammar book or dictionary of any Western language existed in the Muslim world. By contrast, Western scholarship on the Middle East steadily advanced. By the early seventeenth century, a curious European student could find an extensive literature on the history, religion, and culture of the Muslim peoples. In 1633, a professorship in Arabic studies was founded at Cambridge University in England.)[35]

As in language and literature, so in science, engineering, and medicine: the medieval West had no influence on the Muslim world. Muslims had only contempt for Western science. Here is a twelfth-century account of a Muslim's impression of European medical practice:

The Lord of Munaytira (a Crusading Baron) wrote to my uncle asking him to send a physician to treat one of his companions who was sick. He sent him a . . . physician called Thabit. He had hardly been away for ten days, when he returned, and we said to him: "How quickly you have healed the sick!" and he replied, "They brought me two patients, a knight with an abscess on his leg, and a woman afflicted with a mental disorder. I made the knight a poultice, and the abscess burst and he felt better. I put the woman on a diet and kept her humour moist. Then a Frankish physician came to them and said to them: 'This man knows nothing about how to treat them!' Then he said to the knight: 'Which do you prefer, to live with one leg or to die with two?' and the knight said: 'To live with one.' Then the physician said: 'Bring me a strong knight and an ax,' and they brought them. Meanwhile I stood by. Then he put the sick man's leg on a wooden block and said to the knight: 'Strike his leg with the ax and cut it off with one blow!' Then, while I watched, he

struck one blow, but the leg was not severed; then he struck a second blow, and the marrow of the leg spurted out, and the man died at once.

"The physician then turned to the woman, and said: 'This woman has a devil in her head who has fallen in love with her. Shave her hair off.' So they shaved her head, and she began once again to eat their usual diet, with garlic and mustard and such like. Her disorder got worse, and he said:

" 'The devil has entered her head.' Then he took a razor, incised a cross on her head and pulled off the skin in the middle until the bone of the skull appeared; this he rubbed with salt, and the woman died forthwith.

"Then I said to them: 'Have you any further need of me?' and they said no and so I came home, having learned things about their medical practice which I did not know before." [36]

Only in the art of warfare did Muslims show an interest in European knowledge. During the Crusades, the Muslims adopted Frankish weapons and methods of fortification. Overall, though, medieval Muslims considered Christian Europe a backward land and almost always described Europeans as "ignorant infidels."[37]

SUMMARY

Islam is an extraordinary phenomenon in world history. Its universal monotheistic creed helps to explain its initial attractiveness to Bedouin tribes. Driven by the religious zeal of the *jihad*, Muslims carried their faith from the Arabian peninsula through the Middle East to North Africa, Spain, and southern France in the west and to the borders of China and northern India in the east—within the short span of one hundred years. Economic need, the political weaknesses of their enemies, strong military organization, and the practice of establishing army cities in newly conquered territories account for their expansion.

Two successive dynasties—the Umayyad, centered at Damascus in Syria, and the Abbasid, located at Baghdad in Iraq—governed the Islamic state. A large imperial bureaucracy headed by a vizier supervised the administration of the state. All government agencies evolved from the diwan. As provincial governors acquired independent power, which the caliphs could not check, centralized authority within the Islamic state disintegrated.

Commerce and trade also spread the faith of Muhammad. Although its first adherents were nomads, Islam developed and flourished in a mercantile milieu. By land and sea, Muslim merchants transported a rich variety of goods across Asia, the Middle East, Africa, and western Europe. Muslim business procedures and terminology have greatly influenced the West.

On the basis of the wealth that trade generated, a gracious, sophisticated, and cosmopolitan culture developed with centers at Baghdad and Cordoba. In the tenth and eleventh centuries, the Islamic world witnessed enormous intellectual vitality and creativity. Muslim scholars produced important work in many disciplines, especially mathematics, medicine, and philosophy. Muslim civilization in the Middle Ages was far in advance of that of Christian Europe, and Muslims, with some justification, looked on Europeans as ignorant barbarians.

NOTES

1. See F. McG. Donner, *The Early Islamic Conquests* (Princeton, N.J.: Princeton University Press, 1981), pp. 14–37.
2. J. L. Esposito, *Islam: The Straight Path* (New York: Oxford University Press, 1988), pp. 6–17. The quotation is on p. 15.
3. Donner, pp. 57–60.
4. Quoted in J. O'Faolain and L. Martines, eds., *Not in God's Image: Women in History from the Greeks to the Victorians* (New York: Harper & Row, 1973), pp. 108–115.
5. Quoted in P. K. Hitti, *The Near East in History* (Princeton, N.J.: Van Nostrand, 1961), p. 211.
6. Quoted in B. Lewis, ed. and trans., *Islam: From the Prophet Muhammad to the Capture of Constantinople,* vol. 1, *Politics and War* (New York: Harper & Row, 1974), p. 239.
7. Donner, pp. 92–101.
8. Quoted ibid., p. 217.
9. See B. Lewis, *The Muslim Discovery of Europe* (New York: Norton, 1982), pp. 59–63. Discussion herein is based heavily on this important work by Lewis.
10. See G. E. von Grunebaum, *Medieval Islam: A Study in Cultural Orientation* (Chicago: University of Chicago Press, 1954), pp. 142–150.
11. Quoted in Lewis, *Politics and War,* p. 201.
12. L. I. Conrad, "Caliphate," in *Dictionary of the Middle Ages,* vol. 3, ed. J. R. Strayer (New York: Scribner's, 1983), p. 45.
13. Quoted in R. Levy, *The Social Structure of Islam,* 2d ed. (Cambridge, England: Cambridge University Press, 1957), p. 55.
14. Ibid.
15. Hitti, *Near East in History,* p. 229.
16. B. Lewis, ed. and trans., *Islam: From the Prophet Muhammad to the Capture of Constantinople,* vol. 2, *Religion and Society* (New York: Harper & Row, 1975), pp. 219–221.
17. Quoted in Levy, p. 67.
18. N. Coulson and D. Hinchcliffe, "Women and Law Reform in Contemporary Islam," in *Women in the Muslim World,* ed. L. Beck and N. Keddie (Cambridge, Mass.: Harvard University Press, 1982), p. 37.
19. Quoted in B. F. Stowasser, "The Status of Women in Early Islam," in *Muslim Women,* ed. F. Hussain (New York: St. Martin's Press, 1984), p. 25.
20. Quoted ibid., pp. 25–26.
21. Quoted ibid., p. 26.
22. Quoted ibid., p. 16.
23. G. Nashat, "Women in Pre-Revolutionary Iran: A Historical Overview," in *Women and Revolution in Iran,* ed. G. Nashat (Boulder, Colo.: Westview Press, 1983), pp. 47–48.
24. F. Mernissi, *Beyond the Veil: Male-Female Dynamics in Modern Muslim Society* (New York: Schenkman, 1975), p. 16.
25. Ibid.
26. Quoted in D. J. Gerner, "Roles in Transition: The Evolving Position of Women in Arab Islamic Countries," in Hussain, *Muslim Women,* p. 73.
27. Lewis, *Religion and Society,* pp. 126–127.
28. Adapted from Lewis, *Religion and Society,* pp. 154–157.
29. Hitti, p. 278.
30. M. Rodinson, *Islam and Capitalism,* trans. Brian Pearce (Austin: University of Texas Press, 1981), p. 56.
31. R. Hillenbrand, "Cordoba," in Strayer, *Dictionary of the Middle Ages,* vol. 3, pp. 597–601.
32. P. Brown, "Understanding Islam," *The New York Review of Books,* February 22, 1979, pp. 30–33.
33. Quoted in R. W. Southern, *The Making of the Middle Ages* (New Haven, Conn.: Yale University Press, 1961), p. 55.
34. Lewis, *The Muslim Discovery of Europe,* p. 297.
35. Ibid., pp. 296–297.
36. Quoted ibid., p. 222.
37. Ibid.

SUGGESTED READING

In recent years, the literature on classical Islam has expanded greatly, and many studies are available in English. In addition to the works cited in the Notes, the curious student should see A. Hourani, *A History of the Arab Peoples* (1991), a highly readable and profound synthesis, and S. Fisher and W. Ochsenwald, *The Middle East: A History* (1990), which contains excellent bibliographical sections. The older studies of H. A. R. Gibb, *Mohammedanism: An Historical Survey,* 2d ed. (1970), and J. J. Saunders, *A History of Medieval Islam* (1965), are still useful. For the Prophet, see W. M. Watt, *Muhammad at Mecca* (1953) and *Muhammad at Medina* (1956), and M. Rodinson, *Mohammed* (trans. A. Carter, 1971). M. G. S. Hodgson, *The Classical Age of Islam,* vol. 1 of *The Venture of Islam* (1964), is comprehensive but written for the specialist. K. Cragg and R. M. G. Speight, eds., *Islam from Within: Anthology of a Religion* (1980), offers a fine collection of primary material on the beginnings of Islam. For the cultural impact of Islam, G. E. von Grunebaum, *Classical Islam: A History, 600–1258* (trans. K. Watson, 1970), remains valuable.

For law and religious authority within Islam, see N. J. Coulson, *A History of Islamic Law* (1964); J. N. D. Anderson, *Islamic Law in the Modern World* (1959); R. P. Mottahedeh, *Loyalty and Leadership in an Early Islamic Society* (1986); C. Cahen, "The Body Politic," in G. E. von Grunebaum, ed., *Unity and Variety in Muslim Civilization* (1955); A. K. S. Lambton, *State and Government in Medieval Islam (1981);* and S. D. Gottein, *Studies in Islamic History and Institutions* (1966). The best recent study of Muslim expansion is F. M. Donner, *The Early Islamic Conquests* (1986).

A. M. Watson, *Agricultural Innovation in the Early Islamic World* (1983) provides the best study of farming techniques and the diffusion of crops before 1100, while A. L. Udovitch, *Partnership and Profit in Medieval Islam* (1970) treats commercial practices in light of Islamic law and should be compared with the title by Rodinson cited in the Notes. For slavery in the Arab world, see B. Lewis, *Race and Slavery in the Middle East* (1990), which demythologizes the Western view of the Middle East as free of racial prejudice, and G. Murray, *Slavery in the Arab World* (1989), which explains the persistence of slavery in Muslim societies in sexual, not economic, terms.

W. M. Watt, *Islam and the Integration of Society* (1961), is an important sociological study of the economic and social factors that led to the unity of very diverse peoples. A. Talbot Rice, *Islamic Art,* rev. ed. (1985), provides a solid and well-illustrated introduction to the many media of Islamic art. O. Grabar, *The Formation of Islamic Art* (1973), offers a critical analysis of the themes in the development of Islamic art. R. E. Dunn, *The Adventures of Ibn Battuta: A Muslim Traveler of the Fourteenth Century* (1987), contains a fascinating account of Asian and African societies by a Muslim world traveler.

On the Mongols, see D. Morgan, *The Mongols* (1986), a highly readable sketch, and M. Rossabi, *Khubilai Khan: His Life and Times* (1988), which combines biography with a fine appreciation of Eurasian history in the thirteenth century.

11

Tradition and Change in Asia, ca 320–1400

Portrait of the poet Kodai-no-Kimi, or Koogimi

etween approximately 320 and 1400 the various societies of Asia continued to evolve their own distinct social, political, and religious institutions. These years saw momentous changes sweep across Asia. The tide of change surged back and forth between East and West. In the first half of the period Arab conquerors and their new Muslim faith reached the Indian subcontinent and Afghanistan. In central Asia they met the Turks moving westward from the borders of China. The result of this contact was widespread conversion of the Turks to Islam. Muslim Turks then spread their new religion to northern India, which they conquered. Others continued westward, settling in Anatolia and sinking the ethnic and cultural roots of modern Turkey. Meanwhile, Japan emerged into the light of history. Although affected by Chinese culture, philosophy, and religion, the Japanese adapted these influences to their way of life.

In the second half of the period the Mongols swept from their homeland north of China. They conquered China and unsuccessfully hurled two vast fleets at Japan. Toward the end of the period, the travels of the Venetian merchant Marco Polo to Peking gave promise of a new era of East-West contact.

This chapter explores three main questions:

- What effect did these great movements of peoples have on the traditional societies of Asia?

- How were new religious and cultural ideas received by the long-established cultures of the East?

- What political and economic effects did these events have on newcomer and native alike?

INDIA, FROM TRIUMPH TO INVASION (CA 320–1400)

Under the Gupta kings, India enjoyed one of the most magnificent cultural flowerings in its long history. By about 800 the caste system had fully evolved, dividing Indian society into thousands of self-contained subcastes. The incursion of the Muslim Turks—the second permanent foreign influence on India—introduced a new religion that also accelerated the decline of Buddhism in India.

The Gupta Empire (ca 320–480)

For years after the fall of Mauryan power, India suffered fragmentation and foreign domination, but even political turmoil did not interrupt the evolution of Indian culture. Not until about 320 did another line of Indian kings, the Guptas, extend their authority over much of the subcontinent. Founded by Chandragupta—unrelated to the founder of the Mauryan Empire by the same name—the Guptas' original home was in the area of modern Bihar in the Ganges Valley. The Guptas consciously modeled their rule after that of the Mauryan Empire. Although the Guptas failed to restore Ashoka's empire, they united northern India and received tribute from states in Nepal and the Indus Valley. They also gave large parts of India a period of peace and political unity.

The real creator of the Gupta Empire was Chandragupta's son Samudragupta (ca 335–375), who defeated many of the rulers of southern India and then restored them to their thrones as his subjects. With frontier states he made alliances, and over them he extended his protection. By means of military conquest and political shrewdness, Samudragupta brought much of India from the Himalayas in the north to the Vindhya Mountains in the south under his government (Map 11.1).

Once firmly in power, Samudragupta preferred leniency and diplomacy to force of arms. Like Ashoka, he adhered to the ideal of a just king who ruled according to *dharma* (the moral law). Following Ashoka's example (see page 81), he proclaimed the glories of his reign on rocks and pillars throughout the land. In one of his most important pronouncements, inscribed on a stone pillar erected by Ashoka some six hundred years earlier, Samudragupta extolled his own fame, power, and personal qualities:

His far-reaching fame, deep-rooted in peace, emanated from the restoration of the sovereignty of many fallen royal families. . . . He, who had no equal in power in the world, eclipsed the fame of the other kings by the radiance of his versatile virtues, adorned by innumerable good actions. He, who was enigmatic, was the real force that generated good and destroyed the evil. Having a compassionate heart, he could easily be won over by faithfulness, loyalty, and homage.[1]

Samudragupta had reason to boast of his accomplishments. By putting an end to weakness and

Gupta Empire
States tributary to the Guptas
Kushan Empire

Ghur Ghazni

PUNJAB

HIMALAYA MTS.

Delhi

Indus

MAKRAN

Ganges

BIHAR

BENGAL

VINDHYA MTS.

SIND

0   300   600 Km.
0   300   600 Mi.

Ghazni

PUNJAB

HIMALAYA MTS.

Indus

MAKRAN

Delhi

Ganges

BIHAR

BENGAL

VINDHYA MTS.

SIND

0   300 Km.
0   300 Mi.

The Sultanate of Delhi (ca 1294)

INDIAN OCEAN

MAP 11.1 Political Map of India, ca 400–ca 1294   This map and inset show the political face of India from the time of the imperial Guptas to the arrival of Muslim invaders. They also demonstrate the importance of the Indus and Ganges river valleys, perhaps the most coveted area in India.

fragmentation, he laid the foundations of India's golden age.

Samudragupta's many achievements were matched by those of his son Chandragupta II (ca 375–415), under whom the glory of the Guptas reached its height. Perhaps Chandragupta's most significant exploit was the overthrow of the Shakas (invaders from the borders of China) in western India. As a result of that victory, the busy maritime trade conducted by the rich seaports of western India with the Middle East and China came under the protection of the Guptas. Chandragupta II put the Indian people into direct touch with the wider world once again, and as in the past this contact involved ideas as well as goods.

The great crisis of the Gupta Empire was the invasion of the Huns, the nomads whose migration

from central Asia shook the known world. By at least 450 a group of them known as the "White Huns" thundered into India. Mustering his full might, the ruler Skandagupta (ca 455–467) threw back the invaders; only a few Huns settled in northern India, where they were in time absorbed by the native population. Although the Huns failed to uproot the Gupta Empire, they dealt the dynasty a fatal blow. By 500 the glory of the Gupta kings was past. Later kings, like the great Harsha (ca 606–647), made valiant efforts to reunite the Gupta Empire, but the country once again reverted to a pattern of local kingdoms in constant conflict.

Even though they failed to unite India permanently, the Guptas set the stage for one of the most splendid epochs in Indian cultural history. Interest

The Mriga Jataka The Buddhist caves at Ajanta contain the most important surviving collection of wall paintings from the Gupta period. Religious in inspiration, they are also spontaneous and unrestrained, as this detail of a royal servant holding an energetic dog on a leash reflects. *(Source: Satish Pavashav/Dinodia Picture Agency)*

in Sanskrit literature, the literature of the Aryans, was a prominent feature. Sanskrit was also the spoken language of India, one that was written in its own script. Sanskrit masterpieces were preserved, and traditional epic poems and verses on mythological themes were reworked and polished to a higher sheen. The Gupta period also saw the rise of Indian drama. India's greatest poet, Kalidasa (ca 380–450), like Shakespeare, melded poetry and drama. Poets composed epics for the courts of the Gupta kings, and other writers experimented with prose romances and popular tales.

In science, too, the Gupta period could boast of impressive intellectual achievements. Science never appealed to the Indians as much as religion, but Indian mathematicians arrived at the concept of zero, which is necessary for higher mathematics. Other scientific thinkers wrestled with the concept of gravitation long before the day of Sir Isaac Newton.

The greatness of the Guptas is neither limited to their political achievements nor diminished by their ultimate failure. They saved India for a period from political fragmentation, foreign domination, and confusion. The peace they established released cultural and intellectual energies that shaped one of the sunniest epochs in India's long history.

Daily Life in India

The first reliable and abundant information about the daily life of the Indian people dates from the period of the Gupta Empire. One of the most instructive and, to modern minds, amazing characteristics of Indian society is its remarkable stability and veneration for its age-old customs and traditions. Since Indian society changed slowly and gradually, it is possible to take a good long look at daily life and social customs in the millennium between the fourth and the fourteenth centuries.

Although Indian agriculture ranged from subsistence farming to the working of huge estates, agricultural life ordinarily meant village life. The average farmer worked a small plot of land outside the village, aided by the efforts of the extended family. All the family members pooled their resources—human, animal, and material—under the direction of the head of the family. Shared work, shared sacrifice, and joint confrontation of hazards strengthened family ties. The Indian farming family usually lived close to the bone: bad weather and heavy taxes frequently condemned its members to a lean year of poverty and hardship.

To all Indian farmers, rich and poor, water supply was crucial. India's great scourge is its merciless droughts, which cause plants to wither, the earth to crack, and famine to stalk the countryside. Indian farmers quickly learned to drill deep into the ground to tap permanent sources of water. They also irrigated their fields by diverting rivers and digging reservoirs and canals. As in Hammurabi's Mesopotamia, maintenance of waterworks demanded constant effort, and disputes over water rights often led to local quarrels.

The agricultural year began with spring plowing. The ancient plow, drawn by two oxen wearing yokes and collars, had an iron-tipped share and a handle with which the farmer guided it. Similar plows are still used in parts of India. Once plowed and sown, the land yielded a rich variety of crops. Rice, the most important and popular grain, was sown at the beginning of the long rainy season. Beans, lentils, and peas were the farmer's friends, since they grew during the cold season and were harvested in the spring when fresh food was scarce. Cereal crops like wheat, barley, and millet provided carbohydrates and other nutrients, and large estates grew sugar cane. Some families cultivated vegetables, spices, and flowers in their gardens. Village orchards kept people supplied with fruit, and the inhabitants of well-situated villages could eat their fill of fresh and dried fruit and sell the surplus at a nearby town.

Indian farmers raised and bred livestock, the most highly valued of which were cattle. Cattle were used for plowing and esteemed for their milk. Their hides and horns were precious raw materials, as were the fleeces of sheep. All the animals of the community were in the hands of the village cowherd or shepherd, who led them to and from pasture and protected them from wild animals and thieves.

Farmers fortunate enough to raise surpluses found ready markets in towns and cities. There they came into contact with merchants and traders, some of whom dealt in local commodities and others in East-West trade. Like their Muslim counterparts, Indian merchants enjoyed a respectable place in society. Given India's central geographical position between China and the West, there were huge profits to be made in foreign commerce. Daring Indian sailors founded new trading centers along the coasts of Southeast Asia, and in the process spread Indian culture. Other Indian merchants specialized in the caravan trade that continued to link China, Iran, India, and the West. These hardy merchants conducted cargoes from Indian seaports northward to the overland routes across central Asia.

Local craftsmen and tradesmen lived and worked in specific parts of the town or village. Their shops were open to the street; the family lived on the floor above. The busiest tradesmen dealt in milk and cheese, oil, spices, and perfumes. Equally prominent but disreputable were tavern-keepers. Indian taverns were haunts of criminals and con artists, and in the worst of them fighting was as common as drinking. In addition to these tradesmen and merchants a host of peddlers shuffled through towns and villages selling everything from bath salts to fresh-cut flowers.

Although leatherworkers were economically important, their calling was considered beneath the dignity of anyone but *outcastes* (those without places in the traditional social structure). Indian religious and social customs condemned those who made a living handling the skins of dead animals. Masons, carpenters, and brickmakers were more highly respected. As in all agricultural societies, blacksmiths were essential. Pottery was used in all households, but Indian potters, unlike their counterparts in the ancient Near East and the Greco-Roman world, neither baked their wares in kilns nor decorated them. Indian potters restricted themselves to the functional. The economic life of the village, then, consisted of a harmonious balance of agriculture and small business.

What of the village itself—its people and its daily sights? Encircled by walls, the typical village was divided into quarters by two main streets that intersected at the center of the village. The streets were unpaved, and the rainy season turned them into a muddy soup. Cattle and sheep roamed as freely as people. The villagers shared their simple houses with such household pets as cats, parrots, and geese. Half-wild mongooses served as effective protection against snakes. The pond outside the village, which served as its main source of water, also bred fish, birds, and mosquitoes. Women drawing water frequently encountered water buffaloes wallowing in the shallows. After the farmers returned from the fields in the evening, the village gates were closed until morning.

Towns and cities were also typically laid out in a square or rectangular pattern, always situated near a lake or river. They, too, were fortified by walls and towers and entered through gates. A city was usually surrounded by a moat, into which the gutters flowed; the moat often served as a source of drinking water. The streets of cities and towns were paved and flanked by gutters. Every sizable city or town had a marketplace where villagers could sell their surplus to townspeople and peddlers hawked their wares. Nearby were temples, houses, and the usual shops and craftsmen's stalls. Part of every major city was devoted to parks, fountains, and gardens. The populations of particularly prosperous cities often spilled over outside the walls into crowded and squalid slums. Here worked some of the most despised elements of the population: butchers, public executioners, and undertakers. Sometimes the slums evolved into cities that ringed the original city.

The period following the fall of the Guptas saw the slow proliferation and hardening of the caste system. Early Indian society was divided into four major groups: priests (Brahmans), warriors (Kshatriyas), peasants (Vaishyas) and serfs (Shudras) (see page 70). Further subdivisions arose, reflecting differences in trade or profession, tribal or racial affiliation, religious belief, and place of residence. By about 800 these distinctions had solidified into an approximation of the caste system as it is known today. Eventually Indian society comprised perhaps as many as three thousand castes. A caste sustained its members, giving them a sense of belonging and helping to define their relations to members of other castes. Yet the caste system further fragmented society. Each caste had its own governing body, which enforced the rules of the caste. Those incapable of living up to the rules were expelled, becoming outcastes. These unfortunates lived hard lives, performing tasks that others considered unclean or lowly.

For all members of Indian society, regardless of caste, marriage and the family were the focus of life. Once again, far more is known about the upper levels of society than about the lower. As in earlier eras, the Indian family of this period was an extended family: grandparents, uncles and aunts, cousins, and nieces and nephews lived together in the same house or compound. The joint family was under the authority of the eldest male, who might take several wives. The family affirmed its

Indian Monastic Life   Some of the most important duties in a monastery were purely ritualistic. Students often had the duty to keep the sacred fire burning. Some students chopped wood and others carried the logs, which still others placed on the fire. Each played a part in the symbolic ritual. *(Source: Musée Guimet, Cliché des Musées Nationaux)*

solidarity by the religious ritual of honoring its dead ancestors, which linked the living and the dead.

Special attention was devoted to the raising of sons, but all children were pampered. The great poet Kalidasa depicts children as the greatest joy of their father's life:

With their teeth half-shown in causeless laughter,
and their efforts at talking so sweetly uncertain,
when children ask to sit on his lap
a man is blessed, even by the dirt on their bodies.[2]

In poor households children worked as soon as they were able. In wealthier homes children faced the age-old irritations of reading, writing, and arithmetic. Less attention was paid to daughters, though in the most prosperous families they were usually literate.

The three upper castes welcomed boys fully into the life of the caste and society with a religious initiation symbolizing a second birth. Ideally, a boy then entered into a period of asceticism and religious training during which he mastered at least part of one Veda. Such education was at the hands of *gurus*, Brahman teachers with whom the boys boarded. In reality, relatively few went through this expensive education.

Having completed their education, young men were ready to lead adult lives, the first and foremost step in which was marriage. Child-marriage, unknown in earlier periods, later became customary. Indians considered child-marriage desirable, in part because of their attitudes toward women. Girls were thought to be unusually fascinated by sex. Lawgivers feared that young girls left to their own whims would take lovers as soon as they reached puberty and become pregnant before they were married. Girls who had lost their virginity could seldom hope to find good husbands; most became financial burdens and social disgraces to their families. Indian law even warned fathers that they sinned grievously unless they betrothed a daughter before her first menstrual period. Indian custom also held that in the best marriages the husband was at least three times as old as his wife. Daughters were customarily betrothed before they reached puberty, often to men whom they had never seen. The wedding and consummation of the marriage did not take place, however, until after a girl had reached puberty and could start a family.

After an elaborate wedding ceremony, a newly married couple set up quarters in the house or compound of the bridegroom's father. In contrast to ancient Jewish practice, newlyweds were not expected to consummate their marriage on the first night. Indian custom delicately acknowledged that two strangers, though married, might need some time to adjust to their new mode of life. Hindu ritual advised couples to forgo sex for the first three nights so that they could become acquainted.

An Indian wife had two main duties: to manage the house and to produce children, preferably sons. Her husband was her master, to whom she owed obedience; Indian women spent their entire lives, from childhood to old age, under the authority of men. Indian law was blunt:

A woman is not independent, the males are her masters. . . . Their fathers protect them in childhood, their husbands protect them in youth, and their sons protect them in age; a woman is never fit for independence.[3]

Denied a significant role in life outside the home, wives made the household their domain. All domestic affairs were under their control. As a rule, women rarely left the house, and then only with a chaperone. They did accompany their husbands to weddings, great festivals, and quiet outings with the family. Among one stratum of high-caste Hindus, the Kshatriyas, wives' bonds with their husbands were so strong that a widow was expected to perform the act of *sati*, throwing herself on his fu-

neral pyre. In medieval periods it was strongly felt that a true and faithful wife—a *sati,* for whom the practice of self-immolation was named—should have no life apart from her husband, yet there is reason to think that this custom did not become common practice.

Within the home, the position of a wife often depended chiefly on her own intelligence and strength of character. In the best of cases a wife was considered a part of her husband, his friend and comforter as well as his wife. Wives were traditionally supposed to be humble, cheerful, and diligent even toward worthless husbands. In reality, some women took matters into their own hands. Far from being docile, they ruled the roost. An Indian verse paints a vivid picture of what a henpecked husband could expect:

But when she has him in her clutches
*   it's all housework and errands!*
"Fetch a knife to cut this gourd!"
*   "Get me some fresh fruit!"*

"We want wood to boil the greens,
*   and for a fire in the evening!"*
"Now paint my feet!"
*   "Come and massage my back!"*

So . . . resist the wiles of women,
*   avoid their friendship and company*
The little pleasure you get from them
*   will only lead you into trouble!*[4]

Most women, however, were frankly and unashamedly subservient to their husbands. Nevertheless, despite the severe limitations of her society, the typical wife lived her days honored, cherished, and loved by her husband and family.

The most eagerly desired event was the birth of children. Marriage had no other purpose. Before consummating their marriage, the newlyweds repeated traditional prayers for the wife immediately to become pregnant. While pregnant, the wife was treated like a queen, nearly suffocated with affection and attention, and rigorously circumscribed by religious ritual. Members of the family carefully watched her diet and exercise, and women of her caste prayed that she would bear sons. Labor and birth were occasions of religious ceremony. While the women of the household prepared for the birth, the husband performed rituals intended to guarantee an easy delivery and a healthy child. After the child's birth, the parents performed rituals intended to bring the baby happiness, prosperity, and desirable intellectual, physical, and moral qualities. Infants were pampered until they reached the age of schooling and preparation for the adult world.

India and Southeast Asia

Between about 650 and 1250, Indian merchants and missionaries disseminated Indian culture throughout Southeast Asia, the area stretching eastward roughly from Burma to Vietnam and southward to Malaysia and Indonesia. The earlier history of the area is the product of archeological studies. So far the evidence has allowed scholars to trace the movements of numerous peoples without being able to tell very much about them. It is known that Indian penetration of Southeast Asia changed things considerably, and Sanskrit gave peoples a common mode of written expression.

The impact of the Indians was so pervasive that historians often refer to this phenomenon as the "Indianization of Southeast Asia." The phrase, though useful, must not be applied too sweepingly. The demands of trade frequently led to small Indian settlements, generally located on the coast, stretching from modern Thailand in the west to the Mekong Delta of modern Vietnam (Map 11.2). In these trading posts Indians met natives, and the result was often intermarriage and the creation of a culture fertilized by both. The greatest influence of India on Southeast Asian societies came in the courts of local rulers, who often adopted Indian customs and values, embraced Hinduism and Buddhism, and learned Sanskrit.

Although there is no denying Indian influence on Southeast Asia, its strength should not be exaggerated. Indian culture never supplanted the various native cultures that it encountered. Outside the courts of the rulers, native societies maintained their own cultural identity, even when they assimilated various Indian customs. Perhaps two

MAP 11.2 The States of Southeast Asia This map illustrates the greatest extent of several major Southeast Asian states between ca 650 and ca 1250. The boundaries are somewhat approximate, for states gained and lost territory several times during this long period.

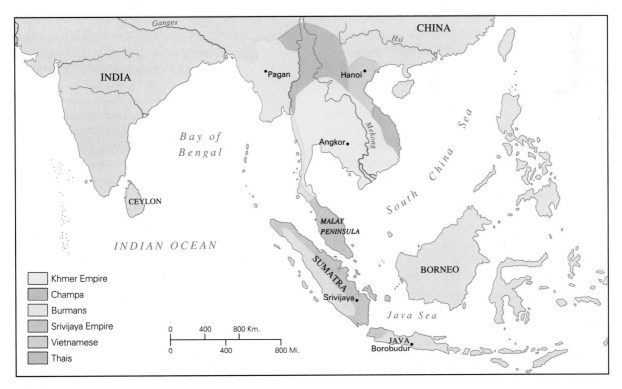

examples can illustrate the process. Among other things, Indian merchants brought to Java their literary epics. There they introduced the *Ramayana,* an epic poem describing the deeds of the Vedic heroes. The tale appealed to the Javanese, who retained the essentials of the Indian narrative but added to it native Javanese legends, thus creating a work that did not belong solely to either culture. So, too, with religion. Early peoples in the region of Cambodia (modern Kampuchea) adapted Buddhism to their own customs and beliefs, as did the peoples of ancient Tibet. They both became Buddhist societies, but their forms of Buddhism varied markedly because each people applied its native values and attitudes to the imported religion. In both cases local tradition changed Buddhism in its own likeness.

When the Indians entered Southeast Asia, they encountered both indigenous peoples and newcomers moving southward from the frontiers of China. Their relations with these peoples varied greatly. Contact with the vigorous tribes moving into the southern areas of the mainland was generally peaceful. But with the native states in the Malay Peninsula and the islands of the Indian Ocean, commercial rivalry sometimes led to active warfare. Although many of the events of these years are imperfectly known, a fairly clear picture has emerged of the Indianization of the Vietnamese, Thais, Burmans, Kampucheans, and the native peoples of the islands (see Map 11.2).

On the mainland three major groups of newcomers pushed southward toward the Indian Ocean from the southern borders of China. Their movements entailed prolonged fighting as each people strove to win a homeland. As in other such extensive migrations, the newcomers fought one another as often as they fought the native populations. The Vietnamese established themselves on the eastern coast of the mainland. In 939 they became independent of China and extended their power southward along the coast of present-day Vietnam. Of all these peoples, the Vietnamese were the least influenced by Indian culture. The Thais lived to the west in what is today southwestern China and northern Burma. In the eighth century the Thai tribes united in a confederacy and even expanded northward against T'ang China; like China, however, the Thai confederacy fell to the Mongols in 1253. Still farther west another tribal people, the Burmans, migrated in the eighth century to the area of modern Burma. They too

established a state, which they ruled from their capital, Pagan, and came into contact with India and Ceylon.

The most important mainland state was the Khmer Empire of Kampuchea, which controlled the heart of the region. The Khmers were indigenous to the area, and around 400 they had created an independent state. Their empire, founded in 802, eventually extended its southern borders to the sea and the northeastern Malay Peninsula. Generally successful in a long series of wars with the Vietnamese, Khmer power reached its peak, then declined after 1219.

Far different from these land-based states was the maritime empire of Srivijaya, which originated as a city-state on the island of Sumatra. Like the Khmers, the people of Srivijaya were indigenous. Their wealth was based on seaborne trade and tolls on ships passing through their waters. To protect their commercial interests, they created a navy strong enough to rule the waters around Sumatra, Java, and Borneo. At its height the Srivijaya Empire controlled the eastern coast of Sumatra, the southern half of the Malay Peninsula, and the western tip of Java. Though long predominant in the area, Srivijaya suffered a stunning blow in 1025: a commercial rival in southern India launched a large naval raid that succeeded in capturing the king and capital of the empire. Unable to hold their gains, the Indians retreated, but the Srivijaya Empire never recovered its former vigor. By the mid-thirteenth century it was further weakened by the arrival of Chinese traders and eventually fell to local rivals.

Although the political histories of all these peoples varied, their responses to Indian culture were similar. The coastal states, influenced by the presence of trading stations, were the first to adopt and adapt Indian ways. The very concept of kingship came from India. Local rulers and their elites, like good Indian kings, began to observe dharma and to govern their peoples by its precepts. Sanskrit, both the Indian language and the script in which it was written, surmounted the barriers raised by the many different native languages of the region. Indian mythology took hold, as did Indian architecture and sculpture. Some of the world's greatest edifices were erected in central Java and Kampuchea, inspired by Indian building principles, techniques, and cultural ideals. Kings and their courts, the first to embrace Indian culture, consciously spread it to their subjects.

Angkor Wat The great artistic achievement of the Khmers was the planning and building of Angkor Wat, an enormous and lavishly decorated temple. The temple also reflects Indian influence, for the god chiefly honored here is Vishnu. *(Source: Jean-Claude Labbé/Gamma-Liaison)*

Indian religion was also instrumental in this process. Certain aspects of Hinduism proved popular, but Buddhism took Southeast Asia by storm. Buddhism emphasized the value of popular education, and its temples, monasteries, and missionaries helped bring education to the common people. Especially influential was the Buddhist concept of the *bodhisattva,* a buddha-in-becoming (see page 78). Inspired by this ideal, many kings and local rulers strove to give their subjects good and humane government. Buddhist missionaries from India played a prominent role in these developments. Local converts continued the process by making pilgrimages to India and Ceylon to worship and to observe Indian life for themselves.

By the twelfth century, Indian culture, secular and religious, had found a permanent new home in Southeast Asia. A major consequence was that the Indianization of Southeast Asia was for the most part peaceful in that unlike western newcomers in modern times no truly forced colonization seems to have occurred. Chinese influence flourished more strongly among the Vietnamese, and Islam would later rival Buddhism; but Indian culture persisted, especially in the southern part of the region. Seldom has the world seen such a protracted and pervasive cultural diffusion. It stands as a monument to the vitality and magnetism of Indian civilization.

India Under Siege

Between roughly 650 and 1400 India experienced turmoil and invasion, as wave after wave of foreign armies moved into the subcontinent. Arabs, Turks, and Mongols all swept into India. Particularly during the six centuries from 636 to 1296, invaders beat against India and its neighbors. This complex and imperfectly understood phenomenon had four distinct phases. The Muslim Arabs' attack on the Sind area (636–713) was followed by the battle for Afghanistan (643–870). Muslims next pushed into the Punjab (870–1030) and finally conquered the valley of the Ganges (1175–1206). Between onslaughts, conflict persisted between newcomer and native.

Arabs under the leadership of Muhammad ibn-Qasim reached the western coast of modern Pakistan in 636 and pushed on into the Sind and the Indus Valley (see Map 11.1). But the Islamic conquest of northern India came at the hands of Turkish converts to Islam, not these first Arab invaders. While huge numbers of Turks advanced on the Byzantine Empire and won control of Asia Minor, others also remained in the East. One group established a small kingdom in northeastern Iran and Afghanistan, with its capital at Ghazni. In 986 Sabuktigin, a Turkish chieftain and devout Muslim, launched his initial raid into the Punjab. Once again, India suffered its age-old fate: invasion by a strong and confident power through the northwestern corridor. Sabuktigin's son Mahmud stepped up the frequency and intensity of the raids until he had won the Punjab. Then, like other invaders before him, he began pushing toward the Ganges. Mahmud systematically looted secular palaces and Hindu shrines, and he destroyed Indian statues as infidel idols. Even the Arab conquerors of the Sind fell to him. The Indus Valley, the Punjab, and the rest of northwestern India were in the grip of the invader.

Mahmud's death gave India roughly a century and a half of fitful peace marred by local conflicts. Then a new line of Turkish rulers that had arisen in Afghanistan, with its capital at Ghur (see Map 11.1), southwest of modern Kabul, renewed Muslim attacks on India. Muhammad of Ghur planned to annex the land he attacked, rather than merely plunder it. After conquering Mahmud's Indian holdings, he struck eastward toward the Ganges in 1192. Muhammad's generals captured Delhi and by the end of the twelfth century had extended their control nearly throughout northern India. Like Mahmud, Muhammad and his generals considered Hindu and Buddhist religious statues nothing more than idols; Muslim troops destroyed them in vast numbers. Buddhist centers of worship and learning suffered grievously. The great Buddhist university at Nalanda in Bihar was destroyed by a Turkish raiding party in 1193. Most Buddhists took refuge from this dual military and religious assault in Tibet and places farther east. Buddhism, which had thrived so long in peaceful and friendly competition with Hinduism, was pushed out of its native soil by the invaders.

When Muhammad fell to an assassin in 1206, one of his generals, the former slave Qutb-ud-din, seized the reins of power and made his capital at Delhi. Qutb-ud-din established the sultanate of Delhi, a Muslim kingdom that ruled northern India from the Indus to Bengal from 1206 to 1526 (see inset, Map 11.1). As early as 1327 the Muslim sultans of Delhi had brought a large portion of India under their control. The Muslims, like the Aryans centuries before them (see pages 68–73), were a conquering minority. To prevent assimilation by the far more numerous Indians, they recruited Turks and Iranians from outside India; they also provided a haven for elite Muslim refugees fleeing the widespread Mongol devastation of Iran and

Arab Invasion Arab cavalry, mounted on camels, stormed into India. The camels allowed the Arabs, who were armed with lances and swords, to strike quickly over great distances. (*Source: Edinburgh University Library*)

INDIA, CA 320–CA 1400

ca 320–480	Gupta Empire
ca 380–450	Kalidasa, India's greatest poet
636–1206	Muslim invasions of India
1192	Destruction of Buddhism in India
1290–1320	Sultanate of Delhi
1398	Timur conquers the Punjab and Delhi

---

the Middle East. Both groups of newcomers reinforced the Islamic impact on India. Under the sultanate of Delhi, Iranian influences deeply affected Hindu art and architecture. Iranians introduced the minaret—an essential architectural feature of the mosque—as well as the arch and the dome. So great was the impact of Iranian Muslims that Urdu, the official language of modern Pakistan, evolved as a mixture of Persian with Arabic and Hindi.

The most lasting impact of the invader was religious. Islam replaced Hinduism and Buddhism in the Indus Valley (modern Pakistan) and in Bengal at the mouth of the Ganges (modern Bangladesh). Elsewhere in India, where Muslim influence was far less powerful, Hinduism resisted the newcomers and their religion. Most Indians looked on the successful invaders simply as a new ruling caste, capable of governing and taxing them but otherwise peripheral to their lives. Hinduism was bolstered in this attitude by the caste system: the myriad castes largely governed themselves, isolating the newcomers. Hinduism also enjoyed profound devotion on the part of the Indian people. The years of war and invasion had not hindered the development of a pious, devotional Hinduism called Bhakti. Bhakti emphasized personal reverence for and worship of a Hindu deity such as Krishna, Shiva, or Rama. Bhakti nourished impassioned love of the Hindu gods among ordinary folk. In some instances the Bhakti tradition sought synthesis with Islam; in others, converts to Islam retained much of Hindu tradition. In all cases there was a certain amount of mutual borrowing. In general, Hinduism's beliefs and social organization had a strong hold over the people of India; roughly 75 percent remained Hindu.

Muslim control over most of the subcontinent was short-lived. By 1336 a native Indian kingdom in the south effectively resisted the Muslims. In the north, the Muslims were dominant longer but still suffered the traditional fate of foreign conquerors of the north. In 1398 the Turkish chieftain Timur, lord of central Asia, Iran, and Mesopotamia, pushed into the Punjab and captured Delhi. To Timur, India was merely a source of loot. When his troops were sated with destruction and slaughter, Timur retired from India, leaving the Muslims and Hindus to pick up the pieces.

By about 1400 India was as politically divided as it had been before the Gupta Empire. Yet the events of the preceding millennium had had more than political and military significance. The march of armies had brought Islam into India and driven Buddhism out. Meanwhile Hinduism had flourished. These developments were to be critically important for the future of the entire region, for in them lie the origins of the modern nations of India, Pakistan, and Bangladesh.

CHINA'S GOLDEN AGE (580–CA 1400)

The years between the fall of the Han Dynasty in the third century and the rise of the Ming in the fourteenth brought some of China's brightest days and some of its darkest. During this period the Chinese absorbed foreign influences, notably Buddhism, that fundamentally shaped their society. Chinese cultural traditions, especially Confucianism, drew new strength and vitality from abroad. This was a golden era of enormous intellectual and artistic creativity in Chinese history.

Sui, T'ang, and Sung emperors and statesmen reunited the empire, repaired the foundations of national strength, and once again made China one of the world's unrivaled states. Even later political disruption, particularly the invasion of the Mongols, could not undo the achievements of those who shaped the history of these years. Nor were invasions and internal chaos enough to break the spirit of the Chinese people. The Mongols were the first foreigners ever to rule all of China, but their domination lasted only ninety-seven years, until the Ming emperors once again united the land under a native dynasty.

Buddhism Reaches China

Between the fall of the Han Dynasty in 220 and the rise of the Sui in 589, Buddhism reached China from the west. Merchants and travelers from India spread word of the new religion in the north while Indian sailors were introducing it into China's southern ports. Buddhism reached China at a time when many thinkers were doubting the value of traditional Confucian thought and many ordinary people wanted a message of hope. Buddhism initially won a place for itself in China because it offered a refreshing and novel solution to social disruption and political chaos (see pages 76–78). Buddhism was ultimately successful in China because it had powerful appeal for many different segments of society. To Chinese scholars, the Buddhist concepts of transmigration of souls, karma, and nirvana posed a stimulating intellectual challenge. For rulers the Buddhist church was a source of magical power and a political tool: since it was neither barbarian nor Chinese, this foreign faith could embrace both groups equally. To the middle and lower classes, Buddhism's egalitarianism—the teaching that enlightenment was available to all—came as a breath of fresh air. Buddhism spoke to all, regardless of their social class. Thus the lower orders of society believed that they had as much chance as the elites to live according to Buddha's precepts. For them especially, simple faith and devotion alone could win salvation. For many, regardless of social status, Buddhism's promise of eternal bliss as the reward for a just and upright life was deeply comforting. In a rough and tumultuous age, moreover, Buddhism's emphasis on kindness and the value of human life offered hope of a better future on earth. Similarly, Buddhist teachings on the value of charity and good works had a profound impact on Chinese morality. Besides holding out a path to salvation in the next world, Buddhism offered a practical program for improving life in this world.

If Buddhism changed Chinese life, China likewise changed Buddhism. Mahayana Buddhism, the more flexible and widespread of Buddhism's two schools (see page 78), gave rise to several new sects responsive to specific Chinese needs. The T'ien-t'ai sect, which later gave rise to the Tendai sect in Japan (see page 325), was favored by Chinese scholars, who attempted to resolve the numerous intellectual problems in Buddhism and to organize its doctrines in keeping with traditional Chinese thought. Most popular was the Pure Land sect, which retained many of the most appealing aspects of Mahayana Buddhism. It too would later have a vast impact on Japanese society. Like its Indian counterpart, this sect was very lenient. Instead of following Buddha's Eightfold Path, people had only to declare their sincere faith in Buddha to reach paradise, the "pure land." Many simple and uneducated people found in the Pure Land sect a comforting route to joy scarcely attainable on earth. Meanwhile the True Word sect, which won more popularity in Japan than in China, promised adherents immortality through magic, rituals, and chants. Last, the Ch'an sect, the forerunner of Zen Buddhism in Japan, combined elements of Taoism and Buddhism. Like Taoism itself, Ch'an dreamed of a return to nature and simplicity and preached that individuals were responsible for their own ultimate enlightenment. In this respect Ch'an was quite similar to Buddha's teaching that each person must tread the path of enlightenment alone. Ch'an emphasized meditation and the individual search for enlightenment instead of the learning and scholarship of the T'ien-t'ai sect. One of the prime reasons for Buddhism's success in China was its extraordinary ability to accommodate itself to local thought, beliefs, and conditions.

Buddhist monks from abroad introduced monasticism to China, and the resulting monasteries became more than merely centers for religious practice and study. Like their Christian counterparts in medieval Europe (see pages 355–357), Buddhist monasteries played an active role in social, economic, and political life. Buddhist missionary monks traveled the trade routes with Buddhist merchants, who gave the newly formed

Buddhism Reaches China   This scene brilliantly illustrates the spread of Buddhism from India to China. The writing at the left, printed in Chinese characters, is a translation of a Buddhist text originally written in Sanskrit. This scene of Buddha addressing a follower is also the earliest dated example of blockprinting. *(Source: The British Library)*

monasteries a secular function: increasingly, they entrusted their money and wares to the monasteries for safekeeping, in effect transforming the monasteries into banks and warehouses. Buddhist merchants often endowed monks with money or land to support temples and monasteries. The monks, who thus became powerful landlords, hired peasants to work the monastic and temple lands, and the tenants in turn became ready converts to Buddhism. Formidable in wealth and numbers, monasteries became influential participants in politics, rivaling the power of the traditional Chinese landlords. The monasteries' prosperity and political power further protected converts from local Chinese lords and reinforced the spread of Buddhism.

Buddhism also had a profound impact on the artistic life of China. Buddhist art, like the faith's religious message, first reached China along the Silk Road. At Tun-huang in northwestern China, thousands of artists worked for centuries to transform a mile-long stretch of hillside into a monumental shrine. The life of Buddha also offered Chinese painters and sculptors a wealth of new themes. From the fourth century on, Buddha and his life became inseparable from Chinese art.

Thus Buddhism's appeal to the Chinese was religious, social, and artistic. Its message struck a sympathetic chord among nobles and peasants alike. It endowed China with a new view of human dignity, the promise of personal salvation, and a compelling vision of peace.

The T'ang Dynasty (618–907)

The T'ang emperors rose to greatness on the shoulders of their predecessors, the Sui Dynasty (ca 581–618). The Sui resembled the Ch'in of the third century B.C. (see pages 99–100) in that both were short-lived dynasties that restored political order to a storm-tossed land and set the stage for splendid successors. Sui land reforms helped to restore prosperity, and Sui waterworks strengthened ties between northern and southern China. The crowning achievement of the Sui was the Grand

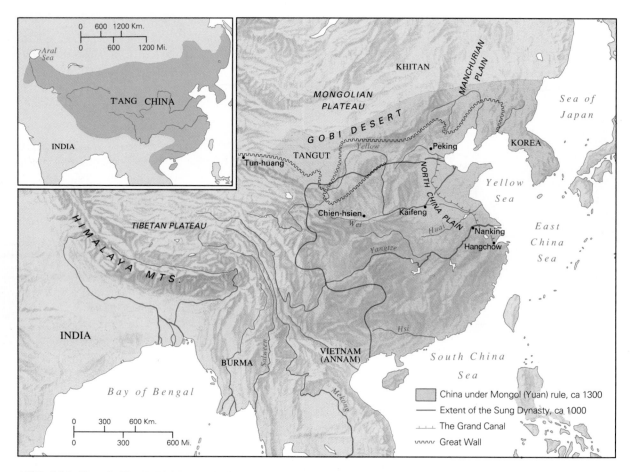

MAP 11.3 The Political Divisions of China from the T'ang to Yuan Dynasties, 618–1368 This map and inset illustrate how the T'ang Dynasty and its successors were able to sustain the expanded frontiers of the Han Dynasty, although their hold in the west was always somewhat tenuous.

Canal, connecting the eastern reaches of the Yellow River to the eastern waters of the Huai and Yangtze rivers (Map 11.3). The canal facilitated the shipping of tax grain from the recently developed Yangtze Delta to the centers of political and military power in northern China. Henceforth the rice-growing Yangtze Valley and southern China generally played an ever more influential role in the country's economic and political life, strengthening China's internal cohesion.

Though successful as reformers, the Sui emperors fell prey to a grim combination of military defeat and massive peasant uprisings. From these unlikely conditions rose the T'ang Dynasty (618–907), probably the greatest dynasty in Chinese history. Its founder, who took the imperial name T'ai Tsung, was far more than a mere upstart who eliminated the last Sui emperor. In addition

to being an able general and astute politician, T'ai Tsung was also an educated and far-sighted administrator who followed conscientiously the lessons of Chinese history. Having seen the results of oppression, T'ai Tsung avoided extravagance and continued Sui reforms.

T'ai Tsung tried first to alleviate the poverty of the peasants. Building on the Sui system, he ordered that land be divided among the peasants as equally as possible and that imperial officials safeguard the peasants' holdings. A prosperous peasantry, in T'ai Tsung's view, would provide a secure and steady base of income for the empire. In practice, the attempt to equalize landholdings quickly broke down, and by 780 the law was revoked. Even so, T'ai Tsung's efforts were not entirely in vain: he had done enough to give agriculture a much-needed boost, and productivity increased in both grain and livestock. Not since the Han Dynasty had the peasants been so well off.

In the civil sphere, T'ang accomplishments far outstripped anything known in Europe until the growth of national states in the seventeenth century (see Chapter 19). T'ang emperors subdivided the administration of the empire into departments, much like the numerous agencies of modern governments. T'ang departments oversaw military organization, maintenance and supply of the armies, foreign affairs, administration of justice, finance, building and transportation, education, and much else. During this period no other state on earth was as politically sophisticated as the T'ang Empire.

A bureaucracy of this scope demanded huge numbers of educated and trained personnel; as in earlier eras of strong central government, the imperial administration offered a lucrative career to talented Chinese. T'ang emperors revived and expanded the Han method of hiring and promoting government officials on the basis of education, ability, and merit. This process reinforced Confucian values, ethics, and emphasis on scholarship. Candidates for official positions were expected to learn the Confucian classics, to master the rules of poetry, and to discuss practical administrative and political matters. Universities were founded to train able and dedicated young men. Graduates passed a demanding battery of oral and written examinations to prove their ability. Training was hard and long; although students did not endure the physical discipline of Mesopotamian scribes, they sacrificed much to achieve success.

Students who passed the official examinations had unlimited futures ahead of them. Talent, education, and a bureaucracy theoretically based on merit promised them high office, wealth, and prestige. Although the rich and powerful often sidestepped the system of formal examinations, the T'ang created an effective civil service long before anything comparable developed elsewhere in the world. The T'ang emperors deserve full credit for the mandarin system of professional public service. Despite weaknesses and loopholes for the influential, the T'ang administrative system was so effective that it lasted into the twentieth century.

Mandarin scholar-officials also played an important cultural role. Since much of an official's training involved the study of literature, history, and politics, China's literary heritage became integral to contemporary life. Because nearly any literate man in the empire could take the examinations, centers for study sprouted throughout China. Knowledge of the classics spread throughout the empire, encouraging cultural unity. The weakness of the mandarin system was its narrow outlook and inflexibility, which stifled originality

Portrait of T'ai Tsung The founder of the T'ang dynasty, T'ai Tsung was an emperor possessing character and vision. He initiated reforms that were intended to help the peasants and increase agricultural productivity. Here he is portrayed as a determined and cultured leader. *(Source: Wan-go Weng/National Palace Museum, Taipei)*

and independence of thought. Nonetheless, the mandarin system was an institution in which people from every part of China could meet on a common ground.

In foreign affairs the T'ang turned their attention first to the Turks, who had spread their power from the northern borders of China to the Byzantine Empire in Asia Minor. By T'ai Tsung's death in 649, Chinese armies had conquered all of Turkestan in the west. The T'ang also turned to Korea, but they had much less success there than the Han had had seven centuries earlier. Chinese influence in Tibet came somewhat more peacefully, despite some Sino-Tibetan rivalries and wars. For years the Tibetans had lived a partly nomadic and partly agricultural life on China's western border. Then in the early seventh century one of their chieftains unified the Tibetan tribes and sought a marriage alliance with T'ai Tsung. The emperor sent his daughter to Tibet with musicians, craftsmen, and technicians to introduce new tools and techniques, along with books on Chinese agricultural methods. The Tibetans modeled their culture partially on the T'ang; the Koreans and Japanese adopted Chinese culture more enthusiastically. China's script and literature, Buddhism, crafts, and political ideas and techniques spread widely, making Chinese culture dominant throughout eastern Asia.

The Sung Dynasty (960–1279)

In the middle of the eighth century, T'ang foreign policy collapsed in rout and rebellion. The defeat of Chinese armies in central Asia and on the southwestern border undercut the emperor's authority. The sources of this crisis varied from the changing demands of frontier defense to stupid imperial decisions. At last in 755 a powerful general, An Lu-shan, revolted in response to imperial maltreatment. An Lu-shan was defeated, but other generals followed his example. The T'ang Dynasty ended in a conflagration of military rebellions, peasant uprisings, and barbarian invasions. The period from 907 to 960, known as the "Era of the Five Dynasties," resembled the age of the barracks emperors of the Roman Empire (see page 217). In northern China rival generals struggled against barbarians and against one another to establish permanent dynasties. Southern China fragmented into ten independent states. Weak and distracted, China presented an easy target to the barbarians, and one group of nomads, known as the "Khitan," captured Peking and most of northeastern China and Manchuria.

The founder of the Sung Dynasty, the northern general Chao K'uang-yin, made his bid for empire in 960. Unsuccessful against the Khitans in the northeast and the Tanguts, a now-extinct ethnic group, in the northwest, Chao K'uang-yin recognized that he lacked the resources to engage all his enemies simultaneously. He thus sought peace with the Khitan and Tanguts by paying them both annual tribute. He then mapped out a broad strategy to annex the economically prosperous southern states, most of which fell to him easily. Gradually Chao K'uang-yin—known as "Emperor Sung T'ai Tsu"—unified southern China and extended his influence as far as Indonesia.

Despite sporadic warfare, the early Sung period enjoyed broad-based economic prosperity for a variety of demographic and economic reasons. The population had increased to an unprecedented 100 million. Rapidly increasing urbanization went hand in hand with greatly expanded agricultural productivity. Advances in the technology and production of coal and iron also played quite a significant part, as did improvements in communications. Efficient water transport fostered the development of a national market for domestic products. The tea trade boomed: in the Han period tea had been a luxury item, but under the T'ang period tea had become immensely popular throughout China. Trade was brisk in other commodities as well. Porcelain continued to be a prime export and domestic product. Salt continued to be a state monopoly. By bringing political stability to southern China, the Sung fostered commercial expansion.

The political and economic success of the Sung permitted the technological innovations of the T'ang period to reach full growth. Foremost among them was the invention of printing, which changed the history of China and the entire world. T'ang craftsmen developed the art of carving words and pictures onto wooden blocks, inking them, and then pressing the blocks onto paper. Each block consisted of an entire page of text and illustrations. Such whole-page blocks were being printed as early as the middle of the ninth century, and in the eleventh century movable type was invented. Movable type was never widely used in China, but when this Chinese invention reached

Europe in the fifteenth century (see page 520), it revolutionized the communication of ideas. In China as in Europe, the invention and spread of printing dramatically increased the availability of books and lowered their price. Scholarship flourished, and literacy spread rapidly among the general population.

The T'ang and Sung periods were rich in technological innovation. The T'ang invented gunpowder, originally for use in fireworks. By the early Sung period people were using gunpowder to propel arrows—in effect, the first rockets. Later, projectiles were given a gunpowder charge so that they exploded on impact. Although the cannon still lay in the future, the Chinese began to develop artillery long before it was known in other parts of the world.

Other inventions included the abacus, which allowed quick computation of complicated sums. The combination of the water wheel and the bellows enabled smelters to increase the output of pig iron. Under the Sung, government-operated spinning and weaving mills produced cheap, durable, and comfortable cotton clothing.

Economic vitality and the consolidation of Sung rule gave a great impetus to urbanization. In fact, city dwellers were becoming economically more important than the landed gentry. Rich urbanites indulged in increasingly costly dress and food. Women suffered a severe decline in social standing, the most obvious expression of which was the custom of footbinding. As long as women's labor was needed to help keep starvation from the door, women possessed a certain status, albeit lowly. In prosperous urban households, however, women no longer fulfilled an economic function and became ornaments of status. To show the world that they need not work, mothers bound the feet of their infant daughters until the arches broke and the foot healed to half its normal growth. Not until the twentieth century was this custom abandoned.

Although the Sung unified central and southern China and created the climate for new prosperity, they never fully solved the problem of political relations with the Khitan and Tangut states in the north.

Whenever possible, the Sung used diplomacy to avoid war and play off one state against the other. In 1114, however, the political situation became more complex. The Jurchen, a people from the northeastern frontier, threw off the yoke of the

Head of the Dragon This elaborate tower is the creation of the astronomer Guo Shoujing, who in 1283 used it to calculate the length of the solar year. He was accurate to within twenty seconds. *(Source: Patrick Lui & Associates)*

Khitan state and in 1125 toppled their former overlords. Flushed with success, the Jurchen marched against the Sung, and in 1126 they sacked the Sung capital and drove the remnants of the imperial court to the southern city of Hangchow.

The Sung emperors who governed from Hangchow, commonly known as the "Southern Sung Dynasty," held on to the area below the Yangtze River from 1127 to 1279. The Southern Sung resisted the northerners but established a stable border with them. Although there never was genuine peace between the two, fighting was usually limited to border areas. For 152 years the Southern Sung flourished, despite the annual tribute they paid to the northerners.

CHINA, CA 320–CA 1400

220–589	Buddhism reaches China
580–618	Sui Dynasty and restoration of public order
618–907	T'ang Dynasty: economic, political, and artistic flowering
907–960	Era of the Five Dynasties: warfare and revolt
960–1279	Sung Dynasty and Neo-Confucian thought
1021–1086	Wang An-shih, author and political reformer
1215–1368	Mongol conquest of China
ca 1300	Marco Polo travels in China

The Southern Sung period is especially notable for a great increase in the volume of maritime trade, both oceanic and coastal. Chinese shipwrights built large, stable junks with huge cargo capacity. These ships enabled Chinese merchants to sail directly to Korea and Japan, which became eager importers of Chinese goods. Ocean voyages were rendered considerably easier and safer by the Chinese invention of the magnetic compass, which was widely used in China at least two centuries earlier than in the rest of the world. The shipping of Chinese goods to the West was mostly in the hands of Arabs, who like their Roman and Indian predecessors, used the annual monsoon winds to sail to ports in India and East Africa. Thus southern China under the Sung entered fully and prosperously into a commercial network that stretched from Japan all the way to the Mediterranean.

The invention of printing and the increased volume of trade led to two momentous innovations: the use of paper money and the development of banking. The standardized currency introduced under the First Emperor in the third century had been bulky copper coinage (see page 99). Paper money originated under the Sung as notes of deposit—documents certifying that a person had deposited a specific amount of copper coinage with the government. Notes of deposit rapidly gave way to true paper money, which anyone could cash in for copper coins. The legendary Venetian merchant and adventurer Marco Polo (ca 1254–1342) wrote one of the earliest descriptions of how Chinese paper money was issued:

The coinage of this paper money is authenticated with as much form and ceremony as if it were actually of pure gold or silver; for to each note a number of officers, specially appointed, not only subscribe their names, but affix their signets also; and when this has been regularly done by the whole of them, the principal officer . . . having dipped into vermillion the royal seal committed to his custody, stamps with it the piece of paper, so that the form of the seal tinged with the vermillion remains impressed upon it.[5]

To this day American paper money carries the signatures of federal officials, the seals of the Federal Reserve Bank, and the Great Seal of the United States; only the vermillion is absent.

Merchants increasingly used the convenient and portable paper money as a medium of exchange. The popularity of paper money also gave rise to the new profession of counterfeiting; Chinese counterfeiters risked their heads, for those inept or unlucky enough to be caught were decapitated. Paper money in turn gave rise to a system of credit and banking that enabled merchants to deposit money, take out loans, and invest in commercial ventures. Facilitated by the new monetary and banking systems, trade burgeoned so much that the Sung government derived more revenue from trade and taxes on trade than from the traditional land tax.

Yet despite their political and economic success, the Southern Sung emperors were living in the twilight of a great era: in the north a new and unforeseen danger, the Mongols, was on the verge of shaking the world from China to Hungary.

Cultural Blossoming of the T'ang and Sung

The economic reforms, political stability, and military successes of the T'ang and Sung nourished a splendid era in the history of Chinese culture. Although the T'ang period is best known for its poetry, many forms of art flourished during these years. Potters produced porcelain of extraordinarily high quality and delicate balance. The finest porcelain was produced in state factories for use at court or as royal gifts to foreign dignitaries. Later, porcelain of uniformly high quality became a major item of export to western Asia and Europe.

Within the past seventeen years the excavations of T'ang imperial tombs at Chien-hsien in Shensi province have shed welcome light on the sculpture and painting of this vibrant period. T'ang emperors were customarily accompanied to their graves by a crowd of monumental stone figures and ceramic statuettes. At Chien-hsien scores of life-size statues of horses and warriors guard the tombs while rows of statues of dignitaries, lions, and sheep stand in silent audience. Inside the tombs, ceramic statuettes of ceremonial troops serve as guardians.

The royal tombs display T'ang painting at its best. The walls are graced with the painted figures of respectful mandarins, court ladies, and warrior guards. Scenes of hunting and polo lend an air of energy and vivacity. Mythological creatures ward off evil spirits. Realistic and graceful in form, the paintings exhibit a sophisticated sense of perspective. The total effect is joyous, even gay. T'ang painters captured life accurately and with a deft touch.

New developments in the T'ang period widened the horizons of prose writing. The translation of Buddhist texts originally written in Indian and central Asian languages introduced new concepts, styles of writing, and literary devices to the Chinese language. In turn, translators had to adapt Chinese to these foreign languages. Mandarins, too, needed a flexible literary medium in which to write their official reports. Writers consciously

Chinese River Festival   All of the beauty and delicacy of Chinese painting is obvious in this lively scene of people enjoying a river festival. Like the great poets, Chinese painters delighted in scenes from daily life. *(Source: The Metropolitan Museum of Art, Fletcher Fund, 1947, The A. W. Bahr Collection)*

aimed at greater clarity and easier means of expression. Some writers used this new flexibility to create the prose essay as a literary form. Prose in the T'ang period became a more useful tool for the bureaucracy and a distinctive literary genre.

The glory of T'ang literature was its poetry, which achieved unmatched elegance and brilliance. T'ang poetry was sophisticated, urbane, and learned. Thoroughly familiar with earlier poetry and with history, T'ang poets were also influenced by Chinese and foreign folk songs. They were consummate masters of meter and rhythm, their poems often gemlike. Though formal and rigorous in composition, T'ang poetry expresses genuine emotion, frequently with humor and sensitivity. Some poets strung songs together to accompany drama, in effect creating Chinese opera. T'ang poets created new vehicles for verse, and they themselves became the models for their Sung successors and all later Chinese poets.

One of the most delightful of the T'ang poets was Li Po (701–762), whose poetry is polished, learned, and good-natured. Unlike most T'ang poets, Li Po was never a mandarin official, although he was familiar with the cultivated life of the imperial court. He was a member in good standing of the literary circle known as the "Eight Immortals of the Wine Cup," and his poems allude often to his love of wine. Even banishment from the court did not dampen his spirits, for Li Po loved his wine, his art, and all of nature too much ever to become morose. One of his most famous poems describes an evening of drinking with only the moon and his shadow for company:

A cup of wine, under the flowering trees;
I drink alone, for no friend is near.
Raising my cup I beckon the bright moon,
For he, with my shadow, will make three men.
The moon, alas, is no drinker of wine;
Listless, my shadow creeps about at my side.

      .   .   .

Now we are drunk, each goes his way.
May we long share our odd, inanimate feast,
And we meet at last on the cloudy River of the sky.[6]

Another poem captures a moment of joy while walking in the mountains on a summer day:

Gently I stir a white feather fan,
With open shirt sitting in a green wood.

I take off my cap and hang it on a jutting stone;
A wind from the pine-trees trickles on my bare head.[7]

Li Po is said to have died one night in the company of his old friend the moon.

Less cheerful but no less talented was Po Chü-i (772–846), whose poems often reflect the concerns of a scholar-official. He felt the weight of his responsibilities as governor of several small provinces and sympathized with the people whom he governed. At times Po Chü-i worried about whether he was doing his job justly and well:

From my high castle I look at the town below
Where the natives of Pa cluster like a swarm of flies.
How can I govern these people and lead them
   aright?
I cannot even understand what they say.

But at least I am glad, now that the taxes are in,
To learn that in my province there is no discontent.[8]

Watching the reapers in the fields, he described their work and wondered about their fate and his:

Tillers of the soil have few idle months;

      .   .   .

Suddenly the hill is covered with yellow corn.
Wives and daughters shoulder baskets of rice;
Youths and boys carry the flasks of wine.
Following after they bring a wage of meat
To the strong reapers toiling on the southern hill,
Whose feet are burned by the hot earth they tread,
Whose backs are scorched by flames of the shining
   sky.

      .   .   .

And I to-day . . . by virtue of what right
Have I never once tended field or tree?

      .   .   .

Thinking of this, secretly I grew ashamed;
And all day the thought lingered in my head.[9]

Like most other T'ang poets, Po Chü-i keenly appreciated nature. Though a high official, he enjoyed such simple things as the pine trees growing around his house and a river babbling over its stony bed. Forced to retire from official life because of ill health, he took discomfort and retirement in graceful stride. At age seventy-four he died of a stroke, comforted by his wine and poetry. He had lived a long life with few regrets.

The artists and thinkers of the Sung period brought to fulfillment what the T'ang had so brilliantly begun. Buoyed by political stability and economic prosperity, the Sung explosion of learning and thought was a direct result of the invention of printing. The availability of books enabled scholars to amass their own libraries and thus to pursue their studies more easily and deeply. Sung scholars formed circles to discuss their interests and ideas and to share their work with others. Sung publishers printed the classics of Chinese literature in huge editions to satisfy scholarly appetites. Works on philosophy, science, and medicine were also consumed avidly. Han and T'ang poetry and historical works became the models for Sung writers' own work. One popular literary innovation was the encyclopedia, which first appeared in the Sung period, at least five centuries before publication of a European encyclopedia.

One of the most influential Sung schools of thought (which gave rise to an intellectual trend known as Neo-Confucianism) was that of Wang An-shih (1021–1086), whose interests embraced economics, politics, literary style, and the classics of Chinese literature. As a Sung minister of state, Wang An-shih launched a series of political and economic innovations with his "New Laws." The "Young Shoots" law extended low-interest loans to poor farmers, as some governments do today. Another law substituted a graduated tax for forced labor on state work projects. Like the Roman emperor Diocletian (see page 218), Wang An-shih introduced official price controls and limitations on profits; he went further than Diocletian by coupling this measure with a plan to equalize the land tax. Though marked by realism and good sense, Wang An-shih's innovations ultimately failed. When his imperial patron died, he was left powerless and defenseless. Ideological warfare and heavy bureaucratic infighting among officials stifled action. The New Laws also met with serious opposition from wealthy merchants and great landowners.

Other schools of Neo-Confucian thought confronted purely intellectual problems and left a more enduring imprint. The Ch'eng-Chu school achieved one of the greatest intellectual feats of a great age by adding a metaphysical dimension to traditional Confucianism's secular approach to human life and the universe. Metaphysics—the theoretical philosophy of being—gave Confucianism an intellectual depth and sophistication that equipped it to challenge what had long been a Buddhist monopoly of ultimate truth.

Neo-Confucians mined Confucian, Buddhist, and Taoist thought to create this new metaphysics. Meanwhile one of the finest minds of the age, Chu Hsi (1120–1200), addressed himself to the metaphysical problem of evil, evolving ideas that correspond roughly to Plato's theory of forms (see page 141). Like Plato, Chu Hsi concluded that everything that exists has a specific form, or *li*. *Ch'i*, or matter, combines with li to make up the material world. When the two are out of balance, the result is evil. People can correct this imbalance, Chu Hsi taught, through Confucian study and Buddhist meditation. In effect, Chu Hsi explained not only how evil develops in the world but how it can be corrected.

Chu Hsi's talents extended to the classics of Chinese literature, on which he wrote learned commentaries. He was also the premier historian of his day. In striving for a unified view of life and the universe, he interpreted history and literature in support of his philosophical ideas. Unparalleled among Neo-Confucians, Chu Hsi's writings became classics; they have been read, revered, and imitated for centuries. He and other intellectuals breathed new life into Confucianism to meet the challenge of Buddhism.

Sung poets and painters matched the greatness of their T'ang predecessors. The Sung particularly excelled at painting. Two dramatically dissimilar approaches to art arose: some painters, like Li Lung-mien (ca 1040–1106), stressed exact realism; others, like Mi Fei (ca 1051–1107), pursued a mystical romanticism in which space and natural elements were suggested with a few brush strokes.

The culture of the T'ang and Sung periods is remarkable for its breadth and variety, as well as its brilliance. From painting to poetry, from philosophy to history, these years gave rise to exquisite masterpieces.

The Mongol Conquest (1215–1368)

In 1215 the Southern Sung and their northern neighbors felt the first tremor of what was to be among the most remarkable movements of people in all history. Jenghiz Khan (1162–1227) and his huge band of Mongols, Tatars, and Turks (see pages 278–279) burst into northern China. Marco Polo left a vivid description of their endurance and military skill:

They are brave in battle, almost to desperation, setting little value upon their lives, and exposing themselves without hesitation to all manner of danger. Their disposition is cruel. They are capable of supporting every kind of privation, and when there is a necessity for it, can live for a month on the milk of their mares, and upon such wild animals as they may chance to catch. Their horses are fed upon grass alone, and do not require barley or other grain. The men are habituated to remain on horseback during two days and two nights, without dismounting, sleeping in that situation whilst their horses graze. No people on earth can surpass them in fortitude under difficulties, nor show greater patience under wants of every kind.[10]

In 1215 the Mongols overwhelmed the Jurchens in the north and captured Peking. All

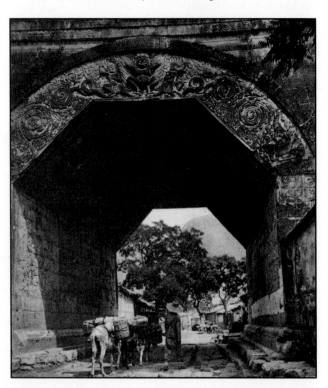

Marble Gate near the Great Wall This majestic arch, erected in 1345, marks the site where the Mongol leader Jenghiz Khan fought and won a major battle against the Chinese. Although it is the monument of a foreign ruler, the arch is typically Chinese in its design and decoration. *(Source: Courtesy Smith College)*

of northern China fell in 1234. The Southern Sung held out tenaciously against the invaders, but Jenghiz Khan's grandson Kublai Khan (1216–1294) extinguished the dynasty and annexed all of southern China by 1279 (see Map 11.3). For the first time in history, all of China was ruled by foreigners. By 1271 Kublai Khan (also known as the Great Khan) had proclaimed himself emperor of China and founder of the Yuan Dynasty (1271–1368).

The Mongols distrusted the traditional mandarin class yet needed their bureaucratic system. They compromised by assigning foreigners—Turks, Muslims from central Asia, and even a handful of European adventurers—to the highest administrative posts and allowing Chinese to hold lower offices. The Mongol conquest did not hinder China's trade, which continued the expansion begun under the Sung. By establishing his capital at Peking, Kublai Khan helped reunite northern and southern China commercially: the wealth of the south flowed north to sustain the capital.

A conquering minority, the Mongols proclaimed repressive laws against the far more numerous Chinese. They divided society into four classes with varying rights, privileges, and legal protection. The Mongols themselves enjoyed full protection under the law; below them were their foreign administrators. The northern Chinese, who had been conquered first, had broader political and legal rights than the southerners but bore a far heavier burden of taxes and services. The southern Chinese shouldered a very light tax load but suffered heavy legal and political discrimination. The Mongols disarmed the Chinese people and forbade them to assemble in large numbers and even to travel by night. The Chinese were captives in their own country.

Yet in internal affairs the Mongols welcomed contact with the outside world. Historians have begun to debate whether Mongol rule was really as harsh as it is usually depicted. Some scholars argue that the Mongols provided a climate of peace and toleration that facilitated friendly relations with those involved in long-distance trade. They see the Mongols as opening China to the West. Other historians point to the restrictions placed on the Chinese as evidence that the Mongols were anything but philanthropists. A realistic, or even cynical, view is that it served the Mongols, who were outsiders, very handsomely to seek outside economic support for their rule, all the while

The Silk Road The Mongol conquest at least secured the safety of merchants traveling the Silk Road. There were few inns or hostels along the route, except in the cities, and most merchants, like those here, pitched camp each night by their camels. *(Source: National Palace Museum, Taiwan)*

keeping the Chinese in their place. The Mongols were hardly altruists, but they did keep the peace in China.

Into this world wandered Marco Polo with his father and uncle. The three Polos had journeyed by land across Asia to the court of Kublai Khan, who received them with warmth and curiosity. Adept in four Asian languages, Marco Polo was uniquely equipped to collect accurate information about China. He probably never traveled far from Peking but instead drew heavily on Chinese accounts. He trained his insatiable curiosity on the land of China, its people and their customs, and everything likely to stimulate commerce. After seventeen years in China, the Polos returned to Italy, where Marco wrote a vivid account of their travels. At first considered sheer fantasy, his book

was widely read and contributed enormously to familiarizing Europeans with Asia.

Mongol repression bred bitter resentment throughout China. By the middle of the fourteenth century, moreover, the Mongol hold on East Asia was weakening. Struggles among claimants to the Yuan throne seriously compromised the Great Khan's power and prestige, and Kublai Khan's successors proved weak and incompetent. In this atmosphere of crisis, some Chinese formed secret societies—underground resistance groups dedicated to overthrowing the oppressor. The most effective secret society, known as the "Red Turbans," consisted of peasants and artisans, who had suffered the most from Mongol rule. In 1351 the rebels were ready to strike. Their rebellion caught the Mongols totally off guard. One of the rebels, a poor peasant and former monk best known to history as Hung Wu, later became the first Ming emperor.

In 1356 Hung Wu and his followers stormed the important city of Nanking. Securing control over southern and central China, they pushed the Mongols northward, and by 1368 the Chinese had driven the Mongols completely out of China. Hung Wu established the Ming Dynasty (1368–1644). Once again China was united under one of its sons. In the following years Ming emperors would continue to push the Mongols north. They also rebuilt the Chinese economy by reclaiming abandoned farmland, by repairing neglected dikes and canals that were essential to fruitful agriculture, and by reforesting the countryside. As a result, under Ming rule China again prospered.

JAPAN, DAWN OF THE RISING SUN

Japan entered the light of history late, and Japanese historical writing originated even later. The earliest reliable information on Japan comes from sporadic notices in Chinese histories, the first of which dates only from A.D. 57. Little is known about the origins and formative years of the Japanese people. By the time of their first appearance in history, they had already had extensive exposure to Chinese culture. Yet though the Japanese derived much from the Chinese, they molded their borrowings to suit their special needs. Early Japan saw the growth of an indigenous culture that was influenced but never overwhelmed by the Chinese.

The Japanese Islands

The heart of Japan is four major islands, the largest and most important of which is Honshu. The three southern islands surround the Inland Sea, a narrow stretch of water dotted with smaller islands (Map 11.4). All four major islands are mountainous, with craggy interiors and some active volcanoes. Rugged terrain divides the land into numerous small valleys watered by streams. There is little flat land, and only 16 percent of the total area is arable. Japan's climate ranges from subtropical in the south, which the Pacific bathes in warm cur-

rents, to a region of cold winters in the north. Rainfall is abundant, favoring rice production. Yet nature can be harsh: Japan is a land buffeted by earthquakes, typhoons, and tidal waves.

Despite occasional rages, the sea provides a rich harvest, and the Japanese have traditionally been fishermen and mariners. Since the land is rugged and lacking in navigable waterways, political unification by land was difficult until the modern period. The Inland Sea, like the Aegean in Greece, was the readiest avenue of communication. Hence the land bordering the Inland Sea developed as the political and cultural center of early Japan. Geography also blessed Japan with a moat, the Korean Strait, and the Sea of Japan. Great powers like the Han and T'ang dynasties and the Mongols might overrun the Asian continent, but their grasp never reached to the Japanese islands. Japan did not suffer a single successful invasion until the Second World War, when American and Allied troops stepped ashore after the Japanese surrender in 1945. Consequently, the Japanese have for long periods been free to develop their way of life without external interference. Continuity has been a hallmark of Japanese history.

Early Japan and the Yamato State

The beginnings of Japanese history are lost in the mists of legend. The Chinese historian Wei Chih wrote one of the earliest reliable descriptions of Japanese life in A.D. 297:

The land of Wa [Japan] is warm and mild. In winter as in summer the people live on raw vegetables and go barefooted. They live in houses; father and mother, elder and younger, sleep separately. They smear their bodies with pink and scarlet, just as the Chinese use powder. They serve food on bamboo and wooden trays, helping themselves with their fingers.[11]

The society that Wei Chih and other Chinese sources portray was based on agriculture and dominated by a warrior aristocracy. Clad in helmet and armor, these warriors wielded swords and battle-axes and often the bow. Some of them rode into battle on horseback. Social stratification was rigid, peasants serving at the command of nobles. At the bottom of the social scale were slaves—usually house servants. Slaves may have accounted for about 5 percent of the total population.

Early Japan was divided into numerous political units, although by about 513 their number had been greatly reduced. Each pocket of local authority was under the rule of a particular clan—a large group of families that claimed descent from a common ancestor and worshiped a common deity. Each clan had its own chieftain, who marshaled clan forces for battle and served as clan chief priest. In Japan as in many other ancient societies, political power was a function of family strength, organization, and cohesion.

By the third century A.D. the Yamato clan had seized the fertile area south of Kyoto, near Osaka Bay (see Map 11.4). At the center of the Yamato holdings was a rich plain, which constituted the chief economic resource of the clan. Gradually the Yamato clan, which traced its descent from the sun-goddess, subordinated a huge number of other clans to create the Yamato state. The chieftain of the Yamato clan proclaimed himself emperor and ruler over the other chieftains. The Yamato harnessed the loyalty of their subordinates by giving them specific duties, functions, and gifts and by including them in a religious hierarchy. Clans that recognized Yamato dominion continued to exercise local authority, and some clans were given specific military or religious functions to fulfill. In an effort to centralize further the administration of the state, the emperor created a council of chieftains, whose members were treated as though they were appointed officials.

The Yamato also used their religion to subordinate the gods of their supporters, much as Hammurabi had used Marduk (see page 19). Creating a hierarchy of gods under the authority of their sun-goddess, the Yamato established her chief shrine in eastern Honshu, where the sun-goddess could catch the first rays of the rising sun. Around the shrine there grew up local clan cults, giving rise to a native religion known as "Shinto," the Way of the Gods. Shinto was a unifying force: the chief deity of Shinto, the sun-goddess, became the nation's protector. Shinto also stressed the worship of ancestors, thus strengthening the link between the present and the past. Much of its appeal rose from the fact that it was a happy religion. Its rituals celebrated the beauty of nature instead of invoking the hazards of fate or divine wrath. Shinto emphasized ritual cleanliness, and its festivals were marked by wine, song, and good cheer.

By the sixth century the powerful Yamato state was struggling to dominate Korea. From the dawn

MAP 11.4 The Islands of Japan, ca 1185 The map illustrates the importance of the island of Honshu and the Inland Sea in the development of early Japanese society.

of their history the Japanese had held parts of Korea, but by 562 the Koreans had driven them out. Yet Japanese-Korean contact was not entirely hostile or limited to warfare. Early Japanese society easily absorbed migrating Koreans, and its holdings in Korea enriched the Japanese economically.

Much more important, however, was Korea's role as the avenue through which Chinese influence reached Japan. Chinese impact on the Japanese was profound and wide ranging. The Japanese adapted the Chinese systems of writing and record keeping, which allowed for bureaucratic administration along Chinese lines and set the stage for literature, philosophy, and written history.

Another influence was of lasting importance to the Japanese: Buddhism. In 538 a Korean king sent the Yamato court Buddhist images and scriptures. The new religion immediately became a political football, one faction of the ruling clan

Creation of Japan   This Japanese painting portrays two deities standing in the clouds above the Pacific Ocean. The god, sword at his side, stirs the waters with a lance and thereby creates the home islands of Japan. (*Source: Courtesy, Museum of Fine Arts, Boston, Bigelow Collection*)

favoring its official adoption and other factions opposing it. The resulting turmoil, both religious and political, ended only in 587, when the pro-Buddhists defeated their opponents on the battlefield. Buddhism proved important to Japanese life for three broad reasons. First, it was a new and sophisticated but appealing religion that met needs not envisaged by Shinto. Second, it served as an influential carrier of Chinese culture. Finally, its acceptance by Japan's rulers enabled it to play an influential role in politics.

The victorious pro-Buddhists undertook a sweeping reform of the state, partly to strengthen Yamato rule and partly to introduce Chinese political and bureaucratic concepts. The architect of this effort was Prince Shotoku (574–622), the author of the "Seventeen Article Constitution," a triumph of Buddhist ethical and Confucian political thought. Issued in 604, the constitution was not a blueprint for government but a list of moral and ethical Buddhist precepts stressing righteous political conduct. It upheld the rights of the ruler and commanded his subjects to obey him. The constitution recommended an intricate bureaucracy like China's and admonished the nobility to avoid strife and opposition. Although the Seventeen Article Constitution never became the law of the entire land, it spelled out what Shotoku considered the proper goals of government and pointed the way to future reform.

Shotoku realized that Japan lacked the trained personnel to put his reforms into effect. To build a corps of professional administrators he sent a large group of talented Japanese to T'ang China in 607 to learn Chinese methods and arts at the source. Other students studied at Buddhist monasteries in China and then carried the message of Buddha accurately and fully to Japan. At first their numbers were small, but over the course of years thousands of young men studied in China and returned home to share what they had learned.

The death of Shotoku in 622 set off some twenty years of political chaos. Finally in 645 supporters of his policies, aided by students trained in China, overthrew the government. The following year they proclaimed the "Taika Reforms," a bold effort to create a complete imperial and bureaucratic system like that of the T'ang Empire. For all their hopes, the Taika Reforms failed to make Japan a small-scale copy of T'ang China. Nonetheless, the reformers created a nation with all the political trappings of its neighbors. The symbol of this new political awareness was the establishment in 710 of Japan's first true capital and first city, modeled on the T'ang capital, at Nara, just north of modern Osaka. Nara gave its name to an era that lasted until 794, an era characterized by the continued importation of Chinese ideas and methods. Buddhism triumphed both religiously and politically. The Buddhist monasteries that ringed the capital were both religious centers and wealthy landlords, and the monks were active in the political life of the capital. In the Nara era, Buddhism and the imperial court went hand in hand.

The Heian Era (794–1185)

Buddhist influence at Nara showed its dark side when in 770 a Buddhist priest tried to usurp the throne. The results were twofold. The imperial family removed the capital to Heian—modern Kyoto—where it remained until 1867. And a strong reaction against Buddhism and Chinese culture soon set in, strikingly symbolized by the severance of relations with China after 838. Thereafter the Japanese assimilated and adapted what they had imported. In a sense their intellectual and cultural childhood had come to an end, and they were ready to go their own way.

Though under a cloud, Buddhism not only survived the reaction but actually made gains. Before closing the door on China, the Japanese admitted two new Buddhist cults that gradually became integral parts of Japanese life. In 805 a Japanese monk introduced the Tendai (Chinese T'ien-t'ai) sect (see page 310). Though a complex product of China's high culture, Tendai proved popular because it held out the possibility of salvation to all. In addition to its religious message, Tendai preached the Confucian ideal of service to the state. The Shingon (True Word) sect arrived in 806 on the heels of Tendai. Like its Chinese precursor, this Japanese sect promised salvation through ritual, magical incantations, and masses for the dead.

Patronized initially by the nobility, both sects held the seeds of popular appeal. The common people cared nothing for Tendai and Shingon as metaphysical and intellectual systems but were strongly attracted by their magic and the prospect of personal salvation. As Tendai and Shingon spread Buddhism throughout Japan, they were gradually transformed into distinctively Japanese

religions. Furthermore, Buddhist art extended an esthetic appeal to the Japanese people.

Only later, during the Kamakura Shogunate (1185–1333), did Buddhism begin a vigorous proselytizing campaign. The emphasis on equality and salvation that was the hallmark of both Tendai and Shingon prepared the way for two sects that promised their followers sure and immediate salvation. The Pure Land sect (see page 310) preached that Buddha's paradise of eternal bliss, the pure land, could be reached through simple faith in Buddha. Neither philosophical understanding of Buddhist scriptures nor devotion to rituals was necessary. People had only to repeat Buddha's name to be saved. The second sect, an offshoot of the first, was the Lotus sect of Nichiren

Prince Shotoku Prince Shotoku, the author of the "Seventeen Article Constitution," is shown here with many of the attributes of a Chinese mandarin official. His sword shows that he was more than a mere administrator, and was ready to resist those who opposed his reforms. *(Source: Imperial Household Collection, Kyoto)*

(1222–1281), a fiery and intolerant preacher who reduced Buddhism to a single moment of faith. To be saved, according to Nichiren, people had only to call sincerely on Buddha. Nothing else was necessary. Stripped of its intellectual top-weight, Buddhism made greater headway in the countryside than ever before.

The eclipse of Chinese influence liberated Japanese artistic and cultural impulses. The Japanese continued to draw on Chinese models but forged new paths of their own. Japanese architects evolved a light, simple, and graceful style of building beautifully in keeping with the country's natural surroundings. The Heian era fostered a unique development in painting, the "Yamato pictures," paintings of everyday scenes in which figures and objects are outlined and then painted with bright colors. Equally great strides were made in writing. In order to express themselves more easily and clearly, Japanese scholars modified the Chinese script that they had adopted during the Yamato period. The Japanese produced two *syllabaries,* sets of phonetic signs that stand for syllables instead of whole words or letters. This development made it possible for the first time to write the Japanese language in the native syntax.

The reform of their written language unshackled Japanese writers. No longer bound in the straitjacket of Chinese, they created their own literary style and modes of expression. The writing of history, which had begun in the Nara era, received a huge boost, as did poetry. Completely original was the birth of the novel, one of the finest of which is *The Tale of Genji.* This ageless novel by the court lady Murasaki Shikibu (978–ca 1016) treats court life, paying minute attention to dialogue and exploring personalities. Not merely a novelist, Murasaki also wrote about the mission of the novelist and the purpose of the novel. The novel was taken up by other writers; Sei Shonagon's *Pillow Book* is another masterpiece. These works bore no resemblance to any works in Chinese literature. The Japanese had launched their own independent and fertile literary tradition.

Politically, the Heian era gave rise to two opposing tendencies: while the emperors were trying to extend their power and centralize their authority, aristocrats were striving to free themselves from imperial control. The aristocrats quickly won out over the emperors. The biggest winners were the Fujiwara family, who in the ninth century had regularly served as regents for the emperors. They were also the most successful, for they married and connived their way into almost complete domination of the imperial line of rulers. As other families too rose to prominence, setting the stage for intrigue and infighting at court, the effectiveness of the imperial government was further diminished.

The emperors contributed to their own eclipse by decreeing disastrous land laws. The imperial government's efforts to appropriate land and redistribute it to peasants wrecked its own economic base. The government was too weak to overcome widespread resistance and evasion of the laws, and the emperors themselves permitted too many loopholes. The result was precisely the opposite of what the central government intended: vast tracts of land were made exempt from taxation and imperial control, and land became consolidated in fewer hands. Those who profited most were local lords and high government officials, members of the imperial court and Buddhist monasteries, all of whom became great landlords at the emperor's expense. Instead of a peasantry of small landholders paying taxes to the imperial treasury, the emperors and even the Fujiwara regents had to contend with strong aristocratic families who were increasingly difficult to control.

In 1156, fed by declining central power, feuds among the great families, and the ambitions of local lords, open rebellion and civil war erupted. The two most powerful contenders in the struggle were the Taira and Minamoto clans, who quickly outstripped both the emperor and the Fujiwara. The Taira drew their political strength from their vast landholdings; the Minamoto dominated the Kanto Plain, a rich agricultural area near modern Tokyo. Both clans relied on *samurai,* skilled warriors who were rapidly consolidating as a new social class. By 1192 the Minamoto had vanquished all opposition, and their leader Yoritomo (1147–1199) became *shogun,* or general-in-chief. With him began the Kamakura Shogunate, which lasted until 1333.

The Land and the Samurai

The twelfth-century events that culminated in the Kamakura Shogunate involved a new relation between the samurai and the land that eventually led to a fusion of the military, civil, and judicial aspects of government into a single authority. The Japanese samurai were a very important part of a larger system. Without an independent income of its own, a warrior class needs the economic support of others, and here the samurai were no different. They depended economically on the *shoen,* a private domain outside imperial control. The shoen typically consisted of a village and its farmland, normally land capable of growing rice. Land was essential to the maintenance of the samurai.

Samurai and shoen were basic elements of early Japanese history, but what conditions bonded them so closely? Both owed their origins directly to the gradual breakdown of central authority in the Heian era. The shoen had its roots in the ninth century, when local lords began escaping imperial taxes and control by formally giving their land to a Buddhist monastery, which was exempt from taxes, or to a court official who could get special privileges from the emperor. The local lord then received his land back as a tenant who paid his protector a nominal rent. The monastery or official received a steady income from the land, and the tenant was thereafter free of imperial taxes and jurisdiction. The local lord continued to exercise actual authority over the land—all the more so, in fact, since imperial officials could no longer touch him. In spite of his legal status as a tenant, he was the real boss of the estate.

The many other people who were economically, politically, and legally dependent on the shoen, and who had various and often overlapping rights and functions within it, enjoyed the rights of the *shiki,* a share of the produce of the land. The lord often entrusted the actual running of the estate to a manager, who received a share of the estate's produce in payment. The shoen was cultivated by independent farmers *(myoshu)* who owned specific fields, by dependent farmers, or, typically, by a combination of both. Unlike peasants in medieval Europe, dependent farmers never became serfs.

To keep order on the shoen and to protect it from harm, lords organized private armies. As the central government weakened, local lords and their armies—the only source of law and order in the countryside—grew stronger. Thus the inability of central authority to defend its subjects sparked the rise of local armies of professional soldiers—the samurai.

The samurai and his lord had a double bond. The lord extended his authority over the samurai in return for the latter's loyalty and service. The samurai originally received from his lord only *shiki rights*—a certain portion of an estate's produce—

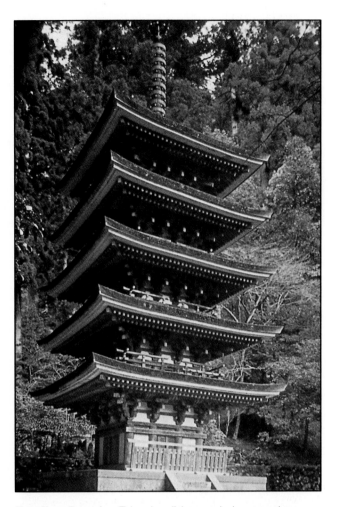

Five-Story Pagoda   This splendid pagoda is a good example of Japanese architecture of the Heian period. Such buildings were intended to complement their natural surroundings. *(Source: Courtesy, Horyuji Temple)*

not a grant of land. Only later did samurai receive land for their service. Each samurai entered into his lord's service in a formal ceremony that included a religious element. Initially, the lord-samurai relationship existed alongside the anemic imperial system. Not until the Ashikaga Shogunate, which lasted from 1338 to 1573 (see page 330), did the military aristocracy take over from imperial officers.

The samurai had his own military and social code of conduct, later called *Bushido,* or "Way of the Warrior." The bedrock of the samurai's code was loyalty to his lord, to which everything else was secondary. Yoritomo founded the Kamakura

JAPAN, CA 320–CA 1400

3d century A.D.	Creation of the Yamato state
538	Introduction of Buddhism
604	Shotoku's Seventeen Article Constitution
655	Taika reforms
710	Establishment of Nara as Japan's first capital and first city
710–784	Nara era
794–1185	Heian era and literary flowering
1185–1333	Kamakura Shogunate and Japanese feudalism
1274 and 1281	Unsuccessful Mongol invasions of Japan

Shogunate on the samurai and his code, and attitudes that blossomed in Yoritomo's lifetime long outlasted the political system he built. Perhaps the scholar George Sansom has best caught the flavor of the samurai's devotion to lord and duty:

The warrior does not question the commands of his lord, but obeys them regardless of his own life, his family, and all his private interests. In defeat he must bear in mind what he owes for past favors and must be ready to die in the cause of his lord, or in the cause of the family or clan of which he is a member. It follows that a warrior's life belongs to his lord, and he may not dispose of it to suit his own ends, or merely to preserve his own reputation.[12]

Preferring death to dishonor, the samurai showed complete dedication in the act of *seppuku* (sometimes incorrectly called *harakiri*), ritual suicide by disemboweling oneself.

By the end of the twelfth century the samurai had left their mark on cultural life as well as on military affairs. They constituted the ruling class at the local level, warrior-aristocrats who were close to the land and to those who worked it. Although samurai's values were not the values of the court aristocracy, their code of conduct was by no means rude or vulgar. The principles of the samurai embraced religion, personal conduct, and practical affairs. As articulated in the *Bushido,* samurai were expected to respect the gods, keep honorable company, be fair and even generous to others, and be sympathetic to the weak and helpless.

The symbols of the samurai were their swords, with which they were expected to be expert, and the cherry blossom, which falls with the spring wind, signifying the way in which samurai gave

their lives for their lords. Like knights, samurai went into battle in armor and often on horseback. Like the ancient Spartans, samurai were expected to make do with little and like it. Physical hardship became routine, and soft living was despised as weak and unworthy. Although the full-blown samurai code did not take final shape until the later Ashikaga Shogunate, samurai were making an irresistible impact on Japanese life by the end of the twelfth century.

The Kamakura Shogunate (1185–1333)

The Kamakura Shogunate derives its name from Kamakura, the seat both of the Minamoto clan and of Yoritomo's shogunate. Yoritomo's victory meant that the emperor was still an ornament, honored and esteemed but mostly powerless.

Based on the loyalty of his followers, Yoritomo's rule was an extension of the way in which he ran his own estate. Having established his *bakufu* (tent government) at Kamakura, Yoritomo created three bodies, staffed by his retainers, to handle political and legal matters. His administrative board drafted government policy. Another board regulated lords and samurai, and a board of inquiry served as the court of the land.

For administration at the local level, Yoritomo created two groups of officials: military land stewards and military governors. The military land stewards were responsible for the collection of taxes. Charged with governing most estates, they saw to the estates' proper operation and maintained law and order in return for a share of the produce. The military governors oversaw the military and police protection of the provinces. They supervised the conduct of the military land stewards in peacetime and commanded the provincial samurai in war.

Yoritomo's system suffered from a weakness. Before the end of the twelfth century, the military land stewards and military governors had become hereditary officials—local rulers in their own right—whose allegiance to the Kamakura Shogunate was waning.

Yoritomo's successors did not inherit his ability, and in 1219 the Hojo family, a powerful vassal, reduced the shogun to a figurehead. Until 1333, the Hojo family held the reins of power by serving as regents of the shogun. The shogun had joined the emperor as a political figurehead.

Internal affairs continued unchanged during the Hojo Regency, but a formidable challenge appeared from abroad. Japan's self-imposed isolation was rudely interrupted in the thirteenth century by a massive seaborne invasion whose lingering effects weakened the Hojo Regency and eventually led to the downfall of the Kamakura Shogunate. The Mongol leader Kublai Khan, having overrun China and Korea, turned his eyes toward Japan. In 1274 and again in 1281 he sent huge numbers of ships and men to storm the islands. On both occasions the Mongols managed to land but were beaten back by samurai. What proved decisive, however, were two fierce storms that destroyed the Mongol fleets. Marco Polo recounted what he heard about one invasion force:

The expedition sailed from the ports of Zai-tun and Kin-sai, and crossing the intermediate sea, reached the island in safety. . . . It happened, after some time, that a north wind began to blow with great force, and the ships of the Tartars, which lay near the shore of the island, were driven foul of each other. . . . The gale, however, increased to so violent a degree that a number of vessels foundered. The people belonging to them, by floating upon the pieces of the wreck, saved themselves upon an island lying about four miles from the coast of Zipangu [Japan].[13]

The Japanese claimed that they were saved by the *kamikaze,* the "Divine Wind"—which lent its name to the thousands of Japanese aviators who tried to become a second divine wind in World War Two by crashing their airplanes on American warships.

Although the Hojo regents had successfully defended Japan, they could not reward their vassals satisfactorily because little booty was found among the wreckage. Discontent grew among the samurai, and by the fourteenth century the entire

Resisting the Mongols   Although this scene shows the Japanese samurai prepared behind a defensive wall for an attack by the Mongols, Kubla Khan's invasion plans were actually ruined by fierce storms, which the Japanese called the *kamikaze,* or "Divine Wind." *(Source: Imperial Household Collection, Tokyo)*

political system was breaking down. Both the imperial and the shogunate families were divided among themselves, and discontent increased among the samurai, who were rapidly growing in number. Since the land could not adequately support more samurai, many samurai families became increasingly impoverished. This phenomenon had two results. First, poverty created a pool of warriors ready for plunder. Second, the samurai shifted their loyalty from the Kamakura Shogunate to local officials who could offer them adequate maintenance.

The combination of factional disputes among Japan's leading families and the samurai remained explosive until 1331, when the emperor Go-Daigo tried to recapture real power. His attempt sparked an uprising by the great families, local lords, samurai, and even Buddhist monasteries, which commanded the allegiance of thousands of samurai. Go-Daigo destroyed the Kamakura Shogunate in 1333 but lost the loyalty of his followers. One of his most important military leaders, Ashikaga Takauji, made his own bid for power. By 1338 the rebel had defeated the emperor and established the Ashikaga Shogunate, which lasted until 1573. Takauji's victory was also a victory for the samurai, who took over civil authority throughout Japan. The day of the samurai had fully dawned.

SUMMARY

By about 1400, traditional religious, social, and intellectual values had been challenged and fertilized by new peoples and new ideas throughout Asia. Most of India clung to Hinduism while Islam took root in modern Pakistan and Bangladesh. China incorporated and distilled Buddhism, which won a place next to Confucianism in Chinese life. Japan imported much of Chinese culture only to mold it into something distinctly Japanese. Finally, firm economic and cultural links made it virtually impossible for any Asian people to continue to develop in isolation.

NOTES

1. O. P. Singh Bhatia, trans., *The Imperial Guptas* (New Delhi: New India Press, 1962), p. 79.

2. A. L. Basham, trans., *The Wonder That Was India* (New York: Grove Press, 1954), p. 161.

3. *Vasishtha,* 4.5.1–2, trans. G. Bühler, in *The Sacred Laws of the Aryas,* part 2, *Vasishtha and Baudhayana* (Oxford: Clarendon Press, 1882), p. 31.

4. *Sutrakritanga,* 1.4.2, quoted in Basham, *The Wonder That Was India,* pp. 459–460.

5. *The Travels of Marco Polo, the Venetian* (London: J. M. Dent and Sons, 1908), p. 203.

6. A. Waley, trans., *More Translations from the Chinese* (New York: Knopf, 1919), p. 27.

7. Ibid., p. 29.

8. Ibid., p. 71.

9. Ibid., p. 41.

10. *The Travels of Marco Polo,* p. 128.

11. R. Tsunoda et al., *Sources of the Japanese Tradition* (New York: Columbia University Press, 1958), p. 6.

12. G. Sansom, *A History of Japan to 1334* (Stanford, Calif.: Stanford University Press, 1958), p. 360.

13. *The Travels of Marco Polo,* pp. 325–326.

SUGGESTED READING

The reign of the Guptas is especially well documented. O. P. Singh Bhatia, *The Imperial Guptas* (1962), treats the entire dynasty. In a series of works S. K. Maity covers many facets of the period: *Gupta Civilization: A Study* (1974), *The Imperial Guptas and Their Times* (1975), and *Economic Life in North India in the Gupta Period* (1975). D. H. H. Ingalls, "Kalidasa and the Attitudes of the Golden Age," *Journal of the American Oriental Society* 96 (1976): 15–26, studies the writings of India's greatest poet and dramatist in their historical context.

Good treatments of Indian society and daily life can be found in A. L. Basham, *The Wonder That Was India* (1954), chap. 6, and J. Auboyer, *Daily Life in Ancient India from 200 B.C. to A.D. 700* (1965).

O. W. Wolters, *Early Indonesian Commerce: A Study of the Origins of Srivijaya* (1967), is perhaps the most comprehensive treatment of that kingdom. Much broader in scope are two books by H. G. Q. Wales: *The Indianization of China and of South-East Asia* (1967), and *The Making of Greater India,* 3d ed. (1974).

An extensive survey of the Islamic invasions of India is J. F. Richards, "The Islamic Frontier in the East: Expansion into South Asia," *South Asia* 4 (1974): 90–109, in which Richards makes the point that many Indian princes put up stiff resistance to the invaders. Much broader studies of the impact of Islam on the subcontinent are A. Embree, ed., *Muslim Civilization in India* (1964), and I. H. Qureshi, *History of the Muslim Community of the Indo-Pakistan Subcontinent* (1961), which is very pro-Pakistan. A good treatment of early Islam in

India is K. A. Nizami, *Some Aspects of Religion and Politics in India During the Thirteenth Century* (reprinted 1970). In two books, *Islam in the Indian Subcontinent* (1980) and *Islam in India and Pakistan* (1982), A. Schimmel surveys many aspects of Islam, including architecture, life, art, and traditions in the subcontinent. G. S. Pomerantz, "The Decline of Buddhism in India," *Diogenes* 96 (1976): 38–66, treats the demise of Buddhism on its native soil.

Two works concentrate on the sultanate of Delhi: M. Habib and K. A. Nizami, eds., *Comprehensive History of India,* vol. 5, *Delhi Sultanate* (1970), and P. Hardy, "The Growth of Authority over a Conquered Political Elite: The Early Delhi Sultanate as a Possible Case Study," in J. F. Richards, ed., *Kingship and Authority in South Asia* (1978).

The standard work on the arrival of Buddhism in China is E. Zürcher, *The Buddhist Conquest of China,* 2 vols. (1959). Also good on the intellectual climate of the time are E. Balazs, *Chinese Civilization and Bureaucracy* (1964), and H. Welch and A. Seidel, eds., *Facets of Taoism* (1979). Shorter and more popular is A. Wright, *Buddhism in Chinese History* (1959). Two books by K. Ch'en, *Buddhism in China* (1964) and *The Chinese Transformation of Buddhism* (1973), cover the early evolution of Buddhism in China. B. Gray, *Buddhist Cave Paintings at Tunhuang* (1959), is the place to begin study of the artistic impact of Buddhism on China.

Political events from the time of the Sui to the Sung Dynasty are particularly well covered. A. F. Wright, *The Sui Dynasty* (1978), has become the standard work on this important dynasty. Though old, W. Bingham, *The Founding of the T'ang Dynasty: The Fall of Sui and Rise of T'ang* (1941), is still useful. C. P. Fitzgerald, *Son of Heaven: A Biography of Li Shih-min, Founder of the T'ang Dynasty* (1933), is likewise an old treatment of the first T'ang emperor. Newer and broader is J. Perry and B. Smith, eds., *Essays on T'ang Society* (1976). The career of An Lu-shan is admirably discussed by E. G. Pullyblank, *The Background of the Rebellion of An Lu-shan* (1955). The difficult period of the Five Dynasties is well covered by G. Wang, *The Structure of Power in North China During the Five Dynasties* (1963). Various aspects of Sung developments receive attention in J. T. C. Liu and P. Golas, eds., *Changes in Sung China* (1969), and E. A. Kracke, Jr., *Civil Service in Early Sung China (960–1067)* (1953).

A brief treatment of the T'ang tombs at Chien-hsien, well illustrated with color plates, is N. H. Dupree, "T'ang Tombs in Chien County, China," *Archaeology* 32, no. 4 (1979): 34–44. Those interested in further discussion of the great poets of the period can find no better place to start than the work of A. Waley, a gifted translator: *The Life and Times of Po Chü-i* (1949) and *The Poetry and Career of Li Po, 701–762* (1950). Wang

An-shih still generates controversy, and a variety of views can be found in J. T. C. Liu, *Reform in Sung China: Wang An-shih (1021–1086) and His New Policies* (1959), and J. Meskill, ed., *Wang An-shih—Practical Reformer?* (1963).

For the Mongols in their native setting, see L. Kwanten, *Imperial Nomads: A History of Central Asia, 500–1500 A.D.* (1979), a comprehensive picture of central Asian developments. H. D. Martin, *The Rise of Chinghis Khan and His Conquest of North China* (1950), studies the rise of the Mongols to greatness. J. Dardess's "From Mongol Empire to Yuan Dynasty: Changing Forms of Imperial Rule in Mongolia and Central Asia," *Monumenta Serica* 30 (1972–1973): 117–165, traces the evolution of Mongol government. His *Conquerors and Confucians: Aspects of Political Change in Late Yuan China* (1973) continues the study for a somewhat later period. Dardess's "The Transformations of Messianic Revolt and the Founding of the Ming Dynasty," *Journal of Asian Studies* 29 (1970): 539–558, treats some of the factors behind the overthrow of the Yuan Dynasty.

Among the many fine general works on Japan, the following are especially recommended in addition to those cited in the Notes: G. Trewartha, *Japan: A Geography* (1965); and E. O. Reischauer and J. K. Fairbank, *East Asia: The Great Tradition* (1960). More recent works include C. Schirokauer, *A Brief History of Chinese and Japanese Civilizations,* 2d ed. (1989); J. K. Fairbank, E. O. Reischauer, and A. Craig, *East Asia: Tradition and Transformation,* rev. ed. (1989); C. Totman, *Japan Before Perry* (1981); and A. Tiedmann, ed., *An Introduction to Japanese Civilization* (1974)

For early Japanese history, G. J. Groot, *The Prehistory of Japan* (1951), is still useful though rapidly becoming dated. The same is true of J. E. Kidder, *Japan Before Buddhism* (1959). Newer and quite readable is Kidder, *Early Buddhist Japan* (1972), which is well illustrated. J. M. Kitagawa, *Religion in Japanese History* (1966), discusses both Shinto and Buddhism.

Early Japanese literary flowering has attracted much attention. I. Morris, *The World of the Shining Prince: Court Life in Ancient Japan* (1964), provides a general treatment of the climate in which early Japanese artists lived. Murasaki Shikibu, *The Tale of Genji* has been recently translated by R. Bowring (1988); I. Morris translated *The Pillow Book of Sei Shonagon,* 2 vols. (1967).

Japanese feudalism, like its medieval European counterpart, continues to excite discussion and disagreement. Some provocative works include K. Asakawa, *Land and Society in Medieval Japan* (1965); P. Duus, *Feudalism in Japan,* 2d ed. (1976); J. W. Hall, *Government and Local Power in Japan: 500–1700: A Study Based on Bizen Province* (1966); and E. O. Reischauer, "Japanese Feudalism," in R. Coulborn, ed., *Feudalism in History* (1956), pp. 26–48.

12

Europe in the Early and High Middle Ages

St. Bernard, Abbot of Clairvaux, preaching to his fellow Cistercians

The Frankish chieftain Charles Martel defeated Muslim invaders in 733 at the Battle of Tours in central France.[1] Although at the time the battle seemed only another skirmish in the struggle between Christians and Muslims, in retrospect it looms as one of the great battles of history: this Frankish victory halted Muslim expansion in northern Europe.

Between 733 and 843 a distinctly European society emerged. A new kind of social and political organization, later called "feudalism," appeared. And for the first time since the collapse of the Roman Empire, most of western Europe was united under one government, which reached its peak under Charles Martel's grandson, Charlemagne. Christian missionary activity among the Germanic peoples continued, and strong ties were forged with the Roman papacy. A revival of study and learning, sometimes styled the "Carolingian Renaissance," occurred under Charlemagne.

In 843 Charlemagne's three grandsons, after a bitter war, concluded the Treaty of Verdun, dividing the European continent among themselves. Against this background, invasion and disorder wracked Europe for about 150 years.

By the last quarter of the tenth century, after a long and bitter winter of discontent, the first signs of European spring appeared. That spring lasted from the early eleventh century to the end of the thirteenth. This period from about 1050 to 1300 has often been called the "High Middle Ages." The term designates a time of crucial growth and remarkable cultural achievement between two eras of economic, political, and social crisis.

- How did Charlemagne acquire and govern his vast empire?
- What was the Carolingian Renaissance?
- What factors contributed to the disintegration of the Carolingian Empire?
- What was feudalism, and how did it begin?
- What were the ingredients of the revival that followed the great invasions of the ninth century?
- What was the social and political impact of the recovery of Europe?
- How did the Christian church's development during the early and High Middle Ages affect relations between the church and civil authorities?
- What were the Crusades, and how did they manifest the influence of the church and the ideals of medieval society?

These are the questions that frame discussion in this chapter.

THE FRANKISH ARISTOCRACY AND THE RISE OF THE CAROLINGIAN DYNASTY

Through a series of remarkable victories over other Germanic tribes, the Franks under Clovis (r. 481–511) had emerged as the most powerful people in Europe by the early sixth century (see page 247). The Frankish kingdom included most of what is now France and a large section of the southern half of western Germany. Clovis's baptism into orthodox Christianity in 496 won him church support against other Germanic tribes, most of them Arian Christians. Clovis died in 511, and the Merovingian dynasty went on to rule for the next two centuries.

Rule is, of course, too strong a verb. Conquering the vast territories proved easier than governing them for the Merovingians, given their inadequate political institutions. The size of Clovis's kingdom forced him to divide it among his four sons, because no one person could govern it effectively. Practically, however, Clovis's decision was disastrous. The Merovingians bitterly hated one another, and each king fought to deprive his relatives of their portions of the kingdom. Violence and assassination ceased only when one man had killed off all his rivals. Thus in 558 Clovis's youngest son, Lothair, acquired the whole kingdom after he had murdered two nephews and eliminated one rebellious son by burning him and his family alive. After Lothair died, his sons continued the civil war until one king survived.

Civil war in the Frankish kingdom may have provided the opportunity for a distinct aristocratic class to emerge. Recent research in Frankish family history has revealed that a noble ruling class existed before the mid-sixth century. Members of this class belonged to families of high reputation who gradually intermarried with members of the old Gallo-Roman senatorial class. They possessed wealth and great villas where they led an aristo-

Merovingian Army This sixth- or seventh-century ivory depicts a nobleman in civilian dress followed by seven warriors. Note that the mounted men do not have stirrups and that they seem to have fought with spears and bows and arrows. The power of the Frankish aristocracy rested on these private armies. *(Source: Rheinisches/Landesmuseum, Trier)*

cratic lifestyle. They exercised rights of lordship over their lands and tenants, dispensing local customary, not royal, law. These families provided almost all the bishops of the church. Because they had a self-conscious awareness of their social, economic, and political distinctiveness, they constituted a noble class.[2]

In the seventh century, the central government of the Merovingians could not control these nobles. Primitive and disorganized, the government consisted of a few household officials, the most important of whom was the mayor of the palace. He was in charge of administration and acted as the king's deputy; he also represented the interests of the nobility. Because the Frankish kingdom was divided into East Frankland, West Frankland, and Burgundy, and because some territories such as Bavaria were virtually independent, the Merovingian kingdom slowly disintegrated.

Reconstruction of the Frankish kingdom began with the efforts of Pippin of Landen, a member of one aristocratic family. In the early seventh century, he was mayor of the palace in East Frankland. His grandson, Pippin II (d. 714), gained the posi-tion of mayor of the palace in both East and West Frankland. It was Pippin II's son Charles Martel (714–741) who defeated the Muslims at Tours and thus checked Arab expansion in northern Europe. Charles's wars against the Saxons, Burgundians, and Frisians broke those weakening forces. His victory over the Muslims and his successful campaigns in the Frankish kingdom added to his family's prestige a reputation for great military strength. Charles Martel held the real power in the Frankish kingdom; the Merovingians were kings in name only.

The rise of the Carolingian dynasty, whose name derives from the Latin *Carolus,* meaning "Charles," was partly due to papal support. In the early eighth century, missionaries supported Charles Martel and his son Pippin III as they attempted to bring the various Germanic tribes under their jurisdiction. The most important missionary was the Anglo-Saxon Wynfrith, or Boniface (680–754), as he was later called. Given the semibarbaric peoples with whom he was dealing, Boniface's achievements were remarkable. He helped shape the structure of the German church.

He established *The Rule of Saint Benedict* in all the monasteries that he founded or reformed. And with the full support of Pippin III, he held several councils that reformed the Frankish church.

Saint Boniface preached throughout Germany against divorce, polygamous unions, and incest. On these matters German custom and ecclesiastical law completely disagreed. The Germans allowed divorce simply by the mutual consent of both parties. The Germanic peoples also practiced polygamy (the practice of having more than one wife) and incest (sexual relations between brothers and sisters or parents and children) on a wide scale. Church councils and theologians stressed that marriage, validly entered into, could not be ended, and they firmly condemned incest.

Boniface's preaching was not without impact, for in 802 Charlemagne prohibited incest and decreed that a husband might separate from an adulterous wife. The woman could be punished, and the man could not remarry in her lifetime. Charlemagne also encouraged severe punishment for adulterous men. In so doing, he contributed to the dignity of marriage, the family, and women.

Charles Martel and Pippin III protected Boniface, and he preached Christian obedience to rulers. Because of Boniface's staunch adherence to Roman ideas and the Roman pope, the Romanization of Europe accompanied its Christianization.

Charles Martel had been king of the Franks in fact but not in title. His son Pippin III (r. 751–768) made himself king in title as well as in fact. In Germanic custom—and custom was law—the kingship had to pass to someone of royal blood. Pippin did not want to murder the ineffectual Merovingian king, but he did want the kingship. Because the missionary activity of Boniface had enhanced papal influence in the Frankish kingdom, Pippin decided to consult the pope. Accordingly, Pippin sent envoys to Rome to ask the pope whether the man with the power was entitled to be king. Pope Zacharias (r. 741–752), guided by the Augustinian principle that the real test of kingship is whether it provides for order and justice, responded in 751 that he who has the power should also have the title. This answer constituted recognition of the Carolingians. The Merovingian king was deposed and forced to become a monk.

Just as the emperors Constantine and Theodosius had taken actions in the fourth century that would later be cited as precedents in church-state relations (see pages 221, 231), so Pippin III in the mid-eighth century took papal confirmation as official approval of his title. In 751 Pippin III was formally elected king of the Franks by the *magnates*, or great lords, of the Frankish territory. Three years later, Pope Stephen II (r. 752–757)—who needed Pippin's protection from the Lombards—came to Gaul and personally anointed Pippin king at Paris. Thus an important alliance was struck between the papacy and the Frankish ruler. In 754 Pope Stephen gave Pippin the title "Protector of the Roman Church." Pippin in turn agreed to restore to the papacy territories in northern Italy recently seized by the Lombards, and he promptly marched into Italy and defeated the Lombards. The Carolingian family had received official recognition and anointment from the leading spiritual power in Europe, and the papacy had gained a powerful military protector.

On a second successful campaign in Italy in 756, Pippin made a large donation to the papacy. The gift was estates in central Italy that technically belonged to the Byzantine emperor. Known as the "Papal States," they existed over a thousand years, until the newly formed kingdom of Italy abolished them in 1870.

Because of Pippin's anointment, his kingship took on a special spiritual and moral character. Before Pippin, only priests and bishops had received anointment. Pippin became the first to be anointed with the sacred oils and acknowledged as *rex et sacerdos* ("king and priest"). Anointment, rather than royal blood, set the Christian king apart. Pippin also cleverly eliminated possible threats to the Frankish throne, and the pope promised him support in the future. When Pippin died, his son Charles succeeded him.

THE EMPIRE OF CHARLEMAGNE

Charles the Great (r. 768–814) built on the military and diplomatic foundations of his ancestors. Charles's secretary and biographer, a Saxon by the name of Einhard, wrote a lengthy description of this warrior-ruler. It has serious flaws, partly because it is modeled directly on the Roman author Suetonius's *Life of the Emperor* Augustus. Still, it is the earliest medieval biography of a layman, and historians consider it generally accurate:

Charles was large and strong, and of lofty stature, though not disproportionately tall . . . the upper part of his head was round, his eyes very large and animated, nose a little long, hair fair, and face laughing and merry. Thus his appearance was always stately and dignified . . . although his neck was thick and somewhat short, and his belly rather prominent; but the symmetry of the rest of his body concealed these defects. His gait was firm, his whole carriage manly, and his voice clear, but not so strong as his size led one to expect. In accordance with the national custom, he took frequent exercise on horseback and in the chase, accomplishments in which scarcely any people in the world can equal the Franks. He enjoyed the exhalations from natural warm springs, and often practiced swimming, in which he was such an adept that none could surpass him.[3]

Though crude and brutal, Charlemagne was a man of enormous intelligence. He appreciated good literature, such as Saint Augustine's *City of God,* and Einhard considered him an unusually effective speaker. On the other hand, he could not even write his own name.

The security and continuation of his dynasty and the need for diplomatic alliances governed Charlemagne's complicated marriage pattern. The high rate of infant mortality required many sons. Married first to the daughter of Desiderius, king of the Lombards, Charlemagne divorced her on grounds of sterility. His second wife, Hildegard, produced nine children in twelve years. When she died, Charlemagne married Fastrada, daughter of an East Frankish count whose support Charles needed in his campaign against the Saxons. Charlemagne had a total of four legal wives and six concubines, and even after the age of sixty-five continued to sire children. Though three sons reached adulthood, only one outlived him. His three surviving grandsons, however, ensured perpetuation of the family.

Territorial Expansion

The most striking feature of Charlemagne's character was his phenomenal energy, which helps to explain his tremendous military achievements.[4]

Continuing the expansionist policies of his ancestors, Charlemagne fought more than fifty campaigns and became the greatest warrior of the early Middle Ages. He subdued all of the north of modern France (Map 12.1). In the south, the lords of the mountainous ranges of Aquitaine—

Equestrian Statue of Charlemagne A medieval king was expected to be fierce (and successful) in battle, to defend the church and the poor, and to give justice to all. This majestic and idealized figure of Charlemagne conveys these qualities. The horse is both the symbol and the means of his constant travels. *(Source: Girandon/Art Resource)*

MAP 12.1 The Carolingian World The extent of Charlemagne's nominal jurisdiction was extraordinary: it was not equaled until the nineteenth century.

what is now called "Basque country"—fought off his efforts at total conquest. The Muslims in northeastern Spain were checked by the establishment of strongly fortified areas known as *marches.*

Charlemagne's greatest successes occurred in modern-day Germany. There his concerns were basically defensive. In the course of a thirty-year war against the semibarbaric Saxons, he added most of the northwestern German tribes to the Frankish kingdom. Because of their repeated rebellions, Charlemagne (according to Einhard) ordered more than four thousand Saxons slaughtered in one day.

To the south, he also achieved spectacular results. In 773 and 774 the Lombards in northern Italy again threatened the papacy. Charlemagne marched south, overran fortresses at Pavia and Spoleto, and incorporated Lombardy into the Frankish kingdom. Charlemagne also ended Bavarian independence and defeated the nomadic Avars, opening the plain of the Danube for later settlement. He successfully fought the Byzantine Empire for Venetia (excluding the city of Venice itself), Istria, and Dalmatia and temporarily annexed those areas to his kingdom.

Charlemagne tried to occupy Basque territory in northwestern Spain between the Ebro River and the Pyrenees. When he was forced to retreat, his rear guard under Count Roland was annihilated by the Basques at Roncevalles (778). Although the foray had little political significance, the campaign in Spain inspired the great medieval epic, *The Song of Roland.* Based on legend and written down around 1100 at the beginning of the European crusading movement, the poem portrays Roland as the ideal chivalric knight and Charlemagne as having devoted his life to fighting the Muslims. Although considerably removed from the historical evidence, *The Song of Roland* is important because it reveals the popular image of Charlemagne in later centuries.

By around 805, the Frankish kingdom included all of continental Europe except Spain, Scandinavia, southern Italy, and the Slavic fringes of the East (see Map 12.1). Not since the third century A.D. had any ruler controlled so much of the Western world. Not until Napoleon Bonaparte's era in the early nineteenth century was the feat to be repeated.

The Government of the Carolingian Empire

Charlemagne ruled a vast rural world dotted with isolated estates and characterized by constant petty violence. His empire was definitely not a state as people today understand that term; it was a collection of primitive peoples and semibarbaric tribes. Apart from a small class of warrior-aristocrats and clergy, almost everyone engaged in agriculture. Trade and commerce played only a small part in the economy. Cities served as the headquarters of bishops and as ecclesiastical centers.

By constant travel, personal appearances, and the sheer force of his personality, Charlemagne sought to awe conquered peoples with his fierce presence and terrible justice. By confiscating the estates of great territorial magnates, he acquired lands and goods with which to gain the support of lesser lords, further expanding the territory under his control.

The political power of the Carolingians rested on the cooperation of the dominant social class, the Frankish aristocracy. By the seventh century, through mutual cooperation and frequent marriage alliances, these families exercised great power that did not derive from the Merovingian kings. The Carolingians themselves had emerged from this aristocracy, and their military and political success depended on its support. The lands and booty with which Charles Martel and Charlemagne rewarded their followers in these noble families enabled the nobles to improve their economic position; but it was only with noble help that the Carolingians were able to wage wars of expansion and suppress rebellions. In short, Carolingian success was a matter of reciprocal help and reward.[5]

Two or three hundred counts, powerful members of the imperial nobility, governed at the local level. They had full military and judicial power and held their offices for life but could be removed for misconduct. As a link between local authorities and the central government of the emperor, Charlemagne appointed officials called *missi dominici,* "agents of the lord king." The empire was divided into visitorial districts. Each year, beginning in 802, two missi, usually a count and a bishop or abbot, visited assigned districts. They held courts and investigated the district's judicial, financial, and clerical activities. They held commissions to regulate crime, moral conduct, education, the clergy, the poor, and many other matters. The missi checked up on the counts and worked to prevent the counts' positions from becoming hereditary: strong counts with hereditary estates would have weakened the emperor's power. In especially barbarous regions, such as the Spanish and Danish borders, Charles set up areas called "marks," where officials called "margraves" had extensive powers to govern.

A modern state has institutions of government, such as a civil service, courts of law, financial agencies for apportioning and collecting taxes, and police and military powers with which to maintain order internally and defend against foreign attack. These did not exist in Charlemagne's empire.

A Dual Investiture As Christ gave authority to St. Peter (Matthew 16:18–20), so Peter invests Pope Leo III (r. 795–816) with the pallium, symbol of archiepiscopal authority, and Charlemagne with the Roman standard, representing civil authority in the West. Leo III commissioned this mosaic to celebrate papal power. *(Source: Scala/Art Resource)*

What held society together were dependent relationships cemented by oaths promising faith and loyalty.

Although the empire lacked viable institutions, some Carolingians involved in governing did have vigorous political ideas. The abbots and bishops who served as Charlemagne's advisers worked out what was for their time a sophisticated political ideology based on high ideals of behavior and of government. They wrote that a ruler may hold power from God but is responsible to the law. Just as all subjects of the empire were required to obey him, so he, too, was obliged to respect the law. They envisioned a unified Christian society presided over by a king who was responsible for maintaining peace. These views derived largely from Saint Augustine's theories of kingship (see page 241). Inevitably, they could not be realized in an illiterate, half-Christianized, preindustrial society. But they were the foundations from which medieval and even modern ideas of government were to develop.

The Imperial Coronation of Charlemagne (800)

In the autumn of the year 800, Charlemagne paid a momentous visit to Rome. Einhard gave this account of what happened:

His last journey there to Rome was due to another factor, namely that the Romans, having inflicted many injuries on Pope Leo—plucking out his eyes and tearing out his tongue, he had been compelled to beg the assistance of the king. Accordingly, coming to Rome in order that he might set in order those things which had exceedingly disturbed the condition of the Church, he remained there the whole winter. It was at the time that he accepted the name of Emperor and Augustus. At first he was so much opposed to this that he insisted that although that day was a great [Christian] feast, he would not have entered the Church if he had known beforehand the pope's intention. But he bore very patiently the jealousy of the Roman Emperors [that is, the Byzantine rulers] who were indignant when he received these titles. He overcame their arrogant haughtiness with magnanimity, a virtue in which he was considerably superior to them, by sending frequent ambassadors to them and in his letters addressing them as brothers.[6]

Did Charles plan the imperial coronation ceremony in Saint Peter's Cathedral on Christmas Day or did he merely accept the imperial title? What did he have to gain from it? Did Charlemagne use the imperial title? Did Pope Leo III (r. 795–816) arrange the coronation in order to identify the Frankish monarchy with the papacy and papal policy? Final answers will probably never be found, but several things seem certain.

First, Charlemagne considered himself a Christian king ruling a Christian people. His motto, *Renovatio Romani Imperi* ("Revival of the Roman Empire"), "implied a revival of the Western Empire in the image of Augustinian political philosophy," according to one historian.[7] Charles was consciously perpetuating old Roman imperial notions while at the same time identifying with the new Rome of the Christian church. Charlemagne and his government represented a combination of Frankish practices and Christian ideals, the two basic elements of medieval European society.

Second, later German rulers were eager to gain the imperial title and to associate themselves with the legends of Charlemagne and ancient Rome. Finally, ecclesiastical authorities continually cited the event as proof that the dignity of the imperial crown could be granted only by the pope. Whether planned by the Carolingian court or by the pope, the imperial coronation of Charlemagne was to have a profound effect on the course of German history and on the later history of Europe.

THE CAROLINGIAN INTELLECTUAL REVIVAL

It is ironic that Charlemagne's most enduring legacy was the stimulus he gave to scholarship and learning. Barely literate himself, preoccupied with the control of vast territories, much more a warrior than a thinker, he nevertheless set in motion a cultural revival that had "international" and long-lasting consequences. The revival of learning associated with Charlemagne and his court at Aachen drew its greatest inspiration from seventh- and eighth-century intellectual developments in the Anglo-Saxon kingdom of Northumbria, situated at the northernmost tip of the old Roman world (see Map 12.1).

Northumbrian Culture

Despite the victory of the Roman forms of Christian liturgy at the Synod of Whitby in 664 (see page 235), Irish-Celtic culture permeated the Roman church in Britain and resulted in a flowering of artistic and scholarly activity. Northumbrian creativity owes a great deal to the intellectual curiosity and collecting zeal of Saint Benet Biscop (ca 628–689). A strong supporter of Benedictine monasticism, Benet Biscop introduced the Roman ceremonial form into new religious houses that he founded and encouraged it in older ones. Benet Biscop made five dangerous trips to Italy, raided libraries, and brought back to Northumbria manuscripts, relics, paintings, and other treasures that formed the libraries on which much later study was based.

Northumbrian monasteries produced scores of books: missals (used for the celebration of the mass), psalters (which contained the 150 psalms and other prayers used by the monks in their devotions), commentaries on the Scriptures, illuminated manuscripts, law codes, and letters and sermons. The finest product of Northumbrian art is probably the Gospel book produced at Lindisfarne around 700. The incredible expense involved in the publication of such a book—for vellum, coloring, gold leaf—represents in part an aristocratic display of wealth. The script, *uncial,* is a Celtic version of contemporary Greek and Roman handwriting. The illustrations have an Eastern quality, combining the abstract style of the Christian Middle East and the narrative approach of classical Roman art. Likewise, the use of geometrical decorative designs shows the influence of Syrian art. Many scribes, artists, and illuminators must have participated in the book's preparation.

The finest representative of Northumbrian and indeed all Anglo-Saxon scholarship is the Venerable Bede (ca 673–735). Bede spent his life in Benet Biscop's monastery, surrounded by the books Benet Biscop had brought from Italy. Bede's scrupulous observance of *The Rule of Saint Benedict* showed his deep piety. As a scholar, his patience and diligence reflected a profound love of learning. Contemporaries revered Bede for his learned commentaries on the Scriptures and for the special holiness of his life, which earned him the title "Venerable." He was the most widely read author in the Middle Ages.

St. Hilda The superior of a mixed monastery of men and women at Whitby in Northumbria, St. Hilda (614–680) here receives a copy of the scholar Aldhelm's treatise *In Praise of Holy Virgins.* The simple drapery of the nuns' clothing with its nervous quality is characteristic of the eleventh-century Anglo-Saxon scriptoria. *(Source: His Grace the Archbishop of Canterbury and the Trustees of Lambeth Palace Library)*

Modern scholars praise Bede for his *Ecclesiastical History of the English Nation.* Broader in scope than the title suggests, it is the chief source of information about early Britain. Bede searched far and wide for his information, discussed the validity of his evidence, compared various sources, and exercised a rare critical judgment. For these reasons, he has been called the "first scientific intellect among the Germanic peoples of Europe."[8]

Bede also popularized the system of dating events from the birth of Christ. He introduced the term *anno Domini,* "in the year of the Lord" (abbreviated A.D.), and fit the entire history of the world into this new dating method. Saint Boniface introduced this system of reckoning time throughout the Frankish kingdom.

The physical circumstances of life in the seventh and eighth centuries make Northumbrian cultural achievements all the more remarkable. Learning was pursued under terribly primitive conditions.

Monasteries such as Jarrow and Lindisfarne stood on the very fringes of the European world (see Map 12.1). The barbarian Picts, just an afternoon's walk from Jarrow, were likely to attack at any time.

Food was not the greatest problem. The North Sea and nearby rivers, the Tweed and the Tyne, yielded abundant salmon and other fish, which could be salted or smoked for winter, a nutritious if monotonous diet. Climate was another matter. Winter could be extremely harsh. In 664, for example, deep snow was hardened by frost from early winter until mid-spring. When it melted away, many animals, trees, and plants were found dead. To make matters worse, disease could take terrible tolls, as Bede described: "Also in that year 664 a sudden pestilence first depopulated the southern parts of Britain and then attacked the kingdom of the Northumbrians as well. Raging far and wide for a long time with cruel devastation it struck down a great multitude of men."[9] Damp cold with bitter winds blowing across the North Sea must have pierced everything, even stone monasteries. Inside, only one room, the *calefactory,* or "warming room," had a fire. Scribes in the *scriptorium,* or "writing room," had to stop frequently to rub circulation back into their numb hands. These monk-artists and monk-writers paid a high physical price for what they gave to posterity.

Had Northumbrian cultural achievements remained entirely insular, they would have been of slight significance. As it happened, an Englishman from Northumbria played a decisive role in the transmission of English learning to the Carolingian Empire and continental Europe.

The Carolingian Renaissance

Charlemagne's empire began to disintegrate shortly after his death in 814. But the support Charlemagne gave to education and learning helped preserve the writings of the ancients and laid the foundations for all subsequent medieval culture in Europe. Charlemagne promoted a revival that scholars have named the "Carolingian Renaissance."

At his court at Aachen, Charlemagne assembled learned men from all over Europe. The most important scholar and the leader of the palace school was a Northumbrian, Alcuin (ca 735–804). From 781 until his death, Alcuin was the emperor's chief adviser on religious and educational matters. An unusually prolific scholar, Alcuin prepared some of the emperor's official documents and wrote many moral *exempla,* or "models," which set high standards for royal behavior and constitute a treatise on kingship. Alcuin's letters to Charlemagne set forth political theories on the authority, power, and responsibilities of a Christian ruler.

What did the scholars at Charlemagne's court do? They copied books and manuscripts and built up libraries. They developed the beautifully clear handwriting known as "Carolingian minuscule," from which modern Roman type is derived. (This script is called "minuscule" because it has lower-case letters; the Romans had only capitals.) They established schools all across Europe, attaching them to monasteries and cathedrals. They placed great emphasis on the education of priests, trying to make all of them at least able to read, write, and do simple arithmetic.

The revival of learning inspired by Charlemagne and directed by Alcuin halted the threat of barbaric illiteracy on the European continent. Although hardly widespread by later standards, basic literacy was established among the clergy and even among some of the nobility. The greatest contribution of the scholars at Aachen was not so much the originality of their ideas as their hard work of salvaging and preserving the language, thought, and writings of classical Greece and Rome.

Meanwhile, the common people spoke their local vernacular languages. Thus the Saxons and Bavarians, for example, despite their geographical

The Venerable Bede This twelfth-century representation of the eighth-century monk cannot pretend to an accurate likeness but shows that later ages respected Bede as a scholar. Note the knife in one hand to sharpen the pen in the other. *(Source: The British Library)*

Plan for an Ideal Monastery This is a ninth-century architectural design for a self-supporting monastic community of two hundred and seventy members. The monks' lives mainly focused on the church and the cloister, which appropriately appear in the center of the plan. Note the herb garden close to the physician's quarters. The western entrance for visitors was surrounded by the hostel for poor guests and pens for farm animals—with all the inevitable smells. *(Source: Kenneth John Conant,* Carolingian and Romanesque Architecture, 800–1200. *Pelican History of Art, 2nd rev. ed. (New York: Pelican, 1978), p. 57)*

proximity (see Map 12.1), could not understand each other. Communication among the diverse peoples of the Carolingian Empire was possible only through the medium of Latin.

Once basic literacy was established, monastic and other scholars went on to more difficult work. By the middle years of the ninth century, there was

a great outpouring of more sophisticated books. Ecclesiastical writers, imbued with the legal ideas of ancient Rome and the theocratic ideals of Saint Augustine, instructed the semibarbaric rulers of the West. And it is no accident that systematic medical study in the West began, at Salerno in southern Italy, in the late ninth century, *after* the Carolingian Renaissance.

Alcuin completed the work of his countryman Boniface: the Christianization of northern Europe. Latin Christian attitudes penetrated deeply into the consciousness of European peoples. By the tenth century, the patterns of thought and lifestyles of educated Western Europeans were those of Rome and Latin Christianity. Even the violence and destruction of the great invasions of the ninth century and the conflicts of the tenth could not destroy the strong foundations laid by Alcuin and his colleagues.

HEALTH AND MEDICAL CARE IN THE EARLY MIDDLE AGES

In a society devoted to fighting, warriors and civilians alike stood a strong chance of wounds from sword, spear, battle-ax, or blunt instrument. Trying to eke a living from poor soil with poor tools, perpetually involved in pushing back forest and wasteland, the farmer and his family daily ran the risk of accidents. Poor diet weakened everyone's resistance to disease. People bathed rarely. Low standards of personal hygiene increased the danger of infection. This being the case, what medical attention was available to medieval people? Scholars' examination of medical treatises, prescription (or herbal) books, manuscript illustrations, and archeological evidence has recently revealed a surprising amount of information about medical treatment in the early Middle Ages.

The Germanic peoples had no rational understanding of the causes and cures of disease. They believed that sickness was due to one of three factors: elf-shot, darts hurled by elves, that produced disease and pain; wormlike creatures in the body; and the number 9. Treatments included charms, amulets, priestly incantations, and potions. Drinks prepared from mistletoe, for example, were thought to serve as an antidote to poison and to make women fertile.

Medical practice consisted primarily of drug and prescription therapy. Through the monks' efforts and recovery of Greek and Arabic manuscripts, a large body of the ancients' prescriptions was preserved and passed on. For almost any ailment, several recipes were likely to exist in the prescription lists. Balsam was recommended for coughs. For asthma, an ointment combining chicken, wormwood, laurel berries, and oil of roses was rubbed on the chest. The scores of prescriptions to rid the body of lice, fleas, and other filth reflect frightful standards of personal hygiene. The large number of prescriptions for eye troubles suggests that they, too, must have been common. This is understandable, given the widespread practice of locating the fireplace in the center of the room. A lot of smoke and soot filtered into the room, rather than going up the chimney. One remedy calls for bathing the eyes in a solution of herbs mixed with honey, balsam, rainwater, salt water, or wine.

Poor diet caused frequent stomach disorders and related ailments such as dysentery, constipation, and diarrhea. The value of dieting and avoiding greasy foods was recognized. For poor circulation, a potion of meadow wort, oak rind, and lustmock was recommended. Pregnant women were advised to abstain from eating the flesh of almost all male animals because their meat might deform the child. Men with unusually strong sexual appetites were advised to fast and to drink at night the juice of agrimony (an herb of the rose family) boiled in ale. If a man suffered from lack of drive, the same plant boiled in milk gave him "courage."

Physicians did not examine patients. The physician, or "leech," as he was known in Anglo-Saxon England, treated only what he could see or deduce from obvious symptoms. The physician knew little about physiological functions, internal medicine, or the pathology of disease. He had no accurate standards of weights and measures. Prescriptions called for "a pinch" or "a handful" or "an eggshell full."

All wounds and open injuries invited infection, and infection invited gangrene. Several remedies were known for wounds. Physicians appreciated the antiseptic properties of honey, and prescriptions recommended that wounds be cleaned with it. When an area or limb had become gangrenous, a good technique of amputation existed. The physician was instructed to cut above the diseased flesh—that is, to cut away some healthy tissue and

bone—in order to hasten cure. The juice of white poppy plants—the source of heroin—could be added to wine and drunk as an anesthetic. White poppies, however, grew only in southern Europe and North Africa. If a heavy slug of wine was not enough to dull the patient, he or she had to be held down forcibly while the physician cut. Butter and egg whites, which have a soothing effect, were prescribed for burns.

Teeth survive long periods of burial and give reasonably good information about disease. Evidence from early medieval England shows that in the adult population, the rate of cavities was only

The Wound Man This illustration from a fifteenth-century manuscript depicts a "wound man" displaying weapons, sources of injuries, and sores. It may have been used to prompt the aspiring surgeon's memory. *(Source: Courtesy, The Wellcome Institute)*

one-sixth that of today. Cavities below the gum line, however, were very common because of the prevalence of carbohydrates in the diet. The resulting abscesses of the gums, and other forms of periodontal disease, were widespread after the age of thirty.[10]

The spread of Christianity in the Carolingian era had a beneficial effect on medical knowledge and treatment. Several of the church fathers expressed serious interest in medicine. Some of them even knew something about it. The church was deeply concerned about human suffering, whether physical or mental. Christian teaching vigorously supported concern for the poor, sick, downtrodden, and miserable. Churchmen taught that, while all knowledge came from God, he had supplied it so that people could use it for their own benefit.

In the sixth and seventh centuries, the period of the bloodiest violence, medical treatment was provided by monasteries. No other places offered the calm, quiet atmosphere necessary for treatment and recuperation. Monks took care of the sick. They collected and translated the ancient medical treatises. They cultivated herb gardens from which medicines were prepared.

The founding of a school at Salerno sometime in the ninth century gave a tremendous impetus to medical study by lay people. Its location attracted Arabic, Greek, and Jewish physicians from all over the Mediterranean region. Students flocked there from northern Europe. The Jewish physician Shabbathai Ben Abraham (931–982) left behind pharmacological notes that were widely studied in later centuries.

By the eleventh century, the medical school at Salerno enjoyed international fame. Its most distinguished professor was Constantine the African. A native of Carthage, he had studied medicine throughout the Middle East and, because of his thorough knowledge of Oriental languages, served as an important transmitter of Arabic culture to the West. Constantine taught and practiced medicine at Salerno for some years before becoming a monk.

Several women physicians also contributed to the celebrity of the school. Trotula, for example, an authority on gynecological problems, wrote a book called *On Female Disorders*. Though not connected with the Salerno medical school, the abbess Hildegard (1098–1179) of Rupertsberg in Hesse, Germany, reputedly treated the emperor Frederick Barbarossa. Hildegard's treatise *On the Physical*

Elements shows a remarkable degree of careful scientific observation.

How available was medical treatment? Most people lived on isolated rural estates and had to take such advice and help as were available locally. Physicians were few in the early Middle Ages. They charged a fee that only the rich could afford. Apparently, most illnesses simply took their course. People had to develop a stoical attitude. Death came early. A person of forty was considered old. People's vulnerability to ailments for which there was no cure contributed to a fatalistic acceptance of death at a young age. Early medical literature shows that attempts to relieve pain were crude; still, they *were* made.

DIVISION AND DISINTEGRATION OF THE CAROLINGIAN EMPIRE (814–987)

Charlemagne left his vast empire to his only surviving son, Louis the Pious (r. 814–840), who had actually been crowned emperor in his father's lifetime. Deeply religious and well educated, Louis was no soldier. Thus he could not retain the respect and loyalty of the warrior-aristocracy on whom he depended for troops and for administration of his territories. Disintegration began almost at once.

The basic reason for the collapse of the Carolingian Empire is simply that it was too big. In Charlemagne's lifetime it was held together by the sheer force of his personality and driving energy. After his death, it began to fall apart. The empire lacked a bureaucracy like that of the Roman Empire—the administrative machinery necessary for strong and enduring government. It was a collection of tribes held together at the pleasure of warrior-aristocrats, men most interested in strengthening their own local positions and ensuring that they could pass on to their sons the offices and estates that they had amassed. Counts, abbots, bishops—both lay and ecclesiastical magnates—needed estates to support themselves and reward their followers. In their localities, they simply assumed judicial, military, and financial functions. Why should they obey an unimpressive distant ruler who represented a centralizing power that threatened their local interests?

Bad roads swarming with thugs and rivers infested with pirates made communication within the empire very difficult. Added to this was the Frankish custom of dividing estates among all male heirs. Between 817 and his death in 840, Louis the Pious made several divisions of the empire. Dissatisfied with their portions and anxious to gain the imperial title, Louis's sons—Lothair, Louis the German, and Charles the Bald—fought bitterly among themselves. Finally, in the Treaty of Verdun of 843, the brothers agreed to partition the empire (Map 12.2).

Lothair, the eldest, received the now-empty title of emperor and the "middle kingdom," which included Italy and the territories bordered by the Meuse, Saône, and Rhône rivers in the west and the Rhine in the east. Almost immediately, this kingdom broke up into many petty principalities extending diagonally across Europe from Flanders to Lombardy. From the tenth century to the twelfth and thirteenth centuries, when French and German monarchs were trying to build strong central governments, this area was constantly contested between them. Even in modern times, the "middle kingdom" of Lothair has been blood-soaked.

The eastern and most Germanic part of the Carolingian Empire passed to Louis the German. The western kingdom went to Charles the Bald; it included the provinces of Aquitaine and Gascony and formed the basis of medieval and modern France. The descendants of Charles the Bald held on in the west until 987, when the leading magnates elected Hugh Capet as king. The heirs of Louis the German ruled the eastern kingdom until 911, but real power was in the hands of local chieftains. Everywhere in the tenth century, fratricidal warfare among the descendants of Charlemagne accelerated the spread of feudalism.

FEUDALISM

The adjective *feudal* is often used disparagingly today to describe something antiquated and barbaric. It is similarly commonplace to think of medieval feudalism as a system that let a small group of lazy military leaders exploit the producing class, the tillers of the soil. This is not a very useful approach. Preindustrial societies ranging from ancient Greece to the American South before the Civil War to some twentieth-century Latin American countries have been characterized by sharp di-

MAP 12.2 Division of the Carolingian Empire, 843 The Treaty of Verdun (843), which divided the empire among Charlemagne's grandsons, is frequently taken as the start of the separate development of Germany, France, and Italy. The "middle kingdom" of Lothair, however, lacking defensive borders and any political or linguistic unity, quickly broke up into numerous small territories.

visions between "exploiters" and "exploited." To call all such societies "feudal" strips the term of significant meaning and distorts understanding of medieval feudalism. Many twentieth-century scholars have demonstrated that, when feudalism developed, it served the needs of medieval society.

The Two Levels of Feudalism

Webster's *Third New International Dictionary* defines *government* as "the officials collectively comprising the governing body of a political unit and constituting the organization as an active agency." Although the term *feudalism* was not coined until the seventeenth century, feudalism emerged in western Europe in the ninth century and was a type of government "in which political power was treated as a private possession and was divided among a large number of lords."[11] This kind of government characterized western Europe from about 900 to 1300.

Feudalism actually existed at two social levels: first, at the level of armed retainers who became knights; second, at the level of royal officials, such as counts, who ruled great feudal principalities. A wide and deep gap in social standing and political function separated these armed retainers and royal officials.

In the early eighth century, the Carolingian kings and other powerful men needed bodyguards and retainers, armed men who could fight effectively on horseback. The arrival in western Europe around this time of a Chinese technological invention, the stirrup, revolutionized warfare. The stirrup welded horse and rider into a powerful fighting unit. A rider without stirrups could seldom impale an adversary, but a rider in stirrups could utilize the force of the galloping animal to strike and wound the enemy. Charles Martel recognized the potential of heavily armed cavalry equipped with stirrups, and the invention prompted him to gather a large number of retainers. Horses and armor were terribly expensive, and few could afford them. It also took considerable time to train a man to be an effective cavalryman. As the value of retainers increased, Charles Martel and other powerful men bound their retainers by oaths of loyalty and ceremonies of homage. Here is an oath of *fealty* (or faithfulness) from the ninth century:

Thus shall one take the oath of fidelity:
By the Lord before whom this sanctuary [some religious place] is holy, I will to N. be true and faithful, and love all which he loves and shun all which he shuns, according to the laws of God and the order of the world. Nor will I ever with will or action, through word or deed, do anything which is unpleasing to him, on condition that he will hold to me as I shall deserve it, and that he will perform everything as it was in our agreement when I submitted myself to him and chose his will.[12]

Lords also tried to ensure the support of their retainers with gifts of weapons and jewelry. Some great lords gave their armed cavalrymen, or *vassals,* estates, or *fiefs,* that produced income to maintain the retainer and his family. Because knights were not involved in any government activity, and because only men who exercised political power were considered noble, knights were not part of the noble class. Down to the eleventh century, political power was concentrated in a small group of counts.

This group of counts, descended from the old Frankish aristocracy (see page 334), constituted the second level of feudalism. Under Charles Martel and his heirs, counts monopolized the high offices in the Carolingian Empire. At the local level, they had full judicial, military, and financial power. They held courts that dispensed justice, waged wars, and collected taxes. For most ordinary people, the counts were the government. Charlemagne regularly sent missi to inspect the activities of the counts, but there was slight chance of a corrupt count being removed from office.

Although countships were not hereditary in the eighth century, they tended to remain within the same family. In the eighth and early ninth centuries, regional concentrations of power depended on family connections and political influence at the king's court. The disintegration of the Carolingian Empire, however, served to increase the power of regional authorities. Civil wars weakened the power and prestige of kings because they could do little about domestic violence. Likewise, the great invasions of the ninth century, especially the Viking invasions (see pages 350–352), weakened royal authority. The West Frankish kings could do little to halt the invaders, and the aristocracy had to assume responsibility for defense. Common people turned for protection to the strongest local power, the counts, whom they considered their rightful rulers. Thus, in the ninth and tenth centuries, great aristocratic families governed virtually independent territories in which distant and weak kings could not interfere. "Political power had become a private, heritable property for great counts and lords."[13] This is what is meant by feudalism as a form of government.

Because feudal society was a military society, men held the dominant positions in it. The legal and social position of women was not as insignificant as might be expected, however. Charters recording gifts to the church indicate that women held land in many areas. Women frequently endowed monasteries, churches, and other religious establishments. The possession of land obviously meant economic power. Moreover, women inherited land. In southern France and Catalonia in Spain, women inherited feudal property as early as the tenth century. Other kinds of evidence attest to women's status. For example, in parts of northern France, children sometimes identified themselves in legal documents by their mother's name rather than their father's, indicating that the mother's social position in the community was higher than the father's.

Commendation and Initiation   Just as the spiritual power of priests is bequeathed by the laying of the priests' hands on the candidate's head at ordination, so the military virtues of strength and loyalty were conveyed to the warrior by the act of commendation when he placed his clasped hands between the hands of his lord. A kiss, symbolizing peace, often concluded the ceremony. *(Source: Universitätsbibliothek, Heidelberg)*

In a treatise he wrote in 822 on the organization of the royal household, Archbishop Hincmar of Reims placed the queen directly above the treasurer. She was responsible for giving the knights their annual salaries. She supervised the manorial accounts. Thus, in the management of large households with many knights to oversee and complicated manorial records to supervise, the lady of the manor had highly important responsibilities. With such responsibility went power and influence.[14]

Manorialism

Feudalism concerned the rights, powers, and lifestyle of the military elite; *manorialism* involved the services and obligations of the peasant classes. The economic power of the warring class rested on landed estates worked by peasants. Hence feudalism and manorialism were inextricably linked. Peasants needed protection, and lords demanded something in return for providing that protection. Free peasants surrendered themselves and their lands to the lord's jurisdiction. The land was given back, but the peasants became tied to the land by various payments and services. In France, England, Germany, and Italy, local custom determined precisely what those services were, but certain practices became common everywhere. The peasant was obliged to turn over to the lord a percentage of the annual harvest, usually in produce, sometimes in cash. The peasant paid a fee to marry someone from outside the lord's estate. He paid a fine, often his best beast, to inherit property. Above all, the peasant became part of the lord's permanent labor force. With vast stretches of uncultivated virgin land and a tiny labor population, lords encouraged population growth and immigration. The most profitable form of capital was not land but laborers.

In entering into a relationship with a feudal lord, a free farmer lost status. His position became servile, and he became a *serf*—that is, he was bound to the land and could not leave it without the lord's permission. He was also subject to the jurisdiction of the lord's court in any dispute over property or if he was suspected of criminal behavior.

The transition from freedom to serfdom was slow; its speed was closely related to the degree of

Scandinavian Sword Hilt   (late sixth century) Scandinavian artists attained a high level of achievement in the zoomorphic (or animal) style, though the animals are not recognizable in this fine example of metalwork. The Scandinavians later learned to work in wood and leather from Merovingian, Northumbrian, and Irish artists, but few examples of these techniques survive. *(Source: University Museum of National Antiquities, Oslo)*

political order in a given region. Even in the late eighth century there were still many free peasants. And within the legal category of serfdom there were many economic levels, ranging from the highly prosperous to the desperately poor. Nevertheless, a social and legal revolution was taking place. By the year 800, perhaps 60 percent of the population of western Europe—completely free a century before—had been reduced to serfdom. The ninth-century Viking assaults on Europe created extremely unstable conditions and individual insecurity, leading to additional loss of personal freedom. The lives of the peasants are described in detail on pages 374–385.

GREAT INVASIONS OF THE NINTH CENTURY

After the Treaty of Verdun (843) and the division of Charlemagne's empire among his grandsons, continental Europe presented an easy target for foreign invaders. All three kingdoms were torn by domestic dissension and disorder. No European political power was strong enough to put up effective resistance to external attacks. Frontier and coastal defenses erected by Charlemagne and maintained by Louis the Pious were completely neglected.

From the moors of Scotland to the mountains of Sicily there arose in the ninth century the Christian prayer "Save us, O God, from the violence of the Northmen." The Northmen, also known as "Normans" or "Vikings," were Germanic peoples from Norway, Sweden, and Denmark who had remained beyond the sway of the Christianizing and civilizing influences of the Carolingian Empire. Some scholars believe that the name "Viking" derives from the Old Norse word *vik,* meaning "creek." A *Viking,* then, was a pirate who waited in a creek or bay to attack passing vessels.

Charlemagne had established marches, fortresses, and watchtowers along his northern coasts to defend his territory against Viking raiders. Their assaults began around 787, and by the mid-tenth century they had brought large chunks of continental Europe and Britain under their sway (Map 12.3). In the east they pierced the rivers of Russia as far as the Black Sea. In the west they sailed as far as Iceland, Greenland, and even

MAP 12.3 The Great Invasions of the Ninth Century Note the Viking penetration of eastern Europe and their probable expeditions to North America. What impact did their various invasions have on European society?

the coast of North America, perhaps as far south as Long Island Sound.

The Vikings were superb seamen. Advanced construction methods gave their ships great speed and maneuverability. Propelled either by oars or by sails, deckless, and about 65 feet long, a Viking ship could carry between forty and sixty men—quite enough to harass an isolated monastery or village. These boats, navigated by thoroughly experienced and utterly fearless sailors, moved through the most complicated rivers, estuaries, and waterways in Europe. The Carolingian Empire, with no navy and no notion of the importance of sea power, was helpless. The Vikings moved swiftly, attacked, and escaped to return again.

Scholars disagree about the reasons for these migrations. Some maintain that overpopulation forced the Vikings to emigrate. Others argue that climatic conditions and crop failures forced migration. Still others insist that the Northmen were looking for trade and new commercial contacts, as well as plunder.

Plunder they did. Viking attacks were savage. At first they attacked and sailed off laden with booty. Later, on returning, they settled down and colonized the areas they had conquered. For example, the Vikings overran a large part of northwestern France and called the territory "Norsemanland," from which the word *Normandy* derives (see Map 12.3).

Scarcely had the savagery of the Viking assaults begun to subside when Europe was hit from the east and south. Beginning about 890, Magyar tribes crossed the Danube and pushed steadily westward. (Since people thought of them as returning Huns, the Magyars came to be known as "Hungarians.") They subdued northern Italy, compelled Bavaria and Saxony to pay tribute, and penetrated even into the Rhineland and Burgundy. These roving bandits attacked isolated villages and monasteries, taking prisoners and selling them in the Eastern slave markets. The Magyars were not colonizers; their sole object was booty and plunder.

The Vikings and Magyars depended on fear. In their initial attacks on isolated settlements, every man, woman, and child was put to the sword. A few attractive women might be spared to satisfy the conquerors' lusts or to be sold into slavery. The Scandinavians and Hungarians struck such terror in defenseless rural peoples that those peoples often gave up without a struggle. Many communities bought peace by paying tribute.

From the south the Muslims began new encroachments, concentrating on the two southern European peninsulas, Italy and Spain. They drove northward and sacked Rome in 846. Expert seamen, they sailed around the Iberian Peninsula and braved the notoriously dangerous shoals and winds of the Atlantic coast. In 859 they attacked the settlements along the coast of Provence. Muslim attacks on the European continent in the ninth and tenth centuries were less destructive than those of the Vikings and Magyars. Compared to the rich, sophisticated culture of the Arab capitals, northern Europe was primitive, backward, and offered little.

What was the effect of these invasions on the structure of European society? Viking, Magyar, and Muslim attacks accelerated the development of feudalism. Lords capable of rallying fighting men, supporting them, and putting up resistance to the invaders did so. They also assumed political power in their territories. Weak and defenseless people sought the protection of local strongmen. Free men sank to the level of serfs. Consequently, European society became further fragmented. Public power became increasingly decentralized.

POLITICAL REVIVAL

The eleventh century witnessed the beginnings of political stability in western Europe. People grew increasingly secure in their persons and property. Political stability and security contributed to a slow increase in population and provided the foundation for economic recovery.

The Decline of Invasion and Civil Disorder

The most important factor in the revival of Europe after the disasters of the ninth century was the gradual decline in foreign invasions and the reduction of domestic violence. In France, for example, the Norwegian leader Rollo in 911 subdued large parts of what was later called "Normandy." The West Frankish ruler Charles the Simple, unable to oust the Northmen, went along with that territorial conquest. He recognized Rollo as duke of Normandy on the condition that Rollo swear allegiance to him and hold the territory as a sort of barrier against future Viking assaults. This agreement, embodied in the Treaty of Saint-Clair-sur-Epte, marks the beginning of the rise of Normandy.

Rollo kept his word. He exerted strong authority over Normandy and in troubled times supported the weak Frankish king. Rollo and his soldiers were baptized as Christians. Although additional Viking settlers arrived, they were easily pacified. The tenth and eleventh centuries saw the steady assimilation of Normans and French. Major attacks on France ended. By 1066—the year Rollo's descendant Duke William I (1035–1087) and the Normans invaded England—the duchy of Normandy was the strongest and most peaceful territory in western Europe.

The civil wars and foreign invasions of the ninth and tenth centuries left the territories now called "France" divided into provinces and counties where local feudal lords held actual power. After the death of the last Carolingian ruler in 987, an assembly of nobles met to choose a successor. The nobles selected Hugh Capet, head of a powerful clan in the West Frankish kingdom. The Capetian kings subsequently saved France from further division. But that they would do so was hardly apparent in 987. Compared with the dukes of Normandy and Aquitaine, the first Capetians were weak, but by hanging on to what they had, they laid the foundations for later political stability.

Recovery followed a different pattern in Anglo-Saxon England. The Danes (or Vikings) had made a concerted effort to conquer and rule the whole island, and probably no region of Europe suffered more. By 877 only parts of Wessex survived. The victory of the remarkable Alfred, king of the West Saxons (or Wessex), over Guthrun the Dane at Edington in 878 inaugurated a great political revival. Alfred and his immediate successors built a system of local defenses and slowly extended royal rule beyond Wessex to other Anglo-Saxon peoples until one law, royal law, replaced local custom.

The Danish ruler Canute, king of England (r. 1016–1035) and after 1030 king of Norway as well, made England the center of his empire. Canute promoted a policy of assimilation and reconciliation between Anglo-Saxons and Vikings. Slowly the two peoples were molded together. The assimilation of Anglo-Saxon and Viking was personified by King Edward the Confessor (r. 1042–1066), the son of an Anglo-Saxon father and a Norman mother who had taken Canute as her second husband.

In the east, the German king Otto I (r. 936–973) inflicted a crushing defeat on the Hungarians at the banks of the Lech River in 955. This battle halted the Magyars' westward expansion and threat to Germany and made Otto a great hero to the Germans. It also signified the revival of the German monarchy and demonstrated that Otto was a worthy successor to Charlemagne.

When chosen king, Otto had selected Aachen as the site of his coronation to symbolize his intention to continue the tradition of Charlemagne.

Vikings Invade Britain   In this twelfth-century representation of the Viking invasions, warriors appear to be armed with helmets, spears, and shields. Crossing the rough North Sea and English Channel in open, oar-propelled boats, they had great courage. *(Source: The Pierpont Morgan Library)*

The basis of his power was to be alliance with and control of the church. Otto asserted the right of effective control over ecclesiastical appointments. Before receiving religious consecration, bishops and abbots had to perform feudal homage for the lands that accompanied the church office. (This practice was to create a grave crisis in the eleventh century; see pages 359–361.)

Otto realized that he had to use the financial and military resources of the church to halt feudal anarchy. He used the higher clergy extensively in

Christ Enthroned with Saints and the Emperor Otto I
(tenth century) Between 933 and 973, Emperor Otto I founded the church of St. Mauritius in Magdeburg. As a memorial to the event, Otto commissioned the production of this ivory plaque showing Christ accepting a model of the church from the emperor. Ivory was a favorite medium of Ottonian artists, and squat figures in a simple geometrical pattern characterize their work. *(Source: The Metropolitan Museum of Art, Bequest of George Blumenthal, 1941 (41.100.157))*

his administration, and the bulk of his army came from monastic and other church lands. Between 936 and 955, Otto succeeded in breaking the territorial power of the great German dukes.

Otto's coronation by the pope in 962 revived the imperial dignity and laid the foundation for what was later called the "Holy Roman Empire." The coronation showed that Otto had the support of the church in Germany and Italy. The uniting of the kingship with the imperial crown advanced German interests. Otto filled a power vacuum in northern Italy and brought peace among the great aristocratic families. The level of order there improved for the first time in over a century. Peace and political stability in turn promoted the eco-

nomic revival of Venice and other northern Italian cities.

By the start of the eleventh century, the Italian maritime cities were seeking a place in the rich Mediterranean trade. Pisa and Genoa fought to break Muslim control of the trade and shipping with the Byzantine Empire and the Far East. Once the Muslim fleets had been destroyed, the Italian cities of Venice, Genoa, and Pisa embarked on the road to prosperity. The eleventh century witnessed a steady rise in their strength and wealth. Freedom from invasion and domestic security made economic growth possible all over western Europe. In Spain, the *reconquista*—the reconquest of Muslim-controlled lands—gained impetus.

Increasing Population and Mild Climate

A steady growth of population also contributed to Europe's general recovery. The decline of foreign invasions and internal civil disorder reduced the number of people killed and maimed. Feudal armies in the eleventh through thirteenth centuries continued their destruction, but they were very small by modern standards and fought few pitched battles. Most medieval conflicts consisted of sieges on castles or fortifications. As few as twelve men could defend a castle. Monastic chroniclers, frequently bored and almost always writing from hearsay evidence, tended to romanticize medieval warfare (as long as it was not in their own neighborhoods). Most conflicts were petty skirmishes with slight loss of life. The survival of more young people, those most often involved in war and usually the most sexually active, meant a population rise.

Nor did nature or biology hinder population expansion. Between the tenth and fourteenth centuries, no major plague or other medical scourge hit Europe, though leprosy and malaria did strike down some people. Leprosy had entered Europe in the early Middle Ages. Caused by a virus, the disease was not very contagious and, if contracted, worked slowly. Lepers presented a frightful appearance: the victim's arms and legs rotted away, and gangrenous sores emitted a horrible smell. Physicians had no cure. Eventually, medieval lepers were segregated in hospitals called "leprosaria." Malaria, spread by protozoa-carrying mosquitoes that infested swampy areas, is characterized by alternate chills and fevers and leaves the afflicted person extremely weak.

During the High Middle Ages, relatively few people caught leprosy or malaria. Crop failure and the ever-present danger of starvation were much more pressing threats. Here, the weather cooperated with the revival. The century between 1080 and 1180 witnessed exceptionally clement weather in England, France, and Germany, with mild winters and dry summers. Good weather helps to explain advances in land reclamation and agricultural yield. And increased agricultural output had a profound impact on society: it affected Europeans' health, commerce, industry, and general lifestyle.

REVIVAL AND REFORM IN THE CHRISTIAN CHURCH

The eleventh century witnessed the beginnings of a remarkable religious revival. Monasteries, always the leaders in ecclesiastical reform, remodeled themselves under the leadership of the Burgundian abbey of Cluny. Subsequently, new religious orders, such as the Cistercians, were founded and became a broad spiritual movement.

The papacy itself, after a century of corruption and decadence, was cleaned up. The popes worked to clarify church doctrine and codify church law. They and their officials sought to communicate with all the clergy and peoples of Europe through a clearly defined, obedient hierarchy of bishops. The popes wanted the basic loyalty of all members of the clergy. Ultimately, assertions of papal power caused profound changes and serious conflicts with secular authorities. The revival of the church was manifested in the twelfth and thirteenth centuries by a flowering of popular piety and the building of magnificent cathedrals (see pages 429–432).

Monastic Decline and Revival

In the early Middle Ages, the best Benedictine monasteries had been citadels of good Christian living and centers of learning. Between the seventh and ninth centuries, religious houses copied and preserved manuscripts, maintained schools, and set high standards of monastic observance. Charlemagne had encouraged and supported these monastic activities, and the collapse of the Carolingian Empire had disastrous effects.

Viking, Magyar, and Muslim invaders attacked and ransacked many monasteries across Europe. Some communities fled and dispersed. In the period of political disorder that followed the disintegration of the Carolingian Empire, many religious houses fell under the control of local feudal lords. Powerful laymen appointed themselves or their relatives as abbots, while keeping their wives or mistresses. They took for themselves the lands and goods of monasteries, spending monastic revenues and selling monastic offices. All over Europe, temporal powers dominated the monasteries. The level of spiritual observance and intellectual activity declined.

In 909 William the Pious, duke of Aquitaine, established the abbey of Cluny near Mâcon in Burgundy. In his charter of endowment, Duke William declared that Cluny was to enjoy complete independence from all feudal or secular lordship. The new monastery was to be subordinate only to the authority of Saints Peter and Paul as represented by the pope. The duke then renounced his own possession of and influence over Cluny.

In the church as a whole, Cluny gradually came to stand for clerical celibacy and the suppression of *simony*—the sale of church offices. In the eleventh century, Cluny was fortunate in having a series of highly able abbots who ruled for a long time. These abbots paid careful attention to sound economic management. In a disorderly world, Cluny gradually came to represent religious and political stability. Moreover, properties and monasteries under Cluny's jurisdiction enjoyed special protection, at least theoretically, from violence.[15] Thus laypersons placed lands in its custody and monastic priories under its jurisdiction for reform. In this way hundreds of monasteries, primarily in France and Spain, came under Cluny's authority.

By the last quarter of the eleventh century, some monasteries enjoyed wide reputations for the beauty and richness of their chant and the piety of their monks' lives. Deeply impressed laymen showered gifts on them. Jewelry, rich vestments, elaborately carved sacred vessels, even lands and properties poured into some houses. With this wealth came lay influence. As the monasteries grew richer, the monks' lifestyle became increasingly

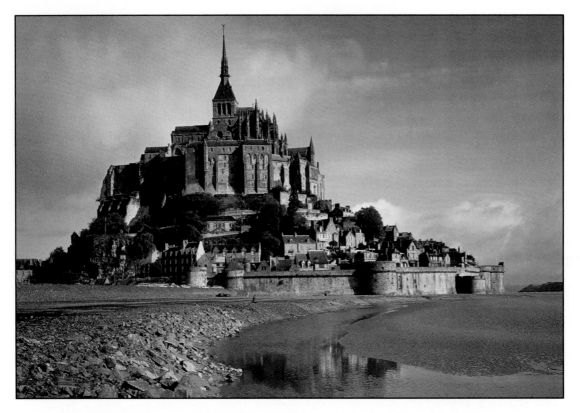

Mont St.-Michel   At the summit of a 250-foot cone of rock rising out of the sea and accessible only at low tide, Mont St.-Michel combined fortified castle and monastery. Thirteenth-century monarchs considered it crucial to their power in northwestern France, and it played a decisive role in French defenses against the English during the Hundred Years' War. The abbots so planned the architecture that monastic life went on undisturbed by military activity. *(Source: Giraudon/Art Resource)*

luxurious. Conversely, monastic observance and spiritual fervor declined.

Once again the ideals of the pristine Benedictine life were threatened. Fresh demands for reform were heard, and the result was the founding of new religious orders in the late eleventh and early twelfth centuries. The best representatives of the new reforming spirit were the Cistercians.

In 1098 a group of monks left the rich abbey of Molesmes in Burgundy and founded a new house in the swampy forest of Cîteaux. They planned to avoid all involvement with secular feudal society. They decided to accept only uncultivated lands far from regular habitation. They intended to refuse all gifts of mills, serfs, tithes, and ovens—the traditional manorial sources of income. The early Cistercians determined to avoid elaborate liturgy and ceremony and to keep their chant simple. Finally, because they knew that lay influence was usually harmful to careful observance, they refused to allow the presence of powerful laymen in their monasteries. The Cistercians were creating a new kind of commune. It was to be simple, isolated, austere, and purified of all the economic and religious complexities found in the Benedictine houses.

These Cistercian goals coincided perfectly with the needs of twelfth-century society. The late eleventh and early twelfth centuries witnessed energetic agricultural expansion and land reclamation all across Europe. The early Cistercians wanted to farm only land that had previously been uncultivated, swampland, or fenland, and that was exactly what needed to be done. They thus became the great pioneers of the twelfth century.

The first monks at Cîteaux experienced sickness, a dearth of recruits, and terrible privations. But their obvious sincerity and high idealism eventually attracted attention. In 1112, a twenty-three-year-old nobleman called Bernard and thirty of his aristocratic companions joined the community at Cîteaux. Thereafter, this reforming movement gained impetus. The Cistercians founded 525 new monasteries in the course of the twelfth century, and their influence on European society was profound. Unavoidably, however, the Cistercians' success brought wealth, and wealth brought power. By the end of the twelfth century, economic prosperity and political power had begun to compromise the primitive Cistercian ideals.

Reform of the Papacy

In the tenth century the papacy provided little leadership to the Christian peoples of Western Europe. Factions in Rome sought to control the papacy for their own material gain. Popes were ap-

pointed to advance the political ambitions of their families—the great aristocratic families of the city—and not because of special spiritual qualifications. The office of pope, including its spiritual powers and influence, was frequently bought and sold even though the crime of simony had been condemned by Saint Peter. The licentiousness and debauchery of the papal court weakened the popes' religious prestige and moral authority. According to a contemporary chronicler, for example, Pope John XII (r. 955–963), who had secured the papal office at the age of eighteen, wore himself out with sexual excesses before he reached his twenty-eighth year.

At the local parish level there were many married priests. Taking Christ as the model for the priestly life, the Roman church had always encouraged clerical celibacy, and celibacy had been an obligation for ordination since the fourth century.

Consecration of the Church of Cluny Pope Urban II surrounded by mitred bishops appears on the left, Abbot Hugh of Cluny with cowled monks on the right. A French nobleman who had been a monk at Cluny, Urban coined the term *curia* as the official designation of the central government of the church. *(Source: Bibliothèque Nationale, Paris)*

But in the tenth and eleventh centuries, probably a majority of European priests were married or living with a woman. Such priests were called "Nicolaites," from a reference in the Book of Revelation to early Christians who advocated a return to pagan sexual practices.

Several factors may account for the lack of clerical celibacy. The explanation may lie in the basic need for warmth and human companionship. Perhaps village priests could not survive economically on their small incomes and needed the help of a mate. Perhaps the tradition of a married clergy was so deep-rooted by the tenth century that each generation simply followed the example of its predecessor. In any case, the disparity between law and reality shocked the lay community and bred disrespect for the clergy.

Serious efforts at reform began under Pope Leo IX (r. 1049–1054). Not only was Leo related to Holy Roman Emperor Henry III (r. 1039–1056)

but, as bishop of Toul and a German, he was also an outsider who owed nothing to any Roman faction. Leo traveled widely and at Pavia, Reims, and Mainz held councils that issued decrees against simony, Nicolaism, and violence. Leo's representatives held church councils across Europe, pressing for moral reform. They urged those who could not secure justice at home to appeal to the pope, the ultimate source of justice.

Papal reform continued after Leo IX. In the short reign of Nicholas II (r. 1058–1061), a council held in Rome in the ancient church of Saint John Lateran in 1059 devised a new method for electing the pope. Since the eighth century, the priests of the major churches in and around Rome had constituted a special group, called a "college," that advised the pope. These chief priests were called "cardinals" from the Latin *cardo*, meaning "hinge." The Lateran Synod of 1059 decreed that the authority and power to elect the pope rested

Rievaulx Abbey   Taking its name from the nearby Rie River and the valley in which it is situated, both this vast abbey church (completed in 1145) and the accompanying monastic complex were financed by the extremely fine wool produced from the sheep who grazed on these hillsides. The wool clip also supported a monastic community of over 600 in the mid-twelfth century. *(Source: English Heritage. Crown Copyright)*

solely in this college of cardinals. The college retains that power today.

The object of this decree was to reduce royal influence and remove this crucial decision from the secular squabbling of Roman aristocratic factions. When the office of pope was vacant, the cardinals were responsible for governing the church. By 1073 the progress of reform in the Christian church was well advanced. The election of Cardinal Hildebrand as Pope Gregory VII (r. 1073–1085) changed the direction of reform from a moral to a political one.

THE GREGORIAN REVOLUTION

The papal reform movement of the eleventh century is frequently called the "Gregorian reform movement," after Pope Gregory VII. The label is not accurate, for reform began long before Gregory's pontificate and continued after it. Gregory's reign, however, did inaugurate a radical or revolutionary phase that had important political and social consequences.

Pope Gregory VII's Ideas

Once Hildebrand became pope, the reform of the papacy took on a new dimension. Its goal was not just the moral regeneration of the clergy and centralization of the church under papal authority. Gregory and his assistants began to insist on the "freedom of the church." By this they meant freedom from control and interference by laymen.

The concept of freedom of the church signaled the end of *lay investiture*—the selection and appointment of church officials by secular authority. Traditionally, bishops and abbots were invested with a staff representing pastoral jurisdiction and a ring signifying union with a diocese or monastic community. Laymen, such as kings, who gave these symbols appeared to be distributing spiritual authority. Ecclesiastical opposition to lay investiture had been part of church theory for centuries. But Gregory's attempt to put theory into practice was a radical departure from tradition. Because feudal monarchs depended on churchmen for the operation of their governments, Gregory's program seemed to spell disaster for stable royal administration. It provoked a terrible crisis.

The Controversy over Lay Investiture

In February 1075, Pope Gregory held a council at Rome. It published decrees not only against Nicolaism and simony but also against lay investiture:

If anyone henceforth shall receive a bishopric or abbey from the hands of a lay person, he shall not be considered as among the number of bishops and abbots. . . . Likewise if any emperor, king. . . . or any one at all of the secular powers, shall presume to perform investiture with bishoprics or with any other ecclesiastical dignity . . . he shall feel the divine displeasure as well with regard to his body as to his other belongings.[16]

In short, clerics who accepted investiture from laymen were to be deposed, and laymen who invested clerics were to be *excommunicated*—that is, cut off from the sacraments and from all Christian worship.

The church's penalty of excommunication relied for its effectiveness on public opinion. Since most Europeans favored Gregory's moral reforms, he believed that excommunication would compel rulers to abide by his changes. Immediately, however, Henry IV in the Holy Roman Empire, William the Conqueror in England, and Philip I in France protested.

The strongest reaction came from the Holy Roman Empire. Most eleventh-century rulers could not survive without the literacy and administrative knowledge of bishops and abbots. Naturally, then, kings selected and invested most of the bishops and abbots. In this respect, as recent research has shown, German kings scarcely varied from other rulers. In two basic ways, however, the German kings had the most to lose from the prohibition on lay investiture, for the pope granted the imperial crown, and both the empire and the Papal States claimed northern Italy.

Over and above the subject of lay investiture, a more fundamental issue was at stake. Gregory's decree raised the question of the proper role of the monarch in a Christian society. Did a king have ultimate jurisdiction over all his subjects, including the clergy? For centuries, tradition had answered this question in favor of the ruler. Thus it is no wonder that Henry protested the papal assertions about investiture. Indirectly, they undermined imperial power and sought to make papal authority supreme.

Henry IV and Gregory VII   The twelfth-century Cistercian chronicler Otto at Freising depicts Gregory VII expelled from Rome while Henry IV sits beside an anti-pope. Grandson of Henry IV, Otto did not sympathize with Gregory, whom he thought had sown disorder in the church. *(Source: Sächsische Landesbibliothek/Deutsche Fotothek)*

An increasingly bitter exchange of letters ensued. Gregory accused Henry IV (r. 1056–1106) of lack of respect for the papacy and insisted that disobedience to the pope was disobedience to God. Henry protested in a now-famous letter beginning, "Henry King not by usurpation, but by the pious ordination of God, to Hildebrand, now not Pope, but false monk."

Within the empire, those who had most to gain from the dispute quickly took advantage of it. In January 1076, the German bishops who had been invested by Henry withdrew their allegiance from the pope. Gregory replied by excommunicating them and suspending Henry from the kingship. With Henry IV excommunicated and cast outside the Christian fold, lay nobles did not have to obey him and could advance their own interests. Gregory hastened to support the nobles. The Christmas season of 1076 witnessed an ironic situation in Germany: the clergy supported the king, and the great nobility favored the pope.

Henry outwitted Gregory. Crossing the Alps in January 1077, he approached the pope's residence at Canossa in northern Italy. According to legend, for three days Henry stood in the snow seeking forgiveness. As a priest, Pope Gregory was obliged to grant absolution and to readmit the emperor to the Christian community.

Henry's trip to Canossa is often described as the most dramatic incident in the High Middle Ages. Some historians claim that it marked the peak of papal power because the most powerful ruler in Europe, the emperor, had bowed before the pope. Actually, Henry scored a temporary victory. When the sentence of excommunication was lifted, Henry regained the kingship and authority over his rebellious subjects. But in the long run, in Germany and elsewhere, secular rulers were reluctant to pose a serious challenge to the papacy for the next two hundred years.

For Germany the incident at Canossa settled nothing. In 1080 Gregory VII again excommunicated and deposed Henry IV; Henry then invaded Italy, captured Rome, and controlled the city when Gregory died in exile in 1085. But Henry's victory did not last. Gregory's successors encouraged Henry's sons to revolt against their father. With lay investiture the ostensible issue, the conflict between the papacy and Henry IV's successors continued into the twelfth century.

The struggle did have profound social consequences for Germany. The nobility triumphed. Recent research has revealed that by the eleventh century many great German families had achieved a definite sense of themselves as noble. The long struggle between pope and emperor preoccupied the monarchy and allowed emerging noble dynasties to enhance their position. When the papal-imperial conflict ended in 1122, the nobility held the balance of power in Germany.[17] Later efforts by Frederick Barbarossa (r. 1152–1190) (see page 409) and other German kings to strengthen the monarchy against the princely families failed. For centuries, the German nobility remained the dominant social class and political force. The German aristocracy subordinated the knights and reinforced their dependency with strong feudal ties. The aristocracy reduced free men and serfs to servile position. Henry IV and then Henry V (r. 1106–1125) were compelled to surrender rights and privileges to the nobility. Particularism, localism, and feudal independence characterized the Holy Roman Empire in the High Middle Ages. The investiture controversy had a catastrophic effect there, severely retarding the development of a strong centralized monarchy.

A long and exhausting propaganda campaign followed the confrontation at Canossa. Finally in 1122, at a conference held at Worms, the issue was settled by compromise. Bishops were to be chosen according to *canon law*—that is, church law—in the presence of the emperor or his delegate. The emperor surrendered the right of investing bishops with the ring and staff. But since lay rulers were permitted to be present at ecclesiastical elections and to accept or refuse feudal homage from the new prelates, they still possessed an effective veto over ecclesiastical appointments. At the same time, the papacy achieved technical success, because rulers could no longer invest. Papal power was enhanced and neither side won a clear victory. The real winners in Germany were the great princes and the lay aristocracy.

William the Conqueror of England and Philip I of France were just as guilty of lay investiture as the German emperor, and both quarreled openly with Gregory. However, Rome's conflict with the Western rulers never reached the proportions of the dispute with the German emperor. Gregory VII and his successors had the diplomatic sense to avoid creating three enemies at once.

The Papacy in the High Middle Ages

In the late eleventh century and throughout the twelfth, the papacy pressed Gregory's campaign for reform of the church. Pope Urban II (r. 1088–1099) laid the real foundations for the papal monarchy by reorganizing the central government of the Roman church, the papal writing office (the chancery), and papal finances. He recognized the college of cardinals as a definite consultative body. These agencies, together with the papal chapel, constituted the papal court, or *curia*—the papacy's administrative bureaucracy and its court of law. The papal curia, although not fully developed until the mid-twelfth century, was the first well-organized institution of monarchial authority in medieval Europe.

The Roman curia had its greatest impact as a court of law. As the highest ecclesiastical tribunal, it formulated canon law for all of Christendom. It was the instrument with which the popes pressed the goals of reform and centralized the church. The curia sent legates to hold councils in various parts of Europe. Councils published decrees and sought to enforce the law. When individuals in any part of Christian Europe felt that they were being denied justice in their local church courts, they could appeal to Rome. Slowly but surely, in the High Middle Ages the papal curia developed into the court of final appeal for all of Christian Europe.

In the course of the twelfth century, appeals to the curia steadily increased. The majority of cases related to disputes over church property or ecclesiastical elections and above all to questions of marriage and annulment. Significantly, most of the popes in the twelfth and thirteenth centuries were canon lawyers. The most famous of them, the man whose pontificate represented the height of medieval papal power, was Innocent III (r. 1198–1216).

Innocent judged a vast number of cases and exerted papal authority in many areas. He compelled King Philip Augustus of France to take back his wife, Ingeborg of Denmark. He arbitrated the rival claims of two disputants to the imperial crown of Germany. He forced King John of England to accept as archbishop of Canterbury a man whom John did not really want.

By the early thirteenth century, papal efforts at reform begun more than a century before had attained phenomenal success. The popes themselves were men of high principles and strict moral behavior. The frequency of clerical marriage and the level of violence had declined considerably. Simony was much more the exception than the rule.

Yet the seeds of future difficulties were being planted. As the volume of appeals to Rome multiplied, so did the size of the papal bureaucracy. As the number of lawyers increased, so did concern for legal niceties and technicalities, fees, and church offices. As early as the mid-twelfth century, John of Salisbury, an Englishman working in the papal curia, had written that the people condemned the curia for its greed and indifference to human suffering. Nevertheless, the power of the curia continued to grow, as did its bureaucracy.

Thirteenth-century popes devoted their attention to the bureaucracy and their conflicts with the German emperor Frederick II (see pages 411–412). Some, like Gregory IX (r. 1227–1241), abused their prerogatives to such an extent that their moral impact was seriously weakened. Even worse, Innocent IV (r. 1243–1254) used secular weapons, including military force, to maintain his leadership. These popes badly damaged papal prestige and influence. By the early fourteenth century, the seeds of disorder would grow into a vast and sprawling tree, and once again cries for reform would be heard.

THE CRUSADES

The Crusades of the eleventh and twelfth centuries were the most obvious manifestation of the papal claim to the leadership of Christian society. The enormous popular response to papal calls for crusading reveals Europe's religious enthusiasm and the influence of the reformed papacy. The Crusades also reflect the church's new understanding of the noble warrior class. As a distinguished scholar of the Crusades wrote:

At around the turn of the millennium [the year 1000], the attitude of the church toward the military class underwent a significant change. The contrast between militia Christi *[war for Christ] and* militia saecularis *[war for worldly purposes] was overcome and just as rulership earlier had been Christianized . . . , so now was the military profession; it acquired a direct eccle-*

siastical purpose, for war in the service of the church or for the weak came to be regarded as holy and was declared to be a religious duty not only for the king but also for every individual knight.[18]

The Crusades in the late eleventh and early twelfth centuries were holy wars sponsored by the papacy for the recovery of the Holy Land from the Muslim Arabs or the Turks. They grew out of the long-standing conflict between Christians and Muslims in Spain, where by about 1250 Christian kings had regained roughly 90 percent of the peninsula. Throughout this period, Christians alone and in groups left Europe in a steady trickle for the Middle East. Although people of all ages and classes participated in the Crusades, so many knights did so that crusading became a distinctive feature of the upper-class lifestyle. In an aristocratic military society, men coveted reputations as Crusaders; the Christian knight who had been to the Holy Land enjoyed great prestige. The Crusades manifested the religious and chivalric ideals—as well as the tremendous vitality—of medieval European society.

By the late eleventh century the Roman papacy had strong reasons for wanting to launch an expedition against Muslim infidels in the Middle East. The papacy had been involved in a bitter struggle over investiture with the German emperors. If the pope could muster a large army against the enemies of Christianity, his claim to be leader of Christian society in the West would be strengthened.

Moreover, in 1054 a serious theological disagreement had split the Greek church of Byzantium and the Roman church of the West. The pope believed that a crusade would lead to strong Roman influence in Greek territories and eventually the reunion of the two churches. Then, in 1071 at Manzikert in eastern Anatolia (Map 12.4), Turkish soldiers in the pay of the Arabs defeated a Greek army and occupied much of Asia Minor. The emperor at Constantinople appealed to the West for support. Shortly afterward, the holy city of Jerusalem, the scene of Christ's preaching and burial, fell to the Turks. Pilgrimages to holy places in the Middle East became very dangerous, and the papacy was outraged that the holy city was in the hands of infidels.

In 1095 Pope Urban II (r. 1088–1099) journeyed to Clermont in France and called for a great

EUROPE IN THE MIDDLE AGES

ca 700	Publication of the Lindisfarne Gospel, Bede's *Ecclesiastical History of the English Nation*, and *Beowulf*
ca 710–750	Missionary work of Wynfrith (Boniface) supports the efforts of Charles Martel and Pippin III to assimilate Germanic tribes
733	Charles Martel defeats Muslims at Battle of Tours
752	Pippin III elected king by Frankish magnates
754	Pope Stephen anoints Pippin III king at Paris, establishing an important alliance between the Christian church and the Frankish ruler
756	Pippin III donates the Papal States to the papacy
768	Charlemagne succeeds to the Frankish crown
768–805	Charlemagne conquers all of continental Europe except Spain, Scandinavia, southern Italy, and Slavic fringes of the East
781	Alcuin enters Charlemagne's court at Aachen as chief adviser on religious and educational matters; encourages Christianization of northern Europe and directs the revival of learning inspired by Charlemagne
ca 787	Viking raids of Carolingian territories begin
800	Imperial coronation of Charlemagne
814	Louis the Pious succeeds to Charlemagne's empire
843	Treaty of Verdun: Charlemagne's empire divided among his grandsons Lothair, Louis the German, and Charles the Bald
ca 845–900	Series of Viking, Magyar, and Muslim invasions complete the disintegration of the Carolingian Empire
878	King Alfred's victory over Guthrun inaugurates political recovery in Anglo-Saxon England
909	Abbey of Cluny, a source of vast religious influence, founded; first step in the revival of monasticism and reform of the Church
955	Otto I's victory at Lech River ends Magyar incursions in Germany
962	Otto's coronation lays the foundation for the Holy Roman Empire
987	Election of Hugh Capet as king of the West Frankish kingdom
1049	Pope Leo IX begins serious reform of the Church
1059	Lateran Synod gives power of papal election to the college of cardinals
1073	Cardinal Hildebrand becomes Pope Gregory VII
1075	Church issues decree against lay investiture that leads to conflict between the pope and the rulers of Germany, England, and France
1096–1099	The First Crusade
1098	The Cistercians found an austere order of monks that would influence societies throughout Europe
1122	Compromise at Worms removes power of investiture from lay rulers but grants them effective veto over eccleciastical appointments
1147–1149	The Second Crusade
1189–1192	The Third Crusade
1202–1204	The Fourth Crusade; sacking of Constantinople cements the split between Eastern and Western churches

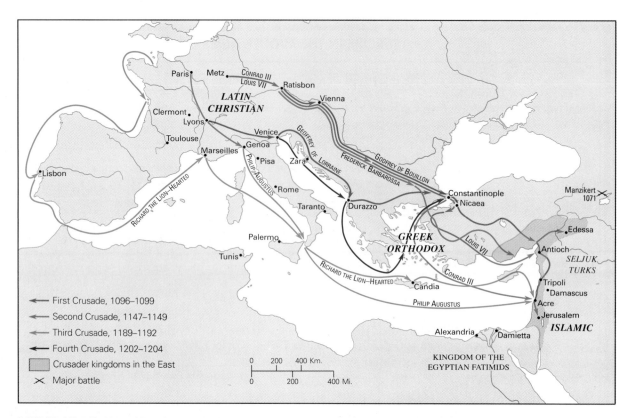

MAP 12.4 The Routes of the Crusades The Crusades led to a major cultural encounter between Muslim and Christian values. What significant intellectual and economic effects resulted?

Christian holy war against the infidels. He stressed the sufferings and persecution of Christians in Jerusalem. He urged Christian knights who had been fighting one another to direct their energies against the true enemies of God, the Muslims. Urban proclaimed an *indulgence*, or remission of the temporal penalties imposed by the church for sin, to those who would fight for and regain the holy city of Jerusalem. Few speeches in history have had such a dramatic effect as Urban's call at Clermont for the First Crusade.

The response was fantastic. Godfrey of Bouillon, Geoffrey of Lorraine, and many other great lords from northern France immediately had the cross of the Crusader sewn on their tunics. Encouraged by popular preachers like Peter the Hermit and by papal legates in Germany, Italy, and England, thousands of people of all classes joined the crusade. Although most of the Crusaders were French, pilgrims from all countries streamed southward from the Rhineland, through Germany and the Balkans.

Religious convictions inspired many, but mundane motives were also involved. Except for wives, who had to remain at home to manage estates, many people expected to benefit from the crusade. For the curious and the adventurous, it offered foreign travel and excitement. The crusade provided kings, who were trying to establish order and build states, the perfect opportunity to get rid of trouble-making knights. It gave land-hungry younger sons a chance to acquire fiefs in the Middle East. Even some members of the middle class who stayed at home profited from the crusade. Many nobles had to borrow money from the townspeople to pay for their expeditions, and they put up part of their land as security. If a noble did not return home or could not pay the interest on the loan, the middle-class creditor took over the land.

The First Crusade (1096–1099) was successful mostly because of the dynamic enthusiasm of the participants. The Crusaders had little more than religious zeal. They knew nothing about the geography or climate of the Middle East. Although there were several counts with military experience among the throng, the Crusaders could never agree on a leader, and the entire expedition was marked by disputes among the great lords. Lines of supply were never set up. Starvation and disease wracked the army, and the Turks slaughtered hundreds of noncombatants. Nevertheless, convinced that "God wills it"—the war cry of the Crusaders—the army pressed on and in 1099 captured Jerusalem. Although the Crusaders fought bravely, Arab disunity was a chief reason for their victory. At Jerusalem, Edessa, Tripoli, and Antioch (see Map 12.4), Crusader kingdoms were founded on the Western feudal model.

Between 1096 and 1270, the crusading ideal was expressed in eight papally approved expeditions to the East. In addition, in 1208 two expedi-

tions of children set out on a crusade to the Holy Land. One contingent turned back; the other was captured and sold into slavery. None of the crusades against the Muslims achieved very much. The third (1189–1192) was precipitated by the recapture of Jerusalem by the sultan Saladin in 1187. Frederick Barbarossa of the Holy Roman Empire, Richard the Lion-Hearted of England, and Philip Augustus of France participated. The Third Crusade was better financed than previous ones, but disputes among the leaders and strategic problems prevented any lasting results.

During the Fourth Crusade (1202–1204), careless preparation and inadequate financing had disastrous consequences for Byzantine-Latin relations. Hoping to receive material support from the Greeks, the leaders of the crusade took the expedition to Constantinople. Once there, they sacked

Crusading Scene Heavily armored Western knights face unencumbered Muslims. Some scholars believe that their dress gave the Muslims a decided advantage in certain battles. *(Source: Bibliothèque Nationale, Paris)*

the city and established the Latin Empire of Constantinople. The empire lasted only from 1204 to 1261. This assault by one Christian people on another, when one of the goals of the Crusades was the reunion of the Greek and Latin churches, made the split between the Western and Eastern churches permanent. It also helped to discredit the entire crusading movement. Two later crusades, undertaken by King Louis IX of France (r. 1226–1270), added to his prestige as a pious ruler.

Apart from that, the last of the official crusades accomplished nothing at all.

Crusades were also mounted against groups perceived as Christian Europe's social enemies. In 1208 Pope Innocent III (r. 1198–1216) proclaimed a crusade against the Albigensians, a heretical sect in southern France (see page 435). The popes in the mid-thirteenth century, fearful of encirclement by imperial territories, promoted crusades against Emperor Frederick II (r. 1215–

The Capture of Jerusalem in 1099   As engines hurl stones to breach the walls, Crusaders enter on scaling ladders. Scenes from Christ's passion (above) identify the city as Jerusalem. *(Source: Bibliothèque Nationale, Paris)*

1250). This use of force against a Christian ruler backfired, damaging the credibility of the papacy as the sponsor of peace.

Although the Crusades introduced some Europeans to Eastern luxury goods, the Crusades' overall cultural impact on the West remains debatable. By the late eleventh century, strong economic and intellectual ties with the East had already been made. The Crusades testify to the religious enthusiasm of the High Middle Ages. But, as Steven Runciman, a distinguished scholar of the Crusades, concluded in his three-volume history:

The triumphs of the Crusade were the triumphs of faith. But faith without wisdom is a dangerous thing. . . . In the long sequence of interaction and fusion between Orient and Occident out of which our civilization has grown, the Crusades were a tragic and destructive episode. . . . High ideals were besmirched by cruelty and greed, enterprise and endurance by a blind and narrow self-righteousness; and the Holy War itself was nothing more than a long act of intolerance in the name of God, which is the sin against the Holy Ghost.[19]

From the Muslim perspective, the Western assaults on the eastern Mediterranean from the eleventh to the thirteenth century represented only a minor event: the Crusades were never a serious threat to Islam. Pressures within European society launched and continued the Crusades, and the European historical tradition has portrayed the relationship between Christianity and Islam in terms of glamorous military conflict. Islam, however, considered the Crusades merely a nuisance.

The feudal states set up by the Crusades along the Syrian and Palestinian coasts (see Map 12.4) managed to survive for about two centuries before the Muslims reconquered them. The Crusaders, however, left in the Middle East two more permanent legacies. First, the long struggle between Islam and Christendom and the example of persecution set by Christian kings and prelates left an inheritance of deep bitterness; relations between Muslims and their Christian and Jewish subjects worsened. Second, European merchants, primarily Italians, had established communities in the Crusader states. After those kingdoms collapsed, Muslim rulers still encouraged trade with European businessmen. Commerce with the West benefited both Muslims and Europeans, and it continued to flourish.[20]

SUMMARY

The civilization that emerged in Europe between 733 and 843 had definite characteristics: it was feudal, Christian, and infused with Latin ideas and models. Despite the disasters of the ninth and tenth centuries, these features remained basic aspects of European culture for centuries to come.

The century and a half after the death of Charlemagne in 814 witnessed a degree of disintegration, destruction, and disorder unparalleled in Europe until the twentieth century. No civil or religious authority could maintain stable government over a very wide area. Local strongmen provided what little security existed. Commerce and long-distance trade were drastically reduced. Leadership of the church became the political football of aristocratic Roman families. The rich became warriors; the poor sought protection. The result was that society became feudal.

The end of the great invasions signaled the beginning of profound changes in European society. In the year 1000, having enough to eat was the rare privilege of a few nobles, priests, and monks. But in the eleventh century, manorial communities slowly improved their agricultural equipment; this advance, aided by warmer weather, meant more food and increasing population.

In the eleventh century also, rulers and local authorities gradually imposed some degree of order within their territories. Peace and domestic security, vigorously promoted by the church, meant larger crops and improved trading conditions. The church overthrew the domination of lay influences, and the spread of the Cluniac and Cistercian orders marked the ascendancy of monasticism. Having put its own house in order, the Roman papacy in the twelfth and thirteenth centuries built the first strong government bureaucracy in medieval Europe. In the High Middle Ages, the church exercised general leadership of European society. The early Crusades exhibited that leadership and the enormous, if misguided, vitality of medieval society.

NOTES

1. For the date of this battle, October 17, 733, see L. White, *Medieval Technology and Social Change* (Oxford: Clarendon Press, 1962), p. 3, n. 3, and p. 12.

2. See F. Irsigler, "On the Aristocratic Character of Early Frankish Society," in *The Medieval Nobility: Studies on the Ruling Class of France and Germany from the Sixth to the Twelfth Century,* ed. and trans. T. Reuter (New York: North-Holland, 1978), pp. 105–136, esp. p. 123.

3. Einhard, *The Life of Charlemagne,* with a foreword by S. Painter (Ann Arbor: University of Michigan Press, 1960), pp. 50–51.

4. P. Stafford, *Queens, Concubines, and Dowagers: The King's Wife in the Early Middle Ages* (Athens, Ga.: University of Georgia Press, 1983), pp. 60–62.

5. See K. F. Werner, "Important Noble Families in the Kingdom of Charlemagne," in Reuter, pp. 174–184.

6. Quoted in B. D. Hill, ed., *Church and State in the Middle Ages* (New York: Wiley, 1970), pp. 46–47.

7. P. Geary, "Carolingians and the Carolingian Empire," in *Dictionary of the Middle Ages,* vol. 3, ed. J. R. Strayer (New York: Scribner's, 1983), p. 110.

8. R. W. Southern, *Medieval Humanism and Other Studies* (Oxford: Basil Blackwell, 1970), p. 3.

9. L. Sherley-Price, trans., *Bede: A History of the English Church and People* (Baltimore: Penguin Books, 1962), bk. 3, chap. 27, p. 191.

10. See S. Rubin, *Medieval English Medicine, 500–1300* (New York: Barnes & Noble, 1974).

11. J. R. Strayer, "The Two Levels of Feudalism," in *Medieval Statecraft and the Perspectives of History,* ed. J. R. Strayer (Princeton, N.J.: Princeton University Press, 1971), p. 63. This section leans heavily on Strayer's seminal study.

12. E. P. Cheney, trans., in *University of Pennsylvania Translations and Reprints,* vol. 4, no. 3 (Philadelphia: University of Pennsylvania Press, 1898), p. 3.

13. Strayer, "Two Levels of Feudalism," pp. 65–76, esp. p. 71.

14. See D. Herlihy, "Land, Family, and Women in Continental Europe, 701–1200," in *Women in Medieval Society,* ed. S. M. Stuart (Philadelphia: University of Pennsylvania Press, 1976), pp. 13–45.

15. See B. Rosenwein, *Rhinoceros Bound: Cluny in the Tenth Century* (Philadelphia: University of Pennsylvania Press, 1982), chap. 2.

16. Quoted in Hill, p. 68.

17. See J. B. Freed, "The Counts of Falkenstein: Noble Self-Consciousness in Twelfth Century Germany," *Transactions of the American Philosophical Society,* vol. 74, pt. 6 (1984): 9–11.

18. C. Erdmann, *The Origin of the Idea of the Crusade,* trans. M. Baldwin and W. Goffart (Princeton, N.J.: Princeton University Press, 1977), p. 57.

19. S. Runciman, *A History of the Crusades,* vol. 3, The Kingdom of Acre (Cambridge, England: Cambridge University Press, 1955), p. 480.

20. B. Lewis, *The Muslim Discovery of Europe* (New York: Norton, 1982), pp. 23–25.

SUGGESTED READING

A good general introduction to the entire period is C. Dawson, *The Formation of Christendom* (1967). The same author's *Religion and the Rise of Western Culture* (1958) emphasizes the religious bases of Western culture. C. H. Talbot, ed., *The Anglo-Saxon Missionaries in Germany* (1954), gives an exciting picture, through biographies and correspondence, of the organization and development of the Christian church in the Carolingian Empire. J. B. Russell, *A History of Medieval Christianity: Prophesy and Order* (1968), describes the mind of the Christian church and how it gradually had an impact on pagan Germanic peoples. The monumental work of F. Kempf et al., *The Church in the Age of Feudalism* (trans. A. Biggs, 1980), volume 3 of the *History of the Church* series edited by H. Jedin and J. Dolan, contains a thorough treatment of the institutional church in both East and West based on the latest scholarship; this book is primarily for scholars. Significant aspects of spirituality are traced in B. McGinn and J. Meyendorff, eds., *Christian Spirituality: From the Apostolic Fathers to the Twelfth Century* (1985).

Einhard's *The Life of Charlemagne* (see Notes) is a good starting point for study of the great chieftain. The best general biography of Charlemagne is D. Bullough, *The Age of Charlemagne* (1965). P. Riché, *Daily Life in the World of Charlemagne* (trans. J. McNamara, 1978), is a richly detailed study of many facets of Carolingian society. The same scholar's *Education and Culture in the Barbarian West: From the Sixth Through the Eighth Century* (trans. J. J. Contreni, 1976) provides an excellent, if technical, treatment of Carolingian intellectual activity. Both volumes contain solid bibliographies. For agricultural and economic life, G. Duby, *Early Growth of the European Economy: Warriors and Peasants from the Seventh to the Twelfth Century* (1977), relates economic behavior to other aspects of human experience in a thoroughly readable style. He also shows how social structure and attitudes evolved. The importance of technological developments in the Carolingian period is described by L. White, *Medieval Technology and Social Change* (1962), now a classic work. For the meaning of war to the Merovingian and Carolingian kings, see "War and Peace in the Early Middle Ages," in J. M. Wallace-Hadrill, *Early Medieval History* (1975). The book also contains interesting essays on Bede, Boniface, Charlemagne, and England. As the title implies, G. Barraclough, *The Crucible of Europe: The Ninth and Tenth Centuries in European History* (1976), sees those centuries as crucial in the formation of European civilization. The author also stresses the importance of stable government. E. James, *The Origins of France: From Clovis to the Capetians, 500–1000* (1982), is a solid introductory survey of early French history, with emphasis on family relationships.

For the eighth-century revival of learning, see M. L. W. Laistner, *Thought and Letters in Western Europe, 500–900* (1931), and the beautifully written evocation by P. H. Blair, *Northumbria in the Days of Bede* (1976). The best treatment of the theological and political ideas of the period is probably K. F. Morrison, *The Two Kingdoms: Ecclesiology in Carolingian Political Thought* (1964), a difficult book.

Those interested in the role of women and children in early medieval society should see the article by D. Herlihy cited in the Notes, as well as E. Coleman, "Infanticide in the Early Middle Ages," in the same volume. The best available study of women in this period is S. F. Wemple, *Women in Frankish Society: Marriage and the Cloister, 500 to 900* (1981). In addition to the work by Stafford cited in the Notes, the following studies are also useful: J. McNamara, "A Legacy of Miracles: Hagiography and Nunneries in Merovingian Gaul," in J. Kirshner and S. Wemple, eds., *Women of the Medieval World: Essays in Honor of John H. Mundy* (1985); and C. Fell, *Women in Anglo-Saxon England* (1984).

For health and medical treatment in the early Middle Ages, the curious student should consult S. Rubin, *Medieval English Medicine, A.D. 500–1300* (1974), especially pp. 97–149; W. H. McNeill, *Plagues and Peoples* (1976); A. Castiglioni, *A History of Medicine* (trans. E. B. Krumbhaar, 1941); and the important article by J. M. Riddle, "Theory and Practice in Medieval Medicine," *Viator* 5 (1974): 157–184. J. C. Russell, *The Control of Late Ancient and Medieval Population* (1985), discusses diet, disease, and demography.

For feudalism and manorialism see, in addition to the references given in the Notes, F. L. Ganshof, *Feudalism* (1961), and J. R. Strayer, "Feudalism in Western Europe," in R. Coulborn, ed., *Feudalism in History* (1956). M. Bloch, *Feudal Society* (trans. L. A. Manyon, 1961), remains important. The more recent treatment of P. Anderson, *Passages from Antiquity to Feudalism* (1978), stresses the evolution of social structures and mental attitudes. For the significance of the ceremony of vassalage, see J. Le Goff, "The Symbolic Ritual of Vassalage," in his *Time, Work, & Culture in the Middle Ages* (trans. A. Goldhammer, 1982). The best broad treatment of peasant life and conditions is G. Duby, *Rural Economy and Country Life in tne Medieval West* (trans. C. Postan, 1968).

J. Brondsted, *The Vikings* (1960), is an excellently illustrated study of the culture of the Northmen. G. Jones, *A History of the Vikings,* rev. ed. (1984), provides

a comprehensive survey of the Viking world based on archeological findings and numismatic evidence.

In addition to the references in the Notes, the curious student will find a fuller treatment of the High Middle Ages in the following works:

C. D. Burns, *The First Europe* (1948), surveys the entire period and emphasizes the transformation from a time of anarchy to one of great creativity. G. Barraclough, *The Origins of Modern Germany* (1963), is essential for central and eastern Europe.

For the Christian church, the papacy, and ecclesiastical developments, the best recent study is I. S. Robinson, *The Papacy, 1073–1198: Continuity and Innovation* (1990), while G. Barraclough's richly illustrated *The Medieval Papacy* (1968) is a good general survey that emphasizes the development of administrative bureaucracy. W. Ullmann's *The Growth of Papal Government in the Middle Ages,* rev. ed. (1970), traces the evolution of papal law and government. G. Tellenbach, *Church, State, and Christian Society at the Time of the Investiture Contest* (1959), emphasizes the revolutionary aspects of the Gregorian reform program. The relationship of the monks to the ecclesiastical crisis of the late eleventh century is discussed by N. F. Cantor, "The Crisis of Western Monasticism," *American Historical Review* 66 (1960), but see also the essential analysis of J. Van Engen, "The 'Crisis of Cenobitism' Reconsidered: Benedictine Monasticism in the Years 1050–1150," *Speculum,* vol. 61, no. 2 (1986): 269–304, as well as H. E. J. Cowdrey, *The Cluniacs and the Gregorian Reform* (1970), an impressive but difficult study. Cowdrey's recent *The Age of Abbot Desiderius: Monte Cassino, the Papacy, and the Normans in the Eleventh and Early Twelfth Centuries* (1983) focuses on Monte Cassino. J. B. Russell, *A History of Medieval Christianity* (1968), offers an important and sensitively written survey. The advanced student will benefit considerably from the works by C. Erdmann, J. B. Freed, and B. Rosenwein that are cited in the Notes.

The following studies provide exciting and highly readable general accounts of the Crusades: J. Riley-Smith, *What Were the Crusades?* (1977); R. C. Finucane, *Soldiers of the Faith: Crusaders and Muslims at War* (1983); and R. Payne, *The Dream and the Tomb: A History of the Crusades* (1984). There are excellent articles on many facets of the Crusades, including "The Children's Crusade," "Crusade Propaganda," "Crusader Art and Architecture," and "The Political Crusades," all written by authorities and based on the latest research, in J. R. Strayer, ed., *Dictionary of the Middle Ages,* vol. 4 (1984). These articles also contain good bibliographies. C. M. Brand, *Byzantium Confronts the West, 1180–1204* (1968), provides the Greek perspective on the Crusades. Serious students will eventually want to consult the multivolume work of K. M. Setton, gen. ed., *A History of the Crusades* (1955–1977).

PERIOD (CA 200–1200)	AFRICA AND THE MIDDLE EAST	THE AMERICAS
200	Camel first used for trans-Saharan transport, ca 200 Expansion of Bantu people, ca 200–900 Axum (Ethiopia) controls Red Sea trade, ca 250	Olmec civilization, ca 1500 B.C.–A.D. 300
300	Axum accepts Christianity, ca 4th century	Maya civilization in Central America, ca 300–1500 Classic period of Teotihuacán civilization in Mexico, ca 300–900
500	Political and commercial ascendency of Axum, ca 6th–7th centuries Muhammad, 570–632; the *hijra,* 622 Extensive slave trade from sub-Saharan Africa to Mediterranean, ca 600–1500 Umayyad Dynasty, 661–750; continued expansion of Islam	Tiahuanaco civilization in South America, ca 600–1000
700	Abbasid Dynasty, 750–1258; Islamic capital moved to Baghdad Decline of Ethiopia, ca 9th century Golden age of Muslim learning, ca 900–1100 Kingdom of Ghana, ca 900–1100 Mahmud of Ghazna, 998–1030	"Time of Troubles" in Mesoamerica, 800–1000
1000	Islam penetrates sub-Saharan Africa, ca 11th century Kingdom of Benin, ca 1100–1897 Kingdom of Mali, middle Niger region, ca 1200–1450 Mongol invasion of Middle East, ca 1220	Inca civilization in South America, ca 1000–1500 Toltec hegemony, ca 1000–1300 Aztecs arrive in Valley of Mexica, ca 1325

EAST ASIA	INDIA AND SOUTHEAST ASIA	EUROPE
Creation of Yamato state in Japan, ca 3rd century Buddhism gains popularity in China and Japan, ca 220–590 Fall of Han Dynasty, 220 Three Kingdoms Era in China, 221–280	Kushan rule in northwestern India, A.D. 2nd–3rd centuries Fall of the Parthian Empire, rise of the Sassanids, ca 225	Breakdown of the *Pax Romana*, ca 180–284; civil wars, economic decline, invasions Reforms by Diocletian, 284–305
Barbarian invasions, 4th–5th centuries	Chandragupta I founds Gupta Dynasty in India, ca 320–500 Chandragupta II conquers western India, establishes trade with Middle East and China, ca 400 Huns invade India, ca 450	Reign of Constantine, 306–337; Edict of Milan, 313; Council of Nicaea, 325; founding of Constantinople, 330 Theodosius recognizes Christianity as official state religion, 380 Germanic raids of Western Europe, 5th century Clovis unites Franks and rules Gauls, 481–511
Sui Dynasty in China, 580–618; restoration of public order "Constitution" of Shotoku in Japan, 604 T'ang Dynasty, 618–907; cultural flowering	Sanskrit drama, ca 600–1000 Muslim invasions of India, ca 636–1206	St. Benedict publishes his *Rule*, 529 Law Code of Justinian, 529 Synod of Whitby, 664
Taika Reform Edict in Japan, 655 Nara era, creation of Japan's first capital, 710–784 Heian era in Japan, 794–1185; literary flowering Era of the Five Dynasties in China, 907–960; warfare, revolt Sung Dynasty, 960–1279	Khmer Empire (Kampuchea) founded, 802	Charles Martel defeats Muslims at Tours, 733 Charles the Great (Charlemagne), 768–814 Invasions of Carolingian Empire, 9th–10th centuries Treaty of Verdun divides Carolingian Empire, 843 Cluny monastery founded, 910
Vietnam gains independence from China, ca 1000 China divided between empires of Sung (south) and Chin (north), 1127 Kamakura Shogunate, 1185–1333 Mongol conquest of China, 1215–1368	Construction of Angkor Wat, ca 1100–1150 Muslim conquerors end Buddhism in India, 1192 Peak of Khmer Empire in southeast Asia, ca 1200 Turkish sultanate at Delhi, 1206–1526; Indian culture divided into Hindu and Muslim	Yaroslav the wise, 1019–1054; peak of Kievan Russia Schism between Latin and Greek churches, 1054 Norman Conquest of England, 1066 Investiture struggle, 1073–1122 The Crusades, 1096–1270 Growth of trade and towns, 12th–13th centuries Frederick Barbarossa invades Italy, 1154–1158

13

Life in Christian Europe in the High Middle Ages

"April," from *Hours of the Virgin*

Close links existed between educated circles on both sides of the English Channel. In one of the writings produced at the court of the late-ninth-century Anglo-Saxon king, Alfred (r. 871–899), Christian society is said to be composed of those who work (the peasants), those who fight (the nobles), and those who pray (the monks). In France, Bishop Adalbero of Laon used the same three social divisions in a poem written about 1028. This image of a society in which function determined social classification gained wide circulation in the High Middle Ages.[1] It did not take into consideration the emerging commercial classes; but that omission is not surprising, for traders and other city dwellers were not typical members of early medieval society. Moreover, medieval Europeans were usually contemptuous (at least officially) of profit-making activities; and even after the appearance of urban commercial groups, the general sociological view of medieval Christian society remained the one first formulated during the ninth century and given expression in King Alfred's court.

In the High Middle Ages, the most representative figures of Christian society were peasants, nobles, and monks.

- How did these people actually live?
- What were their preoccupations and lifestyles?
- To what extent was social mobility possible for them?

These are among the questions that are explored in this chapter.

THOSE WHO WORK

The largest and economically most productive group in medieval European society was the peasants. The men and women who worked the land in the twelfth and thirteenth centuries made up the overwhelming majority of the population, probably more than 90 percent. Yet it is difficult to form a coherent picture of them. The records that serve as historical sources were written by and for the aristocratic classes. Since peasants did not perform what were considered "noble" deeds, the aristocratic monks and clerics did not waste time or precious writing materials on them. When peasants were mentioned, it was usually with contempt or in terms of the services and obligations they owed.

Usually—but not always. In the early twelfth century, Honorius, a monk and teacher at Autun, France, wrote: "What do you say about the agricultural classes? Most of them will be saved because they live simply and feed God's people by means of their sweat."[2] This sentiment circulated widely. Honorius's comment suggests that peasant workers may have been appreciated and in a sense respected more than is generally believed.

In the past twenty-five years, historians have made remarkable advances in their knowledge of the medieval European peasantry. They have been able to do so by bringing fresh and different questions to old documents, by paying greater attention to such natural factors as geography and climate, and by studying demographic changes. Nevertheless, this new information raises additional questions, and a good deal remains unknown.

In 1932 a distinguished economic historian wrote, "The student of medieval social and economic history who commits himself to a generalization is digging a pit into which he will later assuredly fall and nowhere does the pit yawn deeper than in the realm of rural history."[3] This remark is as true today as when it was written. It is therefore important to remember that peasants' conditions varied widely across Europe, that geographical and climatic features as much as human initiative and local custom determined the peculiar quality of rural life. The problems that faced the English farmer in Yorkshire, where the soil was rocky and the climate rainy, were very different from those that faced the Italian peasant in the sun-drenched Po Valley.

Another difficulty has been historians' tendency to group all peasants into one social class. Doing so is a serious mistake. Even though medieval theologians lumped everyone who worked the land into the category of "those who work," there were many levels of peasants, ranging from complete slaves to free and very rich farmers. The period from 1050 to 1250 was one of considerable fluidity with no little social mobility. The status of the peasantry varied widely all across Europe.

The Three Classes Medieval people believed that their society was divided among warriors, clerics, and workers, here represented by a monk, a knight, and a peasant. The new commercial class had no recognized place in the agrarian military world. *(Source: The British Library)*

Slavery, Serfdom, and Upward Mobility

Slaves were found in western Europe in the High Middle Ages, but in steadily declining numbers. That the word *slave* derives from "Slav" attests to the widespread trade in men and women from the Slavic areas in the early Middle Ages. Around the year 1200, there were in aristocratic and upper-middle-class households in Provence, Catalonia, Italy, and Germany a few slaves—blond Slavs from the Baltic, olive-skinned Syrians, and blacks from Africa.

Since ancient times, it had been a universally accepted practice to enslave conquered peoples. The church had long taught that all baptized Christians were brothers in Christ and that all Christians belonged to one "international" community. Although the church never issued a blanket condemnation of slavery, it vigorously opposed the enslaving of Christians. In attacking the enslavement of Christians and in criticizing the reduction of pagans and infidels to slavery, the church made a contribution to the development of human liberty.

In Western Europe during the Middle Ages, legal language differed considerably from place to place, and the distinction between slave and serf was not always clear. Both lacked freedom—the power to do as one wished—and were subject to the arbitrary will of one person, the lord. A serf, however, could not be bought and sold like an animal or an inanimate object, as the slave could.

A serf was required to perform labor services on the lord's land. The number of workdays per week varied, but it was usually three days except in the planting or harvest seasons, when it was more. Serfs had to pay many arbitrary levies. When a man married, he had to pay his lord a fee. When he died, his son or heir had to pay an inheritance tax to inherit his parcels of land. The precise amounts of tax paid to the lord on these important occasions depended on local custom and tradition. Every manor had its particular obligations. A free peasant had to do none of those things. For his or her landholding, rent had to be paid to the lord, and that was often the sole obligation. A free person could move and live as he or she wished.

Serfs were tied to the land, and serfdom was a hereditary condition. A person born a serf was likely to die a serf, though many did secure their freedom. About 1187 Glanvill, an official of King Henry II and an expert on English law, described how *villeins* (literally, "inhabitants of small villages")—as English serfs were called—could be made free:

A person of villein status can be made free in several ways. For example, his lord, wishing him to achieve freedom from the villeinage by which he is subject to him, may quit-claim [release] him from himself and his heirs; or he may give or sell him to another with intent to free him. It should be noted, however, that no person of villein status can seek his freedom with his own money, for in such a case he could, according to the law and custom of the realm, be recalled to villeinage by his lord, because all the chattels of a villein are deemed to such an extent the property of his lord that he cannot redeem himself from villeinage with his own money, as against his lord. If, however, a third party provides the money and buys the villein in order to free him, then he can maintain himself for ever in a state of freedom as against his lord who sold him. . . . If any villein stays peaceably for a year and a day in a privileged town and is admitted as a citizen into their commune, that is to say, their gild, he is thereby freed from villeinage.[4]

Many energetic and hard-working serfs acquired their freedom in the High Middle Ages. More than anything else, the economic revival that began in the eleventh century advanced the cause of individual liberty (see pages 417–426). The revival saw the rise of towns, increased land productivity, the growth of long-distance trade, and the development of a money economy. With the advent of a money economy, serfs could save money and, through a third-person intermediary, buy their freedom.

Another opportunity for increased personal freedom, or at least for a reduction in traditional manorial obligations and dues, was provided by the reclamation of wasteland and forest land in the eleventh and twelfth centuries. Resettlement on newly cleared land offered unusual possibilities for younger sons and for those living in areas of acute land shortage or on overworked, exhausted soil. Historians still do not know very much about this movement: how the new frontier territory was advertised, how men were recruited, how they and their households were transported, and how the new lands were distributed. It is certain, however, that there was significant migration and that only a lord with considerable authority over a wide territory could sponsor such a movement. Great lords supported the fight against the marshes of northern and eastern Germany and against the sea in the Low Countries (present-day Holland, Belgium, and French Flanders). For example, in the twelfth century the invitation of German and Slavic rulers led to peasant settlements in "the territory between the Saale and the upper Elbe" rivers.[5] The thirteenth century witnessed German peasant migrations into Brandenburg, Pomerania, Prussia, and the Baltic states.

In the thirteenth century, the noble class frequently needed money to finance crusading building, or other projects. For example, in 1240 when Geoffrey de Montigny became abbot of Saint-Pierre-le-Vif in the Senonais region of France, he found the abbey church in disrepair. Geoffrey also discovered that the descendants of families who had once owed the abbey servile obligations now refused to recognize their bondage. Some of these peasants had grown wealthy. When the abbot determined to reclaim these peasants in order to get the revenues to rebuild his church, a legal struggle ensued. In 1257 a compromise was worked out whereby Geoffrey manumitted 366 persons who in turn agreed to pay him 500 pounds a year over a 12-year period.[6]

As land long considered poor was brought under cultivation, there was a steady nibbling away at the wasteland on the edges of old villages. Clearings were made in forests. Marshes and fens were drained and slowly made arable. This type of agricultural advancement improved many peasants' social and legal condition. A serf could clear a patch of fen or forest land, make it productive, and, through prudent saving, buy more land and eventually purchase freedom. There were in the thirteenth century many free tenants on the lands of the bishop of Ely in eastern England, tenants who had moved into the area in the twelfth century and drained the fens. Likewise, settlers on the lowlands of the abbey of Bourbourg in Flanders, who had erected dikes and extended the arable lands, possessed hereditary tenures by 1159. They secured personal liberty and owed their overlord only small payments.

Peasants who remained in the villages of their birth often benefited because landlords, threatened with the loss of serfs, relaxed ancient obligations and duties. While it would be unwise to exaggerate the social impact of the settling of new territories, frontier lands in the Middle Ages did provide opportunities for upward mobility.

The Manor

In the High Middle Ages, most European peasants, free and unfree, lived on estates called "manors." The word *manor* derives from a Latin term meaning "dwelling," "residence," or "homestead." In the twelfth century it meant the estate of a lord and his dependent tenants.

The manor was the basic unit of medieval rural organization and the center of rural life. All other generalizations about manors and manorial life have to be limited by variations in the quality of the soil, local climatic conditions, and methods of cultivation. Some manors were vast, covering several thousand acres of farmland; others were no

larger than 120 acres. A manor might include several villages or none at all, but usually it contained a single village and was subject to one lord (Figure 13.1).

The arable land of the manor was divided into two sections. The *demesne,* or home farm, was cultivated for the lord. The other part was held by the peasantry. Usually, the peasants' portion was larger, held on condition that they cultivate the lord's demesne. All the arable land, both the lord's and the peasants', was divided into strips, and the strips belonging to any given individual were scattered throughout the manor. All peasants cooperated in the cultivation of the land, working it as a group. This meant that all shared in any disaster as well as in any large harvest.

A manor usually held pasture or meadow land for the grazing of cattle, sheep, and sometimes goats. Many manors had some forest land as well. Forests had enormous economic importance. They were the source of wood for building and fuel, bark for the manufacture of rope, resin for lighting, ash for candles, and ash and lime for fertilizers and all sorts of sterilizing products. The forests were also used for feeding pigs, cattle, and domestic animals on nuts, roots, and wild berries. If a manor was intersected by a river, it had a welcome source of fish and eels.

Agricultural Methods

The fundamental objective of all medieval agriculture was the production of an adequate food supply. According to the method that historians have called the "open-field system," at any one time half of the manorial land was under cultivation and the other half lay fallow; the length of the fallow period was usually one year. Every peasant farmer had strips scattered in both halves. One part of the land under cultivation was sown with winter cereals, such as wheat and rye, the other with spring crops, such as peas, beans, and barley. What was planted in a particular field varied each year, when the crops were rotated.

Local needs, the fertility of the soil, and dietary customs determined what was planted and the method of crop rotation. Where one or several manors belonged to a great aristocratic establishment, such as the abbey of Cluny, that needed large quantities of oats for horses, more of the ar-

FIGURE 13.1 A Medieval Manor   The basic unit of rural organization and the center of life for most people, the manor constituted the medieval peasants' world. Since manors had to be economically self-sufficient, life meant endless toil.

able land would be planted in oats than in other cereals. Where the land was extremely fertile, such as the Alsace region of Germany, a biennial cycle was used: one crop of wheat was sown and harvested every other year, and in alternate years all the land lay fallow. The author of an English agricultural treatise advised his readers to stick to a two-field method of cultivation and insisted that a rich harvest every second year was preferable to two mediocre harvests every three years.

Farmers were aware of the value of animal fertilizers. Chicken manure, because of its high nitrogen content, was the richest but was limited in quantity. Sheep manure was also valuable. Gifts to English Cistercian monasteries were frequently given on condition that the monks' sheep be allowed to graze at certain periods on the benefactor's demesne. Because cattle were fed on the com-

mon pasture and were rarely stabled, gathering their manure was laborious and time consuming. Nevertheless, whenever possible, animal manure was gathered and thinly spread. So also was house garbage—eggshells, fruit cores, onion skins—that had disintegrated on a compost heap.

Tools and farm implements are often shown in medieval manuscripts. But accepting such representations at face value is unwise. Rather than going out into a field to look at a tool, medieval artists simply copied drawings from classical and other treatises. Thus a plow or harrow (used to smooth out the soil after it had been broken up) pictured in a book written in the Île-de-France may actually have been used in England or Italy a half-century before.

In the early twelfth century, the production of iron increased greatly. There is considerable evidence for the manufacture of iron plowshares (the part of the plow that cuts the furrow into and grinds up the earth). In the thirteenth century, the wooden plow continued to be the basic instrument of agricultural production, but its edge was strengthened with iron. Only after the start of the fourteenth century, when lists of manorial equipment began to be kept, is there evidence for pitchforks, spades, axes, and harrows. Harrows were usually made of wood and weighted down with stones to force a deeper cut into the earth.

Plow and harrow were increasingly pulled by horses. The development of the padded horse collar, resting on the horse's shoulders and attached to the load by shafts, led to an agricultural revolution. The horse collar meant that the animal could put its entire weight into the task of pulling. The use of horses, rather than oxen, spread in the twelfth century. Horses' greater strength brought greater efficiency to farming.[7] Horses were an enormous investment, perhaps comparable to a modern tractor. They had to be shod (another indication of increased iron production), and the

oats they ate were costly. But horses were a crucial element in the improvement of the medieval agricultural economy. Some scholars believe that the use of the horse in agriculture is one of the decisive ways in which western Europe advanced over the rest of the world. But horses were not universally adopted. The Mediterranean countries, for example, did not use horsepower. And tools and farm implements still remained primitive.

Agricultural yields varied widely from place to place and from year to year. Even with good iron tools, horsepower, and careful use of seed and fertilizer, medieval peasants were at the mercy of the weather. Even today, lack of rain or too much rain can cause terrible financial loss and extreme hardship. How much more vulnerable was the medieval peasant with his primitive tools! By twentieth-century standards, medieval agricultural yields were very low. Inadequate soil preparation, poor seed selection, lack of manure—all made this virtually inevitable.

Yet there was striking improvement over time. Between the ninth and early thirteenth centuries,

Late Medieval Wheelless Plow This plow has a sharp-pointed colter, which cut the earth while the attached mold-board lifted, turned, and pulverized the soil. As the man steers the plow, his wife prods the oxen. The caption reads, "God speed the plow, and send us corn (wheat) enough." *(Source: Trinity College Library, Cambridge)*

it appears that yields of cereals approximately doubled, and on the best-managed estates, for every bushel of seed planted, the farmer harvested five bushels of grain. This is a tentative conclusion. Because of the scarcity of manorial inventories before the thirteenth century, the student of medieval agriculture has great difficulty determining how much the land produced. The author of a treatise on land husbandry, Walter of Henley, who lived in the mid-thirteenth century, wrote that the land should yield three times its seed; that amount was necessary for sheer survival. The surplus would be sold to grain merchants in the nearest town. Townspeople were wholly dependent on the surrounding countryside for food, which could not be shipped a long distance. A poor harvest meant that both town and rural people suffered.

Grain yields were probably greatest on large manorial estates, where there was more professional management. For example, the estates of Battle Abbey in Sussex, England, enjoyed a very high yield of wheat, rye, and oats in the century and a half between 1350 and 1499. This was due to heavy seeding, good crop rotation, and the use of manure from the monastery's sheep flocks. Battle Abbey's yields seem to have been double those of smaller, less efficiently run farms. A modern Illinois farmer expects to get 40 bushels of soybeans, 150 bushels of corn, and 50 bushels of wheat for every bushel of seed planted. Of course, modern costs of production in labor, seed, and fertilizer are quite high, but this yield is at least ten times that of the farmer's medieval ancestor. The average manor probably got a yield of 5 to 1 in the thirteenth century.[8] As low as that may seem by current standards, it marked a rise in productivity equal to that of the years just before the great agricultural revolution of the eighteenth century.

Life on the Manor

Life for most people in medieval Europe meant country life. Most people's horizons were restricted to the manor on which they were born. True, peasants who colonized such sparsely settled regions as eastern Germany must have traveled long distances. But most people rarely traveled more than twenty-five miles beyond their villages. Everyone's world was small, narrow, and provincial in the original sense of the word: limited by the boundaries of the province. This way of life did not have entirely unfortunate results. A farmer had a strong sense of family and the certainty of its support and help in time of trouble. People knew what their life's work would be—the same as their mother's or father's. They had a sense of place, and pride in that place was reflected in adornment of the village church. Religion and the village gave people a sure sense of identity and with it psychological peace. Modern people—urban, isolated, industrialized, rootless, and thoroughly secularized—have lost many of these reinforcements.

On the other hand, even aside from the unending physical labor, life on the manor was dull. Medieval men and women must have had a crushing sense of frustration. They lived lives of quiet desperation. Often they sought escape in heavy drinking. English judicial records of the thirteenth century reveal a surprisingly large number of "accidental" deaths. Strong, robust, commonsensical farmers do not ordinarily fall on their knives and stab themselves, or slip out of boats and drown, or get lost in the woods on a winter's night, or fall from horses and get trampled. They were probably drunk. Many of these accidents occurred, as the court records say, "coming from an ale." Brawls and violent fights were frequent at taverns.

Scholars have recently spent much energy investigating the structure of medieval peasant households. Because little concrete evidence survives, conclusions are very tentative. It appears, however, that a peasant household consisted of a simple nuclear family: a married couple alone, a couple with children, or widows or widowers with children. Peasant households were *not* extended families containing grandparents or married sons and daughters and their children, as was common in Asian countries, such as China. The simple family predominated in thirteenth-century England, in northern France in the fourteenth century, and in fifteenth-century Tuscany. Before the first appearance of the Black Death, perhaps 94 percent of peasant farmers married, and bride and groom were both in their twenties. The "typical" household numbered about five people: the parents and three children.[9]

Women played a significant role in the agricultural life of medieval Europe. This obvious fact is often overlooked by historians. Women shared with their fathers and husbands the backbreaking labor in the fields, work that was probably all the more difficult for them because of weaker muscular development and frequent pregnancies. The adage from the Book of Proverbs "Houses and riches are the inheritances of fathers: but a prudent wife is from the Lord" was seldom more true than in an age when the wife's prudent management was often all that separated a household from starvation in a year of crisis. And starvation was a very real danger to the peasantry until the eighteenth century.

Women managed the house. The size and quality of peasants' houses varied according to their relative prosperity, and that prosperity usually depended on the amount of land held. Poorer peasants lived in windowless cottages built of wood or wattle (poles intertwined with twigs or reeds) and clay and thatched with straw. These cottages consisted of one large room that served as the kitchen and living quarters for all. Everyone slept there. The house had an earthen floor and a fireplace. The lack of windows meant that the room was very sooty. A trestle table, several stools, one or two beds, and a chest for storing clothes constituted the furniture. A shed attached to the house provided storage for tools and shelter for animals. Prosperous peasants added rooms and furniture as they could be afforded, and some wealthy peasants in the early fourteenth century had two-story houses with separate bedrooms for parents and children.

Every house had a small garden and an outbuilding. Onions, garlic, turnips, and carrots were grown and stored through the winter in the main room of the dwelling or in the shed attached to it. Cabbage was raised almost everywhere and, after being shredded, salted, and packed in vats in hot water, was turned into kraut. Peasants ate vegetables, not because they appreciated their importance for good health but because there was usually little else. Some manors had fruit trees—apple, cherry, and pear in northern Europe; lemon, lime, and olive in the south. But because of the high price of sugar, when it was available, fruit could not be preserved. Preserving and storing other foods were the basic responsibility of the women and children.

Women also had to know the correct proportions of barley, water, yeast, and hops to make beer—the universal drink of the common people in northern Europe. By modern American standards the rate of beer consumption was heroic. Each monk of Abingdon Abbey in England in the twelfth century was allotted three gallons a day,

Woman's Work Carrying a heavy sack of grain to the mill was part of this medieval woman's everyday work. *(Source: The Pierpoint Morgan Library)*

and a man working in the fields for ten or twelve hours a day probably drank much more.[10]

The mainstay of the diet for peasants everywhere—and for all other classes—was bread. It was a hard, black substance made of barley, millet, and oats, rarely of expensive wheat flour. The housewife usually baked the household supply once a week. Where sheep, cows, or goats were raised, she also made cheese. In places like the Bavarian Alps of southern Germany, where hundreds of sheep grazed on the mountainsides, or at Cheddar in southwestern England, cheese was a staple.[11]

The diet of those living in an area with access to a river, lake, or stream was supplemented with fish, which could be preserved by salting. In many places there were severe laws against hunting and trapping in the forests. Deer, wild boars, and other game were strictly reserved for the king and nobles. These laws were flagrantly violated, however, and stolen rabbits and wild game often found their way to the peasants' tables. Woods and forests also provided nuts, which housewives and small children would gather in the fall.

Lists of peasant obligations and services to the lord, such as the following from Battle Abbey, commonly included the payment of chickens and eggs:

John of Coyworth holds a house and thirty acres of land, and owes yearly 2 p at Easter and Michaelmas; and he owes a cock and two hens at Christmas, of the value of 4 d.[12]

Chicken and eggs must have been highly valued in the prudently managed household. Except for the rare chicken or illegally caught wild game, meat appeared on the table only on the great feast days of the Christian year: Christmas, Easter, and Pentecost. Then the meat was likely to be pork from the pig slaughtered in the fall and salted for the rest of the year. Some scholars believe that by the mid-thirteenth century there was a great increase in the consumption of meat generally. If so, this change in diet is further evidence of an improved standard of living.

Breakfast, eaten at dawn before the farmer departed for his work, might consist of bread, an onion (easily stored through the winter months), and a piece of cheese, washed down with milk or beer. Farmers, then as now, ate their main meal around noon. This was often soup—a thick *potage* of boiled cabbage, onions, turnips, and peas, seasoned with a bone or perhaps a sliver of meat. The evening meal, taken at sunset, consisted of leftovers from the noon meal, perhaps with bread, cheese, milk, or beer.

Once children were able to walk, they helped their parents in the hundreds of chores that had to be done. Small children were set to collecting eggs, if the family had chickens, or gathering twigs and sticks for firewood. As they grew older, children had more responsibility—weeding the family vegetable garden, milking the cows, shearing the sheep, cutting wood for fires, helping with the planting or harvesting, and assisting their mothers in the endless tasks of baking, cooking, and preserving. Because of poor diet, terrible sanitation, and lack of medical care, the death rate among children was phenomenally high.

Popular Religion

Apart from the land, the weather, and the peculiar conditions that existed on each manor, the Christian religion had its greatest impact on the daily lives of ordinary people in the High Middle Ages. Religious practices varied widely from country to country and even from province to province. But nowhere was religion a one-hour-on-Sunday or only-on-high holy days affair. Christian practices and attitudes permeated virtually all aspects of everyday life.

In the ancient world, participation in religious rituals was a public and social duty. As the Germanic and Celtic peoples were Christianized, their new religion became a fusion of Jewish, pagan, Roman, and Christian practices. By the High Middle Ages, religious rituals and practices represented a synthesis of many elements, and all people shared as a natural and public duty in the religious life of the community.

The village church was the center of manorial life—social, political, and economic as well as religious. Most of the important events in a person's life took place in or around the church. A person was baptized there, within hours of birth. Men and women confessed their sins to the village priest there and received, usually at Easter and Christmas, the sacrament of the Eucharist. In front of the church, the bishop reached down from his horse and confirmed a person as a Christian by placing his hands over the candidate's head and making the sign of the cross on the forehead. (Bishops Thomas Becket of Canterbury and Hugh of Lincoln were considered especially holy men because they got down from their horses to confirm.) Young people courted in the churchyard and, so the sermons of the priests complained, made love in the church cemetery. Priests urged couples to marry publicly in the church, but many married privately, without witnesses (see page 450).

The stone in the church altar contained relics of the saints, often a local saint to whom the church itself had been dedicated. In the church, women and men could pray to the Virgin and the local saints. The saints had once lived on earth and thus could well understand human problems. They could be helpful intercessors with Christ or God the Father. According to official church doctrine, the center of the Christian religious life was the mass, the re-enactment of Christ's sacrifice on the cross. Every Sunday and on holy days, villagers stood at mass or squatted on the floor (there were no chairs), breaking the painful routine of work. Finally, people wanted to be buried in the church cemetery, close to the holy place and the saints believed to reside there.

The church was the center of village social life. The feasts that accompanied baptisms, weddings, funerals, and other celebrations were commonly held in the churchyard. Medieval drama originated within the church. Mystery plays, based on biblical episodes, were performed first in the sanctuary, then on the church porch, and finally in the village square, which was often in front of the west door.

From the church porch the priest read to his parishioners orders and messages from royal and ecclesiastical authorities. Royal judges traveling on circuit opened their courts on the church porch. The west front of the church, with its scenes of the Last Judgment, was the background against which the justices disposed of civil and criminal cases. Farmers from outlying districts pushed their carts to the marketplace in the village square near the west front. In busy mercantile centers such as London, business agreements and commercial exchanges were made in the aisles of the church itself, as at Saint Paul's.

Popular religion consisted of rituals heavy with symbolism. Before slicing a loaf of bread, the good wife tapped the sign of the cross on it with her knife. Before the planting, the village priest customarily went out and sprinkled the fields with holy water, symbolizing refreshment and life. Shortly after a woman had successfully delivered a child, she was "churched" in a ceremony of thanksgiving based on the Jewish rite of purification. When a child was baptized, a few grains of salt were dropped on its tongue. Salt had been the symbol of purity, strength, and incorruptibility for the ancient Hebrews, and the Romans had used it in their sacrifices. It was used in Christian baptism to drive away demons and to strengthen the infant in its new faith.

The entire calendar was designed with reference to Christmas, Easter, and Pentecost. Saints' days were legion. Everyone participated in village processions. The colored vestments worn by the priests at mass gave the villagers a sense of the changing seasons of the church's liturgical year. The signs and symbols of Christianity were visible everywhere.

Was popular religion entirely a matter of ritualistic formulas and ceremonies? What did the peasants actually *believe*? They accepted what family, custom, and the clergy ingrained in them. They learned the fundamental teachings of the church from the homilies of the village priests. The mass was in Latin, but the priest delivered sermons on the Gospel in the vernacular. People grasped the meaning of biblical stories and church doctrines

from the paintings on the village church wall. If their parish was wealthy, scenes depicted in the church's stained-glass windows instructed them. Illiterate and uneducated, they certainly could not reason out the increasingly sophisticated propositions of clever theologians. Still, scriptural references and proverbs dotted everyone's language. The everyday English farewell, "Goodbye" (French *adieu,* Spanish *adios*), meaning "God be with you" or "Godspeed," reflects the religious influence in ordinary speech. Christianity was a basic element in the common people's culture; indeed, it was a foundation of their culture.

Christianity has always absorbed the rituals and practices of other faiths, investing them with Christian significance. The rosary provides a good example of the adaptation of an Asian device. Since the beginnings of Christianity, one feature of everyday Christian spirituality was the continuous repetition of prayers and biblical verses. Pebbles, beads, and gems strung on a rope or chain were used to assist in counting these repetitions. This rope of beads originated in Hindu India (see page 73) and from Hinduism it spread to Buddhism and later to Islam. Muslims finger tasseled worry beads to calm their nerves, and in the twelfth century Western Crusaders returning from the Middle East spread this practice, which they had learned from the Muslims. In the Muslim world the beads have a secular character; in the West the practice is strictly religious.[13]

Scholars do not know when the practice of reciting the rosary actually entered Western Christianity. A rosary was found in the grave of the Abbess Gertrude (d. 659), daughter of King Pippin I of the Franks; and when Lady Godiva of Coventry died in 1041, her will mentioned a circlet of gems on which she had said her prayers. Popular tradition holds that Saint Dominic (1170?–1221) (see page 435) invented the rosary after a miraculous vision of the Virgin Mary, but this religious practice obviously existed much earlier.

Christians had long had special reverence and affection for the Virgin Mary as the Mother of Christ. In the eleventh century, theologians began to emphasize the depiction of Mary at the crucifixion in the Gospel of John:

But standing by the cross of Jesus were his mother, and his mother's sister, Mary the wife of Clopas, and Mary Magdalene. When Jesus saw his mother and the disciple whom he loved standing near, he said to his

Medieval Vision of Hell (Winchester Psalter) Frightful demons attack the damned souls—including kings, queens, and monks—in this twelfth-century portrayal of hell. The inscription at the top reads, "Here is hell and the angel closes the gates." *(Source: The British Library)*

mother, "Woman, behold, your son!" Then he said to the disciple, "Behold, your mother!"[14]

Medieval scholars interpreted this passage as expressing Christ's compassionate concern for all humanity and Mary's spiritual motherhood of all Christians. The huge outpouring of popular devotions to Mary concentrated on her role as Queen of Heaven and, because of her special relationship to Christ, as all-powerful intercessor with him. Masses on Saturdays specially commemorated her; sermons focused on her unique influence with Christ; and hymns and prayers to her multiplied. The most famous prayer, "Salve Regina," perfectly expresses the confidence that medieval people placed in Mary, their advocate with Christ:

Hail, holy Queen, Mother of Mercy! Our life, our sweetness, and our hope. To thee we cry, poor banished children of Eve; to thee we send up our sighs, mourning and weeping in this valley of tears. Turn, then, most gracious advocate, thy merciful eyes upon us; and after this our exile show us the blessed fruit of thy womb, Jesus. O merciful, O loving, O sweet Virgin Mary!

Peasants had a strong sense of the universal presence of God. They believed that God intervened directly in human affairs and could reward the virtuous and bring peace, health, and material prosperity. They believed, too, that God punished men and women for their sins with disease, poor harvests, and the destructions of war. Sin was caused by the Devil, who lurked everywhere. The Devil constantly incited people to evil deeds and sin, especially sins of the flesh. Sin frequently took place in the dark. Thus evil and the Devil were connected in the peasant's mind with darkness or blackness. In medieval literature the Devil is sometimes portrayed as a black, an identification that has had a profound and sorry impact on Western racial attitudes.

For peasants, life was not only hard but short. Few lived beyond the age of forty. They had a great fear of nature: storms, thunder, and lightning terrified them. They had a terror of hell, whose geography and awful tortures they knew from sermons. And they certainly saw that the virtuous were not always rewarded but sometimes suffered considerably on earth. These things, which they could not explain, bred a deep pessimism.

No wonder, then, that pilgrimages to shrines of the saints were so popular. They offered hope in a world of gloom. They satisfied a strong emotional need. They meant change, adventure, excitement. The church granted indulgences to those who visited the shrines of great saints. *Indulgences* were remissions of the penalties that priests imposed on penitents for grave sin. People, however, equated indulgences with salvation itself. They generally believed that an indulgence cut down the amount of time one would spend in hell. Thus indulgences and pilgrimages "promised" salvation. Vast numbers embarked on pilgrimages to the shrines of Saint James at Santiago de Compostella in Spain, Thomas Becket at Canterbury, Saint-Gilles de Provence, and Saints Peter and Paul at Rome.

THOSE WHO FIGHT

The nobility, though a small fraction of the total population, strongly influenced all aspects of medieval culture—political, economic, religious, educational, and artistic. For that reason, European society in the twelfth and thirteenth centuries may be termed "aristocratic." Despite political, scientific, and industrial revolutions, the nobility continued to hold real political and social power in Europe down to the nineteenth century. In order to account for this continuing influence, it is important to understand its development in the High Middle Ages.

During the past twenty years, historians have discovered a great deal about the origins and status of the medieval European nobility. It is now known, for example, that ecclesiastical writers in the tenth and eleventh centuries frequently used the term *nobilitas* in reference to the upper classes but did not define it. Clerical writers, however, had no trouble distinguishing who was and was not noble. By the thirteenth century, nobles were broadly described as "those who fight"—those who had the profession of arms. What was a noble? How did the social status and lifestyle of the nobility in the twelfth and thirteenth centuries differ from their tenth-century forms? What political and economic role did the nobility play?

First, in the tenth and eleventh centuries, the social structure in different parts of Europe varied considerably. There were distinct regional customs and social patterns. Broad generalizations about the legal and social status of the nobility, therefore, are dangerous, because they are not universally applicable. For example, in Germany until about 1200, approximately one thousand families, descended from the Carolingian imperial aristocracy and perhaps from the original German tribal nobility, formed the ruling social group. The members of this group intermarried and held most of the important positions in church and state.[15] Between free and nonfree individuals there were rigid distinctions, which prevented the absorption of those of servile birth into the ranks of the nobility.

Likewise, in the region around Paris from the tenth century on, a group of great families held public authority, was self-conscious about its ancestry and honorable status, was bound to the royal house, and was closed to the self-made man. From this aristocracy descended the upper nobility of the High Middle Ages.[16] To the west, however, in the provinces of Anjou and Maine, men of fortune who gained wealth and power became part of the closely related web of noble families by marrying into those families; in these regions, considerable upward mobility existed. Some scholars argue that before the thirteenth century the French nobility was an open caste.[17] Across the English Channel, the English nobility in the High Middle Ages derived from the Norman, Breton, French, and Flemish warriors who helped Duke William of Normandy defeat the Anglo-Saxons at the Battle of Hastings in 1066 (see page 405).

In most places, for a son or daughter to be considered a noble, both parents had to be noble. Non-noble women could not usually enter the nobility through marriage, though evidence from Germany shows that some women were ennobled because they had married nobles. There is no evidence of French or English women being raised to the nobility.

Members of the nobility enjoyed a special legal status. A noble was free personally and in his possessions. He had immunity from almost all outside authorities. He was limited only by his military obligation to king, duke, or prince. As the result of his liberty, he had certain rights and responsibilities. He raised troops and commanded them in the field. He held courts that dispensed a sort of justice. Sometimes he coined money for use within his territories. He conducted relations with outside powers. He was the political, military, and judicial lord of the people who settled on his lands. He made political decisions that affected them, resolved disputes among them, and protected them in time of attack. The liberty of the noble and the privileges that went with his liberty were inheritable, perpetuated by blood and not by wealth alone.

The noble was a professional fighter. His social function, as churchmen described it, was to protect the weak, the poor, and the churches by force of arms. He possessed a horse and a sword. These, and the leisure time in which to learn how to use them in combat, were the visible signs of his nobility. He was encouraged to display chivalric virtues. Chivalry was a code of conduct originally devised by the clergy to transform the crude and brutal behavior of the knightly class. A knight was sup-

posed to be brave, eager to win praise, courteous, loyal to his commander, generous, and gracious. The medieval nobility developed independently of knighthood and preceded it; all nobles were knights, but not all knights were noble.[18]

During the eleventh century, the term *chevalier,* meaning "horseman" or "knight," gained wide currency in France. Non-French people gradually adopted it to refer to the nobility, "who sat up high on their war-horses, looking down on the poor masses and terrorizing the monks."[19] In France and England by the twelfth century, the noble frequently used the Latin term *miles,* or "knight." By this time the word connoted moral values, a consciousness of family, and participation in a superior hereditary caste.

Those who aspired to the aristocracy desired a castle, the symbol of feudal independence and military lifestyle. Through military valor, a fortunate marriage, or outstanding service to king or lord, poor knights could and did achieve positions in the upper nobility. This was not so in Germany, however, where a large class of unfree knights, or *ministerials,* existed. Recruited from the servile dependents of great lords, ministerials were stewards who managed nobles' estates or households or who fought as warriors. In the twelfth century, ministerials sometimes acquired fiefs and wealth. The most important ministerials served the German kings and had significant responsibilities. Legally, however, they remained of servile status: they were not noble.[20]

Infancy and Childhood

Most information about childbirth in the Middle Ages comes from manuscript illuminations that depict the birth process from the moment of coitus through pregnancy to delivery. An interesting thirteenth-century German miniature from Vienna shows a woman in labor. She is sitting on a chair or stool surrounded by four other women, who are present to help her in the delivery. They could be relatives or neighbors. If they are midwives, the woman in labor is probably noble or rich, since midwives charged a fee. Two midwives seem to be shaking the mother up and down to hasten delivery. One of the women is holding a coriander seed near the mother's vagina. Coriander is an herb of the carrot family, and its seeds were used for cleaning purposes. They were thought to be helpful for expelling gas from the alimentary canal—hence their purported value in speeding up delivery.

The rate of infant mortality (the number of babies who would die before their first birthday) in the High Middle Ages must have been staggering. Such practices as jolting a pregnant woman up and down and inserting a seed into her surely contributed to the death rate of both the newborn and the mother. Natural causes—disease and poor or insufficient food—also resulted in many deaths. Infanticide, however, which was common in parts of the ancient world, seems to have declined in the High Middle Ages. Ecclesiastical pressure worked steadily against it. Infanticide in medieval Europe is another indication of the slow and very imperfect Christianization of European peoples. High mortality due to foreign invasions and the generally violent and unstable conditions of the ninth and tenth centuries made unnecessary the deliberate killing of one's own children. On the other hand, English court records from the counties of Warwickshire, Staffordshire, and Gloucestershire for 1221 reveal a suspiciously large number of children dying from "accidental" deaths—drowning, falling from carts, disappearing into the woods, falling into the fire. Still, accidental deaths in rural conditions are more common than is usually thought. More research is needed to determine the actual prevalence of infanticide in the High Middle Ages.

The abandonment of infant children seems to have been the most favored form of family limitation, widely practiced throughout the entire Middle Ages. Abandonment was "the voluntary relinquishing of control over children by their natal parents or guardians, whether by leaving them somewhere, selling them, or legally consigning authority to some other person or institution."[21] Why did parents do this? What became of the children? What was the rate of abandonment? What attitudes did medieval society have toward this practice?

Poverty or local natural disaster led some parents to abandon their children because they could not support them. Before the eleventh century, food was so scarce that few parents could feed themselves, let alone children. Thus Saint Patrick wrote that, in times of famine, fathers would sell their sons and daughters so that the children could

be fed. Parents sometimes gave children away because they were illegitimate or the result of incestuous unions. An eighth-century penitential collection describes the proper treatment for a woman who exposes her unwanted child—that is, leaves it in the open to die—because she has been raped by an enemy or is unable to nourish it. She is not to be blamed, but she should do penance.[22]

Sometimes parents believed that someone of greater means or status might find the child and bring it up in better circumstances than the natal parents could provide. Disappointment in the sex of the child, or its physical weakness or deformity, might also lead parents to abandon it. Finally, some parents were indifferent—they "simply could not be bothered" with the responsibilities of parenthood.[23]

The Christian Middle Ages witnessed a significant development in the disposal of superfluous children: they were given to monasteries as *oblates*.

Children Given to Creditors Ecclesiastical laws against lending money at interest were widely flouted, and many nobles, having borrowed beyond their ability to repay, fell heavily into debt. As illustrated here, the selling or giving of children to creditors was one solution to indebtedness. *(Source: The Bodleian Library, Oxford)*

The word *oblate* derives from the Latin *oblatio,* meaning "offering." Boys and girls were given to monasteries or convents as permanent gifts. Saint Benedict (see pages 242–244), in the fifty-ninth chapter of his *Rule,* takes oblation as a normal method for entrance into the monastic life. By the seventh century, church councils and civil codes had defined the practice: "Parents of any social status could donate a child, of either sex, at least up to the age of ten." Contemporaries considered oblation a religious act, since the child was offered to God often in recompense for parental sin. But oblation also served social and economic functions. The monastery nurtured and educated the child in a familial atmosphere, and it provided career opportunities for the mature monk or nun despite his or her humble origins. Oblation has justifiably been described as "in many ways the most humane form of abandonment ever devised in the West."[24]

The fragmentary medieval evidence prevents the modern student from gaining precise figures on the rate of abandonment. Recent research suggests, however, that abandonment was very common until about the year 1000. The next two hundred years, which saw great agricultural change and relative prosperity, witnessed a low point in abandonment. On the other hand, in the twelfth and thirteenth centuries, the incidence of noble parents giving their younger sons and daughters to religious houses increased dramatically; nobles wanted to preserve the estate intact for the eldest son. Consequently, oblates composed a high percentage of monastic populations. At Winchester in England, for example, 85 percent of the new monks between 1030 and 1070 were oblates. In the early thirteenth century, the bishop of Paris observed that children were

> . . . *cast into the cloister by parents and relatives just as if they were kittens or piglets whom their mothers could not nourish; so that they may die to the world not spiritually but . . . civilly, that is—so that they may be deprived of their hereditary position and that it may devolve on those who remain in the world.*

The abandonment of children remained a socially acceptable practice. Ecclesiastical and civil authorities never legislated against it. Moralists reproached parents for abandoning children because they viewed the child as proof of careless sexuality—not because parents had special obligations to the child. By stressing that all sexual acts have a procreational purpose, and by providing a monastic oblation a humane solution for abandonment, the Christian church may have actually increased the rate of abandonment.[25]

For children of aristocratic birth, the years from infancy to around the age of seven or eight were primarily years of play. Infants had their rattles, as the twelfth-century monk Guibert of Nogent reports, and young children their special toys. Of course, then as now, children would play with anything—handballs, rings, pretty stones, horns, any small household object. Gerald of Wales, who later became a courtier of King Henry II, describes how as a child he built monasteries and churches in the sand while his brothers were making castles and palaces. Vincent of Beauvais, who composed a

Child Oblate   As St. Benedict allowed (*Rule,* Chap. 59), medieval monasteries frequently received oblates, or children offered by their parents, as permanent members. In this twelfth-century manuscript, a father presents his young son, along with the required dowry, to the abbot (shown with staff). *(Source: Giraudon/Art Resource)*

great encyclopedia around 1250, recommended that children be bathed twice a day, fed well, and given ample play time.

Guibert of Nogent speaks in several places in his autobiography of "the tender years of childhood"—the years from six to twelve. Describing the severity of the tutor whom his mother assigned to him, Guibert wrote:

Placed under him, I was taught with such purity and checked with such honesty from the vices which commonly spring up in youth that I was kept from ordinary games and never allowed to leave my master's company, or to eat anywhere else than at home, or to accept gifts from anyone without his leave; in everything I had to show self-control in word, look, and deed, so that he seemed to require of me the conduct of a monk rather than a clerk. While others of my age wandered everywhere at will and were unchecked in the indulgence of such inclinations as were natural at their age, I, hedged in with constant restraints and dressed in my clerical garb, would sit and look at the troops of players like a beast awaiting sacrifice. Even on Sundays and saints' days I had to submit to the severity of school exercises.[26]

Guibert's mother had intended him for the church. Other boys and girls had more play time and freedom.

Nobles naturally wanted to ensure the continuation of the family and to preserve intact its landed patrimony. Scholars disagree about how nobles achieved this. According to one authority, "The struggle to preserve family holdings intact led them to primogeniture [the exclusive right of the first-born son to inherit] and its corollary, wet nursing, which guaranteed a considerable number of children, males among them."[27] Another student has argued persuasively that nobles deliberately married late or limited the number of their children who could marry by placing them in the church or forbidding them to marry while still laypersons. Or, nobles may have practiced birth control. For example, the counts of Falkenstein, who held lordships in upper Bavaria and lower Austria, adopted the strategy of late marriages and few children. This custom plus a violent lifestyle ultimately backfired and extinguished the dynasty.[28] Another student, using evidence from tenth-century Saxony, maintains that parents while alive commonly endowed sons with estates.

This practice allowed sons to marry at a young age and to demonstrate their military prowess.[29] Until more is known about family size and local customs in the High Middle Ages, generalizations about child-rearing practices must be avoided.

Parents decided on the futures of their children as soon as they were born or when they were still toddlers. Sons were prepared for one of the two positions considered suitable to their birth and position. Careers for the youngest sons might be found in the church; for the rest, a suitable position meant a military career. Likewise, parents determined early which daughters would be married—and to whom—and which would become nuns.

At about the age of seven, a boy of the noble class who was not intended for the church was placed in the household of one of his father's friends or relatives. There he became a servant to the lord and received his formal training in arms. He was expected to serve the lord at the table, to assist him as a private valet when called on to do so, and, as he gained experience, to care for the lord's horses and equipment. The boy might have a great deal of work to do, depending on the size of the household and the personality of the lord. The work that children did, medieval people believed, gave them experience and preparation for later life.

Training was in the arts of war. The boy learned to ride and to manage a horse. He had to acquire skill in wielding a sword, which sometimes weighed as much as twenty-five pounds. He had to be able to hurl a lance, shoot with a bow and arrow, and care for armor and other equipment.

Increasingly, in the eleventh and twelfth centuries, noble youths learned to read and write some Latin. Still, on thousands of charters from that period nobles signed with a cross (+) or some other mark. Literacy for the nobility became more common in the thirteenth century. Formal training was concluded around the age of twenty-one with the ceremony of knighthood.

The custom of knighting, though never universal, seems to have been widespread in France and England but not in Germany. The ceremony of knighthood was one of the most important in a man's life. Once knighted, a young man was supposed to be courteous, generous, and, if possible, handsome and rich. Above all, he was to be loyal to his lord and brave in battle. In a society lacking

A Knightly Tournament or the Battle of the Sexes The lid of this exquisitely carved French ivory casket shows ladies and gentlemen on a balcony watching a tournament among mounted knights, while men storm the castle of love (left) and a lady and knight tilt with branches of flowers (right). *(Source: Walters Art Gallery, Baltimore)*

strong institutions of government, loyalty was the cement that held aristocratic society together. That is why the greatest crime was called a "felony," which meant treachery to one's lord.

Power and Responsibility

A member of the nobility became an adult when he came into the possession of his property. He then acquired vast authority over lands and people. With it went responsibility. In the words of Honorius of Autun:

Soldiers: You are the arm of the Church, because you should defend it against its enemies. Your duty is to aid the oppressed, to restrain yourself from rapine and fornication, to repress those who impugn the Church with evil acts, and to resist those who are rebels against priests. Performing such a service, you will obtain the most splendid of benefices from the greatest of Kings.[30]

Nobles rarely lived up to this ideal, and there are countless examples of nobles attacking the church. In the early thirteenth century, Peter of Dreux, count of Brittany, spent so much of his time attacking the church that he was known as the "Scourge of the Clergy."

The nobles' conception of rewards and gratification did not involve the kind of postponement envisioned by the clergy. They wanted rewards immediately. Since by definition a military class is devoted to war, those rewards came through the pursuit of arms. When nobles were not involved in local squabbles with neighbors—usually disputes over property or over real or imagined slights—they participated in tournaments.

Complete jurisdiction over properties allowed the noble, at long last, to gratify his desire for display and lavish living. Since his status in medieval society depended on the size of his household, he would be eager to increase the number of his household retainers. The elegance of his clothes, the variety and richness of his table, the number of his horses and followers, the freedom with which he spent money—all were public indications of his social standing. The aristocratic lifestyle was luxurious and extravagant. To maintain it, nobles often had to borrow from financiers or wealthy monasteries.

At the same time, nobles had a great deal of work to do. The responsibilities of a noble in the High Middle Ages depended on the size and extent of his estates, the number of his dependents, and his position in his territory relative to others of his class and to the king. As a vassal he was required to fight for his lord or for the king when called on to do so. By the mid-twelfth century, this service was limited in most parts of western Europe to forty days a year. He might have to perform guard duty at his lord's castle for a certain number of days a year. He was obliged to attend his lord's court on important occasions when the lord wanted to put on great displays, such as at Easter, Pentecost, and Christmas. When the lord knighted his eldest son or married off his eldest daughter, he called his vassals to his court. They were expected to attend and to present a contribution known as a "gracious aid."

Throughout the year, a noble had to look after his own estates. He had to appoint prudent and honest overseers and make sure that they paid him the customary revenues and services. Since a great lord's estates were usually widely scattered, he had to travel frequently.

Until the late thirteenth century, when royal authority intervened, nobles in France and England had great power over the knights and peasants on their estates. They maintained order among them and dispensed justice to them. Holding the manorial court, which punished criminal acts and settled disputes, was one of their gravest obligations. The quality of justice varied widely: some lords were vicious tyrants who exploited and persecuted their peasants; others were reasonable and evenhanded. In any case, the quality of life on the manor and its productivity were related in no small way to the temperament and decency of the lord—and his lady.

Women played a large and important role in the functioning of the estate. They were responsible for the practical management of the household's "inner economy"—cooking, brewing, spinning, weaving, overseeing servants, caring for yard animals. The lifestyle of the medieval warrior-nobles required constant travel, both for purposes of war and for the supervision of distant properties. When the lord was away for long periods, the women frequently managed the herds, barns, granaries, and outlying fields as well.

Frequent pregnancies and reluctance to expose women to hostile conditions kept the lady at home and therefore able to assume supervision of the family's fixed properties. When a husband went away on crusade—his absence could last anywhere from two to five years, if he returned at all—his wife was often the sole manager of the family properties. When her husband went to the Holy Land between 1060 and 1080, the lady Hersendis was the sole manager of the family properties in northern France.

Women's activities were not confined to managing households and estates in their husbands' absence. Medieval warfare was largely a matter of brief skirmishes, and few men were killed in any single encounter. But altogether the number slain ran high, and there were many widows. Aristocratic widows frequently controlled family properties and fortunes and exercised great authority. Although the evidence is scattered and sketchy, there are indications that women performed many of the functions of men. In Spain, France, and Germany they bought, sold, and otherwise transferred property. Gertrude, labeled "Saxony's almighty widow" by the chronicler Ekkehard of Aura, took a leading role in conspiracies against the emperor Henry V. And Eilika Billung, widow of Count Otto of Ballenstedt, built a castle at Burgwerben on the Saale River and, as advocate of the monastery of Goseck, removed one abbot and selected his successor. From her castle at Bernburg, the countess Eilika was also reputed to ravage the countryside.

Throughout the High Middle Ages, fighting remained the dominant feature of the noble lifestyle. The church's preachings and condemnations reduced but did not stop violence. Late inheritances, which deprived the nobles of constructive outlets for their energy, together with the military ethos of their culture, encouraged petty warfare and disorder (see pages 346–347). The nobility thus were a constant source of trouble for the monarchy. In the thirteenth century, kings drew on the financial support of the middle classes to build the administrative machinery that gradually laid the foundations for strong royal government.

The Crusades relieved the rulers of France, England, and the German Empire of some of their most dangerous elements. Complete royal control of the nobility, however, came only in modern times.

THOSE WHO PRAY

Medieval Europeans believed that monks performed the most important social service, prayer. In the Middle Ages, prayer was looked on as a vital social service, as crucial as the labor of peasants and the military might of nobles. Just as the peasants provided sustenance through their toil and the knights protected and defended society with the sword, so the monks with their prayers and chants worked to secure God's blessing for society.

Monasticism represented some of the finest aspirations of medieval civilization. The monasteries were devoted to prayer, and their standards of Christian behavior influenced the entire church. The monasteries produced the educated elite that was continually drawn into the administrative service of kings and great lords. Monks kept alive the remains of classical culture and experimented with new styles of architecture and art. They introduced new techniques of estate management and land reclamation. Although relatively few in number in the High Middle Ages, the monks played a significant role in medieval society.

Recruitment

Toward the end of his *Ecclesiastical History of England and Normandy,* when he was well into his sixties, Orderic Vitalis (ca 1075–1140), a monk of the Norman abbey of Saint Evroul, interrupted his narrative to explain how he happened to become a monk:

And so, O glorious God, you didst inspire my father Odeleric to renounce me utterly and submit me in all things to thy governance. So, weeping, he gave me, a weeping child, into the care of the monk Reginald, and sent me away into exile for love of thee, and never saw me again. And I, a mere boy, did not presume to oppose my father's wishes, but obeyed him in all things, for he promised me for his part that if I became a monk I should taste of the joys of Heaven with the In-

nocents after my death.... And so, a boy of ten, I crossed the English channel and came into Normandy as an exile, unknown to all, knowing no one. Like Joseph in Egypt I heard a language which I could not understand. But thou didst suffer me through thy grace to find nothing but kindness among strangers. I was received as an oblate in the abbey of St. Evroul by the venerable abbot Mainier in the eleventh year of my life.... The name of Vitalis was given me in place of my English name, which sounded harsh to the Normans.[31]

Orderic Vitalis was one of the leading scholars of his times. As such, he is not a representative figure or even a typical monk. Intellectuals, those who earn their living or spend most of their time working with ideas, are never typical figures of their times. In one respect, however, Orderic was quite representative of the monks of the High Middle Ages: although he had no doubt that God wanted him to be a monk, the decision was actually made by his parents, who gave him to a monastery as a child-oblate. Orderic was the third son of Odeleric, a knight who fought for William the Conqueror at the Battle of Hastings (1066). For his participation in the Norman conquest of England, Odeleric was rewarded with lands in western England. Concern for the provision of his two older sons probably led him to give his youngest to the monastery.

Medieval monasteries were religious institutions whose organization and structure fulfilled the social needs of the feudal nobility. Between the tenth and thirteenth centuries, economic necessities compelled great families, or aspiring ones, to seek a life in the church for some members. There simply were not sufficient resources or career opportunities to provide suitable, honorable positions in life for all the children in aristocratic families. The monasteries provided these children with both an honorable and aristocratic life and opportunities for ecclesiastical careers.[32]

Until well into modern times, and certainly in the Middle Ages, almost everyone believed in the thorough subjection of children to their parents. This belief was the logical consequence of the fact that young noblemen were not expected to work and were therefore totally dependent on their fathers. Some men did become monks as adults, apparently for a wide variety of reasons: belief in a direct call from God, disgust with the materialism and violence of the secular world, the encourage-

French Castle Under Siege Most medieval warfare consisted of small skirmishes and the besieging of castles. If surrounded by a moat and supplied with food and water, a few knights could hold a castle against large armies for a long time. Notice the use of engines to hurl missiles. *(Source: The British Library)*

ment and inspiration of others, economic failure or lack of opportunity, poverty, sickness, fear of hell. However, most men who became monks, until about the early thirteenth century, seem to have been given as child-oblates by their parents.

In the thirteenth century, the older Benedictine and Cistercian orders had to compete with the new orders of friars—the Franciscans and Dominicans (see pages 435–437). More monks had to be recruited from the middle class—that is, from small landholders or traders in the district near the abbey. As medieval society changed economically, and as European society ever so slowly developed middle-class traits, the monasteries almost inevitably drew their manpower, when they were able, from the middle classes. Until that time, they were preserves of the aristocratic nobility.

The Nuns

Throughout the Middle Ages, social class also defined the kinds of religious life open to women. Kings and nobles usually established convents for their daughters, sisters, aunts, or aging mothers. Entrance was restricted to women of the founder's class. Since a well-born lady could not honorably be apprenticed to a tradesperson, and since her dignity did not permit her to do any kind of manual labor, the sole alternative to life at home was the religious life.

The founder's endowment and support greatly influenced the later social, economic, and political status of the convent. Social and religious bonds between benefactors and communities of nuns frequently continued over many generations. A few

Hildegard of Bingen To describe her gift of visions, Hildegard wrote *Scivias (Know the Ways)*, an encyclopedia of Christian salvation. In this first vision, God, enthroned in light at the top of a mountain symbolizing the divine kingdom, embraces all of creation and promises eternal life. *(Source: Rheinisches Bildarchiv)*

convents received large endowments and could accept many women. Amesbury Priory in Wiltshire, England, for example, received a handsome endowment from King Henry II in 1177, and his successors Henry III and Edward I also made lavish gifts. In 1256 Amesbury supported a prioress and 76 nuns, 7 priests, and 16 lay brothers. It owned 200 oxen, 23 horses, 7 cows, 4 calves, 300 pigs, and 4,800 sheep. The convent raised 100 pounds in annual rents and 40 pounds from the wool clip, very large sums at the time. The entrance of such high-born ladies as the dowager queen Eleanor (widow of Henry III), Edward I's daughter Mary, and his niece Isabella of Lancaster stimulated the gift of additional lands and privileges. By 1317 Amesbury had 177 nuns.[33] Most houses of women, however, possessed limited resources and remained small in numbers.

The office of abbess or prioress, the house's superior, customarily went to a nun of considerable social standing. Thus William the Conqueror's daughter Cecelia became abbess of her mother's foundation, Holy Trinity Abbey in Caen, and Henry II's daughter became abbess of Barking. Since an abbess or prioress had responsibility for governing her community and for representing it in any business with the outside world, she was a woman of local power and importance. Sometimes her position brought national prominence. In 1306 Edward I of England summoned several abbesses to Parliament; he wanted their financial support for the expenses connected with knighting his eldest son.

What kind of life did the nuns lead? Religious duties held prime importance. Then there were business responsibilities connected with lands, properties, and rents that preoccupied those women of administrative ability. Sewing, embroidery, and fine needlework were considered the special pursuits of gentlewomen. Nuns in houses with an intellectual tradition copied manuscripts. Although the level of intellectual life in the women's houses varied widely, the careers of two nuns—Hildegard of Bingen and Isabella of Lancaster—suggest the activities of some nuns in the High Middle Ages.

The tenth child of a lesser noble family, Hildegard (1098–1179) was given when eight years old as an oblate to an abbey in the Rhineland, where she learned Latin and received a good education. Obviously possessed of leadership and administrative talents, Hildegard was sent in 1147 to found the convent of Rupertsberg near Bingen. There she produced a body of writings including the *Scivias (Know the Ways)*, a record of her mystical visions that incorporates vast theological learning; the *Physica (On the Physical Elements)*, a classification of the natural elements, such as plants, animals, metals, and the movements of the heavenly bodies; a mystery play; and a medical work that led a distinguished twentieth-century historian of science to describe Hildegard as "one of the most original writers of the Latin West in the twelfth century." At the same time, she carried on a vast correspondence with scholars, prelates, and ordinary people and had such a reputation for wisdom that a recent writer has called her "the Dear Abby of the twelfth century to whom everyone came or wrote for advice or comfort."[34] An exceptionally gifted person, Hildegard represents the Benedictine ideal of great learning combined with a devoted monastic life.

Like intellectual monks, however, intellectual nuns were not typical of the era. The life of the English nun Isabella of Lancaster better exemplifies the careers of high-born women who became nuns. The niece of King Edward I, she was placed at Amesbury Priory in early childhood, grew up there, made her profession of commitment to the convent life, and became abbess in 1343. Isabella seems to have been a conventional but not devout nun. She traveled widely, spent long periods at the royal court, and with the support of her wealthy relations maintained a residence apart from the priory. She was, however, an able administrator who handled the community finances with prudent skill. Amesbury lacked the intellectual and spiritual standards of Bingen. Isabella's interests were secular and her own literary production was a book of romances.

Prayer and Other Work

The pattern of life within individual monasteries varied widely from house to house and from region to region. Each monastic community was shaped by the circumstances of its foundation and endowment, by tradition, by the interests of its abbots and members, and by local conditions. It would thus be a mistake to think that Christian monasticism in the High Middle Ages was every-

where the same. One central activity, however—the work of God—was performed everywhere. Daily life centered around the liturgy.

Seven times a day and once during the night, the monks went to choir to chant the psalms and other prayers prescribed by Saint Benedict. Prayers were offered for peace, rain, good harvests, the civil authorities, and the monks' families and benefactors. Monastic patrons in turn lavished gifts on the monasteries, which often became very wealthy.

Prayer justified the monks' spending a large percentage of their income on splendid objects to enhance the liturgy; monks praised God, they believed, not only in prayer but in everything connected with prayer. They sought to accumulate priestly vestments of the finest silks, velvets, and embroideries, and sacred vessels of embossed silver and gold. Thuribles (vessels) containing sweet-smelling incense brought at great expense from the East were used for the incensing of the altars, following ancient Jewish ritual. The pages of Gospel books were richly decorated with gold leaf, and the books' bindings were ornamented and bejeweled. Every monastery tried to acquire the relics of its patron saint, which if acquired needed to be housed in a beautifully crafted reliquary. The liturgy inspired a great deal of art, and the monasteries became the storehouses of art in Western Christendom.

The monks fulfilled their social responsibility by praying. It was generally agreed that they could best carry out this duty if they were not distracted by worldly matters. Thus great and lesser lords gave the monasteries lands that would supply the community with necessities. Each manorial unit was responsible for provisioning the local abbey for a definite period of time, and the expenses of each abbey were supposed to equal its income.

The administration of an abbey's estates and properties consumed considerable time. The operation of a large establishment, such as Cluny in Burgundy or Bury Saint Edmunds in England, which by 1150 had several hundred monks, involved planning, prudence, and wise management. Although the abbot or prior had absolute authority in making assignments, common sense advised that tasks be allotted according to the talents of individual monks.

The usual method of economic organization was the manor. Many monastic manors were small enough and close enough to the abbey to be supervised directly by the abbot. But if a monastery held and farmed vast estates, the properties were divided into administrative units under the supervision of one of the monks of the house. The lands of the German abbey of Saint Emmeran at Regensburg, for example, were divided into thirty-three manorial centers.

Because the *choir monks* were aristocrats, they did not till the land themselves. In each house one monk, the *cellarer* or general financial manager, was responsible for supervising the lay brothers or peasants who did the actual agricultural labor. *Lay brothers* were vowed religious drawn from the servile classes; they had simpler religious and intellectual obligations than those of the choir monks. The cellarer had to see to it that the estates of the monastery produced enough income to cover its expenses. Another monk, the *almoner,* was responsible for feeding and caring for the poor of the neighborhood. At the French abbey of Saint-Requier in the eleventh century, 110 persons were fed every day. At Corbie, fifty loaves of bread were distributed daily to the poor.

The *precentor* or *cantor* was responsible for the library and the careful preservation of books. The *sacristan* of an abbey had in his charge all the materials and objects connected with the liturgy—vestments, candles, incense, sacred vessels, altar cloths, and hangings. The *novice master* was responsible for the training of recruits, instructing them in the *Rule,* the chant, the Scriptures, and the history and traditions of the house. For a few of the monks, work was some form of intellectual activity, such as the copying of books and manuscripts, the preparation of manuals, and the writing of letters.

Although several orders forbade monks to study law and medicine, that rule was often ignored. In the twelfth and thirteenth centuries, many monks gained considerable reputations for their knowledge and experience in the practice of both the canon law of the church and the civil law of their countries. For example, the Norman monk Lanfranc, because of his legal knowledge and administrative ability, became the chief adviser of William the Conqueror.

Although knowledge of medicine was primitive by twentieth-century standards, monastic practitioners were less ignorant than one would suspect. Long before 1066, a rich medical literature had been produced in England. The most important of these treatises was *The Leech Book of Bald* (*leech* means "medical"). This work exhibits a wide knowledge of herbal prescriptions, ancient authorities, and empirical practice. Bald discusses diseases of the lungs and stomach together with their remedies and demonstrates his acquaintance with surgery. Medical knowledge was sometimes rewarded. King Henry I of England (r. 1100–1135) enriched several of his physicians, and Henry II (r. 1154–1189) made his medical adviser, the monk Robert de Veneys, abbot of Malmesbury.

The religious houses of medieval Europe usually took full advantage of whatever resources and opportunities their location offered. For example, the raising of horses could produce income in a world that depended on horses for travel and for warfare. Some monasteries, such as the Cistercian abbey of Jervaulx in Yorkshire, became famous for and quite wealthy from their production of prime breeds. In the eleventh and twelfth centuries, a period of considerable monastic expansion, large tracts of swamp, fen, forest, and wasteland were brought under cultivation—principally by the Cistercians (see page 356).

The Cistercians, whose constitution insisted that they accept lands far from human habitation and forbade them to be involved in the traditional feudal-manorial structure, were ideally suited to the agricultural needs and trends of their times. In the Low Countries they built dikes to hold back the sea, and the reclaimed land was put to the production of cereals. In the eastern parts of Germany—Silesia, Mecklenburg, and Pomerania—they took the lead in draining swamps and cultivating wasteland. Because of a labor shortage, they advertised widely across Europe for monks and lay brothers. Through their efforts, the rich, rolling land of French Burgundy was turned into lush vineyards. In northern and central England, the rocky soil and damp downs of Lincolnshire, poorly suited to agriculture, were turned into sheep runs. By the third quarter of the twelfth century, the Cistercians were raising sheep and playing a large role in the production of England's staple crop, wool.

Some monasteries got involved in iron and lead mining. In 1291 the Cistercian abbey of Furness operated at least forty forges. The German abbeys of Königsbronn, Waldsassen, and Saabergen also mined iron in the thirteenth century. The monks entered this industry first to fill their own needs, but in an expanding economy they soon discovered a large market. Iron had hundreds of uses. Nails, hammers, plows, armor, axes, stirrups, horseshoes, and spears and many other weapons of war were all made from this basic metal. When King Richard of England was preparing to depart on crusade in 1189, he wanted to take fifty thousand horseshoes with him. Lead also had a great variety of uses. It could be used for roofing; as an alloy for strengthening silver coinage; for framing pane-glass windows in parish, monastery, and cathedral churches; and even for lavatory drainpipes.

Whatever work particular monks did and whatever economic activities individual monasteries were involved in, monks also performed social services and exerted an influence for the good. Monasteries often ran schools that gave primary education to young boys. Abbeys like Saint Albans, situated north of London on a busy thoroughfare, served as hotels and resting places for travelers. Monasteries frequently operated "hospitals" and leprosaria, which provided care— primitive care, it is true, but often all that was available—and attention to the sick, the aged, and the afflicted. In short, monasteries performed a variety of social services in an age when there was no "state" and no conception of social welfare as a public responsibility.

Economic Difficulties

In the twelfth century, expenses in the older Benedictine monastic houses increased more rapidly than did income. The result was a steadily worsening economic situation. Cluny is a good example. Life at Cluny was lavish and extravagant. There were large quantities of rich food. The monks' habits were made of the best cloth available. Cluny's abbots and priors traveled with sizable retinues, as great lords were required to do. The abbots worked to make the liturgy ever more magnificent, and large sums were spent on elaborate vestments and jeweled vessels. Abbot Hugh embarked on an extraordinarily expensive building program. He entirely rebuilt the abbey church, and when Pope Urban II consecrated it in 1095, it was the largest church in Christendom. The monks lived like lords, which in a sense they were.

Revenue came from the hundreds of monasteries scattered across France, Italy, Spain, and England that Cluny had reformed in the eleventh century; each year they paid Cluny a cash sum. Novices were expected to make a gift of land or cash when they entered. For reasons of security, knights departing on crusade often placed their estates under Cluny's authority. Still this income was not enough. The management of Cluny's manors across Europe was entrusted to bailiffs or wardens who were not monks. Many of these bailiffs were poor managers and produced no profits; but, because they had lifetime contracts, they could not be removed and replaced. In order to meet expenses, Cluny had to rely on cash reserves. Cluny's estates produced only a small percentage of needed food supplies; the rest had to be paid for from cash reserves.

Cluny had two basic alternatives: improve management to cut costs or borrow money. The abbey could have placed the monastic manors under the jurisdiction of monks, rather than hiring bailiffs who would grow rich as middlemen. It could have awarded annual rather than lifetime contracts, supervised all revenues, and tried to cut costs within the monastery. Cluny chose the second alter-

Bee Keeping at Monte Cassino   Because of the scarcity and expense of sugar, honey was the usual sweetener for pastries and liquids throughout the Middle Ages. This illustrator had never actually seen the process: without veils, nets, and gloves, the bee keepers would be badly stung. (*Source: Biblioteca Apostolica Vaticana*)

Cluny, ca 1157   Begun in 1085 and supported by the generosity of kings and peasants, the church (right center) and monastery of Cluny was the administrative center of a vast monastic and feudal empire. Note the apse around the east end of the church and the large foreground complex, which served as monastic infirmary and guest hostel. *(Source: The Medieval Academy of America)*

native—borrowing. Consequently, the abbey spent hoarded reserves of cash and fell into debt.

In contrast to the abbot of Cluny, Suger (1122–1151), the superior of the royal abbey of Saint-Denis near Paris, was a shrewd manager. Though he, too, spared no expense to enhance the beauty of his monastery and church, Suger kept an eye on costs and made sure that his properties were soundly managed. But the management of Saint-Denis was unusual. Far more typical was the economic mismanagement at Cluny. By the later twelfth century, small and great monasteries were facing comparable financial difficulties.

SUMMARY

Generalizations about peasant life in the High Middle Ages must always be qualified by manorial

customs, by the weather in a given year, and by the personalities of local lords. Everywhere, however, the performance of agricultural services and the payment of rents preoccupied peasants. Though they led hard lives, peasants could achieve some social mobility through exceedingly hard work, luck, or flight to a town.

By 1100 the knightly class was united in its ability to fight on horseback, its insistence that each member was descended from a valorous ancestor, its privileges, and its position at the top of the social hierarchy. The nobility possessed a strong class consciousness. Aristocratic values and attitudes shaded all aspects of medieval culture. However, these characteristics were not typical of Germany, where a sharp distinction existed between nobles and their servile warriors, the ministerials.

Monks exercised a profound influence on matters of the spirit. In their prayers, monks battled for the Lord just as chivalrous knights fought on the battlefield. In their chant and rich ceremonial, in their architecture, and in the example of many monks' lives, the monasteries inspired Christian peoples to an incalculable degree. As the storehouses of sacred art, the monasteries became cultural centers of Christian Europe.

NOTES

1. G. Duby, *The Chivalrous Society,* trans. C. Postan (Berkeley: University of California Press, 1977), pp. 90–93.
2. Honorius of Autun, "Elucidarium sive Dialogus de Summa Totius Christianae Theologiae," in *Patrologia Latina,* vol. 172, ed. J. P. Migne (Paris: Garnier Brothers, 1854), col. 1149.
3. E. Power, "Peasant Life and Rural Conditions," in *The Cambridge Medieval History,* vol. 7, eds. J. R. Tanner et al. (Cambridge, England: Cambridge University Press, 1958), p. 716.
4. Glanvill, "De Legibus Angliae," bk. 5, chap. 5, in *Social Life in Britain from the Conquest to the Reformation,* ed. G. G. Coulton (London: Cambridge University Press, 1956), pp. 338–339.
5. J. B. Freed, *The Friars and German Society in the Thirteenth Century* (Cambridge, Mass.: Mediaeval Academy of America, 1977), p. 55.
6. See W. C. Jordan, *From Servitude to Freedom: Manumission in the Senonais in the Thirteenth Century* (Philadelphia: University of Pennsylvania Press, 1986), esp. chap. 3, pp. 37–58.
7. See L. White, Jr., *Medieval Technology and Social Change* (Oxford: Clarendon Press, 1962), pp. 59–63.
8. G. Duby, *Early Growth of the European Economy: Warriors and Peasants from the Seventh to the Twelfth Century* (Ithaca, N.Y.: Cornell University Press, 1978), pp. 213–219.
9. See B. A. Hanawalt, *The Ties That Bound: Peasant Families in Medieval England* (New York: Oxford University Press, 1986), pp. 90–100.
10. On this quantity and medieval measurements, see "The Measures of Monastic Beverages," in D. Knowles, *The Monastic Order in England* (Cambridge, England: Cambridge University Press, 1962), p. 717.
11. G. Duby, *Rural Economy and Country Life in the Medieval West,* trans. C. Postan (London: Edward Arnold, 1968), pp. 146–147.
12. S. R. Scargill-Bird, ed., *Custumals of Battle Abbey in the Reigns of Edward I and Edward II* (London: Camden Society, 1887), p. 213.
13. M. Warner, *Alone of Her Sex: The Myth and Cult of the Virgin Mary* (New York: Knopf, Wallaby Books, 1978), pp. 305–306 and p. 390.
14. John 19:25–27.
15. J. B. Freed, "The Origins of the European Nobility: The Problem of the Ministerials," *Viator 7* (1976): 213.
16. Duby, *Chivalrous Society,* pp. 104–105.
17. See C. Bouchard, "The Origins of the French Nobility," *The American Historical Review,* vol. 86 (1981): 501–532.
18. Duby, *Chivalrous Society,* p. 98.
19. G. Duby, *The Age of the Cathedrals: Art and Society, 980–1420,* trans. E. Levieux and B. Thompson (Chicago: University of Chicago Press, 1981), p. 38.
20. Freed, "Origins of European Nobility," p. 214.
21. J. Boswell, *The Kindness of Strangers: The Abandonment of Children in Western Europe from Late Antiquity to the Renaissance* (New York: Pantheon Books, 1989), p. 24. This section relies heavily on Boswell's important work.
22. Ibid., pp. 214, 223.
23. Ibid., pp. 428–429.
24. Ibid., pp. 238–239.
25. Ibid., pp. 297, 299, and the Conclusion.
26. F. Benton, ed. and trans., *Self and Society in Medieval France: The Memoirs of Abbot Guibert Nogent* (New York: Harper & Row, 1970), p. 46.
27. J. C. Russell, *Late Ancient and Medieval Population Control* (Philadelphia: American Philosophical Society, 1985), p. 180.
28. See J. B. Freed, "The Counts of Falkenstein: Noble Self-Consciousness in Twelfth-Century Germany," *Transactions of the American Philosophical Society,* vol. 74, pt. 6 (1984): 63–67.
29. See R. J. Leyser, *Rule and Conflict in an Early Medieval Society: Ottonian Saxony* (Bloomington, Ind.: Indiana University Press, 1979), pp. 49–62, esp. p. 59.
30. Honorius of Autun, in *Patrologia Latina,* vol. 172, col. 1148.
31. M. Chibnall, ed. and trans., *The Ecclesiastical History of Orderic Vitalis,* vol. 2 (Oxford: Oxford University Press, 1972), p. xiii.
32. R. W. Southern, *Western Society and the Church in the Middle Ages* (Baltimore: Penguin Books, 1970), pp. 224–230, esp. p. 228.
33. See M. W. Labarge, *A Small Sound of the Trumpet: Women in Medieval Life* (Boston: Beacon Press, 1986), pp. 104–105.
34. J. M. Ferrante, "The Education of Women in the Middle Ages in Theory, Fact, and Fantasy," in *Beyond Their Sex: Learned Women of the European Past,* ed. P. H. Labalme (New York: New York University Press, 1980), pp. 22–24.

SUGGESTED READING

The best short introduction to the material in this chapter is C. Brooke, *The Structure of Medieval Society* (1971), a beautifully illustrated book. The student interested in aspects of medieval slavery, serfdom, or the peasantry should begin with M. Bloch, "How Ancient Slavery Came to an End" and "Personal Liberty and Servitude in the Middle Ages, Particularly in France," in *Slavery and Serfdom in the Middle Ages: Selected Essays* (trans. W. R. Beer, 1975). There is an excellent discussion of these problems in the magisterial work of G. Duby, *Rural Economy and Country Life in the Medieval West* (see the Notes). G. C. Homans, *English Villagers of the Thirteenth Century* (1975), is a fine combination of sociological and historical scholarship; and the older study of H. S. Bennett, *Life on the English Manor: A Study of Peasant Conditions* (1960), contains much useful information presented in a highly readable fashion. E. L. Ladurie, *Montaillou: Cathars and Catholics in a French Village, 1294–1324* (trans. B. Bray, 1978), is a fascinating glimpse of village life. Also cited in the Notes, G. Duby, *Early Growth of the European Economy,* is a superb synthesis by a leading authority. Advanced students should see the same author's *The Three Orders: Feudal Society Imagined* (1980), a brilliant but difficult book.

For the religion of the people, two recent studies are highly recommended: R. Brooke and C. Brooke, *Popular Religion in the Middle Ages* (1984), a highly readable synthesis, and B. Ward, *Miracles and the Medieval Mind* (1982), an important and scholarly study. For the development of lay literacy, see M. T. Clanchy, *From Memory to Written Record: England, 1066–1307* (1979).

For the origins and status of the nobility in the High Middle Ages, students are strongly urged to see the recent and important studies by Bouchard, Duby, and Freed cited in the Notes. See, in addition, the following articles, which appear in F. L. Cheyette, ed., *Lordship and Community in Medieval Europe: Selected Readings* (1968): L. Genicot, "The Nobility in Medieval Francia: Continuity, Break, or Evolution?"; A. Borst, "Knighthood in the High Middle Ages: Ideal and Reality"; and two studies by G. Duby, "The Nobility in Eleventh and Twelfth Century Maconnais" and "Northwestern France: The 'Youth' in Twelfth Century Aristocratic Society." Social mobility among both peasants and nobles is discussed in T. Evergates, *Feudal Society in the Bailliage of Troyes Under the Counts of Champagne, 1152–1284* (1976). Also fundamental are K. F. Bosl, "Kingdom and Principality in Twelfth-Century France" and "'Noble Unfreedom': The Rise of the Ministerials in Germany," in T. Reuter, ed., *The Medi-*

eval Nobility: Studies on the Ruling Classes of France and Germany from the Sixth to the Twelfth Century (1978), are also fundamental. The older study of M. Bloch, *Feudal Society* (1966), is now somewhat dated. The career of the man described by contemporaries as "the greatest of knights" is celebrated in G. Duby, *William Marshal: The Flowering of Chivalry* (trans. R. How ard, 1985), a remarkable rags-to-riches story.

E. Power, *Medieval Women* (1976), is a nicely illustrated sketch of the several classes of women. For women, marriage, and the family in the High Middle Ages, see D. Herlihy, *Medieval Households* (1985), which describes how medieval families developed ties of kinship and emotional unity; J. McNamara and S. F. Wemple, "Sanctity and Power: The Dual Pursuit of Medieval Women," in R. Bridenthal and C. Koonz, eds., *Becoming Visible: Women in European History* (1977); and E. R. Coleman, "Medieval Marriage Characteristics: A Neglected Factor in the History of Medieval Serfdom," in T. K. Rabb and R. I. Rotberg, eds., *The Family in History: Interdisciplinary Essays* (1973). For health and medical care, see B. Rowland, *Medieval Woman's Guide to Health* (1981).

There is no dearth of good material on the monks in medieval society. The titles listed in Suggested Reading for Chapter 9 represent a good starting point for study. A. Boyd, *The Monks of Durham* (1975), is an excellently illustrated introductory sketch of many facets of monastic culture in the High Middle Ages. B. D. Hill, "Benedictines" and "Cistercian Order," in J. R. Strayer, ed., *Dictionary of the Middle Ages,* vols. 2 and 3 (1982 and 1983), provide broad surveys of the premier monastic orders and contain useful bibliographies. L. J. Lekai, *The Cistercians: Ideals and Reality* (1977), synthesizes recent research on the Cistercians and carries their story down to the twentieth century. P. D. Johnson, *Prayer, Patronage, and Power: The Abbey of La Trinité, Vendôme, 1032–1187* (1981), examines one important French monastery in its social environment; this book is a valuable contribution to medieval local history. T. Verdon, ed., *Monasticism and the Arts* (1984), is a rich compilation of papers on various aspects of monastic culture, some of them written by leading scholars. J. Leclercq, *Monks on Marriage: A Twelfth Century View* (1982), studies marital love literature and gives new insights on medieval attitudes toward sex and marital love. Duby's *The Age of the Cathedrals,* cited in the Notes, is especially strong on the monastic origins of medieval art. Both W. Braunfels, *Monasteries of Western Europe: The Architecture of the Orders* (1972), and C. Brooke, *The Monastic World* (1974), have splendid illustrations and good bibliographies. The best study of medieval English Cistercian architecture is P. Fergusson, *Architecture of Solitude: Cistercian Abbeys in Twelfth Century England* (1984).

14

Creativity and Crisis in the High and Later Middle Ages

Caracassone, southern France

*T*he High Middle Ages witnessed several of the most remarkable achievements in the entire history of Western society. Political rulers tried to establish contact with all their peoples, developed new legal and financial institutions, and slowly consolidated power in the hands of the monarchy. The kings of France and England succeeded in laying the foundations of modern national states. The European economy underwent a remarkable recovery, as towns grew and long-distance trade revived. In arts and letters, medieval people expressed their appreciation for the worlds of nature, man, and God, and in the Gothic cathedral they manifested their sense of community and their deep Christian faith.

In the fourteenth century, however, a string of disasters sapped the vitality of European society. Between 1300 and 1450, Europeans experienced a frightful series of shocks: economic dislocation, plague, war, and social upheaval. During the later Middle Ages, the last book of the New Testament—the Book of Revelation, dealing with visions of the end of the world, disease, war, famine, and death—inspired thousands of sermons and hundreds of religious tracts. Death and preoccupation with death make the fourteenth century one of the most wrenching periods of Western civilization.

The progression from the vitality of the High Middle Ages to the crisis of the later Middle Ages brings to mind a number of questions:

- How did medieval rulers in England, France, and Germany work to solve their problems of government, thereby laying the foundations of the modern state?
- How did medieval towns originate, and how do they reveal the beginnings of radical change in medieval society?
- What social needs and attitudes did the development of universities, the Gothic cathedral, and a vernacular literature indicate?
- Why did medieval towns become the center of religious heresy, and what was the church's response?
- How did economic difficulties, plague, and war affect Europeans socially, economically, and politically in the fourteenth century?
- What provoked the division of the church in the fourteenth century, and how did the schism affect the faith of medieval people?
- What dominant features characterized the lives of ordinary people in the late Middle Ages?

This chapter focuses on these questions.

MEDIEVAL ORIGINS OF THE MODERN STATE

Rome's great legacies to Western civilization were the concepts of the state and the law; but for almost five hundred years after the disintegration of the Roman Empire in the West, the state as a reality did not exist. Political authority was completely decentralized. Power was spread among many feudal lords, who gave their localities such protection and security as their strength allowed. The fiefdoms, kingdoms, and territories that covered the continent of Europe did not have the qualities or provide the services of a modern state. They did not have jurisdiction over many people, and their laws affected a relative few. In the mid-eleventh century, there existed many layers of authority—earls, counts, barons, knights—between a king and the ordinary people.

In these circumstances, medieval kings had common goals. The rulers of England, France, and Germany wanted to strengthen and extend royal authority within their territories. They wanted to establish an effective means of communication with all peoples in order to increase public order. They wanted more revenue and efficient bureaucracies. The solutions they found to these problems laid the foundations for modern national states.

The modern state is an organized territory with definite geographical boundaries that are recognized by other states. It has a body of law and institutions of government. If the state claims to govern according to law, it is guided in its actions by the law. The modern national state counts on the loyalty of its citizens, or at least on that of a majority of them. In return, it provides order so that citizens can go about their daily work and other activities. It protects its citizens in their persons and property. The state tries to prevent violence and to apprehend and punish those who commit it. It supplies a currency or medium of exchange that permits financial and commercial transactions. The state conducts relations with foreign governments. In order to accomplish even these minimal functions, the state must have officials, bureaucracies, laws, courts of law, soldiers, information, and money. States with these attributes are relatively recent developments.

Unification and Communication

Under the pressure of the Danish (or Viking) invasions of the ninth and tenth centuries, the seven kingdoms of Anglo-Saxon England united under one king (see page 353). At the same time, England was divided into local units called *shires,* or counties, each under the jurisdiction of a sheriff appointed by the king. The Danish king Canute (r. 1016–1035) and his successor, Edward the Confessor (r. 1042–1066), exercised broader authority than any contemporary ruler on the Continent. All the English *thegns,* or local chieftains, recognized the central authority of the kingship. The

kingdom of England, therefore, had a political head start on the rest of Europe.

When Edward the Confessor died, his cousin Duke William of Normandy—known in English history as "William the Conqueror"—claimed the English throne and in 1066 he defeated the Anglo-Saxon claimant on the battlefield of Hastings. As William subdued the rest of the country, he distributed lands to his Norman followers and assigned specific military quotas to each estate. He also required all feudal lords to swear an oath of allegiance to him as king.

William the Conqueror (r. 1066–1087) preserved the Anglo-Saxon institution of sheriffs representing the king at the local level but replaced Anglo-Saxon sheriffs with Normans. A sheriff had heavy duties. He maintained order in the shire. He caught criminals and punished them in the shire court, over which he presided. He collected taxes and, when the king ordered him to do so, raised an army of foot soldiers. The sheriff also organized adult males in groups of ten, with each member liable for the good behavior of the others. William thus made local people responsible for order in

The Bayeux Tapestry   Measuring 231 feet by 19½ inches, the Bayeux Tapestry gives a narrative description of the events surrounding the Norman Conquest of England. The tapestry provides an important historical source for the clothing, armor, and lifestyles of the Norman and Anglo-Saxon warrior class. *(Source: Tapisserie de Bayeux et avec autorisation spéciale de la Ville de Bayeux)*

MAP 14.1 Domesday Population and Agriculture, 1086 The incomparably rich evidence of *Domesday Book* enables modern demographers and historians to calculate the English population and land under cultivation in the eleventh century.

their communities. For all his efforts, the sheriff received no pay. This system, whereby unpaid officials governed the county, served as the basic pattern of English local government for many centuries. It cost the Crown nothing, but it restricted opportunities for public service to the well-to-do.

William also retained another Anglo-Saxon device, the *writ*. This brief administrative order, written in the vernacular (Anglo-Saxon) by a government clerk, was the means by which the central government communicated with people at the local level. Sheriffs were empowered to issue writs relating to matters in their counties.

William introduced into England a major innovation, the Norman inquest. To determine how much wealth there was in his new kingdom, who held what land, and what lands had been disputed among his vassals since the conquest of 1066, William in 1086 sent groups of royal officials or judges to every part of the country. In every village and farm, the priest and six local people were put under oath to answer the questions of the king's commissioners truthfully. In the words of a contemporary chronicler:

He sent his men over all England into every shire and had them find out how many hundred hides there were in the shire [a hide was a measure of land large enough to support one family], or what land and cattle the king himself had, or what dues he ought to have in twelve months from the shire. Also . . . what or how much everybody had who was occupying land in England, in land or cattle, and how much money it was worth. So very narrowly did he have it investigated, that there was no single hide nor yard of land, nor indeed . . . one ox nor one cow nor one pig was there left out, and not put down in his record: and all these records were brought to him afterwards.[1]

The resulting record, called *Domesday Book* from the Anglo-Saxon word *doom* meaning "judgment," still survives. It is an invaluable source of social and economic information about medieval England (Map 14.1).

Domesday Book, a unique document, provided William and his descendants with information vital for the exploitation and government of the country. Knowing the amount of wealth every area possessed, the king could tax accordingly. Knowing the amount of land his vassals had, he could allot knight service fairly. The inclusion of material covering all of England helped English kings to regard their country as one unit.

In 1128 William's granddaughter Matilda married Geoffrey of Anjou. Their son, who became Henry II of England and inaugurated the Angevin (from Anjou, his father's county) dynasty, inherited the French provinces of Normandy, Anjou, Maine, and Touraine in northwestern France. When Henry married the great heiress Eleanor of Aquitaine in 1152, he claimed lordships over Aquitaine, Poitou, and Gascony in southwestern France. The territory some students call the "Angevin empire" included most of the British Isles and half of France (see Map 14.2). The histories of England and France in the High Middle Ages were thus closely intertwined.

In the early twelfth century, France consisted of a number of virtually independent provinces. Each was governed by its local ruler; each had its own laws and customs; each had its own coinage; each had its own dialect. Unlike the king of England, the king of France had jurisdiction over a very small area. Chroniclers called King Louis VI (r. 1108–1137) *roi de Saint-Denis,* king of Saint-Denis, because the territory he controlled was limited to Paris and the Saint-Denis area surrounding the city. This region, called the *Île-de-France* or royal domain, became the nucleus of the French state. The term *Saint-Denis* had political and religious charisma, which the Crown exploited. Saint Denis was a deeply revered saint whom the French believed protected the country from danger. The Capetian kings identified themselves with the cult of Saint Denis in order to tap "national" devotion to him and tie that devotion and loyalty to the monarchy.[2] The clear goal of the medieval French king was to increase the royal domain and extend his authority (Map 14.2).

The work of unifying France began under Louis VI's grandson Philip II (r. 1180–1223). Rigord, Philip's biographer, gave him the title "Augustus" (from a Latin word meaning "to increase") because he vastly enlarged the territory of the kingdom of France. By defeating a baronial plot against the Crown, Philip Augustus acquired the northern counties of Artois and Vermandois. When King John of England, who was Philip's vassal for the rich province of Normandy, defaulted on his feudal obligation to come to the French court, Philip declared Normandy forfeit to the French crown. He enforced his declaration militarily, and in 1204 Normandy fell to the French. Within two years Philip also gained the farmlands of Maine, Touraine, and Anjou. By the end of his reign Philip was effectively master of northern France.

In the thirteenth century, Philip Augustus's descendants acquired important holdings in the south, including the county of Poitou, the Mediterranean province of Provence, and Languedoc. By the end of the thirteenth century, most of the provinces of modern France had been added to the royal domain through diplomacy, marriage, war, and inheritance. The king of France was stronger than any group of nobles who might try to challenge his authority.

Philip Augustus devised a method of governing the provinces and providing for communication between the central government in Paris and local communities. Philip decided that each province would retain its own institutions and laws. But royal agents, called *baillis* in the north and *seneschals* in the south, were sent from Paris into the provinces as the king's official representatives with authority to act for him. Often middle-class lawyers, these men possessed full judicial, financial, and military jurisdiction in their districts. The baillis and seneschals were appointed by, paid by, and responsible to the king. Unlike the English sheriffs, they were never natives of the provinces to which they were assigned, and they could not own land there. This policy reflected the fundamental principle of French administration: royal interests superseded local interests.

English government administration was based on the services of unpaid local officials, but France was administered by a professional royal bureaucracy. As new territories came under royal control, the bureaucracy expanded. So great was the variety of customs, laws, and provincial institutions that any attempt to impose uniformity would have touched off a rebellion. The French system was

MAP 14.2 The Growth of the Kingdom of France Some scholars believe that Philip II received the title "Augustus" (from a Latin word meaning "to increase") because he vastly expanded the territories of the kingdom of France.

characterized by diversity at the local level and centralization at the top. Although it sometimes fell into disrepair, the basic system that Philip Augustus created worked so well that it survived until the Revolution of 1789.

The political problems of Germany were considerably different from those of France and England. The eleventh-century investiture controversy

between the German emperor and the Roman papacy had left Germany shattered and divided (see pages 359–361). In the twelfth and thirteenth centuries, Germany was split into hundreds of independent provinces, principalities, bishoprics, duchies, and free cities. Princes, dukes, and local rulers maintained power over small areas.

There were several barriers to the development of a strong central government. The German rulers lacked a strong royal domain, like that of the French kings, to use as a source of revenue and a base from which to expand royal power. No accepted principle of succession to the throne existed; as a result, the death of the emperor was often followed by disputes, civil war, and anarchy. Moreover, German rulers were continually attracted south by the wealth of the northern Italian cities or by dreams of restoring the imperial glory of Charlemagne. Time after time the German kings got involved in Italian affairs, and in turn the papacy, fearful of a strong German power in northern Italy, interfered in German affairs. German princes took bribes from whichever authority—the emperor or the pope—best supported their own particular ambitions. Consequently, in medieval Germany, power remained in the hands of numerous princes instead of the king.

When Conrad III died in 1152, the resulting anarchy was so terrible that the *electors*—the seven princes responsible for choosing the emperor—decided the only alternative to continued chaos was the selection of a strong ruler. They chose Frederick Barbarossa of the house of Hohenstaufen.

Frederick Barbarossa (r. 1152–1190) tried valiantly to unify the empire. Just as the French rulers branched out from their compact domain in the Île-de-France, Frederick tried to use his family duchy of Swabia in southwestern Germany as a power base (Map 14.3). Just as William the Conqueror had done, Frederick required all vassals in Swabia to take an oath of allegiance to him as emperor, no matter who their immediate lord might be. He appointed ministerials (see page 386) to exercise the full imperial authority over administrative districts of Swabia. Ministerials linked the emperor and local communities.

Outside of Swabia, Frederick tried to make feudalism work as a system of government. He made alliances with the great lay princes and the great churchmen, who acknowledged that their lands were fiefs of the emperor. Frederick solved the problem of chronic violence by making the princes responsible for the establishment of peace within their territories. At a great assembly held at Roncaglia in 1158, private warfare was forbidden in Italy, and severe penalties were laid down for violations of the peace.

Unfortunately, Frederick Barbarossa did not concentrate his efforts and resources in one area. He, too, wanted to restore the Holy Roman Empire, joining Germany and Italy and cashing in on the wealth of the northern Italian trading cities. Frederick saw that although the Italian cities were populous and militarily strong, they lacked stable governments and were often involved in struggles with one another. The emperor did not realize that the merchant oligarchs who ran the city governments of Milan, the Venetian republic, and Florence prized their independence and were determined to fight for it. Frederick's desire to control the papacy also attracted him southward. Between 1154 and 1188, Frederick made six expeditions into Italy. After some initial success, he was defeated in 1176 at Legnano (see Map 14.3). Frederick was forced to recognize the municipal autonomy of the northern Italian cities. Germany and Italy remained separate countries and followed separate courses of development.

Frederick Barbarossa's Italian ventures contributed nothing to the unification of the German states. Because the empire lacked a stable bureaucratic system of government, his presence was essential for the maintenance of peace. In Frederick's absences, the fires of independence and disorder spread. The princes and magnates consolidated their power, and the unsupervised royal ministerials gained considerable independence. By 1187 Frederick had to accept again the reality of private warfare. The power of the princes cost the growth of a centralized monarchy.

Finance

As medieval rulers expanded territories and extended authority, they required more officials, larger armies, and more money. Officials and armies had to be paid, and kings had to find ways to raise revenue.

In England, William the Conqueror's son Henry I (r. 1100–1135) established a bureau of finance called the "Exchequer" (for the checkered cloth at which his officials collected and audited royal accounts). Henry's income came from a variety of sources, including taxes paid by peasants living on the king's estates and money paid to the Crown for settling disputes. Henry also received income because of his position as feudal lord, and from the knights he took *scutage,* money paid in lieu of the performance of military service. With the scutage collected, Henry could hire mercenary

0	100	200	300 Km.
0	100	200	300 Mi.

Lübeck

HOLSTEIN

POMERANIA

Bremen

BRANDENBURG

POLAND

FRISIA

SAXONY

Brandenburg

LUSATIA

Goslar

LOWER
LORRAINE

Cologne

Aix-la-Chapelle

THURINGIA

MEISSEN

FRANCONIA

Prague

Trier

Mainz

BOHEMIA

MORAVIA

Worms

Verdun

UPPER
LORRAINE

Toul

Augsburg

BAVARIA

AUSTRIA

FRANCE

SWABIA

Salzburg

STYRIA

Besançon

CARINTHIA

BURGUNDY-
ARLES

VERONA

CARNIOLA

HUNGARY

Legnano 1176

LOMBARDY

Milan

Pavia

Venice

Roncaglia

Avignon

Arles

Florence

Marseilles

TUSCANY

PAPAL
STATES

REPUBLIC OF VENICE

CORSICA

Rome

Capua

APULIA

Naples

Salerno

SARDINIA

KINGDOM OF SICILY

✕ Major battle

Holy Roman Empire, ca 1200

Kingdom of Sicily

Republic of Venice

Messina

Palermo

SICILY

troops. The sheriff in each county was responsible for collecting all these sums and paying them twice a year to the king's Exchequer. Henry, like other medieval kings, made no distinction between his private income and state revenues.

An accurate record of expenditures and income is needed to ensure a state's solvency. Henry assigned a few of the barons and bishops at his court to keep careful records of the moneys paid into and out of the royal treasury. These financial officials, called "barons of the Exchequer," gradually developed a professional organization with its own rules, procedures, and esprit de corps. The Exchequer, which sat in London, became the first institution of England's government bureaucracy.

The development of royal financial agencies in most continental countries lagged behind the English Exchequer. Twelfth-century French rulers derived their income from their royal estates in the Île-de-France. As Philip Augustus and his successors added provinces to the royal domain, the need for money became increasingly acute. Philip made the baillis and seneschals responsible for collecting taxes in their districts, primarily from fines and confiscations imposed by the courts.

In the thirteenth century, French rulers found additional sources of revenue. They acquired some income from the church, and townspeople paid *tallage* or the *taille*—a tax arbitrarily laid by the king. Louis IX converted feudal vassals' military obligation into a cash payment, called "host tallage." Moreover, pervasive anti-Semitism allowed Philip Augustus, Louis VIII, and Louis IX to tax their Jewish subjects mercilessly.

Medieval people believed that a good king lived on the income of his own land and taxed only in time of a grave emergency—a just war. Taxation meant war financing. The French monarchy could not continually justify taxing the people for the needs of war. Thus French kings were slow to develop an efficient bureau of finance. French localism—in contrast to England's early unification—also retarded the growth of a central financial agency. Not until the fourteenth century, as a result of the Hundred Years' War, did a state financial bureau emerge—the Chamber of Accounts.

In the twelfth century, in finance, law, and bureaucratic development, the papal curia repre-

sented the most advanced government. The one secular government other than England that developed a financial bureaucracy was the kingdom of Sicily. Sicily is a good example of how strong government could be built on a feudal base by determined rulers.

Like England, Sicily had come under Norman domination. Between 1061 and 1091, a bold Norman knight, Roger de Hauteville, with a small band of mercenaries had defeated the Muslims and Greeks who controlled the island. Like William the Conqueror in England, Roger introduced Norman feudalism in Sicily and made it work as a system of government. Roger distributed scattered fiefs to his followers, so no vassal had a centralized power base. He took an inquest of royal properties and rights, and he forbade private warfare. Roger adapted his Norman experience to Arabic and Greek government practices. Thus he retained the Muslims' main financial agency, the *diwan,* a sophisticated bureau for record keeping.

His son and heir, Count Roger II (r. 1130–1154), continued the process of state building. He had himself crowned king of Sicily and organized the economy in the interests of the state; for example, the Crown secured a monopoly on the sale of salt and lumber. With the revenues thus acquired, Roger hired mercenary troops. His judiciary welcomed appeals from local communities. The army, the judiciary, and the diwan were staffed by Greeks and Muslims as well as Normans.

Frederick II Hohenstaufen (r. 1212–1250), grandson of Roger II and grandson and heir of Frederick Barbarossa, was a brilliant legislator and administrator, and he constructed the most advanced bureaucratic state in medieval Europe. The institutions of the kingdom of Sicily were harnessed in the service of the state as represented by the king.

Frederick banned private warfare and placed all castles and towers under royal administration. He also replaced town officials with royal governors. In 1231 he published the *Constitutions of Melfi,* a collection of laws that vastly enhanced royal authority. Both feudal and ecclesiastical courts were subordinated to the king's courts. Thus churchmen accused of crimes were tried in the royal courts. Royal control of the nobility, of the towns, and of the judicial system added up to great centralization, which required a professional bureaucracy and sound state financing.

MAP 14.3 The Holy Roman Empire, ca 1200

Frederick's financial experts regulated agriculture, public works, even business. His customs service supervised all imports and exports, collecting taxes on all products. Moreover, Frederick secured the tacit consent of his people to regular taxation. This was an amazing achievement, for most people believed that taxes should be levied only in time of grave emergency, the just war. Frederick defined *emergency* broadly. For much of his reign he was involved in a bitter dispute with the papacy. Churchmen hardly considered the emperor's wars with the popes as just, but Frederick was so strong that he could ignore criticism and levy taxes.

Frederick's contemporaries called him the "Transformer of the World." He certainly transformed the kingdom of Sicily, creating a state that was in many ways modern. But Frederick was highly ambitious: he wanted to control the entire peninsula of Italy. The popes, fearful of being encircled, waged a long conflict to prevent that. The kingdom of Sicily required constant attention, and Frederick's absences took their toll. Shortly after he died, the unsupervised bureaucracy that he had built fell to pieces. The pope, as the feudal overlord of Sicily, called in a French prince to rule.

Frederick showed little interest in Germany. He concentrated on Sicily rather than on the historic Hohenstaufen stronghold in Swabia, and the focus of imperial concerns shifted southward. When he visited the empire, expecting to secure German support for his Italian policy, he made sweeping concessions to the princes, bishops, duchies, and free cities. In 1220, for example, he exempted German churchmen from taxation and from the jurisdiction of imperial authorities. In 1231 he gave lay princes the same exemptions and even threw in the right to coin money. Frederick gave away so much that imperial authority was seriously weakened. In the later Middle Ages, lay and ecclesiastical princes held sway in the Holy Roman Empire. The centralizing efforts of Frederick Barbarossa were destroyed by his grandson Frederick II.

The Chancellery at Palermo Reflecting the fact that Vandals, Ostrogoths, Greeks, Muslims, and Normans had left their imprint on Sicily, the imperial court bureaucracy kept official records in Greek, Arabic, and Latin, as this manuscript illustration shows. *(Source: Burgerbibliothek Bern)*

Law and Justice

Throughout Europe in the twelfth and thirteenth centuries, the law was a hodgepodge of Germanic customs, feudal rights, and provincial practices. Kings wanted to blend these elements into a uniform system of rules acceptable and applicable to all their peoples. In France and England, kings successfully contributed to the development of national states through the administration of their laws. Legal developments in continental countries like France were strongly influenced by Roman law. England slowly built up a unique, unwritten common law.

The French king Louis IX (r. 1226–1270) was famous in his time for his concern for justice. Each French province, even after being made part of the kingdom of France, retained its unique laws and procedures, but Louis IX created a royal judicial system. He established the Parlement of Paris, a kind of supreme court that welcomed appeals from local administrators and from the courts of feudal lords throughout France. By the very act of appealing the decisions of feudal courts to the Parlement of Paris, French people in far-flung provinces were recognizing the superiority of royal justice.

Louis sent royal judges to all parts of the country to check up on the work of the baillis and seneschals and to hear complaints of injustice. He was the first French monarch to publish laws for the entire kingdom. The Parlement of Paris registered (or announced) these laws, which forbade private warfare, judicial duels, gambling, blaspheming, and prostitution. Louis sought to identify justice with the kingship, and gradually royal justice touched all parts of the kingdom.

Under Henry II (r. 1154–1189), England developed and extended a *common law,* a law common to and accepted by the entire country. No other country in medieval Europe did so. Henry I had occasionally sent out *circuit judges* (royal officials who traveled a given circuit or district) to hear civil and criminal cases. Henry II made this way of extending royal justice an annual practice. Every year, royal judges left London and set up court in the counties. Wherever the king's judges sat, there sat the king's court. Slowly, the king's court gained jurisdiction over all property disputes and criminal actions.

Henry also improved procedure in criminal justice. In 1166 he instructed the sheriffs to summon local juries to conduct inquests and draw up lists of known or suspected criminals. These lists, sworn to by the juries, were to be presented to the royal judges when they arrived in the community. This accusing jury is the ancestor of the modern grand jury.

An accused person formally charged with a crime did *not* undergo trial by jury. He or she was tried by ordeal. The accused was tied hand and foot and dropped in a lake or river. People believed that water was a pure substance and would reject anything foul or unclean. Thus a person who sank was considered innocent, and a person who floated was considered guilty. God determined innocence or guilt, and a priest had to be present to bless the water.

Henry II and others considered this ancient Germanic method irrational and a poor way of determining results, but they knew no alternative. In 1215 the Fourth Lateran Council of the church forbade the presence of priests at trials by ordeal and thus effectively abolished them. Gradually, in the course of the thirteenth century, the king's judges adopted the practice of calling on twelve people (other than the accusing jury) to consider the question of innocence or guilt. This became the jury of trial, but it was very slowly accepted because medieval people had more confidence in the judgment of God than in the judgment of twelve ordinary people.

One aspect of Henry's judicial reforms encountered stiff resistance from an unexpected source: a friend and former chief adviser whom Henry had made archbishop of Canterbury—Thomas Becket. In the 1160s many literate people accused of crimes claimed "benefit of clergy" even though they were not clerics and often had no intention of being ordained. Benefit of clergy gave the accused the right to be tried in church courts, which meted out mild punishments. A person found guilty in the king's court might suffer mutilation—loss of a hand or foot, castration—or even death. Ecclesiastical punishments tended to be an obligation to say certain prayers or to make a pilgrimage. In 1164 Henry II insisted that everyone, including clerics, be subject to the royal courts. Becket vigorously protested that church law required clerics to be subject to church courts. The disagreement dragged on for years. The king grew increasingly bitter that his appointment of Becket had proved to be such a mistake. Late in December 1170, in a fit of rage, Henry expressed the wish that Becket

The Martyrdom of Thomas Becket Becket's murder evoked many illustrations in the thirteenth century. This illumination faithfully follows the manuscript sources: while one knight held off the archbishop's defenders, the other three attacked. With a powerful stroke, the crown of Becket's head was slashed off and his brains scattered on the cathedral floor. *(Source: Walters Art Gallery, Baltimore)*

be destroyed. Four knights took the king at his word, went to Canterbury, and killed the archbishop in his cathedral as he was leaving evening services.

What Thomas Becket could not achieve in life, he gained in death. The assassination of an archbishop in his own church during the Christmas season turned public opinion in England and throughout western Europe against the king. Within months, miracles were recorded at Becket's tomb, and in a short time Canterbury Cathedral became a major pilgrimage and tourist site. Henry had to back down. He did public penance for the

murder and gave up his attempts to bring clerics under the authority of the royal court.

Henry II's sons Richard I, who was known as "the Lion-Hearted" (r. 1189–1199), and John (r. 1199–1216) lacked their father's interest in the work of government. Handsome, athletic, and with an international reputation for military prowess, Richard looked on England as a source of revenue for his military enterprises. Soon after his accession, he departed on a crusade to the Holy Land. During his reign he spent only six months in England, and the government was run by ministers trained under Henry II.

Unlike Richard, King John was incompetent as a soldier and unnecessarily suspicious that the barons were plotting against him. His basic problems, however, were financial. King John inherited a heavy debt from his father and brother. The country had paid dearly for Richard's crusading zeal. While returning from the Holy Land, Richard had been captured, and England had paid an enormous ransom to secure his release. In 1204 John lost the rich province of Normandy to Philip Augustus of France and then spent the rest of his reign trying to get it back. To finance that war, John squeezed as much money as possible from his position as feudal lord. He took scutage and each time increased the amount due. He forced widows to pay exorbitant fines to avoid unwanted marriages. He sold young girls who were his feudal wards to the highest bidder. These actions antagonized the nobility.

John also alienated the church and the English townspeople. He rejected Pope Innocent III's nominee to the see of Canterbury. And he infuriated the burghers of the towns by extorting money from them and threatening to revoke their charters of self-government.

All the money that John raised did not bring him success. In July 1214, John's coalition of Flemish, German, and English cavalry suffered a severe defeat at the hands of Philip Augustus of France at Bouvines in Flanders (see Map 14.2). This battle ended English hopes for the recovery of territories from France and also strengthened the barons' opposition to John. On top of his heavy taxation, his ineptitude as a soldier in a society that idealized military glory was the final straw. Rebellion begun by a few hotheaded northern barons eventually grew to involve many of the English nobility. After lengthy negotiations, John was forced to sign the treaty called "Magna

THE EMERGENCE OF STATES

1066	Norman Conquest of England; William the Conqueror requires oath of allegiance from all feudal lords
1085	William introduces the Norman inquest, thereby enabling a systematic investigation of the whole of England
1086	Publication of *Domesday Book*
1095	Pope Urban II calls for the First Crusade
1096–1270	Papacy sponsors the Crusades to recover Jerusalem from the Muslims
1120	Publication of Abelard's *Sic et Non*
1130	Henry I of England establishes the Exchequer, the first governmental bureau of finance in England
	Roger II crowned king of Sicily; establishes a professional royal army
1144	Consecration of the first Gothic church, the abbey church of Saint-Denis
ca 1150–1300	Expansion of church building throughout Europe mirrors growth of towns and expansion of commerce
1152	Henry II marries Eleanor of Aquitaine, thereby gaining control over half of France as well as most of the British Isles (the "Angevin empire")
	Frederick Barbarossa chosen emperor by the German princes; requires oath of allegiance from his vassals
1154–1158	Frederick Barbarossa attempts to restore Holy Roman Empire by invading Italy
1159	Founding of the city of Lübeck, origin of the Hanseatic League
1166	Institution of the accusing jury in England
1170	Assassination of Thomas Becket by Henry II's knights
1176	Battle of Legnano, the first defeat of armed knights by bourgeois infrantrymen; Frederick Barbarossa forced to recognize the autonomy of the northern Italian cities
1180–1223	Philip II (Augustus) extends authority of the French monarchy by conquering most of northern France; hires agents to represent the Crown's interests in the provinces, thus establishing a professional royal bureaucracy
1200	Philip Augustus officially recognizes the University of Paris
1214	John of England defeated by Philip Augustus at Battle of Bouvines; baronial opposition to John increases
1215	Signing of the Magna Carta
1224	Frederick II Hohenstaufen founds the University of Naples
1231	Frederick II enhances royal authority in Sicily by publishing the Constitutions of Melfi, which subordinate feudal and ecclesiastical to royal courts; to gain German support of his efforts to control Italy, he exempts princes from taxation and imperial jurisdiction, thereby weakening royal authority in Germany
1235	Publication of Aquinas's *Summa Theologica*
1296	War opens between Edward I of England and Philip the Fair of France; Pope Boniface VIII attempts to deny kings the power to levy taxes on the Church
1302	Boniface writes *Unam Sanctam*, a letter asserting papal supremacy over monarchies
1303	Philip the Fair orders the arrest of Boniface at Anagni

Carta," which became the cornerstone of English justice and law.

Magna Carta set forth the principle that everyone—including the king and the government—must obey the law. It defends the interests of widows, orphans, townspeople, free men, and the church. Some clauses contain the germ of the ideas of due process of law and the right to a fair and speedy trial. Every English king in the Middle Ages reissued Magna Carta as evidence of his promise to observe the law. Later generations appealed to it as a written statement of English liberties, and it acquired an almost sacred importance as a guarantee of law and justice.

In the thirteenth century, the judicial precedents set under Henry II slowly evolved into permanent institutions. English people found the king's justice more rational and evenhanded than the justice meted out in the baronial courts. Respect for the king's law and courts promoted loyalty to the Crown. By the time of Henry's great-grandson Edward I (r. 1272–1307), one law, the common law, operated all over England.

In the later Middle Ages, the English common law developed features that differed strikingly from the system of Roman law operative in continental Europe. The common law relied on precedents: a decision in an important case served as an authority for deciding similar cases. By contrast, continental judges, trained in Roman law, used the fixed legal maxims of the Justinian *Code* (see pages 256–257) to decide their cases. Thus the common-law system evolved according to the changing experience of the people, and the Roman-law tradition tended toward an absolutist approach. In countries influenced by the common law, such as Canada and the United States, the court is open to the public; in countries with Roman-law traditions, such as France and the Latin American nations, courts need not be public. Under the common law, people accused in criminal cases have a right to access to the evidence against them; under the other system, they need not see the evidence. The common law urges judges to be impartial; in the Roman-law system, judges interfere freely in activities in their courtrooms. Finally, whereas torture is foreign to the common-law tradition, it was once widely used in the Roman legal system.

The extension of law and justice led to a phenomenal amount of legal codification all over Europe. Legal texts and encyclopedias exalted royal authority, consolidated royal power, and emphasized political and social uniformity. The pressure for social conformity in turn contributed to a rising hostility toward minorities, Jews, and homosexuals.

By the late eleventh century, many towns in western Europe had small Jewish populations. Jews typically earned their livelihoods in the lesser trades or by lending money at interest. The laws of most countries forbade Jews to own land, though they could hold land pledged to them for debts. By the twelfth century, many Jews were usurers: they lent to consumers but primarily to new or growing business enterprises. New towns and underdeveloped areas where cash was scarce welcomed Jewish settlers. Like other business people, the Jews preferred to live near their work; they also settled close to their synagogue or school. Thus originated the Jews' street or quarter or ghetto. Such neighborhoods gradually became legally defined sections where Jews were required to live.

Through the twelfth century, Jews had been generally tolerated and had become important participants in urban economies through trade and finance. The later twelfth and entire thirteenth centuries, however, witnessed increasingly ugly anti-Semitism. Shifting agricultural and economic patterns aggravated social tensions. The indebtedness of peasants and nobles to Jews in an increasingly cash-based economy; the xenophobia that accompanied and followed the Crusades; Christian merchants' and financiers' resentment of Jewish business competition; the spread of vicious accusations of ritual murders or sacrileges against Christian property and persons; royal and papal legislation aimed at social conformity—these factors all contributed to rising anti-Semitism. Thus, from 1180 to 1182, Philip Augustus of France used hostility to Jews as an excuse to imprison them and then to demand heavy ransom for their release. The Fourth Lateran Council (1215) forbade Jews to hold public office, restricted their financial activities, and required them to wear distinctive clothing. In 1290 Edward I of England capitalized on mercantile and other resentment of Jews to expel them from the country in return for a large parliamentary grant. In 1302 Philip IV of France followed suit by expelling the Jews from his kingdom and confiscating their property. Fear, ignorance, greed, stupidity, and the pressure for social conformity all played a part in anti-Semitism of the High Middle Ages.

Early Christians displayed no special prejudice against homosexuals (see page 239). Some of the church fathers, such as Saint John Chrysostom (347–407), preached against them, but a general indifference to homosexual activity prevailed throughout the early Middle Ages. In the early twelfth century, a large homosexual literature circulated. Publicly known homosexuals such as Ralph, archbishop of Tours (1087–1118), and King Richard I of England held high ecclesiastical and political positions.

Beginning in the late twelfth century, however, a profound change occurred in public attitudes toward homosexual behavior. Why did this happen, if prejudice against homosexuals cannot be traced to early Christianity? Scholars have only begun to investigate this question, and the root cause of intolerance rarely yields to easy analysis. In the thirteenth century, heretics were the most despised minority in an age that stressed religious and social uniformity, and the notion spread that both Muslims and heretics—the great foreign and domestic menaces to the security of Christian Europe—were inclined to homosexual relations. Finally, the systematization of law and the rising strength of the state made any religious or sexual distinctiveness increasingly unacceptable. Whatever the precise cause, "between 1250 and 1300 homosexual activity passed from being completely legal in most of Europe to incurring the death penalty in all but a few legal compilations."[3] Spain, France, England, Norway, and several Italian city-states adopted laws condemning homosexual acts. Most of these laws remained on statute books until the twentieth century. Anti-Semitism and hostility to homosexuals reflect a dark and evil side to high medieval culture, not the general creativity and vitality of the period.

ECONOMIC REVIVAL

A salient manifestation of Europe's recovery after the tenth-century disorders and of the vitality of the High Middle Ages was the rise of towns and the development of a new business and commercial class. This development was to lay the foundations for Europe's transformation, centuries later, from a rural agricultural society into an industrial urban society—a change with global implications.

Why and how did these developments occur when they did? Part of the answer has already been given. Without increased agricultural output, there would not have been an adequate food supply for new town dwellers. Without a rise in population, there would have been no one to people the towns. Without a minimum of peace and political stability, merchants could not have transported and sold goods.

The Rise of Towns

Early medieval society was traditional, agricultural, and rural. The emergence of a new class that

was none of these constituted a social revolution. The new class—artisans and merchants—came from the peasantry. They were landless younger sons of large families, driven away by land shortage. Or they were forced by war and famine to seek new possibilities. Or they were unusually enterprising and adventurous, curious and willing to take a chance.

Some scholars believe that towns began as *boroughs*—that is, as fortifications erected during the ninth-century Viking invasions. According to this view, towns were at first places of defense into which farmers from the surrounding countryside moved when their area was attacked. Most residents of early towns made their living by farming outside the town.

Later, merchants were attracted to the fortifications because they had something to sell and wanted to be where customers were. Usually traders settled just outside the walls, in the *faubourgs* or *suburbs*—both of which mean "outside" or "in the shelter of the walls." As their markets prospered and as their number outside the walls grew, the merchants built a new wall around themselves, every century or so. According to Belgian historian Henri Pirenne, a medieval town consisted architecturally of a number of concentric walls.

The great cathedrals and monasteries, too, played a part, representing a demand for goods and services. Cathedrals such as Notre Dame in Paris conducted schools that drew students from far and wide. Consequently, traders and merchants settled near religious establishments to cater to the residents' economic needs.

Few towns of the tenth and eleventh centuries were "new" in the sense that American towns and cities were new in the seventeenth and eighteenth centuries. They were not carved out of forest and wilderness. Some medieval towns that had become flourishing centers of trade by the mid-twelfth century had originally been Roman army camps. York in northern England and Cologne in west central Germany are good examples of ancient towns that underwent revitalization in the eleventh century. Some Italian seaport cities, such as Venice, Pisa, and Genoa, had been centers of shipping and commerce in earlier times. Muslim attacks and domestic squabbles had cut their populations and drastically reduced the volume of their trade in the early Middle Ages, but trade with Constantinople and the East had never stopped entirely. The restoration of order and political stability promoted rebirth and new development. The twelfth century also witnessed the foundation of completely new towns, such as Lübeck, Berlin, and Munich.

Whether evolving from a newly fortified place or an old Roman army camp, from a cathedral site or a river junction or a place where several overland routes met, medieval towns had a few common characteristics. Walls enclosed the town. The terms *burgher* and *bourgeois* derive from the Old English and Old German words *burg, burgh, borg,* and *borough* for "a walled or fortified place." Thus a burgher or bourgeois was originally a person who lived or worked inside the walls. The town had a marketplace. It often had a mint for the coining of money and a court to settle disputes.

In each town, many people inhabited a small, cramped area. As population increased, towns rebuilt their walls, expanding the living space to accommodate growing numbers. Through an archeological investigation of the amount of land gradually enclosed by walls, historians have gained a rough estimate of medieval town populations. For example, the walled area of the German city of Cologne equaled 100 hectares in the tenth century (1 hectare = 2.471 acres), about 185 hectares in 1106, about 320 in 1180, and 397 in the fourteenth century. In 1180 Cologne's population was at least 32,000; in the mid-fourteenth century, perhaps 40,000.[4] (By contrast, in the twelfth century some cities in the western Sudan in Africa such as Kumbi, Timbuctu, and Gao may have had populations of between 15,000 and 20,000.) The concentration of the textile industry in the Netherlands brought into being the most populous cluster of cities in western Europe: Ghent with about 56,000 people, Bruges with 27,000, Tournai and Brussels, each with perhaps 20,000.[5] Paris, together with Milan, Venice, and Florence, each with about 80,000, led all Europe in population.

In their backgrounds and abilities, townspeople represented diversity and change. They constituted an entirely new element in medieval society. They fit into none of the traditional categories. Their occupations, their preoccupations, were different from those of the feudal nobility and the laboring peasantry.

The aristocratic nobility glanced down with contempt and derision at the money-grubbing townspeople but were not above borrowing from them. The rural peasantry peered up with suspicion and fear at the town dwellers. Though some

fled to the towns seeking wealth and freedom, what was the point, most farmers wondered, of making money? Only land had real permanence. Nor did the new commercial class make much sense initially to churchmen. The immediate goal of the middle class was obviously not salvation. It was to be a good while before churchmen developed a theological justification for the new class.

Town Liberties

In the words of the Greek poet Alcaeus, "Not houses finely roofed or well built walls, nor canals or dockyards make a city, but men able to use their opportunity."[6] Men and opportunity. That is fundamentally what medieval towns meant—concentrations of people and varieties of chances. No matter where groups of traders congregated, they settled on someone's land and had to secure from king or count, abbot or bishop, permission to live and trade. Aristocratic nobles and churchmen were suspicious of and hostile to the middle class. They soon realized, however, that profits and benefits flowed to them and their territories from the markets set up on their land.

The history of towns in the eleventh through thirteenth centuries consists largely of merchants' efforts to acquire liberties. In the Middle Ages, *liberties* meant special privileges. For the town dweller, liberties included the privilege of living and trading on the lord's land. The most important privilege a medieval townsperson could gain was personal freedom. It gradually developed that an individual who lived in a town for a year and a day, and was accepted by the townspeople, was free of servile obligations and status. More than anything else, perhaps, the liberty of personal freedom that came with residence in a town contributed to the emancipation of the serfs in the High Middle Ages. Liberty meant citizenship, and citizenship in a town implied the right to buy and sell goods there. Unlike foreigners and outsiders of any kind, a full citizen did not have to pay taxes and tolls in the market. Obviously, this increased profits.

In the twelfth and thirteenth centuries, towns fought for, and slowly gained, legal and political rights. Since the tenth century, some English boroughs had held courts with jurisdiction over members of the town in civil and criminal matters. In the twelfth century, such English towns as Lon-

Hammering Cobblestones into place on a roadbed made of loose earth, laborers pave the highways leading from the walled city of Bavay in France. Upkeep of the roads and walls were often a town's greatest expenses. (*Source: Bibliothèque royale Albert 1er, Brussels*)

don and Norwich developed courts that applied a special kind of law, called "law merchant." It dealt with commercial transactions, debt, bankruptcy, proof of sales, and contracts. Gradually, towns across Europe acquired the right to hold municipal courts that alone could judge members of the town. In effect, this right gave them judicial independence.[7]

In the acquisition of full rights of self-government, the *merchant guilds* played a large role. Medieval people were long accustomed to communal enterprises. In the late tenth and early eleventh centuries, those who were engaged in foreign trade joined together in merchant guilds; united enterprise provided them greater security and less

risk of losses than did individual action. At about the same time, the artisans and craftsmen of particular trades formed their own guilds. These were the butchers, bakers, and candlestick makers. Members of the *craft guilds* determined the quality, quantity, and price of the goods produced and the number of apprentices and journeymen affiliated with the guild.

Recent research indicates that by the fifteenth century, women composed the majority of the adult urban population. Many women were heads of households.[8] They engaged in every kind of urban commercial activity, both as helpmates to their husbands and independently. Craft guilds provided greater opportunity for women than did merchant guilds. In many manufacturing trades women predominated, and in some places women were a large percentage of the labor force. In fourteenth-century Frankfurt, for example, about 33 percent of the crafts and trades were entirely female. In late-twelfth-century Cologne, women and men had equal rights in the turners' guild (the guild for those who made wooden objects on a lathe). Most members of the Paris silk and woolen trades were women, and some achieved the mastership. Widows frequently followed their late husbands' professions, but if they remarried outside the craft, they lost the mastership. Guild records show that women received lower wages than men for the same work, on the grounds that they needed less income.

By the late eleventh century, especially in the towns of the Low Countries and northern Italy, the leaders of the merchant guilds were quite rich and powerful. They constituted an oligarchy in their towns, controlling economic life and bargaining with kings and lords for political independence. Full rights of self-government included the right to hold a town court, the right to select the mayor and other municipal officials, and the right to tax and collect taxes. Kings often levied on their serfs and unfree townspeople the arbitrary tax, tallage. Such a tax (also known as "customs") called attention to the fact that men were not free. Citizens of a town much preferred to levy and collect their own taxes.

A charter that King Henry II of England granted to the merchants of Lincoln around 1157 nicely illustrates the town's rights. The passages that follow clearly suggest that the merchant guild had been the governing body in the city for almost a century and that anyone who lived in Lincoln for a year and a day was considered free:

Henry, by the grace of God, etc. . . . Know that I have granted to my citizens of Lincoln all their liberties and customs and laws which they had in the time of Edward [King Edward the Confessor] and William and Henry, kings of England. And I have granted them their gild-merchant, comprising men of the city and other merchants of the shire, as well and freely as they had it in the time of our aforesaid predecessors, kings of England. . . . I also confirm to them that if anyone has lived in Lincoln for a year and a day without dispute from any claimant, and has paid the customs, and if the citizens can show by the laws and customs of the city that the claimant has remained in England during

that period and has made no claim, then let the defendant remain in peace in my city of Lincoln as my citizen, without [having to defend his] right.[9]

Kings and lords were reluctant to grant towns self-government, fearing loss of authority and revenue if they gave the merchant guilds full independence. But the lords discovered that towns attracted increasing numbers of people to an area—people whom the lords could tax. Moreover, when burghers bargained for a town's political independence, they offered sizable amounts of ready cash. Consequently, feudal lords ultimately agreed to self-government.

Town Life

Protective walls surrounded almost all medieval towns and cities. The valuable goods inside a town were too much of a temptation to marauding bands for the town to be without the security of bricks and mortar. The walls were pierced by gates, and visitors waited at the gates to gain entrance to the town. When the gates were opened early in the morning, guards inspected the quantity and quality of the goods brought in and collected the customary taxes. Part of the taxes went to the king or lord on whose land the town stood, part to the town council for civic purposes. Constant repair of the walls was usually the town's greatest expense.

Peasants coming from the countryside and merchants traveling from afar set up their carts as stalls just inside the gates. The result was that the road nearest the gate was the widest thoroughfare. It was the ideal place for a market, because everyone coming in or going out used it. Most streets in a medieval town were marketplaces as much as passages for transit. Yet they were generally narrow, just wide enough to transport goods.

Medieval cities served, above all else, as markets. In some respects the entire city was a marketplace. The place where a product was made and sold was also typically the merchant's residence. Usually the ground floor was the scene of production. A window or door opened from the main workroom directly onto the street. The window displayed the finished product, and passers-by could look in and see the goods being produced. The merchant's family lived above the business on the second or third floor. As the business and the family expanded, the merchant built additional stories on top of the house.

Because space within the town walls was limited, expansion occurred upward. Second and third stories were built jutting out over the ground floor and thus over the street. Neighbors on the opposite side did the same. Since the streets were narrow to begin with, houses lacked fresh air and light. Initially, houses were made of wood and thatched with straw. Fire represented a constant danger, and because houses were built so close together, fires spread rapidly. Municipal governments consequently urged construction in stone or brick.

Most medieval cities developed haphazardly. There was little town planning. As the population increased, space became more and more limited. Air and water pollution presented serious problems. Many families raised pigs for household consumption in sties next to the house. Horses and oxen, the chief means of transportation and power, dropped tons of dung on the streets every

Hamburg Cattle Market In the twelfth and thirteenth centuries, Hamburg, located on the Elbe near the river's mouth on the North Sea, gained great commercial importance, and its alliance (1241) with Lübek became the basis of the Hanseatic League. Pigs and cattle were among the vast merchandise offered for sale. The market court (background) sold licenses, set prices, and settled disputes. *(Source: Staatsarchiv Hamburg)*

Textile and manufacturing areas

— Northern sea routes
— Venetian sea routes
— Genoese sea routes
— Overland routes

ATLANTIC OCEAN

North Sea

Baltic Sea

Black Sea

Mediterranean Sea

Adriatic Sea

Aegean Sea

Sea of Azov

Bay of Biscay

Ireland

Gotland

Corsica

Sardinia

Sicily

Balearic Is.

Crete

Rhodes

Cyprus

Bergen — Fish, Pitch
Oslo — Copper
Stockholm — Copper
Edinburgh
Carlisle — Lead
Durham — Lead
York — Wool, Iron
Chester — Tin
Bristol — Lead
Southampton — Salt
London — Fish
Calais
Bruges
Brussels
Rouen — Wine
Paris — Paper
Orléans — Wheat
Tours — Wine
Rennes — Flax
Nantes — Salt
Bordeaux — Iron
Bayonne — Wool
Limoges
Clermont — Wine
Toulouse — Wool
Lyons — Wine
Avignon — Wine
Marseilles — Mfd. wares
Bergen
Copenhagen — Fish
Lübeck — Grain
Hamburg — Flax
Bremen — Hemp
Amsterdam — Wine
Cologne — Iron
Strasbourg — Salt
Basel — Iron
Geneva — Mfd. wares
Frankfurt — Hemp
Magdeburg — Salt
Leipzig — Copper
Prague — Wheat, Silver
Nuremberg — Paper
Augsburg — Salt
Danzig — Grain
Königsberg
Warsaw
Breslau — Iron
Krakow — Silver
Kiev
Novgorod — Flax, Hemp, Wax
Riga — Flax
Reval — Fish
Rostov — Fish
Caffa
Sinope
Trebizond
Constantinople — Horses
Belgrade — Silver
Buda — Horses
Pest — Wheat, Skins + hides
Vienna — Wine
Ragusa
Venice — Glass, Mfd. wares, Artwares
Milan — Mfd. wares
Genoa
Pisa
Bologna
Florence
Rome
Naples — Cotton, Olives
Taranto
Messina
Palermo — Olives, Wine
Syracuse
Tripoli — Fish
Tunis — Fish, Olives
Algiers — Olives
Ceuta
Lisbon — Cork, Cotton
Santiago — Wine, Fruits+foodstuffs
Leon — Wool
Toledo — Metalwares, Leather, Paper
Cordoba — Copper, Olives
Seville — Silk
Granada — Horses, Olives
Almeira — Silk
Cartagena
Valencia — Fruits+foodstuffs
Barcelona
Ankara — Cotton, Carpets + rugs
Sivas — Fruits+foodstuffs
Smyrna — Fruits + foodstuffs
Antioch — Fruits+foodstuffs
Tripoli — Iron, Glassware
Beirut
Sidon — Paper, Horses
Tyre — Silk
Damascus — Precious woods
Jerusalem
Cairo — Indigo, Cotton
Alexandria — Slave market, Cotton, Fish

Olives
Currants
Raisins
Wine
Opium
Slave market
Silver
Iron
Pitch, Tar
Furs, Honey
Wheat
Horses
Skins + hides
Wool
Dates
Timber, Pitch
Silver

400 Mi.
400 Km.

year. It was universal practice in the early towns to dump household waste, both animal and human, into the road in front of one's house. The stench must have been abominable. In 1298 the burgesses of the town of Boutham in Yorkshire, England, received the following order (one long, vivid sentence):

To the bailiffs of the abbot of St. Mary's York, at Boutham. Whereas it is sufficiently evident that the pavement of the said town of Boutham is so very greatly broken up . . . , and in addition the air is so corrupted and infected by the pigsties situated in the king's highways and in the lanes of that town and by the swine feeding and frequently wandering about . . . and by dung and dunghills and many other foul things placed in the streets and lanes, that great repugnance overtakes the king's ministers staying in that town and also others there dwelling and passing through, the advantage of more wholesome air is impeded, the state of men is grievously injured, and other unbearable inconveniences . . . , to the nuisance of the king's ministers aforesaid and of others there dwelling and passing through, and to the peril of their lives . . . : the king, being unwilling longer to tolerate such great and unbearable defects there, orders the bailiffs to cause the pavement to be suitably repaired within their liberty before All Saints next, and to cause the pigsties, aforesaid streets and lanes to be cleansed from all dung and dunghills, and to cause them to be kept thus cleansed hereafter, and to cause proclamation to be made throughout their bailiwick forbidding any one, under pain of grievous forfeiture, to cause or permit their swine to feed or wander outside his house in the king's streets or the lanes aforesaid.[10]

A great deal of traffic passed through Boutham in 1298 because of the movement of English troops to battlefronts in Scotland. Conditions there were probably not typical. Still, this document suggests that space, air pollution, and sanitation problems bedeviled urban people in medieval times, as they do today.

As members of the bourgeoisie gained in wealth, they expressed their continuing Christian

MAP 14.4 Trade and Manufacturing in Medieval Europe Note the number of cities and the sources of silver, iron, copper, lead, paper, wool, carpets and rugs, and slaves.

faith by refurbishing old churches, constructing new ones, and giving stained-glass windows, statues, and carvings. The twelfth-century chronicler William of Newburgh could proudly boast that the city of London had 126 parish churches, in addition to 13 monastic churches and the great cathedral of Saint Paul's.

The Revival of Long-Distance Trade

The eleventh century witnessed a remarkable revival of trade as artisans and craftsmen manufactured goods for local and foreign consumption (Map 14.4). Because long-distance trade was risky and required large investments of capital, it could be practiced only by professionals. The transportation of goods involved serious risks. Shipwrecks were common. Pirates infested the sea lanes, and robbers and thieves roamed virtually all of the land routes. Since the risks were so great, merchants preferred to share them. A group of people would thus pool some of their capital to finance an expedition to a distant place. When the ship or caravan returned and the goods brought back were sold, the investors would share the profits. If disaster struck the caravan, an investor's loss was limited to the amount of that individual's investment.

In the late eleventh century, the Italian cities, especially Venice, led the West in trade in general and completely dominated the Eastern market. Ships carried salt from the Venetian lagoon, pepper and other spices from North Africa, and silks and purple textiles from the East to northern and western Europe. In the thirteenth century, Venetian caravans brought slaves from the Crimea and Chinese silks from Mongolia to the West. Lombard and Tuscan merchants exchanged those goods at the town markets and regional fairs of France, Flanders, and England. (Fairs were periodic gatherings that attracted buyers, sellers, and goods from all over Europe.) Flanders controlled the cloth industry. The towns of Bruges, Ghent, and Ypres built up a vast industry in the manufacture of cloth. Italian merchants exchanged their products for Flemish tapestries, fine broadcloth, and various other textiles.

Two circumstances help to explain the lead in long-distance trade gained by Venice and the Flemish towns. Both enjoyed a high degree of peace and political stability. Geographical factors were equally, if not more, important. Venice was ideally located at the northwestern end of the Adriatic Sea, with easy access to the transalpine land routes as well as the Adriatic and Mediterranean sea lanes. The markets of North Africa, Byzantium, and Russia and the great fairs of Ghent in Flanders and Champagne in France provided commercial opportunities that Venice quickly seized. The geographical situation of Flanders also offered unusual possibilities. Just across the channel from England, Flanders had easy access to English wool. Indeed, Flanders and England developed a very close economic relationship.

Wool was the cornerstone of the English medieval economy. Population growth in the twelfth century and the success of the Flemish and Italian textile industries created foreign demand for English wool. This demand stimulated Flemish manufacturing, and the expansion of the Flemish cloth industry in turn spurred the production of English wool. The availability of raw wool also encouraged the development of cloth manufacture in England. The towns of Lincoln, York, Leicester, Northampton, Winchester, and Exeter became important cloth-producing towns. The port cities of London, Hull, Boston, and Bristol thrived on the wool trade. In the thirteenth century, commercial families in these towns grew fabulously rich.

The wool and cloth trades serve as a good barometer of the economic growth and decline of English towns. The supply of wool depended on such natural factors as weather, the amount of land devoted to grazing, and the prevalence of sheep disease, or *scab*. The price of wool, unlike the price of wheat or other foodstuffs, was determined not by supply but by demand. Changes in demand—often the result of political developments over which merchants had no control—could severely damage the wool trade. In the 1320s, for example, violent disorder exploded in the Flemish towns, causing a sharp drop in demand for English wool. When wool exports fell, the economies of London, Hull, and Southampton slumped. Then, during the Hundred Years' War (see pages 441–446), the English crown laid increasingly high export taxes on raw wool, and again the wool trade suffered. On the other hand, the decline of wool exports encouraged the growth of domestic cloth manufacturing and led in the fourteenth century to some population growth along with considerable prosperity in English centers of cloth production.

The Commercial Revolution

A steadily expanding volume of international trade from the late eleventh through the thirteenth centuries was a sign of the great economic surge, but it was not the only one. In cities all across Europe, trading and transportation firms opened branch offices. Credit was widely extended, considerably facilitating exchange. Merchants devised the letter of credit, which made unnecessary the slow and dangerous shipment of coin for payment.

A new capitalistic spirit developed. Professional merchants were always on the lookout for new markets and opportunities. They invested surplus capital in a wide variety of operations. The typical prosperous merchant in the late thirteenth century might be involved in buying and selling, shipping, lending some capital at interest, and engaging in other types of banking. Medieval merchants were fiercely competitive.

Some scholars consider capitalism a modern phenomenon, beginning in the fifteenth or sixteenth century. But in their use of capital to make more money, in their speculative pursuits and willingness to gamble, in their competitive spirit, and in the variety of their interests and operations, medieval businessmen displayed capitalistic traits.

The ventures of the German Hanseatic League illustrate these impulses. The Hanseatic League was a mercantile association of towns. Though scholars trace the league's origin to the foundation of the city of Lübeck in 1159, the mutual protection treaty later signed between Lübeck and Hamburg marks the league's actual expansion. During the next century, perhaps two hundred cities from Holland to Poland, including Cologne, Brunswick, Dortmund, Danzig, and Riga, joined the league, but Lübeck always remained the dominant member. From the thirteenth to the sixteenth century, the Hanseatic League controlled trade over a Novgorod-Reval-Lübeck-Hamburg-Bruges-London axis—that is, the trade of northern Europe (see Map 11.4). In the fourteenth century, Hanseatic merchants branched out into southern Germany and Italy by land and into French, Spanish, and Portuguese ports by sea.

Across regular, well-defined trade routes along the Baltic and North seas, the ships of league cities carried furs, wax, copper, fish, grain, timber, and wine. These goods were exchanged for finished products, mainly cloth and salt, from western cities. At cities such as Bruges and London, Hanseatic merchants secured special trading concessions exempting them from all tolls and allowing them to trade at local fairs. Hanseatic merchants established foreign trading centers called "factories." The most famous of these was the London Steelyard, a walled community with warehouses, offices, a church, and residential quarters for company representatives.[11]

By the late thirteenth century, Hanseatic merchants had developed an important business technique, the business register. Merchants publicly recorded their debts and contracts and received a league guarantee for them. This device proved a decisive factor in the later development of credit and commerce in northern Europe.[12] These activities required capital, risk taking, and aggressive pursuit of opportunities—the essential ingredients of capitalism. They also yielded fat profits.

These developments added up to what one modern scholar who knows the period well has called "a commercial revolution, . . . probably the greatest turning point in the history of our civilization."[13] This is not a wildly extravagant statement. In the long run, the commercial revolution of the High Middle Ages brought about radical change in European society. One remarkable aspect of this change is that the commercial classes did not constitute a large part of the total population—never more than 10 percent. They exercised an influence far in excess of their numbers.

The commercial revolution created a great deal of new wealth. Wealth meant a higher standard of living. The new availability of something as simple as spices, for example, allowed for variety in food. Dietary habits gradually changed. Tastes became more sophisticated. Contact with Eastern civilizations introduced Europeans to eating utensils such as forks. Table manners improved. Nobles learned to eat with forks and knives instead of tearing the meat from a roast with their hands. They began to use napkins instead of wiping their greasy fingers on the dogs lying under the table.

The existence of wealth did not escape the attention of kings and other rulers. Wealth could be taxed, and through taxation kings could create strong and centralized states. In the years to come, alliances with the middle classes were to enable kings to defeat feudal powers and aristocratic interests and to build the states that came to be called "modern."

The commercial revolution also provided the opportunity for thousands of serfs to improve

Hanseatic League Merchants at Hamburg In the thirteenth century, the merchants of Hamburg and other cities in northern Germany formed an association for the suppression of piracy and the acquisition of commercial privileges in foreign countries. Members of the Hansa traded in furs, fish, wax, and oriental luxury goods. *(Source: Staatsarchiv Hamburg)*

their social position. The slow but steady transformation of European society from almost completely rural and isolated to relatively more sophisticated constituted the greatest effect of the commercial revolution that began in the eleventh century.

Even so, merchants and business people did not run medieval communities, except in central and northern Italy and in the county of Flanders. Most towns remained small. The castle, the manorial village, and the monastery dominated the landscape. The feudal nobility and churchmen determined the preponderant social attitudes, values, and patterns of thought and behavior. The commercial changes of the eleventh through thirteenth centuries did, however, lay the economic foundations for the development of urban life and culture.

MEDIEVAL UNIVERSITIES

Just as the first strong secular states emerged in the thirteenth century, so did the first universities. This was no coincidence. The new bureaucratic states and the church needed educated administrators, and universities were a response to this need. The word *university* derives from the Latin *universitas,* meaning "corporation" or "guild." Medieval universities were educational guilds that produced educated and trained individuals. They were also an expression of the tremendous vitality and creativity of the High Middle Ages. Their organization, methods of instruction, and goals continue to influence institutionalized learning in the Western world.

Origins

In the early Middle Ages, anyone who received education got it from a priest. Few boys acquired elementary literacy, and girls did not obtain even that. Few schools were available. Society was organized for war and defense and gave slight support to education. But by the late eleventh century, social conditions had markedly improved. There was greater political stability, and favorable economic conditions had advanced many people beyond the level of bare subsistence. The curious and able felt the lack of schools and teachers.

Since the time of the Carolingian Empire, monasteries and cathedral schools had offered the only formal instruction available. Monasteries, geared to religious concerns, wished to maintain an atmosphere of seclusion and silence and were unwilling to accept large numbers of noisy lay students. In contrast, schools attached to cathedrals and run by the bishop and his clergy were frequently situated in bustling cities, and by the eleventh century in Italian cities like Bologna, wealthy businessmen had established municipal schools. Cities inhabited by peoples of many backgrounds and "nationalities" stimulated the growth and exchange of ideas. In the course of the twelfth century, cathedral schools in France and municipal

schools in Italy developed into universities (Map 14.5). The first European universities appeared in Italy, at Bologna and Salerno.

The growth of the University of Bologna coincided with a revival of interest in Roman law. The study of Roman law as embodied in the Justinian *Code* had never completely died out in the West, but this sudden burst of interest seems to have been inspired by Irnerius (d. 1125), a great teacher at Bologna. His fame attracted students from all over Europe. Irnerius not only explained the Roman law of the Justinian *Code,* he applied it to difficult practical situations.

At Salerno, interest in medicine had persisted for centuries. Greek and Muslim physicians there had studied the use of herbs as cures and experimented with surgery. The twelfth century ushered in a new interest in Greek medical texts and in the work of Arab and Greek doctors. Students of medicine poured into Salerno and soon attracted royal attention. In 1140, when King Roger II of Sicily took the practice of medicine under royal control, his ordinance stated:

Who, from now on, wishes to practice medicine, has to present himself before our officials and examiners, in order to pass their judgment. Should he be bold enough to disregard this, he will be punished by imprisonment and confiscation of his entire property. In this way we are taking care that our subjects are not endangered by the inexperience of the physicians.[14]

In the first decades of the twelfth century, students converged on Paris. These men crowded into the cathedral school of Notre Dame and spilled over into the area later called the "Latin Quarter"—whose name probably reflects the Italian origin of many of the students attracted to Paris by the surge of interest in the classics, logic, and theology. The cathedral school's international reputation had already drawn to Paris scholars from all over Europe. One of the most famous of them was the teacher Peter Abelard.

Peter Abelard (1079–1142) was fascinated by logic, which he believed could be used to solve most problems. He had a brilliant mind and, al-

Map 14.5 Intellectual Centers of Medieval Europe Universities provided more sophisticated instruction than did monastic and cathedral schools.

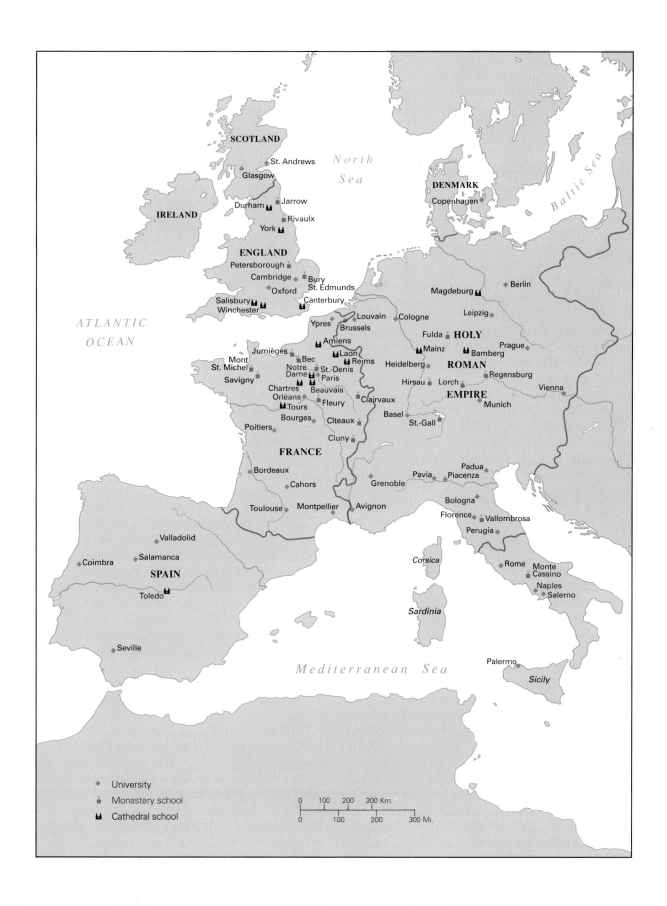

SCOTLAND

St. Andrews

Glasgow

*North
Sea*

DENMARK

Copenhagen

Baltic Sea

IRELAND

Jarrow
Durham
Rivaulx
York

ENGLAND

Petersborough

Cambridge
Bury
St. Edmunds
Oxford
Canterbury
Salisbury
Winchester

Berlin

Magdeburg

Leipzig

Cologne

*ATLANTIC
OCEAN*

Ypres
Louvain
Brussels

Fulda
HOLY

Amiens
Mont
St. Michel
Jumièges
Bec
Laon
Reims
St.-Denis
Paris
Savigny
Notre
Dame
Chartres
Beauvais
Orléans
Fleury
Tours
Bourges
Clairvaux
Poitiers
Citeaux
Cluny

Mainz
Prague
Bamberg

Heidelberg
ROMAN
Regensburg
Hirsau
Lorch
Vienna
Basel
EMPIRE
St.-Gall
Munich

FRANCE

Bordeaux
Cahors

Grenoble

Padua
Pavia
Piacenza

Toulouse
Montpellier
Avignon

Bologna
Florence
Vallombrosa
Perugia

Valladolid

Salamanca

Coimbra

SPAIN

Toledo

Corsica

Rome
Monte
Cassino
Naples
Salerno

Seville

Sardinia

Mediterranean Sea

Palermo

Sicily

◆ University

■ Monastery school

⛪ Cathedral school

0   100   200   300 Km.

0   100   200   300 Mi.

though orthodox in his philosophical teaching, appeared to challenge ecclesiastical authorities. His book *Sic et Non (Yes and No)* was a list of apparently contradictory propositions drawn from the Bible and the writings of the church fathers. One such proposition, for example, stated that sin is pleasing to God and is not pleasing to God. Abelard used a method of systematic doubting in his writing and teaching. As he put it in the preface of *Sic et Non,* "By doubting we come to questioning, and by questioning we perceive the truth." While other scholars merely asserted theological principles, Abelard discussed and analyzed them. Through reasoning he even tried to describe the attributes of the three persons of the Trinity, the central mystery of the Christian faith. Abelard was severely censured by a church council, but his cleverness, boldness, and imagination made him a highly popular figure among students.

The influx of students eager for learning, together with dedicated and imaginative teachers, created the atmosphere in which universities grew. In northern Europe—at Paris and later at Oxford and Cambridge in England—associations or guilds of professors organized universities. They established the curriculum, set the length of time for study, and determined the form and content of examinations.

Instruction and Curriculum

University faculties grouped themselves according to academic disciplines, called "schools"—law, medicine, arts, and theology. The professors, known as "schoolmen" or "Scholastics," developed a method of thinking, reasoning, and writing in which questions were raised and authorities cited on both sides of the issue. The goal of the Scholastic method was to arrive at definitive answers and to provide a rational explanation for what was believed on faith. Schoolmen held that reason and faith constitute two harmonious realms in which the truths of faith and reason complement each other. The Scholastic approach rested on the recovery of classical philosophical texts.

Ancient Greek and Arabic texts had come into Europe in the early twelfth century, primarily through Toledo in Muslim Spain. Thirteenth-century philosophers relied on Latin translations of these texts, especially translations of Aristotle.

Aristotle had stressed direct observation of nature, as well as the principles that theory must follow fact and that knowledge of a thing requires an explanation of its causes. The schoolmen reinterpreted Aristotelian texts in a Christian sense.

In exploration of the natural world, Aristotle's axioms were not precisely followed. Medieval scientists argued from authority—such as the Bible, the Justinian *Code,* or an ancient scientific treatise—rather than from direct observation and experimentation, as modern scientists do. Thus the conclusions of medieval scientists were often wrong. Nevertheless, natural science gradually emerged as a discipline distinct from philosophy. Scholastics made important contributions to the advancement of knowledge. They preserved the Greek and Arabic texts that contained the body of ancient scientific knowledge, which would otherwise have been lost. And, in asking questions about nature and the universe, Scholastics laid the foundations for later scientific work.

Many of the problems raised by Scholastic philosophers dealt with theological issues. For example, they addressed the question that interested all Christians, educated and uneducated: how is a person saved? Saint Augustine's thesis—that, as a result of Adam's fall, human beings have a propensity to sin—had become a central feature of medieval church doctrine. The church taught that it possessed the means to forgive the sinful: grace conveyed through the sacraments. However, although grace provided a predisposition to salvation, the Scholastics held that one must *decide to use* the grace received. In other words, a person must use his or her reason to advance to God.

Thirteenth-century Scholastics devoted an enormous amount of time to collecting and organizing knowledge on all topics. These collections were published as *summa,* or reference books. There were summa on law, philosophy, vegetation, animal life, and theology. Saint Thomas Aquinas (1225–1274), a professor at Paris, produced the most famous collection, the *Summa Theologica,* which deals with a vast number of theological questions.

Aquinas drew an important distinction between faith and reason. He maintained that although reason can demonstrate many basic Christian principles such as the existence of God, other fundamental teachings such as the Trinity and original sin cannot be proved by logic. That reason cannot establish them does not, however, mean that they are contrary to reason. Rather, people understand such doctrines through revelation embodied in Scripture. Scripture cannot contradict reason, nor reason Scripture:

The light of faith that is freely infused into us does not destroy the light of natural knowledge [reason] implanted in us naturally. For although the natural light of the human mind is insufficient to show us these things made manifest by faith, it is nevertheless impossible that these things which the divine principle gives us by faith are contrary to these implanted in us by nature [reason]. Indeed, were that the case, one or the other would have to be false, and, since both are given to us by God, God would have to be the author of untruth, which is impossible. . . . It is impossible that those things which are of philosophy can be contrary to those things which are of faith.[15]

Aquinas also investigated *epistemology,* which is the branch of philosophy concerned with how a person knows something. Aquinas stated that one knows, first, through sensory perception of the physical world—seeing, hearing, touching, and so on. He maintained that there can be nothing in the mind that is not first in the senses. Second, knowledge comes through reason, the mind exercising its natural abilities. Aquinas stressed the power of human reason to know, even to know God. Proofs of the existence of God exemplify the Scholastic method of knowing.

At all universities, the standard method of teaching was the *lecture*—that is, a reading. The professor read a passage from the Bible, the Justinian *Code,* or one of Aristotle's treatises. He then explained and interpreted the passage; his interpretation was called a *gloss.* Students wrote down everything. Texts and glosses were sometimes collected and reproduced as textbooks. But because books had to be copied by hand, they were extremely expensive and few students could afford them. Thus students depended for study on their own or friends' notes accumulated over a period of years. The choice of subjects was narrow. The syllabus at all universities consisted of a core of ancient texts that all students studied and, if they wanted to get ahead, mastered.

There were no examinations at the end of a series of lectures. Examinations were given after three, four, or five years of study, when the student applied for a degree. The professors determined the amount of material students had to know for each degree, and students frequently insisted that the professors specify precisely what that material was. When a candidate for a degree believed himself prepared, he presented himself to a committee of professors for examination. (No evidence survives of women sitting for an examination.)

Examinations were oral and very difficult. If the candidate passed, he was awarded the first, or bachelor's, degree. Further study, about as long, arduous, and expensive as it is today, enabled the graduate to try for the master's and doctor's degrees. All degrees certified competence in a given subject, and degrees were technically licenses to teach. Most students, however, did not become teachers.

THE CREATIVE OUTBURST

The creative energy that characterized the High Middle Ages was manifested in ways sacred and secular. As architecture, drama, art, and literature evolved in adaptation to the changing conditions of the High and late Middle Ages, they both expressed and satisfied the needs of medieval people.

From Romanesque Gloom to "Uninterrupted Light"

Medieval churches stand as the most spectacular manifestations of medieval vitality and creativity. It is difficult for twentieth-century people to appreciate the extraordinary amounts of energy, imagination, and money involved in building them. Between 1180 and 1270 in France alone, eighty cathedrals, about five hundred abbey churches, and tens of thousands of parish churches were constructed. This construction represents a remarkable investment for a country of scarcely eighteen million people. More stone was quarried for churches in medieval France than had been mined in ancient Egypt, where the Great Pyramid alone consumed 40.5 million cubic feet of stone. All these churches displayed a new architectural style. Fifteenth-century critics called the new style "Gothic" because they mistakenly believed that the fifth-century Goths had invented it. It actually developed partly in reaction to the earlier "Romanesque" style, which resembled ancient Roman architecture.

Gothic cathedrals were built in towns and reflect both bourgeois wealth and enormous civic pride. The manner in which a society spends its wealth expresses its values. Cathedrals, abbeys, and village churches testify to the religious faith and piety of medieval people. If the dominant aspect of medieval culture had not been Christianity, the builder's imagination and the merchant's money would have been used otherwise.

The relative political stability and increase of ecclesiastical wealth in the eleventh century encouraged the arts of peace. In the ninth and tenth centuries, the Vikings and Magyars had burned hundreds of wooden churches. In the eleventh century, the abbots wanted to rebuild in a more permanent fashion, and after the year 1000, church building increased on a wide scale. Because fireproofing was essential, ceilings had to be made of stone. The stone ceilings, called "vaults," were heavy; only thick walls would support them. Because the walls were so thick, the windows were small, allowing little light into the interior of the church. In northern Europe, twin bell towers often crowned these Romanesque churches, giving them a powerful, fortresslike appearance, reflecting the quasi-military, aristocratic, and pre-urban society that built them.

The inspiration for the Gothic style originated in the brain of one monk, Suger, abbot of Saint-Denis (1122–1151). When Suger became abbot, he decided to reconstruct the old Carolingian abbey church at Saint-Denis. Work began in 1137. On June 11, 1144, King Louis VII and a large crowd of bishops, dignitaries, and common people witnessed the solemn consecration of the first Gothic church in France.

The basic features of Gothic architecture—the pointed arch, the ribbed vault, and the flying buttress—were not unknown before 1137. What was without precedent was the interior lightness they made possible. Since the ceiling of a Gothic church weighed less than that of a Romanesque church, the walls could be thinner. Stained-glass windows were cut into the stone, flooding the church with light. The bright interior was astounding. Suger, describing his achievement, exulted at "the wonderful and uninterrupted light of most sacred windows, pervading the interior beauty."[16]

Begun in the Île-de-France, Gothic architecture spread throughout France with the expansion of royal power. French architects were soon invited to design and supervise the construction of churches in other parts of Europe, and the new style traveled rapidly over the continent.

Community Expression

The construction of a Gothic cathedral represented a gigantic investment of time, money, and corporate effort. The bishop and the clergy of the cathedral made the decision to build, but they depended on the support of all the social classes. Bishops raised revenue from contributions by people in their dioceses, and the clergy appealed to the king and the nobility. The French kings, for example, were generous patrons of many cathedrals. Noble families often gave contributions in order to have their crests in the stained-glass windows. Above all, the church relied on the financial help of those with the greatest amount of ready cash, the commercial classes.

Money was not the only need. A great number of craftsmen had to be assembled, from quarrymen and sculptors, to blacksmiths and glassmakers, and unskilled laborers had to be recruited for the heavy work. The construction of a large cathedral was rarely completed in one lifetime; many cathedrals were never finished at all. Because generation after generation added to the building, many Gothic churches show the architectural influences of two or even three centuries.

Since cathedrals were symbols of bourgeois civic pride, towns competed to build the largest and most splendid church. The people of Beauvais, in France, exceeded everyone: their church, started in 1247, reached the exceptional height of 157 feet. Unfortunately, the weight imposed on the vaults was too great, and the building collapsed in

1284. Medieval people built cathedrals to glorify God—and if mortals were impressed, so much the better.[17]

Cathedrals served secular as well as religious purposes. The sanctuary containing the altar and the bishop's chair belonged to the clergy, but the rest of the church belonged to the people. In addition to marriages, baptisms, and funerals, there were scores of feast days on which the entire town gathered in the cathedral for festivities. Local guilds met in the cathedrals, and magistrates and municipal officials held political meetings there. Some towns never built town halls because all civic functions took place in the cathedral. Pilgrims

West Front of Notre Dame Cathedral   In this powerful vision of the Last Judgment, Christ sits in judgment surrounded by angels, the Virgin, and Saint John. Scenes of paradise fill the arches on Christ's right, scenes of hell on the left. In the lower lintel, the dead arise incorruptible, and in the upper lintel (below Christ's feet), the saved move off to heaven, while devils push the damned to hell. Below, the twelve apostles line the doorway. *(Source: Alinari/Scala/Art Resource)*

slept there, lovers courted there, traveling actors staged plays there. The cathedral belonged to all.

First and foremost, however, the cathedral was intended to teach the people the doctrines of Christian faith through visual images. Architecture became the servant of theology. The main altar was at the east end, pointing toward Jerusalem, the city of peace. The west front of the cathedral faced the setting sun, and its wall was usually devoted to the scenes of the Last Judgment. The north side, which received the least sunlight, displayed events from the Old Testament. The south side, washed in warm sunshine for much of the day, depicted scenes from the New Testament. This symbolism implied that the Jewish people of the Old Testament lived in darkness and that the Gospel brought by Christ illuminated the world. Every piece of sculpture, furniture, and stained glass had some religious or social significance.

Stained glass beautifully reflects the creative energy of the High Middle Ages. It is both an integral part of Gothic architecture and a distinct form of painting. The glassmaker "painted" the picture with small fragments of glass held together with strips of lead. As Gothic churches became more skeletal and had more windows, stained glass replaced manuscript illumination as the leading kind of painting. Thousands of scenes in the cathedrals celebrate nature, country life, and the activities of ordinary people. All members of medieval society had a place in the City of God, which the Gothic cathedral represented. No one, from king to peasant, was excluded.

Tapestry making also came into its own in the fourteenth century. Heavy woolen tapestries were first made in the monasteries and convents as wall hangings for churches. Because they could be moved and lent an atmosphere of warmth, they subsequently replaced mural paintings. Early tapestries depicted religious scenes, but later hangings produced for the knightly class bore secular designs, especially romantic forests and hunting spectacles.

During the same period drama, derived from the church's liturgy, emerged as a distinct art form. For centuries, skits based on Christ's Nativity and Resurrection had been performed in monasteries and cathedrals. Beginning in the thirteenth century, plays based on these and other biblical themes and on the lives of the saints were performed in the church square and later in the town marketplace. Guilds financed these "mystery plays," so called because they were based on the mysteries of the Christian faith. By combining comical farce based on ordinary life with serious religious scenes, they allowed the common people to understand and identify with religious figures and the mysteries of their faith. Provoking the individual conscience to reform, mystery plays were also an artistic manifestation of local civic pride.

Vernacular Literature

Few developments expressed the emergence of national consciousness more vividly than the emergence of national literatures. Across Europe people spoke the language and dialect of their particular locality and class. In England, for example, the common people spoke regional English dialects, and the upper classes conversed in French. Official documents and works of literature were written in Latin or French. Beginning in the fourteenth century, however, national languages—the vernacular—came into widespread use not only in verbal communication but in literature as well. Three masterpieces of European culture, Dante's *Divine Comedy* (1310–1320), Chaucer's *Canterbury Tales* (1387–1400), and Villon's *Grand Testament* (1461), brilliantly manifested this new national pride.

Dante Alighieri (1265–1321) descended from an aristocratic family in Florence, where he held several positions in the city government. Dante called his work a "comedy" because he wrote it in Italian and in a different style from the "tragic" Latin; a later generation added the adjective "divine," referring both to its sacred subject and to Dante's artistry. The *Divine Comedy* is an allegorical trilogy of one hundred cantos (verses) whose three equal parts (1 + 33 + 33 + 33) each describe one of the realms of the next world: Hell, Purgatory, and Paradise. Dante recounts his imaginary journey through these regions toward God. The Roman poet Virgil, representing reason, leads Dante through Hell, where he observes the torments of the damned and denounces the disorders of his own time, especially ecclesiastical ambition and corruption. Passing up into Purgatory, Virgil shows the poet how souls are purified of their disordered inclinations. From Purgatory, Beatrice, a woman whom Dante once loved and the symbol of divine revelation in the poem, leads him to Paradise. In Paradise, home of the angels and saints,

Dante Alighieri In this fifteenth-century fresco the poet, crowned with the wreath of poet laureate, holds the book containing the opening lines of his immortal *Commedia*. On the left is Hell and the mountain of purgatory; on the right, the city of Florence. *(Source: Scala/Art Resource)*

Saint Bernard—representing mystic contemplation—leads Dante to the Virgin Mary. Through her intercession Dante at last attains a vision of God.

The *Divine Comedy* portrays contemporary and historical figures, comments on secular and ecclesiastical affairs, and draws on Scholastic philosophy. Within the framework of a symbolic pilgrimage to the City of God, the *Divine Comedy* embodies the psychological tensions of the age. A profoundly Christian poem, it also contains bitter criticism of some church authorities. In its symmetrical structure and use of figures from the ancient world, such as Virgil, the poem perpetuates the classical tradition, but as the first major work of literature in the Italian vernacular, it is distinctly modern.

Geoffrey Chaucer (1340–1400), the son of a London wine merchant, was an official in the administrations of the English kings Edward III and Richard II and wrote poetry as an avocation. Chaucer's *Canterbury Tales* is a collection of stories in lengthy, rhymed narrative. On a pilgrimage to the shrine of Saint Thomas Becket at Canterbury (see page 413), thirty people of various social backgrounds each tell a tale. The Prologue sets the scene and describes the pilgrims, whose characters are further revealed in the story each one tells. For example, the gentle Christian Knight relates a chivalric romance; the gross Miller tells a vulgar story about a deceived husband; the earthy Wife of Bath, who has buried five husbands, sketches a fable about the selection of a spouse. In depicting the interests and behavior of all types of people, Chaucer presents a rich panorama of English social life in the fourteenth century. Like the *Divine Comedy*, *Canterbury Tales* reflects the cultural tensions of the times. Ostensibly Christian, many of the pilgrims are also materialistic, sensual, and worldly, suggesting the ambivalence of the broader society's concern for the next world and frank enjoyment of this one.

Present knowledge of François Villon (1431–1463), probably the greatest poet of late medieval France, derives from Paris police records and his own poetry. Although born to desperately poor parents, Villon earned the master of arts degree at the University of Paris. A rowdy and free-spirited student, in 1455 he killed a man in a street brawl. Banished from Paris, he joined one of the bands of wandering thieves that harassed the countryside after the Hundred Years' War. For his fellow bandits he composed ballads in thieves' jargon.

Villon's *Lais* (1456), a pun on the word *legs* ("legacy"), is a series of farcical bequests to friends and enemies. "Ballade des Pendus" ("Ballad of the Hanged") was written while Villon was contemplating that fate in prison. (His execution was commuted.) Villon's greatest and most self-revealing work, the *Grand Testament,* contains another string of bequests, including a legacy to a prostitute, and describes his unshakable faith in the beauty of life on earth. The *Grand Testament* possesses elements of social rebellion, bawdy humor, and rare emotional depth. The themes of Dante's and Chaucer's poetry are distinctly medieval, but Villon's celebration of the human condition brands him as definitely modern. He used medieval forms of versification, but his language was the vernacular of the poor and the criminal.

Perhaps the most versatile and prolific French writer of the later Middle Ages was Christine de Pisan (1363?–1434?). The daughter of a professor of astrology at Bologna whose international reputation won him a post at the French royal court where she received her excellent education, Christine had a broad knowledge of Greek, Latin, French, and Italian literature. The deaths of her father and husband left her with three small children and her mother to support, and she resolved to earn her living with her pen. In addition to poems and books on love, religion, and morality, Christine produced the *Livre de la mutacion de fortune,* a major historical work; a biography of King Charles V; the *Ditié,* celebrating Joan of Arc's victory; and many letters. *The City of Ladies* lists the great women of history and their contributions to society, and *The Book of Three Virtues* provides prudent and practical advice on household management for women of all social classes and at all stages of life. Christine de Pisan's wisdom and wit are illustrated in her autobiographical *Avison-*

Christine. She records that a man told her that an educated woman is unattractive, since there are so few, to which she responded that an ignorant man was even less attractive, since there are so many.

HERESY AND THE FRIARS

As the commercial revolution of the High Middle Ages fostered urban development, the towns experienced an enormous growth of heresy. In fact, in the twelfth and thirteenth centuries, "the most economically advanced and urbanized areas: northern Italy, southern France, Flanders-Brabant, and the lower Rhine Valley" witnessed the strongest heretical movements.[18] Why did heresy flourish in such places? The bishops, usually drawn from the feudal nobility, did not understand urban culture and were suspicious of it. Christian theology, formulated for an earlier, rural age, did not address the problems of the more sophisticated mercantile society. The new monastic orders of the twelfth century, deliberately situated in remote, isolated areas, had little relevance to the towns.[19] Finally, townspeople wanted a pious clergy capable of preaching the Gospel in a manner that satisfied their spiritual needs. They disapproved of clerical ignorance and luxurious living. Critical of the clergy, neglected, and spiritually unfulfilled, townspeople turned to heretical sects.

The term *heresy,* which derives from the Greek *hairesis,* meaning "individual choosing," is older than Christianity. Civil authority in early Christian times could (and did) punish heresy (see page 232). In the early Middle Ages, the term came to be applied to the position of a Christian who chose and stubbornly held to doctrinal error in defiance of church authority.[20]

Ironically, the eleventh-century Gregorian reform movement, which had worked to purify the church of disorder, led to some twelfth- and thirteenth-century heretical movements. Papal efforts to improve the sexual morality of the clergy, for example, had largely succeeded. But Gregory VII did not foresee the consequences of his order forbidding married priests to celebrate church ceremonies. Laypersons assumed that they could remove immoral priests. Critics and heretics accused clergymen of immorality and thus weakened their influence. The clergy's inability to provide adequate instruction weakened its position.

In northern Italian towns, Arnold of Brescia, a vigorous advocate of strict clerical poverty, denounced clerical wealth. In France, Peter Waldo, a rich merchant of Lyon, gave his money to the poor and preached that only prayers, not sacraments, were needed for salvation. The "Waldensians"—as Peter Waldo's followers were called—bitterly attacked the sacraments and church hierarchy, and they carried these ideas across Europe.

Another group, known as the "Cathars" (from the Greek *katharos,* meaning "pure") and as the "Albigensians" (from the town of Albi in southern France), rejected not only the hierarchical organization and the sacraments of the church but the Roman church itself. The Albigensians' primary tenet was the dualist belief that God had created spiritual things and the Devil had created material things; thus the soul was good and the body evil. Albigensians believed that forces of good and evil battled constantly and that leading a perfect life meant being stripped of all physical and material things. Thus sexual intercourse was evil because it led to the creation of more physical bodies. Albigensians were divided into the "perfect," who followed the principles of Catharism, and the "believers," who led ordinary lives until their deaths, when they repented and were saved.

The Albigensian heresy won many adherents in southern France. Townspeople admired the virtuous lives of the "perfect," which contrasted very favorably with the luxurious living of the Roman clergy. Women were attracted because the Albigensians treated them as men's equals. Nobles were drawn because they coveted the clergy's wealth.

Faced with widespread defection in southern France, in 1208 Pope Innocent III proclaimed a crusade against the Albigensian heretics. When the papal legate was murdered by a follower of Count Raymond of Toulouse, the greatest lord in southern France and a suspected heretic, the crusade took on a political character; heretical beliefs became fused with feudal rebellion against the French crown. Northern French lords joined the crusade and inflicted severe defeats on the towns of the large southern province of Languedoc. The Albigensian crusade, however, was a political rather than a religious success; the heresy simply went underground.

In its continuing struggle against heresy, the church gained the support of two remarkable men, Saint Dominic and Saint Francis, and of the orders they founded.

Born in Castile, the province of Spain famous for its zealous Christianity and militant opposition to Islam, Domingo de Gúzman (1170?–1221) received a sound education and was ordained a priest. In 1206 he accompanied his bishop on a mission to preach to the Albigensian heretics in Languedoc. Although the austere simplicity in

St. Dominic and the Inquisition The fifteenth-century court painter to the Spanish rulers Ferdinand and Isabella, Pedro Berruguete here portrays an event from the life of St. Dominic: Dominic presides at the trial of Count Raymond of Toulouse, who had supported the Albigensian heretics. Raymond, helmeted and on horseback, repented and was pardoned; his companions, who would not repent, were burned. Smoke from the fire has put one of the judges to sleep, and other officials, impervious to the human tragedy, chat among themselves. *(Source: Museo del Prado, Madrid)*

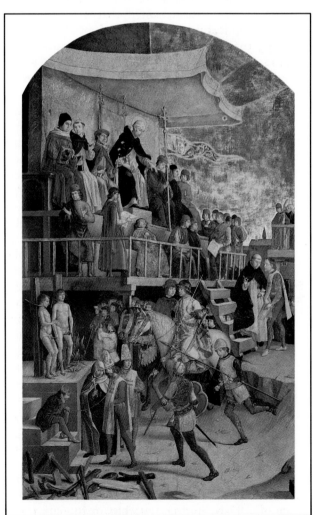

which they traveled contrasted favorably with the pomp and display of the papal legate in the area, Dominic's efforts had little practical success. Determined to win the heretics back with ardent preaching, Dominic subsequently returned to France with a few followers. In 1216 the group—known as the "Preaching Friars"—won papal recognition as a new religious order. Their name indicates their goal: they were to preach. In order to preach effectively, they had to study; so Dominic sent his recruits to the universities for training in theology.

Francesco di Bernardone (1181–1226), son of a wealthy cloth merchant from the northern Italian town of Assisi, was an extravagant wastrel until he had a sudden conversion. Then he determined to devote himself entirely to living the Gospel. Directed by a vision to rebuild the dilapidated chapel of Saint Damiano in Assisi, Francis sold some of his father's cloth to finance the reconstruction. His enraged father insisted that he return the money and enlisted the support of the bishop. When the bishop told Francis to obey his father, Francis took off all his clothes and returned them to his father. Thereafter he promised to obey only his Father in heaven.

Francis was particularly inspired by two biblical texts: "If you seek perfection, go, sell your possessions, and give to the poor. You will have treasure in heaven. Afterward, come back and follow me" (Matthew 19:21); and Jesus's advice to his disciples as they went out to preach, "Take nothing for the journey, neither walking staff nor travelling bag, no bread, no money" (Luke 9:3). Over the centuries, these words had stimulated countless young people. Francis, however, intended to observe them literally and without compromise. He set out to live and preach the Gospel in absolute poverty.

The simplicity, humility, and joyful devotion with which Francis carried out his mission soon attracted companions. Although he resisted pressure to establish an order, his followers became so numerous that he was obliged to develop some formal structure. In 1221 the papacy approved the "Rule of the Little Brothers of Saint Francis," as the Franciscans were known.

The new Dominican and Franciscan orders differed significantly from older monastic orders such as the Benedictines and the Cistercians. First, the Dominicans and Franciscans were friars, not monks. They lived and worked in the cities and

university towns, the busy centers of commercial and intellectual life, not in the secluded and cloistered world of the monastery. Second, the friars stressed apostolic poverty, a life based on the Gospel's teachings. They owned no property and depended on Christian people for their material needs; thus they were called *mendicants,* begging friars. Benedictine and Cistercian abbeys, by contrast, held land—not infrequently great tracts of land. Finally, the friars drew most of their members from the burgher class, from small property owners and shopkeepers. The monastic orders, by contrast, gathered their members (at least until the thirteenth century) overwhelmingly from the nobility.[21]

The friars represented a response to the spiritual and intellectual needs of the thirteenth century. Research on the German friars has shown that although the Franciscans initially accepted uneducated men, the Dominicans always showed a marked preference for university graduates.[22] A more urban and sophisticated society required a highly educated clergy. The Dominicans soon held professorial chairs at leading universities, and they count Thomas Aquinas, probably the greatest medieval philosopher in Europe, as their most famous member. But the Franciscans followed suit at the universities and also produced intellectual leaders. The Franciscans' mission to the towns and the poor, their ideal of poverty, and their compassion for the human condition made them vastly popular. The friars interpreted Christian doctrine for the new urban classes. By living Christianity as well as by preaching it, they won the respect of the medieval bourgeoisie.

Dominic started his order to combat heresy. Francis's followers were motivated by the ideal of absolute poverty. The papacy used the friars to staff a new (1233) ecclesiastical court, the Inquisition. Popes selected the friars to direct the Inquisition because bishops proved unreliable and because special theological training was needed. *Inquisition* means "investigation," and the Franciscans and Dominicans developed expert methods of rooting out unorthodox thought. Modern Americans consider the procedures of the Inquisition exceedingly unjust, and there was substantial criticism of it in the Middle Ages. The accused did not learn the evidence against them or see their accusers; they were subjected to lengthy interrogations often designed to trap them; and torture could be used to extract confessions. Those who supported the Inquisition, however, believed that heretics destroyed the souls of their neighbors. By attacking religion, it was also thought, heretics destroyed the very bonds of society. So successful was the Inquisition that heresy was virtually extinguished within a century.

THE BLACK DEATH

Societies, like individuals, cannot maintain a high level of energy indefinitely. In the later years of the thirteenth century, Europeans seemed to run out of steam. The crusading movement gradually fizzled out. Few new cathedrals were constructed, and if a cathedral had not been completed by

1300, the chances were high that it never would be. The vigor of the strong rulers of England and France did not pass to their immediate descendants. And the church, which for two centuries had guided Christian society, began to face grave difficulties.

Economic problems originating in the later thirteenth century were fully manifest by the start of the fourteenth. In the first decade, the countries of northern Europe experienced considerable price inflation. The costs of grain, livestock, and dairy products rose sharply. Bad weather made a serious situation worse. An unusual number of storms brought torrential rains, ruining the wheat, oat, and hay crops on which people and animals depended almost everywhere. Poor harvests—and one in four was likely to be poor—led

MAP 14.6 The Course of the Black Death in Fourteenth-Century Europe   Note the routes that the bubonic plague took across Europe. How do you account for the fact that several regions were spared the "dreadful death"?

The Plague-Stricken Even as the dead were wrapped in shrouds and collected in carts for mass burial, the disease struck others. The man collapsing has the symptomatic buba on his neck. As Saint Sebastian pleads for mercy (above), a winged devil, bearer of the plague, attacks an angel. *(Source: Walters Art Gallery, Baltimore)*

to scarcity and starvation. Almost all of northern Europe suffered a terrible famine in the years 1315 to 1317. Meanwhile, an epidemic of typhoid fever carried away thousands. In 1316, 10 percent of the population of the city of Ypres may have died between May and October alone. Then in 1318 disease hit cattle and sheep, drastically reducing the herds and flocks. Another bad harvest in 1321 brought famine, starvation, and death.

These catastrophes had devastating social consequences. Population had steadily increased in the twelfth and thirteenth centuries, and large amounts of land had been put under cultivation. The amount of food yielded, however, did not keep up with the level of population growth. Bad weather had disastrous results, and population fell. Meanwhile, the international character of trade and commerce meant that a disaster in one country had serious implications elsewhere. For example, the infection that attacked English sheep in 1318 caused a sharp decline in wool exports in the following years. Without wool, Flemish weavers could not work. Without woolen cloth, the businesses of Flemish, French, and English merchants suffered. Unemployment encouraged many men to turn to crime. Economic and social problems were aggravated by the appearance in western Europe of a frightful disease.

Scholars dispute the origins of the bubonic plague, often known as the "Black Death." Some students hold that it broke out in China or central Asia around 1331 and that during the next fifteen years merchants and soldiers carried it over the caravan routes until in 1346 it reached the Crimea in southern Russia. Other scholars believe that the plague was endemic in southern Russia. In either case, from the Crimea the plague had easy access to Mediterranean lands and western Europe.

In October 1347, Genoese ships brought the plague to Messina. From there it spread across Sicily. Venice and Genoa were hit in January 1348, and from the port of Pisa the disease spread south to Rome and east to Florence and all Tuscany. By late spring, southern Germany was attacked. Frightened French authorities chased a galley bearing the disease from the port of Marseilles, but not before plague had infected the city, from where it spread to Languedoc and Spain. In June 1348 two ships entered the Bristol Channel and introduced it into England. All Europe felt the scourge of this horrible disease (Map 14.6).

Pathology

Modern understanding of the bubonic plague rests on the research of two bacteriologists, one French and one Japanese, who in 1894 independently identified the bacillus that causes the plague, *Pasteurella pestis* (so labeled after the French scientist's teacher, Louis Pasteur). The bacillus liked to live in the bloodstream of an animal or, ideally, in the stomach of a flea. The flea in turn resided in the hair of a rodent, sometimes a squirrel but preferably the hardy, nimble, and vagabond black rat. Why the host black rat moved so much, scientists still do not know, but it often traveled by ship. There the black rat could feast for months on a cargo of grain or live snugly among bales of cloth. Fleas bearing the bacillus also had no trouble nesting in saddlebags.[23] Comfortable, well fed, and often having greatly multiplied, the black rats ended their ocean voyage and descended on the great cities of Europe. Once in the population, the plague also was communicated directly from one person to another.

Although by the fourteenth century urban authorities from London to Paris to Rome had begun to try to achieve a primitive level of sanitation, urban conditions remained ideal for the spread of disease. In the narrow streets filled with mud, refuse, and human excrement, dead animals and sore-covered beggars greeted the traveler. Extreme overcrowding was commonplace. All members of an aristocratic family lived and slept in one room. In a middle-class or poor household, six or eight persons slept in one bed—if they had one. Closeness, after all, provided warmth. Houses were beginning to be constructed of brick, but many remained of wood, clay, and mud. A determined rat had little trouble entering such a house.

Standards of personal hygiene remained frightfully low. Most large cities had public bathhouses, but there is no way of knowing how frequently ordinary people used them. People probably bathed rarely. Lack of personal cleanliness, combined with any number of temporary ailments such as diarrhea and the common cold, weakened the body's resistance to serious disease. Fleas and body lice were universal afflictions: everyone from peasants to archbishops had them. One more bite did not cause much alarm. But if that nibble came from a bacillus-bearing flea, an entire household or area was doomed.

The symptoms of the bubonic plague started with a growth the size of a nut or an apple in the armpit, in the groin, or on the neck. This was the boil, or *buba,* that gave the disease its name and caused agonizing pain. If the buba was lanced and the pus thoroughly drained, the victim had a chance of recovery. The secondary stage was the appearance of black spots or blotches caused by bleeding under the skin. Finally, the victim began to cough violently and spit blood. This stage, indicating the presence of thousands of bacilli in the bloodstream, signaled the end, and death followed in two or three days. Rather than evoking compassion for the victim, a French scientist has written, everything about the bubonic plague provoked horror and disgust: "All the matter which exuded from their bodies let off an unbearable stench; sweat, excrement, spittle, breath, so fetid as to be overpowering; urine turbid, thick, black or red."[24]

Medieval people had no rational explanation for the disease nor any effective medical treatment for it. Most people—lay, scholarly, and medical—believed that the Black Death was caused by some "vicious property in the air" that carried the disease from place to place. When ignorance was joined to fear and ancient bigotry, savage cruelty sometimes resulted. Many people believed that the Jews had poisoned the wells of Christian communities and thereby infected the drinking water. This charge led to the murder of thousands of Jews across Europe.

The Italian writer Giovanni Boccaccio (1313–1375), describing the course of the disease in Florence in the preface to his book of tales, *The Decameron,* pinpointed the cause of the spread:

Moreover, the virulence of the pest was the greater by reason that intercourse was apt to convey it from the sick to the whole, just as fire devours things dry or greasy when they are brought close to it. Nay, the evil went yet further, for not merely by speech or association with the sick was the malady communicated to the healthy with consequent peril of common death, but any that touched the clothes of the sick or aught else that had been touched or used by them, seemed thereby to contract the disease.[25]

The rat that carried the disease-bearing flea avoided travel outside the cities. Thus the countryside was relatively safe. City dwellers who could afford to move fled to the country districts.

Only educated guesses, subject to enormous scholarly controversy, can be made about the plague's mortality rate. Of a total English population of perhaps 4.2 million, probably 1.4 million died of the Black Death in its several visits.[26] Densely populated Italian cities endured incredible losses. Florence, for example, lost between half and two-thirds of its 1347 population of 85,000 when the plague visited in 1348. The disease recurred intermittently in the 1360s and 1370s and reappeared many times down to 1700. There have been twentieth-century outbreaks in such places as Hong Kong, Bombay, and Uganda.

Social and Psychological Consequences

Predictably, the poor died more rapidly than the rich, because the rich enjoyed better health to begin with; but the powerful were not unaffected. In England two archbishops of Canterbury fell victim to the plague in 1349, King Edward III's daughter Joan died, and many leading members of the London guilds followed her to the grave.

It is noteworthy that in an age of mounting criticism of clerical wealth, the behavior of the clergy during the plague was often exemplary. Priests, monks, and nuns cared for the sick and buried the dead. In places like Venice, from where even physicians fled, priests remained to give what ministrations they could. Consequently, their mortality rate was phenomenally high. The German clergy, especially, suffered a severe decline in personnel in the years after 1350. With the ablest killed off, the wealth of the German church fell into the hands of the incompetent and weak. The situation was ripe for reform.

Economic historians and demographers sharply dispute the impact of the plague on the economy in the late fourteenth century. The traditional view that the plague had a disastrous effect has been greatly modified. The clearest evidence comes from England, where the agrarian economy showed remarkable resilience. Although the severity of the disease varied from region to region, it appears that by about 1375 most landlords enjoyed revenues near those of the pre-plague years. By the early fifteenth century seigneurial prosperity reached a medieval peak. Why? The answer appears to lie in the fact that England and many parts of Europe suffered from overpopulation in the early fourteenth century. Population losses caused by the Black Death "led to increased productivity by restoring a more efficient balance between labour, land, and capital."[27] Population decline meant a sharp increase in per capita wealth. Increased demand for labor meant greater mobility among peasant and working classes. Wages rose, providing better distribution of income and putting landlords on the defensive. Some places, such as Florence, experienced economic prosperity as a long-term consequence of the plague.

Even more significant than the social effects were the psychological consequences. The knowledge that the disease meant almost certain death provoked the most profound pessimism. Imagine an entire society in the grip of the belief that it was at the mercy of a frightful affliction about which nothing could be done, a disgusting disease from which family and friends would flee, leaving one to die alone and in agony. It is not surprising that some sought release in orgies and gross sensuality while others turned to the severest forms of asceticism and frenzied religious fervor. Some extremists joined groups of *flagellants,* men and women who collectively whipped and scourged themselves as penance for their and society's sins, in the belief that the Black Death was God's punishment for humanity's wickedness.

The literature and art of the fourteenth century reveal a terribly morbid concern with death. One highly popular artistic motif, the Dance of Death, depicted a dancing skeleton leading away a living person. No wonder survivors experienced a sort of shell shock and a terrible crisis of faith. Lack of confidence in the leaders of society, lack of hope for the future, defeatism, and malaise wreaked enormous anguish and contributed to the decline of the Middle Ages. A prolonged international war added further misery to the frightful disasters of the plague.

THE HUNDRED YEARS' WAR (CA 1337–1453)

On and off from 1337 to 1453, another phase of the centuries-old struggle between the English and French monarchies was fought. The Hundred Years' War had both distant and immediate causes. In 1259 France and England signed the Treaty of Paris, in which the English king agreed to become—for himself and his successors—vassal of the French crown for the duchy of Aquitaine. The English claimed Aquitaine as an ancient inheritance. French policy, however, was strongly expansionist, and the French kings resolved to absorb the duchy into the kingdom of France. In 1329 Edward III (r. 1327–1377) paid homage to Philip VI (r. 1328–1350) for Aquitaine. In 1337 Philip, determined to exercise full jurisdiction there, confiscated the duchy. This was the immediate cause of the war. Edward III maintained that the only way he could exercise his rightful sovereignty over Aquitaine was by assuming the title of king of France.[28] As the eldest surviving male descendant of the French king Philip the Fair (r. 1285–1314), he believed that he could rightfully make this claim. Moreover, the dynastic argument had feudal implications: in order to increase their independent power, French vassals of Philip VI used the excuse that they had to transfer their loyalty to a more legitimate overlord, Edward III. One reason the war lasted so long was that it became a French civil war, with French barons supporting English monarchs in order to thwart the centralizing goals of the French crown.

Economic factors involving the wool trade and the control of Flemish towns had served as justifications for war between France and England for centuries. The causes of the conflicts known as the "Hundred Years' War" were thus dynastic, feudal, political, and economic. Recent historians have stressed economic factors. The wool trade between England and Flanders served as the cornerstone of both countries' economies; they were closely interdependent. Flanders was a fief of the French crown, and the Flemish aristocracy was highly sympathetic to the monarchy in Paris. But the wealth of Flemish merchants and cloth manufacturers depended on English wool, and Flemish burghers strongly supported the claims of Edward III. The disruption of commerce with England threatened their prosperity.

It is impossible to measure the precise influence of the Flemings on the cause and course of the war. Certainly Edward could not ignore their influence, because it represented money he needed to carry on the war. Although the war's impact on commerce fluctuated, over the long run it badly hurt the wool trade and the cloth industry.

One historian has written in jest that if Edward III had been locked away in a castle with a pile of toy knights and archers to play with, he would have done far less damage.[29] The same might be said of Philip VI. Both rulers glorified war and saw it as the perfect arena for the realization of their chivalric ideals. Neither king possessed any sort of policy for dealing with his kingdom's social, economic, or political ills.

The Popular Response

The governments of both England and France manipulated public opinion to support the war. Whatever significance modern students ascribe to the economic factor, public opinion in fourteenth-century England held that the war was waged for one reason: to secure for King Edward the French crown that he had been denied.[30] Edward III issued letters to the sheriffs describing in graphic terms the evil deeds of the French and listing royal needs. Kings in both countries instructed the clergy to deliver sermons filled with patriotic sentiment. The royal courts sensationalized the wickedness of the other side and stressed the great fortunes to be made from the war. Philip VI sent agents to warn communities about the dangers of invasion and to stress the French crown's revenue needs to meet the attack.

The royal campaign to rally public opinion was highly successful, at least in the early stage of the war. Edward III gained widespread support in the 1340s and 1350s. The English developed a deep hatred of the French and feared that King Philip intended "to have seized and slaughtered the entire realm of England." As England was successful in the field, pride in the country's military proficiency increased.

Most important of all, the Hundred Years' War was popular because it presented unusual opportunities for wealth and advancement. Poor knights and knights who were unemployed were promised regular wages. Criminals who enlisted were granted pardons. The great nobles expected to be rewarded with estates. Royal exhortations to the troops before battles repeatedly stressed that, if victorious, the men might keep whatever they seized. The French chronicler Jean Froissart wrote that at the time of Edward III's expedition of 1359, men of all ranks flocked to the English king's banner. Some came to acquire honor, but many came in order "to loot and pillage the fair and plenteous land of France."[31]

The Course of the War to 1419

Armies in the field were commanded by rulers themselves; by princes of the blood such as Edward III's son Edward, the "Black Prince"—so called because of the color of his armor—or by great aristocrats. Knights formed the cavalry; the peasantry served as infantrymen, pikemen, and archers. By medieval standards, the force was astronomically large. The costs of these armies stretched French and English resources to the breaking point.

The war was fought almost entirely in France and the Low Countries (Map 14.7). It consisted mainly of a series of random sieges and cavalry raids. In 1335 the French began supporting Scottish incursions into northern England, ravaging the countryside in Aquitaine, and sacking and burning Southampton and other English coastal towns. Naturally such tactics lent weight to Edward III's propaganda campaign. In fact, royal propaganda on both sides fostered a kind of early nationalism.

During the war's early stages, England was highly successful. At Crécy in northern France in 1346, English longbowmen scored a great victory over French knights and crossbowmen. Although the fire of the longbow was not very accurate, the longbow could be reloaded rapidly; thus English archers could send off three arrows to the French crossbowmen's one. The result was a blinding shower of arrows that unhorsed the French knights and caused mass confusion. The firing of cannon—probably the first use of artillery in the West—created further panic; thereupon the English horsemen charged and butchered the French.

This was not war according to the chivalric rules that Edward III would have preferred. The English victory at Crécy rested on the skill and swiftness of the yeomen archers, who had nothing at all to do with the chivalric ideals of aristocratic military glory for which the war was being fought. Ten years later, Edward the Black Prince, using the same tactics as at Crécy, smashed the French at

MAP 14.7 English Holdings in France During the Hundred Years' War The year 1429 marked the greatest extent of English holdings in France. Why was it unlikely that England could have held these territories permanently?

ENGLAND
Southampton
English Channel
Calais
FLANDERS
NORMANDY
CHAMPAGNE
Paris
Seine
BRITTANY
HOLY
ROMAN
EMPIRE
ANJOU
Loire
BLOIS
BURGUNDY
POITOU
Rhone
AQUITAINE
Bordeaux
Garonne
GASCONY
TOULOUSE

SPAIN
Mediterranean
Sea

1337
(before the Battle of Crécy)
Held by the kings
of England

0   100 Km.
0   100 Mi.

ENGLAND
English Channel
Calais
FLANDERS
Crécy
1346
Rouen
NORMANDY
CHAMPAGNE
Paris
Seine
BRITTANY
HOLY
ROMAN
EMPIRE
ANJOU
Loire
BLOIS
BURGUNDY
Poitiers
1356
POITOU
Rhone
AQUITAINE
Bordeaux
Garonne
GASCONY
TOULOUSE

SPAIN
Mediterranean
Sea

1360
(after the Battle of Poitiers)
Held by the kings
of England
✕ Major battles

0   100 Km.
0   100 Mi.

ENGLAND
Calais
FLANDERS
English Channel
Agincourt
1415
Rouen
Reims
NORMANDY
CHAMPAGNE
Paris
Seine
Domrémy
BRITTANY
Orléans
HOLY
ROMAN
EMPIRE
ANJOU
Loire
BLOIS
BURGUNDY
POITOU
Rhone
AQUITAINE
Bordeaux
Garonne
GASCONY
TOULOUSE

SPAIN
Mediterranean
Sea

ca 1429
(after the siege of Orléans)
Held by the kings
of England
✕ Major battle

0   100 Km.
0   100 Mi.

ENGLAND
Calais
FLANDERS
English Channel
NORMANDY
CHAMPAGNE
Paris
Seine
BRITTANY
HOLY
ROMAN
EMPIRE
ANJOU
Loire
BLOIS
BURGUNDY
POITOU
Rhone
AQUITAINE
Bordeaux
Garonne
GASCONY
TOULOUSE

SPAIN
Mediterranean
Sea

1453
(end of war)
Held by the kings
of England

0   100 Km.
0   100 Mi.

Poitiers, captured the French king, and held him for ransom. Again, at Agincourt in 1415, the chivalric English soldier-king Henry V (r. 1413–1422) gained the field over vastly superior numbers. Henry followed up his triumph at Agincourt with the reconquest of Normandy. By 1419 the English had advanced to the walls of Paris (see Map 14.7).

The French cause, however, was not lost. Although England had scored the initial victories, France won the war.

Joan of Arc and France's Victory

The ultimate success of France rests heavily on the actions of an obscure French peasant girl, Joan of Arc, whose vision and work revived French fortunes and led to victory. A great deal of pious and popular legend surrounds Joan the Maid because of her peculiar appearance on the scene, her astonishing success, her martyrdom, and her canonization by the Catholic church. The historical fact is that she saved the French monarchy.

Born in 1412 to well-to-do peasants in the village of Domrémy in Champagne, Joan of Arc grew up in a religious household. During adolescence she began to hear voices, which she later said belonged to Saint Michael, Saint Catherine, and Saint Margaret. In 1428 these voices spoke to her with great urgency, telling her that the dauphin (the uncrowned King Charles VII) had to be crowned and the English expelled from France. Joan went to the French court, persuaded the king to reject the rumor that he was illegitimate, and secured his support for her relief of the besieged city of Orléans.

Joan arrived before Orléans on April 28, 1429. Seventeen years old, she knew little of warfare and believed that if she could keep the French troops from swearing and frequenting whorehouses, victory would be theirs. On May 8 the English, weakened by disease and lack of supplies, withdrew from Orléans. Ten days later, Charles VII was crowned king at Reims. These two events marked the turning point in the war.

In 1430 England's allies, the Burgundians, captured Joan and sold her to the English. When the English handed her over to the ecclesiastical authorities for trial, the French court did not intervene. The English wanted Joan eliminated for obvious political reasons, but sorcery (witchcraft)

was the ostensible charge at her trial. Her claim of direct inspiration from God, thereby denying the authority of church officials, constituted heresy. In 1431 the court condemned her as a heretic and burned her at the stake in the marketplace at Rouen. A new trial in 1456 rehabilitated her name. In 1920 she was canonized and declared a holy maiden, and today she is revered as the second patron saint of France.

The relief of Orléans stimulated French pride and rallied French resources. At the same time, as the war dragged on, English demoralization increased. Slowly the French reconquered Normandy and, finally, ejected the English from Aquitaine. At the war's end in 1453, only the town of Calais remained in English hands.

Costs and Consequences

For both France and England, the war proved a disaster. In France the English had slaughtered thousands of soldiers and civilians. In the years after the sweep of the Black Death, this additional killing meant a grave loss of population. The English had laid waste to hundreds of thousands of acres of rich farmland, leaving the rural economy of many parts of France a shambles. The war had disrupted trade and the great fairs, drastically reducing French participation in international commerce. Defeat in battle and heavy taxation contributed to widespread dissatisfaction and aggravated peasants' grievances.

In England only the southern coastal ports experienced much destruction, and the demographic effects of the Black Death actually worked to restore the land-labor balance (see pages 440–441). The costs of the war, however, were tremendous. England spent over £5 million on the war effort, a huge sum in the fourteenth and fifteenth centuries. Manpower losses had great social consequences. The knights who ordinarily handled the work of local government as sheriffs, coroners, jurymen, and justices of the peace were abroad, and their absence contributed to the breakdown of order at the local level. The English government attempted to finance the war effort by raising taxes on the wool crop. Because of steadily increasing costs, the Flemish and Italian buyers could not afford English wool. Consequently, exports of raw wool slumped drastically between 1350 and 1450.

The long war also had a profound impact on the political lives of the two countries. Most notably, it stimulated the development of the English Parliament. Between 1250 and 1450, representative assemblies from several classes of society flourished in many European countries. Edward III's constant need for money to pay for the war compelled him to summon not only the great barons and bishops but knights of the shires and burgesses from the towns as well. Between the outbreak of the war in 1337 and the king's death in 1377, parliamentary assemblies met twenty-seven times.[32]

The frequency of the meetings is significant. Representative assemblies were becoming a habit. Knights and burgesses—or the "Commons," as they came to be called—recognized their mutual interests and began to meet apart from the great lords. The Commons gradually realized that they held the country's purse strings, and a parliamentary statute of 1341 required that all nonfeudal levies have parliamentary approval. When Edward III signed the law, he acknowledged that the king of England could not tax without Parliament's consent. Increasingly, during the war, money grants were tied to royal redress of grievances: if the government was to raise money, it had to correct the wrongs that its subjects protested.

In England theoretical consent to taxation and legislation was given in one assembly for the entire country. France had no such single assembly; instead, there were many regional or provincial assemblies. Why did a national representative assembly fail to develop in France? In fact, no one in France wanted a national assembly. Provincial differences and identities were very strong and provincial assemblies highly jealous of their independence. The French monarchy found the idea of representative assemblies thoroughly distasteful. Large gatherings of the nobility potentially or actually threatened the king's power. The advice of a councilor to King Charles VI (r. 1380–1422), "above all things be sure that no great assemblies of nobles or of *communes* take place in your kingdom," was accepted.[33] Charles VII (r. 1422–1461) even threatened to punish those proposing a national assembly.

The English Parliament was above all else a court of law, a place where justice was done and grievances remedied. No French assembly (except that of Brittany) had such competence. The national assembly in England met frequently. In France general assemblies were so rare that they never got the opportunity to develop precise procedures or to exercise judicial functions.

In both countries, however, the war did promote the growth of *nationalism*—the feeling of unity and identity that binds together a people who speak the same language, have a common ancestry and customs, and live in the same area. In the fourteenth century, nationalism took the form of hostility toward foreigners. Both Philip VI and Edward III drummed up support for the war by portraying the enemy as an alien, evil people. Edward III sought to justify his personal dynastic quarrel by linking it with England's national interests. As the Parliament Roll of 1348 states:

The Knights of the shires and the others of the Commons were told that they should withdraw together

Joan of Arc   This is how the court scribe who made this sketch in 1429, the year Joan raised the siege of Orleans, imagined her. He had never seen her. *(Source: Archives Nationales, Paris)*

and take good counsel as to how, for withstanding the malice of the said enemy and for the salvation of our said lord the King and his Kingdom of England . . . the King could be aided.[34]

After victories, each country experienced a surge of pride in its military strength. Just as English patriotism ran strong after Crécy and Poitiers, so French national confidence rose after Orléans. French national feeling demanded the expulsion of the enemy not merely from Normandy and Aquitaine but from French soil. Perhaps no one expressed this national consciousness better than Joan of Arc, when she exulted that the enemy had been "driven out of *France.*"

THE DECLINE OF THE CHURCH'S PRESTIGE

In times of crisis or disaster, people of all faiths have sought the consolation of religion. In the fourteenth century, however, the official Christian church offered very little solace. In fact, the leaders of the church added to the sorrow and misery of the times.

First, a violent dispute between the papacy and the kings of England and France badly damaged the prestige of the pope. In 1294 King Edward I of England and Philip the Fair of France declared war on each other. To finance this war, both kings laid taxes on the clergy. Kings had been taxing the church for decades. Pope Boniface VIII (r. 1294–1303), arguing from precedent, insisted that kings gain papal consent for taxation of the clergy and forbade churchmen to pay the taxes. But Edward and Philip refused to accept this decree, partly because it hurt royal finances and partly because the papal order threatened royal authority within their countries. Edward immediately denied the clergy the protection of the law, an action that meant its members could be attacked with impunity. Philip halted the shipment of all ecclesiastical revenue to Rome. Boniface had to back down.

Philip the Fair and his ministers continued their attack on all powers in France outside royal authority. Philip arrested a French bishop who was also the papal legate. When Boniface defended the ecclesiastical status and diplomatic immunity of the bishop, Philip replied with the trumped-up charge that the pope was a heretic. The papacy and the French monarchy waged a bitter war of propaganda. Finally, in 1302, in a letter entitled *Unam Sanctam* (because its opening sentence spoke of one holy Catholic church), Boniface insisted that all Christians are subject to the pope. Although the letter made no specific reference to Philip, it held that kings should submit to papal authority. Philip's university-trained advisers responded with an argument drawn from Roman law. They maintained that the king of France was completely sovereign in his kingdom and responsible to God alone. French mercenary troops went to Italy and arrested the aged pope. Although Boniface was soon freed, he died shortly afterward.

In order to control the church and its policies, Philip pressured Pope Clement V (r. 1305–1314) to settle in the city of Avignon, in southeastern France. Clement, critically ill with cancer, lacked the will to resist Philip.

The Babylonian Captivity

From 1309 to 1376, the popes lived in Avignon. This period in church history is often called the "Babylonian Captivity" (referring to the seventy years the ancient Hebrews were held captive in Mesopotamian Babylon). The Babylonian Captivity badly damaged papal prestige. The Avignon papacy reformed its financial administration and centralized its government. But the seven popes who resided at Avignon concentrated on bureaucratic matters to the exclusion of spiritual objectives. Some of them led austere lives there, but the general atmosphere was one of luxury and extravagance. The leadership of the church was cut off from its historic roots and the source of its ancient authority, the city of Rome. In the absence of the papacy, the Papal States in Italy lacked stability and good government. As long as the French crown dominated papal policy, papal influence in England (with which France was intermittently at war) and in Germany declined.

Many devout Christians urged the popes to return to Rome, and in 1377 Pope Gregory XI (r. 1370–1378) brought the papal court back to Rome. Unfortunately, he died shortly after the return. At Gregory's death, Roman citizens demanded an Italian pope who would remain in Rome. Determined to influence the papal *conclave* (the assembly of cardinals who chose the new pope) to elect an Italian, a Roman mob surrounded Saint Peter's Basilica, blocked the roads leading out of the city, and seized all boats on the Tiber River. Between the time of Gregory's death and the opening of the conclave, great pressure was put on the cardinals to elect an Italian. At the time, none of them protested this pressure. On April 7, 1378, after two ballots, they unanimously chose a distinguished administrator, the archbishop of Bari, Bartolomeo Prignano, who took the name Urban VI. Each of the cardinals swore that Urban had been elected "sincerely, freely, genuinely, and canonically."

Urban VI (r. 1378–1389) had excellent intentions for church reform. He wanted to abolish simony, *pluralism* (holding several church offices at the same time), absenteeism, clerical extravagance, and ostentation. These were the very abuses being increasingly criticized by Christian people across Europe. Unfortunately, Pope Urban went about the work of reform in a tactless, arrogant, and bullheaded manner. In the weeks following his coronation, Urban attacked clerical luxury, denouncing individual cardinals by name. He threatened to strike the cardinal archbishop of Amiens. Urban even threatened to excommunicate certain cardinals, and when he was advised that such excommunications would not be lawful unless the guilty had been warned three times, he shouted, "I can do anything, if it be my will and judgment."[35] Urban's quick temper and irrational behavior have led scholars to question his sanity. Whether he was medically insane or just drunk with power is a moot point. In any case, Urban's actions brought on disaster.

The cardinals declared Urban's election invalid because it had come about under threats from the Roman mob, and they asserted that Urban himself was excommunicated. Then they elected Cardinal Robert of Geneva, the cousin of King Charles V of France, as pope. Cardinal Robert took the name Clement VII. There were thus two popes: Urban at Rome and the "antipope" Clement VII (r. 1378–1394), who set himself up at Avignon in opposition to the legally elected Urban. So began the Great Schism, which divided Western Christendom until 1417.

The Great Schism

The powers of Europe aligned themselves with Urban or Clement along strictly political lines. France naturally recognized the French antipope, Clement. England, France's historic enemy, recognized Pope Urban. Scotland, whose attacks on England were subsidized by France, followed the French and supported Clement. The Holy Roman emperor, who bore ancient hostility to France, recognized Urban VI. At first the Italian city-states recognized Urban; but when he alienated them, they opted for Clement.

John of Spoleto, a professor at the law school at Bologna, eloquently summed up intellectual opinion of the schism: "The longer this schism lasts, the more it appears to be costing, and the more harm it does; scandal, massacres, ruination, . . . wars, rising tyranny, decreasing freedom.[36] The scandal "rent the seamless garment of Christ," as the church was called, and provoked horror and vigorous cries for reform. The common people, wracked by inflation, wars, and plague, were thoroughly confused about which pope was legitimate. At a time when ordinary Christians needed the consolation of religion and confidence in religious leaders, church officials were fighting among themselves for power.

The Conciliar Movement

Calls for church reform were not new. A half-century before the Great Schism, in 1324, Marsiglio of Padua, then rector of the University of Paris, had published *Defensor Pacis (The Defender of the Peace)*. Dealing as it did with the authority of state and church, *Defensor Pacis* proved to be one of the most controversial works written in the Middle Ages.

Marsiglio argued that the state was the great unifying power in society and that the church was subordinate to the state. He put forth the revolutionary ideas that the church had no inherent jurisdiction and should own no property. Authority in the Christian church, according to Marsiglio, should rest in a general council made up of laymen as well as priests and superior to the pope. These ideas directly contradicted the medieval notion of a society governed by the church and the state, with the church supreme. *Defensor Pacis* was condemned by the pope, and Marsiglio was excommunicated.

Even more earthshaking than the theories of Marsiglio of Padua were the ideas of the English scholar and theologian John Wyclif (1329–1384). Wyclif wrote that papal claims of temporal power had no foundation in the Scriptures and that the Scriptures alone should be the standard of Christian belief and practice. Sincere Christians, according to Wyclif, should read the Bible for themselves. In response to that idea, the first English translation of the Bible was produced and circulated.

Wyclif's views had broad social and economic significance. Wyclif urged that the church be stripped of its property. His idea that every Christian free of mortal sin possessed lordship was seized on by peasants in England during a revolt in 1381 and used to justify their goals. In advancing these views, Wyclif struck at the roots of medieval church structure and religious practices. Consequently, he has been hailed as a precursor of the Reformation of the sixteenth century. Although Wyclif's ideas were vigorously condemned by ecclesiastical authorities, they were widely disseminated by humble clerics and enjoyed great popularity in the early fifteenth century. In Bohemia, they were spread by John Hus (1369?–1415), rector of the University of Prague.

In response to continued calls throughout Europe for a council, the two colleges of cardinals—one at Rome, the other at Avignon—summoned a council at Pisa in 1409. A distinguished gathering of prelates and theologians deposed both popes and selected another. Neither the Avignon pope nor the Roman pope would resign, however, and the appalling result was a threefold schism.

Finally, because of the pressure of the German emperor Sigismund (r. 1411–1437), a great council met at the imperial city of Constance from 1414 to 1418. It had three objectives: to end the schism, to reform the church "in head and members" (from top to bottom), and to wipe out heresy. The council condemned John Hus, and he was burned at the stake. The council accepted the resignation of the Roman pope and deposed the pope chosen at Pisa and the antipope at Avignon. A conclave elected a new leader, the Roman cardinal Colonna, who took the name Martin V (r. 1417–1431).

Martin proceeded to dissolve the council. Nothing was done about reform. The schism was over, and though councils subsequently met at Basel and at Ferrara-Florence, in 1450 the papacy held a jubilee, celebrating its triumph over the conciliar movement. Later in the fifteenth century, the papacy concentrated on Italian problems to the exclusion of universal Christian interests. But the schism and the conciliar movement had exposed the crying need for ecclesiastical reform, thus laying the foundations for the great reform efforts of the sixteenth century.

THE LIFE OF THE PEOPLE

In the fourteenth century, economic and political difficulties, disease, and war profoundly affected the lives of European peoples. Decades of slaughter and destruction, punctuated by the decimating visits of the Black Death, made a grave economic situation virtually disastrous. In many parts of France and the Low Countries, fields lay in ruin or untilled for lack of labor power. In England, as taxes increased, criticisms of government policy and mismanagement multiplied. Crime, always a factor in social history, aggravated economic troubles, and throughout Europe the frustrations of the common people erupted into revolts. Nevertheless, marriage and the local parish church continued to be the center of life for most people.

Marriage

Life for those who were not clerics or nuns meant married life. The community expected people to marry. For a boy, childhood and youth included farm experience or training in a trade or skill; for a girl, childhood was preparation for marriage. In addition to the thousands of chores involved in running a household, girls learned obedience, or at least subordination. Adulthood for women meant living as a wife or widow.

In any case, sweeping statements about marriage in the Middle Ages have limited validity. Most peasants were illiterate and left slight record of their feelings toward their spouses or about marriage as an institution. The gentry, however, often could write, and letters exchanged between Margaret and John Paston, upper-middle-class people who lived in Norfolk, England, in the fifteenth century, provide important evidence of the experience of one couple.

John and Margaret Paston were married about 1439, after an arrangement concluded entirely by their parents. John spent most of his time in London fighting through the law courts to increase his family properties and business interests. Margaret remained in Norfolk to supervise the family lands. Her responsibilities involved managing the Paston estates, hiring workers, collecting rents, ordering supplies for the large household, hearing complaints and settling disputes among tenants, and marketing her crops. In these duties she proved herself a shrewd business person. Moreover, when an army of over a thousand men led by the aristocratic thug Lord Moleyns attacked her house, she successfully withstood the siege. When the Black Death entered her area, Margaret moved her family to safety.

Margaret Paston did all this on top of raising eight children (there were probably other children who did not survive childhood). Her husband died before she was forty-three, and she later conducted the negotiations for the children's marriages. Her children's futures, like her estate management, were planned with an eye toward economic and social advancement. When one daughter secretly married the estate bailiff, an alliance considered beneath her, the girl was cut off from the family as if she were dead.[37]

The many letters surviving between Margaret and John reveal slight tenderness toward their children. They seem to have reserved their love for each other, and during many of John's frequent absences they wrote to express mutual affection and devotion. How typical the Paston relationship was, modern historians cannot say, but the marriage of John and Margaret, though completely arranged by their parents, was based on respect, responsibility, and love.[38]

At what age did people usually marry? For girls, population surveys at Prato, in Italy, place the age at 16.3 years in 1372 and 21.1 in 1470. Chaucer's Wife of Bath says that she married first in her twelfth year. Recent research has indicated that in the Hohenzollern family in the later Middle Ages "five brides were between 12 and 13; five about 14, and five about 15."

Men were older when they married. An Italian chronicler writing about 1354 says that men did not marry before the age of 30. Chaucer's Wife of Bath describes her first three husbands as "goode

Prostitute Invites a Traveling Merchant Poverty and male violence drove women into prostitution, which, though denounced by moralists, was accepted as a normal part of the medieval social fabric. In the cities and larger towns where prostitution flourished, public officials passed laws requiring prostitutes to wear a special mark on their clothing, regulated hours of business, forbade women to drag men into their houses, and denied business to women with the "burning sickness," gonorrhea. (Source: The Bodleian Library, Oxford)

men, and rich, and old." Among seventeen males in the noble Hohenzollern family, eleven were over 20 years when married, five between 18 and 19, one 16. The general pattern in late medieval Europe was marriage between men in their middle or late twenties and women under twenty.[39] The later marriage age of men affected the number of children a couple had.

With marriage for men postponed, was there any socially accepted sexual outlet? Recent research on the southern French province of Languedoc in the fourteenth and fifteenth centuries has revealed the establishment of legal houses of prostitution.[40] Municipal authorities in Toulouse, Montpellier, Albi, and other towns set up houses or red-light districts either outside the city walls or away from respectable neighborhoods. The towns of Languedoc were not unique. In the cities and larger towns where prostitution flourished, public officials passed laws requiring prostitutes to wear a special mark on their clothing, regulating hours of business, forbidding women to drag men into their houses, and denying business to women with the "burning sickness," gonorrhea. Prostitution thus passed from being a private concern to a social matter requiring public supervision. Prostitution was an urban phenomenon because only populous towns had large numbers of unmarried young men, communities of transient merchants, and a culture accustomed to a cash exchange.

Although the risk of disease limited the number of years a woman could practice this profession, many women prospered. Archives in several cities show expensive properties bought by women who named their occupation as prostitution. Legalized prostitution suggests that public officials believed the prostitute could make a positive contribution to the society; it does not mean the prostitute was respected. Rather, she was scorned and distrusted. Legalized brothels also reflect a greater tolerance for male than for female sexuality.[41]

In the later Middle Ages, as earlier—indeed, until the late nineteenth century—economic factors rather than romantic love or physical attraction determined whom and when a person married. A young agricultural laborer on a manor had to wait until he had sufficient land. A journeyman craftsman in an urban guild faced the same material difficulties. Most men had to wait until their fathers died or yielded their holding. Prudent young men selected (or their parents selected for them) girls who would bring the most land or money to the union. Once a couple married, the union ended only with the death of one partner.

Deep emotional bonds knit members of medieval families. Most parents delighted in their children, and the church encouraged a cult of paternal care. The church stressed its right to govern and sanctify marriage, and it emphasized monogamy. Tight moral and emotional unity within marriages resulted.[42]

Divorce did not exist in the Middle Ages, although annulments were granted in extraordinary circumstances, such as male impotence, on the grounds that a lawful marriage had never existed. The church held that a marriage validly entered into could not be dissolved. A valid marriage consisted of the mutual oral consent or promise of two parties. Church theologians of the day urged that marriage be publicized by *banns*, or announcements made in the parish church, and that the couple's union be celebrated and witnessed in a church ceremony and blessed by a priest.

A great number of couples did not observe the church's regulations. Some treated marriage as a private act. They made the promise and spoke the words of marriage to each other without witnesses and then proceeded to enjoy the sexual pleasures of marriage. This practice led to a great number of disputes, for one or the other of the two parties could later deny having made a marriage agreement. The records of the ecclesiastical courts reveal many cases arising from privately made contracts. Evidence survives of marriages contracted in a garden, in a blacksmith's shop, at a tavern, and, predictably, in a bed.[43]

Life in the Parish

In the later Middle Ages, the land and the parish remained the focus of life for the European peasantry. Work on the land continued to be performed collectively. All men, for example, cooperated in the annual tasks of planting and harvesting. The close association of the cycle of agriculture and the liturgy of the Christian calendar endured. The parish priest blessed the fields before the annual planting, offering prayers on behalf of the people for a good crop. If the harvest was a rich one, the priest led the processions and celebrations of thanksgiving.

How did the common people feel about their work? Since the vast majority were illiterate and inarticulate, it is difficult to say. It is known that the peasants hated the ancient services and obligations on the lords' lands and tried to get them commuted for money rents. When lords attempted to reimpose service duties, the peasants revolted.

In the thirteenth century, the craft guilds provided the small minority of men and women living in towns and cities with the psychological satisfaction of involvement in the manufacture of a superior product. The craft guilds set high standards for their merchandise. Guild members also had economic security. The guilds looked after the sick, the poor, the widowed, and the orphaned. Masters and employees worked side by side.

In the fourteenth century, those ideal conditions began to change. The fundamental objective of the craft guild was to maintain a monopoly on its product, and to do so recruitment and promotion were carefully restricted. Some guilds required a high entrance fee for apprentices; others admitted only relatives of members. Apprenticeship increasingly lasted a long time, seven years. Even after a young man had satisfied all the tests for full membership in the guild and had attained the rank of master, he might need special connections just to join a guild. Women began to experience exclusion. A careful study of the records of forty-two craft guilds in Cologne, for example, shows that in the fifteenth century all but six became virtual male preserves, either greatly restricting women's participation or allowing so few female members that they cannot be considered mixed guilds.[44] The larger a particular business was, the greater was the likelihood that the master did not know his employees. The separation of master and journeyman and the decreasing number of openings for master craftsmen created serious frustrations. Strikes and riots occurred in the Flemish towns, in France, and in England.

The recreation of all classes reflected the fact that late medieval society was organized for war and violence was common. The aristocracy engaged in tournaments or jousts; archery and wrestling were popular among ordinary people. Everyone enjoyed the cruel sports of bullbaiting and bearbaiting. The hangings and mutilations of criminals were exciting and well-attended festive events. Chroniclers exulted in describing executions, murders, and massacres. Here a monk gleefully describes the gory execution of William Wallace in 1305:

Wilielmus Waleis, a robber given to sacrilege, arson and homicide . . . was condemned to most cruel but justly deserved death. He was drawn through the streets of London at the tails of horses, until he reached a gallows of unusual height, there he was suspended by a halter; but taken down while yet alive, he

Domestic Brawl In all ages the hen-pecked husband has been a popular subject for jests. This elaborate woodcarving from a fifteenth-century English choir stall shows the husband holding distaff and ball of thread, symbolic of wife's work as "spinster," while his wife thrashes him. *(Source: Royal Commission on the Historical Monuments of England)*

was mutilated, his bowels torn out and burned in a fire, his head then cut off, his body divided into four, and his quarters transmitted to four principal parts of Scotland.[45]

Violence was as English as roast beef and plum pudding, as French as bread, cheese, and *potage.*

If violent entertainment was not enough to dispel life's cares, alcohol was also available. Beer or ale commonly provided solace to the poor, and the frequency of drunkenness reflects their terrible frustrations.

Upper-class violence and crime played a part in parish life. Many nobles turned to crime as a way of raising money. The fourteenth and fifteenth centuries witnessed a great deal of "fur-collar crime," so called for the miniver fur that members of the nobility alone were allowed to wear on their collars. England provides a good case study of upper-class crime.

Fur-collar crime rarely involved such felonies as homicide, robbery, rape, and arson. Instead, nobles used their superior social status to rob and extort from the weak and then to corrupt the judicial process. The rich suffered too. Attacks on the rich often took the form of kidnapping and extortion. Individuals were grabbed in their homes, and wealthy travelers were seized on the highways and held for ransom.[46]

Fur-collar criminals were terrorists, but like some twentieth-century white-collar criminals who commit nonviolent crimes, medieval aristocratic criminals got away with their outrages. When accused of wrongdoing, fur-collar criminals intimidated witnesses. They threatened jurors. They used "pull" or cash to bribe judges. As a fourteenth-century English judge wrote to a young nobleman, "For the love of your father I have hindered charges being brought against you and have prevented execution of indictment actually made."[47] Criminal activity by nobles continued decade after decade because governments were too weak to stop it.

During the fourteenth and fifteenth centuries, the laity began to exercise increasing control over parish affairs. Churchmen were criticized. The constant quarrels of the mendicant orders (the Franciscans and Dominicans), the mercenary and grasping attitude of the parish clergy, the scandal of the Great Schism and a divided Christendom—all these did much to weaken the spiritual mystique of the clergy in the popular mind. The laity steadily took responsibility for the management of parish lands. Lay people organized associations to vote on and purchase furnishings for the church. And ordinary lay people secured jurisdiction over the structure of the church building, its vestments, books, and furnishings. These new responsibilities of the laity reflect the increased dignity of parishioners in the late Middle Ages.[48]

Peasant Revolts

Peasant revolts occurred often in the Middle Ages. Early in the thirteenth century, the French preacher Jacques de Vitry asked rhetorically, "How many serfs have killed their lords or burnt their castles?"[49] And in the fourteenth and fifteenth centuries, social and economic conditions caused a great increase in peasant uprisings (Map 14.8).

In 1358, when French taxation for the Hundred Years' War fell heavily on the poor, the frustrations of the French peasantry exploded in a massive uprising called the *Jacquerie,* after a supposedly happy agricultural laborer, Jacques Bonhomme (Good Fellow). Peasants in Picardy and Champagne went on the rampage. Crowds swept through the countryside slashing the throats of nobles, burning their castles, raping their wives and daughters, killing or maiming their horses and cattle. Peasants blamed the nobility for oppressive taxes, for the criminal brigandage of the countryside, for defeat in war, and for the general misery. Artisans, small merchants, and parish priests joined the peasants. Urban and rural groups committed terrible destruction, and for several weeks the nobles were on the defensive. Then the upper class united to repress the revolt with merciless ferocity. Thousands of the "Jacques," innocent as well as guilty, were cut down.

This forcible suppression of social rebellion, without some effort to alleviate its underlying causes, could only serve as a stopgap measure and drive protest underground. Between 1363 and 1484, serious peasant revolts swept the Auvergne; in 1380 uprisings occurred in the Midi; and in 1420 they erupted in the Lyonnais region of France.

The Peasants' Revolt in England in 1381, involving perhaps a hundred thousand people, was probably the largest single uprising of the entire Middle Ages (see Map 14.8). The causes of the rebellion were complex and varied from place to

The Jacquerie Because social revolt on the part of the war-weary, frustrated poor seemed to threaten the natural order of Christian society during the fourteenth and fifteenth centuries, the upper classes everywhere exacted terrible vengeance on peasants and artisans. In this scene some *jacques* are cut down, some beheaded, and others drowned. *(Source: Bibliothèque Nationale, Paris)*

place. In general, though, the thirteenth century had witnessed the steady commutation of labor services for cash rents, and the Black Death had drastically cut the labor supply. As a result, peasants demanded higher wages and fewer manorial obligations. Thirty years earlier the parliamentary Statute of Laborers (1351) had declared:

Whereas to curb the malice of servants who after the pestilence were idle and unwilling to serve without securing excessive wages, it was recently ordained . . . that such servants, both men and women, shall be bound to serve in return for salaries and wages that were customary . . . five or six years earlier.[50]

This statute was an attempt by landlords to freeze wages and social mobility. It could not be enforced. As a matter of fact, the condition of the English peasantry steadily improved in the course of the fourteenth century. Some scholars believe that the peasantry in most places was better off in the period 1350 to 1450 than it had been for centuries before or was to be for four centuries after.

Why then was the outburst in 1381 so serious? It was provoked by a crisis of rising expectations. The relative prosperity of the laboring classes led to demands that the upper classes were unwilling to grant. Unable to climb higher, the peasants found release for their economic frustrations in revolt. But economic grievances combined with other factors. The south of England, where the revolt broke out, had been subjected to frequent and destructive French raids. The English government did little to protect the south, and villages grew increasingly scared and insecure. Moreover, decades of aristocratic violence, much of it perpetrated against the weak peasantry, had bred hostility and bitterness.

MAP 14.8 Fourteenth-Century Peasant Revolts In the later Middle Ages and early modern times, peasant and urban uprisings were endemic, as common as factory strikes in the industrial world. The threat of insurrection served to check unlimited exploitation.

The straw that broke the camel's back in England was the reimposition of a head tax on all adult males. Although the tax met widespread opposition in 1380, the royal council ordered the sheriffs to collect it again in 1381 on penalty of a huge fine. Beginning with assaults on the tax collectors, the uprising in England followed much the same course as had the Jacquerie in France. Castles and manors were sacked; manorial records were destroyed. Many nobles, including the archbishop of Canterbury, who had ordered the collection of the tax, were murdered.

Although the center of the revolt lay in the highly populated and economically advanced south and east, sections of the north and the Midlands also witnessed rebellions. Violence took different forms in different places. The townspeople of Cambridge expressed their hostility toward the university by sacking one of the colleges and building a bonfire of academic property. In towns containing skilled Flemish craftsmen, fear of competition led to their being brutalized. Urban discontent merged with rural violence. Apprentices and journeymen, frustrated because the highest guild positions were closed to them, rioted.

The boy-king Richard II (r. 1377–1399) met the leaders of the revolt, agreed to charters ensuring peasants' freedom, tricked them with false promises, and then proceeded to crush the uprising. Although the nobility tried to restore ancient duties of serfdom, virtually a century of freedom had elapsed, and the commutation of manorial services continued. Rural serfdom had disappeared in England by 1550.

Albrecht Dürer: The Four Horsemen of the Apocalypse   From right to left, representatives of war, strife, famine, and death gallop across Christian society, leaving thousands dead or in misery. The horrors of the age made this subject extremely popular in art, literature, and sermons. *(Source: Courtesy, Museum of Fine Arts, Boston)*

Conditions in England and France were not unique. In Florence in 1378, the *ciompi,* the poor propertyless workers, revolted. Serious social trouble also occurred in Lübeck, Brunswick, and other German cities. In Spain in 1391, aristocratic attempts to impose new forms of serfdom, combined with demands for tax relief, led to massive working-class and peasant uprisings in Seville and Barcelona. These took the form of vicious attacks on Jewish communities. Rebellions and uprisings everywhere reveal deep peasant and working-class frustration and the general socioeconomic crisis of the time.

SUMMARY

The High Middle Ages was one of the most creative periods in the history of Western society. Advances were made in the evolution of strong government and urban life, economic development, architectural design, and education. Through the instruments of justice and finance, the kings of England and France attacked feudal rights and provincial practices and built centralized bureaucracies. In so doing, these rulers laid the foundations for modern national states. The German emperors, preoccupied with Italian affairs and with a quest for the imperial crown, allowed feudal and local interests to triumph.

Medieval cities recruited people from the countryside and brought into being a new social class, the middle class. Cities provided economic opportunity, which, together with the revival of long-distance trade and a new capitalistic spirit, led to greater wealth, a higher standard of living, and upward social mobility. Medieval townspeople built soaring Gothic cathedrals, and universities, institutions of higher learning unique to the West, emerged from cathedral and municipal schools.

By the later Middle Ages, however, preachers likened the crises of their times to the Four Horsemen of the Apocalypse in the Book of Revelation, who brought famine, war, disease, and death. The crises of the fourteenth and fifteenth centuries were acids that burned deeply into the fabric of traditional medieval European society. Bad weather brought poor harvests, which contributed to the international economic depression. Disease, over which people also had little control, fostered widespread depression and dissatisfaction. Population losses caused by the Black Death and the Hundred Years' War encouraged the working classes to try to profit from the labor shortage by selling their services higher: they wanted to move up the economic ladder. The ideas of thinkers like John Wyclif fanned the flames of social discontent. When peasant frustrations exploded in uprisings, the frightened nobility and upper middle class joined to crush the revolts and condemn heretical preachers as agitators of social rebellion. But the war had heightened social consciousness among the poor.

The Hundred Years' War served as a catalyst for the development of representative government in England. The royal policy of financing the war through Parliament-approved taxation gave the middle classes an increased sense of their economic power. They would pay taxes in return for some influence in shaping royal policies.

In France, by contrast, the war stiffened opposition to national assemblies. The disasters that wracked France decade after decade led the French people to believe that the best solutions to complicated problems lay not in an assembly but in the hands of a strong monarch.

Religion remained the cement that held society together. European culture was a Christian culture. But although the Church exercised leadership of Christian society in the High Middle Ages, the clash between the papacy and the kings of France and England at the end of the thirteenth century seriously challenged papal power. And the Great Schism weakened the prestige of the church and people's faith in papal authority. The conciliar movement, by denying the church's universal sovereignty, strengthened the claims of secular rulers to jurisdiction over all their peoples. The later Middle Ages witnessed a steady shift of basic loyalty from the church to the emerging national states.

NOTES

1. D. C. Douglas and G. E. Greenaway, eds., *English Historical Documents,* vol. 2 (London: Eyre & Spottiswoode, 1961), p. 853.
2. See G. M. Spiegel, "The Cult of Saint Denis and Capetian Kingship," *Journal of Medieval History* 1 (April 1975): 43–65, esp. 59–64.

3. J. Boswell, *Christianity, Social Tolerance, and Homosexuality: Gay People in Western Europe from the Beginning of the Christian Era to the Fourteenth Century* (Chicago: University of Chicago Press, 1980), pp. 270–293; the quotation is from p. 293. For alternative interpretations, see K. Thomas, "Rescuing Homosexual History," *New York Review of Books,* December 4, 1980, pp. 26ff.; and J. DuQ. Adams, *Speculum* 56 (April 1981): 350ff. For the French monarchy's persecution of the Jews, see J. W. Baldwin, *The Government of Philip Augustus: Foundations of French Royal Power in the Middle Ages* (Berkeley: University of California Press, 1986), pp. 51–52; and W. C. Jordan, *The French Monarchy and the Jews* (Philadelphia: University of Pennsylvania Press, 1989).

4. J. C. Russell, *Medieval Regions and Their Cities* (Bloomington: University of Indiana Press, 1972), p. 91.

5. Ibid., pp. 113–117.

6. Quoted in R. S. Lopez, "Of Towns and Trade," in *Life and Thought in the Early Middle Ages,* ed. R. S. Hoyt (Minneapolis: University of Minnesota Press, 1967), p. 33.

7. H. Pirenne, *Economic and Social History of Medieval Europe* (New York: Harcourt, Brace, 1956), p. 53.

8. See D. Herlihy, *Medieval and Renaissance Pistoia: The Social History of an Italian Town, 1200–1430* (New Haven, Conn.: Yale University Press, 1967), p. 257.

9. Douglas and Greenaway, pp. 969–970.

10. H. Rothwell, ed., *English Historical Documents,* vol. 3 (London: Eyre & Spottiswoode, 1975), p. 854.

11. See P. Dollinger, *The German Hansa,* trans. and ed. D. S. Ault and S. H. Steinberg (Stanford, Calif.: Stanford University Press, 1970).

12. C. M. Cipolla, *Before the Industrial Revolution: European Society and Economy, 1000–1700,* 2d ed. (New York: Norton, 1980), p. 197.

13. R. S. Lopez, "The Trade of Medieval Europe: The South," in *The Cambridge Economic History of Europe,* vol. 2, ed. M. M. Postan and E. E. Rich (Cambridge, England: Cambridge University Press, 1952), p. 289.

14. Quoted in H. E. Sigerist, *Civilization and Disease* (Chicago: University of Chicago Press, 1943), p. 102.

15. Quoted in J. H. Mundy, *Europe in the High Middle Ages, 1150–1309* (New York: Basic Books, 1973), pp. 474–475.

16. E. Panofsky, trans. and ed., *Abbot Suger on the Abbey Church of St. Denis and Its Art Treasures* (Princeton, N.J.: Princeton University Press, 1946), p. 101.

17. See J. Gimpel, *The Cathedral Builders* (New York: Grove Press, 1961), pp. 42–49.

18. J. B. Freed, *The Friars and German Society in the Thirteenth Century* (Cambridge, Mass.: Mediaeval Academy of America, 1977), p. 8.

19. Ibid., p. 9.

20. See F. Oakley, *The Western Church in the Later Middle Ages* (Ithaca, N.Y.: Cornell University Press, 1979), p. 175.

21. See Freed, pp. 119–128.

22. Ibid., esp. p. 125.

23. W. H. McNeill, *Plagues and Peoples* (New York: Doubleday, 1976), pp. 151–168.

24. Quoted in P. Ziegler, *The Black Death* (Harmondsworth, England: Pelican Books, 1969), p. 20.

25. J. M. Rigg, trans., *The Decameron of Giovanni Boccaccio* (London: J. M. Dent & Sons, 1903), p. 6.

26. Ziegler, pp. 232–239.

27. J. Hatcher, *Plague, Population and the English Economy, 1348–1530* (London: Macmillan Education, 1986), p. 33.

28. See G. P. Cuttino, "Historical Revision: The Causes of the Hundred Years' War," *Speculum* 31 (July 1956): 463–472.

29. N. F. Cantor, *The English: A History of Politics and Society to 1760* (New York: Simon & Schuster, 1967), p. 260.

30. J. Barnie, *War in Medieval English Society: Social Values and the Hundred Years' War* (Ithaca, N.Y.: Cornell University Press, 1974), p. 6.

31. Quoted in Barnie, p. 34.

32. See M. M. Postan, "The Costs of the Hundred Years' War," *Past and Present* 27 (April 1964): 34–63; G. O. Sayles, *The King's Parliament of England* (New York: Norton, 1974), esp. pp. 137–141.

33. Quoted in P. S. Lewis, "The Failure of the Medieval French Estates," *Past and Present* 23 (November 1962): 6.

34. C. Stephenson and G. F. Marcham, eds., *Sources of English Constitutional History,* rev. ed. (New York: Harper & Row, 1972), p. 217.

35. Quoted in J. H. Smith, *The Great Schism 1378: The Disintegration of the Medieval Papacy* (New York: Weybright & Talley, 1970), p. 141.

36. Ibid., p. 15.

37. A. S. Haskell, "The Paston Women on Marriage in Fifteenth Century England," *Viator* 4 (1973): 459–469.

38. Ibid., p. 471.

39. See D. Herlihy, *Medieval Households* (Cambridge, Mass.: Harvard University Press, 1985), pp. 103–111.

40. L. L. Otis, *Prostitution in Medieval Society: The History of an Urban Institution in Languedoc* (Chicago: University of Chicago Press, 1987), p. 2.

41. Ibid., pp. 25–27, 64–66, 100–106.

42. Herlihy, *Medieval Households,* pp. 118–130.

43. See R. H. Helmholz, *Marriage Litigation in Medi-*

eval England (Cambridge: Cambridge University Press, 1974), pp. 28–29, et passim.

44. See M. C. Howell, *Women, Production, and Patriarchy in Late Medieval Cities* (Chicago: University of Chicago Press, 1986), pp. 134–135.

45. A. F. Scott, ed., *Everyone a Witness: The Plantagenet Age* (New York: Thomas Y. Crowell, 1976), p. 263.

46. B. A. Hanawalt, "Fur Collar Crime: The Pattern of Crime Among the Fourteenth-Century English Nobility," *Journal of Social History* 8 (Spring 1975): 1–14.

47. Quoted ibid., p. 7.

48. See E. Mason, "The Role of the English Parishioner, 1000–1500," *Journal of Ecclesiastical History* 27 (January 1976): 17–29.

49. Quoted in M. Bloch, *French Rural History,* trans. J. Sondeimer (Berkeley: University of California Press, 1966), p. 169.

50. Stephenson and Marcham, p. 225.

SUGGESTED READING

The achievements of the High Middle Ages have attracted considerable scholarly attention. Three general surveys of the period 1050 to 1300 are especially recommended: J. R. Strayer, *Western Europe in the Middle Ages* (1955), a masterful synthesis; J. W. Baldwin, *The Scholastic Culture of the Middle Ages* (1971); and F. Heer, *The Medieval World* (1963).

R. A. Brown, *The Normans* (1983), revitalizes the old thesis that the conquerors of England and Sicily were an exceptionally creative force in the eleventh and twelfth centuries. D. Howarth, *1066: The Year of the Conquest* (1981), is a lively and cleverly written account, from Norman, Scandinavian, and English perspectives, of the Norman conquest of England. G. O. Sayles, *The Medieval Foundations of England* (1961), traces political and social conditions to the end of the twelfth century.

Students interested in crime, society, and legal developments will find the following works useful and sound: J. B. Given, *Society and Homicide in Thirteenth-Century England* (1977); J. M. Carter, *Rape in Medieval England: An Historical and Sociological Study* (1985); R. C. Palmer, *The County Courts of Medieval England, 1150–1350* (1982); and the same scholar's *The Whilton Dispute, 1264–1380: A Social-Legal Study of Dispute Settlement in Medieval England* (1984). Elizabeth M. Hallam, *Domesday Book Through Nine Centuries* (1986), is an excellent recent appreciation of that important document. J. R. Strayer, *On the Medieval Origins of the Modern State* (1970), is a fine synthesis of political, legal, and administrative developments.

For France, both E. Hallam, *The Capetian Kings of France, 987–1328* (1980), and R. Fawtier, *The Capetian Kings of France* (1962), are readable introductions. On Germany, G. Barraclough, *The Origins of Modern Germany* (1963), provides an excellent explanation of the problems and peculiarities of the Holy Roman Empire; this is a fine example of the Marxist interpretation of medieval history. M. Pacaut, *Frederick Barbarossa* (trans. A. J. Pomerans, 1980), is perhaps the best one-volume treatment of that important ruler, but P. Munz, *Frederick Barbarossa* (1979), is also important.

For the economic revival of Europe, see, in addition to the titles by Dollinger, Herlihy, Lopez, and Russell given in the Notes, G. J. Hodgett, *A Social and Economic History of Medieval Europe* (1974), a broad survey; C. M. Cipolla, *Before the Industrial Revolution: European Society and Economy, 1000–1700* (1980), which draws on recent research to treat demographic shifts, technological change, and business practices; and R. Lopez, *The Commercial Revolution of the Middle Ages* (1976). The effect of climate on population and economic growth is discussed in the remarkable work of E. L. Ladurie, *Times of Feast, Times of Famine: A History of Climate Since the Year 1000* (trans. B. Bray, 1971).

Students interested in the origins of medieval towns and cities will learn how historians use the evidence of coins, archeology, tax records, geography, and laws in J. F. Benton, ed., *Town Origins: The Evidence of Medieval England* (1968). H. Pirenne, *Early Democracy in the Low Countries* (1932), is an important and standard work. H. Saalman, *Medieval Cities* (1968), gives a fresh description of the layouts of medieval cities, with an emphasis on Germany, and shows how they were places of production and exchange. R. Muir, *The English Village* (1980), surveys many aspects of ordinary people's daily lives. For readability, few works surpass J. and F. Gies, *Life in a Medieval City* (1973).

For the new currents of thought in the High Middle Ages, see C. Brooke, *The Twelfth Century Renaissance* (1970), a splendidly illustrated book with copious quotations from the sources; E. Gilson, *Héloise and Abélard* (1960), which treats the medieval origins of modern humanism against the background of Abelard the teacher; C. H. Haskins, *The Renaissance of the Twelfth Century* (1971), a classic; and C. W. Hollister, ed., *The Twelfth Century Renaissance* (1969), a well-constructed anthology with source materials on many aspects of twelfth-century culture. N. Orme, *English Schools in the Middle Ages* (1973), focuses on the significance of schools and literacy in English medieval society. J. Leclercq, *The Love of Learning and the Desire of God* (1974), discusses monastic literary culture. For the development of literacy among lay people and the formation of a literate mentality, the advanced student should see M. T. Clanchy, *From Memory to Written Record: England, 1066–1307* (1979).

On the medieval universities, C. H. Haskins, *The Rise of the Universities* (1959), is a good introduction; H.

Rashdall, *The Universities of Europe in the Middle Ages* (1936), is the standard scholarly work. G. Leff, *Paris and Oxford Universities in the Thirteenth and Fourteenth Centuries* (1968), includes a useful bibliography.

N. Pevsner, *An Outline of European Architecture* (1963), provides a good general introduction to Romanesque and Gothic architecture. The following studies are all valuable for the evolution and development of the Gothic style: J. Harvey, *The Gothic World* (1969); the same author's *The Master Builders* (1971); P. Frankl, *The Gothic* (1960); O. von Simson, *The Gothic Cathedral* (1973); and J. Bony, *French Gothic Architecture of the 12th and 13th Centuries* (1983). D. Grivot and G. Zarnecki, *Gislebertus, Sculptor of Autun* (1961), is the finest appreciation of Romanesque architecture written in English. For the actual work of building, see D. Macaulay, *Cathedral: The Story of Its Construction* (1973), a prize-winning, simply written, and cleverly illustrated re-creation of the problems and duration of cathedral building. J. Gimpel, *The Cathedral Builders* (1961), explores the engineering problems involved in cathedral building and places the subject within its social context. E. G. Holt, ed., *A Documentary History of Art* (1957), contains source materials useful for writing papers. J. Gimpel, *The Medieval Machine: The Industrial Revolution of the Middle Ages* (1977), an extremely useful book, discusses the mechanical and scientific problems involved in early industrialization.

For the Black Death, see P. Ziegler, *The Black Death* (1969), a fascinating and highly readable study. For the social implications of disease, see W. H. McNeill, *Plagues and Peoples* (1976); F. F. Cartwright, *Disease and History* (1972); and H. E. Sigerist, *Civilization and Disease* (1970). For the economic effects of the plague, see J. Hatcher, *Plague, Population, and the English Economy, 1348–1550* (1977).

The standard study of the long military conflicts of the fourteenth and fifteenth centuries remains E. Perroy, *The Hundred Years' War* (1959). J. Barnie's *War in Medieval English Society,* treats the attitudes of patriots, intellectuals, and the general public. D. Seward, *The Hundred Years' War: The English in France, 1337–1453* (1981), tells an exciting story, and J. Keegan, *The Face of Battle* (1977), chap. 2, "Agincourt," describes what war meant to the ordinary soldier. B. Tuchman, *A Distant Mirror: The Calamitous Fourteenth Century* (1980), gives a vivid picture of many facets of fourteenth-century life while concentrating on the war. The best treatment of the financial costs of the war is probably M. M. Postan, "The Costs of the Hundred Years' War." E. Searle and R. Burghart, "The Defense of England and the Peasants' Revolt," *Viator* 3 (1972), is a fascinating study of the peasants' changing social attitudes. R. Barber, *The Knight and Chivalry* (1982), and M. Keen, *Chivalry* (1984), give fresh interpretations of the cultural importance of chivalry.

For political and social conditions in the fourteenth and fifteenth centuries, see the works by Lewis, Sayles, Bloch, Hanawalt, and Helmholz cited in the Notes. The following studies are also useful: P. S. Lewis, *Later Medieval France: The Polity* (1968); L. Romier, *A History of France* (1962); A. R. Meyers, *Parliaments and Estates in Europe to 1789* (1975); R. G. Davies and J. H. Denton, eds., *The English Parliament in the Middle Ages* (1981); I. Kershaw, "The Great Famine and Agrarian Crisis in England, 1315–1322," *Past and Present* 59 (May 1973); K. Thomas, "Work and Leisure in Pre-industrial Society," *Past and Present* 29 (December 1964); R. Hilton, *Bond Men Made Free: Medieval Peasant Movements and the English Rising of 1381* (1973), a comparative study; M. Keen, *The Outlaws of Medieval Legend* (1961) and "Robin Hood—Peasant or Gentleman?" *Past and Present* 19 (April 1961): 7–18; and P. Wolff, "The 1391 Pogrom in Spain: Social Crisis or Not?" *Past and Present* 50 (February 1971): 4–18. Students are especially encouraged to consult the brilliant achievement of E. L. Ladurie, *The Peasants of Languedoc* (trans. J. Day, 1976). R. H. Hilton, ed., *Peasants, Knights, and Heretics: Studies in Medieval English Social History* (1976), contains a number of valuable articles primarily on the social implications of agricultural change. J. C. Holt, *Robin Hood* (1982), is a soundly researched and highly readable study of the famous outlaw.

For women's economic status in the late medieval period, see the important study of M. C. Howell, *Women, Production, and Patriarchy in Late Medieval Cities* (1986). B. Hanawalt, *The Ties That Bind: Peasant Families in Medieval England* (1986), gives a living picture of the family lives of ordinary people in rural communities. D. Nicholas, *The Domestic Life of a Medieval City: Women, Children, and the Family in Fourteenth-Century Ghent* (1985), focuses on an urban society.

The poetry of Dante, Chaucer, and Villon may be read in the following editions: D. Sayers, trans., *Dante: The Divine Comedy,* 3 vols. (1963); N. Coghill, trans., *Chaucer's Canterbury Tales* (1977); P. Dale, trans., *The Poems of Villon* (1973). The social setting of *Canterbury Tales* is brilliantly evoked in D. W. Robertson, Jr., *Chaucer's London* (1968).

For the religious history of the period, F. Oakley, *The Western Church in the Later Middle Ages* (1979), is an excellent introduction, while R. N. Swanson, *Church and Society in Late Medieval England* (1989) provides a good synthesis of English conditions. S. Ozment, *The Age of Reform, 1250–1550* (1980), discusses the Great Schism and the conciliar movement in the intellectual context of the ecclesio-political tradition of the Middle Ages. Students seeking a highly detailed and comprehensive work should consult H. Beck et al., *From the High Middle Ages to the Eve of the Reformation,* trans. A. Biggs, vol. 14 in the History of the Church series edited by H. Jedin and J. Dolan (1980).

15

Africa Before European Intrusion, ca 400–1500

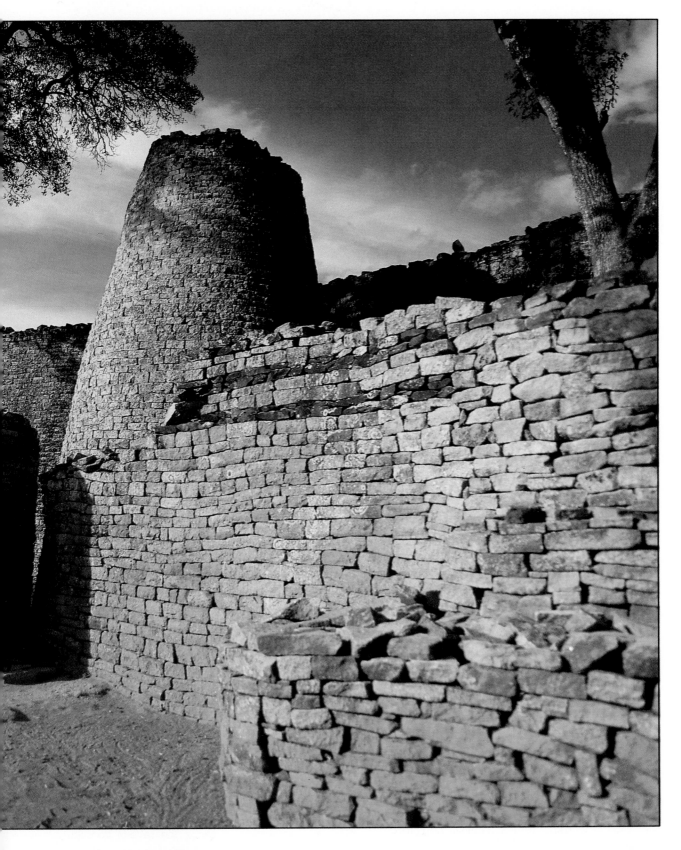

Ruins of Great Zimbabwe

Between about 400 and 1500, Africa witnessed the development of highly sophisticated civilizations alongside a spectrum of more simply organized societies. Until fairly recently, ethnocentrism, Eurocentrism, and white racism have limited what Asians, Europeans, and Americans have known about Africa. The more that historians, sociologists, and anthropologists have learned about early African civilizations, the more they have come to appreciate the richness, diversity, and dynamism of those cultures.

In a discussion of the major civilizations of Africa before 1500, this chapter explores the following questions:

- What patterns of social and political organization prevailed among the peoples of Africa?

- What types of agriculture and commerce did Africans engage in?

- What values do Africans' art, architecture, and religions express?

THE LAND AND PEOPLES OF AFRICA

Africa is immense. The world's second largest continent (after Asia), it is three times as big as Europe and covers 20 percent of the earth's land surface. Since much of the continent lies far from the ocean, Africa's peoples tend to be isolated from the populations of other continents. Five climatic zones roughly divide the continent (Map 15.1). Fertile land though with unpredictable rainfall borders parts of the Mediterranean coast in the north and the southwestern coast of the Cape of Good Hope in the south. Inland from these areas lies dry steppe country with little plant life. The southern fringe of this area is called the "Sabel." The steppes gradually give way to Africa's great deserts: the Sahara in the north and the Namib and Kalahari to the south. The vast Sahara—3.5 million square miles—takes its name from the Arabic word for "tan," the color of the desert. (Folk etymology ascribes the word *Sahara* to an ancient Arabic word that sounds like a parched man's gasp for water.) Dense, humid, tropical rain forests stretch along coastal West Africa and on both sides of the equator in central Africa until they are stopped by volcanic mountains two-thirds of the way across the continent. Savanna—flat grasslands—extends in a swath across the widest part of the continent, as well as across parts of south central Africa and along the eastern coast. One of the richest habitats in the world, the savanna has always invited migration and cultural contacts. Thus it is the most important region of West Africa historically.

The climate in most of Africa is tropical. Subtropical climates are limited to the northern and southern coasts and to regions of high elevation. Rainfall is seasonal in most parts of the continent and is very sparse in desert and semidesert areas.

Geography and climate have shaped the economic development of the peoples of Africa just as they have shaped the lives of people everywhere else. In the eastern African plains, the earliest humans hunted wild animals. The drier steppe regions favored the development of herding. Wetter savanna regions, like the Nile Valley, encouraged the rise of grain-based agriculture. The tropical forests favored hunting and gathering and, later, root-based agriculture. Regions around rivers and lakes supported economies based on fishing.

The peoples of Africa are as diverse as the topography of the continent. In North Africa, contacts with Asian and European civilizations date back to the ancient Phoenicians, Greeks, and Romans. The native Berbers, who lived along the Mediterranean, intermingled with many different peoples—with Muslim Arabs, who first conquered the region of North Africa in the seventh and eighth centuries A.D.; with Spanish Muslims and Jews, many of whom settled in North Africa after their expulsion from Spain in 1492 (see pages 532–533); and with sub-Saharan blacks.[1]

The Egyptians were a cultural rather than a racial group. Geography isolated them from the rest of the continent and brought them into contact with the ancient Greeks and other Mediterranean civilizations.

Black Africans inhabited the region south of the Sahara, an area of savanna and rain forest. In describing them, the ancient Greeks used the term

MAP 15.1 Africa Before 1500 For centuries trade linked West Africa with Mediterranean and Asian societies. Note the major climatic zones, the several trans-Saharan trade routes, and the routes along the East African coast.

EUROPE

Azores

Aral Sea

Black Sea

Caspian Sea

Madeira Islands

Mediterranean Sea

Lisbon

Cadiz

Canary Islands

BERBERS

Fez

ATLAS MTS.

Sijilmassa

Tripoli

Tajura

Alexandria

Cairo

PERSIA

IRAQ

Basra

Shiraz

Persian Gulf

Taghaza

Ghat

S A H A R A

EGYPT

Nile

Red Sea

ARABIA

Mecca

Awdaghost

Walata

Senegal

Timbuktu

Gao

Takedda

Agades

Dongola

Meroë

Adulis

Aden

Gulf of Aden

GHANA

Kumbi
(Kumbi-Saleh)

M A L I

Jenne

S A H E L

Lake Chad

Cape Guardafui

Niani

JOS
PLATEAU

NIGERIA

AXUM

ETHIOPIA

Berbera

SOMALIA

Congo (Zaire)

Gulf of Guinea

PORTUGUESE ROUTE

Mogadishu

Brava

MUSLIM ROUTE

ATLANTIC OCEAN

Olduvai Gorge

Malindi

Mombasa

TANGANYIKA

Pemba

Zanzibar

Mafia

KATANGA

Kilwa

Cape Delgado

Zambezi

MUTAPA REGION

MADAGASCAR

NAMIB DESERT

Great Zimbabwe

Sofala

— Trans-Saharan trade routes

— Coastal trade routes

Major Climatic Zones of Africa

Wet equatorial

Humid tropical and subtropical

Tropical with long dry season (6–9 months)

Sahelian or subdesert

Desert

Mediterranean

Highland (climate moderated by altitude)

Savannah

KALAHARI DESERT

Cape of Good Hope

INDIAN OCEAN

0   500   1000 Km.

0   500   1000 Mi.

Ethiopians, which meant "people with burnt faces." The Berbers coined the term *Akal-n-Iquina-wen,* which survives today as *Guinea.* The Arabs introduced another term, *Bilad al-Sudan,* which survives as *Sudan.* The Berber and Arab words both mean the "land of the blacks." Short-statured peoples sometimes called "Pygmies" inhabited the equatorial rain forests. South of those forests, in the southern third of the continent, lived the Khoisan, a small people of yellow-brown skin color who primarily were hunters.

EARLY AFRICAN SOCIETIES

Africa was one of the sites where agriculture began. Archeological investigations suggest that knowledge of cultivation moved west from ancient

Settled Agriculture This scene of cattle grazing near the group of huts (represented by stylized white ovals) reflects the domestication of animals and the development of settled pastoral agriculture. Note that it is the women and children (background) who perform the domestic chores. *(Source: Henri Lhote, Montrichard, France)*

Judaea (southern Palestine) and arrived in the Nile Delta in Egypt about the fifth millennium before Christ. Settled agriculture then traveled down the Nile Valley and moved west across the southern edge of the Sahara to the central and western Sudan. By the first century B.C. settled agriculture existed in West Africa. From there it spread to the equatorial forests. African farmers learned to domesticate plants, including millet, sorghum, and yams. Cereal-growing people probably taught forest people to plant regular fields. Gradually African farmers also learned to clear land by burning. Slowly they evolved a sedentary way of life: living in villages, clearing fields, relying on root crops, and fishing. As the importance of hunting declined in their lives, so did the need for periodic migrations.

Between 1500 and 1000 B.C., settled agriculture also spread southward from Ethiopia along the Rift Valley of present-day Kenya and Tanzania. Archeological evidence reveals that the peoples of this region grew cereals, raised cattle, and used tools made of wood and stone. Cattle raising spread more quickly than did planting. Early African peoples prized cattle highly. Many trading agreements, marriage alliances, political compacts, and treaties were negotiated in terms of cattle.

Scholars speculate that traders brought bananas, taros (a type of yam), sugar cane, and coconut palms to Africa from Southeast Asia. Because tropical forest conditions were ideal for banana trees, their cultivation spread rapidly; they were easier to raise than cereal grains. Donkeys, pigs, chickens, geese, and ducks were also domesticated.

The evolution to a settled life had profound effects. In contrast to nomadic conditions, settled societies made shared or common needs more apparent, and those needs strengthened ties among extended families. Population also increased:

The change from a hunter-gatherer economy to a settled farming economy affected population numbers. . . . Certainly in the agricultural economy there was more food available, if only because . . . it enabled more food to be extracted from a given piece of land. What remains uncertain is whether in the agricultural economy there were more people, better fed, or more people, less well fed. . . . In precolonial Africa agricultural and pastoral populations may not have increased steadily over time, but fluctuated cyclically, growing and declining, though overall slowly growing.[2]

Scholars dispute the route by which ironworking spread to sub-Saharan Africa. Some believe that the Phoenicians brought the technique for smelting iron to northwestern Africa and that from the north it spread southward. Others insist that it spread from the Meroe region on the Nile westward. Since most of West Africa had acquired knowledge of ironworking by 250 B.C., and since archeologists believe that Meroe achieved pre-eminence as an iron-smelting center only in the first century B.C., a stronger case can probably be made for the Phoenicians. The great African overland trade routes may have carried a knowledge of ironworking southward; in any case, by about A.D. 600 it was widely understood in sub-Saharan Africa. Ancient iron tools found at the village of Nok on the Jos Plateau in present-day Nigeria seem to prove a knowledge of ironworking in West Africa. Nok culture (ca 800 B.C.–A.D. 200) enjoys enduring fame for its fine terra-cotta (baked clay) sculptures.

Around the time of Christ, Bantu-speakers—a small group of people who had long occupied modern-day Nigeria on Africa's west coast—began to move southeastward, settling for a time in central Africa, south of the equatorial rain forests. Because much of central Africa is a plateau, its topsoil is thin and ground water is scarce. These conditions promote migratory rather than settled agriculture. The Bantu continued to move gradually south and east, reaching present-day Zimbabwe by the eighth century and the southeastern coast by the sixteenth century. Knowledge of ironworking gave the Bantu a distinct advantage over hunters and gatherers such as the Pygmy and Khoisan people they encountered, whom they absorbed and displaced.

Describing the village life of Bantu people in the nineteenth century, the Scottish missionary-explorer David Livingstone (1813–1873) wrote, "Food abounds, and very little labor is required for its cultivation. . . . When a garden becomes too poor for good crops . . . the owner removes a little farther into the forest, applies fire round the roots of the larger trees to kill them, cuts down the smaller, and a new, rich garden is ready for the seed."[3] One must be cautious in accepting at face value Livingstone's evaluation of the slight effort involved in cultivating the soil. Farming always requires considerable skill and labor—even more effort if performed by women, as much of it was in Africa.

AFRICAN KINGDOMS IN THE WESTERN SUDAN (CA 1000 B.C.–A.D. 200)

The region bounded on the north by the Sahara, on the south by the Gulf of Guinea, on the west by the Atlantic, and on the east by the mountains of Ethiopia is known as the "Sudan." In the savanna lands of the western Sudan—where the Bantu migrations originated—a series of dynamic kingdoms emerged in the millennium before European intrusion.

Between 1000 B.C. and A.D. 200, the peoples of the western Sudan made the momentous shift from nomadic hunting to settled agriculture. They cultivated crops with iron tools and domesticated animals for food. The rich savanna proved ideally suited to the production of cereals, especially rice, millet, and sorghum, and people situated near the Senegal River and Lake Chad supplemented their diet with fish. Food supply tends to affect population, and the peoples of the region—known as the "Mande" and the "Chadic speakers," or "Sao"—increased dramatically in number. By A.D. 400 the entire savanna, particularly the areas around Lake Chad, the Niger River bend, and present-day central Nigeria (see Map 15.1) had a large population.

Families and clans affiliated by blood kinship lived together in villages or small city-states. The basic social unit was the extended family. The village was governed by a chief in consultation with a council of elders. Some city-states and villages seem to have formed kingdoms. Village chiefs were responsible to regional heads, who answered to provincial governors, who were in turn responsible to a king. The various chiefs and their families formed an aristocracy. Kingship in the Sudan may have emerged from the priesthood, whose members were believed to make rain and to have contact with spirit powers. African kings always had religious sanction or support for their authority and were often considered divine. (In this respect, early African kingship bears a strong resemblance to Germanic kingship of the same period: the authority of the king rested in part on the ruler's ability to negotiate with outside powers, such as the gods.) The most prominent feature of early African society was a strong sense of community, based on the blood relationship and on religion.

African religions were animistic. Most people believed that a supreme being had created the universe and was the source of all life but individual men and women could not know or communicate with that being. The supreme being breathed spirit into all living things, and the *anima,* or spirit, residing in such things as trees, water, and earth had to be appeased. In the cycle of the agricultural year, for example, all the spirits had to be propitiated from the time of clearing the land through sowing the seed to the final harvest. Because special ceremonies and rituals were necessary to satisfy the spirits, special priests with the knowledge and power to communicate with them were needed. Thus the practice of African religion consisted primarily of sacred rituals performed by priests who were also the heads of families and villages. The head of each family was also responsible for maintaining the family ritual cults—ceremonies honoring the dead and living members of the family.[4]

In sum, extended families made up the villages that collectively formed small kingdoms. What spurred the expansion of these small kingdoms into formidable powers controlling sizable territory was the development of long-distance trade. And what made long-distance or trans-Saharan trade possible was the camel.

THE TRANS-SAHARAN TRADE

The camel had an impact on African trade comparable to the impact of the horse on European agriculture (see page 379). Although scholars dispute exactly when the camel was introduced from central Asia—first into North Africa, then into the Sahara and the Sudan—they agree that it was before A.D. 200. Camels can carry about 500 pounds as far as 25 miles a day and can go for days without drinking, living on the water stored in their stomachs. Camels were (and are) stupid and vicious. They had to be loaded on a daily, sometimes twice-daily, basis. And much of the cargo for a long trip consisted of provisions for the journey itself. Nevertheless, camels proved more efficient for desert transportation than horses or oxen. The use of this beast to carry heavy and bulky freight affected not only African economic and social change but the development of world commerce.

Sometime in the fifth century the North African Berbers adopted a saddle for use on the camel. The North African saddle had no direct effect on commercial operations, for a merchant usually walked and guided the camel on foot. But the saddle gave the Berbers and later the Arabian inhabitants of the region maneuverability on the animal and thus a powerful political and military advantage: they came to dominate the desert and to create lucrative routes across it. The Berbers determined who could enter the desert, and they levied heavy protection money on merchant caravans.

Between A.D. 700 and 900 the Berbers developed a network of caravan routes between the Mediterranean coast and the Sudan (see Map 15.1). The Morocco-Niger route ran from Fez to Sijilmasa on the edge of the desert and then south by way of Taghaza and Walata and back to Fez. Another route originated at Sijilmasa and extended due south to Timbuktu with a stop at Taghaza. A third route ran south from Tripoli to Lake Chad. A fourth ran from Egypt to Gao by way of the Saharan oases of Ghat and Agades and then on to Takedda.

The long expedition across the Sahara testifies to the spirit of the traders and to their passion for wealth. Ibn Battuta, an Arab traveler who made the journey in the fourteenth century when trans-Saharan traffic was at its height, wrote an account of the experience. Because of the blistering sun and daytime temperatures of 110, the caravan drivers preferred to travel at night, when the temperature might drop to the low 20s. Nomadic raiders, the Tuareg Berbers, posed a serious threat. The Tuaregs lived in the desert uplands and preyed on the caravans as a way of life. Consequently, merchants made safe-conduct agreements with them and selected guides from among them. Caravans of twelve thousand camels were reported in the fourteenth century. Large numbers of merchants crossed the desert together to discourage attack. Blinding sandstorms often isolated part of a line of camels and on at least one occasion buried alive some camels and drivers. Water was the biggest problem. The Tuaregs sometimes poisoned wells to wipe out caravans and steal their goods. In order to satisfy normal thirst and to compensate for constant sweating, a gallon of water a day per person was required. Desperate thirst sometimes forced the traders to kill camels and drink the foul, brackish water in their stomachs. It took Ibn Battuta twenty-five days to travel from Sijilmasa to the oasis of Taghaza and another sixty-five days to travel from Taghaza to the important market town of Walata. The entire trip took almost three months.

The Arab-Berber merchants from North Africa who controlled the caravan trade carried manufactured goods—silk and cotton cloth, beads, mirrors—as well as dates and salt (essential in tropical climates to replace the loss from perspiration) from the Saharan oases and mines to the Sudan. These products were exchanged for the much-coveted commodities of the West African savanna—gold, ivory, gum, kola nuts (eaten as a stimulant), and slaves.

The steady growth of trans-Saharan trade had three important effects on West African society. The trade stimulated gold mining and the search for slaves. Parts of modern-day Senegal, Nigeria, and Ghana contained rich veins of gold. Both sexes shared in mining it: the men sank the shafts and hacked out gold-bearing rocks and crushed them, separating the gold from the soil; the women washed the gold in gourds. Alluvial gold (mixed with soil, sand, or gravel) was separated from the soil by panning. Scholars estimate that by the eleventh century nine tons were exported to Europe annually, a prodigious amount, since even with modern machinery and sophisticated techniques the total gold exports from the same region in 1937 amounted to only twenty-one tons. A large percentage of this metal went to Egypt. From there it was transported down the Red Sea to India to pay for the spices and silks demanded by Mediterranean commerce. West African gold proved "absolutely vital for the monetization of the medieval Mediterranean economy and for the maintenance of its balance of payments with South Asia."[5] African gold linked the entire world, exclusive of the Western Hemisphere.

West Africa's second most valuable export was slaves. It seems that African slaves, like their early European and Asian counterparts, were peoples captured in war. In the Muslim cities of North Africa, southern Europe, and southwestern Asia, the demand for household slaves was high among the elite. Slaves were also needed to work the gold and salt mines. Recent research suggests, moreover, that large numbers of black slaves were recruited through the trans-Saharan trade for Muslim military service. The armed forces of medieval Islamic regimes in Morocco and Egypt consisted largely of slaves. High death rates from disease, manumission, and the assimilation of some blacks into Muslim society meant that the demand for

Ashanti Weight The Ashanti of Ghana used brass or bronze weights to measure gold dust, their major export. This weight, one of the largest found, probably was used in a chief's treasury. The weights often illustrated folk legends, proverbs, or scenes from everyday life. *(Source: Museum of Mankind (British Museum)/ Michael Holford)*

slaves remained high for centuries. Table 15.1 shows one scholar's tentative conclusions, based on many kinds of evidence, about the scope of the trans-Saharan slave trade. The total number of blacks enslaved over an 850-year period may be tentatively estimated at over 4 million.[6]

Slavery in Muslim societies, as in European and Asian countries before the fifteenth century, was not based strictly on skin color. The slaves exported from West Africa were all black, but Muslims also enslaved Caucasians who had been purchased, seized in war, or kidnapped from Europe. The households of wealthy Muslims in Cordoba, Alexandria, or Tunis often included slaves of a number of races, all of whom had been completely cut off from their cultural roots. Likewise, West African kings who sold blacks to traders from the north also bought a few white slaves—Slavic, British, and Turkish—for their domestic needs. Race had very little to do with the phenomenon of slavery.[7]

The trans-Saharan trade also stimulated the development of vigorous urban centers in West Africa. Scholars date the growth of African cities

TABLE 15.1 ESTIMATED MAGNITUDE OF TRANS-SAHARAN SLAVE TRADE, 650–1500

Years	Annual Average of Slaves Traded	Total
650–800	1,000	150,000
800–900	3,000	300,000
900–1100	8,700	1,740,000
1100–1400	5,500	1,650,000
1400–1500	4,300	430,000

Source: From R. A. Austen, "The Trans-Saharan Slave Trade: A Tentative Census," in The Uncommon Market: Essays in the Economic History of the Atlantic Slave Trade, *ed. H. A. Gemery and J. S. Hogendorn (New York: Academic Press, 1979). Used with permission.*

from around the beginning of the ninth century. Families that had profited from trade tended to congregate in the border zones between the savanna and the Sahara. They acted as middlemen between the miners to the south and Muslim merchants from the north. By the early thirteenth century, these families had become powerful black merchant dynasties. Muslim traders from the Mediterranean settled permanently in the trading depots, from which they organized the trans-Saharan caravans. The concentration of people stimulated agriculture and the craft industries. Gradually cities of sizable population emerged. Jenne, Gao, and Timbuktu, which enjoyed commanding positions on the Niger River bend, became centers of the export-import trade. Sijilmasa grew into a thriving market center. Kumbi, with between 15,000 and 20,000 inhabitants, was probably the largest city in the western Sudan in the twelfth century. (By European standards Kumbi was a metropolis; London and Paris achieved its size only in the late thirteenth century.) Between 1100 and 1400 these cities played a dynamic role in the commercial life of West Africa and Europe and became centers of intellectual creativity.

Perhaps the most influential consequence of the trans-Saharan trade was the introduction of Islam to West African society. Muslim expansion began soon after Muhammad's death in 632 (see pages 268–270). By the tenth century, Muslim Berbers controlled the north-south trade routes to the savanna. By the eleventh century, African rulers of Gao and Timbuktu had accepted Islam. The king of Ghana was also influenced by Islam. Muslims quickly became integral to West African government and society.

Conversion to Islam introduced West Africans to a rich and sophisticated culture. By the late eleventh century, Islam encompassed not only theological doctrines and a way of life but a body of legal traditions and writings, efficient techniques of government and statecraft, advanced scientific knowledge and engineering skills, and collections of lyric poetry and popular romances (see pages 289–292). At approximately the same time, Muslims were aiding Roger of Sicily in the construction of his state bureaucracy (see page 411) and guiding the ruler of Ghana in the operation of his administrative machinery. The king of Ghana adopted the Muslim *diwan*, the agency for keeping financial records. Because efficient government depends on the preservation of records, the arrival of Islam in West Africa marked the advent of written documents there. Arab Muslims also taught the rulers of Ghana how to manufacture bricks, and royal palaces and mosques began to be built of brick. African rulers corresponded with Muslim architects, theologians, and other intellectuals, who advised them on statecraft and religion. In sum, Islam accelerated the development of the African empires of the ninth through fifteenth centuries.

AFRICAN KINGDOMS AND EMPIRES (CA 800–1450)

All African societies shared one basic feature: a close relationship between political and social organization. Ethnic or blood ties bound clan members together. What scholars call "stateless societies" were culturally homogeneous ethnic societies. The smallest ones numbered fewer than a hundred people and were nomadic hunting groups. Larger stateless societies of perhaps several thousand people lived a settled and often agricultural or herding life.

The period from about 800 to 1450 witnessed the flowering of several powerful African states. In the western Sudan, the large empires of Ghana and Mali developed, complete with massive royal bureaucracies. On the east coast emerged powerful city-states based on sophisticated mercantile activities and, like the Sudan, very much influenced by Islam. In Ethiopia, in central East Africa, kings relied on the Christian faith of their people to strengthen political authority. In South Africa the empire of Great Zimbabwe, built on the gold trade with the east coast, flourished.

The Kingdom of Ghana (ca 900–1100)

So remarkable was the kingdom of Ghana during the age of Africa's great empires that writers throughout the medieval world, such as the fourteenth-century Muslim historian Ibn Khaldun, praised it as a model for other rulers. Medieval Ghana also holds a central place in the historical consciousness of the modern state of Ghana. Since this former British colony attained independence in 1957, its political leaders have hailed the medieval period as a glorious heritage. The name of the modern republic of Ghana—which in fact lies far from the site of the old kingdom—was selected to signify the rebirth of an age of gold in black Africa.

The nucleus of the territory that became the kingdom of Ghana was inhabited by Soninke people who called their ruler *ghana*, or war chief. By the late eighth century Muslim traders and other foreigners applied the word to the region where the Soninke lived, the black kingdom south of the Sahara. The Soninke themselves called their land "Aoukar" or "Awkar," by which they meant the region north of the Senegal and Niger rivers. Only the southern part of Aoukar received enough rainfall to be agriculturally productive, and it was in this area that the civilization of Ghana developed. Skillful farming and an efficient system of irrigation led to the production of abundant crops, which eventually supported a population of as many as 200,000.

The Soninke name for their king—war chief—aptly describes the king's major preoccupation in the tenth century. In 992 Ghana captured the Berber town of Awdaghast, strategically situated on the trans-Saharan trade route. Thereafter Ghana controlled the southern portion of a major caravan route. Before the year 1000 the rulers of Ghana

had extended their influence almost to the Atlantic coast and had captured a number of small kingdoms in the south and east. By the beginning of the eleventh century, the king exercised sway over a vast territory approximately the size of Texas. No other African power could successfully challenge him.

Throughout this vast area, all authority sprang from the king. The people considered him semisacred. Religious ceremonies and court rituals emphasized his sacredness and were intended to strengthen his authority. The king's position was hereditary in the matrilineal line—that is, the heir of the ruling king was one of his sister's sons (presumably the eldest or fittest for battle). According to the eleventh-century Spanish Muslim geographer al-Bakri (1040?–1094): "This is their custom . . . the kingdom is inherited only by the son of the

Arab Merchant-Scholars The Islamic faith and the Arabic language lent the Muslim world a unity that fostered the wide circulation of trade and ideas. *(Source: Bibliothèque Nationale/Sonia Halliday)*

king's sister. He the king has no doubt that his successor is a son of his sister, while he is not certain that his son is in fact his own."[8]

A council of ministers assisted the king in the work of government, and from the ninth century on most of these ministers were Muslims. Detailed evidence about the early Ghanaian bureaucracy has not survived, but scholars suspect that separate agencies were responsible for taxation, royal property, foreigners, forests, and the army. The royal administration was well served by Muslim ideas, skills, and especially literacy. The king and his people, however, clung to their ancestral religion, and the basic political institutions of Ghana remained African.

The king of Ghana held his court in Kumbi. Al-Bakri provides a valuable picture of the city in the eleventh century:

The city of Ghana consists of two towns lying on a plain, one of which is inhabited by Muslims and is large, possessing twelve mosques—one of which is a congregational mosque for Friday prayer; each has its imam, its muezzin and paid reciters of the Quran. The town possesses a large number of jurisconsults and learned men.[9]

The town inhabited by the king is six miles from the Muslim one and is called Al Ghana. . . . The residence of the king consists of a palace and a number of dome-shaped dwellings, all of them surrounded by a strong enclosure, like a city wall. In the town . . . is a mosque, where Muslims who come on diplomatic missions to the king pray. The town where the king lives is surrounded by domed huts, woods, and copses where priest-magicians live; in these woods also are the religious idols and tombs of the kings. Special guards protect this area and prevent anyone from entering it so that no foreigners know what is inside. Here also are the king's prisons, and if anyone is imprisoned there, nothing more is heard of him.[10]

The Muslim community in Ghana must have been large and prosperous to have supported twelve mosques. Either for their own protection or to preserve their special identity, the Muslims lived separate from the African artisans and tradespeople. The *imam* was the religious leader who conducted the ritual worship, especially the main prayer service on Fridays. Since Islamic worship had political connotations as well as religious

meaning, the imam was then, as now, both a political and a religious authority in the community. The *muezzin* leads the prayer responses after the imam; he must have a strong voice so that those at a distance and the women in the harem, or enclosure, can hear. Muslim religious leaders exercised civil authority over their coreligionists. Their presence and that of other learned Muslims also suggests vigorous intellectual activity.

Al-Bakri also describes the royal court:

The king adorns himself, as do the women here, with necklaces and bracelets; on their heads they wear caps decorated with gold, sewn on material of fine cotton stuffing. When he holds court in order to hear the people's complaints and to do justice, he sits in a pavilion around which stand ten horses wearing golden trappings; behind him ten pages stand, holding shields and swords decorated with gold; at his right are the sons of the chiefs of the country, splendidly dressed and with their hair sprinkled with gold. The governor of the city sits on the ground in front of the king with other officials likewise sitting around him. Excellently pedigreed dogs guard the door of the pavilion: they never leave the place where the king is; they wear collars of gold and silver studded with bells of the same material. The noise of a sort-of drum, called a daba, and made from a long hollow log, announces the start of the royal audience. When the king's coreligionists appear before him, they fall on their knees and toss dust on their heads—this is their way of greeting their sovereign. Muslims show respect by clapping their hands.[11]

What sort of juridical system did Ghana have? How was the guilt or innocence of an accused person determined? Justice derived from the king, who heard cases at court or on travels throughout his kingdom. As al-Bakri recounts:

When a man is accused of denying a debt or of having shed blood or some other crime, a headman (village chief) takes a thin piece of wood, which is sour and bitter to taste, and pours upon it some water which he then gives to the defendant to drink. If the man vomits, his innocence is recognized and he is congratulated. If he does not vomit and the drink remains in his stomach, the accusation is accepted as justified.[12]

This appeal to the supernatural for judgment was very similar to the justice by ordeal that prevailed among the English and Germanic peoples of western Europe at the same time. Complicated cases in Ghana seem to have been appealed to the king, who often relied on the advice of Muslim legal experts.

The king's elaborate court, the administrative machinery he built, and the extensive territories he governed were all expensive. The king of Ghana needed a lot of money, and he apparently had four main sources of support. The royal estates—some hereditary, others conquered in war—produced annual revenue, mostly in the form of foodstuffs for the royal household. The king also received tribute annually from subordinate chieftains. (Lack of evidence prevents an estimate of the value of this tax.) The third and probably largest source of income was customs duties on goods entering and leaving the country. Salt was the largest import. According to al-Bakri, "for every donkey that enters the country, the king takes a duty of one gold dinar and two for one that leaves."[13] Berber merchants paid a tax to the king on the cloth, metalwork, weapons, and other goods that they brought into the country from North Africa; in return these traders received royal protection from bandits. African traders bringing gold into Ghana from the south also paid the customs duty.

Finally, the royal treasury held a monopoly on the export of gold. The gold industry was undoubtedly the king's largest source of income. It was on gold that the fame of medieval Ghana rested. The eighth-century astronomer al-Fazari called Ghana the "land of gold"; the ninth-century geographer al-Ya-qubi wrote, "its king is mighty, and in his lands are gold mines. Under his authority are various other kingdoms—and in all this region there is gold."[14]

The governing aristocracy—the king, his court, and Muslim administrators—occupied the highest rank on the Ghanaian social ladder. The next rung consisted of the merchant class. Considerably below the merchants stood the farmers, cattle breeders, supervisors of the gold mines, and skilled craftsmen and weavers—what today might be called the "middle class." Some merchants and miners must have enjoyed great wealth, but, as in all aristocratic societies, money alone did not suffice. High status was based on blood and royal service. At the bottom of the social scale were the slaves, who worked in households, on farms, and in the mines. As in Asian and European societies

Royal Woman from Benin The elaborate gold headdress, the gold braided in her hair, and the heavy gold necklace indicate that this woman is from the royal class and attest to the wealth of the region. *(Source: Courtesy of the Trustees of the British Museum)*

of the time, slaves accounted for only a small percentage of the population.

Apart from these social classes stood the army. According to al-Bakri, "the king of Ghana can put 200,000 warriors in the field, more than 40,000 being armed with bow and arrow."[15] Like most medieval estimates, this is probably a gross exaggeration. Even a modern industrialized state with sophisticated means of transportation, communication, and supply lines would have enormous difficulty mobilizing so many men for battle. The king of Ghana, however, was not called "war chief" for nothing. He maintained at his palace a crack standing force of a thousand men, comparable to the Roman Praetorian Guard (see page 207). These thoroughly disciplined, well-armed,

Mali Horsemen Recent archeological excavations have uncovered evidence of an ancient artistic tradition in wood carving. In spite of the threats of weather, termites, and other insects, these wooden horses survived—showing that they were extensively decorated. *(Source: Australian National Gallery, Canberra)*

totally loyal troops protected the king and the royal court. They lived in special compounds, enjoyed the favor of the king, and sometimes acted as his personal ambassadors to subordinate rulers. In wartime, this regular army was augmented by levies of soldiers from conquered peoples and by the use of slaves and free reserves. The force that the king could field was sizable, if not as huge as al-Bakri estimated.

The Kingdom of Mali (ca 1200–1450)

During the century after the collapse of Kumbi, a cloud of obscurity hung over the western Sudan. The kingdom of Ghana split into several small

kingdoms that feuded among themselves. One people, the Mandinke, lived in the kingdom of Kangaba on the upper Niger River. The Mandinke had long been part of the Ghanaian empire, and the Mandinke and Soninke belonged to the same language group. Kangaba formed the core of the new empire of Mali. Building on Ghanaian foundations, Mali developed into a better-organized and more powerful state than Ghana.

The kingdom of Mali (Map 15.2) owed its greatness to two fundamental assets. First, its strong agricultural and commercial base provided for a large population and enormous wealth. Second, Mali had two rulers, Sundiata and Mansa Musa, who combined military success with exceptionally creative personalities.

The earliest surviving evidence about the Mandinke, dating from the early eleventh century, indicates that they were extremely successful at agriculture. Consistently large harvests throughout the twelfth and thirteenth centuries meant a plentiful supply of food, which encouraged steady population growth. The geographical location of Kangaba also placed the Mandinke in an ideal position in West African trade. Earlier, during the period of Ghanaian hegemony, the Mandinke had acted as middlemen in the gold and salt traffic flowing north and south. In the thirteenth century Mandinke traders formed companies, traveled widely, and gradually became a major force in the entire West African trade.

Sundiata (ca 1230–1255) set up his capital at Niani, transforming the city into an important financial and trading center. He then embarked on a policy of imperial expansion. Through a series of military victories, Sundiata and his successors absorbed into Mali other territories of the former kingdom of Ghana and established hegemony over the trading cities of Gao, Jenne, and Walata.

These expansionist policies were continued in the fourteenth century by Sundiata's descendant Mansa Musa (ca 1312–1337), early Africa's most famous ruler. In the language of the Mandinke, *mansa* means "emperor." Mansa Musa fought many campaigns and checked every attempt at rebellion. Ultimately his influence extended northward to several Berber cities in the Sahara, eastward to Timbuktu and Gao, and westward as far as the Atlantic Ocean. Throughout his territories he maintained strict royal control over the rich trans-Saharan trade. Thus this empire, roughly twice the size of the Ghanaian kingdom and containing perhaps 8 million people, brought Mansa Musa fabulous wealth.

Mansa Musa built on the foundations of his predecessors. The stratified aristocratic structure of Malian society perpetuated the pattern set in Ghana, as did the system of provincial administration and annual tribute. The emperor took responsibility for the territories that formed the heart of the empire and appointed governors to rule the outlying provinces or dependent kingdoms. Here Mansa Musa made a significant innovation: in a practice strikingly similar to the French *appanages* of the time, he chose members of the royal family as provincial governors. He could count on their loyalty, and they received valuable experience in the work of government.

In another aspect of administration, Mansa Musa also differed from his predecessors. He became a devout Muslim. While most of the Mandinke clung to their ancestral animism, Islamic practices and influences in Mali multiplied.

The most celebrated event of Mansa Musa's reign was his pilgrimage to Mecca in 1324–1325, during which he paid a state visit to the sultan of Egypt. Mansa Musa's entrance into Cairo was magnificent. Preceded by five hundred slaves, each carrying a six-pound staff of gold, he followed with a huge host of retainers including one hundred elephants each bearing one hundred pounds of gold. Several hundred additional camels carrying food, supplies, and weapons brought up the rear. The emperor lavished his wealth on the citizens of the Egyptian capital. Writing twelve years later, al-Omari, one of the sultan's officials, recounts:

This man Mansa Musa spread upon Cairo the flood of his generosity: there was no person, officer of the court, or holder of any office of the Sultanate who did not receive a sum of gold from him. The people of Cairo earned incalculable sums from him, whether by buying and selling or by gifts. So much gold was current in Cairo that it ruined the value of money. . . . Let me add that gold in Egypt had enjoyed a high rate of exchange up to the moment of their arrival. . . . But from that day onward, its value dwindled; the exchange was ruined, and even now it has not recovered.[16]

Mansa Musa's gold brought about terrible inflation throughout Egypt. For the first time, the Mediterranean world gained concrete knowledge

of the wealth and power of the black kingdom of Mali, and it began to be known as one of the great empires of the world. Mali retained this international reputation into the fifteenth century.

Musa's pilgrimage also had significant consequences within Mali. He gained some understanding of the Mediterranean countries and opened diplomatic relations with the Muslim rulers of Morocco and Egypt. His zeal for the Muslim faith and Islamic culture increased. Musa brought back from Arabia the distinguished architect al-Saheli, whom he commissioned to build new mosques at Timbuktu and other cities. These mosques served as centers for the conversion of Africans. Musa employed Muslim engineers to build in brick where pounded clay had formerly been used. He also encouraged Malian merchants and traders to wear the distinctive flowing robes and turbans of Muslim males.

Timbuktu began as a campsite for desert nomads. Under Mansa Musa it grew into a thriving entrepôt, attracting merchants and traders from

MAP 15.2 The Kingdom of Mali   The economic strength of the kingdom of Mali rested heavily on the trans-Saharan trade.

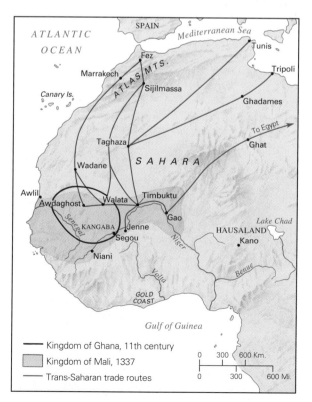

North Africa and all parts of the Mediterranean world. These people brought with them cosmopolitan attitudes and ideas. In the fifteenth century Timbuktu developed into a great center for scholarship and learning. Architects, astronomers, poets, lawyers, mathematicians, and theologians flocked there. One hundred and fifty schools were devoted to the study of the Qur'an. The school of Islamic law enjoyed a distinction in Africa comparable to the prestige of the law school at Bologna. A vigorous trade in books flourished in Timbuktu. Leo Africanus, a sixteenth-century Muslim traveler and writer who later converted to Christianity, recounts that around 1500 Timbuktu had a "great store of doctors, judges, priests, and other learned men that are bountifully maintained at the king's cost and charges. And hitherto are brought diverse manuscripts or written books out of Barbarie the north African states, from Egypt to the Atlantic Ocean which are sold for more money than any

other merchandise." It is easy to understand why the university at Timbuktu was called by a contemporary writer "the Queen of the Sudan." Timbuktu's tradition and reputation for scholarship lasted until the eighteenth century.

In the fourteenth and fifteenth centuries many Muslim intellectuals and Arabic traders married native African women. These unions brought into being a group of racially mixed people. The necessity of living together harmoniously, the traditional awareness of diverse cultures, and the cosmopolitan atmosphere of Timbuktu all contributed to a rare degree of racial toleration and understanding. After visiting the court of Mansa Musa's successor in 1352–1353, Ibn Battuta observed that

the Negroes possess some admirable qualities. They are seldom unjust, and have a greater abhorrence of injustice than any other people. Their sultan shows no

Timbuktu Begun as a Tuareg seasonal camp in the eleventh century, Timbuktu emerged as a great commercial entrepôt in the fourteenth century and as an important Muslim educational center in the sixteenth. A strong agricultural base, watered by the nearby Niger River, supported a sizable population. *(Source: Library of Congress)*

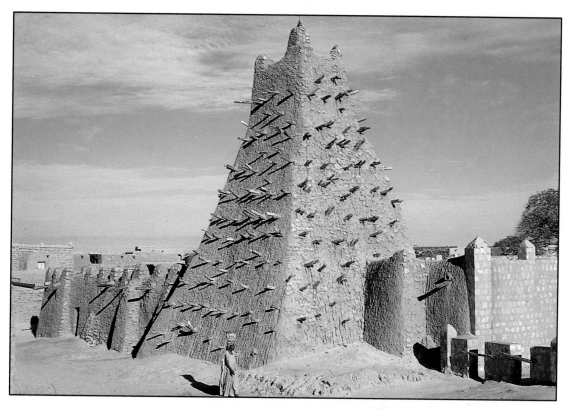

Mosque at Timbuktu This fascinating piece of architecture attests to the strong Muslim religious and intellectual influence at Timbuktu. Another mosque served as the university center there. (*Source: George Holton/Photo Researchers*)

mercy to anyone who is guilty of the least act of it. There is complete security in their country. Neither traveler nor inhabitant in it has anything to fear from robbers. . . . They do not confiscate the property of any white man who dies in their country, even if it be un-counted wealth. On the contrary, they give it into the charge of some trustworthy person among the whites, until the rightful heir takes possession of it. They are careful to observe the hours of prayer, and assiduous in attending them in congregations, and in bringing up their children to them. On Fridays, if a man does not go early to the mosque, he cannot find a corner to pray in, on account of the crowd.[17]

The East African City-States

In the first century A.D., a merchant-seaman from Alexandria in Egypt, possibly acting as an agent of the Roman imperial government, sailed down the Red Sea and out into the Indian Ocean. Along the coasts of East Africa and India he found seaports. He took careful notes on all he observed, and the result, *Periplus of the Erythraean Sea* (as the Greeks called the Indian Ocean), is the earliest surviving literary evidence of the city-states of the East African coast. Although primarily preoccupied with geography and navigation, the *Periplus* includes accounts of the local peoples and their commercial activities. Even in the days of the Roman emperors, the *Periplus* testifies, the East African coast had strong commercial links with India and the Mediterranean.

Greco-Roman ships traveled from Adulis on the Red Sea around the tip of the Gulf of Aden and down the African coast that the Greeks called "Azania," in modern-day Kenya and Tanzania (see Map 15.3). These ships carried manufactured goods—cotton cloth, copper and brass, iron tools, and gold and silver plate. At the African coastal emporiums, Mediterranean merchants exchanged these goods for cinnamon, myrrh and frankincense, slaves, and animal by-products such as ivory, rhinoceros horns, and tortoise shells. Somewhere around Cape Guardafui on the Horn of Africa, the ships caught the monsoon winds eastward to India, where ivory was in great demand.

An omission in the *Periplus* has created a debate over the racial characteristics of the native peoples in East Africa and the dates of Bantu migrations into the area. The author, writing in the first century, did not describe the natives; apparently he did not find their skin color striking enough to comment on. Yet in the fifth century, there are references to these peoples as "Ethiopians." Could this mean that migrating black Bantu-speakers reached the east coast between the first and the fifth centuries? Possibly. The distinguished archeologist Neville Chittick, however, thinks not:

The *Periplus* . . . *tells us nothing about the physical characteristics of the native inhabitants of the East African coast save that they were very tall. The fact that nothing is said about their color has been taken as indicating that they were not Negroid. But we are not really justified in drawing such a conclusion. The writer of the* Periplus *made few comments on the physical nature of the inhabitants of the countries which he described . . . therefore nothing can be based on the mere omission of any mention of skin color.*[18]

In the first few centuries of the Christian era, many merchants and seamen from the Mediterranean settled in East African coastal towns. Succeeding centuries saw the arrival of more traders. The great emigration from Arabia after the death of Muhammad accelerated Muslim penetration of the area, which the Arabs called the *Zanj,* "land of the blacks." Arabic Muslims established along the coast small trading colonies whose local peoples were ruled by kings and practiced various animistic religions. Eventually—whether through Muslim political hegemony or gradual assimilation—the coastal peoples slowly converted to Islam. Indigenous African religions, however, remained strong in the interior of the continent.

Beginning in the late twelfth century, fresh waves of Arabs and of Persians from Shiraz poured down the coast, first settling at Mogadishu, then pressing southward to Kilwa (see Map 15.3). Everywhere they landed, they introduced Islamic culture to the indigenous population. Similarly, Indonesians crossed the Indian Ocean and settled on

the African coast and on the large island of Madagascar or Malagasy, an Indonesian word from the earliest Christian centuries through the Middle Ages. All these immigrants intermarried with Africans, and the resulting society combined Asian, African, and especially Islamic traits.

The East African coastal culture was called "Swahili," after a Bantu language whose vocabulary and poetic forms exhibit a strong Arabic influence. The thirteenth-century Muslim mosque at Mogadishu and the fiercely Muslim populations of Mombasa and Kilwa in the fourteenth century attest to strong Muslim influence.

Much current knowledge about life in the East African trading societies rests on the account of Ibn Battuta. The coastal cities were great commercial empires in the fourteenth and fifteenth centuries, comparable to Venice and Genoa. Like those Italian city-states, Kilwa, Mombasa, and Mafia were situated on offshore islands; the tidal currents that isolated them from the mainland also protected them from landside attack.

When Ibn Battuta arrived at Mogadishu, he was impressed, in the words of a modern historian,

with the size of the town, the . . . richly appointed palace. Traveling on to Kilwa, he found the city large and elegant, its buildings, as was typical along the coast, constructed of stone and coral rag [roofing slate]. Houses were generally single storied, consisting of a number of small rooms separated by thick walls supporting heavy stone roofing slabs laid across mangrove poles. Some of the more formidable structures contained second and third stories, and many were embellished with cut stone decorative borders framing the entranceways. Tapestries and ornamental niches covered the walls and the floors were carpeted. Of course, such appointments were only for the wealthy; the poorer classes occupied the timeless mud and straw huts of Africa, their robes a simple loincloth, their dinner a millet porridge.[19]

On the mainland were fields and orchards of rice, millet, oranges, mangoes, and bananas, and pastures and yards for cattle, sheep, and poultry. Yields were apparently high; Ibn Battuta noted that the rich enjoyed three enormous meals a day and were very fat.

From among the rich mercantile families that controlled the coastal cities arose a ruler who by the fourteenth century had taken the Arabic title *sheik,* which by this time had come to mean "sultan." The sheik governed both the island city and the nearby mainland. Farther inland, tribal chiefs ruled with the advice of councils of elders. By the late thirteenth century Kilwa had become the most powerful city on the coast, exercising political hegemony as far north as Pemba and as far south as Sofala (see Map 15.3).

The Portuguese, approaching the East African coastal cities in the late fifteenth century (see Map 15.1), were astounded at their enormous wealth and prosperity. This wealth rested on monopolistic control of all trade in the area. Some coastal cities manufactured goods for export: Mogadishu produced a cloth for the Egyptian market; Mom-

Church of St. George, Lalibela   Shortly before A.D. 1100 the political capital of Ethiopia was moved south from Axum to Lalibela. Legend holds that St. George, the third-century Christian martyr, ordered villagers here to construct a church in his honor. They carved it from a hillside of volcanic rock. Worshipers entered through the subterranean trench to the left of the building, while concentric Greek crosses, formed of four equal arms and symbolizing the universal Christian Church, made up the roof. *(Source: Kal Mueller/Woodfin Camp & Associates)*

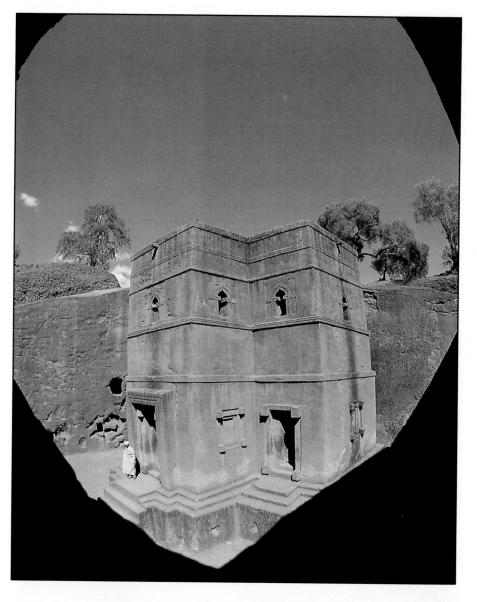

basa and Malindi processed iron tools; and Sofala made Cambay cottons for the interior trade. The bulk of the cities' exports, however, were animal products—leopard skins, tortoise shell, ambergris, ivory, and gold. The gold originated in the Mutapa region south of the Zambezi River, where the Bantu mined it. As in tenth-century Ghana, gold was a royal monopoly in the fourteenth-century coastal city-states. The Mutapa kings received it as annual tribute, prohibited outsiders from entering the mines or participating in the trade, and controlled shipments down the Zambezi to the coastal markets. The prosperity of Kilwa rested on its traffic in gold.

African goods satisfied the widespread aristocratic demand for luxury goods. In Arabia, leopard skins were made into saddles and shells into combs, and ambergris was used in the manufacture of perfumes. Because the tusks of African elephants were larger and more durable than the tusks of Indian elephants, African ivory was in great demand in India for sword and dagger handles, carved decorative objects, and the ceremonial bangles used in Hindu marriage rituals. In China, the wealthy valued African ivory for use in the construction of sedan chairs.

In exchange for these natural products, the Swahili cities bought pottery, glassware and beads, and many varieties of cloth. Swahili kings imposed enormous duties on imports, perhaps more than 80 percent of the value of the goods themselves. Even so, traders who came to Africa made fabulous profits.

Slaves were another export from the East African coast. Reports of slave trading began with the *Periplus,* accelerated with the establishment of Muslim settlements in the eighth century, and continued down to the arrival of the Portuguese in the late fifteenth century. (In fact, the East African coastal trade in slaves persisted at least to the beginning of the twentieth century.) The Arabs called the northern Somali coast *Ras Assir* ("Cape of Slaves"). From the ports of Brava, Mogadishu, Berbera, and Tajura, Arab traders transported slaves northward up the Red Sea and the Caspian Sea to the markets of Arabia, Persia, and Iraq. Muslim dealers also shipped blacks from the region of Zanzibar across the Indian Ocean to markets in India. Rulers of the Deccan in central India used large numbers of black soldier-slaves in their military campaigns. Slaves also worked on the docks and *dhows* (typical Arab lateen-rigged ves-

sels) in the Muslim-controlled Indian Ocean and as domestic servants and concubines throughout South and East Asia. As early as the tenth century, sources mention persons with "lacquer-black bodies" in the possession of wealthy families in Sung China.[20]

As in West Africa, African merchants recruited slaves primarily through raids and kidnappings in the interior. These businessmen responded to the demand for slaves: profit was their obvious motive. In the East African, Indian, and Chinese markets, however, slaves were never as valuable a commodity as ivory. Thus the volume of the eastern slave trade never approached that of the trans-Saharan trade.

Ethiopia: The Christian Kingdom of Axum

Egyptian culture exerted a profound influence on the sub-Saharan kingdom of Nubia in northeastern Africa (see Map 15.3). Nubia's capital was at Meroe; thus the country is often referred to as the Nubian kingdom of Meroe. The elaborate pyramids and temples that survive at Meroe attest to the strong Egyptian influence. As part of the Roman Empire, Egypt was naturally subject to Hellenistic and Roman cultural forces, and it became an early center of Christianity. Nubia, however, was never part of the Roman Empire; its people clung to ancient Egyptian religious ideas. Christian missionaries went to the upper Nile region and succeeded in converting the Nubian rulers around A.D. 600. By that time there were three separate Nubian states, of which the kingdom of Nobatia, centered at Dongola, was the strongest. The Christian rulers of Nobatia had close ties with the kingdom of Ethiopia.

The kingdom of Ethiopia, centered at Axum (Map 15.3), had had important commercial contacts with the Roman world. Perhaps partly for that reason, Axum officially adopted Christianity in A.D. 350, just a short time after Christianity became legal within the Roman Empire itself. Ethiopia adopted the Egyptian or Coptic form of Christianity. According to its Monophysitic doctrine, Christ has only one, divine, nature. Orthodox teaching holds that Christ's nature is both human and divine. The Egyptian partriarch of Alexandria appointed the first bishop of Axum, an appointment that led to close religious ties between Egypt and Ethiopia. At the time Axum was a powerful

MAP 15.3 Trade Routes Between East Africa and India   The Indian Ocean, controlled by the Muslim merchant fleet until the arrival of the Portuguese in the late fifteenth century, was of far greater importance for world trade than the Mediterranean. Gold from Great Zimbabwe passed through the cities on the East African coast before shipment north to the Middle East and east to India and China.

cosmopolitan center whose mercantile activities played a major part in international commerce and whose military and political power was the dominant influence in East Africa.

The expansion of Islam in the eighth century severed Axum's commercial contacts with the Byzantine Empire and ended its control of the Red Sea routes. The kingdom declined as a major power. Ethiopia's high mountains encouraged an inward concentration of attention and hindered access from the outside. Twelfth-century crusaders returning from the Middle East told of a powerful Christian ruler, Prester John, whose lands lay behind Muslim lines and who was eager to help restore the Holy Land to Christian control. Europeans identified that kingdom with Ethiopia. In the later thirteenth century, the dynasty of the Solomonid kings witnessed a literary and artistic

AFRICA, CA 400–1500

ca 1st century A.D.	Beginning of Bantu migrations
ca A.D. 200	First use of the camel for trans-Saharan transportation
4th century	Ethiopia accepts Christianity
600–1500	Extensive slave trade from sub-Saharan Africa to the Mediterranean
6th and 7th centuries	Political and commercial ascendancy of Ethiopia
9th century	Decline of Ethiopia
11th century	Islam penetrates sub-Saharan Africa
	Height of the kingdom of Ghana
13th and 14th centuries	Kingdom of Mali
1312–1337	Mansa Musa, medieval Africa's most famous ruler
14th and 15th centuries	Height of the Swahili (East African) city-states

renaissance particularly notable for works of hagiography (biographies of saints), biblical exegesis, and manuscript illumination. The most striking feature of Ethiopian society in the period from 500 to 1500 was the close relationship between the church and the state. Coptic Christianity inspired a fierce devotion and tended to equate doctrinal heresy with political rebellion, thus reinforcing central monarchial power.

South Africa

South Africa, the region bordered on the northwest by tropical grasslands and on the northeast by the Zambezi River (see Map 15.3), enjoys a mild and temperate climate. Desert conditions prevail along the Atlantic coast, which gets less than five inches of annual rainfall. Eastward rainfall increases, though some areas still receive less than twenty inches a year. Although the Limpopo Valley in the east is very dry, temperate grasslands characterize the highlands of the region of the modern Orange Free State, the Transvaal, and Zimbabwe. Considerable climatic variations occur throughout much of South Africa from year to year.

Located at the southern extremity of the Afro-Eurasian land mass, South Africa has a history that is very different from the histories of West Africa, the Nile Valley, and the east coast. Over the centuries, North and West Africa felt the influences of Phoenician, Greek, Roman, and Muslim cultures; the Nile Valley experienced the impact of major Egyptian, Assyrian, Persian, and Muslim civilizations; and the East African coast had important contacts across the Indian Ocean with southern and eastern Asia and across the Red Sea with Arabia and Persia. South Africa, however, remained far removed from the outside world until the arrival of the Portuguese in the late fifteenth century. With an important exception. Bantu-speaking people reached South Africa in the eighth century. They brought with them skills in ironworking and mixed farming (settled crop production plus cattle and sheep raising) and an immunity to the kinds of diseases that later decimated the Amerindians of South America (see pages 573–574).

The earliest residents of South Africa were hunters and gatherers. In the first millennium after the birth of Christ, new farming techniques from the north arrived. A lack of water and timber (which were needed to produce the charcoal used in iron smelting) slowed the spread of iron technology and tools and thus of crop production in western South Africa. These advances, however, reached the western coastal region by 1500. By that date Khoisan-speakers were farming in the arid western regions. To the east, descendants of Bantu immigrants grew sorghum, raised sheep and cattle, and fought with iron-headed spears. They practiced polygamy and traced their descent in the male line.

In 1871 a German explorer discovered the ruined city of Great Zimbabwe southeast of the modern Rhodesian town of Fort Victoria. Archeologists consider Great Zimbabwe the most powerful monument in Africa south of the Nile Valley and the Ethiopian highlands. The ruins consist of two vast complexes of dry-stone buildings, a fortress, and an elliptically shaped enclosure commonly called "the Temple." Stone carvings, gold and copper ornaments, and Asian ceramics once decorated the buildings. The ruins extend over sixty acres and are encircled by a massive wall. The entire city was built from local granite between the eleventh and fifteenth centuries without any outside influence.

These ruins tell a remarkable story. Great Zimbabwe was the political and religious capital of a vast empire. During the first millennium A.D., settled crop cultivation, cattle raising, and work in metal led to a steady build-up in population in the Zambezi-Limpopo region. The area also contained a rich gold-bearing belt. Gold ore lay near the surface; alluvial gold lay in the Zambezi River tributaries. In the tenth century the inhabitants collected the alluvial gold by panning and washing; after the year 1000 the gold was worked in open mines with iron picks. Traders shipped the gold eastward to Sofala (see Map 15.3). The wealth and power of Great Zimbabwe rested on this gold trade.[21]

Great Zimbabwe declined in the fifteenth century, perhaps because the area had become agriculturally exhausted and could no longer support the large population. Some people migrated northward and settled in the valley of the Mazoe River, a tributary of the Zambezi. This region also contained gold. The settlers built a new empire in the tradition of Great Zimbabwe. Rulers of this

Ruins of Great Zimbabwe Considered the most impressive monument in the African interior south of the Ethiopian highlands, these ruins of Great Zimbabwe consist of two complexes of dry-stone buildings, some surrounded by a massive serpentine wall 32 feet high and 17 feet thick at its maximum. Great Zimbabwe was the center of a state whose wealth rested on gold. *(Source: Robert Aberman/Werner Forman Archive)*

empire were called "Mwene Mutapa," and their power too was based on the gold trade carried on by means of the Zambezi River and Indian Ocean ports. It was this gold that the Portuguese sought when they arrived on the East African coast in the late fifteenth century.

SUMMARY

In the fifteenth century, the African continent contained a number of very different societies and civilizations. In West Africa, Mali continued the brisk trade in gold, salt, and slaves that had originated many centuries earlier. Islam, which had spread to sub-Saharan Africa through the caravan trade, had tremendous influence on the peoples of the western Sudan, their administrative forms, and their cities. The impact of the Islamic faith was also felt in East Africa, whose bustling port cities were in touch with the cultures of the Mediterranean and the Indian Ocean. While the city-states of the eastern coast conducted complicated mercantile activities with foreign powers, the Christian kingdom of Ethiopia led an isolated, inward-looking existence. In South Africa, the vast empire of Great Zimbabwe was giving way to yet another kingdom whose power was based on precious gold.

NOTES

1. See J. Hiernaux, *The People of Africa* (New York: Scribner's, 1975), pp. 46–48.
2. "African Historical Demography" (Proceedings of a seminar held in the Centre of African Studies, University of Edinburgh, April 29–30, 1977), p. 3.
3. Quoted in R. W. July, *Precolonial Africa: An Economic and Social History* (New York: Scribner's, 1975), p. 135.
4. J. S. Trimingham, *Islam in West Africa* (Oxford: Oxford University Press, 1959), pp. 6–9.
5. R. A. Austen, *Africa in Economic History* (London: James Currey/Heinemann, 1987), p. 36
6. R. A. Austen, "The Trans-Saharan Slave Trade: A Tentative Census," in *The Uncommon Market: Essays in the Economic History of the Atlantic Slave Trade,* ed. H. A. Gemery and J. S. Hogendorn

(New York: Academic Press, 1979), pp. 1–71, esp. p. 66.
7. July, pp. 124–129.
8. Quoted in J. O. Hunwick, "Islam in West Africa, A.D. 1000–1800," in *A Thousand Years of West African History,* ed. J. F. Ade Ajayi and I. Espie (New York: Humanities Press, 1972), pp. 244–245.
9. Quoted in A. A. Boahen, "Kingdoms of West Africa, c. A.D. 500–1600," in *The Horizon History of Africa* (New York: American Heritage, 1971), p. 183.
10. Al-Bakri, *Kitab al-mughrib fdhikr bilad Ifriqiya wa'l-Maghrib (Description de l'Afrique Septentrionale),* trans. De Shane (Paris: Adrien-Maisonneuve, 1965), pp. 328–329.
11. Quoted in R. Oliver and C. Oliver, eds., *Africa in the Days of Exploration* (Englewood Cliffs, N.J.: Prentice-Hall, 1965), p. 10.
12. Quoted in Boahen, p. 184.
13. Quoted in ibid.
14. Quoted in E. J. Murphy, *History of African Civilization* (New York: Delta, 1972), p. 109.
15. Quoted ibid., p. 111.
16. Quoted ibid., p. 120.
17. Quoted in Oliver and Oliver, p. 18.
18. H. N. Chittick, "The Peopling of the East African Coast," in *East Africa and the Orient: Cultural Syntheses in Pre-Colonial Times.* ed. H. N. Chittick and R. I. Rotberg (New York: Africana Publishing, 1975), p. 19.
19. July, p. 209.
20. See Austen, "The Trans-Saharan Slave Trade," p. 65; J. H. Harris, *The African Presence in Asia* (Evanston, Ill.: Northwestern University Press, 1971), pp. 3–6, 27–30; and P. Wheatley, "Analecta Sino-Africana Recensa," in *East Africa and the Orient,* ed. Chittick and Rotberg, p. 109.
21. P. Curtin et al., *African History* (New York: Longman, 1984), rev. ed., pp. 284–287.

SUGGESTED READING

The titles by Austen, Chittick, Curtin et al., Hiernaux, and Wheatley listed in the Notes represent some of the recent scholarship on early African history, and they are especially recommended. Most contain useful bibliographies. In addition, the enterprising student should see H. P. White and M. B. Gleave, *An Economic Geography of West Africa* (1971), and N. C. Pollock and S. Agnew, *An Historical Geography of South Africa* (1963). Colin M. Turnbull, *Man in Africa* (1976), and R. E. Leakey and R. Lewin, *Origins: What New Discoveries Reveal*

About the Emergence of Our Species and Its Possible Future (1977), are important for the discoveries of the earliest human skeletons. R. Olaniyan, *African History and Culture* (1982), is a useful general survey. For the importance of the camel to African trade, see R. W. Bulliet, *The Camel and the Wheel* (1975).

For specific topics raised in early African history, see, in addition to the titles listed in the Notes, R. Oliver and G. Mathew, eds., *History of East Africa* (1963), the standard work on the eastern part of the continent, which has a valuable chapter on the coastal city-states; G. S. P. Freeman-Grenville, *The East African Coast: Select Documents from the First to the Earlier Nineteenth Century* (1962), which contains excellent material from Arabic, Chinese, and Portuguese perspectives; D. Conrad and H. Fisher, "The Conquest That Never Was: Ghana and the Almoravids," *History of Africa* 9 (1982): 21–59; M. Klein and P. E. Lovejoy, "Slavery in West Africa," in Gemery and Hogendorn's *The Uncommon Market* (see the Notes); and R. S. Smith, *Warfare and Diplomacy in Pre-colonial West Africa* (1976). On the important topic of Islam, see J. S. Trimingham's *A History of Islam in West Africa* (1970) and *Islam in East Africa* (1974), which are standard works. J. Kritzeck and W. H. Lewis, eds., *Islam in Africa* (1969), and M. Lombard, *The Golden Age of Islam* (1975), are also helpful.

16

The Americas Before European Intrusion, ca 400–1500

Toltec statuary

*I*n 1501–1502 the Florentine explorer Amerigo Vespucci (1451–1512) sailed down the eastern coast of South America to Brazil. Convinced that he had found a new world, Vespucci published an account of his voyage. Shortly thereafter the German geographer Martin Waldseemüller proposed that this new world be called "America" to preserve Vespucci's memory. Initially applied only to South America, by the end of the sixteenth century the term *America* was used for both continents in the Western Hemisphere.

To the people of the Americas, the notion of a discovery meant nothing. The New World was, in a sense, a European invention. And even for Europeans the concept of discovery presented problems. In matters of geography, as in other branches of knowledge, medieval Europeans believed that all human knowledge was contained in the Scriptures, the writings of the church fathers, and the Greek and Roman authors, none of whom mentioned a new world. The adventurous explorers of the fifteenth and sixteenth centuries sailed west searching for Asia and Africa because Europeans believed that those continents and Europe were the only world that existed. They did not expect to find new continents. Long before the arrival of Europeans, however, sophisticated civilizations were flourishing in Central and South America.

- What is the geography of the Americas and how did it shape the lives of the peoples?
- What patterns of social and political organization did Amerindian peoples display before the European intrusion?
- What are the significant cultural achievements of the Mayas, Aztecs, and the Incas?

This chapter considers these questions.

THE GEOGRAPHY AND PEOPLES OF THE AMERICAS

The distance from the Bering Strait, which separates Asia from North America, to the southern tip of South America is about eleven thousand miles. A mountain range extends all the way from Alaska to the tip of South America, crossing Central America from northwest to southeast and making for rugged country along virtually the entire western coast of both continents.

Scholars use the term *Mesoamerica* to designate the area of present-day Mexico and Central America. Mexico is dominated by high plateaus bounded by coastal plains. Geographers have labeled the plateau regions "cold lands," the valleys between the plateaus "temperate lands," and the Gulf and Pacific coastal regions "hot lands." The Caribbean coast of Central America—modern Belize, Guatemala, Honduras, Nicaragua, El Salvador, Costa Rica, and Panama—is characterized by thick jungle lowlands, heavy rainfall, and torrid heat; it is an area generally unhealthy for humans. Central America's western uplands, with their more temperate climate and good agricultural land, support the densest population in the region.

The continent of South America, south of the Isthmus of Panama, contains thirteen nations: in descending order of size, Brazil, Argentina, Peru, Colombia, Bolivia, Venezuela, Paraguay, Chile, Ecuador, Guyana, Uruguay, Surinam, and French Guiana. Brazil—three times the size of Argentina and almost one hundred times larger than French Guiana—is about the same size as the United States including Alaska.

Like Africa, South America is a continent of extremely varied terrain. The entire western coast is edged by the Andes, the highest mountain range in the Western Hemisphere. Mount Alcanqua in Argentina rises 23,000 feet, 3,000 feet higher than the tallest mountain in the United States. On the east coast another mountain range, called the "Brazilian Highlands," accounts for one-fourth of the area of Brazil. Yet three-fourths of South America—almost the entire periphery of the continent—is plains. The Amazon River, at 4,000 miles the second longest river in the world, bisects the north central part of the continent. The Amazon drains 2.7 million square miles of land in Brazil, Colombia, and Peru. Tropical lowland rain forests, characterized by dense growth and annual rainfall in excess of 80 inches, extend from the Amazon and Orinoco river basins northward all the way to southern Mexico. This jungle, the largest in the world, covers parts of Brazil, Venezuela, and Ecuador.

Most scholars believe that people began crossing the Bering Strait from Russian Siberia between

50,000 and 20,000 years ago, when the strait was narrower than it is today. Skeletal finds indicate that these immigrants belonged to several ethnic groups. Anthropologists classify the earliest of them as Amurians, short-statured people with long flat heads and coppery skin—a physical type once common in Asia and Europe. The last to arrive, at about the time of Christ, had strong Mongoloid features, large faces, and yellowish skin. The American Indians, or Amerindians, represent a hybrid of Amurians and Mongoloids.

Nomadic and technologically primitive, Amerindians lived by hunting small animals, fishing, and gathering wild fruits. As soon as an area had been exploited and the group had grown too large for the land to support, some families moved on, usually southward. Gradually the newcomers spread throughout the Americas, losing contact with one another.

At the time the Europeans arrived, most of the peoples of North America and the huge Amazon Basin were Neolithic hunters and farmers, some migratory and some living in villages. Big-game hunters, armed with heavy stone missiles, necessarily traveled in small groups. Sizable populations, however, grew among the peoples who learned to cultivate the soil. By necessity or experimentation or accident, they discovered how to domesticate plants. Archeological excavations in Mexico City indicate that corn was grown there around 2500 B.C. Before 2300 B.C. the Amerindians also were raising beans, squash, pumpkins, and, in the area of modern Peru, white potatoes.

In central Mexico, the Amerindians built *chinampas,* floating gardens, by dredging soil from the bottom of a lake or pond, placing the soil on mats of woven twigs, and planting crops in the soil. Chinampas were enormously productive, yielding up to three harvests a year. So extensive was this method of agriculture that central Mexico became known as the "chinampas region." In Peru, meanwhile, the Andean mountain slopes were terraced with stone retaining walls to keep the hillsides from sliding. Both chinampas and terraced slopes required large labor forces, making stable settlement essential.

Careful cultivation of the land meant a reliable and steady food supply, which contributed to a relatively high fertility rate and in turn to a population boom. Because corn and potatoes require much less labor than does grain, Amerindian civilizations were able to use their large labor forces in the construction of religious and political buildings and as standing armies.[1] Agricultural advancement thus had definitive social and political consequences.

MESOAMERICAN CIVILIZATIONS FROM THE OLMEC TO THE TOLTEC

The period between ca 1500 B.C. and ca 900 A.D. witnessed the rise of several ancient American civilizations. Archeological investigations of these civilizations are still under way, and more questions

Olmec Mother and Child The Olmecs excelled in sculpture and modeled in clay, jade, and basalt. Much of their work reflects a religious impulse. *(Source: The Metropolitan Museum of Art)*

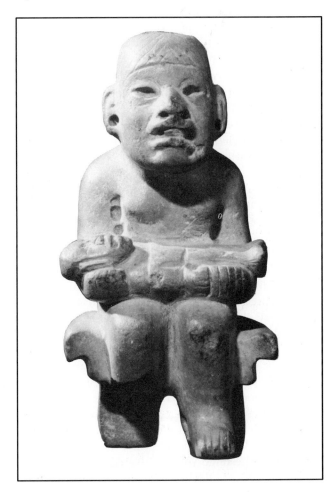

than answers about them remain, but students generally accept a few basic conclusions. Scholars believe the Olmec represent the most ancient advanced Amerindian civilization. Their culture spread over regions in central Mexico that lie thousands of miles apart. The Olmec tradition of building scattered ceremonial centers based on an extensive agricultural foundation found its highest cultural expression in the civilization of the Maya. The Maya occupied an area comprising the present-day Yucatán, the highland crescent of eastern Chiapas in Mexico, much of Guatemala and western Honduras. In the central plateau of Mexico an "empire" centered at Teotihuacán arose. Scholars hotly debate whether the Teotihuacán territory constituted an empire, but they agree that Teotihuacán society was heavily stratified and that it exercised military, religious, and political power over a wide area. The Toltec, whose culture adopted many features of Teotihuacán and Olmec civilizations, was the last advanced Amerindian civilization before the rise of the Aztec.

The Olmec

Population growth led to the development of the first distinct Mesoamerican civilization, the Olmec, which scholars estimate to have thrived from approximately 1500 B.C. to A.D. 300. All subsequent Mesoamerican cultures have rested on the Olmec. Originating at present-day San Lorenzo in the region of southern Veracruz and Tabasco (see Map 16.2), Olmec society revolved around groups of large stone buildings where the political elite and the priestly hierarchy resided with their retainers. Peasant farmers inhabited the surrounding countryside. From careful study of the surviving architectural monuments and their richly carved jade sculptures, scholars have learned that a small hereditary elite governed the mass of workers and that the clustered buildings served as sites for religious ceremonies and as marketplaces for the exchange of agricultural produce and manufactured goods. The Olmecs also possessed a form of writing. Around 900 B.C. San Lorenzo was destroyed, probably by migrating peoples from the north, and power passed to La Venta in Tabasco.

At La Venta, archeological excavation has uncovered the huge volcano-shaped Great Pyramid. Built 110 feet high at an inaccessible site on an island in the Tonala River, the Great Pyramid was the center of the Olmec religion. The upward thrust of this monument, like that of the cathedrals of medieval Europe, may have represented the human effort to get closer to the gods. Built of huge stone slabs, the Great Pyramid required, scholars have estimated, some 800,000 man-hours of labor. It testifies to the region's bumper harvests, which supported a labor force large enough to build such a monument. Around 300 B.C., however, La Venta fell. Tres Zapotes, 100 miles to the northwest, became the leading Olmec site. Olmec ceremonialism, magnificent sculpture, skillful stone work, social organization, and writing were important cultural advances that paved the way for the developments of the Classic period (A.D. 300–900), the golden age of Mesoamerican civilization.

The Maya of Central America

In the Classic period another Amerindian people, the Maya, attained a level of intellectual and artistic achievement equaled by no other Indian people in the Western Hemisphere and by few peoples throughout the world. The Maya developed a sophisticated system of writing perhaps derived partly from the Olmec. They also invented a calendar considered more accurate than the European Gregorian calendar. And the Maya made advances in mathematics that Europeans did not match for several centuries. Who were the Maya and where did they come from? What was the basis of their culture? What is the significance of their intellectual and artistic achievement?

The word *Maya* seems to derive from *Zamna,* the early Maya culture god. On the basis of linguistic evidence, scholars believe that the first Maya were a small North American Indian group who emigrated from southern Oregon and northern California to the western highlands of Guatemala. Between the third and second millennia B.C. various groups, including the Cholans and Tzeltalans, broke away from the parent group, moving north and east into the Yucatán Peninsula. The Cholan-speaking Maya, who occupied the area during the time of great cultural achievement, apparently created the culture.

Maya culture rested on agriculture. As rice proved the staple of the diet in Asia and wheat in

Europe, so in Mesoamerica maize (corn) became the basic or staple crop. In 1972, a geographer and an aerial photographer studying the Campeche region (Map 16.1) proved that the Maya practiced intensive agriculture in raised fields, narrow rectangular plots built above the low-lying, seasonally inundated lands bordering rivers. Because of poor soil caused by heavy tropical rainfall and the fierce sun, farmers may also have relied on *milpa* for growing maize. Using this method, farmers cut down a patch of forest land and set the wood and brush afire. They then used a stick to poke holes through the ash and planted maize seed in the holes. A milpa (meaning both the area and the method) produced for only two years, after which it had to lie fallow for between four and seven years.

In addition to maize, the Maya grew beans, squash, chili peppers, some root crops, and fruit trees. Turkeys were domesticated, but barkless dogs that were fattened on corn seem to have been the main source of protein. In the Yucatán, men trapped fish along the shores. Cotton was widely exported, as the discovery of rich Maya textiles all over Mesoamerica attests.

The raised-field and milpa systems of intensive agriculture yielded food sufficient to support large population centers. The entire Maya region could have had as many as 14 million inhabitants. At Uxmal, Uaxactún, Copan, Piedras Negras, Tikal, Palenque, and Chichén Itza (see Map 16.1), archeologists have uncovered the palaces of nobles, elaborate pyramids where nobles were buried, engraved steles (stone-slab monuments), masonry temples, altars, sophisticated polychrome pottery, and courts for games played with a rubber ball. The largest site, Tikal, may have had 40,000 people. Since these centers lacked commercial and industrial activities, scholars avoid calling them "cities." Rather they were religious and ceremonial centers.

Although Maya sources rarely mention marketplaces in Maya population centers, the Maya carried on extensive long-distance trade with other Mesoamerican peoples. The shipment of products from various local regions to areas where they were needed helped hold the Maya settlements together. Wealth seems to have been concentrated in a few hands, probably in one clan or lineage that enjoyed great power, but the Maya apparently had no distinct mercantile class. They did have sharply

MAP 16.1 The Maya World, A.D. **300–900**   Archeologists have discovered the ruins of dozens of Maya city-states, only the largest of which are shown here. Called the "Greeks of the New World," the Maya perfected the only written language in the Western Hemisphere, developed a sophisticated political system and a flourishing trade network, and created elegant art.

defined social classes, however. A hereditary elite owned private land, defended society, carried on business activities, directed religious rituals, and held all political power. The intellectual class also belonged to the ruling nobility. The rest of the people were free workers, serfs, and slaves.

The Maya developed a system of hieroglyphic writing with 850 characters and used it to record chronology, religion, and astronomy in books made of bark paper and deerskin. The recent deciphering of this writing has demonstrated that inscriptions on steles are actually historical documents recording the births, accessions, marriages, wars, and deaths of Maya kings. An understanding of the civilization's dynastic history allows scholars to interpret more accurately Maya pictorial imagery and to detect patterns in Maya art. They are finding that the imagery explicitly portrays the text in pictorial scenes and on stelar carvings.[2]

Cylindrical Vessel Because the Maya suffered a high death rate from warfare, sacrificial ritual, and natural causes, the subject of death preoccupied them. Many art objects depict death as a journey into Xibalba, the Maya hell, and to rebirth for the Maya in children and grandchildren who replace them. Here three Xibalbans receive a sacrificial head on a drum. The scrawny torso of one has the look of starvation, and the excrement implies a revolting smell. The next figure, with a skeletal head, insect wings, and a distended stomach suggests a parasitic disease. A common if nauseating scene. *(Source: © Justin Kerr 1985. Courtesy Houston Art Museum)*

A method of measuring and recording time to arrange and commemorate events in the life of a society and to plan the agricultural and ceremonial year is a basic feature of all advanced societies. From careful observation of the earth's movements around the sun, the Maya invented a calendar of eighteen 20-day months and one 5-day month, for a total of 365 days. Using a system of bars (— = 5) and dots (° = 1), the Maya devised a form of mathematics based on the vigesimal (20) rather than the decimal (10) system. The Maya proved themselves masters of abstract knowledge—notably in astronomy, mathematics, calendric development, and the recording of history.

Maya civilization lasted about a thousand years, reaching its peak in about A.D. 500–800, the period when the T'ang Dynasty was flourishing in China, Islam was spreading in the Middle East, and Carolingian rulers were extending their sway in Europe. Between the eighth and tenth centuries, the Maya abandoned their cultural and ceremonial centers, and Maya civilization collapsed. Why?

Archeologists and historians have advanced several theories: foreign invasions led by peoples attracted to the wealth of the great centers, domestic revolts of subject peoples, disease, overpopulation caused by crop failures, the acquisition of such broad territories by expansionist kings that rulers could not govern them effectively. Just as students give no single reason for the decline and fall of the Roman Empire in Europe, so current scholarship holds that the fall of Maya civilization involved many factors. But the Maya were not totally vanquished. Having resisted Indian invaders and the encroachments of Spanish American civilization, about two million Maya survive today in the Yucatán peninsula of Mexico.

Teotihuacán and Toltec Civilizations

During the Classic period the Teotihuacán Valley in central Mexico witnessed the flowering of a remarkable civilization. The culture of Teotihuacán seems to have been built by a new people from regions east and south of the Valley of Mexico. The city of Teotihuacán had a population of over 200,000—larger than any European city at the time. The inhabitants were stratified into distinct social classes. The rich and powerful elite resided in a special precinct, in houses of palatial splendor. Ordinary working people, tradespeople, artisans, and obsidian craftsmen lived in apartment compounds, or *barrios,* on the edge of the city. Around A.D. 600 each of these compounds housed about a hundred people; archeological research is slowly yielding information about their standard of living. The inhabitants of the barrios seem to have been very poor and related by kinship ties and perhaps by shared common ritual interests. Agricultural laborers lived outside the city. Teotihuacán was a great commercial center, the entrepôt for trade and culture for all of Mesoamerica. It was also the ceremonial center of an entire society, a capital filled with artworks, a mecca that attracted thousands of pilgrims a year.

In the center of the city stood the pyramids of the Sun and Moon. The Pyramid of the Sun, each of whose sides is 700 feet long and 200 feet high, was built of sun-dried bricks and faced with stone. The smaller Pyramid of the Moon was similar in construction. In lesser temples, natives and outlanders worshiped the rain-god and the feathered serpent, later called "Quetzalcoatl." These gods were associated with the production of corn, the staple of the people's diet.

Although Teotihuacán dominated Mesoamerican civilization during the Classic period, other centers also flourished. In the isolated valley of Oaxaca at modern-day Monte Albán (see Map 16.2), for example, Zapotecan-speaking peoples established a great religious center whose temples and elaborately decorated tombs testify to the wealth of the nobility. The art—and probably the entire culture—of Monte Albán and other centers derived from Teotihuacán.

As had happened to San Lorenzo and La Venta, Teotihuacán collapsed before invaders. Around A.D. 700 semibarbarian hordes from the southwest burned Teotihuacán; Monte Albán fell shortly afterward. By 900 the golden age of Mesoamerica had ended.

There followed an interregnum known as the "Time of Troubles" (ca A.D. 800–1000), characterized by disorders and an extreme militarism. Whereas nature gods and their priests seem to have

governed the great cities of the earlier period, militant gods and warriors dominated the petty states that now arose. Among these states, the most powerful heir to Teotihuacán was the Toltec confederation, a weak union of strong states. The Toltecs admired the culture of their predecessors and sought to absorb and preserve it; through intermarriage, they assimilated with the Teotihuacán people. In fact, every new Mesoamerican confederation became the cultural successor of earlier ones.

Under Toliptzin (ca 980–1000), the Toltecs extended their hegemony over most of central Mexico. He established his capital at Tula, whose splendor and power became legendary during his reign. Apparently Toliptzin took the name "Quetzalcoatl," signifying his position as high priest of the Teotihuacán god worshiped by the Toltecs. According to the "Song of Quetzalcoatl," a long Aztec glorification of Toliptzin,

he was very rich and had everything necessary to eat and drink, and the corn under his reign was in abundance, and the squash very fat, an arm's length around, and the ears of corn were so tall that they were carried with both arms. . . . And more than that the said Quetzalcoatl had all the wealth of the world, gold and silver and green stones jade and other precious things and a great abundance of coca trees in different colors, and the said vassals of the said Quetzalcoatl were very rich and lacked nothing. . . . Nor did they lack corn, nor did they eat the small ears but rather they used them like firewood to heat up their baths.[3]

Later, Aztec legends would describe a powerful struggle between the Toltecs' original tribal god, Tezcatlipoca, who required human sacrifices, and the newer Toltec-Teotihuacán god, Quetzalcoatl, who gave his people bumper corn crops, fostered learning and the arts, and asked only the sacrifice of animals like butterflies and snakes. Tezcatlipoca won this battle, and the priest-king Toliptzin-Quetzalcoatl was driven into exile. As he departed, he promised to return and regain his kingdom.

Whatever reality lies behind this legend, it became a cornerstone of Aztec tradition. It also played a profound role in Mexican history: by a remarkable coincidence, the year that Quetzalcoatl had promised to return happened to be the year when the Spanish explorer Hernando Cortés landed in Mexico. Belief in the Quetzalcoatl legend helps explain the Aztec emperor Montezuma's indecisiveness about the Spanish adventurers and his ultimate fate (pages 571–572).

After the departure of Toliptzin-Quetzalcoatl, troubles beset the Toltec state. Drought led to crop failure. Northern barbarian peoples, the Chichimec, attacked the borders in waves. Weak, in-

competent rulers could not quell domestic uprisings. When the last Toltec king committed suicide in 1174, the Toltec state collapsed. In 1224 the Chichimec captured Tula.

The last of the Chichimec to arrive in central Mexico were the Aztecs. As before, the vanquished strongly influenced the victors: the Aztecs ab-

Tezcatlipoca and Quetzalcoatl The Aztecs were deeply concerned with the passage of time, and like the Maya they had a solar year of 365 days divided into 18 months of 20 days each. The Aztec *tonalamatl*, or sacred "book of days," included a ritual calendar that portrayed thirteen Lords of the Day and nine Lords of the Night, each of them associated with a particular bird. This early sixteenth-century illustration of a book of days shows Tezcatlipoca and Quetzalcoatl, who were major Lords of the Day. *(Source: Bibliothèque de l'Assemblée, Paris)*

MAP 16.2 The Aztec Empire, 1519   Aztecs controlled much of central Mexico, while the Maya survived in the Yucatán Peninsula and some of present-day Guatemala. Note the number of cities.

sorbed the cultural achievements of the Toltecs. The Aztecs—building on Olmec, Maya, Teotihuacán, and Toltec antecedents—created the last unifying civilization in Mexico before the arrival of the Europeans.

AZTEC SOCIETY: RELIGION AND WAR

When the Aztecs appeared in the Valley of Mexico, they spoke the same Nahuatl language as the Toltecs; otherwise, they had nothing in common with their advanced predecessors. Poor, unwelcome, looked on as foreign barbarians, they had to settle on a few swampy islands in Lake Texcoco. There, in 1325, they founded a city consisting of a few huts and an altar for their war-god Huitzilopochtli, who had protected them during 150 years of wandering. From these unpromising beginnings the Aztecs rapidly assimilated the cultural legacy of the Toltecs and in 1428 embarked on a policy of territorial expansion. By the time Cortés arrived in 1519, the Aztec confederation encompassed all of central Mexico from the Gulf of Mexico to the Pacific Ocean as far south as Guatemala (Map 16.2). The rulers of neighboring Texcoco

and Tlacopan bowed to the Aztec king, and thirty-eight subordinate provinces paid tribute to him.

The growth of a strong mercantile class led to an influx of tropical wares and luxury goods: cotton, feathers, cocoa, skins, turquoise jewelry, and gold. The upper classes enjoyed an elegant and extravagant life style; the court of Emperor Montezuma II (r. 1502–1520) was more magnificent than anything in Western Europe. How, in less than two hundred years, had the Mexicans (from the Aztec word *mizquitl,* meaning "desolate land," or from *Mixitli,* the Aztec god of war) grown from an insignificant tribe of wandering nomads to a people of vast power and fabulous wealth?

The Aztecs' pictorial records attribute their success to the power of Huitzilopochtli and to the Aztecs' drive and indomitable will power. Will and determination they unquestionably had, but there is another explanation: the Aztec state was geared for war. In the course of the fifteenth century, the primitive tribesmen who had arrived in the Valley of Mexico in 1325 transformed themselves into professional soldiers. As the territory under Aztec control gradually expanded and military campaigns continued, warriors had to be in perpetual readiness. They were constantly subduing new states and crushing rebellions. A strong standing army was the backbone of the Mexican state, and war had become the central feature of Mexican culture.

War and Human Sacrifice

In Aztec society, war shaped the social hierarchy, education, and economic prosperity. War was also an article of religious faith.

Chief among the Aztecs' many gods was Huitzilopochtli, who symbolized the sun blazing at high noon. The sun, the source of all life, had to be kept moving in its orbit if darkness was not to overtake the world. To keep it moving, Aztecs believed, the sun had to be frequently fed precious fluids—that is, human blood. Human sacrifice was a sacred duty, essential for the preservation and prosperity of humankind. Black-robed priests carried out the ritual:

The victim was stretched out on his back on a slightly convex stone with his arms and legs held by four priests, while a fifth ripped him open with a flint knife and tore out his heart. The sacrifice also often took place in a manner which the Spanish described as gladiatorio: *the captive was tied to a huge disk of stone . . . by a rope that left him free to move; he was armed with wooden weapons, and he had to fight several normally-armed Aztec warriors in turn. If, by an extraordinary chance, he did not succumb to their attacks, he was spared; but nearly always the "gladiator" fell, gravely wounded, and a few moments later he died on the stone, with his body opened by the black-robed, long-haired priests.*[4]

Mass sacrifice was also practiced:

Mass sacrifices involving hundreds and thousands of victims could be carried out to commemorate special events. The Spanish chroniclers were told, for example, that at the dedication in 1487, of the great pyramid of Tenochititlán four lines of prisoners of war stretching for two miles each were sacrificed by a team of executioners who worked night and day for four days. Allotting two minutes for sacrifice, the demographer and historian Sherbourne Cook estimated that the number of victims associated with that single event was 14,100. The scale of these rituals could be dismissed as exaggerations were it not for the encoun-

ters of Spanish explorers with . . . rows of human skulls in the plazas of the Aztec cities. . . . In the plaza of Xocotlan "there were . . . more than one hundred thousand of them."[5]

Anthropologists have proposed several explanations, none of them completely satisfactory, of the Aztecs' practice of human sacrifice and the cannibalism that often accompanied it. Some suggest that human sacrifice served to regulate population growth. Yet ritual slaughter had been practiced by earlier peoples—the Olmecs, the Maya, the dwellers of Teotihuacán, and the Toltecs—in all likelihood before population density had reached the point of threatening the food supply. Moreover, since almost all those sacrificed were men—warriors captured in battle—population growth could still have exceeded the death rate. Executing women of child-bearing age would have had more effect on population growth.

According to a second hypothesis, the ordinary people were given victims' bodies as a source of protein.[6] These people lived on a diet of corn, beans, squash, tomatoes, and peppers. Wildlife was scarce, and dog meat, chicken, turkey, and fish were virtually restricted to the upper classes. The testimony of modern nutritionists that beans supply ample protein, and the evidence that, in an area teeming with wild game, the Huron Indians of North America ritually executed captives and feasted on their stewed bodies, weaken the validity of this theory.

A third, more plausible, theory holds that ritual human sacrifice was an instrument of state terrorism—that the Aztec rulers crushed dissent with terror. The Aztecs controlled a large confederation of city-states by sacrificing prisoners seized in battle; by taking hostages from among defeated peoples as ransom against future revolt; and by demanding from subject states an annual tribute of people to be sacrificed to Huitzilopochtli. Unsuccessful generals, corrupt judges, and careless public officials, even people who accidentally entered forbidden precincts of the royal palaces, were routinely sacrificed. When the supply of such victims ran out, slaves, plebeians, even infants torn from their mothers suffered ritual execution. The emperor Montezuma II, who celebrated his coronation with the sacrifice of 5,100 people, could be said to have ruled by holocaust. Trumpets blasted and drums beat all day long announcing the sacrifice of yet another victim. Blood poured down the steps of the pyramids. Death and fear stalked everywhere. Ordinary people appear to have endured this living nightmare by escaping into intoxicating drink and drugs.[7]

The Life of the People

A wealth of information has survived about fifteenth- and sixteenth-century Mexico. The Aztecs were deeply interested in their own past, and in their pictographic script they wrote many books recounting their history, geography, and religious practices. They loved making speeches, and every public or social occasion gave rise to lengthy orations, which scribes copied down. The Aztecs also preserved records of their legal disputes, which alone amounted to vast files. The Spanish conquerors subsequently destroyed much of this material. But enough documents remain to construct a picture of the Mexican people at the time of the Spanish intrusion.

During their early migrations, no sharp social distinctions existed among the Aztecs. All were equally poor. The head of a family was both provider and warrior, and a sort of tribal democracy prevailed in which all adult males participated in important decision making. By the early sixteenth century, however, a stratified social structure had come into being, and the warrior aristocracy exercised great authority.

Scholars do not yet understand precisely how this social stratification evolved. According to Aztec legend, the Mexicans admired the Toltecs and chose their first king, Acamapichti, from among them. The many children he fathered with Aztec women formed the nucleus of the noble class. At the time of the Spanish intrusion into Mexico, men who had distinguished themselves in war occupied the highest military and social positions in the state. Generals, judges, and governors of provinces were appointed by the emperor from among his servants who had earned reputations as war heroes. These great lords, or *tecuhtli*, dressed luxuriously and lived in palaces. Like feudal lords, the provincial governors exercised full political, judicial, and military authority on the emperor's behalf. In their territories they maintained order, settled disputes and judged legal cases; oversaw the cultivation of land; and made sure that trib-

ute—in food or gold—was paid. The governors also led troops in wartime. These functions resembled those of feudal lords in western Europe during the Middle Ages (see pages 347–348). Just as only nobles of France and England could wear fur and carry a sword, so in Aztec society, only the tecuhtli could wear jewelry and embroidered cloaks.

Beneath the great nobility of soldiers and imperial officials was the class of warriors. Theoretically every freeman could be a warrior, and parents dedicated their male children to war: parents buried a male child's umbilical cord with some arrows and a shield on the day of his birth. In actuality the sons of nobles enjoyed advantages deriving from their fathers' position and influence in the state. At the age of six, boys entered a school that trained them for war. Future warriors were taught to fight with a *macana*, a paddle-shaped wooden club edged with bits of obsidian (a volcanic rock similar to granite but as sharp as glass). This weapon could be brutally effective: during the Spanish invasion, Aztec warriors armed with macanas slashed off the heads of horses at one blow. Youths were also trained in the use of spears, bows and arrows, and lances fitted with obsidian points. They learned to live on little food and sleep and to accept pain without complaint. At about age eighteen a warrior fought his first campaign. If he captured a prisoner for ritual sacrifice, he acquired the title iyac, or warrior; if in later campaigns he succeeded in killing or capturing four of the enemy, he became a *tequiua*—one who shared in the booty and thus was a member of the nobility. Warriors enjoyed a privileged position in Mexican society because they provided the state with the victims necessary for its survival. If a young man failed in several campaigns to capture the required four prisoners, he joined the *maceualtin*, the plebeian or working class.

The maceualtin were the ordinary citizens, the backbone of Aztec society and the vast majority of the population. The word *maceualti* means "worker" and implied boorish speech and vulgar behavior. Members of this class performed all sorts of agricultural, military, and domestic services and carried heavy public burdens not required of noble warriors. Government officials assigned the maceualtin work on the temples, roads, and bridges. Army officers called them up for military duty, but Mexicans considered this an honor and a religious rite, not a burden. Unlike nobles, priests, orphans, and slaves, maceualtin paid taxes. Maceualtin in the capital, however, possessed certain rights: they held their plots of land for life, and they received a small share of the tribute paid by the provinces to the emperor. Maceualtin in subject provinces enjoyed none of those rights.

Beneath the maceualtin were the *thalmaitl*, the landless workers or serfs. Some social historians speculate that this class originated during the

The Goddess Tlazolteotl   The Aztecs believed that Tlazolteotl (sometimes called "Mother of the Gods"), in her eating refuse, consumed the sins of humankind, thus leaving them pure. As the goddess of childbirth, Tlazolteotl was extensively worshiped. Note the squatting position for childbirth, then common all over the world. (*Source: Dumbarton Oaks Research Library and Collections, Washington, D.C.*)

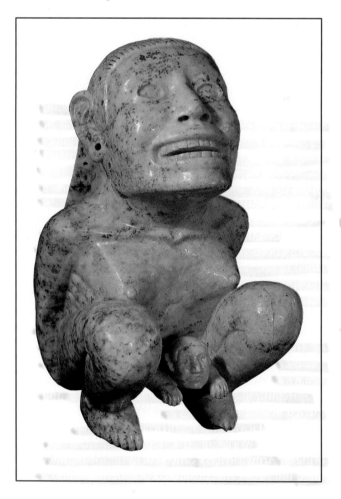

"Time of Troubles," a period of migrations and upheavals in which weak and defenseless people placed themselves under the protection of strong warriors. The thalmaitl provided agricultural labor at times of planting and harvesting, paid rents in kind, and were bound to the soil—they could not move off the land. The thalmaitl resembled in many ways the serfs of Western Europe, but unlike serfs they performed military service when called on to do so. They enjoyed some rights as citizens and generally were accorded more respect than slaves.

Slaves were the lowest social class. Like European and African slaves, most were prisoners captured in war or kidnapped from enemy tribes. Aztecs who stole from a temple or private house or plotted against the emperor could also be enslaved. Also people in serious debt sometimes voluntarily sold themselves into slavery. Female slaves often became their masters' concubines. Mexican slaves, however, differed fundamentally from European ones: "Tlatlocotin slaves could possess goods, save money, buy land and houses and even slaves for their own service."[8] Slaves could purchase their freedom. If a male slave married a free woman, their offspring were free, and a slave who escaped and managed to enter the emperor's palace was automatically free. Most slaves eventually gained their freedom. Mexican slavery, therefore, had humane qualities, in marked contrast with the methods that the Spanish later introduced into South America and those that the English imposed in North America.

Alongside the secular social classes stood the temple priests. Huitzilopochtli and each of the numerous lesser gods had many priests to oversee the upkeep of the temple, assist at religious ceremonies, and perform ritual sacrifices. The priests also did a brisk business in divination, foretelling the future on the basis of signs and omens. Aztecs were deeply concerned about coming events. They consulted priests on the selection of wives and husbands, on the future careers of newborn babies, and before leaving on journeys or for war. Because the emperor and the wealthy showered gifts on the gods, temples possessed enormous wealth in gold and silver ceremonial vessels, statues, buildings, and land. For example, fifteen provincial villages had to provide food for the temple at Texcoco and wood for its eternal fires. The priests who had custody of all this property did not marry and were expected to live moral and upright lives. From the temple revenues and resources, the priests supported schools, aided the poor, and maintained hospitals. The chief priests had the ear of the emperor and often exercised great power and influence.

At the peak of the social pyramid stood the emperor. The various Aztec historians contradict one another about the origin of the imperial dynasty, but modern scholars tend to accept the verdict of one sixteenth-century authority that the "custom has always been preserved among the Mexicans (that) the sons of kings have not ruled by right of inheritance, but by election."[9] The monarchy passed from the emperor to the ablest son of one of his legitimate wives (not his many concubines); a small oligarchy of the chief priests, warriors, and state officials made the selection. If none of the sons proved satisfactory, a brother or nephew of the emperor was chosen, but election was always restricted to the royal family.

The Aztec emperor was expected to be a great warrior; one of his titles was *tlacatecuhtli,* "lord of the men." He led Mexican and allied armies into battle. All his other duties pertained to the welfare of his people. It was up to the emperor to see that justice was done—he was the final court of appeal. He also held ultimate responsibility for ensuring an adequate food supply and for protecting against famine and other disasters. The emperor Montezuma I (r. 1440–1467) distributed twenty thousand loads of stockpiled grain when a flood hit the city. The records show that the Aztec emperors took their public duties seriously.

The Cities of the Aztecs

When the Spanish entered Tenochtitlán (which they called "Mexico City") in November 1519, they could not believe their eyes. According to Bernal Díaz, one of Cortés's companions,

when we saw all those cities and villages built in the water, and other great towns on dry land, and that straight and level causeway leading to Mexico, we were astounded. These great towns and cues (temples) and buildings rising from the water, all made of stone, seemed like an enchanted vision. . . . Indeed, some of our soldiers asked whether it was not all a dream.[10]

Tenochtitlán had about 60,000 households. The upper class practiced polygamy and had many children, and many households included servants and slaves. The total population probably numbered at least 500,000. At the time, no European city and few Asian ones could boast a population even half that size. The total Aztec empire has been estimated at around 5 million inhabitants.

Originally built on salt marshes, Tenochtitlán was approached by four great highways that connected it with the mainland. Wide straight streets and canals crisscrossed the city, and the bridges over the canals were so broad and solidly built that ten horsemen could ride abreast over them. Boats and canoes plied the canals. Lining the roads and canals stood thousands of rectangular one-story houses of mortar faced with stucco. Although space was limited, many houses had small gardens, which along with the numerous parks dazzled with the colors and scents of flowers. The Mexicans loved flowers and used them in ritual ceremonies.

A large aqueduct whose sophisticated engineering astounded Cortés carried pure water from distant springs and supplied fountains in the parks. Streets and canals opened onto public squares and marketplaces. Tradespeople offered every kind of merchandise: butchers hawked turkeys, ducks, chickens, rabbits, and deer, while grocers sold kidney beans, squash, avocados, corn, and all kinds of peppers. Artisans sold intricately designed gold, silver, and feathered jewelry. Seamstresses offered sandals, loincloths and cloaks for men, and blouses and long skirts for women—the traditional dress of ordinary people—and embroidered robes and cloaks for the rich. Slaves for domestic service, wood for building, herbs for seasoning and medicinal purposes, honey and sweets, knives, jars and utensils, smoking tobacco, even human excrement used to cure animal skins—all these wares made a dazzling spectacle.

At one side of the central square of Tenochtitlán stood the great temple of Huitzilopochtli. Built as a pyramid and approached by three flights of 120 steps each, the temple was about 100 feet high and dominated the city's skyline. According to Cortés it was

so large that within the precincts, which are surrounded by a very high wall, a town of some five hundred inhabitants could easily be built. All round

Tenochtitlán The great Mexican archeologist Ignacio Marquina reconstructed the central plaza of the Aztec capital as it looked in 1519. The huge temple of the God of War dominates the area, with royal palaces on each side. On the right stands the rack with tens of thousands of human skulls; in the center is the platform where captives met sacrificial death. *(Source: Library of Congress)*

inside this wall there are very elegant quarters with very large rooms and corridors where their priests live. There are as many as forty towers, all of which are so high that in the case of the largest there are fifty steps leading up to the main part of it . . . They are so well constructed in both their stone and woodwork that there can be none better in any place.[11]

Describing the Aztec way of life for the emperor Charles V, Cortés concluded: "I will say only that these people live almost like those in Spain, and in such harmony and order as there, and considering that they are barbarous and so far from the knowledge of God and cut off from all civilized nations, it is truly remarkable to see what they have achieved in all things."[12] Certainly Cortés's views reflect his own culture and outlook, but it is undeniable that Aztec culture was remarkable.

THE INCAS OF PERU

In the late 1980s archeologists working in the river valleys on the west coast of Peru uncovered stunning evidence of complex societies that flourished between 5,000 and 3,000 years ago—roughly the same period as the great pyramids of Egypt (see page 28). In spite of the altitude and aridity of the semidesert region, scores of settlements existed, perhaps the largest being at Cardal south of Lima, Aspero on the coast, Sechin Alto north of Lima, and the most spectacular, Pampa de las Llamas-Moxeke in the Casma Valley (Map 16.3). Stepped pyramids and U-shaped buildings, some more than ten stories high, dominated these settlements. Were these monuments warehouses for storing food or cultic temples? Were these settlements connected in some sort of political association? Was there sufficient commercial activity to justify calling them cities? Further investigation may answer these questions. The people depended on the sea for food and lived on a diet of fish, sweet potatoes, beans, and peanuts. Why did these peoples suddenly abandon their settlements and move into the Andean highlands? Scholars have only begun to process these vast remains, but radio carbon dating has already demonstrated that the settlements are older than the Maya and Aztec monuments.[13]

The Aztec civilization of Mexico had already passed its peak when the Spanish landed in America. So too had a greater culture to the south, that of the Incas of Peru. Like the Aztecs, the Incas were "a small militaristic group that came to power late, conquered surrounding groups, and established one of the most extraordinary empires in the world."[14] Gradually, Inca culture spread throughout Peru. Modern knowledge of the Incas is concentrated on the last century before Spanish intrusion (1438–1532); today's scholars know far less about earlier developments.

Peru consists of three radically different geographical regions: a 2,000-mile-long semidesert coastland skirting the Pacific Ocean; tropical jungle lowlands bordering modern Bolivia and Brazil; and, in the center, the cold highlands of the Andes Mountains. Six valleys of fertile and wooded land at altitudes of 8,000 to 11,000 feet punctuate highland Peru. The largest of these valleys are Huaylas, Cuzco, and Titicaca. It was there that Inca civilization developed and flourished.

Archeologists still do not understand how people of the Andean region acquired a knowledge of agriculture. Around 2500 B.C. they were relying on fish and mussels for food. Early agriculture seems to have involved cultivating cotton for ordinary clothing, ceremonial dress, and for fish nets. Beautifully dyed cotton textiles, swatches of which have been found in ancient gravesites, may also have served as articles for trade. The central highland region of the Andes is much less suited to agriculture than is Mesoamerica; in the Andes arable land is scarce. Yet between A.D. 600 and 1000, remarkable agricultural progress was made.

The Incas constructed great terraces along the mountain slopes and shored them up with walls to retain moisture. Terracing proved ideal for the cultivation of white potatoes. With only a foot plow, bronze hoe, and *guano* (the dried excrement of sea birds) as fertilizer, the Amerindians of Peru produced bumper crops of potatoes. They also learned an excellent method of preserving them. Potatoes ordinarily cannot be stored for long periods, but the Inca of the Andean highlands developed a product called *chuñu,* freeze-dried potatoes, made by subjecting potatoes alternately to nightly frosts and daily sun. Chuñu will keep unspoiled for several years. The construction of irrigation channels also facilitated the cultivation of corn, the other important Andean crop (much less important than the potato, however). Potatoes and corn required

MAP 16.3 The Inca Empire, 1463–1532 South America, which extends 4,750 miles in length and 3,300 miles from east to west at its widest point, contains every climatic zone and probably the richest variety of vegetation on earth. Note the system of Inca roads that linked most of the Andean region.

THE AMERICAS, CA 400–1500

ca 20,000 B.C.	Migration across the Bering Sea to the Americas
ca 1500 B.C.–A.D. 300	Rise of Olmec culture
A.D. 300–900	Classic period of Teotihuacán civilization
ca 600–900	Peak of Maya civilization
ca 800–1000	"Time of Troubles" in Mesoamerica
ca 1000	Beginning of Inca expansion
ca 1000–1300	Toltec hegemony
ca 1325	Arrival of the Aztecs in the Valley of Mexico
mid-15th century	Height of Aztec culture
1438–1493	Great Age of Inca imperialism
1519	Arrival of the Spanish
1521	Collapse of the Aztecs
1532	Spanish execution of the Inca king and collapse of Inca empire

far less labor and time than did the cultivation of wheat in Europe or rice in China.

By the fifteenth century, enough corn, beans, chili peppers, squash, tomatoes, sweet potatoes, peanuts, avocados, and white potatoes were harvested to feed not only the farmers themselves but also massive armies and administrative bureaucracies and thousands of industrial workers. Wild animals had become almost extinct in the region and were the exclusive preserve of the nobility; common people rarely ate any meat other than guinea pigs, which most families raised. Chicha, a beer fermented from corn, was the staple drink.

Inca Imperialism

Who were the Incas? *Inca* was originally the name of the governing family of an Amerindian group that settled in the basin of Cuzco (see Map 16.3). From that family, the name was gradually extended to all Indians living in the Andes valleys. The Incas themselves used the word to identify their chief or emperor. Here the term is used for both the ruler and the people.

Around A.D. 1000 the Incas were one of many small groups fighting among themselves for land and water. As they began to conquer their neighbors, a body of religious lore came into being that ascribed divine origin to their earliest king, Manco Capac (ca 1200) and promised warriors the gods' favor and protection. Strong historical evidence dates only from the reign of Pachacuti Inca (1438–1471), who launched the imperialist phase of Inca civilization. By threats, promises, and brute conquest, Pachacuti and his son Topa Inca (1471–1493) extended the Incas' domination to the frontier of present-day Ecuador and Colombia in the north and to the Maule River in present-day Chile in the south (see Map 16.3), an area of about 350,000 square miles. Some authorities rank Pachacuti and Topa Inca with Alexander the Great and Napoleon among the world's great conquerors. By the time of the Spanish conquest in 1532, about 16 million people owed allegiance to the Inca ruler.

Inca civilization was the culmination of the fusion and assimilation of earlier Amerindian cultures in the Andes valleys. Each group that had entered the region had its own distinct language. These languages were not written and have become extinct. Scholars will probably never understand the linguistic condition of Peru before the fifteenth century when Pachacuti made Quechua (pronounced "keshwa") the official language of his people and administration. Quechua-speaking peoples were sent as colonists to subject regions, and conquered peoples were forced to adopt the language. Quechua thus superseded native dialects and spread the Inca way of life throughout the

Andes. Although not written until the Spanish in Peru adopted it as a second official language, Quechua had replaced local languages by the seventeenth and eighteenth centuries and is still spoken by most Peruvians today.

Whereas the Aztecs controlled their subject peoples through terror, the Incas governed by means of imperial unification. They imposed not only their language but their entire panoply of gods: the sun-god, divine ancestor of the royal family; his wife the moon-god; and the thunder-god, who brought life-giving rain. Magnificent temples scattered throughout the expanding empire housed idols of these gods and the state-appointed priests who attended them. Priests led prayers and elaborate rituals, and, on such occasions as a terrible natural disaster or a great military victory, they sacrificed human beings to the gods. Subject peoples were required to worship the state gods. Imperial unification was also achieved through the forced participation of local chieftains in the central bureaucracy and through a policy of colonization called *mitima*. To prevent rebellion in newly conquered territories, Pachacuti transferred all their inhabitants to other parts of the empire, replacing them with workers who had lived longer

Machu Picchu   The citadel of Machu Picchu, surrounded by mountains in the clouds, clings to a spectacular crag in upland Peru. It was discovered only in 1911, by the young American explorer Hiram Bingham. Both its origin and the reason for its abandonment remain unknown. *(Source: Carl Frank/Photo Researchers)*

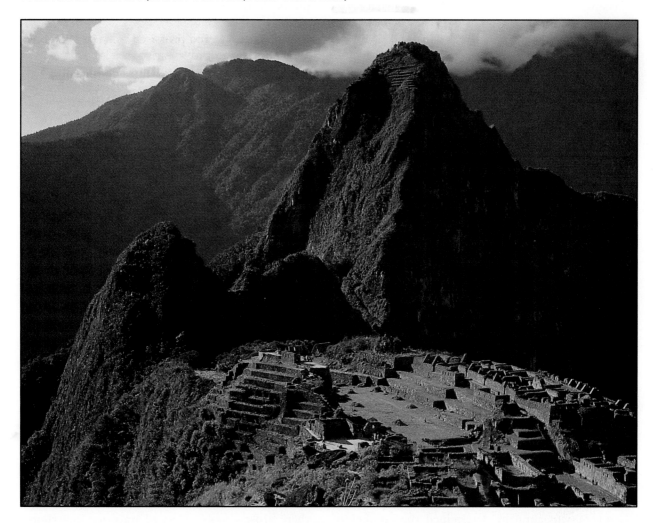

under Inca rule and whose independent spirit had been broken.[15] An excellent system of roads—averaging three feet in width, some paved and others not—provided for the transportation of armies and the rapid communication of royal orders by runners. Inca roads followed straight lines wherever possible, but they also crossed marshes and causeways and rivers and streams on pontoon bridges and tunneled through hills. This great feat of engineering bears striking comparison with ancient Roman roads, which also linked an empire.

Inca Society

The fundamental unit of early Inca society was the *ayllu,* or clan, which consisted of all those who claimed a common male ancestor. A village typically consisted of several ayllus. Each ayllu had its own farmland and woodland, which all members tended. The chief, or *curacas,* of an ayllu, to whom all members owed allegiance, conducted relations with outsiders.

In the fifteenth century, Pachacuti and Topa Incas superimposed imperial institutions on those of kinship. The Incas ordered allegiance to be paid to the ruler at Cuzco rather than to the curacas. They drafted local men for distant wars and changed the entire populations of certain regions through the system of mitima. Entirely new ayllus were formed, based on residence rather than kinship.

The emperors sometimes gave newly acquired lands to victorious generals, distinguished civil servants, and favorite nobles. These lords subsequently exercised authority previously held by the native curacas. Whether long-time residents or new colonists, all had the status of peasant farmers, which entailed heavy agricultural or other obligations. Just as in medieval Europe peasants worked several days each week on their lord's lands, so the Inca people had to work on state lands (that is, the emperor's lands) or on lands assigned to the temple. Peasants also labored on roads and bridges; terraced and irrigated new arable land; served on construction crews for royal palaces, temples, and public buildings such as fortresses; acted as runners on the post roads; and excavated in the imperial gold, silver, and copper mines. The imperial government annually determined the number of laborers needed for these various undertakings,

and each district had to supply an assigned quota. The government also made an ayllu responsible for the state-owned granaries and for the production of cloth for army uniforms.

The state required everyone to marry, and even decided when and sometimes whom a person should marry. A person was not considered an adult until he or she married, started a household, and became liable for public responsibilities. Men married around the age of twenty, women a little younger. A young man who wanted a certain girl "hung around" her father's house and shared in the work. The Incas did not especially prize virginity; premarital sex was common. The marriage ceremony consisted of the joining of hands and the exchange of a pair of sandals. This ritual was followed by a large wedding feast, at which the state presented the bride and groom with two complete sets of clothing, one for everyday wear and one for festive occasions. If a man or woman did not find a satisfactory mate, the provincial governor selected one for him or her. Travel was forbidden, so couples necessarily came from the same region. Like most warring societies with high male death rates, the Incas practiced polygamy, though the cost of supporting many wives restricted it largely to the upper classes.

In many aspects of daily life, the common people were regimented, denied both choice and initiative. The Incas, however, took care of the poor and aged who could not look after themselves, distributed grain in time of shortage and famine, and supplied assistance in natural disasters. Scholars have debated whether Inca society was socialistic, totalitarian, or a forerunner of the welfare state; it may be merely a matter of definition. Although the Inca economy was strictly regulated, there certainly was not an equal distribution of wealth. Everything above and beyond the masses' basic needs went to the emperor and the nobility. The backbreaking labor of ordinary people in the fields and mines made possible the luxurious lifestyle of the great Inca nobility. The nobles—called "Big Ears," or *Orejones* by the Spanish, because they pierced their ears and distended the lobes with heavy jewelry—were the ruling Inca's kinsmen. Lesser nobles included the curacas, royal household servants, public officials, and entertainers. As the empire expanded in the fifteenth century, there arose a noble class of warriors, governors, and local officials, whose support the ruling Inca

Inca Tunic This colorful Inca fabric of many designs, perhaps once part of an emperor's tunic, suggests the remarkable Inca expertise in the dyeing and weaving of textiles. *(Source: Dumbarton Oaks Research Library and Collections, Washington, D.C.)*

secured with gifts of land, precious metals, and llamas and alpacas (llamas were used as beasts of burden; alpacas were raised for their long fine wool). The nobility was exempt from agricultural work and other kinds of public service.

heavily on the Toltec heritage and distinguished by achievements in engineering, sculpture, and architecture. The Incas revealed a genius for organization, and their state was virtually unique in its time in assuming responsibility for the social welfare of all its people.

SUMMARY

Across the Atlantic, several great Amerindian cultures had flourished in the years between 400 and 1500. The Maya are justly renowned for their art and their accomplishments in abstract thought. The Aztecs built a unified civilization based

NOTES

1. See F. Braudel, *The Structures of Everyday Life: Civilization and Capitalism, 15th–18th Century,* vol. I, trans. S. Reynolds (New York: Harper & Row, 1981), pp. 160–161.

2. See L. Schele and M. E. Miller, *The Blood of Kings: Dynasty and Ritual in Maya Art* (New York: Braziller, 1986), pp. 14–15, *passim.*

3. Quoted in I. Bernal, *Mexico Before Cortez: Art, History, and Legend,* rev. ed., trans. Willis Barnstone (New York: Anchor Books, 1975), p. 68.

4. J. Soustelle, *Daily Life of the Aztecs on the Eve of the Spanish Conquest,* trans. P. O'Brian (Stanford, Calif.: Stanford University Press, 1970), p. 97.

5. See M. Harris, *Cannibals and Kings* (New York: Random House, 1977), pp. 99–110; the quotation is from p. 106.

6. Ibid., pp. 109–110.

7. See R. Padden, *The Hummingbird and the Hawk* (Columbus, Ohio: Ohio State University Press, 1967), pp. 76–99.

8. Soustelle, p. 74.

9. Quoted ibid., p. 89.

10. B. Díaz, *The Conquest of New Spain,* trans. J. M. Cohen (New York: Penguin Books, 1978), p. 214.

11. Quoted in J. H. Perry, *The Discovery of South America,* (New York: Taplinger, 1979), pp. 161–163.

12. Quoted ibid., p. 163.

13. William K. Stevens, "Andean Culture Found to Be as Old as the Great Pyramids," in *The New York Times,* October 3, 1989, p. C1.

14. J. A. Mason, *The Ancient Civilizations of Peru* (New York: Penguin Books, 1978), p. 108.

15. Ibid., p. 123

SUGGESTED READING

Students interested in exploring aspects of pre-Columbian Central and South America will have no trouble finding a rich literature. F. Katz, *The Ancient American Civilisations* (1972), is now a standard study by a distinguished historian and anthropologist. G. C. Vaillant, *Aztecs of Mexico* (1979), Michael D. Coe, *The Maya,* 4th ed. (1987), and the work by Mason cited in the Notes are all sound and well-illustrated surveys. Coe's *Mexico* (1977) is probably the most comprehensive treatment of Mexican civilizations, with excellent illustrations and a good bibliography. The clever sketches of V. W. Von Hagen, *Realm of the Incas* (1961) and *The Aztec: Man and Tribe* (1961), are popular archeological accounts. Bernal's *Mexico Before Cortez* (listed in the Notes) brings out the social significance of Mexican art. P. Westheim, *The Sculpture of Ancient Mexico,* trans. U. Bernard (1963), also focuses on the importance of art and sculpture for an understanding of Mexican civilization. For any facet of Maya culture and civilization, see the splendid achievement of Schele and Miller cited in the Notes, which is superbly illustrated and the recent treatment of L. Schele and D. Freidel, *A Forest of Kings: The Untold Story of the Ancient Maya* (1990).

More specialized recent studies include M. P. Weaver, *The Aztec, Maya and Their Predecessors* (1981), which is highly readable and splendidly illustrated; K. W. Luckert, *Olmec Religion: A Key to Middle America and Beyond* (1976), an iconographical study of Olmec and Aztec religious symbolism; B. C. Brundage, *A Rain of Darts: The Mexican Aztecs* (1973); N. Davies, *The Aztecs Until the Fall of Tula* (1977), a highly detailed but fascinating book; E. R. Wolf, ed., *The Valley of Mexico: Studies in Pre-Hispanic Ecology and Society* (1976), an important collection of significant articles; L. Baudin, *A Socialist Empire: The Incas of Peru* (1961); and J. Soustelle, *The Olmecs: The Oldest Civilization in Mexico* (1984). Students interested in the importance of the environment to Inca history and development should see S. Masuda, I. Shimada, and C. Morris, eds., *Andean Ecology and Civilization* (1985).

17

European Society in the Age of the Renaissance and Reformation

Andrea Mantegna, *The Court of the Gonzaga Family*

The fourteenth century witnessed the beginnings of remarkable changes in many aspects of Italian society. In the fifteenth century, these phenomena spread beyond Italy and gradually influenced society in northern Europe. These cultural changes have collectively been labeled the "Renaissance."

Many present-day scholars interpret the sixteenth-century Reformation against the background of reforming trends begun in the fifteenth century. The idea of reform is as old as Christianity itself: the need for reform of the individual Christian and of the institutional church is central to the Christian faith. The Christian humanists of the late fifteenth and early sixteenth centuries called for reform of the church on the pattern of the early church, primarily through educational and social change. Men and women of every period believed the early church represented a golden age, and critics in every period called for reform. In the sixteenth century, demands for religious reform became so strong that they became enmeshed with social, political, and economic factors.

- What does the term *renaissance* mean?
- How did the Renaissance manifest itself in politics, government, art, and social organization?
- Why did the theological ideas of Martin Luther trigger political, social, and economic reactions?
- What response did the Catholic church make to the movements for reform?

This chapter explores these questions.

THE EVOLUTION OF THE ITALIAN RENAISSANCE

Economic growth laid the material basis for the Italian Renaissance. The period extending roughly from 1050 to 1300 witnessed phenomenal commercial and financial development, the growing political power of self-governing cities, and great population expansion. Then the period from the late thirteenth to the late sixteenth century was characterized by an incredible efflorescence of artistic energies.[1] Scholars commonly use the term

Renaissance to describe the cultural achievements of the fourteenth through sixteenth centuries; those achievements rest on the economic and political developments of earlier centuries.

In the great commercial revival of the eleventh century, northern Italian cities led the way. By the middle of the twelfth century, Venice, supported by a huge merchant marine, had grown enormously rich through overseas trade. It profited tremendously from the diversion of the Fourth Crusade to Constantinople (see page 365). Genoa and Milan also enjoyed the benefits of a large volume of trade with the Middle East and northern Europe. These cities fully exploited their geographical positions as natural crossroads for mercantile exchange between the East and West. In the early fourteenth century, furthermore, Genoa and Venice made important strides in shipbuilding, allowing their ships for the first time to sail all year long. Most goods were purchased directly from the producers and sold a good distance away. For example, Italian merchants bought fine English wool directly from the Cistercian abbeys of Yorkshire in northern England. The wool was transported to the bazaars of North Africa either overland or by ship through the Strait of Gibraltar. The risks in such an operation were great, but the profits were enormous. These profits were continually reinvested to earn more.

Scholars tend to agree that the first artistic and literary manifestations of the Italian Renaissance appeared in Florence, which possessed enormous wealth despite geographical constraints: it was an inland city without easy access to water transportation. Toward the end of the thirteenth century, Florentine merchants and bankers acquired control of papal banking. From their position as tax collectors for the papacy, Florentine mercantile families began to dominate European banking on both sides of the Alps. These families had offices in Paris, London, Bruges, Barcelona, Marseilles, Tunis and other North African ports, and, of course, Naples and Rome. The profits from loans, investments, and money exchanges that poured back to Florence were pumped into urban industries. Such profits contributed to the city's economic vitality.

The wool industry, however, was the major factor in Florence's financial expansion and population increase. Florence purchased the best-quality wool from England and Spain, developed remarkable techniques for its manufacture, and employed thousands of workers to turn it into cloth. Florentine weavers produced immense quantities of superb woolen cloth, which brought the highest prices in the fairs, markets, and bazaars of Europe, Asia, and Africa.

By the first quarter of the fourteenth century, the economic foundations of Florence were so strong that even severe crises could not destroy the city. In 1344 King Edward III of England repudiated his huge debts to Florentine bankers and forced some of them into bankruptcy. Florence suffered frightfully from the Black Death, losing perhaps half of its population. Serious labor unrest, such as the ciompi revolts of 1378 (see page 456), shook the political establishment. Still, the basic Florentine economic structure remained stable. Driving enterprise, technical know-how, and competitive spirit saw Florence through the difficult economy of the late fourteenth century.

Communes and Republics

The northern Italian cities were *communes,* sworn associations of free men seeking complete political and economic independence from local nobles. The merchant guilds that formed the communes built and maintained the city walls, regulated trade, raised taxes, and kept civil order. In the course of the twelfth century, communes at Milan, Florence, Genoa, Siena, and Pisa fought for and won their independence from surrounding feudal nobles. The nobles, attracted by the opportunities of long-distance and maritime trade, the rising value of urban real estate, the new public offices available in the expanding communes, and the chances for advantageous marriages into rich commercial families, frequently settled within the cities. Marriage vows often sealed business contracts between the rural nobility and the mercantile aristocracy. This merger of the northern Italian feudal nobility and the commercial aristocracy constituted the formation of a new social class, an urban nobility. Within the nobility, groups tied by blood, economic interests, and social connections formed tightly knit alliances to defend and expand their rights.

This new class made citizenship in the communes dependent on a property qualification, years of residence within the city, and social con-

Business Activities in a Florentine Bank The Florentines early developed new banking devices. One man (left) presents a letter of credit or a bill of exchange, forerunners of the modern check, which allowed credit in distant places. A foreign merchant (right) exchanges one kind of currency for another. The bank profited from the fees it charged for these services. *(Source: Prints Division, New York Public Library; Astor, Lenox and Tilden Foundation)*

nections. Only a tiny percentage of the male population possessed these qualifications and thus could hold office in a commune's political councils. The *pòpolo,* or middle class, bitterly resented its exclusion from power. The pòpolo wanted places in the city government and equality of taxation. Throughout most of the thirteenth century, in city after city, the pòpolo used armed forces and violence to assume power and establish republican governments. However, the pòpolo could not establish civil order within the cities, and these movements for republican government failed. By 1300 *signori* (despots, or one-man rulers) or *oligarchies* (the rule of merchant aristocracies) had triumphed everywhere.[2]

For the next two centuries, the Italian city-states were ruled by signori or by constitutional oligarchies. In the signories, despots pretended to observe the law while actually manipulating it to conceal their basic illegality. Oligarchic regimes possessed constitutions, but through a variety of schemes, a small, restricted class of wealthy merchants exercised the judicial, executive, and legislative functions of government.

In the fifteenth century, political power and elite culture centered at the princely courts of despots and oligarchs. "A court was the space and personnel around a prince as he made laws, received ambassadors, made appointments, took his meals, and proceeded through the streets."[3] At his court a prince flaunted his patronage of learning and the arts by munificent gifts to writers, philosophers, and artists. The princely court afforded the despot or oligarch the opportunity to display his wealth. Ceremonies connected with family births, baptisms, marriages, funerals, or triumphant entrances into the city served as occasions for magnificent pageantry and elaborate ritual—all designed to assert the ruler's wealth and power.

The Balance of Power Among the Italian City-States

Renaissance Italians had a passionate attachment to their individual city-states: political loyalty and feeling centered on the local city. This intense local feeling perpetuated dozens of small states and hindered the development of a unified state. Italy, consequently, was completely disunited.

In the fifteenth century, five powers dominated the Italian peninsula: Venice, Milan, Florence, the Papal States, and the kingdom of Naples (Map 17.1). The rulers of the city-states—whether despots or oligarchs—governed as monarchs. They crushed urban revolts, levied taxes, killed their enemies, and used massive building programs to employ the masses and the arts to overawe them.

Venice, with enormous trade and a vast colonial empire, ranked as an international power. Though Venice had a sophisticated constitution and was a republic in name, an oligarchy of merchant-aristocrats actually ran the city. Milan was also called a "republic," but despots of the Sforza family ruled harshly and dominated the minor city-states of the north. Likewise in Florence the form of government was republican, with authority vested in several councils of state. In reality, however, between 1434 and 1494, power in Florence was held by the great Medici banking family. Though not public officers, Cosimo de' Medici (r. 1434–1464) and Lorenzo de' Medici (r. 1469–1492) ruled from behind the scenes.

Central Italy consisted mainly of the Papal States, which during the Babylonian Captivity had come under the sway of important Roman families (see pages 446–447). Pope Alexander VI (r. 1492–1503), aided militarily and politically by his son Cesare Borgia, reasserted papal authority in the papal lands. Cesare Borgia became the model for Machiavelli's *The Prince* because he began the work of uniting the peninsula by ruthlessly conquering and exacting total obedience from the principalities making up the Papal States.

South of the Papal States was the kingdom of Naples, consisting of virtually all of southern Italy and, at times, Sicily. The kingdom of Naples had long been disputed by the Aragonese of Spain and by the French. In 1435 it passed to Aragon.

The major Italian city-states controlled the smaller ones, such as Siena, Mantua, Ferrara, and Modena, and competed furiously among themselves for territory. The large cities used diplomacy, spies, paid informers, and any other means to get information that could be used to advance their ambitions. While the states of northern Europe were moving toward centralization and consolidation, the world of Italian politics resembled a jungle where the powerful dominated the weak.

In one significant respect, however, the Italian city-states anticipated relations among competing European states after 1500. Whenever one Italian state appeared to gain a predominant position within the peninsula, other states combined to establish a balance of power against the major threat. In 1450, for example, Venice went to war against Milan to protest Francesco Sforza's acquisition of the title of duke of Milan. Cosimo de' Medici of Florence, a long-time supporter of a Florentine-Venetian alliance, switched his position and aided Milan. Florence and Naples combined with Milan against powerful Venice and the papacy. In the peace treaty signed at Lodi in 1454, Venice received territories in return for recognizing Sforza's right to the duchy. This pattern of shifting alliances continued until 1494. In the formation of these alliances, Renaissance Italians invented the machinery of modern diplomacy: permanent embassies with resident ambassadors in capitals where political relations and commercial ties needed continual monitoring. The resident ambassador is one of the great achievements of the Italian Renaissance.

At the end of the fifteenth century, Venice, Florence, Milan, and the Papal States possessed tremendous wealth and represented high cultural achievement. However, their imperialistic ambitions at one another's expense and their inability

MAP 17.1 The Italian City-States, ca 1494   In the fifteenth century the Italian city-states represented great wealth and cultural sophistication. The political divisions of the peninsula invited foreign intervention.

to form a common alliance against potential foreign enemies made Italy an inviting target for invasion. When Florence and Naples entered into an agreement to acquire Milanese territories, Milan called on France for support.

At Florence the French invasion had been predicted by the Dominican friar Girolamo Savona-

rola (1452–1498). In a number of fiery sermons between 1491 and 1494, Savonarola attacked what he considered the paganism and moral vice of the city, the undemocratic government of Lorenzo de' Medici, and the corruption of Pope Alexander VI. For a time Savonarola enjoyed wide popular support among the ordinary people; he

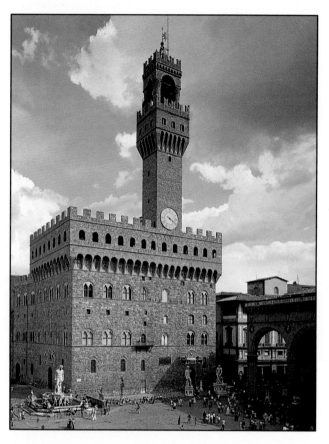

Pallazzo Vecchio, Florence Built during the late thirteenth and early fourteenth centuries as a fortress of defense against both popular uprising and foreign attack, the building housed the *podesta,* the city's highest magistrate, and all the offices of the government. *(Source: Scala/Art Resource)*

fore him. When Piero de' Medici, Lorenzo's son, went to the French camp seeking peace, the Florentines exiled the Medicis and restored republican government.

Charles's success simply whetted French appetites. In 1508 his son Louis XII (r. 1498–1515) formed the League of Cambrai with the pope and the German emperor Maximilian (r. 1486–1519) for the purpose of stripping rich Venice of its mainland possessions. Pope Leo X (r. 1513–1521) soon found the French a dangerous friend, and in a new alliance called on the Spanish and Germans to expel the French from Italy. This anti-French combination was temporarily successful. In 1519 Charles V (r. 1519–1556) succeeded his grandfather Maximilian as Holy Roman emperor. When the French returned to Italy in 1522, there began the series of conflicts called the "Habsburg-Valois Wars" (named for the German and French dynasties), whose battlefield was Italy.

In the sixteenth century, the political and social life of Italy was upset by the relentless competition for dominance between France and the empire. The Italian cities suffered severely from the continual warfare, especially in the frightful sack of Rome in 1527 by imperial forces under Charles V. Thus the failure of the city-states to form some federal system, to consolidate, or at least to establish a common foreign policy led to the continuation of the centuries-old subjection of the peninsula by outside invaders. Italy was not to achieve unification until 1870.

became the religious leader of Florence and as such contributed to the fall of the Medici. Eventually, however, people wearied of his moral denunciations, and he was excommunicated by the pope and executed. Savonarola stands as proof that the common people did not share the worldly outlook of the commercial and intellectual elite. His career also illustrates the internal instability of Italian cities such as Florence, an instability that invited foreign interference.

The invasion of Italy in 1494 by the French king Charles VIII (r. 1483–1498) inaugurated a new period in Italian and European power politics. Italy became the focus of international ambitions and the battleground of foreign armies. Charles swept down the peninsula with little opposition, and Florence, Rome, and Naples soon bowed be-

INTELLECTUAL HALLMARKS OF THE RENAISSANCE

Some fourteenth- and fifteenth-century Italians were aware that they were living in a new era. The realization that something new and unique was happening first came to men of letters in the fourteenth century such as Francesco Petrarch (1304–1374), a poet, humanist, and diplomat. Petrarch thought that he was living at the start of a new age, a period of light following a long night of Gothic gloom.

Petrarch believed that the first two centuries of the Roman Empire had represented the peak in the development of human civilization and that the Germanic invasions had caused a sharp cultural break with the glories of Rome and inaugurated what he called the "Dark Ages." Medieval people had believed that they were continuing in the glorious tradition of ancient Rome, and they had perceived no cultural division between the era of the emperors and their own times. But for Petrarch and many of his contemporaries, the thousand-year period between the fourth and the fourteenth centuries constituted a barbarian, or Gothic, or "middle" age. Sculptors, painters, and writers in the fourteenth and fifteenth centuries, contemptuous of their medieval predecessors, identified themselves with the thinkers and artists of Greco-Roman civilization. Petrarch believed that he was witnessing a new golden age of intellectual achievement—a rebirth or, to use the French word that came into English, a *renaissance*.

The division of historical time into periods is often arbitrary and done for the convenience of historians. In terms of the way most people lived and thought, no sharp division existed between the Middle Ages and the Renaissance. Nevertheless, some important writers and artists believed that they were living in a new age.

Characteristic of the Renaissance was a new attitude toward men, women, and the world—an attitude that may be described as "individualism." Humanism characterized by a deep interest in the Latin classics and a deliberate attempt to revive antique lifestyles emerged, as did a bold new secular spirit.

Individualism

The Middle Ages had seen the appearance of remarkable individuals, but recognition of such persons was limited. The examples of Saint Augustine in the fifth century and Peter Abélard and Guibert of Nogent in the twelfth—men who perceived of themselves as unique and produced autobiographical statements—stand out, for Christian humility discouraged self-absorption. In the Renaissance, in contrast, intellectuals developed a new sense of historical distance from earlier periods. A large literature specifically concerned with the nature of individuality emerged. This literature represented the flowering of a distinctly Renaissance individualism.

The Renaissance witnessed the emergence of many distinctive personalities who gloried in their uniqueness. Italians of unusual abilities were self-consciously aware of their singularity and

unafraid to be unlike their neighbors; they had enormous confidence in their ability to achieve great things. Leon Battista Alberti (1404–1474), a writer, architect, and mathematician, remarked, "Men can do all things if they will."[4] The Florentine goldsmith and sculptor Benvenuto Cellini (1500–1574) prefaced his *Autobiography* with a sonnet that declares:

My cruel fate hath warr'd with me in vain:
Life, glory, worth, and all unmeasur'd skill,
Beauty and grace, themselves in me fulfill
That many I surpass, and to the best attain.[5]

Cellini, certain of his genius, wrote so that the whole world might appreciate it.

Individualism stressed personality, genius, uniqueness, and the fullest development of capabilities and talents. Athlete, painter, scholar, sculptor, whatever—a thirst for fame, a driving ambition, a burning desire for success drove such people to the complete achievement of their potential. The quest for glory was central to Renaissance individualism.

The Revival of Antiquity

In the cities of Italy, especially Rome, civic leaders and the wealthy populace showed phenomenal archeological zeal for the recovery of manuscripts, statues, and monuments. Pope Nicholas V (r. 1447–1455), a distinguished scholar, planned the Vatican Library for the nine thousand manuscripts he had collected. Pope Sixtus IV (r. 1471–1484) built that library, which remains one of the richest repositories of ancient and medieval documents.

Patrician Italians consciously copied the lifestyle of the ancients and even searched out pedigrees dating back to ancient Rome. Aeneas Silvius Piccolomini, a native of Siena who became Pope Pius II (r. 1458–1464), once pretentiously declared, "Rome is as much my home as Siena, for my House, the Piccolomini, came in early times from the capital to Siena, as is proved by the constant use of the names Aeneas and Silvius in my family."[6]

The revival of antiquity also took the form of profound interest in and study of the Latin classics. This feature of the Renaissance became known as the "new learning," or simply *humanism,* the term used by the Florentine rhetorician and historian Leonardo Bruni (1370–1444). The words *humanism* and *humanist* derived ultimately from the Latin *humanitas,* which Cicero used to mean the literary culture needed by anyone who would be considered educated and civilized. Humanists studied the Latin classics to learn what they reveal about human nature. Humanism emphasized human beings—their achievements, interests, and capabilities. Although churchmen supported the new learning, by the later fifteenth century Italian humanism was increasingly a secular phenomenon.

Appreciation for the literary culture of the Romans had never died in the West. Scholars like Bede and John of Salisbury had studied and imitated the writings of the ancients. Medieval thinkers, however, had studied the ancients in order to come to know God. They had interpreted the classics in a Christian sense and invested the ancients' poems and histories with Christian meaning.

Renaissance humanists approached the classics differently. Where medieval writers accepted pagan and classical authors uncritically, Renaissance humanists were skeptical of their authority, conscious of the historical distance separating themselves from the ancients, and fully aware that classical writers often disagreed among themselves. Renaissance humanists rejected classical ideas that were opposed to Christianity, or they sought through reinterpretation an underlying harmony between the pagan and secular and the Christian faith.

Deeply Christian like their medieval predecessors, Renaissance humanists studied the classics to understand human nature, and although they fully grasped the moral thought of pagan antiquity, they viewed man from a strongly Christian perspective. In a remarkable essay, "On the Dignity of Man," the Florentine writer Pico della Mirandola (1463–1494) stressed that man possesses great dignity because he was made as Adam in the image of God before the Fall and as Christ after the Resurrection. Man's place in the universe is somewhere between the beasts and the angels, but because of the divine image planted in man, there are no limits to what he can accomplish. The fundamental difference between Renaissance humanists and medieval humanists is that the former were more self-conscious about what they were doing.[7]

The fourteenth- and fifteenth-century humanists loved the language of the classics and considered it superior to the corrupt Latin of the medieval schoolmen. Eventually, Renaissance writers became concerned more about form than about content, more about the way an idea was expressed than about the significance and validity of the idea. Literary humanists of the fourteenth century wrote one another highly stylized letters imitating ancient authors, and they held witty philosophical dialogues in conscious imitation of Plato's Academy of the fourth century B.C. The leading humanists of the early Renaissance were rhetoricians, seeking effective and eloquent communication, both written and oral.

Brunelleschi: Abraham's Sacrifice of Isaac When the Florentine textile merchants' guild held a competition for designs of the bronze doors of the city Baptistery, Brunelleschi entered this design based on the story in Genesis 22. The Roman altar and the boy removing a thorn from his foot (lower right) show conscious Roman elements in this dramatic, even violent scene. *(Source: Alinari/Art Resource)*

A New Secular Spirit

Secularism is a basic concern with the material world instead of with eternal and spiritual considerations. A secular way of thinking tends to find the ultimate explanation of everything and the final end of human beings within the limits of what the senses can discover. Medieval business people ruthlessly pursued profits while medieval monks fought fiercely over property. Yet medieval society was religious, not secular: the dominant ideals focused on the otherworldly, on life after death. In a secular society, attention is concentrated on the here-and-now, often on the acquisition of material things. The fourteenth and fifteenth centuries witnessed the slow but steady growth of secularism in Italy.

The economic changes and rising prosperity of the Italian cities in the thirteenth century worked a fundamental change in social and intellectual attitudes and values. Worries about shifting rates of interest, shipping routes, personnel costs, and employee relations did not leave much time for thoughts about penance and purgatory. The busy bankers and merchants of the Italian cities calculated ways of making money. Money allowed greater material pleasures, a more comfortable life, leisure to appreciate and patronize the arts. Money could buy many sensual gratifications, and the patricians of Venice, Florence, Genoa, and Rome came to see life more as something to enjoy than as a painful pilgrimage to the City of God.

In *On Pleasure,* the humanist Lorenzo Valla (1406–1457) defended the pleasures of the senses as the highest good. Scholars praise Valla as a father of modern historical criticism. His study *On the False Donation of Constantine* (1444) demonstrated by careful textual examination that an anonymous eighth-century document supposedly giving the papacy jurisdiction over vast territories in western Europe was a forgery. Medieval people had accepted "the donation of Constantine" as a reality, and the proof that it was an invention weakened the foundations of papal claims to temporal authority. Lorenzo Valla's work exemplifies the application of critical scholarship to old and almost-sacred writings, as well as the new secular spirit of the Renaissance. The tales in *The Decameron* (1353) by the Florentine Giovanni Boccaccio (1313–1375), which describe ambitious merchants, lecherous friars, and cuckolded husbands, portray a frankly acquisitive, sensual, and worldly society. The "contempt of the world" theme, so pervasive in medieval literature, had disappeared. Renaissance writers justified the accumulation and enjoyment of wealth with references to ancient authors.

Church leaders did little to combat the new secular spirit. In the fifteenth and early sixteenth centuries, the papal court and the households of the cardinals were just as worldly as those of great urban patricians. Most of the popes and high church officials had come from the bourgeois aristocracy. Renaissance popes beautified the city of Rome and patronized artists and men of letters, expending enormous enthusiasm and huge sums of money. A new papal chancellery, begun in 1483 and finished in 1511, stands as one of the architectural masterpieces of the period that art historians describe as the "High Renaissance" (1500–1527). Pope Julius II (r. 1503–1513) tore down the old Saint Peter's Basilica and began work on the present structure in 1506. Michelangelo's dome for Saint Peter's Basilica is still considered his greatest work. Papal interests, far removed from spiritual concerns, fostered rather than discouraged the new worldly attitude.

The broad mass of the people and the intellectuals and leaders of society remained faithful to the Christian church. Few people questioned the basic tenets of the Christian religion. Italian humanists and their aristocratic patrons were antiascetic, antischolastic, and ambivalent, but they were not agnostics or skeptics. Thousands of pious paintings, sculptures, processions, and pilgrimages prove that strong religious feeling persisted in the Renaissance.

ART AND THE ARTIST

No feature of the Renaissance evokes greater admiration than the masterpieces in painting, architecture, and sculpture created in the 1400s and 1500s. In all the arts, the city of Florence led the way. According to the Renaissance art historian Giorgio Vasari (1511–1574), the painter Perugino once asked why it was in Florence and not elsewhere that men achieved perfection in the arts. The first answer he received was, "There were so many good critics there, for the air of the city makes men quick and perceptive and impatient of mediocrity."[8] But Florence was not the only artistic center. In the High Renaissance Rome took the lead. The main characteristics of High Renaissance art—classical balance, harmony, and restraint—are revealed in the masterpieces of Leonardo da Vinci

(1452–1519), Raphael (1483–1520), and Michelangelo (1475–1564), all of whom worked in Rome at this time.

Art and Power

The subject matter of art through the early fifteenth century, as in the Middle Ages, remained overwhelmingly religious. Religious themes appeared in all media—wood carvings, painted frescoes, stone sculptures, paintings. As in the Middle Ages, art served an educational purpose. A religious picture or statue was intended to spread a particular doctrine, act as a profession of faith, or recall sinners to a moral way of living.

In early Renaissance Italy, art was a sign of corporate power. Powerful urban groups such as guilds and religious confraternities commissioned works of art. The Florentine cloth merchants, for example, delegated Brunelleschi (1377–1466) to build the magnificent dome on the cathedral of Florence and selected Lorenzo Ghiberti (1378–1455) to design the bronze doors of the baptistry. These works represented the merchants' dominant influence in the community. Corporate patronage is also reflected in the Florentine government's decision to hire Michelangelo to sculpt David, the great Hebrew hero and king.

Increasingly in the later fifteenth century, individuals and oligarchs, rather than corporate groups, sponsored works of art. Patrician merchants and bankers, popes, and princes supported the arts as a means of glorifying themselves and their families. Vast sums were spent on family chapels, frescoes, religious panels, and tombs. Paintings cost money and thus were also means of displaying wealth. Writing about 1470, the Florentine oligarch Lorenzo de' Medici, called "the Magnificent," declared that over the past thirty-five years his family had spent the astronomical sum of 663,755 gold florins for artistic and architectural commissions. Yet, he observed, "I think it casts a brilliant light on our estate [public reputation] and it seems to me that the monies were well spent and I am very pleased with this." Powerful men wanted to glorify themselves, their families, and their offices. A magnificent style of living, enriched by works of art, served to prove the greatness and the power of the despot or oligarch.[9]

As the fifteenth century advanced, the subject matter of art became steadily more secular. The study of classical texts deepened understanding of ancient ideas. Classical themes and motifs, such as the lives and loves of pagan gods and goddesses, figured increasingly in painting and sculpture. Religious topics, such as the Annunciation of the Virgin and the Nativity, remained popular among both patrons and artists, but frequently the patron had himself and his family portrayed. People were conscious of their physical uniqueness and wanted their individuality immortalized.

The style of Renaissance art was decidedly different from the style of Medieval art. The individual portrait emerged as a distinct artistic genre. In the fifteenth century, members of the newly rich middle class often had themselves painted in a scene of romantic chivalry or in courtly society. Rather than reflecting a spiritual ideal, as medieval painting and sculpture tended to do, Renaissance portraits mirrored reality. The Florentine painter Giotto (1276–1337) led the way in the depiction of realism; his treatment of the human body and face replaced the formal stiffness and artificiality that had for so long characterized the representation of human features. The sculptor Donatello (1386–1466) probably exerted the greatest influence of any Florentine artist before Michelangelo. His many statues express an appreciation of the incredible variety of human nature. Medieval artists had depicted the nude human body only in a spiritualized and moralizing context. Donatello revived the classical figure with its balance and self-awareness. The short-lived Florentine Masaccio (1401–1428), sometimes called the "father of modern painting," inspired a new style characterized by great realism, narrative power, and remarkable use of light and dark.

Narrative artists depicted the body in a more scientific and natural manner. The female figure is voluptuous and sensual. The male body, as in Michelangelo's David and The Last Judgment, is strong and heroic. The Last Supper of Leonardo da Vinci, with its stress on the tension between Christ and the disciples, is an incredibly subtle psychological interpretation. Brunelleschi and Piero della Francesca (1420–1492) seem to have pioneered artistic perspective, the linear representation of distance and space on a flat surface.

As important as realism was the new "international style," so called because of the wandering careers of influential artists, the close communications and rivalry of princely courts, and the increased trade in works of art. Rich color, decorative detail, curvilinear rhythms, and swaying forms characterized the international style. The Venetian painter Titian's portrait of the emperor Charles V (page 543) is a good example of the international style. As the term *international* implies, this style was European, not merely Italian.

The Status of the Artist

In the Renaissance the social status of the artist improved. The lower-middle-class medieval master mason had been viewed in the same light as a mechanic. The artist in the Renaissance was considered a free intellectual worker. An artist did not produce unsolicited pictures or statues for the general public, for doing so could mean loss of status.

Benozzo Gozzoli: Journey of the Magi   Few Renaissance paintings better illustrate art in the service of the princely court, in this case the Medici. Commissioned by Piero de' Medici to adorn his palace chapel, everything in this fresco—the large crowd, the feathers and diamonds adorning many of the personages, the black servant in front—serve to flaunt the power and wealth of the House of Medici. There is nothing especially religious about it; the painting could more appropriately be called "Journey of the Medici." The artist has discreetly placed himself in the crowd, the name Benozzo embroidered on his cap. *(Source: Scala/Art Resource)*

He usually worked on commission from a powerful prince. An artist's reputation depended on the support of powerful patrons, and through them some artists and architects achieved not only economic security but very great wealth. All aspiring artists received a practical (not theoretical) education in a recognized master's workshop. For example, Michelangelo was apprenticed at age thirteen to the artist Ghirlandaio (1449–1494), although he later denied the fact to make it appear that he never had any formal training. The more famous the artist, the more he attracted assistants or apprentices. Ghiberti had twenty assistants during the period he was working on the bronze doors of the baptistry in Florence, his most famous achievement.

Ghiberti's salary of two hundred florins a year compared very favorably with that of the head of the city government, who earned five hundred florins. Moreover, at a time when a man could live in a princely fashion on three hundred ducats a year, Leonardo da Vinci was making two thousand annually. Michelangelo was paid three thousand ducats for painting the ceiling of the Sistine Chapel. When he agreed to work on Saint Peter's Basilica, he refused a salary; he was already a wealthy man.[10]

Renaissance society respected and rewarded the distinguished artist. In 1537 the prolific letter writer, humanist, and satirizer of princes Pietro Aretino (1492–1556) wrote to Michelangelo while he was painting the Sistine Chapel:

To the Divine Michelangelo:
Sir, just as it is disgraceful and sinful to be unmindful of God so it is reprehensible and dishonourable for any man of discerning judgement not to honour you as a brilliant and venerable artist whom the very stars use as a target at which to shoot the rival arrows of their favour. You are so accomplished, therefore, that hidden in your hands lives the idea of a new king of creation. . . . And it is surely my duty to honour you with this salutation, since the world has many kings but only one Michelangelo.[11]

When the Holy Roman emperor Charles V visited the workshop of the great Titian (1477–1576) and stooped to pick up the artist's dropped paintbrush, the emperor was demonstrating that the patron himself was honored in the act of honoring the artist. The social status of the artist of genius was immortally secured.

Renaissance artists were not only aware of their creative power; they boasted about it. Describing his victory over five others, including Brunelleschi, in the competition to design Florence's baptistry doors, Ghiberti exulted, "The palm of victory was conceded to me by all the experts and by all my fellow-competitors. By universal consent and without a single exception the glory was conceded to me."[12] Some medieval painters and sculptors had signed their works. Renaissance artists almost universally did so, and many of them incorporated self-portraits, usually as bystanders, in their paintings.

The Renaissance, in fact, witnessed the birth of the concept of the artist as genius. In the Middle Ages, people believed that only God created, albeit through individuals; the medieval conception recognized no particular value in artistic originality. Renaissance artists and humanists came to think that a work of art was the deliberate creation of a unique personality, of an individual who transcended traditions, rules, and theories. A genius had a peculiar gift that ordinary laws should not inhibit. Cosimo de' Medici described a Renaissance painter, because of his genius, as "divine," implying that the artist shared in the powers of God. The word *divine* was widely applied to Michelangelo.

Italian Renaissance culture must not be interpreted in twentieth-century democratic terms. The culture of the Renaissance was that of a small mercantile elite, a business patriciate with aristocratic pretensions. Renaissance culture did not directly affect the broad middle classes, let alone the vast urban proletariat. A small, highly educated minority of literary humanists and artists created the culture of and for an exclusive elite. They cared little for ordinary people, and some thoroughly despised the masses. Renaissance humanists were a smaller and narrower group than the medieval clergy had ever been. High churchmen had commissioned the construction of the Gothic cathedrals but, once finished, the buildings were for all to enjoy. Modern visitors can still see the deep ruts in the stone floors of Chartres and Canterbury where the poor pilgrims slept at night. Nothing comparable was built in the Renaissance by the insecure, social-climbing merchant princes.[13] The Renaissance maintained the gulf between the learned minority and the uneducated multitude—a gulf that has survived for century after century.

SOCIAL CHANGE

The new developments of the Renaissance brought about real breaks with the medieval past. In education, in politics, through printing, and in the experience of women and blacks, the Renaissance changed many aspects of Italian, and subsequently European, society.

Education and Political Thought

One of the central preoccupations of the humanists was education and moral behavior. Humanists poured out treatises, often in the form of letters, on the structure and goals of education and the training of rulers. In one of the earliest systematic programs for the young, Peter Paul Vergerio (1370–1444) wrote Ubertinus, the ruler of Carrara:

For the education of children is a matter of more than private interest; it concerns the State, which indeed regards the right training of the young as, in certain aspects, within its proper sphere.... Tutors and comrades alike should be chosen from amongst those likely to bring out the best qualities, to attract by good example, and to repress the first signs of evil.... Above all, respect for Divine ordinances is of the deepest importance; it should be inculcated from the earliest years....

We call those studies liberal which are worthy of a free man; those studies by which we attain and practise virtue and wisdom; that education which calls forth, trains and develops those highest gifts of body and of mind which ennoble men, and which are rightly judged to rank next in dignity to virtue only.[14]

Part of Vergerio's treatise specifies subjects for the instruction of young men in public life: history teaches virtue by examples from the past; ethics focuses on virtue itself; and rhetoric or public speaking trains for eloquence.

No book on education had broader influence than Baldassare Castiglione's *The Courtier* (1528). This treatise sought to train, discipline, and fashion the young man into the courtly ideal, the gentleman. According to Castiglione (1478–1529), the educated man of the upper class should have a broad background in many academic sub-

jects, and his spiritual and physical, as well as intellectual, capabilities should be trained. The courtier should have easy familiarity with dance, music, and the arts. Castiglione envisioned a man who could compose a sonnet, wrestle, sing a song and accompany himself on an instrument, ride expertly, solve difficult mathematical problems, and above all speak and write eloquently. With these accomplishments, he would be the perfect Renaissance man. In the sixteenth and seventeenth centuries, *The Courtier* was widely read. It influenced the social mores and patterns of conduct of elite groups in Renaissance and early modern Europe. The courtier became the model of the European gentleman.

No Renaissance book on any topic, however, has been more widely read and studied in all the centuries since its publication in 1513 than the short political treatise *The Prince,* by Niccolò Machiavelli (1469–1527). Some political scientists maintain that Machiavelli was describing the actual competitive framework of the Italian states with which he was familiar. Other thinkers praise *The Prince* because it revolutionized political theory and destroyed medieval views of the nature of the state. Still other scholars consider this work a classic because it deals with eternal problems of government and society.

Born to a modestly wealthy Tuscan family, Machiavelli received a good education in the Latin classics. He entered the civil service of the Florentine government and served on thirty diplomatic missions. When the exiled Medicis returned to power in the city in 1512, they expelled Machiavelli from his position as officer of the city government. In exile he wrote *The Prince.*

The subject of *The Prince* is political power: how a ruler should gain, maintain, and increase it. In this, Machiavelli implicitly addresses the question of the citizen's relationship to the state. As a good humanist, he explores the problems of human nature and concludes that human beings are selfish and out to advance their own interests. This pessimistic view of humanity leads him to maintain that a prince may have to manipulate the people in any way he finds necessary:

For a man who, in all respects, will carry out only his professions of good, will be apt to be ruined amongst so many who are evil. A prince therefore who desires to maintain himself must learn to be not always good, but to be so or not as necessity may require.[15]

A prince should combine the cunning of a fox with the ferocity of a lion to achieve his goals. Asking rhetorically whether it is better for a ruler to be loved or feared, Machiavelli wrote:

This, then, gives rise to the question "whether it be better to be loved than feared, or to be feared than loved." It will naturally be answered that it would be desirable to be both the one and the other; but as it is difficult to be both at the same time, it is much more safe to be feared than to be loved, when you have to choose between the two. For it may be said of men in general that they are ungrateful and fickle, dissemblers, avoiders of danger, and greedy of gain. So long as you shower benefits upon them, they are all yours.[16]

Medieval political theorists and theologians had stressed the way government *ought* to be; they set high moral and Christian standards for the ruler's conduct. Machiavelli maintained that the ruler should be concerned *not* with the way things ought to be but with the way things actually are. The sole test of a "good" government was whether it was effective, whether the ruler increased his power. Machiavelli did not advocate amoral behavior, but he believed that political action cannot be restricted by moral considerations. Amoral action might be the most effective approach in a given situation. In *Discourses on the Ten Books of Titus Livy,* however, Machiavelli showed his strong commitment to republican government. Nevertheless, on the basis of a crude interpretation of *The Prince,* the word *Machiavellian* entered the language as a synonym for devious, corrupt, and crafty politics in which the end justifies the means. Machiavelli's ultimate significance rests on two ideas: first, that one permanent social order reflecting God's will cannot be established; second, that politics has its own laws and ought to be a science.[17]

The Printed Word

Sometime in the thirteenth century, paper money and playing cards from China reached the West. They were *block printed*—that is, Chinese characters or pictures were carved into a wooden block, inked, and the words or illustrations put on paper. Since each word, phrase, or picture was on a separate block, this method of reproduction was extraordinarily expensive and time consuming.

Around 1455, probably through the combined efforts of three men—Johann Gutenberg, Johann Fust, and Peter Schöffer, all experimenting at Mainz—movable type came into being. The mirror image of each letter (rather than entire words or phrases) was carved on relief on a small block. Individual letters, easily movable, were put together to form words in lines of type that made up a page. Since letters could be arranged into any format, an infinite variety of texts could be printed by reusing and rearranging pieces of type.

By the middle of the fifteenth century, paper too was widely available in Europe. Originating in China, the knowledge of manufacturing paper reached the West in the twelfth century, when the Arabs introduced the process into Spain. Europeans quickly learned that durable paper was far less expensive than the vellum (calfskin) and parchment (sheepskin) on which medieval scribes had relied for centuries.

The effects of the invention of movable-type printing were not felt overnight. Nevertheless, within a half century of the publication of Gutenberg's Bible in 1456, movable type brought about radical changes. Between the sixteenth and eighteenth centuries, printing transformed both the private and the public lives of Europeans. Governments that "had employed the cumbersome methods of manuscripts to communicate with their subjects switched quickly to print to announce declarations of war, publish battle accounts, promulgate treaties or argue disputed points in pamphlet form." Printing made propaganda possible, emphasizing differences between various groups, such as crown and nobility, church and state. These differences laid the basis for the formation of distinct political parties. Printed materials reached an invisible public, allowing silent individuals to join causes and groups of individuals widely separated by geography to form a common identity. This new group consciousness could compete with older, localized loyalties.

Printing also stimulated the literacy of lay people and eventually came to have a deep effect on their private lives. Although most of the earliest books and pamphlets dealt with religious subjects, students, housewives, businessmen, and upper- and middle-class people sought books on all subjects. Printers responded with moralizing, medi-

The Print Shop Sixteenth-century printing involved a division of labor. Two persons (left) at separate benches set the pieces of type. Another (center, rear) inks the chase (or locked plate containing the set type). Another (right) operates the press, which prints the sheets. The boy removes the printed pages and sets them to dry. Meanwhile, a man carries in fresh paper on his head. *(Source: Bettman/Hulton)*

cal, practical, and travel manuals. Pornography as well as piety assumed new forms. Broadsides and fly sheets allowed great public festivals, religious ceremonies, and political events to be experienced vicariously by those who stayed at home. Since books and printed materials were read aloud to the illiterate, print bridged the gap between written and oral cultures.[18]

Women in Renaissance Society

The status of upper-class women declined during the Renaissance. If women in the High Middle Ages are compared with those of fifteenth- and sixteenth-century Italy with respect to the kind of work they performed, their access to property and political power, and the role they played in shap-

ing the outlook of their society, it is clear that ladies in the Renaissance ruling classes generally had less power than comparable ladies of the feudal age.

In the cities of Renaissance Italy, girls and boys received a similar education. Young ladies learned their letters and studied the classics. Many read Greek as well as Latin, knew the poetry of Ovid and Virgil, and could speak one or two "modern" languages, such as French or Spanish. In this respect, Renaissance humanism represented a real educational advance for women.

Some women, though a small minority among humanists, acquired great learning and achieved fame in typically humanist genres—letters, orations, treatises, and poems. Laura Cereta (1469–1499) illustrates the successes and failures of educated Renaissance women. Educated by her father,

Sofonisba Anguissola: The Artist's Sister Minerva A nobleman's daughter and one of the first Italian women to become a recognized artist, Sofonisba did portraits of her five sisters and of prominent people. The coiffure, elegant gown, necklaces, and rings depict aristocratic dress in the mid-sixteenth century. *(Source: Milwaukee Art Museum, Gift of the family of Fred Vogel, Jr.)*

study. However, she had to bear the envy of other women and the hostility of men who felt threatened. In response, Laura condemned "empty women, who strive for no good but exist to adorn themselves . . . these women of majestic pride, fantastic coiffures, outlandish ornament, and necks bound with gold or pearls [which] bear the glittering symbols of their captivity to men." For Laura Cereta, women's inferiority was derived not from the divine order of things but from women themselves: "For knowledge is not given as a gift, but through study. . . . The free mind, not afraid of labor, presses on to attain the good."[19] Despite Laura's faith in women's potential, men frequently believed that a woman in becoming learned violated nature and thus ceased to be a woman. Brilliant women such as Laura Cereta were severely attacked by men who feared threats to male dominance in the intellectual realm.

Laura Cereta was a prodigy. Ordinary girls of the urban upper middle class, in addition to a classical education, received some training in painting, music, and dance. What were they to do with this training? They were to be gracious, affable, charming—in short, decorative. Renaissance women were better educated than their medieval counterparts. But whereas education trained a young man to rule and to participate in the public affairs of the city, it prepared a woman for the social functions of the home. An educated lady was supposed to know how to attract artists and literati to her husband's court and grace her husband's household.

Whatever the practical reality, a striking difference also exists between the medieval literature of courtly love—the etiquette books and romances—and the widely studied Renaissance manual on courtesy and good behavior, Castiglione's *The Courtier*. In the medieval books, manners shaped the man to please the lady; in *The Courtier* the lady was to make herself pleasing to the man. With respect to love and sex, the Renaissance witnessed a downward shift in women's status. In contrast to the medieval tradition of relative sexual equality, Renaissance humanists laid the foundations for the bourgeois double standard. Men, and men alone, operated in the public sphere; women belonged in the home. Castiglione, the foremost spokesman of Renaissance love and manners, completely separated love from sexuality. For women, sex was restricted entirely to marriage. Ladies were bound to chastity, to the roles of wife and mother

who was a member of the governing elite of Brescia in Lombardy, she learned languages, philosophy, theology, and mathematics. She also gained self-confidence and a healthy respect for her own potential. By the age of fifteen, when she married, her literary career was already launched, as her letters to several cardinals attest. For Laura Cereta, however, as for all educated women of the period, the question of marriage forced the issue: she could choose a husband, family, and full participation in social life, or she could study and withdraw from the world. Marriage brought domestic responsibilities and usually prevented women from fulfilling their scholarly potential. Laura chose marriage, but she was widowed at eighteen and spent the remaining twelve years of her life in in a politically arranged marriage. Men, however, could pursue sensual indulgence outside marriage.[20]

Official attitudes toward rape provide another index of the status of women in the Renaissance. A careful study of the legal evidence from Venice in the years 1338 to 1358 is informative. The Venetian shipping and merchant elite held economic and political power and made the laws. Those laws reveal that rape was not considered a particularly serious crime against either the victim or society. Noble youths committed a higher percentage of rapes than their small numbers in Venetian society would imply, despite government-regulated prostitution. The rape of a young girl of marriageable age or a child under twelve was considered a graver crime than the rape of a married woman. Still, the punishment for the rape of a noble, marriageable girl was only a fine or about six months' imprisonment. In an age when theft and robbery were punished by mutilation, and forgery and sodomy by burning, this penalty was very mild indeed. When a youth of the upper class was convicted of the rape of a non-noble girl, his punishment was even lighter. By contrast, the sexual assault on a noblewoman by a man of working-class origin, which was extraordinarily rare, resulted in severe penalties because the crime had social and political overtones.

In the eleventh century, William the Conqueror had decreed that rapists be castrated, implicitly according women protection and a modicum of respect. But in the early Renaissance, Venetian laws and their enforcement show that the governing oligarchy believed that rape damaged, but only slightly, men's property—women.[21]

Evidence from Florence in the fifteenth century sheds light on infanticide, which historians are only now beginning to study in the Middle Ages and the Renaissance. Early medieval penitentials and church councils had legislated against abortion and infanticide, though it is known that Pope Innocent III (r. 1198–1216) was moved to establish an orphanage "because so many women were throwing their children into the Tiber."[22] In the fourteenth and early fifteenth centuries, a considerable number of children died in Florence under suspicious circumstances. Some were simply abandoned outdoors. Some were said to have been crushed to death while sleeping in bed with their parents. Some died from "crib death" or suffocation. These deaths occurred too frequently to

have all been accidental. And far more girls than boys died, thus reflecting societal discrimination against girl children as inferior and less useful than boys. The dire poverty of parents led them to do away with unwanted children.

The gravity of the problem of infanticide, which violated both the canon law of the church and the civil law of the state, forced the Florentine government to build the Foundling Hospital. Supporters of the institution maintained that, without public responsibility, "many children would soon be found dead in the rivers, sewers, and ditches, unbaptized."[23] The unusually large size of the hospital suggests that great numbers of children were abandoned.

Blacks in Renaissance Society

Ever since the time of the Roman Republic, a few black people had lived in Western Europe. They had come, along with white slaves, as the spoils of war. Even after the collapse of the Roman Empire, Muslim and Christian merchants continued to import them. The evidence of medieval art attests to the presence of Africans in the West and Europeans' awareness of them. In the twelfth and thirteenth centuries, a large cult surrounded Saint Maurice, martyred in the fourth century for refusing to renounce his Christian faith, who was portrayed as a black knight. Saint Maurice received the special veneration of the nobility.

The numbers of blacks in Europe had always been small. Beginning in the late fifteenth century, however, hordes of black slaves entered Europe. Portuguese explorers imported perhaps a thousand a year and sold them at the markets of Seville, Barcelona, Marseilles, and Genoa. By the mid-sixteenth century, blacks, slave and free, constituted about 10 percent of the populations of the Portuguese cities of Lisbon and Évora; other cities had smaller percentages. The Venetians controlled the slave trade, which until this time had involved the import of white slaves from southern Russia and the Balkans. But blacks were greatly in demand at the Renaissance courts of northern Italy. What roles did blacks play in Renaissance society? What image did Europeans have of Africans?

The medieval interest in curiosities, the exotic, and the marvelous continued into the Renaissance. Because of their rarity, black servants were highly prized and much sought after. In the late fifteenth century, Isabella, the wife of Gian Galazzo Sforza, took pride in the fact that she had ten blacks. In 1491 Isabella of Este, duchess of Mantua, instructed her agent to secure a black girl between four and eight years old, "shapely and as black as possible." The duchess saw the child as a source of entertainment: she hoped that the little girl would become "the best buffoon in the world."[24] The cruel ancient tradition of a noble household retaining a professional "fool" for the family's amusement persisted through the Renaissance—and even down to the twentieth century.

Adult black slaves filled a variety of positions. Many served as maids, valets, and domestic servants. The Venetians employed blacks—slave and free—as gondoliers and stevedores on the docks. Tradition, stretching back at least as far as the thirteenth century, connected blacks with music and dance. In Renaissance Spain and Italy, blacks performed as dancers, as actors and actresses in courtly dramas, and as musicians, sometimes composing full orchestras.[25]

Until the exploration and observation of the sixteenth, seventeenth, and nineteenth centuries allowed, ever so slowly, for the development of scientific knowledge, the Western conception of Africa and black people remained bound up with religious notions.[26] During the Renaissance, Europeans had little concrete knowledge of Africans and African culture beyond biblical accounts.

The European attitude toward Africans was ambivalent. On the one hand, Europeans perceived Africa as a remote place, the home of strange people isolated by heresy and Islam from "superior" European civilization. They believed that contact, even as slaves with Christian Europeans could only "improve" black Africans. Most Europeans' knowledge of the black as a racial type was based entirely on theological speculation. Theologians taught that God is light. Blackness, the opposite of light, thus represented the hostile forces of the underworld: evil, sin, and the Devil. The Devil was commonly represented as a black man in medieval and early Renaissance art. On the other hand, blackness was also associated with certain positive qualities. It symbolized the vanity of worldly goods, the humility of the monastic way of life. Black clothes permitted a conservative and discreet display of wealth. Black vestments and funeral trappings indicated grief, and Christ had said that those who mourn are blessed. In Renaissance society, blacks, like women, were signs of wealth; both

were used for display. Europeans' image of blacks remained one based on theological ideas.

THE RENAISSANCE IN THE NORTH

In the last quarter of the fifteenth century, students from the Low Countries, France, Germany, and England flocked to Italy, imbibed the "new learning," and carried it back to their countries. Northern humanists interpreted Italian ideas about and attitudes toward classical antiquity, individualism, and humanism in terms of their own traditions. The culture of northern Europe had tended to remain more distinctly Christian, or at least pietistic, than that of Italy. Italians certainly were strongly Christian, but in Italy secular and pagan themes and Greco-Roman motifs received more attention from the humanists than they received in northern Europe. North of the Alps, the Renaissance had a distinctly religious character, and humanists stressed biblical and early Christian themes. What fundamentally distinguished Italian humanists from northern humanists is that the latter had a program for broad social reform based on Christian ideals.

Christian humanists in northern Europe were interested in the development of an ethical way of life. To achieve it, they believed that the best elements of classical and Christian cultures should be combined. For example, the classical ideals of calmness, stoical patience, and broad-mindedness should be joined in human conduct with the Christian virtues of love, faith, and hope. Northern humanists also stressed the use of reason, rather than acceptance of dogma, as the foundation for an ethical way of life. Like the Italians, they were impatient with Scholastic philosophy. Northern humanists had a profound faith in the power of human intellect to bring about moral and institutional reform. They believed that, although human nature had been corrupted by sin, it was fundamentally good and capable of improvement through education, which would lead to piety and an ethical way of life.

The work of the French priest Jacques Lefèvre d'Étaples (ca 1455–1536) is one of the early attempts to apply humanistic learning to religious problems. A brilliant thinker and able scholar, he believed that more accurate texts of the Bible would lead people to live better lives. According to

Lefèvre, a solid education in the Scriptures would increase piety and raise the level of behavior in Christian society. Lefèvre produced an edition of the Psalms and a commentary on Saint Paul's letters.

The Englishman Thomas More (1478–1535) towers above other figures in sixteenth-century English social and intellectual history. More's troubles at the time of the Reformation with King Henry VIII (see page 551) have tended to obscure his contribution to Christian humanism. Trained as a lawyer, More lived as a student in the London Charterhouse, a Carthusian monastery. He subsequently married and practiced law but became deeply interested in the classics. His household served as a model of warm Christian family life and a mecca for foreign and English humanists. In a career pattern similar to that of Italian humanists such as Petrarch, More entered government service. Under Henry VIII he was sent as ambassador to Flanders. There More found the time to write *Utopia* (1516), which presented a revolutionary view of society.

Utopia, which literally means "nowhere," describes an ideal socialistic community on an island somewhere off the mainland of the New World. All its children receive a good education, primarily in the Greco-Roman classics, and learning does not cease with maturity, for the goal of all education is to develop rational faculties. Adults divide their days equally between manual labor or business pursuits and various intellectual activities.

Because the profits from business and property are held strictly in common, there is absolute social equality. The Utopians use gold and silver to make chamber pots or to prevent wars by buying off their enemies. By this casual use of precious metals, More meant to suggest that the basic problems in society were caused by greed. Utopian law exalts mercy above justice. Citizens of Utopia lead an ideal, nearly perfect existence because they live by reason; their institutions are perfect. More punned on the word *Utopia*—which he termed "a good place. A good place which is no place."

More's ideas were profoundly original in the sixteenth century. Contrary to the long-prevailing view that vice and violence exist because women and men are basically corrupt, More maintained that acquisitiveness and private property promoted all sorts of vices and civil disorders. Since society protected private property, *society's* flawed institutions were responsible for corruption and war.

Baldung: Adoration of the Magi Early sixteenth-century German artists produced thousands of adoration scenes depicting a black man as one of the three kings: these paintings were based on direct observation, reflecting the increased presence of blacks in Europe. The elaborate costumes, jewelry, and landscape expressed royal dignity, Christian devotion, and oriental luxury. *(Source: Gemäldegalerie, Staatliche Museen Preusischer Kulturbesitz, Berlin)*

Today people take this view so much for granted that it is difficult to appreciate how radical it was in the sixteenth century. According to More, the key to improvement and reform of the individual was reform of the social institutions that mold the individual.

Better known by his contemporaries than Thomas More was the Dutch humanist Desiderius Erasmus of Rotterdam (1466?–1536). Orphaned as a small boy, Erasmus was forced to enter a monastery. Although he intensely disliked the monastic life, he developed there an excellent knowledge of the Latin language and a deep appreciation for the Latin classics. The application of the best humanistic learning to the study and explanation of the Bible became Erasmus's life work. As a mature scholar with an international reputation stretching from Cracow to London, Erasmus could boast with truth, "I brought it about that humanism, which among the Italians . . . savored of nothing but pure paganism, began nobly to celebrate Christ."[27]

Erasmus's long list of publications includes *The Adages* (1500), a list of Greek and Latin precepts on ethical behavior; *The Education of a Christian Prince* (1504), which combines idealistic and practical suggestions for the formation of a ruler's character through the careful study of Plutarch, Aristotle, Cicero, and Plato; *The Praise of Folly* (1509), a satire on worldly wisdom and a plea for the simple and spontaneous Christian faith of children; and, most important of all, a critical edition of the Greek New Testament (1516). In the preface to the New Testament, Erasmus explained the purpose of his great work:

Only bring a pious and open heart, imbued above all things with a pure and simple faith. . . . For I utterly dissent from those who are unwilling that the sacred Scriptures should be read by the unlearned translated into their vulgar tongue, as though Christ had taught such subtleties that they can scarcely be understood even by a few theologians. . . . Christ wished his mysteries to be published as openly as possible. I wish that even the weakest woman should read the Gospel—should read the epistles of Paul. And I wish these were translated into all languages, so that they might be read and understood, not only by Scots and Irishmen, but also by Turks and Saracens. . . . Why do we prefer to study the wisdom of Christ in men's writings rather than in the writing of Christ himself?[28]

Two fundamental themes pervade all of Erasmus's scholarly work. First, education was the means to reform, the key to moral and intellectual improvement. The core of education ought to be study of the Bible and the classics. Second, the essence of Erasmus's thought is, in his own phrase, "the philosophy of Christ." By this Erasmus meant that Christianity is an inner attitude of the heart or spirit. Christianity is not formalism, special ceremonies, or law. Christianity is Christ—his life and what he said and did—not what theologians have written about him.

The writings of Lefèvre, More, and Erasmus have strong Christian themes and have drawn the attention primarily of scholars. In contrast, the stories of the French humanist François Rabelais (1490?–1553) possess a distinctly secular flavor and have attracted broad readership among the literate public. Rabelais's *Gargantua* and *Pantagruel* (serialized between 1532 and 1552) belong among the great comic masterpieces of world literature. These stories' gross and robust humor introduced the adjective *Rabelaisian* into English.

Gargantua and *Pantagruel* can be read on several levels: as comic romances about the adventures of the giant Gargantua and his son, Pantagruel; as spoofs on contemporary French society; as a program for educational reform; as illustrations of Rabelais's prodigious learning. The reader enters a world of Renaissance vitality, ribald joviality, and intellectual curiosity. On his travels Gargantua meets various absurd characters, and within their hilarious exchanges there occur serious discussions on religion, politics, philosophy, and education. Rabelais had received an excellent humanistic education in a monastery, and Gargantua discusses the disorders of contemporary religious and secular life.

Like Erasmus and More, Rabelais did not denounce institutions directly. Like Erasmus, he satirized hypocritical monks, pedantic academics, and pompous lawyers. But where Erasmus employed intellectual cleverness and sophisticated wit, Rabelais applied wild and gross humor. Like More, Rabelais believed that institutions molded individuals and that education was the key to a moral and healthy life. The middle-class inhabitants of More's Utopia lived lives of restrained moderation. The aristocratic residents of Rabelais's Thélème lived for the full gratification of their physical instincts and rational curiosity.

Thélème, the abbey that Gargantua establishes, parodies traditional religion and other social institutions. Thélème, whose motto is "Do as Thou Wilt," admits men *and* women; allows all to eat, drink, sleep, and work when they choose; provides excellent facilities for swimming, tennis, and football; and encourages sexual experimentation and marriage. Rabelais believed profoundly in the basic goodness of human beings and in the rightness of instinct.

The most roguishly entertaining Renaissance writer, Rabelais was convinced that "laughter is the essence of manhood." A believer in the Roman Catholic faith, he included in Gargantua's education an appreciation for simple and reasonable prayer. Rabelais combined the Renaissance zest for life and enjoyment of pleasure with a classical insistence on the cultivation of the body and the mind.

The distinctly religious orientation of the literary works of the Renaissance in the north also characterized northern art and architecture. Some Flemish painters, notably Jan van Eyck (1366–1441), were the equals of Italian painters. One of the earliest artists successfully to use oil-based paints, van Eyck, in paintings such as *Ghent Altarpiece* and the portrait *Giovanni Arnolfini and His Bride,* shows the Flemish love for detail; the effect is great realism. Van Eyck's paintings also demonstrate remarkable attention to human personality, as is shown in his *Madonna of the Chancellor Rodin.*

Another Flemish painter, Jerome Bosch (ca 1450–1516), frequently used religious themes, but in combination with grotesque fantasies, colorful imagery, and peasant folk legends. Many

Jan van Eyck: Madonna of the Chancellor Rodin The tough and shrewd chancellor who ordered this rich painting visits the Virgin and Christ-Child (though they seem to be visiting him). An angel holds the crown of heaven over the Virgin's head while Jesus, the proclaimed savior of the world, holds a globe in his left hand and raises his right hand in blessing. Through the colonnade, sculpted with scenes from Genesis, is the city of Bruges. Van Eyck's achievement in portraiture is extraordinary; his treatment of space and figures and his ability to capture the infinitely small and very large prompted the art historian Erwin Panofsky to write that "his eye was at one and the same time a microscope and a telescope." *(Source: Louvre/Cliché des Musées Nationaux, Paris)*

of Bosch's paintings reflect the confusion and anguish often associated with the end of the Middle Ages. In *Death and the Miser,* Bosch's dramatic treatment of the Dance of Death theme, diabolical rats and toads control the miser's gold, increased by usury, and the miser's guardian angel urges the bedfast miser to choose the crucifix, not worldly wealth.

A quasi-spiritual aura likewise infuses architectural monuments in the north. The city halls of wealthy Flemish towns like Bruges, Brussels, Louvain, and Ghent seem more like shrines to house the bones of saints than like settings for the mundane decisions of politicians and businessmen. Northern architecture was little influenced by the classical revival so obvious in Renaissance Rome and Florence.

POLITICS AND THE STATE IN THE RENAISSANCE (1450–1521)

Many basic institutions of the modern state have their origins in the High Middle Ages (see pages 404–417). The linchpin for the development of states, however, was strong monarchy. But in the era of the Hundred Years' War (1337–1453), no ruler in western Europe provided effective leadership. As a result, the resurgent power of feudal nobilities weakened the centralizing work begun in the twelfth and thirteenth centuries.

Beginning in the fifteenth century, however, rulers utilized the aggressive methods implied by Renaissance political ideas to rebuild their governments. First in Italy, then in France, England, and Spain, rulers began to reduce violence, curb unruly nobles and other troublesome elements, and establish domestic order. Within the Holy Roman Empire of Germany, the lack of centralization helps to account for later German distrust of the Roman papacy. Divided into scores of independent principalities, Germany could not deal as an equal with the Roman church.

Jerome Bosch: Death and the Miser   Dutch painters frequently used symbolism, and Bosch (ca 1450–1516) is considered the master artist of symbolism and fantasy. Here rats, which symbolize evil, control the miser's gold. Bosch's imagery appealed strongly to twentieth-century surrealist painters. *(Source: National Gallery of Art, Washington, D.C., Samuel H. Kress Collection)*

The dictators and oligarchs of the Italian city-states, however, together with Louis XI of France, Henry VII of England, and Ferdinand and Isabella of Spain, were tough, cynical, calculating rulers. In their ruthless push for power and strong governments, they subordinated morality to hard results. They preferred to be secure, though feared, rather than loved. They could not have read Machiavelli's *The Prince,* but they acted as if they understood its ideas.

Some historians have called Louis XI (r. 1461–1483), Henry VII (r. 1485–1509), and Ferdinand and Isabella (r. 1474–1516) "new monarchs." The term is only partly appropriate. What was new was a marked acceleration in the acquisition and expansion of power. Renaissance rulers spent precious little time seeking religious justification for their actions. They stressed that monarchy was the one institution that linked all classes and peoples within definite territorial boundaries. Rulers emphasized royal majesty and royal sovereignty and insisted that all must respect and be loyal to them. They ruthlessly suppressed opposition and rebellion, especially from the nobility. They loved the business of kingship and worked hard at it.

In other respects, however, the methods of these rulers, which varied from country to country, were not so new. They reasserted long-standing ideas and practices of strong monarchs in the Middle Ages, seizing on a maxim of the Justinian *Code,* "What pleases the prince has the force of law," to advance their authority. Like some medieval rulers, Renaissance rulers tended to rely on middle-class civil servants. Using tax revenues, medieval rulers had built armies to crush feudal anarchy. Renaissance townspeople with commercial and business interests naturally wanted a reduction of violence and usually were willing to be taxed in order to achieve it. These qualifications of the term "new monarchs" are important in understanding the development of national monarchies in France, England, and Spain in the period 1450 to 1521 and the growth in "international" power of Austria's house of Habsburg.

France

The Hundred Years' War left France badly divided, drastically depopulated, commercially ruined, and agriculturally weak. Nonetheless, the seemingly feeble ruler whom Joan of Arc had seen crowned at Reims, Charles VII (1422–1461), revived the monarchy and France. Charles reorganized the royal council, giving increased influence to middle-class men, and strengthened royal finances through such taxes as the *gabelle* (on salt) and the *taille* (a land tax). Charles created France's first permanent royal army by establishing regular companies of cavalry and archers—recruited, paid, and inspected by the state. In 1438 Charles published the Pragmatic Sanction of Bourges, asserting the superiority of a general church council over the papacy, giving the French crown major control over the appointment of bishops, and depriving the pope of French ecclesiastical revenues. Greater control over the army and the church helped to consolidate the authority of the French crown.

Charles's son Louis XI (r. 1461–1483), called the "Spider King" because of his treacherous and cruel character, was very much a Renaissance prince. Facing the perpetual French problems of unification of the realm and reduction of feudal disorder, he saw money as the answer. Louis promoted new industries, such as silk weaving at Lyon and Tours, and entered into commercial treaties with other countries. The revenues raised through these economic activities and severe taxation went into improving the army, which Louis used to stop aristocratic brigandage and to undercut urban independence.

Luck favored Louis's goal of expanding royal authority and unifying the kingdom. On the timely death of Charles the Bold, duke of Burgundy, in 1477, Louis invaded Burgundy and gained some territories. Three years later, the extinction of the house of Anjou brought Louis the counties of Anjou, Bar, Maine, and Provence.

Some scholars have credited Louis XI with laying the foundations for later French royal absolutism. Indeed, he worked tirelessly to remodel and strengthen the government. In his reliance on finances supplied by the middle classes to fight the feudal nobility, Louis was typical of the new monarchs.

England

English society suffered severely from the disorders of the fifteenth century. The aristocracy came to dominate the government and regularly in-

French Tradesmen   A bootmaker, a cloth merchant (with bolts of material on shelves), and a dealer in gold plate and silver share a stall. Through sales taxes, the French crown received a portion of the profits. *(Source: Giraudon/Art Resource)*

dulged in mischievous violence at the local level. Then, between 1455 and 1471, adherents of the ducal houses of York and Lancaster waged civil war, commonly called the "Wars of the Roses" because the symbol of the Yorkists was a white rose and that of the Lancastrians a red rose. Although only a small minority of the nobility participated in the conflict, the chronic disorder hurt trade, agriculture, and domestic industry. Under the pious but mentally disturbed Henry VI (r. 1422–1461), the authority of the monarchy sank lower than it had been in centuries.

The Yorkist Edward IV (r. 1461–1483) defeated the Lancastrian forces and after 1471 began to re-establish domestic tranquillity, reconstruct the monarchy, and consolidate royal power. Edward, his brother Richard III (r. 1483–1485), and Henry VII (r. 1485–1509) of the Welsh house of Tudor worked to restore royal prestige, to crush the power of the nobility, and to establish order

and law at the local level. All three used methods that Machiavelli would have praised: ruthlessness, efficiency, and secrecy.

The Hundred Years' War had cost the nation dearly, and the money to finance it had been raised by Parliament. Dominated by various baronial factions, Parliament had been the arena where the nobility exerted its power. As long as the monarchy depended on the Lords and Commons for revenue for war, the king had to call Parliament. Thus Edward IV reluctantly established a policy that the monarchy was to follow with rare exceptions down to 1603. Edward, and subsequently the Tudors, except Henry VIII, conducted foreign policy on the basis of diplomacy, avoiding expensive wars and thus undercutting a major source of aristocratic influence.

Although Henry VII did summon several meetings of Parliament in the early years of his reign, the center of royal authority was the royal council, which governed at the national level. There Henry VII revealed his distrust of the nobility. Very few great lords were among the king's closest advisers. Most representatives on the council were from the lesser landowning class, and their education was in law. They were, in a sense, middle class.

In addition to handling the executive, legislative, and judicial business of government, the royal council dealt with real or potential aristocratic threats through a judicial offshoot, the "Court of Star Chamber," so called because of the stars painted on the ceiling of the room in which it met. This court applied principles of Roman law, and its methods were sometimes terrifying: the accused was not entitled to see evidence against him or her; sessions were secret; torture could be applied to extract confessions; and juries were not called. These procedures ran directly counter to English common-law precedents, but they effectively reduced aristocratic troublemaking.

Unlike the continental countries of Spain and France, England had no standing army or professional civil service bureaucracy. The Tudors relied on the support of unpaid local officials, the justices of the peace, who were appointed and supervised by the royal council. These influential landowners in the shires handled all the work of local government. From the royal point of view, they were an inexpensive method of government.

The Tudors won the support of the influential upper middle class because the Crown linked government policy with that group's interests. A commercial or agricultural upper class fears and dislikes disorder and violence. If the Wars of the Roses served any purpose, it was killing off dangerous nobles and thus making the Tudors' work easier. The Tudors promoted peace and social order; and because the government had halted the long period of anarchy, the gentry did not object to methods like those used by the Court of Star Chamber.

Grave, secretive, cautious, and always thrifty, Henry VII rebuilt the monarchy. He encouraged the cloth industry and built up the English merchant marine. English exports of wool and the royal export tax on that wool steadily increased. Henry crushed an invasion from Ireland and secured peace with Scotland through the marriage of his daughter Margaret to the Scottish king. When Henry VII died in 1509, he left a country at peace both domestically and internationally, a substantially augmented treasury, and the dignity and role of the royal majesty much enhanced.

Spain

Political development in Spain followed a pattern different from that in France and England. The central theme in the history of medieval Spain—or, more accurately, of the separate kingdoms that Spain comprised—was disunity and plurality. The various peoples who lived in the Iberian Peninsula lacked a common cultural tradition. Different languages, laws, and religious communities made for a rich diversity. Adding to the Hispanic, Roman, and Visigothic heritage, Muslims and Jews had significantly affected the course of Spanish society.

By the middle of the fifteenth century, the kingdoms of Castile and Aragon dominated the weaker Navarre, Granada, and Portugal (Map 17.2), and the reconquista had won the Iberian Peninsula (except for Granada) for Christianity. The wedding in 1469 of the dynamic and aggressive Isabella, heiress of Castile, and the crafty and persistent Ferdinand, heir of Aragon, was the final major step in the unification and Christianization of Spain. This marriage, however, constituted a dynastic union of two royal houses, not the political union of two peoples. Although Ferdinand and Isabella pursued a common foreign policy, Spain under their rule remained a loose confederation of separate states. Each kingdom continued to maintain its own *cortes* (parliament), laws, courts, bureaucracies, and systems of coinage and taxation.

Isabella and Ferdinand were determined to strengthen royal authority. To curb rebellious and warring aristocrats, they revived an old medieval institution. Popular groups in the towns, called *hermandades,* or "brotherhoods," were given the authority to act both as local police forces and as judicial tribunals. The hermandades repressed violence with such savage punishments that by 1498 they could be disbanded.

The decisive step that Ferdinand and Isabella took to curb aristocratic power was the restructuring of the royal council. The king and queen appointed to the council only people of middle-class background, excluding aristocrats and territorial magnates. The council and various government boards recruited men trained in Roman law, a system that exalted the power of the crown as the embodiment of the state.

In the extension of royal authority and the consolidation of the territories of Spain, the church was the linchpin. The major issue confronting Isabella and Ferdinand was the appointment of the higher clergy. Through a diplomatic alliance with the papacy, especially with the Spanish pope Alexander VI (r. 1492–1503), the Spanish monarchs secured the right to appoint bishops in Spain and in the Hispanic territories in America. This power enabled the "Catholic Kings of Spain," a title granted Ferdinand and Isabella by the papacy, to establish, in effect, a national church and to influence ecclesiastical policy, wealth, and military resources.[29] The Spanish rulers used their power to reform the church, and they used some of the church's wealth for national purposes.

Revenues from ecclesiastical estates provided the means to raise an army to continue the reconquista. The victorious entry of Ferdinand and Isabella into Granada on January 6, 1492, signaled the culmination of eight centuries of Spanish struggle against the Arabs in southern Spain and the conclusion of the reconquista (see Map 17.2). Granada in the south was incorporated into the Spanish kingdom, and in 1512 Ferdinand conquered Navarre in the north.

Although the Arabs had been defeated, there still remained a sizable and, in the view of the Catholic sovereigns, potentially dangerous minority, the Jews. Since ancient times, religious faiths that differed from the official state religion had been considered politically dangerous. Medieval writers quoted the fourth-century Byzantine theologian Saint John Chrysostom, who had asked rhetorically, "Why are the Jews degenerate? Because of their odious assassination of Christ." John Chrysostom and his admirers in the Middle Ages chose to ignore two facts: that it was the Romans who had killed Christ (because they considered him a *political* troublemaker) and that Christ had forgiven his executioners from the cross. France and England had expelled their Jewish populations in the Middle Ages, but in Spain Jews had been tolerated. In fact, Jews had played a decisive role in the economic and intellectual life of the several Spanish kingdoms.

Anti-Semitic riots and pogroms in the late fourteenth century had led many Jews to convert; they were called *conversos*. By the middle of the fifteenth century, many conversos held high positions in Spanish society as financiers, physicians, merchants, tax collectors, and even officials of the church hierarchy. Numbering perhaps 200,000 in a total population of about 7.5 million, Jews exercised an influence quite disproportionate to their numbers. Aristocratic grandees (nobles) who borrowed heavily from Jews resented their financial dependence, and churchmen questioned the sincerity of Jewish conversions. At first, Isabella and Ferdinand continued the policy of royal tolera-

MAP 17.2 The Christianization and Unification of Spain   The political unification of Spain was inextricably tied up with conversion or expulsion of the Muslims and the Jews.

tion—Ferdinand himself had inherited Jewish blood from his mother. But many conversos apparently reverted to the faith of their ancestors, prompting Ferdinand and Isabella to secure Rome's permission to revive the Inquisition, a medieval judicial procedure for the punishment of heretics (see page 436).

Although the Inquisition was a religious institution established to ensure the Catholic faith in Spain, it was controlled by the Crown and served primarily as a politically unifying force. Because the Spanish Inquisition commonly applied torture to extract confessions, it gained a notorious reputation. Thus the word *inquisition,* meaning "any judicial inquiry conducted with ruthless severity," came into the English language. The methods of the Spanish Inquisition were cruel, though not as cruel as the investigative methods of certain twentieth-century governments. In 1478 the deeply pious Ferdinand and Isabella introduced the Inquisition into their kingdoms to handle the problem of backsliding conversos. They solved the problem in a dire and drastic manner. Shortly after the reduction of the Moorish stronghold at Granada in 1492, Isabella and Ferdinand issued an edict expelling all practicing Jews from Spain. Of the community of perhaps 200,000 Jews, 150,000 fled. (Efforts were made, through last-minute conversions, to retain good Jewish physicians.) Absolute Catholic orthodoxy served as the foundation of the Spanish national state.

The diplomacy of the Catholic rulers of Spain achieved a success they never anticipated. Partly out of hatred for the French and partly to gain international recognition for their new dynasty, Ferdinand and Isabella in 1496 married their second daughter, Joanna, heiress to Castile, to the archduke Philip, heir through his mother to the Burgundian Netherlands and through his father to the Holy Roman Empire.

Germany and the Rise of the Habsburg Dynasty

The history of the Holy Roman Empire in the later Middle Ages is a story of dissension, disintegration, and debility. Unlike France, England, and Spain, the empire lacked a strong central power. The Golden Bull of 1356 legalized what had long existed—government by an aristocratic federation. Each of seven electors—the archbishops of Mainz, Trier, and Cologne, the margrave of Brandenburg, the duke of Saxony, the count palatine of the Rhine, and the king of Bohemia—gained virtual sovereignty in his own territory. The agreement ended disputed elections in the empire; it also reduced the central authority of the emperor. Germany was characterized by weak borders, localism, and chronic disorder. The nobility strengthened its territories while imperial power declined.

The marriage in 1477 of Maximilian I of the house of Habsburg and Mary of Burgundy was a decisive event in early modern European history. Through this union with the rich and powerful duchy of Burgundy, the Austrian house of Habsburg, already the strongest ruling family in the empire, became an international power.

"Other nations wage war; you, Austria, marry." Historians dispute the origins of the adage, but no one questions its accuracy. It was the heir of Mary and Maximilian, Philip of Burgundy, who married Joanna of Castile. Through a series of accidents and unexpected deaths, Philip and Joanna's son Charles V (r. 1519–1556) inherited Spain from his mother, together with her possessions in the New World and the Spanish dominions in Italy (Sicily, Sardinia, and the kingdom of Naples). From his father he inherited the Habsburg lands in Austria, southern Germany, the Low Countries, and Franche-Comté in east central France (Map 17.3).

Charles's inheritance was an incredibly diverse collection of states and peoples, each governed in a different manner and held together only by the person of the emperor. Charles's Italian adviser, the grand chancellor Gattinara, told the young ruler: "God has set you on the path toward world monarchy." Charles not only believed this; he was convinced that it was his duty to maintain the political and religious unity of Western Christendom. In this respect Charles V was the last medieval emperor.

Charles needed and in 1519 secured the imperial title. Forward-thinking Germans proposed government reforms. They urged placing the administration in the hands of an imperial council whose president, the emperor's appointee, would have ultimate executive power. Reforms of the imperial finances, the army, and the judiciary were also recommended. Such ideas did not interest the young emperor at all. When he finally arrived in Germany from Spain and opened his first *diet* (assembly of the estates of the empire) at Worms in January 1521, he naively announced that "the

MAP 17.3 The European Empire of Charles V Charles V exercised theoretical jurisdiction over more territory than anyone since Charlemagne. This map does not show his Latin American and Asian possessions.

empire from of old has had not many masters, but one, and it is our intention to be that one." Charles went on to say that he was to be treated as of greater account than his predecessors because he was more powerful than they had been. In view of Germany's long history of aristocratic power, Charles's notions were pure fantasy.

THE CONDITION OF THE CHURCH (1400–1517)

The papal conflict with the German emperor Frederick II (r. 1215–1250) in the thirteenth century, followed by the Babylonian Captivity and then the Great Schism (see pages 446–447), badly damaged the prestige of church leaders. In the fourteenth and fifteenth centuries, conciliarists (proponents of the conciliar view of church government) reflected educated public opinion when they called for the reform of the church "in head and members." The secular humanists of Italy and the Christian humanists of the north denounced and satirized corruption in the church. The records of episcopal visitations of parishes, civil court records, and even such literary masterpieces as Chaucer's *Canterbury Tales* and Boccaccio's *The Decameron* tend to confirm the sarcasms of the humanists.

Signs of Disorder

In the early sixteenth century, critics of the church concentrated their attacks on three disorders: clerical immorality, clerical ignorance, and clerical pluralism and the related problem of absenteeism. There was little pressure for doctrinal change; the emphasis was on moral and administrative reform.

Since the fourth century, church law had required candidates for the priesthood to accept absolute celibacy. The law had always been difficult to enforce. Many priests, especially those ministering to country people, had concubines, and reports of neglect of the rule of celibacy were common. Immorality, of course, included more than sexual transgressions. Clerical drunkenness, gambling, and indulgence in fancy dress were frequent charges. There is no way of knowing how many priests were guilty of such behavior. But because such conduct was so much at odds with the church's rules and moral standards, it scandalized the educated faithful.

The bishops only casually enforced regulations regarding the education of priests. As a result, standards for ordination were shockingly low. Many priests could barely read and write, and critics laughed at illiterate priests mumbling the Latin words to the mass, which they could not understand. Predictably, clerical ignorance was the disorder that the Christian humanists, with their concern for learning, particularly condemned.

Pluralism and absenteeism constituted the third major abuse. Many clerics, especially higher ecclesiastics, held several benefices simultaneously but seldom visited them, let alone performed the spiritual responsibilities that they entailed. Instead, absentees collected revenues from all of their benefices and paid a poor priest a fraction of the income to fulfill the spiritual duties of a particular local church. King Henry VIII's chancellor Thomas Wolsey was archbishop of York for fifteen years before he set foot in his diocese. The French king Louis XII's famous diplomat Antoine du Prat is perhaps the most notorious example of absenteeism: as archbishop of Sens, the first time he entered his cathedral was in his own funeral procession. Many Italian officials in the papal curia held benefices in England, Spain, and Germany. Revenues from those countries paid the Italian priests' salaries, provoking not only charges of absenteeism but nationalistic resentment. Critics condemned pluralism, absenteeism, and the way money seemed to change hands when a bishop entered into his office.

Although royal governments strengthened their positions and consolidated their territories in the fifteenth and sixteenth centuries, rulers lacked sufficient revenues to pay and reward able civil servants. The Christian church, with its dioceses and abbeys, possessed a large proportion of Europe's wealth. What better way to reward government officials than with high church offices? After all, the practice was sanctioned by centuries of tradition. Thus in Spain, France, England, and the Holy Roman Empire—in fact, all over Europe—church officials who served their monarchs were allowed to govern the church.

The spectacle of proud, aristocratic prelates living in magnificent splendor contrasted very unfavorably with the simple fishermen who were Christ's disciples. Nor did the popes of the period 1450 to 1550 set much of an example. They lived like secular Renaissance princes. Pius II (r. 1458–1464), although deeply learned and a tireless worker, enjoyed a reputation as a clever writer of love stories and Latin poetry. Sixtus IV (r. 1471–1484) beautified the city of Rome, built the Sistine Chapel, and generously supported several artists. Innocent VIII (r. 1484–1492) made the papal court a model of luxury and scandal. All three popes used papal power and wealth to advance the material interests of their own families.

The court of the Spanish pope Rodrigo Borgia, Alexander VI (r. 1492–1503), who publicly acknowledged his mistress and children, reached new heights of impropriety. Because of the prevalence of intrigue, sexual promiscuity, and supposed poisonings, the name *Borgia* became a synonym for moral corruption. Julius II (r. 1503–1513), the nephew of Sixtus IV, donned military armor and personally led papal troops against the French invaders of Italy in 1506. After him, Giovanni de' Medici, the son of Lorenzo the Magnificent, carried on as Pope Leo X (r. 1513–1521) the Medicean tradition of being a great patron of the arts. Reputedly, Leo opened his pontificate with the words "Now that God has given us the papacy, let us enjoy it."

Signs of Vitality

Calls for reform testify to the spiritual vitality of the church as well as to its problems. In the late fifteenth and early sixteenth centuries, both individuals and groups within the church were working actively for reform. In Spain, Cardinal Jiménez visited religious houses, encouraged the monks and friars to keep their rules and constitutions, and set high standards for the training of the diocesan clergy.

In Holland, beginning in the late fourteenth century, a group of pious lay people called the "Brethren of the Common Life" lived in stark simplicity while daily carrying out the Gospel teaching of feeding the hungry, clothing the naked, and

The Church Contrasted Satirical woodcuts as well as the printed word attacked conditions in the church. Here the attitude of Christ toward money changers is contrasted with the mercenary spirit of the sixteenth-century papacy: Christ drove them from the temple, but the pope kept careful records of revenues owed to the church. *(Source: The Pierpont Morgan Library)*

visiting the sick. The Brethren also taught in local schools. Their goal was to prepare devout candidates for the priesthood and the monastic life. Through prayer, meditation, and the careful study of Scripture, the Brethren sought to make religion a personal, inner experience. The spirituality of the Brethren of the Common Life found its finest expression in the classic *The Imitation of Christ* by Thomas à Kempis. Like later Protestants, the Brethren stressed the centrality of Scripture in the spiritual life.[30] In the mid-fifteenth century, the movement had houses in the Netherlands, central Germany, and the Rhineland; it was a true religious revival.

So, too, were the activities of the Oratories of Divine Love in Italy. The oratories were groups of priests living in communities who worked to revive the church through prayer and preaching. They did not withdraw from the world as medieval monks had done but devoted themselves to pastoral and charitable activities such as founding hospitals and orphanages. Oratorians served God in an active ministry.

The papacy also expressed concern for reform. Pope Julius II summoned an ecumenical (universal) council, which met in the church of Saint John Lateran in Rome from 1512 to 1517. Since most of the bishops were Italian and did not represent a broad cross-section of international opinion, the term *ecumenical* was not appropriate. Nevertheless, the bishops and theologians present strove earnestly to reform the church. They criticized the ignorance of priests and condemned superstitions believed by many of the laity. The council recommended higher standards for education of the clergy and instruction of the common people. The bishops placed the responsibility for eliminating bureaucratic corruption squarely on the papacy and suggested significant doctrinal reforms. But many obstacles stood in the way of ecclesiastical change. The actions of an obscure German friar did not immediately force the issue.

MARTIN LUTHER AND THE BIRTH OF PROTESTANTISM

As the result of a personal religious struggle, a German Augustinian friar named Martin Luther (1483–1546) launched the Protestant Reformation of the sixteenth century. Luther articulated both the widespread desire for reform of the Christian church and a deep yearning for salvation. To the extent that concern for salvation was an important motivating force for Luther and other reformers, the sixteenth-century Reformation was in part a continuation of the medieval religious search.

Martin Luther was born at Eisleben in Saxony, the second son of a hard-working and ambitious copper miner. At considerable sacrifice, his father sent him to school and then to the University of Erfurt. Hans Luther intended his son to proceed to the study of law and a legal career. Badly frightened during a thunderstorm, however, Martin Luther vowed to become a friar. Without consulting his father, he entered the monastery at Erfurt in 1505. Luther was ordained a priest in 1507 and after additional study earned the doctorate of theology. From 1512 until his death in 1546, he served as professor of Scripture at the new University of Wittenberg.

Martin Luther was exceedingly scrupulous in his monastic observances and devoted to prayer, penances, and fasting; nevertheless, the young friar's conscience troubled him constantly. The doubts and conflicts felt by any sensitive young person who has just taken a grave step were especially intense in young Luther. He had terrible anxieties about sin and worried continually about his salvation. Luther intensified his monastic observances but still found no peace of mind.

Luther's wise and kindly professor, Staupitz, directed him to the study of Saint Paul's letters. Gradually, Luther arrived at a new understanding of the Pauline letters and of all Christian doctrine. He came to believe that salvation comes not through external observances and penances but through a simple faith in Christ. Faith is the means by which God sends humanity his grace, and faith is a free gift that cannot be earned. Thus Martin Luther discovered himself, God's work for him, and the centrality of faith in the Christian life.

The Ninety-five Theses

What propelled Martin Luther onto the stage of history was the issue of indulgences. Wittenberg lay within the archdiocese of Magdeburg. Albert, the archbishop of Magdeburg, also held two other high ecclesiastical offices. Such blatant pluralism required papal dispensation, and Pope Leo X, anxious for funds with which to complete Saint Peter's Basilica, allowed Albert to pay for his dispensation by borrowing money from the Fuggers, a wealthy German banking family. Leo also authorized Albert to sell indulgences in Germany to repay the Fuggers.

According to Catholic theology, individuals who sin alienate themselves from God and his love. In order to be reconciled to God, a sinner must confess his or her sins to a priest and do the penance assigned. For example, a man who steals must first return the stolen goods and then perform a penance given by a priest, which is usually certain prayers or good works. The penance given by a priest is known as a "temporal (or earthly) penance," for no one knows what penance God will ultimately require.

The doctrine of indulgence rested on three principles. First, God is merciful but he is also just. Second, Christ and the saints, through their infinite virtue, established a "treasury of merits" on which the church can draw. Third, the church has the authority to grant sinners the spiritual benefits of those merits. Originally an indulgence was a remission of the temporal (priest-imposed) penalties for sin. Beginning in the late eleventh century, popes and bishops had given Crusaders such indulgences. By the later Middle Ages people widely believed that an indulgence secured total remission of penalties for sin—on earth or in purgatory—and ensured swift entry into heaven.

Archbishop Albert hired the Dominican friar John Tetzel to sell indulgences. Tetzel mounted an advertising blitz. One of his slogans—"As soon as coin in coffer rings, the soul from purgatory springs"—brought phenomenal success. Men and women could buy indulgences not only for themselves but for deceased parents, relatives, or friends.

That ignorant people believed that they had no further need for repentance once they had purchased an indulgence severely troubled Luther. Thus, according to historical tradition, on the eve of All Saints' Day (October 31) in 1517, he attached to the door of the church at Wittenberg Castle a list of ninety-five theses (or propositions) on indulgences. By this act Luther intended only to start a theological discussion of the subject and to defend the theses publicly.

Luther firmly rejected the notion that salvation could be achieved by good works, such as indul-

gences. Some of his theses challenged the pope's power to grant indulgences, and others criticized papal wealth: "Why does not the Pope, whose riches are at this day more ample than those of the wealthiest of the wealthy, build the one Basilica of St. Peter's with his own money, rather than with that of poor believers?"[31]

The theses were soon translated into German, printed, and read throughout the empire. Immediately, broad theological issues were raised. When questioned, Luther rested his fundamental argument on the principle that there was no biblical basis for indulgences. But, replied Luther's opponents, to deny the legality of indulgences was to deny the authority of the pope who had authorized them. The issue was drawn: where did authority lie in the Christian church?

In 1519, in a large public debate with the Catholic theologian John Eck at Leipzig, Luther denied both the authority of the pope and the infallibility of a general council. The Council of Constance, he said, had erred when it condemned John Hus (see page 448). The papacy responded with a letter condemning some of Luther's propositions, ordering that his books be burned, and giving him two months to recant or be excommunicated. Luther retaliated by publicly burning the letter. By January 3, 1521, when the excommunication was supposed to become final, the controversy involved more than theological issues. The papal legate wrote, "All Germany is in revolution. Nine-tenths shout 'Luther' as their war-cry; and the other tenth cares nothing about Luther, and cries 'Death to the court of Rome.'"[32]

In this highly charged atmosphere the twenty-one-year-old emperor Charles V held his first diet at Worms and summoned Luther to appear before it. When ordered to recant, Luther replied in language that rang all over Europe:

Unless I am convinced by the evidence of Scripture or by plain reason—for I do not accept the authority of the Pope or the councils alone, since it is established that they have often erred and contradicted themselves—I am bound by the Scriptures I have cited and my conscience is captive to the word of God. I cannot and will not recant anything, for it is neither safe nor right to go against conscience. God help me. Amen.[33]

Charles published the Edict of Worms, in which Luther was declared an outlaw of the empire: he was denied legal protection.

Protestant Thought

Between 1520 and 1530, Luther worked out the basic theological tenets that became the articles of faith for his new church and later for all Protestant groups. The word *Protestant* derives from the protest drawn up by a small group of reforming German princes at the diet of Speyer in 1529. The princes "protested" the decisions of the Catholic majority. At first *Protestant* meant "Lutheran," but with the appearance of many protesting sects, it was applied to all non-Catholic Christians. Lutheran Protestant thought was officially formulated in the Confession of Augsburg in 1530. Ernst Troeltsch, a German student of the sociology of religion, has defined *Protestantism* as a "modification of Catholicism, in which the Catholic formulation of questions was retained, while a different answer was given to them." Luther gave new answers to four basic theological issues.

First, how is a person to be saved? Traditional Catholic teaching held that salvation was achieved by *both* faith *and* good works. Luther held that salvation comes *by faith alone*. Women and men are saved, said Luther, by the arbitrary decision of God, irrespective of good works or the sacraments.

Second, where does religious authority reside? Christian doctrine had long maintained that authority rests both in the Bible and in the traditional teaching of the church. Luther maintained that authority rests in the Word of God as revealed in the Bible alone and as interpreted by an individual's conscience. He urged that each person read and reflect on the Scriptures.

Third, what is the church? Medieval churchmen had identified the church with the clergy. Luther reiterated the Catholic teaching that the church is the entire Christian community.

Finally, what is the highest form of Christian life? The medieval church had stressed the superiority of the monastic and religious life over the secular. Luther argued that all vocations have equal merit, whether ecclesiastical or secular, and that every person should serve God in his or her individual calling.[34] Protestantism, in sum, represented a reformulation of the Christian heritage.

The Social Impact of Luther's Beliefs

As early as 1521, Luther had a vast following. Every encounter with ecclesiastical or political au-

Lucas Cranach the Younger: Luther and the Wittenberg Reformers The massive figure of John Frederick, Elector of Saxony, who protected and supported Luther, dominates this group portrait. Luther is on the far left, his associate Philip Melancthon in the front row on the right. Luther's face shows a quiet determination. *(Source: The Toledo Museum of Art, Toledo, Ohio; Gift of Edward Drummond Libbey)*

thorities attracted attention to him. Pulpits and printing presses spread his message all over Germany. By the time of his death, people of all social classes had become Lutheran. What was the immense appeal of Luther's religious ideas?

Recent historical research on the German towns has shown that two significant late medieval developments prepared the way for Luther's ideas. First,

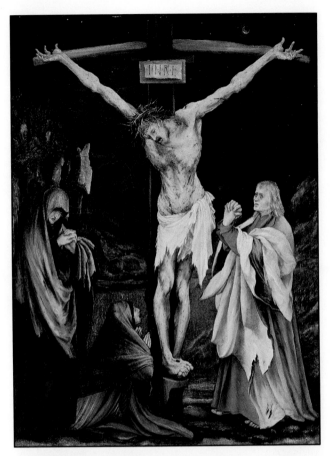

Grünewald: Crucifixion (ca 1510) The bloodless hands, tortured face, and lacerated body contain an unprecedented depiction of the horrors of physical suffering and reflect the deep emotional piety of northern Europe. Court painter to Albert of Brandenburg, Grünewald later was strongly attracted to Luther's ideas. *(Source: National Gallery of Art, Washington, D.C.; Samuel H. Kress Collection)*

controlled, and placed priests and monks under the jurisdiction of the civil courts.

Preacherships also spread Luther's ideas. Critics of the late medieval church, especially informed and intelligent townspeople, condemned the irregularity and poor quality of sermons. As a result, prosperous burghers in many towns established preacherships. Preachers were men of superior education who were required to deliver about a hundred sermons a year, each lasting about forty-five minutes. Luther's ideas attracted many preachers, and in several towns preachers became Protestant leaders. Preacherships also encouraged the Protestant form of worship, in which the sermon, not the Eucharist, was the central part of the service.[35]

In the countryside the attraction of the German peasants to Lutheran beliefs was almost predictable. Luther himself came from a peasant background, and he admired their ceaseless toil. Peasants respected Luther's defiance of church authority. Moreover, they thrilled to the words Luther used in his treatise *On Christian Liberty* (1520): "A Christian man is the most free lord of all and subject to none." Taken by themselves, those words easily contributed to social unrest.

In the early sixteenth century, the economic condition of the peasantry varied from place to place but was generally worse than it had been in the fifteenth century and was deteriorating. Crop failures in 1523 and 1524 aggravated an explosive situation. In 1525 representatives of the Swabian peasants met at the city of Memmingen and drew up the Twelve Articles, which expressed their grievances. The Twelve Articles condemn lay and ecclesiastical lords and summarize the agrarian crisis of the early sixteenth century. The articles complain that nobles had seized village common lands, which traditionally had been used by all; that they had imposed new rents on manorial properties and new services on the peasants working those properties; and that they had forced the poor to pay unjust death duties in the form of the peasants' best horses or cows. Wealthy, socially mobile peasants especially resented these burdens, which they emphasized as new.[36] The peasants believed that their demands conformed to Scripture and cited Luther as a theologian who could prove that they did.

Luther wanted to prevent rebellion. Initially he sided with the peasants, and in a tract, *On Admonition to Peace*, he blasted the lords:

since the fifteenth century, city governments had expressed resentment at clerical privileges and immunities. Priests, monks, and nuns paid no taxes and were exempt from civic responsibilities such as defending the city, yet religious orders frequently held large amounts of urban property. At Zurich in 1467, for example, religious orders held one-third of the city's taxable property. City governments grew determined to integrate the clergy into civic life by reducing clerical privileges and giving the clergy public responsibilities. Accordingly, the Zurich magistracy subjected the religious to taxes, inspected wills so that legacies to the church and legacies left by churchmen could be

We have no one on earth to thank for this mischievous rebellion, except you lords and princes, especially you blind bishops and mad priests and monks. . . . In your government you do nothing but flay and rob your subjects in order that you may lead a life of splendor and pride, until the poor common folk can bear it no longer.[37]

But, Luther warned the peasants, nothing justified the use of armed force: "The fact that rulers are unjust and wicked does not excuse tumult and rebellion; to punish wickedness does not belong to everybody, but to the worldly rulers who bear the sword."[38] As for biblical support for the peasants' demands, he maintained that Scripture had nothing to do with earthly justice or material gain.

Massive revolts first broke out near the Swiss frontier and then swept through Swabia, Thuringia, the Rhineland, and Saxony. The crowds' slogans came directly from Luther's writings. "God's righteousness" and the "Word of God" were invoked in the effort to secure social and economic justice. The peasants who expected Luther's support were soon disillusioned. He had written of the "freedom" of the Christian, but he had meant the freedom to obey the word of God. "Freedom" for Luther meant independence from the authority of the Roman church; it did not mean opposition to legally established secular powers. The nobility ferociously crushed the revolt. Historians estimate that over 75,000 peasants were killed in 1525.

As it developed, Lutheran theology exalted the state, subordinated the church to the state, and everywhere championed the "powers that be." The consequences for German society were profound and have redounded into the twentieth century. The revolt of 1525 strengthened the authority of lay rulers. Peasant economic conditions, however, moderately improved. For example, in many parts of Germany enclosed fields, meadows, and forests were returned to common use.

Scholars in many disciplines have attributed Luther's fame and success to the invention of the printing press, which rapidly reproduced and made known his ideas. Equally important was Luther's skill with language. Language proved to be the weapon with which this peasant's son changed the world. Like the peasants, educated people and humanists were much attracted by Luther's words. He advocated a simpler, personal religion based on faith, a return to the spirit of the early church, the

centrality of the Scriptures in the liturgy and in Christian life, and abolition of elaborate ceremonial—precisely the reforms that the northern humanists had been calling for. Ulrich Zwingli (1484–1531), for example, a humanist of Zurich, was strongly influenced by Luther's bold stand; it stimulated Zwingli's reforms in that Swiss city. The nobleman Ulrich von Hutten (1488–1523), who had published several humanistic tracts, in 1519 dedicated his life to the advancement of Luther's reformation. And the Frenchman John Calvin (1509–1564), often called "the organizer of Protestantism," owed a great deal to Luther's thought.

The publication of Luther's German translation of the New Testament in 1523 democratized religion. His insistence that everyone should read and reflect on the Scriptures attracted the literate and thoughtful middle classes, partly because Luther appealed to their intelligence. Moreover, the business classes, preoccupied with making money, envied the church's wealth, disapproved of the luxurious lifestyle of some churchmen, and resented tithes and ecclesiastical taxation. Luther's doctrines of salvation by faith and the priesthood of all believers not only raised the religious status of the commercial classes but protected their pocketbooks as well.

For his time Luther held enlightened views on matters of sexuality and marriage. He wrote to a young man, "Dear lad, be not ashamed that you desire a girl, nor you my maid, the boy. Just let it lead you into matrimony and not into promiscuity, and it is no more cause for shame than eating and drinking."[39] Luther was confident that God took delight in the sexual act, and he denied that original sin affected the goodness of creation.

Luther believed, however, that marriage was a woman's career. A student recorded Luther as saying, early in his public ministry, "Let them bear children until they are dead of it; that is what they are for." A happy marriage to a former nun, Katharine von Bora, mellowed him somewhat. Another student later quoted him as saying, "Next to God's Word there is no more precious treasure than holy matrimony. God's highest gift on earth is a pious, cheerful, God-fearing, home-keeping wife, with whom you may live peacefully, to whom you may entrust your goods, and body and life."[40]

Luther deeply loved his "dear Katie," but he believed that women's concerns should revolve exclusively around the children, the kitchen, and the

Battle of Gaisbeuren during the Peasants' War, 1525   When peasants' economic and social grievances merged with religious discontent, Luther wrote that the peasants misunderstood the Gospel and could not use it to change the social order. Because his appeal did not persuade the peasants to stop the violence, Luther called on the princes to exercise their right to the sword to end the disorder. A couple of peasants have guns, but most seem armed only with staves. *(Source: Siegfried Lauterwasser)*

church. A happy woman was a patient wife, an efficient manager, and a good mother. Kate was an excellent financial manager (which Luther—much inclined to give money and goods away—was not). A stern if often indulgent father, Luther held that the father should rule his household while the wife controlled its economy. With many relatives and constant visitors, Luther's was a large and happy household, a model for Protestants if an abomination for Catholics.

The Political Impact of Luther's Beliefs

In the sixteenth century, the practice of religion remained a public matter. Everyone participated in the religious life of the community, just as almost everyone shared in the local agricultural work.

Whatever spiritual convictions individuals held in the privacy of their consciences, the emperor, king, prince, magistrate, or other civil authority determined the official form of religious practice within his jurisdiction. Almost everyone believed that the presence of a faith different from that of the majority represented a political threat to the security of the state. Only a tiny minority, and certainly none of the princes, believed in religious liberty.

Against this background, the religious storm launched by Martin Luther swept across Germany. Several elements in his religious reformation stirred patriotic feelings. Anti-Roman sentiment ran high. Humanists lent eloquent intellectual support. And Luther's translation of the New Testament from Latin into German evoked national pride.

For decades devout laymen and churchmen had called on the German princes to reform the church. In 1520 Luther took up the cry in his *Appeal to the Christian Nobility of the German Nation.* Unless the princes destroyed papal power in Germany, Luther argued, reform was impossible. He urged the princes to confiscate ecclesiastical wealth and to abolish indulgences, dispensations, pardons, and clerical celibacy. He told them that it was their public duty to bring about the moral reform of the church. Luther based his argument in part on the papacy's financial exploitation of Germany:

How comes it that we Germans must put up with such robbery and such extortion of our property at the hands of the pope? If the Kingdom of France has pre-vented it, why do we Germans let them make such fools and apes of us? It would all be more bearable if in this way they only stole our property; but they lay waste the churches and rob Christ's sheep of their pious shepherds, and destroy the worship and the Word of God. As it is they do nothing for the good of Christendom; they only wrangle about the incomes of bishoprics and prelacies, and that any robber could do.[41]

Luther's appeal to German patriotism gained him strong support, and national feeling influenced many princes otherwise confused by or indifferent to the complexities of the religious issues.

The church in Germany possessed great wealth. And, unlike other countries, Germany had no strong central government to check the flow of

Titian: The Emperor Charles V   (1548) Court painter to Charles V, Titian portrayed him shortly after the emperor's defeat of the league of German Protestant princes at the battle of Mühlberg near Leipzig. In this idealization, one of the earliest equestrian portraits, Charles appears as heroic victor, chivalric knight, and defender of the church. *(Source: Museo del Prado, Madrid)*

Lutheran

Calvinist (Reformed)

Church of England

Roman Catholic

▲ Huguenot centers

→ Spread of Calvinism

0   150   300 Km.
0   150   300 Mi.

Black Sea

OTTOMAN EMPIRE

LITHUANIA

Helsinki

Riga

PRUSSIA

Warsaw

POLAND

TRANSYLVANIA

Stockholm

Baltic Sea

MORAVIA

Buda• •Pest

HUNGARY

BRANDENBURG

Vienna

AUSTRIA

Bari

S W E D E N

NORWAY
1536/1607

DENMARK

Hamburg•
Copenhagen•

Wittenberg•
Birthplace of
Martin Luther

Leipzig

Eisleben,
1483–1546
Martin Luther,

Erfurt•

Prague
John Hus,
1369–1415

BOHEMIA

Nuremburg•

Munich•

Augsburg•

Stuttgart•

Council of Trent,
1545–1563

Trent•

Rome•
Roman Inquisition
established, 1542

Naples•

Sicily

Adriatic Sea

Mediterranean Sea

Bergen•

North Sea

Amsterdam•

NETHERLANDS

Antwerp•

Brussels•

Münster•

SAXONY

HOLY ROMAN
EMPIRE

Marburg•

Worms•
Edict of Worms,
1521

Speyer•

Zurich
Ulrich Zwingli,
1484–1531

Basel•

Milan•

Pavia•

Genoa•

Pisa•

Florence•

Venice•

ITALY

Corsica

Sardinia

Strasbourg•

Geneva
John Calvin

Avignon•

Marseilles•

Birthplace of
John Calvin,
1509–1564

Noyon•

Paris•

Edinburgh
John Knox,
1505–1572

SCOTLAND
1560

Penetration of Calvinism
to England after 1558

ENGLAND
1536

Oxford•
John Wyclif,
1320–1384

London•

Plymouth•

IRELAND

Dublin•

Rennes•

Orléans•

FRANCE

Nantes•
Edict of Nantes,
1598

La Rochelle•

Bordeaux•

Toulouse•

Barcelona•

Balearic Is.

Loyola
Birthplace of
Ignatius Loyola,
1491

Valencia•

SPAIN

Madrid•

Toledo•

Granada•

PORTUGAL

Seville•

Lisbon•

*ATLANTIC
OCEAN*

MUSLIM STATES

gold to Rome. Rejection of Roman Catholicism and adoption of Protestantism would mean the legal confiscation of lush farmland, rich monasteries, and wealthy shrines. Some German princes were sincerely attracted to Lutheranism, but many civil authorities realized that they had a great deal to gain by embracing the new faith. A steady stream of duchies, margraviates, free cities, and bishoprics secularized church property, accepted Lutheran theological doctrines, and adopted simpler services conducted in German. The Edict of Worms in 1521, which condemned Luther and his teaching, was not enforced because the German princes did not want to enforce it.

Charles V was a vigorous defender of Catholicism, and contemporary social and political theory denied the possibility of two religions coexisting peacefully in one territory. Thus many princes used the religious issue to extend their financial and political independence. With doctrinal differences linked to political ambitions and financial receipts, the Protestant movement ultimately proved disastrous for Germany.

Charles V must share blame with the German princes for the disintegration of imperial authority in the empire. He neither understood nor took an interest in the constitutional problems of Germany, and he lacked the material resources to oppose Protestantism effectively there. Throughout his reign he was preoccupied with his Flemish, Spanish, Italian, and American territories. Moreover, the Turkish threat prevented him from acting effectively against the Protestants; Charles's brother Ferdinand needed Protestant support against the Turks who besieged Vienna in 1529.

Five times between 1521 and 1555, Charles V went to war with the Valois kings of France. The issue each time was the Habsburg lands acquired by the marriage of Maximilian and Mary of Burgundy. Much of the fighting occurred in Germany. The cornerstone of French foreign policy in the sixteenth and seventeenth centuries was the desire to keep the German states divided. Thus Europe witnessed the paradox of the Catholic king

of France supporting the Lutheran princes in their challenge to his fellow Catholic, Charles V. French policy was successful. The long dynastic struggle commonly called the "Habsburg-Valois Wars" advanced the cause of Protestantism and promoted the political fragmentation of the German empire.

Finally, in 1555, Charles agreed to the Peace of Augsburg, which, in accepting the status quo, officially recognized Lutheranism. Each prince was permitted to determine the religion of his territory. Most of northern and central Germany became Lutheran, while the south remained Roman Catholic (Map 17.4). There was no freedom of religion, however. Princes or town councils established state churches to which all subjects of the area had to belong. Dissidents, whether Lutheran or Catholic, had to convert or leave. The political difficulties that Germany inherited from the Middle Ages had been compounded by the religious crisis of the sixteenth century.

THE GROWTH OF THE PROTESTANT REFORMATION

By 1555 much of northern Europe had broken with the Roman Catholic church. All of Scandinavia, England, Scotland, and such self-governing cities as Geneva and Zurich in Switzerland and Strasbourg in Germany had rejected the religious authority of Rome and adopted new faiths. A common religious faith had been the one element uniting all of Europe for almost a thousand years, so the fragmentation of belief led to profound changes in European life and society. The most significant new form of Protestantism was Calvinism, of which the Peace of Augsburg had made no mention at all.

Calvinism

In 1509, while Luther was studying for the doctorate at Wittenberg, John Calvin (1509–1564) was born in Noyon in northeastern France. Calvin's theological writings would profoundly influence the social thought and attitudes of Europeans and English-speaking peoples all over the world, especially in Canada and the United States.

MAP 17.4 The Protestant and the Catholic Reformations The reformations shattered the religious unity of Western Christendom. What common cultural traits predominated in regions where a particular branch of the Christian faith was maintained or took root?

Prior to his ecclesiastical career, Calvin studied law. In 1533 he experienced a religious crisis, as a result of which he converted to Protestantism.

Convinced that God selects certain people to do his work, Calvin believed that God had specifically called him to reform the church. Accordingly, he accepted an invitation to assist in the reformation of the city of Geneva. There, beginning in 1541, Calvin worked assiduously to establish a Christian society ruled by God through civil magistrates and reformed ministers. Geneva, "a city that was a Church," became the model of a Christian community for sixteenth-century Protestant reformers.

To understand Calvin's Geneva, it is necessary to understand Calvin's ideas. These he embodied in *The Institutes of the Christian Religion,* first published in 1536 and definitively issued in 1559. The cornerstone of Calvin's theology was his belief in the absolute sovereignty and omnipotence of God and the total weakness of humanity. Before the infinite power of God, he asserted, men and women are as insignificant as grains of sand.

Calvin did not ascribe free will to human beings because free will would detract from the sovereignty of God. Calvin maintained that men and women cannot actively work to achieve salvation; rather, God in his infinite wisdom decided at the beginning of time who would be saved and who damned. This viewpoint constitutes the theological principle called "predestination":

Predestination we call the eternal decree of God, by which he has determined in himself, what he would have become of every individual of mankind. . . . God has once for all determined, both whom he would admit to salvation, and whom he would condemn to destruction. We affirm that this counsel, as far as concerns the elect, [that is, those whom God has chosen to save], is founded on his gratuitous mercy, totally irrespective of human merit; but that to those whom he devotes to condemnation, the gate of life is closed by a just and irreprehensible, but incomprehensible, judgment. . . . For the will of God is the highest justice; so that what he wills must be considered just, for this very reason, because he wills it.[42]

The doctrine of predestination dates back to Saint Augustine and Saint Paul, but many people have found it a pessimistic view of the nature of God, who they feel revealed himself in the Old and New Testaments as merciful as well as just.

Calvin maintained that although individuals cannot know whether they will be saved—and the probability is that they will be damned—good works are a "sign" of election. In any case, people should concentrate on worshiping God and doing his work and not waste time worrying about whether they will receive salvation.

The Calvinist ethic of the "calling" dignified all work by giving it a religious aspect. Hard work, well done, was believed to be pleasing to God. This doctrine encouraged an aggressive, vigorous activism in the sixteenth and later centuries.

Calvin aroused Genevans to a high standard of morality. His powerful sermons delivered the word of God and thereby monopolized the strongest contemporary means of communication, preaching. Through his *Genevan Catechism,* published in 1541, children and adults memorized set questions and answers and acquired a summary of their faith and a guide for daily living. Calvin's sermons and his *Catechism* gave a whole generation of Genevans thorough instruction in the reformed religion.[43]

In the reformation of the city, the Genevan *consistory* also exercised a powerful role. This body consisted of twelve laymen, plus the Company of Pastors, of which Calvin was the permanent moderator (presider). The duties of the consistory were "to keep watch over every man's life and to admonish amiably those whom they see leading a disorderly life." Although Calvin emphasized that the consistory's activities should be thorough and "its eyes may be everywhere," corrections were only "medicine to turn sinners to the Lord."[44] Thus austere living, public fasting, and evening curfew became the order of the day. Fashionable clothes, dancing, card playing, and heavy drinking were absolutely prohibited. The consistory investigated the private morals of citizens but was unwilling to punish the town prostitutes as severely as Calvin would have preferred. Calvin exercised some political influence through the consistory, but the civil magistrates in Geneva maintained firm control.

Calvin reserved his harshest condemnation for religious dissenters, declaring them "dogs and swine":

God makes plain that the false prophet is to be stoned without mercy. We are to crush beneath our heel all affections of nature when His honor is concerned. The father should not spare his child, nor brother his brother, nor husband his own wife or the friend who is dearer to him than life. No human relationship is more than animal unless it be grounded in God.[45]

Calvin translated his words into action. Executions for heresy were regular occurrences. One example was the Spanish humanist Michael Servetus, who, persecuted by the Spanish Inquisition, escaped to Geneva. In addition to denying the Trinity—which identifies God as three divine persons, Father, Son, and Holy Spirit—Servetus insisted that a person under twenty cannot commit a mortal sin. The city fathers considered this idea dangerous to public morality, "especially in these days when the young are so corrupted." Servetus was burned at the stake.

To many sixteenth-century Europeans, Calvin's Geneva seemed "the most perfect school of Christ since the days of the Apostles." Religious refugees from France, England, Spain, Scotland, and Italy poured into the city. Subsequently, the reformed church of Calvin served as the model for the Presbyterian church in Scotland, the Huguenot church in France, and the Puritan churches in England and New England.

In the *Institutes* Calvin provided a systematic theology for Protestantism. The reformed church of Calvin had a strong and well-organized machinery of government. These factors, together with the social and economic applications of Calvin's theology, made Calvinism the most dynamic force in the sixteenth- and seventeenth-century evolution of Protestantism.

Calvinist Worship   A converted house in Lyons, France, serves as a church for the simple Calvinist service. Although Calvin's followers believed in equality and elected officials administered the church, here men and women are segregated, and some people sit on hard benches while others sit in upholstered pews. Beside the pulpit an hourglass hangs to time the preacher's sermon. (Could the dog sit still for that long?) *(Source: Bibliothèque publique et universitaire, Geneva)*

THE LATER MIDDLE AGES, RENAISSANCE, AND PROTESTANT AND CATHOLIC REFORMATIONS, 1300–1600

As is evident in this chronology, early manifestations of the Renaissance and Protestant Reformation coincided in time with major events of the Later Middle Ages.

1300–1321	Dante, *The Divine Comedy*
1304–1374	Petrarch
1309–1376	Babylonian Captivity of the papacy
1337–1453	Hundred Years' War
1347–1351	The Black Death (returned intermittently until ca 1700)
ca 1350	Boccaccio, *The Decameron*
1356	Golden Bull: transforms the Holy Roman Empire into an aristocratic confederation
1358	The Jacquerie
ca 1376	John Wyclif publishes *Civil Dominion* attacking the church's temporal power and asserting the supremacy of the Scripture
1377–1417	The Great Schism
1378	Laborers' (ciompi) revolt in Florence
1381	Peasants' Revolt in England
1385–1400	Chaucer, *Canterbury Tales*
1414–1418	Council of Constance: ends the schism, postpones reform, executes John Hus
1431	Joan of Arc is burned at the stake
1434	Medici domination of Florence begins
1438	Pragmatic Sanction of Bourges: declares autonomy of the French church from papal jurisdiction
1453	Capture of Constantinople by the Ottoman Turks, ending the Byzantine Empire
1455–1471	Wars of the Roses in England
1456	Gutenberg Bible
1492	Unification of Spain under Ferdinand and Isabela; expulsion of Jews and Muslims from Spain Columbus reaches the Americas
1494	France invades Italy, inaugurating sixty years of war on Italian soil Florence expels the Medici and restores republican government

The Anabaptists

The name *Anabaptist* derives from a Greek word meaning "to baptize again." The Anabaptists, sometimes described as the "left wing of the Reformation," believed that only adults could make a free choice about religious faith, baptism, and entry into the Christian community. Thus they considered the practice of baptizing infants and children preposterous and claimed there was no scriptural basis for it. They wanted to rebaptize believers who had been baptized as children. Anabaptists took the Gospel absolutely literally and favored a return to the kind of church that had existed among the earliest Christians—a voluntary association of believers who had experienced an inner light.

Anabaptists believed in the separation of church and state and in religious tolerance. They almost never tried to force their values on others. In an age that believed in the necessity of state-established churches, Anabaptist views on religious liberty were thought to undermine that idea.

Each Anabaptist community or church was entirely independent; it selected its own ministers and ran its own affairs. In 1534 the Anabaptist community at Münster in Germany, for example, established a legal code that decreed the death penalty for insubordinate wives. The Münster community also practiced polygamy and forced all women under a certain age to marry or face expulsion or execution.

However, Anabaptists admitted women to the priesthood. They also shared goods as the early

1509	Erasmus, *The Praise of Folly*
1512	Restoration of the Medici in Florence
1512–1517	Lateran Council undertakes reform of clerical abuses
1513	Balboa discovers the Pacific
	Machiavelli, *The Prince*
1516	Thomas More, *Utopia*
1517	Martin Luther publishes the Ninety-five Theses
1519–1522	Magellan's crew circumnavigates the earth
1523	Luther's translation of the New Testament into German
1525	Peasants' Revolt in Germany
1527	Sack of Rome by mercenaries of Holy Roman Emperor Charles V
1528	Castiglione, *The Courtier*
1530	Confession of Augsburg, official formulation of Lutheran theology
1533	Act in Restraint of Appeals inaugurates the English Reformation
1534–1541	Michelangelo, *The Last Judgment*
1535	Execution of Thomas More for treason
1536	John Calvin, *Institutes of the Christian Religion*
1540	Loyola founds the Society of Jesus (Jesuits)
1541	Calvin establishes a theocracy in Geneva
1543	Copernicus, *On the Revolutions of the Heavenly Spheres*
1545–1563	Council of Trent
1555	Peace of Augsburg: German princes determine the religion of their territories; in effect, official recognition of Lutheranism
1572	St. Bartholemew's Day Massacre
1588	Spanish Armada
1598	Edict of Nantes grants French Protestants freedom of worship in certain towns
1603	Shakespeare, *Hamlet*
1605	Sir Francis Bacon, *The Advancement of Learning*

Christians had done, refused all public offices, and would not serve in the armed forces. In fact, they laid great stress on pacifism. Such beliefs tended to attract the poor, the unemployed, and the uneducated. Geographically, Anabaptists drew their members from depressed urban areas.

Ideas such as absolute pacifism and the distinction between the Christian community and the state brought down on these unfortunate people fanatical hatred and bitter persecution. Both Protestants and Catholics saw—quite correctly—the separation of church and state as leading ultimately to the complete secularization of society. The powerful rulers of Swiss and German society immediately saw the connection between religious heresy and economic dislocation and feared that the combination would lead to civil disturbances.

In Swiss and German cities, Anabaptists were either banished or cruelly executed. Their community spirit and the edifying example of their lives, however, contributed to the survival of Anabaptist ideas.

The English Reformation

As on the Continent, the Reformation in England had social and economic causes as well as religious ones. As elsewhere, too, Christian humanists had for decades been calling for the purification of the church. When the political matter of the divorce of King Henry VIII (r. 1509–1547) became enmeshed with other issues, a complete break with Rome resulted.

Demands for ecclesiastical reform dated back at least to the fourteenth century. The vigorously anticlerical Lollards had been driven underground in the fifteenth century but survived in parts of London, East Anglia, western Kent, and southern England. The work of the English humanist William Tyndale (ca 1494–1536) stimulated cries for reform. In 1525, at Antwerp, Tyndale began printing an English translation of the New Testament. From Antwerp, merchants carried the New Testament into England, where it was distributed by Lollards. Fortified with copies of Tyndale's English Bible and some of Luther's ideas, the Lollards represented the ideal of "a personal, scriptural, non-sacramental, and lay-dominated religion."[46] In this manner, doctrines that would later be called "Protestant" flourished underground in England before any official or state-approved changes.

In the early sixteenth century, the ignorance of much of the parish clergy, and the sexual misbehavior of some, compared unfavorably with the education and piety of lay people. Even more than the ignorance of the lower clergy, the wealth of the English church fostered resentment and anticlericalism. The church controlled perhaps 20 percent of the land and also received an annual tithe of the produce of lay people's estates. Since the church had jurisdiction over wills, the clergy also received mortuary fees, revenues paid by the deceased's relatives. Mortuary fees led to frequent lawsuits, since the common lawyers nursed a deep jealousy of the ecclesiastical courts.

The career of Thomas Wolsey (1474?–1530) provides an extreme example of pluralism in the English church in the early sixteenth century. The son of a butcher, Wolsey became a priest and in 1507 secured an appointment as chaplain to Henry VII. In 1509 Henry VIII made Wolsey a privy councillor. His remarkable ability and energy won him rapid advancement: in 1515 he became a cardinal and lord chancellor; in 1518, papal legate. Wolsey had more power than any previous royal minister, and he used that power to amass a large number of rich church offices. He displayed the vast wealth that these positions brought him with ostentation and arrogance, which in turn fanned the embers of anticlericalism. The divorce of Henry VIII ignited all these glowing coals.

Having fallen in love with Anne Boleyn, Henry wanted to divorce his wife, Catherine of Aragon, the third daughter of Ferdinand and Isabella of Spain. Legal, diplomatic, and theological problems stood in his way, however. When Henry married Catherine, he had secured a dispensation from Pope Julius II to eliminate all doubts and legal technicalities about Catherine's previous marriage to Henry's dead brother, Arthur. For eighteen years Catherine and Henry lived together in what contemporaries thought a happy marriage. Catherine produced six children, but only the princess Mary survived childhood.

Around 1527 Henry began to insist, citing a passage in the Old Testament Book of Leviticus, that God was denying him a male heir to punish him for marrying his brother's widow. Henry claimed that he wanted to spare England the dangers of a disputed succession. He warned that the anarchy and disorders of the Wars of the Roses would surely be repeated if a woman, the princess Mary, inherited the throne.

Henry went about the business of ensuring a peaceful succession in an extraordinary manner. He petitioned Pope Clement VII (r. 1523–1534) to declare that a legal marriage with Catherine had never existed, in which case Princess Mary was illegitimate and thus ineligible to succeed to the throne. Henry argued that Pope Julius's dispensation had contradicted the law of God—that a man may not marry his brother's widow. The English king's request reached Rome at the very time that Luther was widely publishing tracts condemning the papacy as the core of wickedness. By granting Henry's annulment and thereby admitting that a pope had erred, Clement would have given support to the Lutheran assertion that popes substitute their own evil judgments for the law of God. Clement therefore delayed acting on Henry's request.[47] The capture and sack of Rome in 1527 by the emperor Charles V, Queen Catherine's nephew, thoroughly tied the pope's hands.

Henry determined to get his divorce in England. The convenient death of the archbishop of Canterbury allowed Henry to appoint a new archbishop, Thomas Cranmer (1489–1556). Cranmer heard the case in his archiepiscopal court, granted the annulment, and thereby paved the way for Henry's marriage to Anne Boleyn on May 28, 1533. In September the princess Elizabeth was born.

Since Rome had refused to support Henry's matrimonial plans, he decided to remove the English church from papal jurisdiction. Henry used Parliament to legalize the Reformation in Eng-

Henry VIII's "Victory"   This cartoon shows Henry VIII, assisted by Cromwell and Cranmer, triumphing over Pope Clement VII. Though completely removed from the historical facts, such illustrations were effectively used to promote antipapal feeling in late sixteenth-century England. *(Source: Fotomas Index)*

land. The Act in Restraint of Appeals (1533) declared the king to be the supreme sovereign in England and went on to forbid all judicial appeals to the papacy, thus establishing the Crown as the highest legal authority in the land. The Act for the Submission of the Clergy (1532) required churchmen to submit to the king and forbade the publication of all ecclesiastical laws without royal permission. The Supremacy Act of 1534 declared the king the supreme head of the Church of England.

Some opposed the king. John Fisher, the bishop of Rochester, a distinguished scholar and humanist, lashed out at the clergy for their cowardice. Another humanist, Thomas More, resigned the chancellorship in protest and would not take an oath recognizing Anne's daughter as heir. Fisher, More, and other dissenters were beheaded.

When Anne Boleyn failed to produce a male child, Henry VIII in 1536 had her beheaded. Parliament promptly proclaimed the princess Elizabeth illegitimate. Henry's third wife, Jane Seymour, gave him the desired son, Edward, and then died in childbirth. Henry went on to three more wives. Before he passed to his reward in 1547, he got Parliament to relegitimate Mary and Elizabeth and fixed the succession first in his son and then in his daughters.

Between 1535 and 1539, under the influence of his chief minister Thomas Cromwell, Henry decided to dissolve the English monasteries because he wanted their wealth. Abruptly, the king ended nine hundred years of English monastic life, dispersed the monks and nuns, and confiscated their lands. Hundreds of properties were later sold to the middle and upper classes and the proceeds spent on war. The dissolution of the monasteries brought the loss of a valuable esthetic and cultural force in English life. The redistribution of land, however, greatly strengthened the upper classes and tied them to the Tudor dynasty.

Holbein: Sir Thomas More This powerful portrait (1527), revealing More's strong character and humane sensitivity, shows Holbein's complete mastery of detail—down to the stubble on More's chin. The chain was an emblem of More's service to Henry VIII. *(Source: The Frick Collection, New York)*

Recent scholarly research has emphasized that the English Reformation came from above. The surviving evidence does not allow us to gauge the degree of opposition to (or support for) Henry's break with Rome. Sentiment for reform was strong, though only a minority held distinctly Protestant doctrinal views, but certainly many lay people wrote to the king, begging him to spare the monasteries. Most lay people "acquiesced in the Reformation because they hardly knew what was going on, were understandably reluctant to jeopardise life or limb, a career or the family's good name."[48] But all did not quietly acquiesce. Rebellions in 1536 and 1546, despite possessing economic and Protestant components, reflected considerable public opposition to the state-ordered religious changes.[49]

Henry's motives combined personal, political, social, and economic elements. Theologically he retained such traditional Catholic practices and doctrines as auricular confession, clerical celibacy, and *transubstantiation* (the doctrine of the real presence of Christ in the bread and wine of the Eucharist). Meanwhile, Protestant literature circulated, and Henry approved the selection of men with known Protestant sympathies as tutors for his son.

The nationalization of the church and the dissolution of the monasteries led to important changes in government administration. Vast tracts of land came temporarily under the Crown's jurisdiction, and new bureaucratic machinery had to be developed to manage those properties.

Thomas Cromwell reformed and centralized the king's household, the council, the secretariats, the Exchequer (see page 409), and the distribution of government funds. New departments of state were set up. This balancing resulted in greater efficiency and economy. In Henry VIII's reign can be seen the growth of the modern centralized bureaucratic state.

For several decades after Henry's death in 1547, the English church shifted left and right. In the short reign of Henry's sickly son Edward VI (r. 1547–1553), the strongly Protestant ideas of Archbishop Thomas Cranmer exerted a significant influence on the religious life of the country. Cranmer simplified the liturgy, invited Protestant theologians to England, and prepared the first *Book of Common Prayer* (1549). In stately and dignified English, the *Book of Common Prayer* included, together with the Psalter, the order for all services of the Church of England.

The equally brief reign of Mary Tudor (r. 1553–1558) witnessed a sharp move back to Catholicism. The devoutly Catholic daughter of Catherine of Aragon, Mary rescinded the Reformation legislation of her father's reign and fully restored Roman Catholicism. Mary's marriage to her cousin Philip II of Spain (r. 1556–1598), son of the emperor Charles V, proved highly unpopular in England, and her persecution and execution of several hundred devout Protestants further alienated her subjects. During her reign, many Protestants fled to the Continent. Mary's death raised to the throne her sister Elizabeth (r. 1558–1603) and inaugurated the beginnings of religious stability.

At the start of her reign, Elizabeth's position was insecure. Although the populace cheered her accession, many questioned her legitimacy. On the one hand, Catholics wanted a Roman Catholic ruler. On the other hand, a vocal number of returned English exiles—called "Puritans" because they wanted to "purify" the church—wanted all Catholic elements in the Church of England destroyed.

Elizabeth had been raised a Protestant, but if she had genuine religious convictions she kept them to herself. Probably one of the shrewdest politicians in English history, Elizabeth chose a middle course between Catholic and Puritan extremes. She insisted on dignity in church services and political order in the land. She did not care what people believed as long as they kept quiet about it. Avoiding precise doctrinal definitions, Elizabeth had herself styled "Supreme Governor of the Church of England, Etc.," and left it to her subjects to decide what the "Etc." meant.

The parliamentary legislation of the early years of Elizabeth's reign—laws sometimes labeled the "Elizabethan Settlement"—required outward conformity to the Church of England and uniformity in all ceremonies. Everyone had to attend Church of England services; those who refused were fined. In 1563 a convocation of bishops approved the Thirty-nine Articles, a summary in thirty-nine short statements of the basic tenets of the Church of England. During Elizabeth's reign, the "Anglican church" (for the Latin *Ecclesia Anglicana*), as the Church of England was called, moved in a moderately Protestant direction. Serv-

ices were conducted in English, monasteries were not re-established, and the clergy were allowed to marry. But the bishops remained as church officials, and, apart from language, the services were quite traditional.

THE CATHOLIC AND THE COUNTER-REFORMATIONS

Between 1517 and 1547, the reformed versions of Christianity known as "Protestantism" made remarkable advances. Still, the Catholic church made a significant comeback. After about 1540, no new large areas of Europe, except the Netherlands, accepted Protestant beliefs (see Map 17.4).

Historians distinguish between two types of reform within the Catholic church in the sixteenth and seventeenth centuries: the Catholic Reformation and the Counter-Reformation. The Catholic Reformation began before 1517 and sought renewal through the stimulation of a new spiritual fervor. The Counter-Reformation started in the 1530s as a reaction to the rise and spread of Protestantism. The Counter-Reformation involved Catholic efforts to convince or coerce dissidents or heretics to return to the church. The Catholic Reformation and the Counter-Reformation were not mutually exclusive; in fact, after about 1540 they progressed simultaneously.

The Slowness of Institutional Reform

The Renaissance princes who sat on the throne of Saint Peter were not blind to the evils that existed. Modest reform efforts had begun with the Lateran Council called in 1512 by Pope Julius II. The Dutch pope Adrian VI (r. 1522–1523) had instructed his legate in Germany to

say that we frankly confess that God permits this Lutheran persecution of his church on account of the sins of men, especially those of the priests and prelates. . . . We know that in this Holy See now for some years there have been many abominations, abuses in spiritual things, excesses in things commanded, in short that all has become perverted. . . . We have all turned aside in our ways, nor was there, for a long time, any who did right—no, not one.[50]

Why did the popes, spiritual leaders of the Western church, move so slowly? The answers lie in the personalities of the popes themselves, their preoccupation with political affairs in Italy, and the awesome difficulty of reforming so complicated a bureaucracy as the Roman curia.

Clement VII, a true Medicean, was far more interested in elegant tapestries and Michelangelo's painting of the Last Judgment than in theological disputes in barbaric Germany. Indecisive and vacilating, Pope Clement must bear much of the responsibility for the great spread of Protestantism. While Emperor Charles V and the French king Francis I competed for the domination of divided Italy, the papacy worried about the security of the Papal States. Clement tried to follow a middle course, first backing the emperor, then switching from Charles and the Spaniards to Francis I shortly before the emperor's mercenaries sacked Rome in 1527 and captured the pope. Obviously, papal concern about Italian affairs and the Papal States diverted attention from reform.

The idea of reform was closely linked to the idea of a general council representing the entire church. A strong contingent of countries beyond the Alps—Spain, Germany, and France—wanted to reform the vast bureaucracy of Latin officials, reducing offices, men, and revenues. However, popes from Julius II to Clement VII, remembering fifteenth-century conciliar attempts to limit papal authority, resisted calls for a council. The papal bureaucrats who were the popes' intimates warned the popes against a council, fearing loss of power, revenue, and prestige.

The Council of Trent

In the papal conclave that followed the death of Clement VII, Cardinal Alexander Farnese promised two German cardinals that if he were elected pope he would summon a council. He won the election and ruled as Pope Paul III (r. 1534–1549). This Roman aristocrat, humanist, and astrologer, who immediately made his teenage grandsons cardinals, seemed an unlikely person to undertake serious reform. Yet Paul III appointed as cardinals several learned churchmen, such as Caraffa (later Pope Paul IV); established the Inquisition in the Papal States; and—true to his word—called a council, which finally met at Trent, an imperial city close to Italy.

The Council of Trent met intermittently from 1545 to 1563. Lutherans and Calvinists were invited to participate, but their insistence that the Scriptures be the sole basis for discussion made reconciliation impossible. Trent had been selected as the site for the council in the hope it would attract Protestants. In fact, Italian bishops predominated, and no Protestants came; and a number of factors combined to reduce attendance drastically. Portugal, Poland, Hungary, and Ireland sent representatives, but very few German bishops attended.

Other problems bedeviled all the sessions of the council. International politics repeatedly cast a shadow over the theological debates. Charles V opposed discussions on any matter that might further alienate his Lutheran subjects. And the French kings worked against the reconciliation of Roman Catholicism and Lutheranism because they wanted to keep the German states divided.

In spite of these obstacles, the achievements of the Council of Trent are impressive. It established the centralizing tenet that all acts of the council required papal approval, and it dealt with both doctrinal and disciplinary matters. The council gave equal validity to the Scriptures and to tradition as sources of religious truth and authority. It reaffirmed the seven sacraments and the traditional Catholic teaching on transubstantiation, thus rejecting Lutheran and Calvinist positions.

The council tackled the problems arising from ancient abuses by strengthening ecclesiastical discipline. It issued decrees requiring bishops to reside in their own dioceses, suppressing pluralism and simony, and forbidding the sale of indulgences. Clerics who kept concubines were to give them up. The jurisdiction of bishops over all the clergy of their dioceses was made almost absolute, and bishops were ordered to visit every religious house within their dioceses at least once every two years. In a highly original canon, the council required every diocese to establish a seminary for the education and training of the clergy; and it laid great emphasis on preaching and instructing the laity, especially the uneducated.

The Council of Trent did not meet everyone's expectations. Reconciliation with Protestantism was not achieved, nor was reform brought about immediately. Nevertheless, the council laid a solid basis for the spiritual renewal of the church and for the enforcement of correction. For four centuries, the doctrinal and disciplinary legislation of Trent served as the basis for Roman Catholic faith, organization, and practice.

New Religious Orders

The establishment of new religious orders within the church reveals a central feature of the Catholic Reformation. These new orders developed in response to one crying need: to raise the moral and intellectual level of the clergy and people. Education was a major goal of them all.

The Ursuline order of nuns founded by Angela Merici (1474–1540) attained enormous prestige for the education of women. The daughter of a country gentleman, Merici worked for many years among the poor, sick, and uneducated around her native Brescia in northern Italy. In 1535 she established the Ursuline order to combat heresy through Christian education. The first religious order concentrating exclusively on teaching young girls, the Ursulines sought to re-Christianize society by training future wives and mothers. Approved as a religious community by Paul III in

The Council of Trent   This seventeenth-century engraving depicts one of the early and sparsely attended sessions of the Council of Trent. The tridentine sessions of 1562–1563 drew many more bishops and laymen, but there were never many representatives from northern Europe. *(Source: Photo Vatican Museums)*

Pope Paul III's Confirmation of the Jesuit Constitutions   On the right Ignatius Loyola receives the constitutions of the Society of Jesus by direct illumination from God. At left the pope approves them. When the constitutions were read to him, Paul III supposedly murmured, "There is the finger of God." *(Source: Historical Picture Service, Chicago)*

1544, the Ursulines rapidly grew and spread to France and the New World. Their schools in North America, stretching from Quebec to New Orleans, provided superior education for young women and inculcated the spiritual ideals of the Catholic Reformation.

The Society of Jesus, founded by Ignatius Loyola (1491–1556), a former Spanish soldier, played a powerful international role in resisting the spread of Protestantism, converting Asians and Latin American Indians to Catholicism, and spreading Christian education all over Europe. While recuperating from a severe battle wound in his legs, Loyola studied a life of Christ and other religious books and decided to give up his military career and become a soldier of Christ. During a year spent in seclusion, prayer, and personal mortification, he gained the religious insights that went into his *Spiritual Exercises*. This work, intended for

study during a four-week period of retreat, directed the individual imagination and will to the reform of life and a new spiritual piety.

Loyola was apparently a man of considerable personal magnetism. After study at the universities in Salamanca and Paris, he gathered a group of six companions and in 1540 secured papal approval of the new Society of Jesus, whose members were called "Jesuits." Their goal was the reform of the church through education, preaching the Gospel to pagan peoples, and fighting Protestantism. Within a short time, the Jesuits attracted many recruits.

The Society of Jesus was a centralized, tightly knit organization. Candidates underwent a two-year novitiate, in contrast to the usual one-year probation required of candidates in most religious orders. Although new members took the traditional vows of poverty, chastity, and obedience, the emphasis was on obedience. Carefully selected members made a fourth vow of obedience to the pope and the governing members of the society. As faith was the cornerstone of Luther's life, so obedience became the bedrock of the Jesuit tradition.

The Jesuits had a modern, quasi-military quality; they achieved phenomenal success for the papacy and the reformed Catholic church. Jesuit schools adopted modern teaching methods. They first concentrated on the children of the poor, but they were soon educating the sons of the nobility. As confessors and spiritual directors to kings, Jesuits exerted great political influence. Indifferent to physical comfort and personal safety and operating on the principle that the end sometimes justifies the means, they were not above spying. Within Europe, the Jesuits brought southern Germany and much of eastern Europe back to Catholicism.

The Sacred Congregation of the Holy Office

In 1542 Pope Paul III established the Sacred Congregation of the Holy Office with jurisdiction over the Roman Inquisition, a powerful instrument of the Counter-Reformation. The Inquisition was a committee of six cardinals with judicial authority over all Catholics and the power to arrest, imprison, and execute. Under the direction of the fanatical Cardinal Caraffa, it vigorously attacked heresy.

The Roman Inquisition operated under the principles of Roman law. It accepted hearsay evidence, was not obliged to inform the accused of charges against them, and sometimes applied torture. Echoing one of Calvin's remarks about heresy, Cardinal Caraffa wrote, "No man is to lower himself by showing toleration towards any sort of heretic, least of all a Calvinist."[51] The Holy Office published the *Index of Prohibited Books,* a catalog of forbidden reading that included the publications of many printers.

Within the Papal States, the Inquisition effectively destroyed heresy (and many heretics). Outside the papal territories, however, its influence was slight. Governments had their own judicial systems for the suppression of treasonable activity, as religious heresy was then considered. In Venice,

for instance, authorities cooperated with the Holy Office only when heresy became a great threat to the security of the republic. The *Index* had no influence on scholarly research in nonreligious areas, such as law, classical literature, and mathematics. As a result of the Inquisition, Venetians and Italians were not cut off from the main currents of European learning.[52]

SUMMARY

The Italian Renaissance, spanning the period from the eleventh through sixteenth centuries, developed in two broad stages. In the first stage, from about 1050 to 1300, a new economy emerged, based on Venetian and Genoese shipping and long-distance trade and on Florentine banking and cloth manufacture. These commercial activities, combined with the struggle of urban communes for political independence from surrounding feudal lords, led to the appearance of a new wealthy aristocratic class. The second stage, extending roughly from 1300 to 1600, witnessed a remarkable intellectual efflorescence. Based on a strong interest in the ancient world, the Renaissance had a classicizing influence on many facets of culture. In the city-states of fifteenth- and sixteenth-century Italy, oligarchic or despotic powers governed; Renaissance culture was manipulated to enhance the power of those rulers. Expanding outside Italy, the intellectual features of this movement affected the culture of all Europe.

In northern Europe, city merchants and rural gentry allied with rising monarchies. Using taxes provided by business people, kings provided a greater degree of domestic peace and order, conditions essential for trade. In Spain, France, and England, rulers also emphasized royal dignity and authority. Feudal monarchies gradually evolved in the direction of nation-states.

In the sixteenth century and through most of the seventeenth, religion and religious issues continued to play a major role in the lives of individuals and in the policies and actions of governments. The age of the Reformation presents very real paradoxes. The break with Rome and the rise of Lutheran, Anglican, Calvinist, and other faiths destroyed the unity of Europe as an organic Christian society. The strength of religious convictions caused political fragmentation, and religion, whether Protestant or Catholic, decisively influenced the growth of national states. Although most reformers rejected religious toleration, they helped pave the way for it.

Scholars have maintained that the sixteenth century witnessed the beginnings of the modern world. They are both right and wrong. The sixteenth-century revolt from the church paved the way for the eighteenth-century revolt from the Christian God, one of the strongest supports of life in Western culture. In this respect, the Reformation marks the beginning of the modern world, with its secularism and rootlessness. At the same time, it can be argued that the sixteenth century represents the culmination of the Middle Ages. Martin Luther's anxieties about salvation show him to be very much a medieval man. His concerns had deeply troubled serious individuals since the time of Saint Augustine. Modern people tend to be less troubled by them.

NOTES

1. See L. Martines, *Power and Imagination: City-States in Renaissance Italy* (New York: Vintage Books, 1980), esp. pp. 332–333.
2. Ibid., pp. 22–61.
3. Ibid., pp. 221–237, esp. p. 221.
4. Quoted in J. Burckhardt, *The Civilization of the Renaissance in Italy* (London: Phaidon Books, 1951), p. 89.
5. *Memoirs of Benvenuto Cellini: A Florentine Artist: Written by Himself* (London: J. M. Dent & Sons, Everyman's Library, 1927), p. 2.
6. Quoted in Burckhardt, p. 111.
7. See C. Trinkaus, *In Our Image and Likeness: Humanity and Divinity in Italian Humanist Thought,* vol. 2 (London: Constable, 1970), pp. 505–529.
8. B. Burroughs, ed., *Vasari's Lives of the Artists* (New York: Simon & Schuster, 1946), pp. 164–165.
9. See Martines, chap. 13, esp. pp. 241, 243.
10. See "The Social Status of the Artists," in A. Hauser, *The Social History of Art,* vol. 2 (New York: Vintage Books, 1959), chap. 3, esp. pp. 60, 68.
11. G. Bull, trans., *Aretino: Selected Letters* (Baltimore: Penguin Books, 1976), p. 109.
12. Quoted in P. Murray and L. Murray, *A Dictionary of Art and Artists* (Baltimore: Penguin Books, 1963), p. 125.
13. Hauser, pp. 48–49.
14. Quoted in W. H. Woodward, *Vittorino da Feltre and Other Humanist Educators* (Cambridge, England: Cambridge University Press, 1897), pp. 96–97.
15. C. E. Detmold, trans., *The Historical, Political and Diplomatic Writings of Niccolò Machiavelli* (Boston: J. R. Osgood & Co., 1882), pp. 51–52.
16. Ibid., pp. 54–55.
17. See F. Gilbert, *Machiavelli and Guicciardini: Politics and History in Sixteenth Century Florence* (New York: Norton, 1985), pp. 197–200.
18. E. L. Eisenstein, *The Printing Press as an Agent of Change: Communications and Cultural Transformations in Early Modern Europe,* vol. 1 (New York: Cambridge University Press, 1979), pp. 126–159, esp. p. 135.
19. M. L. King, "Book-lined Cells: Women and Humanism in the Early Italian Renaissance," in *Beyond Their Sex: Learned Women of the European Past,* ed. P. H. Labalme (New York: New York University Press, 1980), pp. 66–81, esp. p. 73.
20. This account rests on J. Kelly-Gadol, "Did Women Have a Renaissance?" in *Becoming Visible: Women in European History,* ed. R. Bridenthal and C. Koonz, (Boston: Houghton Mifflin, 1977), pp. 137–161, esp. p. 161.
21. G. Ruggerio, "Sexual Criminality in Early Renaissance Venice, 1338–1358," *Journal of Social History* 8 (Spring 1975): 18–31.
22. Quoted in R. C. Trexler, "Infanticide in Florence: New Sources and First Results," *History of Childhood Quarterly,* vol. 1, no. 1 (Summer 1973): 99.
23. Ibid., pp. 100–120.
24. J. Devisse and M. Mollat, *The Image of the Black in Western Art,* vol. 2, trans. W. G. Ryan (New York: Morrow, 1979), pt. 2, pp. 187–188.
25. Ibid., pp. 190–194.
26. Ibid., pp. 255–258.
27. Quoted in E. H. Harbison, *The Christian Scholar and His Calling in the Age of the Reformation* (New York: Scribner's, 1956), p. 109.
28. Quoted in F. Seebohm, *The Oxford Reformers* (London: J. M. Dent & Sons, Everyman's Library, 1867), p. 256.
29. See J. H. Elliott, *Imperial Spain, 1469–1716* (New York: Mentor Books, 1963), esp. pp. 75, 97–108.
30. See R. R. Post, *The Modern Devotion: Confrontation with Reformation and Humanism* (Leiden: E. J. Brill, 1968), esp. pp. 237–238, 255, 323–348.
31. T. C. Mendenhall et al., eds., *Ideas and Institutions in European History: 800–1715* (New York: Henry Holt, 1948), p. 220.
32. Quoted in O. Chadwick, *The Reformation* (Baltimore: Penguin Books, 1976), p. 55.
33. Quoted in E. H. Harbison, *The Age of Reformation* (Ithaca, N.Y.: Cornell University Press, 1963), p. 52.

34. Based heavily on Harbison, *The Age of Reformation,* pp. 52–55.

35. See S. E. Ozment, *The Reformation in the Cities: The Appeal of Protestantism to Sixteenth-Century Germany and Switzerland* (New Haven, Conn.: Yale University Press, 1975), pp. 32–45.

36. See S. E. Ozment, *The Age of Reform, 1250–1550: An Intellectual and Religious History of Late Medieval and Reformation Europe* (New Haven, Conn.: Yale University Press, 1980), pp. 273–279.

37. Quoted ibid., p. 280.

38. Ibid., p. 281.

39. Quoted in H. G. Haile, *Luther: An Experiment in Biography* (Garden City, N.Y.: Doubleday, 1980), p. 272.

40. Quoted in J. Atkinson, *Martin Luther and the Birth of Protestantism* (Baltimore: Penguin Books, 1968), pp. 247–248.

41. *Martin Luther: Three Treatises* (Philadelphia: Muhlenberg Press, 1947), pp. 28–31.

42. J. Allen, trans., *John Calvin: The Institutes of the Christian Religion* (Philadelphia: Westminster Press, 1930), bk. 3, chap. 21, paras. 5, 7.

43. E. W. Monter, *Calvin's Geneva* (New York: Wiley, 1967), pp. 98–108.

44. Ibid., p. 137.

45. Quoted in R. Bainton, *The Travail of Religious Liberty* (New York: Harper & Brothers, 1958), pp. 69–70.

46. A. G. Dickens, *The English Reformation* (New York: Schocken Books, 1964), p. 36.

47. See R. Marius, *Thomas More: A Biography* (New York: Knopf, 1984), pp. 215–216.

48. See J. J. Scarisbrick, *The Reformation and the English People* (Oxford: Basil Blackwell, 1984), pp. 81–84, esp. p. 81.

49. Ibid.

50. Ibid., p. 84.

51. Quoted in Chadwick, p. 270.

52. See P. Grendler, *The Roman Inquisition and the Venetian Press, 1540–1605* (Princeton, N.J.: Princeton University Press, 1977).

SUGGESTED READING

There are many exciting studies available on virtually all aspects of the Renaissance and the Reformation. In addition to the titles given in the Notes, the curious student should see J. H. Plumb, *The Italian Renaissance* (1965), a superbly written book and perhaps the best starting point. J. R. Hales, *Renaissance Europe: The Individual and Society, 1480–1520* (1978), is an excellent treatment of individualism. F. H. New, *The Renaissance and Reformation: A Short History* (1977), gives a balanced, concise, and up-to-date account; however, the older study of M. P. Gilmore, *The World of Humanism* (1962), is still useful. For the city where much of the Renaissance originated, G. A. Brucker, *Renaissance Florence* (1969), provides a fine description of Florentine economic, political, social, and cultural history.

For Machiavelli, the following works are helpful: J. R. Hale, *Machiavelli and Renaissance Italy* (1966), a short, sound biography; G. Bull, trans., *Machiavelli: The Prince* (1975), a readable and easily accessible edition of the political thinker's major work; and F. Guilbert, *Machiavelli and Guicciardini* (1984), a superb analysis of the thought of the two writers.

Renaissance art has inspired vast research. The following titles give some introduction to an enormous literature: A. Martindale, *The Rise of the Artist in the Middle Ages and Early Renaissance* (1972); B. Berenson, *Italian Painters of the Renaissance* (1957); E. Panofsky, *Meaning in the Visual Arts* (1955), by one of the great art historians of the century; L. Steinberg, *The Sexuality of Christ in Renaissance Art and Modern Oblivion* (1983), a brilliant study that relates Christ's sexuality to incarnational theology; C. Hibbert, *Rome: The Biography of a City* (1985), an elegant and entertaining work; and I. A. Richter, ed., *The Notebooks of Leonardo da Vinci* (1985), which gives the artist's scientific and naturalistic ideas and drawings. The magisterial achievement of J. Pope-Hennessy, *Cellini* (1985), is a brilliant evocation of the artist's life and work.

The following works should prove useful for various aspects of Renaissance social history: C. Singleton, trans., *The Courtier* (1959); E. L. Eisenstein, *The Printing Press as an Agent of Change: Communications and Cultural Transformations in Early Modern Europe,* 2 vols. (1979); G. Ruggerio, *Violence in Early Renaissance Florence* (1980), a pioneering study of crime and punishment; D. Weinstein and R. M. Bell, *Saints and Society: The Two Worlds of Christendom, 1000–1700* (1982), an essential work for an understanding of the social origins of saints; and J. C. Brown, *Immodest Acts: The Life of a Lesbian Nun in Renaissance Italy* (1985), and I. Maclean, *The Renaissance Notion of Women* (1980), which are useful for an understanding of the role and status of women. For blacks, see the rich and original achievement of J. Devisse and M. Mollat, *The Image of the Black in Western Art,* vol. 2, pt. 1, *From the Demonic Threat to the Incarnation of Sainthood,* and pt. 2, *Africans in the Christian Ordinance of the World: Fourteenth to Sixteenth Century* (trans. W. G. Ryan, 1979).

The best introduction to the Renaissance in northern Europe and a work that has greatly influenced twentieth-century scholarship is J. Huizinga, *The Waning of the Middle Ages: A Study of the Forms of Life, Thought, and Art in France and the Netherlands in the*

Dawn of the Renaissance (1954), which challenges the whole idea of the Renaissance. French Renaissance civilization is brilliantly evoked in L. Febvre, *Life in Renaissance France* (trans. and ed. M. Rothstein, 1977). The Marius biography of More cited in the Notes is an original study of the English humanist and statesman, but the student may also want to consult E. E. Reynolds, *Thomas More* (1962), and R. W. Chambers, *Thomas More* (1935). Erasmas, the leading northern humanist, is sensitively treated by M. M. Phillips, *Erasmus and the Northern Renaissance* (1956), and J. Huizinga, *Erasmus of Rotterdam* (1952). J. Leclercq, trans., *The Complete Works of Rabelais* (1963), is also easily accessible.

The works by Chadwick and Harbison cited in the Notes are good general introductions to the Reformation, as is H. Hillerbrand, *Men and Ideas in the Sixteenth Century* (1969). L. W. Spitz, *The Protestant Reformation, 1517–1559* (1985), provides a sound and comprehensive survey incorporating much of the latest research. For studies that interpret the Reformation against the background of fifteenth-century reforming developments, see the works by Post and by Ozment *(The Age of Reform)* cited in the Notes and G. Strauss, *Manifestations of Discontent in Germany on the Eve of the Reformation (1971),* an exciting collection of documents.

For the central figure of the early Reformation, see, in addition to the works by Atkinson and Haile cited in the Notes, H. Boehmer, *Martin Luther, Road to Reformation* (1960), a well-balanced work on Luther's formative years. Haile's perceptive study focuses on the mature and aging reformer. Students may expect thorough analyses of Luther's theology in J. Pelikan, *Reformation of Church and Dogma, 1300–1700* (1986); A. E. McGrath, *Luther's Theology of the Cross: Martin Luther on Justification* (1985); and H. Bornkamm, *Luther in Mid-Career, 1521–1530* (1983). The best introduction to Calvin is probably W. J. Bouwsma, *John Calvin: A Sixteenth-Century Portrait* (1988), an authoritative study that situates Calvin within Renaissance culture; R. T. Kendall, *Calvinism and English Calvinism to 1649* (1981), focuses on English conditions; and R. M. Mitchell, *Calvin and the Puritan's View of the Protestant Ethic* (1979), gives the socioeconomic implications of Calvin's thought. For the Anabaptists and the "left wing" of the Reformation, see the profound but difficult work of G. H. Williams, *The Radical Reformers* (1962).

For England, in addition to the fundamental works by Dickens and Scarisbrick cited in the Notes, see for popular religion K. Thomas, *Religion and the Decline of Magic* (1971), and S. T. Bindoff, *Tudor England* (1959). The best works on the king's divorce are J. J. Scarisbrick, *Henry VIII* (1968); G. Mattingly, *Catherine of Aragon* (1949); and H. A. Kelly, *The Matrimonial Trials of Henry VIII* (1975). On the dissolution of the English monasteries, D. Knowles, *The Religion Orders in England,* vol. 3 (1959), is a superb example of English historical prose. Many aspects of English social history are discussed in J. Youings, *Sixteenth Century England* (1984), a sound and beautifully written work.

For the social history of the Reformation period, see L. P. Buc and J. W. Zophy, eds., *The Social History of the Reformation* (1972), and K. von Greyerz, ed., *Religion and Society in Early Modern Europe, 1500–1800* (1984), both of which contain interesting and important essays; S. E. Ozment, *The Reformation in the Cities* (see the Notes); and G. Strauss, *Luther's House of Learning: The Indoctrination of the Young in the German Reformation* (1978). For women in the period, M. Wiesner, *Women in the Sixteenth Century: A Bibliography* (1983), is a useful reference tool, and S. M. Wyntjes, "Women in the Reformation Era," in Bridenthal and Koonz's *Becoming Visible* (see the Notes), is a good general survey. The best recent treatment of marriage and the family is probably S. E. Ozment, *When Fathers Ruled: Family Life in Reformation Europe* (1983). Ozment's edition of *Reformation Europe: A Guide to Research* (1982) contains many useful articles.

P. Janelle, *The Catholic Reformation* (1951), is a comprehensive treatment of the Catholic Reformation from a Catholic point of view, and A. G. Dickens, *The Counter-Reformation* (1969), gives the Protestant standpoint in a splendidly illustrated book. The virtually definitive study of the Council of Trent is H. Jedin, *A History of the Council of Trent,* 3 vols. (1957–1961). For the Jesuits, see M. Foss, *The Founding of the Jesuits, 1540* (1969), and W. B. Bangert, *A History of the Society of Jesus* (1972).

18

The Age of European Expansion and Religious Wars

Hans Holbein the Younger, *Jean de Dinteville and George de Seluc (The Ambassadors)*

etween 1450 and 1650 two developments dramatically altered the world in which Europeans lived: overseas expansion and the reformations of the Christian churches. Overseas expansion broadened Europeans' geographical horizons and brought them into confrontation with ancient civilizations in Africa, Asia, and the Americas. These confrontations led first to conquest, then to exploitation, and finally to profound social changes in both Europe and the conquered territories. Likewise, the Renaissance and the reformations drastically changed intellectual, political, religious, and social life in Europe. War and religious issues dominated the politics of European states. Although religion was commonly used to rationalize international conflict, wars were fought for power and territorial expansion.

- Why, in the sixteenth and seventeenth centuries, did a relatively small number of people living on the edge of the Eurasian land mass gain control of the major sea lanes of the world and establish political and economic hegemony on distant continents?

- How were a few Spaniards, fighting far from home, able to overcome the powerful Aztec and Inca empires in America?

- What effect did overseas expansion have on Europe and on conquered societies?

- What were the causes and consequences of the religious wars in France, the Netherlands, and Germany?

- How did the religious crises of this period affect the status of women?

- How and why did African slave labor become the dominant form of labor organization in the New World?

- What religious and intellectual developments led to the growth of skepticism?

- What literary masterpieces of the English-speaking world did this period produce?

This chapter addresses these questions.

The Cantino Map (1502), named for the agent secretly commissioned to design it in Lisbon for the duke of Ferrara, an avid Italian map collector, reveals such a good knowledge of the African continent, of the islands of the West Indies, and of the shoreline of present-day Venezuela, Guiana, and Brazil in South America that modern scholars suspect there may have been clandestine voyages to the Americas shortly after Columbus's. *(Source: Biblioteca Estense Universitaria, Modena)*

DISCOVERY, RECONNAISSANCE, AND EXPANSION

Historians have called the period from 1450 to 1650 the "Age of Discovery," the "Age of Reconnaissance," and the "Age of Expansion." All three labels are appropriate. "Age of Discovery" refers to the era's phenomenal advances in geographical knowledge and technology, often achieved through trial and error. In 1350 it still took as long to sail from the eastern end of the Mediterranean to the western end as it had taken a thousand years earlier. Even in the fifteenth century, Europeans knew little more about the earth's surface than the Romans had known. By 1650, however, Europeans had made an extensive reconnaissance—or preliminary exploration—and had sketched fairly accurately the physical outline of the whole earth. Much of the geographical information they had gathered was tentative and not fully understood—hence the appropriateness of the label "Age of Reconnaissance."

"Age of Expansion" refers to the migration of Europeans to other parts of the world. This colonization resulted in political control of much of South and North America; of coastal regions of Africa, India, China, and Japan; and of many Pacific islands. Political hegemony was accompanied by economic exploitation, religious domination, and the introduction of European patterns of social and intellectual life. The sixteenth-century expansion of European society launched a new age in world history.

Overseas Exploration and Conquest

The outward expansion of Europe began with the Vikings' voyages across the Atlantic in the ninth and tenth centuries. Vikings led by Eric the Red and Leif Ericson discovered Greenland and the eastern coast of North America. The Crusades of the eleventh through thirteenth centuries were another phase in Europe's attempt to explore, Christianize, and exploit peoples on the periphery of the Continent. But these early thrusts outward resulted in no permanent settlements. The Vikings made only quick raids in search of booty. Lacking stable political institutions in Scandinavia, they had no workable forms of government to impose on distant continents. In the twelfth and thir-

teenth centuries, the lack of a strong territorial base, weak support from the West, and sheer misrule combined to make the medieval Crusader kingdoms short-lived. Even in the mid-fifteenth century, Europe seemed ill prepared for international ventures. By 1450 a grave new threat had appeared in the East—the Ottoman Turks.

Combining excellent military strategy with efficient administration of their conquered territories, the Turks had subdued most of Anatolia and begun to settle on the western side of the Bosporus. The Ottoman Turks under Sultan Muhammad II (r. 1451–1481) captured Constantinople in 1453, pressed into the Balkans. By the early sixteenth century, the eastern Mediterranean was under Turkish control. The Turkish menace badly frightened Europeans. In France in the fifteenth and sixteenth centuries, twice as many books were printed about the Turkish threat as about the American discoveries. The Turks imposed a military blockade on eastern Europe, thus forcing Europeans' attention westward. Yet the fifteenth and sixteenth centuries witnessed a fantastic continuation, on a global scale, of European expansion.

Portugal, situated on the extreme southwestern edge of the European continent, got the start on the rest of Europe. Its taking of Ceuta, an Arab city in northern Morocco, in 1415 marked the beginning of European exploration and control of overseas territory. The objectives of Portuguese policy included the Christianization of Muslims and the search for gold, for an overseas route to the spice markets of India, and for the mythical Christian ruler of Ethiopia, Prester John.

In the early phases of Portuguese exploration, Prince Henry (1394–1460), called "the Navigator" because of the annual expeditions he sent down the western coast of Africa, played the leading role. In the fifteenth century, most of the gold that reached Europe came from the Sudan in West Africa and from Ashanti blacks living near the area of present-day Ghana. Muslim caravans brought the gold from the African cities of Niani and Timbuktu and carried it north across the Sahara to Mediterranean ports. Then the Portuguese muscled in on this commerce in gold. Prince Henry's carefully planned expeditions succeeded in reaching Guinea, and, under King John II (r. 1481–1495), the Portuguese established trading posts and forts on the Guinea coast and penetrated into the continent all the way to Timbuktu (Map 18.1). Portuguese ships brought gold to Lisbon,

PACIFIC OCEAN

ARCTIC OCEAN

ASIA

JAPAN
1542

Kyushu

Canton
1513

Macao
1517

CHINA

PHILIPPINES

1521

New
Guinea

Malacca 1509

Borneo

Sumatra

Java

AUSTRALIA

Goa 1510

Ceylon
1505

INDIA

Calicut
1498

INDIAN

OCEAN

Ormuz
1507

PERSIA

Muscat

ARABIA

Aden 1513

MADAGASCAR
1500

1522

Constantinople

EUROPE

Amsterdam
Antwerp

AFRICA

ETHIOPIA

Mombasa
1498

Mozambique

Lisbon
Seville
Ceuta
1415

SAHARA

Timbuktu

Niani

GUINEA

GOLD COAST

CAPE
VERDE

Cape of Good Hope

1522

1497

ATLANTIC

OCEAN

Azores

Canary Is.

1493

1492

Cape Verde Is.
1456

1519

Newfoundland
1497

GREENLAND

Rio de Janeiro
1516

Strait of Magellan

Quebec
1608

St. Augustine 1565

San Salvador 1492

Cuba

Puerto Rico

Hispaniola
1492

Jamaica

HONDURAS

Trinidad
1498

**SPANISH
MAIN**

BRAZIL

Vera Cruz
1519

Cartagena

Panama

**SOUTH
AMERICA**

Potosi

Buenos Aires
1535

**NORTH
AMERICA**

Zacatecas

Guanajuato

Mexico City
1519

**NEW
SPAIN**

Quito
1534

PERU

Lima
1535

Santiago

Cape Horn

1520

*PACIFIC
OCEAN*

1520

Magellan and crew

Columbus

Da Gama

Other

Spanish holdings

Portuguese holdings

0   1500   3000 Km.

0   1500   3000 Mi.

the Portugese capital, and by 1500 Portugal controlled the flow of gold to Europe. The golden century of Portuguese prosperity had begun.

Still the Portuguese pushed farther south down the west coast of Africa. In 1487 Bartholomew Diaz rounded the Cape of Good Hope at the southern tip, but storms and a threatened mutiny forced him to turn back. On a second expedition (1497–1499), the Portuguese mariner Vasco da Gama reached India and returned to Lisbon loaded with samples of Indian wares. King Manuel (r. 1495–1521) promptly dispatched thirteen ships under the command of Pedro Alvares Cabral, assisted by Diaz, to set up trading posts in India. On April 22, 1500, the coast of Brazil in South America was sighted and claimed for the crown of Portugal. Cabral then proceeded south and east around the Cape of Good Hope and reached India. Half of the fleet was lost on the return voyage, but the six spice-laden vessels that dropped anchor in Lisbon harbor in July 1501 more than paid for the entire expedition. Thereafter, convoys were sent out every March. Lisbon became the entrance port for Asian goods into Europe—but not without a fight.

For centuries the Muslims had controlled the rich spice trade of the Indian Ocean, and they did not surrender it willingly. Portuguese commercial activities were accompanied by the destruction or seizure of strategic Muslim coastal forts, which later served Portugal as both trading posts and military bases. Alfonso de Albuquerque, whom the Portuguese crown appointed as governor of India (r. 1509–1515), decided that these bases and not inland territories should control the Indian Ocean. Accordingly, his cannon blasted open the ports of Calicut, Ormuz, Goa, and Malacca, the vital centers of Arab domination of South Asian trade (see Map 18.1). This bombardment laid the foundation for Portuguese imperialism in the sixteenth and seventeenth centuries—a strange way to bring Christianity to "those who were in darkness." As one scholar wrote about the opening of

China to the West, "while Buddha came to China on white elephants, Christ was borne on cannon balls."[1]

Political centralization in Spain helps to explain that country's outward push. In the fifteenth century, Isabella and Ferdinand had consolidated their several kingdoms to achieve a more united Spain. The Catholic rulers reduced the powers of the nobility, revamped the Spanish bureaucracy, and humbled dissident elements, notably the Muslims and the Jews. The Spanish monarchy was stronger than ever before and in a position to support foreign ventures; it could bear the costs and dangers of exploration.

In March 1493, Spanish ships entered Lisbon harbor bearing a triumphant Italian explorer in the service of the Spanish monarchy. Christopher Columbus (1451–1506), a Genoese mariner, had secured Spanish support for an expedition to the East. He sailed from Palos, Spain, to the Canary Islands and crossed the Atlantic to the Bahamas, landing in October 1492 on an island that he named "San Salvador" and believed to be off the coast of India. Like most people of his day, Columbus was deeply religious. The crew of his flagship, *Santa Maria,* recited vespers every night and sang a hymn to the Virgin before going to bed. Nevertheless, the Spanish fleet, sailing westward to find the East, sought wealth as well as souls to convert.

Between 1492 and 1502, Columbus made four voyages to America, discovering all the major islands of the Caribbean—Haiti (which he called "Dominica" and the Spanish named "Hispaniola"), San Salvador, Puerto Rico, Jamaica, Cuba, Trinidad—and Honduras in Central America. Columbus believed until he died that the islands he found were off the coast of India. In fact, he had opened up for the rulers of Spain a whole new world. The Caribbean islands—the West Indies—represented to Spanish missionary zeal millions of Indian natives for conversion to Christianity. Hispaniola, Puerto Rico, and Cuba also offered gold.

The search for precious metals determined the direction of Spanish exploration and expansion into South America. When it became apparent that placer mining (in which ore is separated from soil by panning) in the Caribbean islands was slow and the rewards slim, new routes to the East and new sources of gold and silver were sought.

In 1519 Charles V of Spain commissioned Ferdinand Magellan (1480–1521) to find a direct

MAP 18.1 Overseas Exploration and Conquest in the Fifteenth and Sixteenth Centuries The voyages of discovery marked another phase in the centuries-old migrations of European peoples. Consider the major contemporary significance of each of the three voyages depicted on the map.

route to the Moluccan Islands off the southeast coast of Asia. Magellan sailed southwest across the Atlantic to Brazil and then south around Cape Horn into the Pacific Ocean (see Map 18.1). He crossed the Pacific, sailing west, to the Malay Archipelago, which he called the "Western Isles." (These islands were conquered in the 1560s and named the "Philippines" for Philip II of Spain.)

Though Magellan was killed, the expedition continued, returning to Spain in 1522 from the east by way of the Indian Ocean, the Cape of Good Hope, and the Atlantic. Terrible storms, mutiny, starvation, and disease haunted this voyage. Nevertheless, it verified Columbus's theory that the earth was round and brought information about the vastness of the Pacific. Magellan also proved that the earth was much larger than Columbus and others had believed.

In the West Indies, the slow recovery of gold, the shortage of a healthy labor force, and sheer restlessness speeded up Spain's search for wealth. In 1519, the year Magellan departed on his worldwide expedition, a brash and very determined Spanish adventurer, Hernando Cortés (1485–1547), crossed from Hispaniola to mainland Mexico with six hundred men, seventeen horses, and ten cannon. Within three years, Cortés conquered the fabulously rich Aztec Empire, took captive the Aztec emperor Montezuma, and founded Mexico City as the capital of New Spain. The subjugation of northern Mexico took longer, but between 1531 and 1550 the Spanish gained control of Zacatecas and Guanajuato, where rich silver veins were soon tapped.

Francisco Pizarro (1470–1541), another Spanish *conquistador* (explorer), repeated Cortés's feat in Peru. Between 1531 and 1536, with even fewer resources, Pizarro crushed the Inca Empire in northern South America and established the Spanish viceroyalty of Peru with its center at Lima. In 1545 Pizarro opened at Potosí in the Peruvian highlands what became the richest silver mines in the New World.

Between 1525 and 1575, the riches of the Americas poured into Lisbon and the Spanish port of Seville. For all their new wealth, however, Lisbon and Seville did not become important trading centers. It was the Flemish city of Antwerp, controlled by the Spanish Habsburgs, that developed into the great entrepôt for overseas bullion and Portuguese spices and served as the commercial and financial capital of the entire European world.

Since the time of the great medieval fairs, cities of the Low Countries had been important sites for the exchange of products from the Baltic and Italy. Antwerp, ideally situated on the Scheldt River at the intersection of many trading routes (see Map 18.3), steadily expanded as the chief intermediary for international commerce and finance. English woolens; Baltic wheat, fur, and timber; Portuguese spices; German iron and copper; Spanish fruit; French wines and dyestuffs; Italian silks, marble, and mirrors, together with vast amounts of cash—all were exchanged at Antwerp. The city's harbor could dock 2,500 vessels at once, and 5,000 merchants from many nations gathered daily in the *bourse* (exchange).

By the end of the sixteenth century, Amsterdam had overtaken Antwerp as the financial capital of Europe (see page 652). The Dutch had also embarked on foreign exploration and conquest. The Dutch East India Company, founded in 1602, became the major organ of Dutch imperialism and within a few decades expelled the Portuguese from Ceylon and other East Indian islands. By 1650 the Dutch West India Company had successfully intruded on the Spanish possessions in America and gained control of much of the African and American trade.

English and French explorations lacked the immediate, sensational results of the Spanish and Portuguese. In 1497 John Cabot, a Genoese merchant living in London, sailed for Brazil but discovered Newfoundland. The next year he returned and explored the New England coast and perhaps as far south as present-day Delaware. Since these expeditions found no spices or gold, the English king Henry VII lost interest in exploration. Between 1534 and 1541, the Frenchman Jacques Cartier made several voyages and explored the Saint Lawrence region of Canada, but the first permanent French settlement, at Quebec, was not founded until 1608.

The Explorers' Motives

The expansion of Europe was not motivated by demographic pressures. The Black Death had caused serious population losses from which Europe had not recovered in 1500. Few Europeans immigrated to North or South America in the sixteenth century. Half of those who did sail to begin a new life in the Americas died en route; half of

Market of Cartagena   Founded in 1533 as a port on the Caribbean Sea, Cartagena (modern Colombia) became the storage depot for precious metals waiting shipment to Spain. In this fanciful woodcut, male Indians, wearing tunics composed of overlapping feathers, and nude females sell golden necklaces, fish, fruit, and grain. *(Source: Rare Book Division, New York Public Library; Astor, Lenox and Tilden Foundations)*

those who reached the New World eventually returned to their homeland. Why, then, did explorers brave the Atlantic and Pacific oceans, risking their lives to discover new continents and spread European culture?

The reasons are varied and complex. People of the sixteenth century were still basically medieval in the sense that their attitudes and values were shaped by religion and expressed in religious terms. In the late fifteenth century, crusading fervor remained a basic part of the Portuguese and Spanish national ideal. The desire to Christianize Muslims and pagan peoples played a central role in European expansion, as evidenced by Columbus's explanation of his first voyage:

And Your Highnesses, as Catholic Christians and Princes devoted to the Holy Christian Faith and the propagators thereof, and enemies of the sect of Mahomet and of all idolatries and heresies, resolved to send me . . . to the said regions of India, to see the said princes and peoples and lands and to observe the disposition of them and of all, and the manner in which may be undertaken their conversion to our Holy Faith, and ordained that I should not go by land (the usual way) to the Orient, but by the route of the Occident, by which no one to this day knows for sure that anyone has gone.[2]

Queen Isabella of Spain showed a fanatical zeal for converting the Muslims to Christianity, but she concentrated her efforts on the Arabs in Granada in southern Spain. After the abortive crusading attempts of the thirteenth century, Isabella and other rulers realized that they lacked the material resources to mount the full-scale assault on Islam necessary for victory. Crusading impulses thus shifted from the Muslims to the pagan peoples of India, Africa, and the Americas.

Moreover, after the reconquista, enterprising young men of the Spanish upper classes found economic and political opportunities severely limited.

As a recent study of the Castilian city of Ciudad Real shows, the ancient aristocracy controlled the best agricultural land and monopolized urban administrative posts. Great merchants and a few nobles (surprisingly, since Spanish law forbade noble participation in commercial ventures) dominated the textile and leather glove manufacturing industries. Consequently, many ambitious men immigrated to the Americas to seek their fortunes.[3]

Government sponsorship and encouragement of exploration also help to account for the results of the various voyages. Mariners and explorers as private individuals, could not afford the massive sums needed to explore mysterious oceans and to control remote continents. The strong financial support of Prince Henry the Navigator led to Portugal's phenomenal success in the spice trade. Even the grudging and modest assistance of Isabella and Ferdinand eventually brought untold riches—and complicated problems—to Spain. The Dutch in the seventeenth century, through the Dutch East India Company and other government-sponsored trading companies, reaped enormous wealth. Although the Netherlands was a small country in size, it dominated the European economy in 1650. In England, by contrast, Henry VII's lack of interest in exploration delayed English expansion for a century.

Scholars have frequently described the European discoveries as a manifestation of Renaissance curiosity about the physical universe, the desire to know more about the geography and peoples of the world. There is truth to this explanation. Cosmography, natural history, and geography aroused enormous interest among educated people in the fifteenth and sixteenth centuries. Just as science fiction and speculation about life on other planets excite readers today, quasi-scientific literature about Africa, Asia, and the Americas captured the imaginations of literate Europeans. Spanish chronicler Oviedo's *General History of the Indies* (1547), a detailed eyewitness account of plants, animals, and peoples, was widely read.

Spices were another important incentive to voyages of discovery. Introduced into western Europe by the Crusaders in the twelfth century, nutmeg, mace, ginger, cinnamon, and pepper added flavor and variety to the monotonous diet of Europeans. Spices were also used in the preparation of medicinal drugs and incense for religious ceremonies. In the late thirteenth century, the Venetian Marco Polo (ca 1254–1324) had visited the court of the Chinese emperor. The widely publicized account of his travels in the *Book of Various Experiences* stimulated a rich trade in spices between Asia and Italy. The Venetians came to hold a monopoly on the spice trade in western Europe.

Spices were grown in India and China, shipped across the Indian Ocean to ports on the Persian Gulf, and then transported by Arabs across the Arabian Desert to Mediterranean ports. But the rise of the Ming Dynasty in China in the late fourteenth century resulted in the expulsion of foreigners. And the steady penetration of the Ottoman Turks into the eastern Mediterranean and of hostile Muslims across North Africa forced Europeans to seek a new route to the Asian spice markets.

The basic reason for European exploration and expansion, however, was the quest for material profit. Mariners and explorers frankly admitted this. As Bartholomew Diaz put it, his motives were "to serve God and His Majesty, to give light to those who were in darkness and to grow rich as all men desire to do." When Vasco da Gama reached the port of Calicut, India, in 1498, a native asked what the Portuguese wanted. Da Gama replied, "Christians and spices."[4] The bluntest of the Spanish conquistadors, Hernando Cortés, announced as he prepared to conquer Mexico, "I have come to win gold, not to plow the fields like a peasant."[5]

Portuguese and Spanish explorers carried the fervent Catholicism and missionary zeal of the Iberian Peninsula to the New World, and once in America they urged home governments to send clerics. At bottom, however, wealth was the driving motivation. A sixteenth-century diplomat, Ogier Gheselin de Busbecq, summed up this paradoxical attitude well: in expeditions to the Indies and the Antipodes, he said, "religion supplies the pretext and gold the motive."[6] The mariners and explorers were religious and "medieval" in justifying their actions while remaining materialistic and "modern" in their behavior.

Technological Stimuli to Exploration

Technological developments were the key to Europe's remarkable outreach. By 1350 cannon had been fully developed in western Europe. These pieces of artillery emitted frightening noises and great flashes of fire and could batter down fortresses and even city walls. Sultan Muhammad II's siege of Constantinople in 1453 provides a classic illustration of the effectiveness of cannon fire.

Constantinople had very strong walled fortifications. The sultan secured the services of a Western technician who built fifty-six small cannon and a gigantic gun that could hurl stone balls weighing about eight hundred pounds. The gun could be moved only by several hundred oxen and loaded and fired only by about a hundred men working together. Reloading took two hours. This awkward but powerful weapon breached the walls of Constantinople before it cracked on the second day of the bombardment. Lesser cannon finished the job.

Early cannon posed serious technical difficulties. Iron cannon were cheaper than bronze to construct, but they were difficult to cast effectively and were liable to crack and injure the artillerymen. Bronze guns, made of copper and tin, were less subject than iron to corrosion, but they were very expensive. All cannon were extraordinarily difficult to move, required considerable time for reloading, and were highly inaccurate. They thus proved inefficient for land warfare. However, they could be used at sea.

The mounting of cannon on ships and improved techniques of shipbuilding gave impetus to European expansion. Since ancient times, most seagoing vessels had been narrow, open galleys propelled by manpower. Slaves or convicts who had been sentenced to the galleys manned the oars of the ships that sailed the Mediterranean, and both cargo vessels and warships carried soldiers for defense. Though well suited to the placid and thoroughly explored waters of the Mediterranean, galleys could not withstand the rough winds and uncharted shoals of the Atlantic. The need for sturdier craft, as well as population losses caused by the Black Death, forced the development of a new style of ship that would not require soldiers for defense.

In the course of the fifteenth century, the Portuguese developed the *caravel,* a small, light, three-masted sailing ship. Though somewhat slower than the galley, the caravel held more cargo and was highly maneuverable. When fitted with cannon, it could dominate larger vessels, such as the round ships commonly used as merchantmen. The substitution of wind power for manpower, and artillery fire for soldiers, signaled a great tech-

nological advance and gave Europeans navigational and military ascendancy over the rest of the world.[7]

Other fifteenth-century developments in navigation helped make possible the conquest of the Atlantic. The magnetic compass, brought to Europe from China by the Muslims, enabled sailors to determine their direction and position at sea. The astrolabe, an instrument developed by Muslim navigators in the twelfth century and used to determine the altitude of the sun and other celestial bodies, permitted mariners to plot their *latitude* (position north or south of the equator). Steadily improved maps and sea charts provided information about distance, sea depths, and general geography.

The Conquest of Aztec Mexico and Inca Peru

Technological development also helps to explain the Spanish conquest of Aztec Mexico and Inca Peru. The strange end of the Aztec nation remains one of the most fascinating events in the annals of human societies. The Spanish adventurer Hernando Cortés landed at Vera Cruz in February 1519. In November he entered Tenochtitlán (Mexico City) and soon had the emperor Montezuma II in custody. In less than two years Cortés destroyed the monarchy, gained complete control of the Mexican capital, and extended his jurisdiction over much of the Aztec Empire. Why did a strong people defending its own territory succumb so quickly to a handful of Spaniards fighting in dangerous and completely unfamiliar circumstances? How indeed, since Montezuma's scouts sent him detailed reports of the Spaniards' movements? The answer lies in the Spaniards' boldness and timing and in the Aztecs' psychology, political structure, attitude toward war, and technology.

The Spaniards arrived in late summer, when the Aztecs were preoccupied with harvesting their crops and not thinking of war. From the Spaniards' perspective, their timing was ideal. A series of natural phenomena, signs, and portents seemed to augur disaster for the Aztecs. A comet was seen in daytime, a column of fire had appeared every midnight for a year, and two temples were suddenly destroyed, one by lightning unaccompanied by thunder. These and other apparently inexplicable events raised the specter of the return of Quetzalcoatl (see page 491) and had a pervasively unnerving effect on the Aztecs. They looked on the Europeans riding "wild beasts" as extraterrestrial forces coming to establish a new social order. Defeatism swept the nation and paralyzed its will.

The Aztecs had never developed an effective method of governing subject peoples. The empire was actually a group of subject communities lacking legal or government ties to what today is called the "state." The Aztecs controlled them through terror, requiring from each clan an annual tribute of humans to be sacrificed to the gods. Tributary peoples seethed with revolt. When the Spaniards appeared, the Totonacs greeted them as liberators, and other subject groups joined them in battle against the Aztecs.

Montezuma refrained from attacking the Spaniards as they advanced toward his capital and welcomed Cortés and his men into Tenochtitlán. Historians have often condemned the Aztec ruler for vacillation and weakness. Is this a fair assessment? Montezuma relied on the advice of his state council, itself divided, and on the dubious loyalty of tributary communities. When Cortés—with incredible boldness—took Montezuma hostage, the emperor's influence over his people crumbled.

But the major explanation for the collapse of the Aztec Empire to six hundred Spaniards lies in the Aztec's notion of warfare and level of technology. Forced to leave Tenochtitlán to settle a conflict elsewhere, Cortés placed his lieutenant, Alvarado, in charge. Alvarado's harsh rule drove the Aztecs to revolt, and they almost succeeded in destroying the Spanish garrison. When Cortés returned just in time, the Aztecs allowed his reinforcements to join Alvarado's besieged force. No threatened European or Asian state would have conceived of doing such a thing: dividing an enemy's army and destroying the separate parts was basic to European and Asian military tactics. But for the Aztecs warfare was a ceremonial act, in which "divide and conquer" had no place.

Having allowed the Spanish forces to reunite, the entire population of Tenochtitlán attacked the invaders. The Aztecs killed many Spaniards, who in retaliation executed Montezuma. The Spaniards escaped from the city and inflicted a crushing defeat on the Aztec army at Otumba near Lake Texcoco on July 7, 1520. The Spaniards won because "the simple Indian methods of mass warfare were of little avail against the manoeuvring of a well-drilled force."[8] Aztec weapons proved no match for the terrifyingly noisy and lethal Spanish cannon, muskets, crossbows, and steel swords. European technology decided the battle. Cortés began the systematic conquest of Mexico.

In 1527 the Inca ruled as a benevolent despot. His power was limited only by custom. His millions of subjects looked on him as a god, firm but just to his people, merciless to his enemies. ("Looked on" is figurative. Only a few of the Inca's closest relatives dared look at his divine face: nobles approached him on their knees, and the masses kissed the dirt as he rode by in his litter.) The borders of his vast empire were well fortified, threatened by no foreign invaders. No sedition or civil disobedience disturbed the domestic tranquillity. Grain was plentiful, and apart from an outbreak of smallpox in a distant province—introduced by the Spaniards—no natural disaster upset the general peace. An army of 50,000 loyal troops stood at the Inca's instant disposal. Why, then, did this powerful empire fall so easily to Francisco Pizarro and his band of 175 men armed with one small ineffective cannon? This question has troubled students for centuries. There can be no definitive answers, but several explanations have been offered.

First, the Incas were totally isolated. They had no contact with other Amerindian cultures and knew nothing at all of Aztec civilization or its collapse to the Spaniards in 1521. Since about the year 1500, Inca scouts had reported "floating houses" on the seas, manned by white men with beards. Tradesmen told of strange large animals with feet of silver (as horseshoes appeared in the brilliant sunshine). Having observed a border skirmish between Indians and white men, intelligence sources advised the Inca that the Europeans' swords were as harmless as women's weaving battens. A coastal chieftain had poured chicha, the native beer, down the barrel of a gun to appease the god of thunder. These incidents suggest that Inca culture provided no basis for understanding the Spaniards and the significance of their arrival. Moreover, if the strange pale men planned war, there were very few of them, and the Incas believed that they could not be reinforced from the sea.[9]

At first the Incas did not think that the strangers intended trouble. They believed the old Inca legend that the creator-god Virocha—who had brought civilization to them, become displeased, and sailed away promising to return someday—

had indeed returned. Belief in a legend prevented the Incas, like the Aztecs, from taking prompt action.

A political situation may also have lain at the root of their difficulty. The Incas apparently had no definite principle for the succession of the emperor. The reigning emperor, with the advice of his council, chose his successor—usually the most capable son of his chief wife. In 1527, however, the Inca Huayna Capac died without naming his heir. The council chose Huascar, son of Huayna's chief wife, who was accordingly crowned at Cuzco with the imperial *borla,* the fringed headband symbolizing the imperial office. The people and the generals, however, supported Atahualpa, son of a secondary wife and clearly Huayna's favorite son. A bitter civil war ensued. Atahualpa emerged victorious, but the five-year struggle may have exhausted him and damaged his judgment.

Soon after Pizarro landed at Tumbes on May 13, 1532—the very day Atahualpa won the decisive battle against his brother—he learned of all these events. As Pizarro advanced across the steep Andes toward the capital at Cuzco, Atahualpa—simultaneously proceeding to the capital for his coronation—stopped at the provincial town of Cajamarca. He, like Montezuma, was kept fully informed of the Spaniards' movements. The Inca's strategy was to lure the Spaniards into a trap, seize their horses and ablest men for his army, and execute the rest. What had the Inca, surrounded by his thousands of troops, to fear? Atahualpa thus accepted Pizarro's invitation to come with his bodyguards "unarmed so as not to give offense" into the central plaza of Cajamarca. He rode right into the Spaniard's trap. Pizarro knew that if he could capture that Inca, from whom all power devolved, he would have the "Kingdom of Gold" for which he had come to the New World.

The Inca's litter arrived in the ominously quiet town square. One cannon blast terrified the Indians. The Spaniards rushed out from hiding and ruthlessly slaughtered the Indians. Atahualpa's headband was instantly torn from his head. He offered to purchase his freedom with a roomful of gold. Pizarro agreed to this ransom, and an appropriate document was drawn up and signed. After the gold had been gathered from all parts of the empire to fill the room—17 feet by 22 feet by 9 feet—the Spaniards trumped up charges against the Inca and strangled him. The Inca Empire lay at Pizarro's feet.

The South American Holocaust

In the sixteenth century, about 200,000 Spaniards immigrated to the New World. Soldiers demobilized from the Spanish and Italian campaigns, adventurers and drifters unable to find work in Spain, they did not intend to work in the New World either. After having assisted in the conquest of the Aztecs and the subjugation of the Incas, these drifters wanted to settle down and become a ruling class. In temperate grazing areas they carved out vast estates and imported Spanish sheep, cattle, and horses for the kinds of ranching with which they were familiar. In the coastal tropics, unsuited for grazing, the Spanish erected huge sugar plantations. Columbus had introduced sugar into the West Indies; Cortés, into Mexico. Sugar was a great luxury in Europe, and demand for it was high. Around 1550 the discovery of silver at Zacatecas and Guanajuato in Mexico and Potosí in present-day Bolivia stimulated silver rushes. How were the cattle ranches, sugar plantations, and silver mines to be worked? Obviously, by the Indians.

The Spanish quickly established the *encomiendas* system, whereby the Crown granted the conquerors the right to employ groups of Indians in a town or area as agricultural or mining laborers or as tribute-payers. Theoretically, the Spanish were forbidden to enslave the Indian natives; in actuality, the encomiendas were a legalized form of slavery. The European demand for sugar, tobacco, and silver prompted the colonists to exploit the Indians mercilessly. Unaccustomed to forced labor, especially in the blistering heat of tropical cane fields or the dark, dank, and dangerous mines, Indians died like flies. Recently scholars have tried to reckon the death rate of the Amerindians in the sixteenth century. Some historians maintain that when Columbus landed at Hispaniola in 1492, the island's population stood at 100,000; in 1570, 300 people survived. The Indian population of Peru is estimated to have fallen from 1.3 million in 1570 to 600,000 in 1620; central Mexico had 25.3 million Indians in 1519 and 1 million in 1605.[10] Some demographers dispute these figures, but all agree that the decline of the native Indian population in all of Spanish-occupied America amounted to a catastrophe greater in scale than any that has occurred even in the twentieth century.

What were the causes of this devastating slump in population? Students of the history of medicine have suggested the best explanation: disease. The major cause of widespread epidemics is migration, and those peoples isolated longest from other societies suffer most. Contact with disease builds up bodily resistance. At the beginning of the sixteenth century, American Indians probably had the unfortunate distinction of longer isolation from the rest of humankind than any other people on earth. Crowded concentrations of laborers in the mining camps bred infection, which was then carried by the miners back to their home villages. With little or no resistance to diseases brought from the Old World, the inhabitants of the highlands of Mexico and Peru, especially, fell victim to smallpox. According to one expert, smallpox caused "in all likelihood the most severe single loss of aboriginal population that ever occurred."[11]

Disease was the prime cause of the Indian holocaust, but the Spaniards contributed heavily to the Indians' death rate.[12] According to the Franciscan missionary Bartolomé de Las Casas (1474–1566), the Spanish maliciously murdered thousands:

This infinite multitude of people [the Indians] was . . . without fraud, without subtilty or malice . . . toward the Spaniards *whom they serve, patient, meek and peaceful. . . .*

To these quiet Lambs . . . came the Spaniards *like most c(r)uel Tygres, Wolves and Lions, enrag'd with a sharp and tedious hunger; for these forty years past, minding nothing else but the slaughter of these unfortunate wretches, whom with divers kinds of torments neither seen nor heard of before, they have so cruelly and inhumanely butchered, that of three millions of people which* Hispaniola *it self did contain, there are left remaining alive scarce three hundred persons. And for the Island of* Cuba . . . *it lies wholly desert, until'd and ruin'd. The Islands of St. John and Jamaica lie waste and desolate. The Lucayan Islands . . . are now totally unpeopled and destroyed; the inhabitants thereof amounting to above 5,000,000 souls, partly killed, and partly forced away to work in other places.*[13]

Las Casas's remarks concentrate on the tropical lowlands, but the death rate in the highlands was also staggering.

The Christian missionaries who accompanied the conquistadors and settlers—Franciscans, Dominicans, and Jesuits—played an important role in converting the Indians to Christianity, teaching them European methods of agriculture, and inculcating loyalty to the Spanish crown. In terms of numbers of people baptized, missionaries enjoyed phenomenal success, though the depth of the Indians' understanding of Christianity remains debatable. Missionaries, especially Las Casas, asserted that the Indians had human rights, and through Las Casas's persistent pressure the emperor Charles V abolished the worst abuses of the encomiendas system.

Some scholars offer a psychological explanation for the colossal death rate of the Indians: they simply lost the will to survive. Their gods appeared to have abandoned them to a world over which they had no control. Hopelessness, combined with abusive treatment and overwork, pushed many men to suicide, many women to abortion or infanticide. Whatever its precise causes, the astronomically high death rate created a severe labor shortage in Spanish America. As early as 1511, King Ferdinand of Spain observed that the Indians seemed to be "very frail" and that "one black could do the work of four Indians."[14] Thus was born an absurd myth and the massive importation of black slaves from Africa (see pages 595–598).

Colonial Administration

Having seized the great Indian ceremonial centers in Mexico and Peru, the Spanish conquistadors proceeded to subdue the main areas of native American civilization in the New World. Columbus, Cortés, and Pizarro claimed the lands they had "discovered" for the crown of Spain. How were these lands to be governed?

According to the Spanish theory of absolutism, the Crown was entitled to exercise full authority over all imperial lands. In the sixteenth century the Crown divided Spain's New World territories into four *viceroyalties,* or administrative divisions: New Spain, with its capital at Mexico City, consisted of Mexico, Central America, and present-day California, Arizona, New Mexico, and Texas. Peru, with its viceregal seat at Lima, originally consisted of all the lands in continental South America but later was reduced to the territory of modern Peru, Chile, Bolivia, and Ecuador. New Granada, with Bogotá as its administrative center, included present-day Venezuela, Colombia, Panama, and after 1739 Ecuador. La Plata, with Buenos Aires as its capital, consisted of Argentina, Uruguay, and Paraguay. Within each territory a *viceroy* or imperial governor, had broad military and civil authority as the Spanish sovereign's direct representative. The viceroy presided over the *audiencia*, twelve to fifteen judges who served as advisory council and as the highest judicial body.

From the early sixteenth century to the beginning of the nineteenth, the Spanish monarchy acted on the mercantilist principle that the colonies existed for the financial benefit of the mother country. The mining of gold and silver was always the most important industry in the colonies. The Crown claimed the *quinto*, one-fifth of all precious metals mined in the Americas. Gold and silver yielded the Spanish monarchy 25 percent of its total income. In return, Spain shipped manufactured goods to the New World and discouraged the development of native industries.

The Portuguese governed their colony of Brazil in a similar manner. After the union of the crowns of Portugal and Spain in 1580, Spanish administrative forms were introduced. Local officials called *corregidores* held judicial and military powers. Mercantilist policies placed severe restrictions on Brazilian industries that might compete with those of Portugal. In the seventeenth century the use of black slave labor made possible the cultivation of coffee, cotton, and sugar; and in the eighteenth century Brazil led the world in the production of sugar. The unique feature of colonial Brazil's culture and society was its thoroughgoing mixture of Indians, whites, and blacks.

The Economic Effects of Spain's Discoveries in the New World

The sixteenth century has often been called the "Golden Century" of Spain. The influence of Spanish armies, Spanish Catholicism, and Spanish wealth was felt all over Europe. This greatness rested largely on the influx of precious metals from the New World.

The mines at Zacatecas and Guanajuato in Mexico and Potosí in Peru poured out huge quantities of precious metals. To protect this treasure from French and English pirates, armed convoys transported it each year to Spain. Between 1503 and 1650, 16 million kilograms of silver and 185,000 kilograms of gold entered Seville's port. Spanish predominance, however, proved temporary.

In the sixteenth century, Spain experienced a steady population increase, creating a sharp rise in the demand for food and goods. Spanish colonies in the Americas also represented a demand for products. Since Spain had expelled some of the best farmers and businessmen, the Muslims and the conversos, in the fifteenth century, the Spanish economy was suffering and could not meet the new demands. Prices rose. Because the cost of manufacturing cloth and other goods increased, Spanish products could not compete in the international market with cheaper products made elsewhere. The textile industry was badly hurt. Prices spiraled upward, faster than the government could levy taxes to dampen the economy. (Higher taxes would have cut the public's buying power; with fewer goods sold, prices would have come down.)

Did the flood of American silver bullion cause the inflation? Prices rose most steeply before 1565, but bullion imports reached their peak between 1580 and 1620. Thus there is no direct correlation between silver imports and the inflation rate. Did the substantial population growth accelerate the inflation rate? Perhaps, since when the population pressure declined after 1600, prices gradually stabilized. One fact is certain: the price revolution severely strained government budgets. Several times between 1557 and 1647, Philip II and his successors repudiated the state debt, in turn undermining confidence in the government and leading the economy into shambles.

As Philip II paid his armies and foreign debts with silver bullion, the Spanish inflation was transmitted to the rest of Europe. Between 1560 and 1600, much of Europe experienced large price increases. Prices doubled and in some cases quadrupled. Spain suffered most severely, but all European countries were affected. People who lived on fixed incomes, such as the continental nobles, were badly hurt because their money bought less. Those who owed fixed sums of money, such as the middle class, prospered: in a time of rising prices, debts had less value each year. Food costs rose most sharply, and the poor fared worst of all.

Seaborne Trading Empires

By 1550, European overseas reconnaissance had led to the first global seaborne trade. For centuries the Muslims had conducted sophisticated commercial activities that spanned continents. Although they controlled the rich spice trade of the Indian Ocean, most Muslim expeditions had been

NORTH AMERICA

NEW SPAIN

Mexico City
Acapulco
Vera Cruz

FLORIDA

CUBA
HAITI

PUERTO RICO
CURAÇAO (Neth)

Cartagena
Panama

SPANISH MAIN
NEW GRANADA
GUIANA

Quito
PERU
Lima

SOUTH AMERICA

Santiago
Buenos Aires

BRAZIL
Bahia
Rio de Janeiro

Strait of Magellan
Cape Horn

PACIFIC OCEAN

ATLANTIC OCEAN

ARCTIC OCEAN

EUROPE

Amsterdam
NETHERLANDS

Madrid
SPAIN
Seville

PORTUGAL
Lisbon

Constantinople

Alexandria
Cairo

Mediterranean Sea

Red Sea

AFRICA

CAPE VERDE

GOLD COAST

Luanda
ANGOLA

Mombasa

Mozambique

Sofala

Cape Town
Cape of Good Hope

MADAGASCAR

MAURITIUS (Neth)

ASIA

PERSIA
ARABIA
Aden
Arabian Sea

INDIA
GUJARAT
Goa
COROMANDEL
Calcutta

CHINA
Canton
Macao

JAPAN
Nagasaki

Manila
PHILIPPINES

Malacca
SUMATRA
Sunda Strait
BORNEO
INDONESIA
JAVA
MOLUCCAS
NEW GUINEA

AUSTRALIA

INDIAN OCEAN

PACIFIC OCEAN

ATLANTIC OCEAN

Silk
Silver
Silk
Silver
Sugar
Slaves
Slaves
Slaves
Spices
Spices
Homeward Trade
Silk

Equator

0°

Portuguese control
Spanish control
Dutch control

Portuguese trade routes
Spanish trade routes
Dutch trade routes

0   1500   3000 Km.
0   1500   3000 Mi.

across Asian and African land routes. The Europeans' discovery of the Americas and their exploration of the Pacific for the first time linked the entire world by intercontinental seaborne trade. That trade brought into being three successive commercial empires: the Portuguese, the Spanish, and the Dutch.

In the sixteenth century, naval power and ship-borne artillery gave the Portuguese hegemony over the sea route to India. Their fleet brought spices to Lisbon, which the Portuguese paid for with textiles produced at Gujarat and Coromandel in India and with gold and ivory from East Africa. From their fortified bases at Goa on the Arabian Sea and at Malacca in the Malay Peninsula, ships of Malabar teak carried goods to the Portuguese settlement at Macao on the South China Sea. From Macao, loaded with Chinese silks and porcelains, Portuguese ships sailed to the Japanese port of Nagasaki and to the Philippine port of Manila, where Chinese goods were exchanged for Spanish (that is, Latin American) silver. Throughout Asia, the Portuguese traded in slaves—blacks from Africa, Chinese, and Japanese. The Portuguese imported to India horses from Mesopotamia and copper from Arabia; they exported from India hawks and peacocks for the Chinese and Japanese markets. Across the Atlantic, Portuguese Brazil provided most of the sugar consumed in Europe in the sixteenth and early seventeenth centuries. African slave labor produced the sugar on the plantations of Brazil, and Portuguese merchants, many of them Jewish, controlled both the slave trade between West Africa and Brazil (see pages 734–740) and the commerce in sugar between Brazil and Portugal. The Portuguese were the first worldwide traders, and Portuguese was the language of the Asian maritime trade (Map 18.2).

Spanish possessions in the New World constituted basically a land empire and, as already described, in the sixteenth century the Spaniards devised a method of governing that empire. But across the Pacific the Spaniards also built a sea-

MAP 18.2 Seaborne Trading Empires in the Sixteenth and Seventeenth Centuries In the sixteenth century, for the first time the entire globe was linked by seaborne trade. In the seventeenth century American silver paid for Asian silks and spices; African slaves in Latin America produced sugar for the tables of Europe.

borne empire, centered at Manila in the Philippines, which had been discovered by Magellan in 1563. Between 1564 and 1571, the Spanish navigator Miguel Lopez de Legazpi sailed from Mexico and through a swift and almost bloodless conquest took over the Philippine Islands. Legazpi founded Manila, which served as the trans-Pacific bridge between Spanish America and the extreme Eastern trade. Chinese silk, sold by the Portuguese in Manila for American silver, was transported to Acapulco in Mexico, from which it was carried overland to Vera Cruz for re-export to Spain. Because hostile Pacific winds prohibited direct passage from the Philippines to Peru, large shipments also went south from Acapulco to Peru (see Map 18.2). Spanish merchants could never satisfy the European demand for silk, which meant that huge amounts of bullion went from Acapulco to Manila. For example, in 1597, 12 million pesos of silver, almost the total value of the transatlantic trade, crossed the Pacific. After about 1640, the Spanish silk trade declined because it could not compete with Dutch imports.

In the latter half of the seventeenth century, the worldwide Dutch seaborne trade predominated. The Dutch Empire was built on spices. In 1599 a Dutch fleet returned to Amsterdam carrying 600,000 pounds of pepper and 250,000 pounds of cloves and nutmeg. Those who had invested in the expedition received a 100 percent profit. The voyage led to the establishment in 1602 of the Dutch East India Company, founded with the stated intention of capturing the spice trade from the Portuguese. The Dutch fleet, sailing from the Cape of Good Hope and avoiding the Portuguese forts in India, steered directly for the Sunda Strait in Indonesia. The Dutch wanted direct access to and control of the Indonesian sources of spices. In return for assisting Indonesian princes in local squabbles and disputes with the Portuguese, the Dutch won broad commercial concessions. Through agreements, seizures, and outright war, they gained control of the western access to the Indonesian archipelago. Gradually, they acquired political domination over the archipelago itself. Exchanging European manufactured goods— armor, firearms, linens, and toys—the Dutch soon had a monopoly on the very lucrative spice trade.[15]

The seaborne empires profited from the geographical reconnaissance and technological developments of the sixteenth century. The empires of

Portugal, Spain, and Holland had strong commercial ambitions. They also paved the way for the eighteenth-century mercantilist empires of France and Great Britain (see page 832).

The Chinese and Japanese Discovery of the West

The desire to Christianize pagan peoples was a major motive in Europeans' overseas expansion. The Indians of Central and South America, the Muslims and polytheistic peoples of the Pacific, and the Confucian, Buddhist, and Shinto peoples of China and Japan became objects of Christianizing efforts. In this missionary activity the new Jesuit Order was dominant and energetic.

In 1582 the Jesuit Matteo Ricci (1552–1610) settled at Macao on the mouth of the Canton River. Like the Christian monks who had converted the Germanic tribes of early medieval Europe (see page 236), Ricci sought first to convert the emperor and elite groups and then, through gradual assimilation, to win the throngs of Chinese. Ricci tried to present Christianity to the Chinese in Chinese terms. He understood the Chinese respect for learning and worked to win converts among the scholarly class. When Ricci was admitted to the Imperial City at Peking, he addressed the emperor Wan-li:

Li Ma-tou [Ricci's name transliterated into Chinese], your Majesty's servant, comes from the Far West, addresses himself to Your Majesty with respect, in order to offer gifts from his country. Your Majesty's servant comes from a far distant land which has never exchanged presents with the Middle Kingdom [the Chinese name for China, based on the belief that the Chinese empire occupied the middle of the earth and was surrounded by barbarians]. Despite the distance, fame told me of the remarkable teaching and fine institutions with which the imperial court has endowed all its peoples. I desired to share these advantages and live out my life as one of Your Majesty's subjects, hoping in return to be of some small use.[16]

Ricci presented the emperor with two clocks, one of them decorated with dragons and eagles in the Chinese style. The emperor's growing fascination with clocks gave Ricci the opportunity to display other examples of Western technology. He instructed court scholars about astronomical equipment and the manufacture of cannons and drew for them a map of the world—with China at its center. These inventions greatly impressed the Chinese intelligentsia. Over a century later a Jesuit wrote, "The Imperial Palace is stuffed with clocks . . . watches, carillons, repeaters, organs, spheres, and astronomical clocks of all kinds—there are more than four thousand pieces from the best masters of Paris and London."[17] The Chinese first learned about Europe from the Jesuits.

But the Christians and the Chinese did not understand one another. Because the Jesuits served the imperial court as mathematicians, astronomers, and cartographers, the Chinese emperors allowed them to remain in Peking. For the Jesuits, however, their service was only a means for converting the Chinese to Christianity. The missionaries thought that by showing the pre-eminence of Western science, they were demonstrating the superiority of Western religion. This was a relationship that the Chinese did not acknowledge. They could not accept a religion that required total commitment and taught the existence of an absolute. Only a small number of the highly educated, convinced of a link between ancient Chinese tradition and Christianity, became Christians. Most Chinese were hostile to the Western faith. They accused Christians of corrupting Chinese morals because they forbade people to honor their ancestors—and corruption of morals translated into disturbing the public order—of destroying Chinese sanctuaries, of revering a man (Christ) who had been executed as a public criminal, and of spying on behalf of the Japanese.

The "Rites Controversy," a dispute over ritual between the Jesuits and other Roman Catholic religious orders, sparked a crisis. The Jesuits supported the celebration of the Mass in Chinese and the performance of other ceremonies in terms understandable by the Chinese. The Franciscans and other missionaries felt that the Jesuits had sold out the essentials of the Christian faith in order to win converts. One burning issue was whether Chinese reverence for ancestors was homage to the good that the dead had done during their lives or an act of worship. The Franciscans secured the support of Roman authorities who considered themselves authorities on Chinese culture and decided against the Jesuits. In 1704 and again in 1742 Rome decreed that Roman ceremonial practice (that is, in Latin) was to be the law for Chinese missions. (This decision continued to govern Roman Catholic missionary activity until the Second Vatican Council in 1962.) Papal letters also forbade Chinese Christians from participating in the rites of ancestor worship. The emperor in turn banned Christianity in China, and the missionaries were forced to flee.

The Christian West and the Chinese world learned a great deal from each other. The Jesuits probably were "responsible for the rebirth of Chinese mathematics in the seventeenth and eighteenth centuries," and Western contributions stimulated the Chinese development of other sciences.[18] From the Chinese, Europeans got the idea of building bridges suspended by chains. The first Western experiments in electrostatics and magnetism in the seventeenth century derived from Chinese models. Travel accounts about Chinese society and customs had a profound impact on Europeans, making them more sensitive to the beautiful diversity of peoples and manners, as the essays of Montaigne (see pages 598–599) and other Western thinkers reveal.

Initial Japanese contacts with Europeans paralleled those of the Chinese. In 1542, Portuguese merchants arrived in Japan and quickly won large profits carrying goods between China and Japan. Dutch and English ships followed, also enjoying the rewards of the East Asian trade. The Portuguese merchants vigorously supported Christian missionary activity, and in 1547 the Jesuit missionary Saint Francis Xavier landed at Kagoshima, preached widely, and in two short years won many converts. From the beginning, however, the Japanese government feared that native converts might have conflicting political loyalties. Divided allegiance could encourage European invasion of the islands—the Japanese authorities had the example of the Philippines, where Spanish conquest followed missionary activity.

Convinced that European merchants and missionaries had contributed to the general civil disorder, which the regime was trying to eradicate, the Japanese government decided to expel the Spanish and Portuguese, to destroy every trace of Christianity, and to close Japan to all foreign influence. A decree of 1635 was directed at the commissioners of the port of Nagasaki, a center of Japanese Christianity:

If there is any place where the teachings of the padres (Catholic priests) is practiced, the two of you must order a thorough investigation. . . .

If there are any Southern Barbarians (Westerners) who propagate the teachings of the padres, or otherwise commit crimes, they may be incarcerated in the prison. . . .[19]

In 1639, an imperial memorandum decreed: "hereafter entry by the Portuguese galeota (galleon or large ocean going warship) is forbidden. If they insist on coming (to Japan), the ships must be destroyed and anyone aboard those ships must be beheaded. . . ."[20]

When tens of thousands of Japanese Christians made a stand on the peninsula of Shimabara, the Dutch lent the Japanese government cannon. As Protestants, the Dutch hated Catholicism, and as businessmen they hated Portuguese, their great commercial rivals. Thus convinced that the Dutch had come only for trade and did not want to proselytize, the imperial government allowed the Dutch to remain. But Japanese authorities ordered them to remove their factory-station from Hirado on the western tip of Kyushu to the tiny island of Deshima, which covered just 2,100 square feet. The government limited Dutch trade to one ship a year, watched the Dutch very closely, and required Dutch officials to pay an annual visit to the capital to renew their loyalty. The Japanese also compelled the Dutch merchants to perform servile acts that other Europeans considered humiliating.

Long after Christianity ceased to be a potential threat to the Japanese government, the fear of Christianity sustained a policy of banning all Western books on science or religion. Until well into the eighteenth century, Japanese intellectuals were effectively cut off from Western developments. The Japanese view of Westerners was not high. What little the Japanese knew derived from the few Dutch businessmen at Deshima. Very few Japanese people ever saw Europeans. If they did, they considered them "a special variety of goblin that bore only a superficial resemblance to a normal human being." The widespread rumor was that when Dutchmen urinated they raised one leg like dogs.[21]

POLITICS, RELIGION, AND WAR

In 1559 France and Spain signed the Treaty of Cateau-Cambrésis, which ended the Habsburg-Valois Wars. This event marks a watershed in early modern European history. Spain was the victor. France, exhausted by the struggle, had to acknowledge Spanish dominance in Italy, where much of the war had been fought. Spanish governors ruled in Sicily, Naples, and Milan, and Spanish influence was strong in the Papal States and Tuscany.

Emperor Charles V had divided his attention between the Holy Roman Empire and Spain. Under his son Philip II (r. 1556–1598), however, the center of the Habsburg Empire and the political center of gravity for all of Europe shifted westward to Spain. Before 1559, Spain and France had fought bitterly for control of Italy; after 1559, the two Catholic powers aimed their guns at Protestantism. The Treaty of Cateau-Cambrésis ended an era of strictly dynastic wars and initiated a period of conflicts in which politics and religion played the dominant roles.

Because a variety of issues were stewing, it is not easy to generalize about the wars of the late sixteenth century. Some were continuations of struggles between the centralizing goals of monarchies and the feudal reactions of nobilities. Some were crusading battles between Catholics and Protestants. Some were struggles for national independence or for international expansion.

These wars differed considerably from earlier wars. Sixteenth- and seventeenth-century armies were bigger than medieval ones; some forces numbered as many as fifty thousand men. Because large armies were expensive, governments had to reorganize their administrations to finance them. The use of gunpowder altered both the nature of war and popular attitudes toward it. Guns and cannon killed and wounded from a distance, indiscriminately. Gunpowder weakened the notion, common during the Hundred Years' War, that warfare was an ennobling experience. Governments had to utilize propaganda, pulpits, and the printing press to arouse public opinion to support war.[22]

Late-sixteenth-century conflicts fundamentally tested the medieval ideal of a unified Christian society governed by one political ruler, the emperor, to whom all rulers were theoretically subordinate, and one church, to which all people belonged. The Protestant Reformation had killed this ideal, but few people recognized it as dead. Catholics continued to believe that Calvinists and Lutherans could be reconverted. Protestants persisted in thinking that the Roman church should be destroyed. Most people believed that a state could survive only if its

members shared the same faith. Catholics and Protestants alike feared people of the other faith living in their midst. The settlement finally achieved in 1648, known as the "Peace of Westphalia," signaled acknowledgment of the end of the medieval ideal.

The Origins of Difficulties in France (1515–1559)

In the first half of the sixteenth century, France continued the recovery begun under Louis XI (see page 529). The population losses caused by the plague and the disorders accompanying the Hundred Years' War had created such a labor shortage that serfdom virtually disappeared. Cash rents replaced feudal rents and servile obligations. This development clearly benefited the peasantry. Meanwhile, the declining buying power of money hurt the nobility. The steadily increasing French population brought new lands under cultivation, but the division of property among sons meant that most peasant holdings were very small. Domestic and foreign trade picked up; mercantile centers such as Rouen and Lyon expanded; and in 1517 a new port city was founded at Le Havre.

The charming and cultivated Francis I (r. 1515–1547) and his athletic, emotional son Henry II (r. 1547–1559) governed through a small, efficient council. Great nobles held titular authority in the provinces as governors, but Paris-appointed baillis and seneschals continued to exercise actual fiscal and judicial responsibility (see page 407). In 1539 Francis issued an ordinance that placed the whole of France under the jurisdiction of the royal law courts and made French the language of those courts. This act had a powerful centralizing impact. The taille land tax provided what strength the monarchy had and supported a strong standing army. Unfortunately, the tax base was too narrow for France's extravagant promotion of the arts and ambitious foreign policy.

Deliberately imitating the Italian Renaissance princes, the Valois monarchs lavished money on a magnificent court, a vast building program, and Italian artists. Francis I commissioned the Paris architect Pierre Lescot to rebuild the palace of the Louvre. Francis secured the services of Michelangelo's star pupil, Il Rosso, who decorated the wing of the Fontainebleau chateau, subsequently called

Rossi and Primaticcio: The Gallery of Francis I   Flat paintings alternating with rich sculpture provide a rhythm that directs the eye down the long gallery at Fontainebleau, constructed between 1530 and 1540. Francis I sought to re-create in France the elegant Renaissance lifestyle found in Italy. *(Source: Art Resource)*

the "Gallery Francis I," with rich scenes of classical and mythological literature. After acquiring Leonardo da Vinci's *Mona Lisa,* Francis brought Leonardo himself to France, where he soon died. Henry II built a castle at Dreux for his mistress, Diana de Poitiers, and a palace in Paris, the Tuileries, for his wife, Catherine de' Medici. Art historians credit Francis I and Henry II with importing Italian Renaissance art and architecture to France. Whatever praise these monarchs deserve for their cultural achievement, they spent far more than they could afford.

The Habsburg-Valois Wars, waged intermittently through the first half of the sixteenth century, also cost more than the government could afford. Financing the war posed problems. In addition to the time-honored practices of increasing taxes and heavy borrowing, Francis I tried two new devices to raise revenue: the sale of public

offices and a treaty with the papacy. The former proved to be only a temporary source of money. The offices sold tended to become hereditary within a family, and once a man bought an office he and his heirs were exempt from taxes. The sale of public offices thus created a tax-exempt class called the "nobility of the robe," whose members were beyond the jurisdiction of the Crown.

The treaty with the papacy was the Concordat of Bologna (1516), which in effect rescinded the Pragmatic Sanction of Bourges (see page 529). In it Francis agreed to recognize the supremacy of the papacy over a universal council. In return, the French crown gained the right to appoint all French bishops and abbots. This understanding gave the monarchy a rich supplement of money and offices and power over the church that lasted until the Revolution of 1789. The Concordat of Bologna helps to explain why France did not later

Triple Profile Portrait This portrait from the late sixteenth century exemplifies the very high finish and mannered sophistication of the School of Fontainebleau. These courtiers served Henry III, one of the weak sons of Henry II. *(Source: Milwaukee Art Museum, Gift of Women's Exchange)*

become Protestant: in effect, the concordat established Catholicism as the state religion. Because French rulers possessed control over appointments and had a vested financial interest in Catholicism, they had no need to revolt from Rome.

However, the Concordat of Bologna perpetuated disorders within the French church. Ecclesiastical offices were used primarily to pay and reward civil servants. Churchmen in France, as elsewhere, were promoted to the hierarchy not because of any special spiritual qualifications but because of their services to the state. Such bishops were unlikely to work to elevate the intellectual and moral standards of the parish clergy. Few of the many priests in France devoted scrupulous attention to the needs of their parishioners. The teachings of Luther and Calvin found a receptive audience.

Luther's tracts first appeared in France in 1518, and his ideas attracted some attention. After the publication of Calvin's *Institutes* in 1536, sizable numbers of French people were attracted to the "reformed religion," as Calvinism was called. Be-

cause Calvin wrote in French rather than Latin, his ideas gained wide circulation. Initially, Calvinism drew converts from among reform-minded members of the Catholic clergy, the industrious middle classes, and artisan groups. Most Calvinists lived in major cities, such as Paris, Lyon, Meaux, and Grenoble.

In spite of condemnation by the universities, government bans, and massive burnings at the stake, the numbers of Protestants grew steadily. When Henry II died in 1559, there were 40 well-organized churches and 2,150 mission churches in France. Perhaps one-tenth of the population had become Calvinist (see Map 17.4).

Religious Riots and Civil War in France (1559–1589)

For thirty years, from 1559 to 1589, violence and civil war divided and shattered France. The feebleness of the monarchy was the seed from which the weeds of civil violence germinated. The three weak sons of Henry II who occupied the throne could not provide the necessary leadership. Francis II (r. 1559–1560) died after seventeen months. Charles IX (r. 1560–1574) succeeded at the age of ten and was thoroughly dominated by his opportunistic mother, Catherine de' Medici, who would support any party or position to maintain her influence. The intelligent and cultivated Henry III (r. 1574–1589) divided his attention between debaucheries with his male lovers and frantic acts of repentance.

The French nobility took advantage of this monarchial weakness. In the second half of the sixteenth century, between two-fifths and one-half of the nobility at one time or another became Calvinist. Just as German princes in the Holy Roman Empire had adopted Lutheranism as a means of opposition to the emperor Charles V, so French nobles frequently adopted the "reformed religion" as a religious cloak for their independence. No one believed that peoples of different faiths could coexist peacefully within the same territory. The Reformation thus led to a resurgence of feudal disorder. Armed clashes between Calvinist antimonarchial lords and Catholic royalist lords occurred in many parts of France.

Among the upper classes the Calvinist-Catholic conflict was the surface issue, but the fundamental object of the struggle was power. Working-class

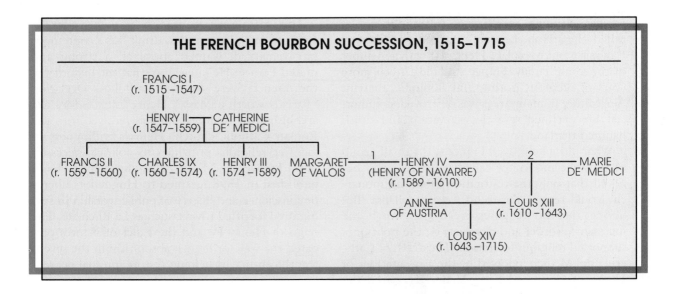

THE FRENCH BOURBON SUCCESSION, 1515–1715

FRANCIS I
(r. 1515 –1547)

HENRY II — CATHERINE
(r. 1547–1559) | DE' MEDICI

FRANCIS II | CHARLES IX | HENRY III | MARGARET | 1 — HENRY IV — 2 — MARIE
(r. 1559 –1560) | (r. 1560 –1574) | (r. 1574 –1589) | OF VALOIS | (HENRY OF NAVARRE) | DE' MEDICI
| | | | (r. 1589 –1610) |

ANNE — LOUIS XIII
OF AUSTRIA | (r. 1610 –1643)

LOUIS XIV
(r. 1643 –1715)

crowds composed of skilled craftsmen and the poor wreaked terrible violence on people and property. Both Calvinists and Catholics believed that the others' books, services, and ministers polluted the community. Preachers incited violence, and ceremonies (baptisms, marriages, funerals) triggered it. Protestant pastors encouraged their followers to destroy statues and liturgical objects in Catholic churches. Catholic priests urged their flocks to shed the blood of the Calvinist heretics.

In 1561 in the Paris church of Saint-Médard, a Protestant crowd cornered a baker guarding a box containing the consecrated Eucharistic bread. Taunting "Does your God of paste protect you now from the pains of death?" the mob proceeded to kill the poor man.[23] Calvinists believed that the Catholics' emphasis on symbols in their ritual desecrated what was truly sacred and promoted the worship of images. In scores of attacks on Catholic churches, religious statues were knocked down, stained-glass windows smashed, and sacred vestments, vessels, and Eucharistic elements defiled. In 1561 a Catholic crowd charged a group of just-released Protestant prisoners, killed them, and burned their bodies in the street. Hundreds of Huguenots, as French Calvinists were called, were tortured, had their tongues or throats slit, were maimed or murdered.

In the fourteenth and fifteenth centuries, crowd action—attacks on great nobles and rich prelates—had expressed economic grievances. Religious rioters of the sixteenth century believed that they could assume the power of public magistrates and rid the community of corruption. Municipal officials criticized the crowds' actions, but the participation of pastors and priests in these riots lent them some legitimacy.[24]

A savage Catholic attack on Calvinists in Paris on August 24, 1572 (Saint Bartholomew's Day), followed the usual pattern. The occasion was a religious ceremony, the marriage of the king's sister Margaret of Valois to the Protestant Henry of Navarre, which was intended to help reconcile Catholics and Huguenots. Among the many Calvinists present for the wedding festivities was the admiral of Coligny, head of one of the great noble families of France and leader of the Huguenot party. Coligny had recently replaced Catherine de' Medici in influence over the young king Charles IX. The night before the wedding, Henry of Guise, the leader of the Catholic aristocracy, had Coligny murdered. Rioting and slaughter then followed. Huguenot gentry in Paris were massacred, and religious violence spread to the provinces. Between August 25 and October 3, perhaps twelve thousand Huguenots perished at Meaux, Lyon, Orléans, and Paris. The contradictory orders of the unstable Charles IX worsened the situation.

The Saint Bartholomew's Day Massacre led to fighting that launched the "War of the Three Henrys," a civil conflict among factions led by the Catholic Henry of Guise, the Protestant Henry of Navarre, and King Henry III, who succeeded the tubercular Charles IX. Though he remained Catholic, King Henry realized that the Catholic Guise group represented his greatest danger. The Guises wanted, through an alliance of Catholic nobles called the "Holy League," not only to destroy Calvinism but to replace Henry III with a member of the Guise family. France suffered fifteen more years of religious rioting and domestic anarchy. Agriculture in many areas was destroyed; commercial life declined severely; starvation and death haunted the land.

What ultimately saved France was a small group of Catholic moderates called *politiques,* who believed that only the restoration of strong monarchy could reverse the trend toward collapse. Believing that no religious creed was worth the incessant disorder and destruction, the politiques supported religious toleration. The death of Catherine de' Medici, followed by the assassinations of Henry of Guise and King Henry III, paved the way for the accession of Henry of Navarre, a politique who became Henry IV (r. 1589–1610).

This glamorous prince, "who knew how to fight, to make love, and to drink," as a contemporary remarked, wanted above all a strong and united France. He knew, too, that the majority of the French were Roman Catholics. Declaring "Paris is worth a Mass," Henry knelt before the archbishop of Bourges and was received into the Roman Catholic church. Henry's willingness to sacrifice religious principles to political necessity saved France. The Edict of Nantes, which Henry published in 1598, granted to Huguenots liberty of conscience and liberty of public worship in two hundred fortified towns, such as La Rochelle. The reign of Henry IV and the Edict of Nantes prepared the way for French absolutism in the seventeenth century by helping restore internal peace.

The Netherlands Under Charles V

In the last quarter of the sixteenth century, the political stability of England, the international prestige of Spain, and the moral influence of the Roman papacy all became mixed up with the religious crisis in the Low Countries. The Netherlands was the pivot around which European money, diplomacy, and war revolved. What began as a movement for church reformation developed into a struggle for Dutch independence.

The emperor Charles V (r. 1519–1556) had inherited the seventeen provinces that compose present-day Belgium and Holland (Map 18.3). Ideally situated for commerce between the Rhine and Scheldt rivers, the great towns of Bruges, Ghent, Brussels, Arras, and Amsterdam made their living by trade and industry. The French-speaking southern towns produced fine linens and woolens; the wealth of the Dutch-speaking northern cities rested on fishing, shipping, and international banking. The city of Antwerp was the largest port and the greatest money market in Europe. In the cities of the Low Countries, trade and commerce had produced a vibrant cosmopolitan atmosphere, which was well personified by the urbane Erasmus of Rotterdam (see page 525).

Each of the seventeen provinces of the Netherlands possessed historical liberties: each was self-governing and enjoyed the right to make its own laws and collect its own taxes. Only the recognition of a common ruler in the person of the emperor Charles V united the provinces. Delegates from each province met together in the Estates

MAP 18.3 The Netherlands, 1578–1609   Though small in geographical size, the Netherlands held a strategic position in the religious struggles of the sixteenth century.

General, but important decisions had to be referred back to each province for approval. In the middle of the sixteenth century, the provinces of the Netherlands had a limited sense of federation.

In the Low Countries, as elsewhere, corruption in the Roman church and the critical spirit of the Renaissance provoked pressure for reform. Lutheran tracts and Dutch translations of the Bible flooded the seventeen provinces in the 1520s and 1530s, attracting many people to Protestantism. Charles V's government responded with condemnation and mild repression. This policy was not particularly effective, however, because ideas circulated freely in the cosmopolitan atmosphere of the commercial centers. But Charles's Flemish loyalty checked the spread of Lutheranism. Charles had been born in Ghent and raised in the Netherlands; he was Flemish in language and culture. He identified with the Flemish and they with him.

In 1556, however, Charles V abdicated, dividing his territories between his brother Ferdinand, who received Austria and the Holy Roman Empire, and his son Philip, who inherited Spain, the Low Countries, Milan and the kingdom of Sicily, and the Spanish possessions in America. Charles delivered his abdication speech before the Estates General at Brussels. The emperor was then fifty-five years old, white haired, and so crippled in the legs that he had to lean for support on the young Prince William of Orange. According to one contemporary account of the emperor's appearance:

His under lip, a Burgundian inheritance, as faithfully transmitted as the duchy and county, was heavy and hanging, the lower jaw protruding so far beyond the upper that it was impossible for him to bring together the few fragments of teeth which still remained, or to speak a whole sentence in an intelligible voice.[25]

Charles spoke in Flemish. His small, shy, and sepulchral son Philip responded in Spanish; he could speak neither French nor Flemish. The Netherlanders had always felt Charles one of themselves. They were never to forget that Philip was a Spaniard.

The Revolt of the Netherlands (1566–1587)

By the 1560s, there was a strong, militant minority of Calvinists in most of the cities of the Netherlands. The seventeen provinces possessed a large middle-class population, and the "reformed religion," as a contemporary remarked, had a powerful appeal "to those who had grown rich by trade and were therefore ready for revolution."[26] Calvinism appealed to the middle classes because of its intellectual seriousness, moral gravity, and emphasis on any form of labor well done. It took deep root among the merchants and financiers in Amsterdam and the northern provinces. Working-class people were also converted, partly because their employers would hire only fellow Calvinists. Well organized and with the backing of wealthy merchants, Calvinists quickly gained a wide following. Lutherans taught respect for the powers that be. The reformed religion, however, tended to encourage opposition to "illegal" civil authorities.

In 1559 Philip II appointed his half-sister Margaret as regent of the Netherlands (1559–1567). A proud, energetic, and strong-willed woman, who once had Ignatius Loyola as her confessor, Margaret pushed Philip's orders to wipe out Protestantism. She introduced the Inquisition. Her more immediate problem, however, was revenue to finance the government of the provinces. Charles V had steadily increased taxes in the Low Countries. When Margaret appealed to the Estates General, they claimed that the Low Countries were more heavily taxed than Spain. Nevertheless, Margaret raised taxes. In so doing, she quickly succeeded in uniting opposition to the government's fiscal policy with opposition to official repression of Calvinism.

In August 1566, a year of very high grain prices, fanatical Calvinists, primarily of the poorest classes, embarked on a rampage of frightful destruction. As in France, Calvinist destruction in the Low Countries was incited by popular preaching, and attacks were aimed at religious images as symbols of false doctrines, not at people. The cathedral of Notre Dame at Antwerp was the first target. Begun in 1124 and finished only in 1518, this church stood as a monument to the commercial prosperity of Flanders, the piety of the business classes, and the artistic genius of centuries. On six successive summer evenings, crowds swept through the nave. While the town harlots held tapers to the greatest concentration of art works in northern Europe, people armed with axes and sledgehammers smashed altars, statues, paintings, books, tombs, ecclesiastical vestments, missals, manuscripts, ornaments, stained-glass windows,

To Purify the Church   The destruction of pictures and statues representing biblical events, Christian doctrine, or sacred figures was a central feature of the Protestant Reformation. Here Dutch Protestant soldiers destroy what they consider idols in the belief that they are purifying the church. *(Source: Fotomas Index)*

and sculptures. Before the havoc was over, thirty more churches had been sacked and irreplaceable libraries burned. From Antwerp the destruction spread to Brussels and Ghent and north to the provinces of Holland and Zeeland.

From Madrid, Philip II sent twenty thousand Spanish troops under the duke of Alva to pacify the Low Countries. To Alva, "pacification" meant the ruthless extermination of religious and political dissidents. On top of the Inquisition he opened his own tribunal, soon called the "Council of Blood." On March 3, 1568, fifteen hundred men were executed. Alva resolved the financial crisis by levying a 10 percent sales tax on every transaction. In the commercial Dutch society, this tax caused widespread hardship and confusion.

For ten years, between 1568 and 1578, civil war raged in the Netherlands between Catholics and Protestants and between the seventeen provinces

and Spain. A series of Spanish generals could not halt the fighting. In 1576 the seventeen provinces united under the leadership of Prince William of Orange, called "the Silent" because of his remarkable discretion. In 1578 Philip II sent his nephew Alexander Farnese, duke of Parma, to crush the revolt once and for all. A general with a superb sense of timing, an excellent knowledge of the geography of the Low Countries, and a perfect plan, Farnese arrived with an army of German mercenaries. Avoiding pitched battles, he fought by patient sieges. One by one the cities of the south fell— Maastricht, Tournai, Bruges, Ghent, and finally the financial capital of northern Europe, Antwerp. Calvinism was forbidden in these territories, and Protestants were compelled to convert or leave. The collapse of Antwerp marked the farthest extent of Spanish jurisdiction and ultimately the religious division of the Netherlands.

The ten southern provinces, the Spanish Netherlands (the future Belgium), remained under the control of the Spanish Habsburgs. The seven northern provinces, led by Holland, formed the Union of Utrecht and in 1581 declared their independence from Spain. Thus was born the United Provinces of the Netherlands (see Map 18.3).

Geography and sociopolitical structure differentiated the two countries. The northern provinces were ribboned with sluices and canals and therefore were highly defensible. Several times the Dutch had broken the dikes and flooded the countryside to halt the advancing Farnese. In the southern provinces the Ardennes Mountains interrupt the otherwise flat terrain. In the north the commercial aristocracy possessed the predominant power; in the south the landed nobility had the greater influence. The north was Protestant; the south remained Catholic.

Philip II and Alexander Farnese did not accept this geographical division, and the struggle continued after 1581. The United Provinces repeatedly begged the Protestant queen Elizabeth of England for assistance.

The crown on the head of Elizabeth I (r. 1558–1603) did not rest easily. She had steered a moderately Protestant course between the Puritans, who sought the total elimination of Roman Catholic elements in the English church, and the Roman Catholics, who wanted full restoration of the old religion (see page 553). Elizabeth survived a massive uprising by the Catholic north in 1569 to 1570. She survived two serious plots against her life. In the 1570s the presence in England of Mary, Queen of Scots, a Roman Catholic and the legal heir to the English throne, produced a very embarrassing situation. Mary was the rallying point of all opposition to Elizabeth, yet the English sovereign hesitated to set the terrible example of regicide by ordering Mary executed.

Elizabeth faced a grave dilemma. If she responded favorably to Dutch pleas for military support against the Spanish, she would antagonize Philip II. The Spanish king had the steady flow of silver from the Americas at his disposal, and Elizabeth, lacking such treasure, wanted to avoid war. But if she did not help the Protestant Netherlands and they were crushed by Farnese, the likelihood was that the Spanish would invade England.

Three developments forced Elizabeth's hand. First, the wars in the Low Countries—the chief market for English woolens—badly hurt the English economy. When wool was not exported, the Crown lost valuable customs revenues. Second, the murder of William the Silent in July 1584 eliminated not only a great Protestant leader but the chief military check on the Farnese advance. Third, the collapse of Antwerp appeared to signal a Catholic sweep through the Netherlands. The next step, the English feared, would be a Spanish invasion of their island. For these reasons, Elizabeth pumped £250,000 and two thousand troops into the Protestant cause in the Low Countries between 1585 and 1587. Increasingly fearful of the plots of Mary, Queen of Scots, Elizabeth finally signed her death warrant. Mary was beheaded on February 18, 1587. Sometime between March 24 and 30, the news of her death reached Philip II.

Philip II and the Spanish Armada

Philip pondered the Dutch and English developments at the Escorial northwest of Madrid. Begun in 1563 and completed under the king's personal supervision in 1584, the monastery of Saint Lawrence of the Escorial served as a monastery for Jeromite monks, a tomb for the king's Habsburg ancestors, and a royal palace for Philip and his family. The vast buildings resemble a gridiron, the instrument on which Saint Lawrence (d. 258) had supposedly been roasted alive. The royal apartments were in the center of the Italian Renaissance building complex. King Philip's tiny bedchamber possessed a concealed sliding window that opened directly onto the high altar of the monastery church so he could watch the services and pray along with the monks. In this somber atmosphere, surrounded by a community of monks and close to the bones of his ancestors, the Catholic ruler of Spain and much of the globe passed his days.

Philip of Spain considered himself the international defender of Catholicism and the heir to the medieval imperial power. Hoping to keep England within the Catholic church when his wife Mary Tudor died, Philip had asked Elizabeth to marry him. She had emphatically refused. Several popes had urged him to move against England. When Pope Sixtus V (r. 1585–1590) heard of the death of the queen of Scots, he promised to pay Philip one million gold ducats the moment Spanish troops landed in England. Alexander Farnese had repeatedly warned that to subdue the Dutch, he would have to conquer England and cut off the source of Dutch support. Philip worried that the vast amounts of South American silver that he was pouring into the conquest of the Netherlands seemed to be going into a bottomless pit. Two plans for an expedition were considered. Philip's naval adviser recommended that a fleet of 150 ships sail from Lisbon, attack the English navy in the Channel, and invade England. Another proposal was to assemble a collection of barges and troops in Flanders to stage a cross-Channel assault. With the expected support of English Catholics, Spain would achieve a great victory. Farnese opposed the latter plan as militarily unsound.

Philip compromised. He prepared a vast armada to sail from Lisbon to Flanders, fight off Elizabeth's navy if it attacked, rendezvous with Farnese, and escort his barges across the English Channel. The expedition's purpose was to transport the Flemish army to England.

On May 9, 1588, *la felicissima armada*—"the most fortunate fleet," as it was called in official documents—sailed from Lisbon harbor on the last

medieval crusade. The Spanish fleet of 130 vessels carried 123,790 cannon balls and perhaps 30,000 men, every one of whom had confessed his sins and received the Eucharist. An English fleet of about 150 ships met the Spanish in the Channel. It was composed of smaller, faster, more maneuverable ships, many of which had greater firing power. A combination of storms and squalls, spoiled food and rank water, inadequate Spanish ammunition, and, to a lesser extent, English fire ships that caused the Spanish to panic and scatter gave England the victory. Many Spanish ships went to the bottom of the ocean; perhaps 65 managed to crawl home by way of the North Sea.

The battle in the Channel has frequently been described as one of the decisive battles in world history. In fact, it had mixed consequences. Spain soon rebuilt its navy, and the quality of the Spanish fleet improved. The destruction of the armada did not halt the flow of silver from the New World. More silver reached Spain between 1588 and 1603 than in any other fifteen-year period.

Defeat of the Spanish Armada   The crescent-shaped Spanish formation was designed to force the English to fight at close quarters—by ramming and boarding. When the English sent burning ships against the Spaniards, the crescent broke up, the English pounced on individual ships, and an Atlantic gale swept the Spaniards into the North Sea, finishing the work of destruction. *(Source: National Maritime Museum, London)*

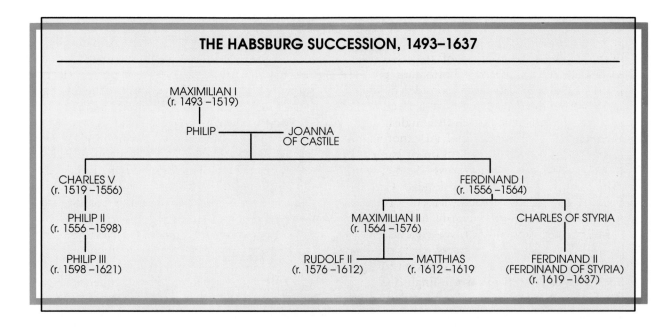

THE HABSBURG SUCCESSION, 1493–1637

MAXIMILIAN I
(r. 1493–1519)

PHILIP ———— JOANNA
OF CASTILE

CHARLES V
(r. 1519–1556)

FERDINAND I
(r. 1556–1564)

PHILIP II
(r. 1556–1598)

MAXIMILIAN II
(r. 1564–1576)

CHARLES OF STYRIA

PHILIP III
(r. 1598–1621)

RUDOLF II ———— MATTHIAS
(r. 1576–1612)   (r. 1612–1619)

FERDINAND II
(FERDINAND OF STYRIA)
(r. 1619–1637)

The war between England and Spain dragged on for years.

The defeat of the Spanish Armada was decisive, however, in the sense that it prevented Philip II from reimposing unity on western Europe by force. He did not conquer England, and Elizabeth continued her financial and military support of the Dutch. In the Netherlands, however, neither side gained significant territory. The borders of 1581 tended to become permanent. In 1609 Philip III of Spain (r. 1598–1621) agreed to a truce, in effect recognizing the independence of the United Provinces. In seventeenth-century Spain memory of the defeat of the armada contributed to a spirit of defeatism.

The Thirty Years' War (1618–1648)

While Philip II dreamed of building a second armada and Henry IV began the reconstruction of France, the political-religious situation in central Europe deteriorated. An uneasy truce had prevailed in the Holy Roman Empire since the Peace of Augsburg of 1555 (see page 545). The Augsburg settlement, in recognizing the independent power of the German princes, had destroyed the authority of the central government. The Habsburg ruler in Vienna enjoyed the title "emperor" but had no power.

According to the Augsburg settlement, the faith of the prince determined the religion of his subjects. Later in the century, though, Catholics grew alarmed because Lutherans, in violation of the Peace of Augsburg, were steadily acquiring north German bishoprics. The spread of Calvinism further confused the issue. The Augsburg settlement had pertained only to Lutheranism and Catholicism, but Calvinists ignored it and converted several princes. Lutherans feared that the Augsburg principles would be totally undermined by Catholic and Calvinist gains. Also, the militantly active Jesuits had reconverted several Lutheran princes to Catholicism. In an increasingly tense situation, Lutheran princes formed the Protestant Union (1608), and Catholics retaliated with the Catholic League (1609). Each alliance was determined that the other should make no religious (that is, territorial) advance. The empire was composed of two armed camps.

Dynastic interests were also involved in the German situation. When Charles V abdicated in 1556, he had divided his possessions between his son Philip II and his brother Ferdinand I. This partition began the Austrian and Spanish branches of the Habsburg family. Ferdinand inherited the imperial title and the Habsburg lands in central Europe, including Austria. Ferdinand's grandson Matthias had no direct heirs and promoted the candidacy of his fiercely Catholic cousin,

RUSSIA

FINLAND

ESTONIA

LIVONIA

SWEDEN

NORWAY

Vilna

POLAND

Warsaw

PRUSSIA

Danzig

Baltic Sea

Copenhagen

DENMARK

JUTLAND

SCHLESWIG

Lübeck

Hamburg

Bremen

POMERANIA

MECKLENBURG

BRANDENBURG

Berlin

SILESIA

White Mountain 1620

Prague

BOHEMIA

MORAVIA

Vienna

STYRIA

CARNIOLA

MOLDAVIA

TRANSYLVANIA

WALLACHIA

CRIMEA

Black Sea

Constantinople

OTTOMAN EMPIRE

Athens

CRETE
(To Rep. of Venice)

Belgrade

Buda

Pest

Danube

Breitenfeld

1631

SAXONY

Lützen 1632

Magdeburg

Münster

Osnabrück

Essen

Cologne

Nördlingen 1634

Augsburg

BAVARIA

Rhine

Elbe

REPUBLIC OF VENICE

FLORENCE

PAPAL STATES

Rome

Naples

NAPLES

Palermo

SICILY

Mediterranean Sea

GENOA

MILAN

PIEDMONT

SAVOY

Geneva

SWITZERLAND

Zurich

ALSACE

FRANCHE-COMTÉ

Metz

Paris

FRANCE

Loire

Nantes

SPANISH NETHERLANDS

Antwerp

UNITED NETHERLANDS

Amsterdam

North Sea

ENGLAND

London

Edinburgh

SCOTLAND

IRELAND

Dublin

ATLANTIC OCEAN

SPAIN

Madrid

Ebro

Tagus

PORTUGAL

Lisbon

CORSICA
(To Genoa)

SARDINIA

BALEARIC IS.

Dnieper

Dniester

Vistula

Austrian Habsburg lands

Spanish Habsburg lands

Prussian lands

German states

Swedish lands

Boundary of Holy Roman Empire

Major battles

0   150   300 Mi.

0   150   300 Km.

Ferdinand of Styria for the imperial crown. The Spanish Habsburgs strongly supported the goals of their Austrian relatives: the unity of the empire and the preservation of Catholicism within it.

In 1617 Ferdinand of Styria secured election as king of Bohemia, a title that gave him jurisdiction over Silesia and Moravia as well as Bohemia. The Bohemians were Czech and German in nationality and Lutheran, Calvinist, Catholic, and Hussite in religion; all these faiths enjoyed a fair degree of religious freedom. When Ferdinand proceeded to close some Protestant churches, the heavily Protestant Estates of Bohemia protested. On May 23, 1618, Protestants hurled two of Ferdinand's officials from a castle window in Prague. They fell seventy feet but survived. Catholics claimed that angels had caught them; Protestants said the officials fell on a heap of soft horse manure. Called the "defenestration of Prague," this event marked the beginning of the Thirty Years' War (1618–1648).

Historians traditionally divide the war into four phases. The first, or Bohemian, phase (1618–1625) was characterized by civil war in Bohemia between the Catholic League, led by Ferdinand, and the Protestant Union, headed by Prince Frederick of the Palatinate. The Bohemians fought for religious liberty and independence from Habsburg rule. In 1618 the Bohemian Estates deposed Ferdinand and gave the crown of Bohemia to Frederick, thus uniting the interests of German Protestants with those of the international enemies of the Habsburgs. Frederick wore his crown only a few months. In 1620 he was totally defeated by Catholic forces at the Battle of the White Mountain (Map 18.4). Ferdinand, who had recently been elected Holy Roman emperor as Ferdinand II, followed up his victories by wiping out Protestantism in Bohemia through forcible conversions and the activities of militant Jesuit missionaries. Within ten years, Bohemia was completely Catholic.

The second, or Danish, phase of the war (1625–1629)—so called because of the participation of King Christian IV of Denmark (r. 1588–1648), the ineffective leader of the Protes-

MAP 18.4 Europe in 1648 Which country emerged from the Thirty Years' War as the strongest European power? What dynastic house was that country's major rival in the early modern period?

tant cause—witnessed additional Catholic victories. The Catholic imperial army led by Albert of Wallenstein scored smashing victories. It swept through Silesia, north through Schleswig and Jutland to the Baltic Sea, and east into Pomerania. Wallenstein had made himself indispensable to the emperor Ferdinand, but he was an unscrupulous opportunist who used his vast riches to build an army loyal only to himself. The general seemed interested more in carving out an empire for himself than in aiding the Catholic cause. He quarreled with the league, and soon the Catholic forces were divided. Religion was eclipsed as a basic issue of the war.

The year 1629 marked the peak of Habsburg power. The Jesuits persuaded the emperor to issue the Edict of Restitution, whereby all Catholic properties lost to Protestantism since 1552 were to be restored and only Catholics and Lutherans (not Calvinists, Hussites, or other sects) were to be allowed to practice their faiths. Ferdinand appeared to be embarked on a policy to unify the empire. When Wallenstein began ruthless enforcement of the edict, Protestants throughout Europe feared collapse of the balance of power in the north central region.

The third, or Swedish, phase of the war (1630–1635) began with the arrival in Germany of the Swedish king Gustavus Adolphus (r. 1594–1632). The ablest administrator of his day and a devout Lutheran, Gustavus Adolphus intervened to support the oppressed Protestants within the empire and to assist his relatives, the exiled dukes of Mecklenburg. Cardinal Richelieu, the chief minister of King Louis XIII of France (r. 1610–1643), subsidized the Swedes, hoping to weaken Habsburg power in Europe. In 1631, with a small but well-disciplined army equipped with superior muskets and warm uniforms, Gustavus Adolphus won a brilliant victory at Breitenfeld. In 1632 he was victorious again, at Lützen, though he was fatally wounded in the battle.

The participation of the Swedes in the Thirty Years' War proved decisive for the future of Protestantism and later German history. When Gustavus Adolphus landed on German soil, he had already brought Denmark, Poland, Finland, and the smaller Baltic States under Swedish influence. The Swedish victories ended the Habsburg ambition of uniting all the German states under imperial authority.

The death of Gustavus Adolphus, followed by the defeat of the Swedes at the Battle of Nördlingen in 1634, prompted the French to enter the war on the side of the Protestants. Thus began the French, or international, phase (1635–1648) of the Thirty Years' War. For almost a century, French foreign policy had been based on opposition to the Habsburgs, because a weak empire divided into scores of independent principalities enhanced France's international stature. In 1622, when the Dutch had resumed the war against Spain, the French had supported Holland. Now, in 1635, Cardinal Richelieu declared war on Spain and again sent financial and military assistance to the Swedes and the German Protestant princes. The war dragged on. French, Dutch, and Swedes, supported by Scots, Finns, and German mercenaries, burned, looted, and destroyed German agriculture and commerce. The Thirty Years' War lasted so long because neither side had the resources to win a quick, decisive victory. Finally, in October 1648, peace was achieved.

The treaties signed at Münster and Osnabrück, commonly called the "Peace of Westphalia," mark a turning point in European political, religious, and social history. The treaties recognized the sovereign, independent authority of the German princes. Each ruler could govern his particular territory and make war and peace as well. With power in the hands of more than three hundred princes, and no central government or courts to control them, the Holy Roman Empire as a real state was effectively destroyed (see Map 18.4).

The independence of the United Provinces of the Netherlands was acknowledged. The international stature of France and Sweden was also greatly improved. The political divisions within the empire, the weak German frontiers, and the acquisition of the province of Alsace increased France's size and prestige. The treaties allowed France to intervene at will in German affairs. Sweden received a large cash indemnity and jurisdiction over German territories along the Baltic Sea. The powerful Swedish presence in northeastern Germany subsequently posed a major threat to the future kingdom of Brandenburg-Prussia. The treaties also denied the papacy the right to participate in German religious affairs—a restriction symbolizing the reduced role of the church in European politics.

In religion, the Westphalian treaties stipulated that the Augsburg agreement of 1555 should stand permanently. The sole modification was that Calvinism, along with Catholicism and Lutheranism, would become a legally permissible creed. In practice, the north German states remained Protestant, the south German states Catholic. The war settled little. Both sides had wanted peace, and with remarkable illogic they fought for thirty years to get it.

Germany After the Thirty Years' War

The Thirty Years' War was a disaster for the German economy and society, probably the most destructive event in German history before the twentieth century. Population losses were frightful. Perhaps one-third of the urban residents and two-fifths of the inhabitants of rural areas died. Entire areas of Germany were depopulated, partly by military actions, partly by disease—typhus, dysentery, bubonic plague, and syphilis accompanied the movements of armies—and partly by the flight of thousands of refugees to safer areas.

In the late sixteenth and early seventeenth centuries, all Europe experienced an economic crisis caused primarily by the influx of silver from the Americas. Because the Thirty Years' War was fought on German soil, these economic difficulties were badly aggravated in the empire. Scholars still cannot estimate the value of losses in agricultural land and livestock, in trade and commerce. The trade of southern cities like Augsburg, already hard hit by the shift in transportation routes from the Mediterranean to the Atlantic, was virtually destroyed by the fighting in the south. Meanwhile, towns like Lübeck, Hamburg, and Bremen in the north and Essen in the Ruhr area actually prospered because of the many refugees they attracted. The destruction of land and foodstuffs, compounded by the flood of Spanish silver, brought on severe price increases. During and after the war, inflation was worse in Germany than anywhere else in Europe.

Agricultural areas suffered catastrophically. The population decline caused a rise in the value of labor, so owners of great estates had to pay more for agricultural workers. Farmers who needed only small amounts of capital to restore their lands started over again. Many small farmers, however, lacked the revenue to rework their holdings and had to become day laborers. Nobles and landlords bought up many small holdings and acquired great estates. In some parts of Germany, especially east of the Elbe River in areas like Mecklenburg and Pomerania, peasants' loss of land led to a new serfdom.[27] Thus the war contributed to the legal and economic decline of the largest segment of German society.

CHANGING ATTITUDES

The age of religious wars revealed extreme and violent contrasts. While some Europeans indulged in gross sensuality, the social status of women declined. The exploration of new continents reflected deep curiosity and broad intelligence, yet Europeans believed in witches and burned thousands at the stake. Europeans explored new continents, partly with the missionary aim of Christianizing native peoples. Yet the Spanish, Portuguese, Dutch, and English proceeded to enslave the Indians and blacks they encountered. It was a deeply religious period in which men fought passionately for their beliefs, and 70 percent of the books printed dealt with religious subjects. Yet the times saw the stirring of religious skepticism, and sexism, racism, and skepticism, all present since antiquity, began to take on their familiar modern forms.

The Status of Women

Did new ideas about women appear in this period? Theological and popular literature on marriage in Reformation Europe helps to answer this question. Manuals emphasized the qualities expected of each partner. A husband was obliged to provide for the material welfare of his wife and children, to protect his family while remaining steady and self-controlled. He was to rule his household firmly but justly; he was not to behave like a tyrant, a guideline counselors repeated frequently. A wife was to be mature, a good household manager, and subservient and faithful to her spouse. The husband also owed fidelity. Both Protestant and Catholic moralists rejected the double standard of sexual morality, viewing it as a threat to family unity. Counselors believed that marriage should be based on mutual respect and trust. Although they discouraged impersonal unions arranged by parents, they did not think romantic attachments—based on physical attraction and emotional love—a sound basis for an enduring relationship.

Moralists held that the household was a woman's first priority. She might assist in her own or her husband's business and do charitable work. Involvement in social or public activities, however, was inappropriate because it distracted the wife from her primary responsibility: her household. If women suffered under their husbands' yoke, writers explained, that submission was their punishment inherited from Eve; it included the pain of childbearing. Moreover, they said, a woman's lot was no worse than a man's: he must earn the family's bread by the sweat of his brow.[28]

Catholics viewed marriage as a sacramental union, which, validly entered into, could not be dissolved. Protestants stressed a contractual form of marriage, whereby each partner promised the other support, companionship, and the sharing of mutual goods. Protestants recognized a mutual right to divorce and remarry for various reasons, including adultery and irreparable breakdown.[29] Society in the early modern period was patriarchal. Women neither lost their identity nor lacked meaningful work, but the all-pervasive assumption was that men ruled. Leading students of the Lutherans, Catholics, French Calvinists, and English Puritans tend to concur that there was no improvement of women's definitely subordinate status.

There are some remarkable success stories, however. Elizabeth Hardwick, the orphaned daughter of an obscure English country squire, made four careful marriages. Each of them brought her more property and carried her higher up the social ladder. She managed her estates, amounting to more than a hundred thousand acres, with a degree of business sense rare in any age. The two great mansions she built, Chatsworth and Hardwick, stand today as monuments to her acumen. As countess of Shrewsbury, "Bess of Hardwick" so thoroughly enjoyed the trust of Queen Elizabeth that Elizabeth appointed her jailer of Mary, Queen of Scots. Having established several aristocratic dynasties, the countess of Shrewsbury died in 1608, past her eightieth year, one of the richest people in England.[30]

Artists' drawings of plump, voluptuous women and massive, muscular men reveal the contemporary standards of physical beauty. It was a sensual age that gloried in the delights of the flesh. Some people found sexual satisfaction with both sexes.

Reformers and public officials simultaneously condemned and condoned sexual "sins." The oldest profession had many practitioners, and, when in 1566 Pope Pius IV expelled all the prostitutes from Rome, so many people left and the city suffered such a loss of revenue that in less than a month the pope was forced to rescind the order. Scholars debated Saint Augustine's notion that whores serve a useful social function by preventing worse sins.

Prostitution was common because desperate poverty forced women and young men into it. The general public took it for granted. Consequently, civil authorities in both Catholic and Protestant countries licensed houses of public prostitution. These establishments were intended for the convenience of single men, and some Protestant cities, such as Geneva and Zurich, installed officials in the brothels with the express purpose of preventing married men from patronizing them. Moralists naturally railed against prostitution. For example, Melchior Ambach, the Lutheran editor of many tracts against adultery and whoring, wrote in 1543 that if "houses of women" for single and married men were allowed, why not provide a "house of boys" for women folk who lack a husband to service them? "Would whoring be any worse for the poor, needy female sex?"[31] Ambach, of course, was not being serious: by treating infidelity from the perspective of female rather than male customers, he was still insisting that prostitution destroyed the family and society.

What became of the thousands of women who left their convents and nunneries during the Reformation? The question concerns primarily women of the upper classes, who formed the dominant social group in the religious houses of late medieval Europe. (Single women of the middle and working classes in the sixteenth and seventeenth centuries worked in many occupations and professions—as butchers, shopkeepers, nurses, goldsmiths, and midwives and in the weaving and printing industries. Those who were married normally assisted in their husbands' businesses.) Luther and the Protestant reformers believed that the monastic cloister symbolized antifeminism, that young girls were forced by their parents into convents and once there were bullied by men into staying. Thus reformers favored the suppression of women's religious houses and encouraged former nuns to marry. Marriage, the reformers maintained, not only gave women emotional and sexual

satisfaction but freed them from clerical domination, cultural deprivation, and sexual repression.[32] It would appear, consequently, that women passed from clerical domination to subservience to husbands.

If some nuns in the Middle Ages lacked a genuine religious vocation and if some religious houses witnessed financial mismanagement and moral laxness, convents nevertheless provided women of the upper classes with scope for their literary, artistic, medical, or administrative talents if they could not or would not marry. Marriage became virtually the only occupation for Protestant women. This helps explain why Anglicans, Calvinists, and Lutherans established communities of religious women, such as the Lutheran one at Kaiserwerth in the Rhineland, in the eighteenth and nineteenth centuries.[33]

The Great European Witch Hunt

The period of the religious wars witnessed a startling increase in the phenomenon of witch-hunting, whose prior history was long but sporadic. "A witch," according to Chief Justice Edward Coke of England (1552–1634), "was a person who hath conference with the Devil to consult with him or to do some act." This definition by the highest legal authority in England demonstrates that educated people, as well as the ignorant, believed in *witches*—individuals who could mysteriously injure other people by, for instance, causing them to become blind or impotent and who could harm animals by, for example, preventing cows from giving milk.

Belief in witches dates back to the dawn of time. For centuries, tales had circulated about old women who made nocturnal travels on greased broomsticks to assemblies of witches, where they participated in sexual orgies and feasted on the flesh of infants. In the popular imagination witches had definite characteristics. The vast majority were married women or widows between fifty and seventy years old, crippled or bent with age, with pockmarked skin. They often practiced midwifery or folk medicine, and most had sharp tongues.

In the sixteenth century, religious reformers' extreme notions of the Devil's powers and the insecurity created by the religious wars contributed to the growth of belief in witches. The idea developed that witches made pacts with the Devil in return for the power to work mischief on their enemies. Since pacts with the Devil meant the renunciation of God, witchcraft was considered heresy, and all religions persecuted it.

Fear of witches took a terrible toll of innocent lives in parts of Europe. In southwestern Germany, 3,229 witches were executed between 1561 and 1670, most by burning. The communities of the Swiss Confederation tried 8,888 persons between 1470 and 1700 and executed 5,417 of them as witches. In all the centuries before 1500, witches in England had been suspected of causing perhaps "three deaths, a broken leg, several destructive storms and some bewitched genitals." Yet between 1559 and 1736, witches were thought to have caused thousands of deaths, and almost 1,000 witches were executed in England.[34]

Historians and anthropologists have offered a variety of explanations for the great European witch hunt. Some scholars maintain that charges of witchcraft were a means of accounting for inexplicable misfortunes. Just as the English in the fifteenth century had blamed their military failures in France on Joan of Arc's sorcery, so in the seventeenth century the English Royal College of Physicians attributed undiagnosable illnesses to witchcraft. Some scholars hold that in small communities, which typically insisted on strict social conformity, charges of witchcraft were a means of attacking and eliminating nonconformists. Witches, in other words, served the collective need for scapegoats. Some writers suggest that the evidence of witches' trials shows that women were accused not because they harmed or threatened their neighbors but because their communities believed that they worshiped the Devil, engaged in wild sexual activities with him, and ate infants. Other scholars argue the exact opposite: that women were tried and executed as witches because their neighbors feared their evil powers. Finally, there is a theory that the unbridled sexuality attributed to women accused of witchcraft was a psychological projection made by the women's accusers, and resulting from Christianity's repression of sexuality.

The reasons for the persecution of women as witches probably varied from place to place. Though several hypotheses exist, scholars still cannot fully understand the phenomenon. Nevertheless, given the broad strand of *misogyny* (hatred of women) in Western religion, the ancient belief in the susceptibility of women (so-called weaker vessels) to the Devil's allurements, and the pervasive seventeenth-century belief about women's multiple and demanding orgasms and thus their sexual insatiability, it is not difficult to understand why women were accused of all sorts of mischief and witchcraft. Charges of witchcraft provided a legal basis for the execution of tens of thousands of women. As the most important capital crime for women in early modern times, witchcraft has significance for the history and status of women.[35]

European Slavery and the Origins of American Racism

Almost all peoples in the world have enslaved other human beings at some time in their histo-

Witches Worshiping the Devil In medieval Christian art, a goat symbolizes the damned at the Last Judgment, following Christ's statement that the Son of Man would separate believers from nonbelievers, as a shepherd separates the sheep from the goats (Matthew 25: 31–32). In this illustration, a witch arrives at a sabbat and prepares to venerate the devil in the shape of a goat by kissing its anus. *(Source: Bodleian Library, Oxford)*

ries. Since ancient times, victors in battle have enslaved conquered peoples. In the later Middle Ages slavery was deeply entrenched in southern Italy, Sicily, Crete, and Mediterranean Spain. The bubonic plague, famines, and other epidemics created severe shortages of agricultural and domestic workers in parts of northern Europe, encouraging Italian merchants to buy slaves from the Balkans, Thrace, southern Russia, and central Anatolia for sale in the West. In 1364 the Florentine government allowed the unlimited importation of slaves, so long as they were not Roman Catholics. Between 1414 and 1423, at least ten thousand slaves were sold in Venice alone. Where profits were lucrative, papal threats of excommunication completely failed to stop Genoese slave traders. The Genoese set up colonial stations in the Crimea and along the Black Sea. According to an international authority on slavery, these outposts were "virtual laboratories" for the development of slave plantation agriculture in the New World.[36] This form of slavery had nothing to do with race; almost all slaves were white. How, then, did black African slavery enter the European picture and take root in the New World?

In 1453 the Ottoman capture of Constantinople halted the flow of white slaves from the Black Sea region and the Balkans. Mediterranean Europe, cut off from its traditional source of slaves, had no alternative source for slave labor but sub-Saharan Africa. The centuries-old trans-Saharan trade was greatly stimulated by a ready market in the vineyards and sugar plantations of Sicily and Majorca. By the later fifteenth century, the Mediterranean had developed an "American" form of slavery before the discovery of America.

Meanwhile, the Genoese and other Italians had colonized the Canary Islands off the western coast of Africa. Prince Henry the Navigator's sailors discovered the Madeira Islands and made settlements there. In this stage of European expansion, "the history of slavery became inextricably tied up with the history of sugar." Although sugar was an expensive luxury that only the affluent could afford, population increases and monetary expansion in the fifteenth century led to a growing demand for it. Resourceful Italians provided the capital, cane, and technology for sugar cultivation on plantations in southern Portugal, Madeira, and the Canary Islands. In Portugal between 1490 and 1530, between 300 and 2,000 black slaves were annually imported into the port of Lisbon (Map

18.5). From Lisbon, where African slaves performed most of the manual labor and constituted about 10 percent of the city's population, slaves were transported to the sugar plantations of Madeira, the Azores, the Cape Verdes, and then Brazil. Sugar and the small Atlantic islands gave New World slavery its distinctive shape.[37]

As already discussed, European expansion across the Atlantic led to the economic exploitation of the Americas. In the New World the major problem faced by settlers was a shortage of labor. As early as 1495 the Spanish solved the problem by enslaving the native Indians. In the next two centuries, the Portuguese, Dutch, and English followed suit.

Unaccustomed to any form of forced labor, certainly not to panning gold for more than twelve hours a day in the broiling sun, the Amerindians died "like fish in a bucket."[38] In 1517 Las Casas urged King Charles V to end Indian slavery in his American dominions (see page 574). Las Casas recommended the importation of blacks from Africa, both because church law did not strictly forbid black slavery and because blacks could better survive under South American conditions. The king agreed, and in 1518 the African slave trade began. Columbus's introduction of sugar plants into Santo Domingo, moreover, stimulated the need for black slaves; and the experience and model of plantation slavery in Portugal and the Atlantic islands encouraged a similar agricultural pattern in the New World.

Several European nations participated in the African slave trade. Portugal brought the first slaves to Brazil; by 1600, about 4,000 were being imported annually. After its founding in 1621, the Dutch West India Company, with the full support of the government of the United Provinces, transported thousands of Africans to Brazil and the Caribbean. Only in the late seventeenth century, with the chartering of the Royal African Company, did the English get involved. Thereafter, large numbers of African blacks poured into the West Indies and North America (see Map 18.5). In 1790 there were 757,181 blacks in a total U.S. population of 3,929,625. When the first census was taken in Brazil in 1798, blacks numbered about 2 million among 3.25 million people.

Settlers brought to the Americas the racial attitudes they had absorbed in Europe. Their beliefs about and attitudes toward blacks derived from two basic sources: Christian theological specula-

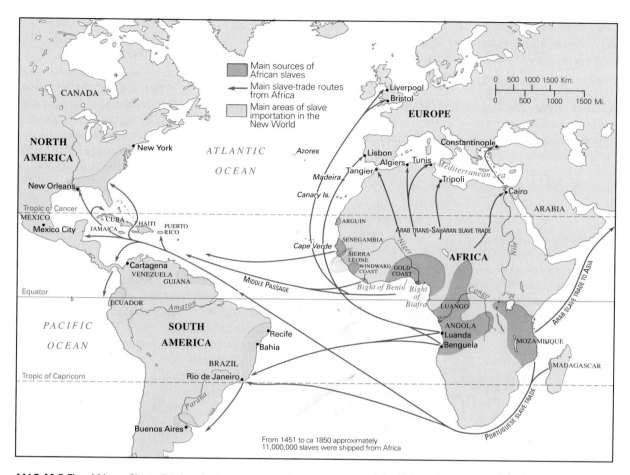

MAP 18.5 The African Slave Trade   Decades before the discovery of America, Greek, Russian, Bulgarian, Armenian, and then black slaves worked the plantation economies of southern Italy, Sicily, Portugal, and Mediterranean Spain—thereby serving as models for the American form of slavery.

tion (see page 524) and Muslim ideas. In the sixteenth and seventeenth centuries, the English, for example, were extremely curious about Africans' lives and customs, and slavers' accounts were extraordinarily popular. Travel literature depicted Africans as savages because of their eating habits, morals, clothing, and social customs; as barbarians because of their language and methods of war; and as heathens because they were not Christian. English people saw similarities between apes and Africans; thus the terms *bestial* and *beastly* were frequently applied to Africans. Africans were believed to possess a potent sexuality. One seventeenth-century observer considered African men "very lustful and impudent . . . their members' extraordinary greatness . . . is a token of their lust." African women were considered sexually aggressive with a "temper hot and lascivious."[39]

"At the time when Columbus sailed to the New World, Islam was the largest world religion, and the only world religion that showed itself capable of expanding rapidly in areas as far apart and as different from each other as Senegal in northwest Africa, Bosnia in the Balkans, Java, and the Philippines."[40] Medieval Arabic literature characterized blacks as physically repulsive, mentally inferior, and primitive. In contrast to civilized peoples from the Mediterranean to China, Muslim writers claimed, sub-Saharan blacks were the only peoples who had produced no sciences or stable states. The fourteenth-century Arab historian Ibn Khaldun wrote that the "only people who accept slavery are the Negroes, owing to their low degree of humanity and their proximity to the animal stage." Though black kings, Ibn Khaldun alleged, sold their subjects without even a pretext of crime or war, the victims bore no resentment because they gave no thought to the future and have "by nature few cares and worries; dancing and rhythm are for them inborn."[41] It is easy to see how such absurd images would develop into the classic stereotypes used to justify black slavery in South and North America in the seventeenth, eighteenth, and nineteenth centuries. Medieval Christians and Muslims had similar notions of blacks as inferior and primitive people ideally suited to enslavement.

African Slave and Indian Woman A black slave approaches an Indian prostitute. Unable to explain what he wants, he points with his finger; she eagerly grasps for the coin. The Spanish caption above moralizes on the black man using stolen money—yet the Spaniards ruthlessly expropriated all South American mineral wealth. (Source: New York Public Library)

Perhaps centuries of commercial contacts between Muslim and Mediterranean peoples had familiarized the latter with Muslim racial attitudes.

The biased racial attitudes of fourteenth- and fifteenth-century European and Muslim intellectuals, however, did not automatically become the views of the general populace in eighteenth-century America. It was the institutionalization of slavery, as manifested by slave plantation society in the Americas, that served as the laboratory of modern racism.[42]

The Origin of Modern Skepticism: Michel de Montaigne

Decades of religious fanaticism, bringing in their wake death, famine, and civil anarchy, caused both Catholics and Protestants to doubt that any one faith contained absolute truth. The late sixteenth and early seventeenth centuries witnessed the beginnings of modern skepticism. *Skepticism* is an attitude of thought based on doubt that total certainty or definitive knowledge is ever attainable. A skeptic is cautious and critical and suspends judgment. Perhaps the finest representative of early modern skepticism is the Frenchman Michel de Montaigne (1533–1592).

Montaigne came from a bourgeois family that had made a fortune selling salted herring and in 1477 had purchased the title and property of Montaigne in Gascony. Montaigne received a classical education before studying law and securing a judicial appointment in 1554. Though a member of the nobility, in embarking on a judicial career, he identified with the new nobility of the robe. He condemned the ancient nobility of the sword for being concerned more with war and sports than with the cultivation of the mind.

At the age of thirty-eight, Montaigne resigned his judicial post, retired to his estate, and devoted the rest of his life to study, contemplation, and the effort to understand himself. Like the Greeks, he believed that the object of life was to "know thyself," for self-knowledge teaches men and women how to live in accordance with nature and God. Montaigne developed a new literary genre, the essay—from the French *essayer,* meaning "to test" or "to try"—to express his thoughts and ideas.

Montaigne's *Essays* provide insight into the mind of a remarkably humane, tolerant, and civilized man. He was a humanist; he loved the Greek and Roman writers and was always eager to learn from them. In his essay "On Solitude," he quoted the Roman poet Horace:

Reason and sense remove anxiety,
Not villas that look out upon the sea

Some said to Socrates that a certain man had grown no better by his travels. "I should think not," he said; "he took himself along with him. . . ."
We should have wife, children, goods, and above all health, if we can; but we must not bind ourselves to them so strongly that our happiness depends on them. We must reserve a back shop all our own, entirely free, in which to establish our real liberty and our principal retreat and solitude.[43]

From the ancient authors, especially the Roman Stoics, Montaigne acquired a sense of calm, inner peace, and patience. The ancient authors also inculcated in him tolerance and broad-mindedness.

Montaigne came of age during the French civil wars, perhaps the worst kind of war. He wrote:

In this controversy . . . France is at present agitated by civil wars, the best and soundest side is undoubtedly that which maintains both the old religion and the old government of the country. However, among the good men who follow that side . . . we see many whom passion drives outside the bounds of reason, and makes them sometimes adopt unjust, violent, and even reckless courses.[44]

Though he remained a Catholic, Montaigne possessed a detachment, an independence, and a willingness to look at all sides of a question: "I listen with attention to the judgment of all men; but so far as I can remember, I have followed none but my own. Though I set little value upon my own opinion, I set no more on the opinions of others."

In the book-lined tower where Montaigne passed his days, he became a deeply learned man. Yet he was not ignorant of world affairs, and he criticized scholars and bookworms who ignored the life around them. Montaigne's essay "On Cannibals" reflects the impact of overseas discoveries on Europeans' consciousness. His tolerant mind rejected the notion that one culture is superior to another:

I long had a man in my house that lived ten or twelve years in the New World . . . in . . . Brazil. . . .

I find that there is nothing barbarous and savage in that nation, by anything that I can gather, excepting, that every one gives the title of barbarism to everything that is not in use in his own country. As, indeed, we have no other level of truth and reason, than the example and idea of the opinions and customs of the place wherein we live.[45]

In his belief in the nobility of human beings in the state of nature, uncorrupted by organized society, and in his cosmopolitan attitude toward different civilizations, Montaigne anticipated many eighteenth-century thinkers.

The thought of Michel de Montaigne marks a sharp break with the past. Faith and religious certainty had characterized the intellectual attitudes of Western society for a millennium. Montaigne's rejection of any kind of dogmatism, his secularism, and his skepticism represented a basic change. In his own time and throughout the seventeenth century, few would have agreed with him. The publication of his ideas, however, anticipated a basic shift in attitudes. Montaigne inaugurated an era of doubt. "Wonder," he said, "is the foundation of all philosophy, research is the means of all learning, and ignorance is the end."[46]

ELIZABETHAN AND JACOBEAN LITERATURE

The age of the religious wars and European expansion also experienced an extraordinary degree of intellectual ferment. In addition to the development of the essay as a distinct literary genre, the late sixteenth and early seventeenth centuries fostered remarkable creativity in other branches of literature. England, especially in the latter part of Elizabeth's reign and the first years of the reign of her successor, James I (r. 1603–1625), witnessed unparalleled brilliance. The terms *Elizabethan* and *Jacobean* (referring to the reign of James) are used to designate the English music, poetry, prose, and drama of this period. The poems of Sir Philip Sidney (1554–1586), such as *Astrophel and Stella*, strongly influenced later poetic writing. *The Faerie Queene* of Edmund Spenser (1552–1599) endures as one of the greatest moral epics in any language. The rare poetic beauty of the plays of Christopher Marlowe (1564–1593), such as *Tamburlaine* and *The Jew of Malta*, paved the way for

A Royal Hunt In the sixteenth and seventeenth centuries, hunting remained an aristocratic pastime. Here a courtier, having slain a deer, presents the dagger to Queen Elizabeth I. *(Source: By permission of the Folger Shakespeare Library)*

the work of Shakespeare. Above all, the immortal dramas of Shakespeare and stately prose of the Authorized or King James Bible mark the Elizabethan and Jacobean periods as the golden age of English literature.

William Shakespeare (1564–1616), the son of a successful glove manufacturer who rose to the highest municipal office in the Warwickshire town of Stratford-on-Avon, chose a career on the London stage. By 1592 he had gained recognition as an actor and playwright. Between 1599 and 1603, Shakespeare performed in the Lord Chamberlain's Company and became co-owner of the Globe Theatre, which after 1603 presented his plays.

Shakespeare's genius lies in the originality of his characterizations, the diversity of his plots, his understanding of human psychology, and his unexcelled gift for language. Shakespeare was a Renaissance man in his deep appreciation for classical culture, individualism, and humanism. Such plays as *Julius Caesar, Pericles,* and *Antony and Cleopatra* deal with classical subjects and figures. Several of his comedies have Italian Renaissance settings. The nine history plays, including *Richard II, Richard III,* and *Henry IV,* enjoyed the greatest popularity among Shakespeare's contemporaries. Written during the decade after the defeat of the Spanish Armada, the history plays express English national consciousness. Lines such as these from *Richard II* reflect this sense of national greatness with unparalleled eloquence:

This royal Throne of Kings, this sceptre'd Isle,
This earth of Majesty, this seat of Mars,
This other Eden, demi-paradise,
This fortress built by Nature for herself,
Against infection and the hand of war:
This happy breed of men, this little world,
This precious stone, set in the silver sea,
Which serves it in the office of a wall,
Or as a moat defensive to a house,
Against the envy of less happier Lands,
This blessed plot, this earth, this Realm,
   this England.

Shakespeare's later plays, above all the tragedies *Othello, Macbeth,* and *Hamlet,* explore an enormous range of human problems and are open to an almost infinite variety of interpretations. *Othello,* which the nineteenth-century historian Thomas Macaulay called "perhaps the greatest work in the world," portrays an honorable man destroyed by a flaw in his own character and the satanic evil of his supposed friend. The central theme of *Macbeth* is exorbitant ambition. Shakespeare analyzes the psychology of sin in the figures of Macbeth and Lady Macbeth, whose mutual love under the pressure of ambition leads to their destruction. The central figure in *Hamlet,* a play suffused with individuality, wrestles with moral problems connected with revenge and with man's relationship to life and death. The soliloquy in which Hamlet debates suicide is perhaps the most widely quoted passage in English literature:

To be, or not to be: that is the question:
Whether 'tis nobler in the mind to suffer
The slings and arrows of outrageous fortune,
Or to take arms against a sea of troubles,
And by opposing end them? . . .

Hamlet's sad cry, "There is nothing either good or bad but thinking makes it so," expresses the anguish and uncertainty of modern man. *Hamlet* has always enjoyed great popularity because in Hamlet's many-faceted personality people have seen an aspect of themselves.

Shakespeare's dynamic language bespeaks his extreme sensitivity to the sounds and meanings of words. Perhaps no phrase better summarizes the reason for his immortality than these lines, slightly modified, from *Antony and Cleopatra:* "Age cannot wither [him], nor custom stale/[his] infinite variety."

The other great masterpiece of the Jacobean period was the Authorized Bible. At a theological conference in 1604, a group of Puritans urged James I to support a new translation of the Bible. The king assigned the task to a committee of scholars, who published their efforts in 1611. Based on the best scriptural research of the time and divided into chapters and verses, the "Authorized Version," so called because it was produced under royal sponsorship—it had no official ecclesiastical endorsement—is actually a revision of earlier Bibles more than an original work. Yet it provides a superb expression of the mature English vernacular in the early seventeenth century. Thus Psalm 37:

> *Fret not thy selfe because of evill doers, neither bee*
> *thou envious against the workers of iniquitie.*
> *For they shall soone be cut downe like the grasse;*
> *and wither as the greene herbe.*
> *Trust in the Lord, and do good, so shalt thou dwell in*
> *the land, and verely thou shalt be fed.*
> *Delight thy selfe also in the Lord; and he shall give*
> *thee the desires of thine heart.*
> *Commit thy way unto the Lord: trust also in him, and*
> *he shall bring it to passe.*
> *And he shall bring forth thy righteousness as the*
> *light, and thy judgement as the noone day.*

The Authorized Version represented the Anglican and Puritan desire to encourage laypeople to read the Scriptures. It quickly achieved great popularity and displaced all earlier versions. British settlers carried this Bible to the North American colonies, where it became known as the "King James Bible." For centuries the King James Bible has had a profound influence on the language and lives of English-speaking peoples.

BAROQUE ART AND MUSIC

Throughout European history, the cultural tastes of one age have often seemed quite unsatisfactory to the next. So it was with the baroque. The term *baroque* itself may have come from the Portuguese word for an "odd-shaped, imperfect pearl" and was commonly used by late-eighteenth-century art critics as an expression of scorn for what they considered an overblown, unbalanced style. The hostility of these critics, who also scorned the Gothic style of medieval cathedrals in favor of a classicism inspired by antiquity and the Renaissance, has long since passed. Specialists agree that the

Veronese: Mars and Venus United by Love (ca 1580) Taking a theme from classical mythology, the Venetian painter Veronese celebrates in clothing, architecture, and landscape the luxurious wealth of the aristocracy. The lush and curvaceous Venus and the muscular and powerfully built Mars suggest the anticipated pleasures of sexual activity and the frank sensuality of the age. *(Source: The Metropolitan Museum of Art, New York, John Stewart Kennedy Fund, 1910)*

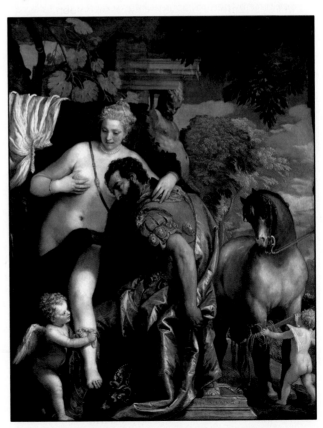

triumphs of the baroque marked one of the high points in the history of Western culture.

The early development of the baroque is complex, but most scholars stress the influence of Rome and the revitalized Catholic church of the later sixteenth century. The papacy and the Jesuits encouraged the growth of an intensely emotional, exuberant art. These patrons wanted artists to go beyond the Renaissance focus on pleasing a small, wealthy cultural elite. They wanted artists to appeal to the senses and thereby touch the souls and kindle the faith of ordinary churchgoers, while proclaiming the power and confidence of the reformed Catholic church. In addition to this underlying religious emotionalism, the baroque drew its sense of drama, motion, and ceaseless striving from the Catholic Reformation. The interior of the famous Jesuit Church of Jesus in Rome—the Gesù—combined all these characteristics in its lavish, shimmering decorations and frescoes.

Velázquez: Juan de Pareja   This portrait (1650) of the Spanish painter Velázquez's one-time assistant, a black man of obvious intellectual and sensual power and himself a renowned religious painter, suggests the integration of some blacks in seventeenth-century society. The elegant lace collar attests to his middle-class status. (Source: The Metropolitan Museum of Art)

Taking definite shape in Italy after 1600, the baroque style in the visual arts developed with exceptional vigor in Catholic countries—in Spain and Latin America, Austria, southern Germany, and Poland. Yet baroque art was more than just "Catholic art" in the seventeenth century and the first half of the eighteenth. True, neither Protestant England nor the Netherlands ever came fully under the spell of the baroque, but neither did Catholic France. And Protestants accounted for some of the finest examples of baroque style, especially in music. The baroque style spread partly because its tension and bombast spoke to an agitated age, which was experiencing great violence and controversy in politics and religion.

In painting, the baroque reached maturity early with Peter Paul Rubens (1577–1640), the most outstanding and representative of baroque painters. Studying in his native Flanders and in Italy, where he was influenced by masters of the High Renaissance, such as Michelangelo, Rubens developed his own rich, sensuous, colorful style, which was characterized by animated figures, melodramatic contrasts, and monumental size. Although Rubens excelled in glorifying monarchs such as Queen Mother Marie de' Medici of France, he was also a devout Catholic. Nearly half of his pictures treat Christian subjects. Yet one of Rubens's trademarks was fleshy, sensual nudes, who populate his canvases as Roman goddesses, water nymphs, and remarkably voluptuous saints and angels.

Rubens was enormously successful. To meet the demand for his work, he established a large studio and hired many assistants to execute his rough sketches and gigantic murals. Sometimes the master artist added only the finishing touches. Rubens's wealth and position—on occasion he was given special diplomatic assignments by the Habsburgs—attest that distinguished artists continued to enjoy the high social status they had won in the Renaissance.

In music, the baroque style reached its culmination almost a century later in the dynamic, soaring lines of the endlessly inventive Johann Sebastian Bach (1685–1750), one of the greatest composers the Western world has ever produced. Organist and choir master of several Lutheran churches across Germany, Bach was equally at home writing secular concertos and sublime religious cantatas. Bach's organ music, the greatest ever written, combined the baroque spirit of invention, tension, and emotion in an unforgettable striving toward the infinite. Bach was not fully appreciated in his lifetime, but since the early 1800s his reputation has grown steadily.

SUMMARY

In the sixteenth and seventeenth centuries, Europeans for the first time gained access to large parts of the globe. European peoples had the intellectual curiosity, driving ambition, and scientific technology to attempt feats that were as difficult and expensive then as going to the moon is today. Exploration and exploitation contributed to a more sophisticated standard of living in the form of spices and Asian luxury goods and to a terrible international inflation resulting from the influx of South American silver and gold. Governments, the upper classes, and especially the peasantry were badly hurt by the inflation. Meanwhile the middle class of bankers, shippers, financiers, and manufacturers prospered for much of the seventeenth century.

Europeans' technological development contributed to their conquest of Aztec Mexico and Inca Peru. Along with technology, Europeans brought disease to the New World, which caused a terrible holocaust among the Indians. Overseas reconnaissance led to the first global seaborne commercial empires of the Portuguese, the Spanish, and the Dutch.

European expansion and colonization took place against a background of religious conflict and rising national consciousness. The sixteenth and seventeenth centuries were by no means a secular period. Although the medieval religious framework had broken down, people still thought largely in religious terms. Europeans explained what they did politically and economically in terms of religious doctrine. Religious ideology served as a justification for a variety of conflicts: the French nobles' opposition to the Crown, the Dutch struggle for political and economic independence from Spain. In Germany, religious pluralism and foreign ambitions added to political difficulties. After 1648 the divisions between Protestant and Catholic tended to become permanent. Sexism, racism, and religious skepticism were harbingers of developments to come.

NOTES

1. Quoted in C. M. Cipolla, *Guns, Sails, and Empires: Technological Innovation and the Early Phases of European Expansion, 1400–1700* (New York: Minerva Press, 1965), pp. 115–116.
2. Quoted in S. E. Morison, *Admiral of the Ocean Sea: A Life of Christopher Columbus* (Boston: Little, Brown, 1946), p. 154.
3. See C. R. Phillips, *Ciudad Real, 1500–1750: Growth, Crisis, and Readjustment in the Spanish Economy* (Cambridge, Mass.: Harvard University Press, 1979), pp. 103–104, 115.
4. Quoted in Cipolla, p. 132.
5. Quoted in F. H. Littell, *The Macmillan Atlas History of Christianity* (New York: Macmillan, 1976), p. 75.
6. Quoted in Cipolla, p. 133.
7. J. H. Parry, *The Age of Reconnaissance: Discovery, Exploration and Settlement, 1450–1650* (Berkeley: University of California Press, 1981), chaps. 3, 5.
8. G. C. Vaillant, *Aztecs of Mexico* (New York: Penguin Books, 1979), p. 241. Chapter 15, on which this section leans, is fascinating.
9. V. W. Von Hagen, *Realm of the Incas* (New York: New American Library, 1961), pp. 204–207.
10. N. Sanchez-Albornoz, *The Population of Latin America: A History,* trans. W. A. R. Richardson (Berkeley: University of California Press, 1974), p. 41.
11. Quoted in A. W. Crosby, *The Columbian Exchange: Biological and Cultural Consequences of 1492* (Westport, Conn.: Greenwood Publishing, 1972), p. 39.
12. Ibid., chap. 2, pp. 35–59.
13. Quoted in C. Gibson, ed., *The Black Legend: Anti-Spanish Attitudes in the Old World and the New* (New York: Knopf, 1971), pp. 74–75.
14. Quoted in L. B. Rout, Jr., *The African Experience in Spanish America* (New York: Cambridge University Press, 1976), p. 23.
15. See Parry, chaps. 12, 14, 15.
16. Quoted in S. Neill, *A History of Christian Missions* (New York: Penguin Books, 1977), p. 163.
17. Quoted in C. M. Cipolla, *Clocks and Culture: 1300–1700* (New York: Norton, 1978), p. 86.
18. J. Gernet, *A History of Chinese Civilization* (New York: Cambridge University Press, 1982), p. 458.
19. Quoted in A. J. Andrea and J. H. Overfield, *The Human Record,* vol. 1, Boston: Houghton Mifflin, 1990), pp. 406–407.
20. Ibid., p. 408.
21. See Donald Keene, *The Japanese Discovery of Europe,* rev. ed. (Stanford, Calif.: Stanford University Press, 1969), pp. 1–17. The quotation is on page 16.
22. See J. Hale, "War and Public Opinion in the Fifteenth and Sixteenth Centuries," *Past and Present* 22 (July 1962): 18–32.

23. Quoted in N. Z. Davis, "The Rites of Violence: Religious Riots in Sixteenth Century France," *Past and Present* 59 (May 1973): 59.

24. See ibid., pp. 51–91.

25. Quoted in J. L. Motley, *The Rise of the Dutch Republic,* vol. 1 (Philadelphia: David McKay, 1898), p. 109.

26. Quoted in P. Smith, *The Age of the Reformation* (New York: Henry Holt, 1951), p. 248.

27. H. Kamen, "The Economic and Social Consequences of the Thirty Years' War," *Past and Present* 39 (April 1968): 44–61.

28. Based heavily on S. Ozment, *When Fathers Ruled: Family Life in Reformation Europe* (Cambridge, Mass.: Harvard University Press, 1983), pp. 50–99.

29. Ibid., pp. 85–92.

30. See D. Durant, *Bess of Hardwick: Portrait of an Elizabethan Dynasty* (London: Weidenfeld & Nicolson, 1977).

31. Quoted in Ozment, p. 56.

32. Ibid., pp. 9–14.

33. See F. Biot, *The Rise of Protestant Monasticism* (Baltimore: Helicon Press, 1968), pp. 74–78.

34. N. Cohn, *Europe's Inner Demons: An Enquiry Inspired by the Great Witch-Hunt* (New York: Basic Books, 1975), pp. 253–254; K. Thomas, *Religion and the Decline of Magic* (New York: Scribner's, 1971), pp. 450–455.

35. See E. W. Monter, "The Pedestal and the Stake: Courtly Love and Witchcraft," in *Becoming Visible: Women in European History,* ed. R. Bridenthal and C. Koonz (Boston: Houghton Mifflin, 1977), pp. 132–135, and A. Fraser, *The Weaker Vessel* (New York: Random House, 1985), pp. 100–103.

36. See C. Verlinden, *The Beginnings of Modern Colonization,* trans. Y. Freccero (Ithaca, N.Y.: Cornell University Press, 1970), pp. 5–6, 80–97.

37. This section leans heavily on D. B. Davis, *Slavery and Human Progress* (New York: Oxford University Press, 1984), pp. 54–62.

38. Quoted in D. P. Mannix with M. Cordley, *Black Cargoes: A History of the Atlantic Slave Trade* (New York: Viking, 1968), p. 5.

39. Ibid., p. 19.

40. Quoted in Davis, p. 40.

41. Ibid., pp. 43–44.

42. W. Rodney, "Africa, Europe and the Americas," in R. Gray, ed., *Cambridge History of Africa,* vol. 4 (Cambridge, England: Cambridge University Press, 1975), pp. 580–581, 590.

43. Quoted in D. M. Frame, trans., *The Complete Works of Montaigne* (Stanford, Calif.: Stanford University Press, 1958), pp. 175–176.

44. Ibid., p. 177.

45. Quoted in C. Cotton, trans., *The Essays of Michel de Montaigne* (New York: A. L. Burt, 1893), pp. 207, 210.

46. Ibid., p. 523.

SUGGESTED READING

Perhaps the best starting point for the study of European society in the age of exploration is Parry's *Age of Reconnaissance,* cited in the Notes, which treats the causes and consequences of the voyages of discovery. Parry's splendidly illustrated *The Discovery of South America* (1979) examines Europeans' reactions to the maritime discoveries and treats the entire concept of new discoveries. For the earliest British reaction to the Japanese, see *A World Elsewhere: Europe's Encounter with Japan in the Sixteenth and Seventeenth Centuries* (1990). The urbane studies of C. M. Cipolla present fascinating material on technological and sociological developments written in a lucid style: In addition to the titles cited in the Notes, see *Cristofano and the Plague: A Study in the History of Public Health in the Age of Galileo* (1973) and *Public Health and the Medical Profession in the Renaissance* (1976). Morison's *Admiral of the Ocean Sea,* also listed in the Notes, is the standard biography of Columbus. The advanced student should consult F. Braudel, *Civilization and Capitalism, 15th–18th Century,* trans. S. Reynolds, vol. 1, *The Structures of Everyday Life* (1981); vol. 2, *The Wheels of Commerce* (1982); and vol. 3, *The Perspective of the World* (1984). These three fat volumes combine vast erudition, a global perspective, and remarkable illustrations. For the political ideas that formed the background of the first Spanish overseas empire, see A. Pagden, *Spanish Imperialism and the Political Imagination* (1990).

For the religious wars, in addition to the references in the Suggested Reading for Chapter 17 and the Notes to this chapter, see J. H. M. Salmon, *Society in Crisis: France in the Sixteenth Century* (1975), which traces the fate of French institutions during the civil wars. A. N. Galpern, *The Religions of the People in Sixteenth-Century Champagne* (1976), is a useful case study in religious anthropology, and W. A. Christian, Jr., *Local Religion in Sixteenth Century Spain* (1981), traces the attitudes and practices of ordinary people.

A cleverly illustrated introduction to the Low Countries is K. H. D. Kaley, *The Dutch in the Seventeenth Century* (1972). The old study of J. L. Motley cited in the Notes still provides a good comprehensive treatment and makes fascinating reading. For Spanish military operations in the Low Countries, see G. Parker, *The Army of Flanders and the Spanish Road, 1567–1659: The Logistics of Spanish Victory and Defeat in the Low Countries' Wars* (1972). The same author's *Spain and the Nether-*

lands, 1559–1659: Ten Studies (1979) contains useful essays, of which students may especially want to consult "Why Did the Dutch Revolt Last So Long?" For the later phases of the Dutch-Spanish conflict, see J. I. Israel, *The Dutch Republic and the Hispanic World, 1606–1661* (1982), which treats the struggle in global perspective.

Of the many biographies of Elizabeth of England, W. T. MacCaffrey, *Queen Elizabeth and the Making of Policy, 1572–1588* (1981), examines the problems posed by the Reformation and how Elizabeth solved them. J. E. Neale, *Queen Elizabeth I* (1957), remains valuable, and L. B. Smith, *The Elizabethan Epic* (1966), is a splendid evocation of the age of Shakespeare with Elizabeth at the center. The best recent biography is C. Erickson, *The First Elizabeth* (1983), a fine, psychologically resonant portrait.

Nineteenth- and early twentieth-century historians described the defeat of the Spanish Armada as a great victory for Protestantism, democracy, and capitalism, which those scholars tended to link together. Recent historians have treated the event in terms of its contemporary significance. For a sympathetic but judicious portrait of the man who launched the armada, see G. Parker, *Philip II* (1978). The best recent study of the leader of the armada is P. Pierson, *Commander of the Armada: The Seventh Duke of Medina Sidonia* (1989). D. Howarth, *The Voyage of the Armada* (1982), discusses the expedition largely in terms of the individuals involved, and G. Mattingly, *The Armada* (1959), gives the diplomatic and political background; both Howarth and Mattingly tell very exciting tales. M. Lewis, *The Spanish Armada* (1972), also tells a good story, but strictly from the English perspective. Significant aspects of Portuguese culture are treated in A. Hower and R. Preto-Rodas, eds., *Empire in Transition: The Portuguese World in the Time of Camões* (1985).

C. V. Wedgwood, *The Thirty Years' War* (1961), must be qualified in light of recent research on the social and economic effects of the war, but it is still a good (if detailed) starting point on a difficult period. Various opinions on the causes and results of the war are given in T. K. Rabb's anthology, *The Thirty Years' War* (1981). In addition to the articles by Hale and Kamen cited in the Notes, the following articles, both of which appear in the scholarly journal *Past and Present*, provide some of the latest important findings: J. V. Polisensky, "The Thirty Years' War and the Crises and Revolutions of Sixteenth Century Europe," 39 (1968), and M. Roberts, "Queen Christina and the General Crisis of the Seventeenth Century," 22 (1962).

As background to the intellectual changes instigated by the Reformation, D. C. Wilcox, *In Search of God and Self: Renaissance and Reformation Thought* (1975), contains a perceptive analysis, and T. Ashton, ed., *Crisis in Europe, 1560–1660* (1967), is fundamental. For women, marriage, and the family, see L. Stone, *The Family, Sex, and Marriage in England, 1500–1800* (1977), an important but controversial work; D. Underdown, "The Taming of the Scold," and S. Amussen, "Gender, Family, and the Social Order," in A. Fletcher and J. Stevenson, eds., *Order and Disorder in Early Modern England* (1985); A. Macfarlane, *Marriage and Love in England: Modes of Reproduction, 1300–1848* (1986); C. R. Boxer, *Women in Iberian Expansion Overseas, 1415–1815* (1975), an invaluable study of women's role in overseas immigration; and S. M. Wyntjes, "Women in the Reformation Era," in Bridenthal and Koonz's *Becoming Visible* (see the Notes), a quick survey of conditions in different countries. Ozment's *When Fathers Ruled*, cited in the Notes, is a seminal study concentrating on Germany and Switzerland.

On witches and witchcraft see, in addition to the titles by Cohn and Thomas in the Notes, J. B. Russell, *Witchcraft in the Middle Ages* (1976) and *Lucifer: The Devil in the Middle Ages* (1984); M. Summers, *The History of Witchcraft and Demonology* (1973); and H. R. Trevor-Roper, *The European Witch-Craze of the Sixteenth and Seventeenth Centuries* (1967), an important collection of essays.

As background to slavery and racism in North and South America, students should see J. L. Watson, ed., *Asian and African Systems of Slavery* (1980), a valuable collection of essays. Davis's *Slavery and Human Progress*, cited in the Notes, shows how slavery was viewed as a progressive force in the expansion of the Western world. For North American conditions, interested students should consult W. D. Jordan, *The White Man's Burden: Historical Origins of Racism in the United States* (1974), and the title by Mannix listed in the Notes, a hideously fascinating account. For Caribbean and South American developments, see F. P. Bowser, *The African Slave in Colonial Peru* (1974); J. S. Handler and F. W. Lange, *Plantation Slavery in Barbados: An Archeological and Historical Investigation* (1978); and R. E. Conrad, *Children of God's Fire: A Documentary History of Black Slavery in Brazil* (1983).

The leading authority on Montaigne is D. M. Frame. In addition to his translation of Montaigne's works cited in the Notes, see his *Montaigne's Discovery of Man* (1955).

19

Absolutism and Constitutionalism in Europe, ca 1589–1725

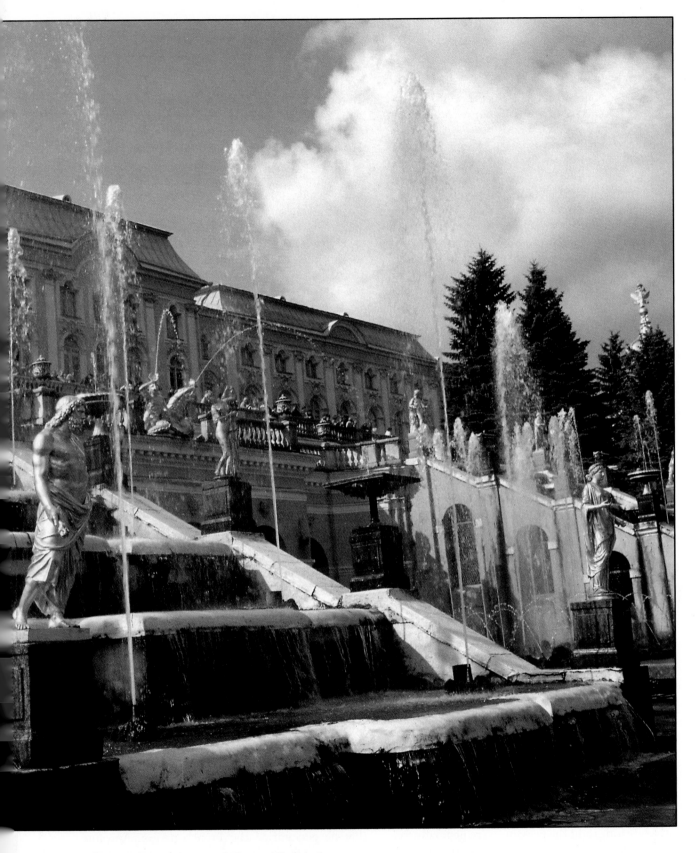

Peter the Great's Summer Palace at Peterhof

*T*he seventeenth century in Europe was an age of intense conflict and crisis. The crisis had many causes, but the era's almost continuous savage warfare—which led governments to build enormous armies and levy ever higher taxes on an already hard-pressed, predominately peasant population—was probably the most important factor. Deteriorating economic conditions also played a major role, although economic depression was not universal and it struck different regions at different times and in varying degrees. An unusually cold and wet climate over many years resulted in smaller harvests, periodic food shortages, and even starvation. Not least, the combination of war, increased taxation, and economic suffering triggered social unrest and widespread peasant revolts, which were both a cause and an effect of profound dislocation.

The many-sided crisis of the seventeenth century posed a grave challenge to European governments: how were they to maintain order? Although there were significant variations in timing and tactics, the most basic response of monarchical governments was to seek more power to deal with the problems and the threats that they perceived. Indeed, European rulers in this period generally sought to attain complete or "absolute" power and build absolutist states. Thus monarchs fought to free themselves from the restrictions of custom, competing institutions, and powerful social groups. Above all, monarchs sought freedom from the nobility and from traditional representative bodies—most commonly known as Estates or Parliament—that were usually dominated by the nobility. The monarchical demand for freedom of action upset the status quo and it led to furious political battles; but in most countries the monarch was largely successful.

Not surprisingly, there were important national variations in the development of absolutism. The most spectacular example occurred in western Europe, where Louis XIV built upon the heritage of a well-developed monarchy and a strong royal bureaucracy. Moreover, when Louis XIV came to the throne, the powers of the nobility were already somewhat limited, the French middle class was relatively strong, and the peasants were generally free from serfdom. In eastern Europe and Russia, absolutism emerged out of a very different social reality: a powerful nobility, a weak middle class, and an oppressed peasantry composed of serfs. Thus eastern monarchs generally had to compromise with their nobilities as they fashioned absolutist states. Finally, royal absolutism did not triumph in Holland and England. In England especially the opponents of unrestrained monarchical authority succeeded in firmly establishing a constitutional state, which guaranteed that henceforth Parliament and the monarch would share power.

Thus in the period between roughly 1589 and 1725, two basic patterns of government emerged in Europe: absolute monarchy and the constitutional state. Almost all subsequent governments in the West have been modeled on one of these patterns, which have also influenced greatly the rest of the world in the last three centuries.

- How did absolute monarchy and the constitutional state differ from the feudal and dynastic monarchies of earlier centuries?

- How and why did Louis XIV of France lead the way in forging the absolute state?

- Why did the basic structure of society in eastern Europe move away from that of western Europe in the early modern period?

- How did Austrian, Prussian, and Russian rulers build powerful absolute monarchies more durable than the monarchy of Louis XIV?

- How did the absolute monarchs' interaction with artists, architects, and writers contribute to the splendid cultural achievements of both western and eastern Europe in this period?

- What were the characteristics of the constitutional state, and why did it rather than absolutism triumph in Holland and England?

This chapter explores these questions.

ABSOLUTISM: AN OVERVIEW

In an *absolutist* state, the ultimate political power—what legal theorists call sovereignty—is embodied in the person of the ruler. Whether or not Louis XIV actually said, "L'état, c'est moi!" ("I am the state!"), the remark expresses his belief that he personified the French nation. Absolute kings claim to rule by *divine right:* they believe that they are responsible to God alone.

Claiming that they alone possessed sovereignty, absolute rulers tried to control competing jurisdictions, institutions, or interest groups in their territories. They regulated religious sects. They abolished the liberties long held by certain areas, groups, or provinces. They also curtailed or eliminated the traditional representative bodies that had frequently consulted and sometimes even legislated with the monarchs. Absolute kings also secured the cooperation of the one class that had posed the greatest threat to monarchy: the nobility. Medieval governments, restrained by the church, the feudal nobility, and their own financial limitations, had been able to exert none of these controls.

In some respects, the key to the power and success of absolute monarchs lay in how they solved their financial problems. Medieval kings frequently had found temporary financial support through bargains with the nobility: the nobility would agree to an ad hoc grant in return for freedom from future taxation. In contrast, the absolutist solution was the creation of new state bureaucracies, which directed the economic life of the country in the interests of the king, either forcing taxes ever higher or devising alternative methods of raising revenue.

Bureaucracies were composed of career officials appointed by and solely accountable to the king. The backgrounds of these civil servants varied. Absolute monarchs sometimes drew on the middle class, as in France, or they utilized members of the nobility, as in Spain and eastern Europe. Where there was no middle class or an insignificant one, as in Austria, Prussia, Spain, and Russia, the government of the absolutist state consisted of an interlocking elite of monarchy, aristocracy, and bureaucracy.

Royal agents in medieval and Renaissance kingdoms had used their public offices and positions to benefit themselves and their families. Seventeenth-century civil servants, however, served the state as represented by the king. Bureaucrats recognized that the offices they held were public, or state, positions. The state paid them salaries to handle revenues that belonged to the Crown, and they were not supposed to use their positions for private gain. Bureaucrats gradually came to distinguish between public duties and private property.

Absolute monarchs also won the right to maintain permanent standing armies. Medieval armies had been raised by feudal lords for particular wars or campaigns, after which the troops were disbanded. In the seventeenth century, monarchs alone recruited and maintained armies—in peacetime as well as during war. Kings deployed their troops both inside and outside the country in the interests of the monarchy. Absolute rulers also invented new methods of compulsion. They concerned themselves with the private lives of potentially troublesome subjects, often through the use of secret police.

The rule of absolute monarchs was not all-embracing because they lacked the financial and military resources and the technology to make it so. Thus the absolutist state was not the same as a totalitarian state. *Totalitarianism* is a twentieth-century phenomenon; it seeks to direct all facets of a state's culture—art, education, religion, the economy, and politics—in the interests of the state. By definition totalitarian rule strives for *total* regulation. By twentieth-century standards, the ambitions of absolute monarchs were quite limited. Yet the absolutist state did foreshadow recent totalitarian regimes in two fundamental respects: in the glorification of the state over all other aspects of the culture and in the use of war and an expansionist foreign policy to divert attention from domestic ills.

All of this is well illustrated by the experience of France, aptly known as the model of absolute monarchy.

FRANCE: THE MODEL OF ABSOLUTE MONARCHY

France had a long history of unifying and centralizing monarchy, although the actual power and effectiveness of the French kings had varied enormously over time. Passing through a time of troubles and civil war after the death of Henry II in 1559, both France and the monarchy recovered under Henry IV and Cardinal Richelieu in the early seventeenth century. They laid the foundations for fully developed French absolutism under the "Great Monarch," Louis XIV. Having provided inspiration for rulers all across Europe, Louis XIV and the mighty machine he fashioned deserve special attention.

The Foundations of French Absolutism: Henry IV and Richelieu

Henry IV, the ingenious Huguenot-turned-Catholic, ended the French religious wars with the Edict of Nantes (1598). The first of the Bourbon dynasty, and probably the first French ruler since Louis IX in the thirteenth century genuinely to care about the French people, Henry IV and his great minister Maximilian de Béthune, duke of Sully (1560–1641), laid the foundations of later French absolutism. Henry denied influence on the royal council to the nobility, which had harassed the countryside for half a century. Maintaining that "if we are without compassion for the people, they must succumb and we all perish with them," Henry also lowered taxes paid by the overburdened peasantry.

Sully reduced the crushing royal debt accumulated during the era of religious conflict and began to build up the treasury. One of the first French officials to appreciate the significance of overseas trade, Sully subsidized the Company for Trade with the Indies. He started a countrywide highway system and even dreamed of an international organization for the maintenance of peace.

In twelve years, Henry IV and Sully restored public order in France and laid the foundation for economic prosperity. By the standards of the time, Henry IV's government was progressive and promising. His murder in 1610 by a crazed fanatic led to a severe crisis.

After the death of Henry IV, the queen-regent Marie de' Medici led the government for the child-king Louis XIII (r. 1610–1643), but feudal nobles and princes of the blood dominated the political scene. In 1624 Marie de' Medici secured the appointment of Armand Jean du Plessis—Cardinal Richelieu (1585–1642)—to the council of ministers. It was a remarkable appointment. The next year Richelieu became president of the council, and after 1628 he was first minister of the French crown. Richelieu used his strong influence over King Louis XIII to exalt the French monarchy as the embodiment of the French state. One of the greatest servants of the French state, Richelieu set in place the cornerstone of French absolutism, and his work served as the basis for France's cultural domination of Europe in the later seventeenth century.

Richelieu's policy was the total subordination of all groups and institutions to the French monar-chy. The French nobility, with its selfish and independent interests, had long constituted the foremost threat to the centralizing goals of the Crown and to a strong national state. Therefore, Richelieu tried to break the power of the nobility. He leveled castles, long the symbol of feudal independence. He crushed aristocratic conspiracies with quick executions, and he never called a session of the Estates General—the ancient representative body of the medieval orders that was primarily a representative of the nobility.

The constructive genius of Cardinal Richelieu is best reflected in the administrative system he established. He extended the use of the royal commissioners called *intendants,* each of whom held authority in one of France's thirty-two *généralités* ("districts"). The intendants were authorized "to decide, order and execute all that they see good to do." Usually members of the upper middle class or minor nobility, the intendants were appointed directly by the monarch, to whom they were solely responsible. The intendants recruited men for the army, supervised the collection of taxes, presided over the administration of local law, checked up on the local nobility, and regulated economic activities—commerce, trade, the guilds, marketplaces—in their districts. They were to use their power for two related purposes: to enforce royal orders in the généralités of their jurisdiction and to weaken the power and influence of the regional nobility. As the intendants' power grew during Richelieu's administration, so did the power of the centralized state.

The cardinal perceived that Protestantism often served as a cloak for the political intrigues of ambitious lords. When the Huguenots revolted in 1625, under the duke of Rohan, Richelieu personally supervised the siege of their walled city, La Rochelle, and forced it to surrender. Thereafter, fortified cities were abolished. Huguenots were allowed to practice their faith, but they no longer possessed armed strongholds or the means to be an independent party in the state.

French foreign policy under Richelieu was aimed at the destruction of the fence of Habsburg territories that surrounded France. Consequently, Richelieu supported the Habsburgs' enemies. In 1631 he signed a treaty with the Lutheran king Gustavus Adolphus, promising French support against the Catholic Habsburgs in what has been called the Swedish phase of the Thirty Years' War (see page 591). French influence became an important factor in the political future of the German Empire.

These new policies, especially war, cost money. Richelieu fully realized that revenues determine a government's ability to inaugurate and enforce policies and programs. A state secures its revenues through taxation. But seventeenth-century France remained "a collection of local economies and local societies dominated by local elites." The government's power to tax was limited by the rights of assemblies in some provinces (such as Brittany) to vote their own taxes, the hereditary exemption from taxation of many wealthy members of the nobility and the middle class, and the royal pension system. Richelieu—and later Louis XIV—temporarily solved their financial problems by securing the cooperation of local elites. But because the French monarchy could not tax at will, it never completely controlled the financial system. Thus French absolutism was restrained by its need to compromise with the financial interests of well-entrenched groups.[1]

In building the French state, Richelieu believed that he had to take drastic measures against persons and groups within France and conduct a tough anti-Habsburg foreign policy. He knew that his approach sometimes seemed to contradict traditional Christian teaching. As a priest and bishop, how did he justify his policies? He developed his own *raison d'état* ("reason of state"): "What is done for the state is done for God, who is the basis and foundation of it." Richelieu had no doubt that "the French state was a Christian state . . . governed by a Christian monarch with the valuable aid of an enlightened Cardinal Minister." "Where the interests of the state are concerned," the cardinal himself wrote, "God absolves actions which, if privately committed, would be a crime."[2]

Richelieu persuaded Louis XIII to appoint his protégé Jules Mazarin (1602–1661) as his successor. When Louis XIII followed Richelieu to the grave in 1643 and a regency headed by Queen Anne of Austria governed for the child-king Louis XIV, Mazarin became the dominant power in the government. He continued the centralizing policies of Richelieu, but his attempts to increase royal revenues led to the civil wars known as the "Fronde." The word *fronde* means "slingshot" or "catapult," and a *frondeur* was originally a street urchin who threw mud at the passing carriages of the rich. The term came to be used for anyone who opposed the policies of the government.

Philippe de Champaigne: Cardinal Richelieu This portrait, with its penetrating eyes, expression of haughty and imperturbable cynicism, and dramatic sweep of red robes, suggests the authority, grandeur, and power that Richelieu wished to convey as first minister of France. *(Source: Reproduced by courtesy of the Trustees, The National Gallery, London)*

By 1660 the state bureaucracy included about sixty thousand officeholders, who represented a great expansion of the royal presence. These officeholders and state bureaucrats extracted the wealth of the working people and were the bitter targets of the exploited peasants and artisans. But these officials, who considered their positions the path to economic and social advancement, felt that they were being manipulated by the Crown and their interests ignored.[3] When in 1648 Mazarin proposed new methods of raising state income, bitter civil war ensued between the monarchy and the frondeurs (the nobility and middle class). Riots and turmoil wracked Paris and the nation. Violence continued intermittently for the next twelve years.

The conflicts of the Fronde had three significant results for the future. First, it became apparent that the government would have to compromise with the bureaucrats and social elites who controlled local institutions and constituted the state bureaucracy. These groups were already largely exempt from taxation, and Louis XIV confirmed their privileged social status. Second, the French economy was badly disrupted and would take years to rebuild. Finally, the Fronde had a traumatic effect on the young Louis XIV. The king and his mother were frequently threatened and sometimes treated as prisoners by aristocratic factions. This period formed the cornerstone of Louis's political education and of his conviction that the sole alternative to anarchy was to concentrate as much power as possible in his hands.

Coysevox: Louis XIV (1687–1689) The French court envisioned a new classical age with the Sun King as emperor and his court as a new Rome. This statue depicts Louis in a classical pose, clothed (except for the wig) as for a Roman military triumph. *(Source: Caisse Nationale des Monuments Historiques et des Sites, Paris. Copyright 1990 ARS N.Y./SPADEM)*

The Absolute Monarchy of Louis XIV

In the reign of Louis XIV (r. 1643–1715), the longest in European history, the French monarchy reached the peak of its absolutist development. In the magnificence of his court, in his absolute power, in the brilliance of the culture over which he presided and which permeated all of Europe, and in his remarkably long life, the "Sun King" dominated his age. It was said that when Louis sneezed, all Europe caught cold.

Born in 1638, king at the age of five, Louis entered into personal, or independent, rule in 1661. He imbibed the devout Catholicism of his mother, Anne of Austria, and throughout his life scrupulously performed his religious duties. Religion, Anne, and Mazarin all taught Louis that God had established kings as his rulers on earth. The royal coronation consecrated Louis to God's service, and he was certain that although kings were a race apart, they had to obey God's laws and rule for the good of the people.

Louis's education was more practical than formal. Under Mazarin's instruction, he conscientiously studied state papers as they arrived, and he attended council meetings. He learned by direct experience, and the misery he suffered during the Fronde gave Louis an eternal distrust of the nobility and a profound sense of his own isolation. Accordingly, silence, caution, and secrecy became political tools for the achievement of his goals. His characteristic answer to requests of all kinds became the enigmatic "Je verrai" ("I shall see").

Louis grew up with a strong sense of his royal dignity. Contemporaries considered him tall and distinguished in appearance but inclined to heaviness because of the gargantuan meals in which he indulged. A highly sensual man easily aroused by an attractive female face and figure, Louis nonetheless ruled without the political influence of either his wife, Queen Maria Theresa, or his mistresses. A consummate actor, he worked extremely hard and succeeded in being "every moment and every inch a king."

Historians have often said that Louis XIV was able to control completely the nobility, which historically had opposed the centralizing goals of the French monarchy. Recent research, however, has demonstrated that Louis XIV actually secured the cooperation or collaboration of the nobility. The nobility agreed to participate in projects that both exalted the monarchy and reinforced the aristocrats' ancient prestige. Through collaboration, the nobility and the king achieved goals that neither could have won alone. Thus French government in the seventeenth century rested on a social and political structure in which the nobility exercised great influence. In this respect, French absolutism was not so much modern as the last phase of a feudal society.[4]

Louis XIV installed his royal court at Versailles, a small town 10 miles from Paris. Louis XIII began Versailles as a hunting lodge, a retreat from a queen he did not like. His son's architects, Le Nôtre and Le Vau, turned what the duke of Saint-Simon called "the most dismal and thankless of sights" into a veritable paradise. Louis XIV required all the great nobility of France—at the peril of social, political, and sometimes economic disaster—to live at Versailles for at least part of the year. Today Versailles stands as the best surviving museum of a vanished society. In the seventeenth century, it became a model of rational order, the center of France and thus the center of Western civilization, the perfect symbol of the king's power. In the gigantic Hall of Mirrors, later to reflect so much of German as well as French history, hundreds of candles illuminated the domed ceiling, where allegorical paintings celebrated the king's victories. Thus Louis skillfully used the art and architecture of Versailles to overawe his subjects and foreign visitors and reinforce his power. Many monarchs subsequently imitated Louis XIV's example.

As in architecture, so too in language. Beginning in the reign of Louis XIV, French became the language of polite society and the vehicle of diplomatic exchange. French gradually replaced Latin as the language of international scholarship and learning. The wish of other kings to ape the courtly style of Louis XIV spread the language all over Europe. The royal courts of Sweden, Russia, Poland, and Germany all spoke French. France inspired a cosmopolitan European culture in the late seventeenth century, and that culture was inspired by the king.

Against this background of magnificent splendor, as Saint-Simon describes him, Louis XIV

> . . . reduced everyone to subjection, and brought to his court those very persons he cared least about. Whoever was old enough to serve did not dare demur. It was still another device to ruin the nobles by accustoming them to equality and forcing them to mingle with everyone indiscriminately. . . .
>
> Upon rising, at bedtime, during meals, in his apartments, in the gardens of Versailles, everywhere the courtiers had a right to follow, he would glance right and left to see who was there; he saw and noted everyone; he missed no one, even those who were hoping they would not be seen. . . .
>
> Louis XIV took great pains to inform himself on what was happening everywhere, in public places, private homes, and even on the international scene. . . . Spies and informers of all kinds were numberless. . . .
>
> But the King's most vicious method of securing information was opening letters.[5]

Although this passage was written by one of Louis's severest critics, all agree that the king used court ceremonial to curb the great nobility. By excluding the highest nobles from his councils, he weakened their ancient right to advise the king and to participate in government; they became mere instruments of royal policy. Operas, fêtes, balls, gossip, and trivia occupied the nobles' time and attention. Thus Louis XIV separated power from status and grandeur: he secured the nobles' cooperation, and the nobility enjoyed the status and grandeur in which they lived.

In government Louis utilized several councils of state, which he personally attended, and the intendants, who acted for the councils throughout France. A stream of questions and instructions flowed between local districts and Versailles, and under Louis XIV a uniform and centralized administration was imposed on the country. The councilors of state came from the upper middle class or from the recently ennobled, who were popularly known as the "nobility of the robe" (because of the long judicial robes many of them wore). These ambitious professional bureaucrats served the state in the person of the king, but they clearly did not share power with the monarch, as great nobles had in the past.

Throughout Louis's long reign and despite increasing financial problems, he never called a meeting of the Estates General. Thus the nobility had no means of united expression or action. Nor did Louis have a first minister; he kept himself free from worry about the inordinate power of a Richelieu. Louis's use of spying and terror—a secret police force, a system of informers, and the practice of opening private letters—foreshadowed some of the devices of the modern state. French government remained highly structured, bureaucratic, centered at Versailles, and responsible to Louis XIV.

Financial and Economic Management Under Louis XIV: Colbert

Louis XIV's bureaucracy, court, and army cost a great amount of money, and the French method of collecting taxes consistently failed to produce the necessary revenue. Tax collectors pocketed a good portion of what they raked in. In addition, an old agreement between the Crown and the nobility permitted the king to tax the common people if he did not tax the nobles. That agreement weakened the nobility's role in government: since they did not pay taxes, they could not legitimately claim a say in how tax money was spent. Louis, however, lost enormous potential revenue. The middle classes, moreover, secured many tax exemptions. With the rich and prosperous classes exempt, the tax burden fell heavily on those least able to pay: the poor peasants.

The king named Jean-Baptiste Colbert (1619–1683), the son of a wealthy merchant-financier of Reims, as controller-general of finances. Colbert came to manage the entire royal administration and proved himself a financial genius. Colbert's central principle was that the wealth and the economy of France should serve the state. He did not invent the system called "mercantilism," but he rigorously applied it to France.

Mercantilism is a collection of government policies for the regulation of economic activities, especially commercial activities, by and for the state. In seventeenth- and eighteenth-century economic theory, a nation's international power was thought to be based on its wealth, and specifically the gold so necessary for fighting wars. To accumulate gold, a country should always sell more goods abroad than it bought. Colbert, however, insisted that France should be self-sufficient, able to produce within its borders everything needed by the subjects of the French king. Consequently, the outflow of gold would be halted; debtor states would pay in bullion; and, with the wealth of the nation increased, its power and prestige would be enhanced.

Colbert attempted to accomplish self-sufficiency through state support for both old industries and newly created ones. He subsidized the established cloth industries at Abbeville, Saint-Quentin, and Carcassonne. New factories at Saint-Antoine in Paris manufactured mirrors to replace Venetian imports, and foundries at Saint-Étienne made steel and firearms that reduced Swedish imports. To ensure a high-quality finished product, Colbert set up a system of state inspection and regulation. He compelled all craftsmen to organize into guilds, and within every guild he gave the masters absolute power over their workers. Colbert encouraged skilled foreign craftsmen and manufacturers to immigrate to France, and he gave them special privileges. To improve communications, he built roads and canals, the most famous linking the Mediterranean and the Bay of Biscay. To protect French goods, he abolished many domestic tariffs and enacted high foreign tariffs, which prevented foreign products from competing with French ones.

Colbert's most important work was the creation of a powerful merchant marine to transport French goods. He gave bonuses to French shipowners and shipbuilders and established maritime conscription, arsenals, and academies for the training of sailors. In 1661 France possessed 18 unseaworthy vessels; by 1681 it had 276 frigates, galleys, and ships of the line. Colbert tried to organize and regulate the entire French economy for the glory of the French state as embodied in the king.

Colbert's achievement in the development of manufacturing was prodigious. The textile industry, especially in woolens, expanded enormously, and "France . . . had become in 1683 the leading nation of the world in industrial productivity."[6] The commercial classes prospered, and between 1660 and 1700 their position steadily improved.

The national economy, however, rested on agriculture. Although French peasants were not serfs, as were the peasants of eastern Europe, they were mercilessly taxed. After 1685 other hardships afflicted them: poor harvests, continuing deflation of the currency, and fluctuation in the price of grain. Many peasants emigrated. With the decline in population and thus in the number of taxable people, the state's resources fell. A totally inadequate tax base and heavy expenditure for war in the later years of Louis's reign made Colbert's goals unattainable.

Revocation of the Edict of Nantes

In 1685, Louis XIV revoked the Edict of Nantes. The new law ordered the destruction of churches, the closing of schools, the Catholic baptism of Huguenots, and the exile of Huguenot pastors who refused to renounce their faith. Why? During previous years there had been so many mass conversions (many of them forced) that Madame de Maintenon, Louis's second wife, could say that "nearly all the Huguenots were converted." Some Huguenots had emigrated. Richelieu had already deprived French Calvinists of political rights. Why, then, did Louis, by revoking the edict, persecute some of his most loyal and industrially skilled subjects, force others to flee abroad, and provoke the outrage of Protestant Europe?

Recent scholarship has convincingly shown that Louis XIV was basically tolerant. He insisted on religious unity not for religious but for political reasons. His goal was "one king, one law, one faith." He hated division within the realm and insisted that religious unity was essential to his royal dignity and to the security of the state. The seventeenth century, moreover, was not a tolerant one. France in the early years of Louis's reign permitted religious liberty, but it was not a popular policy. In fact, aristocrats had petitioned Louis to crack down on Protestants. The revocation, however, was solely the king's decision, and it won him enormous praise: "If the flood of congratulation means anything, it . . . was probably the one act of his reign that, at the time, was popular with the majority of his subjects."[7]

Although contemporaries applauded Louis XIV, writers in the eighteenth century and later damned him for intolerance and for the adverse impact that revocation had on the economy and foreign af-

The Spider and the Fly In reference to the insect symbolism (upper left), the caption on the lower left side of this illustration states, "The noble is the spider, the peasant the fly." The other caption (upper right) notes, "The more people have, the more they want. The poor man brings everything—wheat, fruit, money, vegetables. The greedy lord sitting there ready to take everything will not even give him the favor of a glance." This satirical print summarizes peasant grievances. *(Source: New York Public Library)*

fairs. They claimed that tens of thousands of Huguenot craftsmen, soldiers, and business people emigrated, depriving France of their skills and tax revenues and carrying their bitterness to Holland, England, and Prussia. Modern scholarship has greatly modified this picture. Huguenot settlers in northern Europe did aggravate Protestant hatred for Louis, but the revocation of the Edict of Nantes had only minor and scattered effects on French economic development.[8]

French Classicism

Scholars characterize French art and literature during the age of Louis XIV as "French classicism." French artists and writers of the late seventeenth century deliberately imitated the subject matter and style of classical antiquity; their work resembled that of Renaissance Italy. French art possessed the classical qualities of discipline, balance, and restraint. Classicism was the official style of Louis's court.

After Louis's accession to power, the principles of absolutism molded the ideals of French classicism. Individualism was not allowed, and artists glorified the state as personified by the king. Precise rules governed all aspects of culture. Formal and restrained perfection was the goal.

Contemporaries said that Louis XIV never ceased playing the role of grand monarch on the stage of his court, and he used music and theater as a backdrop for court ceremonial. Louis favored

Jean-Baptiste Lully (1632–1687), whose orchestral works combine lively animation with the restrained austerity typical of French classicism. Lully also composed court ballets, and his operatic productions were a powerful influence throughout Europe. Louis also supported François Couperin (1668–1733), whose harpsichord and organ works possess the grandeur the king loved, and Marc-Antoine Charpentier (1634–1704), whose solemn religious music entertained him at meals.

Louis XIV loved the stage, and in the plays of Molière and Racine his court witnessed the finest achievements of the French theater. When Jean-Baptiste Poquelin (1622–1673), the son of a pros-

Poussin: The Rape of the Sabine Women (ca 1636) Considered the greatest French painter of the seventeenth century, Poussin in this dramatic work shows his complete devotion to the ideals of classicism. The heroic figures are superb physical specimens, but hardly lifelike. *(Source: The Metropolitan Museum of Art, New York, Harris Brisbane Dick Fund, 1946 (46.160)).*

perous tapestry maker, refused to join his father's business and entered the theater, he took the stage name "Molière." As playwright, stage manager, director, and actor, Molière produced comedies that exposed the hypocrisies and follies of society through brilliant caricature. *Tartuffe* satirized the religious hypocrite; *Les Femmes Savantes (The Learned Women)* mocked the fashionable pseudo-intellectuals of the day. In structure Molière's plays followed classical models, but they were based on careful social observation. Molière made the bourgeoisie the butt of his ridicule; he stopped short of criticizing the nobility, thus reflecting the policy of his royal patron.

While Molière dissected social mores, his contemporary Jean Racine (1639–1699) analyzed the power of love. Racine based his tragic dramas on Greek and Roman legends, and his persistent theme is the conflict of good and evil. Several of his plays—*Andromaque, Bérénice, Iphigénie,* and *Phèdre*—bear the names of women and deal with the power of passion in women. For simplicity of language, symmetrical structure, and calm restraint, the plays of Racine represent the finest examples of French classicism. His tragedies and Molière's comedies are still produced today.

Louis XIV's Wars

Visualizing himself as a great military hero, Louis XIV used almost endless war to exalt himself above the other rulers of Europe. "The character of a conqueror," he remarked, "is regarded as the noblest and highest of titles." Military glory was his aim. In 1666 Louis appointed François le Tellier (later marquis of Louvois) secretary of war. Louvois created a professional army, which was modern in the sense that the French state, rather than private nobles, employed the soldiers. The king himself took personal command of the army and directly supervised all aspects and details of military affairs.

A commissariat was established to feed the troops, taking the place of the usual practice of living off the countryside. An ambulance corps was formed to look after the wounded. Uniforms and weapons were standardized. A rational system of recruitment, training, discipline, and promotion was imposed. With this new military machine, one national state, France, was able to dominate the politics of Europe for the first time.

Louis continued on a broader scale the expansionist policy begun by Cardinal Richelieu. In 1667, using a dynastic excuse, he invaded Flanders, part of the Spanish Netherlands, and Franche-Comté. He thus acquired twelve towns, including the important commercial centers of Lille and Tournai (Map 19.1). Five years later, Louis personally led an army of over 100,000 men into Holland, and the Dutch ultimately saved themselves only by opening the dikes and flooding the countryside. This war, which lasted six years and eventually involved the Holy Roman Empire and Spain, was concluded by the Treaty of Nijmegen (1678). Louis gained additional Flemish towns and all of Franche-Comté.

Encouraged by his successes, by the weakness of the German Empire, and by divisions among the other European powers, Louis continued his aggression. In 1681 he seized the city of Strasbourg and three years later sent his armies into the province of Lorraine. At that moment the king seemed invincible. In fact, Louis had reached the limit of his expansion at Nijmegen. The wars of the 1680s and 1690s brought him no additional territories. In 1689 the Dutch prince William of Orange, a bitter foe, became king of England. William joined the League of Augsburg—which included the Habsburg emperor, the kings of Spain and Sweden, and the electors of Bavaria, Saxony, and the Palatinate—adding British resources and men to the alliance. Neither the French nor the league won any decisive victories. France lacked the means to win; it was financially exhausted.

Louis was attempting to support an army of 200,000 men, in several different theaters of war. The weight of taxation fell on the already overburdened peasants. The frustrated workers revolted all over France late in the century.

A series of bad harvests between 1688 and 1694 brought catastrophe. Cold, wet summers reduced the harvests by an estimated one-third to two-thirds. The price of wheat skyrocketed. The result was widespread starvation, and in many provinces the death rate rose to several times the normal figure. Rising grain prices, new taxes for war on top of old ones, a slump in manufacturing and thus in exports, and the constant nuisance of pillaging troops—all these meant great suffering for the French people. France wanted peace at any price. Louis XIV granted a respite for five years while he prepared for the conflict later known as the "War of the Spanish Succession."

MAP 19.1 The Acquisitions of Louis XIV, 1668–1713 The desire for glory and the weakness of his German neighbors encouraged Louis's expansionist policy. But he paid a high price for his acquisitions.

This struggle (1701–1713), provoked by the territorial disputes of the past century, also involved the dynastic question of the succession to the Spanish throne. It was an open secret in Europe that the king of Spain, Charles II (r. 1665–1700), was mentally defective and sexually impotent. In 1698 the European powers, including France, agreed by treaty to partition, or divide, the vast Spanish possessions between the king of France and the Holy Roman emperor, who were Charles II's brothers-in-law. When Charles died in 1700, however, his will left the Spanish crown and the worldwide Spanish Empire to Philip of Anjou, Louis XIV's grandson. Louis, who obviously would gain power in Spain, reneged on the treaty and accepted the will.

The Dutch and the English would not accept French acquisition of the Spanish Netherlands and of the rich trade with the Spanish colonies. The union of the Spanish and French crowns, moreover, would have totally upset the European balance of power. The Versailles declaration that "the Pyrenees no longer exist" provoked the long-anticipated crisis.

In 1701 the English, Dutch, Austrians, and Prussians formed the Grand Alliance against Louis XIV. They claimed that they were fighting to prevent France from becoming too strong in Europe, but the allied powers also wanted to check France's expanding commercial power in North America, Asia, and Africa. In the ensuing series of conflicts, Louis suffered major defeats at Blenheim in Bavaria and at Ramillies near Namur in Brabant.

The war was finally concluded at Utrecht in 1713, where the principle of partition was applied.

Louis's grandson Philip remained the first Bourbon king of Spain on the understanding that the French and Spanish crowns would never be united. France surrendered Newfoundland, Nova Scotia, and the Hudson Bay territory to England, which also acquired Gibraltar, Minorca, and control of the African slave trade from Spain. The Dutch gained little because Austria received the former Spanish Netherlands (Map 19.2).

The Peace of Utrecht had important international consequences. It represented the balance-of-power principle in operation, setting limits on the extent to which any one power, in this case France, could expand. The treaty completed the decline of Spain as a great power. It vastly expanded the British Empire. Finally, Utrecht gave European powers experience in international cooperation, thus preparing them for the alliances against France at the end of the century.

The Peace of Utrecht marked the end of French expansionist policy. In Louis's thirty-five-year quest for military glory, his main territorial acquisition was Strasbourg. Even revisionist historians, who portray the aging monarch as responsible in negotiation and moderate in his demands, acknowledge "that the widespread misery in France during the period was in part due to royal policies, especially the incessant wars."[9]

THE DECLINE OF ABSOLUTIST SPAIN IN THE SEVENTEENTH CENTURY

Spanish absolutism and greatness had preceded that of the French. In the sixteenth century, Spain (or, more precisely, the kingdom of Castile) had developed the standard features of absolute monarchy: a permanent bureaucracy staffed by professionals employed in the various councils of state, a standing army, and national taxes, the *servicios,* which fell most heavily on the poor.

France depended on financial and administrative unification within its borders; Spain had developed an international absolutism on the basis of silver bullion from Peru. Spanish gold and silver, armies, and glory had dominated Europe for most of the sixteenth century, but by the 1590s the seeds of disaster were sprouting. While France in the seventeenth century represented the classic model of the modern absolute state, Spain was experiencing steady decline. The lack of a strong

middle class (largely the result of the expulsion of the Jews and Moors), agricultural crisis and population decline, failure to invest in productive enterprises, intellectual isolation and psychological malaise—by 1715 all combined to reduce Spain to a second-rate power.

The fabulous and seemingly inexhaustible flow of silver from Mexico and Peru had led Philip II (see page 587) to assume the role of defender of Roman Catholicism in Europe. In order to humble the Dutch and to regain control of all the Low Countries, Philip believed that England, the Netherlands' greatest supporter, had to be crushed. He poured millions of Spanish ducats and all of Spanish hopes into the vast fleet that sailed in 1588. When the "Invincible Armada" went down, a century of Spanish pride and power went with it. After 1590 a spirit of defeatism and disillusionment crippled most reform efforts.

Philip II's Catholic crusade had been financed by the revenues of the Spanish-Atlantic economy. These included, in addition to silver and gold bullion, money from the sale of cloth, grain, oil, and wine to the colonies. In the early seventeenth century, the Dutch and English began to trade with the Spanish colonies, cutting into the revenues that had gone to Spain. Mexico and Peru themselves developed local industries, further lessening their need to buy from Spain. Between 1610 and 1650, Spanish trade with the colonies fell 60 percent.

At the same time, the native Indians and African slaves, who worked the South American silver mines under conditions that would have shamed the ancient Egyptian pharaohs, suffered frightful epidemics of disease. Moreover, the lodes started to run dry. Consequently, the quantity of metal produced for Spain steadily declined. Nevertheless, in Madrid royal expenditures constantly exceeded income. The remedies applied in the face of a mountainous state debt and declining revenues were devaluation of the coinage and declarations of bankruptcy. In 1596, 1607, 1627, 1647, and 1680, Spanish kings found no solution to the problem of an empty treasury other than to cancel the national debt. Given the frequency of cancellation, public confidence in the state deteriorated.

Spain, in contrast to the other countries of western Europe, had only a tiny middle class. The Spanish disdain for money, in a century of increasing commercialism and bourgeois attitudes, reveals a significant facet of the Spanish national

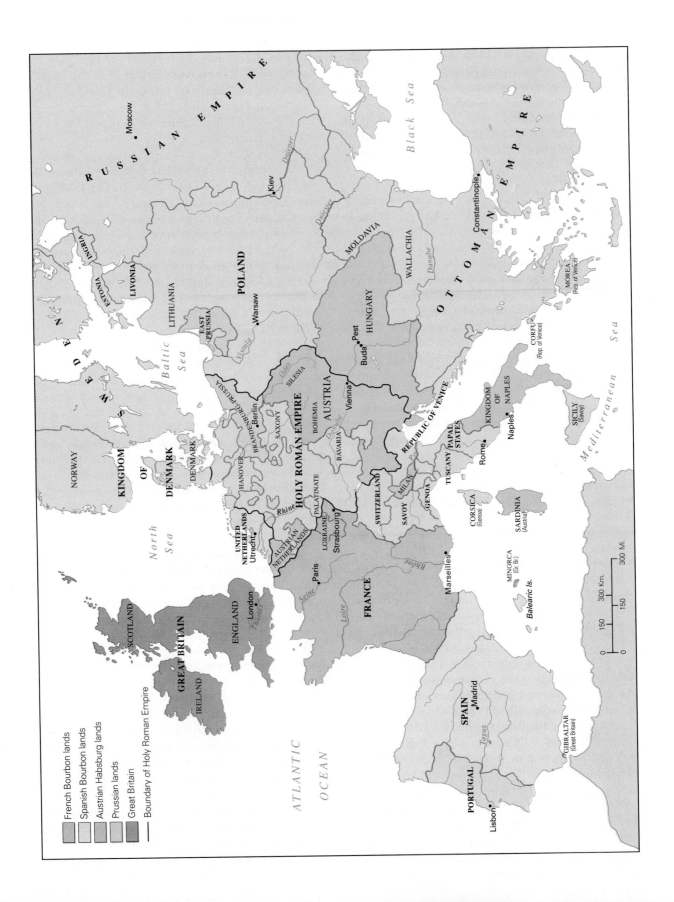

RUSSIAN EMPIRE

Moscow

Black Sea

OTTOMAN EMPIRE

Constantinople

Kiev

Dnieper

Dniester

POLAND

MOLDAVIA

WALLACHIA

Danube

Warsaw

Vistula

LITHUANIA

EAST PRUSSIA

ESTONIA

INGRIA

LIVONIA

HUNGARY

Pest

Buda

MOREA
(Rep. of Venice)

CORFU
(Rep. of Venice)

Baltic Sea

SILESIA

Oder

WEST PRUSSIA

AUSTRIA

Vienna

HOLY ROMAN EMPIRE

BOHEMIA

SAXONY

Berlin

BRANDENBURG

Mediterranean Sea

REPUBLIC OF VENICE

KINGDOM OF NAPLES

SICILY
(Savoy)

HANOVER

BAVARIA

Danube

PAPAL STATES

Naples

NORWAY

KINGDOM OF DENMARK

DENMARK

MILAN

TUSCANY

Rome

SWITZERLAND

SAVOY

GENOA

North Sea

Rhine

PALATINATE

UNITED NETHERLANDS

Utrecht

AUSTRIAN NETHERLANDS

LORRAINE

Strasbourg

CORSICA
(Genoa)

SARDINIA
(Austria)

SWEDEN

Paris

Seine

FRANCE

Loire

Rhone

Marseilles

MINORCA
(Gr. Br.)

Balearic Is.

SCOTLAND

GREAT BRITAIN

ENGLAND

London

Thames

IRELAND

ATLANTIC OCEAN

SPAIN

Madrid

Tagus

PORTUGAL

Lisbon

GIBRALTAR
(Great Britain)

French Bourbon lands
Spanish Bourbon lands
Austrian Habsburg lands
Prussian lands
Great Britain
Boundary of Holy Roman Empire

300 Mi.

300 Km.

150

150

0

character. Public opinion, taking its cue from the aristocracy, condemned moneymaking as vulgar and undignified. Those with influence or connections sought titles of nobility and social prestige or became priests, monks, and nuns. The flood of gold and silver had produced severe inflation, pushing the costs of production in the textile industry higher and higher, to the point that Castilian cloth could not compete in colonial and international markets. Many businessmen found so many obstacles in the way of profitable enterprise that they simply gave up.[10]

Spanish aristocrats, attempting to maintain an extravagant lifestyle that they could no longer afford, increased the rents on their estates. High rents and heavy taxes in turn drove the peasants from the land. Agricultural production suffered, and the peasants departed for the large cities, where they swelled the ranks of beggars.

Their most Catholic majesties, the kings of Spain, had no solutions to these dire problems. If one can discern personality from pictures, the portraits of Philip III (r. 1598–1622), Philip IV (r. 1622–1665), and Charles II hanging in the Prado (the Spanish national museum in Madrid) reflect the increasing weakness of the dynasty. Their faces—the small, beady eyes, the long noses, the jutting Habsburg jaws, the pathetically stupid expressions—tell a story of excessive inbreeding and decaying monarchy.

Philip IV left the management of his several kingdoms to Count Olivares. An able administrator, the count did not lack energy and ideas. He devised new sources of revenue, but he clung to the grandiose belief that the solution to Spain's difficulties rested in a return to the imperial tradition. Unfortunately, the imperial tradition demanded the revival of war with the Dutch, at the expiration of a twelve-year truce in 1622, and a long war with France over Mantua (1628–1659). Spain thus became embroiled in the Thirty Years' War. These conflicts, on top of an empty treasury, brought disaster.

In 1640 Spain faced serious revolts in Catalonia and Portugal; in 1643 the French inflicted a crushing defeat on a Spanish army in Belgium. By the Treaty of the Pyrenees of 1659, which ended the French-Spanish wars, Spain was compelled to surrender extensive territories to France. This treaty marked the end of Spain as a great power.

Seventeenth-century Spain was the victim of its past. It could not forget the grandeur of the sixteenth century and look to the future. The most cherished Spanish ideals were military glory and strong Roman Catholic faith. In the seventeenth century, Spain lacked the finances and the manpower to fight the expensive wars in which it foolishly got involved. Spain also ignored the new mercantile ideas and scientific methods because they came from heretical nations, Holland and England.

In the brilliant novel *Don Quixote*, the Spanish writer Miguel de Cervantes (1547–1616) produced one of the masterpieces of world literature. *Don Quixote*—on which the modern play *Man of La Mancha* is based—delineates the whole fabric of sixteenth-century Spanish society. The main character, Don Quixote, lives in a dream world, traveling about the countryside seeking military glory. A leading scholar wrote, "The Spaniard convinced himself that reality was what he felt, believed, imagined. He filled the world with heroic reverberations. Don Quixote was born and grew."[11]

MAP 19.2 Europe in 1715 The series of treaties commonly called the Peace of Utrecht (April 1713–November 1715) ended the War of the Spanish Succession and redrew the map of Europe. A French Bourbon king succeeded to the Spanish throne on the understanding that the French not attempt to unite the French and Spanish crowns. France surrendered to Austria the Spanish Netherlands (later Belgium), then in French hands; and France recognized the Hohenzollern rulers of Prussia. Spain ceded Gibraltar to Great Britain, for which it has been a strategic naval station ever since. Spain also granted to Britain the *asiento*, the contract for supplying African slaves to America.

LORDS AND PEASANTS IN EASTERN EUROPE (CA 1050–1650)

The rulers of eastern Europe also struggled to build strong absolutist states in the seventeenth century. But they built on different social and economic foundations, which were laid between 1400 and 1650. In those years, the princes and the landed nobility of eastern Europe rolled back the gains made by the peasantry during the High Middle Ages and reimposed serfdom on the rural masses. The nobility also reduced the importance of the towns and the middle classes. This process—another manifestation of the shattered unity of medieval Latin Christendom—differed profoundly from developments in western Europe at the same time. In the West, peasants were winning greater freedom and the rise of the urban capitalistic middle class was continuing.

The Medieval Background

Between roughly 1400 and 1650, nobles and rulers re-established serfdom in Bohemia, Silesia, Hungary, eastern Germany, Poland, Lithuania, and Russia. The east—the land east of the Elbe River in Germany, which historians often call "East Elbia"—gained a certain social and economic unity in the process. But eastern peasants lost their rights and freedoms. They became bound first to the land they worked and then, by degrading obligations, to the lords they served.

This development was a tragic reversal of trends in the High Middle Ages. The period from roughly 1050 to 1300 had been a time of general economic expansion characterized by the growth of trade, towns, and population. Expansion had also meant clearing the forests and colonizing the frontier beyond the Elbe River. Eager to attract German settlers to their sparsely populated lands, the rulers and nobles of eastern Europe had offered potential newcomers economic and legal incentives. Large numbers of incoming settlers had obtained land on excellent terms and gained much personal freedom. These benefits were gradually extended to the local Slavic populations, even those of central Russia. Thus by 1300 peasant conditions in eastern Europe had improved. Serfdom had all but disappeared. Peasants were able to bargain freely with their landlords and move about as they pleased. Opportunities and improvements east of the Elbe had a positive impact on western Europe, where the weight of serfdom was also reduced between 1100 and 1300.

After about 1300, however, as Europe's population and economy declined grievously, mainly because of the Black Death, eastern and western Europe went in different directions. In both east and west landlords sought to solve their tough economic problems by more heavily exploiting the peasantry. In the west this attempt generally failed. In many western areas by 1500, almost all of the peasants were completely free, and in the rest of

western Europe the obligations of serfs had declined greatly. East of the Elbe, however, the landlords were successful. By 1500 eastern peasants were on their way to becoming serfs again.

Throughout eastern Europe, as in western Europe, the drop in population and prices in the fourteenth and fifteenth centuries caused severe labor shortages and hard times for the nobles. Yet rather than offer better economic and legal terms to keep old peasants and attract new ones, eastern landlords used political and police power to turn the tables on peasants. They did this in two ways.

First, the lords made their kings and princes issue laws that restricted or eliminated the peasants' right of free movement. As a result, a peasant could no longer move to take advantage of better opportunities elsewhere without the lord's permission, and the lord had no reason to make such a concession. In Prussian territories by 1500, the law required that runaway peasants be hunted down and returned to their lords, and a runaway servant was to be nailed to a post by one ear and given a knife to cut himself loose. Until the middle of the fifteenth century, medieval Russian peasants had been free to move wherever they wished and seek the best landlord. This freedom was gradually curtailed, and by 1497 a Russian peasant had the right to move only during a two-week period after the fall harvest. Eastern peasants were losing their status as free and independent men and women.

Second, lords steadily took more and more of their peasants' land and imposed heavier and heavier labor obligations. Instead of being independent farmers paying reasonable, freely negotiated rents, peasants tended to become forced laborers on the lords' estates. By the early 1500s, lords in many territories could command their peasants to work for them without pay as many as six days a week.

The gradual erosion of the peasantry's economic position was bound up with manipulation of the legal system. The local lord was also the local prosecutor, judge, and jailer. He generally ruled in his own favor in disputes with his peasants. There were no independent royal officials to provide justice or uphold the common law.

The Consolidation of Serfdom

Between 1500 and 1650, the social, legal, and economic conditions of peasants in eastern Europe

Punishing Serfs This seventeenth-century illustration from Olearius's famous *Travels to Moscovy* suggests what eastern serfdom really meant. The scene is set in eastern Poland. There, according to Olearius, a common command of the lord was, "Beat him till the skin falls from the flesh." *(Source: University of Illinois, Champaign)*

continued to decline. In Poland, for example, nobles gained complete control over their peasants in 1574. They could legally inflict the death penalty on their serfs whenever they wished. In Prussia a series of oppressive measures reached a culmination in 1653. All the old privileges of the lords were reaffirmed, and peasants were assumed to be in "hereditary subjugation" to their lords unless they could prove the contrary in the lords' courts (doing so was practically impossible). Prussian peasants were serfs tied to their lords as well as to the land.

In Russia the right of peasants to move from a given estate was "temporarily" suspended in the 1590s and permanently abolished in 1603. In 1649 a new law code completed the legal re-establishment of permanent hereditary serfdom. Henceforth runaway peasants were to be returned to their lords whenever they were caught, as long as they lived. The new law code set no limits on the lords' authority over their peasants, so control of serfs was strictly the lords' own business. Although the political development of the various eastern states differed, the common fate of peasants in eastern Europe and Russia by the middle of the seventeenth century was serfdom.

The consolidation of serfdom between 1500 and 1650 was accompanied by the growth of estate agriculture, particularly in Poland and eastern Germany. In the sixteenth century, European economic expansion and population growth resumed after the great declines of the late Middle Ages. Prices for agricultural commodities also rose sharply as gold and silver flowed in from the New World. Thus Polish and German lords had powerful economic incentives to increase the production of their estates, and they did so.

Lords seized more and more peasant land for themselves and then demanded ever more unpaid serf labor on their enlarged estates. Generally, the estates were inefficient and technically backward. Nevertheless, the great Polish nobles and middle-rank German lords squeezed sizable, cheap, and profitable surpluses out of their impoverished peasants. These surpluses in wheat and timber were sold to foreign merchants, who exported them to the growing western cities. The poor east helped feed the much wealthier west.

The re-emergence of serfdom in eastern Europe in the early modern period was a momentous human development, and historians have advanced a variety of explanations for it. Some scholars have stressed an economic interpretation. According to this view, agricultural depression and population decline in the fourteenth and fifteenth centuries led to a severe labor shortage, and thus eastern landlords naturally tied their peasants to the land. In the sixteenth century, when prosperity returned, they grabbed the peasants' land and made them work as unpaid serfs on the enlarged estates. This explanation by itself is not very convincing, for almost identical economic developments "caused" the opposite result in western Europe.

It seems fairly clear that political rather than economic factors were crucial in the simultaneous rise of serfdom in the east and decline of serfdom in the west. Specifically, eastern lords enjoyed much greater political power than their western counterparts. In the late Middle Ages, when much of eastern Europe was experiencing innumerable wars and general political chaos, the noble landlord class greatly increased its political power at the expense of the ruling monarchs. Because many royal successions were disputed, weak eastern kings were forced to grant political favors to win the support of the nobility, and such weak kings could not resist the lords' demands for their peasants. Moreover, most eastern monarchs did not want to resist. The typical king was only first among equals in the noble class. He, too, thought mainly in private rather than public terms. He, too, wanted to squeeze as much as he could out of his peasants and enlarge his estates. The western concept and reality of sovereignty, as embodied in a king who protected the interests of all his people, was not well developed in eastern Europe before 1650.

The political power of the peasants was also weaker in eastern Europe and declined steadily after about 1400. Although there were occasional bloody peasant uprisings against the oppression of the landlords, they never succeeded. Nor did eastern peasants effectively resist their landlords' day-by-day infringements on their liberties. One reason for their predicament was that the lords, rather than the kings, ran the courts, control of the legal system being one of the important concessions that nobles extorted from weak monarchs.

Finally, with the approval of weak kings, the landlords systematically undermined the medieval privileges of the towns and the power of the urban classes. Instead of selling their products to local merchants in the towns, as required in the Middle Ages, the landlords sold directly to foreign capitalists. For example, Dutch ships sailed up the rivers of Poland and eastern Germany to the loading docks of the great estates, completely by-passing the local towns. Moreover, "town air" no longer "made people free," for the eastern towns had lost their medieval right of refuge and were compelled to return runaways to their lords. The population of the towns and the importance of the urban middle classes declined greatly. This development both reflected and promoted the supremacy of noble landlords in most of eastern Europe in the sixteenth century.

THE RISE OF AUSTRIA AND PRUSSIA

Despite the strength of the nobility and the weakness of many monarchs before 1600, strong kings did begin to emerge in many eastern European lands in the course of the seventeenth century. War and the threat of war aided rulers greatly in their attempts to build absolute monarchies. There was an endless struggle for power, as eastern rulers not only fought each other but also battled with hordes of Asiatic invaders. In this atmosphere of continuous wartime emergency, monarchs reduced the political power of the landlord nobility. Cautiously leaving the nobles the unchallenged masters of their peasants, the absolutist monarchs of eastern Europe gradually gained and monopolized political power in three key areas. They imposed and collected permanent taxes without consent. They maintained permanent standing armies, which policed their subjects in addition to fighting abroad. And they conducted relations with other states as they pleased.

There were important variations on the absolutist theme in eastern Europe. The royal absolutism created in Prussia was stronger and more effective than that established in Austria. This advantage gave Prussia a thin edge over Austria in the struggle for power in east-central Europe in the eighteenth century. That edge had enormous long-term political significance, for it was a rising Prussia that unified the German people in the nineteenth century and imposed on them a fateful Prussian stamp.

Austria and the Ottoman Turks

Like all the other peoples and rulers of central Europe, the Habsburgs of Austria emerged from the Thirty Years' War (see pages 589–592) impoverished and exhausted. The effort to root out Protestantism in the German lands had failed utterly, and the authority of the Holy Roman Empire and its Habsburg emperors had declined almost to the vanishing point. Yet defeat in central Europe also opened new vistas. The Habsburg monarchs were forced to turn inward and eastward to try to fuse their diverse holdings into a strong unified state.

An important step in this direction had actually been taken in Bohemia during the Thirty Years' War. Protestantism had been strong among the Czechs, a Slavic people concentrated in Bohemia. In 1618 the Czech nobles who controlled the Bohemian Estates—the semiparliamentary body of Bohemia—had risen up against their Habsburg king. Not only was this revolt crushed, but the old Czech nobility was wiped out as well. Those Czech nobles who did not die in 1620 at the Battle of the White Mountain (see page 591), a momentous turning point in Czech history, had their landholdings confiscated. The Habsburg king, Ferdinand II (r. 1619–1637), then redistributed the Czech lands to a motley band of aristocratic soldiers of fortune who had nothing in common with the Czech-speaking peasants.

With the help of this new nobility, the Habsburgs established strong direct rule over reconquered Bohemia. The condition of the enserfed peasantry worsened: three days per week of unpaid labor—the *robot*—became the norm, and a quarter of the serfs worked for their lords every day but Sundays and religious holidays. Serfs also paid the taxes, which further strengthened the alliance between the Habsburg monarch and the Bohemian nobility. Protestantism was also stamped out, and religious unity began to emerge. The reorganization of Bohemia was a giant step toward absolutism.

After the Thirty Years' War, Ferdinand III centralized the government in the hereditary German-speaking provinces, most notably Austria, Styria, and the Tyrol. For the first time, Ferdinand III's reign saw the creation of a permanent standing army ready to put down any internal opposition. The Habsburg monarchy was then ready to turn toward the vast plains of Hungary, in opposition to the Ottoman Turks.

The Ottomans had come out of Anatolia, in present-day Turkey, to create one of history's greatest military empires. At their peak in the middle of the sixteenth century under Suleiman the Magnificent (r. 1520–1566), their possessions stretched from western Persia across North Africa and up into the heart of central Europe (Map 23.2, page 751). Apostles of Islam, the Ottoman Turks were old and determined foes of the Catholic Habsburgs. Their armies had almost captured Vienna in 1529, and for more than 150 years thereafter the Ottomans ruled all of the Balkan territories, almost all of Hungary, and part of southern Russia.

In the late seventeenth century, under vigorous reforming leadership, the Ottoman Empire succeeded in marshaling its forces for one last mighty blow at Christian Europe. After wresting territory from Poland, fighting a long inconclusive war with Russia, and establishing an alliance with Louis XIV of France, the Turks turned again on Austria. A huge Turkish army surrounded Vienna and laid siege to it in 1683. After holding out against great odds for two months, the city was relieved at the last minute by a mixed force of Habsburg, Saxon, Bavarian, and Polish troops. The Ottomans were forced to retreat, and the retreat soon became a rout. As their Russian and Venetian allies attacked on other fronts, the Habsburgs conquered all of Hungary and Transylvania (part of present-day Romania) by 1699 (Map 19.3).

The Turkish wars and this great expansion strengthened the Habsburg army and promoted some sense of unity in the Habsburg lands. The Habsburgs moved to centralize their power and make it as absolute as possible. These efforts to create a fully developed, highly centralized, absolutist state were only partly successful.

The Habsburg state was composed of three separate and distinct territories: the old "hereditary provinces" of Austria, the kingdom of Bohemia, and the kingdom of Hungary. These three parts were tied together primarily by their common ruler, the Habsburg monarch. Each part had its own laws and political life, for the three noble-dominated Estates continued to exist, though with reduced powers. The Habsburgs themselves were well aware of the fragility of the union they had forged.

The Hungarian nobility, despite its reduced strength, effectively thwarted the full development of Habsburg absolutism. Time and again

The Siege of Vienna, 1683   Seeking to tunnel under the city walls and blow them up with mines, a huge Turkish army besieged the Habsburg capital and penetrated the outer fortifications on September 2, 1683. As the Turks launched the final assault on the city ten days later, a relief army led by John Sobieski, the King of Poland (shown in foreground), arrived and delivered a successful surprise attack. This painting shows the battle at its height. *(Source: Heeresgeschichtliches Museum, Vienna)*

throughout the seventeenth century, Hungarian nobles—the most numerous in Europe, making up 5 to 7 percent of the Hungarian population—rose in revolt against the attempts of Vienna to impose absolute rule. They never triumphed decisively, but neither were they ever crushed and replaced, as the Czech nobility had been in 1620.

Hungarians resisted because many of them were Protestants, especially in the area long ruled by the more tolerant Turks, and they hated the heavy-handed attempts of the conquering Habsburgs to re-Catholicize everyone. Moreover, the lords of Hungary often found a powerful military ally in Turkey. Finally, the Hungarian nobility, and even part of the Hungarian peasantry, had become attached to a national ideal long before most of the other peoples of eastern Europe. They were determined to maintain as much independence and local control as possible. Thus when the Habs-

burgs were bogged down in the War of the Spanish Succession (see page 617), the Hungarians rose in one last patriotic rebellion under Prince Francis Rákóczy in 1703. Rákóczy and his forces were eventually defeated, but this time the Habsburgs had to accept a definitive compromise. Charles VI restored many of the traditional privileges of the Hungarian aristocracy in return for Hungarian acceptance of hereditary Habsburg rule. Thus Hungary, unlike Austria or Bohemia, never came close to being fully integrated into a centralized, absolute Habsburg state.

Prussia in the Seventeenth Century

After 1400 the status of east German peasants declined steadily; their serfdom was formally spelled out in the early seventeenth century. While the local princes lost political power and influence, a revitalized landed nobility became the undisputed ruling class. The Hohenzollern family, which ruled through its senior and junior branches as the electors of Brandenburg and the dukes of Prussia, had little real princely power. The Hohenzollern rulers were nothing more than the first among equals, the largest landowners in a landlord society.

Nothing suggested that the Hohenzollerns and their territories would ever play an important role in European or even German affairs. The right of the elector of Brandenburg to help choose the Holy Roman emperor with six other electors was of little practical value, and the elector had no military strength whatsoever. The territory of his cousin, the duke of Prussia, was actually part of the kingdom of Poland. Moreover, geography

conspired against the Hohenzollerns. Brandenburg, their power base, was completely cut off from the sea (see Map 19.3), lacked natural frontiers, and lay open to attack from all directions. The land was poor, a combination of sand and swamp. Contemporaries contemptuously called Brandenburg the "sand-box of the Holy Roman Empire."[12]

Brandenburg was a helpless spectator in the Thirty Years' War, its territory alternately ravaged by Swedish and Habsburg armies. Population fell drastically, and many villages disappeared. The power of the Hohenzollerns reached its lowest point. Yet the country's devastation made the way for Hohenzollern absolutism, because foreign armies dramatically weakened the political power of the Estates—the representative assemblies of

MAP 19.3 The Growth of Austria and Brandenburg-Prussia to 1748   Austria expanded to the southwest into Hungary and Transylvania at the expense of the Ottoman Empire. It was unable to hold the rich German province of Silesia, however, which was conquered by Brandenburg-Prussia.

THE RISE OF WESTERN ABSOLUTISM AND CONSTITUTIONALISM

1581	Formation of the United Provinces of the Netherlands
1588	Defeat of the Spanish Armada
1589–1610	Reign of Henry IV of France; economic reforms help to restore public order, lay foundation for absolutist rule
1598	Edict of Nantes: Henry IV ends the French wars of religion
1608	France establishes its first Canadian settlement, at Quebec
1609	Philip III of Spain recognizes Dutch independence
1610–1650	Spanish trade with the New World falls by 60 percent
1618–1648	Thirty Years' War
1624–1643	Richelieu dominates French government
1625	Huguenot revolt in France; siege of La Rochelle
1629–1640	Eleven Years' Tyranny: Charles I attempts to rule England without the aid of Parliament
1640–1660	Long Parliament in England
1642–1646	English civil war
1643–1661	Mazarin dominates France's regency government during Louis XIV's minority
1643–1715	Reign of Louis XIV
1648–1660	The Fronde: French nobility opposes centralizing efforts of monarchy
1648	Peace of Westphalia confirms Dutch independence from Spain
1649	Execution of Charles I; beginning of the Interregnum in England
1653–1658	The Protectorate: Cromwell heads military rule of England
1659	Treaty of the Pyrenees forces Spain to cede extensive territories to France, marks end of Spain as a great power
1660	Restoration of the English monarchy: Charles II returns from exile
1661	Louis XIV enters into independent rule
ca 1663–1683	Colbert directs Louis XIV's mercantilist economic policy
1670	Treaty of Dover: Charles II secretly agrees with Louis XIV to re-Catholicize England
1673	Test Act excludes Roman Catholics from public office in England
	France invades Holland
1678	Treaty of Nijmegen: Louis XIV acquires Franche-Comté
1681	France acquires Strasbourg
1685	Louis XIV revokes the Edict of Nantes
1685–1688	James II rules England, attempts to restore Roman Catholicism as state religion
1688	The Glorious Revolution establishes a constitutional monarchy in England under Mary and William III
1689	Enactment of the Bill of Rights
1701–1713	War of the Spanish Succession
1713	Peace of Utrecht ends French territorial acquisitions, expands the British Empire

the realm. The weakening of the Estates helped the very talented young elector Frederick William (r. 1640–1688), later known as the "Great Elector," to ride roughshod over traditional parliamentary liberties and to take a giant step toward royal absolutism. This constitutional struggle, often unjustly neglected by historians, was the most crucial in Prussian history for hundreds of years, until that of the 1860s.

When Frederick William came to power in 1640, the twenty-year-old ruler was determined to unify his three quite separate provinces and to add to them by diplomacy and war. These provinces were Brandenburg itself, the area around Berlin; Prussia, inherited in 1618 when the junior branch of the Hohenzollern family died out; and completely separate, scattered holdings along the Rhine in western Germany, inherited in 1614 (see

THE RISE OF ABSOLUTISM IN EASTERN EUROPE

1050–1300	Increasing economic development in eastern Europe encourages decline in serfdom
1054	Death of Great Prince Iaroslav the Wise, under whom the Kievan principality reached its height of unity
1054–1237	Kiev is divided into numerous territories ruled by competing princes
1237–1242	Mongol invasion of Russia
1252	Alexander Nevsky, prince of Moscow, recognizes Mongol overlordship
1327–1328	Suppression of the Tver revolt; Mongol khan recognizes Ivan I as great prince
1400–1650	The nobility reimposes serfdom in eastern Europe
ca 1480	Ivan III rejects Mongol overlordship and begins to use the title of tsar
1520–1566	Rule of Suleiman the Magnificent: Ottoman Empire reaches its height
1533–1584	Rule of Tsar Ivan IV (the Terrible): defeat of the khanates of Kazan and Astrakhan; subjugation of the boyar aristocracy
1574	Polish nobles receive the right to inflict the death penalty on their serfs
1598–1613	Time of Troubles in Russia
1613	Election of Michael Romanov as tsar: re-establishment of autocracy
1620	Battle of the White Mountain in Bohemia: Ferdinand II initiates Habsburg confiscation of Czech estates
1640–1688	Rule of Frederick William, the Great Elector, who unites Brandenburg, Prussia, and western German holdings into one state, Brandenburg-Prussia
1649	Tsar Alexis lifts the nine-year limit on the recovery of runaway serfs
1652	Patriarch Nikon's reforms split the Russian Orthodox church
1653	Principle of peasants' hereditary subjugation to their lords affirmed in Prussia
1670–1671	Cossack revolt of Stenka Razin in Russia
1683	Siege of Vienna by the Ottoman Turks
1683–1699	Habsburg conquest of Hungary and Transylvania
1689–1725	Rule of Tsar Peter the Great
1700–1721	Great Northern War between Russia and Sweden, resulting in Russian victory and territorial expansion
1701	Elector Frederick III crowned king of Prussia
1703	Founding of St. Petersburg
	Rebellion of Prince Francis Rakoczy in Hungary
1713	Pragmatic Sanction: Charles VII guarantees Maria Theresa's succession to the Austrian empire
1713–1740	Rule of King Frederick William I in Prussia

Map 19.3). Each of the three provinces was inhabited by Germans; but each had its own Estates, whose power had increased until about 1600 as the power of the rulers declined. Although the Estates had not met regularly during the chaotic Thirty Years' War, they still had the power of the purse in their respective provinces. The Estates of Brandenburg and Prussia were dominated by the nobility and the landowning classes, known as the "Junkers."

The struggle between the Great Elector and the provincial Estates was long, complicated, and intense. After the Thirty Years' War, the representatives of the nobility zealously reasserted the right of the Estates to vote taxes, a right the Swedish armies of occupation had simply ignored. Yet first in Brandenburg in 1653 and then in Prussia between 1661 and 1663, the Great Elector eventually had his way.

To pay for the permanent standing army that he first established in 1660, Frederick William forced the Estates to accept the introduction of permanent taxation without consent. The soldiers doubled as tax collectors and policemen, becoming the core of the expanding state bureaucracy. The power of the Estates declined rapidly thereafter, for the Great Elector had both financial independence and superior force. He turned the screws of taxation: the state's total revenue tripled during his reign. The size of the army leaped about tenfold.

In accounting for the Great Elector's fateful triumph, two factors appear central. First, as in the formation of every absolutist state, war was a decisive factor. The ongoing struggle between Sweden and Poland for control of the Baltic after 1648 and the wars of Louis XIV in western Europe created an atmosphere of permanent crisis. The Tartars of southern Russia swept through Prussia in the winter of 1656 to 1657, killing and carrying off as slaves more than fifty thousand people, according to an old estimate. This invasion softened up the Estates and strengthened the urgency of the elector's demands for more money for more soldiers. It was no accident that, except in commercially minded Holland, constitutionalism won out only in England, the only major country to escape devastating foreign invasions in the seventeenth century.

Second, the nobility had long dominated the government through the Estates but only for its own narrow self-interest. The nobility was all too concerned with its own rights and privileges, especially its freedom from taxation and its unlimited control over the peasants. When, therefore, the Great Elector reconfirmed these privileges in 1653 and after, even while reducing the political power of the Estates, the nobility accepted a compromise whereby the bulk of the new taxes fell on towns, and royal authority stopped at the landlords' gates. The elector could and did use naked force to break the liberties of the towns. The main leader of the urban opposition in the key city of Königsberg, for example, was simply arrested and imprisoned for life without trial.

The Consolidation of Prussian Absolutism

By the time of his death in 1688, the Great Elector had created a single state out of scattered principalities. But his new creation was still small and

Molding the Prussian Spirit Discipline was strict and punishment brutal in the Prussian army. This scene, from an eighteenth-century book used to teach school children, shows one soldier being flogged while another is being beaten with canes as he walks between rows of troops. The officer on horseback proudly commands. *(Source: University of Illinois, Champaign)*

fragile. Moreover, the Great Elector's successor, Elector Frederick III, "the Ostentatious" (r. 1688–1713), was weak of body and mind. His only real political accomplishment was to gain the title of king from the Holy Roman emperor, a Habsburg, in return for military aid in the War of the Spanish Succession, and in 1701 he was crowned King Frederick I.

The tendency toward luxury-loving, happy, and harmless petty tyranny was completely reversed by Frederick William I, "the Soldiers' King" (r. 1713–1740). A crude, dangerous psychoneurotic, Frederick William I was nevertheless the most talented reformer ever produced by the Hohenzollern family. It was he who truly established Prussian absolutism and gave it its unique character. It was he who created the best army in Europe, for its size, and who infused military values into a whole society.

Frederick William's attachment to the army and military life was intensely emotional. He had, for example, a bizarre, almost pathological love for tall soldiers, whom he credited with superior strength and endurance. Austere and always faithful to his wife, he confided to the French ambassador: "The most beautiful girl or woman in the world would be a matter of indifference to me, but tall soldiers—they are my weakness." Like some fanatical modern-day basketball coach in search of a championship team, he sent his agents throughout both Prussia and all of Europe, tricking, buying, and kidnapping top recruits. Neighboring princes sent him their giants as gifts to win his gratitude. Prussian mothers told their sons: "Stop growing or the recruiting agents will get you."[13]

Frederick William's love of the army was also based on a hardheaded conception of the struggle for power and a dog-eat-dog view of international politics. Even before ascending the throne, he bitterly criticized his father's ministers: "They say that they will obtain land and power for the king with the pen; but I say it can be done only with the sword."[14] Throughout his long reign he never wavered in his conviction that the welfare of king and state depended above all else on the army.

As in France, the cult of military power provided the rationale for a great expansion of royal absolutism. As the ruthless king himself put it: "I must be served with life and limb, with house and wealth, with honour and conscience, everything must be committed except eternal salvation—that belongs to God, but all else is mine."[15] To make good these extraordinary demands, Frederick William created a strong centralized bureaucracy. More commoners probably rose to top positions in the civil government than at any other time in Prussia's history. The last traces of the parliamentary Estates and local self-government vanished.

The king's grab for power brought him into considerable conflict with the noble landowners, the Junkers. In his early years, he even threatened to destroy them; yet in the end the Prussian nobility was not destroyed but enlisted—into the army. Responding to a combination of threats and opportunities, the Junkers became the officer caste. By 1739 all but 5 of 245 officers with the rank of major or above were aristocrats, and most of them were native Prussians. A new compromise had been worked out: the nobility imperiously commanded the peasantry in the army as well as on its estates.

Coarse and crude, penny-pinching and hard working, Frederick William achieved results. Above all, he built a first-rate army on the basis of third-rate resources. The standing army increased from 38,000 to 83,000 during his reign. Prussia, twelfth in Europe in population, had the fourth largest army by 1740, behind France, Russia, and Austria. Moreover, soldier for soldier, the Prussian army became the best in Europe, astonishing foreign observers with its precision, skill, and discipline. For the next two hundred years, Prussia and then Prussianized Germany almost always won the crucial military battles.

Frederick William and his ministers also built an exceptionally honest and conscientious bureaucracy, which not only administered the country but tried with some success to develop it economically. Finally, like the miser he was, living very frugally off the income of his own landholdings, the king loved his "blue boys" so much that he hated to "spend" them. This most militaristic of kings was, paradoxically, almost always at peace.

Nevertheless, the Prussian people paid a heavy and lasting price for the obsessions of the royal drillmaster. Civil society became rigid and highly disciplined. Prussia became the "Sparta of the North"; unquestioning obedience was the highest virtue. As a Prussian minister later summed up, "To keep quiet is the first civic duty."[16] Thus the absolutism of Frederick William I combined with harsh peasant bondage and Junker tyranny to lay the foundations for probably the most militaristic country of modern times.

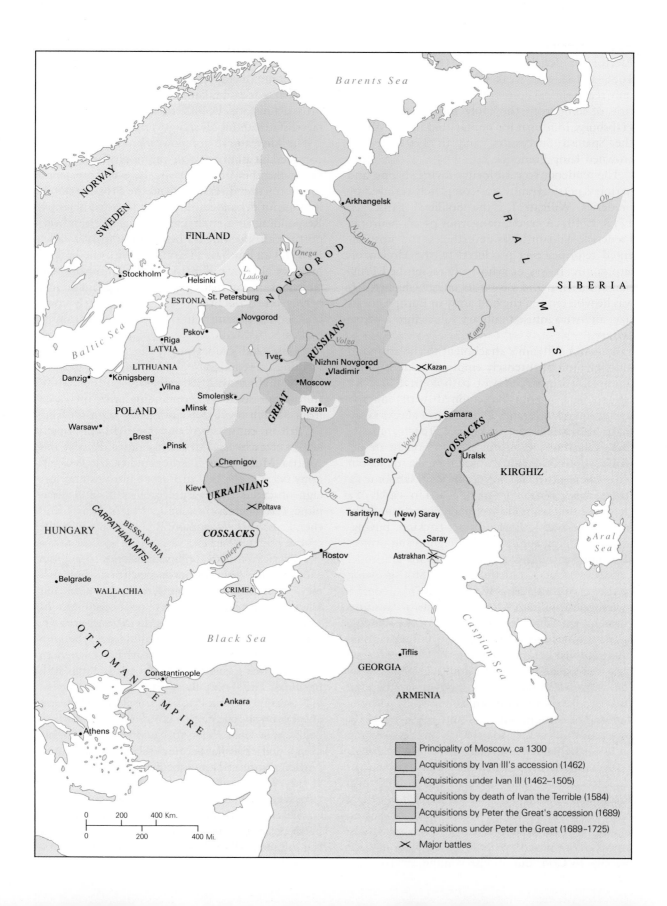

Barents Sea

NORWAY

SWEDEN

FINLAND

•Stockholm
Helsinki•
ESTONIA
•Riga   •St. Petersburg
LATVIA   Psków•   Novgorod•
LITHUANIA
Danzig•   •Königsberg   Tver•
          •Vilna
Smolensk•
POLAND   •Minsk
Warsaw•
     •Brest
          •Pinsk
     •Chernigov
Kiev•   UKRAINIANS
HUNGARY   COSSACKS
BESSARABIA
CARPATHIAN MTS.
•Belgrade
     WALLACHIA   CRIMEA
               Black Sea
OTTOMAN EMPIRE
     •Constantinople
          •Ankara
•Athens

•Arkhangelsk

L. Onega
L. Ladoga

NOVGOROD

RUSSIANS
Nízhni Novgorod•
Vladimir•
•Moscow
GREAT   Ryazan•

Volga

×Kazan

SIBERIA

U R A L   M T S.

Ob

Kama

Samara•

COSSACKS
Uralsk•
KIRGHIZ

Saratov•   •Tsaritsyn   (New) Saray
          Don
Rostov•   •Saray
          Astrakhan×

Tiflis•
GEORGIA
ARMENIA

×Poltava   •Dnieper

Ural
Volga

Caspian Sea

Aral Sea

	Principality of Moscow, ca 1300
	Acquisitions by Ivan III's accession (1462)
	Acquisitions under Ivan III (1462–1505)
	Acquisitions by death of Ivan the Terrible (1584)
	Acquisitions by Peter the Great's accession (1689)
	Acquisitions under Peter the Great (1689–1725)
×	Major battles

0   200   400 Km.
0   200   400 Mi.

THE DEVELOPMENT OF RUSSIA

One of the favorite parlor games of nineteenth-century Russian (and non-Russian) intellectuals was debating whether Russia was a Western and European or a non-Western Asiatic society. This question was particularly fascinating because it was unanswerable. To this day Russia differs fundamentally from the West in some basic ways, though Russian history has paralleled that of the West in other ways: thus the hypnotic attraction of Russian history.

The differences between Russia and Western Europe were particularly striking before 1700, when Russia's overall development began to draw progressively closer to that of its western neighbors. These early differences and Russia's long isolation from Europe explain why little has so far been said here about Russia. Yet it is impossible to understand how Russia has increasingly influenced and been influenced by western European civilization since roughly the late seventeenth century without looking at the course of early Russian history. Such a brief survey will also help explain how, when absolute monarchy finally and decisively triumphed under the rough guidance of Peter the Great in the early eighteenth century, it was a type of absolute monarchy quite different from that of France or even Prussia.

The Vikings and the Kievan Principality

In antiquity the Slavs lived as a single people in central Europe. With the start of the mass migrations of the late Roman Empire, the Slavs moved in different directions and split into three groups. Between the fifth and ninth centuries, the eastern Slavs, from whom the Ukrainians, the Russians, and the White Russians descend, moved into the vast and practically uninhabited area of present-day European Russia and the Ukraine (Map 19.4).

This enormous area consisted of an immense virgin forest to the north, where most of the east-

MAP 19.4 The Expansion of Russia to 1725 After the disintegration of the Kievan state and the Mongol conquest, the princes of Moscow and their descendants gradually extended their rule over an enormous territory.

ern Slavs settled, and an endless prairie grassland to the south. Probably organized as tribal communities, the eastern Slavs, like many North American pioneers much later, lived off the great abundance of wild game and a crude "slash and burn" agriculture. After clearing a piece of the forest to build log cabins, they burned the stumps and brush. The ashes left a rich deposit of potash and lime, and the land gave several good crops before it was exhausted. The people then moved on to another untouched area and repeated the process.

In the ninth century, the Vikings, those fearless warriors from Scandinavia, appeared in the lands of the eastern Slavs. Called "Varangians" in the old Russian chronicles, the Vikings were interested primarily in international trade, and the opportunities were good because the Muslim conquests of the eighth century had greatly reduced Christian trade in the Mediterranean. Moving up and down the rivers, the Vikings soon linked Scandinavia and northern Europe to the Black Sea and to the Byzantine Empire with its capital at Constantinople. Along the rivers they built a few strategic forts, from which they raided the neighboring Slavic tribes and collected tribute. Slaves were the most important article of tribute, and *Slav* even became the word for "slave" in a number of European languages.

In order to increase and protect their international commerce, the Vikings declared themselves the rulers of the eastern Slavs. The Varangian ruler Oleg (r. 878–912) established his residence at Kiev. He and his successors ruled over a loosely united confederation of Slavic territories—the Kievan state—until 1054. The Viking prince and his clansmen quickly became assimilated into the Slavic population, taking local wives and emerging as the noble class.

Assimilation and loss of Scandinavian ethnic identity was speeded up by the conversion of the Vikings and local Slavs to Eastern Orthodox Christianity by missionaries from the Byzantine Empire. Thus the rapidly Slavified Vikings left two important legacies for the future. They created a loose unification of Slavic territories under a single ruling prince and a single ruling dynasty. And they imposed a basic religious unity by accepting Orthodox Christianity (as opposed to Roman Catholicism) for themselves and the eastern Slavs.

Even at its height under Great Prince Iaroslav the Wise (r. 1019–1054), the unity of the Kievan principality was extremely tenuous. Trade, not government, was the main concern of the rulers. Moreover, the Slavified Vikings failed to find a way of peacefully transferring power from one generation to the next. In medieval western Europe this fundamental problem of government was increasingly resolved by resort to the principle of *primogeniture:* the king's eldest son received the crown as his rightful inheritance when his father died. In early Kiev, however, there were apparently no fixed rules, and much strife accompanied each succession.

After Iaroslav's death in 1054, Kiev disintegrated into more and more competing units, each ruled by a prince. Even when only one prince was claiming to be the great prince, the whole situation was very unsettled.

The princes divided their land like private property because they thought of it as private property. A given prince owned a certain number of farms or landed estates and had them worked directly by his people, mainly slaves, called *kholops* in Russian. Outside of these estates, which constituted the princely domain, the prince exercised limited authority in his principality. Excluding the clergy, two kinds of people lived there: the noble *boyars* and the commoner peasants.

The boyars were the descendants of the original Viking warriors, and they also held their lands as free and clear private property. Although the boyars normally fought in princely armies, the customary law declared that they could serve any prince they wished. The ordinary peasants were also truly free; they could move at will wherever opportunities were greatest. In the touching phrase of the times, theirs was "a clean road, without boundaries."[17] In short, fragmented princely power, private property, and personal freedom all went together.

The Mongol Yoke and the Rise of Moscow

The eastern Slavs, like the Germans and the Italians, might have emerged from the Middle Ages weak and politically divided had it not been for the Mongol conquest of the Kievan state. Wild nomadic tribes from present-day Mongolia, the Mongols were temporarily unified in the thirteenth century by Jenghiz Khan (1162–1227), one of history's greatest conquerors. In five years

his armies subdued all of China. His successors then wheeled westward, smashing everything in their path and reaching the plains of Hungary victorious before they pulled back in 1242. The Mongol army—the Golden Horde—was savage in the extreme, often slaughtering the entire populations of cities before burning them to the ground. A chronicler passing in 1245 through Kiev, which the Mongols had sacked in 1242, wrote,

When we passed through that land, we found lying in the field countless heads and bones of dead people; for this city had been extremely large and very populous, whereas now it has been reduced to nothing: barely two hundred houses stand there, and those people are held in the harshest slavery.[18]

Having devastated and conquered, the Mongols ruled the eastern Slavs for more than two hundred years. They forced all the bickering Slavic princes to submit to their rule and to give them tribute and slaves. If the conquered peoples rebelled, the Mongols were quick to punish with death and destruction. Thus the Mongols unified the eastern Slavs, for the Mongol khan was acknowledged by all as the supreme ruler.

Beginning with Alexander Nevsky in 1252, the previously insignificant princes of Moscow became particularly adept at serving the Mongols. They loyally put down popular uprisings and collected the khan's harsh taxes. By way of reward, the princes of Moscow emerged as hereditary great princes. Eventually the Muscovite princes were able to destroy their princely rivals and even to replace the khan as supreme ruler. In this complex process, two princes of Moscow after Alexander Nevsky—Ivan I and Ivan III—were especially noteworthy.

Ivan I (r. 1328–1341) was popularly known as "Ivan the Moneybag." A bit like Frederick William of Prussia, he was extremely stingy and built up a large personal fortune. This enabled him to buy more property and to increase his influence by loaning money to less frugal princes to pay their Mongol taxes. Ivan's most serious rival was the prince of Tver, whom the Mongols at one point appointed as great prince.

In 1327 the population of Tver revolted against Mongol oppression, and the prince of Tver joined his people. Ivan immediately went to the Mongol capital of Saray, where he was appointed commander of a large Russian-Mongol army, which then laid waste to Tver and its lands. For this proof of devotion, the Mongols made Ivan the general tax collector for all the Slavic lands they had subjugated and named him great prince. Ivan also convinced the metropolitan of Kiev, the leading churchman of all eastern Slavs, to settle in Moscow. Ivan I thus gained greater prestige. The church gained a powerful advocate before the khan.

In the next hundred-odd years, in the course of innumerable wars and intrigues, the great princes of Moscow significantly increased their holdings. Then, in the reign of Ivan III (r. 1462–1505), the process of gathering the territories around Moscow was largely completed. After purchasing Rostov, Ivan conquered and annexed other principalities, of which Novgorod with its lands extending almost to the Baltic Sea was most crucial (see Map 19.4). Thus, more than four hundred years after Iaroslav the Wise had divided the embryonic Kievan state, the princes of Moscow defeated all rivals to win complete princely authority.

Another dimension to princely power developed. Not only was the prince of Moscow the *unique* ruler, he was the *absolute* ruler, the autocrat, the *tsar*—the Slavic contraction for "caesar," with all its connotations. This imperious conception of absolute power is expressed in a famous letter from the aging Ivan III to Holy Roman Emperor Frederick III (r. 1440–1493). Frederick had offered Ivan the title of king in conjunction with the marriage of his daughter to Ivan's nephew. Ivan proudly refused:

We by the grace of God have been sovereigns over our domains from the beginning, from our first forebears, and our right we hold from God, as did our forebears. . . . As in the past we have never needed appointment from anyone, so now do we not desire it.[19]

The Muscovite idea of absolute authority was powerfully reinforced by two developments. First, about 1480 Ivan III stopped acknowledging the khan as his supreme ruler. There is good evidence to suggest that Ivan and his successors saw themselves as khans. Certainly they assimilated the Mongol concept of kingship as the exercise of unrestrained and unpredictable power.

Second, after the fall of Constantinople to the Turks in 1453, the tsars saw themselves as the heirs of both the caesars and Orthodox Christianity, the one true faith. All the other kings of Europe were heretics: only the tsars were rightful and holy rulers. This idea was promoted by Orthodox churchmen, who spoke of "holy Russia" as the "Third Rome." Ivan's marriage to the daughter of the last Byzantine emperor further enhanced the aura of an imperial inheritance for Moscow. Worthy successor to the mighty khan and the true Christian emperor, the Muscovite tsar was a king above all others.

Tsar and People to 1689

By 1505 the great prince of Moscow, the tsar, had emerged as the single hereditary ruler of "all the Russias"—all the lands of the eastern Slavs—and he was claiming unrestricted power as his God-given right. In effect, the tsar was demanding the same kind of total authority over all his subjects that the princes had long exercised over their slaves on their own landed estates.

As peasants had begun losing their freedom of movement in the fifteenth century, so had the noble boyars begun losing power and influence. Ivan III pioneered in this regard, as in so many others. When Ivan conquered the principality of Novgorod in the 1480s, he confiscated fully 80 percent of the land, executing the previous owners or resettling them nearer Moscow. He then kept more than half of the confiscated land for himself and distributed the remainder to members of a newly emerging service nobility, who held the tsar's land on the explicit condition that they serve in the tsar's army. Moreover, Ivan III began to require boyars outside of Novgorod to serve him if they wished to retain their lands. Since there were no competing princes left to turn to, the boyars had to yield.

The rise of the new service nobility accelerated under Ivan IV (r. 1533–1584), the famous Ivan the Terrible. Having ascended the throne at age three, Ivan suffered insults and neglect at the hands of the haughty boyars after his mother mysteriously died, possibly poisoned, when he was just eight. At age sixteen he suddenly pushed aside his hated boyar advisers, crowned himself, and officially took the august title of tsar for the first time.

Selecting the beautiful and kind Anastasia of the popular Romanov family for his wife and queen, the young tsar soon declared war on the remnants of Mongol power. He defeated the faltering khanates of Kazan and Astrakhan between 1552 and

1556, adding vast new territories to Russia. In the course of these wars, Ivan virtually abolished the old distinction between hereditary boyar private property and land granted temporarily for service. All nobles, old and new, had to serve the tsar in order to hold any land.

The transformation of the entire nobility into a service nobility was completed in the second part of Ivan the Terrible's reign. In 1557 Ivan turned westward, and for the next twenty-five years Muscovy waged an exhausting, unsuccessful war primarily with the large Polish-Lithuanian state, which controlled not only Poland but much of the Ukraine in the sixteenth century. Quarreling with the boyars over the war and blaming them for the sudden death of his beloved Anastasia in 1560, the increasingly cruel and demented Ivan turned to strike down all who stood in his way.

Above all, he reduced the ancient Muscovite boyar families with a reign of terror. Leading boyars, their relatives, and even their peasants and servants were executed en masse by a special corps of unquestioning servants. Dressed in black and riding black horses, they were forerunners of the modern dictator's secret police. Large estates were confiscated, broken up, and reapportioned to the lower service nobility. The service nobility, still less than half a percent of the total population, was totally dependent on the autocrat.

Ivan also took giant strides toward making all commoners servants of the tsar. His endless wars and demonic purges left much of central Russia depopulated. It grew increasingly difficult for the lower service nobility to squeeze a living for themselves out of the peasants left on their landholdings. As the service nobles demanded more from the remaining peasants, more and more peasants fled toward the wild, recently conquered territories to the east and south. There they formed free groups and outlaw armies known as "Cossacks." The Cossacks maintained a precarious independence beyond the reach of the oppressive landholders and the tsar's hated officials. The solution to this problem was to complete the tying of the peasants to the land, making them serfs perpetually bound to serve the noble landholders, who were bound in turn to serve the tsar.

In the time of Ivan the Terrible, urban traders and artisans were also bound to their towns and jobs so that the tsar could tax them more heavily. The urban classes had no security in their work or property, and even the wealthiest merchants were basically dependent agents of the tsar. The royal monopolization of many of the best commercial activities was in sharp contrast to developments in western Europe, where the capitalist middle classes were gaining strength and security in their private property. The Russian urban classes remained weak and divided.

Ivan the Terrible's system of autocracy and compulsory service struck foreign observers forcibly. Jean Bodin, the French thinker who did so much to develop the modern concept of sovereignty, concluded that Russia's political system was fundamentally different from the systems of all other European monarchies and comparable only to that of the Turkish empire. In both Turkey and Russia, as in other parts of Asia and in Africa, "the prince is become lord of the goods and persons of his subjects . . . governing them as a master of a family does his slaves."[20] The Mongol inheritance weighed heavily on Russia.

As has so often occurred in Russia, the death of an iron-fisted tyrant—in this case, Ivan the Terrible in 1584—ushered in an era of confusion and violent struggles for power. Events were particularly chaotic after Ivan's son Theodore died in 1598 without an heir. The years 1598 to 1613 are aptly called the "Time of Troubles."

Close relatives of the deceased tsar intrigued against and murdered each other, alternately fighting and welcoming the invading Swedes and Poles, who even occupied Moscow. Most serious for the cause of autocracy, there was a great social upheaval as Cossacks marched northward, rallying peasants and slaughtering nobles and officials.

This social explosion from below, which combined with a belated surge of patriotic opposition to Polish invaders, brought the nobles to their senses. In 1613 they elected Ivan's sixteen-year-old grandnephew, Michael Romanov, the new hereditary tsar and rallied around him in the face of common internal and external threats. Michael's election was a real restoration, and his reign saw the gradual re-establishment of tsarist autocracy. Michael was understandably more kindly disposed toward the supportive nobility than toward the sullen peasants. Thus, while the peasants were further ground down, Ivan's heavy military obligations on the nobility were relaxed considerably, a trend that continued in the long reign of Michael's successor, the pious Alexis (r. 1645–1676).

The result was a second round of mass upheaval and protest. In the later seventeenth century, the

St. Basil's Cathedral in Moscow, with its sloping roofs and colorful onion-shaped domes, is a striking example of powerful Byzantine influences on Russian culture. According to tradition, an enchanted Ivan the Terrible blinded the cathedral's architects to ensure that they would never duplicate their fantastic achievement, which still dazzles the beholder in today's Red Square. *(Source: George Holton/Photo Researchers)*

unity of the Russian Orthodox church was torn apart by a great split. The surface question was the religious reforms introduced in 1652 by the patriarch Nikon, a dogmatic purist who wished to bring "corrupted" Russian practices of worship into line with the Greek Orthodox model. The self-serving church hierarchy quickly went along, but the intensely religious common people resisted. They saw Nikon as the anti-Christ, who was stripping them of the only thing they had—the true religion of "holy Russia." Great numbers left the church and formed illegal communities of "Old Believers," who were hunted down and persecuted. After the great split, the Russian masses were alienated from the established church, which became totally dependent on the state for its authority.

Again the Cossacks revolted against the state, which was doggedly trying to catch up with them on the frontiers and reduce them to serfdom. Under Stenka Razin they moved up the Volga River in 1670 and 1671, attracting a great undisciplined army of peasants, murdering landlords and high church officials, and proclaiming freedom from oppression. In response to this rebellion, finally defeated by the government, the thoroughly scared upper classes tightened the screws of serfdom even further. Holding down the peasants and thereby maintaining the tsar became almost the principal obligation of the nobility until 1689.

The Reforms of Peter the Great

It is now possible to understand the reforms of Peter the Great (r. 1682–1725) and his kind of monarchial absolutism. Contrary to some historians' assertions, Peter was interested primarily in

"The Bronze Horseman"   This equestrian masterpiece of Peter the Great, finished for Catherine the Great in 1783, dominates the center of St. Petersburg (modern Leningrad). The French sculptor Falconnet has captured the tsar's enormous energy, power, and determination. *(Source: Courtesy of The Conway Library, Courtauld Institute of Art)*

military power and not in some grandiose westernization plan. A giant for his time, at six feet seven inches, and possessing enormous energy and will power, Peter was determined to redress the defeats that the tsar's armies had occasionally suffered in their wars with Poland and Sweden since the time of Ivan the Terrible. And although Russia had gained a large mass of the Ukraine in 1667 and completed the conquest of Siberia in the seventeenth century, the tsar's vast kingdom had been built on a fierce drive for territorial expansion. Thus it was natural that the seventeen-year-old Peter would seek further gains when he overturned the regency in 1689 and assumed personal rule. The thirty-six years of that rule knew only one year of peace.

When Peter took control in 1689, the heart of his part-time army still consisted of cavalry made up of boyars and service nobility. The Russian army was lagging behind the professional standing armies being formed in Europe in the seventeenth

century. The core of such armies was a highly disciplined infantry—an infantry that fired and refired rifles as it fearlessly advanced, until it charged with bayonets fixed. Such a large, permanent army was enormously expensive and could be created only at the cost of great sacrifice. Given the desire to conquer more territory, Peter's military problem was serious.

Peter's solution was, in essence, to tighten up Muscovy's old service system and really make it work. He put the nobility back in harness with a vengeance. Every nobleman, great or small, was once again required to serve in the army or in the civil administration—for life. Since a more modern army and government required skilled technicians and experts, Peter created schools and even universities. One of his most hated reforms required five years of compulsory education away from home for every young nobleman. Peter established a merit-based military-civilian bureaucracy in which some people of non-noble origin rose to high positions. He also searched out talented foreigners—twice in his reign he went abroad to study and observe—and placed them in his service. These measures combined to make the army and government more powerful and efficient.

Peter also greatly increased the service requirements of the commoners. He established a regular standing army of more than 200,000 soldiers, made up mainly of peasants commanded by officers from the nobility. In addition, special forces of Cossacks and foreigners numbered more than 100,000. The departure of a drafted peasant boy was regarded by his family and village as almost like a funeral, as indeed it was, since the recruit was drafted for life. The peasantry also served with its taxes, which increased threefold during Peter's reign, as people—"souls"—replaced land as the primary unit of taxation. Serfs were also arbitrarily assigned to work in the growing number of factories and mines.

The constant warfare of Peter's reign consumed 80 to 85 percent of all revenues but brought only modest territorial expansion. Yet after initial losses in the Great Northern War with Sweden, which lasted from 1700 to 1721, Peter's new war machine crushed the smaller army of Sweden's Charles XII in the Ukraine at Poltava in 1709, one of the most significant battles in Russian history. Sweden never really regained the offensive, and Russia eventually annexed Estonia and much of present-day Latvia (see Map 19.4), lands that had never before been under Russian rule. Russia became the dominant power on the Baltic Sea and very much a European Great Power. If victory or defeat is the ultimate historical criterion, Peter's reforms were a success.

There were other important consequences of Peter's reign. Because of his feverish desire to use modern technology to strengthen the army, many Westerners and Western ideas flowed into Russia for the first time. A new class of educated Russians began to emerge. At the same time, vast numbers of Russians, especially among the poor and weak, hated Peter's massive changes. The split between the enserfed peasantry and the educated nobility thus widened, even though all were caught up in the endless demands of the sovereign.

A new idea of state interest, distinct from the tsar's personal interests, began to take hold. Peter himself fostered this conception of the public interest by claiming time and again to be serving the common good. For the first time, a Russian tsar attached explanations to his decrees in an attempt to gain the confidence and enthusiastic support of the populace. Yet, as before, the tsar alone decided what the common good was. Here was a source of future tension between tsar and people.

In sum, Peter built on the service obligations of old Muscovy. His monarchial absolutism was truly the culmination of the long development of a unique Russian civilization. Yet the creation of a more modern army and state introduced much that was new and Western to that civilization. This development paved the way for Russia to move much closer to the European mainstream in its thought and institutions during the Enlightenment, especially under that famous administrative and sexual lioness, Catherine the Great.

ABSOLUTISM AND THE BAROQUE IN EASTERN EUROPE

The rise of royal absolutism in eastern Europe had many consequences. Nobles served their powerful rulers in new ways while the great inferiority of the urban middle classes and the peasants was reconfirmed. Armies became larger and more professional; taxes rose. Royal absolutism also interacted with baroque culture and art. Inspired in part by Louis XIV of France, the great and not-so-great rulers called on the artistic talent of the age to glo-

rify their power and magnificence. This exaltation of despotic rule was particularly striking in the lavish masterpieces of architecture.

Palaces and Power

As soaring Gothic cathedrals expressed the idealized spirit of the High Middle Ages, so dramatic baroque palaces symbolized the age of absolutist power. By 1700 palace building had become a veritable obsession for the rulers of central and eastern Europe. Their baroque palaces were clearly intended to overawe the people with the monarch's strength. The great palaces were also visual declarations of equality with Louis XIV and were therefore modeled after Versailles to a greater or lesser extent. One such palace was Schönbrunn, an enormous Viennese Versailles begun in 1695 by Emperor Leopold to celebrate Austrian military victories and Habsburg might.

Petty princes also contributed mightily to the mania of palace-building. The not-very-important elector-archbishop of Mainz, the ruling prince of that city, confessed apologetically that "building is a craze which costs much, but every fool likes his own hat."[21] The archbishop of Mainz's own "hat" was an architectural gem, like that of another churchly ruler, the prince-bishop of Würzburg.

In central and eastern Europe, the favorite noble servants of royalty became extremely rich and powerful, and they, too, built grandiose palaces in the capital cities. These palaces were in part an extension of the monarch, for they surpassed the buildings of less favored nobles. Take, for example, the palaces of Prince Eugene of Savoy. A French nobleman by birth and education, Prince Eugene entered the service of Emperor Leopold I with the relief of the besieged Vienna in 1683, and he became Austria's most famous military hero. It was he who smashed the Turks and fought Louis XIV to a standstill. Rewarded with great wealth by his grateful royal employer, Eugene called on the leading architects of the day, J. B. Fischer von Erlach and Johann Lukas von Hildebrandt, to consecrate his glory in stone and fresco. Fischer built Eugene's Winter (or Town) Palace in Vienna, and he and Hildebrandt collaborated on the prince's Summer Palace on the city's outskirts.

The Summer Palace was actually two enormous buildings, the Lower Belvedere and the Upper Belvedere, completed in 1713 and 1722 respectively and joined by one of the most exquisite gardens in Europe. The Upper Belvedere, Hildebrandt's masterpiece, stood gracefully, even playfully, behind a great sheet of water. One entered through magnificent iron gates into a hall where sculptured giants crouched as pillars; then one moved on to a great staircase of dazzling whiteness and ornamentation. Even today, the emotional impact of this building is great: here art and beauty create a sense of immense power and wealth.

Palaces like the Upper Belvedere were magnificent examples of the baroque style. They expressed the baroque delight in bold, sweeping statements intended to provide a dramatic emotional experience. To create this experience, baroque masters dissolved the traditional artistic frontiers: the architect permitted the painter and the artisan to cover the undulating surfaces with wildly colorful paintings, graceful sculptures, and fanciful carvings. Space was used in a highly original way, to blend everything together in a total environment. These techniques shone in all their glory in the churches and palaces of southern Germany. Artistic achievement and political statement reinforced each other.

Royal Cities

Not content with fashioning ostentatious palaces, absolute monarchs and baroque architects remodeled existing capital cities or built new ones to reflect royal magnificence and the centralization of political power. Karlsruhe, founded in 1715 as the capital city of a small German principality, is one extreme example. There, broad, straight avenues radiated out from the palace, so that all roads—like all power—were focused on the ruler. More typically, the monarch's architects added new urban areas alongside the old city, and these areas became the real heart of the expanding capital.

The distinctive features of the new additions were their broad avenues, their imposing government buildings, and their rigorous mathematical layout. Along major thoroughfares the nobles built elaborate townhouses; stables and servants' quarters were built on the alleys behind. Wide avenues facilitated the rapid movement of soldiers through the city to quell any disturbance (the king's planners had the needs of the military constantly in mind). Under arcades along the avenues

appeared smart and expensive shops, the first department stores, with plate-glass windows and fancy displays.

The new avenues brought reckless speed to the European city. Whereas everyone had walked through the narrow, twisting streets of the medieval town, the high and mighty raced down the broad boulevards in elegant carriages. A social gap opened between the wealthy riders and the gaping, dodging pedestrians. "Mind the carriages!" wrote one eighteenth-century observer in Paris:

Here comes the black-coated physician in his chariot, the dancing master in his coach, the fencing master in his surrey—and the Prince behind six horses at the gallop as if he were in the open country. . . . The threatening wheels of the overbearing rich drive as rapidly as ever over stones stained with the blood of their unhappy victims.[22]

Speeding carriages on broad avenues, an endless parade of power and position: here were the symbol and substance of the baroque city.

The Growth of St. Petersburg

No city illustrates better than St. Petersburg the close ties among politics, architecture, and urban development in this period. In 1702 Peter the Great's armies seized a desolate Swedish fortress on one of the water-logged islands at the mouth of the Neva River on the Baltic Sea. Within a year the tsar had decided to build a new city there and to make it, rather than ancient Moscow, his capital.

Since the first step was to secure the Baltic coast, military construction was the main concern for the next eight years. The land was swampy and uninhabited, the climate damp and unpleasant. But Peter cared not at all. For him, the inhospitable northern marshland was a future metropolis gloriously bearing his name.

After the decisive Russian victory at Poltava in 1709 greatly reduced the threat of Swedish armies, Peter moved into high gear. In one imperious decree after another, he ordered his people to build a city that would equal any in the world. Such a city had to be Western and baroque, just as Peter's army had to be Western and permanent. From such a new city, his "window on Europe," Peter believed that it would be easier to reform the country militarily and administratively.

These general political goals matched Peter's architectural ideas, which had been influenced by his travels in western Europe. First, Peter wanted a comfortable, "modern" city. Modernity meant broad, straight, stone-paved avenues, houses built in a uniform line and not haphazardly set back from the street, large parks, canals for drainage, stone bridges, and street lighting. Second, all building had to conform strictly to detailed architectural regulations set down by the government. Finally, each social group—the nobility, the merchants, the artisans, and so on—was to live in a certain section of town. In short, the city and its population were to conform to a carefully defined urban plan of the baroque type.

Peter used the traditional but reinforced methods of Russian autocracy to build his modern capital. The creation of St. Petersburg was just one of the heavy obligations he dictatorially imposed on all social groups in Russia. The peasants bore the heaviest burdens. Just as the government drafted peasants for the army, it also drafted from 25,000 to 40,000 men each summer to labor in St. Petersburg for three months, without pay. Every ten to fifteen peasant households had to furnish one such worker each summer and then pay a special tax in order to feed that worker in St. Petersburg.

Peasants hated forced labor in the capital, and each year one-fourth to one-third of those sent risked brutal punishment and ran away. Many

Würzburg, the Prince-Bishop's Palace The baroque style brought architects, painters, and sculptors together in harmonious, even playful partnership. This magnificent monumental staircase, designed by Johann Balthasar Neumann in 1735, merges into the vibrant ceiling frescos by Giovanni Battista Tiepolo. A man is stepping out of the picture, and a painted dog resembles a marble statue. *(Source: Erich Lessing Culture and Fine Arts Archive)*

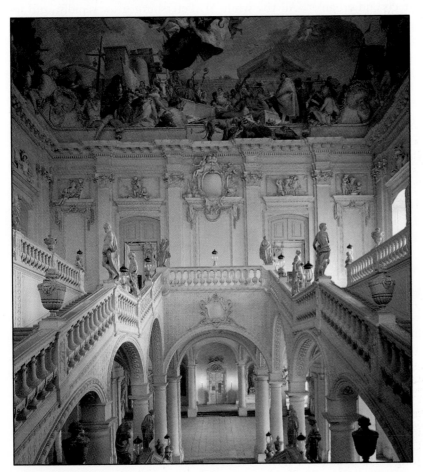

peasant construction workers died each summer from hunger, sickness, and accidents. Many also died because peasant villages tended to elect old men or young boys to labor in St. Petersburg, since strong and able-bodied men were desperately needed on the farm in the busy summer months. Thus beautiful St. Petersburg was built on the shoveling, carting, and paving of a mass of conscripted serfs.

Peter also drafted more privileged groups to his city, but on a permanent basis. Nobles were summarily ordered to build costly stone houses and palaces in St. Petersburg and to live in them most of the year. Merchants and artisans were also commanded to settle and build in St. Petersburg. These nobles and merchants were then required to pay for the city's avenues, parks, canals, embankments, pilings, and bridges, all of which were very costly in terms of both money and lives because they were built on a swamp. The building of St. Petersburg was, in truth, an enormous direct tax levied on the wealthy, who in turn forced the peasantry to do most of the work. The only immediate beneficiaries were the foreign architects and urban planners. No wonder so many Russians hated Peter's new city.

Yet the tsar had his way. By the time of his death in 1725, there were at least six thousand houses and numerous impressive government buildings in St. Petersburg. Under the remarkable women who ruled Russia throughout most of the eighteenth century, St. Petersburg blossomed completely as a majestic and well-organized city, at least in its wealthy showpiece sections. Peter's youngest daughter, the quick-witted, sensual beauty Elizabeth (r. 1741–1762), named as her chief architect Bartolomeo Rastrelli, who had come to Russia from Italy as a boy of fifteen in 1715. Combining Italian and Russian traditions into a unique, wildly colorful St. Petersburg style, Rastrelli built many palaces for the nobility and all the larger government buildings erected during Elizabeth's reign. He also rebuilt the Winter Palace as an enormous, aqua-colored royal residence, now the Hermitage Museum. There Elizabeth established a flashy, luxury-loving, and slightly crude court, which Catherine the Great in turn made truly imperial. All the while St. Petersburg grew rapidly, and its

St. Petersburg, ca 1760 Rastrelli's remodeled Winter Palace, which housed the royal family until the Russian Revolution of 1917, stands on the left along the Neva River. The Navy Office with its famous golden spire and other government office buildings are nearby and across the river. Russia became a naval power and St. Petersburg a great port. *(Source: Michael Holford)*

almost 300,000 inhabitants in 1782 made it one of the world's largest cities. Peter and his successors had created out of nothing a magnificent and harmonious royal city, which unmistakably proclaimed the power of Russia's rulers and the creative potential of the absolutist state.

CONSTITUTIONALISM: AN OVERVIEW

The march toward absolutism seemed almost irresistible in seventeenth-century Europe. Yet while France, Austria, Prussia, and Russia responded to the challenge of war and social unrest by forging the absolutist state, England and Holland evolved toward limited monarchial power and the constitutional state.

Constitutionalism is the limitation of government by law. Constitutionalism implies a balance between (1) the authority and power of the government and (2) the rights and liberties of the subjects. The balance is often very delicate.

A nation's constitution may be written or unwritten. It may be embodied in one basic document, occasionally revised by amendment or judicial decision, like the Constitution of the United States. Or it may be partly written and partly unwritten and include parliamentary statutes, judicial decisions, and a body of traditional procedures and practices, like the English and Canadian constitutions. Whether written or unwritten, a constitution gets its binding force from the government's acknowledgment that it must respect that constitution—that is, that the state must be governed according to the laws. Men and women living in a constitutional state look on the law and the constitution as the protectors of their rights, liberties, and property.

Modern constitutional governments may take either a republican or a monarchial form. In a constitutional republic, sovereign power resides in the electorate and is exercised by the electorate's representatives. In a constitutional monarchy, a king or queen serves as the head of state and may possess considerable political authority but sovereign power rests in the electorate.

A constitutional government is not necessarily a democratic government. In a complete democracy, *all* the people have the right to participate in the government of the state. Their participation is either indirect, through their elected representatives, or direct. Thus democratic government is intimately tied up with the *franchise* (the vote). Most European men could not vote until the later nineteenth century. Women gained the right to vote only in the twentieth century. Consequently, although constitutional government developed in the seventeenth century, full democracy was achieved only in recent times.

ENGLAND: THE TRIUMPH OF CONSTITUTIONAL MONARCHY

In 1588 Queen Elizabeth I of England exercised great personal power, but by 1689 the power of the English monarchy was severely limited. Change in England was anything but orderly. Seventeenth-century England displayed little political stability. It executed one king, experienced a bloody civil war, experimented with military dictatorship, then restored the son of the murdered king, and finally, after a bloodless revolution, established constitutional monarchy. Political stability came only in the 1690s. How do we account for the fact that out of this violent and tumultuous century England built the foundations for a strong and enduring constitutional monarchy?

The Decline of Royal Absolutism in England (1603–1649)

Elizabeth I's extraordinary success was the result of her political shrewdness and flexibility, her careful management of finances, her wise selection of ministers, her clever manipulation of Parliament, and her sense of royal dignity and devotion to hard work. After her Scottish cousin James Stuart succeeded her as James I (r. 1603–1625), Elizabeth's strengths seemed even greater.

King James was well educated, learned, and, with thirty-five years' experience as king of Scotland, politically shrewd. But he was not as interested in displaying the majesty and mystique of monarchy as Elizabeth had been. He also lacked the common touch. Urged to wave at the crowds who waited to greet their new ruler, James complained that he was tired and threatened to drop his breeches "so they can cheer at my arse." The new king failed to live up to the role expected of him in England.

James was devoted to the theory of divine right of kings. He expressed his ideas about divine right in his essay "The Trew Law of Free Monarchy." According to James I, a monarch has a divine (or God-given) right to authority and is responsible only to God. Rebellion is the worst of political crimes. If a king orders something evil, the subject should respond with passive disobedience but should be prepared to accept any penalty for noncompliance. "There are no privileges and immunities," said James, "which can stand against a divinely appointed King." This typically absolutist notion implied total royal jurisdiction over the liberties, persons, and properties of English men and women. Such a view ran directly counter to many long-standing English ideas, including the belief that a person's property could not be taken away without due process of law. And in the House of Commons the English had a strong representative body to question these absolutist pretensions.

The House of Commons guarded the state's pocketbook, and James and later Stuart kings badly needed to open that pocketbook. Elizabeth had bequeathed to James a sizable royal debt, but James I looked on all revenues as a windfall to be squandered on a lavish court and favorite courtiers. The extravagance displayed in James's court, as well as the public flaunting of his male lovers, weakened respect for the monarchy. These actions also stimulated the knights and burgesses who sat in the House of Commons at Westminster to press for a thorough discussion of royal expenditures, religious reform, and foreign affairs. In short, the Commons aspired to sovereignty—the ultimate political power in the realm.

During the reigns of James I and his son Charles I (r. 1625–1649) the English House of Commons was very different from the assembly that Henry VIII had manipulated into passing his Reformation legislation. The class that dominated the Commons during the Stuarts' reign wanted political power corresponding to its economic strength. A social revolution had brought about the change.

Agricultural techniques like the draining of wasteland and the application of fertilizer had improved the land and increased its yield. In the seventeenth century old manorial common land was enclosed and profitably turned into sheep runs. The dissolution of the monasteries and the sale of monastic land had enriched many people. Many invested in commercial ventures at home, such as the expanding cloth industry, and through partnerships and joint stock companies engaged in foreign enterprises. Many also made prudent marriages. These developments increased social mobility. The typical pattern was for the commercially successful to set themselves up as country gentry. This elite group possessed a far greater proportion of the land and of the nation's wealth in 1640 than in 1540. Increased wealth resulted in a better-educated and more articulate House of Commons.

In England, unlike France, no social stigma was attached to paying taxes. Members of the House of Commons were willing to tax themselves provided they had some say in the expenditure of those taxes and in the formulation of state policies. The Stuart kings, however, considered such ambitions intolerable presumption and a threat to their divine-right prerogative. Consequently, at every Parliament between 1603 and 1640, bitter squabbles erupted between Crown and Commons. Like the Great Elector in Prussia, Charles I tried to govern without Parliament (1629–1640) and to finance his government by arbitrary levies. And as in Prussia these absolutist measures brought intense political conflict.

An issue graver than royal extravagance and Parliament's desire to make law was religion. In the early seventeenth century, increasing numbers of English people felt dissatisfied with the Church of England established by Henry VIII and reformed by Elizabeth. Many Puritans (see page 553) believed that Reformation had not gone far enough. They wanted to "purify" the Anglican church of Roman Catholic elements—elaborate vestments and ceremonial, the position of the altar in the church, even the giving and wearing of wedding rings.

It is very difficult to establish what proportion of the English population was Puritan. But it seems clear that many English men and women were attracted by the socioeconomic implications of John Calvin's theology. Calvinism emphasized hard work, sobriety, thrift, competition, and postponement of pleasure, and it tended to link sin and poverty with weakness and moral corruption. These attitudes, which have frequently been called the "Protestant ethic," "middle-class ethic," or "capitalist ethic," fit in precisely with the economic approaches and practices of many (successful) business people and farmers. Although it is hazardous to identify capitalism and progress with Protestantism—there were many successful Catholic capitalists—the "Protestant virtues" represented the prevailing values of members of the House of Commons.

James I and Charles I both gave the impression of being highly sympathetic to Roman Catholicism. Charles supported the policies of Archbishop of Canterbury William Laud (1573–1645), who tried to impose elaborate ritual and rich ceremonial on all churches. Laud insisted on complete uniformity of church services and enforced that uniformity through an ecclesiastical court called the "Court of High Commission." People believed that the country was being led back to Roman Catholicism. In 1637 Laud attempted to impose two new elements on the church organization in Scotland: a new prayer book, modeled on the Anglican Book of Common Prayer, and bishoprics, which the Presbyterian Scots firmly rejected. The Scots revolted. To finance an army to put down the Scots, King Charles was compelled to summon Parliament in November 1640. It was a fatal decision.

For eleven years Charles I had ruled without Parliament, financing his government through extraordinary stopgap levies considered illegal by the majority of the English people. For example, the king had revived a medieval law that required coastal districts to help pay the cost of ships for defense, and he levied the tax, called "ship money," on both inland and coastal counties. Most members of Parliament believed that such taxation without consent amounted to absolute despotism. Thus they were not willing to trust the king with an army. Accordingly, the Parliament summoned in November 1640 (commonly called the "Long Parliament" because it sat from 1640 to 1660) enacted legislation that limited the power of the monarch and made arbitrary government impossible.

In 1641 the Commons passed the Triennial Act, which compelled the king to summon Parliament every three years. The Commons impeached Archbishop Laud and abolished the Court of High Commission. King Charles, fearful of a Scottish invasion—the original reason for summoning Parliament—accepted these measures. Understanding and peace were not achieved, however, partly because radical members of the Commons pushed increasingly revolutionary propositions, partly because Charles maneuvered to rescind those he had already approved. An uprising in Ireland precipitated civil war.

Ever since Henry II had conquered Ireland in 1171, English governors had mercilessly ruled the land, and English landlords had ruthlessly exploited the Irish people. The English Reformation had made a bad situation worse: because the Irish remained Catholic, religious differences united with economic and political oppression. Without an army, Charles I could neither come to terms with the Scots nor put down the Irish rebellion, and the Long Parliament remained unwilling to place an army under a king it did not trust. Charles thus instigated military action against parliamentary forces. He recruited an army drawn from the nobility and the nobility's cavalry staff, the rural gentry, and mercenaries. The parliamentary army was composed of the militia of the city of London, country squires with business connections, and men with a firm belief that serving was their spiritual duty.

The English civil war (1642–1649) tested whether ultimate political power in England was to reside in the king or in Parliament. The civil war did not resolve that problem, although it ended in 1649 with the execution of King Charles on the charge of high treason and thus dealt a severe blow to the theory of divine-right, absolute monarchy in England. The years from 1649 to 1660, called the "Interregnum" because it separated two monarchial periods, was a transitional period of military dictatorship.

Puritanical Absolutism in England: Cromwell and the Protectorate

In the middle years of the seventeenth century, the problem of sovereignty was vigorously debated. In *Leviathan,* the English philosopher and political theorist Thomas Hobbes (1588–1679) maintained that sovereignty is ultimately derived from the people, who transfer it to the monarchy by implicit contract. The power of the ruler is absolute, but kings do not hold their power by divine right. This abstract theory pleased no one in the seventeenth century.

When Charles I was beheaded on January 30, 1649, the kingship was abolished in England. A *commonwealth,* or republican form of government, was proclaimed. In fact, the army that had defeated the royal forces controlled the government, and Oliver Cromwell controlled the army. Though called the "Protectorate," the rule of

Cromwell Dismisses the Rump Parliament In 1648 the army disposed of its enemies in Parliament; those who remained were known as the Rump Parliament. After the execution of Charles I and the establishment of the Commonwealth, legislative power in England theoretically rested in Parliament. But in 1653, concluding that he could not work with this body, Cromwell turned out the Rump. In this satirical Dutch print, Cromwell ordered members to go home. The sign on the wall reads, "This house is to let." *(Source: The British Library/Pat Hodgson Library)*

Cromwell (1653–1658) constituted military dictatorship.

Oliver Cromwell (1599–1658) came from the country gentry, the class that dominated the House of Commons in the early seventeenth century. He had sat in the Long Parliament. Cromwell rose in the parliamentary army and achieved nationwide fame by infusing the army with his Puritan convictions and molding it into the highly effective military machine, called the "New Model Army," that defeated the royalist forces.

The army had prepared a constitution, the Instrument of Government (1653), that invested executive power in a lord protector (Cromwell) and a council of state. The instrument provided for triennial parliaments and gave Parliament the sole power to raise taxes. But after repeated disputes, Cromwell tore up the document and proclaimed quasi-martial law.

On the issue of religion, Cromwell favored broad toleration, and the Instrument of Government gave all Christians, except Roman Catholics, the right to practice their faith. Toleration, however, meant state protection of many different Protestant sects, and most English people had no enthusiasm for such a notion; the idea was far ahead of its time. As for Irish Catholicism, Cromwell identified it with sedition. In 1649 he crushed rebellion in Ireland with merciless savagery, leaving a legacy of Irish hatred for England. He also rigorously censored the press, forbade sports, and kept the theaters closed in England.

Cromwell pursued mercantilist economic policies, similar to those that Colbert established in France. Cromwell enforced a navigation act requiring that English goods be transported on English ships. The navigation act was a great boost to the development of an English merchant marine and brought about a short but successful war with the commercially threatened Dutch. Cromwell also welcomed the immigration of Jews, because of their skills, and they began to return to England after four centuries of absence.

Military government collapsed when Cromwell died in 1658. Fed up with military rule, the English longed for a return to civilian government, restoration of the common law, and social stability. Moreover, the strain of creating a community of puritanical saints proved too psychologically exhausting. Government by military dictatorship was an unfortunate experiment that the English never forgot or repeated. By 1660 they were ready to try a restoration of monarchy.

The Restoration of the English Monarchy

The Restoration of 1660 re-established the monarchy in the person of Charles II (r. 1660–1685), eldest son of Charles I. At the same time both houses of Parliament were also restored, together with the established Anglican church. The Restoration failed to resolve two serious problems. What was to be the attitude of the state toward Puritans, Catholics, and dissenters from the established church? And what was to be the constitutional position of the king—that is, what was to be the relationship between the king and Parliament?

About the first of these issues, Charles II, a relaxed, easygoing, and sensual man, was basically indifferent. He was not interested in doctrinal issues. But the new members of Parliament were, and they proceeded to enact a body of laws that sought to compel religious uniformity. Those who refused to receive the sacrament of the Church of England could not vote, hold public office, preach, teach, attend the universities, or even assemble for meetings, according to the Test Act of 1673. These restrictions could not be enforced. When the Quaker William Penn held a meeting of his Friends and was arrested, the jury refused to convict him.

In politics, Charles II was determined to get along with Parliament and share power with it.

His method for doing so had profound importance for later constitutional development. The king appointed a council of five men who served both as his major advisers and as members of Parliament, thus acting as liaison agents between the executive and the legislature. This body was an ancestor of the cabinet system (see page 649). It gradually came to be accepted that the council of five was answerable in Parliament for the decisions of the king. This development gave rise to the concept of ministerial responsibility: royal ministers must answer to the Commons.

Harmony between the Crown and Parliament rested on the understanding that Charles would summon Parliament frequently and Parliament would vote him sufficient revenues. However, although Parliament believed that Charles should have large powers, it did not grant him an adequate income. Accordingly, in 1670 Charles entered into a secret agreement with Louis XIV. The French king would give Charles £200,000 annually. In return Charles would relax the laws against Catholics, gradually re-Catholicize England, support French policy against the Dutch, and convert to Catholicism himself.

When the details of this secret treaty leaked out, a wave of anti-Catholic fear swept England. This fear was compounded by a crucial fact: although Charles had produced several bastards, he had no legitimate children. It therefore appeared that his brother and heir, James, duke of York, who had publicly acknowledged his Catholicism, would inaugurate a Catholic dynasty. The combination of hatred for the French absolutism embodied in Louis XIV, hostility to Roman Catholicism, and fear of a permanent Catholic dynasty produced virtual hysteria. The Commons passed an exclusion bill denying the succession to a Roman Catholic, but Charles quickly dissolved Parliament and the bill never became law.

James II (r. 1685–1688) indeed succeeded his brother. Almost at once the worst English anti-Catholic fears, already aroused by Louis XIV's revocation of the Edict of Nantes, were realized. In direct violation of the Test Act, James appointed Roman Catholics to positions in the army, the universities, and local government. When these actions were tested in the courts, the judges, whom James had appointed, decided for the king. The king was suspending the law at will and appeared to be reviving the absolutism of his father (Charles I) and grandfather (James I). He went further. Attempting to broaden his base of support with Protestant dissenters and nonconformists, James issued a declaration of indulgence granting religious freedom to all.

Two events gave the signals for revolution. First, seven bishops of the Church of England petitioned the king that they not be forced to read the declaration of indulgence because of their belief that it was an illegal act. They were imprisoned in the Tower of London but subsequently acquitted amid great public enthusiasm. Second, in June 1688 James's second wife produced a male heir. A Catholic dynasty seemed assured. The fear of a Roman Catholic monarchy, supported by France and ruling outside the law, prompted a group of eminent persons to offer the English throne to James's Protestant daughter, Mary, and her Dutch husband, Prince William of Orange. In December 1688 James II, his queen, and their infant son fled to France and became pensioners of Louis XIV. Early in 1689, William and Mary were crowned king and queen of England.

Constitutional Monarchy and Cabinet Government

The English call the events of 1688 to 1689 the "Glorious Revolution." The revolution was indeed glorious in the sense that it replaced one king with another with a minimum of bloodshed. It also represented the destruction, once and for all, of the idea of divine-right absolutism in England. William and Mary accepted the English throne from Parliament and in so doing explicitly recognized the supremacy of Parliament. The revolution of 1688 established the principle that sovereignty, the ultimate power in the state, was divided between king and Parliament and that the king ruled with the consent of the governed.

The men who brought about the revolution quickly framed their intentions in the Bill of Rights, the cornerstone of the modern British constitution. The basic principles of the Bill of Rights were formulated in direct response to Stuart absolutism. Law was to be made in Parliament; once made, it could not be suspended by the Crown. Parliament had to be called at least every three years. Both elections to and debate in Parliament were to be free, in the sense that the Crown was not to interfere in them (this aspect of the bill was widely disregarded in the eighteenth century).

Judges would hold their offices "during good behavior," a provision that assured judicial independence. No longer could the Crown get the judicial decisions it wanted by threats of removal.

In striking contrast to continental states, there was to be no standing army that could be used against the English population in peacetime. The Bill of Rights granted "that the subjects which are Protestants may have arms for their defense suitable to their conditions and as allowed by law,"[23] meaning that Catholics could not possess firearms because the Protestant majority feared them. Additional legislation granted freedom of worship to Protestant dissenters and nonconformists and required that the English monarch always be Protestant.

The Glorious Revolution found its best defense in John Locke's *Second Treatise of Civil Government* (1690). The political philosopher Locke (1632–1704) maintained that people set up civil governments in order to protect life, liberty, and property. A government that oversteps its proper function—protecting the natural rights of life, liberty, and property—becomes a tyranny. (By "natural" rights, Locke meant rights basic to all men because all have the ability to reason.) Under a tyrannical government, the people have the natural right to rebellion. Rebellion can be avoided if the government carefully respects the rights of citizens and if the people zealously defend their liberty. Recognizing the close relationship between economic and political freedom, Locke linked economic liberty and private property with political freedom.

Locke served as the great spokesman for the liberal English revolution of 1688 to 1689 and for representative government. His idea, inherited from ancient Greece and Rome, that there are natural or universal rights equally valid for all peoples and societies, played a powerful role in eighteenth-century Enlightenment thought. His ideas on liberty and tyranny were especially popular in colonial America.

The events of 1688 to 1689 did not constitute a *democratic* revolution. The revolution formalized Parliament's great power, and Parliament represented the upper classes. The great majority of English people had little say in their government. The English revolution established a constitutional monarchy; it also inaugurated an age of aristocratic government, which lasted at least until 1832 and in many ways until 1914.

In the course of the eighteenth century, the cabinet system of government evolved. The term *cabinet* derives from the small private room in which English rulers consulted their chief ministers. In a cabinet system, the leading ministers, who must have seats in and the support of a majority of the House of Commons, formulate common policy and conduct the business of the country. During the administration of one royal minister, Sir Robert Walpole, who led the cabinet from 1721 to 1742, the idea developed that the cabinet was responsible to the House of Commons. Walpole enjoyed the favor of the monarchy and of the House of Commons and came to be called the king's first, or "prime," minister. In the English cabinet system, both legislative and executive power are held by the leading ministers, who form the government.

THE DUTCH REPUBLIC IN THE SEVENTEENTH CENTURY

In the late sixteenth century, the seven northern provinces of the Netherlands, of which Holland and Zeeland were the most prosperous, had thrown off Spanish domination. This success was based on their geographical lines of defense, the wealth of their cities, the military strategy of William the Silent, the preoccupation of Philip II of Spain with so many additional concerns, and the northern provinces' vigorous Calvinism. In 1581 the seven provinces of the Union of Utrecht had formed the United Provinces (see page 587). The Peace of Westphalia in 1648 confirmed the Dutch republic's independence. The seventeenth century witnessed an unparalleled flowering of Dutch scientific, artistic, and literary achievement. In this period, often called the "golden age of the Netherlands," Dutch ideas and attitudes played a profound role in shaping a new and modern world view.

The Republic of the United Provinces of the Netherlands represents a variation in the development of the modern constitutional state. Within each province an oligarchy of wealthy merchants called "regents" handled domestic affairs in the local Estates. The provincial Estates held virtually all the power. A federal assembly, or States General, handled matters of foreign affairs, such as war. But the States General did not possess sovereign authority, since all issues had to be referred back to the local Estates for approval. The regents in each province jealously guarded local independence and resisted efforts at centralization. Nevertheless, Holland, which had the largest navy and the most wealth, dominated the republic and the States General. Significantly, the Estates assembled at Holland's capital, The Hague.

The government of the United Provinces conforms to none of the standard categories of seventeenth-century political organization. The Dutch were not monarchial but fiercely republican. The government was controlled by wealthy merchants and financiers. Though rich, their values were not aristocratic but strongly middle class, emphasizing thrift, hard work, and simplicity in living. The Dutch republic was not a strong federation but a confederation—that is, a weak union of strong provinces. The provinces were a temptation to powerful neighbors, yet the Dutch resisted the Spanish effort at reconquest and withstood both French and English attacks in the second half of the century. Louis XIV's hatred of the Dutch was proverbial. They represented all that he despised—middle-class values, religious toleration, and independent political institutions.

The political success of the Dutch rested on the phenomenal commercial prosperity of the Netherlands. The moral and ethical bases of that commercial wealth were thrift, frugality, and religious toleration. John Calvin had written, "From where do the merchant's profits come except from his own diligence and industry." This attitude undoubtedly encouraged a sturdy people who had waged a centuries-old struggle against the sea.

Alone of all European peoples in the seventeenth century, the Dutch practiced religious toleration. Peoples of all faiths were welcome within their borders. Although there is scattered evidence of anti-Semitism, Jews enjoyed a level of acceptance and absorption in Dutch business and general culture unique in early modern Europe. It is a testimony to the urbanity of Dutch society that in a century when patriotism was closely identified with religious uniformity, the Calvinist province of Holland allowed its highest official, Jan van Oldenbarneveldt, to continue to practice his Roman Catholic faith. As long as business people conducted their religion in private, the government did not interfere with them.

Toleration paid off. It attracted a great amount of foreign capital and investment. The Bank of

Amsterdam became Europe's best source of cheap credit and commercial intelligence and the main clearinghouse for bills of exchange. People of all races and creeds traded in Amsterdam, at whose docks on the Amstel River five thousand ships were berthed. Joost van den Vondel, the poet of Dutch imperialism, exulted:

God, God, the Lord of Amstel cried, hold every
conscience free;

And Liberty ride, on Holland's tide, with billowing
sails to sea,
And run our Amstel out and in; let freedom gird the
bold,
And merchant in his counting house stand elbow
deep in gold.[24]

The fishing industry was the cornerstone of the Dutch economy. For half the year, from June to December, fishing fleets combed the dangerous

Vermeer: A Woman Weighing Gold   (ca 1657) Vermeer painted pictures of middle-class women involved in ordinary activities in the quiet interiors of their homes. Unrivaled among Dutch masters for his superb control of light, in this painting Vermeer illuminates a pregnant woman weighing gold on her scales, as Christ in the painting on the wall weighs the saved and the damned. *(Source: National Gallery of Art, Washington; Widener Collection)*

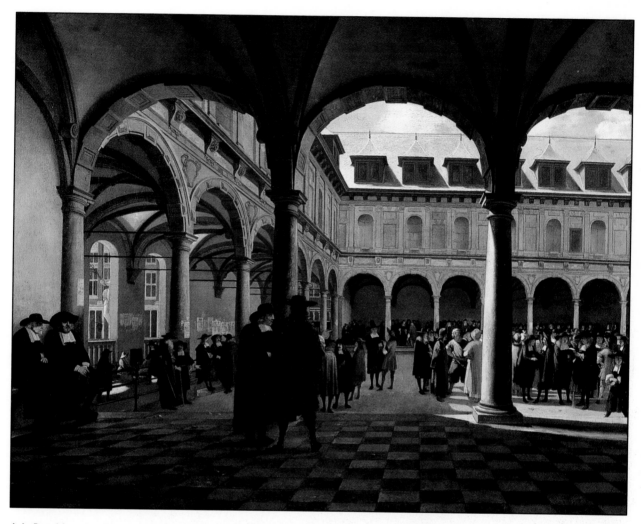

Job Berckheyde: The Amsterdam Stock Exchange Small shareholders (through brokers) as well as rich capitalists could buy and sell and, by various combinations, speculate without having any money at all in the Amsterdam stock market. Shares in the Dutch East India Company were major objects of speculation. The volume, fluidity, and publicity of the Exchange were its new and distinctly modern features. *(Source: Museum Boymans-van Beuningen, Rotterdam)*

English coast and the North Sea, raking in tiny herring. Profits from herring stimulated shipbuilding, and even before 1600 the Dutch were offering the lowest shipping rates in Europe. The merchant marine was the largest in Europe. In 1650 contemporaries estimated that the Dutch had sixteen thousand merchant ships, half the European total. All the wood for these ships had to be imported: the Dutch bought whole forests from Norway. They also bought entire vineyards from French growers before the grapes were harvested. They controlled the Baltic grain trade,

buying entire wheat and rye crops in Poland, east Prussia, and Swedish Pomerania. Because they dealt in bulk, nobody could undersell the Dutch. Foreign merchants coming to Amsterdam could buy anything from precision lenses for the newly invented microscope to muskets for an army of five thousand. Although Dutch cities became famous for their exports—diamonds and linens from Haarlem, pottery from Delft—Dutch wealth depended less on exports than on transport.

In 1602 a group of the regents of Holland formed the Dutch East India Company, a joint

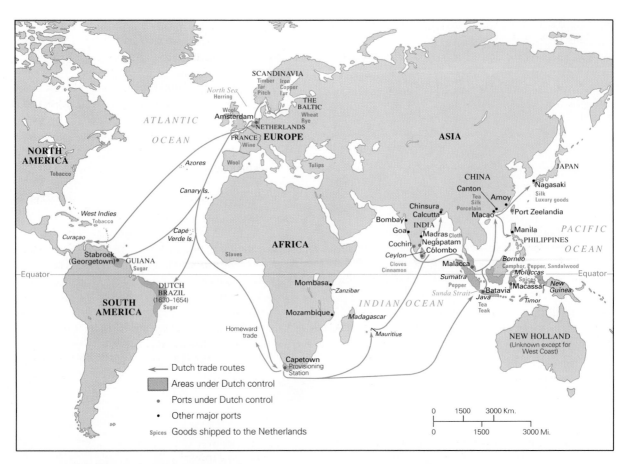

MAP 19.5 Seventeenth-Century Dutch Commerce   Dutch wealth rested on commerce, and commerce depended on the huge Dutch merchant marine, manned by perhaps 48,000 sailors. The fleet carried goods from all parts of the globe to Amsterdam.

stock company. Each investor received a percentage of the profits proportional to the amount of money he had put in. Within half a century, the Dutch East India Company had cut heavily into Portuguese trading in East Asia. The Dutch seized the Cape of Good Hope, Ceylon, and Malacca and established trading posts in each place. In the 1630s the Dutch East India Company was paying its investors about a 35 percent annual return on their investments. The Dutch West India Company, founded in 1621, traded extensively with Latin America and Africa (Map 19.5).

Trade and commerce brought the Dutch prodigious wealth. In the seventeenth century, the Dutch enjoyed the highest standard of living in Europe, perhaps in the world. Amsterdam and Rotterdam built massive granaries where the surplus of one year could be stored against possible shortages the next. Thus food prices fluctuated very little, except during the 1650s when bad harvests reduced supplies. By the standards of Cologne, Paris, or London, salaries were high for all workers, except women. All classes of society, including unskilled laborers, ate well. The low price of bread meant that, compared with other places in Europe, a higher percentage of the worker's income could be spent on fish, cheese, butter, vegetables, even meat. A scholar recently described the Netherlands as "an island of plenty in a sea of want."[25]

Although the initial purpose of the Dutch East and West India companies was commercial—the import of spices and silks to Europe—the Dutch found themselves involved in the imperialist exploitation of parts of East Asia and Latin America, with great success. In 1652 the Dutch founded Cape Town on the southern tip of Africa as a fueling station for ships planning to cross the Pacific.

But war with France and England in the 1670s hurt the United Provinces. The long War of the Spanish Succession, in which the Dutch supported England against France, was a costly drain on Dutch manpower and financial resources. The peace signed in 1713 to end the war marked the beginning of Dutch economic decline.

SUMMARY

War, religious strife, economic depression, and peasant revolts were all aspects of a deep crisis in seventeenth-century Europe. Rulers responded by aggressively seeking to expand their power, which they claimed was essential to meet emergencies and quell disorders. Claiming also that they ruled by divine right, monarchs sought the freedom to wage war, levy taxes, and generally make law as they saw fit. Although they were limited by technology and inadequate financial resources, monarchial governments on the continent succeeded to a large extent, overpowering organized opposition and curbing the power of the nobility and the traditional representative institutions.

The France of Louis XIV led the way to royal absolutism. France developed a centralized bureaucracy, a professional army, a state-directed economy, all of which Louis personally supervised. The king saw himself as the representative of God on earth and accountable to no one here below. His majestic bearing and sumptuous court dazzled contemporaries. Yet behind the grand façade of unchallenged personal rule and obedient bureaucrats working his will there stood major limitations on Louis XIV's power, most notably the financial independence of some provinces and the nobility's traditional freedom from taxation, which Louis himself was compelled to reaffirm.

Within a framework of resurgent serfdom and entrenched nobility, Austrian and Prussian monarchs also fashioned absolutist states in the seventeenth and early eighteenth centuries. These monarchs won absolutist control over standing armies, permanent taxes, and legislative bodies. But they

Pieter Claesz: Still Life   The term "still life" became popular after 1650 as a reference to paintings of inanimate objects—flowers, fruit, all kinds of food, tableware, musical instruments—and the term was usually applied to Dutch paintings. As this scene suggests, the enormously successful Dutch commercial society took great pleasure in sensuous materialism. Yet the tortoise, a symbol of long life, and the watch, a reminder of the passage of time, imply that all is vanity. *(Source: Louvre/Cliché des Musées Nationaux, Paris)*

did not question the underlying social and economic relationships. Indeed, they enhanced the privileges of the nobility, which furnished the leading servitors for enlarged armies and growing government bureaucracies.

In Russia, social and economic trends were similar to those in Austria and Prussia. Unlike those two states, however, Russia had a long history of powerful princes. Tsar Peter the Great succeeded in tightening up Russia's traditional absolutism and modernizing it by reforming the army, the bureaucracy, and the defense industry. In Russia and throughout eastern Europe, war and the needs of the state in time of war weighed heavily in the triumph of absolutism.

Holland and England defied the general trend toward absolute monarchy. While Holland prospered under a unique republican confederation that placed most power in the hands of the different provinces, England—fortunately shielded from continental armies and military emergencies by its navy and the English Channel—evolved into the first modern constitutional state. The bitter conflicts between Parliament and the first two Stuart rulers, James I and Charles I, tested where sovereign power would rest in the state. The resulting civil war deposed the king, but it did not settle the question. A revival of absolutist tendencies under James II brought on the Glorious Revolution of 1688 to 1689, and the people who made that revolution settled three basic issues. Sovereign power was divided between king and Parliament, with Parliament enjoying the greater share. Government was to be based on the rule of law. And the liberties of English people were to be made explicit in written form, in the Bill of Rights. This constitutional settlement marked an important milestone in world history, although the framers left to later generations the task of making constitutional government work.

Triumphant absolution interacted spectacularly with the arts. It molded the ideals of French classicism, which glorified the state as personified by Louis XIV. Baroque art, which had grown out of the Catholic Reformation's desire to move the faithful and exalt the faith, admirably suited the secular aspirations of eastern European rulers. Thus baroque art attained magnificent heights in eastern Europe, symbolizing the ideal and harmonizing with the reality of imperious royal absolutism.

NOTES

1. J. B. Collins, *Fiscal Limits of Absolutism: Direct Taxation in Early Seventeenth Century France* (Berkeley: University of California Press, 1988), pp. 1, 3–4, 215–222.
2. Quoted in J. H. Elliot, *Richelieu and Olivares* (Cambridge: Cambridge University Press, 1984), p. 135; and in W. F. Church, *Richelieu and Reason of State* (Princeton, N.J.: Princeton University Press, 1972), p. 507.
3. D. Parker, *The Making of French Absolutism* (New York: St. Martin's Press, 1983), pp. 146–148.
4. See W. Beik, *Absolutism and Society in Seventeenth Century France: State Power and Provincial Aristocracy in Languedoc* (Cambridge: Cambridge University Press, 1985), pp. 279–302.
5. S. de Gramont, ed., *The Age of Magnificence: Memoirs of the Court of Louis XIV by the Duc de Saint Simon* (New York: Capricorn Books, 1964), pp. 141–145.
6. Quoted in A. Trout, *Jean-Baptiste Colbert* (Boston: Twayne, 1978), p. 128.
7. Ibid.
8. See W. C. Scoville, *The Persecution of the Huguenots and French Economic Development: 1680–1720* (Berkeley: University of California Press, 1960).
9. W. F. Church, *Louis XIV in Historical Thought: From Voltaire to the Annales School* (New York: Norton, 1976), p. 92.
10. J. H. Elliott, *Imperial Spain, 1469–1716* (New York: Mentor Books, 1963), pp. 306–308.
11. B. Bennassar, *The Spanish Character: Attitudes and Mentalities from the Sixteenth to the Nineteenth Century,* trans. B. Keen (Berkeley: University of California Press, 1979), p. 125.
12. F. L. Carsten, *The Origins of Prussia* (Oxford: Clarendon Press, 1954), p. 175.
13. Quoted in R. Ergang, *The Potsdam Fuhrer: Frederick William I, Father of Prussian Militarism* (New York: Octagon Books, 1972), pp. 85, 87.
14. Ibid., pp. 6–7, 43.
15. Quoted in R. A. Dorwart, *The Administrative Reforms of Frederick William I of Prussia* (Cambridge, Mass.: Harvard University Press, 1953), p. 226.
16. Quoted in H. Rosenberg, *Bureaucracy, Aristocracy, and Autocracy: The Prussian Experience, 1660–1815* (Boston: Beacon Press, 1966), p. 38.
17. Quoted in R. Pipes, *Russia Under the Old Regime* (New York: Scribner, 1974), p. 48.
18. Quoted in N. V. Riasanovsky, *A History of Russia* (New York: Oxford University Press, 1963), p. 79.
19. Quoted in I. Grey, *Ivan III and the Unification of Russia* (New York: Collier Books, 1967), p. 39.

20. Quoted in Pipes, p. 85.
21. Quoted in J. Summerson, in *The Eighteenth Century: Europe in the Age of Enlightenment,* ed. A. Cobban (New York: McGraw-Hill, 1969), p. 80.
22. Quoted in L. Mumford, *The Culture of Cities* (New York: Harcourt Brace Jovanovich, 1938), p. 97.
23. C. Stephenson and G. F. Marcham, *Sources of English Constitutional History* (New York: Harper & Row, 1937), p. 601.
24. Quoted in D. Maland, *Europe in the Seventeenth Century* (New York: Macmillan, 1967), pp. 198–199.
25. S. Schama, *The Embarrassment of Riches: An Interpretation of Dutch Culture in the Golden Age* (New York: Knopf, 1987), pp. 165–170.

SUGGESTED READING

Students who wish to explore the problems presented in this chapter will find a rich and exciting literature with many works available in paperback editions. The following surveys provide good background material. G. Parker, *Europe in Crisis, 1598–1618* (1980), provides a sound introduction to the social, economic, and religious tensions of the period. R. S. Dunn, *The Age of Religious Wars, 1559–1715,* 2d ed. (1979), examines the period from the perspective of the confessional strife between Protestants and Catholics, but there is also stimulating material on absolutism and constitutionalism. T. Aston, ed., *Crisis in Europe, 1560–1660* (1967), contains essays by leading historians. P. Anderson, *Lineages of the Absolutist State* (1974), is a Marxist interpretation of absolutism in western and eastern Europe. M. Beloff, *The Age of Absolutism* (1967), concentrates on the social forces that underlay administrative change. H. Rosenberg, "Absolute Monarchy and Its Legacy," in N. F. Cantor and S. Werthman, eds., *Early Modern Europe, 1450–1650* (1967), is a seminal study. The classic treatment of constitutionalism remains that of C. H. McIlwain, *Constitutionalism: Ancient and Modern* (1940), written by a great scholar during the rise of German fascism. S. B. Crimes, *English Constitutional History* (1967), is an excellent survey with useful chapters on the sixteenth and seventeenth centuries.

Louis XIV and his age have attracted the attention of many scholars. J. Wolf, *Louis XIV,* cited in the Notes, remains the best available biography. Two works of W. H. Lewis, *The Splendid Century* (1957) and *The Sunset of the Splendid Century* (1963), make delightful light reading, especially for the beginning student. The advanced student will want to consult the excellent historiographical analysis by W. F. Church mentioned in the Notes, *Louis XIV in Historical Thought.* Perhaps the best works of the Annales school on the period are P. Goubert, *Louis XIV and Twenty Million Frenchmen* (1972), and Goubert's heavily detailed *The Ancien Régime: French Society, 1600–1750,* 2 vols. (1969–1973), which contains invaluable material on the lives and work of ordinary people. For the French economy and financial conditions, the old study of C. W. Cole, *Colbert and a Century of French Mercantilism,* 2 vols. (1939), is still valuable but should be supplemented by R. Bonney, *The King's Debts: Finance and Politics in France, 1589–1661* (1981), and by the works of Trout and Scoville listed in the Notes. R. Hatton, *Europe in the Age of Louis XIV* (1979), is a splendidly illustrated survey of many aspects of seventeenth-century European culture. O. Ranum, *Paris in the Age of Absolutism* (1968), describes the geographical, political, economic, and architectural significance of the cultural capital of Europe. V. L. Tapie, *The Age of Grandeur: Baroque Art and Architecture* (1960), also emphasizes the relationship between art and politics with excellent illustrations.

For Spain, in addition to the works in the Notes, see M. Defourneaux, *Daily Life in Spain in the Golden Age* (1976), highly useful for an understanding of ordinary people and of Spanish society. See also C. R. Phillips, *Ciudad Real, 1500–1750: Growth, Crisis, and Readjustment in the Spanish Economy* (1979), a significant case study

The following works offer solid material on English political and social issues of the seventeenth century: M. Ashley, *England in the Seventeenth Century,* rev. ed. (1980), and *The House of Stuart: Its Rise and Fall* (1980); C. Hill, *A Century of Revolution* (1961); J. P. Kenyon, *Stuart England* (1978); and K. Wrightson, *English Society, 1580–1680* (1982). Perhaps the most comprehensive treatments of Parliament are C. Russell, *Crisis of Parliaments, 1509–1660* (1971), and Russell, *Parliaments and English Politics, 1621–1629* (1979). On the background of the English civil war, L. Stone, *The Crisis of the Aristocracy* (1965), and Stone, *The Causes of the English Revolution* (1972), are standard works. Both B. Manning, *The English People and the English Revolution* (1976), and D. Underdown, *Revel, Riot, and Rebellion* (1985), discuss the extent of popular involvement. For English intellectual currents, see J. O. Appleby, *Economic Thought and Ideology in Seventeenth Century England* (1978), and C. Hill, *Intellectual Origins of the English Revolution* (1966).

For the several shades of Protestant sentiment in the early seventeenth century, see P. Collinson, *The Religion of Protestants* (1982). C. M. Hibbard, *Charles I and the Popish Plot* (1983), treats Roman Catholic influence and may be compared with W. Haller, *The Rise of Puritanism* (1957). For women, see R. Thompson, *Women in Stuart England and America* (1974), and A. Fraser, *The Weaker Vessel* (1985). For Cromwell and the Interregnum, C. Firth, *Oliver Cromwell and the Rule of the Puritans in England* (1956), and A. Fraser, *Cromwell, the Lord Protector* (1973), are both valuable. J. Morrill, *The Revolt of the Provinces,* 2d ed. (1980), is the best study of religious neutralism. C. Hill, *The World Turned Upside Down* (1972), discusses radical thought during the period.

For the Restoration and the Glorious Revolution, see R. Hutton, *Charles II: King of England, Scotland and Ireland* (1989), and A. Fraser, *Royal Charles: Charles II and the Restoration* (1979), two highly readable biographies; R. Ollard, *The Image of the King: Charles I and Charles II* (1980), which examines the nature of monarchy; J. Miller, *James II: A Study in Kingship* (1977); J. Childs, *The Army, James II, and the Glorious Revolution* (1980); J. R. Jones, *The Revolution of 1688 in England* (1972); and L. G. Schwoerer, *The Declaration of Rights, 1689* (1981), a fine assessment of that fundamental document. The ideas of John Locke are analyzed by J. P. Kenyon, *Revolution Principles: The Politics of Party, 1689–1720* (1977).

On Holland, K. H. D. Haley, *The Dutch Republic in the Seventeenth Century* (1972), is a splendidly illustrated appreciation of Dutch commercial and artistic achievements, and J. L. Price, *Culture and Society in the Dutch Republic During the Seventeenth Century* (1974), is a sound scholarly work. R. Boxer, *The Dutch Seaborne Empire* (1980), and the appropriate chapters of D. Maland, *Europe in the Seventeenth Century,* cited in the Notes, are useful for Dutch overseas expansion and the reasons for Dutch prosperity. The following works focus on the economic and cultural life of the leading Dutch city: V. Barbour, *Capitalism in Amsterdam in the Seventeenth Century* (1950), and D. Regin, *Traders, Artists, Burghers: A Cultural History of Amsterdam in the Seventeenth Century* (1977). The leading statesmen of the period may be studied in these biographies: H. H. Rowen, *John de Witt, Grand Pensionary of Holland, 1625–1672* (1978); S. B. Baxter, *William the III and the Defense of European Liberty, 1650–1702* (1966); and J. den Tex, *Oldenbarnevelt,* 2 vols. (1973).

The best study on early Prussian history is Carsten, *The Origin of Prussia* (see the Notes). Rosenberg, *Bureaucracy, Aristocracy, and Autocracy* is a masterful analysis of the social context of Prussian absolutism. In addition to Ergang, *The Potsdam Fuhrer,* an exciting and critical biography of ramrod Frederick William I, there is G. Ritter, *Frederick the Great* (1968), a more sympathetic study of the talented son by one of Germany's leading conservative historians. G. Craig, *The Politics of the Prussian Army, 1640–1945* (1964), expertly traces the great influence of the military on the Prussian state over three hundred years. R. J. Evans, *The Making of the Habsburg Empire, 1550–1770* (1979), and R. A. Kann,

A History of the Habsburg Empire, 1526–1918 (1974), analyze the development of absolutism in Austria, as does A. Wandruszka, *The House of Habsburg* (1964). J. Stoye, *The Siege of Vienna* (1964), is a fascinating account of the last great Ottoman offensive, which is also treated in the interesting study by P. Coles, *The Ottoman Impact on Europe, 1350–1699* (1968). The Austro-Ottoman conflict is also a theme of L. S. Stavrianos, *The Balkans Since 1453* (1958), and D. McKay, *Prince Eugene of Savoy* (1978), a fine biography. A good general account is provided in D. McKay and H. Scott, *The Rise of the Great Powers, 1648–1815* (1983), and R. Vierhaus, *Germany in the Age of Absolutism* (1988), offers a good survey of the different German states.

On eastern European peasants and serfdom, D. Chirot, ed., *The Origins of Backwardness in Eastern Europe: Economics and Politics from the Middle Ages Until the Twentieth Century* (1989), is a wide-ranging introduction that may be compared with J. Blum, "The Rise of Serfdom in Eastern Europe," *American Historical Review* 62 (July 1957): 807–836. E. Levin, *Sex and Society in the World of the Orthodox Slavs, 900–1700* (1989), carries family history to eastern Europe. R. Mousnier, *Peasant Uprisings in Seventeenth-Century France, Russia, and China* (1970), is a fine comparative study. J. Blum, *Lord and Peasant in Russia from the Ninth to the Nineteenth Century* (1961), provides a good look at conditions in rural Russia, and P. Avrich, *Russian Rebels, 1600–1800* (1972), treats some of the violent peasant upheavals those conditions produced. R. Hellie, *Enserfment and Military Change in Muscovy* (1971), is outstanding, as is A. Yanov, *Origins of Autocracy: Ivan the Terrible in Russian History* (1981). In addition to the fine surveys by Pipes and Riasanovsky cited in the Notes, J. Billington, *The Icon and the Axe* (1970), is a stimulating history of early Russian intellectual and cultural developments, such as the great split in the church. M. Raeff, *Origins of the Russian Intelligentsia* (1966), skillfully probes the mind of the Russian nobility in the eighteenth century. B. H. Sumner, *Peter the Great and the Emergence of Russia* (1962), is a fine brief introduction, which may be compared with the brilliant biography by Russia's greatest prerevolutionary historian, V. Klyuchevsky, *Peter the Great* (English trans., 1958), and with N. Riasanovsky, *The Image of Peter the Great in Russian History and Thought* (1985). G. Vernadsky and R. Fisher, eds., *A Source Book of Russian History from Early Times to 1917,* 3 vols. (1972), is an invaluable, highly recommended collection of documents and contemporary writings.

Three good books on art and architecture are E. Hempel, *Baroque Art and Architecture in Central Europe* (1965); G. Hamilton, *The Art and Architecture of Russia* (1954); and N. Pevsner, *An Outline of European Architecture,* 6th ed. (1960).

20

Toward a New World
View in the West

An early library in a British coastal town, 18th century. T. Malton, *Hall's Library at Margate*

*M*ost people are not philosophers, but nevertheless they have a basic outlook on life, a more or less coherent world view. At the risk of oversimplification, one may say that the world view of people in medieval and early modern Europe was primarily religious and theological. Not only did Christian or Jewish teachings form the core of their spiritual and philosophical beliefs, but religious teachings permeated all the rest of human thought and activity. Political theory relied on the divine right of kings, for example, and activities ranging from marriage and divorce to eating habits and hours of business were regulated by churches and religious doctrines.

In the course of the eighteenth century, the religious and theological world view of the educated classes of western Europe underwent a fundamental transformation. Many educated people came to see the world primarily in secular and scientific terms. Few abandoned religious beliefs altogether, but many became openly hostile toward established Christianity. The role of churches and of religious thinking in earthly affairs and in the pursuit of knowledge was substantially reduced. Among many in the upper and middle classes, a new critical, scientific, and very "modern" world view took shape.

- Why did the momentous change in world view occur?
- How did the new outlook on life affect society and politics?

This chapter focuses on those questions.

THE SCIENTIFIC REVOLUTION

The foremost cause of the change in world view was the scientific revolution. Modern science—precise knowledge of the physical world based on the union of experimental observations with sophisticated mathematics—crystallized in the seventeenth century. In medieval intellectual life, science had been secondary and subordinate; for many educated people in the eighteenth century, it became independent and even primary.

The emergence of modern science was a development of tremendous long-term significance. A noted historian has even said that the scientific revolution of the late sixteenth and seventeenth centuries "outshines everything since the rise of Christianity and reduces the Renaissance and Reformation to the rank of mere episodes, mere internal displacements, within the system of medieval Christendom." The scientific revolution was "the real origin both of the modern world and the modern mentality."[1] This statement is an exaggeration, but not by much. Of all the great civilizations, only that of the West developed modern science. It was with the scientific revolution that Western society began to acquire its most distinctive traits.

Although historians agree that the scientific revolution was enormously important, they approach it in quite different ways. Some scholars believe that scientific achievement in this period had its own basic "internal" logic and that "nonscientific" factors had quite limited significance. These scholars write brilliant, often highly technical, intellectual studies, but they neglect the broader historical context. Other historians stress "external" economic, social, and religious factors, brushing over the scientific developments themselves. Historians of science now realize that these two approaches need to be brought together, but they are only beginning to do so. Thus it is best to examine the milestones on the fateful march toward modern science first and then search for nonscientific influences along the route.

Scientific Thought in 1500

Developments in astronomy and physics were at the heart of the scientific revolution. In the early 1500s, traditional European ideas about the universe were still based primarily on the ideas of Aristotle, the great Greek philosopher of the fourth century B.C. These ideas had gradually been recovered during the Middle Ages and then brought into harmony with Christian doctrines by medieval theologians. According to this revised Aristotelian view, a motionless earth was fixed at the center of the universe. Around it moved ten separate, transparent, crystal spheres. In the first eight spheres were embedded, in turn, the moon, the sun, the five known planets, and the fixed stars. Then followed two spheres added during the Middle Ages to account for slight changes in the positions of the stars over the centuries. Beyond the tenth sphere was heaven, with the throne of God and the souls of the saved. Angels kept the spheres moving in perfect circles.

Aristotle's views, suitably revised by medieval philosophers, also dominated thinking about physics and motion on earth. Aristotle had distinguished sharply between the world of the celestial spheres and that of the earth—the sublunar world. The spheres consisted of a perfect, incorruptible "quintessence," or fifth essence. The sublunar world, however, was made up of four imperfect, changeable elements. The "light" elements—air and fire—naturally moved upward; the "heavy" elements—water and earth—naturally moved downward. The natural directions of motion did not always prevail, however, for elements were often mixed together and could be affected by an outside force such as a human being. Aristotle and his followers also believed that a uniform force moved an object at a constant speed and that the object would stop as soon as that force was removed.

Aristotle's ideas about astronomy and physics were accepted with minor revisions for two thousand years, and with good reason. First, they offered an understandable, common-sense explanation for what the eye actually saw. Second, Aristotle's science, as interpreted by Christian theologians, fit neatly with Christian doctrines. It established a home for God and a place for Christian souls. It put human beings at the center of the universe and made them the critical link in a "great chain of being" that stretched from the throne of God to the most lowly insect on earth. Thus science was primarily a branch of theology, and it reinforced religious thought. At the same time, medieval "scientists" were already providing closely reasoned explanations of the universe, explanations that they felt were worthy of God's perfect creation.

The Copernican Hypothesis

The desire to explain and thereby glorify God's handiwork led to the first great departure from the medieval system. This departure was the work of the Polish clergyman and astronomer Nicolaus

Ptolemy's System This 1543 drawing shows how the changing configurations of the planets moving around the earth form the twelve different constellations, or "signs," of the zodiac. The learned astronomer on the right is using his knowledge to predict the future for the king on the left. *(Source: Mary Evans Picture Library/ Photo Researchers)*

Copernicus (1473–1543). As a young man, Copernicus studied church law and astronomy in various European universities. He saw how professional astronomers were still dependent for their most accurate calculations on the work of Ptolemy, the last great ancient astronomer, who had lived in Alexandria in the second century A.D. Ptolemy's achievement had been to work out complicated rules to explain the minor irregularities in the movement of the planets. These rules enabled stargazers and astrologers to track the planets with greater precision. Many people then (and now) believed that the changing relationships between planets and stars influenced and even determined the future.

The young Copernicus was uninterested in astrology and felt that Ptolemy's cumbersome and occasionally inaccurate rules detracted from the majesty of a perfect Creator. He preferred an old Greek idea being discussed in Renaissance Italy: that the sun rather than the earth was at the center of the universe. Finishing his university studies and returning to a church position in east Prussia, Copernicus worked on his hypothesis from 1506 to 1530. Never questioning the Aristotelian belief in crystal spheres or the idea that circular motion was most perfect and divine, Copernicus theorized that the stars and planets, including the earth, revolve around a fixed sun. Yet Copernicus was a cautious man. Fearing the ridicule of other astronomers, he did not publish his *On the Revolutions of the Heavenly Spheres* until 1543, the year of his death.

Copernicus's theory had enormous scientific and religious implications, many of which the conservative Copernicus did not anticipate. First, it put the stars at rest, their apparent nightly movement simply a result of the earth's rotation. Thus it destroyed the main reason for believing in crystal spheres capable of moving the stars around the earth. Second, Copernicus's theory suggested a universe of staggering size. If in the course of a year the earth moved around the sun and yet the stars appeared to remain in the same place, then the universe was unthinkably large or even infinite. Finally, by characterizing the earth as just another planet, Copernicus destroyed the basic idea of Aristotelian physics—that the earthly world was quite different from the heavenly one. Where, then, was the realm of perfection? Where were heaven and the throne of God?

The Copernican theory quickly brought sharp attacks from religious leaders, especially Protestants. Hearing of Copernicus's work even before it was published, Martin Luther spoke of him as the "new astrologer who wants to prove that the earth moves and goes round. . . . The fool wants to turn the whole art of astronomy upside down." Luther noted that "as the Holy Scripture tells us, so did Joshua bid the sun stand still and not the earth." John Calvin also condemned Copernicus, citing as evidence the first verse of Psalm 93: "The world also is established that it cannot be moved." "Who," asked Calvin, "will venture to place the authority of Copernicus above that of the Holy Spirit?"[2]

Catholic reaction was milder at first. The Catholic church had never been hypnotized by literal interpretations of the Bible, and not until 1616 did it officially declare the Copernican theory false. This slow reaction also reflected the slow progress of Copernicus's theory for many years.

Other events were almost as influential as Copernican theory in creating doubts about traditional astronomical ideas. In 1572 a new star appeared and shone very brightly for almost two years. The new star, which was actually a distant exploding star, made an enormous impression on people. It seemed to contradict the idea that the heavenly spheres were unchanging and therefore perfect. In 1577 a new comet suddenly moved through the sky, cutting a straight path across the supposedly impenetrable crystal spheres. It was time, as a typical scientific writer put it, for "the radical renovation of astronomy."[3] One astronomer who agreed was Tycho Brahe.

From Tycho Brahe to Galileo

Born into a leading Danish noble family and earmarked for a career in government, Tycho Brahe (1546–1601) was at an early age tremendously impressed by a partial eclipse of the sun. It seemed to him "something divine that men could know the motions of the stars so accurately that they were able a long time beforehand to predict their places and relative positions."[4] Completing his studies abroad and returning to Denmark, Brahe established himself as Europe's leading astronomer with his detailed observations of the new star of 1572. Aided by generous grants from the king of Denmark, which made him one of the richest men in the country, Brahe built the most sophisticated observatory of his day. For twenty years he meticulously observed the stars and planets with the naked eye. An imposing man who had lost a piece of his nose in a duel and replaced it with a special bridge of gold and silver alloy, a noble who exploited his peasants arrogantly and approached the heavens humbly, Brahe's great contribution was his mass of data. His limited understanding of mathematics, however, prevented him from making much sense out of his data. Part Ptolemaic, part Copernican, he believed that all the planets revolved around the sun and that the entire group of sun and planets revolved in turn around the earth-moon system.

It was left to Brahe's brilliant young assistant, Johannes Kepler (1571–1630), to go much further. Kepler was a medieval figure in many ways. Coming from a minor German noble family and trained for the Lutheran ministry, he long believed that the universe was built on mystical mathematical relationships and a musical harmony among the heavenly bodies. Working and reworking Brahe's mountain of observations in a staggering sustained effort after the Dane's death, this brilliant mathematician eventually went beyond mystical intuitions.

Kepler formulated three famous laws of planetary motion. First, building on Copernican theory, he demonstrated in 1609 that the orbits of the planets around the sun are elliptical rather than circular. Second, he demonstrated that the planets do not move at a uniform speed in their orbits. Third, in 1619 he showed that the time a planet takes to make its complete orbit is precisely related to its distance from the sun. Kepler's contribution was monumental. Whereas Copernicus had speculated, Kepler proved mathematically the precise relations of a sun-centered (solar) system. His work demolished the old system of Aristotle and Ptolemy, and in his third law he came close to formulating the idea of universal gravitation.

Galileo's Paintings of the Moon When Galileo published the results of his telescopic observations of the moon, he added these paintings to illustrate the marvels he had seen. Galileo made two telescopes, which are shown here. The larger one magnifies 14 times, the smaller 20 times. *(Source: Biblioteca Nazionale Centrale, Florence; Museum of Science, Florence/Scala/Art Resource)*

While Kepler was unraveling planetary motion, a young Florentine named Galileo Galilei (1564–1642) was challenging all the old ideas about motion. Like so many early scientists, Galileo was a poor nobleman first marked for a religious career. However, he soon became fascinated by mathematics. A brilliant student, Galileo became a professor of mathematics in 1589 at age twenty-five. He proceeded to examine motion and mechanics in a new way. Indeed, his great achievement was the elaboration and consolidation of the modern experimental method. Rather than speculate about what might or should happen, Galileo conducted controlled experiments to find out what actually did happen.

In an acceleration experiment, he showed that a uniform force—in this case, gravity—produces a uniform acceleration. Here is how Galileo described his pathbreaking method and conclusion late in life in his *Two New Sciences* (1638):

A piece of wooden moulding . . . was taken; on its edge was cut a channel a little more than one finger in breadth. Having made this groove very straight, smooth and polished, and having lined it with parchment, also as smooth and polished as possible, we rolled along it a hard, smooth and very round bronze ball. . . . Noting . . . the time required to make the descent . . . we now rolled the ball only one-quarter the length of the channel; and having measured the time of its descent, we found it precisely one-half of the former. . . . In such experiments [over many distances], repeated a full hundred times, we always found that the spaces traversed were to each other as the squares of the times, and that this was true for all inclinations of the plane.[5]

With this and other experiments, Galileo also formulated the law of inertia: an object continues in motion forever unless stopped by some external force; being at rest is not the natural state of objects. Aristotelian physics was in a shambles.

In the tradition of Brahe, Galileo also applied the experimental method to astronomy. His astronomical discoveries had a great impact on scientific development. On hearing of the invention of the telescope in Holland, Galileo made one for himself and trained it on the heavens. He quickly discovered the first four moons of Jupiter, which clearly suggested that Jupiter could not possibly be embedded in any impenetrable crystal sphere. This discovery provided new evidence for the Copernican theory, in which Galileo already believed.

Galileo then pointed his telescope at the moon. He wrote in 1610 in *Siderus Nuncius:*

I feel sure that the moon is not perfectly smooth, free from inequalities, and exactly spherical, as a large school of philosophers considers with regard to the moon and the other heavenly bodies. On the contrary, it is full of inequalities, uneven, full of hollows and protuberances, just like the surface of the earth itself, which is varied. . . . The next object which I have observed is the essence or substance of the Milky Way. By the aid of a telescope anyone may behold this in a manner which so distinctly appeals to the senses that all the disputes which have tormented philosophers through so many ages are exploded by the irrefutable evidence of our eyes, and we are freed from wordy disputes upon the subject. For the galaxy is nothing else but a mass of innumerable stars planted together in clusters. Upon whatever part of it you direct the telescope straightway a vast crowd of stars presents itself to view; many of them are tolerably large and extremely bright, but the number of small ones is quite beyond determination.[6]

Reading these famous lines, one feels that a crucial corner in Western civilization is being turned. The traditional religious and theological world view, which rested on determining and accepting the proper established authority, is beginning to give way in certain fields to a critical, scientific method. This new method of learning and investigating was the greatest accomplishment of the scientific revolution, for it has proved capable of great extension. A historian investigating documents of the past, for example, is not much different from a Galileo studying stars and rolling balls.

Galileo was employed in Florence by the Medici grand dukes of Tuscany, and his work eventually aroused the ire of some theologians. The issue was presented in 1624 to Pope Urban VII, who permitted Galileo to write about different possible systems of the world as long as he did not presume to judge which system actually did exist. After the publication in Italian of his widely read *Dialogue on the Two Chief Systems of the World* (1632), which too openly lampooned the traditional views of Aristotle and Ptolemy and defended those of Copernicus, Galileo was tried for heresy by the papal Inquisition. Imprisoned and threatened with torture, the aging Galileo recanted, "renouncing and cursing" his Copernican errors. Of minor importance in the development of science, Galileo's trial later became for some writers the perfect symbol of the inevitable conflict between religious belief and scientific knowledge.

Newton's Synthesis

The accomplishments of Kepler, Galileo, and other scientists had taken effect by about 1640. The old astronomy and physics were in ruins, and several fundamental breakthroughs had been made. The new findings, however, had not been fused together in a new synthesis, a single explanatory system that would comprehend motion both on earth and in the skies. That synthesis, which prevailed until the twentieth century, was the work of Isaac Newton (1642–1727).

Newton was born into lower English gentry and attended Cambridge University. A great genius who spectacularly united the experimental and theoretical-mathematical sides of modern science, Newton was also fascinated by alchemy. He sought the elixir of life and a way to change base metals into gold and silver. Not without reason did the twentieth-century economist John Maynard Keynes call Newton the "last of the magicians." Newton was intensely religious. He had a highly suspicious nature, lacked all interest in women and sex, and in 1693 suffered a nervous breakdown from which he later recovered. He was far from being the perfect rationalist so endlessly eulogized by so many writers in the eighteenth and nineteenth centuries.

Of his intellectual genius and incredible powers of concentration there can be no doubt. Arriving at some of his most basic ideas about physics in 1666 at age twenty-four, but unable to prove these theories mathematically, he attained a professorship and studied optics for many years. In 1684 Newton returned to physics for eighteen extraordinarily intensive months. For weeks on end he seldom left his room except to read his lectures. His meals were sent up, but he usually forgot to eat them, his mind fastened like a vise on the laws of the universe. He opened the third book of his immortal *Mathematical Principles of Natural Philosophy,* published in Latin in 1687 and generally known as the *Principia,* with these lines:

In the preceding books I have laid down the principles of philosophy [that is, science]. . . . These principles are the laws of certain motions, and powers or forces, which chiefly have respect to philosophy. . . . It remains that from the same principles I now demonstrate the frame of the System of the World.

Newton made good his grandiose claim. His towering accomplishment was to integrate in a single explanatory system the astronomy of Copernicus, as corrected by Kepler's laws, with the physics of Galileo and his predecessors. Newton did this by means of a set of mathematical laws that explain motion and mechanics. These laws of dynamics are complex, and it took scientists and engineers two hundred years to work out all their implications. Nevertheless, the key feature of the Newtonian synthesis was the law of universal gravitation. According to this law, every body in the universe attracts every other body in the universe in a precise mathematical relationship: the force of attraction is proportional to the quantity of matter of the objects and inversely proportional to the square of the distance between them. Newton unified in one majestic system the whole universe—from Kepler's elliptical orbits to Galileo's rolling balls.

Causes of the Scientific Revolution

With a charming combination of modesty and self-congratulation, Newton once wrote: "If I have seen further [than others], it is by standing on the shoulders of Giants."[7] Surely the path from Copernicus to Newton confirms the "internal" view of the scientific revolution as a product of towering individual genius. The problems of science were inherently exciting, and solution of those problems was its own reward for inquisitive, high-powered minds. Yet there were certainly broader causes as well.

The long-term contribution of medieval intellectual life and medieval universities to the scientific revolution was much more considerable than historians unsympathetic to the Middle Ages once believed. By the thirteenth century, permanent universities with professors and large student bodies had been established in western Europe. The universities were supported by society because they trained the lawyers, doctors, and church lead-

State Support Governments supported scientific research because they thought it might be useful. Here Louis XIV visits the French Royal Academy of Sciences in 1671 and examines a plan for better military fortifications. The great interest in astronomy, anatomy, and geography is evident. *(Source: Bibliothèque Nationale, Paris)*

ers that society required. By 1300 philosophy had taken its place alongside law, medicine, and theology. Medieval philosophers developed a limited but real independence from theologians and a sense of free inquiry. They nobly pursued a body of knowledge and tried to arrange it meaningfully by means of abstract theories.

Within this framework, science was able to emerge as a minor but distinct branch of philosophy. In the fourteenth and fifteenth centuries, first in Italy and then elsewhere in Europe, leading universities established new professorships of mathematics, astronomy, and physics (natural philosophy) within their faculties of philosophy. The prestige of the new fields was still low among both professors and students. Nevertheless, this pattern of academic science, which grew out of the medieval commitment to philosophy and did not change

substantially until the late eighteenth century, undoubtedly promoted scientific development. Rational, critical thinking was applied to scientific problems by a permanent community of scholars. And an outlet existed for the talents of a Galileo or a Newton: all the great pathfinders either studied or taught at universities.

The Renaissance also stimulated scientific progress. One of the great deficiencies of medieval science was its rather rudimentary mathematics. The recovery of the finest works of Greek mathematics—a by-product of Renaissance humanism's ceaseless search for the knowledge of antiquity—greatly improved European mathematics well into the early seventeenth century. The recovery of more texts also showed that classical mathematicians had their differences, and Europeans were forced to try to resolve these ancient controversies by means of their own efforts. Finally, the Renaissance pattern of patronage, especially in Italy, was often scientific as well as artistic and humanistic. Various rulers and wealthy business people supported scientific investigations, just as the Medicis of Florence supported those of Galileo.

The navigational problems of long sea voyages in the age of overseas expansion were a third factor in the scientific revolution. Ship captains on distant shores needed to be able to chart their positions as accurately as possible so that reliable maps could be drawn and the risks of international trade reduced. As early as 1484, the king of Portugal appointed a commission of mathematicians to perfect tables to help seamen find their latitude. The result was the first European navigation manual.

The problem of fixing longitude was much more difficult. In England, the government and the great capitalistic trading companies turned to science and scientific education in an attempt to solve this pressing practical problem. When the famous Elizabethan financier Sir Thomas Gresham left a large amount of money to establish Gresham College in London, he stipulated that three of the college's seven professors had to concern themselves exclusively with scientific subjects. The professor of astronomy was directed to teach courses on the science of navigation. A seventeenth-century popular ballad took note of the new college's calling:

This college will the whole world measure
Which most impossible conclude,
And navigation make a pleasure
By finding out the longitude.[8]

At Gresham College, for the first time in history, scientists had an important, honored role. They enjoyed close ties with the top officials of the Royal Navy and with the leading merchants and shipbuilders. Gresham College became the main center of scientific activity in England in the first half of the seventeenth century. The close tie between practical men and scientists led to the establishment in 1662 of the Royal Society of London, which published scientific papers and sponsored scientific meetings.

Navigational problems were also critical in the development of many new scientific instruments, such as the telescope, the barometer, the thermometer, the pendulum clock, the microscope, and the air pump. Better instruments permitting more accurate observations often led to important new knowledge. Galileo with his telescope was by no means unique.

Better instruments were part of a fourth factor in the scientific revolution, the development of improved ways of obtaining knowledge about the world. Two important thinkers, Francis Bacon (1561–1626) and René Descartes (1596–1650), represented key aspects of this improvement in scientific methodology.

The English politician and writer Francis Bacon was the greatest early propagandist for the new experimental method, as Galileo was its greatest early practitioner. Rejecting the Aristotelian and medieval method of using speculative reasoning to build general theories, Bacon argued that new knowledge had to be pursued through empirical, experimental research. According to Bacon, the researcher who wants to learn more about leaves or rocks, for example, should not speculate about the subject but rather collect a multitude of specimens and then compare and analyze them. Freed from sterile medieval speculation, the facts will speak for themselves, and important general principles will emerge. Knowledge will increase. Bacon's contribution was to formalize the empirical method, which had already been used by Brahe and Galileo, into the general theory of inductive reasoning known as *empiricism.*

Bacon claimed that the empirical method would result not only in more knowledge but in highly practical, useful knowledge. According to Bacon, scientific discoveries like those so avidly sought at Gresham College would bring about much greater control over the physical environment and make people rich and nations powerful. Thus Bacon helped provide a radically new and effective justification for private and public support of scientific inquiry.

The French philosopher René Descartes was a genius who made his first great discovery in mathematics. As a twenty-three-year-old soldier serving in the Thirty Years' War, he experienced on a single night in 1619 a life-changing intellectual vision. Descartes saw that there was a perfect correspondence between geometry and algebra and that geometrical, spatial figures could be expressed as algebraic equations and vice versa. A great step forward in the history of mathematics, Descartes's discovery of analytic geometry provided scientists with an important new tool. Descartes also made contributions to the science of optics, but his greatest achievement was to develop his initial vision into a whole philosophy of knowledge and science.

Like Bacon, Descartes scorned traditional science and had great faith in the powers of the human mind. Yet Descartes was much more systematic and mathematical than Bacon. He decided that it was necessary to doubt everything that could reasonably be doubted and then, as in geometry, to use deductive reasoning from self-evident principles to ascertain scientific laws. Descartes's reasoning ultimately reduced all substances to "matter" and "mind"—that is, to the physical and the spiritual. His view of the world as consisting of two fundamental entities is known as *Cartesian dualism*. Descartes was a profoundly original and extremely influential thinker.

It is important to realize that the modern scientific method, which began to crystallize in the late seventeenth century, has combined Bacon's inductive experimentalism and Descartes's deductive, mathematical rationalism. Neither of these extreme approaches was sufficient by itself. Bacon's inability to appreciate the importance of mathematics and his obsession with practical results clearly showed the limitations of antitheoretical empiricism. Likewise, some of Descartes's positions—he believed, for example, that it was possible to deduce the whole science of medicine from first principles—aptly demonstrated the inadequacy of rigid, dogmatic rationalism. Significantly, Bacon faulted Galileo for his use of abstract formulas, and Descartes criticized the great Italian for being too experimental and insufficiently theoretical. Thus the modern scientific method has typically combined Bacon and Descartes. It has joined precise observations and experimentalism with the search for general laws that may be expressed in rigorously logical, mathematical language.

Finally, there is the question of science and religion. Just as some historians have argued that Protestantism led to the rise of capitalism, others have concluded that Protestantism was a fundamental factor in the rise of modern science. In this view, Protestantism, particularly in its Calvinist varieties, made scientific inquiry a question of individual conscience and not of religious doctrine; and the Catholic church, in contrast, suppressed scientific theories that conflicted with its teachings and thus discouraged scientific progress. The truth of the matter is more complicated.

All religious authorities—Catholic, Protestant, and Jewish—opposed the Copernican system to a greater or lesser extent until about 1630, by which time the scientific revolution was definitely in progress. The Catholic church was initially less hostile than Protestant and Jewish religious leaders. This early Catholic toleration and the scientific interests of Renaissance Italy help account for the undeniable fact that Italian scientists played a crucial role in scientific progress right up to the trial of Galileo in 1633. Thereafter, the Counter-Reformation church became more hostile to science, a change that helps account for the decline of science in Italy (but not in Catholic France) after 1640. At the same time, some Protestant countries became quite "pro-science," especially if the country lacked a strong religious authority capable of imposing religious orthodoxy on scientific questions.

This was the case with England after 1630. English religious conflicts became so intense that it was impossible for the authorities to impose religious unity on anything, including science. It is significant that the forerunners of the Royal Society agreed to discuss only "neutral" scientific questions so as not to come to blows over closely related religious and political disputes. The work of Bacon's many followers during Cromwell's commonwealth helped solidify the neutrality and independence of science. Bacon advocated the experimental approach precisely because it was open-minded and independent of any preconceived religious or philosophical ideas. Neutral and useful, science became an accepted part of life and developed rapidly in England after about 1640.

Some Consequences of the Scientific Revolution

The rise of modern science had many consequences, some of which are still unfolding. First, it went hand in hand with the rise of a new and expanding social group—the scientific community. Members of this community were linked together by learned societies, common interests, and shared values. Expansion of knowledge was the primary goal of this community, and scientists' material and psychological rewards depended on their success in this endeavor. Thus science became quite competitive, and more advances were inevitable.

Second, the scientific revolution introduced not only new knowledge about nature but also a new and revolutionary way of obtaining such knowledge—the modern scientific method. In addition to being both theoretical and experimental, this method was highly critical, and it differed profoundly from the old way of getting knowledge about nature. It refused to base conclusions on tradition and established sources, on ancient authorities and sacred texts.

The scientific revolution had few consequences for economic life and the living standards of the masses until the late eighteenth century at the very earliest. True, improvements in the techniques of navigation facilitated overseas trade and helped enrich leading merchants. But science had relatively few practical economic applications, and the hopes of the early Baconians were frustrated. The close link between theoretical, or pure, science and applied technology—a link that we take for granted today—did not exist before the nineteenth century. Thus the scientific revolution of the seventeenth century was first and foremost an intellectual revolution. For more than a hundred years its greatest impact was on how people thought and believed.

THE ENLIGHTENMENT

The scientific revolution was the single most important factor in the creation of the new world view of the eighteenth-century Enlightenment. This world view, which played a large role in shaping the modern mind, was based on a rich mix of ideas, sometimes conflicting, for intellectuals delight in playing with ideas just as athletes delight in playing games. Despite this diversity, three central concepts stand out.

The most important and original idea of the Enlightenment was that the methods of natural science could and should be used to examine and understand all aspects of life. The "methods of natural science" were what intellectuals meant by *reason,* a favorite word of Enlightenment thinkers. Nothing was to be accepted on faith. Everything was to be submitted to the rational, critical, scientific way of thinking. This approach brought the Enlightenment into a conflict with the established churches, which rested their beliefs on the special authority of the Bible and Christian theology.

A second important Enlightenment concept was that the scientific method was capable of discovering the laws of human society as well as the laws of nature. Thus was social science born. Its birth led to the third key idea, that of progress. Armed with the proper method of discovering the laws of human existence, Enlightenment thinkers believed that it was at least possible to create better societies and better people. Their belief was strengthened by some genuine improvements in economic and social life during the eighteenth century (see Chapter 21).

The Enlightenment was therefore profoundly secular. It revived and expanded the Renaissance concentration on worldly explanations. In the course of the eighteenth century, the Enlightenment had a profound impact on the thought and culture of the urban middle and upper classes. It did not have much appeal for the poor and the peasants.

The Emergence of the Enlightenment

The Enlightenment did not reach maturity until about 1750. Yet it was the generation that came of age between the publication of Newton's masterpiece in 1687 and the death of Louis XIV in 1715 that tied the crucial knot between the scientific revolution and a new outlook on life. Talented writers of that generation popularized hard-to-understand scientific achievements for the educated elite.

The most famous and influential popularizer was a versatile French man of letters, Bernard de Fontenelle (1657–1757). Fontenelle practically invented the technique of making highly complicated scientific findings understandable to a broad nonscientific audience. He set out to make science witty and entertaining, as easy to read as a novel. This was a tall order, but Fontenelle largely succeeded.

His most famous work, *Conversations on the Plurality of Worlds* (1686), begins with two elegant figures walking in the gathering shadows of a large park. One is a woman, a sophisticated aristocrat, and the other is her friend, perhaps even her lover. They gaze at the stars, and their talk turns to a passionate discussion of . . . astronomy! He confides that "each star may well be a different world." She is intrigued by his novel idea: "Teach me about these stars of yours." And he does, gently but persistently stressing how error is giving way to truth. At one point he explains:

There came on the scene . . . one Copernicus, who made short work of all those various circles, all those solid skies, which the ancients had pictured to themselves. The former he abolished; the latter he broke in pieces. Fired with the noble zeal of a true astronomer, he took the earth and spun it very far away from the center of the universe, where it had been installed, and in that center he put the sun, which had a far better title to the honor.[9]

Rather than tremble in despair in the face of these revelations, Fontenelle's lady rejoices in the advance of knowledge. Fontenelle thus went beyond entertainment to instruction, suggesting that the human mind could make great progress.

This idea of progress was essentially a new idea of the later seventeenth century. Medieval and Reformation thinkers had been concerned primarily with sin and salvation. The humanists of the Renaissance had emphasized worldly matters, but they had been backward-looking. They had believed it might be possible to equal the magnificent accomplishments of the ancients, but they did not ask for more. Fontenelle and like-minded writers had come to believe that, at least in science and mathematics, their era had gone far beyond antiquity. Progress, at least intellectual progress, was clearly possible. During the eighteenth century, this idea would sink deeply into the consciousness of the European elite.

Fontenelle and other literary figures of his generation were also instrumental in bringing science into conflict with religion. Contrary to what is often assumed, many seventeenth-century scientists, both Catholic and Protestant, believed that their work exalted God. They did not draw antireligious implications from their scientific findings. The greatest scientist of them all, Isaac Newton, was a devout if unorthodox Christian who saw all of his studies as directed toward explaining God's message. Newton devoted far more of his time to angels and biblical prophecies than to universal gravitation, and he was convinced that all of his inquiries were equally scientific.

Fontenelle, in contrast, was skeptical about absolute truth and cynical about the claims of organized religion. Since such unorthodox views could not be stated openly in Louis XIV's France, Fontenelle made his point through subtle editorializing about science. His depiction of the cautious Copernicus as a self-conscious revolutionary was typical. In *Eulogies of Scientists,* Fontenelle exploited with endless variations the basic theme of rational, progressive scientists versus prejudiced, reactionary priests. Time and time again, Fontenelle's fledgling scientists attended church and studied theology; then, at some crucial moment, each was converted from the obscurity of religion to the clarity of science.

The progressive and antireligious implications that writers like Fontenelle drew from the scientific revolution reflected a very real crisis in European thought at the end of the seventeenth century. This crisis had its roots in several intellectual uncertainties and dissatisfactions, of which the demolition of Aristotelian-medieval science was only one.

A second uncertainty involved the question of religious truth. The destructive wars of religion had been fought, in part, because religious freedom was an intolerable idea in the early seventeenth century. Both Catholics and Protestants had believed that religious truth was absolute and therefore worth fighting and dying for. It was also generally believed that a strong state required unity in religious faith. Yet the disastrous results of the many attempts to impose such religious unity, such as Louis XIV's expulsion of the French Huguenots in 1685, led some people to ask if ideological conformity in religious matters was really necessary. Others skeptically asked if religious truth could ever be known with absolute certainty and concluded that it could not.

The most famous of these skeptics was Pierre Bayle (1647–1706), a French Huguenot who took refuge in Holland. A teacher by profession and a crusading journalist by inclination, Bayle critically examined the religious beliefs and persecutions of the past in his *Historical and Critical Dictionary* (1697). Demonstrating that human beliefs had been extremely varied and very often mistaken, Bayle concluded that nothing can ever be known beyond all doubt. In religion as in philosophy, humanity's best hope was open-minded toleration. Bayle's skeptical views were very influential. Many eighteenth-century writers mined his inexhaustible vein of critical skepticism for ammunition in their attacks on superstition and theology. Bayle's four-volume *Dictionary* was found in more private libraries of eighteenth-century France than any other book.

The rapidly growing travel literature on non-European lands and cultures was a third cause of uncertainty. In the wake of the great discoveries, Europeans were learning that the peoples of China, India, Africa, and the Americas all had their own very different beliefs and customs. Europeans shaved their faces and let their hair grow. The Turks shaved their heads and let their beards grow. In Europe a man bowed before a woman to show respect. In Siam a man turned his back on a woman when he met her because looking directly at her was disrespectful. Countless similar examples discussed in the travel accounts helped change the perspective of educated Europeans. They began to look at truth and morality in relative rather than absolute terms. Anything was possible, and who could say what was right or wrong? As one Frenchman wrote: "There is nothing that opinion, prejudice, custom, hope, and a sense of honor cannot do." Another wrote disapprovingly of religious skeptics who were corrupted "by extensive travel and lose whatever shreds of religion that remained with them. Every day they see a new religion, new customs, new rites."[10]

A fourth cause and manifestation of European intellectual turmoil was John Locke's epoch-making *Essay Concerning Human Understanding.* Published in 1690—the year in which Locke published his *Second Treatise of Civil Government* (see page 648)—Locke's essay set forth a new theory about how human beings learn and form their ideas. Locke rejected the prevailing view of Descartes, who had held that all people are born with certain basic ideas and ways of thinking. Locke insisted that all ideas are derived from experience. The human mind is like a blank tablet *(tabula rasa)* at birth, a tablet on which environment writes the individual's understanding and beliefs. Human development is therefore determined by education and social institutions, for good or for evil. Locke's *Essay Concerning Human Understanding* passed through many editions and translations. It was, along with Newton's *Principia,* one of the dominant intellectual inspirations of the Enlightenment.

The Philosophes and Their Ideas

By the death of Louis XIV in 1715, many of the ideas that would soon coalesce into the new world view had been assembled. Yet Christian Europe

Popularizing Science The frontispiece illustration of Fontenelle's *Conversations on the Plurality of Worlds* invites the reader to share the pleasures of astronomy with an elegant lady and an entertaining teacher. *(Source: University of Illinois, Champaign)*

was still strongly attached to its traditional beliefs, as witnessed by the powerful revival of religious orthodoxy in the first half of the eighteenth century. By the outbreak of the American Revolution in 1775, however, a large portion of western Europe's educated elite had embraced many of the new ideas. This acceptance was the work of one of history's most influential groups of intellectuals, the philosophes, who proudly and effectively proclaimed that they, at long last, were bringing the light of knowledge to their ignorant fellow creatures in a great age of enlightenment.

Philosophe is the French word for "philosopher," and it was in France that the Enlightenment reached its highest development. The French philosophes were indeed philosophers. They asked fundamental philosophical questions about the meaning of life, God, human nature, good and evil, and cause and effect. But, in the tradition of Bayle and Fontenelle, they were not content with abstract arguments or ivory-tower speculations among a tiny minority of scholars and professors. They wanted to influence and convince a broad audience.

The philosophes were intensely committed to reforming society and humanity, yet they were not free to write as they wished, since it was illegal in France to criticize openly either church or state. Their most radical works had to circulate in France in manuscript form, very much as critical works have been passed from hand to hand in unpublished form in modern dictatorships. Knowing that direct attacks would probably be banned or burned, to spread the message the philosophes wrote novels and plays, histories and philosophies, dictionaries and encyclopedias, all filled with satire and double meanings.

One of the greatest philosophes, the baron de Montesquieu (1689–1755), brilliantly pioneered this approach in *The Persian Letters,* an influential social satire published in 1721. Montesquieu's work consisted of amusing letters supposedly written by Persian travelers, who see European customs in unique ways and cleverly criticize existing practices and beliefs.

Having gained fame using wit as a weapon against cruelty and superstition, Montesquieu settled down on his family estate to study history and politics. His interest was partly personal, for, like many members of the high French nobility, he was dismayed that royal absolutism had triumphed in France under Louis XIV. But Montesquieu was also inspired by the example of the physical sciences, and he set out to apply the critical method to the problem of government in *The Spirit of Laws* (1748). The result was a complex comparative study of republics, monarchies, and despotisms—a great pioneering inquiry in the emerging social sciences.

Showing that forms of government were related to history, geography, and customs, Montesquieu focused on the conditions that would promote liberty and prevent tyranny. He argued that despotism could be avoided if political power were divided and shared by a diversity of classes and orders holding unequal rights and privileges. A strong, independent upper class was especially important, according to Montesquieu, because in

order to prevent the abuse of power, "it is necessary that by the arrangement of things, power checks power." Admiring greatly the English balance of power among the king, the houses of Parliament, and the independent courts, Montesquieu believed that in France the thirteen high courts—the *parlements*—were front-line defenders of liberty against royal despotism. Apprehensive about the uneducated poor, Montesquieu was clearly no democrat, but his theory of separation of powers had a great impact on France's wealthy, well-educated elite. The constitutions of the young United States in 1789 and of France in 1791 were based in large part on this theory.

The most famous and in many ways most representative philosophe was François Marie Arouet, known by the pen name Voltaire (1694–1778). In his long career, this son of a comfortable middle-class family wrote over seventy witty volumes, hobnobbed with kings and queens, and died a millionaire because of shrewd business speculations. His early career, however, was turbulent. In 1717 Voltaire was imprisoned for eleven months in the Bastille in Paris for insulting the regent of France. In 1726 a barb from his sharp tongue led a great French nobleman to have him beaten and arrested. This experience made a deep impression on Voltaire. All his life he struggled against legal injustice and class inequalities before the law.

Released from prison after promising to leave the country, Voltaire lived in England for three years. Sharing Montesquieu's enthusiasm for English institutions, Voltaire then wrote various works praising England and popularizing English scientific progress. Newton, he wrote, was history's greatest man, for he had used his genius for the benefit of humanity. "It is," wrote Voltaire, "the man who sways our minds by the prevalence of reason and the native force of truth, not they who reduce mankind to a state of slavery by force and downright violence . . . that claims our reverence and admiration."[11] In the true style of the Enlightenment, Voltaire mixed the glorification of science and reason with an appeal for better people and institutions.

Yet, like almost all of the philosophes, Voltaire was a reformer and not a revolutionary in social and political matters. Returning to France, he was eventually appointed royal historian in 1743, and his *Age of Louis XIV* portrayed Louis as the dignified leader of his age. Voltaire also began a long correspondence with Frederick the Great, and he accepted Frederick's invitation to come brighten up the Prussian court in Berlin. The two men later quarreled, but Voltaire always admired Frederick as a free thinker and an enlightened monarch.

Unlike Montesquieu, Voltaire pessimistically concluded that the best one could hope for in the way of government was a good monarch, since human beings "are very rarely worthy to govern themselves." Nor did he believe in social equality in human affairs. The idea of making servants equal to their masters was "absurd and impossible." The only realizable equality, Voltaire thought, was that "by which the citizen only depends on the laws which protect the freedom of the feeble against the ambitions of the strong."[12]

Voltaire's philosophical and religious positions were much more radical. In the tradition of Bayle, his voluminous writings challenged—often indirectly—the Catholic church and Christian theology at almost every point. Although he was considered by many devout Christians to be a shallow blasphemer, Voltaire's religious views were influential and quite typical of the mature Enlightenment. The essay on religion from his widely read *Philosophical Dictionary* sums up many of his criticisms and beliefs:

I meditated last night; I was absorbed in the contemplation of nature; I admired the immensity, the course, the harmony of these infinite globes which the vulgar do not know how to admire.

I admired still more the intelligence which directs these vast forces. I said to myself: "One must be blind not to be dazzled by this spectacle; one must be stupid

Voltaire leans forward at left to exchange ideas with Frederick the Great across the table, as Prussian officials look on. As this painting suggests, Voltaire's radicalism was mainly intellectual and philosophical, not social or political. *(Source: Bildarchiv Preussischer Kulturbesitz)*

not to recognize its author; one must be mad not to worship the Supreme Being."

I was deep in these ideas when one of those genii who fill the intermundane spaces came down to me . . . and transported me into a desert all covered with piles of bones. . . . He began with the first pile. "These," he said, "are the twenty-three thousand Jews who danced before a calf, with the twenty-four thousand who were killed while lying with Midianitish women. The number of those massacred for such errors and offences amounts to nearly three hundred thousand.

"In the other piles are the bones of the Christians slaughtered by each other because of metaphysical disputes. . . ."

"What!" I cried, "brothers have treated their brothers like this, and I have the misfortune to be of this brotherhood! . . . Why assemble here all these abominable monuments to barbarism and fanaticism?"

"To instruct you. . . . Follow me now." . . .

I saw a man with a gentle, simple face, who seemed to me to be about thirty-five years old. From afar he looked with compassion upon those piles of whitened bones, through which I had been led to reach the sage's dwelling place. I was astonished to find his feet swollen and bleeding, his hands likewise, his side pierced, and his ribs laid bare by the cut of the lash. "Good God!" I said to him, "is it possible for a just man, a sage, to be in this state? . . . Was it . . . by priests and judges that you were so cruelly assassinated?"

With great courtesy he answered, "Yes."

"And who were these monsters?"

"They were hypocrites."

"Ah! that says everything; I understand by that one word that they would have condemned you to the cruelest punishment. Had you then proved to them, as Socrates did, that the Moon was not a goddess, and that Mercury was not a god?"

"No, it was not a question of planets. My countrymen did not even know what a planet was; they were all arrant ignoramuses. Their superstitions were quite different from those of the Greeks."

"Then you wanted to teach them a new religion?"

"Not at all; I told them simply: 'Love God with all your heart and your neighbor as yourself, for that is the whole of mankind's duty.' Judge yourself if this precept is not as old as the universe; judge yourself if I brought them a new religion." . . .

"Did you not say once that you were come not to bring peace, but a sword?"

"It was a scribe's error; I told them that I brought

peace and not a sword. I never wrote anything; what I said can have been changed without evil intention."

"You did not then contribute in any way by your teaching, either badly reported or badly interpreted, to those frightful piles of bones which I saw on my way to consult with you?"

"I have only looked with horror upon those who have made themselves guilty of all these murders."

. . . [Finally] I asked him to tell me in what true religion consisted.

"Have I not already told you? Love God and your neighbor as yourself." . . .

"Well, if that is so, I take you for my only master."[13]

This passage requires careful study, for it suggests several Enlightenment themes of religion and philosophy. As the opening paragraphs show, Voltaire clearly believed in a God. But the God of Voltaire and most philosophes was a distant, deistic God, a great Clockmaker who built an orderly universe and then stepped aside and let it run. The passage also reflects the philosophes' hatred of all forms of religious intolerance. They believed that people had to be wary of dogmatic certainty and religious disputes, which often led to fanaticism and savage, inhuman action. Simple piety and human kindness—the love of God and the golden rule—were religion enough, even Christianity enough, as Voltaire's interpretation of Christ suggests.

The ultimate strength of the philosophes lay in their numbers, dedication, and organization. The philosophes felt keenly that they were engaged in a common undertaking that transcended individuals. Their greatest and most representative intellectual achievement was, quite fittingly, a group effort—the seventeen-volume *Encyclopedia: The Rational Dictionary of the Sciences, the Arts, and the Crafts,* edited by Denis Diderot (1713–1784) and Jean le Rond d'Alembert (1717–1783). Diderot and d'Alembert made a curious pair. Diderot began his career as a hack writer, first attracting attention with a skeptical tract on religion that was quickly burned by the judges of Paris. D'Alembert, the orphaned and illegitimate son of celebrated aristocrats, was one of Europe's leading scientists and mathematicians. Moving in different circles and with different interests, the two men set out to find coauthors who would examine the rapidly expanding whole of human knowledge. Even more fundamentally, they set out to instruct peo-

figure . 1.re

Canal with Locks The articles on science and the industrial arts in the *Encyclopedia* carried lavish explanatory illustrations. This typical engraving from the section on water and its uses shows advances in canal building and reflects the encyclopedists' faith in technical progress. *(Source: University of Illinois, Champaign)*

ple how to think critically and objectively about all matters. As Diderot stated, he wanted the *Encyclopedia* to "change the general way of thinking."[14]

The editors of the *Encyclopedia* had to conquer innumerable obstacles. After the appearance in 1751 of the first volume, which dealt with such controversial subjects as atheism, the soul, and blind people—all words beginning with the letter *a* in French—the government temporarily banned publication. The pope later placed the work on the Index and pronounced excommunication on all who read or bought it. In an attempt to appease the authorities, the timid publisher mutilated some of the articles in the last ten volumes without the editors' consent. Yet Diderot's unwavering belief in the importance of his mission held the encyclopedists together for fifteen years, and the enormous work was completed in 1765. Hundreds

of thousands of articles by leading scientists and famous writers, skilled workers and progressive priests, treated every aspect of life and knowledge.

Not every article was daring or original, but the overall effect was little short of revolutionary. Science and the industrial arts were exalted, religion and immortality questioned. Intolerance, legal injustice, and out-of-date social institutions were openly criticized. More generally, the writers of the *Encyclopedia* showed that human beings could use reason to expand human knowledge. The encyclopedists were convinced that greater knowledge would result in greater human happiness, for knowledge was useful and made possible economic, social, and political progress. The *Encyclopedia* was widely read and extremely influential in France and throughout western Europe as well. It summed up the new world view of the Enlightenment.

The Later Enlightenment

After about 1770, the harmonious unity of the philosophes and their thought began to break down. As the new world view became increasingly accepted by the educated public, some thinkers sought originality by exaggerating certain ideas of the Enlightenment to the exclusion of others. These latter-day philosophes often built rigid, dogmatic systems.

In *System of Nature* (1770) and other works, the wealthy, aristocratic baron Paul d'Holbach (1723–1789) argued that human beings were machines completely determined by outside forces. Free will, God, and immortality of the soul were foolish myths. D'Holbach's aggressive atheism and determinism, which were coupled with deep hostility toward Christianity and all other religions, dealt the unity of the Enlightenment movement a severe blow. Deists such as Voltaire, who believed in God but not in established churches, were repelled by the inflexible atheism they found in the *System of Nature*. They saw in it the same dogmatic intolerance that they had been fighting all their lives.

D'Holbach published his philosophically radical works anonymously to avoid possible prosecution, and in his lifetime he was best known to the public as the generous patron and witty host of writers and intellectuals. At his twice-weekly dinner parties, an inner circle of regulars who knew the baron's secret exchanged ideas with aspiring philosophes and distinguished visitors. One of the most important was the Scottish philosopher David Hume (1711–1776), whose carefully argued skepticism had a powerful long-term influence.

Building on John Locke's teachings on learning, Hume argued that the human mind is really nothing but a bundle of impressions. These impressions originate only in sense experiences and our habits of joining these experiences together. Since our ideas ultimately reflect only our sense experiences, reason cannot tell us anything about questions like the origin of the universe or the existence of God, questions that cannot be verified by sense experience (in the form of controlled experiments or mathematics). Paradoxically, Hume's rationalistic inquiry ended up undermining the Enlightenment's faith in the very power of reason itself.

Another French aristocrat, Marie-Jean Caritat, the marquis de Condorcet (1743–1794), transformed the Enlightenment belief in gradual, hard-won progress into fanciful utopianism. In his *Progress of the Human Mind,* written in 1793 during the French Revolution, Condorcet tracked the nine stages of human progress that had already occurred and predicted that the tenth would bring perfection. Ironically, Condorcet wrote this work while fleeing for his life. Caught and condemned by revolutionary extremists, he preferred death by his own hand to the blade of the guillotine.

Other thinkers and writers after about 1770 began to attack the Enlightenment's faith in reason, progress, and moderation. The most famous of these was the Swiss Jean-Jacques Rousseau (1712–1778), a brilliant but difficult thinker, an appealing but neurotic individual. Born into a poor family of watchmakers in Geneva, Rousseau went to Paris and was greatly influenced by Diderot and Voltaire. Always extraordinarily sensitive and suspicious, Rousseau came to believe that his philosophe friends were plotting against him. In the mid-1750s he broke with them personally and intellectually, living thereafter as a lonely outsider with his uneducated common-law wife and going in his own highly original direction.

Like other Enlightenment thinkers, Rousseau was passionately committed to individual freedom. Unlike them, however, he attacked rationalism and civilization as destroying rather than liberating the individual. Warm, spontaneous feeling had to complement and correct the cold intellect. Moreover, the individual's basic goodness had to be protected from the cruel refinements of civilization. These ideas greatly influenced the early romantic movement (see pages 876–881), which rebelled against the culture of the Enlightenment in the late eighteenth century.

Applying his heartfelt ideas to children, Rousseau had a powerful impact on the development of modern education. In his famous pedagogical novel *Émile* (1762), he argued that education must shield the naturally unspoiled child from the corrupting influences of civilization and too many books. According to Rousseau, children must develop naturally and spontaneously, although the sexes were by nature intended for different occupations. At the proper time, Émile might tackle difficult academic subjects and enter a demanding profession. But Sophie, his future wife, needed to learn only how to manage the home and to be a good mother and an obedient wife. This idea—that girls and boys should be educated to operate in "separate spheres"—was to gain wide acceptance in Europe among the middle classes in the nineteenth century.

Rousseau also made an important contribution to political theory in *The Social Contract* (1762). He believed that sovereign power is vested in the people, not in the monarch. According to Rousseau, the general will, reflecting the common interests of the people, is sacred and absolute. The general will is not necessarily the will of the majority, however, although minorities have to subordinate themselves to it without question. Little noticed before the French Revolution, Rousseau's concept of the general will appealed greatly to democrats and nationalists after 1789. The concept has also been used since 1789 by many dictators, who have claimed that they, rather than some momentary majority of the voters, represent the general will and thus the true interests of democracy and the sovereign masses.

The Social Setting of the Enlightenment

The philosophes were splendid talkers as well as effective writers. Indeed, sparkling conversation in private homes spread Enlightenment ideas to Europe's upper middle class and aristocracy. Paris set the example, and other French cities and European capitals followed. In Paris a number of talented and often rich women presided over regular social gatherings of the great and near-great in their elegant drawing rooms, or *salons*. There they encouraged a d'Alembert and a Fontenelle to exchange witty, uncensored observations on literature, science, and philosophy with great aristocrats, wealthy middle-class financiers, high-ranking officials, and noteworthy foreigners. Talented hostesses brought the various French elites together and mediated the spread of Enlightenment thought.

Elite women also exercised an unprecedented feminine influence on artistic taste. Soft pastels, ornate interiors, sentimental portraits, and starry-eyed lovers protected by hovering Cupids were hallmarks of the style they favored. And it has been argued that feminine influence in the drawing room went hand in hand with the emergence of polite society and the general attempt to civilize a rough military nobility. Similarly, some philosophes championed greater rights and expanded education for women, claiming that the position and treatment of women were the best indicators of a society's level of civilization and decency.[15] To be sure, for these male philosophes, greater rights for women did not mean equal rights, except perhaps in a very abstract, theoretical way. Elite women remained legally subordinate to men in economic and political affairs.

One of the most famous salons was that of Madame Geoffrin, the unofficial godmother of the *Encyclopedia*. Having lost her parents at an early age, the future Madame Geoffrin was married at fifteen by her well-meaning grandmother to a rich and boring businessman of forty-eight. It was the classic marriage of convenience—the poor young girl and the rich old man—and neither side ever pretended that love was a consideration. After dutifully raising her children, Madame Geoffrin sought to break out of her gilded cage as she entered middle age. The very proper businessman's wife became friendly with a neighbor, the marquise de Tencin, an aristocratic beauty who had settled down to run a salon that counted Fontenelle and the philosopher Montesquieu among its regular guests.

When the marquise died in 1749, Madame Geoffrin tactfully transferred these luminaries to her spacious mansion for regular dinners. At first Madame Geoffrin's husband loudly protested the arrival of this horde of "parasites." But his wife's will was much stronger than his, and he soon opened his purse and even appeared at the twice-weekly dinners. "Who was that old man at the end of the table who never said anything?" an innocent newcomer asked one evening. "That," replied Madame Geoffrin without the slightest emotion, "was my husband. He's dead."[16]

When Monsieur Geoffrin's death became official, Madame Geoffrin put to good use the large fortune and spacious mansion that she inherited. She welcomed the encyclopedists, and her generous financial aid helped to save their enterprise from collapse, especially after the first eight volumes were burned by the authorities in 1759. She also corresponded with the king of Sweden and with Catherine the Great of Russia. Madame Geoffrin was, however, her own woman. She remained a practicing Christian and would not tolerate attacks on the church in her house. The plain and long-neglected Madame Geoffrin managed to become the most renowned hostess of the eighteenth century.

There were many other hostesses, but Madame Geoffrin's greatest rival, Madame du Deffand, was one of the most interesting. Madame Geoffrin was middle-class, pious, and chaste; Madame du Deffand, in contrast, was a skeptic from the nobility who lived fast and easy, at least in her early years. In Madame du Deffand's intellectual salon, women—mostly highly intelligent, worldly members of the nobility—were fully the equal of men. Forever pursuing fulfillment in love and life, Madame du Deffand was an accomplished and liberated woman. An exceptionally fine letter writer, she carried on a vast correspondence and counted Voltaire as her most enduring friend.

The salons seem to have functioned as informal schools where established hostesses bonded with younger women and passed their skills on to them. Madame du Deffand's closest female friend was Julie de Lespinasse, a beautiful, talented young woman whom she befriended and made her protégée. The never-acknowledged illegitimate daughter of noble parents, Julie de Lespinasse had a hard youth, but she flowered in Madame du Deffand's drawing room—so much so that she was eventually dismissed by her jealous patron. Her friends, however, gave her money so that she could form her own salon. Julie de Lespinasse's highly informal gatherings—she was not rich enough to supply more than tea and cake—eventually attracted the keenest minds in France and Europe. As one philosophe wrote:

She could unite the different types, even the most antagonistic, sustaining the conversation by a well-aimed phrase, animating and guiding it at will.... Politics, religion, philosophy, news: nothing was excluded. Her circle met daily from five to nine. There one found men of all ranks in the State, the Church, and the Court, soldiers and foreigners, and the leading writers of the day.[17]

Thus in France the ideas of the Enlightenment thrived in a social setting that graciously united members of the intellectual, economic, and social

Madame Geoffrin's Salon   In this stylized group portrait a famous actor reads to a gathering of leading philosophes and aristocrats in 1755. Third from the right presiding over her gathering is Madame Geoffrin, next to the sleepy ninety-eight-year-old Bernard de Fontenelle. *(Source: Giraudon/Art Resource)*

elites. Never before and never again would social and intellectual life be so closely and so pleasantly joined. In such an atmosphere, the philosophes, the French nobility, and the upper middle class intermingled and increasingly influenced one another. Critical thinking became fashionable and flourished alongside hopes for human progress through greater knowledge.

THE DEVELOPMENT OF ABSOLUTISM

How did the Enlightenment influence political developments? To this important question there is no easy answer. On the one hand, the philosophes were primarily interested in converting people to critical scientific thinking and were not particularly concerned with politics. On the other hand, such thinking naturally led to political criticism and interest in political reform. Educated people, who belonged mainly to the nobility and middle class, came to regard political change as both possible and desirable. A further problem is that Enlightenment thinkers had different views on politics. Some, led by the nobleman Montesquieu, argued for curbs on monarchial power in order to promote liberty, and some French judges applied such theories in practical questions.

Until the American Revolution, however, most Enlightenment thinkers believed that political change could best come from above—from the ruler—rather than from below, especially in central and eastern Europe. There were several reasons for this essentially moderate belief. First, royal absolutism was a fact of life, and the kings and queens of Europe's leading states clearly had no intention of giving up their great powers. Therefore, the philosophes realistically concluded that benevolent absolutism offered the best opportunities for improving society. Critical thinking was turning the art of good government into an exact science. It was necessary only to educate and "enlighten" the monarch, who could then make good laws and promote human happiness. Second, philosophes turned toward rulers because rulers seemed to be listening, treating them with respect, and seeking their advice. Finally, although the philosophes did not dwell on this fact, they distrusted the masses. Known simply as "the people" in the eighteenth century, the peasant masses and the urban poor were, according to the philosophes, still enchained by religious superstitions and violent passions. No doubt the people were maturing, but in the philosophes' eyes they were still children in need of firm parental guidance.

Encouraged and instructed by the philosophes, several absolutist rulers of the late eighteenth century tried to govern in an "enlightened" manner. Yet, because European monarchs had long been locked in an intense international competition, a more enlightened state often meant in practice a more effective state, a state capable of expanding its territory and defeating its enemies. Moreover, reforms from above had to be grafted onto previous historical developments and existing social structures. Little wonder, then, that the actual programs and accomplishments of the "enlightened" rulers varied greatly. Thus the evolution of monarchial absolutism must be examined at close range before any overall judgment about the meaning of what historians have often called the "enlightened absolutism" of the late eighteenth century can be attempted.

The "Greats": Frederick of Prussia and Catherine of Russia

Just as the French culture and absolutism of Louis XIV provided models for European rulers in the late seventeenth century, the Enlightenment teachings of the French philosophes inspired European monarchs in the second half of the eighteenth century. French was the international language of the educated classes, and the education of future kings and queens across Europe lay in the hands of French tutors espousing Enlightenment ideas. France's cultural leadership was reinforced by the fact that France was still the wealthiest and most populous country in Europe.

Absolutist monarchs in several west German and Italian states, as well as in Spain and Portugal, proclaimed themselves "enlightened." But by far the most influential of the new-style monarchs were Frederick II of Prussia and Catherine II of Russia, both styled "the Great."

Frederick the Great Frederick II (r. 1740–1786) built masterfully on the work of his father, Frederick William I (see pages 630–631). This was somewhat surprising for, like many children with tyrannical parents, he rebelled against his family's wishes in his early years. Rejecting the crude life of the barracks, Frederick embraced culture and literature, even writing poetry and fine prose in French, a language his father detested. He threw off his father's dour Calvinism and dabbled with atheism. After trying unsuccessfully to run away at age eighteen in 1730, he was virtually imprisoned and even compelled to watch his companion in flight beheaded at his father's command. Yet, like many other rebellious youths, Frederick eventually reached a reconciliation with his father, and by the time he came to the throne, in 1740, Frederick was determined to use the splendid army that his father had left him.

When, therefore, the emperor of Austria, Charles VI, died in 1740 and his young and beautiful daughter, Maria Theresa, became ruler of the Habsburg dominions, Frederick suddenly and without warning invaded her rich, all-German province of Silesia. This action defied solemn Prussian promises to respect the Pragmatic Sanction, which guaranteed Maria Theresa's succession—but no matter. For Frederick, it was the opportunity of a lifetime to expand the size and power of Prussia. Although Maria Theresa succeeded in dramatically rallying the normally quarrelsome Hungarian nobility, her multinational army was no match for Prussian precision. In 1742, as other greedy powers were falling on her lands in the general European War of the Austrian Succession (1740–1748), she was forced to cede all of Silesia to Prussia (see Map 19.3). In one stroke, Prussia doubled its population to six million. Now Prussia unquestionably towered above all the other German states and stood as a European Great Power.

Though successful in 1742, Frederick had to spend much of his reign fighting against great odds to save Prussia from total destruction. Maria Theresa was determined to regain Silesia, and when the ongoing competition between Britain and France for colonial empire brought renewed conflict in 1756, her able chief minister fashioned an aggressive alliance with France and Russia. During the Seven Years' War (1756–1763), the aim of the alliance was to conquer Prussia and divide its territory, just as Frederick II and other monarchs had so recently sought to partition the Austrian Empire. Frederick led his army brilliantly, striking repeatedly at vastly superior forces invading from all sides. At times he believed all was lost, but he fought on with stoic courage. In the end,

he was miraculously saved: Peter III came to the Russian throne in 1762 and called off the attack against Frederick, whom he greatly admired.

In the early years of his reign, Frederick II had kept his enthusiasm for Enlightenment culture strictly separated from a brutal concept of international politics. He wrote:

Of all States, from the smallest to the biggest, one can safely say that the fundamental rule of government is the principle of extending their territories. . . . The passions of rulers have no other curb but the limits of their power. Those are the fixed laws of European politics to which every politician submits.[18]

But the terrible struggle of the Seven Years' War tempered Frederick and brought him to consider how more humane policies for his subjects might also strengthen the state.

Thus Frederick went beyond a superficial commitment to Enlightenment culture for himself and his circle. He tolerantly allowed his subjects to believe as they wished in religious and philosophical matters. He promoted the advancement of knowledge, improving his country's schools and universities. Moreover, Frederick tried to improve the lives of his subjects more directly. As he wrote his friend Voltaire, "I must enlighten my people, cultivate their manners and morals, and make them as happy as human beings can be, or as happy as the means at my disposal permit." The legal system and the bureaucracy were Frederick's primary tools. Prussia's laws were simplified; torture of prisoners was abolished; and judges decided cases quickly and impartially. Prussian officials became famous for their hard work and honesty. After the Seven Years' War ended in 1763, Frederick's government also energetically promoted the reconstruction of agriculture and industry in his war-torn country. In all this Frederick set a good example. He worked hard and lived modestly, claiming that he was "only the first servant of the state." Thus Frederick justified monarchy in terms of practical results and said nothing of the divine right of kings.

Frederick's dedication to high-minded principles went only so far, however. He never tried to change Prussia's existing social structure. True, he condemned serfdom in the abstract, but he accepted it in practice and did not even free the serfs on his own estates. He accepted and extended the

Catherine as Equestrian   Catherine took advantage of her intelligence and good looks to maneuver her husband Peter III off the throne and get herself crowned as Russia's new monarch. Strongly influenced by the Enlightenment, she cultivated the French philosophes and instituted moderate domestic reforms only to reverse them in the aftermath of Pugachev's rebellion. *(Source: Sovfoto)*

privileges of the nobility, which he saw as his primary ally in the defense and extension of his realm. It became practically impossible for a middle-class person to gain a top position in the government. The Junker nobility remained the backbone of the army and the entire Prussian state.

Catherine the Great   Catherine the Great of Russia (r. 1762–1796) was one of the most remarkable rulers who ever lived, and the philosophes adored her. Catherine was a German princess from Anhalt-Zerbst, a totally insignificant principality sandwiched between Prussia and Saxony. Her father commanded a regiment of the Prussian army, but her mother was related to the Romanovs of Russia, and that relationship proved to be her chance.

Peter the Great had abolished the hereditary succession of tsars so that he could name his suc-

cessor and thus preserve his policies. This move opened a period of palace intrigue and a rapid turnover of rulers until Peter's youngest daughter, Elizabeth, came to the Russian throne in 1741. A crude, shrewd woman noted for her hard drinking and hard loving—one of her official lovers was an illiterate shepherd boy—Elizabeth named her nephew Peter heir to the throne and chose Catherine to be his wife in 1744. It was a mismatch from the beginning. The fifteen-year-old Catherine was intelligent and attractive; her husband was stupid and ugly, his face badly scarred by smallpox. Ignored by her childish husband, Catherine carefully studied Russian, endlessly read writers like Bayle and Voltaire, and made friends at court. Soon she knew what she wanted. "I did not care about Peter," she wrote in her *Memoirs,* "but I did care about the crown."[19]

As the old empress Elizabeth approached death, Catherine conspired against her own unpopular husband. A dynamic, sensuous woman, Catherine used her sexuality to good political advantage. She selected as her new lover a tall, dashing young officer, Gregory Orlov, who with his four officer brothers commanded considerable support among the soldiers stationed in St. Petersburg. When Peter came to the throne in 1762, his decision to withdraw Russian troops from the coalition against Prussia alienated the army. Nor did Peter III's attempt to gain support from the Russian nobility by freeing it from compulsory state service succeed. At the end of six months, Catherine and the military conspirators deposed Peter III in a palace revolution. Then the Orlov brothers murdered him. The German princess became empress of Russia.

Catherine had drunk deeply at the Enlightenment well. Never questioning the common assumption that absolute monarchy was the best form of government, she set out to rule in an enlightened manner. One of her most enduring goals was to bring the sophisticated culture of western Europe to backward Russia. To do so, she imported Western architects, sculptors, musicians, and intellectuals. She bought masterpieces of Western art in wholesale lots and patronized the philosophes. An enthusiastic letter writer, she corresponded extensively with Voltaire and praised him as the "champion of the human race." When the French government banned the *Encyclopedia,* she offered to publish it in St. Petersburg. She discussed reform with Diderot in St. Petersburg; and when Diderot needed money, she purchased his library for a small fortune but allowed him to keep it during his lifetime. With these and countless similar actions, Catherine skillfully won a good press for herself and for her country in the West. Moreover, this intellectual ruler, who wrote plays and loved good talk, set the tone for the entire Russian nobility. Peter the Great westernized Russian armies, but it was Catherine the Great who westernized the thinking of the Russian nobility.

Catherine's second goal was domestic reform, and she began her reign with sincere and ambitious projects. Better laws were a major concern. In 1767 she drew up enlightened instructions for the special legislative commission that she appointed to prepare a new law code. No new unified code was ever produced, but Catherine did restrict the practice of torture and allowed limited religious toleration. She also tried to improve education and strengthen local government. The phi-

losophes applauded these measures and hoped more would follow.

Such was not the case. In 1773 a simple Cossack soldier named Emelian Pugachev sparked a gigantic uprising of serfs, very much as Stenka Razin had done a century earlier (see page 637). Proclaiming himself the true tsar, Pugachev issued "decrees" abolishing serfdom, taxes, and army service. Thousands joined his cause, slaughtering landlords and officials over a vast area of southwestern Russia. Pugachev's untrained hordes eventually proved no match for Catherine's noble-led regular army. Betrayed by his own company, Pugachev was captured and savagely executed.

Pugachev's rebellion was a decisive turning point in Catherine's domestic policy. On coming to the throne, she had condemned serfdom in theory but was smart enough to realize that any changes would have to be gradual or else she would quickly follow her departed husband. Pugachev's rebellion put an end to any illusions she might have had about reforming serfdom. The peasants were clearly dangerous, and her empire rested on the support of the nobility. After 1775 Catherine gave the nobles absolute control of their serfs. She extended serfdom into new areas, such as the Ukraine. In 1785 she formalized the nobility's privileged position, freeing the nobles forever from taxes and state service. She also confiscated the lands of the Russian Orthodox church and gave them to favorite officials. Under Catherine, the Russian nobility attained its most exalted position, and serfdom entered its most oppressive phase.

Catherine's third goal was territorial expansion, and in this respect she was extremely successful. Her armies subjugated the last descendants of the Mongols, the Crimean Tartars, and began the conquest of the Caucasus.

Her greatest coup was the partitioning of Poland. Poland showed the dangers of failure to build a strong absolutist state. For decades all important decisions had required the unanimous agreement of all the Polish nobles, which meant that nothing could ever be done. When between 1768 and 1772 Catherine's armies scored unprecedented victories against the Turks and thereby threatened to disturb the balance of power between Russia and Austria in eastern Europe, Frederick of Prussia obligingly came forward with a deal. He proposed that Turkey be let off easily and that Prussia, Austria, and Russia each compensate itself by taking a gigantic slice of Polish territory. Catherine jumped at the chance. The first partition of Poland took place in 1772. Two more partitions, in 1793 and 1795, gave all three powers more Polish territory, and the kingdom of Poland simply vanished from the map (Map 20.1).

Expansion helped Catherine keep the nobility happy, for it provided her with vast new lands to give to her faithful servants. Expansion also helped Catherine reward her lovers, of whom twenty-one have been definitely identified. On all these royal favorites she lavished large estates with many serfs, as if to make sure there were no hard feelings when her interest cooled. Until the end, this remarkable woman—who always believed that, in spite of her domestic setbacks, she was slowly civilizing Russia—kept her zest for life. Fascinated by a new twenty-two-year-old flame when she was a rolypoly grandmother in her sixties, she happily reported her good fortune to a favorite former lover: "I have come back to life like a frozen fly; I am gay and well."[20]

Absolutism in France and Austria

The Enlightenment's influence on political developments in France and Austria was complex. In France, the monarchy maintained its absolutist claims, and some philosophes like Voltaire believed that the king was still the best source of needed reform. At the same time, discontented nobles and learned judges drew on thinkers such as Montesquieu for liberal arguments, and they sought with some success to limit the king's power. In Austria, two talented rulers did manage to introduce major reforms, although traditional power politics were more important than Enlightenment teachings.

Louis XV of France   In building French absolutism, Louis XIV had successfully drawn on the middle class to curb the political power of the nobility. As long as the Grand Monarch lived, the nobility could only grumble and, like the duke of Saint-Simon in his *Memoirs,* scornfully lament the

MAP 20.1 The Partition of Poland and Russia's Expansion, 1772–1795   Though all three of the great eastern absolutist states profited from the division of large but weak Poland, Catherine's Russia gained the most.

rise of "the vile bourgeoisie." But when Louis XIV finally died in 1715, to be succeeded by his five-year-old great-grandson, Louis XV (r. 1715–1774), the Sun King's elaborate system of absolutist rule was challenged in a general reaction. Favored by the duke of Orléans, who governed as regent until 1723, the nobility made a strong comeback.

Most important, the duke gave back to the high court of Paris—the Parlement—the right to "register" and thereby approve the king's decrees. This was a fateful step. The judges of the Parlement of Paris had originally come from the middle class, and their high position reflected the way that Louis XIV (and earlier French monarchs) had chosen to use that class to build the royal bureaucracy so necessary for an absolutist state. By the eighteenth century, however, these middle-class judges had risen to become hereditary nobles. Moreover, although Louis XIV had curbed the political power of the nobility, he had never challenged its enormous social prestige. Thus high position in the government continued to bestow the noble status that middle-class officials wanted, either immediately or after three generations of continuous service. The judges of Paris, like many high-ranking officials, actually owned their government jobs and freely passed them on as private property from father to son. By supporting the claim of this well-entrenched and increasingly aristocratic group to register the king's laws, the duke of Orléans sanctioned a counterweight to absolute power.

These implications became clear when the heavy expenses of the War of the Austrian Succession plunged France into financial crisis. In 1748 Louis XV appointed a finance minister who decreed a 5 percent income tax on every individual, regardless of social status. Exemption from most taxation had long been a hallowed privilege of the nobility, and other important groups—the clergy, the large towns, and some wealthy bourgeoisie—had also gained special tax advantages. The result was a vigorous protest from many sides, and the Parlement of Paris refused to ratify the tax law. The monarchy retreated; the new tax was dropped.

Following the disastrously expensive Seven Years' War, the conflict re-emerged. The government tried to maintain emergency taxes after the war ended. The Parlement of Paris protested and even challenged the basis of royal authority, claiming that the king's power must necessarily be limited to protect liberty. Once again the government caved in and withdrew the wartime taxes in 1764. Emboldened by its striking victory and by widespread support from France's educated elite, the judicial opposition in Paris and the provinces pressed its demands. In a barrage of pamphlets and legal briefs, it asserted that the king could not levy taxes without the consent of the Parlement of Paris, acting as the representative of the entire nation.

Indolent and sensual by nature, more interested in his many mistresses than in affairs of state, Louis XV finally roused himself for a determined defense of his absolutist inheritance. "The magistrates," he angrily told the Parlement of Paris in a famous face-to-face confrontation, "are my officers. . . . In my person only does the sovereign power rest."[21] In 1768 Louis appointed a tough career official named René de Maupeou as chancellor and ordered him to crush the judicial opposition.

Maupeou abolished the Parlement of Paris and exiled its members to isolated backwaters in the provinces. He created a new and docile parlement of royal officials, and he began once again to tax the privileged groups. A few philosophes like Voltaire applauded these measures: the sovereign was using his power to introduce badly needed reforms that had been blocked by a self-serving aristocratic elite. Most philosophes and educated public opinion as a whole sided with the old parlements, however, and there was widespread dissatisfaction with royal despotism. Yet the monarchy's power was still great enough for Maupeou simply to ride over the opposition, and Louis XV would probably have prevailed—if he had lived to a very ripe old age. But Louis XV died in 1774.

The new king, Louis XVI (r. 1774–1792), was a shy twenty-year-old with good intentions. Taking the throne, he is reported to have said: "What I should like most is to be loved."[22] The eager-to-please monarch decided to yield in the face of such strong criticism from so much of France's elite. He dismissed Maupeou and repudiated the strong-willed minister's work. The old Parlement of Paris was reinstated as enlightened public opinion cheered and people hoped for moves toward representative government. Such moves were not forthcoming. Instead, a weakened but unrepentant monarchy faced a judicial opposition that claimed to speak for the entire French nation. Increasingly locked in stalemate, the coun-

Maria Theresa and her husband pose with eleven of their sixteen children at Schönbrunn palace. Joseph, the heir to the throne, stands at the center of the star pattern. Wealthy women often had very large families, in part because they seldom nursed their babies as poor women usually did. *(Source: Kunsthistorisches Museum, Vienna)*

try was drifting toward renewed financial crisis and political upheaval.

The Austrian Habsburgs Joseph II (r. 1780–1790) was a fascinating individual. For an earlier generation of historians he was the "revolutionary emperor," a tragic hero whose lofty reforms were undone by the landowning nobility he dared to challenge. More recent scholarship has revised this romantic interpretation and stressed how Joseph II continued the state-building work of his mother, the empress Maria Theresa, a remarkable but old-fashioned absolutist.

Maria Theresa's long reign (1740–1780) began with her neighbors, led by Frederick II of Prussia,

invading her lands and trying to dismember them (see page 680). Emerging from the long War of the Austrian Succession in 1748 with only the serious loss of Silesia, Maria Theresa and her closest ministers were determined to introduce reforms that would make the state stronger and more efficient. Three aspects were most important in these reforms. First, Maria Theresa introduced measures to bring relations between church and state under government control. Like some medieval rulers, the most devout and very Catholic Maria Theresa aimed at limiting the papacy's political influence in her realm. Second, a whole series of administrative reforms strengthened the central bureaucracy, smoothed out some provincial differences, and

THE ENLIGHTENMENT

1686	Fontenelle, *Conversations on the Plurality of Worlds*
1687	Newton, *Principia*
1690	Locke, "Essay Concerning Human Understanding" and "Second Treatise on Civil Government"
1697	Bayle, *Historical and Critical Dictionary*
1715–1774	Rule of Louis XV in France
1721	Montesquieu, *The Persian Letters*
1740–1748	War of the Austrian Succession
1740–1780	Rule of Maria Theresa in Austria
1740–1786	Rule of Frederick II (the Great) in Prussia
1742	Austria cedes Silesia to Prussia
1743	Voltaire, *Age of Louis XIV*
1748	Montesquieu, *The Spirit of the Laws*
	Hume, *An Enquiry Concerning Human Understanding*
1751–1765	Publication of the *Encyclopedia*, edited by Diderot and d'Alembert
1756–1763	Seven Years' War
1762	Rousseau, *Social Contract*
1762–1796	Rule of Catherine II (the Great) in Russia
1767	Catherine the Great appoints commission to prepare a new law code
1770	D'Holbach, *The System of Nature*
1771	Maupeou, Louis XV's chancellor, abolishes Parlement of Paris
1772	First partition of Poland among Russia, Prussia, and Austria
1774	Ascension of Louis XVI in France; restoration of Parlement of Paris
1780–1790	Rule of Joseph II in Austria
1781	Abolition of serfdom in Austria
1785	Catherine the Great issues the Russian Charter of Nobility, which frees the nobles from taxes and state service
1790–1792	Rule of Leopold II in Austria; serfdom is re-established
1793	Second partition of Poland
1795	Third partition of Poland, which completes its absorption

revamped the tax system, taxing even the lands of nobles without special exemptions. Finally, the government sought to improve the lot of the agricultural population, cautiously reducing the power of lords over both their hereditary serfs and their partially free peasant tenants.

Co-regent with his mother from 1765 onward and a strong supporter of change, Joseph II moved forward rapidly when he came to the throne in 1780. He controlled the established Catholic church even more closely, in an attempt to ensure that it produced better citizens. He granted religious toleration and civic rights to Protestants and Jews—a radical innovation that impressed his contemporaries. In even more spectacular peasant re-

forms, Joseph abolished serfdom in 1781, and in 1789 he decreed that all peasant labor obligations be converted into cash payments. This ill-conceived measure was violently rejected not only by the nobility but by the peasants it was intended to help, since their primitive barter economy was woefully lacking in money. When a disillusioned Joseph died prematurely at forty-nine, the entire Habsburg empire was in turmoil. His brother Leopold (r. 1790–1792) was forced to cancel Joseph's radical edicts in order to re-establish order. Peasants lost most of their gains obtained under Joseph, and once again they were required to do forced labor for their lords, as in the 1770s under Maria Theresa.

An Overall Evaluation

Having examined the evolution of monarchial absolutism in four leading states, we can begin to look for meaningful generalizations and to evaluate the overall influence of Enlightenment thought on politics. That thought was clustered in two distinct schools: (1) the liberal critique of unregulated monarchy promoted by Montesquieu and (2) the defense of royal absolutism led by Voltaire.

It is clear that France diverged from its eastern neighbors in its political development in the eighteenth century. Although neither the French monarchy nor the eastern rulers abandoned the absolutist claims and institutions they had inherited, the monarch's capacity to govern in a truly absolutist manner declined substantially in France, and this was not the case in eastern Europe. The immediate cause of this divergence was the political resurgence of the French nobility after 1715 and the growth of judicial opposition, led by the Parlement of Paris. More fundamentally, however, the judicial and aristocratic opposition in France achieved its still rather modest successes because it received major support from educated public opinion, which increasingly made the liberal critique of unregulated royal authority its own. In France, then, the proponents of absolute monarchy were increasingly on the defensive, as was the French monarchy itself.

The situation in eastern Europe was different. The liberal critique of absolute monarchy remained an intellectual curiosity, and proponents of reform from above held sway. Moreover, despite their differences, the leading eastern European monarchs of the later eighteenth century all claimed that they were acting on the principles of the Enlightenment. The philosophes generally agreed with this assessment and cheered them on. Beginning in the mid-nineteenth century, historians developed the idea of a common "enlightened despotism" or "enlightened absolutism," and they canonized Frederick, Catherine, and Joseph as its most outstanding examples. More recent research has raised doubts about this old interpretation and has led to a fundamental re-evaluation.

First, there is general agreement that these absolutists, especially Catherine and Frederick, did encourage and spread the cultural values of the Enlightenment. Perhaps this was their greatest achievement. Skeptical in religion and intensely secular in basic orientation, they unabashedly accepted the here and now and sought their happiness in the enjoyment of it. At the same time, they were proud of their intellectual accomplishments and good taste, and they supported knowledge, education, and the arts. No wonder the philosophes felt the monarchs were kindred spirits.

Historians also agree that the absolutists believed in change from above and tried to enact needed reforms. Yet the results of these efforts brought only very modest improvements, and the life of the peasantry remained very hard in the eighteenth century. Thus some historians have concluded that these monarchs were not really sincere in their reform efforts. Others disagree, arguing that powerful nobilities blocked the absolutists' genuine commitment to reform. (The old interpretation of Joseph II as the tragic "revolutionary emperor" forms part of this argument.)

The emerging answer to this confusion is that the later eastern absolutists were indeed committed to reform but that humanitarian objectives were of secondary importance. Above all, the absolutists wanted reforms that would strengthen the state and allow them to compete militarily with their neighbors. Modern scholarship has stressed, therefore, how Catherine, Frederick, and Joseph were in many ways simply continuing the state building of their predecessors, reorganizing their armies and expanding their bureaucracies to raise more taxes and troops. The reason for this continuation was simple. The international political struggle was brutal, and the stakes were high. First Austria under Maria Theresa, and then Prussia under Frederick the Great, had to engage in bitter fighting to escape dismemberment. Decentralized Poland was coldly divided and eventually liquidated.

Yet, in their drive for state power, the later absolutists were also innovators, and the idea of an era of enlightened absolutism retains a certain validity. Sharing the Enlightenment faith in critical thinking and believing that knowledge meant power, these absolutists really were more enlightened because they put their state-building reforms in a new, broader perspective. Above all, they considered how more humane laws and practices could help their populations become more productive and satisfied and thus more able to contribute substantially to the welfare of the state. From this perspective, they introduced many of their most progressive reforms—tolerating religious minorities, simplifying legal codes, and promoting practical education.

The primacy of state as opposed to individual interests—a concept foreign to North Americans long accustomed to easy dominion over a vast continent—also helps to explain some puzzling variations in social policies. For example, Catherine the Great took measures that worsened the peasants' condition because she looked increasingly to the nobility as her natural ally and sought to strengthen it. Frederick the Great basically favored the status quo, limiting only the counterproductive excesses of his trusted nobility against its peasants. Joseph II believed that greater freedom for peasants was the means to strengthen his realm, and he acted accordingly. Each enlightened absolutist sought greater state power, but each believed a different policy would attain it.

In conclusion, the eastern European absolutists of the late eighteenth century combined old-fashioned state building with the culture and critical thinking of the Enlightenment. In doing so, they succeeded in expanding the role of the state in the life of society. Unlike the successors of Louis XIV, they perfected bureaucratic machines that were to prove surprisingly adaptive and capable of enduring into the twentieth century.

SUMMARY

This chapter focuses on the complex development of a new world view in Western civilization. The new view of the world was essentially critical and secular, drawing its inspiration from the scientific revolution and crystallizing in the Enlightenment.

The decisive breakthroughs in astronomy and physics in the seventeenth century demolished the imposing medieval synthesis of Aristotelian philosophy and Christian theology but had only limited practical consequences despite the expectations of scientific enthusiasts like Bacon. Yet the impact of new scientific knowledge on intellectual life became great. Interpreting scientific findings and Newtonian laws in an antitraditional, antireligious manner, the French philosophes of the Enlightenment extolled the superiority of rational, critical

thinking. This new method, they believed, promised not just increased knowledge but even the discovery of the fundamental laws of human society. Although they reached different conclusions when they turned to social and political realities, the philosophes nevertheless succeeded in spreading their radically new world view. That was a momentous accomplishment.

NOTES

1. H. Butterfield, *The Origins of Modern Science* (New York: Macmillan, 1951), p. viii.
2. Quoted in A. G. R. Smith, *Science and Society in the Sixteenth and Seventeenth Centuries* (New York: Harcourt Brace Jovanovich, 1972), p. 97.
3. Quoted in Butterfield, p. 47.
4. Quoted in Smith, p. 100.
5. Ibid., pp. 115–116.
6. Ibid., p. 120.
7. Quoted in A. R. Hall, *From Galileo to Newton, 1630–1720* (New York: Harper & Row, 1963), p. 290.
8. Quoted in R. K. Merton, *Science, Technology and Society in Seventeenth-Century England*, rev. ed. (New York: Harper & Row, 1970), p. 164.
9. Quoted in P. Hazard, *The European Mind, 1680–1715* (Cleveland: Meridian Books, 1963), pp. 304–305.
10. Quoted ibid., pp. 11–12.
11. Quoted in L. M. Marsak, ed., *The Enlightenment* (New York: Wiley, 1972), p. 56.
12. Quoted in G. L. Mosse et al., eds., *Europe in Review* (Chicago: Rand McNally, 1964), p. 156.
13. F. M. Arouet de Voltaire, *Oeuvres completes*, vol. 8 (Paris: Firmin–Didot, 1875), pp. 188–190, translated by J. P. McKay.
14. Quoted in P. Gay, "The Unity of the Enlightenment," *History* 3 (1960): 25.
15. See E. Fox-Genovese, "Women in the Enlightenment," in *Becoming Visible: Women in European History*, 2d ed., ed. R. Bridenthal, C. Koonz, and S. Stuard (Boston: Houghton Mifflin, 1987), esp. pp. 252–259 and 263–265.
16. Quoted in G. P. Gooch, *Catherine the Great and Other Studies* (Hamden, Conn.: Archon Books, 1966), p. 112.
17. Ibid., p. 149.
18. Quoted in L. Krieger, *Kings and Philosophers, 1689–1789* (New York: Norton, 1970), p. 257.
19. Ibid., p. 15.
20. Ibid., p. 53.

21. Quoted in R. R. Palmer, *The Age of Democratic Revolution,* vol. 1 (Princeton, N.J.: Princeton University Press, 1959), pp. 95–96.
22. Quoted in G. Wright, *France in Modern Times* (Chicago: Rand McNally, 1960), p. 42.

SUGGESTED READING

The first three authors cited in the Notes—H. Butterfield, A. G. R. Smith, and A. R. Hall—have written excellent general interpretations of the scientific revolution. These may be compared with an outstanding recent work by M. Jacob, *The Cultural Meaning of the Scientific Revolution* (1988), which has a useful bibliography. The older study of England by R. K. Merton, mentioned in the Notes, also analyzes ties between science and the larger community. A. Debus, *Man and Nature in the Renaissance* (1978), is good on the Copernican revolution. M. Boas, *The Scientific Renaissance, 1450–1630* (1966), is especially insightful about the influence of magic on science and about Galileo's trial. T. Kuhn, *The Structure of Scientific Revolutions* (1962), is a challenging, much-discussed attempt to understand major breakthroughs in scientific thought. E. Andrade, *Sir Isaac Newton* (1958), is a good short biography, which may be compared with F. Manuel, *The Religion of Isaac Newton* (1974).

The work of P. Hazard listed in the Notes is a classic study of the formative years of Enlightenment thought, and his *European Thought in the Eighteenth Century* (1954) is also recommended. A famous controversial interpretation of the Enlightenment is that of C. Becker, *The Heavenly City of the Eighteenth Century Philosophers* [*sic*] (1932), which maintains that the world view of medieval Christianity continued to influence the philosophes greatly. Becker's ideas are discussed interestingly in R. O. Rockwood, ed., *Carl Becker's Heavenly City Revisited* (1958). P. Gay has written several major studies on the Enlightenment: *Voltaire's Politics* (1959) and *The Party of Humanity* (1971) are two of the best. I. Wade, *The Structure and Form of the French Enlightenment* (1977), is a major synthesis. F. Baumer, *Religion and the Rise of Skepticism* (1969), H. Payne, *The Philosophes and the People* (1976), and H. Chisick, *The Limits of Reform in the Enlightenment: Attitudes Toward the Education of the Lower Classes in Eighteenth-Century France* (1981), are interesting studies of important aspects of Enlightenment thought. On women, see the stimulating study by E. Fox-Genovese cited in the Notes, as well as S. Spencer, ed., *French Women and the Age of Enlightenment* (1984), and K. Rogers, *Feminism in Eighteenth-Century England* (1982). Above all, one should read some of the philosophes and let them speak for themselves. Two good anthologies are C. Brinton, ed., *The Portable Age of Reason* (1956), and F. Manuel, ed., *The Enlightenment* (1951). Voltaire's most famous and very amusing novel, *Candide,* is highly recommended, as are S. Gendzier, ed., *Denis Diderot: The Encyclopedia: Selections* (1967), and A. Wilson, *Diderot* (1972), a biography.

The monarchies of Europe are examined in the works mentioned in the Suggested Reading for Chapter 19. In addition, they are carefully analyzed in C. Tilly, ed., *The Formation of National States in Western Europe* (1975), and in J. Gagliardo, *Enlightened Despotism* (1967), both of which have useful bibliographies. M. Anderson, *Historians and Eighteenth-Century Europe* (1979), is a valuable introduction to modern scholarship. Other recommended studies on the struggle for power and reform in different countries are F. Ford, *Robe and Sword* (1953), which discusses the resurgence of the French nobility after the death of Louis XIV; R. Herr, *The Eighteenth-Century Revolution in Spain* (1958), on the impact of Enlightenment thought in Spain; and P. Bernard, *Joseph II* (1968). There are several fine works on Russia. J. Alexander, *Catherine the Great: Life and Legend* (1989), is the best biography of the famous ruler. Also recommended are I. de Madariaga, *Russia in the Age of Catherine the Great* (1981), and D. Ransel, *Politics of Catherinean Russia* (1975). The ambitious reader should also look at A. N. Radishchev, *A Journey from St. Petersburg to Moscow* (English trans., 1958), a famous 1790 attack on Russian serfdom and an appeal to Catherine the Great to free the serfs, for which Radishchev was exiled to Siberia.

The culture of the time may be approached through A. Cobban, ed., *The Eighteenth Century* (1969), a richly illustrated work with excellent essays, and C. B. Behrens, *The Ancien Régime* (1967). C. Rosen, *The Classical Style: Haydn, Mozart, Beethoven* (1972), brilliantly synthesizes music and society, as did Mozart himself in his great opera *The Marriage of Figaro,* where the count is the buffoon and his servant the hero.

21

The Life of the People in Europe

People in the Paris marketplace celebrating the news of the birth of the Dauphin

The world of absolutism and aristocracy, a combination of raw power and elegant refinement, was a world apart from that of ordinary men and women. Weakness and uncertainty, poverty and pain—these enduring realities weighed heavily on the vast majority. Yet the common people were by no means helpless victims of fate, ignorance, and inequality. With courage and intelligence, with hard work and family loyalties, ordinary men and women struggled and survived. There is a human dignity in the efforts of these people that is deeply moving.

This, then, is the story of those ordinary lives at a time when the idea of far-reaching scientific and material progress was only the sweet dream of a privileged elite in fashionable salons.

- How did the common people wring a living out of the land, and how was cottage industry growing to complement these efforts?
- What changes in marriage and the family were occurring in the eighteenth century?
- What was life like for children?
- What did people eat, and how did diet and medical care affect people's health?
- What were the patterns of popular religion in the era of Enlightenment?

The answers to these questions help reveal how European peasants and the urban poor really lived before the age of revolution at the end of the eighteenth century.

AGRICULTURE AND POPULATION

At the end of the seventeenth century, at least 80 percent of the people of all western European countries, with the possible exception of Holland, drew their livelihood from agriculture. In eastern Europe the percentage was considerably higher. Men and women lavished their attention on the land, and the land repaid their efforts, yielding the food and most of the raw materials for industry that made life possible. Yet the land was stingy and capricious. Yields were low even in good years, and finding enough to eat was an endless challenge. If there were too many mouths to feed, some would

go hungry or die from starvation or disease when harvests were bad or failed completely. As a result, peasant communities had generally learned to keep family size under control. If total population grew even modestly, as it did in the eighteenth century, people had to find new sources of food and income.

Working the Land

The greatest accomplishment of medieval agriculture was the open-field system of village agriculture developed by European peasants (see page 377). That system divided the land to be cultivated by the peasants into a few large fields, which were in turn cut up into long narrow strips. The fields were open, and the strips were not enclosed into small plots by fences or hedges. An individual peasant family—if it was fortunate—held a number of strips scattered throughout the large fields. The land of those who owned but did not till—primarily the nobility, the clergy, and wealthy townsmen—was also in scattered strips. The peasants farmed each large field as a community. Each family followed the same pattern of plowing, sowing, and harvesting in accordance with tradition and the village leaders.

The ever-present problem was exhaustion of soil. If a community planted wheat year after year in a field, the nitrogen in the soil was soon depleted, and crop failure and starvation were certain. Since the supply of manure for fertilizer was limited, the only way for land to recover its life-giving fertility was for a field to lie fallow for a period of time. In the early Middle Ages, a year of fallow was alternated with a year of cropping, so that half of the land stood idle in a given year. Eventually, three-year rotations were introduced, especially on the most fertile lands. This system permitted a year of wheat or rye followed by a year of oats or beans or peas, and only then a year of fallow. Even so, results were modest. In a rich agricultural region like the Po Valley in northern Italy, every bushel of wheat sown yielded on average only five or six bushels of grain at harvest during the seventeenth century. The average French yield in the same period was somewhat less. Such yields were no more than those attained in fertile, well-watered areas in the thirteenth century or in ancient Greece. By modern standards, output in 1700 was distressingly low. (Today an American or

French farmer with similar land can expect roughly fifty bushels of wheat for each bushel of wheat sown.) Only awareness of the tragic consequences of continuous cropping forced undernourished populations to let a third of their land lie constantly idle.

Traditional rights reinforced the traditional pattern of farming. In addition to rotating the field crops in a uniform way, villages held open meadows in common to provide animals with hay and natural pasture. After the harvest, the people of the village also pastured their animals on the wheat or rye stubble. In many places such pasturing followed a brief period, also established by tra-dition, for the gleaning of grain. Poor women would go through the fields picking up the few single grains that had fallen to the ground in the course of the harvest. The subject of a great nineteenth-century painting, *The Gleaners* by Jean François Millet, this backbreaking labor by hard-working but impoverished women provided the slender margin of survival for some people in the winter months.

In the age of absolutism and nobility, state and landlord levied heavy taxes and high rents as a matter of course. In so doing, they stripped the peasants of much of their meager earnings. Generally speaking, the peasants of eastern Europe were

Millet: The Gleaners   Poor French peasant women search for grains and stalks that the harvesters (in the background) have missed. The open-field system here could still be found in parts of Europe in 1857, when this picture was painted. Millet is known for his great paintings expressing social themes. *(Source: Louvre/Cliché des Musées Nationaux, Paris)*

worst off. As discussed in Chapter 19, they were serfs, bound to their lords in hereditary service. There were few limitations on the amount of forced labor that the lord could require, and five or six days of unpaid work per week on the lord's land was not uncommon. Well into the nineteenth century, individual Russian serfs and serf families were regularly sold with and without land. Serfdom was often very close to slavery.

Social conditions were considerably better in western Europe. Peasants were generally free from serfdom. In France and western Germany, they owned land and could pass it on to their children. Yet life in the village was unquestionably hard, and poverty was the great reality for most people. For the Beauvais region of France at the beginning of the eighteenth century, it has been carefully estimated that in good years and bad only a tenth of the peasants could live satisfactorily off the fruits of their landholdings. Owning less than half of the land, the peasants had to pay heavy royal taxes, the church's tithe, and dues to the lord, as well as set aside seed for the next season. Left with only half of their crop for their own use, they had to toil and till for others and seek work far afield in a constant scramble for a meager living.

One possible way for European peasants to improve their difficult position was to seize land from those who owned but did not labor. Yet the social and political conditions that squeezed the peasants were ancient and deep-rooted, and powerful forces stood ready to crush any protest. Only with the coming of the French Revolution were European peasants able to improve their position by means of radical mass action.

Technological progress offered another possibility. The great need was for new farming methods that would enable Europeans to produce more and eat more. The uncultivated fields were the heart of the matter. If peasants could replace the fallow with crops, they could increase the land under cultivation by 50 percent. The secret was to eliminate the fallow by alternating grain with certain nitrogen-storing crops, such as turnips and potatoes, clovers and grasses. Such crops not only rejuvenate the soil better than fallowing but give more produce as well. Technological progress had its price, though.

Enclosing the Fields   This remarkable aerial photograph captures key aspects of the agricultural revolution. Though the long ridges and furrows of the old open-field system still stretch across the whole picture, hedge rows now cut through the long strips to divide the land into several enclosed fields. *(Source: © British Crown copyright/MOD reproduced with the permission of the Controller of Her Britannic Majesty's Stationery Office)*

New rotations, based primarily on nitrogen-storing clovers and grasses, were scarcely possible within the traditional framework of open fields and common rights. A farmer who wanted to experiment with new methods would have to control the village's pattern of rotation. To wait for the entire village to agree to a new rotation might mean waiting forever. Thus an innovating agriculturalist sought to enclose and consolidate his scattered holdings into a compact, fenced-in field. In doing so, he also sought to enclose his share of the natural pasture, the common. Yet the common rights, like gleaning, were precious to many rural people, and when small landholders and the poor could effectively oppose the enclosure of the open fields, they did so. Only powerful social and political pressures could overcome the traditionalism of rural communities.

The old system of open fields held on tenaciously. Indeed, until the end of the eighteenth century, the promise of the new system was extensively realized only in the Low Countries and in England. Across the rest of Europe, technological progress was limited largely to the introduction of a single new but extremely important crop—the potato (see page 712).

The Balance of Numbers

Many commonly held ideas about population in the past are wrong. One is that past societies were so ignorant that they could do nothing to control their numbers, that population was always growing too fast. On the contrary, until 1700 the total population of Europe grew slowly much of the time and by no means constantly (Figure 21.1).

In seventeenth-century Europe, births and deaths and fertility and mortality were in a crude but effective balance. The birthrate—annual births as a proportion of the population—was fairly high but far lower than it would have been if all women between ages fifteen and forty-four had been having as many children as biologically possible. The death rate in normal years was also high, though somewhat lower than the birthrate. As a result, the population grew modestly in normal years at a rate of perhaps .5 to 1 percent. Yet even fairly modest population growth of 1 percent per year produces a very large increase over a long period—a fourfold increase in 150 years, for example. Such gigantic increases did not occur in agrar-

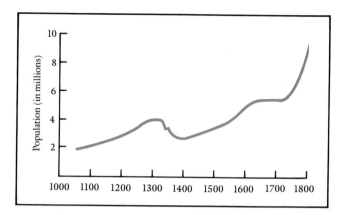

FIGURE 21.1 The Growth of Population in England 1000–1800 England is a good example of both the uneven increase of European population before 1700 and the third great surge of growth, which began in the eighteenth century. *(Source: Data from E. A. Wrigley,* Population and History, *McGraw-Hill, New York, 1969)*

ian Europe before the eighteenth century. In certain abnormal years and tragic periods, many more people died than were born; total population fell sharply, even catastrophically. A number of years of modest growth would then be necessary to make up for those who had died. Increases in deaths helped check total numbers and kept the population from growing rapidly for long periods.

The grim reapers of demographic crisis were famine, epidemic disease, and war. Famine was the tragic result of low yields and periodic crop failures. In most regions of Europe in the sixteenth and seventeenth centuries, harvests were poor or failed completely every eight or nine years. The rural population might survive a single bad harvest by eating less and drawing on its reserves of grain. But when the land combined with persistent bad weather—too much rain rotting the seed or drought withering the young stalks—the result was catastrophic. Meager grain reserves were soon exhausted, and the price of grain soared.

In these crisis years, which periodically stalked Europe even into the eighteenth century, a terrible tightening knot in the belly forced people to tragic substitutes—the "famine foods" of a desperate population. They gathered chestnuts and stripped bark in the forests; they cut dandelions and grass; and they ate these substitutes to escape starvation. Such unbalanced and inadequate food made people weak and extremely susceptible to illness and

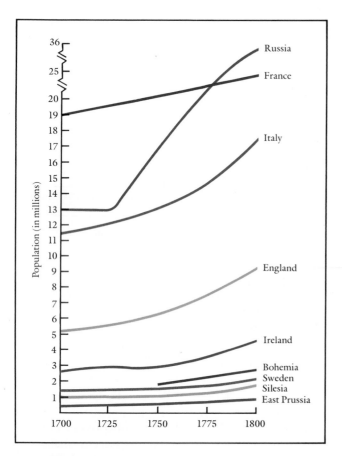

FIGURE 21.2 The Increase of Population in the Eighteenth Century France's large population continued to support French political and intellectual leadership. Russia emerged as Europe's most populous state because natural increase was complemented by growth from territorial expansion.

epidemics. Eating material unfit for human consumption, such as bark or grass, resulted in dysentery and intestinal ailments. Influenza and smallpox preyed with particular savagery on a population weakened by famine. With a brutal one-two punch, famine stunned and weakened the population and disease finished it off.

In years of famine and disease, the number of deaths soared far above normal. A third of a village's population might disappear in a year or two. The 1690s were as dismal as many of the worst periods of earlier times. One county in Finland, probably typical of the entire country, lost fully 28 percent of its inhabitants in 1696 and 1697. Certain well-studied villages in the Beauvais region of northern France suffered a similar fate.

Disease could also ravage independently, even in years of adequate harvests. Bubonic plague returned again and again in Europe for more than three hundred years after the onset of the Black Death in the fourteenth century. Not until the late 1500s did most countries have as many people as in the early 1300s. Epidemics of dysentery and smallpox could also operate independently of famine.

War was another scourge. The indirect effects were more harmful than the organized killing. War spread disease. Soldiers and camp followers passed venereal disease through the countryside to scar and kill. Armies requisitioned scarce food supplies for their own use and disrupted the agricultural cycle. The Thirty Years' War (see pages 589–592) witnessed all possible combinations of distress. In the German states, the number of inhabitants declined by more than two-thirds in some large areas and by at least one-third almost everywhere else. The Thirty Years' War reduced total German population by no less than 40 percent.

The brutal but effective balance considered here tipped decisively in favor of births in the eighteenth century. The population of Europe began to grow markedly, a development that had major consequences for millions of ordinary people. This increase in numbers occurred in all areas of Europe—western and eastern, northern and southern, dynamic and stagnant. Growth was especially dramatic after about 1750, as Figure 21.2 shows.

Although it is certain that Europe's population grew greatly, it is less clear why. Because population grew everywhere, it is best to look for general factors and not those limited to individual countries or areas. Whereas in some families women may have had more babies than before, the basic cause was a decline in mortality—fewer deaths.

Of great importance, the bubonic plague mysteriously disappeared. After the Black Death in the fourteenth century, plagues had remained a part of the European experience, striking again and again with savage force, particularly in towns. As late as 1720, a ship from Syria and the eastern Mediterranean, where plague was ever present, brought the monstrous disease to Marseilles. In a few weeks, forty thousand of the city's ninety thousand inhabitants died. The epidemic swept southern France, killing one-third, one-half, even three-fourths of those in the larger towns.

Once again an awful fear swept across Europe. But the epidemic passed, and that was the last time plague fell on western and central Europe. The final disappearance of plague was due in part to stricter measures of quarantine in Mediterranean ports and along the Austrian border with Turkey. Human carriers of plague were carefully isolated. Chance and plain good luck were more important, however.

It is now understood that bubonic plague is, above all, a disease of rats. More precisely, it is the black rat that spreads major epidemics, for the black rat's flea is the principal carrier of the plague bacillus. After 1600, for reasons unknown, a new rat of Asiatic origin—the brown, or wander, rat—began to drive out and eventually eliminate its black competitor. In the words of a noted authority, "This revolution in the animal kingdom must have gone far to break the lethal link between rat and man."[1] Although the brown rat also carries the plague bacillus, another kind of flea is its main parasite. That flea carries the plague poorly and, for good measure, has little taste for human blood.

Advances in medical knowledge did not contribute much to reducing the death rate in the eighteenth century (see pages 712–717). But human beings were more successful in their efforts to safeguard the supply of food and protect against famine. The eighteenth century was a time of considerable canal and road building in western Europe. These advances in transportation, which were among the positive aspects of strong absolutist states, lessened the impact of local crop failure and famine. Emergency supplies could be brought in. The age-old spectacle of localized starvation became less frequent. War became more gentlemanly and less destructive than it had been in the seventeenth century and spread fewer epidemics. New foods, particularly the potato, were introduced. Potatoes served especially well when the grain crops were skimpy or failed. In short, population grew in the eighteenth century primarily because years of abnormal death rates were less catastrophic. Famines, epidemics, and wars continued to occur, but their severity moderated.

The growth of population in the eighteenth century cannot be interpreted as a sign of human progress, however. Serious population pressure on resources in Europe as a whole existed by 1600 and continued throughout the seventeenth century. Thus renewed population growth in the eighteenth century maintained or even increased the imbalance between the number of people and the economic opportunities available to them. Agriculture could not provide enough work for the rapidly growing labor force, and poor people in the countryside had to look for new ways to make a living.

The Growth of Cottage Industry

The growth of population increased the number of rural workers with little or no land, and this in turn contributed to the development of industry in rural areas. The poor in the countryside needed

Doctor in Protective Clothing Most doctors believed, incorrectly, that poisonous smells carried the plague. This doctor has placed strong-smelling salts in his "beak" to protect himself against deadly plague vapors. *(Source: Germanisches Nationalmuseum, Nuremberg)*

increasingly to supplement their earnings from agriculture with other types of work, and capitalists from the city were eager to employ them, often at wages lower than those usually commanded by urban workers. Manufacturing with hand tools in peasant cottages and worksheds grew markedly in the eighteenth century. Rural industry became a crucial feature of the European economy.

To be sure, peasant communities had always made some clothing, processed some food, and constructed some housing for their own use. But in the Middle Ages, peasants did not produce manufactured goods on a large scale for sale in a market. Industry was dominated and organized by urban craft guilds and urban merchants, who jealously regulated handicraft production and sought to maintain it as an urban monopoly. By the eight-

eenth century, however, the pressures of rural poverty and the need for employment in the countryside had proved too great, and a new system was expanding lustily.

The new system had many names. It has often been called "cottage industry" or "domestic industry," to distinguish it from the factory industry that came later. In recent years, some scholars have preferred to speak of "protoindustrialization," by which they usually mean a stage of rural industrial development with wage workers and hand tools that necessarily preceded the emergence of large-scale factory industry. This focus has sparked renewed interest in Europe's early industrial development and shown again that the mechanized factories grew out of a vibrant industrial tradition. However, the evolving concept of protoindustrial-

The Weaver's Repose   This painting by Decker Cornelis Gerritz (1594-1637) captures the pleasure of release from long hours of toil in cottage industry. The loom realistically dominates the cramped living space and the family's modest possessions. *(Source: Musées Royaux des Beaux-Arts, Brussels. Copyright A.C.I.)*

ization has different versions; thus the phrase "putting-out system," widely used by contemporaries to describe the key features of eighteenth-century rural industry, still seems an appropriate term for the new form of industrial production.

The two main participants in the *putting-out system* were the merchant-capitalist and the rural worker. The merchant loaned or "put out" raw materials—raw wool, for example—to several cottage workers. Those workers processed the raw material in their own homes, spinning and weaving the wool into cloth in this case, and returned the finished product to the merchant. The merchant then paid the workers by the piece and sold the finished products. There were endless variations on this basic relationship. Sometimes rural workers would buy their own materials and work as independent producers before they delivered finished goods to the merchant. Sometimes several workers toiled together in a workshop to perform a complicated process. The relative importance of earnings from the land and from industry varied greatly for handicraft workers. In all cases, however, the putting-out system was a kind of capitalism. Merchants needed large amounts of capital, which they held in the form of goods being worked up and sold in distant markets. They sought to make profits and increase their capital in their businesses. Rural workers were selling their labor.

The putting-out system grew because it offered competitive advantages. Underemployed labor was abundant, and poor peasants and landless laborers would work for low wages. Since production in the countryside was unregulated, workers and merchants could change procedures and experiment as they saw fit. Because cottage industry did not need to meet rigid guild standards, which maintained quality but discouraged the development of new methods, it became capable of producing many kinds of goods. Textiles, all manner of knives, forks, and housewares, buttons and gloves, and clocks and musical instruments could be produced quite satisfactorily in the countryside. The manufacture of luxury goods for the rich, such as exquisite tapestries and fine porcelain, demanded special training, close supervision, and centralized workshops. Yet such goods were as exceptional as those who used them. The skills of rural industry were sufficient for many everyday articles.

Rural manufacturing did not spread across Europe at an even rate. It appeared first in England and developed most successfully there, particularly for the spinning and weaving of woolen cloth. Continental countries developed rural industry more slowly. In France at the time of Louis XIV, Colbert had revived the urban guilds and used them as a means to control the cities and collect taxes (see page 508). But the pressure of rural poverty proved too great. In 1762 the special privileges of urban manufacturing were abolished in France, and the already-developing rural industries were given free rein from then on. Thus in France, as in Germany and other areas, the later part of the eighteenth century witnessed a remarkable expansion of rural industry in certain densely populated regions (Map 21.1). The pattern established in England was spreading to the Continent.

Cottage industry, like peasant agriculture from which it evolved, was based on family enterprise. All the members of the family helped in the work, especially in textiles, the most important cottage industry. While the women and children prepared the raw material and spun the thread, the man of the house wove the cloth. There was work for everyone, even the youngest. After the dirt was beaten out of the raw material, for example, it had to be thoroughly cleaned with strong soap in a tub, where tiny feet took the place of the agitator in a washing machine. A famous English textile inventor recalled that "soon after I was able to walk I was employed in the cotton manufacture. . . . My mother tucked up my petticoats about my waist, and put me into the tub to tread upon the cotton at the bottom."[2] Slightly older children and aged relatives carded and combed the cotton or wool so that the mother and the older daughter whom she had taught could spin it into thread. Each member had a task, and family life overlapped with the work experience.

MARRIAGE AND THE FAMILY

The family is the basic unit of social organization. It is within the structure of the family that human beings love, mate, and reproduce themselves. It is primarily the family that teaches each child, imparting values and customs that condition an individual's behavior for a lifetime. The family is also an institution woven into the web of history.

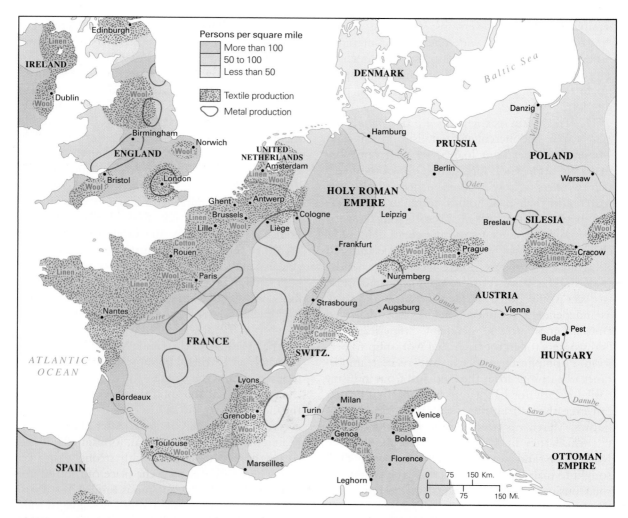

MAP 21.1 Industry and Population in Eighteenth-Century Europe   The growth of cottage manufacturing in rural areas helped country people to increase their income and contributed to increases in the population. This putting-out system began in England, and most of the work was in the textile industry.

Extended and Nuclear Families

In many traditional Asian and African societies, the typical family has often been an extended family. A newly married couple goes to live with either the bride's or the groom's family. Wife and husband raise their children while living under the same roof with their own brothers and sisters, who may also be married. The family is a three- or four-generation clan headed by a patriarch or a matriarch and encompassing everyone from the youngest infant to the oldest grandparent. Extended families, it is often said, provide security for adults and children in traditional agrarian peasant economies. From cradle to grave, everyone has a place within an extended family.

In societies characterized by nuclear families, couples establish their own households and their own family identities when they marry. They live with the children they raise, apart from their parents. Sociologists frequently assume that, with the advent of industrialization and urbanization, the extended family gives way to the nuclear family. Something like this has been happening in much of Asia and Africa in recent years. And since Europe was once agrarian and preindustrial, it has often been believed that the extended family must also have prevailed in Europe before being destroyed by the Industrial Revolution.

In fact, by 1700 the extended three-generational family was a rarity in western and central Europe. Indeed, the extended family may never have been common in Europe, although it is hard to know about the Middle Ages because so few records survive. When young European couples married, they normally established their own households and lived apart from their parents. When a three-generation household came into existence, usually a parent moved in with a married child, rather than a newly married couple moving in with either set of parents. A married couple, and the children who were sure to follow, were on their own from the beginning.

Perhaps because European couples set up separate households when they married, people did not marry young in the seventeenth and early eighteenth centuries. Indeed, the average person, who was neither rich nor aristocratic, married surprisingly late. In one well-studied, typical English village, both men and women married for the first time at an average age of twenty-seven or older in the seventeenth and eighteenth centuries. A similar pattern existed in early-eighteenth-century France. Moreover, a substantial portion of men and women never married at all.

Between two-fifths and three-fifths of European women capable of bearing children—that is, women between fifteen and forty-four—were unmarried at any given time. The contrast with traditional non-Western societies is once again striking. In those societies, the pattern has very often been almost universal and very early marriage. The union of a teenage bride and her teenage groom has been the general rule.

Late marriage and the nuclear family were distinctive characteristics of European society. The consequences have been tremendous, though still only partially explored. It seems likely that the aggressive dynamism and creativity that have characterized European society were due in large part to the pattern of marriage and family, which fostered and required self-reliance and independence. In preindustrial western Europe in the sixteenth through eighteenth centuries, marriage normally joined a mature man and a mature woman—two adults who had already experienced a great deal of life and could transmit self-reliance and real skills to the next generation.

Why was marriage delayed? The main reason was that couples normally could not marry until they could support themselves economically. Land remained the main source of income. The peasant son often needed to wait until his father's death to inherit the family farm and marry his sweetheart. Similarly, the peasant daughter and her family had to accumulate a small dowry to help her boyfriend buy land or build a house.

There were also laws and regulations to temper impetuous love and physical attraction. In some areas, couples needed the legal permission or tacit approval of the local lord or landowner in order to marry, and poor couples had particular difficulty securing that approval. Local officials believed that freedom to marry for the lower classes would mean more paupers, more abandoned children, and more money for welfare. Thus prudence, custom, and law combined to postpone the march to the altar. This pattern helped society maintain some kind of balance between the number of people and the available economic resources.

Work Away from Home

Many young people worked within their families until they could start their own households. Girls tended the cows and spun; boys plowed and wove. Many others left home to work elsewhere. In the towns, a lad might be apprenticed to a craftsman for seven or fourteen years to learn a trade. During that time he would not be permitted to marry. In most trades he earned little and worked hard, but if he were lucky he might eventually be admitted to a guild and establish his economic independence. More often, a young man would drift from one tough job to another: hired hand for a small farmer, laborer on a new road, water carrier in a nearby town. He was always subject to economic fluctuations, and unemployment was a constant threat.

Girls also left their families to work, at an early age and in large numbers. The range of opportunities open to them was more limited, however. Service in another family's household was by far the most common job. Even middle-class families often sent their daughters into service and hired others as servants in return. Thus, a few years away from home as a servant was a normal part of growing up. If all went well, a girl (or boy) would work hard and save some money for parents and marriage. At the least, there would be one less mouth to feed at home.

Legions of young servant girls worked hard but had little real independence. Sometimes the employer paid a girl's wages directly to her parents. Constantly under the eye of her mistress, her tasks were many—cleaning, shopping, cooking, caring for the baby—and often endless, for there were no laws to limit her exploitation. Few girls were so brutalized that they snapped under the strain, like the Russian servant girl Varka in Chekhov's chilling story "Sleepy," who, driven beyond exhaustion, finally quieted her mistress's screaming child by strangling it in its cradle. But court records are full of complaints by servant girls of physical mistreatment by their mistresses. There were many others like the fifteen-year-old English girl in the early eighteenth century who told a judge that her

Chardin: The Kitchen Maid Lost in thought as she pauses in her work, perhaps this young servant is thinking about her village and loved ones there. Chardin was one of eighteenth-century France's greatest painters, and his scenes from everyday life provide valuable evidence for the historian. *(Source: National Gallery of Art, Washington, D.C. Samuel H. Kress Collection)*

mistress had not only called her "very opprobrious names, as Bitch, Whore and the like," but also "beat her without provocation and beyond measure."[3]

There was also the pressure of seducers and sexual attack. In theory, domestic service offered protection and security for a young girl leaving home. The girl had food, lodging, and a new family. She did not drift in a strange and often dangerous environment. But in practice, she was often the easy prey of a lecherous master, or his sons, or his friends. Indeed, "the evidence suggests that in all European countries, from Britain to Russia, the upper classes felt perfectly free to exploit sexually girls who were at their mercy."[4] If the girl became pregnant, she was quickly fired and thrown out in disgrace to make her own way. Prostitution and petty thievery were often the harsh alternatives that lay ahead. "What are we?" exclaimed a bitter Parisian prostitute. "Most of us are unfortunate women, without origins, without education, servants and maids for the most part."[5]

Premarital Sex and Birth-Control Practices

Did the plight of some former servant girls mean that late marriage in preindustrial Europe went hand in hand with premarital sex and many illegitimate children? For most of western and central Europe, until at least 1750, the answer seems to be *no*. English parish registers, in which the clergy recorded the births and deaths of the population, seldom list more than one bastard out of every twenty children baptized. Some French parishes in the seventeenth century had extraordinarily low rates of illegitimacy, with less than 1 percent of the babies born out of wedlock. Illegitimate babies were apparently a rarity, at least as far as the official church records are concerned.

At the same time, premarital sex was clearly commonplace. In one well-studied English village, one-third of all first children were conceived before the couple was married, and many were born within three months of the marriage ceremony. No doubt many of these couples were already betrothed, or at least "going steady," before they entered into an intimate relationship. But the very low rates of illegitimate birth also reflect the powerful social controls of the traditional village, particularly the open-field village with its pattern of cooperation and common action. Irate parents and village elders, indignant priests and authoritative landlords, all combined to pressure any young people who wavered about marriage in the face of unexpected pregnancy. These controls meant that premarital sex was not entered into lightly. In the countryside it was generally limited to those contemplating marriage.

Once a woman was married, she generally had several children. This does not mean that birth control within marriage was unknown in western and central Europe before the nineteenth century. But it was primitive and quite undependable. The most common method was coitus interruptus—withdrawal by the male before ejaculation. The French, who were apparently early leaders in contraception, were using this method extensively to limit family size by the end of the eighteenth century. Withdrawal as a method of birth control was in keeping with the European pattern of nuclear family, in which the father bore the direct responsibility of supporting his children. Withdrawal—a male technique—was one way to meet that responsibility.

Mechanical and other means of contraception were not unknown in the eighteenth century, but they appear to have been used mainly by certain sectors of the urban population. The "fast set" of London used the "sheath" regularly, although primarily to protect against venereal disease, not pregnancy. Prostitutes used various contraceptive techniques to prevent pregnancy, and such information was probably available to anyone who really sought it. The second part of an indictment for adultery against a late-sixteenth-century English vicar charged that the wayward minister was "also an instructor of young folks in how to commit the sin of adultery or fornication and not to beget or bring forth children."[6]

New Patterns of Marriage and Illegitimacy

In the second half of the eighteenth century, the pattern of late marriage and few illegitimate children began to break down. It is hard to say why. Certainly, changes in the economy had a gradual but profound impact. The growth of cottage industry created a way to earn a living that was not tied to limited and hard-to-get land. Because a scrap of ground for a garden and a cottage for the loom and spinning wheel could be quite enough for a modest living, young people had greater

independence and did not need to wait for a good-size farm. A contemporary observer of an area of rapidly growing cottage industry in Switzerland at the end of the eighteenth century described these changes: "The increased and sure income offered by the combination of cottage manufacture with farming hastened and multiplied marriages and encouraged the division of landholdings, while enhancing their value; it also promoted the expansion and embellishment of houses and villages."[7]

As a result, cottage workers married not only earlier but frequently for different reasons. Nothing could be so businesslike, so calculating, as a peasant marriage that was dictated by the needs of the couple's families. After 1750, however, courtship became more extensive and freer as cottage industry grew. It became easier to yield to the attraction of the opposite sex and fall in love. Members of the older generation were often shocked by the lack of responsibility they saw in the early marriages of the poor, the union of "people with only two spinning wheels and not even a bed." But the laws and regulations they imposed, especially in Germany, were often disregarded. Unions based on love rather than on economic considerations were increasingly the pattern for cottage workers. Factory workers, numbers of whom first began to appear in England after about 1780, followed the path blazed by cottage workers.

Changes in the timing and motivation of marriage went hand in hand with a rapid increase in illegitimate births between about 1750 and 1850. Some historians even speak of an "illegitimacy explosion." In Frankfurt, Germany, for example, only about 2 percent of all births were illegitimate in the early 1700s; this figure rose to about 25 percent around 1850. In Bordeaux, France, illegitimate births rose steadily until by 1840 one out of every three babies was born out of wedlock. Small towns and villages less frequently experienced such startlingly high illegitimacy rates, but increases from a range of 1 to 3 percent initially to 10 to 20 percent between 1750 and 1850 were commonplace. A profound sexual and cultural transformation was taking place. Fewer girls were abstaining from premarital intercourse, and fewer boys were marrying the girls they got pregnant.

It is hard to know exactly why this change occurred and what it meant. The old idea of a safe, late, economically secure marriage did not reflect economic and social realities. The growing freedom of thought in the turbulent years beginning with the French Revolution in 1789 influenced sexual and marital behavior. Illegitimate births, particularly in Germany, were also the result of open rebellion against class laws limiting the right of the poor to marry. More fundamentally, the need to seek work outside farming and the village made young people more mobile. Mobility in turn encouraged new sexual and marital relationships, which were less subject to parental pressure and village tradition. As in the case of young servant girls who became pregnant and were then forced to fend for themselves, some of these relationships promoted loose living or prostitution. This resulted in more illegitimate births and strengthened an urban subculture of habitual illegitimacy.

It has been suggested that the increase in illegitimate births represented a stage in the emancipation of women. According to this view, new economic opportunities outside the home, in the city and later in the factory, revolutionized women's attitudes about themselves. Young working women became individualistic and rebelled against old restrictions like late marriage. They sought fulfillment in the pleasure of sexuality. Since there was little birth control, freer sex for single women meant more illegitimate babies.

No doubt single working women in towns and cities were of necessity more independent and self-reliant. Yet, until at least the late nineteenth century, it seems unlikely that such young women were motivated primarily by visions of emancipation and sexual liberation. Most women were servants or textile workers. These jobs paid poorly, and the possibility of a truly independent "liberated" life was correspondingly limited. Most women in the city probably looked to marriage and family life as an escape from hard, poorly paid work and as the foundation of a satisfying life.

Hopes and promises of marriage from men of the working girl's own class led naturally enough to sex.[8] In one medium-size French city in 1787 to 1788, the great majority of unwed mothers stated that sexual intimacy had followed promises of marriage. Many soldiers, day laborers, and male servants were no doubt sincere in their proposals. But their lives were insecure, and many hesitated to take on the heavy economic burdens of wife and child. Nor were their backbones any longer stiffened by the traditional pressures of the village.

In a growing number of cases, therefore, the intended marriage did not take place. The romantic yet practical dreams and aspirations of many young working women and men were frustrated by low wages, inequality, and changing economic and social conditions. Old patterns of marriage and family were breaking down among the common people. Only in the late nineteenth century would more stable patterns reappear.

WOMEN AND CHILDREN

In the traditional framework of preindustrial Europe, women married late but then began bearing children rapidly. If a woman married before she was thirty, and if both she and her husband lived to forty-five, the chances were roughly one in two that she would give birth to six or more children. The newborn child entered a dangerous world. Infant mortality was high: one in five was sure to die and in the poorest areas one in three was quite likely to. Newborn children were very likely to catch infectious diseases of the stomach and chest. Because such diseases were not understood, little could be done for an ill child, even in rich families. Childhood itself was dangerous. Parents in preindustrial Europe could count themselves fortunate if half of their children lived to adulthood.

Child Care and Nursing

Women of the lower classes generally breast-fed their infants, and for much longer periods than is customary today. Breast-feeding decreases the likelihood of pregnancy for the average woman by delaying the resumption of ovulation. Although women may have been only vaguely aware of the link between nursing and not getting pregnant, they were spacing their children—from two to three years apart—and limiting their fertility by nursing their babies. If a newborn baby died, nursing stopped and a new life could be created. Nursing also saved lives: the breast-fed infant was more likely to survive on its mother's milk than on any other foods.

In contrast to the laboring poor, women of the aristocracy and upper middle class seldom nursed their own children. The upper-class woman felt that breast-feeding was crude, common, and beneath her dignity. Instead she hired a wet nurse to suckle her child. The urban mother of more mod-

Peasants Begging In seventeenth-century France, many heavily taxed peasants found it very difficult to afford enough to eat. Although charity was becoming more fashionable, many peasant families were reduced to begging. *(Source: The Metropolitan Museum of Art)*

est means—the wife of a shopkeeper or artisan—also commonly used a wet nurse, sending her baby to some poor woman in the country as soon as possible.

Wet-nursing was a widespread and flourishing business in the eighteenth century, a dismal business within the framework of the putting-out system. The traffic was in babies rather than in wool and cloth, and two or three years often passed before the wet nurse finished her task. The great French historian Jules Michelet described with compassion the plight of the wet nurse, who was still plying her trade in early-nineteenth-century France:

People do not know how much these poor women are exploited and abused, first by the vehicles which transport them (often barely out of their confinement), and afterward by the employment offices which place them. Taken as nurses on the spot, they must send their own child away, and consequently it often dies. They have no contact with the family that hires them, and they may be dismissed at the first caprice of the mother or doctor. If the change of air and place should dry up their milk, they are discharged without any compensation. If they stay here in the city they pick up the habits of the easy life, and they suffer enormously when they are forced to return to their life of rural poverty. A good number become servants in order to stay in the town. They never rejoin their husbands, and the family is broken.[9]

Other observers noted the flaws of wet-nursing. It was a common belief that a nurse passed her bad traits to the baby with her milk. When a child turned out poorly, it was assumed that "the nurse changed it." Many observers charged that nurses were often negligent and greedy. They claimed

Abandoned Children At this Italian foundlings' home a frightened, secretive mother could discreetly deposit her baby. *(Source: The Bettmann Archive)*

that there were large numbers of "killing nurses" with whom no child ever survived because the nurse let the child die quickly so that she could take another child and collect another fee. No matter how the adults in the wet-nurse business fared, the child was a certain loser.

Foundlings and Infanticide

In the ancient world and in some Asian societies it was not uncommon to allow or force newborn babies, particularly girl babies, to die when there were too many mouths to feed. In Europe, the early medieval church, strongly influenced by Jew-

ish law, denounced infanticide as a pagan practice and insisted that every human life was sacred. The willful destruction of newborn children became a crime punishable by death. And yet, as the reference to killing nurses suggests, direct and indirect methods of eliminating unwanted babies did not disappear. Severe poverty on the one hand and increasing illegitimacy on the other conspired to force the very poor to thin their own ranks. There were, for example, many cases of "overlaying" parents rolling over in bed and suffocating a child placed between them. Such parents usually claimed that they were drunk and had acted unintentionally. In Austria in 1784, suspicious authorities made it illegal for parents to take children under five into bed with them.

A young girl—very likely a servant—who could not provide for her child had few choices. If she would not resort to abortion or to the services of a killing nurse, she could bundle up her baby and leave it on the doorstep of a church. In the late seventeenth century, Saint Vincent de Paul was so distressed by the number of babies brought to the steps of Notre Dame in Paris that he established a home for foundlings. By the 1770s one-third of all babies born in Paris were immediately abandoned to the foundling home by their mothers. Fully a third of all those foundlings were abandoned by married couples, for whom an additional mouth to feed often meant tragedy. Other countries followed the French example. In England the government acted on a petition calling for a foundling hospital "to prevent the frequent murders of poor, miserable infants at birth" and "to suppress the inhuman custom of exposing newborn children to perish in the streets."

In much of Europe in the eighteenth century, foundling homes became a favorite charity of the rich and powerful. Great sums were spent on them. The foundling home in St. Petersburg, perhaps the most elaborate and lavish of its kind, occupied the former palaces of two members of the high nobility. In the early nineteenth century it had 25,000 children in its care and was receiving 5,000 new babies a year. At their best, the foundling homes of the eighteenth century were a good example of Christian charity and social concern in an age of tremendous poverty and inequality.

Yet the foundling home was no panacea. Great numbers of babies entered, but few left. Even in the best of these homes, half of the babies died within a year. In the worst, fully 90 percent did not survive. They succumbed to long journeys over rough roads, the intentional and unintentional neglect of wet nurses, and the customary childhood illnesses. So great was the carnage that some contemporaries called the foundling hospitals "legalized infanticide."

Certainly some parents and officials looked on the hospitals as dumps for unwanted babies. In the early 1760s, when the London Foundling Hospital was obliged to accept all babies offered, it was deluged with babies from the countryside. In order to reduce the cost of welfare at the local level, many parish officers placed with the foundling home the abandoned children in their care. Throughout the eighteenth century, millions of children of the poor exited life after the briefest of appearances on the earthly stage.

Attitudes Toward Children

What were the typical circumstances of children's lives? Did the treatment of foundlings reflect the attitudes of all parents? Although some scholars argue otherwise, it seems that young children were often of little concern to their parents and to society in the eighteenth century. This indifference toward children was found in all classes; rich children were by no means exempt. The practice of using wet nurses, who were casually selected and often negligent, is one example of how even the rich and prosperous put children out of sight and out of mind. One French moralist, writing in 1756 about how to improve humanity, observed that "one blushes to think of loving one's children." It has been said that the English gentleman of the period "had more interest in the diseases of his horses than of his children."[10]

Parents believed that the world of the child was uninteresting. When parents did stop to notice their offspring, they often treated them as dolls or playthings—little puppies to fondle and cuddle in a moment of relaxation. The psychological distance between parent and child remained vast.

Much of the indifference was due to the terrible frequency, the terrible banality, of death among children of all classes. Parents simply could not afford to become too emotionally involved with children who were so unlikely to survive. The great eighteenth-century English historian Edward Gibbon (1737–1794) wrote that "the death of a new born child before that of its parents may seem unnatural but it is a strictly probable event, since of any given number the greater part are extinguished before the ninth year, before they possess the faculties of the mind and the body." Gibbon's father named all his boys Edward, hoping that at least one of them would survive to carry his name. His prudence was not misplaced. Edward the future historian and eldest survived. Five brothers and sisters all died in infancy.

Doctors were seldom interested in the care of children. One contemporary observer quoted a famous doctor as saying that "he never wished to be called to a young child because he was really at a loss to know what to offer for it." There were "physicians of note who make no scruple to assert that there is nothing to be done for children when they are ill." Children were caught in a vicious circle: they were neglected because they were very likely to die, and they were likely to die because they were neglected.

Indifference toward children often shaded off into brutality. When parents and other adults did turn toward children, it was normally to discipline and control them. The novelist Daniel Defoe (1660?–1731), always delighted when he saw very young children working hard in cottage industry, coined the axiom "Spare the rod and spoil the child." He meant it. So did Susannah Wesley, mother of John Wesley (1703–1791), the founder of Methodism. According to her, the first task of a parent toward her children was "to conquer the will, and bring them to an obedient temper." She reported that her babies were "taught to fear the rod, and to cry softly; by which means they escaped the abundance of correction they might otherwise have had, and that most odious noise of the crying of children was rarely heard in the house."[11]

It was hardly surprising that, when English parish officials dumped their paupers into the first factories late in the eighteenth century, the children were beaten and brutalized (see page 855). That was part of the child-rearing pattern—widespread indifference on the one hand and strict physical discipline on the other—that prevailed through most of the eighteenth century.

From the middle of the eighteenth century, this pattern came under attack. Critics like Jean-Jacques Rousseau called for greater love, tenderness, and understanding toward children. In addition to supporting foundling homes to discourage infanticide and urging wealthy women to nurse their own babies, these new voices ridiculed the practice of swaddling. Wrapping youngsters in tight-fitting clothes and blankets was generally believed to form babies properly by "straightening them out." By the end of the century, small children were often dressed in simpler, more comfortable clothing, allowing much greater freedom of movement. More parents expressed a delight in the love of and intimacy with their children and found real pleasure in raising their offspring. These changes were part of the general growth of humanitarianism and optimism about human potential that characterized the eighteenth-century Enlightenment.

Schools and Education

The role of formal education outside the home, in those special institutions called "schools," was growing more important. The aristocracy and the rich had led the way in the sixteenth century with special colleges, often run by the Jesuits. But "little schools," charged with elementary education of the children of the masses, did not appear until the seventeenth century. Unlike medieval schools, which mingled all age groups, the little schools specialized in boys and girls from seven to twelve, who were instructed in basic literacy and religion.

Although large numbers of common people got no education at all in the eighteenth century, the beginnings of popular education are recognizable. For example, France made a start in 1682 with the establishment of Christian schools that taught the catechism and prayers as well as reading and writing. The Church of England and the dissenting congregations established "charity schools" to instruct the children of the poor. As early as 1717, Prussia made attendance at elementary schools

The Five Senses   Published in 1774, J. B. Basedow's *Elementary Reader* helped spread new attitudes toward child development and education. Drawing heavily on the theories of Locke and Rousseau, the German educator advocated nature study and contact with everyday life. In this illustration for Basedow's reader, gentle teachers allow uncorrupted children to learn about the five senses through direct experience. *(Source: Caroline Buckler)*

compulsory. Inspired by the old Protestant idea that every believer should be able to read and study the Bible in the quest for personal salvation and by the new idea of a population capable of effectively serving the state, Prussia led the way in the development of universal education. Religious motives were also important elsewhere. From the middle of the seventeenth century, Presbyterian Scotland was convinced that the path to salvation lay in careful study of the Scriptures, and this belief led to an effective network of parish schools for rich and poor alike. The Enlightenment commitment to greater knowledge through critical thinking reinforced interest in education in the eighteenth century.

The result of these efforts was a remarkable growth of basic literacy between 1600 and 1800. Whereas in 1600 only one male in six was barely literate in France and Scotland and one in four in England, by 1800 almost 90 percent of the Scottish male population was literate. At the same time, almost two out of three males were literate in France; and in advanced areas such as Normandy, literacy approached 90 percent (Map 21.2). More than half of English males were literate by 1800. In all three countries the bulk of the jump occurred in the eighteenth century. Women were also increasingly literate, although they probably lagged behind men somewhat in most countries. Some elementary education was becoming a reality for European peoples, and schools were of growing significance in everyday life.

FOOD AND MEDICINE

Plague and starvation, which recurred often in the seventeenth century, gradually disappeared in the eighteenth century. This change probably accounted in large part for the rapid growth in the total number of Europeans and for their longer lives. The increase in the average life span, allowing for regional variations, was remarkable. In 1700 the average European could expect at birth to live only twenty-five years. A century later, a newborn European could expect to live fully ten years longer, to age thirty-five. The doubling of the adult life span meant that there was more time to produce and create—and more reason for parents to stress learning and preparation for adulthood.

MAP 21.2 Literacy in France on the Eve of the French Revolution Literacy rates varied widely between and within states in eighteenth-century Europe. Northern France was clearly ahead of southern France.

Precisely how and why did health and life expectancy improve? What was the role of diet and food in this improvement? What were the differences between rich and poor? What was the contribution of doctors, hospitals, and medical science? To answer these questions, it is necessary first to follow the eighteenth-century family to the table.

Diets and Nutrition

Although the accomplishments of doctors and hospitals are constantly in the limelight today, the greater, if less spectacular, part of medicine is preventive medicine. The great breakthrough of the second half of the nineteenth century was the development of public health techniques—proper sanitation and mass vaccinations—to prevent outbreaks of communicable diseases. Even before the nineteenth century, prevention was the key to longer life. Good clothing, warm, dry housing, and plentiful food make for healthier populations, much more capable of battling off disease. Clothing and housing for the masses probably improved only modestly in the eighteenth century, but the limited modification of the three-field system and increased agricultural output had a beneficial effect. The average European ate more and better food and was healthier as a result in 1800 than in 1700. This pattern is apparent in the fare of the laboring poor.

At the beginning of the eighteenth century, ordinary men and women depended on grain as fully as they had in the past. Bread was quite literally the staff of life. Peasants in the Beauvais region of France ate two pounds of bread a day, washing it down with water, green wine, beer, or a little skimmed milk. Their dark bread was made from a mixture of rough-ground wheat and rye—the standard flour of the poor. The poor also ate grains in soup and gruel. In rocky northern Scotland, for example, people depended on oatmeal, which they often ate half-cooked so it would swell in their stomachs and make them feel full. No wonder, then, that the supply of grain and the price of bread were always critical questions for most of the population.

The poor, rural and urban, also ate a fair quantity of vegetables. Indeed, vegetables were considered "poor people's food." Peas and beans were probably the most common; grown as field crops in much of Europe since the Middle Ages, they were eaten fresh in late spring and summer. Dried, they became the basic ingredients in the soups and stews of the long winter months. In most regions, other vegetables, primarily cabbages, carrots, and wild greens, appeared in season on the tables of the poor. Fruit was uncommon and limited to the summer months.

The European poor loved meat and eggs, but they seldom ate their fill. Meat was too expensive. When the poor did eat meat—on a religious holiday or at a wedding or other special occasion—it was most likely lamb or mutton. Sheep could survive on rocky soils and did not compete directly with humans for the slender resources of grain.

Milk was rarely drunk. It was widely believed that milk caused sore eyes, headaches, and a variety of ills, except among the very young and very old. Milk was used primarily to make cheese and butter, which the poor liked but could afford only occasionally. Medical and popular opinion considered whey, the watery liquid left after milk was churned, "an excellent temperate drink."

The diet of the rich—aristocrats, officials, and the comfortable bourgeoisie—was traditionally quite different from that of the poor. The men and women of the upper classes were rapacious carnivores, and a person's standard of living and economic well-being were often judged by the amount of meat eaten. A truly elegant dinner among the great and powerful consisted of one rich meat after another—a chicken pie, a leg of lamb, a grilled steak, for example. Three separate meat courses might be followed by three fish courses, laced with piquant sauces and complemented with sweets, cheeses, and nuts of all kinds. Fruits and vegetables were not often found on the tables of the rich. The long-standing dominance of meat and fish in the diet of the upper classes continued throughout the eighteenth century. There was undoubtedly great overeating.

There was also an enormous amount of overdrinking among the rich. The English squire, for example, who loved to ride with his hounds, loved drink with a similar passion. He became famous as the "four-bottle man." With his dinner he drank red wine from France or white wine from the Rhineland, and with his dessert he took sweet but strong port or Madeira from Portugal. Sometimes he ended the evening under the table in a drunken stupor.

The diet of small traders, master craftsmen, minor bureaucrats—the people of the towns and cities—was probably less monotonous than that of the peasantry. The markets, stocked by market gardens in the outskirts, provided a substantial variety of meats, vegetables, and fruits, although bread and beans still formed the bulk of the poor family's diet.

There were also regional dietary differences in 1700. Generally speaking, northern Atlantic Europe ate better than southern Mediterranean Europe. The poor of England probably ate best of all. Contemporaries on both sides of the English Channel often contrasted the Englishman's consumption of meat with the French peasant's greater dependence on bread and vegetables. The Dutch were also considerably better fed than the average European, in large part because of their advanced agriculture and diversified gardens.

The Impact of Diet on Health

How were the poor and the rich served by their quite different diets? Good nutrition depends on a balanced supply of food as well as on an adequate number of calories. Modern research has shown that the chief determinant of nutritional balance is the relationship between carbohydrates (sugar and starch) and proteins. A diet consisting primarily of carbohydrates is seriously incomplete.

At first glance, the diet of the laboring poor, relying as it did on carbohydrates, seems unsatisfactory. Even when a peasant got his daily two or three pounds of bread, his supply of protein and essential vitamins would seem too low. A closer look reveals a brighter picture. Most bread was "brown" or "black," made from wheat or rye. The flour of the eighteenth century was a whole-meal flour produced by stone grinding. It contained most of the bran—the ground-up husk—and the all-important wheat germ. The bran and germ contain higher proportions of some minerals, vitamins, and good-quality proteins than does the rest of the grain. Only when they are removed does bread become a foodstuff providing relatively more starch and less of the essential nutrients.

In addition, the field peas and beans eaten by poor people since Carolingian days contained protein that complemented the proteins in whole-meal bread. The proteins in whey, cheese, and eggs, which the poor ate at least occasionally, also supplemented the value of the protein in the bread and vegetables. Indeed, a leading authority concludes that if a pint of milk and some cheese and whey were eaten each day, the balance of the poor people's diet "was excellent, far better indeed than in many of our modern diets."[12]

The basic bread-and-vegetables diet of the poor in normal times was satisfactory. It protected effectively against most of the disorders associated

Le Nain: Peasant Family   A little wine and a great deal of dark bread: the traditional food of the poor French peasantry accentuates the poetic dignity of this masterpiece, painted about 1640 by Louis Le Nain. *(Source: Louvre/Cliché des Musées Nationaux, Paris)*

with a deficiency of the vitamin B complex, for example. The lack of sugar meant that teeth were not so plagued by cavities. Constipation was almost unknown to peasants and laborers living on coarse cereal breads, which provided the roughage that modern diets lack. The common diet of the poor also generally warded off anemia, although anemia among infants was not uncommon.

The key dietary problem was probably getting enough green vegetables (or milk), particularly in the late winter and early spring, to ensure adequate supplies of vitamins A and C. A severe deficiency of vitamin C produces scurvy, a disease that leads to rotting gums, swelling of the limbs, and weakness. Before the season's first vegetables, many people had used up their bodily reserves of vitamin C and were suffering from mild cases of scurvy. Sailors on long voyages suffered most. By the end of the sixteenth century the exceptional antiscurvy properties of lemons and limes led to the practice of supplying some crews with a daily ration of lemon juice, which had highly beneficial effects.

The practice of gorging on meat, sweets, and spirits caused the rich their own nutritional problems. They, too, were very often deficient in vitamins A and C because of their great disdain for fresh vegetables. Gout was a common affliction of the overfed and underexercised rich. No wonder they were often caricatured dragging their flabby limbs and bulging bellies to the table, to stuff their swollen cheeks and poison their livers. People of moderate means, who could afford some meat and dairy products with fair regularity but who had not abandoned the bread and vegetables of the poor, were probably best off from a nutritional standpoint.

New Foods and New Knowledge

In nutrition and food consumption, Europe in the early eighteenth century had not gone beyond its medieval accomplishments. This situation began to change markedly as the century progressed. Although the introduction of new methods of farming was confined largely to the Low Countries and England, a new food—the potato—came to the aid of the poor everywhere.

Introduced into Europe from the Americas, along with corn, squash, tomatoes, chocolate, and many other useful plant products, the humble potato is an excellent food. It contains a good supply of carbohydrates and calories and is rich in vitamins A and C, especially if it is not overcooked and the skin is eaten. The lack of green vegetables was one of the biggest deficiencies in a poor person's winter and early spring diet. Potatoes, which gave a much higher caloric yield than grain for a given piece of land, provided the needed vitamins and helped prevent scurvy. Doctors, increasingly aware of the dietary benefits of potatoes, prescribed them for the general public and in institutions such as schools and prisons.

For some poor people with little land the potato replaced grain as the primary food in the eighteenth century. This happened first in Ireland, where in the seventeenth century rebellion had led to English repression and the perfection of a savage system of exploitation. The foreign (and Protestant) English landlords took the best land, forcing large numbers of poor (and Catholic) peasants to live off tiny scraps of rented ground. By 1700 the poor in Ireland lived almost exclusively on the bountiful fruits of the potato plot. This dependence placed the Irish in a precarious position, and when the usually dependable potato crop failed in 1845 and 1846, there was widespread famine and starvation.

Elsewhere in Europe, potatoes took hold more slowly. Because many people did not like to eat them, potatoes were first fed to pigs and livestock, and there was considerable debate over whether they were fit for humans. In Germany the severe famines caused by the Seven Years' War (1756–1763) settled the matter: potatoes were edible and not famine food. By the end of the century, the potato was an important dietary supplement in much of Europe.

There was also a general growth of market gardening and a greater variety of vegetables in towns and cities. Potatoes, cabbages, peas, beans, radishes, spinach, asparagus, lettuce, parsnips, carrots, and other vegetables were sold in central markets and streets. In the course of the eighteenth century, the large towns and cities of maritime Europe began to receive, from Portugal and the West Indies, semitropical fruit such as oranges, lemons, and limes.

The growing variety of food was matched by some improvement in knowledge about diet and nutrition. For the poor, such improvement was limited primarily to the insight that the potato and other root crops improved health in the winter and helped to prevent scurvy. The rich began to be aware of the harmful effects of their meat-laden, wine-drowned meals.

The waning influence of ancient medical teachings was another aspect of progress. The Roman synthesis of ancient medical doctrines held that the four basic elements—air, fire, water, and earth—combine to produce in each person a complexion and a corresponding temperament. Foods were grouped into four categories appropriate for each complexion. Galen's notions dominated the dietary thinking of the seventeenth-century medical profession. Galen had said, for instance, that "the flesh of a hare preventeth fatness, causeth sleep and cleanseth the blood," and so on for a thousand maladies.

The growth of scientific experimentation in the seventeenth century led to a generally beneficial questioning of the old views. Haphazardly, by trial and error, and influenced by advances in chemistry, saner ideas developed. Not all changes in the eighteenth century were for the better, however. Bread began to change, most noticeably in England. Rising incomes and new tastes led to a shift from whole-meal black or brown bread to white bread made from finely ground and sifted flour. On the Continent, such white bread was generally limited to the well-to-do. To the extent that the preferred wheaten flour was stone-ground and sifted for coarse particles only, white bread remained satisfactory. But the desire for "bread as white as snow" was already leading to a deterioration in quality.

The coarser bran and at least some of the germ were already being sifted out to some extent. Bakers in English cities added the chemical alum to their white loaves to make them smoother, whiter, and larger. In the nineteenth century, "improvements" in milling were to lead to the removal of almost all the bran and germ from the flour, leaving it perfectly white and greatly reduced in nutritional value.

Another sign of nutritional decline was the growing consumption of sweets in general and sugar in particular. Initially a luxury, sugar dropped rapidly in price as slave-based production increased in the Americas, and it was much more widely used in the eighteenth century. This development probably led to an increase in cavities and to other ailments as well. Of course the poverty of the laboring poor saved most of them from the problems of the rich and well-to-do.

The Medical Professionals

Advances in medical science played a very small part in improving the health and lengthening the lives of people in the eighteenth century. Such seventeenth-century advances as William Harvey's discovery of the circulation of blood were not soon translated into better treatment. The sick had to await the medical revolution of the later nineteenth century for much help from doctors.

Yet developments in medicine reflected the general thrust of the Enlightenment. The focus on discovering the laws of nature and on human problems gave rise to a great deal of research and experimentation. The century saw a remarkable rise in the number of doctors, and a high value was placed on their services. Thus when the great breakthroughs in knowledge came in the nineteenth century, they could be rapidly diffused and applied.

Care of the sick was the domain of several competing groups—faith healers, apothecaries, surgeons, and physicians. Since the great majority of common ailments have a tendency to cure themselves, each group could point to successes and win adherents. When a doctor's treatment made a patient worse, as it often did, the original medical problem could always be blamed.

Faith healers, who had been one of the most important kinds of physicians in medieval Europe, remained active. They and their patients believed that demons and evil spirits caused disease by lodging in people and that the proper treatment was to exorcise or drive out the offending devil. This demonic view of disease was strongest in the countryside, as was faith in the healing power of religious relics, prayer, and the laying on of hands. Faith healing was particularly effective in the treatment of mental disorders like hysteria and depression, where the link between attitude and illness is most direct.

Apothecaries, or pharmacists, sold a vast number of herbs, drugs, and patent medicines for every conceivable "temperament and distemper." Early pharmacists were seldom regulated, and they frequently diagnosed as freely as the doctors whose prescriptions they filled. Their prescriptions were incredibly complex—a hundred or more drugs might be included in a single prescription—and often very expensive. Some of the drugs undoubtedly worked: strong laxatives were routinely administered to the rich for their constipated bowels.

Much purging was clearly harmful, and only bloodletting for the treatment of disease was more effective in speeding patients to their graves.

Drugs were prescribed and concocted in a helter-skelter way. With so many different drugs being combined, it was impossible to isolate cause and effect. Nor was there any standardization. A complicated prescription filled by ten different pharmacists would result in ten different preparations with different medical properties.

Surgeons competed vigorously with barbers and "bone benders," the forerunners of chiropractors. The eighteenth-century surgeon (and patient) labored in the face of incredible difficulties. Almost all operations were performed without any pain-killer, for anesthesia was believed too dangerous. The terrible screams of people whose limbs were being sawed off shattered hospitals and battle-fields. Such operations were common because a surgeon faced with an extensive wound sought to obtain a plain surface that he could cauterize with fire. Thus, if a person broke an arm or a leg and the bone stuck out, off came the limb. Many patients died from the agony and shock of these operations.

Surgery was also performed in the midst of filth and dirt. There simply was no knowledge of bacteriology and the nature of infection. The simplest wound treated by a surgeon festered, often fatally. In fact, surgeons encouraged wounds to fester in the belief that the pus was beneficially removing the base portions of the body.

Physicians, the fourth major group, were trained like surgeons. They were apprenticed in their teens to a practicing physician for several years of on-the-job training. This training was then rounded out with hospital work or some university courses. To their credit, physicians in the eighteenth century were increasingly willing to experiment with new methods, but tradition lay heavily on them. Bloodletting was still considered a medical cure-all. It was the way "bad blood," the cause of illness, was removed and the balance of humors necessary for good health restored. According to a physician practicing medicine in Philadelphia in 1799, bleeding was proper at the onset of all inflammatory fevers, in all inflammations, and for "asthma, sciatic pains, coughs, headaches, rheumatisms, the apoplexy, epilepsy, and bloody fluxes."[13] It was also necessary after all falls, blows, and bruises.

Physicians, like apothecaries, laid great stress on purging. They also generally believed that disease was caused by bad odors, and for this reason they carried canes whose heads contained ammonia salts. As they made their rounds in the filthy, stinking hospitals, physicians held their canes to their noses to protect themselves from illness.

While faith healers were praying, apothecaries purging, surgeons sawing, and physicians bleeding, the growth of scientific experimentation from the seventeenth century onward led to a generally beneficial questioning of old views. In the eighteenth century, the leading medical thinkers attempted to pull together and assimilate all the accumulated information and misinformation, to systematize medicine around simple, basic principles, as Newton had done in physics. But the schools of thought resulting from such speculation and theorizing did little to improve medical care. Proponents of animism explained life and disease in terms of *anima,* the "sensitive soul," which they believed was present throughout the body and prevented its decay and self-destruction. Proponents of vitalism stressed "the vital principle," which they believed inhabited all parts of the body. Vitalists tried to classify diseases systematically.

More interesting was the homeopathic system of Samuel Hahnemann of Leipzig. Hahnemann believed that very small doses of drugs that produce certain symptoms in a healthy person would cure a sick person with those symptoms. This theory was probably preferable to most eighteenth-century treatments, in that it was a harmless alternative to the extravagant and often fatal practices of bleeding, purging, drug taking, and induced vomiting. The patient gained confidence, and the body had at least a fighting chance of recovering.

Hospitals and Mental Illness

Hospitals were terrible throughout most of the eighteenth century. There was no isolation of patients. Operations were performed in the patient's bed. The nurses were old, ignorant, greedy, and often drunk women. Fresh air was considered harmful, and infections of every kind were rampant. Diderot's article in the *Encyclopedia* on the Hôtel-Dieu in Paris, the "richest and most terrify-

Hospital Life   Patients crowded into hospitals like this one in Hamburg in 1746 had little chance of recovery. A priest by the window administers last rites, while in the center a surgeon coolly saws off the leg of a man who has received no anesthesia. *(Source: Germanisches Nationalmuseum, Nuremberg)*

ing of all French hospitals," vividly describes normal conditions of the 1770s:

Imagine a long series of communicating wards filled with sufferers of every kind of disease who are sometimes packed three, four, five or even six into a bed, the living alongside the dead and dying, the air polluted by this mass of unhealthy bodies, passing pestilential germs of their afflictions from one to the other, and the spectacle of suffering and agony on every hand. That is the Hôtel-Dieu.

The result is that many of these poor wretches come out with diseases they did not have when they went in, and often pass them on to the people they go back to live with. Others are half-cured and spend the rest of their days in an invalidism as hard to bear as the illness itself; and the rest perish, except for the fortunate few whose strong constitutions enable them to survive.[14]

No wonder the poor of Paris hated hospitals and often saw them as a plot to kill paupers.

In the last years of the century, the humanitarian concern already reflected in Diderot's description of the Hôtel-Dieu led to a movement for hospital reform throughout western Europe. Efforts were made to improve ventilation and eliminate filth, on the grounds that bad air caused disease. The theory was wrong, but the results were beneficial: the spread of infection was somewhat reduced.

Mental hospitals, too, were incredibly savage institutions. The customary treatments for mental illness were bleeding and cold water, administered more to maintain discipline than to effect a cure. Violent persons were chained to the wall and forgotten. A breakthrough of sorts occurred in the 1790s, when William Tuke founded the first humane sanatorium in England. In Paris an innovative warden, Philippe Pinel, took the chains off the mentally disturbed in 1793 and tried to treat them as patients rather than as prisoners.

In the eighteenth century, there were all sorts of wildly erroneous ideas about mental illness. One was that moonlight caused madness, a belief reflected in the word *lunatic*—someone harmed by lunar light. Another mid-eighteenth-century theory, which persisted until at least 1914, was that masturbation caused madness, not to mention acne, epilepsy, and premature ejaculation. Thus parents, religious institutions, and schools waged relentless war on masturbation by males, although they were curiously uninterested in female masturbation. In the nineteenth century, this misguided idea was to reach its greatest height, resulting in increasingly drastic medical treatment. Doctors ordered their "patients" to wear mittens, fitted them with wooden braces between the knees, or simply tied them up in straitjackets.

Medical Experiments and Research

In the second half of the eighteenth century, medicine in general turned in a more practical and experimental direction. Some of the experimentation was creative quackery involving the recently discovered phenomenon of electricity. One magnificent quack, James Graham of London, opened a great hall filled with the walking sticks, crutches, eyeglasses, and ear trumpets of supposedly cured patients, which he kept as symbols of his victory over disease. Graham's principal treatment involved his Celestial Bed, which was lavishly decorated with electrical devices and which cost £100 for a single night—a great sum of money.

The rich could buy expensive treatments, but the prevalence of quacks and the general lack of knowledge meant that they often got little for their money. Because so many treatments were harmful, the poor were probably much less deprived by their almost total lack of access to medical care than one might think.

Renewed experimentation and the intensified search for solutions to human problems also led to some real, if still modest, advances in medicine after 1750. The eighteenth century's greatest medical triumph was the conquest of smallpox.

With the progressive decline of bubonic plague, smallpox became the most terrible of the infectious diseases. In the words of the nineteenth-century historian Thomas Macaulay, "smallpox was always present, filling the churchyard with corpses, tormenting with constant fears all whom it had not stricken." It is estimated that 60 million Europeans died of it in the eighteenth century and

that fully 80 percent of the population was stricken at some point in life. If ever a human problem cried out for solution, it was smallpox.

The first step in the conquest of this killer came in the early eighteenth century. Lady Mary Wortley Montague, an English aristocrat whose great beauty had been marred by the pox, learned about the practice of inoculation in the Ottoman Empire while her husband was serving there as British ambassador. She had her son successfully inoculated in Constantinople and was instrumental in spreading the practice in England after her return in 1722.

Inoculation against smallpox had long been practiced in the Middle East. The skin was deliberately broken, and a small amount of matter taken from a pustule of a smallpox victim was applied. The person thus contracted a mild case of smallpox that gave lasting protection against further attack. Inoculation was risky, however, and about one person in fifty died from it. In addition, people who had been inoculated often spread the disease, so the practice of inoculation against smallpox was widely condemned in the 1730s.

Success in overcoming this problem in British colonies led the British College of Physicians in 1754 to strongly advocate inoculation. Moreover, a successful search for cheaper methods led to something approaching mass inoculation in England in the 1760s. On the Continent, the well-to-do were also inoculated, beginning with royal families like those of Maria Theresa and Catherine the Great. The practice then spread to the middle classes. Smallpox inoculation played some part in the decline of the death rate in the late eighteenth century and the increase in population.

The final breakthrough against smallpox came at the end of the century. Edward Jenner (1749–1823), a talented country doctor, noted that in the English countryside there was a long-standing belief that dairy maids who had contracted cowpox did not get smallpox. Cowpox produces sores on the cow's udder and on the hands of the milker. The sores resemble those of smallpox, but the disease is mild and not contagious.

For eighteen years Jenner practiced a kind of Baconian science, carefully collecting data on protection against smallpox by means of cowpox. Finally, in 1796 he performed his first vaccination on a young boy, using matter taken from a milkmaid with cowpox. Two months later he inoculated the boy with smallpox pus, but the disease did not develop. In the next two years, twenty-three successful vaccinations were performed, and in 1798 Jenner published his findings. There was some skepticism and hostility, but after Austrian medical authorities replicated Jenner's results, the new method of treatment spread rapidly. Smallpox soon declined to the point of disappearance in Europe and then throughout the world. Jenner eventually received a prize of £30,000 from the British government for his great discovery, a fitting recompense for a man who gave an enormous gift to humanity and helped lay the foundation for the science of immunology in the nineteenth century.

RELIGION AND CHRISTIAN CHURCHES

Although the critical spirit of the Enlightenment spread among the educated elite in the eighteenth century, the great mass of ordinary men and women remained firmly committed to the Christian religion, especially in rural areas. Religion offered answers to life's mysteries and gave comfort and courage in the face of sorrow and fear. Religion also remained strong because it was embedded in local traditions and everyday social experience.

Yet the popular religion of village Europe was everywhere enmeshed in church hierarchies and state power—powerful outside forces that sought to regulate religious life at the local level. The resulting tensions helped set the scene for a vigorous religious revival in Germany and England.

The Institutional Church

As in the Middle Ages, the local parish church remained the basic religious unit all across Europe. Still largely coinciding with the agricultural village, the parish fulfilled many needs. The parish church was the focal point of religious devotion, which went far beyond sermons and Holy Communion. In Roman Catholic and Orthodox areas, the parish church organized colorful processions and pilgrimages to local shrines. Even in Protestant countries, where such activities were severely restricted, congregations gossiped and swapped stories after services, and neighbors came together in church for baptisms, marriages, funerals, and

special events. The local church was woven into the very fabric of community life.

Moreover, the local church had important administrative tasks. Priests and parsons were truly the bookkeepers of agrarian Europe, and it is because the parish registers are so complete that historians have learned so much about population and family life. Parishes also normally distributed charity to the destitute, looked after orphans, and provided whatever primary education was available.

The many tasks of the local church were usually the responsibility of a resident priest or pastor, a full-time professional working with assistants and lay volunteers. Moreover, all clerics—whether Catholic, Protestant, or Orthodox—shared the fate of middlemen in a complicated institutional system. Charged most often with ministering to poor peasants, the priest or parson was the last link in a powerful church-state hierarchy that was everywhere determined to control religion down to the grassroots. However, the regulatory framework of belief, which went back at least to the fourth century, when Christianity became the official religion of the Roman Empire, had undergone important changes since 1500.

The Protestant Reformation had begun as a culmination of medieval religiosity and a desire to purify Christian belief. Martin Luther, the greatest of the reformers (see pages 537–545), preached that all men and women were saved from their sins and from God's damnation only by personal faith in Jesus Christ. The individual could reach God directly, without need of priestly intermediaries. Luther's revolutionary concept of a "priesthood of all believers" broke forever the monopoly of the priestly class over medieval Europe's most priceless treasure—eternal salvation.

As the Reformation gathered force, with peasant upheaval and doctrinal competition, Luther turned more conservative. The monkish professor called on willing German princes to put themselves at the head of official churches in their territories. Other monarchs in northern Europe followed suit. Protestant authorities, with generous assistance from state-certified theologians like Luther, then proceeded to regulate their "territorial churches" strictly, selecting personnel and imposing detailed rules. They joined with Catholics to crush the Anabaptists (see page 548), who with their belief in both freedom of conscience and separation of church and state had become the real revolutionaries. Thus the Reformation, initially so radical in its rejection of Rome and its stress on individual religious experience, eventually resulted in a bureaucratization of the church and local religious life in Protestant Europe.

The Reformation era also increased the practical power of Catholic rulers over "their" churches, but only in the eighteenth century did some Catholic monarchs begin to impose striking reforms. These reforms, which had their counterparts in Orthodox Russia, had a very "Protestant" aspect. They increased state control over the Catholic church, making it less subject to papal influence.

Spain provides a graphic illustration of changing church-state relations in Catholic lands. A deeply Catholic country with devout rulers, Spain nevertheless took firm control of ecclesiastical appointments. Papal proclamations could not even be read in Spanish churches without prior approval from the government. Spain also asserted state control over the Spanish Inquisition (see page 533), which had been pursuing heretics as an independent agency under Rome's direction for two hundred years. In sum, Spain went far toward creating a "national" Catholic church, as France had done earlier.

A more striking indication of state power and papal weakness was the fate of the Society of Jesus. As the most successful of the Catholic Reformation's new religious orders (see page 556), the well-educated Jesuits were extraordinary teachers, missionaries, and agents of the papacy. In many Catholic countries, the Jesuits exercised tremendous political influence because individual members held high government positions. Jesuit colleges formed the minds of Europe's Catholic nobility. Yet, by playing politics so effectively, the Jesuits eventually raised a broad coalition of enemies, which destroyed their order. Especially bitter controversies over the Jesuits rocked the entire Catholic hierarchy in France. Following the earlier example of Portugal, Louis XV (1715–1774) ordered the Jesuits out of France in 1763 and confiscated their property. France and Spain then pressured Rome to dissolve the Jesuits completely. In 1773, reluctantly, Pope Clement XIV caved in, although the order was revived after the French Revolution.

Some Catholic rulers also turned their reforming efforts on monasteries and convents, believing that the large monastic clergy should make a more practical contribution to social and religious life.

Austria, a leader in controlling the church (see page 680), showed how far the process could go. Whereas Maria Theresa sharply restricted entry into "unproductive" orders, Joseph II recalled the radical initiatives of the Protestant Reformation. In his Edict on Idle Institutions, Joseph abolished contemplative orders, henceforth permitting only orders engaged in teaching, nursing, or other practical work. The number of monks plunged from 65,000 to 27,000. The state also expropriated the dissolved monasteries and used their great wealth for charitable purposes and higher salaries for ordinary priests.

Catholic Piety

Catholic territorial churches also sought to purify religious practice somewhat. As might be expected, Joseph II went the furthest. Above all, he and his agents sought to root out what they considered to be idolatry and superstition. Yet pious peasants saw only an incomprehensible attack on the true faith and drew back in anger. Joseph's sledgehammer approach and the resulting reaction dramatized an underlying tension between Christian reform and popular piety after the Reformation.

Protestant reformers had taken very seriously the commandment that "Thou shalt not make any graven image" (Exodus 20:4), and their radical reforms had reordered church interiors. Relics and crucifixes had been permanently removed from crypt and altar, and stained-glass windows had been smashed and walls and murals covered with whitewash. Processions and pilgrimages, saints and shrines—all such nonessentials had been rigorously suppressed in the attempt to recapture the vital core of the Christian religion. Such revolutionary changes had often troubled ordinary churchgoers, but by the late seventeenth century, these reforms had been thoroughly routinized by official Protestant churches.

The situation was quite different in Catholic Europe around 1700. First of all, the visual contrast was striking. Baroque art (see pages 601–603) had lavished rich and emotionally exhilarating figures and images on Catholic churches just as Protestants had removed theirs. From almost every indication, people in Catholic Europe remained intensely religious. More than 95 percent of the population probably attended church

"Clipping the Church"   The ancient English ceremony of dancing around the church once each year on the night before Lent undoubtedly had pre-Christian origins, for its purpose was to create a magical protective chain against evil spirits and the devil. The Protestant reformers did their best to stamp them out, but such "pagan practices" sometimes lingered on. *(Source: Somerset Archaeological and Natural History Society)*

for Easter Communion, the climax of the Catholic church year.

Much of the tremendous popular strength of religion in Catholic countries reflected that its practice went far beyond Sunday churchgoing and was an important part of community life. Thus, although Catholics reluctantly confessed their sins to the priest, they enthusiastically joined together in public processions to celebrate the passage of the liturgical year. In addition to the great proces-sional days—such as Palm Sunday, the joyful re-enactment of Jesus's triumphal entry into Jerusa-lem, and Rogations, with its chanted supplications and penances three days before the bodily ascent of Jesus into heaven on Ascension Day—each par-ish had its own local processions. Led by its priest, a congregation might march around the village or across the countryside to a local shrine or chapel. There were endless variations. In the southern French Alps, the people looked forward to "high-mountain" processions in late spring. Parishioners from miles around came together on some high mountain. The assembled priests asked God to bless the people with healthy flocks and pure waters, and then all joined together in an enormous picnic. Before each procession, the priest explained its religious significance to kindle group piety. But processions were also folklore and tradition, an escape from work and a form of recreation. A holiday atmosphere sometimes reigned on longer processions, with drinking and dancing and couples disappearing into the woods.

Devout Catholics held many religious beliefs that were marginal to the Christian faith, often of obscure or even pagan origin. On the Feast of Saint Anthony, priests were expected to bless salt and bread for farm animals to protect them from disease. One saint's relics could help cure a child of fear, and there were healing springs for many ailments. The ordinary person combined a strong Christian faith with a wealth of time-honored superstitions.

Parish priests and Catholic hierarchies were frequently troubled by the limitations of their parishioners' Christian understanding. One parish priest in France, who kept a daily diary, lamented that his parishioners were "more superstitious than devout . . . and sometimes appear as baptized idolators."[15]

Many parish priests in France, often acting on instructions from their bishops, made an effort to purify popular religious culture. One priest tried to abolish pilgrimages to a local sacred spring of Our Lady reputed to revive dead babies long enough for a proper baptism. French priests denounced particularly the "various remnants of paganism" found in popular bonfire ceremonies during Lent, in which young men, "yelling and screaming like madmen," tried to jump over the bonfires in order to help the crops grow and protect themselves from illness. One priest saw rational Christians turning back into pagan animals—"the triumph of Hell and the shame of Christianity."[16]

Yet, whereas Protestant reformers had already used the power of the territorial state to crush such practices, Catholic church leaders generally proceeded cautiously in the eighteenth century. They knew that old beliefs—such as the belief common throughout Europe that the priest's energetic ringing of church bells and his recitation of ritual prayers would protect the village from hail and thunderstorms—were an integral part of the

people's religion. Thus Catholic priests and hierarchies generally preferred a compromise between theological purity and the people's piety, realizing perhaps that the line between divine truth and mere superstition is not easily drawn.

Protestant Revival

By the late seventeenth century, official Protestant churches had completed their vast reforms and had generally settled into complacency. In the Reformation heartland, one concerned German minister wrote that the Lutheran church "had become paralyzed in forms of dead doctrinal conformity" and badly needed a return to its original inspiration.[17] This voice was one of many that would prepare and then guide a powerful Protestant revival, a revival largely successful because it answered the intense but increasingly unsatisfied needs of common people.

The Protestant revival began in Germany. It was known as "Pietism," and three aspects help explain its powerful appeal. First, Pietism called for warm emotional religion that everyone could experience. Enthusiasm—in prayer, in worship, in preaching, in life itself—was the key concept. "Just as a drunkard becomes full of wine, so must the congregation become filled with spirit," exclaimed one writer. Another stated simply, "The heart must burn."[18]

Second, Pietism reasserted the earlier radical stress on the "priesthood of all believers," thereby reducing the large gulf between the official clergy and the Lutheran laity—a gulf that continued to exist after the Reformation. Bible reading and study were enthusiastically extended to all classes and provided a powerful spur for popular education as well as for individual religious development. Finally, Pietists believed in the practical power of Christian rebirth in everyday affairs. Reborn Christians were expected to lead good, moral lives and come from all walks of life.

Pietism had a major impact on John Wesley (1703–1791), who served as the catalyst for popular religious revival in England. Wesley came from a long line of ministers, and when he went to Oxford University to prepare for the clergy, he mapped a fanatically earnest "scheme of religion." Like some students during final exam period, he organized every waking moment. After becoming a teaching fellow at Oxford, he organized the

Holy Club for similarly minded students, who were soon known contemptuously as "Methodists" because they were so methodical in their devotion. Yet, like the young Luther, Wesley remained intensely troubled about his own salvation, even after his ordination as an Anglican priest in 1728.

Wesley's anxieties related to grave problems of the faith in England. The Church of England was shamelessly used by the government to provide favorites with high-paying jobs and sinecures. The building of churches practically stopped although the population grew, and in many parishes there was a grave shortage of pews. Services and sermons had settled into an uninspiring routine. That the properly purified religion had been separated from local customs and social life was symbolized by church doors that were customarily locked on weekdays. Moreover, the skepticism of the Enlightenment was making inroads among the educated classes, and deism was becoming popular. Some bishops and church leaders acted as if they believed that doctrines like the Virgin Birth and the Ascension were little more than elegant superstitions.

Living in an atmosphere of religious decline and uncertainty, Wesley became profoundly troubled by his lack of faith in his own salvation. Yet spiritual counseling from a sympathetic Pietist minister from Germany prepared Wesley for a mystical, emotional "conversion" in 1738. He described this critical turning point in his *Journal:*

In the evening I went to a Christian society in Aldersgate Street where one was reading Luther's preface to the Epistle to the Romans. About a quarter before nine, while he was describing the change which God works in the heart through faith in Christ, I felt my heart strangely warmed. I felt I did trust in Christ, Christ alone for salvation; and an assurance was given me that he had taken away my sins, even mine, and saved me from the law of sin and death.[19]

Wesley's emotional experience resolved his intellectual doubts. Moreover, he was convinced that any person, no matter how poor or simple, might have a similar heartfelt conversion and gain the same blessed assurance.

Wesley took the good news to the people. Since existing churches were often overcrowded and the church-state establishment was hostile, Wesley preached in open fields. People came in large numbers. Of critical importance, Wesley expanded on earlier Dutch theologians' views and emphatically rejected Calvinist predestination—the doctrine of salvation granted only to a select few (see page 546). He preached that all men and women who earnestly sought salvation might be saved. It was a message of hope and joy, of free will and universal salvation. Traveling some 225,000 miles by horseback and preaching more than 40,000 sermons in fifty years, Wesley's ministry won converts, formed Methodist cells, and eventually resulted in a new denomination.

Evangelicals in the Church of England and in the old dissenting groups also followed Wesley's example, giving impetus to an even broader awakening among the lower classes. In England, as throughout Europe, despite different churches and different practices, religion remained a vital force in the lives of the people.

John Wesley preached that all who truly believe in Christ may gain eternal salvation. Shown here preaching from his father's tomb, Wesley waited until the 1780s to organize the Methodists into a separate denomination. *(Source: E. T. Archive)*

SUMMARY

In recent years, imaginative research has greatly increased understanding of ordinary life and social patterns in the past. The human experience, as recounted by historians, has become richer and more meaningful, and many mistaken ideas have fallen. This has been particularly true of eighteenth-century preindustrial Europe. The world of everyday labor, the intimacies of family life, the contours of women's history and of childhood, and vital problems of medicine and religion are emerging from obscurity. This deepened understanding of the common people can shed light on the great political and economic developments that occurred in the West in the late eighteenth and early nineteenth centuries (developments considered in Chapters 25 and 26).

NOTES

1. Quoted in E. E. Rich and C. H. Wilson, eds., *Cambridge Economic History of Europe,* vol. 4 (Cambridge: Cambridge University Press, 1967), p. 85.
2. Quoted in S. Chapman, *The Lancashire Cotton Industry* (Manchester, England: Manchester University Press, 1903), p. 13.
3. Quoted in J. M. Beattie, "The Criminality of Women in Eighteenth-Century England," *Journal of Social History* 8 (Summer 1975): 86.
4. W. L. Langer, "Infanticide: A Historical Survey," *History of Childhood Quarterly* 1 (Winter 1974): 357
5. Quoted in R. Cobb, *The Police and the People: French Popular Protest, 1789–1820* (Oxford: Clarendon Press, 1970), p. 238.
6. Quoted in E. A. Wrigley, *Population and History* (New York: McGraw-Hill, 1969), p. 127.
7. Quoted in D. S. Landes, ed., *The Rise of Capitalism* (New York: Macmillan, 1966), pp. 56–57.
8. See L. A. Tilly, J. W. Scott, and M. Cohen, "Women's Work and European Fertility Patterns," *Journal of Interdisciplinary History* 6 (Winter 1976): 447–476.
9. J. Michelet, *The People,* trans. with an introduction by J. P. McKay (Urbana, Ill.: University of Illinois Press, 1973; original publication, 1846), pp. 38–39.
10. Quoted in B. W. Lorence, "Parents and Children in Eighteenth-Century Europe," *History of Childhood Quarterly* 2 (Summer 1974): 1–2.
11. Ibid., pp. 13, 16.
12. J. C. Drummond and A. Wilbraham, *The Englishman's Food: A History of Five Centuries of English Diet,* 2d ed. (London: Jonathan Cape, 1958), p. 75.
13. Quoted in L. S. King, *The Medical World of the Eighteenth Century* (Chicago: University of Chicago Press, 1958), p. 320.
14. Quoted in R. Sand, *The Advance to Social Medicine* (London: Staples Press, 1952), pp. 86–87.
15. Quoted in I. Woloch, *Eighteenth-Century Europe: Tradition and Progress, 1715–1789* (New York: Norton, 1982), p. 292.
16. Quoted in T. Tackett, *Priest and Parish in Eighteenth-Century France* (Princeton, N.J.: Princeton University Press, 1977), p. 214.
17. Quoted in K. Pinson, *Pietism as a Factor in the Rise of German Nationalism* (New York: Columbia University Press, 1934), p. 13.
18. Quoted ibid., pp. 43–44.
19. Quoted in S. Andrews, *Methodism and Society* (London: Longmans, Green, 1970), p. 327.

SUGGESTED READING

Though long ignored in many general histories of the world, social topics of the kind considered in this chapter have come into their own in recent years. The articles cited in the Notes are typical of the exciting work being done, and the reader is strongly advised to take time to look through recent volumes of some leading journals: *Journal of Social History, Past and Present, History of Childhood Quarterly,* and *Journal of Interdisciplinary History.* In addition, the number of book-length studies has expanded rapidly and continues to do so.

Two fine books on the growth of population are C. Cipolla's short and lively *The Economic History of World Population* (1962) and T. McKeown's scholarly *The Modern Rise of Population* (1977). W. McNeill, *Plagues and Peoples* (1976), is also noteworthy. B. H. Slicher van Bath, *The Agrarian History of Western Europe, A.D. 500–1850* (1963), is a wide-ranging general introduction to the gradual transformation of European agriculture. J. Blum, *The End of the Old Order in Rural Europe* (1978), is an impressive comparative study. Two recommended and complementary studies on landowning nobilities are R. Forster, *The Nobility of Toulouse in the Eighteenth Century* (1960), and G. E. Mingay, *English Landed Society in the Eighteenth Century* (1963). E. L. R. Ladurie, *The Peasants of Languedoc* (1976), a brilliant and challenging study of rural life in southern France for several centuries, complements J. Goody et al., eds., *Family and Inheritance: Rural Society in Western Europe, 1200–1800* (1976). Life in small-town preindustrial France comes alive in P. Higonnet, *Pont-de-Montvert:*

Social Structure and Politics in a French Village, 1700–1914 (1971), and O. Hufton deals vividly and sympathetically with rural migration, work, women, and much more in *The Poor in Eighteenth-Century France* (1974). F. Braudel, *Civilization and Capitalism, 15th–18th Century* (1981–1984), is a monumental and highly recommended three-volume synthesis of social and economic development. Another exciting work is J. Nef, *War and Human Progress* (1968), which examines the impact of war on economic and industrial development in European history between about 1500 and 1800 and may be compared with M. Gutmann, *War and Rural Life in the Early Modern Low Countries* (1980).

Among general introductions to the history of the family, women, and children, J. Casey, *The History of the Family* (1989), is recommended. P. Laslett, *The World We Have Lost* (1965), is an exciting, pioneering investigation of England before the Industrial Revolution, though some of his conclusions have been weakened by further research. L. Stone, *The Family, Sex and Marriage in England, 1500–1800* (1977), is a brilliant general interpretation, and L. Tilly and J. Scott, *Women, Work and Family* (1978), is excellent. Two valuable works on women, both with good bibliographies, are M. Boxer and J. Quataert, eds., *Connecting Spheres: Women in the Western World, 1500 to the Present* (1987), and R. Bridenthal, C. Koonz, and S. Stuard, eds., *Becoming Visible: Women in European History*, 2d ed. (1987). P. Ariès, *Centuries of Childhood: A Social History of Family Life* (1962), is another stimulating study. E. Shorter, *The Making of the Modern Family* (1975), is a lively controversial interpretation, which should be compared with the excellent study by M. Segalen, *Love and Power in the Peasant Family: Rural France in the Nineteenth Century* (1983). T. Rabb and R. I. Rothberg, eds., *The Family in History* (1973), is a good collection of articles dealing with both Europe and the United States. A. MacFarlane, *The Family Life of Ralph Josselin* (1970), is a brilliant re-creation of the intimate family circle of a seventeenth-century English clergyman who kept a detailed diary; MacFarlane's *Origins of English Individualism: The Family, Property and Social Transition* (1978) is a major work. I. Pinchbeck and M. Hewitt, *Children in English*

Society (1973), is a good introduction. Various aspects of sexual relationships are treated imaginatively by M. Foucault, *The History of Sexuality* (1981), and R. Wheaton and T. Hareven, eds., *Family and Sexuality in French History* (1980).

J. Burnett, *A History of the Cost of Living* (1969), has a great deal of interesting information about what people spent their money on in the past and complements the fascinating work of J. C. Drummond and A. Wilbraham, *The Englishman's Food: A History of Five Centuries of English Diet* (1958). D. and R. Porter, *Patient's Progress: Doctors and Doctoring in Eighteenth-Century England* (1989), and M. Romsey, *Professional and Popular Medicine in France, 1770–1830* (1988) are recommended. Good introductions to the evolution of medical practices are B. Ingles, *History of Medicine* (1965); O. Bettmann, *A Pictorial History of Medicine* (1956); and H. Haggard's old but interesting *Devils, Drugs, and Doctors* (1929). W. Boyd, *History of Western Education* (1966), is a standard survey, which may be usefully supplemented by an important article by L. Stone, "Literacy and Education in England, 1640–1900," *Past and Present* 42 (February 1969): 69–139. M. D. George, *London Life in the Eighteenth Century* (1965), is a delightfully written book, and L. Chevalier, *Labouring Classes and Dangerous Classes* (1973), is a keen analysis of the poor people of Paris in a slightly later period. G. Rudé, *The Crowd in History, 1730–1848* (1964), is an innovative effort to see politics and popular protest from below. An important series edited by R. Forster and O. Ranum considers neglected social questions such as diet, abandoned children, and deviants, as does P. Burke's excellent study, *Popular Culture in Early Modern Europe* (1978). J. Gillis, *For Better, for Worse: Marriage in Britain Since 1500* (1985), admirably covers the subject.

Good works on religious life include J. Delumeau, *Catholicism Between Luther and Voltaire: A New View of the Counter-Reformation* (1977); B. Semmel, *The Methodist Revolution* (1973); and J. Bettey, *Church and Community: The Parish Church in English Life* (1979). Also see the work by Tackett cited in the Notes.

22

African Kingdoms and Societies, ca 1450–1800

The Oba of Benin flanked by his chieftains

frican states and societies of the fifteenth through eighteenth centuries represented a wide variety of languages, cultures, and kinds of economic and political development. European intrusion into Africa led to the transatlantic slave trade, one of the great forced migrations in world history. Africa helped substantially in building the West's industrial civilization. In the seventeenth century, an increasing desire for sugar in Europe resulted in an increasing demand for slave labor in South America and the West Indies. In the eighteenth century, Western technological changes created a demand for cotton and other crops that required extensive human labor. As a result, the West's "need" for slaves from Africa increased dramatically.

Africa's relationship with Asia, the Islamic world, and the West stretches back a very long time (see Chapter 15), but only recently have anthropologists, economists, and historians begun to ask critical questions about African societies in early modern times.

- What kinds of economic and social structures did African societies have?

- What impact did Islam have on African societies?

- What kinds of literary sources survive?

- What role did slavery play in African societies before European intrusion?

- What were the geographical and societal origins of the African slaves shipped to America and to Asia?

This chapter explores these questions.

SENEGAMBIA AND BENIN

In Africa in the mid-fifteenth century there were societies held together by family or kinship ties and kingdoms and states ruled by princes who governed defined areas through bureaucratic hierarchies. Along the 2,000-mile west coast between Senegambia and modern Cameroon, a number of kingdoms flourished. Because much of the coastal region is covered by tropical rain forest, in contrast to the western Sudan, it is called the "West African Forest Region" (Map 22.1). The Sene-

gambian states in the north possessed a homogeneous culture and a common history. For centuries Senegambia—named for the Senegal and Gambia rivers—had served as an important entrepôt for desert caravan contact with the Islamic civilizations of North Africa and the Middle East. Through the transatlantic slave trade, Senegambia contributed heavily to New World population in the early seventeenth century. That trade brought Senegambia into contact with Europe and the Americas. Thus Senegambia felt the impact of Islamic culture from the north and of European influences from the maritime West.

In the thirteenth century, the kingdoms of Ghana and Mali (see pages 469–475) had incorporated parts of Senegambia, but by 1450 several northern states, such as Wolof, were completely independent. Southern states like Kantora remained under Mali's hegemony. Mali's influence disintegrated after 1450, and successor kingdoms that were independent but connected to one another through family ties emerged. Stronger states rose and temporarily exercised power over weaker ones.

Scholars are still exploring the social and political structures of the various Senegambian states. The peoples of Senegambia spoke Wolof, Serer, and Pulaar, which are all members of the West African language group. Both the Wolof-speakers and the Serer-speakers had clearly defined classes: royalty, nobility, warriors, peasants, low-caste artisans such as blacksmiths and leatherworkers, and slaves. Slaves were individuals who were pawned for debt, house servants who could not be sold, and people who were acquired through war or purchase. Senegambian slavery varied from society to society but generally was not a benign institution. In some places the treatment of slaves was as harsh as treatment in the Western world later would be. However, many Senegambian slaves were not considered property to be bought and sold, and some served as royal advisers and enjoyed great power and prestige.[1]

The king of the Wolof was elected by the nobility. After his election the king immediately acquired authority and a special religious charisma. He commanded contingents of soldier-slaves and appointed village chiefs. The king gained his revenue from the chiefs, from merchants, and from taxes levied on defeated peoples.[2] The Wolof had a well-defined government hierarchy.

Among the stateless societies of Senegambia, where kinship and lineage groups tended to frag-

RrWPAS.

MAP 22.1 West African Kingdoms and Slave Trade, ca 1500–1800 Consider the role that rivers and other geographical factors played in the development of the West African slave trade. Why would Luanda and Benguela be the logical Portuguese source for slaves?

ment communities, age-grade systems evolved. Age-grades were groups of men and women whom the society initiated into adulthood at the same time. Age-grades cut across family ties, created communitywide loyalties, and provided a means of local law enforcement, since the group was responsible for the behavior of all its members.

The typical Senegambian community was a small self-supporting agricultural village of closely related families. Custom assigned a high value to cultivation of the land, the shared objective of the group; work was understood more in terms of social relationships than as labor in the abstract. Fields were cut from the surrounding forest, and the average farm of six or eight acres supported a moderate-size family. Often the family worked the land for a common harvest; sometimes individuals had their own private fields. Millet and sorghum were the staple grains in northern Senegambia; farther south, forest dwellers cultivated yams as a staple. Senegambians supplemented their diet with plantains, beans, and bananas. Fish, oysters, and small game such as rabbits and monkeys provided protein. Along the Guinea coast rice was the basic cereal, and okra, onions, melons, and pepper spiced the regular diet. Frequent fairs in neighboring villages served as markets for the exchange of produce and opportunities for outside news and social diversion. As one scholar has put it, "Life was simple, government largely limited to the settlement of disputes by family heads or elders, the basic economy scarcely more than the production and consumption of food, social life centered on the ceremony accompanying birth, death, and

The Oba of Benin The walls of the Oba's palace were decorated with bronze plaques that may date to the sixteenth to eighteenth centuries. This plaque vividly conveys the Oba's power, majesty, and authority. The necklace (or choker) is his symbol of royalty. Attendants hold up his hands, while warriors raise shields over his head as sunshades. *(Source: The Metropolitan Museum of Art, The Michael C. Rockefeller Memorial Collection, Gift of Nelson A. Rockefeller, 1965)*

family alliance, recreation preoccupied with the eternal round of visit and gossip which were the main pursuits of leisure time."[3]

The fifteenth and sixteenth centuries saw the emergence of the great forest kingdom of Benin in what is now southern Nigeria. Although scholars still know little about Benin's origins, its history seems to have been characterized by power struggles between the king and the nobility that neither side ever completely won. An elaborate court ceremonial exalted the position of the *oba*, or king, and brought stability to the state. In the later fifteenth century, the oba Ewuare played off his palace chiefs against the village chiefs and thereby maintained a balance of power. A great warrior, Ewuare strengthened his army and pushed Benin's borders as far as the Niger River on

the east, westward into Yoruba country, and south to the Gulf of Guinea (see Map 22.1). During the late sixteenth and seventeenth centuries the office of the oba evolved from a warrior kingship to a position of spiritual leadership.

At its height in the late sixteenth century, Benin controlled a vast territory, and European visitors described a sophisticated society. According to a modern historian, the capital, Benin City, "was a stronghold twenty-five miles in circumference, protected by walls and natural defenses, containing an elaborate royal palace and neatly laid-out houses with verandas and balustrades, and divided by broad avenues and smaller intersecting streets."[4] Visitors also noted that Benin City was kept scrupulously clean and had no beggars and that public security was so effective that theft was unknown.

In 1485 the Portuguese and other Europeans in pursuit of trade began to appear in Benin. A small exchange in pepper and slaves developed but never acquired importance in the Benin economy. Nor did the Portuguese have much success in converting the staunchly animistic people to Christianity. Europe's impact on Benin was minimal. In the late seventeenth century, Benin's tributary states seceded, and stronger neighbors nibbled at its frontiers. The exact reasons for Benin's decline in the eighteenth and nineteenth centuries remain uncertain.

THE SUDAN: SONGHAY, KANEM-BORNU, AND HAUSALAND

The kingdom of Songhay, a successor state of Ghana and Mali, dominated the whole Niger region of the western and central Sudan (see Map 22.1). Muhammad Toure (1492–1528) completed the expansionist and administrative consolidation begun by his predecessors. Muhammad Toure's power rested on his successful military expeditions. From his capital at Gao he extended his lordship as far north as the salt-mining center at Taghaz in the mid-Sahara and as far east as Agada and Kano. A convert to Islam, Muhammad made a pilgrimage to Mecca. Impressed by what he saw there, he tried to bring about greater centralization in his own territories. In addition to building a strong army and improving taxation procedures, he replaced local Songhay officials with more efficient Arab ones in an effort to substitute royal institutions for ancient kinship ties.

What kind of economy existed in the Songhay empire? What social structures? What role did women play in Songhay society? What is known of Songhay education and culture? The lack of written records and the paucity of surviving artifacts prevent scholars from satisfactorily exploring these questions. Some information is provided by Leo Africanus (ca. 1465–1550), a Moroccan captured by pirates and given as a slave to Pope Leo X. Leo Africanus became a Christian, taught Arabic in Rome, and in 1526 published an account of his many travels, including a stay in the Songhay kingdom.

As a scholar Leo was naturally impressed by Timbuktu, the second city of the empire, which he visited in 1513. "Here [is] a great store of doctors, judges, priests, and other learned men, that are bountifully maintained at the King's court," Leo reported.[5] Many of these Islamic scholars had studied in Cairo and other centers of Muslim learning. They gave Timbuktu a reputation for intellectual sophistication, religious piety, and moral justice.

Songhay under Muhammad Toure seems to have enjoyed economic prosperity. Leo Africanus noted the abundant food supply, which was produced in the southern savanna and carried to Timbuktu by a large fleet of canoes controlled by the king. The Sudanese had large amounts of money to spend, and expensive North African and European luxuries were much in demand: clothes, copperware, glass and stone beads, perfumes, and horses. The existence of many shops and markets implies the development of an urban culture. At Timbuktu, merchants, scholars and judges, and artisans constituted a distinctive bourgeoisie. The presence of many foreign merchants, including Jews and Italians, gave the city a cosmopolitan atmosphere. Jews largely controlled the working of gold, and after the expulsion of the Jews from Spain in 1492 (see page 532), Jewish refugees became active in the trade with the Sudan.

Slaves played a very important part in the economy of Songhay. On the royal farms scattered throughout the kingdom, slaves produced the staple crop, rice, for the royal granaries. Although slaves could possess their own slaves, land, and cattle, they could not bequeath any of this property; the king inherited all of it. Muhammad Toure greatly increased the number of royal slaves

through raids on the pagans (non-Muslims). He gave slaves to favorite Muslim scholars, who thus gained a steady source of income. Or the slaves were sold at the large market at Gao. Traders from North Africa bought them for sale in Cairo, Istanbul, Lisbon, Naples, Genoa, and Venice. The sugar plantations of Sicily and the domestic households of Portugal and northern Italy (see page 508) had a constant demand for slaves, some of whom came from Songhay.

Sixteenth-Century Ivory Salt Cellar Mande-speaking people of Bullom (modern Sierra Leone in West Africa) carved this beautiful egg-shaped salt container, which is supported by intricately carved African men and women. *(Source: Courtesy of the Trustees of the British Museum)*

The kingdom of Songhay had considerable economic and cultural strengths, but it also had serious internal problems. Islamic institutions never took root in the countryside, and Muslim officials alienated the king from his people. Muhammad Toure's reforms were a failure. He governed a diverse group of peoples—Tuareg, Malinke, Fulani, as well as Songhai—who were often hostile to one another, and no cohesive element united them. Finally, the Songhai never developed an effective method of transferring power. Revolts, conspiracies, and palace intrigues followed the deaths of every king, and only three of the nine rulers in the dynasty begun by Muhammad Toure died natural deaths. Muhammad himself was murdered by one of his sons. His death began a period of political instability that led to the slow disintegration of the kingdom.[6]

In 1582 the sultanate of Morocco began to press southward in search of a greater share of the trans-Saharan trade. The people of Songhay, lacking effective leadership and believing the desert to be a sure protection against invasion, took no defensive precautions. In 1591 a Moroccan army of three thousand soldiers—many of whom were slaves of European origin equipped with European muskets—crossed the Sahara and inflicted a crushing defeat on the Songhai at Tondibi. This battle spelled the end of the Songhay Empire. Although a moderate-size kingdom lingered on in the south for a century or so and weak political units arose, not until the eighteenth century did kingdoms able to exercise wide authority emerge again.

To the east of Songhay lay the kingdoms of Kanem-Bornu and Hausaland (see Map 22.1). Under the dynamic military leader Idris Alooma (1571–1603), Kanem-Bornu subdued weaker peoples and gained jurisdiction over an extensive area. Well drilled and equipped with firearms, camel-mounted cavalry and a standing army decimated warriors fighting with spears and arrows. Idris Alooma perpetuated the feudal pattern of government in which lands were granted to able fighters in return for loyalty and the promise of future military assistance. Meanwhile agriculture occupied most people, peasants and slaves alike. Kanem-Bornu shared in the trans-Saharan trade, shipping eunuchs and young girls to North Africa in return for horses and firearms. A devout Muslim, Idris Alooma elicited high praise from Ibn Fartura, who wrote a history of his reign called *The Kanem Wars:*

So he made the pilgrimage and visited Medina with delight. . . . He was enriched by visiting the tomb of the pious Companions of the Prophet, the chosen, the perfect ones. . . . Then he prepared to return to the kingdom of Bornu. When he reached the land called Barak east of Lake Chad he killed all the inhabitants who were warriors. They were strong but after this they became weak. . . . Among the benefits which God . . . conferred upon the Sultan Idris Alooma was the acquisition of Turkish musketeers and numerous household slaves who became skilled in firing muskets.

Hence the Sultan was able to kill the people of Amsaka with muskets, and there was no need for other weapons, so that God gave him great victory by reason of his superiority in arms.

Among the most surprising of his acts was the stand he took against obscenity and adultery, so that no such thing took place openly in his time. Formerly the people had been indifferent to such offences. . . . In fact he was a power among his people and from him came their strength.

The Sultan was intent on the clear path laid down by the Qur'an . . . in all his affairs and actions.[7]

Idris Alooma built mosques at his capital city of N'gazargamu and substituted Muslim courts and Islamic law for African tribunals and ancient customary law. His eighteenth-century successors lacked his vitality and military skills, however, and the empire declined.

Between Songhay and Kanem-Bornu were the lands of the Hausa. An agricultural people living in small villages, the Hausa grew millet, sorghum, barley, rice, cotton, and citrus fruit and raised livestock. Some Hausa merchants carried on a heavy trade in slaves and kola nuts with North African communities across the Sahara. Obscure trading posts evolved into important Hausa city-states like Kano and Katsina, through which Islamic influences entered the region. Kano and Katsina became Muslim intellectual centers and in the fifteenth century attracted scholars from Timbuktu. The Muslim chronicler of the reign of King Muhammad Rimfa of Kano (r. 1463–1499) records that Muhammad introduced the Muslim practices of *purdah*, or seclusion of women, of the *idal-fitr*, or festival after the fast of Ramadan, and of assigning eunuchs to the high offices of state.[8] The expansion of Islam into sub-Saharan Africa may have slightly reduced the slave trade, since the Qur'an forbade Muslims to enslave fellow Muslims. As in Songhay and Kanem-Bornu, however, Islam made no strong imprint on the mass of the Hausa people until the nineteenth century.

ETHIOPIA

At the beginning of the sixteenth century, the powerful East African Christian kingdom of Ethiopia extended from Massawa in the north to several tributary states in the south (see Map 15.1). The ruling Solomonid dynasty, however, faced serious troubles. Adal, a Muslim state along the southern base of the Red Sea, began incursions into Ethiopia, and in 1529 the Adal general Ahmad ibn-Ghazi inflicted a disastrous defeat on the Ethiopian emperor Lebna Dengel (r. 1508–1540). Ahmad followed up his victory with systematic devastation of the land, destruction of many Ethiopian artistic and literary works, and the forced conversion of thousands to Islam. Lebna Dengel fled to the mountains and appealed to Portugal for assistance. The Portuguese, eager for a share in the wealth of the East African coast and interested in the conversion of Ethiopia to Roman Catholicism, responded with a force of musketeers. In 1541 they decisively defeated the Muslims near Lake Tana.

St. George in Ethiopian Art   This image of a black St. George slaying a dragon from a seventeenth-century Ethiopian manuscript attests to the powerful and pervasive Christian influence in Ethiopian culture. *(Source: The British Library)*

MAP 22.2 East Africa, Sixteenth Century In early modern times, the Christian kingdom of Ethiopia, first isolated and then subjected to Muslim and European pressures, played an insignificant role in world affairs. But the East African city-states, which stretched from Sofala in the south to Mogadishu in the north, had powerfully important commercial relations with Mughal India, China, the Ottoman world, and southern Europe.

No sooner had the Muslim threat ended than Ethiopia encountered three more dangers. The Galla, Cushitic-speaking peoples, moved northward in great numbers, occupying portions of Harar, Shoa, and Amhara. The Ethiopians could not defeat them militarily, and the Galla were not interested in assimilation. For the next two centuries the two peoples lived together in an uneasy truce. Simultaneous with the Galla migrations was the Ottoman Turks' seizure of Massawa and other coastal cities; the Ethiopian emperor could not dislodge them. Then the Jesuits arrived, eager to capitalize on earlier Portuguese support, and attempted to force Roman Catholicism on a proud people whose form of Christianity long antedated the European version. The overzealous Jesuit missionary Alphonse Mendez tried to revamp the Ethiopian liturgy, rebaptize the people, and replace ancient Ethiopian customs and practices with Roman ones. Since Ethiopian national sentiment was closely tied to Coptic Christianity, violent rebellion and anarchy ensued. In 1633 the Jesuit missionaries were expelled. For the next two centuries hostility to foreigners, weak political leadership, and regionalism characterized Ethiopia. Civil conflicts between the Galla and the Ethiopians erupted continually. The Coptic church, though lacking strong authority, survived as the cornerstone of Ethiopian national identity.

THE SWAHILI CITY-STATES

The Swahili city-states on the east coast of Africa enjoyed a worldwide reputation for commercial prosperity in the late fifteenth century (Map 22.2). Mogadishu, Mombasa, Kilwa, and Sofala continued their ancient trade with the Arabian and Persian Gulf ports and also exchanged ivory, gold, and slaves for Indian beads and Chinese silks, textiles, and porcelains. Kilwa dominated the lesser states, including Sofala, through which poured gold from the inland mines. The cities' culture was cosmopolitan, and their standard of living, based on inland agriculture, was very high.

The arrival of the Portuguese explorer Vasco da Gama (see Map 18.1) in 1498 spelled the end of the Swahili cities' independence. Da Gama wanted to build a Portuguese maritime empire in the Indian Ocean, and between 1502 and 1507 the

Dutch Colony, Cape of Good Hope Founded in 1657, by the mid-eighteenth century the Cape Colony had 15,000 inhabitants and may have been the largest European settlement on the African continent. Here crews took on fresh provisions, repaired their ships, and awaited favorable winds for crossing the Indian Ocean. *(Source: William Fehr Collection)*

southern ports of Kilwa, Zanzibar, and Sofala fell before Portuguese guns and became Portuguese tributary states. The better-fortified northern cities, such as Mogadishu, survived as important entrepôts for goods to India. But the Portuguese victory in the south proved hollow: rather than accept Portuguese commercial restrictions, the residents deserted the towns and the town economies crumbled. Large numbers of Kilwa's people, for example, immigrated to northern cities. The flow of gold from inland mines to Sofala slowed to a trickle. Swahili passive resistance successfully prevented the Portuguese from gaining control of the local coastal trade.

Initially lured to the Indian Ocean by the spice trade, the Portuguese wanted a station on the East African coast. After the intermittent bombardment of several cities, Portugal finally won an administrative stronghold near Mombasa in 1589. Called Fort Jesus, it remained a Portuguese base for over a century. In the late seventeenth century, pressures from the northern European maritime powers—the Dutch, French, and English—aided greatly by the Arabs of Oman, combined with local African rebellions to bring about the collapse of Portuguese influence in Africa. A Portuguese presence remained only at Mozambique in the far south.

TABLE 22.1 ESTIMATED SLAVE IMPORTS BY DESTINATION, 1451–1870

Destination	Estimated Total Slave Imports
British North America	399,000
Spanish America	1,552,100
British Caribbean	1,665,000
French Caribbean	1,600,200
Dutch Caribbean	500,000
Danish Caribbean	28,000
Brazil	3,646,800
Old World	175,000
	9,566,100

Source: P. D. Curtin, The Atlantic Slave Trade: A Census (Madison, Wis.: University of Wisconsin Press, 1969), p. 268. Used with permission.

The Portuguese made no religious or cultural impact on the Swahili cities. Their sole effect was the cities' economic decline.

THE TRANSATLANTIC SLAVE TRADE

By the sixteenth century, slavery had a long history in Africa; and the transatlantic slave trade is properly understood against that background even though the transatlantic slave trade actually began in 1493, when Christopher Columbus returned to Spain from the West Indies with a few hundred Indian slaves. "Slavery was . . . fundamental to the social, political, and economic order of parts of the northern savanna, Ethiopia and the East African coast. . . . Enslavement was an organized activity, sanctioned by law and custom. Slaves were a principal commodity in trade, including the export sector, and slaves were important in the domestic sphere" as concubines, servants, soldiers and ordinary laborers[9] (see page 467).

Islam had heavily influenced African slavery, partly because before 1500 the major foreign market for slaves was North Africa and the Middle East and partly because Islam had exerted a strong cultural influence in many of the states and societies of the northern savanna, the Ethiopian highlands, and the East African coast. African rulers justified enslavement with the Muslim argument

that prisoners of war could be sold; and, since captured peoples were considered chattel, they could be used in the same positions that prevailed in the Muslim world. Between 650 and 1600, Muslims transported perhaps as many as 4.82 million black slaves across the trans-Saharan trade route.[10] When the transatlantic slave trade began, it represented little that was new.

Until recently scholars advanced two basic theories about the transatlantic slave trade. One school of thought, proposed by the defenders, held that the transatlantic slave trade "freed" Africans from the "barbarism" of their own society, which sanctioned human sacrifice, cannibalism, and its own form of slavery. This thesis was a self-serving rationalization of economic exploitation. The other school of thought, first set forth by abolitionists, pointed out that the Atlantic slave trade destroyed African kingdoms that had had well-developed civilizations since the time of the Egyptian pharaohs and maintained that the slave trade itself was a form of barbarism and the source of Africa's woes. This theory oversimplified very complicated issues and failed to address significant questions. For one thing, the later Egyptian pharaohs were of Macedonian, not black, sub-Saharan descent. Furthermore, what regions of Africa were the sources of slaves? How were the slaves treated? What goods and business procedures were involved in the exchange of slaves? What were the economic, social, political, and demographic effects of the slave trade on African societies?

The search for a sea route to India led the Portuguese in the fifteenth century to explore the West African coast. Having "discovered" Brazil in 1500, the Portuguese founded a sugar colony at Bahia in 1551. Between 1551 and 1575, before the traffic to North America had gotten under way, the Portuguese delivered more African slaves to Brazil than would ever reach British North America (Table 22.1). Portugal essentially monopolized the slave trade until 1600 and continued to play a large role in the seventeenth century, though increasingly threatened by the Dutch, French, and English. From 1690 until the House of Commons abolished the slave trade in 1807, England was the leading carrier of African slaves.

Population density and supply conditions along the African coast and the sailing time to New World markets determined the sources of slaves. As the demand for slaves rose, slavers moved down the West African coast from Senegambia to the more densely populated hinterlands of the Bights of Benin and Biafra. In the sixteenth and early seventeenth centuries, the Senegambian coast and the area near the mouth of the Congo River yielded the greatest numbers. By the late seventeenth century the British found the Ivory Coast region the most profitable territory. A century later the Bight of Benin and the Gold Coast had become the largest suppliers. The abundant supply of slaves in Angola, the region south of the Congo River (see Map 18.5), however, and the quick passage from Angola to Brazil and the Caribbean had established that region as the major coast for slavers. The Portuguese acquired the bulk of their slaves from Angola.

Transatlantic wind patterns partly determined the routes of exchange. Shippers naturally preferred the swiftest crossing—that is, from the African port nearest the latitude of the intended American destination. Thus Portuguese shippers carried their cargoes from Angola to Brazil, and British merchants sailed from the Bight of Benin to the Caribbean. The great majority of slaves were intended for the sugar and coffee plantations extending from the Caribbean islands to Brazil.[11]

Angola produced 26 percent of all African slaves and 70 percent of all Portuguese slaves. Trading networks extending deep into the interior culminated at two major ports on the Angolan coast, Luanda and Benguela (see Map 22.1). Between the 1730s and 1770s Luanda shipped between 8,000 and 10,000 slaves each year; at the end of the eighteenth century Benguela's numbers equaled those of Luanda. In 1820, the peak year, 18,957 blacks left Luanda. Although a few slaves were acquired through warfare, the Portuguese secured the vast majority through trade with African dealers. Whites did not participate in the inland

City of Luanda, Angola Founded by the Portuguese in 1575, Luanda was a center of the huge slave trade to Brazil. In this eighteenth-century print, offices and warehouses line the streets, while (right foreground) slaves are dragged to the ships for transportation to America. *(Source: New York Public Library, Astor, Lenox, and Tilden Foundations)*

Cross Section of a Slave Ship Packed, literally like sardines in a can, and forced to endure this method of transportation for weeks at sea (or until death): thus were thousands of blacks shipped from Angola to Brazil. *(Source: Library of Congress)*

markets. Almost all Portuguese shipments went to satisfy the virtually insatiable Brazilian demand for slaves.[12]

The slave trade lasted for almost four centuries and involved the brutalization and exploitation of millions of human beings. Here is an excerpt from the report in 1793 of a Portuguese doctor with experience on the Middle Passage between Angola and Brazil:

When the slaves coming from many different parts of the interior reach the maritime ports of Africa, they are there once more traded for goods and merchandise. . . .

Here takes place the second round of hardships that these unlucky people are forced to suffer. . . . They are terribly handled and most scantily provided for . . . their human nature entirely overlooked. The dwelling

place of the slave is simply the dirt floor of the compound, and he remains there exposed to harsh conditions and bad weather, and at night there are only a lean-to and some sheds . . . which they are herded into like cattle.

Their food continues scarce as before . . . limited at times to badly cooked beans, at other times to corn, also boiled, and at other times to beans mixed with corn to provide variety. They also add to the diet a small amount of salted fish, which abounds in Luanda and the kingdom of Angola. . . .

They suffer in other ways. When they are first traded, they are made to bear the brand mark of the backlander who enslaved them, so that they can be recognized in case they run away. And when they reach a port . . . , they are branded on the right breast with the coat of arms of the king and nation, of whom they have become vassals. . . . This mark is made with a hot silver instrument in the act of paying the king's duties, and this brand mark is called a carimbo.

They are made to bear one more brand mark. This one is ordered by their private master, under whose name they are transported to Brazil. . . .

In this miserable and deprived condition the terrified slaves remain for weeks and months, and the great number of them who die is unspeakable. With some ten or twelve thousand arriving at Luanda each year, it often happens that only six or seven thousand are finally transported to Brazil. . . .

Shackled in the holds of ships, the black slaves . . . are far more deprived than when on land. First of all, with two or three hundred slaves placed under the deck, there is hardly room enough to draw a breath. . . . The captains, aware of their own (financial) interests, recognize the seriousness of the problem, and they try to remedy it to some extent. . . . Each day they order a certain number of slaves brought on deck in chains to get some fresh air, not allowing more because of their fear of rebellion. However, very little is accomplished in this way, because the slaves must go down again into the hold. . . .

Second, the slaves are afflicted with a very short ration of water, of poor quality and lukewarm because of the climate—hardly enough to water their mouths. The suffering that this causes is extraordinary, and their dryness and thirst cause epidemics which, beginning with one person, soon spread to many others. Thus, after only a few days at sea, they start to throw the slaves into the ocean.

Third, they are kept in a state of constant hunger. Their small ration of food, brought over from Brazil on the outward voyage, is spoiled and damaged. . . . They add to each ration a small portion of noxious fish from the Atlantic Ocean, which decays during the voyage.[13]

Unlike Great Britain, France, and the Netherlands, Portugal did not have a strong mercantile class involved in slaving in the eighteenth century. Instead the Portuguese colony of Brazil provided the ships, capital, and goods for the slave trade. Credit played a major role in the trade: Brazilian-controlled firms in Luanda extended credit to African operators, who had to make payments in slaves six or eight months later. Portuguese ironware and wine, Brazilian tobacco and brandies, European and Asian textiles, firearms, and beads were the main goods exchanged for slaves. All commodities entered Angola from Brazil. The

Luandan (or Benguelan) merchants pegged the value of the goods to the value of prime young slaves, but then undervalued the worth of the slaves and overpriced the goods. As a result, the African operators frequently ended up in debt to the merchants.

Although the demand was great, Portuguese merchants in Angola and Brazil sought to maintain only a steady trickle of slaves from the African interior to Luanda and across the ocean to Bahia and Rio de Janeiro: a flood of slaves would have depressed the American market. Rio, the port capital through which most slaves passed, commanded the Brazilian trade. Planters and mine operators from the provinces traveled to Rio to buy slaves. Between 1795 and 1808, approximately 10,000 Angolans per year stood in the Rio slave market. In 1810 the figure rose to 18,000; in 1828 it reached 32,000.[14]

The English ports of London, Bristol, and particularly Liverpool dominated the British slave trade. In the eighteenth century Liverpool was the world's greatest slave-trading port. In all three cities, small and cohesive merchant classes exercised great public influence. The cities also had huge stores of industrial products for export, growing shipping industries, and large amounts of ready cash for investment abroad. Merchants generally formed partnerships to raise capital and to share risks; each voyage was a separate enterprise.

Slaving ships from Bristol searched the Gold Coast, the Bight of Benin, Bonny, and Calabar. The ships of Liverpool drew slaves from Gambia, the Windward Coast, and the Gold Coast. To Africa, British ships carried textiles, gunpowder and flint, beer and spirits, British and Irish linens, and woolen cloth. African dealers wanted to trade their slaves for an equivalent value in consumer goods. European traders wanted to sell their goods at a profit calculated in their own national currencies. Thus a system based on both barter and monetary exchange developed. A collection of goods was grouped together into what was called the "sorting." An English sorting might include bolts of cloth, firearms, alcohol, tobacco, and hardware; this batch of goods would be traded for an individual slave or a quantity of gold, ivory, or dyewood. When Europeans added a markup for profit, Africans followed suit. Currency was not exchanged; instead it served as a standard of value and a means of keeping accounts.[15]

Ashanti Staff Top In the early eighteenth century, the Ashanti of central Ghana expanded northward, subdued various peoples, and established a powerful successor state to the medieval African kingdoms of Ghana and Mali. The gold trade was the linchpin of its economic and political power. A splendid example of the Ashanti's superb skill in goldworking, this staff top reflects the region's proverbial wealth. *(Source: Lee Boltin Picture Library)*

European traders had two systems for exchange. First, especially on the Gold Coast, they established factory-forts. These fortified trading posts were expensive to maintain but proved useful for fending off rival Europeans. In the second, or shore, method of trading, European ships sent boats ashore or invited African dealers to bring traders and slaves out to the ships. The English captain John Adams, who made ten voyages to Africa between 1786 and 1800, described the shore method of trading at Bonny:

This place is the wholesale market for slaves, as not fewer than 20,000 are annually sold here; 16,000 of whom are natives of one nation called Ibo. . . . Fairs where the slaves of the Ibo nation are obtained are held every five or six weeks at several villages, which are situated on the banks of the rivers and creeks in the interior, and to which the African traders of Bonny resort to purchase them.

The preparation necessary for going to these fairs generally occupies the Bonny people some days. Large canoes . . . are launched and stored for the voyage. The traders augment the quantity of their merchandise, by obtaining from their friends, the captains of the slave ships, a considerable quantity of goods on credit. . . . Evening is the period chosen for the time of departure, when they proceed in a body, accompanied by the noise of drums, horns, and gongs. At the expiration of the sixth day, they generally return bringing with them 1,500 or 2,000 slaves, who are sold to Europeans the evening after their arrival, and taken on board the ships. . . .

It is expected that every vessel, on her arrival at Bonny, will fire a salute the instant the anchor is let go, as a compliment to the black monarch who soon afterwards makes his appearance in a large canoe, at which time, all those natives who happen to be alongside the vessel are compelled to proceed in their canoes to a respectful distance, and make way for his Majesty's barge. After a few compliments to the captain, he usually enquires after brother George, meaning the King of England, George III, and hopes he and his family are well. He is not pleased unless he is regaled with the best the ship affords. . . . His power is absolute; and the surrounding country, to a considerable distance, is subject to his dominion.[16]

The shore method of buying slaves allowed the ship to move easily from market to market. The final prices of the slaves depended on their ethnic origin, their availability when the shipper arrived, and their physical health when offered for sale in the West Indies or the North or South American colonies.

Meanwhile, according to one student, the northbound trade in slaves across the Sahara (see page 467) "continued without serious disruption until the late nineteenth century, and in a clandestine way and on a much reduced scale it survived well into the twentieth century."[17] Estimates of the numbers of slaves exported north to Algiers, Tripoli, and Cairo have ranged as high as 15 million for the sixteenth century alone, but that figure has been sharply disputed. The present scholarly consensus is that the trans-Saharan slave trade in the seventeenth and eighteenth centuries was never as important as the transatlantic trade. But it persisted.

Supplying slaves for the foreign market was in the hands of a small wealthy merchant class or was a state monopoly. Gathering a band of raiders and the capital for equipment, guides, and tolls, and maintaining raiders and captives before they reached the European or Muslim dealers, involved considerable expense. By contemporary standards, slave raiding was a costly operation. Only black entrepreneurs with sizable capital and labor could afford to finance and direct raiding drives. They exported slaves because the profits on exports were greater than the profits to be made from using labor in the domestic economy:

The export price of slaves never rose to the point where it became cheaper for Europeans to turn to alternative sources of supply, and it never fell to the point where it caused more than a temporary check to the trade. Consequently, Africa was able consistently to undercut all other potential suppliers. . . . The remarkable expansion of the slave trade in the eighteenth century provides a horrific illustration of the rapid response of producers in an underdeveloped economy to price incentives.[18]

Europeans initiated the Atlantic slave trade, but its continuation was made possible through an alliance between European shippers and African suppliers.

What economic impact did European trade have on African societies? Africans possessed technology well suited to their environment. Over the centuries they had cultivated a wide variety of plant foods, developed plant and animal husbandry techniques, and mined, smelted, and otherwise worked a great variety of metals. Apart from firearms, American tobacco and rum, and the cheap brandy brought by the Portuguese, European goods presented no novelty to Africans. What made foreign products desirable to Africans was their price. Traders of Indian hand-woven cotton textiles, Venetian imitations of African beads, and iron bars from European smelters could undersell African manufacturers. Africans exchanged slaves, ivory, gold, pepper, and animal skins for those goods. Their earnings usually were not retained in Africa. African states eager to expand or to control commerce bought European firearms, although the difficulty of maintaining guns often gave gun owners only marginal superiority over skilled bowmen.[19] The kingdom of Dahomey, however, built its power on the effective use of firearms.

The African merchants who controlled the production of exports gained from foreign trade. The king of Dahomey, for example, had a gross income in 1750 of £250,000 from the overseas export of slaves. A portion of his profits was spent on goods that improved the living standards of his people. Slave-trading entrepôts, which provided opportunities for traders and for farmers who supplied foodstuffs to towns, caravans, and slave ships, prospered. But such economic returns did not spread very far.[20] International trade did not lead to the economic development of Africa. Neither technological growth nor the gradual spread of economic benefits occurred in Africa in early modern times.

The arrival of Europeans did cause basic social changes in some West African societies. In Senegambia, chattel slavery seems to have been unknown before the growth of the transatlantic trade (see page 726). By the late eighteenth century, however, chiefs were using the slave labor of craftsmen, sailors, and farm workers. If the price was right, they were sold off. Those who committed crimes had traditionally paid fines, but because of the urgent demand for slaves, many misdemeanors became punishable by sale to slave dealers. Europeans introduced corn, pineapple, cassava, and sweet potatoes to West Africa, which had important consequences for population growth.

The intermarriage of French traders and Wolof women in Senegambia created a *métis* or mulatto class. In the emerging urban centers at Saint-Louis, this small class adopted the French lan-

TABLE 22.2 THE TRANSATLANTIC SLAVE TRADE, 1450–1900

Period	Volume	Percent
1450–1600	367,000	3.1
1601–1700	1,868,000	16.0
1701–1800	6,133,000	52.4
1801–1900	3,330,000	28.5
Total	11,698,000	100.0

Source: P. E. Lovejoy, Transformations in Slavery: A History of Slavery in Africa *(Cambridge: Cambridge University Press, 1983), p. 19. Used with permission.*

guage, the Roman Catholic faith, and a French manner of life. The métis exercised considerable political and economic power. When granted French citizenship in the late eighteenth century, its members sent Senegalese grievances to the Estates General of 1789.[21] However, European cultural influences did not penetrate West African society beyond the seacoast.

The political consequences of the slave trade varied from place to place. In the kingdom of the Congo the perpetual Portuguese search for slaves undermined the monarchy, destroyed political unity, and led to constant disorder and warfare; power passed to the village chiefs. Likewise in Angola, which became a Portuguese proprietary colony, the slave trade decimated and scattered the population and destroyed the local economy. By contrast, the military kingdom of Dahomey, which entered into the slave trade in the eighteenth century and made it a royal monopoly, prospered enormously from trading in slaves. The economic strength of the state rested on the slave trade. The royal army raided deep into the interior, and in the late eighteenth century Dahomey became one of the major West African sources of slaves. When slaving expeditions failed to yield sizable catches, and when European demands declined, the resulting depression in the Dahomeyan economy caused serious political unrest. Iboland inland from the Niger Delta, from whose great port cities of Bonny and Brass the British drained tens of thousands of slaves, experienced minimal political effects and suffered no permanent population loss. A high birthrate kept pace with the incursions of the slave

trade, and Ibo societies remained demographically and economically strong.

What of the overall demographic impact? Tables 22.1 and 22.2 report the somewhat divergent recent findings of two careful scholars. The total number of slaves who left Africa over a 400-year period seems to lie somewhere between 9 and 12 million. These numbers represent only the transatlantic slave trade. They do not include slaves exported from East Africa to Asia or across the Sahara to the Mediterranean and Europe. Furthermore, these are export figures; they do not include the approximately 10 to 15 percent who died during procurement or in transit. The demographic impact varied with time and place: the effect was obviously less severe in places where fewer blacks were enslaved, and African societies that raided the interior for slaves suffered less than did those that sold their own members. West Africa, a large supplier of slaves, lost an enormous labor supply, primarily of strong young men. The slaving coast of Angola suffered the greatest losses. Many African societies, particularly those organized in strong kingdoms, suffered no significant population loss.

The Atlantic slave trade was one of the great forced migrations of world history. It caused terrible misery and degradation, but the present scholarly consensus seems to be that the long-term demographic effects of the slave trade on the course of African history were slight.

SUMMARY

The period between 1400 and 1800 saw the rise of several different African societies. French culture influenced the coastal fringes of Senegambia; the English maintained factories along the Gold Coast; and the Portuguese held Angola as a colony and maintained an insecure grip on Mozambique in East Africa. Yet European influence hardly penetrated the African interior. And despite the export of as many as 12 million slaves from Africa to meet the labor needs of South and North America, the overall impact of the slave trade on Africa was marginal. It appeared around 1810 that Africa's development would be entirely autonomous.

NOTES

1. P. D. Curtin, *Economic Change in Precolonial Africa: Senegambia in the Era of the Slave Trade* (Madison, Wis.: University of Wisconsin Press, 1975), pp. 34–35; and J. A. Rawley, *The Transatlantic Slave Trade: A History* (New York: Norton, 1981), p. 12.
2. R. W. July, *A History of the African People,* 3d ed. (New York: Scribner's, 1980), pp. 128–129.
3. R. W. July, *Precolonial Africa: An Economic and Social History* (New York: Scribner's, 1975), p. 99.
4. July, *A History of the African People,* p. 141.
5. Quoted in R. Hallett, *Africa to 1875* (Ann Arbor: University of Michigan Press, 1970), p. 151.
6. See *The Cambridge History of Africa,* vol. 3, ca 1050 to 1600, ed. R. Oliver (Cambridge, England: Cambridge University Press, 1977), pp. 427–435.
7. A. ibn-Fartura, "The Kanem Wars," in *Nigerian Perspectives,* ed. T. Hodgkin (London: Oxford University Press, 1966), pp. 111–115.
8. "The Kano Chronicle," quoted in Hodgkin, pp. 89–90.
9. P. E. Lovejoy, *Transformations in Slavery: A History of Slavery in Africa* (Cambridge, England: Cambridge University Press, 1983), p. 19. This section leans heavily on Lovejoy's work.
10. See Table 2.1, "Trans-Saharan Slave Trade, 650–1600," in Lovejoy, p. 25.
11. Rawley, p. 45.
12. Ibid., pp. 41–47.
13. R. E. Conrad, *Children of God's Fire: A Documentary History of Black Slavery in Brazil* (Princeton, N.J.: Princeton University Press, 1983), pp. 20–23.
14. Rawley, pp. 45–47.
15. July, *A History of the African People,* p. 208.
16. J. Adams, "Remarks on the Country Extending from Cape Palmas to the River Congo," in Hodgkin, pp. 178–180.
17. A. G. Hopkins, *An Economic History of West Africa* (New York: Columbia University Press, 1973), p. 83.
18. Ibid., p. 105.
19. July, *Precolonial Africa,* pp. 269–270.
20. Hopkins, p. 119.
21. July, *A History of the African People,* pp. 201–202.

SUGGESTED READING

Students should have little difficulty finding interesting and sound material on the topics raised in this chapter. For Africa in the era of the slave trade, in addition to the titles given in the Notes, see D. Gamble, *The Wolof of Senegambia* (1967), which discusses Wolof economy, political structure, and social organization; A. F. C. Ryder, *Benin and the Europeans, 1485–1897* (1969); R. E. Bradbury, *Benin Studies* (1973), which contains useful articles on government, art, and society; and E. Isichei, *The Ibo People and the Europeans* (1973), which treats internal migrations and the impact of the slave trade on society. L. W. Henderson, *Angola: Five Centuries of Conflict* (1979), provides a good survey of the Portuguese in Angola. G. J. Bender, *Angola Under the Portuguese: The Myth and the Reality* (1978), focuses on the nineteenth and twentieth centuries with some background sections. For the Swahili city-states, C. S. Nicholls, *The Swahili Coast* (1971), is an important work. W. Bascom and M. J. Herskovits, eds., *Continuity and Change in African Cultures* (1959), treats many facets of African cultures with emphasis on linguistics and ethnohistory. The standard reference works on African history are R. Oliver, ed., *The Cambridge History of Africa,* vol. 3, ca 1050–1600 (1977), and R. Gray, ed., *The Cambridge History of Africa,* vol. 4, ca 1600–ca 1870 (1975).

23

The Middle East and India, ca 1450–1800

A marriage procession passing through a bazaar, Bilaspur or Mandi

The spiritual descendants of Muhammad controlled three vast and powerful empires around 1450: the Ottoman Empire centered in Anatolia, the Safavid Empire of Persia, and the Mughal Empire of India. From West Africa to central Asia, from the Balkans to Southeast Asia, Muslim arms pursued policies of territorial expansion. Between 1450 and 1800, these powerful Muslim kingdoms reached the zenith of their territorial extension and of their intellectual and artistic vitality. With the conquest of Constantinople in 1453 the Ottoman Turks gained an impregnable capital and the respect of all Islam. The Ottomans soon overran much of Anatolia, North Africa, and the Balkans. Lasting almost five hundred years (1453–1918), the Ottoman Empire was one of the largest and most enduring political entities in world history. In Persia the Safavid dynasty created a theocracy and presided over a brilliant culture. A theological dispute between the Ottomans and the Safavids brought bitter division in the Islamic world and weakened both powers. Meanwhile, the Mughal leader Babur and his successors conquered the Indian subcontinent, and Mughal rule inaugurated a period of radical administrative reorganization in India and the flowering of intellectual and architectural creativity.

In 1450 all the great highways of international trade were in Muslim hands, and the wealth of the Muslim states derived largely from commerce. By 1750 the Muslims had lost that control, and the Muslim states were declining economically, politically, and culturally.

- Who were the Ottomans and the Safavids?
- What political and religious factors gave rise to the Ottoman and Safavid empires?
- What were the sources of Ottoman and Safavid power, and how were the two empires governed?
- What intellectual developments characterized the Ottoman and Safavid cultures?
- What external and domestic difficulties caused the decline of the Ottoman Empire and Safavid Persia?
- How did Muslim government reform and artistic inspiration affect the dominant Hindu population in India?

- What political and social conditions in India enabled the British to expand their empire by gaining power there?

These are the questions explored in this chapter.

THE SPLENDOR OF THE OTTOMAN STATE

The Ottomans took their name from Osman (1299–1326), the ruler of a Turkish-speaking people in western Anatolia who began expansionist moves in the fourteenth century. The Ottomans gradually absorbed other peoples on the Anatolian peninsula, and the Ottoman state emerged as one of many small Turkish states during the breakup of the empire of the Seljuk Turks. The first Ottoman state thus occupied the border between Islam and Byzantine Christendom. The Ottoman ruler called himself "border chief," or leader of the *gazis,* frontier fighters in the *jihad,* or holy war. The earliest Ottoman historical source, a fourteenth-century saga, defines the *gazis* as the "instrument of God's religion . . . God's scourge who cleanses the earth from the filth of polytheism . . . God's pure sword."[1]

The principle of *jihad* was the cornerstone of Ottoman political theory and then of the Ottoman state. Europe was the frontier of the Muslim crusading mission. In 1389 in what is today southern Yugoslavia the Ottomans defeated a combined force of Serbs and Bosnians. In 1396, on the Danube in modern Bulgaria, they crushed King Sigismund of Hungary, who was supported by French, German, and English knights. The reign of Sultan Mehmet II (r. 1451–1481) saw the end of all Turkish dynasties in Anatolia and the Ottoman conquest of Constantinople, capital of the Byzantine Empire.

The six-week siege of Constantinople in 1453 remains one of the dramatic events in world history because Constantinople symbolized the continuation of imperial Rome. The Byzantine emperor Constantine IX Palaeologus (r. 1449–1453), with only about 10,000 men, relied on the magnificent system of circular walls and stone fortifications that had protected the city for a thousand years. Mehmet II had over 100,000 men and a large fleet, but iron chains spanning the harbor kept him out of the Golden Horn.

Western technology eventually decided the battle. A Hungarian working for the Ottomans cast huge bronze cannon on the spot (bringing raw materials to the scene of military action was easier than moving guns long distances).[2] When a cannon shot shattered a city gate, the Turks forced an entry. For three days the city suffered looting and rape. The Muslim historian Oruc described the conquest of Constantinople:

Sultan Mehmet, the son of Sultan Murad, inspired by zeal, said "in the cause of God" and commanded plunder. The gazis, entering by force on every side, found a way in through the breaches in the fortress made by the guns and put the infidels in the fortress to the sword. The way was opened to the rest of the soldiers. They came through the trenches and set up ladders. They threw these against the walls of the towers and climbed up them. Mounting on the tower they destroyed the infidels who were inside and entered the city. They looted and plundered. They seized their money and possessions and made their sons and daughters slaves. Sultan Mehmet also gave orders to plunder the houses. In this way what could be taken was taken. The Muslims took so much booty that the wealth gathered in Istanbul Constantinople since it was built 2400 years before became the portion of the gazis. They plundered for three days, and after three days plunder was forbidden.[3]

The conquest of Constantinople inaugurated the imperial phase of the Ottoman military state. The Ottoman emperors considered themselves successors of the Byzantine emperor—as their title *Sultan-i-Rum* ("Sultan of Rome") attests. They also continued to expand. In 1453 the Ottomans controlled only the northwest quadrant of Anatolia. Mehmet II completed the conquest of Anatolia. From Constantinople, their new capital, the Ottomans pushed down the Aegean and up the Adriatic. They so severely threatened Italy and southeastern Europe that the aged Pope Pius II himself shouldered the cross of the Crusader in 1464. The Ottoman Turks inspired such fear that even in distant Iceland the Lutheran Book of Common Prayer begged God for protection from "the cunning of the Pope and the terror of the Turk."

In 1480 a fleet took the Italian port of Otranto, and serious plans were laid for the conquest of all Italy. Only a disputed succession following the death of Mehmet II in 1481 caused the postponement of that conquest and, later, the cancellation of those plans. The political vacuum that characterized Italy in the late fifteenth century, and the ease with which the French conquered several Italian states after 1494 (see page 512) suggest that the history of Renaissance Italy and of all Europe would have been vastly different if the Turks had persisted.

Procession of Suleiman In 1533 the Dutch painter and print maker Pieter Coecke van Aelst visited Constantinople, where he sketched the design for this elegant scene. The triumphant procession of the sultan, with his officials and courtiers, through monuments brought from all over the Mediterranean world (notice the column with Egyptian hieroglyphics) captures the power of the Grand Turk. *(Source: The Metropolitan Museum of Art, Harris Brisbane Dick Fund, 1928)*

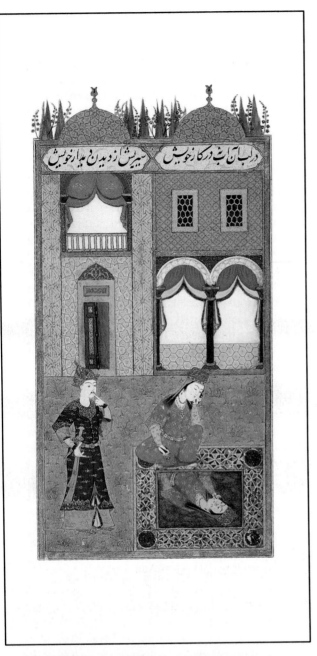

Royal Ottoman Couple This scene from a palace courtyard appears in a five-volume illustrated history (1560) of the rulers of the Ottoman house. The man's ivory-handled dagger, the lady's embroidered cap, and the jeweled belts of both display their fabulous wealth. Islamic painting very rarely showed a mirror image. *(Source: Courtesy of The Harvard University Art Museums (The Edward Binney 3rd Collection of Turkish Art))*

Selim the Grim (r. 1512–1520) gained the Ottoman throne by forcing his father's abdication and murdering his brother. A bloodthirsty and inflexible despot, Selim was, however, a superb military commander. Under his leadership, the Ottomans added Syria and Palestine (1516) and Egypt (1517) to their empire, and Ottoman rule was extended across North Africa to Cyrenaica, Tripolitania, Tunisia, and Algeria. Selim's reign marks the beginning of four centuries when most Arabs were under Ottoman rule.

Suleiman (r. 1520–1566), who brought to the throne great experience as a provincial administrator and enormous energy as a soldier, extended Ottoman jurisdiction to its widest geographical extent. He led his armies on thirteen major campaigns and many minor ones and spent ten years in the field. With Greece and the Balkans already under Ottoman domination, Suleiman's army crushed the Hungarians at Mohács in 1526, killing the king and thousands of his nobles. Suleiman seems to have taken this victory entirely as his due. Not long after the battle he recorded laconically in his diary, "The emperor, seated on a golden throne, receives the homage of the viziers and beys: massacre of 2,000 prisoners: the rains fall in torrents." Three years later the Turks besieged the Habsburg capital at Vienna. Once again, only an accident—the army's insistence on returning home before winter—prevented Muslim control of all central Europe. In virtually every area, the Ottomans' success was due to the weakness and political disunity of their enemies and to the superiority of Turkish military organization and artillery. Gunpowder, invented by the Chinese and adapted to artillery use by Europeans, played an influential role in the expansion of the Ottoman state.

Although victorious on land, the Ottomans did not enjoy complete dominion on the sea. The middle decades of the sixteenth century witnessed a titanic struggle between the Ottoman and Habsburg empires for control of the Mediterranean. In September 1538 an Ottoman naval victory at Preveze, the chief Turkish port in Albania, assured Turkish control of the Ionian and Aegean seas. Meanwhile, attacks from the island of Cyprus by Christian pirates on Ottoman shipping in the eastern Mediterranean provoked the sultan to conquer Cyprus in 1570. He introduced Ottoman administration and settled thousands of Turks from Anatolia there. (Thus began the large Turkish presence on Cyprus that continues to the present day.) In response, Pope Pius V organized the Holy League against the Turks. An armada of over 200 Spanish, Venetian, and papal galleys under the command of Don John of Austria, illegitimate son of Holy Roman Emperor Charles V sailed against a Turkish fleet under Uluç Ali Pasha. On October 7, 1571, the allied fleet smashed the Turks at Lepanto at the mouth of the Gulf of Patras in Greece. About 15,000 Turks were killed or captured, 10,000 Christian galley slaves were liberated, and the victors lost about 7,000 men. Scholars consider Lepanto the greatest naval battle since the Battle of Actium in 31 B.C. European churches rang with victory celebrations for the first major Ottoman defeat by Christian forces. Lepanto, however, marked no decisive change in Turkish hegemony: the Turks remained supreme on land and quickly rebuilt their entire fleet. Mastery of the sea continued to be contested.

Military organization dominated the Ottoman social and administrative systems, which reached classic form under Suleiman I. The seventeenth-century Ottoman historian Mustafa Naima divided Muslim society into producers of wealth, Muslim and non-Muslim, and the military. In Naima's view there could be no state without the military; wealth was needed to support the military; the state's subjects raised the wealth; subjects could prosper only through justice; and without the state there could be no justice.[4]

The ruling class consisted exclusively of Muslims, theoretically totally loyal to the sultan and fully immersed in the complex Islamic culture. Under Suleiman I, the Ottoman ruling class consisted in part of descendants of Turkish families that had formerly ruled parts of Anatolia. In return for bureaucratic service to the sultan, they held *trimars* (landed estates) on *sipahinek* (property) for the duration of their lifetimes. The ruling class had the usufruct but not the ownership of the land. Since all property belonged to the sultan and reverted to him on the holder's death, Turkish nobles—unlike their European counterparts—could not put down roots. Because there was no security of landholding and no hereditary nobility, the Ottoman Empire did not develop a feudal structure before 1600.

Slaves who had been purchased from Spain, North Africa, and Venice, captured in battle, and acquired through the system known as *devshirme*—by which the sultan's agents swept the provinces for Christian youths—were recruited for the imperial civil service and the army. Southern Europeans did not shrink from selling people into slavery, and, as the Ottoman *jihad* advanced in the fifteenth and sixteenth centuries, Albanian, Bosnian, Wallachian, and Hungarian slave boys filled Ottoman imperial needs. Moreover, because *devshirme* recruitment often meant social advancement, some Christian and Muslim parents bribed government officials to accept their children. All were converted to Islam. (Islamic law forbade the enslavement of Muslims but not of converts.) The brightest 10 percent entered the palace school, where they learned to read and write Arabic, Ottoman Turkish, and Persian, received special religious instruction, and were trained for the civil service. Other boys were sent to Turkish farms, where they acquired physical toughness in preparation for military service. Known as *janissaries* (Turkish for "recruits"), they formed the elite army corps. Thoroughly indoctrinated and absolutely loyal to the sultan, the janissary slave corps eliminated the influence of old Turkish families and played the central role in Ottoman military affairs in the sixteenth century. Some converted slaves of Slavic, Greek, and Armenian origin rose to high positions in the Ottoman state as theologians, poets, jurists, and generals.

All authority theoretically emanated from the sultan and flowed from him to his state servants: police officers, provincial governors, heads of the treasury, generals. The sultan frequently designated these men *pashas,* a title of distinction.

The reign of Suleiman I witnessed an extraordinary artistic flowering and represents the peak of Ottoman influence and culture (Map 23.1). In Turkish history Suleiman is known as *Kanuni* ("Lawgiver") because of his profound influence on the civil law. Suleiman ordered Lütfi Paşa (d. 1562), a poet of slave origin and juridical scholar, to draw up a new general code of laws. Published in Suleiman's name, this sultanic legal code prescribed penalties for such routine criminal acts as robbery, adultery, and murder. It also sought to reform bureaucratic and financial corruption in such areas as harem intervention in administrative affairs, foreign merchants' payment of bribes to avoid customs duties, imprisonment without trial, and promotion in the provincial administration according to ability rather than favoritism. The code also introduced the idea of a balanced financial budget. Issued as decrees, the *Kanuns* became

MAP 23.1 The Ottoman Empire at Its Height, 1566   The Ottomans, like their great rivals the Habsburgs, rose to rule a vast dynastic empire encompassing many different peoples and ethnic groups. The army and the bureaucracy served to unite the disparate territories into a single state.

the laws of the empire.[5] Suleiman's legal acts influenced many legal codes, including that of the United States. Today, Suleiman's image, along with the images of other great lawgivers such as Solon, Moses, and Thomas Jefferson, appears in the chamber of the U.S. House of Representatives.

Europeans called Suleiman "the Magnificent" because of the grandeur of his court. With annual state revenues of about $80 million (when Elizabeth I of England could expect $150,000 and Francis I of France perhaps $1 million), with thousands of servants to cater to his whims, and with a lifestyle no European monarch could begin

to rival, Suleiman was indeed magnificent. He used his fabulous wealth and power to adorn Constantinople with palaces and mosques. Some of his undertakings, such as his reconstruction of the water systems of the great pilgrimage sites at Mecca and Jerusalem, also benefited his subjects.

The Ottomans under Suleiman demonstrated splendid creativity in carpet weaving, textiles, ceramics, and, above all, architecture. In the buildings of Pasha Sinan (1491–1588), a Christian slave who rose to become imperial architect, the Ottoman spirit is powerfully expressed. A contemporary of Michelangelo, Sinan designed 312 public buildings—mosques, schools, hospitals, public baths, palaces, and burial chapels. His masterpieces, the Shehzade and Suleimaniye mosques at Constantinople, represented solutions to spatial problems unique to domed buildings and expressed the discipline, power, and devotion to Islam that characterized the Ottoman Empire under Suleiman the Magnificent. With pardonable exaggeration, Suleiman began a letter to the king of France, with whom he was allied against the Habsburgs after 1536, by saying, "I who am the sultan of sultans, the sovereign of sovereigns, the dispenser of crowns to the monarchs on the face of the earth . . . to thee who are Francis, King of the land of France."[6]

European prejudice against Islam propagated the notions that Ottoman strength rested entirely on military achievement and that military activity was the Ottoman state's dominant characteristic. In fact, the age of Suleiman witnessed a tremendous cultural explosion that may have rivaled the artistic and literary achievements of the European Renaissance. In addition to architecture, Ottoman scholars and artists showed great distinction in poetry, painting, history, mathematics, geographical literature, astronomy, medicine, and the religious sciences.

Poetry, rather than prose, was the main vehicle of Ottoman literary expression. *Diwan* poetry, so called because it consisted of collections of poems, though written by intellectuals in Turkish, followed classical Islamic (Arabic) forms and rules and addressed the ruling class. Şeyhi of Kütahya (d. 1429) compiled a large Diwan collection and in his *Book of the Donkey* used animals to personify and satirize his political enemies. Modern scholars consider Bursah Ahmet Paşa, an imperial judge and confidential adviser to the sultan Mehmet II, to be the greatest Ottoman poet of the fifteenth century. Bursah Ahmet Paşa's beautiful odes and diversified style won him widespread popularity.

Folk literature, produced by traveling troubadours, described the traditions and wisdom of the people in humorous short stories and anecdotes. The folk collection of Dede Korkut, set down in Turkish prose, includes tribal epics describing the conflicts with the Georgians, Circassians, and Byzantines and serves as a major source for the history of the fourteenth century.

Just as Western historical writing in the early modern period often served to justify the rights of ruling dynasties, so Ottoman historical scholarship under Mehmet II and Suleiman promoted the claims of the family of Osman. Perhaps the greatest historian of the early sixteenth century was Ahmet Semseddin Iba-i Kemal, or Kemalpaşazêde (d. 1526), the Muslim judge and administrator whose *History of the House of Osman* gives original source material for the reigns through which he himself lived. Building on the knowledge of earlier Islamic writers and stimulated by Ottoman naval power, the geographer and cartographer Piri Reis produced a map that showed all the known world (1513); another of his maps detailed Columbus's third voyage to the New World. Piri Reis's *Book of the Sea* (1521) contained 129 chapters, each with a map incorporating all Islamic (and Western) knowledge of the seas and navigation and describing harbors, tides, dangerous rocks and shores, and storm areas. Takiyuddin Mehmet (1521–1585), who served as the sultan's chief astronomer, built an observatory at Constantinople. His *Instruments of the Observatory* catalogued astronomical instruments and described an astronomical clock that fixed the location of heavenly bodies with greater precision than ever before.

The large number of hospitals in Istanbul during Suleiman's reign testifies not only to the sultan's concern for the sick but also to his support for medical sciences. In the fifteenth century and partly through the inspiration of physicians imported from central Asia, Şabuncuoghlu Şerefeddin, the chief doctor at a public hospital, wrote an important treatise on surgery based on his own experience. Under Suleiman, Abi Ahmet Celebi (1436–1523), the chief physician of the empire, produced a study on kidney and bladder stones and supported the research of the Jewish doctor Musa Colinus ul-Israili on the application of drugs. Celebi founded the first Ottoman medical school, which served as a training institution for physicians of the entire empire.[7]

In the seventeenth and eighteenth centuries, grave political, social, and economic difficulties afflicted the Ottoman Empire. Ottoman government depended heavily on the sultan, and the matter of the dynastic succession posed a major political problem. In earlier centuries heirs to the throne had gained administrative experience as governors of provinces and military experience on the battlefield as part of their education. Following Suleiman's reign, however, this tradition was abandoned. In order to prevent threats of usurpation, heirs were brought up in the harem and were denied a role in government. By the time a prince succeeded his father, years of dissipation often had rendered the prince alcoholic, insane, or exhausted from excessive sexual activity. Selim II (r. 1566–1574), whom the Turks called "Selim the Drunkard," left the conduct of public affairs to his vizier while he pursued the pleasures of the harem. Turkish sources attribute his death to a fall in his bath caused by dizziness when he tried to stop drinking. The Ottomans, moreover, abandoned the system whereby the eldest son inherited and instead gave the throne to the member of the dynasty with the greatest political influence at the time of the sultan's death. As the sultan's brothers and sons formed factions, harem coalitions conspired for the throne.

A series of incompetent rulers enabled the janissaries to destroy the influence of the old Turkish families. Members of the elite army corps secured permanent military and administrative offices for their sons through bribery, making their positions hereditary. The janissaries thus became the powerful feudal class in Ottoman Turkey.

Under the very competent vizier Muhammad Kuprili (ca 1570–1661) Ottoman fortunes revived. Kuprili abolished the corruption pervasive throughout the imperial administration, maintained domestic peace, and pursued a vigorous foreign policy. When Kuprili died, his brother-in-law Kara Mustafa directed the empire's military operations. His object was an attack on the Habsburg capital, Vienna. When battle came on September 12, 1683, the combination of a strong allied Christian force (see page 625) and Habsburg heavy artillery, which the Turks lacked, gave the Europeans the victory. The Ottomans rallied again, but defeat at Vienna and domestic disorders led to the decline of Ottoman power in the Balkans. "The Ottoman state was predicated upon, committed to, and organized for conquest. . . . An end to significant and sustained conquest rocked the entire state structure and sent aftershocks through all its institutions."[8]

The peace treaty signed at Karlowitz (1699) marks a watershed in Ottoman history. By it the empire lost (to Austria) the major European provinces of Hungary and Transylvania with the vast tax revenues they had represented. Karlowitz also shattered Ottoman morale. Eighteenth-century wars against European powers—Venice (1714–1718), Austria and Russia (1736–1739), and Russia (1768–1774 and 1787–1792)—proved indecisive but contributed to general Ottoman internal disintegration.

Rising population caused serious social problems. A long period of peace in the later sixteenth century and again in the mid-eighteenth century—while the War of the Austrian Succession (1740–1748) and the Seven Years' War (1756–1763) were preoccupying the European powers (see pages 679–680)—and a decline in the frequency of visits of the plague, led to a doubling of population. The land could not sustain so many people, nor could the towns provide jobs for the thousands of agricultural workers who fled to them. The return of demobilized soldiers from the West aggravated the situation. Inflation, famine, and widespread revolts resulted.

Inability to respond to European and worldwide economic changes contributed to Ottoman weakness and decline. The empire did not modernize and thus could not compete effectively with European capitalistic powers. European trade with the Americas, Asia, and Africa via the Atlantic meant that the ancient Middle Eastern trade routes—with their heavy customs duties—were by-passed. The Ottoman state lost vast revenues. Moreover, Ottoman guilds and craft industries resisted change. Guilds set the prices of such commodities as wheat, wool, copper, and precious metals, and European willingness to pay high prices pulled these commodities out of the Ottoman Empire. The result was scarcity, which led to a decline in Turkish industrial production. Likewise in the craft industries, Europeans bought Ottoman raw materials, used them to manufacture textiles and metallurgical goods, and sold them in Turkish lands—destroying Ottoman craft industries in the early nineteenth century. Prices rose; inflation increased; and the government devalued the currency, causing new financial crises.

More than any other single factor, a series of agreements known as *capitulations,* which the Ottoman government signed with European powers, contributed to the Ottoman decline. A trade compact signed in 1536 virtually exempted French merchants from Ottoman law and allowed them to travel and buy and sell throughout the sultan's dominions and to pay low customs duties on French imports and exports. Renewed in 1569, this agreement temporarily established French pre-eminence in the Middle East. In 1590, in spite of strong French opposition, a group of English merchants gained the right to trade in Ottoman territory, in return for supplying the sultan with iron, steel, brass, and tin for his war with Persia. In 1615, as part of a twenty-year peace treaty, the capitulation rights already given to French and English businessmen were extended to the Habsburgs. In 1802, as part of the treaties known as the "Peace of Amiens" during the wars that accompanied the French Revolution (see page 819), the Ottoman economic capitulations to France were again renewed. These capitulations progressively gave European merchants an economic stranglehold on Ottoman trade and commerce. At the beginning of the nineteenth century, the loss of territory, the pressures of European capitalistic imperialism, and unresolved internal problems all combined to weaken the Ottoman world. It was labeled "the sick man of Europe."[9]

THE PERSIAN THEOCRATIC STATE

Persia, after a long period of Arab and Mongol domination, emerged as a powerful Muslim state under the Safavid dynasty in the early sixteenth century (Map 23.2). (Since 1935 Persia has been known as Iran.) Between 1502 and 1510, Ismail (r. 1502–1524), the founder of the dynasty, defeated petty Turkish leaders, united all of Persia under his sovereign rule, and proclaimed himself shah, or king.

The strength of the Safavid state rested on three crucial features. First, it had the loyalty and military support of Qizilbash nomadic tribesmen. (*Qizilbash,* a Turkish word meaning "red-heads," was applied to these people because of the red hats they wore.) The shah secured the loyalty of the Qizilbash by granting them vast grazing lands, especially on the troublesome Ottoman frontier. In return, the Qizilbash supplied him troops. Second, the Safavid state utilized the skills of urban bureaucrats and made them an essential part of the government civil machinery. The highest offices in they administration, especially that of *wakel,* or deputy to the shah, was always held by a Persian.

The third source of Safavid strength was the Shi'ite faith. The Shi'ites claimed descent from Ali, Muhammad's cousin and son-in-law, and believed

MAP 23.2 The Safavid Empire   In the late sixteenth century, the power of the Safavid kingdom of Persia rested on its strong military force, its Shi'ite Muslim faith, and its extraordinarily rich trade in rugs and pottery. Many of the cities on the map, such as Tabriz, Qum, and Shiraz, were great rug-weaving centers.

Persian Merchant with Servant   Persian narrative literature frequently depicted black people (together with whites) as servants and attendants, and painting illustrated that literature. In this delicate miniature attendants lead the heavily laden mules. *(Source: The British Library)*

that leadership among Muslims rightfully belonged to the Prophet's descendants (see pages 274–275). Ismail claimed descent from a line of twelve infallible *imans* beginning with Ali and was officially regarded as their representative on earth. When Ismail conquered Tabriz in 1501, he declared Shi'ism the official and compulsory religion of his new empire under penalty of death. Today, in the late twentieth century, Iran remains the only Muslim state in which Shi'ism is the official religion.

Scholars have long debated the reasons for Ismail's decision; definitive explanations remain unavailable. The great majority of the Persian people in the sixteenth century belonged to the Sunni branch of Islam, and there was no Shi'ite religious establishment in Persia by whom Ismail could have been influenced and to whom he could have appealed for assistance. Nevertheless, Shi'ism gradually shaped the cultural and political identity of Persia (and later Iran). Recent scholarship asserts that Ismail was not "motivated by cynical notions

of political manipulation."[10] Shah Ismail imported Shi'ite *ulema* from other Arab lands to instruct and guide his people. With its puritanical emphasis on the holy law and on self-flagellation in penance for any disloyalty to Ali, the Safavid state represented theocracy triumphant throughout the first half century of its existence.

Safavid power reached its height under Shah Abbas (r. 1587–1629), whose military achievements, support for trade and commerce, and endowment for the arts earned him the epithet "the Great." The Persian army had hitherto consisted of tribal units under tribal leadership. Shah Abbas built a national army on the Ottoman model, composed of Armenian and Georgian recruits paid by and loyal to himself. Utilizing the engineering skills of the English adventurer Sir Anthony Sherley, who supplied the Persian army with cannon, Shah Abbas campaigned against the Turks and captured Baghdad, Mosul, and Diarbakr in Mesopotamia.

Military victories account for only part of Shah Abbas's claim to greatness. Determined to improve his country's export trade, he built the small cottage business of carpet weaving into a national industry. In the capital city of Isfahan alone, factories employed over 25,000 weavers who produced woolen carpets, brocades, and silks of brilliant color, design, and quality. Armenians controlled the carpet industry; the Safavids had brought them to Isfahan to protect them from Turkish persecution. Three hundred Chinese potters were imported to make glazed building tiles, which adorned the great Safavid buildings. They captured much of the European tile market.

The jewel of the empire was Isfahan, whose prosperity and beauty rested on trade and industry. Shah Abbas himself supervised the reconstruction of the city. A seventeenth-century English visitor described Isfahan's bazaar as "the surprisingest piece of Greatness in Honour of commerce the world can boast of." Besides splendid rugs, stalls displayed pottery and fine china, metalwork of exceptionally high quality, silks and velvets of stunning weave and design. A city of perhaps 750,000 people, Isfahan contained 162 mosques, 48 seminaries where future members of the *ulema* learned the sacred Muslim sciences, 273 public baths, and the vast imperial palace. Private houses had their own garden courts; and public gardens, pools, and parks adorned the wide streets. Tales of the beauty of Isfahan circulated worldwide, attracting thousands of tourists annually in the seventeenth and eighteenth centuries.

Shah Abbas was succeeded by inept rulers whose heavy indulgence in wine and the pleasures of the harem weakened the monarchy and fed the slow disintegration of the state. The harem dominated the court. Shi'ite theologians seized power. Internal weakness encouraged foreign aggression. In the eighteenth century the Turks, Afghans, and Russians invaded and divided Persia among themselves. Political anarchy and social chaos characterized Persian life.

INDIA: FROM MUGHAL DOMINATION TO BRITISH DOMINION (CA 1498–1805)

While African societies were experiencing their first large-scale contacts with Europeans, the Asian subcontinent of India was achieving a remarkable culture under the domination of the Mughals. In 1504 Babur (r. 1483–1530), ruler of the small Mughal territory in central Asia, captured Kabul and established a kingdom in Afghanistan. From Kabul he moved southward into India. In 1525 Babur launched a serious invasion; a year later, with a force of only twelve thousand men, he defeated the decrepit sultan of Delhi at Panipat. Babur's capture of the cities of Agra and Delhi paved the way for further conquests in northern India. Thus began Mughal rule, which lasted until the eighteenth century, when domestic disorder and incompetent government opened the door to lengthy European intervention. (*Mughal* refers to the Muslim empire of India. However, the name *Mughal*, which is a variant of *Mongol*, is a misnomer because the founders of the Mughal Empire were mainly Turks and Afghans, not Mongol descendants of Jenghiz Khan.)

The Rule of the Mughals

By the start of the sixteenth century, India had been the object of foreign conquest for almost a millennium. Muslims first invaded India in the seventh century (see pages 307–309). The Turkish chieftain Mahmud conquered the Punjab in the tenth century, and in the thirteenth century the Turkish Muslim Qutb-ud-din established the sultanate of Delhi, which ruled northern India. In the next century, the sultanate of Delhi gained control over most of the subcontinent. In 1398, central Asian armies under Timur the Lame (Tamerlane) swept down through the northwest, looted Delhi, and seized tens of thousands of slaves as booty. Timur left Delhi completely destroyed with "not a bird moving" and all India politically fragmented. Although the vast majority of the people remained Hindu, Islam had a strong impact on the culture of India, especially in art and architecture.

The conquests of Babur, the great-grandson of Timur, laid the foundation for Mughal control of India. Babur's son Humayun reigned from 1530 to 1540 and from 1555 to 1556. When the Afghans of northern India rebelled, he lost most of the territories that his father had acquired. Humayun went into temporary exile in Persia, where he developed a deep appreciation for Persian art and literature. This interest led to a remarkable flowering of Mughal art under his son Akbar.

The reign of Akbar (r. 1556–1605) may well have been the greatest in the history of India. Under his dynamic leadership the Mughal state took

The Vizier at Work Sitting cross-legged on two beautiful Persian carpets, the vizier dictates to one scribe while another calculates on what appears to be an abacus. The portrait suggests the importance of the office of vizier in Mughal India, as throughout the Islamic world. *(Source: Courtesy of The Harvard University Art Museums (Gift of John Goelet))*

definite form. A boy of thirteen when he became *badshah,* or imperial ruler, Akbar was ably assisted during his early years by his father's friend Bairam Khan, a superb military leader. In 1555 Bairam Khan had defeated Hindu forces at Panipat and shortly afterward recaptured Delhi and Agra, the key fortresses of the north. Before falling from power in 1560, Bairam Khan took the great for-

tress of Gwalior, annexed the rich city of Janupur, and prepared for war against Malwa. Akbar continued this expansionist policy, gradually adding the territories of Malwa, Gondwana, and Gujarat. Because the Afghan tribesmen put up tremendous resistance, it took Akbar several years to acquire Bengal. The Mughal Empire under Akbar eventually included most of the subcontinent north of the Godavari River (see Map 23.3).

To govern this vast region, Akbar developed an efficient bureaucracy staffed by able and well-trained officials, both Muslim and non-Muslim. As in the early modern nations of Europe (see page 411), solvency in the Mughal state depended on the establishment of a careful system for recording income and expenditures. Under Akbar's finance minister Raja Todar Mal, a Hindu, a *diwan* (bureau of finance) and royal mint came into existence. Raja Todar Mal devised methods for the assessment and collection of taxes that were applied throughout the empire. To administer the provinces, Akbar appointed about 800 *mansabdars,* or imperial officials, who performed a wide variety of financial, military, and judicial functions at the local level. The central government, however, rarely interfered in the life of village communities. Akbar's policies laid the basis for all later Mughal administration in India.

The cornerstone of Akbar's policies was religious toleration: he sought the peaceful mutual assimilation of Hindus and Muslims, especially in his government. Although this was not a radical innovation—a few Hindus had long been employed in the imperial army and in the administration—very deep prejudices divided the two peoples. When the refusal of many Hindus to serve under a Muslim ruler or to learn Persian, the court language, thwarted Akbar's goal, he took decisive steps to heal the breach. According to his principle of *sulahkul,* or universal tolerance, the *badshah* assumed responsibility for all the people, regardless of religion. In 1564 Akbar ended the pilgrim tax, which won him the gratitude of the many Hindus who traveled to various pilgrimage sites. Akbar's most widely acclaimed act was to abolish the *jizya,* a tax imposed on non-Muslim adult males. He immediately earned the support of the Hindu warrior class and the good will of the general Hindu population. Twice Akbar married Hindu princesses, one of whom became the mother of his heir Jahangir. Hindus eventually accounted for 30 percent of the imperial bureaucracy.

Scholars have heatedly debated Akbar's own religious beliefs. He considered himself an orthodox Muslim and demonstrated great devotion to the shrine of an Islamic mystic at Ajmer. Yet he supported an eclectic assortment of theological ideas, a policy that caused serious domestic difficulties. In 1575 Akbar sponsored public theological debates among the Muslim *ulema*. When the discussions degenerated into mutual recriminations, Akbar declared himself the final interpreter of Islamic law. Orthodox Muslims became alarmed. After 1579 Akbar invited Jains, Zoroastrians, Hindus, and Jesuits to join the Muslim *ulema* in debate. From these discussions Akbar created the *Din-i-Ilahi* (literally, "divine discipleship"), which some advisers called a "syncretic religion" (a religion that reconciles different beliefs).

The Din-i-Ilahi borrowed the concept of great respect for animal life from the Jains and reverence for the sun from the Zoroastrians, but it was primarily based on the rationalistic elements in the Islamic tradition and stressed the emperor as a Perfect Man. Some scholars interpret it as a reflection of Akbar's "cult of personality," intended to serve as a common bond for the court nobility. In any case, the Din-i-Ilahi antagonized all sects and provoked serious Muslim rebellions. Although misinterpreted by contemporaries and misunderstood later, the Din-i-Ilahi established Akbar's reputation as a philosopher-king.

The birth of his son Jahangir, which Akbar saw as fulfillment of a prophecy, inspired Akbar to build a new city, Fatehpur-Sikri. Akbar personally supervised the construction of the new city. It

City of Fatehpur-Sikri   In 1569 Akbar founded the city of Fatehpur-Sikri to honor the Muslim holy man Shaikh Salim Chishti, who had foretold the birth of Akbar's son and heir, Jahangir. The red sandstone city, probably the finest example of Mughal architecture still intact, was Akbar's capital for fifteen years. *(Source: Nrupen Madhvani/Dinodia Picture Agency, Bombay)*

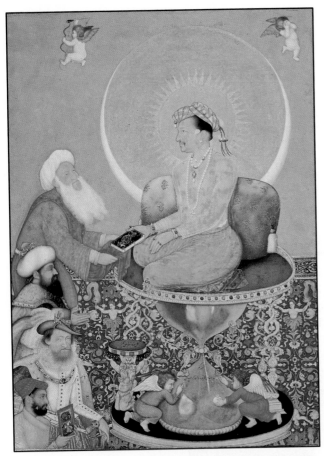

Sufism Triumphant Illuminated manuscript, ca 1615–1618. In this remarkable vignette, the emperor Jahangir celebrates the spiritual side of his reign while rejecting a merely wordly mode of government. The angels above bemoan his choice; the cherub on the left clutches a broken arrow symbolic of the power Jahangir has spurned. The ruler offers a book to the venerable Sufi sheik Husain, to whom he owed his birth. The sheik had offered prayers on behalf of Jahangir's father, Akbar the Great, for a son and heir to the throne. Beneath Husain is a Turkish sultan, depicted in general rather than individual fashion. Next is James I of England, whose presence underscores the inferior status given to monarchy untempered by the chastening force of piety. The royal portrait had reached India through the English merchant Thomas Roe, who had come to make a commercial treaty. According to Roe's memoirs, a picture of James I was displayed in the New Year's Durbar (state reception) of 1616. At the bottom the Hindu painter Bichitr advertises his respects with a placard of himself paying obeisance. Other elements emphasize the glory of Jahangir's reign: the dazzling sun around his head and the pair of industrious angels writing on the hourglass throne pedestal: 'O, Shah, may the span of your life be a thousand years.' *(Source: Courtesy of the Freer Gallery of Art, Smithsonian Institution)*

combined the Muslim tradition of domes, arches, and spacious courts with the Hindu tradition of flat stone beams, ornate decoration, and solidity. According to Abu-l-Fazl, the historian of Akbar's reign, "His majesty plans splendid edifices, and dresses the work of his mind and heart in the garment of stone and clay."[11] Completed in 1578, the city included an imperial palace, a mosque, lavish gardens, and a hall of worship, as well as thousands of houses for ordinary people. Along with the ancient cities of Delhi and Agra, Fatehpur-Sikri served as an imperial capital and the center of Akbar's lavish court. Its construction reflects Akbar's desire to assimilate Hindus and Muslims and the vaunting power of his empire.

Akbar was gifted with a creative intellect and imagination. He enthusiastically supported artists who produced magnificent paintings and books in the Indo-Persian style. In Mughal India, as throughout the Muslim world, books were regarded as precious objects. Time, talent, and expensive materials went into their production, and they were highly coveted because they reflected wealth, learning, and power. Akbar reportedly possessed 24,000 books when he died. Abu-l-Fazl described the library and Akbar's love of books:

His Majesty's library is divided into several parts. . . . Each part . . . is subdivided, according to the value of the books and the estimation in which the sciences are held of which the books treat. Prose works, poetical works, Hindi, Persian, Greek, Kashmirian, Arabic, are all separately placed. In this order they are also inspected. Experienced people bring them daily and read them before His Majesty, who hears every book from beginning to end. At whatever page the reader stops, His Majesty makes with his own pen a sign, according to the number of pages; and rewards the readers with presents of cash either in gold or silver, according to the number of leaves read out by them. Among books of renown there are few that are not read in His Majesty's assembly hall; and there are no historical facts of past ages, or curiosities of science, or interesting points of philosophy, with which His Majesty, a leader of impartial sages, is unacquainted.[12]

Official court biographies almost always exaggerate the achievements of their subjects, but Akbar's library attests to his sincere appreciation for learning.

Akbar's son Jahangir (r. 1605–1628) lacked his father's military abilities and administrative genius but did succeed in consolidating Mughal rule in Bengal. His patronage of the arts and lavish court have led scholars to characterize his reign as the "age of splendor."

Jahangir's son Shah Jahan (r. 1628–1658) launched fresh territorial expansion. Faced with dangerous revolts by the Muslims in Ahmadnagar and the resistance of the newly arrived Portuguese in Bengal, Shah Jahan not only crushed them but strengthened his northwestern frontier. He reasserted Mughal authority in the Deccan and Golkunda.

The new capital that Shah Jahan founded at Delhi superseded Agra, Akbar's main capital. Situated on the rich land linking the Indus and Ganges valleys, Delhi eventually became one of the great cities of the Muslim world. The city boasted one of the finest mosques in Islam, the Juma Masjid, and magnificent boulevards. The Red Fort, named for its red sandstone walls, housed the imperial palace, the headquarters of the imperial administration, the imperial treasury, an arsenal, and a garrison. Subsequent Mughal rulers held their *durbar,* or court, at Delhi.

Shah Jahan also ordered the construction of the Peacock Throne. This famous piece, actually a cot resting on golden legs, was encrusted with emeralds, diamonds, pearls, and rubies. It took seven years to fashion and cost the equivalent of five million dollars. It served as the imperial throne of India until 1739, when the Persian warrior Nadir Shah seized it as plunder and carried it to Persia.

Shah Jahan's most enduring monument is the Taj Mahal, the supreme example of the garden tomb. The English word *paradise* derives from the old Persian *pairidaeza,* a walled garden. The Mughals sought to bring their vision of paradise alive in the walled garden tombs in which they buried their dead. Twenty thousand workers toiled eighteen years to build this memorial in Agra to Shah Jahan's favorite wife, Mumtaz Mahal, who died giving birth to their fifteenth child. One of the most beautiful structures in the world, the Taj Mahal is both an expression of love and a superb architectural blending of Islamic and Indian culture. It also asserted the power of the Mughal dynasty.

The Mughal state never developed a formal procedure for the imperial succession, and a crisis occurred toward the end of Shah Jahan's reign. Competition among his sons ended with the victory of Aurangzeb, who executed his elder brother and locked his father away until death in 1666. A puritanically devout and strictly orthodox Muslim, a skillful general and a clever diplomat, Aurangzeb (r. 1658–1707) ruled more of India than did any previous *badshah.* His reign witnessed the culmination of Mughal power and the beginning of its decline (Map 23.3).

A combination of religious zeal and financial necessity seems to have prompted Aurangzeb to introduce a number of reforms. He appointed censors of public morals in important cities to enforce Islamic laws against gambling, prostitution, drinking, and the use of narcotics. He forbade *sati*—the self-immolation of widows on their husbands' funeral pyres—and the castration of boys to be sold as eunuchs. He also abolished all taxes not authorized by Islamic law. This measure led to a serious loss of state revenues. To replace them, Aurangzeb in 1679 reimposed the *jizya,* the tax on non-Muslims. It fell most on the Hindu majority.

Regulating Indian society according to Islamic law meant modifying the religious toleration and cultural cosmopolitanism instituted by Akbar. Aurangzeb ordered the destruction of some Hindu temples. He required Hindus to pay higher customs duties than Muslims. Out of fidelity to Islamic law, he even criticized his mother's tomb, the Taj Mahal: "The lawfulness of a solid construction over a grave is doubtful, and there can be no doubt about the extravagance involved."[13] On the other hand, Aurangzeb employed more Hindus in the imperial administration than any previous Mughal ruler. But his religious policy proved highly unpopular with the majority of his subjects. Although his indomitable military strength and persistent activity staved off difficulties and maintained the unity of the empire, Aurangzeb created problems that weaker successors could not handle.

Aurangzeb's military ventures also had mixed results. A tireless general, he pushed the conquest of the south and annexed the Golkunda and Bijapur sultanates. The stiffest opposition came from the Marathas, a militant Hindu group centered in the western Deccan. From 1681 until his death in 1707 at the age of ninety, Aurangzeb led repeated sorties through the Deccan. He took many forts and won several battles. But total destruction of the Maratha guerrilla bands eluded him, and after his death they played an important role in the collapse of the Mughal Empire.

Aurangzeb's eighteenth-century successors faced formidable problems. Repeated disputes over

MAP 23.3 India, 1707–1805 In the eighteenth century Mughal power gradually yielded to the Hindu Marathas, and the British East India Company.

the succession contributed to the instability of the monarchy. Court intrigues replaced the battlefield as the testing ground for the nobility. Mughal provincial governors began to rule independently, giving only minimal allegiance to the *badshah* at Delhi. The Marathas, who revolted and pressed steadily northward, constituted the gravest threat to Mughal authority. No ruler could defeat them.

In 1739 the Persian adventurer Nadir Shah invaded India, defeated the Mughal army, looted Delhi, and after a savage massacre carried off a huge amount of treasure, including the Peacock Throne. When Nadir Shah withdrew to Afghanistan, he took with him the Mughal government's prestige. Constant skirmishes between the Afghans and the Marathas for control of the Punjab and northern India ended in 1761 at Panipat, where the Marathas were crushingly defeated. India no longer had any power capable of imposing order on the subcontinent or of checking the rapacious penetration of the Europeans.

European Rivalry for the Indian Trade

Shortly before Babur's invasion of India, the Portuguese under the navigator Pedro Alvares Cabral had opened the subcontinent to Portuguese trade. In 1510 they established the port of Goa on the Arabian Sea as their headquarters and through a policy of piracy and terrorism swept the Muslims off the Indian and Arabian oceans. The Portuguese historian Barrões attempted to justify Portugal's seizure of commercial traffic that the Muslims had long dominated:

It is true that there does exist a common right to all to navigate the seas and in Europe we recognize the rights which others hold against us; but the right does not extend beyond Europe and therefore the Portuguese as Lords of the Sea are justified in confiscating the goods of all those who navigate the seas without their permission.[14]

In short, Western principles of international law did not apply in Asia. For almost a century the Portuguese controlled the spice trade over the Indian Ocean.

In 1602 the Dutch formed the Dutch East India Company with the stated goal of wresting the enormously lucrative spice trade from the Portuguese. The scent of fabulous profits also attracted the English. With a charter signed by Queen Elizabeth, eighty London merchants organized the British East India Company: their objective also was the Indian spice and cotton trade. Although the English initially had no luck, in 1619 Emperor Jahangir granted a British mission led by Sir Thomas Roe important commercial concessions at the port of Surat on the western coast of India. Gifts, medical services, and bribes to Indian rulers enabled the British to set up twenty-seven other

Taj Mahal at Agra   The finest example of Muslim architecture in India. Its white marble exterior is inlaid with semi-precious stones in Arabic inscriptions and floral designs. The oblong pool reflects the building, which asserts the power of the Mughal dynasty. *(Source: Ira Kirschenbaum/Stock, Boston)*

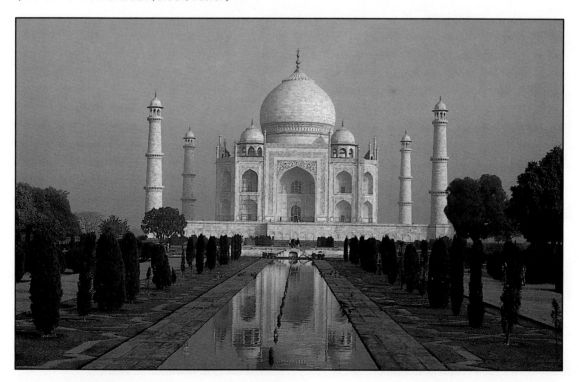

forts along the coasts. Fort St. George on the eastern coast became the modern city of Madras. In 1668 the city of Bombay—given to England when the Portuguese princess Catherine of Braganza married King Charles II—was leased to the company, marking the virtually total British absorption of Portuguese power in India. In 1690 Job Charnock, a company official, founded a fort that became the city of Calcutta. Thus the three places that later became centers of British economic and political imperialism—Madras, Bombay, and Calcutta—existed before 1700. The Dutch concentrated their efforts in Indonesia.

Factory-Fort Societies

The British called their trading post at Surat a "factory," and the word was later used for all European settlements in India. The term did not signify manufacturing; it designated the walled compound containing the residences, gardens, and offices of British East India Company officials and the warehouses where goods were stored before being shipped to Europe. The company president exercised political authority over all residents.

Factory-forts existed to make profits from the Asian-European trade, and they evolved into flourishing centers of economic profit. The British East India Company sold silver, copper, zinc, lead, and fabrics to the Indians and bought cotton goods, silks, pepper and other spices, sugar, and opium from them. By the late seventeenth century the company was earning substantial profits. Profitability increased after 1700 when it began to trade with China. Some Indian merchants in Calcutta and Bombay made gigantic fortunes from the country trade—that is, trade within Asia.

English Factory at Surat   The factory began as a storage place for goods before they were bought and transported abroad; it gradually expanded to include merchants' residences and some sort of fortification. By 1650, the English had twenty-three factories in India. Surat, in the Gujarat region on the Gulf of Cambay, was the busiest factory and port until it was sacked by the Mahrattas in 1664. *(Source: The Mansell Collection)*

Because the directors of the British East India Company in London discouraged all unnecessary expenses and financial risks, they opposed any interference in local Indian politics and even missionary activities. Indian conditions, however, brought about a fundamental change in the nature of the company's factories. The violent disorders and political instability that wracked India during Aurangzeb's reign and in the early eighteenth century caused the factories to evolve into forts and then into territorial settlements. In order to protect British East India trading interests, company officials transformed the factories into defensive installations manned by small garrisons of native troops. When warlords appeared or an uprising occurred, people from the surrounding countryside flocked into the fort. Because there was no strong central government and because local princes were unable to provide security, the company factory-forts gradually came to exercise political authority over the territories around them.

Indian and Chinese wares enjoyed great popularity in England and on the European continent in the late seventeenth and early eighteenth centuries. The middle classes wanted Indian textiles, which were colorful, durable, cheap, and washable. The upper classes desired Chinese wallpaper and porcelains, Indian silks and brocades. In the European economies, however, Asian goods created serious problems. As early as 1695 English manufacturers called for an embargo on Indian cloth, and silk weavers picketed the House of Commons. Trade with Asia was one-way: Asians had little interest in European manufactured articles. Finding the Siamese completely uninterested in traditional Dutch goods, the Dutch East India Company tried to interest them in collections of pornography. Europeans had to pay for everything they bought from Asia with precious metals. Thus there was insistent pressure in England, France, and the Netherlands against the importation of Asian goods. As one authority explains it:

The root of the argument from which grew a tree of many branches was the old fear of the drain of gold. When the English pamphleteers professed to be shocked by the transparency of Indian fabrics, their care for the modesty of English females was a disguise, not less transparent than muslin, for the objections of those who on general grounds deplored sending gold and silver abroad or on particular grounds were anxious to protect domestic industries.[15]

The Rise of the British East India Company

The French were the last to arrive in India. Louis XIV's financial wizard Colbert (see pages 614–615) planned the French East India Company for trade in the Eastern Hemisphere, and in the 1670s the company established factories at Chandernagore in Bengal, Pondicherry, and elsewhere. Joseph Dupleix (1697–1764), who was appointed governor general at Pondicherry in 1742, was the first European to appreciate fully the political as well as the economic potential of India. He understood the instability of the Mughal Empire and realized that one European power would eventually govern India. Dupleix also knew that since the French East India Company could expect no support from the government in Paris, it would have to be economically self-sufficient and acquire territory. He made allies with Indian princes and built an army of native troops, called *sepoys,* who were trained as infantrymen. The British likewise built an army with Indian surrogates trained in Western military drill and tactics. War broke out at midcentury.

From 1740 to 1763 Britain and France were almost continually engaged in a tremendous global struggle. India, like North America in the Seven Years' War, became a battlefield and a prize. Both the French and the English bid for the support of the rulers of the Deccan. In 1746 Dupleix captured Madras, and in 1751 the French gained control of the huge Deccan and Carnatic regions. The French won land battles, but English seapower decided the first phase of the war. Then in 1757, the English commander Robert Clive, having bought up most of the officers of the French-supported *nawab* (Muslim governor) of Bengal, defeated the nawab at Plassey. In a series of brilliant victories Clive went on to destroy French power in southern India. By preventing French reinforcements from arriving, British seapower again proved to be the determining factor, and Clive soon extended British jurisdiction over the important northern province of Bengal. The Treaty of Paris of 1763 recognized British control of much of India, and scholars acknowledge the treaty as the beginning of the British Empire in India.

How was the vast subcontinent to be governed? Parliament believed that the British East India Company had too much power and considered the company responsible for the political disorders in India, which were bad for business. Parliament attempted to solve Indian problems with special legislation. The Regulating Act of 1773 deprived the company of some of its political power. The newly created office of governor general, with an advisory council, would exercise political authority over the territory controlled by the company. The India Act of 1784 required that the governor general be chosen from outside the company and made company directors subject to parliamentary supervision.

Implementation of these reforms fell to Warren Hastings, the governor of Bengal and first governor general (r. 1774–1785) with jurisdiction over Bombay and Madras. Hastings tried to build an effective administrative system and to turn the British East India Company into a government. He laid the foundations for the first Indian civil service, abolished tolls to facilitate internal trade, placed the salt and opium trades under government control, and planned a codification of Muslim and Hindu laws. He sought allies among Indian princes and, in imitation of Dupleix, built an army of sepoy troops trained as infantrymen to support the British artillery. The biggest problem facing Hastings's administration was a coalition of the rulers of Mysore and the Marathas aimed at the expulsion of the British. Hastings's skillful diplomacy offset this alliance temporarily. In 1785, however, Hastings resigned his office and returned to England. Charges that he had interfered in provincial administrations, extorted money from Indian princes, and ordered the murder of an Indian merchant led to his impeachment. He was finally acquitted in 1795.

Hastings's successor Lord Charles Cornwallis (whom George Washington had defeated at Yorktown) served as governor general of India from 1786 to 1794. Cornwallis continued the work of building a civil service and the war against Mysore. His introduction of the British style of property relations in effect converted a motley collection of former Mughal officers, tax collectors, and others into English-style landlords. A new system of landholding, with the landlords supported by the rents of tenant farmers, resulted.

The third governor general, the marquess Richard Wellesley (r. 1797–1805), defeated the Mysore in 1799 and four years later crushed the Marathas at the Battle of Assaye. Building on the work of his predecessors, he vastly extended British influence in India. Like most nineteenth-century British governors of India, Wellesley believed that British rule strongly benefited the Indians. With supreme condescension he wrote that British power should be established over the Indian princes in order "to deprive them of the means of prosecuting any measure or of forming any confederacy hazardous to the security of the British empire, and to enable us to preserve the tranquility of India by exercising a general control over the restless spirit of ambition and violence which is characteristic of every Asiatic government."[16]

By the beginning of the nineteenth century, the authority and power of the British East India Company had yielded to the government in London. Subsequent British rule of India rested on three foundations: the support of puppet Indian princes, who exercised the trappings but not the reality of power; a large army of sepoys of dubious loyalty; and an increasingly effective civil service, staffed largely by Englishmen with Hindus and Muslims in minor positions.

SUMMARY

In the eighteenth century, the Ottoman Turks lived almost entirely within a closed Islamic environment. Very few knew European languages or had firsthand knowledge of Europe. Diplomatic relations with any European power did not exist before 1793. When the Ottomans thought of Europe at all, they believed it inferior to Islamic civilization, despite the plea in 1653 of Katib Chelebi, a renowned Ottoman historian, for greater Muslim knowledge of geography: "Sufficient and compelling proof of the necessity for learning this science is the fact that the unbelievers, by their application to and esteem for those branches of learning, have discovered the New World and have overrun the ports of India and the East Indies."[17] Everyone looked backward to the period of Suleiman the Magnificent, when the empire was at its height. There was little thought of innovation or experimentation. Some scholars believe that Islam's hostility to innovation is traceable to a saying of the Prophet: "The worst things are those that are novelties, every novelty is an innovation, every innovation is an error, and every error leads to Hell-fire." After war with Russia (1736–1739), in which the Turks were largely successful, the Ottomans entered a long period of peace on their western frontier. Only with the reforms of Sultan

Selim III (r. 1761–1808), in which the imperial administration and the army were restructured, European languages studied, and relations established with European powers, did the Ottoman Empire begin to become a modern state.

In the seventeenth century, the Shi'ite state of Persia enjoyed military success, economic boom, and cultural preeminence. The wealth and magnificence of the shah was a legend in sophisticated China and in primitive North America. In the eighteenth century, however, political weakness attracted Russian and Ottoman invasion and led, ultimately, to Persia's dismemberment.

The contemporary Indian writer V. S. Naipaul has called India "a wounded civilization." For centuries the economic prize of European commercial interests, in the 1700s the Indian subcontinent began to experience British political domination. Bitter hostility between Hindus and Muslims persisted as a dominant theme of Indian life.

NOTES

1. Quoted in B. Lewis, *The Muslim Discovery of Europe* (New York: Norton, 1982), p. 29.
2. W. H. McNeill, *The Pursuit of Power: Technology, Armed Force, and Society Since A.D. 1000* (Chicago: University of Chicago Press, 1982), p. 87.
3. Quoted in Lewis, p. 30.
4. F. Robinson, *Atlas of the Islamic World Since 1500* (New York: Facts on File, 1982), p. 72.
5. See S. J. Shaw, History of the Ottoman Empire and Modern Turkey, vol. 1, *Empire of the Gazis: The Rise and Decline of the Ottoman Empire, 1208–1808* (Cambridge, England: Cambridge University Press, 1988), pp. 10–101.
6. Quoted in P. K. Hitti, *The Near East in History* (Princeton, N.J.: Van Nostrand, 1961), p. 336.
7. Shaw, pp. 139–151.
8. N. Itzkowitz, *Ottoman Empire and Islamic Tradition* (Chicago: University of Chicago Press, 1980), p. 95.
9. Shaw, pp. 171–175, 225, 246–227; V. H. Parry, H. Inalcik, A. N. Kurat, and J. S. Bromley, *A History of the Ottoman Empire to 1715* (New York: Cambridge University Press, 1976), pp. 126, 139–140.
10. D. Morgan, *Medieval Persia, 1040–1797* (New York: Longman's, 1988), pp. 112–113.
11. Quoted in V. A. Smith, *The Oxford History of India* (Oxford: Oxford University Press, 1967), p. 398.
12. Quoted in M. C. Beach, *The Imperial Image: Paintings for the Mughal Court* (Washington, D.C.: Freer Gallery of Art, Smithsonian Institution, 1981), pp. 9–10.
13. Quoted in S. K. Ikram, *Muslim Civilization in India* (New York: Columbia University Press, 1964), p. 202.
14. Quoted in K. M. Panikkar, *Asia and Western Domination* (London: George Allen & Unwin, 1965), p. 35.
15. Quoted ibid., p. 53.
16. Quoted in W. Bingham, H. Conroy, and F. W. Ikle, *A History of Asia,* vol. 2 (Boston: Allyn and Bacon, 1967), p. 74.
17. Quoted ibid., p. 106.

SUGGESTED READING

The best up-to-date accounts of Ottoman history are H. Inalcik, *The Ottoman Empire: The Classical Age, 1300–1600* (1973), and the work by Itzkowitz cited in the Notes. O. G. de Busbecq, *Turkish Letters* (trans. E. S. Foster, 1967), is a firsthand report of the court of Suleiman the Magnificent. G. Goodwin, *A History of Ottoman Architecture* (1971), is probably the best available general study, and the famous architect has found his biographer in A. Stratton, Sinan (1972). I. Andric, *The Bridge on the Drina* (trans. L. F. Edwards, 1959), is a brilliant novel evoking Balkan life under Turkish rule; it earned its author the Nobel Prize for literature. Islam's understanding of the West is studied in the excellent work by Lewis listed in the Notes; and R. W. Southern, *Western Views of Islam* (1962), is a fine summary of the Western viewpoint.

The best general introduction to the history and civilization of India is S. Wolpert's elegant appreciation *India* (1990). There is no up-to-date treatment of Mughal India, but the curious student might start with P. M. Holt et al., eds., *The Cambridge History of Islam,* 2 vols. (1970). M. Mujeeb, *The Indian Muslims* (1967), and I. Habib, *The Agrarian System of Mughal India, 1556–1707* (1963), are both useful. B. Gascoigne, *The Great Moghuls* (1971), and G. Hambly, *The Cities of Mughal India: Delhi, Agra, and Fatehpur Sikri* (1968), are well illustrated and highly readable. For the impact of Portuguese, Dutch, and English mercantile activities on India, see M. N. Pearson, *Merchants and Rulers in Gujarat: The Response to the Portuguese in the Sixteenth Century* (1976).

PERIOD (CA 1200–1700)	AFRICA AND THE MIDDLE EAST	THE AMERICAS
1200	Kingdom of Mali, ca 1200–1450 Mongols conquer Baghdad, 1258; fall of Abbasid Dynasty	Maya civilization in Central America, ca 300–1500 Inca civilization in South America, ca 1000–1500 Toltec hegemony, ca 1000–1300
1300	Rise of Yoruba states, West Africa, ca 1300 Height of Swahili (East African) city-states, ca 1300–1500 Mansa Musa rules Mali, 1312–1337	Tenochtitlán (Mexico City) founded by Aztecs, 1325
1400	Zara Yakob rules Ethiopia, 1434–1468 Arrival of Portugese in Benin, ca 1440 Songhay Empire, West Africa, ca 1450–1591 Atlantic slave trade, ca 1450–1850 Ottoman Empire, 1453–1918 Da Gama arrives on East African coast, 1498	Height of Inca Empire, 1438–1493 Reign of Montezuma I, 1440–1468; height of Aztec culture Columbus reaches the Americas, 1492
1500	Portugal dominates East Africa, ca 1500–1650 Peak of Ottoman power under Suleiman the Magnificent, 1520–1566 Height of Kanem-Bornu under Idris Alooma, 1571–1603 Portuguese found Angola, 1571 Battle of Lepanto, 1571, signals Ottoman naval weakness in the eastern Mediterranean	South American holocaust, ca 1500–1600 First African slaves, ca 1510 Cortés arrives in Mexico, 1519; Aztec Empire falls, 1521 Pizarro reaches Peru, 1531; conquers Incas Spanish conquer the Philippines, 1571
1600	Dutch West India Co. supplants Portuguese in West Africa, ca 1630 Dutch settle Cape Town, 1651 Rise of Ashanti Empire, founded on Gold Coast trade, ca 1700–1750	British settle Jamestown, 1607 Champlain founds Quebec, 1608 Dutch found New Amsterdam, 1624 Black labor allows tenfold increase in production of Carolinian rice and Virginian tobacco, ca 1730–1760 Silver production quadruples in Mexico and Peru, ca 1700–1800

EAST ASIA	INDIA AND SOUTHEAST ASIA	EUROPE
Kamakura Shogunate, 1185–1333 Unsuccessful Mongol invasions of Japan, 1274, 1281 Yüan (Mongol) Dynasty, 1279–1368	Peak of Khmer Empire in southeast Asia, ca 1200 Turkish sultanate at Delhi, 1206–1526; Indian culture divided into Hindu and Muslim	Magna Carta, 1215 Thomas Aquinas, *Summa Theologica*, 1253 Prince Alexander Nevsky recognizes Mongol overlordship of Moscow, 1252
Marco Polo arrives at Kublai Khan's court, ca 1275 Ashikaga Shogunate, 1336–1408 Hung Wu drives Mongols from China, 1368; founds Ming Dynasty, 1368–1644	Mongol chieftain, Timur the Lame (Tamerlame) conquers the Punjab, 1398	Babylonian Captivity of the papacy, 1309–1376 Tver revolt in Russia, 1327–1328 Hundred Years' War, 1337–1453 Bubonic plague, 1347–1352 Ottoman Turks invade Europe, 1356 Peasants' Revolt in England, 1381
Early Ming policy encourages foreign trade, ca 15th century Ming maritime expeditions to India, Middle East, Africa, 1405–1433	Sultan Mehmed II, 1451–1481 Pasha Sinon, Ottoman architect, 1491–1588 Da Gama reaches India, 1498	Beginnings of representative government, ca 1350–1500 Italian Renaissance, ca 1400–1530 Voyages of discovery, ca 1450–1600 Ottomans capture Constantinople, 1453; end of Byzantine Empire War of the Roses in England, 1455–1485 Unification of Spain completed, 1492
Portuguese trade monopoly in East Asia, ca 16th century Christian missionaries active in China and Japan, ca 1550–1650 Unification of Japan, 1568–1600	Safavid Empire, 1501–1722 Barbur defeats Delhi sultanate, 1526–1527; founds Mughal Empire Akbar expands Mughal Empire, 1556–1605 Height of Safavid power under Shah Abbas, 1587–1629	Martin Luther, Ninety-five Theses, 1517 Charles V elected Holy Roman Emperor, 1519 Henry VIII leads English Reformation, 1534 Council of Trent, 1545–1563 Dutch United Provinces declare independence, 1581 Spanish Armada, 1588
Tokugawa Shogunate, 1600–1867 Japan expels all Europeans, 1637 Manchus establish Ch'ing Dynasty, 1644 Height of Manchu Dynasty under K'ang–hsi, 1662–1722 Height of Edo urban culture in Japan, ca 1700	Height of Mughal Empire under Shah Jahan, 1628–1658 British found Calcutta, 1690 Decline of Mughal Empire, ca 1700–1800 Persian invaders sack Delhi, 1739	Romanov Dynasty in Russia, 1613 Thirty Years' War, 1618–1648 Brandenburg-Prussia unified, 1640–1688 English Civil War, 1642–1646 Louis XIV, king of France, 1643–1715 Ottoman Turks besiege Vienna, 1683 Revocation of Edict of Nantes, 1685 The Glorious Revolution in England, 1688 War of Spanish Succession, 1701–1713; Treaty of Utrecht, 1713

24

China and Japan,
ca 1400–1800

Inside the Meridian Gate, looking southwest, Forbidden City

The period from about 1400 to 1800 witnessed growth and dynamic change in East Asia. In China the native Ming Dynasty had replaced the Yuan (see page 322) and was in turn replaced by the foreign Manchu, or Ch'ing, Dynasty. The early Ming period was a time of remarkable economic reconstruction and of the establishment of new and original social institutions. Over time, however, the bureaucracy prevented the changes necessary to meet new demands on the empire. The Ch'ing Dynasty inaugurated a long period of peace, relative prosperity, and population expansion. Under the Ch'ing, the Chinese Empire reached its greatest territorial extent, and literary and artistic creativity reached their apogee.

The Japanese islands, united by Nobunaga and later the Tokugawa Shogunate, underwent further evolution of the feudal military aristocracy (see page 328). Although Japan developed in near-total isolation from outside influences, its sociopolitical system bore striking similarities to medieval European feudalism. The period of the Tokugawa Shogunate, like that of the Ming Dynasty in China, was marked by remarkable agricultural productivity and industrial growth.

- What features characterized the governments of the Ming and Ch'ing in China and the Tokugawa Shogunate in Japan?
- How were Chinese and Japanese societies affected by agricultural and commercial developments?
- How did Chinese thinkers interpret and explain the shift from the Ming to the Ch'ing?

This chapter explores these questions.

CHINA: FROM THE MING TO THE MID-MANCHU DYNASTY (CA 1368–1795)

Mongol repression, rapid inflation of the currency, disputes over succession among the khans, and the growth of peasant secret societies led to the decay of Mongol government in China (see page 322). By 1368, Hung Wu, the leader of a secret society called the "Red Turbans," had pushed the Mongols out of China. Hung Wu (r. 1368–1398),

founder of the Ming Dynasty, and Liu Pang (r. 206–195 B.C.), founder of the Han Dynasty, are the only peasants to found major dynasties in China. The Ming Dynasty (1368–1644) is the only dynasty that originated south of the Yangtze River (see Map 24.1).

Under the Ming, China experienced remarkable change. Agricultural development and commercial reconstruction followed a long period of chaos and disorder. Hung Wu introduced far-reaching social and political institutions that he intended to be hereditary. By the middle of the fifteenth century, however, his administrative framework had begun to decay. Ming government tended to be harshly autocratic. Externally, the Ming emperors strove to push back the Mongols in the north, but Chinese defeats in Mongolia in the later fifteenth century led to a long period of Chinese withdrawal. Nevertheless, the Ming period stands out because of its social and cultural achievements.

The Ming Agricultural and Commercial Revolutions

Mongol exploitation and the civil disorders that accompanied the breakdown of Yuan rule left China in economic chaos in the mid-fourteenth century. Vast stretches of farmland were laid waste, some entirely abandoned. Damaged dikes and canals proved unusable, causing trade to decline.

A profound economic reconstruction occurred between 1370 and 1398. The agricultural revolution that China underwent in the Ming period was in part a gigantic effort at recovery after the disaster of Mongol rule and in part a continuation of developments begun under the Sung (see pages 314–322). At the heart of this revolution was radical improvement in methods of rice production.

More than bread in Europe, rice supplied almost the total nourishment of the population in central and south China. (In north China, wheat, made into steamed or baked bread or into noodles, served as the staple of the diet.) Terracing and irrigation of mountain slopes, introduced in the eleventh century, had increased rice harvests. The introduction of Indochinese, or Champa, rice proved an even greater boon. Champa rice was drought resistant, yielded larger harvests, and could be sown earlier in the year than traditional Chinese rice. Although Champa rice was of lower nutritional quality, it considerably increased the

Chinese Peasants at Work   The Western artist who sketched this picture in the seventeenth century seems to be telling us that human power in agriculture was as common in China as animal power. Note that a woman also pulls the plow; she might have been pregnant. Coco palms (left) are not usually found as far north as China. The pigtailed men date the picture from the Manchu period. *(Source: Caroline Buckler)*

total output of food. Ming farmers experimented with Champa rice that required only sixty days from planting to harvesting, instead of the usual hundred days. Peasants soon reaped two harvests a year, an enormous increase in production.

Other innovations also brought good results. Because the roots of rice plants require a rich supply of oxygen, the water in which rice grows must be kept in motion so that oxygenation can occur. Ming-era peasants introduced irrigation pumps worked by pedals. Farmers also began to stock the rice paddies with fish, which continuously fertilized the rice fields, destroyed malaria-bearing mosquitoes, and enriched the diet. Fish farming in the paddies eventually enabled large, previously uninhabitable parts of southern China to be brought under cultivation. Farmers discovered the possibilities of commercial cropping in cotton, sugar cane, and indigo. Finally, new methods of crop rotation allowed for continuous cultivation and more than one harvest per year from a single field.

The Ming rulers promoted the repopulation and colonization of devastated regions through massive transfers of people. Immigrants received large plots of land and exemption from taxation for many years. Table 24.1, based on fourteenth-century records of newly reclaimed land, helps tell the story.[1]

Reforestation was a dramatic aspect of the agricultural revolution. In 1391 the Ming government ordered 50 million trees planted in the Nanking area. Lumber from the trees was intended for the construction of a maritime fleet. In 1392 each family holding colonized land in Anhwei province had to plant 200 mulberry trees, 200 jujube trees, and 200 persimmon trees. In 1396 peasants in the present-day provinces of Hunan and Hupei in the east planted 84 million fruit trees. Historians have estimated that 1 billion trees were planted during Hung Wu's reign.[2]

What were the social consequences of agricultural development? Increased food production led to steady population growth. Demographers date

TABLE 24.1 LAND RECLAMATION IN EARLY MING CHINA

Year	Reclaimed Land (in hectares; 1 hectare = 2.5 acres)
1371	576,000
1373	1,912,000
1374	4,974,000
1379	1,486,000

Source: J. Gernet, A History of Chinese Civilization, trans. J. R. Foster (Cambridge: Cambridge University Press, 1982), p. 391. Used with permission.

the start of the Chinese population boom at about 1550, as a direct result of improved methods of rice production. Increases in total yields differed fundamentally, however, from comparable agricultural growth in Europe: Chinese grain harvests were improved through intensification of peasant labor. This meant lower income per capita.

Population increase seems to have led to the multiplication of towns and small cities. Urbanization in the Ming era (and, later, in the Ch'ing period) meant the proliferation of market centers and small towns rather than the growth of "large" cities like those in Europe in the High Middle Ages and China in the Sung period. Most people lived in tiny hamlets or villages that had no markets. What distinguished a village from a town was the existence of a market in a town.

Towns held markets twice a week; in southern China, where a week was ten days long, markets were held three times a week. Town markets consisted of little open-air shops that sold essential goods—pins, matches, oil for lamps, candles, paper, incense, tobacco—to country people from surrounding hamlets. The market usually included a tearoom or tavern where tea and rice wine were sold, entertainers performed, and moneylenders and pawnshops sometimes did business. Because itinerant salesmen depended on the city market for their wares, town markets were not held on days when the nearest city had its market.

Tradesmen, who carried their wares on their backs, and craftsmen—carpenters, barbers, joiners, locksmiths—moved constantly from market to market. In large towns and cities foodstuffs from

the countryside and rare and precious goods from distant places were offered for sale. Cities gradually became islands of sophistication in the highly localized Chinese economy. Nanking, for example, spread out enormously because of the presence of the imperial court and bureaucracy. The concentration of people in turn created demand for goods and services. Industrial development was stimulated. Small businesses manufactured textiles, paper, and luxury goods such as silks and porcelains. Nanking and Shanghai became centers for the production of cotton and silks; Hsin-an specialized in the grain and salt trade and in silver. Small towns remained embedded in peasant culture, but large towns and cities pursued contacts with the wider world.

The Government of Hung Wu

Hung Wu's government reforms rested on a few strong centralizing principles. Hung Wu established China's capital at Nanking (literally, "southern capital"), his old base on the Yangtze River. He stripped many nobles of their estates and divided the estates among the peasantry. Although Hung Wu had been a monk, he confiscated many of the temples' tax-exempt lands, thereby increasing the proceeds of the state treasury. In the Sung period, commercial taxes had fed the treasury. In the Ming and, later, the Ch'ing periods, imperial revenues came mainly from agriculture: farmers produced the state's resources.

Hung Wu ordered a general survey of all China's land and several censuses of the population. The data gathered were recorded in official registers, which provided valuable information about the taxes that landlords, temples, and peasants owed. According to the registers, the capital was owed 8 million *shih,* or 160,000 tons, of rice per year. Such thorough fiscal information contributed to the efficient operation of the state.

To secure soldiers for the army and personnel for his administration and to generate revenue, Hung Wu adopted the Yuan practice of requiring service to the state. He made all occupations hereditary. The entire Chinese population was classified into three hereditary categories: peasants, artisans, and soldiers. The state ministry that had jurisdiction over a particular category designated an individual's obligations to the state. The ministry of finance oversaw the peasants, who provided the bulk of the taxes and performed public labor services. The ministry of public works supervised artisans and all people who had special skills and crafts. The ministry of the army controlled the standing army of 2 million men. Each social category prevailed in a particular geographical region: peasants lived in the countryside; craftsmen lived mainly in the neighborhoods of the cities for which they produced goods; army families lived along the coasts and lengthy frontiers that they defended. At birth, every person entered the state category determined by his or her father's occupation; one's descendants belonged to the same category. When a soldier died or proved unable to fight, his family had to provide a replacement.

The Ming emperor wielded absolute and despotic power. Access to his personal favor was the only means of acquiring privilege or some limited derivative power. The complex ceremonial and court ritual surrounding any public appearance by the emperor, the vast imperial palace staffed only by servile women and eunuchs, and the precise procedures of the imperial bureaucracy, which blamed any difficulties on the emperor's advisers—all lent the throne a rarefied aura and exalted the emperor's authority. In addition, Hung Wu demanded that the military nobles (his old rebel comrades-in-arms) live at his court in Nanking, where he could keep an eye on them. He raised many generals to the nobility, a position that be-

Chinese Marketplace This busy scene of commercial activity shows camels, horses, donkeys, and humans used to transport goods. The rich are carried in sedan chairs, while tea shops and restaurants provide a variety of refreshments. *(Source: Werner Forman Archive)*

stowed honor and financial benefits but no political power whatsoever.

Late in his reign Hung Wu executed many nobles and divided China into principalities, putting one of his sons in charge of each. Suspicious even of his sons' loyalty, he carefully circumscribed their power. Positions in the imperial administration were filled in part by civil service examinations, whose re-establishment proved to be Hung Wu's most enduring reform. The examination system, which lasted until the twentieth century, later became the exclusive channel for official recruitment. In the Ming period the examinations required minute knowledge of the ancient Chinese classics and a formal and precise literary style, and they discouraged all originality. They promoted conservatism and opposition to innovation in the bureaucrats who passed them.

After 1426 the eunuch-dominated secret police controlled the palace guards and the imperial workshops, infiltrated the civil service, and headed all foreign missions. Through blackmail, espionage, and corruption, the secret police exercised enormous domestic power. How did eunuchs acquire such power? Without heirs, they had no immediate family concerns. Drawn from the lowest classes of society, viewed with distaste by respectable people, eunuchs had no hope of gaining status except by satisfying every whim of the emperor. They were indifferent to public opinion. Because of their total submission to the emperor, the emperors believed them absolutely trustworthy. Several eunuchs—Wang Chih in the 1470s, Liu Chin in the 1500s, and Wei Chung-hsien in the 1620s—gained dictatorial power when their emperors lost interest in affairs of state.

Foreign affairs occupied much of Hung Wu's attention. He sought to control all Chinese contacts with the outside world, and he repeatedly invaded Mongolia. But the strengthening and extension of

Chinese Coal Miner   In every society mining has been (and is) a hard, dangerous, and dirty work—which helps to explain why in Ming China miners had trouble finding wives. The undesirability of the occupation also helps explain why Hung Wu made all work hereditary: to ensure a continuing workforce. The well-dressed official with sunshade and the half-naked barefoot miner tells an important social story. *(Source: Jean-Loup Charmet)*

the Great Wall stands as Hung Wu's and his Ming successors' most visible achievement. According to one record, the defense system of the Great Wall throughout the Ming period "stretched 10,000 *li* (a *li* is about one-third of a mile) in an unbroken chain from the Yalu River in the east to Jiayuguan in the west."[3] The wall served as a protective girdle around the northern parts of the empire, sheltering towns, cities, and the inner countryside. The forts, beacon towers, and garrisons that pierced the wall at militarily strategic spots kept in close contact with the central government of the emperor. Because of the steady pressure of Mongol attacks in the fifteenth century, Hung Wu's successors continued the work of reinforcing the Great Wall.

Hung Wu forbade free commercial contacts along the coasts between Chinese and foreign merchants. He insisted that foreign states eager to trade with China acknowledge his suzerainty by offering tribute. The early Ming emperors displayed greater military and diplomatic efficiency than had Chinese rulers for centuries. By the mid-fifteenth century, however, the emperors could not restrict the commercial demands of Chinese and foreign traders within tight commercial channels. Mongol raids by land and Japanese piracy at sea, often with the hidden cooperation of the local Chinese, were commonplace. Along the coasts of Kiangsu, Chekiang, and Fukien provinces, Koreans, Vietnamese, Malays, Sumatrans, and Japanese entered China disguised as merchants. If they were dissatisfied with the official rates of exchange, they robbed and destroyed. Neither fortresses and the transfer of coastal settlements inland nor precautionary attacks on pirate merchant raiders and their Chinese allies could suppress the problem. The imperial court came to regard foreigners arriving by ship as barbarians. When Europeans arrived in the sixteenth century, they too were commonly called "barbarians."

Maritime Expansion

Another dramatic development of the Ming period was the series of naval expeditions sent out between 1405 and 1433 under Hung Wu's son Yung Lo and Yung Lo's successor. China had a strong maritime history stretching back to the eleventh century, and these early fifteenth-century voyages were a continuation of that tradition. The Ming expeditions established China as the greatest maritime power in the world—considerably ahead of Portugal, whose major seafaring reconnaissances began a half-century later. The expeditions revealed the scale of Chinese naval power in Asia and exalted the majesty and power of the Chinese emperor.

In contrast to Hung Wu, whose isolationist policy sought to close China to foreign trade, Yung Lo took a positive approach to foreign contacts and foreign trade: he favored overseas exploration and broadened diplomatic and commercial contacts within the tribute system. Yung Lo had two basic motives for launching the voyages. First, he sent them in search of Chien Wen, a serious contender for the throne whom he had defeated but who, rumor claimed, had escaped to Southeast Asia. Second, he launched the expeditions to explore, to expand trade, and to provide the imperial court with luxury objects. Led by the Muslim eunuch admiral Cheng Ho and navigating by compass, seven fleets sailed to East and South Asia. The first expedition (which carried 27,800 men) involved 62 major ships, the largest of which was 440 feet in length and 180 feet in the beam and had 9 masts. The expeditions crossed the Indian Ocean to Ceylon, the Persian Gulf, and the east coast of Africa.

These voyages had important consequences. They extended the prestige of the Ming Dynasty throughout Asia. Trade, in the form of tribute from nineteen states including Java, Sumatra, Malacca, and even Cochin on the west coast of southern India, greatly increased. Diplomatic contacts with the distant Middle East led to the arrival in Nanking of embassies from Egypt. These maritime expeditions also led to the publication of such geographical works as the *Treatise on the Barbarian Kingdoms on the Western Oceans* (1434) and *The Marvels Discovered by the Boat Bound for the Galaxy* (1436). The information acquired from these voyages served as the basis of Chinese knowledge of the maritime world until the nineteenth century. Finally, these expeditions resulted in Chinese emigration to the countries of Southeast Asia and the ports of southern India. The voyages were terminated because Confucian court intellectuals persuaded the emperor that his quest for strange and exotic things signaled the collapse of the dynasty.[4] After 1435, China returned to a policy of isolation.

Decline of the Ming Dynasty

A bitter struggle for the throne ensued when Hung Wu died. Eventually his fourth son prevailed, taking the regnal name Yung Lo (r. 1403–1424). The bloody wars that brought Yung Lo to the throne devastated the territory between the Yellow River and the Yangtze, and he promoted a policy of resettlement there. Yung Lo continued his father's policies of requiring civil service examinations, controlling the nobility, and trying to restrain pirates. His most significant act, however, proved to be the transfer of the capital back to Peking. Yung Lo had served as governor *(wang)* of the north during his father's reign, and he felt greater support there than in the south. Peking was also closer to the northern frontier and thus was a better place for strategic defense against China's ancient enemies, the Mongols. The move pleased the military faction but hurt the new gentry and mercantile groups whose economic interests centered around Nanking.

The extravagance of the imperial court caused economic difficulties. Hung Wu had exercised fiscal restraint, but Yung Lo and his successors tried to outdo the splendor and magnificence of the Mongols. Yung Lo rebuilt his palaces and temples in a monumental style; their grandeur surpassed that of Louis XIV's Versailles. The emperor and his court lived in the Forbidden City, a quarter-mile compound filled with palatial buildings, ceremonial halls, marbled terraces, and lengthy galleries. The Forbidden City was surrounded

by the Imperial City, an area of no less than three square miles, also closed to the public. Within the enclosure were numerous avenues and artificial lakes. In addition to imperial villas, temples, and residences of eunuch officials inside the compound, there were also supply depots and material-processing plants. Among them was the court of Imperial Entertainments, which had the capacity to serve banquets for up to 15,000 men on short notice. Next to the bakery, distillery, and confectionery were the emperor's stable, armory, printing-office, and book depository. In sum, the palace was completely self-sufficient.[5]

A century and a half later, in the reign of the emperor Wan-li, everything required for the maintenance of the Imperial City was manufactured or deposited there. Approximately 20,000 eunuchs, some of whom held top positions in the imperial entourage, worked there. Some 3,000 female domestics performed household tasks. The emperor's immediate court—councilors, bodyguards, relatives, official wives, and concubines—numbered several thousand people. Supporting so many people on a lavish scale placed a great burden on the treasury. Financial difficulties thus played a major role in the decline of the Ming.

Yung Lo's successors lacked his drive and ability. The Mongols continued to press on the northern borders, and the Chinese had to yield some territory. In 1449 an ill-prepared and thoroughly inexperienced expedition launched by the eunuch Wang Zhen, with the participation of the young emperor Ying-tsung (r. 1436–1450 and 1457–1464), met total disaster. The emperor was captured and remained a prisoner of the Mongols for seven years. He regained his throne only with great difficulty. In the south, a Chinese army of 200,000 had pressed into northern Vietnam in 1406. This imperialistic move led to temporary Chinese domination of the Red River basin and of much of central Vietnam. A Vietnamese liberation movement retaliated and by 1427 had driven the occupiers out. In the sixteenth century the Japanese accelerated their coastal raids and even sacked the cities of Ningpo and Yangchow. Difficulties in collecting taxes hindered the government's ability to strengthen the army. It was commonplace in the eleven hundred counties of Ming China for people to delay or refuse to pay taxes, aware that no magistrate could prosecute thousands of delinquents. Their taxes were eventually written off. Without adequate revenues, the empire could not maintain a strong army to defend itself.

In spite of these pressures, the empire did not fall apart. In fact, southern China enjoyed considerable prosperity in the late sixteenth and early seventeenth centuries. Why? Japanese, Portuguese, and Dutch merchants paid in silver for the Chinese silks and ceramics they bought. The steady flow of silver into China from the trade with Japan—and, later, from the mines of Mexico and Peru via Spain—had momentous consequences. The value of Chinese paper currency, which had been in circulation since the eleventh century, drastically declined. Unable to control either the state economy or local commercial activity, the imperial government had to adopt a more liberal attitude and simply acquiesce in foreign trade. The emperor also had to recognize the triumph of silver as a medium of exchange.

In the southern maritime provinces, where trade flourished with Japan, the Philippines, and Indonesia, merchants invested surplus capital in new ventures in the towns. So many peasants migrated to the towns seeking employment that agriculture declined. Some businesses employed several hundred workers, many of them women. According to a French scholar, "Peasant women took jobs at Sung-chiang, southwest of Shanghai in the cotton mills. According to contemporary descriptions, in the big workshops the employees were already the anonymous labor force that we regard as characteristic of the industrial age."[6]

Sung-chiang developed into a large cotton-weaving center; Soochow became famous for its luxury silks; and by the end of the sixteenth century paper factories in Kiangsi employed 50,000 workers.

By the late sixteenth century China was participating in the emerging global economy. Portuguese ships carried Chinese silks and ceramics to Nagasaki and returned with Japanese silver. The huge Ming merchant marine, built from the trees planted by Hung Wu and more technically proficient for long sea voyages than were the Spanish and Portuguese fleets, transported textiles, porcelains, silk, and paper to Manila in the Philippines

Porcelain Manufacture   In the eighteenth century the city of Jingdezhen expanded as a commercial center, based on the manufacture of porcelain for the elite and for the Western export market. Chinese porcelain, already imitated by Muslim craftsmen at Baghdad and Isfahan, was soon copied by Westerners, such as the Wedgwoods of England. The word "china," meaning porcelain, entered the English language in 1579. (*Source: Reprinted by permission of the Cornell University Library, Wason Collection*)

and brought back sweet potatoes, tobacco, fire-arms, and silver. From Manila the Spanish fleet carried Chinese goods to the markets of Barcelona, Antwerp, and Venice. The Dutch transported tea by the boatload from Fukien and Chekiang for the castles and drawing rooms of Europe.[7] Europeans paid for most of their imports with silver. Recent scholars argue that between one-third and one-half of all the silver mined in the Americas between 1527 and 1821 wound up in China. Spanish galleons carried it from Acapulco to Manila and thence to Chinese ports[8] (see page 577).

In the middle of the sixteenth century, China showed many signs of developing into an urban mercantile society. Merchants and businessmen had large amounts of capital, and they invested it not in land, as in the past, but in commercial and craft industries. Silk making, cotton weaving, porcelain manufacture, printing, and steel production assumed a definite industrial character. Technical treatises reveal considerable progress in manufacturing procedures. For example, silk looms had three or four shuttle winders. Printers could produce a sheet of paper with three or four different colors, similar to the page of a modern magazine. Chinese ceramics displayed astonishing technology—which helps explain the huge demand for them. Likewise, agricultural treatises described new machines for working the soil, sowing seed, and irrigation. Population, which stood at roughly 70 million at the start of the Ming period, increased to about 130 million by 1600.

With population, technology, and ready capital, why did China fail to develop something comparable to what Westerners later called an industrial or commercial revolution? The answer lies in the financial and political crises and the external threats that the state faced. The traditional Chinese value system, moreover, did not esteem commerce, industry, or social change.

In 1600 the Ming Dynasty faced grave political and economic problems. The Manchus, a Tungusic people from Manchuria, threatened from the north. Wars against the Japanese and Koreans had depleted the imperial treasury. As rich landowners bought up the lands assigned to farm families, the social structures set up by Hung Wu broke down. The government had to hire mercenaries; the military, considered a disreputable profession, drew the dregs of society. According to the Italian Jesuit missionary Matteo Ricci (1552–1610), "All those

under arms lead a despicable life, for they have not embraced this profession out of love of their country or devotion to their king or love of honour and glory, but as men in the service of a provider of employment."[9]

Maintenance of the army placed a heavy burden on the state. Meanwhile, the imperial court continued to squander vast sums on an ostentatious lifestyle and the allowances of the extended imperial family. Under the emperor Wan-li, forty-five princes of the first rank received annual incomes of 10,000 *shih* (the money equivalent of 10,000 tons of grain), and 21,000 lesser nobles also received large allowances. The emperors increased domestic sales taxes, established customs posts for export-import duties, and laid ever-more-crushing taxes on the peasants. New taxes provoked violent riots in the large commercial centers of Soochow, Hangchow, and Peking. Between 1619 and 1627, greedy court eunuchs helped precipitate a crisis. The eunuch Wei Chung-hsien (1568–1627) exercised a two-year reign of terror and sent hundreds of honest civil servants to their deaths as conspirators. The bureaucracy, which the eunuchs controlled, was so torn by factions that it could not function.

Finally, the emperors became victims of their training and servants rather than masters of the bureaucracy. A Ming emperor was taught that his primary duties were to venerate Heaven (the Chinese deity) and to follow the precedents set by his ancestors. As long as the emperor performed certain time-honored rituals, he retained the Mandate of Heaven, the traditional legitimization of Chinese rulers. In a society lacking a strong army and effective bureaucratic institutions, it was imperial ritual that connected the ordinary person to the state by imbuing awe, respect, and loyalty. Thus the emperors spent a large part of each day in the performance of imperial ceremonies that they began to resent.

The reign of Emperor Wan-li (r. 1573–1619), who ruled longer than any other member of the dynasty, illustrates what happened when the emperor was at odds with the system. An intelligent man with some good ideas, Wan-li felt that the bureaucrats opposed everything he wanted to do. When he tried to increase the size of the army and to improve its effectiveness through drills and maneuvers, civil service officials sent him lengthy petitions calling for an end to such exercises. When he wanted to take personal command of the army at a time of foreign invasion, bureaucrats told him that precedent forbade his leaving the Imperial City. Wan-li gradually reached the conclusion that the monarchy had become no more than a set of stylized performances. Stymied in whatever he wanted to do, he simply refused to make state decisions. He devoted his time to his horses and, while still a young man, to the construction of his tomb. Imperial decisions were postponed. Factional strife among the court eunuchs and bureaucrats increased. The wheels of government ground to a halt.[10]

Meanwhile, the Manchus pressed against China's northeastern border. Under their leader Nurhachi (1559–1626), they built a powerful military and administrative organization and gained the allegiance of the Mongols and other tribes. As the Ming government in Peking floundered, public anger at bureaucratic corruption mounted. Ming troops, their pay in arrears, turned outlaw. Droughts led to crop failures, which in turn caused widespread famines. Starving peasants turned to banditry, and entire provinces revolted. The general decay paved the way for Manchu conquest.

The dynastic shift from the Ming to the Ch'ing (Manchu) seemed to fulfill the Han Confucian doctrine that history operates in a cyclical fashion. The Ming emperor apparently had forfeited the Mandate of Heaven (see page 104). According to Han Confucian scholars, a wise ruler satisfies Heaven's mandate by observing the proper Confucian rites of social intercourse. If the emperor is respectful to his parents, attentive to his ministers, and concerned for his subjects, then the empire and the civilized world will flourish. Because Chinese government lacked adequate checks on bureaucratic performance, imperial dynasties relied on Confucian modes of behavior—that is, on officials' sense of self-restraint. The emperor was supposed to be a model. If he was virtuous, his officials were likely to be so too. If he looked to his own self-interest, his civil servants would probably do likewise, to the cost of the general welfare: corruption would spread, taxes would become oppressive, and peasants would revolt.

In the popular understanding of the Mandate of Heaven, the natural and political orders were closely linked, and events such as droughts, famines, earthquakes, floods, and volcanic eruptions were signs of Heaven's displeasure and signaled that conditions were ripe for the appearance of a new dynasty. Predictably, when it seemed that the Mandate of Heaven had been withdrawn from the Ming emperor and was about to redescend on someone worthy, ambitious generals, bandit warlords, and popular movements appeared. "The prospect of a new mandate feverishly excited rebellions, which seemed in turn to prove that the previous dynastic cycle had reached its term."[11] Such events had accompanied the collapse of the Yuan and the rise of the Ming, and similar developments greeted the fall of the Ming and the emergence of the Ch'ing.

Manchu Rule

In 1644 the Manchus declared a new dynasty, the Ch'ing. They went on to capture Peking and slowly gain control of all China. Their initial success was due more to the internal weaknesses of the Ming than to special strengths of their own. Other developments help explain their ultimate victory and rule. The gentry and business classes, centered in the south around Nanking, had been alienated by the Ming court's fiscal mismanagement and demands for more taxes. Although various Ming princelings and local bandit groups had risen against the Manchus, the army lacked good equipment and staying power and gradually collapsed. The entry of the Manchus' imperial armies into Yunnan in 1681 marked their complete military triumph.

By purging the civil service of the old court eunuchs and troublesome factions, and by offering Chinese intellectuals positions in the bureaucracy, the Manchus gained the support of the influential academic and intellectual classes. Chinese scholars flocked to Peking. The Manchu government, staffed by able and honest Chinese, became much more efficient than the Ming.

The Ch'ing Dynasty—the name adopted by the Manchus means "pure" or "unsullied"—ruled until 1912. In its heyday in the eighteenth century, the Ch'ing Empire covered much of Asia—China proper, Manchuria, Mongolia, Tibet, and Sinkiang—and enjoyed tribute from Burma, Nepal, Laos, Siam, Annam, and Korea (Map 24.1). China had the largest population on earth and achieved an unprecedented degree of prosperity.

How did 1 million Manchus govern 350 million Chinese? The Ch'ing Dynasty retained the basic structures of Ming and Confucian government.

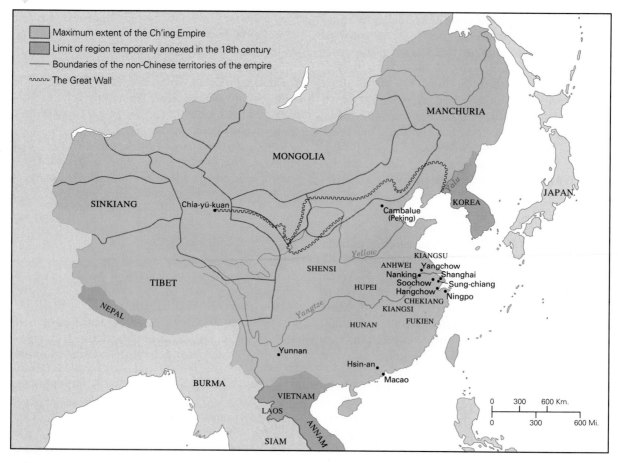

MAP 24.1 China: Ch'ing Empire, 1759 The sheer size of the Ch'ing Empire in China almost inevitably led to its profound cultural influence on the rest of Asia. What geographical and political factors limited the extent of the empire?

The emperor governed as supreme and autocratic ruler with the Mandate of Heaven. The bureaucracies continued as they had in Ming and earlier times: the imperial household bureaucracy managed the emperor's palaces and households; the central bureaucracy administered his vast empire. Most positions in the empire were assigned on the basis of candidates' performances in the civil service examinations in the Confucian classics. The highest positions in Peking and in the provinces of China were open to Chinese as well as to Manchus. These measures pacified the Chinese economic and intellectual elites. The Manchus, however, maintained a privileged status in society. They wore distinctive clothes, did not practice foot binding, retained their own language and alphabet, and maintained ethnic separatism by forbidding intermarriage with the Chinese. The Manchus required Chinese males to wear their hair in a pigtail as a sign of subservience.

The agricultural improvements begun in the Ming period had profound social effects in the eighteenth century. China experienced a population explosion, as the statistics in Table 24.2 illustrate.

Internal peace, relative prosperity, and engineering methods that prevented flooding of the countryside contributed to the steady growth of population. But in the late eighteenth century growth without increased agricultural output led to rebellions and uprisings that eventually weakened the Ch'ing Dynasty.

The reign of the emperor K'ang-hsi (r. 1662–1722) launched a period of great achievement. A contemporary of the Indian ruler Aurang-zeb, the French king Louis XIV, and the Russian tsar Peter the Great, K'ang-hsi demonstrated exceptional intelligence, energy, and concern for the welfare of his people. He also enjoyed much greater freedom of action than had the Ming emperor Wan-li a century earlier. Whereas Wan-li had been a captive of precedent, incapable of making changes, K'ang-hsi cut both court expenses and taxes and traveled extensively throughout his domain. On these trips he investigated the conduct of local bureaucrats in an effort to prevent them from oppressing the people. Where Wan-li had vacillated in the face of domestic revolt and foreign invasion, K'ang-hsi squarely faced a massive rebellion in southern China in 1678 and thoroughly crushed it. He personally led an army into Mongolia and smashed the forces of the Mongol leader Galdan. This victory permanently eliminated the danger of a reinvigorated Mongolian empire on China's borders.

K'ang-hsi also cultivated the arts of peace. He invited scholars to his court and subsidized the compilation of a huge encyclopedia and two monumental dictionaries. *The Complete Library of the Four Treasuries,* a collection of all of Chinese literature, required the work of 15,000 calligraphers and 361 editors. It preserved the Chinese literary tradition. K'ang-hsi's contributions to literature hold a distinguished place in the long history of Chinese culture. Europeans and Americans, however, appreciate this period primarily for its excellent porcelain. The word *china* entered the English language and became synonymous with fine pottery and tableware. An imperial factory at Kiangsi, directly controlled by K'ang-hsi's court, produced porcelain masterpieces. Monochrome vases, bowls, and dishes in oxblood, pale green, and dark blue, and polychromes in blue and white, enjoyed enormous popularity in Paris, London, and New York in the eighteenth century and ever since.

The long reign of the Ch'ien-lung emperor (r. 1736–1795) marked the zenith of the Ch'ing Dynasty. The cultivation of new crops from the Americas, such as white potatoes, corn, and peanuts, on marginal lands helped to support the steadily expanding population. Chinese rule was extended into central Asia. The imperial court continued to support arts and letters. In the last two decades of his reign, however, Ch'ien-lung showered titles, gifts, and offices on a handsome young Manchu named Ho-shen. Contemporaries

TABLE 24.2 POPULATION OF CHINA, 1578–1989

Year	Government	Population (in millions)	
		Families	Individuals
1578	Ming Dynasty	10.6	60.7
1662	Ch'ing Dynasty	19.2	100.0
1710		23.3	116.0
1729		25.5	127.0
1741			143.4
1754			184.5
1778			243.0
1796			275.7
1814			374.6
1850			414.5
1953	People's Republic		601.9
1974			800.0
1989			1,064.1

considered him uncultured, greedy, and ambitious. The corruption of the imperial civil service under Ho-shen, combined with heavy taxation, sparked revolts that continued to the end of the dynasty in 1912.

The Life of the People

The family is the fundamental unit of every society. In Ming and Ch'ing China, however, the family exercised greater social influence than it did anywhere else—and far more than in Western societies. The family directed the moral education of the child, the economic advancement and marriage of the young, and religious life through ceremonial rites honoring family ancestors. The Chinese family discharged many of the roles that the Christian church performed in Europe in the Middle Ages and that the state carries out today. It assumed total responsibility for the sick, the indigent, and the aged. The family expected and almost invariably received the full devotion and loyalty of its members. A person without a family had no material or psychological support.

Poor families tended to be nuclear: couples established their own households and raised their own children. The educated, the middle class, and the wealthy frequently resided in extended families: several generations of patrilineal relatives and their wives lived together in one large house or compound, individual families occupying different sections. In both kinds of families, the paternal head of the family held autocratic power over all members of the household. When he died, his authority passed to his eldest son.

The father led the family in the ancient Confucian rites honoring the family ancestors. If these ceremonies were not continued by the next generation, the family suffered social disgrace and, it was believed, the dead endured great misery. Thus marriage and childbearing were extremely important.

Almost everyone married. Reverence for one's parents, maintenance of the family, and perpetua-

tion of the line required that sons marry shortly after reaching puberty. The father and family elders discussed the possibilities and employed a local go-between to negotiate with the prospective bride's family. The go-between drew up a marriage contract specifying the property, furniture, clothing, and gifts that the two young people would bring to the union. As elsewhere, parents wanted to make the most economically and socially advantageous union for their children. The couple had no part in these arrangements. Often they had never seen each other until the groom lifted the bride's veil on their wedding day. But they had been brought up to accept this custom.

A Chinese bride became part of her husband's family, subject to him and to her in-laws. Her first duty was to bear sons. If she did not, she might adopt one. Failure to provide heirs gave her hus-

Children Playing in a Garden Produced on silk, this charming scene of children (obviously upper class) playing reflects both the brilliance of Chinese manufacture and use of silk and the affection in which children were held. (*Source: Courtesy of the Freer Gallery of Art, Smithsonian Institution*)

band grounds for divorce, which brought great disgrace on her family. A woman, however, could not divorce her husband for any reason. Divorce was extremely rare in Chinese society, but a wealthy man with a "nonproductive" wife might bring concubines to live in the house along with his wife.

Because males performed the all-important ceremonies in honor of the family ancestors, they held a much higher position in society than did women. The desperately poor often killed girl babies or sold their daughters as servants or concubines. Young brides came under the direct control of their mothers-in-law, whose severity and cruelty are a common theme in Chinese literature. Once a strong-willed woman had sons, she gained increasing respect as the years went by. The Chinese deeply respected age. Some women of the wealthy classes, with servants to do the household chores, spent their days in semiseclusion nibbling dainties, smoking opium, and gambling. Women who brought large dowries to their marriages could dispose of part of those dowries as they wished. Some invested in profitable business activities. Poor women worked in the fields beside their husbands, in addition to bearing children and managing the household.

The educational system during the Ming and Ch'ing periods had both virtues and weaknesses. Most villages and all towns and cities operated schools that prepared boys for the all-important civil service examinations. Boys learned to write with a brush the approximately three thousand commonly used characters of literary Chinese; and they learned from memory the standard texts of Confucian philosophy, ethics, and history. The curriculum was very limited, and the instructional method stressed memorization and discouraged imagination. The successful civil service candidate received no practical training in the work of government. But the system yielded a high percentage of literate men (relative to Europe at the same time), preserved the ethical values of Chinese culture, and gave Chinese society cohesion and stability. All educated Chinese shared the same basic literary culture, much as medieval Europeans were formed by Latin Christian culture.

In China, as in medieval Europe, educational opportunities for girls were severely limited. Rich men occasionally hired tutors for their daughters, and a few women achieved exceptional knowledge. Most women of all classes received training that

Chinese Scholars The civil service examinations, the chief means of access to governmental positions and social status, inculcated total submission to the autocratic state. The largest number of candidates took the examinations in general knowledge and literary ability. Here candidates stand at writing desks, composing essays. (*Source: Bibliothèque Nationale, Paris*)

prepared them for roles as wives and mothers: courteous behavior, submission to their husbands, and the administration of a household.

In sharp contrast to the social structure of Europe, Chinese society had few hard-and-fast lines. The emperors fought the development of a hereditary aristocracy, which would have worked against the interest of absolute monarchy. Few titles of nobility were granted in perpetuity. Meanwhile, the state bureaucracy provided opportunities and motivation for upward mobility. The entire family supported and encouraged intelligent sons to prepare for the civil service examinations, and the work and self-sacrifice of the parents bore fruit in the sons. Positions in the bureaucracy brought salaries and gifts, which the family invariably invested in land. The competitive examinations—

open, with few exceptions, to all classes—prevented the formation of a ruling caste. Since everyone accepted the Confucian principle that the nation should be led by the learned and civilized, scholars ranked highest in the social order. They, along with Heaven, Earth, the emperor, and parents, deserved special veneration. With the possible exception of the Jewish people, no people has respected learning as much as the Chinese, who gave special deference to the teacher-scholar. Farmers merited esteem because they produced food, merchants less so because they were believed to live off the profits of others' toil. Merchants tried to marry into the scholar class in order to rise on the social ladder, but China did not develop an articulate bourgeoisie. At the bottom of society were actors, prostitutes, and the many beggars.

The Chinese found recreation and relaxation in many ways. All classes gambled at cards and simple numbers games. The teahouse served as the local meeting place to exchange news and gossip and to listen to the tales of professional storytellers, who enjoyed great popularity. The affluent indulged in an alcoholic drink made from fermented and distilled rice, and both men and women liked pipes and tobacco. Everyone who could afford to went to theaters, which were a central part of Chinese culture. The actors wore happy and sad masks like their ancient Greek counterparts, and their gestures were formal and heavily stylized; the plays typically dramatized episodes from Chinese history and literature. The Chinese associated athletics, riding, and horse racing with soldiers, at best a necessary evil, and regarded the active life as the direct antithesis of the scholarly contemplation they most valued.

JAPAN (CA 1400–1800)

The Ashikaga Shogunate lasted from the middle of the fourteenth to the late sixteenth century. During this period, Japanese society experienced almost continual violence and civil war. Weak central governments could not maintain order.

Chinese Cookery Everywhere in the world, until very recently, meat was scarce and thus a luxury. In China, the shortage of meat encouraged great sophistication in the preparation of foods, especially vegetables. Although European travelers interpreted the frequency of vegetables and fish as a sign of poverty, the Chinese, if we can trust modern nutritionists, probably had the healthier diet. Notice the variety of dishes. Women obviously ate separately. *(Source: Roger-Viollet)*

Women Husking Rice   Rice was basic to Japanese culture. Farmers paid their taxes to the daimyo's agent in rice, and the daimyo paid the salaries of the samurai in rice. It was the staple of the diet eaten by all classes. Here women husk the rice, separate the grains from the chaff using a primitive machine, and clean and pack the rice in bales made of rice stalks. *(Source: Laurie Platt Winfrey, Inc.)*

Throughout the islands, local strong men destroyed weak ones. Around 1450, 250 *daimyos,* or lords, held power; by 1600, only 12 survivors could claim descent from daimyo families of the earlier date. Successful military leaders carved out large territories and governed them as independent rulers. Political and social conditions in fifteenth- and sixteenth-century Japan strongly resembled conditions in western Europe in the tenth and eleventh centuries. Political power was in the hands of a small group of military leaders. Historians often use the same term—*feudalism*—to describe the Japanese and the European experience. As in medieval Europe, feudalism paved the way for the rise of a strong centralized state in seventeenth-century Japan.

Feudalism in Japan

Feudalism played a powerful role in Japanese culture until the nineteenth century. The similarities between feudalism in Japan and in medieval Europe have fascinated scholars, as have the very significant differences. In Europe, feudalism emerged out of the fusion of Germanic and Roman social institutions and flowered under the impact of Muslim and Viking invasions. Likewise in Japan, feudalism evolved from a combination of the native warrior tradition and Chinese Confucian ethics. Japanese society had adopted the Confucian emphasis on filial respect for the head of the family, for the local civil authorities, and for the supreme authority at the head of the state.

The two constituent elements of Japanese feudalism appeared between the eighth and the twelfth centuries: (1) the *shoen,* or land, with its *shiki,* or rights, and (2) the military warrior clique. Some scholars have equated the shoen with the European manor, but the comparison needs careful qualification. A manor corresponded to one composite village; a particular family's shoen was widely scattered. Those who held shoen possessed the shiki there—that is, the right to the income or rice produced by the land. On the other hand, just as several persons might hold rights—military, judicial, grazing—on a medieval European manor and all these rights yielded income, so several persons frequently held shiki on a Japanese estate.

By the sixteenth century, however, most warriors had no connection with the estate. Only a small proportion of samurai attained the rank of daimyo and possessed a shoen. Most warriors received from their daimyos stipends in rice, not in land. In this respect they resembled European knights, who were supported by cash or money fiefs. They were salaried fighters with no connection to land.

The Japanese samurai warrior resembled the knight of twelfth-century France in other ways as well. Both were armed with expensive weapons, and both fought on horseback. Just as the knight was supposed to live according to the chivalric code (see page 386), so Japanese samurai were expected to live according to *Bushido,* a code that stressed military honor, courage, stoic acceptance of hardship, and, above all, loyalty. Disloyalty brought social disgrace, which the samurai could avoid only through *seppuku* (or *hara-kiri*), ritual suicide by slashing his belly. Samurai and knights were both highly conscious of themselves as aristocrats. But knights fought as groups, and samurai fought as individuals.

By the middle of the sixteenth century Japanese feudalism had taken on other distinctive features. As the number of shoen decreased and the powerful daimyos consolidated their territories, the practice of primogeniture became common. Instead of being divided among all of a lord's children, the estate was kept intact and assigned to the eldest or ablest son. Moreover, the nature of warfare changed. As in medieval Europe, the typical method of warfare had been to besiege a castle and wait for it to surrender. Around 1540 the introduction of the musket from Europe made infantrymen effective against mounted samurai, and the use of Western cannon required more elaborately fortified castles. Thus, in addition to armed cavalrymen, daimyos began to employ large numbers of foot soldiers equipped with spears. The countryside also saw the construction of new castles. These military and social developments occurred during a century of turbulence and chronic disorder, out of which emerged a leader who ended the chaos and began the process of unification, laying the foundation of the modern Japanese national state.

Nobunaga and National Unification

Oda Nobunaga, a samurai of the lesser daimyo class, won control of his native province of Owari in 1559. He began immediately to extend his power and made himself lord of the eastern province of Mikawa. Nobunaga defeated a powerful daimyo in 1560 and eight years later seized Kyoto, the capital city, where the emperor and his court resided. As a result, Nobunaga became the virtual ruler of central Japan.

Scholars have called the years 1568 to 1600 the period of "national unification." During this time Japan underwent aggressive and dynamic change. Adopting the motto "Rule the empire by force," Nobunaga set out to subdue all real and potential enemies of unification. With the support of Toyotomi Hideyoshi, a brilliant but low-born general, he subdued most of western Japan. In 1575 Nobunaga's use of firearms at the Battle of Nagashino led to a decisive victory that added the province of Totomi to his domain. When Hideyoshi smashed the great fortress of Odawara, eastern and northern Japan came under Nobunaga's control as well.

The great Buddhist temple-fortresses proved to be Nobunaga's biggest problem. Some of these monasteries possessed vast wealth and armed retainers, and they actively intervened in secular affairs. During the civil wars the Buddhists had supported various daimyos in their private wars, but Nobunaga would tolerate no such interference. The strategically located monastery on Mount Hiei near Kyoto had long provided sanctuary for political factions, but previous daimyos had refused to attack it because it was sacred. Nobunaga had his troops surround Mount Hiei and set fire to the thickets on the lower slopes of the mountain. As the monks and lay people fled the fire, Nobunaga's men slaughtered them by the thousands. The destruction of Japan's most powerful monastery ended Buddhist influence as a political force.

Although Nobunaga won control of most of Japan by the sword, he backed up his conquests with government machinery and a policy of conciliation. He gave lands and subordinate positions in the army to his defeated enemies. Trusted daimyos received complete civil jurisdiction over entire provinces. At strategic points, such as Nijo near Kyoto and Azuchi on the shore of Lake Biwa, Nobunaga built castles to serve as key administrative and defensive centers for the surrounding territories. He opened the little fishing village of Nagasaki to foreign commerce; it soon grew into the nation's largest port. He standardized the currency, eliminated customs barriers, and encouraged the development of trade and industry. In

1582, when Nobunaga was murdered by one of his vassals, his general and staunchest adherent, Hideyoshi, carried on his work.

The son of a peasant, Hideyoshi had risen to power by his military bootstraps: he was an exceptionally able field commander. Hideyoshi advanced the unification and centralization of Japan in two important ways. First, in 1582 he attacked the great fortress at Takamatsu; when direct assault failed, his troops flooded the castle (which stood on marshy ground) and forced its surrender. When Takamatsu fell, so did the large province of Mori. A successful siege of the town of Kagoshima then brought the southern island of Kyushu under his domination. Hideyoshi soothed the vanquished daimyos as Nobunaga had done—with lands and military positions—but he also required them to swear allegiance and to obey him "down to the smallest particular."[12]

Having reduced his most dangerous adversaries and taken steps to control the daimyos, Hideyoshi ordered a survey of the entire country. The military power of the unified Japanese state depended on a strong agricultural base, and Hideyoshi wanted to exploit the peasantry fully. His agents collected detailed information about the daimyos' lands and about towns, villages, agricultural produce, and industrial output all over Japan. A sort of Japanese equivalent of the *Domesday Book* (see page 407), this material enabled Hideyoshi to assess military quotas and taxable property. His surveys tied the peasant population to the land and tightened the collection of the land tax. When Hideyoshi died in 1598, he left a strong centralized state. Brute force had created a unified Japan.

On his deathbed the old soldier had set up a council of regents to govern during the minority of his infant son. The strongest regent was Hideyoshi's long-time supporter, Tokugawa Ieyasu, who ruled vast territories around Edo, modern-day Tokyo. Ieyasu quickly eliminated the young ruler, and in 1600 at Sekigahara he smashed a coalition of daimyo defenders of the heir. This battle was the beginning of the Tokugawa regime.

Tokugawa Ieyasu A short, stocky man who had spent most of his life on horseback, Ieyasu was sixty-two when he secured appointment as shogun. Having unified Japan and established a peace that lasted two hundred and fifty years, he ranks with George Washington and Peter the Great of Russia as one of the great nation builders in world history. In this iconic style of Shinto painting, the elderly Ieyasu is depicted as a deity. *(Source: The Tokugawa Foundation)*

The Tokugawa Regime

Japanese children are taught that "Ieyasu ate the pie that Nobunaga made and Hideyoshi baked." As the aphorism suggests, Ieyasu took over and completed the work begun by his able predecessors. He took decisive steps to solidify his dynasty and control the feudal nobility and to maintain peace and prosperity in Japan. The Tokugawa regime that Ieyasu fashioned worked remarkably well, lasting until 1867.

Ieyasu obtained from the emperor the title of *shogun*, which meant that he and his heirs had the right to command everyone. Constitutionally, the emperor exercised sovereign authority. In practice, authority and power—both the legal right and the physical means—were held by the Tokugawa shogun. Ieyasu declared the emperor and his court at Kyoto "very precious and decorative, like gold and silver," and surrounded the imperial court with all the ceremonial trappings but none of the realities of power.

In a scheme reminiscent of Louis XIV (see pages 612–614) and Peter the Great (see page 642), Ieyasu forced the feudal lords to establish "alternate residence" at his capital city of Edo, to spend every other year there, and to leave their wives and sons there—essentially as hostages. This requirement had obvious advantages: the shogun could keep close tabs on the daimyos, control them through their children, and weaken them financially with the burden of maintaining two residences. Ieyasu justified this course of action by invoking the *Bushido* code, with its emphasis on loyalty. He forbade members of the nobility to marry without his consent, thus preventing the formation of dangerous alliances. The Tokugawa shoguns also severely restricted the construction of castles—symbols, in Japan as in medieval Europe, of feudal independence. Members of the aristocratic samurai class, however, possessed the right to wear two swords, and they exercised full administrative powers within their own domains. In effect, the country was governed by martial law in peacetime. Only warriors could hold official positions in the state bureaucracy. Finally, a network of spies kept close watch on the nobility.

As in medieval Europe and early modern China, the agricultural class held a respected position because its members provided Japanese society with sustenance. Even so, farmers had to mind their betters, and they bore a disproportionate share of the tax load. According to the survey made by Hideyoshi, taxes were imposed on villages, not on individuals; the tax varied between 30 and 40 percent of the rice crop.

As in the social ideologies of Europe and China, so in Japan the commercial classes occupied the lowest rungs on the social ladder because they profited from the toil of others. The peace that the Tokugawa Shogunate imposed in the seventeenth century brought a steady rise in population and prosperity. As demand for goods grew, so did the numbers of merchants. To maintain stability, the early Tokugawa shoguns froze the four social

categories: imperial court nobility, samurai, peasants, and merchants. Laws rigidly prescribed what each class could and could not do. Nobles, for example, were "strictly forbidden whether by day or by night, to go sauntering through the streets or lanes in places where they have no business to be." Daimyos were prohibited from moving troops outside their frontiers, making alliances, and coining money. Designated dress and stiff rules of etiquette distinguished one class from another.[13] This kind of stratification was successful in its purpose: it protected the Tokugawa shoguns from daimyo attack and inaugurated a long era of peace.

To maintain dynastic stability and internal peace, Ieyasu's descendants imposed measures called *sakoku,* or the "closed country policy," which sealed Japan's borders around 1636. Japanese were forbidden to leave the country. Foreigners were excluded.

In 1549 the Jesuit missionary Francis Xavier had landed at Kagoshima. He soon made many converts among the poor and even some among the daimyos. By 1600 there were 300,000 baptized Christians, most of them on the southernmost island of Kyushu, where the shogun's power was weakest and the loyalty of the daimyos most doubtful (Map 24.2). In 1615 bands of Christian samurai supported Ieyasu's enemies at the fierce Battle of Osaka. In 1637 30,000 peasants in the heavily Catholic area of northern Kyushu revolted. The shoguns thus came to associate Christianity with domestic disorder and feudal rebellion. Accordingly, what had been mild persecution became ruthless repression after 1639. Foreign priests were expelled or tortured, and thousands of Japanese Christians suffered crucifixion. The "closed country policy" remained in force for almost two centuries as a means of controlling religious organizations and securing political order. The shogunate kept Japan isolated—but not totally.

Through the Dutch factory on the tiny island of Deshima in Nagasaki harbor (see page 577), a stream of Western ideas and inventions trickled into Japan in the eighteenth century. Western writings, architectural illustrations, calendars, watches, medicine, and paintings deeply impressed the Japanese. Their curiosity about things Western gave rise to an intellectual movement known as *rangaku,* foreign studies. For example, Western portraits and other paintings introduced the Japanese to perspective and shading, a profound discovery to them. When the Swedish scientist C. P. Thunberg, physician to the Dutch at Deshima, visited Nagasaki and Edo, the Japanese looked on him as a scientific oracle and plied him with questions. Japanese scholars believed Western inventions were more efficient than their Japanese equivalents and contributed to the prosperity of European nations. Thus the rangaku movement urged that these ideas and inventions be adopted by the Japanese. Japanese understanding of the West was severely limited and often fanciful, as was Western knowledge of Asian civilizations. Like eighteenth-century Europeans who praised Chinese and Persian customs to call attention to shortcomings at home, so Japanese scholars idealized Western conditions. Both peoples wanted to create within their countries the desire for reform and progress.[14]

The Life of the People

Two hundred years of peace is no mean achievement in the history of world societies. There is nothing comparable to it in all of medieval and modern times. Moreover, profound social and economic development occurred in spite of Japan's near-total isolation. The lives of the Japanese people changed profoundly in the seventeenth and eighteenth centuries.

The Tokugawa Shogunate subdued the nobility by emasculating it politically. Stripped of power and required to spend every other year at Edo, the daimyos and samurai passed their lives pursuing pleasure. They spent frantically on fine silks, paintings, concubines, boys, the theater, and the redecoration of their castles. Around 1700 one scholar observed that the entire military class was

MAP 24.2 Tokugawa Japan   Consider the cultural and political significance of the fact that Japan is an island. How did the concentration of shogunate lands affect its government of Japan?

living "as in an inn, that is, consuming now and paying later."[15] Eighteenth-century Japanese novels, plays, and histories portray the samurai engrossed in tavern brawls and sexual orgies. These frivolities, plus the heavy costs of maintaining an alternate residence at Edo, traveling with their retinues, and the sophisticated pleasures of the capital, gradually ruined the warrior class.

In traditional Japanese society, women were subordinate to men, and the civil disorders of the sixteenth century strengthened male domination. Parents in the samurai class arranged their daughters' marriages to advance family interests. Once a woman married, her life centered on her children and domestic chores. The management of a large household with several children and many servants imposed heavy responsibilities on women. But the focus of an upper-class wife's attention was the home, and she rarely left it unchaperoned. "Middle class" women, however, began to emerge from the home. The development of an urban commercial culture in the cities (see page 790) in the Tokugawa period led to the employment of women in silk and textile manufacture, in publishing, in the food and restaurant business, as clerks in various shops, and especially in entertainment.

All major cities contained amusement quarters with teahouses, theaters, restaurants, and houses of prostitution where men could find diversion. Desperately poor parents sometimes sold their daughters to entertainment houses, and the most attractive or talented girls, trained in singing, dancing, and conversational arts, became courtesans called *geishas,* or "accomplished persons," in modern times. The Tokugawa period saw the beginnings for men of the separation of family and business life on the one hand, and leisure and amusement on the other, that still characterizes Japanese society.[16]

The samurai spent heavily on kabuki theater. An art form created by townspeople, *kabuki* consisted of crude, bawdy skits dealing with love and romance or aspects of prostitution, an occupation in which many actors and actresses had professional experience. Performances featured elaborate costumes, song, dance, and poetry. Because female actresses were thought to be corrupting the public morals, the Tokugawa government banned them from the stage in 1629. From that time men played all the parts. Male actors in female dress and makeup performed as seductively as possible in order to entice the burly samurai who thronged the theaters. Homosexuality, long accepted in Japan, was widely practiced among the samurai, who pursued the actors and spent profligately on them. According to one seventeenth-century writer:

Ladies at Their Leisure   This six-paneled screen showing nine women in brilliantly patterned kimonos might have been used as a window advertisement for a textile shop. The elaborate hairstyles reflect a very complex art. *(Source: The Museum Yamato Bunkakan)*

"Youth's kabuki" began with beautiful youths being made to sing and dance, whereupon droll fools . . . had their hearts captivated and their souls stolen. . . . There were many of these men who soon had run through their fortunes. . . . Even though the lineage of every one of the youths was extremely base, these beautiful youths were respected by the stupid; they flapped about like kites and owls and, going into the presence of the exalted distinguished persons, befouled the presence; and these were scoundrels who, saying insolent things as it pleased them, ruined men and held them in contempt.[17]

Some moralists and bureaucrats complained from time to time, but the Tokugawa government decided to accept kabuki and prostitution as necessary evils. The practices provided employment, gratified the tastes of samurai and townspeople, and diverted former warriors from potential criminal and political mischief.[18] And how did the samurai pay for their costly pleasures? In the same way their European counterparts did—by fleecing the peasants and borrowing from the merchants.

According to Japanese tradition, farmers deserved respect. In practice, peasants were sometimes severely oppressed and led miserable lives. It was government policy to tax them to the level of bare subsistence, and official legislation repeatedly defined their duties. In 1649 every village in Japan received these regulations:

Peasants are people without sense or forethought. Therefore they must not give rice to their wives and children at harvest time, but must save food for the future. They should eat millet, vegetables, and other coarse food instead of rice. Even the fallen leaves of plants should be saved as food against famine. . . . During the seasons of planting and harvesting, however, when the labor is arduous, the food taken may be a little better. . . .

They must not buy tea or sake [a fermented liquor made from rice] to drink nor must their wives.

The husband must work in the fields, the wife must work at the loom. Both must do night work. However good-looking a wife may be, if she neglects her household duties by drinking tea or sightseeing or rambling on the hillsides, she must be divorced.

Peasants must wear only cotton or hemp—no silk. They may not smoke tobacco. It is harmful to health, it takes up time, and costs money. It also creates a risk of fire.[19]

The state demanded that peasants work continually and live frugally.

The conspicuous consumption of the upper classes led them during the seventeenth and eighteenth centuries to increase taxes from 30 or 40 percent of the rice crop to 50 percent. Mountains cover much of Japan, and only 20 percent of its land is arable. Although the amount of cultivated land rose from about 5 million acres in 1600 to roughly 11.5 million in 1860, the long period of peace brought a great increase in population. Merchants who bought farm produce fixed the price of rice so low that it seemed to farmers that the more they produced, the less they earned. They found release only by flight or revolt.

After 1704, peasant rebellions were chronic. Oppressive taxation provoked 84,000 farmers in the province of Iwaki to revolt in 1739. Following widespread burning and destruction, their demands were met. In other instances the shoguns ordered savage repression. Natural disasters also added to the peasants' misery. In the 1770s fires, floods, and volcanic eruptions hit all parts of Japan. Drought and torrential rain led to terrible famines between 1783 and 1788 and again between 1832 and 1836. Oppressive taxation, bad weather, and the contempt of lords and the central government often combined to make the lot of peasants one of virtually unrelieved wretchedness.

This picture of the Japanese peasantry tells only part of the story, however. In the Tokugawa period the Japanese peasantry was not a single homogeneous class. Recent scholarship has demonstrated that peasant society was more "a pyramid of wealth and power . . . that rose from the tenant farmer at the bottom through small landholders to wealthy peasants at the top."[20] Agricultural productivity increased substantially during the Tokugawa period, and, although assessed taxes remained high, they were fixed. Peasants who improved their lands and increased their yields continued to pay the same assessed tax, but they paid proportionately less and pocketed the surplus as profit. Their social situation accordingly improved. By the early nineteenth century there existed a large class of relatively wealthy, educated, and ambitious peasant families. This upper stratum of village peasants resembled the middle ranks of the warrior class more than it did the peasantry.

The Tokugawa period witnessed a major transformation of agriculture, a great leap in productivity and specialization. The rural population in-

Heroes of Suikoden The artist Utagawa Kuniyoshi (1797–1861) found inspiration for his prints in the rich repertoire of Japanese legends, especially those dealing with the warfare of the samurai. Here Tameijiro dan Shogo, one of the heroes of the Suikoden collection of tales, grapples with an enemy underwater. Such melodramatic drawings were imitated by Western cartoonists in the development of the comic book. *(Source: The Bridgeman Art Library)*

many peasants worked in the manufacture of silk, cotton, or vegetable oil as in the production of rice.[21]

In theory, the urban commercial classes, scorned for benefiting from the misery of the peasants and the appetites of the samurai, occupied the bottom rung of the social ladder. Merchants had no political power, but they accumulated wealth, sometimes great wealth. They also demonstrated the possibility of social mobility and thus the inherent weakness of the regime's system of strict social stratification.

The commercial class grew in response to the phenomenal development of urban life. In the seventeenth century, the surplus rural population, together with underemployed samurai, desperately poor peasants, and the ambitious and adventurous, thronged to the cities. All wanted a better way of life than could be found in the dull farming villages. Japan's cities grew tremendously: Kyoto, the imperial capital of the emperor and his pleasure-loving court; Edo (modern Tokyo), the political capital, with its multitudes of government bureaucrats, daimyos in alternate residence, intellectuals, and police; and Osaka, by this time the greatest commercial city in Japan, with its huge grain exchange and commercial banks. In the eighteenth century, Edo's population of almost 1 million represented the largest demand for goods and services in the world.

The Tokugawa shoguns provided order and political stability and turned the samurai into urban consumers by denying them military opportunities. Merchants stood ready to serve them. Towns offered all kinds of luxury goods and catered to every extravagant and exotic taste. By marketing the daimyos' grain, town merchants gave the aristocrats the cash they needed to support their rich establishments. Merchants formed guilds and banks and lent money to the samurai. Those who defaulted on their debts found themselves cut off from further credit.[22]

As the ruling samurai with their fixed stipends became increasingly poorer, the despised merchants grew steadily wealthier. By contemporary standards anywhere in the world, the Japanese "middle" class lived very well. In 1705 the shogunate confiscated the property of a merchant in Osaka "for conduct unbecoming a member of the commercial class." In fact, the confiscation was at the urging of influential daimyos and samurai who owed the merchant gigantic debts. The gov-

creased, but surplus labor was drawn to other employment and to the cities. The agricultural population did not increase. In fact, Japan suffered an acute shortage of farm labor from 1720 to 1868. In some villages, industry became almost as important as agriculture. At Hirano near Osaka, for example, 61.7 percent of all arable land was sown in cotton. The peasants had a thriving industry: they ginned the cotton locally before transporting it to wholesalers in Osaka. In many rural places, as ernment seized 50 pairs of gold screens, 360 carpets, several mansions, 48 granaries and warehouses scattered around the country, and hundreds of thousands of gold pieces. This merchant possessed fabulous wealth, but other merchants too enjoyed a rich lifestyle.[23]

SUMMARY

In the eighteenth and early nineteenth centuries China experienced a rapid increase in both prosperity and population. On the basis of highly developed agriculture, the Ch'ing Empire supported a population of 200 million in 1762 and 374 million in 1812, compared with only 193 million in all of Europe in 1800. Ch'ing China was geographically larger than the People's Republic of China today, encompassing some of the present-day Soviet Union.

China's political and economic systems began to deteriorate in the late eighteenth and early nineteenth centuries. The country suffered from excessive centralization: all local questions had to be referred to Peking. The extravagant court placed an intolerable drain on the state treasury. Graft and corruption pervaded the imperial bureaucracy, provincial administration, and army. The population explosion led to a severe land shortage, causing tension and revolts in the countryside. The massive opium trade also had a disastrous effect on Chinese society. The volume of opium smuggled by the British East India Company into China increased tenfold between 1790 and 1820. So vast was the amount of opium imported, relative to Chinese exports of tea and silk, that China suffered a highly unfavorable balance of trade. The outflow of silver severely damaged the Chinese economy and thus the Ch'ing Dynasty.

In 1800 Tokugawa Japan was reaping the rewards of two centuries of peace and social order. Steady economic growth and improved agricultural technology had swelled the population. The samurai had been transformed into peaceful city dwellers and civil bureaucrats. The wealth of the business classes grew, and the samurai, dependent on fixed agricultural rents or stipends in rice in a time of rising standards of living, fell into debt. The Tokugawa regime formed submissive citizens whose discipline is apparent even today.

Japanese Netsukes During the Edo period, wealthy people commissioned the production of *netsukes,* small highly decorated carvings in wood or ivory that were used to attach to the girdle such everyday objects as keys, purses, tobacco pouches, or scent bottles. These small objects often show a very high degree of craftsmanship. *(Source: The Metropolitan Museum of Art)*

Although the shogunate maintained a policy of national isolation, and no foreign power influenced Japan's political or social life, Japan was not really cut off from outside cultural contacts. Through the port of Nagasaki, Western scientific ideas and some Western technology entered Japan in response to the persistent interest of Japanese scholars. The Japanese readily absorbed foreign technological ideas.

NOTES

1. J. Gernet, *A History of Chinese Civilization* (New York: Cambridge University Press, 1982), p. 391.
2. Ibid.
3. L. Zewen et al., *The Great Wall* (New York: McGraw-Hill, 1981), p. 140.
4. See E. L. Dreyer, *Early Ming China: A Political History, 1355–1435* (Stanford, Calif.: Stanford University Press, 1982), pp. 194–205.

5. R. Huang, *1587: A Year of No Significance: The Ming Dynasty in Decline* (New Haven, Conn.: Yale University Press, 1981), p. 13.

6. Gernet, pp. 425–426.

7. J. E. Wills, Jr., "Maritime China from Wang Chih to Shih Long," in *From Ming to Ch'ing: Conquest, Region, and Continuity in Seventeenth-Century China,* ed. J. D. Spence and J. E. Wills, Jr. (New Haven, Conn.: Yale University Press, 1979), pp. 203–216.

8. F. Braudel, *The Wheels of Commerce: Civilization and Capitalism, 15th–18th Century,* vol. 2, trans. S. Reynolds (New York: Harper & Row, 1982), pp. 198–199.

9. Quoted in Gernet, p. 431.

10. See Huang, pp. 120–129.

11. F. Wakeman, Jr., *The Fall of Imperial China* (New York: Free Press, 1975), pp. 58–64.

12. See G. B. Sansom, *A History of Japan, 1344–1615,* vol. 2 (Stanford, Calif.: Stanford University Press, 1961), chaps. 20–21.

13. Ibid., chap. 25.

14. See D. Keene, *The Japanese Discovery of Europe, 1720–1830* (Stanford, Calif.: Stanford University Press, 1969), pp. 24–25, chap. 4, and passim.

15. Quoted in D. H. Shively, "Bakufu Versus Kabuki," in *Studies in the Institutional History of Early Modern Japan,* ed. J. W. Hall (Princeton, N.J.: Princeton University Press, 1970), p. 236.

16. E. O. Reischauer and A. M. Craig, *Japan: Tradition and Transformation,* rev. ed. (Boston: Houghton Mifflin, 1989), pp. 104–105.

17. Quoted in Shively, pp. 241–242.

18. Ibid.

19. Quoted in G. B. Sansom, *A History of Japan, 1615–1867,* vol. 3 (Stanford, Calif.: Stanford University Press, 1978), p. 99.

20. T. C. Smith, "The Japanese Village in the Seventeenth Century," in Hall, p. 280.

21. T. C. Smith, *The Agrarian Origins of Modern Japan* (Stanford, Calif.: Stanford University Press, 1959), pp. 78–79.

22. See W. Bingham, H. Conroy, and F. W. Ikle, *A History of Asia,* vol. 2 (Boston: Allyn and Bacon, 1967), pp. 140–142.

23. G. B. Sansom, *Japan: A Short Cultural History,* rev. ed. (New York: Appleton-Century-Crofts, 1962), p. 472.

SUGGESTED READING

In recent years a considerable number of expert treatments of the traditional cultures of East Asia have appeared, many of them in paperback editions. The best starting point for the weaknesses of Yuan rule and the early development of the Ming Dynasty in China is C. O. Hucker, *The Ming Dynasty: Its Origins and Evolving Institutions* (1978); but see also Dreyer's *Early Ming China* (listed in the Notes), which contains a valuable up-to-date bibliography. Hucker's *The Traditional Chinese State in Ming Times, 1368–1644* (1962), is a standard study written in simple, untechnical language. J. D. Spence, *Ts'ao Yin and the K'ang-hsi Emperor: Bondservant and Master* (1966), uses the life of an official in the Chinese bureaucracy to describe the era and institutional framework in which he operated. The best appreciation of the emperor K'ang-hsi is J. D. Spence, *Emperor of China: Self-Portrait of K'ang-hsi* (1988). Spence and Wills, *From Ming to Ch'ing,* cited in the Notes, focuses on the transition from Ming to Ch'ing in a collection of wide-ranging essays by leading scholars. For social change in China, see S. Naquin and E. S. Rawski, *Chinese Society in the Eighteenth Century* (1987). J. D. Spence's widely acclaimed *The Search for Modern China* (1990), is probably the best general survey of Chinese history from the late Ming period to the 1980s.

The best one-volume survey of Japanese history and culture is E. O. Reischauer, *Japan: The Story of a Nation,* 4th ed. (1990), which combines expert knowledge with superb readability. Sansom's *Japan: A Short Cultural History* (see the Notes) is an older but still useful account. More detailed treatments of Japanese history are Reischauer and Craig's, *Japan: Tradition and Transformation* (see the Notes), and Sansom's *A History of Japan,* 3 vols. (1958–1978). For Japanese feudalism, see P. Duus, *Feudalism in Japan* (1976), and J. W. Hall and J. P. Mass, eds., *Medieval Japan: Essays in Institutional History* (1974). The sophisticated study of H. Ooms, *Tokugawa Ideology: Early Constructs, 1570–1680* (1985), describes how early Tokugawa rulers developed ideological constructs and military values to create a highly disciplined people and a stable society. M. Cooper, ed., *They Came to Japan. An Anthology of European Reports on Japan, 1543–1640* (1981), gives first European impressions of Japan and the Japanese. G. Elison and B. L. Smith, eds., *Warlords, Artists, and Commoners: Japan in the Sixteenth Century* (1987), is an excellent collection of articles by leading scholars. D. Massarella, *A World Elsewhere: Europe's Encounter with Japan in the Sixteenth and Seventeenth Centuries* (1990) is an almost definitive study of the early English and Dutch in Japan.

The following studies are valuable for specific topics: M. Colcutt, *Five Mountains: The Zen Monastic Institution in Medieval Japan* (1980); C. R. Boxer, *The Christian Century in Japan, 1549–1650* (1967); R. P. Dore, *Education in Tokugawa Japan* (1965); and C. D. Sheldon, *The Rise of the Merchant Class in Tokugawa Japan, 1600–1868* (1958). Also see A. B. Jannetta, *Epidemics and Mortality in Early Modern Japan,* (1986), for disease and health; and H. P. Bix, *Peasant Protest in Japan, 1590–1884* (1986), a Marxist interpretation of peasant uprisings primarily in the eighteenth century.

25

The Revolution in
Western Politics,
1775–1815

The Tennis Court Oath. Members of the Third Estate meet at an indoor tennis court, June 20, 1789

The last years of the eighteenth century were a time of great upheaval. A series of revolutions and revolutionary wars challenged the old order of kings and aristocrats. The ideas of freedom and equality, ideas that have not stopped shaping the world since that era, flourished and spread. The revolution began in North America in 1775. Then in 1789 France, the most influential country in Europe, became the leading revolutionary nation. It established first a constitutional monarchy, then a radical republic, and finally a new empire under Napoleon. The armies of France also joined forces with patriots and radicals abroad in an effort to establish new governments based on new principles throughout much of Europe. The world of modern domestic and international politics was born.

- What caused this era of revolution?
- What were the ideas and objectives of the men and women who rose up violently to undo the established system?
- What were the gains and losses for privileged groups and for ordinary people in a generation of war and upheaval?

These are the questions underlying this chapter's examination of the French and American revolutions.

LIBERTY AND EQUALITY

Two ideas fueled the revolutionary period in both America and Europe: liberty and equality. What did eighteenth-century politicians and other people mean by liberty and equality, and why were those ideas so radical and revolutionary in their day?

The call for liberty was first of all a call for individual human rights. Even the most enlightened monarchs customarily claimed that it was their duty to regulate what people wrote and believed. Liberals of the revolutionary era protested such controls from on high. They demanded freedom to worship according to the dictates of their consciences instead of according to the politics of their prince. They demanded the end of censorship and the right to express their beliefs freely in print and at public meetings. They demanded freedom from arbitrary laws and from judges who simply obeyed orders from the government.

These demands for basic personal freedoms, which were incorporated into the American Bill of Rights and other liberal constitutions, were very far-reaching. Indeed, eighteenth-century revolutionaries demanded more freedom than most governments today believe it is desirable to grant. The Declaration of the Rights of Man, issued at the beginning of the French Revolution, proclaimed, "Liberty consists in being able to do anything that does not harm another person." A citizen's rights had, therefore, "no limits except those which assure to the other members of society the enjoyment of these same rights." Liberals called for the freedom of the individual to develop and to create to the fullest possible extent. In the context of the aristocratic and monarchial forms of government that then dominated Europe, this was a truly radical idea.

The call for liberty was also a call for a new kind of government. The revolutionary liberals believed that the people were sovereign—that is, that the people alone had the authority to make laws limiting an individual's freedom of action. In practice, this system of government meant choosing legislators who represented the people and who were accountable to them. Moreover, liberals of the revolutionary era believed that every people—in other words, every ethnic group—had this right of self-determination and, thus, the right to form a free nation.

By equality, eighteenth-century liberals meant that all citizens were to have identical rights and civil liberties. Above all, the nobility had no right to special privileges based on the accident of birth.

Liberals did not define equality as meaning that everyone should be equal economically. Quite the contrary. As Thomas Jefferson wrote in an early draft of the American Declaration of Independence, before changing "property" to the more noble-sounding "happiness," everyone was equal in "the pursuit of property." Jefferson and other liberals certainly did not expect equal success in that pursuit. Great differences in wealth and income between rich and poor were perfectly acceptable to liberals. The essential point was that everyone should legally have an equal chance. French liberals and revolutionaries said that they wanted "careers opened to talent." They wanted employment in government, in business, and in the professions to be based on ability, not on family background or legal status.

Equality of opportunity was a very revolutionary idea in eighteenth-century Europe. Legal inequality between classes and groups was the rule, not the exception. Society was still legally divided into groups with special privileges, such as the nobility and the clergy, and groups with special burdens, like the peasantry. In many countries, various middle-class groups—professionals, business people, townspeople, and craftsmen—enjoyed privileges that allowed them to monopolize all sorts of economic activity. It was this kind of economic inequality, an inequality based on artificial legal distinctions, against which liberals protested.

The Roots of Liberalism

The ideas of liberty and equality—the central ideas of classical liberalism—have deep roots in Western history. The ancient Greeks and the Judeo-Christian tradition had affirmed for hundreds of years the sanctity and value of the individual human being. The Judeo-Christian tradition, reinforced by the Reformation, had long stressed the personal responsibility of both common folk and exalted rulers, thereby promoting the self-discipline without which liberty becomes anarchy. The hounded and persecuted Protestant radicals of the late sixteenth century had died for the revolutionary idea that individuals were entitled to their own religious beliefs.

Although the liberal creed had roots deep in the Western tradition, classical liberalism first crystallized at the end of the seventeenth century and during the Enlightenment of the eighteenth century. Liberal ideas reflected the Enlightenment's stress on human dignity and human happiness on earth. Liberals shared the Enlightenment's general faith in science, rationality, and progress: the adoption of liberal principles meant better government and a better society for all. Almost all the writers of the Enlightenment were passionately committed to greater personal liberty. They preached religious toleration, freedom of press and speech, and fair and equal treatment before the law.

Certain English and French thinkers were mainly responsible for joining the Enlightenment's concern for personal freedom and legal equality to a theoretical justification of liberal self-government. The two most important were John Locke and the baron de Montesquieu. Locke (see page 648) maintained that England's long political tradition rested on "the rights of Englishmen" and on representative government through Parliament. Locke admired especially the great Whig nobles who had made the bloodless revolution of 1688 to 1689, and he argued that if a government oversteps its proper function of protecting the natural rights of life, liberty, and private property, it becomes a tyranny. Montesquieu (see page 672) was also inspired by English constitutional history. He, too, believed that powerful "intermediary groups"—such as the judicial nobility of which he was a proud member—offered the best defense of liberty against despotism.

The Marquis de Lafayette was the most famous great noble to embrace the liberal revolution. Shown here directing a battle in the American Revolution, he returned to champion liberty and equality in France. For admirers he was the "hero of two worlds." *(Source: Jean-Loup Charmet)*

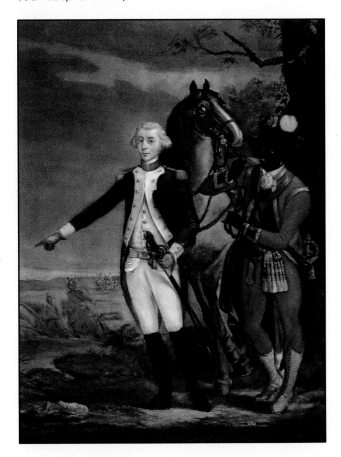

The Attraction of Liberalism

The belief that representative institutions could defend their liberty and interests appealed powerfully to ambitious and educated bourgeois. Yet it is important to realize that liberal ideas about individual rights and political freedom, as formulated by Montesquieu, also appealed to much of the aristocracy, at least in western Europe. Representative government did not mean democracy, which liberal thinkers tended to equate with mob rule. Rather, they envisioned voting for representatives as being restricted to those who owned property, those with a stake in society. England had shown the way. After 1688 it had combined a parliamentary system and considerable individual liberty with a restricted franchise and unquestionable aristocratic pre-eminence. During the eighteenth century, many French nobles, led by a judicial nobility inspired by Montesquieu, were increasingly eager to follow the English example.

Eighteenth-century liberalism, then, appealed not only to the middle class but also to some aristocrats. It found broad support among the educated elite and the substantial classes in western Europe. What it lacked from the beginning was strong mass support. For comfortable liberals, the really important questions were theoretical and political. They had no need to worry about their stomachs and the price of bread. For the much more numerous laboring poor, the great questions were immediate and economic. Getting enough to eat was the crucial challenge. These differences in outlook and well-being were to lead to many misunderstandings and disappointments for both groups in the revolutionary era.

THE AMERICAN REVOLUTION (1775–1789)

The era of liberal revolution began in the New World. The thirteen mainland colonies of British North America revolted against their home country and then succeeded in establishing a new unified government.

Americans have long debated the meaning of their revolution. Some have even questioned whether it was a real revolution, as opposed to a war for independence. According to some scholars, the Revolution was conservative and defensive in that its demands were for the traditional liberties of English citizens; Americans were united against the British, but otherwise they were a satisfied people, not torn by internal conflict. Other scholars have argued that, on the contrary, the American Revolution was quite radical. It split families between patriots and loyalists and divided the country. It achieved goals that were fully as advanced as those obtained by the French in their great revolution a few years later.

How does one reconcile these positions? Both contain large elements of truth. The American revolutionaries did believe that they were demanding only the traditional rights of English men and women. But those traditional rights were liberal rights, and in the American context they had very strong democratic and popular overtones. Thus the American Revolution was fought in the name of established ideals that were still quite radical in the context of the times. And in founding a government firmly based on liberal principles, the Americans set an example that had a forceful impact on Europe and speeded up political development there.

The Origins of the Revolution

The American Revolution had its immediate origins in a squabble over increased taxes. The British government had fought and decisively won the Seven Years' War (see page 680) on the strength of its professional army and navy. The American colonists had furnished little real aid. The high cost of the war to the British, however, had led to a doubling of the British national debt. Anticipating further expense defending its recently conquered western lands from Indian uprisings like that of Pontiac, the British government in London set about reorganizing the empire with a series of bold, largely unprecedented measures. Breaking with tradition, the British decided to maintain a large army in North America after peace was restored in 1763. Moreover, they sought to exercise strict control over their newly conquered western lands and to tax the colonies directly. In 1765 the government pushed through Parliament the Stamp Act, which levied taxes on a long list of commercial and legal documents, diplomas, pamphlets, newspapers, almanacs, dice, and playing cards. A stamp glued to each article indicated that the tax had been paid.

The Boston Tea Party   This contemporary illustration shows men disguised as Indians dumping East India Company tea into Boston's harbor. The enthusiastic crowd cheering from the wharf indicates widespread popular support. *(Source: Library of Congress)*

The effort to increase taxes as part of tightening up the empire seemed perfectly reasonable to the British. Heavier stamp taxes had been collected in Great Britain for two generations, and Americans were being asked only to pay a share of their own defense costs. Moreover, Americans had been paying only very low local taxes. The Stamp Act would have doubled taxes to about 2 shillings per person per year. No other people in the European or colonial world (except the Poles) paid so little. The British, meanwhile, paid the highest taxes in the Western world in about 1765—26 shillings per person. Nevertheless, the colonists protested the Stamp Act vigorously and violently; and after riots and boycotts against British goods, Parliament reluctantly repealed the new tax.

As the fury of the Stamp Act controversy revealed, much more was involved than taxes. The key question was political. To what extent could the home government refashion the empire and reassert its power while limiting the authority of colonial legislatures and their elected representatives? Accordingly, who should represent the colonies, and who had the right to make laws for Americans? While a troubled majority of Americans searched hard for a compromise, some radicals began to proclaim that "taxation without representation is tyranny." The British government replied that Americans were represented in Parliament, albeit indirectly (like most English people themselves), and that the absolute supremacy of Parliament throughout the empire could not be questioned. Many Americans felt otherwise. As John Adams put it, "A Parliament of Great Britain can have no more rights to tax the colonies than a Parliament of Paris." Thus imperial reorganization and parliamentary supremacy came to appear as grave threats to Americans' existing liberties and time-honored institutions.

Americans had long exercised a great deal of independence and gone their own way. In British North America, unlike England and Europe, no powerful established church existed, and personal freedom in questions of religion was taken for granted. The colonial assemblies made the important laws, which were seldom overturned by the home government. The right to vote was much more widespread than in England. In many parts of colonial Massachusetts, for example, as many as 95 percent of the adult males could vote.

Moreover, this greater political equality was matched by greater social and economic equality. Neither a hereditary nobility nor a hereditary serf population existed, although the slavery of the Americas consigned blacks to a legally oppressed caste. Independent farmers were the largest group in the country and set much of its tone. In short, the colonial experience had slowly formed a people who felt themselves separate and distinct from the home country. The controversies over taxation intensified those feelings of distinctiveness and separation and brought them to the fore.

In 1773 the dispute over taxes and representation flared up again. The British government had permitted the financially hard-pressed East India Company to ship its tea from China directly to company agents in the colonies, rather than through London middlemen who sold to independent merchants in the colonies. Thus the company secured a vital monopoly on the tea trade, and colonial merchants were suddenly excluded from a highly profitable business. The colonists were quick to protest.

In Boston, men disguised as Indians had a rowdy "tea party" and threw the company's tea into the harbor. This led to extreme measures. The so-called Coercive Acts closed the port of Boston, curtailed local elections and town meetings, and greatly expanded the royal governor's power. County conventions in Massachusetts protested vehemently and urged that the acts be "rejected as the attempts of a wicked administration to enslave America." Other colonial assemblies joined in the denunciations. In September 1774, the First Continental Congress met in Philadelphia, where the most radical members argued successfully against concessions to the Crown. Compromise was also rejected by the British Parliament; and in April 1775, fighting began at Lexington and Concord in Massachusetts.

The Signing of the Declaration, July 4, 1776   John Trumbull's famous painting shows the dignity and determination of America's revolutionary leaders. An extraordinarily talented group, they succeeded in rallying popular support without losing power to more radical forces in the process. *(Source: Yale University Art Gallery)*

Independence

The fighting spread, and the colonists moved slowly but inevitably toward open rebellion and a declaration of independence. The uncompromising attitude of the British government and its use of German mercenaries helped dissolve longstanding loyalties to the home country and rivalries among the separate colonies. *Common Sense* (1775), a brilliant attack by the recently arrived English radical Thomas Paine (1737–1809), also mobilized public opinion in favor of independence. A runaway best-seller with sales of 120,000 copies in a few months, Paine's tract ridiculed the idea of a small island ruling a great continent. In his call for freedom and republican government, Paine expressed Americans' growing sense of separateness and moral superiority.

On July 4, 1776, the Second Continental Congress adopted the Declaration of Independence. Written by Thomas Jefferson, the Declaration of Independence boldly listed the tyrannical acts committed by George III (r. 1760–1820) and confidently proclaimed the natural rights of humankind and the sovereignty of the American states. Sometimes called the world's greatest political editorial, the Declaration of Independence in effect universalized the traditional rights of English people and made them the rights of all humanity. It stated that "all men are created equal . . . they are endowed by their Creator with certain unalienable rights . . . among these are life, liberty, and the pursuit of happiness." No other American political document has ever caused such excitement, both at home and abroad.

Many American families remained loyal to Britain; many others divided bitterly. After the Declaration of Independence, the conflict often took the form of a civil war—pitting patriot against loyalist. The loyalists tended to be wealthy and politically moderate. Many patriots, too, were wealthy—individuals such as John Hancock and George Washington—but willingly allied themselves with farmers and artisans in a broad coalition. This coalition harassed the loyalists and confiscated their property to help pay for the American war effort. The broad social base of the revolutionaries tended to make the liberal revolution democratic. State governments extended the right to vote to many more people in the course of the war and re-established themselves as republics.

On the international scene, the French sympathized with the rebels from the beginning. They wanted revenge for the humiliating defeats of the Seven Years' War. Officially neutral until 1778, they supplied the great bulk of guns and gunpowder used by the American revolutionaries, very much as neutral great powers supply weapons for "wars of national liberation" in our day. By 1777 French volunteers were arriving in Virginia, and a dashing young nobleman, the marquis de Lafayette (1757–1834), quickly became one of Washington's most trusted generals. In 1778 the French government offered a formal alliance to the American ambassador in Paris, Benjamin Franklin, and in 1779 and 1780 the Spanish and Dutch declared war on Britain. Catherine the Great of Russia helped organize a League of Armed Neutrality in order to protect neutral shipping rights, which Britain refused to recognize.

Thus by 1780 Great Britain was engaged in an imperial war against most of Europe as well as against the thirteen colonies. In these circumstances, and in the face of severe reverses in India, the West Indies, and at Yorktown in Virginia, a new British government decided to cut its losses. American negotiators in Paris were receptive. They feared that France wanted a treaty that would bottle up the new United States east of the Alleghenies and give British holdings west of the Alleghenies to France's ally, Spain. The American negotiators ditched the French and accepted the extraordinarily favorable terms offered by Britain.

By the Treaty of Paris of 1783, Britain recognized the independence of the thirteen colonies and ceded all its territory between the Appalachians and the Mississippi River to the Americans. Out of the bitter rivalries of the Old World, the Americans snatched dominion over half a continent.

Framing the Constitution

The liberal program of the American Revolution was consolidated by the federal Constitution, the Bill of Rights, and the creation of a national republic. Assembling in Philadelphia in the summer of 1787, the delegates to the Constitutional Convention were determined to end the period of economic depression, social uncertainty, and very weak central government that had followed independence. The delegates decided, therefore, to grant the federal, or central, government important powers: regulation of domestic and foreign trade, the right to levy taxes, and the means to enforce its laws.

Strong rule was placed squarely in the context of representative self-government. Senators and congressmen would be the lawmaking delegates of the voters, and the president of the republic would be an elected official. The central government was to operate in Montesquieu's framework of checks and balances. The executive, legislative, and judicial branches would systematically balance each other. The power of the federal government would in turn be checked by the powers of the individual states.

When the results of the secret deliberations of the Constitutional Convention were presented to the states for ratification, a great public debate began. The opponents of the proposed constitution—the Anti-Federalists—charged that the framers of the new document had taken too much power from the individual states and made the federal government too strong. Moreover, many Anti-Federalists feared for the personal liberties and individual freedoms for which they had just fought. In order to overcome these objections, the Federalists solemnly promised to spell out these basic freedoms as soon as the new constitution was adopted. The result was the first ten amendments to the Constitution, which the first Congress passed shortly after it met in New York in March 1789. These amendments formed an effective bill of rights to safeguard the individual. Most of them—trial by jury, due process of law, right to assemble, freedom from unreasonable search—had their origins in English law and the English Bill of Rights of 1689. Others—the freedoms of speech, the press, and religion—reflected natural-law theory and the American experience.

The American Constitution and the Bill of Rights exemplified the great strengths and the limits of what came to be called "classical liberalism." Liberty meant individual freedoms and political safeguards. Liberty also meant representative government but did not necessarily mean democracy with its principle of one person, one vote.

Equality—slaves excepted—meant equality before the law, not equality of political participation or economic well-being. Indeed, economic inequality was resolutely defended by the elite who framed the Constitution. The right to own property was guaranteed by the Fifth Amendment, and if the government took private property, the owner was to receive "just compensation." The radicalism of liberal revolution in America was primarily legal and political, not economic or social.

The Revolution's Impact on Europe

Hundreds of books, pamphlets, and articles analyzed and romanticized the American upheaval. Thoughtful Europeans noted, first of all, its enormous long-term implications for international politics. A secret report by the Venetian ambassador to Paris in 1783 stated what many felt: "If only the union of the Provinces is preserved, it is reasonable to expect that, with the favorable effects of time, and of European arts and sciences, it will become the most formidable power in the world."[1] More generally, American independence fired the imaginations of the few aristocrats who were uneasy with their privileges and of commoners who yearned for greater equality. Many Europeans believed that the world was advancing and that America was leading the way. As one French writer put it in 1789: "This vast continent which the seas surround will soon change Europe and the universe."

Europeans who dreamed of a new era were fascinated by the political lessons of the American Revolution. The Americans had begun with a revolutionary defense against tyrannical oppression, and they had been victorious. They had then shown how rational beings could assemble together to exercise sovereignty and write a permanent constitution—a new social contract. All this gave greater reality to the concepts of individual liberty and representative government. It reinforced one of the primary ideas of the Enlightenment, the idea that a better world was possible.

THE FRENCH REVOLUTION (1789-1791)

No country felt the consequences of the American Revolution more directly than France. Hundreds of French officers served in America and were inspired by the experience. The most famous of these, the young and impressionable marquis de Lafayette, left home as a great aristocrat determined only to fight France's traditional foe, England. He returned with a love of liberty and firm republican convictions. French intellectuals and publicists engaged in passionate analysis of the federal Constitution and the constitutions of the various states of the new United States. The American Revolution undeniably hastened upheaval in France. Yet the French Revolution did not mirror the American example. It was more violent and more complex, more influential and more controversial, more loved and more hated. For Europeans and most of the rest of the world, it was the great revolution of the eighteenth century, the revolution that opened the modern era in politics.

The Breakdown of the Old Order

Like the American Revolution, the French Revolution had its immediate origins in the financial difficulties of the government. The efforts of Louis XV's ministers to raise taxes had been thwarted by the Parlement of Paris, strengthened in its opposition by widespread popular support (see pages 683–684). When renewed efforts to reform the tax system met a similar fate in 1776, the government was forced to finance all of its enormous expenditures during the American war with borrowed money. The national debt and the annual budget deficit soared. By the 1780s fully half of France's annual budget went for ever-increasing interest payments on the ever-increasing debt. Another quarter went to maintain the military, and 6 percent was absorbed by the costly and extravagant king and his court at Versailles. Less than one-fifth of the entire national budget was available for the productive functions of the state, such as transportation and general administration. It was an impossible financial situation.

One way out would have been for the government to declare partial bankruptcy, forcing its creditors to accept greatly reduced payments on the debt. The powerful Spanish monarchy had regularly repudiated large portions of its debt in earlier times, and France had done likewise after an attempt to establish a French national bank ended in financial disaster in 1720. Yet by the 1780s the French debt was held by an army of aristocratic and bourgeois creditors, and the French monarchy, though absolute in theory, had become far too weak for such a drastic and unpopular action.

Nor could the king and his ministers, unlike modern governments, print money and create inflation to cover their deficits. Unlike England and Holland, which had far larger national debts relative to their populations, France had no central bank, no paper currency, and no means of creating credit. French money was good gold coin. Therefore, when a depressed economy and a lack of public confidence made it increasingly difficult for the government to obtain new gold loans in 1786, it had no alternative but to try to increase taxes. And since France's tax system was unfair and out of date, increased revenues were possible only through fundamental reforms. Such reforms, which would affect all groups in France's complex and fragmented society, opened a Pandora's box of social and political demands.

Legal Orders and Social Realities

As in the Middle Ages, France's 25 million inhabitants were still legally divided into three orders, or "estates"—the clergy, the nobility, and everyone else. As the nation's first estate, the clergy numbered about 100,000 and had important privileges. It owned about 10 percent of the land and paid only a "voluntary gift" to the government every five years; moreover, the church levied on landowners a tax (the tithe) that averaged somewhat less than 10 percent. Much of the church's income was drained away from local parishes by political appointees and worldly aristocrats at the top of the church hierarchy, to the intense dissatisfaction of the poor parish priests.

The second legally defined estate consisted of some 400,000 noblemen and noblewomen—the descendants of "those who fought" in the Middle Ages. The nobles owned outright about 25 percent of the land in France, and they, too, were taxed very lightly. Moreover, nobles continued to enjoy certain manorial rights, or privileges of lordship, that dated back to medieval times and allowed them to tax the peasantry for their own profit—through exclusive rights to hunt and fish, village monopolies on baking bread and pressing grapes for wine, fees for justice, and other "useful privileges." Nobles also had "honorific privileges," such as the right to precedence on public occasions and the right to wear a sword. These rights conspicuously proclaimed the nobility's legal superiority and exalted social position.

Everyone else was a commoner, a member of the third estate. A few commoners were rich merchants or highly successful doctors and lawyers. Many more were urban artisans and unskilled day laborers. The vast majority of the third estate consisted of the peasants and agricultural workers in the countryside. Thus the third estate was a conglomeration of vastly different social groups, united only by their shared legal status as distinct from the privileged nobility and clergy.

In discussing the long-term origins of the French Revolution, historians have long focused on growing tensions between the nobility and the comfortable members of the third estate, usually known as the *bourgeoisie,* or middle class. A dominant historical interpretation has held sway for at least two generations. According to this interpretation, the bourgeoisie was basically united by economic position and class interest. Aided by the general economic expansion discussed in Chapter 21, the middle class grew rapidly in the eighteenth century, tripling to about 2.3 million persons, or about 8 percent of France's population. Increasing in size, wealth, culture, and self-confidence, this rising bourgeoisie became progressively exasperated by archaic "feudal" laws restraining the economy and by the growing pretensions of a reactionary nobility, which was closing ranks against middle-class needs and aspirations. As a result, the French bourgeoisie eventually rose up to lead the entire third estate in a great social revolution, a revolution that destroyed feudal privileges and established a capitalist order based on individualism and a market economy.

In recent years, a flood of new research has challenged these views, and once again the French Revolution is a subject of heated scholarly debate. Above all, revisionist historians have questioned the existence of a growing social conflict between a progressive capitalistic bourgeoisie and a reactionary feudal nobility in eighteenth-century France. Instead, these historians see both bourgeoisie and nobility as highly fragmented, riddled with internal rivalries. The great nobility, for example, was profoundly separated from the lesser nobility by differences in wealth, education, and world view. Moreover, the old military nobility—known as the "nobility of the sword"—eyed with suspicion the more recent bureaucratic and judicial nobility—the so-called "nobility of the robe." Differences within the bourgeoisie—between wealthy financiers and local lawyers, for example—were no less profound. Rather than standing as unified blocs against each other, nobility and bourgeoisie formed two parallel social ladders, increasingly linked together at the top by wealth, marriage, and Enlightenment culture.

Revisionist historians stress three developments in particular. First, the nobility remained a fluid and relatively open order. Throughout the eighteenth century, substantial numbers of successful commoners continued to seek and obtain noble status through government service and purchase of expensive positions conferring nobility. Thus the nobility of the robe continued to attract the wealthiest members of the middle class and to permit social mobility. Second, key sections of the nobility were no less liberal than the middle class, which, until revolution actually began, generally supported the judicial opposition led by the Parlement of Paris. Finally, the nobility and the bourgeoisie were not really at odds in the economic sphere. Both looked to investment in land and to government service as their preferred activities, and the ideal goal of the merchant-capitalist was to gain enough wealth to retire from trade, purchase estates, and live nobly as a large landowner. At the same time, wealthy nobles often acted as aggressive capitalists, investing especially in mining, metallurgy, and foreign trade.

The revisionists have clearly shaken the belief that the bourgeoisie and the nobility were inevitably locked in growing conflict before the Revolution. But in stressing the similarities between the two groups, especially at the top, revisionists have also reinforced the view, long maintained by historians, that the Old Regime had ceased to reflect social reality by the 1780s. Legally, society was still based on rigid orders inherited from the Middle Ages. In reality, France had moved far toward being a society based on wealth and economic achievement, and an emerging elite that included both aristocratic and bourgeois notables was frustrated by a bureaucratic monarchy that had long claimed the right to absolute power.

The Formation of the National Assembly

The Revolution was under way by 1787, though no one could have realized what was to follow. Spurred by a depressed economy and falling tax receipts, Louis XVI's minister of finance revived old proposals to impose a general tax on all landed property and to develop provincial assemblies to help administer the tax, and he convinced the king to call an Assembly of Notables to gain support for the idea. The assembled notables, who were mainly important noblemen and high-ranking clergy, were not in favor of it. In return for their support, they demanded that control over all government spending be given to the provincial assemblies, which they expected to control. When the government refused, the notables responded that such sweeping tax changes required the approval of the Estates General, the representative body of all three estates, which had not met since 1614.

Facing bankruptcy, the king tried to reassert his authority. He dismissed the notables and established new taxes by decree. In stirring language, the Parlement of Paris promptly declared the royal initiative null and void. The Parlement went so far as to specify some of the "fundamental laws" against which no king could transgress, such as national consent to taxation and freedom from arbitrary arrest and imprisonment. When the king tried to exile the judges, a wave of protest swept the country. Frightened investors also refused to advance more loans to the state. Finally, in July 1788, a beaten Louis XVI called for a spring session of the Estates General. Absolute monarchy was collapsing.

What would replace it? Throughout the unprecedented election campaign of 1788 and 1789, that question excited France. All across the country, clergy, nobles, and commoners came together in their respective orders to draft petitions for change and to elect their respective delegates to the Estates General. The local assemblies of the clergy showed considerable dissatisfaction with the church hierarchy, and two-thirds of the delegates were chosen from among the poorest parish priests, who were commoners by birth. The nobles, already badly split by wealth and education, remained politically divided. A conservative majority was drawn from the poorest and most numerous provincial nobility, but fully a third of the nobility's representatives were liberals committed to major changes.

As for the third estate, there was great popular participation in the elections. Almost all male commoners twenty-five years or older had the right to vote. However, voting required two stages, which meant that most of the representatives finally selected by the third estate were well-educated, prosperous members of the middle class. Most were not businessmen but lawyers and

Fan: Opening of the Legislature   In 1789 the first meeting of the Estates General since 1614 was recorded not only in the annals of French history but in the most ordinary objects, including this painted fan. *(Source: Musée Carnavalet/Bulloz)*

government officials. Status and prestige were of particular concern to this elite. There were no delegates from the great mass of laboring poor, which included the peasants and the artisans.

The petitions for change from the three estates showed a surprising degree of agreement on most issues, as recent research has clearly revealed. There was general agreement that royal absolutism should give way to constitutional monarchy, in which laws and taxes would require the consent of an Estates General meeting regularly. All agreed that, in the future, individual liberties must be guaranteed by law and that the position of the parish clergy had to be improved. It was generally acknowledged that economic development required reforms, such as the abolition of internal trade barriers. The striking similarities in the grievance petitions of the clergy, nobility, and third estate reflected the broad commitment of France's elite to liberalism.

Yet an increasingly bitter quarrel undermined this consensus during the intense campaign: how would the Estates General vote, and precisely who would lead in the political reorganization that was generally desired? The Estates General of 1614 had sat as three separate houses. Any action had required the agreement of at least two branches, a requirement that had guaranteed control by the privileged orders—the nobility and the clergy. Immediately after its victory over the king, the aristocratic Parlement of Paris, mainly out of respect for tradition but partly to enhance the nobility's political position, ruled that the Estates General should once again sit separately. The ruling was quickly denounced by certain middle-class intellectuals and some liberal nobles. They demanded instead a single assembly dominated by representatives of the third estate, to ensure fundamental reforms. Reflecting a growing hostility toward aristocratic aspirations, the abbé Sieyès argued in 1789, in his famous pamphlet *What Is the Third Estate?*, that the nobility was a tiny, overprivileged minority and that the neglected third estate constituted the true strength of the French nation. When the government agreed that the third estate should have as many delegates as the clergy and the nobility combined but then rendered its act meaningless by upholding voting by separate order, middle-class leaders saw fresh evidence of an aristocratic conspiracy.

In May 1789 the twelve hundred delegates of the three estates paraded in medieval pageantry through the streets of Versailles to an opening session resplendent with feudal magnificence. The estates were almost immediately deadlocked. Delegates of the third estate refused to transact any business until the king ordered the clergy and nobility to sit with them in a single body. Finally, after a six-week war of nerves, a few parish priests began to go over to the third estate, which on June 17 voted to call itself the "National Assembly." On June 20, excluded from their hall because of "repairs," the delegates of the third estate moved to a large indoor tennis court. There they swore the famous Oath of the Tennis Court, pledging never to disband until they had written a new constitution.

The king's actions were then somewhat contradictory. On June 23 he made a conciliatory speech to a joint session, urging reforms, and then ordered the three estates to meet together. At the same time, he apparently followed the advice of relatives and court nobles who urged him to dissolve the Estates General by force. The king called an army of eighteen thousand troops toward Versailles, and on July 11 he dismissed his finance minister and his other more liberal ministers. Faced with growing opposition since 1787, Louis XVI had resigned himself to bankruptcy. Now he sought to reassert his divine and historic right to rule. The middle-class delegates had done their best, but they were resigned to being disbanded at bayonet point. One third-estate delegate reassured a worried colleague: "You won't hang—you'll only have to go back home."[2]

The Revolt of the Poor and the Oppressed

While the third estate pressed for symbolic equality with the nobility and clergy in a single legislative body at Versailles, economic hardship gripped the masses of France. Grain was the basis of the diet of ordinary people, and in 1788 the harvest had been extremely poor. The price of bread, which had been rising gradually since 1785, began to soar. By July 1789 the price of bread in the provinces climbed as high as eight sous per pound. In Paris, where bread was subsidized by the government in an attempt to prevent popular unrest, the price rose to four sous. The poor could scarcely afford to pay two sous per pound, for even at that price a laborer with a wife and three children had to spend half of his wages to buy bread.

Storming the Bastille   This representation by an untrained contemporary artist shows civilians and members of the Paris militia—the "conquerors of the Bastille"—on the attack. This successful action had enormous practical and symbolic significance, and July 14 has long been France's most important national holiday. *(Source: Musée Carnavalet/ Photo Hubert Josse)*

Harvest failure and high bread prices unleashed a classic economic depression of the preindustrial age. With food so expensive and with so much uncertainty, the demand for manufactured goods collapsed. Thousands of artisans and small traders were thrown out of work. By the end of 1789, almost half of the French people would be in need of relief. One person in eight was a pauper, living in extreme want. In Paris the situation was desperate in July 1789: perhaps 150,000 of the city's 600,000 people were without work.

Against this background of dire poverty and excited by the political crisis, the people of Paris entered decisively onto the revolutionary stage. They believed in a general, though ill-defined, way that the economic distress had human causes. They believed that they should have steady work and enough bread to survive. Specifically, they feared

that the dismissal of the king's moderate finance minister would throw them at the mercy of aristocratic landowners and grain speculators. Stories like one quoting the wealthy financier Joseph François Foulon as saying that the poor "should eat grass, like my horses," and rumors that the king's troops would sack the city began to fill the air. Angry crowds formed, and passionate voices urged action. On July 13 the people began to seize arms for the defense of the city, and on July 14 several hundred of the most determined people marched to the Bastille to search for gunpowder.

A medieval fortress with walls 10 feet thick and eight great towers each 100 feet high, the Bastille had long been used as a prison. It was guarded by eighty retired soldiers and thirty Swiss guards. The governor of the fortress-prison refused to hand over the powder, panicked, and ordered his men to fire, killing ninety-eight people attempting to enter. Cannon were brought to batter the main gate, and fighting continued until the governor of the prison surrendered. While he was being taken under guard to city hall, a band of men broke through and hacked him to death. His head and that of the mayor of Paris, who had been slow to give the crowd arms, were stuck on pikes and paraded through the streets. The next day, a committee of citizens appointed the marquis de Lafayette commander of the city's armed forces. Paris was lost to the king, who was forced to recall the finance minister and to disperse his troops. The uprising had saved the National Assembly.

As the delegates resumed their long-winded and inconclusive debates at Versailles, the people in the countryside sent them a radical and unmistakable message. All across France, peasants began to rise in spontaneous, violent, and effective insurrection against their lords, ransacking manor houses and burning feudal documents that recorded the peasants' obligations. Neither middle-class landowners, who often owned manors and village monopolies, nor the larger, more prosperous farmers were spared. In some areas, the nobles and bourgeoisie combined forces and organized patrols to protect their property. Yet the peasant insurrection went on. Recent enclosures were undone; old common lands were reoccupied; and the forests were seized. Taxes were not paid. Fear of vagabonds and outlaws—the so-called Great Fear—seized the countryside and fanned the flames of rebellion. The long-suffering peasants were doing their best to free themselves from aristocratic privilege and exploitation.

Faced with chaos yet afraid to call on the king to restore order, some liberal nobles and middle-class delegates at Versailles responded to peasant demands with a surprise maneuver on the night of August 4, 1789. The duke of Aiguillon, one of France's greatest noble landowners, declared that

in several provinces the whole people forms a kind of league for the destruction of the manor houses, the ravaging of the lands, and especially for the seizure of the archives where the title deeds to feudal properties are kept. It seeks to throw off at last a yoke that has for many centuries weighted it down.[3]

He urged equality in taxation and the elimination of feudal dues. In the end, all the old exactions were abolished, generally without compensation:

serfdom where it still existed, exclusive hunting rights for nobles, fees for justice, village monopolies, the right to make peasants work on the roads, and a host of other dues. Though a clarifying law passed a week later was less generous, the peasants ignored the "fine print." They never paid feudal dues again. Thus the French peasantry, which already owned about 30 percent of all the land, quickly achieved a great and unprecedented victory. Henceforth, the French peasants would seek mainly to consolidate their triumph. As the Great Fear subsided, they became a force for order and stability.

A Limited Monarchy

The National Assembly moved forward. On August 27, 1789, it issued the Declaration of the Rights of Man. This great liberal document had a very American flavor, and Lafayette even discussed his draft in detail with the American ambassador in Paris, Thomas Jefferson, the author of the American Declaration of Independence. According to the French declaration, "men are born and remain free and equal in rights." Humankind's natural rights are "liberty, property, security, and resistance to oppression." Also, "every man is presumed innocent until he is proven guilty." As for law, "it is an expression of the general will; all citizens have the right to concur personally or through their representatives in its formation. . . . Free expression of thoughts and opinions is one of the most precious rights of mankind: every citizen may therefore speak, write, and publish freely." In short, this clarion call of the liberal revolutionary ideal guaranteed equality before the law, representative government for a sovereign people, and individual freedom. This revolutionary credo, only two pages long, was propagandized throughout France and Europe and around the world.

Moving beyond general principles to draft a constitution proved difficult. The questions of how much power the king should retain and whether he could permanently veto legislation led to another deadlock. Once again the decisive answer came from the poor, in this instance the poor women of Paris.

To understand what happened, one must remember that the work and wages of women and children were essential in the family economy of the laboring poor. In Paris great numbers of women worked, particularly within the putting-out system in the garment industry—making lace, fancy dresses, embroidery, ribbons, bonnets, corsets, and so on. Many of these goods were beautiful luxury items destined for an aristocratic and international clientele.[4] Immediately after the fall of the Bastille, many of France's great court nobles began to leave Versailles for foreign lands, so a plummeting demand for luxuries intensified the general economic crisis. International markets also declined, and the church was no longer able to give its traditional grants of food and money to the poor. Unemployment and hunger increased further, and the result was another popular explosion.

On October 5 some seven thousand desperate women marched the 12 miles from Paris to Versailles to demand action. A middle-class deputy looking out from the Assembly saw "multitudes arriving from Paris including fishwives and bullies from the market, and these people wanted nothing but bread." This great crowd invaded the Assembly, "armed with scythes, sticks and pikes." One coarse, tough old woman directing a large group of younger women defiantly shouted into the debate: "Who's that talking down there? Make the chatterbox shut up. That's not the point: the point is that we want bread."[5] Hers was the genuine voice of the people, essential to any understanding of the French Revolution.

The women invaded the royal apartments, slaughtered some of the royal bodyguards, and furiously searched for the despised queen, Marie Antoinette. "We are going to cut off her head, tear out her heart, fry her liver, and that won't be the end of it," they shouted, surging through the palace in a frenzy. It seems likely that only the intervention of Lafayette and the National Guard saved the royal family. But the only way to calm the disorder was for the king to go and live in Paris, as the crowd demanded.

The next day, the king, the queen, and their son left for Paris in the midst of a strange procession. The heads of two aristocrats, stuck on pikes, led the way. They were followed by the remaining members of the royal bodyguard, unarmed and surrounded and mocked by fierce men holding sabers and pikes. A mixed and victorious multitude surrounded the king's carriage, hurling crude insults at the queen. There was drinking and eating among the women. "We are bringing the baker, the baker's wife, and the baker's boy," they joy-fully sang. The National Assembly followed the king to Paris. Reflecting the more radical environment, it adopted a constitution that gave the virtually imprisoned "baker" only a temporary veto in the lawmaking process. And, for a time, he and the government made sure that the masses of Paris did not lack bread.

The next two years, until September 1791, saw the consolidation of the liberal Revolution. Under middle-class leadership, the National Assembly abolished the French nobility as a legal order and pushed forward with the creation of a constitutional monarchy, which Louis XVI reluctantly agreed to accept in July 1790. In the final constitution, the king remained the head of state, but all lawmaking power was placed in the hands of the National Assembly, elected by the economic upper half of French males. Eighty-three departments of approximately equal size replaced the complicated old patchwork of provinces with their many historic differences. The jumble of weights and measures that varied from province to province was reformed, leading to the introduction of the simple, rational metric system in 1793. The National Assembly promoted economic freedom. Monopolies, guilds, and workers' combinations were prohibited, and barriers to trade within France were abolished in the name of economic liberty. Thus the National Assembly applied the critical spirit of the Enlightenment to reform France's laws and institutions completely.

The Assembly also threatened nobles who had emigrated from France with the loss of their lands. It nationalized the property of the church and abolished the monasteries as useless relics of a distant past. The government used all former church property as collateral to guarantee a new paper currency, the *assignats*, and then sold these properties in an attempt to put the state's finances on a solid footing. Although the church's land was sold in large blocks, a procedure that favored nimble speculators and the rich, peasants eventually purchased much of it as it was subdivided. These purchases strengthened their attachment to the revolutionary state.

The most unfortunate aspect of the reorganization of France was that it brought the new government into conflict with the Catholic church. Many middle-class delegates to the National Assembly, imbued with the rationalism and skepticism of the eighteenth-century philosophes, harbored a deep distrust of popular piety and "superstitious religion." They were interested in the church only to the extent that they could seize its land and use the church to strengthen the new state. Thus they established a national church, with priests chosen by voters. In the face of resistance, the National Assembly required the clergy to take a loyalty oath to the new government. The clergy became just so many more employees of the state. The pope formally condemned this attempt to subjugate the church. Against such a backdrop, it is not surprising that only half of the priests of France took the oath of allegiance. The result was a deep division within both the country and the clergy itself on the religious question, and confusion and hostility among French Catholics were pervasive. The attempted reorganization of the Catholic church was the revolutionary government's first important failure.

WORLD WAR AND REPUBLICAN FRANCE (1791–1799)

When Louis XVI accepted the final version of the completed constitution in September 1791, a young and still obscure provincial lawyer and member of the National Assembly named Maximilien Robespierre (1758–1794) evaluated the work of two years and concluded, "The Revolution is over." Robespierre was both right and wrong. He was right in the sense that the most constructive and lasting reforms were in place. Nothing substantial in the way of liberty and equality would be gained in the next generation, though much would be lost. He was wrong in the sense that a much more radical stage lay ahead. New heroes and new ideologies were to emerge in revolutionary wars and international conflict.

Foreign Reactions and the Beginning of War

The outbreak and progress of revolution in France produced great excitement and a sharp division of opinion in Europe and the United States. Liberals and radicals saw a mighty triumph of liberty over despotism. In Great Britain especially, they hoped that the French example would lead to a fundamental reordering of the political system. That system, which had been consolidated in the revo-

lution of 1688 to 1689 (see pages 643–649), placed Parliament in the hands of the aristocracy and a few wealthy merchants; the great majority of people had very little say in the government. After the French Revolution began, conservative leaders like Edmund Burke (1729–1797) were deeply troubled by the aroused spirit of reform. In 1790 Burke published *Reflections on the Revolution in France,* one of the great intellectual defenses of European conservatism. He defended inherited privileges in general and those of the English monarchy and aristocracy in particular. He glorified the unrepresentative Parliament and predicted that thoroughgoing reform like that occurring in France would lead only to chaos and tyranny. Burke's work sparked vigorous debate.

One passionate rebuttal came from a young writer in London, Mary Wollstonecraft (1759–1797). Born into the middle class, Wollstonecraft was schooled in adversity by a mean-spirited father who beat his wife and squandered his inherited fortune. Determined to be independent in a society that generally expected women of her class to become homebodies and obedient wives, she struggled for years to earn her living as a governess and teacher—practically the only acceptable careers for single, educated women—before attaining success as a translator and author. Interested in politics and believing that "A desperate disease requires a powerful remedy" in Great Britain as well as France, Wollstonecraft was incensed by Burke's book. She immediately wrote a blistering, widely read attack, *A Vindication of the Rights of Man* (1790).

Then, fired up on controversy and commitment, she made a daring intellectual leap. She developed for the first time the logical implications of natural-law philosophy in her masterpiece, *A Vindication of the Rights of Woman* (1792). To fulfill the liberating promise of the French Revolution and to eliminate the economic and sexual inequality she had felt so keenly, she demanded that

the Rights of Women be respected . . . [and] JUSTICE for one-half of the human race. . . . It is time to effect a revolution in female manners, time to restore to them their lost dignity, and make them, as part of the human species, labor, by reforming themselves, to reform the world.

Setting high standards for women—"I wish to persuade women to endeavor to acquire strength, both of mind and body"—Wollstonecraft broke with those who had a low opinion of women's intellectual potential. She advocated rigorous coeducation, which would make women better wives and mothers, good citizens, and even economically independent. "Women might certainly study the art of healing, and be physicians, as well as nurses." Women could manage businesses and enter politics. Men themselves would benefit from women's rights, for Wollstonecraft believed that "the two sexes mutually corrupt and improve each other."[6] Marking the birth of the modern women's movement for equal rights, Wollstonecraft's strikingly original analysis testified to the power of the Revolution to excite and inspire outside of France.

The kings and nobles of continental Europe, who had at first welcomed the revolution in France as weakening a competing power, began to feel no less threatened than Burke and his supporters. At their courts they listened to the diatribes of great court nobles who had fled France and were urging intervention in France's affairs. When Louis XVI and Marie Antoinette were arrested and returned to Paris after trying unsuccessfully to slip out of France in June 1791, the monarchs of Austria and Prussia issued the Declaration of Pillnitz. This carefully worded statement declared their willingness to intervene in France, but only with the unanimous agreement of all the Great Powers, which they did not expect to receive. Austria and Prussia expected their threat to have a sobering effect on revolutionary France without causing war.

The crowned heads of Europe misjudged the revolutionary spirit in France. When the National Assembly disbanded, it sought popular support by decreeing that none of its members would be eligible for election to the new Legislative Assembly. As a result, the new representative body that was duly elected and convened in October 1791 had a different character. The great majority of members were still prosperous, well educated, and middle class, but they were younger and less cautious than their predecessors. Loosely allied as "Jacobins," so named after their political club, the new representatives to the Assembly were passionately committed to liberal revolution.

The Jacobins increasingly lumped "useless aristocrats" and "despotic monarchs" together, and they easily whipped themselves into a patriotic fury with bombastic oratory. Were the courts of

Mary Wollstonecraft Painted by an unknown artist when Mary Wollstonecraft was thirty-two and writing her revolutionary *Vindication of the Rights of Woman,* this portrait highlights the remarkable strength of character that energized Wollstonecraft's brilliant intellect. *(Source: The Board of Trustees of the National Museums and Galleries on Merseyside, Walker Art Gallery)*

Europe attempting to incite a war of kings against France? Well then, "we will incite a war of people against kings. . . . Ten million Frenchmen, kindled by the fire of liberty, armed with the sword, with reason, with eloquence would be able to change the face of the world and make the tyrants tremble on their thrones."[7] Only Robespierre and a very few others argued that people do not welcome liberation at the point of a gun. Such warnings were brushed aside. France would "rise to the full height of her mission," as one deputy urged. In April 1792 France declared war on Francis II, archduke of Austria and king of Hungary and Bohemia.

France's crusade against tyranny went poorly at first. Prussia joined Austria in the Austrian Netherlands (present-day Belgium), and French forces broke and fled at their first encounter with armies of this First Coalition. The road to Paris lay open, and it is possible that only conflict between the eastern monarchs over the division of Poland saved France from defeat.

Military reversals and Austro-Prussian threats caused a wave of patriotic fervor to sweep France. The Legislative Assembly declared the country in danger. Volunteer armies from the provinces streamed through Paris, fraternizing with the people and singing patriotic songs like the stirring "Marseillaise," later the French national anthem.

In this supercharged wartime atmosphere, rumors of treason by the king and queen spread in Paris. Once again, as in the storming of the Bastille, the common people of Paris acted decisively. On August 10, 1792, a revolutionary crowd attacked the royal palace at the Tuileries, capturing it after heavy fighting with the Swiss guards. The king and his family fled for their lives to the nearby Legislative Assembly, which suspended the king from all his functions, imprisoned him, and called for a new National Convention to be elected by universal male suffrage. Monarchy in France was on its deathbed, mortally wounded by war and revolt.

The Second Revolution

The fall of the monarchy marked a rapid radicalization of the Revolution, a phase that historians often call the "second revolution." Louis's imprisonment was followed by the September Massacres, which sullied the Revolution in the eyes of most of its remaining foreign supporters. Wild stories spread through the city that imprisoned counter-revolutionary aristocrats and priests were plotting with the allied invaders. As a result, angry crowds invaded the prisons of Paris and summarily slaughtered half of the men and women they found. In late September 1792, the new, popularly elected National Convention proclaimed France a republic. The republic adopted a new revolutionary calendar, and citizens were expected to address each other with the friendly "thou" of the people, rather than with the formal "you" of the rich and powerful.

All of the members of the National Convention were Jacobins and republicans, and the great majority continued to come from the well-educated middle class. But the convention was increasingly divided into two well-defined, bitterly competitive groups—the Girondists, named after a department in southwestern France, and the Mountain, led by Robespierre and another young lawyer, Georges Jacques Danton. The "Mountain" was so called because its members sat on the uppermost left-hand benches of the assembly hall. Many indecisive Convention members seated in the "Plain" below floated between the rival factions.

This division was clearly apparent after the National Convention overwhelmingly convicted Louis XVI of treason. By a single vote, 361 of the 720 members of the Convention then unconditionally sentenced him to death in January 1793. Louis died with tranquil dignity on the newly invented guillotine. One of his last statements was, "I am innocent and shall die without fear. I would that my death might bring happiness to the French, and ward off the dangers which I foresee."[8]

Both the Girondists and the Mountain were determined to continue the "war against tyranny." The Prussians had been stopped at the indecisive Battle of Valmy on September 20, 1792, one day before the First Republic was proclaimed. Republican armies then successfully invaded Savoy and captured Nice. A second army corps invaded the German Rhineland and took the city of Frankfurt. To the north, the revolutionary armies won their first major battle at Jemappes and occupied the entire Austrian Netherlands by November 1792. Everywhere they went, French armies of occupation chased the princes, "abolished feudalism," and found support among some peasants and middle-class people.

But the French armies also lived off the land, requisitioning food and supplies and plundering local treasures. The liberators looked increasingly like foreign invaders. International tensions mounted. In February 1793 the National Convention, at war with Austria and Prussia, declared war on Britain, Holland, and Spain as well. Republican France was now at war with almost all of Europe, a great war that would last almost without interruption until 1815.

As the forces of the First Coalition drove the French from the Austrian Netherlands, peasants in western France revolted against being drafted into the army. They were supported and encouraged in their resistance by devout Catholics, royalists, and foreign agents.

In Paris the quarrelsome National Convention found itself locked in a life-and-death political struggle between the Girondists and the Mountain. The two groups were in general agreement on questions of policy. Sincere republicans, they hated privilege and wanted to temper economic liberalism with social concern. Yet personal hatreds ran deep. The Girondists feared a bloody dictatorship by the Mountain, and the Mountain was no less convinced that the more moderate Girondists would turn to conservatives and even royalists in order to retain power. With the middle-class delegates so bitterly divided, the laboring poor of Paris emerged as the decisive political factor.

The great mass of the Parisian laboring poor always constituted—along with the peasantry in the summer of 1789—the elemental force that drove the Revolution forward. It was the artisans, shopkeepers, and day laborers who had stormed the Bastille, marched on Versailles, driven the king from the Tuileries, and carried out the September Massacres. The petty traders and laboring poor were often known as the *sans-culottes,* "without breeches," because they wore trousers instead of the knee breeches of the aristocracy and the solid middle class. The immediate interests of the sans-culottes were mainly economic, and in the spring of 1793 the economic situation was as bad as the military situation. Rapid inflation, unemployment, and food shortages were again weighing heavily on the poor.

In addition, by the spring of 1793, the sans-culottes were keenly interested in politics. Encouraged by the so-called angry men, such as the passionate young former priest and journalist Jacques Roux, the sans-culottes were demanding radical political action to guarantee them their daily bread. At first the Mountain joined the Girondists in violently rejecting these demands. But in the face of military defeat, peasant revolt, and hatred of the Girondists, the Mountain and especially Robespierre became more sympathetic. The Mountain joined with sans-culottes activists in the city government to engineer a popular uprising that forced the Convention to arrest thirty-one Girondist deputies for treason on June 2. All power passed to the Mountain.

Robespierre and others from the Mountain joined the recently formed Committee of Public Safety, to which the Convention had given dictatorial power to deal with the national emergency. These developments in Paris triggered revolt in leading provincial cities, such as Lyons and Marseilles, where moderates denounced Paris and demanded a decentralized government. The peasant revolt spread, and the republic's armies were driven back on all fronts. By July 1793 only the areas around Paris and on the eastern frontier were firmly controlled by the central government. Defeat appeared imminent.

Total War and the Terror

A year later, in July 1794, the Austrian Netherlands and the Rhineland were once again in the hands of conquering French armies, and the First Coalition was falling apart. This remarkable change of fortune was due to the revolutionary government's success in harnessing in a total war effort, for perhaps the first time in history, three explosive forces: a planned economy, revolutionary terror, and modern nationalism.

Robespierre and the Committee of Public Safety advanced with implacable resolution on several fronts in 1793 and 1794. In an effort to save revolutionary France, they collaborated with the fiercely patriotic and democratic sans-culottes. They established, as best they could, a planned economy with egalitarian social overtones. Rather than let supply and demand determine prices, the government decreed the maximum allowable prices, fixed in paper assignats, for a host of key products. Although the state was too weak to enforce all its price regulations, it did fix the price of bread in Paris at levels the poor could afford. Rationing and ration cards were introduced to make sure that the limited supplies of bread were shared fairly. Quality was also controlled. Bakers were permitted to make only the "bread of equality"—a rough brown bread made of a mixture of all available flours. Fine wheat bread and pastries were outlawed as frivolous luxuries. The poor of Paris may not have eaten well, but at least they ate.

They also worked, mainly to produce arms and munitions for the war effort. Craftsmen and small manufacturers were told what to produce and when to deliver. The government nationalized many small workshops and requisitioned raw materials and grain from the peasants. Sometimes planning and control did not go beyond orders to meet the latest emergency: "Ten thousand soldiers lack shoes. You will take the shoes of all the aristocrats in Strasbourg and deliver them ready for transport to headquarters at 10 A.M. tomorrow."

Failures to control and coordinate were failures of means and not of desire: seldom if ever before had a government attempted to manage an economy so thoroughly. The second revolution and the rise of the sans-culottes had produced an embryonic emergency socialism, which was to have great influence on the development of socialist ideology.

While radical economic measures supplied the poor with bread and the armies with weapons, a Reign of Terror (1793–1794) was solidifying the home front. Special revolutionary courts, responsible only to Robespierre's Committee of Public Safety, tried rebels and "enemies of the nation" for political crimes. Drawing on popular, sans-culottes support in the local Jacobin clubs, these local courts ignored normal legal procedures and judged severely. Some 40,000 French men and women were executed or died in prison. Another 300,000 suspects crowded the prisons and often brushed close to death in a revolutionary court.

Robespierre's Reign of Terror was one of the most controversial phases of the French Revolution. Most historians now believe that the Reign of Terror was not directed against any single class. Rather, it was a political weapon directed impartially against all who might oppose the revolutionary government. For many Europeans of the time, however, the Reign of Terror represented a terrifying perversion of the generous ideals that existed in 1789. It strengthened the belief that France had foolishly replaced a weak king with a bloody dictatorship.

The third and perhaps most decisive element in the French republic's victory over the First Coalition was its ability to continue drawing on the explosive power of patriotic dedication to a national state and a national mission. This dedication is the essence of modern nationalism. With a common language and a common tradition newly reinforced by the ideas of popular sovereignty and democracy, the French people were stirred by a common loyalty. The shared danger of foreign foes and internal rebels unified all classes in a heroic defense of the nation.

The Reign of Terror   A man, woman, and child accused of political crimes are brought before a special revolutionary committee for trial. The Terror's iron dictatorship crushed individual rights as well as treason and opposition. *(Source: Photo Flammarion)*

In such circumstances, war was no longer the gentlemanly game of the eighteenth century but a life-and-death struggle between good and evil. Everyone had to participate in the national effort. According to a famous decree of August 23, 1793,

The young men shall go to battle and the married men shall forge arms. The women shall make tents and clothes, and shall serve in the hospitals; children shall tear rags into lint. The old men will be guided to the public places of the cities to kindle the courage of the young warriors and to preach the unity of the Republic and the hatred of kings.

Like the wars of religion, war in 1793 was a crusade; this war, though, was fought for a secular rather than a religious ideology.

Because all unmarried young men were subject to the draft, the French armed forces swelled to one million men in fourteen armies. A force of this size was unprecedented in the history of European warfare. The soldiers were led by young, impetuous generals, many of whom had risen rapidly from the ranks and personified the opportunities that the Revolution seemed to offer gifted sons of the people. These generals used mass attacks at bayonet point by their highly motivated forces to overwhelm the enemy. By the spring of 1794, French armies were victorious on all fronts. The republic was saved.

The Thermidorian Reaction and the Directory (1794–1799)

The success of the French armies led Robespierre and the Committee of Public Safety to relax the emergency economic controls, but they extended the political Reign of Terror. Their lofty goal was increasingly an ideal democratic republic, where justice would reign and there would be neither rich nor poor. Their lowly means were unrestrained despotism and the guillotine, which struck down any who might seriously question the new order. In March 1794, to the horror of many sans-culottes, Robespierre's Terror wiped out many of the "angry men," led by the radical social democrat Jacques Hébert. Two weeks later, several of Robespierre's long-standing collaborators, led by the famous orator Danton, marched up the steps to the guillotine. Knowing that they might be next, a strange assortment of radicals and mod-

erates in the Convention organized a conspiracy. They howled down Robespierre when he tried to speak to the National Convention on 9 Thermidor (July 27, 1794). On the following day, it was Robespierre's turn to be shaved by the revolutionary razor.

As Robespierre's closest supporters followed their leader, France unexpectedly experienced a thorough reaction to the despotism of the Reign of Terror. In a general way, this "Thermidorian reaction" recalled the early days of the Revolution. The respectable middle-class lawyers and professionals who had led the liberal revolution of 1789 reasserted their authority, drawing support from their own class, the provincial cities, and the better-off peasants. The National Convention abolished many economic controls, printed more paper currency, and let prices rise sharply. It severely restricted the local political organizations where the sans-culottes had their strength. And all the while, the wealthy bankers and newly rich speculators celebrated the sudden end of the Terror with an orgy of self-indulgence and ostentatious luxury.

The collapse of economic controls, coupled with runaway inflation, hit the working poor very hard. The gaudy extravagance of the rich wounded their pride. The sans-culottes accepted private property, but they believed passionately in small business and the right of all to earn a decent living. Increasingly disorganized after Robespierre purged their radical leaders, the common people of Paris finally revolted against the emerging new order in early 1795. The Convention quickly used the army to suppress these insurrections. For the first time since the fall of the Bastille, bread riots and uprisings by Parisians living on the edge of starvation were effectively put down by a government that made no concessions to the poor.

In the face of all these catastrophes, the revolutionary fervor of the laboring poor finally subsided. As far as politics was concerned, their interest and influence would remain very limited until 1830. There arose, especially from the women, a great cry for peace and a turning toward religion. As the government looked the other way, the women brought back the Catholic church and the worship of God. In one French town, women fought with each other over which of their children should be baptized first. After six tumultuous years, the women of the poor concluded that the Revolution was a failure.

THE FRENCH REVOLUTION

May 5, 1789	Estates General convene at Versailles
June 17, 1789	Third Estate declares itself the National Assembly
June 20, 1789	Oath of the Tennis Court
July 14, 1789	Storming of the Bastille
July–August 1789	The Great Fear in the countryside
August 4, 1789	National Assembly abolishes feudal privileges
August 27, 1789	National Assembly issues Declaration of the Rights of Man
October 5, 1789	Parisian women march on Versailles and force royal family to return to Paris
November 1789	National Assembly confiscates church lands
July 1790	Civil Constitution of the Clergy establishes a national church
	Louis XVI reluctantly agrees to accept a constitutional monarchy
June 1791	Arrest of the royal family while attempting to flee France
August 1791	Declaration of Pillnitz by Austria and Prussia
April 1792	France declares war on Austria
August 1792	Parisian mob attacks palace and takes Louis XVI prisoner
September 1792	September Massacres
	National Convention declares France a republic and abolishes monarchy
January 1793	Execution of Louis XVI
February 1793	France declares war on Britain, Holland, and Spain
	Revolts in provincial cities
March 1793	Bitter struggle in the National Convention between Girondists and the Mountain
April–June 1793	Robespierre and the Mountain organize the Committee of Public Safety and arrest Girondist leaders
September 1793	Price controls to aid the sans-culottes and mobilize war effort
1793–1794	Reign of Terror in Paris and the provinces
Spring 1794	French armies victorious on all fronts
July 1794	Execution of Robespierre
	Thermidorean Reaction begins
1795–1799	The Directory
1795	End of economic controls and suppression of the sans-culottes
1797	Napoleon defeats Austrian armies in Italy and returns triumphant to Paris
1798	Austria, Great Britain, and Russia form the Second Coalition against France
1799	Napoleon overthrows the Directory and seizes power

As for the middle-class members of the National Convention, they wrote yet another constitution, which they believed would guarantee their economic position and political supremacy. The mass of the population could vote only for electors, who were men of means. Electors then elected the members of a reorganized Legislative Assembly, and key officials throughout France. The Assembly chose a five-man executive—the Directory.

The Directory continued to support French military expansion abroad. War was no longer so much a crusade as a means to meet the ever-present, ever-unsolved economic problem. Large, victorious French armies reduced unemployment at home, and they were able to live off the territories they conquered and plundered.

The unprincipled action of the Directory reinforced widespread disgust with war and starvation. This general dissatisfaction revealed itself clearly in the national elections of 1797, which returned a large number of conservative and even monarchist deputies who favored peace at almost any price. Fearing for their skins, the members of the Directory used the army to nullify the elections and began to govern dictatorially. Two years later, Napoleon Bonaparte ended the Directory in a coup d'état and substituted a strong dictatorship for a weak one. Truly, the Revolution was over.

THE NAPOLEONIC ERA (1799–1815)

For almost fifteen years, from 1799 to 1814, France was in the hands of a keen-minded military dictator of exceptional ability. One of history's most fascinating leaders, Napoleon Bonaparte realized the need to put an end to civil strife in France in order to create unity and consolidate his rule. And he did. But Napoleon saw himself as a man of destiny, and the glory of war and the dream of universal empire proved irresistible. For years he spiraled from victory to victory; but in the end he was destroyed by a mighty coalition united in fear of his restless ambition.

Napoleon's Rule of France

In 1799, when he seized power, young General Napoleon Bonaparte was a national hero. Born in Corsica into an impoverished noble family in 1769, Napoleon left home to become a lieutenant in the French artillery in 1785. After a brief and unsuccessful adventure fighting for Corsican independence in 1789, he returned to France as a French patriot and a dedicated revolutionary. Rising rapidly in the new army, Napoleon was placed in command of French forces in Italy and won brilliant victories there in 1796 and 1797. His next campaign, in Egypt, was a failure, but Napoleon made his way back to France before the fiasco was well-known. His reputation remained intact.

Napoleon soon learned that some prominent members of the Legislative Assembly were plotting against the Directory. The dissatisfaction of these plotters stemmed not so much from the fact that the Directory was a dictatorship as from the fact that it was a weak dictatorship. Ten years of upheaval and uncertainty had made firm rule much more appealing than liberty and popular politics to these disillusioned revolutionaries. The abbé Sieyès personified this evolution in thinking. In 1789 he had written in *What Is the Third Estate?* that the nobility was grossly overprivileged and that the entire people should rule the French nation. Now Sieyès's motto was "confidence from below, authority from above."

Like the other members of his group, Sieyès wanted a strong military ruler. The flamboyant thirty-year-old Napoleon was ideal. Thus the conspirators and Napoleon organized a takeover. On November 9, 1799, they ousted the Directors, and the following day soldiers disbanded the Assembly at bayonet point. Napoleon was named first consul of the republic, and a new constitution consolidating his position was overwhelmingly approved in a plebiscite in December 1799. Republican appearances were maintained, but Napoleon was already the real ruler of France.

The essence of Napoleon's domestic policy was to use his great and highly personal powers to maintain order and put an end to civil strife. He did so by working out unwritten agreements with powerful groups in France, whereby these groups received favors in return for loyal service. Napoleon's bargain with the solid middle class was codified in the famous Civil Code of 1804, which reasserted two of the fundamental principles of the liberal and essentially moderate revolution of 1789: equality of all citizens before the law and absolute security of wealth and private property. Napoleon and the leading bankers of Paris established a privately owned Bank of France, which loyally served the interests of both the state and the financial oligarchy. Napoleon's defense of the economic status quo also appealed to the peasants, who had bought some of the lands confiscated from the church and nobility. Thus Napoleon reconfirmed the gains of the peasantry and reassured the middle class, which had already lost a large number of its revolutionary illusions in the face of social upheaval.

At the same time, Napoleon accepted and strengthened the position of the French bureaucracy. Building on the solid foundations that revolutionary governments had inherited from the Old Regime, he perfected a thoroughly centralized state. A network of prefects, subprefects, and centrally appointed mayors depended on Napoleon and served him well. Nor were members of the old nobility slighted. In 1800 and again in 1802, Napoleon granted amnesty to a hundred thousand émigrés on the condition that they return to France and take a loyalty oath. Members of this returning elite soon ably occupied many high posts in the expanding centralized state. Only a thousand diehard monarchists were exempted and remained abroad. Napoleon also created a new imperial nobility in order to reward his most talented generals and officials.

Napoleon's great skill in gaining support from important and potentially hostile groups is illustrated by his treatment of the Catholic church in

THE NAPOLEONIC ERA

November 1799	Napoleon overthrows the Directory
December 1799	French voters overwhelmingly approve Napoleon's new constitution
1800	Napoleon founds the Bank of France
1801	France defeats Austria and acquires Italian and German territories in the Treaty of Lunéville
	Napoleon signs a concordat with the pope
1802	Treaty of Amiens with Britain
December 1804	Napoleon crowns himself emperor
October 1805	Battle of Trafalgar: Britain defeats the French and Spanish fleets
December 1805	Battle of Austerlitz: Napoleon defeats Austria and Prussia
1807	Treaties of Tilsit: Napoleon redraws the map of Europe
1810	Height of the Grand Empire
June 1812	Napoleon invades Russia with 600,000 men
Winter 1812	Disastrous retreat from Russia
March 1814	Russia, Prussia, Austria, and Britain form the Quadruple Alliance to defeat France
April 1814	Napoleon abdicates and is exiled to Elba
February–June 1815	Napoleon escapes from Elba and rules France until suffering defeat at the Battle of Waterloo

France. In 1800 the French clergy was still divided into two groups: those who had taken an oath of allegiance to the revolutionary government and those in exile or hiding who had refused to do so. Personally uninterested in religion, Napoleon wanted to heal the religious division so that a united Catholic church in France could serve as a bulwark of order and social peace. After long and arduous negotiations, Napoleon and Pope Pius VII (r. 1800–1823) signed the Concordat of 1801. The pope gained for French Catholics the precious right to practice their religion freely, but Napoleon gained the most politically. His government now nominated bishops, paid the clergy, and exerted great influence over the church in France.

The domestic reforms of Napoleon's early years were his greatest achievement. Much of his legal and administrative reorganization has survived in France to this day. More generally, Napoleon's domestic initiatives gave the great majority of French people a welcome sense of order and stability. And when Napoleon added the glory of military victory, he rekindled a spirit of national unity that would elude France throughout most of the rest of the nineteenth century.

Order and unity had their price: Napoleon's authoritarian rule. Women, who had participated actively in revolutionary politics, had no political rights under the Napoleonic Code. Under the law, women were dependents, of either their fathers or their husbands, and they could not make contracts or even have bank accounts in their own names. Free speech and freedom of the press—fundamental rights of the liberal revolution enshrined in the Declaration of the Rights of Man—were continually violated. Napoleon constantly reduced the number of newspapers in Paris. By 1811 only four were left—organs of government propaganda. The occasional elections were a farce. Later laws prescribed harsh penalties for political offenses.

These changes in the law were part of the creation of a police state in France. Since Napoleon was usually busy making war, this task was largely left to Joseph Fouché, an unscrupulous opportunist who had earned a reputation for brutality during the Reign of Terror. As minister of police, Fouché organized a ruthlessly efficient spy system, which kept thousands of citizens under continuous police surveillance. People suspected of subversive activities were arbitrarily detained, placed under house arrest, or even consigned to insane asylums. After 1810 political suspects were held in state prisons, as during the Terror. There were about 2,500 such political prisoners in 1814.

Napoleon's Wars and Foreign Policy

Napoleon was above all a military man, and a great one. After coming to power in 1799, he sent peace feelers to Austria and Great Britain, the two remaining members of the Second Coalition, which had been formed against France in 1798. When these overtures were rejected, French armies led by Napoleon decisively defeated the Austrians. In the Treaty of Lunéville (1801) Austria accepted the loss of its Italian possessions, and German territory on the west bank of the Rhine was incorporated into France. Once more, as in 1797, the British were alone, and war-weary, like the French.

Still seeking to consolidate his regime domestically, Napoleon concluded the Treaty of Amiens with Great Britain in 1802. Britain agreed to return Trinidad and the Caribbean islands, which it had seized from France in 1793. The treaty said very little about Europe, though. France remained in control of Holland, the Austrian Netherlands, the west bank of the Rhine, and most of the Italian peninsula. Napoleon was free to reshape the German states as he wished. To the dismay of British business people, the Treaty of Amiens did not provide for expansion of the commerce between Britain and the Continent. It was a diplomatic triumph for Napoleon, and peace with honor and profit increased his popularity at home.

In 1802 Napoleon was secure but unsatisfied. Ever a romantic gambler as well as a brilliant administrator, he could not contain his power drive. Aggressively redrawing the map of Germany so as to weaken Austria and attract the secondary states of southwestern Germany toward France, Napoleon was also mainly responsible for renewed war with Great Britain. Regarding war with Britain as inevitable, he threatened British interests in the eastern Mediterranean and tried to restrict British trade with all of Europe. Britain had technically violated the Treaty of Amiens by failing to evacuate the island of Malta, but it was Napoleon's decision to renew war in May 1803. He concentrated his armies in the French ports on the English Channel in the fall of 1803 and began making preparations to invade England. Yet Great Britain remained dominant on the seas. When Napoleon tried to bring his Mediterranean fleet around Gibraltar to northern France, a combined French and Spanish fleet was, after a series of mishaps, virtually annihilated by Lord Nelson at the Battle of Trafalgar on October 21, 1805. Invasion of England was henceforth impossible. Renewed fighting had its advantages, however, for the first consul used the wartime atmosphere to have himself proclaimed emperor in late 1804.

Austria, Russia, and Sweden joined with Britain to form the Third Coalition against France shortly before the Battle of Trafalgar. Actions like Napoleon's assumption of the Italian crown had convinced both Alexander I of Russia and Francis II of Austria that Napoleon was a threat to their interests and to the European balance of power. Yet the Austrians and the Russians were no match for Napoleon, who scored a brilliant victory over them at the Battle of Austerlitz in December 1805. Alexander I decided to pull back, and Austria accepted large territorial losses in return for peace as the Third Coalition collapsed.

Victorious at Austerlitz, Napoleon proceeded to reorganize the German states to his liking. In

David: Napoleon Crossing the Alps Bold and commanding, with flowing cape and surging stallion, the daring young Napoleon Bonaparte leads his army across the Alps from Italy to battle the Austrians in 1797. This painting by the great Jacques-Louis David (1748–1825) is a stirring glorification of Napoleon, a brilliant exercise in mythmaking. *(Source: Louvre/Cliché des Musées Nationaux, Paris)*

KINGDOM OF NORWAY AND DENMARK

KINGDOM OF SWEDEN

RUSSIAN EMPIRE

OTTOMAN EMPIRE

AUSTRIAN EMPIRE

GRAND DUCHY OF WARSAW

PRUSSIA

GREAT BRITAIN

SCOTLAND

IRELAND

ENGLAND

FRANCE

SPAIN

PORTUGAL

CONFEDERATION OF THE RHINE

WESTPHALIA

SAXONY

BAVARIA

WÜRTTEMBERG

BADEN

SWITZERLAND

KINGDOM OF ITALY

ILLYRIAN PROVINCES

KINGDOM OF NAPLES

KINGDOM OF SICILY

SARDINIA

Black Sea

Baltic Sea

North Sea

ATLANTIC OCEAN

Mediterranean Sea

Moscow
Borodino 1812
St. Petersburg
Smolensk
Kiev
Stockholm
Tilsit
Friedland 1807
Königsberg
Warsaw
Danzig
Constantinople
Athens
Pest
Buda
Pressburg
Austerlitz 1805
Wagram 1809
Vienna
Lübeck
Hamburg
Berlin
Bremen
Auerstädt 1806
Jena 1806
Leipzig 1813
Copenhagen
Brussels
Waterloo 1815
Antwerp
Amiens
Paris
Lunéville
Zurich
Milan
Marengo 1800
Genoa
Rome
Naples
Marseilles
Madrid
Lisbon
Trafalgar 1805
London
Dnieper
Dniester
Dnieper
Vistula
Oder
Danube
Rhine
Rhône
Loire
Seine
Tagus
Thames

Elba
Corsica
Cyprus
Crete
IONIAN IS. (Gr. Br.)
MALTA (Gr. Br.)
GIBRALTAR (Gr. Br.)
HELGOLAND (Gr. Br.)

French empire
Dependent states
Allied with Napoleon
At war with Napoleon
✕ Major battles

0   150   300 Km.
0   150   300 Mi.

1806 he abolished many of the tiny German states, as well as the ancient Holy Roman Empire, whose emperor had traditionally been the ruler of Austria. Napoleon established by decree a German Confederation of the Rhine, a union of fifteen German states minus Austria, Prussia, and Saxony. Naming himself "protector" of the confederation, Napoleon firmly controlled western Germany.

Napoleon's intervention in German affairs alarmed the Prussians, who had been at peace with France for more than a decade. Expecting help from his ally Russia, Frederick William III of Prussia mobilized his armies. Napoleon attacked and won two more brilliant victories in October 1806 at Jena and Auerstädt, where the Prussians were outnumbered two to one. The war with Prussia and Russia continued into the following spring, and after Napoleon's larger armies won another victory, Alexander I of Russia wanted peace.

For several days in June 1807, the young tsar and the French emperor negotiated face to face on a raft anchored in the middle of the Niemen River. All the while, the helpless Frederick William rode back and forth on the shore, anxiously awaiting the results. As the German poet Heinrich Heine said later, Napoleon had but to whistle and Prussia would have ceased to exist. In the subsequent treaties of Tilsit, Prussia lost half of its population while Russia accepted Napoleon's reorganization of western and central Europe. Alexander also promised to enforce Napoleon's recently decreed economic blockade against British goods and to declare war on Britain if Napoleon could not make peace on favorable terms with his island enemy.

After the victory of Austerlitz and even more after the treaties of Tilsit, Napoleon saw himself as the emperor of Europe, not just of France. The so-called Grand Empire he built had three parts. The core was an ever-expanding France, which by 1810 included Belgium, Holland, parts of northern Italy, and much German territory on the east bank of the Rhine (Map 25.1). Beyond French borders Napoleon established a number of dependent satellite kingdoms, on the thrones of which he placed (and replaced) the members of his large family. Last, there were the independent but allied states of Austria, Prussia, and Russia. Both satellites and allies were expected after 1806 to support Napoleon's continental system and cease trade with Britain.

The impact of the Grand Empire on the peoples of Europe was considerable. In the areas incorporated into France and in the satellites, Napoleon introduced many French laws, abolishing feudal dues and serfdom where French revolutionary armies had not already done so. Some of the peasants and middle class benefited from these reforms. Yet while he extended progressive measures to his cosmopolitan empire, Napoleon had to put the prosperity and special interests of France first in order to safeguard his power base. Levying heavy taxes in money and men for his armies, Napoleon came to be regarded more as a conquering tyrant than as an enlightened liberator.

The first great revolt occurred in Spain. In 1808 a coalition of Catholics, monarchists, and patriots rebelled against Napoleon's attempts to make Spain a French satellite with a Bonaparte as its king. French armies occupied Madrid, but the foes of Napoleon fled to the hills and waged uncompromising guerrilla warfare. Spain was a clear warning. Resistance to French imperialism was growing.

Yet Napoleon pushed on, determined to hold his complex and far-flung empire together. In 1810, when the Grand Empire was at its height, Britain still remained at war with France, helping the guerrillas in Spain and Portugal. The continental system, organized to exclude British goods from the Continent and force that "nation of shopkeepers" to its knees, was a failure. Instead, it was France that suffered from Britain's counter-blockade, which created hard times for French artisans and the middle class. Perhaps looking for a scapegoat, Napoleon turned on Alexander I of Russia, who had been fully supporting Napoleon's war of prohibitions against British goods.

Napoleon's invasion of Russia began in June 1812 with a force that eventually numbered 600,000, probably the largest force yet assembled in a single army. Only one-third of this force was French, however; nationals of all the satellites and allies were drafted into the operation. Originally planning to winter in the Russian city of Smolensk if Alexander did not sue for peace, Napoleon reached Smolensk and recklessly pressed on. The great battle of Borodino that followed was a draw, and the Russians retreated in good order. Alexander ordered the evacuation of Moscow, which then

MAP 25.1 Napoleonic Europe in 1810

burned, and refused to negotiate. Finally, after five weeks in the burned-out city, Napoleon ordered a retreat. That retreat was one of the great military disasters in history. The Russian army and the Russian winter cut Napoleon's army to pieces. Only 30,000 men returned to their homelands.

Leaving his troops to their fate, Napoleon raced to Paris to raise yet another army. Possibly he might still have saved his throne if he had been willing to accept a France reduced to its historical size—the proposal offered by Austria's foreign minister Metternich. But Napoleon refused. Austria and Prussia deserted Napoleon and joined Russia and Great Britain in the Fourth Coalition. All across Europe, patriots called for a "war of liberation" against Napoleon's oppression, and the well-disciplined regular armies of Napoleon's enemies closed in for the kill. This time the coalition held together, cemented by the Treaty of Chaumont, which created a Quadruple Alliance to last for twenty years. Less than a month later, on April 4, 1814, a defeated, abandoned Napoleon abdi-

cated his throne. After this unconditional abdication, the victorious allies granted Napoleon the island of Elba off the coast of Italy as his own tiny state. Napoleon was even allowed to keep his imperial title, and France was required to pay him a large yearly income of 2 million francs.

The allies also agreed to the restoration of the Bourbon dynasty, in part because demonstrations led by a few dedicated French monarchists indicated some support among the French people for that course of action. The new monarch, Louis XVIII (r. 1814–1824), tried to consolidate that support by issuing the Constitutional Charter, which accepted many of France's revolutionary changes and guaranteed civil liberties. Indeed, the Charter gave France a constitutional monarchy roughly similar to that established in 1791, although far fewer people had the right to vote for representatives to the resurrected Chamber of Deputies. Moreover, after Louis XVIII stated firmly that his government would not pay any war reparations, France was treated leniently by the al-

Goya: The Third of May, 1808 This great painting screams in outrage at the horrors of war, which Goya witnessed in Spain. Spanish rebels, focused around the Christ-like figure at the center, are gunned down by anonymous French soldiers, grim forerunners of modern death squads and their atrocities. *(Source: Museo del Prado, Madrid)*

lies, who agreed to meet in Vienna to work out a general peace settlement.

Louis XVIII—old, ugly, and crippled by gout—totally lacked the glory and magic of Napoleon. Hearing of political unrest in France and diplomatic tensions in Vienna, Napoleon staged a daring escape from Elba in February 1815. Landing in France, he issued appeals for support and marched on Paris with a small band of followers. French officers and soldiers who had fought so long for their emperor responded to the call. Louis XVIII fled, and once more Napoleon took command. But Napoleon's gamble was a desperate long shot, for the allies were united against him. At the end of a frantic period known as the Hundred Days, they crushed his forces at Waterloo on June 18, 1815, and imprisoned him on the rocky island of St. Helena, far off the western coast of Africa. Old Louis XVIII returned again—this time "in the baggage of the allies," as his detractors scornfully put it—and recommenced his reign. The allies now dealt more harshly with the apparently incorrigible French (see pages 865–868). And Napoleon, doomed to suffer crude insults at the hands of sadistic English jailers on distant St. Helena, could take revenge only by writing his memoirs, nurturing the myth that he had been Europe's revolutionary liberator, a romantic hero whose lofty work had been undone by oppressive reactionaries. An era had ended.

SUMMARY

The revolution that began in America and spread to France was a liberal revolution. Inspired by English history and some of the teachings of the Enlightenment, revolutionaries on both sides of the Atlantic sought to establish civil liberties and equality before the law within the framework of representative government. Success in America was subsequently matched by success in France. There, liberal nobles and an increasingly class-conscious middle class overwhelmed declining monarchial absolutism and feudal privilege, thanks to the common people—the sans-culottes and the peasants. The government and society established by the Declaration of the Rights of Man and the French constitution of 1791 were remarkably similar to those created in America by the federal Constitution and the Bill of Rights. Thus the new political system, based on electoral competition and civil equality, came into approximate harmony with France's evolving social structure, which had become increasingly based on wealth and achievement rather than on tradition and legal privileges.

Yet the Revolution in France did not end with the liberal victory of 1789 to 1791. As Robespierre led the determined country in a total war effort against foreign foes, French revolutionaries became more democratic, radical, and violent. Their effort succeeded, but at the price of dictatorship—first by Robespierre himself and then by the Directory and Napoleon. Some historians blame the excesses of the French revolutionaries for the emergence of dictatorship; others hold the conservative monarchs of Europe responsible. In any case, historians have often concluded that the French Revolution ended in failure.

This conclusion is highly debatable, though. After the fall of Robespierre, the solid middle class, with its liberal philosophy and Enlightenment world view, reasserted itself. Under the Directory, it salvaged a good portion of the social and political gains that it and the peasantry had made between 1789 and 1791. In so doing, the middle-class leaders repudiated the radical social and economic measures associated with Robespierre, but they never re-established the old pattern of separate legal orders and absolute monarchy. Napoleon built on the policies of the Directory. With considerable success he sought to add the support of the old nobility and the church to that of the middle class and the peasantry. And though Napoleon sharply curtailed thought and speech, he effectively promoted the reconciliation of old and new, of centralized government and careers open to talent, of noble and bourgeois in a restructured property-owning elite. Louis XVIII had no choice but to accept a French society solidly based on wealth and achievement. In granting representative government and civil liberties to facilitate his restoration to the throne in 1814, Louis XVIII submitted to the rest of the liberal triumph of 1789 to 1791. The core of the French Revolution had survived a generation of war and dictatorship. Old Europe would never be the same.

NOTES

1. Quoted in R. R. Palmer, *The Age of the Democratic Revolution,* vol. 1 (Princeton, N.J.: Princeton University Press, 1959), p. 239.

2. Quoted in G. Lefebvre, *The Coming of the French Revolution* (New York: Vintage Books, 1947), p. 81.

3. Quoted in P. H. Beik, ed., *The French Revolution* (New York: Walker, 1970), p. 89.

4. O. Hufton, "Women in Revolution," *Past and Present* 53 (November 1971): 91–95.

5. Quoted in G. Pernoud and S. Flaisser, eds., *The French Revolution* (Greenwich, Conn.: Fawcett, 1960), p. 61.

6. Quotations from Wollstonecraft are drawn from E. W. Sunstein, *A Different Face: The Life of Mary Wollstonecraft* (New York: Harper & Row, 1975), pp. 208, 211; and H. R. James, *Mary Wollstonecraft: A Sketch* (London: Oxford University Press, 1932), pp. 60, 62, 69.

7. Quoted in L. Gershoy, *The Era of the French Revolution, 1789–1799* (New York: Van Nostrand, 1957), p. 150.

8. Quoted in Pernoud and Flaisser, pp. 193–194.

SUGGESTED READING

For fascinating eyewitness reports on the French Revolution, see the edited works by Beik and Pernoud and Flaisser mentioned in the Notes. In addition, A. Young *Travels in France During the Years 1787, 1788 and 1789* (1969), offers an engrossing contemporary description of France and Paris on the eve of revolution. Edmund Burke, *Reflections on the Revolution in France,* first published in 1790, is the classic conservative indictment. The intense passions generated by the French Revolution may be seen in the nineteenth-century French historians, notably the enthusiastic Jules Michelet, *History of the French Revolution;* the hostile Hippolyte Taine; and the judicious Alexis de Tocqueville, whose masterpiece, *The Old Regime and the French Revolution,* was first published in 1856. Important general studies include the work of R. R. Palmer, cited in the Notes, which paints a comparative international picture; E. J. Hobsbawm, *The Age of Revolution, 1789–1848* (1962); C. Breunig, *The Age of Revolution and Reaction, 1789–1850* (1970); O. Connelly, *French Revolution—Napoleonic Era* (1979); and L. Dehio, *The Precarious Balance: Four Centuries of the European Power Struggle* (1962).

Recent decades have seen a wealth of new scholarship and interpretation, culminating in a profusion of works published to coincide with the French Revolution's bicentenary of 1989. A. Cobban, *The Social Interpretation of the French Revolution* (1964), and F. Furet, *Interpreting the French Revolution* (1981), are major reassessments of long-dominant ideas that are admirably presented in N. Hampson, *A Social History of the French Revolution* (1963), and in the volume by Lefebvre listed in the Notes. R. Chartier, *The Cultural Origins of the*

French Revolution (1989), and W. Doyle, *Origins of the French Revolution* (1981), are excellent on long-term developments. Among recent studies, which generally are often quite critical of revolutionary developments, several are noteworthy: J. Bosher, *The French Revolution* (1988); S. Schama, *Citizens: A Chronicle of the French Revolution* (1989); W. Doyle, *The Oxford History of the French Revolution* (1989); and D. Sutherland, *France, 1789–1815: Revolution and Counterrevolution* (1986).

Two valuable anthologies concisely presenting a range of interpretations are F. Kafker and J. Laux, eds., *The French Revolutions: Conflicting Interpretations,* 4th ed. (1989), and G. Best, ed., *The Permanent Revolution: The French Revolution and Its Legacy, 1789–1989* (1988). G. Rude makes the men and women of the great days of upheaval come alive in his *The Crowd in the French Revolution* (1959), and R. R. Palmer studies sympathetically the leaders of the Terror in *Twelve Who Ruled* (1941). Four other particularly interesting, detailed works are D. Jordan, *The Revolutionary Career of Maximilien Robespierre* (1985); J. P. Bertaud, *The Army of the French Revolution: From Citizen-Soldier to Instrument of Power* (1988); C. L. R. James, *The Black Jacobins* (1938, 1980), on black slave revolt in Haiti; and J. C. Herold, *Mistress to an Age* (1955), on the remarkable Madame de Staël. Other significant studies on aspects of revolutionary France include P. Jones's pathbreaking *The Peasantry in the French Revolution* (1988); D. Jordan's vivid *The King's Trial: Louis XVI vs. the French Revolution* (1979); W. Sewell Jr.'s imaginative *Work and Revolution in France: The Language of Labor from the Old Regime to 1848* (1980); and L. Hunt's innovative *Politics, Culture, and Class in the French Revolution* (1984). Mary Wollstonecraf is the subject of several biographies, including those by Sunstein and James cited in the Notes.

Two important works placing political developments in a comparative perspective are P. Higonnet, *Sister Republics: The Origins of French and American Republicanism* (1988), and E. Morgan, *Inventing the People: The Rise of Popular Sovereignty in England and America* (1988). B. Bailyn, *The Ideological Origins of the American Revolution* (1967), is also noteworthy.

The best synthesis on Napoleonic France is L. Bergeron, *France Under Napoleon* (1981). P. Geyl, *Napoleon, For and Against* (1949), is a delightful discussion of changing historical interpretations of Napoleon, which may be compared with a more recent treatment by R. Jones, *Napoleon: Man and Myth* (1977). Good biographies are J. M. Thompson, *Napoleon Bonaparte: His Rise and Fall* (1952); F. H. M. Markham, *Napoleon* (1964); and V. Cronin, *Napoleon Bonaparte* (1972). Wonderful novels inspired by this period include Raphael Sabatini's *Scaramouche,* a swashbuckler of revolutionary intrigue with accurate historical details; Charles Dickens's classic *Tale of Two Cities;* and Leo Tolstoy's saga of Napoleon's invasion of Russia, *War and Peace.*

26

The Industrial Revolution in Europe

Paddington Station, London. William-Powell Frith, *The Railway Station* (detail)

While the Revolution in France was opening a new political era, another revolution was transforming economic and social life. This was the Industrial Revolution, which began in England around the 1780s and started to influence continental Europe and the rest of the world after 1815. Because the Industrial Revolution was less dramatic than the French Revolution, some historians see industrial development as basically moderate and evolutionary. From a long perspective, however, it was rapid and brought about radical changes. Perhaps only the development of agriculture during Neolithic times had a similar impact and significance.

The Industrial Revolution profoundly modified much of human experience. It changed patterns of work, transformed the social class structure, and even altered the international balance of political and military power, giving added impetus to ongoing Western expansion into non-Western lands. The Industrial Revolution also helped ordinary people gain a higher standard of living as the widespread poverty of the preindustrial world was gradually reduced.

Unfortunately, improvement in the European standard of living was quite limited until about 1850, for at least two reasons. First, even in England only a few key industries experienced a technological revolution. Many more industries continued to use old methods, especially on the Continent, and this held down the increase in total production. Second, the increase in total population, which began in the eighteenth century (see pages 695–697), continued all across Europe as the era of the Industrial Revolution unfolded. As a result, the rapid growth in population threatened—quite literally—to eat up the growth in production and to leave individuals poorer than ever. Thus rapid population growth formed a somber background for European industrialization and made the wrenching transformation even more difficult.

- What was the Industrial Revolution?
- What were the origins of the Industrial Revolution, and how did it develop?
- How did the changes brought by the Industrial Revolution affect people and society in an era of continued rapid population growth?

These are the questions that this chapter seeks to answer. Chapter 28 examines in detail the emergence of accompanying changes in urban civilization, and Chapter 30 probes the consequences of industrialization in Europe for non-Western peoples.

THE INITIAL BREAKTHROUGH IN ENGLAND

The Industrial Revolution began in England. It was something new in history, and it was quite unplanned. With no models to copy and no idea of what to expect, England had to pioneer not only in industrial technology but also in social relations and urban living. Between 1793 and 1815, these formidable tasks were complicated by almost constant war with France. The trailblazer in economic development, as France was in political change, England must command special attention.

Eighteenth-Century Origins

Although many aspects of the Industrial Revolution are still matters for scholarly debate, it is generally agreed that the industrial changes that did occur grew out of a complex combination of factors. These factors came together in eighteenth-century England and initiated a decisive breakthrough, a breakthrough that many place in the 1780s—after the American war for independence and just before the French Revolution.

In analyzing the causes of the late-eighteenth-century acceleration in the English economy, historians have paid particular attention to dramatic changes in agriculture, foreign trade, technology, energy supplies, and transportation. Although this chapter focuses on those issues, one must first understand that England had other, less conspicuous, assets that favored the long process of development that culminated in industrial breakthrough.

Relatively good government was one such asset. The monarchy and the aristocratic oligarchy, which jointly ruled the country after the constitutional settlement of 1688 (see pages 648–649), provided stable and predictable government. Neither civil strife nor invading armies threatened the peace of the realm. Thus the government let the domestic economy operate fairly freely and with few controls, encouraging personal initiative, technological change, and a free market.

A related asset was an experienced business class with very modern characteristics. This business class, which traced its origins to the High Middle Ages, eagerly sought to make profits and to accumulate capital.

England also had a large class of hired agricultural laborers, whose numbers were further increased by agricultural changes in the eighteenth century. These rural wage earners were relatively mobile—compared with village-bound peasants in France and western Germany, for example—and along with cottage workers they formed a potential labor force for capitalist entrepreneurs.

Several other assets supporting English economic growth stand out. First, unlike France and most other countries, England had an effective central bank and well-developed credit institutions. Second, although England may seem a rather small country today, it undoubtedly enjoyed the largest effective domestic market in eighteenth-century Europe. In an age when shipping goods by water was much cheaper than shipping goods by land, no part of England was more than twenty miles from navigable water. Beginning in the 1770s, a canal-building boom greatly enhanced this natural advantage (Map 26.1). Nor were there any tariffs within the country to hinder trade, as there were in France before 1789 and in politically fragmented Germany and Italy. Finally, only in Holland did the lower classes appear to live as well as in England. The ordinary English family did not have to spend almost everything it earned just to buy bread. It could spend more on other items, thereby adding significantly to the total demand for manufactured goods. And growing demand for manufactured goods was probably the critical factor in initiating England's industrial breakthrough.

All these factors combined to initiate the Industrial Revolution, a term first coined by awed contemporaries in the 1830s to describe the burst of major inventions and technical changes that they had witnessed in certain industries. This technical revolution went hand in hand with an impressive quickening in the annual rate of industrial growth in England. Thus industry grew at only 0.7 per-

MAP 26.1 Cottage Industry and Transportation in Eighteenth-Century England   England had an unusually good system of navigable waterways even before river-linking canals made it better.

cent per year between 1700 and 1760—before the Industrial Revolution—but it grew at the much higher rate of 3 percent between 1801 and 1831, when industrial transformation was in full swing.[1] The decisive quickening of growth probably came in the 1780s, after the American war of independence and just before the French Revolution.

The great economic and political revolutions that shaped the modern world occurred almost simultaneously, though they began in different countries. The Industrial Revolution, however, was a longer process. It was not complete in England until 1830 at the earliest, and it had no real impact on continental countries until after the Congress of Vienna ended the era of revolutionary wars in 1815.

The Agricultural Revolution

According to an older generation of historians, England's industrial transformation depended on an earlier revolution in agriculture and rural life. Although scholars no longer believe that radical agricultural change was a necessary precondition for the industrial breakthrough, the general stress on the importance of agricultural improvement remains valid. A gradual but profound revolution in agricultural methods did promote accelerated economic growth, and that revolution mirrored the general economic leadership underpinning England's epoch-making industrial surge.

In essence, the Agricultural Revolution eliminated the traditional pattern of village agriculture found in northern and central Europe. It replaced the medieval open-field system (see page 692) with a new system of continuous rotation that resulted in more food for humans and their animals. The new agricultural system had profound implications, for it eliminated long-standing common rights as well as the fallow. But whereas peasants and rural laborers checked the spread of the new system on the Continent in the eighteenth century, large landowners and powerful market forces overcame such opposition in England.

The new methods of agriculture originated in the Low Countries. The vibrant, dynamic middle-class society of seventeenth-century republican Holland was the most advanced in Europe in many areas of human endeavor, including agriculture. By 1650 intensive farming was well established throughout much of the Low Countries. Enclosed fields, continuous rotation, heavy manuring, and a wide variety of crops—all these innovations were present. Agriculture was highly specialized and commercialized. The same skills that grew turnips produced flax to be spun into linen for clothes and tulip bulbs to lighten the heart with beautiful flowers. The fat cattle of Holland, so beloved by Dutch painters, gave the most milk in Europe.

The reasons for early Dutch leadership in farming were basically threefold. First, the Low Countries were densely populated, and the Dutch were forced at an early date to seek maximum yields from their land and to increase land area through the steady draining of marshes and swamps. Second, the growth of towns and cities—Amsterdam grew from 30,000 to 200,000 in its golden seventeenth century—provided Dutch peasants with good markets and encouraged each region to specialize in what it did best. Finally, there was the quality of the people. Oppressed by neither grasping nobles nor war-minded monarchs, the Dutch could develop their potential in a free and capitalistic society. The Low Countries became "the Mecca of foreign agricultural experts who came . . . to see Flemish agriculture with their own eyes, to write about it and to propagate its methods in their home lands."[2]

The English were the best students. They learned about water control from the Dutch, the world's leaders after centuries of effort in the skills of drainage. In the seventeenth century, Dutch experts made a great contribution to draining the extensive marshes, or fens, of wet and rainy England. On such new land, where traditions and common rights were not established, farmers introduced new crops and new rotations fairly easily.

Dutch experience was also important to Viscount Charles Townsend (1674–1738), one of the pioneers of English agriculture improvement. This lord from the upper reaches of the English aristocracy learned about turnips and clover while serving as English ambassador to Holland. In the 1710s, he was growing these crops in the sandy soil of his large estates in Norfolk in eastern England, already one of the most innovative agricultural areas in the country. When Lord Charles retired from politics in 1730 and returned to Norfolk, it was said that he spoke of turnips, turnips, and nothing but turnips. This led some wit to nickname his lordship "Turnip" Townsend. But Townsend had the last laugh. Draining extensively, manuring heavily, and sowing crops in regular rotation without fallowing, the farmers who leased Townsend's lands produced larger crops. They and he earned higher incomes. Those who had scoffed reconsidered. By 1740 agricultural improvement had become a craze among the English aristocracy.

Jethro Tull (1674–1741), part crank and part genius, was another important English innovator. A true son of the early Enlightenment, Tull constantly tested accepted ideas about farming in an effort to develop better methods through empirical research. He was especially enthusiastic about using horses for plowing, in preference to slower-moving oxen. He also advocated sowing seed with drilling equipment rather than scattering it by hand. Drilling distributed seed evenly and at the proper depth. There were also improvements in livestock, inspired in part by the earlier successes of English country gentlemen in breeding ever-faster horses for the races and fox hunts that were their passions. Selective breeding of ordinary livestock was a marked improvement over the old pattern, which has been graphically described as little more than "the haphazard union of nobody's son with everybody's daughter."

By the mid-eighteenth century, English agriculture was in the process of a radical and technologically desirable transformation. The eventual result was that by 1870 English farmers produced 300 percent more food than they had produced in 1700, although the number of people working the land had increased by only 14 percent. This great surge of agricultural production provided food for England's rapidly growing urban population. It was a tremendous achievement.

The Cost of Enclosure

What was the cost of technical progress in England, and to what extent did its payment result in social injustice? Scholars agree that the impetus for enclosing the fields came mainly from the powerful ruling class, the English landowning aristocracy. Owning large estates, the aristocracy benefited directly from higher yields that could support higher rents, and it was able and ready to make expensive investments in the new technology. Beyond these certainties, there are important differences of interpretation among historians.

Many historians contrast the initiative and enterprise of the big English landowners with the inertia and conservatism of continental landowners, big and small. They also assert that the open fields were enclosed fairly and that both large and small owners received their fair share after the strips were surveyed and consolidated.

Other historians argue that fairness was more apparent than real. The large landowners controlled Parliament, which made the laws. They had Parliament pass hundreds of "enclosure acts," each of which authorized the fencing of open fields in a given village and the division of the common in proportion to one's property in the open fields. The heavy legal and surveying costs of enclosure were also divided among the landowners. This meant that many peasants who had small holdings had to sell out to pay their share of the expenses. Similarly, the landless cottagers lost their age-old

access to the common pasture but received no compensation whatsoever. Landless families were dealt a serious blow, for women were deprived of the means to raise animals for market and to earn vital income. In the spirited words of one critical historian, "Enclosure (when all the sophistications are allowed for) was a plain enough case of class robbery, played according to the fair rules of property and law laid down by a Parliament of property-owners and lawyers."[3]

In assessing these conflicting interpretations, one needs to put eighteenth-century developments in a longer historical perspective. In the first place, as much as half of English farmland was already enclosed by 1750. A great wave of enclosure of English open fields into sheep pastures had occurred in the sixteenth and early seventeenth centuries, a wave that had dispossessed many English peasants in order to produce wool for the thriving textile industry. In the later seventeenth and early eighteenth centuries, many open fields were enclosed fairly harmoniously by mutual agreement among all classes of landowners in English villages. Thus parliamentary enclosure, the great bulk of which occurred after 1760 and particularly during the Napoleonic wars, only completed a process that was in full swing. Nor did an army of

Surveyors Measuring Enclosing open farmland met with much resistance, especially from poorer peasants and some nobility. It was more successful in England as illustrated in this scene from a nineteenth-century map of Bedfordshire. *(Source: Courtesy, Bedfordshire County Council)*

landless cottagers and farm laborers appear only in the last years of the eighteenth century. Much earlier, and certainly by 1700, there were perhaps two landless agricultural workers in England for every independent farmer.

Indeed, by 1700 a highly distinctive pattern of landownership and production existed in England. At one extreme were a few large landowners, at the other a large mass of landless cottagers who labored mainly for wages and who could graze only a pig or a cow on the village common. In between stood two other groups: small, independent peasant farmers who owned their own land, and substantial tenant farmers who rented land from the big landowners, hired wage laborers, and sold their output on a cash market. Yet the small, independent English farmers had been declining in numbers since the sixteenth-century enclosures (and even before), and they continued to do so in the eighteenth century. They could not compete with the profit-minded, market-oriented tenant farmers.

These tenant farmers, many of whom had formerly been independent owners, were the key to mastering the new methods of farming. Well financed by the large landowners, the tenant farmers fenced fields, built drains, and improved the soil with fertilizers. Such improvements and new methods of farming actually increased employment opportunities for wage workers. Thus enclosure did not force people off the land by eliminating jobs.

At the same time, by eliminating common rights and greatly reducing the access of poor men and women to the land, the eighteenth-century enclosure movement marked the completion of two major historical developments in England: the rise of market-orientated estate agriculture and the emergence of a landless proletariat. By 1815 a tiny minority of wealthy English (and Scottish) landowners held most of the land and pursued profits aggressively, leasing their holdings through agents at competitive prices to middle-sized farmers. These farmers produced mainly for cash markets and relied on landless laborers for their workforce. In strictly economic terms, these landless laborers may have lived as well in 1800 as in 1700, but they had lost that bit of independence and self-respect that common rights had provided. They had become completely dependent on cash wages. In no other European country had this "proletarianization"—this transformation of large numbers of

small peasant farmers into landless rural wage earners—gone so far as it had in England by the late eighteenth century. And, as in the earlier English enclosure movement, the village poor found the cost of economic change and technical progress heavy and unjust.

The Growth of Foreign Trade

In addition to leading Europe in agricultural improvement, Great Britain (formed in 1707 by the union of England and Scotland into a single kingdom) gradually became the leading maritime power. In the eighteenth century, British ships and merchants succeeded in dominating long-distance trade, particularly intercontinental trade across the Atlantic. This foreign trade stimulated the economy.

Britain's commercial leadership in the eighteenth century had its origins in the mercantilism of the seventeenth century (see page 614). European mercantilism was a system of economic regulations aimed at increasing the power of the state. What distinguished English mercantilism was the unusual idea that government economic regulations could and should serve the private interest of individuals and groups as well as the public needs of the state. As Josiah Child, a very wealthy brewer and director of the East India Company, put it, in the ideal economy "Profit and Power ought jointly to be considered."[4]

The seventeenth-century Navigation Acts reflected the desire of Great Britain to increase both its military power and its private wealth. The initial target of these instruments of economic warfare was the Dutch, who were far ahead of the English in shipping and foreign trade in the mid-seventeenth century. The Navigation Acts, in conjunction with three Anglo-Dutch wars between 1652 and 1674, did seriously damage the Dutch. By the later seventeenth century, the Netherlands was falling behind England in shipping, trade, and colonies. France then stood clearly as England's most serious rival in the competition for overseas empire. Rich in natural resources and endowed with a population three or four times that of England, continental Europe's leading military power was already building a powerful fleet and a worldwide system of rigidly monopolized colonial trade. And France, aware that Great Britain coveted large parts of Spain's American em-

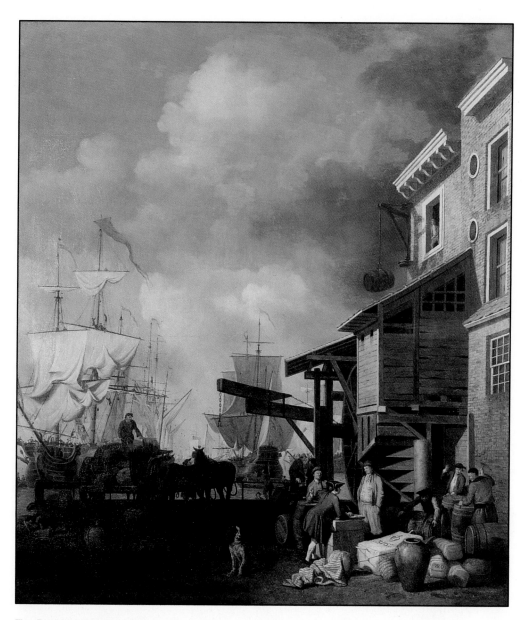

The East India Dock, London This painting by Samuel Scott captures the spirit and excitement of British maritime expansion. Great sailing ships line the quay, bringing profit and romance from far-off India. London grew in population from 350,000 in 1650 to 900,000 in 1800, when it was twice as big as Paris, its nearest rival. *(Source: Courtesy of Board of Trustees of the Victoria & Albert Museum)*

pire, was determined to revitalize its Spanish ally. Thus from 1701 to 1763, Britain and France were locked in a series of wars to decide, in part, which nation would become the leading maritime power and claim the lion's share of the profits of Europe's overseas expansion (Map 26.2).

The first round was the War of the Spanish Succession (see page 617), which resulted in major gains for Great Britain in the Peace of Utrecht (1713). France ceded Newfoundland, Nova Scotia, and the Hudson Bay territory to Britain. Spain was compelled to give Britain control of the lucrative West African slave trade—the so-called *asiento*—and to let Britain send one ship of merchandise into the Spanish colonies annually. In the course of the War of the Austrian Succession

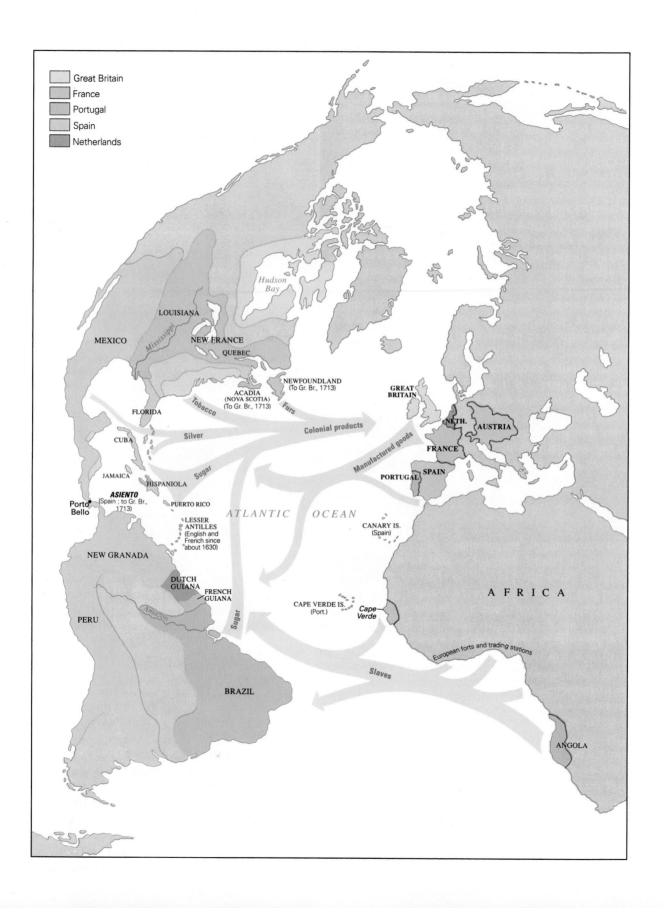

Great Britain
France
Portugal
Spain
Netherlands

Hudson
Bay

LOUISIANA

MEXICO   NEW FRANCE

QUEBEC

NEWFOUNDLAND
(To Gr. Br., 1713)

ACADIA
(NOVA SCOTIA)
(To Gr. Br., 1713)

GREAT
BRITAIN

Tobacco

Furs

FLORIDA

NETH.   AUSTRIA

Silver

Colonial products

Manufactured goods

FRANCE

CUBA

PORTUGAL   SPAIN

JAMAICA

Sugar

HISPANIOLA

ASIENTO
(Spain ; to Gr. Br.,
1713)

Porto
Bello

PUERTO RICO

ATLANTIC   OCEAN

CANARY IS.
(Spain)

LESSER
ANTILLES
(English and
French since
about 1630)

NEW GRANADA

DUTCH
GUIANA

FRENCH
GUIANA

AFRICA

CAPE VERDE IS.
(Port.)

Cape
Verde

Amazon

PERU

Sugar

European forts and trading stations

Slaves

BRAZIL

ANGOLA

(1740–1748), New England colonists momentarily seized French territory in Canada.

This stand-off helped set the stage for the Seven Years' War (1756–1763), which was the decisive round in the Franco-British competition for colonial empire. Led by William Pitt, whose grandfather had made a fortune as a trader in India, the British concentrated on using superior sea power to destroy the French fleet and choke off French commerce around the world. With the Treaty of Paris (1763), France lost all its possessions on the mainland of North America and gave up most of its holdings in India as well. By 1763, Britain had realized its goal of monopolizing a vast trade and colonial empire for its benefit.

This interconnected expansion of trade and empire marked a major step toward the Industrial Revolution, although people could not know it at the time. Since the late Middle Ages, England had successfully manufactured woolen cloth, which had provided an outstanding opportunity for profit and economic growth. By 1700 much of this cloth was exported abroad, and fully 90 percent of it was sold to Europeans. In the course of the eighteenth century, however, the states of continental Europe were trying to develop their own cottage textile industries in an effort to deal with the growth of rural poverty and population. Like England earlier, these states adopted protectionist, mercantilist policies. They tried, with some success, by means of tariffs and other measures to exclude competing goods from abroad, and by 1773 England was selling only about two-thirds as much woolen cloth to northern and western Europe as it had sold in 1700. The English economy badly needed new markets and new products in order to develop and prosper.

Protected colonial markets came to the rescue and provided a great stimulus for many branches of English manufacturing. The value of sales of manufactured products to the Atlantic economy—primarily the mainland colonies of North America and the West Indian sugar islands, with an important assist from West Africa and Latin America—soared from £475,000 in 1700 to £3.9 million in 1773 (Figure 26.1). English exports of manufac-

MAP 26.2 The Economy of the Atlantic Basin in 1701 The growth of trade encouraged both economic development and military conflict in the Atlantic Basin.

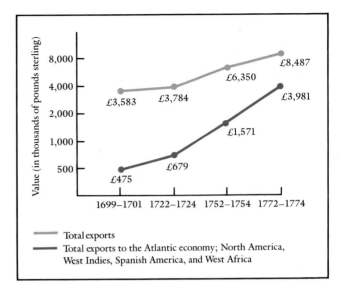

FIGURE 26.1 Exports of English Manufactured Goods, 1700–1774 While trade between England and Europe stagnated after 1700, English exports to Africa and the Americas boomed and greatly stimulated English economic development. *(Source: Based on information from R. Davis, "English Foreign Trade, 1700–1774," Economic History Review, 2d series, 15 (1962): 302–303. Used with permission of Basil Blackwell Ltd.)*

tured goods to continental Europe grew hardly at all in these years.

English exports became much more balanced and diversified. To America and Africa went large quantities of metal items—axes to frontiersmen, firearms, chains for slaveowners. Also exported were clocks and coaches, buttons and saddles, china and furniture, musical instruments and scientific equipment, and a host of other things. By 1750 half of the nails made in England were going to the colonies. Foreign trade became the bread and butter of some industries. Thus the mercantile system established in the seventeenth century to attack the Dutch and to win power and profit for England continued to shape trade in the eighteenth century. The English concentrated in their hands much of the demand for manufactured goods from the growing Atlantic economy. Sales to other "colonies"—Ireland and India—also rose substantially in the eighteenth century. Nor was this all. Demand from the well-integrated home market was also rising. The English were relatively well-off, and their population was growing. Moreover, new methods of farming and good weather brought a period of bountiful crops and low food prices, especially before 1760. Ordinary people could buy more manufactured goods. Rising demand from home and abroad put intense pressure on the whole system of production.

Land and Wealth in North America

Britain's colonies on the North American mainland proved particularly valuable in the long run (Map 26.3). Because the settlements along the Atlantic coast provided an important outlet for surplus population, migration abroad limited poverty in England, Scotland, and Northern Ireland. The settlers benefited because for most of the eighteenth century they had privileged access to virtually free and unlimited land. The abundance of almost-free land resulted in a rapid increase in the white population, which multiplied a staggering ten times between 1700 and 1774 as immigrants arrived and colonial couples raised large families. In 1774, 2.2 million whites and 330,000 blacks inhabited what would soon become the independent United States.

Rapid population growth did not reduce the settlers to poverty. On the contrary, agricultural development resulted in fairly high standards of living. It has been estimated that between 1715 and 1775 the real income of the average American was increasing about 1 percent per year per person, almost two-thirds as fast as it increased with massive industrialization between 1840 and 1959.[5] There was also an unusual degree of economic equality, by European standards. Few people were extremely rich and few were extremely poor. On the eve of the American Revolution, the average white man or woman in the mainland British colonies probably had the highest income and standard of living in the world.

The availability of land made labor expensive. This encouraged the growth of black slavery in the southern colonies and created a wealthy planter class with a taste for home-country luxuries.

The First Factories

The pressure to produce more goods for a growing market was directly related to the first decisive breakthrough of the Industrial Revolution—the creation of the world's first large factories in the English cotton textile industry. Technological innovations in the manufacture of cloth led to a whole new pattern of production and social relationships. Since no other industry experienced such a rapid or complete transformation before 1830, these trailblazing developments deserve special consideration.

Although the putting-out system of merchant capitalism (see page 699) was expanding all across Europe in the eighteenth century, this pattern of rural industry was most fully developed in England. Thus it was in England, under the pressure of growing demand, that the system's shortcomings first began to outweigh its advantages—especially in the cottage textile industry after about 1760.

There was always a serious imbalance in this family enterprise: the work of four or five spinners was needed to keep one weaver steadily employed. The wife and the husband had constantly to try to find more thread and more spinners. Widows and unmarried women—"spinsters" who spun for their living—were recruited by the wife. Or perhaps the weaver's son went off on horseback to seek thread. The need for thread might even lead the weaver and his wife to become small capitalist employers, putting out raw wool or cotton to other cottagers.

Deep-seated conflict between workers and employers complicated increased production. In "The Clothier's Delight, or the Rich Men's Joy and the Poor Men's Sorrow," an English popular song written about 1700, a merchant boasts of his countless tricks used to "beat down wages":

We heapeth up riches and treasure great store
Which we get by griping and grinding the poor.
And this is a way for to fill up our purse
Although we do get it with many a curse.[6]

There were constant disputes over the weights of materials and the quality of the cloth. Merchants accused workers of stealing raw materials, and weavers complained that merchants delivered underweight bales. Both were right; each tried to cheat the other, even if only in self-defense.

There was another problem, at least from the merchant-capitalist's point of view. Rural labor was cheap, scattered, and poorly organized; thus it was hard to control. Cottage workers tended to work in spurts. After they got paid on Saturday af-

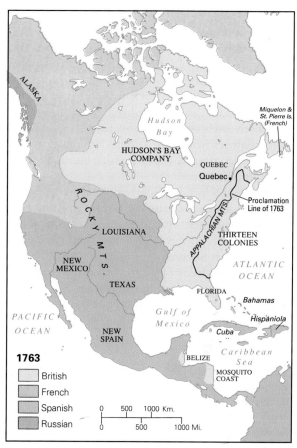

MAP 26.3 European Claims in North America Before and After the Seven Years' War, 1756–1763 France lost its vast claims in North America, though the British government then prohibited colonists from settling west of a line drawn in 1763. The British wanted to avoid costly wars with Indians living in the newly conquered territory.

ternoon, the men in particular tended to drink and carouse for two or three days. Indeed, Monday was called "holy Monday" because inactivity was so religiously observed. By the end of the week the weaver was probably working feverishly to make his quota. But if he did not succeed, there was little the merchant could do. When times were good and the merchant could easily sell everything produced, the weaver and his family did fairly well and were particularly inclined to loaf, to the dismay of the capitalist. Thus, in spite of its early virtues, the putting-out system in the textile industry revealed growing limitations, and the merchant-capitalist's search for more efficient methods of production intensified.

Attention focused on ways to improve spinning. Many a merchant and tinkering worker knew that

a better spinning wheel promised rich rewards. Spinning of the traditional raw materials—wool and flax—proved hard to change, but cotton was different. Cotton textiles had first been imported into England from India by the East India Company, and by 1760 there was a tiny domestic industry in northern England. After many experiments over a generation, a gifted carpenter and jack-of-all-trades, James Hargreaves, invented his cotton-spinning jenny about 1765. At almost the same moment a barber-turned-manufacturer, Richard Arkwright, invented (or possibly pirated) another kind of spinning machine, the water frame. These breakthroughs produced an explosion in the infant industry. By 1790 the new machines produced ten times as much cotton yarn as had been made in 1770. By 1800 the production of cotton thread had become England's most important industry.

Hargreaves's jenny was simple and inexpensive. It was also operated by hand. In early models, from six to twenty-four spindles were mounted on a sliding carriage, and each spindle spun a fine, slender thread. A woman moved the carriage back and forth with one hand and turned a wheel to supply power with the other. Now it was the weaver who could not keep up with his vastly more efficient wife.

Arkwright's water frame employed a different principle. It quickly acquired a capacity of several hundred spindles and demanded much more power—water power. The water frame thus required large specialized mills, factories that employed hundreds of workers from the very beginning. The water frame could spin only coarse, strong thread, which was then put out for respinning on hand-powered cottage jennies. Around

1790 another innovation, Samuel Crompton's "mule"— which combined the best aspects of the jenny and the water frame—began to require more power than the human arm could supply. Thus all cotton spinning gradually became concentrated in factories.

The first consequences of these revolutionary developments were more beneficial than is generally believed. Cotton goods became much cheaper, and they were bought and treasured by all classes. In the past, only the wealthy could afford the comfort and cleanliness of underwear, which was called "body linen" because it was made from expensive linen cloth. Now millions of poor people, who had earlier worn nothing underneath their coarse, filthy outer garments, could afford to wear cotton slips and underpants.

Families using cotton in cottage industry were freed from their constant search for adequate yarn from scattered, part-time spinners, since all the

Hargreave's Spinning Jenny The loose cotton strands on the slanted bobbins passed up to the sliding carriage and then on to the spindles in back for fine spinning. By 1783 one woman could spin by hand a hundred threads at a time on an improved model. *(Source: University of Illinois, Champaign)*

thread needed could be spun in the cottage on the jenny or obtained from a nearby factory. The wages of weavers, now hard pressed to keep up with the spinners, rose markedly until about 1792. Weavers were among the best-paid workers in England. They were known to walk proudly through the streets with £5 notes stuck in their hatbands, and they dressed like the middle class.

One result of this unprecedented prosperity was that large numbers of agricultural laborers became weavers. Meanwhile, however, mechanics and capitalists were seeking to invent a power loom to save on labor costs. This Edmund Cartwright achieved in 1785. But the power looms of the factories worked poorly at first, and handloom weavers continued to receive good wages until at least 1800.

Working conditions in the early factories were less satisfactory than those of cottage weavers and spinners. But until the late 1780s, most English factories were in rural areas, where they had access to water power. These factories employed a relatively small percentage of all cotton textile workers. Since people were reluctant to work in them, factory owners often turned to children who had been abandoned by their parents and put in the care of local parishes. The parish officers often "apprenticed" such unfortunate orphans to factory owners. The parish thus saved money, and the factory owners gained workers over whom they exercised almost the authority of slaveowners.

Apprenticed as young as five or six years of age, the boy and girl workers were forced by law to labor for their "master" for as many as fourteen years. Clothed, fed, and locked up nightly in factory dormitories, the young workers received little or no pay for their toil. Hours were appalling—commonly thirteen or fourteen hours a day, six days a week. Harsh physical punishment maintained brutal discipline. To be sure, poor children had typically worked long hours from an early age in the eighteenth century—and frequently outside the home for a brutal master. But the wholesale coercion of orphans as factory apprentices constituted exploitation on a truly unprecedented scale. This exploitation ultimately piqued the conscience of reformers and reinforced humanitarian attitudes toward children and their labor in the early nineteenth century.

The creation of the world's first modern factories in the English cotton textile industry in the 1770s and 1780s, which grew out of the putting-out system of cottage production, was a momentous development. Both symbolically and in substance, the big new cotton mills marked the beginning of the Industrial Revolution in England. By 1831 the largely mechanized cotton textile industry towered above all others, accounting for fully 22 percent of the country's entire industrial production.

ENERGY AND TRANSPORTATION

If water from rivers and streams had remained the primary source of power for the new factories, the growth of the cotton textile industry might have been stunted or cut short. This did not occur because an epoch-making solution was found to the age-old problem of energy and power. This solution to the energy problem—a problem that has reappeared in recent times—permitted continued rapid development in cotton textiles, the gradual generalization of the factory system, the revolution in transportation, and the triumph of the Industrial Revolution.

The Problem of Energy

Human beings, like all living organisms, require energy. Adult men and women need 2,000 to 4,000 calories (units of energy) daily simply to fuel their bodies, work, and survive. Energy comes from a variety of sources; it also takes different forms, and one form may be converted into another. Plants have been converting solar energy into caloric matter for eons. Human beings have used their toolmaking abilities to construct machines that convert one form of energy into another for their own benefit.

Prehistoric people relied on plants and plant-eating animals as their sources of energy. With the development of agriculture, early civilizations were able to increase the number of useful plants and thus the supply of energy. Some plants could be fed to domesticated animals, like the horse. Stronger than human beings, these animals converted the energy in the plants into work. In the medieval period, people began to develop water mills to grind their grain and windmills to pump water and drain swamps. In the sixteenth and seventeenth centuries, more efficient use of water and wind enabled human beings, especially Europeans, to accomplish somewhat more; intercontinental sailing ships are a prime example. Nevertheless, even into the eighteenth century, European society continued to rely for energy mainly on plants, and human beings and animals continued to perform most work. This dependence meant that Western civilization remained poor in energy and power.

Lack of power lay at the heart of the poverty that afflicted the large majority of people worldwide. The man behind the plow and the woman at the spinning wheel could employ only horsepower and human muscle in their labor. No matter how hard they worked, they could not produce very much. What people needed were new sources of energy and more power at their disposal; then they would be able to work more efficiently, produce more, and live better.

Where was more energy to be found? Almost all energy came directly or indirectly from plants and therefore from the land: grain for people, hay for animals, and wood for heat. The land was also the principal source of raw materials needed for industrial production: wool and flax for clothing; leather for shoes; wood for housing, tools, and ironmaking. Although the land's yield could be increased—through the elimination of fallow, for example—there were definite limits to such improvements.

The shortage of energy was becoming particularly severe in England by the eighteenth century. Because of the growth of population, most of the great forests of medieval England had long ago been replaced by fields of grain and hay. Wood was in ever shorter supply; yet it remained tremendously important. In addition to serving as the primary source of heat and as a basic raw material, processed wood (charcoal) was mixed with iron ore in a blast furnace to produce pig iron. The iron industry's appetite for wood was enormous, and by 1740 the English iron industry was stagnating. Vast forests enabled Russia in the eighteenth century to become the world's leading producer of iron, much of which was exported to England. But Russia's potential for growth was limited, too, and in a few decades Russia would reach the barrier of inadequate energy that was already holding back England.

The Steam Engine Breakthrough

As this early energy crisis grew worse, England looked toward its abundant and widely scattered reserves of coal as an alternative to wood. Coal was first used in England in the late Middle Ages as a source of heat. By 1640 most homes in London were heated with it, and it also provided heat for making beer, glass, soap, and other products. Coal was not used, however, to produce mechanical energy or to power machinery. It was there that coal's potential was enormous, as a simple example shows.

One pound of good bituminous coal contains about 3,500 calories of heat energy. A miner who eats 3,500 calories of food can produce about 1 horsepower-hour as he digs out 500 pounds of coal in the course of a day using hand tools. Even an extremely inefficient converter, which transforms only 1 percent of the heat energy in coal into mechanical energy, will produce 27 horsepower-hours of work from the 500 pounds of coal that the miner cut out of the earth. Much more energy is consumed by the converter, but much more work can be done. Early steam engines were just such inefficient converters.

As more coal was produced, mines were dug deeper and deeper and were constantly filling with water. Mechanical pumps, usually powered by animals walking in circles at the surface, had to be installed. At one mine, fully five hundred horses were used for pumping. Such power was expensive and bothersome. In an attempt to overcome these disadvantages, Thomas Savery in 1698 and Thomas Newcomen in 1705 invented the first primitive steam engines.

These engines were extremely inefficient. Both burned coal to produce steam, which was then injected into a cylinder or reservoir. In Newcomen's engine, the steam in the cylinder was cooled, creating a partial vacuum in the cylinder. This vacuum allowed the pressure of the earth's atmosphere to push the piston in the cylinder down and operate a pump. By the early 1770s, many of the Savery engines and hundreds of the Newcomen engines were operating successfully, though inefficiently, in English and Scottish mines.

In the early 1760s, a gifted young Scot named James Watt (1736–1819) was drawn to a critical study of the steam engine. Watt was employed at

Making Charcoal After wood was carefully cut and stacked, iron masters slowly burned it to produce charcoal. Before the Industrial Revolution, a country's iron industry depended greatly on the size of its forests. *(Source: University of Illinois, Champaign)*

the time by the University of Glasgow as a skilled craftsman making scientific instruments. The Scottish universities were pioneers in practical technical education, and in 1763 Watt was called on to repair a Newcomen engine being used in a physics course. After a series of observations, Watt saw why the Newcomen engine wasted so much energy: the cylinder was being heated and cooled for every single stroke of the piston. To remedy this problem, Watt added a separate condenser, where the steam could be condensed without cooling the cylinder. This splendid invention greatly increased the efficiency of the steam engine.

To invent something in a laboratory is one thing; to make it a practical success is quite another. Watt needed skilled workers, precision parts, and capital. The relatively advanced nature of the English economy proved essential. A partnership with a wealthy, progressive toymaker provided risk capital and a manufacturing plant. In the craft tradition of locksmiths, tinsmiths, and millwrights, Watt found skilled mechanics who could install, regulate, and repair his sophisticated engines. From ingenious manufacturers like the cannonmaker John Wilkinson, who learned to bore cylinders with a fair degree of accuracy, Watt was gradually able to purchase precision parts. This support allowed him to create an effective vacuum and regulate a complex engine. In more than twenty years of constant effort, Watt made many further improvements. By the late 1780s, the steam engine was a practical and commercial success in England.

The steam engine of Watt and his followers was the Industrial Revolution's most fundamental advance in technology. For the first time in history, humanity had—at least for a few generations—almost unlimited power at its disposal. For the first time, inventors and engineers could devise and implement all kinds of power equipment to aid people in their work. For the first time, abundance was at least possible for ordinary men and women.

The steam engine was quickly put to use in many industries in England. It made possible the production of even more coal to feed steam engines elsewhere. The steam-power plant began to replace the use of waterpower in the cotton-spinning mills during the 1780s, as well as in the flour, malt, and sugar mills.

Steam power promoted important breakthroughs in other industries. The English iron industry was radically transformed. The use of powerful, steam-driven bellows in blast furnaces helped ironmakers switch over rapidly from limited charcoal to unlimited coke (which is made from coal) in the smelting of pig iron after 1770. In the 1780s Henry Cort developed the puddling furnace, which allowed pig iron to be refined in turn with coke. Strong, skilled ironworkers—the puddlers—"cooked" molten pig iron in a great vat, raking off globs of refined iron for further processing. Cort also developed heavy-duty steam-powered rolling mills capable of spewing out finished iron in every shape and form.

The economic consequence of these technical innovations was a great boom in the English iron industry. In 1740 annual British iron production was only 17,000 tons. With the spread of coke smelting and the first impact of Cort's inventions, production reached 68,000 tons in 1788, 125,000 tons in 1796, and 260,000 tons in 1806. In 1844 Britain produced 3 million tons of iron. This was truly phenomenal expansion. Once scarce and expensive, iron became the cheap, basic building block of the economy.

The Coming of the Railroads

Sailing ships had improved noticeably since the Age of Discovery, and the second half of the eighteenth century saw extensive construction of hard and relatively smooth roads in Europe. Yet passenger traffic benefited most from this construction. Overland shipment of freight, relying solely on horsepower, was still quite limited and frightfully expensive; shippers used rivers and canals for heavy freight whenever possible. It was logical therefore that inventors would try to use steam power.

As early as 1800, an American ran a "steamer on wheels" through city streets. Other experiments followed. In the 1820s, English engineers perfected steam cars capable of carrying fourteen passengers at ten miles an hour—as fast as the mail coach. But the noisy, heavy steam automobiles frightened passing horses and damaged themselves as well as the roads with their vibrations. For the rest of the century, horses continued to reign on highways and city streets.

The coal industry had long been using plank roads and rails to move coal wagons within mines and at the surface. Rails reduced friction and allowed a horse or a human being to pull a heavier load. Thus, once a rail capable of supporting a heavy locomotive was developed in 1816, all sorts of experiments with steam engines on rails went forward. In 1825, after ten years of work, George Stephenson built an effective locomotive. In 1830 his Rocket sped down the track of the just-completed Liverpool and Manchester Railway at sixteen miles per hour. This was the world's first important railroad, fittingly steaming in the heart of industrial England.

The line from Liverpool to Manchester was a financial as well as a technical success, and many private companies were quickly organized to build more rail lines. These companies had to get permission for their projects from Parliament and pay for the rights of way they needed; otherwise, their freedom was great. Within twenty years, they had completed the main trunk lines of Great Britain. Other countries were quick to follow.

The significance of the railroad was tremendous. The railroad dramatically reduced the cost and uncertainty of shipping freight overland. This advance had many economic consequences. Previously, markets had tended to be small and local. As the barrier of high transportation costs was lowered, they became larger and even nationwide. Larger markets encouraged larger factories with more sophisticated machinery. Such factories could make goods cheaper, enabling people to pay less for them. They also tended to drive most cottage workers, many urban artisans, and other manufacturers out of business.

In all countries, the construction of railroads contributed to the growth of a class of urban workers. Cottage workers, farm laborers, and small peasants did not generally leave their jobs and homes to go directly to work in factories. However, the building of railroads created a strong demand for labor, especially unskilled labor, throughout a country. Like farm work, hard work on construction gangs was done in the open air with animals and hand tools. Many farm laborers and poor peasants, long accustomed to leaving their villages for temporary employment, went to build railroads. By the time the work was finished, life back home in the village often seemed dull and unappealing, and many men drifted to towns in search of work with the railroad companies, in construction, in factories. By the time they sent for their wives and sweethearts to join them, they had become urban workers.

The railroad changed the outlook and values of the entire society. The last and culminating invention of the Industrial Revolution, the railroad dramatically revealed the power and increased the speed of the new age. Racing down a track at sixteen miles per hour or, by 1850, at a phenomenal fifty miles per hour was a new and awesome experience. As a noted French economist put it after a ride on the Liverpool and Manchester in 1833, "There are certain impressions that one cannot put into words!"

The Liverpool and Manchester Railway This hand-colored engraving celebrates the opening of the world's first major railroad on September 15, 1830. Railroad construction reshaped the built environment and proclaimed the coming of a new age. *(Source: Mr. and Mrs. M. G. Powell)*

The Third-Class Carriage   The French artist Honoré Daumier was fascinated by the railroad and its human significance. This great painting focuses on the peasant grandmother, absorbed in memories. The nursing mother represents love and creativity; the sleeping boy, innocence. *(Source: The Metropolitan Museum of Art. Bequest of Mrs. H. O. Havemeyer, 1929. The H. O. Havemeyer Collection (29.100.129))*

Some great painters, notably J. M. W. Turner (1775–1851) and Claude Monet (1840–1926), succeeded in expressing this sense of power and awe. So did the massive new train stations, the cathedrals of the industrial age. Leading railway engineers like Isambard Kingdom Brunel and Thomas Brassey, whose tunnels pierced mountains and whose bridges spanned valleys, became public idols—the astronauts of their day. Everyday speech absorbed the images of railroading. After you got up a "full head of steam," you "highballed" along. And if you did not "go off the track," you might "toot your own whistle." The railroad fired the imagination.

Industry and Population

In 1851 London was the site of a famous industrial fair. This Great Exposition was held in the newly built Crystal Palace, an architectural masterpiece made entirely of glass and iron, both of which were now cheap and abundant. For the millions who visited, one fact stood out. The little island of Britain—England, Wales, and Scotland—was the "workshop of the world." It alone produced two-thirds of the world's coal and more than half of its iron and cotton cloth. More generally, it has been carefully estimated that, in 1860, Britain produced a truly remarkable 20 percent of the entire world's output of industrial goods, whereas it had produced only about 2 percent of the world's total in 1750.[7] Experiencing revolutionary industrial change, Britain became the first industrial nation (Map 26.4).

As the British economy significantly increased its production of manufactured goods, the gross national product (GNP) rose roughly fourfold at constant prices between 1780 and 1851. In other words, the British people increased their wealth and their national income dramatically. At the same time, the population of Great Britain boomed, growing from about 9 million in 1780 to almost 21 million in 1851. Thus growing numbers consumed much of the increase in total production. According to one recent study, average consumption per person increased by only 75 percent between 1780 and 1851, as the growth in the total population ate up a large part of the fourfold increase in gross national product in those years.[8]

Although the question is still debated, many economic historians now believe that rapid population growth in Great Britain was not harmful because it facilitated industrial expansion. More people meant a more mobile labor force, with a wealth of young workers in need of employment and ready to go where the jobs were. Contemporaries were much less optimistic. In his influential *Essay on the Principle of Population* (1798), Thomas Malthus (1766–1834) argued that population would always tend to grow faster than the food supply. In Malthus's opinion, the only hope of warding off such "positive checks" to population growth as war, famine, and disease was "prudential restraint"—that is, young men and women had to limit the growth of population by the old tried-and-true means of marrying late in life. But Malthus was not optimistic about this possibility. The powerful attraction of the sexes would cause most people to marry early and have many children.

The wealthy English stockbroker and leading economist David Ricardo (1772–1823) coldly spelled out the pessimistic implications of Malthus's thought. Ricardo's depressing "iron law of wages" posited that, because of the pressure of population growth, wages would always sink to the subsistence level—that is, wages would be just high enough to keep the workers from starving. With Malthus and Ricardo setting the tone, there

is little wonder that economics was soon dubbed "the dismal science."

Malthus, Ricardo, and their many followers were proved wrong—in the long run. However, as the great economist John Maynard Keynes quipped in the Great Depression of the 1930s, "we are all dead in the long run." Those who lived through the Industrial Revolution could not see the long run in advance. As modern quantitative studies show, until the 1820s, or even the 1840s, contemporary observers might reasonably conclude that the economy and the total population were racing neck and neck, with the outcome very much in doubt. The closeness of the race added to

MAP 26.4   The Industrial Revolution in England, ca 1850   Industry concentrated in the rapidly growing cities of the north and the Midlands, where rich coal and iron deposits were in close proximity.

the difficulties inherent in the unprecedented journey toward industrial civilization.

There was another problem as well. Perhaps workers, farmers, and ordinary people did not get their rightful share of the new wealth. Perhaps only the rich got richer while the poor got poorer or made no progress at all. We will turn to this great issue after looking at the process of industrialization in continental countries in the nineteenth century.

INDUSTRIALIZATION IN CONTINENTAL EUROPE

The new technologies developed in the British Industrial Revolution were adopted rather slowly by businesses in continental Europe. Yet by the end of the nineteenth century several European countries, as well as the United States, had industrialized their economies to a considerable but variable degree. This meant that the process of Western industrialization proceeded gradually, with uneven jerks and national (and regional) variations.

Scholars are still struggling to explain these variations, especially since good answers may offer valuable lessons in our own time for poor countries seeking to improve their material condition through industrialization and economic development. The latest findings on the Western experience are encouraging. They suggest that there were alternative paths to the industrial world in the nineteenth century and that, today as then, there is no need to follow a rigid, predetermined British model.

National Variations

European industrialization, like most economic developments, requires some statistical analysis as part of the effort to understand it. Comparative data on industrial production in different countries over time help to give an overview of what happened. One set of data, the work of a Swiss scholar, compares the level of industrialization on a per capita basis in several countries from 1750 to 1913. These data are far from perfect because there are gaps in the underlying records. But they reflect basic trends and are presented in Table 26.1 for closer study.

As the heading of Table 26.1 makes clear, this is a per capita comparison of levels of industrialization—a comparison of how much industrial product was available, on average, to each person in a given country in a given year. Thus, all the numbers in the table are expressed in terms of a single index number of 100, which equals the per capita level of industrial goods in Great Britain (and Ireland) in 1900. Every number is a percentage of the 1900 level in Great Britain and is directly comparable with every other number in the table. The countries are listed in roughly the order in which they began to use large-scale, power-driven technology.

What does this overview of European industrialization tell us? First, and very significantly, in 1750 all countries were fairly close together and Britain was only slightly ahead of its archenemy, France. Second, by 1800 Britain had opened up a noticeable lead over all continental countries, and that gap progressively widened as the British Industrial Revolution accelerated to 1830 and reached full maturity by 1860. In 1830, the British level of per capita industrialization was twice the French level, for example; in 1860, it was more than three times the French level. At both dates, all other large countries, except the United States, had fallen even further behind Britain than France had. Sophisticated quantitative history confirms the primacy and relative rapidity of Britain's Industrial Revolution.

Third, variations in the timing and in the extent of industrialization among the continental powers and the United States are also apparent. Belgium, independent in 1831 and rich in iron and coal, led in adopting Britain's new technology. France developed factory production more gradually, and most historians now detect no burst in French mechanization and no acceleration in the growth of overall industrial output that may accurately be called revolutionary. They stress instead France's relatively good pattern of early industrial growth, which has been unjustly tarnished by the spectacular rise of Germany and the United States after 1860. By 1913 Germany was rapidly closing in on Britain and the United States had already passed Britain in per capita production.

	1750	1800	1830	1860	1880	1900	1913
Great Britain	10	16	25	64	87	100	115
Belgium	9	10	14	28	43	46	88
United States	4	9	14	21	38	69	126
France	9	9	12	20	28	39	59
Germany	8	8	9	15	25	52	85
Austria-Hungary	7	7	8	11	15	23	32
Italy	8	8	8	10	12	17	26
Russia	6	6	7	8	10	15	20

Note: All entires are based on an index value of 100, equal to the per capita level of industrialization in Great Britain in 1900.

Source: P. Bairoch, "International industrialization Levels from 1750 to 1980," *Journal of European Economic History* 11 (Spring 1982): 294. Used with permission. Data for Great Britain are actually for the United Kingdom, thereby including Ireland with England, Wales,and Scotland.

TABLE 26.1 Per Capita Levels of Industrialization, 1750–1913

All European states (as well as the United States, Canada, and Japan) managed to raise per capita industrial levels in the nineteenth century. These continent-wide increases stood in stark contrast to the large and tragic decreases that occurred at the same time in most non-Western countries, and most notably in China and India. European countries industrialized to a greater or lesser extent even as most of the non-Western world deindustrialized. Thus differential rates of wealth- and power-creating industrial development, which heightened disparities within Europe, also greatly magnified existing inequalities between Europe and the rest of the world. We return to this momentous change in Chapter 30.

The Challenge of Industrialization

The different patterns of industrial development suggest that the process of industrialization was far from automatic. Indeed, building modern industry was an awesome challenge. To be sure, the eighteenth century was throughout Europe an era of agricultural improvement, population increase, expanding foreign trade, and growing cottage industry. England led in these developments, but other countries participated in the general trend. Thus, when the pace of English industry began to accelerate in the 1780s, continental businesses began to adopt the new methods as they proved their profitability. English industry enjoyed clear superiority, but at first the Continent was not very far behind.

By 1815, however, the situation was quite different. In spite of wartime difficulties, English industry maintained the momentum of the 1780s and continued to grow and improve between 1789 and 1815. On the Continent, the unending political and economic upheavals that began with the French Revolution had another effect. They disrupted trade, created runaway inflation, and fostered social anxiety. War severed normal communications between England and the Continent, severely handicapping continental efforts to use new British machinery and technology. Moreover, the years from 1789 to 1815 were, even for the privileged French economy, a time of "national catastrophe"—in the graphic words of a leading French scholar.[9] Thus, whatever the French Revolution and the Napoleonic era meant politically, economically and industrially they meant that France and the rest of Europe were further behind Britain in 1815 than in 1789.

The Crystal Palace The Great Exhibition of 1851 attracted more than six million visitors, many of whom journeyed to London on the newly built railroads. Companies and countries displayed their products and juries awarded prizes in the strikingly modern Crystal Palace. *(Source: The Bridgeman Art Library)*

This widening gap made it more difficult if not impossible for other countries to follow the British pattern in energy and industry after 1815. Above all, in the newly mechanized industries British goods were being produced very economically, and these goods had come to dominate world markets completely while the continental states were absorbed in war between 1792 and 1815. Continental firms had little hope of competing with mass-produced British goods in foreign markets for a long time. In addition, British technology had become so advanced and complicated that very few engineers or skilled technicians outside England understood it. Moreover, the technology of steam power had grown much more expensive. It involved large investments in the iron and coal industries and, after 1830, required the existence of railroads, which were very costly. Continental business people had great difficulty finding the large sums of money demanded by the new methods, and there was a shortage of laborers accustomed to working in factories. Landowners and government officials were often so suspicious of the new form of industry and the changes it brought that they did little at first to encourage it. All these disadvantages slowed the spread of modern industry (Map 26.5).

After 1815, however, when continental countries began to face up to the British challenge, they had at least three important advantages. First, most continental countries had a rich tradition of putting-out enterprise, merchant-capitalists, and skilled urban artisans. Such a tradition gave continental firms the ability to adapt and survive in the face of new market conditions. Second, continental capitalists did not need to develop, ever so slowly and expensively, their own advanced technology. Instead, they could simply "borrow" the new methods developed in Great Britain, as well as engineers and some of the financial resources they lacked. European countries like France and Russia also had a third asset that many non-Western areas lacked in the nineteenth century. They had strong independent governments, which did not fall under foreign political control. These governments could fashion economic policies to serve their own interests, and they proceeded to do so. They would eventually use the power of the state to promote the growth of industry and catch up with Britain.

Agents of Industrialization

The British realized the great value of their technical discoveries and tried to keep their secrets to themselves. Until 1825 it was illegal for artisans and skilled mechanics to leave Britain; until 1843 the export of textile machinery and other equipment was forbidden. Many talented, ambitious workers, however, slipped out of the country illegally and introduced the new methods abroad.

MAP 26.5 Continental Industrialization, ca 1850 Although continental countries were beginning to make progress by 1850, they still lagged far behind England. For example, continental railroad building was still in an early stage, whereas the English rail system was essentially complete.

One such man was William Cockerill, a Lancashire carpenter. He and his sons began building cotton-spinning equipment in French-occupied Belgium in 1799. In 1817 the most famous son, John Cockerill, purchased the old summer palace of the deposed bishops of Liège in southern Belgium. Cockerill converted the palace into a large industrial enterprise that produced machinery, steam engines, and then railway locomotives. He also established modern ironworks and coal mines.

Cockerill's plants in the Liège area became an industrial nerve center, continually gathering new information and transmitting it across Europe. Many skilled British workers came, illegally, to work for Cockerill, and some went on to found their own companies throughout Europe. Newcomers brought the latest plans and secrets and Cockerill could boast that ten days after an industrial advance occurred in Britain, he knew all about it in Belgium. Thus British technicians and skilled workers were a powerful force in the spread of early industrialization.

Another agent of industrialization was Fritz Harkort, a pioneer in the German machinery industry. Serving in England as a Prussian army officer during the Napoleonic wars, Harkort was impressed and enchanted with what he saw. He concluded that Germany had to match all these English achievements as quickly as possible. Setting up shop in an abandoned castle in the still-tranquil Ruhr Valley, Harkort felt an almost religious calling to build steam engines and become the "Watt of Germany."

Harkort's basic idea was simple, but it was enormously difficult to carry out. Lacking skilled laborers to do the job, Harkort turned to England for experienced, though expensive, mechanics. He could not be choosy, and he longed for the day when he could afford to replace the haughty foreigners with his fellow Germans. Getting materials

A Silesian Ironworks, 1841   This plant is using the new British method of smelting iron with coke. Silesia and the Ruhr region emerged as the main centers of German heavy industry in the nineteenth century, but that development was only beginning when this picture was painted. *(Source: Deutsches Museum, Munich)*

also posed a great problem. At great cost, he had to import from England the thick iron boilers that he needed. Moreover, German roads were so bad that steam engines had to be built at the works, dismantled and shipped piece by piece to the buyer, and then reassembled by Harkort's technicians. In spite of all these problems, Harkort built and sold engines, winning fame and praise. His ambitious efforts over sixteen years also resulted in large financial losses for himself and his partners, and in 1832 he was forced out of his company by his financial backers, who cut back operations to reduce losses. His career illustrates both the great efforts of a few important business leaders to duplicate the British achievement and the difficulty of the task.

Entrepreneurs like Harkort were obviously exceptional. Most continental businesses adopted factory technology slowly, and handicraft methods lived on. Recent research on France has shown that continental industrialization usually brought substantial but uneven expansion of handicraft industry in both rural and urban areas for a time. Artisan production of luxury items grew in France, as the rising income of the international middle class created foreign demand for silk scarfs, embroidered needlework, perfumes, and fine wines.

Support from the government often helped business people in continental countries to overcome some of their difficulties. Tariff protection was one such support. For example, after Napoleon's wars ended in 1815, France was suddenly flooded with cheaper and better English goods. In order to protect the French economy, the French government responded by laying high tariffs on many English imports. After 1815 continental governments bore the cost of building roads and canals to improve transportation, and they also bore to a significant extent the cost of building railroads.

The career of the German journalist and thinker Friedrich List (1789–1846) reflects government's greater role in industrialization on the Continent than in England. List considered the growth of modern industry of the utmost importance because manufacturing was a primary means of increasing people's well-being and relieving their poverty. Moreover, List was a dedicated nationalist. He wrote that the "wider the gap between the backward and advanced nations becomes, the more dangerous it is to remain behind," for an ag-

ricultural nation was not only poor but weak, increasingly unable to defend itself and maintain its political independence. To promote industry was to defend the nation.

The practical policy that List focused on in articles and in his *National System of Political Economy* (1841) was the tariff. He supported the formation of a customs union, or *Zollverein,* among the separate German states. Such a tariff union came into being in 1834. It allowed goods to move between the German member states without tariffs, and a single uniform tariff was erected against all other nations. List wanted a high protective tariff, which would encourage infant industries, allowing them to develop and eventually to hold their own against their more advanced British counterparts. List denounced the English doctrine of free trade as little more than England's attempt "to make the rest of the world, like the Hindus, its serfs in all industrial and commercial relations." By the 1840s List's ideas were increasingly popular in Germany and elsewhere.

Banks, like governments, also played a larger and more creative role on the Continent than in England. Previously, almost all banks in Europe had been private, organized as secretive partnerships. Such banks were content to deal with a few rich clients and a few big merchants. They avoided industry. In the 1830s two important Belgian banks pioneered in a new direction. They operated as big corporations with many stockholders, large and small. Thus their financial resources were large. The banks were able to use that money to develop industrial companies. They became, in short, industrial banks.

Similar banks became important in France and Germany in the 1850s. They established and developed many railroads and many companies working in heavy industry. The most famous such bank was the Crédit Mobilier of Paris, founded by Isaac and Émile Pereire, two young Jewish journalists from Bordeaux. The Crédit Mobilier advertised extensively. It used the savings of thousands of small investors, as well as the resources of big ones. The activities of the bank were far-reaching; it built railroads all over France and Europe. As Émile Pereire had said in 1835, "It is not enough to outline gigantic programs on paper. I must write my ideas on the earth."

Industrial banks like the Crédit Mobilier mobilized the savings of thousands of small investors and invested those savings in industry and transportation, particularly in the 1850s. In doing so, the directors of these banks helped their countries find the capital needed for industrialization. They also often made themselves very wealthy.

CAPITAL AND LABOR

Industrial development brought new social relations and intensified problems between capital and labor. A new group of factory owners and industrial capitalists arose. These men strengthened the wealth and size of the middle class, which had previously been made up mainly of merchants and professional people. The nineteenth century became the golden age of the middle class. Modern industry also created a much larger group, the factory workers. For the first time, large numbers of men and women came together under one roof to work with complicated machinery for major capitalists and large companies. What was the nature of relations between these two new groups—capital and labor? Did the new industrial middle class ruthlessly exploit the workers, as Karl Marx and others have charged?

The New Class of Factory Owners

Early industrialists operated in a highly competitive economic system. As the careers of Watt and Harkort illustrate, there were countless production problems, and success and large profits were by no means certain. Manufacturers, therefore, waged a constant battle to cut their production costs and stay afloat. Much of the profit had to go back into the business for new and better machinery. "Dragged on by the frenzy of this terrible life," according to one of the dismayed critics, the struggling manufacturer had "no time for niceties. He must conquer or die, make a fortune or drown himself."[10]

The early industrialists came from a variety of backgrounds. Many, like Harkort, were from well-established merchant families who provided capital and contacts. Others, like Watt and Cockerill, were of modest means, especially in the early days. Artisans and skilled workers of exceptional ability had unparalleled opportunities. The ethnic

and religious groups that had been discriminated against in the traditional occupations controlled by the landed aristocracy jumped at the new chances. Quakers and Scots were tremendously important in England; Protestants and Jews dominated banking in Catholic France. Many of the industrialists were newly rich, and, not surprisingly, they were very proud and self-satisfied.

As factories grew larger, opportunities declined, at least in well-developed industries. It became considerably harder for a gifted but poor young mechanic to end up as a wealthy manufacturer. Formal education became more important as a means of advancement, and formal education at the advanced level was expensive. In England by 1830 and in France and Germany by 1860, leading industrialists were more likely to have inherited their well-established enterprises, and they were financially much more secure than their fathers and grandfathers. They were also aware of a greater gap between themselves and their workers.

The New Factory Workers

The social consequences of the Industrial Revolution have long been hotly debated. The condition of English workers during the transformation has always generated the most controversy among historians because England was the first country to industrialize and because the social consequences seem harshest there. Before 1850, other countries had not proceeded very far with industrialization, and almost everyone agrees that the economic conditions of European workers improved after 1850. The countries that followed England were able to benefit from English experience in social as well as technical matters. Thus the experience of English workers to about 1850 deserves special attention. (Industrial growth also promoted rapid European urbanization with its own awesome problems, as is shown in Chapter 28.)

From the beginning, the Industrial Revolution in England had its critics. Among the first were the romantic poets. William Blake (1757–1827) called the early factories "satanic mills" and protested against the hard life of the London poor. William Wordsworth (1770–1850) lamented the destruction of the rural way of life and the pollution of the land and water. Some handicraft workers—notably the Luddites, who attacked whole factories in northern England in 1812 and after—smashed the new machines, which they believed were putting them out of work. Doctors and reformers wrote eloquently of problems in the factories and new towns, and Malthus and Ricardo (see page 845) concluded that workers would earn only enough to stay alive.

This pessimistic view was accepted and reinforced by Friedrich Engels (1820–1895), the future revolutionary and colleague of Karl Marx. After studying conditions in northern England, this young middle-class German published in 1844 *The Condition of the Working Class in England,* a blistering indictment of the middle classes. "At the bar of world opinion," he wrote, "I charge the English middle classes with mass murder, wholesale robbery, and all the other crimes in the calendar."[11] The new poverty of industrial workers was worse than the old poverty of cottage workers and agricultural laborers, according to Engels. The culprit was industrial capitalism, with its relentless competition and constant technical change. Engels's charge of middle-class exploitation and increasing worker poverty was embellished by Marx and later socialists. It was extremely influential.

Meanwhile, other observers believed that conditions were improving for the working class. Andrew Ure wrote in 1835 in his study of the cotton industry that conditions in most factories were not harsh and were even quite good. Edwin Chadwick, a great and conscientious government official well acquainted with the problems of the working class, concluded that the "whole mass of the laboring community" was increasingly able "to buy more of the necessities and minor luxuries of life."[12] Nevertheless, if all the contemporary assessments were counted up, those who thought conditions were getting worse for working people would probably be the majority.

In an attempt to go beyond the contradictory judgments of contemporaries, some historians have looked at different kinds of sources. Statistical evidence is one such source. If working people suffered a great economic decline, as Engels and later socialists asserted, then they must have bought less and less food, clothing, and other necessities as time went on. The purchasing power of the working person's wages must have declined drastically.

Scholarly statistical studies, which continue to multiply rapidly in an age of easy calculations with computer technology, have weakened the idea that the condition of the working class got much worse with industrialization. On the other hand, the most recent studies also confirm the view that the early years of the Industrial Revolution were hard ones for English and Scottish workers. There was little or no increase in the purchasing power of the average British worker from about 1780 to about 1820. The years from 1792 to 1815, a period of almost constant warfare with France, were particularly difficult. Food prices rose faster than wages, and the living conditions of the laboring poor declined. Only after 1820, and especially after 1840, did real wages rise substantially, so that the average worker earned and consumed roughly 50 percent more in real terms in 1850 than in 1770.[13] In short, there was considerable economic improvement for workers throughout Great Britain by 1850, but that improvement was hard-won and slow in coming.

This important conclusion must be qualified, though. Increased purchasing power meant more goods, but it did not necessarily mean greater happiness. More goods may have provided meager compensation for work that was more dangerous and monotonous. Also, statistical studies do not say anything about how the level of unemployment may have risen, for the simple reason that there are no good unemployment statistics from this period. Furthermore, the hours in the average workweek increased; to an unknown extent, workers earned more simply because they worked more. Finally, the wartime decline was of great importance. The war years were formative years for the new factory labor force. They were also some of the hardest yet experienced. They colored the early experience of modern industrial life in somber tones.

Another way to consider workers' standard of living is to look at the goods that they purchased. Again the evidence is somewhat contradictory. Speaking generally, workers ate somewhat more food of higher nutritional quality as the Industrial Revolution progressed, except during wartime. Diets became more varied; people ate more potatoes, dairy products, fruits, and vegetables. Clothing improved, but housing for working people probably deteriorated somewhat. Per capita use of specific goods supports the position that the standard of living of the working classes rose, at least moderately, after the long wars with France.

Cotton Mill Workers Family members often worked side by side in industry. Here women and children are combing raw cotton and drawing it into loose strands called rovings, which will then be spun into fine thread. *(Source: The Mansell Collection)*

Conditions of Work

What about working conditions? Did workers eventually earn more only at the cost of working longer and harder? Were workers exploited harshly by the new factory owners?

The first factories were cotton mills, which began functioning along rivers and streams in the 1770s. Cottage workers, accustomed to the putting-out system, were reluctant to work in factories even when they received relatively good wages, because factory work was different from what they were used to and unappealing. In the factory, workers had to keep up with the machine and follow its tempo. They had to show up every day and work long, monotonous hours. Factory workers had to adjust their daily lives to the shrill call of the factory whistle.

Cottage workers were not used to that kind of life and discipline. All members of the family worked hard and long, but in spurts, setting their own pace. They could interrupt their work when they wanted to. Women and children could break up their long hours of spinning with other tasks. On Saturday afternoon the head of the family delivered the week's work to the merchant-manufacturer and got paid. Saturday night was a time of relaxation and drinking, especially for the men. Recovering from his hangover on Tuesday, the weaver bent to his task on Wednesday and then worked frantically to meet his deadline on Saturday. Like some students today, he might "pull an all-nighter" on Thursday or Friday in order to get his work in.

Also, early factories resembled English poorhouses, where totally destitute people went to live on welfare. Some poorhouses were industrial prisons, where the inmates had to work in order to receive their food and lodging. The similarity between large brick factories and large stone poorhouses increased the cottage workers' fear of factories and their hatred of factory discipline.

It was cottage workers' reluctance to work in factories that prompted the early cotton mill owners to turn to abandoned and pauper children for their labor (see page 707). They contracted with local officials to employ large numbers of these children, who had no say in the matter. Pauper children were often badly treated and terribly overworked in the mills, as they were when they were apprenticed as chimney sweeps, market girls, shoemakers, and so forth. In the eighteenth century, semiforced child labor seemed necessary and was socially accepted. From our modern point of view, it was cruel exploitation and a blot on the record of the new industrial system.

By 1790 the early pattern was rapidly changing. The use of pauper apprentices was in decline, and in 1802 it was forbidden by Parliament. Many more factories were being built, mainly in urban areas, where they could use steam rather than waterpower and attract a workforce more easily than in the countryside. The need for workers was great. Indeed, people came from near and far to work in the cities, both as factory workers and as laborers, builders, and domestic servants. Yet, as they took these new jobs, working people did not simply give in to a system of labor that had formerly repelled them. Rather, they helped modify the system by carrying over old, familiar working traditions.

For one thing, they often came to the mills and the mines as family units. This was how they had worked on farms and in the putting-out system. The mill or mine owner bargained with the head of the family and paid him or her for the work of the whole family. In the cotton mills, children worked for their mothers or fathers, collecting wastes and "piecing" broken threads together. In the mines, children sorted coal and worked the ventilation equipment. Their mothers hauled coal in the narrow tunnels below the surface while their fathers hewed with pick and shovel at the face of the seam.

The preservation of the family as an economic unit in the factories from the 1790s on made the new surroundings more tolerable, both in Great Britain and in other countries during the early stages of industrialization. Parents disciplined their children, making firm measures socially acceptable, and directed their upbringing. The presence of the whole family meant that children and adults worked the same long hours (twelve-hour shifts were normal in cotton mills in 1800). In the early years, some very young children were employed solely to keep the family together. Jedediah Strutt, for example, believed children should be at least ten years old to work in his mills, but he reluctantly employed seven-year-olds to satisfy their parents. Adult workers were not particularly interested in limiting the minimum working age or hours of their children as long as they worked side by side. Only when technical changes threatened to place control and discipline in the hands of impersonal managers and foremen did they protest against inhuman conditions in the name of their children.

Some enlightened employers and social reformers in Parliament argued that more humane standards were necessary, and they used widely circulated parliamentary reports to influence public opinion. For example, Robert Owen (1771–1858), a very successful manufacturer in Scotland, testified in 1816 before an investigating committee on the basis of his experience. He stated that "very strong facts" demonstrated that employing children under ten years of age as factory workers was "injurious to the children, and not beneficial to the proprietors." The parliamentary committee asked him to explain, and the testimony proceeded as follows:

"Seventeen years ago, a number of individuals, with myself, purchased the New Lanark establishment from the late Mr. Dale, of Glasgow. At that period I find that there were 500 children, who had been taken from poor-houses, chiefly in Edinburgh. . . . The hours of work at that time were thirteen, inclusive of meal times, and an hour and a half was allowed for meals. I very soon discovered that although those children were very well fed, well clothed, well lodged, and very great care taken of them when out of the mills, their growth and their minds were materially injured by being employed at those ages within the cotton mills for eleven and a half hours per day. . . . Their limbs were generally deformed, their growth was stunted, and although one of the best school-masters upon the old plan was engaged to instruct those children every night, in general they made but a very slow progress, even in learning the common alphabet. . . ."

"Do you think the age of ten the best period for the admission of children into full and constant employment for ten or eleven hours per day, within woollen, cotton, and other mills or manufactories?"

"I do not."

"What other period would you recommend for their full admission to full work?"

"Twelve years." [14]

Owen's testimony rang true because he had already raised the age of employment in his mills and was promoting education for young children. Workers also provided graphic testimony at such hearings as the reformers pressed Parliament to pass corrective laws. The reformers scored some important successes.

Their first major accomplishment was the Factory Act of 1833. It limited the factory workday for children between nine and thirteen to eight hours and that of adolescents between fourteen and eighteen to twelve hours, although the act made no effort to regulate hours of work for children at home or in small businesses. The law also prohibited the factory employment of children under nine; they were to be enrolled in the elementary schools that factory owners were required to establish. The employment of children declined rapidly. The Factory Act broke the pattern of whole families working together in the factory because efficiency required standardized shifts for all workers.

Ties of blood and kinship were important in other ways in Great Britain in the formative years between about 1790 and 1840. Many manufacturers and builders hired workers not directly but through subcontractors. They paid the subcontractors on the basis of what the subcontractors and their crews produced—for smelting so many tons of pig iron or moving so much dirt or gravel for a canal or roadbed. Subcontractors in turn hired and fired their own workers, many of whom were friends and relations. The subcontractor might be as harsh as the greediest capitalist, but the relationship between subcontractor and work crew was close and personal. This kind of personal relationship had traditionally existed in cottage industry and in urban crafts, and it was more acceptable to many workers than impersonal factory discipline. This system also provided people an easy way to find a job. Even today, a friend or relative who is a supervisor is frequently worth a hundred formal application forms.

Ties of kinship were particularly important for newcomers, who often traveled considerable distances to find work. Many urban workers in Great Britain were from Ireland. Forced out of rural Ireland by population growth and deteriorating economic conditions from 1817 on, Irish in search of jobs could not be choosy; they took what they could get. As early as 1824, most of the workers in the Glasgow cotton mills were Irish; in 1851 one-sixth of the population of Liverpool was Irish. Even when Irish workers were not related directly by blood, they were held together by ethnic and religious ties. Like other immigrant groups elsewhere, they worked together, formed their own neighborhoods, and not only survived but thrived.

It is important to remember that many kinds of employment changed slowly during and after the Industrial Revolution in Great Britain. Within industry itself, the pattern of small-scale production with artisan skills lived on in many trades even as some other trades were revolutionized. For example, as in the case of cotton and coal, the British iron industry was completely dominated by large-scale capitalist firms by 1850. One iron magnate in Wales employed six thousand workers in his plant, and many large ironworks had over a thousand people on their payroll. Yet the firms that fashioned iron into small metal goods, such as tools, tableware, and toys, employed on average fewer than ten workers, who used time-honored handicraft skills. Only gradually after 1850 did some owners find ways to reorganize such handicraft industries with new machines and new patterns of work. The survival of small workshops and artisan crafts gave many workers an alternative to factory employment.

Old, familiar jobs outside industry provided other alternatives for individual workers. In 1850 more British people still worked on farms than in any other occupation. The second largest occupation was domestic service, which counted more than a million household servants, 90 percent of whom were women. Thus many traditional jobs lived on, and this also helped ease the transition to industrial civilization.

In Great Britain and in other countries later on, workers gradually built a labor movement to improve working conditions and to serve their needs. In 1799, partly in panicked reaction to the French Revolution, Parliament had passed the Combination Acts outlawing unions and strikes. These acts were widely disregarded by workers. Societies of skilled factory workers organized unions, as printers, papermakers, carpenters, and other such craftsmen had long since done. The unions sought to control the number of skilled workers, limit apprenticeship to members' own children, and bargain with owners over wages. They were not afraid to strike; there was, for example, a general strike of adult cotton spinners in Manchester in 1810. In the face of widespread union activity, Parliament repealed the Combination Acts in 1824, and unions were tolerated though not fully accepted after 1825.

The next stage in the development of the British trade-union movement was the attempt to create a single large national union. This effort was led not so much by working people as by social reformers like Robert Owen. Owen, the self-made cotton manufacturer quoted earlier, had pioneered in industrial relations by combining firm discipline with concern for the health, safety, and hours of his workers. After 1815 he experimented with cooperative and socialist communities, including one at New Harmony, Indiana. Then, in 1834, Owen organized one of the largest and most visionary of the early national unions, the Grand National Consolidated Trades Union. When this and other grandiose schemes collapsed, the British labor movement moved once again after 1851 in the direction of craft unions. The most famous of these "new model unions" was the Amalgamated Society of Engineers. These unions won real benefits for members by fairly conservative means and thus became an accepted part of the industrial scene.

British workers also engaged in direct political activity in defense of their own interests. After the collapse of Owen's national trade union, a great deal of the energy of working people went into the Chartist movement, whose goal was political democracy. The key Chartist demand—that all men be given the right to vote—became the great hope of millions of aroused people. Workers were also active in campaigns to limit the workday in the factories to ten hours and to permit duty-free importation of wheat into Great Britain to secure cheap bread. Thus working people played an active role in shaping the new industrial system. Clearly, they were neither helpless victims nor passive beneficiaries.

The Sexual Division of Labor

The era of the Industrial Revolution witnessed major changes in the sexual division of labor. In preindustrial Europe most people generally worked in family units. By tradition, certain jobs were defined by sex—women and girls for milking and spinning, men and boys for plowing and weaving. But many tasks might go to either sex

Girl Dragging Coal Tubs Published by reformers in Parliament in 1842, this picture shocked public opinion and contributed to the Mines Act of 1842. *(Source: The British Library)*

because particular circumstances dictated a family's response in its battle for economic survival. This pattern of family employment carried over into early factories and subcontracting, but it collapsed as child labor was restricted and new attitudes emerged. A different sexual division of labor gradually arose to take its place. The man emerged as the family's primary wage earner, and the woman found only limited job opportunities. Generally denied good jobs at good wages in the growing urban economy, women were expected to concentrate on unpaid housework, child care, and craft work at home.

"Be United and Industrious" This handsome membership certificate of the "new model" Amalgamated Society of Engineers exalts the nobility of skilled labor and the labor movement. Union members are shown rejecting the call of Mars, the God of War, and accepting well-deserved honors from the Goddess of Peace. Other figures represent the strength of union solidarity, famous English inventors, and the trades of the members. (*Source: E. T. Archive*)

This new pattern of "separate spheres" had several aspects. First, all studies agree that married women were much less likely to work full-time for wages outside the house after the first child arrived, although they often earned small amounts doing putting-out handicrafts at home and taking in boarders. Second, when married women did work for wages outside the house, they usually came from the poorest, most desperate families, where the husbands were poorly paid, sick, unemployed, or missing. Third, these poor married (or widowed) women were joined by legions of young unmarried women, who worked full-time but only in certain jobs. Fourth, all women were generally confined to low-paying, dead-end jobs. Virtually no occupation open to women paid a living wage—a wage sufficient for a person to live independently. Men predominated in the better-paying, more promising employments. Evolving gradually as family labor declined, but largely in place in the urban sector of the British economy by 1850, the new sexual division of labor constituted a major development in the history of women and of the family.

If the reorganization of paid work along gender lines is widely recognized, there is as yet no agreement on its causes. One school of scholars sees little connection with industrialization and finds the answer in the deeply ingrained sexist attitudes of a "patriarchal tradition" that predated the economic transformation. These scholars stress the role of male-dominated craft unions in denying women access to good jobs and in reducing them to unpaid maids dependent on their husbands. Other scholars, believing that the gender roles of women and men can vary enormously with time and culture, look more to a combination of economic and biological factors in order to explain why the mass of women were either unwilling or unable to halt the emergence of a sex-segregated division of labor.

Three ideas stand out in this more recent interpretation. First, the new and unfamiliar discipline of the clock and the machine was especially hard on married women. Above all, relentless factory discipline conflicted with child care in a way that labor on the farm or in the cottage had not. A woman operating ear-splitting spinning machinery could mind a child of seven or eight working beside her (until such work was outlawed), but she could no longer pace herself through pregnancy, even though overwork during pregnancy heightened the already high risks of childbirth. Nor could a woman breast-feed her baby on the job, although breast-feeding saved lives. Thus a working-class woman had strong incentives to concentrate on child care within her home, if her family could afford for her to do so.

Second, running a household in conditions of primitive urban poverty was an extremely demanding job in its own right. There were no supermarkets or discount department stores; there was no running water or public transportation. Everything had to be done on foot. As in the poor sections of many inner cities today, shopping and feeding the family constituted a never-ending challenge. The woman marched from one tiny shop to another, dragging her tired children (for who was to watch them?) and struggling valiantly with heavy sacks, tricky shopkeepers, and walk-up apartments. Yet another brutal job outside the house—a "second shift"—had limited appeal for the average married woman. Thus women might well accept the emerging division of labor as the best available strategy for family survival in the industrializing society.[15]

Third, why were the women who did work for wages outside the home segregated and confined to certain "women's jobs"? No doubt the desire of males to monopolize the best opportunities and hold women down provides part of the answer. Yet, as the English women's historian Jane Humphries has argued, sex-segregated employment also formed a collective response to the new industrial system. Previously, at least in theory, young people worked under a watchful parental eye. The growth of factories and mines brought unheard-of opportunities for girls and boys to mix on the job, free of familial supervision. Continuing to mix after work, they were "more likely to form liaisons, initiate courtships, and respond to advances."[16] Such intimacy also led to more unplanned pregnancies and fueled the illegitimacy explosion that had begun in the late eighteenth century and that gathered force until at least 1850 (see pages 702–704). Thus segregation of jobs by gender was partly an effort by older people to help control the sexuality of working-class youth.

Parliamentary investigations into the British coal industry before 1842 provide a graphic example of this concern. The middle-class men leading the inquiry often failed to appreciate the physical effort of the girls and women who dragged with belt and chain the unwheeled carts of coal along narrow underground passages. But they professed horror at the sight of girls and women working without shirts, which was a common practice because of the heat, and they quickly assumed the prevalence of licentious sex with the male miners, who also wore very little clothing. In fact, most girls and married women worked for related males in a family unit that provided considerable protection and restraint. Yet many witnesses from the working class believed that "blackguardism and debauchery" were common and that "They are best out of the pits, the lasses." Some miners stressed particularly the sexual danger of letting girls work past puberty. As one explained when corrective legislation was being considered,

"I consider it a scandal for girls to work in the pits. Till they are 12 or 14 they may work very well but after that it's an abomination. . . . The work of the pit does not hurt them, it is the effect on their morals that I complain of, and after 14 they should not be allowed to go. . . . [A]fter that age it is dreadful for them."[17]

The Mines Act of 1842 prohibited underground work for all women, as well as for boys under ten.

Some women who had to support themselves protested against being excluded from coal mining, which paid higher wages than most other jobs open to women. But if they were part of families that could manage economically, the girls and the women who had worked underground were generally pleased with the law. In explaining her satisfaction in 1844 to a follow-up investigator, one mother of four provided a real insight into why many women accepted the emerging sexual division of labor:

While working in the pit I was worth to my [miner] husband seven shillings a week, out of which we had to pay 2 1/2 shillings to a woman for looking after the younger children. I used to take them to her house at 4 o'clock in the morning, out of their own beds, to put them into hers. Then there was one shilling a week for washing; besides, there was mending to pay for, and other things. The house was not guided. The other children broke things; they did not go to school when they were sent; they would be playing about, and get ill-used by other children, and their clothes torn. Then when I came home in the evening, everything was to do after the day's labor, and I was so tired I had no heart for it; no fire lit, nothing cooked, no water fetched, the house dirty, and nothing comfortable for my husband. It is all far better now, and I wouldn't go down again.[18]

SUMMARY

Western society's industrial breakthrough grew out of a long process of economic and social change in which the rise of capitalism, overseas expansion, and the growth of rural industry stand out as critical preparatory developments. Eventually taking the lead in all of these developments, and also profiting from stable government, abundant natural resources, and a flexible labor force, England experienced between roughly the 1780s and the 1850s an epoch-making transformation that is still aptly termed the "Industrial Revolution."

Building on technical breakthroughs, power-driven equipment, and large-scale enterprise, the Industrial Revolution in England greatly increased output in certain radically altered industries, stimulated the large handicraft and commercial sectors, and speeded up overall economic growth. Rugged Scotland industrialized at least as fast as England, and Great Britain became the first industrial nation. By 1850 the level of British per capita industrial production surpassed continental levels by a growing margin, and Britain savored a near monopoly in world markets for mass-produced goods. Thus continental countries inevitably took rather different paths to the urban industrial society. They relied more on handicraft production in both towns and villages, and only in the 1840s did railroad construction begin to create a strong demand for iron, coal, and railway equipment that speeded up the process of industrialization.

The rise of modern industry had a profound impact on people and their lives. In the early stages Britain again led the way, experiencing in a striking manner the long-term social changes accompanying the economic transformation. Factory discipline and Britain's stern capitalist economy weighed heavily on working people, who, however, actively fashioned their destinies, refusing to be passive victims. Improvements in the standard of living came slowly, although they were substantial by 1850. The era of industrialization fostered new attitudes toward child labor, encouraged protective factory legislation, and called forth an as-

sertive labor movement. Within the family it also promoted a more rigid division of roles and responsibilities that was detrimental to women, another gradual but profound change of revolutionary proportions.

NOTES

1. N. F. R. Crafts, *British Economic Growth During the Industrial Revolution* (Oxford: Oxford University Press, 1985), p. 32. These estimates are for Great Britain as a whole.
2. B. H. Slicher van Bath, *The Agrarian History of Western Europe, A.D. 500–1850* (New York: St. Martin's Press, 1963), p. 240.
3. E. P. Thompson, *The Making of the English Working Class* (New York: Vintage Books, 1966), p. 218.
4. Quoted in C. Wilson, *England's Apprenticeship, 1603–1763* (London: Longmans, Green, 1965), p. 169.
5. G. Taylor, "America's Growth Before 1840," *Journal of Economic History* 24 (December 1970): 427–444.
6. Quoted in P. Mantoux, *The Industrial Revolution in the Eighteenth Century* (New York: Harper & Row, 1961), p. 75.
7. P. Bairoch, "International Industrialization Levels from 1750 to 1980," *Journal of European Economic History* 11 (Spring 1982): 269–333.
8. Crafts, pp. 45, 95–102.
9. M. Lévy-Leboyer, *Les banques européennes et l'industrialisation dans la première moitié du XIXe siècle* (Paris: Presses Universitaires de France, 1964), p. 29.
10. J. Michelet, *The People*, trans. with an introduction by J. P. McKay (Urbana: University of Illinois Press, 1973; original publication, 1846), p. 64.
11. F. Engels, *The Condition of the Working Class in England*, trans. and ed. W. O. Henderson and W. H. Chaloner (Stanford, Calif.: Stanford University Press, 1968), p. xxiii.
12. Quoted in W. A. Hayek, ed., *Capitalism and the Historians* (Chicago: University of Chicago Press, 1954), p. 126.
13. Crafts, p. 95.
14. Quoted in E. R. Pike, *"Hard Times": Human Documents of the Industrial Revolution* (New York: Praeger, 1966), p. 109.
15. See especially J. Brenner and M. Rama, "Rethinking Women's Oppression," *New Left Review* 144 (March–April 1984): 33–71, and sources cited there.
16. J. Humphries, " '. . . The Most Free from Objection . . .' The Sexual Division of Labor and Wom-

en's Work in Nineteenth-Century England," *Journal of Economic History* 47 (December 1987): 948.
17. Quoted in Ibid., p. 941; quoted in Pike, p. 266.
18. Quoted in Pike, p. 208.

SUGGESTED READING

There is a vast and exciting literature on the Industrial Revolution. R. Cameron, *A Concise Economic History of the World* (1989), provides an introduction to the issues and has a carefully annotated bibliography. J. Goodman and K. Honeyman, *Gainful Pursuits: The Making of Industrial Europe, 1600–1914* (1988); D. S. Landes, *The Unbound Prometheus: Technological Change and Industrial Development in Western Europe from 1750 to the Present* (1969); and S. Pollard, *Peaceful Conquest: The Industrialization of Europe* (1981), are excellent general treatments of European industrial growth. These studies also suggest the range of issues and interpretations. M. Berg, *The Age of Manufactures: Industry, Innovation and Work in Britain, 1700–1820* (1985); P. Mathias, *The First Industrial Nation: An Economic History of Britain, 1700–1914* (1969); and P. Mantoux, *The Industrial Revolution in the Eighteenth Century* (1961), admirably discuss the various aspects of the English breakthrough and offer good bibliographies, as does the work by Crafts mentioned in the Notes. J. de Vries, *The Dutch Rural Economy in the Golden Age, 1500–1700* (1974), examines the causes of early Dutch Leadership in farming, and E. L. Jones, *Agriculture and Economic Growth in England* (1967), shows the importance of the Agricultural Revolution for England. W. Rostow, *The Stages of Economic Growth: A Non-Communist Manifesto* (1960), is a well-known, provocative study.

H. Kirsch, *From Domestic Manufacturing to Industrial Revolution: The Case of the Rhineland Textile Districts* (1989), and M. Neufield, *The Skilled Metalworkers of Nuremberg: Craft and Class in the Industrial Revolution* (1985), examine the persistence and gradual transformation of handicraft techniques. R. Cameron brilliantly traces the spread of railroads and industry across Europe in *France and the Economic Development of Europe, 1800–1914* (1961). The works of A. S. Milward and S. B. Saul, *The Economic Development of Continental Europe, 1780–1870* (1973) and *The Development of the Economies of Continental Europe, 1850–1914* (1977), may be compared with J. Clapham's old-fashioned classic, *Economic Development of France and Germany* (1963). C. Kindleberger, *Economic Growth in France*

and Britain, 1851–1950 (1964), is a stimulating study, especially for those with some background in economics. Other important works on industrial developments are C. Tilly and E. Shorter, *Strikes in France, 1830–1848* (1974); D. Ringrose, *Transportation and Economic Stagnation in Spain, 1750–1850* (1970); L. Schofer, *The Formation of a Modern Labor Force* (1975), which focuses on the Silesian part of Germany; and W. Blackwell, *The Industrialization of Russia*, 2d ed. (1982). L. Moch, *Paths to the City: Regional Migration in Nineteenth-Century France* (1983), and W. Schivelbusch, *Disenchanted Night: The Industrialization of Light in the Nineteenth Century* (1983), imaginatively analyze different aspects of industrialization's many consequences.

The debate between "optimists" and "pessimists" about the consequences of industrialization in England goes on. P. Taylor, ed., *The Industrial Revolution: Triumph or Disaster?* (1970), is a useful introduction to different viewpoints. Hayek's collection of essays, cited in the Notes, stresses positive aspects. It is also fascinating to compare Friedrich Engels's classic condemnation, *The Condition of the Working Class in England,* with Andrew Ure's optimistic defense, *The Philosophy of Manufactures,* first published in 1835 and reprinted recently. E. P. Thompson continues and enriches the Engels tradition in *The Making of the English Working Class* (1963), an exciting book rich in detail and early working-class lore. E. R. Pike's documentary collection, *"Hard Times,"* cited in the Notes, provides fascinating insights into the lives of working people. An unorthodox but moving account of a doomed group is D. Bythell, *The Handloom Weavers* (1969). F. Klingender, *Art and the Industrial Revolution,* rev. ed. (1968), is justly famous, and M. Ignatieff, *A Just Measure of Pain* (1980), is an engrossing study of prisons during English industrialization. D. S. Landes, *Revolution in Time: Clocks and the Making of the Modern World* (1983), is a brilliant integration of industrial and cultural history.

Among general studies, G. S. R. Kitson Clark, *The Making of Victorian England* (1967), is particularly imaginative. A. Briggs, *Victorian People* (1955), provides an engrossing series of brief biographies. H. Ausubel discusses a major reformer in *John Bright* (1966), and B. Harrison skillfully illuminates the problem of heavy drinking in *Drink and the Victorians* (1971). The most famous contemporary novel dealing with the new industrial society is Charles Dickens's *Hard Times,* an entertaining but exaggerated story. *Mary Barton* and *North and South* by Elizabeth Gaskell are more realistic portrayals, and both are highly recommended, as is Émile Zola's *Germinal,* a grim, powerful story of love and hate during a violent strike by French coal miners.

27

Ideologies and Upheavals in Europe, 1815–1850

Citizens of Vienna astride the barricades during the revolution of 1848

The momentous economic and political transformation of modern times began in the late eighteenth century with the Industrial Revolution in England and then the French Revolution. Until about 1815, these economic and political revolutions were separate, involving different countries and activities and proceeding at very different paces. The Industrial Revolution created the factory system and new groups of capitalists and industrial workers in northern England, but almost continuous warfare with France checked its spread to continental Europe. Meanwhile, England's ruling aristocracy suppressed all forms of political radicalism at home and joined with crowned heads abroad to oppose and eventually defeat revolutionary and Napoleonic France. The economic and political revolutions worked at cross-purposes and even neutralized each other.

After peace returned in 1815, the situation changed. Economic and political changes tended to fuse, reinforcing each other and bringing about what the historian Eric Hobsbawm has incisively called the "dual revolution." For instance, the growth of the industrial middle class encouraged the drive for representative government, while the demands of the French sans-culottes in 1793 and 1794 inspired many socialist thinkers. Gathering strength and threatening almost every aspect of the existing political and social framework, the dual revolution rushed on to alter completely first Europe and then the entire world. Much of world history in the last two centuries can be seen as the progressive unfolding of the dual revolution.

Yet three qualifications must be kept firmly in mind. In Europe in the nineteenth century, as in Asia and Africa in more recent times, the dual revolution was not some inexorable mechanical monster grinding peoples and cultures into a homogenized mass. The economic and political transformation it wrought was built on complicated histories, strong traditions, and highly diverse cultures. Radical change was eventually a constant, but the particular results varied enormously.

Nor should the strength of the old forces be underestimated. In central and eastern Europe especially, the traditional elites—the monarchs, noble landowners, and bureaucrats—long proved capable of defending their privileges and even of redirecting the dual revolution to serve their interests.

Finally, the dual revolution posed a tremendous intellectual challenge. The meanings of the economic, political, and social changes that were occurring, as well as the ways they could be shaped by human action, were anything but clear. These questions fascinated observers and stimulated new ideas and ideologies.

- What ideas did thinkers develop to describe and shape the transformation going on?
- How did the artists and writers of the romantic movement reflect and influence changes in this era?
- How did the political revolution, derailed in France and resisted by European monarchs, eventually break out again after 1815?
- Why did the revolutionary surge triumph briefly in 1848, then fail almost completely?

These are the questions explored in this chapter.

PEACE SETTLEMENT

The eventual triumph of revolutionary economic and political forces was by no means certain in 1814. Quite the contrary. The conservative, aristocratic monarchies with their preindustrial armies and economies (Great Britain excepted) appeared firmly in control once again. France had been decisively defeated by the off-again, on-again alliance of Russia, Prussia, Austria, and Great Britain. That alliance had been strengthened and reaffirmed in March 1814, when the allies pledged not only to defeat France but to hold it in line for twenty years thereafter. The Quadruple Alliance had then forced Napoleon to abdicate in April 1814 and restored the Bourbon dynasty to the French throne (see page 822). But there were many other international questions outstanding, and the allies agreed to meet in Vienna to fashion a general peace settlement. Interrupted by Napoleon's desperate gamble during the Hundred Days, the allies concluded their negotiations at the Congress of Vienna after Napoleon's defeat at Waterloo.

Most people felt a profound longing for peace. The great challenge for political leaders in 1814

The Great Powers   negotiated the main questions of the peace settlement in intimate sessions at the Congress of Vienna. This painting shows the Duke of Wellington, standing at the far left; seated at far left is the Prussian Prince of Hardinberg. Wellington had just led the allied forces to victory against Napoleon at Waterloo. *(Source: Windsor Castle, Royal Library © 1990. Her Majesty Queen Elizabeth II)*

was to construct a peace settlement that would last and not sow the seeds of another war. Their efforts were largely successful and contributed to a century unmarred by destructive, generalized war (Map 27.1).

The Congress of Vienna

The allied powers were concerned first and foremost with the defeated enemy, France. Agreeing to the restoration of the Bourbon dynasty, the allies signed the first Peace of Paris with Louis XVIII on May 30, 1814.

The allies were quite lenient toward France. France was given the boundaries it possessed in 1792, which were larger than those of 1789.

France lost only the territories it had conquered in Italy, Germany, and the Low Countries, in addition to a few colonial possessions. Although there was some sentiment for levying a fine on France to pay for the war, the allies did not press the matter when Louis XVIII stated firmly that his government would not pay any reparations. France was even allowed to keep the art treasures that Napoleon's agents had looted from the museums of Europe. Thus the victorious powers did not punish harshly, and they did not foment a spirit of injustice and revenge in the defeated country.

When the four allies met together at the Congress of Vienna, assisted in a minor way by a host of delegates from the smaller European states, they also agreed to raise a number of formidable barriers against renewed French aggression. The Low

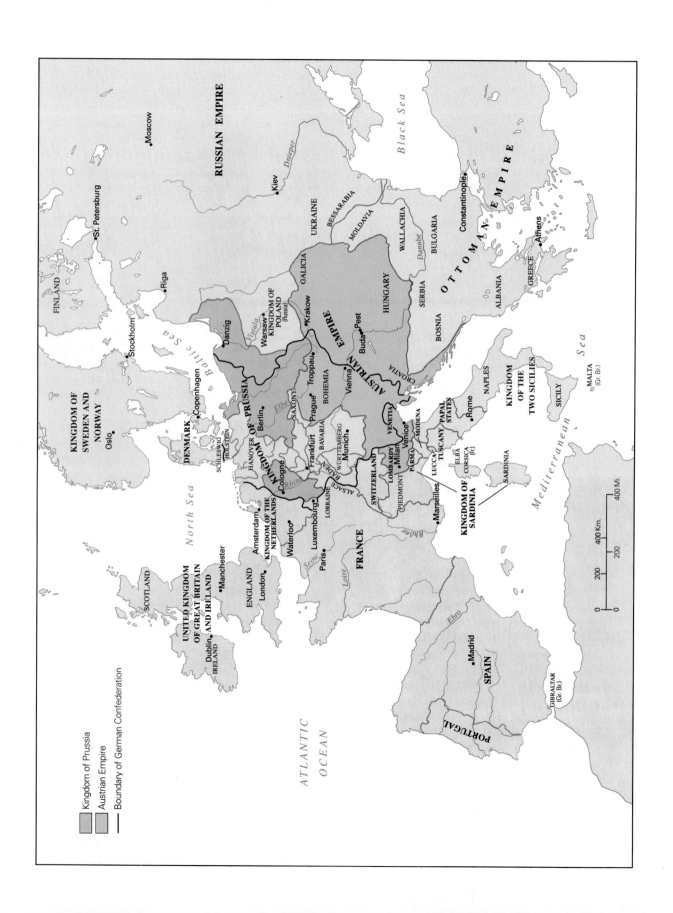

Kingdom of Prussia

Austrian Empire

Boundary of German Confederation

RUSSIAN EMPIRE

OTTOMAN EMPIRE

AUSTRIAN EMPIRE

KINGDOM OF PRUSSIA

FRANCE

SPAIN

PORTUGAL

UNITED KINGDOM OF GREAT BRITAIN AND IRELAND

KINGDOM OF SWEDEN AND NORWAY

DENMARK

KINGDOM OF THE NETHERLANDS

KINGDOM OF SARDINIA

KINGDOM OF THE TWO SICILIES

PAPAL STATES

FINLAND

Moscow

St. Petersburg

Riga

Kiev

Stockholm

Copenhagen

Oslo

Danzig

Warsaw

KINGDOM OF POLAND (Russia)

Krakow

GALICIA

UKRAINE

BESSARABIA

MOLDAVIA

WALLACHIA

BULGARIA

SERBIA

BOSNIA

ALBANIA

GREECE

Athens

Constantinople

HUNGARY

Buda Pest

CROATIA

VENETIA

Venice

Berlin

HANOVER

SAXONY

BOHEMIA

Prague

Troppau

Vienna

BAVARIA

WÜRTTEMBERG

Munich

Frankfurt

Cologne

BADEN

ALSACE

LORRAINE

SWITZERLAND

LOMBARDY

Milan

PIEDMONT

PARMA

MODENA

LUCCA

TUSCANY

ELBA

CORSICA (Fr.)

SARDINIA

NAPLES

SICILY

ROME

Rome

MALTA (Gr. Br.)

Marseilles

Luxembourg

Waterloo

Amsterdam

Paris

London

Manchester

ENGLAND

SCOTLAND

IRELAND

Dublin

Madrid

GIBRALTAR (Gr. Br.)

SCHLESWIG

HOLSTEIN

Black Sea

Baltic Sea

North Sea

ATLANTIC OCEAN

Mediterranean Sea

Dnieper

Danube

Vistula

Elbe

Rhine

Seine

Loire

Rhône

Ebro

400 Mi.

400 Km.

200

0

Countries—Belgium and Holland—were united under an enlarged Dutch monarchy capable of opposing France more effectively. Moreover, Prussia received considerably more territory on France's eastern border so as to stand as "sentinel on the Rhine" against France. In these ways the Quadruple Alliance combined leniency toward France with strong defensive measures. They held out a carrot with one hand and picked up a bigger stick with the other.

In their moderation toward France the allies were motivated by self-interest and traditional ideas about the balance of power. To Metternich and Castlereagh, the foreign ministers of Austria and Great Britain, as well as their French counterpart Talleyrand, the balance of power meant an international equilibrium of political and military forces that would preserve the freedom and independence of each of the Great Powers. Such a balance would discourage aggression by any combination of states or, worse, the domination of Europe by any single state. As they saw it, the task of the powers was thus twofold. They had to make sure that France would not dominate Europe again, and they also had to arrange international relations so that none of the victors would be tempted to strive for domination in its turn. Such a balance involved many considerations and all of Europe.

The balance of power was the mechanism used by the Great Powers—Austria, Britain, Prussia, Russia, and France—to settle their own dangerous disputes at the Congress of Vienna. There was general agreement among the victors that each of them should receive compensation in the form of territory for their successful struggle against the French. Great Britain had already won colonies and strategic outposts during the long wars, and these it retained. Metternich's Austria gave up territories in Belgium and southern Germany but expanded greatly elsewhere, taking the rich provinces of Venetia and Lombardy in northern Italy as well as its former Polish possessions and new lands on the eastern coast of the Adriatic (see Map 27.1). There was also agreement that Prussia and Russia should be compensated. But where, and to

what extent? That was the ticklish question that almost led to renewed war in January 1815.

The vaguely progressive, impetuous Alexander I of Russia had already taken Finland and Bessarabia on his northern and southern borders. Yet he burned with ambition to restore the ancient kingdom of Poland, on which he expected to bestow the benefits of his rule. The Prussians were willing to go along and give up their Polish territories, provided they could swallow up the large and wealthy kingdom of Saxony, their German neighbor to the south.

These demands were too much for Castlereagh and Metternich, who feared an unbalancing of forces in central Europe. In an astonishing about-face, they turned for diplomatic support to the wily Talleyrand and the defeated France he represented. On January 3, 1815, Great Britain, Austria, and France signed a secret alliance directed against Russia and Prussia. As Castlereagh concluded somberly, it appeared that the "peace we have so dearly purchased will be of short duration."[1]

The outcome, however, was compromise rather than war. When rumors of the alliance were intentionally leaked, the threat of war caused the rulers of Russia and Prussia to moderate their demands. They accepted Metternich's proposal: Russia established a small Polish kingdom, and Prussia received two-fifths rather than all of Saxony (see Map 27.1). This compromise was very much within the framework of balance-of-power ideology and eighteenth-century diplomacy: Great Powers became greater, but not too much greater. In addition, France had been able to intervene and tip the scales in favor of the side seeking to prevent undue expansion of Russia and Prussia. In so doing, France regained its Great Power status and was no longer isolated, as Talleyrand gleefully reported to Louis XVIII.

Unfortunately for France, as the final touches were being put on the peace settlement at Vienna, Napoleon suddenly reappeared on the scene. Escaping from his "comic kingdom" on the island of Elba in February 1815 and rallying his supporters for one last campaign during the Hundred Days, Napoleon was defeated at Waterloo and exiled to St. Helena. Yet the resulting peace—the second Peace of Paris—was still relatively moderate toward France. Fat old Louis XVIII was restored to his throne for a second time. France lost some

MAP 27.1 Europe in 1815 Europe's leaders re-established a balance of political power after the defeat of Napoleon.

territory, had to pay an indemnity of 700 million francs, and had to support a large army of occupation for five years.

The rest of the settlement already concluded at the Congress of Vienna was left intact. The members of the Quadruple Alliance, however, did agree to meet periodically to discuss their common interests and to consider appropriate measures for the maintenance of peace in Europe. This agreement marked the beginning of the European "congress system," which lasted long into the nineteenth century and settled international crises through diplomatic conferences.

Intervention and Repression

There was also a domestic political side to the re-establishment of peace. Within their own countries, the leaders of the victorious states were much less flexible. In 1815, under Metternich's leadership, Austria, Prussia, and Russia embarked on a crusade against the ideas and politics of the dual revolution. The crusade lasted until 1848.

The first step was the Holy Alliance, formed by Austria, Prussia, and Russia in September 1815. First proposed by Russia's Alexander I, the alliance proclaimed the intention of the three eastern monarchs to rule exclusively on the basis of Christian principles and to work together to maintain peace and justice on all occasions. Castlereagh refused to sign, characterizing the vague statement of principle as "a piece of sublime mysticism and nonsense." Yet it soon became a symbol of the repression of liberal and revolutionary movements all over Europe.

In 1820 revolutionaries succeeded in forcing the monarchs of Spain and the southern Italian kingdom of the Two Sicilies to grant liberal constitutions against their wills. Metternich was horrified: revolution was rising once again. Calling a conference at Troppau in Austria, under the provisions of the Quadruple Alliance he and Alexander I proclaimed the principle of active intervention to maintain all autocratic regimes whenever they were threatened. Austrian forces then marched into Naples and restored Ferdinand I to the throne of the Two Sicilies. The French armies of Louis XVIII likewise restored the Spanish regime—after the Congress of Troppau had rejected Alexander's offer to send his Cossacks across Europe to teach the Spanish an unforgettable lesson.

Great Britain remained aloof, arguing that intervention in the domestic politics of foreign states was not an object of British diplomacy. In particular, Great Britain opposed any attempts by the restored Spanish monarchy to reconquer its former Latin American possessions, which had gained their independence during and after the Napoleonic wars. Encouraged by the British position, the young United States proclaimed its celebrated Monroe Doctrine in 1823. This bold document declared that European powers were to keep their hands off the New World and in no way attempt to re-establish their political system there. In the United States, constitutional liberalism, which was an ongoing challenge to the conservatism of continental Europe, retained its cutting edge.

In the years following the crushing of liberal revolution in southern Italy in 1821 and in Spain in 1823, Metternich continued to battle against liberal political change. Sometimes he could do little, as in the case of the new Latin American republics. Nor could he undo the dynastic changes of 1830 and 1831 in France and Belgium. Nonetheless, until 1848 Metternich's system proved quite effective in central Europe, where his power was the greatest.

Metternich's policies dominated not only Austria and the Italian peninsula but the entire German Confederation, which the peace settlement of Vienna had called into being. The confederation was composed of thirty-eight independent German states, including Prussia and Austria. (Neither Prussia's eastern territories nor the Hungarian half of the Austrian Empire was included in the confederation.) These states met in complicated assemblies dominated by Austria, with Prussia a willing junior partner in the planning and execution of repressive measures.

It was through the German Confederation that Metternich had the infamous Carlsbad Decrees issued in 1819. The decrees required the thirty-eight German member states to root out subversive ideas in their universities and newspapers. The decrees also established a permanent committee with spies and informers to investigate and punish any liberal or radical organizations. Metternich's ruthless imposition of repressive internal policies on the governments of central Europe contrasted with the intelligent moderation he had displayed in the general peace settlement of 1815.

Metternich and Conservatism

Metternich's determined defense of the status quo made him a villain in the eyes of most progressive, optimistic historians of the nineteenth century. Yet rather than denounce the man, it is more useful to try to understand him and the general conservatism he represented.

Born into the middle ranks of the landed nobility of the Rhineland, Prince Klemens von Metternich (1773–1859) was an internationally oriented aristocrat. In 1795 his splendid marriage to Eleonora von Kaunitz, granddaughter of a famous Austrian statesman and heiress to vast estates, opened the door to the highest court circles and a brilliant diplomatic career. Austrian ambassador to Napoleon's court in 1806 and Austrian foreign minister from 1809 to 1848, the cosmopolitan Metternich always remained loyal to his class and jealously defended its rights and privileges to the day he died. Like most other conservatives of his time, he did so with a clear conscience. The nobility was one of Europe's most ancient institutions, and conservatives regarded tradition as the basic source of human institutions. In their view, the proper state and society remained that of pre-1789 Europe, which rested on a judicious blend of monarchy, bureaucracy, and aristocracy.

Metternich's commitment to conservatism was coupled with a passionate hatred of liberalism. He firmly believed that liberalism, as embodied in revolutionary America and France, had been responsible for a generation of war with untold bloodshed and suffering. Liberal demands for representative government and civil liberties had unfortunately captured the imaginations of some middle-class lawyers, business people, and intellectuals. Metternich thought that these groups had been and still were engaged in a vast conspiracy to impose their beliefs on society and destroy the existing order. Like many other conservatives then and since, Metternich blamed liberal revolutionaries for stirring up the lower classes, whom he believed to be indifferent or hostile to liberal ideas, desiring nothing more than peace and quiet.

The threat of liberalism appeared doubly dangerous to Metternich because it generally went with national aspirations. Liberals, especially liberals in central Europe, believed that each people, each national group, had a right to establish its own independent government and seek to fulfill its own destiny. The idea of national self-determination was repellent to Metternich. It not only threatened the existence of the aristocracy, but it also threatened to destroy the Austrian Empire and revolutionize central Europe.

The vast Austrian Empire of the Habsburgs was a great dynastic state. Formed over centuries by war, marriage, and luck, it was made up of many peoples speaking many languages (Map 27.2). The Germans, long the dominant element, had supported and profited by the long-term territorial expansion of Austria, yet they accounted for only a quarter of the population. The Magyars (Hungarians), a substantially smaller group, dominated the kingdom of Hungary—which was part of the Austrian Empire—though they did not account for a majority of the population even there.

The Czechs, the third major group, were concentrated in Bohemia and Moravia. There were

Metternich   This portrait by Sir Thomas Lawrence reveals much of Metternich the man. Handsome, refined, and intelligent, Metternich was a great aristocrat passionately devoted to the defense of his class and its interests. *(Source: Copyright reserved to Her Majesty Queen Elizabeth II)*

GERMAN
STATES

RUSSIA

POLAND

SILESIA

GALICIA

Danube

MORAVIA

•Prague
BOHEMIA

BAVARIA

SWITZERLAND

TYROL

SALZBURG

AUSTRIA

•Vienna

Danube

Tisza

Budapest•

HUNGARY

TRANSYLVANIA

ROMANIA

OTTOMAN EMPIRE

SERBIA

BOSNIA

CROATIA-SLAVONIA

STYRIA

CORINTHIA

ILLYRIA

VENETIA

Venice•

Po

LOMBARDY

Milan•

ITALIAN
STATES

Adriatic Sea

0   50   100 Km.
0   50   100 Ml.

Germans

Hungarians

Italians

Romanians

Poles

Czechs

Carpatho-Ukrainians
(Ruthenians)

Serbs and Croats

Slovaks

Slovenes

— Habsburg Monarchy
     boundaries

also large numbers of Italians, Poles, and Ukrainians, as well as smaller groups of Slovenes, Croats, Serbs, Ruthenians, and Romanians. The various Slavic peoples, together with the Italians and the Romanians, represented a widely scattered and completely divided majority in an empire dominated by Germans and Hungarians. Different ethnic groups often lived in the same provinces and even the same villages. Thus the different parts and provinces of the empire differed in languages, customs, and institutions. They were held together primarily by their ties to the Habsburg emperor.

The multinational state that Metternich served was both strong and weak. It was strong because of its large population and vast territories; it was weak because of its many and potentially dissatisfied nationalities. In these circumstances, Metternich virtually had to oppose liberalism and nationalism, for Austria was simply unable to accommodate those ideologies of the dual revolution. Other conservatives supported Austria because they could imagine no better fate for the jumble of small nationalities wedged precariously between masses of Germans and hordes of Russians in east central Europe. Castlereagh even went so far as to say that Austria was the "great hinge upon which the fate of Europe must ultimately depend." Metternich's repressive conservatism may not hold appeal for many people today, but it had understandable roots in the dilemma of a multinational state in an age of rising nationalism.

RADICAL IDEAS AND EARLY SOCIALISM

The years following the peace settlement of 1815 were years of profound intellectual activity. Intellectuals and social observers were seeking to understand the revolutionary changes that had occurred and were still taking place. These efforts led to ideas that still motivate the world.

Almost all of these basic ideas were radical. In one way or another they opposed the old, deeply

MAP 27.2 Peoples of the Habsburg Monarchy, 1815 The old dynastic state was a patchwork of nationalities. Notice the widely scattered pockets of Germans and Hungarians.

felt conservatism that Metternich exemplified so well. The revived conservatism, with its stress on tradition, a hereditary monarchy, a strong and privileged landowning aristocracy, and an official church, was rejected by radicals. Instead, radicals developed and refined alternative visions—alternative ideologies—and tried to convince society to act on them. With time, they were very successful.

Liberalism

The principal ideas of liberalism—liberty and equality—were by no means defeated in 1815. First realized successfully in the American Revolution and then achieved in part in the French Revolution, this political and social philosophy continued to pose a radical challenge to revived conservatism. Liberalism demanded representative government as opposed to autocratic monarchy, equality before the law as opposed to legally separate classes. The idea of liberty also continued to mean specific individual freedoms: freedom of the press, freedom of speech, freedom of assembly, and freedom from arbitrary arrest. In Europe, only France with Louis XVIII's Constitutional Charter and Great Britain with its Parliament and historic rights of English men and women had realized much of the liberal program in 1815. Even in those countries, liberalism had not fully succeeded; and elsewhere, liberal demands were still a call for revolutionary change.

Although liberalism still had its cutting edge, it was not as sharp a tool as it had been. This was true because liberalism in the early nineteenth century resolutely opposed government intervention in social and economic affairs, even if the need for action seemed great to social critics and reformers. This form of liberalism is often called "classical" liberalism in the United States, in order to distinguish it sharply from modern American liberalism, which usually favors more government programs to meet social needs and to regulate the economy. Classical liberalism's decline in radicalism was especially evident in its economic principles, which called for unrestricted private enterprise and no government interference in the economy. This philosophy was popularly known as the doctrine of *laissez faire*.

The idea of a free economy had first been persuasively formulated by a Scottish professor of philosophy, Adam Smith (1723–1790). Smith, whose *Inquiry into the Nature and Causes of the Wealth of Nations* (1776) founded modern economics, was highly critical of eighteenth-century mercantilism. Mercantilism, he said, meant stifling government regulations as well as unjust privileges for private monopolies and government favorites. Far preferable was free competition, which would give all citizens an equal opportunity to do what they did best. Smith argued effectively that freely competitive private enterprise would bring greater income for everyone, not just the rich.

Unlike some of his contemporaries, Smith applauded the modest rise in real wages of British workers in the eighteenth century and went so far as to say, "No society can surely be flourishing and happy, of which the far greater part of the members are poor and miserable." Smith also believed that greater competition meant higher wages for workers, since manufacturers and "masters are always and everywhere in a sort of tacit, but constant and uniform, combination, not to raise the wages of laborers above their actual rate." In short, Adam Smith was a spokesman for general economic development, not narrow business interests.

In the early nineteenth century, the British economy was progressively liberalized as old restrictions on trade and industry were relaxed or eliminated. This liberalization promoted continued economic growth in the Industrial Revolution. At the same time, however, economic liberalism and laissez-faire economic thought were tending to become a doctrine serving business interests. Businessmen used the doctrine to defend their right to do exactly as they wished in their factories. Labor unions were outlawed because they supposedly restricted free competition and the individual's "right to work."

The teachings of Thomas Malthus (1766–1834) and David Ricardo (1772–1823) helped especially to make economic liberalism an ideology of business interests in many people's minds (see page 845). Malthus argued that population would always tend to grow faster than the supply of food. This led Ricardo to formulate his "iron law of wages," which said that, because of the pressure of population growth, wages would be just high enough to keep the workers from starving. Malthus and Ricardo thought of themselves as objective social scientists. Yet their teachings were often used by industrial and middle-class in-

terests in England, the Continent, and the United States to justify opposing any kind of government action to protect or improve the lot of workers: if workers were poor, it was their own fault, the result of their breeding like rabbits.

In the early nineteenth century, liberal political ideals also became more closely associated with narrow class interests. Early-nineteenth-century liberals favored representative government, but they generally wanted property qualifications attached to the right to vote. In practice, this meant limiting the vote to well-to-do aristocratic landowners, substantial businessmen, and successful members of the professions. Workers and peasants as well as the lower middle class of shopkeepers, clerks, and artisans did not own the necessary property and thus could not vote.

As liberalism became increasingly middle class after 1815, some intellectuals and foes of conservatism felt that it did not go nearly far enough. Inspired by memories of the French Revolution and the contemporary example of exuberant Jacksonian democracy in the young American republic, they called for universal voting rights, at least for males. Giving all men the vote, they felt, would allow the masses to join in government and would lead to democracy.

Many people who believed in democracy also believed in the republican form of government. They detested the power of the monarchy, the privileges of the aristocracy, and the great wealth of the upper middle class. These democrats and republicans were more radical than the liberals. Taking for granted much of the liberal program, they sought to go beyond it. Democrats and republicans were also more willing than most liberals to endorse violent upheaval to achieve goals. All of this meant that liberals and radical, democratic republicans could join forces against conservatives only up to a point.

Nationalism

Nationalism was a second radical idea in the years after 1815, an idea destined to have an enormous influence in the modern world. In a summation of this complex ideology, three points stand out. First, nationalism has normally evolved from a real or imagined cultural unity, manifesting itself especially in a common language, history, and territory. Second, nationalists have usually sought to turn this cultural unity into political reality so that the territory of each people coincides with its state boundaries. It was this goal that made nationalism so potentially explosive in central and eastern Europe after 1815, when there were either too few states (Austria, Russia, and the Ottoman Empire) or too many (the Italian peninsula and the German Confederation) and when different peoples overlapped and intermingled. Third, modern nationalism had its immediate origins in the French Revolution and the Napoleonic wars. Nationalism was effectively harnessed by the French republic during the Reign of Terror to help repel foreign foes, and all across Europe patriots tried to kindle nationalist flames in the war against Napoleon. Thus by 1815 there were already hints of nationalism's remarkable ability to spread and develop.

Between 1815 and 1850, most people who believed in nationalism also believed in either liberalism or radical, democratic republicanism. In more recent times, however, many governments have been very nationalistic without favoring liberty and democracy. Why, then, was love of liberty almost synonymous with love of nation in the early nineteenth century?

A common faith in the creativity and nobility of the people was perhaps the single most important reason for linking these two concepts. Liberals and especially democrats saw the people as the ultimate source of all government. The people (or some of them) elected their officials and governed themselves within a framework of personal liberty. Yet such self-government would be possible only if the people were united by common traditions and common loyalties. In practice, common loyalties rested above all on a common language. Thus liberals and nationalists agreed that a shared language forged the basic unity of a people, a unity that transcended local or provincial interests and even class differences.

Early nationalists usually believed that every nation, like every citizen, had the right to exist in freedom and to develop its character and spirit. They were confident that the independence and freedom of other nations, as in the case of other citizens within a nation, would not lessen the freedom of their own country. Rather, the symphony of nations would promote the harmony and ultimate unity of all peoples. As the French historian Jules Michelet put it in *The People* in 1846, each

citizen "learns to recognize his country . . . as a note in the grand concert; through it he himself participates and loves the world." Similarly, the Italian patriot Giuseppe Mazzini believed that "in laboring according to the true principles of our country we are laboring for Humanity." Thus individual liberty and love of a free nation overlapped greatly in the early nineteenth century.

Nationalism also had a negative side to it. Even as they talked of serving the cause of humanity, early nationalists stressed the differences among peoples. The German pastor and philosopher Johann Herder (1744–1803) had argued that every people has its own particular spirit and genius, which it expresses through its culture and language. Yet Herder (and others after him) could not define the uniqueness of the French, German, and Slavic peoples without comparing and contrasting one people with another. Thus, even early nationalism developed a strong sense of "we" and "they."

"They" were often the enemy. The leader of the Czech cultural revival, the passionate democrat and nationalist historian Francis Palacký, is a good example of this tendency. In his histories he lauded the achievements of the Czech people, which he characterized as a long struggle against brutal German domination. To this "we-they" outlook, it was all too easy for nationalists to add two other highly volatile ingredients: a sense of national mission and a sense of national superiority. As Mazzini characteristically wrote, "Peoples never stop before they have achieved the ultimate aim of their existence, before having fulfilled their mission." Even Michelet, so alive to the aspirations of other peoples, could not help speaking in 1846 of the "superiority of France"; the principles espoused in the French Revolution had made France the "salvation of mankind."

German and Spanish nationalists had a very different opinion of France. To them the French often seemed as oppressive as the Germans seemed to the Czechs, as hateful as the Russians seemed to the Poles. The despised enemy's mission might seem as oppressive as the American national mission seemed to the Mexicans after the U.S. annexation of Texas. In 1845 the American journalist and strident nationalist John Louis O'Sullivan wrote that taking land from an "imbecile and distracted Mexico" was a laudable step in the "fulfillment of our manifest destiny to overspread the continent allotted by Providence for the free development of our yearly multiplying millions."[2]

Early nationalism was thus ambiguous. Its main thrust was liberal and democratic. But below the surface lurked ideas of national superiority and national mission that could lead to aggressive crusades and counter-crusades, as had happened in the French Revolution and in the "wars of liberation" against Napoleon.

French Utopian Socialism

Despite the fact that France lagged far behind Great Britain in developing modern industry, almost all the early socialists were French. Although they differed on many specific points, these French thinkers were acutely aware that the political revolution in France and the rise of modern industry in England had begun a transformation of society. Yet they were disturbed by what they saw. Liberal practices in politics and economics appeared to be fomenting selfish individualism and splitting the community into isolated fragments. There was, they believed, an urgent need for a further reorganization of society to establish cooperation and a new sense of community. Starting from this shared outlook, individual French thinkers went in many different directions. They searched the past, analyzed existing conditions, and fashioned luxurious utopias. Yet certain ideas tied their critiques and visions together.

Early French socialists believed in economic planning. Inspired by the emergency measures of 1793 and 1794 in France, they argued that the government should rationally organize the economy and not depend on destructive competition to do the job. Early socialists also shared an intense desire to help the poor and to protect them from the rich. With passionate moral fervor, they preached that the rich and the poor should be more nearly equal economically. Finally, socialists believed that most private property should be abolished and replaced by state or community ownership. Planning, greater economic equality, and state ownership of property: these were the key ideas of early French socialism and of all socialism since.

One of the most influential early socialist thinkers was a nobleman, Count Henri de Saint-Simon (1760–1825). A curious combination of radical thinker and successful land speculator, Saint-Simon optimistically proclaimed the tremendous possibilities of industrial development: "The age of gold is before us!" The key to progress was proper social organization. Such an arrangement of society required the "parasites"—the court, the aristocracy, lawyers, churchmen—to give way, once and for all, to the "doers"—the leading scientists, engineers, and industrialists. The doers would carefully plan the economy and guide it forward by undertaking vast public works projects and establishing investment banks. Saint-Simon also stressed in highly moralistic terms that every social institution ought to have as its main goal improved conditions for the poor. Saint-Simon's stress on industry and science inspired middle-class industrialists and bankers, like the Pereire brothers, founders of the Crédit Mobilier (see page 851).

After 1830 the socialist critique of capitalism became sharper. Charles Fourier (1772–1837), a lonely, saintly man with a tenuous hold on reality, described a socialist utopia in lavish mathematical detail. Hating the urban wage system, Fourier envisaged self-sufficient communities of 1,620 people living communally on 5,000 acres devoted to a combination of agriculture and industry. Although Fourier waited in vain each day at noon in his apartment for a wealthy philanthropist to endow his visionary schemes, he was very influential. Several utopian communities were founded along the lines he prescribed, mainly in the United States.

Fourier was also an early proponent of the total emancipation of women. Extremely critical of middle-class family life, Fourier believed that most marriages were only another kind of prostitution. According to Fourier, young single women were shamelessly "sold" to their future husbands for dowries and other financial considerations. Thus Fourier called for the abolition of marriage, free unions based only on love, and complete sexual freedom. Many middle-class men and women found these ideas, which were shared and even practiced by some followers of Saint-Simon, shocking and immoral. The socialist program for the liberation of women as well as workers appeared to them as doubly dangerous and revolutionary.

Louis Blanc (1811–1882), a sharp-eyed, intelligent journalist, was much more practical. In his *Organization of Work* (1839), he urged workers to agitate for universal voting rights and to take control of the state peacefully. Blanc believed that the full power of the state should be directed at setting up government-backed workshops and factories to guarantee full employment. The right to work had to become as sacred as any other right. Finally, there was Pierre Joseph Proudhon (1809–1865), a self-educated printer, who wrote a pamphlet in 1840 entitled *What Is Property?* His answer was that it was nothing but theft. Property was profit that was stolen from the worker, who was the source of all wealth. Unlike most socialists, Proudhon feared the power of the state and was often considered an anarchist.

Thus a variety of French thinkers blazed the way with utopian socialism in the 1830s and 1840s. Their ideas were very influential, particularly in Paris, where poverty-stricken workers with a revolutionary tradition were attentive students. Yet the economic arguments of the French utopians were weak, and their specific programs usually seemed too fanciful to be taken seriously. To Karl Marx was left the task of establishing firm foundations for modern socialism.

The Birth of Marxian Socialism

In 1848 the thirty-year-old Karl Marx (1818–1883) and the twenty-eight-year-old Friedrich Engels (1820–1895) published the *Communist Manifesto,* the bible of socialism. The son of a Jewish lawyer who had converted to Christianity, the atheistic young Marx had studied philosophy at the University of Berlin before turning to journalism and economics. He read widely in French socialist thought and was influenced by it. He shared Fourier's view of middle-class marriage as legalized prostitution, and he too looked forward to the emancipation of women and the abolition of the family. But by the time he was twenty-five, he was developing his own socialist ideas.

Early French socialists often appealed to the middle class and the state to help the poor. Marx ridiculed such appeals as naive. He argued that the interests of the middle class and those of the industrial working class are inevitably opposed to each other. Indeed, according to the *Manifesto,* the "history of all previously existing society is the history of class struggles." In Marx's view, one class had always exploited the other, and with the advent of modern industry, society was split more clearly than ever before: between the middle class—the *bourgeoisie*—and the modern working

The Marx Family In 1849 the exiled Marx settled in London. There he wrote *Capital,* the weighty exposition of his socialist theories, and worked to organize the working class. With his coauthor and financial supporter Friedrich Engels (right), Marx is shown here with his daughters, ironically a picture of middle-class respectability. *(Source: Culver Pictures)*

class—the *proletariat.* Moreover, the bourgeoisie had reduced everything to a matter of money and "naked self-interest." "In a word, for exploitation, veiled by religious and political illusions, the bourgeoisie had substituted naked, shameless, direct brutal exploitation."

Just as the bourgeoisie had triumphed over the feudal aristocracy, Marx predicted, the proletariat was destined to conquer the bourgeoisie in a violent revolution. While a tiny minority owned the means of production and grew richer, the ever-poorer proletariat was constantly growing in size and in class consciousness. In this process, the proletariat was aided, according to Marx, by a portion of the bourgeoisie who had gone over to the proletariat and who (like Marx and Engels) "had raised themselves to the level of comprehending theoretically the historical moment." And the critical moment was very near. "Let the ruling classes tremble at a Communist revolution. The proletarians have nothing to lose but their chains. They have a world to win. WORKING MEN OF ALL COUNTRIES, UNITE!" So ends the *Communist Manifesto.*

In brief outline, Marx's ideas may seem to differ only slightly from the wild and improbable ideas of the utopians of his day. Yet whatever one may think of the validity of Marx's analysis, he must be taken seriously. He united sociology, economics, and all human history in a vast and imposing edifice. He synthesized in his socialism not only French utopian schemes but English classical economics and German philosophy—the major intellectual currents of his day. Moreover, after the young Marx fled to England as a penniless political refugee after the revolutions of 1848, he continued to show a rare flair for combining complex theorization with both lively popular writing and practical organizational ability. This combination of theoretical and practical skills contributed greatly to the subsequent diffusion of Marx's socialist synthesis after 1860 (see pages 953–956).

Marx's debt to England was great. He was the last of the classical economists. Following David Ricardo, who had taught that labor was the source of all value, Marx went on to argue that profits were really wages stolen from the workers. Moreover, Marx incorporated Engels's charges of terrible oppression of the new class of factory workers in England; thus his doctrines seemed to be based on hard facts.

Marx's theory of historical evolution was built on the philosophy of the German Georg Hegel (1770–1831). Hegel believed that history is "ideas in motion": each age is characterized by a dominant set of ideas, which produces opposing ideas and eventually a new synthesis. The idea of *being* had been dominant initially, for example, and it had produced its antithesis, the idea of *nonbeing.* This idea in turn had resulted in the synthesis of *becoming.* Thus history has pattern and purpose.

Marx retained Hegel's view of history as a dialectic process of change but made economic relationships between classes the driving force. This dialectic explained the decline of agrarian feudalism and the rise of industrial capitalism. And Marx stressed again and again that the "bourgeoisie, historically, has played a most revolutionary part. . . . During its rule of scarcely one hundred years the bourgeoisie has created more massive and more colossal productive forces than have all preceding generations together." Here was a convincing explanation for people trying to make sense of the dual revolution. Marx's next idea, that it was now the bourgeoisie's turn to give way to the socialism of revolutionary workers, appeared to many the irrefutable capstone of a brilliant interpretation of humanity's long development. Thus Marx pulled together powerful ideas and insights to create one of the great secular religions out of the intellectual ferment of the early nineteenth century.

THE ROMANTIC MOVEMENT

Radical concepts of politics and society were accompanied by comparable changes in literature and other arts during the dual revolution. The early nineteenth century marked the acme of the romantic movement, which profoundly influenced the arts and enriched European culture immeasurably.

The romantic movement was in part a revolt against classicism and the Enlightenment. Classicism was essentially a set of artistic rules and standards that went hand in glove with the Enlightenment's belief in rationality, order, and restraint. The classicists believed that the ancient Greeks and Romans had discovered eternally valid esthetic rules and that playwrights and painters should continue to follow them. Classicists could enforce these rules in the eighteenth century because they dominated the courts and academies for which artists worked.

Forerunners of the romantic movement appeared from about 1750 on. Of these, Rousseau (see page 676)—the passionate advocate of feeling, freedom, and natural goodness—was the most influential. Romanticism then crystallized fully in the 1790s, primarily in England and Germany. The French Revolution kindled the belief that radical reconstruction was also possible in cultural and artistic life (even though many early English and German romantics became disillusioned with events in France and turned from liberalism to conservatism in politics). Romanticism gained strength until the 1840s.

Romanticism

Romanticism was characterized by a belief in emotional exuberance, unrestrained imagination, and spontaneity in both art and personal life. In Germany early romantics of the 1770s and 1780s called themselves the "Storm and Stress" *(Sturm und Drang)* group, and many romantic artists of the early nineteenth century lived lives of tremendous emotional intensity. Suicide, duels to the death, madness, and strange illnesses were not uncommon among leading romantics. Romantic artists typically led bohemian lives, wearing their hair long and uncombed in preference to powdered wigs and living in cold garrets rather than frequenting stiff drawing rooms. They rejected materialism and sought to escape to lofty spiritual heights through their art. Great individualists, the romantics believed the full development of one's unique human potential to be the supreme purpose in life. The romantics were driven by a sense of an unlimited universe and by a yearning for the unattained, the unknown, the unknowable.

Nowhere was the break with classicism more apparent than in romanticism's general conception of nature. Classicism was not particularly interested in nature. In the words of the eighteenth-century English author Samuel Johnson, "A blade of grass is always a blade of grass; men and women are my subjects of inquiry." Nature was

Constable: The Hay Wain Constable's love of a spiritualized and poetic nature radiates from this masterpiece of romantic art. Exhibited in Paris in 1824, *The Hay Wain* created a sensation and made a profound impression on the young Delacroix. *(Source: Courtesy of the Trustees, The National Gallery, London)*

portrayed by classicists as beautiful and chaste, like an eighteenth-century formal garden. The romantics, on the other hand, were enchanted by nature. Sometimes they found it awesome and tempestuous, as in Théodore Géricault's painting *The Raft of the Medusa,* which shows the survivors of a shipwreck adrift in a turbulent sea. Others saw nature as a source of spiritual inspiration. As the great English landscape artist John Constable declared, "Nature is Spirit visible."

Most romantics saw the growth of modern industry as an ugly, brutal attack on their beloved nature and on the human personality. They sought escape—in the unspoiled Lake District of northern England, in exotic North Africa, in an idealized Middle Ages. Yet some romantics found a vast, awesome, terribly moving power in the new industrial landscape. In ironworks and cotton mills they saw the flames of hell and the evil genius of Satan himself. One of John Martin's last and greatest paintings, *The Great Day of His Wrath* (1850), vividly depicts the Last Judgment foretold in Revelation 6, when the "sun became black as sackcloth of hair, and the moon became as blood; and the stars of heaven fell unto the earth." Martin's romantic masterpiece was inspired directly by a journey through the "Black country" of the industrial Midlands in the dead of night. According to Martin's son:

The glow of the furnaces, the red blaze of light, together with the liquid fire, seemed to him truly sublime and awful. He could not imagine anything more terrible even in the regions of everlasting punishment. All he had done or attempted in ideal painting fell far short, very far short, of the fearful sublimity.[3]

Fascinated by color and diversity, the romantic imagination turned toward the study and writing of history with a passion. For romantics, history was not a minor branch of philosophy from which philosophers picked suitable examples to illustrate their teachings. History was beautiful, exciting, and important in its own right. It was the art of change over time—the key to a universe that was now perceived to be organic and dynamic. It was no longer perceived to be mechanical and static as it had seemed to the philosophers of the eighteenth-century Enlightenment.

Historical studies supported the development of national aspirations and encouraged entire peoples to seek in the past their special destinies. This trend was especially strong in Germany and eastern Europe. As the famous English historian Lord Acton put it, the growth of historical thinking associated with the romantic movement was a most fateful step in the story of European thought.

Literature

Britain was the first country where romanticism flowered fully in poetry and prose, and the British romantic writers were among the most prominent in Europe. William Wordsworth, Samuel Taylor Coleridge, and Sir Walter Scott were all active by 1800, to be followed shortly by Percy Bysshe Shelley, John Keats, and George Gordon, Lord Byron. All were poets: romanticism found its distinctive voice in poetry, as the Enlightenment had in prose.

A towering leader of English romanticism, William Wordsworth (1770–1850) traveled in France after his graduation from Cambridge. There he fell passionately in love with a French woman, who bore him a daughter. He was deeply influenced by the philosophy of Rousseau and the spirit of the early French Revolution. Back in England, prevented by war and the Terror from returning to France, Wordsworth settled in the countryside with his sister Dorothy and Samuel Taylor Coleridge (1772–1834).

In 1798 the two poets published their *Lyrical Ballads,* one of the most influential literary works in the history of the English language. In defiance of classical rules, Wordsworth and Coleridge abandoned flowery poetic conventions for the language of ordinary speech, simultaneously endowing simple subjects with the loftiest majesty. This twofold rejection of classical practice was at first ignored and then harshly criticized, but by 1830 Wordsworth had triumphed.

One of the best examples of Wordsworth's romantic credo and genius is "Daffodils":

I wandered lonely as a cloud
That floats on high o'er vales and hills,
When all at once I saw a crowd,
A host, of golden daffodils;
Beside the lake, beneath the trees,
Fluttering and dancing in the breeze.

. . .

The waves beside them danced, but they
Out-did the sparkling waves in glee:

Heroes of Romanticism   Observed by a portrait of Byron and a bust of Beethoven, Liszt plays for friends. From left to right sit Alexandre Dumas, George Sand (characteristically wearing men's garb), and Marie d'Agoult, Liszt's mistress. Standing are Victor Hugo, Paganini, and Rossini. *(Source: Bildarchiv Preussischer Kulturbesitz)*

A poet could not but be gay,
In such a jocund company:
I gazed—and gazed—but little thought
What wealth the show to me had brought:

For oft, when on my couch I lie
In vacant or in pensive mood,
They flash upon that inward eye
Which is the bliss of solitude;
And then my heart with pleasure fills,
And dances with the daffodils.

Here are simplicity and love of nature in commonplace forms. Here, too, is Wordsworth's romantic conviction that nature has the power to elevate and instruct, especially when interpreted by a high-minded poetic genius. Wordsworth's conception of poetry as the "spontaneous overflow of powerful feeling recollected in tranquility" is well illustrated by the last stanza.

At first, the strength of classicism in France inhibited the growth of romanticism there. Then, between 1820 and 1850, the romantic impulse broke through in the poetry and prose of Alphonse de Lamartine, Alfred de Vigny, Victor Hugo, Alexandre Dumas, and George Sand. Of these, Victor Hugo (1802–1885) was the greatest in both poetry and prose.

Son of a Napoleonic general, Hugo achieved an amazing range of rhythm, language, and image in his lyric poetry. His powerful novels exemplified the romantic fascination with fantastic characters, strange settings, and human emotions. The hero of Hugo's famous *Hunchback of Notre Dame* (1831) is the great cathedral's deformed bell-ringer, a "human gargoyle" overlooking the teeming life of fifteenth-century Paris. A great admirer of Shakespeare, whom classical critics had derided as undisciplined and excessive, Hugo also championed romanticism in drama. His play *Hernani* (1830) consciously broke all the old rules as Hugo renounced his early conservatism and equated freedom in literature with liberty in politics and society. Hugo's political evolution was thus exactly the opposite of Wordsworth's, in whom youthful radicalism gave way to middle-aged caution. As the contrast between the two artists suggests, romanticism was a cultural movement compatible with many political beliefs.

Amadine Aurore Lucie Dupin (1804–1876), a strong-willed and gifted woman generally known by her pen name, George Sand, defied the narrow conventions of her time in an unending search for self-fulfillment. After eight years of unhappy marriage in the provinces, she abandoned her dullard of a husband and took her two children to Paris to pursue a career as a writer. There Sand soon achieved fame and wealth, eventually writing over eighty novels on a variety of romantic and social themes. All were shot through with a typically romantic love of nature and moral idealism. George Sand's striking individualism went far beyond her flamboyant preference for men's clothing and cigars and her notorious affairs with the poet Alfred de Musset and the composer Frédéric Chopin, among others. Her semi-autobiographical novel *Lélia* was shockingly modern, delving deeply into her tortuous quest for sexual and personal freedom.

In central and eastern Europe, literary romanticism and early nationalism often reinforced each other. Seeking a unique greatness in every people, well-educated romantics plumbed their own histories and cultures. Like modern anthropologists, they turned their attention to peasant life and transcribed the folk songs, tales, and proverbs that the cosmopolitan Enlightenment had disdained. The brothers Jacob and Wilhelm Grimm were particularly successful at rescuing German fairy tales from oblivion. In the Slavic lands, romantics played a decisive role in converting spoken peasant languages into modern written languages. The greatest of all Russian poets, Alexander Pushkin (1799–1837), rejecting eighteenth-century attempts to force Russian poetry into a classical straitjacket, used his lyric genius to mold the modern literary language.

Art and Music

The greatest and most moving romantic painter in France was Eugène Delacroix (1798–1863), probably the illegitimate son of the French foreign minister Talleyrand. Delacroix was a master of dramatic, colorful scenes that stir the emotions. He was fascinated with remote and exotic subjects, whether lion hunts in Morocco or the languishing, sensuous women of a sultan's harem. Yet he was also a passionate spokesman for freedom. His masterpiece, *Liberty Leading the People,* celebrated the nobility of popular revolution in general and revolution in France in particular.

In England the most notable romantic painters were J. M. W. Turner (1775–1851) and John Constable (1776–1837). Both were fascinated by nature, but their interpretations of it contrasted sharply, aptly symbolizing the tremendous emotional range of the romantic movement. Turner depicted nature's power and terror; wild storms and sinking ships were favorite subjects. Constable painted gentle Wordsworthian landscapes in which human beings were at one with their environment, the comforting countryside of unspoiled rural England.

It was in music that romanticism realized most fully and permanently its goals of free expression and emotional intensity. Whereas the composers of the eighteenth century had remained true to well-defined structures like the classical symphony, the great romantics used a great range of forms to create a thousand musical landscapes and evoke a host of powerful emotions. Romantic composers also transformed the small classical orchestra, tripling its size by adding wind instruments, percussion, and more brass and strings. The crashing chords evoking the surge of the masses in Chopin's "Revolutionary" etude, the bottomless despair of the funeral march in Beethoven's Third Symphony, the solemn majesty of a great religious event in Schumann's *Rhenish* Symphony—such were the modern orchestra's musical paintings that plumbed the depths of human feeling.

This range and intensity gave music and musicians much greater prestige than in the past. Music no longer simply complemented a church service or helped a nobleman digest his dinner. Music became a sublime end in itself. It became for many the greatest of the arts, precisely because it achieved the most ecstatic effect and most perfectly realized the endless yearning of the soul. It was worthy of great concert halls and the most dedicated sacrifice. The unbelievable one-in-a-million performer—the great virtuoso who could transport the listener to ecstasy and hysteria—became a cultural hero. The composer Franz Liszt (1811–1886) vowed to do for the piano what Nicolo Paganini (1782–1840) had done for the violin, and he was lionized as the greatest pianist of his age. People swooned for Liszt as they scream for rock stars today.

Though romanticism dominated music until late in the nineteenth century, no composer ever surpassed its first great master, Ludwig van Beethoven (1770–1827). Extending and breaking open classical forms, Beethoven used contrasting themes and tones to produce dramatic conflict and inspiring resolutions. As the contemporary German novelist Ernst Hoffmann (1776–1822) wrote, "Beethoven's music sets in motion the lever of fear, of awe, of horror, of suffering, and awakens just that infinite longing which is the essence of Romanticism." Beethoven's range was tremendous; his output included symphonies, chamber music, sonatas for violin and piano, masses, an opera, and a great many songs.

At the peak of his fame, in constant demand as a composer and recognized as the leading concert pianist of his day, Beethoven began to lose his hearing. He considered suicide but eventually overcame despair: "I will take fate by the throat; it will not bend me completely to its will."[4] Beethoven continued to pour out immortal music. Among other achievements, he fully exploited for the first time the richness and beauty of the piano. Beethoven never heard much of his later work, including the unforgettable choral finale to the Ninth Symphony, for his last years were silent, spent in total deafness.

REFORMS AND REVOLUTIONS

While the romantic movement was developing, liberal, national, and socialist forces battered against the conservatism of 1815. In some countries, change occurred gradually and peacefully. Elsewhere, pressure built up like steam in a pressure cooker without a safety valve and eventually caused an explosion—in 1848. Three important countries—Greece, Great Britain, and France—experienced variations on this basic theme.

National Liberation in Greece

National, liberal revolution, frustrated in Italy and Spain by conservative statesmen, succeeded first after 1815 in Greece. Since the fifteenth century, the Greeks had been living under the domination of the Ottoman Turks. In spite of centuries of foreign rule, the Greeks had survived as a people, united by their language and the Greek Orthodox religion. It was perfectly natural that the general growth of national aspirations and a desire for independence would inspire some Greeks in the early nineteenth century. This rising national movement led to the formation of secret societies and then to revolt in 1821, led by Alexander Ypsilanti, a Greek patriot and a general in the Russian army.

The Great Powers, particularly Metternich, were opposed to all revolution, even revolution against the Islamic Turks. They refused to back Ypsilanti and supported the Ottoman Empire. Yet for many Europeans the Greek cause became a holy one. Educated Americans and Europeans were in love with the culture of classical Greece; Russians were stirred by the piety of their Orthodox brethren. Writers and artists, moved by the romantic impulse, responded enthusiastically to the Greek struggle. The flamboyant, radical poet Lord Byron went to Greece and died there in the struggle "that Greece might still be free." Turkish atrocities toward the rebels fanned the fires of European outrage and Greek determination. One of Delacroix's romantic masterpieces memorialized the massacre at Chios, where the Turks slaughtered nearly 100,000 Greeks.

The Greeks, though often quarreling among themselves, battled on against the Turks and hoped for the eventual support of European governments. In 1827 Great Britain, France, and Russia responded to popular demands at home and directed Turkey to accept an armistice. When the Turks refused, the navies of these three powers trapped the Turkish fleet at Navarino and destroyed it. Russia then declared another of its

Delacroix: Massacre at Chios　The Greek struggle for freedom and independence won the enthusiastic support of liberals, nationalists, and romantics. The Ottoman Turks were seen as cruel oppressors holding back the course of history, as in this powerful masterpiece by Delacroix. *(Source: Louvre/Cliché des Musées Nationaux, Paris)*

periodic wars of expansion against the Turks. This led to the establishment of a Russian protectorate over much of present-day Romania, which had also been under Turkish rule. Great Britain, France, and Russia finally declared Greece independent in 1830 and installed a German prince as king of the new country in 1832. In the end the Greeks won: a small nation gained its independence in a heroic war against a foreign empire.

Liberal Reform in Great Britain

Eighteenth-century British society had been both flexible and remarkably stable. It was dominated by the landowning aristocracy, but that class was neither closed nor rigidly defined. Successful business and professional people could buy land and become gentlefolk, and the common people had more than the usual opportunities of the preindustrial world. Basic civil rights for all were balanced by a tradition of deference to one's social superiors. Parliament was manipulated by the king and was thoroughly undemocratic. Only about 6 percent of the population could vote for representatives to Parliament, and by the 1780s there was growing interest in some kind of political reform.

But the French Revolution threw the aristocracy into a panic for a generation, making it extremely hostile to any attempts to change the status quo. The Tory party, completely controlled by the landed aristocracy, was particularly fearful of radical movements at home and abroad. Castlereagh initially worked closely with Metternich to restrain France and restore a conservative balance in central Europe. This same intense conservatism motivated the Tory government at home. After 1815 the aristocracy defended its ruling position by repressing every kind of popular protest.

The first step in this direction began with revision of the Corn Laws in 1815. Corn Laws to regulate the foreign grain trade had long existed, but they were not needed during a generation of war with France because the British had been unable to import cheap grain from eastern Europe. As shortages occurred and agricultural prices skyrocketed, a great deal of marginal land had been brought under cultivation. This development had been a bonanza for the landed aristocracy, whose fat rent rolls became even fatter. Peace meant that grain could be imported again and that the price of wheat and bread would go down. To almost everyone except the aristocracy, lower prices seemed highly desirable. The aristocracy, however, rammed far-reaching changes in the Corn Laws through Parliament. The new law prohibited the importation of foreign grain unless the price at home rose above 80 shillings per quarter-ton—a level reached only in time of harvest disaster before 1790. Seldom has a class legislated more selfishly for its own narrow economic advantage.

The change in the Corn Laws, coming at a time of widespread unemployment and postwar adjustment, led to protests and demonstrations by urban laborers. They were supported by radical intellectuals, who campaigned for a reformed House of Commons that would serve the nation and not just the aristocracy. In 1817 the Tory government responded by temporarily suspending the traditional rights of peaceable assembly and habeas corpus. Two years later, Parliament passed the infamous Six Acts, which among other things controlled a heavily taxed press and practically eliminated all mass meetings. These acts followed an enormous but orderly protest, at Saint Peter's Fields in Manchester, that had been savagely broken up by armed cavalry. Nicknamed the "Battle of Peterloo," in scornful reference to the British victory at Waterloo, this incident expressed the government's determination to repress and stand fast.

Ongoing industrial development was not only creating urban and social problems but also strengthening the upper middle classes. The new manufacturing and commercial groups insisted on a place for their new wealth alongside the landed wealth of the aristocracy in the framework of political power and social prestige. They called for certain kinds of liberal reform: reform of town government, organization of a new police force, and more rights for Catholics and dissenters. In the 1820s a less frightened Tory government moved in the direction of better urban administration, greater economic liberalism, and civil equality for Catholics. The prohibition on imports of foreign grain was replaced by a heavy tariff. These actions encouraged the middle classes to press on for reform of Parliament so that they could have a larger say in government and perhaps repeal the revised Corn Laws, that symbol of aristocratic domination.

The Whig party, though led like the Tories by great aristocrats, had by tradition been more responsive to commercial and manufacturing interests. In 1830 a Whig ministry introduced "an act to amend the representation of the people of England and Wales." Defeated, then passed by the House of Commons, this reform bill was rejected by the House of Lords. But when in 1832 the Whigs got the king to promise to create enough new peers to pass the law, the House of Lords reluctantly gave in rather than see its snug little club ruined by upstart manufacturers and plutocrats. A mighty surge of popular protest had helped the king and lords make up their minds.

The Reform Bill of 1832 had profound significance. The House of Commons emerged as the all-important legislative body. In the future, an obstructionist House of Lords could always be brought into line by the threat of creating new peers. The new industrial areas of the country gained representation in the Commons, and many

THE PRELUDE TO 1848

March 1814	Russia, Prussia, Austria, and Britain form the Quadruple Alliance to defeat France
April 1814	Napoleon abdicates
May–June 1814	Restoration of the Bourbon monarchy; Louis XVIII issues Constitutional Charter providing for civil liberties and representative government
	First Peace of Paris: allies combine leniency with defensive posture toward France
October 1814–June 1815	Congress of Vienna peace settlement: establishes balance-of-power principle and creates the German Confederation
February 1815	Napoleon escapes from Elba and marches on Paris
June 1815	Battle of Waterloo
September 1815	Austria, Prussia, and Russia form the Holy Alliance to repress liberal and revolutionary movements
November 1815	Second Peace of Paris and renewal of Quadruple Alliance: punishes France and establishes the European "congress system"
1819	Carlsbad Decrees: Metternich imposes harsh measures throughout the German Confederation
1820	Revolution in Spain and the Kingdom of the Two Sicilies
	Congress of Troppau: Metternich and Alexander I of Russia proclaim principle of intervention to maintain autocratic regimes
1821	Austria crushes liberal revolution in Naples and restores the Sicilian autocracy
	Greek revolt against the Ottoman Turks
1823	French armies restore the Spanish regime
	United States proclaims the Monroe Doctrine
1824	Reactionary Charles X succeeds Louis XVIII in France
1830	Charles X repudiates the Constitutional Charter; insurrection and collapse of government; Louis Philippe succeeds to the throne and maintains a narrowly liberal regime until 1848
	Greece wins independence from the Ottoman Empire
1832	Reform Bill expands British electorate and encourages the middle class
1839	Louis Blanc, *Organization of Work*
1840	Pierre Joseph Proudhon, *What Is Property?*
1846	Jules Michelet, *The People*
1848	Karl Marx and Friedrich Engels, *The Communist Manifesto*

old "rotten boroughs"—electoral districts with very few voters that the landed aristocracy had bought and sold—were eliminated.

The redistribution of seats reflected the shift in population to the northern manufacturing counties and the gradual emergence of an urban society. As a result of the Reform Bill of 1832, the number of voters increased about 50 percent. Comfortable middle-class groups in the urban population, as well as some substantial farmers who leased their land, received the vote. Thus the pressures building in Great Britain were successfully—though only temporarily—released. A major reform had been achieved peacefully,

without revolution or civil war. More radical reforms within the system appeared difficult but not impossible.

The principal radical program was embodied in the "People's Charter" of 1838 and the Chartist movement (see page 857). Partly inspired by the economic distress of the working class, the Chartists' core demand was universal male (not female) suffrage. They saw complete political democracy and rule by the common people as the means to a good and just society. Hundreds of thousands of people signed gigantic petitions calling on Parliament to grant all men the right to vote, first and most seriously in 1839, again in 1842, and yet again in 1848. Parliament rejected all three petitions. In the short run, the working poor failed with their Chartist demands, but they learned a valuable lesson in mass politics.

While calling for universal male suffrage, many working-class people joined with middle-class manufacturers in the Anti–Corn Law League, founded in Manchester in 1839. Mass participation made possible a popular crusade against the tariff on imported grain and against the landed aristocracy. People were fired up by dramatic popular orators such as John Bright and Richard Cobden. These fighting liberals argued that lower food prices and more jobs in industry depended on repeal of the Corn Laws. Much of the working class agreed. The climax of the movement came in 1845. In that year Ireland's potato crop failed, and rapidly rising food prices marked the beginning of the Irish famine. Famine prices for food and even

famine itself also seemed likely in England. To avert the impending catastrophe, the Tory prime minister Robert Peel joined with the Whigs and a minority of his own party to repeal the Corn Laws in 1846. England escaped famine. Thereafter, free trade became almost sacred doctrine in Great Britain.

The following year, the Tories passed a bill designed to help the working classes, but in a different way. This was the Ten Hours Act of 1847, which limited the workday for women and young people in factories to ten hours. Tory aristocrats continued to champion legislation regulating factory conditions. They were competing vigorously with the middle class for the support of the working class. This healthy competition between a still-vigorous aristocracy and a strong middle class was a crucial factor in Great Britain's peaceful evolution. The working classes could make temporary

Evictions of Irish Peasants who could not pay their rent continued for decades after the famine. Surrounded by a few meager possessions, this family has been turned out of its cottage in the 1880s. The door is nailed shut to prevent their return. *(Source: Lawrence Collection, National Library of Ireland, Dublin)*

alliances with either competitor to better their own conditions.

The people of Ireland did not benefit from this political competition. Long ruled as a conquered people, the great mass of the population (outside the northern counties of Ulster, which were partly Presbyterian) were Irish Catholic peasants who rented their land from a tiny minority of Church of England Protestants, many of whom lived in England (see page 642). Ruthlessly exploited and growing rapidly in numbers, Irish peasants depended on the potato crop, the size of which varied substantially from year to year. Potato failures cannot be detected in time to plant other crops, nor can potatoes be stored for more than a year. Moreover, Ireland's precarious potato economy was a subsistence economy, which therefore lacked a well-developed network of roads and trade capable of distributing other foods in time of disaster. When the crop failed in 1845, the Irish were very vulnerable.

In 1846, 1848, and 1851, the potato crop failed again in Ireland and throughout much of Europe. The general result was high food prices, widespread suffering, and, frequently, social upheaval. In Ireland, the result was unmitigated disaster—the Great Famine. Blight attacked the young plants, and the tubers rotted. Widespread starvation and mass fever epidemics followed. Total losses of population were staggering. Fully 1 million emigrants fled the famine between 1845 and 1851, going primarily to the United States and Great Britain, and at least 1.5 million people died or went unborn because of the disaster. The British government's efforts at famine relief were too little and too late. At the same time, the government energetically supported the heartless demands of landowners with armed force. Tenants who could not pay their rents were evicted and their homes broken up or burned. Famine or no, Ireland remained a conquered province, a poor agricultural land that had gained little from the liberal reforms and the industrial developments that were transforming Great Britain.

The Revolution of 1830 in France

Louis XVIII's Constitutional Charter of 1814—theoretically a gift from the king but actually a response to political pressures—was basically a liberal constitution (see page 822). The economic gains of the middle class and the prosperous peasantry were fully protected; great intellectual and artistic freedom was permitted; and a real parliament with upper and lower houses was created. Immediately after Napoleon's abortive Hundred Days, the moderate, worldly wise king refused to bow to the wishes of diehard aristocrats like his brother Charles, who wished to sweep away all the revolutionary changes and return to a bygone age of royal absolutism and aristocratic pretension. Instead, Louis appointed as his ministers moderate royalists who sought and obtained the support of a majority of the representatives elected to the lower Chamber of Deputies between 1816 and Louis's death in 1824.

Louis XVIII's charter was anything but democratic. Only about 100,000 of the wealthiest people out of a total population of 30 million had the right to vote for the deputies who, with the king and his ministers, made the laws of the nation. Nonetheless, the "notable people" who did vote came from very different backgrounds. There were wealthy businessmen, war profiteers, successful professionals, former revolutionaries, large landowners from the middle class, Bourbons, and Bonapartists.

The old aristocracy with its pre-1789 mentality was a minority within the voting population. It was this situation that Louis's successor, Charles X (r. 1824–1830), could not abide. Crowned in a lavish, utterly medieval, five-hour ceremony in the cathedral of Reims in 1824, Charles was a true reactionary. He wanted to re-establish the old order in France. Increasingly blocked by the opposition of the deputies, Charles finally repudiated the Constitutional Charter in an attempted coup in July 1830. He issued decrees stripping much of the wealthy middle class of its voting rights, and he censored the press. The reaction was an immediate insurrection. In "three glorious days" the government collapsed. Paris boiled with revolutionary excitement, and Charles fled. Then the upper middle class, which had fomented the revolt, skillfully seated Charles's cousin, Louis Philippe, duke of Orléans, on the vacant throne.

Louis Philippe (r. 1830–1848) accepted the Constitutional Charter of 1814, adopted the red, white, and blue flag of the French Revolution, and admitted that he was merely the "king of the French people." In spite of such symbolic actions, the situation in France remained fundamentally unchanged. Casimir Périer, a wealthy banker and

Delacroix: Liberty Leading the People   This great romantic painting glorifies the July Revolution in Paris in 1830. Raising high the revolutionary tricolor, Liberty unites the worker, bourgeois, and street child in a righteous crusade against privilege and oppression. *(Source: Louvre/Cliché des Musées Nationaux, Paris)*

Louis Philippe's new chief minister, bluntly told a deputy who complained when the vote was extended only from 100,000 to 170,000 citizens, "The trouble with this country is that there are too many people like you who imagine that there has been a revolution in France."[5] The wealthy "notable" elite actually tightened its control as the old aristocracy retreated to the provinces to sulk harmlessly. For the upper middle class there had been a change in dynasty in order to protect the status quo and the narrowly liberal institutions of 1815. Republicans, democrats, social reformers, and the poor of Paris were bitterly disappointed.

They had constructed a revolution, but it seemed for naught.

THE REVOLUTIONS OF 1848

In 1848 revolutionary political and social ideologies combined with economic crisis and the romantic impulse to produce a vast upheaval. Only the most advanced and the most backward major countries—reforming Great Britain and immobile Russia—escaped untouched. Governments toppled; monarchs and ministers bowed or fled. National independence, liberal-democratic constitutions, and social reform: the lofty aspirations of a generation seemed at hand. Yet, in the end, the revolutions failed. Why was this so?

A Democratic Republic in France

The late 1840s in Europe were hard economically and tense politically. The potato famine in Ireland in 1845 and in 1846 had echoes on the Continent. Bad harvests jacked up food prices and caused misery and unemployment in the cities. "Prerevolutionary" outbreaks occurred all across Europe: an abortive Polish revolution in the northern part of Austria in 1846, a civil war between radicals and conservatives in Switzerland in 1847, and an armed uprising in Naples, Italy, in January 1848. Revolution was almost universally expected, but it took revolution in Paris—once again—to turn expectations into realities.

From its beginning in 1830, Louis Philippe's "bourgeois monarchy" was characterized by stubborn inaction. There was a glaring lack of social legislation, and politics was dominated by corruption and selfish special interests. The king's chief minister in the 1840s, François Guizot, was complacency personified. Guizot was especially satisfied with the electoral system. Only the rich could vote for deputies, and many of the deputies were docile government bureaucrats. It was the government's stubborn refusal to consider electoral reform that touched off popular revolt in Paris. Barricades went up on the night of February 22, 1848, and by February 24 Louis Philippe had abdicated in favor of his grandson. But the common people in arms would tolerate no more monarchy. This refusal led to the proclamation of a provisional republic headed by a ten-man executive committee and certified by cries of approval from the revolutionary crowd.

In the flush of victory, there was much about which Parisian revolutionaries could agree. A generation of historians and journalists had praised the First French Republic, and their work had borne fruit: the revolutionaries were firmly committed to a republic as opposed to any form of constitutional monarchy, and they immediately set about drafting a constitution for France's Second Republic. Moreover, they wanted a truly popular and democratic republic so that the healthy, life-giving forces of the common people—the peasants and the workers—could reform society with wise legislation. In practice, building such a republic meant giving the right to vote to every adult male, and this was quickly done. Revolutionary compassion and sympathy for freedom were expressed in the freeing of all slaves in French colonies, abolition of the death penalty, and the establishment of a ten-hour workday for Paris.

Yet there were profound differences within the revolutionary coalition in Paris. On the one hand, there were the moderate, liberal republicans of the middle class. They viewed universal manhood suffrage as the ultimate concession to be made to popular forces, and they strongly opposed any further radical social measures. On the other hand were the radical republicans. Influenced by the critique of capitalism and unbridled individualism elaborated by a generation of utopian socialists, and appalled by the poverty and misery of the urban poor, the radical republicans were committed to socialism. To be sure, socialism came in many utopian shapes and sizes for the Parisian working poor and their leaders, but that did not make their commitment to it any less real. Finally, wedged in between these groups were individuals like the poet Lamartine and the democrat Alexandre Auguste Ledru-Rollin, who were neither doctrinaire socialists nor stand-pat liberals and who sought to escape an impending tragedy.

Worsening depression and rising unemployment brought these conflicting goals to the fore. Louis Blanc (see page 874), who along with a worker named Albert represented the republican socialists in the provisional government, pressed for recognition of a socialist right to work. Blanc asserted that permanent government-sponsored cooperative workshops should be established for workers. Such workshops would be an alternative to capitalist employment and a decisive step toward a new social order.

The moderate republicans wanted no such thing. They were willing to provide only temporary relief. The resulting compromise set up national workshops—soon to become a vast program of pick-and-shovel public works—and established a special commission under Louis Blanc to "study the question." This satisfied no one. As bad as the national workshops were, though, they were better than nothing. An army of desperate poor from the French provinces and even from foreign countries streamed into Paris to sign up. The number enrolled in the workshops soared from 10,000 in March to 120,000 by June, and another 80,000 were trying unsuccessfully to join.

While the workshops in Paris grew, the French masses went to the polls in late April. Voting in most cases for the first time, the people elected to the new Constituent Assembly about five hundred moderate republicans, three hundred monarchists, and one hundred radicals who professed various brands of socialism. One of the moderate republicans was the author of *Democracy in America,* Alexis de Tocqueville (1805–1859), who had predicted the overthrow of Louis Philippe's government. To this brilliant observer, socialism was the most characteristic aspect of the revolution in Paris.

This socialist revolution was evoking a violent reaction not only among the frightened middle and upper classes but also among the bulk of the population—the peasants. The French peasants owned land, and according to Tocqueville, "private property had become with all those who owned it a sort of bond of fraternity."[6] The countryside, Tocqueville wrote, had been seized with a universal hatred of radical Paris. Returning from Normandy to take his seat in the new Constituent Assembly, Tocqueville saw that a majority of the members were firmly committed to the republic and strongly opposed to the socialists, and he shared their sentiments.

The clash of ideologies—of liberal capitalism and socialism—became a clash of classes and arms after the elections. The new government's executive committee dropped Louis Blanc and thereafter included no representative of the Parisian working class. Fearing that their socialist hopes were about to be dashed, the workers invaded the Constituent Assembly on May 15 and tried to proclaim a new revolutionary state. But the government was ready and used the middle-class National Guard to squelch this uprising. As the workshops continued to fill and grow more radical, the fearful but powerful propertied classes in the Assembly took the offensive. On June 22 the government dissolved the national workshops in Paris, giving the workers the choice of joining the army or going to workshops in the provinces.

The result was a spontaneous and violent uprising. Frustrated in their attempts to create a socialist society, masses of desperate people were now

Daumier: The Legislative Belly Protected by freedom of the press after 1830, French radicals bitterly attacked the do-nothing government of Louis Philippe. Here Daumier savagely ridicules the corruption of the Chamber of Deputies. *(Source: © 1990 The Art Institute of Chicago. All Rights Reserved)*

losing even their life-sustaining relief. As a voice from the crowd cried out when the famous astronomer François Arago counseled patience, "Ah, Monsieur Arago, you have never been hungry!"[7] Barricades sprang up in the narrow streets of Paris, and a terrible class war began. Working people fought with the courage of utter desperation, but the government had the army and the support of peasant France. After three terrible "June Days" and the death or injury of greater than ten thousand people, the republican army under General Louis Cavaignac stood triumphant in a sea of working-class blood and hatred.

The revolution in France thus ended in spectacular failure. The February coalition of the middle and working classes had in four short months become locked in mortal combat. In place of a generous democratic republic, the Constituent Assembly completed a constitution featuring a strong executive. This allowed Louis Napoleon, nephew of Napoleon Bonaparte, to win a landslide victory in the election of December 1848. The appeal of his great name, as well as the desire of the propertied classes for order at any cost, had produced a semi-authoritarian regime.

The Austrian Empire in 1848

Throughout central Europe, news of the upheaval in France evoked feverish excitement and eventually revolution. Liberals demanded written constitutions, representative government, and greater civil liberties. When governments hesitated, popular revolts followed. Urban workers and students served as the shock troops, but they were allied with middle-class liberals and peasants. In the face of this united front, monarchs collapsed and granted almost everything. The popular revolutionary coalition, having secured great and easy victories, then broke down as it had in France. The traditional forces—the monarchy, the aristocracy, and the regular army—recovered their nerve, reasserted their authority, and took back many though not all of the concessions. Reaction was everywhere victorious.

The revolution in the Austrian Empire began in Hungary. Nationalism had been growing among Hungarians since about 1790. In 1848, under the leadership of Louis Kossuth, the Hungarians demanded national autonomy, full civil liberties, and universal suffrage. When the monarchy in Vienna

hesitated, Viennese students and workers took to the streets on March 13 and added their own demands. Peasant disorders broke out in parts of the empire. The Habsburg emperor Ferdinand I (r. 1835–1848) capitulated and promised reforms and a liberal constitution. Metternich fled in disguise toward London. The old order seemed to be collapsing with unbelievable rapidity.

The coalition of revolutionaries was not completely stable, though. The Austrian Empire was overwhelmingly agricultural, and serfdom still existed. On March 20, as part of its capitulation before upheaval, the monarchy abolished serfdom with its degrading forced labor and feudal services. Peasants throughout the empire felt that they had won a victory reminiscent of that in France in 1789. Newly free, men and women of the land lost interest in the political and social questions agitating the cities. The government had in the peasants a potential ally of great importance, especially since, in central Europe as in France, the army was largely composed of peasants.

The coalition of March was also weakened—and ultimately destroyed—by conflicting national aspirations. In March the Hungarian revolutionary leaders pushed through an extremely liberal, almost democratic, constitution granting widespread voting rights and civil liberties and ending feudal obligations. So far, well and good. Yet the Hungarian revolutionaries were also nationalists with a mission. They wanted the ancient Crown of Saint Stephen, with its mosaic of provinces and nationalities, transformed into a unified, centralized Hungarian nation. To the minority groups that formed half of the population of the kingdom of Hungary—the Croats, the Serbs, and the Romanians—such unification was completely unacceptable. Each felt entitled to political autonomy and cultural independence. The Habsburg monarchy in Vienna exploited the fears of the minority groups, and they were soon locked in armed combat with the new Hungarian government.

In a somewhat different way, Czech nationalists based in Bohemia and the city of Prague, led by the Czech historian Palacký, came into conflict with German nationalists. Like the minorities in Hungary, the Czechs saw their struggle for autonomy as a struggle against a dominant group, the Germans. Thus the national aspirations of different peoples in the Austrian Empire came into sharp conflict, and the monarchy was able to play off one group against the other.

THE REVOLUTIONS OF 1848

February	Revolt in Paris against Louis Philippe's "bourgeois monarchy"; Louis Philippe abdicates; proclamation of a provisional republic
February–June	Establishment and rapid growth of government-sponsored workshops in France
March 3	Hungarians under Kossuth demand autonomy from Austrian Empire
March 13	Uprising of students and workers in Vienna; Metternich flees to London
March 19–21	Frederick William IV of Prussia is forced to salute the bodies of slain revolutionaries in Berlin and agrees to a liberal constitution and merger into a new German state
March 20	Ferdinand I of Austria abolishes serfdom and promises reforms
March 26	Workers in Berlin issue a series of socialist demands
April 22	French voters favor moderate republicans over radicals 5:1
May 15	Parisian socialist workers invade the Constitutional Assembly and unsuccessfully proclaim a new revolutionary state
May 18	Frankfurt National Assembly begins writing a new German constitution
June 17	Austrian army crushes working-class revolt in Prague
June 22–26	French government abolishes the national workshops, provoking an uprising June Days: republican army defeats rebellious Parisian working class
October	Austrian army besieges and retakes Vienna from students and working–class radicals
December	Conservatives force Ferdinand I of Austria to abdicate in favor of young Francis Joseph
	Frederick William IV disbands Prussian Constituent Assembly and grants Prussia a conservative constitution
	Louis Napoleon wins a landslide victory in French presidential elections
March 1849	Frankfurt Assembly elects Frederick William IV of Prussia emperor of the new German state; Frederick William refuses and reasserts royal authority in Prussia
June–August 1849	Habsburg and Russian forces defeat the Hungarian independence movement

Nor was this all. The urban working classes of poor artisans and day laborers were not as radical in the Austrian Empire as they were in France, but then neither were the middle class and lower middle class. Throughout Austria and the German states, where Metternich's brand of absolutism had so recently ruled supreme, the middle class wanted liberal reform, complete with constitutional monarchy, limited voting rights, and modest social measures. They wanted a central European equivalent of the English Reform Bill of 1832 and the Corn Laws repeal of 1846. When the urban poor rose in arms—as they did in the Austrian cities of Vienna, Prague, and Milan and throughout the German Confederation as well, presenting their own demands for socialist workshops and universal voting rights for men—the prosperous middle classes recoiled in alarm. As in Paris, the union of

the urban poor and the middle class was soon a mere memory, and a bad memory at that.

Finally, the conservative aristocratic forces gathered around Emperor Ferdinand I regained their nerve and reasserted their great strength. The archduchess Sophia, a conservative but intelligent and courageous Bavarian princess married to the emperor's brother, provided a rallying point. Deeply ashamed of the emperor's collapse before a "mess of students,"[8] she insisted that Ferdinand, who had no heir, abdicate in favor of her eighteen-year-old son, Francis Joseph. Powerful nobles who held high positions in the government, the army, and the church agreed completely. They organized around Sophia in a secret conspiracy to reverse and crush the revolution.

Their first breakthrough came when one of the most dedicated members of the group, Prince

Alfred Windischgrätz, bombarded Prague and savagely crushed a working-class revolt there on June 17. Other Austrian officials and nobles began to lead the minority nationalities of Hungary against the revolutionary government proclaimed by the Hungarian patriots. In late July 1848 another Austrian army reconquered Austria's possessions in northern Italy, where Italian patriots had seized power in March. Thus revolution failed as miserably in Italy as everywhere else. At the end of October, the well-equipped, predominantly peasant troops of the regular Austrian army attacked the student and working-class radicals in Vienna and retook the city at the cost of more than four thousand casualties. Thus the determination of the Austrian aristocracy and the loyalty of its army were the final ingredients in the triumph of reaction and the defeat of revolution.

Sophia's son Francis Joseph (r. 1848–1916) was crowned emperor of Austria immediately after his eighteenth birthday in December 1848. Only in Hungary were the Austrian forces at first unsuccessful in establishing control on the new emperor's behalf. Yet another determined conservative, Nicholas I of Russia (r. 1825–1855), obligingly lent his iron hand. On June 6, 1849, 130,000 Russian troops poured into Hungary. After bitter fighting—in which the Hungarian army supported the revolutionary Hungarian government—they subdued the country. For a number of years the Habsburgs ruled Hungary as a conquered territory.

Prussia and the Frankfurt Assembly

The rest of the states in the German Confederation generally recapitulated the ebb and flow of developments in France and Austria. The key difference was the additional goal of unifying the thirty-eight states of the German Confederation, with the possible exception of Austria, into a single sovereign nation. Thus events in Germany were extraordinarily complex, for they were occurring not only in the individual principalities but at the all-German level as well.

After Austria, Prussia was the largest and most influential German kingdom. Prior to 1848, the goal of middle-class Prussian liberals had been to transform absolutist Prussia into a liberal constitutional monarchy. Such a monarchy would then take the lead in merging itself and all the other German states into a liberal, unified nation. The agitation following the fall of Louis Philippe encouraged Prussian liberals to press their demands. When these were not granted, the artisans and factory workers in Berlin exploded, joining temporarily with the middle-class liberals in the struggle against the monarchy. The autocratic yet paternalistic Frederick William IV (r. 1840–1861), already displaying the instability that later became insanity, vacillated. Humiliated by the revolutionary crowd, which forced him to salute from his balcony the blood-spattered corpses of workers who had fallen in an uprising on March 18, the nearly hysterical king finally caved in. On March 21 he promised to grant Prussia a liberal constitution and to merge it into a new national German state. He appointed two wealthy businessmen from the Rhineland—perfect representatives of moderate liberalism—to form a new government.

The situation might have stabilized at this point if the workers had not wanted much more and the Prussian aristocracy much less. On March 26 the workers issued a series of radical and vaguely socialist demands that troubled their middle-class allies: universal voting rights, a ministry of labor, a minimum wage, and a ten-hour day. At the same time, a wild-tempered Prussian landowner and aristocrat, Otto von Bismarck, joined the conservative clique gathered around the king to urge counter-revolution. While these tensions in Prussia were growing, an elected assembly met in Berlin to write a constitution for the Prussian state.

To add to the complexity of the situation, a self-appointed committee of liberals from various German states successfully called for the formation of a national constituent assembly to begin writing a federal constitution for a unified German state. That body met for the first time on May 18 in Saint Paul's Church in Frankfurt. The Frankfurt National Assembly was a most curious revolutionary body. It was really a serious middle-class body whose 820 members included some 200 lawyers; 100 professors; many doctors, judges, and officials; and 140 businessmen for good measure.

Convened to write a constitution, the learned body was soon absorbed in a battle with Denmark over the provinces of Schleswig and Holstein. Jurisdiction over them was a hopelessly complicated issue from a legal point of view. Britain's foreign minister Lord Palmerston once said that only three people had ever understood the Schleswig-Holstein question, and of those one had died, another had gone mad, and he himself had forgotten the answer. The provinces were inhabited primarily by Germans but were ruled by the king of Denmark, although Holstein was a member of the German Confederation. When Frederick VII, the new nationalistic king of Denmark, tried to integrate both provinces into the rest of his state, the Germans there revolted.

Hypnotized by this conflict, the National Assembly at Frankfurt debated ponderously and fi- nally called on the Prussian army to oppose Denmark in the name of the German nation. Prussia responded and began war with Denmark. As the Schleswig-Holstein issue demonstrated, the national ideal was a crucial factor motivating the German middle classes in 1848.

Almost obsessed with the fate of Germans under Danish rule, many members of the National Assembly also wanted to bring the German-speaking provinces of Austria into the new German state.

Revolutionary Justice in Vienna   As part of the conservative resurgence, in October 1848 the Austrian minister of war ordered up reinforcements for an army marching on Hungary. In a last defiant gesture the outraged revolutionaries in Vienna seized the minister and lynched him from a lamppost for treason. The army then reconquered the city in a week of bitter fighting. *(Source: Mary Evans Picture Library/Photo Researchers)*

Yet resurgent Austria resolutely opposed any division of its territory. Once this Austrian action made a "big German state" impossible, the National Assembly completed its drafting of a liberal constitution. Finally, in March 1849, the Assembly elected King Frederick William of Prussia emperor of the new German national state (minus Austria and Schleswig-Holstein).

By early 1849, however, reaction had been successful almost everywhere. Frederick William reasserted his royal authority, disbanded the Prussian Constituent Assembly, and granted his subjects a limited, essentially conservative, constitution. Reasserting that he ruled by divine right, Frederick William contemptuously refused to accept the "crown from the gutter." The reluctant revolutionaries in Frankfurt had waited too long and acted too timidly.

When Frederick William, who really wanted to be emperor but only on his own authoritarian terms, tried to get the small monarchs of Germany to elect him emperor, Austria balked. Supported by Russia, Austria forced Prussia to renounce all its schemes of unification in late 1850. The German Confederation was re-established. After two turbulent years, the political map of the German states remained unchanged. Attempts to unite the Germans—first in a liberal national state and then in a conservative Prussian empire—had failed completely.

SUMMARY

In 1814 the victorious allied powers sought to restore peace and stability in Europe. Dealing moderately with France and wisely settling their own differences, the allies laid the foundations for beneficial international cooperation throughout much of the nineteenth century. Led by Metternich, the conservative powers also sought to prevent the spread of subversive ideas and radical changes in domestic politics. Yet European thought has seldom been more powerfully creative than after 1815, and ideologies of liberalism, nationalism, and socialism all developed to challenge the existing order. The romantic movement, breaking decisively with the dictates of classicism, reinforced the spirit of change and revolutionary anticipation.

All of these forces culminated in the liberal and nationalistic revolutions of 1848. Political, economic, and social pressures that had been building since 1815 exploded dramatically, but the upheavals of 1848 were abortive and very few revolutionary goals were realized. The moderate, nationalistic middle classes were unable to consolidate their initial victories in France or elsewhere in Europe. Instead, they drew back when artisans, factory workers, and radical socialists rose up to present their own much more revolutionary demands. This retreat facilitated the efforts of dedicated aristocrats in central Europe and made possible the crushing of Parisian workers by a coalition of solid bourgeoisie and landowning peasantry in France. A host of fears, a sea of blood, and a torrent of disillusion had drowned the lofty ideals and utopian visions of a generation. The age of romantic revolution was over.

NOTES

1. Quoted in A. J. May, *The Age of Metternich, 1814–1848*, rev. ed. (New York: Holt, Rinehart & Winston, 1963), p. 11.
2. Quoted in H. Kohn, *Nationalism* (New York: Van Nostrand, 1955), pp. 141–142.
3. Quoted in F. D. Klingender, *Art and the Industrial Revolution* (St. Albans, England: Paladin, 1972), p. 117.
4. Quoted in F. B. Artz, *From the Renaissance to Romanticism: Trends in Style in Art, Literature, and Music, 1300–1830* (Chicago: University of Chicago Press, 1962), pp. 276, 278.
5. Quoted in G. Wright, *France in Modern Times* (Chicago: Rand McNally, 1960), p. 145.
6. A. de Tocqueville, *Recollections* (New York: Columbia University Press, 1949), p. 94.
7. M. Agulhon, *1848* (Paris: Éditions du Seuil, 1973), pp. 68–69.
8. Quoted in W. L. Langer, *Political and Social Upheaval, 1832–1852* (New York: Harper & Row, 1969), p. 361.

SUGGESTED READING

All of the works cited in the Notes are highly recommended. May's book is a good brief survey, and Kohn has written perceptively on nationalism in many books. Wright's *France in Modern Times* is a lively introduction to French history with stimulating biographical discussions; Langer's work is a balanced synthesis with an excellent bibliography. Among general studies, C. Moraze, *The Triumph of the Middle Classes* (1968), a wide-ranging procapitalist interpretation, may be compared with E. J. Hobsbawm's flexible *Marxism in the Age of Revolution, 1789–1848* (1962). For English history, A. Briggs, socially oriented *The Making of Modern England, 1784–1867* (1967), and D. Thomson, *England in the Nineteenth Century, 1815–1914* (1951), are excellent. Restoration France is sympathetically portrayed by G. de Bertier de Sauvigny in *The Bourbon Restoration* (1967), and R. Price, *A Social History of Nineteenth-Century France* (1987), is a fine synthesis incorporating recent research. T. Hamerow studies the social implications of the dual revolution in *Germany in Restoration, Revolution, Reaction 1815–1871* (1966), which may be compared with H. Treitschke's bombastic, pro-Prussian *History of Germany in the Nineteenth Century* (1915–1919), a classic of nationalistic history, and L. Snyder, *Roots of German Nationalism* (1978). H. James, *A German Identity, 1770–1990* (1989), and J. Sheehan, *Germany, 1770–1866* (1989), are stimulating general histories that skillfully incorporate recent research. E. Kedourie, *Nationalism* (1960), is a stimulating critique of the new faith. H. Kissinger, *A World Restored* (1957), offers not only a provocative interpretation of the Congress of Vienna but also insights into the mind of Richard Nixon's famous secretary of state. Compare that volume with H. Nicolson's entertaining *The Congress of Vienna* (1946). On 1848, L. B. Namier's highly critical *1848: The Revolution of the Intellectuals* (1964) and P. Robertson's *Revolutions of 1848: A Social History* (1960) are outstanding. I. Deak, *The Lawful Revolution: Louis Kossuth and the Hungarians, 1848–49* (1979), is a noteworthy study of an interesting figure.

On early socialism and Marxism, there are A. Lindemann's stimulating survey, *A History of European Socialism* (1983), and W. Sewell Jr.'s *Work and Revolution in France: The Language of Labor from the Old Regime to 1848* (1980), as well as G. Lichtheim's high-powered *Marxism* (1961) and his *Short History of Socialism* (1970). Fourier is treated sympathetically in J. Beecher, *Charles Fourier* (1986). J. Schumpeter, *Capitalism, Socialism and Democracy* (1947), is magnificent but difficult, a real mind-stretcher. Also highly recommended is B. Taylor, *Eve and the New Jerusalem: Socialism and Feminism in the Nineteenth Century* (1983), which explores fascinating English attempts to emancipate workers and women at the same time. On liberalism, there are R. Heilbroner's entertaining *The Worldly Philosophers* (1967) and G. de Ruggiero's classic *History of European Liberalism* (1959). J. Barzun, *Classic, Romantic and Modern* (1961), skillfully discusses the emergence of romanticism. R. Stromberg, *An Intellectual History of Modern Europe,* 3d ed. (1981), and F. Baumer, *Modern European Thought: Continuity and Change in Ideas, 1600–1950* (1970), are valuable surveys. The important place of religion in nineteenth-century thought is considered from different perspectives in H. McLeod, *Religion and the People of Western Europe* (1981), and O. Chadwick, *The Secularization of the European Mind in the Nineteenth Century* (1976). Two good church histories with useful bibliographies are J. Altholz, *The Churches in the Nineteenth Century* (1967), and A. Vidler, *The Church in an Age of Revolution: 1789 to the Present Day* (1961).

The thoughtful reader is strongly advised to delve into the incredibly rich writing of contemporaries. J. Bowditch and C. Ramsland, eds., *Voices of the Industrial Revolution* (1961), is an excellent starting point, with well-chosen selections from leading economic thinkers and early socialists. H. Hugo, ed., *The Romantic Reader,* is another fine anthology. Mary Shelley's *Frankenstein,* a great romantic novel, draws an almost lovable picture of the famous monster and is highly recommended. Jules Michelet's compassionate masterpiece *The People,* a famous historian's anguished examination of French social divisions on the eve of 1848, draws one into the heart of the period and is highly recommended. Alexis de Tocqueville covers some of the same ground less romantically in his *Recollections,* which may be compared with Karl Marx's white-hot "instant history," *Class Struggles in France, 1848–1850* (1850). Great novels that accurately portray aspects of the times are Victor Hugo, *Les Misérables,* an exciting story of crime and passion among France's poor; Honoré de Balzac, *La Cousine Bette* and *Le Père Goriot;* and Thomas Mann, *Buddenbrooks,* a wonderful historical novel that traces the rise and fall of a prosperous German family over three generations during the nineteenth century.

28

Life in European Urban Society

Nineteenth-century London. John O'Connor, *St. Pancras Hotel and Station from Pentonville Road*

The era of intellectual and political upheaval that culminated in the revolutions of 1848 was also an era of rapid urbanization. After 1848, Western political development veered off in a novel and uncharted direction, but the growth of towns and cities rushed forward with undiminished force. Thus Western society was urban and industrial in 1900, as surely as it had been rural and agrarian in 1800. The urbanization of society was both a result of the Industrial Revolution and a reflection of its enormous long-term impact.

- What was life like in the cities, and how did it change?
- What did the emergence of urban industrial society mean for rich and poor and those in between?
- How did families cope with the challenges and respond to the opportunities of the developing urban civilization?
- What changes in science and thought inspired and gave expression to this new urban society?

These questions are investigated in this chapter.

TAMING THE CITY

The growth of industry posed enormous challenges for all elements of Western society, from young factory workers confronting relentless discipline to aristocratic elites maneuvering to retain political power. As we saw in Chapter 26, the early consequences of economic transformation were mixed and far-reaching and by no means wholly negative. By 1850 at the latest, working conditions were improving and real wages were definitely rising for the mass of the population, and they continued to do so until 1914. Thus, given the poverty and uncertainty of preindustrial life, some historians maintain that the history of industrialization in the nineteenth century is probably better written in terms of increasing opportunities than of greater hardships.

Critics of this relatively optimistic view of industrialization claim that it neglects the quality of life in urban areas. They stress that the new industrial towns and cities were awful places, where people,

especially poor people, suffered from bad housing, lack of sanitation, and a sense of hopelessness. They ask if these drawbacks did not more than cancel out higher wages and greater opportunity. An examination of urban development provides some answers to this complex question.

Industry and the Growth of Cities

Since the Middle Ages, European cities had been centers of government, culture, and large-scale commerce. They had also been congested, dirty, and unhealthy. People were packed together almost as tightly as possible within the city limits. The typical city was a "walking city": for all but the wealthiest classes, walking was the only available form of transportation.

Infectious disease spread with deadly speed in cities, and people were always more likely to die in the city than in the countryside. In the larger towns, more people died each year than were born, on the average, and urban populations were able to maintain their numbers only because newcomers were continuously arriving from rural areas. Little could be done to improve these conditions. Given the pervasive poverty, absence of urban transportation, and lack of medical knowledge, the deadly and overcrowded conditions could only be accepted fatalistically. They were the urban equivalents of bad weather and poor crops, the price of urban excitement and opportunity.

Clearly, deplorable urban conditions did not originate with the Industrial Revolution. What the Industrial Revolution did was to reveal those conditions more nakedly than ever before. The steam engine freed industrialists from dependence on the energy of fast-flowing streams and rivers, so that by 1800 there was every incentive to build new factories in urban areas. Cities had better shipping facilities than the countryside and thus better supplies of coal and raw materials. There were also many hands wanting work in the cities, for cities drew people like a magnet. And it was a great advantage for a manufacturer to have other factories nearby to supply the business's needs and buy its products. Therefore, as industry grew, there was also a rapid expansion of already overcrowded and unhealthy cities.

The challenge of the urban environment was felt first and most acutely in Great Britain. The number of people living in cities of 20,000 or more in

MAP 28.1 European Cities of 100,000 or More, 1800 and 1900 There were more large cities in Great Britain in 1900 than in all of Europe in 1800.

England and Wales jumped from 1.5 million in 1801 to 6.3 million in 1851 and reached 15.6 million by 1891. Such cities accounted for 17 percent of the total English population in 1801, for 35 percent as early as 1851, and for fully 54 percent in 1891. Other countries duplicated the English pattern as they industrialized. An American observer was hardly exaggerating when he wrote in 1899 that "the most remarkable social phenomenon of the present century is the concentration of population in cities" (Map 28.1).[1]

In the 1820s and 1830s, people in Britain and France began to worry about the condition of their cities. In those years, the populations of a number of British cities were increasing by 40 to 70 percent each decade. With urban areas expanding at such previously undreamed-of rates, people's fatalistic acceptance of overcrowded, unsanitary urban living conditions began to give way to active concern. Something had to be done.

On one point everyone could agree: except on the outskirts, each town and city was using every scrap of land to the fullest extent. Parks and open areas were almost nonexistent. A British parliamentary committee reported in 1833 that "with a rapidly increasing population, lodged for the most part in narrow courts and confined streets, the means of occasional exercise and recreation in fresh air are every day lessened, as inclosures [of

vacant areas] take place and buildings spread themselves on every side."[2] Buildings were erected on the smallest possible lots in order to pack the maximum number of people into a given space. Narrow houses were built wall to wall, in long rows. These row houses had neither front nor back yards, and only a narrow alley in back separated one row from the next. Or buildings were built around tiny courtyards completely enclosed on all four sides. Many people lived in cellars and attics. These tiny rooms were often overcrowded. "Six, eight, and even ten occupying one room is anything but uncommon," wrote a doctor from Aberdeen in Scotland for a government investigation in 1842.

These highly concentrated urban populations lived in extremely unsanitary and unhealthy conditions. Open drains and sewers flowed alongside or down the middle of unpaved streets. Because of poor construction and an absence of running water, the sewers often filled with garbage and excrement. Toilet facilities were primitive in the extreme. In parts of Manchester, as many as two hundred people shared a single outhouse. Such privies filled up rapidly, and since they were infrequently emptied, sewage often overflowed and seeped into cellar dwellings.

The extent to which filth lay underfoot and the smell of excrement filled the air is hard to believe,

A COURT FOR KING CHOLERA.

Filth and Disease This 1852 drawing from *Punch* tells volumes about the unhealthy living conditions of the urban poor. In the foreground children play with a dead rat and a woman scavenges a dungheap. Cheap rooming houses provide shelter for the frightfully overcrowded population. *(Source: The British Library)*

yet it was abundantly documented between 1830 and 1850. One London construction engineer found, for example, that the cellars of two large houses on a major road were "full of night-soil [human excrement], to the depth of three feet, which had been permitted for years to accumulate from the overflow of the cesspools." Moreover, some courtyards in poorer neighborhoods became dunghills, collecting excrement that was sometimes sold as fertilizer. In the provocative words of a leading historian, by the 1840s there was among the better-off classes a growing, shocking "realization that, to put it as mildly as possible, millions of English men, women, and children were living in shit."[3]

Who or what was responsible for these awful conditions? The crucial factors were the tremendous pressure of more people and the total ab-

sence of public transportation. People simply had to jam themselves together if they were to be able to walk to shops and factories. Another factor was that government in Great Britain, both local and national, was slow to provide sanitary facilities and establish adequate building codes. This slow pace was probably attributable more to a need to explore and identify what precisely should be done than to rigid middle-class opposition to government action. Certainly Great Britain had no monopoly on overcrowded and unhealthy urban conditions; many continental cities were as bad.

Most responsible of all was the sad legacy of rural housing conditions in preindustrial society, combined with appalling ignorance. As the author of a major study concludes, there "were rural slums of a horror not surpassed by the rookeries of London. . . . The evidence shows that the decent cottage was the exception, the hovel the rule."[4] Thus housing was far down on the newcomer's list of priorities, and it is not surprising that many people carried the filth of the mud floor and the dung of the barnyard with them to the city.

Indeed, ordinary people generally took dirt and filth for granted, and some even prized it. One English miner told an investigator, "I do not think it usual for the lasses [in the coal mines] to wash their bodies; my sisters never wash themselves." As for the men, "their legs and bodies are as black as your hat." When poor people were admitted to English workhouses, they often resisted the required bath. One man protested that it was "equal to robbing him of a great coat which he had had for some years."[5]

The Public Health Movement

Although cleanliness was not next to godliness in most people's eyes, it was becoming so for some reformers. The most famous of these was Edwin Chadwick, one of the commissioners charged with the administration of relief to paupers under the revised Poor Law of 1834. Chadwick was a follower of the radical philosopher Jeremy Bentham (1748–1832). Bentham had taught that public problems ought to be dealt with on a rational, scientific basis and according to the "greatest good for the greatest number." Applying these principles, Chadwick soon saw that much more than economics was involved in the problems of poverty and the welfare budget. Indeed, he soon became convinced that disease and death actually caused poverty, simply because a sick worker was an unemployed worker and orphaned children were poor children. Most important, Chadwick believed that disease could be prevented by quite literally cleaning up the urban environment. That was his "sanitary idea."

Building on a growing number of medical and sociological studies, Chadwick collected detailed reports from local Poor Law officials on the "sanitary conditions of the laboring population." After three years of investigation, these reports and Chadwick's hard-hitting commentary were published in 1842 to wide publicity. This mass of evidence proved that disease was related to filthy environmental conditions, which were in turn caused largely by lack of drainage, sewers, and garbage collection. Putrefying, smelly excrement was no longer simply disgusting. For reformers like Chadwick, it was a threat to the entire community. It polluted the atmosphere and caused disease.

The key to the energetic action that Chadwick proposed was an adequate supply of clean piped water. Such water was essential for personal hygiene, public bathhouses, street cleaning, firefighting, and industry. Chadwick correctly believed that the stinking excrement of communal outhouses could be carried off by water through sewers at less than one-twentieth the cost of removing it by hand. The cheap iron pipes and tile drains of the industrial age would provide running water and sewerage for all sections of town, not just the wealthy ones. In 1848, with the cause strengthened by the cholera epidemic of 1846, Chadwick's report became the basis of Great Britain's first public health law, which created a national health board and gave cities broad authority to build modern sanitary systems.

The public health movement won dedicated supporters in the United States, France, and Germany from the 1840s on. As in Great Britain, governments accepted at least limited responsibility for the health of all citizens. Moreover, they adopted increasingly concrete programs of action, programs that broke decisively with the age-old fatalism of urban populations in the face of shockingly high mortality. Thus, despite many people's skepticism about sanitation, European cities were making real progress toward adequate water supplies and sewage systems by the 1860s and 1870s. And city dwellers were beginning to reap the reward of better health.

The Bacterial Revolution

Effective control of communicable disease required a great leap forward in medical knowledge and biological theory as well as a clean water supply and good sewers. Reformers like Chadwick were seriously handicapped by the prevailing *miasmatic theory* of disease—the belief that people contract disease when they breathe the bad odors of decay and putrefying excrement; in short, the theory that smells cause disease. The miasmatic theory was a reasonable deduction from empirical observations: cleaning up filth did produce laudable results. Yet the theory was very incomplete.

Keen observation by doctors and public health officials in the 1840s and 1850s pinpointed the role of bad drinking water in the transmission of disease and suggested that contagion was spread through filth and not caused by it. Moreover, some particularly horrid stenches, such as that of the sewage-glutted Thames River at London in 1858, did not lead to widely feared epidemics, and this fact also weakened the miasmatic idea.

The breakthrough was the development of the *germ theory* of disease by Louis Pasteur (1822–1895), a French chemist who began studying fermentation in 1854. For ages people had used fermentation to make bread and wine, beer and cheese, but without really understanding what was going on. And from time to time, beer and wine would mysteriously spoil for no apparent reason. Responding to the calls of big brewers for help, Pasteur used his microscope to develop a simple test that brewers could use to monitor the fermentation process and avoid spoilage. Continuing his investigations, Pasteur found that fermentation depended on the growth of living organisms and that the activity of these organisms could be sup-

pressed by heating the beverage—by pasteurizing it. The breathtaking implication was that specific diseases were caused by specific living organisms—germs—and that those organisms could be controlled in people as well as in beer, wine, and milk.

By 1870 the work of Pasteur and others had demonstrated the general connection between germs and disease. When, in the middle of the 1870s, the German country doctor Robert Koch and his coworkers developed pure cultures of harmful bacteria and described their life cycles, the dam broke. Over the next twenty years, researchers—mainly Germans—identified the organisms responsible for disease after disease, often identifying several in a single year. These discoveries led to the development of a number of effective vaccines and the emergence of modern immunology.

Acceptance of the germ theory brought about dramatic improvements in the deadly environment of hospitals and surgery. The English surgeon Joseph Lister (1827–1912) had noticed that patients with simple fractures were much less likely to die than those with compound fractures, in which the skin was broken and internal tissues were exposed to the air. In 1865, when Pasteur showed that the air was full of bacteria, Lister immediately grasped the connection between aerial bacteria and the problem of wound infection. He reasoned that a chemical disinfectant applied to a wound dressing would "destroy the life of the floating particles." Lister's "antiseptic principle" worked wonders. In the 1880s, German surgeons developed the more sophisticated practice of sterilizing not only the wound but everything—hands, instruments, clothing—that entered the operating room.

The achievements of the bacterial revolution coupled with the ever-more-sophisticated public health movement saved millions of lives, particularly after about 1890. As the awful death sentences of the past—diphtheria, typhoid and typhus, cholera, yellow fever—became vanishing diseases, mortality rates began to decline dramatically in European countries (Figure 28.1). City dwellers benefited especially from these developments. By 1910 the death rates for people of all ages in urban areas were generally no greater than in rural areas, and sometimes they were less. Particularly striking was the decline in infant mortality in the cities after 1890. By 1910, in many countries, an urban mother was less likely than a

FIGURE 28.1 The Decline of Death Rates in England and Wales, Germany, France, and Sweden, 1840–1913 A rising standard of living, improvements in public health, and better medical knowledge all contributed to the dramatic decline of death rates in the nineteenth century.

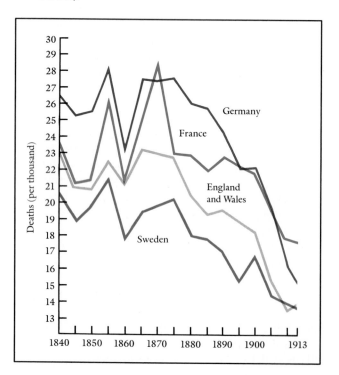

rural mother to see her child die before its first birthday. A great silent revolution had occurred: the terrible ferocity of death from disease-carrying bacteria in the cities had almost been tamed.

Urban Planning and Public Transportation

Public health was only part of the urban challenge. Overcrowding, bad housing, and lack of transportation could not be solved by sewers and better medicine; yet in these areas, too, important transformations significantly improved the quality of urban life after midcentury.

More effective urban planning was one of the keys to improvement. Urban planning was in decline by the early nineteenth century, but after 1850 its practice was revived and extended. France took the lead during the rule of Napoleon III (r. 1848–1870), who sought to stand above class conflict and promote the welfare of all his subjects through government action (see pages 930–933). He believed that rebuilding much of Paris would provide employment, improve living conditions, and testify to the power and glory of his empire. In the baron Georges Haussmann, an aggressive, impatient Alsatian whom he placed in charge of Paris, Napoleon III found an authoritarian planner capable of bulldozing both buildings and opposition. In twenty years Paris was quite literally transformed (Map 28.2).

The Paris of 1850 was a labyrinth of narrow, dark streets, the results of desperate overcrowding. In a central city not twice the size of New York's Central Park lived more than one-third of the city's one million inhabitants. Terrible slum conditions and extremely high death rates were facts of life. There were few open spaces and only two public parks for the entire metropolis. Public transportation played a very small role in this enormous walking city.

Haussmann and his fellow planners proceeded on many interrelated fronts. With a bold energy that often shocked their contemporaries, they razed old buildings in order to cut broad, straight, tree-lined boulevards through the center of the city as well as in new quarters on the outskirts. These boulevards, designed in part to prevent the easy construction and defense of barricades by revolutionary crowds, permitted traffic to flow freely. Their creation also demolished some of the worst slums. New streets stimulated the construction of

better housing, especially for the middle classes. Small neighborhood parks and open spaces were created throughout the city, and two very large parks suitable for all kinds of holiday activities were developed on either side of the city. The city also improved its sewers, and a system of aqueducts more than doubled the city's supply of good fresh water.

Haussmann and Napoleon III tried to make Paris a more beautiful city, and to a large extent they succeeded. The broad, straight boulevards, such as those radiating out like the spokes of a wheel from the Arch of Triumph and those centering on the new Opera House, afforded impressive vistas. If for most people Paris remains one of the world's most beautiful and enchanting cities, it is in part because of the transformations of Napoleon III's Second Empire.

Rebuilding Paris provided a new model for urban planning and stimulated modern urbanism throughout Europe, particularly after 1870. In city after city, public authorities mounted a coordinated attack on many of the interrelated problems of the urban environment. As in Paris, improvements in public health through better water supplies and waste disposal often went hand in hand with new boulevard construction. Cities like Vienna and Cologne followed the Parisian example of tearing down old walled fortifications and replacing them with broad, circular boulevards on which office buildings, town halls, theaters, opera houses, and museums were erected. These ring roads and the new boulevards that radiated out from them toward the outskirts eased movement and encouraged urban expansion (see Map 28.2).

The development of mass public transportation was also of great importance in the improvement of urban living conditions. Such transportation came late but in a powerful rush. In the 1870s, many European cities authorized private companies to operate horse-drawn streetcars, which had been developed in the United States, to carry riders along the growing number of major thoroughfares. Then, in the 1890s, occurred the real revolution: European countries adopted another American transit innovation, the electric streetcar.

Electric streetcars were cheaper, faster, more dependable, and more comfortable than their horse-drawn counterparts. Service improved dramatically. Millions of Europeans—workers, shoppers, schoolchildren—hopped on board during the workweek. And on weekends and holidays,

Apartment Living in Paris This drawing shows how different social classes lived close together in European cities about 1850. Passing the middle-class family on the first (American second) floor, the economic condition of the tenants declined until one reached abject poverty in the garret. *(Source: Bibliothèque Nationale, Paris)*

MAP 28.2 The Modernization of Paris, ca 1850–1870 Broad boulevards, large parks, and grandiose train stations transformed Paris. The cutting of the new north-south axis—known as the Boulevard Saint-Michel—was one of Haussmann's most controversial projects. It razed much of Paris's medieval core and filled the Île de la Cité with massive government buildings.

streetcars carried millions on happy outings to parks and countryside, racetracks and music halls. In 1886 the horse-drawn streetcars of Austria-Hungary, France, Germany, and Great Britain were carrying about 900 million riders. By 1910 electric streetcar systems in those four countries were carrying 6.7 billion riders. Each man, woman, and child was using public transportation four times as often in 1910 as in 1886.[6]

Good mass transit helped greatly in the struggle for decent housing. The new boulevards and horse-drawn streetcars had facilitated a middle-class move to better housing in the 1860s and 1870s; similarly, after 1890, electric streetcars gave people of modest means access to new, improved housing. The still-crowded city was able to expand and become less congested. In England in 1901, only 9 percent of the urban population was "overcrowded" in terms of the official definition of more than two persons per room. On the Continent, many city governments in the early twentieth century were building electric streetcar systems that provided transportation for the working classes to new public and private housing developments in outlying areas of the city. Poor, overcrowded housing, long one of the blackest blots on the urban landscape, was in retreat—another example of the gradual taming of the urban environment.

RICH AND POOR AND IN BETWEEN

General improvements in health and in the urban environment had beneficial consequences for all kinds of people. Yet differences in living conditions between social classes remained gigantic.

Social Structure

How much had the almost-completed journey to an urban, industrialized world changed the social framework of rich and poor? The first great change was a substantial and undeniable increase in the standard of living for the average person. The real wages of British workers, for example, which had already risen by 1850, almost doubled between 1850 and 1906. Similar unmistakable increases occurred in continental countries as industrial development quickened after 1850. Ordinary people took a major step forward in the centuries-old battle against poverty, reinforcing efforts to improve many aspects of human existence.

There is another side to the income coin, however, and it must be stressed as well. Greater economic rewards for the average person did not eliminate poverty, nor did they make the wealth and income of the rich and the poor significantly more nearly equal. In almost every advanced country around 1900, the richest 5 percent of all households in the population received one-third of all national income. The richest one-fifth of households received anywhere from 50 to 60 percent of all national income, and the entire bottom four-fifths received only 40 to 50 percent. Moreover, the bottom 30 percent of households received 10 percent or less of all income. These

enormous differences are illustrated in Figure 28.2.

The middle classes, smaller than they are today, accounted for less than 20 percent of the population; thus the statistics show that the upper and middle classes alone received more than one-half of all income. The poorest four-fifths—the working classes, including peasants and agricultural laborers—received less altogether than the two richest classes. And since many wives and teenagers in poor families worked for wages, these figures actually understate the enduring gap between rich and poor. Moreover, income taxes on the wealthy were light or nonexistent. Thus the gap between rich and poor remained enormous at the beginning of the twentieth century. It was probably almost as great as it had been in the age of agriculture and aristocracy, before the Industrial Revolution.

The great gap between rich and poor endured, in part, because industrial and urban development made society more diverse and less unified. By no means did society split into two sharply defined opposing classes, as Marx had predicted. Instead, economic specialization enabled society to produce more effectively and in the process created more new social groups than it destroyed. There developed an almost unlimited range of jobs, skills, and earnings; one group or subclass shaded off into another in a complex, confusing hierarchy. Thus the tiny elite of the very rich and the sizable mass of the dreadfully poor were separated from each other by many subclasses, each filled with individuals struggling to rise or at least to hold their own in the social order. In this atmosphere of competition and hierarchy, neither the middle classes nor the working classes acted as a unified force. The age-old pattern of great economic inequality remained firmly intact.

The Middle Classes

By the beginning of the twentieth century, the diversity and range within the urban middle class were striking. Indeed, it is more meaningful to think of a confederation of middle classes, loosely united by occupations requiring mental rather than physical skill. At the top stood the *upper middle class,* composed mainly of the most successful business families from banking, industry, and large-scale commerce. These families were the prime beneficiaries of modern industry and scientific progress. As people in the upper middle class gained in income and progressively lost all traces of radicalism after the trauma of 1848, they were strongly drawn toward the aristocratic lifestyle.

As the aristocracy had long divided the year between palatial country estates and lavish townhouses during "the season," so the upper middle class purchased country places or built beach houses for weekend and summer use. (Little wonder that a favorite scenario in late-nineteenth-century middle-class novels was a mother and children summering gloriously in the country home, with only sporadic weekend intrusions by a distant, shadowy father.) The number of servants was an important indicator of wealth and standing for the middle class, as it had always been for the aristocracy. Private coaches and carriages, ever an expensive item in the city, were also signs of rising social status. More generally, the rich businessman and certainly his son devoted less time to business and more to "culture" and easy living than was the case in less wealthy or well-established commercial families.

The topmost reaches of the upper middle class tended to shade off into the old aristocracy to form a new upper class. This was the 5 percent of the population that received roughly one-third of the national income in European countries before 1914. Much of the aristocracy welcomed this development. Having experienced a sharp decline in its relative income in the course of industrialization, the landed aristocracy had met big business coming up the staircase and was often delighted to trade titles, country homes, and snobbish elegance for good hard cash. Some of the best bargains were made through marriages to American heiresses. Correspondingly, wealthy aristocrats tended increasingly to exploit their agricultural and mineral resources as if they were business people. Bismarck was not the only proud nobleman to make a fortune distilling brandy on his estates.

Below the wealthy upper middle class were much larger, much less wealthy, and increasingly diversified middle-class groups. Here one found the moderately successful industrialists and merchants, as well as professionals in law and medicine. This was the *middle middle class,* solid and quite comfortable but lacking great wealth. Below them were independent shopkeepers, small traders, and tiny manufacturers—the *lower middle class.* Both of these traditional segments of the

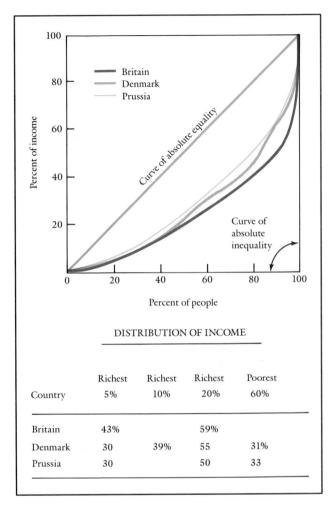

Country	Richest 5%	Richest 10%	Richest 20%	Poorest 60%
Britain	43%		59%	
Denmark	30	39%	55	31%
Prussia	30		50	33

DISTRIBUTION OF INCOME

FIGURE 28.2 The Distribution of Income in Britain, Denmark, and Prussia in 1913   The so-called Lorenz curve is useful for showing the degree of economic inequality in a given society. The closer the actual distribution of income lies to the (theoretical) curve of absolute equality, where each 20 percent of the population receives 20 percent of all income, the more nearly equal are incomes. European society was very far from any such equality before the First World War. Notice that incomes in Prussia were somewhat more equal than those in Britain. (*Source: Based on information from S. Kuznets,* Modern Economic Growth, Yale University Press, New Haven, 1966, pp. 208–209. Copyright © 1966 by Yale University Press. Used with permission.)

middle class expanded modestly in size with economic development.

Meanwhile, the traditional middle class was gaining two particularly important additions. The expansion of industry and technology created a growing demand for experts with specialized knowledge. The most valuable of the specialties became solid middle-class professions. Engineering, for example, emerged from the world of skilled labor as a full-fledged profession of great importance, considerable prestige, and many branches. Architects, chemists, accountants, and surveyors—to name only a few—first achieved professional standing in this period. They established criteria for advanced training and certification and banded together in organizations to promote and defend their interests.

Management of large public and private institutions also emerged as a kind of profession, as governments provided more services and as very large corporations like railroads came into being. Government officials and many private executives were not capitalists in the sense that they owned business enterprises. But public and private managers did have specialized knowledge and the capacity to earn a good living. And they shared most of the values of the business-owning entrepreneurs and the older professionals.

Industrialization also expanded and diversified the lower middle class. The number of independent, property-owning shopkeepers and small business people grew and so did the number of white-collar employees—a mixed group of traveling salesmen, bookkeepers, store managers, and clerks who staffed the offices and branch stores of large corporations. White-collar employees were propertyless and often earned no more than the better-paid skilled or semiskilled workers did. Yet white-collar workers were fiercely committed to the middle class and to the ideal of moving up in society. In the Balkans, for example, clerks let their fingernails grow very long to distinguish themselves from people who worked with their hands. The tie, the suit, and soft clean hands were no-less-subtle marks of class distinction than wages.

Relatively well educated but without complex technical skills, many white-collar groups aimed at achieving professional standing and the accompanying middle-class status. Elementary school teachers largely succeeded in this effort. From being miserably paid part-time workers in the early nineteenth century, teachers rode the wave of mass education to respectable middle-class status and income. Nurses also rose from the lower ranks of unskilled labor to precarious middle-class standing. Dentistry was taken out of the hands of the working-class barbers and placed in the hands of highly trained (and middle-class) professionals.

In spite of their growing occupational diversity and conflicting interests, the middle classes were loosely united by a certain style of life. Food was the largest item in the household budget, for middle-class people liked to eat very well. In France and Italy, the middle classes' love of good eating meant that, even in large cities, activity ground almost to a halt between half past twelve and half past two on weekdays, as husbands and schoolchildren returned home for the midday meal. Around eight in the evening, the serious business of eating was taken up once again.

The English were equally attached to substantial meals, which they ate three times a day if income allowed. The typical English breakfast of bacon and eggs, toast and marmalade, and stewed fruits—not to mention sardines, kidneys, or fresh fish—always astonished French and German travelers, though large-breakfast enthusiasts like the Dutch and Scandinavians were less awed. The European middle classes consumed meat in abundance, and a well-off family might spend 10 percent of its substantial earnings on meat alone. In the 1890s, even a very prosperous English family—with an income of, say, $10,000 a year (the average working-class family earned perhaps $400 a year)—spent fully a quarter of its income on food and drink.

Spending on food was also great because the dinner party was the favored social occasion of the middle classes. A wealthy family might give a lavish party for eight to twelve almost every week; more modest households would settle for once a month. Throughout middle-class Europe, such dinners were served in the "French manner" (which the French had borrowed from the Russian aristocracy): eight or nine separate courses, from appetizers at the beginning to coffee and liqueurs at the end. In summer, a picnic was in order. But what a picnic! For a party of ten, one English cookbook suggested 5 pounds of cold salmon, a quarter of lamb, 8 pounds of pickled brisket, a beef tongue, a chicken pie, salads, cakes, and 6 pounds of strawberries. An ordinary family meal normally consisted of only four courses—soup, fish, meat, and dessert.

A middle-class wife could cope with this endless procession of meals, courses, and dishes because she had both servants and money at her disposal. The middle classes were solid members of what some contemporary observers called the "servant-keeping classes." Indeed, the employment of

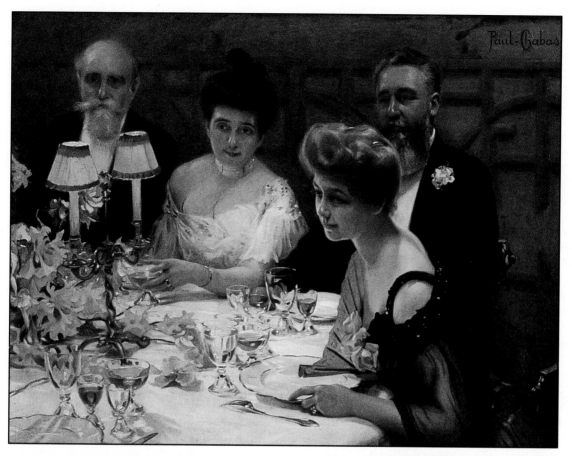

"A Corner of the Table"   With photographic precision this 1904 oil painting by French academic artist Paul-Émile Chabas (1867–1937) skillfully idealizes the elegance and intimacy of a sumptuous dinner party. *(Source: Bibliothèque des Arts Decoratifs/Jean-Loup Charmet)*

at least one enormously helpful full-time maid to cook and clean was the best single sign that a family had crossed the vague line separating the working classes from the middle classes. The greater its income, the greater was the number of servants a family employed. The all-purpose servant gave way to a cook and a maid, then to a cook, a maid, and a boy, and so on. A prosperous English family, far up the line with $10,000 a year, in 1900 spent fully one-fourth of its income on a hierarchy of ten servants: a manservant, a cook, a kitchen maid, two housemaids, a serving maid, a governess, a gardener, a coachman, and a stable boy. Domestic servants were the second largest item in the budget of the middle classes. Food and servants together absorbed about one-half of income at all levels of the middle classes.

Well fed and well served, the middle classes were also well housed by 1900. Many quite prosperous families rented rather than owned their homes. Apartment living, complete with tiny rooms for servants under the eaves of the top floor, was commonplace (outside Great Britain), and wealthy investors and speculative builders found good profits in middle-class housing. By 1900 the middle classes were also quite clothes-conscious. The factory, the sewing machine, and the department store had all helped to reduce the cost and expand the variety of clothing. Middle-class women were particularly attentive to the fickle dictates of fashion.

Education was another growing expense, as middle-class parents tried to provide their children with ever-more-crucial advanced education. The keystones of culture and leisure were books, music, and travel. The long realistic novel, the heroics of Wagner and Verdi, the diligent striving of the dutiful daughter on a piano, and the packaged tour to a foreign country were all sources of middle-class pleasure.

Finally, the middle classes were loosely united by a shared code of expected behavior and morality. This code was strict and demanding. It laid great stress on hard work, self-discipline, and personal achievement. Men and women who fell into crime or poverty were generally assumed to be responsible for their own circumstances. Traditional Christian morality was reaffirmed by this code and preached tirelessly by middle-class people who took pride in their own good conduct and regular church attendance. Drinking and gambling were denounced as vices; sexual purity and fidelity were celebrated as virtues. In short, the middle-class person was supposed to know right from wrong and was expected to act accordingly.

The Working Classes

About four out of five people belonged to the working classes at the turn of the century. Many members of the *working classes*—that is, people whose livelihoods depended on physical labor and who did not employ domestic servants—were still small landowning peasants and hired farm hands. This was especially true in eastern Europe. In western and central Europe, however, the typical worker had left the land. In Great Britain, less than 8 percent of the people worked in agricul-

ture, and in rapidly industrializing Germany only one person in four was employed in agriculture and forestry. Even in less industrialized France, less than half of the people depended on the land in 1900.

The urban working classes were even less unified and homogeneous than the middle classes. In the first place, economic development and increased specialization expanded the traditional range of working-class skills, earnings, and experiences. Meanwhile, the old sharp distinction between highly skilled artisans and unskilled manual workers was gradually breaking down. To be sure, highly skilled printers and masons, as well as unskilled dock workers and common laborers, continued to exist. But between these extremes there were ever-more semiskilled groups, many of which were composed of factory workers and machine tenders (Figure 28.3).

In the second place, skilled, semiskilled, and unskilled workers had widely divergent lifestyles and cultural values, and their differences contributed to a keen sense of social status and hierarchy within the working classes. The result was great variety and limited class unity.

Highly skilled workers, who constituted about 15 percent of the working classes, were a real "labor aristocracy." By 1900 they were earning about £2 a week in Great Britain, or roughly $10 a week and $500 per year. This was only about two-thirds the income of the bottom ranks of the servant-keeping classes. But it was fully twice as much as the earnings of unskilled workers, who averaged about $5 per week, and substantially more than the earnings of semiskilled workers, who averaged perhaps $7 per week. Other European countries had a similar range of earnings.

The most "aristocratic" of the highly skilled workers were construction bosses and factory foremen, men who had risen from the ranks and were fiercely proud of their achievement. The labor aristocracy also included members of the traditional highly skilled handicraft trades that had not been mechanized or placed in factories. These included makers of scientific and musical instruments, cabinetmakers, potters, jewelers, bookbinders, engravers, and printers. This group as a whole was under constant long-term pressure. Irregularly but inexorably, factory methods were being extended to more crafts, and many skilled artisans were being replaced by lower-paid semiskilled factory workers. Traditional woodcarvers and watchmakers virtu-

FIGURE 28.3 The Urban Social Hierarchy

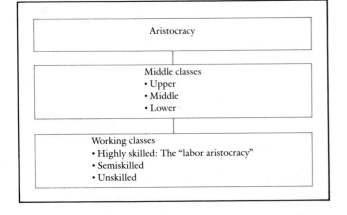

Aristocracy

Middle classes
• Upper
• Middle
• Lower

Working classes
• Highly skilled: The "labor aristocracy"
• Semiskilled
• Unskilled

Sweated Industry About 1900   This moving photograph shows an English family making cheap toys at home for low wages. Women and children were the backbone of sweated industry, and this husband may be filling in while unemployed. *(Source: University of Reading, Institute of Agricultural History and Museum of English Rural Life)*

ally disappeared, for example, as the making of furniture and timepieces was put into the factory.

At the same time, a contrary movement was occurring. The labor aristocracy was consistently being enlarged by the growing need for highly skilled workers, such as shipbuilders, machine-tool makers, railway locomotive engineers, fine cotton textile spinners, and some metalworkers. Thus the labor elite was in a state of flux as individuals and whole crafts moved in and out of it.

To maintain its precarious standing, the upper working class adopted distinctive values and strait-laced, almost puritanical, behavior. Like the middle classes, the labor aristocracy was strongly committed to the family and to economic improvement. Families in the upper working class saved money regularly, worried about their children's education, and valued good housing. Despite these similarities, which superficial observers were quick to exaggerate, skilled workers viewed themselves not as aspirants to the middle class but as the pacesetters and natural leaders of all the working classes. Well aware of the degradation not

so far below them, they practiced self-discipline and stern morality.

The upper working class in general frowned on heavy drinking and sexual permissiveness. The organized temperance movement was strong in the countries of northern Europe, such as Great Britain, where a generation advocated tea as the "cup that cheers but does not inebriate." As one German labor aristocrat somberly warned, "the path to the brothel leads through the tavern" and from there quite possibly to drastic decline or total ruin for person and family.[7]

Below the labor aristocracy stood *semiskilled* and *unskilled urban workers* (see Figure 28.3). The enormous complexity of this sector of the world of labor is not easily summarized. Workers in the established crafts—carpenters, bricklayers, pipefitters—stood near the top of the semiskilled hierarchy, often flirting with (or having backslid from) the labor elite. A large number of the semiskilled were factory workers, who earned highly variable but relatively good wages and whose relative importance in the labor force was increasing.

Below the semiskilled workers was the larger group of unskilled, who included day laborers such as longshoremen, wagon-driving teamsters, teenagers, and every kind of "helper." Many of these people had real skills and performed valuable services, but they were unorganized and divided, united only by the common fate of meager earnings. The same lack of unity characterized street vendors and market people—self-employed workers who competed savagely with each other and with the established shopkeepers of the lower middle class.

One of the largest components of the unskilled group was domestic servants, whose numbers grew steadily in the nineteenth century. In Great Britain, for example, in 1911 one out of every seven employed persons was a domestic servant. The great majority were women; indeed, one out of every three girls in Britain between the ages of fifteen and twenty was a domestic servant. Throughout Europe and America, a great many female domestics in the cities were recent migrants from rural areas. As in earlier times, domestic service was still hard work at low pay with limited personal independence.

Nonetheless, domestic service had real attractions for "rough country girls" with strong hands and few specialized skills. Marriage prospects were better, or at least more varied, in the city. And though wages were low, they were higher and more regular than in hard agricultural work. Finally, as one London observer noted, young girls and other migrants were drawn to the city by "the contagion of numbers, the sense of something going on, the theaters and the music halls, the brightly lighted streets and busy crowds—all, in short, that makes the difference between the Mile End fair on a Saturday night, and a dark and muddy country lane, with no glimmer of gas and with nothing to do."[8]

Many young domestics from the countryside made a successful transition to working-class wife and mother. Yet, with an unskilled or unemployed husband and a growing family, such a woman often had to join the broad ranks of working women in the "sweated industries." These industries resembled the old putting-out and cottage industries of the eighteenth and early nineteenth centuries. The women normally worked at home, though sometimes together in some loft or garret, for tiny merchant-manufacturers. Paid by the piece and not by the hour, these women (and their

young daughters), for whom organization was impossible, earned pitiful wages and lacked any job security.

Some women did hand-decorating of every conceivable kind of object; the majority, however, made clothing, especially after the advent of the sewing machine. Foot-powered sewing machines allowed the poorest wife or widow in the foulest dwelling to rival and eventually supplant the most highly skilled male tailor. By 1900 only a few such tailors lingered on in high-priced "tailor-made" shops. An army of poor women accounted for the bulk of the inexpensive "ready-made" clothes displayed on department store racks and in tiny shops. All of these considerations graphically illustrate the rise and fall of groups and individuals within the working classes.

The urban working classes sought fun and recreation, and they found it. Across the face of Europe, drinking was unquestionably the favorite leisure-time activity of working people. For many middle-class moralists, as well as moralizing historians since, love of drink has been a curse of the modern age—a sign of social dislocation and popular suffering. Certainly, drinking was deadly serious business. One English slum dweller recalled that "drunkenness was by far the commonest cause of dispute and misery in working class homes. On account of it one saw many a decent family drift down through poverty into total want."[9]

Generally, however, heavy "problem" drinking declined by the late nineteenth century, as it became less and less socially acceptable. This decline reflected in part the moral leadership of the upper working class. At the same time, drinking became more public and social, especially as on-the-job drinking, an ancient custom of field laborers and urban artisans, declined. Cafés and pubs became increasingly bright, friendly places. Working-class political activities, both moderate and radical, were also concentrated in taverns and pubs. Moreover, social drinking by married couples and sweethearts became an accepted and widespread practice for the first time. This greater participation by women undoubtedly helped to civilize the world of drink and hard liquor.

The two other leisure-time passions of the working classes were sports and music halls. By the late nineteenth century there had been a great decline in "cruel sports," such as bullbaiting and cockfighting, throughout Europe. Their place was filled by modern spectator sports, of which racing and soccer were the most popular. There was a great deal of gambling on sports events, and for many a working person the desire to decipher the racing forms was a powerful incentive toward literacy. Music halls and vaudeville theaters, the working-class counterparts of middle-class opera and classical theater, were enormously popular throughout Europe. In the words of one English printer, "It is to the music halls that the vast body of working people look for recreation and entertainment."[10] In 1900 there were more than fifty in London alone. Music hall audiences were thoroughly mixed, which may account for the fact that drunkenness, sexual intercourse and pregnancy before marriage, marital difficulties, and problems with mothers-in-law were favorite themes of broad jokes and bittersweet songs.

In more serious moments, religion and the Christian churches continued to provide working people with solace and meaning. The eighteenth-century vitality of popular religion in Catholic countries and the Protestant rejuvenation exemplified by German Pietism and English Methodism (see pages 720–721) carried over into the nineteenth century. Indeed, many historians see the early nineteenth century as an age of religious revival. Yet historians also recognize that, by the last two or three decades of the nineteenth century, a considerable decline in both church attendance and church donations was occurring in

Renoir: Le Moulin de la Galette à Montmartre In this 1876 masterpiece the impressionist painter Auguste Renoir (1841–1919) has transformed a popular outdoor dance hall of the Parisian masses into an enchanted fairyland. Renoir was a joyous artist, and his work optimistically affirmed the beauty and value of modern life. (Source: Musée d'Orsay/ Cliché des Musées Nationaux, Paris)

most European countries. And it seems clear that this decline was greater for the urban working classes than for their rural counterparts or for the middle classes.

What did the decline in working-class church attendance really mean? Some have argued that it accurately reflected a general decline in faith and religious belief. Others disagree, noting correctly that most working-class families still baptized their children and considered themselves Christians. Although more research is necessary, it appears that the urban working classes in Europe did become more secular and less religious in the late nineteenth and early twentieth centuries. They rarely repudiated the Christian religion, but it tended to play a diminishing role in their day-to-day lives.

Part of the reason was that the construction of churches failed to keep up with the rapid growth of urban population, especially in new working-class neighborhoods. Thus the vibrant, materialistic urban environment undermined popular religious impulses, which were poorly served in the cities. Equally important, however, was the fact that throughout the nineteenth century both Catholic and Protestant churches were normally seen as they saw themselves—as conservative institutions defending social order and custom. Therefore, as the European working classes became more politically conscious, they tended to see the established (or quasi-established) "territorial church" as defending what they wished to change and allied with their political opponents. Especially the men of the urban working classes developed vaguely antichurch attitudes, even though they remained neutral or positive toward religion. They tended to regard regular church attendance as "not our kind of thing"—not part of urban working-class culture.

The pattern was different in the United States. There, most churches also preached social conservatism in the nineteenth century. But because church and state had always been separate and because there was always a host of competing denominations and even different religions, working people identified churches much less with the political and social status quo. Instead, individual churches in the United States were often closely identified with an ethnic group rather than with a social class; and churches thrived, in part, as a means of asserting ethnic identity.

THE FAMILY

Urban life wrought many fundamental changes in the family. Although much is still unknown, it seems clear that by the late nineteenth century the family had stabilized considerably after the disruption of the late eighteenth and early nineteenth centuries. The home became more important for both men and women. The role of women and attitudes toward children underwent substantial change, and adolescence emerged as a distinct stage of life. These are but a few of the transformations that affected all social classes in varying degrees.

Premarital Sex and Marriage

By 1850 the preindustrial pattern of lengthy courtship and mercenary marriage was pretty well dead among the working classes. In its place, the ideal of romantic love had triumphed. Couples were ever more likely to come from different, even distant, towns and to be more nearly the same age, further indicating that romantic sentiment was replacing tradition and financial considerations.

Economic considerations in marriage long remained much more important to the middle classes than to the working classes. In France, dowries and elaborate legal marriage contracts were standard practice among the middle classes, and marriage was for many families life's most crucial financial transaction. A popular author advised young Frenchmen that "marriage is in general a means of increasing one's credit and one's fortune and of insuring one's success in the world."[11] This preoccupation with money led many middle-class men, in France and elsewhere, to marry late, after they were established economically, and to choose women considerably younger and less sexually experienced than themselves. These differences between husband and wife became a source of tension in many middle-class marriages.

A young woman of the middle class found her romantic life carefully supervised by her well-meaning mother, who schemed for a proper marriage and guarded her daughter's virginity like the family's credit. After marriage, middle-class morality sternly demanded fidelity.

Middle-class boys were watched, too, but not as vigilantly. By the time they reached late adolescence, they had usually attained considerable sexual experience with maids or prostitutes. With marriage a distant, uncertain possibility, it was all too easy for a young man of the middle classes to turn to the urban underworld of whoredom and sexual exploitation to satisfy his desires.

Sexual experimentation before marriage had also triumphed, as had illegitimacy. There was an "illegitimacy explosion" between 1750 and 1850 (see page 703). By the 1840s, as many as one birth in three was occurring outside of wedlock in many large cities. Although poverty and economic uncertainty undoubtedly prevented many lovers from marrying, there were also many among the poor and propertyless who saw little wrong with having illegitimate offspring. One young Bavarian woman answered happily when asked why she kept having illegitimate children: "It's O.K. to make babies. . . . The king has o.k.'d it!"[12] Thus the pattern of romantic ideals, premarital sexual activity, and widespread illegitimacy was firmly established by midcentury among the urban working classes.

It is hard to know how European couples managed sex, pregnancy, and marriage after 1850, because such questions were considered improper both in polite conversation and in public opinion polls. Yet there are many telltale clues. In the second half of the century the rising rate of illegitimacy was reversed: more babies were born to married mothers. Some observers have argued that this shift reflected the growth of puritanism and a lessening of sexual permissiveness among the unmarried. This explanation, however, is unconvincing.

The percentage of brides who were pregnant continued to be high and showed little or no tendency to decline. In many parts of urban Europe around 1900, as many as one woman in three was going to the altar an expectant mother. Moreover, unmarried people almost certainly used the cheap condoms and diaphragms that the industrial age had made available to prevent pregnancy, at least in predominantly Protestant countries.

Unmarried young people were probably engaging in just as much sexual activity as their parents and grandparents who had created the illegitimacy explosion of 1750 to 1850. But toward the end of the nineteenth century, pregnancy usually meant marriage and the establishment of a two-parent household. This important development reflected the growing respectability of the working classes, as well as their gradual economic improvement. Skipping out was less acceptable, and marriage was less of an economic disaster. Thus the urban working-class couple became more stable, and this stability strengthened the family as an institution.

Prostitution

In Paris alone, 155,000 women were registered as prostitutes between 1871 and 1903, and 750,000 others were suspected of prostitution in the same years. Men of all classes visited prostitutes, but the middle and upper classes supplied much of the motivating cash. Thus, though many middle-class men abided by the publicly professed code of stern puritanical morality, others indulged their appetites for prostitutes and sexual promiscuity.

My Secret Life, the anonymous eleven-volume autobiography of an English sexual adventurer from the servant-keeping classes, provides a remarkable picture of such a man. Beginning at an early age with a maid, the author becomes progressively obsessed with sex and devotes his life to living his sexual fantasies. In almost every one of his innumerable encounters all across Europe, this man of wealth simply buys his pleasure. Usually meetings are arranged in a businesslike manner: regular and part-time prostitutes quote their prices; working-class girls are corrupted by hot meals and baths.

At one point, he offers a young girl six pence for a kiss and gets it. Learning that the pretty, unskilled working girl earns nine pence a day, he offers her the equivalent of a week's salary for a few moments of fondling. When she finally agrees, he savagely exults that "her want was my opportunity."[13] Later he offers more money for more gratification, and when she refuses, he tries unsuccessfully to rape her in a hackney cab.

Obviously atypical in its excesses, the encyclopedic thoroughness of *My Secret Life* does reveal the dark side of sex and class in urban society. Thinking of their wives largely in terms of money and social position, the men of the comfortable classes often purchased sex and even affection from poor girls both before and after marriage. Moreover, the great continuing differences between rich and poor made for every kind of debauchery and sexual exploitation, including the brisk trade in poor virgins that the author of *My Secret Life* particularly relished. Brutal sexist behavior was part of life—a part the sternly moral women (and men) of the upper working class detested and tried to shield their daughters from. For many poor young women, prostitution, like domestic service, was a stage of life. Having passed through it for two or three years in their early twenties, they went on in their mid-twenties to marry (or live with) men of their own class and establish homes and families.

Kinship Ties

Within working-class homes, ties to relatives after marriage—kinship ties—were in general much stronger than superficial social observers have recognized. Most newly-weds tried to live near their parents, though not in the same house. Indeed, for many married couples in the cities, ties to mothers and fathers, uncles and aunts, became more important, and ties to nonrelated acquaintances became weaker.

People turned to their families for help in coping with sickness, unemployment, death, and old age. Although governments were generally providing more welfare services by 1900, the average couple and their children inevitably faced crises. Funerals, for example, were an economic catastrophe requiring a sudden large outlay for special clothes, carriages, and burial services. Unexpected death or desertion could leave the bereaved or abandoned, especially widows and orphans, in need of financial aid or perhaps a foster home. Relatives responded to such crises, knowing full well that their own time of need would come.

Relatives were also valuable at less tragic moments. If a couple was very poor, an aged relation often moved in to cook and mind the children so the wife could earn badly needed income outside the home. Sunday dinners were often shared, as were outgrown clothing and useful information. Often the members of a large family group all lived in the same neighborhood.

Women and Family Life

Industrialization and the growth of modern cities brought great changes to the lives of European women. These changes were particularly consequential for married women, and in the nineteenth century most women did marry.

The work of most wives became quite distinct and separate from the work of their husbands. Husbands became wage earners in factories and offices; wives tended to stay home and manage the household and care for the children. The preindustrial pattern among both peasants and cottage workers, in which husbands and wives worked together and divided up household duties and child rearing, declined. Only in a few occupations, such as retail trade, did married couples live where they worked and struggle together to make their mom-and-pop operations a success. Factory employment for married women also declined as the early practice of hiring entire families in the factory disappeared.

As economic conditions improved late in the nineteenth century, only married women in poor families tended to work outside the home. One old English worker recalled that "the boy wanted to get into a position that would enable him to keep a wife and family, as it was considered a thoroughly unsatisfactory state of affairs if the wife had to work to help maintain the home."[14] The ideal was a strict division of labor by sex: the wife as mother and homemaker, the husband as wage earner.

This rigid division of labor meant that married women faced great injustice if they tried to move into the man's world, the world of employment outside the home. Husbands were unsympathetic or hostile. Well-paying jobs were off-limits to women, and a woman's wage was almost always less than a man's, even for the same work.

Moreover, married women were subordinated to their husbands by law and lacked many basic legal rights. In England, the situation was summed up in a famous line from the jurist William Blackstone: "In law husband and wife are one person, and the husband is that person." Thus a wife in England had no legal identity and hence no right to own property in her own name. Even the wages she might earn belonged to her husband. In France, the Napoleonic Code also enshrined the principle of female subordination and gave the wife few legal rights regarding property, divorce, and custody of the children. Legal inferiority for women permeated Western society.

With middle-class women suffering, sometimes severely, from a lack of legal rights and with all

Women Workers Founded in 1869, the German Social Democratic party became the strongest socialist party in Europe. Women were active in the socialist movement, as this engraving from 1890 of a meeting of workers in Berlin illustrates. *(Source: Bildarchiv Preussischer Kulturbesitz)*

women facing discrimination in education and employment, there is little wonder that some women rebelled and began the long-continuing fight for equality of the sexes and the rights of women. Their struggle proceeded on two main fronts. First, following in the steps of women like Mary Wollstonecraft (see page 810), organizations founded by middle-class feminists campaigned for equal legal rights for women as well as access to higher education and professional employment. These organizations scored some significant victories, like the law giving English married women full property rights in 1882. In the years before 1914, middle-class feminists increasingly shifted their attention to securing the right to vote for women.

Women inspired by utopian and particularly Marxian socialism blazed a second path. Often scorning the programs of middle-class feminists, socialist women leaders argued that the liberation of (working-class) women would come only with the liberation of the entire working class through revolution. In the meantime, they championed the cause of working women and won some practical improvements, especially in Germany, where the socialist movement was most effectively organized. In a general way, these different approaches to women's issues reflected the diversity of classes in the urban society.

If the ideology and practice of rigidly separate roles undoubtedly narrowed women's horizons and caused some women to rebel, there was a brighter side to the same coin. As home and children became the typical wife's main concerns, her control and influence there apparently became increasingly strong throughout Europe. Among the English working classes, it was the wife who generally determined how the family's money was spent. In many families the husband gave all his earnings to his wife to manage, whatever the law might read. She returned to him only a small allowance for carfare, beer, tobacco, and union dues. All the major domestic decisions, from the children's schooling and religious instruction to the selection of new furniture or a new apartment, were hers. In France women had even greater power in their assigned domain. One English feminist noted in 1908 that "though legally women occupy

A Working-Class Home, 1875 Emotional ties within ordinary families grew stronger in the nineteenth century. *(Source: Illustrated London News, LXVI, 1875. Photo courtesy of Boston Public Library)*

a much inferior status than men [in France], in practice they constitute the superior sex. They are the power behind the throne."[15]

Women ruled at home partly because running the urban household was a complicated, demanding, and valuable task. Twice-a-day food shopping, penny-pinching, economizing, and the growing crusade against dirt—not to mention child rearing—constituted a full-time occupation. Nor were there any labor-saving appliances to help. Working yet another job for wages outside the home had limited appeal for most married women, unless such earnings were essential for family survival.

The wife also guided the home because a good deal of her effort was directed toward pampering her husband as he expected. In humble households she saw that he had meat while she ate bread, that he relaxed by the fire while she did the dishes.

The woman's guidance of the household went hand in hand with the increased emotional importance of home and family. The home she ran was idealized as a warm shelter in a hard and impersonal urban world. By the 1820s one observer of the comfortable middle classes in Marseilles had noted, for example, that "the family father, obliged to occupy himself with difficult business

problems during the day, can relax only when he goes home. . . . Family evenings together are for him a time of the purest and most complete happiness."[16]

In time the central place of the family spread down the social scale. For a child of the English slums in the early 1900s,

home, however poor, was the focus of all love and interests, a sure fortress against a hostile world. Songs about its beauties were ever on people's lips. "Home, sweet home," first heard in the 1870s, had become "almost a second national anthem." Few walls in lower-working-class houses lacked "mottoes"—colored strips of paper, about nine inches wide and eighteen inches in length, attesting to domestic joys: EAST, WEST, HOME'S BEST; BLESS OUR HOME; GOD IS MASTER OF THIS HOUSE; HOME IS THE NEST WHERE ALL IS BEST.[17]

By 1900 home and family were what life was all about for millions of people of all classes.

Women also developed stronger emotional ties to their husbands. Even in the comfortable classes, marriages were increasingly founded on sentiment and sexual attraction rather than on money and calculation. Affection and eroticism became more central to the couple after marriage. Gustave Droz, whose best seller *Mr., Mrs., and Baby* went through 121 editions between 1866 and 1884, saw love within marriage as the key to human happiness. He condemned men who made marriage sound dull and practical, men who were exhausted by prostitutes and rheumatism and who wanted their young wives to be little angels. He urged women to follow their hearts and marry a man more nearly their own age:

A husband who is stately and a little bald is all right, but a young husband who loves you and who drinks out of your glass without ceremony, is better. Let him, if he ruffles your dress a little and places a kiss on your neck as he passes. Let him, if he undresses you after the ball, laughing like a fool. You have fine spiritual qualities, it is true, but your little body is not bad either and when one loves, one loves completely. Behind these follies lies happiness.[18]

Many French marriage manuals of the late 1800s stressed that women had legitimate sexual needs, such as the "right to orgasm." Perhaps the French were a bit more enlightened in these matters than other nationalities. But the rise of public socializing by couples in cafés and music halls, as well as franker affection within the family, suggest a more erotic, pleasurable intimate life for women throughout Western society. This, too, helped make the woman's role as mother and homemaker acceptable and even satisfying.

Child Rearing

One of the most striking signs of deepening emotional ties within the family was the mother's love and concern for her tiny infants. This was a sharp break with the past. It may seem scarcely believable today that the typical mother in preindustrial Western society was very often indifferent toward her baby. This indifference—unwillingness to make real sacrifices for the welfare of the infant—was giving way among the comfortable classes by the later part of the eighteenth century, but the ordinary mother adopted new attitudes only as the nineteenth century progressed. The baby became more important, and women became better mothers.

Mothers increasingly breast-fed their infants, for example, rather than paying wet nurses to do so. Breast-feeding involved sacrifice—a temporary loss of freedom, if nothing else. Yet in an age when there was no good alternative to mother's milk, it saved lives. The surge of maternal feeling also gave rise to a wave of specialized books on child rearing and infant hygiene, such as Droz's phenomenally successful book. Droz urged fathers to get into the act and pitied those "who do not know how to roll around on the carpet, play at being a horse and a great wolf, and undress their baby."[19] Another sign, from France, of increased affection is that fewer illegitimate babies were abandoned as foundlings, especially after about 1850. Moreover, the practice of swaddling disappeared completely. Instead, ordinary mothers allowed their babies freedom of movement and delighted in their spontaneity.

The Drawing Room The middle-class ideal of raising cultured, educated, and properly protected young women is captured in this illustration. A serious mother lovingly teaches her youngest child while the older daughters practice their genteel skills. A drawing room was a kind of nineteenth-century family room, mercifully spared the tyranny of television. *(Source: Bettmann/Hulton)*

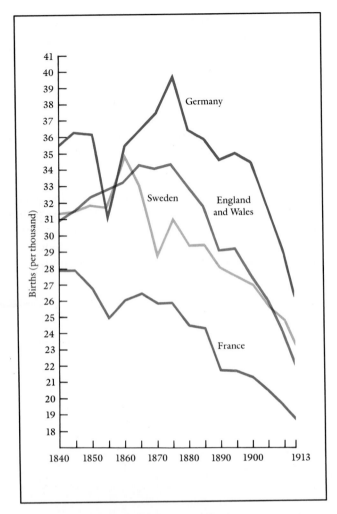

FIGURE 28.4 The Decline of Birthrates in England and Wales, France, Germany, Sweden, 1840–1913 Women had fewer babies for a variety of reasons, including the fact that their children were increasingly less likely to die before reaching adulthood. Compare with Figure 28.1.

The loving care lavished on infants was matched by greater concern for older children and adolescents. They, too, were wrapped in the strong emotional ties of a more intimate and protective family. For one thing, European women began to limit the number of children they bore, in order to care adequately for those they had. It was evident by the end of the century that the birthrate was declining across Europe, as Figure 28.4 shows, and it continued to do so until after the Second World War. An Englishwoman who married in the 1860s, for example, had an average of about six children; her daughter marrying in the 1890s had

only four; and her granddaughter marrying in the 1920s had only two or possibly three.

The most important reason for this revolutionary reduction in family size, in which the comfortable and well-educated classes took the lead, was parents' desire to improve their economic and social position and that of their children. Children were no longer an economic asset. By having fewer youngsters, parents could give those they had valuable advantages, from music lessons and summer vacations to long, expensive university educations and suitable dowries. A young German skilled worker with only one child spoke for many in his class when he said, "We want to get ahead, and our daughter should have things better than my wife and sisters did."[20] Thus the growing tendency of couples in the late nineteenth century to use a variety of contraceptive methods—rhythm, withdrawal, and mechanical devices—certainly reflected increased concern for children.

Indeed, many parents were probably too concerned about their children, unwittingly subjecting them to an emotional pressure cooker of almost unbearable intensity. The result was that many children and especially adolescents came to feel trapped, longing for greater independence.

Biological and medical theories led parents to believe in the possibility that their own emotional characteristics were passed on to their offspring and that they were thus directly responsible for any abnormality in a child. The moment a child was conceived was thought to be of enormous importance. "Never run the risk of conception when you are sick or over-tired or unhappy," wrote one influential American woman. "For the bodily condition of the child, its vigor and magnetic qualities, are much affected by conditions ruling this great moment."[21] So might the youthful "sexual excess" of the father curse future generations. Although this was true in the case of syphilis, which could be transmitted to unborn children, the rigid determinism of such views left little scope for the child's individual development.

Another area of excessive parental concern was the sexual behavior of the child. Masturbation was viewed with horror, for it represented an act of independence and even defiance. Diet, clothing, games, and sleeping were carefully regulated. Girls were discouraged from riding horses and bicycling because rhythmic friction simulated masturbation. Boys were dressed in trousers with shallow and widely separated pockets.

These and less blatant attempts to repress the child's sexuality were a source of unhealthy tension, often made worse by the rigid division of sexual roles within the family. It was widely believed that mother and child love each other easily but relations between father and child are necessarily difficult and often tragic. The father was a stranger; his world of business was far removed from the maternal world of spontaneous affection. Moreover, the father was demanding, often expecting the child to succeed where he himself had failed and making his love conditional on achievement. Little wonder that the imaginative literature of the late nineteenth century came to deal with the emotional and destructive elements of father-son relationships. In the Russian Feodor Dostoevsky's great novel *The Brothers Karamazov* (1880–1881), for example, four sons work knowingly or unknowingly to destroy their father. Later, at the murder trial, one of the brothers claims to speak for all mankind and screams out: "Who doesn't wish his father dead?"

Sigmund Freud (1856–1939), the Viennese founder of psychoanalysis, formulated the most striking analysis of the explosive dynamics of the family, particularly the middle-class family in the late nineteenth century. A physician by training, Freud began his career treating mentally ill patients. He noted that the hysteria of his patients appeared to originate in bitter early childhood experiences, wherein the child had been obliged to repress strong feelings. When these painful experiences were recalled and reproduced under hypnosis or through free association of ideas, the patient could be brought to understand his or her unhappiness and eventually to deal with it.

One of Freud's most influential ideas concerned the Oedipal tensions resulting from the son's instinctive competition with the father for the mother's love and affection. More generally, Freud postulated that much of human behavior is motivated by unconscious emotional needs, whose nature and origins are kept from conscious awareness by various mental devices that he called "defense mechanisms." Freud concluded that much unconscious psychological energy is sexual energy, which is repressed and precariously controlled by rational thinking and moral rules. If Freud exaggerated the sexual and familial roots of adult behavior, that exaggeration was itself a reflection of the tremendous emotional intensity of family life in the late nineteenth century.

The working classes probably had more avenues of escape from such tensions than did the middle classes. Unlike their middle-class counterparts, who remained economically dependent on their families until a long education was finished or a proper marriage secured, working-class boys and girls went to work when they reached adolescence. Earning wages on their own, by the time they were sixteen or seventeen they could bargain with their parents for greater independence within the household. If they were unsuccessful, they could and did leave home, to live cheaply as paying lodgers in other working-class homes. Thus a young person from the working classes broke away from the family more easily when emotional ties became oppressive. In the twentieth century, middle-class youth would follow this lead.

SCIENCE AND THOUGHT

Major changes in Western thought accompanied the emergence of urban society. Two aspects of these complex intellectual developments stand out as especially significant. Scientific knowledge expanded rapidly and came to influence the Western world view even more profoundly than it had since the scientific revolution and the early Enlightenment. And, between about the 1840s and the 1890s, European literature underwent a shift from soaring romanticism to tough-minded realism.

The Triumph of Science

As the pace of scientific advance quickened and as theoretical advances resulted in great practical benefits, science exercised growing influence on human thought. The intellectual achievements of the scientific revolution had resulted in few such benefits, and theoretical knowledge had also played a relatively small role in the Industrial Revolution in England. But breakthroughs in industrial technology enormously stimulated basic scientific inquiry, as researchers sought to explain theoretically how such things as steam engines and blast furnaces actually worked. The result was an explosive growth of fundamental scientific discoveries from the 1830s onward. And in contrast to earlier periods, these theoretical discoveries were increasingly transformed into material improvements for the general population.

A perfect example of the translation of better scientific knowledge into practical human benefits was the work of Pasteur and his followers in biology and the medical sciences. Another was the development of the branch of physics known as "thermodynamics." Building on Newton's laws of mechanics and on studies of steam engines, thermodynamics investigated the relationship between heat and mechanical energy. By midcentury, physicists had formulated the fundamental laws of thermodynamics, which were then applied to mechanical engineering, chemical processes, and many other fields. The *law of conservation of energy* held that different forms of energy—such as heat, electricity, and magnetism—could be converted but neither created nor destroyed. Nineteenth-century thermodynamics demonstrated that the physical world is governed by firm, unchanging laws.

Chemistry and electricity were two other fields characterized by extremely rapid progress. Chemists devised ways of measuring the atomic weight of different elements, and in 1869 the Russian chemist Dmitri Mendeleev (1834–1907) codified the rules of chemistry in the periodic law and the periodic table. Chemistry was subdivided into many specialized branches, such as organic chemistry—the study of the compounds of carbon. Applying theoretical insights gleaned from this new field, researchers in large German chemical companies discovered ways of transforming the dirty, useless coal tar that accumulated in coke ovens into beautiful, expensive synthetic dyes for the world of fashion. The basic discoveries of Michael Faraday (1791–1867) in electromagnetism in the 1830s and 1840s resulted in the first dynamo (generator) and opened the way for the subsequent development of electric motors, electric lights, and electric streetcars.

The triumph of science and technology had at least three significant consequences. First, though ordinary citizens continued to lack detailed scientific knowledge, everyday experience and innumerable popularizers impressed the importance of science on the popular mind.

As science became more prominent in popular thinking, the philosophical implications of science formulated in the Enlightenment spread to broad sections of the population. Natural processes appeared to be determined by rigid laws, leaving little room for either divine intervention or human will. Yet scientific and technical advances had also fed the Enlightenment's optimistic faith in human progress, which now appeared endless and automatic to many middle-class minds.

Finally, the methods of science acquired unrivaled prestige after 1850. For many, the union of careful experiment and abstract theory was the only reliable route to truth and objective reality. The "unscientific" intuitions of poets and the revelations of saints seemed hopelessly inferior.

Social Science and Evolution

From the 1830s onward, many thinkers tried to apply the objective methods of science to the study of society. In some ways these efforts simply perpetuated the critical thinking of the philosophes. Yet there were important differences. The new "social scientists" had access to the massive sets of numerical data that governments had begun to collect on everything from children to crime, from population to prostitution. In response, they developed new statistical methods to analyze these facts "scientifically" and supposedly to test their theories. And the systems of the leading nineteenth-century social scientists were more unified, all-encompassing, and dogmatic than those of the philosophes. Marx was a prime example (see pages 875–876).

Another extremely influential system builder was the French philosopher Auguste Comte (1798–1857). Initially a disciple of the utopian socialist Saint-Simon (see page 874), Comte wrote the six-volume *System of Positive Philosophy* (1830–1842), largely overlooked during the romantic era. But when the political failures of 1848 completed the swing to realism, Comte's philosophy came into its own. Its influence has remained great to this day.

Comte postulated that all intellectual activity progresses through predictable stages:

The great fundamental law . . . is this:—that each of our leading conceptions—each branch of our knowledge—passes successively through three different theoretical conditions: the Theological, or fictitious; the Metaphysical, or abstract; and the Scientific, or positive. . . . The first is the necessary point of departure of human understanding, and the third is the fixed and definitive state. The second is merely a transition.[22]

By way of example, Comte noted that, as knowledge of astronomy developed, the prevailing explanation of cosmic patterns had shifted from the will of God (the theological) to the will of an orderly Nature (the metaphysical) to the rule of unchanging laws (the scientific). Later, this same intellectual progression took place in increasingly complex fields—physics, chemistry, and finally the study of society. By applying the scientific or positivist method, Comte believed, his new discipline of sociology would soon discover the eternal laws of human relations. This colossal achievement would in turn enable expert social scientists to impose a disciplined harmony and well-being on less enlightened citizens. Dismissing the "fictions" of traditional religions, Comte became the chief priest of the religion of science and rule by experts.

Comte's stages of knowledge exemplify the nineteenth-century fascination with the idea of evolution and dynamic development. Thinkers in many fields, like the romantic historians and "scientific" Marxists, shared and applied this basic concept. In geology, Charles Lyell (1797–1875) effectively discredited the long-standing view that the earth's surface had been formed by short-lived cataclysms, such as biblical floods and earthquakes. Instead, according to Lyell's principle of uniformitarianism, the same geological processes that are at work today slowly formed the earth's surface over an immensely long time. The evolutionary view of biological development, first proposed by the Greek Anaximander in the sixth century B.C., re-emerged in a more modern form in the work of Jean Baptiste Lamarck (1744–1829). Lamarck asserted that all forms of life had arisen through a long process of continuous adjustment to the environment.

Lamarck's work was flawed—he believed that characteristics that parents acquired in the course of their lives could be inherited by their children—and was not accepted, but it helped prepare the way for Charles Darwin (1809–1882), the most influential of all nineteenth-century evolutionary thinkers. As the official naturalist on a five-year scientific cruise to Latin America and the South Pacific beginning in 1831, Darwin carefully collected specimens of the different animal species that he encountered on the voyage. Back in England, convinced by fossil evidence and by his friend Lyell that the earth and life on it were immensely ancient, Darwin came to doubt the general belief in a special divine creation of each species of animals. Instead, he concluded, all life had gradually evolved from a common ancestral origin in an unending "struggle for survival." After long hesitation, Darwin published his research, which immediately attracted wide attention.

Darwin's great originality lay in suggesting precisely how biological evolution might have occurred. His theory is summarized in his title, *On the Origin of Species by the Means of Natural Selection* (1859). Decisively influenced by Malthus's gloomy theory that populations naturally grow faster than their food supplies, Darwin argued that chance differences among the members of a given species help some to survive while others die. Thus the variations that prove useful in the struggle for survival are selected naturally and gradually spread

Attracting Females was an integral part of the struggle for survival, according to Charles Darwin. He theorized that those males who were most attractive to females would have the most offspring, like this type of monkey that had developed ornamental hair with devastating sex appeal. Darwin used this illustration in *The Descent of Man* (1871). *(Source: Library of Congress)*

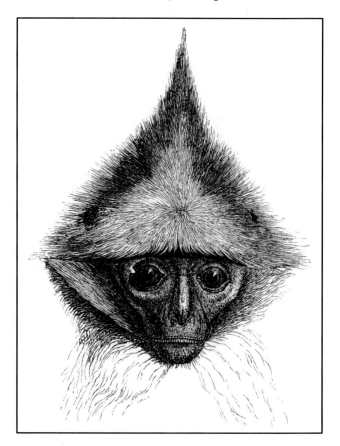

to the entire species through reproduction. Darwin did not explain why such variations occurred in the first place, and not until the early twentieth century did the study of genetics and the concept of mutation provide some answers.

As the capstone of already-widespread evolutionary thinking, Darwin's theory had a powerful and many-sided influence on European thought and the European middle classes. Darwin was hailed as the great scientist par excellence, the "Newton of biology," who had revealed once again the powers of objective science. Darwin's findings also reinforced the teachings of secularists like Comte and Marx, who scornfully dismissed religious belief in favor of agnostic or atheistic materialism. In the great cities especially, religion was on the defensive. Finally, many writers applied the theory of biological evolution to human affairs. Herbert Spencer (1820–1903), an English disciple of Auguste Comte, saw the human race as driven forward to ever-greater specialization and progress by the brutal economic struggle that efficiently determined the "survival of the fittest." The poor were the ill-fated weak, the prosperous the chosen strong. Understandably, Spencer and other Social Darwinists were especially popular with the upper middle class.

Realism in Literature

In 1868 Émile Zola (1840–1902), the giant of the realist movement in literature, defended his violently criticized first novel against charges of pornography and corruption of morals. Such accusations were meaningless, Zola claimed: he was only a purely objective scientist using "the modern method, the universal instrument of inquiry of which this age makes such ardent use to open up the future":

I chose characters completely dominated by their nerves and their blood, deprived of free-will, pushed to each action of their lives by the fatality of their flesh. . . . I have simply done on living bodies the work of analysis which surgeons perform on corpses.[23]

Zola's literary manifesto articulated the key themes of realism, which had emerged in the 1840s and dominated Western culture and style until the 1890s. Realist writers believed that literature should depict life exactly as it was. Forsaking poetry for prose and the personal, emotional viewpoint of the romantics for strict, scientific objectivity, the realists simply observed and recorded—content to let the facts speak for themselves.

The major realist writers focused their extraordinary powers of observation on contemporary everyday life. Emphatically rejecting the romantic search for the exotic and the sublime, they energetically pursued the typical and the commonplace. Beginning with a dissection of the middle classes, from which most of them sprang, many realists eventually focused on the working classes, especially the urban working classes, which had been neglected in imaginative literature before this time. They put a microscope to many unexplored and taboo subjects—sex, strikes, violence, alcoholism—and hastened to report that slums and factories teemed with savage behavior. Many shocked middle-class critics denounced realism as ugly sensationalism wrapped provocatively in pseudoscientific declarations and crude language.

The realists' claims of objectivity did not prevent the elaboration of a definite world view. Unlike the romantics, who had gloried in individual freedom and an unlimited universe, realists such as Zola were strict determinists. Human beings, like atoms, were components of the physical world, and all human actions were caused by unalterable natural laws. Heredity and environment determined human behavior; good and evil were merely social conventions.

The realist movement began in France, where romanticism had never been completely dominant, and three of its greatest practitioners—Balzac, Flaubert, and Zola—were French. Honoré de Balzac (1799–1850) spent thirty years writing a vastly ambitious panorama of postrevolutionary French life. Known collectively as *The Human Comedy,* this series of nearly one hundred books vividly portrays more than two thousand characters from virtually all sectors of French society. Balzac pictures urban society as grasping, amoral, and brutal, characterized by a Darwinian struggle for wealth and power. In *Le Père Goriot* (1835), the hero, a poor student from the provinces, eventually surrenders his idealistic integrity to feverish ambition and society's all-pervasive greed.

Madame Bovary (1857), the masterpiece of Gustave Flaubert (1821–1880), is far narrower in scope than Balzac's work but unparalleled in its depth and accuracy of psychological insight. Unsuccessfully prosecuted as an outrage against public morality and religion, Flaubert's carefully crafted novel tells the ordinary, even banal, story of a frustrated middle-class housewife who has an adulterous love affair and is betrayed by her lover. Without moralizing, Flaubert portrays the provincial middle class as petty, smug, and hypocritical.

Zola was most famous for his seamy, animalistic view of working-class life. But he also wrote gripping, carefully researched stories featuring the stock exchange, the big department store, and the army, as well as urban slums and bloody coal strikes. Like many later realists, Zola sympathized with socialism, a sympathy evident in his overpowering *Germinal* (1885).

Realism quickly spread beyond France. In England, Mary Ann Evans (1819–1880), who wrote under the pen name George Eliot, brilliantly achieved a more deeply felt, less sensational kind of realism. "It is the habit of my imagination," George Eliot wrote, "to strive after as full a vision of the medium in which a character moves as one of the character itself." Her great novel *Middlemarch: A Study of Provincial Life* examines masterfully the ways in which people are shaped by their social medium as well as by their own inner strivings, conflicts, and moral choices. Thomas Hardy (1840–1928) was more in the Zola tradition. His novels, such as *Tess of the D'Urbervilles* and *Return of the Native,* depicted men and women frustrated and crushed by fate and bad luck.

The greatest Russian realist, Count Leo Tolstoy (1828–1910), combined realism in description and character development with an atypical moralizing, which came to dominate his later work. Tolstoy's greatest work was *War and Peace,* a monumental novel set against the historical background of Napoleon's invasion of Russia in 1812. Tolstoy probes deeply into the lives of a multitude of unforgettable characters: the ill-fated Prince Andrei; the shy, fumbling Pierre; and the enchanting, level-headed Natasha. Tolstoy goes to great pains to develop his fatalistic theory of history, which regards free will as an illusion and the achievements of even the greatest leaders as only the channeling of historical necessity. Yet Tolstoy's central message is one that most of the people discussed in this chapter would readily accept: human love, trust, and everyday family ties are life's enduring values.

Degas: Women Ironing   Realism replaced romanticism as the dominant trend in the visual arts for a long generation after 1850. This French work by Edgar Degas (1834–1917) accurately captures the hard work and fatigue of unskilled labor. *(Source: Musée d'Orsay/Cliché des Musées Nationaux, Paris)*

SUMMARY

The Industrial Revolution had a decisive influence on the urban environment. The populations of towns and cities grew rapidly because it was economically advantageous to locate factories and offices in urban areas. This rapid growth worsened long-standing overcrowding and unhealthy living conditions and posed a frightening challenge for society. Eventually government leaders, city planners, reformers, scientists, and ordinary citizens responded. They took effective action in public health and provided themselves with other badly needed urban services. Gradually they tamed the ferocious savagery of the traditional city.

As urban civilization came to prevail, there were major changes in family life. Especially among the lower classes, family life became more stable, more loving, and less mercenary. These improvements had a price, though. Sex roles for men and women became sharply defined and rigidly separate.

Women especially tended to be locked into a subordinate and stereotypical role. Nonetheless, on balance, the quality of family life improved for all family members. Better, more stable family relations reinforced the benefits for the masses of higher real wages, increased social security, political participation, and education.

While the quality of urban and family life improved, the class structure became more complex and diversified than before. Urban society featured many distinct social groups, which existed in a state of constant flux and competition. In mature urban society, the gap between rich and poor remained enormous and really quite traditional, although there were countless gradations between the extremes. Large numbers of poor women in particular continued to labor as workers in sweated industries, as domestic servants, and as prostitutes in order to satisfy the demands of their masters in the servant-keeping classes. Urban society in the late nineteenth century represented a great step forward for humanity, but it remained very unequal.

Inequality was a favorite theme of realist novelists like Balzac and Zola. More generally, literary realism reflected Western society's growing faith in science, progress, and evolutionary thinking. The emergence of urban, industrial civilization accelerated the secularization of the Western world view.

NOTES

1. A. Weber, *The Growth of Cities in the Nineteenth Century* (New York: Columbia University Press, 1899), p. 1.
2. Quoted in W. Ashworth, *The Genesis of Modern British Town Planning* (London: Routledge & Kegan Paul, 1954), p. 17.
3. S. Marcus, "Reading the Illegible," in *The Victorian City: Images and Realities,* vol. 1, ed. H. J. Dyos and Michael Wolff, (London: Routledge & Kegan Paul, 1973), p. 266.
4. E. Gauldie, *Cruel Habitations: A History of Working-Class Housing, 1780–1918* (London: Allen & Unwin, 1974), p. 21.
5. Quoted in E. Chadwick, *Report on the Sanitary Condition of the Labouring Population of Great Britain,* ed. M. Flinn (Edinburgh: University of Edinburgh Press, 1965; original publication, 1842), pp. 315–316.
6. J. P. McKay, *Tramways and Trolleys: The Rise of Urban Mass Transport in Europe* (Princeton, N.J.: Princeton University Press, 1976), p. 81.
7. Quoted in R. P. Neuman, "The Sexual Question and Social Democracy in Imperial Germany," *Journal of Social History* 7 (Winter 1974): 276.
8. Quoted in J. A. Banks, "The Contagion of Numbers," in Dyos and Wolff, vol. 1, p. 112.
9. Quoted in R. Roberts, *The Classic Slum: Salford Life in the First Quarter of the Century* (Manchester, England.: University of Manchester Press, 1971), p. 95.
10. Quoted in B. Harrison, "Pubs," in Dyos and Wolff, vol. 1, p. 175.
11. Quoted in T. Zeldin, *France, 1848–1945,* vol. 1 (Oxford, England.: Clarendon Press, 1973), p. 288.
12. Quoted in J. M. Phayer, "Lower-Class Morality: The Case of Bavaria," *Journal of Social History* 8 (Fall 1974): 89.
13. Quoted in S. Marcus, *The Other Victorians: A Study of Sexuality and Pornography in Mid-Nineteenth-Century England* (New York: Basic Books, 1966), p. 142.
14. Quoted in G. S. Jones, "Working-Class Culture and Working-Class Politics in London, 1870–1900: Notes on the Remaking of a Working Class," *Journal of Social History* 7 (Summer 1974): 486.
15. Quoted in Zeldin, vol. 1, p. 346.
16. Quoted in E. Shorter, *The Making of the Modern Family* (New York: Basic Books, 1975), pp. 230–231.
17. Roberts, p. 35.
18. Quoted in Zeldin, vol. 1, p. 295.
19. Ibid., p. 328.
20. Quoted in Neuman, p. 281.
21. Quoted by S. Kern, "Explosive Intimacy: Psychodynamics of the Victorian Family," *History of Childhood Quarterly* 1 (Winter 1974): 439.
22. A. Comte, *The Positive Philosophy of Auguste Comte,* vol. 1, trans. H. Martineau (London: J. Chapman, 1853), pp. 1–2.
23. Quoted in G. J. Becker, ed., *Documents of Modern Literary Realism* (Princeton, N.J.: Princeton University Press, 1963), p. 159.

SUGGESTED READING

All of the books and articles cited in the Notes are highly recommended; each in its own way is an important contribution to social history and the study of life in the urban society. Note that the *Journal of Social History,* which has a strong European orientation, is excellent both for its articles and for its reviews of new books.

The book by T. Zeldin, *France, 1848–1945,* 2 vols. (1973, 1977), is a pioneering social history that opens many doors, as is the ambitious synthesis by T. Hamerow, *The Birth of a New Europe: State and Society in the Nineteenth Century* (1983).

On the European city, D. Harvey, *Consciousness and the Urban Experience* (1985), is provocative, and D. Pickney, *Napoleon III and the Rebuilding of Paris* (1972), is fascinating, as are G. Masur, *Imperial Berlin* (1970), and M. Hamm, ed., *The City in Russian History* (1976). So also are N. Evenson's beautifully illustrated *Paris: A Century of Change, 1878–1978* (1979) and D. Grew's authoritative *Town in the Ruhr: A Social History of Bochum, 1860–1914* (1979). J. Siegel, *Bohemian Paris: Culture, Politics, and the Boundaries of Bourgeois Life, 1830–1930* (1986), and J. Merriman, ed., *French Cities in the Nineteenth Century: Class, Power, and Urbanization* (1982), are important works on France. D. Olsen's scholarly *Growth of Victorian London* (1978) complements H. Mayhew's wonderful contemporary study, *London Labour and the Labouring Poor* (1861), reprinted recently. M. Crichton's realistic historical novel on organized crime, *The Great Train Robbery* (1976), is excellent. J. J. Tobias, *Urban Crime in Victorian England* (1972), is a lively, scholarly approach to declining criminal activity in the nineteenth century, with a wealth of detail. J. P. Goubert, *The Conquest of Water: The Advent of Health in the Industrial Age* (1989), and G. Rosen, *History of Public Health* (1958), are excellent introductions to sanitary and medical developments. For society as a whole, J. Burnett, *History of the Cost of Living* (1969), cleverly shows how different classes spent their money, and B. Tuchman, *The Proud Tower* (1966), draws an unforgettable portrait of people and classes before 1914. J. Laver's handsomely illustrated *Manners and Morals in the Age of Optimism, 1848–1914* (1966) investigates the urban underworld and relations between the sexes. Sexual attitudes are also examined by E. Trudgill, *Madonnas and Magdalenas: The Origin and Development of Victorian Sexual Attitudes* (1976), and J. Phayer, *Sexual Liberation and Religion in Nineteenth Century Europe* (1977). G. Alter, *Family and Female Life Course: The Women of Verviers, Belgium, 1849–1880* (1988), and A. McLaren, *Sexuality and Social Order: Birth Control in Nineteenth-Century France* (1982), explore attitudes toward family planning.

Women are coming into their own in historical studies. In addition to the general works by Shorter, Wrigley, Stone, and Tilly and Scott cited in Chapter 21, there are a growing number of eye-opening specialized investigations. These include L. Davidoff, *The Best Circles* (1973), and P. Jalland, *Women, Marriage and Politics, 1860–1914* (1986), on upper-class society types; O.

Banks, *Feminism and Family Planning in Victorian England* (1964); and P. Branca, *Women in Europe Since 1750* (1978). M. J. Peterson, *Love and Work in the Lives of Victorian Gentlewomen* (1989), and L. Holcombe, *Victorian Ladies at Work* (1973), examine middle-class women at work. M. Vicinus, ed., *Suffer and Be Still* (1972), and *A Widening Sphere* (1981), are far-ranging collections of essays on women's history, as is R. Bridenthal, C. Koonz, and S. Stuard, eds., *Becoming Visible: Women in European History,* 2d ed. (1987). Feminism is treated perceptively in R. Evans, *The Feminists: Women's Emancipation in Europe, America, and Australia* (1979); K. Blair, *The Clubwoman as Feminist: True Womanhood Redefined, 1868–1914* (1980); and C. Moses, *French Feminism in the Nineteenth Century* (1984). J. Gillis, *Youth and History* (1974), is a good introduction. D. Ransel, ed., *The Family in Imperial Russia* (1978), is an important work on the subject, as is J. Donzelot, *The Policing of Families* (1979), which stresses the loss of family control of all aspects of life to government agencies.

Among studies of special groups, J. Scott, *The Glass-Workers of Carmaux* (1974), is outstanding on skilled French craftsmen, and D. Lockwood, *The Black-coated Worker* (1958), carefully examines class consciousness in the English lower middle class. J. R. Wegs, *Growing Up Working Class: Continuity and Change Among Viennese Youth, 1890–1938* (1989), is recommended. Two fine studies on universities and their professors are S. Rothblatt, *Revolution of the Dons: Cambridge and Society in Victorian England* (1968), and F. Ringer, *The Decline of the German Mandarins* (1969). Servants and their employers receive excellent treatment in T. McBride, *The Domestic Revolution: The Modernization of Household Service in England and France, 1820–1920* (1976), and B. Smith, *Ladies of the Leisure Class: The Bourgeoises of Northern France in the Nineteenth Century* (1981), which may be compared with the innovative study by M. Miller, *The Bon Marché: Bourgeois Culture and the Department Store, 1869–1920* (1981).

On Darwin, M. Ruse, *The Darwinian Revolution* (1979), is a good starting point, as are P. Bowler, *Evolution: The History of an Idea,* rev. ed. (1989), and G. Himmelfarb, *Darwin and the Darwinian Revolution* (1968). O. Chadwick, *The Secularization of the European Mind in the Nineteenth Century* (1976), analyzes the impact of science (and other factors) on religious belief. The masterpieces of the great realist social novelists remain one of the best and most memorable introductions to nineteenth-century culture and thought. In addition to the novels discussed in this chapter and those cited in the Suggested Reading for Chapters 26 and 27, I. Turgenev's *Fathers and Sons* and Zola's *The Dram-Shop (L'Assommoir)* are especially recommended.

29

The Age of Nationalism
in Europe, 1850–1914

The meeting of Garibaldi and Victor Emmanuel

The revolutions of 1848 closed one era and opened another. Urban industrial society began to take strong hold on the Continent, as it already had in Great Britain. Internationally, the repressive peace and diplomatic stability of Metternich's time was replaced by a period of war and rapid change. In thought and culture, soaring romanticism gave way to tough-minded realism. In the European economy, the hard years of the 1840s were followed by good times and prosperity throughout most of the 1850s and 1860s. Perhaps most important of all, European society progressively found, for better or worse, a new and effective organizing principle, capable of coping with the many-sided challenge of the dual revolution and the emerging urban civilization. That principle was *nationalism:* dedication to and identification with the nation-state.

The triumph of nationalism in Europe after 1850 is a development of enormous historical significance. It was by no means completely predictable. After all, nationalism had been a powerful force since at least 1789. Yet it had repeatedly failed to realize its goals, most spectacularly so in 1848.

- Why did nationalism become in one way or another an almost universal faith in Europe between 1850 and 1914?

- How did nationalism evolve so that it appealed not only to predominantly middle-class liberals but to the broad masses of society as well?

These are the weighty questions that this chapter seeks to answer.

NAPOLEON III IN FRANCE

Early nationalism was at least liberal and idealistic and was often democratic and radical as well. The ideas of nationhood and popular sovereignty posed an awesome revolutionary threat to conservatives like Metternich. Yet from the vantage point of the twentieth century, it is clear that nationalism wears many masks. It may be democratic and radical, as it was for Mazzini and Michelet; but it can also flourish in dictatorial states, which may be conservative, fascist, or communist. Napoleon I's France had already combined national devotion with authoritarian rule. Significantly, it was Napoleon's nephew, Louis Napoleon, who revived and extended this merger. It was he who showed how governments could reconcile popular and conservative forces in an authoritarian nationalism. In doing so, he provided a model for political leaders elsewhere.

The Second Republic and Louis Napoleon

The overwhelming victory of Louis Napoleon Bonaparte in the French presidential elections of December 1848 has long puzzled historians. The nephew of Napoleon I, Louis Napoleon had lived most of his life outside of France and played no part in French politics before 1848. Why did universal manhood suffrage give such an unproven nobody 5.5 million votes while the runner-up, General Cavaignac of June Days fame, polled only 1.5 million and the other three candidates (including the poet Lamartine) received insignificant support?

The usual explanation is that, though Louis Napoleon had only his great name in common with his uncle, that was enough. According to some historians, the Napoleonic legend—a monument to the power of romanticism between 1820 and 1848—had transformed a dictator into a demigod in the minds of the unsophisticated French masses. Another explanation, popularized by Karl Marx, has stressed the fears of middle-class and peasant property owners in the face of the socialist challenge of urban workers. These classes wanted protection. They wanted a tough cop with a big stick on the beat. They found him in Louis Napoleon, who had indeed served briefly as a special constable in London during the Chartist agitation.

These explanations are not wrong, but there was more to Louis Napoleon's popularity than stupidity and fear. In late 1848, Louis Napoleon had a positive "program" for France—a plan that was to guide him throughout most of his long reign. He had elaborated his program in two pamphlets, *Napoleonic Ideas* and *The Elimination of Poverty,* which he had written while imprisoned for a farcical attempt to overthrow Louis Philippe's government. The pamphlets had been widely circulated prior to the presidential election.

Louis Napoleon believed that the government should represent the people and that it should also try hard to help them economically. How was this to be done? Parliaments and political parties were not the answer, according to Louis Napoleon. Politicians represented special-interest groups, particularly middle-class ones. When they ran a parliamentary government, they stirred up class hatred because they were not interested in helping the poor. This had occurred under Louis Philippe, and it was occurring again under the Second Republic. The answer was a strong, even authoritarian, national leader, like the first Napoleon, who would serve all the people, rich and poor. This leader would be linked to the people by direct democracy and universal male suffrage. Sovereignty would flow from the entire population to the leader and would not be diluted or corrupted by politicians and legislative bodies.

These political ideas went hand in hand with Louis Napoleon's vision of national unity and social progress. Unlike his uncle, who had reduced unemployment and social tensions by means of foreign wars, Louis Napoleon favored peaceful measures to relieve the awful poverty of the poor. Rather than doing nothing or providing only temporary relief, the state and its leader had a sacred duty to provide jobs and stimulate the economy. All classes would benefit by such action.

Louis Napoleon's political and social ideas were at least vaguely understood by large numbers of French peasants and workers in December 1848. To many common people he appeared to be both a strong man and a forward-looking champion of their interests, and that is why they voted for him.

Elected to a four-year term, President Louis Napoleon had to share power with a conservative National Assembly. With some misgivings he signed a bill to increase greatly the role of the Catholic church in primary and secondary education. In France as elsewhere in Europe after 1848, the anxious well-to-do saw religion as a bulwark against radicalism. As one leader of the church in France put it, "There is only one recipe for making those who own nothing believe in property-rights: that is to make them believe in God, who dictated the Ten Commandments and who promises eternal punishment to those who steal."[1] Very reluctantly, Louis Napoleon also signed another conservative law, depriving many poor men of the right to vote. He took these conservative measures for two main

reasons: he wanted the Assembly to vote funds to pay his personal debts, and he wanted it to change the constitution so he could run for a second term.

The Assembly did neither. Thus in 1851, Louis Napoleon began to organize a conspiracy with key army officers. On December 2, 1851, he illegally dismissed the Assembly and seized power in a coup d'état. There was some armed resistance in Paris and other cities, but the conservative actions of the Assembly had left the Second Republic with few defenders. Restoring universal male suffrage, Louis Napoleon called on the French people to legalize his actions as his uncle had done. They did: 92 percent voted to make him a strong president for ten years. A year later, 97 percent agreed in a national plebiscite to make him hereditary emperor. For the third time, and by the greatest margin yet, the authoritarian Louis Napoleon was overwhelmingly elected to lead the French nation.

Napoleon III's Second Empire

Louis Napoleon—now Emperor Napoleon III—experienced both success and failure between 1852 and 1870. His greatest success was with the economy, particularly in the 1850s. His government encouraged the new investment banks and massive railroad construction that were at the heart of the Industrial Revolution on the Continent. General economic expansion was also fostered by the government's ambitious program of public works, which included the rebuilding of Paris to improve the urban environment (see pages 903–906). The profits of businessmen soared with prosperity, and the working classes did not fare poorly either. Their wages more than kept up with inflation, and jobs were much easier to find. France's economy benefited from a worldwide economic boom and from other external events, such as gold discoveries in California and Australia. Yet the contribution of Napoleon III's economic policies was real all the same.

Louis Napoleon always hoped that economic progress would reduce social and political tensions. This hope was at least partially realized. Until the mid-1860s, there was little active opposition and even considerable support for his government from France's most dissatisfied group, the urban workers. Napoleon III's regulation of pawnshops and his support of credit unions and

Rebuilding Paris Expensive and time consuming, boulevard construction in Paris brought massive demolition, considerable slum clearance, and protests of ruin to the old city. In addition to expecting economic benefits, Napoleon III rightly believed that broad boulevards would be harder for revolutionaries to barricade than narrow twisting streets. *(Source: The Monsell Collection)*

better housing for the working class were evidence of positive concern in the 1850s. In the 1860s, he granted workers the right to form unions and the right to strike—important economic rights denied by earlier governments.

At first, political power remained in the hands of the emperor. He alone chose his ministers, and they had great freedom of action. At the same time, Napoleon III restricted but did not abolish the Assembly. To be sure, the French parliament in the 1850s had little power. It could not initiate legislation, and it did not control the budget. Yet the members of the Assembly were elected by universal male suffrage every six years, and Louis Napoleon and his government took the parliamentary elections very seriously. They tried to entice notable people, even those who had opposed the

regime, to stand as government candidates in order to expand its base of support. Moreover, the government used its officials and appointed mayors to spread the word that the election of the government's candidates—and the defeat of the opposition—was the key to roads, schools, tax rebates, and a thousand other local concerns.

In 1857 and again in 1863, Louis Napoleon's system worked well and produced overwhelming electoral victories. The poet-politician Alphonse de Lamartine was convinced that Louis Napoleon was France's greatest politician since Talleyrand, and possibly even greater than he. Yet in the course of the 1860s Napoleon III's electoral system gradually disintegrated, for several reasons. France's problems in Italy and the rising power of Prussia led to increasing criticism at home from his

Catholic and nationalist supporters. With increasing effectiveness, the middle-class liberals who had always detested his dictatorship denounced his rule as a disgrace to France's republican tradition.

Napoleon III was always sensitive to the public mood. Public opinion, he once said, always wins the last victory. Thus in the 1860s, he progressively "liberalized" his empire. He gave the Assembly greater powers and the opposition candidates greater freedom, which they used to good advantage. In 1869 the opposition, consisting of republicans, monarchists, and liberals, polled almost 45 percent of the vote.

The following year, a sick and weary Louis Napoleon once again granted France a new constitution, which combined a basically parliamentary regime with a hereditary emperor as chief of state. In a final great plebiscite on the eve of a disastrous war with Prussia, 7.5 million Frenchmen voted in favor of the new constitution, and only 1.5 million opposed it. Napoleon III's attempt to reconcile a strong national state with universal manhood suffrage was still evolving, in a democratic direction.

NATION BUILDING IN ITALY AND GERMANY

Louis Napoleon's triumph in 1848 and his authoritarian rule in the 1850s provided the old ruling classes of Europe with a new model in politics. To what extent was it possible that the expanding urban middle classes and even the growing working classes might, like people in rural areas, rally to a strong and essentially conservative national state? This was one of the great political questions in the 1850s and 1860s. In central Europe, a resounding and definitive answer came with the national unification of Italy and Germany.

Italy to 1850

Italy had never been a united nation prior to 1860. Part of Rome's great empire in ancient times, the Italian peninsula was divided in the Middle Ages into competing city-states, which led the commercial and cultural revival of the West with amazing creativity. A battleground for great powers after 1494, Italy had been reorganized in 1815 at the Congress of Vienna. The rich northern provinces of Lombardy and Venetia were taken by Metternich's Austria. Sardinia and Piedmont were under the rule of an Italian monarch, and Tuscany with its famous capital of Florence shared north central Italy with several smaller states. Central Italy and Rome were ruled by the papacy, which had always considered an independent political existence necessary to fulfill its spiritual mission. Naples and Sicily were ruled, as they had been for almost a hundred years, by a branch of the Bourbons. Metternich was not wrong in dismissing Italy as "a geographical expression" (Map 29.1).

Between 1815 and 1848, the goal of a unified Italian nation captured the imaginations of increasing numbers of Italians. There were three basic approaches. The first was the radical program of the idealistic patriot Giuseppi Mazzini (1805–1872), who preached a centralized democratic republic based on universal suffrage and the will of the people. The second was that of Vincenzo Gioberti (1801–1852), a Catholic priest, who called for a federation of existing states under the presidency of a progressive pope. Finally, there were those who looked for leadership toward the autocratic kingdom of Sardinia-Piedmont, much as many Germans looked toward Prussia.

The third alternative was strengthened by the failures of 1848, when Austria smashed and discredited Mazzini's republicanism. Almost by accident, Sardinia's monarch Victor Emmanuel II (1849–1878) retained the liberal constitution granted under duress in March 1848. This constitution provided for a fair degree of civil liberties and real parliamentary government, complete with elections and parliamentary control of taxes. To the Italian middle classes, Sardinia appeared to be a liberal, progressive state, ideally suited to achieve the goal of national unification. By contrast, Mazzini's brand of democratic republicanism seemed quixotic and too radical. As for the papacy, the initial cautious support by Pius IX (r. 1846–1878) for unification had given way to fear and hostility after he was temporarily driven from Rome during the upheavals of 1848. For a long generation, the papacy would stand resolutely opposed not only to national unification but to most modern trends. In 1864, in the *Syllabus of Errors,* Pius IX strongly denounced rationalism, socialism, separation of church and state, and religious liberty, denying that "the Roman pontiff can and ought to reconcile and align himself with progress, liberalism, and modern civilization."

MAP 29.1 The Unification of Italy, 1859–1870   The leadership of Sardinia-Piedmont and nationalist fervor were decisive factors in the unification of Italy.

Cavour and Garibaldi

The kingdom of Sardinia (see Map 29.1) had the good fortune of being led by a brilliant statesman, Count Camillo Benso di Cavour (1810–1861), the dominant figure in the Sardinian government from 1850 until his death. Cavour's rise to promi-nence presaged the coming tacit alliance between the aristocracy and the solid middle class through-out much of Europe. Beginning as a successful manager of his father's landed estates in Piedmont, Cavour was also an economic liberal. He turned toward industry and made a fortune in sugar mills, steamships, banks, and railroads. Economically secure, he then entered the world of politics and became chief minister in the liberalized Sardinian monarchy. Cavour's national goals were limited and realistic. Until 1859 he sought unity only for the states of northern and perhaps central Italy in a greatly expanded kingdom of Sardinia. It was *not* one of his goals to incorporate the papal states or the kingdom of the Two Sicilies, with their very different cultures and governments, into an Italy of all the Italians. Cavour was a moderate nationalist.

In the 1850s Cavour worked to consolidate the kingdom of Sardinia as a liberal state capable of leading northern Italy. His program of highways and railroads, of civil liberties and opposition to clerical privilege, increased support for Sardinia throughout northern Italy. Yet Cavour realized that Sardinia could not drive Austria out of Lombardy and Venetia and unify northern Italy under Victor Emmanuel without the help of a powerful ally. He sought that ally in the person of Napoleon III, who sincerely believed in the general principle of nationality as well as in modest expansion for France.

In a complicated series of diplomatic maneuvers, Cavour worked for a diplomatic alliance with Napoleon III against Austria. Finally, in July 1858, he succeeded and goaded Austria into attacking Sardinia. Napoleon III came to Sardinia's defense. Then, after the victory of the combined Franco-Sardinian forces, Napoleon III did a complete about-face. Nauseated by the gore of war and criticized by French Catholics for supporting the pope's declared enemy, Napoleon III abandoned Cavour. He made a compromise peace with the Austrians at Villafranca in July 1859. The kingdom of Sardinia received only Lombardy, the area around Milan. The rest of the map of Italy remained essentially unchanged. Cavour resigned in a rage.

Garibaldi and His Red Shirts Four days after landing in western Sicily, Garibaldi's forces won the Battle of Calatafimi, pictured here with the flamboyant patriot exhorting his troops at the center. Within two weeks Garibaldi took Palermo and established a provisional government in Sicily. *(Source: Museo del Risorgimento, Milan. Photo: Giancarlo Costa)*

Yet Cavour's plans were salvaged by popular revolts and Italian nationalism. While the war against Austria had raged in the north, dedicated nationalists in central Italy had risen and driven out their rulers. Nationalist fervor seized the urban masses. Large crowds demonstrated, chanting, "Italy and Victor Emmanuel!" and singing passionately, "Foreigners, get out of Italy!" Buoyed by this enthusiasm, leaders of the nationalist movement in central Italy ignored the compromise peace of Villafranca and called for fusion with Sardinia. This was not at all what France and the other Great Powers wanted, but the nationalists held firm and eventually had their way. Cavour returned to power in early 1860 and worked out a diplomatic deal with Napoleon III. The people of central Italy voted overwhelmingly to join a greatly enlarged kingdom of Sardinia. Cavour had achieved his original goal of a north Italian state (see Map 29.1).

Superpatriots like Giuseppe Garibaldi (1801–1882) believed that the job of unification was still only half done. The son of a poor sailor, Garibaldi personified the romantic, revolutionary nationalism of Mazzini and 1848. As a lad of seventeen, he had traveled to Rome and been converted to the "New Italy, the Italy of all the Italians." As he later wrote in his *Autobiography,* "The Rome that I beheld with the eyes of youthful imagination was the Rome of the future—the dominant thought of my whole life." Sentenced to death in 1834 for his part in an uprising in Genoa, Garibaldi escaped to South America. For twelve years he led a guerrilla band in Uruguay's struggle for independence. "Shipwrecked, ambushed, shot through the neck," he found in a tough young woman, Anna da Silva, a mate and companion in arms. Their first children nearly starved in the jungle while Garibaldi, clad in a long red shirt, fashioned a legend not unlike that of the Cuban Che Guevara in recent times. He returned to Italy to fight in 1848 and led a corps of volunteers against Austria in 1859. By the spring of 1860, Garibaldi had emerged as a powerful independent force in Italian politics.

Partly to use Garibaldi and partly to get rid of him, Cavour secretly supported Garibaldi's bold plan to "liberate" Sicily. Landing in Sicily in May 1860, Garibaldi's guerrilla band of a thousand "Red Shirts" captivated the Sicilian peasantry. Outwitting the 20,000-man royal army, the guerrilla leader took Palermo. Then he and his men crossed to the mainland, marched triumphantly toward Naples, and prepared to attack Rome and the pope. But the wily Cavour quickly sent Sardinian forces to occupy most of the Papal States (but not Rome) and to intercept Garibaldi.

Cavour realized that an attack on Rome would bring about war with France, and he also feared Garibaldi's popular appeal. Thus he immediately organized a plebiscite in the conquered territories. The patriotic Garibaldi did not oppose Cavour, despite the urging of some of his more radical supporters, and the people of the south voted to join the kingdom of Sardinia. When Garibaldi and Victor Emmanuel rode through Naples to cheering crowds, they symbolically sealed the union of north and south, of monarch and people.

Cavour had succeeded. He had controlled Garibaldi and had turned popular nationalism in a conservative direction. The new kingdom of Italy, which did not include Venice until 1866 or Rome until 1870, was neither radical nor democratic. Italy was a parliamentary monarchy under Victor Emmanuel, but in accordance with the Sardinian constitution only a small minority of Italians had the right to vote. There was a definite division between the propertied classes and the common people. There was also a great social and cultural gap between the progressive, industrializing north and the stagnant, agrarian south. This gap would increase, since peasant industries in the south would not be able to survive. Italy was united politically. Other divisions remained.

Germany Before Bismarck

In the aftermath of 1848, while Louis Napoleon consolidated his rule and Cavour schemed, the German states were locked in a political stalemate. With Russian diplomatic support, Austria had blocked the halfhearted attempt of Frederick William IV of Prussia (r. 1840–1861) to unify Germany "from above" This action contributed to growing tension between Austria and Prussia, as each power sought to block the other within the reorganized German Confederation (pages 868 and 894). Stalemate also prevailed in the domestic politics of the individual states, as Austria, Prussia, and the smaller German kingdoms entered a period of reaction and immobility.

At the same time, powerful economic forces were undermining the political status quo. Modern industry grew rapidly in Europe throughout the 1850s (see pages 846–852). Nowhere was this growth more rapid than within the German customs union *(Zollverein)*. Developing gradually under Prussian leadership after 1818 and founded officially in 1834 to stimulate trade and increase the revenues of member states, the Zollverein did not include Austria. After 1848 it became a crucial factor in the Austro-Prussian rivalry.

Prussia convinced the Zollverein to reduce substantially its tariff duties, so that Austria's highly protected industry could not afford to join the customs union. In retaliation, Austria tried to destroy the Zollverein by inducing the south German states to leave it, but without success. Indeed, by the end of 1853 all the German states except Austria had joined the customs union. A new Germany excluding Austria was becoming an economic reality, and the middle class and business groups were finding solid economic reasons to bolster their idealistic support of national unification. Thus economic developments helped Prussia greatly in its struggle against Austria's traditional supremacy in German affairs.

The national uprising in Italy in 1859 made a profound impression in the German states. In Prussia, great political change and war—perhaps with Austria, perhaps with France—seemed quite possible. The tough-minded William I of Prussia (r. 1861–1888), had replaced the unstable Frederick William IV as regent in 1858 and become king in 1861. He and his top military advisers were convinced of the need for major army reforms. William I wanted to double the size of the highly disciplined regular army. He also wanted to reduce the importance of the reserve militia, a semipopular force created during the Napoleonic wars. Of course, reform of the army meant a bigger defense budget and higher taxes.

Prussia had emerged from 1848 with a parliament of sorts, and by 1859 the Prussian parliament was in the hands of the liberal middle class. The middle class, like the landed aristocracy, was overrepresented by the Prussian electoral system, and it wanted society to be less, not more, militaristic. Above all, middle-class representatives wanted to establish once and for all that parliament, not the king, had the ultimate political power. They also wanted to ensure that the army was responsible to the people and not a "state within a state." These demands were popular. The parliament rejected the military budget in 1862,

Otto von Bismarck A fierce political fighter with a commanding personality and a brilliant mind, Bismarck was devoted to Prussia and its king and aristocracy. Uniforms were worn by civilian officials as well as by soldiers in Prussia. *(Source: Brown Brothers)*

and the liberals triumphed so completely in new elections that the conservatives "could ride to the parliament building in a single coach." King William considered abdicating in favor of his more liberal son. In the end, he called on Count Otto von Bismarck to head a ministry and defy the parliament. It was a momentous choice.

Bismarck Takes Command

The most important figure in German history between Luther and Hitler, Otto von Bismarck (1815–1898) has been the object of enormous interest and debate. Like his contemporary Abraham Lincoln, who successfully led the North against the South in the American Civil War between

1861 and 1865, Bismarck used military victory to forge a strong, unified national state.

A great hero to some, a great villain to others, Bismarck was above all a master of politics. Born into the Prussian landowning aristocracy, the young Bismarck was a wild and tempestuous student, given to duels and drinking. Proud of his Junker heritage—"my fathers have been born and have lived and died in the same rooms for centuries"—and always devoted to his Prussian sovereign, Bismarck had a strong personality and an unbounded desire for power.

Bismarck entered the civil service—the only socially acceptable career, except the army, for a Prussian aristocrat. But he soon found bureaucratic life unbearable and fled to his ancestral estate. The civil servant was like a musician in an orchestra, he said, and, "I want to play the tune the way it sounds to me or not at all. . . . My pride bids me command rather than obey."[2] Yet in his drive for power, power for himself and for Prussia, Bismarck was extraordinarily flexible and pragmatic. "One must always have two irons in the fire," he once said. He kept his options open, pursuing one policy and then another as he moved with skill and cunning toward his goal.

Bismarck first honed his political skills as a diplomat. Acquiring a reputation as an ultraconservative in the Prussian assembly in 1848, he fought against Austria as the Prussian ambassador to the German Confederation from 1851 to 1859. Transferred next to St. Petersburg and then to Paris, Bismarck had an excellent opportunity to evaluate Tsar Alexander II and Emperor Napoleon III at close range. A blunt, expansive talker, especially after a few drinks, Bismarck's basic goal was well known in 1862: to build up Prussia's strength and consolidate Prussia's precarious Great Power status.

To achieve this goal, Bismarck was convinced that Prussia had to control completely the northern, predominantly Protestant part of the German Confederation. He saw three paths open before him. He might work with Austria to divide the smaller German states lying between them (see Map 29.2). Or he might combine with foreign powers—France and Italy, or even Russia—against Austria. Or he might ally with the forces of German nationalism to defeat and expel Austria from German affairs. Each possibility was explored in many complicated diplomatic maneuvers, but in the end the last path was the one Bismarck took.

That Bismarck would join with the forces of German nationalism to increase Prussia's power seemed unlikely when he took office in 1862. Bismarck's appointment made a strong but unfavorable impression. One of the liberal middle-class members of the Prussian parliament expressed enlightened public opinion throughout Prussia and the other German states: "Bismarck, that is to say: government without budget, rule by the sword in home affairs, and war in foreign affairs. I consider him the most dangerous Minister for Prussia's liberty and happiness."[3]

Bismarck's speeches were a sensation and a scandal. Declaring that the government would rule without parliamentary consent, Bismarck lashed out at the middle-class opposition: "The great questions of the day will not be decided by speeches and resolutions—that was the blunder of 1848 and 1849—but by blood and iron." In 1863 he told the Prussian parliament, "If a compromise cannot be arrived at and a conflict arises, then the conflict becomes a question of power. Whoever has the power then acts according to his opinion." Denounced for his view that "might makes right," Bismarck and the bureaucracy went right on collecting taxes, even though the parliament refused to approve the budget, and reorganized the army. And for four years, from 1862 to 1866, the voters of Prussia continued to express their opposition by sending large liberal majorities to the parliament.

The Austro-Prussian War of 1866

Opposition at home spurred the search for success abroad. The ever-knotty question of Schleswig-Holstein (see page 892) provided a welcome opportunity. When the Danish king tried again, as in 1848, to bring the provinces into a centralized Danish state against the will of the German Confederation, Prussia joined Austria in a short and successful war against Denmark in 1864. Then, rather than following nationalist sentiment and allowing the conquered provinces to become another medium-size independent state within the German Confederation, Bismarck maneuvered Austria into a tricky position. Prussia and Austria agreed to joint administration of the conquered provinces, thereby giving Bismarck a weapon he could use either to force Austria into peacefully accepting Prussian domination in northern Germany or to start a war against Austria.

MAP 29.2 The Unification of Germany, 1866–1871 Prussian expansion, Austrian expulsion from the old German Confederation, and the creation of a new German Empire all went together. Austria lost no territory, but Prussia's neighbors in the north suffered grievously or simply disappeared.

Bismarck knew that a war with Austria would have to be localized war. He had to be certain that Prussian expansion did not provoke a mighty armed coalition, such as the coalition that had almost crushed Frederick the Great in the eighteenth century. Russia, the great bear to the east,

was no problem. Bismarck had already gained Alexander II's gratitude by supporting Russia's repression of a Polish uprising in 1863. Napoleon III—the "sphinx without a riddle," according to Bismarck—was another matter. But Bismarck charmed him into neutrality with vague promises of more territory along the Rhine. Thus, when Austria proved unwilling to give up its historic role in German affairs, Bismarck was in a position to engage in a war of his own making.

The Austro-Prussian War of 1866 lasted only seven weeks. Utilizing railroads to mass troops and the new breechloading needle gun for maximum firepower, the reorganized Prussian army overran northern Germany and defeated Austria decisively at the battle of Sadowa in Bohemia. Anticipating Prussia's future needs, Bismarck offered Austria realistic, even generous, peace terms. Austria paid no reparations and lost no territory to Prussia, although Venice was ceded to Italy. But Hanover was seized by Prussia, the German Confederation was dissolved, and Austria agreed to withdraw from German affairs. The states north of the Main River were grouped in a new North German Confederation led by an expanded Prussia. The mainly Catholic states of the south were permitted to remain independent while forming military alliances with Prussia. Bismarck's fundamental goal of Prussian expansion was being realized (Map 29.2).

The Taming of Parliament

Bismarck had long been convinced that the old order he so ardently defended should make peace—on its own terms—with the liberal middle class and the nationalist movement. Inspired somewhat by Louis Napoleon, he realized that nationalism was not necessarily hostile to conservative, authoritarian government. Moreover, Bismarck believed that, because of the events of 1848, the German middle class could be led to prefer the reality of national unity to a long, uncertain battle for truly liberal institutions. During the constitutional struggle over army reform and parliamentary authority, he had delayed but not abandoned this goal. Thus, during the attack on Austria in 1866, he increasingly identified Prussia's fate with the "national development of Germany."

In the aftermath of victory, Bismarck fashioned a federal constitution for the new North German Confederation. Each state retained its own local government, but the king of Prussia was to be president of the confederation and the chancellor—Bismarck—was to be responsible only to the president. The federal government—William I and

Bismarck—controlled the army and foreign affairs. There was also a legislature, consisting of an upper house, whose delegates were appointed by the different states, and a lower house. Both houses shared equally in the making of laws. Members of the lower house were elected by universal, equal manhood suffrage. With this radical innovation, Bismarck opened the door to popular participation and went over the head of the middle class directly to the people. All the while, however, ultimate power rested as securely as ever in the hands of Prussia and its king and army.

Events within Prussia itself were even more significant than those at the federal level. In the flush of victory, the ultraconservatives expected Bismarck to suspend the Prussian constitution or perhaps abolish the Prussian parliament altogether. Yet he did nothing of the sort. Instead, he held out an olive branch to the parliamentary opposition. Marshaling all his diplomatic skill, Bismarck asked the parliament to pass a special indemnity bill to approve after the fact all of the government's spending between 1862 and 1866. Most of the liberals snatched at the chance to cooperate. For four long years, they had opposed and criticized Bismarck's "illegal" measures. And what had happened? Bismarck, the king, and the army had persevered, and in the end these conservative forces had succeeded beyond the wildest dreams of the liberal middle class. In 1866 German unity was in sight, and the people were going to be allowed to participate actively in the new state. Many liberals repented their "sins" and were overjoyed that Bismarck would forgive them.

None repented more ardently or more typically than Hermann Baumgarten, a mild-mannered, thoroughly decent history professor and member of the liberal opposition. In an essay entitled "A Self Criticism of German Liberalism," he confessed in 1866:

We thought by agitation we could transform Germany. But . . . almost all the elements of our political system have been shown erroneous by the facts themselves. . . . Yet we have experienced a miracle almost without parallel. The victory of our principles would have brought us misery, whereas the defeat of our principles has brought boundless salvation.[4]

The constitutional struggle was over. The German middle class was bowing respectfully before

Bismarck and the monarchial authority and aristocratic superiority that he represented. They did not stand upright again in the years before 1914.

The Franco-Prussian War of 1870 to 1871

The rest of the story of German unification is anticlimactic. In 1867 Bismarck brought the four south German states into the customs union and established a customs parliament. The south Germans, led by the anti-Prussian Bavarians, were reluctant to go further because of their different religious and political traditions. Bismarck realized that a patriotic war with France would drive the south German states into Prussia's arms. The French obligingly played their part. The apparent issue—whether a distant relative of Prussia's William I (and France's Napoleon III) might become king of Spain—was only a diplomatic pretext. By 1870 the French leaders of the Second Empire, alarmed by their powerful new neighbor on the Rhine, had decided on a war to teach Prussia a lesson.

As soon as war against France began in 1870, Bismarck had the wholehearted support of the south German states. With other governments standing still—Bismarck's generosity to Austria in 1866 was paying big dividends—German forces under Prussian leadership decisively defeated Louis Napoleon's armies at Sedan on September 1, 1870. Three days later, French patriots in Paris proclaimed yet another French republic (the third) and vowed to continue fighting. But after five months, in January 1871, a starving Paris surrendered and France went on to accept Bismarck's harsh peace terms. By this time, the south German states had agreed to join a new German Empire. The victorious William I was proclaimed emperor of Germany in the Hall of Mirrors in the palace of Versailles. Europe had a nineteenth-century German "sun king." As in the 1866 constitution, the king of Prussia and his ministers had ultimate power in the new empire, and the lower house of the legislature was elected popularly by universal male suffrage.

The Franco-Prussian War of 1870 to 1871, which Europeans generally saw as a test of nations in a pitiless Darwinian struggle for existence, released an enormous surge of patriotic feeling in Germany. Bismarck's genius, the invincible Prus-

sian army, the solidarity of king and people in a unified nation—these and similar themes were trumpeted endlessly during and after the war. The weakest of the Great Powers in 1862—after Austria, Britain, France, and Russia—Prussia (fortified by the other German states) had become the most powerful state in Europe in less than a decade. Most Germans were enormously proud, enormously relieved. And they were somewhat drunk with success, blissfully imagining themselves the fittest and best of the European species.

"His First Thought" This 1896 cartoon provides a brilliant commentary on German middle-class attitudes. Suddenly crippled, the man's first thought is "Disaster! Now I can no longer be an army reserve officer." Being a part-time junior officer, below the dominant aristocratic career officers, became a great middle-class status symbol. *(Source: Caroline Buckler)*

Semi-authoritarian nationalism had triumphed. Only a few critics remained dedicated to the liberal ideal of truly responsible parliamentary government.

THE MODERNIZATION OF RUSSIA

In Russia, unlike in Italy and Germany, there was no need to build a single state out of a jumble of principalities. The Russian Empire was already an enormous multinational state, a state that contained all the ethnic Russians and many other nationalities as well. The long-term challenge facing the government was to hold the existing state together, either by means of political compromise or by military force. Thus Russia's rulers saw nationalism as a subversive ideology in the early nineteenth century, and they tried with some success to limit its development among their non-Russian subjects.

Yet old, autocratic Russia found itself in serious trouble after 1853. It became clear to Russia's leaders that the country had to embrace the process of modernization. A vague and often overworked term, "modernization" is a great umbrella under which some writers place most of the major developments of the last two hundred or even five hundred years. Yet defined narrowly—as changes that enable a country to compete effectively with the leading countries at a given time—modernization can be a useful concept. It fits Russia after the Crimean War particularly well.

The "Great Reforms"

In the 1850s Russia was a poor agrarian society. Industry was little developed, and almost 90 percent of the population lived on the land. Agricultural techniques were backward: the ancient open-field system reigned supreme. Serfdom was still the basic social institution. Bound to the lord on a hereditary basis, the peasant serf was little more than a slave. In the early nineteenth century, individual serfs and serf families were regularly sold, with and without land. Serfs were obliged to furnish labor services or money payments as the lord saw fit. Moreover, the lord could choose freely among them for army recruits, who had to serve for twenty-five years, and he could punish a serf with deportation to Siberia whenever he wished. Sexual exploitation of female serfs by their lords was common.

Serfdom had become the great moral and political issue for the government by the 1840s, but it might still have lasted many more years had it not been for the Crimean War of 1853 to 1856. The war began as a dispute with France over who should protect certain Christian shrines in the Ottoman Empire. Because the fighting was concentrated on the Crimean peninsula in the Black Sea, Russia's transportation network of rivers and wagons failed to supply the distant Russian armies adequately. France and Great Britain, aided by Sardinia, inflicted a humiliating defeat on Russia.

The military defeat marked a turning point in Russian history. The Russian state had been built on the military, and Russia had not lost a major war for a century and a half. This defeat demonstrated that Russia had fallen behind the rapidly industrializing nations of western Europe in many areas. At the very least, Russia needed railroads, better armaments, and reorganization of the army if it was to maintain its international position as a Great Power. Moreover, the disastrous war had caused hardship and raised the specter of massive peasant rebellion. Reform of serfdom was imperative. And, as the new tsar, Alexander II (r. 1855–1881), told the serf owners, it would be better if reform came from above rather than from below. Military disaster thus forced Alexander II and his ministers along the path of rapid social change and general modernization.

The first and greatest of the reforms was the freeing of the serfs in 1861. Human bondage was abolished forever, and the emancipated peasants received, on the average, about half of the land. Yet they had to pay fairly high prices for their land, and because the land was owned collectively, each peasant village was jointly responsible for the payments of all the families in the village. The government hoped that collective responsibility would strengthen the peasant village as a social unit and prevent the development of a class of landless peasants. In practice, collective ownership and responsibility made it very difficult for individual peasants to improve agricultural methods or leave their villages. Thus the effects of the reform were limited, for it did not encourage peasants to change their old habits and attitudes.

Most of the later reforms were also halfway measures. In 1864 the government established a new institution of local government, the *zemstvo*. Members of this local assembly were elected by a three-class system of towns, peasant villages, and noble landowners. A zemstvo executive council dealt with local problems. The establishment of the zemstvos marked a significant step toward popular participation, and Russian liberals hoped that it would lead to a national parliament. They were soon disappointed. The local zemstvo remained subordinate to the traditional bureaucracy and the local nobility, which were heavily favored by the property-based voting system. More successful was reform of the legal system, which established independent courts and equality before the law. Education was also liberalized somewhat, and censorship was relaxed but not removed.

The Industrialization of Russia

Until the twentieth century, Russia's greatest strides toward modernization were economic rather than political. Industry and transport, both so vital to the military, were transformed in two industrial surges. The first came after 1860. The government encouraged and subsidized private railway companies, and construction boomed. In 1860 the empire had only about 1,250 miles of railroads; by 1880 it had about 15,500 miles. The railroads enabled agricultural Russia to export grain and thus earn money for further industrialization. Domestic manufacturing was stimulated, and by the end of the 1870s Russia had a sophisticated and well-developed railway-equipment industry. Industrial suburbs grew up around Moscow and St. Petersburg, and a class of modern factory workers began to take shape.

Industrial development strengthened Russia's military forces and gave rise to territorial expansion to the south and east. Imperial expansion greatly excited many ardent Russian nationalists and superpatriots, who became some of the government's most enthusiastic supporters. Industrial development also contributed mightily to the spread of Marxian thought and the transformation of the Russian revolutionary movement after 1890.

In 1881 Alexander II was assassinated by a small group of terrorists. The era of reform came to an abrupt end, for the new tsar, Alexander III (r. 1881–1894), was a determined reactionary. Russia, and indeed all of Europe, experienced hard times economically in the 1880s. Political modernization remained frozen until 1905, but economic modernization sped forward in the 1890s, in the massive second industrial surge. As it had after the Crimean War, nationalism played a decisive role. The key leader was Sergei Witte (1849–1915), the tough, competent minister of finance from 1892 to 1903. Early in his career, Witte had found in the writings of Friedrich List (page 851) an analysis and a program for action. List had stressed the peril for Germany of remaining behind England in the 1830s and 1840s. Witte saw the same threat of industrial backwardness hindering Russia's power and greatness.

Witte moved forward on several fronts. A railroad manager by training, he believed that railroads were "a very powerful weapon . . . for the direction of the economic development of the country."[5] Thus the Russian government built railroads rapidly, doubling the network to 35,000 miles by the end of the century. The gigantic trans-Siberian line connecting Moscow with Vladivostok on the Pacific Ocean 5,000 miles away was Witte's pride, and it was largely completed during his term of office. Following List's advice, Witte raised high protective tariffs to build Russian industry, and he put the country on the gold standard of the "civilized world" in order to strengthen Russian finances.

Witte's greatest innovation, however, was to use the West to catch up with the West. He aggressively encouraged foreigners to use their abundant capital and advanced technology to build great factories in backward Russia. As he told the tsar, "The inflow of foreign capital is . . . the only way by which our industry will be able to supply our country quickly with abundant and cheap products."[6] This policy was brilliantly successful, especially in southern Russia. There, in the eastern Ukraine, foreign capitalists and their engineers built an enormous and very modern steel and coal industry almost from scratch in little more than a decade. By 1900 only the United States, Germany, and Great Britain were producing more steel than Russia. The Russian petroleum industry had even pulled up alongside that of the United States and was producing and refining half of the world's output of oil.

Novgorod Merchants Drinking Tea This late nineteenth-century photograph suggests how Russian businessmen were slow to abandon traditional dress and attitudes. Stern authoritarians and staunchly devoted to church and tsar, they were often suspicious of foreigners as well as the lawyers and journalists who claimed to speak for the nation's middle class. *(Source: Bettmann/Hulton)*

Witte knew how to keep foreigners in line. Once a leading foreign businessman came to him and angrily demanded that the Russian government fulfill a contract that it had signed and pay certain debts immediately. Witte asked to see the contract. He read it and then carefully tore it to pieces and threw it in the wastepaper basket without a word of explanation. It was just such a fiercely independent Russia that was catching up with the advanced nations of the West.

The Revolution of 1905

In part, catching up meant vigorous territorial expansion, for this was the age of Western imperialism (see Chapter 30). By 1903 Russia had established a sphere of influence in Chinese Man-churia and was casting greedy eyes on northern Korea. When the protests of equally imperialistic Japan were ignored, the Japanese launched a surprise attack in February 1904. To the world's amazement, Russia suffered repeated losses and was forced in August 1905 to accept a humiliating defeat.

As is often the case, military disaster abroad brought political upheaval at home. The business and professional classes had long wanted to match economic with political modernization. Their minimal goal was to turn the last of Europe's absolutist monarchies into a liberal, representative regime. Factory workers, strategically concentrated in the large cities, had all the grievances of early industrialization and were organized in a radical labor movement. Peasants had gained little from the era of reforms and were suffering from poverty and overpopulation. Nationalist sentiment was emerging among the empire's minorities. The politically and culturally dominant ethnic Russians were only about 45 percent of the population, and by 1900 some intellectuals among the subject nationalities were calling for self-rule and autonomy. Separatist nationalism was strongest among the Polish and Ukrainians. With the army pinned down in Manchuria, all these currents of discontent converged in the revolution of 1905.

The beginning of the revolution pointed up the incompetence of the government. On a Sunday in January 1905, a massive demonstration of workers and their families converged peacefully on the Winter Palace in St. Petersburg to present a petition to the tsar. The workers were led by a trade-unionist priest named Father Gapon, who had been secretly supported by the police as a preferable alternative to more radical unions. Carrying icons and respectfully singing "God Save the Tsar," the workers did not know that Nicholas II had fled the city. Suddenly troops opened fire, killing and wounding hundreds. The "Bloody Sunday" massacre turned ordinary workers against the tsar and produced a wave of general indignation.

Outlawed political parties came out into the open, and by the summer of 1905 strikes, peasant uprisings, revolts among minority nationalities, and troop mutinies were sweeping the country. The revolutionary surge culminated in October 1905 in a great paralyzing general strike, which forced the government to capitulate. The tsar issued the October Manifesto, which granted full civil rights and promised a popularly elected *Duma* (parliament) with real legislative power. The manifesto split the opposition. It satisfied most moderate and liberal demands, but the Social Democrats rejected it and led a bloody workers' uprising in Moscow in December 1905. Frightened middle-class moderates helped the government repress the uprising and survive as a constitutional monarchy.

On the eve of the opening of the first Duma in May 1906, the government issued the new constitution, the Fundamental Laws. The tsar retained great powers. The Duma, elected indirectly by universal male suffrage, and a largely appointive upper house could debate and pass laws, but the tsar had an absolute veto. As in Bismarck's Germany, the

emperor appointed his ministers, who did not need to command a majority in the Duma.

The disappointed, predominantly middle-class liberals, the largest group in the newly elected Duma, saw the Fundamental Laws as a great step backward. Efforts to cooperate with the tsar's ministers soon broke down. The government then dismissed the Duma, only to see a more hostile and radical opposition elected in 1907. After three months of deadlock, the second Duma was also dismissed. Thereupon the tsar and his reactionary advisers unilaterally rewrote the electoral law so as to increase greatly the weight of the propertied classes at the expense of workers, peasants, and national minorities.

The new law had the intended effect. With landowners assured half of the seats in the Duma, the government secured a loyal majority in 1907 and again in 1912. Thus armed, the tough, energetic chief minister, Peter Stolypin, pushed through important agrarian reforms designed to break down collective village ownership of land and to encourage the most enterprising peasants—the so-called wager on the strong. On the eve of the First World War, Russia was partially modernized, a conservative constitutional monarchy with a peasant-based but industrializing economy.

THE RESPONSIVE NATIONAL STATE (1871–1914)

For central and western Europe, the unification of Italy and Germany by "blood and iron" marked the end of a dramatic period of nation building. After 1871 the heartland of Europe was organized in strong national states. Only on the borders of Europe—in Ireland and Russia, in Austria-Hungary and the Balkans—did subject peoples still strive for political unity and independence. Despite national differences, European domestic politics after 1871 had a common framework: the firmly established national state. The common themes within that framework were the emergence of mass politics and growing mass loyalty toward the national state.

For good reason, ordinary people—the masses of an industrializing, urbanizing society—felt increasing loyalty to their governments. More and more people could vote. By 1914 universal manhood suffrage was the rule rather than the exception. This development had as much psychological as political significance. Ordinary men were no longer denied the right to vote because they lacked wealth or education. They counted; they could influence the government to some extent. They could feel that they were becoming "part of the system."

Women began to demand the right to vote. The women's suffrage movement achieved its first success in the western United States, and by 1913 women could vote in twelve states. Europe, too, moved slowly in this direction. In 1914 Norway gave the vote to most women. Elsewhere, women like the English Emmeline Pankhurst were very militant in their demands. They heckled politicians and held public demonstrations. These efforts generally failed before 1914, but they prepared the way for the triumph of the women's suffrage movement immediately after the First World War.

As the right to vote spread, politicians and parties in national parliaments represented the people more responsively. Most countries soon had many political parties. The multiparty system meant that parliamentary majorities were built on shifting coalitions, which were unstable but did give parties leverage. They could obtain benefits for their supporters. Governments increasingly passed laws to alleviate general problems and to help specific groups. Governments seemed to care, and they seemed more worthy of support.

The German Empire

Politics in Germany after 1871 reflected many of these developments. The new German Empire was a federal union of Prussia and twenty-four smaller states. Much of the everyday business of government was conducted by the separate states, but there was a strong national government with a chancellor—until 1890, Bismarck—and a popularly elected parliament, called the *Reichstag*. Although Bismarck refused to be bound by a parliamentary majority, he tried nonetheless to maintain such a majority. This situation gave the political parties opportunities. Until 1878 Bismarck relied mainly on the National Liberals, who had rallied to him after 1866. They supported legislation useful for further economic and legal unification of the country.

Less wisely, they backed Bismarck's attack on the Catholic church, the so-called *Kulturkampf,* or "struggle for civilization." Like Bismarck, the middle-class National Liberals were particularly alarmed by Pius IX's declaration of papal infallibility in 1870. That dogma seemed to ask German Catholics to put loyalty to their church above loyalty to their nation. Only in Protestant Prussia did the Kulturkampf have even limited success. Catholics throughout the country generally voted for the Catholic Center party, which blocked passage of national laws hostile to the church. Finally in 1878, Bismarck abandoned his attack. Indeed, he and the Catholic Center party entered into an uneasy but mutually advantageous alliance. The reasons were largely economic.

After a worldwide financial bust in 1873, European agriculture was in an increasingly difficult position. Wheat prices plummeted as cheap grain poured in from the United States, Canada, and Russia. New lands were opening up in North America and Russia, and the combination of railroads and technical improvements in shipping cut freight rates for grain drastically. European peasants with their smaller, less efficient farms could not compete in cereal production, especially in western and southern Germany. The peasantry there was largely Catholic, and the Catholic Center party was thus converted to the cause of higher tariffs to protect the economic interests of its supporters.

The same competitive pressures caused the Protestant Junkers, who owned large estates in eastern Germany, to embrace the cause of higher tariffs. They were joined by some of the iron and steel magnates of the Prussian Rhineland and Westphalia, who had previously been for free trade. With three such influential groups lobbying energetically, Bismarck was happy to go along with a new protective tariff in 1879. In doing so, he won new supporters in the Reichstag—the Center party of the Catholics and the Conservative party of the Prussian landowners—and he held on to most of the National Liberals.

Bismarck had been looking for a way to increase taxes and raise more money for the government. The solution was higher tariffs. Many other governments acted similarly. The 1880s and 1890s saw a widespread return to protectionism. France in particular established very high tariffs to protect agriculture and industry, peasants and manufacturers. Thus the German government and other

Bismarck and William II Shown here visiting Bismarck's country estate in 1888, shortly after he became emperor of Germany (and king of Prussia), the young and impetuous William II soon quarrelled with his chief minister. Determined to rule, not merely to reign, his dismissal of Bismarck in 1890 was a fatal decision. *(Source: Bildarchiv Preussicher Kulturbesitz)*

governments responded to a major economic problem and simultaneously won greater loyalty.

At the same time, Bismarck tried to stop the growth of German socialism because he genuinely feared its revolutionary language and allegiance to a movement transcending the nation-state. In 1878, after two attempts on the life of William I by radicals (though not socialists), Bismarck succeeded in ramming through the Reichstag a law repressing socialists. Socialist meetings and publications were strictly controlled. The Social Democratic party was outlawed and driven underground. However, German socialists displayed a discipline and organization worthy of the Prussian army itself. Bismarck had to try another tack.

Thus Bismarck's state pioneered with social measures that were designed to win the support of working-class people. In 1883 he pushed through parliament the first of several modern social security laws to help wage earners. The laws of 1883 and 1884 established national sickness and acci-

dent insurance; the law of 1889 established old-age pensions and retirement benefits. Henceforth sick, injured, and retired workers could look forward to regular weekly benefits from the state. This national social security system, paid for through compulsory contributions by wage earners and employers as well as grants from the state, was the first of its kind anywhere. It was to be fifty years before similar measures would be taken in the United States. Bismarck's social security system did not wean workers from socialism, but it did protect them from some of the uncertainties of the complex urban industrial world. This enormously significant development was a product of political competition and government efforts to win popular support.

Increasingly, the great issues in German domestic politics were socialism and the Marxian Social Democratic party. In 1890 the new emperor, the young, idealistic, and unstable William II (r. 1888–1918), opposed Bismarck's attempt to renew the law outlawing the Social Democratic party. Eager to rule in his own right, as well as to earn the support of the workers, William II forced Bismarck to resign. After the "dropping of the pilot," German foreign policy changed profoundly and mostly for the worse, but the government did pass new laws to aid workers and to legalize socialist political activity.

Yet William II was no more successful than Bismarck in getting workers to renounce socialism. Indeed, socialist ideas spread rapidly, and more and more Social Democrats were elected to the parliament in the 1890s. After opposing a colonial war in German Southwest Africa in 1906 and thus suffering important losses in the general elections of 1907, the German Social Democratic party broadened its base in the years before the First World War. In the elections of 1912, the party scored a great victory, becoming the largest single party in the Reichstag. The "revolutionary" socialists, however, were becoming less and less revolutionary in Germany. In the years before the First World War, the strength of socialist opposition to greater military spending and imperialist expansion declined greatly. German socialists marched under the national banner.

Republican France

In 1871 France seemed hopelessly divided once again. The patriotic republicans who proclaimed the Third Republic in Paris after the military disaster at Sedan refused to admit defeat. They defended Paris with great heroism for weeks, living off rats and zoo animals, until they were quite literally starved into submission by German armies in January 1871. When national elections then sent a large majority of conservatives and monarchists to the National Assembly, the traumatized Parisians exploded and proclaimed the Paris Commune in March 1871. Vaguely radical, the leaders of the Commune wanted to govern Paris without interference by the conservative French countryside. The National Assembly, led by the aging politician Adolphe Thiers, would hear none of it. The Assembly ordered the French army into Paris and brutally crushed the Commune. Twenty thousand people died in the fighting. As in June 1848, it was Paris against the provinces, French against French.

Out of this tragedy France slowly formed a new national unity, achieving considerable stability before 1914. How is one to account for this? Luck played a part. Until 1875 the monarchists in the "republican" National Assembly had a majority but could not agree about who should be king. The compromise Bourbon candidate refused to rule except under the white flag of his ancestors—a completely unacceptable condition. In the meantime, Thiers's slaying of the radical Commune and his other firm measures showed the fearful provinces and the middle class that the Third Republic might be moderate and socially conservative. France therefore retained the republic, though reluctantly. As President Thiers cautiously said, it was "the government which divides us least."

Another stabilizing factor was the skill and determination of the moderate republican leaders in the early years. The most famous of these was Léon Gambetta, the son of an Italian grocer, a warm, easygoing, unsuccessful lawyer turned professional politician. A master of emerging mass politics, Gambetta combined eloquence with the personal touch as he preached a republic of truly equal opportunity. Gambetta was also instrumental in establishing absolute parliamentary supremacy between 1877 and 1879, when the somewhat autocratic president Marie Edmé MacMahon was forced to resign. By 1879 the great majority of members of both the upper and the lower houses of parliament were republicans. Although these republicans were split among many parliamentary groups and later among several parties—a situation that led to constant coalition politics and the rapid turnover of ministers—the Third Republic had firm foundations after almost a decade.

The moderate republicans sought to preserve their creation by winning the hearts and minds of the next generation. Trade unions were fully legalized, and France acquired a colonial empire. More important, under the leadership of Jules Ferry, the moderate republicans of small towns and villages passed a series of laws between 1879 and 1886 establishing free compulsory elementary education for both girls and boys. At the same time, they greatly expanded the state system of public tax-supported schools. Thus France shared fully in the general expansion of public education that served as a critical nation-building tool throughout the Western world in the late nineteenth century.

In France most elementary and much secondary education had traditionally been in the parochial schools of the Catholic church, which had long been hostile to republics and to much of secular life. Free compulsory elementary education in France became secular republican education. The pledge of allegiance and the national anthem replaced the catechism and the Ave Maria. Militant young elementary teachers carried the ideology of patriotic republicanism into every corner of France. In their classes, they sought to win the loyalty of the young citizens to the republic so that France would never again vote en masse for dictators like Napoleon I and Napoleon III.

Although these educational reforms disturbed French Catholics, many of them rallied to the republic in the 1890s. The limited acceptance of the modern world by Pope Leo XIII (r. 1878–1903) eased tensions between church and state. Unfortunately, the Dreyfus affair changed all that.

Alfred Dreyfus, a Jewish captain in the French army, was falsely accused and convicted of treason. His family never doubted his innocence and fought unceasingly to reopen the case, enlisting the support of prominent republicans and intellectuals such as the novelist Émile Zola. In 1898 and 1899, the case split France apart. On one side was the army, which had manufactured evidence against Dreyfus, joined by anti-Semites and most of the Catholic establishment. On the other side stood the civil libertarians and most of the more radical republicans.

This battle, which eventually led to Dreyfus's being declared innocent, revived republican feeling against the church. Between 1901 and 1905, after centuries of close relations, the government severed all ties between the state and the Catholic church. The salaries of priests and bishops were no longer paid by the government, and all churches were given to local committees of lay Catholics.

Captain Alfred Dreyfus Leaving an 1899 reconsideration of his original court martial, Dreyfus receives an insulting "guard of dishonor" from soldiers whose backs are turned. Top army leaders were determined to brand Dreyfus as a traitor. *(Source: Bibliothèque Nationale, Paris)*

Catholic schools were put completely on their own financially, and in a short time they lost a third of their students. The state school system's power of indoctrination was greatly strengthened. In France, only the growing socialist movement, with its very different and thoroughly secular ideology, stood in opposition to patriotic, republican nationalism.

Great Britain and Ireland

Britain in the late nineteenth century has often been seen as a shining example of peaceful and successful political evolution. Germany was stuck with a manipulated parliament that gave an irresponsible emperor too much power. France had a quarrelsome parliament that gave its presidents too little power. Great Britain, in contrast, seemed to enjoy an effective two-party parliament that skillfully guided the country from classical liberalism to full-fledged democracy with hardly a misstep.

This view of Great Britain is not so much wrong as incomplete. After the right to vote was granted to males of the solid middle class in 1832, opinion leaders and politicians wrestled long and hard with the uncertainties of a further extension of the franchise. In his famous "Essay on Liberty," published in 1859, the philosopher John Stuart Mill (1806–1873), the leading heir to the Benthamite tradition (page 901), probed the problem of how to protect the rights of individuals and minorities in the emerging age of mass electoral participation. Mill pleaded eloquently for the practical and moral value inherent in safeguarding individual differences and unpopular opinions. In 1867 Prime Minister Benjamin Disraeli and the Conservatives extended the vote to all middle-class males and the best-paid workers in the Second Reform Bill. The son of a Jewish stockbroker, himself a novelist and urban dandy, the ever-fascinating Disraeli (1804–1881) was willing to risk this "leap in the dark" in order to gain new supporters. The Conservative party, he believed, needed to broaden its traditional base of aristocratic and landed support if it was to survive. After 1867 English political parties and electoral campaigns became more modern, and the "lower orders" appeared to vote as responsibly as their "betters." Hence in 1884 the Third Reform Bill gave the vote to almost every adult male.

While the House of Commons was drifting toward democracy, the House of Lords was content to slumber nobly. Between 1901 and 1910, however, that bastion of aristocratic conservatism tried to reassert itself. Acting as supreme court of the land, it ruled against labor unions in two important decisions. And after the Liberal party came to power in 1906, the Lords vetoed several measures passed by the Commons, including the so-called People's Budget. The Lords finally capitulated, as they had done in 1832, when the king threatened to create enough new peers to pass the new legislation.

Aristocratic conservatism yielded once and for all to popular democracy. The result was that extensive social welfare measures, slow to come to Great Britain, were passed in a spectacular rush between 1906 and 1914. During those years, the Liberal party, inspired by the fiery Welshman David Lloyd George (1863–1945), substantially raised taxes on the rich as part of the People's Budget. This income helped the government pay for national health insurance, unemployment benefits, old-age pensions, and a host of other social measures. The state was integrating the urban masses socially as well as politically.

This record of accomplishment was only part of the story, though. On the eve of the First World War, the ever-emotional, ever-unanswered question of Ireland brought Great Britain to the brink of civil war. In the 1840s, Ireland had been decimated by famine, which fueled an Irish revolutionary movement. Thereafter, the English slowly granted concessions, such as the abolition of the privileges of the Anglican church and rights for Irish peasants. The Liberal prime minister William Gladstone (1809–1898), who had proclaimed twenty years earlier that "my mission is to pacify Ireland," introduced bills to give Ireland self-government in 1886 and in 1893. They failed to pass. After two decades of relative quiet, Irish nationalists in the British Parliament saw their chance. They supported the Liberals in their battle for the People's Budget and received passage of a home-rule bill for Ireland in return.

Thus Ireland, the emerald isle, achieved self-government—but not quite, for Ireland is composed of two peoples. As much as the Irish Catholic majority in the southern counties wanted home rule, precisely that much did the Irish Protestants of the northern counties of Ulster come to oppose it. Motivated by the accumulated fears and hostilities of generations, the Protestants of Ulster refused to submerge themselves in a Catholic Ireland, just as Irish Catholics had refused to submit to a Protestant Britain.

The Ulsterites vowed to resist home rule in northern Ireland. By December 1913, they had raised 100,000 armed volunteers, and they were supported by much of English public opinion. Thus in 1914, the Liberals in the House of Lords introduced a compromise home-rule law that did not apply to the northern counties. This bill, which openly betrayed promises made to Irish nationalists, was rejected, and in September the original home-rule plan was passed but simultaneously suspended. The momentous Irish question was overtaken by cataclysmic world war in August 1914.

Irish developments illustrated once again the power of national feeling and national movements in the nineteenth century. Moreover, they were proof that European states, which traced their development far back in history, could not elicit greater loyalty unless they could capture and control that elemental current of national feeling. Thus, even though Great Britain had much going for it—power, Parliament, prosperity—none of these availed in the face of the conflicting nationalisms espoused by Catholics and Protestants in Northern Ireland.

Similarly, progressive Sweden was powerless to stop the growth of the Norwegian national movement, which culminated in Norway breaking away from Sweden and becoming a fully independent nation in 1905. One can also see how hopeless was the cause of the Ottoman Empire in Europe in the later nineteenth century. The Ottoman Empire was an old dynastic state without ethnic or linguistic unity. It was only a matter of time before the Serbs, Bulgarians, and Romanians would break away to form their own independent nation-states (see pages 1042–1043).

The Austro-Hungarian Empire

The dilemma of conflicting nationalisms in Ireland highlights how desperate the situation in the Austro-Hungarian Empire had become by the early twentieth century. In 1849 Magyar nationalism had driven Hungarian patriots to declare an independent Hungarian republic, which was savagely crushed by Russian and Austrian armies (see

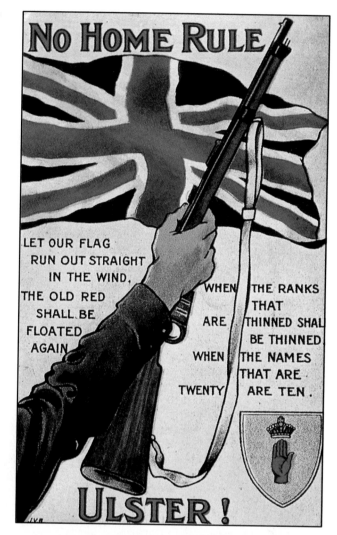

"No Home Rule" Posters like this one helped to foment pro-British, anti-Catholic sentiment in the northern Irish counties of Ulster before the First World War. The rifle raised defiantly and the accompanying rhyme are a thinly veiled threat of armed rebellion and civil war. *(Source: Reproduced with kind permission of the Trustees of the Ulster Museum)*

pages 890–892). Throughout the 1850s, Hungary was ruled as a conquered territory, and Emperor Francis Joseph and his bureaucracy tried hard to centralize the state and Germanize the language and culture of the different nationalities.

Then, in the wake of defeat by Prussia in 1866, a weakened Austria was forced to strike a compromise and establish the so-called dual monarchy. The empire was divided in two, and the nationalistic Magyars gained virtual independence for Hungary. Henceforth each half of the empire agreed to

THE SPREAD OF NATIONALISM IN EUROPE, 1850–1914

1851	Louis Napoleon dismisses French National Assembly in coup d'état
1852–1870	Second Empire in France
1853–1856	Crimean War
1859	Mill, *Essay on Liberty*
1859–1870	Unification of Italy
1861	Abolition of serfdom in Russia
1862–1890	Bismarck's reign of power in German affairs
1864–1871	First Socialist International
1866	Prussia wins decisive victory in Austro-Prussian War
1866–1871	Unification of the German Empire
1867	Magyar nobility increases its power by restoring the constitution of 1848 in Hungary, thereby further dividing the Austro-Hungarian Empire
	Marx, *Capital*
	Second Reform Bill passed by British Parliament
1870–1871	Prussia wins decisive victory in Franco-Prussian War; William I proclaimed emperor of a united Germany
1871	Paris Commune
1871–1914	Third Republic in France
1878	Suppression of Social Democrats in Germany
1881	Assassination of Tsar Alexander II
1883–1889	Enactment of social security laws in Germany
1884	Third Reform Bill passed by British Parliament
1889–1914	Second Socialist International
1890	Repeal of anti-Social Democrat law in Germany
1892–1903	Witte directs modernization of Russian economy
1904–1905	Japan wins decisive victory in Russo-Japanese War
1905	Revolution in Russia: Tsar Nicholas II forced to issue the October Manifesto promising a popularly elected Duma
1906–1914	Liberal reform in Great Britain
1907–1912	Stolypin's agrarian reforms in Russia
1912	German Social Democratic party becomes largest party in the German Reichstag
1914	Irish Home Rule bill passed by British Parliament but immediately suspended with outbreak of First World War

deal with its own "barbarians"—its own minorities—as it saw fit. The two states were joined only by a shared monarch and common ministries for finance, defense, and foreign affairs. After 1867 the disintegrating force of competing nationalisms continued unabated, for both Austria and Hungary had several "Irelands" within their borders.

In Austria, ethnic Germans were only one-third of the population, and by the late 1890s many Germans saw their traditional dominance threatened by Czechs, Poles, and other Slavs. A particularly emotional and divisive issue in the Austrian parliament was the language used in government and elementary education at the local level. From 1900 to 1914, the parliament was so divided that ministries generally could not obtain a majority and ruled instead by decree. Efforts by both conservatives and socialists to defuse national antagonisms by stressing economic issues cutting across ethnic lines—which led to the introduction of universal male suffrage in 1907—proved largely unsuccessful.

One aspect of such national antagonisms was anti-Semitism, which was particularly virulent in Austria. After Jews obtained full legal equality in

1867, the Jewish populations of Austrian cities grew very rapidly, reaching 10 percent of the population of Vienna by 1900. Many Jewish businessmen were quite successful in banking and retail trade; and Jewish artists, intellectuals, and scientists, like the world-famous Sigmund Freud, played a major role in making Vienna a leading center of European culture and modern thought. When extremists charged the Jews with controlling the economy and corrupting German culture with alien ideas and ultramodern art, anxious Germans of all classes tended to listen. The popular mayor of Vienna from 1897 to 1910, Dr. Karl Lueger, combined anti-Semitic rhetoric with calls for "Christian socialism" and municipal ownership of basic services. Lueger appealed especially to the German lower middle class—and to an unsuccessful young artist named Adolf Hitler.

In Hungary, the Magyar nobility in 1867 restored the constitution of 1848 and used it to dominate both the Magyar peasantry and the minority populations until 1914. Only the wealthiest one-fourth of adult males had the right to vote, making parliament the creature of the Magyar elite. Laws promoting use of the Magyar (Hungarian) language in schools and government were rammed through and bitterly resented, especially by the Croatians and Romanians. While Magyar extremists campaigned loudly for total separation from Austria, the radical leaders of the subject nationalities dreamed of independence from Hungary. Unlike most major countries, which harnessed nationalism to strengthen the state after 1871, the Austro-Hungarian Empire was progressively weakened and destroyed by it.

MARXISM AND THE SOCIALIST MOVEMENT

Nationalism served, for better or worse, as a new unifying principle. But what about socialism? Did the rapid growth of socialist parties, which were generally Marxian parties dedicated to an international proletarian revolution, mean that national states had failed to gain the support of workers? Certainly, many prosperous and conservative citizens were greatly troubled by the socialist movement. And many historians have portrayed the years before 1914 as a time of increasing conflict between revolutionary socialism on the one hand and a nationalist alliance between conservative aristocracy and the prosperous middle class on the other. This question requires close examination.

The Socialist International

The growth of socialist parties after 1871 was phenomenal. Neither Bismarck's antisocialist laws nor his extensive social security system checked the growth of the German Social Democratic party, which espoused the Marxian ideology. By 1912 it had attracted millions of followers and was the largest party in the Reichstag. Socialist parties also grew in other countries, though nowhere else with quite such success. In 1883 Russian exiles in Switzerland founded a Russian Social Democratic party, which grew rapidly in the 1890s and thereafter, despite internal disputes. In France, various socialist parties re-emerged in the 1880s after the carnage of the Commune. In 1905 most of them were finally unified in a single, increasingly powerful Marxian party called the "French Section of the Workers International." Belgium and Austria-Hungary also had strong socialist parties of the Marxian persuasion.

As the name of the French party suggests, Marxian socialist parties were eventually linked together in an international organization. As early as 1848, Marx had laid out his intellectual system in the *Communist Manifesto* (see pages 875–876). He had declared that "the working men have no country," and he had urged proletarians of all nations to unite against their governments. Joining the flood of radicals and republicans who fled continental Europe for England and America after the revolutions of 1848, Marx settled in London. Poor and depressed, he lived on his meager earnings as a journalist and on the gifts of his friend Engels. Marx never stopped thinking of revolution. Digging deeply into economics and history, he concluded that revolution follows economic crisis and tried to prove it in *Critique of Political Economy* (1859) and his greatest theoretical work, *Capital* (1867).

The bookish Marx also excelled as a practical organizer. In 1864 he played an important role in founding the First International of socialists—the International Working Men's Association. In the following years, he battled successfully to control the organization and used its annual meetings as a means of spreading his realistic, "scientific" doctrines of inevitable socialist revolution. Then Marx enthusiastically embraced the passionate, vaguely radical patriotism of the Paris Commune and its terrible conflict with the French National Assembly as a giant step toward socialist revolution. This impetuous action frightened many of his early supporters, especially the more moderate British labor leaders. The First International collapsed.

Yet international proletarian solidarity remained an important objective for Marxists. In 1889, as the individual parties in different countries grew stronger, socialist leaders came together to form the Second International, which lasted until 1914. Although the International was only a federation of various national socialist parties, it had great psychological impact. Every three years,

delegates from the different parties met to interpret Marxian doctrines and plan coordinated action. May 1—May Day—was declared an annual international one-day strike, a day of marches and demonstrations. A permanent executive for the International was established. Many feared and many others rejoiced in the growing power of socialism and the Second International.

Unions and Revisionism

Was socialism really radical and revolutionary in these years? On the whole, it was not. Indeed, as socialist parties grew and attracted large numbers of members, they looked more and more toward gradual change and steady improvement for the working class, less and less toward revolution. The

Socialist Clubs helped spread Marxian doctrines among the working classes. There workers (and intellectuals) from different backgrounds debated the fine points and developed a sense of solidarity. *(Source: Bildarchiv Preussischer Kulturbesitz)*

mainstream of European socialists became militantly moderate—that is, they increasingly combined radical rhetoric with sober action.

Workers themselves were progressively less inclined to follow radical programs. There were several reasons for this reluctance. As workers gained the right to vote and to participate politically in the nation-state, their attention focused more on elections than on revolutions. And as workers won real, tangible benefits, this furthered the process. Workers were not immune to patriotic education and indoctrination during military service, however ardently socialist intellectuals might wish the contrary. Nor were workers a unified social group (see pages 910–914).

Perhaps most important of all, workers' standard of living rose substantially after 1850 as the promise of the Industrial Revolution was at least partially realized. In Great Britain, workers could buy almost twice as much with their wages in 1906 as in 1850, and most of the increase came after 1870. Workers experienced similar increases in most continental countries after 1850, though much less strikingly in late-developing Russia. Improvement in the standard of living was much more than merely a matter of higher wages. The quality of life improved dramatically in urban areas. For all these reasons, workers tended more and more to become militantly moderate: they demanded gains, but they were less likely to take to the barricades in pursuit of them.

The growth of labor unions reinforced this trend toward moderation. In the early stages of industrialization, modern unions were generally prohibited by law. A famous law of the French Revolution had declared all guilds and unions illegal in the name of "liberty" in 1791. In Great Britain, attempts by workers to unite were considered criminal conspiracies after 1799. Other countries had similar laws, and these obviously hampered union development. In France, for example, about two hundred workers were imprisoned each year between 1825 and 1847 for taking part in illegal combinations. Unions were considered subversive bodies, only to be hounded and crushed.

From this sad position workers struggled to escape. Great Britain led the way in 1824 and 1825, when unions won the right to exist but (generally) not the right to strike. After the collapse of Robert Owen's attempt to form one big union in the 1830s (see page 857), new and more practical

kinds of unions appeared. Limited primarily to highly skilled workers such as machinists and carpenters, the "new model unions" avoided both radical politics and costly strikes. Instead, their sober, respectable leaders concentrated on winning better wages and hours for their members through collective bargaining and compromise. This approach helped pave the way to full acceptance in Britain in the 1870s, when unions won the right to strike without being held legally liable for the financial damage inflicted on employers. After 1890 unions for unskilled workers developed, and between 1901 and 1906, the legal position of British unions was further strengthened.

Germany was the most industrialized, socialized, and unionized continental country by 1914. German unions were not granted important rights until 1869, and until the antisocialist law was repealed in 1890, they were frequently harassed by the government as socialist fronts. Nor were socialist leaders particularly interested in union activity, believing as they did in the iron law of low wages and the need for political revolution. The result was that, as late as 1895, there were only about 270,000 union members in a male industrial workforce of nearly 8 million. Then, with German industrialization still storming ahead and almost all legal harassment eliminated, union membership skyrocketed to roughly 3 million in 1912.

This great expansion both reflected and influenced the changing character of German unions. Increasingly, unions in Germany focused on concrete bread-and-butter issues—wages, hours, working conditions—rather than on instilling pure socialist doctrine. Genuine collective bargaining, long opposed by socialist intellectuals as a "sellout," was officially recognized as desirable by the German Trade Union Congress in 1899. When employers proved unwilling to bargain, a series of strikes forced them to change their minds.

Between 1906 and 1913, successful collective bargaining was gaining a prominent place in German industrial relations. In 1913 alone, over ten thousand collective bargaining agreements affecting 1.25 million workers were signed. Further gradual improvement, not revolution, was becoming the primary objective of the German trade-union movement.

The German trade unions and their leaders were—in fact if not in name—thoroughgoing revisionists. Revisionism—that most awful of sins in the eyes of militant Marxists in the twentieth century—was an effort by various socialists to update Marxian doctrines to reflect the realities of the time. Thus the socialist Edward Bernstein argued in 1899 in his *Evolutionary Socialism* that Marx's predictions of ever-greater poverty for workers and ever-greater concentration of wealth in ever-fewer hands had been proved false. Therefore, Bernstein suggested, socialists should reform their doctrines and tactics. They should combine with other progressive forces to win gradual evolutionary gains for workers through legislation, unions, and further economic development. These views were formally denounced as heresy by the German Social Democratic party and later by the entire Second International. Nevertheless, the revisionist, gradualist approach continued to gain the tacit acceptance of many German socialists, particularly in the trade unions.

Moderation found followers elsewhere. In France, the great humanist and socialist leader Jean Jaurès formally repudiated revisionist doctrines in order to establish a unified socialist party, but he remained at heart a gradualist. Questions of revolutionary versus gradualist policies split Russian Marxists.

Socialist parties before 1914 had clear-cut national characteristics. Russians and socialists in the Austro-Hungarian Empire tended to be the most radical. The German party talked revolution and practiced reformism, greatly influenced by its enormous trade-union movement. The French party talked revolution and tried to practice it, unrestrained by a trade-union movement that was both very weak and very radical. In England, the socialist but non-Marxian Labour party, reflecting a well-established union movement, was formally committed to gradual reform. In Spain and Italy, Marxian socialism was very weak. There anarchism, seeking to smash the state rather than the bourgeoisie, dominated radical thought and action.

In short, socialist policies and doctrines varied from country to country. Socialism itself was to a large extent "nationalized" behind the imposing façade of international unity. This helps explain why, when war came in 1914, socialist leaders almost without exception supported their governments.

SUMMARY

From the mid-nineteenth century on, Western society became nationalistic as well as urban and industrial. Nation-states and strong-minded national leaders gradually enlisted widespread support and gave men and women a sense of belonging. Even socialism became increasingly national in orientation, gathering strength as a champion of working-class interests in domestic politics. Yet, while nationalism served to unite peoples, it also drove them apart. Though most obvious in Austria-Hungary and Ireland, this was in a real sense true for all of Western civilization. The universal national faith, which reduced social tensions within states, promoted a bitter, almost Darwinian competition between states and thus ominously threatened the progress and unity that it had helped to build.

NOTES

1. Quoted in G. Wright, *France in Modern Times* (Chicago: Rand McNally, 1960), p. 179.
2. Quoted in O. Pflanze, *Bismarck and the Development of Germany: The Period of Unification, 1815–1871* (Princeton, N.J.: Princeton University Press, 1963), p. 60.
3. Quoted in E. Eyck, *Bismarck and the German Empire* (New York: W. W. Norton, 1964), p. 59.
4. Quoted in H. Kohn, *The Mind of Germany: The Education of a Nation* (New York: Scribner, 1960), pp. 156–161.
5. Quoted in T. von Laue, *Sergei Witte and the Industrialization of Russia* (New York: Columbia University Press, 1963), p. 78.
6. Quoted in J. P. McKay, *Pioneers for Profit: Foreign Entrepreneurship and Russian Industrialization, 1885–1913* (Chicago: University of Chicago Press, 1970), p. 11.

SUGGESTED READING

The general works mentioned in the Suggested Reading for Chapter 27 treat the entire nineteenth century. In addition, G. Craig, *Germany, 1866–1945* (1980), and B. Moore, *Social Origins of Dictatorship and Democracy*

(1966), are outstanding. R. Anderson, *France, 1870–1914* (1977), provides a good introduction and has a useful blibliography.

Among specialized works of high quality, R. Williams, *Gaslight and Shadows* (1957), brings the world of Napoleon III vibrantly alive. Karl Marx's *The Eighteenth Brumaire of Louis Napoleon* is a famous contemporary denunciation of the coup d'état. E. Weber, *France, Fin de Siècle* (1986), and the engaging collective biography by R. Shattuck, *The Banquet Years* (1968), capture the spirit of artistic and intellectual Paris at the end of the century. E. Weber, *Peasants into Frenchmen* (1976), stresses the role of education and modern communications in the transformation of rural France after 1870. E. Thomas, *The Women Incendiaries* (1966), examines radical women in the Paris Commune. G. Chapman, *The Dreyfus Case: A Reassessment* (1955), and D. Johnson, *France and the Dreyfus Affair* (1967), are careful examinations of the famous case. In *Jean Barois*, Nobel Prize winner R. M. Du Gard accurately recreates in novel form the Dreyfus affair, and Émile Zola's novel *The Debacle* treats the Franco-Prussian War realistically.

D. M. Smith has written widely on Italy, and his *Garibaldi* (1956) and *Italy: A Modern History*, rev. ed. (1969), are recommended. P. Schroeder, *Austria, Great Britain and the Crimean War* (1972), is an outstanding and highly original diplomatic study. In addition to the important studies on Bismarck and Germany by Pflanze, Eyck, and Kohn cited in the Notes, F. Stern, *Gold and Iron* (1977), is a fascinating examination of relations between Bismarck and his financial adviser, the Jewish banker Bleichröder. L. Cecil, *Wilhelm II: Prince and Emperor, 1859–1900* (1989), probes the character and politics of Germany's ruler. G. Iggers, *The German Conception of History* (1968); K. D. Barkin, *The Controversy over German Industrialization, 1890–1902* (1970); and E. Spencer, *Management and Labor in Imperial Germany: Ruhr Industrialists as Employers* (1984), are valuable in-depth investigations. H. Glasser, ed., *The German Mind in the Nineteenth Century* (1981), is an outstanding anthology, as are R. E. Joeres and M. Maynes, eds., *German History in the Eighteenth and Nineteenth Centuries* (1986), and P. Mendès-Flohr, *The Jew in the Modern World: A Documentary History* (1980). C. Schorske, *Fin de Siècle Vienna: Politics and Culture* (1980), and P. Gay, *Freud, Jews, and Other Germans* (1978), are brilliant on aspects of modern culture. A. Sked, *The Decline and Fall of the Habsburg Empire, 1815–1918* (1989), and R. Kann, *The Multinational Empire*, 2 vols. (1950, 1964), probe the intricacies of the nationality problem in Austria-Hungary. S. Stavrianos has written extensively on southeastern Europe, including *The Balkans, 1815–1914* (1963).

In addition to the studies on Russian industrial development by von Laue and McKay cited in the Notes, W. Blackwell, *The Industrialization of Russia*, 2d ed. (1982), and A. Rieber, *Merchants and Entrepreneurs in Imperial Russia* (1982), are recommended. Among fine studies on Russian social development and modernization, H. Rogger, *Russia in the Age of Modernization and Revolution, 1881–1917* (1983), which has an extensive bibliography; T. Emmons, *The Russian Landed Gentry and the Peasant Emancipation of 1861* (1968); R. Zelnik, *Labor and Society in Tsarist Russia, 1855–1870* (1971); R. Johnson, *Peasant and Proletarian: The Working Class of Moscow at the End of the Nineteenth Century* (1979); and H. Troyat, *Daily Life in Russia Under the Last Tsar* (1962), are especially recommended. T. Friedgut, *Iuzovka and Revolution: Life and Work in Russia's Donbass, 1869–1924* (1989); R. Zelnik, *Labor and Society in Tsarist Russia, 1855–1870* (1971); and R. Johnson, *Peasant and Proletarian: The Working Class of Moscow at the End of the Nineteenth Century* (1979), skillfully treat different aspects of working-class life and politics. W. E. Mosse, *Alexander II and the Modernization of Russia* (1958), provides a good discussion of midcentury reforms. C. Black, ed., *The Transformation of Russian Society* (1960), offers a collection of essays on Russian modernization. I. Turgenev's great novel *Fathers and Sons* probes the age-old conflict of generations as well as nineteenth-century Russian revolutionary thought.

G. Dangerfield, *The Strange Death of Liberal England* (1961), brilliantly examines social tensions in Ireland as well as Englishwomen's struggle for the vote before 1914. W. Arnstein convincingly shows how the Victorian aristocracy survived and even flourished in nineteenth-century Britain in F. Jaher, ed., *The Rich, the Well-Born, and the Powerful* (1973), an interesting collection of essays on social elites in history. The theme of aristocratic strength and survival is expanded in A. Mayer's provocative *Persistence of the Old Regime: Europe to the Great War* (1981).

On late-nineteenth-century socialism, C. Schorske, *German Social Democracy, 1905–1917* (1955), is a modern classic. V. Lidtke, *The Outlawed Party* (1966), and J. Quataert, *Reluctant Feminists in German Social Democracy, 1885–1917* (1979), are also recommended for the study of German socialists. H. Goldberg, *The Life of Jean Jaurès* (1962), is a sympathetic account of the great French socialist leader. P. Stearns, who has written several books on European labor history, considers radical labor leaders in *Revolutionary Syndicalism and French Labor* (1971). D. Geary, ed., *Labour and Socialist Movements in Europe Before 1914* (1989), contains excellent studies on developments in different countries and has up-to-date bibliographies.

30

The World and the West

Flags of various countries flying in front of factories at Canton Harbor

While industrialization and nationalism were transforming urban life and Western society, Western society itself was reshaping the world. At the peak of its power and pride, the West entered the third and most dynamic phase of the aggressive expansion that began with the Crusades and continued with the great discoveries and the rise of seaborne colonial empires. An ever-growing stream of products, people, and ideas flowed out of Europe in the nineteenth century. Hardly any corner of the globe was left untouched. The most spectacular manifestations of Western expansion came in the late nineteenth century, when the leading European nations established or enlarged their far-flung political empires. The political annexation of territory in the 1880s—the "new imperialism," as it is often called by historians—was the capstone of a profound underlying economic and technological process.

- How and why did this many-sided, epoch-making expansion occur in the nineteenth century?
- What were some of its consequences for the West and for the rest of the world?

These are the questions examined in this chapter.

INDUSTRIALIZATION AND THE WORLD ECONOMY

The Industrial Revolution created, first in Great Britain and then in continental Europe and North America, a growing and tremendously dynamic economic system. In the course of the nineteenth century, that system was extended across the face of the earth. Some of the extension into non-Western areas was peaceful and beneficial for all concerned, for the West had many products and techniques desired by the rest of the world. If peaceful methods failed, however, Europeans did not stand on ceremony. They used their superior military power to force non-Western nations to open their doors to Western economic interests, and they did not worry when their aggression caused bitter resentment. In general, Westerners fashioned the global economic system so that the largest share of the ever-increasing gains from trade, technology, and migration flowed to the West and its propertied classes.

The Rise of Global Inequality

The Industrial Revolution in Europe marked a momentous turning point in world history. Indeed, only when Europe's economic breakthrough is placed in a world perspective can its revolutionary implications and consequences be fully appreciated. From a world perspective, the ultimate significance of the Industrial Revolution was that it allowed those regions of the globe that industrialized in the nineteenth century to increase their wealth and power enormously in comparison with those that did not. As a result, a gap between the industrializing regions—mainly Europe and North America—and the nonindustrializing regions—mainly Africa, Asia, and Latin America—opened up and grew steadily throughout the nineteenth century. This pattern of uneven global development became institutionalized, or built into the structure of the world economy. Thus evolved a "lopsided world," a world of rich lands and poor.

Historians have long been aware of this gap, but only recently have historical economists begun to chart its long-term evolution with some precision. Their findings are extremely revealing, although they contain a margin of error and other limitations as well. The findings of one such study are summarized in Figure 30.1. This figure compares the long-term evolution of average income per person in today's "developed" (or industrialized) regions—defined as western and eastern Europe, North America, and Japan—with that found in the "Third World," a term that is now widely used by international organizations and by scholars to group Africa, Asia, and Latin America into a single unit. To get these individual income figures, researchers estimate a country's gross national product (GNP) at different points in time, convert those estimates to some common currency, and divide by the total population.

Figure 30.1 highlights three main points. First, in 1750 the average standard of living was no higher in Europe as a whole than in the rest of the world. In 1750 Europe was still a poor agricultural society. Moreover, the average per person income in the wealthiest western European country (Great

Britain) was less than twice that in the poorest non-Western (or eastern European) land. By 1970, however, the average person in the wealthiest countries had an income fully twenty-five times as great as that received by the average person in the poorest countries of Africa and Asia.

Second, it was industrialization that opened the gap in average wealth and well-being between countries and regions. By 1830, Great Britain, the first industrial nation, had jumped well above the European average and was well in advance of its continental competitors. Great Britain's lead eventually narrowed, reflecting the industrialization of some other European countries and the United States in the course of the nineteenth century.

Finally, income per person stagnated in the Third World before 1913, in striking contrast to income per person in the industrializing regions. Only after 1945, in the era of political independence and decolonialization, did Third World countries finally make some real economic progress, beginning in their turn the critical process of industrialization.

These enormous income disparities are poignant indicators of equal disparities in food and clothing, health and education, life expectancy, and general material well-being. The rise of these disparities has generated a great deal of debate. One school of interpretation stresses that the West used science, technology, capitalist organization, and even its critical world view to create its wealth and greater physical well-being. Another school argues that the West used its political and economic power to steal much of its riches, continuing in the nineteenth (and twentieth) century the rapacious colonialism born of the era of expansion.

These issues are complex, and there are few simple answers. As noted in Chapter 26, the wealth-creating potential of technological improvement and more intensive capitalist organization was indeed great. At the same time, those breakthroughs rested, in part, on Great Britain having already used military power to dominate world trade and the Atlantic economy for its own great advantage. Great Britain, the United States, and the other Western powers continued to use force and the threat of force to tilt the expanding world economy in their favor in the nineteenth century. Wealth—unprecedented wealth—was indeed created, but the lion's share of that new wealth flowed to the West and to a tiny non-

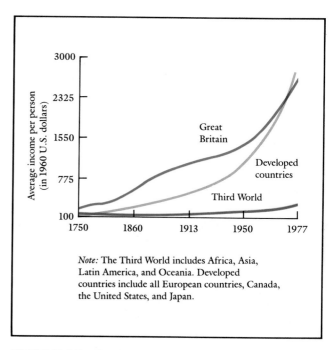

FIGURE 30.1 The Growth of Average Income per Person in the Third World, Developed Countries, and Great Britain, 1750–1970, in 1960 U.S. dollars and prices. *(Source: Data from P. Bairoch and M. Lévy-Leboyer, eds.,* Disparities in Economic Development Since the Industrial Revolution. *St. Martin's Press, New York, 1981, pp. 7–8, 10)*

Western elite of cooperative rulers, landowners, and big merchants.

Trade and Foreign Investment

Commerce between nations has always been a powerful stimulus to economic development. Never was this more true than in the nineteenth century, when world trade grew prodigiously. World trade grew modestly until about 1840, and then it took off. After a slowdown in the last years of the century, another surge lasted until the First World War. In 1913 the value of world trade was roughly $38 billion, or about *twenty-five* times what it had been in 1800. (This amount actually understates the growth, since average prices of both manufactured goods and raw materials were lower in 1913 than in 1800.) In a general way, the enormous increase in international commerce summed up the growth of an interlocking world economy, centered in and directed by Europe.

Great Britain played a key role in using trade to tie the world together economically. In 1815 Britain already had a colonial empire, for India, Canada, Australia, and other scattered areas remained British possessions after American independence. The technological breakthroughs of the Industrial Revolution allowed Britain to manufacture cotton textiles, iron, and other goods cheaply and to far outstrip domestic demand for such products. Thus British manufacturers sought export markets, first in Europe and then around the world.

Take the case of cotton textiles. India was by far the largest producer of cotton textiles in the seventeenth century, when the East India trading companies began exporting beautiful printed cloths to Europe to meet a rapidly growing demand. Worried European governments then passed mercantilist laws to limit these imports, which competed directly with domestic silk and woolen production. British merchants in the putting-out system searched for new techniques and patterns of organization that would enable them to compete with Indian cottons and lower-cost Indian labor. These efforts were highly successful in the late eighteenth century, as we saw in Chapter 26. By 1820 a revolutionized factory industry in Britain was exporting half of its production. Europe bought half of Britain's cotton-textile exports; India bought only 6 percent. Then, as European nations and the United States exercised sovereignty to erect protective tariff barriers and promote domestic industry, British cotton-textile manufacturers aggressively sought and found other foreign markets in non-Western areas. By 1850 India was buying 25 percent and Europe only 16 percent of a much larger total. As a British colony, India had no right to raise tariffs to protect its ancient cotton-textile industry. The Indian economy thus suffered a heavy blow, and thousands of Indian weavers lost their livelihoods.

Attaining undisputed world leadership in the revolutionized industries in the early nineteenth century, prosperous and powerful Britain also became the world's single best market after the repeal of the Corn Laws in 1846 (see page 885). A key argument in the battle against tariffs on imported grain had been that Britain had to buy from foreigners if foreigners were to obtain money to buy from Britain. Until 1914 Britain thus remained the world's emporium, where not only agricultural products and raw materials but also manufactured goods entered freely. Free access to the enormous market of Britain stimulated the development of mines and plantations in many non-Western areas.

The growth of trade was facilitated by the conquest of distance. The earliest railroad construction occurred in Europe (including Russia) and in America north of the Rio Grande; other parts of the globe saw the building of rail lines after 1860. By 1920 more than one-quarter of the world's railroads were in Latin America, Asia, Africa, and Australia. Wherever railroads were built, they drastically reduced transportation costs, opened new economic opportunities, and pulled people into a market economy. Moreover, in the areas of massive European settlement—North America and Australia—they were built in advance of the population and provided a means of settling the land.

The power of steam revolutionized transportation by sea as well as by land. In 1807 inhabitants of the Hudson Valley in New York saw the "Devil on the way to Albany in a saw-mill," as Robert Fulton's steamship *Clermont* traveled 150 miles upstream in thirty-two hours. Steam power, long used to drive paddle-wheelers on rivers, particularly in Russia and North America, finally began to supplant sails on the oceans of the world in the late 1860s. Lighter, stronger, cheap steel replaced iron, which had replaced wood. Screw propellers superseded paddle wheels, and mighty compound steam engines cut fuel consumption by half. Passenger and freight rates tumbled, and the intercontinental shipment of low-priced raw materials became feasible. In addition to the large passenger liners and freighters of the great shipping companies, there were innumerable independent tramp steamers searching endlessly for cargo around the world.

An account of an actual voyage by a typical tramp freighter highlights nineteenth-century developments in global trade. The ship left England in 1910, carrying rails and general freight to western Australia. From there, it carried lumber to Melbourne in southeastern Australia, where it took on harvester combines for Argentina. In Buenos Aires it loaded wheat for Calcutta, and in Calcutta it took on jute for New York. From New York it carried a variety of industrial products to Australia before returning to England with lead, wool, and wheat after a voyage of approximately

The Suez Canal Completed in 1869, the hundred-mile canal cut in half the length of the journey between Europe and Asia. This picture from a popular weekly newspaper shows a line of ships passing through the canal on the opening day. *(Source: Giraudon/ Art Resource)*

72,000 miles to six continents in seventeen months.

The revolution in land and sea transportation helped European pioneers to open up vast new territories and to produce agricultural products and raw materials there for sale in European markets. Moreover, the development of refrigerated railway cars and, from the 1880s, refrigerator ships enabled first Argentina and then the United States, Australia, and New Zealand to ship mountains of chilled or frozen beef and mutton to European (mainly British) consumers. From Asia, Africa, and Latin America came not only the traditional tropical products—spices, tea, sugar, coffee—but new raw materials for industry, such as jute, rubber, cotton, and coconut oil.

Intercontinental trade was enormously facilitated by the Suez and Panama canals. Of great importance, too, was large and continuous investment in modern port facilities, which made loading and unloading cheaper, faster, and more dependable. Finally, transoceanic telegraph cables inaugurated rapid communication among the financial centers of the world. While a British tramp freighter steamed from Calcutta to New York, a broker in London was arranging, by telegram, for it to carry an American cargo to Australia. World

commodity prices were also instantaneously conveyed by the same network of communication.

The growth of trade and the conquest of distance encouraged the expanding European economy to make massive foreign investments. Beginning about 1840, European capitalists started to invest large sums in foreign lands. They did not stop until the outbreak of the First World War in 1914. By that year, Europeans had invested more than $40 billion abroad. Great Britain, France, and Germany were the principal investing countries, although by 1913 the United States was emerging as a substantial foreign investor. The sums involved were enormous (Map 30.1). In the decade before 1914, Great Britain was investing 7 percent of its annual national income abroad, or slightly more than it was investing in its entire domestic economy. The great gap between rich and poor within Europe meant that the wealthy and moderately well-to-do could and did send great sums abroad in search of interest and dividends.

Most of the capital exported did not go to European colonies or protectorates in Asia and Africa. About three-quarters of total European investment went to other European countries, the United States and Canada, Australia and New Zealand, and Latin America. This was because

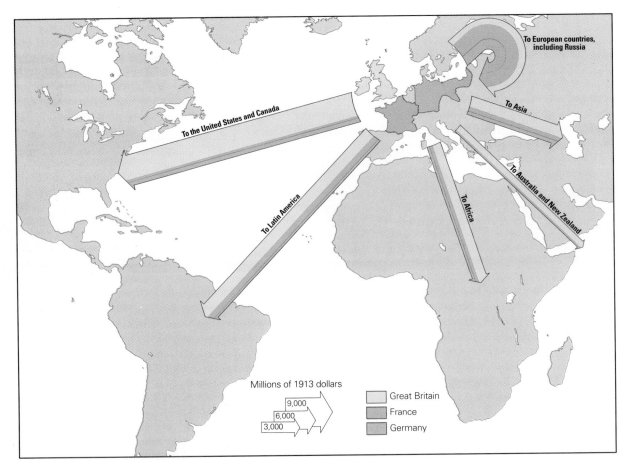

MAP 30.1 European Investment to 1914 Foreign investment grew rapidly after 1850, and Britain, France, and Germany were the major investing nations. Most European investment was not directed to the area seized by the "new imperialism."

Europe found many of its most profitable opportunities for investment in construction of the railroads, ports, and utilities that were necessary to settle and develop those almost-vacant lands. By loaning money for a railroad in Argentina or in Canada's prairie provinces, Europeans not only collected interest but also enabled settlers to buy European rails and locomotives, developed sources of cheap wheat, and opened still more territory for European settlement. Much of this investment—such as in American railroads, fully a third of whose capital in 1890 was European, or in Russian railroads, which drew heavily on loans from France—was peaceful and mutually beneficial. The victims were native American Indians and Australian aborigines, who were decimated by the diseases, liquor, and weapons of an aggressively expanding Western society.

The Opening of China and Japan

Europe's relatively peaceful development of robust offshoots in sparsely populated North America, Australia, and much of Latin America absorbed huge quantities of goods, investments, and migrants. From a Western point of view, that was perhaps the most important aspect of Europe's global thrust. Yet Europe's economic and cultural penetration of old, densely populated civilizations was also profoundly significant for the non-European peoples affected by it. With such civilizations Europeans also increased their trade and profit. Moreover, as had been the case ever since Vasco da Gama and the Spanish conquistadors, the expanding Western society was prepared to use force to attain its desires, if necessary. This was what happened in China and Japan, two crucial examples of the general pattern of intrusion into non-Western lands.

Traditional Chinese civilization was self-sufficient. For centuries China had sent more to Europe in the way of goods and inventions than it received, and this was still the case in the eighteenth century. Europeans and the English in particular had developed a taste for Chinese tea, but they had to pay for it with hard silver because China was supremely uninterested in European wares. Trade with Europe was carefully regulated by the Chinese imperial government—the Manchu Dynasty, which was more interested in isolating and controlling the strange "sea barbarians" than in pursuing commercial exchange. The imperial government refused to establish diplomatic relations with the "inferior" European states, and it required all foreign merchants to live in the southern city of Canton and to buy and sell only from the local merchant monopoly. Practices considered harmful to Chinese interests, such as the sale of opium and the export of silver from China, were strictly forbidden.

For years the little community of foreign merchants in Canton had to accept the Chinese system. By the 1820s, however, the dominant group, the British, was flexing its muscles. Moreover, in the smoking of opium—that "destructive and ensnaring vice" denounced by Chinese decrees—the British had found something that the Chinese really wanted. Grown legally in British-occupied India, opium was smuggled into China by means of fast ships and bribed officials. The more this rich trade developed, the greedier British merchants became and the more they resented the patriotic attempts of the Chinese government to stem the tide of drug addiction. By 1836 the aggressive goal of the British merchants in Canton was an independent British colony in China and "safe and unrestricted liberty" in trade. They pressured the British government to take decisive action and enlisted the support of British manufacturers with visions of vast Chinese markets to be opened.

At the same time, the Manchu government decided that the opium trade had to be stamped out. It was ruining the people and stripping the empire of its silver, which was going to British merchants to pay for the opium. The government began to prosecute Chinese drug dealers vigorously and in 1839 sent special envoy Lin Tse-hsü to Canton. Lin Tse-hsü ordered the foreign merchants to

East Meets West   This painting gives a Japanese view of the first audience of the American Consul and his staff with the shogun, Japan's hereditary military governor, in 1859. The Americans appear strange and ill at ease. (*Source: Laurie Platt Winfrey, Inc.*)

obey China's laws, "for our great unified Manchu Empire regards itself as responsible for the habits and morals of its subjects and cannot rest content to see any of them become victims of a deadly poison."[1] The British merchants refused and were expelled, whereupon war soon broke out.

Using troops from India and in control of the seas, the British occupied several coastal cities and forced China to surrender. In the Treaty of Nanking in 1842, the imperial government was forced to cede the island of Hong Kong to Britain, pay an indemnity of $21 million, and open up five cities to foreign trade with low tariffs.

Thereafter the opium trade flourished, and Hong Kong rapidly became an Anglo-Chinese enclave. China continued to nurture illusions of superiority and isolation, however, and refused to accept foreign diplomats to Peking, the imperial capital. Finally, there was a second round of foreign attacks between 1856 and 1860, culminating in the occupation of Peking by seventeen thousand British and French troops and the intentional burning of the emperor's summer palace. Another round of harsh treaties gave European merchants and missionaries greater privileges and protection. Thus did Europeans use military aggression to blow a hole in the wall of Chinese seclusion. Blasting away at Chinese sovereignty as well, they forced the Chinese to accept trade and investment on unfavorable terms for the foreseeable future.

China's neighbor Japan had its own highly distinctive civilization and even less use for Westerners. European traders and missionaries first arrived in Japan in the sixteenth century. By 1640 Japan had reacted quite negatively to their presence. The government decided to seal off the country from all European influences, in order to preserve traditional Japanese culture and society. It ruthlessly persecuted Japanese Christians and expelled all but a few Dutch merchants, who were virtually imprisoned in a single port and rigidly controlled. When American and British whaling ships began to appear off Japanese coasts almost two hundred years later, the policy of exclusion was still in effect. An order of 1825 commanded Japanese officials to "drive away foreign vessels without second thought."[2]

Japan's unbending isolation seemed hostile and barbaric to the West, particularly to the United States. It complicated the practical problems of shipwrecked American sailors and the provisioning of whaling ships and China traders sailing in the eastern Pacific. It also thwarted the hope of trade and profit. Moreover, Americans shared the self-confidence and dynamism of expanding Western society. They had taken California from Mexico in 1848 and felt destined to play a great role in the Pacific. Americans convinced themselves that it was their duty to force the Japanese to share their ports and behave like a "civilized" nation.

After several unsuccessful American attempts to establish commercial relations with Japan, Commodore Matthew Perry steamed into Edo (now Tokyo) Bay in 1853 and demanded diplomatic negotiations with the emperor. Japan entered a grave crisis. Some Japanese warriors urged armed resistance, but senior officials realized how defenseless their cities were against naval bombardment. Shocked and humiliated, they reluctantly signed a treaty with the United States that opened two ports and permitted trade. Over the next five years, more treaties spelled out the rights and privileges of the Western nations and their merchants in Japan. Japan was "opened." What the British had done in China with war, the Americans had done in Japan with the threat of war.

Western Penetration of Egypt

Egypt's experience illustrates not only the explosive power of the expanding European economy and society but also their seductive appeal for some modernizing elites in non-Western lands. Of great importance in African and Middle Eastern history, the ancient land of the pharaohs had since 525 B.C. been ruled by a succession of foreigners, most recently by the Ottoman Turks. In 1798 French armies under young General Napoleon Bonaparte invaded the Egyptian part of the Ottoman Empire and occupied the territory for three years. Into the power vacuum left by the French withdrawal stepped an extraordinary Albanian-born Ottoman general, Muhammad Ali (1769–1849).

First appointed governor of Egypt by the Ottoman sultan, Muhammad Ali soon disposed of his political rivals. Impressed by Western military might, he set out to build his own state on the strength of a large, powerful army organized along European lines. He drafted for the first time the illiterate peasant masses of Egypt, and he hired

French and Italian army officers to train these raw recruits and their Ottoman officers. By the time of his death, Muhammad Ali had established a strong and virtually independent Egyptian state, to be ruled by his family on a hereditary basis within the Ottoman Empire.

Muhammad Ali's policies of modernization attracted large numbers of European fortune seekers to the banks of the Nile. As one Arab sheik of the Ottoman Empire remarked in the 1830s, "Englishmen are like ants; if one finds a bit of meat, hundreds follow."[3] The port city of Alexandria had more than fifty thousand Europeans by 1864, most of them Italians, Greeks, French, and English. Europeans served not only as army officers but also as engineers, doctors, high government officials, and policemen. Others found their "meat" in trade, finance, and shipping.

To pay for a modern army as well as for European services and manufactured goods, Muhammad Ali encouraged the development of commercial agriculture geared to the European market. This development had profound implications. Egyptian peasants had been poor but largely self-sufficient, growing food for their own consumption on state-owned lands allotted to them by tradition. Faced with the possibility of export agriculture, high-ranking officials and members of Muhammad Ali's family began carving large private landholdings out of the state domain. The new landlords made the peasants their tenants and forced them to grow cash crops like cotton for foreign markets. Borrowing money from European lenders at high rates, the landlords still made large profits, accumulated fortunes, and often lived like wealthy Europeans. The big landowners were "modernizing" agriculture, but to the detriment of peasant well-being.

These trends continued under Muhammad Ali's grandson Ismail, who in 1863 began his sixteen-year rule as Egypt's *khedive,* or "prince." Educated at France's leading military academy, Ismail was a Westernizing autocrat. He dreamed of using European technology and capital to accelerate Egyptian modernization and build a vast empire in northwest Africa. The large irrigation networks he promoted caused the further growth of large estates and commercial agriculture. Cotton production and exports to Europe boomed. Ismail also borrowed large sums to install modern communications, and with his support the Suez Canal

was completed by a French company in 1869. The Arabic of the masses rather than the Turkish of the conquerors became the official language, and young Egyptians educated in Europe helped spread new skills and new ideas in the bureaucracy. Cairo acquired modern boulevards, Western hotels, and an opera house. As Ismail proudly declared: "My country is no longer in Africa, we now form part of Europe."[4]

Yet Ismail was too impatient and too reckless. His projects were enormously expensive, and the sale of his stock in the Suez Canal to the British government did not relieve the situation. By 1876 Egypt owed foreign bondholders a colossal $450 million and could not pay the interest on its debt. Rather than let Egypt go bankrupt and repudiate its loans, as had some Latin American countries and U.S. state governments in the early nineteenth century, the governments of France and Great Britain intervened politically to protect the European bankers who held the Egyptian bonds. They forced Ismail to appoint French and British commissioners to oversee Egyptian finances, in order that the Egyptian debt would be paid in full. This was a momentous decision. It implied direct European political control and was a sharp break with the previous pattern of trade and investment. Throughout most of the nineteenth century, Europeans had used naked military might and political force primarily to make sure that non-Western lands would accept European trade and investment. Now Europeans were going to determine the state budget and effectively rule Egypt.

Foreign financial control evoked a violent nationalistic reaction among Egyptian religious leaders, young intellectuals, and army officers. In 1879, under the leadership of Colonel Ahmed Arabi, they formed the Egyptian Nationalist party. Continuing European pressure, which forced Ismail to abdicate in favor of his weak son Tewfiq (r. 1879–1892), resulted in bloody anti-European riots in Alexandria in 1882. A number of Europeans were killed, and Tewfiq and his court had to flee to British ships for safety. When the British fleet bombarded Alexandria, more riots swept the country, and Colonel Arabi declared that "an irreconcilable war existed between the Egyptians and the English." But a British expeditionary force decimated Arabi's forces and occupied Egypt.

The British said that their occupation was temporary, but British armies remained in Egypt until

Ellis Island in New York's harbor was the main entry point into the United States after 1892. For millions of immigrants the first frightening experience in the new land was being inspected and processed through its crowded "pens." *(Source: Culver Pictures)*

1956. They maintained the façade of the khedive's government as an autonomous province of the Ottoman Empire, but the khedive was a mere puppet. The British consul general Evelyn Baring, later Lord Cromer, ruled the country after 1883. Once a vocal opponent of involvement in Egypt, Baring was an authoritarian reformer who had come to believe that "without European interference and initiative reform is impossible here." Baring's rule did result in somewhat better conditions for peasants as well as tax reforms necessary to ensure revenues to pay foreign bondholders. But Egypt's

British rulers discouraged education because they feared it would lead to political unrest. Thus Cromer blocked all efforts to establish a university in Cairo until 1907 because, he said, it would only "manufacture demagoges."[5] Europeans knew what was best for Egyptians.

In Egypt, Baring and the British provided a new model for European expansion in densely populated lands. Such expansion was based on military force, political domination, and a self-justifying ideology of good administration. This model was to flourish until 1914. Thus did European industrialization lead to tremendous political as well as economic expansion throughout the world.

THE GREAT MIGRATION

Before considering European political empires, it is well to realize that a poignant human drama was part of the West's global expansion: literally millions of people picked up stakes and left their ancestral lands in the course of history's greatest migration. To millions of ordinary people, for whom the opening of China and the interest on the Egyptian debt had not the slightest significance, this great movement was the central experience in the saga of Western expansion. It was, in part, because of this great migration that the West's impact on the world in the nineteenth century was so powerful and many-sided.

The Pressure of Population

In the early eighteenth century, the growth of European population entered its third and decisive stage, which continued unabated until the twentieth century (see page 696). Birthrates eventually declined in the nineteenth century, but so did death rates, mainly because of the rising standard of living and secondarily because of the medical revolution. Thus the population of Europe (including Asiatic Russia) more than doubled, from approximately 188 million in 1800 to roughly 432 million in 1900.

These figures actually understate Europe's population explosion, for between 1815 and 1932 more than 60 million people left Europe. These migrants went primarily to the "areas of European settlement"—North and South America, Australia, New Zealand, and Siberia—where they contributed to a rapid growth of numbers. The population of North America (the United States and Canada) alone grew from 6 million to 81 million between 1800 and 1900 because of continuous immigration and the high fertility rates of North American women. Since population grew more slowly in Africa and Asia than in Europe, as Figure 30.2 shows, Europeans and people of European origin jumped from about 22 percent of the world's total to about 38 percent on the eve of the First World War.

The growing number of Europeans provided further impetus for Western expansion. It was a driving force behind emigration. As in the eighteenth century, the rapid increase in numbers put pressure on the land and led to land hunger and relative overpopulation in area after area. In most countries, migration increased twenty years after a rapid growth in population, as many children of the baby boom grew up, saw little available land and few opportunities, and migrated. This pattern was especially prevalent when rapid population increase predated extensive industrial development, which offered the best long-term hope of creating jobs within the country and reducing poverty. Thus millions of country folk went abroad, as well as to nearby cities, in search of work and economic opportunity.

Before looking at the people who migrated, let us consider three facts. First, the number of men and women who left Europe increased steadily until the First World War. As Figure 30.3 shows, more than 11 million left in the first decade of the twentieth century, over five times the number departing in the 1850s. The outflow of migrants was clearly an enduring characteristic of European society for the entire period.

Second, different countries had very different patterns of movement. As Figure 30.3 also shows, people left Britain and Ireland (which are not distinguished in the British figures) in large numbers from the 1840s on. This emigration reflected not only rural poverty but also the movement of skilled, industrial technicians and the preferences shown to British migrants in the British Empire. Ultimately, about one-third of all European migrants between 1840 and 1920 came from the British Isles. German migration was quite different. It grew irregularly after about 1830, reaching

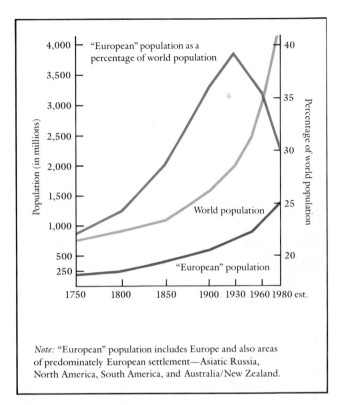

Note: "European" population includes Europe and also areas of predominately European settlement—Asiatic Russia, North America, South America, and Australia/New Zealand.

FIGURE 30.2 The Increase of European and World Populations, 1750–1980 *(Source: Data from W. Woodruff,* Impact of Western Man: A Study of Europe's Role in the World Economy. *St. Martin's Press, New York, 1967, p. 103; United Nations, Statistical Yearbook, 1982, 1985, pp. 2–3)*

a first peak in the early 1850s and another in the early 1880s. Thereafter it declined rapidly, for Germany's rapid industrialization was providing adequate jobs at home. This pattern contrasted sharply with that of Italy. More and more Italians left the country right up to 1914, reflecting severe problems in Italian villages and relatively slow industrial growth. In sum, migration patterns mirrored social and economic conditions in the various European countries and provinces.

Third, although the United States absorbed the largest number of European migrants, only slightly less than half went to the United States. Asiatic Russia, Canada, Argentina, Brazil, and Australia also attracted large numbers, as Figure 30.4 shows. Moreover, migrants accounted for a larger proportion of the total population in Argentina, Brazil, and Canada than in the United States. Between 1900 and 1910, for example, new

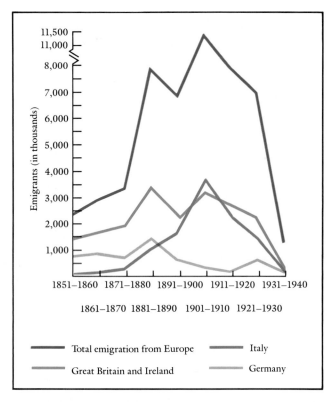

FIGURE 30.3 Emigration from Europe by Decades, 1851–1940 *(Source: Data from W. Woodruff,* Impact of Western Man: A Study of Europe's Role in the World Economy. *St. Martin's Press, New York, 1967, pp. 106–107 and references cited therein)*

arrivals represented 3 percent of Argentina's population each year, as opposed to only 1 percent for the United States. The common American assumption that European migration meant migration to the United States is quite inaccurate.

European Migrants

What kind of people left Europe, and what were their reasons for doing so? Most were poor people from rural areas, though seldom from the poorest classes. Indeed, the European migrant was most often a small peasant landowner or a village craftsman whose traditional way of life was threatened by too little land, estate agriculture, and cheap, factory-made goods. German peasants who left the Rhineland and southwestern Germany between 1830 and 1854, for example, felt trapped by what Friedrich List (see page 851) called the "dwarf economy," with its tiny landholdings and declining craft industries. Selling out and moving to buy much cheaper land in the American Midwest became a common response.

Determined to maintain or improve their status, migrants were a great asset to the countries that received them. This was doubly so because the vast majority were young and very often unmarried. Fully two-thirds of those admitted to the United States were under thirty-one years of age, and 90 percent were under forty. They came in the prime of life and were ready to work hard in the new land, at least for a time.

Many Europeans, especially by the end of the nineteenth century, were truly migrants as opposed to immigrants—that is, they returned home after some time abroad. One in two migrants to Argentina, and probably one in three to the United States, eventually returned to their native land. The likelihood of repatriation varied greatly by nationality. Seven out of eight people who migrated from the Balkans to the United States in the late nineteenth century returned to their countries. At the other extreme, only one in ten from Ireland and only one in twenty among eastern European Jews returned to the country of origin.

Once again, the possibility of buying land in the old country was of central importance. Land in Ireland (as well as in England and Scotland) was tightly held by large, often absentee landowners, and little land was available for purchase. In Russia, Jews were left in relative peace until the assassination of Alexander II by non-Jewish terrorists in 1881 brought a new tsar and an official policy of pogroms and savage discrimination. Russia's 5 million Jews were already confined to the market towns and small cities of the so-called Pale of Settlement, where they worked as artisans and petty traders. Most land was held by non-Jews. When, therefore, Russian Jewish artisans began in the 1880s to escape both factory competition and oppression by migrating—a migration that eventually totaled 2 million people—it was basically a once-and-for-all departure. Non-Jewish migrants from Russia, who constituted a majority of those leaving the tsar's empire after 1905, had access to land and thus returned much more frequently to their peasant villages in central Russia, Poland, and the Ukraine.

The mass movement of Italians illustrates many of the characteristics of European migration. As late as the 1880s, three in every four Italians depended on agriculture. With the influx of cheap North American wheat, the long-standing problems of the Italian village became more acute. And since industry was not advancing fast enough to provide jobs for the rapidly growing population, many Italians began to leave their country for economic reasons. Most Italian migrants were not landless laborers from areas dominated by large estates; such people tended to stay in Italy and turned increasingly toward radical politics. Instead, most were small landowning peasants whose standard of living was falling because of rural overpopulation and agricultural depression. Migration provided them both an escape valve and a possible source of income to buy more land.

Many Italians went to the United States, but before 1900 more went to Argentina and Brazil. Indeed, two out of three migrants to those two developing countries came from Italy. Other Italians migrated to other European countries. France was a favorite destination. In 1911 the Italian-born population of France was roughly a third as large as that in the United States.

Ties of family and friendship played a crucial role in the movement of peoples. There are many examples of people from a given province or village settling together in rural enclaves or tight-knit urban neighborhoods thousands of miles away. Very often a strong individual—a businessman, a religious leader—would blaze the way and others would follow.

Many landless young European men and women were spurred to leave by a spirit of revolt and independence. In Sweden and in Norway, in Jewish Russia and in Italy, these young people felt frustrated by the small privileged classes, who often controlled both church and government and resisted demands for change and greater opportunity. Many a young Norwegian seconded the passionate cry of their national poet, Björnstjerne Björnson (1832–1910): "Forth will I! Forth! I will be crushed and consumed if I stay."[6]

Many young Jews wholeheartedly agreed with a spokesman of Kiev's Jewish community in 1882, who declared, "Our human dignity is being trampled upon, our wives and daughters are being dishonored, we are looted and pillaged: either we get decent human rights or else let us go wherever our eyes may lead us."[7] Thus, for many, migration was a radical way to "get out from under." Migration slowed when the people won basic political and social reforms, such as the right to vote and social security.

FIGURE 30.4 Origin and Destination of European Emigrants, 1851–1960 *(Source: Data from W. Woodruff, Impact of Western Man: A Study of Europe's Role in the World Economy. St. Martin's Press, New York, 1967, pp. 108–109 and references cited therein)*

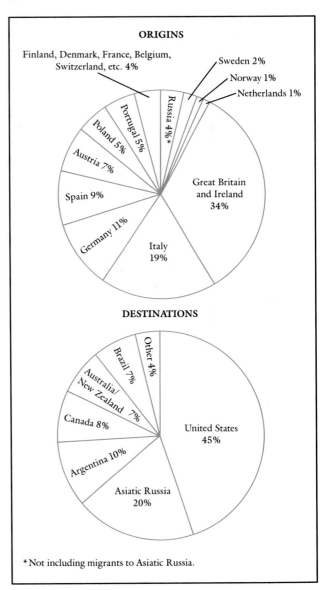

* Not including migrants to Asiatic Russia.

Asian Migrants

Not all migration was from Europe. A substantial number of Chinese, Japanese, Indians, and Filipinos—to name only four key groups—responded to rural hardship with temporary or permanent migration. At least 3 million Asians (as opposed to more than 60 million Europeans) moved abroad before 1920. Most went as indentured laborers to work under incredibly difficult conditions on the plantations or in the gold fields of Latin America, southern Asia, Africa, California, Hawaii, and Australia. White estate owners very often used Asians to replace or supplement blacks after the suppression of the slave trade.

In the 1840s, for example, there was a strong demand for field hands in Cuba, and the Spanish government actively recruited Chinese laborers. They came under eight-year contracts, were paid about twenty-five cents a day, and were fed potatoes and salted beef. Between 1853 and 1873, when such migration was stopped, more than 130,000 Chinese laborers went to Cuba. The majority spent their lives as virtual slaves. The great landlords of Peru also brought in more than 100,000 workers from China in the nineteenth century, and there were similar movements of Asians elsewhere.

Such migration from Asia would undoubtedly have grown to much greater proportions if planters and mine owners in search of cheap labor had had their way. But they did not. Asians fled the plantations and gold fields as soon as possible, seeking greater opportunities in trade and towns. There they came into conflict with other brown-skinned peoples—such as in Malaya and East Africa—and with white settlers in areas of European settlement.

These settlers demanded a halt to Asian migration. One Australian brutally summed up the typical view: "The Chinaman knows nothing about Caucasian civilization. It would be less objectionable to drive a flock of sheep to the poll than to allow Chinamen to vote. The sheep at all events would be harmless."[8] By the 1880s Americans and Australians were building "great white walls"—discriminatory laws designed to keep Asians out. Thus a final, crucial factor in the migrations before 1914 was the general policy of "whites only" in the rich open lands of possible permanent settlement. This, too, was part of West-ern dominance in the increasingly lopsided world. Largely successful in monopolizing the best overseas opportunities, Europeans and people of European ancestry reaped the main benefits from the great migration. By 1913 people in Australia, Canada, and the United States all had higher average incomes than people in Great Britain, still Europe's wealthiest nation.

WESTERN IMPERIALISM

The expansion of Western society reached its apex between about 1880 and 1914. In those years, the leading European nations not only continued to send massive streams of migrants, money, and manufactured goods around the world, but also rushed to create or enlarge vast political empires abroad. This political empire building contrasted sharply with the economic penetration of non-Western territories between 1816 and 1880, which had left a China or a Japan "opened" to European economic interests but still politically independent. By contrast, the empires of the late nineteenth century recalled the old European colonial empires of the seventeenth and eighteenth centuries and led contemporaries to speak of the "new imperialism."

Characterized by a frantic rush to plant the flag over as many people and as much territory as possible, the new imperialism had momentous consequences. It resulted in new tensions among competing European states, and it led to wars and rumors of war with non-European powers. The new imperialism was aimed primarily at Africa and Asia. It put millions of black, brown, and tan peoples directly under the rule of whites. How and why did whites come to rule these peoples?

The Scramble for Africa

The most spectacular manifestation of the new imperialism was the seizure of Africa, which broke sharply with previous patterns and fascinated contemporary Europeans and Americans.

As late as 1880, European nations controlled only 10 percent of the African continent, and their possessions were hardly increasing. The French had begun conquering Algeria in 1830, and within fifty years substantial numbers of French, Italian, and Spanish colonists had settled among the overwhelming Arab majority.

At the other end of the continent, in southern Africa, the British had taken possession of the Dutch settlements at Cape Town during the wars with Napoleon I. This takeover had led disgruntled Dutch cattlemen and farmers in 1835 to make their so-called Great Trek into the interior, where they fought the Zulu and Xhosa peoples for land. After 1853, while British colonies like Canada and Australia were beginning to evolve toward self-government, the Boers, or Afrikaners (as the descendants of the Dutch in the Cape Colony were beginning to call themselves), proclaimed their political independence and defended it against British armies. By 1880 Afrikaner and British settlers, who detested each other, had wrested control of much of the southern tip of Africa from the Zulu, Xhosa, and other African peoples.

European trading posts and forts dating back to the Age of Discovery and the slave trade dotted the coast of West Africa. The Portuguese proudly but ineffectively held their old possessions in Angola and Mozambique. Elsewhere, over the great mass of the continent, Europeans did not rule.

Between 1880 and 1900, the situation changed drastically. Britain, France, Germany, and Italy scrambled for African possessions as if their lives depended on them. By 1900 nearly the whole continent had been carved up and placed under European rule: only Ethiopia in northeast Africa and Liberia on the west African coast remained independent. Even the Afrikaner settler republics of southern Africa were conquered by the British in the bloody Boer War (1899–1902). In the years before 1914, the European powers tightened their control and established colonial governments to rule their gigantic empires (Map 30.2).

In the complexity of the European seizure of Africa, certain events and individuals stand out. Of enormous importance was the British occupation of Egypt, which established the new model of formal political control. There was also the role of Leopold II of Belgium (r. 1865–1909), an energetic, strong-willed monarch with a lust for distant territory. "The sea bathes our coast, the world lies before us," he had exclaimed in 1861. "Steam and electricity have annihilated distance, and all the non-appropriated lands on the surface of the globe can become the field of our operations and

of our success."[9] By 1876 Leopold was focusing on central Africa. Subsequently he formed a financial syndicate under his personal control to send Henry Morton Stanley, a sensation-seeking journalist and part-time explorer, to the Congo basin. Stanley established trading stations, signed "treaties" with African chiefs, and planted Leopold's flag. Leopold's actions alarmed the French, who quickly sent out an expedition under Pierre de Brazza. In 1880 de Brazza signed a treaty of protection with the chief of the large Teke tribe and began to establish a French protectorate on the north bank of the Congo River.

Leopold's buccaneering intrusion into the Congo area raised the question of the political fate of black Africa—Africa south of the Sahara. By the time the British successfully invaded and occupied Egypt, the richest and most developed land in Africa in 1882, Europe had caught "African fever." There was a gold-rush mentality, and the race for territory was on.

To lay down some basic rules for this new and dangerous game of imperialist competition, Jules Ferry of France and Bismarck of Germany arranged an international conference on Africa in Berlin in 1884 and 1885. The conference established the principle that European claims to African territory had to rest on "effective occupation" in order to be recognized by other states. This principle was very important. It meant that Europeans would push relentlessly into interior regions from all sides and that no single European power would be able to claim the entire continent. The conference recognized Leopold's personal rule over a neutral Congo Free State and declared all of the Congo basin a free-trade zone. The conference also agreed to work to stop slavery and the slave trade in Africa.

The Berlin conference coincided with Germany's sudden emergence as an imperial power. Prior to about 1880, Bismarck, like many European leaders at the time, had seen little value in colonies. Colonies reminded him, he said, of a poor but proud nobleman who wore a fur coat when he could not afford a shirt underneath. Then, in 1884 and 1885, as political agitation for expansion increased, Bismarck did an abrupt about-face, and Germany established protectorates over a number of small African kingdoms and tribes in Togoland, Cameroons, German Southwest Africa, and later in German East Africa.

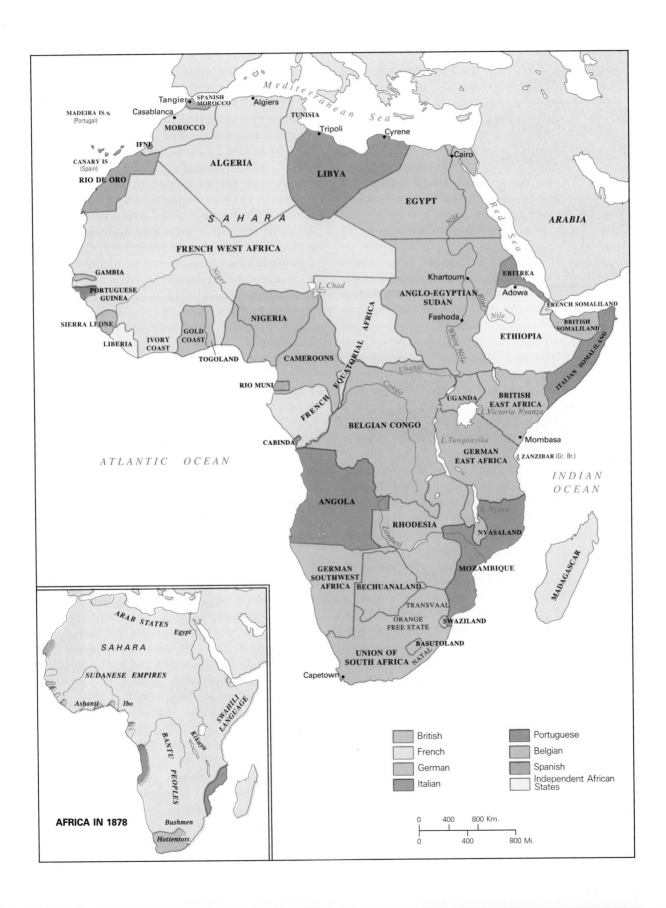

Mediterranean Sea

MADEIRA IS. (Portugal)

SPANISH MOROCCO
Tangier
Casablanca
MOROCCO
IFNI

CANARY IS (Spain)
RIO DE ORO

Algiers

ALGERIA

TUNISIA
Tripoli

LIBYA

Cyrene

Cairo

EGYPT

Nile

Red Sea

ARABIA

SAHARA

FRENCH WEST AFRICA

GAMBIA
PORTUGUESE GUINEA

SIERRA LEONE
LIBERIA

IVORY COAST

GOLD COAST

TOGOLAND

Niger

L. Chad

NIGERIA

CAMEROONS

RIO MUNI

FRENCH EQUATORIAL AFRICA

Ubangi

Congo

Khartoum

ANGLO-EGYPTIAN SUDAN

Fashoda

Blue Nile

White Nile

ERITREA

Adowa

FRENCH SOMALILAND

BRITISH SOMALILAND

ETHIOPIA

ITALIAN SOMALILAND

ATLANTIC OCEAN

CABINDA

BELGIAN CONGO

ANGOLA

UGANDA

BRITISH EAST AFRICA

L. Victoria Nyanza

L. Tanganyika

GERMAN EAST AFRICA

Mombasa

ZANZIBAR (Gr. Br.)

INDIAN OCEAN

RHODESIA

Zambesi

L. Nyasa

NYASALAND

MOZAMBIQUE

MADAGASCAR

GERMAN SOUTHWEST AFRICA

BECHUANALAND

TRANSVAAL

ORANGE FREE STATE

SWAZILAND

BASUTOLAND

UNION OF SOUTH AFRICA

NATAL

Capetown

AFRICA IN 1878

ARAB STATES

Egypt

SAHARA

SUDANESE EMPIRES

Ashanti

Ibo

BANTU PEOPLES

Kikuyu

SWAHILI LANGUAGE

Bushmen

Hottentots

British
French
German
Italian

Portuguese
Belgian
Spanish
Independent African States

0   400   800 Km.

0   400   800 Mi.

Omdurman, 1898 European machine guns cut down the charging Muslim tribesmen again and again. "It was not a battle but an execution," said one witness. Thus the Sudan was conquered and one million square miles added to the British empire. *(Source: E. T. Archive)*

In acquiring colonies, Bismarck cooperated against the British with France's Jules Ferry, who was as ardent for empire as he was for education. With Bismarck's tacit approval, the French pressed vigorously southward from Algeria, eastward from their old forts on the Senegal coast, and northward from de Brazza's newly formed protectorate on the Congo River. The object of these three thrusts was Lake Chad, a malaria-infested swamp on the edge of the Sahara.

Meanwhile, the British began enlarging their west African enclaves and impatiently pushing northward from the Cape Colony and westward

MAP 30.2 The Partition of Africa European nations carved up Africa after 1880 and built vast political empires.

from the island of Zanzibar in the Indian Ocean. Their thrust southward from Egypt was blocked in the Sudan by an uprising of fiercely independent Muslims, who decimated a British force at Khartoum in 1885. The peoples of the Sudan maintained the Islamic state that they had established in 1881 in a revolt against foreign control of Egypt, and the British retreated to Cairo. Sudanese Muslims were deeply committed to Islam, and for them the struggle to preserve Islam and the struggle for freedom were one and the same thing.

The invaders bided their time, and in 1896 a British force under General Horatio H. Kitchener moved cautiously and more successfully up the Nile River, building a railroad to supply arms and reinforcements as it went. Finally, in 1898, these British troops met their foe at Omdurman, where

Sea of
Okhotsk

Sakhalin   KARAFUTO
(Jap. 1905)

PACIFIC

OCEAN

AMUR DISTRICT
(1858)

Khabarovsk
(1858)

JAPANESE EMPIRE

New Guinea

Vladivostok
(1860)

Tokyo

Sea of

Japan

Harbin

MANCHURIA

KOREA
(1905, 1910)

Ryūkyū Is. (Jap.)

Chita

INNER
MONGOLIA

Mukden

Port Arthur
(Rus. 1898, Jap. 1905)

East
China
Sea

Irkutsk

Peking
Tientsin

Kiaochow
(Ger. 1898)

Weihaiwei
(Gr. Br. 1898)

Pescadores
(Jap. 1895)

Formosa
(Jap. 1895)

PHILIPPINE IS.
(U.S. from Spain 1898)

Timor
(Port. 1859)

RUSSIAN EMPIRE

OUTER MONGOLIA
(Autonomous, Russian sphere 1912)

L. Baikal

Yenisei

Nanking

Shanghai
(Gr. Br. 1842)

Foochow
Amoy
(Gr. Br. 1842)

Manila

DUTCH EAST INDIES

Celebes

Timor
(Neth.)

Hankow

Canton
(Gr. Br. 1842)

Hong Kong
(Gr. Br. 1842)

Macao
(Port. 1557)

Kwangshowan
(Fr. 1898)

South

China

Sea

BRITISH
NORTH BORNEO
(1888)

Borneo

SARAWAK
(1888)

CHINA

Chungking

Yangtze

Ob

Huang Ho

SINKIANG

Hanoi

FRENCH
INDOCHINA
(1884, 1907)

Saigon

MALAY STATES
(1800, 1824)

Singapore
(Gr. Br. 1819)

Sumatra

Java

Tobolsk

SIBERIA

Omsk

Trans-Siberian Railway

Tashkent
(1864)

Lhasa

TIBET

BHUTAN

SIAM

Bangkok

Yenisei

Irtysh

BURMA
(1852, 1885)

HIMALAYAS

NEPAL

KASHMIR
(1846)

PUNJAB

Delhi

Ganges

Calcutta

Rangoon

Bay

of

Bengal

Andaman Is.
(Gr. Br.)

Mery
(1884)

AFGHANISTAN

BALUCHISTAN
(1883)

Indus

INDIA

Bombay

BRITISH INDIA

Madras

Pondichéry
(Fr.)

Karikal
(Fr.)

Ceylon

Yanaon
(Fr.)

1000 Mi.

1000 Km.

*Aral
Sea*
(1873)

BRITISH
SPHERE
(1907)

Karachi

Diu
(Port.)

Goa
(Port.)

INDIAN

OCEAN

500

500

0

0

L. Balkhash
(1854)

PERSIA

RUSSIAN SPHERE
(1907)

Teheran

Caspian Sea

Arabian

Sea

Territories held by:

Great Britain
Netherlands
France
United States
Russia
Japan
Railroads

brave Muslim tribesmen of the Sudan charged time and time again only to be cut down by the recently invented machine gun. For one smug participant, the young British officer Winston Churchill, it was "like a pantomime scene" in a play. "These extraordinary foreign figures . . . march up one by one from the darkness of Barbarism to the footlights of civilization . . . and their conquerors, taking their possessions, forget even their names. Nor will history record such trash." For another more somber English observer, "It was not a battle but an execution. The bodies were not in heaps . . . but they spread evenly over acres and acres."[10] In the end, eleven thousand Muslim tribesmen lay dead, and only twenty-eight Britons had been killed.

Continuing up the Nile after the battle of Omdurman, Kitchener's armies found that a small French force had already occupied the village of Fashoda. Locked in imperial competition ever since Britain had occupied Egypt, France had tried to beat the British to one of Africa's last unclaimed areas—the upper reaches of the Nile. The result was a serious diplomatic crisis and even the threat of war. Eventually, wracked by the Dreyfus affair (see page 949) and unwilling to fight, France backed down and withdrew its forces.

The reconquest of the Sudan exemplified some general characteristics of empire building in Africa. The fate of the Muslim force at Omdurman was usually inflicted on all native peoples who resisted European invaders: they were blown away by ruthless and vastly superior military force. But however much the Western powers lusted for territory and dominion around the world, they always had the sense to stop short of actually fighting each other for it. Imperial ambitions were not worth a great European war.

Imperialism in Asia

Although the conquest of Africa was more spectacular, Europeans also extended their political control in Asia. In 1815 the Dutch ruled little more than the island of Java in the East Indies. There-

after they gradually brought almost all of the 3,000-mile archipelago under their political authority, though—in good imperialist fashion—they had to share some of the spoils with Britain and Germany. In the critical decade of the 1880s, the French under the leadership of Jules Ferry took Indochina. India, Japan, and China also experienced a profound imperialist impact (Map 30.3).

Two other great imperialist powers, Russia and the United States, also seized rich territories in Asia. Russia, whose history since the later Middle Ages had been marked by almost continuous expansion, moved steadily forward on two fronts throughout the nineteenth century. Russians conquered Muslim areas to the south in the Caucasus and in central Asia and also proceeded to nibble greedily on China's provinces in the Far East, especially in the 1890s.

The United States's great trophy was the Philippines, taken from Spain in 1898 after the Spanish-American War. When it quickly became clear that the Americans had no intention of granting self-rule, Philippine patriots rose against the United States in a war of independence. They were eventually defeated after thousands died in long, bitter fighting. Some Americans protested the taking of the Philippines, but they had no impact on government policy. Thus another big Western power joined the imperialist ranks in Asia.

Causes of the New Imperialism

Many factors contributed to the late nineteenth-century rush for territory and empire, which was in turn one aspect of Western society's generalized expansion in the age of industry and nationalism. Little wonder that controversies have raged over interpretation of the new imperialism, especially since authors of every persuasion have often exaggerated particular aspects in an attempt to prove their own theories. Yet despite complexity and controversy, basic causes are identifiable.

Economic motives played an important role in the extension of political empires, especially the British Empire. By the late 1870s, France, Germany, and the United States were industrializing rapidly behind rising tariff barriers. Great Britain was losing its early lead and facing increasingly tough competition in foreign markets. In this new

MAP 30.3 Asia in 1914 India remained under British rule while China precariously preserved its political independence.

economic situation, Britain came to value old possessions, such as India and Canada, more highly. The days when a leading free-trader like Richard Cobden could denounce the "bloodstained fetish of Empire" and statesman Benjamin Disraeli could call colonies a "millstone round our necks" came to an abrupt end. When continental powers began to grab unclaimed territory in the 1880s, the British followed suit immediately. They feared that France and Germany would seal off their empires with high tariffs and restrictions and that future economic opportunities would be lost forever.

Actually, the overall economic gains of the new imperialism proved limited before 1914. The new colonies were usually too poor to buy many manufactured goods, and they offered few immediately profitable investments. Nonetheless, even the poorest, most barren desert was jealously prized, and no territory was ever abandoned. Colonies became important for political and diplomatic reasons. Each leading country saw colonies as crucial to national security, military power, and international prestige. For instance, safeguarding the Suez Canal played a key role in the British occupation of Egypt, and protecting Egypt provided in turn a justification for the bloody reconquest of the Sudan. Military security was a major factor in the United States's decision to establish firm control over the Panama Canal Zone in 1903. Far-flung possessions guaranteed ever-growing navies the safe havens and the dependable coaling stations that they needed in time of crisis or war.

Many people in the West were convinced that colonies were essential to great nations. "There has never been a great power without great colonies," wrote one French publicist in 1877. "Every virile people has established colonial power," echoed the famous nationalist historian of Germany, Heinrich von Treitschke. "All great nations in the fullness of their strength have desired to set their mark upon barbarian lands and those who fail to participate in this great rivalry will play a pitiable role in time to come."[11]

Treitschke's harsh statement reflects not only the increasing aggressiveness of European nationalism after Bismarck's wars of German unification but also Social Darwinian theories of brutal competition between races. As one prominent English economist argued, the "strongest nation has always been conquering the weaker . . . and the strongest tend to be best." Thus European nations, which were seen as racially distinct parts of

the dominant white race, had to seize colonies to show that they were strong and virile. Moreover, since racial struggle was nature's inescapable law, the conquest of inferior peoples was just. "The path of progress is strewn with the wreck . . . of inferior races," wrote one professor in 1900. "Yet these dead peoples are, in very truth, the stepping stones on which mankind has risen to the higher intellectual and deeper emotional life of today."[12] Social Darwinism and racial doctrines fostered imperial expansion.

Finally, certain special-interest groups in each country were powerful agents of expansion. Shipping companies wanted lucrative subsidies, and promoters wanted mining concessions. White settlers on dangerous, turbulent frontiers constantly demanded ever more land and greater protection. Missionaries and humanitarians wanted to spread religion and stop the slave trade. Explorers and adventurers sought knowledge and excitement. Military men and colonial officials, whose role has often been overlooked by writers on imperialism, foresaw rapid advancement and high-paid positions in growing empires. The actions of such groups and the determined individuals who led them thrust the course of empire forward.

Western society did not rest the case for empire solely on naked conquest and a Darwinian racial struggle, or on power politics and the need for naval bases on every ocean. In order to satisfy their consciences and answer their critics, imperialists developed additional arguments. A favorite idea was that Europeans could and should "civilize" nonwhites. According to this view, nonwhites would receive the benefits of modern economies, cities, advanced medicine, and higher standards of living; and eventually they might be ready for self-government and Western democracy. Thus the French spoke of their sacred "civilizing mission." Rudyard Kipling (1865–1936), who wrote masterfully of Anglo-Indian life and was perhaps the most influential writer of the 1890s, exhorted Europeans to unselfish service in distant lands:

Take up the White Man's Burden—
 Send forth the best ye breed—
Go bind your sons to exile
 To serve your captives' need,
To wait in heavy harness,
 On fluttered folk and wild—
Your new-caught, sullen peoples
 Half-devil and half-child.[13]

"The Administration of Justice"   In this 1895 illustration from a popular magazine, a Belgian official, flanked by native soldiers, settles a tribal dispute in the Congo State. This flattering view of Europe's "civilizing mission" suggests how imperial rule rested on more than just brute force. *(Source: Bettmann/Hulton)*

Many Americans accepted the ideology of the white man's burden. It was an important factor in the decision to rule rather than liberate the Philippines after the Spanish-American War. Like their European counterparts, these Americans believed that their civilization had reached unprecedented heights and that they had unique benefits to bestow on all "less-advanced" peoples. Another argument was that imperial government protected natives from tribal warfare as well as from the crudest forms of exploitation by white settlers and businessmen.

Some Westerners also sought the peace and stability of imperial rule in order to spread Christianity. In Africa, Catholic and Protestant missionaries competed with Islam south of the Sahara, seeking converts and building schools to spread the Gospel. Many Africans' first real contact with whites was in mission schools. As late as 1942, for example, 97 percent of Nigeria's small student population was in mission schools. Some peoples, like the Ibos in Nigeria, became highly Christianized.

Such occasional successes in black Africa contrasted with the general failure of missionary efforts in India, China, and the Islamic world. There, Christians often preached in vain to peoples with ancient, complex religious beliefs. Yet the number of Christian believers around the world did increase substantially in the nineteenth century, and missionary groups kept trying. Unfortunately, "many missionaries had drunk at the well of European racism," and this probably prevented them from doing better.[14]

Critics of Imperialism

The expansion of empire aroused sharp, even bitter, critics. A forceful attack came in 1902, after the unpopular Boer War, by the radical English

THE SPREAD OF WESTERN IMPERIALISM

1800–1913	World trade increases 25-fold
1816–1880	European economic penetration of non-Western countries
1835	Great Trek: Boers proclaim independence from Great Britain in the South African hinterland
1840s	European capitalists begin large-scale foreign investment
1842	Treaty of Nanking: Manchu government of China cedes Hong Kong to Great Britain
1846	Repeal of Corn Laws: Great Britain declares its strong support of free trade
1848	British defeat of last independent native state in India
1853	Perry's arrival in Tokyo: Japan opened to European influence
1857–1858	Great Rebellion in India
1858–1863	Anti-foreign reaction in Japan
1867	Meiji Restoration in Japan: adoption of Western reforms
1869	Completion of Suez Canal
1871	Abolition of feudal domains in Japan
1876	Ismail, khedive of Egypt, appoints British and French commissioners to oversee government finances
1880	Establishment of French protectorate on the northern bank of the Congo
1880–1900	European powers intensify their "scramble for Africa"
1882	British occupation of Egypt
1883	Formation of the Indian National Congress
1884–1885	International conference on Africa in Berlin: European powers require "effective occupation"; Germany acquires protectorates in Togo, Cameroon, South West Africa, and East Africa; Belgium acquires the Congo Free State
1890	Establishment of an authoritarian constitution in Japan
1893	France completes its acquisition of Indochina
1894	Sino-Japanese War: Japan acquires Formosa
1898	Battle of Omdurman: under Kitchener, British forces reconquer the Sudan Spanish-American War: United States acquires the Philippines "Hundred Days of Reform" in China
1899–1902	Boer War: British defeat Dutch settlers in South Africa
1900–1903	The Boxer Rebellion in China
1903	American occupation of the Panama Canal zone
1904–1905	Russo-Japanese War: Japan wins protectorate over Port Arthur in China
1910	Japanese annexation of Korea
1912	Fall of Manchu dynasty in China

economist J. A. Hobson (1858–1940) in his *Imperialism,* a work that influenced Lenin and others. Hobson contended that the rush to acquire colonies was due to the economic needs of unregulated capitalism, particularly the need of the rich to find profitable outlets for their surplus capital. Yet, Hobson argued, imperial possessions do not pay off economically for the country as a whole. Only unscrupulous special-interest groups profit from them, at the expense of both the European taxpayer and the natives. Moreover, the quest for empire diverts attention from domestic reform and closing the gap between rich and poor. These and sim-

ilar arguments were not very persuasive. Most people then (and now) believed that imperialism was economically profitable for the homeland, and a broad and genuine enthusiasm for empire developed among the European masses.

Hobson and many other critics struck home, however, with their moral condemnation of whites imperiously ruling nonwhites. They rebelled against crude Social Darwinian thought. "O Evolution, what crimes are committed in thy name!" cried one foe. Another sardonically coined a new beatitude: "Blessed are the strong, for they shall prey on the weak."[15] Kipling and his kind were lampooned as racist bullies, whose rule rested on brutality, racial contempt, and the Maxim machine gun. Henri Labouchère, a member of Parliament and prominent spokesman for this position, mocked Kipling's famous poem:

Pile on the Brown Man's burden!
And if ye rouse his hate,
Meet his old-fashioned reasons
With Maxims up to date,
With shells and Dum-Dum bullets
A hundred times plain
The Brown Man's loss must never
Imply the White Man's gain.[16]

Similarly, in *Heart of Darkness,* the Polish-born novelist Joseph Conrad (1857–1924) castigated the "pure selfishness" of Europeans in "civilizing" Africa. The main character, once a liberal scholar, turns into a savage brute.

Critics charged Europeans with applying a degrading double standard and failing to live up to their own noble ideals. At home, Europeans had won or were winning representative government, individual liberties, and a certain equality of opportunity. In their empires, Europeans imposed military dictatorships on Africans and Asians, forced them to work involuntarily, almost like slaves, and discriminated against them shamelessly. Only by renouncing imperialism, critics insisted, and giving captive peoples the freedoms that Western society had struggled for since the French Revolution would Europeans be worthy of their traditions. Europeans who denounced the imperialist tide provided colonial peoples with a Western ideology of liberation.

RESPONSES TO WESTERN IMPERIALISM

To peoples in Africa and Asia, Western expansion represented a profoundly disruptive assault. Everywhere it threatened traditional ruling classes, traditional economies, and traditional ways of life. Christian missionaries and European secular ideologies attacked established beliefs and values. Non-Western peoples experienced a crisis of identity, a crisis made all the more painful by the power and arrogance of the white intruders.

The initial response of African and Asian rulers was to try to drive the unwelcome foreigners away.

This was the case in China, Japan, and the upper Sudan. Violent antiforeign reactions also exploded elsewhere again and again, but the superior military technology of the industrializing West almost invariably prevailed. Beaten in battle, many Africans and Asians concentrated on preserving their cultural traditions at all costs. Others found themselves forced to reconsider their initial hostility. Some (like Ismail of Egypt) concluded that the West was indeed superior in some ways and that it was therefore necessary to reform their societies and copy European achievements. Thus it is possible to think of responses to the Western impact as a spectrum, with "traditionalists" at one end, "Westernizers" or "modernizers" at the other, and many shades of opinion in between. Both before and after European domination, the struggle among these groups was often intense. With time, however, the modernizers tended to gain the upper hand.

When the power of both the traditionalists and the modernizers was thoroughly shattered by brute force, the great majority of Asians and Africans accepted imperial rule. Political participation in non-Western lands was historically limited to small elites, and the masses were accustomed to doing what their rulers told them to do. In these circumstances Europeans, clothed in power and convinced of their righteousness, governed smoothly and effectively. They received considerable support from both traditionalists (local chiefs, landowners, and non-Muslim religious leaders) and modernizers (the Western-educated merchants, professional classes, and civil servants).

Nevertheless, imperial rule was in many ways a hollow shell built on sand. Support for European rule among the conforming and accepting millions was shallow and weak. Thus the conforming masses followed with greater or lesser enthusiasm a few determined personalities who came to oppose the Europeans. Such leaders always arose, both when Europeans ruled directly and when they manipulated native governments, for at least two basic reasons.

First, the nonconformists—the eventual anti-imperialist leaders—developed a burning desire for human dignity. They came to feel that such dignity was incompatible with foreign rule—with its smirks and smiles, its paternalism and condescension. Second, potential leaders found in the West the ideologies and justification for their protest. They discovered liberalism with its credo of civil liberty and political self-determination. They echoed the demands of anti-imperialists in Europe and America that the West live up to its own ideals. More important, they found themselves attracted to modern nationalism, which asserted that every people had the right to control its own destiny. After 1917, anti-imperialist revolt would find another weapon in Lenin's version of Marxian socialism.

That the anti-imperialist search for dignity drew strength from Western culture is apparent in the development of three major Asian countries: India, Japan, and China.

Empire in India

India was the jewel of the British Empire, and no colonial area experienced a more profound British impact. Unlike Japan and China, which maintained a real or precarious independence, and unlike African territories, which were annexed by Europeans only at the end of the nineteenth century, India was ruled more or less absolutely by Britain for a very long time.

Arriving in India on the heels of the Portuguese in the seventeenth century, the British East India Company had conquered the last independent native state by 1848. The last "traditional" response to European rule—the attempt by the established ruling classes to drive the white man out by military force—was broken in India in 1857 and 1858. Those were the years of the Great Rebellion (which the British called a "mutiny"), when an insurrection by Muslim and Hindu mercenaries in the British army spread throughout northern and central India before it was finally crushed, primarily by loyal native troops from southern India. Thereafter Britain ruled India directly. India illustrates, therefore, for better and for worse, what generations of European domination could produce.

After 1858 India was ruled by the British Parliament in London and administered by a tiny, all-white civil service in India. In 1900 this elite consisted of fewer than 3,500 top officials, for a population of 300 million. The white elite, backed by white officers and native troops, was competent and maintained reasonably good authoritarian rule. Yet it practiced strict job discrimination and social segregation, and most of its members quite frankly considered the jumble of Indian peoples

and castes to be racially inferior. As Lord Kitchener, one of the most distinguished top military commanders of India, stated:

It is this consciousness of the inherent superiority of the European which has won for us India. However well educated and clever a native may be, and however brave he may prove himself, I believe that no rank we can bestow on him would cause him to be considered an equal of the British officer.[17]

When, for example, the British Parliament in 1883 was considering a major bill to allow Indian judges to try white Europeans in India, the British community rose in protest and defeated the measure. The idea that they might be judged by Indians was inconceivable to Europeans, for it was clear to the Europeans that the empire in India rested squarely on racial inequality.

In spite of (perhaps even because of) their strong feelings of racial and cultural superiority, the British acted energetically and introduced many desirable changes to India. Realizing that they needed well-educated Indians to serve as skilled subordinates in the government and army, the British established a modern system of progressive secondary education, in which all instruction was in English. Thus, through education and government service the British offered some Indians excellent opportunities for both economic and social advancement. High-caste Hindus were particularly quick to respond and emerged as skillful intermediaries between the British rulers and the Indian people—a new elite profoundly influenced by Western thought and culture.

This new bureaucratic elite played a crucial role in modern economic development, which was a second result of British rule. Irrigation projects for agriculture, the world's third largest railroad network for good communication, and large tea and jute plantations geared to the needs of the *international* economy were all developed. Unfortunately, the lot of the Indian masses improved little, for the increase in agricultural production was quite literally eaten up by population increase.

Finally, with a well-educated, English-speaking Indian bureaucracy and modern communications, the British created a unified, powerful state. They placed under the same general system of law and administration the different Hindu and Muslim peoples and the vanquished kingdoms of the entire subcontinent—groups that had fought each

The British in India   This photo suggests not only the incredible power and luxury of the British ruling class in India but also its confidence and self-satisfaction. As one British viceroy said, "We are all British gentlemen engaged in the magnificent work of governing an inferior race." *(Source: Bettmann/Hulton)*

other for centuries during the Middle Ages and had been repeatedly conquered by Muslim and Mongol invaders. It was as if Europe, with its many states and varieties of Christianity, had been conquered and united in a single great empire.

In spite of these achievements, the decisive reaction to European rule was the rise of nationalism among the Indian elite. No matter how Anglicized and necessary a member of the educated classes became, he or she could never become the white ruler's equal. The top jobs, the best clubs, the modern hotels, and even certain railroad compartments were sealed off to brown-skinned men and women. The peasant masses might accept such inequality as the latest version of age-old oppression, but the well-educated, English-speaking elite eventually could not. For the elite, racial discrimination meant not only injured pride but bitter injustice. It flagrantly contradicted the cherished Western concepts of human rights and equality. Moreover, it was based on dictatorship, no matter how benign.

By 1885, when educated Indians came together to found the predominantly Hindu Indian National Congress, demands were increasing for the equality and self-government that Britain enjoyed and had already granted white-settler colonies, such as Canada and Australia. By 1907, embold-

ened in part by Japan's success (see pages 983–985), the radicals in the Indian National Congress were calling for complete independence. Even the moderates were demanding home rule for India through an elected parliament. Although there were sharp divisions between Hindus and Muslims, Indians were finding an answer to the foreign challenge. The common heritage of British rule and Western ideals, along with the reform and revitalization of the Hindu religion, had created a genuine movement for national independence.

The Example of Japan

When Commodore Perry arrived in Japan in 1853 with his crude but effective gunboat diplomacy, Japan was a complex feudal society. At the top stood a figurehead emperor, but for more than two hundred years, real power had been in the hands of a hereditary military governor, the *shogun*. With the help of a warrior nobility known as *samurai*, the shogun governed a country of hard-working, productive peasants and city dwellers. Often poor and restless, the intensely proud samurai were deeply humiliated by the sudden American intrusion and the unequal treaties with Western countries. When foreign diplomats and merchants began to settle in Yokohama, radical samurai reacted with a wave of antiforeign terrorism and antigovernment assassinations between 1858 and 1863. The imperialist response was swift and unambiguous. An allied fleet of American, British, Dutch, and French warships bombarded and demolished key forts, which further weakened the power and prestige of the shogun's government. Then, in 1867, a coalition led by patriotic samurai seized control of the government with hardly any bloodshed and restored the power of the emperor. This was the Meiji Restoration, a great turning point in Japanese development.

The immediate, all-important goal of the new government was to meet the foreign threat. The battle cry of the Meiji reformers was "enrich the state and strengthen the armed forces." Yet how was this to be done? In an about-face that was one of history's most remarkable chapters, the young but well-trained, idealistic but flexible leaders of Meiji Japan dropped their antiforeign attacks. Convinced that Western civilization was indeed superior in its military and industrial aspects, they initiated from above a series of measures to reform Japan along modern lines. They were convinced that "Japan must be reborn with America its mother and France its father."[18] In the broadest sense, the Meiji leaders tried to harness the power inherent in Europe's dual revolution, in order to protect their country and catch up with the West.

Japanese Industrialization   The famous Tomioka silk reeling factory pioneered with mass-production techniques and women factory workers in the 1870s. The combination shown here of European technology with native dress symbolizes Japan's successful integration of Western practices into the traditional culture of its society. *(Source: Laurie Platt Winfrey, Inc.)*

In 1871 the new leaders abolished the old feudal structure of aristocratic, decentralized government and formed a strong, unified state. Following the example of the French Revolution, they dismantled the four-class legal system and declared social equality. They decreed freedom of movement in a country where traveling abroad had been a most serious crime. They created a free, competitive, government-stimulated economy. Japan began to build railroads and modern factories. Thus the new generation adopted many principles of a free, liberal society; and, as in Europe, such freedom resulted in a tremendously creative release of human energy.

Yet the overriding concern of Japan's political leadership was always a powerful state, and to achieve this, more than liberalism was borrowed from the West. A powerful modern navy was created, and the army was completely reorganized along French and German lines, with three-year military service for all males and a professional officer corps. This army of draftees effectively put down disturbances in the countryside, and in 1877 it was used to crush a major rebellion by feudal elements protesting the loss of their privileges. Japan also borrowed rapidly and adopted skillfully the West's science and modern technology, particularly in industry, medicine, and education. Many Japanese were encouraged to study abroad, and the government paid large salaries to attract foreign experts. These experts were always carefully controlled, though, and replaced by trained Japanese as soon as possible.

By 1890, when the new state was firmly established, the wholesale borrowing of the early restoration had given way to more selective emphasis on those things foreign that were in keeping with Japanese tradition. Following the model of the German Empire, Japan established an authoritarian constitution and rejected democracy. The power of the emperor and his ministers was vast, that of the legislature limited.

Japan successfully copied the imperialism of Western society. Expansion not only proved that Japan was strong; it also cemented the nation together in a great mission. Having "opened" Korea with the gunboat diplomacy of imperialism in 1876, Japan decisively defeated China in a war over Korea in 1894 and took Formosa. In the next years, Japan competed aggressively with the leading European powers for influence and territory in China, particularly Manchuria. There Japanese

and Russian imperialism met and collided. In 1904 Japan attacked Russia without warning, and at the end of a bloody war Japan emerged with a valuable foothold in China—Russia's former protectorate over Port Arthur (Map 30.4). By 1910, when it annexed Korea, Japan was a major imperial power, continuously expanding its influence in China.

Japan became the first non-Western country to use an ancient love of country to transform itself and thereby meet the many-sided challenge of Western expansion. Moreover, Japan demonstrated convincingly that a modern Asian nation could defeat and humble a great Western power. Many Chinese nationalists were fascinated by Japan's achievement. A group of patriots in French-ruled southern Vietnam sent Vietnamese students to Japan to learn the island empire's secret of success. Japan provided patriots in Asia and Africa with an inspiring example of national recovery and liberation.

Toward Revolution in China

In 1860 the 200-year-old Manchu Dynasty in China appeared on the verge of collapse. Efforts to repel the foreigners had failed, and rebellion and chaos wracked the country. Yet the government drew on its traditional strengths and made a surprising comeback that lasted more than thirty years.

Two factors were crucial in this reversal. First, the traditional ruling groups temporarily produced new, effective leadership. Loyal scholar-statesmen and generals quelled disturbances like the great Tai Ping Rebellion. A remarkable woman, the empress dowager Tzu Hsi, governed in the name of her young son and combined shrewd insight with vigorous action to revitalize the bureaucracy.

Second, destructive foreign aggression lessened, for the Europeans had achieved their primary goal of advantageous commercial and diplomatic relations. Indeed, some Europeans even contributed to the dynasty's recovery. A talented Irishman effectively reorganized China's customs office and increased the government tax receipts, and a sympathetic American diplomat represented China in foreign lands and helped strengthen the central government. Such efforts dovetailed with the dynasty's efforts to adopt some aspects of Western government and technology while maintaining traditional Chinese values and beliefs.

The parallel movement toward domestic reform and limited cooperation with the West collapsed under the blows of Japanese imperialism. The Sino-Japanese war of 1894–1895 and the subsequent harsh peace treaty revealed China's helplessness in the face of aggression, triggering a rush for foreign concessions and protectorates in China. At the height of foreign pressure in 1898, it appeared that the Western powers and Japan might actually divide China among themselves, as they had recently divided Africa. Probably only the jealousy that each nation felt toward its imperial competitors saved China from partition, although the U. S. Open Door policy, which opposed formal annexation of Chinese territory, may have helped tip the balance. In any case, the tempo and the impact of foreign penetration greatly accelerated after 1894.

MAP 30.4 The Expansion and Modernization of Japan, 1868–1918   Japan was uniquely successful among Asian states in responding to the challenge of Western imperialism before 1914. Japan made great progress in building a modern economy and in creating a political empire beyond the home islands.

The Empress Dowager Tzu Hsi   drew on conservative forces, like the court eunuchs surrounding her here, to maintain her power. Three years after her death in 1908, a revolution broke out and forced the last Chinese emperor, a boy of six, to abdicate. *(Source: Courtesy of the Freer Gallery of Art, Smithsonian Institution, Washington, D.C.)*

So, too, did the intensity and radicalism of the Chinese reaction. Like the men of the Meiji Restoration, some modernizers saw salvation in Western institutions. In 1898 the government launched a desperate "hundred days of reform" in an attempt to meet the foreign challenge. Radical reformers like the revolutionary Sun Yat-sen (1866–1925), who came from the peasantry and was educated in Hawaii by Christian missionaries, sought to overthrow the dynasty altogether and establish a republic.

On the other side, some traditionalists turned back toward ancient practices, political conservatism, and fierce hatred of the "foreign devils." "Protect the country, destroy the foreigner" was their simple motto. Such conservative, antiforeign

patriots had often clashed with foreign missionaries, whom they charged with undermining reverence for ancestors and thereby threatening the Chinese family and the entire society. In the agony of defeat and unwanted reforms, secret societies like the Boxers rebelled. In northeastern China, more than two hundred foreign missionaries and several thousand Chinese Christians were killed. Once again, the imperialist response was swift and harsh. Peking was occupied and plundered by foreign armies. A heavy indemnity was imposed.

The years after the Boxer Rebellion (1900–1903) were even more troubled. Anarchy and foreign influence spread as the power and prestige of the Manchu Dynasty declined still further. Antiforeign, antigovernment revolutionary groups agitated and plotted. Finally, in 1912, a spontaneous uprising toppled the Manchu Dynasty. After thousands of years of emperors and empires, a loose coalition of revolutionaries proclaimed a Western-style republic and called for an elected parliament. The transformation of China under the impact of expanding Western society entered a new phase, and the end was not in sight.

SUMMARY

In the nineteenth century the industrializing West entered the third and most dynamic phase of its centuries-old intrusion into non-Western lands. In so doing, Western nations profitably subordinated those lands to their economic interests, sent forth millions of emigrants, and established political influence in Asia and vast political empires in Africa. The reasons for this culminating surge were many, but the economic thrust of robust industrial capitalism, an ever-growing lead in technology, and the competitive pressures of European nationalism were particularly important.

Western expansion had far-reaching consequences. For the first time in human history, the world became in many ways a single unit. Moreover, European expansion diffused the ideas and techniques of a highly developed civilization. Yet the West imposed inequality in commercial relations, and it relied on military might to conquer and rule. It treated non-Western peoples as racial inferiors.

Non-Western elites, often armed with Western doctrines, gradually responded to the Western challenge. They launched a national, anti-imperialist struggle for dignity, genuine independence, and modernization. This struggle would emerge as a central drama of world history after the great European civil war of 1914 to 1918, which reduced the West's technological advantage and shattered its self-confidence and complacent moral superiority.

NOTES

1. Quoted in A. Waley, *The Opium War Through Chinese Eyes* (New York: Macmillan, 1958), p. 29.

2. Quoted in J. W. Hall, *Japan, from Prehistory to Modern Times* (New York: Delacorte Press, 1970), p. 250.
3. Quoted in R. Hallett, *Africa to 1875* (Ann Arbor: University of Michigan Press, 1970), p. 109.
4. Quoted in Earl of Cromer, *Modern Egypt* (London: 1911), p. 48.
5. Quoted in G. Jensen, *Militant Islam* (New York: Harper & Row, 1979), p. 70.
6. Quoted in T. Blegen, *Norwegian Migration to America* (Northfield, Minn.: Norwegian-American Historical Association, 1940), 2.468
7. Quoted in I. Howe, *World of Our Fathers* (New York: Harcourt Brace Jovanovich, 1976), p. 25.
8. Quoted in C. A. Price, *The Great White Walls Are Built: Restrictive Immigration to North America and Australia, 1836–1888* (Canberra: Australian National University Press, 1974), p. 175.
9. Quoted in W. L. Langer, *European Alliances and Alignments, 1871–1890* (New York: Vintage Books, 1931), p. 290.
10. Quoted in J. Ellis, *The Social History of the Machine Gun* (New York: Pantheon Books, 1975), pp. 86, 101.
11. Quoted in G. H. Nadel and P. Curtis, eds., *Imperialism and Colonialism* (New York: Macmillan, 1964), p. 94.
12. Quoted in W. L. Langer, *The Diplomacy of Imperialism*, 2d ed. (New York: Knopf, 1951), pp. 86, 88.
13. Rudyard Kipling, *The Five Nations* (London: 1903), quoted by the permission of Mrs. George Bambridge, Methuen & Company, and Doubleday & Company, Inc.
14. E. H. Berman, "African Responses to Christian Mission Education," *African Studies Review* 17:3 (1974): 530.
15. Quoted in Langer, *Diplomacy of Imperialism*, p. 88.
16. Quoted in Ellis, pp. 99–100.
17. Quoted in K. M. Panikkar, *Asia and Western Dominance* (London: George Allen & Unwin, 1959), p. 116.
18. Quoted in Hall, p. 289.

SUGGESTED READING

General surveys of European expansion in a broad perspective include R. Betts, *Europe Overseas* (1968); A. Thornton, *Imperialism in the 20th Century* (1977); T. Smith, *The Patterns of Imperialism* (1981); and W. Woodruff, *Impact of Western Man* (1967), which has an extensive bibliography. D. K. Fieldhouse has also written two fine surveys, *Economics and Empire, 1830–1914* (1970), and *Colonialism, 1870–1945* (1981). G. Barraclough, *An Introduction to Contemporary History* (1964), argues powerfully that Western imperialism and the non-Western reaction to it have been crucial in world history since about 1890. J. A. Hobson's classic *Imperialism* (1902) is readily available, and the Marxist-Leninist case is effectively presented in V. G. Kieran, *Marxism and Imperialism* (1975). Two excellent anthologies on the problem of European expansion are G. Nadel and P. Curtis, eds., *Imperialism and Colonialism* (1964), and H. Wright, ed., The *"New Imperialism,"* rev. ed. (1975).

Britain's leading position in European imperialism is examined in a lively way by B. Porter, *The Lion's Share* (1976); J. Morris, *Pax Britannica* (1968); and D. Judd, *The Victorian Empire* (1970), a stunning pictorial history. B. Semmel has written widely on the intellectual foundations of English expansion, as in *The Rise of Free Trade Imperialism* (1970). J. Gallagher and R. Robinson, *Africa and the Victorians: The Climax of Imperialism* (1961), is an influential reassessment. H. Brunschwig, *French Colonialism, 1871–1914* (1966), and W. Baumgart, *Imperialism: The Idea and Reality of British and French Colonial Expansion* (1982), are well-balanced studies. A. Moorehead, *The White Nile* (1971), tells the fascinating story of the European exploration of the mysterious upper Nile. Volumes 5 and 6 of K. Latourette, *History of the Expansion of Christianity, 7 vols.* (1937–1945), examine the powerful impulse for missionary work in non-European areas. D. Headrick stresses Western technical superiority in *Tools of Empire: Technology and European Imperialism in the Nineteenth Century* (1981).

G. Perry, *The Middle East: Fourteen Islamic Centuries* (1983), concisely surveys nineteenth-century developments and provides up-to-date bibliographies. B. Lewis, *The Middle East and the West* (1963), is a standard older analysis of the impact of Western ideas on Middle Eastern thought, which may be compared with the more sympathetic view of G. Jansen, *Militant Islam* (1979). Hallett, cited in the Notes, and R. July, *A History of the African People* (1970), contain excellent introductions to Africa in the age of imperialism. D. Lamb, *The Africans* (1984), and J. D. Fage, *A History of Africa* (1978), are also recommended. B. Davidson, *The African Genius: An Introduction to African Social and Cultural History* (1969), imaginatively looks at Western expansion from an African point of view. A classic study of that same expansion from an Indian viewpoint is found in K. M. Panikkar, *Asia and Western Dominance: A Survey of the Vasco da Gama Epoch of Asian History* (1959). S. Wolpert, *A New History of India,* 2d ed. (1982), incorporates recent scholarship in a wide-ranging study that is highly recommended. On Africa and India, see also the Suggested Reading for Chapters 22, 23, and 33.

A. Waley, cited in the Notes, has written extensively and well on China. Valuable surveys of Chinese history include J. Spence, *The Search for Modern China* (1990), I. Hsü, *The Rise of Modern China,* 2d ed. (1975), and K. Latourette, *The Chinese: Their History and Culture,* rev. ed. (1964). All three have many suggestions for further reading. The most comprehensive scholarly work is the multivolume series edited by J. Fairbank and D. Twitchett, *The Cambridge History of China.* In addition to Hall, cited in the Notes, E. Reischauer's topical survey, *Japan: The Story of a Nation* (1981), is recommended. Excellent social studies include M. Hane, *Peasants, Rebels and Outcasts: The Underside of Modern Japan* (1982), and Y. Fukuzawa, *Autobiography* (1966), the personal account of a leading intellectual who witnessed the emergence of modern Japan. E. Sugimoto, *A Daughter of the Samurai* (1966), is another fascinating autobiography. E. Wolf, *Europe and the People Without History* (1982), considers the impact of imperialism on non-Western peoples with skill and compassion.

Two unusual and provocative studies on personal relations between European rulers and non-European subjects are D. Mannoni, *Prospero and Caliban: The Psychology of Colonialization* (1964), and F. Fanon, *The Wretched of the Earth* (1965), a bitter attack on white racism by a black psychologist active in the Algerian revolution. The Indian work by A. Nandy, *The Intimate Enemy: Loss and Recovery of Self Under Colonialism* (1983), is another stimulating psychological study, as is K. Ballhatchet, *Race, Sex and Class Under the Raj* (1980). Novels also bring the psychological and human dimensions of imperialism alive. H. Rider Haggard, *King Solomon's Mines,* portrays the powerful appeal of adventure in exotic lands, and Rudyard Kipling, the greatest writer of European expansion, is at his stirring best in *Kim* and *Soldiers Three.* Joseph Conrad unforgettably probes European motives in *Heart of Darkness,* and André Gide, in *The Immoralist,* closely examines European moral corruption in North Africa.

31

Nation Building in the Western Hemisphere and in Australia

Governor's Palace, Plaza de Armas, Lima, Peru

In the Western Hemisphere and in Australia, as in Europe, the nineteenth century was a period of nation building, geographic expansion, and industrial and commercial growth. Waves of emigrants moved from Europe and Asia to the Americas and to Australia. The millions who braved the oceans populated and built new nations also linked the Western Hemisphere and Australia with the rest of the globe.

The countries of North and South America became highly diverse ethnically and culturally, and the issue of race created serious tensions throughout the hemisphere. In the United States it helped to bring on the Civil War. In the late nineteenth and early twentieth centuries, European immigration directly affected the ways with which the United States and the Latin American nations coped with racial situations.

At the end of the eighteenth century, Canada and the countries of South America remained colonies. Their European mother countries looked on the democratic experiment of the infant United States with suspicion and scorn. The island continent of Australia, remote from Europe and economically undeveloped, served as a dumping ground for English criminals. By 1914 the Latin American states, Canada, and Australia were enjoying political independence and playing a crucial role in the world economy. The United States had become a colossus on which the Old World depended in the First World War.

- Why and how did the Spanish colonies of Latin America shake off European domination and develop into national states?

- What role did the concept of manifest destiny play in the evolution of the United States?

- How did slavery affect the black family in the United States?

- How did the Americas and Australia absorb new peoples, and what was the social impact of the immigrants?

- What geographical, economic, and political conditions shaped the development of Canada?

- What factors aided the economic growth of Australia?

These are among the questions that this chapter addresses.

LATIN AMERICA (1800–1929)

In 1800 the Spanish Empire in the Western Hemisphere stretched from the headwaters of the Mississippi River in present-day Minnesota to the tip of Cape Horn in the Antarctic (see Map 31.1). The Spanish crown claimed 7 million square miles, roughly one-third of the entire hemisphere. According to the Kentucky statesman Henry Clay (1777–1852), "Within this vast region, we behold the most sublime and interesting objects of creation: the loftiest mountains, the most majestic rivers in the world; the richest mines of precious metals, the choicest productions of the earth."[1] Spain believed that this great wealth existed for its benefit, and Spanish policies fostered bitterness and the desire for independence in the colonies.

Between 1806 and 1825 the Spanish colonies in Latin America were convulsed by upheavals that ultimately resulted in their separation from Spain. Some scholars regard these insurrections as wars of revolution; others call them wars of independence; still others consider them civil wars. All three characterizations contain elements of truth.

The Latin American wars were revolutions in the sense that the colonists revolted against the domination of Spain and fought for direct self-government. They were wars of independence in the sense that the colonies sought economic liberation and management of their own commercial affairs. They were civil wars in the sense that social and racial groups fought one another. The *Creoles*—people of Spanish descent born in America—resented the economic and political dominance of the *peninsulares,* as natives of Spain or Portugal were called. Peninsulares controlled the rich export-import trade, intercolonial trade, and the mining industries. At the same time *mestizos* of mixed Spanish and Indian background and *mulattos* of mixed Spanish and African heritage sought an end to their systematic subordination.

Between 1850 and the worldwide depression of 1929, the countries of Latin America developed into national states. The predominant factors in this evolution were the heritage of colonial exploitation, a neocolonial economic structure, massive immigration from Europe and Asia, and the fusion of Amerindian, Caucasian, African, and Asian peoples. The Latin American societies that emerged in the twentieth century can best be understood against this background.

The Origins of the Revolutions

Because of regional, geographic, and racial differences, the Latin American movements for independence took different forms in different places. Everywhere, however, they grew out of recent colonial economic grievances. By the late seventeenth century the Spanish colonies had achieved a high degree of economic diversity and independence. The mercantilist imperialism of the days of Cortés and Pizarro (see pages 568–575), which held that the colonies existed for Spain's financial benefit and should be economically dependent on Spain, had faded away. The colonies had become agriculturally and commercially self-sufficient producers of foodstuffs, wine, textiles, and consumer goods. What was not produced domestically was secured through trade between colonies. A healthy intercolonial trade had developed independent of Spain, despite formidable geographic obstacles and colonial policies designed to restrict it.

In Peru, for example, domestic agriculture supported the large mining settlements, and the colony did not have to import food. Craft workshops owned by the state or by private individuals produced consumer goods for the working class; what was not manufactured locally was bought from Mexico and transported by the Peruvian merchant marine. By 1700 Mexico and Peru were sending shrinking percentages of their revenues to Spain and retaining more for public works, defense, and administration. The colonies lived for themselves, not for Spain.

The reforms of the Spanish Bourbons radically reversed this economic independence. Spain's humiliating defeat in the War of the Spanish Succession prompted demands for sweeping reform of all of Spain's institutions, including colonial policies and practices (see page 617). To improve administrative efficiency, the enlightened monarch Charles III (r. 1759–1788) carved the region of modern Colombia, Venezuela, and Ecuador out of the vast viceroyalty of Peru; it became the new viceroyalty of New Granada with its capital at Bogotá. The Crown also created the viceroyalty of Rio de la Plata (present-day Argentina) with its capital at Buenos Aires (Map 31.1).

Far more momentous was Charles III's radical overhaul of colonial trade policies, to enable Spain to compete with Great Britain and Holland in the great eighteenth-century struggle for empire. The Spanish crown intended the colonies to serve as sources of raw materials and as markets for Spanish manufactured goods. Charles III's free-trade policies cut duties drastically for Spanish merchants. All Iberian ports, no longer just Cadiz, were allowed to trade with the colonies. In Latin America these actions stimulated the production of crops in demand in Europe: coffee in Venezuela; sugar in Cuba and throughout the Caribbean; hides, leather, and salted beef in the Rio de la Plata viceroyalty. In Mexico and Peru, production of silver climbed steadily in the last quarter of the century. The volume of Spain's trade with the colonies soared, possibly as much as 700 percent between 1778 and 1788.[2]

Colonial manufacturing, which had been growing steadily, suffered severely. Better-made and cheaper European goods drove colonial goods out of the marketplace. Colonial textiles, chinaware, and wine, for example, could not compete with cheap Spanish products. For one thing, Latin American free laborers were paid more than European workers in the eighteenth century; this helps explain the great numbers of immigrants to the colonies. Also, intercolonial transportation costs were higher than transatlantic costs. In Buenos Aires, for example, Spanish wines were actually cheaper than locally produced Mendoza wine. In the Rio de la Plata region, heavy export taxes and light import duties shattered the wine industry. When the wine merchants complained of "tyrannical taxes" and asked an end to the import of Spanish wines, the imperial government rejected their appeal.

Geographic obstacles also hampered the economic development of Latin America. Mountains, deserts, jungles, and inadequate natural harbors frustrated colonial efforts to promote economic integration.

Having made the colonies dependent on essential Spanish goods, however, Spain found that it could not keep the sea routes open. After 1789 the French Revolution and Napoleonic wars isolated Spain from Latin America. Foreign traders, especially from the United States, swarmed into Spanish-American ports. In 1796 the Madrid government lifted the restrictions against neutrals trading with the colonies, thus acknowledging Spain's inability to supply the colonies with needed goods and markets.[3] All these difficulties spelled disaster for colonial trade and industry.

At the end of the eighteenth century colonists also complained bitterly that only peninsulares

Disputed by Great Britain, Spain, and Russia

Effective frontier of Spanish settlement

COAHUILA

VICEROYALTY OF NEW SPAIN

BAJIO LEÓN

Mexico City• •Veracruz

Havana

CUBA

JAMAICA

SAINT DOMINGUE (HAITI)

SANTO DOMINGO

PUERTO RICO

Caribbean Sea

•Guatemala

ATLANTIC OCEAN

•Caracas

Magdalena *Suarez*

•Bogotá

VICEROYALTY OF NEW GRANADA

GUIANA

Amazon

PACIFIC OCEAN

ANDES

Lima•

VICEROYALTY OF PERU

VICEROYALTY OF BRAZIL

•Bahia

Parana

ANDES

São Paulo• •Rio de Janeiro

Spanish colonies

Viceroyalty of New Spain

Viceroyalty of New Granada

Viceroyalty of Peru

Audiencia of Chile

Viceroyalty of Rio de la Plata

Portuguese colony

Viceroyalty of Brazil

Disputed territory

Disputed by Great Britain, Spain, and Russia

VICEROYALTY OF RIO DE LA PLATA

Santiago• Buenos Aires• •Montevideo

AUDIENCIA OF CHILE

0   500   1000 Km.

0   500   1000 Mi.

ISLAS MALVINAS (FALKLAND ISLANDS)

Cape Horn

were appointed to the *audiencias*—the colonies' highest judicial bodies, which also served as councils to the viceroys—and to other positions in the colonial governments. According to the nineteenth-century Mexican statesman and historian Lucas Alamán (1792–1853),

this preference shown to Spaniards in political offices and ecclesiastical benefices has been the principal cause of the rivalry between the two classes; add to this the fact that Europeans possessed great wealth, which although it may have been the just reward of effort and industry, excited the envy of Americans and was considered as so much usurpation from them; consider that for all these reasons the Spaniards had obtained a decided preponderance over those born in the country; and it will not be difficult to explain the increasing jealousy and rivalry between the two groups which culminated in hatred and enmity.[4]

In the late seventeenth and early eighteenth centuries, large numbers of Creoles had been appointed to government positions, including the audiencias. Then, beginning in 1751, the Crown drastically reduced the appointments of Creoles, and the upper levels of colonial bureaucracies became overwhelmingly Spanish. Between 1730 and 1750, fully 53 percent of appointees to the audiencias had been Creoles; from 1751 to 1775, only 13 percent were Creoles.[5] This change in imperial policy provoked outrage. To the Creole elite of Spanish America, the world seemed "upside down."[6] Creoles hungered for political office and resented their successful Spanish rivals.

Madrid's tax reforms also aggravated discontent. In the 1770s and 1780s the Spanish crown needed income to finance imperial defense. Colonial ports had to be fortified and standing armies built. Like Great Britain, Spain believed its colonies should bear some of the costs of their own defense. Accordingly, Madrid raised the prices of tobacco and liquor and increased the *alcabala* (a sales tax of Arabic origin) on many items. Improved government administration made tax collection more efficient. Creole business and agri-cultural interests resented the Crown's monopoly of the tobacco industry and opposed new taxes.

As in the thirteen North American colonies a decade earlier, protest movements in Latin America claimed that the colonies were being taxed unconstitutionally. Merchants in Boston and Philadelphia had protested taxation without representation; the Spanish colonies, however, had no tradition of legislative approval of taxes. Creole mercantile leaders argued instead that the constitutional system was being violated because taxes were being imposed without consultation. They asserted that relations between imperial authorities and colonial interests stayed on an even keel through consultation and compromise and that when the Crown imposed taxes without consultation, it violated ancient constitutional practice.

North American ships calling at South American ports had introduced the subversive writings of Thomas Paine and Thomas Jefferson. The imperial government recognized the potential danger of the North American example. Although Spain had joined France on the side of the rebel colonies against Great Britain during the American Revolution, the Madrid government refused in 1783 to grant diplomatic recognition to the new United States. For decades the ideas of Voltaire, Rousseau, and Montesquieu had also trickled into Latin America. In 1794 the Colombian Antonio Nariño translated and published the French *Declaration of the Rights of Man and the Citizen*. Although Spanish authorities sentenced him to ten years in an African prison, Nariño lived to become the father of Colombian independence. By 1800 the Creole elite throughout Latin America was familiar with liberal Enlightenment political thought.[7] The Creoles assumed, however, that the "rights of man" were limited, and they did not share such rights with Indians and blacks.

Race in the Colonial Period

The racial complexion of Latin American societies is one of the most complicated in the world. Because few European women emigrated to the colonies, Spanish men had relations with Indian and African women. African men deprived of black women sought Indian women. The result was a population composed of every possible combination of Indian, Spanish, and African blood.

MAP 31.1 Latin America Before Independence Consider the factors that led to the boundaries of the various Spanish and Portuguese colonies in North and South America.

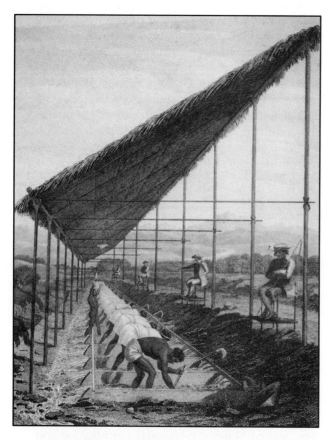

Diamond Mining in Brazil The discovery of gold and diamonds in Brazil in the seventeenth century increased the demand for slave labor. The English geologist John Mawe made this dramatic engraving of slaves washing for diamonds in the early nineteenth century. *(Source: Courtesy, Oliveira Lima Library, The Catholic University of America. Photo: Paul McKane, OSB)*

Spanish theories of racial purity rejected people of mixed blood, particularly those of African descent. A person's social status depended on the degree of European blood he or she possessed or appeared to possess. Peninsulares and Creoles reinforced their privileged status by showing contempt for people who were not white. As the great nineteenth-century German scientist Alexander von Humboldt put it, having spent five years traveling throughout South America, "Any white person, although he rides his horse barefoot, imagines himself to be of the nobility of the country."[8] Coupled with the Spaniard's aristocratic disdain for manual labor, a 300-year tradition had instilled in the minds of Latin Americans the notion that dark skin and manual labor went together. Owners of mines, plantations, and factories had a vested interest in keeping blacks and Indians in servile positions. Racism and discrimination pervaded all the Latin American colonies.

In spite of the catastrophes that had befallen them in the sixteenth and seventeenth centuries, Indians still constituted the majority of the population of Latin America at the end of the colonial period. Demographers estimate that Indians accounted for between three-fifths and three-fourths of the total population. The colonies that became Peru and Bolivia had Indian majorities; the regions that became Argentina and Chile had European majorities. As the Indians declined in the seventeenth century, the Spanish grabbed Indian lands for wheat, corn, cattle, and sheep raising. Indians and black slaves toiled in the silver and gold mines of Mexico, Colombia, and Peru, in the wheat fields of Chile, in the humid, mosquito-ridden cane brakes of Mexico and the Caribbean, and in the diamond mines and coffee and sugar plantations of Brazil.

Nevertheless, nonwhites did experience some social mobility in the colonial period, certainly more than in North America. In Mexico, decreasing reliance on slaves led to a great increase in manumissions. Once freed, however, Negroes immediately became subject to the payment of a money tribute, as were the Indians. Freedmen also incurred the obligation of military service. A few mulattos rose in the army, some as high as the rank of colonel. The army and the church seem to have offered the greatest opportunities for social mobility. Many black slaves gained their freedom by fleeing to the jungles or mountains, where they established self-governing communities. Around the year 1800 Venezuela counted 24,000 fugitive slaves in a total population of 87,000.

Many Indians were still subject to the mita and repartimiento. The *mita,* a system of forced labor requiring all adult Indian males to work for part of each year in the silver mines, was thinly disguised slave labor; the silver mines were deathtraps. The law of *repartimiento* required Indians to buy goods solely from local *corregidores,* officials who collected taxes. The new taxes of the 1770s and 1780s fell particularly heavily on the Indians. When Indian opposition to these taxes and to oppressive conditions exploded into violence, Creoles organized the protest movements and assumed leadership of them.

The Comunero Revolution

In Peru in November 1779 the wealthy, well-educated mestizo Tupac Amaru (1742–1781), a descendant of the Inca kings, captured, tried, and executed the local corregidor. Tupac Amaru and his mostly Indian followers demanded the abolition of the alcabala tax and the mita and replacement of the corregidores with Indian governors. Proclaiming himself liberator of the people, Tupac Amaru waged a war of blood and fire against the Spanish governors. Violence swept the Peruvian highlands. Thousands lost their lives, and a vast amount of private property was destroyed. Poor communication among the rebel forces and the superior organization of the imperial armies enabled the Spanish to crush the revolt. Tupac Amaru, his family, and his captains were captured and savagely executed. Frightened colonial administrators, however, did grant some reforms. The Crown repealed the repartimiento, reduced the mita, and replaced the corregidores with a lighter system of intendants. The condition of the Indians temporarily improved.

News of the rebellion of Tupac Amaru trickled northward, where it helped stimulate revolution in the New Granada viceroyalty. Disorders occurred first at Socorro in modern Colombia (Map 31.2). Throughout the eighteenth century Socorro had prospered. Sugar cane, corn, and cattle flourished on its exceptionally fertile soil. Large cotton crops stimulated the production of textiles, mostly in a primitive cottage industry worked by women. Socorro's location on the Suarez River made it an agricultural and manufacturing center and an entrepôt for trade with the hinterland. Hardworking Spanish immigrants had prospered and often intermarried with the Indians.

When the viceroy published new taxes on tobacco and liquor and reorganized the alcabala, riots broke out in Socorro in March 1781 and spread to other towns. Representatives of peasants and artisan groups from many towns elected a *comun,* or central committee, to lead the insurrection. Each town elected its local comun and the captain of its militia. Known as the "Comunero Revolution," the insurrection in New Granada enjoyed broad-based support and good organization and appeared far more threatening to government authorities than had the uprising in Peru.

An Indian peasant army commanded by Creole captains marched on Bogotá. Government officials, lacking adequate military resources, sent a commission to play for time by negotiating with the comuneros. On June 4 the commission agreed to the rebels' terms: reduction of the alcabala and of the Indians' forced tribute, abolition of the new taxes on tobacco, and preference for Creoles over peninsulares in government positions. The joyful Indian army disbanded and went home. What they did not know was that the commission had already secretly disclaimed the agreement with the rebels on the grounds that it had been taken by force. Having succeeded in dispersing the Indians, the government at Bogotá won over the Creole leaders with promise of pardons and then moved in reserve troops who captured large numbers of rebels. When the last rebel holdout—that of José Antonio Galan—had been captured, a kangaroo court tried Galan and condemned him

to be taken out of jail, dragged and taken to the place of execution where he will be hung until dead, that his head be removed from his dead body, that the rest of his body be quartered, that his torso be committed to flames for which purpose a fire shall be lit in front of the platform. His head shall be sent to Guaduas, the scene of his scandalous insults, his right arm shall be displayed in the main square of Socorro, his left arm shall be displayed in the square of San Gil, his right leg shall be displayed in Charala his birthplace, and his left leg in the parish of Mogotes. All his descendants shall be declared infamous, all his property shall be confiscated by the royal treasury, his home shall be burnt, and the ground salted, so that in this fashion his infamous name may be forgotten.[9]

Thus ended the revolt of the comuneros in New Granada. They failed to win self-rule, but they forced the authorities to act in accordance with the spirit of the "unwritten constitution," whose guiding principle was consultation and compromise. Although the authorities used Galan's execution as a stick to kill social revolution, over the next twenty years they extended the carrot of government concern to promote colonial prosperity.

Independence

Napoleon Bonaparte lit the fuse of the Latin American powder keg. In 1808, as part of his effort to rule Europe, Napoleon deposed the Spanish king Ferdinand VII and placed his own brother

UNITED STATES

ATLANTIC
OCEAN

MEXICO

Havana
CUBA
Mexico City• •Veracruz
DOMINICAN REP.
JAMAICA
BR. HONDURAS
GUATEMALA•
Guatemala• HONDURAS
EL SALVADOR NICARAGUA
COSTA
RICA
PANAMA

HAITI
PUERTO RICO

Caribbean Sea

Suarez
Caracas•
VENEZUELA
BR. GUIANA
DUTCH GUIANA
FR. GUIANA

•Bogotá
COLOMBIA

Quito•
ECUADOR
Amazon

PACIFIC
OCEAN

PERU

BRAZIL

Lima•

•La Paz
BOLIVIA

•Bahia

MINAS GERAIS

PARAGUAY
Paraná
SÃO PAULO
São Paulo•
RIO DE JANEIRO
•Rio de Janeiro

RIO GRANDE
DO SUL

Valparaiso•
•Santiago
CHILE
Buenos Aires•
ARGENTINA
URUGUAY
•Montevideo

•Bahía Blanca

Independent nations
Colonial possessions

PATAGONIA

0   500   1000 Km.
0   500   1000 Mi.

ISLAS MALVINAS
(FALKLAND ISLANDS)

on the Spanish throne (see page 821). In Latin America the Creoles subsequently seized the opportunity. Since everything in Spanish America was done in the name of the king, the Creoles argued that the removal of the legitimate king shifted sovereignty to the people—that is, to themselves. In 1810 the small, wealthy Creole aristocracy used the removal of the Spanish king as justification for their seizure of political power and their preservation of that power.

Thus began the war for independence. An able scholar has described it as

a prolonged, confused, and in many ways contradictory movement. In Mexico it began as a popular social movement and ended many years later as a conservative uprising against a liberal Spanish constitution. In Venezuela it came to be a war unto the death; in other places it was a war between a small Creole minority and the Spanish authorities. It was not an organized movement with a central revolutionary directorate. It had no Continental Congress. . . . If there was no central direction, no centrally recognized leadership, likewise there was no formally accepted political doctrine.[10]

The Creoles who led the various movements for independence did not intend a radical redistribution of property or reconstruction of society; they merely rejected the authority of the Spanish crown.

In the final battle . . . the soldiers on the field came from Venezuela, Colombia, Ecuador, Peru, Argentina, and Chile, and among the officers there were Frenchmen and Englishmen who had opposed each other in the Napoleonic Wars. . . . The war stopped but did not officially end. There was no treaty of peace. There was no recognition of the new states. There was no definite agreement as to the form of government or even as to national boundaries. . . . In Latin America each separate area went its own way. Central America broke way from Mexico and then splintered into five separate nations. Uruguay, Paraguay, and Bolivia separated themselves from Argentina, Chile from Peru,

MAP 31.2 Latin America in 1830 What geographical factors have led to the relative political power of the United States and the Latin American nations?

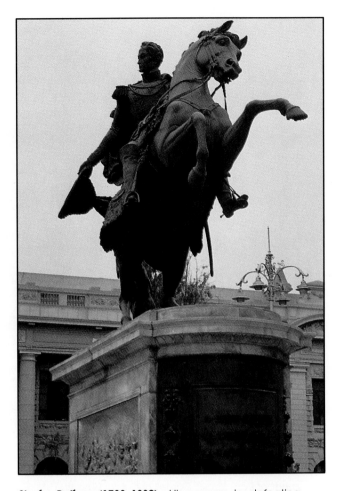

Simón Bolívar (1783–1830) His success in defeating Spanish armies earned him the title "the Liberator." President of Greater Colombia, Bolívar organized the government of Peru, created Bolivia, and dreamt of a United Spanish America. He is respected as the greatest Latin American hero. *(Source: Stuart Cohen/Comstock)*

and [Simón] Bolívar's attempt to federate the state of Greater Colombia (Venezuela, Colombia, and Ecuador) with Peru and Bolivia under a centralized government broke down.*[11]

The great hero of the movement for independence was Simón Bolívar (1783–1830), who is considered the Latin American George Washington. A very able general, Bolívar's victories over the royalist armies won him the presidency of Greater Colombia in 1819. Bolívar dreamed of a continental union, and in 1826 he summoned a conference of the American republics at Panama. The meeting

Street Scene in Rio de Janeiro   Soldiers, planter-aristocrats, merchants, slaves, friars, and carriages thronged the cobblestone streets of the capital of Brazil. *(Source: Department of Rare Books, Cornell University Library)*

achieved little. Bolívar organized the government of Bolivia and became the head of the new state of Peru. The territories of Greater Colombia splintered apart, however, and a sadly disillusioned Bolívar went into exile, saying, "America is ungovernable. Those who served the revolution plowed the seas." The failure of pan-Americanism isolated individual countries, prevented collective action, and later paved the way for the political and economic intrusion of the United States and other powers.

Brazil's quest for independence from Portugal was unique: Brazil won its independence without violent upheaval. When Napoleon's troops entered Portugal, the royal family fled to Brazil and made Rio de Janeiro the capital of the Portuguese Empire. The new government immediately lifted the old mercantilist restrictions and opened Brazilian ports to the ships of all friendly nations. Under popular pressure, King Pedro I (r. 1822–1831),

proclaimed Brazil's independence in 1822 and published a constitution. Pedro's administration was wracked by factional disputes between Portuguese courtiers and Brazilian Creoles, a separatist movement in the Rio Grande do Sul region, and provincial revolts. His successor, Pedro II (r. 1831–1889), restored order and laid the foundations of the modern Brazilian state. His reign witnessed the expansion of the coffee industry, the beginnings of the rubber industry, and massive immigration.

The Consequences of Independence

The wars of independence ended around 1825. What effects did they have on Latin American societies? How were Latin American countries governed in the nineteenth century? What factors worked against the development of modern nations? Because the movements for independence differed in character and course in different regions and countries, generalizations about Mexico, the Caribbean islands, and South America are likely to be misleading. Significant changes did occur, however, throughout Latin America.

The newly independent nations did not achieve immediate political stability when the wars of independence ended. The Spanish crown had served as a unifying symbol, and its disappearance left a power vacuum. Civil disorder typically followed. The Creole leaders of the revolutions had no experience in government, and the wars had left a legacy of military, not civilian, leadership. Throughout the continent, idealistic but impractical leaders proclaimed republics—independent states governed by an assembly of representatives of the electorate. In practice, the generals ruled.

In Argentina, for example, Juan Manuel de Rosas (r. 1835–1852) assumed power amid widespread public disorder and ruled as dictator. In Mexico, liberals declared a federal republic, but incessant civil strife led to the rise of the dictator Antonio López de Santa Anna in the mid-nineteenth century. Likewise in Venezuela, strongmen, dictators, and petty aristocratic oligarchs governed from 1830 to 1892. Some countries suffered constant revolutions. In the course of the century Bolivia had sixty and Venezuela fifty-two. The rule of force prevailed almost everywhere. Enlightened dictatorship was the typical form of government.

The wars of liberation disrupted the economic life of most Latin American countries. The prosperity that many areas had achieved toward the end of the colonial period was destroyed. Mexico and Venezuela in particular lost large percentages of their populations and suffered great destruction of farmland and animals. Even areas that saw relatively little violence, such as Chile and New Granada, experienced a weakening of economic life. Armies were frequently recruited by force, and when the men were demobilized many did not return home. The consequent population dislocation hurt agriculture and mining. Guerrilla warfare disrupted trade and communications. Forced loans and the seizure of private property for military use ruined many people. In the 1820s Peru's economy staggered under the burden of supporting large armies. Isolated territories such as Paraguay and much of Central America suffered little damage, but most countries gained independence at the price of serious economic problems.

Brazil, which had a large slave population, did not free the slaves until 1888. Spain abolished slavery in its Cuban colony in a series of measures between 1870 and 1886; Cuba itself became independent in 1903, a consequence of the Spanish-American War. Elsewhere, however, independence accelerated the abolition of slavery. The destruction of agriculture in countries such as Mexico and Venezuela caused the collapse of the plantation system, and fugitive slaves could not be recaptured. Also, the royalists and patriot generals such as Bolívar offered slaves their freedom in exchange for military service. The result was that slaves constituted a large part of the military forces. Finally, most of the new independent states adopted republican constitutions declaring the legal equality of all men. For Indians and blacks, however, these noble words were meaningless, for the revolution brought about no redistribution of property. Nor could long-standing racist attitudes be eliminated by the stroke of a pen.

Although the edifice of racism persisted in the nineteenth century, Latin America experienced much more assimilation and offered Negroes greater economic and social mobility than did the United States. As a direct result of their heroic military service in the wars of independence, a substantial number of Negroes improved their social status. Some even attained the political heights: the Mexican revolutionary Vicente Guerrero, served as president of his country in 1829; Antonio Guzmán governed Venezuela as a benevolent dictator (r. 1870–1888); Ramón Castilla served as president of Peru (r. 1845–1851 and 1855–1862) and made great improvements in state financing.

What accounts for the relative racial permeability of Latin America in contrast with the severe segregation in the United States? As the Dutch scholar H. Hoetink points out, Latin American countries evolved a three-tiered socioracial structure, in contrast to the two-tiered racial edifice in the United States. Legally and socially, Latin American societies classified people as white, colored, or black, and marriages between whites and light-skinned colored people were commonly accepted. Legislative discrimination against colored people proved unenforceable. Thus light skin allowed for gradual assimilation into the middle and upper social echelons. In the United States, by contrast, anyone who was not "pure" white was classified as black.

Hoetink explains the problem partly in terms of the large population of poor whites in the United States: "Nowhere, but in the North American mainland, did the number of extremely poor whites always exceed the number of slaves. Nowhere, but in the U.S. South, were special police forces predominantly manned by poor whites."[12] Also, Latin American elites' definition of "whiteness" and perception of physical beauty seem to have been broader than those of the white majority in the United States.

Nevertheless, the advantages of assimilation did not (and do not) apply to dark-skinned people in Latin America. While substantial numbers of light-skinned colored people rose economically and socially, the great mass of dark-skinned blacks continued to experience all the consequences of systematic and insistent racism.

Neocolonialism

The leaders of the Latin American revolutions had hoped that their nations, once independent, would attract European and North American investment. Instead, political instability and the preoccupation of European and North American financiers with industrial expansion in their own countries discouraged investment. The advent of stable dictatorships, however, eventually paved the way for economic growth. After 1870 capital began to flow south and across the Atlantic. In Mexico, North American capital supported the production of hemp (used in the United States for grain harvesting), sugar, bananas, and rubber, frequently on American-owned plantations. British and American interests backed the development of tin, copper, and gold mining in Mexico. Oil drilling leaped forward, and by 1911 Mexico had taken third place among the world's oil producers. British financiers built Argentina's railroads, meatpacking industry, and utilities. British businessmen in Chile developed the copper and nitrate industries (nitrate is used in the production of pharmaceuticals and fertilizers); by 1890 the British controlled 70 percent of the nitrate industry. Likewise in Brazil, foreign capital—primarily British—flowed into coffee, cotton, and sugar production and manufacturing. In 1889 Brazil produced 56 percent of the world's coffee; by 1904 that figure had risen to 76 percent. When massive overproduction of coffee led to a sharp

drop in prices in 1906, a commission of British, American, German, and French bankers rescued the Brazilian government from near disaster.

The price paid for economic development by Latin America at the end of the nineteenth century was a new form of economic domination. Foreign investors acquired control of the railroads, mineral resources, and banking, and they made heavy inroads into real estate. British investments led all others, but beginning in 1898 the United States flexed its imperialistic muscles and sent gunboats and troops to defend its dollars in the Caribbean and Central America. By the turn of the century the Latin American nations were active participants in the international economic order, but foreigners controlled most of their industries.

Another distinctive feature of the neocolonial order was the cultivation of one crop. Each country's economy revolved around only one or two products: sugar in Cuba, nitrates and copper in Chile, meat in Argentina, coffee in Brazil. A sharp drop in the world market demand for a product could destroy the industry and with it the nation's economic structure. The outbreak of the First World War in 1914 drastically reduced exports of Latin American raw materials and imports of European manufactured goods, provoking general economic crisis.[13]

Throughout the eighteenth century the Spanish-owned *haciendas*—large landed estates—and plantations had continued to expand to meet the needs of commercial agriculture: wheat for the cities, corn for the Indians' consumption, sugar for export to Europe and North America. By means of purchase, forced removal of Indians, and outright seizure, the Spanish continued to take Indian land, as they had done in the seventeenth century. Some land was acquired merely to eliminate competition by depriving Indians of their fields, which were then left fallow.

The late nineteenth century witnessed ever greater concentrations of land in ever fewer hands. In places like the Valley of Mexico in southern Mexico, a few large haciendas controlled all the land. Under the dictatorship of General Porfirio Díaz, the Mexican government in 1883 passed a law allowing real estate companies (controlled by Díaz's political cronies) to survey public and "vacant" lands and to retain one-third of the land they surveyed. An 1894 law provided that land could be declared vacant if legal title to it could

Mexico Today, Mexico Tomorrow   In this detail from a huge mural cycle completed for the National Palace of Mexico City, the naturalist painter Diego Rivera (1886–1957), in the style of traditional Mexican folk art, celebrates the triumph of creative labor in farming, mining, and industry, and denounces the evils of capitalism. A member of the Mexican Communist party, Rivera condemned through his art what he considered the oppression of both communism and fascism. (Source: Robert Frerck/Odyssey)

not be produced. Since few Indians had deeds to the land that their ancestors had worked for centuries, the door swung open to wholesale expropriation of small landowners and entire villages. Shrewd speculators tricked illiterate Indians into selling their lands for trifling sums. Thousands of litigants clogged the courts. Indians who dared armed resistance were crushed by government troops and carried off to virtual slave labor. Vast stretches of land came into the hands of private individuals—in one case, 12 million acres. Stripped of their lands, the Indians were a ready labor supply. They were mercilessly exploited. Debt peonage became common: landowners paid their laborers not in cash but in vouchers redeemable only at the company store, whose high prices and tricky bookkeeping kept the peons permanently in debt.

Some scholars maintain that the hacienda owners usually let their land lie fallow until it rose in value or attracted American investors. The lack of cultivation, they assert, kept the prices of corn and other crops artificially high. The owners themselves, supported by rents, passed indolent lives in extravagant luxury in Mexico City and other cities.

Other scholars argue that the haciendas were efficient enterprises whose owners sought to maximize profits on invested capital. The Sanchez Navarro family of northwestern Mexico, for instance, engaged in a wide variety of agricultural and commercial pursuits, exploiting their lands and resources as fully as possible. The Sanchez Navarros controlled 800,000 acres in 1821 and continued to acquire land; ultimately their *latifundio*—a

LATIN AMERICA, CA 1760–1900

1764–1780	Charles III of Spain's administrative and economic reforms
1781	Communero revolution in New Granada
1810–1825	Latin American wars of independence against Spain
1822	Proclamation by Portugal of Brazil's independence
1826	Call by Simón Bolívar for Panama Conference on Latin American union
1825–ca 1870	Political instability in most Latin American nations
ca 1870–1919	Latin American neocolonialism
1876–1911	Porfirio Diaz' control of Mexico
1888	Emancipation of slaves in Brazil; final abolition of slavery in Western Hemisphere
1880–1914	Massive immigration from Europe and Asia to Latin America
1898	Spanish American War; end of Spanish control over Cuba; transfer of Puerto Rico to United States

large landed estate—was about the size of West Virginia. Along with vast cattle ranches and sheep runs containing as many as 250,000 sheep, the Sanchez Navarros cultivated maize, wheat, and cotton. They invested heavily and profitably in silver mining and manufacturing and lent sizable sums at high interest. Although they brutally exploited their peons and practiced debt peonage, the Sanchez Navarros lived very modestly on their own estates rather than luxuriating in Mexico City. A final determination of whether the Sanchez Navarros were unique or representative of a type of magnate prevalent in the agricultural and business communities of nineteenth-century Mexico[14] must await further investigation.

The Impact of Immigration

In 1852 the Argentine political philosopher Juan Bautista Alberdi published *Bases and Points of Departure for Argentine Political Organization,* arguing that "to govern is to populate." Alberdi meant that the development of his country—and, by extension, all of Latin America—depended on immigration. Argentina had an adequate labor supply, but it was unevenly distributed throughout the country. Moreover, Alberdi maintained, Indians and blacks lacked basic skills, and it would take too long to train them. Therefore he pressed for massive immigration from the "advanced" countries of northern Europe and the United States. Alberdi's ideas won immediate acceptance and were even incorporated into the Argentine constitu-

tion, which declared that "the Federal government will encourage European immigration." Other Latin American countries adopted similar policies promoting immigration.[15]

European needs coincided perfectly with those of Latin America (see pages 938–940). After 1880, Ireland, Great Britain, Germany, Italy, Spain, and the central European nations experienced greater population growth than their labor markets could absorb. Meanwhile the growing industries of Europe needed South American raw materials and markets for their finished goods, and South American countries wanted European markets for their minerals, coffee, sugar, beef, and manufactured goods. Italian, Spanish, and Portuguese peoples poured into Latin America.

Immigration led to rapid urbanization, which meant Europeanization and industrialization. By 1900, Buenos Aires and Rio de Janeiro had populations of more than 500,000 people; Mexico City, Montevideo, Santiago, and Havana also experienced spectacular growth. Portuguese, Italian, French, Chinese, and Japanese immigrants gave an international flavor to the cities, and a more vigorous tempo replaced the somnolent Spanish atmosphere.

By 1914 Buenos Aires had emerged as one of the most cosmopolitan cities in the world. In less than half a century, the population of the city and its province had grown from 500,000 to 3.6 million. As Argentina's political capital, the city housed all its government bureaucracies and agencies. The meatpacking, food-processing, flour-milling, and wool industries were concentrated in

Buenos Aires. Half of all overseas tonnage passed through the city, which was also the heart of the nation's railroad network. The University of Buenos Aires was the intellectual hub of the nation. Elegant shops near the Plaza de Mayo catered to the expensive tastes of the elite upper classes, who constituted about 5 percent of the population.

Meanwhile the thousands of immigrants who toiled twelve hours a day, six days a week, on the docks and construction sites and in the meatpacking plants crowded into the city's *conventillos*, or tenements:

The one-room dwelling . . . served a family with two to five children or a group of four or five single men. At the door to each room stood a pile of wooden boxes. One generally held a basin for washing; another a charcoal brazier on which to cook the daily watery stew, or puchero; *and garbage accumulated in a third. Two or three iron cots, a pine table, a few wooden chairs, an old trunk, perhaps a sewing machine, and more boxes completed the furnishings. Light came from the open door and one window, from an oil or gas lamp, or occasionally from a bare electric light bulb. On the once-whitewashed walls were tacked pictures of popular heroes, generals, or kings torn from magazines, an image of the Madonna and a couple of saints, perhaps a faded photograph of family members in Europe. The women often eked out miserable incomes by taking in laundry and washing and drying it in the patios. Others ironed or sewed on a piecework basis. Some men worked here: in one corner a shoemaker might ply his trade, in another a man might bend over a small table repairing watches.*[16]

Domestic Scenes in Mid-Nineteenth-Century Rio The servants, lace tablecloth, and fancy dress of the mistress imply that this is a well-to-do household. The meal, consisting of meat, bread, fruit, and wine, seems to be eaten on imported china. *(Source: Courtesy, Oliveira Lima Library, The Catholic University of America. Photo: Paul McKane, OSB)*

Immigrants dreamed of rapid economic success in the New World, and there was in fact plenty of upward social mobility. The first generation almost always did manual labor, but its sons often advanced to upper blue-collar or white-collar jobs. The rare Genoese or Neapolitan immigrant whose labor and thrift made his son a millionaire quickly learned the meaning of assimilation: the son typically assumed the dress, style, and values of the Spanish elite. Hispanic attitudes toward class, manual labor, and egalitarianism prevailed, and the new immigrant rich imitated the Spanish nobility.[17]

Europeans gave an enormous boost to the development of industry and commerce. Italian and Spanish settlers in Argentina stimulated the ex-

pansion of the cattle industry and the development of the wheat and shoe industries. In Brazil, English investments facilitated the growth of the iron industry and the railroads. Swiss immigrants built the cheese business; Italians gained a leading role in the coffee industry; and the Japanese pioneered the development of the cotton industry. In Peru, the British controlled railroad construction, Italians became influential in banking and the restaurant business, and the French dominated jewelry, dressmaking, and pharmaceutical ventures. The arrival of millions of migrants changed the entire commercial structure of South America.

Immigration promoted further ethnic integration. The vast majority of migrants were unmarried males; seven out of ten people who landed in

Argentina between 1857 and 1924 were single males between thirteen and forty years old. Many of those who stayed sought out Indian or other low-status women. This kind of assimilation also occurred in Brazil, Mexico, Peru, and other South American countries. Male settlers from eastern Europe and women of all nationalities preferred to marry within their own ethnic groups. But men greatly outnumbered women, and a man who chose to marry usually had to marry an Indian.[18] Immigration, then, furthered the racial mixture of Europeans, Asians, and native South Americans.

For Latin America's sizable black population, immigration proved a calamity. Slavery had been technically abolished in Spanish America after independence and in Portuguese Brazil by 1888, but the economic and social status of the Negro population had scarcely changed. Accustomed to working the rural coffee plantations and the mines, blacks sometimes had little preparation for urban living. Many former slaves had skills, even for factory work, but racism explains the greater presence of immigrants in factories. In 1893, 71.2 percent of the working population of São Paulo was foreign-born. Anxious to adapt to America and to climb the economic ladder, immigrants quickly learned the traditional racial prejudices. Negro women usually found work as domestics, but employers excluded black males from good jobs. Racial prejudice kept the vast bulk of the South American black population in a wretched socioeconomic position until the Second World War.

Independence did little to change the basic social, economic, and political structure of Latin American countries. Although republican constitutions declared all men (but not women) equal under law, the elite continued to control status, wealth, and power almost everywhere as Creoles moved into positions formerly held by peninsulares. European and United States neocolonial support for steps to modernize the area's commerce and industry during the last half of the nineteenth century served to strengthen the position of the elite and allow it to use capitalistic values and ideals as a shield against demands for fundamental socioeconomic reforms. European styles in art, clothing, housing, and literature became highly popular, particularly among the elite, as they sought acceptance and approval by their economic masters. Meaningful structural change would await the revolutions and violent confrontations of the twentieth century.

THE UNITED STATES (1789–1929)

The victory of the North American colonies and the founding of the United States seemed to validate the Enlightenment idea that a better life on earth was possible (see pages 669–675). Americans carried over into the nineteenth and twentieth centuries an unbounded optimism about the future. The vastness of the land and its untapped resources reinforced that faith. The young nation, confident of its "manifest destiny," pushed relentlessly across the continent. Westward movement, however, threatened to extend black slavery, which generated increasing disagreement between the industrialized North and the agricultural South. The ensuing Civil War cost more American lives than any other war the nation was to fight. The victory of the North did not resolve the racial issue that had caused the war, but it did preserve the federal system.

The years between 1865 and 1917 witnessed the building of a new industrialized nation. Immigrants pursued the frontier to its end, provided the labor to exploit the country's mineral resources, turned small provincial towns into sophisticated centers of ethnic and cultural diversity, and built the railroads that tied the country together. However, the American economy absorbed immigrants faster than American society did. The ideology of manifest destiny lived on after the frontier closed and considerably affected relations between the United States and Latin America. In the First World War, American aid and American troops were the deciding factor in the Allied victory. After the war, "normalcy" and the façade of prosperity supported a persistent optimism. Only the Great Depression, beginning in 1929 and bringing enormous unemployment and terrible social problems, shook Americans' confidence in their potential and their future.

Manifest Destiny

In an 1845 issue of the *United States Magazine and Democratic Review,* editor John L. O'Sullivan boldly declared that foreign powers were trying to prevent American annexation of Texas in order to impede "the fulfillment of our manifest destiny to overspread the continent allotted by Providence for the free development of our yearly multiplying millions." O'Sullivan was articulating a sentiment prevalent in the United States since early in its history: that God had foreordained the nation to cover the entire continent. After a large-circulation newspaper picked up the phrase "manifest destiny," it was used on the floor of Congress and soon entered the language as a catchword for and justification of expansion. The concept of manifest destiny played an important role in some basic developments in American history: the settlement of peoples of diverse nationalities, the issue of slavery, the conflict over whether the United States was to remain agrarian or become a commercial and industrial society.

When George Washington took office in 1789, fewer than 4 million people inhabited the thirteen states on the eastern seaboard. By the time Abraham Lincoln became the sixteenth president in 1861, the United States stretched across the continent and had 31 million inhabitants.

During the colonial period, pioneers had pushed westward to the Appalachian Mountains. After independence, westward movement accelerated. The eastern states claimed all the land from the Atlantic to the Mississippi River, but two forces blocked immediate expansion. The Indians, trying to save their lands, allied with the British in Canada to prevent further American encroachment. However, the federal government, with an almost empty treasury, wanted revenue from land sales. In 1794 Britain agreed to evacuate border forts in the Northwest Territory and thereby end British support for the Indians. A similar treaty with Spain paved the way for southeastern expansion (Map 31.3).

Events in Europe and the Caribbean led to a massive increase in American territory. In 1800 Spain ceded the Louisiana Territory—the land between the Mississippi River and the Rocky Mountains—to France. Napoleon intended to use the Louisiana Territory to make France an imperial power in America, but a black revolution on the island of Hispaniola (present-day Haiti and Santo Domingo) upset his plans. Led by Toussaint L'Ouverture, Haiti's 500,000 slaves revolted against their 40,000 white owners. Napoleon quickly dispatched troops with orders to crush the revolt, seize New Orleans, and take possession of the Louisiana Territory. Alarmed, President Thomas Jefferson ordered the American minister in Paris, Robert Livingston, to negotiate to buy the Louisiana Territory.

When yellow fever and Haitian bullets carried off most of the French troops in Haiti, Napoleon relinquished his grandiose plans. He was planning war with Great Britain and realized that France's weakness at sea meant that Britain might be able to take Louisiana.

On the day Napoleon opened hostilities with England, his foreign minister Talleyrand casually asked Livingston, "What would you give us for the whole of Louisiana?" The astonished American proposed four million dollars. "Too low!" said Talleyrand. "Reflect and see me tomorrow." Less than three weeks later the deed of sale was signed. The United States paid only twelve million dollars for millions of acres of some of the world's richest farmland; the Louisiana Purchase was the greatest bargain in U.S. history.

Scarcely was the ink dry on the treaty when pressure rose for war with England. Repeated British attacks on American vessels on the high seas and British interference in American trade provided diplomatic justification for the War of 1812. Western settlers wanted further expansion. "War hawks" in the old Northwest Territory, Kentucky, Tennessee, and the southern frontier believed that a war with Britain would yield Canada, permanently end Indian troubles, and open up vast forest lands for settlement. The Treaty of Ghent (1814) ended the conflict, and the prewar boundaries were unchanged.

After the restoration of peace, settlers poured into the Northwest and the Gulf Plains (the region of Georgia, Alabama, and Mississippi). Congress sold land in lots of 160 acres at two dollars an acre; only eighty dollars was needed as down payment. Irish and German immigrants rapidly put the black earth of Indiana and Illinois under cultivation. Pioneers of American stock planted cotton in the lush delta of the Gulf Plains. Scandinavian and German settlers found the softly rolling hills of the Wisconsin country ideal for cattle.

Spain, preoccupied with rebellions in South America, sold the Florida territory to the United States government; and beginning in 1821, American settlers poured into the Mexican territory of Texas, whose soil proved excellent for the production of cotton and sugar. Contemptuous of the government of the Mexican president Santa Anna, Texans rebelled and proclaimed Texas an independent republic in 1836. Southern politicians, fearing that Texas would become a refuge for fugitive slaves, pressured President John Tyler to admit

NORTHWEST TERRITORY

Boston
New York
Philadelphia
Baltimore
Washington
Charleston
Savannah

Erie Canal
BOSTON POST ROAD

Pittsburgh
Columbus
CUMBERLAND ROAD
Indianapolis
St. Louis
GREAT VALLEY ROAD
Chattanooga
NATCHEZ TRACE
New Orleans

Duluth
Council Bluffs
St. Joseph
Kansas City
Topeka
Dodge City
Houston
San Antonio

Fargo
Bismarck
NORTHERN PACIFIC RAILROAD
Omaha
UNION PACIFIC RAILROAD
Denver
Albuquerque
El Paso

Butte
OREGON TRAIL
Cheyenne
Salt Lake City

Spokane
Seattle
CENTRAL PACIFIC RAILROAD
Virginia City
Sacramento
San Francisco
Portland
Los Angeles

400 Mi.
400 Km.
200
200
0
0

United States 1783
Louisiana Purchase 1803
Ceded by Great Britain 1818
Treaty with Spain 1819
Annexation of Texas 1845
Oregon Country 1846
Ceded by Mexico 1848
Gadsden Purchase 1853

Texas to the United States. A joint resolution of Congress, hastily signed by Tyler, did so in 1845.

The absorption of Texas's 267,339 square miles (France, by comparison, covers 211,200 square miles) whetted American appetites for the rest of the old Spanish Empire in North America. Some expansionists even dreamed of taking Cuba and Central America. President James Polk tried to buy California from Mexico, but the Mexicans harbored a grudge over the annexation of Texas and refused to do business.

Exploiting Mexico's political instability, Polk goaded Mexico into war. Mexico suffered total defeat and in the Treaty of Guadalupe Hidalgo (1848) surrendered its claims to Texas, yielded New Mexico and California, and recognized the Rio Grande as the international border. A treaty with Great Britain in 1846 had already recognized the American settlement in the Oregon territory. The continent had been acquired. The nation's "manifest destiny" was fulfilled. But what of the millions of Indians—the only native Americans—who inhabited this vast territory?

The Fate of the Indians

The Indians faithfully observed their treaties with the United States, but "white pioneers in the Northwest committed the most wanton and cruel murders of them, for which it was almost impossible to obtain a conviction from a pioneer jury."[19] Government officials frequently manipulated the Indians by gathering a few chiefs, plying them with cheap whiskey, and then inducing them to hand over their tribes' hunting grounds. By this method William Henry Harrison, superintendent of the Indians of the Northwest Territory and a future president, got the Native Americans to part with 48 million acres. He had the full backing of President Jefferson.

MAP 31.3 Territorial Growth of the United States The Cumberland Road between Cumberland, Maryland, and—by 1833—Columbus, Ohio, and the Erie Canal, which linked New York City and the Great Lakes region, carried thousands of easterners and immigrants to the Old Northwest and the frontier beyond. Transcontinental railroads subsequently made all the difference.

War News from Mexico, 1848 In this scene of everyday life, the front porch of the "American Hotel" represents a microcosm of American society. The man reading the newspaper bursts with excitement, as the well-dressed white men (and woman, partly hidden) eagerly listen to the news from the front. In showing the black child in a tattered dress while the seated black man drinks whiskey (a jug is half hidden under his hat) from a silver cup, Woodville makes a stereotypically racist statement. But Woodville did not witness such a scene: he painted this in Dusseldorf, Germany. *(Source: National Academy of Design)*

The policy of pushing the Indians westward across the Mississippi, which President James Monroe's administration had adopted early in the century, accelerated during Andrew Jackson's presidency (1829–1837). Thousands of Delawares, Shawnees, and Wyandots, tricked into moving from the Northwest Territory to reservations west of Missouri, died of cholera and measles during the journey. The survivors found themselves hopelessly in debt for supplies and farming equipment. The state of Georgia, meanwhile, was nibbling away at Cherokee lands, which were theoretically protected by treaty with the United States government. Then gold was discovered on the Cherokee lands, and a gold rush took place. A Vermont

Passage of the Choctaw The Choctaw were the only Native Americans in the southeast whose economy rested on agriculture, and they were considered very competent farmers. But the United States government forced them to sell their lands and to move west of the Mississippi. The Choctaw and other tribes endured such sufferings on the journey west in the winter of 1831 that it became known as the "Trail of Tears." This painting romanticizes the event. *(Source: New Orleans Museum of Art: Gift of William E. Groves)*

missionary, the Reverend Samuel C. Worcester, carried the Indians' case to the Supreme Court. Chief Justice John Marshall ruled that the laws of Georgia had no force within the Cherokee territory and that white settlers and gold rustlers had to leave. President Jackson retorted, "John Marshall has made his decision. Now let him enforce it." The Creek, Cherokee, and other tribes were rounded up, expelled, and sent beyond the western boundaries of Missouri and Arkansas. They were guaranteed complete possession of their new reservations "as long as grass grows and water runs."[20] The shameful price of westward expansion was the dislocation and extermination of millions of Native Americans (Map 31.4).

Black Slavery in the South

Dutch traders brought the first black people as prisoners to Virginia in 1619 as one solution to the chronic shortage of labor in North America (white indentured servants who worked for a term of years was another solution). Black penal servitude became rooted in three regions: in the Chesapeake Bay area of Virginia and Maryland, where

MAP 31.4 Indian Cession of Lands to the United States Forced removal of the Creek, Cherokee, and Chickasaw Indians led to the deaths of thousands on the Trail of Tears to reservations in Oklahoma, and to the destruction of their cultures.

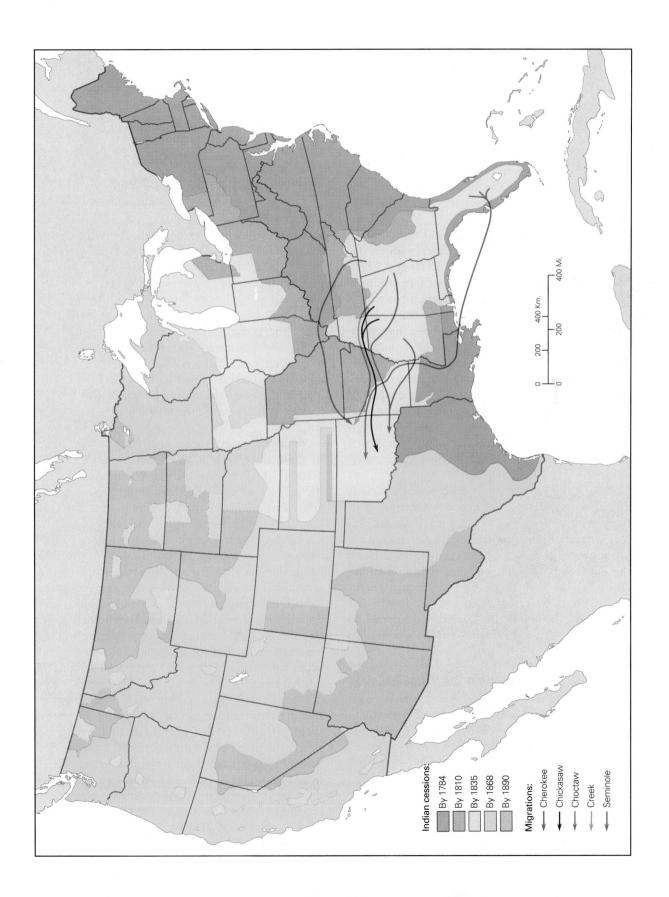

Indian cessions:

By 1784
By 1810
By 1835
By 1868
By 1890

Migrations:

Cherokee
Chickasaw
Choctaw
Creek
Seminole

400 Mi.

400 Km.

0   200   400

0   200

tobacco was the staple crop; in the coastal settlements of South Carolina and Georgia, where rice and indigo (a plant from which a blue dye is made) were raised; and in some of the northern colonies such as New York, where in the eighteenth century slaves and free blacks eventually totaled 15 percent of the population. The first black arrivals, however, were not slaves. In the seventeenth century, a system of racial servitude and discrimination did not exist. Some blacks themselves acquired property and indentured servants.

As rice cultivation expanded in the Carolinas in the early eighteenth century, however, planters demanded more laborers. Between 1720 and 1770, black prisoners poured into the southern colonies. In South Carolina they came to outnumber whites by almost two to one. White fears of black revolts pushed colonial legislatures to pass laws that established tight white control and blacks' legal position as slaves. Only in the decades 1730–1760 just before the publication of the Declaration of Independence did the slave system become enshrined in law. Economic demands led to the legal and social institutionalization of black slavery in North America. Racist arguments of blacks' supposed inferiority were used to justify that institutionalization.

Slavery and race relations have posed a serious dilemma for the American majority for more than two centuries. Powerful moral, legal, political, and sociological arguments have characterized slavery as a great evil, a violation of the central principle of the Declaration of Independence that all men are created equal. Eighteenth- and nineteenth-century Americans, however, could not decide whether the ringing words of the Declaration applied to blacks. One scholar recently posed the question in this way:

How did the slave-holding class, which was molded by the same forces that shaped the nation, which fought America's wars and helped inspire its Revolution, a class which boasted of its patriotism, its devotion to freedom, its adherence to the major tenets of liberalism—how did such a class justify its continuing commitment to slavery?[21]

The answer can be given in two words: *profit* and *status*.

The system of slavery involved many factors—the size of a plantation or farm and the number of slaves working it, the arability of the soil and the quantity of rainfall, the efficiency of plantation management, and individual initiative. Nevertheless, many slaveowners realized reasonable, sometimes handsome, profits in the decades before the Civil War. For white planters and farmers, slavery proved lucrative, and ownership of slaves was a status symbol as well as a means of social control. Slavery "was at the center of a well-established way of life to which [slaveowners] were accustomed and attached, and the disruption or demise of which they feared above all else."[22] Millions of whites, whether or not they owned many slaves, would have agreed with the South Carolina planter who wrote, "Slavery informs all our modes of life, all our habits of thought, lies at the basis of our social existence, and of our political faith." Since the possession of slaves brought financial profit *and* conferred social status and prestige, struggling small farmers had a material and psychological interest in maintaining black bondage. Slavery provided the means by which they might rise, and the floor beneath which they could not fall.

American society subsequently paid a high price in guilt and psychological conflict. Some slaveholders, like President George Washington, found the subject of slavery too uncomfortable even to talk about: "I shall frankly declare to you that I do not like even to think, much less talk of it."[23] In the half-century before the Civil War, most slaveowners were deeply religious. On the one hand, they taught their children to get rich by the accumulation of land and slaves; on the other hand, they taught that God would punish the greedy with eternal damnation. Slaveholders justified slavery by dismissing blacks as inferior, but religion preached that in the eyes of God black and white were equal and would ultimately be judged on that basis.

Some slaveowners felt completely trapped by the system. One master wrote, "I cannot just take them up and sell them though that would be clearly the best I could do for myself. I cannot free them. I cannot keep them with comfort. . . . What would I not give to be freed from responsibility for these poor creatures." Perhaps to an even greater extent than men, women of the planter class felt troubled by slavery. The South Carolina aristocrat Mary Boykin Chesnut confided to her diary in 1861:

The Cotton Pickers   Considered one of the most original American painters of the nineteenth century, Winslow Homer painted these sharecroppers on a visit to the South in 1876. The vastness of the field in that age before the invention of machines to pick the cotton suggests the enormity of the women's work. As their faces imply, Homer depicted black Americans as a psychologically complex people with beauty, strength, and dignity. *(Source: Winslow Homer,* The Cotton Pickers, *1876. Los Angeles County Museum of Art. Acquisition made possible through Museum Trustees)*

I wonder if it be a sin to think slavery a curse to any land. Sumner (the Massachusetts senator and abolitionist who bitterly denounced slavery in the U.S. Senate) said not one word of this hated institution which is not true. Men and women are punished when their masters and mistresses are brutes and not when they do wrong. . . . God forgive us, but ours is a monstrous system and wrong and iniquity. Perhaps the rest of the world is as bad—this only I see. Like the patriarchs of old our men live all in one house with their wives and their concubines, and the mulattoes one sees in every family exactly resemble the white children—and every lady tells you who is the father of all the mulatto children in everybody's household, but those in her own she seems to think drop from the clouds, or pretends so to think.[24]

Mary Chesnut believed that most white women of the South were abolitionists in their hearts. Although she enjoyed the attentions and services of her slaves, when Lincoln issued the Emancipation Proclamation she welcomed it with "an unholy joy."[25]

Westward Expansion and Civil War

Cotton was king in the mid-nineteenth century, and cotton carried slavery westward. It was westward expansion, not moral outrage, that brought the controversy over slavery to a head. As Congress created new territories, the question of whether slavery would be extended arose again and again (Map 31.5). For years elaborate compromises were worked out, but the North increasingly feared that the South was intent on controlling the nation. The South was afraid that free territories would harbor fugitive slaves. Issues of sectional political power became more and more heated.

In the 1850s the question of the further expansion of slavery agitated the nation. Perhaps no statesman better summarized the dilemma than Abraham Lincoln in a speech in 1854:

When they [southern proponents of expansion] remind us of their constitutional rights, I acknowledge them, not grudgingly, but fully, and fairly; and I would give them any legislation for the reclaiming of their fugitives, which should not, in its stringency, be more likely to carry a free man into slavery, than our ordinary criminal laws are to hang an innocent one. . . . But all this, to my judgment, furnishes no more excuse

for permitting slavery to go into our own free territory, than it would for reviving the African slave trade by law.

Slavery is founded in the selfishness of man's nature—opposition to it, in his love of justice. These principles are in eternal antagonism; and when brought into collision so fiercely, as slavery extension brings them, shocks, and throes, and convulsions must ceaselessly follow.[26]

Accepting the Republican party nomination for a seat in the United States Senate in 1858, Lincoln predicted the tragic events ahead:

A house divided against itself cannot stand.

I believe this government cannot endure, permanently half slave and half free.

I do not expect the Union to be dissolved—I do not expect the house to fall—but I do expect it will cease to be divided.

MAP 31.5 Slavery in the United States, 1860 The Confederacy waged a heroic struggle, but the North's industrial might and the waves of immigrants who fought in the Union army decided the war. Note the slave populations of such states as South Carolina and Mississippi, and consider how they influenced the later social and economic history of those regions.

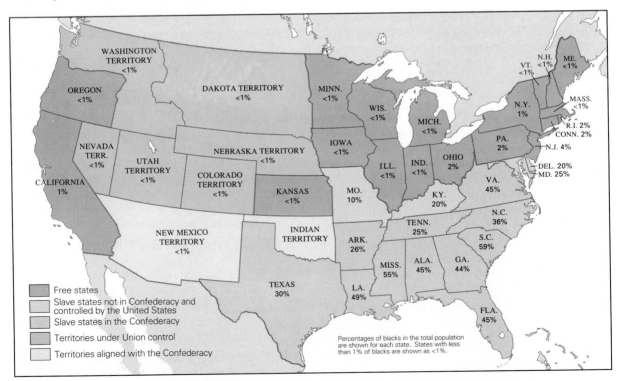

It will become all *one thing, or* all *the other.*

Either the opponents of slavery will arrest the further spread of it, and place it where the public mind shall rest in the belief that it is in the course of ultimate extinction; or its advocates *will push it forward, till it shall become alike lawful in* all *the States, old as well as new—North as well as* South.[27]

In this and every other speech that Lincoln made between 1854 and his election to the presidency in 1860, he argued against slavery less on moral or legal grounds than in terms of free labor's self-interest.

If slavery continued to expand, Lincoln insisted, it would become a nationwide institution. He appealed to both immigrants and native-born whites when he declared that slavery should be excluded from new territories so that they could be "an outlet for free white people everywhere, the world over—in which Hans, and Baptiste, and Patrick, and all other men from all the world, may find new homes and better their condition in life."[28] Free white workers, in other words, could not compete in the labor market against blacks; therefore, the territories should be kept open.

To protest Lincoln's victory in the election of 1860, South Carolina seceded from the Union in December 1860. Ten southern states soon followed South Carolina's example and formed the Confederacy. Its capital was at Richmond, Virginia.

The Civil War began in 1861. Lincoln fought it to preserve the Union and to maintain the free labor system; the abolition of slavery was a secondary outcome, which he in fact tried to avoid. When a Union general in the field declared the slaves of South Carolina and Georgia free, Lincoln overruled the order. He wanted to bring the seceding states back into the Union with their institutions intact. To many people it seemed absurd to fight the Confederacy, which depended on slavery to wage the war, without abolishing slavery. In the words of one historian, Lincoln wanted "to conduct the war for the preservation of *status quo,* which had produced the war."[29] Only after the war had dragged on and the slaughter had become frightful on both sides, only when it appeared that Great Britain might recognize the Confederacy, and only when it had been proved that the southern war effort benefited considerably from slave labor—only then did Lincoln, reluctantly, resolve on emancipation.

The Emancipation Proclamation became effective on January 1, 1863. It expressed no moral indignation. It freed slaves only in states and areas that were in rebellion against the United States. It preserved slavery in states that were loyal to the United States or under military jurisdiction. The London *Spectator* sneered, "The principle is not that a human being cannot justly own another, but that he cannot own him unless he is loyal to the United States."[30] The Emancipation Proclamation nevertheless spelled the doom of North American slavery. It transformed the Civil War from a political struggle to preserve the Union into a moral crusade for the liberty of all Americans.

European and English liberals greeted the proclamation with great joy. A gathering of working people in Manchester, England, wrote President Lincoln:

The erasure of that foul blot upon civilization and Christianity—chattel slavery—during your Presidency will cause the name of Abraham Lincoln to be honoured and revered by posterity. Accept our high admiration of your firmness in upholding the proclamation of freedom.[31]

As Lincoln acknowledged, this was a magnanimous statement, for the Civil War hurt working people in Manchester. In fact, it had a worldwide impact socially and economically.

Because the English and continental textile industries relied on raw American cotton, the Confederacy sought European help. In 1861, however, England had a 50 percent oversupply of fiber and cotton cloth. A huge crop, 23 billion pounds, shipped before the Union blockade of Confederate ports, filled British warehouses. By 1862, however, the picture in England had changed. Deprived of American cotton because of the blockade, the mills of Lancashire closed. Tens of thousands of workers were thrown out of work and nearly starved. Many emigrated to the United States. Between 1862 and 1864, efforts to alleviate the terrible suffering severely taxed the resources of the British government. English manufacturers were forced to find new suppliers. They found them in Egypt, India, and Brazil, where cotton production had been stimulated by the Union blockade of the South. The demands of English industry for Egyptian and Indian cotton played a significant role in the expansion of the English merchant marine fleet. Although England initially opposed construction of the Suez Canal, it later became a major shareholder. The canal was the swiftest route to Indian cotton.

The war also had important political consequences in Europe. In 1861 British and European opinion had divided along class lines. The upper classes sympathized with the American South; the commercial classes and working people sided with the North. The English people interpreted the northern victory as a triumph of the democratic experiment over aristocratic oligarchy. The Union success proved that popular government worked. Thus the United States gave a powerful stimulus to those in Britain and elsewhere who supported the cause of political democracy. When parliaments debated the extension of suffrage, the American example was frequently cited.

Military historians describe the American Civil War as the first modern war:

It was the first conflict in which the massive productive capacities of the Industrial Revolution were placed at the disposal of the military machine. It witnessed the first prominent use of mass production of goods to sustain mass armies, mass transportation on railroads, and telegraphic communication between different theaters and on the battlefield. It saw also the first use of such devices of the future as armored warships, breech-loading and repeating rifles, rifled artillery, land and sea mines, submarines, balloons, precursors of the machine gun, and trench warfare. . . . In its material manifestations alone, in its application of the resources of technology to the business of killing, the Civil War presaged the later world wars.[32]

In April 1865, the Confederate general Robert E. Lee surrendered his army at Appomattox Court House in Virginia, ending the war. Lincoln had called for "malice toward none and charity for all" in his second inaugural address in 1864 and planned a generous policy toward the defeated South. The bullet that killed him brought on a different kind of reconstruction, the central figure in which was the Negro.

During the period called "Reconstruction" (1865–1877), the vanquished South adjusted to a new social and economic order without slavery, and the eleven Confederate states rejoined the Union. Congress and the nation debated the political and social status of the Negro in the reconstructed South. The experience of slavery cast a deep and perhaps permanent mark in the collective memory of American blacks. Black people resented the abuse, the humiliation and subordination, the separation of families, the entire badge of servitude. For former slaves, Reconstruction represented an opportunity to exercise their new freedom, though southerners detested the very notion of social equality and northerners were ambivalent on the subject.

In practical terms, Reconstruction meant the reunion of black families separated before emancipation. Blacks wanted land to farm but, lacking cash, they soon accepted the sharecropping system: farmers paid landowners about half of a year's crops at harvest time in return for a cabin, food, mules, seed, and tools the rest of the year. Believing that education was the key to economic advancement, blacks flocked to country schools and to colleges supported by northern religious groups. Although the Fifteenth Amendment to the United States Constitution forbade states to deny anyone the vote "on account of race, color, or previous condition of servitude," whites used violence, terror, and, between 1880 and 1920, so-called Jim Crow laws to prevent blacks from voting and to enforce rigid racial segregation. Lacking strong northern support, blacks did not gain legal equality or suffrage in many parts of the old Confederacy until the 1960s. Racist assumptions and attitudes thwarted their legal, social, and economic advance.

In the construction of a black community, no institution played a larger role than the black Protestant churches. Local black churches provided hope to the oppressed, education to the illiterate when financially possible, and a forum for the spread of political ideas and platforms. During Reconstruction and ever since, black preachers, esteemed for their oratorical skill, organizational ability, and practical judgment, held important positions in black politics. In a racist and exploitative society, the black church gave support, security, and a sense of solidarity.

The Black Family

What impact did slavery have on the black family? Able scholars, both black and white, have long maintained that the enslavement of Africans in the eighteenth century led to the deterioration of the black family as a social unit in the nineteenth and twentieth centuries. As two authorities put it,

The Battle of Gettysburg, July 1–3, 1863 marked the high point of the Confederate advance and was the greatest battle of the war. This painting commemorates the climax on the third day, when Confederate General Robert E. Lee commanded Pickett's division to charge the Union center. Coming toward the viewer in the face of terrible fire, the brave Southerners have reached the first Union line. But General Hancock, shown with arm extended in the left foreground, is ordering the Northern counterattack that will decimate Pickett's troops and force the Confederates back into Virginia. *(Source: Photograph by Al Freni © 1985 Time-Life Books, Inc. Courtesy, The Seventh Regiment Fund, Inc.)*

"The most rudimentary type of family organization was not permitted to survive, to say nothing of the extensions of the family. The mother-child family, with the father either unknown, absent, or, if present, incapable of wielding influence, was the only type of family that could survive."[33] However, Herbert G. Gutman's authoritative *The Black Family in Slavery and Freedom, 1750–1925* has demonstrated that such theories are not supported by fact. In spite of the destructive effects of slavery, African-Americans established strong family units.

Most slave couples had long marriages. A study of the entire adult slave population of North Carolina in 1860 has shown that 25 percent of slave marriages lasted between ten and nineteen years, 20 percent lasted at least twenty years, and almost 10 percent endured thirty years or more. Most slave women spent their entire adult lives in settled unions with the same husband. Planters encouraged slave marriages, because, as one owner put it, "marriage adds to the comfort, happiness, and health of those entering upon it, besides insuring a greater increase." Large slave families advanced owners' economic interests, and planters rewarded slave women who had many children.[34]

Forcible separation due to the sale of one partner proved the greatest threat to the permanence of slave marriages. In spite of illiteracy, separated

The Oblate Sisters of Providence of Baltimore   In 1929 the Oblate Sisters of Providence, the oldest order of black nuns in the United States, gathered to celebrate a century of educational, missionary, and social work—operating orphanages, day care centers, schools, and homes for the elderly. Limited only by numbers, their work continues today. *(Source: The Oblate Sisters of Providence of Baltimore)*

spouses tried to remain in touch with one another. Once slavery had been abolished, separated couples went to enormous lengths to reunite their families. Evidence from all parts of the South reveals that this was the common pattern.

Women often had to resist the attentions of the slaveowners themselves; in addition, owners not infrequently supplied slave women with black men who had reputations for sexual prowess. Slave women, however, made choices: they tried to select their own husbands, rejecting—up to the point of risking being sold—mates chosen by their owners.

Historians of medicine know little about the birth-control methods used by slave couples. Considerable information survives, however, about abortion. In 1860 a Tennessee physician reported that slave women tried to abort by "medicine," "violent exercise," and other means. Cotton plants were "habitually and effectively resorted to by slaves of the South for producing abortion."[35]

Typically, slave women had their first child around the age of nineteen. The continual labor shortage in the South led slaveowners to encourage slaves to produce children. Owners urged teenage slaves to begin bearing children and to have more children soon thereafter. On the Good Hope plantation in South Carolina, for example, 80 percent of slave couples had at least four children. Almost all women had all their children by one husband, and most children grew to their teens in households with both parents present. Although premarital intercourse was common among slaves—though not as common as among young American adults during the 1970s—the weight of the evidence shows that women rarely engaged in extramarital sexual activity.

Settled slave marriages provided models for growing children. The pattern of stable black marriages lasted well into the present century. Research on black households in New York City in 1925 shows that 85 percent were headed by two parents.[36] The period since the Great Depression of 1929 has witnessed a general decline in the stability of American families, both white and black. Shifting values throughout American society, such as changed sexual attitudes and an enormous in-crease in the divorce rate, have increased the pro-portion of black families headed by one parent. In recent decades, the 1990 census shows, the differ-ence between black and white wages has nar-rowed, but the total income of black households and white households has remained highly diver-gent because so many black households depend on the income of a single parent. The decline in fam-ily stability has proved an obstacle to black eco-nomic advancement.

Industrialization and Immigration

After the Civil War the United States underwent an industrial boom based on exploitation of the country's natural resources. The federal govern-ment turned over vast amounts of land and min-eral resources to industry for development. In par-ticular, the railroads—the foundation of industrial expansion—received 130 million acres. By 1900 the American railroad system was 193,000 miles long, connected every part of the nation, and rep-resented 40 percent of the railroad mileage of the entire world. Immigrant workers built it.

The late nineteenth and early twentieth centu-ries witnessed the immigration of unprecedented numbers of Europeans and Asians to the United States (see page 969). Between 1860 and 1900, 14 million immigrants came, and during the peak years between 1900 and 1914, another 14 million passed through the U.S. Customs inspection sta-tion at Ellis Island in New York City. All sought a better life and higher standard of living.

The immigrants' ambitions precisely matched the labor needs of the times. Chinese, Scandina-vian, and Irish immigrants laid 30,000 miles of railroad tracks between 1867 and 1873 and an-other 73,000 miles in the 1880s. Poles, Hungari-ans, Bohemians, and Italians poured into the coal and iron mines of western Pennsylvania and Appa-lachia. The steel magnate Andrew Carnegie re-cruited southern and eastern European immi-grants for his smoking mills around Pittsburgh, Cleveland, and Gary, Indiana. At the Carnegie Steel Corporation (later USX), Slavs and Italians produced one-third of the world's total steel sup-ply in 1900. John D. Rockefeller, whose Standard Oil Company earned tens of billions of dollars, employed thousands of Czechs, Poles, and other Slavs in his oil fields around the country. Lithua-nians, Poles, Croats, Scandinavians, Irish, and Ne-groes entered the Chicago stockyards and built the meatpacking industry. Irish immigrants con-tinued to operate the spinning frames and knitting machines of New England's textile mills. Indus-trial America developed on the sweat and brawn—the cheap labor—of its immigrant millions.

As industrial expansion transformed the eastern half of the United States, settlers conquered the trans-Mississippi West. Thousands of land-hungry farmers moved westward, where land was still only $1.25 an acre. In the final third of the nineteenth century, pioneers acquired 430 million acres and put 225 million of them under cultivation.

The West also held precious metals. The discov-ery of gold and silver in California, Colorado, Ari-zona, and Montana, and on the reservations of the Sioux Indians of South Dakota, precipitated huge rushes. Even before 1900, miners had extracted $1.24 billion in gold and $901 million in silver from western mines. Some miners left the West as soon as they had made their piles, but others settled down to farm and help their territories to-ward statehood. By 1912 the West had been won and the last frontier closed.

In the entire movement westward, women shared with men the long and dangerous journey and then the dawn-to-dusk, backbreaking work of carving a homestead out of the wilderness. Gener-ally speaking, the frontier blurred sex roles: women commonly did the same agricultural work as men.[37] In addition, it fell to women to make a home out of crude log cabins that had no windows or doors or out of tarpaper shacks that had mud floors—if they were lucky; more frequently, settlers lacked even a roof over their heads. One "gently reared" bride of seventeen took one look at her mud roof and dirt floor and indignantly an-nounced, "My father had a much better house for his hogs!" Lacking cookstoves, they had to prepare food over open fireplaces, using all kinds of substi-tutes for ingredients easily available back east. Be-fore they could wash clothes, women had to make soap out of lye and carefully saved household ashes.

Considered the carriers of "high culture," women organized whatever educational, religious, musical, and recreational activities the frontier so-ciety possessed. Frontier women also had to de-fend their homes against prairie fires and Indian attacks. These burdens were accompanied by fre-quent pregnancies and, often, the need to give birth without medical help or even the support of other women. Many frontier women used such contraceptive devices as spermicides, condoms, and, after 1864, vaginal diaphragms. The death rate for infants and young children ran as high as 30 percent in the mid-nineteenth century. Even so, frontier women had large families.

As in South America, immigration led to rapid urbanization. In 1790 only 5.1 percent of Americans were living in centers of 2,500 or more people. By 1860 this figure had risen to 19.9 percent, and by 1900 almost 40 percent were living in cities. The overwhelming majority of the southern and eastern Europeans who came to North America at the turn of the century became urban industrial workers, their entire existence framed by the factory and the tenement. Newly uprooted from rural Europe, Italians, Greeks, Croats, Hungari-

ans, Czechs, Poles, Russians, and Jews contrasted sharply with their urban neighbors and with each other. Older residents saw only "a sea of strange faces, babbling in alien tongues and framed by freakish clothes. Walking through these multitudes now was really like a voyage round the globe."[38]

Between 1880 and 1920 industrial production soared. New inventions such as the steam engine, the dynamo (generator), and the electric light were given industrial and agricultural applications. Transcontinental railroads and innovations like the sewing machine and the assembly line made large-scale production possible. Large factories replaced small ones. Large factories could buy large machines, operate them at full capacity, and take advantage of railroad discount rates. In the automobile industry, for example, Henry Ford of De-

Chinese Laborers Chinese immigrant laborers, who laid thousands of miles of railroad track across the United States in the nineteenth century, played a major role in industrial expansion. (*Source: California State Railroad Museum, Southern Pacific Collection*)

troit set up assembly lines. Each worker working on the line performed only one task instead of assembling an entire car. In 1910 Ford sold 10,000 cars; in 1914, a year after he inaugurated the first moving assembly line, he sold 248,000 cars. Such developments changed the face of American society. Sewing machines made cheap, varied, mass-produced clothing available to city people in department stores and to country people through mail-order catalogs. The automobile increased opportunities for travel, general mobility, and change.

By the 1890s factory managers were stressing industrial efficiency and the importance of time. Management engineers wanted to produce more at lower cost. They aimed to reduce labor costs by eliminating unnecessary workers. As the quantity rather than the quality of goods produced became the measure of acceptability, workers' skills were less valued. As assembly-line workers more and more performed only monotonous and time-determined work, in effect they became interchangeable parts of the machines they operated.

Despite accelerated production, and perhaps because of overproduction, the national economy experienced repeated cycles of boom and bust in the late nineteenth century. Serious depressions in 1873, 1884, and 1893 slashed prices and threw many people out of work. Leading industrialists responded by establishing larger corporations and trusts. Trusts granted control of their stock to a board of trustees, which then managed the operation of all the companies owned by the trust. The legalization of trusts led to huge conglomerates, such as John D. Rockefeller's Standard Oil Company, which as a result of the merger of several smaller oil companies controlled 84 percent of the nation's oil in 1898. Standard Oil also controlled most American pipelines and was involved in natural gas production. Standard Oil monopolized the oil industry; J. P. Morgan's United States Steel, the iron and steel industries; and Swift & Co. of Chicago, the meat-processing industry.

Industrialization led to the creation of a vast class of salaried workers who depended totally on their employers for work. Corporate managers, however, were always preoccupied with cutting labor costs. Thus employers paid workers piecemeal for the number of articles produced, to encourage the use of the new machines; and managers hired more women and children and paid them much less than they paid men. Most women worked in the textile industry. Some earned as little as $1.56 for seventy hours of work, while men received $7 to $9 for the same work. Employers reduced wages, forcing workers to toil longer and harder to maintain a certain level of income. Owners fought in legislatures and courts against the installation of safety devices, so working conditions in mines and mills were frightful. In 1913, even after some safety measures had been taken, 25,000 people died in industrial accidents. Between 1900 and 1917, 72,000 railroad worker deaths occurred. Workers responded with strikes, violence, and, gradually, unionization.

Urbanization brought serious problems. In *How the Other Half Lives* (1890), Jacob Riis, a newspaper reporter and recent immigrant from Denmark, drew national attention to what he called "the foul core of New York's slums." His phrase "the other half" soon became a synonym for the urban poor. Riis estimated that 300,000 people inhabited a single square mile on New York's Lower East Side. Overcrowding, poor sanitation, and lack of health services caused frequent epidemics. The blight of slums increased crime, prostitution, alcoholism, and other drug-related addictions. Riis attacked the vicious economic exploitation of the poor.

New York City was not unique; slums and the social problems resulting from them existed in all large American cities. Reformers fought for slum clearance, but public apathy and vested economic interests delayed massive urban renewal until after the Second World War. In spite of all these industrial and urban difficulties, immigrants continued to come: the United States offered opportunity, upward social mobility, and a better life.

European and Asian immigrants aroused nativist sentiments—that is, intense hostility to their foreign and "un-American" looks, behavior, and loyalties—on the part of native-born Americans. Some of this antagonism sprang from the deep-rooted Anglo-Saxon racism of many Americans. Some grew out of old Protestant suspicions of Roman Catholicism, the faith of most of the new arrivals. A great deal of the dislike of the foreign-born sprang from fear of economic competition. To most Americans, the Chinese with their exotic looks and willingness to work for very little seemed the most dangerous. Increasingly violent agitation against Asians led to race riots in California and finally culminated in the Chinese Exclusion Act of 1882, which denied Chinese laborers entrance to the country.

Harlem Hellfighters Returning to New York in 1919 aboard the U.S.S. *Stockholm*, these black men of the famed U.S. 369th Division had fought in the bloody battle of the Meuse-Argonne during the First World War. The French government awarded 150 of them the coveted Croix de Guerre. *(Source: Springer/Bettmann Film Archive)*

Immigrants from Europe seized on white racism as a way of improving themselves in the job market: they could compensate for their immigrant status by claiming superiority to former slaves and their descendants. The arrival of thousands of Irish immigrants in the 1850s, followed by millions of Italians and Slavs between 1880 and 1914, aggravated an already bad situation. What the German scientist Alexander von Humboldt wrote about the attitude of peninsulares toward Creoles in Latin America in the early nineteenth century—"the lowest, least educated, and uncultivated European believes himself superior to the white born in the New World"[39]—precisely applies to the outlook of Irish, Italian, or Slavic immigrants to the United States at the turn of this century if one merely substitutes *black* for *white*. In the eyes of all ethnic groups, the social status of blacks remained the lowest while that of immigrants rose. As the United States underwent expansion and industrialization in the course of the nineteenth century, blacks remained the worst off *because of immigration.*[40]

In the 1890s the nation experienced a severe economic depression. Faced with overproduction, the rich and politically powerful owners of mines, mills, and factories fought the organization of labor unions, laid off thousands, slashed wages, and ruthlessly exploited their workers. Workers in turn feared that immigrant labor would drive salaries lower. The frustrations provoked by pitifully low salaries in "good times," by unemployment during the depression, and by all the unresolved problems of industrial urban society boiled over into savage attacks on the foreign-born. One of the bloodiest incidents took place in western Pennsylvania in 1897, when about 150 unarmed Polish and Hungarian coal miners tried to persuade others to join their walkout. The mine owners convinced the local sheriff that the strike was illegal. As the strikers approached, the sheriff panicked and ordered his deputies to shoot. Twenty-one immigrants died and forty were wounded. The sheriff subsequently explained that the miners were only "infuriated foreigners . . . like wild beasts." Local people agreed that if the strikers had been American-born, no blood would have been shed.[41]

Pressure to restrict immigration varied with economic conditions: it slackened in times of relative prosperity and increased in periods of recession. After the First World War, labor leaders lobbied Congress for restrictions because they feared losing the wage gains achieved during the war. Some intellectuals argued that immigrants from southern and eastern Europe, with their unfamiliar cultural traditions, threatened to destroy American society. Italians were feared because of possible Cosa Nostra connections. Eastern Europeans were thought to have communist connections. In the 1920s Congress responded with laws that set severe quotas—2 percent of resident nationals as of the 1890 census—on immigration from southern and eastern Europe. The Japanese were completely excluded. These racist laws remained on the books until 1965.

CANADA: FROM FRENCH COLONY TO NATION

In 1608 the French explorer Samuel de Champlain (1567–1635) sailed down the St. Lawrence River and established a trading post on the site of present-day Quebec. Thus began the permanent colony of New France. The fur-trading monopolies subsequently granted to Champlain by the French crown attracted settlers, and Jesuit missionaries to the Indians further increased the French population. The British, however, vigorously challenged French control of the lucrative fur trade, and the long mid-eighteenth century global struggle for empire between the British and the French, known in North America as the "French and Indian Wars" because of Indian border warfare, tested French control (see pages 609–619). In 1759, on the Plains of Abraham, a field next to the city of Quebec, the English under General James Wolfe defeated the French under General Louis Montcalm. This battle ended the French Empire in North America. By the Treaty of Paris of 1763, France ceded Canada to Great Britain.

British Colony (1763–1839)

For the French Canadians, who in 1763 numbered about 90,000, the British conquest was a tragedy and the central event in their history. British governors replaced the French; English-speaking merchants from Britain and the thirteen American colonies to the south took over the colony's economic affairs. The Roman Catholic church remained and until about 1960 played a powerful role in the political and cultural, as well as religious, life of French Canadians. Most of the French Canadians engaged in agriculture, though a small merchant class sold furs and imported manufactured goods.

Intending to establish a permanent administration for Canada, in 1774 the British Parliament passed the Quebec Act. This law granted religious freedom to French Canadians and recognized French law in civil matters, but it denied Canadians a legislative assembly, a traditional feature of British colonial government. Parliament held that French Canadians had no experience in elective institutions; moreover, the example of the assemblies of the thirteen American colonies, which were then demanding more political power than the British wanted to grant, discouraged the establishment of a Canadian counterpart. Therefore, Parliament placed power in the hands of an appointed governor and an appointed council; the latter, however, was composed of French Canadians as well as English-speaking members. English Canadian businessmen protested that they were being denied a basic right of Englishmen—representation.

During the American Revolution, about 40,000 Americans demonstrated their loyalty to Great Britain and its empire by emigrating to Canada. These "loyalists" not only altered the French-English ratio in the population but also pressed for a representative assembly. In 1791 Parliament responded with the Constitution Act, which divided the province of Quebec at the Ottawa River into

Lower Canada (present-day Quebec, predominantly French and Catholic) and Upper Canada (present-day Ontario, primarily English and Protestant). The act also provided for an elective assembly in each of the two provinces. Because the assemblies' decisions could be vetoed by an appointed upper house or by the governor and his council, general discontent continued. Finally, in 1837, disputes over control of revenue, the judiciary, and the established churches erupted into open rebellion in both Upper and Lower Canada. The British government, fearful of a repetition of the American events of 1776, decided on a full investigation and appointed Lord Durham, a prominent liberal reformer, to make recommendations for reform. Lord Durham published his *Report on the Affairs of British North America,* later called the "Magna Carta" of British colonial administration, in 1839.

The Age of Confederation (1840–1905)

Lord Durham proposed the union of Upper and Lower Canada and the establishment in Canada of "responsible government," meaning that Canadians should manage their own local affairs through ministries responsible to their legislatures. The imperial government in London was to retain control over trade, foreign affairs, public lands, and the colonial constitution.

Accordingly, Parliament in 1840 passed the Union Act, which united Ontario and Quebec under one government composed of a governor, an appointed legislative council, and an elective assembly in which the two provinces had equal representation. The Union Act marks an important milestone toward confederation. When Lord Durham's son-in-law, Lord Elgin, was appointed governor in 1847, he made it clear that his cabinet (council) would be chosen from the party with the majority in the elected assembly; and, following the British model, the cabinet had to retain the support of that majority in order to stay in office.

The idea of a union or confederation of the other Canadian provinces persisted in the 1860s. During the American Civil War, English-American relations were severely strained, and "Canada found herself in the centre of the storm. The resulting fear of American aggression was a powerful factor in bringing confederation to completion."[42] Parliament's passage of the British North America

Act in 1867 brought the Canadian constitution to its modern form. By the act the traditional British parliamentary system was adapted to the needs of the new North American nation. The provinces of New Brunswick and Nova Scotia joined Ontario and Quebec to form the Dominion of Canada. A governor-general, who represented the British crown and fulfilled ceremonial functions, governed through the Dominion cabinet, which, like the British cabinet, was composed of members selected from the lower house of the legislature, to which it was responsible.

Legislative power rested in a parliament of two houses: a Senate, whose members were appointed for life by the governor-general, and a House of Commons, whose members were elected by adult males. (Canadian women won the right to vote in national elections in 1917, shortly before women in the United States and Great Britain but after women in Australia.) In theory, the two houses had equal power, though money bills had to originate in the House of Commons; in practice, the Senate came to serve only as a deliberative check on hasty legislation and as a means of rewarding elder statesmen for their party services.

The Dominion cabinet received complete jurisdiction over internal affairs. Britain retained control over foreign policy. (In 1931 the British Statute of Westminster officially recognized Canadian autonomy in foreign affairs.) The constitution of 1982 abolished the power of the London Parliament to amend Canada's constitution and ended all appeals from the provinces to London. Because Quebec did not sign the 1982 document, however, federal-provincial relationships remain under study.

Believing that the American system of the division of powers between the states and the federal government left the states too strong and helped to bring on the Civil War, the framers of the Canadian constitution intended to create a powerful central government. Provincial legislatures, therefore, were assigned powers explicitly stated and applicable only to local conditions. With the implementation of the British North America Act, Canada attained "responsible government." John A. Macdonald (1815–1891), the strongest advocate of confederation, became the Dominion's first prime minister.

Macdonald vigorously pushed Canada's "manifest destiny" to absorb all the northern part of the continent. In 1869 his government purchased for

$1,500,000 the vast Northwest Territories of the Hudson Bay Company. From this territory the province of Manitoba emerged to become part of the Dominion in 1870. Fearful that the sparsely settled colony of British Columbia would join the United States, Macdonald lured British Columbia into the confederation with a subsidy to pay its debts and the promise of a transcontinental railroad to be completed between 1873 and 1883. Likewise, the debt-ridden little maritime province of Prince Edward Island was drawn into confederation with a large subsidy. In five short years, between 1868 and 1873, through Macdonald's imagination and drive, Canadian sovereignty stretched from coast to coast.

Believing that a transcontinental railroad was essential to Canada's survival as a nation, Macdonald declared that "until this great work is completed our Dominion is little more than a 'geographical expression.' We have as much interest in British Columbia as in Australia, and no more. The railroad, once finished, we become a great united country with a large interprovincial trade and a common interest."[43] On November 7, 1885, Macdonald received a telegram announcing that the first train from Montreal in Quebec was

Prospectors in the Klondike The discovery of gold in 1896 in the Canadian Klondike (in the Yukon Territory just east of the Alaskan border) drew thousands, including these hardy women prospectors. *(Source: Library of Congress)*

approaching the Pacific; traveling at 24 miles per hour, the train had made the coast-to-coast trip in a little over five days. The completion of the railroad led to the formation of two new prairie provinces, Alberta and Saskatchewan, which in 1905 entered the Dominion. (Only in 1949 did the island of Newfoundland renounce colonial status and join the Dominion.) The Canadian Pacific Railroad was Macdonald's greatest achievement.

Growth, Development, and National Maturity

Macdonald's hopes for large numbers of immigrants to people the thinly populated country did not immediately materialize. Between 1897 and 1912, however, 961,000 entered Canada from the British Isles, 594,000 from Europe, and 784,000 from the United States. Some immigrants went to work in the urban factories of Hamilton, Toronto, and Montreal. Most immigrants from continental Europe—Poles, Germans, Scandinavians, and Russians—flooded the Midwestern plains and soon transformed the prairies into one of the world's greatest grain-growing regions.

Because of Canada's small population, most of which in the early twentieth century was concentrated in Ontario and Quebec, the assimilation of the immigrants to the older English-Canadian culture occurred more slowly than in the "melting pot" of the United States. French Canadians remained the largest minority in the population. Distinctively different in language, law, and religion, and fiercely proud of their culture, they resisted assimilation. Since the 1950s, Italian and Hungarian immigration has contributed to the evolution of a more cosmopolitan culture.

Supported by population growth, Canada experienced an agricultural and industrial boom between 1891 and 1914. In those years wheat production rocketed from 2 million bushels per year to 150 million bushels. The discovery of gold, silver, copper, and nickel in northern Ontario led to the full exploitation of those mineral resources. British Columbia, Ontario, and Quebec produced large quantities of wood pulp, much of it sold to the United States. Canada's great rivers were harnessed to supply hydroelectric power for industrial and domestic use. Meanwhile the government erected tariffs to protect Canadian industry, estab-

lished a national civil service, and built a sound banking system.

Canada's powerful support of the Allied cause in the First World War demonstrated its full maturity as a nation. In 1914 the British government still controlled the foreign policy of all parts of the empire. When Britain declared war on Germany, Canada unhesitatingly followed. More than 600,000 Canadian soldiers served with distinction in the army, some of them in the bloodiest battles in France; the 60,661 Canadians killed represent a greater loss than that experienced by the more populous United States. Canadian grain and foodstuffs supplied much of the food of the Allied troops, and Canadian metals were in demand for guns and shells. Canadian resentment, therefore, over lack of voice in the formulation of Allied war policies was understandable.

In 1917 the British government established the Imperial War Cabinet, a body composed of the chief British ministers and the prime ministers of the Dominions (Australia, Canada, New Zealand, and South Africa) to set policy. In 1918 Canada demanded and received—over the initial opposition of Britain, France, and the United States—the right to participate in the Versailles Peace Conference and in the League of Nations. Canada had become a respected and independent nation. Since 1939, Canada has been a member of the British Commonwealth of Nations.

AUSTRALIA: FROM PENAL COLONY TO NATION

In April 1770, James Cook, the English explorer, navigator, and captain of H.M.S. *Endeavor,* dropped anchor in a wide bay about ten miles south of the present city of Sydney on the coast of eastern Australia. Because the young botanist on board the ship, Joseph Banks, subsequently discovered 30,000 specimens of plant life in the bay, 1,600 of them unknown to European science, Captain Cook called the place Botany Bay. Totally unimpressed by the flat landscape and its few naked inhabitants—the Aborigines, or native people—Cook sailed north along the coast. Finally, the ship rounded Cape York Peninsula, the northernmost point of Australia. On August 21, on a rock later named Possession Island, Cook formally claimed the entire land south of where he stood for King George III, 16,000 miles away. Cook called the land "New South Wales." Australia (Map 31.6) became part of the British Empire.

The world's smallest continent, Australia is located southeast of Asia between the Pacific and Indian oceans. It is about half the size of Europe and almost as large as the United States (excluding Alaska and Hawaii). Three topographical zones roughly divide the continent. The Western Plateau, a vast desert and semidesert region, covers almost two-thirds. The Central Eastern Lowlands extend from the Gulf of Carpentaria in the north to western Victoria in the south. The Eastern Highlands are a complex belt of tablelands. Australia is one of the world's driest continents. It has a temperate climate and little intense cold.

The British Admiralty had sent Cook to chart the transit of the planet Venus across the sun—information that would help establish the earth's distance from the sun. Cook had completed the task at Tahiti in 1769. He had also been charged with finding or disproving the existence of "the

MAP 31.6 Australia The vast deserts in western Australia meant that cities and industries would develop mainly in the east. Australia's early geographical and cultural isolation bred a sense of inferiority. Air travel, the communications revolution, and the massive import of Japanese products and cheap American pop culture have changed that.

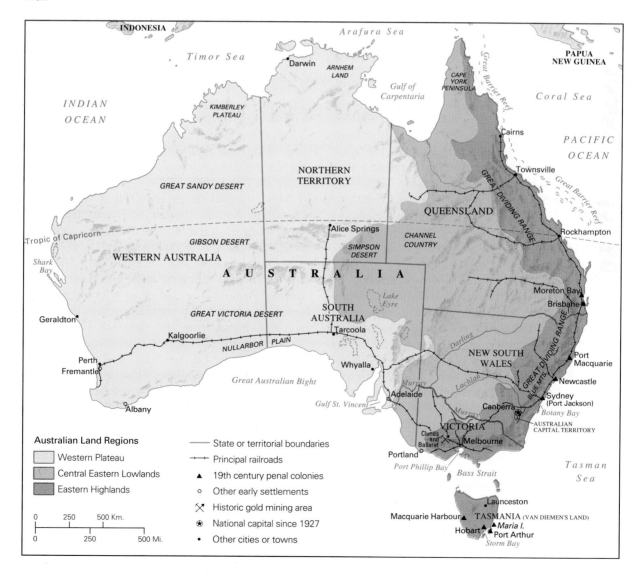

southern continent," a land first mentioned by the seventeenth-century Dutch explorer Abel Tasman. Scurvy, the common sailors' disease caused by vitamin C deficiency, and maritime ignorance of longitude had prevented Tasman and a series of eighteenth-century navigators from accurately charting the location of Australia.

When Cook arrived in Australia, about 300,000 Aborigines inhabited the continent. A peaceful and nomadic people who had emigrated from southern Asia millennia before, the Aborigines lived entirely by food gathering, fishing, and hunting. They had no domestic agriculture. Tribal customs governed their lives. Although they used spears and bows and arrows in hunting, they never practiced warfare as it was understood by more technologically advanced peoples such as the Aztecs of Mexico (see pages 571–572) or the Mandinke of West Africa (see pages 472–478). When white settlers arrived and occupied the Aborigines' lands, they never directed any concerted opposition to them. According to one Australian scholar, from 1788 to the present "Australian governments have been much more concerned with protecting the Aborigines than with fighting them."[44] Like the Indians of Central and South America, the Aborigines fell victim to the white peoples' diseases and to a spiritual malaise caused by the breakdown of their tribal life. Today, only about 45,000 pureblood Aborigines survive.

Penal Colony

The victory of the thirteen North American colonies in 1783 inadvertently contributed to the establishment of a colony in Australia five years later. Before 1775, the British government had shipped about one thousand convicts annually to Georgia. Crime in England was increasing in the 1770s and 1780s, and the transportation of felons "beyond the seas" seemed the answer to the problem of overcrowded prisons. Moreover, the establishment of a colony in Australia would provide a home for dispossessed loyalists who had fled America during the Revolution.

Some recent students of early Australian history deny those motivations. These scholars claim that other factors led to the founding of the colony: the British goal of checking French political and economic power in India, anxiety about the Dutch trading monopoly in the southwest Pacific, the

desire to set up strategic supply bases in the region, and the need to acquire pine trees and flax, which were essential for the construction of eighteenth-century ships and sails. But these arguments for the strategic potential of an Australian colony did not influence eighteenth-century British politicians. By the late 1760s French ships posed an insignificant threat to British interests. Moreover, Australia was thousands of miles away from the area of French and Dutch interests.

In England, the prisons were so full that old transport ships in southern naval ports were being used to house criminals, and pressure on the government to do something was intense. Finally, in August 1786, the British cabinet approved the establishment of a penal colony at Botany Bay to serve as "a remedy for the evils likely to result from the late alarming and numerous increase of felons in this country, and more particularly in the metropolis (London)."[45] The name "Botany Bay" became a byword for the forced and permanent exile of criminals. A competent but undistinguished semiretired navy officer, Captain Arthur Phillip, was appointed to lead the first expedition and to be governor of New South Wales. In May 1787 a fleet of eleven ships packed with one thousand felons and their jailers sailed for Australia. After an eight-month voyage it landed in Sydney Cove on January 28, 1788.

Mere survival in an alien world was the first challenge. Because the land at Botany Bay proved completely unsuited for agriculture and lacked decent water, Governor Phillip moved the colony ten miles north to Port Jackson, later called Sydney after the British Colonial Secretary Lord Thomas Sydney. Announcing that those who did not work would not eat, Phillip set the prisoners to planting seeds. Coming from the slums of London, the convicts knew nothing of agriculture, and some were too ill or old to work. The colony lacked draft animals and plows. The army and (after 1792) marine detachments sent to guard the prisoners considered it below their dignity to work the land. For years the colony of New South Wales tottered on the brink of starvation.

For the first thirty years, men far outnumbered women. Because the British government refused to allow wives to accompany their convict-husbands, prostitution flourished. Many women convicts, if not professional prostitutes when they left England, became such during the long voyage south. Army officers, government officials, and

Convicts Embarking for Botany Bay   The English printmaker and caricaturist Thomas Rowlandson (1756–1827) sketched this scene with ink and watercolor wash. In the background the gibbet with hanging felons shows the legal alternative to transportation to Australia. (*Source: National Library of Australia*)

free immigrants chose favorite convicts as mistresses. The vast majority of children born in the colony were illegitimate. Officers and jailers, although descended from the middle and lower middle classes, tried to establish a colonial gentry and to impose the rigid class distinctions that they had known in England. Known as *exclusionists,* this self-appointed colonial gentry tried to exclude from polite society all freed or emancipated persons, called *emancipists.* Deep and bitter class feeling took root.

Economic Development

For eighty long years after 1787, Britain continued to transport convicts to New South Wales. Transportation rested on two premises: that criminals should be punished and that they should not be a financial burden on the state. Just as convicts

had been sold to planters in Georgia and Maryland before the revolt of the American colonies, so after 1787 the government maintained that convicts should build and strengthen the colonial economy of New South Wales.

Convicts became free when their sentences expired or were remitted, and few returned to England. Governor Phillip and his successors urged the Colonial Office to send free settlers. The Napoleonic war slowed emigration before 1815, but thereafter a steady stream of people relocated. The end of the European wars also released capital for potential investment. But investment in what? What was the economy of New South Wales to rest on? What commodity could be developed and exported to England?

Immigrants explored several economic enterprises. In the last decade of the eighteenth century, for example, sealing seemed a likely possibility. Sealing merchants hired aboriginal women to swim out to the seal rocks, lie down among the seals until their suspicions were dulled, and then at a signal rise up and club the seals to death. In 1815, a single ship carried 60,000 seal skins to London (a normal cargo contained at least 10,000 skins). Such destruction rapidly depleted the seals.

Credit for the development of the product that was to be Australia's staple commodity for export—wool—goes to John Macarthur (1767–1834), who first saw the economic potential of sheep farming in New South Wales. Granted a large tract of crown lands and assigned thirty convicts to work for him, Macarthur conducted experiments in the production of fine merino wool. In 1800 he sent sample fleeces to England to determine their quality. He also worked to change the government's penal view of New South Wales to a commercial one and to attract the financial support of British manufacturers.

The report of J. T. Bigge, an able lawyer sent out in 1819 to evaluate the colony, proved decisive. Persuaded by large landowners like Macarthur, Bigge reported that wool was the country's future staple. He recommended that convicts be removed from the temptations of towns and seaports and dispersed to work on the estates of men of capital. He also urged that British duties on colonial wool be suspended. The Colonial Office accepted this advice, and the pastoral economy of Australia, as the continent was beginning to be called, began.

Australia's temperate though capricious climate is ideally suited to sheep farming. Moreover, wool production requires much land and little labor—precisely the situation in Australia. In 1820 the sheep population was 120,000; by 1830 it reached a half-million. After 1820 the commercial importance of Australia exceeded its significance as a penal colony, and wool export steadily increased: From 75,400 pounds in 1821, to 2 million pounds in 1830, to 10 million pounds in 1839, to 24 million pounds in 1845.

Settlers also experimented with wheat farming. Soil deficiencies and the dry climate slowed early production, but farmers eventually developed a white-grained variety (in contrast to the red-grained variety grown in the Northern Hemisphere) planted during the Australian winter from May through July and harvested from September to January. By 1900 wheat proved Australia's second most valuable crop.

Population shortage remained a problem. In this area, the development of Australia owes some-

thing to the vision of Edward Gibbon Wakefield (1769–1862), a theorist of colonization. Between 1825 and 1850, 3 million people emigrated from Great Britain. In the quest for immigrants, Australia could not really compete with North America. The 12,000-mile journey to Australia cost between £20 and £25 and could take five weary months. By contrast, the trip to Canada or the United States cost only £5 and lasted just ten weeks. Wakefield proposed that Australian land be sold relatively cheaply and that proceeds from the sale be used to pay the passages of free laborers and mechanics. That eliminated the disadvantage of cost. Although over 2,500,000 British immigrants went to North America, 223,000 industrious English and Irish people chose Australia.

Population in the early nineteenth century concentrated on the eastern coast of the continent most of which remained unexplored. The growth of sheep farming stimulated exploration and led to the opening of the interior. In 1813 explorers discovered a route over the Blue Mountains. New settlements were made in Hobart, Tasmania, in 1813; in Queensland on the Brisbane River in 1824; and on the Swan River in Western Australia in 1829. Melbourne was established on Port Phillip Bay in 1835 and Adelaide on Gulf St. Vincent in 1836. These settlements served as the bases for further exploration and settlement. Population continued to grow with the arrival of more convicts (a total of 161,000 when the system was finally abolished in 1868). The Ripon Land Regulation Act of 1831, which provided land grants, attracted free settlers. By 1850 Australia had 500,000 inhabitants. The discovery of gold in Victoria in 1851 quadrupled that in a few years.

From Colony to Nation

On February 12, 1851, Edward Hargraves, an Australian-born prospector who had returned to Australia after unsuccessful digging in the California gold rush of 1849, discovered gold in a creek on the western slopes of the Blue Mountains. Hargraves gave the district the biblical name Ophir (Job 22:24), and the newspapers said the region was "one vast gold field." In July a miner found gold at Clunes, 100 miles west of Melbourne, and in September gold was found in what proved to be the richest field of all, Ballarat, just 75 miles west of Melbourne. Gold fever convulsed Australia. Although the government charged prospectors a very high license fee, men and women from all parts of the globe flocked to Australia to share in the fabulous wealth.

Besides the enormous population growth, what impact did the gold rush of 1851–1861 have on Australian society? Contemporaries agreed with explorer and politician W. C. Wentworth, who said that the gold rush opened a new era "which must in a very few years precipitate us from a colony to a nation."[46] Although recent scholars have disputed Wentworth, there is much truth to his viewpoint. The gold rush led to an enormous improvement in transportation within Australia. People customarily traveled by horseback and used two-wheel ox-drawn carts to bring wool from inland ranches to coastal cities. Gold prospectors ordinarily walked the 100-odd miles from Sydney or Melbourne to the gold fields. Then two newly arrived Americans, Freeman Cobb and James Rutherford, built sturdy four-wheel coaches capable of carrying heavy cargo and of negotiating the bush tracks. With stops to change horses, Cobb and Co. carried passengers and mail up to 80 miles

a day, a week's work for ox-drawn vehicles. By 1870 company coaches covered 28,000 miles per week. Railroad construction began in the 1870s, and between 1870 and 1890 9,000 miles of track were laid. Railroad construction, financed by British investors, stimulated agricultural growth.

The gold rush also provided the financial means for the promotion of education and culture. The 1850s witnessed the establishment of universities at Sydney and Melbourne and later at Adelaide and Hobart. Public libraries, museums, art galleries, and schools opened in the thirty years after 1851. In keeping with the overwhelmingly British ethnic origin of most immigrants to Australia, these institutions dispensed a distinctly British culture, though a remote and provincial version.

On the negative side, the large numbers of Asians in the gold fields—in Victoria in 1857 one adult male in seven was Chinese—sparked bitter racial prejudice. Scholars date the "white Australia policy" to the hostility, resentment, and fear that whites showed the Chinese.

Although Americans numbered only about 5,000 in Victoria and Asians 40,000, Americans

Sheepshearing Sheep farming was introduced early into Australia, and wool (with wheat and minerals) became the foundation of the nation's economy. The sheep were sheared in vast sheds like this one. (*Source: Tom Roberts,* Shearing the Rams, *1890. Reproduced by permission of the National Gallery of Victoria, Melbourne*)

with their California gold-rush experience, aggressive ways, and "democratic" frontier outlook, exercised an influence on Australian society far out of proportion to their numbers. "There was evidence to suggest that some Americans, bringing with them their pre–Civil War racist attitudes, had an appreciable influence on the growth of color prejudice in Australia."[47] On the Fourth of July in 1852, 1854, and 1857 (anniversaries of the American Declaration of Independence), anti-Chinese riots occurred in the gold fields of Victoria. After the gold-rush decade, public pressure for the exclusion of all colored peoples increased. Nevertheless, Asian peoples continued to arrive. Chinese and Japanese built the railroads and ran the market gardens near, and the shops in, the towns. Filipinos and Pacific Islanders did the hard work in the sugar-cane fields. Afghani and their camels controlled the carrying trade in some areas.

"Colored peoples" (as all nonwhites were called in Australia) adapted more easily than the British to the tropical climate and worked for lower wages. Thus they proved essential to the country's economic development in the nineteenth century. But fear that colored labor would lower living standards and undermine Australia's distinctly British culture triumphed. The Commonwealth Immigration Restriction Act of 1901 closed immigration to Asians and established the "white Australia policy." Australia achieved racial and cultural unity only at the price of Asian resentment at discrimination and the retardation of the economic development of the northern colonies, which desperately needed labor. The laws of 1901 remained on the books until the 1970s.

The gold rush had a considerable political impact. In 1850 the British Parliament had passed the Australian Colonies Government Act, which allowed the four most populous colonies—New South Wales, Tasmania, Victoria, and South Australia—to establish colonial legislatures, determine the franchise, and frame their own constitutions. The gold rush, vastly increasing population, accelerated the movement for self-government. Acknowledging this demand, the Colonial Secretary in London wrote that the gold discoveries "imparted new and unforeseen features to (Australia's) political and social condition." The British Parliament approved the constitutions of Victoria, New South Wales, South Australia, and Queensland. Western Australia's decision to remain a penal colony delayed responsible government there,

but by 1859 all other colonies were self-governing. The provincial parliament of South Australia was probably the most democratic in the world, since it was elected by universal manhood suffrage and by secret ballot. Other colonies soon adopted the secret ballot. In 1909 Australia became the first country in the world to adopt woman suffrage.

The government of Australia combines features of the British and American systems. In the later nineteenth century, pressure for continental federation culminated in meetings of the premiers (governors) of the colonies. They drafted a constitution that the British Parliament approved in the Commonwealth of Australia Constitution Act of 1900. The Commonwealth of Australia came into existence on January 1, 1901. From the Westminster model, Australia adopted the parliamentary form of government in which a cabinet is responsible to the House of Commons. From the American system, Australia took the concept of decentralized government whereby the states and the federal government share power. The states in Australia, as in the United States, retain considerable power, especially in local or domestic affairs.

Deep loyalty to the mother country led Australia to send 329,000 men and vast economic aid to Britain in the First World War. The issue of conscription, however, bitterly divided the country, partly along religious lines. About one-fourth of Australia's population was (and is) Irish and Roman Catholic. Although the Catholic population, like the dominant Anglican one, split over conscription, the powerful, influential, and long-lived Catholic archbishop of Melbourne, Daniel Mannix (r. 1917–1963) publically supported the Sinn Fein, the Irish nationalist (and later terrorist) movement. Mannix also denounced the English and the European war.

Twice submitted to public referendum, conscription twice failed. When the Australian poet Frank Wilmot wrote, "The fumes of ancient hells have invaded your spirit," he meant that English wrongs in Ireland had become part of Australian culture.

Australian troops fought valiantly in the Dardenelles campaign, where more than 10,000 died. During the long nightmare of trench warfare on the western front (see page 1045), Australian soldiers were brilliantly led by Sir John Monash, a Jewish Australian whose planning led to the Allied breakthrough and the ultimate defeat of Germany. With 213,850 casualties, however, the death toll proved so staggering that the war exerted a severely traumatic effect on Australian life and society. With the young men died the illusion that remote Australia could escape the problems and sins of the Old World. But the experience of the Great War drew the disparate colonies together; the war forged a sense of national identity among the states of Australia.

At the Paris Peace Conference in 1919, Australian delegates succeeded in excluding recognition of the principle of racial equality in the League of Nations Covenant. Australians did not want Asian immigrants. The treaties that followed the war allowed Australia a mandate over German New Guinea and the equatorial island of Nauru. Nauru had vast quantities of phosphates that Australian wheatfields needed as fertilizer. The former penal colony had become a colonial power.

cated culture and had been Christians for three centuries.

The notion of manifest destiny had swept the United States into the Caribbean and across the Pacific. Between 1900 and 1929 the United States intervened in Latin American affairs whenever it felt its economic interests were threatened. Americans secured control of the Panama Canal on their own terms, and in 1912 and 1926 U.S. Marines intervened in Nicaragua to bolster conservative governments. The result has been a bitter legacy of anti-American feeling throughout Latin America. Only with the launching of President Franklin D. Roosevelt's Good Neighbor Policy did relations between the United States and Latin America begin to improve.

Canada and Australia achieved political and economic maturity.

SUMMARY

In the later years of the nineteenth century, industrialization, expansion, and the assimilation of foreign peoples preoccupied the nations of the Western Hemisphere. Political instability slowed the development of most Latin American countries. A few reformers sought closer relations between North and South America, but little of significance was accomplished. In 1889, for example, a Pan-American Conference in Washington rejected a proposal to settle disputes among nations by arbitration.

A revolt in Cuba against incompetent Spanish administration had more far-reaching consequences. The American "yellow press" luridly described the horrors of the concentration camps where the Spanish incarcerated the rebels. When the battleship *Maine* was mysteriously blown up in Havana harbor, inflamed public opinion swept the United States into war. The Spanish-American War of 1898—the "splendid little war," as Secretary of State John Hay called it—lasted just ten weeks and resulted in the United States acquiring Cuba and the Philippine Islands. Denying any imperialistic ambitions in the Philippines, President William McKinley declared that the United States wanted only "to take them all and educate the Filipinos and uplift and civilize and Christianize them." McKinley, like most Americans, did not know that the Filipinos had an old and sophisti-

NOTES

1. Quoted in W. S. Robertson, *Rise of the Spanish American Republics* (New York: Free Press, 1965), p. 19.
2. See B. Keen and M. Wasserman, *A Short History of Latin America* (Boston: Houghton Mifflin, 1980), pp. 109–115.
3. J. Lynch, *The Spanish-American Revolutions, 1808–1826* (New York: Norton, 1973), pp. 13–14; Keen and Wasserman, pp. 145–146.
4. Quoted in Lynch, p. 18.
5. M. Burkholder and D. S. Chandler, *From Impotence to Authority: The Spanish Crown and the American Audiencias, 1687–1808* (Columbia, Mo.: University of Missouri Press, 1977), p. 145.
6. Ibid., p. 141.
7. Keen and Wasserman, p. 146.
8. Quoted in J. L. Phelan, *The People and the King: The Comunero Revolution in Colombia, 1781* (Madison, Wis.: University of Wisconsin Press, 1978), p. 62; see also L. B. Rout, *The African Experience in Spanish America* (New York: Cambridge University Press, 1977), p. 165.
9. Quoted in Phelan, pp. 206–207.
10. F. Tannenbaum, *Ten Keys to Latin America* (New York: Random House, 1962), pp. 69–71.
11. Ibid.
12. H. Hoetink, *Slavery and Race Relations in the Americas* (New York: Harper & Row, 1973), p. 14.
13. Keen and Wasserman, pp. 201–204.
14. See C. H. Harris, *A Mexican Family Empire: The Latifundio of the Sanchez Navarros, 1765–1867* (Austin:

University of Texas Press, 1975).

15. N. Sanchez-Albornoz, *The Population of Latin America: A History,* trans. W. A. R. Richardson (Berkeley: University of California Press, 1974), pp. 151–152.

16. J. R. Scobie, "Buenos Aires as a Commercial-Bureaucratic City, 1880–1910: Characteristics of a City's Orientation," *American Historical Review 77* (October 1972): 1046.

17. Ibid., p. 1064.

18. See M. Morner, ed., *Race and Class in Latin America. Part II: Immigration, Stratification, and Race Relations* (New York: Columbia University Press, 1971), pp. 73–122; Sanchez-Albornoz, pp. 160–167.

19. S. E. Morison, *The Oxford History of the American Peeople* (New York: Oxford University Press, 1965), pp. 380–381.

20. Ibid., pp. 446–452.

21. J. Oakes, *The Ruling Race: A History of American Slaveholders* (New York: Knopf, 1982), pp. x–xi.

22. See P. Parish, *Slavery: History and Historians* (New York: Harper & Row, 1989), pp. 45–46.

23. Quoted in Oakes, p. 120.

24. C. V. Woodward, ed., *Mary Chesnut's Civil War* (New Haven, Conn.: Yale University Press, 1981), p. 29.

25. Ibid., pp. xlix–l.

26. R. P. Basler, ed., *The Collected Works of Abraham Lincoln,* vol. II (New Brunswick, N.J.: Rutgers University Press, 1953), pp. 255–256, 271.

27. Ibid., pp. 461–462.

28. Quoted in R. Hofstadter, *The American Political Tradition* (New York: Random House, 1948), p. 114.

29. T. H. Williams, quoted in Hofstadter, pp. 128–129.

30. Quoted in Hofstadter, p. 132.

31. Quoted in Morison, p. 654.

32. T. H. Williams, *The History of American Wars: From Colonial Times to World War I* (New York: Alfred A. Knopf, 1981), p. 202.

33. A. Kardiner and L. Ovesey quoted in H. G. Gutman, *The Black Family in Slavery and Freedom, 1750–1925* (New York: Random House, 1977), p. xvii.

34. Quoted in R. W. Fogel and S. L. Engerman, *Time on the Cross: The Economics of American Negro Slavery* (Boston: Little, Brown, 1974), p. 84.

35. Ibid., pp. 81–82.

36. Gutman, p. xix.

37. S. L. Myres, *Westering Women and the Frontier Experience, 1800–1915* (Albuquerque: University of New Mexico Press, 1982), chaps. 6 and 7.

38. G. Barth, *City People: The Rise of Modern City Culture in the Nineteenth Century* (New York: Oxford University Press, 1980), p. 15.

39. Quoted in Lynch, p. 18.

40. Hoetink, p. 18.

41. Quoted in J. Higham, *Strangers in the Land: Patterns of American Nativism, 1860–1925* (New York: Atheneum, 1971), pp. 89–90.

42. Quoted in R. Cook, *Canada: A Modern Study* (Toronto: Clarke, Irwin, 1971), p. 89.

43. Quoted ibid., p. 127.

44. R. Ward, *Australia* (Englewood Cliffs, N.J.: Prentice-Hall, 1965, p. 21.

45. Quoted in R. Hughes, *The Fatal Shore* (New York: Knopf, 1987), p. 66.

46. Quoted in Ward, p. 60.

47. Ward, *op. cit.,* p. 59.

SUGGESTED READING

Perhaps the best introduction to the independence movements in Latin America is J. Lynch, *The Spanish-American Revolutions* (1973), which is soundly researched and includes a good bibliography. The most useful biographies of Simón Bolívar are those of G. Masur, *Simón Bolívar,* 2d ed. (1969), and J. J. Johnson and D. M. Ladd, *Simón Bolívar and Spanish American Independence, 1783–1830* (1968); the latter contains good selections of Bolívar's writings. For Brazil, see K. R. Maxwell, *Conflicts and Conspiracies: Brazil and Portugal, 1750–1808* (1973), and A. J. R. Russell-Wood, ed., *From Colony to Nation: Essays in the Independence of Brazil* (1975). A. P. Whitaker, *The United States and the Independence of Latin America, 1800–1830* (1941), remains the standard study of the role of the United States. The essays in E. Viotti da Costa, *The Brazilian Empire: Myths and Histories* (1985), are sound and penetrating.

J. Bazant, *A Concise History of Mexico* (1978), is a good starting point for the study of Mexican history, but M. C. Meyer and W. L. Sherman, *The Course of Mexican History* (1979), is the most thorough treatment. T. Halperin-Donghi, *The Aftermath of Revolution in Latin America* (1973), and C. C. Griffin, "Economic and Social Aspects of the Era of Spanish-American Independence," *Hispanic American Historical Review* 29 (1949), provide important interpretations of the consequences of the revolutions.

The following studies offer good treatments of society and politics in Latin America in the nineteenth century: R. Graham and P. H. Smith, eds., *New Approaches to Latin American History* (1974); R. Roeder, *Juarez and His Mexico,* 2 vols. (1947), perhaps the best available work in English; H. S. Ferns, *Argentina* (1969); J. Kinsbruner, *Chile: A Historical Interpretation* (1973); A. J. Bauer, *Chilean Rural Society from the Spanish Conquest to 1930* (1975); E. B. Burns, *A History of Brazil* (1970); Robert Conrad, *The Destruction of Brazilian Slavery,*

1850–1888 (1973); and R. B. Toplin, *The Abolition of Slavery in Brazil* (1972). C. N. Degler, *Neither Black Nor White: Slavery and Race Relations in Brazil and the United States* (1971) remains the best comparative study of race in the two societies.

For social and economic developments and the triumph of neocolonialism, the following titles are useful: R. C. Conde, *The First Stages of Modernization in Spanish America* (1967); J. Bazant, *A Concise History of Mexico from Hidalgo to Cardenas, 1805–1940* (1978); R. Knowlton, *Church Property and the Mexican Reform, 1856–1910* (1976); R. D. Anderson, *Outcasts in Their Own Land: Mexican Industrial Workers, 1906–1911* (1976); J. Scobie, *Argentina: A City and a Nation*, 2d ed. (1971); M. J. Mamalakis, *The Growth and Structure of the Chilean Economy from Independence to Allende* (1976), which provides an excellent economic overview; A. G. Frank, *Capitalism and Underdevelopment in Latin America: Historical Studies of Chile and Brazil* (1969); D. Rock, *Politics in Argentina, 1890–1930: The Rise and Fall of Radicalism* (1975); R. Graham, *Britain and the Onset of Modernization in Brazil, 1850–1914* (1968).

The major themes in United States history have been extensively treated by many able scholars, and students will have no difficulty finding a wealth of material. J. M. Burns, *The Vineyard of Liberty* (1982), traces the origins and development of American society, politics, and culture, emphasizing the growth of liberty, from the 1780s to 1863; this work is a classic achievement. The standard study of manifest destiny remains F. Merk, *Manifest Destiny and Mission in American History: A Reinterpretation* (1963), but see also K. Jack Bauer, *The Mexican-American War, 1846–1848* (1976). In *The Only Land They Knew: The Tragic Story of the American Indians in the Old South* (1981), J. Leitch Wright recounts the interaction of Native Americans, Africans, and Europeans in the American South.

The best recent study of the pre–Civil War years is K. M. Stampp, *American in 1857: A Nation on the Brink* (1990). For slavery, see the elegant study by P. J. Parish cited in the Notes; Parish surveys an enormous body of scholarship. W. Jordan, *White over Black: American Attitudes Towards the Negro, 1550–1812* (1969), remains the best treatment of the relationship of racism to slavery; S. M. Elkins, *Slavery: A Problem in American Institutional and Intellectual Life*, 3d. rev. ed (1976), provides a good comparison of slavery in the United States and in Latin America. C. N. Degler, *Neither Black nor White: Slavery and Race Relations in Brazil and the United States* (1971), also treats the two continents. E. D. Genovese, *Roll, Jordan, Roll: The World the Slaves Made* (1974), gives the comprehensive Marxist treatment.

On black culture and black women and the family, see, in addition to Gutman's work cited in the Notes, J. Jones, *Labor of Love, Labor of Sorrow: Black Women,* *Work, and the Family from Slavery to the Present* (1985); C. Neverdon-Morton, *Afro-American Women of the South and the Advancement of the Race, 1895–1925* (1989); M. R. Malson et al., *Black Women in America: Social Science Perspectives* (1988), offers useful essays for classroom discussion. W. S. McFeely, *Frederick Douglass* (1991); and I. Berlin et al. eds., *Freedom: A Documentary History of Emancipation* (1990). For the powerful influence of the black church see E. Lincoln and C. H. Mamiya, *The Black Church in the African American Experience* (1990).

The literature on the Civil War and Reconstruction is mammoth. The following titles treat important aspects of them: D. Donald, ed., *Why the North Won the Civil War* (1977); J. H. Franklin, *Reconstruction* (1965); H. M. Hyman, *A More Perfect Union* (1973); and J. McPherson, *The Abolitionist Legacy* (1975). E. Foner, *Reconstruction: America's Unfinished Revolution, 1863–1877* (1988), has probably superseded previous works.

T. C. Cochrane, *Business in American Life* (1977); A. D. Chandler, *Strategy and Structure: Chapters in the History of American Industrial Enterprise* (1966); H. C. Livesay, *Andrew Carnegie and the Rise of Big Business* (1975); and D. F. Hawkes, *John D.: The Founding Father of the Rockefellers* (1980), are fine studies of industrialism and corporate growth in the late nineteenth century.

On the lives of Jews and other immigrants in American cities, see I. Howe's brilliant achievement, *World of Our Fathers* (1976), which is splendidly illustrated and contains a good bibliography, and S. S. Weinberg, *The World of Our Mothers: The Lives of Jewish Immigrant Women (1988).*

For developments in Canada, see, in addition to the highly readable sketch by R. Cook cited in the Notes, K. McNaught, *The Pelican History of Canada* (1976), a sound survey that emphasizes those cultural traits that are distinctly Canadian. For the Age of Confederation, J. M. S. Careless, *The Union of the Canadas, 1841–1857* (1967), offers a solid treatment by a distinguished scholar. D. G. Creighton, *John A. Macdonald*, 2 vols. (1952, 1955), is probably the best study of the great prime minister. The critical years of expansion and development are discussed in the full accounts of R. C. Brown and G. R. Cook, *Canada, 1896–1921* (1974), and R. Graham, *Canada, 1922–1939* (1979).

Perhaps the best starting point for the study of Australian history is the title by R. Hughes, cited in the Notes. M. Clark, *A Short History of Australia* (1987), is a highly readable general sketch, while C. M. H. Clark, *A History of Australia*, 6 vols. (1962–1987), is the standard political history. R. Terrill, *The Australians* (1987), offers an attractive appreciation of the Australian people and the society they made, from the first settlers to the present.

32

The Great Break:
War and Revolution

World War One trench warfare (John Nash, *Over the Top*)

In the summer of 1914 the nations of Europe went willingly to war. They believed they had no other choice. Moreover, both peoples and governments confidently expected a short war leading to a decisive victory. Such a war, they believed, would "clear the air," and European society would go on as before.

These expectations were almost totally mistaken. The First World War was long, indecisive, and tremendously destructive. To the shell-shocked generation of survivors, it was known simply as the "Great War": the war of unprecedented scope and intensity. From today's perspective it is clear that the First World War marked a great break in the course of world historical development. The war accelerated the growth of nationalism in Asia (see Chapter 33), and it consolidated the position of the United States as a global power. Yet the war's greatest impact was on Europe, the focus of this chapter. A noted British political scientist has gone so far as to say that even in victorious and relatively fortunate Great Britain, the First World War was *the* great turning point in government and society "as in everything else in modern British history. . . . There's a much greater difference between the Britain of 1914 and, say, 1920, than between the Britain of 1920 and today."[1]

That is a strong statement, but it contains much truth, for all of Europe as well as for Britain. It suggests three questions that this chapter tries to answer:

- What caused the Great War?
- How and why did war and revolution have such enormous and destructive consequences?
- How did the years of trauma and bloodshed form elements of modern life that people now accept and even cherish?

THE FIRST WORLD WAR

The First World War was so long and destructive because it involved all the Great Powers in Europe and because it spread to envelop several non-European states and peoples. Moreover, it quickly degenerated into a senseless military stalemate.

Like two evenly matched boxers in a championship bout, each side tried to wear down its opponent. There was no referee to call a draw, only the blind hammering of a life-or-death struggle until one combatant fell prostrate.

The Bismarckian System of Alliances

In examining the complex origins of the First World War, one needs to begin with the Franco-Prussian War and the foundation of the German Empire, which opened a new era in international relations. France was decisively defeated in 1871 and forced to pay a large war indemnity and give up Alsace-Lorraine. In ten short years, from 1862 to 1871, Bismarck had made Prussia-Germany—traditionally the weakest of the Great Powers—the most powerful nation in Europe (see pages 937–940). Had Bismarck been a Napoleon I or a Hitler, for whom no gain was ever sufficient, continued expansion would no doubt sooner or later have raised a powerful coalition against the new German Empire. But he was not. As Bismarck never tired of repeating after 1871, Germany was a "satisfied" power. Germany had no territorial ambitions and only wanted peace in Europe.

But how was peace to be preserved? The most serious threat to peace came from the east, from Austria-Hungary and from Russia. Those two enormous multinational empires had many conflicting interests, particularly in the Balkans, where the Ottoman Empire—the "sick man of Europe"—was ebbing fast. There was a real threat that Germany might be dragged into a great war between the two rival empires. Bismarck's solution was a system of alliances (Figure 32.1) to restrain both Russia and Austria-Hungary, to prevent conflict between them, and to isolate a hostile France.

A first step was the creation in 1873 of the conservative Three Emperors' League, which linked the monarchs of Austria-Hungary, Germany, and Russia in an alliance against radical movements. In 1877 and 1878, when Russia's victories over the Ottoman Empire threatened the balance of Austrian and Russian interests in the Balkans and the balance of British and Russian interests in the Middle East, Bismarck played the role of sincere peacemaker. At the Congress of Berlin in 1878, he saw that Austria obtained the right to "occupy and

The Congress of Berlin, 1878 With the Austrian representative on his right and with other participants looking on, Bismarck the mediator symbolically seals the hard-won agreement by shaking hands with the chief Russian negotiator. The Great Powers often relied on such special conferences to settle their international disputes. *(Source: The Bettmann Archive)*

administer" the Ottoman provinces of Bosnia and Herzegovina to counterbalance Russian gains, while independent Balkan states were also carved from the disintegrating Ottoman Empire.

Bismarck's balancing efforts at the Congress of Berlin infuriated Russian nationalists. Their anger led Bismarck to conclude a defensive military alliance with Austria against Russia in 1879. Motivated by tensions with France, Italy joined Germany and Austria in 1882, thereby forming the Triple Alliance.

Bismarck continued to work for peace in eastern Europe, seeking to neutralize tensions between Austria-Hungary and Russia. In 1881 he capitalized on their mutual fears and cajoled them both into a secret alliance with Germany. This Alliance of the Three Emperors lasted until 1887. It established the principle of cooperation among all three powers in any further division of the Ottoman Empire, and each state pledged friendly neutrality in case one of the three found itself at war with a fourth power (except the Ottoman Empire).

Bismarck also maintained good relations with Britain and Italy, while cooperating with France in Africa but keeping France isolated in Europe. In 1887 Russia declined to renew the Alliance of the Three Emperors because of new tensions in the Balkans. Bismarck craftily substituted a Russian-German Reinsurance Treaty, by which both states promised neutrality if the other were attacked.

Bismarck's accomplishments in foreign policy after 1871 were great. For almost a generation, he maintained German leadership in international affairs, and he worked successfully for peace by managing conflicts and by restraining Austria-Hungary and Russia with defensive alliances.

The Rival Blocs

In 1890 the young, impetuous emperor William II (r. 1888–1941) dismissed Bismarck, in part because of the chancellor's friendly policy toward

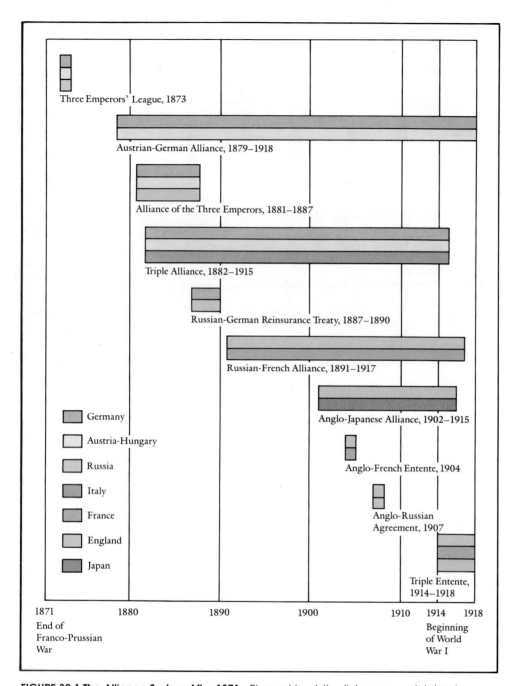

FIGURE 32.1 The Alliance System After 1871 Bismarck's subtle diplomacy maintained reasonably good relations among the eastern monarchies—Germany, Russia, and Austria-Hungary—and kept France isolated. The situation changed dramatically in 1891, when the Russian-French Alliance divided the Great Powers into two fairly equal military blocs.

Russia since the 1870s. William then adamantly refused to renew the Russian-German Reinsurance Treaty, in spite of Russian willingness to do so. This fateful departure in foreign affairs prompted long-isolated republican France to court absolutist Russia, offering loans, arms, and friendship. In both countries there were enthusiastic public demonstrations, and in St. Petersburg the autocratic Alexander III stood bareheaded on a French battleship while a band played the "Marseillaise," the hymn of the French Revolution. A preliminary agreement between the two countries was reached in 1891, and in early 1894 France and Russia became military allies. This alliance (see Figure 32.1) was to remain in effect as long as the Triple Alliance of Austria, Germany, and Italy: continental Europe was dangerously divided into two rival blocs.

The policy of Great Britain became increasingly crucial. Long content with "splendid isolation" and no permanent alliances, Britain after 1891 was Europe's only uncommitted Great Power. Could Britain afford to remain isolated, or would it feel compelled to take sides? Alliance with France or Russia certainly seemed highly unlikely. With its vast and rapidly expanding empire, Britain was often in serious conflict with these countries around the world in the heyday of imperialism.

Britain also squabbled with Germany, but many Germans and some Britons still believed that their statesmen would eventually formalize the "natural alliance" that they felt already united the advanced, racially related Germanic and Anglo-Saxon peoples. Such an understanding never materialized. Instead, the generally good relations that had prevailed between Prussia and Great Britain ever since the mid-eighteenth century, and certainly under Bismarck, gave way to a bitter Anglo-German rivalry.

There were several reasons for this tragic development. The hard-fought Boer War (1899–1902) between the British and the tiny Dutch republics of South Africa had a major impact on British policy. British statesmen saw that Britain was overextended around the world. The Boer War also brought into the open widespread anti-British feeling, as editorial writers in many nations denounced the latest manifestation of British imperialism. There was even talk of Germany, Austria, France, and Russia forming a grand alliance against the bloated but insatiable British Empire. Therefore British statesmen prudently set about shoring up their exposed position with alliances and agreements.

Britain improved its often-strained relations with the United States and in 1902 concluded a formal alliance with Japan (see Figure 32.1). Britain then responded favorably to the advances of France's skillful foreign minister, Théophile Delcassé, who wanted better relations with Britain and was willing to accept British rule in Egypt in return for British support of French plans to dominate Morocco. The resulting Anglo-French Entente of 1904 (see Figure 32.1) settled all outstanding colonial disputes between Britain and France.

Frustrated by Britain's turn toward France in 1904, Germany decided to test the strength of the entente and drive Britain and France apart. First Germany threatened and bullied France into dismissing Delcassé. However, rather than accept the typical territorial payoff of imperial competition— a slice of French jungle in Africa or a port in Morocco—in return for French primacy in Morocco, the Germans foolishly rattled their swords in 1905. Without presenting any precise or reasonable demands, the Germans insisted on an international conference in the Spanish city of Algeciras to examine all aspects of European influence in Morocco. Germany's crude bullying forced France and Britain closer together, and Germany left the Algeciras Conference of 1906 empty-handed and isolated (except for Austria-Hungary).

The result of the Moroccan crisis and the Algeciras Conference was something of a diplomatic revolution. Britain, France, Russia, and even the United States began to see Germany as a potential threat that might seek to dominate all Europe. At the same time, German leaders began to see sinister plots to "encircle" Germany and block its development as a world power. In 1907 Russia, battered by the disastrous war with Japan and the revolution of 1905, agreed to settle outstanding imperialist quarrels with Great Britain in Persia and in central Asia with a special Anglo-Russian Agreement (see Figure 32.1). As a result of that agreement, Germany's blustering paranoia increased and so did Britain's thinly disguised hostility.

Germany's decision to add a large, enormously expensive fleet of big-gun battleships to its already expanding navy also heightened tensions after 1907. German nationalists, led by the all-too-persuasive Admiral Alfred von Tirpitz, saw a large navy as the legitimate mark of a great world power. But British leaders like David Lloyd George saw it as a detestable military challenge, which forced them to spend the People's Budget on battleships rather than on social welfare. As Germany's rapid industrial growth allowed it to overcome Britain's early lead, economic rivalry also contributed to distrust and hostility between the two nations. Unscrupulous journalists and special-interest groups in both countries portrayed healthy competition in foreign trade and investment as a form of economic warfare.

In Britain and Germany, many educated shapers of public opinion and ordinary people were increasingly locked in a fateful love-hate relationship with the two countries. Proud nationalists in both countries simultaneously admired and feared the power and accomplishments of their nearly equal rival. In 1909 the mass-circulation London *Daily Mail* hysterically informed its readers in a series of reports that "Germany is deliberately preparing to destroy the British Empire."[2] By then, Britain was psychologically, if not officially, in the Franco-Russian camp. The leading nations of Europe were divided into two hostile blocs, both ill prepared to deal with upheaval on Europe's southeastern frontier.

The Outbreak of War

In the early years of the twentieth century, war in the Balkans was as inevitable as anything can be in human history. The reason was simple: nationalism was destroying the multinational Ottoman Empire and threatening to break up the Austro-Hungarian Empire. The only questions were what kinds of wars would occur and where they would lead.

Greece had long before led the struggle for national liberation, winning its independence in 1832. In 1875 widespread nationalist rebellion in the Ottoman Empire's European possessions resulted in Turkish repression, Russian intervention, and Great Power tensions. Bismarck helped resolve this crisis at the 1878 Congress of Berlin, which worked out the partial division of Ottoman holdings in Europe. Austria-Hungary obtained the right to "occupy and administer" Bosnia and Herzegovina. Serbia and Romania won complete independence, and a part of Bulgaria won local autonomy. The Ottoman Empire retained important

Balkan holdings, for Austria-Hungary and Russia each feared the other's domination of totally independent states in the area (Map 32.1).

After 1878 the siren call of imperialism lured European energies, particularly Russian energies, away from the Balkans. This division helped preserve the fragile balance of interests in southeastern Europe. By 1903, however, nationalism in the Balkans was on the rise once again. Serbia led the way, becoming openly hostile toward both Austria-Hungary and the Ottoman Empire. The Serbs, a Slavic people, looked to Slavic Russia for support of their national aspirations. To block Serbian expansion and to take advantage of Russia's weakness after the revolution of 1905, Austria in 1908 formally annexed Bosnia and Herzegovina with their predominantly Serbian populations. The kingdom of Serbia erupted in rage but could do nothing without Russian support.

Then in 1912, in the First Balkan War, Serbia turned southward. With Greece and Bulgaria it took Macedonia from the Ottoman Empire and then quarreled with its ally Bulgaria over the spoils of victory—a dispute that led in 1913 to the Second Balkan War. Austria intervened in 1913 and forced Serbia to give up Albania. After centuries, nationalism had finally destroyed the Ottoman Empire in Europe (Map 32.2). This sudden but long-awaited event elated the Balkan nationalists and dismayed the leaders of multinational Austria-Hungary. The former hoped and the latter feared that Austria might be next to be broken apart.

Within this tense context, Archduke Francis Ferdinand, heir to the Austrian and Hungarian thrones, and his wife Sophie were assassinated by Bosnian revolutionaries on June 28, 1914, during a state visit to the Bosnian capital of Sarajevo. The assassins were closely connected to the ultranationalist Serbian society The Black Hand. This revolutionary group was secretly supported by members of the Serbian government and was dedicated to uniting all Serbians in a single state. Although the leaders of Austria-Hungary did not and could not know all the details of Serbia's involvement in the assassination plot, they concluded after some hesitation that Serbia had to be severely punished once and for all. After a month of maneuvering, on July 23 Austria-Hungary presented Serbia with an unconditional ultimatum.

The Serbian government had just forty-eight hours in which to agree to cease all subversion in Austria and all anti-Austrian propaganda in

MAP 32.1 The Balkans After the Congress of Berlin, 1878 The Ottoman Empire suffered large territorial losses but remained a power in the Balkans.

MAP 32.2 The Balkans in 1914 Ethnic boundaries did not follow political boundaries, and Serbian national aspirations threatened Austria-Hungary.

Serbia. Moreover, a thorough investigation of all aspects of the assassination at Sarajevo was to be undertaken in Serbia by a joint commission of Serbian and Austrian officials. These demands amounted to control of the Serbian state. When Serbia replied moderately but evasively, Austria began to mobilize and then declared war on Serbia on July 28. Thus a desperate multinational Austria-Hungary deliberately chose war in a last-ditch attempt to stem the rising tide of hostile nationalism. The "Third Balkan War" had begun.

Of prime importance in Austria-Hungary's fateful decision was Germany's unconditional support. Emperor William II and his chancellor, Theobald von Bethmann-Hollweg (Bismarck had resigned in 1890), gave Austria-Hungary a "blank check" and urged aggressive measures in early July even

though they realized that war between Austria and Russia was the most probable result. They knew that Russian pan-Slavs saw Russia not only as the protector but also as the eventual liberator of southern Slavs. As one pan-Slav had said much earlier, "Austria can hold her part of the Slavonian mass as long as Turkey holds hers and vice versa."[3] At the very least a resurgent Russia could not stand by, as in the Bosnian crisis, and simply watch the Serbs be crushed. Yet Bethmann-Hollweg apparently hoped that while Russia (and therefore France) went to war, Great Britain would remain neutral, unwilling to fight over "Russian aggression" in the distant Balkans. After all, Britain had only "friendly understandings" with France and Russia on colonial questions and had no alliance with either power.

In fact, the diplomatic situation was already out of control. Military plans and timetables began to dictate policy. Russia, a vast country, would require much longer to mobilize its armies than Germany and Austria-Hungary. On July 28, as Austrian armies bombarded Belgrade, Tsar Nicholas II ordered a partial mobilization against Austria-Hungary. Almost immediately he found that this was impossible. All the complicated mobilization plans of the Russian general staff had assumed a war with both Austria and Germany: Russia could not mobilize against one without mobilizing against the other. On July 29, therefore, Russia ordered full mobilization and in effect declared general war.

The same tragic subordination of political considerations to military strategy descended on Germany. The German general staff had also thought only in terms of a two-front war. The German plan for war called for knocking out France first with a lightning attack through neutral Belgium before turning on Russia.

On August 2, 1914, General Helmuth von Moltke, "acting under a dictate of self-preservation," demanded that Belgium permit German armies to pass through its territory. Belgium, whose neutrality was solemnly guaranteed by all the great states including Prussia, refused. Germany attacked. Thus Germany's terrible, politically disastrous response to a war in the Balkans was an all-out invasion of France by way of the plains of neutral Belgium on August 3. In the face of this act of aggression, Great Britain declared war on Germany the following day. The First World War had begun.

Reflections on the Origins of the War

Although few events in history have aroused such interest and controversy as the coming of the First World War, the question of immediate causes and responsibilities can be answered with considerable certainty. Austria-Hungary deliberately started the "Third Balkan War." A war for the right to survive was Austria-Hungary's desperate, if understandable, response to the aggressive, yet also understandable, revolutionary drive of Serbian nationalists to unify their people in a single state. In spite of Russian intervention in the quarrel, it was clear from the beginning of the crisis that Germany not only pushed and goaded Austria-Hungary but was

also responsible for turning a little war into the Great War by means of its sledgehammer attack on Belgium and France. Why was this so?

After Bismarck's resignation in 1890, German leaders lost control of the international system. They felt increasingly that Germany's status as a world power was declining while that of Britain, France, Russia, and the United States was growing. Indeed, the powers of what officially became in August 1914 the Triple Entente (see Figure 32.1)—Great Britain, France, and Russia—were checking Germany's vague but real aspirations as well as working to strangle Austria-Hungary, Germany's only real ally. Germany's aggression in 1914 reflected the failure of all European statesmen, not just German leaders, to incorporate Bismarck's mighty empire permanently and peacefully into the international system.

There were other underlying causes. The new overseas expansion—imperialism—did not play a direct role, since the European powers always settled their colonial conflicts peacefully. Yet the easy imperialist victories did contribute to a general European overconfidence and reinforced national rivalries. In this respect imperialism was influential.

The triumph of nationalism was a crucial underlying precondition of the Great War. Nationalism—in the form of Serbian aspirations and the grandiose pan-German versus pan-Slavic racism of some fanatics—was at the heart of the Balkan wars. Nationalism drove the spiraling arms race. More generally, the aristocracy and middle classes arrived at nationalistic compromises while ordinary people looked toward increasingly responsive states for psychological and material well-being (see pages 945–953).

Broad popular commitment to "my country right or wrong" weakened groups that thought in terms of international communities and consequences. Thus the big international bankers, who were frightened by the prospect of war in July 1914, and the extreme-left socialists, who believed that the enemy was at home and not abroad, were equally out of step with national feeling.

Finally, the wealthy governing classes underestimated the risk of war in 1914. They had forgotten that great wars and great social revolutions very often go together in history. Metternich's alliance of conservative forces in support of international peace and the domestic status quo had become only a distant memory.

The First Battle of the Marne

When the Germans invaded Belgium in August 1914, they and everyone else believed that the war would be short, for urban society rested on the food and raw materials of the world economy: "The boys will be home by Christmas." The Belgian army heroically defended its homeland, however, and fell back in good order to join a rapidly landed British army corps near the Franco-Belgian border. This action complicated Germany's plan of concentrating its armies on the right wing and boldly capturing Paris in a vast encircling movement. By the end of August dead-tired German soldiers were advancing along an enormous front in the scorching summer heat. The neatly designed prewar plan to surround Paris from the north and west had been thrown into confusion.

French armies totaling 1 million, reinforced by more than 100,000 British troops, had retreated in orderly fashion before Germany's 1.5 million men in the field. Under the leadership of the steel-nerved General Joseph Joffre, the French attacked a gap in the German line at the Battle of the Marne on September 6. For three days, France threw everything into the attack. At one point, the French government desperately requisitioned all the taxis of Paris to rush reserves to the troops at the front. Finally, the Germans fell back. Paris and France had been miraculously saved.

Stalemate and Slaughter

The attempts of French and British armies to turn the German retreat into a rout were unsuccessful, and so were moves by both sides to outflank each other in northern France. As a result, both sides began to dig trenches to protect themselves from machine-gun fire. By November 1914, an unbroken line of trenches extended from the Belgian ports through northern France past the fortress of Verdun and on to the Swiss frontier.

In the face of this unexpected stalemate, slaughter on the western front began in earnest. Troops on both sides dug in behind rows of trenches, mines, and barbed wire. For weeks ceaseless shelling by heavy artillery supposedly "softened up" the enemy in a given area (and also signaled the coming attack). Then young draftees and their junior officers went "over the top" of the trenches in frontal attacks on the enemy's line.

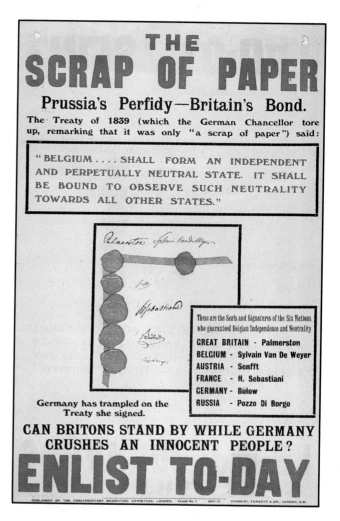

This British Poster shows the signature page of the 1839 treaty guaranteeing the neutrality of Belgium. When German armies invaded Belgium in 1914, Chancellor Bethmann-Hollweg cynically dismissed the treaty as a "scrap of paper"—a perfect line for anti-German propaganda. *(Source: By courtesy of the Trustees of the Imperial War Museum)*

The cost in lives was staggering, the gains in territory minuscule. The massive French and British offensives during 1915 never gained more than three miles of blood-soaked earth from the enemy. In the Battle of the Somme in the summer of 1916, the British and French gained an insignificant 125 square miles at the cost of 600,000 dead or wounded, while the Germans lost half a million men. That same year, the unsuccessful German campaign against Verdun cost 700,000 lives on both sides. The British poet Siegfried Sassoon

Preparing the Attack   The great offenses of the First World War required the mobilization of men and material on an unprecedented scale. This photo shows American troops moving up. *(Source: U.S. Army Signal Corps)*

(1886–1967) wrote of the Somme offensive: "I am staring at a sunlit picture of Hell."

Terrible 1917 saw General Robert Nivelle's French army almost destroyed in a grand spring attack at Champagne, while at Passchendaele in the fall, the British traded 400,000 casualties for fifty square miles of Belgian Flanders. The hero of Erich Maria Remarque's great novel *All Quiet on the Western Front* (1929) describes one such attack:

We see men living with their skulls blown open; we see soldiers run with their two feet cut off. Still the little piece of convulsed earth in which we lie is held. We have yielded no more than a few hundred yards of it as a prize to the enemy. But on every yard there lies a dead man.

Such was war on the western front.

The war of the trenches shattered an entire generation of young men. Millions who could have provided political creativity and leadership after the war were forever missing. Moreover, those who lived through the holocaust were maimed, shell-shocked, embittered, and profoundly disillusioned. The young soldiers went to war believing in the world of their leaders and elders, the pre-1914 world of order, progress, and patriotism. Then, in Remarque's words, the "first bombardment showed us our mistake, and under it the world as they had taught it to us broke in pieces." For many, the sacrifice and comradeship of the battlefield became life's crucial experience, an experience that "soft" civilians could never understand. A chasm opened up between veterans and civilians, making the difficult postwar reconstruction all the more difficult.

The Widening War

On the eastern front, slaughter did not degenerate into suicidal trench warfare. With the outbreak of the war, the "Russian steamroller" immediately moved into eastern Germany. Very badly damaged by the Germans under Generals Paul von Hindenburg and Erich Ludendorff at the battles of Tannenberg and the Masurian Lakes in August and September 1914, Russia never threatened Germany again. On the Austrian front, enormous armies seesawed back and forth, suffering enormous losses. Austro-Hungarian armies were repulsed twice by little Serbia in bitter fighting. But with the help of German forces, they reversed the Russian advances of 1914 and forced the Russians to retreat deep into their own territory in the eastern campaign of 1915. A staggering 2.5 million Russians were killed, wounded, or taken prisoner that year.

These changing tides of victory and hopes of territorial gains brought neutral countries into the war (Map 32.3). In Europe Italy, a member of the Triple Alliance since 1882, had declared its neutrality in 1914 on the grounds that Austria had launched a war of aggression. Then, in May 1915, Italy joined the Triple Entente of Great Britain, France, and Russia in return for promises of Austrian territory. Bulgaria also declared its neutrality in 1914. But after the Ottoman Empire joined in October 1914 with Austria and Germany, now known as the Central Powers, Bulgaria weighed enticing promises from all sides. In September 1915 it decided to follow the Ottoman Empire's lead in order to settle old scores with Serbia. Bulgarian and German armies were successful, and

The Fruits of War The extent of carnage, the emotional damage, and the physical destruction were equally unprecedented. Once great cathedrals standing in ruin symbolized the disaster. *(Source: UPI/Bettmann Newsphotos)*

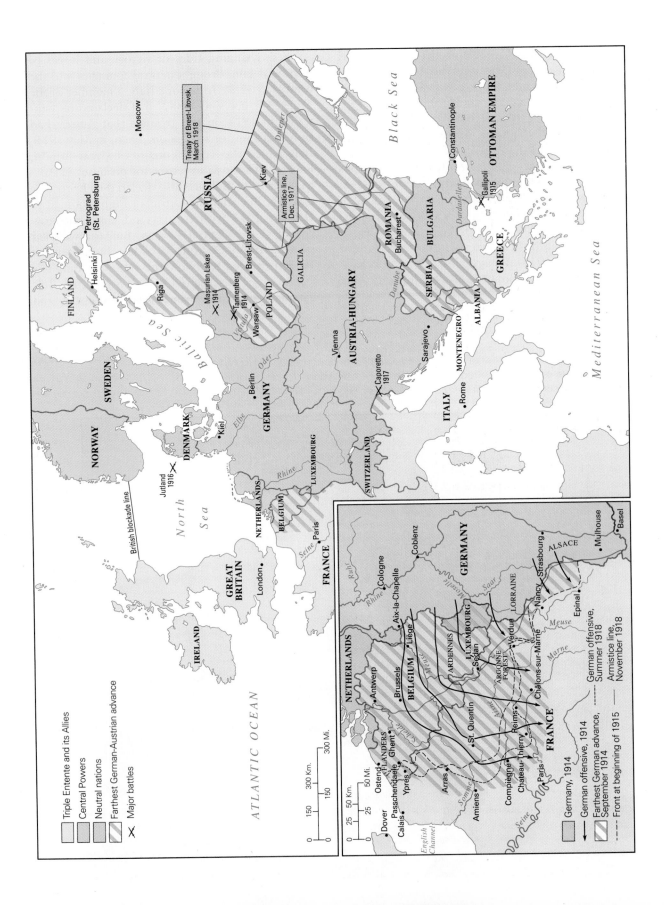

Treaty of Brest-Litovsk, March 1918

Armistice line, Dec. 1917

Main map labels:

Moscow

Petrograd (St. Petersburg)

Helsinki

FINLAND

RUSSIA

Kiev

Riga

Masurian Lakes 1914

Tannenberg 1914

Warsaw

POLAND

Brest-Litovsk

GALICIA

Vienna

AUSTRIA-HUNGARY

Caporetto 1917

ROMANIA

Bucharest

BULGARIA

SERBIA

Sarajevo

MONTENEGRO

ALBANIA

GREECE

Constantinople

OTTOMAN EMPIRE

Gallipoli 1915

Dardanelles

Black Sea

Mediterranean Sea

Danube

SWEDEN

NORWAY

Baltic Sea

Berlin

GERMANY

Kiel

Elbe

Oder

Vistula

Dnieper

DENMARK

Jutland 1916

North Sea

British blockade line

NETHERLANDS

BELGIUM

LUXEMBOURG

Rhine

SWITZERLAND

ITALY

Rome

Paris

Seine

FRANCE

GREAT BRITAIN

London

IRELAND

ATLANTIC OCEAN

Legend (main map):

- Triple Entente and its Allies
- Central Powers
- Neutral nations
- Farthest German-Austrian advance
- ✕ Major battles

Scale:

0 150 300 Km.

0 150 300 Mi.

Inset map labels:

NETHERLANDS

Antwerp

Brussels

BELGIUM

Ghent

FLANDERS

Ostend

Passchendaele

Ypres

Dover

Calais

English Channel

GERMANY

Coblenz

Cologne

Aix-la-Chapelle

Liège

Ruhr

Rhine

Moselle

Alsace

Saar

LUXEMBOURG

ARDENNES

Sedan

ARGONNE FOREST

Verdun

LORRAINE

Nancy

Strasbourg

ALSACE

Mulhouse

Basel

Épinal

Meuse

Marne

Châlons-sur-Marne

Château-Thierry

Reims

Compiègne

St. Quentin

Somme

Arras

Amiens

Meuse

Scheldt

Aisne

Seine

Paris

FRANCE

Legend (inset map):

- Germany, 1914
- → German offensive, 1914
- Farthest German advance, September 1914
- --- Front at beginning of 1915
- --- German offensive, Summer 1918
- — Armistice line, November 1918

Scale (inset):

0 25 50 Km.

0 25 50 Mi.

the Central Powers occupied all of the Balkans, with the exception of Greece.

The entry of the Ottoman Turks carried the war into the Middle East, a momentous development. Heavy fighting with Russia saw bloody battle lines seesawing back and forth. In 1915 British forces tried to take the Dardanelles and Constantinople from Turkey, but they were badly defeated. The British were more successful at inciting Arab nationalists against their Turkish overlords. An enigmatic British colonel, soon known to millions as Lawrence of Arabia, helped lead the Arab revolt in early 1917. In 1918 British armies totally smashed the old Ottoman state, drawing primarily on imperial forces from Egypt, India, Australia, and New Zealand. Thus war brought revolutionary change to the Middle East (see pages 1075–1079).

War also spread to some parts of East Asia and Africa. Instead of revolting as the Germans hoped, the colonial subjects of the British and French supported their foreign masters, providing critical supplies and fighting in armies in Europe and in the Ottoman Empire. They also helped local British and French commanders seize Germany's colonies around the globe. The Japanese, allied in Asia with the British since 1902, similarly used the war to grab German outposts in the Pacific Ocean and on the Chinese mainland, infuriating Chinese patriots and heightening long-standing tensions between the two countries.

Another crucial development in the expanding conflict came in April 1917, when the United States declared war on Germany. American intervention grew out of the war at sea, sympathy for the entente, and the increasing desperation of total war. At the beginning of the war, Britain and France had established a total naval blockade to strangle the Central Powers and prevent deliveries of food and raw materials. No neutral ship could sail to Germany with any cargo. The blockade irked Americans, but effective propaganda over German atrocities in occupied Belgium and lush profits from selling war supplies to Britain and France blunted American indignation.

MAP 32.3 The First World War in Europe The trench war on the western front was concentrated in Belgium and northern France. The war in the east encompassed an enormous territory.

Moreover, in early 1915 Germany launched a counter-blockade using the murderously effective submarine, a new weapon that violated traditional niceties of fair warning under international law. In May 1915, after sinking about ninety ships in the British war zone, a German submarine sank the British passenger liner *Lusitania,* which was carrying arms and munitions as well as passengers. More than a thousand lives, among them 139 Americans, were lost. President Woodrow Wilson protested vigorously, forcing Germany to relax its submarine warfare for almost two years; the alternative would have been almost certain U.S. entry into the war.

Early in 1917, the German military command—confident that improved submarines could starve its island enemy, Britain, into submission before the United States could come to Britain's rescue—resumed unrestricted submarine warfare. Like the invasion of Belgium, this was a reckless gamble. British shipping losses reached staggering proportions, though by late 1917 naval strategists came up with the inevitable effective response: the convoy system for safe transatlantic shipping. In the meantime, President Wilson had told a sympathetic Congress and people that the "German submarine warfare against commerce is a warfare against mankind." Thus the last uncommitted great nation, as fresh and enthusiastic as Europe had been in 1914, entered the world war in April 1917, almost three years after it had begun. Eventually the United States was to tip the balance in favor of the Triple Entente and its allies.

THE HOME FRONT

The widening Great War had significant economic, social, and political repercussions for the people on the home front. The people behind the lines were tremendously involved in the titanic struggle. War's impact on them was no less massive than on the men crouched in the trenches.

Mobilizing for Total War

In August 1914 most people in Europe greeted the outbreak of hostilities enthusiastically. The masses in every country believed that their nation was in the right and defending itself from aggression. With the exception of a few extreme left-wingers, even socialists supported the war. Tough standby plans to imprison socialist leaders and break general strikes protesting the war proved quite unnecessary in 1914. Everywhere patriotic support of the masses and the working class contributed to national unity and an energetic war effort.

By mid-October generals and politicians began to realize that more than patriotism would be needed to win the war, whose end was not in sight. Each country experienced a relentless, desperate demand for men and weapons. Countless shortages quickly developed. In each European country economic life and organization had to change and change fast to keep the war machine from sputtering to a stop. And change they did.

In each country a government of national unity began to plan and control economic and social life in order to wage "total war." Free-market capitalism was abandoned, at least "for the duration." Instead, government planning boards established priorities and decided what was to be produced and consumed. Rationing, price and wage controls, and even restrictions on workers' freedom of movement were imposed by government. Only through such regimentation could a country make the greatest possible military effort. Thus, though there were national variations, the great nations all moved toward planned economies commanded by the established political leadership.

The economy of total war blurred the old distinction between soldiers on the battlefield and civilians at home. The war was a war of whole peoples and entire populations, and the loser would be the society that cracked first. Interestingly enough, the ability of governments to manage and control highly complicated economies strengthened the cause of socialism. With the First World War, socialism became for the first time a realistic economic blueprint rather than a utopian program.

Germany illustrates the general trend. It also went furthest in developing a planned economy to wage total war. As soon as war began, Walter Rathenau, the talented, foresighted Jewish industrialist in charge of Germany's largest electrical company, convinced the government to set up a War Raw Materials Board to ration and distribute raw materials. Under Rathenau's direction, every useful material from foreign oil to barnyard manure was inventoried and rationed. Moreover, the board launched spectacularly successful attempts to produce substitutes, such as synthetic rubber and synthetic nitrates, which were essential to the German war machine.

Food was also rationed in accordance with physical need. Men and women doing hard manual work were given extra rations. During the last two years of the war, only children and expectant mothers received milk rations. At the same time, Germany failed to tax the war profits of private firms heavily enough. This failure contributed to massive deficit financing, inflation, the growth of a black market, and the eventual re-emergence of class conflict.

Following the terrible battles of Verdun and the Somme in 1916, the military leaders Hindenburg and Ludendorff became the real rulers of Germany, and they decreed the ultimate mobilization for total war. Germany, said Hindenburg, could win only "if all the treasures of our soil that agriculture and industry can produce are used exclusively for the conduct of War. . . . All other considerations must come second."[4] This goal, they believed, required that every German man, woman, and child be drafted into the service of the war. Thus, in December 1916, the military leaders rammed through the parliament the Auxiliary Service Law, which required all males between seventeen and sixty to work only at jobs considered critical to the war effort.

Although women and children were not specifically mentioned, this forced-labor law was also aimed at them. Many women already worked in war factories, mines, and steel mills, where they labored like men at the heaviest and most dangerous jobs. With the passage of the Auxiliary Service Law, many more women followed. Children were organized by their teachers into garbage brigades to collect every scrap of useful material: grease strained from dishwater, coffee grounds, waste paper, tin cans, metal door knockers, bottles, rags, hair, bones, and so forth, as well as acorns, chestnuts, pine cones, and rotting leaves. Potatoes gave way to turnips, and people averaged little more than a thousand calories a day. Thus in Germany total war led to the establishment of history's first "totalitarian" society, and war production increased while some people literally starved to death.

Great Britain mobilized for total war less rapidly and less completely than Germany, for it could im-

Waging Total War   A British war plant strains to meet the insatiable demand for trench-smashing heavy artillery shells. Quite typically, many of these defense workers are women. *(Source: By courtesy of the Trustees of the Imperial War Museum)*

port materials from its empire and from the United States. By 1915, however, a serious shortage of shells led to the establishment of a Ministry of Munitions under David Lloyd George. The ministry organized private industry to produce for the war, controlled profits, allocated labor, fixed wage rates, and settled labor disputes. By December 1916, when Lloyd George became prime minister, the British economy was largely planned and regulated. More than two hundred factories and 90 percent of all imports were bought and allocated directly by the state. Subsequently, even food was strictly rationed. War production continued to soar. Great Britain followed successfully in Germany's footsteps.

The Social Impact

The social impact of total war was no less profound than the economic impact, though again there were important national variations. The millions of men at the front and the insatiable needs of the military created a tremendous demand for workers. Jobs were available for everyone. This situation had seldom if ever been seen before 1914, when unemployment and poverty had been facts of urban life. The exceptional demand for labor brought about momentous changes.

One such change was greater power and prestige for labor unions. Having proved their loyalty in August 1914, labor unions became an indispensable partner of government and private industry in the planned war economies. Unions cooperated with war governments on work rules, wages, and production schedules in return for real participation in important decisions. This entry of labor leaders and unions into policy-making councils paralleled the entry of socialist leaders into the war governments.

The role of women changed dramatically. In every country, large numbers of women left home and domestic service to work in industry, transportation, and offices. By 1917 women formed fully 43 percent of the labor force in Russia. Moreover, women became highly visible—not only as munitions workers but as bank tellers, mail carriers, even police officers.

At first, the male-dominated unions were hostile to women moving into new occupations, believing that their presence would lower wages and change work rules. But government pressure and the principle of equal pay for equal work (at least until the end of the war) overcame these objections. Women also served as nurses and doctors at the front. In general, the war greatly expanded the range of women's activities and changed attitudes toward them. As a direct result of women's many-sided war effort, Britain, Germany, and Austria granted women the right to vote immediately after the war. Women also showed a growing spirit of independence during the war as they started to bob their hair, shorten their skirts, and smoke in public.

War also promoted social equality, blurring class distinctions and lessening the gap between rich and poor. This blurring was most apparent in Great Britain, where wartime hardship was never extreme. In fact, the bottom third of the population generally lived better than ever before, for the poorest gained most from the severe shortage of labor. The English writer Robert Roberts recalled how his parents' tiny grocery store in the slums of Manchester thrived as never before during the war, when people who had scrimped to buy bread and soup bones were able to afford fancy cakes and thick steaks. In continental countries greater equality was reflected in full employment, ration-

Wartime Propaganda was skillful and effective. The poster on the left spurred men to volunteer for military service before the draft was introduced in Britain in 1916. The poster on the right appeals to patriotism and the love of family as it urges the French to buy another batch of war bonds. *(Source: By courtesy of the Trustees of the Imperial War Museum)*

ing according to physical need, and a sharing of hardship. There, too, society became more uniform and more egalitarian, in spite of some war profiteering.

Death itself had no respect for traditional social distinctions. It savagely decimated the young aristocratic officers who led the charge, and it fell heavily on the mass of drafted peasants and unskilled workers who followed. Yet death often spared the aristocrats of labor, the skilled workers and foremen. Their lives were too valuable to squander at the front, for they were needed to train and direct the newly recruited women and older unskilled men laboring valiantly in war plants at home.

Growing Political Tensions

During the first two years of war, most soldiers and civilians supported their governments. Even in Austria-Hungary—the most vulnerable of the belligerents, with its competing nationalities—loyalty to the state and monarchy remained astonishingly strong through 1916. Belief in a just cause, patriotic nationalism, the planned economy, and a sharing of burdens united peoples behind their various national leaders. Furthermore, each government did its best to control public opinion to bolster morale. Newspapers, letters, and public addresses were rigorously censored. Good news was overstated; bad news was repressed or distorted.

Each government used both crude and subtle propaganda to maintain popular support. German propaganda hysterically pictured black soldiers from France's African empire raping German women, and German atrocities in Belgium and elsewhere were ceaselessly recounted and exaggerated by the French and British. Patriotic posters and slogans, slanted news, and biased editorials inflamed national hatreds and helped sustain superhuman efforts.

By the spring of 1916, however, people were beginning to crack under the strain of total war. In April 1916, Irish nationalists in Dublin tried to take advantage of this situation and rose up against British rule in their Easter Rebellion. A week of bitter fighting passed before the rebels were crushed and their leaders executed. Strikes and protest marches over inadequate food began to flare up on every home front. Soldiers' morale began to decline. Italian troops mutinied. Numer-

ous French units refused to fight after General Nivelle's disastrous offensive of May 1917. A rising tide of war-weariness and defeatism also swept France's civilian population before Georges Clemenceau emerged as a ruthless and effective wartime leader in November 1917. Clemenceau established a virtual dictatorship, pouncing on strikers and jailing without trial journalists and politicians who dared to suggest a compromise peace with Germany.

The strains were worse for the Central Powers. In October 1916, the chief minister of Austria was assassinated by a young socialist crying, "Down with Absolutism! We want peace!"[5] The following month, when the feeble old Emperor Francis Joseph died sixty-eight years after his mother Sophia had pushed him onto the throne in 1848 (see page 891), a symbol of unity disappeared. In spite of absolute censorship, political dissatisfaction and conflicts among nationalities grew. In April 1917, Austria's chief minister summed up the situation in the gloomiest possible terms. The country and army were exhausted. Another winter of war would bring revolution and disintegration, he predicted. The allied blockade kept tightening; people were starving.

The strain of total war and of the Auxiliary Service Law was also evident in Germany. In the winter of 1916 to 1917, Germany's military position appeared increasingly desperate. Stalemates and losses in the west were matched by temporary Russian advances in the east. Thus the military insisted on the all-or-nothing gamble of unrestricted submarine warfare when the Entente refused in December 1916 to consider peace on terms favorable to the Central Powers.

Also, the national political unity of the first two years of war was collapsing as the social conflict of prewar Germany re-emerged. A growing minority of socialists in the parliament began to vote against war credits, calling for a compromise "peace without annexations or reparations." In July 1917, a coalition of socialists and Catholics passed a resolution in the parliament to that effect. Such a peace was unthinkable for conservatives and military leaders. So also was the surge in revolutionary agitation and strikes by war-weary workers that occurred in early 1917. When the bread ration was further reduced in April, more than 200,000 workers struck and demonstrated for a week in Berlin, returning to work only under the threat of prison and military discipline. Thus militaristic Germany, like its ally Austria-Hungary (and its enemy France), was beginning to crack in 1917. Yet it was Russia that collapsed first and saved the Central Powers, for a time.

THE RUSSIAN REVOLUTION

The Russian Revolution of 1917 was one of modern history's most momentous events. Directly related to the growing tensions of the First World War, its significance went far beyond the wartime agonies of a single European nation. The Russian Revolution opened a new era. For some it was Marx's socialist vision come true; for others, it was the triumph of dictatorship. To all, it presented a radically new prototype of state and society.

The Fall of Imperial Russia

Like its allies and its enemies, Russia embraced war with patriotic enthusiasm in 1914. At the Winter Palace, while throngs of people knelt and sang "God Save the Tsar," Tsar Nicholas II (r. 1894–1917) repeated the oath that Alexander I had made in 1812 and vowed never to make peace as long as the enemy stood on Russian soil. Russia's lower house, the Duma, voted war credits. Conservatives anticipated expansion in the Balkans, while liberals and most socialists believed alliance with Britain and France would bring democratic reforms. For a moment, Russia was united.

Soon, however, the strains of war began to take their toll. Unprecedented artillery barrages used up Russia's supplies of shells and ammunition, and better-equipped German armies inflicted terrible losses. For a time in 1915, substantial numbers of Russian soldiers were sent to the front without rifles; they were told to find their arms among the dead. There were 2 million Russian casualties in 1915 alone. Morale declined among soldiers and civilians. Nonetheless, Russia's battered peasant army did not collapse but continued to fight courageously until early 1917.

Under the shock of defeat, Russia moved toward full mobilization on the home front. The Duma and organs of local government took the lead, setting up special committees to coordinate defense, industry, transportation, and agriculture. These efforts improved the military situation, and Rus-

sian factories produced more than twice as many shells in 1916 as in 1915. Yet there were many failures, and Russia mobilized less effectively for total war than the other warring nations.

The great problem was leadership. Under the constitution resulting from the revolution of 1905 (see pages 944–945), the tsar had retained complete control over the bureaucracy and the army. Legislation proposed by the Duma, which was weighted in favor of the wealthy and conservative classes, was subject to the tsar's veto. Moreover, Nicholas II fervently wished to maintain the sacred inheritance of supreme royal power, which with the Orthodox church was for him the key to Russia's greatness. A kindly, slightly stupid man, Nicholas failed to form a close partnership with his citizens in order to fight the war more effectively. He relied instead on the old bureaucratic apparatus, distrusting the moderate Duma, rejecting popular involvement, and resisting calls to share power.

As a result, the Duma, the educated middle classes, and the masses became increasingly critical of the tsar's leadership. Following Nicholas's belated dismissal of the incompetent minister of war, demands for more democratic and responsive government exploded in the Duma in the summer of 1915. In September, parties ranging from conservative to moderate socialist formed the Progressive Bloc, which called for a completely new government responsible to the Duma instead of to the tsar. In answer, Nicholas temporarily adjourned the Duma and announced that he was traveling to the front in order to lead and rally Russia's armies.

His departure was a fatal turning point. With the tsar in the field with the troops, control of the government was taken over by the hysterical empress, Tsarina Alexandra, and a debauched adventurer, the monk Rasputin. A minor German princess and granddaughter of England's Queen Victoria, Nicholas's wife was a devoted mother with a sick child, a strong-willed woman with a hatred of parliaments. Having constantly urged her husband to rule absolutely, Alexandra tried to do so herself in his absence. She seated and unseated the top ministers. Her most trusted adviser was "our Friend Grigori," an uneducated Siberian preacher who was appropriately nicknamed Rasputin—the "Degenerate."

Rasputin began his career with a sect noted for mixing sexual orgies with religious ecstasies, and his influence rested on mysterious healing powers.

Alexis, Alexandra's fifth child and heir to the throne, suffered from a rare disease, hemophilia. The tiniest cut meant uncontrollable bleeding, terrible pain, and possible death. Medical science could do nothing. Only Rasputin could miraculously stop the bleeding, perhaps through hypnosis. The empress's faith in Rasputin was limitless. "Believe more in our Friend," she wrote her husband in 1916. "He lives for you and Russia." In this atmosphere of unreality, the government slid steadily toward revolution.

In a desperate attempt to right the situation and end unfounded rumors that Rasputin was the empress's lover, three members of the high aristocracy murdered Rasputin in December 1916. The empress went into semipermanent shock, her mind haunted by the dead man's prophecy: "If I die or you desert me, in six months you will lose your son

and your throne."[6] Food shortages in the cities worsened, morale declined. On March 8, women in Petrograd (formerly St. Petersburg) calling for bread started riots, which spontaneously spread to the factories and throughout the city. From the front the tsar ordered the troops to restore order, but discipline broke down and the soldiers joined the revolutionary crowd. The Duma responded by declaring a provisional government on March 12, 1917. Three days later, Nicholas abdicated without protest.

The Provisional Government

The March revolution was the result of an unplanned uprising of hungry, angry people in the capital, but it was joyfully accepted throughout the

Mass Demonstrations in Petrograd in June 1917 showed a surge of working-class support for the Bolsheviks. In this photo a few banners of the Mensheviks and other moderate socialists are drowned in a sea of Bolshevik slogans. *(Source: Sovfoto)*

country. The patriotic upper and middle classes rejoiced at the prospect of a more determined and effective war effort, while workers happily anticipated better wages and more food. All classes and political parties called for liberty and democracy. They were not disappointed. As Lenin said, Russia became the freest country in the world. After generations of arbitrary authoritarianism, the provisional government quickly established equality before the law; freedom of religion, speech, and assembly; the right of unions to organize and strike; and the rest of the classic liberal program.

Yet both the liberal and the moderate socialist leaders of the provisional government rejected social revolution. The reorganized government formed in May 1917, which included the fiery agrarian socialist Alexander Kerensky, refused to confiscate large landholdings and give them to peasants, fearing that such drastic action in the countryside would only complete the disintegration of Russia's peasant army. For the patriotic Kerensky, as for other moderate socialists, the continuation of war was still the all-important national duty. There would be plenty of time for land reform later, and thus all the government's efforts were directed toward a last offensive in July. Human suffering and war-weariness grew, sapping the limited strength of the provisional government.

From its first day, the provisional government had to share power with a formidable rival—the Petrograd Soviet (or council) of Workers' and Soldiers' Deputies. Modeled on the revolutionary soviets of 1905, the Petrograd Soviet was a huge, fluctuating mass meeting of two to three thousand workers, soldiers, and socialist intellectuals. Seeing itself as a true grass-roots revolutionary democracy, this counter- or half-government suspiciously watched the provisional government and issued its own radical orders, further weakening the provisional government. The most famous of these orders was Army Order No. 1, issued to all Russian military forces as the provisional government was forming.

Order No. 1 stripped officers of their authority and placed power in the hands of elected committees of common soldiers. Designed to protect the revolution from some counter-revolutionary Bonaparte on horseback, Army Order No. 1 instead led to a total collapse of army discipline. Many an officer was hanged for his sins. Meanwhile, following the foolhardy summer offensive,

masses of peasant soldiers began "voting with their feet," to use Lenin's graphic phrase. They began returning to their villages to help their families get a share of the land, land that peasants were simply seizing as they settled old scores in a great agrarian upheaval. All across the country, liberty was turning into anarchy in the summer of 1917. It was an unparalleled opportunity for the most radical and most talented of Russia's many socialist leaders, Vladimir Ilyich Lenin (1870–1924).

Lenin and the Bolshevik Revolution

Lenin's whole life was dedicated to the cause of revolution. He was born into the middle class and at seventeen became an implacable enemy of imperial Russia when his older brother was executed for plotting to kill the tsar in 1887. As a law student he began searching for a revolutionary faith. He found it in Marxian socialism, which began to win converts among radical intellectuals as industrialization surged forward in Russia in the 1890s. Exiled to Siberia for three years because of socialist agitation, Lenin studied Marxist doctrines with religious intensity. After his release, he joined fellow believers in western Europe. There Lenin lived for seventeen years and developed his own revolutionary interpretations of the body of Marxian thought.

Three interrelated ideas were central for Lenin. First, turning to the early fire-breathing Marx of 1848 and the *Communist Manifesto* for inspiration, Lenin stressed that capitalism could be destroyed only by violent revolution. He tirelessly denounced all revisionist theories of a peaceful evolution to socialism as betraying Marx's message of unending class conflict. Lenin's second, more original, idea was that under certain conditions a socialist revolution was possible even in a relatively backward country like Russia. Though capitalism was not fully developed there and the industrial working class was small, the peasants were poor and thus potential revolutionaries.

Lenin believed that at a given moment revolution was determined more by human leadership than by vast historical laws. Thus came Lenin's third basic idea: the necessity of a highly disciplined workers' party, strictly controlled by a dedicated elite of intellectuals and full-time revolutionaries like Lenin himself. Unlike ordinary workers and trade-union officials, this elite would never be seduced by short-term gains. It would not stop until revolution brought it to power.

Lenin's theories and methods did not go unchallenged by other Russian Marxists. At the meetings of the Russian Social Democratic Labor party in London in 1903, matters came to a head. Lenin demanded a small, disciplined, elitist party; his opponents wanted a more democratic party with mass membership. The Russian party of Marxian socialism promptly split into two factions. Lenin's camp was called Bolsheviks, or "Majority group"; his opponents were Mensheviks, or "Minority group." Lenin's majority did not last, but Lenin did not care. He kept the fine-sounding name Bolshevik and developed the party he wanted: tough, disciplined, revolutionary.

Unlike most socialists, Lenin did not rally round the national flag in 1914. Observing events from neutral Switzerland, he saw the war as a product of imperialistic rivalries and a marvelous opportunity for class war and socialist upheaval. The March revolution was, Lenin felt, a step in that direction. Since propaganda and internal subversion were accepted weapons of total war, the German government graciously provided the impatient Lenin, his wife, and about twenty trusted colleagues with safe passage across Germany and back into Russia in April 1917. The Germans hoped that Lenin would undermine the sagging war effort of the world's freest society. They were not disappointed.

Arriving triumphantly at Petrograd's Finland Station on April 3, Lenin attacked at once. To the great astonishment of the local Bolsheviks, he rejected all cooperation with the "bourgeois" provisional government of the liberals and moderate socialists. His slogans were radical in the extreme: "All power to the Soviets." "All land to the peasants." "Stop the war now." Never a slave to Marxist determinism, the brilliant but not unduly intellectual Lenin was a superb tactician. The moment was now.

Yet Lenin almost overplayed his hand. An attempt by the Bolsheviks to seize power in July collapsed, and Lenin fled and went into hiding. He was charged with being a German agent, and indeed he and the Bolsheviks were getting money from Germany.[7] But no matter. Intrigue between Kerensky, who became prime minister in July, and his commander in chief General Lavr Kornilov, a popular war hero "with the heart of a lion and the brains of a sheep," resulted in Kornilov's leading a feeble attack against the provisional government in

Vladimir Lenin *Dramatically displaying both his burning determination and his skill as a revolutionary orator, Lenin addresses the victorious May Day celebration of 1918 in Moscow's Red Square. (Source: Culver Pictures)*

September. In the face of this rightist "counter-revolutionary" threat, the Bolsheviks were rearmed and redeemed. Kornilov's forces disintegrated, but Kerensky lost all credit with the army, the only force that might have saved him and democratic government in Russia.

Trotsky and the Seizure of Power

Throughout the summer, the Bolsheviks had appealed very effectively to the workers and soldiers of Petrograd, markedly increasing their popular support. Party membership had soared from

THE RUSSIAN REVOLUTION

1914	Russia enthusiastically enters the First World War
1915	Two million Russian casualties
	Progressive Bloc calls for a new government responsible to the Duma rather than to the tsar
	Tsar Nicholas adjourns the Duma and departs for the front; control of the government falls to Alexandra and Rasputin
December 1916	Murder of Rasputin
March 8, 1917	Bread riots in Petrograd (St. Petersburg)
March 12, 1917	Duma declares a provisional government
March 15, 1917	Tsar Nicholas abdicates without protest
April 3, 1917	Lenin returns from exile and denounces the provisional government
May 1917	Reorganized provisional government, including Kerensky, continues the war
	Petrograd Soviet issues Army Order no. 1, granting military power to committees of common soldiers
Summer 1917	Agrarian upheavals: peasants seize estates, peasant soldiers desert the army to participate
October 1917	Bolsheviks gain a majority in the Petrograd Soviet
November 6, 1917	Bolsheviks seize power; Lenin heads the new "provisional workers' and peasants' government"
November 1917	Lenin ratifies peasant seizure of land and worker control of factories; all banks nationalized
January 1918	Lenin permanently disbands the Constituent Assembly
February 1918	Lenin convinces the Bolshevik Central Committee to accept a humiliating peace with Germany in order to pursue the revolution
March 1918	Treaty of Brest-Litovsk: Russia loses one-third of its population
	Trotsky as war commissar begins to rebuild the Russian army
	Government moves from Petrograd to Moscow
1918–1920	Great Civil War
Summer 1918	Eighteen competing regional governments; White armies oppose the Bolshevik revolution
1919	White armies on the offensive but divided politically; they receive little benefit from Allied intervention
1920	Lenin and Red armies victorious, retaking Belorussia and the Ukraine

50,000 to 240,000, and in October the Bolsheviks gained a fragile majority in the Petrograd Soviet. Moreover, Lenin had found a strong right arm—Leon Trotsky, the second most important person in the Russian Revolution.

A spellbinding revolutionary orator and independent radical Marxist, Trotsky (1877–1940) supported Lenin wholeheartedly in 1917. It was he who brilliantly executed the Bolshevik seizure of power. Painting a vivid but untruthful picture of German and counter-revolutionary plots, Trotsky first convinced the Petrograd Soviet to form a special Military-Revolutionary Committee in October and make him its leader. Military power in the capital passed into Bolshevik hands. Trotsky's second master stroke was to insist that the Bolsheviks reduce opposition to their coup by taking power in the name, not of the Bolsheviks, but of the more popular and democratic soviets, which were meeting in Petrograd from all over Russia in early November. On the night of November 6, militants from Trotsky's committee joined with trusty Bolshevik soldiers to seize government buildings and pounce on members of the provisional government. Then on to the congress of soviets! There a Bolshevik majority—roughly

THE RUSSIAN REVOLUTION 1059

390 of 650 turbulent delegates—declared that all power had passed to the soviets and named Lenin head of the new government.

The Bolsheviks came to power for three key reasons. First, by late 1917 democracy had given way to anarchy: power was there for those who would take it. Second, in Lenin and Trotsky the Bolsheviks had an utterly determined and truly superior leadership, which both the tsarist government and the provisional government lacked. Third, in 1917 the Bolsheviks succeeded in appealing to many soldiers and urban workers, people who were exhausted by war and eager for socialism. With time, many workers would become bitterly disappointed, but for the moment they had good reason to believe that they had won what they wanted.

Dictatorship and Civil War

History is full of short-lived coups and unsuccessful revolutions. The truly monumental accomplishment of Lenin, Trotsky, and the rest of the Bolsheviks was not taking power but keeping it. In the next four years, the Bolsheviks went on to conquer the chaos they had helped to create, and they began to build their kind of socialist society. How was this done?

Lenin had the genius to profit from developments over which he and the Bolsheviks had no control. Since summer, a peasant revolution had been sweeping across Russia as the tillers of the soil invaded and divided among themselves the great and not-so-great estates of the landlords and the church. Peasant seizure of the land—a Russian 1789—was not very Marxist, but it was quite unstoppable in 1917. Thus Lenin's first law, which supposedly gave land to the peasants, actually merely approved what peasants were already doing. Urban workers' great demand in November was direct control of individual factories by local workers' committees. This, too, Lenin ratified with a decree in November.

Unlike many of his colleagues, Lenin acknowledged that Russia had lost the war with Germany, that the Russian army had ceased to exist, and that the only realistic goal was peace at any price. The price was very high. Germany demanded in December 1917 that the Soviet government give up all its western territories. These areas were inhabited by Poles, Finns, Lithuanians, and other non-

Russians—all those peoples who had been conquered by the tsars over three centuries and put into the "prisonhouse of nationalities," as Lenin had earlier called the Russian Empire.

At first, Lenin's fellow Bolsheviks would not accept such great territorial losses. But when German armies resumed their unopposed march into Russia in February 1918, Lenin had his way in a very close vote in the Central Committee of the party. In the words of a noted American scholar, "Not even his greatest enemy can deny that at this moment Lenin towered like a giant over his Bolshevik colleagues."[8] A third of old Russia's population was sliced away by the German meat ax in the Treaty of Brest-Litovsk in March 1918. With peace, Lenin escaped the certain disaster of continued war and could uncompromisingly pursue his goal of absolute political power for the Bolsheviks—now renamed Communists—within Russia.

In November 1917, the Bolsheviks had proclaimed their regime only a "provisional workers' and peasants' government," promising that a freely elected Constituent Assembly would draw up a new constitution. But the freest elections in Russia's history—both before and after 1917—produced a stunning setback for the Bolsheviks, who won less than one-fourth of the elected delegates. The Socialist Revolutionaries—the peasants' party—had a clear majority. The Constituent Assembly met for only one day, on January 18, 1918. It was then permanently disbanded by Bolshevik soldiers acting under Lenin's orders. Thus, even before the peace with Germany, Lenin was forming a one-party government.

The dissolution of the democratically elected Constituent Assembly helped feed the flames of civil war. People who had risen up for self-rule in November saw that once again they were getting dictatorship from the capital. For the next three years, "Long live the democratic soviets; down with the Bolsheviks" was to be a popular slogan. The officers of the old army took the lead in organizing the "White" opposition to the Bolsheviks in southern Russia and the Ukraine, in Siberia, and to the west of Petrograd. The Whites came from many social groups and were united only by their hatred of the Bolsheviks—the Reds.

By the summer of 1918, fully eighteen self-proclaimed regional governments—several of which represented minority nationalities—competed with Lenin's Bolsheviks in Moscow. By the end of the year, White armies were on the attack.

In October 1919, it appeared that they might triumph as they closed in on Lenin's government from three sides. Yet they did not. By the spring of 1920, the White armies had been almost completely defeated, and the Bolshevik Red Army had retaken Belorussia and the Ukraine. The following year, the Communists also reconquered the independent nationalist governments of the Caucasus. The civil war was over; Lenin had won.

Lenin and the Bolsheviks won for several reasons. Strategically, they controlled the center while the Whites were always on the fringes and disunited. Moreover, the poorly defined political program of the Whites was vaguely conservative, and it did not unite all the foes of the Bolsheviks under a progressive, democratic banner. Most important, the Communists quickly developed a better army, an army for which the divided Whites were no match.

Once again, Trotsky's leadership was decisive. The Bolsheviks had preached democracy in the army and had elected officers in 1917. But beginning in March 1918, Trotsky as war commissar re-established the draft and drastic discipline for the newly formed Red Army. Soldiers deserting or disobeying an order were summarily shot. Moreover, Trotsky made effective use of former tsarist army officers, who were actively recruited and given unprecedented powers of discipline over their troops. In short, Trotsky formed a disciplined and effective fighting force.

The Bolsheviks also mobilized the home front. Establishing "war communism"—the application of the total-war concept to a civil conflict—they seized grain from peasants, introduced rationing, nationalized all banks and industry, and required everyone to work. These measures served to maintain labor discipline and to keep the Red Army supplied.

"Revolutionary terror" also contributed to the Communist victory. The old tsarist secret police was re-established as the Cheka, which hunted down and executed thousands of real or supposed foes, like the tsar's family and other "class enemies." Moreover, people were shot or threatened with being shot for minor nonpolitical failures. The Cheka sowed fear, and fear silenced opposition.

Finally, foreign military intervention in the civil war ended up helping the Communists. After Lenin made peace with Germany, the Allies (the Americans, British, and Japanese) sent troops to Archangel and Vladivostok to prevent war matériel that they had sent the provisional government from being captured by the Germans. After the Soviet government nationalized all foreign-owned factories without compensation and refused to pay all of Russia's foreign debts, Western governments and particularly France began to support White armies. Yet these efforts were small and halfhearted. In 1919 Western peoples were sick of war, and few Western politicians believed in a military crusade against the Bolsheviks. Thus Allied intervention in the civil war did not aid the Whites effectively, though it did permit the Communists to appeal to the patriotic nationalism of ethnic Russians, which was particularly strong among former tsarist army officers. Allied intervention was both too little and too much.

The Russian Revolution and the Bolshevik triumph was, then, one of the reasons the First World War was such a great turning point in modern history. A radically new government, based on socialism and one-party dictatorship, came to power in a great European state, maintained power, and encouraged worldwide revolution. Although halfhearted constitutional monarchy in Russia was undoubtedly headed for some kind of political crisis before 1914, it is hard to imagine the triumph of the most radical proponents of change and reform except in a situation of total collapse. That was precisely what happened to Russia in the First World War.

THE PEACE SETTLEMENT

Victory over revolutionary Russia boosted sagging German morale, and in the spring of 1918 the Germans launched their last major attack against France. Yet this offensive failed like those before it. With breathtaking rapidity, the United States, Great Britain, and France decisively defeated Germany militarily. Bulgaria also collapsed. Austria-Hungary and the Ottoman Empire broke apart and ceased to exist. The guns of world war finally fell silent. Then, as civil war spread in Russia and as chaos engulfed much of eastern Europe and the Middle East, the victorious Western Allies came together in Paris to establish a lasting peace.

Expectations were high; optimism was almost unlimited. The Allies labored intensively and soon worked out terms for peace with Germany and for the creation of the peace-keeping League of Nations. Nevertheless, the hopes of peoples and politicians were soon disappointed, for the peace settlement of 1919 turned out to be a terrible failure. Rather than creating conditions for peace, it sowed the seeds of another war. Surely this was the ultimate tragedy of the Great War, a war that left 10 million dead and another 20 million wounded. How did it happen? Why was the peace settlement unsuccessful?

The End of the War

In early 1917, the strain of total war was showing everywhere. After the Russian Revolution in March, there were major strikes in Germany. In July a coalition of moderates passed a "peace resolution" in the German parliament, calling for peace without territorial annexations. To counter this moderation born of war-weariness, the German military established a virtual dictatorship. The military also aggressively exploited the collapse of Russian armies after the Bolshevik Revolution. Advancing almost unopposed on the eastern front in early 1918, the German high command won great concessions from Lenin in the Treaty of Brest-Litovsk in March 1918.

With victory in the east quieting German moderates, General Ludendorff and company fell on France once more in the spring offensive of 1918. For a time, German armies pushed forward, coming within thirty-five miles of Paris. But Ludendorff's exhausted, overextended forces never broke through. They were decisively stopped in July at the second Battle of the Marne, where 140,000 fresh American soldiers saw action. Adding 2 million men in arms to the war effort by August, the late but massive American intervention decisively tipped the scales in favor of Allied victory.

By September, British, French, and American armies were advancing steadily on all fronts, and a panicky General Ludendorff realized that Germany had lost the war. Yet he insolently insisted that moderate politicians shoulder the shame of defeat, and on October 4, the emperor formed a new, more liberal German government to sue for peace. As negotiations over an armistice dragged on, an angry and frustrated German people finally rose up. On November 3, sailors in Kiel mutinied, and throughout northern Germany, soldiers and workers began to establish revolutionary councils on the Russian soviet model. The same day, Austria-Hungary surrendered to the Allies and began breaking apart. Revolution broke out in Germany, and masses of workers demonstrated for peace in Berlin. With army discipline collapsing, the emperor was forced to abdicate and fled to Holland. Socialist leaders in Berlin proclaimed a German republic on November 9 and simultaneously agreed to tough Allied terms of surrender. The armistice went into effect November 11, 1918. The war was over.

Revolution in Germany

Military defeat brought political revolution to Germany and Austria-Hungary, as it had to Russia and the old Ottoman Empire (see pages 1078–

Rosa Luxemburg A brilliant writer and a leader in the German Social Democratic party, Luxemburg scorned moderate socialism and stressed the revolutionary character of Marxism. Murdered by army officers in 1919, she was canonized by the faithful as a communist saint. *(Source: Courtesy, Centralne Archiwum KCPZPR, Warsaw, Poland)*

1081). In Austria-Hungary, the revolution was primarily nationalistic and republican in character. Having started the war to preserve an antinationalist dynastic state, the Habsburg Empire had perished in the attempt. In its place, independent Austrian, Hungarian, and Czechoslovakian republics were proclaimed, while a greatly expanded Serbian monarchy united the south Slavs and took the name of Yugoslavia. The prospect of firmly establishing the new national states overrode class considerations for most people in east central Europe.

The German Revolution of November 1918 resembled the Russian Revolution of March 1917. In both cases, a genuine popular uprising toppled an authoritarian monarchy and established a liberal provisional republic. In both countries, liberals and moderate socialists took control of the central government while workers' and soldiers' councils formed a counter-government. In Germany, however, the moderate socialists won and the Lenin-like radical revolutionaries in the councils lost. In communist terms, the liberal, republican revolution in Germany in 1918 was only half a revolution: it was a bourgeois political revolution without a communist second installment; it was Russia without Lenin's Bolshevik triumph.

There were several reasons for the German outcome. The great majority of Marxian socialist leaders in the Social Democratic party were, as before the war, really pink and not red. They wanted to establish real political democracy and civil liberties, and they favored the gradual elimination of capitalism. They were also German nationalists, appalled by the prospect of civil war and revolutionary terror. Moreover, there was much less popular support among workers and soldiers for the extreme radicals than in Russia. Nor did the German peasantry, which already had most of the land, at least in western Germany, provide the elemental force that has driven all great modern revolutions, from the French to the Chinese.

Of crucial importance also was the fact that the **moderate German Social Democrats,** unlike Kerensky and company, accepted defeat and ended the war the day they took power. This act ended the decline in morale among soldiers and prevented the regular army with its conservative officer corps from disintegrating. When radicals, led by Karl Liebknecht and Rosa Luxemburg and their supporters in the councils, tried to seize control of the government in Berlin in January, the moderate socialists called on the army to crush the uprising. Liebknecht and Luxemburg were arrested and then brutally murdered by army leaders. In reaction, the radicals in the Social Democratic party broke away in anger and formed a pro-Lenin German Communist party shortly thereafter. Finally, even if the moderate socialists had followed Liebknecht and Luxemburg on the Leninist path, it is very unlikely that they would have succeeded. Civil war in Germany would certainly have followed, and the Allies, who were already occupying western Germany according to the terms of the armistice, would have marched on to Berlin and ruled Germany directly. Historians have often been unduly hard on Germany's moderate socialists.

The Treaty of Versailles

The peace conference on Germany opened in Paris in January 1919 with seventy delegates representing twenty-seven victorious nations. There were great expectations. A young British diplomat later wrote that the victors "were convinced that they would never commit the blunders and iniquities of the Congress of Vienna of 1815." Then the "misguided, reactionary, pathetic aristocrats" had cynically shuffled populations; now "we believed in nationalism, we believed in the self-determination of peoples." Indeed, "we were journeying to Paris . . . to found a new order in Europe. We were preparing not Peace only, but Eternal Peace."[9] The general optimism and idealism had been greatly strengthened by President Wilson's January 1918 peace proposal, the Fourteen Points, which stressed national self-determination and the rights of small countries.

The real powers at the conference were the United States, Great Britain, and France, for defeated Germany was not allowed to participate and Russia was locked in civil war and did not attend. Italy was considered part of the Big Four, but its role was quite secondary. Almost immediately the three great allies began to quarrel. President Wilson, who was wildly cheered by European crowds as the spokesman for a new idealistic and democratic international cooperation, was almost obsessed with creating a League of Nations. Wilson insisted that this question come first, for he believed that only a permanent international organization could protect member states from aggres-

The Treaty of Versailles   was signed in the magnificent Hall of Mlrrors, part of the vast palace that Louis XIV had built to celebrate his glory. The Allies did not allow Germany to participate in the negotiation of the treaty. *(Source: National Archives, Washington)*

sion and avert future wars. Wilson had his way, although Lloyd George of Great Britain and especially Clemenceau of France were unenthusiastic. They were primarily concerned with punishing Germany.

Playing on British nationalism, Lloyd George had already won a smashing electoral victory in December on the popular platform of making Germany pay for the war. "We shall," he promised, "squeeze the orange until the pips squeak." Personally inclined to make a somewhat moderate peace with Germany, Lloyd George was to a considerable extent a captive of demands for a total victory worthy of the sacrifices of total war against a totally depraved enemy. As Rudyard Kipling summed up the general British feeling at the end of the war, the Germans were "a people with the heart of beasts."[10]

France's Georges Clemenceau, "the Tiger" who had broken wartime defeatism and led his country to victory, wholeheartedly agreed. Like most French people, Clemenceau wanted old-fashioned revenge. But he also wanted lasting security for

France. This, he believed, required the creation of a buffer state between France and Germany, the permanent demilitarization of Germany, and vast German reparations. He feared that sooner or later Germany with its 60 million people would attack France with its 40 million, unless the Germans were permanently weakened. Moreover, France had no English Channel (or Atlantic Ocean) as a reassuring barrier against German aggression. Wilson, supported by Lloyd George, would hear none of it. Clemenceau's demands seemed vindictive, violating morality and the principle of national self-determination. By April the conference was deadlocked on the German question, and Wilson packed his bags to go home.

Clemenceau's obsession with security reflected his anxiety about France's long-term weakness. In the end, convinced that France should not break with its allies because France could not afford to face Germany alone in the future, he agreed to a compromise. He gave up the French demand for a Rhineland buffer state in return for a formal defensive alliance with the United States and Great

Britain. Under the terms of this alliance, both Wilson and Lloyd George promised that their countries would come to France's aid in the event of a German attack. Thus Clemenceau appeared to win his goal of French security, as Wilson had won his of a permanent international organization. The Allies moved quickly to finish the peace settlement, believing that necessary adjustments would later be possible within the dual framework of a strong Western alliance and the League of Nations (Map 32.4).

The Treaty of Versailles between the Allies and Germany was the key to the settlement, and the terms were not unreasonable as a first step toward re-establishing international order. Germany's colonies were given to France, Britain, and Japan as League of Nations mandates. Germany's territorial losses within Europe were minor, thanks to Wilson. Alsace-Lorraine was returned to France. Parts of Germany inhabited primarily by Poles were ceded to the new Polish state, in keeping with the principle of national self-determination. Predominantly German Danzig was also placed within the Polish tariff lines, but as a self-governing city under League of Nations protection. Germany had to limit its army to 100,000 men and agree to build no military fortifications in the Rhineland.

More harshly, the Allies declared that Germany (with Austria) was responsible for the war and had therefore to pay reparations equal to all civilian damages caused by the war. This unfortunate and much-criticized clause expressed inescapable popular demands for German blood, but the actual figure was not set and there was the clear possibility that reparations might be set at a reasonable level in the future, when tempers had cooled.

When presented with the treaty, the German government protested vigorously. But there was no alternative, especially in that Germany was still starving because the Allies had not yet lifted their naval blockade. On June 28, 1919, German representatives of the ruling moderate Social Democrats and the Catholic party signed the treaty in the Sun King's Hall of Mirrors at Versailles, where Bismarck's empire had been joyously proclaimed almost fifty years before.

Separate peace treaties were concluded with the other defeated powers—Austria, Hungary, Bulgaria, and Turkey (the successor to the Ottoman Empire). For the most part, these treaties merely ratified the existing situation in east central Europe following the breakup of the Austro-Hungarian Empire. Like Austria, Hungary was a particularly big loser, as its "captive" nationalities (and some interspersed Hungarians) were ceded to Romania, Czechoslovakia, Poland, and Yugoslavia. Italy got some Austrian territory. The Ottoman Empire was broken up. France received control of Lebanon and Syria. Britain took Iraq and Palestine, which was to include a Jewish national homeland first promised by Britain in 1917. Officially League of Nations mandates, these acquisitions of the Western powers were one of the more imperialistic elements of the peace settlement. Another was mandating Germany's holdings in China to Japan. The age of Western imperialism lived on (see pages 1072–1075). National self-determination remained a reality only for Europeans and their offspring.

American Rejection of the Versailles Treaty

The rapidly concluded peace settlement of early 1919 was not perfect, but within the context of war-shattered Europe it was an acceptable beginning. The principle of national self-determination, which had played such a large role in starting the war, was accepted and served as an organizing framework. Germany had been punished but not dismembered. A new world organization complemented a traditional defensive alliance of satisfied powers. The remaining problems could be solved in the future. The Allied leaders had seen speed as essential because they detested Lenin and feared that his Bolshevik Revolution might spread. They realized that their best answer to Lenin's unending calls for worldwide upheaval was peace and tranquillity for war-weary peoples.

There were, however, two great interrelated obstacles to such peace: Germany and the United States. Plagued by communist uprisings, reactionary plots, and popular disillusionment with losing the war at the last minute, Germany's moderate socialists and their liberal and Catholic supporters faced an enormous challenge. Like French republicans after 1871, they needed time (and luck) if they were to establish firmly a peaceful and democratic republic. Progress in this direction required understanding yet firm treatment of Germany by the victorious Western Allies, and particularly by the United States.

MAP 32.4 Shattered Empires and Territorial Changes After the First World War The Great War brought tremendous changes in eastern Europe. New nations were established, and a dangerous power vacuum was created between Germany and Soviet Russia.

However, the United States Senate and, to a lesser extent, the American people rejected President Wilson's handiwork. Republican senators led by Henry Cabot Lodge refused to ratify the Treaty of Versailles without changes in the articles creating the League of Nations. The key issue was the league's power—more apparent than real—to require member states to take collective action against aggression.

Lodge and others believed that this requirement gave away Congress's constitutional right to declare war. No doubt Wilson would have been wise to accept some reservations. But, in failing health, Wilson with narrow-minded self-righteousness rejected all attempts at compromise. He instructed loyal Democratic senators to vote against any reservations whatsoever to the Treaty of Versailles. In doing so, Wilson assured that the treaty was never ratified by the United States in any form and that the United States never joined the League of Nations. Moreover, the Senate refused to ratify Wilson's defensive alliance with France and Great Britain. America turned its back on Europe.

Perhaps understandable in the light of American traditions and the volatility of mass politics, the Wilson-Lodge fiasco and the newfound gospel of isolationism nevertheless represented a tragic renunciation of America's responsibility. Using America's action as an excuse, Great Britain, too, refused to ratify its defensive alliance with France. Bitterly betrayed by its allies, France stood alone. Very shortly, France was to take actions against Germany that would feed the fires of German resentment and seriously undermine democratic forces in the new German republic. The great hopes of early 1919 were turning to ashes by the end of the year. The Western alliance had collapsed, and a grandiose plan for permanent peace had given way to a fragile truce. For this and for what came later, the United States must share a large part of the guilt.

SUMMARY

Why did the First World War have such revolutionary consequences? Why was it such a great break with the past? The Great War was, first of all, a war of committed peoples. In France, Britain, and Germany in particular, governments drew on genuine popular support. This support reflected not only the diplomatic origins of the war but also the way western European society had been effectively unified under the nationalist banner in the later nineteenth century. The relentlessness of total war helps explain why so many died, why so many were crippled physically and psychologically, and why Western civilization would in so many ways never be the same again. More concretely, the war swept away monarchs and multinational empires. National self-determination apparently triumphed, not only in Austria-Hungary but in much of Russia's western borderlands as well. Except in Ireland

and parts of Soviet Russia, the revolutionary dream of national unity, born of the French Revolution, had finally come true.

Two other revolutions were products of the war. In Russia, the Bolsheviks established a radical regime, smashed existing capitalist institutions, and stayed in power with a new kind of authoritarian rule. Whether the new Russian regime was truly Marxian or socialist was questionable, but it indisputably posed a powerful, ongoing revolutionary challenge in Europe and its colonial empires.

More subtle, but quite universal in its impact, was an administrative revolution. This revolution, born of the need to mobilize entire societies and economies for total war, greatly increased the power of government. And after the guns grew still, government planning and wholesale involvement in economic and social life did not disappear in Europe. Liberal market capitalism and a well-integrated world economy were among the casualties of the administrative revolution, and greater social equality was everywhere one of its results. Thus, even in European countries where a communist takeover never came close to occurring, society still experienced a great revolution.

Finally, the "war to end war" did not bring peace but only a fragile truce. In the West the Allies failed to maintain their wartime solidarity. Germany remained unrepentant and would soon have more grievances to nurse. Moreover, the victory of national self-determination in eastern Europe created a power vacuum between a still-powerful Germany and a potentially mighty communist Russia. A vast area lay open to military aggression from two sides.

NOTES

1. M. Beloff, *U.S. News & World Report,* March 8, 1976, p. 53.
2. Quoted in J. Remak, *The Origins of World War I* (New York: Holt, Rinehart & Winston, 1967), p. 84.
3. Quoted in W. E. Mosse, *Alexander II and the Modernization of Russia* (New York: Collier Books, 1962), pp. 125–126.
4. Quoted in F. P. Chambers, *The War Behind the War, 1914–1918* (London: Faber & Faber, 1939), p. 168.
5. Quoted in R. O. Paxton, *Europe in the Twentieth Century* (New York: Harcourt Brace Jovanovich, 1975), p. 109.

6. Quoted in Chambers, pp. 302, 304.
7. A. B. Ulam, *The Bolsheviks* (New York: Collier Books, 1968), p. 349.
8. Ibid., p. 405.
9. H. Nicolson, *Peacemaking 1919* (New York: Grosset & Dunlap Universal Library, 1965), pp. 8, 31–32.
10. Quoted ibid., p. 24.

SUGGESTED READING

O. Hale, *The Great Illusion, 1900–1914* (1971), is a thorough account of the prewar era. Both J. Remak, *The Origins of World War I* (1967), and L. Lafore, *The Long Fuse* (1971), are highly recommended studies of the causes of the First World War. A. J. P. Taylor, *The Struggle for Mastery in Europe, 1848–1919* (1954), is an outstanding survey of diplomatic developments with an exhaustive bibliography. V. Steiner, *Britain and the Origins of the First World War* (1978), and G. Kennan, *The Decline of Bismarck's European Order: Franco-Russian Relations, 1875–1890* (1979), are also major contributions. K. Jarausch, *The Enigmatic Chancellor* (1973), is an important study on Bethmann-Hollweg and German policy in 1914. C. Falls, *The Great War* (1961), is the best brief introduction to military aspects of the war. B. Tuchman, *The Guns of August* (1962), is a marvelous account of the dramatic first month of the war and the beginning of military stalemate. G. Ritter provides an able study in *The Schlieffen Plan* (1958). J. Winter, *The Experience of World War I* (1988), is a strikingly illustrated history of the war, and A. Horne, *The Price of Glory: Verdun 1916* (1979), is a moving account of the famous siege. J. Ellis, *Eye-Deep in Hell* (1976), is a vivid account of trench warfare. Vera Brittain's *Testament of Youth,* the moving autobiography of a nurse in wartime, shows lives buffeted by new ideas and personal tragedies.

F. L. Carsten, *War Against War* (1982), considers radical movements in Britain and Germany. The best single volume on the home fronts is still F. Chambers, *The War Behind the War, 1914–1918* (1939). Chambers drew heavily on the many fine books on the social and economic impact of the war in different countries published by the Carnegie Endowment for International Peace under the general editorship of J. T. Shotwell. A. Marwick, *The Deluge* (1970), is a lively account of war and society in Britain. G. Feldman, *Army, Industry, and Labor in Germany, 1914–1918* (1966), shows the impact of total war and military dictatorship on Germany. Three excellent collections of essays, R. Wall and J. Winter, eds., *The Upheaval of War: Family, Work, and Welfare in Europe, 1914–1918* (1988), J. Roth, ed., *World War I* (1967), and R. Albrecht-Carrié, ed., *The Meaning of the First World War* (1965), deftly probe the enormous consequences of the war for people and society. The debate over Germany's guilt and aggression, which has been reopened in recent years, may be best approached through G. Feldman, ed., *German Imperialism, 1914–1918* (1972), and A. Hillgruber, *Germany and the Two World Wars* (1981). M. Fainsod, *International Socialism and the World War* (1935), ably discusses the splits between radical and moderate socialists during the conflict. In addition to Erich Maria Remarque's great novel *All Quiet on the Western Front,* Henri Barbusse's *Under Fire* (1917) and Jules Romain's *Verdun* (1939) are highly recommended for their fictional yet realistic recreations of the war. P. Fussell, *The Great War and Modern Memory* (1975), probes all the powerful literature inspired by the war.

R. Suny and A. Adams, eds., *The Russian Revolution and Bolshevik Victory,* 3d ed. (1990), presents a wide range of old and new interpretations. A. Ulam's work cited in the Notes, which focuses on Lenin, is a masterful introduction to the Russian Revolution: S. Fitzpatrick, *The Russian Revolution* (1982), provides a provocative reconsideration. B. Wolfe, *Three Who Made a Revolution* (1955), a collective biography of Lenin, Trotsky, and Stalin, and R. Conquest, *V. I. Lenin* (1972), are recommended. Leon Trotsky himself wrote the colorful and exciting *History of the Russian Revolution* (1932), which may be compared with the classic eyewitness account of the young, pro-Bolshevik American John Reed, *Ten Days That Shook the World* (1919). R. Daniels, *Red October* (1969), provides a clear account of the Bolshevik seizure of power, and R. Pipes, *The Formation of the Soviet Union* (1968), is recommended for its excellent treatment of the nationality problem during the revolution. D. Koenker, W. Rosenberg, and R. Suny, eds., *Party, State and Society in the Russian Civil War* (1989), probes the social foundation of Bolshevik victory. A. Wildman, *The End of the Russian Imperial Army* (1980), is a fine account of the soldiers' revolt, and G. Leggett, *The Cheka: Lenin's Secret Police* (1981), shows revolutionary terror in action. Boris Pasternak's justly celebrated *Doctor Zhivago* is a great historical novel of the revolutionary era. R. Massie, *Nicholas and Alexandra* (1971), is a moving popular biography of Russia's last royal family and the terrible health problem of the heir to the throne. H. Nicolson's study listed in the Notes captures the spirit of the Versailles settlement. T. Bailey, *Woodrow Wilson and the Lost Peace* (1963), and W. Widenor, *Henry Cabot Lodge and the Search for an American Foreign Policy* (1981), are also highly recommended. A. Mayer provocatively stresses the influence of domestic social tensions and widespread fear of further communist revolt in *The Politics and Diplomacy of Peacemaking* (1969).

PERIOD (CA 1700–1920)	AFRICA AND THE MIDDLE EAST	THE AMERICAS
1700	Approximately 11,000,000 slaves shipped from Africa, ca 1450–1850 Dutch found Cape Colony, 1657 Rise of the Ashanti, West Africa, ca 1700 Decline of the Safavid Empire under Nadir Shah, 1737–1747	Spain's defeat in War of the Spanish Succession, 1701–1714, prompts trade reform, leading to colonial dependence on Spanish goods, 18th century
1750	Sultan Selim III establishes first diplomatic relations between Ottoman Empire and Europe, introduces administrative and military reforms, 1761–1808 British seize Cape town, 1795 Napoleon's campaign in Egypt, 1798	"French and Indian wars," 1756–1763 Quebec Act, 1774 American Revolution, 1775–1783 Comunero revolution, New Granada, 1781
1800	Muhammad Ali founds dynasty in Egypt, 1805–1848 Slavery abolished in British Empire, 1807 Peak year of African transatlantic slave trade, 1820 European capitalists begin large-scale investment in Africa, 1840s	Latin American wars of independence from Spain, 1806–1825 Brazil wins independence from Portugal, 1822 Monroe Doctrine, 1823 Political instability in most Latin American countries, 1825–1870 Mexican War, 1846–1848
1850	Crimean War, 1853–1856 Suez Canal opens, 1869 Europeans intensify "scramble for Africa," 1880–1900 Battle of Omdurman, 1898 Boer War, 1899–1902	American Civil War, 1861–1865 British North America Act, 1867, for Canada Porfirio Diaz controls Mexico, 1876–1911 U.S. practices "dollar diplomacy" in Latin America, 1890–1920s Spanish-American War, 1898; U.S. gains Philippines
1900	Union of South Africa formed, 1910 French annex Morocco, 1912 Ottoman Empire enters World War One on Germany's side Treaty of Sèvres dissolves Ottoman Empire, 1919; Mustafa Kemal mounts nationalist struggle in Turkey	Massive immigration from Europe and Asia to the Americas, 1880–1914 Mexican Revolution, 1910 Panama Canal opens, 1914 U.S. enters World War One, 1917 Mexico adopts constitution, 1917

EAST ASIA	INDIA AND SOUTHEAST ASIA	EUROPE
Tokugawa Regime in Japan, characterized by political stability and economic growth, 1600–1867 Manchus establish Ch'ing Dynasty, 1644–1911 Height of Ch'ing Dynasty under Emperor Ch'ien-lung, 1736–1799	Mughal power contested by Hindus and Muslims, 18th century Persian invaders defeat Mughal army, loot Delhi, 1739 French and British fight for control of India, 1740–1763	Growth of absolutism in central and eastern Europe, ca 1680–1790 The Enlightenment, ca 1680–1800 Development of Cabinet system in England, 1714–1742 Height of land enclosure in England, ca 1760–1810
Maximum extent of Ch'ing Empire, 1759	Battle of Plassey, 1757 Treaty of Paris, 1763; French colonies to Britain Cook in Australia, 1768–1771; first British prisoners to Australia, 1788 East India Act, 1784	Englishman James Watt produces first steam engine, 1769 Louis XVI of France, 1774–1792 Outbreak of French Revolution, 1789 National Convention declares France a republic, 1792
Java War, 1825–1830 Anglo-Chinese Opium War, 1839–1842 Treaty of Nanking, 1842: Manchus surrender Hong Kong to British	British found Singapore, 1819 British defeat last independent native state in India, 1848	Napoleonic Empire, 1804–1814 Congress of Vienna, 1814–1815 European economic penetration of non-Western countries, ca 1816–1880 Greece wins independence from Ottoman Empire, 1829 Revolutions in France, Prussia, Italy, and Austria, 1848–1849
Taiping Rebellion, 1850–1864 Perry's arrival opens Japan to U.S. and Europe, 1853 Meiji Restoration in Japan, 1867 Adoption of constitution in Japan, 1890 Sino-Japanese War, 1894–1895 "Hundred Days of Reform" in China, 1898	Great Rebellion in India, 1857–1858 French seize Saigon, 1859 Indian National Congress formed, 1885 French acquire Indochina, 1893	Second and Third Empires in France, 1852–1914 Unification of Italy, 1859–1870 Otto von Bismarck's reign of power in German affairs, 1862–1890 Franco-Prussian War, 1870–1871; foundation of the German Empire Parliamentary Reform Bill, Great Britain, 1867 Second Socialist International, 1889–1914
Boxer Rebellion in China, 1900–1903 Russian-Japanese War, 1904–1905 Chinese Revolution; fall of Ch'ing Dynasty, 1911 Chinese Republic, 1912–1949	Commonwealth of Australia, 1900 Muslim League formed, 1906 Radicals make first calls for Indian independence, 1907 Amritsar Massacre in India, 1919 Intensification of Indian nationalism, 1919–1947	Revolution in Russia; Tsar Nicholas II forced to issue October Manifesto, 1905 Triple Entente (Britain, Russia, France), 1914–1918 World War One, 1914–1918 Treaty of Versailles, 1919

33

Nationalism in Asia, 1914–1939

Turks celebrating victory at Smyrna, October 1922

From Asia's perspective the First World War was largely a European civil war that shattered the united front of Western imperialism and convulsed prewar relationships throughout Asia. Most crucially, the war speeded the development of modern nationalism in Asia. Before 1914, the nationalist gospel of anti-imperialist political freedom and racial equality had already won converts among Asia's Westernized, educated elites. In the 1920s and 1930s it increasingly won the souls of the masses. As in Europe in the nineteenth century, nationalism in Asia between 1914 and 1939 became a mass movement with potentially awesome power.

There were at least three reasons for the upsurge of nationalism in Asia. First and foremost, nationalism provided the most effective means of organizing the anti-imperialist resistance both to direct foreign rule and to indirect Western domination. Second, nationalism called for fundamental changes and challenged old political practices and beliefs. Thus modernizers used it as a weapon in their ongoing contest for influence and power with conservative traditionalists. Modernizers also used nationalism as a conduit to spread other values, like industrialization, or the European secular world view with its faith in science, critical thinking, and progress. Third, nationalism spread because it gave both leaders and followers a vision of a shining future for a rejuvenated people. Thus nationalism provided an ideology to ennoble the sacrifices that the struggle for rejuvenation would require.

The spread of nationalism also had its dark side. As in Europe (see page 873), nationalists in Asia developed a strong sense of "we" and "they." "They" were often the enemy—the oppressor. White-skinned European imperialists were just such a "they," and nationalist feeling generated the power to destroy European empires and successfully challenge widespread foreign economic domination. But, as in Europe, nationalism in Asia also stimulated bitter conflicts and wars between peoples, in two different ways. First, it stimulated conflicts between relatively homogeneous peoples in large states, rallying, for example, Chinese against Japanese and vice versa. Second, nationalism often heightened tensions between ethnic (or religious) groups within states, especially states with a variety of peoples, like British India or the Ottoman Empire. Such states had been formed by authoritarian rulers and their armies and bureaucracies, very much like the Austrian or Russian empires before 1914. When their rigid rule declined or snapped, increasingly self-conscious and nationalistic peoples might easily quarrel, seeking to divide the existing state or to dominate the enemy "they" within its borders.

Although modern nationalism has everywhere exhibited certain shared characteristics, it has never been monolithic. In Asia especially, the range of historical experience has been enormous, and the new and often narrow ideology of nationalism was grafted onto old, rich, and complex civilizations. Between the outbreak of the First and Second World Wars each Asian country developed a distinctive national movement, rooted in its unique culture and history. Each nation's people created its own national reawakening, which renovated thought and culture as well as politics and economics.

- How did modern nationalism—the dominant force in most of the world in the twentieth century—develop in Asia between the First and Second World Wars?
- How did national movements arise in different countries, and how did some of these parallel movements come into brutal conflict?

These are the questions that this chapter seeks to answer.

THE FIRST WORLD WAR AND WESTERN IMPERIALISM

Every Asian national movement shared in a burning desire for genuine freedom from foreign imperialism. The First World War had a profound effect on these aspirations by altering relations between Asia and Europe.

In the words of a distinguished Indian historian, "the Great War of 1914–1918 was from the Asian point of view a civil war within the European community of nations."[1] For four years Asians watched the haughty bearers of the "white man's burden" vilifying and destroying each other. Far from

Delegates to the Peace Conference of 1919   Standing in the foreground is Prince Faisal, third son of King Hussein of Hejaz and frustrated spokesman for the Arab cause at Versailles. The British officer T. E. Lawrence—popularly known as Lawrence of Arabia—is second from the right in the middle row. *(Source: Imperial War Museum)*

standing united and supremely self-confident in an apparently unbeatable imperialistic phalanx, the Western nations were clawing at each other in total disarray. The impact of this spectacle was enormous. Japan's defeat of imperial Russia in 1904 (see page 944) had shown that an Asian power could beat a European great power; now for the first time Asians saw the entire West as divided and vulnerable.

In the East Asian countries of China and Japan few people particularly cared who won the vicious family quarrel in distant Europe. In India and French Indochina enthusiasm was also limited, but the impact of the war was unavoidably greater. The British and the French were driven by the harsh logic of total war to draft their colonial subjects into the conflict. They uprooted hundreds of thousands of Asians to fight the Germans and the Ottoman Turks. This too had major consequences. An Indian or Vietnamese soldier who fought in France and came in contact there with democratic and republican ideas was likely to be less willing to accept foreign rule when he returned home.

The British and the French also made rash promises to gain the support of colonial peoples during the war. British leaders promised Jewish nationalists in Europe a homeland in Palestine even as they promised Arab nationalists independence from the Ottoman Empire. In India the British were forced in 1917 to announce a new policy of self-governing institutions in order to counteract Indian popular unrest fanned by wartime inflation and heavy taxation. After the war the nationalist genie that the colonial powers had called on refused to slip meekly back into the bottle.

The war aims of President Wilson also raised the hopes of peoples under imperial rule. In January 1918 Wilson proposed to make peace on the basis of his Fourteen Points (see page 1062), whose key idea was national self-determination for the peoples of Europe and of the Ottoman Empire. Wilson also proposed that in all colonial questions "the interests of native populations be given equal weight with the desires of European governments." Wilson's program seemed to call for national self-rule, preservation of the rights of weak nations, and international justice. This subversive message was broadcast around the world by American propagandists in 1918 and 1919. It had enormous appeal for educated Asians, fueling their hopes of freedom and dignity.

Military service and Wilsonian self-determination also fired the hopes of some Africans and some visionary American black supporters of African freedom. The First World War, however, had less impact on European imperialism in black Africa—Africa south of the Sahara—than in Asia and the Arab world. Because the European conquest of black Africa was not completed until 1900, Africans outside of certain coastal areas had not experienced foreign domination long enough for nationalist movements to develop. Moreover, European rulers customarily grouped many tribes and peoples into a single administrative unit, and ethnic diversity slowed the development of a common national loyalty. For black Africa, the Great Depression and the Second World War were to prove much more influential in the growth of nationalist movements (see pages 1237–1238).

Once the Allies had won the war, they tried to shift gears and re-establish or increase their political and economic domination in Asia and Africa. Although fatally weakened, Western imperialism remained very much alive in 1918. Part of the reason for its survival was that President Wilson was certainly no revolutionary. At the Versailles Peace Conference he proved willing to compromise on colonial questions in order to achieve some of his European goals and the creation of the League of Nations. Also, Allied statesmen and ordinary French and British citizens quite rightly believed that their colonial empires had contributed to

their ultimate victory over the Central Powers. They were in no mood to give up such valuable possessions voluntarily. Finally and very importantly, the victors remained convinced of the superiority of their civilization. They believed that their rule was best for colonial peoples. A few "discontented" Asian or African intellectuals might agitate for self-rule; but Europeans in general, and colonial officials in particular, believed that the humble masses were grateful for the law and order brought by the white man's administration. If pressed, Europeans said that such administration was preparing colonial subjects for eventual self-rule, but only in the distant future.

The compromise at Versailles between Wilson's vague, moralistic idealism and the European preoccupation with "good administration" was the establishment of a system of League of Nations mandates over Germany's former colonies and the old Ottoman Empire. Article 22 of the League of Nations Covenant, which was part of the Treaty of Versailles, assigned territories "inhabited by peoples incapable of governing themselves" to various "developed nations." "The well-being and development of such peoples" was declared "a sacred trust of civilization." A Permanent Mandates Commission was created to oversee the developed nations' fulfillment of their international responsibility; most of the members of the Permanent Mandates Commission came from European countries that had colonies. Thus the League elaborated a new principle, development toward the eventual goal of self-government, but left its implementation to the colonial powers themselves.

The mandates system clearly demonstrated that Europe was determined to maintain its imperial power and influence. It is no wonder that patriots throughout Asia were bitterly disappointed after the First World War. They saw France, Great Britain, and other nations—industrialized Japan was the only Asian state to obtain mandates—grabbing Germany's colonies as spoils of war and extending the existing system of colonial protectorates in Muslim North Africa into the territories of the old Ottoman Empire. Yet Asian patriots were not about to give up. They preached the nationalist creed and struggled to build mass movements capable of achieving freedom and independence.

In this struggle they were encouraged and sometimes inspired by Soviet communism. Immediately after seizing power in 1917, Lenin and his fellow Bolsheviks declared that the Asian peoples conquered by the tsars, now inhabitants of the Soviet Union, were complete equals of the Russians with a right to their own development. (In actuality this equality hardly existed, but the propaganda was effective nonetheless.) The Communists also denounced European and American imperialism and pledged to support revolutionary movements in all colonial countries, even when they were primarily movements of national independence led by "middle-class" intellectuals instead of by revolutionary workers. Foreign political and economic exploitation was the immediate enemy, they said, and socialist revolution could wait until after Western imperialism had been defeated.

The example, ideology, and support of Russian Communists exerted a powerful influence in the 1920s and 1930s, particularly in China and French Indochina. Middle-class nationalists were strengthened in their battle with foreign rule, and the ranks of communist nationalists also swelled. A nationalistic young Vietnamese man, who had pleaded the cause of Vietnamese independence unsuccessfully at the Versailles Peace Conference, described his feelings when he read Lenin's statement on national self-determination for colonial peoples, adopted by the Communist Third International in 1920:

These resolutions filled me with great emotion, enthusiasm, and faith. They helped me see the problem clearly. My joy was so great I began to cry. Alone in my room I wrote the following words, as if I were addressing a great crowd: "My dear compatriots, so miserable and oppressed, here is what we need. Here is the path to our liberation." [2]

The young nationalist was Ho Chi Minh (1890–1969), who was to fight a lifetime to create an independent, communist Vietnam.

The appeal of nationalism in Asia was not confined to territories under direct European rule, like French Indochina and League of Nations mandates. The extraordinary growth of international trade after 1850 had drawn millions of peasants and shopkeepers throughout Asia into the Western-dominated world economy, disrupting local markets and often creating hostility toward European businessmen. Moreover, Europe and the United States had forced even the most solid Asian states, China and Japan, to accept unequal

treaties and humiliating limitations on their sovereignty. Thus the nationalist promise of genuine economic independence and true political equality with the West appealed as powerfully in old but weak states like China as in colonial territories like British India.

Finally, as in Russia after the Crimean War or in Japan after the Meiji Restoration, the nationalist creed went hand in hand with acceptance of modernization by the educated elites. Modernization promised changes that would enable old societies to compete effectively with the world's leading nations.

THE MIDDLE EAST

The most flagrant attempt to expand the scope of Western imperialism occurred in what is usually called the Middle East, but which is perhaps more accurately termed West Asia—that vast expanse that stretches eastward from the Suez Canal and Turkey's Mediterranean shores across the Tigris-Euphrates Valley and the Iranian Plateau to the Arabian Sea and the Indus Valley. There the British and the French successfully encouraged an Arab revolt in 1916 and destroyed the Ottoman Empire. The conquering Europeans then sought to replace the Turks as principal rulers throughout the region, even in Turkey itself. Turkish, Arab, and Iranian nationalists, as well as Jewish nationalists arriving from Europe, reacted violently. They struggled to win dignity and nationhood, and as the Europeans were forced to make concessions, they sometimes came into sharp conflict with each other, most notably in Palestine.

The First World War and the Arab Revolt

The Ottoman Empire, like neighboring Egypt (see pages 966–968), had long been subject to European pressure and had also adopted European military and educational reforms in the 1820s and 1830s. In the late nineteenth century, however, the Ottoman Empire became increasingly weak and autocratic. The combination of declining international stature and domestic tyranny eventually led to an upsurge of revolutionary activity among idealistic exiles and nationalistic young army officers who wanted to seize power and save the Ottoman state. These fervent patriots, the so-called Young Turks, succeeded in the revolution of 1908, and subsequently they were determined to hold the remnants of the vast multiethnic empire together. Defeated by Bulgaria, Serbia, and Greece in the Balkan War of 1912, stripped of practically all territory in Europe, the Young Turks redoubled their efforts in Asia. The most important of their Asian possessions were Syria—consisting of modern-day Lebanon, Syria, Israel, and Jordan—and Iraq. The Ottoman Turks also claimed the Arabian peninsula but exercised only a loose control there.

For centuries the largely Arabic populations of Syria and Iraq had been tied to their Ottoman rulers by their common faith in Islam (though there were Christian Arabs as well). Yet beneath the surface, ethnic and linguistic tensions simmered between Turks and Arabs, who were as different as Chinese and Japanese or French and Germans. As early as 1883, a Frenchman who had traveled widely in the Arab provinces claimed:

Everywhere I came upon the same abiding and universal sentiment: hatred of the Turks. The notion of concerted action to throw off the detested yoke is gradually shaping itself. . . . An Arab movement, newly-risen, is looming in the distance; a race hitherto downtrodden will presently claim its due place in the destinies of Islam.[3]

Europeans like this French traveler often encouraged Arabs in the Ottoman Empire to see their situation in nationalistic terms. Nationalism was part of the Western world view and it undermined the all-encompassing nature of Islam, the traditional defense against European expansion in West Africa and North Africa. Arab nationalism appealed particularly to the Ottoman Empire's sizable minority of Arab Christians, who were most numerous in the province of Syria and who were increasingly attracted by French power and culture.

The actions of the Young Turks after 1908 made the embryonic "Arab movement" a reality. Although some Turkish reformers argued for an Ottoman liberalism that would give equal political rights to all ethnic and religious groups within the empire, the majority successfully insisted on a narrow Turkish nationalism. They further centralized the Ottoman Empire and extended the sway of the Turkish language, culture, and race. In 1909 the Turkish government brutally slaughtered thousands of Armenian Christians, a prelude to the wholesale destruction of more than a million Armenians during the heavy fighting with Russia in the First World War. Meanwhile the Arab revolt gathered strength. By 1914 the great majority of Arab leaders believed that armed conflict with their Turkish masters was inevitable.

In close contact with Europeans for centuries, the Turks willingly joined forces with Germany and Austria-Hungary in late 1914. The Young Turks were pro-German because Germans had helped reform Ottoman armies before the war and had built important railroads, like the one to Baghdad. Alliance with Germany permitted the Turks to renounce immediately the limitations on Ottoman sovereignty that the Europeans had imposed in the nineteenth century, and it offered the prospect of settling old scores with Russia, the historic enemy.

The Young Turks' fatal decision to side with the Central Powers pulled the entire Middle East into the European civil war and made it truly a world conflict. While Russia attacked the Ottomans in the Caucasus, the British had to protect Egypt and the Suez Canal, the life line to India. Thus Arab leaders opposed to Ottoman rule suddenly found an unexpected ally in Great Britain. The foremost Arab leader was Hussein Ibn-Ali (1856–1931), a direct descendant of the prophet Muhammad through the house of Quraysh. As the *sharif*, or chief magistrate of Mecca, the most holy city in the Muslim world, Hussein governed much of the Ottoman Empire's territory along the Red Sea, an area known as the Hejaz. Basically anti-Turkish, Hussein refused to second the Turkish sultan's call for a holy war against the Triple Entente. His refusal pleased the British, who feared that such calls would trigger a Muslim revolt in India.

In 1915 Hussein managed to win vague British commitments for an independent Arab kingdom. The British attempt to take the Dardanelles and capture Constantinople in 1915 failed miserably, and Britain (and Russia) badly needed a new ally on the Ottoman front. Thus in 1916 Hussein revolted against the Turks, proclaiming himself king of the Arabs. Hussein joined forces with the British under T. E. Lawrence, who in 1917 led Arab tribesmen and Indian soldiers in a highly successful guerrilla war against the Turks on the Arabian peninsula. In September 1918, British armies and their Arab allies smashed into Syria. This offensive culminated in the triumphal entry of Hussein's son Faisal into Damascus.

Similar victories were eventually scored in the Ottoman province of Iraq. Britain had established a protectorate over the emirate of Kuwait in 1899, and from there British troops occupied the southern Iraqi city of Basra in 1914. Moving up the Tigris-Euphrates Valley, British armies from India and armed forces from Australia and New Zealand were repulsed by Ottoman forces at Kut el Amara in 1916, but they smashed through to capture Baghdad in 1917. Throughout Syria and Iraq there was wild Arab rejoicing. Many patriots expected a large, unified Arab state to rise from the dust of the Ottoman collapse.

Within two years, however, many Arab nationalists felt bitterly betrayed by Great Britain and its allies. The issues involved are complex, controversial, and highly emotional, but it is undeniable that this bitterness left an enduring legacy of hatred toward the West. Part of the reason for the Arabs's bitterness was that Britain and France had signed secret wartime treaties to divide and rule the old Ottoman Empire. In the Sykes-Picot Agreement of 1916, Britain and France had secretly agreed that France would receive modern-day Lebanon, Syria, and much of southern Turkey and Britain would receive Palestine, Jordan, and Iraq. The Sykes-Picot treaties, drawn up to reinforce Allied determination to fight on, contradicted British (and later Wilsonian) promises concerning Arab independence after the war. When Britain and France set about implementing these secret plans, Arab nationalists felt cheated and betrayed.

A related source of Arab bitterness was Britain's wartime commitment to a Jewish homeland in Palestine. The famous Balfour Declaration of November 1917, made by the Britsh foreign secretary Arthur Balfour, declared:

His Majesty's Government views with favor the establishment in Palestine of a National Home for the Jewish People, and will use their best endeavors to facilitate the achievement of this object, it being clearly understood that nothing shall be done which may prejudice the civil and religious rights of existing non-Jewish communities in Palestine, or the rights and political status enjoyed by Jews in any other country.

As careful reading reveals, the Balfour Declaration made contradictory promises to European Jews and Middle Eastern Arabs. It has been a subject of passionate debate ever since 1917.

Some British Cabinet members apparently believed such a declaration would appeal to German, Austrian, and American Jews and thus help the British war effort. Others sincerely supported the Zionist vision of a Jewish homeland. These supporters also believed that such a homeland would be grateful to Britain and help maintain British control of the Suez Canal. In any event, Arabs were dismayed. In 1914 Jews accounted for about 11 percent of the predominantly Arab population in the three Ottoman administrative units that would subsequently be lumped together by the British to form Palestine. A "National Home for the Jewish People" implied to the Arabs—and to the Zionist Jews as well—the establishment of some kind of Jewish state that would be incompatible with majority rule. Also, a state founded on religious and ethnic exclusivity was out of keeping with both Islamic and Ottoman tradition, which had historically been more tolerant of religious diversity and minorities than had the Christian monarchs or nation-states in Europe.

Despite strong French objections, Hussein's son Faisal (1885–1933) was allowed to attend the Paris Peace Conference. The Allies, however, made clear that he represented only the recently proclaimed kingdom of Hejaz, not all Arabs. Faisal invoked Wilson's idea of self-determination, but despite Wilson's lukewarm support Faisal's effort to secure an independent state embracing all Arabs came to nothing. The independence of the kingdom of Hejaz was confirmed, but in return Faisal was forced to accept Franco-British demands for mandates in Syria, Iraq, and Palestine. (The Saudis had attacked Hussein in 1916 and they conquered his kingdom of Hejaz in 1924–1925, incorporating it with the Nejd in 1932 to form Saudi Arabia.) The British mandate in Palestine formally incorporated the Balfour Declaration and its commitment to a Jewish national home. On his return to Syria, Faisal's followers repudiated the agreement he had reluctantly accepted. In March 1920 they met as the Syrian National Congress and proclaimed Syria independent with Faisal as king. A similar congress declared Iraq an independent kingdom.

Western reaction to events in Syria and Iraq was swift and decisive. France and Britain convened the League of Nations to approve the mandates they wanted. Then a French army stationed in Lebanon attacked Syria, taking Damascus in July

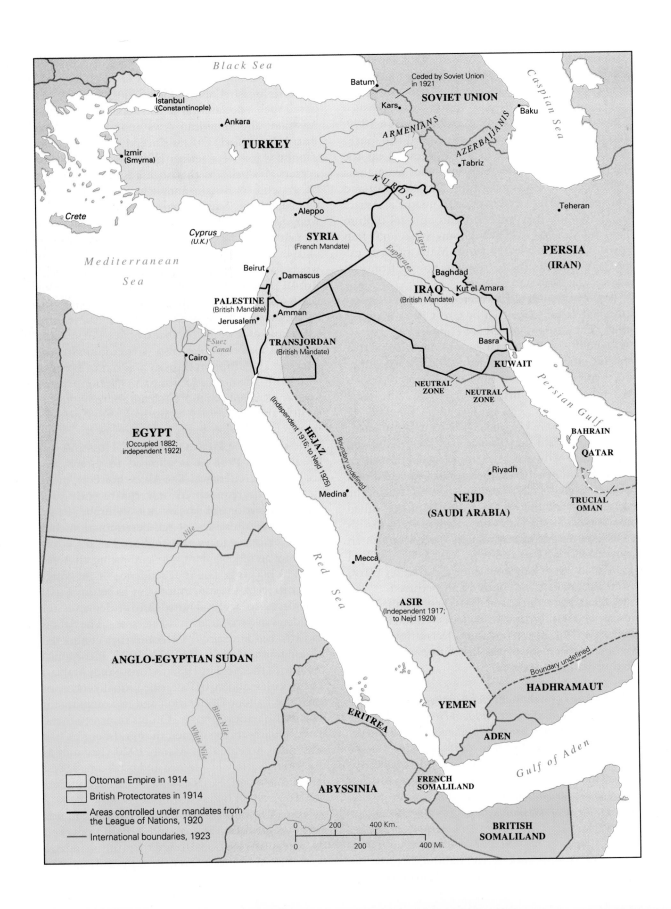

Black Sea

Batum
Ceded by Soviet Union
in 1921
SOVIET UNION
Kars
Baku
Caspian Sea

Istanbul
(Constantinople)

Ankara
ARMENIANS
AZERBAIJANIS

TURKEY
Tabriz
Teheran

Izmir
(Smyrna)
KURDS
PERSIA
(IRAN)

Crete
Aleppo
Tigris

Cyprus
(U.K.)
SYRIA
(French Mandate)
Euphrates
Baghdad

Mediterranean
Sea
Beirut
Damascus
IRAQ
(British Mandate)
Kut el Amara

PALESTINE
(British Mandate)
Amman
Basra

Jerusalem
TRANSJORDAN
(British Mandate)
KUWAIT

Suez
Canal
NEUTRAL
ZONE
NEUTRAL
ZONE
Persian Gulf

Cairo
BAHRAIN

EGYPT
(Occupied 1882;
independent 1922)
HEJAZ
(Independent 1916; to Nejd 1925)
Boundary undefined
Riyadh
QATAR

Medina
NEJD
(SAUDI ARABIA)
TRUCIAL
OMAN

Nile

Red Sea
Mecca

ASIR
(Independent 1917;
to Nejd 1920)

ANGLO-EGYPTIAN SUDAN
Boundary undefined
HADHRAMAUT

Blue Nile
YEMEN

White Nile
ERITREA
ADEN

Gulf of Aden

Ottoman Empire in 1914
FRENCH
SOMALILAND

British Protectorates in 1914
ABYSSINIA

Areas controlled under mandates from
the League of Nations, 1920
BRITISH
SOMALILAND

International boundaries, 1923

0   200   400 Km.

0   200   400 Mi.

1920. Faisal fled and the French took over. Meanwhile the British put down an uprising in Iraq with bloody fighting and established military rule there. Western imperialism appeared to have replaced Turkish rule in the Middle East (Map 33.1).

The Turkish Revolution

In November 1918 the Allied fleet entered Constantinople, the Ottoman capital. A young English official vividly described the strange and pathetic situation he encountered:

I found the Ottoman Empire utterly smashed, her vast territories stripped into pieces, and her conquered populations blinded and bewildered by their sudden release. The Turks were worn out, dead-tired, and without bitterness awaited their fate. . . . The debris of the old order waited to be constructed into a new system.[4]

The Allies' "new system" was blatant imperialism, and it proved harsher for the defeated Turks than for the "liberated" Arabs. A treaty forced on the helpless sultan dismembered Turkey and reduced it to a puppet state. Great Britain and France occupied parts of Turkey, and Italy and Greece claimed shares as well. There was a sizable Greek minority in western Turkey, and Greek nationalists cherished the "Great Idea" of incorporating this territory into a modern Greek empire modeled on long-dead Christian Byzantium. In 1919 a Greek army carried by British ships landed on the Turkish coast at Smyrna. The sultan ordered his exhausted troops not to resist, and Greek

Mustafa Kemal explains his radical reform of the written language. Impeccably elegant European dress symbolizes Kemal's conception of a modernized Turkey. *(Source: Historical Pictures Service, Chicago)*

MAP 33.1 The Partition of the Ottoman Empire, 1914–1923 The decline of the mighty Ottoman Empire had begun in 1699, when the Habsburgs conquered Hungary, and it had accelerated after 1805, when Egypt became virtually independent. By 1914 the Ottoman Turks had been pushed out of the Balkans and their Arab provinces were on the edge of revolt; that revolt erupted in the First World War and contributed greatly to the Ottomans' defeat. When the Allies then attempted to implement their plans, including independence for the Armenian people, Mustafa Kemal arose to forge in battle the modern Turkish state.

armies advanced into the interior. Turkey seemed finished.

But Turkey produced a great leader and revived to become an inspiration to the entire Middle East. Mustafa Kemal (1881–1938), the father of modern Turkey, was a military man. The son of a petty government official and sympathetic to the Young Turk movement, Kemal had distinguished himself in the Great War by directing the successful defense of the Dardanelles against British attack, the most famous Turkish victory of the war. Back in Constantinople after the armistice, Mustafa Kemal watched with anguish the Allies' aggression and the sultan's cowardice. In early 1919 he moved to central Turkey and began working to unify the Turkish resistance.

The sultan, bowing to Allied pressure, initially denounced Kemal, but the cause of national liberation proved more powerful. The catalyst was the Greek invasion and attempted annexation of much of western Turkey. A young woman who was to play a major role in the Turkish revolution described feelings she shared with countless others:

After I learned about the details of the Smyrna occupation by Greek armies, I hardly opened my mouth on any subject except when it concerned the sacred struggle. . . . I suddenly ceased to exist as an individual. I worked, wrote and lived as a unit of that magnificent national madness.[5]

Refusing to acknowledge the Allied dismemberment of their country, the Turks battled on through 1920 despite staggering defeats. The next year the Greeks, egged on by the British, advanced almost to Ankara, the nationalist stronghold in central Anatolia. There Mustafa Kemal's forces took the offensive and won a great victory. The Greeks and their British allies sued for peace. After long negotiations, the resulting Treaty of Lausanne (1923) solemnly abolished the hated Capitulations imposed by European powers in the nineteenth century to give their citizens special privileges in the Ottoman Empire, and recognized the territorial integrity of a truly independent Turkey. Turkey lost only its former Arab provinces.

Mustafa Kemal, a nationalist without religious faith, believed that Turkey should modernize and secularize along Western lines. His first moves were political. Drawing on his prestige as a war hero, Kemal called on the somewhat reluctant National Assembly to depose the sultan and establish a republic. He had himself elected president and moved the capital from cosmopolitan Constantinople (soon to be renamed Istanbul) to Ankara in the Turkish heartland. Kemal savagely crushed the demands for independence of ethnic minorities like the Armenians and the Kurds, but he realistically abandoned all thought of winning back lost Arab territories. He focused instead on internal affairs, creating a one-party system—partly inspired by the Bolshevik example—to work his will.

The most radical of Kemal's changes pertained to religion and culture. For centuries, most of the intellectual and social activities of believers had been sternly regulated by Islamic religious authorities, in keeping with the Sacred Law. Profoundly influenced by the example of western Europe, Mustafa Kemal set out, like the philosophes of the Enlightenment, to limit the place of religion and religious leaders in daily affairs. Like Russia's Peter the Great, he employed dictatorial measures rather than reason to reach his goal. Kemal and his followers simply decreed a revolutionary separation of church and state. Religious courts were abolished, replaced by a completely new legal system based on European law codes. Religious schools gave way to state schools that taught such secular subjects as science, mathematics, and social sciences.

To dramatize the break with the past, Mustafa Kemal struck down many entrenched patterns of behavior. Women, traditionally secluded and dominated by males in Islamic society, received the right to vote. Marriage was now governed by civil law on a European model, rather than by the Islamic code. Women were allowed to seek divorces, and no longer could a wealthy man take a second, third, or fourth wife, as under Islamic law. Men were forbidden to wear the tall red fez as headgear; government employees were ordered to wear business suits and felt hats, erasing the visible differences between Muslims and "infidel" Europeans. The old Arabic script was replaced with a new Turkish alphabet based on Roman letters; it made the written language closer to the spoken vernacular. The new alphabet isolated Turks from their historical heritage and literature, as the radical reformers probably hoped it would. The simpler, more phonetic alphabet facilitated massive government efforts to spread basic literacy after 1928. Finally, in 1935, family names on the European model were introduced. The National Assembly granted Mustafa Kemal the surname Atatürk, which means "father of the Turks."

By the time of his death in 1938, Atatürk and his supporters had consolidated their revolution. Government-sponsored industrialization was fostering urban growth and new attitudes. Turks no longer considered business and science beneath their dignity. Nevertheless, poverty persisted in rural areas, as did some religious discontent among devout Muslims. After the Second World War, this religious discontent caused Turkish governments to modify some of Atatürk's most radical reforms in a conservative direction. But like the

Japanese after the Meiji Restoration, the Turkish people had rallied around the nationalist banner to repulse European imperialism and were building a modern secular nation-state.

Iran and Afghanistan

In Persia (renamed Iran in 1935), strong-arm efforts to build a unified modern nation ultimately proved less successful than in Turkey.

The late nineteenth century had been a sorry period in Iran's long and sometimes glorious history. Iran was subject to extreme foreign pressure: the Russians were pressing relentlessly from the north, and the British were pushing upward from India and the Persian Gulf. Like China in a similar predicament at the same time, Iran managed to play the Great Powers against each other to maintain a precarious independence. However, the spectacle of the shah granting economic privileges to foreigners alienated native merchants. An inspired religious leader, Jamal al-Din al-Afghani (1838–1897), began to preach government reform as a means of reviving Islamic civilization. In 1906 a nationalistic coalition of merchants, religious leaders, and intellectuals revolted. The despotic shah was forced to grant a constitution and establish a national assembly, the *Majlis*. Nationalist hopes ran high.

Yet the Iranian revolution of 1906 was doomed to failure, largely because of European imperialism. Without consulting Iran, Britain and Russia in 1907 simply divided the country into spheres of influence. Britain's sphere ran along the Persian Gulf; the Russian sphere encompassed the whole northern half of Iran. Thereafter Russia intervened constantly. It blocked reforms, occupied cities, and completely dominated the country by 1912. When Russian power temporarily collapsed in the Bolshevik Revolution, British armies rushed into the power vacuum. By bribing corrupt Iranians liberally, Great Britain in 1919 negotiated a treaty allowing the installation of British "advisers" in every department of the government. The Majlis refused to ratify the treaty, which confirmed Iranians' worst suspicions about Britain and the West.

That blatant attempt to make Iran a British satellite was a key event in the development of Iranian nationalism. It aroused the national spirit. In 1921 reaction against the British brought to power a military dictator, Reza Shah Pahlavi (1877–1944), who proclaimed himself shah in 1925 and ruled until 1941.

Inspired throughout his reign by the example of Turkey's Mustafa Kemal, the patriotic, religiously indifferent Reza Shah had three basic goals: to build a modern nation, to free Iran from foreign domination, and to rule with an iron fist. The challenge was enormous. Iran was a vast, backward country of deserts, mountain barriers, and rudimentary communications. Most of the rural population was poor and illiterate, and among the Persian majority were sizable ethnic minorities with their own aspirations. Furthermore, Iran's powerful religious leaders hated Western (Christian) domination but were no less opposed to a more secular, less Islamic society.

To realize his vision of a strong Iran, the energetic shah created a modern army, built railroads, and encouraged commerce and industry. He won control over ethnic minorities such as the Kurds in the north and Arab tribesmen on the border with Iraq. He withdrew many of the privileges granted to foreigners and raised taxes on the powerful Anglo-Persian Oil Company, which had been founded in 1909 to exploit the first great oil strike in the Middle East. Yet Reza Shah was ultimately less successful than Atatürk. Because the European-educated elite in Iran was smaller than in Turkey, the idea of re-creating Persian greatness on the basis of a secularized society attracted fewer determined supporters. Many powerful religious leaders turned against him. Reza Shah became increasingly brutal, greedy, and tyrannical, murdering his enemies and lining his pockets. His support of Hitler's Nazi Germany also exposed Iran's tenuous and fragile independence to the impact of European conflicts.

Afghanistan, meanwhile, was nominally independent in the nineteenth century, but the British imposed political restrictions and constantly meddled in the country. In 1919 the new, violently anti-British amir Amanullah (1892–1960) declared a holy war on the British government in India and won complete independence for the first time. Amanullah then decreed revolutionary reforms designed to hurl his primitive country into the twentieth century. The result was tribal and religious revolt, civil war, and retreat from reform. Islam remained both religion and law. A powerful but primitive patriotism had enabled Afghanistan to win political independence from the West, but modest efforts to build a modern society met little success.

The Arab States and Palestine

The establishment of French and British mandates at gunpoint forced Arab nationalists to seek independence by gradual means after 1920. Arab nationalists were indirectly aided by Western taxpayers, who wanted cheap—that is, peaceful—empires. As a result, Arabs won considerable control over local affairs in the mandated states, except Palestine, though the mandates remained European satellites in international and economic affairs.

The wily British chose Faisal, whom the French had so recently deposed in Syria, as king of Iraq. Faisal obligingly signed an alliance giving British advisers broad behind-the-scenes control. The king also accepted British ownership of Iraq's oil fields, thereby giving the West a stranglehold on the Iraqi economy. Given the limitations imposed on him, Faisal (r. 1921–1933) proved an able ruler, gaining the support of his people and encouraging moderate reforms. In 1932 he secured Iraqi independence at the price of a long-term military alliance with Great Britain.

Egypt, occupied by Great Britain ever since 1882 (see page 967) and a British protectorate since 1914, pursued a similar path. Following intense nationalist agitation after the Great War, Great Britain in 1922 proclaimed Egypt formally independent but continued to occupy the country militarily. In 1936, the British agreed to a treaty restricting their troops to their big bases in the Suez Canal Zone.

The French were less compromising in Syria. They practiced a policy of divide-and-rule, carving out a second mandate in Lebanon and generally playing off ethnic and religious minorities against each other. Lebanon eventually became a republic, dominated by a very slender Christian majority and under French protection. Arab nationalists in Syria finally won promises of Syrian independence in 1936 in return for a treaty of friendship with France.

In short, the Arab states gradually freed themselves from Western political mandates but not from the Western military threat or from pervasive Western influence. Of great importance, large Arab landowners and urban merchants increased their wealth and political power after 1918, and they often supported the Western hegemony from which they benefited greatly. Western control over the newly discovered oil fields by foreign companies helped to convince radical nationalists that economic independence and genuine freedom had not yet been achieved. The struggle against the West had to continue, they believed.

Relations between the Arabs and the West were complicated by the tense situation in the British mandate of Palestine, and that situation deteriorated in the interwar years. Both Arabs and Jews denounced the British, who tried unsuccessfully to compromise with both sides. The anger of Arab nationalists, however, was aimed primarily at Jewish settlers. The key issue was Jewish migration from Europe to Palestine.

A small Jewish community had survived in Palestine ever since the destruction of Jerusalem and the dispersal of the Jews in Roman times. But Jewish nationalism, known as "Zionism," was a recent phenomenon of European origin. The Dreyfus affair (see page 949) and anti-Jewish riots in Russia had convinced a cultured Austrian journalist named Theodore Herzl (1860–1904) that even nonreligious Jews would never be fully accepted in Europe. He believed that only the re-creation of a Jewish state, preferably but not necessarily in Palestine, could guarantee Jews dignity and security. Under Herzl's leadership, the Zionist movement encouraged Jews from all over the world to settle in the Palestine region on lands purchased by Jewish philanthropists with the approval of the relatively tolerant Ottoman rulers. Some Jewish idealists from Russia and central Europe were attracted to Palestine by the Zionist vision, but until 1921 the great majority of Jewish emigrants preferred the United States.

After the First World War the situation changed radically. An isolationist United States drastically limited immigration from eastern Europe, where war and revolution had caused chaos and kindled anti-Semitism. Moreover, the British began honoring the Balfour Declaration despite Arab protests. Thus the number of Jewish immigrants to Palestine from turbulent Europe grew rapidly. The first surge came in the early 1920s. The second came in the 1930s, when German and Polish per-

The Founding of Tel-Aviv, 1908 This rare photo shows Jewish settlers coming together to found Tel-Aviv as a new city on the outskirts of the old port of Jaffa. Tel-Aviv grew modestly at first, but its population surged in the 1930s after Hitler came to power and many European Jews sought refuge in Palestine. (*Source: Zionist Archives and Library*)

secution created a mass of Jewish refugees. By 1939 the Jewish population of Palestine had increased almost fivefold over 1914 and accounted for about 30 percent of all inhabitants.

Jewish settlers in Palestine faced formidable economic and political difficulties. Much of the land purchased by the Jewish National Fund was productive. But many of the sellers of such land were wealthy absentee Arab landowners, the kind who had profited from the rise of commercial agriculture in Egypt and other parts of the Ottoman Empire and who had little interest in the welfare of their Arab tenants (see page 967). When the new Jewish owners subsequently replaced those age-old Arab tenants with Jewish settlers, Arab farmers and intellectuals burned with a sense of injustice. Moreover, most Jewish immigrants came from ur-

ban backgrounds and preferred to establish new cities like Tel Aviv or to live in existing towns, where they competed with the Arabs. The land issue combined with economic and cultural friction to harden Arab protest into hatred. Anti-Jewish riots and even massacres ensued.

The British gradually responded to Arab pressure and tried to slow Jewish immigration. This effort satisfied neither Jews nor Arabs, and by 1938 the two communities were engaged in an undeclared civil war. On the eve of the Second World War, the frustrated British proposed an independent Palestine as well as a cap of 75,000 additional Jewish immigrants. This low number would permanently limit the Jews to being only about one-third of Palestine's total population. Zionists felt themselves in grave danger.

THE MIDDLE EAST, 1914–1939

1914	Ottoman Empire enters First World War on Germany's side
1916	Allies agree secretly to partition Ottoman Empire
1916–1917	Arab revolt against Turkish rule grows
November 1917	Balfour Declaration pledges British support for a Jewish homeland in Palestine
October 1918	Arabs and British triumph as Ottoman Empire collapses
1919	Treaty of Versailles divides old Ottoman Empire into League of Nations mandates
1919	Mustafa Kemal mounts nationalist struggle against foreign occupation
1920	Faisal proclaimed king of Syria but quickly deposed by the French, who establish their mandate in Syria
Early 1920s	Tide of Jewish immigration surges into British mandate of Palestine
1923	Treaty of Lausanne recognizes independent Turkey; Mustafa Kemal begins to secularize Turkish society
1925	Reza Shah takes power in Iran and rules to 1941
1932	Iraq gains political independence in return for long-term military alliance with Great Britain
1936	Syrian nationalists sign treaty of friendship with France in return for promises of independence
late 1930s	Tensions mount between Arabs and Jews in Palestine

In the face of adversity, Jewish settlers from many different countries gradually succeeded in forging a cohesive community. Hebrew, which for centuries had been used only in religious worship, was revived as a living language to bind the Jews in Palestine together. Despite its slow beginnings, rural development achieved often spectacular results. The key unit of agricultural organization was the *kibbutz,* a collective farm on which each member shared equally in the work, rewards, and defense of the farm. Men and women labored side by side; a nursery cared for the children and a common dining hall served meals. Some cooperative farms turned arid grazing land into citrus groves and irrigated gardens. An egalitarian socialist ideology also characterized industry, which grew rapidly and was owned largely by the Jewish trade unions. By 1939 a new but old nation was emerging in the Middle East.

TOWARD SELF-RULE IN INDIA

The national movement in British India grew out of two interconnected cultures, Hindu and Muslim, which came to see themselves as fundamentally different in rising to challenge British rule. Nowhere has the power of modern nationalism, both to unify and to divide, been more strikingly demonstrated than in India.

Promises and Repression (1914–1919)

Indian nationalism had emerged in the late nineteenth century (see page 983), and when the First World War began, the British feared revolt. Instead, somewhat like Europe's equally mistrusted socialist workers, Indians supported the war effort. About 1.2 million Indian soldiers and laborers volunteered for duty and served in Europe, Africa, and the Middle East. The British government in India and the native Indian princes sent large supplies of food, money, and ammunition. In return, the British opened more good government jobs to Indians and made other minor concessions.

As the war in distant Europe ground on, however, inflation, high taxes, food shortages, and a terrible influenza epidemic created widespread suffering and discontent. The prewar nationalist movement revived, stronger than ever, and the moderate and radical wings of the Indian National Congress joined forces. Moreover, in 1916 the

Hindus leading the Congress party hammered out an alliance—the Lucknow Pact—with India's Muslim League. Founded in 1906 to uphold Muslim interests, the league had grown out of fears arising from the fact that under British rule the once-dominant Muslim minority had fallen behind the Hindu majority, especially in the Western education necessary to secure good jobs in the government. The Lucknow Pact forged a powerful united front of Hindus and Muslims and called for putting India on equal footing with self-governing white British dominions like Canada, Australia, and New Zealand.

The British response was contradictory. On the one hand, the secretary of state for India made the unprecedented announcement in August 1917 that British policy in India called for the "gradual development of self-governing institutions and the progressive realization of responsible government." The means of achieving this great step forward were spelled out in late 1919 in the Govern-

ment of India Act, which established a dual administration: part Indian and elected, part British and authoritarian. Such noncontroversial activities as agriculture, health, and education were transferred from British to Indian officials who were accountable to elected provincial assemblies. More sensitive matters like taxes, police, and the courts remained solely in British hands.

The positive impact of this reform, so typical of the British tradition of gradual political change, was seriously undermined by old-fashioned authoritarian rule. Despite the unanimous opposition of the elected Indian members, the British in 1919 rammed the repressive Rowlatt Acts through India's Imperial Legislative Council. These acts indefinitely extended wartime "emergency measures" designed to curb unrest and root out "conspiracy." The result was a wave of rioting across India.

Under these tense conditions an unsuspecting crowd of some ten thousand gathered to celebrate

Toward Self Rule A British and an Indian official oversee efforts to lift an injured camel out of a canal, symbolizing the new policy of joint administration in 1919. Although the Amritsar Massacre undermined Indian faith in British promises, joint administration was a major step toward independence. *(Source: By permission of the British Library)*

a Hindu religious festival in an enclosed square in Amritsar, a city in the northern province of Punjab. The local English commander, General Reginald Dyer, had, unknown to the crowd, banned all public meetings that very day. Dyer marched his native Gurkha troops onto the field and, without warning, ordered them to fire. The soldiers kept firing into the unarmed mass at point-blank range until the ammunition ran out. A total of 1,650 rounds were fired, killing 379 and wounding 1,137; nine of every ten rounds claimed a victim. The Amritsar Massacre shattered wartime hopes in a frenzy of postwar reaction. India seemed to stand on the verge of more violence and repression and, sooner or later, terrorism and guerrilla war. That India took a different path to national liberation was due largely to Mohandas "Mahatma" Gandhi (1869–1948), who became the most fascinating and influential Indian since Ashoka (see pages 81–83).

Hindu Society and Mahatma Gandhi

By the time of Gandhi's birth in 1869, the Indian subcontinent was firmly controlled by the British. Part of the country was directly ruled by British (and subordinate Indian) officials, ultimately answerable to the British Parliament in London. These areas included Bengal and its teeming capital of Calcutta in eastern India, Bombay and its hinterland in western India, the Punjab in the northwest, and Madras on the southeast coast. So-called protected states were more sheltered from European ideas and from the world economy. There many of the old ways remained intact. The native prince—usually known as the *maharaja*—remained the titular ruler, though he was bound to the British by unequal treaties and had to accept the "advice" of the British resident assigned to his court.

It was in just such a tiny backwater protected state that Gandhi grew up. His father was a member of the merchant caste—*gandhi* means "grocer" in the Gujarati language. The Indian caste system has always been more flexible and dynamic than unsympathetic Westerners have wanted to believe, and for six generations the heads of Gandhi's family had served as hereditary prime ministers in various minuscule realms on the Kathiawar peninsula, north of Bombay on the Arabian Sea.

The extended (or joint) family, which had for generations been the most important unit of Indian society, powerfully influenced young Gandhi. Gandhi's father was the well-to-do head of the clan, which included five brothers and their wives, children, and children's children. The big three-story ancestral home swarmed with relatives. A whole community crowded into the labyrinth of tiny rooms and spilled out into the open courtyards. There the entire extended family celebrated holidays and Hindu festivals. There the prime minister routinely entertained a score of dinner guests each day. In such a communal atmosphere, patience, kindness, and a good-natured love of people were essential virtues; the aggressive, solitary individualism so prized in Europe and North America would have threatened group harmony. So it was for Gandhi.

In the Hindu family the woman is subordinate but respected. She is "worshipped as a mother, venerated as a wife, loved as a sister, but not much regarded as a woman. Woman as woman is the handmaid of man; her duty is to worship her husband, to bear and rear his children."[6] Every Hindu girl married young, often before puberty; her husband was chosen by her parents. The young bride moved into her father-in-law's house, where, according to one famous Indian nationalist, it was "the common rule for intercourse to take place on that very night when she has the first menstruation. . . This custom has been practiced for at least 2500 years."[7]

Marriage was a sacrament that could not be dissolved by divorce or even by death. Widows were forbidden by custom to remarry and, until the British abolished the practice in 1829, a dutiful wife from a high-ranking caste was expected to throw herself on her husband's funeral pyre and join him immediately in the world beyond. More generally, a woman's fate was linked to that of the family, in which she was the trusted guardian of orthodox Hindu values.

Gandhi's mother was the ideal Hindu housewife. Married as a young illiterate girl to a forty-two-year-old man whose first wives had died without male children, Putali Ba bore three boys and a girl. According to Gandhi, his ever-cheerful mother was "the first to rise and the last to go to bed . . . and she never made any distinction between her own children and other children in the family."[8] Very devoted but undogmatic in relig-

The March to the Sea   Gandhi repeatedly used nonviolent resistance to challenge British rule and mobilize the Indian masses. Here he leads his supporters in the famous march to the sea in 1929. *(Source: Press Association Limited)*

ious matters, Putali Ba fasted regularly and exercised a strong influence on her precocious son. Gandhi was married at thirteen to a local girl who became his lifelong companion.

After his father's death, Gandhi decided to study law in England. No member of his subcaste had ever done so, and the local elders declared Gandhi an outcaste, claiming that Hindu practices would not be possible in alien England. Gandhi disagreed. To win over his wife and anxious mother, he swore that he would not touch meat, women, or wine in the foreign land. Gandhi kept his word and became a zealous vegetarian, refusing even to eat eggs because they were potential living creatures. After passing the English bar, he returned to India. But his practice in Bombay failed, and in 1893 he decided to try his luck as a lawyer for wealthy Indian merchants in South Africa. It was a momentous decision.

The Roots of Militant Nonviolence

Soon after arriving in South Africa, the elegant young lawyer in Western dress took a business trip by train. A white man entered Gandhi's first-class compartment, took one look, and called the conductor. Gandhi was ordered to ride in the baggage car. When he protested, a policeman threw him off the train. Years later Gandhi recalled this experience as a critical turning point in his life. He had refused to bow to naked racial injustice.

As Gandhi's law practice flourished, he began to examine the plight of Indians in South Africa.

After the British abolished black slavery in the empire, plantation owners in South Africa and elsewhere had developed a "new system of slavery"[9]: they imported desperately poor Indians as indentured laborers on five-year renewable contracts. When some thrifty, hard-working Indians completed their terms and remained in South Africa as free persons and economic competitors, the Dutch and British settlers passed brutally discriminatory laws. The law books called Indians "semi-barbarous Asiatics," and some towns even prohibited Indians from walking on the sidewalks. Poor Indians had to work on white-owned plantations or return to India; rich Indians lost the vote. Gandhi undertook the legal defense of his countrymen, infuriating the whites. In 1896 a hysterical mob almost lynched the "coolie lawyer."

Meanwhile Gandhi was searching for a spiritual theory of social action. Identifying with South Africa's black majority as well as with his own countrymen, he meditated on the Hindu pursuit of spiritual strength through fasting, sexual abstinence, devotion to duty, and reincarnation. He also studied Christian teachings. Gradually Gandhi developed and articulated a weapon for the weak that he called "Satyagraha." *Satya* in Hindu means "spiritual truth," which equals love; *agraha* is "strength" or "force." Gandhi conceived of Satyagraha, loosely translated as "Soul Force," as a means of striving for truth and social justice through love, suffering, and conversion of the oppressor. Its tactic is courageous nonviolent resistance. Satyagraha owed a good deal to the Christian Gospels, for Christ's call to "love your enemies" touched Gandhi to the core.

As the undisputed leader of South Africa's Indians before the First World War, Gandhi put his philosophy into action. When the white government of South Africa severely restricted Asians' immigration and internal freedom of movement, he led a campaign of mass resistance. Thousands of Indian men and women marched across forbidden borders and peacefully withstood beatings, arrest, and imprisonment.

The struggle was hard and the odds long, but Gandhi never wavered. He remarked to a friend at the time, "Men say I am a saint losing myself in politics. The fact is I am a politician trying my hardest to be a saint."[10] In 1914, South Africa's exasperated whites agreed to many of the Indians' demands. A law was passed abolishing discriminatory taxes on Indian traders, recognizing the legality of non-Christian marriages, and permitting the continued immigration of free Indians. Satyagraha—militant nonviolence in pursuit of social justice—had proved itself a powerful force in Gandhi's hands.

Gandhi Leads the Way

In 1915 Gandhi returned to India. His reputation had preceded him: the masses hailed him as a "Mahatma," or "Great Soul"—a Hindu title of veneration for a man of great knowledge and humanity—and the name stuck. Feeling his way into Indian affairs, Gandhi, dressed in peasant garb, crisscrossed India on third-class trains, listening to common folk and talking to Congress party leaders. Moved by the wretched misery of the very poor, he led some sharecroppers against British landowners and organized a strike of textile workers in his native Gujarat. But it was the aftermath of the Amritsar Massacre that catapulted Gandhi to leadership of the national movement in India.

Drawing on his South African experience, Gandhi in 1920 launched a national campaign of nonviolent resistance to British rule. Denouncing British injustice, he urged his countrymen to boycott British goods, jobs, and honors. He returned medals that he had won in South Africa and told peasants not to pay taxes or buy heavily taxed liquor. Gandhi electrified the people.

The result was nothing less than a revolution in Indian politics. The nationalist movement had previously touched only the tiny, prosperous, Western-educated elite. Now both the illiterate masses of village India and the educated classes heard a voice that seemed to be in harmony with their profoundest values. Even Gandhi's renunciation of sex—with his wife's consent—accorded with a popular Hindu belief attributing special power to those who do not squander their life force in sexual intercourse. Gandhi's call for militant nonviolence was particularly appealing to the masses of Hindus who were not members of the warrior caste or the so-called military races and who were traditionally passive and nonviolent. The British had regarded ordinary Hindus as cowards. Gandhi told them that they could be courageous and even morally superior:

Formerly, when people wanted to fight with one another, they measured between them their bodily strength; now it is possible to take away thousands of lives by one man working behind a gun from a hill. . . .

What do you think? Wherein is courage required— in blowing others to pieces from behind a cannon, or with a smiling face to approach a cannon and be blown to pieces? Who is the true warrior—he who keeps death always as a bosom-friend, or he who controls the death of others? Believe me that a man devoid of courage and manhood can never be a passive resister.[11]

Gandhi made Congress into a mass political party, welcoming members from every ethnic group and cooperating closely with the Muslim minority.

In 1922, some Indian resisters turned to violence. A mob murdered twenty-two policemen and savage riots broke out. Gandhi abruptly called off his campaign. Arrested for fomenting rebellion, Gandhi told the British judge that he had committed "a Himalayan blunder to believe that India had accepted nonviolence."[12] Released from prison after two years, Gandhi set up a commune, established a national newspaper, and set out to reform Indian society and improve the lot of the poor. He welcomed the outcaste untouchables into his fellowship. He worked to help child widows, promote cottage industry, and end the use of alcohol. For Gandhi, moral improvement, social progress, and the national movement always went hand in hand.

The resistance campaign of 1920–1922 left the British severely shaken. Although moderate Indians had participated effectively in the system of dual government, the commission formed by the British in 1927 to consider further steps toward self-rule included no Indian members. Indian resentment was intense. In 1929, the radical nationalists, led by the able and aristocratic Jawaharlal Nehru (1889–1964), pushed through the National Congress a resolution calling for virtual independence within a year. The British predictably stiffened, and Indian radicals talked of a bloody showdown.

In this tense situation Gandhi masterfully reasserted his leadership. To satisfy the extremists, he took a hard line toward the British, but he controlled the extremists by insisting on nonviolent methods. He then organized another massive resistance campaign, this time against the hated salt tax, which affected every Indian family. Gandhi himself led 50,000 people in a spectacular march to the sea to make salt without paying a

The Flag of the Indian National Congress flies over this mass political meeting. Gandhi believed that India had to revive its handicraft industry and he chose the Indian spinning wheel—placed in the center of the party's flag—as a symbol of national rejuvenation. *(Source: Wide World Photos)*

tax, in defiance of the law. A Western journalist described their reception:

Suddenly, at a word of command, scores of native policemen rushed upon the advancing marchers and rained blows on their heads. . . . No one of the marchers even raised an arm to fend off the blows. They went down like ten-pins. From where I stood I heard the whack of the clubs on unprotected skulls.... Those struck down fell sprawling, unconscious or writhing with fractured skulls or broken shoulders.... The survivors, without breaking ranks, silently and doggedly marched on until struck down.[13]

Over the next few months 60,000 protesters, including Gandhi, went to jail, but this time there was very little rioting. Finally, in 1931, the frustrated, unnerved British released Gandhi from jail and sat down to negotiate with him, as an equal, over self-rule for India. There were many complications, including the determined opposition of diehard imperialists like Winston Churchill. But in 1935 the negotiations resulted in a new constitution, which greatly strengthened India's parliamentary representative institutions. It was virtually a blueprint for independence.

Gandhi inspired people far beyond India's borders. Martin Luther King, Jr., was later to be deeply influenced by his tactic and philosophy of nonviolent social action. Gandhi did much to transform the elitist nationalism of Indian intellectuals into a mighty mass movement with social as well as political concerns. Above all, Gandhi nurtured national identity and self-respect. As Nehru summed it up, Gandhi "instilled courage and manhood in India's people; . . . courage is the one sure foundation of character, he had said; without courage there is no morality, no religion, no love."[14]

Despite his best efforts, Gandhi failed to heal a widening split between Hindus and Muslims. The development of an Indian nationalism based largely on Hindu symbols and customs increasingly disturbed the Muslim minority. Tempers mounted and atrocities were committed by both sides. By the late 1930s the leaders of the Muslim League were calling for the creation of a Muslim nation in British India, a "Pakistan" or "land of the pure." As in Palestine, the rise of conflicting nationalisms in India was to lead to tragedy (see page 1083).

TURMOIL IN EAST ASIA

Because of the efforts of the Meiji reformers, nationalism and modernization were well developed in Japan by 1914. Not only was Japan capable of competing politically and economically with the world's leading nations, but it had already begun building its own empire and proclaiming its special mission in Asia. China lagged far behind, but after 1912 the pace of nationalist development there began to quicken.

In the 1920s the Chinese nationalist movement managed to win a large measure of political independence from the imperialist West and promoted extensive modernization. But these achievements were soon undermined by internal conflict and war with an expanding Japan. Nationalism also flourished elsewhere in Asia, scoring a major victory in the Philippine Islands.

The Rise of Nationalist China

The revolution of 1911–1912, which overthrew the Manchu Dynasty (see page 987), opened an era of unprecedented change for Chinese society. Before the revolution, many progressive Chinese had realized that fundamental technological and political reforms were necessary to save the Chinese state and to meet the many-sided Western challenge. Most had hoped, however, to preserve the traditional core of Chinese civilization and culture. The fall of the 2,000-year-old dynastic system shattered such hopes. If the emperor himself was no longer sacred, what was? Everything was open to question and to alteration.

The central figure in the revolution was a crafty old military man, Yüan Shih-k'ai (1859–1916). Called out of retirement to save the dynasty, Yüan betrayed the Manchus and convinced the revolutionaries that he was a Chinese Bismarck who could unite the country peacefully and prevent foreign intervention. Once elected president of the republic, however, Yüan concentrated on building his own power. He quarreled with parliament and with Sun Yat-sen (see page 987), the inspiring revolutionary leader who had built the Kuomintang, or Nationalist party. Once again Yüan was a betrayer. In 1914, he used military force to dissolve China's parliament and ruled as a dictator. China's first modern revolution had failed.

The extent of the failure became apparent only after Yüan's death in 1916. The central government in Peking almost disintegrated. For more than a decade power resided in a multitude of local military leaders, the so-called warlords. Most warlords were men of strong, flamboyant personality, capable of building armies by preying on the peas-

antry and of winning legal recognition from Peking. None of them proved able to establish either
a new dynasty or a modern state. Their wars, taxes,
and corruption created only terrible suffering.

Foreign imperialism intensified the agony of
warlordism. Although China declared its neutrality in 1914, Japan used the Great War in Europe as
an opportunity to seize Germany's holdings on
the Shantung Peninsula and in 1915 forced China
to accept Japanese control of Shantung and southern Manchuria (see Map 30.4, page 986). Japan's
expansion angered China's growing middle class
and enraged China's young patriots. On May 4,
1919, five thousand students in Peking exploded
against the decision of the Versailles Peace Conference to leave the Shantung Peninsula in Japanese
hands. This famous incident launched the "May
Fourth Movement," which opposed both foreign
domination and warlord government.

The May Fourth Movement and the anti-imperialism of Bolshevik Russia renewed the hopes of
Chinese nationalists. Struggling for a foothold in

southern China, Sun Yat-sen (1866–1925) decided in 1923 to ally his Nationalist party with the
Communist Third International and the newly
formed Chinese Communist party. The result was
the first of many so-called national liberation
fronts, in keeping with Lenin's blueprint for (temporarily) uniting all anticonservative, anti-imperialist forces in a common revolutionary struggle.
In an effort to develop a disciplined party apparatus and a well-indoctrinated party army, Sun reorganized the Nationalist party along Bolshevik
lines.

Sun, however, was no Communist. In his *Three
Principles of the People,* elaborating on the official
Nationalist party ideology—nationalism, democracy, and people's livelihood—nationalism remained of prime importance:

*For the most part the four hundred million people of
China can be spoken of as completely Han Chinese.
With common habits and customs, we are completely
of one race. But in the world today what position do*

Civil War in China Chiang Kai-shek's move to purge his Communist allies in 1927
marked the beginning of a long bitter conflict. Here dead combatants lie on a main
street in Canton, where in December 1927 a Communist uprising established an independent commune that was soon crushed. *(Source: BBC Hulton/The Bettmann Archive)*

we occupy? Compared to the other peoples of the world we have the greatest population and our civilization is four thousand years old; we should be advancing in the front rank with the nations of Europe and America. But the Chinese people have only family and clan solidarity, they do not have national spirit. Therefore even though we have four hundred million people gathered together in one China, in reality they are just a heap of loose sand. Today we are the poorest and weakest nation in the world, and occupy the lowest position in international affairs. Other men are the carving knife and serving dish; we are the fish and the meat. Our position at this time is most perilous. If we do not earnestly espouse nationalism and weld together our four hundred million people into a strong nation, there is a danger of China's being lost and our people being destroyed. If we wish to avert this catastrophe, we must espouse nationalism and bring this national spirit to the salvation of the country.[15]

Democracy, on the other hand, had a less exalted meaning. Sun equated it with firm rule by the Nationalists, who would promote the people's livelihood through land reform and welfare measures. Sun was in some ways a traditional Chinese rebel and reformer who wanted to re-establish order and protect the peasants.

Sun's plan was to use the Nationalist party's revolutionary army to crush the warlords and reunite China under a strong central government. When Sun unexpectedly died in 1925, this task was assumed by Chiang Kai-shek (1887–1975), the young Japanese-educated director of the party's army training school. In 1926 and 1927, Chiang led enthusiastic Nationalist armies in a highly successful attack on warlord governments in central and northern China. Preceded by teams of party propagandists, the well-disciplined Nationalist armies were welcomed by the people. In a series of complicated moves, the Nationalists consolidated their rule in 1928 and established a new capital at Nanking. Foreign states recognized the Nanking government, and superficial observers believed China to be truly reunified.

In fact, national unification was only skin-deep. China remained a vast agricultural country plagued by foreign concessions, regional differences, and a lack of modern communications. Moreover, Japan was opposed to a China strong enough to challenge Japan's stranglehold on Manchuria. Finally, the uneasy alliance between the Nationalist party and the Chinese Communist party had turned into a bitter, deadly rivalry. Justifiably fearful of Communist subversion of the Nationalist government and encouraged by his military success and by wealthy Chinese capitalists, Chiang decided in April 1927 to liquidate his left-wing "allies" in a bloody purge. Secret agents raided Communist cells without warning, and soldiers gunned down suspects on sight. Chinese Communists went into hiding and vowed revenge.

China's Intellectual Revolution

Nationalism was the most powerful idea in China between 1911 and 1929, but it was only one aspect of a highly complex intellectual revolution that hammered at traditional Chinese thought and practice, advocated cultural renaissance, and led China into the modern world. Two other currents in that intellectual revolution, generally known as the "New Culture Movement," were significant.

The New Culture Movement was founded by young Western-oriented intellectuals in Peking during the May Fourth era. These intellectuals fiercely attacked China's ancient Confucian ethics, which subordinated subjects to rulers, sons to fathers, and wives to husbands. Confucius had lived in a distant feudal age, they said; his teachings were totally inappropriate to modern life. In such widely read magazines as *New Youth* and *New Tide,* the modernists provocatively advocated new and anti-Confucian virtues: individualism, democratic equality, and the critical scientific method. They also promoted the use of simple, understandable written language, a language freed from classical scholarship and literary conventions, as a means to clear thinking and mass education. China, they said, needed a whole new culture, a radically different world view.

The most influential of these intellectuals championing liberalism was Hu Shih (1891–1962). Educated on a scholarship in the United States, Hu had studied with the educational philosopher John Dewey, whose thoroughly American pragmatism stressed compromise and practical problem solving. A master at tearing down old beliefs, the mature Hu Shih envisioned a vague and uninspiring future. The liberation and reconstruction of China was possible, he said, but it would have to occur gradually, "bit by bit, drop by drop." Hu personified the limitations of the Western liberal tradition in China.

The other major current growing out of the New Culture Movement was Marxian socialism. It too was Western in origin, "scientific" in approach, and materialist in its denial of religious belief and Confucian family ethics. But while liberalism and individualism reflected the bewildering range of Western thought since the Enlightenment, Marxian socialism offered Chinese intellectuals the certainty of a single all-encompassing creed. As one young Communist exclaimed:

I am now able to impose order on all the ideas which I could not reconcile; I have found the key to all the problems which appeared to me self-contradictory and insoluble.[16]

Marxism was undeniably Western and therefore modern. But it also provided a means of criticizing Western dominance, thereby salving Chinese pride: China's pitiful weakness was due to rapacious foreign capitalistic imperialism. Also Marxism, as modified by Lenin and applied by the Bolsheviks, appeared to get results. For Chinese believers, it promised salvation soon. Chinese Communists could and did interpret Marxism-Leninism to appeal to the masses—the peasants.

Mao Tse-tung (1893–1976) in particular recognized quickly the enormous revolutionary potential of the Chinese peasantry, impoverished and oppressed by parasitic landlords. A member of a prosperous, hard-working peasant family, Mao converted to Marxian socialism in 1918 while employed as an assistant librarian at Peking University and began his revolutionary career as an urban labor organizer. In 1925 protest strikes by Chinese textile workers against their Japanese employers unexpectedly spread from the big coastal cities to rural China, prompting Mao to reconsider the peasants. Investigating the rapid growth of radical peasant associations in Hunan province, Mao argued passionately in a 1927 report that

the force of the peasantry is like that of the raging winds and driving rain. It is rapidly increasing in violence. No force can stand in its way. The peasantry will tear apart all nets which bind it and hasten along the road to liberation. They will bury beneath them all forces of imperialism, militarism, corrupt officialdom, village bosses and evil gentry. Every revolutionary party, every revolutionary comrade will be subjected to their scrutiny and be accepted or rejected by them.[17]

Mao Tse-tung Adapting Marxian theory to Chinese reality, Mao concentrated on the revolutionary potential of the peasantry. Here the forty-year-old Mao is preaching his gospel to representatives of poor peasants in southern China in 1933. *(Source: Wide World Photos)*

The task of Communists was to harness the peasant hurricane and use its elemental force to destroy the existing order and take power. Mao's first experiment in peasant revolt—the Autumn Harvest Uprising of September 1927—was no more successful than the abortive insurrections of urban workers launched by his more orthodox comrades. But Mao learned quickly. He advocated equal distribution of land and broke up his forces into small guerrilla groups. After 1928 he and his supporters built up a self-governing Communist soviet, centered at Juichin in southeastern China, and dug in against Nationalist attacks.

The Changing Chinese Family

For many generations, Confucian reverence for the family and family ties helped stabilize traditional Chinese society and gave life meaning. The

A Manchu Family   The women of a large, rich Manchu family pose for a solemn group portrait. Coming out of Manchuria and ruling China until 1912, the Manchus sought to preserve a separate cultural identity. Unlike Chinese women, Manchu women did not bind their feet. *(Source: Popperfoto)*

Confucian principle of subordination suffused family life—subordination of the individual to the group, of the young to the old, of the wife to the husband. Given in marriage by her parents at an early age, the wife owed unquestioning obedience to her husband and mother-in-law. Wealthy husbands customarily took additional wives or purchased concubines from poor families, but for women divorce and running away were almost unthinkable. Women of all ages were commonly sold, and they lacked all property rights.

A Daughter of Han, a rare autobiography of a Chinese woman, as told to an American friend, offers an unforgettable glimpse of Chinese family life. Born in 1867 to poor parents in a northern city, Lao T'ai T'ai lived it all. Her foot-binding was delayed to age nine, "since I loved so much to run and play." When the bandages were finally drawn tight, "my feet hurt so much that for two years I had to crawl on my knees."[18] Her arranged marriage at fourteen was a disaster: her husband

was a drug addict—"in those days everyone took opium to some extent"—who grabbed everything to pay for his habit. "There was no freedom then for women," and she endured her situation until her husband sold their four-year-old daughter to buy opium. Taking her remaining baby daughter, Lao T'ai T'ai fled. She became a beggar, a cook in wealthy households, and a peddler of luxury goods to wealthy cooped-up women.

The two unshakable values that buoyed her were a tough, fatalistic acceptance—"Only fortune that comes of itself will come. There is no use to seek for it"—and devotion to her family. Lao T'ai T'ai eventually returned home to her husband, who was "good" in those years, "but I did not miss him when he died. I had my newborn son and I was happy. My house was established. . . . Truly all my life I spent thinking of my family." Her lifelong devotion was reciprocated by her faithful son and granddaughter, who cared for her well in old age.

EAST ASIA, 1911–1939

1911–1912	Revolution in China overthrows Manchu dynasty and establishes republic
1915	Japan seizes German holdings in China and expands into southern Manchuria
May 4, 1919	Demonstration by Chinese students against Versailles peace conference and Japan sparks broad nationalist movement
1920s	New Cultural Movement challenges traditional Chinese values
1922	Japan signs naval agreement with Western powers
1923	Sun Yat-sen allies the Nationalist Party with Chinese Communists
	Kita Ikki advocates ultranationalism in Japan
1925–1928	Chiang Kai-shek, leader of the Nationalist Party, attacks warlord government and seeks to unify China
1927	Chiang Kai-shek purges his Communist allies
	Mao Tse-tung recognizes the revolutionary potential of the Chinese peasantry
1930–1934	Nationalists campaign continually against the Chinese Communists
1931	Mukden Incident leads to Japanese occupation of Manchuria
1932	Japan proclaims Manchuria an independent state
1934	Mao Tse-tung leads Communists on Long March to new base in northwestern China
	The Philippines gain self-governing commonwealth status from United States
1936	Japan allies with Germany in anti-Communist pact
1937	Japanese militarists launch general attack on China

Lao T'ai T'ai's remarkable life history encompasses both old and new Chinese attitudes toward the family. Her son moved to the city, prospered, and had only one wife. Her granddaughter eventually became a college teacher, an anti-Japanese patriot, and a determined foe of arranged marriages, admirably personifying the trend toward greater freedom and equality for Chinese women after 1911. Foot-binding was outlawed and gradually died out unlamented. Marriage for love became increasingly common, and unprecedented educational and economic opportunities opened up for women. Polygamy declined. In the short space of three generations, rising nationalism and the intellectual revolution accomplished monumental changes in Chinese family life.

From Liberalism to Ultranationalism in Japan

The efforts of the Meiji reformers (see page 983) to build a powerful nationalistic state and resist Western imperialism were spectacularly successful and deeply impressive to Japan's fellow Asians. The Japanese, alone among non-Western peoples, had mastered modern industrial technology by 1910 and fought victorious wars against both China and Russia. The First World War brought more triumphs. Japan easily seized Germany's Asian holdings and held on to most of them as League of Nations mandates. The Japanese economy expanded enormously. Profits soared as Japan won new markets that wartime Europe could no longer supply.

In the early 1920s Japan seemed to make further progress on all fronts. Most Japanese nationalists believed that Japan had a semidivine mission to enlighten and protect Asia, but some were convinced that they could achieve their goal peacefully. In 1922, Japan signed a naval arms limitation treaty with the Western powers and returned some of its control over the Shantung Peninsula to China. These conciliatory moves reduced tensions in East Asia. At home, Japan seemed headed toward genuine democracy. The electorate expanded twelve-fold between 1918 and 1925 as all males over twenty-five won the vote. Two-party competition was intense, and cabinet ministers were made responsible to the lower house. Japanese living standards were the highest in Asia. Literacy was universal.

Japan's remarkable rise, however, was accompanied by serious problems. Japan had a rapidly growing population, but natural resources were scarce. As early as the 1920s Japan was exporting manufactured goods in order to pay for imports of food and essential raw materials. Deeply enmeshed in world trade, Japan was vulnerable to every boom and bust. These conditions reinforced the widespread belief that colonies and foreign expansion were matters of life and death for Japan.

Also, rapid industrial development had created an imbalanced "dualistic" economy. The modern sector consisted of a handful of giant conglomerate firms, the *zaibatsu,* or "financial combine." A zaibatsu firm like Mitsubishi employed thousands of workers and owned banks, mines, steel mills, cotton factories, shipyards, and trading companies, all of which were closely interrelated. Zaibatsu firms had enormous economic power and dominated the other sector of the economy, which

Little Samurai Proud to wear the battle dress of Japan's feudal warriors, a group of boys imitate their leader in a patriotic procession on Empire Day in 1934. The values of Japanese nationalism are being passed to the next generation. *(Source: UPI/Bettmann Newsphotos)*

consisted of an unorganized multitude of peasant farmers and craftsmen. The result was financial oligarchy, corruption of government officials, and a weak middle class.

Behind the façade of party politics, the old and new elites—the emperor, high government officials, big businessmen, and military leaders—were jockeying savagely for the real power. Cohesive leadership, which had played such an important role in Japan's modernization by the Meiji reformers, had ceased to exist.

By far the most serious challenge to peaceful progress, however, was fanatical nationalism. As in Europe, ultranationalism first emerged in Japan in the late nineteenth century but did not flower fully until the First World War and the 1930s. Though often vague, Japan's ultranationalists shared several fundamental beliefs.

The ultranationalists were violently anti-Western. They rejected democracy, big business, and Marxian socialism, which they blamed for destroying the older, superior Japanese practices that they wanted to restore. Reviving old myths, they stressed the emperor's godlike qualities and the samurai warrior's code of honor and obedience. Despising party politics, they assassinated moderate leaders and plotted armed uprisings to achieve their goals. Above all else, the ultranationalists preached foreign expansion. Like Western imperialists with their "white man's burden," Japanese ultranationalists thought theirs was a noble mission. "Asia for the Asians" was their self-satisfied rallying cry. As the famous ultranationalist Kita Ikki wrote in 1923:

Our seven hundred million brothers in China and India have no other path to independence than that offered by our guidance and protection. . . . The noble Greece of Asian culture must complete her national reorganization on the basis of her own national polity. At the same time, let her lift the virtuous banner of an Asian league and take the leadership in a world federation which must come.[19]

The ultranationalists were noisy and violent in the 1920s, but it took the Great Depression of the 1930s to tip the scales decisively in their favor. The worldwide depression hit Japan like a tidal wave in 1930. Exports and wages collapsed; unemployment and raw suffering soared. Starving peasants ate the bark off trees and sold their daughters to brothels. The ultranationalists blamed the system, and people listened.

Japan Against China

Among those who listened with particular care were young Japanese army officers in Manchuria. This underpopulated, resource-rich province of northeastern China, controlled by the Japanese army since its victory over Russia in 1905, seemed a particularly valuable asset in the depression. Many junior Japanese officers in Manchuria came from the peasantry and were distressed by the stories of rural suffering they heard from home. They also knew that the budget and prestige of the Japanese army had declined in the prosperous 1920s.

Most worrisome of all to the young officers was the rise of Chinese nationalism. This new political force challenged the control that Japan exercised over Manchuria through Chinese warlord puppets. In response, junior Japanese officers in Manchuria, in cooperation with top generals in Tokyo, secretly manufactured an excuse for aggression in late 1931. They blew up some tracks on a Japanese-owned railroad near the city of Mukden and then quickly occupied all of Manchuria in "self-defense."

In 1932 Japan proclaimed Manchuria an independent state with a Manchu puppet as emperor. When the League of Nations condemned its aggression in Manchuria, Japan resigned in protest. Politics in Japan became increasingly chaotic. The army, though reporting directly to the emperor of Japan, was clearly an independent force subject to no outside control.

For China, the Japanese conquest of Manchuria was disastrous. After unifying most of China in 1928, the Nationalist government had won from the Western powers the right to set tariffs and other marks of sovereignty. The government had also begun to expand higher education, build railroads, and improve the banking system. Japanese aggression in Manchuria drew attention away from these modernizing efforts, which in any event had been none too vigorous. The Nationalist government promoted a massive boycott of Japanese goods but lost interest in social reform.

Above all, the Nationalist government after 1931 completely neglected land reform and the grinding poverty of the Chinese peasants. As in

The Japanese Army in Manchuria Consolidating their hold on China's rich northern province, these Japanese troops are occupying the strategic city of Hailar near the border with the Soviet Union. The Japanese seizure of Manchuria in 1931 was disastrous for China, a prelude to Japan's general attack in 1937. *(Source: Wide World Photos)*

many poor agricultural societies, Chinese peasants paid roughly half of their crops to their landlords as rent. Ownership of land was very unequal. One careful study estimated that fully half of the land was owned by a mere 4 percent of the families, usually absentee landlords living in cities. Poor peasants and farm laborers—70 percent of the rural population—owned only one-sixth of the land.

Peasants were heavily in debt and chronically underfed. Eggs and meat accounted for only 2 percent of the food consumed by poor and middle-income peasants. A contemporary Chinese economist spelled out the revolutionary implications: "It seems clear that the land problem in China today is as acute as that of eighteenth-century France or nineteenth-century Russia."[20] Mao Tse-tung certainly agreed.

Having abandoned land reform, partly because they themselves were often landowners, the Nationalists under Chiang Kai-shek devoted their energies between 1930 and 1934 to five great campaigns of encirclement and extermination against the Communists' rural power base in southeastern China. In 1934 they closed in for the kill, only to miss again. In one of the most incred-

MAP 33.2 The Chinese Communist Movement and the War with Japan, 1927–1938 After urban uprisings ordered by Stalin failed in 1927, Mao Tse-tung succeeded in forming a self-governing Communist soviet in mountainous southern China. Relentless Nationalist attacks between 1930 and 1934 finally forced the Long March to Yenan, where the Communists were well positioned for guerrilla war against the Japanese.

	Scale	
0	250	500 Km.
0	250	500 Mi.

U.S.S.R.

MANCHURIA

OUTER MONGOLIA
(Independent 1924)

Tsitsihar

Kiamusze

Harbin

Amur

Ussuri

Mukden

Chinchow

Paotow

Kalgan

Peking

Tientsin

KOREA
(Japanese 1910–1945)

Port Arthur
(Lüshun)

Taiyuan

Yenan

Lanchow

SHENSI

Sian

Loyang

Yellow

Chengchow

Tsinan

Tsingtao

CHINA

Suchow

Nanking

Shanghai

Chengtu

Yangtze

SZECHWAN

Chungking

Wuhan

Hangchow

Tsunyi

Nanchang

Changsha

Kweiyang

HUNAN

Kiangsi Soviet under
Mao Tse-tung and
Chu Ta, 1929–1934

Kunming

Juichin

TAIWAN
(Japanese
1895–1945)

*PACIFIC
OCEAN*

Amoy

Canton uprising,
Dec. 1927

Swatow

Canton

BURMA

Hailufeng Soviet,
1927–1928

Hong Kong
(British)

**FRENCH
INDO-CHINA**

▨	Areas under Communist control before Nov. 1934
▩	Areas under Communist control, 1929–1938
▨	Areas occupied by Japan by end of 1938
←	Route of the Long March, Oct. 1934–Oct. 1935: Main forces from Juichin
←	Other forces

ible sagas of modern times, the main Communist army broke out of the Nationalist encirclement, beat off attacks, and marched 6,000 miles in twelve months to a remote region on the northwestern border (Map 33.2). Of the estimated 100,000 men and women who began the Long March, only from 8,000 to 10,000 reached the final destination. There Mao Tse-tung built up his forces once again, established a new territorial base, and won the support of local peasants by undertaking land reform.

Mao Tse-tung and his Communists gradually emerged as the more determined nationalists. Once again, the decisive factor in the eyes of ordinary Chinese was Japanese aggression. In 1937, the Japanese military and the ultranationalists were in command and decided to use a minor incident near Peking as a pretext for a general attack. The Nationalist government, which had just formed a united front with the Communists in response to the demands of Chinese patriots, fought hard but could not halt the Japanese.

By late 1938, Japanese armies occupied sizable portions of coastal China (see Map 33.2). The Nationalists and the Communists had retreated to the interior, both refusing to accept defeat. The determination of the Communist guerrillas equaled that of the Nationalists, and their political skill proved superior. In 1939, as Europe (and the United States) edged toward the Second World War, the undeclared war between China and Japan bogged down in a savage stalemate. The bloody clash on the mainland provided a spectacular example of conflicting nationalism, convulsing China and preparing for Communist victory.

Southeast Asia

The tide of nationalism was also rising in Southeast Asia. Like their counterparts in India, China, and Japan, nationalists in Southeast Asia urgently wanted genuine political independence and freedom from foreign rule. In both French Indochina and the Dutch East Indies, local nationalists were inspired by events elsewhere in Asia. Japan's rise to the status of Great Power, the struggle of Gandhi and the Congress party in India, and China's unification under the Nationalists all encouraged Vietnamese and Indonesian patriots to press their own demands. In both cases they ran up against an imperialist stone wall.

In the words of one historian, "Indochina was governed by Frenchmen for Frenchmen, and the great liberal slogans of liberty, equality, and fraternity were not considered to be export goods for overseas dominions."[21] This uncompromising attitude stimulated the growth of an equally stubborn Communist opposition, which emerged despite ruthless repression as the dominant anti-French force.

In the East Indies—modern Indonesia—the Dutch made some concessions after the First World War, establishing a people's council with very limited lawmaking power. But in the 1930s the Dutch cracked down hard, jailing all the important nationalist leaders. Like the French, the Dutch were determined to hold on.

In the Philippines, however, a mature and well-established nationalist movement achieved greater success. As in colonial Latin America, the Spanish in the Philippines had been indefatigable missionaries. By the late nineteenth century 80 percent of the Filipino population was Catholic. Filipinos shared a common cultural heritage as well as a common racial origin. Education, especially for girls, was quite advanced for Southeast Asia, and in 1843 a higher percentage of people could read in the Philippines than in Spain itself. Economic development helped to create a Westernized elite, which turned first to reform and then to revolution in the 1890s. As in Egypt or Turkey, long-standing intimate contact with Western civilization created a strong nationalist movement at an early date.

Filipino nationalists were bitterly disillusioned when the United States, having taken the Philippines from Spain in the Spanish-American War of 1898, ruthlessly beat down a patriotic revolt and denied the universal Filipino desire for independence. The Americans claimed that the Philippines were not ready and might be seized by Germany or Britain. As the imperialist power in the Philippines, the United States encouraged education and promoted capitalistic economic development. As in British India, an elected legislature was given some real powers. In 1919 President Wilson even promised eventual independence, though subsequent Republican administrations saw it as a distant goal.

As in India and French Indochina, demands for independence grew. One important contributing factor was American racial attitudes. Americans treated Filipinos as inferiors and introduced segre-

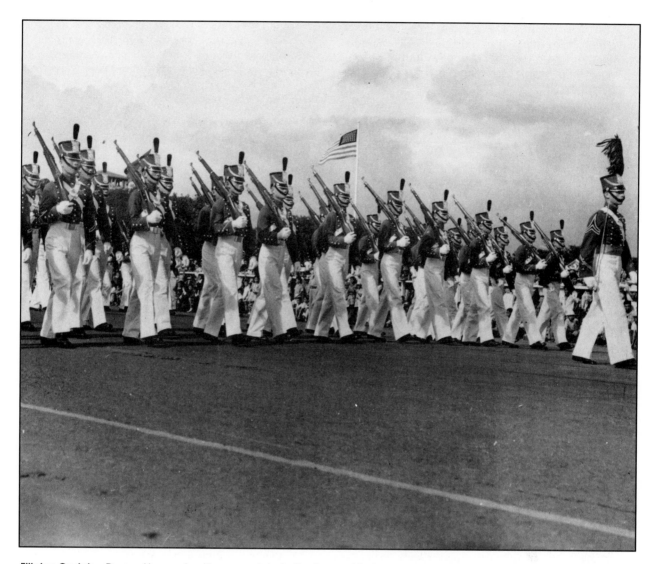

Filipino Cadets Dressed in smart uniforms modeled after those of their West Point counterparts in the United States, these future officers of the Philippine army march with flawless precision. They are passing the reviewing stand in a 1937 parade celebrating American promises of political independence for the Philippines. *(Source: UPI/Bettmann Newsphotos)*

gationist practices borrowed from the American South. American racism made passionate nationalists of many Filipinos.

However, it was the Great Depression that had the most radical impact on the Philippines. As the United States collapsed economically, the Philippines suddenly appeared to be a liability rather than an asset. American farm groups lobbied for protection from cheap Filipino sugar. To protect American jobs, labor unions demanded an end to Filipino immigration. In 1934 Congress made the

Philippines a self-governing commonwealth and scheduled independence for 1944. Sugar imports were reduced, and immigration was limited to only fifty Filipinos per year.

Like Britain and France in the Middle East, the United States was determined to hold on to its big military bases in the Philippines as it permitted increased local self-government and promised eventual political independence. The continued presence of U.S. fleets and armies was denounced by some Filipino nationalists. Others were less certain that the American presence was the immediate problem. Japan was fighting in China and expanding economically into the Philippines and throughout Southeast Asia. By 1939, a new threat to Filipino independence appeared to come from Asia itself.

SUMMARY

The Asian revolt against the West began before the First World War. But only after 1914 did Asian nationalist movements broaden their bases and become capable of challenging Western domination effectively. These mass movements sought human dignity as well as political freedom. Generally speaking, Asian nationalists favored modernization and adopted Western techniques and ideas even as they rejected Western rule. Everywhere Asian nationalists had to fight long and hard, though their struggle gained momentum from the relative decline of European power and confidence, the encouragement of the Soviet Union, and American calls for self-determination.

Asia's nationalist movements arose out of separate historical experiences and distinct cultures. This chapter surveys the variations on the common theme of nationalism in Turkey, the Arab world, India, China, Japan, and the Philippines. This diversity helps explain why Asian peoples became defensive in their relations with one another while rising against Western rule. Like earlier nationalists in Europe, Asian nationalists developed a strong sense of "we" and "they"; "they" included other Asians as well as Europeans. Nationalism meant freedom, modernization, and cultural renaissance, but it nonetheless proved a mixed blessing.

NOTES

1. K. M. Panikkar, *Asia and Western Dominance: A Survey of the Vasco da Gama Epoch of Asian History* (London: George Allen & Unwin, 1959), p. 197.
2. Quoted in Henri Grimal, *La Décolonisation, 1919–1965* (Paris: Armand Colin, 1965), p. 100.
3. Quoted in Peter Mansfield, *The Ottoman Empire and Its Successors* (New York: St. Martin's Press, 1973), p. 18.
4. Harold Armstrong, *Turkey in Travail: The Birth of a New Nation* (London: John Lane, 1925), p. 75.
5. Quoted in Lord Kinross, *Atatürk: A Biography of Mustafa Kemal, Father of Modern Turkey* (New York: Morrow, 1965), p. 181.
6. Percival Spear, *India, Pakistan, and the West,* 3d ed. (Oxford: Oxford University Press, 1958), p. 67.
7. Quoted in Erik Erikson, *Gandhi's Truth: On the Origins of Militant Nonviolence* (New York: Norton, 1969), p. 225.
8. Ibid., p. 105.
9. Hugh Tinker, *A New System of Slavery: The Export of Indian Labour Overseas, 1830–1920* (London: Oxford University Press, 1974).
10. Quoted in Louis Fischer, *Gandhi: His Life and Message for the World* (New York: New American Library, 1954), p. 35.
11. Quoted in Erikson, p. 225.
12. Quoted in Woodbridge Bingham, Hilary Conroy, and Fran Iklé, *A History of Asia,* vol. 1, 2d ed. (Boston: Allyn and Bacon, 1974), p. 447.
13. Webb Miller, *I Found No Peace: The Journal of a Foreign Correspondent* (New York: Simon and Schuster, 1936), p. 193.
14. Quoted in Lloyd Rudolph and Susanne Rudolph, *The Modernity of Tradition: Political Development in India* (Chicago: University of Chicago Press, 1967), p. 248.
15. Quoted in William Theodore deBary, Wing-tsit Chan, and Burton Watson, *Sources of Chinese Tradition* (New York: Columbia University Press, 1964), pp. 768–769.
16. Quoted in John F. Fairbank, Edwin O. Reischauer, and Albert M. Craig, *East Asia: Tradition and Transformation* (Boston: Houghton Mifflin, 1973), p. 774.
17. Quoted in Benjamin I. Schwartz, *Chinese Communism and the Rise of Mao* (Cambridge, Mass.: Harvard University Press, 1951), p. 74.
18. Ida Pruitt, *A Daughter of Han: The Autobiography of a Chinese Working Woman* (New Haven, Conn.: Yale University Press, 1945), p. 22. Other quotations are taken, in order, from pages 83, 71, 182, 166, and 235.
19. Quoted in William Theodore deBary, Ryusaku Tsunoda, and Donald Keene, *Sources of Japanese Tradition,* vol. 2 (New York: Columbia University Press, 1958), p. 269.
20. Quoted in Olga Lang, *Chinese Family and Society* (New Haven, Conn.: Yale University Press, 1946), p. 70.
21. Quoted in Woodbridge Bingham, Hilary Conroy, and Fran Iklé, *A History of Asia,* vol. 2, 2d ed. (Boston: Allyn and Bacon, 1974), p. 480.

SUGGESTED READING

All of the works cited in the Notes are highly recommended. Two important general studies of nationalism and independence movements are H. Kohn, *The Age of Nationalism: The First Era of Global History* (1962), and R. Emerson, *From Empire to Nation: The Rise to Self-Assertion of Asian and African Peoples* (1960). These may be compared with the provocative works of E. Kedourie, *Nationalism in Asia and Africa* (1970) and *England and the Middle East: The Destruction of the Ottoman Empire, 1914–1921* (1956), and with a justly famous global history of the twentieth century by G. Barraclough, *An Introduction to Contemporary History* (1975). Two fine studies of the Middle East are G. Lenczowski, *The Middle East in World Affairs,* 4th ed. (1980), and S. N. Fisher, *The Middle East: A History,* 3d ed. (1979), both of which have detailed bibliographies. On Turkey, in addition to Lord Kinross's *Atatürk* (1965), see B. Lewis, *The Emergence of Modern Turkey* (1961), and D. Kushner, *The Rise of Turkish Nationalism, 1876–1908* (1977). Peter Mansfield, *The Arab World: A Comprehensive History* (1976), and S. G. Haim, ed., *Arab Nationalism: An Anthology* (1964), provide engaging general coverage and important source materials. W. Lacqueur, *A History of Zionism* (1972), and A. Eban, *My People* (1968), discuss the Jewish homeland in Palestine. The Arab viewpoint is presented by G. Antonius, *The Arab Awakening: The Story of the Arab National Movement* (1946). R. Cottam, *Nationalism in Iran*, rev. ed. (1979), complements the classic study of D. Wilbur, *Iran: Past and Present,* 9th ed. (1981).

The historical literature on modern India is very rich. S. Wolpert, *A New History of India,* 2d ed. (1982), is an excellent introduction, with up-to-date scholarship and detailed suggestions for further reading. Also see the handsomely illustrated volume by F. Watson, *A Concise History of India* (1975). In addition to the biographies of Gandhi by Erikson and Fischer cited in the Notes, J. Brown, *Gandhi's Rise to Power: Indian Politics, 1915–1922* (1972), and L. Gordon, *Bengal: The Nationalist Movement, 1876–1970* (1974), are major studies. Developments in the Muslim community are considered by P. Hardy, *The Muslims of British India* (1972); B. Metcalf, *Islamic Revival in British India: Deoband,* 1860–1900 (1982); and F. Robinson, *Atlas of the Islamic World Since 1500* (1982), a beautifully illustrated survey encompassing far more than India.

Studies of China in the twentieth century are also very numerous. J. Spence, *The Search for Modern China* (1990), and I. Hsü, *The Rise of Modern China,* 4th ed. (1990), are comprehensive studies with extensive bibliographies, which may be supplemented by the documentary collection of F. Schurmann and O. Schell, eds., *Republican China: Nationalism, War and the Rise of Communism, 1911–1949* (1967). J. Spence, *The Gate of Heavenly Peace: The Chinese and Their Revolution, 1895–1980* (1981), skillfully focuses on leading literary figures. T. Chow, *The May Fourth Movement: Intellectual Revolution in Modern China* (1960), examines a critical time period. Other important studies of China in this period include R. Hofheinz, Jr., *The Broken Wave: The Chinese Communist Peasant Movement, 1922–1928* (1977); S. Schram, *Mao Tse-tung* (1966); H. Schriffrin, *Sun Yat-sen and the Origins of the Chinese Revolution* (1970); and L. Eastman, *The Abortive Revolution: China Under Nationalist Rule, 1927–1937* (1974). P. Ebrey, ed., *Chinese Civilization and Society: A Sourcebook* (1981), complements the classic studies of the Chinese family by Lang and Pruitt, which may be compared with M. J. Levy, *The Family Revolution in Modern China* (1949). E. Reischauer, *Japan: The Story of a Nation,* rev. ed. (1970), and P. Duus, *The Rise of Modern Japan* (1976), are excellent interpretations of the recent history of the island nation. W. Lockwood, *The Economic Development of Japan, 1868–1938* (1954), and R. Storry, *The Double Patriots: A Story of Japanese Nationalism* (1973), are valuable specialized works. M. Hane, *Peasants, Rebels, and Outcasts: The Underside of Modern Japan* (1982), sees few benefits for the poor before 1945. S. Garon, *The State and Labor in Modern Japan* (1988), skillfully analyzes the history of Japanese labor relations. Two edited collections, J. Morley, *The China Quagmire* (1983), and R. Myers and M. Peattie, *The Japanese Colonial Expansion, 1895–1945* (1984), probe Japan's imperial expansion. For Southeast Asia, see D. G. E. Hall, *A History of South-east Asia,* 4th ed. (1981); J. Pluvier, *South-East Asia from Colonialism to Independence* (1974); and the Suggested Reading for Chapter 37. Two more recommended works are M. Osborne, *Southeast Asia: An Illustrated History,* expanded ed. (1988), and D. R. Sardesa, *Southeast Past and Present,* 2d ed. (1989).

34

The Age of Anxiety in the West

Isaac Soyer, *Employment Agency*, 1937

When Allied diplomats met in Paris in early 1919 with their optimistic plans for building a lasting peace, most people looked forward to happier times. They hoped that life would return to normal after the terrible trauma of total war. They hoped that once again life would make sense in the familiar prewar terms of peace, prosperity, and progress. These hopes were in vain. The Great Break—the First World War and the Russian Revolution—had mangled too many things beyond repair. Life would no longer fit neatly into the old molds or former routines.

Instead, great numbers of men and women in the West felt themselves increasingly adrift in a strange, uncertain, and uncontrollable world. They saw themselves living in an age of anxiety, an age of continuous crisis, which lasted until at least the early 1950s. In almost every area of human experience, people went searching for ways to put meaning back into life.

- What did the doubts and searching mean for Western thought, art, and culture?
- How did political leaders try to re-establish real peace and prosperity between 1919 and 1939?
- Why did those leaders fail?

These questions are explored in this chapter.

UNCERTAINTY IN MODERN THOUGHT

Before the Great War, a complex revolution in thought and ideas was under way in Western society, but only small, unusual groups were aware of it. After the war, new and upsetting ideas began to spread widely. People in the West began to question and even abandon many cherished values and beliefs that had guided Western society since the eighteenth-century Enlightenment and the nineteenth-century triumph of industrial development, scientific advances, and evolutionary thought.

Before 1914 most people in the West still believed in progress, reason, and the rights of the individual. Progress seemed to be a daily reality, apparent in rising standards of living, the taming of the cities, and steady increases in popular education. Such developments encouraged a comforting belief in the logical universe of Newtonian physics, as well as faith in the ability of a rational human mind to understand that universe through intellectual investigation. Just as there seemed to be laws of science, so there seemed to be laws of society that rational human beings could discover and then wisely act on. The rights of the individual were not taken for granted and were actually increasing. Well-established rights were gradually spreading to women and workers, and new "social rights" like old-age pensions were emerging. In short, before the Great War, most Europeans and North Americans had a moderately optimistic view of the world, and with good reason.

Since the 1880s, however, a small band of serious thinkers and creative writers had been attacking these well-worn optimistic ideas. These critics rejected the general faith in progress and the power of the rational human mind. Their views were greatly strengthened by the experience of history's most destructive war. The First World War suggested to many that human beings were a pack of violent, irrational animals quite capable of tearing individuals and their rights to shreds. Pessimism and a general crisis of the mind increased as a growing chorus of thinkers, creative writers, and scientists echoed and enlarged on the themes first expressed between 1880 and 1914. After the war, people did not know what to think. Their disorientation was particularly acute in the 1930s, when the rapid rise of harsh dictatorships and the Great Depression transformed old certainties into bitter illusions.

No one expressed this state of uncertainty better than the French poet and critic Paul Valéry (1871–1945) in the early 1920s. Speaking of the "crisis of the mind," Valéry noted that Europe was looking at its future with dark foreboding:

The storm has died away, and still we are restless, uneasy, as if the storm were about to break. Almost all the affairs of men remain in a terrible uncertainty. We think of what has disappeared, and we are almost destroyed by what has been destroyed; we do not know what will be born, and we fear the future, not without reason. . . . Doubt and disorder are in us and with us. There is no thinking man, however shrewd or learned he may be, who can hope to dominate this anxiety, to escape from this impression of darkness.[1]

"The War, as I Saw It" This was the title of a series of grotesque drawings that appeared in 1920 in *Simplicissimus*, Germany's leading satirical magazine. Nothing shows better the terrible impact of World War One than this profoundly disturbing example of expressionist art. *(Source: Caroline Buckler)*

In the midst of economic, political, and social disruptions Valéry saw the "cruelly injured mind," besieged by doubts and suffering from anxieties. This was the general intellectual crisis of the twentieth century—a crisis that touched almost every field of thought. The implications of new ideas and discoveries in philosophy, physics, psychology, and literature disturbed thinking men and women everywhere in the West.

Modern Philosophy

Among those thinkers in the late nineteenth century who challenged the belief in progress and the general faith in the rational human mind, the German philosopher Friedrich Nietzsche (1844–1900) was particularly influential. Nietzsche believed that Western civilization had lost its creativity and decayed into mediocrity. Christianity's "slave morality" had glorified weakness and humility. Furthermore, human beings in the West had overstressed rational thinking at the expense of passion and emotion. Nietzsche viewed the pillars of conventional morality—reason, democracy, progress, respectability—as outworn social and psychological constructs whose influence was suffocating creativity. The only hope of revival was for a few superior individuals to free themselves from the humdrum thinking of the masses and embrace life passionately. Such individuals would become true heroes, supermen capable of leading the dumb herd of inferior men and women. Nietzsche also condemned both political democracy and greater social equality.

The growing dissatisfaction with established ideas before 1914 was apparent in other important thinkers. In the 1890s, the French philosophy professor Henri Bergson (1859–1941) convinced many young people through his writing that immediate experience and intuition are as important as rational and scientific thinking for understanding reality. Indeed, according to Bergson, a religious experience or a mystical poem is often more accessible to human comprehension than a scientific law or a mathematical equation.

Another thinker who agreed about the limits of rational thinking was the French socialist Georges Sorel (1847–1922). Sorel frankly characterized Marxian socialism as an inspiring but unprovable religion rather than a rational scientific truth. Socialism would come to power, he believed, through a great, violent strike of all working people that would miraculously shatter capitalist society. Sorel rejected democracy and believed that the masses of the new socialist society would have to be tightly controlled by a small revolutionary elite.

The First World War accelerated the revolt against established certainties in philosophy, but that revolt went in two very different directions. In English-speaking countries, the main development was the acceptance of logical empiricism (or logical positivism) in university circles. In continental countries, where esoteric and remote logical empiricism has never won many converts, the primary development in philosophy was existentialism.

Logical empiricism was truly revolutionary. It quite simply rejected most of the concerns of traditional philosophy—from the existence of God to the meaning of happiness—as nonsense and hot air. This outlook began primarily with the Austrian philosopher Ludwig Wittgenstein (1889–1951), who later emigrated to England, where he trained numerous disciples.

Wittgenstein argued in his pugnacious *Tractatus Logico-Philosophicus (Essay on Logical Philosophy)* in 1922 that philosophy is only the logical clarification of thoughts and therefore it becomes the study of language, which expresses thoughts. The great philosophical issues of the ages—God, freedom, morality, and so on—are quite literally senseless, a great waste of time, for statements about them can be neither tested by scientific experiments nor demonstrated by the logic of mathematics. Statements about such matters reflect only the personal preferences of a given individual. As Wittgenstein put it in the famous last sentence of his work, "Of what one cannot speak, of that one must keep silent." Logical empiricism, which has remained dominant in England and the United States to this day, drastically reduced the scope of philosophical inquiry. Anxious people could find few if any answers in this direction.

Highly diverse and even contradictory, existential thinkers were loosely united in a courageous search for moral values in a world of terror and uncertainty. Theirs were true voices of the age of anxiety.

Most existential thinkers in the twentieth century have been atheists. Like Nietzsche, who had already proclaimed that "God is dead," they did not believe that a supreme being had established humanity's fundamental nature and given life its meaning. In the words of the famous French existentialist Jean-Paul Sartre (1905–1980), human beings simply exist: "They turn up, appear on the scene." Only after they "turn up" do they seek to define themselves. Honest human beings are terribly alone, for there is no God to help them. They are hounded by despair and the meaninglessness of life. The crisis of the existential thinker epitomized the modern intellectual crisis: the shattering of traditional beliefs in God, reason, and progress.

Existentialists did recognize that human beings, unless they kill themselves, must act. Indeed, in the words of Sartre, "man is condemned to be free." There is, therefore, the possibility—indeed, the necessity—of giving meaning to life through actions, of defining oneself through choices. To do so, individuals must become "engaged" and choose their own actions courageously, consistently, and in full awareness of their inescapable responsibility for their own behavior. In the end, existentialists argued, human beings can overcome the absurdity that existentialists saw in life.

Modern existentialism developed first in Germany in the 1920s, when the philosophers Martin Heidegger (1889–1976) and Karl Jaspers (1883–1969) found a sympathetic audience among disillusioned postwar university students. But it was in France during the years immediately after the Second World War that existentialism came of age. The terrible conditions of that war reinforced the existential view of life and the existential approach to it. On the one hand, the armies of the German dictator Adolf Hitler had conquered most of Europe and unleashed a hideous reign of barbarism. On the other, men and women had more than ever to define themselves by their actions. Specifically, each individual had to choose whether to join the Resistance against Hitler or to accept and even abet tyranny. The writings of Sartre, who along with Albert Camus (1913–1960) was the leading French existentialist, became enormously influential. Sartre, active in the Resistance, and his colleagues offered a powerful answer to profound moral issues and the contemporary crisis.

The Revival of Christianity

In intellectual circles, Christianity and religion in general had been on the defensive since the Enlightenment and especially during the late nineteenth century. But in the aftermath of the Great Break, the loss of faith in human reason and in continual progress led to renewed interest in the Christian view of the world. A number of thinkers and theologians began to revitalize the fundamentals of Christianity. They had a powerful impact on society. Sometimes described as "Christian existentialists" because they shared the loneliness and despair of atheistic existentialists, they revived the tradition of Saint Augustine. They stressed human beings' sinful nature, the need for faith, and the mystery of God's forgiveness.

This development was a break with the late nineteenth century. In the years before 1914, some theologians, especially Protestant theologians, had felt the need to interpret Christian doctrine and the Bible so that they did not seem to contradict science, evolution, and common sense. Christ was therefore seen primarily as the greatest moral teacher, and the "supernatural" aspects of his divinity were strenuously played down. An important if extreme example of this tendency was the young Albert Schweitzer's *Quest of the Historical Jesus* (1906). A theologian and later a famous medical missionary and musician of note, Schweitzer (1875–1965) argued that Christ while on earth was a completely natural man whose teachings had been only temporary rules to prepare himself and his disciples for the end of the world, which they were erroneously expecting. In short, some modern theologians were embarrassed by the miraculous, unscientific aspects of Christianity and turned away from them.

The revival of fundamental Christian belief after the Great War was fed by rediscovery of the work of the nineteenth-century Danish religious philosopher Sören Kierkegaard (1813–1855), whose ideas became extremely influential. Kierkegaard had rejected formalistic religion and denounced the worldliness of the Danish Lutheran church. He had eventually resolved his personal anguish over his own imperfect nature by making a total religious commitment to a remote and majestic God.

Similar ideas were brilliantly developed by the Swiss Protestant theologian Karl Barth (1886–1968), whose many influential writings after 1920 sought to re-create the religious intensity of the Reformation. For Barth, the basic fact about human beings was that they are imperfect, sinful creatures whose reason and will are hopelessly flawed. Religious truth is therefore made known to human beings only through God's grace. People have to accept God's word and the supernatural revelation of Jesus Christ with awe, trust, and obedience. Lowly mortals should not expect to "reason out" God and his ways.

Among Catholics, the leading existential Christian thinker was Gabriel Marcel (1887–1973). Born into a cultivated French family, where his atheistic father was "gratefully aware of all that . . . art owed to Catholicism but regarded Catholic thought itself as obsolete and tainted with absurd superstitions,"[2] Marcel found in the Catholic church an answer to what he called the postwar "broken world." Catholicism and religious belief provided the hope, humanity, honesty, and piety for which he hungered.

After 1914 religion became much more relevant and meaningful to thinking people, and many illustrious individuals turned to religion between about 1920 and 1950. The poets T. S. Eliot and W. H. Auden, the novelists Evelyn Waugh and Aldous Huxley, the historian Arnold Toynbee, the Oxford professor C. S. Lewis, the psychoanalyst Karl Stern, and the physicist Max Planck were all either converted to religion or attracted to it for the first time. Religion, often of a despairing, existential variety, was one meaningful answer to terror and anxiety. In the words of another famous Roman Catholic convert, English novelist Graham Greene, "One began to believe in heaven because one believed in hell."[3]

The New Physics

Ever since the Scientific Revolution of the seventeenth century, scientific advances and their implications have greatly influenced the beliefs of thinking people. By the late nineteenth century, science was one of the main pillars supporting Western society's optimistic and rationalistic view of the world. The Darwinian concept of evolution had been accepted and assimilated in most intellectual circles. Progressive minds believed that science, unlike religion and philosophical speculation, was based on hard facts and controlled experiments. Science seemed to have achieved an unerring and almost completed picture of reality. Unchanging natural laws seemed to determine physical processes and permit useful solutions to more and more problems. All this was comforting, especially to people who were no longer committed to traditional religious beliefs. And all this was challenged by the new physics.

An important first step toward the new physics was the discovery at the end of the century that atoms were not like hard, permanent little billiard balls. They were actually composed of many far-smaller, fast-moving particles, such as electrons and protons. The Polish-born physicist Marie Curie (1867–1934) and her French husband discovered that radium constantly emits subatomic particles and thus does not have a constant atomic weight. Building on this and other work in radiation, the German physicist Max Planck (1858–1947) showed in 1900 that subatomic energy is emitted in uneven little spurts, which Planck called "quanta," and not in a steady stream as previously believed. Planck's discovery called into question the old sharp distinction between matter and energy; the implication was that matter and

energy might be different forms of the same thing. The old view of atoms as the stable, basic building blocks of nature, with a different kind of unbreakable atom for each of the ninety-two chemical elements, was badly shaken.

In 1905 the German-born Jewish genius Albert Einstein (1879–1955) went further than the Curies and Planck in challenging Newtonian physics. His theory of special relativity postulated that time and space are not absolute. The closed framework of Newtonian physics was quite limited compared to that of Einsteinian physics, which unified an apparently infinite universe with the incredibly small, fast-moving subatomic world. Moreover, Einstein's theory stated clearly that matter and energy are interchangeable and that all matter contains enormous levels of potential energy.

The 1920s opened the "heroic age of physics," in the apt words of one of its leading pioneers, Ernest Rutherford (1871–1937). Breakthrough followed breakthrough. In 1919 Rutherford showed that the atom could be split. By 1944 seven subatomic particles had been identified, of which the most important was the neutron. The neutron's capacity to pass through other atoms allowed for even more intense experimental bombardment of matter, leading to chain reactions of unbelievable force—and to the atomic bomb.

Although few nonscientists understood the revolution in physics, the implications of the new theories and discoveries, as presented by newspapers and popular writers, were disturbing to millions of men and women in the 1920s and 1930s. The new universe was strange and troubling. It lacked any absolute objective reality. Everything was "relative"—that is, dependent on the observer's frame of reference. Moreover, the universe was uncertain and undetermined, without stable building blocks. Instead of Newton's dependable, rational laws, there seemed to be only tendencies and probabilities in an extraordinarily complex and uncertain universe. And that universe, described by abstract mathematical symbols, seemed to have little to do with human experience and human problems.

Freudian Psychology

With physics presenting an uncertain universe so unrelated to ordinary human experience, questions about the power and potential of the human mind assumed special significance. The findings and speculations of the leading psychologist, Sigmund Freud (see page 921), were particularly disturbing.

Before Freud, poets and mystics had probed the unconscious and irrational aspects of human behavior. But most professional, "scientific" psychologists assumed that a single, unified conscious mind processed sense experiences in a rational and logical way. Human behavior in turn was the result of rational calculation—of "thinking"—by the conscious mind. Basing his insights on the analysis of dreams and of hysteria, Freud developed a very different view of the human psyche beginning in the late 1880s.

According to Freud (1856–1939), human behavior is basically irrational. The key to understanding the mind is the primitive, irrational unconscious, which Freud called the *id*. The unconscious is driven by sexual, aggressive, and pleasure-seeking desires and is locked in a constant battle with the other parts of the mind: the rationalizing conscious (the *ego*), which mediates what a person can do, and ingrained moral values (the *superego*), which tell what a person should do. Human behavior is a product of fragile compromise between instinctual drives and the controls of rational thinking and moral values. Since the instinctual drives are extremely powerful, the ever-present danger for individuals and whole societies is that unacknowledged drives will overwhelm the control mechanisms in a violent, distorted way. Yet Freud also agreed with Nietzsche that these mechanisms of rational thinking and

Munch: The Dance of Life Like his contemporary Sigmund Freud, the expressionist painter Edvard Munch studied the turmoil and fragility of human thought and action. Solitary figures struggling with fear and uncertainty dominate his work. Here the girl in white represents innocence, the tense woman in black stands for mourning and rejection and the woman in red evokes the joy of passing pleasure. *(Source: © Nasjonalgalleriet, Oslo. Photo: Jacques Lathion)*

traditional moral values can be too strong. They can repress sexual desires too effectively, crippling individuals and entire peoples with guilt and neurotic fears.

Freudian psychology and clinical psychiatry had become an international movement by 1910, but only after 1918 did they receive popular attention, especially in the Protestant countries of northern Europe and in the United States. Many opponents and even some enthusiasts interpreted Freud as saying that the first requirement for mental health is an uninhibited sex life. Thus, after the First World War, the popular interpretation of Freud reflected and encouraged growing sexual experimentation, particularly among middle-class

Virginia Woolf Her novels captured sensations like impressionist paintings, and her home attracted a circle of artists and writers known as the Bloomsbury Group. Many of Woolf's essays dealt with women's issues and urged greater opportunity for women's creativity. *(Source: © Gisèle Freund/Photo Researchers)*

women. For more serious students, the psychology of Freud and his followers drastically undermined the old, easy optimism about the rational and progressive nature of the human mind.

Twentieth-Century Literature

Literature articulated the general intellectual climate of pessimism, relativism, and alienation. Novelists developed new techniques to express new realities. The great nineteenth-century novelists had typically written as all-knowing narrators, describing realistic characters and their relationship to an understandable if sometimes harsh society. In the twentieth century, most major writers adopted the limited, often confused viewpoint of a single individual. Like Freud, these novelists focused their attention on the complexity and irrationality of the human mind, where feelings, memories, and desires are forever scrambled.

Serious novelists also used the stream-of-consciousness technique to explore the psyche. The novel *Jacob's Room* (1922), by Virginia Woolf (1882–1941), is a series of internal monologues in which ideas and emotions from different periods of time bubble up as randomly as from a patient on a psychoanalyst's couch. William Faulkner (1897–1962), perhaps America's greatest twentieth-century novelist, used the same technique in *The Sound and the Fury* (1929), much of whose intense drama is confusedly seen through the eyes of an idiot. The most famous stream-of-consciousness novel—and surely the most disturbing novel of its generation—is *Ulysses,* which the Irish novelist James Joyce (1882–1941) published in 1922. Into *Ulysses*'s account of an ordinary day in the life of an ordinary man, Joyce weaves an extended ironic parallel between his hero's aimless wanderings through the streets and pubs of Dublin and the adventures of Homer's hero Ulysses on his way home from Troy. Abandoning conventional grammar and blending foreign words, puns, bits of knowledge, and scraps of memory together in bewildering confusion, Joyce intended the language of *Ulysses* to mirror modern life itself: a gigantic riddle waiting to be unraveled.

As creative writers turned their attention from society to the individual and from realism to psychological relativity, they rejected the idea of progress. Some even described "anti-utopias," nightmare visions of things to come. In 1918 an obscure German high school teacher named Oswald Spengler (1880–1936) published *The Decline of the West,* which quickly became an international sensation. According to Spengler, every culture experiences a life cycle of growth and decline. Western civilization, in Spengler's opinion, was in its old age, and death was approaching in the form of conquest by the yellow race. T. S. Eliot (1888–1965), in his famous poem *The Waste Land* (1922), depicted a world of growing desolation, although after his conversion to Anglo-Catholicism in 1927, Eliot came to hope cautiously for humanity's salvation. No such hope appeared in the work of Franz Kafka (1883–1924), whose novels *The Trial* and *The Castle,* as well as several of his greatest short stories, portray helpless individuals crushed by inexplicably hostile forces. The German-Jewish Kafka died young, at forty-one, and so did not see the world of his nightmares materialize in the Nazi state.

MODERN ART AND CULTURE

Throughout the twentieth century, there has been considerable unity in the arts. The "modernism" of the immediate prewar years and the 1920s is still strikingly modern. Manifestations of modernism in art, architecture, and music have of course been highly varied, just as in physics, psychology, and philosophy; yet there are resemblances, for artists, scientists, and original thinkers partake of the same culture. Creative artists rejected old forms and old values. Modernism in art and music meant constant experimentation and a search for new kinds of expression. And though many people find the modern visions of the arts strange, disturbing, and even ugly, the twentieth century, so dismal in many respects, will probably stand as one of Western civilization's great artistic eras.

Architecture and Design

Modernism in the arts was loosely unified by a revolution in architecture. The architectural revolution not only gave the other arts striking new settings, it intended nothing less than to transform the physical framework of the urban society ac-

cording to a new principle: functionalism. Believing that buildings, like industrial products, should be useful and "functional"—that is, they should serve, as well as possible, the purpose for which they were made—some architects and designers worked with engineers, town planners, and even sanitation experts. Moreover, they threw away useless ornamentation and found beauty and esthetic pleasure in the clean lines of practical constructions and efficient machinery.

The United States, with its rapid urban growth and lack of rigid building traditions, pioneered in the new architecture. In the 1890s the Chicago school of architects, led by Louis H. Sullivan (1856–1924), used cheap steel, reinforced concrete, and electric elevators to build skyscrapers and office buildings lacking almost any exterior ornamentation. In the first decade of the twentieth century, Sullivan's student Frank Lloyd Wright (1869–1959) built a series of radically new and truly modern houses featuring low lines, open interiors, and mass-produced building materials. Europeans were inspired by these and other American examples of functional construction such as the massive, unadorned grain elevators of the Midwest.

Around 1905, when the first really modern buildings were going up in Europe, architectural leadership shifted to the German-speaking countries and remained there until Hitler took power in 1933. In 1911 the twenty-eight-year-old Walter Gropius (1883–1969) broke sharply with the past in his design of the Fagus shoe factory at Alfeld, Germany. A clean, light, elegant building of glass and iron, Gropius's new factory represented a jump right into the middle of the century.

After the First World War, the new German republic gave Gropius the authority to merge the schools of fine and applied arts at Weimar into a single, interdisciplinary school, the Bauhaus. In spite of intense criticism from conservative politicians and university professors, the Bauhaus brought together many leading modern architects, artists, designers, and theatrical innovators, who worked as an effective, inspired team. Throwing out traditional teaching methods, they combined the study of fine art, such as painting and sculpture, with the study of applied art in the crafts of printing, weaving, and furniture making. Throughout the 1920s, the Bauhaus, with its stress on functionalism and good design for everyday life, attracted enthusiastic students from all over the world. It had a great and continuing impact.

Another leader in the modern or "international" style was Ludwig Mies van der Rohe (1886–1969), who followed Gropius as director of the Bauhaus in 1930 and emigrated to the United States in 1937. His classic Lake Shore Apartments in Chicago, built between 1948 and 1951, symbolize the triumph of steel-frame and glass-wall modern architecture, which grew out of Sullivan's skyscrapers and German functionalism in the great building boom after the Second World War.

Modern Painting

Modern painting grew out of a revolt against French impressionism. The impressionism of such French painters as Claude Monet (1840–1926),

Frank Lloyd Wright: The "Fallingwater" House Often considered Wright's masterpiece, Falling Water combines modern architectural concepts with close attention to a spectacular site. Anchored to a high rock ledge by means of reinforced concrete, the house soars out over a cascading waterfall at Bear Run in western Pennsylvania. Built in 1937 for a Pittsburgh businessman, Fallingwater is now open to the public and attracts 70,000 visitors each year. *(Source: Western Pennsylvania Conservancy/Art Resource)*

Picasso: Guernica In this rich, complex work a shrieking woman falls from a burning house on the far right. On the left a woman holds a dead child, while toward the center are fragments of a warrior and a screaming horse pierced by a spear. Picasso has used only the mournful colors of black, white, gray, and dark blue. (*Source: Museo del Prado, Madrid. Pablo Picasso, Guernica (1937, May–early June). Oil on canvas. © SPADEM, Paris/VAGA, New York, 1982*)

Pierre Auguste Renoir (1841–1919), and Camille Pissarro (1830–1903) was, in part, a kind of super-realism. Leaving exact copying of objects to photography, these artists sought to capture the momentary overall feeling, or impression, of light falling on a real-life scene before their eyes. By 1890, when impressionism was finally established, a few artists known as "postimpressionists," or "expressionists," were already striking out in new directions. After 1905 art took on the abstract, nonrepresentational character that it generally retains today.

Though individualistic in their styles, postimpressionists were united in their desire to know and depict worlds other than the visible world of fact. Like the early nineteenth-century romantics, they wanted to portray unseen, inner worlds of emotion and imagination. Like modern novelists, they wanted to express a complicated psychological view of reality as well as an overwhelming emotional intensity. In *The Starry Night* (1889), for example, the great Dutch expressionist Vincent van Gogh (1853–1890) painted the vision of his mind's eye. Flaming cypress trees, exploding stars, and a cometlike Milky Way swirl together in one great cosmic rhythm.

Fascination with form, as opposed to light, was characteristic of postimpressionism and expressionism. Paul Cézanne (1839–1906), who had a profound influence on twentieth-century painting, was particularly committed to form and ordered design. He told a young painter, "You must see in nature the cylinder, the sphere, and the cone."[4] As Cézanne's later work became increasingly abstract and nonrepresentational, it also moved away from the traditional three-dimensional perspective toward the two-dimensional plane, which has characterized so much of modern art. The expressionism of a group of painters led by Henri Matisse (1869–1954) was so extreme that an exhibition of their work in Paris in 1905 prompted shocked critics to call them *les fauves*— "the wild beasts." Matisse and his followers were primarily concerned not with real objects but with the arrangement of color, line, and form as an end in itself.

In 1907 a young Spaniard in Paris, Pablo Picasso (1881–1973), founded another movement: cubism. Cubism concentrated on a complex geometry of zigzagging lines and sharp-angled, overlapping planes. About three years later came the ultimate stage in the development of abstract, nonrepresentational art. Artists such as the Russian-born Wassily Kandinsky (1866–1944) turned away from nature completely. "The observer," said Kandinsky, "must learn to look at [my] pictures . . . as form and color combinations . . . as a representation of mood and not as a representation of objects."[5] On the eve of the First World War, extreme expressionism and abstract painting were developing rapidly not only in Paris but also in Russia and Germany. Modern art had become international.

In the 1920s and 1930s, the artistic movements of the prewar years were extended and consolidated. The most notable new developments were dadaism and surrealism. Dadaism attacked all accepted standards of art and behavior, delighting in outrageous conduct. Its name, from the French word *dada,* meaning "hobbyhorse," is deliberately silly. A famous example of dadaism was a reproduction of Leonardo da Vinci's *Mona Lisa* in which the famous woman with the mysterious smile sports a mustache and is ridiculed with an obscene inscription. After 1924 many dadaists were attracted to surrealism, which became very influential in art in the late 1920s and 1930s. Surrealism was inspired to a great extent by Freudian psychology. Surrealists painted a fantastic world of wild dreams and complex symbols where watches melted and giant metronomes beat time in precisely drawn but impossible alien landscapes.

Refusing to depict ordinary visual reality, surrealist painters made powerful statements about the age of anxiety. Picasso's 26-foot-long mural *Guernica* (1937) masterfully unites several powerful strands in twentieth-century art. Inspired by the Spanish Civil War (see page 1157), the painting commemorates the bombing of the ancient Spanish town of Guernica by fascist planes, an attack that took the lives of a thousand people—one out of every eight inhabitants—in a single night of terror. Combining the free distortion of expressionism, the overlapping planes of cubism, and the surrealist fascination with grotesque subject matter, *Guernica* is what Picasso meant it to be: an unforgettable attack on brutality and darkness.

Modern Music

Developments in modern music were strikingly parallel to those in painting. Composers, too, were attracted by the emotional intensity of ex-

pressionism. The ballet *The Rite of Spring* by Igor Stravinsky (1882–1971) practically caused a riot when it was first performed in Paris in 1913 by Sergei Diaghilev's famous Russian dance company. The combination of pulsating, barbaric rhythms from the orchestra pit and an earthy representation of lovemaking by the dancers on the stage seemed a shocking, almost pornographic enactment of a primitive fertility rite.

After the experience of the First World War, when irrationality and violence seemed to pervade the human experience, expressionism in opera and ballet flourished. One of the most famous and powerful examples is the opera *Wozzeck* by Alban Berg (1885–1935), first performed in Berlin in 1925. Blending a half-sung, half-spoken kind of dialogue with harsh, atonal music, *Wozzeck* is a gruesome tale of a soldier driven by Kafka-like inner terrors.

Some composers turned their backs on long-established musical conventions. As abstract painters arranged lines and color but did not draw identifiable objects, so modern composers arranged sounds without creating recognizable harmonies. Led by the Viennese composer Arnold Schönberg (1874–1951), they abandoned traditional harmony and tonality. The musical notes in a given piece were no longer united and organized by a key; instead they were independent and unrelated. Schönberg's twelve-tone music of the 1920s arranged all twelve notes of the scale in an abstract, mathematical pattern, or "tone row." This pattern sounded like no pattern at all to the ordinary listener and could be detected only by a highly trained eye studying the musical score. Accustomed to the harmonies of classical and romantic music, audiences generally resisted modern atonal music. Only after the Second World War did it begin to win acceptance.

Movies and Radio

Until after the Second World War at the earliest, those revolutionary changes in art and music appealed mainly to a minority of "highbrows" and not to the general public. That public was primarily and enthusiastically wrapped up in movies and radio. The long-declining traditional arts and amusements of people in villages and small towns almost vanished and were replaced by standardized, commercial entertainment.

Moving pictures were first shown as a popular novelty in naughty peepshows—"What the Butler Saw"—and penny arcades in the 1890s, especially in Paris. The first movie houses date from an experiment in Los Angeles in 1902. They quickly attracted large audiences and led to the production of short, silent action films like the eight-minute *Great Train Robbery* of 1903. American directors and business people then set up "movie factories," at first in the New York area and after 1910 in Los Angeles. These factories churned out two short films each week. On the eve of the First World War, full-length feature films were suggesting the screen's vast possibilities.

During the First World War the United States became the dominant force in the rapidly expanding silent-film industry. In the 1920s, Mack Sennett (1884–1960) and his zany Keystone Cops specialized in short, slapstick comedies noted for frantic automobile chases, custard-pie battles, and gorgeous bathing beauties. Screen stars such as Mary Pickford and Lillian Gish, and Douglas Fairbanks and Rudolph Valentino became household names, with their own "fan clubs." Yet Charlie Chaplin (1889–1978), a funny little Englishman working in Hollywood, was unquestionably the king of the "silver screen" in the 1920s. In his enormously popular role as a lonely tramp, complete with baggy trousers, battered derby, and an awkward, shuffling walk, Chaplin symbolized the "gay spirit of laughter in a cruel, crazy world."[6] Chaplin also demonstrated that, in the hands of a genius, the new medium could combine mass entertainment and artistic accomplishment.

The early 1920s were also the great age of German films. Protected and developed during the war, the large German studios excelled in bizarre expressionist dramas. Unfortunately, their period of creativity was short-lived. By 1926 American money was drawing the leading German talents to Hollywood and consolidating America's international domination. Film making was big business, and European theater owners were forced to book whole blocks of American films to get the few pictures they really wanted. This system put European producers at a great disadvantage until "talkies" permitted a revival of national film industries in the 1930s, particularly in France.

Whether foreign or domestic, motion pictures became the main entertainment of the masses until after the Second World War. In Great Britain one in every four adults went to the movies twice a week in the late 1930s, and two in five went at least once a week. Continental countries had similar figures. The greatest appeal of motion pictures was that they offered ordinary people a temporary escape from the hard realities of everyday life. For an hour or two a moviegoer could flee the world of international tensions, uncertainty, unemployment, and personal frustrations. The appeal of escapist entertainment was especially strong during the Great Depression. Millions flocked to musical comedies featuring glittering stars such as Ginger Rogers and Fred Astaire and to the fanciful cartoons of Mickey Mouse and his friends.

Radio became possible with the transatlantic "wireless" communication of Guglielmo Marconi (1874–1937) in 1901 and the development of the vacuum tube in 1904, which permitted the transmission of speech and music. But only after 1920 did every major Western country establish national broadcasting networks. In the United States, such networks were privately owned and were financed by advertising. In Great Britain, Parliament set up an independent, high-minded public corporation, the British Broadcasting Corporation (BBC), which was supported by licensing fees. Elsewhere in Europe, the typical pattern was direct control by the government. Whatever the institutional framework, radio became popular and influential. By the late 1930s, more than three out of every four households in both democratic Great Britain and dictatorial Germany had at least one cheap, mass-produced radio. Other European countries were not far behind.

Radio in unscrupulous hands was particularly well suited for political propaganda. Dictators like Mussolini and Hitler controlled the airwaves and could reach enormous national audiences with their frequent, dramatic speeches. In democratic countries, politicians such as President Franklin Roosevelt and Prime Minister Stanley Baldwin effectively used informal "fireside chats" to bolster their support.

Motion pictures also became powerful tools of indoctrination, especially in countries with dictatorial regimes. Lenin himself encouraged the development of Soviet film making, believing that the new medium was essential to the social and ideological transformation of the country. Beginning in the mid-1920s, a series of epic films, the most famous of which were directed by Sergei Eisenstein (1898–1948), brilliantly dramatized the communist view of Russian history.

In Germany, Hitler turned to a young and immensely talented woman film maker, Leni Riefenstahl (b. 1902), for a masterpiece of documentary propaganda, *The Triumph of the Will*, based on the Nazi party rally at Nuremberg in 1934. Riefenstahl combined stunning aerial photography, joyful crowds welcoming Hitler, and mass processions of young Nazi fanatics. Her film was a brilliant and all-too-powerful documentary of Germany's "Nazi rebirth."

THE SEARCH FOR PEACE AND POLITICAL STABILITY

The Versailles settlement had established a shaky truce, not a solid peace. Within the general context of intellectual crisis and revolutionary artistic experimentation, politicians and national leaders struggled to create a stable international order.

The pursuit of real and lasting peace proved difficult. Germany hated the Treaty of Versailles. France was fearful and isolated. Britain was undependable, and the United States had turned its back on European problems. Eastern Europe was in ferment, and no one could predict the future of communist Russia. Moreover, the international economic situation was poor and greatly complicated by war debts and disrupted patterns of trade. Yet for a time, from 1925 to late 1929, it appeared that peace and stability were within reach. When the subsequent collapse of the 1930s mocked these hopes, the disillusionment of liberals in the democracies was intensified.

Germany and the Western Powers

Germany was the key to lasting peace. Only under the pressure of the Allies' naval blockade and threat to extend their military occupation from the Rhineland to the rest of the country had Germany's new republican government signed the Treaty of Versailles in June 1919. To Germans of all political parties, the treaty represented a harsh, dictated peace to be revised or repudiated as soon as possible. The treaty neither broke nor reduced Germany, which was potentially still the strongest country in Europe. Thus the treaty fell between two stools: it was too harsh for a peace of reconciliation, too soft for a peace of conquest.

Moreover, with ominous implications for the future, France and Great Britain did not see eye to eye on Germany. By the end of 1919, France wanted to stress the harsh elements in the Treaty of Versailles. Most of the war in the west had been fought on French soil, and much of rich, industrialized northern France had been devastated. The expected costs of reconstruction were staggering; like Great Britain, France during the war had borrowed large sums from the United States, which had to be repaid. Thus French politicians believed that massive reparations from Germany were a vital economic necessity; and if the Germans had to suffer to make the payments, the French would not be overly concerned. Having compromised with President Wilson only to be betrayed by America's failure to ratify the treaty, many French leaders saw strict implementation of all provisions of the Treaty of Versailles as France's last best hope. Large reparation payments could hold Germany down indefinitely, and France would realize its goal of security.

The British soon felt differently. Prewar Germany had been Great Britain's second-best market in the entire world, and after the war a healthy, prosperous Germany appeared to be essential to the British economy. Indeed, many English people agreed with the analysis of the young English economist John Maynard Keynes (1883–1946), who eloquently denounced the Treaty of Versailles in his *Economic Consequences of the Peace* (1919). According to Keynes's interpretation, astronomical reparations and harsh economic measures would indeed reduce Germany to the position of an impoverished second-rate power, but such impoverishment would increase economic hardship in all countries. Only a complete revision of the foolish treaty could save Germany—and Europe. Keynes's attack exploded like a bombshell and became very influential. It stirred deep guilt feelings about Germany in the English-speaking world, feelings that often paralyzed English and American leaders in their relations with Germany and its leaders between the First and Second World Wars.

The British were also suspicious of France's army—momentarily the largest in Europe—and France's foreign policy. Ever since 1890, France had looked to Russia as a powerful ally against Germany. But with Russia hostile and communist, and with Britain and the United States unwilling to make any firm commitments, France turned to the newly formed states of eastern Europe for diplomatic support. In 1921 France signed a mutual defense pact with Poland and associated itself closely with the so-called Little Entente, an alliance that joined Czechoslovakia, Romania, and Yugoslavia against defeated and bitter Hungary. The British and the French were also on cool terms because of conflicts relating to their League of Nations mandates in the Middle East.

While French and British leaders drifted in different directions, the Allied reparations commission completed its work. In April 1921 it announced that Germany had to pay the enormous sum of 132 billion gold marks ($33 billion) in annual installments of 2.5 billion gold marks. Facing possible occupation of more of its territory, the young German republic, which had been founded in Weimar but moved back to Berlin, made its first payment in 1921. Then in 1922, wracked by rapid inflation and political assassinations, and motivated by hostility and arrogance as well, the Weimar Republic announced its inability to pay more. It proposed a moratorium on reparations for three years, with the clear implication that thereafter reparations would either be drastically reduced or eliminated entirely.

The British were willing to accept this offer, but the French were not. Led by their tough-minded, legalistic prime minister, Raymond Poincaré (1860–1934), they decided that they either had to call Germany's bluff or see the entire peace settlement dissolve to France's great disadvantage. So, despite strong British protests, France and its ally Belgium decided to pursue a firm policy. In early January 1923, French and Belgian armies began to occupy the Ruhr district, the heartland of industrial Germany, creating the most serious international crisis of the 1920s.

The Occupation of the Ruhr

The strategy of Poincaré and his French supporters was simple. Since Germany would not pay reparations in hard currency or gold, France and Belgium would collect reparations in kind—coal, steel, and machinery. If forcible collection proved impossible, France would occupy Germany and force it to accept the Treaty of Versailles.

"Hands Off the Ruhr" The French occupation of the Ruhr to collect reparations payments raised a storm of patriotic protest, including this anti-French poster of 1923. *(Source: Internationaal Instituut voor Sociale Geschiedenis)*

Strengthened by a wave of patriotism, the German government ordered the people of the Ruhr to stop working and start resisting—passively—the French occupation. The coal mines and steel mills of the Ruhr grew silent, leaving 10 percent of Germany's total population in need of relief. The French answer to passive resistance was to seal off not only the Ruhr but the entire Rhineland from the rest of Germany, letting in only enough food to prevent starvation. The French also revived plans for a separate state in the Rhineland.

By the summer of 1923, France and Germany were engaged in a tremendous test of wills. As the

German government had anticipated, French armies could not collect reparations from striking workers at gunpoint. But French occupation was indeed paralyzing Germany and its economy, for the Ruhr district normally produced 80 percent of Germany's steel and coal. Moreover, the occupation of the Ruhr turned rapid German inflation into runaway inflation. Faced with the need to support the striking Ruhr workers and their employers, the German government began to print money to pay its bills. Prices soared. People went to the store with a big bag of paper money and returned home with only a handful of groceries. German money rapidly lost all value, and so did anything else with a stated fixed value.

Runaway inflation brought about a social revolution. The accumulated savings of many retired and middle-class people were wiped out. The old middle-class virtues of thrift, caution, and self-reliance were cruelly mocked by catastrophic inflation. People told themselves that nothing had real value anymore, not even money. The German middle and lower middle classes, feeling cheated, burned with resentment. Many hated and blamed the Western governments, their own government, big business, the Jews, the workers, the communists for their misfortune. They were psychologically prepared to follow radical leaders in a crisis.

In August 1923, as the mark fell and political unrest grew throughout Germany, Gustav Stresemann (1878–1929) assumed leadership of the government. Stresemann adopted a compromising attitude. He called off passive resistance in the Ruhr and in October agreed in principle to pay reparations, but he asked for a re-examination of Germany's ability to pay. Poincaré accepted. His hard line was becoming increasingly unpopular with French citizens, and it was hated in Britain and the United States. Moreover, occupation was dreadfully expensive, and France's own currency was beginning to lose value on foreign exchange markets.

More generally, in both Germany and France, power was finally passing to the moderates, who realized that continued confrontation was a destructive, no-win situation. Thus, after five long years of hostility and tension culminating in a kind of undeclared war in the Ruhr in 1923, Germany and France decided to give compromise and cooperation a try. The British, and even the Americans, were willing to help. The first step was a reasonable compromise on the reparations question.

Hope in Foreign Affairs (1924–1929)

The reparations commission appointed an international committee of financial experts headed by an American banker, Charles G. Dawes, to re-examine reparations from a broad perspective. The committee made a series of recommendations known as the "Dawes Plan" (1924), and the plan was accepted by France, Germany, and Britain. German reparations were reduced and placed on a sliding scale, like an income tax, whereby yearly payments depended on the level of German economic prosperity. The Dawes Plan also recommended large loans to Germany, loans that could come only from the United States. These loans were to help Stresemann's government put its new currency on a firm basis and promote German recovery. In short, Germany would get private loans from the United States and pay reparations to France and Britain, thus enabling those countries to repay the large sums they owed the United States.

This circular flow of international payments was complicated and risky. For a time, though, it worked. The German republic experienced a spectacular economic recovery. By 1929 Germany's wealth and income were 50 percent greater than in 1913. With prosperity and large, continuous inflows of American capital, Germany easily paid about $1.3 billion in reparations in 1927 and 1928, enabling France and Britain to pay the United States. In 1929 the "Young Plan," named after an American businessman, further reduced German reparations and formalized the link between German reparations and French-British debts to the United States. In this way the Americans, who did not have armies but who did have money, belatedly played a part in the general economic settlement, which though far from ideal facilitated the worldwide recovery of the late 1920s.

The economic settlement was matched by a political settlement. In 1925 the leaders of Europe signed a number of agreements at Locarno, Switzerland. Stresemann, who guided Germany's foreign policy until his death in 1929, had suggested a treaty with France's conciliatory Aristide Briand (1862–1932), who had returned to office in 1924 after French voters rejected the bellicose Poincaré. By this treaty Germany and France solemnly pledged to accept their common border, and both Britain and Italy agreed to fight either country if it invaded the other. Stresemann also agreed to settle boundary disputes with Poland and Czecho-slovakia by peaceful means, and France promised those countries military aid if they were attacked by Germany. For their efforts Stresemann and Briand shared the Nobel Peace Prize in 1926. The effect of the treaties of Locarno was far-reaching. For years, a "spirit of Locarno" gave Europeans a sense of growing security and stability in interna-tional affairs.

Hopes were strengthened by other develop-ments. In 1926 Germany joined the League of Nations, where Stresemann continued his peace offensive. In 1928 fifteen countries signed the Kellogg-Briand Pact, which "condemned and re-nounced war as an instrument of national policy." The signing states agreed to settle international disputes peacefully. Often seen as idealistic non-sense because it made no provisions for action in case war actually occurred, the pact was neverthe-less a hopeful step. It grew out of a suggestion by Briand that France and the United States re-nounce the possibility of war between their two

countries. Briand was gently and subtly trying to draw the United States back into involvement with Europe. When Secretary of State Frank B. Kellogg (1856–1937) proposed a multinational pact, Briand appeared close to success. Thus the cautious optimism of the late 1920s also rested on the hope that the United States would accept its responsibilities as a great world power and conse-quently contribute to European stability.

Hope in Democratic Government

Domestic politics also offered reason to hope. During the occupation of the Ruhr and the great inflation, republican government in Germany had appeared on the verge of collapse. In 1923 Com-munists momentarily entered provincial govern-ments, and in November an obscure nobody named Adolf Hitler leaped on a table in a beer hall in Munich and proclaimed a "national socialist revolution." But Hitler's early plot was poorly

The Fruits of Germany's Inflation   In the end, currency had value only as waste paper. Here bank notes are being purchased by the bail for paper mills, along with old rags *(Lumpen)* and bones *(Knochen)*. *(Source: Archiv für Kunst u. Geschichte)*

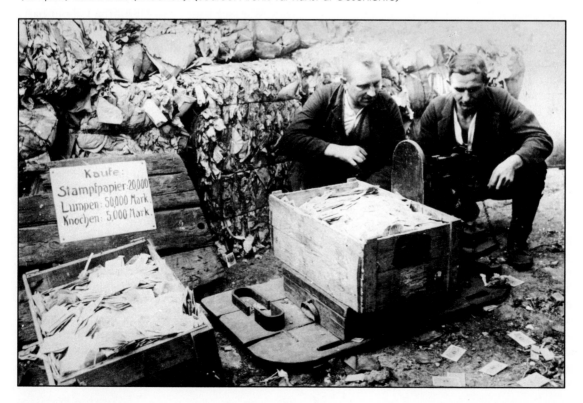

organized and easily crushed, and Hitler was sentenced to prison, where he outlined his theories and program in *Mein Kampf (My Struggle)*. Throughout the 1920s, Hitler's National Socialist party attracted support only from a few fanatical anti-Semites, ultranationalists, and disgruntled former servicemen. In 1928 his party had an insignificant twelve seats in the national parliament. Indeed, after 1923 democracy seemed to take root in Weimar Germany. A new currency was established, and the economy boomed.

The moderate businessmen who tended to dominate the various German coalition governments were convinced that economic prosperity demanded good relations with the Western powers, and they supported parliamentary government at home. Stresemann himself was a man of this class, and he was the key figure in every government until his death in 1929. Elections were held regularly, and republican democracy appeared to have growing support among a majority of Germans.

There were, however, sharp political divisions in the country. Many unrepentant nationalists and monarchists populated the right and the army. Germany's Communists were noisy and active on the left. The Communists, directed from Moscow, reserved their greatest hatred and sharpest barbs for their cousins the Social Democrats, whom they endlessly accused of betraying the revolution. The working classes were divided politically, but most supported the nonrevolutionary but socialist Social Democrats.

The situation in France had numerous similarities to that in Germany. Communists and Socialists battled for the support of the workers. After 1924 the democratically elected government rested mainly in the hands of coalitions of moderates, and business interests were well represented. France's great accomplishment was the rapid rebuilding of its war-torn northern region. The expense of this undertaking led, however, to a large deficit and substantial inflation. By early 1926 the franc had fallen to 10 percent of its prewar value, causing a severe crisis. Poincaré was recalled to office, and Briand became minister for foreign affairs. The Poincaré government proceeded to slash spending and raise taxes, restoring confidence in the economy. The franc was "saved," stabilized at about one-fifth of its prewar value. Good times prevailed until 1930.

Despite its political shortcomings, France attracted artists and writers from all over the world in the 1920s. Much of the intellectual and artistic ferment of the times flourished in Paris. More generally, France appealed to foreigners and the French as a harmonious combination of small businesses and family farms, of bold innovation and solid traditions.

Britain, too, faced challenges after 1920. The wartime trend toward greater social equality continued, however, helping to maintain social harmony. The great problem was unemployment. Many of Britain's best markets had been lost during the war. In June 1921 almost 2.2 million people—23 percent of the labor force—were out of work, and throughout the 1920s unemployment hovered around 12 percent. Yet the state provided unemployment benefits of equal size to all those who were without jobs and supplemented those payments with subsidized housing, medical aid, and increased old-age pensions. These and other measures kept living standards from seriously declining, defused class tensions, and pointed the way toward the welfare state that Britain established after the Second World War.

Relative social harmony was accompanied by the rise of the Labour party as a determined champion of the working classes and of greater social equality. Committed to the kind of moderate, "revisionist" socialism that had emerged before the First World War (see pages 954–956), the Labour party replaced the Liberal party as the main opposition to the Conservatives. The new prominence of the Labour party reflected the decline of old liberal ideals of competitive capitalism, limited government control, and individual responsibility. In 1924 and 1929, the Labour party under Ramsay MacDonald (1866–1937) governed the country with the support of the smaller Liberal party. Yet Labour moved toward socialism gradually and democratically, so that the middle classes were not overly frightened as the working classes won new benefits.

The Conservatives under Stanley Baldwin (1867–1947) showed the same compromising spirit on social issues. The last line of Baldwin's greatest speech in March 1925 summarized his international and domestic programs: "Give us peace in our time, O Lord." Thus, in spite of such conflicts as the 1926 strike by hard-pressed coal miners, which ended in an unsuccessful general strike, social unrest in Britain was limited in the 1920s and in the 1930s as well. In 1922 Britain granted southern, Catholic Ireland full autonomy

An American in Paris The young Josephine Baker suddenly became a star when she brought an exotic African eroticism to French music halls in 1925. American blacks and Africans had a powerful impact on entertainment in Europe in the 1920s and 1930s. *(Source: Bettmann/Hulton)*

after a bitter guerrilla war, thus removing another source of prewar friction. In summary, developments in both international relations and in the domestic politics of the leading democracies gave cause for cautious optimism in the late 1920s.

THE GREAT DEPRESSION (1929–1939)

Like the Great War, the Great Depression must be spelled with capital letters. Economic depression was nothing new. Economic hard times occurred throughout the nineteenth century with predict-

able regularity, as they recur in the form of recessions and slumps to this day. What was new about this depression was its severity and duration. It struck with ever-greater intensity from 1929 to 1933, and recovery was uneven and slow. Moreover, the Great Depression was truly global in scope.

The social and political consequences of prolonged economic collapse were enormous all around the world. Subsequent military expansion in Japan has already been described (see page 1097), and later chapters examine a similarly powerful impact on Latin America and Africa. In Europe and the United States, the depression shat-

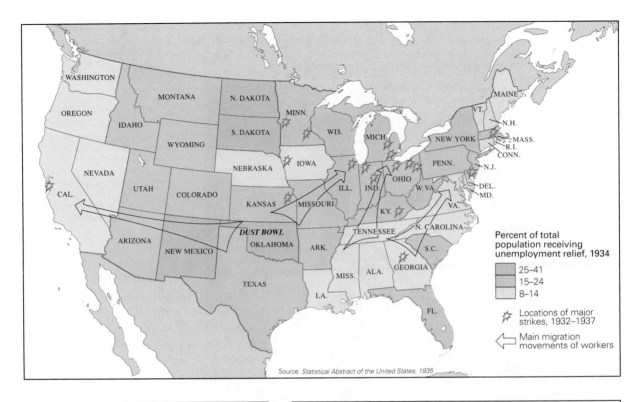

Percent of total
population receiving
unemployment relief, 1934

25–41

15–24

8–14

Locations of major
strikes, 1932–1937

Main migration
movements of workers

Source: *Statistical Abstract of the United States, 1935*

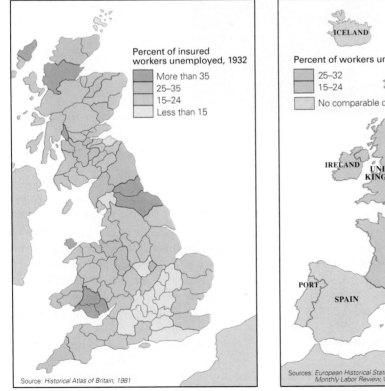

Percent of insured
workers unemployed, 1932

More than 35

25–35

15–24

Less than 15

Source: *Historical Atlas of Britain, 1981*

Percent of workers unemployed, 1932

25–32

15–24

No comparable data available

Sources: *European Historical Statistics, 1790–1970*
Monthly Labor Review, U.S. Dept. of Labor, 1934, vol. 39

MAP 34.1 The Great Depression in the United States, Britain, and Europe National and
regional differences were substantial. Germany, industrial northern Britain, and the
American Middle West were particularly hard-hit.

tered the fragile optimism of political leaders in the late 1920s. Mass unemployment made insecurity a reality for millions of ordinary people, who had paid little attention to the intellectual crisis or to new directions in art and ideas (Map 34.1). In desperation, people looked for leaders who would "do something." They were willing to support radical attempts to deal with the crisis by both democratic leaders and dictators.

The Economic Crisis

There is no agreement among historians and economists about why the Great Depression was so deep and lasted so long. Thus it is best to trace the course of the great collapse before trying to identify what caused it.

Though economic activity was already declining moderately in many countries by early 1929, the crash of the stock market in the United States in October of that year really started the Great Depression. The American stock market boom, which had seen stock prices double between early 1928 and September 1929, was built on borrowed money. Many wealthy investors, speculators, and people of modest means had bought stocks by paying only a small fraction of the total purchase price and borrowing the remainder of the purchase price from their stockbrokers. Such buying "on margin" was extremely dangerous. When prices started falling, the hard-pressed margin buyers either had to put up more money, which was often impossible, or sell their shares to pay their brokers. Thus thousands of people started selling all at once. The result was a financial panic. Countless investors and speculators were wiped out in a matter of days or weeks.

The general economic consequences were swift and severe. Stripped of their wealth and confidence, battered investors and their fellow citizens started buying fewer goods. Production began to slow down, and unemployment began to rise. Soon the entire American economy was caught in a vicious, spiraling decline.

The financial panic in the United States triggered a worldwide financial crisis, and that crisis resulted in a drastic decline in production in country after country. Throughout the 1920s American bankers and investors had lent large amounts of capital not only to Germany but to many other countries. Many of these loans were short-term, and once panic broke, New York bankers began recalling them. Gold reserves thus began to flow out of European countries, particularly Germany and Austria, toward the United States. It became very hard for European business people to borrow money, and the panicky public began to withdraw its savings from the banks. These banking problems eventually led to the crash of the largest bank in Austria in 1931 and then to general financial chaos. The recall of private loans by American bankers also accelerated the collapse in world prices, as business people around the world dumped industrial goods and agricultural commodities in a frantic attempt to get cash to pay what they owed.

The financial crisis led to a general crisis of production: between 1929 and 1933, world output of goods fell by an estimated 38 percent. As this happened, each country turned inward and tried to go it alone. In 1931, for example, Britain went off the gold standard, refusing to convert bank notes into gold, and reduced the value of its money. Britain's goal was to make its goods cheaper and therefore more salable in the world market. But because more than twenty nations, including the United States in 1934, also went off the gold standard, no country gained a real advantage. Similarly, country after country followed the example of the United States when it raised protective tariffs to their highest levels ever in 1930 and tried to seal off shrinking national markets for American producers only. Within this context of fragmented and destructive economic nationalism, recovery finally began in 1933.

Although opinions differ, two factors probably best explain the relentless slide to the bottom from 1929 to early 1933. First, the international economy lacked leadership able to maintain stability when the crisis came. Specifically, as a noted American economic historian concludes, the seriously weakened British, the traditional leaders of the world economy, "couldn't and the United States wouldn't" stabilize the international economic system in 1929.[7] The United States, which had momentarily played a positive role after the occupation of the Ruhr, cut back its international lending and erected high tariffs.

The second factor was poor national economic policy in almost every country. Governments generally cut their budgets and reduced spending when they should have run large deficits in an attempt to stimulate their economies. Since the Second World War, such a "counter-cyclical policy," advocated by John Maynard Keynes, has become a well-established weapon against depression. But in the 1930s Keynes's prescription was generally regarded with horror by orthodox economists.

Mass Unemployment

The need for large-scale government spending was tied to mass unemployment. As the financial crisis led to cuts in production, workers lost their jobs and had little money to buy goods. This led to still more cuts in production and still more unemploy-

Middle-Class Unemployment An English office worker's unusual sandwich board poignantly summarizes the bitter despair of the unemployed in the 1930s. *(Source: Bettmann/Hulton)*

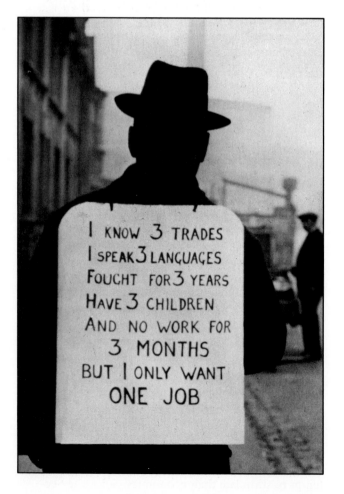

ment, until millions were out of work. In Britain, unemployment had averaged 12 percent in the 1920s; between 1930 and 1935, it averaged more than 18 percent. Far worse was the case of the United States, where unemployment had averaged only 5 percent in the 1920s. In 1932 unemployment soared to about one-third of the entire U.S. labor force: fourteen million people were out of work (see Map 34.1). Only by pumping new money into the economy could the government increase demand and break the vicious cycle of decline.

Along with its economic effects, mass unemployment posed a great social problem that mere numbers cannot adequately express. Millions of people lost their spirit and dignity in an apparently hopeless search for work. Homes and ways of life were disrupted in millions of personal tragedies. Young people postponed marriages they could not afford, and birthrates fell sharply. There was an increase in suicide and mental illness. Poverty or the threat of poverty became a grinding reality. In 1932 the workers of Manchester, England, appealed to their city officials—a typical appeal echoed throughout the Western world:

We tell you that thousands of people . . . are in desperate straits. We tell you that men, women, and children are going hungry. . . . We tell you that great numbers are being rendered distraught through the stress and worry of trying to exist without work. . . .

If you do not do this—if you do not provide useful work for the unemployed—what, we ask, is your alternative? Do not imagine that this colossal tragedy of unemployment is going on endlessly without some fateful catastrophe. Hungry men are angry men.[8]

Mass unemployment was a terrible time bomb preparing to explode.

The New Deal in the United States

Of all the major industrial countries, only Germany was harder hit by the Great Depression, or reacted more radically to it, than the United States. Depression was so traumatic in the United States because the 1920s had been a period of complacent prosperity. The Great Depression and the response to it marked a major turning point in American history.

President Herbert Hoover (1874–1964) and his administration initially reacted to the stock market crash and economic decline with dogged optimism and limited action. In May 1930 Hoover told a group of business and farm leaders, "I am convinced that we have now passed the worst and with continued unity of effort we shall rapidly recover." When, however, the full force of the financial crisis struck Europe in the summer of 1931 and boomeranged back to the United States, people's worst fears became reality. Banks failed; unemployment soared. In 1932 industrial production fell to about 50 percent of its level in 1929. In these tragic circumstances Franklin Delano Roosevelt (1882–1945), an inspiring wheelchair aristocrat previously crippled by polio, won a landslide electoral victory with grand but vague promises of a "New Deal for the forgotten man."

Roosevelt's basic goal was to reform capitalism in order to preserve it. In his words, "A frank examination of the profit system in the spring of 1933 showed it to be in collapse; but substantially everybody in the United States, in public office and out of public office, from the very rich to the very poor, was as determined as was my Administration to save it."[9] Roosevelt rejected socialism and government ownership of industry in 1933. To right the situation, he chose forceful government intervention in the economy.

In this choice, Roosevelt and his advisers were greatly influenced by America's experience in the First World War. During the wartime emergency, the American economy had been thoroughly planned and regulated. Roosevelt and his "brain trust" of advisers adopted similar policies to restore prosperity and reduce social inequality. Roosevelt was flexible, pragmatic, and willing to experiment. Government intervention and experimentation were combined in some of the New Deal's most significant measures.

The most ambitious attempt to control and plan the economy was the National Recovery Administration (NRA), established by Congress right after Roosevelt took office. The key idea behind the NRA was to reduce competition and fix prices and wages for everyone's benefit. This goal required government, business, and labor to hammer out detailed regulations for each industry. Along with this kind of national planning in the private sector of the economy, the government believed it could sponsor enough public works projects to assure recovery. Because the NRA broke with the cherished American tradition of free competition and aroused conflicts among business people, consumers, and bureaucrats, it did not work well. By the time the NRA was declared unconstitutional in 1935, Roosevelt and the New Deal were already moving away from government efforts to plan and control the entire economy.

Instead, Roosevelt and his advisers attacked the key problem of mass unemployment directly. The federal government accepted the responsibility of employing directly as many people as financially possible, something Hoover had consistently rejected. Thus, when it became clear in late 1933 that the initial program of public works was too small, new agencies were created to undertake a vast range of projects.

The most famous of these agencies is the Works Progress Administration (WPA), set up in 1935. At its peak in late 1938, this government agency employed more than three million individuals. One-fifth of the entire labor force worked for the WPA at some point in the 1930s. To this day, thousands of public buildings, bridges, and highways built by the WPA stand as monuments to energetic government efforts to provide people with meaningful work. The WPA was enormously popular in a nation long schooled in self-reliance and the work ethic. The hope of a job with the government helped check the threat of social revolution in the United States.

Other social measures aimed in the same direction. Following the path blazed by Germany's Bismarck in the 1880s, the U.S. government in 1935 established a national social security system, with old-age pensions and unemployment benefits, to protect many workers against some of life's uncertainties. The National Labor Relations Act of 1935 gave union organizers the green light by declaring collective bargaining to be the policy of the United States. Following some bitter strikes, such as the sit-down strike at General Motors in early 1937, union membership more than doubled, from four million in 1935 to nine million in 1940. In general, between 1935 and 1938 government rulings and social reforms chipped away at the privileges of the wealthy and tried to help ordinary people.

Yet, despite its undeniable accomplishments in social reform, the New Deal was only partly successful as a response to the Great Depression. At

President Roosevelt   used his famous "fireside chats" to explain his changing policies and to reassure the American people that the New Deal initiatives were working. This photo captures Roosevelt's forceful personality and contagious confidence, which he conveyed over the air waves. *(Source: Brown Brothers)*

the height of the recovery, in May 1937, seven million workers were still unemployed. The economic situation then worsened seriously in the recession of 1937 and 1938. Production fell sharply, and although unemployment never again reached the fifteen million mark of 1933, it hit eleven million in 1938 and was still a staggering ten million when war broke out in Europe in September 1939.

The New Deal never did pull the United States out of the depression. This failure frustrated Americans then, and it is still puzzling today. Perhaps, as some have claimed, Roosevelt should have used his enormous popularity and prestige in 1933 to nationalize the banks, the railroads, and some heavy industry, so that national economic planning could have been successful. On the other hand, Roosevelt's sharp attack on big business and the wealthy after 1935 had popular appeal but also damaged business confidence and made the great

capitalists uncooperative. Given the low level of profit and the underutilization of many factories, however, it is questionable whether business would have behaved much differently even if the New Deal had catered to it.

Finally, it is often argued that the New Deal did not put enough money into the economy through deficit financing. Like his predecessors in the White House, Roosevelt was attached to the ideal of the balanced budget. His largest deficit was only $4.4 billion in 1936. Compare this figure with deficits of $21.5 billion in 1942 and $57.4 billion in 1943, when the nation was prosperously engaged in total war and unemployment had vanished. By 1945 many economists concluded that the New Deal's deficit-financed public works had been too small a step in the right direction. These Keynesian views were to be very influential in economic policy in Europe and America after the Second World War.

The Scandinavian Response to Depression

Of all the Western democracies, the Scandinavian countries under Socialist leadership responded most successfully to the challenge of the Great Depression. Having grown steadily in number in the late nineteenth century, the Socialists became the largest political party in Sweden and then in Norway after the First World War. In the 1920s they passed important social reform legislation for both peasants and workers, gained practical administrative experience, and developed a unique kind of socialism. Flexible and nonrevolutionary, Scandinavian socialism grew out of a strong tradition of cooperative community action. Even before 1900, Scandinavian agricultural cooperatives had shown how individual peasant families could join together for everyone's benefit. Labor leaders and capitalists were also inclined to work together.

When the economic crisis struck in 1929, Socialist governments in Scandinavia built on this pattern of cooperative social action. Sweden in particular pioneered in the use of large-scale deficits to finance public works and thereby maintain production and employment. Scandinavian governments also increased social welfare benefits, from old-age pensions and unemployment insurance to subsidized housing and maternity allowances. All this spending required a large bureaucracy and high taxes, first on the rich and then on practically everyone. Yet both private and cooperative enterprise thrived, as did democracy. Some observers saw Scandinavia's welfare socialism as an appealing "middle way" between sick capitalism and cruel communism or fascism.

Recovery and Reform in Britain and France

In Britain, MacDonald's Labour government and then, after 1931, the Conservative-dominated coalition government followed orthodox economic theory. The budget was balanced, but unemployed workers received barely enough welfare to live. Despite government lethargy, the economy recovered considerably after 1932. By 1937 total production was about 20 percent higher than in 1929. In fact, for Britain the years after 1932 were actually somewhat better than the 1920s had been, quite the opposite of the situation in the United States and France.

This good, but by no means brilliant, performance reflected the gradual reorientation of the British economy. After going off the gold standard in 1931 and establishing protective tariffs in 1932, Britain concentrated increasingly on the national rather than the international market. The old export industries of the Industrial Revolution, such as textiles and coal, continued to decline, but new industries like automobiles and electrical appliances grew in response to British demand at home. Moreover, low interest rates encouraged a housing boom. By the end of the decade there were highly visible differences between the old, depressed industrial areas of the north and the new, growing areas of the south. These developments encouraged Britain to look inward and avoid unpleasant foreign questions.

Because France was relatively less industrialized and more isolated from the world economy, the Great Depression came later there. But once it hit France, it stayed and stayed. Decline was steady until 1935, and the short-lived recovery never brought production or employment back up to predepression levels. Economic stagnation both reflected and heightened an ongoing political crisis. There was no stability in government. As before 1914, the French parliament was made up of many political parties that could never cooperate for very long. In 1933, for example, five coalition cabinets formed and fell in rapid succession.

The French lost the underlying unity that had made government instability bearable before 1914. Fascist-type organizations agitated against parliamentary democracy and looked to Mussolini's Italy and Hitler's Germany for inspiration. In February 1934, French fascists and semifascists rioted and threatened to overturn the republic. At the same time, the Communist party and many workers opposed to the existing system were looking to Stalin's Russia for guidance. The vital center of moderate republicanism was sapped from both sides.

Frightened by the growing strength of the fascists at home and abroad, the Communists, the Socialists, and the Radicals formed an alliance—the Popular Front—for the national elections of May 1936. Their clear victory reflected the trend toward polarization. The number of Communists in the parliament jumped dramatically from 10 to 72, while the Socialists, led by Léon Blum (1872–1950), became the strongest party in

France with 146 seats. The really quite moderate Radicals slipped badly, and the conservatives lost ground to the semifascists.

In the next few months, Blum's Popular Front government made the first and only real attempt to deal with the social and economic problems of the 1930s in France. Inspired by Roosevelt's New Deal, the Popular Front encouraged the union movement and launched a far-reaching program of social reform, complete with paid vacations and a forty-hour workweek. Popular with workers and the lower middle class, these measures were quickly sabotaged by rapid inflation and cries of revolution from fascists and frightened conservatives. Wealthy people sneaked their money out of the country, labor unrest grew, and France entered a severe financial crisis. Blum was forced to announce a "breathing spell" in social reform.

The fires of political dissension were also fanned by civil war in Spain. The Communists demanded that France support the Spanish republicans, while many French conservatives would gladly have joined Hitler and Mussolini in aiding the attack of Spanish fascists. Extremism grew, and France itself was within sight of civil war. Blum was forced to resign in June 1937, and the Popular Front quickly collapsed. An anxious and divided France drifted aimlessly once again, preoccupied by Hitler and German rearmament.

SUMMARY

After the First World War, Western society entered a complex and difficult era—truly an age of anxiety. Intellectual life underwent a crisis marked by pessimism, uncertainty, and fascination with irrational forces. Ceaseless experimentation and rejection of old forms characterized art and music while motion pictures and radio provided a new, standardized entertainment for the masses. Previously avant-garde intellectual and artistic developments, along with the insecure state of mind they expressed, gained wider currency.

Politics and economics were similarly disrupted. In the 1920s political leaders groped to create an enduring peace and rebuild the prewar prosperity, and for a brief period late in the decade they seemed to succeed. Then the Great Depression shattered the fragile stability. Uncertainty re-

turned with redoubled force in the 1930s. The international economy collapsed, and unemployment struck millions. The democracies turned inward as they sought to cope with massive domestic problems and widespread disillusionment. Generally speaking, they were not very successful. The old liberal ideals of individual rights and responsibilities, elected government, and economic freedom seemed ineffective and outmoded, even when they managed to survive. And in many countries they were abandoned completely.

NOTES

1. P. Valéry, *Variety,* trans. M. Cowley (New York: Harcourt, Brace, 1927), pp. 27–28.
2. G. Marcel, as quoted in S. Hughes, *The Obstructed Path: French Social Thought in the Years of Desperation, 1930–1960* (New York: Harper & Row, 1967), p. 82.
3. G. Greene, *Another Mexico* (New York: Viking Press, 1939), p. 3.
4. Quoted in A. H. Barr, Jr., *What Is Modern Painting?* 9th ed. (New York: Museum of Modern Art, 1966), p. 27.
5. Ibid., p. 25.
6. R. Graves and A. Hodge, *The Long Week End: A Social History of Great Britain, 1918–1939* (New York: Macmillan, 1941), p. 131.
7. C. P. Kindleberger, *The World in Depression, 1929–1939* (Berkeley: University of California Press, 1973), p. 292.
8. Quoted in S. B. Clough et al., eds., *Economic History of Europe: Twentieth Century* (New York: Harper & Row, 1968), pp. 243–245.
9. Quoted in D. Dillard, *Economic Development of the North Atlantic Community* (Englewood Cliffs, N.J.: Prentice-Hall, 1967), p. 591.

SUGGESTED READING

Among general works, E. Wiskemann, *Europe of the Dictators, 1919–1945* (1966), and R. Sontag, *A Broken World, 1919–1939* (1971), are particularly recommended. The latter has an excellent bibliography. A. Bullock, ed., *The Twentieth Century* (1971), is a lavish visual feast combined with penetrating essays on major developments since 1900. Two excellent accounts of contemporary history—one with a liberal and the other with a conservative point of view—are R. Paxton, *Europe in the Twentieth Century* (1975), and P. Johnson, *Modern Times: The World from the Twenties to the Eighties* (1983). Crucial changes in thought before and after the First World War are discussed in three rewarding intellectual histories: G. Masur, *Prophets of Yesterday* (1961); H. S. Hughes, *Consciousness and Society* (1956); and M. Biddiss, *Age of the Masses: Ideas and Society Since 1870* (1977). R. Stromberg, *European Intellectual History Since 1789,* 4th ed. (1986), and F. Baumer, *Modern European Thought: Continuity and Change in Ideas, 1600–1950* (1970), are recommended general surveys.

J. Rewalds, *The History of Impressionism,* rev. ed. (1961), and *Post-Impressionism* (1956) are excellent, as is the work by Barr cited in the Notes. P. Collaer, *A History of Modern Music* (1961), and H. R. Hitchcock, *Architecture: Nineteenth and Twentieth Centuries* (1958), are good introductions. T. Wolfe, *From Bauhaus to Our House* (1981), is a lively critique of modern architecture. L. Barnett, *The Universe and Dr. Einstein* (1952), is a fascinating study of the new physics. A. Storr, *Freud* (1989), and P. Rieff, *Freud* (1956), consider the man and how his theories have stood the test of time. M. White, ed., *The Age of Analysis* (1955), opens up basic questions of twentieth-century psychology and philosophy. H. Liebersohn, *Fate and Utopia in German Sociology* (1988), analyzes developments in German social science, and P. Gay, *Weimar Culture* (1970), is a brilliant exploration of the many-sided artistic renaissance in Germany in the 1920s. M. Marrus, ed., *Emergence of Leisure* (1974), is a pioneering inquiry into an important aspect of mass culture. H. Daniels-Rops, *A Fight for God,* 2 vols. (1966), is a sympathetic history of the Catholic church between 1870 and 1939.

G. Ambrosius and W. Hibbard, *A Social and Economic History of Twentieth-Century Europe* (1989), provides a good survey; C. Maier, *Recasting Bourgeois Europe* (1975), is an ambitious comparative study of social classes and conflicts in France, Germany, and Italy after the First World War. P. Fritzsche, *Rehearsals for Fascism: Populism and Political Mobilization in Weimar Germany* (1990); R. Wohl, *The Generation of 1914* (1979); R. Kuisel, *Capital and State in Modern France: Renovation and Economic Management* (1982); and W. McDougall, *France's Rhineland Diplomacy, 1914–1924* (1978), are four more important studies on aspects of the postwar challenge. M. Childs, *Sweden: The Middle Way* (1961), applauds Sweden's efforts at social reform. W. Neuman, *The Balance of Power in the Interwar Years, 1919–1939* (1968), perceptively examines international politics after the Locarno treaties of 1925. In addition to the contemporary works discussed in the text, the crisis of the interwar period comes alive in R. Crossman, ed., *The God That Failed* (1950), in which famous Western writers tell why they were attracted to and later repelled by communism; J. Ortega y Gasset's renowned *The Revolt of the Masses* (1932); and F. A. Hayek's *The Road to Serfdom* (1944), a famous warning of the dangers to democratic freedoms.

In addition to Kindleberger's excellent study of the Great Depression cited in the Notes, there is J. K. Galbraith's very lively and understandable account of the stock market collapse, *The Great Crash* (1955). J. Garraty, *Unemployment in History* (1978), is noteworthy, though novels best portray the human tragedy of economic decline. Winifred Holtby, *South Riding* (1936), and Walter Greenwood, *Love on the Dole* (1933), are moving stories of the Great Depression in England; Hans Fallada, *Little Man, What Now?* (1932), is the classic counterpart for Germany. Also highly recommended as commentaries on English life between the wars are Robert Graves, *Goodbye to All That,* rev. ed. (1957), and George Orwell, *The Road to Wigan Pier* (1972). Among French novelists, André Gide painstakingly examines the French middle class and its values in *The Counterfeiters,* and Albert Camus, the greatest of the existential novelists, is at his unforgettable best in *The Stranger* and *The Plague.*

35

Dictatorships and the Second World War

Adolf Hitler at Bueckeberg (Westphalia)

The era of anxiety and economic depression was also a time of growing strength for political dictatorship. Popularly elected governments and basic civil liberties declined drastically in Europe. On the eve of the Second World War, liberal democratic government survived only in Great Britain, France, the Low Countries, the Scandinavian nations, and neutral Switzerland. Elsewhere in Europe, various kinds of "strong men" ruled. Dictatorship seemed the wave of the future. Thus the decline in liberal political institutions and the intellectual crisis were related elements in the general crisis of European civilization.

The era of dictatorship is a highly disturbing chapter in the history of Western civilization. The key development was not simply the resurgence of dictatorship but the rise of a new kind of tyranny—the modern totalitarian state. Modern totalitarianism reached its fullest realization in Communist Russia and Nazi Germany in the 1930s. Stalin and Hitler mobilized their peoples for enormous undertakings and ruled with unprecedented severity. Hitler's mobilization was ultimately directed toward racial aggression and territorial expansion, and his ruthless attack on Poland in 1939 started the Second World War.

Nazi armies were defeated by a great coalition, and people today want to believe that the era of totalitarian dictatorship was a terrible accident, that Stalin's slave labor camps and Hitler's gas chambers "can't happen again." Yet the cruel truth is that terrible atrocities continue to plague the world: the Khmer Rouge inflicted genocide on people in Kampuchea in recent times; civil wars in the Horn of Africa have brought horrible man-made famines, and there are many other examples. Thus it is vital to understand Europe's tragic era of totalitarian dictatorship in order to guard against a recurrence.

- What was the nature of the twentieth-century totalitarian state?
- How did totalitarianism affect ordinary people?
- How did the rise of totalitarian states result in another world war?

These are the questions that this chapter seeks to answer.

AUTHORITARIAN AND TOTALITARIAN STATES

The modern totalitarian state differed from the old-fashioned authoritarian state. Completely rejecting liberal values and drawing on the experience of total war, the modern totalitarian state exercised much greater control over the masses and mobilized them for constant action. The nature of this control may be examined by comparing the old and new forms of dictatorship in a general way, before entering the strange worlds of Stalin's Russia and Hitler's Germany.

Conservative Authoritarianism

The traditional form of antidemocratic government in European history has been conservative authoritarianism. Like Catherine the Great in Russia and Metternich in Austria, the leaders of such governments have tried to prevent major changes that would undermine the existing social order. To do so, they have relied on obedient bureaucracies, vigilant police departments, and trustworthy armies. Popular participation in government has been forbidden or else severely limited to such natural allies as landlords, bureaucrats, and high church officials. Liberals, democrats, and socialists have been persecuted as radicals, often finding themselves in jail or exile.

Yet old-fashioned authoritarian governments were limited in their power and in their objectives. Lacking modern technology and communications, they did not have the power to control many aspects of their subjects' lives. Nor did they wish to do so. Preoccupied with the goal of mere survival, these governments largely limited their demands to taxes, army recruits, and passive acceptance. As long as the people did not try to change the system, they often had considerable personal independence.

After the First World War, this kind of authoritarian government revived, especially in the less developed eastern part of Europe. There, the parliamentary regimes that had been founded on the wreckage of empires in 1918 fell one by one. By early 1938 only economically and socially advanced Czechoslovakia remained true to liberal political ideals. Conservative dictators also took over in Spain and Portugal.

There were several reasons for this development. These nations lacked a strong tradition of self-government, with its necessary restraint and compromise. Moreover, many of these new states were torn by ethnic conflicts that threatened their very existence. Dictatorship appealed to nationalists and military leaders as a way to repress such tensions and preserve national unity. Large landowners and the church were still powerful forces in these largely agrarian areas, and they often looked to dictators to save them from progressive land reform or communist agrarian upheaval. So did some members of the middle class, which was small and weak in eastern Europe. Finally, though some kind of democracy managed to stagger through the 1920s in Austria, Bulgaria, Romania, Greece, Estonia, and Latvia, the Great Depression

delivered the final blow in those countries in 1936.

Although some of the authoritarian regimes adopted certain Hitlerian and fascist characteristics in the 1930s, their general aims were not totalitarian. They were concerned more with maintaining the status quo than with forcing society into rapid change or war. This tradition lives on, especially in some of the military dictatorships that ruled in Latin America until quite recently.

Hungary was a good example of conservative authoritarianism. In the chaos of collapse in 1919, Béla Kun formed a Lenin-style government, but communism in Hungary was soon crushed by foreign troops, large landowners, and hostile peasants. Thereafter, a combination of great and medium-size landowners instituted a semi-authoritarian regime, which maintained the status quo in the 1920s. Hungary had a parliament, but

Nazi Mass Rally, 1936 This picture captures the spirit of modern totalitarianism. The uniformed members of the Nazi party have willingly merged themselves into a single force and await the command of the godlike leader. *(Source: Wide World Photos)*

elections were carefully controlled. The peasants did not have the right to vote, and an upper house representing the landed aristocracy was re-established. There was no land reform, no major social change. In the 1930s the Hungarian government remained conservative and nationalistic. Increasingly, it was opposed by a Nazi-like fascist movement, the Arrow Cross, which demanded radical reform and totalitarian measures.

Another example of conservative authoritarianism was newly independent Poland, where democratic government was overturned in 1926 when General Joseph Pilsudski established a military dictatorship. Sandwiched between Russia and Germany, Poland was torn by bitter party politics. Pilsudski silenced opposition and tried to build a strong state. His principal supporters were the army, major industrialists, and dedicated nationalists.

In Yugoslavia, King Alexander (r. 1921–1934) proclaimed a centralized dictatorship in 1929 to prevent ethnic rivalries among Serbs, Croats, and Slovenes from tearing the country apart. An old-style authoritarian, Alexander crushed democracy, jailed separatists, and ruled through the bureaucracy.

Another example of conservative authoritarianism was Portugal, at the westernmost end of the European peninsula. Constantly shaken by military coups and uprisings after a republican revolution in 1910, very poor and backward Portugal finally got a strong dictator in Antonio de Oliveira Salazar in 1932. A devout Catholic, Salazar gave the church the strongest possible position in the country while controlling the press and outlawing most political activity. Yet there was no attempt to mobilize the masses or to accomplish great projects. The traditional society was firmly maintained, and that was enough.

Modern Totalitarianism

Both modern totalitarianism and conservative authoritarianism are dictatorships, but they differ. They may be thought of as two distinct types of political organization that in practice sometimes share certain elements.

Modern totalitarianism burst on the scene with the revolutionary total-war effort of 1914 to 1918. The Great War called forth a tendency to subordinate all institutions and all classes to one supreme objective: victory. Nothing, absolutely nothing, had equal value. People were called to make ever-greater sacrifices, and their personal freedom was constantly reduced by ever-greater government control. As the outstanding French thinker Elie Halévy put it in 1936, the varieties of modern totalitarian tyranny—fascism, Nazism, and communism—may be thought of as "feuding brothers" with a common father, the nature of modern war.[1]

The crucial experience of the First World War was carried further by Lenin and the Bolsheviks during the Russian civil war. Lenin showed how a dedicated minority could make a total effort and achieve victory over a less determined majority. Lenin also demonstrated how institutions and human rights might be subordinated to the needs of a single group—the Communist party—and its leader, Lenin. Thus Lenin provided a model for single-party dictatorship, and he inspired imitators.

Building on its immediate origins in the First World War and the Russian civil war, modern totalitarianism reached maturity in the 1930s in Stalinist Russia and Nazi Germany. Both had several fundamental characteristics of modern totalitarianism.

Armed with modern technology and communications, the true totalitarian state began as a dictatorship exercising complete political power, but it did not stop there. Increasingly, the state took over and tried to control just as completely the economic, social, intellectual, and cultural aspects of life. Although such unlimited control could not be fully realized, individuals' freedom of action was greatly reduced. Deviation from the norm even in art or family behavior could become a crime. In theory, nothing was politically neutral; nothing was outside the scope of the state.

This grandiose vision of total state control broke decisively not only with conservative authoritarianism but also with nineteenth-century liberalism and democracy. Indeed, totalitarianism was a radical revolt against liberalism. Liberalism sought to limit the power of the state and protect the sacred rights of the individual. Moreover, liberals stood for rationality, harmony, peaceful progress, and a strong middle class. All of that disgusted totalitarians as sentimental slop. They believed in will power, preached conflict, and worshiped violence.

They believed that the individual was infinitely less valuable than the state and that there were no lasting rights, only temporary rewards for loyal and effective service. Only a single powerful leader and a single party, both unrestrained by law or tradition, determined the destiny of the totalitarian state.

Unlike old-fashioned authoritarianism, modern totalitarianism was based not on an elite but on the masses. As in the First World War, the totalitarian state sought and sometimes won the support and even the love of ordinary people. Modern totalitarianism built on politically alert masses, on people who had already become engaged in the political process, most notably through commitment to nationalism and socialism. Its character as a mass movement gave totalitarianism much of its elemental force.

The final shared characteristic of real totalitarian states was their boundless dynamism. The totalitarian society was a fully mobilized society, a society moving toward some goal. It was never content merely to survive, like an old-fashioned military dictatorship or a decaying democracy. Paradoxically, totalitarian regimes never reached their goals. Or, more precisely, as soon as one goal was achieved at the cost of enormous sacrifice, another arose at the leader's command to take its place. Thus totalitarianism was in the end a permanent revolution, an unfinished revolution, in which rapid, profound change imposed from on high went on forever.

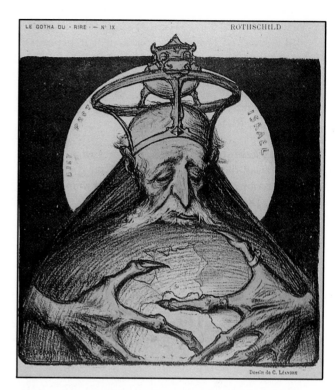

Vicious Anti-Semitism was visible in all European countries before World War One. This 1898 French cartoon shows the Jewish banker Rothschild worshiping gold and exploiting the whole world. Jews were also denounced as revolutionary socialists intent upon destroying private property and the middle class. *(Source: Historical Pictures Service, Chicago)*

Totalitarianism of the Left and the Right

The two most developed totalitarian states—Stalin's Communist Russia and Hitler's Nazi Germany—shared all the central characteristics of totalitarianism. But although those regimes may seem more alike than not, there were at least two major differences between them.

Communism as practiced in Soviet Russia grew out of Marxian socialism. Nazism in Germany grew out of extreme nationalism and racism. This distinction meant that private property and the middle class received very different treatment in the two states. In Soviet Russia, the socialist program of the radical left was realized: all large holdings of private property were taken over by the state, and the middle class lost its wealth and status. In Germany, big landowners and industrialists on the conservative right were sharply criticized but managed to maintain their private wealth. This difference in property and class relations has led some scholars to speak of "totalitarianism of the left"—Stalinist Russia—and "totalitarianism of the right"—Nazi Germany.

More important were the differing possibilities for regeneration. Socialism, with its concern for social justice and human progress, is linked to the living core of Western civilization and the Judeo-Christian tradition. Stalin's communism was an ugly perversion of socialism, but even in its darkest moments it had the potential for reforming itself and creating a more humane society. But Nazism had no such potential. Based on the phobias of anticapitalism, anti-Semitism, and racism, its elements could be found in many a European city before the First World War. Totally negative and devoid of even perverted truth, it promised only destruction and never rebirth.

STALIN'S RUSSIA

Lenin established the basic outlines of a modern totalitarian dictatorship in Russia after the Bolshevik Revolution and during the civil war. Joseph Stalin (1879–1953) finished the job. A master of political infighting, Stalin cautiously consolidated his power and eliminated his enemies in the mid-1920s. Then in 1928, as undisputed leader of the ruling Communist party, he launched the first five-year plan—the "revolution from above," as he so aptly termed it.

The five-year plans were extremely ambitious. Often incorrectly considered a mere set of economic measures to speed up Soviet Russia's industrial development, the five-year plans actually marked the beginning of a renewed attempt to mobilize and transform Soviet society along socialist lines. The goal was to create a new way of life and to generate new attitudes and new loyalties. The means that Stalin and the small Communist party elite chose were constant propaganda, enormous sacrifice, and unlimited violence and state control. In this way the Soviet Union in the 1930s became a dynamic, modern totalitarian state.

Lenin and Stalin in 1922 Lenin re-established limited economic freedom throughout Russia in 1921, but he ran the country and the Communist party in an increasingly authoritarian way. Stalin carried the process much further and eventually built a regime based on harsh dictatorship. *(Source: Sovfoto)*

From Lenin to Stalin

By spring 1921 Lenin and the Bolsheviks had won the civil war, but they ruled a shattered and devastated land. Many farms were in ruins, and food supplies were exhausted. In southern Russia, drought combined with the ravages of war to produce the worst famine in generations. By 1920, according to the government, from 50 to 90 percent of the population in seventeen provinces was starving. Industrial production also broke down completely. In 1921, for example, output of steel and cotton textiles was only about 4 percent of what it had been in 1913. The revolutionary Trotsky later wrote that the "collapse of the productive forces surpassed anything of the kind history had ever seen. The country, and the government with it, were at the very edge of the abyss."[2] The Bolsheviks had destroyed the economy as well as their foes.

In the face of economic disintegration and rioting by peasants and workers, as well as an open rebellion by previously pro-Bolshevik sailors at Kronstadt—a rebellion that had to be quelled with machine guns—the tough but ever-flexible Lenin changed course. In March 1921 he announced the New Economic Policy (NEP), which re-established limited economic freedom in an attempt to rebuild agriculture and industry. During the civil war, the Communists had simply seized grain without payment. Lenin in 1921 substituted a grain tax on the country's peasant producers, who were permitted to sell their surpluses in free markets. Peasants were also encouraged to buy as many goods as they could afford from private traders and small handicraft manufacturers, groups that were now allowed to reappear. Heavy industry, railroads, and banks, however, remained wholly nationalized. Thus NEP saw only a limited restoration of capitalism.

Lenin's New Economic Policy was shrewd and successful, from two points of view. Politically, it was a necessary but temporary compromise with Russia's overwhelming peasant majority. Flushed with victory after their revolutionary gains of 1917, the peasants would have fought to hold onto their land. With fond hopes of immediate worldwide revolution fading by 1921, Lenin realized that his government was not strong enough to take it from them. As he had accepted Germany's harsh terms at Brest-Litovsk in 1918, Lenin made a deal with the only force capable of overturning his government.

Economically, NEP brought rapid recovery. In 1926 industrial output had surpassed the level of 1913, and Russian peasants were producing almost as much grain as before the war. Counting shorter hours and increased social benefits, workers were living somewhat better than they had in the past.

As the economy recovered and the government partially relaxed its censorship and repression, an intense struggle for power began in the inner circles of the Communist party, for Lenin had left no chosen successor when he died in 1924. The principal contenders were the stolid Stalin and the flamboyant Trotsky.

The son of a shoemaker, Joseph Dzhugashvili—later known as "Stalin"—studied for the priesthood but was expelled from his theological seminary, probably for rude rebelliousness. By 1903 he had joined the Bolsheviks. In the years before the First World War, he engaged in many revolutionary activities in the Transcaucasian area of southern Russia, including a daring bank robbery to get money for the Bolsheviks. This raid gained Lenin's attention and approval. Ethnically a Georgian and not a Russian, Stalin in his early writings focused on the oppression of minority peoples in the Russian Empire. Stalin was a good organizer but a poor speaker and writer, with no experience outside of Russia.

Leon Trotsky, a great and inspiring leader who had planned the 1917 takeover (see page 1058) and then created the victorious Red Army, appeared to have all the advantages. Yet it was Stalin who succeeded Lenin. Stalin won because he was more effective at gaining the all-important support of the party, the only genuine source of power in the one-party state. Rising to general secretary of the party's Central Committee just before Lenin's first stroke in 1922, Stalin used his office to win friends and allies with jobs and promises. Stalin also won recognition as commissar of nationalities, a key position in which he governed many of Russia's minorities.

The "practical" Stalin also won because he appeared better able than the brilliant Trotsky to relate Marxist teaching to Russian realities in the 1920s. First, as commissar of nationalities, he built on Lenin's idea of granting minority groups a certain degree of freedom in culture and language while maintaining rigorous political control through carefully selected local Communists. Stalin could loudly claim, therefore, to have found a way to solve the ancient problem of ethnic demands for independence in the multinational state. And of course he did.

Second, Stalin developed a theory of "socialism in one country," which was more appealing to the majority of Communists than Trotsky's doctrine of "permanent revolution." Stalin argued that Russia had the ability to build socialism on its own. Trotsky maintained that socialism in Russia could succeed only if revolution occurred quickly throughout Europe. To many Communists, Trotsky's views seemed to sell Russia short and to promise risky conflicts with capitalist countries by recklessly encouraging revolutionary movements around the world. Stalin's willingness to break with NEP and push socialism at home appealed to young militants. In short, Stalin's theory of socialism in one country provided many in the party with a glimmer of hope in the midst of the capitalist-appearing NEP, which they had come to detest.

With cunning skill Stalin gradually achieved absolute power between 1922 and 1927. First, he allied with Trotsky's personal enemies to crush Trotsky, who was expelled from the Soviet Union in 1929 and eventually was murdered in Mexico in 1940, undoubtedly on Stalin's order. Stalin then aligned with the moderates, who wanted to go slow at home, to suppress Trotsky's radical followers. Finally, having defeated all the radicals, he turned against his allies, the moderates, and destroyed them as well. Stalin's final triumph came at the Party Congress of December 1927, which condemned all "deviation from the general party line" formulated by Stalin. The dictator was then ready to launch his "revolution from above"—the real Russian revolution for millions of ordinary citizens.

The Five-Year Plans

The Party Congress of 1927, which ratified Stalin's seizure of power, marked the end of the New Economic Policy and the beginning of the era of socialist five-year plans. The first five-year plan had staggering economic objectives. In just five years, total industrial output was to increase by 250 percent. Heavy industry, the preferred sector, was to grow even faster; steel production, for example, was to jump almost 300 percent. Agricultural production was slated to increase by 150 percent, and one-fifth of Russia's peasants were scheduled to give up their private plots and join socialist collective farms. In spite of warnings from moderate Communists that these goals were unrealistic, Stalin raised them higher as the plan got under way. By 1930 a whirlwind of economic and social change was sweeping the country.

Stalin unleashed his "second revolution" for a variety of interrelated reasons. There were, first of all, ideological considerations. Like Lenin, Stalin and his militant supporters were deeply committed to socialism as they understood it. Since the country had recovered economically and their rule was secure, they burned to stamp out NEP's private traders, independent artisans, and few well-to-do peasants. Purely economic motivations were also important. Although the economy had recovered, it seemed to have stalled in 1927 and 1928. A new socialist offensive seemed necessary if industry and agriculture were to grow rapidly.

Political considerations were most important. Internationally, there was the old problem, remaining from prerevolutionary times, of catching up with the advanced and presumably hostile capitalist nations of the West. Stalin said in 1931, when he pressed for ever-greater speed and sacrifice: "We are fifty or a hundred years behind the advanced countries. We must make good this distance in ten years. Either we do it, or we shall go under."[3]

Domestically, there was what Communist writers of the 1920s called the "cursed problem"—the problem of the Russian peasants. For centuries, Russian peasants had wanted to own the land, and finally they had it. Sooner or later, the Communists reasoned, the peasants would become conservative little capitalists and pose a threat to the regime. Thus Stalin decided on a preventive war against the peasantry in order to bring it under the absolute control of the state.

That war was *collectivization*—the forcible consolidation of individual peasant farms into large, state-controlled enterprises. Beginning in 1929, peasants all over the Soviet Union were ordered to give up their land and animals and to become members of collective farms, although they continued to live in their own homes. As for the *kulaks*, the better-off peasants, Stalin instructed party workers to "liquidate them as a class." Stripped of their land and livestock, the kulaks

Plastov: Collective Farm Threshing   This example of socialist realism portrays the results of collectivization in positive terms, but the propaganda message does not seem heavy-handed. These peasants have become employees of a large collective farm and are threshing its wheat crop. Socialist realism was expected to depict—and to glorify—the achievements of the New Soviet society. (*Source: Kiev State Museum of Russian Art*)

were generally not even permitted to join the collective farms. Many starved or were deported to forced-labor camps for "re-education."

Since almost all peasants were in fact poor, the term *kulak* soon meant any peasant who opposed the new system. Whole villages were often attacked. One conscience-stricken colonel in the secret police confessed to a foreign journalist: "I am an old Bolshevik. I worked in the underground against the Tsar and then I fought in the Civil War. Did I do all that in order that I should now surround villages with machineguns and order my men to fire indiscriminately into crowds of peasants? Oh, no, no!"[4]

Forced collectivization of the peasants led to economic and human disaster. Large numbers of peasants slaughtered their animals and burned their crops in sullen, hopeless protest. Between 1929 and 1933, the number of horses, cattle, sheep, and goats in the Soviet Union fell by at least half. Nor were the state-controlled collective farms more productive. The output of grain barely increased between 1928 and 1938, when it was al-

most identical to that of 1913. Communist economists had expected collectivized agriculture to pay for new factories. Instead, the state had to invest heavily in agriculture, building thousands of tractors to replace slaughtered draft horses. Collectivized agriculture was unable to make any substantial financial contribution to Soviet industrial development in the first five-year plan. The human dimension of the tragedy was shocking. Collectivization created man-made famine in 1932 and 1933, and many perished. Indeed, Stalin confided to Churchill at Yalta in 1945 that ten million people had died in the course of collectivization.

Yet collectivization was a political victory of sorts. By the end of 1932, fully 60 percent of Russian peasant families had been herded onto collective farms; by 1938, 93 percent. Regimented and indoctrinated as employees of an all-powerful state, the peasants were no longer even a potential political threat to Stalin and the Communist party. Moreover, the state was assured of grain for bread for urban workers, who were much more important politically than the peasants. Collective farmers had to meet their grain quotas first and worry about feeding themselves second. Many collectivized peasants drew much of their own food from tiny, grudgingly tolerated garden plots that they worked in their off hours. No wonder some peasants joked, with that grim humor peculiar to the totalitarian society, that the initials then used by the Communist party actually stood for "The Second Serfdom, That of the Bolsheviks."

The industrial side of the five-year plans was more successful—indeed, quite spectacular. The output of industry doubled in the first five-year plan and doubled again in the second. Soviet industry produced about four times as much in 1937 as it had in 1928. No other major country had ever achieved such rapid industrial growth. Heavy industry led the way; consumer industry grew quite slowly. Steel production—a near-obsession with Stalin, whose name fittingly meant "man of steel" in Russian—increased roughly 500 percent between 1928 and 1937. A new heavy industrial complex was built almost from scratch in western Siberia. Industrial growth also went hand in hand with urban development. Cities rose where nomadic tribes had grazed their flocks. More than twenty-five million people migrated to cities during the 1930s.

The great industrialization drive, concentrated between 1928 and 1937, was an awe-inspiring achievement purchased at enormous sacrifice. The sudden creation of dozens of new factories required a great increase in investment and a sharp decrease in consumption. Few nations had ever invested more than one-sixth of their yearly net national income. Soviet planners decreed that more than one-third of net income go for investment. This meant that only two-thirds of everything being produced could be consumed by the people and the increasingly voracious military. The money was collected from the people by means of heavy, hidden sales taxes.

There was, therefore, no improvement in the average standard of living. Indeed, the most careful studies show that the average nonfarm wage apparently purchased only about half as many goods in 1932 as in 1928. After 1932 real wages rose slowly, so that in 1937 workers could buy about 60 percent of what they had bought in 1928. Thus rapid industrial development went with an unprecedented decline in the standard of living for ordinary people.

Two other factors contributed importantly to rapid industrialization: firm labor discipline and foreign engineers. Between 1930 and 1932, trade unions lost most of their power. The government could assign workers to any job anywhere in the country, and individuals could not move without the permission of the police. When factory managers needed more hands, they called on their counterparts on the collective farms, who sent them millions of "unneeded" peasants over the years.

Foreign engineers were hired to plan and construct many of the new factories. Highly skilled American engineers, hungry for work in the depression years, were particularly important until newly trained Soviet experts began to replace them after 1932. The gigantic mills of the new Siberian steel industry were modeled on America's best. Those modern mills were eloquent testimony to the ability of Stalin's planners to harness even the skill and technology of capitalist countries to promote the surge of socialist industry.

Life in Stalinist Society

The aim of Stalin's five-year plans was to create a new kind of society and human personality, as well as a strong industrial economy and a powerful army. Stalin and his helpers were good Marxian economic determinists. Once everything was owned by the state, they believed, a socialist society and a new kind of human being would inevitably emerge. They were by no means totally successful, but they did build a new society, whose broad outlines existed to the early 1980s. For the people, life in Stalinist society had both good and bad aspects.

The most frightening aspect of Stalinist society was brutal, unrestrained police terrorism. First directed primarily against the peasants after 1929, terror was increasingly turned on leading Communists, powerful administrators, and ordinary people for no apparent reason. As one Soviet woman later recalled, "We all trembled because there was no way of getting out of it. Even a Communist himself can be caught. To avoid trouble became an exception."[5] A climate of fear fell on the land.

In the early 1930s, the top members of the party and government were Stalin's obedient servants, but there was some grumbling in the party. At a small gathering in November 1932, even Stalin's wife complained bitterly about the misery of the people. Stalin showered her with insults, and she died that same night, apparently by her own hand. In late 1934 Stalin's number-two man, Sergei Kirov, was suddenly and mysteriously murdered. Although Stalin himself probably ordered Kirov's murder, he used the incident to launch a reign of terror.

In August 1936 sixteen prominent old Bolsheviks confessed to all manner of plots against Stalin in spectacular public trials in Moscow. Then, in 1937, lesser party officials and newer henchmen were arrested. In addition to party members, union officials, managers, intellectuals, army officers, and countless ordinary citizens were struck down. Local units of the secret police were even ordered to arrest a certain percentage of the people in their districts. In all, at least eight million people were probably arrested, and millions never returned from prisons and forced-labor camps.

Stalin's mass purges were truly baffling, and many explanations have been given for them. Possibly Stalin believed that the old Communists, like the peasants under NEP, were a potential threat to be wiped out in a preventive attack. Yet why did leading Communists confess to crimes they could not possibly have committed? Their lives had been devoted to the party and the socialist revolution. In the words of the German novelist Arthur Koestler, they probably confessed "in order to do a last service to the Party," the party they loved even when it was wrong. Some of them were subjected to torture and brainwashing. It has been argued that the purges indicate that Stalin was sadistic or insane, for his blood bath greatly weakened the government and the army. Others see the terror as an aspect of the fully developed totalitarian state, which must by its nature always be fighting real or imaginary enemies. At the least, the mass purges were a message to the people: no one was secure. Everyone had to serve the party and its leader with redoubled devotion.

Another aspect of life in the 1930s was constant propaganda and indoctrination. Party activists lectured workers in factories and peasants on collective farms, and newspapers, films, and radio broadcasts endlessly recounted socialist achievements and capitalist plots. Art and literature became highly political. Whereas the 1920s had seen considerable experimentation in modern art and theater, the intellectual elite were ordered by Stalin to become "engineers of human minds." Writers and artists who could effectively combine genuine creativity and political propaganda became the darlings of the regime. They often lived better than top members of the political elite. It became increasingly important for the successful writer and artist to glorify Russian nationalism. History was rewritten so that early tsars like Ivan the Terrible and Peter the Great became worthy forerunners of the greatest Russian leader—Stalin.

Stalin seldom appeared in public, but his presence was everywhere—in portraits, statues, books, and quotations from his "sacred" writings. Although the government persecuted religion and turned churches into "museums of atheism," the state had both an earthly religion and a high priest—Marxian socialism and Joseph Stalin.

Life was hard in Stalin's Soviet Russia. The standard of living declined substantially in the 1930s. The masses of people lived primarily on black bread and wore old, shabby clothing. There were constant shortages in the stores, although very heavily taxed vodka was always readily available. A shortage of housing was a particularly serious problem. Millions were moving into the cities, but the government built few new apartments. In 1940 there were approximately 4 people per room in every urban dwelling, as opposed to 2.7 per room in 1926. A relatively lucky family received one room for all its members and shared both a kitchen and a toilet with others on the floor. Less fortunate workers, kulaks, and class enemies built scrap-lumber shacks or underground dugouts in shanty-towns.

Life was hard, but not hopeless. Idealism and ideology appealed to many Russians, who saw themselves heroically building the world's first socialist society while capitalism crumbled in the West. This optimistic belief in the future of Soviet Russia also attracted many disillusioned Western liberals to communism in the 1930s.

On a more practical level, Soviet workers did receive some important social benefits, such as old-age pensions, free medical services, free education, and day-care centers for children. Unemployment was almost unknown. Finally, there was the possibility of personal advancement.

The keys to improving one's position were specialized skills and technical education. Rapid industrialization required massive numbers of trained experts, such as skilled workers, engineers, and plant managers. Thus the state provided tremendous incentives to those who could serve its needs. It paid the mass of unskilled workers and

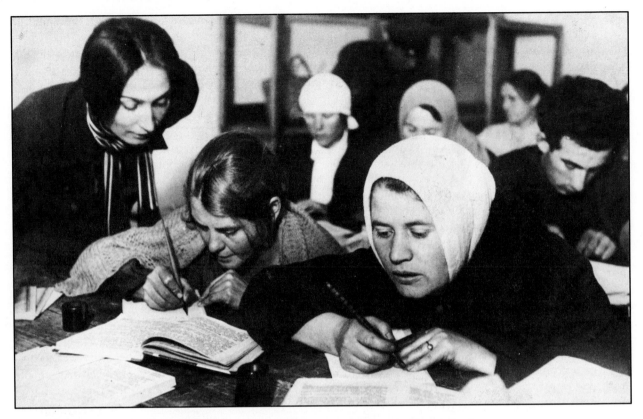

Adult Education Illiteracy, especially among women, was a serious problem after the Russian Revolution. This early photo shows how adults successfully learned to read and write throughout the Soviet Union. *(Source: Sovfoto)*

collective farmers very low wages, but it dangled high salaries and many special privileges before its growing technical and managerial elite. This elite joined with the political and artistic elites in a new upper class, whose members were rich, powerful, and insecure, especially during the purges. Yet the possible gains of moving up outweighed the risks. Millions struggled bravely in universities, institutes, and night schools for the all-important specialized education. One young man summed it up: "In Soviet Russia there is no capital except education. If a person does not want to become a collective farmer or just a cleaning woman, the only means you have to get something is through education."[6]

Women in Soviet Russia

Women's lives were radically altered by Stalinist society. Marxists had traditionally believed that both capitalism and the middle-class husband ex-

ploited women. The Russian Revolution of 1917 immediately proclaimed complete equality of rights for women. In the 1920s divorce and abortion were made very easy, and women were urged to work outside the home and liberate themselves sexually. A prominent and influential Bolshevik feminist, Alexandra Kollontai, went so far as to declare that the sexual act had no more significance than "drinking a glass of water." This observation drew a sharp rebuke from the rather prudish Lenin, who said that "no sane man would lie down to drink from a puddle in the gutter or even drink from a dirty glass."[7] After Stalin came to power, sexual and familial liberation was played down, and the most lasting changes for women involved work and education.

The changes were truly revolutionary. Young women were constantly told that they must be fully equal to men, that they could and should do anything men could do. Russian peasant women had long experienced the equality of backbreaking physical labor in the countryside, and they continued to enjoy that equality on collective farms. With the advent of the five-year plans, millions of women also began to toil in factories and in heavy construction, building dams, roads, and steel mills in summer heat and winter frost. Yet most of the opportunities open to men through education were also opened to women. Determined women pursued their studies and entered the ranks of the better-paid specialists in industry and science. Medicine practically became a woman's profession. By 1950, 75 percent of all doctors in Soviet Russia were women.

Thus Stalinist society gave women great opportunities but demanded great sacrifices as well. The vast majority of women simply had to work outside the home. Wages were so low that it was almost impossible for a family or couple to live on only the husband's earnings. Moreover, the full-time working woman had a heavy burden of household tasks in her off hours, for most Soviet men in the 1930s still considered the home and the children the woman's responsibility. Finally, rapid change and economic hardship led to many broken families, creating further physical, emotional, and mental strains for women. In any event, the often-neglected human resource of women was ruthlessly mobilized in Stalinist society. This, too, was an aspect of the Soviet totalitarian state.

MUSSOLINI'S ITALY

Like all the other emerging dictators, Mussolini hated liberalism, and he destroyed it in Italy. Mussolini and his supporters were the first to call themselves "fascists"—revolutionaries determined to create a certain kind of totalitarian state. As Mussolini's famous slogan of 1926 put it, "Everything in the state, nothing outside the state, nothing against the state." But Mussolini in power, unlike Stalin and Hitler, did not create a real totalitarian state. His dictatorship was rather an instructive hybrid, a halfway house between conservative authoritarianism and modern totalitarianism.

The Seizure of Power

Before the First World War, Italy was a liberal state moving gradually toward democracy. But there were serious problems. Much of the Italian population was still poor, and class differences were extreme. Many peasants were more attached to their villages and local interests than to the national state. Moreover, the papacy and many devout Catholics, as well as the socialists, were strongly opposed to the heirs of Cavour and Garibaldi, middle-class lawyers and politicians who ran the country largely for their own benefit. Relations between church and state were often tense.

The war worsened the political situation. Having fought on the side of the Allies almost exclusively for purposes of territorial expansion, Italian nationalists were bitterly disappointed with Italy's modest gains at Versailles. Workers and peasants also felt cheated: to win their support during the war, the government had promised social and land reform, which it did not deliver after the war.

Encouraged by the Russian Revolution of 1917, radical workers and peasants began occupying factories and seizing land in 1920. These actions scared and radicalized the property-owning classes. The Italian middle classes were already in an ugly mood, having suffered from inflation during the war. Moreover, after the war, the pope lifted his ban on participation by Catholics in Italian politics, and a strong Catholic party quickly emerged. Thus by 1922 almost all the major groups in Italian society were opposed—though for different reasons—to the liberal parliamentary government.

Into these crosscurrents of unrest and frustration stepped the blustering, bullying Benito Mussolini (1883–1945). Son of a village schoolteacher and a poor blacksmith, Mussolini began his political career as a Socialist leader and radical newspaper editor before the First World War. In 1914, powerfully influenced by antiliberal cults of violent action, the young Mussolini urged that Italy join the Allies, a stand for which he was expelled from the Italian Socialist party by its antiwar majority. Later Mussolini fought at the front and was wounded in 1917. Returning home, he began organizing bitter war veterans like himself into a band of Fascists—from the Italian word for "a union of forces."

At first, Mussolini's program was a radical combination of nationalist and socialist demands, including territorial expansion, benefits for workers, and land reform for peasants. As such, it competed with the better-organized Socialist party and failed to get off the ground. When Mussolini saw that his violent verbal assaults on the rival Socialists won him growing support from the frightened middle classes, he shifted gears in 1920. In thought and action, Mussolini was a striking example of the turbulence of the age of anxiety.

Mussolini and his growing private army of Black Shirts began to grow violent. Typically, a band of Fascist toughs would roar off in trucks at night and swoop down on a few isolated Socialist organizers, beating them up and force-feeding them almost deadly doses of castor oil. Few people were killed, but Socialist newspapers, union halls, and local Socialist party headquarters were destroyed. Mussolini's toughs pushed Communists and Socialists out of the city governments of northern Italy.

Mussolini, a skillful politician, refused to become a puppet of frightened conservatives and capitalists. He allowed his followers to convince themselves that they were not just opposing the "reds" but were making a real revolution of their own. Many believed that they were not only destroying parliamentary government but forming a strong, dynamic movement that would help the little people against the established interests.

With the government breaking down in 1922, largely because of the chaos created by his direct-action bands, Mussolini stepped forward as the savior of order and property. Striking a conservative note in his speeches and gaining the sympathetic neutrality of army leaders, Mussolini demanded the resignation of the existing government and his own appointment by the king. In October 1922, to force matters, a large group of Fascists marched on Rome to threaten the king and force him to call on Mussolini. The threat worked. Victor Emmanuel III (r. 1900–1946), who had no love for the old liberal politicians, asked Mussolini to form a new cabinet. Thus, after widespread violence and a threat of armed uprising, Mussolini seized power "legally." He was immediately granted dictatorial authority for one year by the king and the parliament.

The Regime in Action

Mussolini became dictator on the strength of Italians' rejection of parliamentary government, coupled with fears of Russian-style revolution. Yet what he intended to do with his power was by no means clear until 1924. Some of his dedicated supporters pressed for a "second revolution." Mussolini's ministers, however, included old conservatives, moderates, and even two reform-minded Socialists. A new electoral law was passed giving two-thirds of the representatives in the parliament to the party that won the most votes, a change that allowed the Fascists and their allies to win an overwhelming majority in 1924. Shortly thereafter, five of Mussolini's Fascist thugs kidnapped and murdered Giacomo Matteotti, the leader of the Socialists in the parliament. In the face of this outrage, the opposition demanded that Mussolini's armed squads be dissolved and all violence be banned.

Although he may or may not have ordered Matteotti's murder, Mussolini stood at the crossroads of a severe political crisis. After some hesitation, he charged forward. Declaring his desire to "make the nation Fascist," he imposed a series of repressive measures. Freedom of the press was abolished, elections were fixed, and the government ruled by decree. Mussolini arrested his political opponents, disbanded all independent labor unions, and put dedicated Fascists in control of Italy's schools. Moreover, he created a Fascist youth movement, Fascist labor unions, and many other Fascist organizations. By the end of 1926, Italy was a one-party dictatorship under Mussolini's unquestioned leadership.

Yet Mussolini did not complete the establishment of a modern totalitarian state. His Fascist party never became all-powerful. It never destroyed the old power structure, as the Communists did in Soviet Russia, or succeeded in dominating it, as the Nazis did in Germany. Membership in the Fascist party was more a sign of an Italian's respectability than a commitment to radical change. Interested primarily in personal power, Mussolini was content to compromise with the old conservative classes that controlled the army, the economy, and the state. He never tried to purge these classes or even move very vigorously against them. He controlled and propagandized labor but left big business to regulate itself, profitably and securely. There was no land reform.

Mussolini also came to draw on the support of the Catholic church. In the Lateran Agreement of 1929, he recognized the Vatican as a tiny independent state, and he agreed to give the church heavy financial support. The pope expressed his satisfaction and urged Italians to support Mussolini's government.

Nothing better illustrates Mussolini's unwillingness to harness everyone and everything for dynamic action than his treatment of women. He abolished divorce and told women to stay at home and produce children. To promote that goal, he decreed a special tax on bachelors in 1934. In 1938 women were limited by law to a maximum of 10 percent of the better-paying jobs in industry and government. Italian women, as women, appear not to have changed their attitudes or behavior in any important way under Fascist rule.

It is also noteworthy that Mussolini's government did not persecute Jews until late in the Second World War, when Italy was under Nazi control. Nor did Mussolini establish a truly ruthless police state. Only twenty-three political prisoners were condemned to death between 1926 and 1944. In spite of much pompous posing by the

Mussolini loved to swagger and bully. Here in his office he instinctively strikes his favorite theatrical pose, even as he discusses with its painter a less aggressive portrait of himself. *(Source: Courtesy, Gabriele Stocchi, Rome)*

chauvinist leader and in spite of mass meetings, salutes, and a certain copying of Hitler's aggression in foreign policy after 1933, Mussolini's Italy was undemocratic but never really totalitarian.

HITLER'S GERMANY

The most frightening totalitarian state was Nazi Germany. A product of Hitler's evil genius as well as of Germany's social and political situation and the general attack on liberalism and rationality in the age of anxiety, Nazi Germany emerged rapidly after Hitler came to power in 1933. The Nazis quickly smashed or took over most independent organizations, mobilized the economy, and began brutally persecuting the Jewish population. From the start, all major decisions were in the hands of the aggressive dictator Adolf Hitler.

The Roots of Nazism

Nazism grew out of many complex developments, of which the most influential were extreme nationalism and racism. These two ideas captured the mind of the young Hitler, and it was he who dominated Nazism for as long as it lasted.

Born the fourth child of a successful Austrian customs official and an indulgent mother, Adolf Hitler (1889–1945) spent his childhood happily in small towns in Austria. A good student in grade school, Hitler did poorly on reaching high school and dropped out at age fourteen after the death of his father. After four years of unfocused loafing, Hitler finally left for Vienna to become an artist. Denied admission to the Imperial Academy of Fine Arts because he lacked talent, the dejected Hitler stayed on in Vienna. There he lived a comfortable, lazy life on his generous orphan's pension and found most of the perverted beliefs that guided his life.

In Vienna Hitler soaked up extreme German nationalism, which was particularly strong there. Austro-German nationalists, as if to compensate for their declining position in the Austro-Hungarian Empire, believed Germans to be a superior people and the natural rulers of central Europe. They often advocated union with Germany and violent expulsion of "inferior" peoples as the

means of maintaining German domination of the Austro-Hungarian Empire.

Hitler was deeply impressed by Vienna's mayor, Karl Lueger, whom he called the "mightiest mayor of all times." Lueger claimed to be a "Christian socialist." With the help of the Catholic trade unions, he had succeeded in winning the support of the little people of Vienna for an attack on capitalism and liberalism, which he held responsible for un-Christian behavior and excessive individualism. A master of mass politics in the urban world, Lueger showed Hitler the enormous potential of anticapitalist and antiliberal propaganda.

From Lueger and others, Hitler eagerly absorbed virulent anti-Semitism, racism, and hatred of Slavs. He was particularly inspired by the racist ravings of a former monk named Lanz von Liebenfels. Preaching the crudest, most exaggerated distortions of the Darwinian theory of survival, Liebenfels stressed the superiority of Germanic races, the inevitability of racial conflict, and the inferiority of the Jews. Liebenfels even anticipated the breeding and extermination policies of the Nazi state. He claimed that the master race had to multiply its numbers by means of polygamy and breeding stations, while it systematically sterilized and liquidated inferior races. Anti-Semitism and racism became Hitler's most passionate convictions, his explanation for everything. He believed that inferior races—the Slavs and the Jews in particular—were responsible for Austria's woes. The Jews, he claimed, directed an international conspiracy of finance capitalism and Marxian socialism against German culture, German unity, and the German race. Hitler's belief was totally irrational, but he never doubted it.

Although he moved to Munich in 1913 to avoid being drafted in the Austrian army, the lonely Hitler greeted the outbreak of the First World War as a salvation. He later wrote in his autobiography, *Mein Kampf,* that, "overcome by passionate enthusiasm, I fell to my knees and thanked heaven out of an overflowing heart." The struggle and discipline of war gave life meaning, and Hitler served bravely as a dispatch carrier on the western front.

When Germany was suddenly defeated in 1918, Hitler's world was shattered. Not only was he a fanatical nationalist, but war was his reason for living. Convinced that Jews and Marxists had "stabbed Germany in the back," he vowed to fight on. And in the bitterness and uncertainty of postwar Germany, his wild speeches began to attract attention.

In late 1919 Hitler joined the German Workers' party, a tiny extremist group in Munich. In addition to denouncing Jews, Marxists, and democrats, the German Workers' party promised unity under a uniquely German "national socialism," which would abolish the injustices of capitalism and create a mighty "people's community." By 1921 Hitler had gained absolute control of this small but growing party. Moreover, Hitler was already a master of mass propaganda and political showmanship. Party members sported badges and uniforms, gave victory salutes, and marched like robots through the streets of Munich. But Hitler's most effective tool was the mass rally, a kind of political revival meeting. Songs, slogans, and demonstrations built up the tension until Hitler finally arrived. He then often worked his audience into a frenzy with wild, demagogic attacks on the Versailles Treaty, the Jews, the war profiteers, and Germany's Weimar Republic.

Party membership multiplied tenfold after early 1922. In late 1923, when the Weimar Republic seemed on the verge of collapse, Hitler decided on an armed uprising in Munich. Inspired by Mussolini's recent easy victory, Hitler had found an ally in General Ludendorff of First World War fame. After Hitler had overthrown the Bavarian government, Ludendorff was supposed to march on Berlin with Hitler's support. The plot was poorly organized, however, and it was crushed by the police, backed up by the army, in less than a day. Hitler was arrested, tried, and sentenced to five years in prison. He had failed for the moment. But Nazism had been born, and it did not die.

Hitler's Road to Power

At his trial, Hitler violently denounced the Weimar Republic and skillfully presented his own program. In doing so, he gained enormous publicity and attention. Moreover, he learned from his unsuccessful revolt. Hitler concluded that he had to undermine rather than overthrow the government, that he had to use its tolerant democratic framework to intimidate the opposition and come to power through electoral competition. He forced his more violent supporters to accept his new strategy. Finally, Hitler used his brief prison

Hitler in Opposition Hitler returns the salute of his Brown Shirts in this photograph from the third party day rally in Nuremberg in 1927. The Brown Shirts formed a private army within the Nazi movement, and their uniforms, marches, salutes, and vandalism helped keep Hitler in the public eye in the 1920s. *(Source: Courtesy, Bison Books, London)*

term—he was released in less than a year—to dictate *Mein Kampf*. There he expounded on his basic themes: "race," with the stress on anti-Semitism; "living space," with a sweeping vision of war and conquered territory; and the leader-dictator (the *Führer*) with unlimited, arbitary power. Hitler's followers had their bible.

In the years of prosperity and relative stability between 1924 and 1929, Hitler concentrated on building his National Socialist German Workers' party, or Nazi party. By 1928 the party had a hundred thousand highly disciplined members under Hitler's absolute control. To appeal to the middle classes, Hitler de-emphasized the anticapitalist elements of national socialism and vowed to fight Bolshevism.

The Nazis were still a small splinter group in 1928, when they received only 2.6 percent of the vote in the general elections and twelve Nazis won seats in the parliament. There the Nazi deputies pursued the legal strategy of using democracy to destroy democracy. As Hitler's talented future minister of propaganda Joseph Goebbels (1897–1945) explained in 1928 in the party newspaper, "We become Reichstag deputies in order to paralyze the spirit of Weimar with its own aid. . . . We come as enemies! As the wolf breaks into the sheepfold, so we come."[8]

In 1929 the Great Depression began striking down economic prosperity, one of the barriers that had kept the wolf at bay. Unemployment jumped from 1.3 million in 1929 to 5 million in 1930; that year Germany had almost as many unemployed as all the other countries of Europe combined. Industrial production fell by one-half between 1929 and 1932. By the end of 1932, an incredible 43 percent of the labor force was unemployed, and it was estimated that only one in every three union members was working full-time. No factor contributed more to Hitler's success than the economic crisis. Never very interested in economics before, Hitler began promising German voters economic as well as political and military salvation.

Hitler focused his promises on the middle and lower middle class—small business people, office workers, artisans, and peasants. Already disillusioned by the great inflation of 1923, these people were seized by panic as bankruptcies increased, unemployment soared, and the dreaded Communists made dramatic election gains. The middle and lower middle classes deserted the conservative and moderate parties for the Nazis in great numbers.

The Nazis also appealed strongly to German youth. Indeed, in some ways the Nazi movement was a mass movement of young Germans. Hitler himself was only forty in 1929, and he and most of his top aides were much younger than other leading German politicians. "National Socialism is the organized will of the youth," proclaimed the official Nazi slogan, and the battle cry of Gregor

Strasser, a leading Nazi organizer, was "Make way, you old ones."[9] In 1931 almost 40 percent of Nazi party members were under thirty, compared with 20 percent of Social Democrats. Two-thirds of Nazi members were under forty. National recovery, exciting and rapid change, and personal advancement: these were the appeals of Nazism to millions of German youths.

In the election of 1930, the Nazis won 6.5 million votes and 107 seats, which made them second in strength only to the Social Democrats, the moderate socialists. The economic situation continued to deteriorate, and Hitler kept promising that he would bring recovery. In 1932 the Nazi vote leaped to 14.5 million, and the Nazis became the largest party in the Reichstag.

Another reason Hitler came to power was the breakdown of democratic government as early as May 1930. Unable to gain support of a majority in the Reichstag, Chancellor Heinrich Brüning convinced the president, the aging war hero General Hindenburg, to authorize rule by decree. The Weimar Republic's constitution permitted such rule in emergency situations, but the rather authoritarian, self-righteous Brüning intended to use it indefinitely. Moreover, Brüning was determined to overcome the economic crisis by cutting back government spending and ruthlessly forcing down prices and wages. Brüning's ultra-orthodox policies not only intensified the economic collapse in Germany, they also convinced the lower middle classes that the country's republican leaders were stupid and corrupt. These classes were pleased rather than dismayed by Hitler's attacks on the republican system. After President Hindenburg forced Brüning to resign in May 1932, the new government headed by Franz von Papen continued to rule by decree.

The continuation of the struggle between the Social Democrats and Communists, right up until the moment Hitler took power, was another aspect of the breakdown of democratic government. The Communists foolishly refused to cooperate with the Social Democrats, even though the two parties together outnumbered the Nazis in the Reichstag, even after the elections of 1932. German Communists (and the complacent Stalin) were blinded by their ideology and their hatred of the Socialists. They were certain that Hitler's rise represented the last agonies of monopoly capitalism and that a communist revolution would quickly follow his taking power. The Socialist leaders pleaded, even at the Russian embassy, for at least a temporary alliance with the Communists to block Hitler, but to no avail. Perhaps the Weimar Republic was already too far gone, but this disunity on the left was undoubtedly another nail in its coffin.

Finally, there was Hitler's skill as a politician. A master of mass propaganda and psychology, he had written in *Mein Kampf* that the masses were the "driving force of the most important changes in this world" and were themselves driven by hysterical fanaticism and not by knowledge. To arouse such hysterical fanaticism, he believed that all propaganda had to be limited to a few simple, endlessly repeated slogans. Thus, in the terrible economic and political crisis, he harangued vast audiences with passionate, irrational oratory. Men moaned and women cried, seized by emotion. And many uncertain individuals, surrounded by thousands of entranced listeners, found security and a sense of belonging.

At the same time, Hitler excelled at dirty, back-room politics. That, in fact, brought him to power. In 1932 he cleverly succeeded in gaining the support of key people in the army and big business. These people thought that they could use Hitler for their own advantage, to get increased military spending, fat contracts, and tough measures against workers. Conservative and nationalistic politicians like Papen thought similarly. They thus accepted Hitler's demand to join the government only if he became chancellor. There would be only two other National Socialists and nine solid Conservatives as ministers, and in such a coalition government, they reasoned, Hitler could be used and controlled. On January 30, 1933, Hitler was legally appointed chancellor by Hindenburg.

The Nazi State and Society

Hitler moved rapidly and skillfully to establish an unshakable dictatorship. His first step was to continue using terror and threats to gain more power while maintaining legal appearances. He immediately called for new elections and applied the enormous power of the government to restrict his opponents. In the midst of a violent electoral campaign, the Reichstag building was partly destroyed by fire. Although the Nazis themselves may have set the fire, Hitler screamed that the Communist party was responsible. On the strength of this accusation, he convinced President Hindenburg to sign dictatorial emergency acts that practically abolished freedom of speech and assembly, in addition to most personal liberties.

When the Nazis won only 44 percent of the vote in the elections, Hitler immediately outlawed the Communist party and arrested its parliamentary representatives. Then, on March 23, 1933, the Nazis pushed through the Reichstag the so-called Enabling Act, which gave Hitler absolute dictatorial power for four years. Only the Social Democrats voted against this bill, for Hitler had successfully blackmailed the Center party by threatening to attack the Catholic church.

Armed with the Enabling Act, Hitler and the Nazis moved to smash or control all independent organizations. Meanwhile, Hitler and his propagandists constantly proclaimed that their revolution was legal and constitutional. This deceitful stress on legality, coupled with the divide-and-conquer technique, disarmed the opposition until it was too late for effective resistance.

The systematic subjugation of independent organizations and the creation of a totalitarian state had massive repercussions. The Social Democratic and Center parties were soon dissolved, and Germany became a one-party state. Only the Nazi party was legal. Elections were farces. The Reichstag was jokingly referred to as the most expensive glee club in the country, for its only function was to sing hymns of praise to the Führer. Hitler and the Nazis took over the government bureaucracy intact, installing many Nazis in top positions. At the same time, they created a series of overlapping Nazi party organizations, responsible solely to Hitler. Thus Hitler had both an established bureaucracy for normal business and a private, personal "party government" for special duties.

In the economic sphere, strikes were forbidden and labor unions were abolished, replaced by a Nazi Labor Front. Professional people—doctors and lawyers, teachers and engineers—also saw their previously independent organizations swallowed up in Nazi associations. Nor did the Nazis neglect cultural and intellectual life. Publishing houses were put under Nazi control, and universities and writers were quickly brought into line. Democratic, socialist, and Jewish literature was put on ever-growing blacklists. Passionate students and pitiful professors burned forbidden books in public squares. Modern art and architecture were ruthlessly prohibited. Life became violently anti-intellectual. As Hitler's cynical minister of propaganda, Joseph Goebbels, put it, "When I hear the word 'culture' I reach for my gun."[10] By 1934 a totalitarian state characterized by frightening dynamism and obedience to Hitler was already largely in place.

By 1934 only the army retained independence, and Hitler moved brutally and skillfully to establish his control there, too. He realized that the army, as well as big business, was suspicious of the Nazi storm troopers (the S.A.), the quasi-military band of three million toughs in brown shirts who had fought Communists and beaten up Jews before the Nazis took power. These unruly storm troopers expected top positions in the army and even talked of a "second revolution" against capi-

talism. Needing the support of the army and big business, Hitler decided that the S.A. leaders had to be eliminated. On the night of June 30, 1934, he struck.

Hitler's elite personal guard—the S.S.—arrested and shot without trial roughly a thousand S.A. leaders and assorted political enemies. While his propagandists spread lies about S.A. conspiracies, the army leaders and President Hindenburg responded to the purge with congratulatory telegrams. Shortly thereafter, the army leaders swore a binding oath of "unquestioning obedience . . . to the Leader of the German State and People, Adolf Hitler." The purge of the S.A. was another decisive step toward unlimited totalitarian terror. The S.S., the elite guard that had loyally murdered the S.A. leaders, grew rapidly. Under its methodical, inhu-

"Hitler, Our Last Hope"   So reads the vary effective Nazi campaign poster, which is attracting attention with its gaunt and haggard faces. By 1932 almost half of all Germans, like these in Berlin, had come to agree. *(Source: Bildarchiv Preussischer Kulturbesitz. Photo: Herbert Hoffman, 1932)*

man leader, Heinrich Himmler (1900–1945), the S.S. joined with the political police, the *Gestapo,* to expand its network of special courts and concentration camps. Nobody was safe.

From the beginning, the Jews were a special object of Nazi persecution. By the end of 1934, most Jewish lawyers, doctors, professors, civil servants, and musicians had lost their jobs and the right to practice their professions. In 1935 the infamous Nuremberg Laws classified as Jewish anyone having one or more Jewish grandparents and deprived Jews of all rights of citizenship. By 1938 roughly one-fourth of Germany's half-million Jews had emigrated, sacrificing almost all their property in order to leave Germany.

Following the assassination of a German diplomat in Paris by a young Jewish boy trying desperately to strike out at persecution, the attack on the Jews accelerated. A well-organized wave of violence destroyed homes, synagogues, and businesses, after which German Jews were rounded up and made to pay for the damage. It became very difficult for Jews to leave Germany. Some Germans privately opposed these outrages, but most went along or looked the other way. Although this lack of response partly reflected the individual's helplessness in the totalitarian state, it was also a sign of the strong popular support that Hitler's government enjoyed.

Hitler's Popularity

Hitler had promised the masses economic recovery—"work and bread"—and he delivered. Breaking with Brüning's do-nothing policies, Hitler immediately launched a large public works program to pull Germany out of the depression. Work began on superhighways, offices, gigantic sports stadiums, and public housing. In 1936, as Germany rearmed rapidly, government spending began to concentrate on the military. The result was that unemployment dropped steadily, from six million in January 1933 to about one million in late 1936. By 1938 there was a shortage of workers, and women eventually took many jobs previously denied them by the antifeminist Nazis. Thus everyone had work, and between 1932 and 1938 the standard of living for the average employed worker rose more than 20 percent. The profits of business also increased. For millions of people, economic recovery was tangible evidence in their daily lives that the excitement and dynamism of Nazi rule were based on more than show.

For the masses of ordinary German citizens, who were not Jews, Slavs, Gypsies, Jehovah's Witnesses, or Communists, Hitler's government meant greater equality and exceptional opportunities. It must be remembered that in 1933 the position of the traditional German elites—the landed aristocracy, the wealthy capitalists, and the well-educated professional classes—was still very strong. Barriers between classes were generally high. Hitler's rule introduced vast changes in this pattern. For example, stiff educational requirements, which favored the well-to-do, were greatly relaxed. The new Nazi elite was composed largely of young and poorly educated dropouts, rootless lower-middle-class people like Hitler, who rose to the top with breathtaking speed.

More generally, the Nazis, like the Russian Communists, tolerated privilege and wealth only as long as they served the needs of the party. Big business was constantly ordered around, to the point that "probably never in peacetime has an ostensibly capitalist economy been directed as non- and even anti-capitalistically as the German economy between 1933 and 1939."[11] Hitler brought about a kind of social revolution, which was enthusiastically embraced by millions of modest middle-class and lower-middle-class people and even by many workers.

Hitler's extreme nationalism, which had helped him gain power, continued to appeal to Germans after 1933. Ever since the wars against Napoleon, many Germans had believed in a special mission for a superior German nation. The successes of Bismarck had furthered such feelings, and near-victory in the Great World War made nationalists eager for renewed expansion in the 1920s. Thus, when Hitler went from one foreign triumph to another (see pages 1158–1159) and a great German empire seemed within reach, the majority of the population was delighted and praised the Führer's actions.

By no means all Germans supported Hitler, however, and a number of German groups actively resisted him after 1933. Tens of thousands of political enemies were imprisoned, and thousands were executed. Opponents of the Nazis pursued various goals, and under totalitarian conditions they were never unified, a fact that helps account for their ultimate lack of success. In the first years of Hitler's rule, the principal resisters were the

EVENTS LEADING TO WORLD WAR TWO

1919	Treaty of Versailles
	J. M. Keynes, *Economic Consequences of the Peace*
1919–1920	U.S. Senate rejects the Treaty of Versailles
1921	Germany is billed $35 billion in reparations
1922	Mussolini seizes power in Italy
	Germany proposes a moratorium on reparations
January 1923	France and Belgium occupy the Ruhr
	Germany orders passive resistance to the occupation
October 1923	Stresemann agrees to reparations with re-examination of Germany's ability to pay
1924	Dawes Plan: German reparations reduced and put on a sliding scale; large U.S. loans to Germany recommended to promote German recovery; occupation of the Ruhr ends
	Adolf Hitler, *Mein Kampf*
1924–1929	Spectacular German economic recovery; circular flow of international funds enables sizable reparations payments
1925	Treaties of Locarno promote European security and stability
1926	Germany joins the League of Nations
1928	Kellogg-Briand Pact renounces war as an instrument of international affairs
1929	Young Plan further reduces German reparations
	Crash of U.S. stock market
1929–1933	Depths of the Great Depression
1931	Japan invades Manchuria
1932	Nazis become the largest party in the Reichstag
January 1933	Hitler appointed chancellor
March 1933	Reichstag passes the Enabling Act, granting Hitler absolute dictatorial power
October 1933	Germany withdraws from the League of Nations
July 1934	Nazis murder Austrian chancellor
March 1935	Hitler announces German rearmament
June 1935	Anglo-German naval agreement
October 1935	Mussolini invades Ethiopia and receives Hitler's support
1935	Nuremburg Laws deprive Jews of all rights of citizenship
March 1936	German armies move unopposed into the demilitarized Rhineland
July 1936	Outbreak of civil war in Spain
1937	Japan invades China
	Rome-Berlin Axis
March 1938	Germany annexes Austria
September 1938	Munich Conference: Britain and France agree to German seizure of the Sudetenland from Czechoslovakia
March 1939	Germany occupies the rest of Czechoslovakia; the end of appeasement in Britain
August 1939	Russo-German nonaggression pact
September 1, 1939	Germany invades Poland
September 3, 1939	Britain and France declare war on Germany

Communists and the Social Democrats in the trade unions. But the expansion of the S.S. system of terror after 1935 smashed most of these leftists. A second group of opponents arose in the Catholic and Protestant churches. However, their efforts were directed primarily at preserving genuine religious life, not at overthrowing Hitler. Finally, in 1938 (and again in 1942 to 1944), some high-ranking army officers, who feared the consequences of Hitler's reckless aggression, plotted against him, unsuccessfully.

NAZI EXPANSION AND THE SECOND WORLD WAR

Although economic recovery and increased opportunities for social advancement won Hitler support, they were only by-products of Nazi totalitarianism. The guiding concepts of Nazism remained space and race—the territorial expansion of the superior German race. As Germany regained its economic strength and as independent organizations were brought under control, Hitler formed alliances with other dictators and began expanding. German expansion was facilitated by the uncertain, divided, pacific Western democracies, which tried to buy off Hitler to avoid war.

Yet war inevitably broke out, in both the West and the East, for Hitler's ambitions were essentially unlimited. On both war fronts the Nazi soldiers scored enormous successes until late 1942, establishing a horrifyingly vast empire of death and destruction. Hitler's reckless aggression also raised a mighty coalition determined to smash the Nazi order. Led by Britain, the United States, and the Soviet Union, the "Grand Alliance"—to use Winston Churchill's favorite term—functioned quite effectively in military terms. By the summer of 1943, the tide of battle had turned. Two years later, Germany and its allies lay in ruins, utterly defeated. Thus the terrible Nazi empire proved short-lived.

Aggression and Appeasement (1933–1939)

Hitler's tactics in international politics after 1933 strikingly resembled those he used in domestic politics between 1924 and 1933. When Hitler was weak, he righteously proclaimed that he intended to overturn the "unjust system" established by the treaties of Versailles and Locarno—but only by legal means. As he grew stronger, and as other leaders showed their willingness to compromise, he increased his demands and finally began attacking his independent neighbors (Map 35.1).

Hitler realized that his aggressive policies had to be carefully camouflaged at first, for Germany's army was limited by the Treaty of Versailles to only a hundred thousand men. As he told a group of army commanders in February 1933, the early stages of his policy of "conquest of new living space in the East and its ruthless Germanization" had serious dangers. If France had real leaders, Hitler said, it would "not give us time but attack us, presumably with its eastern satellites."[12] To avoid such threats to his plans, Hitler loudly proclaimed his peaceful intentions to all the world. Nevertheless, he felt strong enough to walk out of a sixty-nation disarmament conference and withdraw from the League of Nations in October 1933. Stresemann's policy of peaceful cooperation was dead; the Nazi determination to rearm was out in the open.

Following this action, which met with widespread approval at home, Hitler moved to incorporate independent Austria into a Greater Germany. Austrian Nazis climaxed an attempted overthrow by murdering the Austrian chancellor in July 1934. They were unable to take power, however, because a worried Mussolini, who had initially greeted Hitler as a fascist little brother, massed his troops on the Brenner Pass and threatened to fight. When, in March 1935, Hitler established a general military draft and declared the "unequal" disarmament clauses of the Treaty of Versailles null and void, other countries appeared to understand the danger. With France taking the lead, Italy and Great Britain protested strongly and warned against future aggressive actions.

Yet the emerging united front against Hitler quickly collapsed. Of crucial importance, Britain adopted a policy of appeasement, granting Hitler everything he could reasonably want (and more) in order to avoid war. The first step was an Anglo-German naval agreement in June 1935, which broke Germany's isolation. The second step came in March 1936, when Hitler suddenly marched his armies into the demilitarized Rhineland, brazenly violating the treaties of Versailles and Locarno. This was the last good chance to stop the Nazis, for Hitler had ordered his troops

MAP 35.1 The Growth of Nazi Germany, 1933–1939   Until March 1939, Hitler brought ethnic Germans into the Nazi state; then he turned on the Slavic peoples, whom he had always hated.

to retreat if France resisted militarily. But an uncertain France would not move without British support, and the occupation of German soil by German armies seemed right and just to Britain. Its strategic position greatly improved, Germany had handed France a tremendous psychological defeat.

British appeasement, which practically dictated French policy, lasted far into 1939. It was motivated by British feelings of guilt toward Germany and the pacifism of a population still horrified by the memory of the First World War. Like many Germans, British political leaders seriously underestimated Hitler. They believed that they could use him to stop Russian communism. A leading member of Britain's government personally told Hitler in November 1937 that it was his conviction that Hitler "not only had accomplished great things in Germany itself, but that through the total destruction of Communism in his own country . . . Germany rightly had to be considered as a Western bulwark against Communism."[13] Such rigid anticommunist feelings made an alliance between the Western powers and Stalin very unlikely.

As Britain and France opted for appeasement and Russia watched all developments suspiciously, Hitler found powerful allies. In 1935 the bombastic Mussolini decided that imperial expansion was needed to revitalize fascism. From Italian colonies on the east coast of Africa he attacked the independent African kingdom of Ethiopia. The Western powers and the League of Nations piously condemned Italian aggression—a posture that angered Mussolini—without saving Ethiopia from defeat. Hitler, who had secretly supplied Ethiopia with arms to heat up the conflict, supported Italy energetically and thereby overcame Mussolini's lingering doubts about the Nazis. The result in 1936 was an agreement on close cooperation between Italy and Germany, the so-called Rome-Berlin Axis. Japan, which had been expanding into Manchuria since 1931, soon joined the alliance between Italy and Germany.

At the same time, Germany and Italy intervened in the long, complicated Spanish Civil War, where their support eventually helped General Francisco Franco's fascist movement defeat republican Spain. Spain's only official aid came from Soviet Russia, for public opinion in Britain and especially in France was hopelessly divided on the Spanish question.

By late 1937, as he was proclaiming his peaceful intentions to the British and their gullible prime minister, Neville Chamberlain (1869–1940), Hitler told his generals his real plans. His "unshakable decision" was to crush Austria and Czechoslovakia at the earliest possible moment, as the first step in his long-contemplated drive to the east for "living space." By threatening Austria with invasion, Hitler forced the Austrian chancellor in March 1938 to put local Nazis in control of the government. The next day, German armies moved in unopposed, and Austria became two more provinces of Greater Germany (see Map 35.1).

Simultaneously, Hitler began demanding that the pro-Nazi, German-speaking minority of western Czechoslovakia—the Sudetenland—be turned over to Germany. Yet democratic Czechoslovakia

Cartoonist David Low's biting criticism of appeasing leaders appeared shortly after Hitler remilitarized the Rhineland. Appeasement also appealed to millions of ordinary citizens, who wanted to avoid at any cost another great war. *(Source: Cartoon by David Low. Reproduced by permission of London Evening Standard/Solo)*

was prepared to defend itself. Moreover, France had been Czechoslovakia's ally since 1924; and if France fought, Soviet Russia was pledged to help. As war appeared inevitable—for Hitler had already told the leader of the Sudeten Germans that "we must always ask so much we cannot be satisfied"—appeasement triumphed again. In September 1938 Chamberlain flew to Germany three times in fourteen days. In these negotiations, to which Russia was deliberately not invited, Chamberlain and the French agreed with Hitler that the Sudetenland should be ceded to Germany immediately. Returning to London from the Munich Conference, Chamberlain told cheering crowds that he had secured "peace with honor . . . peace for our time." Sold out by the Western powers, Czechoslovakia gave in.

Confirmed once again in his opinion of the Western democracies as weak and racially degenerate, Hitler accelerated his aggression. In a shocking violation of his solemn assurances that the Sudetenland was his last territorial demand, Hitler's armies occupied the Czech lands in March 1939, and Slovakia became a puppet state. The effect on Western public opinion was electrifying. For the first time, there was no possible rationale of self-determination for Nazi aggression, since Hitler was seizing Czechs and Slovaks as captive peoples. Thus, when Hitler used the question of German minorities in Danzig as a pretext to confront Poland, a suddenly militant Chamberlain declared that Britain and France would fight if Hitler attacked his eastern neighbor. Hitler did not take these warnings seriously and decided to press on.

In an about-face that stunned the world, Hitler offered and Stalin signed a ten-year Nazi-Soviet nonaggression pact in August 1939, whereby each dictator promised to remain neutral if the other became involved in war. Even more startling was the attached secret protocol, which ruthlessly divided eastern Europe into German and Russian zones, "in the event of a political territorial reorganization." Although this top-secret protocol sealing the destruction of Poland and the Baltic states became known only after the war, the nonaggression pact itself was enough to make Britain and France cry treachery, for they too had been negotiating with Stalin. But Stalin had remained distrustful of Western intentions. Moreover, Britain and France had offered him military risk without gain; Hitler had offered territorial gain without risk. For Hitler, everything was set. He told his generals on the day of the nonaggression pact: "My only fear is that at the last moment some dirty dog will come up with a mediation plan." On September 1, 1939, German armies and warplanes smashed into Poland from three sides. Two days later, finally true to their word, Britain and France declared war on Germany. The Second World War had begun.

Hitler's Empire (1939–1942)

Using planes, tanks, and trucks in the first example of the *blitzkrieg,* or "lightning war," Hitler's armies crushed Poland in four weeks. While Soviet Russia quickly took its part of the booty—the eastern half of Poland and the Baltic states of Lithuania, Estonia, and Latvia—French and British armies dug in in the west. They expected another war of attrition and economic blockade.

In spring 1940 the lightning war struck again. After occupying Denmark, Norway, and Holland, German motorized columns broke through southern Belgium, split the Franco-British forces, and trapped the entire British army on the beaches of Dunkirk. By heroic efforts the British withdrew their troops but not their equipment.

France was taken by the Nazis. The aging marshal Henri-Philippe Pétain (1856–1951) formed a new French government—the so-called Vichy government—to accept defeat, and German armies occupied most of France. By July 1940 Hitler ruled practically all of western continental Europe; Italy was an ally, and the Soviet Union was a friendly neutral. Only Britain, led by the uncompromising Winston Churchill (1874–1965), remained unconquered. Churchill proved to be one of history's greatest wartime leaders, rallying his fellow citizens with stirring speeches, infectious confidence, and bulldog determination.

Germany sought to gain control of the air, the necessary first step for an amphibious invasion of Britain. In the Battle of Britain, up to a thousand German planes attacked British airfields and key factories in a single day, dueling with British defenders high in the skies. Losses were heavy on both sides. Then in September Hitler angrily and foolishly changed his strategy, turning from military objectives to indiscriminate bombing of British cities in an attempt to break British morale. British factories increased production of their excellent fighter planes; anti-aircraft defense improved with the help of radar; and the heavily bombed people of London defiantly dug in. In September through October 1940, Britain was beating Germany three to one in the air war. There was no possibility of immediate German invasion of Britain.

In these circumstances, the most reasonable German strategy would have been to attack Britain through the eastern Mediterranean, taking Egypt and the Suez Canal and pinching off Britain's supply of oil. Mussolini's early defeats in Greece had drawn Hitler into the Balkans, where Germany quickly conquered Greece and Yugoslavia while forcing Hungary, Romania, and Bulgaria into alliances with Germany by April 1941. These successes reinforced the logic of a thrust into the eastern Mediterranean. But Hitler was not a reasonable person. His lifetime obsession with a vast eastern European empire for the so-called master race irrationally dictated policy. By late 1940 he had already decided on his next move, and in June 1941 German armies suddenly attacked the Soviet Union along a vast front. With Britain still unconquered, Hitler's decision was a wild, irrational gamble, epitomizing the violent, unlimited ambitions of modern totalitarianism.

Faithfully fulfilling all his obligations under the Nazi-Soviet Pact and even ignoring warnings of impending invasion, Stalin was caught off guard. Nazi armies moved like lightning across the Russian steppe. By October 1941 Leningrad was practically surrounded, Moscow besieged, and most of the Ukraine conquered; yet the Russians did not collapse. When a severe winter struck German armies outfitted in summer uniforms, the invaders were stopped.

While Hitler's armies dramatically expanded the war in Europe, his Japanese allies did the same in Asia. Engaged in a general but undeclared war against China since 1937 (see pages 1097–1100), Japan's rulers had increasingly come into diplomatic conflict with the Pacific Basin's other great power, the United States. When the Japanese occupied French Indochina in July 1941, the United States retaliated by cutting off sales of vital rubber, scrap iron, oil, and aviation fuel. Tension mounted further, and on December 7, 1941, Japan attacked the U.S. naval base at Pearl Harbor in Hawaii. Hitler immediately declared war on the United States even though his treaty obligations with Japan did not require him to initiate this course of action.

As Japanese forces advanced swiftly into Southeast Asia after the crippling surprise attack at Pearl Harbor, Hitler and his European allies continued the two-front war against the Soviet Union and Great Britain. Not until late 1942 did the Nazis suffer their first major defeats. In the meantime, Hitler ruled a vast European empire stretching from the outskirts of Moscow to the English Channel. Hitler and the top Nazi leadership began building their "New Order," and they continued their efforts until their final collapse in 1945. In doing so, they showed what Nazi victory would have meant (Map 35.2).

Hitler's New Order was based firmly on the guiding principle of Nazi totalitarianism: racial imperialism. Within this New Order, the Nordic peoples—the Dutch, the Norwegians, and the Danes—received preferential treatment, for they were racially related to the Germans. The French, an "inferior" Latin people, occupied the middle position. They were heavily taxed to support the Nazi war effort but were tolerated as a race. Once Nazi reverses began to mount in late 1942, however, all the occupied territories of western and northern Europe were exploited with increasing intensity. Material shortages and both mental and physical suffering afflicted millions of people.

Slavs in the conquered territories to the east were treated with harsh hatred as "subhumans." At the height of his success in 1941 to 1942, Hitler painted for his intimate circle the fantastic details of a vast eastern colonial empire, where the Poles, Ukrainians, and Russians would be enslaved and forced to die out while Germanic peasants resettled their abandoned lands. Himmler and the elite corps of S.S. volunteers struggled loyally, sometimes against the German army, to implement part of this general program even before victory was secured. In parts of Poland, the S.S. arrested and evacuated Polish peasants to create a German "mass settlement space." Polish workers and Russian prisoners of war were transported to Germany, where they did most of the heavy labor and were systematically worked to death. The conditions of Russian slave labor in Germany were so harsh that four out of five Russian prisoners did not survive the war.

Finally, Jews were condemned to extermination, along with Gypsies, Jehovah's Witnesses, and captured Communists. By 1939 German Jews had lost all their civil rights, and after the fall of Warsaw the Nazis began deporting them to Poland. There

Legend

- Hitler's Greater Germany
- Allied with Germany
- Occupied by Germany and its allies
- Grand Alliance
- Neutral nations
- X Major battles

ATLANTIC OCEAN

IRELAND

NORTHERN IRELAND

GREAT BRITAIN

Battle of Britain
Fall 1940

London

Dunkirk

North Sea

NETHERLANDS

BELGIUM
Battle of the Bulge
Dec. 1944

Invasion of Normandy
June 6, 1944

Paris

FRANCE

Western front, Feb. 1945

Vichy

VICHY FRANCE
(occupied Nov. 1942)

SWITZERLAND

PORTUGAL

Lisbon

SPAIN

Madrid

GIBRALTAR (Gr. Br.)

SP. MOROCCO

Casablanca
Nov. 1942

FRENCH MOROCCO

Ebro

ALGERIA
(Vichy France)

NORWAY

Oslo

SWEDEN

Stockholm

DENMARK

Copenhagen

Berlin

GERMANY

Elbe

Rhine

Danube

Vienna

SLOVAKIA

Krakow

HUNGARY

Budapest

CROATIA

YUGOSLAVIA

SERBIA

Po

Bologna

Italian front, Feb. 1945

ITALY

Rome

Monte Casino
May 1944

ALBANIA

GREECE

Athens

Crete

Salerno
Sept. 1943

Sicily
July 1943

Sicily

MALTA (Gr. Br.)

Mediterranean Sea

LIBYA

TUNISIA

Rommel defeated
in Tunisia
(May 1943)

FINLAND

Helsinki

Riga

Leningrad

Baltic Sea

Posen

Warsaw

Vistula

Russian front, Feb. 1945

SOVIET UNION

Volga

Volga

Stalingrad

Russian front, Nov. 1942

Russian front, Dec. 1941

Moscow

Tula

Smolensk

Russian front, Spring 1944

Pinsk

Kiev

Dnieper

UKRAINE

Dniester

ROMANIA

Bucharest

Danube

BULGARIA

Sofia

Black Sea

Yalta

Baku

TURKEY

Ankara

CYPRUS

SYRIA

TRANS-JORDAN
(Br. Mandate)

PALESTINE
(Br. Mandate)

Suez Canal

Cairo

Nile

EGYPT

El Alamein
Summer 1942

0   200   400 Km.
0   200   400 Mi.

they and Jews from all over Europe were concentrated in ghettos, compelled to wear the Jewish star, and turned into slave laborers. But by 1941 Himmler's S.S. was carrying out the "final solution of the Jewish question"—the murder of every single Jew. All over Hitler's empire, Jews were arrested, packed like cattle onto freight trains, and dispatched to extermination camps.

There the victims were taken by force or deception to "shower rooms," which were actually gas chambers. These gas chambers, first perfected in the quiet, efficient execution of seventy thousand mentally ill Germans between 1938 and 1941, permitted rapid, hideous, and thoroughly bureaucratized mass murder. For fifteen to twenty minutes came the terrible screams and gasping sobs of men, women, and children choking to death on poison gas. Then, only silence. Special camp workers quickly tore the victims' gold teeth from their jaws and cut off their hair for use as chair stuffing. The bodies were then cremated or sometimes boiled for oil to make soap; the bones were crushed to produce fertilizers. At Auschwitz, the most infamous of the Nazi death factories, as many as twelve thousand human beings were slaughtered each day. On the turbulent Russian front, the S.S. death squads forced the Jewish population to dig giant pits, which became mass graves as the victims were lined up on the edge and cut down by machine guns. The extermination of European Jews was the ultimate monstrosity of Nazi racism and racial imperialism. By 1945 six million Jews had been murdered.

The Grand Alliance

While the Nazis built their savage empire, the Allies faced the hard fact that chance, rather than choice, had brought them together. Stalin had been cooperating fully with Hitler between August 1939 and June 1941, and only the Japanese attack on Pearl Harbor in December 1941 and Hitler's immediate declaration of war had over-

whelmed powerful isolationism in the United States. The Allies' first task was to try to overcome their mutual suspicions and build an unshakable alliance on the quicksand of accident. By means of three interrelated policies they succeeded.

First, President Franklin Delano Roosevelt (1882–1945) accepted Churchill's contention that the United States should concentrate first on defeating Hitler. Only after victory in Europe would the United States turn toward the Pacific for an all-out attack on Japan, the lesser threat. Therefore, the United States promised and sent large amounts of military aid to Britain and Russia, and American and British forces in each combat zone were tightly integrated under a single commander. America's policy of "Europe first" helped solidify the anti-Hitler coalition.

Second, within the European framework, the Americans and the British put immediate military needs first. They consistently postponed tough political questions relating to the eventual peace settlement and thereby avoided, until after the war, conflicts that might have split the alliance.

Third, to further encourage mutual trust, the Allies adopted the principle of the "unconditional surrender" of Germany and Japan. The policy of unconditional surrender cemented the Grand Alliance because it denied Hitler any hope of dividing his foes. It probably also discouraged Germans and Japanese who might have tried to overthrow their dictators in order to make a compromise peace. Of great importance for the postwar shape of Europe, it meant that Russian and Anglo-American armies would almost certainly come together to divide all of Germany, and most of the Continent, among themselves.

The military resources of the Grand Alliance were awesome. The strengths of the United States were its mighty industry, its large population, and its national unity. Even before the attack on Pearl Harbor, President Roosevelt had called America the "arsenal of democracy" and given military aid to Britain and Russia. Now the United States geared up rapidly for all-out war production and drew heavily on a generally cooperative Latin America for resources. It not only equipped its own armies but eventually gave its allies about $50 billion of arms and equipment. Britain received by far the most, but about one-fifth of the total went to Russia in the form of badly needed trucks, planes, and munitions.

Map 35.2 The Second World War in Europe The map shows the extent of Hitler's empire at its height, before the battle of Stalingrad in late 1942, and the subsequent advances of the Allies until Germany surrendered on May 7, 1945.

Prelude to Murder This photo captures the terrible inhumanity of Nazi racism. Frightened and bewildered families from the soon-to-be destroyed Warsaw ghetto are being forced out of their homes by German soldiers for deportation to concentration camps. There they face murder in the gas chambers. *(Source: Roger-Viollet)*

Too strong to lose and too weak to win when it stood alone, Britain, too, continued to make a great contribution. The British economy was totally and effectively mobilized, and the sharing of burdens through rationing and heavy taxes on war profits maintained social harmony. Moreover, as 1942 wore on, Britain could increasingly draw on the enormous physical and human resources of its empire and the United States. By early 1943 the Americans and the British combined small aircraft carriers with radar-guided bombers to rid the Atlantic of German submarines. Britain, the impregnable floating fortress, became a gigantic frontline staging area for the decisive blow to the heart of Germany.

As for Soviet Russia, so great was its strength that it might have defeated Germany without Western help. In the face of the German advance, whole factories and populations were successfully evacuated to eastern Russia and Siberia. There, war production was reorganized and expanded, and the Red Army was increasingly well supplied. The Red Army was also well led, for a new generation of talented military leaders quickly arose to replace those so recently purged. Most important of all, Stalin drew on the massive support and heroic determination of the Soviet people. Broad-based Russian nationalism, as opposed to narrow communist ideology, became the powerful unifying force in what was appropriately called the "Great Patriotic War of the Fatherland."

Finally, the United States, Britain, and Soviet Russia were not alone. They had the resources of much of the world at their command. And, to a greater or lesser extent, they were aided by a growing resistance movement against the Nazis throughout Europe, even in Germany. Thus, although Ukrainian peasants often welcomed the Germans as liberators, the barbaric occupation policies of the Nazis quickly drove them to join and support behind-the-lines guerrilla forces. More generally, after Russia was invaded in June 1941, Communists throughout Europe took the lead in the underground Resistance, joined by a growing number of patriots and Christians. Anti-Nazi leaders from occupied countries established governments-in-exile in London, like that of the "Free French" under the intensely proud General Charles de Gaulle (1890–1970). These governments gathered valuable secret information from Resistance fighters and even organized armies to help defeat Hitler.

The Tide of Battle

Barely halted at the gates of Moscow and Leningrad in 1941, the Germans renewed their Russian offensive in July 1942. This time they drove toward the southern city of Stalingrad in an attempt to cripple communications and seize the crucial oil fields of Baku (see Map 35.2). Reaching Stalingrad, the Germans slowly occupied most of the ruined city in a month of incredibly savage house-to-house fighting.

Then, in November 1942, Soviet armies counterattacked. They rolled over Romanian and Italian troops to the north and south of Stalingrad, quickly closing the trap and surrounding the entire German Sixth Army of 300,000 men. The surrounded Germans were systematically destroyed, until by the end of January 1943 only 123,000 soldiers were left to surrender. Hitler, who refused to allow a retreat, suffered a catastrophic defeat. In the summer of 1943, the larger, better-equipped Soviet armies took the offensive and began moving forward.

In late 1942 the tide also turned in the Pacific and in North Africa. By late spring 1942, Japan had established a great empire in East Asia (Map 35.3). Unlike the Nazis, the Japanese made clever appeals to local nationalists, who sometimes saw Japan and its so-called Greater Asian Co-prosperity Sphere as potent allies against Western domination.

Then, in the Battle of the Coral Sea in May 1942, Allied naval and air power stopped the Japanese advance and also relieved Australia from the threat of invasion. This victory was followed by the Battle of Midway Island, in which American pilots sank all four of the attacking Japanese aircraft carriers and established American naval superiority in the Pacific. In August 1942, American marines attacked Guadalcanal in the Solomon Islands. Badly hampered by the policy of "Europe first"—only 15 percent of Allied resources were going to fight the war in the Pacific in early 1943—the Americans, under General Douglas MacArthur and Admiral Chester Nimitz, and the Australians nevertheless began "island hopping"

Mobilizing the Soviet People Joining the historic Russian warrior and the young Soviet soldier in the common cause, this poster portrays the defense of the nation as a sacred mission and illustrates the way Soviet leaders successfully appealed to Russian nationalism during the war. *(Source: Library of Congress)*

For the Motherland's Sake, Go Forward, Heroes

toward Japan. Japanese forces were on the defensive.

In North Africa, the war had been seesawing back and forth since 1940. In May 1942, combined German and Italian armies, under the brilliant General Erwin Rommel, attacked British-occupied Egypt and the Suez Canal for the second time. After a rapid advance, they were defeated by British forces at the Battle of El Alamein, only seventy miles from Alexandria (see Map 35.2). In Oc-

tober the British counterattacked in Egypt, and almost immediately thereafter an Anglo-American force landed in Morocco and Algeria. These French possessions, which were under the control of Pétain's Vichy French government, quickly went over to the side of the Allies.

Having driven the Axis powers from North Africa by the spring of 1943, Allied forces maintained the initiative by invading Sicily and then mainland Italy. Mussolini was deposed by a

MAP 35.3 The Second World War in the Pacific Japanese forces overran an enormous territory in 1942, which the Allies slowly recaptured in a long bitter struggle. As this map shows, Japan still held a large Asian empire in August 1945, when the unprecedented devastation of atomic warfare suddenly forced it to surrender.

The City of Nagasaki   A second atomic bomb struck Nagasaki on August 9, 1945, three days after the first giant fireball incinerated Hiroshima. Approximately 75,000 Japanese were killed or injured at Nagasaki. In this grim photo, taken about a month after the attack, a Japanese survivor pushes his bicycle along a path cleared through the ruins. (Source: UPI/Bettmann Newsphotos)

war-weary people, and the new Italian government publicly accepted unconditional surrender in September 1943. Italy, it seemed, was liberated. Yet Mussolini was rescued by German commandos in a daring raid and put at the head of a puppet government. German armies seized the city of Rome and all of northern Italy. Fighting continued in Italy.

Indeed, bitter fighting continued in Europe for almost two years. Germany, less fully mobilized for war than Britain in 1941, applied itself to total war in 1942 and enlisted millions of prisoners of war and slave laborers from all across occupied Europe in that effort. Between early 1942 and July 1944, German war production actually tripled. Although British and American bombing raids killed many German civilians, they were surprisingly ineffective from a military point of view. Also, German resistance against Hitler failed. After an un-

successful attempt on Hitler's life in July 1944, thousands of Germans were brutally liquidated by S.S. fanatics. Terrorized at home and frightened by the prospect of unconditional surrender, the Germans fought on with suicidal stoicism.

On June 6, 1944, American and British forces under General Dwight Eisenhower landed on the beaches of Normandy in history's greatest naval invasion. Having tricked the Germans into believing that the attack would come near the Belgian border, the Allies secured a foothold on the coast of Normandy (see Map 35.2). In a hundred dramatic days, more than two million men and almost a half-million vehicles pushed inland and broke through German lines. Rejecting proposals to strike straight at Berlin in a massive attack, Eisenhower moved forward cautiously on a broad front. Not until March 1945 did American troops cross the Rhine and enter Germany.

The Russians, who had been advancing steadily since July 1943, reached the outskirts of Warsaw by August 1944. For the next six months they moved southward into Romania, Hungary, and Yugoslavia. In January 1945, Red armies again moved westward through Poland, and on April 26 they met American forces on the Elbe River. The Allies had closed their vise on Nazi Germany and overrun Europe. As Soviet forces fought their way into Berlin, Hitler committed suicide in his bunker, and on May 7 the remaining German commanders capitulated.

Three months later, the United States dropped atomic bombs on Hiroshima and Nagasaki in Japan (see Map 35.3). Mass bombing of cities and civilians, one of the terrible new practices of the Second World War, had ended in the final nightmare—unprecedented human destruction in a single blinding flash. The Japanese surrendered. The Second World War, which had claimed the lives of more than fifty million soldiers and civilians, was over.

also won enthusiastic supporters by offering tough, ruthless people from modest backgrounds enormous rewards for loyal and effective service. Thus these totalitarian dictatorships rested on considerable genuine popular support, as well as on police terror. This combination gave them their awesome power and dynamism. That dynamism, however, was channeled in quite different directions. Stalin and the Communist party aimed at building their kind of socialism and the new socialist personality at home. Hitler and the Nazi elite aimed at unlimited territorial and racial aggression on behalf of a master race; domestic recovery was only a means to that end.

Unlimited Nazi aggression made war inevitable, first with the western European democracies, then with Germany's totalitarian neighbor, and finally with the United States. Plunging Europe into the ultimate nightmare, unlimited aggression unwittingly forged a mighty coalition that smashed the racist Nazi empire and its leader. In the words of the ancient Greeks, he whom the gods would destroy, they first make mad.

SUMMARY

The Second World War marked the climax of the tremendous practical and spiritual maladies of the age of anxiety, which led in many lands to the rise of dictatorships. Many of these dictatorships were variations on conservative authoritarianism, but there was also a fateful innovation—the modern totalitarian regime, most fully developed in Communist Russia and Nazi Germany. The totalitarian regimes utterly rejected the liberalism of the nineteenth century. Inspired by the lessons of total war and Lenin's one-party rule, they tried to subordinate everything to the state. Although some areas of life escaped them, state control increased to a staggering, unprecedented degree. The totalitarian regimes trampled on basic human rights with unrestrained brutality and police terror. Moreover, these regimes were armed with the weapons of modern technology, rendering opposition almost impossible.

Both Communist Russia and Nazi Germany tried to gain the willing support of their populations. Monopolizing the means of expression and communication, they claimed to represent the masses and to be building new, more equal societies. Many people believed them. Both regimes

NOTES

1. E. Halévy, *The Era of Tyrannies* (Garden City, N.Y.: Doubleday, 1965), pp. 265–316, esp. p. 300.
2. Quoted in P. C. Roberts, " 'War Communism': A Re-Examination," *Slavic Review* 29 (June 1970): 25.
3. Quoted in A. G. Mazour, *Soviet Economic Development: Operation Outstrip, 1921–1965* (Princeton, N.J.: Van Nostrand, 1967), p. 130.
4. Quoted in I. Deutscher, *Stalin: A Political Biography*, 2d ed. (New York: Oxford University Press, 1967), p. 325.
5. Quoted in H. K. Geiger, *The Family in Soviet Russia* (Cambridge, Mass.: Harvard University Press, 1968), p. 123.
6. Ibid., p. 156.
7. Quoted in B. Rosenthal, "Women in the Russian Revolution and After," in *Becoming Visible: Women in European History*, ed. R. Bridenthal and C. Koonz (Boston: Houghton Mifflin, 1976), p. 383.
8. Quoted in K. D. Bracher, "The Technique of the National Socialist Seizure of Power," in T. Eschenburg et al., *The Path to Dictatorship, 1918–1933* (Garden City, N.Y.: Doubleday, 1966), p. 117.
9. Quoted in K. D. Bracher, *The German Dictatorship: The Origins, Structure and Effects of National Socialism* (New York: Praeger, 1970), pp. 146–147.

10. Quoted in R. Stromberg, *An Intellectual History of Modern Europe* (New York: Appleton-Century-Crofts, 1966), p. 393.
11. D. Schoenbaum, *Hitler's Social Revolution: Class and Status in Nazi Germany, 1933–1939* (Garden City, N.Y.: Doubleday, 1967), p. 114.
12. Quoted in Bracher, p. 289.
13. Ibid., p. 306.

SUGGESTED READING

The historical literature on totalitarian dictatorships is rich and fascinating. H. Arendt, *The Origins of Totalitarianism* (1951), is a challenging interpretation. E. Weber, *Varieties of Fascism* (1964), stresses the radical social aspirations of fascist movements all across Europe. F. L. Carsten, *The Rise of Fascism*, rev. ed. (1982), and W. Laqueur, ed., *Fascism* (1976), are also recommended.

R. Stites, *The Women's Liberation Movement in Russia: Feminism, Nihilism, and Bolshevism, 1860–1930* (1978); S. Fitzpatrick, *Cultural Revolution in Russia, 1928–1931* (1978); and the works by Geiger and Deutscher cited in the Notes are all highly recommended, as is Deutscher's sympathetic three-volume study of Trotsky. S. Cohen, *Bukharin and the Bolshevik Revolution* (1973), examines the leading spokesman of moderate communism, who was destroyed by Stalin. R. Conquest, *The Great Terror* (1968), is an excellent account of Stalin's purges of the 1930s. A. Solzhenitsyn, *The Gulag Archipelago* (1964), passionately condemns Soviet police terror, which Solzhenitsyn tracks back to Lenin. A. Koestler, *Darkness at Noon* (1956), is a famous fictional account of Stalin's trials of the Old Bolsheviks. R. Medvedev, *Let History Judge* (1972), is a penetrating and highly recommended history of Stalinism by a Russian dissident. R. Conquest, *The Harvest of Sorrow* (1986), recounts authoritatively Soviet collectivization and the man-made famine. Three other remarkable books are J. Scott, *Behind the Urals* (1942, 1973), an eyewitness account of an American steelworker in Russia in the 1930s; S. Alliluyeva, *Twenty Letters to a Friend* (1967), the amazing reflections of Stalin's daughter, who chose twice to live in the United States before returning home; and M. Fainsod, *Smolensk Under Soviet Rule* (1958), a unique study based on Communist records captured first by the Germans and then by the Americans.

A. De Grand, *Italian Fascism: Its Origins and Development*, 2d ed. (1989), and E. R. Tannebaum, *The Fascist Experience* (1972), are excellent studies of Italy under Mussolini. I. Silone, *Bread and Wine* (1937), is a moving novel by a famous opponent of dictatorship in Italy. Two excellent books on Spain are H. Thomas, *The Spanish Civil War* (1961), and E. Malefakis, *Agrarian Reform and Peasant Revolution in Spain* (1970). In the area of foreign relations, G. Kennan, *Russia and the West Under Lenin and Stalin* (1961), is justly famous, while A. L. Rowse, *Appeasement* (1961), powerfully denounces the policies of the appeasers. R. Paxton, *Vichy France* (1973), tells a controversial story extremely well, and J. Lukac, *The Last European War* (1976), skillfully—and infuriatingly—argues that victory by Hitler could have saved Europe from both Russian and American domination.

On Germany, F. Stern, *The Politics of Cultural Despair* (1963), and G. Mosse, *The Crisis of German Ideology* (1964), are excellent complementary studies on the origins of Nazism. The best single work on Hitler's Germany is Bracher's *The German Dictatorship*, cited in the Notes; W. Shirer, *The Rise and Fall of the Third Reich* (1960), is the best-selling account of an American journalist who experienced Nazi Germany firsthand. J. Fest, *Hitler* (1974), and A. Bullock, *Hitler* (1953), are engrossing biographies of the Führer. In addition to *Mein Kampf*, *Hitler's Secret Conversations, 1941–1944* (1953), reveals the dictator's wild dreams and beliefs. Among countless special studies, E. Kogon, *The Theory and Practice of Hell* (1958), is a chilling examination of the concentration camps; M. Mayer, *They Thought They Were Free* (1955), probes the minds of ten ordinary Nazis and why they believed Hitler was their liberator; and A. Speer, *Inside the Third Reich* (1970), contains the fascinating recollections of Hitler's wizard of the armaments industry. G. Mosse, *Toward the Final Solution* (1978), is a powerful history of European racism. A. Mayer, *Why Did the Heavens Not Darken? The "Final Solution" in History* (1989), and L. Dawidowicz, *The War Against the Jews, 1933–1945* (1975), are moving accounts of the Holocaust. Jørgen Haestrup, *Europe Ablaze* (1978), is a monumental account of wartime resistance movements throughout Europe, and *The Diary of Anne Frank* is a remarkable personal account of a young Jewish girl in hiding during the Nazi occupation of Holland.

J. Campbell's *The Experience of World War II* (1989) is attractively illustrated and captures the drama of global conflict. G. Wright, *The Ordeal of Total War, 1939–1945* (1968), is the best comprehensive study on the Second World War. B. H. Liddell Hart, *The History of the Second World War* (1971), is an overview of military developments. Three dramatic studies of special aspects of the war are A. Dallin, *German Rule in Russia, 1941–1945* (1957), which analyzes the effects of Nazi occupation policies on the Soviet population; L. Collins and D. La Pierre, *Is Paris Burning?* (1965), a best-selling account of the liberation of Paris and Hitler's plans to destroy the city; and J. Toland, *The Last Hundred Days* (1966), a lively account of the end of the war.

36

Recovery and Crisis in Europe and the Americas

An East German border guard at the Berlin Wall in the 1960s

The total defeat of the Nazis and their allies laid the basis for one of Western civilization's most remarkable recoveries. A battered western Europe dug itself out from under the rubble and fashioned a great renaissance in the postwar era. The Western Hemisphere, with its strong European heritage, also made exemplary progress. And the Soviet Union became more humane and less totalitarian after Stalin's death. Yet there was also a tragic setback. Dictatorship settled over eastern Europe, and the Grand Alliance against Hitler gave way to an apparently endless cold war, in which conflict between East and West threatened world peace.

Sometime during the late 1960s or early 1970s, the postwar era of recovery came to an end. Postwar certainties like domestic political stability and social harmony evaporated, and several countries experienced major crises. Moreover, the almost automatic economic improvement of the postwar years was abruptly replaced by serious economic difficulties, which lasted throughout most of the 1970s and 1980s. Of critical importance, this pattern in the industrialized nations of a generation of progress followed by a generation of crisis was shared by much of the world, as the next two chapters show. Thus the knitting together of the peoples and regions of this small planet has been accelerated by similar historical experiences in recent times.

- What were the causes of the cold war?
- How and why, in spite of the sad division of Europe into two hostile camps, did western Europe recover so successfully from the ravages of war and Nazism?
- To what extent did communist eastern Europe and the Americas experience a similar recovery?
- Why, after a generation, did the economy shift into reverse gear, and what were some of the social consequences of the reversal?
- How did political crisis strike many countries from the late 1960s onward?
- Why did a reform movement eventually triumph in eastern Europe in 1989 and bring an end to the cold war?

These are the questions that this chapter seeks to answer.

THE COLD WAR (1942–1953)

In 1945 triumphant American and Russian soldiers came together and embraced on the banks of the Elbe River in the heart of vanquished Germany. At home, in the United States and in the Soviet Union, the soldiers' loved ones erupted in joyous celebration. Yet victory was flawed. The Allies could not cooperate politically in peacemaking. Motivated by different goals and hounded by misunderstandings, the United States and the Soviet Union soon found themselves at loggerheads. By the end of 1947, Europe was rigidly divided. It was West versus East in a cold war that eventually was waged around the world.

The Origins of the Cold War

The most powerful allies in the wartime coalition—the Soviet Union and the United States—began to quarrel almost as soon as the unifying threat of Nazi Germany disappeared. The hostility between the Eastern and Western superpowers was a tragic disappointment for millions of people, but it was not really so surprising. It was the sad but logical outgrowth of military developments, wartime agreements, and long-standing political and ideological differences.

In the early phases of the Second World War, the Americans and the British made military victory their highest priority. They consistently avoided discussion of Stalin's war aims and the shape of the eventual peace settlement. This policy was evident in December 1941 and again in May 1942, when Stalin asked the United States and Britain to agree to the Soviet Union's moving its western border of 1938 farther west at the expense of Poland, in effect ratifying the gains that Stalin had made from his deal with Hitler in 1939.

Stalin's request ran counter to the moralistic Anglo-American Atlantic Charter of August 1941. In good Wilsonian fashion, the Atlantic Charter had called for peace without territorial expansion or secret agreements and for free elections and self-determination for all liberated nations. In this spirit, the British and Americans declined to promise Polish territory to Stalin. He received only a military alliance and no postwar commitments. Yet the United States and Britain did not

The Big Three   In 1945 a triumphant Winston Churchill, an ailing Franklin Roosevelt, and a determined Joseph Stalin met at Yalta in southern Russia to plan for peace. Cooperation soon gave way to bitter hostility. *(Source: F.D.R. Library)*

try to take advantage of the Soviet Union's precarious position in 1942, because they feared that hard bargaining would anger Stalin and encourage him to consider making a separate peace with Hitler. They focused instead on the policy of unconditional surrender to solidify the alliance.

By late 1943, as Allied armies scored major victories, specific issues related to the shape of the postwar world could no longer be postponed. The conference that Stalin, Roosevelt, and Churchill held in the Iranian capital of Teheran in November 1943 thus proved of crucial importance in determining subsequent events. There, the "Big Three" jovially reaffirmed their determination to crush Germany and searched for the appropriate military strategy. Churchill, fearful of the military

dangers of a direct attack and anxious to protect Britain's political interests in the eastern Mediterranean, argued that American and British forces should follow up their North African and Italian campaigns with an indirect attack on Germany through the Balkans. Roosevelt, however, agreed with Stalin that an American-British frontal assault through France would be better. This agreement was part of Roosevelt's general effort to meet Stalin's wartime demands whenever possible, and it had momentous political implications. It meant that the Soviet and the American-British armies would come together in defeated Germany along a north-south line and that only Soviet troops would liberate eastern Europe. Thus the basic shape of postwar Europe was emerging even as the fighting continued. Real differences over questions like Poland were carefully ignored.

When the Big Three met again in February 1945 at Yalta on the Black Sea in southern Russia, advancing Soviet armies were within a hundred miles of Berlin. The Red Army had occupied not only Poland but also Bulgaria, Romania, Hungary, part of Yugoslavia, and much of Czechoslovakia. The temporarily stalled American-British forces had yet to cross the Rhine into Germany. Moreover, the United States was far from defeating Japan. Indeed, it was believed that the invasion and occupation of Japan would cost a million American casualties—an estimate that contributed to the subsequent decision to drop atomic bombs in order to save American lives. In short, the Soviet Union's bargaining position was strong and America's weak.

There was little the increasingly sick and apprehensive Roosevelt could do but double his bet on Stalin's peaceful intentions. It was agreed at Yalta that Germany would be divided into zones of occupation and would pay heavy reparations to the Soviet Union in the form of agricultural and industrial goods, though many details remained unsettled. At American insistence, Stalin agreed to declare war on Japan after Germany was defeated. He also agreed to join the proposed United Nations, which the Americans believed would help preserve peace after the war; it was founded in April 1945 in San Francisco.

For Poland and eastern Europe—"that Pandora's Box of infinite troubles," according to American Secretary of State Cordell Hull—the Big Three struggled to reach an ambiguous compromise at Yalta: eastern European governments were to be freely elected but pro-Russian. As Churchill put it at the time, "The Poles will have their future in their own hands, with the single limitation that they must honestly follow in harmony with their allies, a policy friendly to Russia."[1]

The Yalta compromise over eastern Europe broke down almost immediately. Even before the Yalta Conference, Bulgaria and Poland were controlled by communists who arrived home with the Red Army. Minor concessions to noncommunist groups thereafter did not change this situation. Elsewhere in eastern Europe, pro-Soviet "coalition" governments of several parties were formed, but the key ministerial posts were reserved for Moscow-trained communists.

At the postwar Potsdam Conference of July 1945, the long-ignored differences over eastern Europe finally surged to the fore. The compromising Roosevelt had died and been succeeded by the more determined President Harry Truman, who demanded immediate free elections throughout eastern Europe. Stalin refused pointblank. "A freely elected government in any of these East European countries would be anti-Soviet," he admitted simply, "and that we cannot allow."[2]

Here, then, is the key to the much-debated origins of the cold war. American ideals, pumped up by the crusade against Hitler, and American politics, heavily influenced by millions of voters from eastern Europe, demanded free elections in Soviet-occupied eastern Europe. Stalin, who had lived through two enormously destructive German invasions, wanted absolute military security from Germany and its potential Eastern allies, once and for all. Suspicious by nature, he believed that only communist states could be truly dependable allies, and he realized that free elections would result in independent and possibly hostile governments on his western border. Moreover, by the middle of 1945 there was no way short of war that the United States and its Western allies could determine developments in eastern Europe, and war was out of the question. Stalin was bound to have his way.

West Versus East

The American response to Stalin's exaggerated conception of security was to "get tough." In May 1945 Truman abruptly cut off all aid to Russia. In October he declared that the United States would never recognize any government established by force against the free will of its people. In March 1946 former British prime minister Churchill ominously informed an American audience that an "iron curtain" had fallen across the Continent, dividing Germany and all of Europe into two antagonistic camps. Emotional, moralistic denunciations of Stalin and communist Russia emerged as part of American political life. Yet the United States also responded to the popular desire to "bring the boys home" and demobilized with great speed. When the war against Japan ended in September 1945, there were 12 million Americans in the armed forces; by 1947 there were only 1.5

million, as opposed to 6 million for the Soviet Union. Some historians have argued that American leaders believed that the atomic bomb gave the United States all the power it needed; but "getting tough" really meant "talking tough."

Stalin's agents quickly reheated what they viewed as the "ideological struggle against capitalist imperialism." The large, well-organized Communist parties of France and Italy obediently started to uncover American plots to take over Europe and challenged their own governments with violent criticisms and large strikes. The Soviet Union also put pressure on Iran and Turkey, and while Greek communists battled Greek royalists, another bitter civil war raged in China. By the spring of 1947, it appeared to many Americans that Stalin wanted much more than just puppet regimes in Soviet-occupied eastern Europe. He seemed determined to export communism by subversion throughout Europe and around the world.

The United States responded to this challenge with the Truman Doctrine, which was aimed at "containing" communism in areas already occupied by the Red Army. Truman told Congress in March 1947: "I believe it must be the policy of the United States to support free people who are resisting attempted subjugation by armed minorities or by outside pressure." To begin, Truman asked Congress for military aid to Greece and Turkey. Then, in June, Secretary of State George C. Marshall offered Europe economic aid—the Marshall Plan—to help it rebuild.

Stalin refused Marshall Plan assistance for all of eastern Europe. He purged the last remaining

The Berlin Air Lift   Standing in the rubble of their bombed-out city, a German crowd in the American sector awaits the arrival of a U.S. transport plane flying in over the Soviet blockade in 1948. The crisis over Berlin was a dramatic indication of growing tensions among the Allies, which resulted in the division of Europe into two hostile camps. *(Source: Walter Sanders, LIFE MAGAZINE © Time Inc.)*

noncommunist elements from the coalition governments of eastern Europe and established Soviet-style, one-party communist dictatorships. The seizure of power in Czechoslovakia in February 1948 was particularly brutal and antidemocratic, and it greatly strengthened Western fears of limitless communist expansion, beginning with Germany. Thus, when Stalin blocked all traffic through the Soviet zone of Germany to Berlin, the former capital, which the occupying powers had also divided into sectors at the end of the war, the Western Allies acted firmly but not provocatively. Hundreds of planes began flying over the Soviet roadblocks around the clock, supplying provisions to the people of West Berlin and thwarting Soviet efforts to swallow up the West Berliners. After 324 days the Soviets backed down: containment seemed to work. In 1949, therefore, the United States formed an anti-Soviet military alliance of Western governments: the North Atlantic Treaty Organization (NATO). Stalin countered by tightening his hold on his satellites, later united in the Warsaw Pact. Europe was divided into two hostile blocs.

In late 1949 the communists triumphed in China, frightening and angering many Americans, some of whom saw an all-powerful worldwide communist conspiracy extending even into the upper reaches of the American government. When the Russian-backed communist forces of northern Korea invaded southern Korea in 1950, President Truman acted swiftly. American-led United Nations armies intervened. The cold war had spread around the world and become very hot.

The rapid descent from victorious Grand Alliance to bitter cold war was intimately connected with the tragic fate of eastern Europe. After 1932, when the eastern European power vacuum invited Nazi racist imperialism, the appeasing Western democracies mistakenly did nothing. They did, however, have one telling insight: how, they asked themselves, could they unite with Stalin to stop Hitler without giving Stalin great gains on his western borders? After Hitler's invasion of the Soviet Union, the Western powers preferred to ignore this question and hope for the best. But when Stalin later began to claim the spoils of victory, the United States began to protest and professed outrage. This belated opposition quite possibly encouraged even more aggressive measures by the always-suspicious Stalin, and it helped explode the quarrel over eastern Europe into a global confrontation. This Soviet-American confrontation became institutionalized, and it lasted for decades despite intermittent periods of relaxation. Only when the Soviet Union's policy toward eastern Europe changed dramatically in the 1980s was the original cause of the conflict removed and the long cold war brought to an end (see pages 1194–1200).

THE WESTERN EUROPEAN RENAISSANCE

As the cold war divided Europe into two blocs, the future appeared bleak on both sides of the iron curtain. Economic conditions were the worst in generations. Politically, Europe was weak and divided, a battleground for cold war ambitions. Moreover, European empires were crumbling in the face of nationalism in Asia and Africa. Yet Europe recovered, and the Western nations led the way. In less than a generation, western Europe achieved unprecedented economic prosperity and peaceful social transformation. Moreover, western Europe began moving toward genuine unity and regained much of its traditional prominence in world affairs. It was an amazing rebirth—a true renaissance.

The Postwar Challenge

After the war, economic conditions in western Europe were terrible. Simply finding enough to eat was a real problem. Runaway inflation and black markets testified to severe shortages and hardship. The bread ration in Paris in 1946 was little more than it had been in 1942 under the Nazi occupation. Many people believed that Europe was quite simply finished. The prominent British historian Arnold Toynbee felt that, at best, western Europeans might seek to civilize the crude but powerful Americans, somewhat as the ancient Greeks had civilized their Roman conquerors.

Suffering was most intense in defeated Germany. The major territorial change of the war had moved the Soviet Union's border far to the west. Poland was in turn compensated for this loss to the Soviets with land taken from Germany (Map 36.1). To solidify these changes in boundaries,

MAP 36.1 Europe After the Second World War Both the Soviet Union and Poland took land from Germany, which the Allies partitioned into occupation zones. Those zones subsequently formed the basis of the east and the west German states, as the iron curtain fell to divide both Germany and Europe.

Postwar Reconstruction The Hamburg apartments on the left were bombed-out shells in 1945, along with 300,000 other housing units in the city. Yet by 1951 these same apartments were replaced, or ingeniously rebuilt (right). In half of the shells, crushed rubble mixed with concrete was poured to provide missing walls and to achieve a quick and economical rehabilitation. *(Source: National Archives, Washington)*

thirteen million people were driven from their homes in eastern Germany (and other countries in eastern Europe) and forced to resettle in a greatly reduced Germany. The Russians were also seizing factories and equipment as reparations, even tearing up railroad tracks and sending the rails to the Soviet Union.

In 1945 and 1946, conditions were not much better in the Western zones, for the Western Allies also treated the German population with great severity at first. By February 1946 the average daily diet of a German in the Ruhr had been reduced to two slices of bread, a pat of margarine, a spoonful of porridge, and two small potatoes. Countless Germans sold prized possessions to American soldiers to buy food. By the spring of 1947, refugee-clogged, hungry, prostrate Germany was on the verge of total collapse and threatening to drag down the rest of Europe.

Yet western Europe was not finished. The Nazi occupation and the war had discredited old ideas and old leaders. All over Europe, many people were willing to change and experiment in hopes of building a new and better Europe out of the rubble. New groups and new leaders were coming to the fore to guide these aspirations. Progressive Catholics and revitalized Catholic political parties—the Christian Democrats—were particularly influential.

In Italy, the Christian Democrats emerged as the leading party in the first postwar elections in 1946, and in early 1948 they won an absolute majority in the parliament in a landslide victory. Their very able leader was Alcide De Gasperi, a courageous antifascist and former Vatican librarian, firmly committed to political democracy, economic reconstruction, and moderate social reform. In France, too, the Catholic party provided some of the best postwar leaders, like Robert Schuman. This was particularly true after January 1946, when General Charles de Gaulle, the inspiring wartime leader of the Free French, resigned after having re-established the free and democratic Fourth Republic. As Germany was partitioned by the cold war, a radically purified Federal Republic of Germany (as West Germany was officially known) found new and able leadership among its Catholics. In 1949 Konrad Adenauer, the former mayor of Cologne and a long-time anti-Nazi, began his long, highly successful democratic rule; the Christian Democrats became West Germany's majority party for a generation. In providing effective leadership for their respective countries, the Christian Democrats were inspired and united by a common Christian and European heritage. They steadfastly rejected totalitarianism and narrow nationalism and placed their faith in democracy and cooperation.

The Socialists and the Communists, active in the Resistance against Hitler, also emerged from the war with increased power and prestige, especially in France and Italy. They, too, provided fresh leadership and pushed for social change and economic reform with considerable success. In the immediate postwar years, welfare measures such as family allowances, health insurance, and increased public housing were enacted throughout much of Europe. In Italy social benefits from the state came to equal a large part of the average worker's wages. In France large banks, insurance companies, public utilities, coal mines, and the Renault auto company were nationalized by the government. Britain followed the same trend. The voters threw out Churchill and the Conservatives in 1945, and the socialist Labour party under Clement Attlee moved toward establishment of a "welfare state." Many industries were nationalized, and the government provided each citizen with free medical service and taxed the middle and upper classes more heavily. Thus, all across Europe, social reform complemented political transformation, creating solid foundations for a great European renaissance.

The United States also supplied strong and creative leadership. Frightened by fears of Soviet expansion, the United States provided western Europe with both massive economic aid and ongoing military protection. Economic aid was channeled through the Marshall Plan. Between early 1948 and late 1952, the United States furnished foreign countries roughly $22.5 billion, of which seven-eighths was in the form of outright gifts rather than loans. Military security was provided through NATO, established as a regional alliance for self-defense and featuring American troops stationed permanently in Europe and the American nuclear umbrella. Thus the United States assumed its international responsibilities after the Second World War, exercising the leadership it had shunned after 1919.

Economic "Miracles"

As Marshall Plan aid poured in, the battered economies of western Europe began to turn the corner in 1948. The outbreak of the Korean War in 1950 further stimulated economic activity, and Europe entered a period of rapid economic progress that lasted into the late 1960s. By 1963 western Europe was producing more than two-and-one-half times as much as it had produced before the war. Never before had the European economy grown so fast, and it was a time of loudly proclaimed economic "miracles."

There were many reasons for western Europe's brilliant economic performance. American aid helped the process get off to a fast start. Moreover, economic growth became a basic objective of all western European governments, for leaders and voters were determined to avoid a return to the dangerous and demoralizing stagnation of the 1930s. Thus governments generally accepted Keynesian economics (see page 1126) and sought to stimulate their economies. Some also adopted a number of imaginative strategies. Those in Germany and France were particularly successful and influential.

Under Minister of Economy Ludwig Erhard, a roly-poly, cigar-smoking former professor, postwar West Germany broke decisively with the straitjacketed Nazi economy. Erhard bet on the free-market economy while maintaining the extensive social welfare network inherited from the Hitler era. He and his teachers believed not only that capitalism was more efficient but also that political and social freedom could thrive only if there were real economic freedom. Erhard's first step was to reform the currency and abolish rationing and price controls in 1948. He boldly declared, "The only ration coupon is the Mark."[3] By the late 1950s, West Germany had a prospering economy and full employment, a strong currency and stable prices. West Germany success renewed respect for free-market capitalism and encouraged freer trade among other European nations.

The French innovation was a new kind of planning. Under the guidance of Jean Monnet, an economic pragmatist and apostle of European unity, a planning commission set ambitious but flexible goals for the French economy. It used Marshall Plan aid money and the nationalized banks to funnel money into key industries, several of which were state owned. It also encouraged private enterprise to "think big," and the often-cautious French business community responded. Thus France combined flexible planning and a "mixed" state and private economy to achieve the most rapid economic development in its long history.

Other factors also contributed to western Europe's economic boom. In most countries there were many people ready to work hard for low wages and the hope of a better future. Expanding industries in those countries thus had a great asset to draw on. Moreover, although many consumer products had been invented or perfected since the late 1920s, during the depression and war few Europeans had been able to buy them. In 1945 the electric refrigerator, the washing machine, and the automobile were rare luxuries. There was a great potential demand, which the economic system moved to satisfy.

Finally, ever since 1919 the nations of Europe had suffered from high tariffs and small national markets. In the postwar era, European countries junked many of these economic barriers and gradually created a large unified market known as the "Common Market." This historic action, which certainly stimulated the economy, was part of a larger search for European unity.

Toward European Unity

Western Europe's political recovery was spectacular in the generation after 1945. Republics were re-established in France, West Germany, and Italy. Constitutional monarchs were restored in Belgium, Holland, and Norway. Democratic governments, often within the framework of multiparty politics and shifting parliamentary coalitions, took root again and thrived. National self-determination was accompanied by civil liberties and individual freedom. All of this was an extraordinary achievement.

So also was the still-continuing march toward a united Europe. The Christian Democrats with their shared Catholic heritage were particularly committed to "building Europe," and other groups shared their dedication. Many Europeans believed that narrow, exaggerated nationalism had been a fundamental cause of both world wars and that only through unity could European conflict be avoided in the future. Many western Europeans also realized how weak their countries were in comparison with the United States and the Soviet Union, the two superpowers that had divided Europe from outside and made it into a cold war battleground. Thus the cold war encouraged some visionaries to seek a new "European nation," a superpower capable of controlling western Europe's destiny and reasserting its influence in world affairs.

The close cooperation among European states required by the Marshall Plan led to the creation of both the Organization of European Economic Cooperation (OEEC) and the Council of Europe in 1948. European federalists hoped that the Council of Europe would quickly evolve into a true European parliament with sovereign rights, but this did not happen. Britain, with its empire and its "special relationship" with the United States, consistently opposed giving any real political power—any sovereignty—to the council. Many old-fashioned continental nationalists and communists felt similarly. The Council of Europe became little more than a multinational debating society.

Frustrated in the direct political approach, European federalists turned toward economics as a way of working toward genuine unity. Two far-seeing French statesmen, the planner Jean Monnet and Foreign Minister Robert Schuman, courageously took the lead in 1950. The Schuman Plan called for a special international organization to control and integrate all European steel and coal production. West Germany, Italy, Belgium, the Netherlands, and Luxembourg accepted the French idea in 1952; the British would have none of it. The immediate economic goal—a single competitive market without national tariffs or quotas—was rapidly realized. The more far-reaching political goal was to bind the six-member nations so closely together economically that war among them would become unthinkable and virtually impossible. This brilliant strategy did much to reduce tragic old rivalries, particularly that of France and Germany.

The Coal and Steel Community encouraged further technical and economic cooperation among "the Six." In 1957 the same six nations signed the Treaty of Rome, which created the European Economic Community, generally known as the "Common Market" (Map 36.2). The first goal of the treaty was a gradual reduction of all tariffs among the Six in order to create a single market almost as

MAP 36.2 European Alliance Systems After the cold war divided Europe into two hostile military alliances, six Western European countries formed the Common Market in 1957. The Common Market grew later to include most of Western Europe. The Communist states organized their own economic association—COMECON.

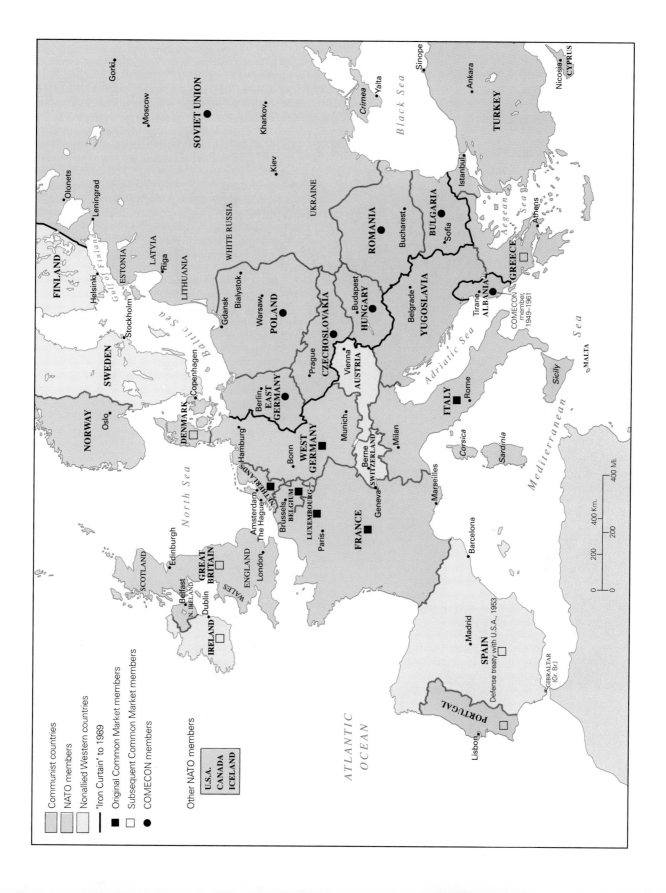

SOVIET UNION

Gorki•

Moscow•

•Olonets

Leningrad•

•Kharkov

•Kiev

FINLAND

Helsinki•

Stockholm•

ESTONIA

LATVIA
•Riga

LITHUANIA

WHITE RUSSIA

UKRAINE

Crimea

•Yalta

Sinope•

Black Sea

•Ankara

Nicosia•
CYPRUS

TURKEY

Istanbul•

Aegean Sea

Athens•

NORWAY

Oslo•

SWEDEN

Copenhagen•

DENMARK

Gdansk•

Bialystok•

Warsaw•
POLAND

Berlin•
EAST GERMANY

Prague•
CZECHOSLOVAKIA

Vienna•
AUSTRIA

Budapest•
HUNGARY

ROMANIA

Bucharest•

BULGARIA
•Sofia

Belgrade•
YUGOSLAVIA

Tirane•
ALBANIA

COMECON
member,
1949–1961

GREECE

Baltic Sea

Gulf of Finland

North Sea

Hamburg•

Bonn•
WEST GERMANY

Munich•

Berne•
SWITZERLAND

Geneva•

Milan•

•Rome
ITALY

Adriatic Sea

Corsica

Sardinia

Sicily

MALTA

Mediterranean Sea

Edinburgh•

SCOTLAND

Belfast•
N. IRELAND
Dublin•

IRELAND

WALES

ENGLAND
London•

GREAT BRITAIN

Amsterdam•
The Hague•
NETHERLANDS

Brussels•
BELGIUM
LUXEMBOURG
Paris•

FRANCE

Marseilles•

Barcelona•

Madrid•

SPAIN

Defense treaty with U.S.A., 1953

GIBRALTAR
(Gr. Br.)

PORTUGAL

Lisbon•

ATLANTIC OCEAN

400 Mi.

400 Km.

200

200

0

0

Communist countries

NATO members

Nonallied Western countries

"Iron Curtain" to 1989

Original Common Market members

Subsequent Common Market members

COMECON members

Other NATO members

U.S.A.
CANADA
ICELAND

Date is year independence was achieved.
Shading indicates former ruler.

Great Britain
France
Netherlands
Italy
Belgium
Portugal
United States

PACIFIC OCEAN

INDIAN OCEAN

ATLANTIC OCEAN

JAPAN

NORTH KOREA 1948
SOUTH KOREA 1948
From Japan

PHILIPPINES 1946

BRUNEI 1984 From Great Britain

INDONESIA 1949

NORTH VIETNAM 1954
Unified 1974
SOUTH VIETNAM 1954
CAMBODIA 1954
MALAYSIA 1963
SINGAPORE 1965

LAOS 1949
MYANMAR (BURMA) 1947

PAKISTAN 1947, BANGLADESH 1973

INDIA 1947

SRI LANKA (CEYLON) 1948

PAKISTAN 1947

CYPRUS 1960
ISRAEL 1948
MALTA 1964 From Great Britain

JORDAN 1946
KUWAIT 1961
BAHRAIN 1971
QATAR 1971
UNITED ARAB EMIRATES 1971
YEMEN P.D.R. OF YEMEN 1967 Unified with Yemen 1990

SOMALIA 1960
DJIBOUTI 1977

MAURITIUS 1968 From Great Britain

MADAGASCAR 1960

KENYA 1963
UGANDA 1962
TANZANIA 1964
MALAWI 1964
MOZAMBIQUE 1974
SWAZILAND 1968
LESOTHO 1966

SUDAN 1956

ZAIRE 1960
RWANDA 1962
BURUNDI 1962
ZAMBIA 1964
ZIMBABWE 1980
BOTSWANA 1966

CHAD 1960
CENTRAL AFRICAN REPUBLIC 1960
CAMEROON 1960
GABON 1960
CONGO 1960
ANGOLA 1975
NAMIBIA 1990
SOUTH AFRICA (Republic 1961)

LIBYA 1951

NIGER 1960
NIGERIA 1960
BENIN 1960
TOGO 1960
EQUATORIAL GUINEA 1968 From Spain

GREAT BRITAIN
NETHERLANDS
BELGIUM
FRANCE
ITALY
PORTUGAL
SPAIN

TUNISIA 1957
ALGERIA 1962
MOROCCO 1956

MALI 1960
BURKINA FASO 1960
CÔTE D'IVOIRE 1960
GHANA 1957

MAURITANIA 1960
SENEGAL 1960
GAMBIA 1965
GUINEA-BISSAU 1974
GUINEA 1958
SIERRA LEONE 1961
LIBERIA 1820s

WESTERN SAHARA (MOROCCO) 1975 From Spain

0   500   1000   1500 Km.
0   500   1000   1500 Mi.

large as that of the United States. Other goals included the free movement of capital and labor and common economic policies and institutions. The Common Market was a great success. Tariffs were rapidly reduced, and companies and regions specialized in what they did best.

The development of the Common Market fired imaginations and encouraged hopes of rapid progress toward political as well as economic union. In the 1960s, however, these hopes were frustrated by a resurgence of more traditional nationalism. Once again, France took the lead. Mired in a bitter colonial war in Algeria, the French turned in 1958 to General de Gaulle, who established the Fifth French Republic and ruled as its president until 1969. The last of the bigger-than-life wartime leaders, de Gaulle was at heart a romantic nationalist dedicated to reasserting France's greatness and glory. Resolving the Algerian conflict, he labored to re-create a powerful, truly independent France. Viewing the United States as the main threat to genuine French (and European) independence, he withdrew all French military forces from the "American-controlled" NATO command as France developed its own nuclear weapons. Within the Common Market, de Gaulle twice vetoed the application of the pro-American British, who were having second thoughts and wanted to join. More generally, he refused to permit the scheduled advent of majority rule within the Common Market, and he forced his partners to accept many of his views. Thus, throughout the 1960s the Common Market thrived economically but remained a union of sovereign states.

Decolonization

The postwar era saw the total collapse of European political empires. Between 1947 and 1962 almost every colonial territory gained formal independence: Europe's long overseas expansion was dramatically reversed. Future generations will almost certainly see this rolling back of Western expansion as one of world history's truly great turning points (Map 36.3).

The most basic cause of imperial collapse—what Europeans called "decolonization"—was the rising demand of Asian and African peoples for national self-determination, racial equality, and personal dignity. This demand spread from intellectuals to the masses in virtually every colonial territory after the First World War. As a result, colonial empires had already been shaken by 1939 and the way was prepared for the eventual triumph of independence movements (see pages 1238–1243). Yet decolonization also involved the imperial powers, and looking at the process from their perspective helps explain why independence came so quickly and why a kind of neocolonialism subsequently took its place in some areas.

European empires had been based on an enormous power differential between the rulers and the ruled, a difference that had declined almost to the vanishing point by 1945. Not only was western Europe poor and battered immediately after the war, but Japan had demonstrated for a second time that whites were not invincible. With its political power and moral authority in tatters, Europe could either submit to decolonization or enter into risky wars of reconquest.

Most Europeans regarded their empires very differently after 1945 than before 1914, or even before 1939. Empire had rested on self-confidence and self-righteousness; Europeans had believed their superiority to be not only technical and military but spiritual and moral as well. The horrors of the Second World War destroyed such complacent arrogance and gave opponents of imperialism much greater influence in Europe. After 1945 many Europeans were willing to let go of their colonies more or less voluntarily and to concentrate on rebuilding at home.

Indian independence played a key role in decolonization. When the Labour party came to power in Great Britain in 1945, it was determined to leave India. British socialists had always opposed imperialism, and the heavy cost of governing India had become an intolerable burden. Empire in India ended in 1947, and most Asian colonies achieved independence shortly thereafter. Although the French obstinately tried to re-establish colonial rule in Indochina, they were defeated in 1954, and two independent Vietnamese states

MAP 36.3 The New States in Africa and Asia Divided primarily along religious lines into two states, British India led the way to political independence in 1947. Most African territories achieved statehood by the mid-1960s, as European empires passed away, unlamented.

came into being. The French also fought a long, dirty war to keep Algeria French, but Algeria won its independence in 1962 (see Map 36.3).

In much of Africa south of the Sahara, decolonization proceeded much more smoothly. Beginning in 1957, Britain's colonies achieved independence with little or no bloodshed and then entered a very loose association with Britain as members of the British Commonwealth of Nations. In 1958 the clever de Gaulle offered the leaders of French black Africa the choice of a total break with France or immediate independence within a kind of French commonwealth. All but one of the new states chose association with France. African leaders did so because they identified with French culture and because they wanted aid from France. The French, buoyed up by economic growth and political recovery, were eager to help—provided their former colonies would accept close ties with France on French terms. As in the past, the French and their Common Market partners, who helped foot the bill, saw themselves as continuing their civilizing mission in black Africa. More importantly, they saw in Africa untapped markets for their industrial goods, raw materials for their factories, outlets for profitable investment, and good temporary jobs for their engineers and teachers. The British acted somewhat similarly, especially after they finally joined the Common Market in 1973.

As a result, western European countries actually managed to increase their economic and cultural ties with their former African colonies in the 1960s and 1970s. Above all, they used the lure of special trading privileges with the Common Market and heavy investment in French- and English-language education to enhance a powerful Western presence in the new African states. This situation led a variety of leaders and scholars to charge that western Europe (and the United States) had imposed a system of neocolonialism on the former colonies. According to this view, *neocolonialism* was a system designed to perpetuate Western economic domination and undermine the promise of political independence, thereby extending to Africa (and much of Asia) the neocolonial subordination that the United States had established in Latin America after the political revolutions of the early nineteenth century (see pages 992–1004). At the very least, enduring influence in black Africa testified to western Europe's resurgent economic and political power in international relations.

The Changing Class Structure

Rapid economic growth, combined with scientific and technological progress, went a long way toward creating a new society in Europe after the Second World War. European society became more mobile and more democratic. Old class barriers relaxed, and class distinctions became fuzzier.

Changes in the structure of the middle class were particularly influential in the general drift toward a less rigid class structure. In the nineteenth and early twentieth centuries, the model for the middle class had been the independent, self-employed individual who owned a business or practiced a liberal profession like law or medicine. Ownership of property—usually inherited property—and strong family ties had often been the keys to wealth and standing within the middle class. After 1945, this pattern declined drastically in western Europe. A new breed of managers and experts replaced traditional property owners as the leaders of the middle class. Ability to serve the needs of a big organization largely replaced inherited property and family connections in determining an individual's social position in the middle and upper middle class. At the same time, the middle class grew massively and became harder to define.

There were several reasons for these developments. Rapid industrial and technological expansion created in large corporations and government agencies a powerful demand for technologists and managers, of whom only a few at best could come from the old property-owning families. Moreover, the old propertied middle class lost control of many family-owned businesses. Even very wealthy families had to call on the general investing public for capital, and many small businesses (including family farms) simply passed out of existence as their former owners joined the ranks of salaried employees.

Top managers and ranking civil servants therefore represented the model for a new middle class of salaried specialists. Well paid and highly trained, often with backgrounds in engineering or accounting, these experts increasingly came from all social classes, even the working class. Pragmatic and realistic, they were primarily concerned with efficiency and practical solutions to concrete problems. Everywhere successful managers and technocrats passed on the opportunity for all-important advanced education to their children, but only in rare instances could they pass on the positions they had attained. Thus the new middle class, which was based largely on specialized skills and high levels of education, was more open, democratic, and insecure than the old propertied middle class.

The structure of the lower classes also became more flexible and open. There was a mass exodus from farms and the countryside, as one of the most traditional and least mobile groups in European society drastically declined. Meanwhile, because of rapid technological change, the industrial working class ceased to expand, and job opportunities for white-collar and service employees grew rapidly. Such employees bore a greater resemblance to the new middle class of salaried specialists than to industrial workers, who were also better educated and more specialized.

While the demands of growing economies and big bureaucracies were breaking down rigid class divisions, European governments were reducing class tensions with a series of social security reforms. Many of these reforms—like increased unemployment benefits and more extensive old-age pensions—simply strengthened social security measures first pioneered in Bismarck's Germany before the First World War. Other programs were new.

Britain's Labour government took the lead immediately after 1945 in establishing a comprehensive national health system; other European governments followed the British example. Depending on the system, patients either received completely free medical care or paid only a small portion of the total cost.

Most countries also introduced family allowances—direct government grants to parents to help them raise their children. These allowances helped many poor families make ends meet. Most European governments also gave maternity grants and built inexpensive public housing for low-income families and individuals. These and other social reforms provided a humane floor of well-being, below which few individuals could fall in the advanced countries of northern and western Europe. Reforms also promoted greater equality

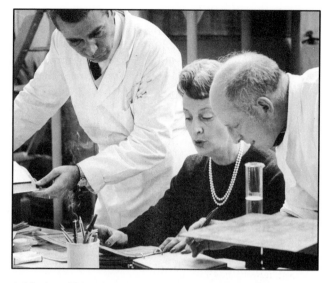

A Modern Manager Despite considerable discrimination, women were increasingly found in the expanding middle class of salaried experts after World War Two, working in business, science, and technology. *(Source: Niépce-Rapho/Photo Researchers)*

because they were expensive and were paid for in part by higher taxes on the rich.

The rising standard of living and the spread of standardized consumer goods also worked to level Western society. In the mid-nineteenth century, food and drink cost roughly two-thirds of the average family's income in western and northern Europe. By the mid-1960s, they took only about one-third to two-fifths of that family's income, and more money was available for consumer goods.

The European automobile industry expanded phenomenally. Automobile ownership was commonplace far down the social scale in the United States by the mid-1920s, but only the rich could generally afford cars in Europe before the Second World War. In 1948 there were only five million cars in western Europe. By 1957 the number of cars had increased to fifteen million, and by 1965 it had tripled again to forty-four million as car ownership was democratized and came within the range of better-paid workers.

Europeans took great pleasure in the products of the "gadget revolution" as well. Like Americans, Europeans filled their houses and apartments with washing machines, vacuum cleaners, refrigerators, dishwashers, radios, TVs, and stereos. The purchase of these and other consumer goods was greatly facilitated by installment purchasing, which allowed people to buy on credit. Before the Second World War, Europeans had rarely bought "on time." But with the expansion of social security safeguards, reducing the need to accumulate savings for hard times, ordinary people were increasingly willing to take on debt. This change had far-reaching consequences.

The most astonishing leisure-time development in the consumer society was the blossoming of mass travel and tourism. Before the Second World War, travel for pleasure and relaxation remained a rather aristocratic pastime. Most people had neither the time nor the money for it. But with month-long paid vacations required by law in most European countries, and widespread automobile ownership, beaches and ski resorts came within the reach of the middle class and many workers. By the late 1960s packaged tours with cheap group flights and bargain hotel accommodations had made even distant lands easily accessible. One-fifth of West Germany's population traveled abroad each year. A French company grew rich building imitation Tahitian paradises around the world. At Swedish nudist colonies on secluded West African beaches, office workers from Stockholm fleetingly worshiped the sun in the middle of the long northern winter. Truly, consumerism had come of age.

Political Upheaval in the Late 1960s

For twenty years after 1945, most Europeans were preoccupied with the possibilities of economic progress and consumerism. The more democratic

Student Protest in Paris These rock-throwing students in the Latin Quarter of Paris are trying to force education reforms or even to topple de Gaulle's government. Throughout May 1968 students clashed repeatedly with France's tough riot police in bloody street fighting. *(Source: Bruno Barbey/Magnum)*

class structure also helped to reduce social tension, and ideological conflict went out of style. In the late 1960s, however, sharp criticism and social conflicts re-emerged, heralding a new era of uncertainty and crisis.

Much of the criticism came from radical students. They rejected the materialism of their parents and claimed that the postwar society was repressive and badly flawed. With their counterparts in North America, they argued that the Vietnam War (see pages 1201–1202) proved that Western civilization was immoral and imperialistic.

The very rapid expansion of European higher education had created problems as well as opportunities for students. Classes were badly overcrowded, and competition for grades was intense. "Practical" areas of study were added to the curriculum, but they were added less quickly than many students wanted. Thus many students felt that they were not getting the kind of education they needed for jobs in the modern economy and that universities as well as society needed fundamental, even revolutionary reforms.

Tensions came to a head in the late 1960s and early 1970s. Following in the footsteps of their American counterparts, European university students rose to challenge their university administrations and even their governments. The most far-reaching of these revolts occurred in France in 1968. Students occupied university buildings, clashed violently with police, and appealed to France's industrial workers for help. A general strike then spread across France in May 1968, and it seemed certain that President De Gaulle's Fifth Republic would collapse. De Gaulle, however, stiffened, moving troops toward Paris and calling for new elections. Thoroughly frightened by the protest-turned-upheaval and fearful that a successful revolution could lead only to an eventual communist takeover, the masses of France voted for a return to law and order. De Gaulle and his party scored the biggest electoral victory in modern French history, and the mini-revolution collapsed. Yet the proud de Gaulle and the confident, though old-fashioned, nationalism that he represented had been cruelly mocked. In 1969, tired and discouraged, he resigned over a minor issue, and within a year he was dead.

The international student revolution of the late 1960s was announcing the end of an era. The social stability and material progress of the postwar years were giving away to conflict and crisis.

The Troubled Economy in Recent Times

The reappearance of economic crisis in the 1970s brought the most serious problems for the average person. The postwar international monetary system, which had proved instrumental in the unprecedented postwar boom, was based on the American dollar. Because foreign governments could exchange dollars for gold at $35 an ounce, the dollar was considered to be "as good as gold." The United States proceeded to make needed dollars readily available to the rest of the world—so readily that by early 1971 it had only $11 billion in gold left, and Europe had accumulated 50 billion American dollars as claims against that gold. Foreigners then panicked and raced to exchange their dollars for gold. President Richard Nixon was forced to stop the sale of American gold, and the value of the dollar declined against many European currencies. Fixed rates of exchange were abandoned, and great uncertainty replaced postwar predictability in international trade and finance.

Even more damaging was the dramatic reversal in the price and availability of energy. The great postwar boom was fueled by cheap oil, especially in western Europe. Cheap oil from the Middle East permitted energy-intensive industries—automobiles, chemicals, and electric power—to expand rapidly and lead other sectors of the economy forward. By 1971, the Arab-led Organization of Petroleum Exporting Countries (OPEC) had watched the price of crude oil decline consistently compared with the price of manufactured goods. OPEC decided to reverse that trend by presenting a united front against the oil companies. The stage was set for a revolution in energy prices during the fourth Arab-Israeli war in October 1973 (see page 1232). In the course of a year crude oil prices quadrupled. It was widely realized that the rapid price rise was economically destructive, but the world's big powers did nothing. The Soviet Union was a great oil exporter and benefited directly. A cautious western Europe looked to the United States for leadership, but the United States was immobilized, its attention absorbed by the Watergate crisis in politics (see page 1202). Without the benefit of organization, therefore, governments, companies, and individuals had no other choice than to deal piecemeal with the so-called oil shock—a "shock" that really turned out to be an earthquake.

Saudi Riches   Saudi Arabia has enormous oil reserves, making it one of the most influential members of the Organization of Petroleum Exporting Countries and giving it one of the world's highest per capita incomes. Oil has also made rich men of Prince Fahd and King Khalid, shown here. *(Source: Robert Azzi/Woodfin Camp & Associates)*

Coming on the heels of upheaval in the international monetary system, the revolution in energy prices plunged the world into its worst economic decline since the 1930s. The energy-intensive industries that had driven the economy up in the 1950s and 1960s now dragged it down. Unemployment rose. Productivity and living standards declined.

By 1976 a modest recovery was in progress, but when Iranian oil production collapsed during Iran's fundamentalist Islamic revolution (see page 1232), the price of crude oil doubled again in 1979 and the world economy succumbed to its second oil shock. Unemployment and inflation rose dramatically before another uneven recovery began in 1982. In the summer of 1985, the unemployment rate in western Europe rose to its highest levels since the Great Depression. Fully nineteen million people were unemployed. Although unemployment declined in the late 1980s, large numbers of people remained out of work.

Anxious observers, recalling the disastrous consequences of the Great Depression, worried that democratic government and steps toward European unity would be destroyed by social conflicts and economic nationalism. But, on the whole, the welfare system fashioned in the postwar era prevented mass suffering and social unrest. Extended benefits for the unemployed, pensions for the aged, free medical care for the needy, surplus food and special allowances for parents with children—all these and a host of lesser supports did their part. The socially responsive national state undoubtedly contributed to the preservation of political stability and democracy in the face of economic disorder that might have been the cause of revolution and dictatorship in earlier times.

Nor did the Common Market disintegrate in the face of severe economic dislocation. Indeed, it continued to exert a powerful attraction on non-members. In 1973, Denmark and Iceland, in addition to Britain, finally joined. In 1977, Greece, Portugal, and Spain applied for membership. The negotiations were long and difficult, especially for Spain. Spain was a big low-cost producer of wine, olive oil, and fresh fruit, which French and Italian farmers feared would come flooding into Common Market countries and drive them out of business. In the end, subsidies to injured farmers and special transition rules for agricultural products achieved a characteristic Common Market compromise. Greece joined in 1981, Portugal and Spain in 1986.

After de Gaulle's death, the nations of the Common Market cooperated more closely in many international undertakings and negotiations. The Common Market decided in 1977, for example, to go ahead with plans for a nuclear breeder reactor to produce electric power, and it tried to develop a common policy on peace in the Middle East, terrorism, and economic negotiations with Third World countries. The movement toward European unity stayed alive. The Common Market countries eventually set 1992 as the year for the attainment of total economic and social integration, and new projects and discussions on the prospects of greater political unity filled the media as the 1990s opened. Some Europeans even believed that the transformation of eastern Europe (see pages 1196–1200) opened the way to genuine unity in the not-so-distant future. This admittedly optimistic vision suggested that western Europe had weathered the storms of the 1970s and 1980s, which contrasted so sharply with the clear sailing of the 1950s and 1960s.

SOVIET EASTERN EUROPE

While western Europe surged ahead economically after the Second World War and regained political independence as American influence gradually waned, eastern Europe followed a different path. The Soviet Union first tightened its grip on the "liberated" nations of eastern Europe under Stalin and then refused to let go. Thus postwar economic recovery in eastern Europe proceeded along Soviet lines, and political and social developments were strongly influenced by changes in the Soviet Union. These changes went forward at a slow and uneven pace, and they appeared to almost halt after Leonid Brezhnev came to power and crushed a socialist reform movement in Czechoslovakia in 1968.

Yet beneath the apparent stagnation of the Brezhnev years Soviet society experienced a major transformation. This transformation encouraged new political thinking in the Soviet Union and in turn enabled the long-frustrated reform movement to triumph spectacularly in eastern Europe in the unexpected revolution of 1989. Thus one must look primarily at the Soviet Union in order to understand the history of eastern European peoples since 1945.

Stalin's Last Years

The unwillingness of the United States to accept Stalin's control of territories occupied by the triumphant Red Army was at least partly responsible for the outbreak and institutionalization of the cold war. Americans, however, were not the only ones who felt betrayed by Stalin's postwar actions.

The Great Patriotic War of the Fatherland had fostered Russian nationalism and a relaxation of totalitarian terror. It also produced a rare but real unity between Soviet rulers and most Russian people. When an American correspondent asked a distinguished sixty-year-old Jewish scientist, who had decided to leave Russia for Israel in 1972, what had been the best period in Russian history, he received a startling answer: the Second World War. The scientist explained: "At that time we all felt closer to our government than at any other time in our lives. It was not their country then, but our country. . . . It was not their war, but our war."[4] Having made such a heroic war effort, the vast majority of the Soviet people hoped in 1945 that a grateful party and government would grant greater freedom and democracy. Such hopes were soon crushed.

Even before the war ended, Stalin was moving his country back toward rigid dictatorship. As early as 1944, the leading members of the Communist party were being given a new motivating slogan: "The war on Fascism ends, the war on capitalism begins."[5] By early 1946, Stalin was publicly singing the old tune that war was inevitable as long as capitalism existed. Stalin's new foreign foe in the West provided an excuse for re-establishing totalitarian measures, for the totalitarian state cannot live without enemies.

One of Stalin's first postwar goals was to repress the millions of Soviet citizens who were living outside Soviet borders when the war ended. Many had been captured by the Nazis; others were ordinary civilians who had been living abroad. Many were opposed to Stalin; some had fought for the Germans. Determined to hush up the fact that large numbers of Soviet citizens hated his regime so much that they had willingly supported the Germans and refused to go home, Stalin demanded that all these "traitors" be given back to him. At Yalta, Roosevelt and Churchill agreed, and roughly 2 million people were delivered to Stalin against their will. Most were immediately arrested and sent to forced-labor camps, where about 50 percent perished. The revival of many forced-labor camps, which had accounted for roughly one-sixth of all new construction in the Soviet Union before the war, was further stimulated by large-scale purges of many people who had never left the Soviet Union, particularly in 1945 and 1946.

Culture and art were also purged. Violent campaigns led by Stalin's trusted henchman Andrei Zhdanov reimposed rigid anti-Western ideological conformity. Zhdanov denounced many artists, including the composers Sergei Prokofiev and Dimitri Shostakovich and the outstanding film director Sergei Eisenstein. The great poet Anna Akhmatova was condemned as "a harlot and nun who mixes harlotry and prayer" and, like many others, driven out of the writers' union. This expulsion practically ensured that her work would not be published. In 1949 Stalin launched a savage verbal attack on Soviet Jews, accusing them of being pro-Western and antisocialist.

In the political realm, Stalin reasserted the Communist party's complete control of the government and his absolute mastery of the party. Five-year plans were reintroduced to cope with the enormous task of economic reconstruction. Once again, heavy and military industry were given top priority, and consumer goods, housing, and still-collectivized agriculture were neglected. Everyday life was very hard: in 1952 the wages of ordinary people still bought 25 to 40 percent less than in 1928. In short, it was the 1930s all over again in the Soviet Union, although police terror was less intense.

Stalin's prime postwar innovation was to export the Stalinist system to the countries of eastern Europe. The Communist parties of eastern Europe had established one-party states by 1948, thanks to the help of the Red Army and the Russian secret police. Rigid ideological indoctrination, attacks on religion, and a lack of civil liberties were soon facts of life. Industry was nationalized, and the middle class was stripped of its possessions. Economic life was then faithfully recast in the Stalinist mold. Forced industrialization, with five-year plans and a stress on heavy industry, lurched forward without regard for human costs. For the sake of ideological uniformity, agriculture had to be collectivized; this process went much faster in Bulgaria and Czechoslovakia than in Hungary and Poland.

Only Josip Tito (1892–1980), the popular resistance leader and Communist chief of Yugoslavia, was able to resist Soviet domination successfully. Tito openly broke with Stalin in 1948, and since there was no Russian army in Yugoslavia, he got away with it. Tito's successful proclamation of Communist independence led the infuriated and humiliated Stalin to purge the Communist parties of eastern Europe. Popular Communist leaders who, like Tito, had led the resistance against Germany, were made to star in reruns of the great show trials of the 1930s (see page 1143). Thus did history repeat itself as Stalin sought to create absolutely obedient instruments of domination in eastern Europe.

Reform and De-Stalinization

In 1953 the aging Stalin finally died, and the totalitarian system that he had built began to change. Even as Stalin's heirs struggled for power, they realized that reforms were necessary. There was widespread fear and hatred of Stalin's political terrorism, and even Stalin's secret-police chief, Lavrenti Beria, publicly favored relaxing controls in an unsuccessful attempt to seize power. Beria was arrested and shot, but the power of the secret police was curbed and many of the forced-labor camps were gradually closed. Change was also necessary for economic reasons. Agriculture was in bad shape, and shortages of consumer goods were

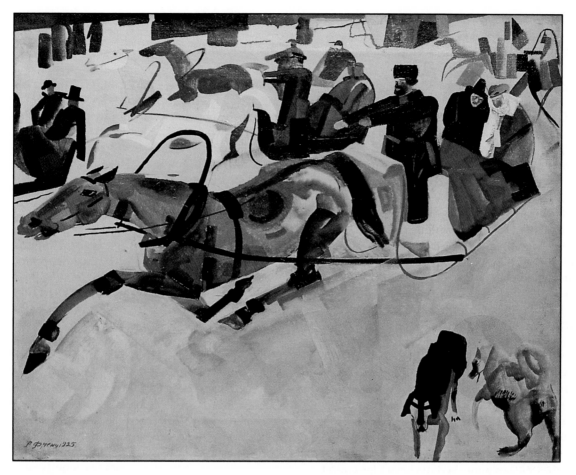

Frenz: Pink Snow This light-hearted, fanciful rendition of traditional Russian themes hardly seems a threat to the Stalinist state. Yet it failed to conform to the official style of socialist realism and thus was suppressed with a host of other works during Zhdanov's brutal cultural purge. *(Source: Sovfoto)*

discouraging hard work and initiative. Moreover, Stalin's belligerent foreign policy had led directly to a strong Western alliance, which isolated and contained the Soviet Union.

On the question of just how much change should be permitted, the Communist leadership was badly split. Conservatives wanted to make as few changes as possible. Reformers, who were led by Nikita Khrushchev, argued for major innovations. Khrushchev (1894–1971), who had joined the party as an uneducated coal miner in 1918 at twenty-four and had risen steadily to a high-level position in the 1930s, was emerging as the new ruler by 1955.

To strengthen his position and that of his fellow reformers within the party, Khrushchev launched an all-out attack on Stalin and his crimes at a closed session of the Twentieth Party Congress in 1956. In gory detail he described to the startled Communist delegates how Stalin had tortured and murdered thousands of loyal Communists, how he had trusted Hitler completely and bungled the country's defense, and how he had "supported the glorification of his own person with all conceivable methods." Khrushchev's "secret speech" was read to Communist party meetings throughout the country and it strengthened the reform movement.

The liberalization—or "de-Stalinization," as it was called in the West—of the Soviet Union was genuine. The Communist party jealously maintained its monopoly on political power, but

Khrushchev shook up the party and brought in new members. The economy was made more responsive to the needs of the people as some resources were shifted from heavy industry and the military toward consumer goods and agriculture. Stalinist controls over workers were relaxed. The Soviet Union's very low standard of living finally began to improve and continued to rise throughout the booming 1960s. By 1970 Soviet citizens were able to buy twice as much food, three times as much clothing, and twelve times as many appliances as in 1950.

De-Stalinization created great ferment among writers and intellectuals who hungered for cultural freedom. The poet Boris Pasternak (1890–1960) finished his great novel *Doctor Zhivago* in 1956. Published in the West but not in Russia, *Doctor Zhivago* is both a literary masterpiece and a powerful challenge to communism. It tells the story of a prerevolutionary intellectual who rejects the violence and brutality of the revolution of 1917 and the Stalinist years. Even as he is destroyed, he triumphs because of his humanity and Christian spirit. Pasternak was denounced—but he was not shot. Other talented writers followed Pasternak's lead, and courageous editors let the sparks fly.

The writer Alexander Solzhenitsyn (b. 1918) created a sensation when his *One Day in the Life of Ivan Denisovich* was published in the Soviet Union in 1962. Solzhenitsyn's novel portrays in grim detail life in a Stalinist concentration camp—a life to which Solzhenitsyn himself had been unjustly condemned—and is a damning indictment of the Stalinist past.

Khrushchev also de-Stalinized Soviet foreign policy. "Peaceful coexistence" with capitalism was possible, he argued, and great wars were not inevitable. Khrushchev made positive concessions, agreeing in 1955 to real independence for a neutral Austria after ten long years of Allied occupation. Thus there was considerable relaxation of cold war tensions between 1955 and 1957. At the same time, Khrushchev began wooing the new nations of Asia and Africa—even if they were not communist—with promises and aid.

De-Stalinization stimulated rebelliousness in the eastern European satellites. Having suffered in silence under Stalin, Communist reformers and the masses were quickly emboldened to seek much greater liberty and national independence. Poland took the lead in March 1956: riots there resulted in the release of more than nine thousand political prisoners, including the previously purged leader Wladyslaw Gomulka. Taking charge of the government, Gomulka skillfully managed to win greater autonomy for Poland while calming anti-Soviet feeling.

Hungary experienced a real and tragic revolution. Led by students and workers—the classic urban revolutionaries—the people of Budapest installed a liberal Communist reformer as their new chief in October 1956. Soviet troops were forced to leave the country. The new government promised free elections and renounced Hungary's military alliance with Moscow. As in 1849, the Russian leaders answered by invading Hungary with a large army and crushing, once again, a national, democratic revolution.

Fighting was bitter until the end, for the Hungarians hoped that the United States would fulfill its earlier propaganda promises and come to their aid. When this did not occur because of American unwillingness to risk a general war, most people in eastern Europe concluded that their only hope was to strive for small domestic gains while following Russia obediently in foreign affairs. This cautious approach produced some results, and east Europeans could hope for still greater freedom in the future.

Brezhnev and Stagnation

By late 1962, opposition in party circles to Khrushchev's policies was strong, and within two years Khrushchev fell in a bloodless palace revolution. Under Leonid Brezhnev (1906–1982), the Soviet Union began a period of stagnation and limited "re-Stalinization." The basic reason for this development was that Khrushchev's Communist colleagues saw de-Stalinization as a dangerous, two-sided threat. How could Khrushchev denounce the dead dictator without eventually denouncing and perhaps even arresting his still-powerful henchmen? In a heated secret debate in 1957, when the conservatives had tried without success to depose the menacing reformer, Khrushchev had pointed at two of Stalin's most devoted followers, Molotov and Kaganovich, and exclaimed: "Your hands are stained with the blood of our party leaders and of innumerable innocent Bolsheviks!" "So are yours!" Molotov and Kaganovich shouted back at him. "Yes, so are mine," Khrushchev replied. "I admit this. But during the purges I was merely carrying out your order. . . . I was not responsible. You were."[6] Moreover, the widening campaign of de-Stalinization posed a clear threat to the dictatorial authority of the party. It was producing growing, perhaps uncontrollable, criticism of the whole communist system. The party had to tighten up while there was still time. It was clear that Khrushchev had to go.

Another reason for conservative opposition was that Khrushchev's policy toward the West was erratic and ultimately unsuccessful. In 1958 he ordered the Western allies to evacuate West Berlin within six months. In response, the allies reaffirmed their unity, and Khrushchev backed down. Then in 1961, as relations with communist China deteriorated dramatically, Khrushchev ordered the East Germans to build a wall between East and West Berlin, thereby sealing off West Berlin in clear violation of existing access agreements between the Great Powers. The recently elected U.S. president, John F. Kennedy, acquiesced to the construction of the Berlin Wall. Emboldened and seeing a chance to change the balance of military power decisively, Khrushchev ordered missiles with nuclear warheads installed in Fidel Castro's communist Cuba in 1962. President Kennedy countered with a naval blockade of Cuba. After a tense diplomatic crisis, Khrushchev agreed to remove the Soviet missiles in return for American pledges not to disturb Castro's regime. Khrushchev looked like a bumbling buffoon; his influence, already slipping, declined rapidly after the Cuban fiasco.

After Brezhnev and his supporters took over in 1964, they started talking quietly of Stalin's "good points" and ignoring his crimes. This informed Soviet citizens that further liberalization could not be expected at home. Russian leaders, determined never to suffer Khrushchev's humiliation in the face of American nuclear superiority,

The End of Reform In August 1968 Soviet tanks rumbled into Prague to extinguish Czechoslovakian efforts to build a humane socialism. Here people watch the massive invasion from the sidewalks, knowing full well the suicidal danger of armed resistance. *(Source: Joseph Koudelka PP/Magnum)*

also launched a massive arms buildup. Yet Brezhnev and company proceeded cautiously in the mid-1960s.

In the wake of Khrushchev's reforms, the 1960s brought modest liberalization and more consumer goods to eastern Europe, as well as somewhat greater national autonomy, especially in Poland and Romania. In January 1968, the reform elements in the Czechoslovak Communist party gained a majority and voted out the long-time Stalinist leader in favor of Alexander Dubček (b. 1921), whose new government launched dramatic reforms.

Educated in Moscow, Dubček was a dedicated Communist. But he and his allies believed that they could reconcile genuine socialism with personal freedom and internal party democracy. Thus local decision making by trade unions, managers, and consumers replaced rigid bureaucratic planning. Censorship was relaxed, and the reform program proved enormously popular.

Although Dubček remembered the lesson of the Hungarian revolution and constantly proclaimed his loyalty to the Warsaw Pact, the determination of the Czech reformers to build what they called "socialism with a human face" created an acute political crisis in eastern Europe. Frightened hard-line Communists, especially in Poland and East Germany, knew full well that they lacked popular support. Moreover, the Soviet Union feared that a liberalized Czechoslovakia would eventually be drawn to neutralism or even to the democratic West. Thus the East bloc countries launched a concerted campaign of intimidation against the Czech leaders, and in August 1968, 500,000 Russian and allied eastern European troops suddenly occupied Czechoslovakia. The Czechs made no attempt to resist militarily, and the arrested Czech leaders were flown to Moscow, where they surrendered to Soviet demands. Gradually but inexorably, the reform program was abandoned and its supporters were removed from office. Thus the Czechoslovak experiment in humanizing communism was aborted.

Shortly after the invasion of Czechoslovakia, Brezhnev declared the so-called Brezhnev Doctrine, according to which the Soviet Union and its allies had the right to intervene in any socialist country whenever they saw the need. The occupation of Czechoslovakia and the ensuing Brezhnev Doctrine raised a storm of protest but did not seriously alter ongoing Western efforts to achieve better relations with the East bloc countries. The reason was simple. The West considered Czechoslovakia to be part of the Soviet sphere of influence, and it believed that change in eastern Europe could only continue to follow developments in the Soviet Union.

The 1968 invasion of Czechoslovakia was the crucial event of the Brezhnev era, which really lasted beyond the aging leader's death in 1982 until the emergence in 1985 of Mikhail Gorbachev. The invasion demonstrated unmistakably the intense conservatism of the Soviet Union's predominately Russian leaders and the determination of the ruling elite to maintain the status quo in the Soviet bloc. That determination resulted in further re-Stalinization of the Soviet Union, though with collective rather than personal dictatorship and without uncontrolled terror. Thus 1968, like 1848, was a fatal year in European history. It brought revolution and repression in both Czechoslovakia and France, and it marked the end of an era for the entire continent.

The compromise inherent in limited re-Stalinization seemed to suit the Soviet leaders and a majority of the Soviet people, and the Soviet Union appeared quite stable in the 1970s and early 1980s. A rising standard of living for ordinary people contributed to stability, although the economic difficulties of the 1970s markedly slowed the rate of improvement, and long lines and innumerable shortages persisted. The enduring differences between the life of the elite and the life of ordinary people also reinforced the system. In order to gain access to special, well-stocked stores, attend special schools, and travel abroad, ambitious individuals still had tremendous incentive to do as the state wished.

Another source of stability was that ordinary citizens in the Russian heartland remained more intensely nationalistic than almost any other people in the world. Party leaders successfully identified themselves with this patriotism, stressing their role in saving the motherland during the Second World War and protecting it now from foreign foes, including eastern European "counterrevolutionaries." Moreover, the politically dominant Great Russians, who are concentrated in central Russia and in Siberia—formally designated the Russian Federation—and who held through the Communist party the commanding leadership

MAP 36.4 Soviet Peoples   Encompassing one-sixth of the earth's land mass, the enormous Soviet Union contained many ethnic groups and fifteen separate republics. The Great Russians dominated the Communist party and the entire country, but they represented less than half of the total population. As Mikhail Gorbachev's reforms undermined the pervasive control of the Communist party, nationalists in the various republics called increasingly for genuine autonomy and even independence.

positions in the non-Russian republics, constituted only half of the total Soviet population. The Great Russian leaders generally feared that greater freedom and open political competition might result in demands for autonomy and even independence, not only by eastern European nationalities but by non-Russian nationalities within the Soviet Union itself (Map 36.4). Thus Western-style liberalism and democracy appeared as alien and divisive political philosophies that would undermine Russia's power and achievements.

The strength of the government was expressed in the re-Stalinization of culture and art. Free ex-

pression and open protest disappeared. Modest acts of open nonconformity and protest were severely punished—but with sophisticated, cunning methods. Most frequently, dissidents were blacklisted and thus rendered unable to find a decent job, for the government was the only employer. This fate was enough to keep most in line. The more determined but unrenowned protesters were quietly imprisoned in jails or mental institutions. Celebrated nonconformists such as Solzhenitsyn were permanently expelled from the country. Thus the worst aspects of Stalin's totalitarianism were eliminated, but a self-perpetuating Communist elite maintained its monopoly on the instruments of power.

Yet beneath the immobility of political life in the Brezhnev era, the Soviet Union experienced profound changes. As a perceptive British journalist put it in 1986, "The country went through a social revolution while Brezhnev slept."[7] Three aspects of this revolution, which was appreciated by few Western observers at the time, were particularly significant.

First, the growth of the urban population, which had raced forward at breakneck speed in the Stalin years, continued rapidly in the 1960s and 1970s. In 1985 two-thirds of all Soviet citizens lived in cities, and one-fourth lived in big cities (see Map 36.4). Of great significance, this expanding urban population lost its old peasant ways. As a result, it acquired more education, better job skills, and greater sophistication.

Second, the number of highly trained scientists, managers, and specialists expanded prodigiously, jumping fourfold between 1960 and 1985. Thus the class of well-educated, pragmatic, and self-confident experts, which played such an important role in restructuring industrial societies after the Second World War (see pages 1182–1183), developed rapidly in the Soviet Union.

Finally, education and freedom for experts in their special areas helped foster the growth of Soviet public opinion. Educated people read, discussed, and formed definite ideas about social questions. Developing definite ideas on such things as environmental pollution or urban transportation, educated urban people increasingly saw themselves as worthy of having a voice in society's decisions, even its political decisions. This, too, was part of the quiet transformation that set the stage for the dramatic reforms of the Gorbachev era.

Newly Elected President Mikhail Gorbachev vowed in his acceptance speech before the Supreme Soviet, the U.S.S.R.'s parliament, to assume "all responsibility" for the success or failure of perestroika. Previous parliaments were no more than tools of the Communist party, but this one has actively debated and frequently opposed government programs. *(Source: Vlastimir Shone/ Gamma-Liaison)*

The Gorbachev Era

Fundamental change in Russian history has often come in short, intensive spurts, which contrast vividly with long periods of immobility. Four of these spurts were the ambitious "Westernization" of Peter the Great in the early eighteenth century (see pages 637–639), the great reforms connected with the freeing of the serfs in the mid-nineteenth century (pages 942–943), the Russian Revolution of 1917 (pages 1054–1060), and Stalin's wrenching "revolution from above" in the 1930s (pages 1138–1142). To this select list of decisive transformations must be added the era of fundamental reforms launched by Mikhail Gorbachev in 1985. Gorbachev's reforms have already had a profound impact, and they have permitted democracy and national self-determination to triumph spectacularly in the old satellite empire.

The Soviet Union's Communist elite seemed secure in the early 1980s, as far as any challenge from below was concerned. The long-established system of administrative controls continued to stretch downward from the central ministries and state committees to provincial cities and from there to factories, neighborhoods, and villages. At each level of this massive state bureaucracy, the overlapping hierarchy of the Communist party, with its 17.5 million members, continued to watch over all decisions and manipulate every aspect of national life. Organized opposition was impossible, and average people simply left politics to the bosses.

The massive state and party bureaucracy was a mixed blessing. It safeguarded the elite, but it promoted apathy in the masses. Discouraging personal initiative and economic efficiency, it was ill suited to secure the effective cooperation of the rapidly growing class of well-educated urban experts. Therefore, when the ailing Brezhnev finally died in 1982, his successor introduced modest reforms to improve economic performance and to combat worker absenteeism and high-level corruption. Little came of these efforts, but they combined with a worsening economic situation to set the stage for the emergence in 1985 of Mikhail Gorbachev (b. 1931), the most vigorous Soviet leader since Stalin.

Gorbachev was smart, charming, and tough. As long-time Soviet foreign minister Andrei Gromyko reportedly said, "This man has a nice smile, but he has got iron teeth."[8] In his first year in office, Gorbachev attacked corruption and incompetence in the upper reaches of the bureaucracy, and he consolidated his power by packing the top level of the party with his supporters. He attacked alcoholism and drunkenness, which were deadly scourges of Soviet society. More basically, he elaborated a series of reform policies designed to revive and even remake the vast Soviet Union.

The first set of reform policies was designed to transform and restructure the economy, which was falling ever further behind the economy of the West and failing to provide for the very real needs of the Soviet population. To accomplish this economic restructuring—this *perestroika*—Gorbachev and his supporters permitted freer prices, more independence for state enterprises, and the setting up of profit-seeking private cooperatives to provide personal services. These reforms initially produced some improvements, but shortages then grew as the economy stalled at an intermediate point between central planning and free-market mechanisms. By 1990 Gorbachev's timid economic initiatives had met with very little success, eroding his support and that of the Communist party.

Gorbachev's bold and far-reaching campaign "to tell it like it is" was much more successful. Very popular in a country where censorship, dull uniformity, and outright lies had long characterized public discourse, the newfound openness—the *glasnost*—of the government and the media marked an astonishing break with the past. A disaster like the Chernobyl nuclear-reactor accident, which devastated part of the Ukraine and showered Europe with radioactive fallout, was investigated and reported with honesty and painstaking thoroughness. The works of long-banned and vilified Russian émigré writers sold millions of copies in new editions, and denunciations of Stalin and his terror became standard fare in plays and movies. Openness in government pronouncements led rather quickly to something approaching free speech and free expression, a veritable cultural revolution.

Democratization was the third element of Gorbachev's reform. Beginning as an attack on corruption in the Communist party and as an attempt to bring the class of educated experts into the decision-making process, it led to the first free elections in the Soviet Union since 1917. Gorbachev and the party remained in control, but a minority of critical independents were elected in April 1989 to a revitalized Congress of People's Deputies. Many top-ranking Communists who ran unopposed saw themselves defeated as a majority of angry voters struck their names from the ballot. Millions of Soviets then watched the new congress for hours on television as Gorbachev and his ministers saw their proposals debated and even rejected.

Democratization also encouraged demands for greater autonomy by non-Russian minorities—demands that certainly went beyond what Gorbachev had envisaged. In April 1989 troops with sharpened shovels charged into a rally of Georgian separatists in Tbilisi and left twenty dead. But whereas China's Communist leaders brutally massacred similar prodemocracy demonstrators in Beijing (Peking) in June 1989 and reimposed rigid authoritarian rule, Gorbachev drew back from

MAP 36.5 Democratic Movements in Eastern Europe, 1989 With Gorbachev's repudiation of the Brezhnev Doctrine, the desire for freedom and democracy spread throughout eastern Europe. Countries that had been satellites in the orbit of the Soviet Union began to set themselves free to establish their own place in the universe of free nations.

repression. Thus nationalist demands continued to grow in the non-Russian Soviet republics, an unexpected consequence of democratization.

Finally, the Soviet leader brought "new political thinking" to the field of foreign affairs—and he acted on it. He withdrew Soviet troops from Afghanistan (see page 1203), encouraged reform movements in Poland and Hungary, and sought to reduce East-West tensions. Of enormous historical importance, Gorbachev pledged to respect the political choices of the peoples of eastern Europe, and he thereby repudiated the Brezhnev Doctrine, which had proclaimed the right of the Soviet

Union and its allies to intervene at will in eastern Europe. By 1989 it seemed that if Gorbachev held to his word, the tragic Soviet occupation of eastern Europe might wither away, taking the long cold war with it.

The Revolutions of 1989

Instead, history accelerated, and 1989 brought a series of largely peaceful revolutions throughout eastern Europe (Map 36.5). These revolutions overturned existing communist regimes and led to the formation of provisional governments dedicated to democratic elections, human rights, and national rejuvenation. The face of eastern Europe changed dramatically, almost overnight.

Solidarity and the Polish people led the way. Poland was an unruly satellite from the beginning, and Stalin said that introducing communism to Poland was like putting a saddle on a cow. Efforts to saddle the cow—really a spirited stallion—had led to widespread riots in 1956. As a result, the Polish Communists dropped efforts to impose Soviet-style collectivization on the peasants and to break the Roman Catholic church. With an independent agriculture and a vigorous church, the Communists failed to monopolize society.

They also failed to manage the economy effectively, and bureaucratic incompetence coupled with worldwide recession put the economy into a nose dive by the mid-1970s. Then the "Polish miracle" occurred: Cardinal Karol Wojtyla, archbishop of Cracow, was elected pope and in June 1979 he returned to his native land to preach the love of Christ and country and the "inalienable rights of man." Pope John Paul II electrified the Polish nation, and the economic crisis became a spiritual crisis as well.

In August 1980, scattered strikes snowballed into a working-class revolt. Led by a feisty electrician and devout Catholic named Lech Walesa, the workers organized a free and democratic trade union that they called "Solidarity." Solidarity became the union of the nation, and cultural and intellectual freedom blossomed in Poland. But Solidarity did not try to take power in 1981. History, the Brezhnev Doctrine, and virulent attacks from communist neighbors all seemed to guarantee the intervention of the Red Army and a terrible blood bath if Solidarity directly challenged the Communist monopoly of political power with a general strike. Then, as economic hardship increased, grassroots radicalism and frustration mounted: a hunger-march banner proclaimed that "A hungry nation can eat its rulers."[9] With an eye on Western public opinion, the Polish Communist leadership shrewdly denounced Solidarity for promoting economic collapse and provoking Soviet invasion. The

The Rise of Solidarity This photograph shows the determination and mass action that allowed Polish workers to triumph in August 1980. Backed by a crowd of enthusiastic supporters, leader Lech Walesa announces the historic Gdansk Agreement to striking workers at the main gate of the Lenin Shipyards. *(Source: Jean Gaumy/Magnum)*

Communist leader General Wojciech Jaruzelski suddenly proclaimed martial law in December 1981, arresting Solidarity's leaders and "saving" the nation.

Outlawed and driven underground, Solidarity fought successfully to maintain its organization and to voice the aspirations of the Polish masses. Thus popular support for outlawed Solidarity remained strong and deep under martial law in the 1980s, preparing the way for its resurgence at the end of the decade.

By 1988 widespread labor unrest, raging inflation, and the outlawed Solidarity's refusal to cooperate with the military government had brought Poland to the brink of economic collapse. Profiting from Gorbachev's tolerant attitude and skillfully mobilizing its forces, Solidarity pressured Poland's frustrated Communist leaders into another round of negotiations that might work out a sharing of power to resolve the political stalemate and the economic depression. The subsequent agreement legalized Solidarity again and declared that a large minority of representatives to the Polish parliament would be chosen by free elections in June 1989. The Communist party was still guaranteed a majority, but Solidarity won every single contested seat in an overwhelming victory. On July 4, 1989, Solidarity members jubilantly entered the 460-member Polish parliament, the first freely elected opposition in a communist country. A month later the editor of Solidarity's weekly newspaper was sworn in as the first noncommunist leader in eastern Europe since Stalin had used Soviet armies to impose his system there after the Second World War.

Hungary followed Poland. Hungary's Communist boss, János Kádár, had permitted liberalization of the rigid planned economy after the 1956 upris-

Celebrating on the Berlin Wall   In a year filled with powerful images, none was more dramatic or more hopeful than the opening of the Berlin Wall, symbol of the harsh division between Eastern and Western Europe. *(Source: Tom Haley/SIPA-PRESS)*

ing, in exchange for political obedience and continued Communist control. In May 1988, in an effort to hang on to power by granting modest political concessions, the party replaced Kádár with a reform Communist. But growing popular resistance rejected piecemeal progress, forcing the Communist party to renounce one-party rule and schedule free elections for early 1990. Welcoming Western investment and moving rapidly toward multiparty democracy, Hungarians gleefully tore down the barbed-wire "iron curtain" that separated Hungary and Austria and opened their border to East German refugees.

As thousands of dissatisfied East Germans began pouring into Hungary, before going on to immediate resettlement in thriving West Germany, growing economic dislocation and huge candlelight demonstrations brought revolution in East Berlin. The Berlin Wall was opened, and people danced for joy atop that grim symbol of the prison state. East Germany's aging Communist leaders were swept aside and in some cases arrested. General elections were scheduled for March 1990. Subsequently, a conservative-liberal "Alliance for Germany," which was closely tied to West German Chancellor Helmut Kohl's Christian Democrats, defeated the East German Social Democrats (the Communists ignominiously fell to minor-party status). The Alliance for Germany quickly negotiated an economic union on favorable terms with Chancellor Kohl, and in July 1990 a historic agreement between Kohl and Gorbachev removed the last obstacles to German unification, which came in October 1990. Communism also died in Czechoslovakia in December 1989, in an almost good-humored ousting of Communist bosses in ten short days.

Only in Romania was revolution violent and bloody. There the iron-fisted Communist dictator, Nicolae Ceauşescu, had long combined Stalinist brutality with stubborn independence from Moscow. Faced with mass protests, Ceauşescu, alone among eastern European bosses, ordered his ruthless security forces to slaughter thousands, thereby sparking a classic armed uprising. After Ceauşescu's forces were defeated, the tyrant and his wife were captured and executed by a military court. A coalition government emerged from the fighting, although the legacy of Ceauşescu's oppression left a troubled country with an uncertain political future.

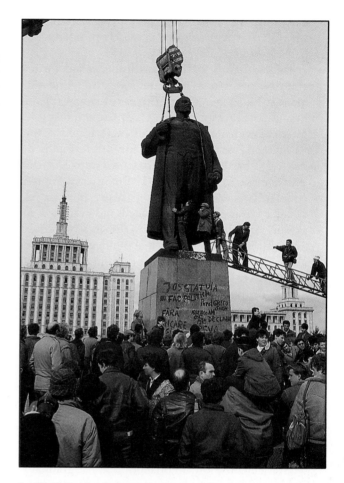

In Bucharest's Palace Square, cranes remove the statue of Lenin that dominated the square during the dictatorship of Nicolae Ceauşescu. Despite Ceauşescu's vow that democratic reform would come to Romania "when pears grow on poplar trees," citizens joined in a mass revolt to topple the despot and his oppressive regime. *(Source: BI/Gamma-Liaison)*

As the 1990s began, the revolutionary changes that Gorbachev had permitted, and even encouraged, had triumphed in all but two eastern European states: tiny Albania and the vast Soviet Union itself. The great question then became whether the Soviet Union would follow its former satellites, and whether reform communism would give way there to a popular anticommunist revolution. Near civil war between Armenians and Azerbaijanis in the Caucasus, assertions of independence in the Baltic states, including Lithuania's bold declaration of national sovereignty, and growing dissatisfaction among the Great Russian masses were all parts of a fluid, unstable political situation (see Map 36.4). Increasingly, the reform-minded Gorbachev stood as a besieged moderate.

As competing Russian politicians called for an end to communist rule and as nationalists demanded independence in the non-Russian republics of the Soviet Union, the Communist old guard also challenged Gorbachev. Defeated at the Communist party congress in July 1990, a gang of desperate hardliners tried to seize control of the government in August 1991. But the attempted coup collapsed in the face of massive popular resistance. Gorbachev was rescued and returned to power. An anticommunist revolution swept Russia. Although uncertainties abounded, it seemed clear that the peoples of the once-unified Soviet Union were making great progress toward personal freedom, national self-determination, and political democracy, a most surprising development in full accord with the noblest traditions of Western society.

THE WESTERN HEMISPHERE

One way to think of what historians used to call the "New World" is as a vigorous offshoot of Western civilization, an offshoot that has gradually developed its own characteristics while retaining European roots. From this perspective can be seen many illuminating parallels and divergences in the histories of Europe and the Americas. After the Second World War, the Western Hemisphere experienced a many-faceted recovery, somewhat similar to that of Europe though it began earlier, especially in Latin America. And when the postwar era drew to a close, the countries of the New World began to experience their own crises.

Postwar Prosperity in the United States

The Second World War cured the depression in the United States and brought about the greatest boom in American history. Unemployment practically vanished and personal income doubled as the well-being of Americans increased dramatically. Despite fears that peace would bring renewed depression, conversion to a peacetime economy went smoothly. The U.S. economy then proceeded to advance fairly steadily for a long generation.

Prosperity helps explain why postwar domestic politics consisted largely of modest adjustments to the status quo until the 1960s. Truman's upset victory in 1948 demonstrated that Americans had no interest in undoing Roosevelt's social and economic reforms. The Congress proceeded to increase social security benefits, subsidize middle- and lower-class housing, and raise the minimum wage. These and other liberal measures consolidated the New Deal. In 1952 the Republican party and the voters turned to General Dwight D. Eisenhower (1890–1969), a national hero and self-described moderate.

The federal government's only major new undertaking during the Eisenhower years (1952–1960) was the interstate highway system, a suitable symbol of the basic satisfaction of the vast majority. Some Americans feared that the United States was becoming a "blocked society," obsessed with stability and incapable of wholesome change. This feeling contributed in 1960 to the election of the young John F. Kennedy (1917–1963), who promised to "get the country moving again." President Kennedy captured the popular imagination, revitalized the old Roosevelt coalition, and modestly expanded existing liberal legislation before he was struck down by an assassin's bullet in 1963.

The Civil Rights Revolution

Belatedly and reluctantly, complacent postwar America experienced a genuine social revolution: after a long struggle, blacks (and their white supporters) threw off a deeply entrenched system of segregation, discrimination, and repression. This civil rights movement advanced on several fronts. Eloquent lawyers from the National Association for the Advancement of Colored People (NAACP) challenged school segregation in the courts. In 1954 they won a landmark decision in the Supreme Court: "separate educational facilities are inherently unequal." Blacks effectively challenged institutionalized inequality with bus boycotts, sit-ins, and demonstrations. As civil rights leader Martin Luther King, Jr. (1929–1968), told the white power structure, "We will not hate you, but we will not obey your evil laws."[10]

In key northern states blacks used their growing political power to gain the support of the liberal wing of the Democratic party. A liberal landslide

The March on Washington   in August 1963 marked a dramatic climax in the civil rights struggle. More than 200,000 people gathered at the Lincoln Memorial to hear the young Martin Luther King, Jr., deliver his greatest address, his "I have a dream" speech. *(Source: Francis Miller, LIFE MAGAZINE © Time Warner Inc.)*

elected Lyndon Johnson (1908–1973) president in 1964. The Civil Rights Act of 1964 categorically prohibited discrimination in public services and on the job. In the follow-up Voting Rights Act of 1965, the federal government firmly guaranteed all blacks the right to vote. By the 1970s, substantial numbers of blacks had been elected to public and private office throughout the southern states, proof positive that dramatic changes had occurred in American race relations.

Blacks enthusiastically supported new social legislation in the mid-1960s. President Johnson solemnly declared "unconditional war on poverty." Congress and the administration created a host of antipoverty projects, such as a domestic peace corps, free preschools for poor children, and community-action programs. Although these programs were directed to all poor Americans—the majority of whom were white—they were also intended to increase economic equality for blacks.

Thus the United States promoted in the mid-1960s the kind of fundamental social reform that western Europe had embraced immediately after the Second World War. The United States became more of a welfare state, as government spending for social benefits rose dramatically and approached European levels.

The Vietnam Trauma and Beyond

President Johnson wanted to go down in history as a master reformer and a healer of old wounds. Instead he opened new ones with the Vietnam War.

American involvement in Vietnam had its origins in the cold war and the ideology of containment (see page 1174). From the late 1940s on, most Americans and their leaders viewed the world in terms of a constant struggle to stop the spread of communism. As Europe began to revive and

China established a communist government in 1949, efforts to contain communism shifted to Asia. The bloody Korean War (1950–1953) ended in stalemate, but the United States did succeed in preventing a communist government in South Korea. After the defeat of the French in Indochina in 1954, the Eisenhower administration refused to sign the Geneva accords that temporarily divided the country into two zones pending national unification by means of free elections. President Eisenhower then acquiesced in the refusal of the anticommunist South Vietnamese government to accept the verdict of elections and provided it with military aid. President Kennedy greatly increased the number of American "military advisers" to sixteen thousand and had the existing South Vietnamese leader deposed in 1963 when he refused to follow American directives.

After successfully depicting his opponent, Barry Goldwater, as a trigger-happy extremist in a nuclear age and resoundingly winning the 1964 election on a peace platform, President Johnson greatly expanded the American role in the Vietnam conflict. As Johnson explained to his ambassador in Saigon, "I am not going to lose Vietnam. I am not going to be the President who saw Southeast Asia go the way China went."[11] American strategy was to "escalate" the war sufficiently to break the will of the North Vietnamese and their southern allies without resorting to "overkill" that might risk war with the entire communist bloc. Thus South Vietnam received massive military aid; American forces in the South gradually grew to a half-million men; and the United States bombed North Vietnam with ever-greater intensity. But there was no invasion of the North, nor did the United States dare to interrupt the seaborne shipment of military supplies from the Soviet Union to the North. In the end, the American strategy of savage but limited warfare backfired. It was the Americans themselves who grew weary and the American leadership that cracked.

The undeclared war in Vietnam, fought nightly on American television, eventually divided the United States in a great political battle. Initial support was strong, but by 1967 a growing number of critics denounced the war as an immoral and unsuccessful intrusion into a complex and distant civil war. There were major protests, often led by college students. Criticism reached a crescendo after the Vietcong "Tet Offensive" in January 1968.

This, the communists' first major attack with conventional weapons on major cities, failed militarily but showed that the communist forces in South Vietnam were still strong. U.S. critics of the Vietnam War interpreted the bloody battle as proof that a Vietcong victory was inevitable. America's leaders lost heart. In 1968, after an ambiguous defeat in the New Hampshire primary, President Johnson called for negotiations with North Vietnam and announced that he would not stand for re-election.

Elected by a razor-slim margin in 1968, President Richard Nixon (b. 1913) sought to gradually disengage America from Vietnam and the accompanying national crisis. Intensifying the continuous bombardment of the enemy while simultaneously pursuing peace talks with the North Vietnamese, Nixon cut American forces in Vietnam from 550,000 to 24,000 in four years. The cost of the war dropped dramatically. Moreover, President Nixon launched a flank attack in diplomacy. He journeyed to China in 1972 and reached a spectacular if limited reconciliation with the People's Republic of China. This reconciliation took advantage of China's growing fears of the Soviet Union and undermined North Vietnam's position. In January 1973, fortified by the overwhelming endorsement of the voters in his 1972 electoral triumph, President Nixon and Secretary of State Henry Kissinger finally reached a peace agreement with North Vietnam. The agreement allowed remaining American forces to complete their withdrawal, and the United States reserved the right to resume bombing if the accords were broken. South Vietnamese forces seemed to hold their own, and the storm of crisis in the United States seemed past.

On the contrary, the country reaped the Watergate whirlwind. Like some other recent American presidents, Nixon authorized spying activities that went beyond the law. Going further than his predecessors, Nixon authorized special units to use various illegal means to stop the leaking of government documents to the press. One such group broke into the Democratic party headquarters in Washington's Watergate complex in June 1972 and was promptly arrested. Nixon and many of his assistants then tried to hush up the bungled job, but the media and the machinery of congressional investigation eventually exposed the administration's web of lies and lawbreaking. In 1974 a beleaguered Nixon was forced to resign in disgrace.

The consequences of renewed political crisis flowing from the Watergate affair were profound. First, Watergate resulted in a major shift of power away from the presidency toward Congress, especially in foreign affairs. Therefore, as American aid to South Vietnam diminished in 1973 and as an emboldened North Vietnam launched a general invasion against South Vietnamese armies in early 1974, first President Nixon and then his successor, President Gerald Ford (b. 1913), stood by because Congress refused to permit any American military response. After more than thirty-five years of battle, the Vietnamese communists unified their country in 1975 as a fledgling totalitarian state—a second consequence of the U.S. crisis. Third, in the wake of Watergate, the belated fall of South Vietnam—generally seen as a disastrous American military defeat—shook America's postwar pride and confidence. The Vietnam aftermath left the United States divided and uncertain about its proper role in world affairs. The postwar belief in worldwide containment of communism was seriously damaged, but no alternative concept generated general support in the 1970s.

One possibility was the policy of *détente*, or progressive relaxation of cold war tensions. Nixon's phased withdrawal from Vietnam was part of détente, which reached its apogee when all European nations (except isolationist Albania), the United States, and Canada signed the Final Act of the Helsinki Conference in 1975. Thirty-five nations agreed that Europe's existing political frontiers could not be changed by force, and they solemnly accepted numerous provisions guaranteeing the human rights and political freedoms of their citizens.

Optimistic hopes for détente in international relations gradually faded in the later 1970s. Brezhnev's Soviet Union ignored the human rights provisions of the Helsinki agreement, and East-West political competition remained very much alive outside Europe. Many Americans became convinced that the Soviet Union was taking advantage of détente, steadily building up its military might and pushing for political gains in Africa, Asia, and Latin America. The Soviet invasion of Afghanistan in December 1979, which was designed to save an increasingly unpopular Marxist regime, was especially alarming. Many Americans feared that the

oil-rich states of the Persian Gulf would be next, and they looked again to the Atlantic alliance and military might to contain communist expansion.

President Jimmy Carter (b. 1924), elected in 1976, tried to lead the Atlantic alliance beyond verbal condemnation, but among the European allies only Great Britain supported the American policy of economic sanctions. The alliance showed the same lack of concerted action when Solidarity rose in Poland. Some observers concluded that the alliance had lost the will to think and act decisively in dealings with the Soviet bloc.

In fact, the Atlantic alliance, formed in the late 1940s to prevent further Soviet expansion in

Nixon in China, 1972 Shown here toasting U.S.–China friendship with Chinese Premier Chou En-lai in Peking in February 1972, President Nixon took advantage of Chinese fears of the Soviet Union to establish good relations with Asia's Communist giant. Arriving after twenty-five years of mutual hostility, reconciliation with China was Nixon's finest achievement. *(Source: John Dominis, LIFE MAGAZINE © Time Inc. 1972)*

Diego Rivera (1886–1957) was one of the great and committed painters of the Mexican Revolution. Rivera believed that art should reflect the "new order of things" and inspire the common people—the workers and the peasants. One of Rivera's many wall paintings, this vibrant central mural in the National Palace in Mexico City, depicts a brutal Spanish conquest and a liberating revolution. *(Source: Robert Frerck/Odyssey Productions)*

Europe, endured and remained true to its original purpose in the 1980s. The U.S. military build-up launched by Jimmy Carter in his last years in office was greatly accelerated by President Ronald Reagan (b. 1911), who was swept into office in 1980 by a wave of patriotism following an agonizing hostage crisis in Iran (see page 1233). The new American leadership acted as if the military balance had tipped in favor of the Soviet Union. Increasing defense spending enormously and starving social welfare programs, the Reagan administration concentrated especially on nuclear arms and an expanded navy as keys to American power in the post-Vietnam age. European governments reluctantly agreed to help strengthen NATO forces and to allow medium-range nuclear warheads on their soil.

Thus the Atlantic alliance bent, but it did not break in the 1980s. In doing so, the United States and its Western allies gave indirect support to ongoing efforts to liberalize authoritarian communist eastern Europe and probably helped convince Mikhail Gorbachev that endless cold war conflict was foolish and dangerous.

Economic Nationalism in Latin America

Although the countries of Latin America share a Spanish-Portuguese heritage, their striking differences make it difficult to generalize meaningfully about modern Latin American history. Yet a growing economic nationalism seems unmistakable. As the early nineteenth century saw Spanish and Portuguese colonies win wars of political independence, so has recent history been an ongoing quest for genuine economic independence through local control and industrialization.

To understand the rise of economic nationalism, one must remember that Latin American countries developed as producers of foodstuffs and raw materials that were exported to Europe and the United States in return for manufactured goods and capital investment. This exchange brought considerable economic development but exacted a heavy price: neocolonialism (see pages 1002–1004). Latin America became very dependent on foreign markets, products, and investments. Industry did not develop, and large landowners tied to production for the world market profited most from economic development and thus enhanced their social and political power.

The old international division of labor was finally destroyed by the Great Depression. Prices and exports of Latin American commodities collapsed as Europe and the United States drastically reduced their purchases and raised tariffs to protect domestic products. With their foreign sales plummeting, Latin American countries could not buy the industrial goods that they needed from abroad.

Latin America suffered the full force of the global depression. Especially in the largest Latin American countries—Argentina, Brazil, Chile, and Mexico—the result was a profound shift toward economic nationalism after 1930. The most popularly based governments worked to reduce foreign influence and gain control of their own economies and natural resources. They energetically promoted national industry by means of high tariffs, government grants, and even state enterprise. They favored the lower middle and urban working classes with social benefits and higher wages in order to increase their purchasing power and gain their support. These efforts at recovery gathered speed during the Second World War and were fairly successful. By the late 1940s, the factories of Argentina, Brazil, and Chile could generally satisfy domestic consumer demand for the products of light industry. In the 1950s, some countries began moving into heavy industry. Economic nationalism and the rise of industry are particularly striking in the two largest and most influential countries, Mexico and Brazil, which together account for half of the population of Latin America.

Mexico Overthrowing the elitist, upper-class rule of the tyrant Porfirio Díaz, the spasmodic, often-chaotic Mexican Revolution of 1910 culminated in 1917 in a new constitution. This radical nationalistic document called for universal suffrage, massive land reform, benefits for labor, and strict control of foreign capital. Actual progress was quite modest until 1934, when a charismatic young Indian from a poor family, Lazaro Cárdenas, became president and dramatically revived the languishing revolution. Under Cárdenas, many large estates were divided up among small farmers or returned undivided to Indian communities.

Meanwhile, state-supported Mexican businessmen built many small factories to meet domestic needs. The government also championed the cause of industrial workers. In 1938, when Mexican workers became locked in a bitter dispute with

British and American oil companies, Cárdenas nationalized the petroleum industry—to the amazement of a world unaccustomed to such bold action. Finally, the 1930s saw the flowering of a distinctive Mexican culture, which proudly embraced its long-despised Indian past and gloried in the modern national revolution.

In 1940 the official, semi-authoritarian party that has governed Mexico continuously since the revolution selected the first of a series of more moderate presidents. These presidents used the full power of the state to promote industrialization through a judicious mixture of public, private, and even foreign enterprise. Following the postwar trend in Europe and the United States, the Mexican economy grew rapidly, at about 6 percent per year from the early 1940s to the late 1960s. However, in Mexico, unlike Europe and the United States, the upper and middle classes reaped the lion's share of the benefits.

Brazil   After the fall of Brazil's monarchy in 1889 (see page 1000), politics was dominated by the coffee barons and by regional rivalries. These rivalries and deteriorating economic conditions allowed a military revolt led by Getulio Vargas, governor of one of Brazil's largest states, to seize control of the federal government in 1930. Vargas, who proved to be a consummate politician, fragmented the opposition and established a mild dictatorship that lasted until 1945. His rule was generally popular, combining effective economic nationalism and moderate social reform.

Vargas decisively tipped the balance of political power away from the Brazilian states to the ever-expanding federal government, which became a truly national government for the first time. Vargas and his allies also set out to industrialize Brazil and gain economic independence. While the national coffee board used mountains of surplus coffee beans to fire railroad locomotives, the government supported Brazilian manufacturers with high tariffs, generous loans, and labor peace. This probusiness policy did not prevent new social legislation: workers received shorter hours, pensions, health and accident insurance, paid vacations, and other benefits. Finally, Vargas shrewdly upheld the nationalist cause in his relations with the giant to the north. Brazil was modernizing rapidly.

Modernization continued for the next fifteen years. The economy boomed. Presidential politics was re-established, though the military kept a watchful eye for extremism among the civilian politicians. Economic nationalism was especially vigorous under the flamboyant President Juscelino Kubitschek. Between 1956 and 1960, the government borrowed heavily from international bankers to promote industry and built the new capital of Brasília in the midst of a wilderness. Kubitschek's slogan was "Fifty Years' Progress in Five," and he meant it.

The Brazilian and Mexican formula of national economic development, varying degrees of electoral competition, and social reform was shared by some other Latin American countries, notably Argentina and Chile. By the late 1950s, optimism was widespread, though cautious. Economic and social progress seemed to be bringing less violent, more democratic politics to the region. These expectations were shaken by the Cuban Revolution.

The Cuban Revolution

Although many aspects of the Cuban Revolution are obscured by controversy, certain background conditions are clear. First, achieving nominal independence in 1898 as a result of the Spanish-American War, Cuba was for many years virtually an American protectorate. The Cuban constitution gave the United States the legal right to intervene in Cuban affairs, a right that was frequently exercised until President Franklin Roosevelt renounced it in 1934. Second, and partly because the American army had often been the real power on the island, Cuba's political institutions were weak and Cuban politicians were extraordinarily corrupt. Third, Cuba was one of Latin America's most prosperous countries by the 1950s, but its sugar-and-tourist economy was completely dependent on the United States. Finally, the enormous differences between rich and poor in Cuba were typical of Latin America. But Cuba also had a strong Communist party, and that was highly unusual.

Fidel Castro (b. 1927), a magnetic leader with the gift of oratory, managed to unify all opposition elements in a revolutionary front, and his guerrilla forces triumphed in late 1958. Castro had promised a "real" revolution, and it soon became clear that "real" meant "communist." Wealthy Cubans fled to Miami, and the middle class began to follow. Cuban relations with the Eisenhower administration deteriorated rapidly. Thus, in April 1961, the newly elected U.S. president, John Kennedy, went ahead with a pre-existing CIA plan to use Cuban exiles to topple Castro. But the Kennedy administration abandoned the exiles as soon as they were put ashore at the Bay of Pigs, and the exiles were quickly captured.

The Bay of Pigs invasion—a triumph for Castro and a humiliating fiasco for the United States—had significant consequences. It freed Castro to build his version of a communist society. Political life in Cuba featured "anti-imperialism," an alliance with the Soviet bloc, the dictatorship of the party, and a Castro cult. Revolutionary enthusiasm was genuine among party activists, much of Cuba's youth, and some of the masses some of the time. Prisons and emigration silenced opposition. The economy was characterized by state ownership, collective farms, and Soviet trade and aid. Early efforts to industrialize ran aground, and sugar production continued to dominate the economy. Socially, the Castro regime pursued equality and the creation of a new socialist personality. In short, revolutionary totalitarianism came to the Americas.

The failure of the United States to derail Castro probably encouraged Khrushchev to start putting nuclear missiles in Cuba and in turn led directly to the most serious East-West crisis since the Korean War. The Soviets backed down (see page 1191), but Castro's survival had major consequences for Latin America. Above all, it heightened both hopes and fears that similar revolutions could spread throughout the region. In the United States, Castro aroused cold war fears of communism in Latin America. Using the Organization of American States to isolate Cuba, the United States in 1961 pledged $10 billion in aid over ten years to a new hemispheric "Alliance for Progress." The Alliance was intended to promote long-term economic development and social reform, which American liberals assumed would immunize the rest of Latin America from the Cuban disease.

Authoritarianism and Democracy in Latin America

U.S. aid contributed modestly to continued Latin American economic development in the 1960s, although population growth canceled out two-thirds of the increase on a per capita basis. Demo-

cratic social reforms—the other half of the Alliance for Progress formula—proceeded slowly, however. Instead, the era following the Cuban Revolution saw increasing conflict between leftist movements and ruling elites contending for power. In most countries the elites and their military allies won the struggle, imposing a new kind of conservative authoritarianism as their collective response to the social and economic crisis. By the late 1970s, only four Latin American countries—Costa Rica, Venezuela, Colombia, and Mexico—retained some measure of democratic government. Brazil, Argentina, and Chile represented the general trend.

Influential Brazil led the way. Intense political competition in the early 1960s prompted President João Goulart to swing to the left to gain fresh support. Castroism appeared to spread in the impoverished northeast, and mass meetings of leftists were answered by huge demonstrations of conservatives. Meanwhile Goulart called for radical change, proposing that the great landed estates be broken up and that Brazil's many illiterates receive the right to vote. When Goulart and his followers appeared ready to use force to implement their program, army leaders took over in 1964. The right-wing military government banned political parties and ruled by decree. Industrialization and urbanization went forward under military rule, but the gap between rich and poor widened as well.

In Argentina, the military had intervened in 1955 to oust the dictatorial populist and economic nationalist Juan Perón, but it had restored elected government. Then, worried by a Peronist revival and heartened by the Brazilian example, the army took control in 1966 and again in 1976 after a brief civilian interlude. Each military takeover was followed by an escalation of repression, and culturally and economically advanced Argentina became a brutal military dictatorship.

If events in Argentina were discouraging, those in Chile were tragic. Chile has a population of predominantly European origin and a long tradition of democracy and moderate reform. Thus when Salvador Allende, a doctor and the Marxist head of a coalition of Communists, Socialists, and Radicals, won a plurality of 36 percent of the vote in fair elections in 1970, he was duly elected president by the Congress. Allende completed the nationalization of the American-owned copper companies—the great majority of Chileans had already

Return to Democracy in Argentina Elected president in 1983 after seven years of increasingly brutal military rule, Raul Alfonsín stands with sash and rod—the symbols of authority—to swear the presidential oath of office in Buenos Aires. Alfonsín's inauguration gave rise to great popular rejoicing. *(Source: Urraca/Sygma)*

embraced economic nationalism—and proceeded to socialize private industry, accelerate the breakup of landed estates, and radicalize the poor.

Marxism in action evoked a powerful backlash in Chile. The middle class struck back, and by 1973 Chile seemed headed for civil war. Then, with widespread conservative support and strong U.S. backing, the traditionally impartial army struck in a well-organized coup. Allende died, probably murdered, and thousands of his supporters were arrested, or worse. As in Argentina, the military imposed a harsh despotism.

The revival of antidemocratic authoritarianism in Latin America challenged not only the Marxist and socialist program but most liberal and moderate reform as well. Thus military governments,

supported by Washington and local big business, effectively defended private capital and halted or reversed radical change. Yet some observers noted that the new military governments grew out of political crises that threatened national unity as well as the upper classes. In such circumstances, the politically conscious officer corps saw the military as the only institution capable of preventing chaos. Moreover, the new authoritarians were determined modernizers. Eager to catch up with the more advanced countries, they were often deeply committed to nationalism, industrialization, technology, and some modest social progress. They even promised free elections in the future.

That time came in the 1980s, when another democratic wave gained momentum throughout

Latin America. In South America the three Andean nations—Peru, Bolivia, and Ecuador—led the way with the re-establishment of elected governments, all of which were committed in varying degrees to genuine social reform. In Argentina, the military government gradually lost almost all popular support because of its "dirty war" against its own citizens, in which it imprisoned, tortured, and murdered thousands whom it arbitrarily accused of opposing the regime. In 1982, in a desperate gamble to rally the people around the nationalist flag, Argentina's military rulers sent nine thousand troops to seize the Falkland (or Malvinas) Islands (see Map 31.2, page 998) from Great Britain. But the British, led by the "iron lady," Prime Minister Margaret Thatcher, retook the islands in a brief war, routing Argentina's poorly led troops and forcing its humiliated generals to schedule national elections. Elected by an overwhelming majority in 1983, President Raul Alfonsín prosecuted former military rulers for their crimes, reformed the currency, and appeared to lay solid foundations for liberty and political democracy.

In 1985, the Brazilian military also turned over power to an elected government, thereby completing a peaceful transition begun in the late 1970s. Relatively successful in its industrialization effort, Brazil's military government had proved unable (or unwilling) to improve the social and economic position of the masses. After twenty-one years of rule, and with even Brazil's richest families calling for reforms to forestall social upheaval, the military leaders were ready to let civilian politicians have a try. Chile also turned from harsh military dictatorship to elected government. Thus Latin America entered the second half of the 1980s with 94 percent of its population living under civilian and constitutional regimes, and a major turn toward democracy and civil liberty appeared under way.

The most dramatic developments in Central America occurred in Nicaragua. In 1979, a broad coalition of liberals, socialists, and Marxist revolutionaries drove long-time dictator Anastasio Somoza from power. The Somoza family had relied on solid U.S. support in its four-decade dictatorship, and the new Sandinista government viewed the United States as an oppressive imperialist power. The new leaders wanted genuine political and economic independence from the United States, as well as throughgoing land reform, some state ownership of industry, and friendly ties with communist countries.

These policies infuriated the Reagan administration, which applied economic sanctions and tried everything short of sending American soldiers to overturn the Sandinista government. The Nicaraguan economy collapsed, and the popularity of the Sandinista government eventually declined. Then, after a decade of rule, the Sandinistas accepted free elections and stepped down when they were defeated by a coalition led by a winsome Violetta Chamorro.

Thus, as the 1990s opened, almost all of Latin America lived under civilian and constitutional governments seeking to mobilize the broad-based support that seemed necessary to deal effectively with the region's enduring economic and social problems.

SUMMARY

The postwar recovery of western Europe and the Americas was a memorable achievement in the long, uneven course of Western civilization. The transition from imperialism to decolonization proceeded rapidly, surprisingly smoothly, and without serious damage to western Europe. Genuine political democracy gained unprecedented strength in the West, and economic progress and social reforms improved the lives of ordinary citizens.

Postwar developments in eastern Europe displayed both similarities to and differences from developments in western Europe and the Americas. Perhaps the biggest difference was that Stalin imposed harsh one-party rule in the lands occupied by his armies, which was a critical factor in the onset of the long and bitter cold war. Nevertheless, the Soviet Union became more liberal and less dictatorial under Khrushchev, and the standard of living in the Soviet Union improved markedly in the 1950s and 1960s.

In the late 1960s and early 1970s, Europe and the Americas entered a new and turbulent time of crisis. Many nations, from France to Czechoslovakia and from Argentina to the United States, experienced major political difficulties, as social conflicts and ideological battles divided peoples and shook governments. Beginning with the oil shocks of the 1970s, severe economic problems added to the turmoil. Yet in western Europe and North America the welfare system held firm, and both democracy and the movement toward European unity successfully passed through the storm. Elsewhere the response to political and economic crisis sent many countries veering off toward repression, as the communist system in eastern Europe was tightened up in the Brezhnev years and a new kind of conservative authoritarianism arose in most of Latin America. Then, in the 1980s, both regions turned back toward free elections and civil liberties, most spectacularly so in the east European revolution of 1989. As the 1990s opened, differences in political organization and human rights were less pronounced in a reuniting Western civilization than at any time since the fateful opening of the First World War.

NOTES

1. Quoted in N. Graebner, *Cold War Diplomacy, 1945–1960* (Princeton, N.J.: Van Nostrand, 1962), p. 17.
2. Ibid.
3. Quoted in J. Hennessy, *Economic "Miracles"* (London: André Deutsch, 1964), p. 5.
4. Quoted in H. Smith, *The Russians* (New York: Quadrangle/New York Times, 1976), p. 303.
5. Quoted in D. Treadgold, *Twentieth Century Russia,* 5th ed. (Boston: Houghton Mifflin, 1981), p. 442.
6. Quoted in I. Deutscher, in *Soviet Society,* ed. A. Inkeles and K. Geiger (Boston: Houghton Mifflin, 1961), p. 41.
7. M. Walker, *The Waking Giant: Gorbachev's Russia* (New York: Pantheon Books, 1987), p. 175.
8. Quoted in *Time,* January 6, 1986, p. 66.
9. T. G. Ash, *The Polish Revolution: Solidarity* (New York: Scribner's, 1983), p. 186.
10. Quoted in S. E. Morison et al., *A Concise History of the American Republic* (New York: Oxford University Press, 1977), p. 697.
11. Ibid., p. 735.

SUGGESTED READING

An excellent way to approach wartime diplomacy is through the accounts of the statesmen involved. Great leaders and matchless stylists, both Winston Churchill and Charles de Gaulle have written histories of the war in the form of memoirs. Other interesting memoirs are those of Harry Truman (1958); Dwight Eisenhower, *Crusade in Europe* (1948); and Dean Acheson, *Present at the Creation* (1969), a beautifully written defense of American foreign policy in the early cold war. W. A. Williams, *The Tragedy of American Diplomacy* (1962), and W. La Feber, *America, Russia, and the Cold War* (1967), claim, on the contrary, that the United States was primarily responsible for the conflict with the Soviet Union. Two other important studies focusing on American policy are J. Gaddis, *The United States and the Origins of the Cold War* (1972), and D. Yergin, *Shattered Peace: The Origins of the Cold War and the National Security Council* (1977). A. Fontaine, a French journalist, provides a balanced general approach in his *History of the Cold War,* 2 vols. (1968). V. Mastny's thorough investigation of Stalin's war aims, *Russia's Road to the Cold War* (1979), is also recommended.

R. Mayne, *The Recovery of Europe, 1945–1973,* rev. ed. (1973), and N. Luxenburg, *Europe Since World War II,* rev. ed. (1979), are recommended general surveys, as are two other important works: W. Laqueur, *Europe Since Hitler,* rev. ed. (1982), and P. Johnson, *Modern Times: The World from the Twenties to the Eighties* (1983). T. White, *Fire in the Ashes* (1953), is a vivid view of European resurgence and Marshall Plan aid by an outstanding journalist. I. and D. Unger, *Postwar America: The United States Since 1945* (1989), and W. Leuchtenberg, *In the Shadow of FDR: From Harry Truman to Ronald Reagan,* rev. ed. (1989), discuss developments in the United States. Postwar economic and technological developments are analyzed in G. Ambrosius and W. Hibbard, *A Social and Economic History of Twentieth-Century Europe* (1989). A. Shonfield, *Modern Capitalism* (1965), provides an engaging, optimistic assessment of the growing importance of government investment and planning in European economic life. The culture and politics of protest are provocatively analyzed in H. Hughes, *Sophisticated Rebels: The Political Culture of European Dissent, 1968–1987* (1988), and W. Hampton, *Guerrilla Minstrels: John Lennon, Joe Hill, Woody Guthrie, Bob Dylan* (1986). Two outstanding works on France are J. Ardagh, *The New French Revolution* (1969), which puts the momentous social changes since 1945 in human terms, and D. L. Hanley et al., eds., *France: Politics and Society Since 1945* (1979). On Germany, H. Turner, *The Two Germanies Since 1945: East and West* (1987), and R. Dahrendorf, *Society and Democracy in Germany* (1971), are recommended. The spiritual dimension of West German recovery is probed by G. Grass in his world-famous novel *The Tin Drum* (1963); W. Laqueur, *The Germans* (1985), is a recent journalistic report by a well-known historian. A. Marwick, *British Society Since 1945* (1982), is good on postwar developments; P. Jenkins, *Mrs. Thatcher's Revolu-*

tion: The End of the Socialist Era (1988), is a provocative critique. Two outstanding books on the Vietnam War are N. Sheehan, *A Bright and Shining Lie: John Paul Vann and America in Vietnam* (1988), and A. Short, *The Origins of the Vietnam War* (1989).

H. Seton-Watson, *The East European Revolution* (1965), is a good history of the communization of eastern Europe, and S. Fischer-Galati, ed., *Eastern Europe in the Sixties* (1963), discusses major developments. P. Zinner, *Revolution in Hungary* (1962), is excellent on the tragic events of 1956. I. Svitak, *The Czechoslovak Experiment, 1968–1969* (1971), and Z. Zeman, *Prague Spring* (1969), are good on Czechoslovakia. T. Ash, *The Polish Revolution: Solidarity* (1983), is the best book on the subject, and M. Kaufman, *Mad Dreams, Saving Graces: Poland, a Nation in Conspiracy* (1989), is recommended. Z. Brzezinski, *The Soviet Bloc: Unity and Conflict* (1967), and J. Hough and M. Fainsod, *How the Soviet Union Is Governed* (1978), are important general studies. A. Amalrik, *Will the Soviet Union Survive Until 1984?* (1970), is a fascinating critique of Soviet history, and A. Lee, *Russian Journal* (1981), is a moving personal account of a young American woman. H. Smith has written two outstanding journalistic reports on the Soviet Union under Brezhnev and Gorbachev, *The Russians* (1976) and *The New Russians* (1990). Gorbachev's reforms are perceptively examined by Walker, *The Waking Giant,* cited in the Notes, and M. Lewin, *The Gorbachev Phenomenon: A Historical Interpretation* (1988).

R. von Albertini, *Decolonialization* (1971), is a good history of the decline and fall of European empires, a theme also considered in T. Vadney, *The World Since 1945* (1988), and H. van der Wee, *Prosperity and Upheaval: The World Economy, 1945–1980* (1986). Two excellent general studies on Latin America are J. E. Fagg, *Latin America: A General History,* 3d ed. (1977), and R. J. Shafer, *A History of Latin America* (1978). Both contain detailed suggestions for further reading. E. Burns, *A History of Brazil* (1970); M. Meyer and W. Sherman, *The Course of Mexican History* (1979); and B. Loveman, *Chile: The Legacy of Hispanic Capitalism* (1979), are recommended studies of developments in three leading nations. W. La Feber, *Inevitable Revolutions: The United States in Central America* (1983), is an important, quite critical assessment of U.S. support of neocolonial patterns in Central America.

37

Asia and Africa in the Contemporary World

Construction of Asia's longest river bridge, spanning the River Ganges in India

When future historians look back at our era, they are likely to be particularly struck by the epoch-making resurgence of Asia and Africa after the Second World War. They will try to explain the astonishingly rapid rise of new or radically reorganized Asian and African countries and their increasingly prominent role in world affairs.

- How did Asian and African countries reassert or establish their political independence in the postwar era?
- How in the postindependence world did leading states face up to the enormous challenges of nation building, challenges that were all the more difficult after the 1960s?

These are the questions that this chapter seeks to answer.

THE RESURGENCE OF EAST ASIA

In 1945 Japan and China, the two great powers of East Asia, lay exhausted and devastated. Japanese aggression had sown extreme misery in China and reaped an atomic whirlwind at Hiroshima and Nagasaki. The future looked bleak. Yet both nations recovered even more spectacularly than western Europe. In the course of recovery the two countries, closely linked since the 1890s, went their separate ways. As China under Mao Tse-tung (Mao Zedong) transformed itself into a strong, self-confident communist state, Japan under American occupation turned from military expansion to democracy and extraordinarily successful economic development. Not until the 1970s did the reborn giants begin moving somewhat closer together.

The Communist Victory in China

There were many reasons for the triumph of communism in China. As a noted historian has forcefully argued, however, "Japanese aggression was . . . the most important single factor in Mao's rise to power."[1] When Japanese armies advanced rapidly in 1938 (see page 1100), the Nationalist gov-

ernment of Chiang Kai-shek (Jiang Jieshi) moved its capital to Chungking, deep in the Chinese interior. The Japanese then occupied an area five hundred miles wide in northern and central China, and the war settled into stalemate in 1939. These wartime conditions enabled the Communists, aided by their uneasy "united front" alliance with the Nationalists, to build up their strength in guerrilla bases in the countryside behind Japanese lines. Mao Tse-tung, at the peak of his creative powers, avoided pitched battles and concentrated on winning peasant support and forming a broad anti-Japanese coalition. By reducing rents, enticing intellectuals, and spreading propaganda, Mao and the Communists emerged in peasant eyes as the true patriots, the genuine nationalists. And the promise of radical redistribution of the land strongly reinforced their appeal to poor peasants and landless laborers.

Meanwhile, the long war with Japan was exhausting the established government and its supporters. American generals were never satisfied with China's war effort, but in fact fully half of Japan's overseas armies were pinned down in China in 1945. Chiang Kai-shek's Nationalists had mobilized 14 million men, and a staggering 3 million Chinese soldiers had been killed or wounded. The war created massive Chinese deficits and runaway inflation, hurting morale and ruining lives.

When Japan suddenly collapsed in August 1945, Communists and Nationalists both rushed to seize evacuated territory. Heavy fighting broke out in Manchuria. The United States, which had steadfastly supported the Nationalists during the Second World War, tried unsuccessfully to work out a political compromise, but civil war resumed in earnest in April 1946. At first Chiang Kai-shek's more numerous Nationalists had the upper hand. Soon the better-led, more determined Communists rallied, and by 1948 the demoralized Nationalist forces were disintegrating. The following year Chiang Kai-shek and a million mainland Chinese fled to the island of Taiwan, and in October 1949 Mao Tse-tung proclaimed the People's Republic of China.

Within three years the Communists had succeeded in consolidating their rule. The Communist government seized the holdings of landlords and rich peasants—10 percent of the farm population had owned between 70 and 80 percent of the land—and distributed it to 300 million poor peasants and landless laborers. This revolutionary land reform was extremely popular. Although the Chinese Communists soon began pushing the development of socialist collectives, they did so less brutally than had the Soviets in the 1930s and retained genuine support in the countryside.

Meanwhile, the Communists were dealing harshly with their foes. Mao admitted in 1957 that 800,000 "class enemies" had been summarily liquidated between 1949 and 1954; the true figure is probably much higher. By means of mass arrests, forced-labor camps, and, more generally, re-education through relentless propaganda and self-criticism sessions, all visible opposition from the old ruling groups was destroyed.

Finally, Mao and the Communists reunited China's 550 million inhabitants in a strong centralized state. They laid claim to a new "Mandate of Heaven" and demonstrated that China was once again a great power. This was the real significance of China's participation in the Korean War. In 1950, when the American-led United Nations forces in Korea crossed the 38th parallel and appeared to threaten China's industrial base in Manchuria, the Chinese attacked, advanced swiftly, and fought the Americans to a bloody standstill on the Korean peninsula. This struggle against "American imperialism" mobilized the masses, and military success increased Chinese self-confidence.

Mao's China

Asserting Chinese power and prestige in the armed conflict with the United States, Mao and the party looked to the Soviet Union for inspiration in the early 1950s. Along with the gradual collectivization of agriculture, China adopted a typical Soviet five-year plan to develop large factories and heavy industry rapidly. Many Chinese plants were built by Russian specialists; Soviet economic aid was also considerable. The first five-year plan was successful, as were associated efforts to redirect higher education away from the liberal arts toward science and engineering.

A People's Court tries a case as local villagers follow the proceedings intently. The man on his knees is accused of selling a young girl living in his household, an old practice that has become a serious crime in revolutionary China. *(Source: Popperfoto)*

People remained very poor, but undeniable economic growth followed on the Communists' social revolution.

In the cultural and intellectual realms too, the Chinese followed the Soviet example. Basic civil and political rights, which had been seriously curtailed by the Nationalists, were simply abolished. Temples and churches were closed; all religion was persecuted. Freedom of the press died, and the government went to incredible lengths to control information. A Soviet-style puritanism took hold. To the astonishment of "old China hands," the Communists quickly eradicated the long-standing scourges of prostitution and drug abuse, which they had long regarded as humiliating marks of exploitation and national decline. More generally, the Communists enthusiastically promoted Soviet-Marxian ideas concerning women and the family. Full equality and freedom from housework and child care became primary goals. Work in fields and factories was hailed as a proud badge of women's liberation rather than a shameful sign of poverty. It became rather easy for a woman to get a divorce, although premarital chastity remained the accepted norm.

By the mid-1950s, the People's Republic of China seemed to be firmly set on the Marxist-Leninist course of development previously perfected in the Soviet Union. In 1958, however, China began to go its own way. Mao had always stressed revolutionary free will and peasant equality. Now he proclaimed a spectacular acceleration of development, a "Great Leap Forward" in which soaring industrial growth was to be based on small-scale backyard workshops run by peasants living in gigantic self-contained communes. Creating an authentic new socialist personality that rejected individualism and traditional family values was a second goal. In extreme cases, commune members ate in common dining halls, nurseries cared for children, and fiery crusaders preached the evils of family ties.

The intended great leap past the Soviets to socialist utopia—true communism—produced an economic disaster in the countryside, for frantic efforts with primitive technology often resulted only in chaos. By 1960, only China's efficient rationing system was preventing starvation. But when Khrushchev criticized Chinese policy, Mao condemned Khrushchev and his Russian colleagues as detestable "modern revisionists"—capitalists and cowards unwilling to risk a world war that would bring communist revolution in the United States. The Russians abruptly cut off economic aid and withdrew their scientists who were helping China build an atomic bomb. A mood of fear and hostility developed in both countries in the 1960s as the communist world split apart.

Mao lost influence in the party after the fiasco of the Great Leap Forward and the Sino-Soviet split, but in 1965 the old revolutionary staged a dramatic comeback. Apprehensive that China was becoming bureaucratic, capitalistic, and "revisionist" like the Soviet Union, Mao launched what he called the "Great Proletarian Cultural Revolution." Its objective was to purge the party of time-serving bureaucrats and to recapture the revolutionary fervor and social equality of the Long March and his guerrilla struggle (see page 1100). The army and the nation's young people, especially students, responded enthusiastically. Encouraged by Mao to organize themselves into radical cadres called "Red Guards," young people denounced their teachers and practiced rebellion in the name of revolution. One Red Guard manifesto, "Long Live the Revolutionary Rebel Spirit of the Proletariat," exulted:

Revolution is rebellion, and rebellion is the soul of Mao Tse-tung's thought. Daring to think, to speak, to act, to break through, and to make revolution—in a word, daring to rebel—is the most fundamental and most precious quality of proletarian revolutionaries; it is fundamental to the Party spirit of the Party of the proletariat! . . .

You say we are too arrogant? "Arrogant" is just what we want to be. Chairman Mao says, "And those in high positions we counted as no more than the dust." We are bent on striking down not only the reactionaries in our school, but the reactionaries all over the world. Revolutionaries take it as their task to transform the world. How can we not be "arrogant"?[2]

The Red Guards also sought to forge a new socialist spirit by purging China of all traces of "feudal" and "bourgeois" culture and thought. Some ancient monuments and works of art were destroyed. Party officials, professors, and intellectuals were exiled to remote villages to purify themselves with the heavy labor of the peasant masses and to rekindle a burning devotion to the semidivine Chairman Mao. The Red Guards attracted enor-

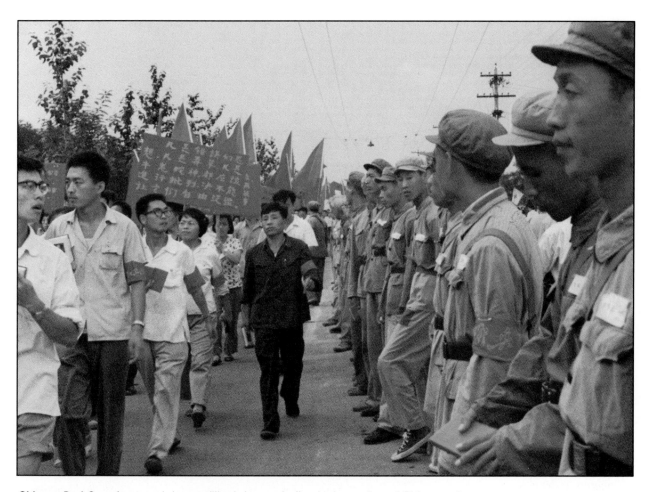

Chinese Red Guards   march in a political demonstration before a line of Chinese soldiers. This photo captures the youth and determination of the Red Guards, who are carrying the "Little Red Book," the world-renowned collection of Chairman Mao's slogans and revolutionary teachings. *(Source: Wide World Photos)*

mous worldwide attention. Many observers were appalled, but China's young revolutionaries inspired radical admirers around the world and served as an extreme model for the student rebellions of the late 1960s.

The Limits of Reform

Mao and the Red Guards succeeded in mobilizing the masses, shaking up the party, and creating greater social equality. But the Cultural Revolution also created growing chaos and a general crisis of confidence, especially in the cities. Intellectuals, technicians, and purged party officials saw themselves as victims of senseless persecution. Fighting back, they launched a counterattack on the radicals and regained much of their influence by 1969. Thus China shifted to the right at the same time that Europe and the United States did. This shift in China, coupled with actual fighting between China and the Soviet Union on the northern border in 1969 and not-so-secret Soviet talk of atomic attack, opened the door to a limited but lasting reconciliation between China and the United States in 1972.

The moderates were led by Deng Xiaoping (b. 1904), a long-time member of the Communist elite who had been branded a dangerous agent of capitalism during the Cultural Revolution. After

China's Peasants benefitted the most from Deng's reforms and the subsequent economic progress. Still clad in the blue cotton jackets of the Maoist era, these peasants are purchasing more expensive synthetic fabrics, which they will sew into brightly colored dresses and fancy shirts. *(Source: Camera Press)*

Mao's death in 1976, Deng and his supporters initiated a series of new policies, embodied in the ongoing campaign of the "Four Modernizations"— agriculture, industry, science and technology, and national defense. The campaign to modernize had a profound effect on China's people, and Deng proudly called it China's "second revolution."

China's 800 million peasants experienced the greatest and most beneficial change from this "second revolution"—a fact that at first glance may seem surprising. The support of the peasantry had played a major role in the Communist victory. After 1949, land reform and rationing undoubtedly improved the diet of poor peasants. Subsequently, literacy campaigns taught rural people how to read, and "barefoot doctors"—local peasants trained to do simple diagnosis and treatment—brought modern medicine to the countryside. The Communists also promoted handicraft industries to provide rural employment. Neverthe-less, rigid collectivized agriculture had failed to provide either the peasants or the country with adequate food, as Chinese documents published in the 1980s made clear. Levels of agricultural production and per capita food consumption were no higher in the mid-1970s than in the mid-1950s, and only slightly higher than in 1937, before the war with Japan.

Determined to prevent a return to Maoist extremism as well as to modernize the economy, Deng and the reformers looked to the peasants as natural allies. Their answer to the stalemate in agricultural production was to let China's peasants farm the land in small family units rather than in large collectives. Peasants were encouraged to produce what they could produce best and "dare to be rich." Peasants responded enthusiastically, increasing food production by more than 50 percent in just six years after 1978. As a result of this achievement, both rural and urban Chinese finally gained enough calories and protein for normal life and growth, although the grain-dominated diet remained monotonous.

The successful use of free markets and family responsibility in agriculture encouraged further economic experimentation. Foreign capitalists were allowed to open factories in southern China, and they successfully exported Chinese products around the world. The private enterprise of Chinese citizens was also permitted in cities. Snack shops, beauty parlors, and a host of small businesses sprang up, along with rock music and a rage for English lessons. As signs of liberalization abounded, the Chinese economy bucked the world trend and grew rapidly at an annual rate of almost 10 percent between 1978 and 1987. The level of per capita income more than doubled in these years.

Yet the extent of change must not be exaggerated. Industry remained largely state owned and centrally planned; only 3 percent of the urban workforce was employed by private enterprise in 1986. Cultural change was limited, and the party maintained its strict control of the media. Above all, under Deng's leadership the Communist party zealously preserved its monopoly of political power.

Dictatorial rule in the midst of economic liberalization helps explain why the worldwide movement for greater democracy and political freedom in the late 1980s also took root in China. Chinese university students led the movement, organizing large demonstrations and calling for genuine political reform in late 1986. The government responded by banning all demonstrations and gradually halting the trend toward a freer economy. Inflation then soared to more than 30 percent a year, and in 1988 consumers cleared the shelves in a buying panic.

The economic reversal and the conviction that Chinese society was becoming more corrupt and unjust led China's idealistic university students to renew their demonstrations in April 1989. The students evoked tremendous popular support, and more than a million people streamed into Beijing's central Tiananmen Square on May 17 in support of their demands. The old men gathered around Deng and then declared martial law and ordered the army to clear the students. Incredibly, masses of courageous Chinese citizens using only their bodies and voices as weapons peacefully blocked the soldiers' entry into the city for two weeks. But after ominous threats from the government gradually reduced the number of protesting students to less than 10,000, the hesitant army finally struck. In the early hours of June 4, 1989, tanks rolled into Tiananmen Square. At least 700 students died as a wave of repression, arrests, and executions descended on China.

China's Communist leaders claimed that they had saved the country from a counter-revolutionary plot to destroy socialism. In fact, they had temporarily saved the Communist monopoly of power and showed the limits of permissible reform. Like so many leading Chinese in modern times, Deng and his circle were most interested in making China strong, and they still saw authoritarian rule as the means to that goal.

Japan's American Revolution

After Japan's surrender in August 1945, American occupation forces began landing in the Tokyo-Yokohama area. Riding through what had been the heart of industrial Japan, the combat-hardened veterans saw an eerie sight. Where mighty mills and factories had once hummed with activity, only smokestacks and giant steel safes remained standing amid miles of rubble and debris. The empty landscape manifested Japan's state of mind as the nation lay helpless before its conqueror.

Japan, like Nazi Germany, was formally occupied by all the Allies, but real power resided in American hands. The commander was General Douglas MacArthur (1880–1964), the five-star hero of the Pacific, who with his advisers exercised almost absolute authority.

MacArthur and the Americans had a revolutionary plan for defeated Japan. Convinced that militaristic, antidemocratic forces were responsible for Japanese aggression and had to be destroyed, they introduced fundamental reforms designed to make Japan a free, democratic society along American lines. The Americans believed in their mission and in the obvious superiority of their civilization. The exhausted, demoralized Japanese, who had feared a worse fate, accepted passively. Long-suppressed liberal leaders emerged to offer crucial support and help carry the reforms forward.

Japan's sweeping American revolution began with demilitarization and a systematic purge.

Twenty-five top government leaders and army officers were tried and convicted as war criminals by a special international tribunal; other courts sentenced hundreds to death and sent thousands to prison. Over 220,000 politicians, businessmen, and army officers were declared ineligible for office.

Many Americans also wanted to try Emperor Hirohito (r. 1926–1989) as a war criminal, but MacArthur wisely decided to let him reign as a useful figurehead. According to the American-dictated constitution of 1946, the emperor was "the symbol of the State and of the people with whom resides sovereign power." The new constitution made the government fully responsible to the Diet, whose members were popularly elected by all adults. A bill of rights granted basic civil liberties and freed all political prisoners, including Communists. The constitution also abolished forever all Japanese armed forces. Japan's resurrected liberals enthusiastically supported this American move to destroy militarism.

The American occupation left Japan's powerful bureaucracy largely intact and used it to implement the fundamental social and economic reforms that were rammed through the Japanese Diet. Many had a New Deal flavor. The occupation promoted the Japanese labor movement, and the number of union workers increased fifteenfold in three years. The occupation also introduced American-style antitrust laws. The gigantic zaibatsu firms (see page 1096) were broken up into many separate companies in order to encourage competition and economic democracy. The American reformers proudly "emancipated" Japanese women, granting them equality before the law.

The occupation also imposed truly revolutionary land reform. MacArthur, often seen in the United States as a rigid conservative, pressured the Japanese Diet into buying up the land owned by absentee landlords and selling it to peasants on very generous terms. This reform strengthened the small, independent peasant, who became a staunch defender of postwar democracy.

The United States's efforts to remake Japan in its own image were powerful but short-lived. By 1948, when the United States began to look at the world through a cold war lens, occupation policy shifted gears. The Japanese later referred to this about-face as "the reverse course." As China went decisively communist, American leaders began to see Japan as a potential ally, not as an object of social reform. The American command began purging leftists and rehabilitating prewar nationalists, many of whom joined the Liberal Democratic party, which became increasingly conservative and emerged as the dominant political organization in postwar Japan. The United States ended the occupation in 1952. Under the treaty terms, Japan regained independence and the United States retained its vast military complex in Japan. In actuality, Japan became a military protectorate, a special ally shielded, and restricted, by America's nuclear capability.

"Japan, Inc."

Restricted to satellite status in world politics, the Japanese people applied their exceptional creative powers to rebuilding their country. Japan's economic recovery, like Germany's, proceeded painfully slowly immediately after the war. At the time of the Korean War, however, the economy took off and grew with spectacular speed for a whole generation. Between 1950 and 1970 the real growth rate of Japan's economy—adjusted for inflation—averaged a breathtaking 10 percent a year—almost three times that of the United States. Even after the shock of much higher energy prices in 1973, the petroleum-poor Japanese did considerably better than most other peoples. In 1986 average per capita income in Japan exceeded that in the United States for the first time. As recently as 1965, the average Japanese had earned only one-fourth of the average American's income.

Japan's emergence as an economic superpower fascinated some outsiders and troubled others. While Asians and Africans looked to Japan for the secrets of successful modernization, some Americans and Europeans whipped up quick recipes for copying Japanese success. Some of Japan's Asian neighbors again feared Japanese exploitation. And in the 1970s and 1980s, some Americans and Europeans bitterly accused "Japan, Inc." of an unholy alliance between government and business. Industries and workers hurt by "unfair" Japanese competition called on their governments for aggressive countermeasures.

Many of the ingredients in western Europe's recovery also operated in Japan. American aid, cheap labor, and freer international trade all helped spark the process. As in western Europe, the government concentrated its energies on economic development. Japanese businessmen recognized the opportunity to replace their bombed-out plants with the latest, most efficient technology.

Japan's astonishing economic surge also seems to have had deep roots in Japanese history, culture, and national character. Restricted by geography to mountainous islands, Japan was for centuries safely isolated from invaders. By the time American and European pressure forced open its gates in the mid-nineteenth century, Japan was politically unified and culturally homogeneous. Agriculture, education, and material well-being were advanced even by European standards. Moreover, Japanese society put the needs of the group before those of the individual. When the Meiji reformers redefined Japan's primary task as catching up with the West, they had the support of a sophisticated and disciplined people. Japan's modernization, even including a full share of aggressive imperialism, was extremely rapid.

By the end of the American occupation, this tight-knit, group-centered society had reassessed its future and worked out a new national consensus. Japan's new task was to build its economy and compete efficiently in world markets. Improved living standards emerged as a related goal after the initial successes of the 1950s. The ambitious "double-your-income" target for the 1960s was ultimately surpassed by 50 percent.

Government and big business shared leading roles in the drama of economic growth. As during the Meiji Restoration (see page 984), capable, respected bureaucrats directed and aided the efforts of cooperative business leaders. The government decided which industries were important, then made loans and encouraged mergers to create powerful firms in those industries. The antitrust policy introduced by the American occupation, based on the very un-Japanese values of individualism and unrestrained competition, was scrapped.

Big business was valued and respected because it served the national goal and mirrored Japanese society. Big companies, and to a lesser extent small ones, traditionally hired workers for life immediately after they finished school. Employees were never fired and seldom laid off, and in return they were loyal and obedient. To an extent difficult for a Westerner to imagine, the business firm in Japan was a big, well-disciplined family. The workday be-

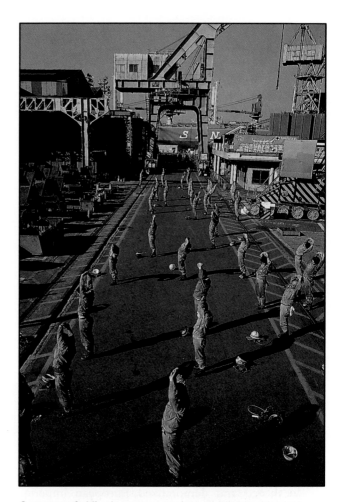

Company Spirit Japanese workers at this big shipping firm shout and sing in unison as they go through their morning exercise routine. Such practices encourage group solidarity in Japan, where the success of the group is placed above the success of the individual. *(Source: Paolo Koch/Photo Researchers, Inc.)*

gan with the company song. Employees' social lives also revolved around the company. Wages were based on age. (Discrimination against women remained severe: wages and job security were strikingly inferior.) Most unions became moderate, agreeable company unions. The social and economic distance between salaried managers and workers was slight and often breached. *Efficiency, quality,* and *quantity* were the watchwords. Management was quick to retrain employees, secure in the knowledge that they would not take their valuable new skills elsewhere. These factors, not "unfair" competition, were most important in accounting for Japan's economic success.

Japanese society, with its inescapable stress on cooperation and compromise, has proved well adapted to the challenges of modern industrial urban civilization. For example, Japan alone among industrial nations has experienced a marked decrease in crime over the last generation. In the 1970s and 1980s the Japanese addressed themselves effectively to such previously neglected problems as serious industrial pollution and their limited energy resources. Highly dependent on imported resources and foreign sales, Japan groped for a new role in world politics. Closer relations with China, increased loans to Southeast Asia, and tough trade negotiations with the United States were all features of that ongoing effort.

NEW NATIONS IN SOUTH ASIA AND THE MUSLIM WORLD

South Asia and the Muslim world have transformed themselves no less spectacularly than China and Japan. The national independence movements, which had been powerful mass campaigns since the 1930s, triumphed decisively over weakened and demoralized European imperialism after the Second World War. Between 1947 and 1962, as decolonization gathered irresistible strength, virtually every colonial territory won its political freedom. The complete reversal of the long process of European expansion was a turning point in world history.

The newly independent nations of South Asia and the revitalized states of the Muslim world exhibited many variations on the dominant themes of national renaissance and modernization, especially as the struggle for political independence receded into the past.

The Indian Subcontinent

After the First World War, Mahatma Gandhi and the Indian Congress party developed the philosophy of militant nonviolence to oppose British rule of India and to lessen oppression of the Indian poor by the Indian rich (see pages 1087–1090). By

1929 Gandhi had succeeded in transforming the Congress party from a narrow, middle-class party into a mass independence movement. Gradually and grudgingly, Britain's rulers introduced reforms culminating in limited self-government in 1937.

The Second World War accelerated the drive toward independence but also pointed it in a new direction. Congress party leaders, humiliated that Great Britain had declared war against Germany on India's behalf without consulting them, resigned their posts in the Indian government and demanded self-rule as the immediate price of political cooperation. In 1942, Gandhi called on the British to "Quit India" and threatened another civil disobedience campaign. He and the other Congress leaders were quickly arrested and jailed for the virtual duration of the war. As a result, India's wartime support for hard-pressed Britain was substantial but not always enthusiastic. Meanwhile, the Congress party's prime political rival skillfully seized the opportunity to increase its influence.

That rival was the Muslim League, led by the brilliant, elegant English-educated lawyer Muhammad Ali Jinnah (1876–1948). Jinnah and the other leaders of the Muslim League feared Hindu domination of an independent Indian state led by the Congress party. Asserting in nationalist terms the right of Muslim areas to separate from the Hindu majority, Jinnah described the Muslims of India as

a nation of a hundred million, and what is more, we are a nation with our distinct culture and civilization, language, literature, arts, and architecture . . . laws and moral codes, customs and special aptitudes and ambitions. In short, we have our own distinctive outlook on life and of life.[3]

Jinnah told 100,000 listeners at the Muslim League's Lahore Conference in March 1940,

If the British Government is really in earnest and sincere to secure the peace and happiness of the people of the subcontinent, the only course open to us all is to allow the major nations separate homelands by dividing India into autonomous national states.[4]

The Muslim League's insistence on the division of India appalled Gandhi. He regarded Jinnah's two-nation theory as simply untrue and as promising the victory of hate over love. Gandhi's argument was most accurate when applied to the Bengali Muslims of northeastern India's Ganges River basin. Their language, dress, racial appearance, food, and social customs were virtually identical to those of Bengali Hindus; only in religion did the two groups differ. The passionate debate between Jinnah and Gandhi continued unabated during the war as millions argued whether India was one nation or two. By 1945 the subcontinent was intellectually and emotionally divided, though still momentarily held together by British rule.

When Britain's Labour government agreed to speedy independence for India after 1945, conflicting Hindu and Muslim nationalisms and religious hatred became obstacles leading to murderous clashes between the two communities in 1946. In a last attempt to preserve the subcontinent's political unity, the British proposed a federal constitution providing for extensive provincial—and thus religious and cultural—autonomy. When after some hesitation Jinnah and the Muslim League would accept nothing less than an independent Pakistan, India's last viceroy—war hero Lord Louis Mountbatten (1900–1979), Queen Victoria's great-grandson—proposed partition. Both sides accepted. At the stroke of midnight on August 14, 1947, one-fifth of humanity gained political independence. As the sumptuous, horse-drawn coach of the last viceroy pulled away from the final ceremony, endless cries of "Long live Mountbatten!" rose from the tremendous crowds —ringing testimony to India's residue of good feeling toward its vanquished conquerors and their splendidly peaceful departure.

Yet independence through partition was to bring tragedy. In the weeks after independence, communal strife exploded into an orgy of massacres and mass expulsions. Perhaps 100,000 Hindus and Muslims were slaughtered, and an estimated 5 million refugees from both communities fled in opposite directions to escape being hacked to death by frenzied mobs.

This wave of violence was a bitter potion for Congress leaders, who were completely powerless to stop it. "What is there to celebrate?" exclaimed Gandhi. "I see nothing but rivers of blood."[5] In January 1948, announcing yet another fast to protest Hindu persecution of Muslims in the Indian capital of New Delhi and to restore "heart friend-ship" between the two communities, Gandhi was gunned down by a Hindu fanatic. As the Mahatma's death tragically testifies, the constructive and liberating forces of modern nationalism have frequently deteriorated into blind hatred.

After the ordeal of independence, relations between India and Pakistan—both members of the British Commonwealth—remained tense. Fighting over the disputed area of Kashmir continued until 1949 and broke out again in 1965–1966 and 1971. Mutual hostility remains deeply ingrained to this day (Map 37.1).

Pakistan Like many newly independent states, Pakistan eventually adopted an authoritarian government in 1958. Unlike most, Pakistan failed to preserve its exceptionally fragile unity, which proved to be the unworkable dream of its Muslim League leaders.

Pakistan's western and eastern provinces were separated by more than a thousand miles of Indian territory, as well as by language, ethnic background, and social custom. They shared only the Muslim faith that had temporarily brought them together against the Hindus. The Bengalis of East Pakistan constituted a majority of the population of Pakistan as a whole but were neglected by the central government, which remained in the hands of West Pakistan's elite after Jinnah's death. In essence, East Pakistan remained a colony of West Pakistan.

Tensions gradually came to a head in the late 1960s. Bengali leaders calling for virtual independence were charged with treason, and martial law was proclaimed in East Pakistan. In 1971 the Bengalis revolted. Despite savage repression— 10 million Muslim Bengalis fled temporarily to India, which provided some military aid—the Bengalis won their independence as the new nation of Bangladesh in 1973. The world's eighth most populous country, Bangladesh remains one of its poorest.

India India was ruled for a generation after 1947 by Jawaharlal Nehru (1889–1964) and the Congress party, which introduced major social reforms. Hindu women and even young girls were granted legal equality, which included the right to vote, to seek a divorce, and to marry outside their caste. The constitution also abolished the untouchable caste and, in an effort to compensate for

MAP 37.1 The Partition of British India, 1947   Violence and fighting were most intense where there were large Hindu and Muslim minorities—in Kashmir, Punjab, and Bengal. The tragic result of partition, which has occurred repeatedly throughout the world in the twentieth century, was a forced exchange of populations and greater homogeneity on both sides of the border.

centuries of the most profound discrimination, established "ex-untouchable" quotas for university scholarships and government jobs. In practice, attitudes toward women and untouchables evolved slowly—especially in the villages, where 85 percent of the people lived.

The Congress leadership tried with modest success to develop the country economically by means of democratic socialism. But population growth of about 2.4 percent per year ate up much of the increase in output, and halfhearted government efforts to promote birth control met with indifference or hostility. Intense poverty remained the lot of most people and encouraged widespread corruption within the bureaucracy.

The Congress party maintained a moralizing neutrality in the cold war and sought to group India and other newly independent states in Asia and Africa into a "third force" of "nonaligned" nations. This effort culminated in the Afro-Asian Conference in Bandung, Indonesia, in 1955.

Nehru's daughter, Indira Gandhi (1917–1984), became prime minister in 1966. Mrs. Gandhi (whose deceased husband was no relation to Mahatma Gandhi) dominated Indian political life for a generation with a combination of charm, tact, and toughness. As it became clear that population growth was frustrating efforts to improve living standards, Mrs. Gandhi's government stepped up measures to promote family planning. Bus posters featuring smiling youngsters proclaimed that "A Happy Family Is a Small Family,"

and doctors and nurses promoted intra-uterine loop rings for women and condoms and surgical vasectomy for men. Most Indian males rejected vasectomy for both psychological and religious reasons. As a doctor in a market town explained to a Western journalist:

They have mostly heard of family planning around here by now, but they are afraid. They are afraid that the sterilizing operation will destroy their male power and make them docile, like castrated animals. Mostly, they are afraid of interfering with God's will.[6]

In the face of such reluctance—and in an effort to clamp down on widespread corruption at all levels of government—Mrs. Gandhi in 1975 subverted parliamentary democracy and proclaimed a state of emergency. Attacking dishonest officials, black marketeers, and tax evaders, she also threw the weight of the government behind a heavy-handed

Indian Refugees Independence and partition brought a wave of bloodshed that sent millions of Hindus and Muslims fleeing for their lives in opposite directions. Here desperate Muslims seek precious space atop a train that will carry them to safety in Pakistan. *(Source: Wide World Photos)*

campaign of mass sterilization to reduce population growth. In some areas, poor men with very large families were rounded up and made to accept a few cents' payment to submit to a simple, almost painless irreversible vasectomy. Everywhere the pressure was intense, and 7 million men were sterilized in 1976.

Many Indian and foreign observers believed that Mrs. Gandhi's emergency measures marked the end of the parliamentary democracy and Western liberties introduced in the last phase of British rule. But Mrs. Gandhi—true to the British tradition—called for free elections, in which she suffered a spectacular defeat, largely because of the vastly unpopular sterilization campaign and her subversion of democracy. But her successors fell to fighting among themselves, and in 1980 Mrs. Gandhi won an equally stunning electoral victory.

Her defeat and re-election undoubtedly strengthened India's democratic tradition.

Mrs. Gandhi's last years in office were plagued by another old political problem, one that cost her her life. Democratic India remained a patchwork of religions, languages, and peoples. This enduring diversity threatened to divide the country along ethnic or religious lines, as conflicting national aspirations had earlier torn British India into two and then three different states. Several peoples developed a strong ethnic consciousness and made political demands, most notably the 15 million Sikhs of the Punjab in northern India.

The Sikhs have their own religion—a blend of Islam and Hinduism—and a distinctive culture, including a warrior tradition and the wearing of elegantly coiled turbans. Industrious and cohesive, most Sikhs wanted (and still want) greater auton-

Sikh Patriots   With the domes of the majestic Golden Temple rising behind them, a mass of Sikhs gather to protest the Indian army's bloody assault on their most holy shrine. The vast majority of Sikhs want greater autonomy at the least. Sikh radicals seek an independent state. *(Source: Bartholomew/Gamma-Liaison)*

ASIA SINCE 1945

1945	Japan surrenders
	Civil war begins in China
1946	Japan receives democratic constitution
	The Philippines gain independence
1947	Communal strife follows independence for India and Pakistan
1948	Civil war between Arabs and Jews in Palestine
1949	Korean War begins
	Mao Tse-tung (Mao Zedong) proclaims the People's Republic of China
	Indonesia under Sukarno wins independence from the Dutch
1950	China enters Korean War
	Japan begins long period of rapid economic growth
1951	Iran tries unsuccessfully to nationalize the Anglo-Iranian Oil Company
1952	American occupation of Japan officially ends
1954	Vietnamese nationalists defeat the French at Dien Bien Phu
1955	First Afro-Asian Conference of non-aligned nations meets at Bandung, Indonesia
1958	Mao Tse-tung announces the Great Leap Forward
1960	Open split between China and the Soviet Union emerges
1965	The Great Proletarian Cultural Revolution begins in China
	Growing American involvement in the Vietnamese civil war
1966	Indira Gandhi becomes Prime Minister of India
1972	President Nixon's visit to China signals improved Sino-American relations
1975	War in Vietnam ends with Communist victory
1976	China pursues modernization after Mao's death
1979	Revolution topples the shah of Iran
1984	Growth of Sikh nationalism in India
1986	Democratic movement in the Philippines brings Corazon Aquino to power
1989	Chinese government uses the army to crush student demonstrations

omy for the Punjab. By 1984, some radicals were fighting for an independent homeland—a Sikh national state. In retaliation, Mrs. Gandhi tightened control in the Punjab and ordered the army to storm the Sikhs' sacred Golden Temple at Amritsar. Six hundred died in the assault. Five months later, two of Mrs. Gandhi's Sikh bodyguards—she prided herself on their loyalty—cut her down with machine-gun fire in her own garden. Violence followed as Hindu mobs slaughtered over a thousand Sikhs throughout India.

Elected prime minister by a landslide sympathy vote, one of Mrs. Gandhi's sons, Rajiv Gandhi (1944–1991), showed considerable skill at effecting a limited reconciliation with a majority of the Sikh population. But slow economic growth, government corruption, and Rajiv Gandhi's lack of warmth gradually undermined his support. In 1989, he was voted out of office, and a fragile coalition of opposition took power. Despite poverty and ethnic tensions, India remained committed to free elections and representative government.

Southeast Asia

The rest of southeast Asia gained independence quickly after 1945, but the attainment of stable political democracy proved a more difficult goal.

Sri Lanka and Malaya Ceylon, renamed Sri Lanka in 1972, quickly and smoothly gained freedom from Britain in 1948. Malaya, however, encountered serious problems not unlike those of British India. The native Malays, an Islamic agricultural people, feared and disliked the Chinese,

President Corazón Aquino Shown here with her infectious smile and dignity, Corazón Aquino led the democratic movement to power in the Philippines and she enjoyed tremendous popular support. For millions of Filipinos she was simply "Cory"—their trusted friend. *(Source: Wide World Photos)*

who had come to the Malaya Peninsula as poor migrant workers in the nineteenth century and stayed on to dominate the urban economy. The Malays having pressured the British into giving them the dominant voice in a multi-ethnic federation of Malayan territories, local Chinese communists launched an all-out guerrilla war in 1948. They were eventually defeated by the British and the Malays, and Malaya became self-governing in 1957 and independent in 1961. Yet two peoples soon meant two nations. In 1965, the largely Chinese city of Singapore was pushed out of the Malayan-dominated Federation of Malaysia. Ethnic tension continued to erupt periodically in Malaysia, which still retained a large Chinese minority. The independent city-state of Singapore prospered on the hard work and inventiveness of its largely Chinese population.

The Philippine Islands The Philippine Islands (see Map 37.2) suffered greatly under Japanese occupation during the Second World War. After the war the United States extended economic aid while retaining its large military bases, and it fol-

lowed through on its earlier promises by granting the Philippines independence in 1946. As in Malaya, communist guerrillas tried unsuccessfully to seize power. The Philippines pursued American-style two-party competition until 1965, when President Ferdinand Marcos (1917–1989) subverted the constitution and ruled as a dictator. Abolishing martial law in 1981 but retaining most of his power, Marcos faced growing opposition as the economy crumbled and land-hungry communist guerrillas made striking gains in the countryside. Led by a courageous Corazón Aquino (b. 1933), whose politician husband had been murdered, probably by Marcos supporters, the opposition won a spectacular electoral victory in 1986 and forced Marcos to take refuge in Hawaii, where he subsequently died.

As president, Mrs. Aquino negotiated a cease-fire with the communist rebels and beat off several attempted takeovers by dissident army officers. But a tiny elite continued to dominate the country, and the gap between rich and poor remained huge. The question of whether U.S. military bases in the Philippines should be closed after September 1991, when their lease came up for renewal, became a passionate and divisive issue. After four turbulent years in office, President Aquino and the Filipino people still faced the tremendous challenge of reconciliation and genuine reform.

Indonesia The Netherlands East Indies, having successfully resisted stubborn Dutch efforts at reconquest, emerged in 1949 as independent Indonesia under the nationalist leader Achmed Sukarno (1901–1970). The populous new nation encompassed a variety of peoples, islands, and religions (Islam was predominant; see Map 37.2). Beginning in 1957, Sukarno tried to forge unity by means of his so-called guided democracy. He rejected parliamentary democracy as politically divisive and claimed to replicate at the national level the traditional deliberation and consensus of the Indonesian village. For a time the authoritarian, anti-Western Sukarno seemed to be under the sway of well-organized Indonesian communists, who murdered and mutilated the seven leading army generals whom they had kidnapped as part of an unsuccessful uprising in 1965. The army immediately retaliated, systematically slaughtering a half-million or more Indonesian communists, radicals, and noncommunist Chinese. Sukarno was forced to resign, and Muslim generals ruled thereafter without any pretense of free and open political competition.

Vietnam, Laos, and Cambodia The most bitterly destructive fighting occurred in French Indochina. The French tried to reimpose imperial rule there after the communist and nationalist guerrilla leader Ho Chi Minh (1890–1969) declared an independent republic in 1945. In spite of considerable aid from the United States, the French were decisively defeated in 1954 in the battle of Dien Bien Phu. At the subsequent international peace conference, French Indochina gained independence. Laos and Cambodia (later known as Kampuchea) became separate states; Vietnam was "temporarily" divided into two hostile sections at the 17th parallel pending elections to select a single unified government within two years (see Map 36.3).

The elections were never held, and the civil war that soon broke out between the two Vietnamese governments, one communist and one anticommunist, became a very hot cold war conflict in the

1960s. The United States invested tremendous military effort but fought its Vietnam War as a deeply divided country (see pages 1201–1205). The tough, dedicated communists eventually proved victorious in 1975. Thus events in Vietnam roughly recapitulated those in China, but in a long, drawn-out fashion: after a bitter civil war worsened by cold war hatreds, the communists succeeded in creating a unified Marxist nation.

The Muslim World

Throughout the vast arc of predominantly Islamic lands that stretches from Indonesia in Southeast Asia to Senegal in West Africa (Map 37.2), change and bewildering internal conflict prevailed after 1945. But everywhere nationalism remained the predominant political force. Although anti-Western and hospitable to radical social reform, nationalism in the Muslim world remained consistently true to Islam and generally anticommunist. Cold war conflicts and enormous oil resources enhanced the region's global standing.

In the Arab countries of North Africa and the Middle East, with their shared but highly differentiated language and culture, nationalism wore two faces. The idealistic, unrealized side focused on the pan-Arab dream, the dream of uniting all Arabs in a single nation that would be strong enough to resist the West and achieve genuine independence. Like German or Italian nationalists in the mid-nineteenth century, pan-Arabs believed that Arabs formed a single people and that they were destined to have their own nation state. This pan-Arab vision contributed to political and economic alliances like the Arab League, but no Arab Bismarck appeared and the vision foundered on intense regional, ideological, and personal rivalries. Thus the practical, down-to-earth side of Arab nationalism focused largely on nation building *within* the particular states that supplanted former League of Nations mandates and European colonies.

Palestine and Israel Before the Second World War, Arab nationalists were loosely united in their opposition to the colonial powers and to Jewish migration to Palestine. The French gave up their League of Nations mandates in Syria and Lebanon in 1945, having been forced by popular uprisings

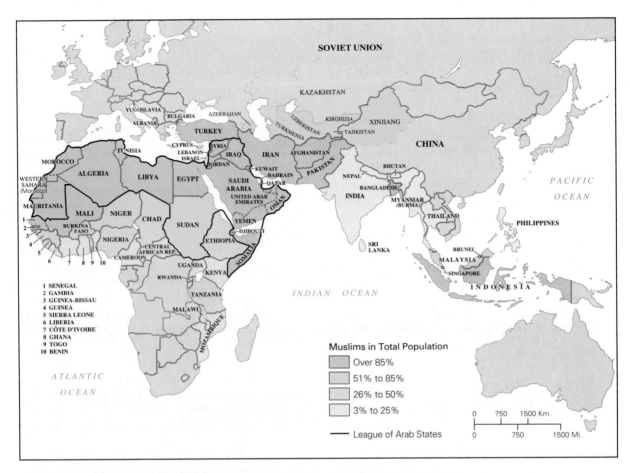

MAP 37.2 Modern Islam, ca 1990 Although the Islamic heartland remains the Middle East and North Africa, Islam is growing steadily in black Africa and is the faith of heavily populated Indonesia.

and British-American pressure to follow the British example. Attention then focused even more sharply on British-mandated Palestine. The situation was volatile. The Jews' demand that the British permit all survivors of Hitler's death camps to settle in Palestine was strenuously opposed by the Palestinian Arabs and the seven independent states of the newly founded Arab League (Egypt, Iraq, Jordan, Lebanon, Saudi Arabia, Syria, and Yemen). Murder and terrorism flourished, nurtured by bitterly conflicting Arab and Jewish nationalisms.

The British—their occupation policies in Palestine condemned by Arabs and Jews, by Russians and Americans—announced in 1947 their intention to withdraw from Palestine in 1948. The insoluble problem was dumped in the lap of the United Nations. In November 1947 the United Nations General Assembly passed a nonbinding

resolution supporting a plan to partition Palestine into two separate states—one Arab and one Jewish (Map 37.3). The Jews accepted but the Arabs rejected partition of Palestine.

By early 1948 an undeclared civil war was raging in Palestine. The departing British looked on impartially. When the British mandate officially ended on May 14, 1948, the Jews proclaimed the state of Israel. Arab countries immediately launched an attack on the new Jewish state. Fighting for their lives, the Israelis drove off the invaders and conquered more territory. Roughly 900,000 Arab refugees—the exact number is disputed—fled or were expelled from old Palestine. This war left an enormous legacy of Arab bitterness toward Israel and its political allies, Great Britain and the United States, and it led to the creation of the Palestine Liberation Organization, a

MAP 37.3 Palestine, Israel, and the Middle East, 1947–1990 Since the British mandate expired on May 14, 1948, there have been five major wars and innumerable armed clashes in what was formerly Palestine. After winning the War of Independence in 1948, Israel achieved spectacular victories in 1967 in the Six-Day War, occupying the Sinai Peninsula, the Golan Heights, and the West Bank. The Yom Kippur War of 1973 eventually led to the Israeli evacuation of the Sinai and peace with Egypt, but there has been no agreement on the West Bank.

loose union of Palestinian refugee groups opposed to Israel.

Egypt   The humiliation of defeat triggered a nationalist revolution in Egypt, where a young army colonel named Gamal Abdel Nasser (1918–1970) drove out the corrupt and pro-Western king Farouk in 1952. A gifted politician and the unchallenged leader of the largest Arab state, Nasser enjoyed powerful influence in the Middle East and throughout Asia and Africa. Perhaps his most successful and widely imitated move was radical land reform: large estates along the Nile were nationalized and divided up among peasants without violence or drastic declines in production. Nasser, who preached the gospel of neutralism in the cold war and jailed Egyptian communists, turned for aid to the Soviet Union to demonstrate Egypt's

A Leader and His People   Millions of ordinary Egyptians were fanatically devoted to Gamal Abdel Nasser. Here he is mobbed by ecstatic supporters at the Cairo railroad station two days after an unsuccessful attempt on his life in 1954. *(Source: Popperfoto)*

independence of the West. Relations with Israel and the West worsened, and in 1956 the United States abruptly canceled its offer to finance a giant new dam on the Nile, intended to promote economic development.

Nasser retaliated by immediately nationalizing the Suez Canal Company, the last remaining vestige and symbol of European power in the Middle East. Outraged, the British and French joined forces with the Israelis and successfully invaded Egypt. That action was to be the last gasp of imperial power in the Middle East in the 1950s. The Americans, suddenly moralistic, reversed course and sided with the Soviets—who were at that very moment crushing the Hungarian revolution—to force the British, French, and Israelis to withdraw from Egypt. This great victory for Nasser encouraged anti-Western radicalism, hopes of pan-Arab political unity, and a vague "Arab socialism." In Iraq radicals overthrew a conservative pro-Western government. In the aftermath of Suez, Egypt merged—temporarily—with Syria.

Yet the Arab world remained deeply divided. The only shared goals were opposition to Israel—war recurred in 1967 and in 1973—and support for the right of Palestinian refugees to return to their homeland. In late 1977, after more than a generation of bitter Arab-Israeli conflict, President Anwar Sadat of Egypt tried another tack: a stunningly unexpected official visit to Israel, where his meeting with Israeli Prime Minister Menachim Begin was watched on television by millions around the world. Sadat's visit led to direct negotiations between Israel and Egypt, which were effectively mediated by U.S. President Jimmy Carter, and a historic if limited peace settlement. Each country gained: Egypt got back the Sinai Peninsula, which Israel had taken in the 1967 Six-Day War (see Map 37.3), and Israel obtained peace and normal relations with Egypt. Sadat's initiative was denounced as treason by other Arab leaders, who continued to support the Palestine Liberation Organization against Israel.

After Sadat was assassinated by Islamic fundamentalists in 1981, Egypt's relations with the Begin government deteriorated badly over the question of ever-increasing Israeli settlement on the West Bank—the area west of the Jordan River inhabited by Palestinian Arabs but taken by Israel from Jordan during the 1967 war and occupied by Israel ever since. Yet Egypt quietly stood by when

Israeli troops occupied southern Lebanon in 1982 in an attempt to destroy the Palestine Liberation Organization. Israel's subsequent withdrawal from Lebanon helped preserve the fragile peace between the former enemies.

Algeria In the French colony of Algeria, Arab nationalism was emboldened by Nasser's great triumph—and by the defeat of the French in Indochina. Neighboring Tunisia and Morocco (see Map 37.2), both more recently colonized and sparsely settled by Europeans than Algeria, had won independence from France in 1956. But Algeria's large European population—1 million French-speaking Europeans lived among 8 million Muslims—considered Algeria home and an integral part of France. When nationalism stirred Algerian Muslims to revolt, they found themselves confronting a solid block of European settlers determined to defend their privileged position.

It was this determination that made the ensuing Algerian war so bitter and bloody. In 1958 a military coup in Algeria, resulting from the fears of the European settlers that a disillusioned, anticolonial majority of French voters would sell them out, brought General de Gaulle back to power in France. Contrary to expectations, de Gaulle accepted the principle of self-determination for Algeria in 1959, and in a national referendum the vast majority of the French population agreed. In 1962, after more than a century of French conquest, Algeria became an independent Arab state. The European population quickly fled.

Turkey, Iran, and Iraq The recent history of the non-Arab states of Turkey and Iran and the Arab state of Iraq (see Map 37.2) testify to the diversity of national development in the Muslim world. That history also dramatically illustrates the intense competition between rival states.

Turkey remained basically true to Atatürk's vision of a thoroughly modernized, secularized, Europeanized state (see page 1080). Islam played a less influential role in daily life and thought there than in other Middle Eastern countries, and Turkey joined NATO to protect itself from possible Soviet aggression.

Iran tried again to follow Turkey's example, as it had before 1939 (see page 1081). Once again, its success was limited. The new shah—Muhammad Reza Pahlavi (r. 1941–1979), the son of Reza Shah

Pahlavi—angered Iranian nationalists by courting Western powers and Western oil companies in the course of freeing his country from Soviet influence after the war. In 1951, however, the shah accepted the effort of the Iranian Majlis and the fiery Prime Minister Muhammad Mossaddeq to nationalize the British-owned Anglo-Iranian Oil Company. In retaliation an effective Western boycott of Iranian oil plunged the economy into chaos. Refusing to compromise or be dismissed, Mossaddeq forced the shah to flee to Europe in 1953. But Mossaddeq's victory was short-lived, for the shah was quickly restored to his throne by loyal army officers and with the help of the American CIA.

The shah set out to build a powerful modern nation to ensure his rule. Iran's gigantic oil revenues provided the necessary cash. The shah undermined the power bases of the traditional politicians—large landowners and religious leaders—by means of land reform, secular education, and increased power for the central government. Modernization surged forward, but at the price of ancient values, widespread corruption, and harsh dictatorship. The result was a violent reaction against secular values: an Islamic revolution in 1978 led by religious leaders grouped around the spellbinding Ayatollah Ruholla Khomeini. After the shah fled Iran in 1979, radicals seized fifty-two American diplomats and imprisoned them for a year as they consolidated their power.

Iran's radical Islamic republic frightened its neighbors. Iraq, especially, feared that Iran—a nation of Shi'ite Muslims (see page 274)—would succeed in getting Iraq's Shi'ite majority to revolt against its Sunnite leaders. Thus in September 1980, Iraq's president Saddam Hussein (b. 1937) launched a surprise attack, expecting his well-equipped armies to defeat an increasingly chaotic Iran. Instead, Iraqi aggression galvanized the Iranian revolutionaries in a fanatical determination to defend their homeland and punish Iraq's leader. Iranians and Iraqis—Persians and Arabs—clashed in one of the bloodiest wars in modern times, a savage stalemate that killed hundreds of thousands of soldiers before finally grinding to a halt in 1988.

Emerging from the eight-year war with a big tough army and a sizable arsenal of weapons from Western countries and the Soviet bloc, Iraq's strong man set out to make himself the leader of a revitalized and radicalized Arab world. Eyeing the great oil wealth of his tiny southern neighbor, Saddam Hussein's forces suddenly overran Kuwait in August 1990 and proclaimed its annexation to Iraq. To Saddam's surprise, his aggression brought a vigorous international response (see page 1287). In early 1991 his troops were chased out of Kuwait by an American led, U.N.-sanctioned military coalition, after American planes had first destroyed most of Iraq's infrastructure with the heaviest bombing since the Second World War. The American troops, accompanied by small British, French, and Italian forces, were joined in ground operations against Iraq by some Arab forces from Egypt, Syria, and Saudia Arabia. Thus the Arab peoples, long wracked by bitter rivalries between nation-building states, came to fight a kind of bloody civil war as the 1990s opened.

IMPERIALISM AND NATIONALISM IN BLACK AFRICA

Most of sub-Saharan Africa won political independence fairly rapidly after the Second World War. Only Portugal's old but relatively underdeveloped African territories and white-dominated southern Africa remained beyond the reach of African nationalists by 1964. The rise of independent states in black Africa—a decisive development in world history—resulted directly from both a reaction against Western imperialism and the growth of African nationalism.

The Imperial System (1900–1930)

European traders had been in constant contact with Africa's coastal regions ever since the Age of Discovery. In the nineteenth century, as trade in so-called legitimate products like peanuts and palm oil increasingly supplanted traffic in human beings, European influence continued to grow. Then came the political onslaught. After 1880 the Great Powers scrambled for territory and pushed into the interior, using overwhelming military force to mow down or intimidate African opposition and establish firm rule (see pages 972–979). By 1900, most of black Africa had been conquered—or, as Europeans preferred to say, "pacified"—and a system of imperial administration was taking shape.

Gradually but relentlessly, this imperial system transformed Africa. Generally, its effect was to weaken or shatter the traditional social order and challenge accepted values. Yet this generalization must be qualified. For one thing, sub-Saharan Africa consisted of an astonishing diversity of peoples and cultures prior to the European invasion. There were, for example, over eight hundred distinct languages and literally thousands of independent political units, ranging all the way from tiny kinship groups to large and powerful kingdoms like Ashanti of central Ghana and Ethiopia. The effects of imperialism varied accordingly.

Furthermore, the European powers themselves took rather different approaches to colonial rule. The British tended to exercise indirect rule through existing chiefs. The French believed in direct rule by appointed officials, both black and white. Moreover, the number of white settlers varied greatly from region to region, and their presence had important consequences. In light of these qualifications, how did imperial systems generally operate in black Africa?

The self-proclaimed political goal of the French and the British—the principal foreign powers in black Africa—was to provide good government for their African subjects, especially after 1919. "Good government" meant, above all, law and order. It meant maintaining a small army and building up an African police force to put down rebellion, suppress tribal warfare, and protect life and property. Good government required a modern bureaucracy capable of taxing and governing the population. Many African leaders and their peoples had chosen not to resist the invader's superior force, and most others had stopped fighting after experiencing crushing military defeat. Thus the goal of law and order was widely achieved. This success was a source of great satisfaction to colonial officials. It strengthened their self-confidence and convinced them that they were serving the common people, who were assumed to want only peace and security.

Colonial governments demonstrated much less interest in providing basic social services than in establishing law and order. Expenditures on education, public health, hospitals, and other social services increased after the First World War but still remained small. Europeans feared the political implications of mass education and typically relied instead on the modest efforts of state-subsidized mission schools. Moreover, they tried to

District Officer on Tour For many Africans, imperialism meant the local colonial official, who might be a vicious, petty tyrant or a relatively enlightened administrator. This humorous wood carving by Thomas Ona grows out of the rich satirical tradition upheld by the Yoruba of western Nigeria. *(Source: Berta Bascom/Lowie Museum of Anthropology, University of California, Berkeley)*

make even their poorest colonies pay for themselves. Thus salaries for government workers normally absorbed nearly all tax revenues.

Economically, the imperialist goal was to draw the vast untapped interior of the continent into the rapidly expanding world economy on terms favorable to the dominant Europeans. The key was railroads, linking coastal trading centers to outposts hundreds of miles into the interior. Cheap, dependable transportation facilitated easy shipment of raw materials out and manufactured goods in. Most African railroads were built after 1900; 5,200 miles were in operation by 1926, when attention turned to road building for trucks. Railroads and roads had two other important outcomes. They allowed the quick movement of troops to put down any local unrest, and they allowed many African peasants to earn wages for the first time.

Efforts to force Africa into the world economy on European terms went hand in hand with the advent of plantations and mines. The Europeans often imposed head taxes, payable in money or labor, to compel Africans to work for their white overlords. No aspect of imperialism was more disruptive and more despised by Africans than forced labor, widespread until about 1920. In some regions, however, particularly in West Africa, African peasants responded freely to the new economic opportunities by voluntarily shifting to export crops on their own farms. Overall, the result was increased production geared to the world market and a gradual decline in both traditional self-sufficient farming and nomadic herding.

In sum, the imposition of bureaucratic Western rule and the gradual growth of a world-oriented cash economy between 1900 and 1930 had a revolutionary impact on large parts of Africa. The experiences of Ghana and Kenya, two very different African countries, dramatically illustrate variations on the general pattern.

Present-day Ghana (see Map 37.4), which takes its name from one of West Africa's most famous early kingdoms, had a fairly complex economy well before British armies smashed the powerful Ashanti kingdom in 1873 and established the Crown colony that they called the "Gold Coast." Precolonial local trade was vigorous and varied,

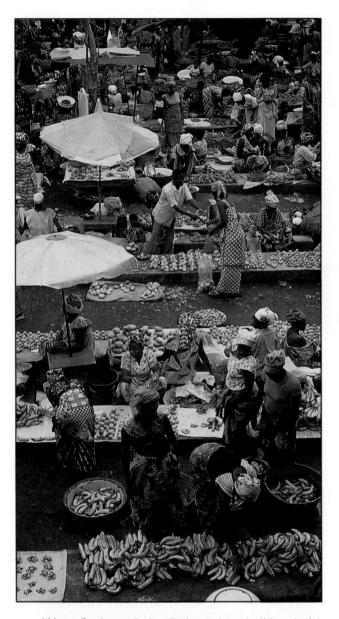

African Traders display their produce in this colorful, contemporary scene, which suggests the competition and the dynamism of a West African market. African traders and peasants have played a key role in the economic development of West Africa since the 1920s. *(Source: Cynthia Johnson/Gamma-Liaison)*

though occasionally disrupted by war and hindered by poor transportation, especially in the rainy season.

Into this sophisticated economy the British introduced production of cocoa beans for the world's chocolate bars. Output rose spectacularly,

from a few hundred tons in the 1890s to 305,000 tons in 1936. British imperialists loved to brag about the railroads to the interior, but recent studies clearly show that independent peasants and energetic African business people—many of the traders were women—were mainly responsible for the spectacular success of cocoa-bean production. Creative African entrepreneurs even went so far as to build their own roads, and they sometimes reaped big profits. During the boom of 1920, "motor cars were purchased right and left, champagne flowed freely, and expensive cigars scented the air."[7] As neighboring West African territories followed the Gold Coast's entrepreneurial example, West Africa took its place in the world economy.

The Gold Coast also showed the way politically and culturally. The Westernized elite—relatively prosperous and well-educated lawyers, professionals, and journalists—and business people took full advantage of opportunities provided by the fairly enlightened colonial regime. The black elite was the main presence in the limited local elections permitted by the British, for few permanent white settlers had ventured to hot and densely populated West Africa.

Across the continent in the British East African colony of Kenya, events unfolded differently. The East African peoples were more self-sufficient, less numerous, and less advanced commercially and politically than Africans in the Gold Coast. Once the British had built a strategic railroad from the Indian Ocean coast across Kenya to Uganda, foreigners from Great Britain and India moved in to exploit the situation. Indian settlers became shopkeepers, clerks, and laborers in the towns. The British settlers dreamed of turning the cool, beautiful, and fertile Kenya highlands into a "white man's country" like Southern Rhodesia or the Union of South Africa. They dismissed the local population of peasant farmers as "barbarians," fit only to toil as cheap labor on their large estates and plantations. By 1929, two thousand white settlers were producing a variety of crops for export.

The white settlers in Kenya manipulated the colonial government for their own interests and imposed rigorous segregation on the black (and Indian) population. Kenya's Africans thus experienced much harsher colonial rule than their fellow Africans in the Gold Coast.

The Growth of African Nationalism

Western intrusion was the critical factor in the development of African nationalism, as it had been in Asia and the Middle East. Yet two things were different about Africa. Because the imperial system and Western education did not solidify in Africa until after 1900, national movements did not come of age there until after 1945. And, too, Africa's multiplicity of ethnic groups, coupled with imperial boundaries that often bore no resemblance to existing ethnic boundaries, greatly complicated the development of political—as distinct from cultural—nationalism. Was a modern national state to be based on ethnic tribal loyalties (as it had been in France and Germany, in China and Japan)? Was it to be founded on an all-African union of all black peoples? Or would such a state have to be built on the multitribal territories arbitrarily carved out by competing European empires? Only after 1945 did a tentative answer emerge.

A few educated West Africans in British colonies had articulated a kind of black nationalism before 1914. But the first real impetus came from the United States and the British West Indies. American blacks struggling energetically for racial justice and black self-confidence early in the twentieth century took a keen interest in their African origins and in the common problems of all black people. Their influence on educated Africans was great.

Of the many persons who participated in this "black nationalism" and in the "Renaissance" of American black literature in the 1920s, the most renowned was W. E. B. Du Bois (1868–1963). The first black to receive a Ph.D. from Harvard, this brilliant writer and historian was stirred by President Woodrow Wilson's promises of self-determination. Thus Du Bois organized pan-African congresses in Paris during the Versailles Peace Conference and in Brussels in 1921. The goals of pan-Africanists were solidarity among blacks everywhere and, eventually, a vast self-governing union of all African peoples.

The European powers were hostile, of course, but so was the tiny minority of educated blacks in French Africa. As the influential Blaise Daigne, a black politician elected to the French parliament by the privileged African "citizens" of Senegal, told Du Bois:

We Frenchmen of Africa wish to remain French, for France has given us every liberty and accepted us without reservation along with her European children. None of us aspire to see French Africa delivered exclusively to the Africans as is demanded, though without any authority, by the American Negroes.[8]

More authoritarian than the British but less racist, French imperialists aimed to create a tiny elite of loyal "black Frenchmen" who would link the uneducated African masses to their white rulers. They were sometimes quite successful.

Many educated French and British Africans, however, experienced a strong surge of pride and cultural nationalism in the 1920s and 1930s, inspired in part by American and West Indian blacks. The Senegalese poet and political leader Léopold Senghor (b. 1906) is an outstanding example.

A gifted interpreter of Catholicism and of the French language in his native Senegal, Senghor discovered his African heritage in the cafés and lecture halls of Paris. He and other black and white students and intellectuals marveled at the accomplishments of American blacks in art, literature, African history, and anthropology. They listened to black musicians—jazz swept Europe by storm—and concluded that "in music American Negroes have acquired since the War a place which one can call pre-eminent; for they have impressed the entire world with their vibrating or melancholy rhythms."[9]

Senghor and his circle formulated and articulated the rich idea of *négritude*, or blackness: racial pride, self-confidence, and joy in black creativity and the black spirit. The powerful cultural nationalism that grew out of the cross-fertilization of African intellectuals and blacks from the United States and the West Indies was an unexpected by-product of European imperialism.

Black consciousness also emerged in the British colonies between the world wars—especially in West Africa. The Westernized elite pressed for more equal access to government jobs, modest steps toward self-government, and an end to humiliating discrimination. This elite began to claim the right to speak for ordinary Africans and to denounce the government-supported chiefs as "Uncle Toms." Yet the great majority of well-educated British and French Africans remained moderate in their demands. They wanted to join the white man's club, not to tear it down.

The Great Depression was the decisive turning point in the development of African nationalism. For the first time, unemployment was widespread among educated Africans, who continued to increase in number as job openings in government and the large foreign trading companies remained stable or even declined. Hostility toward well-paid white officials rose sharply. The Western-educated elite became more vocal, and some real radicals appeared.

Educated Africans ventured into new activities, often out of necessity. Especially in the towns, they supplied the leadership for many new organizations, including not only political parties and trade unions, but also social clubs, native churches, and agricultural cooperatives. Radical journalists published uncompromising attacks on colonial governments in easy-to-read mass-circulation newspapers. The most spectacular of these journalists was the Nigerian Nnamdi Azikiwe, who had attended black colleges in the United States and learned his trade on an African-American weekly in Baltimore. The popular, flamboyant "Zik" was demanding independence for Nigeria as early as the late 1930s.

The Great Depression also produced extreme hardship and profound discontent among the African masses. African peasants and small-business people who had been drawn into world trade, and sometimes profited from booms, felt the agony of decade-long bust. Urban workers, many of whom were disaffiliated from their rural tribal origins, experienced a similar fate. In some areas the result was unprecedented mass protest.

The Gold Coast "cocoa holdups" of 1930–1931 and 1937–1938 are the most famous example. Cocoa completely dominated the Gold Coast's economy. As prices plummeted after 1929, cocoa farmers refused to sell their beans to the large British firms that fixed prices and monopolized the export trade. Instead, the farmers organized cooperatives to cut back production and sell their crops directly to European and American chocolate manufacturers. Small African traders and traditional tribal leaders largely supported the movement, which succeeded in mobilizing much of the population against the foreign companies. Many Africans saw the economic conflict in racial terms. The holdups were only partially successful, but they did force the government to establish an independent cocoa marketing board. They also

demonstrated that mass organization and mass protest had come to advanced West Africa. Powerful mass movements for national independence would not be far behind.

Achieving Independence with New Leaders

The repercussions of the Second World War in black Africa greatly accelerated the changes begun in the 1930s. Mines and plantations strained to meet wartime demands. Towns mushroomed into cities whose tin-can housing, inflation, and shortages of consumer goods created discontent and hardship. Africans had such eye-opening experiences as the curious spectacle of the British denouncing the racism of the Germans. Many African soldiers who served in India were powerfully impressed by Indian nationalism.

The attitudes of Western imperialists changed also. Both the British and the French acknowledged the need for rapid social and economic improvement in their colonies; both began sending money and aid on a large scale for the first time. The French funneled more money into their West African colonies between 1947 and 1957 than during the entire previous half-century. The principle of self-government was written into the United Nations charter and was fully supported by Great Britain's postwar Labour government. As one top British official stated in 1948:

The central purpose of British colonial policy is simple. It is to guide the colonial territories to responsible government within the commonwealth in conditions that ensure to the people concerned both a fair standard of living and freedom from oppression from any quarter.[10]

Thus the key question for Great Britain's various African colonies was their rate of progress toward self-government. The British and the French were in no rush. But a new breed of African leader was emerging. Impatient and insistent, these spokesmen for modern African nationalism were remarkably successful: by 1964 almost all of western, eastern, and central Africa had achieved statehood, usually without much bloodshed.

The new postwar African leaders shared common characteristics. They formed an elite by virtue

NATIONALISM IN BLACK AFRICA

1919	Du Bois organizes first pan-African congress
1920s	Cultural nationalism grows among Africa's educated elites
1929	Great Depression brings economic hardship and discontent
1930–1931	Farmers in the Gold Coast organize first "cocoa hold-ups"
1939–1945	World War Two accelerates political and economic change
1951	Nkrumah and Convention People's Party win national elections
1957	Nkrumah leads Ghana—former Gold Coast—to independence
1958	De Gaulle offers commonwealth status to France's African territories; Guinea alone chooses independence
1960	Mali and Nigeria become independent states
1966	Ghana's Nkrumah deposed in military coup
1967	Eastern Region secedes from Nigeria to form state of Biafra
1975	Nigeria's military rulers permit elected civilian government
1980	Blacks rule Zimbabwe—formerly southern Rhodesia—after long civil war with white settlers
1983	South Africa's whites maintain racial segregation and discrimination
1989–1990	South African government begins process of reform; black leader Nelson Mandela freed from prison

of advanced European (or American) education, and they were profoundly influenced by Western thought. But compared with the interwar generation of educated Africans, they were more radical and humbler in social origin. Among them were former schoolteachers, union leaders, government clerks, and unemployed students, as well as lawyers and prize-winning poets.

Furthermore, the postwar African leaders expressed their nationalism in terms of the existing territorial governments. They accepted prevailing boundaries to avoid border disputes and to facilitate building unified modern states. Sometimes traditional tribal chiefs became their worst political enemies. Skillfully, the new leaders channeled postwar hope and discontent into support for mass political parties. These new parties in turn organized gigantic protests and eventually came to power by winning elections held by the colonial government to choose its successor.

Ghana Shows the Way

Perhaps the most charismatic of this fascinating generation of African leaders was Kwame Nkrumah (1909–1972). Under his leadership the Gold Coast—which he rechristened "Ghana"—became the first independent African state to emerge from colonialism. Having begun his career as a schoolteacher in the Gold Coast, Nkrumah spent ten years studying in the United States, where he was deeply influenced by European socialists and by the Jamaican-born black leader Marcus Garvey (1887–1940). Convinced that blacks could never win justice in countries with white majorities, Garvey had organized a massive "Back to Africa" movement in the 1920s. He also preached "Africa for the Africans," calling for independence. Nkrumah returned to the Gold Coast immediately after the war and entered politics.

And the time was ripe. Economic discontent erupted in rioting in February 1948; angry crowds looted European and Lebanese stores. The British, embarking on their new course, invited African proposals for constitutional reform. These proposals became the basis of the new constitution, which gave more power to Africans within the framework of (eventual) parliamentary democracy.

Meanwhile Nkrumah was building a radical mass party appealing particularly to modern elements—former servicemen, market women, union members, urban toughs, and cocoa farmers. Nkrumah and his party injected the joy and enthusiasm

The Opening of Parliament in Ghana   As part of an ancient ritual, two medicine men pour out sacred oil and call upon the gods to bless the work of the Second Parliament and President Kwame Nkrumah, standing on the right. The combination of time-honored customs and modern political institutions has been characteristic of African states since independence. *(Source: Wide World Photos)*

of religious revivals into their rallies and propaganda: "Self-Government Now" was their credo, secular salvation the promise.

Rejecting halfway measures—"We prefer self-government with danger to servitude in tranquillity"—Nkrumah and his Convention People's party staged strikes and riots. Arrested, the "Deliverer of Ghana" campaigned from jail and saw his party win a smashing victory in the national elections of 1951. Called from prison to head the transitional government, Nkrumah and his nationalist party continued to win victories in free elections, defeating both Westernized moderates and more traditional "tribal" rivals. By 1957 Nkrumah

had achieved worldwide fame and influence as Ghana became the first African state to emerge from colonial control.

After Ghana's breakthrough, independence for other African colonies followed with breathtaking speed. As in Algeria, the main problem was the permanent white settlers, as distinguished from the colonial officials. Wherever white settlers were at all numerous, as in Kenya, they sought to preserve their privileged position. This white hope was fed by a substantial influx of white settlers after 1945, especially in central Africa. Yet only in Southern Rhodesia were whites numerous enough to prevail long. Southern Rhodesian whites declared independence illegally in 1965 and held out for more than a decade until black nationalists won a long guerrilla war and renamed the country Zimbabwe. In Zambia (formerly Northern Rhodesia) and East Africa, white settlers simply lacked the numbers to challenge black nationalists or the British colonial office for long.

French-speaking Regions

Decolonization took a somewhat different course in French-speaking Africa. France tried hard to hold on to Indochina and Algeria after 1945. Thus, although France upped its financial and technical aid to its African colonies, *independence* remained a dirty word until de Gaulle came to power in 1958. Seeking to head off radical nationalists, and receiving the crucial support of moderate black leaders, de Gaulle divided the federations of French West Africa and French Equatorial Africa into thirteen separate governments, thus creating a "French commonwealth." Plebiscites were called in each territory to ratify the new arrangement. An affirmative vote meant continued ties with France; a negative vote signified immediate independence and a complete break with France.

De Gaulle's gamble was shrewd. The educated black elite—as personified by the poet Senghor, who now led the government of Senegal (see Map 37.4)—loved France and dreaded a sudden divorce. They also wanted French aid to continue. France, in keeping with its ideology of assimilation, had given the vote to the educated elite in its colonies after the Second World War, and about forty Africans held seats in the French parliament after 1946. Some of these impressive African politicians exercised real power and influence in metropolitan France. The Ivory Coast's Félix Houphouét-Boigny, for instance, served for a time as France's minister of health. For both cultural and practical reasons, therefore, French Africa's leaders tended to be moderate and in no rush for independence.

Yet political nationalism was not totally submerged. In Guinea (see Map 37.4), an inspiring young radical named Sekou Touré (1922–1984) led his people in overwhelming rejection of the new constitution in 1958. Touré had risen to prominence as a labor leader in his country's rap-

idly expanding mining industry; he had close ties with France's Communist-dominated trade unions and was inspired by Ghana's Nkrumah. Touré laid it out to de Gaulle, face to face:

We have to tell you bluntly, Mr. President, what the demands of the people are. . . . We have one prime and essential need: our dignity. But there is no dignity without freedom. . . . We prefer freedom in poverty to opulence in slavery.[11]

De Gaulle punished Guinea as best he could. French officials and equipment were withdrawn, literally overnight, down to the last man and pencil. Guinea's total collapse was widely predicted—and devoutly hoped for in France. Yet Guinea's new government survived. Following Guinea's lead, Mali asked for independence in 1960. The other French territories quickly followed suit, though the new states retained close ties with France.

Belgium tried belatedly to imitate de Gaulle in its enormous Congo colony, but without success. Long-time practitioners of extreme paternalism, coupled with harsh, selfish rule, the Belgians had discouraged the development of an educated elite. In 1959, therefore, when after wild riots they suddenly decided to grant independence, the fabric of government simply broke down. Independence was soon followed by violent tribal conflict, civil war, and foreign intervention. The Belgian Congo was the great exception to black Africa's generally peaceful and successful transition to independence between 1957 and 1964.

BLACK AFRICA SINCE 1960

The ease with which most of black Africa achieved independence stimulated buoyant optimism in the early 1960s. As Europeans congratulated themselves on having fulfilled their "civilizing mission," Africans and sympathetic Americans anticipated even more rapid progress.

A generation later the outlook was different. In most former colonies, democratic government and civil liberties had given way to one-party rule or military dictatorship. Even where dictatorship did not prevail or was overturned, political conduct in Africa often seemed to slip into reverse gear. In many countries it was routine for the winners in a political power struggle to imprison, exile, or murder the losers. Corruption was widespread; politicians, army officers, and even lowly government clerks used their positions to line their pockets and reward their relatives. Meanwhile, the challenge of constructive economic and social development sometimes appeared overwhelming in a time of global crisis (see Chapter 39).

Some European and American observers, surveying these conditions, went so far as to write off Africa as a lost cause. Such a dismissal betrayed a limited vision and a serious lack of historical perspective. Given the scope of their challenges, the new African countries did rather well after achieving political independence. Nationalism, first harnessed to throw off imperialism, served to promote some degree of unity and ongoing modernization. Fragile states held together and began to emerge as viable modern nation-states with their own distinct personalities.

Building National Unity

The course of African history after independence was complex and often confusing. Yet the common legacy of imperialism resulted in certain basic patterns and problems.

The legacy of imperialism in Africa was by no means all bad. One positive outcome was the creation of about forty well-defined states (see Map 36.3, page 1180). These new states inherited functioning bureaucracies, some elected political leaders, and some modern infrastructure—that is, transportation, schools, hospitals, and the like.

The new African states also inherited relatively modern, diversified social structures. Traditional tribal and religious rulers had generally lost out to a dynamic Westernized elite whose moderate and radical wings faithfully reproduced the twentieth-century political spectrum. Each new state also had the beginnings of an industrial working class (as well as a volatile urban poor population). Each country also inherited the cornerstone of imperial power—a tough, well-equipped army to maintain order.

Other features of the imperialist legacy served to torment independent Africa, however. The disruption of traditional life caused real suffering and resulted in postindependence expectations that could not be met. The prevailing export economies were weak, lopsided, and concentrated in foreign hands. Technical, managerial, and medical skills were in acutely short supply. Above all, the legacy of political boundaries imposed by foreigners without regard to ethnic and cultural groupings weighed heavily on postindependence Africa. Almost all of the new states encompassed a variety of peoples, with different languages, religions, and cultures. In such circumstances, building up the central government and forging a truly unified country could conflict with ethnic loyalties. As in the Austrian Empire in the nineteenth century or in British India before independence, different peoples might easily develop conflicting national aspirations.

The multi-ethnic character of the new states had a powerful impact on African political development after 1960. Great Britain and France had granted Africa democratic government in the belief that, if Africans insisted on independence, they might as well get the best. Yet Western-style democracy served poorly. Political parties often coalesced along regional and ethnic lines, so that political competition encouraged regional and ethnic conflict and promoted political crisis. Many African leaders concluded that democracy threatened to destroy the existing states, which they deemed essential for social and economic progress in spite of their less-than-perfect boundaries. These leaders imposed tough measures to hold their countries together, and free elections often gave way to dictators and one-party rule.

After Ghana won its independence, for instance, Nkrumah jailed without trial his main opponents—chiefs, lawyers, and intellectuals—and outlawed opposition parties. Embracing the totalitarian model, Nkrumah worked to build a dynamic "revolutionary" one-party state. His personality, his calls for African unity, and his bitter attacks on "Western imperialists" aroused both strong support and growing opposition. By the mid-1960s Nkrumah's grandiose economic projects had almost bankrupted Ghana, and in 1966 the army suddenly seized power while Nkrumah was visiting China. Across the continent in East Africa, Kenya and Tanzania likewise became one-party states with strong leaders.

The French-speaking countries also shifted toward one-party government to promote state unity and develop distinctive characteristics that could serve as the basis for statewide nationalism. Mali followed Guinea into fiery radicalism. Senegal and the Ivory Coast stressed moderation and close economic and cultural ties with France.

Like Nkrumah, many of the politicians at the helm of one-party states were eventually overthrown by military leaders. "The man on horseback" became a familiar figure in postindependence Africa. Between 1952, when Egypt's King Farouk was overthrown by Colonel Nasser, and 1968, Africa experienced at least seventy attempted military takeovers, twenty of which succeeded. The trend continued after 1968 with important coups in Ethiopia, Liberia, Uganda, and elsewhere. The rise of would-be Napoleons was lamented by many Western liberals and African intellectuals, who often failed to note that military rule was also widespread in Latin America, Asia, and the Near East.

As elsewhere, military rule in Africa was authoritarian and undemocratic. Sometimes it placed a terrible burden on Africans. In Uganda, for instance, Idi Amin (b. 1925?), a brutal former sergeant, seized power, packed the army with his tribal supporters, and terrorized the population for a decade. Yet military government often had redeeming qualities. African military leaders generally managed to hold their countries together, and they worked to build existing states into viable nations.

Equally important, and like their counterparts in Latin America (see pages 1205–1209), military regimes were usually committed to social and economic modernization. Drawing on a well-educated, well-organized, and highly motivated elite, they sometimes accomplished a good deal. Finally, African military leaders often believed in the ultimate goal of free, representative civilian government, which they sometimes restored after surmounting a grave national crisis. It was a question of priorities: unity came first, democracy second.

Nigeria, Africa's Giant

The history of Nigeria illustrates just how difficult nation building could be when state and ethnic boundaries were at odds with each other. "Nigeria" was a name coined by the British to designate their conquests in the Niger River basin (Map 37.4). The peoples of Nigeria encompassed many ancient kingdoms and hundreds of smaller groupings. The northern region was part of a great open plain, devoted to grazing and intensive farming. The much smaller southern region was a combination of coastal swamp and inland forest belt. Most of the peoples of the north were Muslims; most southerners were Christians or animists. The south was dominated by two very different peoples: in the west the proud Yorubas, with a military tradition and strong, well-defined kingdom; in the east the Ibos, with a tradition of business enterprise and independent villages.

Modern Nigeria came into being in 1914, when the British arbitrarily consolidated the northern and southern territories for administrative convenience. One British governor described Nigeria in 1920 as a

collection of self-contained and mutually independent Native States, separated from one another, as many of them are, by differences of history and traditions, and by ethnological, racial, tribal, political, and religious barriers.[12]

Such a land, the governor believed, could never be welded into a single homogeneous nation.

In spite of its internal divisions, by 1945 Nigeria had spawned a powerful independence movement. The British responded receptively, and Nigeria entered into a period of intense but peaceful negotiation. In 1954, the third constitution in seven years set up the framework within which independence was achieved in 1960.

The key constitutional question was the relationship between the central government and the various regions. Some Nigerians, like the fiery Ibo journalist Azikiwe, wanted a strong centralized state, but the Yorubas in the west and the Muslim Hausa-Fulani leaders in the north wanted real power concentrated at the regional level. Ultimately Nigeria adopted a federal system, whereby the national government at Lagos shared power with three regional or state governments in the north, west, and east. Each region had a dominant tribe and a corresponding political party. The parties were expected to cooperate in the national parliament, and the rights of minorities were protected by law.

With a population of 55 million in 1963, "Africa's Giant" towered over the other new African nations. But after independence, Nigerians' bright

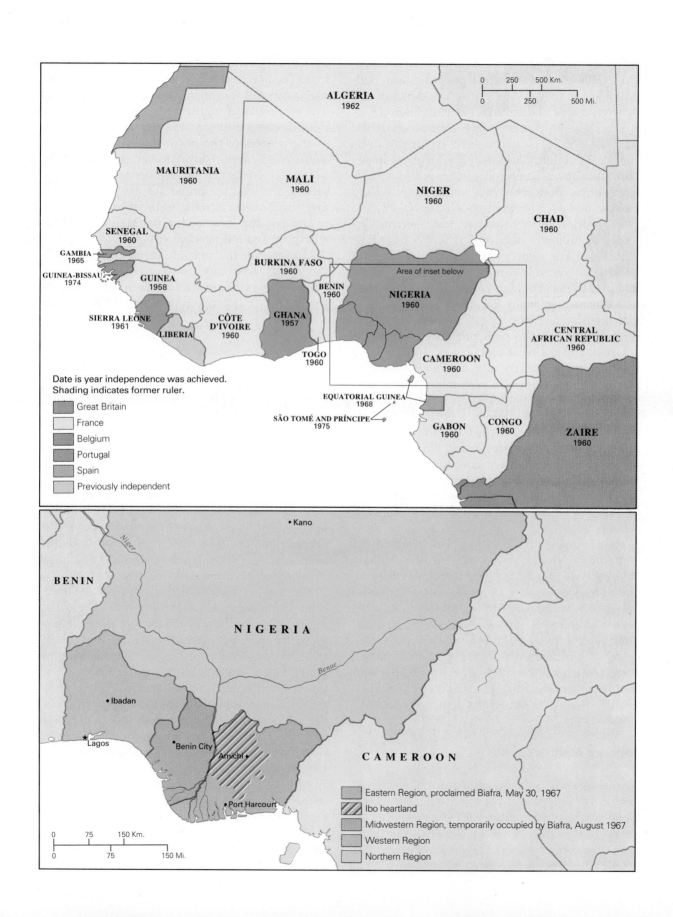

Date is year independence was achieved.
Shading indicates former ruler.

- Great Britain
- France
- Belgium
- Portugal
- Spain
- Previously independent

ALGERIA
1962

MAURITANIA
1960

MALI
1960

NIGER
1960

CHAD
1960

SENEGAL
1960

GAMBIA
1965

GUINEA-BISSAU
1974

GUINEA
1958

SIERRA LEONE
1961

LIBERIA

CÔTE
D'IVOIRE
1960

BURKINA FASO
1960

BENIN
1960

GHANA
1957

TOGO
1960

NIGERIA
1960

Area of inset below

CAMEROON
1960

CENTRAL
AFRICAN REPUBLIC
1960

EQUATORIAL GUINEA
1968

SÃO TOMÉ AND PRÍNCIPE
1975

GABON
1960

CONGO
1960

ZAIRE
1960

0   250   500 Km.
0   250   500 Mi.

BENIN

NIGERIA

Niger

Benue

Kano

Ibadan

Lagos

Benin City

Amichi

Port Harcourt

CAMEROON

- Eastern Region, proclaimed Biafra, May 30, 1967
- Ibo heartland
- Midwestern Region, temporarily occupied by Biafra, August 1967
- Western Region
- Northern Region

0   75   150 Km.
0   75   150 Mi.

Mobilizing in Biafra A Biafran officer, himself only nine years old, drills a column of fresh recruits in 1969 during the Nigerian civil war. The boy soldiers were used for spying and sabotage, as Biafra struggled desperately against encirclement and starvation to win its independence. *(Source: Pictorial Parade)*

hopes gradually dimmed. Ethnic rivalries made for political tensions. In 1964, minorities in the Western Region began forming their own Midwestern Region in an attempt to escape Yoruba domination (see Map 37.4). Tribal battles ensued, and in 1965 law and order broke down completely in the Western Region. At this point a group of young army officers seized power in the capital city of Lagos, executing leading politicians and all officers above the rank of major. In an attempt to end the national crisis, the new military council imposed martial law and abolished the regional governments.

At first the young officers were popular, for the murdered politicians had been widely considered weak, corrupt, and too pro-Western. However,

MAP 37.4 Nationalism and Independence in West Africa Most of West Africa achieved independence by 1960. Borders inherited from the colonial era were generally accepted, although the Ibo people tried unsuccessfully to break away from Nigeria in the bitter Nigerian civil war.

most of the new military leaders were Ibos. The Muslim northerners had long distrusted the hardworking, clannish, non-Muslim Ibos, who under the British had come to dominate business and the professions throughout Nigeria. Thus every town in the Muslim north had its Ibo "strangers' district." When the Ibo-led military council proclaimed a highly centralized dictatorship, angry mobs in northern cities went wild. Thousands of Ibos were brutally massacred, and the panic-stricken survivors fled to their Ibo homeland. When a group of northern officers then seized the national government in a counter-coup, the traumatized Ibos revolted. Like the American South in the Civil War, the Eastern Region seceded from Nigeria in 1967 and proclaimed itself the independent state of Biafra (see Map 37.4).

The war in Biafra lasted three long years. The Ibos fought with heroic determination, believing that political independence was their only refuge from genocide. Heavily outnumbered, the Ibos were gradually surrounded. Perhaps millions starved to death as Biafra became another name for monumental human tragedy.

But Nigeria, like Abraham Lincoln's Union, endured. The civil war entered the history books of the victors as the "War for Nigerian Unity," not the "War for Biafran Independence." Whatever its name, the conflict in Nigeria showed the world that Africa's "artificial" boundaries and states were remarkably durable.

Having preserved the state in the 1960s, Nigeria's military focused on building a nation in the 1970s. Although the federal government held the real power, the country was divided into nineteen small, manageable units to handle local and cultural matters. The defeated Ibos were generously pardoned, not slaughtered, and Iboland was rebuilt with federal money. Modernizing investments of this kind were made possible by soaring oil revenues; Nigeria became the world's seventh largest oil producer.

In 1979, after thirteen years of military rule, Nigeria's army leaders were confident enough to relinquish power to an elected civilian government. Yet four years later the army again seized control, arresting the civilian politicians at the head of Nigeria's Second Republic. Once again, the coup was popular, for the politicians had mismanaged the economy and lined their pockets with bribes and kickbacks. But the military rulers soon imposed a harsh dictatorship that violated human rights as badly as the greedy politicians had abused the public trust. The military dictatorship was dominated by Hausa-Fulani Muslims, and these northerners practiced a tribal favoritism that threatened to reignite regional and ethnic tensions that were never far beneath the surface. Thus a group of reforming officers engineered another coup in 1985, promising more liberty and less favoritism. The new generals showed greater respect for basic rights, but they repeatedly postponed national elections and maintained military rule to hold Nigeria together.

The Struggle in Southern Africa

After the great rush toward political independence, decolonization stalled. Meanwhile, southern Africa remained under white rule, largely because of the numerical strength and determination of its white settlers. In Portuguese Angola and Mozambique, the white population actually increased from 70,000 to 380,000 between 1940 and the mid-1960s as white settlers using forced native labor established large coffee farms.

As economic exploitation grew, so did resentment. Nationalist liberation movements arose to wage unrelenting guerrilla warfare. After a coup overturned the long-established dictatorship in Portugal, African guerrillas managed to take control in Angola and Mozambique in 1975. Shortly thereafter, a coalition of nationalist groups also won in Zimbabwe after a long struggle.

This second round of decolonization in black Africa was bloodier than the first, and a third round in South Africa threatened to be still worse. The racial conflict in the white-ruled Republic of South Africa (Map 37.5) could be traced back in history—to the seventeenth-century Dutch settlers, to complex rivalries between black tribes, to settler wars of extermination and enslavement in the eighteenth and nineteenth centuries, and to the surging British imperialism that resulted in the Boer War (see page 973). Although the British finally conquered the inland Afrikaner republics, they had to compromise to avoid a long guerrilla war. Specifically, the British agreed to grant all of South Africa self-government as soon as possible and to let its government decide which nonwhites, if any, should vote. It was to be a tragic compromise.

Defeated on the battlefield, the embittered Afrikaners elaborated a potently racist nationalism. Between 1910—when South Africa became basically a self-governing dominion, like Canada and Australia—and 1948, the Afrikaners gradually won political power from their English-speaking settler rivals. After their decisive electoral victory in 1948, Afrikaner nationalists spoke increasingly for a large majority of South African whites, who supported the political leadership with varying degrees of enthusiasm.

The goals of Afrikaner nationalism in the twentieth century were remarkably consistent: white supremacy and racial segregation. In 1913, the new South African legislature passed the Native Land Act, which limited black ownership of land to native reserves encompassing a mere one-seventh of the country. Poor, overpopulated, and too small to feed themselves, the native reserves in the countryside served as a pool of cheap, temporary black labor for white farms, gold mines, and urban factories. A black worker—typically a young single person—could leave the reserve only with

MAP 37.5 The Republic of South Africa and Apartheid, ca 1960 Despite repressive apartheid laws, many blacks managed to leave the reserves for South Africa's growing cities, where most Indians and coloureds already lived.

special permission. In the eyes of the law, he or she was only a temporary migrant who could be returned at will by the employer or the government. Thus so-called pass laws required every black outside the reserves to carry at all times an up-to-date pass approved by the white police. The native reserves system, combining racial segregation and indirect forced labor, formed the foundation of white supremacy in South Africa.

After 1948, successive Afrikaner governments wove the somewhat haphazard early racist measures into an authoritarian fabric of racial discrimination and inequality. This system was officially known as *apartheid,* meaning "separation" or "segregation." The population was dogmatically divided into four legally unequal racial groups: whites, blacks, Asians, and racially mixed "col-

oureds." Afrikaner propagandists claimed to serve the interests of all racial groups by preserving separate cultures and racial purity; marriage and sexual relations between races became criminal offenses. Most observers saw apartheid as a way of maintaining the lavish privileges of the white minority, which accounted for only one-sixth of the total population.

After 1940, South Africa's cities grew rapidly in conjunction with its emergence as the most highly industrialized country in Africa. Urbanization changed the face of the country, but good jobs in the cities were reserved for whites. Moreover, the whites lived in luxurious modern central cities; the blacks, legally classified as temporary migrants, were restricted to outlying black townships plagued by poverty, crime, and white policemen.

In spite of pass laws and segregation, the growing cities produced a vibrant urban black culture, largely distinct from that of the tribal reserves. As a black journalist in Johannesburg explained in 1966:

I am supposed to be a Pondo, but I don't even know the language of that tribe. . . . I am just not a tribesman, whether I like it or not. I am, inescapably, a part of the city slums, the factory machines and our beloved shebeens [illegal bars].[13]

South Africa's harsh white supremacy elicited many black nationalist protests from the 1920s onward. Black nationalists began as moderates, seeking gradual reforms. By the 1950s, blacks—and their coloured, white, and Asian allies—were staging large-scale peaceful protests. A high point came in 1960, when police at Sharpeville fired into a crowd of demonstrators and killed sixty-nine blacks. The main black nationalist organization—the African National Congress (ANC)—was outlawed but sent some of its leaders abroad to establish new headquarters. Other members, led by a young black lawyer named Nelson Mandela (b. 1918), stayed in South Africa to set up an underground army to oppose the government. Captured after seventeen months, Mandela was tried for treason and sentenced to life imprisonment. With harsh laws, a powerful police force, and an army of spies, the government defended and strengthened the apartheid system.

By the late 1970s, the white government had apparently destroyed the moderate black opposition within South Africa. Operating out of the sympathetic black states of Zimbabwe and Mozambique to the north (see Map 37.5), the militant ANC turned increasingly to armed struggle. South Africa struck back hard. It used its awesome economic and military strength to support separatist movements that destabilized its neighbors, and it forced Marxist Mozambique in particular to curtail the ANC's guerrilla activities. Fortified by these successes, South Africa's white leaders launched in 1984 a program of "reforms"—changes designed to ensure continued white domination by means of a few strategic concessions.

The main reform was constitutional. The government set up a new parliament consisting of one house for the 5 million whites and, for the first time, two much less powerful houses for the 3 million coloureds and the 1 million South Africans of Asian descent. But no provision was made for any representation of the country's 22 million blacks, on the grounds that they were citizens of "black homelands"—the new name for the tribal reserves. The government also made cosmetic adjustments to apartheid, permitting marriage between races, for example. But the hated pass laws were replaced only by a new identity card, which still controlled black movement and settlement.

The government's self-serving reforms provoked black indignation and triggered a massive reaction. In the segregated townships surrounding white cities, young black militants took to the streets, attacking in particular black civil servants and policemen as traitorous agents of white oppression. White security forces, armed with tear gas, whips, and guns, clashed repeatedly with black protesters, who turned funerals for fallen comrades into mass demonstrations. Foreign governments and opinion leaders urged fundamental changes that would move South Africa toward universal suffrage and black majority rule.

Instead, the white government dug in. In 1985, it imposed a state of emergency, which gave the police and army virtually unlimited powers to put down protest. In late 1986, the government imposed unlimited press censorship and took a gigantic step toward dictatorship for all, regardless of race. The state security force and the secret police hammered away at protesters in the black townships. Between 1985 and 1989, 5,000 died and 50,000 were jailed without charges because of the political unrest.

By 1989, the white government and the black opposition had reached an impasse. Black protesters had been bloodied but not beaten, and their movement for democracy had gathered worldwide support. The U.S. Congress had applied strong sanctions against South Africa in October 1986 and the Common Market had followed. The white government still held power, but the white population was increasingly divided. White South Africans had long prided themselves on their basic freedoms and parliamentary democracy even though they excluded blacks. Being rejected as outcasts by the world community wounded the pride of some whites and, more importantly, harsh repression of the black resistance had obviously failed.

A major step toward breaking the political stalemate came in September 1989 with the election of a new state president, Frederik W. de Klerk, an Afrikaner lawyer and politician. A late-blooming reformer, de Klerk moved cautiously toward reducing tensions and opening a dialogue with the ANC leaders. He began by freeing some prominent black prisoners, lifting the ban on black political demonstrations, and integrating public beaches. Negotiating with Nelson Mandela, whose reputation had soared among urban blacks during his long years in prison, de Klerk then lifted the state of emergency in most of the country, legalized the ANC, and freed Mandela in February 1990. Emerging from prison as a proud and impressive leader, Mandela received a hero's welcome in South Africa and then in the United States and Europe.

In August 1990, Mandela showed again his courage and statesmanship. Overriding the doubts of some militant supporters, he suspended the ANC's armed struggle, thereby meeting de Klerk's condition for more talks and eventual negotiations on South Africa's political future. The two leaders were still far apart, especially on the question of universal adult suffrage and majority rule. But striking progress had been made, more than had been thought possible, and the prospects for a multiracial democratic state in South Africa had never seemed brighter.

Soweto, 1990 Angry black protesters are forced to retreat in the face of tear gas fired by police. With a population today of more than 2 million, the sprawling black township near Johannesburg has for many years been the center of the struggle against the white minority government. *(Source: Wide World Photos)*

SUMMARY

This chapter focuses on the remarkable resurgence of Asian and African peoples after the Second World War, a resurgence that will almost certainly stand as a decisive turning point in world history. The chapter examines how the long-developing nationalist movement in China culminated in a social revolution led by communists who went on to pursue innovative and fiercely independent policies that redeemed China as a great power in world affairs. Meanwhile, Japan, defeated, demilitarized, and democratized, took a completely different path to the rank of economic superpower in a no less spectacular renaissance. Elsewhere—in India, Indonesia, and the Philippines—Asian peoples won their freedom and self-confidently charted independent courses. The Muslim world was also rejuvenated, most notably under Nasser in Egypt. In black Africa, a generation of nationalist leaders guided colonial territories to self-rule so successfully that by the middle of the 1960s only the Soviet Union still retained a large colonial empire.

The resurgence and political self-assertion of Asian and African peoples in revitalized or developing nation-states did not proceed without conflict. Serious regional and ethnic confrontations erupted, notably between Hindus and Muslims in India and between Arabs and Israelis in the Middle East. Moreover, the vestiges of Western colonialism and cold war struggles resulted in atypical but highly destructive conflicts in Algeria, Vietnam, and Zimbabwe. The revitalized peoples of Asia and Africa continued to face tremendous economic and social challenges, which had to be met if the emerging nations were to realize fully the promise of self-assertion and independence.

NOTES

1. S. Schram, *Mao Tse-tung* (New York: Simon and Schuster, 1966), p. 151.
2. Quoted in P. B. Ebrey, ed., *Chinese Civilization and Society: A Source Book* (New York: Free Press, 1981), p. 393.
3. Quoted in W. Bingham, H. Conroy, and F. Iklé, *A History of Asia,* vol. 2, 2d ed. (Boston: Allyn and Bacon, 1974), p. 459.
4. Quoted in S. Wolpert, *A New History of India,* 2d ed. (New York: Oxford University Press, 1982), p. 330.
5. Quoted in K. Bhata, *The Ordeal of Nationhood: A Social Study of India Since Independence, 1947–1970* (New York: Atheneum, 1971), p. 9.
6. Quoted in B. D. Nossiter, *Soft State: A Newspaperman's Chronicle of India* (New York: Harper & Row, 1970), p. 52.
7. G. B. Kay, ed., *The Political Economy of Colonialism in Ghana: A Collection of Documents and Statistics* (Cambridge, England: Cambridge University Press, 1972), p. 48.
8. Quoted in R. W. July, *A History of the African People,* 3d ed. (New York: Scribner's, 1980), pp. 519–520.
9. Quoted in J. L. Hymans, *Léopold Sédar Senghor: An Intellectual Biography* (Edinburgh: University of Edinburgh Press, 1971), p. 58.
10. Quoted in L. H. Gann and P. Duignan, *Colonialism in Africa,* vol. 2 (Cambridge, England: Cambridge University Press, 1970), p. 512.
11. Quoted in R. Hallett, *Africa Since 1875: A Modern History* (Ann Arbor: University of Michigan Press, 1974), pp. 378–379.
12. Ibid., p. 345.
13. Ibid., p. 657.

SUGGESTED READING

Many of the works mentioned in the Suggested Reading for Chapter 33 are also valuable for considering postwar developments in Asia and the Middle East. Three other important studies on developments in China are C. Johnson, *Peasant Nationalism and Communist Power: The Emergence of Revolutionary China, 1937–1945* (1962); L. Dittmer, *China's Continuous Revolution: The Post-Liberation Epoch, 1949–1981* (1987); and W. L. Parish and M. K. Whyte, *Village and Family in Contemporary China* (1978). M. Meisner, *Mao's China: A History of the People's Republic* (1977), is an excellent comprehensive study, and C. P. FitzGerald, *Communism Takes China: How the Revolution Went Red* (1971), is a lively, illustrated account by a scholar who spent many years in China. Recent developments are ably analyzed by J. Spence, *The Search for Modern China* (1990), and F. Butterfield, *China, Alive in a Bitter Sea* (1982), a journalist's perceptive eyewitness account. Yueh, T. and C. Wakeman, *To the Storm: The Odyssey of a Revolutionary Chinese Woman* (1985) is the poignant drama of a participant. R. Lardy, *Agriculture in China's Economic Development* (1983), carefully examines the poor performance that led to Deng's reforms, and A. Smith, ed., *The*

Re-emergence of the Chinese Peasantry (1987), considers the rural transformation.

K. Kawai, *Japan's American Interlude* (1960), and R. P. Dore, *Land Reform in Japan* (1959), consider key problems of occupation policy. Three excellent and thought-provoking studies of contemporary Japanese society are E. Reischauer, *The Japanese* (1977); F. Gibney, *Japan, the Fragile Superpower* (1977); and E. Vogel, *Japan as Number One: Lessons for America* (1979). G. Bernstein, *Haruko's World: A Japanese Farm Woman and Her Community* (1983), probes changing patterns of rural life. Akira Iriye, *The Cold War in Asia: A Historical Introduction* (1974), and M. Schaller, *The United States and China in the Twentieth Century* (1979), analyze international conflicts in the postwar Pacific Basin.

F. G. Hutchins, *India's Revolution: Gandhi and the Quit India Movement* (1973), is an excellent account of wartime developments in India, which may be compared with J. Nehru, *An Autobiography* (1962), the appealing testimony of a principal architect of Indian freedom. F. Frankel, *India's Political Economy, 1947–1977* (1978), intelligently discusses the economic policies of independent India. There is a good biography of Indira Gandhi by D. Moraes (1980). H. Tinker, *South Asia: A Short History,* 2d ed. (1990), is a good guide to the states of the Indian subcontinent. For Southeast Asia there are solid general accounts by C. Dubois, *Social Forces in Southeast Asia* (1967), and R. N. Kearney, *Politics and Modernization in South and Southeast Asia* (1974). C. Cooper, *The Lost Crusade: America in Vietnam* (1972), and F. FitzGerald, *Fire in the Lake* (1973), probe the tragic war in Vietnam. Two valuable works on other Asian countries are B. Dahm, *Sukarno and the Struggle for Indonesian Independence* (1969), and T. Friend, *Between Two Empires: The Ordeal of the Philippines, 1929–1946* (1965).

Recommended studies of the Middle East and Israel include a cultural investigation by R. Patai, *The Arab Mind* (1973); a balanced account by C. Smith, *Palestine and the Arab-Israeli Conflict* (1988); and an excellent biography of Israel's inspiring leader during its war for independence by A. Avi-Hai, *Ben Gurion, State Builder* (1974). A. Goldschmidt, Jr., *Modern Egypt: The Formation of a Nation-State* (1988), treats the post-Nasser years extensively and H. Munson, Jr., *Islam and Revolution in the Middle East* (1988), compares Iran and Arab countries.

The studies by July and Hallett cited in the Notes are outstanding interpretations of modern Africa's rich and complex history. Both have extensive bibliographies. Important works on the colonial era include J. A. Langley, *Pan-Africanism and Nationalism in West Africa, 1900–1945: A Study in Ideology and Social Classes* (1973); R. O. Collins, *Problems in the History of Colonial Africa, 1860–1960* (1970); T. Hodgkin, *Nationalism in Colonial Africa* (1957); and the monumental investigation edited by L. H. Gann and P. Duignan, *Colonialism in Africa, 1870–1960,* 5 vols. (1969–1975). W. E. B. Du Bois, *The World and Africa* (1947), and J. Kenyatta, *Facing Mount Kenya* (1953), are powerful comments on African nationalism by the distinguished American black thinker and Kenya's foremost revolutionary and political leader. R. July, *The African Voice: The Role of the Humanities in African Independence* (1987), focuses on intellectuals and artists struggling against cultural imperialism. A Hopkins, *An Economic History of West Africa* (1973), is a pioneering synthesis. C. Dewey and A. Hopkins, eds., *The Imperial Impact: Studies in the Economic History of Africa and India* (1978), is an innovative comparative study. R. Olaniyan, ed., *African History and Culture* (1982), is a valuable recent collection. M. Crowder, ed., *The Cambridge History of Africa,* vol. 8, examines the struggle for independence and nationhood between 1940 and 1975 in broad perspective. Major works on specific countries include M. Crowder, *The Story of Nigeria,* 4th ed. (1978); P. Hill, *Migrant Cocoa Farmers in Ghana* (1963); and R. W. Johnson, *How Long Will South Africa Survive?* (1977). P. C. Lloyd, *Africa in Social Change* (1972), is a useful study on the contemporary era, and F. Willett, *African Art* (1971), is a good introduction.

38

Life in the Third World

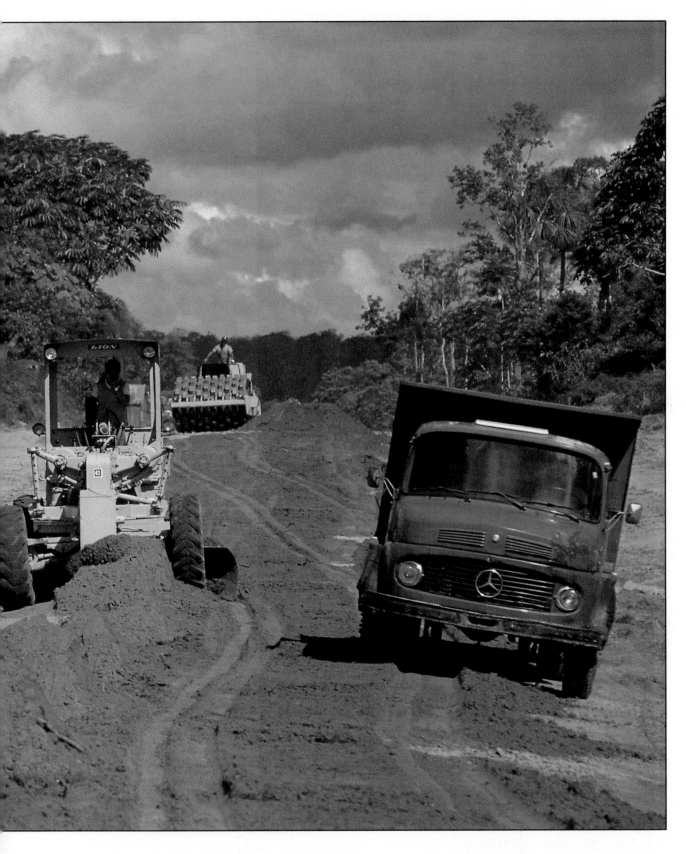

Destruction of the Amazon rain forest, near the Peru border

Everyday life in the emerging nations of Asia and Africa changed dramatically after the Second World War as many peoples struggled to build effective nation-states. Some of the changes paralleled the experiences of Europe and North America: science and modern technology altered individuals' lives in countless ways, and efforts to raise the standard of living by means of industrialization profoundly affected relations among social classes. Yet most observers stressed the differences in development between the emerging nations and the industrialized nations. In the new nations, which—along with the older states of Latin America—suffered widespread poverty and had a heritage of foreign domination, life remained very hard. Moreover, many discerned a widening economic gap between the industrialized nations of Europe and North America on the one hand and most of the emerging nations on the other, especially in the economically difficult 1970s and 1980s. Some writers even argued that the gap between North and South—that is, between rich nations and poor nations — had replaced the cold war between East and West and its immediate aftermath as humankind's most explosive division.

This chapter concentrates on shared problems of development and everyday life in Asia, Africa, and Latin America—a vast geographical expanse commonly known as the "Third World." Three key questions guide the investigation:

■ How have the emerging nations of the Third World sought to escape from poverty, and what have been the results of their efforts?

■ What has caused the prodigious growth of Third World cities, and what does their growth mean for their inhabitants?

■ How have Third World thinkers and artists interpreted the modern world and the experiences of their peoples before, during, and after foreign domination?

DEFINING THE THIRD WORLD

Can Africa, Asia, and Latin America be validly and usefully lumped together as a single entity—the Third World? Some experts prefer to speak of "emerging nations" or of "less developed countries"—deliberately vague terms suggesting a spectrum of conditions ranging from near-hopeless poverty to moderate well-being. Others now add a "Fourth" and even a "Fifth World" in order to distinguish more closely among the less developed nations. Nevertheless, the countries often termed "Third World" share characteristics that make it generally valid to speak of them jointly.

First, virtually all the countries of the Third World experienced political or economic domination, nationalist reaction, and a struggle for independence or autonomy. This shared past gave rise to a common consciousness and a widespread feeling of having been oppressed and victimized in dealings with Europe and North America. This outlook was nurtured by a variety of nationalists, Marxists, and anti-imperialist intellectuals, who argued forcibly that the Third World's problems were the result of past and present exploitation by the wealthy capitalist nations. Precisely because of their shared sense of past injustice, many influential Latin Americans have identified with the Third World, despite their countries' greater affluence. Indeed, "Third World" was first widely used by Latin American intellectuals in the late 1950s. They picked up the term from a French scholar who likened the peoples of Africa, Asia, and Latin America to the equally diverse but no less oppressed and humiliated French third estate before the revolution of 1789. The term also came into global use in the cold war era as a handy way of distinguishing Africa, Asia, and Latin America from the "First" and "Second" worlds—the capitalist and communist industrialized nations, respectively. (With the end of the cold war in 1989 eastern Europe has thrown off its former communist unity and is in flux. Some east European countries like Hungary may succeed in joining the capitalist First World; others like the Soviet Union may fall to Third World status as their planned economies collapse.)

Second, a large majority of men and women in most Third World countries live in the countryside and depend on agriculture for a living. Agricultural goods and raw materials are still the primary exports of Third World countries. In Europe, North America, and Japan, by contrast, most people live in cities and depend mainly on industry and urban services for employment.

Finally, the agricultural countries of Asia, Africa, and most of Latin America are united by awareness

An Indian Family walking barefoot across the countryside captures the human dimension of Third World poverty. Quite possibly they are landless laborers, searching for work, and carrying all their meager belongings. *(Source: Harmit Singh/Black Star)*

of their common poverty. By no means is everyone in the Third World poor; some people are quite wealthy. The average standard of living, however, is low, especially compared with that of people in the wealthy industrial nations, and massive poverty remains ever present.

ECONOMIC AND SOCIAL CHALLENGES IN THE THIRD WORLD

Alongside the tough postindependence task of preserving political unity and building cohesive nation-states, the emerging countries of the Third World faced the enormous challenges of poverty, malnutrition, and disease. These scourges weighed especially heavily on rural people, who depended on agriculture for survival and accounted for most of the Third World's population. Stirred by nationalism and the struggle for political freedom, peasants and landless laborers wanted the brighter future that their leaders had promised them.

Most Third World leaders and their advisers in the 1950s and 1960s saw rapid industrialization and "modernization" as the answer to rural poverty and disease. Industrialization and modernization also kindled popular enthusiasm and thus served nation building, which in turn promised economic self-sufficiency and genuine independence. For these reasons, the leaders and peoples of the Third World in the 1950s and 1960s set themselves the massive task of building modern factories, roads, and public health services like those of Europe and North America. Their considerable success fueled rapid economic progress.

Yet social problems, complicated by surging population growth, almost dwarfed the accomplishment. Disappointments multiplied. By and large, the poorest rural people in the poorest countries gained the least from industrialization, and industrial expansion provided jobs for only a small segment even of the urban population. By the late 1960s, widespread dissatisfaction with policies of all-out industrialization prompted a greater emphasis on rural development. The economic downturn of the 1970s and the crisis of the early 1980s reinforced this trend. More generally, different approaches proliferated from the late 1960s onward, as the Third World became less unified and more complex.

Poverty

It is easy to lose sight of the true dimensions of poverty in the Third World in a fog of economic statistics. In the 1950s and 1960s the United Nations and the emerging nations began collecting national income statistics. Dividing those estimates by total population yields a nation's average per capita income. These figures received enormous attention because they were stunningly low compared with those of wealthy nations. In 1960, for example, average annual income per person in all of Africa and Southeast Asia was about $100. In North America it was $2,500—twenty-five times more. Using such figures, journalists, politicians, and scholars often concluded that Third World people were unspeakably poor and verging on mass starvation.

Such comparisons, however, exaggerated the economic gap between the North and the South. They made a hard, sometimes desperate situation seem utterly hopeless. For example, average income per person in the United States in 1973 was about $5,000; in India it was about $100. Yet the average American was not necessarily fifty times better off than the average Indian. As an English and an Indian economist jointly pointed out, "Merely to survive, to be able to buy enough basic food, clothing and shelter in the United States would cost over $1,000 while $100 would suffice for these in India, so that someone with $1,000 in

America may be worse off than someone in India with $100."[1] Basic necessities cost considerably less in poor countries than in rich countries.

Reliance on national income statistics also promotes distorted comparisons because the statistics on poor countries are less complete and tend to leave out many wage-earning activities. Furthermore, fewer economic activities involve money transactions in poor countries than in rich ones, and only wage-earning work shows up consistently in national income statistics. In industrialized countries, only housewives do not receive money wages and thus do not show up in income statistics; there are many such "housewife" groups in the Third World.

A deeper understanding arises from considering Third World poverty not in statistical terms but in human terms, as did the postwar generation of nationalist leaders. To them, poverty meant, above all, not having enough to eat. For millions, hunger and malnutrition were harsh facts of life. In India, Ethiopia, Bolivia, and other extremely poor countries, the average adult ate fewer than 2,000 calories a day—only 85 percent of the minimal requirement. Although many poor countries fared better, in the 1960s none but Argentina could match the 3,000 or more calories consumed in the more fortunate North. Even Third World people who consumed enough calories often suffered from the effects of unbalanced high-starch diets and inadequate protein. Severe protein deficiency stunts the brain as well as the body, and many of the poorest children grew up mentally retarded.

Poor housing—crowded, often damp, and exposed to the elements—also contributed significantly to the less developed world's high incidence of chronic ill health. So too did scanty education and lack of the fundamentals of modern public health: adequate and safe water, sewage disposal, immunizations, prenatal care, and control of communicable diseases. Infant mortality was savage, and chronic illness weakened and demoralized many adults, making them unfit for the hard labor that their lives required.

Generally speaking, health status in Asia and Latin America was better than in the new states of sub-Saharan Africa. As one authority described the situation in the early 1960s:

In the African social drama, sickness has a strong claim to being archvillain. . . . In tropical Africa, most men, women, and children are habitually unwell.

Many are unwell from the day of their birth to the day of their death. . . . Most of the sick are sick of more than one disease.[2]

The people of poor countries were overwhelmingly concentrated in the countryside, as small farmers and landless laborers. These rural people were often unable to read or write, and they lacked steady employment. Even with hard work, simple tools limited productivity. Basic services like safe running water were uncommon: village women around the world spent much of each day carrying water and searching for firewood or dung to use as fuel, as they must still do in many countries.

Mass poverty represented an awesome challenge to the postwar leaders of the newly emerging nations. Having raised peoples' hopes in the struggle for independence, they had to start delivering on their promises if they were to maintain trust and stay in power. A strong commitment to modern economic and social development, already present in parts of Latin America in the 1930s, took hold in Asia and Africa in the postwar era.

The Medical Revolution and the Population Explosion

The most thoroughgoing success achieved by the Third World after the Second World War was a spectacular, ongoing medical revolution. Immediately after winning independence, the governments of emerging nations began adapting modern methods of immunology and public health.

The One-Child Family China's continued moderate rate of population increase resulted in the early 1980s in drastic laws that generally prohibit Chinese families from having more than one child. The happy grandmother and the government posters behind preach the joys of the one-child family, which is at odds with Chinese tradition. *(Source: Jin Xuqi/Picture Group)*

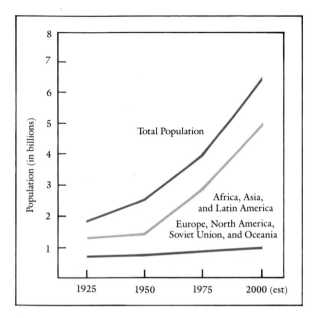

FIGURE 38.1 The Increase of World Population, 1925–2000 Since the first quarter of the twentieth century Africa, Asia, and Latin America—the Third World—have been growing much more rapidly than industrialized Europe, North America, and the Soviet Union. Compare with Figure 30.2 for a long-term perspective. *(Source: Data from United Nations,* Concise Report on the World Population Situation in 1970–1975 and Its Long-Range Implications, *New York, 1974, p. 59.)*

These methods were often simple and inexpensive but extremely effective. One famous measure was spraying DDT in Southeast Asia in order to control mosquitoes bearing malaria, one of the deadliest and most debilitating of tropical diseases. In Sri Lanka (formerly Ceylon), DDT spraying halved the yearly toll of deaths in the very first postwar decade—at a modest cost of $2 per person. According to the U.N. World Health Organization, which helped provide medical expertise to the new states, deaths from smallpox, cholera, and plague declined by more than 95 percent worldwide between 1951 and 1966.

Asian and African countries increased the small numbers of hospitals, doctors, and nurses that they had inherited from the colonial past. Large African cities' biggest, most modern, and most beautiful buildings were often their hospitals. Sophisticated medical facilities became symbols of the commitment to a better life.

Some critics, however, maintained that expensive medical technology was an indulgence that Third World countries could not afford, for it was ill suited to the pressing health problems of most of the population. In recent years, such criticism has prompted greater emphasis on delivering medical services to the countryside. Local people have been successfully trained as paramedics to staff rural outpatient clinics that offer medical treatment, health education, and prenatal and postnatal care. Most of the paramedics are women: many health problems involve childbirth and infancy, and villagers the world over consider it improper for a male to examine a woman's body.

The medical revolution significantly lowered death rates and lengthened life expectancy. In particular, children became increasingly likely to survive their early years, though infant and juvenile mortality remained far higher in the Third World than in rich countries. By 1980 the average inhabitant of the Third World could expect at birth to live about 54 years; life expectancy varied from 40 to 64 years depending on the country. In developed countries, by contrast, life expectancy at birth averaged 71 years.

A much less favorable consequence of the medical revolution was the acceleration of population growth. As in Europe during the nineteenth century, a rapid decline in the death rate was not immediately accompanied by a similar decline in the birthrate. Third World women generally continued to bear from five to seven children, as their mothers and grandmothers had done. The combined populations of Asia, Africa, and Latin America, which had grown relatively modestly from 1925 to 1950, increased between 1950 and 1975 from 1,750 million to 3,000 million (Figure 38.1 and Map 38.1). Barring catastrophe, the population of the three continents is expected to surge to about 5,200 million in the year 2000—an unprecedented explosion.

The population explosion aroused fears of approaching famine and starvation. Thomas Malthus's gloomy late-eighteenth-century conclusion that population always tends to grow faster than the food supply (see page 872) was revived and updated by "neo-Malthusian" social scientists. Such

MAP 38.1 World Population Density

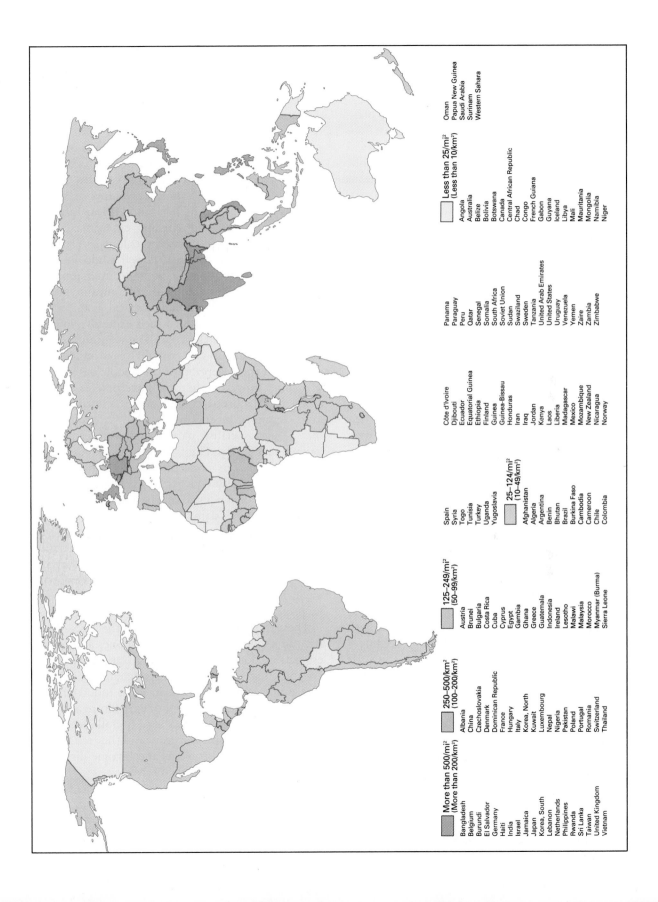

More than 500/mi² (More than 200/km²)
Bangladesh
Belgium
Burundi
El Salvador
Germany
Haiti
India
Israel
Jamaica
Japan
Korea, South
Lebanon
Luxembourg
Nepal
Netherlands
Nigeria
Philippines
Poland
Portugal
Rwanda
Sri Lanka
Taiwan
United Kingdom
Vietnam

250–500/km² (100–200/km²)
Albania
China
Czechoslovakia
Denmark
Dominican Republic
France
Hungary
Italy
Korea, North
Kuwait
Luxembourg
Nepal
Nigeria
Pakistan
Poland
Portugal
Romania
Switzerland
Thailand

125–249/mi² (50–99/km²)
Austria
Brunei
Bulgaria
Costa Rica
Cuba
Cyprus
Gambia
Ghana
Greece
Guatemala
Indonesia
Ireland
Lesotho
Malawi
Malaysia
Morocco
Myanmar (Burma)
Sierra Leone
Spain
Syria
Togo
Tunisia
Turkey
Uganda
Yugoslavia

25–124/mi² (10–49/km²)
Afghanistan
Algeria
Argentina
Benin
Bhutan
Burkina Faso
Cambodia
Cameroon
Chile
Colombia
Côte d'Ivoire
Djibouti
Ecuador
Equatorial Guinea
Ethiopia
Finland
Guinea
Guinea-Bissau
Honduras
Iran
Iraq
Jordan
Kenya
Laos
Liberia
Madagascar
Mexico
Mozambique
New Zealand
Nicaragua
Norway
Panama
Paraguay
Peru
Qatar
Senegal
Somalia
South Africa
Soviet Union
Sudan
Sweden
Tanzania
United Arab Emirates
United States
Uruguay
Venezuela
Yemen
Zaire
Zambia
Zimbabwe

Less than 25/mi² (Less than 10/km²)
Angola
Australia
Belize
Bolivia
Botswana
Canada
Central African Republic
Chad
Congo
French Guiana
Gabon
Guyana
Iceland
Libya
Mali
Mauritania
Mongolia
Namibia
Niger
Oman
Papua New Guinea
Saudi Arabia
Surinam
Western Sahara

fears were exaggerated, but they did produce uneasiness in the Third World, where leaders saw that their countries had to run fast just to maintain already low standards of living.

Some governments began pushing family planning and birth control to slow the growth of population. These measures were not very successful in the 1950s and 1960s. In many countries, Islamic and Catholic religious teachings were hostile to birth control. Moreover, widespread cultural attitudes dictated that a real man keep his wife pregnant. There were also solid economic reasons for preferring large families. Farmers needed the help of plenty of children at planting and harvest times. And sons and daughters were a sort of social security system for their elders; thus a prudent couple wanted several children because some would surely die young.

The Race to Industrialize (1950–1970)

Throughout the 1950s and most of the 1960s, many key Third World leaders, pressed on by their European, American, and Soviet advisers, were convinced that all-out industrialization was the only answer to poverty and population growth. The masses, they concluded, were poor because they were imprisoned in a primitive, inefficient agricultural economy. Farm families' tiny holdings were too small for modern machinery. Large landowners showed more, but still limited, promise. Only modern factory industry appeared capable of creating wealth quickly enough to outrace the growth of numbers.

The two-century experience of the West, Japan, and the Soviet Union seemed to validate this faith in industrialization. Economic history became a popular subject among Third World elites. It taught the encouraging lesson that the wealthy countries had also been agricultural and "underdeveloped" until the Industrial Revolution had lifted them out of poverty, one by one. According to this view, the uneven progress of industrialization was primarily responsible for the great income gap that existed between the rich countries of North America and Europe (including the Soviet Union) and the poor countries of the postindependent Third World.

Theories of modernization, particularly popular in the 1960s, also assumed that all countries were following the path already taken by the industrialized nations and that the task of the elite was to speed the trip. Marxism, with its industrial and urban bias, preached a similar gospel. These ideas reinforced the Third World's desire to industrialize.

Nationalist leaders believed that successful industrialization required state action and enterprise. Many were impressed by socialism in general and by Stalin's forced industrialization in particular, which they saw as having won the Soviet Union international power and prominence, whatever its social costs. In Asia and Africa, furthermore, capitalists and private enterprise were equated with the old rulers and colonial servitude. The reasoning was practical as well as ideological: in addition to high-paying administrative jobs for political allies, modern industry meant ports, roads, schools, and hospitals, as well as factories. Only the state could afford such expensive investments—as, indeed, the colonial governments had begun to realize in the twilight years of colonial rule. With the exception of the People's Republic of China, however, the new governments recognized private property and also tolerated native (and foreign) businessmen. The "mixed economy"—part socialist, part capitalist—became the general rule in the Third World.

Political leaders concentrated state investment in big, highly visible projects that proclaimed the country's independence and stimulated national pride. Enormous dams for irrigation and hydroelectric power were favored undertakings. Nasser's stupendous Aswan Dam harnessed the Nile, demonstrating that modern Egyptians could surpass even the pyramids of their ancient ancestors. The gigantic state-owned steel mill was another favorite project.

These big projects testified to the prevailing faith in expensive advanced technology and modernization along European lines. Nationalist leaders and their economic experts generally believed that money for investment in rapid industrialization would be squeezed out of agriculture and the farm population. They measured overall success by how fast national income grew, and they tended to assume that social problems and income distribution would take care of themselves.

India, the world's most populous noncommunist country, exemplified the general trends. After India achieved independence in 1947, Gandhi's special brand of nationalism was redirected toward economic and social rebirth through state enterprise and planning. Nehru and many Congress

Building the Aswan Dam Financed and engineered by the Soviet Union, the massive high dam at Aswan was Nasser's dream for Egypt's economic future. Here an army of workers lay the stones that will harness the Nile for irrigation and hydroelectric power. *(Source: Popperfoto)*

party leaders believed that unregulated capitalism and free trade under British rule had deepened Indian poverty. Considering themselves democratic socialists, they introduced five-year plans, built state-owned factories and steel mills, and raised tariffs to protect Indian manufacturers. Quite typically, they neglected agriculture, land reform, and village life.

The Third World's first great industrialization drive was in many ways a success. Industry grew faster than ever before, though from an admittedly low base in Africa and most of Asia. According to the United Nations, industry in the noncommunist developing nations grew at more than 7 percent per year between 1950 and 1970. Because

this growth exceeded the average annual population increase of 2.5 percent, Third World industrial production per capita grew about 4.5 percent per year for a generation. This was very solid industrial growth by historical standards: it matched the fastest rates of industrialization in the United States before 1914 and was double the rate of Britain and France in the same years.

Industrial expansion stimulated the other sectors of Third World economies. National income per capita grew about 2.5 percent per year in the 1950s and 1960s. This pace was far superior to the very modest increases that had occurred under colonial domination between 1900 and 1950. Future historians may well see the era after political emancipation as the era of industrial revolution in Asia and Africa.

This was certainly the case for a few small Asian countries that downgraded government control and emphasized private enterprise and the export of manufactured goods. South Korea, Taiwan, the city-state of Singapore, and the British colony of Hong Kong were genuine "economic miracles," industrializing rapidly and remarkably improving the living standards of ordinary people.

South Korea and Taiwan were typical underdeveloped countries after the Second World War—poor, small, agricultural, densely populated, and lacking in natural resources. They had also suffered from Japanese imperialism. How did they manage to make good?

Radical land reform drew the mass of small farmers into a competitive market economy, which proved an excellent school of self-reliance and initiative. As in Japan, probusiness governments in South Korea and Taiwan cooperated with capitalists and helped keep wages low. American aid also helped, as did almost free access to the large American market. And like Japan, both countries succeeded in preserving the fundamentals of their traditional cultures even as they accepted and mastered Western technology. Tough nationalist leaders maintained political stability at the expense of genuine political democracy.

Nevertheless, by the late 1960s, disillusionment with the Third World's relatively rapid industrialization was spreading, for several reasons. In the first place, the experience of a few small states like South Korea and Taiwan was the exception. The countries of Asia, Africa, and Latin America did not as a whole match the "miraculous" concurrent advances of western Europe and Japan, and the great economic gap between the rich and the poor nations continued to widen.

Also, most Third World leaders had genuinely believed that rapid industrial development would help the rural masses. Yet careful studies showed that the main beneficiaries of industrialization were businessmen, bureaucrats, skilled workers, and urban professionals. Peasants and agricultural laborers gained little or nothing. In fast-growing, dynamic Mexico, for instance, it was estimated that about 40 percent of the population was completely excluded from the benefits of industrialization. Moreover, the very poorest countries—such as India and Indonesia in Asia, and Ethiopia and

the Sudan in Africa—were growing most slowly in per capita terms. The industrialization prescription appeared least effective where poverty was most intense. Economic dislocations after 1973, and especially the worldwide economic crisis of the early 1980s, accentuated this trend, visiting particularly devastating effects on the poorest countries.

Perhaps most seriously, industrialization failed to provide the sheer number of jobs needed for the sons and daughters of the population explosion. Statisticians estimated that the growth of Third World manufacturing between 1950 and 1970 provided jobs for only about one-fifth of the 200 million young men and women who entered the exploding labor force in the same period. Most new enterprises employed advanced technology that required few workers. One person on a bulldozer could do the job of hundreds with shovels. For the foreseeable future, most Third World people would have to remain on the farm or work in traditional handicrafts and service occupations. All-out modern industrialization had failed as a panacea.

Agriculture and Village Life

From the late 1960s onward, the limitations of industrial development forced Third World governments to take a renewed interest in rural people and village life. At best, this attention meant giving agriculture its due and coordinating rural development with industrialization and urbanization. At worst, it fostered a resigned second-best approach to the unrelenting economic and social challenge, especially in the very poorest countries. The optimistic vision of living standards approaching those of the wealthy North gave way to the pessimistic conclusion that it was possible to ease only modestly the great hardships.

Nationalist elites had neglected agriculture in the 1950s and the 1960s for various reasons. They regarded an agricultural economy as a mark of colonial servitude, which they were symbolically repudiating by embracing industrialization. They wanted to squeeze agriculture and peasant producers in order to provide capital for industry. Thus governments often established artificially low food prices, which also subsidized their volatile urban supporters at the expense of the farmers.

In addition, the obstacles to more productive farming seemed overwhelming to unsympathetic urban elites and condescending foreign experts: farms were too small and fragmented for mechanization, peasants were too stubborn and ignorant to change their ways, and so on. Little wonder that only big farmers and some plantations received much government support. Wherever large estates and absentee landlords predominated—in large parts of Asia and most of Latin America, excluding Mexico, though not in black Africa— landless laborers and poor peasants who had no other choice than to rent land simply lacked the incentive to work harder. Any increased profits from larger crops went mainly to the absentee landowners.

Most honest observers were convinced that improved farm performance required land reform. Yet ever since the French Revolution, genuine land reform has been a profoundly radical measure, frequently bringing violence and civil war. Powerful landowners and their allies have generally succeeded in blocking or subverting redistribution of land to benefit the poor. Land reform, unlike industrialization, has generally been too hot for most politicians to handle.

Third World governments also neglected agriculture because feeding the masses was deceptively easy in the 1950s and early 1960s. Very poor countries received food from the United States at giveaway prices as part of a U.S. effort to dispose of enormous grain surpluses and help American farmers. Before 1939, the countries of Asia, Africa, and Latin America had collectively produced more grain than they consumed. But after 1945, as their populations soared, they began importing ever increasing quantities. Crops might fail, but starvation seemed a thing of the past. In 1965, when India was urged to build up its food reserves, one top Indian official expressed a widespread attitude: "Why should we bother? Our reserves are the wheat fields of Kansas."[3]

In the short run, the Indian official was right. In 1966 and again in 1967, when the monsoon failed to deliver its life-giving rains to the Indo-Pakistan subcontinent and famine gripped the land, the United States gave India one-fifth of the U.S. wheat crop. More than 60 million Indians lived exclusively on American grain. The effort required a food armada of six hundred ships, the largest fleet assembled since the Normandy in-vasion of 1944. The famine was ultimately contained, and instead of millions of deaths there were only a few thousand.

That close brush with mass starvation sent a shiver down the world's spine. Complacency dissolved in the Third World, and prophecies of disaster multiplied in wealthy nations. Paul Ehrlich, an American scientist, envisioned a grisly future in his polemical 1968 best-seller *The Population Bomb*:

The battle to feed all of humanity is over. In the 1970s the world will undergo famines—hundreds of millions of people are going to starve to death in spite of any crash programs embarked upon now. At this stage nothing can prevent a substantial increase in the world death rate.[4]

Other Western commentators outdid each other with nightmare visions. One portrayed the earth as a crowded lifeboat in a sea of hungry poor who would have to drown in order not to swamp the lifeboat. Another vision compared truly poor countries like Bangladesh, Ethiopia, and Haiti to hopelessly wounded soldiers on a gory battlefield. Such victims were best left to die so that scarce resources could be concentrated on the "walking wounded" who might yet be saved. Such crude and brutal Social Darwinism made it easy for Third World intellectuals to believe the worst about the rich industrialized nations and their economies.

Yet there was another face, a technological face, to the European and American interest in the Third World's food supply. Plant scientists and agricultural research stations had already set out to develop new hybrid seeds genetically engineered to suit the growing conditions of tropical agriculture. Their model was extraordinarily productive hybrid corn developed for the American Midwest in the 1940s. The first breakthrough came in Mexico in the 1950s, when an American-led team developed new high-yielding dwarf wheats. These varieties enabled farmers to double their yields from one year to the next, though they demanded greater amounts of fertilizer and water for irrigation. Mexican wheat production soared. Thus began the transformation of Third World agriculture—the so-called Green Revolution.

In the 1960s an American-backed team of scientists in the Philippines turned their attention to rice, the Asian staff of life; they quickly developed

Peasant Farming in Ecuador   Cultivating the land with simple hand tools, these peasant women in Latin America appear doomed to poverty despite backbreaking labor. In many cases, a high rent to an absentee landlord reduces the peasants' income still further. *(Source: Bernard Pierre Wolff/Photo Researchers, Inc.)*

a "miracle rice." The new hybrid also required more fertilizer and water but yielded more and grew much faster. It permitted the revolutionary advent of year-round farming on irrigated land, making possible two, three, or even four crops a year. The brutal tropical sun of the hot dry season became an agricultural blessing for the first time. Asian scientists, financed by their governments, developed similar hybrids to meet local conditions.

Increases in grain production were rapid and dramatic in some Asian countries. In gigantic India, for example, farmers upped production more than 60 percent in fifteen years. By 1980, thousands of new grain bins dotted the countryside, symbols of the agricultural revolution in India and the country's new-found ability to feed all its people. China followed with its own highly successful version of the Green Revolution under Deng Xiao-ping.

The Green Revolution offered new hope to the Third World, but it was no cure-all. At first it seemed that most of its benefits flowed to large landowners and substantial peasant farmers who could afford the necessary investments in irrigation and fertilizer. Subsequent experience in China and other Asian countries showed, however, that even peasant families with tiny farms could gain substantially. The new techniques of year-round cropping required more work, but they enabled a peasant family to squeeze more food out of its precious land. For any family lucky enough to have even three acres, the ongoing Green Revolution proved a godsend.

After early breakthroughs in Mexico, the Green Revolution's greatest successes have occurred not in Latin America but in Asia, most notably in countries with broad-based peasant ownership of land. The technical revolution has shared relatively few of its benefits with the poorest classes—landless laborers, tenant farmers, and tiny landholders. Lacking even the two or three acres necessary to feed themselves with intensive effort, the very poorest groups have gained only slightly more regular employment from the Green Revolution's demand for more labor. Pakistan, the Philippines, and other countries with large numbers of landless peasants and insecure tenant farmers have experienced less improvement than countries like South Korea and Taiwan, where land is generally owned by peasants. This helps to explain why the Green Revolution failed to spread from Mexico through-out Latin America: as long as 3 or 4 percent of the rural population owned 60 to 80 percent of the land, which is still the case in many Latin American countries, the Green Revolution will probably remain stillborn.

The same fatal equation of property ownership has prevailed in Bangladesh. There an elite tenth of the population owns half of the land, and the poorest half owns nothing at all. People eat less today than in 1970, yet land reform remains a political and social minefield. One member of a big (fifty-acre) landowning family in Bangladesh told an American reporter in 1981: "They talk of removing property markers. It cannot happen. I will kill you if you move my property markers one inch."[5]

Old and New With a fetish statue designed to frighten off evil spirits standing by, the proud owner of a two-acre plot in southern India shows a visiting expert his crop of miracle rice. As this picture suggests, the acceptance of modern technology does not necessarily require the repudiation of cultural traditions. *(Source: Marc and Evelyne Bernheim/Woodfin Camp)*

Black Africa has benefited little from the new agricultural techniques, even though land reform has been a serious problem only in white-ruled South Africa. Poor transportation, inadequate storage facilities, and low government-imposed agricultural prices have to bear much of the blame. Also, the climatic conditions of black Africa have encouraged continued adherence to dry farming and root crops, whereas the Green Revolution has been almost synonymous with intensive irrigation and grain production.

The Green Revolution, like the medical revolution and industrialization, represented a large but uneven step forward for the Third World. Most unfortunately, relatively few of its benefits flowed to the poorest groups—black Africans and the landless peasants of Asia and Latin America. These poor, who lacked political influence and had no clear idea about what needed to be done, increasingly longed to escape from ill-paid, irregular work in somebody else's fields. For many of the bravest and most enterprising, life in a nearby town or city seemed a way out.

THE GROWTH OF CITIES

Life in the less developed countries has been marked by violent contrasts, and it is in urban areas that such contrasts are most striking. Shiny airports, international hotels, and massive government buildings were built next to tar-paper slums. Like their counterparts in the North, these rapidly growing cities were monuments to political independence and industrial development. Unfortunately, they were also testimonials to increasing population, limited opportunities in the countryside, and neocolonial influence. Runaway urban growth has become a distinctive feature of the Third World.

Urbanization in the Third World

The cities of the Third World expanded at an astonishing pace after the Second World War. Many doubled and some even tripled in size in a single decade. The Algerian city of Algiers jumped from 300,000 to 900,000 between 1950 and 1960;

Accra in Ghana, Lima in Peru, and Nairobi in Kenya grew just as fast. Moreover, rapid urban growth has continued. Thus the less developed countries have become far more thoroughly urbanized in recent times than most people realize. In Latin America, three out of four people lived in towns and cities by 1975; in Asia and Africa, as Table 38.1 shows, one in four lived in an urban area by the same year.

The urban explosion continued in the 1980s, so that by 1990 fully 60 percent of the planet's city dwellers lived in the cities of the Third World, according to U.N. estimates. Rapid Third World urbanization represents a tremendous historical change. As recently as 1920, three out of every four of the world's urban inhabitants were concentrated in Europe and North America.

In most Third World countries the largest cities grew fastest. Gigantic "super cities" of 2 to 10 million persons arose. The capital typically emerged as the all-powerful urban center, encompassing all the important elite groups and dwarfing smaller cities as well as villages. Mexico City, for example, grew from 3 million to 12 million people between 1950 and 1975, and it will probably have a staggering 31 million in the year 2000. The pattern of a dominant megalopolis has continued to spread from Latin America to Africa and Asia (though not to Asia's giants, China and India).

In the truly poor countries of Africa and Asia, moreover, the process of urbanization is still in the early stages. However populous the cities, the countryside still holds most of the people. But if present trends continue, a city like Jakarta, the capital of Indonesia, will have about 17 million people by the end of this century. Calcutta and Bombay could be equally large. In the year 2000, the world will have 25 megalopolises with more than 10 million people—20 of them in the Third World, by World Bank estimates. Such growth poses enormous challenges for the future.

This urban explosion has been due, first of all, to the general growth of population in the Third World. Urban residents gained substanially from the medical revolution but only gradually began to reduce the size of their families. At the same time, the pressure of numbers in the countryside encouraged millions to set out for the nearest city. More than half of all urban growth has been due to rural migration.

TABLE 38.1 URBAN POPULATION AS A PERCENTAGE OF TOTAL POPULATION IN THE WORLD AND IN EIGHT MAJOR AREAS, 1925–2025

Area	1925	1950	1975	2000 (est.)	2025 (est.)
World total	21	28	39	50	63
North America	54	64	77	86	93
Europe	48	55	67	79	88
Soviet Union	18	39	61	76	87
East Asia	10	15	30	46	63
Latin America	25	41	60	74	85
Africa	8	13	24	37	54
South Asia	9	15	23	35	51
Oceania	54	65	71	77	87

Little more than one-fifth of the world's population was urban in 1925. In 1990 the urban proportion in the world total was about 45 percent and, according to United Nations experts, it should reach one-half by the century's end and two-thirds by about 2025. The most rapid urban growth will come in Africa and Asia, where the move to cities is still in its early stages. *(Source: United Nations,* Concise Report on the World Population Situation in 1970–1975 and Its Long-Range Implications, *New York, 1974, p. 63.)*

Even more than in Europe and North America in the nineteenth century, great cities became the undisputed centers of industry in the less developed countries. Half of all the industrial jobs in Mexico were concentrated in Mexico City in 1980. The same kind of extreme concentration of industry occurred in many Third World countries. Yet careful study leads scholars to play down industrialization as a cause of urban explosion. In the words of a leading authority:

After about 1930 a new phenomenon which might be termed "urbanization without industrialization" began to appear in the Third World. This phenomenon very rapidly acquired an inflationary character and in the early 1960s began to present most serious problems of urban employment and underemployment.[6]

In short, urban population grew much faster than industrial employment. It was a lucky migrant who found a real factory job.

Nevertheless, newcomers continued to stream to the cities. Many were pushed: they simply lacked enough land to survive. Large landowners found it more profitable to produce export crops, like sugar or coffee, for wealthy industrialized countries, and their increasingly mechanized operations provided few jobs for agricultural laborers. The push factor was particularly strong in Latin America, where the neocolonial pattern of large landowners and foreign companies exporting food and raw materials to the industrialized nations worked against peasant agriculture. More generally, much migration was seasonal or temporary. Many a young person left home for the city to work in construction or serve as a maid, planning to return shortly with a modest nest egg. Higher wages and steadier work in the city also strongly influenced most decisions to migrate.

Yet the magnetic attraction of Third World cities was more than economic. Their attraction rested on the services and opportunities they offered, as well as on changing attitudes and the urge to escape from the traditional restraints of village life. Most of the modern hospitals, secondary schools, and transportation systems in less developed countries were in the cities. So were most banks, libraries, movie houses, and basic conveniences. Safe piped water and processed food were rare in rural areas, for instance, and village women by necessity spent much of their time carrying water and grinding grain.

The city held a special appeal for rural people who had been exposed to the seductive influence of modern education. In Africa, a European economist concluded that "the number of people who are prepared to go back to the land after more than three or four years in the classroom is infinitesimal."[7] One survey from the 1960s in the Ivory Coast found two out of three rural high school graduates planning to move to the city; only one in ten of the illiterates expressed the same intention. Africa was not unique in this. For the young and the ambitious, the allure of the city was the excitement and opportunity of modern life. The village took on the curse of boredom and failure.

Overcrowding and Shantytowns

Rapid population growth placed great pressure on already inadequate urban social services, and in many Third World cities the quality of life deteriorated. Many people lacked running water, paved streets, electricity, and police and fire protection. As in the early days of England's industrial revolution, sanitation was minimal in poor sections of town. Outdoor toilets were shared by many. Raw sewage often ran in streets and streams.

Faced with a rising human tide, government officials and their well-to-do urban allies sometimes tried to restrict internal migration to preserve the cities. Particularly in Africa, politicians talked of sending newcomers "back to the land" in order to reduce urban unemployment, crime rates, congestion, and environmental decline. In Africa as elsewhere, these antimigration efforts proved unsuccessful, and frustrated officials often threw up their hands in despair.

Surging population growth had particularly severe consequences for housing. As in western Europe in the early nineteenth century, overcrowding reached staggering proportions in a great many Third World cities. Old buildings were often divided and redivided until population density reached the absolute saturation point. Take, for example, this vivid description of an old inner-city area, Singapore's Chinatown, in the late 1950s:

Chinatown . . . consists almost entirely of two or three story shop-houses. These shop-houses, originally intended to house one or two families, have been divided by a maze of interior partitions into cubicles, the ma-jority of which are without windows and in permanent semi-darkness. Most of these cubicles are about the size of two double beds, placed side by side. In one such cubicle—dark, confined, unsanitary, and without comfort—may live a family of seven or more persons. Many of them sleep on the floor, often under the bed. Their possessions are in boxes, placed on shelves to leave the floor free for sleeping. Their food . . . is kept in tiny cupboards, which hang from the rafters. Their clothes hang on the walls, or from racks.[8]

Makeshift squatter settlements were another manifestation of the urban housing problem. These shantytowns sprang up continuously, almost overnight, on the worst possible urban land. Mudflats, garbage dumps, railroad sidings, steep hills on the outskirts, even polluted waterfronts—these were the dismal sites that squatters claimed. Typically, a group of urban poor "invaded" unoccupied land and quickly threw up tents or huts. Often beaten off by the police, they invaded again and again until the authorities gave up and a new squatter beachhead had been secured.

Squatter shantytowns grew much faster than more conventional urban areas in most Third World cities. In the giant Brazilian city of Rio de Janeiro, for example, the population of the shantytowns grew four times faster than the population of the rest of the city in the 1950s and 1960s. As a result, the Third World's squatter settlements came to house up to two-fifths of the urban population. The proportion was particularly high in Asia. Such settlements had occasionally grown up in American mining towns and in Europe, but never to the extent of Latin America, Asia, and Africa. The Third World created a new urban form.

The meaning of squatter housing has been hotly debated. For a long time "pessimists" stressed the miseries of squatter settlements—the lack of the most basic services, the pitiful one-room shacks, the hopelessness of disoriented migrants in a strange environment, the revolutionary discontent. More recently, detailed case studies have presented a more "optimistic" interpretation, stressing the vitality of the settlements and the resourcefulness of their inhabitants. In this view, shantytowns appeared to be real neighborhoods, whose residents often share common ethnic origins and kinship ties.

Moreover, the shantytowns themselves evolved, most notably in Latin America, where they have

Shacks and Skyscrapers   This striking view of Bombay, India, has many counterparts in the Third World. Makeshift dwellings coexist with luxurious high-rise apartments, and the urban landscape expands rapidly as newcomers pour into the swollen city from rural areas. *(Source: Camera Press London/Globe Photos. Photograph: Alan Whicker)*

existed longest. There poor but enterprising inhabitants relied on self-help to improve their living conditions. With much sweat labor and a little hard-earned cash, a family replaced its mud walls with concrete blocks and gradually built a real home. Or the community pressured the city to install a central water pump or build a school. Low-paid office workers in search of cheap housing sometimes moved in and continued the upgrading process.

Few members of squatter communities have been particularly attracted to revolutionary doctrines, despite widespread fears (and hopes) to the contrary. Making a living and holding the family together have been challenges enough. Indeed, one observer described squatters' beliefs as resembling those of the classic small businessman:

These beliefs can be summed up in the familiar and accepted maxims: Work hard, save your money, trust only family members (and them not too much), outwit the state, vote conservatively if possible, but always in your own economic self-interest; educate your children for their future and as old-age insurance for yourself.[9]

Thus the optimists have counseled politicians to abandon their hostility to squatter settlements and help them to help themselves. The rush to the city cannot be stopped, they say. However bad life in the city is, it appears desirable to the millions of rural people who "voted with their feet." Since hard-pressed Third World governments can provide only a fraction of the urban masses with subsidized housing, they should support the creativ-

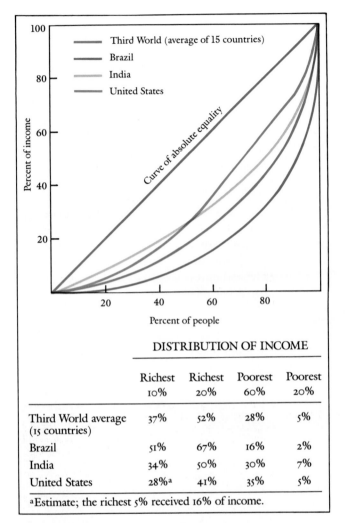

DISTRIBUTION OF INCOME

	Richest 10%	Richest 20%	Poorest 60%	Poorest 20%
Third World average (15 countries)	37%	52%	28%	5%
Brazil	51%	67%	16%	2%
India	34%	50%	30%	7%
United States	28%[a]	41%	35%	5%

[a]Estimate; the richest 5% received 16% of income.

FIGURE 38.2 The Distribution of Income in the Third World, Brazil, India, and the United States, ca 1975 The Lorenz curve is useful for showing the degree of economic inequality in a given country. The closer the actual distribution lies to the (theoretical) curve of absolute equality, the more nearly equal are incomes. In general, Third World countries have a high degree of income inequality, as great as that in Europe before 1914 (see Figure 28.2). However, there are important differences among Third World countries in the degree of income inequality, as may be seen here in the comparison of Brazil and India. *(Source: Data from M. Todaro, Economic Development in the Third World, 4th ed., (New York: Longman, 1989), p. 155 and references cited therein; U.S. Department of Commerce, Historical Statistics of the United States: Colonial Times to 1970, (Washington, D.C.: GPO, 1975), Part I, p. 291.)*

ity of the "spontaneous settlement." However squalid such settlements appear, they are preferable to sleeping on sidewalks.

Rich and Poor

After the less developed countries achieved political independence, massive inequality continued, with few exceptions, to be the reality of life. Rich and poor were separated by a monumental gap, a gap that could be measured, to some extent, as Third World governments began gathering better statistical information. As Figure 38.2 shows, in about 1975 in most developing countries, the top 10 percent of all households received more than one-third of all national income, and the top 20 percent took more than 50 percent. At the other end of the scale, the poorest 60 percent received on average less than 30 percent of all income, and the poorest fifth got about 6 percent. Thus the average household in the top fifth of the population received almost ten times as much monetary income as the average household in the bottom fifth in the 1970s. This situation did not change significantly in the 1980s.

Such differences have been the rule in human history. A comparison of Figure 38.2 with Figure 28.2 on page 907 shows that the situation in the Third World in our time has strongly resembled that of Europe prior to the First World War, before the movement toward greater equality accelerated sharply. It is noteworthy that the usual distinctions between rightist and leftist governments in the Third World, or between capitalist and socialist economies, have had limited significance where shares of income are concerned. For example, in the 1970s income inequality was almost as pronounced in Mexico with its progressive, even revolutionary, tradition, as in Brazil with its rightist military rule.

Differences in wealth and well-being have been most pronounced in the towns and cities of the Third World. Few rich or even middle-class people lived in the countryside. Urban squatters may have been better off than landless rural laborers, but they were light-years away from the luxury of the urban elite.

Consider housing. In the sober words of one careful observer, "The contrast between the opulent housing enjoyed by the tiny minority of the rich and the conditions under which the vast majority of the urban poor must live is extreme."[10] In Asia and Africa, the rich often moved into the luxurious sections previously reserved for colonial administrators and white businessmen. Particularly in Latin America, upper-class and upper-middle-class people built fine mansions in exclusive suburbs, where they lived behind high walls, with many servants, protected from intruders by armed guards and fierce dogs.

A lifestyle in the "modern" mold was almost the byword of the Third World's urban elite. From French perfume and Scotch whiskey to electronic gadgets and the latest rock music, imported luxuries became the unmistakable signs of wealth and privilege. In Swahili-speaking East Africa, the common folk called them *wa Benzi*, "those who ride in a Mercedes-Benz." Even in Mao Tse-tung's relatively egalitarian China, the urban masses saved to buy bicycles while government officials rode in chauffeur-driven state-owned limousines. The automobile became the ultimate symbol of the urban elite.

Education also distinguished the wealthy from the masses. Young people from the elite often studied abroad at leading European and North American universities, or they monopolized openings in local universities. While absorbing the latest knowledge in a prestigious field like civil engineering or economics, they also absorbed foreign customs and values. They mastered the fluent English or French that is indispensable for many top-paying jobs, especially with international agencies and giant multinational corporations. Thus Third World elites often had more in common with the power brokers of the industrialized

A Sleek Automobile fascinates four boys in an African village. The most ambitious youngster may already dream of acquiring power and wealth in the city. (*Source: Marc and Evelyne Bernheim/Woodfin Camp*)

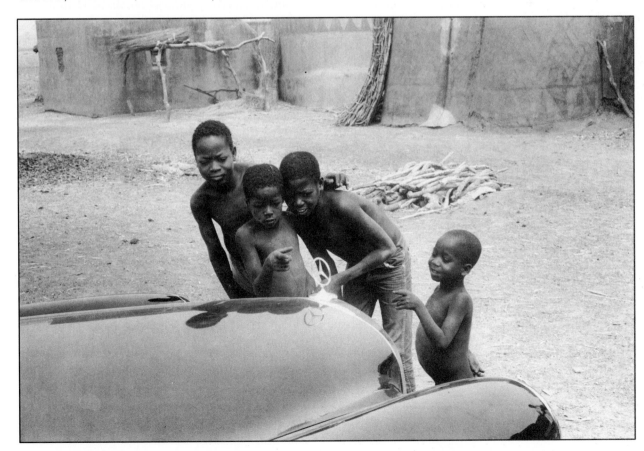

nations than with their own people. Willing tools of neocolonial penetration, they became "white men with black faces," in the words of Frantz Fanon, one angry critic (see page 1275).

The middle classes of the Third World remained quite small relative to the total population. White-collar workers and government bureaucrats joined the traditional ranks of merchants and professionals in the urban middle class. Their salaries, though modest, were wonderfully secure and usually carried valuable fringe benefits. Unlike recent migrants and the rural poor, white-collar workers often received ration cards entitling them to cheap subsidized food.

An unexpected component of the urban middle classes was the modern factory proletariat, a privileged segment of the population in many poor countries. Few in number because sophisticated machines require few workers relative to agriculture or traditional crafts, they received high wages for their skilled work. On the Caribbean island of Jamaica in the late 1960s, for example, aluminum workers in big, modern American-owned plants earned from $60 to $65 a week. Meanwhile, cane cutters on sugar plantations earned $3 a week and many laborers on small farms only $1 a week. Little wonder that modern factory workers tended to be self-satisfied in the Third World.

The great majority, the urban poor, earned precarious livings in a modern yet traditional "bazaar economy"—an economy of petty trades and unskilled labor. Here regular salaried jobs were rare and highly prized, and a complex world of tiny, unregulated businesses and service occupations predominated.

As in industrializing Europe a century ago, irregular armies of peddlers and pushcart operators hawked their wares and squeezed a living from commerce. West African market women, with their colorful dresses and overflowing baskets, provided a classic example of this pattern. Sweatshops and home-based workers manufactured cheap goods for popular consumption. Maids, prostitutes, small-time crooks, and unemployed former students sold all kinds of services. This old-yet-new bazaar economy showed no signs of dying out in the late twentieth century. Indeed, it continued to grow prodigiously as migrants streamed to the cities, as modern industry provided few jobs, and as the wide gap between rich and poor persisted.

Migration and the Family

Large-scale urban migration had a massive impact on traditional family patterns in the Third World. Particularly in Africa and Asia, the great majority of migrants to the city were young men, married and unmarried; women tended to stay in the villages. The result was a sexual imbalance in both places. There were several reasons for this pattern. Much of the movement to cities (and mines) remained temporary or seasonal. At least at first, young men left home to earn hard cash to bring back to their villages. Moreover, the cities were expensive and prospects there were uncertain. Only after a man secured a genuine foothold did he become married or call for his wife and children.

Kinship and village ties helped ease the rigors of temporary migration. Often a young man could go to the city rather easily because his family had close ties with friends and relatives there. Many city neighborhoods were urban versions of their residents' original villages. Networks of friendship and mutual aid helped young men (and some women, especially brides) move back and forth without being overwhelmed.

For rural women, the consequences of male out-migration were mixed. Asian and African women had long been treated as subordinates, if not inferiors, by their fathers and husbands. Rather suddenly, such women found themselves heads of households, faced with managing the farm, feeding the children, and running their own lives. In the east African country of Kenya, for instance, one-third of all rural households were headed by women in the late 1970s.

African and Asian village women had to become unprecedentedly self-reliant and independent. The real beginnings of more equal rights and opportunities, of women's liberation, became readily visible in Africa and Asia. But the price was high and progress uneven. Rural women often had only their children to help in the endless, backbreaking labor. And their husbands, when they returned, often expected their wives to revert to the old subordination.

In economically more advanced Latin America, the pattern of migration was different. Whole families migrated, very often to squatter settlements, much more commonly than in Asia and Africa. These families frequently belonged to the class of landless laborers, which was generally larger in

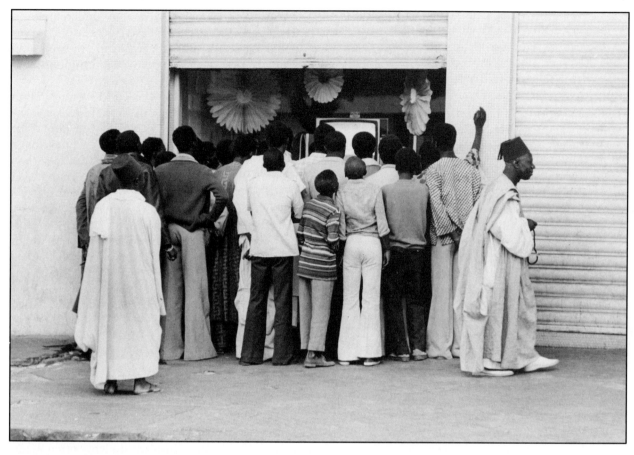

The Power of Television   An enterprising merchant in West Africa uses television to attract a crowd to a tiny shop in Dakar, Senegal. Only the man passing on the right, suggestively clad in the traditional dress of the Muslim believer, appears oblivious to the siren call of the modern age. *(Source: Philip Jon Bailey/Stock, Boston)*

Latin America than in Africa or even Asia. Migration was also more likely to be once-and-for-all. Another difference was that single women were as likely as single men to move to the city. The situation in Mexico in the late 1970s was typical:

They [women] leave the village seeking employment, often as domestic servants. When they do not find work in the cities, they have few alternatives. If they are young, they frequently turn to prostitution; if not, they often resort to begging in the streets. Homeless peasant women, often carrying small children, roam every quarter of Mexico City.[11]

Some women also left to escape the narrow, male-dominated villages. Even so, in Latin America urban migration seemed to have less impact on traditional family patterns and on women's attitudes than in Asia and Africa. This helps explain why the women's movement lagged behind in Latin America.

MASS CULTURE AND CONTEMPORARY THOUGHT

Ideas and beliefs continued to change dramatically in the Third World after independence. Education fostered new attitudes, and mass communications relentlessly spread the sounds and viewpoints of modern life. Third World intellectuals, in their search for the meanings of their countries' experiences, articulated a wide spectrum of independent opinion in keeping with growing national diversity.

Education and Mass Communications

In their efforts to modernize and better their societies, Third World leaders became increasingly convinced of the critical importance of education. They realized that "human capital"—skilled and educated workers, managers, and citizens—played a critical role in the development process.

Faith in education and "book learning" spread surprisingly rapidly to the Third World's masses, for whom education principally meant jobs. Asked how their lives differed from their mothers' and grandmothers' lives, poor and often illiterate peasant women in several countries in the late 1970s testified to the need for an education, along with the need to earn money and have fewer children. A young African woman in Kenya was quite typical of Third World women when she explained it this way.

My mother has eleven children. She is my father's only wife. She works in the fields and grows the food we eat. She plants cabbage, spinach, and corn. She works very hard, but with so many children it is difficult to get enough food or money. All of my brothers and sisters go to school. One is already a teacher....

My life is very different from my mother's.... Women have to get an education. Then if you get a large family and don't know how to feed it, you can find work and get some cash. That's what I will teach my children: "Get an education first." [12]

As this voice suggests, young people in the Third World headed for schools and universities in unprecedented numbers. Latin America, in keeping with its higher incomes and greater urbanization, had the highest percentage of students in all age groups, followed by Asia and then by Africa. There still remained, however, a wide education gap with the rich countries, where more than 90 percent of both sexes attended school through age seventeen.

Moreover, the quality of education in the Third World was often mediocre. African and Asian universities tended to retain the old colonial values, stressing law and liberal arts at the expense of technical and vocational training. As a result, many poor countries found themselves with large numbers of unemployed or underemployed liberal-arts graduates. These "generalists" competed for scarce jobs in the already bloated government bureaucracies while less prestigious technical jobs went begging.

A related problem was the Third World's "brain drain": many gifted students in vital fields like engineering and medicine ended up pursuing their careers in the rich countries of the developed world, which needed their talents far less than their native lands needed them. For example, in the early 1980s, as many Indian-trained doctors practiced abroad, mainly in advanced countries, as served India's entire rural population of 480 million. The threat represented by the brain drain helped explain why the Third World's professional elite received high salaries even in very poor countries.

In recent years many observers have concluded that the education drive, like its forerunner, the industrialization drive, served the rural masses poorly. It sometimes seemed that its greatest beneficiaries were schoolteachers, who profited from the elite status provided by a permanent government job. Instruction was often impractical and mind-numbing. The children of farmers generally learned little about agriculture, animal raising, or practical mechanics. Instead, students often memorized passages from ancient literary works and religious texts and spewed back cut-and-dried answers. No wonder children stayed away from school in droves. Village schools succeeded best at identifying the exceptional pupils, who were then siphoned off to the city for further study and lost forever to the village.

Whatever its shortcomings, formal education spread hand in hand with another influential agent of popular instruction: mass communications. The transistor radio penetrated the most isolated hamlets of the Third World. Governments universally embraced radio broadcasting as a means of power, propaganda, and education. Relentlessly, the transistor radio propagated the outlook and attitudes of urban elites and in the process challenged old values.

Moreover, the second communications revolution—the visual one—is now in the process of reaching rural people everywhere. Television is bringing the whole planet into the bars and meetinghouses of the world's villages. Experience elsewhere—in remote French villages, in Eskimo communities above the Arctic Circle—seems to show that television is likely to have a profound, even revolutionary impact. At the very least the lure of the city seems certain to grow.

Interpreting the Experiences of the Emerging World

Popular education and mass communications compounded the influence of the Third World's writers and thinkers, its purveyors of explanations. Some intellectuals meekly obeyed their employers, whether the ministry of information or a large newspaper. Others simply embellished or reiterated some received ideology like Marxism or free-market capitalism. But some Third World intellectuals led in the search for meanings and direction that has accompanied rapid social change and economic struggle.

Having come of age during and after the struggle for political emancipation, Third World intellectuals have been centrally preoccupied with achieving genuine independence and freedom from outside control. Thus some Third World writers argued that real independence required a total break with the former colonial powers and a total rejection of Western values. This was the message of Frantz Fanon (1925–1961) in his powerful study of colonial peoples, *The Wretched of the Earth.*

Fanon, a French-trained black psychiatrist from the Caribbean island of Martinique, was assigned to a hospital in Algeria during the bloody war for Algerian independence. He quickly came to sympathize with the guerrillas and probed deeply into the psychology of colonial revolt. According to Fanon, decolonization is always a violent and totally consuming process whereby one "species" of men, the colonizers, is completely replaced by an absolutely different species—the colonized, the wretched of the earth. During decolonization the colonized masses mock colonial values, "insult them, and vomit them up," in a psychic purge.

Fanon believed that the battle for formal independence was only the first step. The former imperialists and their local collaborators—the "white men with black faces"—remained the enemy:

The mobilization of the masses, when it arises out of the war of liberation, introduces into each man's consciousness the ideas of a common cause, of a national destiny, and of a collective history. In the same way

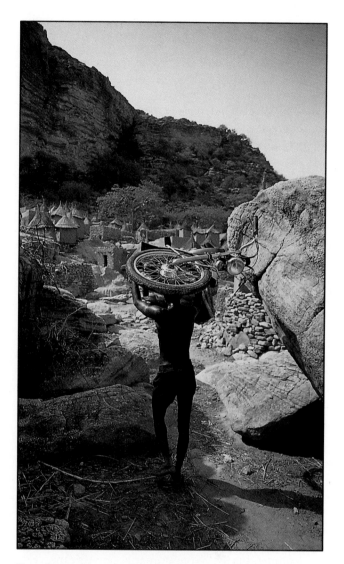

The Revolution in Communications Although this young man must carry his motorbike up a rocky path to reach his home, he has gained access to speed and excitement, to roads and cities. The messages of the modern world easily reach remote villages by transistor radio. *(Source: Pern/Hutchison Library)*

the second phase, that of the building-up of the nation, is helped on by the existence of this cement which has been mixed with blood and anger. . . . During the colonial period the people are called upon to fight against oppression; after national liberation, they are called upon to fight against poverty, illiteracy. and underdevelopment. The struggle, they say, goes on. The people realize that life is an unending contest.

. . . The apotheosis of independence is transformed into the curse of independence, and the colonial

*power through its immense resources of coercion con-
demns the young nation to regression. In plain words,
the colonial power says: "Since you want independence, take it and starve."*

*. . . We are not blinded by the moral reparation of
national independence; nor are we fed by it. The
wealth of the imperial countries is our wealth too. . . .
Europe is literally the creation of the Third World. The
wealth which smothers her is that which was stolen
from the underdeveloped peoples.*[13]

For Fanon, independence and national solidarity went hand in hand with outrage at the mis-
deeds and moral posturings of the former colonial
powers. Fanon's passionate, angry work became a
sacred text for radicals attacking imperialism and
struggling for liberation.

As independence was gained and nationalist
governments were established, some later writers
looked beyond wholesale rejection of the industrialized powers. They too were "anti-imperialist,"
but they saw colonial domination as only one
chapter in the life of their people. Many of these
writers were cultural nationalists who applied their
talents to celebrating the rich histories and cultures of their people. At the same time, they did
not hesitate to criticize their own leaders and fellow citizens, with whom they often disagreed.

The Nigerian writer Chinua Achebe (b. 1930)
rendered these themes with acute insight and vivid
specificity in his short, moving novels. Achebe
wrote in English rather than his native Ibo
tongue, but he wrote primarily for Africans, seeking to restore his people's self-confidence by re-
interpreting the past. For Achebe, the "writer in a
new nation" had first to embrace the "fundamental theme":

*This theme—quite simply—is that the African people
did not hear of culture for the first time from Europeans; that their societies were not mindless but frequently had a philosophy of great depth and volume
and beauty, that they had poetry and above all, they
had dignity. It is this dignity that many African
peoples all but lost in the colonial period, and it is
this that they must now regain. The worst thing that
can happen to any people is the loss of their dignity
and self-respect. The writer's duty is to help them regain it by showing what happened to them, what they
lost.*[14]

In *Things Fall Apart* (1959) Achebe achieves his
goal by bringing vividly to life the men and
women of an Ibo village at the beginning of the
twentieth century, with all their virtues and frail-
ties. The hero, Okonkwo, is a mighty wrestler and
a hard-working, prosperous farmer, but he is stern
and easily angered. Enraged at the failure of his
people to reject newcomers, and especially at the
white missionaries who convert his son to Christianity and provoke the slaying of the sacred py-
thon, Okonkwo kills a colonial messenger. When
his act fails to spark a tribal revolt, he commits suicide. Okonkwo is destroyed by the general breakdown of tribal authority and his own intransigent
recklessness. Woven into the story are the proverbs
and wisdom of a sophisticated people and the
beauty of a vanishing world.

In later novels, especially *A Man of the People*
(1966), Achebe portrays the postindependence
disillusionment of many Third World intellectuals.
The villain is Chief The Honorable Nanga, a politician with the popular touch. This "man of the
people" lives in luxury, takes bribes to build expensive apartment buildings for foreigners, and
flim-flams the voters with celebrations and empty
words. The hero, an idealistic young schoolteacher, tries to unseat Chief Nanga, with disastrous results. Beaten up and hospitalized, the hero
broods that the people "had become even more
cynical than their leaders and were apathetic into
the bargain."[15] Achebe's harsh but considered
judgment reflected trends in many Third World
nations in the 1960s and 1970s: the rulers seemed
increasingly corrupted by Western luxury and es-
tranged from the rural masses, and idealistic intellectuals could only gnash their teeth in frustration.

The celebrated novelist V. S. Naipaul, born in
Trinidad in 1932 of Indian parents, has also castigated Third World governments for corruption,
ineptitude, and self-deception. Another of Naipaul's recurring themes is the poignant loneliness
and homelessness of uprooted people. In *The
Mimic Men* (1967), the blacks and whites and the
Hindus and Chinese who populate the tiny Caribbean islands are all aliens, thrown together by
"shipwreck." As one of the characters says:

*It was my hope in writing to give expression to the
restlessness, the deep disorder, which the great exploration, the overthrow in three continents of established social organizations, the unnatural bringing to-*

On Location Third World countries responded to the overthrow of foreign domination with a renewed interest in their own cultures. Here director Marcela Fernandez Volante is shown shooting a film set in Mexico. *(Source: Courtesy of John Mosier)*

gether of peoples who could achieve fulfillment only within the security of their own societies and the landscapes hymned by their ancestors . . . has brought about. The empires of our time were short-lived, but they altered the world for ever; their passing away is their least significant feature. It was my hope to sketch a subject which, fifty years hence, a great historian might pursue. . . . But this work will not now be written by me; I am too much a victim of that restlessness which was to have been my subject.[16]

Naipaul and Achebe, like many other talented Third World writers and intellectuals, probed Third World experiences in pursuit of understanding and identity. A similar soul-searching went on in other creative fields, from art and dance to architecture and social science, and seemed to reflect the intellectual maturity of genuine independence.

SUMMARY

As Third World leaders and peoples threw off foreign domination after 1945 and reasserted themselves in new or revitalized states, they turned increasingly inward to attack poverty and limited economic development. The collective response was an unparalleled medical revolution and the Third World's first great industrialization drive. Long-neglected agriculture also made progress, and some countries experienced a veritable Green Revolution. Moreover, rapid urbanization, expanding educational opportunities, and greater rights for women were striking evidence of modernization and fundamental human progress. The achievement was great.

Yet so was the challenge, and results fell far short of aspirations. Deep and enduring rural poverty, overcrowded cities, enormous class differences, and the sharp criticisms of leading Third World writers mocked early hopes of quick solutions. Since the late 1960s there has been growing dissatisfaction and frustration in Third World nations. And, as the final chapter will examine, the belief grew that the Third World could meet the challenge only by reordering the entire global system and dissolving the unequal ties that bound it to the rich nations.

NOTES

1. A. MacBean and V. N. Balasubramanyam, *Meeting the Third World Challenge* (New York: St. Martin's Press, 1976), p. 27.
2. P. J. McEwan and R. B. Sutcliffe, eds., *Modern Africa* (New York: Thomas Y. Crowell, 1965), p. 349.
3. Quoted in L. R. Brown, *Seeds of Change: The Green Revolution and Development in the 1970s* (New York: Praeger, 1970), p. 16.
4. P. Ehrlich, *The Population Bomb* (New York: Ballantine, 1968), p. 11.
5. *Wall Street Journal,* April 16, 1981, p. 17.
6. P. Bairoch, *The Economic Development of the Third World Since 1900* (London: Methuen, 1975), p. 144.
7. R. Dumont, *False Start in Africa* (London: André Deutsch, 1966), p. 88.
8. B. Kaye, *Upper Nankin Street, Singapore: A Sociological Study of Households Living in a Densely Populated Area* (Singapore: University of Malaya Press, 1960), p. 2.
9. W. Mangin, "Latin American Squatter Settlements," *Latin American Research Review* 2 (1967): 84–85.
10. D. J. Dwyer, *People and Housing in Third World Cities: Perspectives on the Problem of Spontaneous Settlements* (London: Longman, 1975), p. 24.
11. P. Hudson, *Third World Women Speak Out: Interviews in Six Countries on Change, Development, and Basic Needs* (New York: Praeger, 1979), p. 11.
12. Ibid., p. 22.
13. F. Fanon, *The Wretched of the Earth* (New York: Grove Press, 1968), pp. 43, 93–94, 97, 102.
14. C. Achebe, *Morning Yet on Creation Day* (London: Heinemann, 1975), p. 81.
15. C. Achebe, *A Man of the People* (London: Heinemann, 1966), p. 161.
16. V. S. Naipaul, *The Mimic Men* (New York: Macmillan, 1967), p. 38.

SUGGESTED READING

Many of the suggested readings for Chapter 37 discuss themes considered in this chapter. P. Bairoch, *The Economic Development of the Third World Since 1900* (1975), is a valuable historical study. A. B. Mountjoy, ed., *The Third World: Problems and Perspectives* (1978), and A. MacBean and V. N. Balasubramanyam, *Meeting the Third World Challenge* (1976), are reliable, even-handed introductions to contemporary trends and policies. R. Gamer, *The Developing Nations: A Comparative Perspective,* 2d ed. (1986), is a stimulating synthesis. Two excellent works from a truly Third World perspective are especially recommended: E. Hermassi, *The Third World Reassessed* (1980), and M. ul-Haq, *The Poverty Curtain: Choices for the Third World* (1976). The many clear and compelling works of B. Ward, notably *The Rich Nations and the Poor Nations* (1962) and *The Lopsided World* (1968), movingly convey the hopes and frustrations of sympathetic Western economists in the 1960s. Equally renowned are studies by the Swedish socialist G. Myrdal: *Asian Drama: An Inquiry Into the Poverty of Nations,* 3 vols. (1968), and *The Challenge of World Poverty: A World Anti-Poverty Program in Outline* (1970). Valuable introductions to world agriculture and population are found in various works by L. R. Brown, notably *Seeds of Change: The Green Revolution and Development in the 1970s* (1970) and *In the Human Interest: A Strategy to Stabilize World Population* (1974). R. King, *Land Reform: A World Survey* (1977), is a useful introduction to key problems.

Three valuable studies on African questions are R. Austen, *African Economic History: Internal Development and External Dependency* (1987); K. Patterson, *History and Disease in Africa: An Introductory Survey and Case Studies* (1978); and P. Lloyd, ed., *The New Elites of Tropical Africa* (1966). C. Turnbull, *The Lonely African* (1962), provides intimate portraits of Africans caught up in decolonization and rapid social change; J. Iliffe, *The African Poor: A History* (1987), is an original and important work that is highly recommended. Critical aspects of contemporary Indian economic development are carefully considered by M. Franda, *India's Rural Development: An Assessment of Alternatives* (1980), and A. G. Noble and A. K. Dutt, eds., *Indian Urbanization and Planning: Vehicles of Modernization* (1977). China's economic and social problems are skillfully placed in a broad and somewhat somber perspective by two Chinese-speaking journalists, F. Butterfield, *China: Alive in the Bitter Sea* (1982), and R. Bernstein, *From the Center of the Earth: The Search for the Truth About China* (1982).

For the prodigious growth of Third World cities, J. Abu-Lughod and R. Hay, Jr., eds., *Third World Urban-*

ization (1977), and the lively studies of D. J. Dwyer, *People and Housing in Third World Cities: Perspectives on the Problem of Spontaneous Settlements* (1975) and *The City in the Third World* (1974), are highly recommended. Similarly recommended is a fascinating investigation of enduring urban-rural differences by M. Lipton, *Why Poor People Stay Poor: Urban Bias in World Development* (1977), which may be complemented by C. Elliott, *Patterns of Poverty in the Third World: A Study of Social and Economic Stratification* (1975).

A good introduction to changes within families is P. Hudson, *Third World Women Speak Out: Interviews in Six Countries on Change, Development, and Basic Needs* (1979), a truly remarkable study. Other useful works on Third World women and the changes they are experiencing include L. Iglitzen and R. Ross, *Women in the World: A Comparative Study* (1976); A. de Souza, *Women in Contemporary India and South Asia* (1980); N. J. Hafkin and E. Bay, eds., *Women in Africa* (1977); J. Ginat, *Women in Muslim Rural Society: Status and Role in Family and Community* (1982); and M. Wolf, *Revolution Postponed: Women in Contemporary China* (1985). K. Kakar, *The Inner World: A Psychoanalytic Study of Childhood and Society in India* (1978), is a fascinating interpretation of Indian dependence on family and personal relations, which is provocatively compared with the compulsive individualism of Western society.

The reader is especially encouraged to enter into the contemporary Third World with the aid of the gifted writers discussed in this chapter. F. Fanon, *The Wretched of the Earth* (1968), is a particularly strong indictment of colonialism from the 1960s. The wide-ranging work of C. Achebe illuminates the proud search for a viable past in his classic novel of precolonial Africa, *Things Fall Apart* (1959), and the disillusionment with unprincipled postindependence leaders in *A Man of the People* (1966). G. Moore and U. Beier, eds., *Modern Poetry from Africa* (1963), is a recommended anthology. In addition to his rich and introspective novels like *The Mimic Men* (1967), V. S. Naipaul has reported extensively on life in Third World countries. His *India: A Wounded Civilization* (1978), impressions gleaned from a trip to his family's land of origin, and *A Bend in the River* (1980), an investigation of the high price that postcolonial Africa is paying for modernization, are especially original and thought provoking. Finally, L. Heng and J. Shapiro, *Son of the Revolution* (1983), brilliantly captures the drama of Mao's China through the turbulent real-life story of a young Red Guard.

PERIOD (CA 1920–1990)	AFRICA AND THE MIDDLE EAST	THE AMERICAS
1920	Cultural nationalism in Africa, 1920s Treaty of Lausanne recognizes Turkish Republic, 1923 Reza Shah leads Iran, 1925–1941	U.S. "consumer revolution," 1920s Stock market crash in U.S.; Great Depression begins, 1929
1930	African farmers organize first "cocoa hold-ups," 1930–1931 Iraq gains independence, 1932 Syrian-French friendship treaty, 1936	Revolutions in six South American countries, 1930 New Deal under U.S. President Franklin D. Roosevelt, 1933
1940	Civil war between Arabs and Jews in Palestine; state of Israel is created, 1948 Apartheid system in South Africa, 1948 to 1991 Libya gains independence, 1949	Surprise attack by Japan on Pearl Harbor; U.S. enters World War Two, 1941 U.N. established, 1945 Marshall Plan, 1947 Perón regime in Argentina, 1946–1953
1950	Egypt declared a republic; Nasser named premier, 1954 Morocco, Tunisia, Sudan, and Ghana gain independence, 1956–1957 French-British Suez invasion, 1956	Fidel Castro takes power in Cuba, 1959
1960	French maintain powerful presence in Africa, ca 1960–1980 Mali, Nigeria, and the Congo gain independence, 1960 Biafra declares independence from Nigeria, 1967 Arab-Israeli Six-Day War, 1967	Cuban Missile Crisis, 1962 Military dictatorship in Brazil, 1964–1985 U.S. escalates war in Vietnam, 1964 Separatist movement in Quebec, 1967 to present
1970	"Yom Kippur War," 1973 Mozambique and Angola gain independence, 1975 Islamic revolution in Iran, 1979 Camp David Accords, 1979	Military coup in Chile, 1973 U.S. Watergate scandal, 1974 Revolutions in Nicaragua and El Salvador, 1979
1980	Iran-Iraq War, 1980–1988 Reforms in South Africa, 1989 to present	U.S. military buildup, 1980 to present Argentina restores civilian rule, 1983

EAST ASIA	INDIA AND SOUTHEAST ASIA	EUROPE
Kita Ikki advocates ultranationalism in Japan, 1923 Chiang Kai-shek unites China, 1928	Mohandas "Mahatma" Gandhi launches nonviolent resistance campaign, 1920	Mussolini seizes power in Italy, 1922 Treaties of Locarno, 1925 Stalin takes power in U.S.S.R., 1927 Depths of Great Depression, 1929–1933
Japan invades Manchuria, 1931 Mao Tse-tung's Long March, 1934 Sino-Japanese War, 1937–1945	Mahatma Gandhi's Salt March, 1930 Japanese conquer empire in southeast Asia, 1939–1942	Hitler gains dictatorial power, 1933 Civil war in Spain, 1936–1939 Germany invades Poland; Britain and France declare war on Germany, 1939 World War Two, 1939–1945
U.S. drops atomic bombs on Hiroshima and Nagasaki, 1945 Chinese civil war, 1945–1949 Mao Tse-tung proclaims People's Republic of China, 1949	Philippines gain independence, 1946 Vietnam War, French phase, 1947–1954 India (Hindu) and Pakistan (Muslim) gain independence, 1947; violent clashes continue	Yalta Conference, 1945 NATO alliance, 1949 Soviet Union and Red China sign 30-year alliance treaty, 1949
Korean War, 1950–1953 Japan begins long period of rapid economic growth, 1950 Mao Tse-tung announces Great Leap Forward, 1958	Vietnamese nationalists defeat French at Dien Bien Phu; Vietnam divided, 1954 Islamic Republic of Pakistan declared, 1956	Death of Stalin, 1953 Warsaw Pact, 1955 Revolution in Hungary crushed by Soviets, 1956 Creation of the Common Market, 1957
Sino-Soviet split becomes apparent, 1960 Great Proletarian Cultural Revolution in China, 1965–1969	Vietnam War, American phase, 1963–1975 Indira Gandhi Prime Minister of India, 1966–1977, 1980–1984	Construction of Berlin Wall, 1961 Student revolution in France, 1968 Soviet invasion of Czechoslovakia, 1968 German Chancellor Willy Brandt's Ostpolitik, 1969–1973
Communist victory in Vietnam War, 1975 China pursues modernization after Mao Tse-tung's death, 1976	India-Pakistan war, 1971 Republic of Bangladesh, 1972 Chinese invade Vietnam, 1979	Fall of Polish government of Gomulka, 1970 Détente reaches apogee in Helsinki Agreement, 1975 Soviet invasion of Afghanistan, 1979
Japanese foreign investment surge, 1980 to present China crushes democracy movement, 1989	Sikh nationalism in India, 1984 to present Corazón Aquino takes power in the Philippines, 1986	Soviet reform under Mikhail Gorbachev, 1985–1991 Anticommunist revolutions sweep eastern Europe, 1989

39

One Small Planet

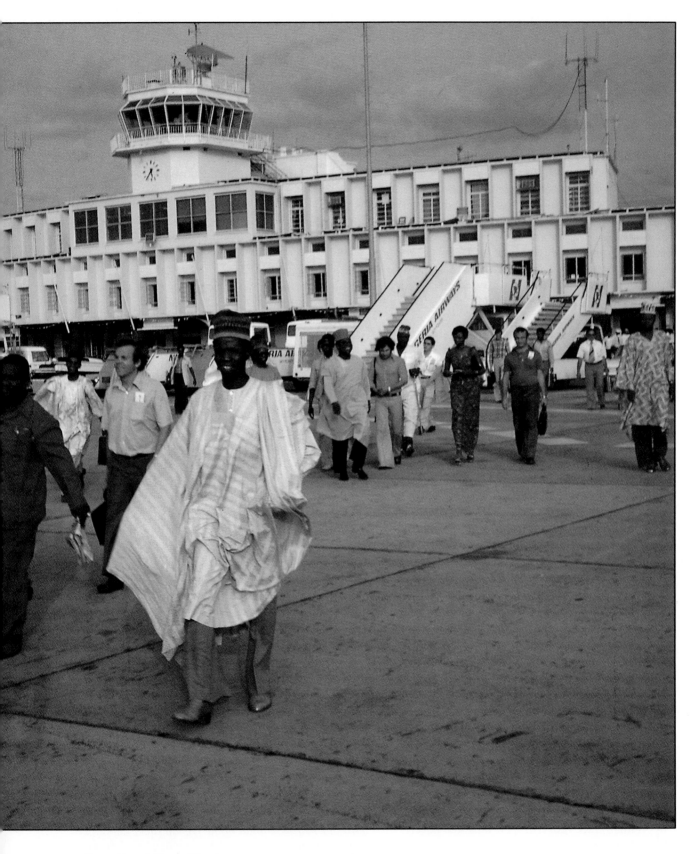

Kano Airport, Kano, Nigeria

The idea of visitors from elsewhere in the universe has kindled the modern imagination. Motorists swear that they have seen unidentified flying objects; the alchemy of imagination even lands the crew of the starship *Enterprise* on our earth in our era. A best-selling author spins preposterous theories about "ancient astronauts" who landed on earth and built everything from the pyramids at Giza to the temples of the Aztecs. It is as if we earthlings, believers in the power of technology but weighed down by apparently insoluble human conflicts, have been yearning for some superior intelligence to decipher our little world and set it straight while there is still time.

Yet perhaps our yearning for enlightened interstellar visitors can be put to good use. We can imagine how superior intelligences, easily able to grasp our world and its complex history, would view the planet and its talented but quarrelsome human race. Surely interstellar observers would take a genuinely global perspective, free from our customary biases of creed and nation. If we try to do the same, perhaps we too can gain insight into our world's ongoing development.

From a global perspective, three questions might seem particularly important.

- How has the planet organized itself politically, and will competing nation-states continue to dominate world politics?

- How has the human race been using its resources to meet its material needs?

- What key ideas are guiding human behavior as our planet moves toward an uncertain future?

WORLD POLITICS

Although many earthlings are deeply impressed by our recent scientific and technological achievements, highly advanced space travelers might be less so. They might instead be astonished that accelerated technological achievement has not been matched by any corresponding change in the way the human race governs—or fails to govern—itself. Sovereign nation-states reign supreme, as assertive and as competitive as ever, and are con-

tinuously reinforced by ever more destructive weapons. The embryonic growth of an effective global political organization, of a government that could protect the world's nations from themselves, appears permanently arrested. The tension generated by powerful, warlike states in a fragile and interdependent world remains one of the most striking—and dangerous—characteristics of this small planet.

Nation-States and the United Nations

The rise of the nation-state and the global triumph of nationalism have been a grand theme of modern world history. The independent territorial nation-state—sometimes containing separatist ethnic groups striving for nationhood in their own right—is clearly the fundamental principle of political organization in our times. Yet from a global perspective we must surely question what we take for granted. Has the nation-state system, with its apparently inevitable conflicts, become a threat to life on the planet?

Some have thought so. It is one of history's ironies that nationalism has been widely condemned in the twentieth century, especially in Europe, just as it has triumphed decisively in world politics. In *Mankind and Mother Earth* (1976), his last work, the renowned British historian Arnold Toynbee (1889–1975) poignantly expressed the post-1914 disillusionment of many European and American intellectuals. At the time of his birth, Toynbee wrote, his middle-class countrymen "supposed Earthly Paradise was just around the corner." They also assumed that the national state was "the natural, normal, rightful political unit."

Toynbee's generation of Europeans, however, lived through an era of "self-inflicted tribulation," war and genocide, largely due to their "explosive, subversive" faith in national self-determination. Toynbee borrowed a term from the ancient Greeks to explain that the spread of the western European political idea of the national state, first to eastern Europe and then to Asia and Africa, had created a fatal discrepancy—

the discrepancy between the political partition of the Oikoumené [the habitat of the human race] into local sovereign states and the global unification of the Oikoumené on technological and economic planes. This misfit is the crux of mankind's present plight. Some form of global government is now needed for keeping the peace . . . and for reestablishing the balance between Man and the rest of the biosphere.[1]

Similar views prevail among a small but articulate group of intellectuals and political scientists. Thus we should probably take the "unrealistic" question of world government seriously. Let us look more closely than usual at the United Nations for signs of the emergence of a global authority transcending sovereign states.

When the United Nations was founded in San Francisco in 1945, the United States was the driving force behind its creation. President Roosevelt and Democrats in the Wilsonian tradition believed that the failure of the United States to join the League of Nations had contributed to the tragic breakdown of "collective security" in the 1930s. A resurrected League, they believed, would facilitate Allied cooperation in the postwar era.

It was to be the prime purpose of the new organization "to maintain international peace and security." Primary responsibility for this awesome task was assigned to the twelve-nation Security Council. According to the U.N. charter, the Security Council had the authority to examine any international conflict, impose economic and political penalties on an aggressor, and even "take such action by air, sea, or land forces as may be necessary to restore international peace and security." In short, the Security Council had the power to police the world.

Yet this theoretical power was severely restricted in practice. China, Great Britain, France, the Soviet Union, and the United States were all made permanent members of the Security Council, and all five had to agree on any peacekeeping action. The veto power of the Big Five has been criticized for preventing the United Nations from ever regulating its most powerful members. But that was precisely the point: none of the Big Five, and certainly not the United States, was willing to surrender sovereign power to a potential world government.

Indeed, the United Nations affirmed and reinforced the primacy of the national state in world politics. The charter directed the United Nations to pursue "friendly relations between nations based on the principle of equal rights and self-determination of peoples." Every "peace-loving" state was eligible to join and to participate in the General Assembly, the United Nations's second main body. Founded with 50 members, the General Assembly reached 122 members in 1965 and 159 in 1990. Each member state, whatever its size, always had one voice and one vote on all resolutions. However, the resolutions of the General Assembly became legally binding on states only if all five of the Security Council's permanent members agreed. The General Assembly was a world debating society for nation-states, not a lawmaking body for the peoples of the planet.

The third express purpose of the United Nations testified to the expanded scope of government tasks since the late nineteenth century, as well as to global interdependence. According to its charter, the United Nations was "to achieve international cooperation in solving international problems of an economic, social, cultural, or humanitarian character, and in promoting and encouraging respect for human rights and for fundamental freedom for all without distinction as to race, sex, language, or religion." This open-ended assignment was the province of an Economic and Social Council, whose eighteen members were to be elected periodically by the General Assembly. The council was also to work with such specialized affiliated agencies as the World Health Organization in Geneva and the Food and Agriculture Organization in Rome.

The scope of its original purposes helps explain the evolution of the United Nations. Hopes of effective Allied cooperation in the Security Council faded as cold war rhetoric and vetoes by the outnumbered Soviet Union began to paralyze that body. The Security Council proved somewhat more successful at quieting bloody conflicts between smaller states where the interests of the superpowers were not directly involved, such as the dispute between India and Pakistan over Kashmir and that between Greece and Turkey over Cyprus. In 1960, it even sent military forces to re-establish order in the former Belgian Congo. This ambitious undertaking, criticized from all sides, marked an early high point of Security Council peacekeeping.

With the Security Council often deadlocked, the rapidly changing General Assembly claimed ever greater authority. As decolonization picked up speed and the number of member states more than doubled by the early 1960s, a nonaligned, anticolonial Afro-Asian bloc emerged. Reinforced by sympathetic Latin American countries, the bloc succeeded in organizing a coherent Third World majority in the General Assembly by the mid-1960s. This majority concentrated on economic and social issues, passing many fiery and fine-sounding resolutions often directed against the former colonial powers, the United States, Israel, imperialist Portugal, and racist South Africa.

The long-term significance of these developments at the United Nations was by no means clear. The Third World majority, predominantly composed of small and poor countries, clearly mistook the illusion of power at the United Nations for the substance of power in world affairs. By the

Learning About Nutrition   The United Nations expert in the center is showing women with hospitalized children in Mali how to prepare meals providing maximum nourishment. *(Source: United Nations/Ray Witlin)*

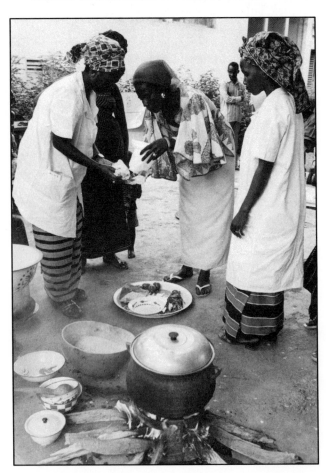

late 1970s, many of the General Assembly's resolutions were simply ignored. Meanwhile, many critical international issues, such as the Arab-Israel conflict, were increasingly resolved by resort to traditional diplomacy or war. In the mid-1980s, the United Nations experienced a serious financial crisis as the United States and other Western countries cut their contributions in order to retaliate against U.N. policies that they opposed.

Nor did the United Nations generate much popular support around the world. Most people continued to identify with their national states, which may even provide adults with a psychological substitute for the family bonds that nurtured them in childhood. Thus nation-states have continued to weave the powerful social bonds necessary for group action. As two American political scientists put it, "The nation-state may all too seldom speak the voice of reason. But it remains the only serious alternative to chaos."[2]

And yet the United Nations has also proved to be a remarkably hardy institution. Particularly significant in long-term perspective was the Third World majority's successful expansion of the scope of the organization's economic, social, and cultural mission. By the early 1980s, an alphabet soup of U.N. committees, specialized agencies, and affiliated international organizations was studying and promoting health, labor, agriculture, industrial development, and world trade, not to mention disarmament, control of narcotics, and preservation of the great whales. These U.N. agencies and affiliated organizations derived their initial authority from treaties and agreements between sovereign states, but once in operation they took on a life of their own.

Staffed by a talented international bureaucracy, U.N. agencies worked tenaciously to consolidate their power and to serve their main constituency—the overwhelming Third World majority in both the General Assembly and the world's total population. Without directly challenging national sovereignty, they exerted a steady pressure for more "international cooperation" in dealing with specific global issues, and the world's big powers sometimes went along. The United Nations also emerged as the central forum for the debate on the world economic order and the relations between rich and poor countries, issues of fundamental importance in the late twentieth century. Thus sharp-eyed observers detected a grad-

Desert Warfare   American soldiers practice the art of desert warfare in Saudi Arabia as the U.N.-authorized coalition builds up its forces and Iraq's army defiantly remains in Kuwait. After Saddam Hussein's forces were smashed and expelled in a lightning attack, the Security Council continued to punish and discipline Iraq. *(Source: U.S. Air Force)*

ual, many-sided enlargement of U.N. involvement in planetary affairs.

This development marked time in the 1980s, but as the 1990s opened the United Nations suddenly took fresh and almost unprecedented action. In response to Iraq's invasion and annexation of the small state of Kuwait, the five permanent members of the Security Council agreed in August 1990 to impose a strict naval blockade on Iraq. Naval forces, led by the United States but augmented by ships from several nations, then enforced the blockade and halted all trade between Saddam Hussein's country and the rest of the world. Receiving the support of ground units from some Arab states as well as from Great Britain and France, the United States also landed first 200,000—and then a total of 500,000—American soldiers in Saudia Arabia near the border of Kuwait. At the same time the United States and its allies pushed a series of resolutions through the

U.N. Security Council, which ordered Iraq to withdraw from Kuwait and pay reparations. When a defiant Saddam Hussein continued to claim that Kuwait had become an Iraqi province, the Security Council authorized the U.S.-led military coalition to attack Iraq.

The subsequent war (Map 39.1) and the Soviet Union's unsuccessful attempt to mediate an Iraqi retreat from Kuwait received saturation coverage in the world's media. But the most notable feature of the war from a truly global perspective was that it could not have occurred—at least under U.N. auspices—without the permission of China and the Soviet Union. Once before, in the Korean War, the United States and its Western allies had fought with U.N. authorization. But that was only because an angry Soviet Union had walked out of the United Nations and was not present to cast its veto—a tactical error that none of the five permanent members ever repeated when their far-flung

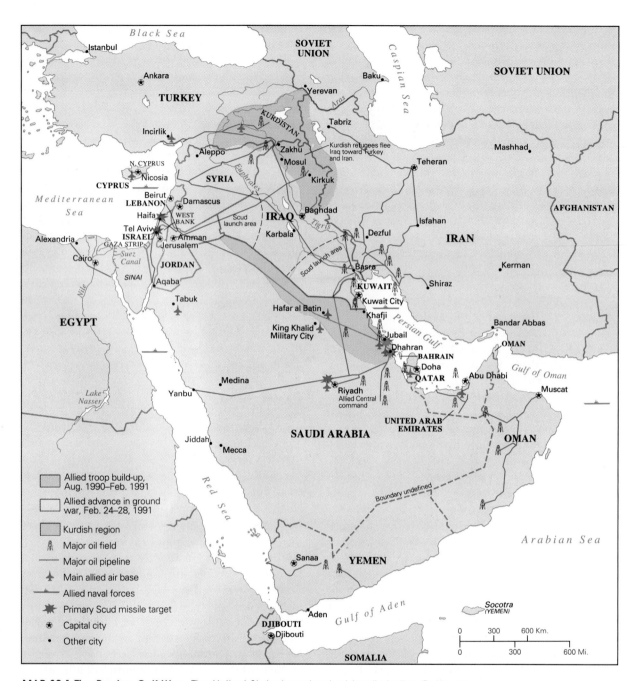

MAP 39.1 The Persian Gulf War The United States' most valuable ally in the Gulf war was the kingdom of Saudia Arabia, which feared it might be next on the list after Iraq suddenly seized Kuwait. Providing U.S. commanders with both bases and troops, Saudi Arabia emerged from the war with increased regional influence and unique superpower status in the world oil industry.

Legend:

■ Allied troop build-up, Aug. 1990–Feb. 1991

□ Allied advance in ground war, Feb. 24–28, 1991

■ Kurdish region

⚒ Major oil field

— Major oil pipeline

✈ Main allied air base

— Allied naval forces

✸ Primary Scud missile target

✹ Capital city

• Other city

interests appeared threatened or even challenged. Did five-power agreement to punish Saddam Hussein severely mean the triumph of the original American idea of using the United Nations as a means for the great states to police the world? Or was the Security Council's unified response to Iraq's Kuwaiti invasion something of a fluke, the result of special circumstances? Only time will tell. In any event it seems possible that dramatic military action in the Persian Gulf has only reinforced the gradual expansion of U.N. action in world affairs, and that the early steps toward some kind of world government have already been taken.

Complexity and Violence

In between territorial nation-states and international organizations that concentrate on specific problems there has stretched a vast middle ground of alliances, blocs, partnerships, and ongoing conflicts and rivalries. Although it is often difficult to make sense of this tangle of associations, certain fundamental developments have structured a complexity sometimes bordering on chaos.

First, East-West competition and the mutual hostility of the bloc leaders, the Soviet Union and the United States, was one of the planet's most enduring realities until very recently. The cold war raged in the 1980s, when Soviet armies decimated Afghanistan and the United States modernized its military might. Yet even then it was clear that neither bloc was as solid as it had been a generation earlier. China had long since broken with the Soviet Union, and Poland's effort to chart its own course testified eloquently to tensions within the East bloc. As for the West, serious differences on military matters surfaced within NATO (which France had long since quit), and economic quarrels flared between the Common Market and the United States. Thus the hostile superpowers were restrained by their allies as well as by the possibility of nuclear self-destruction. When, therefore, Mikhail Gorbachev launched his reforms in the Soviet Union—reforms that unexpectedly snowballed into successful anticommunist revolutions in eastern Europe in 1989—the scene was set for the unification of the two Germanys and the end of the cold war. Joyously welcomed, and rightly so, the sudden end of the cold war removed nonethe-

less a basic principle of global organization and signaled a new era in world politics.

The long cold war contributed to the ideology of Third World solidarity, a second significant factor in planetary affairs. A critical step was taken in 1955, when Asian and African nations came together in Bandung, Indonesia, to form a "third force" of nonaligned nations. The neutralist leaders of Asia and Africa believed that genuine independence and social justice were the real challenges before them, and they considered the cold war a wasteful and irrelevant diversion. African, Asian, and Latin American countries learned to work together at the United Nations, and they called for a restructuring of the world economic system. These efforts have brought mixed results (see below), but a loose majority of Third World countries has coalesced around some global issues.

A striking third development has been the increasingly "multipolar" nature of world politics. Regional conflict and a fluid, complicated jockeying for regional influence have been the keynotes. While the two superpowers were struggling to control their allies and competing for global power and influence, a number of increasingly assertive "middle powers" were arising around the world. Often showing by their actions limited commitment to Third World solidarity, these middle powers strove to be capable of leading or dominating their neighbors and of standing up to the world's superpowers on regional questions. The rise of middle powers reflected the fact that most of the world's countries are small and weak, with fewer than 20 million people. Only a few countries have the large populations, natural resources, and industrial bases necessary for real power on a regional or global scale.

Latin America presented two striking examples of middle powers. Brazil, with more than 140 million people, vast territory and resources, and one of the world's most rapidly industrializing economies, emerged rather suddenly as South America's dominant nation-state. Even more striking was the rapid rise of Mexico, with its population of over 80 million, its substantial industrial base and oil wealth, and its proud nationalism. Although the world recession of the early 1980s hit hard, Mexico clearly saw itself as the natural leader of the Spanish-speaking Americas. As a major regional power, it challenged the long-dominant influence of the United States in Central America.

Strong regional powers like France and West Germany had re-emerged in western Europe by the early 1960s. The unification of Germany in 1990 created a dominant economic power in Europe, with far-reaching implications for the Common Market and Europe's role in world affairs. Resurgent Nigeria was unquestionably the leading power in sub-Saharan Africa. Heavily populated Egypt and much smaller Israel were also regional powerhouses. Iran sought under the shah to dominate the Persian Gulf but came out of the long, bitter war with Iraq in the 1980s a bloodied loser. This defeat encouraged Saddam Hussein to launch his surprise attack on tiny Kuwait as part of Iraq's unsuccessful bid to become the dominant power in the region. China, India, and Japan were all leading regional powers, and several other Asian countries—notably Indonesia, Vietnam, Pakistan, and the Philippines—were determined to join them.

A high degree of conflict and violence characterized the emerging multipolar political system. Conflict in Europe remained mainly verbal, but in Africa, Asia, and Central America blood flowed freely. Of the 145 wars that occurred worldwide between 1945 and 1979, 117 were in the Third World. As Germany was in the Thirty Years' War, some countries were literally torn apart. Lebanon, which had long been considered the most advanced state in the Arab world, was practically destroyed by endless war, civil conflict, and foreign occupation. Cambodia (Kampuchea), invaded by American armies in 1970, then ravaged by the savage Pol Pot regime and finally occupied by Vietnamese armies, became another terrible tragedy.

Beirut: The Fruits of Civil War Savage conflict between rival militias divided and decimated the Lebanese capital in the 1980s. This Muslim family is walking along the previously fortified "green line," which separated the city's warring Muslim and Christian quarters for fifteen years before it was dismantled by a resurgent national government in 1990. *(Source: Wide World Photos)*

The ongoing plague of local wars and civil conflicts caused great suffering. Millions of refugees, like Vietnam's "boat people," fled for their lives. The war for independence in Bangladesh temporarily created over 10 million refugees, who fled into India toward Calcutta. Hungry, homeless people overwhelmed the Indian relief centers, sleeping in trees, huddling in the rain, starving to death. After the Soviet invasion of Afghanistan, fully one-tenth of that country's population of 1.7 million people fled. In 1981, the United Nations's commission for emergency relief counted 10 million refugees in Asia and Africa. It was an appalling commentary on organized violence in our time, which continued unabated in the 1980s.

The Arms Race and Nuclear Proliferation

Regional competition and local hot wars brought military questions once again to the forefront of world attention. Indeed, nearly every country in the world joined the superpowers in the ever-intensifying arms race. In garrison states like Israel, South Africa, and Vietnam, defense expenditures assumed truly fantastic proportions. Unified Vietnam, having defeated the Americans and battled the Chinese to a standstill, emerged as a modern-day Prussia or Sparta. In the early 1980s, Vietnam was spending half of its national income on the military; its standing army of a million men was the world's third largest, after the Soviet Union and China, and one of the best. Vietnam, with its population of 54 million, had achieved the status of a major Asian power for the foreseeable future. In both India and Brazil, there developed a widespread belief that heavy defense spending spurred economic growth because such outlays created more sophisticated weapons for which there was a strong international demand.

A particularly ominous aspect of the global arms race was the threat of nuclear proliferation. For a generation after 1945, nuclear weapons were concentrated mainly in the hands of the two superpowers, who learned a grudging respect for each other. But other states also developed nuclear weapons, and by the 1970s many more were capable of doing so. Some experts then feared that as many as twenty countries might have their own atomic bombs in a few brief years. As the 1990s opened, these fears had not come true. But the specter of nuclear proliferation and ever-increasing chances of nuclear war clearly haunted the planet. How, a superior intelligence would surely ask, had this frightening situation arisen? And what was being done to find a solution?

Having let the atomic genie out of the bottle at Hiroshima and Nagasaki in 1945, a troubled United States immediately proposed that it be recaptured through effective international control of all atomic weapons. As American representative Bernard Baruch told the first meeting of the United Nations Atomic Energy Commission in 1946:

We are here to make a choice between the quick and the dead. . . . We must elect World Peace or World Destruction. . . . Therefore the United States proposes the creation of an International Atomic Development Authority, to which should be entrusted all phases of the development and use of atomic energy.

The Soviets, suspicious that the United States was really trying to preserve its atomic monopoly through its proposal for international control and inspection, rejected the American idea and continued their crash program to catch up with the United States. The Soviet Union exploded its first atomic bomb in 1949. As the cold war raged on in the 1950s, the two superpowers pressed forward with nuclear development. The United States exploded its first hydrogen bomb in 1952; within ten months the Soviet Union did the same. Further American, Soviet, and then British tests aroused intense worldwide concern about nuclear fallout. There was well-founded fear that radioactive fallout entering the food chain would cause leukemia, bone cancer, and genetic damage. Concerned scientists called for an international agreement to stop all testing of atomic bombs.

Partly in response to worldwide public pressure, the United States, the Soviet Union, and Great Britain agreed in 1958 to stop testing for three years. In 1963 these three powers signed an agreement, later signed by more than one hundred countries, banning nuclear tests in the atmosphere. A second step toward control was the 1968 Treaty on the Non-Proliferation of Nuclear Weapons, designed to halt their spread to other states and to reduce stockpiles of existing bombs. It seemed that the nuclear arms race might yet be reversed.

Chernobyl, Five Years Later   A specialist measures the level of deadly radiation in the reactor hall, sixty yards from the center of the nuclear accident. Contaminating a large part of the Soviet Ukraine, the Chernobyl meltdown provided an ominous warning of the dangers of nuclear proliferation. *(Source: V. Ivleva/Magnum)*

Unfortunately, this outcome did not come to pass. De Gaulle's France and Mao's China, seeing themselves as great world powers, simply disregarded the test ban and refused to sign the nonproliferation treaty. By 1968, they too had hydrogen bombs. In 1974, India exploded an atomic device, reversing its previous commitment to nuclear arms limitations.

India's reversal was partly due to the failure of the Soviet Union and the United States to abide by the terms of the 1968 treaty on nuclear nonproliferation. According to the terms of the treaty, the nuclear powers agreed "to pursue negotiations in good faith on effective measures relating to cessation of the nuclear arms race at an early date and to nuclear disarmament, and on a treaty on general and complete disarmament under strict and effective international control." The non-nuclear states, which had seen serious efforts at disarmament by the superpowers as their payoff for promising not to go nuclear, had offered a whole series of proposals ranging from a complete test ban to a freeze or reduction on nuclear weapons before agreeing to sign the treaty.

In fact, the nuclear arms race between the Soviet Union and the United States surged ahead after 1968. According to American officials, the United States was capable in 1974 of dropping 36 bombs on each of the 218 Soviet cities with populations of 100,000 or more. The Soviet Union had 11 nuclear weapons for each American city of comparable size. The much-discussed SALT talks confined themselves to limiting the rate at which the Soviet Union and the United States produced more nuclear warheads. After 1980, when the second Strategic Arms Limitation Treaty failed to be ratified by the United States Senate, the superpowers appeared once again to be locked into a nuclear arms race.

Partly out of fear for their own security, many near-nuclear powers appeared poised to go nuclear in the 1980s. The worldwide energy crisis of the 1970s had played a part: peaceful use of the atom to generate electric power had created as a by-product large quantities of plutonium, the raw material for bombs. Ominously, some countries began to regard nuclear bombs as just another weapon in the struggle for power and survival.

India, for instance, developed its atomic capability out of fear of China, which had manhandled India in a savage border war in 1962. India's nuclear blast in 1974 in turn frightened Pakistan, which regarded India as a bitter enemy after 1947 and which lost Bangladesh because of Indian armies. Pakistan's President Zulfikar Ali Bhutto (1928–1979) was reported to have said that Pakistan must have the bomb even if its people had to eat grass. In the 1980s, Pakistan was clearly on the verge of producing nuclear weapons. It was also widely believed that both Israel and South Africa had arsenals of nuclear bombs. Israel's apparent nuclear superiority was profoundly distasteful to the Arabs. Hence Iraq pushed hard, with help from France, to develop nuclear capability. In June 1981, Israel reponded suddenly, attacking and destroying the Iraqi nuclear reactor. When Iraq subsequently used deadly chemical weapons against Iran and against its own dissatisfied minorities, the terrible dangers of nuclear proliferation were driven home to all.

If countries like Iraq developed nuclear arms, and if regional conflicts remained so intense, would not some nation use the dreadful weapons sooner or later? And if so, was there not a danger that such a nuclear war would spread to the superpowers? And what about nuclear terrorism and blackmail? In a world full of nuclear weapons and nuclear potential, might not fanatical political groups and desperate states resort to nuclear blackmail to gain their demands? None of these ominous possibilities came to pass in the 1980s, but in a world of bitter political rivalries they made the hardheaded observer grimly apprehensive. Was the human race, as one expert on nuclear arms warned, "an endangered species"?[3]

The end of the cold war offered new hopes and dangers. Some observers worried that a disintegrating Soviet Union might lose control of its vast nuclear stockpile, but the likelihood of nuclear war between the United States and the Soviet Union seemed greatly reduced. In addition, effective Soviet-American cooperation presented the possibility of a reduction in existing nuclear arsenals along with a corresponding renunciation of such weapons by non-nuclear countries, as already spelled out in the 1968 Treaty on the Non-Proliferation of Nuclear Weapons. A major step in this direction was quite possibly taken in July 1990, when the Soviet Union, no doubt with U.S. support, required West Germany to renounce forever the manufacture of nuclear arms in return for Soviet agreement to German reunification. That Germany—mighty, unified, and with a tragic history of aggression in the twentieth century—was forever refusing to produce nuclear weapons raised the hope that nuclear proliferation might yet be mastered.

GLOBAL INTERDEPENDENCE

Alongside political competition and the global arms race, a contradictory phenomenon unfolded: as Toynbee suggested, the nations of our small world became increasingly interdependent both economically and technologically. Even the great continental states with the largest land masses and populations and the richest natural resources found that they could not depend only on themselves. The United States required foreign oil, and the Soviet Union needed foreign grain. All countries and peoples had need of each other.

Mutual dependence in economic affairs was often interpreted as a hopeful sign for the human race. Dependence promoted peaceful cooperation and limited the scope of violence. Yet the existing framework of global interdependence also came under intense attack. The poor countries of the South—the Third World—charged that the North continued to receive far more than its rightful share from existing economic relationships, relationships forged to the South's disadvantage in the era of European expansion and political domination. The South demanded a new international economic order. Critics also saw strong evidence of neocolonialism in the growing importance of the North's huge global business corporations—

the so-called multinationals—in world economic development. Thus global interdependence has been widely accepted in principle and hotly debated in practice.

Pressure on Vital Resources

During the postwar economic boom of the 1950s and the 1960s, the nations of the world became ever more dependent on each other for vital resources. Yet resources also seemed abundant, and rapid industrialization was a worldwide article of faith. Only those alarmed by the population explosion predicted grave shortages, and they spoke almost exclusively about food shortages in the Third World.

The situation changed suddenly in the early 1970s. Fear that the world was running out of resources was widely voiced. In a famous study aptly titled *The Limits to Growth* (1972), a group of American and European scholars argued that unlimited growth is impossible on a finite planet. By the early twenty-first century, they predicted, the ever-increasing demands of too many people and factories would exhaust the world's mineral resources and destroy the fragile biosphere with pollution.

Meanwhile, Japan was importing 99 percent of its petroleum, western Europe 96 percent. When the Organization of Petroleum Exporting Countries (OPEC) increased the price of crude oil fourfold in 1973 (see page 1185), there was panic in many industrial countries. Skyrocketing prices for oil and other raw materials seemed to confirm grim predictions that the world was exhausting its vital resources.

In much of the Third World, the pressure to grow more food for more people led to piecemeal destruction of forests and increased soil erosion. Much of the Third World suffered from what has been called "the other energy crisis"—a severe lack of firewood for cooking and heat.

A striking case is the southern edge of the Sahara. Population growth caused the hard-pressed peoples of this region to overgraze the land and denude the forests. As a result, the sterile sand of the Sahara advanced southward as much as thirty [miles a] year along a 3,000-mile front. Thus land [for] cultivation decreased, leaving Africa [more] exposed to terrible droughts in the [1970s. Cr]ops shriveled up and famine stalked the

land. Yet an interdependent world mobilized, and international relief prevented mass starvation.

A recognition of interdependence was also reinforced by a common dependence on the air and the sea. Just as radioactive fallout has no respect for national boundaries, so pollution may sully the whole globe. Deadly chemicals, including mercury, lead, and arsenic, accumulated in the biosphere. Some feared that pollution of the oceans would lead to the contamination of fish, one of the world's main sources of protein. Others, worried that the oceans had been overfished, feared that the significant decline in the worldwide fish catch in the 1970s indicated abuse of the sea, the common heritage of humankind.

Of all the long-term pressures on global resources, the growth of population was probably the most serious. Here recent experience offered some room for cautious optimism. Population growth in the industrialized countries slowed markedly or even stopped. Of much greater importance from a global perspective, the world's poor women began to bear fewer children. Small countries like Barbados, Chile, Costa Rica, South Korea, Taiwan, Tunisia, and the British colony of Hong Kong led the way. Between 1970 and 1975, China had history's fastest five-year decline in the birthrate. The rate fell from 32 births per thousand people to only 19 births per thousand and stayed level thereafter.

There were several reasons for the decline of the birthrate in many Third World countries. Fewer babies were dying of disease or malnutrition; thus couples needed fewer births to guarantee the survival of the number of children they wanted. As had happened earlier in the industrialized nations, better living conditions, urbanization, and more education encouraged women to have fewer children. No wonder that the most rapidly industrializing countries, like Taiwan or South Korea, led the way in birthrate declines. On the other hand, state-run birth control programs proved most successful in authoritarian China. The birth control pill, borrowed from the West but manufactured locally, was widely used in conjunction with heavy financial penalties for couples who exceeded the birth quota, increasingly fixed at one child per couple. As in most communist countries, abortion was free and on demand.

Elsewhere—in Africa, the Muslim world, and North and South America—contraception and abortion remained controversial. This helps ex-

Famine in Ethiopia These desperate Ethiopians, fleeing from drought and starvation in 1985, hoped to find enough food to escape death in makeshift refugee camps sponsored by international relief organizations. Huddling together after a night exposed to the bitter desert cold, the recent arrivals in the foreground are completely exhausted from hunger and fatigue. *(Source: Sebastio Salgado/Magnum)*

plain why birthrates and population growth remained much higher in Africa and South America than in Asia. In 1985, Africa led the world with a population growth of 3.2 percent per year—enough to double the continent's numbers in only twenty-two years.

Indira Gandhi's fiasco with compulsory sterilization (see page 1226) suggests that, barring catastrophe, worldwide population growth will decline only gradually, as a result of billions of private decisions supplemented by government policies. This means that world population will continue to grow for a long time, as the Third World's current huge population of young adults form their own families. Thus the world's population—5 billion in 1987, as opposed to 1.6 billion in 1900—will probably not stabilize until the

mid-twenty-first century at the earliest, when it will have reached 10 to 12 billion people. Such continued growth will put tremendous pressure on global resources.

Yet gloom is not the only possible perspective. Even with 11 billion people, the earth would be less densely populated than Europe is today, and only one-fourth as densely populated as small, prosperous countries like Belgium and the Netherlands, which largely feed themselves (see Map 38.1). Such countries, often overlooked in world politics, are promising models for life on a crowded planet. Moreover, the human race has exhibited considerable skill throughout its history at finding new resources and inventing new technologies. A striking example was the way that conservation, alternative energy sources, and world recession in the early 1980s at least temporarily belied gloomy prophecies about dwindling energy resources. An optimist could conclude that, at least from a quantitative and technical point of view, the adequacy of resources is a serious but by no means insoluble problem.

North-South Relations

The real key to adequate resources is probably global cooperation. Will the world's peoples work together, or will they eventually fight over resources like wild dogs over meat?

Since the late 1960s there has been dissatisfaction in Asia, Africa, and Latin America not only with the fruits of the industrialization drive but also with the world's economic system. Scholars imbued with a Third World perspective and spokesmen for the United Nations majority declared that the international system was unjust and in need of radical change. A brilliant Pakistani, World Bank official, and member of the international bureaucratic elite sympathetically articulated this position in 1976:

The vastly unequal relationship between the rich and the poor nations is fast becoming the central issue of our time. The poor nations are beginning to question the basic premises of an international order which leads to ever-widening disparities between the rich and the poor countries and to a persistent denial of equality of opportunity to many poor nations. They are, in fact, arguing that in international order—just as much as within national orders—all distribution of benefits, credit, services, and decision-making becomes warped in favor of a privileged minority and that this situation cannot be changed except through fundamental institutional reforms.[4]

The subsequent Third World demand for a "new international economic order" had many causes, both distant and immediate. Critics of imperialism like J. A. Hobson (see page 980) and Third World writers on decolonization like Franz Fanon (see page 1275) had long charged that the colonial powers grew rich exploiting Asia, Africa, and Latin America. Beginning in the 1950s, a number of writers, many of them Latin American Marxists, breathed new life into these ideas with their "theory of dependency."

The poverty and so-called underdevelopment of the South, they argued, were not the starting points but the deliberate and permanent results of exploitation by the capitalist industrialized nations in the modern era. Third World countries produced cheap raw materials for wealthy, industrialized countries and were conditioned to buy their expensive manufactured goods. As in the case of Latin America since the nineteenth century, the industrialized nations perpetuated this neocolonial pattern after Third World countries gained political independence. Thus the prevailing economic interdependence was the unequal, unjust interdependence of dominant and subordinate, of master and peon. Declining economic aid, smug pronouncements about the overpopulation of the Third World, and the natural resentment of the poor toward the rich also fostered calls for radical restructuring of the international order.

It was the highly successful OPEC oil coup of 1973–1974 that ignited Third World hopes of actually achieving a new system of economic interdependence. From the industrialized North's point of view, OPEC's action in quadrupling the price of oil was a dangerous attack. It brought an end to the postwar economic boom and created serious social problems. From a global perspective, however, the sudden price rise brought a massive global transfer of wealth unprecedented since the looting of Mexico and Peru by the Spanish conquistadors. Perhaps 2 percent of all the income of the rich nations was suddenly forwarded to the OPEC countries (Map 39.2). Third World critics of dependence and neocolonialism were euphoric. For years the developed countries had gradually been reducing their economic aid. They had never seriously tried to meet the goal suggested by the U.N. General Assembly of earmarking 1 percent of their income each year for foreign aid. OPEC's success suggested that radical change was possible.

In 1974, a special session of the General Assembly rammed through two landmark resolutions calling for a "new international economic order" and a "program of action" to attain it. Among the specific demands were firm control by each country of its own natural resources, higher and more stable prices for raw materials, and equal tariff treatment for manufactured goods from the Third World. These demands were subject to "collective bargaining," but the Third World vigorously insisted on new terms. As one sympathetic scholar observed in 1980:

There has taken place a unionization of the Third World that has marked a profound shift in international relations. It looks as if the confrontation between unions and employers that stirred capitalist societies in the nineteenth century is being reenacted, but this time on a world scale between developed and developing nations. The question this time is whether the new nations command as many assets and opportunities as did the laboring classes of capitalist nations.[5]

That profound question remained unanswered in the late twentieth century. The developing countries did negotiate some victories, notably a Common Fund under U.N. auspices to support the prices of raw materials and a scaling down of their enormous debts to the industrial nations. But the North, deeply troubled by inflation and by its own economic problems, proved a very tough bargainer when it came to basic changes.

For example, in the late 1970s the South laid great hopes on a long, complicated conference to formulate a new Law of the Sea. The proposed new law was based on the principle that the world's oceans are "a common heritage of mankind" and should be exploited only for the benefit of all nations. In practice, this was to mean that a U.N.-sponsored authority would regulate and tax use of the sea and that a global organization would even mine the ocean floor. Some wealthy countries and their business firms were reluctant to accept such an infringement of their economic sovereignty and scope of action. The United States withdrew from the negotiations in 1981, and in 1982 the Reagan administration and the governments of several other developed nations refused to sign the final draft of the new Law of the Sea.

Increasingly frustrated in their desire to fashion a new international economic order quickly, some

MAP 39.2 OPEC and the World Oil Trade Though much of the world depends on imported oil, Western Europe and Japan are OPEC's biggest customers. What major oil exporters remain outside of OPEC?

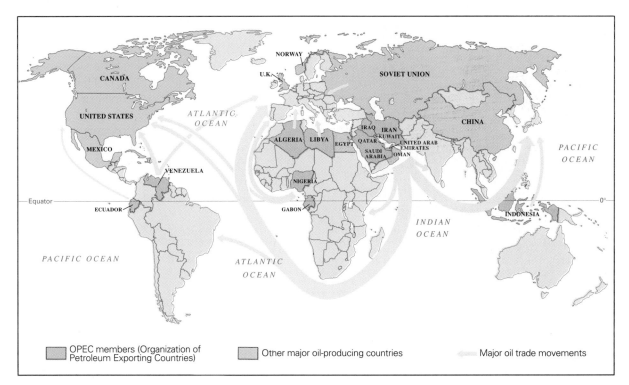

OPEC members (Organization of Petroleum Exporting Countries)   Other major oil-producing countries   Major oil trade movements

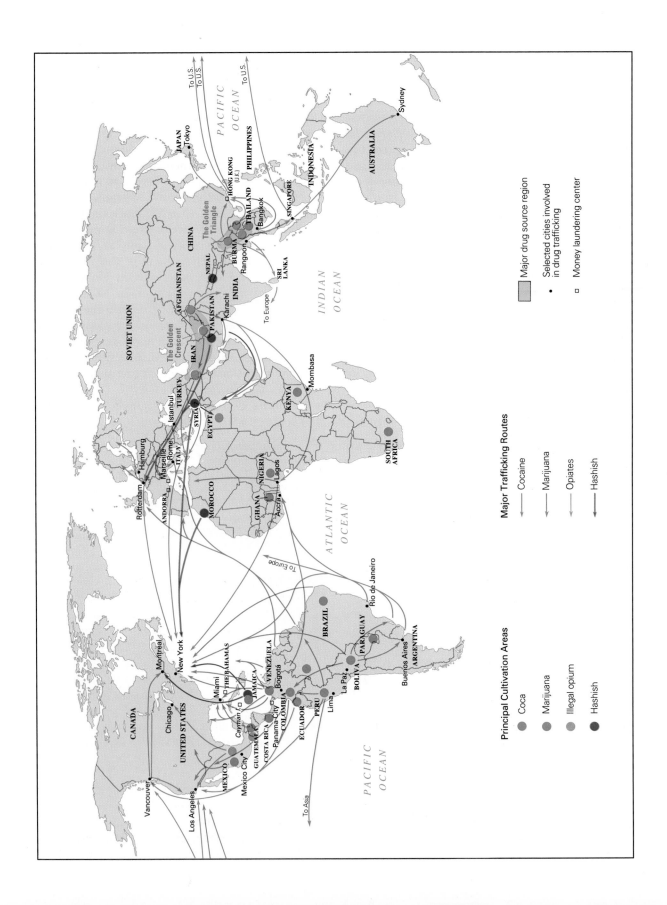

Principal Cultivation Areas

- Coca
- Marijuana
- Illegal opium
- Hashish

Major Trafficking Routes

- Cocaine
- Marijuana
- Opiates
- Hashish

- Major drug source region
- Selected cities involved in drug trafficking
- Money laundering center

Third World leaders predicted more confrontation and perhaps military conflict between North and South. Some alarmists in the North voiced similar concerns. For example, these alarmists charged that many Third World governments secretly condoned the production of illegal drugs for sale in the industrialized nations, and they predicted that this behavior would dangerously increase the tensions existing between the rich and the poor countries (Map 39.3).

In considering these ominous predictions, an impartial observer is initially struck by the great gap between the richest and poorest nations. That gap was built on the coercive power of Western imperialism as well as on the wealth-creating achievements of continuous technological improvement since the Industrial Revolution. In the face of bitter poverty, unbalanced economies, and local elites that often cater to Western interests, Third World peoples have reason for anger.

Yet close examination of our small planet hardly suggests two sharply defined economic camps, a "North" and a "South." Rather, there are several distinct classes of nations in terms of wealth and income, as may be seen in Map 39.4. The former communist countries of eastern Europe form something of a middle-income group, as do the major oil-exporting states, which still lag behind the wealthier countries of western Europe and North America. Latin America is much better off than sub-Saharan Africa, having a number of middle-range countries to match their counterparts in highly diverse Asia.

When one adds global differences in culture, religion, politics, and historical development, the supposed clear-cut split between the rich North and the poor South breaks down further. Moreover, the solidarity of the Third World is fragile, resting largely on the ideas of some Third World intellectuals and their supporters. As one writer put it,

in the advocacy of growth and equalization at the international level . . . Third World states have aston-

MAP 39.3 World Drug Trade As the drug trade has grown, the area of production has greatly expanded from the traditional Asian centers—the Golden Crescent and the Golden Triangle—to include many Third World countries. Poverty provides the drug lords with an army of drug runners.

ished everybody, their enemies and their friends alike, for no one has ever believed that such a diverse congress of countries, separated by geography, geopolitics, cultural traditions, size, ideology, and a host of other factors, could ever manage to build a cohesive alliance.[6]

The oil cartel's achievement rested in large part on regional (and perhaps temporary) Arab solidarity, for example, and duplicating its success with less vital raw materials and more complicated issues proved impossible.

Thus continuing global collective bargaining seems more likely than international class (and race) war. The poorer nations will press to reduce international economic differences through taxation, redistribution measures, and special aid to the most unfortunate countries. And because global interdependence is a reality, they will gradually win concessions, as has occurred domestically for the working classes in the wealthy nations since the late nineteenth century.

The international debt crisis suggests how this global bargaining is already occurring. The economic dislocations of the 1970s and early 1980s worsened the problems of many Third World countries, especially those that had to import the oil they needed. Growing unemployment, unbalanced budgets, and large trade deficits forced many Third World countries to borrow rapidly from the wealthy industrialized nations. By the middle of 1982, Third World nations—led by Mexico, Brazil, and Argentina—owed foreign banks and governments about $600 billion. Moreover, much of this staggering debt was short-term and could not possibly be repaid as it fell due.

When Mexico closed its foreign exchange markets in August 1982, unable to keep up with the payments on $80 billion of foreign debts, default and financial chaos in Mexico seemed at hand. Yet the Reagan administration, consistently opposed to Third World calls for a new international system, quickly organized a gigantic rescue operation to pump new money into Mexico and prevent default. The reason was simple: Mexico's failure to service its foreign debt would cripple or even bankrupt some of the large American banks that had lent Mexico money. Such a failure promised to touch off such massive debt repudiations in the Third World and corporate losses in the industrialized countries that the whole world would be

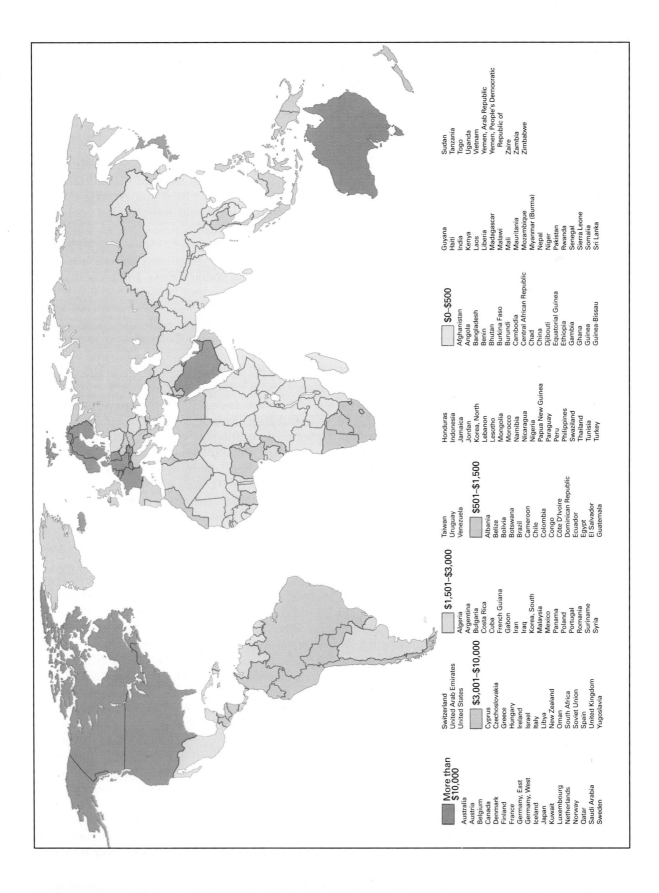

More than $10,000
Australia
Austria
Belgium
Canada
Denmark
Finland
France
Germany, East
Germany, West
Iceland
Japan
Kuwait
Luxembourg
Netherlands
Norway
Qatar
Saudi Arabia
Sweden
Switzerland
United Arab Emirates
United States

$3,001–$10,000
Cyprus
Czechoslovakia
Greece
Hungary
Ireland
Israel
Italy
Libya
New Zealand
Oman
South Africa
Soviet Union
Spain
United Kingdom
Yugoslavia

$1,501–$3,000
Algeria
Argentina
Bulgaria
Costa Rica
Cuba
French Guiana
Gabon
Iran
Iraq
Korea, South
Malaysia
Mexico
Panama
Poland
Portugal
Romania
Suriname
Syria

$501–$1,500
Albania
Belize
Bolivia
Botswana
Brazil
Cameroon
Chile
Colombia
Congo
Côte D'Ivoire
Dominican Republic
Ecuador
Egypt
El Salvador
Guatemala
Honduras
Indonesia
Jamaica
Jordan
Korea, North
Lebanon
Lesotho
Mongolia
Morocco
Namibia
Nicaragua
Nigeria
Papua New Guinea
Paraguay
Peru
Philippines
Swaziland
Thailand
Tunisia
Turkey
Taiwan
Uruguay
Venezuela

$0–$500
Afghanistan
Angola
Bangladesh
Benin
Bhutan
Burkina Faso
Burundi
Cambodia
Central African Republic
Chad
China
Djibouti
Equatorial Guinea
Ethiopia
Gambia
Ghana
Guinea
Guinea-Bissau
Guyana
Haiti
India
Kenya
Laos
Liberia
Madagascar
Malawi
Mali
Mauritania
Mozambique
Myanmar (Burma)
Nepal
Niger
Pakistan
Rwanda
Senegal
Sierra Leone
Somalia
Sri Lanka
Sudan
Tanzania
Togo
Uganda
Vietnam
Yemen, Arab Republic
Yemen, People's Democratic Republic of
Zaire
Zambia
Zimbabwe

plunged into depression and even social turmoil. Thus a series of ongoing negotiations began all over the globe to reduce Third World debts, stretch out repayments far into the future, and grant desperately needed new loans. Lenders and borrowers, rich and poor, North and South, have realized that they are bound together in mutual dependence by the international debt crisis.

The Multinational Corporations

One of the most striking features of global economic interdependence has been the rapid emergence of multinational corporations since the early 1950s. Multinationals are business firms that operate in a number of different countries and tend to adopt a global rather than a national perspective. Multinational corporations themselves were not new, but their great importance was. By 1971, each of the ten largest multinational corporations—the IBMs, the Royal Dutch Shell Petroleums, the General Motors—was selling more than $3 billion worth of goods annually, more than the total national incomes of four-fifths of the world's countries. Multinational corporations accounted for fully a fifth of the noncommunist world's annual income, and they have grown even more important in the last two decades.

The rise of multinationals has aroused a great deal of heated discussion around the world. Defenders see the multinational corporations as building an efficient world economic system and transcending narrow national ties. In the words of a top manager of Royal Dutch Shell, the multinational corporation is

a new form of social architecture, matching the world-girding potential inherent in modern technology. . . .

In an age when modern technology has shrunk the world, and brought us all closer together, the multinational corporation and the nation state must get used to living with each other[7]

Critics worry precisely that the nation-state is getting the worst of the new arrangement. Pro-

vocative book titles portray *Frightening Angels* holding *Sovereignty at Bay,* while building *Invisible Empires* and extending their nefarious *Global Reach.* As usual whenever a major development attracts widespread attention, exaggerations and unreasonable predictions abound on both sides.

The rise of the multinationals was partly due to the general revival of capitalism after the Second World War, relatively free international economic relations, and the worldwide drive for rapid industrialization. The multinationals also had three specific assets, which they used to their advantage. First, "pure" scientific knowledge unrelated to the military was freely available, but its highly profitable industrial applications remained in the hands of the world's largest business firms. These firms held advanced, fast-changing technology as a kind of property and hurried to make profitable use of it wherever they could. Second, the multinationals knew how to sell, as well as how to innovate and produce. They used their advertising and marketing skills to push their products relentlessly, especially the ever-expanding range of consumer products, around the world. Finally, the multinationals developed new techniques to escape from political controls and national policies. Managers found ways to treat the world as one big market, coordinating complex activities across many political boundaries so as to reap the greatest profits.

Multinational industrial corporations began in the last quarter of the nineteenth century. U.S. businessmen took the lead, for reasons rooted in the nature of the American economy and society. Above all, the United States had a vast, unified market and the world's highest standard of living by 1890, so that U.S. businessmen were positioned to pioneer in the mass production of standardized consumer goods. Many of the most famous examples—such as kerosene (John D. Rockefeller and Standard Oil), sewing machines (Singer), and farm machinery (Cyrus McCormick and International Harvester)—date from the 1880s. Others—like the cheap automobile (Henry Ford), the mass retailer (Sears), and standardized food (Coca-Cola, Wrigley's chewing gum)—were thriving by 1914.

Having developed mass-marketing techniques as well as new products, the biggest, most monopolistic American corporations quickly expanded abroad. They created wholly owned subsidiaries to

MAP 39.4 Estimated GNP per Capita Income in the Early 1980s

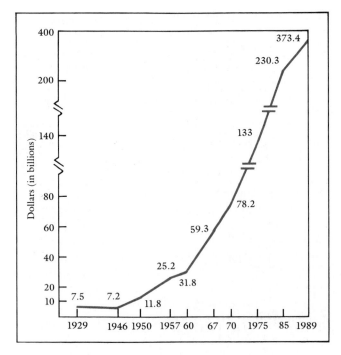

FIGURE 39.1 Total Investment by American Corporations in Foreign Subsidiaries (*Source: Data from U.S. Department of Commerce. Survey of Current Business.*)

American investment had been heavily concentrated in Europe, Canada, and the Middle East, Japanese firms turned at first to Asia for raw materials and cheap, high-quality factory labor. By the 1970s Japanese subsidiaries in Taiwan, Thailand, Hong Kong, and Malaysia were pouring out a torrent of transistor radios, televisions, cameras, and pocket calculators.

Fearful of a growing protectionist reaction in their largest foreign market, the United States, where unemployed autoworkers symbolically demolished a Japanese automobile with sledgehammers in 1979, a host of Japanese firms followed Sony's example and began manufacturing in the United States in the 1980s. The Japanese inflow was so great that by 1989 Japanese multinationals had invested $70 billion in their subsidiaries in the United States, which far surpassed the $19 billion that American multinationals had invested in Japan. In 1989 investment by European multinationals in the United States was also about 50 percent greater than American multinational investment in Europe. The emergence of European and Japanese multinational corporations alongside their American forerunners marked the coming of age of global business in an interdependent world.

The impact of multinational corporations, especially on Third World countries, has been heatedly debated. From an economic point of view, the effects have been mixed. The giant firms have provided advanced technology, but the technology has been expensive and often inappropriate for poor countries with widespread unemployment.

The social consequences have been quite striking. The multinationals helped spread the products and values of consumer society to the elites of the Third World. Moreover, they fostered the creation of islands of Western wealth, management, and consumer culture around the world. After buying up local companies with offers that local business people did not dare to refuse, multinational corporations often hired Third World business leaders to manage their operations abroad. Critics considered this practice an integral part of the process of neocolonialism, whereby local elites abandoned the national interest and made themselves willing tools of continued foreign domination.

Some global corporations have used aggressive techniques of modern marketing to sell products

produce and sell American-style consumer goods in foreign lands before 1914, and they continued to do so between the world wars. With ever more products and the attractions of the European Common Market, there followed a mighty surge of American investment in Europe after 1945. Nor were other parts of the world neglected by the giant American manufacturing firms: there was continued multinational investment in raw-material production in Latin America (particularly copper, sugar, and bananas) as well as in the Middle East and Africa (primarily oil and gold). By 1967, American corporations—mainly the largest, most familiar household names—had sunk $60 billion into their foreign operations (Figure 39.1).

A few European companies, notably German chemical and electrical firms, also became multinationals before 1900. Others emerged in the twentieth century. By the 1970s these European multinationals were in hot pursuit. Some, like Volkswagen, pushed directly into the American heartland and also into the Third World. Big Japanese firms like Sony also rushed to catch up and go multinational in the 1960s and 1970s. Whereas

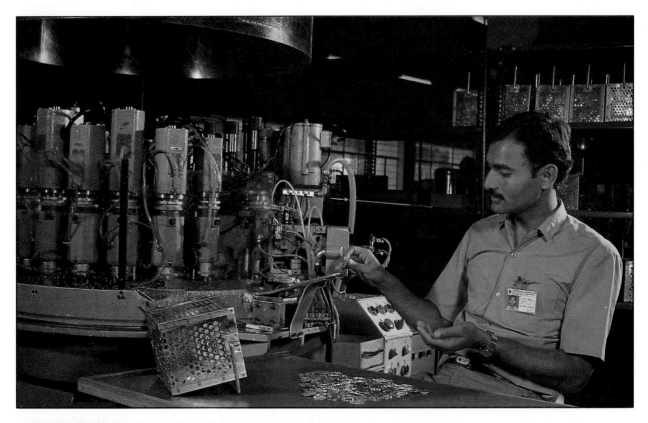

Japanese Investment in India An Indian worker carefully feeds a machine in this Japanese-owned plant. The high cost of labor in Japan encourages Japanese companies to manufacture a growing number of products in low-wage countries like India. *(Source: P. R. Gansham/Dinodia Picture Agency)*

that are not well suited to Third World conditions. For example, Third World mothers have been urged to abandon "old-fashioned, primitive" breast-feeding (which was, ironically, making a strong comeback in rich countries) and to buy powdered milk formulas for their babies. But the use of unsanitary bottles and contaminated water and the dilution of the expensive formula to make it last longer tragically resulted in additional infant deaths. On this and many other issues, the multinationals have come into sharp conflict with host countries.

Far from acting helpless in such conflicts, some poor countries have exercised their sovereign rights over the foreign multinationals. Many foreign mining companies, like the fabulously profitable U.S. oil companies in the Middle East, were simply nationalized by the host countries. More importantly, Third World governments began to learn how to make foreign manufacturing companies conform to some of their plans and desires. Increasingly, multinationals have to share ownership with local investors, hire more local managers, provide technology on better terms, and accept a variety of controls. Governments have learned to play Americans, Europeans, and Japanese off against each other. Frustrated by such treatment, one American managing director in Malaysia pounded his desk in 1979 and sputtered, "This little country and her little people need help, but they must be reasonable, otherwise we will get out of here." A Japanese manager in the same country expressed a more cooperative view: "We came here as guests, and our nation is small and needs natural resources, as well as foreign trade and investment to survive."[8] A growing proliferation of multinationals has opened up new opportunities for Third World countries that want to use these powerful foreign corporations without being dominated by them.

PATTERNS OF THOUGHT

The renowned economist John Maynard Keynes often said that we live by our ideas and by very little else. True or not, a global perspective surely requires keen attention to patterns of collective thinking. As Keynes saw, we need to be aware of the ideas that are shaping the uncertain destiny of this small, politically fragmented, economically interdependent planet.

To be sure, human thought can be baffling in its rich profusion. Nevertheless, in the late twentieth century, three distinct patterns on a global scale can be identified: the enduring strength of the modern world's secular ideologies, a vigorous revival of the world's great religions, and a search for mystical experience. The human race lives by these ideas.

Secular Ideologies

A good deal has been said in this book about the modern world's great secular ideologies. Almost all of these bodies of ideas, including liberalism, nationalism, and Marxian socialism, as well as faith in scientific and technical progress, industrialism, and democratic republicanism, took form in Europe between the eighteenth-century Enlightenment and the revolutions of 1848. These ideologies continued to evolve with the coming of mass society in the late nineteenth century and were carried by imperialism to the highly diverse societies of Asia and Africa. There they won converts among the local elites, who eventually conquered their imperialist masters in the twentieth century. European ideologies became worldwide ideologies, gradually outgrowing their early, specifically European character.

All this can be seen as an aspect of global interdependence. The world has come to live, in part, by shared ideas. These ideas have continued to develop in a complex global dialogue, and champions of competing views now arise from all regions. This has certainly been true of nationalist ideology and also of Marxism. Europe, the birthplace of Marxism, has made few original intellectual contributions to Marxism since Stalin transformed it into a totalitarian ideology of forced industrialization. Since 1945, it has been Marxists from the Third World who have injected new meanings into the old ideology, notably with Mao's brand of peasant-based revolution and the Marxist theory of Third World dependency. Leftist intellectuals in Europe have cheered and said "me too."

It is primarily as critics that Europeans contributed to world Marxism. Yugoslavs were particularly influential. After breaking with Stalin in 1948, they revived and expanded the ideas of Stalin's vanquished rival, Leon Trotsky. Trotsky had claimed that Stalin perverted socialism by introducing "state capitalism" and reactionary bureaucratic dictatorship. According to the influential Yugoslav Milovan Djilas (b. 1911) Lenin's dedicated elite of full-time revolutionaries became Stalin's ruthless bureaucrats, "a new class" that was unprecedented in history. Djilas's powerful impact stemmed from his mastery of the Marxian dialectic:

The social origin of the new class lies in the proletariat just as the aristocracy arose in peasant society, and the bourgeoisie in a commercial and artisans' society. . . .

Former sons of the working class are the most steadfast members of the new class. It has always been the fate of slaves to provide for their masters the most clever and gifted representatives. In this case a new exploiting and governing class is born from the exploited class. . . .

The communists are . . . a new class.

As in other owning classes, the proof that it is a special class lies in its ownership and in its special relations to other classes. In the same way, the class to which a member belongs is indicated by the material and other privileges which ownership brings him.

As defined by Roman law, property constitutes the use, enjoyment, and disposition of material goods. The communist political bureaucracy uses, enjoys, and disposes of nationalized property.[9]

Non-Marxian criticism of communism also continued to develop, as in Jean François Revel's provocative *The Totalitarian Temptation* (1977). According to Revel, the application of the Marxist-Leninist-Maoist model, which came to be adopted by many countries not strictly belonging to the Communist camp, brought about phony revolution. Under the guise of supposedly progressive socialism, it built reactionary totalitarian states of the Stalinist variety. Critics of Marxism-Leninism like Revel and Dijlas undermined the intellectual appeal of communism and thereby contributed to its being overthrown in eastern Europe in 1989.

As the varieties of Marxism lost considerable luster in the 1980s, old-fashioned, long-battered liberalism and democracy survived and even thrived as a global ideology. In every communist country small, persecuted human rights movements bravely demanded the basic liberties first set into law in the American and French revolutions, preparing the way against all odds for the renewed triumph of liberal revolution in eastern Europe in 1989. And there have always been some African and Asian intellectuals, often in exile, calling for similar rights even in the most authoritarian states.

The call for human rights and representative government coincided with a renewed faith in market forces and economic liberalism as effective tools of economic and social development. That countries as highly diverse as Brazil, China, Ghana, and the Soviet Union all moved in this direction in the 1980s was little short of astonishing.

Efforts to combine the best elements of socialism and liberalism in a superior hybrid have also been important. The physicist Andrei Sakharov (1921–1990), the father of the Russian atomic bomb, who in the 1960s became a fearless leader of the human rights movement in the Soviet Union, was an eloquent spokesman for what might be called the "convergence school." According to Sakharov, humanity's best hope lay in the accelerated convergence of liberal capitalism and dictatorial communism on some middle ground of welfare capitalism and democratic socialism, like that which has flourished in the small, close-knit societies of Scandinavia, Iceland, and New Zealand.

Solzhenitsyn in Vermont   After he was forcibly expelled from the Soviet Union in 1974, Solzhenitsyn settled in Vermont, which recalled to him the beauty of Russia. Although an uncompromising opponent of communism, Solzhenitsyn criticized the West for its materialism and restless greed. *(Source: S. Bassouls/Sygma)*

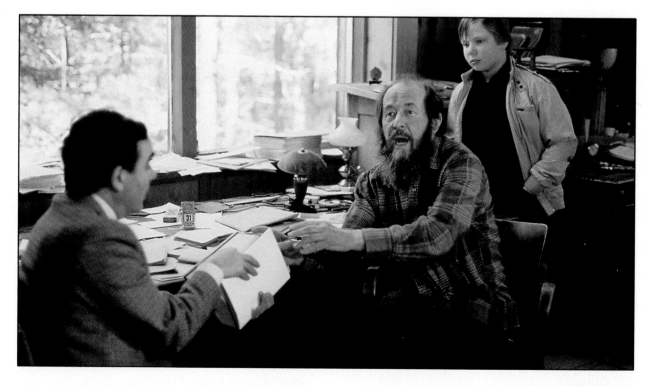

This outlook waxes and wanes in influence, but it has deep historical roots in society and remains a potent force in world thought.

Finally, there has been a many-sided global reaction to the dominant faith in industrialization, consumerism, and unrestrained "modernization." The disillusionment of the Third World has been matched by disillusionment in the developed countries and a search for alternative secular visions of the future. The student revolt of the 1960s (see page 1185), with its vague ideology of broad participation in community decisions, coincided with widespread nostalgia for simple, close-knit rural societies. The great Russian novelist Alexander Solzhenitsyn, caught up in the vanishing-resources doctrine of the 1970s, called on Soviet leaders to renounce Western technology and return to the earth:

Herein lies Russia's hope for winning time and winning salvation: In our vast northeastern spaces, which over four centuries our sluggishness has prevented us from mutilating by our mistakes, we can build anew: not the senseless, voracious civilization of "progress"—no; we can set up a stable economy without pain or delay and settle people there for the first time according to the needs and principles of that economy. These spaces allow us to hope that we shall not destroy Russia in the general crisis of Western civilization.[10]

Communes sprang up in the United States and Europe in the late 1960s. There were many advocates of alternative technologies and lifestyles. E. F. Schumacher, an English disciple of Gandhi, in *Small Is Beautiful* (1973) urged the building of solar-heated houses to conserve nonrenewable oil. Africa and Asia increasingly stressed "appropriate technologies" tailored to village life rather than borrowed from large-scale urban industrialized society—such as small, rugged, three-wheeled motorized carts suited to existing country lanes, rather than large trucks requiring expensive modern highways, elaborate maintenance facilities, and large amounts of imported fuel.

Perhaps the most striking aspect of the worldwide reappraisal of industrialization was the heretical revival of Jean-Jacques Rousseau's belief in the superiority of the simple, frugal "noble savage." As Robert Heilbroner poignantly put it in 1974 in his otherwise gloomy *An Inquiry into the Human Prospect:*

One element [of hope] . . . is our knowledge that some human societies have existed for millennia, and that others can probably exist for future millennia, in a continuous rhythm of birth and coming of age and death, without pressing toward those dangerous ecological limits, or engendering those dangerous social tensions, that threaten present-day "advanced" societies. In our discovery of "primitive" cultures, living out their timeless histories, we may have found the single most important object lesson for future man.[11]

Other writers from the industrialized countries reassessed traditional cultures and found nobility and value similar to that championed by the Nigerian novelist Achebe (see page 1276). It was another striking example of the globalization of intellectual life.

Religious Belief: Christianity and Islam

The reaction to industrialism and consumerism was part of a broader religious response to the dominance of secular ideologies in general. The revival of Christianity among intellectuals after the First World War (see pages 1109–1110) was matched in the 1970s and 1980s by a surge of popular, often fundamentalist, Christianity in many countries. Judaism and Islam also experienced resurgence, and Buddhism and Hinduism stopped losing ground. The continuing importance of religion in contemporary human thought—an importance that has often escaped those fascinated by secular ideology and secular history—must impress the unbiased observer.

Pope John Paul II (r. 1978–) exemplified several aspects of the worldwide Christian revival. A jet-age global evangelist, John Paul journeyed to Africa, Asia, and North and South America, inspiring enthusiatic multitudes with his warm sincerity and unfailing popular touch. John Paul's melding of a liberal social gospel with conservatism in doctrinal matters also seemed to reflect the spirit of the age. Thus the pope boldly urged a more equitable distribution of wealth in plutocratic Brazil and more civil liberties in Marcos's authoritarian Philippines while reaffirming the church's long-standing opposition to mechanical contraception and women in the priesthood. Many of Christianity's most rapidly growing Protestant churches also espoused theological fundamentalism, based on a literal reading of the Bible.

Pope John Paul II   The man of peace and good will arrives in Warsaw in 1983 for a second pilgrimage to his homeland. John Paul drew vast and enthusiastic crowds, demonstrating their opposition to an oppressive system as well as their deep-rooted Christian faith. *(Jean-Claude Francolon/Alain Mingam/Chip Hires/François Lochon/Gamma-Liaison)*

It was also emblematic that the "Polish Pope" came from an officially atheist communist country. Yet after thirty-five years of communist rule, Poland was more intensely Catholic than ever before. Lech Walesa, the courageous leader of Poland's trade union Solidarity, said that he never could be a communist because he was a devout Roman Catholic. Poland illustrated the enduring strength of spiritual life in the face of materialistic culture and secular ideologies, of which communism was only the most openly hostile.

The attempted assassination of the pope in 1981 by a mysterious Turkish terrorist, possibly connected with the Soviet KGB in an effort to undermine the Catholic church in Poland, also dramatized the appeal of religious thinking. In a frightening, violent world, faith and prayer offer comfort and courage.

Islam, the religion of one-seventh of the earth's people, also experienced a powerful resurgence in the 1970s and 1980s. Like orthodox Christianity, Islam had been challenged by the self-confident secular ideologies of the West since the early nineteenth century. And although the acids of modern thought did not eat as deeply as in Europe and North America, they etched a seductive alternative to Islam. Moderate Muslim intellectuals advocated religious reforms; radicals wanted drastic surgery. The most famous and successful of the radicals was the twentieth-century Turkish nationalist Kemal Atatürk (see pages 1079–1081), who reflected and accelerated the impact of secularism on the Muslim world.

The generation of Muslim intellectual and political leaders born in the interwar years, who reached maturity after the Second World War, agreed that Islam required at least some modernizing. They accepted the attractively simple Muslim creed, "There is no god but Allah and Muhammad is his Prophet," but they did not think that the

Ayatollah Khomeini The apostle of Islamic regeneration and the unwavering critic of the shah returns in triumph to Teheran from exile in February 1979. The shah had visions of making Iran a major military power, but all his military might crumbled before the emotional appeal of Islamic revolution. *(Source: Black Star/Sipa Press–Setboun)*

laws of the Qur'an should be taken literally. The prohibition on lending money at interest, the social inferiority of women, even cutting off the hands of thieves and public beheading of murderers, had made sense for the Arabian peninsula in the Middle Ages. But such practices did not suit the modern age. It became necessary for Islam to adapt.

These views were still common among educated elites in the 1970s, and they remained dominant in Turkey and probably in Egypt. Yet throughout much of the Middle East they have had to bow before a revival of Islamic fundamentalism, the critical development of recent years. Like some of their Christian and Jewish counterparts, orthodox Muslim believers wanted to return to unalterable fundamentals. In taking the Qur'an literally, they demanded that the modern world adapt to the Prophet's teachings, not vice versa. And because the masses remained deeply religious and distrustful of change, Islamic fundamentalism aroused a heartfelt popular response.

Iran provided a spectacular manifestation of resurgent Islamic fundamentalism. In the 1970s, Iran's religious leaders, notably the charismatic Ayatollah Khomeini, catalyzed intense popular dissatisfaction with the shah's all-out industrialization and heavy-handed religious reform into a successful revolution. An "Islamic Republic" was established to govern according to the sacred laws of the Qur'an. State and church were tightly bound together. The holy men and their followers were absolutely serious: they sanctioned the stoning to death of prostitutes and adulterers and proposed revising the legal code along strictly Qur'anic lines.

Iran's fundamentalism was exceptionally rigid and antimodern, partly because the country adhered to the minority Shi'ite version of Islam. But similar movements developed in every Muslim country. Even where the fundamentalists are unlikely to take power, as in Indonesia or Pakistan, and where they have been co-opted and neutralized, as in Saudi Arabia, they have found enthusiastic support among the masses and have revitalized the Muslim faith. Islamic religious thought remains extremely vigorous and continues to win converts, especially in black Africa.

Searching for Mystical Experience

Alongside secular ideologies and a revival of the world's great religions, the third powerful current of intellectual attraction has consisted of an enormous variety of religious sects, cults, and spiritual yearnings. Some of these new outpourings welled up within one or another of the great religions; many more did not. Though widely divergent, these movements seemed to share a common urge toward nonrational experiences, such as meditation, spiritual mysteries, and direct communication with supernatural forces.

Not that this is new. So-called primitive peoples have always embraced myths, visions, and continuous revelation. So too have the world's main religions, especially those of the ancient East—Taoism, Hinduism, and the Zen form of Buddhism. What is new is the receptiveness of many people in the rationalistic, scientific industrialized countries (and their disciples, the Third World elite) to ancient modes of mystical experience. Some of this interest stems from the doubt about the power of the rational human mind that blossomed after the First World War. By the 1960s, it had struck deep roots in the mass culture of Europe and North America.

In this sense, the late twentieth century is reminiscent of the initial encounter of West and East in the Hellenistic Age. Then, the rationalistic, humanistic Greeks encountered the Eastern mystery religions and were profoundly influenced by them. Now, various strains of mystical thought are again appearing from the East and from "primitive" peoples. It can be said that the non-Western world is providing intellectual repayment for the powerful secular ideologies that it borrowed in the nineteenth century.

Reflecting on this ongoing encounter, the American social scientist Robert Heilbroner was not alone in suggesting startling implications for the future:

It is therefore possible that a post-industrial society would also turn in the direction of many preindustrial societies—toward the exploration of inner states of experience rather than the outer world of fact and material accomplishment. Tradition and ritual, the pillars of life in virtually all societies other than those of an industrial character, would probably once again assert their ancient claims as the guide to and solace for life.[12]

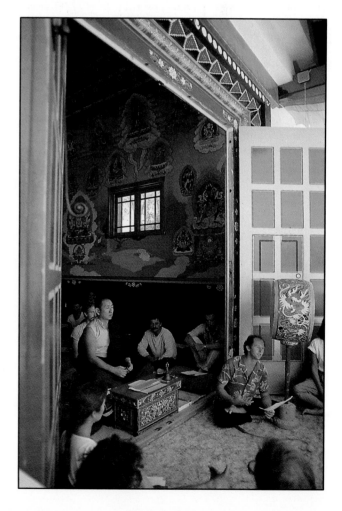

Buddhism in the West Americans from different backgrounds come together for worship in this Buddhist temple in Santa Fe, New Mexico. This temple adheres to the Tibetan form of Buddhism, which combines mysticism and colorful ceremony. *(Source: Mimi Forsyth/Monkmeyer Press)*

Some observers see the onrush of science and technology as actually reinforcing the search for spiritual experience. Electronic communications demolish time and distance; information itself is becoming the new global environment. According to the philosopher William Thompson:

Culture is full of many surprises, because culture is full of the play of opposites. And so there will be scientists and mystics in the New Age. . . . To look at the American counterculture today, one would guess . . . that the East was about to engulf the West. But in fact . . . America is swallowing up and absorbing the traditional Eastern techniques of transformation, because only these are strong enough to humanize its technology. In the days before planetization, when civilization was split between East and West, there were basically two cultural directions. The Westerner went outward to level forests, conquer nations, and walk on the moon; the Easterner went inward and away from the physical into the astral and causal planes. Now . . . we can glimpse the beginnings of a new level of religious experience, neither Eastern nor Western, but planetary.[13]

Many people have doubts about the significance of such views. But it is just possible that the upsurge of mysticism and religious searching will exert a growing influence in the coming era, especially if political conflict and economic difficulties continue to undermine the old secular faith in endless progress.

SUMMARY

Whatever does or does not happen, the study of world history puts the future in perspective. Future developments on this small planet will surely build on the many-layered foundations hammered out in the past. Moreover, the study of world history, of mighty struggles and fearsome challenges, of shining achievements and tragic failures, imparts a strong sense of life's essence: the process of change over time. Again and again we have seen how peoples and societies evolve, influenced by ideas, human passions, and material conditions. Armed with the ability to think historically, students of history are prepared to comprehend this inexorable process of change in their own life-

times, as the world races forward toward an uncertain destiny.

NOTES

1. A. Toynbee, *Mankind and Mother Earth* (New York: Oxford University Press, 1976), pp. 576–577.
2. D. Calleo and B. Rowland, *America and the World Political Economy* (Bloomington: Indiana University Press, 1973), p. 191.
3. W. Epstein, *The Last Chance: Nuclear Proliferation and Arms Control* (New York: Free Press, 1976), p. 274.
4. M. ul-Haq, *The Poverty Curtain: Choices for the Third World* (New York: Columbia University Press, 1976), p. 152.
5. E. Hermassi, *The Third World Reassessed* (Berkeley: University of California Press, 1980), p. 76.
6. Ibid., p. 185.
7. Quoted in H. Stephenson, *The Coming Clash: The Impact of Multinational Corporations on National States* (New York: Saturday Review Press, 1973), p. 60.
8. Quoted in A. R. Negandhi, *The Functioning of the Multinational Corporation: A Global Comparative Study* (New York: Pergamon Press, 1980), p. 142.
9. M. Djilas, *The New Class* (New York: Praeger, 1957), pp. 41–42, 44.
10. A. I. Solzhenitsyn, *Letter to the Soviet Leaders* (New York: Harper & Row, 1974), p. 33.
11. R. L. Heilbroner, *An Inquiry into the Human Prospect* (New York: Norton, 1974), p. 141.
12. Ibid., p. 140.
13. W. I. Thompson, *Evil and World Order* (New York: Harper & Row, 1980), p. 53.

SUGGESTED READING

Many of the books cited in the Suggested Reading for Chapter 38 pertain to the themes of this chapter. Three helpful and stimulating studies on global politics from different viewpoints are R. Barnet, *The Lean Years: The Politics of the Age of Scarcity* (1980); F. M. Lappé and J. Collins, *Food First: Beyond the Myth of Scarcity* (1977); and S. Hoffman, *Primacy or World Order: American Foreign Policy Since the Cold War* (1978). An excellent if ominous introduction to international negotiations for the control of nuclear arms is W. Epstein, *The Last Chance: Nuclear Proliferation and Arms Control* (1976). Two clear and judicious studies on the evolving nuclear policies of the two great superpowers, by relatively impartial British scholars, are D. Holloway, *The Soviet Union and the Arms Race* (1983), and L. Freedman, *The Evolution of Nuclear Strategy* (1982), a history of American thinking about nuclear weapons and nuclear war. J. Hackett, *The Third World War, August 1985* (1978), is a gripping but all-too-optimistic best-selling account of limited nuclear war by a retired British general, writing "in consultation with NATO experts."

M. ul Haq, *The Poverty Curtain: Choices for the Third World* (1976), is an excellent presentation of Third World demands for a new economic order. This position is expanded in J. Tinbergen and A. J. Dolman, eds., *RIO, Reshaping the International Order: A Report to the Club of Rome* (1977), and *North-South: A Program for Survival* (1980), a report calling for increased help for the South by the blue-ribbon Independent Commission on International Development Issues, under the chairmanship of Willy Brandt. Such views do not go unchallenged, and P. T. Bauer, *Equality, the Third World, and Economic Delusion* (1981), is a vigorous defense of the industrialized nations and their wealth. J. K. Galbraith, the witty economist and former U.S. ambassador to India, argues simply and effectively that poor countries have important lessons to teach rich countries in *The Voice of the Poor* (1983). Common problems and aspirations are also the focus of E. Laszlo et al., *Goals for Mankind* (1977). The important study by R. Ayres, *Banking on the Poor: The World Bank and World Poverty* (1983), shows how this international financial organization has emerged as a standard-bearer for the poorest countries. *World Development Report,* which the World Bank publishes annually, is an outstanding source of information about current trends. Valuable studies on multinational corporations and global indebtedness include L. Solomon, *Multinational Corporations and the Emerging World Order* (1978); A. R. Negandhi, *The Functioning of the Multinational Corporation: A Global Comparative Study* (1980); R. Barnet and R. Muller, *Global Reach: The Power of the Multinational Corporations* (1975); and A. Sampson, *The Money Lenders: The People and Politics of the World Banking Crisis* (1983).

Contemporary thought is so rich and diverse that any selection must be highly arbitrary. Among works not mentioned elsewhere, G. Blainey, *The Great Seesaw: A New View of the Western World, 1750–2000* (1988), uncovers a cyclical pattern of optimism and pessimism and is recommended as an introduction to the history of ideas. E. Banfield, *The Unheavenly City Revisited* (1974), is a provocative and influential reassessment of urban problems and solutions in the United States. D. H. Meadows and D. L. Meadows, *The Limits of Growth* (1974), argue that the world will soon exhaust its natural resources. E. F. Schumacher, *Small Is Beautiful: Economics as If People Mattered* (1973), advocates conservation and a scaling down of technology to avoid disaster. R. M. Pirsig, *Zen and the Art of Motorcycle Maintenance: An Inquiry into Values* (1976), is a stimulating exploration of the tie between modern technology and personal development.

E. Rice, *Wars of the Third Kind: Conflict in Underdeveloped Countries* (1988), is a thoughtful inquiry into the dynamics of guerrilla movements. T. R. Gurr, *Why Men Rebel* (1970), skillfully reworks the idea that revolutions occur when rising expectations are frustrated. M. Djilas, *The New Class* (1957), criticizes the ruling Communist bureaucracies from a Marxist point of view. J. Revel, *The Totalitarian Temptation* (1977), claims that many Western intellectuals have been seduced into seeing Communist dictatorships as progressive socialist societies. A. Sakharov, *Progress, Coexistence, and Intellectual Freedom,* rev. ed. (1970), soberly assesses the prospects for improved relations between the Soviet Union and the United States.

The Islamic revival may be approached through the sympathetic work of E. Gellner, *Muslim Society* (1981); and the reservations of V. S. Naipaul, *Among the Believers: An Islamic Journey* (1981); H. Algar, ed., *Islam and Revolution: Writings and Declarations of Imam Khomeini* (1982); and J. Stempel, *Inside the Iranian Revolution* (1981). Muslim writers address issues in the Islamic world in J. Donohue and J. Esposito, eds., *Islam in Transition: Muslim Perspectives* (1982).

Studies of the future are so numerous that M. Marien, *Societal Directions and Alternatives: A Critical Guide to the Literature* (1977), is a useful aid with its annotated bibliography. The many future-oriented works of the members of the Hudson Institute usually combine optimism and conservatism, as in H. Kahn et al., *The Next Two Hundred Years* (1976), and H. Kahn, *The Coming Boom* (1982). J. Lorraine, *Global Signposts to the 21st Century* (1979), and R. L. Heilbroner, *An Inquiry into the Human Prospect* (1974), are especially recommended as stimulating and intelligent studies. L. Stavrianos, *The Promise of the Coming Dark Age* (1976), is especially suited to those with cataclysmic dispositions.

Chapter Opener Credits

Chapter 1: *Courtesy of the Trustees of the British Museum.* The Royal Standard of Ur, peace panel.

Chapter 2: *Ronny Jaques/Photo Researchers.* Audience hall of King Darius, Persepolis.

Chapter 3: *Courtesy of the Freer Gallery of Art, Smithsonian Institution, Washington, D.C.* King Vidudabha visiting the Buddha.

Chapter 4: *J. C. Francolon/Gama-Liaison.* Clay warriors from the tomb of the First Emperor.

Chapter 5: *John Veltri/Photo Researchers.* The Erechtheum, Parthenon.

Chapter 6: *Robert Harding Picture Library.* (Detail) Panel from Alexander Sarcophagus.

Chapter 7: *Michael Holford.* The Pont du Gard, a Roman aqueduct at Nîmes in southern France.

Chapter 8: *TSW/CLICK/Chicago Ltd.* Hadrian's Wall Cuddy's Crag, Northumberland.

Chapter 9: *Scala/Art Resource.* Apse mosaic of S. Apollinare in Classe, Ravenna.

Chapter 10: *© Ric Ergenbright.* Alhambra Palace, Granada.

Chapter 11: *The Museum Yamato Bunkakan.* Portrait of the poet Kodai-no-Kimi, or Koogimi.

Chapter 12: *Giraudon/Art Resource.* St. Bernard, Abbot of Clairvaux, preaching to his fellow Cistercians.

Chapter 13: *The Pierpont Morgan Library.* "April," from *Hours of the Virgin.*

Chapter 14: *Jonathan Blair/Woodfin Camp & Associates.* Carcassonne, southern France.

Chapter 15: *Robert Aberman/Barbara Heller Photo Library.* Ruins of Great Zimbabwe.

Chapter 16: *Photo Jean Mazenod. From L'ART PRECOLOMBIEN, Editions Citadelles, Paris.* Toltec statuary.

Chapter 17: *Scala/Art Resource.* The family and court of Lodovico II Gonzaga, of Mantua.

Chapter 18: *Reproduced by courtesy of the Trustees, The National Gallery, London.* Jean de Dinteville and Bishop Georges de Selve, the French ambassadors, 1533.

Chapter 19: *Robert Harding Picture Library.* Peter the Great's Summer Palace at Peterhof.

Chapter 20: *The British Library.* An early library in a British coastal town, 18th century.

Chapter 21: *Musée Carnavalet/Bulloz.* People in the Paris marketplace celebrating the news of the birth of the Dauphin.

Chapter 22: *© Arnold Newman.* The Oba of Benin flanked by his chieftains.

Chapter 23: *By Courtesy of the Board of Trustees of the Victoria & Albert Museum. Lent by Mr. Howard Hodgkin.* A marriage procession passing through a bazaar, Bilaspur or Mandi.

Chapter 24: *Photograph from PALACES OF THE FORBIDDEN CITY by Yu Zhuoyun (Allen Lane, 1984), © The Commercial Press Ltd., Hong Kong Branch, 1982.* Inside the Meridian Gate, looking southwest, Forbidden City.

Chapter 25: *Musée Carnavalet/Bulloz.* Locked out of their meeting hall, members of the Third Estate meet at an indoor tennis court, June 20, 1789.

Chapter 26: *The Bridgeman Art Library. Reproduced by courtesy of the Royal Holloway & Bedford New College, Surrey.* Paddington Station, London, 1862, bustling with middle-class travellers.

Chapter 27: *Historisches Museen der Stadt Wien.* Citizens of Vienna astride the barricades during the revolution of 1848.

Chapter 28: *Museum of London.* Urban growth, 19th-century London.

Chapter 29: *Fabio Lensini/Madeline Grimoldi.* The meeting of Garibaldi and Victor Emmanuel.

Chapter 30: *Peabody Museum of Salem. Photo: Mark Sexton.* Flags of various countries flying in front of factories at Canton Harbor.

Chapter 31: *E. Williamson/The Picture Cube.* Governor's Palace, Plaza de Armas, Lima, Peru.

Chapter 32: *Trustees of the Imperial War Museum.* World War One trench warfare.

Chapter 33: *Bettmann/Hulton.* Turks surrounding victory flag made to celebrate the victory at Smyrna, October 1922.

Chapter 34: *Collection of Whitney Museum of American Art.* The unemployed seeking jobs during the 1930s Depression in the United States.

Chapter 35: *Archiv/Photo Researchers. Cindy Pardy, Artist.* Adolf Hitler at Bueckeberg (Westphalia).

Chapter 36: *Leonard Freed/Magnum.* A young *Grepo,* an East German border guard, at the Berlin Wall in the 1960s.

Chapter 37: *Gary Sawhney, Hertfordshire, England.* Construction of Asia's longest river bridge, spanning the River Ganges in India.

Chapter 38: *John Maier, Jr./Picture Group.* Destruction of the Amazon rain forest, near the Peru border.

Chapter 39: *Frank T. Wood/Superstock.* Kano Airport, Kano, Nigeria.

Notes on the Illustrations

Pages 2–3: Peace panel of the Royal Standard of Ur, mosaic, ca 2500 B.C. The "standard," a rectangular wooden box 18 inches long, was probably a sounding board of a musical instrument used on ceremonial occasions.

Page 7: Paintings by Stone Age hunters, from Lascaux caves in southern France, 15,000–10,000 B.C.

Page 19: Commemorative stele from Susa of the victory of Naramsin, after the Babylonian conquest of Sippar and other cities, ca 2389–2353 B.C. Pink sandstone; 78⅘ × 41⅓ in.

Page 23: Detail from an inlaid panel from a harp found in the Royal Cemetery at Ur, ca 2500 B.C.

Page 24: The judgments of Hammurabi were inscribed in 3600 lines of cuneiform writing on the 8 ft. high black basalt pillar. Late Larsa period, 1930–1888 B.C.

Page 27: The Narmer Palette was found in the ruins of a temple at Nekhen, ca 3100 B.C. Made of carved schist, h. 29¼ in., it is the earliest example of the Egyptians' hieroglyphic writing. From the Egyptian Museum, Cairo.

Page 30: Detail from a wall painting from an Old Kingdom tomb, ca 2300 B.C.

Page 32: This statue of the Goddess Selket is of gilded and painted wood, h. 90 cm., from the tomb of Tutankhamen, Valley of the Kings, Thebes. New Kingdom, 18th dynasty, 1347–1337 B.C.

Page 35: These four seated figures of Ramses II, h. 67 ft., each weighing 1,200 tons, are part of the façade fronting Ramses' Great Temple at Abu Simbel, 3200 B.C.

Pages 38–39: At Persepolis, Persians and delegations of subject peoples mounted the wide apadana steps with tributes for King Darius I, climbing past the figures of royal guards.

Page 43: A stone relief from Sargon II's palace at Dur-Sharrukin (modern Khorsabad), 8th century B.C.

Page 44: Fresco from a tomb at Beni-Hassan in Upper Egypt, ca 1890 B.C. From the Kunsthistorisches Museum, Vienna.

Page 45: This silver calf and its ceramic byre (ca 1600–1550 B.C.) were found during the Ashkelon excavations by the Leon Levy Expedition.

Pages 49 and 51: Alabaster reliefs from the center palace, Nimrud, ca 745–727 B.C.

Page 54: From the Teheran Bastan Museum, Iran.

Page 55: Cyrus the Great's tomb at Pasargadae, Iran, is of limestone; from the achaemenid Period, ca 530 B.C. From the Iranian Expedition of The Oriental Institute of The University of Chicago, 1932.

Page 56: Attributed to the "painter of Myson," ca 500 B.C.

Page 58: Closeup of relief on the southern wall, Persepolis, B.C., from Achaemenid Period.

Pages 62–63: King Vidudabha visiting the Buddha, from the Bharhut stupa, Shunga, 2nd c. B.C. Red sandstone, h. 18⅞".

Page 66: Statue of a god or priest-king ca 2100 B.C., from the Indus city of Mohenjo-daro.

Page 67: The great bath (39′ × 23′) at Mohenjo-daro, ca 2600–1800 B.C.

Page 70: Bronze sword with forked antennae from North India, ca 1000 B.C.

Page 74: Siva (on a bull) destroys the demon Andhakari. From the MS. of Harivamsa (Mughal, ca 1590), Victoria and Albert Museum, London.

Page 75: The mother goddess Kali Ma from Orissa, India, 9th century A.D. The British Museum. Kali Ma, the fiercest wife of Siva, brings in her train bloodshed, terror, and death. She is frequently depicted wearing a necklace of human skulls.

Page 77: The Great Buddha, cave 10, Jung Kang, China, 5th century A.D.

Page 80: The Sarnath lion-capital with its four lions was carved for the Mauryan Emperer Ashoka in the third century B.C. It was adopted as India's national emblem.

Page 82: North gate to the largest memorial mound in Sanchi, India, the oldest building in India, believed to have been erected by Ashoka in the 3rd century B.C. The carving illustrates Buddhist writings. There are four 18-foot gateways to this mound, or *tope,* which is built like a big compass; the mound is 42 feet high and 103 feet in diameter.

Pages 86–87 and 103: Terracotta figurines of warriors and horses buried in 250 B.C. to guard the tomb of Qin Shih Huang Ti, China's first emperer. Unearthed in 1974 in Lintong County, Shaanxi Province. The tomb itself has not yet been excavated.

Page 94: Bronze ritual vessel in the shape of an animal, excavated in 1959 at Shu-Ch'eng, Anhui. Height 27.5 cm. 7th or early 6th century B.C.

Page 105: Detail of simulated Chinese village with earthenware tomb figures, Han dynasty. The custom of placing pottery models of buildings in tombs began in the 1st century A.D. The village can be seen at the St. Louis Art Museum.

Pages 114–115: The Erechtheum, built during the reconstruction of the Acropolis by Pericles after its devastation by the Persians, is unique among Greek buildings; it has porches on three sides, each quite different in size and rising from different levels. It was constructed as a shrine enclosing the site where the city of Athens had its beginnings.

Page 119: One of the best-preserved of the lavish wall paintings that were covered by a thick layer of ash and pumice when a volcanic explosion tore apart half of the island of Santorini, or Thera, ca 1500 B.C.

Page 120: Funeral games of Patrochus: A fragment of an Athenian bowl from Pharsalus (Thessaly), 6th century B.C., signed by the painter Sophilus.

Page 125: This painting from the "Chigi" vase is the earliest surviving picture of the new style of close-order, heavily-armed infantry adopted by the Greeks, ca end of 8th century B.C. Found at Formello, near Rome; h. 10¼ in.

Page 135: This 5th century B.C. bronze, dredged from the sea near Cape Artemisium, in Attica, is thought to represent Poseidon or Zeus.

Page 138: Black-figured amphora, *Women working wool,* from Lekythos, ca 560 B.C., h. 6¾ in.

Page 146–147: Detail from the Alexander Sarcophagus, ca 325–300 B.C.; h. of Frieze 69 cm; found in the royal cemetery at Sidon, Phoenicia, late 4th century B.C. Alexander, wearing the heroic lion's-scalp helmet, is on horseback at the left. From the Archaeological Museum, Istanbul.

Page 150: This mosaic, found at Pompeii, is thought to be a copy of an original painting of ca 330 B.C.

Page 160: The Tyche (or Fortune) of Antioch; the original probably executed by Eutychides of Sikyon, ca 300 B.C. Marble; h. 37¾ in. Vatican, Galleria Candelabri: Scomparto IV, 48 inv. 2672.

Page 162: Life-size marble genre statue, probably created as a garden sculpture, ca 180 B.C. From the Palazzo dei Conservatori, Rome.

Pages 170–171: The Pont du Gard, at Nîmes in southern France, is the finest example of Roman practical engineering. This great aqueduct, 885 ft. long and made of unadorned stone blocks, was built ca A.D. 14 to bring water to Nîmes from higher ground to the north.

Page 175: This terracotta statue of the Sun god Aplu—known as Apollo to the Greeks—stood on a temple ridgepole in Veii. It was probably made by the sculptor Vulca, or his school, ca 500 B.C.

Page 183: Roman bronze decoration forming part of a horse harness, 3rd century B.C.

Page 190: Stone bas-relief, found in Saint Remy, Provence; 59 × 83 cm. From the Musée de la Civilisation Gallo-Romaine, Lyon.

Pages 194–195: A section of Hadrian's Wall at Cuddy's Crag, Northumberland. Hadrian's Wall was the formidable barrier that wound across northern Britain, 2nd century A.D.

Page 197: From the Museo della Terme, Rome.

Page 198: Detail, the onyx Chalcedony gem (cameo) of Augustus and Roma, early 1st century A.D. From the Kunsthistorisches Museum, Vienna.

Page 201: In this mosaic Virgil is seated between the muses of Epic and Tragedy, and reading from his *Aeneid.* From the Bardo Museum, Tunis.

Page 202: The reliefs adorning the Ara Pacis Augustae, the altar of Augustan peace, are among the greatest works of art of the early Roman empire. The Roman senate had the altar erected on the Campus Martius to commemorate Augustus' return from Gaul, where he had been living for three years.

Page 205: Mosaic from the Sant'Apollinare Nuovo, Ravenna, 6th century A.D.

Page 208: Bas-relief of spoils being carried from the temple in Jerusalem. From the Arch of Titus, Rome, 80–85 A.D.

Page 211: The port of Ostia had been pillaged by pirates in 68 B.C. Augustus made it one of his many rebuilding projects. By A.D. 150 this large cosmopolitan city boasted new harbors, fine public buildings, airy apartments, and had become the largest receiving port in Italy.

Page 218: This 4th century porphyry group shows Diocletian and Maximian with their respective caesars, their sons-in-law. From the Basilica of San Marco, Venice.

Page 220: Roman mosaic of a North African villa, from the Bardo Museum, Tunis, 3rd or 4th century A.D.

Pages 228–229: Apse mosaic, S. Apollinare in Classe, Ravenna; ca A.D. 533–549.

Page 231: This uncolored pen and ink drawing is from the *Utrecht Psalter,* an outstanding example of a new mode of Carolingian illustration developed from a fusion of Anglo-Saxon, Irish, and Frankish techniques, 9th century. MS 32, fol. 90v.

Page 243: Miniature of St. Benedict, founder of the Abbey of Monte Cassino, blessing the Abbot Desiderius, who rebuilt the Abbey and founded a school of Byzantine-influenced mosaicists and painters.

Page 250: Mosaic from Carthage, ca 500 A.D.

Page 253: Emperor Justinian and his court, A.D. 546–548, in mosaic at San Vitale, Ravenna, Italy.

Pages 262–263: Alhambra Palace in Granada, from which the Nasrid sultans ruled southern Spain until Christian armies expelled them in 1492.

Page 266: Arabic manuscript (Persia): 9th-century page from the *Qur'an,* Kufic script. 6½ by 4⁹⁄₁₆ inches.

Page 268: From the Edinburgh Rashid al-Din, Or MS 20, f. 23v.

Page 269: From the Turkish version of the *Siyar-i-Nabi,* 16th c., folio 309 recto.

Page 278: From the Edinburgh Rashid al-Din, Or MS 20, f. 52R.

Page 280: Detail of an ivory casket of Al Mughira, son of the caliph Abd-el-Rahman III, who was assassinated in A.D 176.

Page 281: The slave market in Zabid, in the Yemen, 13th century. From an illustration of the Makamats 635/1237 of Al-Hariri. Bibliothèque Nationale, MS. Ar. 5847.

Page 283: Persian pottery: Seljuk, late 12th–early 13th century bowl. 3¼ by 9 ¹⁄₁₆ inches.

Page 285: Miniature, Iran, Tabriz, 16th c. Sultan-Muhammad, Allegory of Worldly and other Wordly Drunkenness: illustration from *Divan of Hafiz.* Opaque watercolor on paper, 21.5 × 15 cm. (1988.460)

Page 286: A trading boat on the Euphrates: Arab manuscript, Baghdad school, 13th century.

Page 289: The most important monument of Islamic Cordoba is the Great Mosque, or Mezquita Grande, which was converted to a church in later centuries.

Begun by Abd al-Rahman (756–768), it was enlarged three times: in A.D. 848, 961–965, and 987.

Page 290: Miniature from the Makamat of Al-Hariri, a 12th-century historical work showing everyday life. Depicted here is the public library of Hulwan, near Baghdad.

Page 291: Iraqi painting: *Abdallah ibn al-Fadl.* A.D. 1224 (Rajab 621 H.), Baghdad school; 13 $\frac{1}{16}$ by 9 $\frac{13}{16}$ inches. Outdoor scene with mad dog biting man, onlooker with sword on left.

Pages 296–297: Portrait of the poet Kodai-no-kimi, or Koogimi, attributed to Fujiwara-no-Nobuzane (1176–?). Kamakura period, 13th c.; color on paper.

Page 311: Scroll of the Diamond Sutra, the Sanskrit Buddhist work *Vajraccedikā prajña pāramitā* in Chinese translation found at Tunhuang. The earliest specimen of block printing, A.D. 868. Buddha is addressing Subhiti, and aged disciple.

Page 317: (detail #8) Chinese, Ming Dynasty. After Ch'iu Ying (flourished 1622–1660), "Ch'ing Ming (Spring Festival) on the River." (47.18.1)

Page 324: "Creation of Japan: Izanagi and Izanami Standing in Clouds and Creating Island out of Sea Water," Kobayashi, Eitaku (1843–1890). Japanese, Ukiyoe, late 19th-century hanging scroll. Ink on silk, 1.257 by 0.546 m.

Page 325: Shōtoku Taishi in prince regent form. Late Kamakura period, 14th century. Colors on silk, mounted as a panel; 109.5 by 82.0 cm. The full ceremonial court dress, scepter, and sword depicted here identify Shōtoku Taishi as prince regent. His actual regency lasted 29 years, A.D. 592–622.

Page 327: Five-story pagoda, Daigo. Heian period, A.D. 951.

Pages 332–333: Miniature from Jean Fouquet, *Les Heures d'Etienne Chevalier,* ca 1460. From Musée Conde, Chantilly.

Page 337: This bronze statue of the Emperor Charlemagne shows him carrying an orb to symbolize wordly peace. He was the first Chirstian monarch to be sculpted in an equestrian statue. 9th–10th century A.D.; h. 24 cm. (Louvre)

Page 345: Wellcome Institute Western MS 290, ps.-Galen, *Anatomy,* 15th century, fol. 53v.

Page 349: Cod. Pal. Germ. 164, fol. 6v (Heidelberger Sachsenspiegel)

Page 353: The invasion of Danes under Hinguar (Ingrar) and Bubba: Seven shiploads of men in three tiers. From *Life, Passion and Miracles of St. Edmunds, King and Martyr* in Latin, Bury St. Edmund's, ca 1130. Ms. 736, f. 9v.

Page 354: This plaque is one from a series of nineteen, known as the Magdeberg ivories (German or Northern Italian), 10th century; 5 × 4 ½ in. (41.100.157)

Page 356: Benedictine Abbey of Mont-Saint-Michel, founded in 708 in the Department of the Manche in northwestern France, a mile off the French coast in the English Channel and formerly an island at high tide. Heavily fortified.

Page 357: The third and greatest of the abbey churches of Cluny was begun by St. Hugh in 1088.

By 1095 the east end was finished, and was consecrated by Pope Urban II, himself a former Cluniac monk. LAT 177 16, f. 91. Bibliothèque Nationale.

Page 358: Rievaulx Abbey was founded in Yorkshire, England, as a Cistercian house in 1130. By 1175 all of its monastic buildings were complete. The nave of Rievaulx Abbey, dating to 1135–1140, is today the oldest remaining Cistercian structure in the world.

Page 365: Crusaders fighting the Saracens, *Roman de Godefroi,* fol. 19r. Paris, 1337. Bibliothèque Nationale.

Page 366: FR 352, f. 62. Bibliothèque Nationale.

Pages 372–373: "April" miniature from the *Hours of the Virgin,* MS 399 fol. 5v. Flanders, ca 1515.

Page 375: From MS Sloane 2435, fol. 85, British Library.

Page 379: From *Piers Plowman,* MS. R.3, fol. 3v.

Page 381: From Rene I, d'Anjoy, *Le Mortifiement de vaine plaisance.* MS 705, f. 38v. French, 15th century.

Page 384: Miniature from the *Winchester Psalter;* English, painted at Winchester for the Bishop, Henry of Bois, ca 1150–1160. Cott. Ner. CIV, fol. 39r, British Library.

Page 387: From MS Bodley 270b, fol. 176, Bodleian Library, Oxford.

Page 390: This is one of the most famous of a group of finely carved Parisian Caskets for jewels or other precious objects, probably all made in the same workshop. French, first half of the 14th century. L. 9¾ in.

Page 393: Miniature from Jean de Wavrin's *Chronique d'Angleterre,* siege of the castle of Mortagne. Flemish, late fifteenth century. MS Roy. 14. E.IV, fol. 23r. British Library.

Page 394: From MS 13 321, Wiesbaden, Codex B, f lr. Museum of the City of Cologne.

Page 397: From the Exultet Roll (Burberini lat. 592), ca A.D. 1075; w. 11⅜ in.

Page 398: From Kenneth John Conant, *Cluny: Les églises et la maison du chef d'ordre.* The Mediaeval Academy of America Publication No. 77. Cambridge, Mass., 1968.

Pages 402–403: Carcassonne, in south-western France, is the most complete example today of a medieval fortified town. Parts of the walls go back to the Visigothic period, but most of the inner wall, with the citadel, dates from the 11th and 12th centuries, and the outer from the end of the 13th century. Extensive restoration was carried out in the 19th century.

Page 405: Presumed to be the work of Matilda, queen of William the Conqueror, the original tapestry (ca 1100) can be seen in the city of Bayeux, France. A replica is in the Victoria and Albert Museum, London.

Page 412: From Petro d'Eboli, *De Rebus siclis carmen,* Italian, ca 1200. Codex 120, f. 101.

Page 414: Carrow Psalter MS., fol. 15v. Thirteenth century.

Page 419: From Jacques de Guisis, *Chroniques de Hainaut,* Flemish, 1448. Ms 9242, fol. 48 verso.

Pages 421 and 425: Miniatures from the town laws of Hamburg, 1497.

Page 433: Detail, fresco by Domenico di Michelino, *Allegory of the Divine Comedy,* of Dante with *La Divina Commedia* 1465. Florence Cathedral.

Page 435: Pedro Berruguete (Spanish, 1477–1504), *St. Dominick presiding over an Auto da Fé.* Tempera on panel; 5′ ½″ × 3′ ¼″. From the sacristy of Santo Tomás of Avila, where there was a companion panel now believed to be in a private collection in London.

Page 438: *St. Sebastian Interceding for the Plague-Stricken* by Josse Lieferinxe.

Page 445: This is the only known contemporary picture of Joan of Arc. AE[II] 447, f. 27.

Page 449: From MS Bodley 264, fol. 245v, Bodleian Library, Oxford.

Page 451: Misericord from Henry VII's Chapel, Westminster Abbey.

Page 453: During the French peasant rebellion of the 14th century, the most famous uprising was the *Jacquerie,* which began in the Beqauvais region in 1358, when men were killed if they didn't have worker's hands. From Sir Jean Froissart's *Chronicles,* MS Fr. 2643, fol. 226v. Bibliothèque Nationale.

Page 455: *The Four Horsemen of the Apocalypse,* woodcut ca 1498, by Albrecht Dürer, German painter and engraver (1471–1528) regarded as leader of the German Renaissance school of painting.

Page 464: Rock painting from the "Shelter of Horses," Tassili n'Ajjer Range, Algeria, ca 3500–3000 B.C.

Page 467: Brass casting of an armed warrior made for weighing gold dust. It shows a typical Akan warrior holding a shield and a now-broken sword. H. 108 cm.

Page 469: The travelers Abu Zayd and Al Harith arrive in a village. From the Bibliothèque Nationale, Ar. 5847 fol. 138r.

Page 472: Djenneh, Mali. Horse and rider, 14th century. Terracotta, 66.0 × 38.0 cm.

Page 487: Primitive. Mexican, Olmec, 10th–6th c. Stone. Figure on bench with baby. H. 11.3 cm. The Metropolitan Museum of Art, The Michael C. Rockefeller Memorial Collection of Primitive Art, Bequest of Nelson A. Rockefeller, 1979. (1979.206.940)

Page 492: Quetzalcoatl, "Feathered Serpent" (left), and Tezcatlipoca, "Smoking Mirror" (right). Codex Borbonicus, p. 22 (detail). Screenfold manuscript, panel 39 × 39.5 cm.

Page 503: Inca tunic, cotton and wool. Peru, ca A.D. 1500.

Pages 506–507: Andrea Mantegna (Italian, 1431–1506), *The Court of the Gonzaga Family,* 1473–1474. Fresco, w. ca 19′ 8″. From the Palazzo Ducale, Mantua. The Gonzaga family, who reigned over Mantua from 1328 to 1627, invited Mantegna to their court in 1460. He continued to paint there until his death. In this fresco, from the walls of the Camera degli Sposi, Mantegna shows an intimate family festivity, the visit paid by Cardinal Francesco Gonzaga to his parents in Mantua.

Page 509: Woodcut, Italian (Florence), probably late 15th century.

Page 512: The Palazzo Vecchio (1298–1314) is attributed to Arnolfo di Cambio and was built as the seat of the Signoria, the government of the Florentine republic. This fortified palace is also known as the Palazzo della Signoria.

Page 514: Filippo Brunelleschi (1377–1440), *Sacrifice of Isaac,* from the competition to design the north doors of the Baptistry of S. Giovanni, Florence, 1401–1402. Gilded bronze relief, 21 × 17½ in. (inside molding). From the Museo Nazionale del Bargello, Florence. Brunelleschi, trained as a sculptor, was the founder of the Renaissance style in architecture.

Page 517: Benozzo Gozzolli (Italian), *Journey of the Magi,* ca 1459. From the Medici Riccardi Palace, Florence. Nominally of the journey of the Magi, this painting in fact shows the magnificence of the Florentine Renaissance Court, with Lorenzo de' Medici on a hunting expedition in the foreground.

Page 521: Engraving by Johannes Stradanus (J. van der Straet), Belgian painter (1523–1605).

Page 523: Sofonisba Anguissola (Italian, 1532/35–1625), *Portrait of the Artist's Sister,* ca 1559. Oil on canvas; 33½ × 26 in. This prolific artist was the first of Renaissance women artists to establish an international reputation, and the first for whom a substantial body of work exists. In this portrait, her sister Minerva wears a medallion that depicts another Minerva, the ancient Roman goddess of wisdom and the arts.

Page 525: *The Adoration,* 1507, by Hans Baldung (also called Hans Grien or Grün), German painter, engraver, and designer of woodcuts and glass painting (1476?–1545).

Page 527: Jan van Eyck (Flemish, 1422–1441), *Madonna of Chancellor Rodin,* ca 1435.

Page 528: Hieronymus Bosch (Hieronymus van Aeken), Dutch painter (ca 1450–1516), *Death and the Miser.*

Page 530: From *Ethique d'Aristotle,* French, 15th century. MS I.2 (927), fol. 145r. Bibliothèque de la Ville, Rouen.

Page 536: Lucas Cranach the Elder (1472–1553), *Passional Christi und Antichristi,* Wittenberg, 1521.

Page 539: Lucas Cranach the Younger (German, 1515–1586), *Martin Luther and the Wittenberg Reformers,* ca 1543. Oil on panel; 27⅝ × 15⅝ in.

Page 540: *The Small Crucifixion,* ca 1510, by Matthias Grünewald, German painter (ca 1465–1528). Wood; 24¼ × 18⅛ in. (1961.9.19)

Page 542: Detail from the 1528 escutcheon of the town of Überlingen town hall.

Page 543: Titian (Tiziano Vecellio, 1487–1577), *Charles V on Horseback,* 1548. Oil on canvas; 10′ 10½″ × 9′ 2″. The colors of this portrait are dark, perhaps emphasized by restorations that followed damage incurred in a fire in the eighteenth century.

Page 547: Attributed to Jean Perrissin (ca 1530–1611), *Temple de Lyon, nommé Paradis,* 1565.

Page 551: Woodcut from Foxe, 1569 edition, British Library.

Page 552: *Sir Thomas More* (1478–1535), painted in 1527 by Hans Holbein the Younger, German painter (1497?–1543) and court painter to Henry VIII.

Page 555: Council of Trent by an unknown artist; detached fresco, Secretariat of State, Vatican.

Pages 562–563: Hans Holbein the Younger (1497?–1543), *Jean de Dinteville and Georges de Seluc (The Ambassadors),* 1533. 81¼ × 82½ in.

Page 564: *Cantino Planisphere,* Portuguese, color on parchment, ca 1502.

Page 581: Long the site of a royal residence and hunting lodge, Fontainebleau was expanded and transformed by Francis I in 1530–1540. Il Rosso (Giovanni Battista de'Rossi, 1494–1540), Florentine painter; Francesco Primaticcio, Italian painter and architect (1504–1570); and Sebastiano Serlio, Italian architect and writer on art (1475–1554) were called by Francis I from Italy to build and decorate the palace. The gallery of Francis I set a fashion in decoration imitated throughout Europe.

Page 582: School of Fontainebleau (French, 16th century), *Triple Profile Portrait;* oil on slate, ca 1560–1580; 22½ × 22 ½ in. (Acc. no. M1965.55)

Page 595: MS Rawl. D 410, fol. 1, Bodleian Library, Oxford.

Page 601: Paulo Veronese (Paulo Caliari: 1528?–1588), *Mars and Venus United by Love.* Oil on canvas; 81 × 63⅜ in.

Page 602: Diego Rodriguez de Silva y Velázquez (1599–1660), *Juan de Pareja,* ca 1610–1670. Oil on canvas; h. 32 in.; w. 27 ½ in. The Metropolitan Museum of Art, Fletcher Fund, Rogers Fund, and Bequest of Miss Adelaide Milton de Groot (1876–1967), by exchange, supplemented by gifts from friends of the Museum, 1971.

Pages 606–607: Peter the Great brought architects and artists from the West to design and build his Summer Palace at Peterhof.

Page 611: Philippe de Champaigne (French, 1602–1674), *Cardinal Richelieu Swearing the Order of the Holy Ghost.*

Page 612: Antoine Coysevox (French, 1640–1730), *Louis XIV,* statue for the Town Hall of Paris, 1687–1689.

Page 615: "The Noble Is the Spider," from Jacques Lagnier, *Receuil des Proverbes,* 1657–1663.

Page 616: Nicholas Poussin (French, 1594–1665), *The Rape of the Sabine Women,* ca 1636–1637. Oil on canvas; 60⅞ × 82⅝ in. (46.160)

Page 637: The Church of St. Basil (formerly the Cathedral of the Intercession), Moscow, 1555–1560, with 17th century additions.

Page 638: Etienne Falconnet (1716–1791), *The Bronze Horseman, St. Petersburg* (Leningrad), completed in 1783.

Page 641: The grand stairway of the Residenz at Würzburg (built by the powerful Schönborn family) was intended by its architect Balthasar Neumann (1678–1753) to allow a slow ascent to be able to take in gradually the ceiling paintings by Giovanni Battista Tiepolo glorifying Bishop Schönborn, 1750–1753.

Page 650: Johannes Vermeer, known as Jan Vermeer van Delft (Dutch, 1632–1675), *Woman Holding a Balance,* ca 1664. Canvas; 16¾ × 15 in.

Page 651: Hiob Adriaensz Berckheyde, *The Old Stock Exchange, Amsterdam.* Canvas; 85 × 105 cm. (Inv. no. 1043)

Page 653: Pieter Claesz (Dutch, 1597–1660), *Still Life with Musical Instruments.*

Page 673: "Die Tafelrunde" is a copy by Joachim Tietze, Berlin, of the paintings by Adolph von Menzel, 1850. The original belonged to the National Gallery, Berlin, and was destroyed in 1945.

Page 678: *Une Soirée chez Madame Geoffrin* by Anicet-Charles-Gabriel Lemonnier, (French, 1793–1824), depicts the first reading of Voltaire's "L'Orpheline de Chine" in 1755.

Page 681: V. Eriksen, *Catherine II on Horseback,* 1762.

Page 685: Marten Meytens (alternate spelling: Mijtens; Swedish-Austrian, 1695–1770), *Kaiseria Maria Theresie mit Familie.* Meytens was an active court painter; in 1759 he was made director of the Vienna Academy of Art.

Pages 690–691: P. Debucourt, *Celebrations in Les Halls on the Birth of Dauphin, 21st January, 1782.*

Page 693: *Les Glaneuses* by Jean-François Millet (1814–1875), French genre and landscape painter of the Barbizon school. Oil on canvas, 21¼ × 26 in.

Page 702: Jean-Baptiste Siméon Chardin (French, 1699–1779), *The Kitchen Maid,* ca 1738. Canvas; 18¼ × 14¾ in. (1952.5.38(117)) Chardin is now considered to be the most popular eighteenth century French artist. He was a realist in the manner of seventeenth-century Dutch masters.

Page 705: Attr. to Master of the Beguins (french, active ca 1650–1660), *Beggars at a Doorway.*

Page 711: Louis (or Antoine?) Le Nain (French, 1593–1648), *Famille de paysans dans un interieur,* ca 1640.

Page 719: W. W. Wheatley, "Dancing around the Church," 1848.

Page 721: From the City Temple, London.

Pages 724–725; 728: Armed warriors and Oba of Benin with attendants, Benin, Nigeria. Bronze plaque, late 17th or early 18th c.

Page 733: Aernout Smit, "The Africa in Table Bay—1683."

Page 735: Pieter van der Aa, *View of Loango,* Plate 47 from Galérie Agréable du Monde (Vol. 60–67).

Page 745: After Pieter Coecke van Aelst, Flemish, Antwerp (?), 1553. From *Ces Moeurs et fachons de faire de Turez.* Woodcut. The Metropolitan Museum of Art, Harris Brisbane Dick Fund, 1928 (28.85.7ab)

Page 746: From *Rawzat al-Ushshaq* (Garden of Lovers) by Arifi, folio 23a. Artist unknown. Opaque watercolor on paper, Turkey, Ottoman, ca 1560–75.

From the Edward Binney 3rd Collection of Turkish Art at the Harvard University Art Museums.

Page 752: From Jalal al-Din Rumi, Masnavi. Add. 27263, f. 29a. British Library.

Page 754: *A Magnanimous Vizier.* Opaque watercolor on paper, attributed to Manohar. From the Divan of Anvari, dated 1588; 14 × 8 cm.

Page 756: Indian painting; Mughal, school of Jahangir, 17th century, ca 1615–1618; "Jahangir Preferring a Sufi Shaikh to Kings"; color and gold, 10 × 7⅛″.

Page 759: The Taj Mahal is the mausoleum in memory of Arjumand Banu Begum, called Mumtaz Mahal ("chosen one of the palace"), of which Taj Mahal is a corruption. She died in 1631. The building was begun in 1632, after plans were submitted by a council of architects. Credit for the final design is given to Usted Isa, who was either Turkish or Persian. Workmen and materials came from all over India and Central Asia. The mausoleum itself was completed by 1643, although the whole complex—consisting of the mausoleum, central garden square, mosque, and service buildings surrounded by a red sandstone wall—took much longer.

Page 771: Detail of Chinese sik scroll: *Going up the River at the Spring Festival.* Sung Dynasty.

Page 775: From the 1815 edition of *Jingdezhen taolu,* Vol. 1, second half of leaf 26 and first half of leaf 27, housed in the Wason Collection on East Asia, Cornell University Library.

Page 780: Chinese painting, Ming (?), "Children Playing in a Garden." Color on silk fan; 10 × 10⅝″.

Page 783: Detail from Rice Cultivation Scroll, Tawarakasame Kosaku Emaki. Color on paper, late 16th c. Artist unknown. University of Tokyo.

Page 790: *Tanneijiro Grappling Under Water* by Kuniyoshi, 19th century. British Museum.

Pages 794–795: After David, and probably the work of a collaborator of David, *The Tennis Court Oath.* This is a slightly smaller painting than the famous pen drawing with sepia was by David, 1791. It gives some idea of the intended color scheme of David's great project, which remains only as the famous drawing.

Page 800: John Trumbull (American, 1756–1843), *Signing of the Declaration of Independence,* 1786. Oil on canvas, 21⅛ × 31½ in. John Trumbull was considered to be one of the most significant American artists of his time.

Page 807: A primitive but contemporary representation of the taking of the Bastille, by "Cholet" who was a participant in the attack.

Page 811: This was the first portrait of Mary Wollstonecraft, by an unknown artist, commissioned by William Roscoe.

Page 814: "Un Comité révolutionnaire sous la Terreur," after Alexandre Évariste Fragonard, French historical painter (1780–1850).

Page 819: Jacques-Louis David (French, 1748–1825), *Napoleon Crossing the Alps.* Oil on canvas.

Page 822: Francisco de Goya y Lucientes, *The Third of May, 1808* (1814–1815). Oil on canvas; 8 ft. 9 in. × 11 ft. 3½ in. Goya was known in the Spain of his day as a portraitist, history painter, and church painter.

Pages 826–827: William-Powell Frith (British, 1819–1909), *The Railway Station* (detail), completed 1862. Oil on canvas; 45¼ × 98¼ in.

Page 833: Samuel Scott (English, 1702–1772), *Old East India Quay, London,* Victoria and Albert Museum. Samuel Scott was the most distinguished native English topographical view painter in the eighteenth century. Such painting was popularized in England by Canaletto during his residence there from 1746–1755.

Page 844: Honoré Daumier (French, 1808–1879), *The Third-Class Carriage.* Oil on canvas. Daumier was both a caricaturist and a serious painter.

Page 857: From *Parliamentary Papers,* 1842, vol. XV.

Pages 862–863: Anton Ziegler, *Barricade in the Michaeler Square on the Night of 26 to 27 May 1848.* Oil on canvas; 68 × 55 cm.

Page 865: Isabey, *Congress of Vienna.* Royal Library, Windsor Castle, RL.21539.

Page 869: *Count Clemens von Metternich* (1773–1859) by Sir Thomas Lawrence, English painter (1769–1830).

Page 875: Left to right: K. Marx, F. Engels (rear), with Marx's daughters: Jenny, Eleanor, and Laura, photographed in the 1860s.

Page 877: John Constable (English, 1776–1837), *The Hay Wain.* Constable was one of the two great romantic painters of the period (Joseph Turner being the other), and was the first artist of importance to paint outdoors.

Page 879: Joseph Danhauser (German, 1805–1845), *Liszt am Klavier,* 1840.

Page 882: Eugene Delacroix (French, 1789–1863), *Les Massacres de Scio.* Delacroix was leader of the Romantic school. This dramatic interpretation of a contemporary event scandalized Paris Salon visitors in 1824.

Page 887: Eugene Delacroix (French, 1789–1863), *Liberty Leading the People,* 1830. Oil on canvas; 10½ × 128 in. Exhibited at the Paris Salon of 1831, the painting was acquired by the French Government.

Page 889: Honoré Daumier (French, 1808–1879), *Legislative Belly,* lithograph, 1834, 42 × 52.5 cm. Charles Deering Collection (1941.1258)

Pages 896–897: John O'Connor, *St. Pancras Hotel and Station from Pentonville Road.*

Page 900: "The Court for King Cholera," cartoon from *Punch,* XXIII (1852), 139.

Page 904: Cross-section of a Parisian house, about 1850, from Edmund Texier, *Tableauade Paris,* Paris, 1852, vol. I, p. 65.

Page 909: Paul-Emile Chabas (French, 1869–1937), *Un Coin de Table,* 1904. Oil on canvas. Bibliothèque des Arts Decoratifs.

Page 913: Pierre-Auguste Renoir (French, 1841–1919), *Le Moulin de la Galette à Montmartre,*

1876. 4 ft. 3½ in. × 5 ft. 9 in. Bequest of Gustave Caillabotte, 1894.

Page 917: After a drawing by C. Koch, 1890.

Page 925: Hilaire Germaine Edgar Degas (French, 1834–1917), *Les Repasseuses.*

Pages 928–929: Wall painting from the Town Hall and Civic Museum, Siena.

Page 932: Demolition of part of the Latin Quarter in 1860. Engraving from a drawing by Félix Thorigny.

Page 935: R. Legat, *Battle of Calatafim,* 1860.

Page 944: Merchants of Nijni-Novgorod drinking tea. From *L'Illustration,* 29 August 1905.

Pages 958–959: Oil painting on glass, post 1780, by unknown Chinese artist.

Page 965: Townsend Harris, the American Consul, meeting with representatives of the Tokugawa Shogunate. Color on paper, 1857. Artist unknown. Tsuneo Tamba Collection, Yokohama.

Page 975: A. Sutherland, *Battle of Omdurman,* September 2, 1898. Colored lithograph.

Page 979: From "The Graphic," November 9, 1895.

Page 984: Ichiyosai Kuniteru, *Tomioka raw-silk reeling factory,* ca 1875. Painted wood black. Tsuneo Tamba Collection, Yokohama.

Page 1009: Richard Caton Woodville (1815–1855), *War News from Mexico,* 1848. Oil on canvas, 27 × 25".

Page 1010: Alfred Boisseau French (1823–1901), *Louisiana Indians Walking Along a Bayou.* Oil on canvas. (NOMA # 56.34).

Page 1013: Winslow Homer (1836–1910), *The Cotton Pickers,* 1876. Oil on canvas, 26¹⁄₁₆ × 38⅛". Los Angeles County Museum of Art, Acquisition made possible through Museum Trustees: Robert O. Anderson, R. Stanton Avery, B. Gerald Cantor, Edward W. Carter, Justin Dart, Charles E. Ducommun, Mrs. F. Daniel Frost, Julian Ganz, Jr., Dr. Armand Hammer, Harry Lenart, Dr. Franklin D. Murphy, Mrs. Joan Palevsky, Richard E. Sherwood, Maynard J. Toll, and Hal B. Wallis.

Page 1017: Thure de Thulstrup, *The Battle of Gettysburg,* from the *CIVIL WAR, Gettysburg* (Time-Life Books, Inc.). Courtesy, The Seventh Regiment Fund, Inc.

Page 1029: Thomas Rowlandson (1756–1827), *Convicts Embarking for Botany Bay.* Pen and wash drawing, 17.3 × 15.7 cm. Rex Nan Kivell Collection, National Library of Australia.

Pages 1036–1037: John Nash (English), *Over the Top.*

Page 1039: Anton von Werner (German, 1843–1915), *The Congress of Berlin,* 1878.

Pages 1070–1071: Cheering Turks mass around a Turkish victory flag made to celebrate the victory at Smyrna, October 1922.

Page 1091: "Anti-Reds" wrest Canton from the Communists, with over 3,000 casualties. This January 1928 photo shows the dead strewn in the principal streets of Canton.

Page 1101: Philippine "West Pointers" on parade: cadets of the Baguio Military Academy march in a parade to celebrate the second anniversary of the Philippine Commonwealth.

Pages 1104–1105: Isaac Soyer (American, 1907–   ), *Employment Agency,* 1937. Oil on canvas; 34 ¼ × 45 in. Whitney Museum of American Art (Purchase 37.44). Photo: Geoffrey Clements, New York.

Page 1111: Edvard Munch (Norwegian, 1863–1944), *The Dance of Life,* 1899.

Page 1114: Frank Lloyd Wright (American architect, 1869–1959), Falling Water, Bear Run, Pennsylvania—perhaps the greatest modern house in America, 1936. The largely self-taught Wright was an exponent of what he called "organic architecture": the idea that a building should blend in with its setting and be harmonious with nature.

Page 1115: Pablo Picasso (Spanish, 1881–1973), *Guernica,* 1937. The original oil on canvas, 11 ft. 5 ½ in. × 25 ft. 5¾ in., is in the Museo del Prado, Madrid.

Page 1135: 100,000 Nazi Storm Troopers gathered in the Luitpodarena in Nuremberg, Germany, to hear Adolf Hitler on Brown Shirt Day at the Nazi Party convention, September 20, 1936.

Page 1137: French caricature by C. Leavdre, 1898.

Page 1141: Arkady Aleksandrovich Plastov (Russian 1893–1972) *Collective Farm Threshing,* 1949. Oil on canvas, 200 × 382 cm. Plastov's career was entirely in the Soviet era; his great paintings were calls to action—icons of socialism.

Page 1157: The cartoon "Stepping Stones to Glory" by Sir David Low (1891–1963) appeared in the London *Evening Standard* on 8 July 1936.

Page 1163: I. Toidze (Russian), *For the Motherland's Sake, Go Forward, Heroes,* 1942 poster.

Page 1204: Detail from Diego Rivera's monumental fresco painting (8.59 × 12.87 m), *History of Mexico: From the Conquest to the Future,* 1929–1930. From the West Wall, Stairway of the Palacio Nacional, Mexico City. In this detail, the priest Hidalgo presides over the cause of independence. In the center the Mexican eagle, symbol of nationality, holds the Aztec emblem of ceremonial war. Rivera was a painter, printmaker, sculptor, book illustrator, as well as a political activist.

Index

Abacus, invention of, 315

Abbas (Ah-bahs), shah of Persia, 752–753

Abbasids (Ah-bas'-ids), 274, 275, 276; decline of, 277–278

Abelard, Peter, 426, 428, 513

Aborigines, Australian, 1026, 1028

Abortion, 1018, 1144, 1294. *See also* Birth control

Absolutism, 608–609, 628(table), 629(table), 643, 687–688; Spanish theory of, 574; French, 584, 609–614, 683–685, 687; Spanish, decline of, 619, 621; in eastern Europe, 624, 639, 687–688; Habsburg, 625–626, 685–686; Hohenzollern, 627; Prussian, 630–631, 680–681; Russian, 635, 681–683; decline of, in England, 643–645; puritanical, 645–647; Stuart, 648; Enlightenment and, 679–688; Austrian, 683, 685–686; falls in France, 805

Abstract art, 1115–1116

Abu-Bakr (Ah-boo Bak'-eer), 273–274

Abu-l-Fazl (Ab-bool-Fahzl), 756

Ab Urbe Condita (Livy), 201

Academy (Greek school), 141

Acamapichti, 495

Achaens. *See* Mycenaeans

Achebe, Chinua, 1276, 1277, 1306

Acropolis, 122, 131, 132

Act for the Submission of the Clergy, 551

Act in Restraint of Appeals, 551

Actium, Battle of, 747

Acton, Lord, 878

Adages, The (Erasmus), 526

Adalbero of Laon, 374

Adams, John, 738, 799

Adenauer, Konrad, 1176

Adrian VI, pope, 553

Adultery: Hammurabi's code and, 25; Jewish law and, 47; in Roman Republic, 184

Aediles (Ee-diles), 177

Aeneas, legend of, 201

Aeneid (Uh-ne'-id) (Virgil), 201

Aeschylus (Ehs'-kuh-lus), 134

Afghanistan, 64; gains independence, 1081–1082; Soviet invasion of, 1203

Africa, 462–482; spread of Greek culture in, 153, 154; land and peoples of, 462, 464; before 1500, 463(map); early societies of, 464–465; kingdoms of, 465–466, 469–472, 472–475, 726–731; trans-Saharan trade in, 466–468, 468(table); historical periods of, 480(table); Western conception of, during Renaissance, 524; colonization of, 565; Dutch West India Company and, 652; Swahili city-states in, 732–734; economic impact of European trade on, 739; imperialism in, 972–973, 975, 977, 981, 982, 1234–1236, 1242; partition of, 974(map); impact of Great Depression and World War II on, 1074, 1237–1238; Horn of, 1134; decolonization in, 1182; nationalism in, 1234, 1237–1241, 1239(table); since 1960, 1241–1249; deforestation and droughts in, 1294; population growth in, 1295. *See also individual countries*

African National Congress (ANC), 1248, 1249

Afrikaners, 973; racist nationalism of, 1246–1247

Afro-Asian Conference, 1225

Age-grades, 727

Age of Louis XIV (Voltaire), 672

Agincourt, 444

Agora, 122

Agricultural Revolution, 9, 830–831

Agriculture: in Paleolithic Age, 7; Neolithic origins of, 9–10, 11(map), 12(map), 13; Hammurabi's code and, 24–25; in ancient Israel, 47; Persian, 54; Indian, 64, 68, 69, 301; in ancient China, 90, 93–94, 100, 105–106, 108, 109; Hellenic, 137; Hellenistic, 157–158; in Roman Republic, 184–185, 188; in Roman Empire, 212, 220; in medieval Europe, 249–250, 256, 692–693; in Islamic state, 287; Indian, 301; T'ang, 312–313; in Charlemagne's empire, 339; in Middle Ages, 355, 356, 377–380, 450; open-field system of, 377, 692, 830; in early Africa, 462, 464, 465, 466, 480; in early Mexico, 487; Maya, 488–489; Inca, 499–500; German, after Thirty Years' War, 592; French economy and, 615; serfdom and, 623–624; slash-and-burn, 633; in 17th-century England, 644; in Ming China, 768–770, 776; in Tokugawa Japan, 789–790; Industrial Revolution and, 830–831; English enclosure movement and, 831–832; European, after 1873, 946; U.S., black slavery and, 1012; Australian, 1030; collectivized, in Stalinist Russia, 1140–1142; under Deng Xiaoping, 1218–1219; in Third World, 1254, 1262–1266. *See also* Green Revolution

Ahmose (Ah-mo'-zuh), pharaoh, 30

Ahriman (Ah-rih-mahn), 57, 58

Ahuramazda (Ah-hoor-ah-mahz-day), 56, 57, 58

Akbar, *badshah* of Mughal, 753–756

Akhenaten (Ah-ke-na-ten), 31, 32

Akhmatova (Ak-ma'-ta-va), Anna, 1188

Alamán, Lucas, 995

Alaric (Al'-uhr-ick), 241

al-Bakri, 469–470, 471

Albania, 1199

Alberdi, Juan Batista, 1004

Albert, archbishop of Magdeburg, 537–538

Alberti, Leon Battista, 513

Albert of Wallenstein, 591

Albigensians, 366, 435

Albuquerque, Alfonso de, 567

Alcabala tax, 997

Alcaeus (Al-se-us), 418

Alcibiades (Al-se-bi'-uh-deez), 130–131, 135

Alcuin, 343, 344

al-Dawla, Mu'izz, 277

al-Din al-Afghani, Jamal, 1081

Alexander, king of Yugoslavia, 1136

Alexander I, tsar of Russia, 819, 821, 867, 970

Alexander II, tsar of Russia, 939, 942, 943

Alexander III, tsar of Russia, 943, 1041

Alexander VI, pope, 510, 511, 532, 536

Alexander the Great, 79–80, 116; conquests of, 148–150, 155, 172, 500

Alexandra, empress of Russia, 1054

Alexandria, 154, 166; under the Ptolemies, 163, 164; riots in, 967

Alexis, tsar of Russia, 636–637

al-Farabi, 292

al-Fazari, 471

Alfonsín, Raul, 1209

Alfred of Wessex, 252, 353

al-Fustat, 276

Algebra, origins of, 290
Algeciras Conference of 1906, 1041
Algeria, 972; gains independence, 1182, 1233
Ali, Islamic ruler, 751, 752
al-Khwarizmi (al-kwar-ih-ze-me), 290
al-Kindi, 291–292
Allende (Ah-yen′-day), Salvador, 1207, 1208
Alliance for Germany, 1199
Alliance for Progress, 1207
Alliance of the Three Emperors, 1039
Allies: in World War I, 1060–1061, 1064, 1145; Russian Revolution of 1917 and, 1060; in World War II, 1161, 1163, 1164, 1165, 1166
All Quiet on the Western Front (Remarque), 1046
al-Ma'mun, caliph, 291
al-Mansur, caliph, 288
al-Muqtadir, caliph, 288
al-Mustafki, caliph, 277
al-Mu'tasin, caliph, 277
al-Mutawakkil, caliph, 277
Alphabet: development of, 42; Etruscan, 174; Cyrillic, 256
Al-Qanun (Ibn Sina), 291
Al-Razi, physician, 291
Alsace-Lorraine, 1038, 1064
Alva, duke of, 586
al-Ya-qubi, 471
Amalgamated Society of Engineers, 857
Amanullah, amir of Afghanistan, 1081
Amazon River, 486
Ambach, Melchior, 594
Ambassador, resident, 510
Ambrose, bishop of Milan, 232, 252
American Civil War, 937–938, 1015–1016
American Indians, 1009–1010. *See also* Amerindians
American Republic, creation of, 172
American Revolution, 671, 798–802, 836; origins of, 798–800; independence and, 801; framing of Constitution and, 801–802; impact on Europe, 802; liberalism and, 871; emigration to Canada and, 1023
Americas: geography and peoples of, 486–487; historical periods of, 500(table); economic exploitation of, 596; revolutionary totalitarianism in, 1207. *See also* Central America; Latin America; North America; South America; United States
Amerindians, 480, 487, 500; death rate in 16th century, 573–574, 596
Amesbury Priory, 394, 395
Amiens, Peace of, 751
Amiens, Treaty of, 819
Amin, Idi, 1243

Amir al-umara, 277
Amon-Re, 31, 45
Amorites, 43
Amritsar Massacre, 1086, 1088
Amsterdam: as financial capital of Europe, 568; Bank of, 650
Amurians, 487
Anabaptists, 548–549, 717–718
Analects (Confucius), 95
Anastasia, tsarina of Russia, 635
Anatolia, 4, 10, 32, 33, 34; Ottoman Turks and, 625. *See also* Turkey
Anatomy, Hellenistic, 166
Anaximander (Uh-nak′-suh-man-duhr), 140, 923
ANC. *See* African National Congress
Andean region, 499, 500
Andromaque (Racine), 617
Anesthesia, in early Middle Ages, 345
Angevin empire, 407
Anglican church. *See* Church of England
Anglo-Saxons, 245, 249, 251–252, 405; conversion to Christianity, 235
Angola, 735, 740; nationalism in, 1246
Animism, 249, 714
An Lu-Shan, 314
Anna da Silva, 936
Anne of Austria, 612
Anno Domini, 342
"Anticeptic principle," 902
Anticommunism, 1156–1157, 1289
Anti-Corn Law League, 885
Anti-Federalists, 802
Antigone (Sophocles), 134
Antigonus, 149
Anti-imperialists, 981–982
Anti-Semitism: in medieval Europe, 411, 416, 417; in Austria, 952–953; of Hitler, 1148, 1149
Antisthenes (An-tis-thuh-neez), 159
"Anti-utopias," 1112–1113
Antoinette, Marie, 809, 811
Antonines, age of, 208–209, 212, 214, 217
Antony, Marc, 191, 192
Antony and Cleopatra (Shakespeare), 600, 601
Antwerp, 568, 584; collapse of, 586, 587
Apartheid, 1247, 1248
Apocalypse of Baruch, 203, 204
Apollo, statue of, 175(illus.)
Apologists, 253
Apothecaries, 713–714
Apparel. *See* Clothing
Appeal to the Christian Nobility of the German Nation (Luther), 543
Aquinas. *See* St. Thomas Aquinas
Aquino, Corazón, 1228, 1229
Aquitaine, 441
Arab, defined, 264, 280

Arabi, Ahmed (Air-ah-be, Ahk-med), 967
Arabian Nights, The, 289
Arabian peninsula, 264
Arab-Israeli conflict, 1185, 1232
Arab League, 1229
Arabs, 254, 264, 268–269; before Islam, 264–265; political organization of, 265; social organization of, 279–284; invade India, 307, 308; nationalism of, 1075–1077, 1082
Arago, François, 890
Aramaic script, 79
Ara Pacis Augustae (Altar of Augustan Peace), 202(illus.)
Archilochus (Ar-kil-o-kus), 124
Archimedes (Ar-kuh-me-deez), 163, 258
Architecture: Mesopotamian, 16–17; Indian, 66–67, 67(illus.), 79, 82(illus.); Chinese, under Shang Dynasty, 90(illus.); Greek, 131–132, 133, 135, 153; Roman, 211(illus.); Islamic, 289(illus.); Iranian, 309; Japanese, 326; Carolingian, 344(illus.); Gothic, 430, 432; early African, 473; Olmec, 488; Renaissance, 515, 516, 527, 528; in 16th-century France, 580–581; of Versailles, 613; baroque, 639–641; Ottoman, 748–749; 20th-century, 1113–1114. *See also* Cathedrals; Churches; Housing; Mosques; Palaces; Pyramids; Temples
Arch of Constantine, 223(illus.)
Aretino, Pietro, 518
Argentina, 486, 969, 970, 996; consequences of independence in, 1001; economic nationalism in, 1205; under Perón, 1207; Falkland Islands and, 1209
Arianism, 231–232
Aristarchus of Samos, 142, 163
Aristocracy: defined, 122; Hittite, 34; Shang, 90–91; Chou, 92, 93; Mycenaean, 118; Spartan, 125, 126; Athenian, 126–127, 128; Hellenistic, 152; Byzantine, 259; in Islamic state, 279; Japanese, 326, 786; Frankish, 334–335, 339; German, 361; in medieval Europe, 385–386, 393, 418; recreation of, 451; peasant revolts against, 456; in kingdom of Ghana, 471; in kingdom of Mali, 473; Italian, during Renaissance, 509; English, during Renaissance, 529–530; in 17th-century Spain, 621; Parisian, 677; child care among, 704; education of, 708; diet of, 710, 712; liberalism and, 798; American Revolution and, 802; agricultural improvements and, in England, 830, 831; Tory

party and, 883; in 19th-century European cities, 907; Creole, 999. *See also* Nobility

Aristophanes (Ah-ris-tahf'-uh-neez), 135

Aristotle, 122, 141–142, 163, 164, 292, 428, 526, 660–661

Arius, 231–232

Arkwright, Richard, 837, 838

Armagh, monastery at, 235

Armenians, 1199

Arms race: nuclear proliferation and, 1291–1293

Army: Assyrian, 49–51, 52; Mauryan, 80; of First Emperor, 103(illus.); Spartan, 125, 128; under Philip II, 143; under Alexander the Great, 148–149; Roman, 175, 188, 190, 197–198, 209–210, 212, 213; Byzantine, 254–255; Merovingian, 335(illus.); of kingdom of Ghana, 471–472; Aztec, 494; French, during Renaissance, 529; of absolute monarchs, 609; under Frederick William I, 631; Mongol, 634; under Peter the Great, 638, 682; parliamentary, 645; under Catherine the Great, 682; Moroccan, 730; under Suleiman I, 746; in Ming China, 771; French, 815; Prussian, under Bismarck, 941; Japanese, 985; Red, 1060, 1139, 1162, 1166, 1172, 1173, 1187, 1188; German, Treaty of Versailles and, 1064; under Hitler, 1158–1159. *See also* Warfare

Army Order No. 1, 1056

Arnold of Brescia, 435

Arouet, François Marie. *See* Voltaire

Arrow Cross, 1136

Art, 5; Paleolithic, 7(illus.), 8; Egyptian, 31–32, 44(illus.); Hittite, 34; Assyrian, 51(illus.); Persian, 54(illus.), 58(illus.); Indian, 66(illus.), 80(illus.); Chinese, 93(illus.), 94(illus.), 103(illus.), 105(illus.); Greek, 119(illus.), 132–133, 135(illus.), 138(illus.), 157(illus.); Etruscan, 175(illus.); Roman, 183(illus.), 186, 202(illus.), 218(illus.); Visigothic, 245(illus.); Byzantine, 256; Persian, 285(illus.); Gupta, 300(illus.); Buddhist, 311(illus.); T'ang, 317; Sung, 319; Japanese, 324(illus.), 326, 790(illus.); Northumbrian, 341; Ottonian, 354(illus.); monasteries as storehouses of, 395; bubonic plague and, 441; Maya, 489, 490(illus.); Renaissance, 515–518, 527–528, 581; international style of, 516–517; baroque, 601–602, 718; during Louis XIV's rule, 615–616; Ethiopian, 731(illus.); Mughal, 753; in

Indo-Persian style, 756; Chinese, 779; Western, introduction into Japan, 786–787; of romantic movement, 878, 880; modern, 1113, 1114–1116. *See also* Literature; Music

Artisans: Shang, 90; Athenian, 135. *See also* Craftsmen

Artists. *See* Art

Aryans, 53, 68–71, 301

Asceticism, 71

Ashanti kingdom, 1235

Ashikaga Shogunate (Ash-ih-kah-gah Sho-gun-ate), 327, 330, 782–783

Ashoka (Ah-sho'-kah), king of India, 78, 298; reign of, 81, 83

Asia, 298–330; Alexander's conquest of, 148; spread of Greek culture in, 154; Gupta Empire and, 298–301; European trade with, 761; migrations from, 972, 1019; responses to imperialism in, 981, 982; nationalism in, 1072–1102; impact of World War I on, 1072–1075; West, 1075; East, 1214; since 1945, 1227(table). *See also individual countries*

Asiento, 833

Assaye, Battle of, 762

Assembly-line production, 1021

Assembly of Notables, 805

Assignats, 809

Assimilation: Christianity and, 236; in Muslim society, 279–280

Assyrian Empire, 40, 50(map); rise of, 49–51; downfall of, 52

Astaire, Fred, 1117

Astrolabe, 571

Astrology, Roman, 204

Astronomy: in ancient China, 104–105; Hellenistic, 162–163; medieval, 660–661; Ptolemy's rules of, 661–662; Copernican theory of, 662, 664; Brahe's contribution to, 662–663; Kepler's laws of planetary motion and, 663; Galileo's telescope and, 664

Astrophel and Stella (Sidney), 599

Aswan Dam, 1260, 1261(illus.)

Atahualpa (At-a-wal'-pa), 573

Atatürk, Mustafa Kemal (At-uh-turk', Muss-ta-fuh Keh-mahl'), 1079–1081, 1233, 1307

Atheism, 676, 1108, 1143

Athens, 123, 132(map); evolution of, 126–128; Persian attack on, 128–129; war with Sparta, 129–130; arts in, 131–135; daily life in, 135–139

Atlantic alliance. *See* North Atlantic Treaty Organization

Atlantic Charter, 1170, 1171

Atlas, 164(illus.)

Atman, 72

Atomic bomb: development of, 1110; dropped on Japan, 1166; cold war and, 1173; nuclear proliferation and, 1291

Atomic Energy Commission (U.N.), 1291

Atomic physics, 1110

Aton, 31

Attila the Hun, 233

Attlee, Clement, 1177

Auden, W. H., 1110

Audencias, 575, 995

Augsburg, League of, 617

Augsburg, Peace of, 545, 589, 592

Augustine of Canterbury, 248

Augustus, Roman emperor, 191, 192, 201, 208, 210, 212, 218, 252; principate and restored Republic under, 196–198; army under, 197–198, 207; administration of provinces by, 198–199; Roman expansion under, 199, 200(map); literary flowering under, 199, 201–202

Aurangzeb (Awr'-ang-zeb), *badshah* of India, 757, 761

Aurelian (Aw-re'-lee-uhn), 217

Auschwitz, 1161

Austerlitz, Battle of, 819, 821

Australia, 962, 983; Cook's discovery of, 1026–1027; geography of, 1027; under British control, as penal colony, 1028–1029; economic development of, 1029–1030; immigration to, 1030; gold rush in, 1030–1032; Commonwealth of, 1032; in World War I, 1032–1033; as colonial power, 1033

Australian Colonies Government Act, 1032

Austria: baroque art in, 602; War of the Spanish Succession and, 618; rise of, 624–626; attacked by Ottoman Turks, 625; growth of, 627(map); absolutism in, 685–686; Ottoman war against, 750; at war with France, 812; First Coalition and, 813; Treaty of Lunéville and, 819; in Third Coalition, 819; in Fourth Coalition, 822; industrialization of, 847(table); in Quadruple Alliance, 864; Congress of Vienna and, 867; in Holy Alliance, 868; revolution of 1848 in, 890–892; unification of Germany and, 940; independent republic proclaimed, 952; in Balkan Wars, 1042; 1919 peace treaty and, 1064; threatened by Hitler, 1157; gains independence, 1190. *See also* Austro-Hungarian Empire

Austrian Netherlands, 812, 813

Austrian Succession, War of the, 680, 684, 685, 750, 833, 835
Austro-Hungarian Empire, 869–871, 870(map); nationalism in, 951–953; in Balkan Wars, 1042–1043, 1044; in World War I, 1047; surrenders to Allies, 1061; revolution in, 1061–1062
Austro-Prussian War of 1866, 938–940
Authoritarianism, conservative, 1134–1136, 1207. *See also* Absolutism; Dictatorship; Totalitarianism
Autobiography (Cellini), 513
Autobiography (Garibaldi), 936
Autocracy, 636, 641
Automobile industry, postwar expansion of, 1183
Autumn Harvest Uprising, 1093
Auxiliary Service Law (Germany), 1050, 1053
Avars, 254, 339
Averroës, 292
Avicenna (Ibn Sina of Bukhara), 291, 292
Avison-Christine (Pisan), 434
Axis powers, 1164
Axum, 478–479
Ayllu (Inca clan), 502
Azania, 475
Azerbaijanis, 1199
Azikiwe, Nnamdi (Ah-zik-ih-we, Ung-nahm-dee), 1238, 1243
Aztec Empire, 488, 491, 492; religion and war in, 493–495; daily life in, 495–498; cities of, 497–498; Spanish conquest of, 571–572

Baal, 44, 45
Babur (Bah-burr), 753, 759
Babylonia, 18–19, 162; conquest of, by Assyrians, 50; fall of Assyrian Empire and, 52, 55, 56
Babylonian Captivity, 446–447, 510, 535
Bacchus, cult of, 204
Bach, Johann Sebastian, 602
Bacon, Francis, 667, 668
Bacterial revolution, 901–903
Badshah, 754, 757, 758
Baghdad, 264, 288
Baillis, 407
Bairam Khan, 754
Bakufu, 328
Baldwin, Stanley, 1117, 1122
Balfour, Arthur, 1077
Balfour Declaration, 1077
Balkans, 1038, 1039, 1043(maps), 1049
Balkan Wars: First, 1042; Second, 1042; "Third," 1043, 1044; defeat of Young Turks in, 1076

"Ballade des Pendus" (Villon), 434
Balzac, Honoré de, 924
Bangladesh, 309, 1223, 1265, 1291, 1293
Banks, Joseph, 1026
Banks: Industrial Revolution and, 851–852; Great Depression and, 1125
Bantu, 465, 476, 480
Baptism, in medieval Europe, 235
Barbarians, 196, 199, 210, 214, 217–218. *See also* Toba
Barid, 276
Baring, Evelyn, 968
Baroque arts, 601–603, 639–640, 718
Barracks emperors, 217, 218, 221, 314
Barrios, 491
Barrões, 759
Barth, Karl, 1109
Baruch, Bernard, 1291
Bases and Points of Departure for Argentine Political Organization (Alberdi), 1004
Basques, 339
Bastille, 807, 809
Baths, Roman, 67, 186–187
Battle Abbey, 380, 381
Battle of Britain, 1158
Battle of Peterloo, 883
Bauhaus, 1113–1114
Baumgarten, Hermann, 940
Bavaria, 335, 339
Bayle, Pierre, 670, 672, 673
Bay of Pigs invasion, 1207
Bazaar economy, 1272
BBC. *See* British Broadcasting Corporation
Beauvais, 696, 710
Becket, Thomas, 382, 385, 413–414, 433
Bede (the Venerable), 251, 341–342, 343(illus.), 514
Bedouins, 264, 269, 279, 286
Beer, consumption of in medieval Europe, 381
Beethoven, Ludwig van, 880
Begin, Menachim, 1232
Beijing, demonstrations in, 1195, 1219. *See also* Peking
Belgian Congo, 1241
Belgium, 376, 584, 587; in Napoleon's Grand Empire, 821; industrialization of, 847(table), 850; attacked by Germany, 1044; in World War I, 1045; atrocities in, 1049, 1053; occupation of Ruhr and, 1119; Nazi Germany attacks, 1158; following World War II, 1178; population density in, 1295. *See also* Low Countries
Belize, 486
Beloch, K. J., 116

Benedictines, 244, 393
Benefit of clergy, 413
Bengal. *See* Bangladesh
Bengalis, 1223
Bengtson, Hermann, 148
Benin, 728, 735
Bentham, Jeremy, 901
Benthamite tradition, 950
Berbers, 462, 464, 466
Bérénice (Racine), 617
Berg, Alban, 1116
Bergson, Henri, 1108
Bering Strait, 486–487
Berlin, Congress of, 1038–1039, 1042
Berlin Wall, 1191; opening of, 1199
Bernstein, Edward, 956
Bessarabia, 867
Bethmann-Hollweg, Theobald von, 1043
Bevshirme, 747
Bhagavad Gita, 75
Bhakti, 309
Bhutto (Bu'-tow), Zulfikar Ali, 1293
Biafra, 735, 1245
Bible: Mesopotamian culture and, 18, 23; composition of Old Testament and, 43; Vulgate, 239; medieval popularity of Book of Revelation and, 404; Renaissance education and, 526; German translation of New Testament and, 541, 542; Dutch translations of, 585; Authorized (King James) Version, 600, 601; theological fundamentalism and, 1306
Big Five, 1285
Big Four, 1062
Big Three, 1171, 1172
Bigge, J. T., 1030
Bill of exchange, origins of, 287
Bill of Rights (England), 648, 802
Bill of Rights (United States), 796, 802
Birth control: among medieval nobility, 389; in 18th-century Europe; in 19th-century European cities, 915, 920; in India, 1224, 1225–1226; in Third World, 1260; state-run, in China, 1294
Birthrate: in 17th-century Europe, 695; 19th-century decline of, 920(table); modern, 1294
Bishops of Rome, 232–233
Bismarck, Otto von, 892, 907, 953; early career of, 937–938; unification of Germany and, 938–942; German Empire under, 946–948; resigns, 948; imperialism in Africa and, 973, 975; European system of alliances and, 1038–1042, 1040(fig.)
Björnson (Be-yorn'-son), Björnstjerne, 971

Black Death. *See* Bubonic plague
Black Family in Slavery and Freedom, The (Gutman), 1017
Black Hand, 1042
Black Prince, 442
Blacks: in early Africa, 462–463, 474–475, 476, 478; in Renaissance society, 523–524; origins of American racism and, 596–598; proportion in U.S. population, 596; Latin American, immigration and, 1006; Reconstruction and, 1016; impact of slavery on, 1016–1019; immigration and, 1022; civil rights movement and, 1200; in French Africa, 1237
Black Shirts, 1146
Blackstone, William, 916
Blake, William, 852
Blanc, Louis, 874–875, 888, 889
Blinding, Buyid practice of, 277
Blitzkrieg, 1158
Bloodletting, 714
"Bloody Sunday" massacre, 945
Blum, Léon, 1129, 1130
Boat people, 1291
Boccaccio, Giovanni, 440, 515
Bodhisattva, 78, 307
Bodin, Jean, 636
Boers, 973
Boer War, 973, 979, 1041
Bohemia, 869; Thirty Years' War and, 591, 625
Boleyn, Anne, 550, 551
Bolívar, Simón (Bo-lee-vahr, See-mon'), 999–1000
Bolivia, 486; Indians in, 996; elected government in, 1209
Bologna, Concordat of, 581–582
Bolshevik revolution, 1056–1057
Bolsheviks, 1057, 1059, 1139
Bombay, 760
Bonaparte, Louis Napoleon. *See* Napoleon III, emperor of France
Bonaparte, Napoleon. *See* Napoleon I, emperor of France
Bonhomme, Jacques, 452
Boniface III, pope, 446
Book of Common Prayer, 552–553
Book of Revelation, 404
Book of the Donkey (Bursah Ahmet Pasa), 749
Book of the Sea (Piri Reis), 749
Book of Three Virtues, The (Pisan), 434
Book of Various Experiences (Polo), 570
Books. *See* Literature
Borgia (Bor'-zha), Cesare, 510
Borgia, Rodrigo (Pope Alexander VI), 536
Boroughs, 417, 418
Bosch, Jerome, 527–528
Boston Tea Party, 799(illus.), 800

Botany, Hellenistic, 164–165
Botany Bay, 1026, 1028
Bourbons: succession of, 583(chart); restoration of, 822, 864, 865
Bourbourg, abbey of, 377
Bourgeoisie (Bur-zhwa-zee'), 804, 875–876. *See also* Middle class
Boxer Rebellion, 987
Boyars, 634, 636
Brahe (Bray'-e), Tycho, 662–663
Brahma, 72, 73, 75
Brahmanism, 71
Brahmans, 69, 70, 71, 73
Brandenburg, 627, 628
Brandenburg-Prussia, 592, 627(map)
Brassey, Thomas, 844
Brazil, 486, 575, 735, 736–737; black slaves in, 596; gains independence from Portugal, 1000; economic nationalism in, 1205; under Goulart, 1207; elected government in, 1209; as "middle power," 1289
Brazza, Pierre de, 973
Bread: in 18th-century European diet, 710, 713; price of, in France, 806, 813
Breast-feeding: wet nursing and, 705–706, 707; sexual division of labor and, 859; in 19th-century European cities, 919; versus powdered milk formula, in Third World, 1303
Brest-Litovsk, Treaty of, 1039, 1139
Brethren of the Common Life, 536–537
Brezhnev, Leonid, 1187, 1190–1194
Brezhnev Doctrine, 1192, 1196
Briand, Aristide, 1120, 1121
Bridge building, development of, 579
Bright, John, 885
Britain. *See* Battle of Britain; England; Great Britain
British Broadcasting Corporation (BBC), 1117
British Commonwealth of Nations, 1026, 1182, 1223
British East India Company, 760, 761; rise of, 761–762; American Revolution and, 800; British imperialism and, 982
British Isles, 407
British North America Act, 1024
Broadcasting networks, 1117
Bronze, 90, 92, 94(illus.), 107–108
Bronze Age, 30, 118, 120
Brothels, in late Middle Ages, 450
Brothers Karamazov, The (Dostoevsky), 921
Brunel, Isambard Kingdom, 844
Brunelleschi (Bru-nel-les'-ke), Filippo, 516
Bruni, Leonardo, 514

Brünig, Heinrich, 1150, 1153
Bubonic plague (Black Death), 437–441, 437(map), 444, 448, 453, 696–697; population losses caused by, 509, 568, 571, 580
Buddha, 76–78, 77(illus.), 83, 311, 325, 326
Buddhism, 73, 76–78, 81, 83–84, 1306, 1309; in India, 298, 307; in Cambodia, 306; Islam and, 309; in China, 309, 310–311, 319; in Japan, 323–326, 784; rosary and, 383
Bulgaria: in Balkan Wars, 1042; in World War I, 1047, 1060; 1919 peace treaty and, 1064; in World War II, 1159; cold war and, 1172; collectivization in, 1188
Bureaucracy: in Mauryan Empire, 80; in ancient China, 91, 102, 110; in Hellenistic Greece, 152; imperial, in Roman Empire, 207, 209, 346; under T'ang Dynasty, 313; in early Japan, 324; papal, 361, 362; royal, in medieval France, 407–408; Exchequer as, 411; financial, of Sicily, 411; during Reformation, 552, 554; absolutism and, 609, 610, 611; Spanish, 619; under Frederick William I, 631; under Peter the Great, 638; Chinese, 776, 777, 778, 781; Japanese, 786; Napoleon I and, 817; under Hitler, 1151; Soviet, 1195
Burghers, 418, 420, 540
Burgundians, 246, 247, 249
Burgundy, 335, 396
Burke, Edmund, 810
Burmans, 306
Bursah Ahmet Pasa, 749
Bury Saint Edmunds, Abbey of, 395
Busbecq (Buz-beck), Ogier Gheselin de, 570
Bushido, 327–328, 784, 786
Buyids, 277
Byron, George Gordon, 878, 881
Byzantine, defined, 258
Byzantine Empire: as buffer between Europe and East, 230; compared with Germanic West, 252–254; external threats to, 254; internal conflicts in, 255–256; law code of Justinian and, 256–257; intellectual life in, 257–258; private life in, 258–259; and spread of Islam, 270–271

Cabinet system, 647, 649
Cabot, John, 568
Cabral, Pedro Alvarez, 567, 759
Caesar, Julius, Roman emperor, 188, 191–192, 196, 199
Calcutta, 760

Calendar, Maya, 490
Caligula (Kuh-lig'-u-lah), Roman emperor, 207
Caliphate, 273–277
Calvin, John, 541, 545; ideas of, 546–547, 582, 649; condemns Copernicus, 662
Calvinism, 545–547; in 16th-century France, 582–583; revolt of Netherlands and, 585; Thirty Years' War and, 589, 591, 592; status of women and, 594; in 17th-century England, 644
Cambodia, 306, 1229, 1290
Cambrai, League of, 512
Cambridge, University of, 428
Cambyses (Kam-buy'-seez), 58
Camel: African trade and, 466
Campania, 174, 176
Camus, Albert, 1109
Canaanites, 43, 44
Canada: French expansion into, 568; industrialization of, 847; under British control, 962, 983, 1023–1024; union of Upper and Lower, 1024; Dominion of, 1024; age of confederation (1840–1905) in, 1024–1026; growth, development, and national maturity of, 1026
Cannae, Battle of, 181
Cannibalism, in Aztec society, 494
Cannon, 571, 745
Canon law, 231, 361
Canossa (Kan-no-sah), 360
Canterbury Cathedral, 414
Canterbury Tales (Chaucer), 432, 433–434, 535
Canute, king of Denmark, 353, 405
Cape of Slaves, 478
Capet, Hugh, 347, 353Capetians, 353
Capital (Marx), 953
Capitalism: in Muslim society, 288; medieval, 424; Protestantism and, 668; putting-out system and, 699; socialist critique of, 874; New Deal and, 1127
Capitoline Hill, 174
Capitulations, 750–751; abolition of, 1080
Caracalla (Car-ah-cal'-ah), Roman emperor, 212
Caraffa, cardinal. See Paul IV, pope
Caravel, 571
Cárdenas, Lazaro, 1205, 1206
Caritat, Marie-Jean. See Condorcet, marquis de
Carlsbad Decrees, 868
Carnegie, Andrew, 1019
Carolingian Empire, 490; government of, 339–340; communication in, through Latin, 344; division and dis

integration of, 346–347, 347(map), 348, 351, 355
Carolingian minuscule, 343
Carolingian Renaissance, 343–344
Carter, Jimmy, 1203, 1205, 1232
Cartesian dualism, 668
Carthage: founding of, 42; conflict with Rome, 181
Cartier, Jacques, 568
Cassian, John, 242
Cassiodorus (Kah'-see-o-door'-us), 242, 244
Caste system, 70–71, 75, 78, 298, 302, 303
Castiglione, Baldassare, 519
Castilla, Ramón, 1001
Castle, The (Kafka), 1113
Castlereagh, Robert Stewart, 867, 871, 883
Castro, Fidel, 1191, 1206–1207
Cateau-Cambrésis, Treaty of, 579–580
Cathars, 435
Cathedrals, 232, 355, 417, 423, 437; schools attached to, 426; Gothic, in medieval towns, 429–432
Catherine II (the Great), empress of Russia, 639, 642, 677, 681–682, 687, 688, 801, 1134
Catherine of Aragon, 550, 553
Catholic, defined, 233–234
Catholic Center party, 946
Catholic church. See Roman Catholic church
Catholic League, 589, 591
Catholic Reformation, 553, 602, 718
Cato, Marcus, 184, 186
Cato the Elder, 183, 204
Causes of Plants (Theophrastus), 165
Cavaignac (Ka-ven-yak), Louis, 890, 930
Cave paintings, 7(illus.), 8–9
Cavour, Camillo Benso di, 934–936, 1145
Ceauşescu, Nicolae, 1199
Celebi, Abi Ahmet, 749
Celibacy, clerical, 357–358, 535
Cellini, Benvenuto, 513
Celts, sack Rome, 175
Censors (Roman), 177
Center party (Germany), 1151
Central America, 486, 567, 1209; Maya of, 488–490, 489(map); Spanish expansion into, 574
Central Powers, 1047, 1048, 1053, 1054
Centuries (Roman), 176
Cereta, Laura, 521–522
Cervantes, Miguel de, 621
Ceylon (Sri Lanka), 1227, 1258
Cézanne, Paul, 1115
Chadwick, Edwin, 853, 901

Chamberlain, Neville, 1157, 1158
Chamber of Accounts, 411
Chamorro, Violetta, 1209
Champlain, Samuel de, 1023
Chandragupta (Chun'-dra-gup-tah), king of India, 80–81
Chandragupta II, 299
Chang Heng (Chang' Huhng'), 104–105
Ch'an sect, 310
Chao K'uang-yin (Jow' Kwang-yin), 314
Chao Kuo (Jow' Kwo'), 106
Chaplin, Charlie, 1117
Chariot racing, Roman, 211–212
Charlemagne (Charles the Great), 334, 337(illus.), 346, 355; empire of, 336–341, 338(map), 350; territorial expansion under, 337–339; government of empire under, 339–340; imperial coronation of, 340–341; Carolingian Renaissance and, 343–344; empire collapses, 346–347; successor to, 353
Charles I, king of England, 644, 645
Charles II, king of England, 647
Charles II, king of Spain, 618, 621
Charles III, king of Spain, 993
Charles V, Holy Roman emperor, 512, 517, 518, 580; rise of Habsburg dynasty and, 533–535; Luther and, 538; Titian and, 543(illus.); Habsburg-Valois Wars and, 545; black slaves and, 574, 596; Netherlands under, 584–587; abdication of, 585, 589
Charles V, king of Spain, 567–568
Charles VI, Holy Roman emperor, 680
Charles VI, king of France, 445
Charles VII, king of France, 445, 529
Charles VIII, king of France, 512
Charles IX, king of France, 582, 583
Charles X, king of France, 886
Charles XII, king of Sweden, 638
Charles the Bald, 347
Charles the Bold, 529
Charles the Simple, 352
Charpentier, Marc-Antoine, 616
Chartist movement, 857, 884–885
Chaucer, Geoffrey, 432, 433
Chaumont, Treaty of, 822
Checks and balances, framework of, 802
Cheka, 1060
Chekhov, Anton, 702
Chemistry, 922
Ch'eng-Chu, school of, 319
Cheng Ho, 773
Chernobyl nuclear-reactor accident, 1195
Chesnut, Mary Boykin, 1012–1013

Chess, game of, 289

Ch'i, 319

Chiang Kai-shek (Chee-ang' Ki'-shek), 1092

Chicago school of architects, 1113

Chichimec, 492

Chien Wen, 773

Child, Josiah, 832

Child abuse, 707

Childbirth: in Hebrew society, 47; in Byzantine Empire, 259; in Indian society, 304–305; in medieval Europe, 383, 386–387; among black American slaves, 1018; in Third World, 1258

Child labor, 839, 855–856

Child-marriage, 303–304

Child rearing: in 18th century, 704–706; in 19th century, 858–859, 918, 919–921. *See also* Breast-feeding; Children; Family

Children: in Paleolithic Age, 8; Hammurabi's code and, 25; in Hebrew society, 47–48; in Greek polis, 126; infanticide and, 126, 387, 523, 706–707, 781; in Roman Republic, 184; in Islamic society, 282; in Indian society, 303, 304; infant mortality and, 337, 387, 704, 902–903; in feudal society, 348; in medieval Europe, 382, 387–390, 392, 448; abandonment of, 387–388, 919; in Aztec society, 495; in Renaissance society, 523; Rousseau's views on education of, 676–677; employment of, 701–702; illegitimate, 703–704, 915; 18th-century attitudes toward, 707–708; child labor and, 839, 855–856; 19th-century attitudes toward, 918; foundlings and, 919; of American black slaves, 1018; organized during World War I, 1050; in Third World, 1260. *See also* Family

Children of Israel, 42–43. *See also* Hebrews; Jews

Chile, 486, 996; economic nationalism in, 1205; under Allende, 1207–1208; elected government in, 1209

China, 4, 88–110; origins of agriculture in, 10; Buddhism and, 84; geography of, 88, 89(map); under Shang Dynasty, 89–91; under Chou Dynasty, 92–94; philosophies of, 94–99; under Ch'in Dynasty, 99–102; under Han Dynasty, 101(map), 102–110, 768; historical periods of, 109(table), 316(table); golden age of, 309–322; Buddhism and, 310–311; under T'ang Dynasty, 311–314, 316–318, 319; Mongol conquest of, 310, 319–322; under

Sung Dynasty, 314–316, 319; influence on Japan, 322, 323, 324, 326; family structure in, 380; colonization of, 565; European overseas expansion and, 578–579; British East India Company and, 760; agricultural and commercial revolutions, under Ming Dynasty, 768–770; land reclamation in, 769, 770(table); population of, 769–770, 776, 777–778, 779(table); government of Hung Wu in, 770–773; maritime expansion in, 773; decline of Ming Dynasty in, 774–777; Manchu rule in, 777–779; daily life in, 779–782; "opening" of, 964–966; responses to imperialism in, 981, 985–988; revolution in, 985–988; at war with Japan, 985, 986, 1099(map), 1100, 1159, 1214; nationalism in, 1090–1092; intellectual revolution in, 1092–1093; changing family in, 1093–1095; Communist victory in, 1214–1215; under Mao, 1214, 1215–1219; Cultural Revolution in, 1216, 1217; reconciliation with United States, 1217; under Deng Xiaoping, 1217–1219, 1264; U.N. Security Council and, 1285; as regional power, 1290; nuclear arms race and, 1292; state-run birth control in, 1294. *See also* People's Republic of China

Chinampas (floating gardens), 487

Ch'in (Kin') Dynasty: and unification of China, 99–100

Chinese Exclusion Act of 1882, 1021

Chinese writing, 91

Ching Chi, 104

Ch'ing Dynasty: Manchu rule under, 777–779; daily life under, 779–782; educational system of, 781

Ch'in Shih Huang Ti. *See* First Emperor

Chittick, Neville, 476

Chivalry, 386, 784

Chopin (Sho'-pan), Frédéric, 880

Chou (Jo') Dynasty, 92–94, 99

Christ. *See* Jesus of Nazareth

Christian IV, king of Denmark, 591

Christian church. *See* Christianity; Roman Catholic church

Christian Democratic party, 1178

Christian Democratic party (Italy), 1176

Christian Democratic party (West Germany), 1176

"Christian existentialists," 1109

Christianity, 45, 46, 186, 196, 211, 220; Hellenism paves the way for, 148, 152, 159; rise of, in Roman Empire, 202–207; opposition to,

221–224; legalization of, by Constantine, 224, 230, 231, 232, 241; making of European civilization and, 230; in Roman Empire, 231–232, 234(map); conversion and assimilation of pagans and, 236–238; penitential system and, 237–238; classical culture and, 238–241; St. Augustine's impact on, 239–241; monasticism and, 241–244; separation of Byzantine East and Germanic West and, 253–254; attitude toward Islam, 273; Muslim bitterness toward, 292; medicine and, in early Middle Ages, 346; slavery and, 375–376, 596–597; rituals of, in High Middle Ages, 383; oblation and, 388; Babylonian Captivity and, 446–447, 535; Great Schism and, 447, 535; conciliar movement and, 447–448; Coptic (Egyptian) form of, in Ethiopia, 478, 480, 732; humanism and, 514, 524, 535; in Spain, 532; Protestant Reformation and, 539; Catholic and Counter-Reformations and, 553–557; European overseas expansion and, 567, 569, 578–579; hostility toward, 660; in 17th-century Japan, 786; "new imperialism" and, 979; revival in 20th century, 1109–1110, 1306–1307. *See also* Churches; Protestantism; Protestant Reformation; Roman Catholic church

Christine de Pisan, 434

Chu Hsi (Joo' Shee'), 319

Church courts, 231

Churches: split between Western and Eastern, during Crusades, 366; as center of medieval life, 382–383; parish, in 18th century, 717; in 19th-century European cities, 913–914. *See also* Cathedrals; Clergy; Greek Orthodox church; Papacy; Priesthood; Protestantism; Roman Catholic church

Church of England, 553; under Elizabeth I, 587; 17th-century dissatisfaction with, 644; in 18th century, 721

Church General, 207

Churchill, Winston, 977, 1090, 1158; at Teheran conference, 1171; at Yalta, 1188

Church law. *See* Canon law

Church-state relations, in Middle Ages, 231, 232, 336. *See also* Lay investiture

Cicero, 188, 191, 240, 514, 526

Ciompi revolts, 456, 509

Circumcision, 48

Cistercians (Sis-ter-shuns), 355, 356–357, 393, 396

Cîteaux, monastery of, 356–357
Cities: Mesopotamian, 15; Sumerian, 15–16; Libyan, in Nile Delta, 41; Phoenician, 42; in ancient Israel, 47, 48–49; Persian, 52–53; Indian, 65, 66–67, 69, 79, 302; in ancient China, 92, 93, 106–107; in Hellenic Greece, 122; in Hellenistic Greece, 151–152, 153(illus.); Roman, 175, 209(illus.), 212; in Muslim society, 288–289; medieval, 420–421; in early Africa, 468; of the Aztecs, 497–498; baroque, 640, 641; Chinese, 770; in Great Britain, 898–901, 899(map); American, immigration and, 1020; Soviet, growth of, 1194; in South Africa, 1247–1248; Third World, growth of, 1266–1268; migration to, 1267, 1272–1273; overcrowding in, 1268. See also Towns
Citizenship: Athenian, 127; Roman, 176, 179, 188, 190
City of God (St. Augustine), 241, 253, 337
City of Ladies, The (Pisan), 434
City-states: Greek, 116, 121–122, 151; Roman, 189, 191; East African, 475–478; Italian, 510–512, 511(map), 933; Swahili, 732–734. See also Polis
Civil Code of 1804 (France), 817
Civilization, 5–6, 14
Civil law, 178, 257
Civil Rights Act of 1964, 1200–1201
Civil rights movement, 1200–1201
Civil service (China), 93, 95, 313; examinations for, 772, 774, 778, 781–782
Civil War, American, 1015–1016
Civil war, English, 645
Civil war, in Roman Empire, 203, 217
Civil War, Spanish, 1116, 1157
Civitus sine suffragio, 176
Classical Period, 123, 128–143. See also Greece, Hellenic period of
Classicism, 615–617, 877, 879
Classic period of Mesoamerican civilization, 488, 490, 491
Class (social) structure: 19th-century, urban, 906–914; changing, modern, 1182–1184
Claudius, Roman emperor, 207, 251
Clay, Henry, 992
Clay tablets, 20, 21(illus.)
Cleisthenes (Klys'-thuh-neez), 127
Clemenceau (Kle-man-so'), Georges, 1053, 1063–1064
Clement V, pope, 446
Clement VII, pope, 447, 550, 554
Clement XIV, pope, 718
Cleopatra, 192, 202

Clergy, medieval: heresy and, 434; during bubonic plague, 440; in 16th-century Europe, 535–538, 550; Concordat of Bologna and, 582; French, 803, 805, 806, 818. See also Priesthood; Papacy
Climate: of Italy, 172; Northumbrian, 342–343; of medieval Europe, 355
Clive, Robert, 761
"Clothier's Delight, or the Rich Men's Joy and the Poor Men's Sorrow, The," 836
Clothing: in ancient China, 106–107; in medieval Europe, 250(illus.); in kingdom of Mali, 473; Aztec, 497; Inca, 503(illus.); industrial innovations and, 838; 19th-century, 912
Clovis, 235, 247, 249, 334
Cluny, abbey of, 355, 377, 395, 397–398
Coal and Steel Community, 1178
Coal industry, 840, 943
Cobb, Freeman, 1031
Cobden, Richard, 885, 978
Cockerill, William, 850; John, 850, 852
Cocoa-beans, in Gold Coast, 1236, 1238
Code, Justinian, 230, 256–257, 416, 426, 428, 529
Codes of conduct: Bushido, 327–328, 784, 786; chivalric, 386
Coenobitic monasticism, 242
Coercive Acts, 800
Coffee, Brazilian production of, 1002
Coinage, 79, 99–100, 155, 316
Coitus interruptus, 703
Coke, Edward, 594
Colbert, Jean-Baptiste, 614–615, 699, 761
Cold war, 1170–1174, 1187; origins of, 1170–1172; West versus East and, 1172–1174; détente versus, 1203; end of, 1254, 1293; Third World solidarity and, 1289; nuclear development during, 1291
Coleridge, Samuel Taylor, 878
Collectivization: in Russia, 1140–1142; in eastern European countries, 1188; in China, 1215
Colombia, 486, 1207
Colonization: of Mediterranean basin, 123(map), 124; Greek, 123–124, 123(map); Phoenician, 123(map); Seleucid, 154; Roman, 199, 200(map); Viking, 350–352, 351(map); Spanish, 993, 994(map), 995. See also Imperialism; Overseas expansion
Columbus, Christopher, 567, 573, 574, 596, 734

Combinations Act, 857
Comitatus (Germanic war band), 248
Comitia centuriata, 176
Comitia curiata, 176
Commentaries (Caesar), 192
Commerce: in Neolithic Age, 10; Babylonian, 19; in ancient Israel, 49; Hellenic, 119; Hellenistic, 155–156; Roman, disruption of, 221; in Byzantine Empire, 258–259; in Islamic state, 286–288; Indian, 301–302; during Crusades, 367; rise of towns and, 417–418; medieval commercial revolution and, 424–426; 17th-century Dutch, 649–653, 652(map); international, 961–964. See also Merchants; Trade
Committee of Public Safety, 813, 814, 815
Commodus, 217
Common Fund (U.N.), 1297
Common law, 413, 416
Common Market (European Economic Community), 1178, 1179(map), 1181, 1187, 1289; decolonization and, 1182
Common people (commoners): Sumerian, 18; Egyptian, 28; Chinese, 90; Inca, 502; Russian, 638; European, life of, 692–722; agricultural livelihood of, 692–695; population trends among, 692, 695–697; cottage industry and, 697–699; marriage and family patterns of, 699–704; child care among, 704–709; education of, 708–709; French, 804, 806; in 18th-century British society, 882–883. See also Peasantry
Commons. See House of Commons
Common Sense (Paine), 801
Commonwealth, 645
Commonwealth Immigration Restriction Act of 1901, 1032
Commonwealth of Australia Constitution Act of 1900, 1032
Communal living, in medieval Europe, 242
Commune. See Paris Commune
Communes: Italian, 509; in late 1960s, 1306
Communication(s): in Mesopotamia, 16; in Assyrian Empire, 51, 52; in Persian Empire, 60; in Han Empire, 108; in Hellenic Greece, 118; in Roman Republic, 174; between Roman and Chinese empires, 216; among Japanese islands, 322; within Carolingian Empire, 344, 346–347; in Inca empire, 502; revolution in, 1274–1275; electronic, 1310
Communism, 1074, 1137; containment policy toward, 1173, 1174,

1201–1202, 1203; victory in China, 1214–1215, 1216; mass, in Third World, 1273, 1274–1275; non-Marxian criticism of, 1304–1305

Communist Manifesto (Marx and Engels), 875–876, 953, 1056

Communist party (China), 1091, 1195, 1214–1215, 1219

Communist party (Cuba), 1206

Communist party (Czechoslovakia), 1192

Communist party (France), 1129, 1130

Communist party (Germany), 1062, 1122, 1150, 1151

Communist party (Hungary), 1198–1199

Communist party (Poland), 1197–1198

Communist party (Russia), 1075; under Khruschev, 1189–1190

Communist Third International, 1075, 1091

Company for Trade with the Indies, 610

Compass, magnetic, 316, 571

Complete Library of the Four Treasuries, The, 779

Comte, Auguste, 922–923, 924

Comunero Revolution, 997

Conciliar movement, 447–448

Concilium plebis, 176, 178

Concordat of Bologna, 581–582

Concordat of 1801, 818

"Concord of the orders," 191

Concubines, in Islamic society, 282

Condition of the Working Class in England (Engels), 853

Condorcet, marquis de (Marie-Jean Caritat), 676

Conferences (Cassian), 242

Confessions, The (St. Augustine), 240

Confessors, 254

Confucianism, 94–96, 103–104, 309, 313, 319, 325, 777, 783

Confucius, 94–95

Congo, 740, 973; nationalism in, 1241

Congo Free State, 973

Congress of Berlin, 1038–1039, 1042

Congress of Troppau, 868

Congress of Vienna, 864, 865, 867–868, 933

Congress party (India), 1222, 1223, 1225

Congress system, European, 868

Conquistadors, Spanish, 568, 574

Conrad III, 409

Conservatism: Metternich and, 869; Tory party and, 883

Conservative party (Germany), 946

Conservative party (Great Britain), 950

Consistory, 546

Constable, John, 877(cap.), 878, 880

Constantine, 216, 221, 252, 253, 336; reconstruction under, 218, 220; builds Constantinople, 224; legalization of Christianity by, 224, 230, 231, 232, 241

Constantine V, 255

Constantine IX Palaeologus, 744

Constantinople, 224, 258, 571, 596; established, during Crusades, 365–366; Ottoman conquest of, 744–745

Constituent Assembly: French, 889, 890; Prussian, 894; Russian, 1059

Constitution: Roman, 187, 191; Japanese, 324; of United States, 643, 672, 801–802; French, 672, 886; Italian, 933; Sardinian, 936; of North German Confederation, 940; Russian, 945, 1054; Japanese, 985; Argentine, 1004; Canadian, 1024; Mexican, 1205; Cuban, 1206; Japanese, 1220; of India, 1223–1224

Constitution Act, 1023–1024

Constitutional Charter (France), 822, 871; Revolution of 1830 and, 886

Constitutional Convention, 801–802

Constitutionalism, 628(table), 643

Constitutions of Melfi (Frederick II), 411

Consuls, Roman, 176–177

Consumerism, 1184; reactions to, 1306

Consumer protection, in Mesopotamia, 23–24

Containment, policy of, 1173, 1174, 1201, 1203

Continental Congress: First, 800; Second, 801

Contraception. *See* Birth control

Convention People's party, 1240

Convents, in medieval Europe, 244, 388, 393–395

"Convergence school," 1305–1306

Conversations on the Plurality of Worlds (Fontenelle), 669

Conversos, 532–533

Converts, Muslim, 279

Cook, James, 1026–1028

Copernicus, Nicolaus, 142, 163, 661–662, 670

Coptic church, 478, 480, 732

Coral Sea, Battle of, 1163

Cordoba, 264, 288, 289

Corn Laws, 883, 885, 891, 962

Cornwallis, Charles, 762

Corpus juris civilis, 257

Corregidores, 575, 996, 997

Cort, Henry, 842

Cortés, Hernando, 491, 497–498, 568, 570, 571–572, 573, 574, 993

Cosmology, Aristotle's theory of, 141

Cossacks, 636, 637, 638

Costa Rica, 486, 1207

Cottage industry: growth of, 697–699; new patterns of marriage and illegitimacy and, 703; working conditions and, 854–855

Cotton industry, 836, 837–839, 962

Council of Blood, 586

Council of Constance, 538

Council of Europe, 1178

Council of Trent, 554–555

Counter-cyclical policy, 1126

Counterfeiting, 316

Counter-Reformation, 553, 668

Counts, feudalism and, 348

Couperin, François, 616

Courtesans: Athenian, 137; Japanese, 788. *See also* Prostitution

Courtier, The (Castiglione), 519, 522

Court of High Commission, 645

Court of Star Chamber, 531

Courts: church, 231, 361; papal, 361

Covenant, 45

Coventillos, 1005

Craft guilds, 419–420, 450

Craftsmen: in ancient Israel, 49; in ancient China, 93, 107–108; in Hellenic Greece, 118, 119, 135, 136. *See also* Artisans; Guilds

Cranmer, Thomas, 550, 552

Crassus, 191, 192

"Creation of the Pickax, The," 22

Crécy, 442

Credit: in medieval Europe, 316, 424; postwar changes in, 1184

Crédit Mobilier, 851–852, 874

Creoles, 992, 995, 996, 999, 1006

Crete, 118, 596

Crime: in Mesopotamia, 24; in ancient China, 107; in medieval Europe, 448, 452

Crimean War, 942

Critique of Political Economy (Marx), 953

Croesus (Lydian king), 56

Cromer, Lord, 968

Crompton, Samuel, 838

Cromwell, Oliver, 552, 646–647

Crop rotation, in medieval Europe, 377–378, 437

Crown of Saint Stephen, 890

Crusades, 258, 292, 293, 362, 364–367, 392, 565; routes of, 364(map); First, 364–365; Third, 365; Fourth, 365–366, 508; cultural impact of, 367; xenophobia and, 416

Crystal Palace, 844

Cuba, 567; Asian immigration to, 972; Russian nuclear warheads in, 1191. *See also* Cuban Revolution

Cuban Revolution, 1206–1207

Cubism, 1115

Cults, Greek, 139, 158, 159; Roman, 199, 204
Cultural Revolution, 1216, 1217
Culture, defined, 6
Cuneiform (Ku-nay-ih-form) writing, 19, 20, 34, 91
Curia, 361, 411
Curie, Marie, 1110
Currency, standardized, 316. *See also* Coinage; Paper money
Cushitic, 732
Customs union, German. *See* Zollverein
Cybele, cult of, 204
Cynics, 159–160; women as viewed by, 162
Cyprus, settlement of Turks in, 746–747
Cyrillic script, 256
Cyrus the Great, 55–56
Czechoslovakia: revolts against Habsburg king, 625; in Habsburg Empire, 869; Austrian revolution of 1848 and, 890; in Little Entente, 1119; treaties of Locarno and, 1121; Hitler's annexation of, 1158; cold war and, 1172; Stalin's seizure of, 1174; collectivization in, 1188; in Soviet bloc, 1192; communism dies in, 1199

Dadaism, 1116
"Daffodils" (Wordsworth), 878
Dahomey, 739, 740
Daigne, Blaise, 1237
Daimyos, 783, 784, 786, 787
d'Alembert, Jean le Rond, 674–675, 677
Dance of Death, 441, 528
Danes, 353
Dante Alighieri, 292, 432–433
Danton, Georges Jacques, 812
Darius (Dah-ry′-uhs), 58–59, 78
Dark Age of Greece, 120, 121
Dark Ages of India, 69
Dark Ages of medieval Europe, 513
Darwin, Charles, 6, 140, 923
Dating method, of Bede, 342
David (Michelangelo), 516
David of Bethlehem, 44
da Vinci, Leonardo, 515–516, 518, 581
Dawes, Charles G., 1120
Dawes Plan, 1120
Dead Sea Scrolls, 203
Death and the Miser (Bosch), 528
Death rate: among children in High Middle Ages, 382; demographic crisis and, 695–696; 18th-century decline in, 696–697. *See also* Infant mortality
Debt. *See* International debt crisis
Decameron, The (Boccaccio), 440, 515, 535

Deccan Plateau, 64
Decius, 241
Declaration of Independence, 801, 808, 1012
Declaration of the Rights of Man (France), 796, 808, 818
Declaration of the Rights of Man and the Citizen, 995
Decline of the West, The (Spengler), 1113
Decolonization: following World War II, 1181–1182; in Africa, 1241, 1246; Fanon's views on, 1275
Dede Korkut, 749
Defensor Pacis (Marsiglio of Padua), 447–448
Deffand, Madame du, 677–678
Defoe, Daniel, 707
De Gasperi, Alcide, 1176
de Gaulle, Charles, 1163, 1181, 1182; resignation of, 1176, 1185; returns to power, 1233; creates French commonwealth, 1241
Deism, 721
de Klerk, Frederick W., 1249
Delacroix (De-la-krwah), Eugène, 880, 881
Delcassé, Théophile, 1041
Delhi, 757
Delian League, 129, 131
Delos, 156(illus.)
Deme, 127
Demesne, 377
Demobilization, following World War II, 1172–1173
Democracy: defined, 122, 643; Athenian, 126, 127–128; Aztec, 495; liberalism and, 798, 872; Chartist movement and, 857; in France, 888–890; in Great Britain, 950; in Soviet Union, 1194, 1195–1196; authoritarianism and, in Latin America, 1207–1209; parliamentary, 1225, 1226, 1229, 1248; as secular ideology, 1305
Democracy in America (Tocqueville), 889
Democritus, 140, 160
Deng Xiaoping (Deng Chow-ping), 1217–1218
Denmark: Thirty Years' War and, 591; war over Schleswig-Holstein, 892–893; Hitler occupies, 1158
Dental care, in early Middle Ages, 345–346
Dependence, mutual, 1293. *See also* Global interdependence
Dependency, theory of, 1296
Depression of 1929. *See* Great Depression
Descartes, René (Day′-cart, Ray′-nay′), 667–668, 671

Descent of Man, The (Darwin), 6, 923(cap.)
Design, 20th-century, 1113–1114
Despots, Italian, 509–510
De-Stalinization, 1188–1190
Détente, 1203
De Veneys, Robert, 396
Devi, 81
Devil: medieval view of, 385; in medieval and early Renaissance art, 524; belief in witches and, 594–595
Dewey, John, 1092
Dharma, 73, 298
Dhimmis, 273, 280–281, 292
d'Holbach, Paul, 676
Diaghilev (Dyag′-yil-yef), Sergei, 1116
Dialogue on the Two Chief Systems of the World (Galileo), 664
Diana of Poitiers, 581
Diaz, Bartholomew, 567, 570
Díaz, Bernal, 497
Díaz, Porfirio, 1003, 1205
Dictatorship, 1134, 1136; under Mussolini, 1145, 1146; Stalin's move toward, 1187–1188. *See also* Absolutism; Authoritarianism; Totalitarianism
Diderot, Denis (Deed-ro′, Deh-nee′), 674–675, 676, 682, 714–715
Dido, 201
Dien Bien Phu, battle of, 1229
Diet (food), 709–713; in Paleolithic Age, 8; in ancient China, 105–106, 107; in Hellenic Greece, 135, 136; in Roman Republic, 184, 188(illus.); Muslim, 267; Northumbrian, 342; in early Middle Ages, 345; in High Middle Ages, 377–378, 381–382; in early Africa, 465, 476; Maya, 488–489; Aztec, 494, 497; Inca, 499, 500; nutrition and, 709–710; health and, 710–713; Senegambian, 727; Industrial Revolution and, 853; in 19th- century European cities, 908; German, following World War II, 1176; in Third World, 1256
Diet of Worms, 533, 538
Digest (Justinian), 257
Din-i-Ilahi, 755
Dioceses, 218, 232
Diocles, Gaius Appuleius, 212
Diocletian (Dy-uh-klee′-shun), 216, 232, 241, 254, 319; reconstruction under, 218, 220
Diogenes (Dy-ah′-juh-neez) of Sinope, 159–160
Diplomacy: Roman, 176, 177; Italian, during Renaissance, 510
Directory (France), 816, 817
Discourses on the Ten Books of Titus Livy (Machiavelli), 520
Disease: in Middle Ages, 342–343, 344–346, 355; in 16th-century Mex-

ico and Peru, 574; Thirty Years' War and, 592; demographic crisis and, 695–696; in 19th-century European cities, 901–903. *See also* Medicine

Disraeli, Benjamin, 950, 978

Divine Comedy (Dante), 292, 432–433

Divine right, 608, 644

Division of labor, sexual, 857–860, 916

Divorce: in Hebrew society, 47; in Periclean Athens, 138; in Roman Republic, 184; German custom of, 336; in late Middle Ages, 450; in Ming and Ch'ing China, 781; in Stalinist Russia, 1144; abolished, in Mussolini's Italy, 1147

Diwan (Dih-vahn'), 276, 411, 468, 749, 754

Diwan al-kharaj, 276

Djilas, Milovan, 1304, 1305

Doctors. *See* Medicine; Physicians; Surgeons

Doctor Zhivago (Pasternak), 1190

Dogmatic school of medicine, 166

Domesday Book, 406(cap.), 407, 785

Domestication, 10, 487

Domestic service, 702

Dominicans, 393, 452, 574

Dominion of Canada, 1024–1026

Domitian (Doe-me-she-un), 207

Donatello, 516

Donatism, 240

Donatus, 240

Don Quixote (Cervantes), 621

Dooms of Ethelbert, 248

Dorians, 119

Dostoevsky (Das-ta-yef'-ski), Feodor, 921

Doubting, systematic, 428

Draco, 127

Drama: medieval, 383, 432; French, 617; Japanese, 788

Dravidians, 66

Dress. *See* Clothing

Dreyfus, Alfred, 949

Dreyfus affair, 949–950

Drinking: in medieval manor, 380; among 18th-century aristocracy, 710; in 19th-century cities, 912

Droz, Gustave, 919

Drugs, prescription of, 713–714; world trade in, 1298(map)

Dual monarchy, 951

Dual revolution, 864, 868, 876, 984

Dubček (Doob-check), Alexander, 1192

Du Bois, W. E. B., 1237

Duma, 945, 1054

Dumas, Alexandre, 879

Dupin, Amadine Aurore Lucie. *See* Sand, George

du Prat, Antoine, 535

Durham, Lord, 1024

Dutch. *See* Holland; Netherlands

Dutch East India Company, 568, 577, 651–652, 759, 761, 837

Dutch West India Company, 568, 596, 652

"Dwarf economy," 970

Dyer, Reginald, 1086

Dynastic cycle, 104

Dzhugashvili (Ju-gosh'-vyel-yi), Joseph. *See* Stalin, Joseph

East Africa, 1241

East Asia, 1090–1102, 1095(table), 1214–1222. *See also* China; Japan

Eastern Orthodox church: conversion of Vikings and Slavs to, 633. *See also* Greek Orthodox church; Russian Orthodox church

Easter Rebellion, 1053

East Frankland, 335

East Germany, 1191, 1192, 1199

East Indies, 1100. *See also* Southeast Asia

Eating habits, in Roman Republic, 187. *See also* Diet

Ebla tablets, 18

Ecclesiastical History of England and Normandy (Orderic Vitalis), 392

Ecclesiastical History of the English Nation (Bede), 342

Ecclesiastical reform. *See* Religious reforms

Eck, John, 538

Economic Consequences of the Peace (Keynes), 1118

Economic nationalism, in Latin America, 1205–1206

Economics: modern, founding of, 872; Keynesian, 1126, 1177. *See also* Economy, theories of

Economy: Mycenaean, 119; Hellenic, 119, 137; Athenian, 137; Hellenistic, 155–158; Roman, 188; Muslim, 288; in High Middle Ages, 376, 397–398; of medieval monasteries, 397–398; effect of plague on, 440–441; Hundred Years' War and, 444; medieval marriage and, 450; Florentine, during Italian Renaissance, 508–509; mining in New World and, 575; in 16th-century Spain, 575; German, after Thirty Years' War, 592; under Louis XIV, 617; decline of absolutist Spain and, 619, 621; eastern European absolutism and, 622; Dutch, 649–653; French, War of the Austrian succession and, 684; revolt of French peasantry and, 806–807; French, after fall of Bastille, 809; French Revolution and, 813–814, 815; British, Industrial Revolution and, 828–829,

845; of Atlantic Basin, 834(map); after French Revolution, 847; free, 871, 872; theories of, 871–872, 874–876; British, in 19th century, 872; French, Napoleon III, and, 930, 931; unification of Germany and, 936–937; industrialization and, in Russia, 943; European, growth of international trade and, 963; "dwarf," 970; "new imperialism" and, 977–978; international, imperialism and, 982; Japanese, 985, 1095; Spanish, in 18th century, 993; Latin American, 1001, 1002, 1021; of total war, 1050–1051; German, following World War I, 1118, 1119, 1120; Great Depression and, 1125–1126; Russian, Lenin's New Economic Policy and, 1139; rise of Hitler and, 1150; in Nazi Germany, 1151; post–World War II, in Europe, 1174, 1177; free-market, in Germany, 1177; recovery in western Europe, 1177–1178; Europe's political recovery and, 1178, 1179; oil and, 1185–1186; postwar, in United States, 1200; Latin American, economic nationalism and, 1205–1206; Chinese, under Deng Xiaoping, 1219; Japan's emergence as economic superpower and, 1220–1222; rapid industrialization and, in Asia, 1262; bazaar, 1272; "new international economic order" and, 1296–1297, 1299. *See also* Commerce; Inflation; Trade

Ecuador, 486, 1209

Edict of Nantes, 584, 610; revocation of, 615, 647

Edict of Restitution, 591

Edict of Worms, 538, 545

Edict on Idle Institutions, 718

Edo, 785, 786, 790. *See also* Tokyo

Education, 708–709; Sumerian, 20–21; Hebrew, 48; Hellenistic, 161; Roman, 184, 186; Christianity and, 239; in medieval Europe, 240, 382, 389, 397, 426; Byzantine, 257; Indian, 303; T'ang, 313; during Carolingian Renaissance, 343; medieval universities and, 426, 428–429; in early Timbuktu, 474; during Renaissance, 519, 521–522, 526; of priests, 535; Catholic Reformation and, 555–556; of Louis XIV, 612; under Peter the Great, 638; Rousseau's views on, 676–677; in Ming and Ch'ing China, 781; 19th-century, 908, 909–910; French, 948–949; British system of, in India, 982; in Stalinist Russia, 1143–1144, 1145; European, postwar expansion of,

Education *(cont.)*
1185; in Soviet Union, 1194; in Mao's China, 1215; in Third World, 1268; mass communications and, 1274–1275

Education of a Christian Prince, The (Erasmus), 526

Edward I, king of England, 394, 395, 416, 446

Edward III, king of England, 441–442, 445, 509

Edward IV, king of England, 530

Edward VI, king of England, 552

Edward the Black Prince (duke of Aquitaine), 442, 444

Edward the Confessor, 353, 405

Egalitarianism, of Buddhism, 310

Ego, 1111

Egypt, 4; irrigation in, 11; geography of, 25–26; in antiquity, 25–32; pharaohs and Old Kingdom of, 26–28; people of, 28–29; First and Second Intermediate Periods of, 29; Hyksos in, 28, 29–30, 32; New Kingdom of, 30–32; Eighteenth Dynasty of, 30–32, 43; historical periods of, 31(table); Akhenaten and monotheism in, 31–32; Hittites in, 32–36; fall of empire in, 35–36; decline of, 40–41; Third Intermediate Period of, 41; reunification of, 41; under Ptolemies, 154; spread of Islam and, 270; slavery in, 467; Nubia and, 478; in Ottoman empire, 746, 966; British occupation of, 967–968, 973, 978, 1082; in World War II, 1164; nationalist revolution in, 1232; invaded by British, French, and Israelis, 1232; under Nasser, 1232; as regional power, 1290

Egyptian Nationalist party, 967

Eightfold Path, 76–77, 78, 310

Einhard, 337–338, 339, 340–341

Einstein, Albert, 1110

Eiseley, Loren, 7

Eisenhower, Dwight, 1165, 1200, 1202

Eisenstein, Sergei, 1117, 1188

Ekkehard of Aura, 391

El Alamein, 1164

Eleanor, queen of England, 394

Electricity, 922

Electric streetcar, 903, 905–906, 922

Electromagnetism, 922

Electrostatics, first Western experiments in, 579

Elements of Geometry, The (Euclid), 163

Eleusinian mysteries, 206

Elgin, Lord, 1024

Elimination of Poverty, The (Napoleon III), 930

Eliot, George, 925

Eliot, T. S., 1110, 1113

Elite: Maya, 489; Teotihuacán, 491; during Renaissance, 518; Creole, 995; urban, in Third World, 1271–1272. *See also* Aristocracy; Nobility

Elizabeth, empress of Russia, 642, 681

Elizabeth I, queen of England, 553, 587, 589, 593, 599, 643, 748, 759

Elizabethan literature, 599–600

"Elizabethan Settlement" laws, 553

El Salvador, 486

Emancipation Proclamation, 1013, 1015

Emancipists, 1029

Emigration. *See* Migrations

Émile (Rousseau), 676

Emirs, 275–276

Empires. *See* Colonization; Imperialism; Overseas expansion; *individual empires*

Empiricism, 667

Empiric school of medicine, 166

Enabling Act, 1151

Enclosure movement, 831–832

Encomiendas, 573

Encyclopedia, first appearance of, 319

Encyclopedia: The Rational Dictionary of the Sciences, the Arts, and the Crafts (Diderot and d'Alembert), 674–675, 677, 682, 714–715

Energy: requirements for and sources of, 839–840; English Industrial Revolution and, 839–840; steam as source of, 840–842

Energy crisis, 1185–1186

Engels, Friedrich, 853, 875, 876

England: as Roman province, 210(map), 251; conversion to Christianity, 235; Bede's history of, 251; Anglo-Saxon, 251–252, 251(map), 353, 405; Norman invasion of, 353; family structure in, 380; medieval nobility in, 386, 391; custom of knighting in, 389; Cistercians in, 396; development of modern state in, 404, 405–407; unification following Viking invasions, 405; division into shires, 405; medieval finances in, 409, 411; medieval law in, 413–416; Magna Carta signed by, 414–415; wool trade of, 424, 439, 508, 531, 587, 835; bubonic plague in, 440; Hundred Years' War and, 441, 443(map), 444–446; economic crisis of late Middle Ages in, 444; Great Schism and, 447; "fur-collar crime" in, 452; Peasants' Revolt in, 452–453, 455; monarchy of, during Renaissance, 528, 529–530; Wars of the Roses and, 530, 531; Puritan church in, 547; Protestant Reformation in, 549–553; under Elizabeth I,

553, 587, 589, 593, 599, 643, 748, 759; overseas expansion of, 568; defeats Spanish Armada, 588–589; witch-hunting in, 595; slave trade and, 596, 734, 737; Elizabethan and Jacobean literature in, 599–600; under James I, 599, 601, 643–644, 645; War of the Spanish Succession and, 618; constitutional monarchy and cabinet government in, 630, 648–649; decline of royal absolutism in, 643–645; under Charles I, 644, 645; "Long Parliament" and, 645, 646; puritanical absolutism in, 645–647; restoration of monarchy in, 647–648; "Glorious Revolution" in, 648; religious conflicts in, after 1630, 668; cottage industry in, 697–699, 854–855; diet in, during 18th century, 710; Seven Years' War and, 798; individual liberty in, 798; colonies of, 798–800, 801, 836, 837(map); Napoleon I attempts to restrict trade of, 819; war with France, 819; Industrial Revolution in, 828–839, 845(map); united with Scotland, forms Great Britain, 832; growth of foreign trade in, 832–833, 835–836; in competition with France for colonies, 835; trade in manufactured goods, 18th-century, 835–836, 836(fig.); textile industry during 18th century, 836–839; railroads in, 842–844; Continent uses industrial methods of, 847–849; new capital and labor classes in, 852–853; romantic movement in, 878–880; gains control of India, 982–983. *See also* Great Britain

English civil war, 645

English language, 432, 601

English revolution, 648

Enlightenment, 639, 648, 686(table); emergence of, 669–671; philosophes and, 671–675; later phase of, 676–677; social setting of, 677–679; development of absolutism and, 679; child care during, 708; education during, 709; developments in medicine during, 713; popular religion during, 717–721; liberalism and, 797; American Revolution and, 802, 1006

Enlil, 45

Ennius, 186

Entertainment. *See* Recreation

Environmental crisis, population growth and, 1294–1296

Epaminondas, 143

Ephors, 126

Epic of Gilgamesh, 22, 23(illus.)

Epicureans, 160

Epicurus, 160
Epistemology, 429
Equality: revolutionary period and, 796–797; liberalism and, 797; American Revolution and, 800; American Constitution and, 802
Era of the Five Dynasties, 314
Era of the Warring States, 92–93
Erasistratus, 166
Erasmus, Desiderius, 525–526, 584
Eratosthenes, 104–105, 163, 164
Erechtheion, 131, 132, 136
Erhard, Ludwig, 1177
Erlich, Paul, 1263
Eskimos, Caribou, 9
Essay Concerning Human Understanding (Locke), 671
"Essay on Liberty" (Mill), 950
Essay on the Principle of Population (Malthus), 845
Essays (Montaigne), 598–599
Essenes, 203
Estate agriculture, 623
Estates, 608; of Holy Roman Empire, 627–628, 629–630, 631; Dutch, 649; French, 803
Estates General, 610, 612, 740, 805, 806
Estonia, 638–639
Ethelbert, king of Kent, 235, 248
Ethiopia, 469; kingdom of, 478–480, 731–732
Ethiopians, 464, 476
Etruria, 175, 181
Etruscans, 174–175; origins of Roman senate and, 176 Eucharist, 205, 206
Euclid, 163
Eugene, prince of Savoy, 639
Eulogies of Scientists (Fontenelle), 670
Eunuchs, 109, 772, 774
Euphrates River, 13, 15, 16, 26
Euripides, 134, 186
Eurocentrism, 16, 486
Europe: origins of, in Middle East, 4–36, 255(table); civilization of, shaped by Hellenic Greece, 116; Roman expansion into, 199; making of, 230–260; in Middle Ages, 334–367, 363(table), 374–399, 404–456; Christianization of, 336, 344; 9th-century invasions of, 350–352; political revival in, 352–355; Crusades and, 362; economic revival in, 417–426; during Renaissance, 508–545; during Reformation, 545–558; age of expansion and religious wars in, 564–603; in 1648, 590(map); western, absolutism in, 608–621; in 1715, 620(map); eastern, absolutism in, 621–643; constitutionalism in, 643–653; Enlightenment in, 669–679; life of common

people in, 692–722; agriculture in 18th century, 692–695; population growth in 18th century, 695–697; growth of cottage industry in, 697–699; 18th-century family in, 699–708; diet in 18th century, 709–713; victory over Ottoman state, 750; trade with Asia, 761; revolutionary era of, 796–823; impact of American Revolution on, 802; Napoleonic era in, 817–823, 818(table), 820(map); Industrial Revolution in, 828–860; ideologies and upheavals during 1815–1850, 864–894; in 1815, 866(map); Congress of Vienna and, 865, 867–868; balance of power in, 867; during 1814–1848, 884(table); 19th-century urban life in, 898–921; triumph of science and thought in, 921–925; age of nationalism in, 930–956, 952(table); industrialization and world economy and, 961; expansion and imperialism and, 962; growth of international trade and, 962–968; 19th-century population of, 968, 969(fig.); 19th-century migrations from, 968–971, 970(fig.), 971(fig.), 1019; impact of American Civil War on, 1016; in World War I, 1045–1049, 1048(map); Russian Revolution in, 1054–1060; peace settlement and, 1060–1066; age of anxiety (1919–1939) in, 1106–1130; Great Depression in, 1123–1130; conservative authoritarianism in, 1134–1136; rise of totalitarianism in, 1136–1155; in World War II, 1155–1166, 1161(map); cold war and, 1170–1174; following World War II, 1174–1177, 1175(map); economic recovery in, 1177–1178; Common Market and, 1178, 1179(map), 1181; political recovery of, 1178, 1181; decolonization and, 1181–1182; changing class structure in, 1182–1184; rising standard of living in, 1183–1184; student revolts of 1960s in, 1185, 1306; recent economic decline in, 1185–1187; eastern, Soviet, 1187–1200, 1196(map); détente versus cold war in, 1203, 1205; multinational corporations in, 1302. *See also individual countries*
European Economic Community. *See* Common Market
Evangelicals, 721
Evans, Arthur, 118
Evans, Mary Ann. *See* Eliot, George
Evil, metaphysics of, 319
Evolution, theory of, 923–924
Evolutionary Socialism (Bernstein), 956

Ewuare, oba of Benin, 728
Exchequer, 409, 411, 552
Exclusionists, 1029
Excommunication, 359
Executions: medieval, 451–452; ritual, in Aztec society, 494–495
Existentialism, 1108–1109
Exorcism, 713
Expansion. *See* Colonization; Imperialism; Overseas expansion
Experimental method, 667
Expressionism, 1115, 1116

Fabius Pictor, 186
Factories: first, 836–839; child labor in, 839; early owners of, 852; American, 1020–1021
Factory Act of 1833, 856
Factory workers, 852–853, 944; in Third World, 1272. *See also* Working people
Faerie Queen, The (Spenser), 599
Fairbanks, Douglas, 1117
Faisal, king of Iraq, 1077
Faith healers, 713
Falkenstein, counts of, 389
Falkland Islands, 1209
Family, 699–708; in Paleolithic Age, 8; Hammurabi's code and, 25; in Hebrew society, 46–48; Confucius' view of, 95; in Byzantine Empire, 259; in Indian society, 302–303; in medieval Europe, 380, 389, 450; in early Africa, 465, 466; cottage industry and, 699; marriage and, in 18th-century Europe, 699–704; extended and nuclear, 700–701; in M'ing and Ch'ing China, 779–780; factory workers and, 855, 858; in 19th-century European cities, 914–921; reduction in size of, 920; black, impact of American slavery on, 1016–1019; in Hindu society, 1086; Chinese, 1093–1095; urban migration and, in Third World, 1272–1273. *See also* Marriage
Family planning. *See* Birth control
Famine: in 18th-century Europe, 695–696; Irish, 885, 886, 950; in Stalinist Russia, 1139, 1141
Fanon, Frantz, 1272, 1275, 1296
Faraday, Michael, 922
Farming. *See* Agriculture
Farnese, 586, 587–588
Farouk, king of Egypt, 1232
Fascism: French, following Great Depression, 1129; Italian, 1145–1146
Faulkner, William, 1112
Federal Republic of Germany. *See* West Germany
Felony, 390

Feminism, 917–918. *See also* Women's movement

Ferdinand I, emperor of Austria, 890, 891

Ferdinand I, king of Spain, 529, 531–533, 550, 567, 574, 585, 589, 868

Ferdinand II (of Styria), Holy Roman emperor, 591

Ferdinand III, Holy Roman emperor, 625

Ferdinand VII, king of Spain, 997

Ferry, Jules, 948, 973, 975

Fertile Crescent, 11(map), 18, 270

Feudalism, 334, 347, 352; two levels of, 347–348; manorialism and, 349–350; Norman, 411; in Japan, 783–784

Fifth Amendment, to U.S. Constitution, 802

Fifth Republic, 1185

Filipinos, 1100–1102

Films. *See* Motion pictures

Finance, medieval, 409, 411

Finland, 696, 867

"Fireside chats," 1117

First Citizen, 208

First Coalition, 812, 813, 814

First Continental Congress, 800

First Emperor, 99–102, 103

First International, 953–954

First Messenian War, 125

First Punic War, 181

First Triumvirate, 191, 192

First World War. *See* World War I

Fischer von Erlach, J. B., 639

Fisher, John, 551

Fishing industry, Dutch, 650–651

Five good emperors, era of, 207, 208–210

Five-year plans: in Stalinist Russia, 1140; reintroduction of, 1188; in Mao's China, 1215

Flagellants, 441

Flanders, 376, 377; long-distance trade and, 423–424; Hundred Years' War and, 441; invaded by Louis XIV, 617

Flaubert (Flow-bair), Gustave, 924–925

Flavians, 207, 209

Florence: during bubonic plague, 440, 441; ciompi revolts in, 456; during Renaissance, 508–509, 510–511, 515, 523

Fontainebleau chateau, 580–581

Fontenelle, Bernard de, 669–670, 672, 677

Food. *See* Diet

Food and Agriculture Organization, 1285

Foot binding, in China, 315, 778

Forbidden City, 774

Forced-labor camps, 1188

Forced-labor law, 1050

Ford, Gerald, 1203

Ford, Henry, 1021

Foreign investment, European, 963–964, 964(map)

Foreign trade, growth of, 832–836, 834(map)

Forests: use of in medieval Europe, 377; population growth and, 1294

Formosa, 985

Forum Romanum. *See* Roman Forum

Fossil remains, 6–7

Fouché, Joseph, 818

Foulon, Joseph François, 807

Foundlings, 523, 706–707

Fourier, Charles, 874, 875

Four Modernizations, 1218

Four Noble Truths, 76

Fourteen Points, 1062, 1074

Fourth Coalition, 822

Fourth Lateran Council, 413, 416

France: Roman expansion into, 199, 200(map); Muslim conquest of, 269; in Frankish kingdom, 334; Charlemagne's expansion into, 337; medieval and modern basis of, 347; Viking invasion of, 352; after civil wars and invasions of 9th and 10th centuries, 353; medieval family structure in, 380; medieval nobility in, 385–386, 391; custom of knighting in, 389; development of modern state in, 404, 407–408; under Philip II, 407, 408(map); medieval finances in, 411; medieval law in, 413; cathedrals in, 417, 430, 431(illus.); heresy in, 435; Hundred Years' War and, 441, 443(map), 444–446; papal court at Avignon and, 446; Great Schism and, 447; peasant revolt in, 452; invades Italy, 512; monarchy of, during Renaissance, 528, 529; recovery under Charles, autonomy of church in, 529; conflict with Habsburgs, 545; Huguenot church in, 547; opposition to reconciliation of Roman Catholicism and Lutheranism, 554; overseas expansion of, 568, 619; difficulties during 1515–1559, 580–581; Concordat of Bologna and, 581–582; Calvinism in, 582–583; religious riots and civil war in, 582–584; Edict of Nantes signed, 584; Thirty Years' War and, 589, 592; Richelieu and, 591, 592, 610–611, 615, 617; absolutism in, 609–619; under Louis XIV, 612–619; wars with Spain, 621; Enlightenment in, 669–679; philo-sophes of, 671–675, 676; in Seven Years' War, 684, 801, 835; growth of cottage industry in, 699; popular education in, 708; diet in, during 18th century, 710; Ottoman economic capitulations to, 751; liberalism in, 797, 798; individual liberty in, 798; supports American Revolution, 801; national debt of, 803; National Assembly of, 804–806, 808, 809–810; limited monarchy in, 808–810; war with Austria and Prussia, 811–812; First Republic of, 812; monarchy falls, second phase of revolution in, 812–813; Thermidorian reaction and Directory in, 815–816; Napoleon I's rule of, 817–818, 818(table); war with Britain, 819; Bourbon monarchy restored in, 822, 864, 865; War of the Spanish Succession and, 833; loss of holdings in North America and India, 835; competition with England for colonies, 835; Treaty of Paris and, 835; industrialization of, 846, 847(table), 851; tariffs imposed by, 851; Congress of Vienna and, 865, 867–868; Napoleon I reappears, exiled again, 867; utopian socialism in, 874–875; romantic movement in, 879–880; Revolution of 1830 in, 886–887; Second Republic of, 888–890, 931; under Napoleon III, 903, 930–933; 19th-century diet in, 908; in Franco-Prussian War of 1870–1871, 941, 1038; in Crimean War, 942; Paris Commune and, 948–950; Third Republic in, 948; Dreyfus affair in, 949–950; socialism in, 953, 954; foreign investments of, 963, 964; in Africa, 972–973, 1234, 1237; in Asia, 977; reasons for imperialism of, 977, 978; alliance with Russia, 1040(fig.), 1041; in Triple Entente, 1044; in World War I, 1045, 1046, 1060; Treaty of Versailles and, 1062–1064, 1118; Sykes-Picot Agreement and, 1077; German reparations and, 1119; mutual defense pact with Poland, 1119; disagrees with Britain over Germany, 1119; occupies Ruhr, 1119; treaties of Locarno and, 1120; during 1920s, 1122; following Great Depression, 1129–1130; policy of appeasement toward Germany, 1155, 1156; declares war on Germany, World War II begins, 1158; taken by Nazis, 1158; Vichy government of, 1158; Fourth Republic of, 1176; following World War II, 1177; Fifth Republic of,

1181, 1185; decolonization and, 1181–1182; student revolts in, 1185; U.N. Security Council and, 1285; re-emergence as regional power, 1290; nuclear arms race and, 1292. See also French Revolution; Gaul

Francesco di Bernardone, 436

Franche-Comté, 617

Franchise. See Suffrage

Francis I, king of France, 580–581, 748

Francis II, king of France, 582

Franciscans, 393, 452, 574, 578

Francis Ferdinand, archduke of Austria, 1042

Francis Joseph, emperor of Austria, 891, 892, 951, 1053

Franco, Francisco, 1157

Franco-Prussian War of 1870–1871, 941–942, 1038

Frankfurt Assembly, 892–893

Frankish kingdom, territories of, 334, 335, 339

Franks, 217–218, 256, 339, 341; rise of Carolingian dynasty and, 334–336

Frederick I, king of Prussia, 631, 679

Frederick II (Hohenstaufen), Holy Roman emperor, 362, 366–367, 411–412, 535

Frederick II (the Great), king of Prussia, 672–673, 682–683, 687, 688; as absolute monarch, 679–681; starts War of the Austrian Succession, 680, 685

Frederick III, Holy Roman emperor, 635

Frederick III (the Ostentatious), elector of Prussia. See Frederick I, king of Prussia

Frederick VII, king of Denmark, 893

Frederick Barbarossa, 346, 361, 365, 409, 412

Frederick William (Great Elector), 628–631

Frederick William I (Soldiers' King), king of Prussia, 631

Frederick William III, king of Prussia, 821

Frederick William IV, king of Prussia, 892, 894, 936, 937

Freedom, personal: in medieval towns, 376, 377, 418; in American colonies, 799. See also Liberties (freedoms)

Free French, 1163, 1176

Free-market economy, 1177

French and Indian Wars, 1023

French Canadians, 1023, 1026

French commonwealth, 1241

French East India Company, 761

French Guiana, 486

French language, 432, 521, 580, 613, 679, 739–740

French Revolution, 704, 802–810; breakdown of old order and, 803; legal orders and social realities and, 803–804; formation of National Assembly and, 804–806; revolt of poor and oppressed and, 806–808; limited monarchy and, 808–810; foreign reactions to, 810–811; second phase of, 812–813; Reign of Terror and, 814–815; Thermidorian reaction and Directory and, 815–816; historical periods of, 816(table); rise of Napoleon I and, 817; liberalism and, 871

French Section of the Workers International, 953

French-Spanish wars, 621

Freud, Sigmund, 921, 953, 1111–1112

Freudian psychology, 1110–1112, 1116

Friars, medieval, 436

Fronde, 611, 612

Fugger family, 538

Fujiwara family, 326

Fulani, 730

Functionalism, in architecture, 1113–1114

Fundamentalism: theological, 1306; Islamic, 1308

Fundamental Laws, 945

"Fur-collar crime," 452

Furness, abbey of, 396

"Gadget revolution," 1183–1184

Gaius, 189–190

Galan, José Antonio, 997

Galdan, 779

Galen, 713

Galileo Galilei, 664–665

Galla, 732

Gama, Vasco da, 567, 570, 732–733, 964

Gambetta, Léon, 948

Gandersheim, 289

Gandhi (Gahn'-dee), Indira, 1225–1226, 1295

Gandhi, Mahatma, 1086–1087, 1222–1223; militant nonviolence and, 1087–1088; resistance campaign of, 1088–1090

Gandhi, Rajiv, 1227

Ganges River, 64, 65, 69

Gangrene, treatment for, 345

Gao, 468

Gapon, Father, 945

Gargantua (Rabelais), 526

Garibaldi, Giuseppe, 935(illus.), 936, 1145

Garvey, Marcus, 1239

Gaul: sacks Rome, 175; under Rome, 179, 192; under Postumus, 217

Gautama, Siddhartha. See Buddha

Geishas, 788

Gelasius I, pope, 252–253

General Assembly (U.N.), 1285–1286, 1296

General History of the Indies (Oviedo), 570

General will, concept of, 677

Geneva, Calvinism in, 546–547

Geneva accords, 1202

Genevan Catechism (Calvin), 546

Genius, Renaissance artist as, 518

Genoa, 508, 596

Geoffrey de Monigney, 376–377

Geoffrey of Lorraine, 364

Geoffrin, Madame, 677, 678

Geography: Mesopotamian civilization and, 16; Hellenistic, 164

Geometry: Euclidian, 163; analytic, discovery of, 667

George III, king of England, 801

George, David Lloyd, 950

Georgics (Virgil), 201

Gerald of Wales, 388

Géricault (Zhe-re′-ko), Théodore, 878

German Confederation of the Rhine, 821, 892, 893–894; Metternich's policies and, 868; unification of Germany and, 936; re-establishment of, 940

German Empire, 946–948

Germania (Tacitus), 248

Germanic peoples: migrations of, 245; conversion to Christianity, 245, 248; society of, 248–252; marital and sexual customs of, 336

German Trade Union Congress, 955

German Workers' party, 1149

Germany: Roman conquest of, 199; in Frankish kingdom, 334; Charlemagne's expansion into, 339; controversy over lay investiture and, 360–361, 408; medieval nobility in, 385; development of modern state in, 404, 408–409; medieval division of, 408–409; under Frederick II, 411–412; bubonic plague in, 439; monarchy of, during Renaissance, 528; rise of Habsburg dynasty and, 533, 535; Luther and Protestant Reformation in, 537–545; under Charles V, 538, 545; religious division in, 544 (map), 545; in Habsburg-Valois conflict, 545; after Thirty Years' War, 592–593, 696; eastern, serfdom in, 623; famine in, 712; 18th-century Protestant revival in, 720; Napoleon I's reorganization of, 819, 821; industrialization of,

Germany (cont.)
846, 847(table), 850–851; tariffs imposed by, 851; romantic movement in, 877; revolution of 1848 and, 892–894; unification of, 936–942, 939(map), 945, 1290; unions in, 955; foreign investments of, 963; 19th-century migrations from, 969; in Africa, 973, 975; reasons for imperialism of, 977, 978; attempts to drive France and Britain apart, 1041; rivalry with Britain, 1042; in Balkan Wars, 1043; attacks France, 1044; attacks Belgium, World War I begins, 1044, 1045; in World War I, 1045, 1046, 1049, 1050, 1060; demands that Russia give up territories, 1059; Brest-Litovsk treaty and, 1059, 1061; Revolution of November 1918 in, 1061–1062; Treaty of Versailles and, 1062–1064, 1118; reparations by, 1064, 1118, 1119, 1120; modern architecture in, 1113; movies in, 1117, 1118; economy following World War I, 1118, 1119, 1120; Weimar Republic of, 1119, 1149; occupation of Ruhr and, 1119–1120; American loans to, 1120; runaway inflation of, 1120; treaties of Locarno and, 1120–1121; Great Depression and, 1126, 1150; nonaggression pact with Stalin, 1158; in World War II, 1158–1159, 1165; division into zones of occupation, 1172; following World War II, 1174–1176; Federal Republic of, 1176; economic recovery in, 1177; reunification of, 1199, 1293. See also German Confederation of the Rhine; East Germany; Germanic peoples; West Germany
Germinal (Zola), 925
Germ theory of disease, 902
Gertrude, Abbess, 383, 391
Gestapo, 1153
Ghana, 467, 468; kingdom of, 469–472; under Nkrumah, 1239–1240. See also Gold Coast
Ghent, Treaty of, 1007
Ghent Altarpiece (van Eyck), 527
Ghiberti (Ge-ber'-ti), Lorenzo, 516, 518
Ghirlandaio (Gir-lan-di-oh), Domenico, 518
Gibbon, Edward, 210, 212, 707
Gioberti, Vincenzo, 933
Giotto, 516
Giovanni Arnolfini and His Bride (van Eyck), 527
Girondists, 812–813
Gish, Lillian, 1117
Gladiators, Roman, 211
Gladstone, William, 950

Glanvill, 376
Glasnost, 1195
Gleaners, The (Millet), 693
Global interdependence, 1293–1304; vital resources and, 1294–1296; "North-South relations" and, 1296–1297, 1299, 1301; multinational corporations and, 1301–1304; secular ideologies and, 1304
Globe Theatre, 600
Glorious Revolution, 648
Gnosticism, 241
GNP. See Gross national product
God, medieval peasants' view of, 385
Go-Daigo, Japanese emperor, 330
Godfrey of Bouillon, 364
Goebbels (Goerb-als), Joseph, 1150, 1152
Gold Coast, 735, 738; under British control, 1235–1236, 1239
Golden Bull of 1356, 533
Golden Horde, 634
Golden rule, 674
Gold rush: Australian, 1030–1032; U.S., 1009
Gold standard, Britain and United States go off, 1125
Gold trade: in early Africa, 467, 471, 478, 481; European overseas expansion and, 570, 575
Goldwater, Barry, 1202
Gomulka, Wladyslaw, 1190
"Good government," 1234
Good Neighbor Policy, 1033
Gorbachev, Mikhail, 1194–1196, 1205, 1289
Goseck, monastery of, 391
Gospels, 206, 265, 267
Gothic architecture, 430, 639
Goths, 217, 245
Goulart, Joao, 1207
Gout, 712
Government, 14, 347; in ancient China, 93, 99, 105; Confucius' view of, 95; Taoists' view of, 96; Legalists' view of, 98; under Han emperors, 103; constitutional, in Roman Empire, 196; Muslim, 276–277; Japanese, 324, 328–329; of Carolingian Empire, 339–340; feudalism as, 347, 348; of medieval England and France, 407–408; in medieval Sicily, 411; of medieval Europe, 418–420; imperial, in Inca empire, 502; Italian, during Renaissance, 510; of absolutist state, 609, 614; aristocratic, era of, 648; cabinet system of, 649; under Frederick II, 680; of North German Confederation, 940; local, in Russia, 943; Australian, 1032; provisional, during Russian Revolu-

tion of 1917, 1055–1056; antidemocratic (authoritarian), 1134; world, 1285. See also State
Government of India Act, 1085
Gracchi, 188
Graham, James, 716
Granada, 532, 532
Grand Alliance, 618, 1155, 1161–1163
Grand Empire, of Napoleon I, 820(map), 821
Grand Testament (Villon), 432
Gravity, 664; law of universal gravitation and, 663, 665
Great Britain: Seven Years' War and, 798, 833; taxes on colonies, 798–799, 800; Americans revolt against, 798–800; recognizes independence of colonies, 801; Treaty of Paris and, 801; reaction to French Revolution, 810; France declares war on, 812; cedes Caribbean islands to France, 819; defeats Napoleon I at Trafalgar, 819; in Fourth Coalition, 822; formed, 832; foreign trade of, 832–833, 835–836; in War of Spanish Succession, 833; population growth in, 845; industrialization of, 847(table), 961; Continent uses industrial methods of, 849–852; labor unions in, 856–857; in Quadruple Alliance, 864; Congress of Vienna and, 867; Holy Alliance and, 868; liberalism in, 871–872; 19th-century economy of, 872; romantic movement in, 878–880; liberal reform in, 882–886; 19th-century urban life in, 898–901; diet in, during 19th century, 908; domestic servants in, during 19th century, 908–909, 912; in Crimean War, 942; extends suffrage and social welfare measures, 950; Irish demand for home rule and, 950–951; wages in, 955; unions in, 955; colonial empire of, 962; 19th-century growth in trade in, 962–963; foreign investments of, 963; in China, 965–966; in Egypt, 966–968; 19th-century migrations from, 969, 1030; in Africa, 973, 975, 977, 1234; reasons for imperialism of, 977–978; in India, 978; impact of American Civil War on, 1015–1016; alliance with Japan, 1041; rivalry with Germany, 1041; declares war on Germany, 1044; in Triple Entente, 1044; in World War I, 1045, 1046, 1050–1051, 1060; Treaty of Versailles and, 1062–1066, 1118; Sykes-Picot Agreement and, 1077; in Iran, 1081; movies and radio in, 1117; disagrees with France

over Germany, 1119; German reparations and, 1119, 1120; treaties of Locarno and, 1120; during 1920s, 1122; Great Depression in, 1125, 1126; following Great Depression, 1129; in Grand Alliance, 1155, 1160, 1161; policy of appeasement toward Germany, 1155–1157; declares war on Germany, World War II begins, 1158; in World War II, 1158–1159; refuses to promise Polish territory to Stalin, 1170; cold war and, 1170–1171, 1172; following World War II, 1177; Common Market and, 1178, 1181, 1182; de Gaulle's opposition to, 1181; decolonization and, 1181, 1182; national health system of, 1183; supports economic sanctions against Soviet Union, 1203; withdraws from Palestine, 1230; U.N. Security Council and, 1285. *See also* England; Ireland; Scotland

Great Day of His Wrath, The (Martin), 878

Great Depression, 1006, 1101, 1117, 1123–1130, 1124(map), 1294; economic crisis and, 1125; mass unemployment during, 1126; New Deal in United States and, 1126–1128; Scandinavian response to, 1129; Britain and France after, 1129–1130; impact on Latin America, 1205

Greater Colombia, 999, 1000

Great Exposition, 844

Great Famine, 886

Great Fear, 808

Great Leap Forward, 1216

Great Powers, 914

Great Proletarian Cultural Revolution. *See* Cultural Revolution

Great Pyramid, 488

Great Rebellion, 982

Great Russians, 1192–1193

Great Schism, 447, 535

Great Train Robbery, 1117

Great Trek, 973

Great Wall of China, 100(illus.), 101, 773

Great War. *See* World War I

Great Zimbabwe, 469, 480–482, 481(illus.)

Greco-Egyptian culture, 154

Greco-Roman culture, 206, 214, 256, 513, 525; spread of, 196, 199, 252; Christian attitudes toward, 238–239; synthesis of Christianity and, 239–241; Carolingian Renaissance and, 343

Greece: Hellenic period of, 116–144; geography of, 116, 117(map), 118, 137; science in, 116, 139, 141–142, 162–165; Minoan and Mycenaean societies of, 118–120; economy of, 119, 137, 155–158; Dark Age of, 120, 121; poets in, 120–121, 124, 125; polis in, 121–123, 126, 132(illus.), 133, 135, 139, 141, 151, 159, 172, 176; Lyric Age of, 123–128, 139; women in, 123, 128, 135, 136, 137–138, 161–162; growth of Sparta in, 124–126; evolution of Athens in, 126–128; defeat of Persian forces by, 128–129; Classical Period of, 128–143; growth of Athenian empire in, 129; Peloponnesian War and, 130, 135, 142; arts in, 131–135; daily life in, 135–139, 157(illus.); religion in, 138–139, 158–159; philosophy in, 139–142, 159–161, 162; medicine in, 140, 165–167; historical periods of, 142(table); decline of Athens and Sparta in, 142–143; Macedonian conquests and, 143, 148; Hellenistic period of, 148–168; Alexander's conquests and legacy, 148–150, 152(map); spread of Hellenism in, 150–155; Roman conquest of, 154, 182; national liberation in, 881–882; gains independence, 1042; Hitler conquers, 1159. *See also* Byzantine Empire

Greek drama, 133–135, 136(illus.)

"Greek fire," 254, 258

Greek Orthodox church: split with Roman Catholic church, 256, 637; Greek national aspirations and, 881

Greene, Graham, 1110

Green Revolution, 1263–1266

Gregorian reform movement, 434

Gregorian revolution, 359–362

Gregory I, pope, 233

Gregory VII, pope, 359, 360, 361, 434

Gregory IX, pope, 362

Gregory XI, pope, 446–447

Gresham, Thomas, 667

Gresham College, 667

Grimm, Jacob and Wilhelm, 880

Gromyko, Andrei, 1195

Gropius, Walter, 1113, 1114

Gross national product (GNP), 960, 1300(map); English Industrial Revolution and, 845

Guadalcanal, 1163

Guadalupe, Treaty of, 1009

Guatemala, 486

Guernica (Gware'-nih-kah) (Picasso), 1116

Guerrero, Vicente, 1001

Guibert of Nogent, 388, 389, 513

Guilds: Hebrew, 49; in medieval Europe, 419–420, 426, 450–451; during Renaissance, 509

Guinea, 464; nationalism in, 1241

Guise family, 583–584

Guizot, François, 888

Gunpowder, origins of, 315

Gustavus Adolphus, king of Sweden, 591–592, 610

Guthrun the Dane, 353

Gutman, Herbert G., 1017

Guyana, 486

Guzmán, Antonio, 1001

Habiru, 42

Habsburg Dynasty, 529, 685–686, 869, 871; rise of, 533, 534(map), 535; Thirty Years' War and, 589, 591, 592, 610; in opposition to Ottoman Turks, 625; Ottoman capitulations extended to, 751; Austrian revolution of 1848 and, 890; perishes, 1062. *See also* Austro-Hungarian Empire; Holy Roman Empire

Habsburg succession, 589(chart)

Habsburg-Valois Wars, 512, 545, 581; end of, 579–580

Haciendas, 1002–1003

Hadrian, Roman emperor, 208–209

Hahnemann, Samuel, 714

Haiti, 567

Hajib, 274

Halévy, Elie, 1136

Hamlet (Shakespeare), 600–601

Hammurabi, 19; law code of, 21, 23, 24(illus.), 25, 45, 47, 323

Hancock, John, 801

Han Dynasty, 99, 101(map), 216; intellectual thought during, 103–105; daily life during, 105–108; fall of, 109–110, 309

Han Fei-tzu (Han' Fay'-dzuh'), 97, 98

Han Kuang Wu (Han' Kyang' Wu'), 109

Hannibal, 181

Hanover, 940

Hanseatic League, 424–425

Han Wu Ti, 102

Harams, 265

Harappa, 66, 67

Hardy, Thomas, 925

Hardwick, Elizabeth, 593

Harems, 47; Muslim, 259, 282, 284

Hargraves, Edward, 1030

Hargreaves, James, 837

Harkort, Fritz, 850–851, 852

Harnesses, development of, 93

Harrison, William Henry, 1009

Harsha, king of northern India, 299

Harun al-Rashid, caliph, 276, 288, 289

Harvey, William, 713
Hastings, Warren, 762
Hastings, Battle of, 386, 392
Hausa-Fulanis, 1243, 1246
Hausaland, 730–731
Haussmann, Georges, 903
Hay, John, 1033
Hazor (Jewish citadel), 46(illus.)
Health: Hippocrates' view of, 140; in early Middle Ages, 344–346; impact of diet on, 709, 710–713; increased concern for, 901; poverty and, in Third World, 1256–1257
Heart of Darkness (Conrad), 981
Heaven, Muslim vision of, 267
Hébert (A-bair'), Jacques, 815
Hebrew language, 1084
Hebrews: Mesopotamian thought adopted by, 23; in Egypt, 30–31; migrations of, 40, 43–44; enslavement of, in Egypt, 43; in Palestine, 43; religion of, 44–46; law of, 45. *See also* Jews; Judaism
Hegel, Georg, 876
Heian (Hay-ahn) era, in Japan, 325–326, 327
Heidegger, Martin, 1109
Heilbroner, Robert, 1306, 1309
Heine, Heinrich, 821
Hejaz, 1076, 1077
Heliocentric theory, 163
Hell, medieval vision of, 384(illus.)
Hellas. *See* Greece
Hellenism, 80, 83–84, 116, 148, 168; spread of, 155, 165(table); influence of, on Roman life, 186–187. *See also* Greece, Hellenistic period of
Helots, 125, 126
Helsinki Conference, 1203
Hemp, 106, 107, 1002
Henry I, king of England, 396, 409, 411
Henry II, king of England, 394, 396, 413–414, 420, 645
Henry II, king of France, 580, 581
Henry III, Holy Roman emperor, 358
Henry III, king of England, 394
Henry III, king of France, 582, 583–584
Henry IV, Holy Roman emperor, 359, 360
Henry IV (of Navarre), king of France, 583, 584, 609, 610
Henry IV (Shakespeare), 600
Henry V, Holy Roman emperor, 391
Henry V, king of England, 444
Henry VI, king of England, 530
Henry VII, king of England, 529, 530, 531, 568, 570
Henry VIII, king of England, 525, 644; divorce of, 549, 550; Wolsey

and, 550; break with Rome, 550–552
Henry of Guise, 583, 584
Henry of Navarre. *See* Henry IV, king of France
Henry the Navigator, prince of Portugal, 565, 570, 596
Heptarchy, of Anglo-Saxon Britain, 251–252
Hera, 185
Heraclides (Her-e-klid'-ez) of Tarentum, 166
Heraclitus (Hair-uh-clite-us), 140
Heraclius, 254
Herder, Johann, 873
Heresy, 232, 417, 434–437, 533, 549
Hermandades, 531
Hermitage Museum, 642
Hermits, in medieval Europe, 242, 259
Hernani (Hugo), 880
Herod, king of Judea, 203
Herodotus, 5, 25
Heroic age, of Greece, 120
Herophilus, 165–166, 167
Herzl (Hairt-zell), Theodore, 1082
Hideyoshi, Toyotomi (Hid-uh-yo-she, Toe-yo-toe-me), 784, 785
Hieroglyphics, Mayan, 489
High Middle Ages. *See* Middle Ages, High
High Renaissance, 515–516
Hijra, 268
Hildebrand, cardinal (Pope Gregory VII), 359
Hildegard of Bingen, abbess, 346, 394–395
Hillel, 204
Himalayan Mountains, 64
Himmler, Heinrich, 1153, 1159, 1161
Hincmar (Hink-mar), archbishop of Reims, 349
Hindenburg, Paul von, 1047, 1050, 1150, 1151
Hinduism, 69, 71, 73–76, 98, 305, 307, 309, 1306, 1309
Hindu Kush, 59
Hindus, 757, 982, 983, 1085; society of, 1086–1087; division of India and, 1222, 1223
Hippocrates (Hip-pah'-cra-teez), 140, 141, 165, 166, 258
Hippocratic oath, 166
Hirohito (He-ro-he-toe), emperor of Japan, 1220
Hiroshima, 1166, 1214, 1291
Historical and Critical Dictionary (Bayle), 670
History: sources and, 4–5; interpretation of, 5; social, 5; Chinese view of, 104; St. Augustine's view of, 241; generalization and, 374; Hegel's

view of, as "ideas in motion," 876; romanticism and, 878; Tolstoy's fatalistic theory of, 925; study of, 1310
History of Plants (Theophrastus), 165
History of Rome (Fabius Pictor), 186
History of the Goths (Jordanes), 217
History of the House of Osman (Kemal-paşazède), 749
Hitler, Adolph, 179, 953, 1117, 1118, 1121–1122; roots of Nazism and, 1148–1149; road to power, 1149–1151; state and society under, 1151–1153; popularity of, 1153, 1155; opponents of, 1153, 1155; Nazi expansion and, 1155–1159, 1161; alliance with Mussolini, 1157; nonaggression pact with Stalin, 1158; defeat at Stalingrad, 1163
Hittites, 32–33; rise of, 33–34; society of, 34; era of greatness of, 35; fall of empire of, 35–36; migrations of, 40
Hobbes, Thomas, 645
Hobson, J. A., 980, 1296
Ho Chi Minh (Ho' Chee' Minh'), 1075, 1229
Hoetink, H., 1001–1002
Hoffmann, Ernst, 881
Hogsbawm, Eric, 864
Hohenzollern (Ho'-ent-sol-ern) family, 627, 631
Hojo Regency, 329
Holland: 376; church during 14th and 15th centuries, 536–537; invaded by Louis XIV, 617; constitutionalism and economic success in 17th century, 649–653; diet in, during 18th century, 710; France declares war on, 812; Hitler occupies, 1158; following World War II, 1178. *See also* Netherlands
Holy Club, 721
Holy Land: Crusades and, 362, 414
Holy League, 584, 747
Holy persons, 253–254
Holy Roman Empire, 409, 410(map), 412, 589; foundations of, 354; controversy over lay investiture and, 359, 361; lack of centralization in, 528; rise of Habsburg dynasty and, 533; destruction of, 592; Louis XIV's wars and, 617; decline of, 625; abolished by Napoleon I, 821
"Holy Russia," 635, 637
Holy Trinity Abbey, 394
Holy wars. *See* Crusades; *Jihad*
Home farm. *See* Demesne
Homeopathy, 714
Homer, 118, 120–121
Homo sapiens, 6, 8
Homosexuality: Greek acceptance of, 138; Christianity and, 239; medieval

attitudes toward, 416–417; in Reformation Europe, 593; among Japanese samurai, 788–789

Honduras, 486, 567

Hong Kong, 966

Honorius of Autun, 374, 390

Hoover, Herbert, 1127

Hoplites, 125, 128

Horace, 186, 199, 201–202, 599

Horses: medieval agriculture and, 379, 466; raised by medieval monasteries, 396

Horus, 28

Ho-shen, 779

Hospitals: Byzantine, 258; in 18th-century Europe, 714–716; during Suleiman's reign, 749

Hostage crisis, 1205

Hôtel-Dieu, 715–716

Houphouët-Boigny, Félix (Oof-way-bwa-nee, Fay-lix), 1241

House of Commons, 644, 646, 647, 649, 734, 883, 950. *See also* Parliament (England)

House of Lords, 950, 951

House of Wisdom, 291

Housing: Indus, 66–67; Shang, 90(illus.); Athenian, 135; Roman, 210, 211(illus.); Ostrogoth, 250; Byzantine, 259; medieval, 381, 420–421, 439; Teotihuacán, 491; Aztec, 497; in 19th-century European cities, 899–901, 903, 905–906, 909–910; in Stalinist Russia, 1143; in Third World, 1268–1270

How the Other Half Lives (Riis), 1021

Huayna Capac (Wi′-na Cay′-pack), 573

Hugh of Lincoln, bishop, 382

Hugo, Victor, 879–880

Huguenots, 547, 583, 584, 670; revolt of, 610; Louis XIV's campaign to repress, 615

Huitzilopochtli (We′-zih-lo-poacht-lee), Aztec god, 493, 494, 496; temple of, 497–498

Hulagu, 279

Hull, Cordell, 1172

Human Comedy, The (Balzac), 924

Humanism, 513–514, 521; secular, 514–515; Christian, 524–525, 526, 541, 549

Humanitarianism, 708

Human rights, 796, 1305

Human sacrifice, in Aztec society, 494–495

Humayun (Hu-may′-un), Mughal ruler, 753

Humboldt, Alexander von, 996

Hume, David, 676

Hunchback of Notre Dame (Hugo), 880

Hundred Days, 823, 864, 867

Hundred Years' War, 411, 424, 441–442, 528; popular response to, 442; course of, 442, 443(map), 444; Joan of Arc and, 444; costs and consequences of, 444–446, 580; taxation for, 452; France after, 529; England after, 530

Hungary: conquered by Habsburgs, 625–626; industrialization of, 847(table); Magyars and, 869, 951; revolution of 1848 in, 890, 892; independent republic proclaimed, 951–952; in World War II, 1159; cold war and, 1172; collectivization in, 1188; revolution of 1956 in, 1190

Hung Wu, emperor of China, 322, 768, 774; government of, 770–773; 1919 peace treaty and, 1064; conservative authoritarianism of, 1135–1136

Huns, 101, 102, 217, 245; invade Gupta Empire, 299

Hunting: in Paleolithic Age, 8, 9; in Neolithic Age, 9; in Periclean Athens, 137

Huron Indians, 494

Hurrians, 32

Hus, John, 448, 538

Hu Shih (Hoo′ Shur′), 1092

Hussein, Saddam, 1233, 1234, 1287, 1290

Hutten, Ulrich von, 541

Huxley, Aldous, 1110

Hydrogen bomb, 1291

Hydrostatics, 163

Hygiene, in early Middle Ages, 345

Hyksos (Hik′-sos), 26, 29–30, 40, 79

Iaroslav the Wise, 633, 634, 635

Iberian Peninsula, 181, 531

Ibn-Ali, Hussein (Ib′-ahn Ah′-lee, Hu-sayn′), 1076

ibn-Barmak, Khalid, 276

Ibn Battuta, 466, 474, 476

Ibn Fartura, 730

ibn-Ghazi, Ahmad, 731

Ibn-i Kemal, Ahmet Semseddin. *See* Kemalpaşazêde

ibn-Ishaq, Humayn, 291

ibn Jarir al-Tabiri, Abu Ja'far Muhammad, 282

Ibn Khaldun, 469, 597

ibn-Nusayr, Musa, 281

ibn-Ra'ig, 277

Ibn Rushid (Averroës), 292

Ibn Sina of Bukhara (Avicenna), 291, 292

Ibos: Christianization of, 979; in Nigeria, 1243, 1245, 1246

Ice ages, 9

I Ching (*The Book of Changes*), 94, 98–99

Iconoclasm, 255–256

Icons, 255

Id, 1111

Ideograms, 20

Idolatry, 255

Idris Alooma, 730

Ieyasu, Tokugawa (E-ay-ya-su, Toe-ku-gah-wah), 785–786

Ikki, Kita (Ik-kee, Kee-ta), 1097

Île de France, 407, 411, 430

Iliad (Homer), 118, 120, 151, 201

Illegitimacy: new patterns of, in 18th-century Europe, 703–704; in 19th-century European cities, 915

Il Rosso, 580–581

Imam, 274, 470

Imāns, 752

Imitation of Christ, The (Thomas à Kempis), 537

Immigration: impact on Latin America, 1004–1006; U.S. industrialization and, 1019–1023; into Canada, 1023, 1026; Jewish, 1082–1083. *See also* Migrations

Immunology, foundation for, 717

Imperial Academy of Fine Arts, 1148

Imperialism: Persian, 55–56; under Alexander the Great, 148–150, 149(map); Roman, 179, 183; Portuguese, 567; Dutch, 568; "new," 960, 972, 977–979; in Africa, 972–973, 974(map), 975, 977; in Asia, 976(map), 977; critics of, 979–981; Western, responses to, 981–983; Japanese, 983–985; Asia and, following World War I, 1072–1075; in Africa, 1234–1236, 1242. *See also* Colonization; Overseas expansion

Imperialism (Hobson), 980

Imperial War Cabinet, 1026

Impressionism, 1114–1115

Inca empire, 498–503, 499(map); imperialism of, 500–502; society of, 502–503; Spanish conquest of, 571, 572–573

Incest, German custom of, 336

Income: unequal distribution of, 907(fig.), 960–961, 1270(fig.); in Third World, 1256, 1261. *See also* Standard of living; Wages; Wealth

Index of Prohibited Books, 557, 676

India, 4, 52, 64–84, 753–762; geography of, 64–65, 299(map); development of, 65(map); urban culture of, 66–67; shaping of society of, 69–71; religions of, 71–78, 83; Persian Empire and, 78–79; historical periods of, 79(table); Alexander's conquest of, 79–80; invaders of, 83; daily life

India (cont.)
in, 301–305; and Southeast Asia,
305–307; Islamic conquest of,
308–309, 753; historical periods of,
309(table); trade routes between
East Africa and, 479(map); under
Mughals, 753–759; European rivalry
over trade with, 759–760; factory-
forts in, 760–761; rise of British East
India Company and, 761–762; under
British control, 962, 982–983, 1086;
nationalism in, 1084–1086,
1088–1090, 1260; Gandhi and,
1086–1090; decolonization of, 1181;
dispute with Pakistan over Kashmir,
1223; partition of, 1223, 1224
(map); under Nehru, 1223–1224;
industrialization of, after independence, 1260–1261; Green Revolution
in, 1264; as regional power, 1290;
nuclear arms race and, 1291, 1293.
See also Aryans; Indus civilization
India Act of 1784, 762
Indian National Congress, 983, 1084
Indians: in Latin America, during colonial period, 996. See also American
Indians; Amerindians
Individualism, of Renaissance, 513
Indochina, 1073, 1075; Japanese occupation of, 1159; decolonialization of,
1181–1182; defeat of French in,
1202, 1229
Indo-European languages, 32–33, 174
Indonesia, 760, 1229
Indulgences, 364, 385; Luther and,
537–538
Indus civilization, 65–68
Industrial middle class, 852, 853, 864
Industrial Revolution, 828–860;
18th-century origins of, 828–829; in
England, 828–846, 845(map), 872;
Agricultural Revolution and,
830–831; enclosure movement and,
831–832; growth of foreign trade
and, 832; first factories and,
836–839; problem of energy and,
839–840; steam engine and,
840–842; railroads and, 842–844;
population and, 844–846; in continental Europe, 846–852, 849(map);
national variations in industrialization and, 846–847; challenge of industrialization and, 847–849; agents
of industrialization and, 849–852;
factory owners and, 852; factory
workers and, 852–853; working conditions and, 854–857; labor unions
and, 856–857; sexual division of labor and, 857–860; urban conditions
and, 898; global inequality and, 960

Industry: Hellenistic, 157; growth of,
in Roman provinces, 214; cottage,
697–699; putting-out system of,
699, 836, 837, 839, 840, 855; per
capita levels of industrialization and,
847(table); romantic movement and,
878; 19th-century growth of, 898;
growth of cities and, 898–901; German, 937; Russian, 943–944, 1139,
1142; world economy and, 960; colonial, 993; American, 1019,
1020–1021; British, following Great
Depression, 1129; Third World industrialization and, 1260–1262; alternative technologies and lifestyles
and, 1306. See also Coal industry;
Cotton industry; Industrial Revolution; Iron industry; Textile industry;
Wool industry
Inequality, economic, 906, 907(fig.),
960–961, 1270–1272, 1270(fig.);
"North-South relations" and,
1296–1297, 1299, 1301
Inertia, law of, 664
Infanticide, 706–707; in Hellenic
Greece and Rome, 126; in High
Middle Ages, 387; during Renais-
sance, 523; in Ming and Ch'ing
China, 781
Infant mortality: in medieval Europe,
337, 387; in preindustrial England,
704; decline of, after 1890, 902–903
Inflation: in Roman Empire, 221; in
medieval Europe, 437; in 16th-
century Spain, 575; post–World War
I, in Germany, 1120; in China, un-
der Deng Xiaoping, 1219
Information, as new global environ-
ment, 1310
Inheritance, Qu'ran on, 267
Innocent I, pope, 233
Innocent III, pope, 361, 366, 414,
435, 523
Innocent IV, pope, 362
Innocent VIII, 536
Inquiry into the Human Prospect, An
(Heilbroner), 1306
Inquiry into the Nature and Causes of the
Wealth of Nations (Smith), 872
Inquisition: papal, 436–437, 554;
Spanish, 533; Roman, 557; during
revolt of Netherlands, 585, 586
Institutes (Justinian), 257
Institutes of the Christian Religion, The
(Calvin), 546, 547, 582
Instrument of Government, 646
Instruments of the Observatory (Takiyud-
din Mehemet), 749
Intendants, 610
Intermarriage, in early Africa, 474, 476

International debt crisis, 1299, 1301
International style, 516–517; of architecture, 1114
International Working Men's Association, 953–954
Interregnum, 645
Iona, monastery of, 235
Ionians, 128, 139, 140
Iphigénie (Racine), 617
Iran, 216, 309, 751; ancient, 52,
53–55; geography of, 52–53; religion of, 56–58; Parthians and Sassanids of, 214–216; nationalism in,
1081; hostage crisis in, 1205, 1233;
war with Iraq, 1233, 1290; Islamic
fundamentalism in, 1308–1309. See
also Persia
Iraq, 1064, 1077; war with Iran, 1233,
1290; invades Kuwait, 1234, 1287;
nuclear arms race and, 1293
Ireland: conversion to Christianity,
234–235; conquered by Henry II,
645; Cromwell and, 646; importance
of potato in, 712; English factory
workers from, 856; famine in, 885,
886, 950; home rule and, 950–951;
Easter Rebellion in, 1053; southern,
Britain grants autonomy to,
1122–1123
Irnerius (Ir-ner'-i-us), 426
Iron, 33, 42, 54; in ancient China,
93–94; under Han dynasty, 107; in
early Africa, 465, 480
Iron curtain, 1172, 1174, 1199
Iron industry: in High Middle Ages,
378–379, 396–397; English, 840,
842, 856; Russian, 840
Iron law of wages, 845, 872
Irrigation, in Neolithic Age, 11, 13; in
Mesopotamia, 24; in ancient China,
106
Isabella, queen of Spain, 529,
531–533, 550, 567, 569
Isabella of Este, 524
Isabella of Lancaster, 394, 395
Isfahan, 753
Isis (Eye-sis), 27; cult of, 159, 204
Islam, 45, 46, 264–294; Arabs before,
264; Muhammad and, 265–268; origins of, 266; similarities with Christianity, 267; expansion of, 268–273,
270(map), 271(map), 490; attitude
toward Christianity, 273, 367; wom-
en and, 282–284; Sufism and, 284,
286; replaces Hinduism and Buddhism, 309; Crusades and, 367;
rosary and, 383; African converts to,
468, 476; slavery and, 597–598,
730, 734; resurgence in 1970s and
1980s, 1307–1309. See also Muslims

Islamic fundamentalism, 1308–1309
Islamic revolution, 1233
Islamic state: centralization of, 271; consolidation of, 273–277; administration of, 275; historical periods of, 275(table); decentralization of, 277–278; assaults on, 278–279; social equality and, 279; classes of society in, 279–282; women in, 282–284; Sufism in, 284, 286; trade and commerce in, 286–288; urban centers in, 288–289; intellectual life of, 289–292; invades India, 307, 308
Ismail, prince of Egypt, 967, 981
Isolationism, of United States, 1064–1066, 1082
Israel, 42; religion in, 43, 44–46; family relations and marriage in, 46–49; Palestine and, 1230, 1231(map), 1232; as regional power, 1290; nuclear arms race and, 1293
Issus, Battle of, 150(illus.)
Italy: slaves in, 156, 596; geography of, 172, 173(map); Greek immigration into, 174; Roman conquest of, 175–176; colonies of, 198; Lombard conquest of, 247, 252; Papal States in, 336, 359; Magyar invasion of, 352; Muslim invasion of, 352; Frederick Barbarossa's expeditions into, 409; medieval merchant guilds in, 420; evolution of Renaissance in, 508–512; invaded by France, 512; unification of, 512, 933–936, 934(map); growth of secularism in, 515; humanism in, 524; monarchy of, during Renaissance, 528; church during 14th and 15th centuries, 537; industrialization of, 847(table); unification of, 933–936, 945; 19th-century migrations from, 971; in Africa, 973; in World War I, 1047; Treaty of Versailles and, 1062; treaties of Locarno and, 1120; impact of World War I on, 1145; under Mussolini, 1145–1148; in World War II, 1164–1165; following World War II, 1176, 1177. *See also* Roman Empire; Rome
Ius civile, gentium, and *naturale,* 178
Ivan I (the Moneybag), prince of Moscow, 634–635
Ivan III, prince of Moscow, 634, 635
Ivan IV (the Terrible), tsar of Russia, 635–636
Ivory, African, 478

Jackson, Andrew, 1009, 1010
Jacobean literature, 599–600
Jacobins, 811

Jacob's Room (Woolf), 1112
Jacquerie, 452, 453(illus.), 455
Jacques de Vitry, 452
Jahan (Jah-hahn'), shah of Mughal, 757
Jahangir (Jah-hahn'-gear), emperor of India, 756–757, 759
Jainism, 73, 76
Jamaica, 567, 1272
James, duke of York, 647
James I, king of England, 599, 601, 643–644, 645
James II, king of England, 647–648
Janissaries, 747
Japan: writing system of, 91; influence of China on, 322, 323, 324, 326; geography of, 322, 323(map); daily life in, 322; Yamato state and, 322–325; Buddhism in, 323–326; Heian era of, 325–326, 327; samurai and, 326–328; historical periods of, 328(table); under Kamakura Shogunate, 328–330; colonization of, 565; European overseas expansion and, 578, 579; under Ashikaga Shogunate, 782–783; feudalism in, 783–784; during period of national unification, 784–785; under Hideyoshi, 785; Tokugawa regime in, 785–787, 787(map); daily life in, 787–791; industrialization of, 847; attacks Russia, 944; "opening" of, 964–965, 966; responses to imperialism in, 981, 983–984; Meiji Restoration in, 984; imperialism of, 985, 986; at war with China, 985, 986, 1099(map), 1100, 1159, 1214; alliance with Britain, 1040(fig.), 1041; receives Germany's holdings in China, 1064; nationalism in, 1090, 1095–1097; Great Depression and, 1097, 1123; alliance with Germany and Italy, 1157; in World War II, 1159, 1163–1164; East Asian empire of, 1163, 1164(map); surrenders, 1166; Stalin agrees to declare war on, 1172; American occupation of, 1219–1220; regains independence, 1220; as economic superpower, 1220–1222; as regional power, 1290; multinational corporations in, 1302
Jarmo, 10
Jarro monastery, 342
Jaspers, Karl, 1109
Jaurès (Jho'-res), Jean, 956
Javanese, 306
Jazz, 1237
Jefferson, Thomas, 796, 801, 808, 995, 1007, 1009
Jehovah. *See* Yahweh

Jenghiz Khan, 279, 319–320, 634
Jenner, Edward, 716–717
Jericho, 9
Jerusalem, 44, 205, 362, 365
Jervaulx (Zher-vo'), abbey of, 396
Jesuits (Society of Jesus), 556–557, 574, 578, 589, 602, 718
Jesus of Nazareth, 203–207, 231–232, 265; teachings of, 235–236; dating method based on birth of, 342; Virgin Mary and, 383–385; Voltaire's interpretation of, 674. *See also* Christianity
Jew of Malta, The (Marlowe), 599
Jews: ancient, 42–49; rise of Christianity and, 203, 204–207; Roman hatred of, 203, 222–223; under Muslim rule, 280–281; anti-Semitism and, 411, 416, 417, 952–953, 1148, 1149; in medieval towns, 416; blamed for plague, 440; peasant attacks on, 456; expulsion from Spain, 533, 729; in trade with Sudan, 729; in Russia, 970; 19th-century migrations of, 970; in Palestine, 1082–1083; persecuted in Mussolini's Italy, 1147; in Nazi Germany, 1153, 1159, 1161. *See also* Hebrews; Judaism
Jiang Jieshi. *See* Chiang Kai-shek
Jihad, 270, 272, 744
Jim Crow laws, 1016
Jinna, Muhammad Ali (Jin-nah, Mu-ham'-mad Ah-lee), 1222
Jizya, 754, 757
Joanna of Castile, 533
Joan of Arc, 444, 446, 529
Joffre, Joseph, 1045
John, king of England, 407, 414
John II, king of Portugal, 565
John XII, pope, 357
John of Salisbury, 362, 514
John of Spoleto, 447
John Paul II, pope, 1197, 1306–1307
Johnson, Lyndon, 1200; Vietnam War and, 1201, 1202
John the Baptist, 203
Jordanes, 217
Joseph II, king of Austria, 685, 686, 687, 718
Journal (Wesley), 721
Joyce, James, 1112
Judaea, 202, 203
Judah, 44
Judaism, 44; beliefs of, 44–46; rise of Christianity and, 203--207; resurgence of, 1306
Judeo-Christian tradition: liberalism and, 797

Jugurtha (Ju-gur'-tha), 190
Julio-Claudians, 207
Julius II, pope, 515, 536, 550, 553
Julius Caesar (Shakespeare), 600
Juma Masjid mosque, 757
"June Days," 890
Junkers, 629, 631, 681, 946
Juno, 185, 204
Jupiter (Roman god), 185, 204
Jupiter Optimus Maximus, temple of, 174
Jurchen, 315, 320
Jury, origins of, 413
Justinian, Roman emperor, 252, 254, 257. *See also Code,* Justinian
Jutes, 251

Ka, 28
Kabuki, 788
Kádár, János, 1198–1199
Kafka, Franz, 1113
Kaganovich, Lazar Moiseyevich, 1190–1191
Kalidasa (Kahl-ih-dah-sah), 301
Kamakura Shogunate, 325, 326, 327, 328–330
Kamikaze, 329
Kampuchea. *See* Cambodia
Kandinsky, Wassily, 1116
Kanem-Bornu, 730
Kanem Wars, The (Ibn Fartura), 730
Kangaba, 472
K'ang-hsi (Kang-she), emperor of China, 778–779
Kanuns, 747–748
Kan Ying, 216–217
Karma, 71, 73, 77
Kashmir: dispute between India and Pakistan over, 1223
Kassites, 32
Katherine von Bora, 541–542
Kaunitz, Eleanora von, 869
Kautilya, 80
Keats, John, 878
Kellogg, Frank B., 1121
Kellogg-Briand Pact, 1121
Kemal, Mustafa. *See* Atatürk, Mustafa Kemal
Kemalpaşazêde, 749
Kennedy, John F., 1191, 1200; Bay of Pigs invasion and, 1207
Kenya, 475; under British control, 1235
Kepler, Johannes, 663–664
Kerensky, Alexander, 1056, 1057
Keynes, John Maynard, 845, 1118, 1126, 1128, 1304
Keynesian economics, 1177
Keystone Cops, 1117
Khadija, 265
Khalifa. *See* Caliphate

Khedive, 967, 968
Khitans, 314
Khmer Empire, 306
Khmer Rouge, 1134
Khoisan, 464, 465, 480
Kholops, 634
Khomeini, Ayatollah Ruholla, 1233, 1308
Khrushchev, Nikita, 1189–1192, 1207, 1216
Khyber Pass, 64
Kibbutz, 1084
Kierkegaard (Kir'-ke-gor), Sören, 1109
Kiev: Vikings and, 256, 633–634; Mongol conquest of, 634
Kilwa, 477, 478, 732, 733
King, Martin Luther, Jr., 1090
King James Bible, 601
Kingship, 405; Germanic, 336; St. Augustine's theories of, 340; Alcuin's treatise on, 343; in Sudan, 465; abolition of, in England, 645. *See also* Monarchy
Kinship ties: in Germanic society, 248; among factory workers, 856; in 19th-century European cities, 916; urban migration and, in Third World, 1272
Kipling, Rudyard, 978, 980–981, 1063
Kirov, Sergei, 1143
Kissinger, Henry, 1202
Kitchener, Horatio H., 975, 977, 982
Knights and knighthood, 348, 386, 389–390
Koch, Robert, 902
Koestler, Arthur, 1143
Kohl, Helmut, 1199
Kollontai, Alexandra, 1144
Königsbronn, abbey of, 396
Korea: adoption of Chinese writing system by, 91; Japan and, 323; "opening" of, 985. *See also* Korean War; North Korea; South Korea
Korean War, 1177, 1202, 1215, 1287
Kornilov, Lavr, 1057
Kossuth, Louis, 890
Krishna, 75
Kshatriyas, 302, 304
Kublai Khan, 279, 320, 329
Kulaks, 1140–1141
Kulturkampf, 946
Kumbi, 468, 472
Kun, Béla, 1135
K'ung Fu-tzu (Kuhng' Fuh'-dzuh). *See* Confucius
Kuomintang, 1090
Kuprili, Muhammad, 750
Kush, Kingdom of, 41
Kushans, 83
Kuwait, 1077; Iraq invades, 1234, 1287

Labor: child, 839, 855–856; sexual division of, 857–860, 916; demand for, during World War I, 1051–1052. *See also* Labor force; Labor unions
Laborers. *See* Working people
Labor force: women in, 857–860, 1051–1052; in 19th-century European cities, hierarchy of, 910–912, 910(fig.); WPA and, 1127; in Stalinist Russia, 1142
Labor unions: beginnings in Great Britain, 856–857; male domination of, 858; growth of, 955; during World War I, 1051; following Great Depression, 1127; in Mussolini's Italy, 1146; in Nazi Germany, 1151; Polish Solidarity union and, 1197–1198, 1203
Labouchère (Lab-u-sher'), Henri, 981
Labour party, 956, 1122, 1177, 1181
Lacquered ware, Chinese, 106, 107
Lady Godiva, 383
Lafayette, marquis de, 801, 802–803, 808, 809
Lahore Conference, 1222
Lais (Villon), 434
Laissez-faire, doctrine of, 871, 872
Laity, in late Middle Ages, 452
Lake District, 878
Lake Shore Apartments, 1114
Lake Trasimene, Battle of, 181
Lamarck, Jean Baptiste, 923
Lamartine, Alphonse de, 879, 932
Lancaster, ducal house of, 530
Land laws, Japanese, 326
Landlord nobility, 624
Landownership: in Hellenic Greece, 126, 137; in Roman Republic, 188; in medieval Europe, 348; English enclosure movement and, 831, 832; haciendas and, 1002–1003; in South Africa, 1246; in Third World, 1265
Land reform, 1263, 1265, 1266: in China, 100, 311, 312, 1214–1215; in Roman Republic, 189; in Mao's China, 1218–1219; in postwar Japan, 1220; under Nasser, 1232
Land use: in ancient China, 106; in medieval Europe, 376, 380
Lanfranc, 396
Language: Semitic, 15; Indo-European, 32–33, 174; Chinese, 99; Greek, 118, 154, 155, 186; Latin, 186, 251, 239, 292, 344, 432, 521; Urdu, 309; vernacular, 432, 601; English, 432, 601; French, 432, 521, 580; Swahili, 476; Zapotecan, 491; Nahuatl, 493; Quechua, 500–501; Spanish, 521; Greek, 521; Luther's skill with, 541; Wolof, 726; Serer, 726; Pulaar, 726; Cushitic, 732; nationalism and, 873,

953; Magyar (Hungarian), 953; Hebrew, 1084; Gujarati, 1086

Laos, 1229

Lao T'ai T'ai (Low' Tie' Tie'), 1094

Lao-tzu (Lou-dzuh), 96

Las Casas, Bartolomé de, 574, 596

Last Judgment, The (Michelangelo), 516

Last Supper, The (Leonardo), 516

Lateran Agreement of 1929, 1146

Lateran Council, 553

Lateran Palace, 231

Lateran Synod, 358–359

Latifundia, 188, 212

Latin America, 602, 652; growth of international trade and, 962, 964; Spanish colonies in, 992, 993, 994(map), 995; origins of revolutions in, 993, 995; before independence, 994(map); race in the colonial period of, 995–996; Comunero Revolution and, 997; in 1830, 998(map); movement for independence, 999–1000; consequences of independence in, 1000–1002, 1006; neocolonialism and, 1002–1004; historical periods of, 1004(table); impact of immigration on, 1004–1006; economic nationalism in, 1205–1206; authoritarianism in, 1207–1208; democracy in, 1208–1209; Green Revolution fails to spread throughout, 1265. *See also individual countries*

Latin language, 186; Bible translated into, 239; in Anglo-Saxon England, 251; Greek philosophy and, 292; in Carolingian Empire, 344; medieval education and, 389; celebration of Mass in, 578–579

Latin Quarter, 426

Latium, 174, 175, 181

Latvia, 638–639

Laud, William, archbishop of Canterbury, 645

Lausanne, Treaty of, 1080

La Venta, 488

Law(s): Hammurabi's code, 21, 23, 24(illus.), 25, 45, 47; Hebrew, 45, 47; of Persian Empire, 79; of Greek polis, 122, 127; Draco's code, 127; Roman, 176, 178, 256–257; Licinian-Sextian rogations, 178; civil, 178, 257; Justinian *Code* and, 230, 256–257, 416, 426, 428, 529; canon, 231, 361; Germanic, 248–249; Salic, 249; *corpus juris civilis,* 257; Muslim, 273, 276, 284; Arab tribal, 282; Indian, 304; Sung, 319; Young Shoots, 319; medieval, 376, 413–417, 426; common, 413, 416; in kingdom of Ghana, 470–471;

Renaissance, rape and, 523; royal council and, 531; marriage and, in 18th-century Europe, 701; in Ottoman Empire, 747–748; Napoleonic Code and, 916; under Napoleon III, 931; Fundamental Laws and, 945; unions outlawed by, 955; of repartimiento, 996, 997; Jim Crow, 1016; against immigration, 1023; forced-labor, during World War I, 1050

Law merchant, 419

Law of conservation of energy, 922

Law of peoples, 178

Law of the Sea, 1297

Law of the Twelve Tables, 178

Lawrence, T. E., 1076

Laws, The (Plato), 141

Lay investiture, 359–361

Lead mining, 396, 397

League of Armed Neutrality, 801

League of Augsburg, 617

League of Cambrai, 512

League of Nations, 1033, 1061, 1065, 1119, 1155, 1229; Wilson and, 1062, 1074; mandates of, 1064, 1074, 1077; failure of United States to join, 1066, 1285

Lebanon, 1064, 1229, 1233, 1290

Lebna Dengel, emperor of Ethiopia, 731

Lee, Robert E., 1016

Leech Book of Bald, The, 396

Lefèvre d'Étaples, Jacques, 524–525, 526

Legalism, 96–98, 99, 101, 102, 104

Legislative Assembly (France), 816, 817

Lélia (Sand), 880

Lenin, Vladimir Ilyich, 980, 982, 1117, 1136, 1138, 1304; Bolshevik revolution and, 1056–1057; New Economic Policy of, 1139

Leo I, pope, 233, 235

Leo III, emperor, 255

Leo III, pope, 340, 341

Leo IX, pope, 358

Leo X, pope, 512, 536, 538, 729

Leo XIII, pope, 949

Leo Africanus, 474, 729

Leonardo da Vinci, 515–516, 518, 581

Leopold I, Holy Roman emperor, 639

Leopold II, Holy Roman emperor, 686; king of Belgium, 973

Lepanto, battle of, 747

Le Père Goriot (Balzac), 924

Lepidus, 192

Leprosy, in medieval Europe, 354, 355

Lérins, monastery of, 242

Lesbos, 124

Lescot, Pierre, 580

Les Femmes Savantes (Molière), 617

Lespinasse, Julie de, 678

Lessons for Women (Pan Chao), 104

Leviathan (Hobbes), 645

Lewis, C. S., 1110

Lex Canuleia, 178

Lex Hortensia, 178

Li, 319

Liberal Democratic party (Japan), 1220

Liberalism: principal ideas of, 797, 871; roots of, 797; attraction of, 798; constitutional, in United States, 868; Metternich's hatred of, 869; classical, 871; economic, 872

Liberal party (Britain), 1122

Liberties (freedoms): economic revival and, in Middle Ages, 376, 377; of medieval nobility, 386; of merchants, in medieval towns, 418–420; liberalism and, 871

Liberty (concept): revolutionary period and, 796–797; liberalism and, 797–798; meaning of, in American Constitution and Bill of Rights, 802; anti-imperialism and, 981–982; totalitarianism versus, 1136–1137; Mussolini's hatred of, 1145; as secular ideology, 1304, 1305

Liberty Leading the People (Delacroix), 880

Libya, invasion of Egypt by, 41

Licinian-Sextian rogations, 178

Licinius (Lie-sin-e-us), 178

Liebenfels, Lanz von, 1148

Liebknecht (Leep'-knekt), Karl, 1062

Life expectancy, 709; in Third World, 1258

Life of the Emperor Augustus (Suetonius), 336

Liguge, monastery of, 234

Li Lung-mien (Lee' Lung'-myehn), 319

Limits to Growth, The, 1294

Lincoln, Abraham, 937–938, 1007, 1013; American Civil War and, 1014–1015

Lindisfarne monastery, 342

Linear A script, 118

Linear B script, 32, 118

Lin Tse-hsü, 965–966

Li Po (Lee' Po), 318

Li Ssu (Lee' Suh'), 97, 98, 99

List, Friedrich, 851, 943

Lister, Joseph, 902

Liszt, Franz, 881

Literacy: in ancient China, 91; in Hellenic Greece, 120; of Hellenistic women, 161; Carolingian Renaissance and, 343, 344; during Renaissance, 520; 18th-century surge in, 709

Literature: Mesopotamian, 18, 21; Hebrew, 43; Persian, 57; Indian, 69, 72, 73, 74–75, 76, 301, 306; Chinese, 94, 96, 98, 104, 773, 779; Greek, 120–121, 124, 127, 133–135, 140, 141; Roman, 185–186, 199, 201–202; Byzantine, 257; T'ang, 317–318; Japanese, 326; Northumbrian, 341–342; vernacular, of late Middle Ages, 432–434; bubonic plague and, 441; of Renaissance, 513–515, 525–526; Elizabethan and Jacobean, 599–601; under Louis XIV, 615; of romantic movement, 878; realism in, 921, 924–925; 20th-century, 1112–1113; in Nazi Germany, 1151; Stalin's purge of, 1190; *glasnost* and, 1195; of American blacks, 1237; of Third World intellectuals, 1275–1277
Lithuania, national sovereignty declared by, 1199
Little Entente, 1119
Liturgy, in High Middle Ages, 395
Liu Chin, 772
Liu Pang 102, 768
Livingston, Robert, 1007
Livingstone, David, 465
Livre de la mutacion de fortune (Pisan), 434
Livy, 201
Lloyd George, David, 1042, 1051, 1063
Locarno, treaties of, 1120–1121, 1155
Locke, John, 648, 671, 676; liberalism and, 797
Lodge, Henry Cabot, 1065
Loess, 88
Logical empiricism (positivism), 1108
Lollards, 550
Lombards, 233, 249, 252, 336
Lombardy, 933, 935
London Steelyard, 425
Long March, 1100, 1216
Long Parliament, 645, 646
López de Santa Anna, Antonio, 1001
Lord's Supper, 206, 221
Lorenz curve, 907(fig.), 1270(fig.)
Lorenzo the Magnificent, 536
Lothair, 334, 347
Lotus sect, 325–326
Louis (Loo-ee) VI, king of France, 407
Louis IX, king of France, 366, 413
Louis XI (Spider King), king of France, 529, 580
Louis XII, king of France, 512
Louis XIII, king of France, 591, 610, 611
Louis XIV, king of France, 608, 639, 669, 671, 679, 682–683; absolute monarchy of, 609, 612–614; Fronde

and, 612; financial and economic management under, 614–615; revokes Edict of Nantes, 615; French classicism and, 615–617; wars of, 617–619; acquisitions of, 618(map); secret treaty with Charles II, 647; hatred of Dutch, 649; expels French Huguenots, 670
Louis XV, king of France, 684, 718, 803
Louis XVI, king of France, 684, 804, 805, 806, 810, 811, 812
Louis XVIII, king of France, 822–823, 865, 867, 886
Louisiana Purchase, 1007
Louis Napoleon. *See* Napoleon III, emperor of France
Louis Philippe, king of France, 886, 888, 892, 930, 931
Louis the German, 347
Louis the Pious, 346, 347, 350
L'Ouverture, Toussaint (Loo-ver-tuer, Too-san'), 1007
Louvois, marquis of (François le Tellier), 617
Louvre, 580
Low Countries, 376, 396, 420, 584, 587, 568; origination of new agricultural methods in, 830; united under Dutch monarchy, 867. *See also* Belgium; Holland; Netherlands
Lower class. *See* Peasantry; Working people
Loyalists, in American Revolution, 801
Loyola, Ignatius, 556, 585
Lucas von Hildebrandt, Johann, 639
Lucknow Pact, 1085
Luddites, 852–853
Ludendorff, Erich, 1047, 1050, 1061, 1149
Lueger, Karl, 953, 1148
Lully, Jean-Baptiste, 616
Lunéville, Treaty of, 819
Lupercalia, festival of, 236–237
Lusitania, sinking of, 1049
Luther, Martin, 508, 557, 582, 717; early years of, 537; Ninety-five Theses of, 537–538; Protestant thought and, 539; social impact of beliefs of, 539–542; political impact of beliefs of, 542–543, 545, 594; renounces Copernicus, 662
Lutheranism, 539, 541, 582; Peace of Augsburg and, 545; status of women and, 594; Pietism and, 720
Luxemburg, Rosa, 1062
Lyceum, 165
Lycurgan regimen, 126
Lydia, 56
Lyell, Charles, 923
Lyric Age of Greece, 123–128

Lyrical Ballads (Wordsworth and Coleridge), 878

MacArthur, Douglas, 1163, 1219, 1220
Macarthur, John, 1030
Macaulay, Thomas, 600
Macbeth (Shakespeare), 600
MacDonald, John A., 1024–1026
MacDonald, Ramsay, 1122
Macedonia: conquests of, 143, 148, 182; monarchy in, 150; in Balkan Wars, 1042
Maceualtin, 495
Machiavelli, Niccolò, 510, 519–520, 530
Machiavellian, defined, 520
McKinley, William, 1033
MacMahon, Marie Edmé, 948
Madame Bovary (Flaubert), 924–925
Madonna of the Chancellor Rodin (van Eyck), 527
Madras, 760
Magellan, Ferdinand, 567–568
Magi, 56
Magna Carta, 414–415
Magnetism, first Western experiments in, 579
Magyars, 352, 353, 355, 869, 951, 953. *See also* Hungary
Mahabharata (Ma-ha-bah'-ra-ta), 74–75
Mahal, Mumtaz, 757
Mahavira, Vardhamana (Ma-ha-vih-ra, Vard-ha-ma-na), 76
Mahayana Buddhism, 78, 84, 310
Mahmud (Mah-mood'), Turkish chieftain, 308
Majlis, 1081, 1233
Malaria: in medieval Europe, 354–355; in Third World, 1258
Malaya, 1227–1228
Malaysia, Federation of, 1228
Mali: kingdom of, 469, 472–475, 473(map); nationalism in, 1241
Malinke, 730
Malnutrition, in Third World, 1256
Malthus, Thomas, 845, 853, 872, 923, 1258
Malvinas Islands. *See* Falkland Islands
Manchu Dynasty: 776, 777; rule by, 777–779; opium trade and, 965–966; revolution and overthrow of, 985–988, 1090
Manchuria, 1097, 1214
Manco Capac, 500
Mandarin system, 313–314
Mandate of Heaven, 92, 104, 776, 777, 778, 1215
Mandela, Nelson, 1248; freed from prison, 1249

Mandinke, 472

Manetho (Ma-ni-to), 29

Manicheanism, 58

Manifest destiny, 1006–1007, 1009, 1024

Mankind and Mother Earth (Toynbee), 1284–1285

Mannix, Daniel, 1032

Man of La Mancha, 621

Man of the People, A (Achebe), 1276

Manorialism, 349–350

Manors: as basic unit of medieval rural organization, 377, 378(illus.); life on, 380–381; monastic, 395–396

Mansabdars, 754

Mansib, 265

Manuel, king of Portugal, 567

Manumission, 185, 996

Mao Tse-tung (Mow Dze-dong'), 1093

Mao Zedong. *See* Mao Tse-tung

Marathas, 758–759, 762

Marcel, Gabriel, 1109

Marches, of Charlemagne, 339

March revolution, 1055–1056, 1057

Marconi, Guglielmo, 1117

Marcos, Ferdinand, 1228

Marcus Aurelius, 217

Marduk (Mar-duke), god of Babylon, 19, 45

Margaret, regent of Netherlands, 585

Margaret of Valois, 583

Maria Theresa, queen of Austria, 680, 685, 718

Maria Theresa, queen of France, 613

Maritime trade, Chinese, 216, 773

Marius, Gaius, 188, 190

Market: medieval, 420, 421(illus.); Aztec, 497; Chinese, 770, 771(illus.)

Marlowe, Christopher, 599–600

Marne: first battle of, 1045; second battle of, 1061

Marriage: Hammurabi's code and, 25; in Hebrew society, 47; in Periclean Athens, 138; in Roman Republic, 184; in Byzantine Empire, 259; Qu'ran on, 267, 282; in Indian society, 302, 303–304; in medieval Europe, 336, 382, 448–450; nobility and, 386, 389; in Inca society, 502; in Renaissance society, 522–523; Luther's view of, 541; Catholic view of, 593; in Reformation Europe, 594; family and, in 18th-century Europe, 699–704; illegitimacy and, 703–704; in Ming and Ch'ing China, 780–781; in traditional Japanese society, 788; utopian socialism and, 874, 875; in 19th-century European cities, 914–915; among American black slaves, 1017–1018;

in Turkey, under Kemal, 1080; in Hindu society, 1086; changing Chinese family and, 1094

Mars (Roman god), 204

"Marseillaise," 812, 1041

Marshall, George C., 1173

Marshall Plan, 1173, 1177, 1178

Marsiglio of Padua, 447–448

Martel, Charles, 334, 335, 336, 339, 348

Martin, John, 878

Martin V, pope, 448

Martyrs, 242, 254

Marvels Discovered by the Boat Bound for the Galaxy, The, 773

Marx, Karl, 852, 853, 875–876, 906, 922, 924, 930, 953–954

Marxian socialism, 875–876, 982, 1056, 1093, 1137; Socialist International and, 953–954; as secular ideology, 1304. *See also* Communism

Mary, queen of England, 648

Mary, Queen of Scots, 587, 593

Mary of Burgundy, 533, 545

Mary Tudor, 553, 587

Masaccio, 516

Mass, in medieval Europe, 382

Mass communications, 1274; education and, 1274–1275

Master Tseng, 95

Masturbation: mental illness and, 716; 19th-century concern over, 920

Masurian Lakes, battle of, 1047

Mathematical Principles of Natural Philosophy (Newton), 665

Mathematics: Mesopotamian, 21; Hellenistic, 163, 164; in Islamic state, 289, 290; in Gupta Empire, 301; Maya system of, 490; Chinese, 579; Newtonian, 665; development of, during Renaissance, 666–667

Matisse, Henri, 1115

Matteotti, Giacomo, 1146

Maupeou, René de (Mow-poh, Ray'-nay' de), 684

Mauryan Empire, 80Maximilian de Béthune, duke of Sully, 610

Maximilian I, Holy Roman emperor, 512, 533, 545

Maya civilization, 488–490, 489(map), 494

May Day, 954

May Fourth Movement, 1091

Mazarin (Maz-e-ran'), Jules, 611, 612

Mazzini, Giuseppe, 873, 930, 933

Meat, consumption of: in medieval Europe, 382; by 18th-century upper class, 710; in 19th-century European cities, 908

Mecca, 264, 267, 268, 286

Mecklenberg, dukes of, 591

Medes, 52, 53, 54–55

Medici (Med-e-chi'), Catherine de', 581, 583, 584

Medici, Cosimo de', 510, 518

Medici, Giovanni de', 536

Medici, Lorenzo de', 510, 511, 516

Medici, Marie de', 602, 610

Medici, Piero de', 512

Medici family, 512, 519, 664, 667

Medicine, 709, 713–717; Mesopotamian, 21; Chinese, 104; Greek, 140, 165–167; Byzantine, 257; in Islamic state, 289, 290–291; in medieval Europe, 344–345; monastic, 396; medieval study of, 426; 18th-century, 713–714; faith healers and, 713; apothecaries and, 713–714; surgeons and, 713, 714; physicians and, 713, 714; experiments and research in, 716–717; bacterial revolution and, 901–903

Mediterranean region, 172; colonization of, 123(map), 124; spread of Roman culture in, 179; Roman conquest of, 181, 182, 186; medical revolution and, in Third World, 1257–1258

Megalopolises, 1266

Megasthenes, 80–81

Mehmet II, sultan, 744, 745

Meiji Restoration, 984, 987, 1221

Mein Kampf (Hitler), 1122, 1148, 1149, 1151

Memoirs (Elizabeth, empress of Russia), 681

Memoirs (Saint-Simon), 683

Mendeleev, Dmitri, 922

Mendez, Alphonse, 732

Mendicants, 436

Mensheviks, 1057

Mental hospitals, in 18th-century Europe, 715–716

Mental illness, 715–716

Mercantile class, 489; Aztec, 493

Mercantilism, 614, 832, 835, 872

Merchant-capitalists, 836–837

Merchant guilds, 419, 420, 509

Merchant marine: French, 614; Dutch, 651; English, 1015

Merchants: Babylonian, 19; in Persian Empire, 54; Indian, 79, 301–302, 306; in ancient China, 100, 108; in Byzantine Empire, 258–259; Buddhist, 310–311; medieval, 417–421, 424–425; in early Africa, 466, 467, 471, 478; Calvinism and, 585; in St. Petersburg, 642; Japanese, 786, 790–791

Merici, Angela, 555

Merovingian dynasty, 247, 334, 335

Mesoamerica, 486, 487–493
Mesopotamia, 4, 10, 13, 52; geography of, 11(map); civilization of, 15–21; spread of culture of, 18–23; religion of, 21–22; daily life in, 23–25; marriage customs in, 47; trade in, 66; overrun by Sassanids, 218
Messana, 181
Messenia, 125, 126
Messiah: coming of, 203, 204. *See also* Jesus of Nazareth
Mestizos, 992
Metallurgy: in ancient China, 107. *See also* Bronze; Iron
Metaphysics, during Sung period, 319
Metaphysics (Aristotle), 141
Methodism, 707, 721, 913
Métis. *See* Mulattos
Metternich (Met-er-nick), Klemens von, 867, 868, 869(illus.), 881, 883, 890, 933, 1134; conservatism and, 869, 871; nationalism and, 930
Mexican Revolution of 1910, 1205
Mexico, 486, 487; Aztec empire in, 493(map); Spanish conquest of, 495, 497, 571–572; daily life in, 495–497; slavery in, 496; consequences of independence in, 1001; war with United States, 1009; economic nationalism in, 1205–1206; democratic government in, 1207; origins of Green Revolution in, 1263; population growth in, 1266; as "middle power," 1289; foreign debt of, 1299
Meyer, Eduard, 56–57
Miasmatic theory of disease, 901
Michael IV, 259
Michael Romanov, tsar of Russia, 636
Michelangelo, 515, 516, 518, 580, 602, 748
Michelet, Jules, 705, 873, 930
Mickey Mouse, 1117
Middle Ages, 230–259, 260, 334–367, 404–456; state-church relations in, 232; High, 334, 374–399, 405, 416, 425, 426, 432, 528; Frankish aristocracy and rise of Carolingian dynasty, 334–336; Charlemagne's empire in, 336–341, 338(map); Carolingian Empire in, 339–340, 346–347; intellectual revival in, 341–344; health and medical care in, 344–346; feudalism in, 347–350; manorialism in, 349–350; invasions of ninth century, 350–352, 351(map); political revival in, 352–355; increasing population in, 354; church revival and reform in, 355–359; Gregorian revolution in, 359–362; Crusades in, 362,

364–367; historical periods of, 363(map), 415(table), 548(table); peasants in, 374–385, 692–693, 698; nobility in, 376, 385–386, 390–392; late, 404, 412; origins of modern state in, 404–417; economic revival in, 417–426; universities of, 426, 427(map), 428–429; creative outburst in, 429–434; growth of heresy in, 434–437; Black Death in, 437–441; Hundred Years' War, 441–446; decline of church's prestige in, 446–448; daily life in, 448–456; origins of scientific revolution in, 665–666
Middle class: Crusades and, 364; monasteries and, 393; rise of, in medieval towns, 418; in early Africa, 471; Italian, during Renaissance, 509, 518, 522, 531; Calvinism and, 585; French, 614, 684, 806; Spanish, 619; of eastern Europe, 624; Japanese, 788, 790; origins of French Revolution and, 804; Napoleon I and, 817; new industrial, 852, 853, 864; in 19th-century European cities, 906–910; marriage and, 914; Bismarck and, 940–941; changing class structure and, 1182–1183; in Third World, 1272
Middle East: nationalism in, 1075–1084; during 1914–1939, 1084(table); Palestine, Israel, and, 1231(map)
Middlemarch: A Study of Provincial Life (Eliot), 925
Middle powers, 1289
Midway Island, Battle of, 1163
Mies van der Rohe, Ludwig, 1114
Mi Fei, 319
Migrations, 40; of Hebrews, 40, 43–44; of Aryans, 68–69; of Greeks, 124, 150; of barbarians, 217; of Germanic peoples, 244–247, 246(map); of Vikings, 352; of peasants, in Middle Ages, 376; in early Africa, 462, 476, 481; of Aztecs, 495; overseas expansion and, 565, 566(map); disease and, 574; of Galla, 732; Chinese, 773; liberalism and, 798; to North American colonies, 836; Irish potato famine and, 886; European, of 19th century, 968–971; population growth and, 969; of 19th-century Asians, 972; in Latin America, 1004–1006; of Jews from Nazi Germany, 1153; to cities, in Third World, 1267, 1272–1273
Milan, 508, 510–511
Militant nonviolence, 1088

Military. *See* Army; Warfare
Military warrior clique, Japanese, 783–784
Milk, in 18th-century European diet, 710
Mill, John Stuart, 950
Millet, Jean François, 693
Milpa system of agriculture, 489
Mimic Men, The (Naipaul), 1276–1277
Minamoto clan, 326
Minarets, 309
Mines Act of 1842, 859
Ming Dynasty, 309, 310, 570; establishment of, 322; land reclamation under, 769, 770(table); agricultural and commercial revolutions under, 770; government of Hung Wu and, 770–773; maritime expansion under, 773; decline of, 774–777; daily life under, 779–782; educational system under, 781
Ministerials, 386, 409
Ministers, 254
Ministry of Munitions (England), 1051
Minoans, 116, 118–119
"Miracle rice," 1264
Mirandola, Pico della, 514
Misogyny, 595
Missi dominici, 339–340
Missing link, in evolution, 7
Missionaries: of early church, 233–236, 248; in medieval Europe, 335; in Africa, 979
Mita, 996, 997
Mithra (Mih-thrah), sun-god, 56
Mithraism, 206
Modern architecture and design, 1113–1114
Modernism, 1113
Modernization, of Russia, 942–945
Modern music, 1116
Modern painting, 1114–1116
Modern thought: uncertainty in, 1106–1113; philosophy and, 1107–1109; revival of Christianity and, 1109–1110; new physics and, 1110; Freudian psychology and, 1110–1112; literature and, 1112–1113
Mogadishu, 732
Mohenjo-daro, 66, 67(illus.), 68
Moksha, 72, 74
Molesmes, abbey of, 356
Molière, 616–617
Molotov, Vyacheslav, 1190–1191
Moltke, Helmuth von, 1044
Mombasa, 732, 733
Mona Lisa (Leonardo), 581, 1116
Monarchy: defined, 122; Sumerian, 17–18; Babylonian, 19; Hittite, 34;

under Cyrus the Great, 55–56; Mycenaean, 118; in Greek polis, 122, 127; Hellenistic, 149, 150–151, 152(map), 153–154, 155, 156, 161; Macedonian, 150; Roman, constitutional, 196, 202; Antonine, 208–209; Frankish, 256, 335; Indian, 306; German, 359, 361; controversy over lay investiture and, 359–361; of Ghana, 469–470; Aztec, 497; Renaissance, 529–530; Spanish, 567, 575; Valois, 580; French, 581, 582, 683, 687; absolute, in 17th-century Europe, 608–643; English, restoration of, 647–648; constitutional, 648; Prussian, 679–681; Russian, 681–683; "bourgeois," 888. *See also* Absolutism

Monash, John, 1032

Monasteries, 242, 395–397; in Gaul, 234, 242; Irish, 235; in Byzantine Empire, 259; Buddhist, 310–311, 327, 784; Carolingian, 344(illus.); Benedictine, 355, 356; oblation and, 387–388, 392, 393; recruitment into, 392–393; economic difficulties of, 397–398. *See also* Convents

Monasticism, 241–242; and the rule of St. Benedict, 242–247; spread of, in Byzantine Empire, 259; Sufism and, 284; Northumbrian, 341; in Middle Ages, 355–357, 392–397; dissolution by Henry VIII, 552

Monet, Claude, 844, 1114–1115

Money: during Renaissance, 515. *See also* Coinage; Paper money

Money economy: advent of, in High Middle Ages, 376

Mongolia, 109, 772; conquest of, 779

Mongoloids, 487

Mongols, 316; assault Islamic state, 278–279; defeat Thai confederacy, 306; conquer China, 306, 310, 319–322, 634; invade India, 307; decay of government in China, 768

Monks, in medieval Europe, 243. *See also* Monasteries

Monnet, Jean, 1177, 1178

Monotheism: Egyptian, 31, 32; Hebrew, 45, 46

Monroe, James, 1009

Monroe Doctrine, 868

Montague (Mant-eh-gyu), Mary Wortley, 716

Montaigne (Mon-tan'), Michel de, 579, 598–599

Montcalm, Louis, 1023

Monte Albán, 491

Montesquieu (Mon-tes-kyu), Charles-Louis, Baron de, 672, 673,

677, 687, 802, 995; liberalism and, 797–798

Montezuma I, Aztec emperor, 492, 497, 571–572

Montezuma II, Aztec emperor, 493, 494

Morality: Hindu law of, 73; preoccupation with, during Renaissance, 519; in 19th-century European cities, 910

Moravia, 869

More, Thomas, 525, 526, 551, 552(illus.)

Morocco, 467, 1041

Mortality. *See* Death rate

Mosaic law, 23, 45, 267

Moscow: as "Third Rome," 256; rise of, 634–635

Moses, 43, 45, 46, 57

Mosques: Ottoman, 749; Indian, 757

Mossaddeq (Mo-sahd-deck), Muhammad, 1233

Motion pictures, 1116–1118; German, 1117; propaganda and, 1117–1118

Mountain (French political group), 812–813

Mountbatten, Louis, 1223

Movable type, 314–315

Movies. *See* Motion pictures

Mozambique, 733; nationalism in, 1246

Mr., Mrs., and Baby (Droz), 919

Mu'awiya (Mu-ah'-we-ah), 274

Muezzin, 470

Muhammad (Mu-ham'-mad), 264, 273–275, 286, 292, 751–752; and faith of Islam, 265–268

Muhammad II, 565, 571

Muhammad Ali, Ottoman general, 966–967

Muhammad of Ghur, 308

Muhammad Rimfa, king of Kano, 730

Muhammad Toure, 728–730

Mulattos, 739–740, 992

Multinational corporations, 1294, 1301–1304

Mummies, Egyptian, 28

Murasaki Shikibu, 326

Musa, Mansa, 472–473

Music: in ancient China, 107; baroque, 602–603; of romantic movement, 880–881; modern, 1116

Music halls, in 19th-century Europe, 912, 913

Muslim League, 1085, 1222

Muslims, 252, 256, 279–293, 355; end Visigothic rule, 246, 269, 289–292; beliefs of, 265; military organization of, 272; social organization of, 279–282; versus Christians, 280–281, 292–293; view of the

West, 292–293; invade India, 308–309, 753; sack Rome, 352; slavery and, 467; in kingdom of Ghana, 470; under Louis XIV, 616; defeated by Portuguese, 731; Sudanese, 975, 977; nationalism of, 1229, 1233. *See also* Shi'ites; Sunnites

Musset, Alfred de, 880

Mussolini, Benito, 172, 1117, 1145–1148, 1147(illus.); Hitler's attack on Austria and, 1155; alliance with Hitler, 1157; deposed, 1164–1165

Mycenaeans, 32, 33, 116, 118–120

Myoshu, 327

My Secret Life (anonymous), 915, 916

Mysore, 762

Mystery plays, 383, 432

Mystery religions, 139, 158–159, 204, 206

Mystical experience, search for, 1309–1310

Myths, Mesopotamian, 22

NAACP. *See* National Association for the Advancement of Colored People

Nadir (Nah-deer) Shah, 758

Nagasaki, 1166, 1214, 1291

Nagashino, Battle of, 784

Nahuatl, 493

Nahum (Hebrew prophet), 52

Naipaul (Nigh-paul), V. S., 1276–1277

Nanking, Treaty of, 966

Nantes, Edict of, 584, 610; revocation of, 615, 647

Naples, 933

Napoleon I, emperor of France, 172, 179, 339, 500, 816; rules France, 817–818; wars and foreign policy of, 819, 821–823; Grand Empire of, 820(map), 821; abdication of, 822, 864; returns from Elba, exiled again, 823; defeated at Waterloo, 823, 864, 867; invades Egypt, 966; Louisiana Purchase and, 1007

Napoleon III, emperor of France, 930–933, 939; rebuilding of Paris and, 903, 931, 932(illus.); wins election of 1848, 930; political and social ideas of, 931; as president of Second Republic, 931; as emperor, 931–933; unification of Italy and, 936; defeated in Franco-Prussian War of 1870–1871, 941; deposes Ferdinand VII, 997

Napoleonic Code, women and, 818, 916

Napoleonic Ideas (Napoleon III), 930

Nara, 325

Nariño (Na-reen-yo), Antonio, 995

Nasser, Gamal Abdel (Nahs′-ser, Gah-mehl Ab-del), 1232
National Assembly (France): formation of, 804–806; limited monarchy and, 808, 809–810; conflict with church, 809–810; Napoleon III and, 931, 932, 933; Paris Commune and, 948, 954
National Association for the Advancement of Colored People (NAACP), 1200
National Consolidated Trades Union, 857
National Convention (France): declares war on Britain, Holland, and Spain, 812; division in, 812–813; collapse of economic controls and, 815
Nationalism, 872–874, 931–956, 1137, 1178, 1284; Hundred Years' War and, 445; French, 814–815, 873, 930–933, 950; Hungarian, 890; Italian, 933–936; German, 936–942, 1148; Russian, 943–945, 1143; Irish, 950–951, 1053; in Austro-Hungarian Empire, 951–953; Magyar, 951, 953; socialist parties and, 953–954; anti-imperialism and, 982; in colonial India, 983; Balkan, 1042; decline of Ottoman Empire and, 1042; Serbian, 1044; World War I and, 1044; Austrian, 1053; in Asia, 1072–1102; of Arabs, 1076, 1077, 1082, 1229; Turkish, 1076, 1079–1081; Greek, 1079; Iranian, 1081, 1233; in Afghanistan, 1081–1082; Palestinian, 1082–1084; Jewish, 1082; in India, 1084–1090; Chinese, 1090–1092, 1097, 1214; Japanese, 1090, 1095–1097; of Hitler, 1148, 1153; Russian, 1162; economic, in Latin America, 1205–1206; African, 1234, 1237–1241, 1239(table); Afrikaner, racist, 1246–1247; as secular ideology, 1304
Nationalist party (China), 1090, 1214
National Labor Relations Act, 1127
National Liberals, 946
National Recovery Administration (NRA), 1127
National Socialist German Workers' party. See Nazism
National Socialist party (Germany), 1122
National System of Political Economy (List), 851
Nation-states: United Nations and, 1284–1287, 1289; multinational corporations and, 1301
Native Americans, westward expansion and, 1010. See also American Indians

Native Land Act, 1246
Native reserves system, in South Africa, 1247
NATO. See North Atlantic Treaty Organization
Natural law, 178
Natural science, 669
Nature: Indians' fondness for, 68; Aristotle's view of, 141; Cynics' view of, 160; Stoics' view of, 161; direct observation of, in Aristotle's view, 428; Montaigne's thoughts on, 598, 599; scientific method and, 669; conceptions of, during romantic movement, 878, 879
Navigation: Muslim advances in, 288; 15th-century developments in, 571; scientific revolution and, 667, 669. See also Merchant marine; Navy; Ships
Navigation Acts, growth in English trade and, 832
Navy: Athenian, 128; Hellenistic, 153; Roman, 181, 212; Japanese, 985; German, 1041–1042
Nazism, 1137–1138; roots of, 1148–1149; state and society under, 1151–1153; opponents of, 1153, 1155; expansion and, 1155–1159, 1161; World War II and, 1159, 1161
Nazi-Soviet Pact, 1158, 1159
Neanderthal man, 6, 8, 9
Near East: origins of Western world in, 4–36; kingdoms and empires in, 40–60, 42(map), 57(table); spread of Greek culture in, 154
Nefertiti, 31
Négritude, 1237
Nehru, Jawaharlal (Nay′-ru, Jah-wah-har-lal), 1089, 1223
Nelson, Lord, 819
Neocolonialism, 1002, 1182, 1205, 1293–1294
Neo-Confucianism, 319
Neolithic Age, 7, 9–14
NEP. See New Economic Policy
Nepal, 64
Nero, Roman emperor, 207, 215
Nerva, Roman emperor, 216–217
Netherlands: United Provinces of, 584(map), 587, 589, 591; under Charles V, 584–585; revolt of, 585–587; Spanish, 617, 618; War of the Spanish Succession and, 618–619, 618(map), 653; in 17th century, 649–653; trade of, 651–652; commercial prosperity of, 652; Austrian, 812, 813; in First Coalition against France, 812, 813; in Asia, 977; population density in,

1295. See also Holland; Low Countries
Netherlands East Indies. See Indonesia
Nevsky, Alexander, 634
Newcomen, Thomas, 840
New Culture Movement, 1092–1093
New Deal, 1126–1128, 1130, 1200
New Economic Policy (NEP), 1139
New Kingdom (Egypt), 28, 30–32, 35, 41
New Laws, 319
New Order, of Hitler, 1159
New physics, 1110
New South Wales, colony of, 1027, 1028, 1029
New Testament, 404, 432, 526, 541, 542
Newton, Isaac, 301, 665, 669, 670, 672
New World, 486; Spanish immigration to, 573; era of liberal revolution and, 798. See also Americas; Central America; Latin America; North America
Nicaragua, 486; intervention of U.S. Marines in, 1033; Sandinista government in, 1209
Nicene Creed, 232
Nicephorus I Phocas, 258
Nichiren, 325–326
Nicholas I, tsar of Russia, 892
Nicholas II, pope, 358
Nicholas II, tsar of Russia, 945, 1044, 1054
Nicholas V, pope, 513
Nicolaism, 358, 359
Nietzsche (Nee′-cha), Friedrich, 1107–1108, 1111
Nigeria, 465, 467, 728, 979; nation building in, 1243, 1245–1246; as leading power in sub-Saharan Africa, 1290. See also Biafra
Nijmegen, Treaty of, 617
Nikon, 637
Nile River, in Neolithic Age, 13
Nimitz, Chester, 1163
Ninety-five Theses, of Luther, 537–538
Nippur, 15(map), 16
Nirvana, 77
Nivelle, Robert, 1046, 1053
Nixon, Richard, 1185, 1202
Nkrumah, Kwame (Ung′-kroo-mah, Kwah-may), 1239–1240, 1242
Nobel Peace Prize, 1121
Nobility: Sumerian, 18; European, origins of, 248, 334–335; lay investiture and, 361; Crusades and, 364; in High Middle Ages, 376, 385–386, 390–392; in late Middle Ages, 455;

Maya, 489; Aztec, 495; Inca, 502–503; Italian, during Renaissance, 509; French, 582, 610, 613–614, 684, 687, 803, 805, 806, 809; of eastern Europe, 621–624; Czech, 625; Hungarian, 625–626; Prussian, 630, 681; Russian, 635–639, 642, 682, 683, 688; Chinese, 771–772, 781; Japanese, 786, 787; Napoleon I and, 817; conservatism and, 869. See also Aristocracy

Nobunaga, Oda (No-bu-nah-gah, Oh-dah), 784–785

Nomadic lifestyle, 8, 9, 44(illus.), 46, 47, 264–265

Nonviolence, militant, 1087–1088

Nördlingen, Battle of, 592

Normandy, 352, 407, 414

Normandy invasion, 1165

Norman inquest, 406

Normans. See Vikings

North Africa: Roman conquest of, 181, 190; in World War II, 1164

North America, 565, 596; British colonies in, 798, 799, 836; population growth in, 969. See also Canada; United States

North Atlantic Treaty Organization (NATO), 1174, 1177, 1289; détente versus cold war and, 1203

Northern Rhodesia. See Zambia

North German Confederation, 940

North Korea: invades South Korea, 1174; Korean War and, 1202

Northmen. See Vikings

Northumbria, 341–343

North Vietnam: Vietnam War and, 1202, 1203

Norway: independence of, 951; Hitler occupies, 1158; following World War II, 1178

Notre Dame, cathedral of, 417, 431(illus.), 585–586

NRA. See National Recovery Administration

Nubia, 31; Egypt and, 41, 478

Nuclear proliferation, 1291

Nuns: in medieval Europe, 389, 393–395; during Reformation, 555–556

Nuremberg Laws, 1153

Nurhachi, 777

Nursing, of babies. See Breast-feeding

Nutrition, 709–710. See also Diet

Oath of the Tennis Court, 806

Oba, 728

Oblation, 387–388, 392, 393

October Manifesto, 945

Oderic Vitalis, 392

Odyssey (Homer), 118, 120–121, 201

Oedipus at Colonus (Sophocles), 134

Oedipus the King (Sophocles), 134

OEEC. See Organization of European Economic Cooperation

Oil: postwar economy and, 1185; imports of, 1294; global transfer of wealth and, 1296

Oil shocks, 1185, 1186, 1294

Oldenbarneveldt, Jan van, 649

Old Kingdom (Egypt), 27, 28, 31–32

Old Testament, 43, 44, 46, 48, 52, 432, 550

Oleg, Varangian ruler, 256, 633

Oligarchy: defined, 122; Lycurgan regimen and, 126; Italian, during Renaissance, 509–510

Olivares, Count, 621

Olmec civilization, 488, 494

Olympic games, 139

Omdurman, battle of, 975, 977

On Admonition to Peace (Luther), 540–541

On Airs, Waters, and Places (Hippocrates), 140

On Baptism and Against the Donatists (St. Augustine), 240

On Christian Liberty (Luther), 540

One Day in the Life of Ivan Denisovich (Solzhenitsyn), 1190

On Female Disorders (Trotula), 346

On Floating Bodies (Archimedes), 163

On Plane Equilibriums (Archimedes), 163

On Pleasure (Valla), 515

"On Solitude" (Montaigne), 599

"On the Dignity of Man" (Mirandola), 514

On the False Donation of Constantine (Valla), 515

On the Heaven (Aristotle), 141–142

On the Origin of Species by the Means of Natural Selection (Darwin), 6, 923

On the Physical Elements (Hildegard), 346

On the Revolutions of the Heavenly Spheres (Copernicus), 662

OPEC. See Organization of Petroleum Exporting Countries

Open Door policy, 986

Open-field agricultural system, 377, 692, 693(illus.), 694(illus.), 695. See also Enclosure movement

Opium trade, 965–966

Oracles, 91, 98

Oratories of Divine Love, 537

Orderic Vitalis, 392

Oresteia, The (Or-eh-sty-ah) (Aeschylus), 134

Organization of American States, 1207

Organization of European Economic Cooperation (OEEC), 1178

Organization of Petroleum Exporting Countries (OPEC), 1185, 1294, 1296

Organization of Work (Blanc), 874

Orlov, Gregory, 682

Oruc, 745

Osaka, Battle of, 786

Osiris (O-sigh-ris), 27, 28, 159

Osman, 744

Ostracism, 127

Ostrogoths, 245, 246, 247, 250

O'Sullivan, John Louis, 873, 1006–1007

Othello (Shakespeare), 600

Otto I, king of Germany, 353–354

Ottoman Empire, 744–751, 748(map), 951, 1079(map); conquers Constantinople, 744–745; expansion of, 745; under Selim the Grim, 746; under Suleiman I, 746–749; ruling class of, 747; art and culture of, 747–749; government of, 749–750; under Muhammad Kuprili, 750; Karlowitz peace treaty and, 750; Peace of Amiens and, 751; Egypt in, 966–967; in Crimean War, 942; Congress of Berlin and, 1039, 1042; destruction of, 1042, 1049, 1075

Ottoman Turks, 565, 570; Habsburg defeat of, 625; capture Constinople, 744–745; driven from Greece, 881–882

Otto of Ballenstedt, 391

Outcastes, 302

Overpopulation, 40

Overseas expansion: by Greeks, 123–124; by Vikings, 565; Portuguese, 565, 567, 731, 733–734; Spanish, 567–568, 574–575; by Low Countries, 568; English, 568; French, 568, 619. See also Colonization; Imperialism

Ovid, 185–186, 521

Oviedo (O-vya-tho), 570

Owen, Robert, 855–856, 857, 955

Oxford University, 428

Pachacuti (Pah-shah-ku-tee) Inca, Incan king, 500, 501, 502

Pachomius, 242

Pacific islands, colonization of, 565

Paganini, Nicolo, 881

Paganism, Christianity and, 203–204, 221–224, 230, 236; Islam and, 265, 267

Pahlavi, Muhammad Reza, 1233

Paine, Thomas, 801, 995

Pakistan, 64, 65, 309; after independence, 1223; nuclear arms race and, 1293

Palaces: Minoan, 118; baroque, 639–640

Palacký, Francis, 873, 890

Paleoanthropologists, 6, 7

Pale of settlement, 970

Paleolithic Age, 7, 8–9

Palestine, 42, 43, 1230, 1231(map); Crusades and, 367; in Ottoman empire, 746; Jewish nation created in, 1064, 1077, 1082–1083

Palestine Liberation Organization, 1230, 1232, 1233

Palmerston, Lord, 892

Pan-Africanists, 1237

Panama, 486

Panama Canal: growth of intercontinental trade and, 963; U.S. control over, 978

Pan-American Conference, 1033

Pan-Arabs, 1229

Pan Chao, 104

Pankus, 34

Pantagruel (Rabelais), 526

Papacy: rise of Carolingian dynasty and, 335–336; reform of, 355, 357–359, 361–362; controversy over lay investiture and, 359–361; in High Middle Ages, 361–362; Crusades and, 362, 367; dispute between Frederick II and, 412; Inquisition and, 436; 13th-century dispute with kings of England and France, 446; Babylonian Captivity and, 446–447; secularism and, 515; Pragmatic Sanction of Bourges and, 529; in 16th-century Europe, 535–536, 537; Luther's denunciation of, 543; Catholic Reformation and, 554; Concordat of Bologna and, 581; baroque art and, 602; opposition to national unification of Italy, 933. See also individual popes

Papal conclave, 447

Papal court. See Curia

Papal States, 336, 359, 446; during Renaissance, 510–511; during Catholic Reformation, 554

Papen, Franz von, 1150, 1151

Paper: invention of, 107; use of, by Muslims, 289; manufacture of, during Renaissance, 520

Paper money, 316, 520

Paprius Vitalis, 212

Paraguay, 486

Paris: cathedrals in, 417, 431(illus.); medieval schools in, 426; university at, 428; Treaty of, 441, 761, 801,

835, 1023; St. Bartholomew's Day massacre in, 583; salons in, during Enlightenment, 677–678; 19th-century rebuilding of, 903, 931, 932(illus.)

Paris Commune, 948, 953, 954

Paris Peace Conference, 1033, 1077

Parlement of Paris, 413; absolutism and, 684, 687; French Revolution and, 803, 804, 805

Parlements (high courts of France), 672

Parliament (Canada), 1024

Parliament (England), 608, 950; Hundred Years' War and, 445, 530; Elizabeth I and, 643; Triennial Act and, 645; Instrument of Government and, 646; restoration of monarchy and, 647; British East India Company and, 761–762; taxation of American colonies and, 799; child labor and, 855–856; liberal reform of, 883–884; colonial India and, 982; Canada and, 1023, 1024; Australia and, 1032

Parliament (France), 948, 950, 1129

Parliament (Germany), under Bismarck, 940–941, 946, 950

Parliament (Italy), 1146

Parliament (Prussia), unification of Germany and, 937, 938, 940

Parliament (Russia), 945

Parthenon, 131, 132–133, 133(illus.), 134(illus.)

Parthians, 149, 214–215

Pashas, 747

Pass laws, 1247, 1248

Pasternak, Boris, 1190

Pasteur, Louis, 902, 922

Paston, John and Margaret, 449

Paterfamilias, 184

Paternalism, 83

Patriarch, 253; in Paleolithic Age, 8

Patricians, 176; conflict with Plebeians, 178

Paul III, pope, 554, 555, 557

Paul IV, pope, 554

Paul of Tarsus. See St. Paul

Pax Romana, 183, 192, 196–224; economic aspect of, 213(map)

Peacekeeping, by U.N. Security Council, 1285

Peace of Amiens, 751

Peace of Augsburg (Augsburg settlement), 545, 589, 592

Peace of Paris: first (1814), 865; second (1815), 867–868

Peace of Utrecht, 619

Peace of Westphalia, 580, 592

Peace settlement, following World War I, 1060–1066

Peacock Throne, 757

Pearl Harbor, Japanese attack on, 1159

Peasantry: Egyptian, 29, 967; Aryan, 70; Chinese, 102, 105, 109; in ancient Greece, 126; Byzantine, 254–255; during T'ang Dynasty, 312–313; in early Japan, 326; manorialism and, 349–350; in medieval Europe, 374–385, 692–693, 698; revolts during late Middle Ages, 452–456, 454(map); in Inca society, 502; in 16th-century Europe, 540–541; taxation of, under Louis XIV, 614, 615; in 17th-century Spain, 621; in eastern Europe, 622–624, 688, 693–694; Russian, 634, 636, 637, 639, 944–945; forced labor of, in St. Petersburg, 641–642; life of, in 18th-century Europe, 692–721; marriage and families of, 700, 701; child care among, 704; diet of, 711–712; Japanese, 785, 786, 789, 789–790; revolts in France, 808; Napoleon I and, 817; in 19th-century Europe, 946; Chinese, under Mao Tse-tung, 1093; collectivization of, in Stalinist Russia, 1140–1142; Chinese, under Deng Xiaoping, 1218. See also Serfdom

Pedro I, king of Brazil, 1000

Pedro II, king of Brazil, 1000

Peel, Robert, 885

Peking, occupation by British and French, 966. See also Beijing

Peloponnesian War, 130, 135, 142

Peninsulares, 992, 993, 995, 996, 1006

Penitential system, 237–238

Penn, William, 647

People, The (Michelet), 873

People's Budget, 950, 1042

People's Charter, 884

People's Republic of China, 1202, 1214; under Mao, 1215–1219. See also China

Pereire brothers, 874

Perestroika, 1195

Pergamum, 182.

Pericles (Pehr′-uh′-kleez), 129, 130, 131

Pericles (Shakespeare), 600

Périer (Par-ye), Casimir, 886–887

Periplus of the Erythraean Sea, 475, 476, 478

Permanent Mandates Commission, 1074

Perón, Juan, 1207

Perry, Matthew, 966, 983

Persecution, religious, 241–242

Persia, 52–60, 751–753, 1081; geography of, 52, 53(map); background of;

53–55, creation of, 55–56; under Cyrus the Great, 55–56; religion in, 56–58; becomes world empire, 58–60, 78; India and, 78–79; Greek wars with, 128, 148; fall of, 149; Alexander's conquest of, 155; under Ismail, 751–752; under Shah Abbas, 752–753. *See also* Iran

Persian Gulf War, 1287, 1288(map), 1289

Persian Letters, The (Montesquieu), 672

Personal hygiene, bubonic plague and, 439

Peru, 486; Incas of, 498–503; Spanish conquest of, 568, 571, 572–573; Indians in, 996; consequences of independence in, 1001; elected government in, 1209

Pétain (Pay'-tan), Henri-Philippe, 1158, 1164

Peter (Jesus' follower), 205, 206, 230, 233

Peter I (the Great), tsar of Russia, 633, 638(illus.), 682; reforms of, 637–639; St. Petersburg and, 640–643; abolishes hereditary succession of tsars, 681

Peter III, tsar of Russia, 680, 682

"Peterloo." *See* Battle of Peterloo

Peter of Dreux (Scourge of the Clergy), 390

Peter the Hermit, 364

Petrarch (Pe-trark), Francesco, 512–513, 525

Petrine Doctrine, 230

Petrograd Soviet of Workers' and Soldiers' Deputies, 1056, 1058

Pharaohs, 26, 27–28, 29

Phèdre (Racine), 617

Philinus (Fil-eye-nus), 166

Philip I, king of France, 359, 361

Philip II, king of France (Philip Augustus), 407, 408, 411, 416

Philip II, king of Macedonia, 143, 148

Philip II, king of Spain: marries Mary Tudor, 553; Spanish economy and, 575; revolt of Netherlands and, 585–587; Spanish Armada and, 587–589, 619

Philip III, king of Spain, 589, 621

Philip IV (the Fair), king of France, 416, 441, 446

Philip IV, king of Spain, 621

Philip VI, king of France, 441, 442, 445

Philip Augustus, king of France, 361, 365, 414

Philip of Burgundy, 533

Philippine Islands, 1228–1229; nationalism in, 1090, 1100–1102

Philistines, 42, 44

Phillip, Arthur, 1028

Philosophes, 671–675, 676, 679, 687, 922

Philosophical Dictionary (Voltaire), 673–674

Philosophy: Chinese, 93, 94; origins of, in Hellenic Greece, 116, 139–142; Hellenistic, 159–161; Muslim, 291–293; Greek, transmitted to European West, 292, 428; of Enlightenment, philosophes and, 671–675; modern, 1107–1109

Phoenicians (Fo-ne'-shuns), 42, 49

Physica (On the Physical Elements) (Hildegard), 395

Physicians: Hellenistic, 166, 167; Byzantine, 258; Arab, 290–291; in early Middle Ages, 345; child care and, 707; 18th-century, 713, 714

Physics: medieval, 661; Aristotelian, 662, 664; Newtonian, 665; in 20th century, 1110

Physics (Aristotle), 141

Piankhy, 41

Picasso, Pablo, 1115, 1116

Pickford, Mary, 1117

Pictographs, 20

Picts, 251

Piedmont, 933

Pietism, 720, 913

Pigtail, as sign of subservience, 778

Pilate, Pontius, 202–203, 204–205

Pilgrimages: medieval, 385; to Mecca, by Musa, 473

Pillow Book (Sei), 326

Pilsudski, Joseph, 1136

Pinel, Philippe, 715

Pippin II, 335

Pippin III, 335, 336

Pippin of Landen, 335

Piracy, 156, 773, 774

Pirenne, Henri, 417

Piri Reis, 749

Pisistratus (Py-sihs'-trah-tus), 127

Pissarro, Camille, 1115

Pitt, William, 835

Pius II, pope, 513, 536, 745

Pius IV, pope, 594

Pius V, pope, 747

Pius VII, pope, 818

Pius IX, pope, 933, 946

Pizarro, Francisco, 568, 572, 573, 574, 993

Place value, concept of, 21

Plague. *See* Bubonic plague

Planck, Max, 1110

Plato, 141, 292, 319, 526

Plautus (Plawt-us), 186

Playing cards, 520

Plebeians (Ple-be'-ans), 176; conflict with patricians, 178

Plessis, Armand Jean du. *See* Richelieu, Cardinal

Pliny (Plin'-e) the Elder, 216

Plows: in Neolithic Age, 11; in ancient China, 106; in High Middle Ages, 379(illus.)

Pluralism, 550; Luther and, 537–538

Plutarch (Plu-tark), 131, 163, 526

Plutonium, 1293

Po Chü-i (Po Ju-e), 318

Poincaré (Pwan-ca-re'), Raymond, 1119, 1120, 1122

Poland: serfdom in, 623; war with Sweden, 630; partitions of, 682–683, 683(map), 687; Treaty of Versailles and, 1064; conservative authoritarianism in, 1136; Hitler attacks, 1158; in World War II, 1158; United States and Britain refuse to promise territory to Soviet Union, 1170; cold war and, 1170, 1172; following World War II, 1174; collectivization in, 1188; rebellion in, 1190; Solidarity movement in, 1197–1198; revolution of 1989 in, 1198; revival of Christianity in, 1307

Police terrorism, in Stalinist Russia, 1142

Polis, 121–123, 126, 132(illus.), 133, 135, 139, 141, 151, 159, 172, 176

Politics: origins of, in Hellenistic Greece, 116

Politics, The (Aristotle), 141, 292

Politiques, 584

Polk, James, 1009

Polo, Marco, 298, 320, 321, 329; spice trade and, 570

Pol Pot regime, 1290

Polybius (Pol-ib-e-us), 172, 186, 257

Polygamy: in Islamic society, 282–283; German custom of, 336; in Aztec society, 497; in Inca society, 502

Polytheism, Egyptian, 32

Pompeius Trogus, 144

Pompey, 188, 192

Pontifex maximus, 197

Poorhouses, English, 854–855

Popes. *See* Papacy; *individual popes*

Pòpolo (Italian middle class), 509

Popular Front, 1129, 1130

Population: in Neolithic Age, 9, 10; of Rome, in late Republic, 192; of Roman Empire, 198; of ancient Rome, 210; European, in Middle Ages, 352, 354, 417, 418, 439; in early Africa, 464; Maya, 489; Teotihuacán, 491; Aztec, 497; of Peru and Mexico in 16th century, 573–574; of Germany,

Population (cont.)
after Thirty Years' War, 592; demographic crisis and, 695–696; in England during 1000–1800, 695(fig.); in 18th-century Europe, 696(fig.), 697, 968; in Ottoman Empire, 750; in Ming China, 769–770, 776; under Manchu rule, 777–778; growth of, Industrial Revolution and, 828; in Amsterdam, 830; urban, in 19th century, 898–899; pressure of, European migrations of 19th century and, 968–970; North American, in 19th century, 969; increase of European and world, 969(fig.); of Buenos Aires, by 1914, 1004; American, 1007; Australian, 1030; growth of, in India, 1224; of Nigeria, 1243; urban, 1266, 1267(table); of the world, 1295. See also Overpopulation; Population explosion

Population Bomb, The (Erlich), 1263
Population explosion, 1258, 1259(map), 1260, 1262, 1294
Poquelin, Jean-Baptiste. See Molière
Porcelain, Chinese, 317, 775(illus.), 779
Pornography, 521
Portugal: in Africa, 477, 480, 973; overseas expansion of, 565, 567, 731, 733–734; seaborne trade of, 577, 579; slavery and, 596, 729, 734, 735–736; Brazil's independence from, 1000; conservative authoritarianism in, 1136
Positivist method, 923
Postimpressionism, 1115
Postumus, 217
Potatoes: in 18th-century European diet, 712; failure of crop in Ireland, 885, 886
Potsdam Conference, 1172
Pottery: Greek, 138(illus.), 175; Hellenistic, 157; Indian, 302
Po Valley, 172, 174
Poverty: French Revolution and, 806–807; lack of power and, 840; in Third World, 1256–1257; theory of dependency and, 1296
Praetorian (Pree-tawr′-e-uhn) Guard, 207, 471
Praetors, Roman, 177, 178
Pragmatic Sanction of Bourges, 529, 581
Praise of Folly, The (Erasmus), 526
Prayer, in medieval monasteries, 392, 395
Preacherships, 540
"Preaching Friars," 436
Predestination, doctrine of, 546, 721
Pregnancy: in medieval society, 386–387, 391; birth control and,

702–703, 915, 1020; among American frontier women, 1019–1020
Premarital sex: in 18th-century Europe, 702–703; in 19th-century European cities, 915
Presbyterian church, 547
Pre-Socratics, 139, 140
Prester John, 479, 565
Priene, 153(illus.)
Priesthood: Sumerian, 17; Egyptian, 31; Aryan, 70; Chinese, 92; Greek, 138, 158; marriage and, 357–358; in early Africa, 465; Aztec, 496–497; Inca, 501. See also Clergy
Primary sources, 4–5
Primogeniture, 389, 634
Prince, The (Machiavelli), 510, 519–520, 529
Princeps civitatis, 197
Principate, 197
Principia (Newton), 665, 671
Printing: invention of, 107, 314, 319; movable type and, 314–315, 520; spread of Lutheranism and, 541
Private enterprise, 871, 872
Procopius, 257
Progress, idea of: Enlightenment and, 670; belief in, 1106; rejection of, 1106, 1112
Progress of the Human Mind (Condorcet), 676
Prokofiev (Pro-kof′-yef), Sergei, 1188
Proletariat, 832, 875–876
Propaganda: radio and, 1117; movies and, 1117–1118; under Stalin, 1138, 1143; under Hitler, 1151
Prophet. See Muhammad
Prose writing, during T'ang period, 317–318
Prostitution: in Mesopotamia, 24; in Periclean Athens, 137, 138; during late Middle Ages, 449–450; in Renaissance society, 523; in Reformation Europe, 594; use of birth control by, 703; under Tokagawa regime, 789; in 19th-century European cities, 915–916; in Australian penal colony, 1028
Protected people. See Dhimmis
Protectionism, 946
Protectorate, 645–646
Protestantism, 539–542, 545, 550, 580, 644–645; defined, 539; spread of, 553, 555, 582; Thirty Years' War and, 591, 592; status of women and, 593–594; Edict of Nantes and, 615; science and, 662, 668; 18th-century revival of, 720–721; theological fundamentalism and, 1306. See also Calvinism; Lutheranism; Protestant Reformation

Protestant Reformation: birth of, Luther and, 537; Ninety-five Theses and, 537–538; Protestant thought and, 539; social impact of, 539–542; political impact of, 542–543, 545; growth of, 545–553; Calvinism and, 545–547; Anabaptists and, 548–549, 717–718; in England, 549–553
Protestant Union, 589
Protoindustrialization, 698–699
Proudhon (Pru-don′), Pierre Joseph, 875
Prussia, 624; in 17th century, 626–630; absolutism in, 630–631, 679–681; annexation of Silesia to, 680; popular education in, 708–709; at war with France, 812, 821; treaties of Tilsit and, 821; in Fourth Coalition, 822; in Quadruple Alliance, 864; Congress of Vienna and, 867; secret alliance against, 867; in Holy Alliance, 868; revolution of 1848 in, 892–894; war with Denmark, 893–894; unification of Germany and, 937–938; in Franco-Prussian War of 1870–1871, 941
Ptolemaic dynasty, 155
Ptolemais, 154
Ptolemies (Tahl-uh-meez), 151; Egypt under, 154; commerce of, 155; slavery and, 156; agriculture under, 157–158; under Roman rule, 182
Ptolemy, Claudius (mathematician and astronomer), 163, 661–662
Ptolemy, king of Egypt, 149, 163, 166
Publicans, 203
Public health: in 18th century, 709; in 19th century, 901
Publishing, movable type and, 314–315, 520. See also Printing
Puerto Rico, 567
Pugachev, Emelian, 682
Pulaar, 726
Punt (monarchy), 41
Purdah, 284
Pure Land sect, 310, 325
Purging, 714
Puritans, 547, 553, 587, 644
Pushkin, Alexander, 880
Putali Ba, 1086–1087
Putting-out system, 699, 836, 837, 839, 854, 855, 962
Pygmies, 464, 465
Pyramids, 28, 29(illus.), 488, 489, 491, 497, 498
Pyrenees, Treaty of the, 621
Pyrrhus (Pihr-us), king of Epirus, 181
Pythian games, 139

Qadis (Ka-dis), 276
Qizilbash, 751

Quackery, in medicine: Hellenistic, 167; in 18th-century Europe, 716
Quadruple Alliance, 822, 864, 867, 868
Quaestorship, Roman, 177
Quakers, as factory owners, 852
Quanta, 1110
Quebec Act, 1023
Quechua, 500–501
Quest of the Historical Jesus (Schweitzer), 1109
Quetzalcoatl, Aztec god, 491–492, 571–572
Quietism, 160
Qur'an, 265, 268, 273, 274, 292; on marriage, illicit intercourse, and inheritance, 267; on slavery, 281; on women, 282; Sufism and, 284; study of, in kingdom of Mali, 474; on enslavement, 730; Islamic fundamentalism and, 1308
Qutb-ud-din (Kut-bud-den'), 753

Rabelais (Rab-e-lay'), François, 526–527
Rabia, 284
Racine, Jean, 616, 617
Racism, 979, 981, 1012, 1137; American, origins of, 598; in Latin America, 996, 1001, 1002, 1006; immigration and, 1021–1022, 1023; in Australia, 1032; of Afrikaners, 1246–1247
Radical party (France), 1129, 1130
Radio, 1117, 1274
Raft of the Medusa, The (Géricault), 878
Railroads: English Industrial Revolution and, 842–844; in Russia, 943; growth of trade and, 962–963; transcontinental, in Canada, 1025–1026; Australian gold rush and, 1031; African, imperialism and, 1235
Rain forests, 486, 726
Raised-field system of agriculture, 489
Rákáczy (Ra-kot'-see), Francis, prince of Hungary, 626
Ralph, archbishop of Tours, 416
Ramadan, 267
Ramayana, 306
Rameses (Ram'-seez) II, statues of, 35(illus.)
Rangaku movement, 786–787
Rape, Renaissance attitudes toward, 523
Raphael, 516
Rasputin, Grigori Yefimovich, 1054–1055
Rastrelli, Bartolomeo, 642
Rathenau (Ra'-te-nau), Walter, 1050
Rationing, during World War I, 1050

Rats, bubonic plague and, 439, 697
Raymond, count of Toulouse, 435
Razin, Stenka, 637
Reagan, Ronald, 1205
Realism, in literature, 921, 924–925
Reason: Enlightenment and, 669, 676
Reconquista (Ray-con-kis-ta), 269, 354, 531, 532, 569
Reconstruction, after American Civil War, 1016
Records of the Grand Historian (Ssu-ma), 104
Recreation: in ancient China, 107; in Hellenic Greece, 137; in Roman Republic, 186–187; in late Middle Ages, 451–452; in Ming and Ch'ing China, 782; in 19th-century European cities, 912; movies and radio and, 1116–1118; tourism and, 1184
Red Army, 1060, 1139, 1162, 1166, 1172, 1173, 1187, 1188
Red Guards, 1216–1217
Reds. *See* Bolsheviks
Red Shirts, 935(illus.), 936
Red Turbans, 321–322
Reflections on the Revolution in France (Burke), 810
Reform. *See* Land reform; Lycurgan regimen; *Perestroika;* Religious reforms; Taika Reforms
Reformation, 549(table); Protestant, 537–553; Catholic and Counter-, 553–557
Reform Bill of 1832, 883–884, 891
"Reformed religion," 582. *See also* Calvinism
Refugees, 1291
Regulating Act of 1773, 762
Reichstag, under Hitler, 946, 947, 953, 1150, 1151
Reign of Terror, 814, 815, 818
Religion: Mesopotamian, 21–22; Egyptian, 27–28, 31; Jewish, 44–46; Persian, 58; Indian, 68, 71–72, 75–76, 83, 307; Chinese, 91; Greek, 138–139, 158–159; mystery, 139, 158–159, 204, 207; Roman, 185–186, 203–204, 223; in Byzantine Empire, 253–254; for Muslims, 272; Mongol, 278; Yamato, 323; in medieval Europe, 355–367, 380, 382–385, 434–437; in early Africa, 465–466; Aztec, 496–497; in 16th-century Europe, 542; Westphalian treaties and, 592; science and, 665, 668, 670; Voltaire's views on, 673–674; 18th-century, 717–722; 19th-century, 913–914; 20th-century, 1109–1110, 1306–1310. *See also* Christianity; Churches; Greek Orthodox church;

Islam; Judaism; Protestantism; Roman Catholic church
Religious art: icons and, 256; during Middle Ages and Renaissance, 516
Religious communities, for women, 594
Religious reforms, 355, 359, 447, 448, 508, 550
Remarque (Re-mark'), Erich Maria, 1046
Remus, 174
Renaissance, 508–535; defined, 508; Italian, evolution of, 508–512; intellectual hallmarks of, 512–515; individualism of, 513; revival of antiquity during, 513; secularism of, 514–515; art and artists of, 515–518; social change during, 519–524; women in, 521–523; blacks in, 523–524; in northern Europe, 524–528; politics and the state during, 528–535; historical periods of, 548–549(table); origins of scientific revolution during, 666–667
Renoir, Pierre Auguste, 1115
Renovatio Romani Imperi (Charlemagne's motto), 341
Reparations, following World War I, 1064, 1118, 1119, 1120
Repartimiento, law of, 996, 997
Report on the Affairs of British North America (Durham), 1024
Republic, The (Plato), 141, 292
Res Gestae (Augustus), 197, 198
Restoration: of 1660, 647; Meiji, 984, 987
Return of the Native (Hardy), 925
Revel, Jean François, 1304–1305
Revisionism, 804, 956, 1122
Revolution(s): English, 648; scientific, 660–669; ideas of liberty and equality and, 796–797; American Revolution and, 798–802; French Revolution and, 802–810, 816(table); Industrial, 828–860; in agriculture, 830–831; "dual," 864, 868, 876, 984; in Italy, 868; in Spain, 868; Greece, 881–882; in Great Britain, 882–886; of 1830, in France, 886–887; of 1848, 887–894, 891(table); in Austrian Empire, 890–892; bacterial, 901–903; of 1905, in Russia, 944–945, 1054, 1055–1056, 1057; Latin American, origins of, 993, 995; Counero, 997; Russian Revolution of 1917 and, 1054–1060, 1058(table), 1144; Bolshevik, 1056–1057; in Germany, 1061–1062; Turkish, 1079–1081; Iranian, of 1906, 1081; intellectual, in China, 1092–1093; of 1956, in Hungary, 1190; of 1989, in

Revolution(s) *(cont.)*
Poland, 1196–1200; Mexican, 1205; Cuban, 1206–1207; Islamic, 1233; medical, 1257–1258; in communications, 1274–1275
"Revolutionary terror," 1060
"Revolution from above," 1140
Rex et sacerdos, 336
Reza Shah Pahlavi (Ray′-za Shah Pah′-lah-vee), 1081
Ricardo, David, 845, 853, 872, 876
Ricci, Matteo, 578, 776
Rice, in 14th-century China, 768–769; "miracle," 1264
Richard, king of England, 397
Richard I (the Lion-Hearted), king of England, 365, 414, 416
Richard II, king of England, 455
Richard II (Shakespeare), 600
Richard III, king of England, 530
Richard III (Shakespeare), 600
Richelieu (Re-shel-yu′), Cardinal, 591, 592, 610–611, 615, 617
Riefenstahl, Leni, 1118
Rigveda (Rig-vay-duh), 69, 70
Riis, Jacob, 1021
Rio de la Plata, 993. *See also* Argentina
Rite of Spring, The (Stravinsky), 1116
Rites Controversy, 578
Rituals, religious, 383
Rivers, as important resource, 11, 13–14, 16, 88
Roads: in Persian Empire, 60; Roman, 199; English, 842
Roberts, Robert, 1052
Robespierre (Robes′-pi-ehr), Maximilien, 810, 812, 813, 814, 815
Robot, 625
Rockefeller, John D., 1019
Roe, 759
Roger II, king of Sicily, 411, 426, 468
Roger de Hautville, 411
Rogers, Ginger, 1117
Roland, count, 339
Rollo, 352
Roma et Augustus, cult of, 198–199
Roman Catholic church: first popes, 230, 233; Synod of Whitby and, 235, 341; split with Greek Orthodox church, 256; rise of Carolingian Renaissance and, 344; revival and reform in Middle Ages, 355–359; opposition to slavery of, 375–376; as center of medieval life, 382–383; inquisitions and, 436–437, 533, 554, 557, 585, 586; effect of plague on, 440; Babylonian Captivity and, 446–447, 535; Great Schism and, 447, 535; conciliar movement and, 447–448; secularism and, 515; Spanish monarchy and, 531–532; during 1400–1517, 535–537; Luther breaks

with, 545; Church of England and, 553, 587; restored by Mary Tudor, 553; England breaks with, 553; Catholic and Counter-Reformations and, 553–557; Thirty Years' War and, 589, 591; view of marriage, 593; science and, 662, 668; infanticide denounced by, 706; changing relations with state, 717–718; 18th-century reform of, 718–720; conflict with French National Assembly, 809–810; restored after French Revolution, 817–818; Bismarck's attack on, 946; role in French education, 949; opposition to, in France's Third Republic, 949–950; 20th-century revival of, 1109–1110; supports Mussolini, 1146; revival in Poland, 1307. *See also* Cathedrals; Christianity; Churches; Papacy
Roman Empire, 196–224; Huns' invasion of, 101; foundations of, 148, 172, 176; Hellenistic medicine and, 166; Po Valley and, 172; beginning of, 196; under Augustus, 196–202; population of, 198; provinces of, 198–199, 212, 214; literary flowering of, 199, 201–202; expansion of, 199, 200(map), 214; Christianity's ascendancy in, 202–207; civil wars in, 203, 217; under Julio-Claudians and Flavians, 207; during age of "five good emperors," 208–210; golden age of, 210–214; Iranians and, 214–216; trade and contact with, 216–217; barbarian invasions of, 217–218; breakdown of, 217; reconstruction under Diocletian and Constantine in, 218–221; division of, 218, 219(map), 220; inflation and taxes in, 221; legalization of Christianity in, 221–224; historical periods of, after Augustus, 222 (table); construction of Constantinople and, 224; Germanic invasions of, 230, 245–246; division of, 252–254
Roman Forum (Forum Romanum), 174–175, 177(illus.)
Romania, 882; gains independence, 1042; in World War II, 1159; cold war and, 1172; under Ceauşescu, 1199
Roman Republic, 172–192; founding of, 175; social divisions of, 176; historical periods of, 189(table)
Romantic movement, 676, 876–881
Romanus III, 259
Rome: slavery in, 156; rise of, 172–192; geography of, 172, 173(map), 174; Estruscans and, 174–175; conquest of Italy by,

175–176; politics and law in, 176–178; overseas conquests of, 177, 179–182, 180(map), 191; social conflict in, 179; opposing attitudes in, 182–187; daily life in, 184, 186–187; religion in, 185–186; in late Republic, 187–192; under Augustus, 196–202; founding of, according to legend, 201; population of, 210; golden age of, 210–212; and the East, 214–217; bishops of, 232–233; conquest of, 241; sacked by Charles V, 512; Treaty of, 1178, 1181. *See also* Roman Republic; Roman Empire
Rome-Berlin Axis, 1157
Rommel, Erwin, 1164
Romulus, 174, 201
Roosevelt, Franklin D., 1033, 1117, 1128(illus.), 1161, 1206, 1285; New Deal of, 1127–1128; at Teheran Conference, 1171; at Yalta, 1172, 1188
Rosary, origins of, 383
Rousseau (Ru-so′), Jean-Jacques, 676–677, 707, 876, 995, 1306
Rowlatt Acts, 1085
Royal Africa Company, 596
Royal council, 530–531
Royal Road, 60
Royal Society of London, 667, 668
Rubens, Peter Paul, 602
Ruhr, occupation of, 1119–1120
Ruirik, 256
Rule of Saint Benedict, The, 242, 243–244, 336, 341, 388, 396
Rule of the Master, The (St. Benedict), 242–243
Rupertsberg, convent of, 395
Russia, 256, 632(map); serfdom in, 623; development of, 633–639; Vikings and Kievan principality and, 633–634; rise of Moscow and, 634–635; tsars and people in 635–637; reforms of Peter the Great in, 637–639; during Enlightenment, 639; building of St. Petersburg in, 640–643; Seven Years' War and, 680; absolutism in, 681–683; under Catherine the Great, 681–683; expansion of, 683(map); Ottoman wars against, 750; in Third Coalition, 819; Napoleon's invasion of, 819, 821–822; at war with France, 821; treaties of Tilsit and, 821; in Fourth Coalition, 822; industrialization of, 847(table); in Quadruple Alliance, 864; Congress of Vienna and, 867; secret alliance against, 867; in Holy Alliance, 868; romantic movement in, 880; in Crimean War, 942; modernization of, 942–945; "Great Reforms" in,

942–943; industrialization of, 943–944; Japan attacks, 944; revolution of 1905 in, 944–945, 1054; 19th-century European migrations and, 970; in Asia, 977; alliance with France, 1040(fig.), 1041; in Balkan Wars, 1042, 1043; in Triple Entente, 1044; in World War I, 1047; women in labor force of, 1051; Lenin and Bolshevik revolution in, 1056–1057; Treaty of Brest-Litovsk and, 1059, 1061; civil war and, 1059–1060, 1138, 1139; in Iran, 1081; film making in, 1117; Communist, 1137; Stalinist, 1138–1145. *See also* Russian Revolution of 1917; Soviet Union

Russian-French Alliance, 1040(fig.), 1041

Russian-German Reinsurance Treaty, 1039, 1041

Russian Orthodox church, split in, 637. *See also* Eastern Orthodox church

Russian Revolution of 1917, 1054–1060, 1058(table), 1144; fall of imperial Russia and, 1054–1055; provisional government and, 1055–1056; Lenin and Bolshevik revolution and, 1056–1057; Trotsky seizes power, 1057–1059; dictatorship and civil war and, 1059–1060; Lenin and Bolsheviks win, 1060

"Russian steamroller," 1047

Rutherford, Ernest, 1110

Rutherford, James, 1031

S.A. *See* Storm troopers

Saabergen, abbey of, 396

Sabuktigin, 308

Sabuncuoghlu Sereddin, 749

Sacred Congregation of the Holy Office, 557

Sadat, Anwar, 1232

Safavid (Sah-fah-vid) empire, 751(map), 752, 753

Sahara Desert, 462

St. Albans, abbey of, 397

St. Anthony of Egypt, 242

St. Augustine, 239–240, 241, 253, 428, 513, 546, 594

St. Bartholomew's Day massacre, 583

St. Basil's Cathedral, 637(illus.)

St. Benedict, 242–247, 388, 395

St. Benet Biscop, 341

St. Boniface, 335–336, 342, 344

Saint-Clair-sur-Epte, Treaty of, 352

St. Columba, 235

St. Denis, 407

Saint-Denis, abbey of, 398, 430

St. Dominic, 383, 435–436

St. Emmeran, abbey of, 396

St. Evroul, abbey of, 392

St. Francis, 435

St. Francis Xavier, 579

Saint-Gilles de Provence, 385

St. James, 385

St. Jerome, 239

St. John Chrysostom, 416, 532

St. Lawrence, 587

St. Martin of Tours, 234

St. Patrick, 234–235, 242, 387

St. Paul, 205–206, 234, 238–239, 537, 546

St. Paul's Cathedral, 423

St. Peter, 385

St. Peter's Basilica, 515, 518, 538

St. Petersburg, 640–643, 642(illus.)

St. Requier, abbey of, 396

Saint-Simon, Henri de, 613, 683, 874, 922

St. Thomas Aquinas, 428–429, 436

St. Valentine's Day, 236–237

St. Vincent de Paul, 706

St. Wandrille, abbey of, 244

Sakharov, Andrei, 1305

Sakoku, 786

Saladin, sultan, 365

Salazar, Antonio de Oliveira, 1136

Salerno medical school, 346

Salic Law, 249

Sallust, 182–183, 240

Salons, French, 677

SALT. *See* Strategic Arms Limitation Treaty

Samnites, 176

Samnite wars, 181

Samnium, 181

Samsara, 71, 73, 76

Samudragupta (Sa-mu′-dra-gup′-ta), 298–299

Samurai, 326–328, 784, 786, 787–788; and U.S. imperialism, 983–984

Sanchez Navarro family, 1003–1004

Sand-Counter (Archimedes), 163

Sand, George, 879, 880

Sandinistas, 1209

Sangha, 78

Sanhedrin, 203

Sanitation. *See* Public health

San Lorenzo, 488

San Salvador, 567

Sans-culottes, 813, 814, 864

Sanskrit, 301, 305, 306

Santa Maria, 567

Sappho (Saff′-o), 124

Sardinia: unification of Italy and, 933; under Cavour, 934–936; in Crimean War, 942

Sargon (Semitic chieftain), 18

Sartre (Sart′-r), Jean-Paul, 1108–1109

Sassanids, 214, 254, 270

Sassoon, Siegfried, 1045–1046

Sati (self-immolation), 304

Satrapy, 55, 59–60

Satyagraha, 1088

Saudi Arabia, 264

Savannah, 462

Savery, Thomas, 840

Savonarola, Girolamo, 511–512

Saxons, 218; Charlemagne's war against, 339

Saxony, 867

Schism, religious, 256

Schleswig-Holstein, Danish war over, 892–893, 938

Schliemann, Heinrich, 118

Scholarship: Islamic, 289–292; Northumbrian, 341–342. *See also* Education; Schools; Universities

Scholasticism, 292

Scholastic method, 428

Schönberg (Shern′-berg), Arnold, 1116

Schönbrunn palace, 639

Schools, 708–709; Sumerian, 20–21; medieval, 426, 428–429; in kingdom of Ghana, 474; Ursuline, 556; Jesuit, 557. *See also* Education

Schumacher, E. F., 1306

Schuman, Robert (statesman), 1176, 1178

Schumann, Robert (composer), 880

Schuman Plan, 1178

Schweitzer, Albert, 1109

Science: in ancient China, 104–105; origins of, in Hellenic Greece, 116, 139, 141–142; scientific method and, 139, 664, 669; Hellenistic, 162–165; Byzantine, 258; Muslim, 291; in Gupta Empire, 301; Chinese, 579; scientific revolution and, 660–669, 921; Aristotelian view of, 660–661; Copernican hypothesis and, 661–662; Brahe's theory and, 662; Kepler's theory and, 663–664; Galileo's work and, 664; Newton's physics and, 665; religion and, 665, 668, 670; scientific community and, 668; popularization of, 669–670, 671(illus.), 672; scientific experimentation and, 713, 714; bacterial revolution and, 901–903; Freudian psychology and, 921; 19th-century developments in, 921–922; in 20th century, 1110. *See also* Medicine; Scientific revolution

Scientific revolution, 660–669; causes of, 665–668; consequences of, 668–669

Scipio Aemilianus, 181, 183, 186, 187, 188

Scipio Africanus, 181

Scivius (Know the Ways) (Hildegard), 394(cap.), 395

Scotland: as Pict stronghold, 251; Great Schism and, 447

Scots, as factory owners, 852

Scott, Walter, 878

Scribal schools, 20–21

Script. See Writing

Sculpture, Renaissance, 515, 516

Scurvy, 712

Sea Peoples, 36, 40, 41, 42

Seclusion, of Muslim women. See Purdah

Secondary sources, 5

Second Coalition, 819

Second Constitutional Congress, 801

Second Empire, 931–933, 941

Second International, 954

Second Messenian War, 125

Second Punic War, 156, 163, 181

Second Reform Bill, 950

Second Republic, 931

Second Treatise of Civil Government (Locke), 648, 671

Second Triumvirate, 192

Second Vatican Council, 579

Second World War. See World War II

Secret History (Procopius), 257

Secret societies, Chinese, 321

Secular ideologies, 1304–1306

Secularism, during Renaissance, 514–515

Security Council (U.N.), 1285; imposes naval blockade on Iraq, 1287

Segregation, in South Africa, 1247, 1248

Sei Shonagon, 326

Seleucids (Suh-loo′-suhds), 151, 154, 155, 182

Seleucus (Suh-loo′-suhs), 80, 149, 155

"Self Criticism of German Liberalism, A," (Baumgarten), 940

Self-determination, 796; Metternich's views on, 869; Fourteen Points and, 1062, 1074; in Soviet Union, 1195

Self-government, 419, 420

Selim I (the Grim), 746

Selim II (the Drunkard), 750

Seljuk Turks, 278

Selket (Egyptian goddess), 32(illus.)

Semites, 15–16; spread of Mesopotamian culture and, 18–19; in Egypt, 29

Senate, Roman, 176, 177, 190, 191, 196

Senegal, 467, 1241

Senegambia, 726–728, 734, 739

Seneschals, 407

Senghor, Léopold (San′-gawr, Lay′-o-pold), 1237, 1241

Sennett, Mack, 1117

Sepoys, 761

September Massacres, 812

Septimius Severus, 215, 217

Serapion (Ser-uh-pe-on), 166, 167

Serapis (Seh-rap-iss), cult of, 159

Serbia: in Balkan Wars, 1042, 1043; gains independence, 1042; nationalism in, 1044

Serer, 726

Serfdom: in ancient India, 70; in ancient China, 90; in Hellenic Greece, 125; in medieval Europe, 350, 352, 425; emancipation of serfs and, 418; disappears from England, 455; in Aztec society, 496; consolidation of, in eastern Europe, 622–624; in Prussia, 626; in Russia, 637, 642, 682, 942; abolished in Austria, 686, 890; abolished in Russia, 942. See also Feudalism; Peasantry

Servants, in 19th-century urban households, 908–909

Servetus, Michael, 547

Servicios, 619

Servile obligations, in medieval Europe, 376–377, 381–382

Servius Tullius, 176

Seventeen Article Constitution, 324

Seven Years' War, 680, 684, 712, 750, 798, 801

Severan dynasty, 217

Sextus, 178

Sexuality: homosexuality and, 138, 239, 416–417, 593; penitentials and, 237–238; St. Augustine on, 240; in medieval Europe, 259; Qu'ran on, 267; Islamic view of, 283–284; in Indian society, 304; German custom and, 336; priesthood and, 357–358; Christian view of, 388; Albigensians' attitude toward, 435; Incas' view of, 502; Renaissance attitudes toward, 522–523; Luther's view of, 541; marriage and, 593; Reformation attitudes toward, 593–594, 595; birth control and, 702–703; premarital sex and, 702–703, 915; 19th-century labor aristocracy and, 911; 19th-century attempts to repress, 921; Hindu attitude toward, 1088; Freudian psychology and, 1111, 1112; in Stalinist Russia, 1144. See also Prostitution

Şeyhi of Kütahya, 749

Seymour, Jane, 551

Sforza (Sfort′-sa), Francesco, 510

Sforza, Gian Galazzo, 524

Shabbathai Ben Abraham, 346

Shakas, 299

Shakespeare, William, 301, 600

Shamanism, 278

Shang Dynasty: social organization of, 89–91; origins of Chinese writing in, 91; overthrow of, by Chou, 92

Shantytowns, in Third World, 1268–1270

Shapur, Persian king, 215–216

Shari'a, 276

Scheherazade, 289

Shehzade mosque, 749

Sheiks, 476–477

Shelley, Percy Bysshe, 878

Sheriffs, medieval, 405–406, 411

Sherley, Anthony, 752

Shi'ites, 274–275, 279, 751–752, 1233, 1309

Shiki, 327, 783

Shingon sect, 325

Shinto, 323

Ships: Viking, 351; medieval trade and, 423; Italian, 508; cannon on, 571; seaborne trade and, 575, 577; Dutch, 651; navigational problems and, 667; slave trade and, 738; Chinese maritime expansion and, 773; growth of international trade and, 963. See also Navigation; Navy

Shires, 405

Shoen, 327, 783

Shoguns (Show-guns), 326, 785–786, 983

Shostakovich, Dimitri, 1188

Shotoku (Shoe′-toe-ku), 324, 325(illus.)

Shudras, 302

Siberia, 638

Sic et Non (Abelard), 428

Sicily, 172; Roman conquest of, 181; slaves in, 185; medieval finances in, 411–412; slavery in, 596; under Bourbon rule, 933; in World War II, 1164

Siderus Nuncius (Galileo), 664

Sidney, Sir Philip, 599

Sieyès (Sya-yes), abbé, 806, 817

Sigismund, emperor of Germany, 448

Sigismund, king of Hungary, 744

Signori, 509

Sikhs, 1226–1227

Silent-film industry, 1117

Silesia, 680

Silk Road, 215(map), 216, 217

Silk trade, 90, 100, 106, 107, 577

Silver trade, 575, 592

Simony, 355, 357, 359

Sinai Peninsula, 1232

Sinan, Pasha, 748–749

Sinn Fein, 1032

Sino-Japanese war of 1894–1895, 986

Sistine Chapel, 518, 536

Siva, 75

Six Acts, 883

Six-Day War, 1232

Sixtus IV, pope, 513, 536

Sixtus V, pope, 587

Skandagupta, 299

Skepticism, 598–599, 670, 671, 721

Slavery: Sumerian, 18; in ancient Egypt, 28, 30; Hebrews in, 42; in Persian Empire, 54; in ancient India, 71; in ancient China, 90; in Hellenic Greece, 126, 128, 136–137; in Hellenistic Greece, 156; in Roman Republic, 184, 185; in Roman Empire, 212; in Islamic state, 281–282, 283; in early Japan, 322; in Middle Ages, 375–376, 596; in early Africa, 467, 468, 471, 478; in Aztec society, 496; in Renaissance society, 523, 524; European overseas expansion and, 574, 595–598; origins of American racism and, 595–598; Senegambian, 726; in Songhay, 729; in Ottoman Empire, 747; in Latin America, 996, 1001; system of, in American South, 1010, 1012–1013; Emancipation Proclamation and, 1015; impact on black family, 1016–1019

Slave trade, 478; trans-Saharan, 468(table), 596, 734, 739; Venetian control of, 523; transatlantic, 726, 734–740; abolition of, in England, 734; political and demographic consequences of, 740; British control of, 833

Slavs: Byzantine civilization of, 254, 256; as slaves, 375, 633; ruled by Vikings, 633; ruled by Mongols, 634; Hitler's treatment of, 1159

"Sleepy" (Chekhov), 702

Slovakia, 1158Slums, in New York, 1021

Small Is Beautiful (Schumacher), 1306

Smallpox, 574; conquest of, 716–717

Smith, Adam, 872

Social and Economic Council (U.N.), 1285

Social classes. *See* Aristocracy; Common people; Lower class; Middle class; Nobility; Peasantry; Working people

Social Contract, The (Rousseau), 677

Social Darwinism, 924, 978, 980, 1263

Social Democratic Labor party (Russia), 1057

Social Democratic party (Germany), 947–948, 953, 956, 1062, 1150, 1151

Social Democratic party (Russia), 953

Socialism: in ancient China, 108; women and, 874; utopian, French, 874–875; Marxian, 875–876, 953–954, 982, 1056, 1093, 1137, 1304; clashes with liberal capitalism, 889; French revolution of 1848 and, 889–890; in German Empire, 947;

nationalism and, 953; unions and, 955; total-war economy and, 1050; welfare, in Scandinavia, 1129; Stalinist, 1140; as secular ideology, 1304, 1305

Socialist party (France), 1129–1130

Socialist party (Italy), 1145, 1146

Socialist Revolutionaries, 1059

Social science, 669; 19th-century developments in, 922–924

Social security system: in German Empire, 947; in United States, 947, 1127; reforms in, 1183

Society of Jesus. *See* Jesuits

Socrates, 139, 140(illus.), 141, 292

Sofala, 732, 733

Solidarity (Polish trade union), 1197–1198, 1203

Solomon, 44

Solomonid dynasty, 479–480, 731

Solon, 127

Solzhenitsyn, Alexander, 1190, 1305(illus.), 1306

Somme, Battle of the, 1045–1046, 1050

Somoza, Anastasio, 1209

Songhai, 730

Songhay, 728–730

Song of Roland, The, 339

Soninke, 472

Sophia, archduchess of Austria, 891, 1053

Sophists, 141

Sophocles, 134

Sorel, Georges, 1108

Sound and the Fury, The (Faulkner), 1112

South Africa, 480–482; Indians in, 1087–1088; racial conflict in, 1246–1249; nuclear arms race and, 1293

South America, 486, 565; elected governments in, 1209

Southeast Asia: states of, 305(map); India and, 305–307; Buddhism in, 305, 307; nationalism in, 1100–1102

Southern Rhodesia, 1240–1241

Southern Sung Dynasty, 315–316

South Korea: North Korea invades, 1174; Korean War and, 1202; rapid industrialization of, 1262; declining birthrate in, 1294

South Vietnam: Vietnam War and, 1202, 1203

Sovereignty: of Greek polis, 151; absolutism and, 608, 609; Hobbes' view of, 645

Soviet Union, 1075; in Grand Alliance, 1155, 1162; nonaggression pact with Hitler, 1158, 1159; Germany attacks, 1159, 1163; in World War II, 1159,

1162, 1163, 1166; takes Polish territory, 1172; Truman cuts off aid to, 1172; cold war and, 1172–1174; following World War II, 1174, 1176, 1187; de-Stalinization of, 1189–1190; standard of living in, 1190, 1192; re-Stalinization of, 1190–1194; Russian republics in, 1193(map); reform in, 1194–1196; Polish Solidarity and, 1197, 1203; détente versus cold war in, 1203; Helsinki agreement and, 1203; U.N. Security Council and, 1285; Persian Gulf War and, 1287; invades Afghanistan, 1291; nuclear arms race and, 1291, 1292–1293. *See also* Russia; Russian Revolution of 1917

Spain: under Rome, 179, 192; Hannibal in, 181; Augustus's conquest of, 199; Christian reconquest of, 269, 354; Muslim invasion of, 352; women in, 391; peasant uprisings in, 456; monarchy of, during Renaissance, 528, 529, 531–533; overseas expansion of, 567–568, 569, 574–575; viceroyalties of, 574–575; economic effects of New World discoveries, 575; seaborne trade of, 577; Armada defeated, 587–589; black slaves in, 596; baroque art in, 602; absolutist, 17th-century decline of, 619–621, 620(map); Thirty Years' War and, 621; changing church-state relations in, 718; France declares war on, 812; revolts against Napoleon, 821; colonies of, 832–833, 992, 993, 994(map), 995; cedes Louisiana Territory, 1007; following Great Depression, 1130

Spanish-American War, 979, 1033, 1206

Spanish Armada, 587–589, 619

Spanish Civil War, 1116; Germany and Italy intervene in, 1157

Spanish Inquisition, 533, 718

Spanish Netherlands, 617, 618

Spanish Succession, War of the, 617–618, 626, 653, 833, 993

Sparta: 123, 161; growth of, 124–126; war with Athens, 129–130; defeat of, 142–143; women in, 161, 162

Spencer, Herbert, 924

Spengler, Oswald, 1113

Spice trade, European overseas expansion and, 567, 570, 577

Spinning jenny, 837–838, 838(illus.)

Spirit of Laws, The (Montesquieu), 672

Spiritual Exercises (Loyola), 556

Sports, in 19th-century Europe, 912–913

Squatter settlements. *See* Shantytowns

Sri Lanka (Ceylon), 1227, 1258
Srivijaya (Sree-vih-jah-yah) Empire, 306
S.S. (Nazi Germany), 1152–1153, 1155, 1159, 1161, 1165
Ssu-ma Ch'ien (Soo'-ma Chy'-en), 99, 102–103, 104
Stained glass, 432
Stalin, Joseph, 1134, 1137, 1138–1145, 1260; five-year plans of, 1138, 1140–1142; society under, 1142–1145; cold war and, 1170–1174; at Teheran conference, 1171; at Yalta, agrees to declare war on Japan, 1172; moves toward dictatorship, 1187–1188; in postwar era, 1188
Stamp Act, 798–799
Standard of living: of factory workers, 853; inequalities in, 906; in 1750, 960; Japanese, 1095; in Stalinist Russia, 1142, 1143; in Nazi Germany, 1153; in Soviet Union, 1190, 1192; in Third World, 1255. See also Income; Wages; Wealth
Stanley, Henry Morton, 973
Starry Night, The (van Gogh), 1115
State, 340, 404–405; centralization of, in ancient China, 99; medieval origins of, 404–417, 528; medieval finance and, 409, 411–413; medieval law and justice in, 413–417; development of, 528; during Renaissance, 528–535; separation of church from, 949–950; totalitarian, 1136–1137, 1148
Stateless societies, 468
States General, 649
Statute of Laborers, 453
Staupitz, 537
Steam engine, 840–842; growth of trade and, 962–963
Steel industry, 943
Stephen II, pope, 336
Stephenson, George, 842
Sterilization, compulsory, 1226, 1295
Stern, Karl, 1110
Stirrup, invention of, 348
Stoics, 161, 162
Stolypin (Stuh-lip-yin), Peter, 945
Stone Age(s). See Neolithic Age; Paleolithic Age
Storm and Stress (Sturm und Drang) group, 877
Storm troopers, 1152
Strabo, 214–215
Strasser, Gregor, 1150
Strategic Arms Limitation Treaty (SALT), 1292–1293
Strategoi, 254
Stravinsky, Igor, 1116
Stream-of-consciousness technique, 1112

Stresemann, Gustav, 1120, 1121, 1122
Struggle of the Orders, 178–179
Strutt, Jedediah, 855
Stuart kings, 644
Student revolts, 1185, 1306
Styria, 591, 625
Sudan, 464, 465, 469, 472; kingdoms of, 728–731; British conquest of, 975, 977; responses to imperialism in, 981
Sudetenland, 1157
Suetonius, 336
Suez Canal, 963, 967, 978, 1016, 1077, 1164
Suez Canal Company, 1232
Suffrage, 643, 945–946; American colonists and, 799–800; French National Convention and, 812; liberalism and, 872; English Parliamentary reform and, 884–885; Revolution of 1830 in France and, 887; French revolution of 1848 and, 888; under Napoleon III, 931, 932; in Russia, 945; women's, 946, 1032, 1052, 1080; in Great Britain, 950; in Austria, 952
Sufi mysticism, 241
Sufism, 284–286
Sugar: slavery and, 596, 726; in 18th-century European diet, 713
Suger (Sue-zher), abbot of Saint-Denis, 398, 430
Sui Dynasty, 310, 311–312
Sukarno, Achmed (Su-kar'-no, Ahk-mehd), 1229
Sulahkul, principle of, 754
Suleiman (Su'-lay-mahn) I (the Magnificent), 625, 746–749
Suleimaniye mosque, 749
Sulla, 188, 190–191
Sullivan, Louis H., 1113, 1114
Sultans, 278
Sumer, 15, 16
Sumerians, 4, 15–18; schools of, 20–21. See also Mesopotamia
Summa Theologica, (Aquinas) 428
Summer Palace, 639–640
Sundiata, 472
Sung Dynasty, 314–316, 768; Kublai Kahn's defeat of, 279, 319–320
Sunna, 273, 274
Sunnites, 274, 1233
Sun Yat-sen, 987, 1090, 1091–1092
"Super cities," 1266
Superego, 1111
Supremacy Act of 1534, 551
Surgeons: Hellenistic, 166; 18th-century, 713, 714
Surinam, 486
Surrealism, 1116
"Survival of the fittest," 924
Swabia, 409

Swaddling, 708; disappearance of, 919
Swahili, 476, 478; city-states, 732–734
"Sweated industries," 912
Sweden: Thirty Years' War and, 591–592; war with Poland, 630; in Third Coalition, 819; Norway breaks away from, 951; response to Great Depression, 1129
Swiss Confederation, 595
Syagrius, 247
Sydney, Thomas, 1028
Sykes-Picot Agreement, 1077
Syllabaries, 326
Syllabus of Errors (Pope Pius IX), 933
Symmachus, 223
Synod of Whitby, 235, 341
Syracuse, Roman conquest of, 163, 181
Syria, 151, 1064, 1229; spread of Greek culture in, 154; spread of Islam and, 271–272; Crusades and, 367; in Ottoman empire, 746; nationalism in, 1077; independence proclaimed in, 1082
Syrian National Congress, 1077
System of Nature (d'Holbach), 676
System of Positive Philosophy (Comte), 922

Tabula rasa, 671
Tacitus, 221, 248
Taika Reforms, 324
Tai Ping Rebellion, 985
Taira clan, 326
T'ai Tsung (Tie Tsoong), 312, 313(illus.)
Taiwan, 1214; rapid industrialization of, 1262; declining birthrate in, 1294
Taj Mahal, 757
Takauji, Ashikaga (Tack-ah-u-ji, Ah-she-ka-gah), 330
Tale of Genji, The (Murasaki), 326
"Tale of the Eloquent Peasant, The," 28
"Talkies," 1117
Tallage (taille), 411, 420, 580
Talleyrand, Charles de, 867, 880, 932
Tamburlaine (Marlowe), 599
Tamerlane. See Timur the Lame
T'ang Dynasty, 311–314, 316–317, 490
Tannenberg, battle of, 1047
Tanzania, 475
Taoism (Dow'-ism), 94, 96, 310, 319, 1309
Tao Te Ching (Book of the Way and Its Power) (Lao-tzu), 96
Tapestries, in Gothic cathedrals, 432
Tariffs, 851, 962; German Empire and, 946
Tarquin the Proud, 175
Tartuffe (Molière), 617

Tatars, under Jenghiz Khan, 319–320

Taverns, Mesopotamian, 24

Taxes: in Egypt, 28; in India, 70, 80; in ancient China, 100, 102, 105, 109; in Roman Empire, 221; in Islamic state, 276, 280; during Sung period, 319; during Middle Ages, 376, 411, 412, 420, 424, 425, 445, 446, 455, 456, 529; in Aztec society, 496; during Renaissance, 529; on clergy, in Zurich, 540; in 16th-century France, 580; in Low Countries, 585; under Louis XIV, 614, 615; in 17th-century Spain, 619; under Frederick William, 629–630; under Peter the Great, 638; in 17th-century England, 644; under Louis XV, 684; in Western Europe, 694; on non-Muslim adult males, 754, 757; under Ming Dynasty, 770–771, 774; under Tokugawa regime, 786, 789; American Revolution and, 798–799, 800; of British, 799; French national debt and, 803, 804–805; under Napoleon I, 821; in Latin America, during colonial period, 995, 996, 997; under Lenin, 1139; under Mussolini, 1147

Technology: in ancient China, 93; overseas expansion and, 570–571; science and, 669; agriculture and, 694–695; English Industrial Revolution and, 848; 19th-century development of science and, 921, 922. *See also* Industrial Revolution; Industry; Science; Scientific revolution

Telepinus, 35

Telescope, development of, 663(illus.), 664

Television, 1274–1275

Temperance movement, 911

Temples: Sumerian, 16–17; Hebrew, 44; Iranian, 57; Greek, 132, 133(illus.), 139; Aztec, 497–498

Ten Commandments, 45, 236

Tendai sect, 310, 325

Ten Hours Act, 885

Tenochtitlán, 497, 498(illus.), 571, 572

Tensin, marquise de, 677

Teotihuacán civilization, 488, 490–493, 494

Tepe Yahya, 10

Terence, 186, 240

Tertulian, 238

Tess of the D'Urbervilles (Hardy), 925

Test Act, 647

Tet Offensive, 1202

Textile industry, 11, 614, 699, 831, 836, 962. *See also* Cotton industry; Wool industry

Tewfiq, 967

Tezcatlipoca, 491

Thales (Thay-leez), 139, 162

Thalmaitl, 496

Thatcher, Margaret, 1209

Thebans, 142–143

Thegns, 405

Themistocles (Thuh-mist-o-cleez), 128

Theocracy, 17

Theodore of Canterbury, 237–238

Theodoric, 247, 248

Theodosius, 231, 232, 252, 257, 336

Theophrastus, 142, 164–165

Theravada Buddhism, 78, 84

"Thermidorian reaction," 815

Thermodynamics, 922

Thiers, Adolphe, 948

Things Fall Apart (Achebe), 1276

Third Coalition, 819

Third estate, 804, 805

Third International, Communist, 1075, 1091

Third Reform Bill, 950

Third Republic, 948

Third World, 960, 961; defined, 1254–1255; poverty in, 1256–1257; medical revolution and population explosion in, 1257–1260; industrialization of, 1260–1262; agriculture and village life in, 1262–1266; education and mass communications in, 1274–1275; intellectual reflections on, 1275–1277; United Nations and, 1286, 1289; wars in, 1290; demand for "new international economic order," 1296; international debt crisis and, 1299, 1301; multinational corporations and, 1302–1304. *See also individual countries*

Thirty-nine Articles, 553

Thirty Years' War (1618–1648), 589, 591–592, 610, 627; Germany after, 592–593, 696

Thomas à Kempis, 537

Thompson, William, 1310

Thousand and One Nights, A, 288–289

Three Emperors' League, 1038

Three Henrys, War of the, 583

Three Kingdoms Era, 109

Three Principles of the People (Sun), 1091–1092

Thucydides (Thu-sid'-e-dez), 104, 130

Thunberg, C. P., 787

Thutmose (Tuht-mo-zuh) III, 10

Tiananmen Square, 1219

Tiberius, Roman emperor, 202–203, 207

Tiberius Gracchus, 189

Tiber River, 174

Tibet, 308; Chinese influence in, 314

T'ien-t'ai sect, 310, 325

Tiglath-pileser (Tig-lath-pil-le'-zer) III, 51

Tigris River, 13, 15, 16, 26, 50, 52, 88

Tikal, 489

Tilsit, treaties of, 821

Timbuktu, 468, 473–474, 729, 730

Time, Maya method of measuring and recording, 490

"Time of Troubles," 491, 496, 636

Timur the Lame, 753, 309

Tirpitz, Alfred von, 1041

Titian, 517, 518, 543(illus.)

Tito, Josip, 1188

Titus, 207, 208(illus.)

Toba, 109–110

Tocharians, 4

Tocqueville (Tok-vel), Alexis de, 889

Tokugawa regime, 785–787, 787(map)

Tokyo, 785

Toliptzin, 491

Tolstoy, Leo, 925

Toltec civilization, 488, 491, 493, 494, 495

Tools: in Paleolithic Age, 7; in Neolithic Age, 7, 10–11; in ancient China, 106; invented by Archimedes, 163

Topa Inca, 500, 502

Torah, 45, 267

Tory party, 883, 885

Totalitarianism, 609; modern, 1136–1137; of the left and right, 1137–1138; in Stalinist Russia, 1138–1145; in Mussolini's Italy, 1145–1148; in Hitler's Germany, 1148–1155. *See also* Absolutism; Authoritarianism; Dictatorship

Totalitarian Temptation, The (Revel), 1304–1305

Touré, Sekou, 1241

Tourism, 1184

Tours, Battle of, 269, 334, 335

Tower of London, 648

Tower of the Four Winds, 166(illus.)

Towns: in Neolithic Age, 10; growth of, in ancient China, 100; in Roman Empire, 212; Indian, 302; rise of, in Middle Ages, 376, 417–418; liberties of merchants in, 418, 420; daily life in, during Middle Ages, 420–421, 423; in Ming China, 770. *See also* Cities; Villages

Townsend, Charles, 830

Toynbee, Arnold, 1110, 1174, 1284, 1293

Tractatus Logico-Philosophicus (Wittgenstein), 1108

Trade: in Neolithic Age, 9; Egyptian, 41; Phoenician, 42; in ancient Israel, 49; in Persian Empire, 54; in ancient India, 66, 79; in Mesopotamia, 66; in ancient China, 93, 100, 102; Hellenic, 119; Hellenistic, 155–156; in Roman Republic, 175; among

Trade (cont.)
  Roman provinces, 212, 214; between China and West, 216–217; in Islamic state, 286–288; Indian, 301–302, 305, 306; during Sung Dynasty, 314, 316; in medieval Europe, 367, 422(map), 423–426; trans-Saharan, in early Africa, 466–468, 472; among East African city-states, 477–478; Mesoamerican, 489; Antwerp as center of, 568; seaborne, 575–578, 576(map); in Germany, after Thirty Years' War, 592; Spanish, in 17th century, 619; Dutch, 651–652; Chinese, 773, 775–776; growth of, in Atlantic Basin, 834(map); 19th-century international growth in, 961–964; colonial, 993. See also Commerce; Merchants
Trade unions. See Labor unions
Trains. See Railroads
Trajan, Roman emperor, 209, 215
Transportation: in ancient China, 108; in Hellenic Greece, 135; by camel, in Islamic state, 287; 18th-century population growth and, 697; public, in 19th-century European cities, 903, 905–906. See also Railroads; Roads
Transubstantiation, 552
Transylvania, 625
Treatise on Fevers (Ching Chi), 104
Treatise on the Barbarian Kingdoms on the Western Oceans, 773
Treaty of Amiens, 819
Treaty of Brest-Litovsk, 1059, 1139
Treaty of Cateau-Cambrésis, 579–580
Treaty of Chaumont, 822
Treaty of Ghent, 1007
Treaty of Guadalupe, 1009
Treaty of Lausanne, 1080
Treaty of Lunéville, 819
Treaty of Nijmegen, 617
Treaty of Paris, 441, 761, 801, 835, 1023
Treaty of Rome, 1178, 1181
Treaty of Saint-Clair-sur-Epte, 352
Treaty of the Pyrenees, 621
Treaty of Verdun, 334, 350
Treaty of Versailles, 1062–1064; American rejection of, 1066; disagreement over, 1118; Hitler violates, 1155
Treaty on the Non-Proliferation of Nuclear Weapons, 1291, 1293
Trebia, Battle of, 181
Treitschke (Trich'-ke), Heinrich von, 978
Trent, Council of, 554–555
Tres Zapotes, 488
"Trew Law of Free Monarchy, The" (James I), 644
Trial, The (Kafka), 1113

Tribes: in Paleolithic Age, 8; Hebrew, 46–47; Athenian, 127; Germanic, 235, 242, 245, 248, 334; Mongolian, 245; Arab, 264; Magyar, 352
Tribunes, Roman, 178, 197
Tribunicia potestas, 197
Triennial Act, 645
Trinidad, 567
Trinity, denial of, 547
Triple Alliance, 1039, 1041, 1047Triple Entente, 1044, 1047, 1049, 1053, 1076
Triumph of the Will, The (Riefenstahl), 1118
Troppau, Congress of, 868
Trotsky, Leon, 1058–1059, 1139, 1304
Trotula, 346
True Word sect, 310, 325
Truman, Harry, 1172, 1174, 1200
Truman Doctrine, 1173
Ts'ai Lun (Tsigh' Lun'), 107
Tsar, 635
Tuaregs, 466, 730
Tudors, 531
Tuileries, 581
Tuke, William, 715
Tull, Jethro, 830
Tupac Amaru, 997
Turkestan, 314
Turkey: nationalism in, 1079–1081, 1233. See also Anatolia
Turks, 298; invasion of India by, 307, 308; T'ang and, 314; under Jenghiz Khan, 378, 319–320; under Muhammad II, 565; Holy League and, 747; 1919 peace treaty and, 1064. See also Anatolia; Ottoman Turks
Turner, J. M. W., 844, 880
Tuscany, 933; family structure in, 380
Tutankhamen (Toot-onk'-ah-mon) (King Tut), 31
Twelve Articles, 540
Two New Sciences (Galileo), 664
Two Sicilies, 868
Tyche (Tie'-ke), 158, 159, 160(illus.)
Tyler, John, 1007, 1009
Tyndale, William, 550
Tyrants and tyranny, 122–123, 127, 648
Tyrol, 625
Tyrtaeus (Ter-te'-us), 125
Tzu-ch'an, 95
Tzu-Hsi (Dzuh' Shee), 985

Uganda, 1243
Ukraine, 256, 638
Ulama, 752
Ulema, 276, 284, 286, 755
Ulsterites, 951
Ultranationalism, 1097
Ulysses (Joyce), 1112

Umar, 273–274
Umayyad (Um-eye-yed) Dynasty, 274, 275, 277
Umma, 266, 267, 273, 274
Uncial script, 341
Unemployment: British, in 1920s, 1122; during Great Depression, 1126; following Great Depression, 1128; in Nazi Germany, 1150; in postwar United States, 1186; among educated black Africans, following Great Depression, 1238
Unification, national: Japanese, 784; Italian, 933–936, 945; German, 936–942, 939(map), 945
Uniformitarianism, 923
Union Act, 1024
Union of Utrecht, 587
Unions. See Labor unions
United Nations, 1174, 1215, 1230, 1256, 1261, 1285–1289
United Provinces of the Netherlands, 584(map), 587; independence of, 589, 591; government of, 649. See also Holland; Netherlands
United States: influence of Calvinism on, 545; constitution of, 643, 672, 801–802; industrialization of, 836, 846, 847(table); Monroe Doctrine and, 868; constitutional liberalism in, 868; women's suffrage in, 946; 19th-century trade and foreign investments of, 962–963; "opening" of Japan and, 966; European migration to, 969–970; in Asia, 977; control over Panama Canal Zone, 978; reasons for imperialism of, 978, 979; in Philippines, 979; manifest destiny and, 1006–1007, 1009; territorial growth of, 1007–1009, 1008(map); fate of Indians in, 1009–1010; black slavery in, 1010, 1012–1013, 1014(map); Indian cession of land to, 1011(map); Civil War in, 1015–1016; impact of slavery on black family in, 1016–1019; impact of industrialization and immigration in, 1019–1023; pioneers in, 1019–1020; in World War I, 1049, 1060; Treaty of Versailles and, 1062–1066; isolationism of, 1064–1066, 1082; modern architecture in, 1113; movies and radio in, 1117; Great Depression in, 1125, 1126; New Deal in, 1126–1128; in Grand Alliance, 1155, 1161; in World War II, 1159, 1161–1163, 1165–1166; cold war and, 1172–1174; cuts off aid to Russia, 1172; Marshall Plan of, 1173, 1177, 1178; following World War II, 1177;

de Gaulle's opposition to, 1181; changing class structure in, 1183; postwar prosperity in, 1200; civil rights movement in, 1200–1201; Vietnam War and, 1201–1202; Watergate scandal and, 1202–1203; détente versus cold war in, 1203; Cuba and, 1206–1207; reconciliation with China, 1217; in Japan, 1219–1220; at war with Iraq, 1234; U.N. Security Council and, 1285; nuclear arms race and, 1291, 1292–1293; rise of multinational corporations and, 1301–1302. *See also* American Revolution
United States Magazine and Democratic Review, 1006
Universities: medieval, 426, 428–429; Scottish, 841; student revolts at, 1185, 1306
Untouchables, 1223–1224
Upanishads (Oo-pan'-ih-shadz), 72–73
Upper Belvedere palace, 640
Upper class. *See* Aristocracy; Elite; Nobility
Ur, 17(illus.)
Urban II, pope, 361, 362, 364, 397
Urban VI, pope, 447
Urban VII, pope, 664
Urbanization, industrial growth and, 852
Urban life. *See* Cities; Towns
Urban migration, in Third World, 1267, 1272–1273
Urban planning: in ancient India, 67; in 19th-century Europe, 903, 905–906
Urban population, 1266, 1267(table)
Urdu, 309
Ure, Andrew, 853
Ursuline order, 555–556
Uruguay, 486, 936
Uthman, 273–274
Utopia, 141, 525, 526; socialist, 874
Utopia (More), 525
Utrecht, Peace of, 619

Vacuum tube, 1117
Vaishyas, 302
Valens, Roman emperor, 251
Valentino, Rudolph, 1117
Valéry, Paul, 1106–1107
Valla, Lorenzo, 515
Valmy, Battle of, 812
Valois kings, 545
Vandals, 217, 246, 250(illus.)
van Eyck, Jan, 527
van Gogh, Vincent, 1115
Varangians. *See* Vikings
Vasari, Giorgio, 515
Vases, Greek, 138(illus.), 175

Vatican Library, 513
Vedas (Vay-duhz), 69, 72, 73
Vedic society. *See* Aryans
Vegetables, in 18th-century European diet, 710
Veii, 175
Veiling, of Muslim women, 284
Venetia, 933
Venezuela, 486; consequences of independence in, 1001; democratic government in, 1207
Venice, 510–511, 523; as trading center, 423–424; black slaves and, 596; Ottoman war against, 750; ceded to Italy, 940
Verdun (Vair-dun), battle of, 1050
Verdun, Treaty of, 334, 350
Vergerio, Peter Paul, 519
Vernacular literature, 432–434
Versailles, 613, 639; Treaty of, 1062–1066, 1118, 1155
Vespasian (Ve-spa'-zhe-un), 207
Vespucci, Amerigo, 486
Viceroyalties, Spanish, 574–575
Vichy government, 1158, 1164
Victor Emmanuel II, king of Sardinia-Piedmont and Italy, 933, 936
Victor Emmanuel III, king of Italy, 1146
Vienna, Congress of, 864, 865, 867–868, 933
Vietcong, 1202
Vietnam, 102, 306, 774, 1075, 1291. *See also* Vietnam War
Vietnam War, 1202–1203, 1229
Vigny (Ven-ye), Alfred de, 879
Vikings, 245, 252, 256, 355; 9th-century invasions of, 348, 350–352; assimilation of Anglo-Saxons and, 353; overseas expansion of, 565; and Kievan principality, 633–634
Villages, 10; Indian, 69, 76, 80, 302, 1224; in medieval manor, 377, 380; in early Africa, 465, 466; in Third World, 1262–1266. *See also* Cities; Towns
Villeins, 376
Villon, François, 432, 434
Vincent of Beauvais, 388–389
Vindication of the Rights of Man, A (Wollstonecraft), 810
Vindication of the Rights of Woman, A (Wollstonecraft), 810
Virgil, 201, 240, 521
Virgin Mary, popular view of in High Middle Ages, 383–385
Virgins, 254
Virocha, 572–573
Vishnu, Hindu god, 75
Vitalism, 714

Vivarium, 242
Vivisection, 166
Vizier, 276
Völkerwanderungen, 245, 248
Voltaire (François Marie Arouet), 672–674, 676, 678, 680, 683, 687, 995
Voting rights. *See* Suffrage
Voting Rights Act of 1965, 1201
Vulgate, 239

Wager on the strong, 945
Wages: of weavers, 839; "iron law of," 845, 872; of European factory workers, 853; of women in American textile industry, 1021; in Stalinist Russia, 1142; in Third World, 1272. *See also* Income
Wakefield, Edward Gibbon, 1030
Waldassen, abbey of, 396
Waldensians, 435
Waldo, Peter, 435
Waldseemüller, Martin, 486
Wales, 251
Walesa, Lech, 1197, 1307
Wallace, William, 451
Walpole, Robert, 649
Walter of Henley, 380
Wang An-shih (Wang' An'-shur), 319
Wang Chih, 772
Wang Mang, 109
Wang Zhen, 774
Wan-li (Wahn-lee), emperor of China, 774, 776–777, 779
War and Peace (Tolstoy), 925
"War communism," 1060
Warfare: Sumerian, 16, 17; Egyptian weapons and, 30; Hittite, 33; Hebrew, 43; Assyrian, 49–52; Aryan, 69; Mauryan, 81; Shang, 90; Chou, 93; Ch'in, 101; Han, 102; Mycenaean, 119–120; Greek polis and, 123; Spartan, 125, 126; during Classical Period of Greece, 128; Greco-Macedonian, 153; Roman, 175, 179, 181–182, 188, 198; Muslim, 293; in India, 307–309; during T'ang period, 314; Mongol conquests and, 319–322; among Charlemagne's descendants, 347; medieval, 391, 393(illus.), 409, 411, 442, 444; Aztec, 493–494, 495, 572; in 16th-century Europe, 580; in 17th-century Europe, 608; under Peter the Great, 638–639; demographic crisis and, 695, 696; Japanese, 784; during World War I, 1045–1047, 1049; mobilizing for total war, during World War I, 1049–1051; during World War II, 1158–1159. *See also individual wars*

Warlords, 1090–1091
War of 1812, 1007
War of the Austrian Succession, 680, 684, 685, 750, 833, 835
War of the Spanish Succession, 617–618, 626, 653, 833, 993
War of the Three Henrys, 583
War Raw Materials Board, 1050
Warrior-aristocracy, 265, 322, 346, 495
Warsaw Pact, 1174, 1192
Wars of the Roses, 530, 531, 550
Washington, George, 801, 1007; attitude toward slavery, 1012
Waste Land, The (Eliot), 1113
Water frame, 837, 838
Watergate affair, 1185, 1202–1203
Waterloo, Napoleon I's defeat at, 823, 864, 867
Waterworks: Indian, 301; Sui, 311–312
Watt, James, 840–842, 852
Waugh (Waw), Evelyn, 1110
"Way of the Warrior," 327–328
Wealth: in Hellenic Greece, 119, 123–124; of caliphal court, 277; of Cordoba and Baghdad, 289; of Buddhist monasteries, 311; of medieval monasteries, 395, 396, 397; of Florence, during Renaissance, 508; as motive for European overseas expansion, 570; Dutch, 649–652; cotton industry and, 838–839; English Industrial Revolution and, 844–846
Weapons: Egyptian, 30; Aryan, 70(illus.); invented by Archimedes, 163
Weavers, wages of, 839
Wei Chih (Way' Cher'), 322
Wei Chung-hsien, 772, 776
Weights and measures, Chinese system of, 99–100
Weimar Republic, 1119; Hitler's denunciation of, 1149
Wellesley, Richard, 762
Wentworth, W. C., 1031
Wesley, John, 707, 720–721
Wesley, Susannah, 707
Wessex, 353
West Africa, 740, 1236, 1237, 1238; nationalism and independence in, 1244(map)
West African Forest Region, 726, 727(map)
West Asia, 1075
West Frankland, 335
West Germany, 1176, 1177, 1199, 1290; renounces manufacture of nuclear arms, 1293. *See also* Germany
West Indies, black slaves in, 596
Westphalia, Peace of, 580, 592
Wet nursing, 389, 705–706, 707
What Is Property? (Proudhon), 875
What Is the Third Estate? (Sieyès), 806, 817

"What the Butler Saw," 1117
Wheel, invention of, 11
Wheeler, Mortimer, 65–66
Wheel of life, 72, 73, 74
Whig party, 797, 883
White Australia policy, 1031
White-collar workers, in Third World, 1272
"White man's burden," 978–979, 1072, 1097
White Mountain, Battle of, 591, 625
Wife of Bath, 449
Wilkinson, John, 841
William I, duke of Normandy, 352–353
William I: king of Prussia, 937, 940; emperor of Germany, 941, 1039, 1041
William II, emperor of Germany, 947–948, 1043
William II, Prince William of Orange, 585, 586, 587, 617, 648
William of Newburgh, 423
William of Normandy. *See* William the Conqueror
William the Conqueror, 359, 361, 386, 392, 394, 396, 405–406, 409, 411, 523
William the Pious, 355
Wilmot, Frank, 1032
Wilson, Woodrow, 1049, 1062–1063, 1065–1066, 1074, 1100, 1118
Windischgrätz, Alfred, 892
Winter (Town) Palace, 639, 642
"Wireless" communication, 1117
Witchcraft, in Mesopotamia, 23
Witch-hunting, 594–595
Witte, Sergei, 943–944
Wittgenstein (Vit-gen-shtine), Ludwig, 1108
Wojtyla, Karol. *See* John Paul II, pope
Wolfe, James, 1023
Wollstonecraft, Mary, 810–811
Wolof, 726
Wolsey, Thomas, 535, 550
Women: in Paleolithic Age, 8, 9; Hammurabi's code and, 25; in ancient Israel, 47; in India, 69, 304; in ancient China, 105; Hellenic, 123, 128, 135, 136, 137–138; Hellenistic, 161–162; Roman, 184; Jesus' thoughts on, 237–238; in medieval Europe, 244; under Salic Law, 249; Byzantine, 259; in Islamic society, 267, 282–284; during T'ang period, 315; in Germanic society, 336; in early Middle Ages, 336, 346; under feudalism, 348–349; in High Middle Ages, 380–381, 381(illus.), 383, 386–387, 391; as nuns, 389, 393–395, 555–556; in late Middle Ages, 419–420, 448, 449, 451; in

craft guilds, 419–420; Albigensians and, 435; in early Africa, 465, 467; in Renaissance society, 521–523; Luther's appeal to, 541–542; Anabaptists and, 548–549; in Reformation Europe, 555, 593–594; persecuted as witches, 594–595; as rulers of 18th-century Russia, 642; vote granted to, 643, 1032; of Enlightenment, 677; child care and, 704–706, 919–921; breast-feeding and, 705–706, 707, 859, 919, 1303; literacy of, 709; in Ming and Ch'ing China, 774, 775, 781; Japanese, 788; French Revolution and, 808–809; cry for peace by, after French Revolution, 815; Napoleonic Code and, 818, 916; in labor force, 857–860, 1051–1052; utopian socialism and, 874; Fourier, on emancipation of, 874, 875; Marxian socialism and, 875; in 19th-century European cities, 908, 909, 912, 916–919; as domestic servants, 912; vote granted to, 946, 1052; in slavery, 1017, 1018; frontier, 1019–1020; in American textile industry, 1021; during World War I, 1050, 1051–1052; Turkish, under Kemal, 1080; in Hindu society, 1086; in changing Chinese family, 1094; in Stalinist Russia, 1144–1145; Mussolini's treatment of, 1147; in Mao's China, 1216; during economic surge in Japan, 1221; in India, under Nehru, 1223, 1224; in Third World, 1258, 1272, 1273
Women's movement, origins of, 811
Woolf, Virginia, 1112
Wool industry: English, 424, 439, 508, 531, 587, 835; Hundred Years' War and, 441, 444; enclosure movement and, 831; Australian, 1030
Worcester, Samuel C., 1010
Wordsworth, William, 852, 878, 880
Working conditions, 853; in factories, 854–857
Working people: Maya, 489; Teotihuacán, 491; Aztec, 495–496; English, Industrial Revolution and, 852–860; 19th-century wages of, 853; French revolution of 1848 and, 889–890; in 19th-century European cities, 910–914; Napoleon III, and, 932; revolution of 1905 and, 945; unions and revisionism and, 954–956; changing class structure and, 1183. *See also* Common people; Labor; Peasantry
Workshops, national, 888–889
Works Progress Administration (WPA), 1127

World government, 1285, 1289. *See also* United Nations

World Health Organization, 1285

World politics, 1284–1293; United Nations and, 1285–1287, 1289; "middle" and regional powers and, 1290; arms race and nuclear proliferation and, 1291–1293

World view, 660, 664, 675, 676

World War I, 1038–1047, 1048(map), 1049–1054; Bismarck's alliances and, 1038–1039, 1040(fig.); rival blocs and, 1039, 1041–1042; outbreak of, 1042–1044; origins of, 1044; first Battle of the Marne and, 1045; widening of, 1046–1047, 1049; mobilization for, 1049–1051; social impact of, 1051–1053; political tensions and, 1053–1054; Russian Revolution of 1917 and, 1054–1060; end of, 1061; revolution in Germany and, 1061–1062; Treaty of Versailles and, 1062–1066; reparations following, 1064, 1118, 1119, 1120

World War II: events leading to, 1154(table); appeasement by England and France and, 1155–1157; begins, 1158; Japan attacks Pearl Harbor, U.S. enters, 1159; Grand Alliance and, 1161–1163; Hitler defeated at Stalingrad, 1163; in Pacific, 1163–1164, 1164(map); Normandy invasion and, 1165; Japanese surrender and, 1166; end of, 1166

Worms: Diet of, 533, 538; Edict of, 538, 545

Wozzeck (Berg), 1116

WPA. *See* Works Progress Administration

Wretched of the Earth, The (Fanon), 1275

Wright, Frank Lloyd, 1113

Writ, Anglo Saxon, 406; Calvinism and, 585; English Parliamentary reform and, 885

Writing: Sumerian, 4, 20(illus.), 21(illus.); in Neolithic Age, 9, 14; origins of, 19; cuneiform, 19, 20, 34, 91; Mycenaean, 32; Chinese, 91, 99, 323, 326, 781; Greek, 118; Cyrillic, 256; Sanskrit, 301, 305, 306; Japanese, 326; uncial, 341; Carolingian minuscule, 343; Olmec, 488; Maya, 488, 489

Wu Ti, 216

Wyclif (Wik′-lif), John, 448

Wynfrith. *See* Boniface

Xavier, Francis, 786

Xenophon (Zen-o-fon), 52

Xerxes (Zerk-seez), 58–59, 128

Xhosa, 973

Yahweh (Jehovah), 44, 45, 48, 203, 204

Yalta Conference, 1172, 1188

Yamato clan, 323

Yamato pictures, 326

Yangtze (Yang′-tsee) River, 88

Year of the Four Emperors, 207

"Yellow press," 1033

Yellow River, 13, 88, 89(illus.)

Yields, agricultural: in medieval Europe, 380

Yin and Yang, 98–99

Ying-tsung, emperor of China, 774

Yoritomo (Yore-ih-toe-mo), 326; administrative system of, 328–329

York, ducal house of, 530

Yorubas, 1243, 1245

Young Plan, 1120

Young Shoots law, 319

Young Turks, 1076

Ypsilanti, Alexander, 881

Yuan Dynasty, 279; founding of, 320

Yucatán, 488, 490

Yugoslavia: in Little Entente, 1119; conservative authoritarianism in, 1136; Hitler conquers, 1159; cold war and, 1172

Yung Lo, emperor of China, 773, 774

Zacharias, pope, 336

Zaibatsu, 1096–1097

Zambia, 1241

Zamna, 488

Zanj ("land of the blacks"), 476

Zanzibar, 733

Zapotecan, 491

Zarathustra. *See* Zoroaster

Zealots, 203

Zeeland, 649

Zemstvo, 943

Zen Buddhism, 310, 1309

Zend Avesta, 57

Zeno, 161

Zeus, 185

Zhdanov (Zhda′-nef), Andrei, 1188

Ziggurat, 17

Zik. *See* Azikiwe, Nnamdi

Zimbabwe, 465, 1241; nationalism in, 1246. *See also* Great Zimbabwe; Southern Rhodesia

Zionism, 1082

Zola, Émile, 924, 925, 949

Zollverein (Tsoll-fer-ine), 851, 937

Zoology, Aristotle's study of, 142, 165

Zoroaster, 57–58

Zoroastrianism, 206, 280

Zulu, 973

Zwingli, Ulrich (Tsuing-li, Ool′-rikh), 541